Chambers
Spanish
Pocket
Dictionary

GW00598316

Chambers

CHAMBERS

An imprint of Chambers Harrap Publishers Ltd
7 Hopetoun Crescent, Edinburgh, EH7 4AY

Chambers Harrap is an Hachette UK company

© Chambers Harrap Publishers Ltd 2009

Chambers® is a registered trademark of Chambers Harrap Publishers Ltd

First published by Chambers Harrap Publishers Ltd 2009
Previously published as *Harrap's Spanish Paperback Dictionary* in 2001
Second edition published 2007

Database right Chambers Harrap Publishers Ltd (makers)

A CIP catalogue record for this book is available from the British
Library.

ISBN 978 0550 10540 0

10 9 8 7 6 5 4 3 2 1

Editors/Redacción: Teresa Álvarez, Liam Rodger

www.chambers.co.uk

Designed by Chambers Harrap Publishers Ltd, Edinburgh
Typeset in Abadi and Cheltenham by Chambers Harrap Publishers Ltd,
Edinburgh
Printed and bound in Great Britain by Clays Lts, St Ives plc

Contents/Índice

Preface

This dictionary packs a wealth of vocabulary into a pocket-sized book, making it the ideal resource for all students from beginner to intermediate level together with holidaymakers and business travellers.

Comprehensive, accurate and up-to-date, it is packed with information and covers all the basic vocabulary learners will need for everyday communication. It also features terms from a wide range of technical areas (computing, biology, education, finance etc) and offers excellent coverage of colloquial and idiomatic language. In addition, there is detailed treatment of Latin American Spanish and American English.

Useful extra features of the dictionary include boxed notes on false friends, which help the user avoid common translation pitfalls; notes on interesting grammar points to aid correct usage and a detailed pronunciation guide in which special attention is given to the problems English speakers encounter in pronouncing Spanish.

Prefacio

Les presentamos un diccionario de tamaño bolsillo repleto de vocabulario, ideal tanto para principiantes como para estudiantes de nivel intermedio, y de gran utilidad durante las vacaciones o los viajes de trabajo.

Esta es una obra completa, con informacion precisa y actual sobre la lengua, que recoge todo el vocabulario necesario para la comunicacion basica. Se incluyen tambien terminos tecnicos (de informatica, biologia, educacion, finanzas, etc), asi como el vocabulario coloquial y numerosas expresiones idiomaticas. Ademas de esto, se recogen tanto el español de America como el ingles americano.

Otros elementos utiles de este diccionario son las anotaciones sobre falsos amigos, que ayudan al lector a evitar errores habituales; notas sobre puntos gramaticales de interes que facilitan el uso correcto de la lengua y una guia de pronunciacion que presta especial atencion a los problemas que los hispanohablantes encuentran a la hora de pronunciar el ingles.

Structure of entries

> **Amtrak** ['æmtræk] N = compañía ferroviaria estadounidense

- The equals sign = introduces an explanation when there is no direct translation.

> **cupcake** ['kʌpkeɪk] N *(cake)* ≃ magdalena *f*

- The sign ≃ introduces a translation that has a roughly equivalent status but is not identical.

> **alert** [ə'lɜːt] **1** ADJ *(watchful)* alerta; *(lively)* despabilado(a)
> **2** N alerta *m*; **to be on the a.** estar alerta
> **3** VT **to a. sb to sth** avisar a algn de algo

- The different grammatical categories are cleary indicated, introduced by a bold Arabic numeral.

> **depress** [dɪ'pres] VT (**a**) *(person)* deprimir (**b**) *Econ* *(profits)* reducir; *(trade)* dificultar (**c**) *Fml* *(switch, lever etc)* presionar; *(clutch, piano pedal)* pisar

- Usage and field labels are clearly shown.

> **reconocer** [34] VT (**a**) *(identificar)* to recognize (**b**) *(admitir)* to admit (**c**) *Med* *(paciente)* to examine

- A number before an irregular Spanish verb refers the user to the verb tables in the middle of the book for information on how to conjugate it.

> **bland** [blænd] ADJ *(food)* soso(a)
>
> Note that the Spanish word **blando** is a false friend and is never a translation for the English word **bland**. In Spanish **blando** means "soft".

- Usage notes warn the user when a word is a false friend.

> **aback** [ə'bæk] ADV **to be taken a.** quedarse de una pieza (**by** por)

- The most common prepositions used are given after the translation.

> **debris** ['debriː, 'deɪbriː] N SING escombros *mpl*

- The number of a noun is indicated where this is ambiguous.

Estructura de las entradas

> **ceviche** NM = raw fish marinated in lemon and garlic

- Cuando no es posible dar una traducción se ofrece una explicación precedida por el signo igual (=).

> **inocentada** NF *Fam* ≃ April Fool's joke; **hacer una i. a algn** to play an April Fool's joke on sb

- El signo ≃ precede a una traducción que tiene un significado aproximado pero no idéntico.

> **aflojar 1** VT to loosen
> **2** VI *(viento etc)* to abate, to die down
> **3 aflojarse** VPR to come *o* work loose; *(rueda)* to go down

- Las diferentes categorías gramaticales vienen precedidas por un número en negrita.

> **abrir²** *(pp* **abierto)** **1** VI to open
> **2** VT **(a)** *(en general)* to open; *(cremallera)* to undo **(b)** *(gas, grifo)* to turn on **(c)** *Der* **a. (un) expediente** to start proceedings
> **3 abrirse** VPR **(a)** *(en general)* to open; *Fig* **abrirse paso** to make one's way **(b)** *Fam* **¡me abro!** I'm off!

- Las marcas de uso y de campo semántico están claramente indicadas.

> **reconocer** [34] VT **(a)** *(identificar)* to recognize **(b)** *(admitir)* to admit **(c)** *Med (paciente)* to examine

- Los números que aparecen detrás de los verbos irregulares españoles remiten a las conjugaciones que se encuentran en la parte central del diccionario.

> **blando, -a** ADJ soft
>
> Observa que la palabra inglesa **bland** es un falso amigo y no es la traducción de la palabra española **blando**. En inglés **bland** significa "soso".

- Las notas de uso informan sobre los falsos amigos.

> **acodarse** VPR to lean **(en on)**

- Las preposiciones de uso más frecuente aparecen después de las traducciones.

> **acústica** NF acoustics *sing*

- El número de las traducciones sustantivas aparece en los casos en los que éste es ambiguo.

Abbreviations and Symbols
Abreviaturas y símbolos

abbreviation	ABBR, ABR	abreviatura
adjective	ADJ	adjetivo
adverb	ADV	adverbio
agriculture	*Agr*	agricultura
somebody, someone	*algn*	alguien
Latin American	*Am*	hispanoamericano
anatomy	*Anat*	anatomía
Andean Spanish (Bolivia, Chile, Colombia, Ecuador, Peru)	*Andes*	español andino (Bolivia, Chile, Colombia, Ecuador, Perú)
approximately	*aprox*	aproximadamente
architecture	*Archit*	arquitectura
Argentinian Spanish	*Arg*	español de Argentina
architecture	*Arquit*	arquitectura
article	ART	artículo
art	*Art, Arte*	bellas artes
astronomy	*Astron*	astronomía
Australian	*Austr*	australiano
motoring	*Aut*	automóviles
auxiliary	AUX	auxiliar
aviation	*Av*	aviación
biology	*Biol*	biología
Bolivian	*Bol*	español de Bolivia
botany	*Bot*	botánica
British	*Br*	británico
Central American Spanish	*CAm*	español centroamericano
Canary Islands	*Can*	español de Canarias
Caribbean Spanish (Cuba, Puerto Rico, Dominican republic, Venezuela)	*Carib*	español caribeño (Cuba, Puerto Rico, República Dominicana, Venezuela)
chemistry	*Chem*	química
Chilean Spanish	*Chile*	español de Chile
cinema	*Cin*	cine
Colombian Spanish	*Col*	español de Colombia
commerce	*Com*	comercio
comparative	*comp*	comparativo
computers	*Comput*	informática
conjunction	CONJ	conjunción
building industry	*Constr*	construcción
sewing	*Cost*	costura
Costa Rican Spanish	*CRica*	español de Costa Rica
Spanish from the Southern Cone region (Argentina, Uruguay, Paraguay, Chile)	*CSur*	español del Cono Sur (Argentina, Uruguay, Paraguay, Chile)
Cuban Spanish	*Cuba*	español de Cuba
cookery	*Culin*	cocina
definite	DEF	definido
demonstrative	DEM	demostrativo
sport	*Dep*	deporte
law	*Der*	derecho
ecology	*Ecol*	ecología
economics	*Econ*	economía
Ecuadorian Spanish	*Ecuad*	español de Ecuador
education	*Educ*	educación
electricity	*Elec*	electricidad
especially	esp	especialmente
Peninsular Spanish	*Esp*	español de España
specialist term	*Espec*	término especializado

euphemism	*Euph, Euf*	eufemismo
feminine	*f*	femenino
familiar	*Fam*	familiar
railways	*Ferroc*	ferrocarriles
figurative use	*Fig*	uso figurado
finance	*Fin*	finanzas
physics	*Fís*	física
formal use	*Fml*	uso formal
photography	*Fot*	fotografía
feminine plural	*fpl*	plural femenino
football	*Ftb*	fútbol
future	FUT	futuro
geography	*Geog*	geografía
geology	*Geol*	geología
geometry	*Geom*	geometría
Guatemalan Spanish	*Guat*	español de Guatemala
history	*Hist*	historia
humorous	*Hum*	humorístico
imperative	IMPERAT	imperativo
imperfect	IMPERF	imperfecto
impersonal	IMPERS	impersonal
printing	*Impr*	imprenta
industry	*Ind*	industria
indefinite	INDEF	indefinido
indeterminate	INDET	indeterminado
indicative	INDIC	indicativo
infinitive	*infin*	infinitivo
computers	*Inform*	informática
insurance	*Ins*	seguros
inseparable	INSEP	inseparable
interjection	INTERJ	interjección
interrogative	INTERR	interrogativo
invariable	*inv*, INV	invariable
ironic	*Irón*	irónico
law	*Jur*	derecho
linguistics	*Ling*	lingüística
literature	*Lit*	literatura
phrase	LOC	locución
masculine	*m*	masculino
mathematics	*Math, Mat*	matemáticas
medicine	*Med*	medicina
meteorology	*Met*	meteorología
Mexican Spanish	*Méx*	español de México
military	*Mil*	militar
mining	*Min*	minas
masculine plural	*mpl*	plural masculino
music	*Mus, Mús*	música
noun	N	nombre
nautical	*Naut, Náut*	náutica
neuter	NEUT	neutro
feminine noun	NF	nombre femenino
plural feminine noun	NFPL	nombre femenino plural
masculine noun	NM	nombre masculino
masculine and feminine noun	NMF/NM,F	mombre masculino y femenino
plural masculine noun	NMPL	nombre masculino plural
plural noun	NPL	nombre plural
optics	*Opt*	óptica
ornithology	*Orn*	ornitología
Panamanian Spanish	*Pan*	español de Panamá
Paraguayan Spanish	*Par*	español de Paraguay
pejorative	*Pej*	peyorativo
personal	PERS	personal
Peruvian Spanish	*Perú*	español de Perú

Abbreviations/Abreviaturas

pejorative	*Pey*	peyorativo
photography	*Phot*	fotografía
physics	*Phys*	física
plural	*pl*, PL	plural
politics	*Pol*	política
possessive	POS, POSS	posesivo
past participle	*pp*, PP	participio pasado
prefix	PREF	prefijo
preposition	PREP	preposición
present	*pres*	presente
present participle	*pres p*	gerundio
Puerto Rican Spanish	*PRico*	español de Puerto Rico
pronoun	PRON	pronombre
psychology	*Psi*, *Psy*	psicología
past tense	*pt*, PT	pretérito
chemistry	*Quím*	químico
radio	*Rad*	radio
railways	*Rail*	ferrocarriles
Dominican Spanish	*RDom*	español de la República Dominicana
relative	REL	relativo
religion	*Rel*	religión
Spanish from the River Plate region (Argentina, Uruguay, Paraguay)	*RP*	español de los países ribereños del Río de la Plata
Salvadoran Spanish	*Salv*	español de El Salvador
somebody, someone	*sb*	alguien
school	*Sch*	escuela
Scottish	*Scot*	escocés
separable	SEP	separable
singular	*sing*	singular
something	*sth*	algo
subjunctive	SUBJ	subjuntivo
superlative	SUPERL	superlativo
bullfighting	*Taurom*	tauromaquia
technical	*Tech*, *Téc*	técnica
telephones	*Tel*	teléfonos
textiles	*Tex*	textiles
theatre	*Th*	teatro
television	*TV*	televisión
typography	*Typ*	tipografía
university	*Univ*	universidad
Uruguayan Spanish	*Urug*	español de Uruguay
United States	*US*	Estados Unidos
usually	*usu*	usualmente
verb	V	verbo
Venezualan Spanish	*Ven*	español de Venezuela
intransitive verb	VI	verbo intransitivo
reflexive verb	VPR	verbo pronominal
transitive verb	VT	verbo transitivo
vulgar	*Vulg*	vulgar
zoology	*Zool*	zoología
cultural equivalent	≃	equivalente cultural
registered trademark	®	marca registrada

Spanish Pronunciation Guide

The pronunciation of most Spanish words is predictable as there is a close match between spelling and pronunciation. The table below gives an explanation of that pronunciation. In the dictionary text therefore pronunciation is only given when the word does not follow these rules, often because it is a word of foreign origin. In these cases, the IPA (International Phonetic Alphabet) is used (see column 2 of the table below).

Letter in Spanish	IPA Symbol	Example in Spanish	Pronunciation (example in English)
Vowels			
Note that all vowel sounds in Spanish are shorter than in English			
a	a	**a**la	Similar to the sound in "f**a**ther" but more central
e	e	**e**m**e**	Similar to the sound in "m**e**t"
I	i	**i**r**i**s	like the vowel sound in "m**ea**t" but much shorter
o	o	**o**s**o**	**o**ff, **o**n
u	u	**u**va	like the vowel sound in "s**oo**n" but much shorter
Semiconsonants			
"i" in: ia, ie, io, iu	j	h**i**ato, h**i**elo, av**i**ón, v**i**uda	**y**es
"u" in: ua, ue, ui, uo	w	s**u**ave, f**u**ego, h**u**ida	**w**in
Consonants			
b	b	**b**om**b**a (at beginning of word or after "m")	**b**oom
	β	a**b**ajo (all other contexts)	a "**b**" pronounced without quite closing the lips completely
c	θ (in Spain)	**c**eño (before "e") **c**inco (before "i")	**th**anks (in Spain)
	s (in Southern Spain and Latin America)		**s**un (in Southern Spain and Latin America)
	k	**c**asa (all other contexts)	**c**at
ch	t	**ch**au**ch**a	ar**ch**

Spanish Pronunciation Guide

Letter in Spanish	IPA Symbol	Example in Spanish	Pronunciation (example in English)
d	d	**d**on**d**e (beginning of word or after "n") al**d**ea (after "l")	**d**ay
	ð	a**d**orno (all other contexts)	Similar to the sound in "mo**th**er" but less strong
f	f	**f**uria	**f**ire
g	χ	**g**ema (before "e") **g**irasol (before "i")	Like an "**h**" but pronounced at the back of the throat (similar to Scottish "lo**ch**")
	g	**g**ato (beginning of word) len**g**ua (after "n")	**g**oose
	ɣ	a**g**ua (all other contexts)	Like a "**w**" pronounced while trying to say "**g**"
j	χ	**j**abalí	Like an "**h**" but pronounced at the back of the throat (similar to Scottish "lo**ch**")
l	l	**l**ado	**l**ake
ll	j	**ll**uvia	**y**ellow
	ʒ		In some regions (eg the Rio de la Plata area of South America) it is pronounced like the "**s**" in "plea**s**ure"
m	m	**m**ano	**m**an
n	n	**n**ulo	**n**o
ñ	ŋ	**ñ**ato	onion
p	p	**p**a**p**a	**p**ool
q	k	**q**ueso	**c**at
r	r	do**r**ado (in between vowels) habla**r** (at end of syllable or word)	A rolled "**r**" sound (similar to Scottish "**r**")
	rr	**r**osa (beginning of word) al**r**ededor (after "l") en**r**edo (after "n")	A much longer rolled "**r**" sound (similar to Scottish "**r**")
rr	rr	a**rr**oyo	A much longer rolled "**r**" sound (similar to Scottish "**r**")
s	s	**s**aco	**s**ound
sh	ʃ	**sh**ow	**sh**ow
t	t	**t**ela	**t**ea
v	b	**v**aso (beginning of word) in**v**ierno (after "n")	**b**oom
	β	a**v**e (all other contexts)	A "**b**" pronounced without quite closing the lips completely
x	ks	e**x**amen	e**x**tra

Letter in Spanish	IPA Symbol	Example in Spanish	Pronunciation (example in English)
y	j	ayer	**y**es
	ʒ		In some regions (eg the Rio de la Plata area of South America) it is pronounced like the "**s**" in "plea**s**ure"
z	θ (in Spain)	**z**apato	**th**anks (in Spain)
	s (in Southern Spain and Latin America)		**s**un (in Southern Spain and Latin America)

Pronunciación del inglés

Para ilustrar la pronunciación inglesa, en este diccionario utilizamos los símbolos del AFI (Alfabeto Fonético Internacional). En el siguiente cuadro, para cada sonido del inglés hay ejemplos de palabras en inglés y palabras en español donde aparece un sonido similar. En los casos en los que no hay sonido similar en español, ofrecemos una explicación de cómo pronunciarlo.

Carácter AFI	Ejemplo en inglés	Ejemplo en español
Consonantes		
[b]	ba**bb**le	be**b**é
[d]	**d**ig	**d**e**d**o
[dʒ]	**g**iant, **j**ig	se pronuncia como [ʒ] en "plea**s**ure" pero con una "**d**" adelante, o como "**gi**" en italiano: **Gio**vanna
[f]	**f**it, **ph**ysics	**f**aro
[g]	**g**rey, bi**g**	**g**ris
[h]	**h**appy	**h** aspirada
[j]	**y**ellow	se pronuncia como "**y**" o "**ll**" en España: **y**o, **ll**uvia
[k]	**c**lay, **k**i**ck**	**c**li**c**
[l]	**l**ip	**l**abio
	pi**ll**	pape**l**
[m]	**m**u**mm**y	**m**a**m**á
[n]	**n**ip, pi**n**	**n**ada
[p]	**p**i**p**	**p**a**p**á
[ŋ]	si**ng**	se pronuncia como "**n**" antes de "c": ba**n**co
[r]	**r**ig, w**r**ite	sonido entre "**r**" y "**rr**"
[s]	**s**ick, **sc**ience	**s**apo
[ʃ]	**sh**ip, na**ti**on	**sh**ow
[t]	**t**ip, bu**tt**	**t**ela
[tʃ]	**ch**ip, ba**tch**	**ch**au**ch**a
[θ]	**th**ick	**z**apato (como se pronuncia en España)
[ð]	**th**is	se pronuncia como la "**d**" de "ha**d**a" pero más fuerte
[v]	**v**ague, gi**v**e	se pronuncia como antiguamente en español "**v**" de **v**ida, con los dientes apoyados sobre el labio inferior
[w]	**w**it, **wh**y	**wh**isky
[z]	**z**ip, phy**s**ics	"**s**" con sonido zumbante
[ʒ]	plea**s**ure	se pronuncia como "**y**" o "**ll**" en el Río de la Plata: **y**o, **ll**uvia
[χ]	lo**ch**	**j**ota

CarácterAFI	Ejemplo en inglés	Ejemplo en español
Vocales		
[æ]	rag	se pronuncia "a" con posición bucal para "e"
[ɑ:]	large, half	"a" muy alargada
[ʌ]	cup	"a" breve y cerrada
[e]	set	se pronuncia como "e" de elefante pero más corta
[ɜ:]	curtain, were	se pronuncia como una "e" larga con posición bucal entre "o" y "e"
[ə]	utter	se pronuncia como "e" con posición bucal para "o"
[ɪ]	big, women	"i" breve, a medio camino entre "e" e "i"
[i:]	leak, wee	"i" muy alargada
[ɒ]	lock	"o" abierta
[ɔ:]	wall, cork	"o" cerrada y alargada
[ʊ]	put, look	"u" breve
[u:]	moon	"u" muy alargada
Diptongos		
[aɪ]	why, high, lie	aire
[aʊ]	how	aura
[eə]	bear	"ea" pronunciado muy brevemente y con el sonido de "e" más marcado que el de "a"
[eɪ]	day, make, main	reina
[əʊ]	show, go	"ou" como en estadounidense.
[ɪə]	here, gear	hielo pronunciado con el sonido de "i" más marcado y alargado que el de "e"
[ɔɪ]	boy, soil	voy
[ʊə]	poor	cuerno, pronunciado con el sonido de "u" más marcado u alargado que el de "e"

Algunas dificultades de la pronunciación inglesa para el hispanohablante

La vocal neutra

Una de las diferencias más marcadas entre ambas lenguas es que en inglés las vocales no acentuadas a menudo se pronuncian de una forma neutra no comparable a ninguna de las cinco vocales españolas. Esto puede verse claramente, por ejemplo, al comparar los sonidos vocálicos de la palabra **banana** pronunciada en inglés [bə'nɑ:nə] y en español [ba'nana].

Vocales no equivalentes

Algunos sonidos vocálicos ingleses resultan muy difíciles de diferenciar para el oído español, ya que en nuestra lengua hay un único sonido equivalente a varios sonidos ingleses. Quizá la diferencia más notable sea entre:

heat [hi:t] y **hit** [hɪt]

Pronunciación del inglés

El hispanohablante tiende a pronunciar ambos sonidos de una forma semejante, que a oídos ingleses parece siempre más **heat** que **hit**.

Lo mismo ocurre con:

hut [hʌt] y **hat** [hæt]

en cuyo caso nuestra pronunciación a menudo se asemeja más a **hut** que a **hat**.

La "b" y la "v"
A diferencia del español, las consonantes **b** y **v** se distinguen claramente en inglés: para pronunciar la **b** inglesa se cierran totalmente los labios al principio, mientras que la pronunciación de la **v** se asemeja a un zumbido producido al rozar el aire de forma continua. Para ambos sonidos, el hispanohablante tiende a usar el sonido español, más cercano a la **b** inglesa que a la **v**.

La "h"
La **h** inglesa se pronuncia con una ligera aspiración, mucho más suave que el sonido que tiende a pronunciar el hispanohablante, más cercano a la **j** española.

La "s" inicial
Muchas palabras inglesas empiezan por dos o tres consonantes, la primera de las cuales es **s**, por ejemplo "sc-", "sl-", "sp-", "st-" o bien "spr-", "str-", "spl-". En español no se crean palabras que empiecen por dicha agrupación de consonantes, por lo que el hispanohablante suele añadir una **e** inicial al pronunciarla, creando como resultado una sílaba más. De ahí que "sport" se convierta en "esport", "strike" en "estrike", etcétera.

Spanish – English

Español – Inglés

A, a [a] NF *(letra)* A, a

a¹ *(abr* **área)** area

a² PREP

> **a** combines with the article **el** to form the contraction **al** (e.g. **al centro** to the centre).

(**a**) *(dirección)* to; **ir a Colombia** to go to Colombia; **llegar a Valencia** to arrive in Valencia; **subir al tren** to get on the train; **ir al cine** to go to the cinema; **vete a casa** go home (**b**) *(lugar)* at, on; **a la derecha** on the right; **a la entrada** at the entrance; **a lo lejos** in the distance; **a mi lado** at o by my side, next to me; **al sol** in the sun; **a la mesa** at (the) table (**c**) *(tiempo)* at; **a las doce** at twelve o'clock; **a los sesenta años** at the age of sixty; **a los tres meses/la media hora** three months/half an hour later; **al final** in the end; **al principio** at first (**d**) *(distancia)* away; **a 100 km de aquí** 100 km from here (**e**) *(manera)* **a la inglesa** in the English fashion o style; **escrito a máquina** typed, typewritten; **a mano** by hand (**f**) *(proporción)* **a 90 km por hora** at 90 km an hour; **a dos euros el kilo** two euros a kilo; **tres veces a la semana** three times a week (**g**) *Dep* **ganar cuatro a dos** to win four (to) two (**h**) *(complemento indirecto)* to; *(procedencia)* from; **díselo a Javier** tell Javier; **te lo di a ti** I gave it to you; **comprarle algo a algn** to buy sth from sb; *(para algn)* to buy sth for sb; *(complemento directo de persona)* **saludé a tu tía** I said hello to your aunt (**i**) *Fam* **ir a por algn/algo** to go and fetch sb/sth (**j**) *(verbo + a + infin)* to; **aprender a nadar** to learn (how) to swim; **fueron a ayudarle** they went to help him (**k**) *(nombre + a + infin)* **distancia a recorrer** distance to be covered (**l**) *(a decir verdad* to tell (you) the truth; **a no ser por ...** if it were not for ...; **a no ser que** unless; **a ver** let's see; **¡a comer!** lunch/dinner/*etc* is ready!; **¡a dormir!** bedtime!; **¿a que no lo haces?** *(desafío)* I bet you don't do it!

abad NM abbot

abadía NF abbey

abajeño, -a NM,F *Am* lowlander

abajo 1 ADV (**a**) *(en una casa)* downstairs; **el piso de a.** the downstairs flat (**b**) *(dirección)* down, downwards; **ahí/aquí a.** down there/

here; **la parte de a.** the bottom (part); **más a.** further down; **hacia a.** down, downwards; **calle a.** down the street; **echar algo a.** to knock sth down; **venirse a.** *(edificio)* to fall down; *Fig (proyecto)* to fall through

2 INTERJ **¡a. la censura!** down with censorship!

abalanzarse [40] VPR **a. hacia** to rush towards; **a. sobre** to pounce on

abalear VT *Andes, CAm, Ven* to shoot at

abalorio NM (**a**) *(cuenta)* glass bead (**b**) *(baratija)* trinket

abanderado, -a NM,F standard bearer

abandonado, -a ADJ (**a**) *(persona, cosa)* abandoned; **tiene a su familia muy abandonada** he takes absolutely no interest in his family (**b**) *(desaseado)* untidy, unkempt

abandonar 1 VT (**a**) *(lugar)* to leave, to quit; *(persona, cosa)* to abandon; *(proyecto, plan)* to give up (**b**) *Dep (carrera)* to drop out of
2 abandonarse VPR to let oneself go

abandono NM (**a**) *(acción)* abandoning, desertion (**b**) *(de proyecto, idea)* giving up (**c**) *(descuido)* neglect

abanicarse VPR to fan oneself

abanico NM (**a**) *(objeto)* fan (**b**) *(gama)* range; **un amplio a. de posibilidades** a wide range of possibilities

abaratar 1 VT *(precio)* to bring down, to reduce; *(artículo)* to reduce the price of
2 abaratarse VPR to become cheaper, to come down in price

abarcar [44] VT *(incluir)* to cover

abarrotado, -a ADJ *(teatro, autobús)* packed (**de** with); *(desván, baúl)* crammed (**de** with)

abarrotar VT *(teatro, autobús)* to pack (**de** o **con** with); *(desván, baúl)* to cram full (**de** o **con** of)

abarrotería NF *CAm, Méx* grocer's (shop), grocery store

abarrotero, -a NM,F *CAm, Méx* grocer

abarrotes NMPL *CAm, Méx* groceries; **tienda de a.** grocer's (shop), grocery store

abastecedor, -a NM,F supplier

abastecer [33] **1** VT to supply
2 abastecerse VPR **abastecerse de** to stock up on

abastecimiento NM supplying; **a. de agua** water supply

abasto NM (**a**) *Fam* **no doy a.** I can't cope, I can't keep up (**b**) **mercado de abastos** wholesale food market

abatible ADJ folding, collapsible; **asiento a.** reclining seat

abatido, -a ADJ downcast

abatir 1 VT (**a**) (*derribar*) to knock down, to pull down (**b**) (*matar*) to kill; **a. a tiros** to shoot down (**c**) (*desanimar*) to depress, to dishearten
2 abatirse VPR (*desanimarse*) to lose heart, to become depressed

abdicación NF abdication

abdicar [44] VT & VI to abdicate

abdomen NM abdomen

abdominales NMPL sit-ups

abecedario NM alphabet

abedul NM birch

abeja NF bee; **a. reina** queen bee

abejorro NM bumblebee

aberración NF aberration

aberrante ADJ (**a**) (*absurdo*) ridiculous, idiotic (**b**) (*perverso*) perverse

abertura NF (*hueco*) opening, gap; (*grieta*) crack, slit

abertzale [aβerˈtʃale] ADJ & NMF *Esp* Basque nationalist

abeto NM *Bot* fir (tree); **a. rojo** spruce

abierto, -a 1 ADJ (**a**) open; (*grifo*) (turned) on; **a. de par en par** wide open (**b**) (*persona*) open-minded
2 PP *de* **abrir**

abigarrado, -a ADJ (*mezclado*) jumbled, mixed up

abismal ADJ abysmal; **una diferencia a.** a world of difference

abismo NM abyss; *Fig* **al borde del a.** on the brink of ruin; *Fig* **entre ellos media un a.** they are worlds apart

ablandar 1 VT to soften
2 ablandarse VPR (**a**) (*objeto, material*) to soften, to go soft (**b**) *Fig* (*persona*) to mellow

abnegación NF abnegation, self-denial

abnegado, -a ADJ selfless, self-sacrificing

abocado, -a ADJ destined (**a** to); **está a. al fracaso** it is doomed to failure

abochornar VT to embarrass

abofetear VT to slap

abogacía NF legal profession

abogado, -a NM,F *Br* lawyer, *US* attorney; (*en tribunal supremo*) lawyer, *Br* barrister; **a. de oficio** legal aid lawyer; **a. defensor** counsel for the defence; **a. del diablo** devil's advocate; **a. laboralista** union lawyer

abogar [42] VI to plead; **a. a favor de** to plead for, to defend; **a. por algo** to advocate *o* champion sth

abolengo NM lineage

abolición NF abolition

abolir VT to abolish

abolladura NF dent

abollar VT to dent

abominable ADJ abominable

abominar 1 VT (*detestar*) to abhor, to abominate
2 VI **a. de** (*condenar*) to condemn, to criticize

abonado, -a 1 NM,F (*a revista*) subscriber; (*a teléfono, de gas*) customer
2 ADJ *Fin* (*pagado*) paid; **a. en cuenta** credited

abonar 1 VT (**a**) *Agr* to fertilize (**b**) (*pagar*) to pay (for) (**c**) (*subscribir*) to subscribe
2 abonarse VPR to subscribe (**a** to)

abonero, -a NM,F *Méx* hawker, street trader

abono NM (**a**) *Agr* (*producto*) fertilizer; (*estiércol*) manure (**b**) (*pago*) payment (**c**) (*a revista etc*) subscription; (*billete*) season ticket (**d**) *Méx* (*plazo*) instalment; **pagar en abonos** to pay by instalments

abordar VT (*persona*) to approach; (*barco*) to board; **a. un asunto** to tackle a subject

aborigen (*pl* **aborígenes**) **1** ADJ native, indigenous; *esp Austral* aboriginal
2 NMF native; *esp Austral* aborigine

aborrecer [33] VT to detest, to loathe

abortar 1 VI (*involuntariamente*) to miscarry, to have a miscarriage; (*intencionadamente*) to abort, to have an abortion
2 VT to abort

abortista ADJ & NMF abortionist

aborto NM miscarriage; (*provocado*) abortion

abotargado, -a ADJ swollen

abotonar VT (*ropa*) to button (up)

abovedado, -a ADJ vaulted

abracadabra NM abracadabra

abrasador, -a ADJ scorching

abrasar 1 VT to burn oneself
2 abrasarse VPR to burn

abrazadera NF clamp

abrazar [40] **1** VT to embrace, to hug; *Fig* (*doctrina*) to embrace
2 abrazarse VPR **abrazarse a algn** to embrace sb; **se abrazaron** they embraced each other

abrazo NM embrace, hug; **un a., abrazos** (*en carta*) best wishes

abrebotellas NM INV bottle opener

abrecartas NM INV letter-opener, paperknife

abrefácil NM **caja con a.** easy-open carton

abrelatas NM INV can opener, *Br* tin-opener

abreviar [43] **1** VT to shorten; (*texto*) to abridge; (*palabra*) to abbreviate
2 VI to be quick *o* brief; **para a.** to cut a long story short

abreviatura NF abbreviation

abridor NM (*de latas, botellas*) (can-)opener, *Br* (tin-)opener

abrigado, -a ADJ wrapped-up; **ir muy a.** to be well wrapped-up

abrigar [42] VT (**a**) (*dar calor*) to keep warm (**b**) (*proteger*) to protect, to shelter (**c**) (*esperanza*) to cherish; (*duda*) to have, to harbour
2 VI to be warm; **esta chaqueta abriga mucho** this cardigan is very warm

abrigo NM (**a**) *(prenda)* coat, overcoat; **ropa de a.** warm clothes (**b**) **al a. de** protected o sheltered from

abril NM April

abrillantador NM polish

abrillantar VT to polish

abrir¹ NM **en un a. y cerrar de ojos** in the twinkling of an eye

abrir² (*pp abierto*) **1** VI to open
2 VT (**a**) *(en general)* to open; *(cremallera)* to undo (**b**) *(gas, grifo)* to turn on (**c**) *Der* **a. (un) expediente** to start proceedings
3 abrirse VPR (**a**) *(en general)* to open; *Fig* **abrirse paso** to make one's way (**b**) *Fam* **¡me abro!** I'm off!

abrochar 1 VT (**a**) *(botones, camisa)* to do up; *(cinturón)* to fasten (**b**) *RP (papeles)* to staple
2 abrocharse VPR *(botones, camisa)* to do up; *(cinturón)* to fasten; **abrocharse la camisa** to do up one's shirt

abrumado, -a ADJ overwhelmed

abrumador, -a ADJ overwhelming

abrumar VT to overwhelm, to crush; **tantos problemas me abruman** all these problems are getting on top of me

abrupto, -a ADJ (**a**) *(terreno)* steep, abrupt (**b**) *Fig* abrupt, sudden

absceso NM abscess

absentismo NM *Esp* **a. laboral** *(justificado)* absence from work; *(injustificado)* absentee-ism

ábside NM *Arquit* apse

absolución NF (**a**) *Rel* absolution (**b**) *Der* acquittal

absolutamente ADV absolutely, completely; **a. nada** nothing at all

absoluto, -a ADJ absolute; **en a.** not at all, by no means

absolutorio, -a ADJ *Der* **sentencia absoluto-ria** verdict of not guilty

absolver [4] (*pp absuelto*) VT (**a**) *Rel* to absolve (**b**) *Der* to acquit

absorbente ADJ (**a**) *(papel)* absorbent (**b**) *Fig* absorbing, engrossing

absorber VT (**a**) *(líquido, gas)* to absorb (**b**) *(consumir)* to take up, to soak up (**c**) *(empresa)* to absorb by merger

absorción NF (**a**) *(de líquido, gas)* absorption (**b**) *(de empresa)* absorption (by merger)

absorto, -a ADJ absorbed, engrossed (**en** in)

abstemio, -a 1 ADJ teetotal, abstemious
2 NM,F teetotaller

abstención NF abstention

abstenerse [24] VPR to abstain (**de** from); *(privarse)* to refrain (**de** from)

abstinencia NF abstinence; **síndrome de a.** withdrawal symptoms

abstracción NF abstraction

abstracto, -a ADJ abstract

abstraer [25] **1** VT to abstract
2 abstraerse VPR to become lost in thought

abstraído, -a ADJ *(ensimismado)* absorbed, engrossed (**en** in); *(distraído)* absent-minded

absuelto, -a PP *de* **absolver**

absurdo, -a 1 ADJ absurd
2 NM absurdity, absurd thing

abuchear VT to boo, to jeer at

abucheo NM booing, jeering

abuela NF grandmother; *Fam* grandma, granny; *Fig* old woman

abuelo NM (**a**) *(hombre)* grandfather; *Fam* grandad, grandpa; *Fig* old man (**b**) **abuelos** grandparents

abulense 1 ADJ of/from Avila
2 NMF person from Avila

abulia NF apathy, lack of willpower

abultado, -a ADJ bulky, big

abultar 1 VI to be bulky; **abulta mucho** it takes up a lot of space
2 VT to exaggerate

abundancia NF abundance, plenty; *Fig* **nadar en la a.** to be rolling in money

abundante ADJ abundant, plentiful

abundar VI (**a**) *(ser abundante)* to abound, to be plentiful (**b**) **a. en** *(tener)* to be rich in

aburrido, -a ADJ (**a**) **ser a.** to be boring (**b**) **estar a.** to be bored; **estar a. de** *(harto)* to be tired of

aburrimiento NM boredom; **¡qué a.!** how boring!, what a bore!

aburrir 1 VT to bore
2 aburrirse VPR to get bored; **aburrirse como una ostra** to be bored stiff

abusado, -a ADJ *Méx Fam* smart, sharp

abusar VI (**a**) *(propasarse)* to go too far (**b**) **a. de** *(situación, persona)* to take (unfair) advantage of; *(poder, amabilidad)* to abuse too; **a. de la bebida/del tabaco** to drink/smoke too much o to excess; *Der* **a. de un niño/una mujer** to abuse a child/woman

abusivo, -a ADJ *(precio)* exorbitant

abuso NM abuse

abyecto, -a ADJ abject

a. C. *(abr* **antes de Cristo**) BC

a/c *Com (abr* **a cuenta**) on account

acá ADV (**a**) *(lugar)* here, over here; **más a.** nearer; **¡ven a.!** come here! (**b**) **de entonces a.** since then

acabado, -a 1 ADJ (**a**) *(terminado)* finished (**b**) *Fig (persona)* worn-out, spent
2 NM finish

acabar 1 VT to finish (off); *(completar)* to complete
2 VI (**a**) *(en general)* to finish, to end; **a. bien** to have a happy ending; **a. con algo** *(terminarlo)* to finish sth; *(romperlo)* to break sth (**b**) **a. de ...** to have just ...; **acaba de entrar** he has just come in; **no acaba de convencerme** I'm not quite convinced (**c**) **acabaron casándose** o

por casarse they ended up getting married; **acabó en la cárcel** he ended up in jail **3 acabarse** VPR (**a**) to finish, to come to an end; **se 'nos acabó la gasolina** we ran out of *Br* petrol *o US* gas; *Fam* **¡se acabó!** that's that!

acabóse NM *Fam* **esto es el a.** this is the end

acacia NF acacia

academia NF academy; **a. de idiomas** language school

académico, -a ADJ & NM,F academic

acaecer [33] V IMPERS to happen, to occur

acallar VT to silence

acalorado, -a ADJ (**a**) (*por calor*) hot (**b**) *Fig* (*excitado*) worked up, excited; (*debate etc*) heated, angry

acalorarse VPR (**a**) (*por calor*) to get hot (**b**) *Fig* to get excited *o* worked up

acampada NF camping; **ir de a.** to go camping; **zona de a.** camp site, *US* campground

acampanado, -a ADJ bell-shaped; (*prendas*) flared

acampar VI to camp

acantilado NM cliff

acantonar VT (*tropas*) to billet, to quarter (**en** in)

acaparar VT (**a**) (*productos*) to hoard; (*el mercado*) to corner (**b**) *Fig* to monopolize

acápite NM (**a**) *Am* (*párrafo*) paragraph (**b**) *CAm* (*título*) title

acaramelado, -a ADJ (**a**) (*color*) caramel-coloured (**b**) (*pareja*) lovey-dovey, starry-eyed

acariciar [43] VT (**a**) to caress; (*pelo, animal*) to stroke; (*esperanza*) to cherish

acarrear VT (**a**) (*transportar*) to carry, to transport (**b**) (*conllevar*) to entail

acaso ADV perhaps, maybe; **¿a. no te lo dije?** did I not tell you, by any chance?; **por si a.** just in case; **si a. viene …** if he should come …

acatamiento NM respect; (*de la ley*) observance

acatar VT to observe, to comply with

acatarrado, -a ADJ **estar a.** to have a cold

acatarrarse VPR to catch a cold

acaudalado, -a ADJ rich, wealthy

acaudillar VT to lead

acceder VI **a. a** (*consentir*) to accede to, to consent to; (*tener acceso*) to gain admittance to; *Inform* to access

accesible ADJ accessible; (*persona*) approachable

acceso NM (**a**) (*entrada*) access, entry; *Inform* **a. aleatorio** random access; *Univ* **prueba de a.** entrance examination; **a. a Internet** Internet access (**b**) (*carretera*) approach, access (**c**) *Med & Fig* fit

accesorio, -a ADJ & NM accessory

accidentado, -a 1 ADJ (*terreno*) uneven, hilly; (*viaje, vida*) eventful **2** NM,F casualty, accident victim

accidental ADJ accidental; **un encuentro a.** a chance meeting

accidente NM (**a**) (*suceso*) accident; **por a.** by chance; **a. laboral** industrial accident (**b**) *Geog* **accidentes geográficos** geographical features

acción NF (**a**) (*efecto de hacer*) action; **poner en a.** to put into action; **ponerse en a.** to go into action; **campo de a.** field of action; **película de a.** adventure movie *o Br* film (**b**) (*hecho*) deed, act; **una buena a.** a good deed (**c**) *Fin* share

accionar 1 VT (**a**) (*mecanismo, palanca*) to activate (**b**) *Am Der* to bring a suit against **2** VI (*gesticular*) to gesture, to gesticulate

accionariado NM *Fin Br* shareholders, *US* stockholders

accionista NMF *Br* shareholder, *US* stockholder

acebo NM (*hoja*) holly; (*árbol*) holly tree

acechar VT to lie in wait for; **un grave peligro nos acecha** great danger awaits us

acecho NM **estar al a. de** (*esperar*) to lie in wait for

aceite NM oil; **a. de girasol/maíz/oliva** sunflower/corn/olive oil

aceitera NF (**a**) *Culin* **aceiteras** oil and vinegar set (**b**) *Aut* oil can

aceitero, -a 1 ADJ oil **2** NM,F oil merchant

aceitoso, -a ADJ oily

aceituna NF olive; **a. rellena** stuffed olive

aceitunado, -a ADJ olive, olive-coloured

aceitunero, -a NM,F (**a**) (*recolector*) olive picker *o* harvester (**b**) (*vendedor*) olive seller

acelerado, -a ADJ accelerated, fast; *Fam Fig* **estar a.** to be hyper

acelerador NM *Aut* accelerator

acelerar VT & VI to accelerate

acelga NF chard

acento NM (**a**) (*en una palabra*) (*escrito*) accent; (*pronunciado*) stress (**b**) (*entonación*) accent

acentuar [30] **1** VT (**a**) (*palabra*) to stress (**b**) *Fig* to emphasize, to stress **2 acentuarse** VPR *Fig* to become more pronounced *o* noticeable

acepción NF meaning, sense

aceptable ADJ acceptable

aceptación NF acceptance; **tener poca a.** to have little success, not to be popular

aceptar VT to accept

acequia NF irrigation ditch *o* channel

acera NF *Br* pavement, *US* sidewalk; *Fam Pey* **ser de la a. de enfrente** to be gay *o* queer

acerbo, -a ADJ (**a**) (*áspero*) bitter (**b**) (*mordaz*) caustic, cutting

acerca ADV **a. de** about

acercamiento NM bringing together, coming together; *Pol* rapprochement

acercar [44] **1** VT to bring near *o* nearer, to bring (over); *Fig* to bring together; **¿te acerco**

a casa? can I give you a *Br* lift *o US* ride home?
  2 acercarse VPR (**a**) **acercarse (a)** to approach (**b**) *(ir)* to go; *(venir)* to come

acerico NM pincushion

acero NM steel; **a. inoxidable** stainless steel

acérrimo, -a ADJ *(partidario)* staunch; *(enemigo)* bitter

acertado, -a ADJ (**a**) *(solución)* right, correct; *(decisión)* wise (**b**) **no estuviste muy a. al decir eso** it wasn't very wise of you to say that

acertante 1 NMF winner
  2 ADJ winning

acertar [1] **1** VT *(pregunta)* to get right; *(adivinar)* to guess correctly; **a. las quinielas** to win the pools
  2 VI to be right; **acertó con la calle que buscaba** she found the street she was looking for

acertijo NM riddle

acervo NM **a. cultural** cultural tradition *o* heritage

achacar [44] VT to attribute (**a** to)

achacoso, -a ADJ ailing, unwell

achaque NM ailment, complaint

achicar [44] **1** VT (**a**) *(amilanar)* to intimidate (**b**) *(encoger)* to reduce, to make smaller (**c**) *(barco)* to bale out
  2 achicarse VPR (**a**) *(amilanarse)* to lose heart (**b**) *(encogerse)* to get smaller

achicharrar 1 VT to burn to a crisp
  2 achicharrarse VPR *Fam (de calor)* to be boiling (hot)

achicoria NF chicory

achinado, -a ADJ (**a**) *(ojos)* slanting (**b**) *RP (aindiado)* Indian-looking

acholado, -a ADJ *Bol, Chile, Perú Pey (mestizo) (físicamente)* Indian-looking; *(culturalmente)* = who has adopted Indian ways

achuchar VT *Fam (empujar)* to shove; *(abrazar)* to hug

achuchón NM *Fam (empujón)* push, shove; *(abrazo)* big hug

aciago, -a ADJ ill-fated, fateful

acicalado, -a ADJ well-dressed, smart

acicalarse VPR to dress up, to smarten up

acicate NM spur, incentive

acidez NF *(de sabor)* sharpness, sourness; *Quím* acidity; *Med* **a. de estómago** heartburn

ácido, -a 1 ADJ *(sabor)* sharp, tart; *Quím* acidic; *Fig (tono)* harsh
  2 NM *Quím* acid

acierto NM *(buena decisión)* good choice *o* idea; **con gran a.** very wisely

aclamación NF acclamation, acclaim

aclamar VT to acclaim

aclaración NF explanation, clarification

aclarado NM *Esp* rinsing, rinse

aclarar 1 VT (**a**) *(explicar)* to clarify, to explain; *(color)* to lighten, to make lighter (**b**) *Esp (enjuagar)* to rinse

  2 V IMPERS *Met* to clear (up)
  3 aclararse VPR (**a**) *(decidirse)* to make up one's mind; *(entender)* to understand (**b**) *Met* to clear (up)

aclaratorio, -a ADJ explanatory

aclimatación NF *Br* acclimatization, *US* acclimation

aclimatar 1 VT *Br* to acclimatize, *US* to acclimate (**a** to)
  2 aclimatarse VPR *Fig* **aclimatarse a algo** to get used to sth

acné NF acne

acobardar 1 VT to frighten
  2 acobardarse VPR to get frightened, to lose one's nerve

acodarse VPR to lean (**en** on)

acogedor, -a ADJ cosy, warm

acoger [53] **1** VT (**a**) *(recibir)* to receive; *(a invitado)* to welcome (**b**) *(persona desvalida)* to take in; *(en familia)* to foster
  2 acogerse VPR *Fig* **acogerse a** to take refuge in; *(amnistía)* to avail oneself of; **acogerse a la ley** to have recourse to the law

acogida NF (**a**) *(de persona)* reception, welcome (**b**) *(familiar)* fostering; **familia/ hogar de a.** foster parents/home

acojonado, -a ADJ *Esp muy Fam* shit-scared

acojonante ADJ *Esp muy Fam* damn *o Br* bloody great *o* terrific

acojonarse VPR *Esp muy Fam* to shit oneself, to be shit-scared

acolchar VT *(rellenar)* to pad; *(prenda)* to quilt

acometer 1 VT (**a**) *(emprender)* to undertake (**b**) *(atacar)* to attack
  2 VI *(embestir)* **a. contra** to hurtle into

acometida NF attack

acomodado, -a ADJ well-off, well-to-do

acomodador, -a NM,F *(hombre)* usher; *(mujer)* usherette

acomodar 1 VT (**a**) *(alojar)* to lodge, to accommodate (**b**) *(en cine etc)* to find a place for
  2 acomodarse VPR (**a**) *(ponerse cómodo)* to make oneself comfortable (**b**) *(adaptarse)* to adapt

acomodaticio, -a ADJ accommodating, easygoing

acompañamiento NM *Culin & Mús* accompaniment

acompañante 1 NMF companion
  2 ADJ accompanying

acompañar VT (**a**) *(persona)* to accompany; **le acompañó hasta la puerta** she saw him to the door; **me acompañó al médico** he came with me to see the doctor; **¿te acompaño a casa?** can I walk you home?; *Fml* **le acompaño en el sentimiento** my condolences (**b**) *(adjuntar)* to enclose

acompasado, -a ADJ *(crecimiento, desarrollo)* steady; *(pasos)* measured

acomplejado, -a ADJ estar a. to have a complex (por about)

acomplejar 1 VT a. a algn to give sb a complex 2 acomplejarse VPR a. por to develop a complex about

acondicionado, -a ADJ aire a. air conditioning

acondicionador NM conditioner

acondicionar VT to prepare, to set up; (mejorar) to improve; (cabello) to condition

acongojar VT to distress

aconsejable ADJ advisable

aconsejar VT to advise

acontecer [33] V IMPERS to happen, to take place

acontecimiento NM event

acopio NM store, stock; hacer a. de (existencias) to stock up on; (valor, paciencia) to summon up

acoplar 1 VT (a) (encajar) to fit (together), to join (b) Téc to couple, to connect 2 acoplarse VPR (nave espacial) to dock

acorazado, -a 1 ADJ armoured, armour-plated 2 NM battleship

acordado, -a ADJ agreed; según lo a. as agreed

acordar [2] **1** VT to agree; (decidir) to decide 2 acordarse VPR to remember; no me acuerdo (de Silvia) I can't remember (Silvia)

acorde 1 ADJ in agreement 2 NM Mús chord

acordeón NM (a) (instrument) accordion (b) Col, Méx Fam (en examen) crib

acordonado, -a ADJ cordoned off

acordonar VT (zona) to cordon off

acorralar VT to corner

acortar VT to shorten; a. distancias to cut down the distance

acosar VT to harass; Fig a. a algn a preguntas to bombard sb with questions

acoso NM harassment; a. sexual sexual harassment

acostado, -a ADJ (tumbado) lying down; (en la cama) in bed

acostar [2] **1** VT to put to bed 2 acostarse VPR to go to bed; Fam acostarse con algn to sleep with sb, to go to bed with sb

acostumbrado, -a ADJ (a) (habitual) usual, customary; es lo a. it is the custom (b) (habituado) a. al frío/calor used to the cold/heat

acostumbrar 1 VI a. a (soler) to be in the habit of 2 VT a. a algn a algo (habituar) to get sb used to sth 3 acostumbrarse VPR (habituarse) acostumbrarse a algo to get used to sth

acotación NF (a) (en escrito) (marginal) note; Teatro stage direction (b) (en mapa) elevation mark

acotamiento NM Méx (arcén) Br hard shoulder, US shoulder

acotar VT (a) (área) to enclose; Fig (tema) to delimit (b) (texto) to annotate (c) (mapa) to mark with elevations

ácrata ADJ & NM,F anarchist

acre 1 ADJ (a) (sabor) sour, bitter; (olor) acrid (b) (palabras) bitter, harsh; (crítica) biting 2 NM (medida) acre

acrecentar [1] VT to increase

acreditación NF (de periodista) press card; (de diplomático) credentials

acreditado ADJ (a) (médico, abogado) distinguished; (marca) reputable (b) (embajador, representante) accredited

acreditar VT (a) (certificar) to certify; (autorizar) to authorize, to entitle (b) (demostrar) to prove, to confirm (c) (periodista, embajador) to accredit (d) (dar fama a) to be a credit to (e) Fin to credit

acreedor, -a NM,F Com creditor

acribillar VT to riddle, to pepper; a. a algn a balazos to riddle sb with bullets; Fig a. a algn a preguntas to fire questions at sb

acrílico, -a ADJ acrylic

acriollarse VPR Am to adopt local ways

acritud NF acrimony

acrobacia NF acrobatics sing

acróbata NM,F acrobat

acta NF (a) (de reunión) minutes, record (b) (certificado) certificate, official document; a. notarial affidavit; A. Única (Europea) Single European Act

> Takes the masculine articles el and un.

actitud NF attitude

activar VT to activate

actividad NF activity

activista NM,F activist

activo, -a 1 ADJ active; en a. on active service 2 NM Fin assets

acto NM (a) (hecho) act, action; a. sexual sexual intercourse; en el a. at once; a. seguido immediately afterwards; Mil en a. de servicio in action; hacer a. de presencia to put in an appearance (b) (ceremonia) ceremony (c) Teatro act

actor NM actor

actriz NF actress

actuación NF (a) (de artista) performance (b) (conducta, proceder) conduct, behaviour

actual ADJ current, present; (al día) up-to-date; un tema muy a. a very topical subject

actualidad NF current situation; la a. deportiva the sports news; en la a. at present; estar de a. to be topical; temas de a. topical subjects

actualizar [40] VT to update, to bring up to date; Inform (software, hardware) to upgrade

actualmente ADV (hoy en día) nowadays, these days; (ahora) at the moment, at present

Observa que las palabras inglesas **actual** y **actually** son falsos amigos y no son la traducción de las palabras españolas **actual** y **actualmente**. En inglés, **actual** significa "real, verdadero", y **actually** significa "en realidad".

actuar [30] VI (**a**) *(obrar)* to act; **a. como** *o* **de** to act as (**b**) *Cin & Teatro* to perform, to act

acuarela NF watercolour

Acuario NM Aquarius

acuario NM aquarium

acuartelar VT to confine to barracks

acuático, -a ADJ aquatic; **esquí a.** water-skiing

acuchillar VT to knife, to stab

acuciante ADJ urgent, pressing

acuciar [43] VT (**a**) *(instar)* to goad; **el deseo me acuciaba** I was driven by desire (**b**) *(ser urgente)* **le acucia encontrar un trabajo** he urgently needs to find a job

acudir VI *(ir)* to go; *(venir)* to come, to arrive; **nadie acudió en su ayuda** nobody came to help him; **no sé dónde** I don't know where to turn

acueducto NM aqueduct

acuerdo NM agreement; **¡de a.!** all right!, O.K.!; **de a. con** in accordance with; **de común a.** by common consent; **estar de a. en algo** to agree on sth; **ponerse de a.** to agree; **a. marco** framework agreement

acumulación NF accumulation

acumular 1 VT to accumulate
 2 acumularse VPR to accumulate, to build up

acunar VT *(en cuna)* to rock; *(en brazos)* to cradle

acuñar VT *(moneda)* to mint; *(frase)* to coin

acuoso, -a ADJ watery; *(jugoso)* juicy

acupuntura NF acupuncture

acurrucarse [44] VPR to curl up, to snuggle up

acusación NF accusation; *Der* charge

acusado, -a 1 NM,F accused, defendant
 2 ADJ *(marcado)* marked, noticeable

acusar 1 VT (**a**) *(inculpar)* to accuse (**de** of); *Der* to charge (**de** with) (**b**) *(golpe etc)* to feel; *Fig* **su cara acusaba el cansancio** his exhaustion showed in his face (**c**) *Com* **a. recibo** to acknowledge receipt
 2 acusarse VPR (**a**) *(acentuarse)* to become more pronounced (**b**) *(notarse)* to show

acuse NM **a. de recibo** acknowledgment of receipt

acusica ADJ & NMF *Fam* telltale

acústica NF acoustics *sing*

acústico, -a ADJ acoustic

adán NM *Fam* untidy *o* slovenly person

adaptable ADJ adaptable

adaptación NF adaptation

adaptador NM adapter

adaptar 1 VT to adapt
 2 adaptarse VPR to adjust (**a** to)

adecentar VT to tidy (up), to clean (up)

adecuado, -a ADJ appropriate, suitable

adecuar [47] VT to adapt

adefesio NM *(persona)* fright, sight; *(cosa)* monstrosity

a. de J.C. *(abr antes de Jesucristo)* BC

adelantado, -a ADJ (**a**) *(avanzado, precoz)* advanced (**b**) *(reloj)* fast (**c**) **pagar por a.** to pay in advance

adelantamiento NM overtaking; **hacer un a.** to overtake

adelantar 1 VT (**a**) *Aut* to overtake (**b**) *(avanzar)* to move *o* bring forward; *(reloj)* to put forward (**c**) *(fecha)* to bring forward (**d**) *(dinero)* to pay in advance (**e**) *(información)* **no podemos a. nada más por el momento** we can't tell you *o* say any more for the time being (**f**) *(conseguir)* **¿qué adelantas con eso?** what do you hope to gain *o* achieve by that?
 2 VI (**a**) *(progresar)* to make progress (**b**) *(reloj)* to be fast (**c**) *(en carretera)* to overtake
 3 adelantarse VPR (**a**) *(ir delante)* to go ahead (**b**) *(reloj)* to gain, to be fast (**c**) **el verano se ha adelantado** we are having an early summer (**d**) **adelantarse a los acontecimientos** to jump the gun

adelante 1 ADV forward; **más a.** *(lugar)* further on; *(tiempo)* later; **seguir a.** to keep going, to carry on; **llevar a. un plan** to carry out a plan
 2 INTERJ **¡a!** come in!

adelanto NM (**a**) *(técnico, de dinero)* advance (**b**) **el reloj lleva diez minutos de a.** the watch is ten minutes fast

adelfa NF oleander, rosebay

adelgazamiento NM slimming

adelgazar [40] VI to slim, to lose weight

ademán NM *(con las manos)* gesture; *(con la cara)* face, expression

además ADV moreover, furthermore; **a., no lo he visto nunca** what's more, I've never seen him; **a. de él** besides him

adentrarse VPR **a. en** *(bosque)* to go deep into; *(asunto)* to study thoroughly

adentro 1 ADV *(dentro)* inside; **mar a.** out to sea; **tierra a.** inland
 2 adentros NMPL **decir algo para sus adentros** to say sth to oneself

adepto, -a NM,F follower, supporter

Observa que la palabra inglesa **adept** es un falso amigo y no es la traducción de la palabra española **adepto**. En inglés, **adept** significa "experto".

aderezar [40] VT *(comida)* to season; *(ensalada)* to dress

aderezo NM *(de comida)* seasoning; *(de ensalada)* dressing

adeudar 1 VT to owe; *Fin* to debit
  2 adeudarse VPR to get into debt
adherencia NF adherence; *Aut* roadholding
adherente ADJ adhesive, sticky
adherir [5] **1** VT to stick on
  2 adherirse VPR **adherirse a** to adhere to; *(partido)* to join
adhesión NF adhesion; *(a partido)* joining; *(a teoría)* adherence
adhesivo, -a ADJ & NM adhesive
adicción NF addiction; **crear a.** to be addictive
adición NF addition
adicional ADJ additional
adicto, -a 1 NM,F addict
  2 ADJ addicted (**a** to)
adiestrar VT to train
adinerado, -a ADJ wealthy, rich
adiós *(pl* **adioses) 1** INTERJ goodbye; *Fam* bye-bye; *(al cruzarse)* hello
  2 NM goodbye
aditivo, -a ADJ & NM additive
adivinanza NF riddle, puzzle
adivinar VT to guess; **a. el pensamiento de algn** to read sb's mind
adivino, -a NM,F fortune-teller
adjetivo, -a 1 NM adjective
  2 ADJ adjectival
adjudicación NF award; *(en subasta)* sale
adjudicar [44] **1** VT (**a**) *(premio, contrato)* to award (**b**) *(en subasta)* to sell
  2 adjudicarse VPR to appropriate, to take over
adjuntar VT to enclose
adjunto, -a 1 ADJ (**a**) *(en sobre)* enclosed, attached (**b**) *Educ* assistant
  2 NM,F *Educ* assistant teacher
adm., admón. *(abr* **administración)** admin.
administración NF (**a**) *(gobierno)* **la A.** *Br* Government, *US* the Administration; *Pol* **a. central** central government; **a. pública** civil service (**b**) *(de empresa)* administration, management (**c**) *(oficina)* (branch) office
administrador, -a 1 NM,F administrator
  2 NM *Inform* **a. de archivos** file manager
administrar 1 VT (**a**) *(dirigir)* to run, to manage (**b**) *(medicamento, sacramentos)* to administer
  2 administrarse VPR to manage one's own money
administrativo, -a 1 ADJ administrative
  2 NM,F office worker
admirable ADJ admirable
admiración NF (**a**) *(sentimiento)* admiration; **causar a.** to impress (**b**) *Ling Br* exclamation mark, *US* exclamation point
admirador, -a NM,F admirer
admirar 1 VT (**a**) *(persona, obra)* to admire (**b**) *(sorprender)* to amaze, to astonish
  2 admirarse VPR to be amazed, to be astonished
admisible ADJ admissible, acceptable

admisión NF admission; **reservado el derecho de a.** *(en letrero)* the management reserves the right to refuse admission
admitir VT (**a**) *(dejar entrar)* to admit, to let in (**b**) *(aceptar)* to accept; **no se admiten cheques** *(en letrero)* no cheques accepted (**c**) *(tolerar)* to allow (**d**) *(reconocer)* to admit, to acknowledge; **admito que mentí** I admit that I lied
admón. *(abr* **administración)** admin.
admonición NF warning
ADN NM *(abr* **ácido desoxirribonucleico)** DNA
adobar VT *Culin* to marinate
adobe NM adobe
adobo NM marinade
adoctrinar VT to indoctrinate
adolecer [33] VI **a. de** *(enfermedad)* to suffer from; *(defecto)* to be guilty of
adolescencia NF adolescence
adolescente ADJ & NMF adolescent
adonde ADV where
adónde ADV INTERR where (to)?
adondequiera ADV wherever
adopción NF adoption
adoptar VT to adopt
adoptivo, -a ADJ *(hijo)* adopted; *(padres)* adoptive; *Fig* **país a.** country of adoption
adoquín NM cobble, paving stone
adorable ADJ adorable
adoración NF adoration; **sentir a. por algn** to worship sb
adorar VT (**a**) *Rel* to worship (**b**) *Fig* to adore
adormecer [33] **1** VT to lull to sleep
  2 adormecerse VPR to doze off
adormecido, -a ADJ sleepy, drowsy
adormilarse VPR to doze
adornar VT to adorn, to decorate
adorno NM decoration, adornment; **de a.** decorative
adosado, -a ADJ adjacent; *(casa)* semidetached
adquirir [31] VT to acquire; *(comprar)* to purchase
adquisición NF acquisition; *(compra)* buy, purchase
adquisitivo, -a ADJ **poder a.** purchasing power
adrede ADV deliberately, on purpose
adrenalina NF adrenalin
Adriático ADJ & NM **el (Mar) A.** the Adriatic (Sea)
adscribir *(pp* **adscrito) 1** VT (**a**) *(asignar)* to assign (**b**) *(a un trabajo)* to appoint
  2 adscribirse VPR **adscribirse a** *(grupo, partido)* to become a member of; *(ideología)* to subscribe to
aduana NF customs
aduanero, -a 1 ADJ customs
  2 NM,F customs officer

aducir [10] VT *(motivo, pretexto)* to give

adueñarse VPR **a. de** to take over; *(sujeto: pánico)* to take hold of

aduje PT INDEF *de* aducir

adulación NF adulation

adular VT to flatter

adulterar VT to adulterate

adulterio NM adultery

adúltero, -a 1 ADJ adulterous
2 NM,F *(hombre)* adulterer; *(mujer)* adulteress

adulto, -a ADJ & NM,F adult

adusto, -a ADJ harsh, severe

aduzco INDIC PRES *de* aducir

advenedizo, -a ADJ & NM,F upstart

advenimiento NM advent, coming

adverbio NM adverb

adversario, -a 1 NM,F adversary, opponent
2 ADJ opposing

adversidad NF adversity

adverso, -a ADJ *(condiciones)* adverse; *(suerte)* bad; *(viento)* unfavourable

advertencia NF warning

advertido, -a ADJ warned; *(informado)* informed; **estás** *o* **quedas a.** you've been warned

advertir [5] VT (**a**) *(de problema)* to warn; *(informar)* to inform, to advise; *Fam* **te advierto que yo tampoco lo vi** mind you, I didn't see it either (**b**) *(notar)* to realize, to notice

adviento NM Advent

adyacente ADJ adjacent

aéreo, -a ADJ *(del aire)* aerial; *(de la aviación)* **tráfico a.** air traffic; *Com* **por vía aerea** by air

aeróbic NM aerobics *sing*

aerodinámico, -a ADJ aerodynamic; **de línea aerodinámica** streamlined

aeródromo NM aerodrome

aeromodelismo NM aeroplane modelling

aeromozo, -a NM,F *Am* air steward; *(mujer)* air hostess

aeronáutica NF aeronautics *sing*

aeronáutico, -a ADJ **la industria aeronáutica** the aeronautics industry

aeronave NF airship

aeroplano NM light aeroplane

aeropuerto NM airport

aerosol NM aerosol

aerostático, -a ADJ **globo a.** hot-air balloon

afable ADJ affable

afamado, -a ADJ famous, well-known

afán NM (**a**) *(esfuerzo)* effort (**b**) *(celo)* zeal

afanador, -a NM,F (**a**) *Méx (empleado)* (office) cleaner (**b**) *Méx, RP Fam (ladrón)* crook, thief

afanar 1 VT *Fam (robar)* to pinch
2 afanarse VPR **a. por conseguir algo** to do one's best to achieve sth

afanoso, -a ADJ keen, eager

afección NF disease

afectación NF affectation

afectado, -a ADJ affected

afectar VT **a. a** to affect; **le afectó mucho** she was deeply affected; **nos afecta a todos** it concerns all of us

afectivo ADJ *(emocional)* emotional; **tener problemas afectivos** to have emotional problems

afecto NM affection; **tomarle a. a algn** to become fond of sb

afectuoso, -a ADJ affectionate

afeitado NM shave

afeitar 1 VT to shave
2 afeitarse VPR *(uno mismo)* to shave; **se afeitó la barba** he shaved his beard off

afeminado, -a ADJ effeminate

aferrado, -a ADJ **a.** clinging to

aferrarse VPR to clutch, to cling; *Fig* **a. a una creencia** to cling to a belief

Afganistán N Afghanistan

afgano, -a ADJ & NM,F Afghan

afianzamiento NM strengthening, reinforcement

afianzar [40] **1** VT to strengthen, to reinforce
2 afianzarse VPR *(persona)* to establish oneself

afiche NM *Am* poster

afición NF (**a**) *(interés)* liking; **tiene a. por la música** he is fond of music (**b**) *(aficionados)* **la a.** the fans

aficionado, -a 1 NM,F (**a**) *(interesado)* enthusiast; **un a. a la música** a music lover (**b**) *(no profesional)* amateur
2 ADJ (**a**) *(interesado)* keen, fond; **ser a. a algo** to be fond of sth (**b**) *(no profesional)* amateur

aficionarse VPR to become fond (**a** of), to take a liking (**a** to)

afilado, -a ADJ sharp

afilar VT to sharpen

afiliación NF *(a organización)* membership

afiliado, -a NM,F member

afiliarse [43] VPR to become a member

afín ADJ *(semejante)* kindred, similar; *(relacionado)* related

afinar VT (**a**) *(puntería)* to sharpen (**b**) *(instrumento)* to tune

afincarse [44] VPR to settle (**en** in)

afinidad NF affinity

afirmación NF affirmation; **afirmaciones** *(declaración)* statement

afirmar VT (**a**) *(aseverar)* to state, to declare (**b**) *(afianzar)* to strengthen, to reinforce

afirmativo, -a ADJ affirmative; **en caso a. ...** if the answer is yes ...

aflicción NF suffering, sorrow

afligir [57] **1** VT to afflict
2 afligirse VPR to grieve, to be distressed

aflojar 1 VT to loosen
2 VI *(viento etc)* to abate, to die down

3 aflojarse VPR to come o work loose; *(rueda)* to go down

aflorar VI *(río)* to come to the surface; *(sentimiento)* to surface, to show

afluencia NF inflow, influx; **gran a. de público** great numbers of people

afluente NM tributary

afluir [37] VI to flow (**a** into)

afónico, -a ADJ **estar a.** to have lost one's voice

aforismo NM aphorism

aforo NM *(capacidad)* seating capacity

afortunadamente ADV fortunately, luckily

afortunado, -a ADJ fortunate; **las Islas Afortunadas** the Canaries

afrenta NF *Fml* affront

África N Africa

africano, -a ADJ & NM,F African

afrodisíaco, -a ADJ & NM aphrodisiac

afrontar VT to confront, to face; **a. las consecuencias** to face the consequences

afrutado, -a ADJ fruity

afuera 1 ADV outside; **la parte de a.** the outside; **más a.** further out; **salir a.** to come o go out

2 afueras NFPL outskirts

agachar 1 VT to lower

2 agacharse VPR to crouch down

agalla NF (a) *(de pez)* gill (b) *(valor)* guts, pluck; **tiene agallas** she's got guts

agarradera NF *Am* handle

agarrado, -a ADJ (a) *Fam (persona)* stingy, tight (b) **baile a.** cheek-to-cheek dancing

agarrar 1 VT (a) *(asir)* to grasp, to seize; **agárralo fuerte** hold it tight (b) *Am (tomar)* to take; **a. un taxi** to take a taxi (c) *Fam (pillar)* to catch; **a. una borrachera** to get drunk o *Br* pissed

2 agarrarse VPR to hold on; **agárrate bien** hold tight

agarrotarse VPR (a) *(músculo)* to stiffen (b) *(máquina)* to seize up

agasajar VT to smother with attentions

ágata NF agate

Takes the masculine articles **el** and **un**.

agazaparse VPR to crouch (down)

agencia NF agency; *(sucursal)* branch; **a. de viajes** travel agency; **a. de seguros** insurance agency; **a. inmobiliaria** *Br* estate agent's, *US* real estate office

agenciarse [43] VPR to get hold of, to fix oneself up with

agenda NF diary

agente NMF agent; **a. de bolsa** stockbroker; **a. de policía** *(hombre)* policeman; *(mujer)* policewoman; **a. de seguros** insurance broker

agigantado, -a ADJ **a pasos agigantados** by leaps and bounds

ágil ADJ agile

agilidad NF agility

agilización NF speeding up

agilizar [40] VT *(trámites)* to speed up

agitación NF *(intranquilidad)* restlessness; *(social, político)* unrest

agitado, -a ADJ agitated; *(persona)* anxious; *(mar)* rough; **una vida muy agitada** a very hectic life

agitar 1 VT *(botella)* to shake; *(multitud)* to agitate

2 agitarse VPR *(persona)* to become agitated; *(mar)* to become rough

aglomeración NF agglomeration; *(de gente)* crowd

aglomerar 1 VT to bring together

2 aglomerarse VPR to mass o gather together

agnóstico, -a ADJ & NM,F agnostic

agobiado, -a ADJ *Fig* **a. de problemas** snowed under with problems; *Fig* **a. de trabajo** up to one's eyes in work

agobiante ADJ *(trabajo)* overwhelming; *(lugar)* claustrophobic; *(calor)* oppressive; *(persona)* tiresome, tiring

agobiar [43] **1** VT to overwhelm

2 agobiarse VPR *(con problemas)* to get over-anxious; *(por el calor)* to suffocate

agobio NM (a) *(angustia)* anxiety (b) *(sofoco)* suffocation

agolparse VPR to crowd, to throng

agonía NF dying breath, last gasp

agonizante ADJ dying

agonizar [40] VI to be dying

agosto NM August; *Fam* **hacer su a.** to make a packet

agotado, -a ADJ (a) *(cansado)* exhausted, worn out (b) *Com (entradas)* sold out; *(libro, disco)* out of stock

agotador, -a ADJ exhausting

agotamiento NM exhaustion

agotar 1 VT (a) *(cansar)* to exhaust, to wear out (b) *(acabar)* to exhaust, to use up *(completely)*

2 agotarse VPR (a) *(acabarse)* to run out, to be used up; *(libro, disco, entradas)* to sell out (b) *(persona)* to become exhausted o tired out

agraciado, -a ADJ (a) *(atractivo)* attractive, fetching (b) *(ganador)* winning; **ser a. con** to win

agradable ADJ pleasant

agradar VI to please; **no me agrada** I don't like it

agradecer [33] VT (a) *(dar las gracias)* to thank for; **les agradezco su atención** (I) thank you for your attention; **te lo agradezco mucho** thank you very much (b) *(estar agradecido)* to be grateful to; **te agradecería que vinieras** I'd be grateful if you'd come (c) *(uso impers)* **siempre se agradece un descanso** a rest is always welcome

agradecido, -a ADJ grateful; **le estoy muy a.** I am very grateful to you

agradecimiento NM gratitude

agrado NM pleasure; **no es de su a.** it isn't to his liking

agrandar 1 VT to enlarge, to make larger
  2 agrandarse VPR to enlarge, to become larger

agrario, -a ADJ *(reforma)* agrarian; *(producto, política)* agricultural

agravamiento NM aggravation

agravante *Der* **1** ADJ aggravating
  2 NM aggravating circumstance

agravar 1 VT to aggravate
  2 agravarse VPR to worsen, to get worse

agraviar [43] VT to offend, to insult

agravio NM offence, insult

agredir VT to assault

agregación NF addition

agregado, -a 1 ADJ *Educ* **profesor a.** *(escuela)* secondary school teacher; *Univ* assistant teacher
  2 NM,F *Pol* attaché

agregar [42] **1** VT **(a)** *(añadir)* to add **(b)** *(destinar)* to appoint
  2 agregarse VPR **agregarse a** to join

agresión NF aggression

agresividad NF aggressiveness

agresivo, -a ADJ aggressive

agresor, -a 1 NM,F aggressor, attacker
  2 ADJ attacking

agreste ADJ *(abrupto, rocoso)* rough, rugged; *Fig (basto, rudo)* coarse, uncouth

agriarse VPR to turn sour

agrícola ADJ agricultural

agricultor, -a NM,F farmer

agricultura NF agriculture; **a. biológica** o **ecológica** organic farming

agridulce ADJ bittersweet

agrietar 1 VT to crack; *(piel, labios)* to chap
  2 agrietarse VPR to crack; *(piel)* to get chapped

agringarse [42] VPR *Am Pey* = to become like a North American or European

agrio, -a 1 ADJ sour
  2 agrios NMPL citrus fruits

agrónomo, -a NM,F agronomist

agropecuario, -a ADJ farming, agricultural

agroturismo NM rural tourism

agrupación NF association

agrupar 1 VT to group
  2 agruparse VPR **(a)** *(congregarse)* to group together, to form a group **(b)** *(asociarse)* to associate

agua NF water; **a. potable** drinking water; **a. corriente/del grifo** running/tap water; **a. dulce/salada** fresh/salt water; **a. mineral sin/ con gas** still/fizzy o sparkling mineral water; **a. de colonia** (eau de) cologne; *Fig* **estar con el a. al cuello** to be up to one's neck in it;

aguas jurisdiccionales territorial waters; **aguas residuales** sewage

> Takes the masculine articles **el** and **un**.

aguacate NM *(árbol)* avocado; *(fruto)* avocado (pear)

aguacero NM shower, downpour

aguado, -a ADJ watered down

aguafiestas NMF INV spoilsport, wet blanket

aguafuerte NM **(a)** *Arte* etching **(b)** *Quím* nitric acid

aguamala NF *Carib, Col, Ecuad, Méx* jellyfish

aguamarina NF aquamarine

aguamiel NM o NF **(a)** *Am (bebida)* = water mixed with honey or cane syrup **(b)** *Carib, Méx (jugo)* maguey juice

aguanieve NF sleet

aguantar 1 VT **(a)** *(soportar)* to tolerate; **no lo aguanto más** I can't stand it any longer **(b)** *(sostener)* to support, to hold; **aguanta esto** hold this **(c)** **aguanta la respiración** hold your breath
  2 aguantarse VPR **(a)** *(contenerse)* to restrain oneself; *(lágrimas)* to hold back; **no pude aguantarme la risa** I couldn't help laughing **(b)** *(resignarse)* to resign oneself

aguante NM endurance; **tener mucho a.** *(ser paciente)* to be very patient; *(tener resistencia)* to be strong, to have a lot of stamina

aguar [45] VT to water down; *Fig* **a. la fiesta a algn** to spoil sb's fun

aguardar 1 VT to await
  2 VI to wait

aguardiente NM liquor, brandy

aguarrás NM turpentine

aguatero, -a NM,F *Am* water seller

aguaviva NF *RP* jellyfish

agudeza NF **(a)** *(de vista, olfato)* keenness; *(mental)* sharpness, shrewdness **(b)** *(dicho ingenioso)* witticism

agudización NF *(empeoramiento)* worsening

agudizar [40] **1** VT to intensify, to make more acute
  2 agudizarse VPR to intensify, to become more acute

agudo, -a ADJ **(a)** *(vista, olfato)* keen; *(sonido)* high, high-pitched; *(dolor)* sharp; *(crisis, problema, enfermedad)* serious, acute **(b)** *(perspicaz)* keen, sharp; *(ingenioso)* witty

agüero NM **de mal a.** that bodes ill

aguijón NM sting; *Fig (estímulo)* spur

águila NF **(a)** eagle; **á. real** golden eagle **(b)** *Méx (de moneda)* heads; **¿á. o sol?** heads or tails?

> Takes the masculine articles **el** and **un**.

aguileño, -a ADJ aquiline; **nariz aguileña** aquiline nose

aguinaldo NM = tip given at Christmas, *Br* Christmas box; **pedir el a.** to go carol singing

agüita NF *Chile* (herbal) tea

aguja NF (**a**) *(de coser, jeringuilla)* needle; *(de reloj)* hand; *(de tocadiscos)* stylus (**b**) *Arquit* spire (**c**) *Ferroc* point, *US* switch

agujerear VT to make holes in

agujero NM (**a**) *(hueco, abertura)* hole; **a. negro** black hole (**b**) *Econ* deficit, shortfall

agujetas NFPL (**a**) *Esp (en los músculos)* stiffness; **tener a.** to be stiff (**b**) *Méx* shoelaces

agur INTERJ *Fam* bye!, see you!

aguzar [40] VT (**a**) *(afilar)* to sharpen (**b**) *Fig* **a. el oído** to prick up one's ears; **a. la vista** to look attentively; **aguzar el ingenio** to sharpen one's wits

ahí ADV there; **está** there he/she/it is; **ve por a.** go that way; **está por a.** it's over there; **setenta o por a.** seventy or thereabouts; **de a.** hence

ahijado, -a NM,F godchild; *(niño)* godson; *(niña)* goddaughter; **ahijados** godchildren

ahínco NM eagerness; **con a.** eagerly

ahíto, -a ADJ **estar a. de algo** *(saciado)* to be full of sth; *(harto)* to have had enough of sth

ahogado, -a 1 ADJ (**a**) *(en líquido)* drowned; **morir a.** to drown (**b**) *(asfixiado)* suffocated
2 NM,F drowned person

ahogar [42] **1** VT (**a**) *(en líquido)* to drown (**b**) *(asfixiar)* to suffocate
2 ahogarse VPR (**a**) *(en líquido)* to drown, to be drowned; *Fig* **ahogarse en un vaso de agua** to make a mountain out of a molehill (**b**) *(asfixiarse)* to suffocate (**c**) *(motor)* to be flooded

ahondar 1 VT to deepen
2 VI to go deep; *Fig* **a. en un problema** to go into a problem in depth

ahora 1 ADV (**a**) *(en este momento)* now; **a. mismo** right now; **de a. en adelante** from now on; **por a.** for the time being (**b**) **a. voy** I'm coming; **a. vuelvo** I'll be back in a minute (**c**) **hasta a.** *(hasta el momento)* until now, so far; *(hasta luego)* see you later
2 CONJ **a. bien** *(sin embargo)* however; *(y bueno)* well then

ahorcado, -a 1 NM,F hanged person
2 ADJ hanged

ahorcar [44] **1** VT to hang
2 ahorcarse VPR to hang oneself

ahorita, ahoritita ADV *Am salvo RP Fam* (**a**) *(en el presente)* (right) now; **a. voy** I'm just coming (**b**) *(pronto)* in a second (**c**) *(hace poco)* just now, a few minutes ago

ahorrador, -a ADJ thrifty

ahorrar 1 VT to save
2 ahorrarse VPR **ahórrate los comentarios** keep your comments to yourself

ahorrativo, -a ADJ thrifty

ahorro NM (**a**) *(acción)* saving; **a. energético** energy saving (**b**) **ahorros** savings; *Fin* **caja de ahorros** savings bank

ahuecar [44] VT (**a**) *(tronco)* to hollow out; *Fam* **a. el ala** to clear off, to beat it (**b**) *(voz)* to deepen

ahuevado, -a ADJ *CAm, Ecuad, Perú Fam (tonto)* **estar a. con algo** to be bowled over by sth

ahumado, -a ADJ *(cristal, jamón)* smoked; *(bacon)* smoky; **salmón a.** smoked salmon

ahumar 1 VT to smoke
2 ahumarse VPR to get all smoky

ahuyentar VT to scare away

aindiado, -a ADJ Indian *(used of American Indians)*

airado, -a ADJ angry

airar 1 VT to anger
2 airarse VPR to get angry

airbag ['erβaɣ, air'βaɣ] *(pl* **airbags***)* NM airbag

aire NM (**a**) air; **a. acondicionado** air conditioning; **al a.** *(hacia arriba)* into the air; *(al descubierto)* uncovered; **al a. libre** in the open air; **en el a.** *(pendiente)* in the air; *Rad* on the air; **saltar por los aires** to blow up; **tomar el a.** to get some fresh air; **necesito un cambio de aires** I need a change of scene (**b**) *(viento)* wind; **hace a.** it's windy (**c**) *(aspecto)* air, appearance (**d**) *(expresiones)* **va a su a.** he goes his own sweet way; **darse aires** to put on airs

airear VT *(ropa, lugar)* to air; *Fig (asunto)* to publicize

airoso, -a ADJ graceful, elegant; *Fig* **salir a. de una situación** to come out of a situation with flying colours

aislacionismo NM isolationism

aislado, -a ADJ (**a**) *(lugar, suceso)* isolated (**b**) *Téc* insulated

aislamiento NM (**a**) *(de lugar, persona)* isolation (**b**) *Téc* insulation

aislante 1 ADJ **cinta a.** insulating tape
2 NM insulator

aislar VT (**a**) *(persona, virus)* to isolate (**b**) *Téc* to insulate

ajar VT to wear out

ajedrez NM (**a**) *(juego)* chess (**b**) *(piezas y tablero)* chess set

ajeno, -a ADJ belonging to other people; **los bienes ajenos** other peoples' property; **por causas ajenas a nuestra voluntad** for reasons beyond our control

ajetreado, -a ADJ (very) busy, hectic

ajetreo NM activity, hard work, bustle

ají *(pl* **ajís** *o* **ajíes***)* NM (**a**) *Andes, RP (pimiento)* chilli (pepper) (**b**) *Andes, RP (salsa)* = sauce made from oil, vinegar, garlic and chilli

ajiaco NM (**a**) *Andes, Carib (estofado)* = chilli-based stew (**b**) *Méx (estofado con ajo)* = tripe stew flavoured with garlic

ajillo NM *Culin* **al a.** fried with garlic

ajo NM garlic; **cabeza/diente de a.** head/clove of garlic; *Fam* **estar en el a.** to be in on it

ajonjolí *(pl* **ajonjolíes***)* NM sesame

ajuar NM *(de novia)* trousseau

ajustado, -a ADJ tight

ajustador, -a 1 NM,F fitter

  2 ajustadores NMPL *Col, Cuba* bra

ajustar 1 VT (**a**) *(encajar)* *(piezas de motor)* to fit (**b**) *(arreglar)* to adjust (**c**) *(apretar)* to tighten

  2 VI *(venir justo)* to fit properly, to be a good fit; **la ventana no ajusta bien** the window won't close properly

  3 ajustarse VPR (**a**) *(encajarse)* to fit; *Fig* **tu relato no se ajusta a la verdad** your account is at variance with the truth, your account doesn't match the facts (**b**) *(adaptarse)* to fit in (**a** with); **tenemos que ajustarnos al presupuesto del que disponemos** we have to keep within the limits of our budget

ajuste NM *(de pieza)* fitting; *(de mecanismo)* adjustment; *(de salario)* agreement; **a. de cuentas** settling of scores

ajusticiar [43] VT to execute

al *(contracción de a + el)* (**a**) *ver* **a²** (**b**) *(al + infin)* **al salir** on leaving; **está al caer** it's about to happen; **al parecer** apparently

ala 1 NF (**a**) *(de ave, avión, edificio)* wing; *Fig* **cortarle las alas a algn** to clip sb's wings (**b**) *(de sombrero)* brim

  2 NMF *Dep* winger

> Takes the masculine articles **el** and **un**.

alabanza NF praise

alabar VT to praise

alabastro NM alabaster

alacena NF (food) cupboard

alacrán NM scorpion

alambicado, -a ADJ intricate

alambique NM still

alambrada NF, *Am* **alambrado** NM wire fence

alambrar VT to fence with wire

alambre NM wire; **a. de púas** barbed wire

alameda NF (**a**) *(de álamos)* poplar grove (**b**) *(paseo)* avenue, boulevard

álamo NM poplar

alano, -a NM,F (*perro*) **a.** mastiff

alarde NM bragging, boasting; **hacer a. de** to show off

alardear VI to brag, to boast; **a. de rico** *o* **de riqueza** to flaunt one's wealth

alargadera NF *Elec* extension

alargado, -a ADJ long

alargar [42] 1 VT (**a**) *(ropa)* to lengthen; *(estirar)* to stretch; **alargó la mano para cogerlo** she stretched out her hand to get it (**b**) *(prolongar)* to prolong, to extend (**c**) *(dar)* to pass, to hand over; **alárgame ese jersey** can you pass me that sweater?

  2 alargarse VPR (**a**) *(hacerse más largo)* to get longer (**b**) *(prolongarse)* to go on

alarido NM screech, shriek; **dar un a.** to howl

alarma NF alarm; **la a. saltó** the alarm went off; **falsa a.** false alarm; **señal de a.** alarm (signal)

alarmado, -a ADJ alarmed

alarmante ADJ alarming

alarmar 1 VT to alarm

  2 alarmarse VPR to be alarmed

alazán, -ana ADJ & NM,F (*caballo*) **a.** chestnut

alba NF dawn, daybreak

> Takes the masculine articles **el** and **un**.

albacea NMF *(hombre)* executor; *(mujer)* executrix

albahaca NF basil

albanés, -esa 1 ADJ & NM,F Albanian

  2 NM *(idioma)* Albanian

Albania N Albania

albañil NM bricklayer

albañilería NF bricklaying; **pared de a.** *(obra)* brick wall

albarán NM *Esp Com* delivery note, despatch note

albaricoque NM *Esp* apricot

albaricoquero NM *Esp* apricot tree

albatros NM INV albatross

albedrío NM will; **libre a.** free will

alberca NF (**a**) *(depósito)* water tank (**b**) *Col, Méx (piscina)* swimming pool

albergar [42] 1 VT *(alojar)* to house, to accommodate; *Fig (esperanza)* to cherish; *(odio)* to harbour

  2 albergarse VPR to stay

albergue NM hostel; **a. juvenil** youth hostel

albino, -a ADJ & NM,F albino

albóndiga NF meatball

albores NMPL beginning; **en los a. de ...** at the beginning of ...

albornoz NM bathrobe

alborotado, -a ADJ (**a**) *(personas)* worked up, agitated (**b**) *(pelo)* untidy, messy (**c**) *(mar)* rough; *(tiempo)* stormy

alborotar 1 VT (**a**) *(agitar)* to agitate, to work up (**b**) *(desordenar)* to mess up

  2 VI to kick up a racket

  3 alborotarse VPR (**a**) *(personas)* to get excited *o* worked up (**b**) *(mar)* to get rough; *(tiempo)* to get stormy

alboroto NM (**a**) *(jaleo)* din, racket (**b**) *(desorden)* disturbance, uproar

alborozo NM merriment, gaiety

albufera NF lagoon

álbum NM album

alcachofa NF (**a**) *Bot* artichoke (**b**) *Esp (de regadera)* rose, sprinkler; *(de ducha)* shower head

alcalde NM mayor

alcaldesa NF mayoress

alcaldía NF (**a**) *(cargo)* mayorship (**b**) *(oficina)* mayor's office

alcalino, -a ADJ alkaline

alcance NM (**a**) *(de persona)* reach; *(de arma, emisora)* range; **al a. de cualquiera** within everybody's reach; **dar a. a** to catch up with; **fuera del a. de los niños** out of the reach of children (**b**) *(de reformas, medidas)* scope; *(de noticia)* importance

alcancía NF *esp Am* money box

alcanfor NM camphor

alcantarilla NF sewer; *(boca)* drain

alcantarillado NM sewer system

alcanzar [40] **1** VT (**a**) *(llegar a)* to reach; *(persona)* to catch up with; **la producción alcanza dos mil unidades** production is up to two thousand units (**b**) *(pasar)* **alcánzame la sal** pass me the salt (**c**) *(conseguir)* to attain, to achieve
2 VI (**a**) *(ser suficiente)* to be sufficient; **con un kilo no alcanza para todos** one kilo won't be enough for all of us (**b**) *(poder)* **a. a hacer algo** to be able to do sth; **alcancé a verlo unos segundos** I managed to see him for a few seconds (**c**) *(llegar)* **no alcanzo** I can't reach it; **hasta donde alcanza la vista** as far as the eye can see

alcaparra NF *(fruto)* caper; *(planta)* caper bush

alcatraz NM *(ave)* gannet

alcaucil NM *RP* artichoke

alcayata NF hook

alcazaba NF fortress, citadel

alcázar NM (**a**) *(fortaleza)* fortress, citadel (**b**) *(castillo)* castle, palace

alcista ADJ *Fin* **mercado a.** bull market; **tendencia a.** upward tendency

alcoba NF bedroom

> Observa que la palabra inglesa **alcove** es un falso amigo y no es la traducción de la palabra española **alcoba**. En inglés **alcove** significa "hueco".

alcohol NM alcohol

alcoholemia NF blood alcohol level; **prueba de a.** Breathalyzer® test

alcohólico, -a ADJ & NM,F alcoholic

alcoholímetro NM *Br* Breathalyzer®, *US* drunkometer

alcoholismo NM alcoholism

alcoholizado, -a ADJ & NM,F alcoholic

alcoholizarse VPR to become an alcoholic

alcornoque NM cork oak

alcurnia NF lineage, ancestry; **de alta a.** of noble lineage

alcuzcuz NM couscous

aldaba NF door knocker

aldabonazo NM (**a**) *(golpe)* loud knock (**b**) *(advertencia)* warning

aldea NF village

aldeano, -a 1 ADJ village
2 NM,F villager

aleación NF alloy

aleatorio, -a ADJ random

alebrestarse VPR (**a**) *Méx (alborotarse, entusiasmarse)* to get excited (**b**) *Méx, Ven (rebelarse, indisciplinarse)* to rebel (**c**) *Col (ponerse nervioso)* to get nervous

aleccionador, -a ADJ *(instructivo)* instructive; *(ejemplar)* exemplary

aleccionar VT *(instruir)* to teach, to instruct; *(adiestrar)* to train

aledaños NMPL **en los a. de** in the vicinity of

alegar [42] VT *(motivos, pruebas)* to put forward; **a. que** to claim (that)

alegato NM *Der* plea; *Fig* **hacer un a. a favor de/en contra de** to make a case for/against

alegoría NF allegory

alegrar 1 VT (**a**) *(complacer)* to make happy *o* glad; **me alegra que se lo hayas dicho** I am glad you told her (**b**) *Fig (avivar)* to enliven, to brighten up
2 alegrarse VPR to be glad, to be happy; **me alegro de verte** I am pleased to see you; **me alegro por ti** I am happy for you

alegre ADJ (**a**) *(contento)* happy, glad (**b**) *(color)* bright; *(música)* lively; *(lugar)* pleasant, cheerful (**c**) *Fig (borracho)* tipsy, merry

alegremente ADV *(con alegría)* happily, joyfully; *(irreflexivamente)* blithely

alegría NF joy, happiness

alejado, -a ADJ far away, remote

alejar 1 VT to move further away
2 alejarse VPR to go away, to move away; **no te alejes de mí** keep close to me

aleluya NM *o* NF hallelujah, alleluia

alemán, -ana 1 ADJ & NM,F German
2 NM *(idioma)* German

Alemania N Germany; **A. del Este/Oeste** East/West Germany; **A. Occidental/Oriental** West/East Germany

alentador, -a ADJ encouraging; **un panorama poco a.** a rather bleak outlook

alentar [1] VT to encourage

alergia NF allergy

alérgico, -a ADJ allergic

alero NM eaves

alerón NM *Av* aileron

alerta ADJ & NF alert; **estar en estado de a.** to be (on the) alert

alertar VT to alert (**de** to); **nos alertó del peligro** he alerted us to the danger

aleta NF *(de pez)* fin; *(de foca, de nadador)* flipper

aletargado, -a ADJ lethargic

aletargar [42] **1** VT to make lethargic
2 aletargarse VPR to become lethargic

aletear VI to flutter *o* flap its wings

alevín NM *(pescado)* young fish; *Fig (principiante)* beginner

alevosía NF *(traición)* treachery; *(premeditación)* premeditation

alevoso, -a ADJ *(persona)* treacherous; *(acto)* premeditated

alfabético, -a ADJ alphabetical

alfabetización NF teaching to read and write; **campaña de a.** literacy campaign

alfabetizar VT *(personas)* to teach to read and write

alfabeto NM alphabet

alfajor NM *CSur* = large biscuit filled with toffee and coated with coconut

alfalfa NF lucerne, alfalfa

alfarería NF (a) *(arte)* pottery (b) *(taller)* potter's workshop; *(tienda)* pottery shop

alfarero, -a NM,F potter

alféizar NM windowsill

alférez NM second lieutenant

alfil NM bishop

alfiler NM *(para coser)* pin; *(broche)* pin, brooch; *(de corbata)* tiepin; *Andes, RP, Ven* **a. de gancho** *(imperdible)* safety pin

alfiletero NM pin box, pin case

alfombra NF *(grande)* carpet; *(pequeña)* rug; *Am salvo RP* fitted carpet

alfombrar VT to carpet

alfombrilla NF rug, mat; *Inform (para ratón)* mouse mat

alforja NF *(para caballos)* saddlebag; *(para persona)* knapsack

alga NF alga; *(marina)* seaweed

> Takes the masculine articles **el** and **un**.

algarabía NF hubbub, hullabaloo

algarrobo NM carob tree

algazara NF din, row

álgebra NF algebra

> Takes the masculine articles **el** and **un**.

álgido, -a ADJ culminating, critical; **el punto a.** the climax

algo 1 PRON INDEF (a) *(afirmativo)* something; *(interrogativo)* anything; **a. así** something like that; **¿a. más?** anything else?; **por a. será** there must be a reason for it; *Fam* **a. es a.** it's better than nothing (b) *(cantidad indeterminada)* some; **¿queda a. de pastel?** is there any cake left?
2 ADV *(un poco)* quite, somewhat; **se siente a. mejor** she's feeling a bit better

algodón NM cotton; **a. (hidrófilo)** *Br* cotton wool, *US* absorbent cotton; **a. de azúcar** *Br* candy floss, *US* cotton candy

algodonero, -a ADJ cotton

alguacil NM (a) *(del ayuntamiento)* mayor's assistant (b) *(del juzgado)* bailiff

alguien PRON INDEF *(afirmativo)* somebody, someone; *(interrogativo)* anybody, anyone

alguno, -a 1 ADJ (a) *(delante de nombre)* *(afirmativo)* some; *(interrogativo)* any; **algunos días** some days; **algunas veces** some times; **alguna que otra vez** now and then; **¿has tomado alguna medicina?** have you taken any medicine?; **¿le has visto alguna vez?** have you ever seen him? (b) *(después de nombre)* not at all; **no vino persona alguna** nobody came

> **algún** is used instead of **alguno** before masculine singular nouns (e.g. **algún día** some day).

2 PRON INDEF (a) *(singular)* someone, somebody; **a. dirá que …** someone might say that …; **a. que otro** some (b) **algunos, -as** some (people)

alhaja NF jewel

alhelí *(pl* **alhelíes)** NM wallflower, stock

aliado, -a 1 ADJ allied
2 NM,F **los Aliados** the Allies

alianza NF (a) *(pacto)* alliance (b) *(anillo)* wedding ring

aliarse [29] VPR to become allies, to form an alliance

alias ADV & NM INV alias

alicaído, -a ADJ (a) *(débil)* weak, feeble (b) *(deprimido)* down, depressed

alicatar VT *Esp* to tile

alicates NMPL pliers

aliciente NM (a) *(atractivo)* lure, charm (b) *(incentivo)* incentive

alienación NF alienation

alienado, -a ADJ insane, deranged

alienar VT to alienate

alienígena NMF alien

aliento NM (a) *(respiración)* breath; **sin a.** breathless (b) *(ánimo)* encouragement

aligerar 1 VT *(acelerar)* to speed up; **a. el paso** to quicken one's pace
2 VI *Fam* **¡aligera!** hurry up!

alijo NM haul; **un a. de drogas** a consignment of drugs

alimaña NF vermin

alimentación NF *(comida)* food; *(acción)* feeding; *Téc* supply

alimentar 1 VT (a) *(dar alimento)* to feed (b) *Fig (sentimientos)* to nourish (c) *Inform* to feed; *Téc* to supply
2 VI *(ser nutritivo)* to be nutritious
3 alimentarse VPR **alimentarse con** *o* **de** to live on

alimentario, -a ADJ food

alimenticio, -a ADJ nutritious; **productos alimenticios** food products, foodstuffs; **valor a.** nutritional value

alimento NM (a) *(comida)* food (b) *Fig* **tiene poco a.** it is not very nourishing

alimón ADV **al a.** together

alineación NF (a) *(colocación en línea)* alignment (b) *Dep (equipo)* line-up

alineado, -a ADJ aligned, lined-up; **países no alineados** non-aligned countries

alineamiento NM alignment

alinear 1 VT to align, to line up
  2 alinearse VPR to line up

aliñar VT to season, to flavour; *(ensalada)* to dress

aliño NM seasoning, dressing

alioli NM garlic mayonnaise

alisar VT to smooth

aliscafo, alíscafo NM *RP* hydrofoil

alistarse VPR (**a**) *Mil* to enlist (**b**) *Am (prepararse)* to get ready

aliviar [43] **1** VT *(dolor)* to soothe, to relieve; *(carga)* to lighten, to make lighter
  2 aliviarse VPR *(dolor)* to ease (off *o* up), to get better

alivio NM relief

aljibe NM cistern, tank

allá ADV (**a**) *(lugar alejado)* there, over there; **a. abajo/arriba** down/up there; **¡a. voy!** here I go!; **más a.** further on; **más a. de** beyond; **el más a.** the beyond (**b**) *(tiempo)* **a. por los años veinte** back in the twenties (**c**) **a. tú** that's your problem

allanamiento NM *Der* **a. de morada** breaking and entering

allanar VT (**a**) *(terreno)* to level, to flatten; *Fig (camino)* to smooth (**b**) *Am (hacer una redada en)* to raid

allegado, -a 1 ADJ close
  2 NM,F close friend

allende ADV *Fml* beyond; **a. los mares** overseas

allí ADV there, over there; **a. abajo/arriba** down/up there; **de a. para acá** back and forth; **por a.** *(movimiento)* that way; *(posición)* over there

alma NF soul; **no había ni un a.** there was not a soul

> Takes the masculine articles **el** and **un**.

almacén NM (**a**) *(local)* warehouse; *(habitación)* storeroom (**b**) **(grandes) almacenes** department store *sing* (**c**) *Andes, RP (de alimentos)* grocer's (shop), grocery store (**d**) *CAm (de ropa)* clothes shop

almacenaje NM storage, warehousing

almacenamiento NM storage, warehousing; *Inform* storage

almacenar VT to store

almanaque NM calendar

almeja NF clam; *muy Fam* pussy

almena NF merlon

almendra NF almond; **a. garapiñada** sugared almond

almendrado, -a 1 ADJ almond-shaped; **ojos almendrados** almond eyes
  2 NM *Culin* almond paste

almendro NM almond tree

almíbar NM syrup

almidón NM starch

almidonado, -a 1 ADJ starched
  2 NM starching

almidonar VT to starch

alminar NM minaret

almirante NM admiral

almizcle NM musk

almohada NF pillow; *Fam* **consultarlo con la a.** to sleep on it

almohadilla NF (**a**) *(cojín)* small cushion (**b**) *(de animal)* pad

almohadón NM pillowcase

almorranas NFPL piles

almorzar [2] **1** VI to have lunch
  2 VT to have lunch

almuerzo NM lunch

aló INTERJ *Andes, Carib (al teléfono)* hello!

alocado, -a ADJ thoughtless, rash

alocución NF speech, address

alojamiento NM accommodation; **dar a.** to accommodate

alojar 1 VT to accommodate
  2 alojarse VPR to stay

alondra NF lark; **a. común** skylark

alpaca NF alpaca

alpargata NF canvas sandal, espadrille

Alpes NPL **los A.** the Alps

alpinismo NM mountaineering, climbing

alpinista NMF mountaineer, climber

alpino, -a ADJ Alpine; **esquí a.** downhill skiing

alpiste NM (**a**) *(planta)* canary grass (**b**) *(semilla)* birdseed

alquilar VT to hire; *(pisos, casas)* to rent; **se alquila** *(en letrero)* to let

alquiler NM (**a**) *(de pisos, casas)* renting; **a. de coches** *Br* car hire, *US* car rental; **de a.** *(pisos, casas)* to let, rented; *(coche)* for hire; *(televisión)* for rent (**b**) *(precio)* hire, rental; *(de pisos, casas)* rent

alquimia NF alchemy

alquitrán NM tar

alrededor 1 ADV *(lugar)* round, around; **mira a.** look around; **a. de la mesa** round the table; **a. de las dos** around two o'clock; **a. de quince** about fifteen
  2 alrededores NMPL surrounding area; **en los alrededores de Murcia** in the area round Murcia

alta NF **dar de** *o* **el a. a algn** *(a un enfermo)* to discharge sb from hospital

> Takes the masculine articles **el** and **un**.

altamente ADV highly, extremely

altanería NF haughtiness

altanero, -a ADJ haughty

altar NM altar

altavoz NM loudspeaker

alteración NF (**a**) *(cambio)* alteration (**b**) *(alboroto)* quarrel, row; **a. del orden público**

disturbance of the peace (**c**) *(excitación)* agitation

alterar 1 VT to alter, to change; **a. el orden público** to disturb the peace
2 **alterarse** VPR (**a**) *(cambiar)* to change (**b**) *(inquietarse)* to be upset (**c**) *(alimentos)* to go off

altercado NM quarrel, argument

alternar 1 VT to alternate
2 VI *(relacionarse)* to meet people, to socialize
3 **alternarse** VPR to alternate

alternativa NF alternative

alternativo, -a ADJ alternative

alterno, -a ADJ alternate; **días alternos** alternate days

alteza NF Highness; **Su A. Real** His/Her Royal Highness

altibajos NMPL ups and downs

altillo NM (**a**) *(desván)* attic, loft (**b**) *Esp (armario)* = small storage cupboard above head height, usually above another cupboard

altiplano NM high plateau

Altísimo NM *Rel* **el A.** the Almighty

altisonante ADJ grandiloquent

altitud NF altitude

altivez NF haughtiness

altivo, -a ADJ haughty

alto¹, -a 1 ADJ *(persona, árbol, edificio)* tall; *(montaña, techo, presión)* high; *(sonido)* loud; *Fig (precio, tecnología)* high; *(tono)* high-pitched; **los pisos altos** the top floors; **en lo a.** at the top; **alta sociedad** high society; **clase alta** upper class; **en voz alta** aloud, in a loud voice; **a altas horas de la noche** late at night
2 ADV (**a**) *(en posición)* high, high up (**b**) *(en volumen)* loud, loudly; **pon la radio más alta** turn the radio up; **¡habla más a.!** speak up!
3 NM (**a**) *(altura)* height; **¿cuánto tiene de a.?** how tall/high is it?; *Fig* **por todo lo a.** in a grand way (**b**) *(elevación)* hill

alto² NM (**a**) *(interrupción)* stop, break (**b**) *Mil* halt; **dar el a. a algn** to order sb to halt; **un a. el fuego** a cease-fire

altoparlante NM *Am* loudspeaker

altozano NM hillock

altramuz NM lupin

altruismo NM altruism

altruista 1 ADJ altruistic
2 NMF altruist

altura NF (**a**) *(de persona, cosa)* height; **de 10 m de a.** 10 m high (**b**) *(nivel)* level; **a la misma a.** on the same level; *Geog* on the same latitude; **a la a. del cine** by the cinema; *Fig* **estar a la a. de las circunstancias** to meet the challenge; *Fig* **no está a su a.** he does not measure up to him; *Fig* **a estas alturas** at this stage (**c**) *Rel* **alturas** heaven

alubia NF bean

alucinación NF hallucination

alucinado, -a ADJ *Fam* staggered, *Br* gobsmacked

alucinante ADJ *Fam* brilliant, mind-blowing

alucinar VI (**a**) *Med* to hallucinate (**b**) *Fam (gustar)* **le alucinan las motos** he's crazy about motorbikes

alucinógeno, -a 1 ADJ hallucinogenic
2 NM hallucinogen

alud NM avalanche

aludido, -a ADJ *Fig* **darse por a.** to take it personally

aludir VI to allude to, to mention

alumbrado, -a 1 ADJ lit
2 NM *Elec* lighting; **a. público** street lighting

alumbrar 1 VT *(iluminar)* to light, to illuminate
2 VI *(parir)* to give birth

aluminio NM *Br* aluminium, *US* aluminum

alumnado NM *(de colegio)* pupils; *Univ* student body

alumno, -a NM,F (**a**) *(de colegio)* pupil; **a. externo** day pupil; **a. interno** boarder (**b**) *Univ* student

alusión NF allusion, mention

aluvión NM *(de agua)* flood; **un a. de críticas** a barrage of criticism; **un a. de insultos** a torrent of abuse

alverja NF *Am* pea

alza NF rise; **en a.** rising; **jugar al a.** *(bolsa)* to bull the market

> Takes the masculine articles **el** and **un**.

alzado, -a 1 ADJ raised, lifted; **votación a mano alzada** vote by a show of hands
2 NM *Arquit* elevation

alzamiento NM *(rebelión)* uprising

alzar [40] 1 VT to raise, to lift; **a. el vuelo** to take off; **a. los ojos/la vista** to look up; **álzate el cuello** turn your collar up
2 **alzarse** VPR (**a**) *(levantarse)* to get up, to rise (**b**) *(rebelarse)* to rise, to rebel (**c**) **alzarse con la victoria** to win, to be victorious

AM *(abr* **amplitude modulation***)* AM

ama NF *(señora)* lady of the house; *(dueña)* owner; **a. de casa** housewife; **a. de llaves** housekeeper

> Takes the masculine articles **el** and **un**.

amabilidad NF kindness; *Fml* **tenga la a. de esperar** would you be so kind as to wait?

amable ADJ kind, nice; *Fml* **¿sería usted tan a. de ayudarme?** would you be so kind as to help me?

amado, -a 1 ADJ loved, beloved
2 NM,F loved one

amaestrado ADJ *(animal)* trained; *(en circo)* performing

amaestrar VT to train; *(domar)* to tame

amagar [42] VI to threaten; **amaga tormenta** a storm is threatening

amago NM hacer a. de to make as if to; **hizo a. de salir corriendo** he made as if to run off

amainar VI *(viento etc)* to drop, to die down

amalgama NF amalgam

amalgamar VT to amalgamate

amamantar VT to breast-feed; *Zool* to suckle

amancay NM *Andes* golden hurricane lily

amanecer [33] **1** V IMPERS to dawn; **¿a qué hora amanece?** when does it get light?; **amaneció lluvioso** it was rainy in the morning
2 VI **amanecimos en Finlandia** we were in Finland at daybreak; **amaneció muy enfermo** he woke up feeling very ill
3 NM dawn, daybreak; **al a.** at dawn

amanerado, -a ADJ mannered, affected

amansar VT **(a)** *(fiera)* to tame **(b)** *Fig (apaciguar)* to pacify, to calm

amante NMF lover; **a. del arte** art lover

amañar VT to fix, to fiddle; *(elecciones)* to rig

amapola NF poppy

amar **1** VT to love
2 amarse VPR to love each other

amaraje NM *Av* landing at sea

amargado, -a **1** ADJ *(resentido)* bitter; **estar a. de la vida** to be bitter and twisted
2 NM,F bitter person

amargar [42] **1** VT to make bitter; *Fig* to embitter, to sour
2 amargarse VPR *Fig* to become embittered *o* bitter; **no te amargues por eso** don't let that make you bitter

amargo, -a ADJ bitter

amargor NM bitterness

amargura NF *(pena)* sorrow

amarillear **1** VT to turn yellow
2 VI to (turn) yellow

amarillento, -a ADJ yellowish

amarillo, -a ADJ & NM yellow; **prensa amarilla** gutter press

amarilloso, -a ADJ *Col, Méx, Ven* yellowish

amarradero NM mooring

amarrar VT *Náut* to moor, to tie up; *(atar)* to tie (up), to bind

amarras NFPL **soltar a.** to cast off, to let go

amarre NM *Náut* mooring

amarrete, -a ADJ *Andes, RP Fam* mean, tight

amasar VT **(a)** *Culin* to knead **(b)** *(fortuna)* to amass

amasiato NM *CAm, Chile, Méx* **vivir en a.** to live together

amasijo NM *Fam* hotchpotch, jumble

amasio, -a NM,F *CAm, Méx* live-in lover, common-law partner

amateur [ama'ter] *(pl* **amateurs)** ADJ & NMF amateur

amatista NF amethyst

amazona NF **(a)** *(jinete)* horsewoman **(b)** *(en mitología)* Amazon

Amazonas N **el A.** the Amazon

amazónico, -a ADJ Amazonian

ambages NMPL **hablar sin a.** to go straight to the point

ámbar NM amber

Amberes N Antwerp

ambición NF ambition

ambicionar VT to have as an ambition; **ambiciona ser presidente** his ambition is to become president

ambicioso, -a **1** ADJ ambitious
2 NM,F ambitious person

ambidextro, -a **1** ADJ ambidextrous
2 NM,F ambidextrous person

ambientación NF *Cin & Teatro* setting

ambientador NM air freshener

ambiental ADJ environmental

ambientar **1** VT **(a)** *Cin & Teatro* to set **(b)** *(iluminar)* to light; *(decorar)* to decorate
2 ambientarse VPR *(adaptarse)* to adapt, to settle in

ambiente **1** NM **(a)** *(gen)* environment; *Fig (medio)* environment, milieu **(b)** *Andes, RP (habitación)* room
2 ADJ environmental; **temperatura a.** room temperature

ambigüedad NF ambiguity

ambiguo, -a ADJ ambiguous

ámbito NM field, sphere; **empresa de a. nacional** nationwide company

ambos, -as ADJ PL *Fml* both; **por a. lados** on both sides

ambulancia NF ambulance

ambulante ADJ travelling, mobile; **biblioteca a.** mobile library

ambulatorio NM surgery, clinic

amedrentar VT to frighten, to scare

amén¹ NM amen

amén² ADV **a. de** in addition to

amenaza NF threat

amenazador, -a, amenazante ADJ threatening, menacing

amenazar [40] VT to threaten; **a. de muerte a algn** to threaten to kill sb

amenizar [40] VT to liven up

ameno, -a ADJ entertaining

América N America; **A. Central/del Norte/del Sur** Central/North/South America

americana NF *(prenda)* jacket

americano, -a ADJ & NM,F American

amerindio, -a ADJ & NM,F Amerindian, American Indian

ameritar VT *Am* to deserve

amerizar [40] VI *(hidroavión)* to land at sea; *(vehículo espacial)* to splash down

ametralladora NF machine gun

ametrallar VT to machine-gun

amianto NM asbestos

amigable ADJ friendly

amígdala NF tonsil

amigdalitis NF INV tonsillitis

amigo, -a 1 NM,F friend; **hacerse a. de** to make friends with; **hacerse amigos** to become friends; **son muy amigos** they are very good friends

  2 ADJ *(aficionado)* fond (**de** of)

amilanar 1 VT to frighten, to scare

  2 amilanarse VPR to be frightened *o* daunted

aminorar VT to reduce; **a. el paso** to slow down

amistad NF (**a**) *(relación)* friendship (**b**) **amistades** friends

amistoso, -a ADJ friendly

amnesia NF amnesia

amnistía NF amnesty

amo NM (**a**) *(dueño)* owner (**b**) *(señor)* master

amodorrarse VPR to get drowsy

amoldar 1 VT to adapt, to adjust

  2 amoldarse VPR to adapt

amonestación NF (**a**) *(reprimenda)* rebuke, reprimand, *Dep* warning (**b**) *Rel* **amonestaciones** banns

amonestar VT (**a**) *(reprender)* to rebuke, to reprimand; *Dep* to warn (**b**) *Rel* to publish the banns of

amoniaco, amoníaco NM ammonia

amontonar 1 VT to pile up, to heap up

  2 amontonarse VPR to pile up, to heap up; *(gente)* to crowd together

amor NM love; **hacer el a.** to make love; **a. propio** self-esteem; **¡por el a. de Dios!** for God's sake!

amoral ADJ amoral

amoratado, -a ADJ *(de frío)* blue with cold; *(de un golpe)* black and blue

amordazar [40] VT *(perrp)* to muzzle; *(persona)* to gag

amorfo, -a ADJ amorphous

amorío NM love affair, flirtation

amoroso, -a ADJ loving, affectionate

amortajar VT to shroud, to wrap in a shroud

amortiguador NM *Aut* shock absorber

amortiguar [45] VT *(golpe)* to cushion; *(ruido)* to muffle; *(luz)* to subdue

amortización NF repayment

amortizar [40] VT to pay off

amotinado, -a NM,F rioter; *Mil* mutineer

amotinamiento NM riot, rioting; *Mil* mutiny

amotinar 1 VT to incite to riot; *Mil* to incite to mutiny

  2 amotinarse VPR to rise up; *Mil* to mutiny

amparar 1 VT to protect

  2 ampararse VPR to seek refuge

amparo NM protection, shelter; **al a. de la ley** under the protection of the law

amperio NM *Elec* ampère, amp

ampliación NF enlargement; *(de plazo, casa)* extension

ampliar [29] VT to enlarge; *(casa, plazo)* to extend

amplificador NM amplifier

amplificar [44] VT to amplify

amplio, -a ADJ large, roomy; *(ancho)* wide, broad; **en el sentido más a. de la palabra** in the broadest sense of the word

amplitud NF (**a**) *(cualidad)* roominess, spaciousness; **a. de miras** broad-mindedness (**b**) *Fís (de onda)* amplitude

ampolla NF (**a**) *Med* blister; *Fig* **levantar ampollas** to raise people's hackles (**b**) *(de medicina)* ampoule

ampuloso, -a ADJ pompous, bombastic

amputación NF amputation

amputar VT to amputate

amueblado, -a ADJ *(piso)* furnished

amueblar VT to furnish

amuermar VT *Esp Fam (aburrir)* to bore

amuleto NM amulet; **a. de la suerte** lucky charm

amurallar VT to wall, to fortify

anacronismo NM anachronism

ánade NM duck

anales NM PL annals

analfabetismo NM illiteracy

analfabeto, -a NM,F illiterate

analgésico, -a ADJ & NM analgesic

análisis NM INV analysis; **a. de sangre** blood test

analista NMF analyst; **a. financiero** financial analyst; **a. de sistemas** systems analyst

analítico, -a ADJ analytical

analizar [40] VT to analyse

analogía NF analogy

analógico, -a ADJ analogue

análogo, -a ADJ analogous, similar

ananá NM , **ananás** NM INV *RP* pineapple

anaquel NM shelf

anaranjado, -a ADJ & NM orange

anarquía NF anarchy

anárquico, -a ADJ anarchic

anarquismo NM anarchism

anarquista ADJ & NMF anarchist

anatomía NF anatomy

anatómico, -a ADJ anatomical

anca NF haunch; **ancas de rana** frogs' legs

> Takes the masculine articles **el** and **un**.

ancestral ADJ ancestral

ancho, -a 1 ADJ wide, broad; **a lo a.** breadthwise; **te está muy a.** it's too big for you

  2 NM (**a**) *(anchura)* width, breadth; **2 m de a.** 2 m wide; **¿qué a. tiene?** how wide is it? (**b**) *Cost* width

  3 anchas NFPL *Esp Fam* **a mis/tus/sus anchas** at ease, comfortable

anchoa NF anchovy

anchura NF width, breadth

anciano, -a 1 ADJ very old
2 NM,F old person; **los ancianos** old people
ancla NF anchor

> Takes the masculine articles **el** and **un**.

anclar VT & VI to anchor
andadas NFPL **volver a las a.** to go back to one's old ways
andaderas NFPL baby-walker
andadura NF **la a. de un país** the evolution of a country; **el Festival comenzó su a. en 1950** the Festival's history began in 1950
ándale INTERJ *CAm, Méx Fam* come on!
Andalucía N Andalusia
andaluz, -a ADJ & NM,F Andalusian
andamio NM scaffold
andanzas NFPL adventures
andar¹ NM a. *o* andares walk, gait
andar² [8] **1** VI (**a**) *esp Esp (caminar)* to walk (**b**) *(coche etc)* to move; **este coche anda despacio** this car goes very slowly (**c**) *(funcionar)* to work; **esto no anda** this doesn't work (**d**) *Fam* **anda por los cuarenta** he's about forty; **anda siempre diciendo que …** he's always saying that …; **¿cómo andamos de tiempo?** how are we off for time?; **tu bolso debe a. por ahí** your bag must be over there somewhere
2 VT *(recorrer)* to walk
andarín, -ina ADJ **ser muy a.** to be a very keen walker
ándele INTERJ *CAm, Méx Fam* come on!
andén NM (**a**) *(en estación)* platform (**b**) *Andes, CAm (acera) Br* pavement, *US* sidewalk (**c**) *Andes (bancal de tierra)* terrace
Andes NMPL Andes
andinismo NM *Am* mountaineering, mountain climbing
andinista NMF *Am* mountaineer, mountain climber
andino, -a ADJ Andean
andrajo NM rag
andrajoso, -a ADJ ragged, tattered
androide NM android
andurriales NMPL *Fam* out-of-the-way place
anécdota NF anecdote
anecdótico, -a ADJ anecdotal
anegar [42] **1** VT to flood
2 anegarse VPR to flood; **sus ojos se anegaron de lágrimas** tears welled up in his eyes
anejo, -a ADJ *(edificio)* connected (**a** to)
anemia NF anaemia
anémico, -a 1 ADJ anaemic
2 NM,F anaemia sufferer
anestesia NF *(técnica)* anaesthesia; *(sustancia)* anaesthetic
anestésico, -a ADJ anaesthetic
anestesista NMF anaesthetist
anexar VT to annex
anexión NF annexation

anexionar VT to annex
anexo, -a 1 ADJ *(edificio)* connected (**a** to)
2 NM annexe
anfetamina NF amphetamine
anfibio, -a 1 ADJ amphibious
2 NM amphibian
anfiteatro NM (**a**) *(romano)* amphitheatre (**b**) *Cin & Teatro* gallery
anfitrión, -ona NM,F host, *f* hostess
ángel NM (**a**) *(ser)* angel; **á. de la guarda** guardian angel (**b**) *Am (micrófono)* hand-held microphone
angelical ADJ angelic
angina NF angina; **tener anginas** to have tonsillitis; *Med* **a. de pecho** angina pectoris
anglófono, -a 1 ADJ English-speaking
2 NM,F English speaker
anglosajón, -ona ADJ & NM,F Anglo-Saxon
Angola N Angola
angosto, -a ADJ *Fml* narrow
anguila NF eel; **a. de mar** conger eel
angula NF elver
angular ADJ angular; *Fot* **(objetivo) gran a.** wide-angle lens; **piedra a.** cornerstone
ángulo NM angle; *(rincón)* corner
angustia NF anguish
angustiado, -a ADJ anguished, distressed
angustiar [43] VT to distress
angustioso, -a ADJ distressing
anhelar VT to long for, to yearn for
anhelo NM longing, yearning
anhídrido NM **a. carbónico** carbon dioxide
anidar VI to nest
anilla NF ring; **carpeta de anillas** ring-binder
anillo NM ring; **a. de boda** wedding ring
ánima NF soul

> Takes the masculine articles **el** and **un**.

animación NF *(diversión)* entertainment
animado, -a ADJ *(fiesta etc)* lively
animador, -a NM,F (**a**) *(en espectáculo)* compere; *(en fiesta de niños)* children's entertainer; **a. cultural** cultural organizer (**b**) *Dep* cheerleader
animadversión NF ill feeling, animosity
animal 1 NM animal; *Fig (basto)* brute; *(necio)* dunce
2 ADJ animal
animar 1 VT (**a**) *(alentar)* to encourage (**b**) *(alegrar) (persona)* to cheer up; *(fiesta, bar)* to liven up, to brighten up
2 animarse VPR (**a**) *(persona)* to cheer up; *(fiesta, reunión)* to brighten up (**b**) **¿te animas a venir?** do you fancy coming along?
anímico, -a ADJ **estado a.** frame *o* state of mind
ánimo NM (**a**) *(espíritu)* spirit; **estado de á.** frame *o* state of mind (**b**) **con á. de** *(intención)* with the intention of (**c**) *(valor, coraje)*

courage; **dar ánimos a** to encourage; **¡á.!** cheer up!

animosidad NF animosity

animoso, -a ADJ *(valiente)* courageous; *(decidido)* undaunted

aniñado, -a ADJ childlike; *Pey* childish

aniquilación NF annihilation

aniquilar VT to annihilate

anís *(pl* **anises)** NM (**a**) *(bebida)* anisette (**b**) *(grano)* aniseed

anisete NM anisette

aniversario NM anniversary

ano NM anus

anoche ADV last night; *(por la tarde)* yesterday evening; **antes de a.** the night before last

anochecer [33] **1** V IMPERS to get dark; **cuando anochece** at nightfall, at dusk
2 VI to be somewhere at dusk; **anochecimos en Cuenca** we were in Cuenca at dusk
3 NM nightfall, dusk

anodino, -a ADJ *(insustancial)* insubstantial; *(soso)* insipid, dull

anomalía NF anomaly

anómalo, -a ADJ anomalous

anonadado, -a ADJ **me quedé/dejó a.** I was astonished

anonimato NM anonymity; **permanecer en el a.** to remain anonymous o nameless

anónimo, -a 1 ADJ *(desconocido)* anonymous
2 NM *(carta)* anonymous letter

anorak *(pl* **anoraks)** NM anorak

anorexia NF anorexia

anormal 1 ADJ (**a**) *(anómalo)* abnormal; **una situación a.** an irregular situation (**b**) *(como insulto)* moronic
2 NMF *(como insulto)* moron

anotación NF *(nota escrita)* note; *(en registro)* entry; *Com* **a. contable** book entry

anotar 1 VT to take down, to make a note of
2 anotarse VPR *RP (en curso)* to enrol (**en** for); *(para actividad)* to sign up (**en** for)

anquilosado, -a ADJ fossilized; **a. en el pasado** locked in the past

anquilosarse VPR to stagnate

ansia NF (**a**) *(deseo)* longing, yearning (**b**) *(ansiedad)* anxiety (**c**) *Med* sick feeling

Takes the masculine articles **el** and **un**.

ansiar [29] VT to long for, to yearn for

ansiedad NF anxiety; **con a.** anxiously

ansioso, -a ADJ (**a**) *(deseoso)* eager (**por** for) (**b**) *(avaricioso)* greedy

antagónico, -a ADJ antagonistic

antagonismo NM antagonism

antagonista 1 ADJ antagonistic
2 NMF antagonist

antaño ADV in the past, formerly

antártico, -a 1 ADJ Antarctic
2 NM **el A.** the Antarctic

Antártida NF Antarctica

ante¹ NM (**a**) *Zool* elk, moose (**b**) *(piel)* suede

ante² PREP (**a**) *(delante de, en presencia de)* before, in the presence of; *Der* **a. notario** in the presence of a notary; **a. todo** most of all (**b**) *(en vista de)* faced with, in view of; **a. la crisis energética** faced with the energy crisis

anteanoche ADV the night before last

anteayer ADV the day before yesterday

antebrazo NM forearm

antecedente 1 ADJ previous
2 NM antecedent
3 antecedentes NMPL *(historial)* record; *Der* **antecedentes penales** criminal record; **poner en antecedentes** to put in the picture

anteceder VT to precede, to go before

antecesor, -a NM,F (**a**) *(en un cargo)* predecessor (**b**) *(antepasado)* ancestor

antedicho, -a ADJ above-mentioned

antelación NF notice; **con poca a.** at short notice; **con un mes de a.** a month beforehand, with a month's notice

antemano ADV **de a.** beforehand, in advance

antena NF (**a**) *Rad & TV* aerial; **a. parabólica** satellite dish; **en a.** on the air (**b**) *Zool* antenna, feeler

anteojos NMPL *(prismáticos)* binoculars; *Am (gafas)* spectacles, glasses

antepasado, -a NM,F ancestor

antepecho NM *(de ventana)* sill; *(de puente)* parapet

antepenúltimo, -a ADJ antepenultimate; **el capítulo a.** the last chapter but two

anteponer [19] *(pp* **antepuesto)** VT to give preference to

anteproyecto NM *Pol* **a. de ley** draft bill

antepuesto, -a PP *de* anteponer

antepuse PT INDEF *de* anteponer

anterior ADJ (**a**) *(previo)* previous; **el día a.** the day before (**b**) *(delantero)* front; **parte a.** front part

anterioridad NF **con a.** before; **con a. a** prior to, before

anteriormente ADV previously, before

antes ADV (**a**) *(tiempo)* before; **a. de las tres** before three o'clock; **mucho a.** long before; **la noche a.** the night before; **cuanto a.** as soon as possible (**b**) *(antaño)* in the past; **a. llovía más** it used to rain more in the past (**c**) *(lugar)* before; **a. del semáforo** before the traffic lights (**d**) **a. prefiero hacerlo yo** I'd rather do it myself; **a. (bien)** on the contrary

antesala NF antechamber, anteroom; *Fig* **en la a. de** on the eve of

anti- PREF anti-

antiabortista 1 ADJ anti-abortion, pro-life
2 NMF anti-abortion o pro-life campaigner

antiadherente ADJ nonstick

antiaéreo, -a ADJ anti-aircraft

antiarrugas ADJ INV anti-wrinkle

antibiótico, -a ADJ & NM antibiotic

anticaspa ADJ anti-dandruff

anticiclón NM anticyclone, high pressure area

anticipación NF **con a.** in advance

anticipadamente ADV in advance

anticipado, -a ADJ brought forward; **elecciones anticipadas** early elections; **gracias anticipadas** thanks in advance; *Com* **por a.** in advance

anticipar 1 VT (*acontecimiento*) to bring forward; (*dinero*) to pay in advance; **no anticipemos acontecimientos** we'll cross that bridge when we come to it
2 **anticiparse** VPR (**a**) (*adelantarse*) **anticiparse a algn** to beat sb to it; **iba a decírtelo, pero él se me anticipó** I was going to tell you, but he beat me to it (**b**) (*llegar pronto*) to arrive early; *Fig* **anticiparse a su tiempo** to be ahead of one's time

anticipo NM (*adelanto*) advance; **pedir un a.** to ask for an advance (on one's wages)

anticonceptivo, -a ADJ & NM contraceptive

anticongelante ADJ & NM antifreeze

anticonstitucional ADJ unconstitutional

anticuado, -a ADJ antiquated

anticuario, -a NM,F antique dealer

anticucho NM *Andes* (*brocheta*) kebab

anticuerpo NM antibody

antidepresivo, -a 1 ADJ antidepressant
2 NM antidepressant (drug)

antídoto NM antidote

antier ADV *Am Fam* the day before yesterday

antiestético, -a ADJ ugly, unsightly

antifaz NM mask

antigás ADJ **careta/mascarilla a.** gas mask

antigualla NF *Pey* museum piece

antiguamente ADV (*hace mucho*) long ago; (*previamente*) formerly

antigüedad NF (**a**) (*período histórico*) antiquity; **en la a.** in olden days, in former times (**b**) (*en cargo*) seniority (**c**) **tienda de antigüedades** antique shop

antiguo, -a ADJ (**a**) (*viejo*) old, ancient (**b**) (*anterior*) former (**c**) (*pasado de moda*) old-fashioned (**d**) (*en cargo*) senior

antihigiénico, -a ADJ unhygienic, unhealthy

antihistamínico, -a ADJ & NM antihistamine

antiinflamatorio, -a 1 ADJ anti-inflammatory
2 NM anti-inflammatory (drug)

Antillas NFPL **las A.** the West Indies, the Antilles

antílope NM antelope

antinatural ADJ unnatural, contrary to nature

antiniebla ADJ INV **faros a.** fog lamps

antipatía NF antipathy, dislike; **tener a. a** to dislike

antipático, -a ADJ unpleasant; **Pedro me es a.** I don't like Pedro

antípodas NFPL **las A.** the Antipodes

antiquísimo, -a (*superl de* **antiguo**) ADJ very old, ancient

antirrobo 1 ADJ INV antitheft; **alarma a.** burglar alarm; (*para coche*) car alarm
2 NM (*para coche*) car alarm; (*para casa*) burglar alarm

antisemita 1 ADJ anti-Semitic
2 NMF anti-Semite

antiséptico, -a ADJ & NM antiseptic

antítesis NF INV antithesis

antivirus NM INV *Inform* antivirus system

antojadizo, -a ADJ capricious, unpredictable

antojarse VPR (**a**) (*capricho*) **cuando se me antoja** when I feel like it; **se le antojó un helado** he fancied an ice-cream (**b**) (*posibilidad*) **se me antoja que ...** I have a feeling that ... (**c**) *Méx* (*apetecer*) to feel like, to want

antojitos NMPL *Ecuad, Méx* snacks, appetizers

antojo NM (**a**) (*capricho*) whim, caprice; (*de embarazada*) craving; **a su a.** in one's own way, as one pleases (**b**) (*en la piel*) birthmark

antología NF anthology

antónimo NM antonym

antonomasia NF **por a.** par excellence

antorcha NF torch

antro NM dump, hole; *Fig* **a. de perdición** den of iniquity

antropología NF anthropology

antropólogo, -a NM,F anthropologist

anual ADJ annual; **ingresos anuales** yearly income

anualidad NF annual payment, annuity

anuario NM yearbook

anudar VT to knot, to tie

anulación NF cancellation; (*de matrimonio*) annulment; (*de ley*) repeal

anular¹ NM ring finger

anular² VT (**a**) *Com* (*pedido*) to cancel; *Dep* (*gol*) to disallow; (*matrimonio*) to annul; *Der* (*ley*) to repeal (**b**) *Inform* to delete

anunciador, -a ADJ **empresa anunciadora** advertising company

anunciante NM advertiser

anunciar [43] 1 VT (**a**) (*producto etc*) to advertise (**b**) (*avisar*) to announce
2 **anunciarse** VPR to advertise oneself; **anunciarse en un periódico** to put an advert in a newspaper

anuncio NM (**a**) (*comercial*) advertisement, *Br* advert, ad (**b**) (*aviso*) announcement (**c**) (*cartel*) notice, poster

anzuelo NM (fish) hook

añadidura NF addition; **por a.** besides, on top of everything else

añadir VT to add (**a** to)

añejo, -a ADJ (**a**) (*vino, queso*) mature (**b**) (*costumbre*) long-established

añicos NMPL smithereens; **hacer a.** to smash to smithereens

añil ADJ & NM indigo

año NM (**a**) *(periodo)* year; **el a. pasado** last year; **el a. que viene** next year; **hace años** a long time ago, years ago; **los años noventa** the nineties; **todo el a.** all year (round); **a. luz** light year (**b**) *(edad)* **¿cuántos años tienes?** how old are you?; **tiene seis años** he's six (years old); **entrado en años** getting on

añoranza NF longing, yearning

añorar VT *(pasado)* to long for, to yearn for; *(país)* to feel homesick for, to miss

aorta NF *Anat* aorta

APA NF *(abr* **Asociación de Padres de Alumnos)** = Spanish association for parents of schoolchildren, ≃ PTA

> Takes the masculine articles **el** and **un**.

apabullar VT to overwhelm

apacentar [1] VT to put out to pasture, to graze

apache ADJ & NMF Apache

apachurrar VT *Fam* to squash, to crush

apacible ADJ mild, calm

apaciguar [45] **1** VT *(calmar)* to pacify, to appease
  2 apaciguarse VPR *(persona)* to calm down; *(tormenta)* to abate

apadrinar VT (**a**) *(en bautizo)* to act as godfather to; *(en boda)* to be best man for (**b**) *(artista)* to sponsor

apagado, -a ADJ (**a**) *(luz)* out, off; *(cigarro)* out (**b**) *(color)* dull; *(voz)* sad; *(mirada)* expressionless, lifeless; *(carácter, persona)* spiritless

apagar [42] VT *(fuego)* to put out; *(luz, tele etc)* to turn off, to switch off; *(color)* to soften; *(sed)* to quench

apagón NM power cut, blackout

apaisado, -a ADJ *(papel)* landscape

apalabrar VT *(concertar)* to make a verbal agreement on

apalancado, -a ADJ *Esp Fam* **se pasó la tarde a. delante del televisor** he spent the afternoon lounging in front of the television

apalancar [44] **1** VT to lever up
  2 apalancarse VPR *Esp Fam* to install oneself

apalear VT to beat, to thrash

apañado, -a ADJ *Fam* (**a**) *(hábil, mañoso)* clever, resourceful (**b**) **estar a.** to have had it; **¡estamos apañados!** we've had it!

apañar 1 VT to mend, to fix
  2 apañarse VPR *Esp (arreglarse)* to cope, to manage; **apañárselas (para hacer algo)** to manage (to do sth)

apaño NM *Fam* (**a**) *(reparación)* patch (**b**) *(chanchullo)* fix, shady deal (**c**) *(acuerdo)* compromise

apapachar VT *Méx Fam (mimar)* to cuddle; *(consentir)* to spoil

apapacho NM *Méx Fam (mimo)* cuddle

aparador NM *(mueble)* sideboard; *(de tienda)* shop window

aparato NM (**a**) *(dispositivo)* device; *(instrumento)* instrument; **a. de radio/televisión** radio/television set; **a. digestivo** digestive system; **a. eléctrico** thunder and lightning (**b**) *Tel* **¿quién está al a.?** who's speaking? (**c**) *(ostentación)* display

aparatoso, -a ADJ (**a**) *(pomposo)* ostentatious, showy (**b**) *(espectacular)* spectacular

aparcamiento NM *Esp (parking) Br* car park, *US* parking lot; *(hueco)* parking place

aparcar [44] *Esp* **1** VT *(estacionar)* to park; *Fig (posponer)* to shelve
  2 VI to park

apareamiento NM mating

aparear 1 VT to mate
  2 aparearse VPR to mate

aparecer [33] **1** VI (**a**) *(ante la vista)* to appear; **no aparece en mi lista** he is not on my list (**b**) *(algo perdido)* to turn up, to show up; **¿apareció el dinero?** did the money turn up?; **no apareció nadie** nobody turned up
  2 aparecerse VPR to appear

aparejado, -a ADJ **llevar** *o* **traer a.** to entail

aparejador, -a NM,F quantity surveyor

aparejar VT (**a**) *(caballo)* to harness (**b**) *(emparejar)* to pair off

aparejo NM (**a**) *(equipo)* equipment (**b**) *(de caballo)* harness

aparentar 1 VT (**a**) *(fingir)* to affect (**b**) *(tener aspecto)* to look; **no aparenta esa edad** she doesn't look that age
  2 VI to show off

aparente ADJ apparent; **sin motivo a.** for no apparent reason

aparición NF (**a**) *(de persona, cosa)* appearance (**b**) *(de ser sobrenatural)* apparition

apariencia NF appearance; **en a.** apparently; **guardar las apariencias** to keep up appearances

apartado, -a 1 ADJ *(lugar)* remote, isolated; **mantente a. de él** keep away from him
  2 NM (**a**) *(párrafo)* section, paragraph (**b**) **a. de correos** Post Office Box

apartamento NM *esp Am (en edificio) Br* flat, *US* apartment; *Esp (más pequeño)* apartment

apartar 1 VT (**a**) *(alejar)* to move away, to remove; **a. la mirada** to look away (**b**) *(guardar)* to put aside
  2 VI **¡aparta!** move out of the way!
  3 apartarse VPR *(alejarse)* to move over, to move away; **apártate de en medio** move out of the way

aparte 1 ADV (**a**) *(en otro lugar, a un lado)* aside; **ponlo a.** put it aside; **modestia/bromas a.** modesty/joking apart (**b**) *(por separado)* separately; **eso hay que pagarlo a.** you have to pay for that separately (**c**) **a. de eso** from that
  2 NM *Teatro* aside

apasionado, -a 1 ADJ passionate; **a. de la música** very fond of music
2 NM,F enthusiast
apasionante ADJ exciting
apasionar VT to excite, to thrill; **le apasiona el jazz** he is mad about jazz
apatía NF apathy
apático, -a 1 ADJ apathetic
2 NM,F apathetic person
apátrida 1 ADJ stateless
2 NMF stateless person
apdo. (*abr apartado*) P.O. Box
apeadero NM halt
apearse VPR **a. (de)** (*tren*) to alight (from), to get off; (*coche, autobús*) to get out (of); (*caballo*) to dismount (from); **se apeó en Jerez** he got off in Jerez
apechugar [42] VI *Fam* **a. con** to shoulder
apedrear VT (*persona*) to stone; (*cosa*) to throw stones at
apegado, -a ADJ attached (**a** to)
apegarse [42] VPR to become attached (**a** to)
apego NM attachment; **tener a. a** to be attached to
apelación NF appeal
apelar VI (**a**) *Der* to (lodge an) appeal; **a. ante/ contra** to appeal to/against (**b**) (*recurrir*) **a. a** (*sentido común, bondad*) to appeal to
apellidarse VPR to have as a surname, to be called
apellido NM surname; **a. de soltera** maiden name
apelmazado, -a ADJ (*arroz, bizcocho*) stodgy; **el jersey está a.** the jumper has lost its fluffiness
apelotonar 1 VT to bundle up
2 apelotonarse VPR (*gente*) to crowd together
apenado, -a ADJ (**a**) (*entristecido*) sad (**b**) *Am salvo RP* (*avergonzado*) embarrassed; **está muy a. por lo que hizo** he's very embarrassed about what he did
apenar 1 VT to sadden
2 apenarse VPR (**a**) (*entristecerse*) to be saddened (**b**) *Am salvo RP* (*avergonzarse*) to be embarrassed
apenas ADV (**a**) (*casi no*) hardly, scarcely; **a. come** he hardly eats anything; **a. (si) hay nieve** there is hardly any snow (**b**) (*tan pronto como*) scarcely; **a. llegó, sonó el teléfono** no sooner had he arrived than the phone rang
apéndice NM appendix
apendicitis NF INV appendicitis
apercibir 1 VT to warn
2 apercibirse VPR **apercibirse (de)** to notice
aperitivo NM (*bebida*) apéritif; (*comida*) appetizer
aperos NMPL **a. de labranza** farming implements
apertura NF (**a**) (*comienzo*) opening (**b**) *Pol* liberalization

apestar 1 VI to stink (**a** of)
2 VT to infect with the plague
apetecer [33] VI *Esp* **¿qué te apetece para cenar?** what would you like for supper?; **¿te apetece ir al cine?** do you fancy going to the cinema?
apetecible ADJ tempting, inviting
apetito NM appetite; **tengo mucho a.** I'm really hungry
apetitoso, -a ADJ appetizing, tempting; (*comida*) delicious, tasty
apiadarse VPR to take pity (**de** on)
ápice NM **ni un á.** not a bit
apicultura NF beekeeping, apiculture
apilar 1 VT to pile up
2 apilarse VPR to pile up
apiñado, -a ADJ packed, crammed
apiñarse VPR to crowd together
apio NM celery
apisonadora NF roadroller, steamroller
apisonar VT to roll
aplacar [44] **1** VT to placate, to calm
2 aplacarse VPR to calm down
aplanar VT to level
aplastante ADJ (*victoria, derrota*) crushing, overwhelming; (*mayoría, superioridad*) overwhelming
aplastar VT (**a**) (*por el peso*) to flatten, to squash (**b**) *Fig* (*vencer*) to crush
aplatanado, -a ADJ *Esp, Méx Fam* listless
aplaudir 1 VT to applaud
2 VI to applaud, to clap
aplauso NM (*ovación*) round of applause; *Fig* (*alabanza*) applause; **aplausos** applause
aplazamiento NM postponement
aplazar [40] VT to postpone
aplicación NF application
aplicado, -a ADJ hard-working
aplicar [44] **1** VT to apply
2 aplicarse VPR (**a**) (*esforzarse*) to apply oneself, to work hard (**b**) (*norma, ley*) to apply, to be applicable
aplique NM wall light, wall lamp
aplomo NM aplomb
apocado, -a ADJ shy, timid
apocamiento NM timidity
apodar 1 VT to nickname
2 apodarse VPR to be nicknamed
apoderado, -a NM,F (*de torero, deportista*) agent, manager
apoderarse VPR to take possession (**de** of), to seize; *Fig* **el miedo se apoderó de ella** she was seized by fear
apodo NM nickname
apogeo NM height; **estar en pleno a.** (*fama etc*) to be at its height
apolillarse VPR to get moth-eaten
apolítico, -a ADJ apolitical

apología NF apology, defence

apoltronarse VPR *Fam* to vegetate

apoplejía NF apoplexy

apoquinar VT & VI *Esp Fam* to cough up, to fork out

aporrear VT *(puerta)* to bang; **a. el piano** to bang (away) on the piano

aportación NF contribution

aportar VT to contribute

aposentarse VPR to take up lodgings

aposento NM room

aposta ADV *Esp* on purpose, intentionally

apostar¹ [2] **1** VT to bet; **te apuesto una cena a que no viene** I bet you a dinner that he won't come

2 VI to bet (**por** on); **a. a los caballos** to bet on horses; **apuesto a que sí viene** I bet she will come

3 **apostarse** VPR to bet; **me apuesto lo que quieras** I bet you anything

apostar² VT *(situar)* to post, to station

apostilla NF *(nota)* note; *(comentario)* comment

apóstol NM apostle

apóstrofo NM apostrophe

apoteósico, -a ADJ tremendous; **un final a.** a grand finale

apoyacabezas NM INV *Aut* headrest

apoyar **1** VT (**a**) *(inclinar)* to lean, to rest (**b**) *(causa)* to support

2 **apoyarse** VPR (**a**) *(sostenerse)* **apoyarse en** to lean on; **apóyate en mi brazo** take my arm (**b**) *(buscar respaldo)* **apoyarse en** to rely on (**c**) *(basarse)* **apoyarse en** to base one's arguments on

apoyo NM support

apreciable ADJ appreciable, noticeable

apreciación NF appreciation

apreciado, -a ADJ *(querido)* esteemed, highly regarded

apreciar [43] **1** VT (**a**) *(sentir afecto por)* to be fond of (**b**) *(percibir)* to notice, to see (**c**) *(valorar)* to appreciate

2 **apreciarse** VPR to be noticeable

aprecio NM regard, esteem; **tener a. a algn** to be fond of sb

aprehender VT *(persona)* to apprehend; *(alijo, mercancía)* to seize

aprehensión NF *(de persona)* arrest, capture; *(de alijo, mercancía)* seizure

apremiante ADJ urgent, pressing

apremiar [43] VI to be urgent; **el tiempo apremia** time is short

aprender VT to learn; **así aprenderás** that'll teach you

aprendiz, -a NM,F apprentice, trainee

aprendizaje NM (**a**) *(adquisición de conocimientos)* learning (**b**) *(tiempo, situación)* apprenticeship, traineeship

aprensión NF apprehension

aprensivo, -a ADJ apprehensive

apresar VT to seize, to capture

aprestarse VPR **a. a hacer algo** to get ready to do sth

apresurado, -a ADJ *(persona)* in a hurry; *(cosa)* hurried

apresuramiento NM haste, hurry

apresurar **1** VT *(paso etc)* to speed up

2 **apresurarse** VPR to hurry up

apretado, -a ADJ (**a**) *(ropa, cordón)* tight; **íbamos todos apretados en el coche** we were all squashed together in the car (**b**) *(día, agenda)* busy

apretar [1] **1** VT *(botón)* to press; *(nudo, tornillo)* to tighten; **a. el gatillo** to pull the trigger; **me aprietan las botas** these boots are too tight for me

2 VI **apretaba el calor** it was really hot

3 **apretarse** VPR to squeeze together, to cram together; *Fig* **apretarse el cinturón** to tighten one's belt

apretón NM squeeze; **a. de manos** handshake

apretujar **1** VT to squeeze, to crush

2 **apretujarse** VPR to squeeze together, to cram together

aprieto NM tight spot, fix, jam; **poner a algn en un a.** to put sb in an awkward position

aprisa ADV quickly

aprisionar VT *(atrapar)* to trap

aprobación NF approval

aprobado NM *Educ* pass

aprobar [2] VT (**a**) *(autorizar)* to approve (**b**) *(estar de acuerdo con)* to approve of (**c**) *Educ* to pass (**d**) *Pol (ley)* to pass

aprontar **1** VT *(preparar)* to quickly prepare o get ready

2 **aprontarse** VPR *RP (prepararse)* to get ready; **aprontate para cuando llegue tu papá!** just you wait till your father gets home!

apropiado, -a ADJ suitable, appropriate

apropiarse [43] VPR to appropriate

aprovechado, -a ADJ (**a**) *(recurso, tiempo)* wasted; **bien a.** put to good use (**b**) *(espacio)* well-planned (**c**) *(egoísta)* self-seeking

aprovechamiento NM use

aprovechar **1** VT *(tiempo, dinero)* to make the most of; *(oferta, ocasión)* to take advantage of; *(conocimientos, experiencia)* to use, to make use of; **me gustaría a. esta oportunidad para …** I'd like to take this opportunity to …

2 VI **¡que aproveche!** enjoy your meal!, bon appétit!

3 **aprovecharse** VPR to take advantage; **aprovecharse de algn** to take advantage of sb; **aprovecharse de algo** to make the most of sth

aprovisionar 1 VT to supply
2 aprovisionarse VPR **aprovisionarse de algo** to stock up on sth

aproximación NF approximation

aproximadamente ADV approximately, roughly

aproximado, -a ADJ approximate; **un cálculo a.** a rough estimate

aproximar 1 VT to bring *o* put nearer
2 aproximarse VPR **aproximarse (a)** to approach

aproximativo, -a ADJ approximate, rough

aptitud NF aptitude; **prueba de a.** aptitude test

apto, -a ADJ (**a**) *(apropiado)* suitable, appropriate; *Cin* **a. para todos los públicos** *Br* U, *US* G (**b**) *(capacitado)* capable, able (**c**) *Educ* passed

apuesta NF bet, wager

apuesto, -a ADJ good-looking; *(hombre)* handsome

apunado, -a ADJ *Andes* **estar a.** to have altitude sickness

apunarse VPR *Andes* to get altitude sickness

apuntador, -a NM,F *Teatro* prompter

apuntalar VT to shore up

apuntar 1 VT (**a**) *(arma)* to aim; **a. a algn** to aim at sb (**b**) *(señalar)* to point out (**c**) *(anotar)* to note down, to make a note of
2 VI (**a**) *(indicar)* to indicate, to suggest; **todo parece a. a …** everything seems to point to … (**b**) **cuando apunta el día** when day breaks
3 apuntarse VPR (**a**) *(en una lista)* to put one's name down (**b**) *Fam* **¿te apuntas?** are you game?; **me apunto** count me in

apunte NM *(usu pl)* note; **tomar apuntes** to take notes

apuñalar VT to stab

apurado, -a 1 ADJ (**a**) *(necesitado)* in need; **a. de dinero** hard up for money; **a. de tiempo** in a hurry (**b**) *(preocupado)* worried; *(avergonzado)* embarrassed (**c**) *(situación)* awkward, difficult (**d**) *Esp (afeitado)* close (**e**) *Am (con prisa)* **estar a.** to be in a hurry
2 NM *Esp (afeitado)* close shave

apurar 1 VT (**a**) *(terminar)* to finish off, to end (**b**) *(preocupar)* to worry
2 apurarse VPR (**a**) *Esp, Méx (preocuparse)* to worry, to get worried; **no te apures** don't worry (**b**) *Am (darse prisa)* to rush, to hurry, to pester; **apúrate** get a move on

apuro NM (**a**) *(situación difícil)* tight spot, fix, jam; **estar en un a.** to be in a tight spot (**b**) *(escasez de dinero)* hardship; **pasar apuros** to be hard up (**c**) *(vergüenza)* embarrassment; **¡qué a.!** how embarrassing! (**d**) *Am (prisa)* **tener a.** to be in a hurry

aquejado, -a ADJ **a. de** suffering from

aquel, -ella *(pl* **aquellos, -ellas)** ADJ DEM (**a**) *(singular)* that; **a. niño** that boy (**b**) **aquellos, -as** those; **aquellas niñas** those girls

aquél, -élla *(pl* **aquéllos, -éllas)** PRON DEM M,F (**a**) *(singular)* that one; *(el anterior)* the former; **aquél/aquélla … éste/ésta** the former … the latter (**b**) **todo a. que** anyone who, whoever (**c**) **aquéllos, -as** those; *(los anteriores)* the former

> Note that **aquél** and its various forms can be written without an accent when there is no risk of confusion with the adjective.

aquelarre NM coven

aquella ADJ DEM F *ver* **aquel**

aquélla PRON DEM F *ver* **aquél**

aquello PRON NEUT F that, it

aquellos, -as ADJ DEM PL *ver* **aquel**

aquéllos, -as PRON DEM M,F PL *ver* **aquél**

aquí ADV (**a**) *(lugar)* here; **a. arriba/fuera** up/out here; **a. está** here it is; **a. mismo** right here; **de a. para allá** up and down, to and fro; **hasta a.** this far; **por a., por favor** this way please; **está por a.** it's around here somewhere (**b**) *(tiempo)* **de a. en adelante** from now on; **de aquí a junio** between now and June; **hasta a.** up till now

aquietar VT to pacify, to calm down

árabe 1 ADJ *(de Arabia)* Arab
2 NMF *(persona)* Arab
3 NM *(idioma)* Arabic

Arabia N Arabia; **A. Saudí** Saudi Arabia

arado NM plough

Aragón N Aragon

aragonés, -esa ADJ & NM,F Aragonese

arancel NM tariff; **a. aduanero** customs duty

arancelario, -a ADJ tariff; **barreras arancelarias** tariff barriers

arandela NF *Téc* washer; *(anilla)* ring

araña NF (**a**) *(insecto)* spider (**b**) *(lámpara)* chandelier

arañar VT to scratch

arañazo NM scratch

arar VT to plough

aras NFPL *Fml* **en a. de** for the sake of

araucaria NF araucaria, monkey puzzle tree

arbitraje NM (**a**) *Der* arbitration (**b**) *Dep* refereeing; *Ten* umpiring

arbitrar VT & VI (**a**) *Der* to arbitrate (**b**) *Dep* to referee; *Ten* to umpire

arbitrariedad NF (**a**) *(cualidad)* arbitrariness (**b**) *(acto)* arbitrary action

arbitrario, -a ADJ arbitrary

arbitrio NM **dejar algo al a. de algn** to leave sth to sb's discretion

árbitro, -a NM,F (**a**) *Dep* referee; *(de tenis)* umpire (**b**) *(mediador)* arbitrator

árbol NM (**a**) *Bot* tree (**b**) *Téc* shaft (**c**) *Náut* mast (**d**) *(gráfico)* tree (diagram); **á. genealógico** family *o* genealogical tree

arbolado, -a 1 ADJ wooded
2 NM woodland

arboleda NF grove

arbusto NM bush, shrub

arca NF (**a**) *(mueble)* chest (**b**) **arcas públicas** Treasury

> Takes the masculine articles **el** and **un**.

arcada NF (**a**) *(de estómago)* **me dieron arcadas** I retched (**b**) *Arquit (arcos)* arcade

arcaico, -a ADJ archaic

arcángel NM archangel

arcén NM *Esp (en carretera) Br* hard shoulder, *US* shoulder

archi- PREF super-

archiconocido, -a ADJ extremely well-known

archipiélago NM archipelago

archivador NM filing cabinet

archivar VT (**a**) *(documento etc)* to file (away) (**b**) *(caso, asunto)* to shelve (**c**) *Inform* to save

archivo NM (**a**) *(documento)* file (**b**) *(lugar)* archive (**c**) *Inform* file; **a. adjunto** attachment

arcilla NF clay

arco NM (**a**) *Arquit* arch (**b**) *Mat & Elec* arc (**c**) *(de violín)* bow (**d**) *(para flechas)* bow; **tiro con a.** archery (**e**) **a. iris** rainbow (**f**) *esp Am Dep (portería)* goal, goalmouth

arder VI to burn; *Fam* **la conversación está que arde** the conversation is really heating up; **Juan está que arde** Juan is really fuming

ardid NM ruse, trick

ardiente ADJ (**a**) *(encendido)* burning; **capilla a.** chapel of rest (**b**) *Fig (fervoroso)* eager

ardilla NF squirrel

ardor NM (**a**) *(quemazón)* burning (sensation); *Med* **a. de estómago** heartburn (**b**) *(entusiasmo)* fervour

ardoroso, -a ADJ ardent, passionate

arduo, -a ADJ arduous

área NF (**a**) *(extensión)* area; *Dep* penalty area (**b**) *(medida)* are *(100 square metres)*

> Takes the masculine articles **el** and **un**.

arena NF (**a**) *(material)* sand; **playa de a.** sandy beach (**b**) *Taurom* bullring

arengar [42] VT to harangue

arenisca NF sandstone

arenoso, -a ADJ sandy

arenque NM herring; *Culin* **a. ahumado** kipper

arepa NF *Carib, Col* = pancake made of maize flour

arete NM *Andes, Méx (pendiente)* earring; *Esp (en forma de aro)* hoop earring

argamasa NF mortar

Argel N Algiers

Argelia N Algeria

argelino, -a ADJ & NM,F Algerian

Argentina N Argentina

argentino, -a ADJ & NM,F Argentinian, Argentine

argolla NF (**a**) *(aro)* (large) ring (**b**) *Andes, Méx (alianza)* wedding ring (**c**) *Carib (pendiente)* hoop earring

argot *(pl* argots*)* NM *(popular)* slang; *(técnico)* jargon

argucia NF ruse

argüende NM *Méx Fam* (**a**) *(chisme)* gossip (**b**) *(fiesta)* party, *Br* rave-up

argüir [62] VT (**a**) *(deducir)* to deduce (**b**) *(argumentar)* to argue

argumentación NF argument

argumentar 1 VT *(alegar)* to argue

2 VI *(discutir)* to argue

argumento NM (**a**) *Lit & Teatro (trama)* plot (**b**) *(razonamiento)* argument

arguyo INDIC PRES de **argüir**

aria NF *(de ópera)* aria

aridez NF *(de terreno, clima)* aridity, dryness

árido, -a ADJ *(terreno, clima)* arid, dry; *(libro, tema)* dry

Aries NM Aries

ariete NM *Mil* battering ram

ario, -a ADJ & NM,F Aryan

arisco, -a ADJ surly

arista NF edge

aristocracia NF aristocracy

aristócrata NM,F aristocrat

aristocrático, -a ADJ aristocratic

aritmética NF arithmetic

arlequín NM harlequin

arma NF weapon; **a. blanca** knife; **a. de fuego** firearm; **a. homicida** murder weapon; **a. nuclear** nuclear weapon; *Fig* **a. de doble filo** double-edged sword

> Takes the masculine articles **el** and **un**.

armada NF navy

armadillo NM armadillo

armado, -a ADJ armed; **ir a.** to be armed; **lucha armada** armed struggle

armador, -a NM,F shipowner

armadura NF (**a**) *(armazón)* frame (**b**) *Hist* suit of armour

armamentista ADJ arms; **la carrera a.** the arms race

armamento NM armaments; **a. nuclear** nuclear weapons

armar 1 VT (**a**) *(tropa, soldado)* to arm (**b**) *(piezas)* to fit *o* put together, to assemble (**c**) *Fam* **armaron un escándalo** they kicked up a fuss

2 armarse VPR to arm oneself; *Fig* **armarse de paciencia** to summon up one's patience; *Fig* **armarse de valor** to pluck up courage; *Fam* **se armó la gorda** all hell broke loose

armario NM *(para ropa)* wardrobe; *(de cocina)* cupboard; **a. empotrado** built-in wardrobe *o* cupboard

armatoste NM *(mueble, objeto)* unwieldy object; *(máquina)* contraption

armazón NM *(estructura)* framework, frame; *(de avión, coche)* chassis; *(de edificio)* skeleton

Armenia N Armenia

armería NF gunsmith's (shop)

armiño NM ermine

armisticio NM armistice

armonía NF harmony

armónica NF harmonica, mouth organ

armonioso, -a ADJ harmonious

armonizar [40] VT & VI to harmonize

aro NM (a) *(gen)* hoop; *Fam* **pasar por el a.** to knuckle under (b) *Am (pendiente)* earring; *Esp (circular)* hoop earring (c) *Ven (alianza)* wedding ring (d) *Col (montura)* rim (e) *Bol (anillo)* ring

aroma NM aroma; *(de vino)* bouquet

aromático, -a ADJ aromatic

arpa NF harp

> Takes the masculine articles **el** and **un**.

arpía NF *(en mitología)* harpy; *Fig* harpy, old witch

arpón NM harpoon

arquear 1 VT *(madera)* to warp; *(vara, fusta)* to flex; *(cejas, espalda)* to arch
2 **arquearse** VPR to warp

arqueología NF archaeology

arqueólogo, -a NM,F archaeologist

arquero NM,F (a) *(tirador)* archer (b) *Am Ftb* goalkeeper

arquetipo NM archetype

arquitecto, -a NM,F architect

arquitectónico, -a ADJ architectural

arquitectura NF architecture

arrabalero, -a ADJ *Esp Pey* coarse

arrabales NMPL slums

arraigado, -a ADJ deeply rooted

arraigar [42] VI to take root

arraigo NM roots; **una tradición con mucho a.** a deeply-rooted tradition

arrancar [44] 1 VT (a) *(planta)* to uproot, to pull up; **a. de raíz** to uproot (b) *(extraer)* to pull o tear off o out; *(diente, pelo)* to pull out; *Fig (confesión etc)* to extract; **arranca una hoja del cuaderno** tear a page out of the notebook (c) *(coche, motor)* to start; *Inform* to boot
2 VI (a) *Aut & Téc* to start; *Inform* to boot (up) (b) *(empezar)* to begin; **a. a llorar** to burst out crying

arranque NM (a) *Aut & Téc* starting (b) *(comienzo)* start (c) *Fam (arrebato)* outburst, fit

arrasar 1 VT *(edificio, cosecha)* to destroy; *(zona)* to devastate
2 VI (a) **a. con** *(destruir)* to destroy (b) *Fam (triunfar)* to win overwhelmingly

arrastrado, -a ADJ (a) *(vida)* miserable, wretched (b) *Méx, RP (servil)* grovelling
2 NM,F *Méx, RP* groveller

arrastrar 1 VT to pull (along), to drag (along); **vas arrastrando el vestido** your dress is trailing on the ground; **lo arrastró la corriente** he was swept away by the current
2 **arrastrarse** VPR to drag oneself; *Fig (humillarse)* to crawl

arrastre NM (a) *(acción)* pulling, dragging; *Esp Fam* **estar para el a.** to have had it (b) *(pesca de)* **a.** trawling (c) *RP Fam* **tener a.** to have a lot of influence

arrayán NM myrtle

arre INTERJ gee up!, giddy up!

arrear VT (a) *(azuzar)* to gee up (b) *Fam (bofetada)* to give

arrebatador, -a ADJ captivating, fascinating

arrebatar 1 VT *(coger)* to snatch, to seize; *Fig (cautivar)* to captivate, to fascinate
2 **arrebatarse** VPR *(enfurecerse)* to become furious; *(exaltarse)* to get carried away

arrebato NM outburst, fit

arrecho, -a ADJ (a) *CAm, Méx, Ven Fam (furioso)* mad, furious (b) *CAm, Col, Méx, Ven Vulg (sexualmente)* horny

arreciar [43] VI *(viento, tormenta)* to get worse

arrecife NM reef

arreglado, -a ADJ (a) *(reparado)* repaired, fixed (b) *(solucionado)* settled (c) *(habitación)* tidy, neat (d) *(persona)* well-dressed, smart

arreglar 1 VT (a) *(reparar)* to repair, to fix (b) *(solucionar)* to sort out (c) *(ordenar)* to tidy (up)
2 **arreglarse** VPR (a) *(vestirse)* to get ready (b) *Fam* **arreglárselas** to manage

arreglo NM (a) *(reparación)* repair; **no tiene a.** it is beyond repair; *Fam* **¡no tienes a.!** you're hopeless! (b) *(acuerdo)* agreement; *Fml* **con a. a** in accordance with (c) *Mús* **arreglos musicales** musical arrangements

arrellanarse VPR to sit back

arremangarse [42] VPR to roll up one's sleeves

arremeter VI **a. contra** to attack

arremolinarse VPR *(agua, hojas)* to whirl about; *(personas)* **a. alrededor de** o **en torno a** to mill round about, to crowd round

arrendamiento NM (a) *(alquiler)* renting, leasing (b) *(precio)* rent

arrendar [1] VT *(dar en arriendo)* to let on lease; *(tomar en arriendo)* to take on lease; *Am* **se arrienda** *(en letrero)* to let

arrendatario, -a NM,F leaseholder, tenant

arreos NMPL (a) *(de caballería)* harness, trappings (b) *(adornos)* adornments

arrepentido, -a ADJ repentant

arrepentimiento NM repentance

arrepentirse [5] VPR **a. de** to regret; *Rel* to repent

arrestar VT to arrest

arresto NM (**a**) *(detención)* arrest; *Der* **a. domiciliario** house arrest (**b**) **arrestos** courage

arriar [29] VT *(bandera)* to strike; *(velas)* to lower

arriba 1 ADV up; *(encima)* on the top; **ahí a.** up there; **de a. abajo** from top to bottom; *Fam* **mirar a algn de a. abajo** to look sb up and down; **desde a.** from above; **hacia a.** upwards; **de un millón para a.** from one million upwards; **más a.** higher up, further up; **a. del todo** right on *o* at the top; **la parte de a.** the top (part); **vive a.** he lives upstairs; **véase más a.** see above
2 INTERJ get up!, up you get!; **¡a. la República!** long live the Republic!; **¡a. las manos!** hands up!
3 PREP *Am* **a. (de)** on top of

arribar VI **a. a** to reach

arribeño, -a *Am* **1** ADJ highland
2 NM,F highlander

arribista NMF *(profesionalmente)* careerist; *(socialmente)* social climber

arriendo NM lease; *(de un piso)* renting; **dar en a.** to let out on lease; **tomar en a.** to take on lease

arriesgado, -a ADJ (**a**) *(peligroso)* risky (**b**) *(temerario)* fearless, daring

arriesgar [42] **1** VT to risk
2 arriesgarse VPR to risk; **se arriesga demasiado** he's taking too many risks

arrimar 1 VT to move closer, to bring near *o* nearer; *Fam* **a. el hombro** to lend a hand
2 arrimarse VPR to move *o* get close, to come near *o* nearer

arrinconar VT (**a**) *(apartar)* to put in a corner; **a. a algn** to leave sb out in the cold (**b**) *(abandonar)* to discard (**c**) *(acorralar)* to corner

arroba NM *Inform* at, @ sign

arrobo NM rapture, enthralment

arrocero, -a ADJ *(región)* rice-growing; **la industria arrocera** the rice industry

arrodillarse VPR to kneel down

arrogancia NF arrogance

arrogante ADJ arrogant

arrojadizo, -a ADJ **arma arrojadiza** missile

arrojado, -a ADJ bold, daring

arrojar 1 VT (**a**) *(tirar)* to throw, to fling (**b**) *Com (saldo)* to show
2 arrojarse VPR to throw oneself, to fling oneself

arrojo NM daring, courage

arrollador, -a ADJ *(victoria, superioridad)* overwhelming; *(belleza, personalidad)* dazzling

arrollar VT **1** to run over, to knock down
2 VI *Dep & Pol* to win easily

arropar 1 VT (**a**) *(con ropa)* to wrap up; *(en la cama)* to tuck in (**b**) *(proteger)* to support
2 arroparse VPR to wrap up (warm)

arrostrar VT to face up to

arroyo NM brook, stream

arroz NM rice; **a. con leche** rice pudding

arruga NF *(en la piel)* wrinkle; *(en la ropa)* crease

arrugar [42] **1** VT *(piel)* to wrinkle; *(ropa)* to crease; *(papel)* to crumple (up)
2 arrugarse VPR *(piel)* to wrinkle; *(ropa)* to crease

arruinado, -a ADJ ruined

arruinar 1 VT to ruin
2 arruinarse VPR to be ruined

arrullar 1 VT *(bebé)* to lull to sleep
2 VI *(paloma)* to coo

arrullo NM (**a**) *(de paloma)* cooing (**b**) *(nana)* lullaby

arrumacos NMPL *Fam* **hacerse a.** *(amantes)* to kiss and cuddle; **hacer a. a** *(bebé)* to coo at

arsenal NM (**a**) *Esp (de barcos)* shipyard (**b**) *(de armas)* arsenal

arsénico NM arsenic

arte NM *o* NF art; **bellas artes** fine arts; *Fam* **por amor al a.** for the love of it

> Takes the masculine articles **el** and **un**.

artefacto NM device; **a. explosivo** explosive device

arteria NF artery; *(carretera)* highway

artesanal ADJ handmade

artesanía NF (**a**) *(cualidad)* craftsmanship (**b**) *(objetos)* crafts, handicrafts

artesano, -a 1 NM,F *(hombre)* craftsman; *(mujer)* craftswoman
2 ADJ handmade

ártico, -a 1 ADJ arctic; **el océano Á.** the Arctic Ocean
2 NM **el Á.** the Arctic

articulación NF (**a**) *Anat* joint, articulation (**b**) *Téc* joint

articulado, -a ADJ *(tren etc)* articulated

articular VT to articulate

articulista NMF feature writer

artículo NM article; **a. de fondo** leader (article)

artífice NMF architect; **el a. del acuerdo** the architect of the agreement

artificial ADJ artificial; *Tex* man-made, synthetic

artificio NM (**a**) *(falsedad)* artifice; **fuego de a.** firework (**b**) *(artimaña)* ruse

artillería NF artillery; **a. antiaérea** anti-aircraft guns

artillero NM artilleryman

artilugio NM gadget, device

artimaña NF trick, ruse

artista NMF artist; **a. de cine** movie *o Br* film actor

artístico, -a ADJ artistic

artritis NF INV arthritis

arveja NF *RP* pea

arzobispo NM archbishop
as NM ace
asa NF handle

> Takes the masculine articles **el** and **un**.

asado, -a 1 ADJ *Culin* roast; **pollo a.** roast chicken; *Fig* **a. de calor** roasting, boiling hot
  2 NM *Culin* roast; *Col, CSur (barbacoa)* barbecue
asador NM (a) *(aparato)* roaster (b) *(restaurante)* grill, grillroom
asaduras NFPL *(de cordero, ternera)* offal; *(de ave)* giblets
asalariado, -a 1 ADJ salaried
  2 NM,F wage earner, salaried worker
asaltante NMF attacker; *(en un robo)* robber
asaltar VT to assault, to attack; *(banco)* to rob; **le asaltaron las dudas** he was seized by doubts
asalto NM (a) *(ataque)* assault, attack; **a. a un banco** bank robbery (b) *(en boxeo)* round
asamblea NF meeting; **a. general** general meeting
asar 1 VT to roast
  2 asarse VPR *Fig* to be roasting, to be boiling hot
ascendencia NF ancestry, ancestors; **de a. escocesa** of Scottish descent
ascendente 1 ADJ rising
  2 NM *(en astrología)* ascendant
ascender [3] **1** VT *(en un cargo)* to promote
  2 VI (a) *(subir)* to move upward; *(temperatura)* to rise; *(al trono)* to ascend (b) *(de categoría)* to be promoted (c) **a. a** *(totalizar)* to come o amount to; **la factura asciende a ...** the bill adds up o comes to ...
ascendiente NMF ancestor
ascensión NF ascent; *Rel* **A.** Ascension
ascenso NM promotion; *(subida)* rise
ascensor NM *Br* lift, *US* elevator
asco NM disgust, repugnance; **me da a.** it makes me (feel) sick; **¡qué a.!** how disgusting o revolting!
ascua NF ember; *Fig* **en ascuas** on tenterhooks

> Takes the masculine articles **el** and **un**.

aseado, -a ADJ tidy, neat
asear 1 VT to clean, to tidy up
  2 asearse VPR to wash, to get washed
asediar [43] VT *Mil* to lay siege to; *Fig* to pester, to badger
asedio NM siege
asegurado, -a 1 ADJ insured
  2 NM,F policy holder
asegurador, -a 1 ADJ insurance
  2 NM,F insurer
asegurar 1 VT (a) *(contra riesgos)* to insure (b) *(garantizar)* **me aseguró que ...** he assured me that ...; **a. el éxito de un proyecto** to ensure the success of a project (c) *(cuerda)* to fasten

2 asegurarse VPR (a) *(cerciorarse)* to make sure; **asegurarse de que ...** to make sure that ... (b) *(contra riesgos)* to insure oneself
asemejarse VPR **a. a** to look like
asentado, -a ADJ *(establecido)* established, settled
asentamiento NM settlement
asentar [1] **1** VT **a. la cabeza** to settle down
  2 asentarse VPR (a) *(establecerse)* to settle down, to establish oneself (b) *(té, polvo)* to settle
asentimiento NM assent, consent
asentir [5] VI to assent, to agree; **a. con la cabeza** to nod
aseo NM (a) *(limpieza)* cleanliness, tidiness (b) *Esp (habitación)* bathroom; **aseos** *Br* toilets, *US* restroom
aséptico, -a ADJ *Med* aseptic; *Fig (indiferente)* detached
asequible ADJ affordable; *(comprensible)* easy to understand; *(alcanzable)* attainable
asesinar VT to murder; *(rey, ministro)* to assassinate
asesinato NM murder; *(de rey, ministro)* assassination
asesino, -a 1 ADJ murderous
  2 NM,F killer; *(hombre)* murderer; *(mujer)* murderess; *Pol* assassin
asesor, -a 1 NM,F adviser; **a. fiscal** tax adviser
  2 ADJ advisory
asesoramiento NM advice; *(de empresa)* consultancy
asesorar 1 VT to advise; *(empresa)* to provide with consultancy services
  2 asesorarse VPR to seek advice; **asesorarse de** o **con** to consult
asesoría NF (a) *(trabajo)* consultancy (b) *(oficina)* consultant's office
asestar VT to deal; **a. un golpe a algn** to deal sb a blow
aseverar VT to assert
asfaltado, -a 1 ADJ asphalt
  2 NM *(acción)* asphalting, surfacing; *(asfalto)* asphalt, (road) surface
asfaltar VT to asphalt, to surface
asfalto NM asphalt
asfixia NF asphyxiation, suffocation
asfixiante ADJ asphyxiating, suffocating; *Fam* **hace un calor a.** it's stifling
asfixiar [43] **1** VT to asphyxiate, to suffocate
  2 asfixiarse VPR to asphyxiate, to suffocate
así ADV (a) *(de esa manera)* like this o that, this way, thus; **ponlo a.** put it this way; **a. de grande/alto** this big/tall; **algo a.** something like this o that; **¿no es a.?** isn't that so o right?; **a. es la vida** such is life; **a. a.** so-so; **a. sin más,** *Am* **a. no más** o **nomás** just like that (b) **a las seis o a.** around six o'clock; **diez años o a.** ten years more or less (c) **a. como** as well as (d) **a. tenga que ...** *(aunque)* even if I have to

… (**e**) **aun a.** and despite that (**f**) **a. pues** so; **a. que … so …** (**g**) **a. que llegues** as soon as you arrive

Asia N Asia; **A. Menor** Asia Minor

asiático, -a ADJ & NM,F Asian

asidero NM *(asa)* handle; *Fig* pretext, excuse

asiduidad NF frequency; **con a.** frequently, regularly

asiduo, -a ADJ & NM,F regular

asiento NM (**a**) *(silla, butaca)* seat; **a. trasero/ delantero** front/back seat; **tome a.** take a seat (**b**) *(base)* bottom (**c**) *Fin* entry

asignación NF (**a**) *(acción)* allocation, assignment (**b**) *(cantidad)* allocation

asignar VT to allocate, to assign

asignatura NF subject; **a. pendiente** failed subject

asilado, -a NM,F refugee

asilar VT to grant o give political asylum to

asilo NM (**a**) *(amparo)* asylum; *Pol* **a. político** political asylum (**b**) *(hospicio)* home; **a. de ancianos** old people's home

asimilación NF assimilation

asimilar VT to assimilate

asimismo ADV *(también)* also, as well; *(a principio de frase)* likewise

asir [46] **1** VT to grasp, to take hold of
2 asirse VPR *también Fig* to cling (**a** to)

asistencia NF (**a**) *(presencia)* attendance; **falta de a.** absence (**b**) **a. médica/técnica** medical/ technical assistance (**c**) *(público)* audience, public

asistenta NF *Esp* cleaning lady

asistente NM,F (**a**) *(ayudante)* assistant, helper; **a. social** social worker (**b**) *(presente)* person present; **los asistentes** *(el público)* the audience

asistido, -a ADJ assisted; **a. por ordenador** computer-assisted; *Esp Aut* **dirección asistida** power steering

asistir 1 VT to assist, to help
2 VI **a.** (**a**) to attend, to be present (at)

asma NF asthma

Takes the masculine articles **el** and **un**.

asmático, -a ADJ & NM,F asthmatic

asno NM donkey, ass

asociación NF association

asociado, -a 1 ADJ associated
2 NM,F associate, partner

asociar [43] **1** VT to associate
2 asociarse VPR to form a partnership

asolar [2] VT to devastate, to destroy

asomar 1 VT **asomó la cabeza por la ventana** he put his head out of the window
2 VI *(sobresalir)* to peep up; *(del interior de algo)* to peep out
3 asomarse VPR (**a**) **asomarse a la ventana** to

lean out of the window (**b**) *(entrar)* to pop in; *(salir)* to pop out

asombrar 1 VT to amaze, to astonish
2 asombrarse VPR to be astonished; **asombrarse de algo** to be amazed at sth

asombro NM amazement, astonishment

asombroso, -a ADJ amazing, astonishing

asomo NM trace, hint; *(de esperanza)* glimmer; **ni por a.** not under any circumstances

asorocharse VPR *Andes* (**a**) *(por la altitud)* to get altitude sickness (**b**) *(sonrojarse)* to blush

aspa NF (**a**) *(de molino)* arm; *(de ventilador)* blade (**b**) *(cruz)* cross

Takes the masculine articles **el** and **un**.

aspaviento NM **hacer aspavientos** to wave one's arms about

aspecto NM (**a**) *(apariencia)* look, appearance (**b**) *(faceta)* aspect

aspereza NF roughness; *Fig* **limar asperezas** to smooth things over

áspero, -a ADJ rough; *Fig (carácter)* surly

aspersión NF *(de jardín)* sprinkling; *(de cultivos)* spraying

aspersor NM *(para jardín)* sprinkler; *(para cultivos)* sprayer

aspiración NF (**a**) *(de aire)* inhalation, breathing in (**b**) *(pretensión)* aspiration

aspiradora NF vacuum cleaner, *Br* Hoover

aspirante NM,F candidate, applicant

aspirar 1 VT (**a**) *(respirar)* to inhale, to breathe in (**b**) *Téc (absorber)* to suck in, to draw in
2 VI *Fig* **a. a algo** to aspire to sth

aspirina NF aspirin

asquear VT to disgust, to make sick

asquerosidad NF filthy o revolting thing; **¡que a.!** how revolting!

asqueroso, -a 1 ADJ *(sucio)* filthy; *(desagradable)* revolting, disgusting
2 NM,F filthy o revolting person

asta NF (**a**) *(de bandera)* staff, pole; **a media a.** at half-mast (**b**) *Zool (cuerno)* horn

Takes the masculine articles **el** and **un**.

asterisco NM asterisk

astilla NF splinter

astillero NM shipyard

astral ADJ astral; **carta a.** birth chart

astringente ADJ astringent

astro NM star

astrología NF astrology

astrólogo, -a NM,F astrologer

astronauta NM,F astronaut

astronave NF spaceship

astronomía NF astronomy

astronómico, -a ADJ astronomical

astrónomo, -a NM,F astronomer

astucia NF *(trampas)* cunning; *(sagacidad)* astuteness

asturiano, -a ADJ & NM,F Asturian

Asturias N Asturias

astuto, -a ADJ *(tramposo)* cunning; *(listo)* astute

asumir VT to assume

asunción NF assumption

asunto NM (a) *(cuestión)* matter; *(problema)* issue; **no es a. tuyo** it's none of your business (b) **Asuntos Exteriores** Foreign Affairs

asustar 1 VT to frighten, to scare
2 **asustarse** VPR to be frightened, to be scared

atacante NMF attacker, assailant

atacar [44] VT to attack, to assault; *Fig* **me ataca los nervios** he gets on my nerves

atado, -a ADJ tied; *(ocupado)* tied up

atadura NF tie

atajar 1 VI to take a shortcut (**por** across o through)
2 VT *(contener)* to put a stop to; *(hemorragia, inundación)* to stem

atajo NM (a) *(camino corto, medio rápido)* short cut (b) *Esp Pey (panda)* bunch

atalaya NF watchtower

atañer VI to concern, to have to do with; **eso no te atañe** that has nothing to do with you

ataque NM (a) *(acometida)* attack, assault; **a. aéreo** air raid (b) *Med* fit; **a. cardíaco** o **al corazón** heart attack; **a. de nervios/tos** fit of hysterics/coughing

atar 1 VT (a) *(nudo, cuerda)* to tie; *(persona caballo, barco)* to tie up; *Fig* **a. cabos** to put two and two together (b) *Fig (constreñir)* to tie down
2 **atarse** VPR (a) *(uno mismo)* to tie oneself down (b) **se ató el pelo** she tied her hair up; **atarse los zapatos** to tie one's shoes o shoelaces

atardecer [33] 1 V IMPERS to get o grow dark
2 NM evening, dusk

atareado, -a ADJ busy

atascado, -a ADJ stuck

atascar [44] 1 VT to block, to obstruct
2 **atascarse** VPR (a) *(bloquearse)* to become blocked, to become obstructed (b) *Fig (detenerse)* to get stuck

atasco NM traffic jam

ataúd NM coffin

ataviar [29] 1 VT to dress up
2 **ataviarse** VPR to dress up

atavío NM dress, attire

ate NM *Méx* quince jelly

ateísmo NM atheism

atemorizar [40] VT to frighten, to scare

atemperar VT to moderate, to temper

atemporal ADJ timeless

Atenas N Athens

atención 1 NF attention; **llamar la a.** to attract attention; **prestar/poner a.** to pay attention (**a** to); **a. al cliente** customer care, customer services
2 INTERJ attention!

atender [3] 1 VT to attend to; *(petición)* to agree to
2 VI *(alumno)* to pay attention (**a** to)

atenerse [24] VPR **a. a** *(promesa, orden)* to stick to; *(ley, normas)* to observe, to abide by; *(consecuencias)* to bear in mind; **no saber a qué a.** not to know what to expect

atentado NM attack; **a. terrorista** terrorist attack

atentamente ADV **le saluda a.** *(en carta)* yours sincerely/faithfully

atentar VI **a.** o **contra algo** to commit a crime against sth; **a. contra (la vida de) algn** to make an attempt on sb's life

atento, -a ADJ (a) *(pendiente)* attentive; **estar a. a** *(explicación, programa, lección)* to pay attention to; *(ruido, sonido)* to listen out for (b) *(amable)* thoughtful, considerate

atenuante 1 ADJ attenuating
2 NM *Der* extenuating circumstance

atenuar [30] VT *(disminuir, suavizar)* to diminish; *(dolor)* to ease, to alleviate; *(sonido, luz)* to attenuate

ateo, -a 1 ADJ atheistic
2 NM,F atheist

aterciopelado, -a ADJ velvety

aterido, -a ADJ **a. de frío** stiff with cold, numb

aterrador, -a ADJ terrifying

aterrar 1 VT to terrify
2 **aterrarse** VPR to be terrified

aterrizaje NM *Av* landing; **a. forzoso** forced landing

aterrizar [40] VI to land

aterrorizar [40] 1 VT to terrify; *Mil & Pol* to terrorize
2 **aterrorizarse** VPR to be terrified

atesorar VT *(riquezas)* to amass

atestado¹, -a ADJ packed, crammed; **estaba a. de gente** it was full of people

atestado² NM *Der* affidavit, statement; **atestados** testimonials

atestar¹ VT *Der* to testify

atestar² VT *(abarrotar)* to pack, to cram (**de** with)

atestiguar [45] VT (a) *Der* to testify to (b) *Fig* to vouch for

atiborrar 1 VT to pack, to stuff (**de** with)
2 **atiborrarse** VPR *Fam* to stuff oneself (**de** with)

ático NM *(piso)* = attic *Br* flat o *US* apartment, usually with a roof terrace; *(desván)* attic

atinado, -a ADJ *(juicioso)* sensible; *(pertinente)* pertinent

atinar VI to get it right; **a. a hacer algo** to succeed in doing sth; **a. al blanco** to hit the target; **atinó con la solución** he hit on o found the solution

atingencia NF (**a**) *Am, CAm, Chile, Méx (relación)* connection (**b**) *Chile, Méx (adecuación)* appropriateness; **la Cámara está estudiando la a. de esa ley** the House is investigating whether the law is appropriate o acceptable (**c**) *Méx (tino)* good sense

atípico, -a ADJ atypical

atisbar VT to make out

atisbo NM slight sign, inkling

atizar [40] VT (**a**) *(fuego)* to poke, to stir (**b**) *(sospechas, discordias)* to stir up (**c**) *Esp (persona)* **me atizó bien fuerte** *(un golpe)* he hit me really hard; *(una paliza)* he gave me a good hiding

atlántico, -a 1 ADJ Atlantic
   2 NM **el (océano) A.** the Atlantic (Ocean)

atlas NM INV atlas

atleta NMF athlete

atlético, -a ADJ athletic

atletismo NM athletics *sing*

atmósfera NF atmosphere

atmosférico, -a ADJ atmospheric

atole, atol NM *CAm, Méx* = thick hot drink made of corn meal

atolladero NM fix, jam; **estar en un a.** to be in a jam

atolondrado, -a ADJ foolish, thoughtless

atómico, -a ADJ atomic

átomo NM atom

atónito, -a ADJ amazed, astonished

atontado, -a ADJ (**a**) *(tonto)* silly, foolish (**b**) *(aturdido)* bewildered, amazed

atontar 1 VT to confuse, to bewilder
   2 atontarse VPR to be o get confused, to be bewildered

atorarse VPR (**a**) *(atragantarse)* to choke (**con** on) (**b**) *Am (atascarse)* to get stuck (**c**) *Am (meterse en un lío)* to get into a mess

atormentar 1 VT to torment
   2 atormentarse VPR to torment oneself, to suffer agonies

atornillar VT to screw on

atorón NM *Méx* traffic jam

atorrante ADJ *RP Fam* lazy

atosigar [42] VT *(con prisas)* to harass; *(con exigencias)* to pester, to badger

atracador, -a NM,F *(de banco)* (bank) robber; *(en la calle)* attacker, mugger

atracar [44] **1** VT to hold up; *(persona)* to rob
   2 VI *Náut* to come alongside, to tie up
   3 atracarse VPR *(de comida)* to stuff oneself (**de** with), to gorge oneself (**de** on)

atracción NF attraction; **parque de atracciones** funfair

atraco NM hold-up, robbery; **a. a mano armada** armed robbery

atracón NM *Fam* binge, blowout; **darse un a. de comer** to make a pig of oneself

atractivo, -a 1 ADJ attractive, appealing
   2 NM attraction, appeal

atraer [25] VT to attract

atragantarse VPR to choke (**con** on), to swallow the wrong way; *Fig* **esa chica se me ha atragantado** I can't stand that girl

atraigo INDIC PRES *de* atraer

atraje PT INDEF *de* atraer

atrancar [44] **1** VT *(puerta)* to bolt
   2 atrancarse VPR to get stuck; *(al hablar, escribir)* to dry up

atrapar VT to catch

atrás ADV (**a**) *(lugar)* at the back; behind; **hacia/para a.** backwards; **puerta de a.** back o rear door; *Fig* **echarse a.** to back out (**b**) *(tiempo)* previously, in the past, ago; **un año a.** a year ago; **venir de muy a.** to go o date back a long time

atrasado, -a ADJ late, slow; *(pago)* overdue; *(reloj)* slow; *(país)* backward; *Prensa* **número a.** back number

atrasar 1 VT to put back
   2 VI *(reloj)* to be slow
   3 atrasarse VPR (**a**) *(quedarse atrás)* to remain o stay behind, to lag behind (**b**) *(en el tiempo)* to be late (**c**) *(reloj)* to lose time

atraso NM (**a**) *(demora)* delay (**b**) *(de país)* backwardness (**c**) *Fin* **atrasos** arrears

atravesado, -a ADJ *(cruzado)* lying crosswise; **lo tengo a.** I can't stand him

atravesar [1] **1** VT (**a**) *(calle)* to cross (**b**) *(muro)* to pierce, to go through (**c**) *(poner a través)* to lay across, to put across, to put crosswise
   2 atravesarse VPR to get in the way; *Fig* **se me ha atravesado Luis** I can't stand Luis

atrayente ADJ attractive

atreverse VPR to dare; **a. a hacer algo** to dare to do sth

atrevido, -a ADJ (**a**) *(osado)* daring, bold (**b**) *(insolente)* insolent, impudent (**c**) *(ropa etc)* daring, risqué

atrevimiento NM (**a**) *(osadía)* daring, audacity (**b**) *(insolencia)* insolence, impudence

atribución NF (**a**) *(imputación)* attribution (**b**) *(competencia)* responsibility, duty

atribuir [37] **1** VT to attribute, to ascribe
   2 atribuirse VPR to assume

atribular VT to distress

atributo NM attribute

atril NM *(para partituras)* music stand; *(para libros)* lectern

atrio NM (**a**) *(pórtico)* portico (**b**) *(patio interior)* atrium

atrocidad NF atrocity

atrofiar [43] **1** VT to atrophy
   2 atrofiarse VPR to atrophy

atropellado, -a ADJ hasty, impetuous

atropellar VT to knock down, to run over

atropello NM (**a**) *Aut* knocking down, running over (**b**) *(abuso)* abuse

atroz ADJ (**a**) *(bárbaro)* atrocious (**b**) *Fam (hambre, frío)* enormous, tremendous

ATS NMF *Esp (abr* **ayudante técnico sanitario**) qualified nurse

atuendo NM dress, attire

atún NM tuna, tunny

aturdido, -a ADJ stunned, dazed

aturdimiento NM confusion, bewilderment

aturdir VT (**a**) *(con un golpe)* to stun, to daze (**b**) *(confundir)* to bewilder, to confuse

aturrullar VT *Fam* to fluster

atuve PT INDEF *de* atenerse

audacia NF audacity

audaz ADJ audacious, bold

audible ADJ audible

audición NF (**a**) *(acción de oír)* hearing (**b**) *Mús & Teatro* audition

audiencia NF (**a**) *(público)* audience; *TV & Rad* **horas de máxima a.** prime time; **índice de a.** viewing figures, ratings (**b**) *(entrevista)* audience (**c**) *Der* court hearing

audiolibro NM audiobook, talking book

audiovisual ADJ audio-visual

auditivo, -a 1 ADJ auditory; **comprensión auditiva** listening comprehension 2 NM receiver

auditor NM *Fin* auditor

auditoría NF *Fin* (**a**) *(profesión)* auditing (**b**) *(despacho)* auditor's, auditing company (**c**) *(balance)* audit; **a. externa/interna** external/internal audit

auditorio NM (**a**) *(público)* audience (**b**) *(sala)* auditorium, hall

auge NM peak; *Econ* boom; *Fig* **estar en a.** to be thriving *o* booming

augurar VT *(sujeto: persona)* to predict; *(sujeto: suceso)* to augur

augurio NM omen

aula NF *(en colegio)* classroom; *Univ* lecture room; **a. magna** amphitheatre

Takes the masculine articles **el** and **un**.

aullar VI to howl, to yell

aullido NM howl, yell

aumentar 1 VT to increase; *(precios)* to put up; *(producción)* to step up; *Fot* to enlarge; *Opt* to magnify 2 VI *(precios)* to go up, to rise; *(valor)* to appreciate 3 **aumentarse** VPR to increase, to be on the increase

aumento NM increase; *Opt* magnification; **a. de precios** rise in prices; **ir en a.** to be on the increase

aun ADV even; **a. así** even so, even then; **a. más** even more

aún ADV still; *(en negativas)* yet; **a. está aquí** he's still here; **ella no ha venido a.** she hasn't come yet

aunar VT to unite, to join

aunque CONJ although, though; *(enfático)* even if, even though; **a. no vengas** even if you don't come

aúpa INTERJ *Esp (¡levántate!)* up!, get up!; *(al coger a un niño en brazos)* ups-a-daisy!

aura NF aura

Takes the masculine articles **el** and **un**.

aureola NF halo

auricular NM (**a**) *Tel* receiver (**b**) **auriculares** earphones, headphones

aurora NF daybreak, dawn

auscultar VT to sound (with a stethoscope)

ausencia NF absence

ausentarse VPR to leave

ausente 1 ADJ absent 2 NMF absentee

ausentismo NM *Am* **a. laboral** *(justificado)* absence from work; *(injustificado)* absenteeism

austeridad NF austerity

austero, -a ADJ austere

austral 1 ADJ southern 2 NM *Fin* = former standard monetary unit of Argentina

Australia N Australia

australiano, -a ADJ & NM,F Australian

Austria N Austria

austríaco, -a ADJ & NM,F Austrian

autenticidad NF authenticity

auténtico, -a ADJ authentic

autentificar [44] VT to authenticate

autismo NM autism

autista 1 ADJ autistic 2 NMF autistic person

auto¹ NM *esp CSur (vehículo)* car

auto² NM *Der* decree, writ; **autos** *(pleito)* papers, documents

autoadhesivo, -a ADJ self-adhesive

autoayuda NF self-help

autobiografía NF autobiography

autobiográfico, -a ADJ autobiographical

autobombo NM *Fam* self-praise, blowing one's own trumpet

autobús *(pl* **autobuses**) NM bus

autocar NM *Esp* bus, *Br* coach

autocontrol NM self-control

autocrítica NF self-criticism

autóctono, -a ADJ indigenous

autodefensa NF self-defence

autodisciplina NF self-discipline

autoedición NF *Inform* desktop publishing, DTP

autoescuela NF driving school, school of motoring

autogobierno NM self-government

autógrafo NM autograph

autómata NM automaton

automático, -a ADJ automatic

automatización NF automation

automatizar [40] VT to automate

automotor, -triz ADJ self-propelled

automóvil NM car, US automobile

automovilismo NM motoring

automovilista NMF motorist

automovilístico, -a ADJ car; **accidente a.** car accident

autonomía NF (a) (cualidad) autonomy (b) (región) autonomous region

autonómico, -a ADJ autonomous, self-governing; **elecciones autonómicas** elections for the autonomous parliament; **televisión autónomica** regional television

autónomo, -a ADJ autonomous

autopista NF Br motorway, US freeway; Inform **autopista de la información** information superhighway

autopsia NF autopsy, postmortem

autor, -a NM,F (hombre) author; (mujer) authoress; (de crimen) perpetrator

autoría NF (de obra) authorship; (de crimen) perpetration

autoridad NF authority

autoritario, -a ADJ authoritarian

autorización NF authorization; **dar a. a algn (para hacer algo)** to authorize sb (to do sth)

autorizado, -a ADJ authoritative, official

autorizar [40] VT to authorize

autorretrato NM self-portrait

autoservicio NM self-service; (supermercado) supermarket

autostop NM hitch-hiking; **hacer a.** to hitch-hike

autostopista NMF hitch-hiker

autosuficiencia NF self-sufficiency

autosuficiente ADJ self-sufficient

autovía NF Br dual carriageway, US divided highway

auxiliar [43] **1** ADJ auxiliary
2 NMF assistant; **a. de vuelo** flight attendant
3 VT to help, to assist

auxilio NM help, assistance; **primeros auxilios** first aid

auyama NF Carib, Col pumpkin

Av. NF (abr **Avenida**) Ave

aval NM Com & Fin endorsement

avalancha NF avalanche

avalar VT to guarantee, to endorse

avance NM (a) (movimiento, progreso) advance (b) TV (de futura programación) preview; **a.**

informativo news summary, US news in brief (c) Fin (anticipo) advance payment

avanzado, -a ADJ advanced; **de avanzada edad** advanced in years

avanzar [40] VT to advance

avaricia NF greed, avarice

avaricioso, -a ADJ greedy, avaricious

avaro, -a 1 ADJ mean, miserly
2 NM,F miser

avasallar VT (a) (dominar) **dejarse a.** to let oneself be pushed o ordered around (b) (rival, oponente) to overwhelm (c) (pueblo) to subjugate

avatares NMPL **los a. de la vida** the ups and downs of life

Avda. = **Av.**

AVE NF (abr **Alta Velocidad Española**) High Speed Train

ave NF bird; **aves de corral** poultry; **a. de rapiña** bird of prey

> Takes the masculine articles **el** and **un**.

avecinarse VPR to approach, to come near

avellana NF hazelnut

avellano NM hazelnut tree

avena NF oats

avendré INDIC FUT de **avenir**

avenencia NF compromise

avengo INDIC PRES de **avenir**

avenida NF avenue

avenido, -a ADJ **bien/mal avenidos** on good/bad terms

avenirse [27] VPR (llevarse bien) to be on good terms; (consentir) to agree (**en** to)

aventajado, -a ADJ (destacado) outstanding, exceptional

aventajar VT (a) (estar por delante de) to be ahead o in front (**a** of) (b) (superar) to surpass, to outdo

aventar [1] **1** VT (a) Agr to winnow (b) (el fuego) to fan (c) Andes, CAm, Méx Fam (tirar) to throw; **le aventé una bofetada** I slapped him (d) Andes, CAm, Méx (empujar) to push, to shove
2 aventarse VPR Méx (a) (tirarse) to throw oneself (b) (atreverse) **aventarse a hacer algo** to dare to do sth

aventón NM CAm, Méx, Perú **dar a. a algn** to give sb a Br lift o US ride; **pedir a.** to hitch a Br lift o US ride

aventura NF (a) (suceso, empresa) adventure (b) (amorosa) (love) affair

aventurado, -a ADJ risky

aventurarse VPR to venture

aventurero, -a ADJ adventurous

avergonzado, -a ADJ ashamed

avergonzar [63] **1** VT to shame
2 avergonzarse VPR to be ashamed (**de** of)

avería NF breakdown

averiado, -a ADJ out of order; *(coche)* broken down

averiar [29] **1** VT to break

2 averiarse VPR *(estropearse)* to malfunction, to go wrong; *(coche)* to break down

averiguación NF enquiry

averiguar [45] VT to ascertain

aversión NF aversion

avestruz NM ostrich

aviación NF (a) *(navegación)* aviation; **accidente de a.** plane crash; **a. civil** civil aviation (b) *(ejército)* airforce

aviador, -a NM,F aviator, flier; *Mil (piloto)* air force pilot

aviar[1][29] VT *(preparar)* to prepare, to get ready

aviar[2] ADJ *(gripe)* bird

avícola ADJ poultry

avicultura NF poultry farming

avidez NF avidity, eagerness

ávido, -a ADJ avid; **a. de** eager for

avinagrado, -a ADJ sour

avinagrarse VPR *(vino, alimento)* to turn sour; *(persona, carácter)* to become sour o bitter

avión[1] NM aircraft, *Br* aeroplane, *US* airplane; **viajar en a.** to fly, to go by plane; **por a.** *(en carta)* airmail

avión[2] NM *(ave)* martin

avioneta NF light aircraft o plane

avíos NMPL *(equipo)* things

avisar VT (a) *(informar)* to inform; **avísame cuando hayas acabado** let me know when you've finished (b) *(advertir)* to warn; **ya te avisé** I warned you (c) *(llamar)* to call for; **a. a la policía** to notify the police; **a. al médico** to send for the doctor

aviso NM (a) *(advertencia)* warning; **estar sobre a.** to be forewarned (b) *(notificación)* notice; *(en teatros, aeropuertos)* call; **hasta nuevo a.** until further notice; **sin previo a.** without notice (c) *Am (anuncio)* advertisement; **a. clasificado** classified advertisement

avispa NF wasp

avispado, -a ADJ *Fam* quick-witted

avispero NM *(nido)* wasps' nest

avistar VT to see, to sight

avituallamiento NM provisioning

avituallar VT to provide with food

avivar VT *(fuego)* to stoke (up); *(pasión)* to intensify; *(paso)* to quicken

avizor, -a ADJ **estar ojo a.** to be on the alert o on the lookout

axila NF armpit, axilla

axioma NM axiom

ay *(pl* **ayes)** INTERJ *(dolor)* ouch!

aya NF *(niñera)* nanny

> Takes the masculine articles **el** and **un**.

ayer 1 ADV yesterday; **a. por la mañana/por la tarde** yesterday morning/afternoon; **a. por la**

noche last night; **antes de a.** the day before yesterday

2 NM **el a.** yesteryear

ayuda NF help, assistance; **ir en a. de algn** to come/go to sb's assistance; **a. al desarrollo** development aid

ayudante NMF assistant; *Med* **a. técnico-sanitario** qualified nurse

ayudar 1 VT to help; **¿en qué puedo ayudarle?** (how) can I help you?

2 ayudarse VPR (a) *(unos a otros)* to help (b) **ayudarse de** to use, to make use of

ayunar VI to fast

ayunas NFPL **en a.** without having eaten breakfast

ayuno NM fasting; **guardar/hacer a.** to fast

ayuntamiento NM *(institución) Br* town council, *US* city council; *(edificio) Br* town hall, *US* city hall

azabache NM jet; **negro a.** jet black

azada NF hoe

azafata NF (a) *Av* air stewardess, *Br* air hostess (b) *(de congresos)* stewardess; *(de concurso)* hostess

azafate NM *CAm, Carib, Méx, Perú* tray.

azafrán NM saffron

azahar NM *(del naranjo)* orange blossom; *(del limonero)* lemon blossom

azar NM chance; **por a.** by chance; **al a.** at random; **juegos de a.** games of chance; **los azares de la vida** the ups and downs of life

azaroso, -a ADJ hazardous, dangerous

azogue NM mercury, quicksilver

azorado, -a ADJ embarrassed

azorar 1 VT to embarrass

2 azorarse VPR to be embarrassed

Azores NFPL **las (Islas) A.** the Azores

azotar VT *(pegar, golpear)* to beat; *(con látigo)* to whip, to flog; *Fig* to scourge

azote NM (a) *(golpe)* smacking; *(latigazo)* lash, stroke (of the whip) (b) *Fig* scourge

azotea NF flat roof

azteca ADJ & NMF Aztec

azúcar NM o NF sugar

azucarado, -a ADJ sweetened

azucarera NF *(fábrica)* sugar refinery; *(recipiente)* sugar bowl

azucarero, -a 1 NM sugar bowl

2 ADJ sugar

azucena NF white lily

azufre NM sulphur

azul ADJ & NM blue; **a. celeste** sky blue; **a. marino** navy blue; **a. turquesa** turquoise; **sangre a.** blue blood

azulado, -a ADJ bluish

azulejo NM (glazed) tile

azuzar [40] VT **a. los perros a algn** to set the dogs on sb

B, b [be] NF *(letra)* B, b
baba NF dribble; *Fig* **se le caía la b.** he was
delighted
babear VI *(niño)* to dribble; *(adulto, animal)* to
slobber
babel NM o NF bedlam
babero NM bib
Babia N *Fig* **estar en B.** to be daydreaming
babor NM *Náut* port, port side
babosa NF slug
babosada NF *CAm, Méx Fam (disparate)* daft
thing; **¡no digas babosadas!** don't talk *Br*
rubbish o *US* bull!
baboso, -a 1 ADJ (a) *Fam (despreciable)* slimy
(b) *Am Fam (tonto)* daft, stupid
2 NM,F *Fam* (a) *(persona despreciable)* creep
(b) *Am (tonto)* twit, idiot
babucha NF slipper
baca NF *Aut* roof rack
bacalao NM *(pez)* cod
bacán 1 *Cuba, Perú* ADJ cool, wicked
2 *Cuba* NM toff; **como un b.** like a real
gentleman
bache NM (a) *(en carretera)* pot hole (b) *Av* air
pocket (c) *Fig* bad patch; **pasar un b.** to go
through a bad patch
bachillerato NM = academically orientated
Spanish secondary school course for pupils
aged 14-17
bacilo NM bacillus
bacon NM *Esp* bacon
bacteria NF bacterium; **bacterias** bacteria
bacteriológico, -a ADJ bacteriological;
guerra bacteriológica germ warfare
báculo NM *(de obispo)* crosier; **ella será el b. de
mi vejez** she'll comfort me in my old age
badén NM *(de carretera)* ditch
bádminton NM badminton
bafle, baffle ['bafle] NM loudspeaker
bagaje NM background; **b. cultural** cultural
baggage
bagatela NF trifle
Bagdad N Baghdad
Bahamas NPL **las (Islas) B.** the Bahamas
bahía NF bay
bailaor, -a NM,F flamenco dancer
bailar VT & VI to dance; *Fig* **b. al son que le
tocan** to toe the line; *Fam* **¡que me quiten lo
baila(d)o!** but at least I had a good time!

bailarín, -a NM,F dancer; *(clásico)* ballet
dancer
baile NM (a) *(danza)* dance (b) *(fiesta popular)*
dance; *(formal)* ball; **b. de disfraces** fancy
dress ball
baja NF (a) *(descenso)* drop, fall; *Fin* **jugar a la
b.** to bear the market (b) *(cese)* **dar de b. a
algn** *(en una empresa)* to lay sb off; *(en un club,
sindicato)* to expel sb; **darse de b. (de)** *(dimitir)*
to resign (from); *(salirse)* to drop out (of) (c)
Esp (por enfermedad) (permiso) sick leave;
(documento) sick note, doctor's certificate;
estar/darse de b. to be on/take sick leave; **b.
por maternidad** maternity leave (d) *Mil* loss,
casualty; **bajas civiles** civilian casualties
bajada NF (a) *(descenso)* descent (b) *(cuesta)*
slope (c) **b. de bandera** *(de taxi)* minimum fare
bajamar NF low tide
bajar 1 VT (a) *(mover hacia abajo) (libro,
cuadro)* to take/bring down; *(telón, ventanilla,
mano)* to lower; *(persiana)* to let down; *(cabeza)*
to bow o lower (b) *(montaña, escaleras)* to go/
come down (c) *(reducir) (volumen)* to turn
down; *(voz)* to lower; *(precios)* to reduce, to
cut (d) *Fam Inform* to download
2 VI (a) *(descender)* to go/come down (b) **b.
(de)** *(coche)* to get out (of); *(moto, bicicleta,
tren, avión)* to get off; *(caballo)* to get off, to
dismount; *(árbol, escalera, silla, mesa)* to
come/get down (from) (c) *(disminuir)* to fall,
to drop
3 bajarse VPR (a) **bajarse (de)** *(coche)* to get
out (of); *(moto, bicicleta, tren, avión)* to get off;
(caballo) to get off, to dismount (from); *(árbol,
escalera, silla)* to come/get down (from) (b)
Fam Inform to download
bajativo NM *Andes, RP (licor)* digestive liqueur;
(tisana) herbal tea
bajeza NF despicable action
bajial NM *Méx, Perú* lowland
bajinis NM *Fam* **decir algo por lo b.** to whisper
sth, to say sth under one's breath
bajío NM sandbank
bajista 1 ADJ *Fin* bearish; **tendencia b.** downward trend
2 NMF *Mús* bass guitarist
bajo, -a 1 ADJ low; *(persona)* short; *(sonido)*
faint, soft; **en voz baja** in a low voice; **planta
baja** *Br* ground floor, *US* first floor; **de baja
calidad** of poor quality; **la clase baja** the
lower class
2 NM (a) *Mús* bass (b) *(planta baja) (piso)* *Br*

ground floor flat, US first floor apartment
3 ADV low; (hablar) quietly
4 PREP under, underneath; **b. cero** below zero;
b. tierra underground; **b. la lluvia** in the rain

bajón NM (**a**) (bajada) slump (**b**) (de salud)
relapse, deterioration

bajorrelieve NM bas-relief

bajura NF **pesca de b.** coastal fishing

bala NF bullet; Fig **como una b.** like a shot

balacear VT Am to shoot

balacera NF Am shoot-out

balada NF ballad

baladí (pl **baladíes**) ADJ trivial

balance NM (**a**) Fin balance sheet; Fig **hacer b.
de una situación** to take stock of a situation
(**b**) (resultado) outcome

balancear 1 VT to rock
2 balancearse VPR (en mecedora) to rock; (en
columpio, hamaca) to swing; (barco) to roll

balanceo NM (**a**) (de columpio, hamaca)
swinging; (de cuna, mecedora) rocking; (de
barco) roll (**b**) Am Aut wheel balance

balancín NM (**a**) (mecedora) rocking chair; (en
el jardín) swing hammock (**b**) (columpio)
seesaw

balanza NF scales; Fig **estar en la b.** to be in the
balance o in danger; **b. comercial** balance of
trade; **b. de pagos** balance of payments

balar VI to bleat

balaustrada NF balustrade, railing

balazo NM (**a**) (disparo) shot; **matar a algn de
un b.** to shoot sb dead (**b**) (herida) bullet
wound

balboa NM Fin balboa, = standard monetary
unit of Panama

balbucear VT & VI (adulto) to stutter, stammer;
(niño) to babble

balbuceo NM (de adulto) stuttering, stammering; (de niño) babbling

balbucir VT & VI = **balbucear**

Balcanes NMPL **los B.** the Balkans

balcón NM balcony

balda NF Esp shelf

baldado, -a ADJ Esp Fam shattered

balde 1 NM pail, bucket
2 de balde LOC ADV (gratis) free
3 en balde LOC ADV (en vano) in vain

baldío, -a 1 ADJ (terreno) uncultivated, waste;
(esfuerzo) vain, useless
2 NM Méx, RP (terreno) vacant lot

baldosa NF (ceramic) floor tile; (para pavimentar) flagstone, paving stone

balear 1 VT Am (disparar) to shoot
2 ADJ Balearic

Baleares NPL **las (Islas) B.** the Balearic Islands

baleo NM Am shoot-out

balido NM bleating, bleat

balística NF ballistics sing

balístico, -a ADJ ballistic

baliza NF Náut marker buoy; Av beacon; Aut
warning light (for roadworks)

ballena NF whale

ballet [ba'le] (pl **ballets**) NM ballet

balneario NM spa, health resort

balompié NM soccer, Br football

balón NM ball; Fig **b. de oxígeno** boost

baloncesto NM basketball

balonmano NM handball

balonvolea NM volleyball

balsa NF (**a**) Náut raft (**b**) Fig **como una b. de
aceite** very quiet

bálsamo NM balsam, balm

balsero, -a NM,F (de Cuba) = refugee fleeing
Cuba on a raft

Báltico NM **el (Mar) B.** the Baltic (Sea)

baluarte NM Fig stronghold

bambas® NFPL Esp Br plimsolls, US sneakers

bambolear 1 VT to shake
2 bambolearse VPR (árbol, persona) to sway;
(mesa, silla) to wobble; (tren, autobús) to judder

bambú (pl **bambúes** o **bambús**) NM bamboo

banal ADJ banal

banalidad NF banality

banana NF banana

banano NM banana tree

banca NF (**a**) (asiento) bench (**b**) Com & Fin
(sector) (the) banks; (actividad) banking; **b.
electrónica** electronic banking (**c**) (en juegos)
bank

bancario, -a ADJ bank; **crédito b.** bank loan;
sector b. banking sector

bancarrota NF Fin bankruptcy; **estar en b.** to
be bankrupt

banco NM (**a**) (para sentarse) bench; (de iglesia)
pew (**b**) Com & Fin bank (**c**) (depósito) bank;
Inform **b. de datos** data bank; **b. de sangre**
blood bank (**d**) **b. de arena** sandbank (**e**) (de
peces) shoal, school

banda NF (**a**) Mús band (**b**) Inform **b. ancha**
broadband; Cin **b. sonora** sound track (**c**)
(cinta) sash (**d**) (lado) side; Ftb **línea de b.**
touchline; **saque de b.** throw-in

bandada NF (de aves) flock; (de peces) shoal

bandazo NM **dar bandazos** to lurch

bandeja NF tray; Fig **servir algo a algn en b.** to
hand sth to sb on a plate

bandera NF flag; **b. azul** (en playa) blue flag

banderilla NF (**a**) Taurom banderilla, = barbed
dart thrust into bull's back (**b**) Esp (aperitivo) =
hors d'œuvre of pickles and olives on a
cocktail stick

banderín NF pennant, small flag

bandido NM bandit, outlaw

bando¹ NM (**a**) Der (edicto) edict, proclamation
(**b**) **bandos** banns

bando² NM faction, side; **pasarse al otro b.** to
go over to the other side, to change sides

bandolero NM bandit, outlaw

banjo ['banjo] NM banjo

banquero, -a NM,F banker

banqueta NF (a) (asiento) stool (b) (para los pies) foot-stool (c) CAm, Méx (acera) Br pavement, US sidewalk

banquete NM banquet, feast; **b. de bodas** wedding reception

banquillo NM (a) Der dock (b) Dep bench

banquina NF RP (arcén) Br hard shoulder, US shoulder

bañadera NF (a) Arg (bañera) bath (b) RP (vehículo) = old-fashioned school bus

bañado NM Bol, RP (terreno) marshy area

bañador NM Esp (de mujer) swimsuit; (de hombre) swimming trunks

bañar 1 VT (a) (con agua) to bath (b) (cubrir) to coat, cover; **b. en oro** to goldplate

2 bañarse VPR (en baño) to have o take a bath; (en mar, piscina) to go for a swim; Am (ducharse) to have o take a shower

bañera NF bath, bathtub

bañista NMF bather, swimmer

baño NM (a) (acción) (en bañera) bath; (en playa, piscina) swim; **darse un b.** (en bañera) to have o take a bath; (en playa, piscina) to go for a swim; **b. María** bain Marie; **b. de sangre** bloodbath (b) (cuarto de aseo) bathroom; (servicios) Br toilet, US bathroom (c) (de oro etc) coat; (de chocolate etc) coating, covering (d) (bañera) bathtub, bath (e) Am (ducha) shower

bar NM bar, pub

barahúnda NF din, uproar

baraja NF Br pack o US deck (of cards)

barajar VT (cartas) to shuffle; Fig (nombres, cifras) to juggle with

baranda, Esp **barandilla** NF (de escalera) handrail, banister; (de balcón) handrail

baratija NF trinket, knick-knack

baratillo NM (a) (género) junk (b) (tienda) junkshop; (mercadillo) flea market

barato, -a 1 ADJ cheap

2 ADV cheaply

barba NF (a) Anat chin (b) (pelo) beard; Esp **2 euros por b.** 2 euros a head

barbacoa NF barbecue

barbaridad NF (a) (crueldad) atrocity (b) (disparate) piece of nonsense; **no digas barbaridades** don't talk nonsense (c) (montón) **una b.** a lot; **costar una b.** to cost a fortune

barbarie NF savagery, cruelty

bárbaro, -a 1 ADJ (a) Hist barbarian (b) (cruel) barbaric, barbarous (c) Fam (enorme) massive (d) RP Fam (estupendo) tremendous, terrific

2 NM,F Hist barbarian

barbecho NM (sistema) land set-aside; (terreno) fallow field; **dejar en b.** to leave fallow

barbería NF barber's (shop)

barbero NM barber

barbilla NF chin

barbitúrico NM barbiturate

barbudo, -a ADJ with a heavy beard

barca NF small boat

barcaza NF lighter

Barcelona N Barcelona

barcelonés, -esa 1 ADJ of/from Barcelona

2 NM,F person from Barcelona

barco NM boat, ship; **b. de pasajeros** liner; **b. de vapor** steamer

baremo NM (escala) scale; (norma) yardstick

barítono NM baritone

barlovento NM windward (side)

barman (pl barmans) NM barman

barniz NM (a) (en madera) varnish; (en cerámica) glaze (b) Fig veneer

barnizado, -a ADJ (madera) varnished; (cerámica) glazed

barnizar [40] VT (madera) to varnish; (cerámica) to glaze

barómetro NM barometer

barón NM baron

baronesa NF baroness

barquero, -a NM,F (hombre) boatman; (mujer) boatwoman

barquillo NM wafer

barra NF (a) (pieza alargada) bar; **b. de pan** French loaf, baguette; **b. de labios** lipstick (b) (mostrador) bar; **b. americana** = bar where hostesses chat with clients (c) Dep **b. fija** horizontal bar; **barras paralelas** parallel bars (d) (signo gráfico) slash, oblique (e) Andes, RP Fam (de amigos) gang; **b. brava** = group of violent soccer supporters

barraca NF (a) (caseta) shack, hut (b) (en Valencia y Murcia) thatched farmhouse

barracón NM prefabricated hut

barranco NM (despeñadero) cliff, precipice; (torrentera) gully, ravine

barranquismo NM Dep canyoning

barrena NF twist drill

barrenar VT Téc to drill

barrendero, -a NM,F sweeper, street sweeper

barreno NM (a) (taladro) large drill (b) (agujero) (para explosiones) blast hole

barreño NM Esp washing-up bowl

barrer 1 VT to sweep

2 VI (en elecciones) to win by a landslide

barrera NF barrier

barriada NF (a) (barrio popular) neighbourhood, area (b) Am (barrio de chabolas) shanty town

barricada NF barricade

barrida NF sweep

barriga NF belly; Fam tummy

barrigón, -ona, barrigudo, -a ADJ Fam potbellied

barril NM barrel; **cerveza de b.** draught beer

barrillo NM blackhead

barrio NM area, district, *US* neighborhood; **del b.** local; **el B. Gótico** the Gothic Quarter; **b. chino** *(de chinos)* Chinatown; *Esp (de prostitución)* red-light district; **barrios bajos** slums

barrizal NM mire, quagmire

barro NM **(a)** *(lodo)* mud **(b)** *(arcilla)* clay; **objetos de b.** earthenware

barroco, -a ADJ baroque

barruntar VT *(sospechar)* to suspect; *(presentir)* to have a feeling

barrunto NM *(presentimiento)* feeling, presentiment; *(sospecha)* suspicion

bartola: a la bartola LOC ADV *Fam* **tumbarse a la b.** to laze around, to idle away one's time

bártulos NMPL *Fam* things, bits and pieces

barullo NM *(alboroto)* row, din; *(confusión)* confusion

basar 1 VT to base (**en** on)
2 basarse VPR *(teoría, película)* **basarse en** to be based on; **¿en qué te basas para decir eso?** what grounds do you have for saying that?

basca NF *Esp Fam* people, crowd

báscula NF scales; *(para camiones)* weighbridge

bascular VI to tilt

base NF **(a)** *(fundamento, origen)* basis; **en b.** on the basis of; **a b. de estudiar** by studying; **a b. de productos naturales** using natural products **(b)** *(militar, científica)* base **(c)** *Quím, Mat & Geom* base; *Inform* **b. de datos** database **(d)** *(de partido)* **las bases** the grass roots, the rank and file; **miembro de b.** rank and file member **(e)** *(nociones)* grounding

básico, -a ADJ basic

basílica NF basilica

basket, *Am* **básquet** NM basketball

basta INTERJ **¡b.!** that's enough!; **¡b. de chistes/tonterías!** that's enough jokes/of this nonsense!

bastante 1 ADJ **(a)** *(suficiente)* enough; **b. tiempo/comida** enough time/food; **bastantes platos** enough plates **(b)** *(abundante)* quite a lot of; **hace b. calor/frío** it's quite hot/cold; **bastantes amigos** quite a lot of friends
2 ADV **(a)** *(suficiente)* enough; **con esto hay b.** that is enough; **no soy lo b. rico (como) para ...** I am not rich enough to ... **(b)** *(considerablemente)* fairly, quite; **me gusta b.** I quite like it; **vamos b. al cine** we go to the cinema quite *o* fairly often

bastar 1 VI to be sufficient *o* enough, to suffice; **basta con tres** three will be enough; **¡basta de tonterías!** enough of this nonsense!; **basta con tocarlo para que se abra** you only have to touch it and it opens; **¡basta (ya)!** that's enough!, that will do!
2 bastarse VPR **bastarse a sí mismo** to be self-sufficient, to rely only on oneself

bastardilla NF *Impr* italics

bastardo, -a ADJ & NM,F bastard

bastidor NM **(a)** *(armazón)* frame **(b)** *Teatro* **bastidores** wings; *Fig* **entre bastidores** behind the scenes

bastión NM bastion

basto, -a 1 ADJ *(cosa)* rough, coarse; *(persona)* coarse, uncouth
2 bastos NMPL *Naipes* = suit in Spanish deck of cards, with the symbol of a wooden club

bastón NM stick, walking stick

bastoncillo NM *(de algodón)* cotton bud

basura NF *Br* rubbish, *US* garbage, *US* trash

basurero NM **(a)** *(persona) Br* dustman, *US* garbage man **(b)** *(lugar) Br* rubbish tip *o* dump, *US* garbage dump

bata NF *(para casa)* dressing gown; *(de médico etc)* white coat; *(de científico)* lab coat

batacazo NM **(a)** *(golpe)* bump, bang; **los resultados representan un nuevo b. para el partido** the results are another blow for the party **(b)** *CSur Fam (triunfo inesperado)* surprise victory

batalla NF battle; **librar b.** to do *o* join battle; **b. campal** pitched battle

batallar VI **(a)** *(con armas)* to fight **(b)** *(con esfuerzo)* to battle

batallón NM battalion

batata NF *Esp, Arg, Col, Ven* sweet potato

bate NM *Dep* bat; **b. de béisbol** baseball bat

batear *Dep* **1** VI to bat
2 VT to hit

batería 1 NF **(a)** *Elec* battery **(b)** *Mús* drums **(c)** **b. de cocina** pots and pans, set of pans
2 NMF drummer

batiburrillo NM jumble, mess

batida NF **(a)** *(de la policía)* raid **(b)** *(en caza)* beat

batido, -a 1 ADJ **(a)** *Culin* whipped **(b)** *Dep* **tierra batida** clay
2 NM milk shake

batidora NF *(eléctrica)* mixer

batiente ADJ **reírse a mandíbula b.** to laugh one's head off

batín NM short dressing gown

batir 1 VT **(a)** *(huevo)* to beat; *(nata)* to whip, to whisk **(b)** *(récord)* to break **(c)** *(golpear)* to beat against **(d)** *(en caza)* to beat
2 batirse VPR to fight

batuta NF *Mús* baton; *Fig* **llevar la b.** to be in charge

baúl NM **(a)** *(cofre)* trunk **(b)** *Arg, Col (maletero) Br* boot, *US* trunk

bautismo NM baptism, christening

bautizar [40] VT to baptize, to christen; *(vino)* to water down

bautizo NM baptism, christening

Baviera N Bavaria

baya NF berry

bayeta NF floorcloth

bayoneta NF bayonet

baza NF (**a**) *(en naipes)* trick; *Fig* **meter b.** to butt in (**b**) *(ventaja)* advantage

bazar NM bazaar

bazo NM spleen

bazofia NF (**a**) *(comida)* pigswill (**b**) *(libro, película)* **ser (una) b.** to be *Br* rubbish *o US* garbage

be NF (**a**) *Esp (letra)* = name of the letter "b" (**b**) *Am* **be alta** *o* **grande** *o* **larga** *(to distinguish from "v")*

beato, -a ADJ *(piadoso)* devout; *Pey* prudish, sanctimonious

bebe, -a NM,F *Andes, RP* baby

bebé NM baby; **b. probeta** test-tube baby

bebedero NM (**a**) *(abrevadero)* drinking trough, water trough (**b**) *Méx, RP (fuente)* drinking fountain

bebedor, -a NM,F (hard *o* heavy) drinker

beber VT & VI to drink

bebible ADJ drinkable

bebida NF drink; **darse a la b.** to take to drink

bebido, -a ADJ drunk

beca NF *(del gobierno)* grant; *(de organización privada)* scholarship

becar [44] VT *(sujeto: gobierno)* to award a grant to; *(sujeto: organización privada)* to award a scholarship to

becario, -a NM,F (**a**) *(estudiante)* *(del gobierno)* grant holder; *(de organización privada)* scholarship holder (**b**) *(en prácticas)* person on a work placement, *US* intern

becerro NM calf

bechamel NF bechamel; **salsa b.** bechamel sauce, white sauce

bedel NM beadle

begonia NF begonia

beige ADJ & NM INV beige

béisbol NM baseball

Belén N Bethlehem

belén NM nativity scene, crib

belga ADJ & NMF Belgian

Bélgica N Belgium

Belgrado N Belgrade

Belice N Belize

bélico, -a ADJ warlike, bellicose; *(preparativos etc)* war; **material b.** armaments

belicoso, -a ADJ warlike, bellicose; *(agresivo)* aggressive

beligerancia NF belligerence

beligerante ADJ belligerent; **los países beligerantes** the countries at war

bellaco, -a NM,F villain, scoundrel

belleza NF beauty

bello, -a ADJ beautiful

bellota NF *Bot* acorn; *Fig* **animal de b.** blockhead

bemol 1 ADJ *Mús* flat
2 NM *Fam* **esto tiene bemoles** this is a tough one

bencina NF *Chile (gasolina)* *Br* petrol, *US* gas

bencinera NF *Chile* *Br* petrol station, *US* gas station

bendecir [12] VT to bless; **b. la mesa** to say grace; **¡Dios te bendiga!** God bless you!

bendición NF blessing

bendito, -a 1 ADJ blessed; *(maldito)* damned
2 NM,F *(bonachón)* good sort, kind soul; *(tontorrón)* simple soul

beneficencia NF beneficence, charity

beneficiado, -a ADJ favoured; **salir b. de algo** to do well out of sth

beneficiar [43] **1** VT to benefit
2 beneficiarse VPR **beneficiarse de** *o* **con algo** to profit from *o* by sth

beneficiario, -a NM,F beneficiary

beneficio NM (**a**) *Com & Fin* profit (**b**) *(bien)* benefit; **en b. propio** in one's own interest; **un concierto a b. de …** a concert in aid of …

beneficioso, -a ADJ beneficial

benéfico, -a ADJ charitable

beneplácito NM *Fml* approval, consent

benevolencia NF benevolence

benevolente, benévolo, -a ADJ benevolent

bengala NF flare

benigno, -a ADJ *(persona)* gentle, benign; *(clima)* mild; *(tumor)* benign

benjamín, -ina NM,F youngest child

beodo, -a ADJ & NM,F drunk

berberecho NM (common) cockle

berbiquí *(pl* **berbiquíes** *o* **berbiquís)** NM *Téc* brace and bit

berenjena NF *Br* aubergine, *US* eggplant

Berlín N Berlin

berlina NF four-door saloon

berlinés, -esa 1 ADJ of/from Berlin
2 NM,F Berliner

berma NF *Andes (arcén)* *Br* hard shoulder, *US* shoulder

bermejo, -a ADJ reddish

bermellón NM vermilion

Bermudas NFPL **las (Islas) B.** Bermuda

bermudas NMPL *o* NFPL Bermuda shorts

Berna N Bern

berrear VI to bellow, to low

berrido NM bellowing, lowing

berrinche NM *Fam* tantrum

berro NM cress, watercress

berza NF cabbage

besar 1 VT to kiss
2 besarse VPR to kiss

beso NM kiss

bestia 1 NF beast, animal; **b. de carga** beast of burden

2 NMF *Fam (persona)* brute, beast

3 ADJ brutish, boorish; **a lo b.** rudely

bestial ADJ *(brutal)* animal, brutal; *Fam (enorme)* huge, tremendous; *(extraordinario)* fantastic, terrific

bestialidad NF (a) *Fam (estupidez)* stupidity (b) *(brutalidad)* brutality (c) *Fam (montón)* **una b. de** tons of, stacks of

best-seller [bes'seler] *(pl* **best-sellers)** NM best-seller

besugo NM (a) *(pez)* sea bream (b) *Esp (persona)* idiot, half-wit

besuquear *Fam* **1** VT to kiss, to cover with kisses

2 besuquearse VPR to smooch

betabel NF *Méx Br* beetroot, *US* beet

betarraga NF *Andes Br* beetroot, *US* beet

betún NM *(para el calzado)* shoe polish; *Quím* bitumen

biberón NM baby's bottle, feeding bottle

Biblia NF Bible

bíblico, -a ADJ biblical

bibliografía NF bibliography

bibliorato NM *RP* lever arch file

biblioteca NF (a) *(institución)* library; **b. ambulante** mobile library (b) *Chile, Perú, RP (mueble)* bookcase

bibliotecario, -a NM,F librarian

bicameral ADJ *Pol* bicameral, two-chamber

bicarbonato NM bicarbonate; **b. sódico** bicarbonate of soda

bicentenario NM *Br* bicentenary, *US* bicentennial

bíceps NM INV biceps

bicho NM (a) *(animal)* beast, animal; *(insecto)* bug; **¿qué b. le ha picado?** *Br* what's up with him?, *US* what's eating him? (b) *Fam (persona)* **todo b. viviente** every living soul; **un b. raro** a weirdo, an oddball

bici NF *Fam* bike

bicicleta NF bicycle; **montar en b.** to ride a bicycle

bicolor ADJ two-coloured; *Pol* **gobierno b.** two-party government

bidé NM bidet

bidón NM drum

biela NF *Aut* connecting rod

Bielorrusia N Belarus

bien¹ **1** ADV (a) *(correctamente)* well; **habla b. (el) inglés** she speaks English well; **responder b.** to answer correctly; **hiciste b. en decírmelo** you were right to tell me; **las cosas le van b.** things are going well for him; **¡b.! good!, great!; ¡muy b.!** excellent, first class!; **¡qué b.!** great!, fantastic! (b) *(de salud)* well; **sentirse/encontrarse/ estar b.** to feel well (c) **vivir b.** to be comfortably off; **¡está b.! (¿de acuerdo!)** fine!, all right!; **¡ya está b.!** that's (quite) enough!; **aquí se está muy b.** it's really

nice here; **esta falda te sienta b.** this skirt suits you; *Fam* **ese libro está muy b.** that book is very good; *Fam* **su novia está muy b.** his girlfriend is very nice

(d) *(intensificador)* very, quite; **b. temprano** very early, nice and early; **b. caliente** pretty hot; **b. es verdad que …** it's quite clear that … (e) **más b.** rather, a little

(f) **b. podía haberme avisado** she might have let me know

(g) *(de buena gana)* willingly, gladly; **b. me tomaría una cerveza** I'd really love a beer

2 CONJ **ahora b.** now, now then; **o b.** or, or else; **b. … o b. …** either … or …; **no b.** as soon as; **no b. llegó …** no sooner had she arrived than …; **si b.** although, even if

3 ADJ **la gente b.** the wealthy, the upper classes

bien² NM (a) *(bondad)* good; **el b. y el mal** good and evil; **un hombre/familia de b.** a good man/family (b) *(bienestar)* **por el b. de** for the good of; **lo hace por tu b.** he does it for your own good (c) **bienes** goods; **bienes de equipo** capital goods; **bienes inmuebles** real estate, *US* real property; **bienes de consumo** consumer goods

bienal NF biennial exhibition

bienestar NM *(personal)* well-being, contentment; *(comodidad)* ease, comfort; **la sociedad del b.** the affluent society

bienhechor, -a NM,F *(hombre)* benefactor; *(mujer)* benefactress

bienintencionado, -a ADJ well-meaning, well-intentioned

bienio NM biennium, two-year period

bienvenida NF welcome; **dar la b. a algn** to welcome sb

bienvenido, -a ADJ welcome

bife NM (a) *Andes, RP (bistec)* steak (b) *Andes, RP (bofetada)* slap

bifocal ADJ bifocal; **gafas bifocales** bifocals

bifurcación NF *(de la carretera)* fork; *Tel* bifurcation

bifurcarse [44] VPR to fork

bigamia NF bigamy

bígamo, -a **1** ADJ bigamous

2 NM,F bigamist

bigote NM *(de persona)* moustache; *(de animal)* *(usu pl)* whiskers

> Observa que la palabra inglesa **bigot** es un falso amigo y no es la traducción de la palabra española **bigote**. En inglés, **bigot** significa "intolerante".

bigotudo, -a ADJ with a big moustache

bigudí *(pl* **bigudís** *o* **bigudíes)** NM curler

bilateral ADJ bilateral

bilbaíno, -a **1** ADJ of/from Bilbao

2 NM,F person from Bilbao

bilingüe ADJ bilingual

bilis NF INV bile

billar NM (a) *(juego)* billiards *sing*; **b. americano** pool; **b. ruso** snooker (b) *(mesa)* billiard table

billete NM (a) *Esp (transporte)* ticket; **b. de ida** *(en avión)* one-way (ticket); **b. de ida y vuelta** *Br* return (ticket), *US* round-trip (ticket) (b) *(de banco)* *Br* note, *US* bill; **un b. de cinco euros** a five euro note

billetera NF, **billetero** NM wallet, *US* billfold

billón NM trillion

bimensual ADJ twice-monthly, bi-monthly

bimotor 1 ADJ twin-engined
2 NM twin-engined plane

binario, -a ADJ binary

bingo NM (a) *(juego)* bingo (b) *(sala)* bingo hall

binomio NM (a) *Mat* binomial (b) *(de personas)* pairing

biodegradable ADJ biodegradable

biodiversidad NF biodiversity

biofísica NF biophysics *sing*

biografía NF biography

biográfico, -a ADJ biographical

biógrafo, -a NM,F biographer

biología NF biology

biológico, -a ADJ biological; *(agricultura, productos)* organic

biólogo, -a NM,F biologist

biomasa NF bio-mass

biombo NM (folding) screen

biopsia NF biopsy

bioquímica NF biochemistry

bioquímico, -a 1 ADJ biochemical
2 NM,F biochemist

bióxido NM dioxide; **b. de carbono** carbon dioxide

bipartidismo NM two-party system

biquini NM bikini

birlar VT *Fam* to pinch, *Br* to nick

Birmania N *Antes* Burma

birmano, -a ADJ & NM,F *Antes* Burmese

birome NF *RP* Biro®, ballpoint (pen)

birra NF *Fam* beer, *US* brew

birrete NM cap, beret; *Rel* biretta; *Univ* mortarboard

birria NF *Fam Br* rubbish, *US* garbage

bis 1 NM encore
2 ADV twice

bisabuelo, -a NM *(hombre)* great-grandfather; *(mujer)* great-grandmother; **bisabuelos** great-grandparents

bisagra NF hinge; **partido b.** party holding the balance of power

bisbisar, bisbisear VT to whisper

bisexual ADJ & NMF bisexual

bisiesto ADJ **año b.** leap year

bisnieto, -a NM,F *(niño)* great-grandson; *(niña)* great-granddaughter; **mis bisnietos** my great-grandchildren

bisonte NM bison, American buffalo

bisoño, -a ADJ inexperienced

bistec *(pl* **bistecs)** NM steak

bisturí *(pl* **bisturíes)** NM scalpel

bisutería NF imitation jewellery

bit *(pl* **bits)** NM *Inform* bit

bitácora NF *Inform* blog

bíter NM bitters

bizantino, -a ADJ *Hist* Byzantine; *Fig* **discusiones bizantinas** hair-splitting arguments

bizco, -a 1 ADJ cross-eyed
2 NM,F cross-eyed person

bizcocho NM sponge cake

biznieto, -a NM,F = **bisnieto**

blanca NF *Esp* **estar sin b.** to be flat broke

blanco¹, -a 1 ADJ white; *(tez)* fair
2 NM,F *(hombre)* white man; *(mujer)* white woman; **los blancos** whites

blanco² NM (a) *(color)* white (b) *(hueco)* blank; **dejó la hoja en b.** he left the page blank; **votos en b.** blank votes; *Fig* **pasar la noche en b.** to have a sleepless night; **me quedé en b.** my mind went blank (c) *(diana)* target; **dar en el b.** to hit the target; *Fig* **ser el b. de todas las miradas** to be the centre of attention

blancura NF whiteness

blandengue ADJ *Pey* weak, soft

blandir VT to brandish

blando, -a ADJ soft

> Observa que la palabra inglesa **bland** es un falso amigo y no es la traducción de la palabra española **blando**. En inglés **bland** significa "soso".

blanquear VT (a) *(ropa)* to whiten (b) *(casa)* to whitewash (c) *(dinero)* to launder

blanquecino, -a ADJ whitish

blanqueo NM (a) *(de ropa)* whitening (b) *(de casa)* whitewashing (c) *(de dinero)* laundering

blanquillo NM (a) *CAm, Méx (huevo)* egg (b) *Andes (melocotón)* white peach

blasfemar VI to blaspheme (**contra** against)

blasfemia NF blasphemy

blasón NM coat of arms

bledo NM *Fam* **me importa un b.** I couldn't give a damn

blindado, -a ADJ *Mil* armoured, armour-plated; *(antibalas)* bullet-proof; **coche b.** bullet-proof car; **puerta blindada** reinforced door, security door

blindaje NM *(de puerta)* armour-plating; *(de vehículo)* armour

blindar VT to armour-plate

bloc *(pl* **blocs)** NM pad; **b. de notas** notepad

blog [bloɣ] *(pl* **blogs)** NM *Inform* blog

bloomer ['blumer] NM *CAm, Carib* panties, *Br* knickers

bloque NM (a) *(pieza, edificio)* block; **en b.** en bloc; **b. de pisos** *Br* (block of) flats, *US* apartment block (**b**) *Pol* bloc; **el b. comunista** the Communist Bloc

bloquear 1 VT (**a**) *(comunicaciones, carreteras, acuerdo)* to block (**b**) *Mil* to blockade (**c**) *Fin (cuentas)* to freeze (**d**) *Inform (archivo)* to lock **2 bloquearse** VPR (**a**) *(atascarse)* to be stuck (**b**) *(persona)* to freeze (**c**) *Aut (dirección)* to lock; *(frenos)* to jam (**d**) *Inform (pantalla)* to freeze

bloqueo NM (**a**) *(militar, económico)* blockade (**b**) *Fin (de cuentas)* freeze, freezing (**c**) *(de mecanismo)* jamming (**d**) **b. mental** mental block

blues [blus] NM INV *Mús* blues

blúmer (*pl* **blúmers** o **blúmeres**) NM *CAm, Carib* panties, *Br* knickers

blusa NF blouse

blusón NM loose blouse, smock

bluyín NM , **bluyines** NMPL *Andes, Ven* jeans

boato NM show, ostentation

bobada NF nonsense; **decir bobadas** to talk nonsense

bobalicón, -ona *Fam* **1** ADJ simple, stupid **2** NM,F simpleton, idiot

bobería NF = bobada

bobina NF (**a**) *(de hilo)* reel (**b**) *Elec* coil

bobo, -a 1 ADJ *(tonto)* stupid, silly; *(ingenuo)* naïve **2** NM,F fool

boca 1 NF (**a**) *(de persona, animal)* mouth; **b. abajo** face downward; **b. arriba** face upward; *Fig* **a pedir de b.** perfectly; *Fig* **andar de b. en b.** to be the talk of the town; *Fam* **¡cierra la b!** shut up!; *Fam* **con la b. abierta** open-mouthed; *Fam* **se le hizo la b. agua** his mouth watered (**b**) **b. del metro** *Br* tube o underground entrance, *US* subway entrance; **b. de riego** hydrant **2** NM **el b. a b.** the kiss of life, mouth-to-mouth resuscitation

bocacalle NF entrance to a street

bocadillo NM (**a**) *Esp (con pan)* filled roll *(made with a baguette)*; **un b. de jamón/tortilla** a ham/an omelette sandwich (**b**) *(de cómic)* balloon

bocado NM (**a**) *(mordedura)* bite (**b**) *(de caballo)* bit

bocajarro: a bocajarro LOC ADV *(disparar)* at point-blank range; **decir algo a b.** to say sth straight out

bocanada NF *(de humo)* puff; *(de viento)* gust; *Fig* **una b. de aire fresco** a breath of fresh air

bocata NM *Esp Fam* filled roll *(made with a baguette)*

bocazas NM,F INV *Fam* bigmouth, blabbermouth

boceto NM *Arte* sketch, outline; *(esquema)* outline, plan

bochinche NM *Am Fam (ruido)* racket; *(alboroto)* fuss

bochorno NM (**a**) *(tiempo)* sultry o close weather; *(calor sofocante)* stifling heat (**b**) *Fig (vergüenza)* shame, embarrassment

bochornoso, -a ADJ (**a**) *(tiempo)* sultry, close, muggy; *(calor)* stifling (**b**) *Fig (vergonzoso)* shameful, embarrassing

bocina NF horn; **tocar la b.** to blow o sound one's horn

bocinazo NM hoot, toot

bocón, -ona ADJ *Am Fam* **ser b.** to be a bigmouth o blabbermouth

boda NF wedding, marriage; **bodas de plata** silver wedding

bodega NF (**a**) *(cava)* wine cellar; *(tienda)* wine shop (**b**) *Náut* hold (**c**) *Méx (almacén)* warehouse (**d**) *CAm, Carib (colmado)* small grocery store

bodegón NM still-life

bodrio NM *Fam* **un b.** *Br* rubbish, *US* trash

body (*pl* **bodies**) NM body *(garment)*

BOE NM *(abr* **Boletín Oficial del Estado)** = official Spanish gazette

bofetada NF, **bofetón** NM slap on the face; **dar una b./un b. a algn** to slap sb's face

boga NF **estar en b.** to be in vogue

bogar [42] VI (**a**) *(remar)* to row (**b**) *(navegar)* to sail

bogavante NM lobster

bogotano, -a 1 ADJ of/from Bogotá **2** NM,F person from Bogotá

bohemio, -a 1 ADJ (**a**) *(aspecto, vida, barrio)* bohemian (**b**) *(de Bohemia)* Bohemian **2** NM,F (**a**) *(artista, vividor)* bohemian (**b**) *(de Bohemia)* Bohemian

bohío NM *Carib* hut, cabin

boicot (*pl* **boicots**) NM boycott

boicotear VT to boycott

boicoteo NM boycott

bóiler NM *Méx* boiler

boina NF beret

bol NM bowl

bola NF (**a**) *(objeto)* ball; *(canica)* marble; **b. de nieve** snowball; *Fig* **no dar pie con b.** to be unable to do anything right (**b**) *Fam (mentira)* fib, lie; **meter bolas** to tell fibs (**c**) *(rumor)* rumour; **corre la b. por ahí de que te has echado novio** they say you've got yourself a boyfriend

bolchevique ADJ & NM,F Bolshevik

bolear VT *Méx (sacar brillo)* to shine, to polish

bolera NF bowling alley

bolería NF *Méx* shoeshine store

bolero NM bolero

boleta NF (**a**) *Cuba, Méx, RP (para votar)* ballot, voting slip (**b**) *CSur (comprobante) (de venta, de depósito bancario)* receipt (**c**) *CAm, CSur (multa)* parking ticket (**d**) *Méx (de califica- ciones) Br* (school) report, *US* report card

boletería NF *Am (de cine, teatro)* box office; *(de estación)* ticket office

boletero, -a NM,F *Am* box office attendant

boletín NM bulletin; **B. Oficial del Estado** Official Gazette

boleto NM (**a**) *(de lotería, rifa)* ticket (**b**) *Am (para transporte)* ticket (**c**) *Col, Méx (para espectáculo)* ticket

boli NM *Esp Fam* pen, Biro®

boliche NM (**a**) *(juego)* bowling (**b**) *(bola)* jack (**c**) *(lugar)* bowling alley (**d**) *CSur Fam (bar)* cheap bar; *(tienda)* small-town store

bólido NM *Aut* racing car

bolígrafo NM ballpoint (pen), Biro®

bolillo NM (**a**) *(en costura)* bobbin (**b**) *Méx (panecillo)* bread roll

bolita NF *CSur (bola)* marble; **jugar a las bolitas** to play marbles

bolívar NM *Fin* bolivar, = standard monetary unit of Venezuela

Bolivia N Bolivia

boliviano, -a ADJ & NM,F Bolivian

bollería NF (**a**) *(tienda)* cake shop (**b**) *(productos)* cakes

bollo NM (**a**) *Culin* bun, bread roll (**b**) *(abolladura)* dent

bolo¹ NM *(pieza)* skittle, pin; **bolos** *(juego)* (ten-pin) bowling

bolo², -a NM,F *CAm Fam (borracho)* boozer

bolsa¹ NF bag; *Méx (de mano) Br* handbag, *US* purse; *Av* **b. de aire** air pocket; **b. de deportes** sports bag; **b. de la compra** shopping bag; **b. de viaje** travel bag

bolsa² NF *Fin* Stock Exchange; **jugar a la b.** to play the market

bolsillo NM *(en prenda)* pocket; **de b.** pocket, pocket-size; **libro de b.** paperback; **lo pagó de su b.** he paid for it out of his own pocket

bolso NM (**a**) *Esp (de mujer) Br* handbag, *US* purse (**b**) *(de viaje)* bag

boludear VI *RP Fam* (**a**) *(hacer tonterías)* to mess about (**b**) *(decir tonterías)* to talk *Br* rubbish *o US* garbage (**c**) *(perder el tiempo)* to waste one's time

boludo, -a NM,F *RP Fam (estúpido) Br* prat, *US* jerk

bomba¹ NF pump; *Chile, Ecuad, Ven (gasolinera) Br* petrol station, *US* gas station; **b. de aire** air pump; **b. de incendios** fire engine; *Chile, Ecuad, Ven* **b. (de gasolina)** *(surtidor) Br* petrol pump, *US* gas pump

bomba² NF bomb; **b. atómica/de hidrógeno/de neutrones** atomic/hydrogen/neutron bomb; **b. de relojería** time bomb; **b. fétida** stink bomb; *Fam* **noticia b.** shattering piece of news; *Esp Fam* **pasarlo b.** to have a whale of a time

bombacha NF *RP (braga) Br* knickers, *US* panties; **bombachas** *(pantalones)* = loose trousers worn by cowboys

bombardear VT to bomb, to shell; **b. a algn a preguntas** to bombard sb with questions

bombardeo NM bombing, bombardment

bombardero NM *Av* bomber

bombear VT to pump

bombeo NM pumping; **estación de b.** pumping station

bombero, -a NM,F (**a**) *(de incendios)* fire-fighter; *(hombre)* fireman; *(mujer)* firewoman; **cuerpo de bomberos** *Br* fire brigade, *US* fire department; **parque de bomberos** fire station (**b**) *Ven (de gasolinera) Br* petrol-pump *o US* gas-pump attendant

bombilla *Esp* NF (light) bulb

bombillo NM *CAm, Carib, Col, Méx* (light) bulb

bombín NM bowler hat

bombita NF *RP* light bulb

bombo NM (**a**) *Mús* bass drum; *Fig* **a b. y platillo(s)** with a great song and dance; *Fam* **darse b.** to blow one's own trumpet (**b**) *(de sorteo)* lottery drum

bombón NM chocolate

bombona NF cylinder; **b. de butano** butane gas cylinder

bombonera NF chocolate box

bonachón, -ona ADJ good-natured, easy-going

bonaerense 1 ADJ of/from Buenos Aires
2 NMF person from Buenos Aires

bonanza NF (**a**) *Náut (tiempo)* fair weather; *(mar)* calm at sea (**b**) *Fig (prosperidad)* prosperity

bondad NF goodness; *Fml* **tenga la b. de esperar** please be so kind as to wait

bondadoso, -a ADJ kind, good-natured

bonete NM *Rel* cap, biretta; *Univ* mortar-board

boniato NM *Esp, Cuba, Urug* sweet potato

bonificación NF bonus

bonificar [44] VT *Com* to give a bonus to

bonito¹, -a ADJ pretty, nice

bonito² NM tuna

bono NM (**a**) *(vale)* voucher (**b**) *Fin* bond, debenture; **bonos del tesoro** *o* **del Estado** Treasury bonds

bonobús *(pl bonobuses)* NM *Esp* = multiple-journey bus ticket

bonoloto NM = Spanish state-run lottery

bonsái NM bonsai

boñiga NF cowpat

boom [bum] *(pl booms)* NM boom

boquerón NM anchovy

boquete NM hole

boquiabierto, -a ADJ open-mouthed; *Fig* **se quedó b.** he was flabbergasted

boquilla NF (**a**) *(de cigarro)* tip; *(de pipa)* mouthpiece; **decir algo de b.** to pay lip service to sth (**b**) *Mús* mouthpiece (**c**) *(orificio)* opening

borbotar, borbotear VI to bubble

borbotón NM salir a borbotones to gush forth

borda NF *Náut* gunwale; **arrojar** o **echar por la b.** to throw overboard; **fuera b.** *(motor)* outboard motor

bordado, -a 1 ADJ embroidered; *Esp* **el examen me salió b.** I made a good job of that exam
2 NM embroidery

bordar VT (a) *(tejido)* to embroider (b) *Fig* to do excellently

borde¹ NM *(de mesa, camino)* edge; *Cost* hem, edge; *(de vasija)* rim, brim; **al b. de** on the brink of, on the verge of; **al b. del mar** at the seaside

borde² *Fam* 1 ADJ *Esp Fam (antipático)* **ser b.** to be *Br* a ratbag o *US* an s.o.b.
2 NMF *Esp Fam (antipático) Br* ratbag, *US* s.o.b.

bordear VT to go round the edge of, to skirt

bordillo NM *Br* kerb, *US* curb

bordo NM **a b.** on board; **subir a b.** to go on board

bordó ADJ INV *RP* burgundy

borla NF tassel

borne NM *Elec* terminal

borra NF (a) *(pelusa)* fluff (b) *(poso)* sediment, dregs

borrachera NF *(embriaguez)* drunkenness; **agarrarse** o **cogerse una b.** to get drunk

borracho, -a 1 ADJ (a) *(bebido)* drunk; **estar b.** to be drunk (b) *(bizcocho)* with rum
2 NM,F drunkard, drunk

borrador NM (a) *(escrito)* rough copy, first draft (b) *(croquis)* rough o preliminary sketch (c) *(para pizarra)* board duster

borraja NF **quedar en agua de borrajas** to come to nothing, to fizzle o peter out

borrar 1 VT (a) *(con goma) Br* to rub out, *US* to erase; *(pizarra)* to clean (b) *Inform* to delete
2 **borrarse** VPR *(de un club etc)* to drop out, to withdraw

borrasca NF area of low pressure

borrascoso, -a ADJ stormy

borrego, -a NM,F (a) *(animal)* lamb (b) *Fam (persona)* **como borregos** like sheep

borrico NM ass, donkey; *Fam Fig* ass, dimwit

borrón NM blot, smudge

borroso, -a ADJ blurred; **veo b.** I can't see clearly, everything's blurred

Bosnia N Bosnia

bosnio, -a ADJ & NM,F Bosnian

bosque NM wood

bosquejar VT *(dibujo)* to sketch, outline; *(plan)* to draft, to outline

bosquejo NM *(de dibujo)* sketch, study; *(de plan)* draft, outline

bostezar [40] VI to yawn

bostezo NM yawn

bota NF (a) *(calzado)* boot; *Fig* **ponerse las botas** to make a killing (b) *(de vino)* wineskin

botana NF *Méx* snack, appetizer

botánica NF botany

botánico, -a 1 ADJ botanic; **jardín b.** botanic gardens
2 NM,F botanist

botar 1 VI (a) *Esp (saltar)* to jump (b) *(pelota)* to bounce
2 VT (a) *(barco)* to launch (b) *(pelota)* to bounce (c) *Am salvo RP (tirar)* to throw away; **bótalo a la basura** throw it away

botarate NMF madcap, fool

bote NM (a) *(envase) (tarro)* jar; *Esp (lata)* tin, can; *(de champú, pastillas)* bottle; *Am* **b. de la basura** *Br* rubbish bin; *US* garbage can; **b. de humo** smoke canister (b) *(barca)* boat; **b. salvavidas** lifeboat; **b. de remos** rowing boat (c) *(propinas)* tips; **para el bote** as a tip (d) *(salto)* jump; **dar botes** *(saltar)* to jump up and down; *(tren, coche)* to bump up and down; **pegar un b.** *(de susto)* to jump, to give a start (e) *(de pelota)* bounce; **dar botes** to bounce; *Dep* **a b. pronto** on the rebound (f) *(expresiones) Esp* **chupar del b.** to feather one's nest; *Esp* **tener en el b. a algn** to have sb eating out of one's hand; **a b. pronto** *(sin pensar)* off the top of one's head

botella NF (a) *(recipiente)* bottle (b) *Cuba (autoestop)* **dar b. a algn** to give sb a *Br* lift o *US* ride; **hacer b.** to hitchhike

botellín NM small bottle

botepronto NM *Fam* **a b.** all of a sudden

botica NF *Anticuado* pharmacy, *Br* chemist's (shop), *US* drugstore; *Fam* **hay de todo como en b.** there's everything under the sun

boticario, -a NM,F *Anticuado* pharmacist, *Br* chemist, *US* druggist

botijo NM earthenware pitcher *(with spout and handle)*

botín¹ NM *(de un robo)* loot, booty

botín² NM *(calzado)* ankle boot

botiquín NM (a) *(armario)* medicine chest o cabinet; *(portátil)* first-aid kit (b) *(enfermería)* first-aid post

botón NM button; **pulsar el b.** to press the button; **b. de muestra** sample

botones NM INV *(en hotel)* bellboy, *US* bellhop; *(recadero)* messenger, errand boy

bouquet [bu'ke] *(pl bouquets)* NM bouquet

boutique [bu'tik] NF boutique

bóveda NF vault

bovino, -a ADJ bovine; **ganado b.** cattle

box *(pl boxes)* NM (a) *(de caballo)* stall (b) *(de coches)* pit (c) *Am (boxeo)* boxing

boxeador, -a NM boxer

boxear VI to box

boxeo NM boxing

boya NF (a) *Náut* buoy (b) *(corcho)* float

boyante ADJ *(empresa, negocio)* prosperous; *(economía, comercio)* buoyant

boy-scout [bojes'kaut] *(pl boy scouts)* NM boy scout

bozal NM (a) *(para perro)* muzzle (b) *Am (cabestro)* halter

bracero NM (day) labourer

braga NF, **bragas** NFPL *Esp* panties *Br* knickers

bragueta NF *(de pantalón etc) Br* flies, *US* zipper

braguetazo NM *Esp Fam* **dar el b.** to marry for money

braille ['braile] NM braille

bramar VI to low, to bellow

bramido NM lowing, bellowing

brandy *(pl* **brandis**) NM brandy

branquia NF gill

brasa NF ember, red-hot coal; **a la b.** barbecued

brasero NM brazier

brasier NM *Carib, Col, Méx* bra

Brasil N Brazil

brasileño, -a, *RP* **brasilero, -a** ADJ & NM,F Brazilian

bravata NF piece *o* act of bravado

bravo, -a 1 ADJ (a) *(valiente)* brave, courageous (b) *(feroz)* fierce, ferocious; **un toro b.** a fighting bull (c) *(mar)* rough, stormy
2 INTERJ ¡b.! well done!, bravo!

bravucón, -ona NM,F boaster, braggart

bravura NF (a) *(de animal)* ferocity, fierceness (b) *(de persona)* courage, bravery (c) *(de toro)* fighting spirit

braza NF (a) *(medida)* fathom (b) *Esp (en natación)* breaststroke; **nadar a b.** to do the breaststroke

brazada NF *(en natación)* stroke

brazalete NM (a) *(insignia)* armband (b) *(pulsera)* bracelet

brazo NM arm; *(de animal)* foreleg; *(de sillón, tocadiscos)* arm; **en brazos** in one's arms; **ir del b.** to walk arm in arm; *Fig* **con los brazos abiertos** with open arms; *Fig* **no dar su b. a torcer** not to give in, to stand firm; **b. de gitano** *Br* Swiss roll, *US* jelly roll

brea NF tar, pitch

brebaje NM concoction, brew

brecha NF *(en muro)* opening, gap; *Mil & Fig* breach; *Fig* **estar siempre en la b.** to be always in the thick of things

brécol NM broccoli

bregar [42] VI to fight

Bretaña NF (a) *(francesa)* Brittany (b) **Gran B.** Great Britain

brete NM **poner a algn en un b.** to put sb in a tight spot

bretel NM *CSur* strap; **un vestido sin breteles** a strapless dress

breva NF (a) *(fruta)* early fig (b) *Esp Fam* ¡**no caerá esa b.!** some chance (of that happening)!

breve ADJ brief; **en b., en breves momentos** shortly, soon; **en breves palabras** in short

brevedad NF briefness; *(concisión)* brevity; **con la mayor b. posible** as soon as possible

brevet NM *Chile (de avión)* pilot's licence; *Bol, Ecuad, Perú (de automóvil) Br* driving licence, *US* driver's license; *RP (de velero)* sailor's licence

brezo NM heather

bribón, -ona 1 ADJ roguish, dishonest
2 NM,F rogue, rascal

bricolaje NM *Br* DIY, do-it-yourself, *US* home improvement

brida NF (a) *(rienda)* rein, bridle (b) *Téc* flange

bridge [britʃ] NM *Naipes* bridge

brigada 1 NF (a) *Mil* brigade (b) *(de policías)* squad; **b. antiterrorista** anti-terrorist squad
2 NM *Mil* sergeant major

brillante 1 ADJ (a) *(reluciente) (luz, astro)* shining; *(metal, zapatos, pelo)* shiny; *(ojos, joyas)* sparkling (b) *(magnífico)* brilliant
2 NM diamond

brillantez NF brilliance

brillantina NF brilliantine

brillar VI *(resplandecer)* to shine; *(ojos, joyas)* to sparkle; *(lentejuelas etc)* to glitter; **b. por su ausencia** to be conspicuous by one's absence

brillo NM *(resplandor)* shine; *(del sol, de la luna)* brightness; *(de lentejuelas etc)* glittering; *(del cabello, tela)* sheen; *(de color)* brilliance; *(de pantalla)* brightness; *(de zapatos)* shine; **sacar b. a** to shine, to polish

brilloso, -a ADJ *Am* shining

brincar [44] VI to skip

brinco NM skip

brindar 1 VI to drink a toast; **b. por algn/algo** to drink to sb/sth
2 VT (a) *(oportunidad)* to offer, to provide (b) *Taurom* to dedicate (**a** to)
3 brindarse VPR to offer (**a** to), to volunteer (**a** to)

brindis NM INV (a) *(con bebida)* toast (b) *Taurom* dedication (of the bull)

brío NM energy

brioso, -a ADJ energetic, vigorous

brisa NF breeze; **b. marina** sea breeze

británico, -a 1 ADJ British; **las Islas Británicas** the British Isles
2 NM,F Briton; **los británicos** the British

brizna NF *(de hierba)* blade; *(de carne)* string

broca NF *Téc* bit

brocha NF *(para pintar)* paintbrush; **b. de afeitar** shaving brush

broche NM (a) *(joya)* brooch; *Fig* **poner el b. de oro** to finish with a flourish (b) *(de vestido)* fastener

brocheta NF *Culin* shish kebab; *(aguja)* skewer

brócoli NM broccoli

broma NF *(chiste)* joke; **bromas aparte** joking apart; **en b.** as a joke; ¡**ni en b.!** not on your life!; **b. pesada** practical joke; **gastar una b.** to play a joke

bromear VI to joke

bromista 1 ADJ fond of joking o playing jokes **2** NMF joker, prankster

bronca NF (**a**) *(jaleo)* row; **armar (una) b.** to kick up a row (**b**) *Esp (crítica)* scolding, telling-off; **echar una b. a algn** to bawl sb out (**c**) *RP Fam (rabia)* **me da b.** it hacks me off; **el jefe le tiene b.** the boss can't stand him

bronce NM bronze

bronceado, -a 1 ADJ suntanned, tanned **2** NM suntan, tan

bronceador, -a 1 ADJ **leche bronceadora** suntan cream **2** NM suntan cream o lotion

broncearse VPR to get a tan o a suntan

bronco, -a ADJ rough, coarse

bronquio NM bronchial tube

bronquitis NF INV bronchitis

brotar VI *(planta)* to sprout; *(agua)* to spring, to gush; *(lágrimas)* to well up; *(epidemia)* to break out

brote NM (**a**) *Bot (renuevo)* bud, shoot; *(de agua)* gushing (**b**) *(de epidemia, violencia)* outbreak

bruces: de bruces LOC ADV face down; **se cayó de b.** he fell flat on his face

bruja NF witch, sorceress

brujería NF witchcraft, sorcery

brujo 1 NM wizard, sorcerer **2** ADJ *Méx Fam* broke; **estar b.** to be broke

brújula NF compass

bruma NF mist

brumoso, -a ADJ misty

bruñir VT to polish

brusco, -a ADJ (**a**) *(persona)* brusque, abrupt (**b**) *(repentino)* sudden, sharp

Bruselas N Brussels

brusquedad NF brusqueness, abruptness

brutal ADJ brutal

brutalidad NF brutality

bruto, -a 1 ADJ (**a**) *(necio)* stupid, thick; *(grosero)* coarse, uncouth (**b**) *Fin* gross; **peso b.** gross weight (**c**) **un diamante en b.** an uncut diamond **2** NM,F blockhead, brute

bucear VI to swim under water

buche NM maw; *(de ave)* craw; *Fam (estómago)* belly, stomach

bucle NM curl, ringlet

bucólico, -a ADJ (**a**) *(campestre)* **un paisaje b.** a charmingly rural landscape (**b**) *Lit* bucolic

budín NM pudding

budismo NM Buddhism

budista ADJ & NMF Buddhist

buen ADJ good; *ver* **bueno**

buenamente ADV **haz lo que b. puedas** just do what you can; **si b. puedes** if you possibly can

buenaventura NF good fortune, good luck; **echar la b. a algn** to tell sb's fortune

bueno, -a

grammar note: **buen** is used instead of **bueno** before masculine singular nouns (e.g. **buen hombre** good man). The comparative form of **bueno** is **mejor** (better), and the superlative form is **el mejor** (masculine) or **la mejor** (feminine) (the best).

1 ADJ (**a**) *(en calidad)* good; **un alumno muy b.** a very good pupil; **una buena película** a good movie o Br film; **lo b.** the good thing (**b**) *(amable)* (con **ser**) good, kind; **es muy buena persona** he's a very kind soul (**c**) *(sano)* (con **estar**) well, in good health (**d**) *(tiempo)* good; **hoy hace buen tiempo** it's fine today; **mañana hará b.** it will be fine o a nice day tomorrow (**e**) *(conveniente)* good; **no es b. comer tanto** it's not good for you to eat so much; **sería b. que vinieras** it would be a good idea if you came (**f**) *(considerable)* considerable; **un buen número de** a good number of; **una buena cantidad** a considerable amount (**g**) *(grande)* good, big; **un buen trozo de pastel** a nice o good big piece of cake (**h**) *Fam (atractivo)* gorgeous, sexy; **Rosa está muy buena** Rosa's a bit of all right!; **una tía buena** a good-looking girl (**i**) *Irón* fine, real, proper; **¡en buen lío te has metido!** that's a fine mess you've got yourself into! (**j**) **¡buenas!** *(saludos)* hello!; **buenas tardes** *(desde mediodía hasta las cinco)* good afternoon; *(desde las cinco)* good evening; **buenas noches** *(al llegar)* good evening; *(al irse)* good night; **buenos días** good morning (**k**) *(locuciones)* **de buenas a primeras** suddenly, all at once; **estar de buenas** to be in a good mood; **los buenos tiempos** the good old days; **por las buenas** willingly; **por las buenas o por las malas** willy-nilly; *Irón* **¡buena la has hecho!** that's done it!; **un susto de los buenos** a real fright; *Irón* **¡estaría b.!** I should jolly well hope not!; *Irón* **librarse de una buena** to get off scot free **2** NM,F **el b. de Carlos** good old Carlos **3** INTERJ (**a**) *(vale)* all right, OK (**b**) *(expresa sorpresa)* hey! (**c**) *Col, Méx (al teléfono)* hello

buey *(pl* **bueyes***)* NM ox, bullock

búfalo, -a NM,F buffalo

bufanda NF scarf

bufar VI (**a**) *(toro)* to snort; *(gato)* to hiss (**b**) *(persona)* to be fuming

bufé NM buffet; **b. libre** self-service buffet meal

bufete NM *(de abogado)* lawyer's office

buffet *(pl* **buffets***)* NM = **bufé**

bufido NM *(de toro)* snort; *(de gato)* hiss

bufón NM clown, buffoon

buhardilla NF attic, garret

búho NM owl; **b. real** eagle owl

buhonero, -a NM,F pedlar, hawker

buitre NM vulture

bujía NF (**a**) *Aut* spark plug (**b**) *Fís* candlepower

bula NF (*documento*) (papal) bull

bulbo NM bulb

buldog (*pl* **buldogs**) NM bulldog

bulerías NFPL = popular Andalusian song and dance

bulevar NM boulevard

Bulgaria N Bulgaria

búlgaro, -a ADJ & NM,F Bulgarian

bulín NM *RP Fam* (*picadero*) bachelor pad

bulla NF *Fam* (**a**) (*ruido*) racket, uproar; **armar. b.** to kick up a racket (**b**) *Esp* (*prisa*) **meter b. a algn** to hurry sb up

bullicio NM (*de ciudad, mercado*) hustle and bustle; (*de multitud*) hubbub

bullicioso, -a 1 ADJ (**a**) (*agitado*) (*reunión, multitud*) noisy; (*calle, mercado*) busy, bustling (**b**) (*inquieto*) rowdy, boisterous
  2 NM,F boisterous person

bullir VI (**a**) (*hervir*) to boil, to bubble (up) (**b**) **b. de gente** to be teeming with people

bulto NM (**a**) (*cosa indistinta*) shape, form (**b**) (*maleta, caja*) piece of luggage (**c**) *Med* lump (**d**) **hacer mucho b.** to be very bulky; *Fam* **escurrir el b.** to pass the buck

bumerán NM boomerang

bungalow [bunga'lo] (*pl* **bungalows**) NM bungalow

búnker (*pl* **bunkeres**) NM (**a**) (*refugio*) bunker (**b**) *Esp Pol* reactionary forces

buñuelo NM doughnut

BUP NM *Antes* (*abr* **Bachillerato Unificado Polivalente**) = academically orientated Spanish secondary school course for pupils aged 14-17

buque NM ship; **b. de guerra** warship; **b. de pasajeros** liner, passenger ship; **b. insignia** flagship

burbuja NF bubble; **hacer burbujas** to bubble, make bubbles

burbujear VI to bubble

burdel NM brothel

Burdeos N Bordeaux

burdo, -a ADJ coarse, rough

burgalés, -esa 1 ADJ of/from Burgos
  2 NM,F person from Burgos

burgués, -esa ADJ & NM,F bourgeois

burguesía NF bourgeoisie

burla NF gibe, jeer; **hacer b. de algo/algn** to make fun of sth/sb; **hacer b. a algn** to stick one's tongue out at sb.

burladero NM *Taurom* = refuge in bullring

burlar 1 VT (**a**) (*engañar*) to deceive (**b**) (*eludir*) to dodge, to evade

  2 burlarse VPR to make fun (**de** of), to laugh (**de** at)

burlón, -ona ADJ mocking

buró NM (**a**) *Pol* executive committee (**b**) (*escritorio*) bureau, desk (**c**) *Méx* (*mesa de noche*) bedside table

burocracia NF bureaucracy

burócrata NM,F bureaucrat

burocrático, -a ADJ bureaucratic

burrada NF (*comentario*) stupid *o* foolish remark; (*hecho*) stupid *o* foolish act

burro, -a 1 NM,F (**a**) (*animal*) donkey, ass; *Fam Fig* **bajarse del b.** to climb *o* back down (**b**) *Fam* (*estúpido*) dimwit, blockhead (**c**) **b. de carga** dogsbody, drudge
  2 ADJ *Fam* (**a**) (*necio*) stupid, dumb (**b**) (*obstinado*) stubborn

bursátil ADJ stock-market

bus NM bus

busca 1 NF search; **ir en b. de** to go in search of
  2 NM *Esp* (*buscapersonas*) pager

buscador, -a 1 NM,F (*en general*) hunter; **b. de oro** gold prospector
  2 NM *Inform* (*en Internet*) search engine

buscapersonas NM INV pager

buscapleitos NM,F INV troubleseeker

buscar [44] **1** VT to look *o* search for; **b. una palabra en el diccionario** to look up a word in the dictionary; **ir a b. algo** to go and get sth, to fetch sth; **fue a buscarme a la estación** she picked me up at the station
  2 buscarse VPR *Fam* **buscarse la vida** to try and earn one's living; *Fam* **te la estás buscando** you're asking for it; **se busca** (*en anuncios*) wanted

buseta NF *Col, CRica, Ecuad, Ven* minibus

búsqueda NF search, quest; *Inform* search

busto NM bust

butaca NF (**a**) (*sillón*) armchair, easy chair (**b**) *Cin & Teatro* seat; **b. de platea** *o* **patio** seat in the stalls

butano NM butane; (**gas**) **b.** butane gas

butifarra NF sausage

buzo NM (**a**) (*persona*) diver (**b**) *Arg* (*sudadera*) sweatshirt (**c**) *Col, Urug* (*jersey*) sweater,. *Br* jumper

buzón NM post box, *Br* letter box, *US* mailbox; *Inform* (*de correo electrónico*) (electronic) mailbox; **echar una carta al b.** to *Br* post *o US* mail a letter; **b. de voz** voice mail

bypass [bai'pas] NM INV *Med* heart bypass operation

byte [bait] NM *Inform* byte

C, c [θe] NF (*letra*) C, c

C (**a**) (*abr* **Celsius**) C (**b**) (*abr* **centígrado**) C

C., Cª (*abr* **compañía**) Co

c (**a**) (*abr* **calle**) St (**b**) (*abr* **cargo**) cargo, freight (**c**) (*abr* **cuenta**) a/c

cabal 1 ADJ (**a**) (*exacto*) exact, precise (**b**) (*honesto*) honest, upright
2 cabales NMPL *Fam* **no está en sus cabales** he's not in his right mind

cábala NF *Fig* **hacer cábalas sobre algo** to speculate about sth

cabalgadura NF mount

cabalgar [42] VT & VI to ride

cabalgata NF cavalcade; **la c. de los Reyes Magos** the procession of the Three Wise Men

caballa NF mackerel

caballar ADJ **ganado c.** horses

caballería NF (**a**) (*cabalgadura*) mount, steed (**b**) *Mil* cavalry

caballeriza NF stable

caballero NM (**a**) (*hombre*) gentleman; **¿qué desea, c.?** can I help you, sir?; **ropa de c.** menswear (**b**) *Hist* knight (**c**) **caballeros** (*en letrero*) gents

caballeroso, -a ADJ gentlemanly, chivalrous

caballete NM (**a**) (*de pintor*) easel (**b**) *Téc* trestle (**c**) (*de nariz*) bridge

caballito NM (**a**) **c. de mar** seahorse (**b**) **caballitos** merry-go-round, *US* carousel

caballo NM (**a**) (*animal*) horse; **a c.** on horseback; **montar a c.** to ride; *Fig* **a c. entre ...** halfway between ... (**b**) *Téc* **c. de vapor** horse power (**c**) (*pieza de ajedrez*) knight (**d**) *Naipes* queen (**e**) *Fam* (*heroína*) horse, smack

cabaña NF cabin

cabaret (*pl* **cabarets**) NM cabaret

cabecear 1 VI to nod
2 VT *Dep* to head

cabecera NF (**a**) (*de fila, mesa*) head; (*de cama*) headboard (**b**) *Esp* (*de texto*) heading; (*de periódico*) masthead

cabecilla NMF leader

cabellera NF head of hair

cabello NM hair; *Culin* **c. de ángel** = sweet made of gourd and syrup

cabelludo, -a ADJ **cuero c.** scalp

caber [9] VI (**a**) (*haber espacio para*) to fit; **cabe en el maletero** it fits in the *Br* boot *o US* trunk; **¿cabemos todos?** is there room for all of us?; **en este coche/jarro caben ...** this car/jug

holds ...; **no cabe por la puerta** it won't go through the door (**b**) (*expresiones*) **no c. en sí de gozo** to be beside oneself with joy; **no me cabe en la cabeza** I can't understand it; **no cabe duda** there is no doubt; **cabe la posibilidad de que ...** there is a possibility *o* chance that ...; **no está mal, dentro de lo que cabe** it isn't bad, under the circumstances; **cabe señalar que ...** we should point out that ... (**c**) *Mat* **doce entre cuatro caben a tres** four into twelve goes three (times)

cabestrillo NM sling

cabestro NM to nod

cabeza 1 NF head; **en c.** in the lead; **por c.** a head, per person; *Fig* **a la c. de** at the front *o* top of; *Fig* **estar mal de la c.** to be a mental case; **c. de turco** scapegoat; **el** *o* **la c. de familia** the head of the family
2 NM **c. rapada** skinhead

cabezada NF (**a**) (*golpe*) butt, blow on the head (**b**) *Fam* **echar una c.** to have a snooze; **dar cabezadas** to nod

cabezal NM (**a**) (*de aparato*) head (**b**) (*almohada*) bolster

cabezazo NM (*con la cabeza*) headbutt; (*en la cabeza*) blow *o* bump on the head; *Dep* header

cabezón, -ona *Fam* **1** ADJ (**a**) (*persona*) **ser c.** (*de cabeza grande*) to have a big head; (*terco*) to be pigheaded (**b**) *Fam* (*vino*) rough
2 NM,F pigheaded person

cabezota *Fam* **1** ADJ pigheaded
2 NM,F pigheaded person

cabezudo NM = carnival figure with a huge head

cabida NF capacity; **dar c. a** to leave room for

cabildo NM (**a**) (*municipio*) ≃ district council (**b**) *Rel* chapter

cabina NF cabin; **c. telefónica** (*con puerta*) *Br* phone box, *US* phone booth

cabinero, -a NM,F *Col* flight attendant

cabizbajo, -a ADJ crestfallen

cable NM cable; *Fam* **echarle un c. a algn** to give sb a hand

cableoperador NM cable company, cable operator

cabo NM (**a**) (*extremo*) end; **al c. de** after; **de c. a rabo** from start to finish (**b**) *Mil* corporal; (*policía*) sergeant (**c**) *Náut* rope, cable; *Fig* **atar cabos** to put two and two together; *Fig* **no dejar ningún c. suelto** to leave no loose ends (**d**) *Geog* cape; **Ciudad del C.** Cape Town; **C. Verde** Cape Verde

cabra NF goat; *Fam* **estar como una c.** to be off one's head

cabré INDIC FUT *de* **caber**

cabreado, -a ADJ *muy Fam Br* pissed off, *US* pissed

cabrear *muy Fam* **1** VT to make angry, *Br* to piss off
2 cabrearse VPR to get *Br* pissed off *o US* pissed

cabreo NM *muy Fam* rage, fit; **agarrar** *o Esp* **coger un c.** to get really *Br* narked *o US* pissed

cabrío, -a ADJ **macho c.** billy goat; **ganado c.** goats

cabriola NF skip

cabrito NM *Zool* kid

cabro, -a NM,F *Chile Fam* kid

cabrón, -ona NM,F *Vulg* bastard, *f* bitch, *US* asshole

cabronada NF *muy Fam* dirty trick

cabuya NF (**a**) *(planta)* agave (**b**) *(fibra)* fibre hemp (**c**) *CAm, Col, Ven (cuerda)* rope

caca NF *Fam Br* poo, *US* poop

cacahuete, *CAm, Méx* **cacahuate** NM peanut, *US* groundnut

cacao NM (**a**) *Bot* cacao (**b**) *(polvo, bebida)* cocoa (**c**) *Fam (lío)* mess

cacarear 1 VI *(gallina)* to cluck
2 VT *Fig* to boast about

cacareo NM *(de gallina)* clucking

cacatúa NF (**a**) *(ave)* cockatoo (**b**) *Fam (mujer vieja)* old bat

cacereño, -a 1 ADJ of/from Cáceres
2 NM,F person from Cáceres

cacería NF (**a**) *(actividad)* hunting, shooting (**b**) *(partida)* hunt, shoot

cacerola NF saucepan

cacha NF *Fam (muslo)* thigh; *Esp* **estar cachas** to be well-built

cachalote NM sperm whale

cacharro NM (**a**) *(recipiente)* pot; **cacharros** *(de cocina)* pots and pans (**b**) *Fam (trasto)* thing, piece of junk

caché NM *Inform* **(memoria) c.** cache memory

cachear VT to frisk, to search

cachemir NM, **cachemira** NF cashmere

cacheo NM frisk, frisking

cachetada NF slap

cachete NM (**a**) *(bofetada)* slap (**b**) *Am (mejilla)* cheek

cachila NF *RP (automóvil)* vintage car

cachimba NF (**a**) *(pipa)* pipe (**b**) *RP (pozo)* well

cachiporra NF club, truncheon

cachivache NM *Fam* thing, knick-knack

cacho¹ NM *Fam (pedazo)* bit, piece; *Esp* **¡c. tonto!** you idiot!

cacho² NM (**a**) *Andes, Ven (asta)* horn (**b**) *Andes, Guat, Ven (cuento)* story; **no me vengan a contar cachos, que sé lo que pasó** don't start telling me stories, I know what happened (**c**) *Andes, Guat, Ven (burla)* joke

cachondearse VPR *Esp Fam* **c. de algn** to make a fool out of sb, *Br* to take the mickey out of sb

cachondeo NM *Esp Fam* **ser un c.** to be a laugh; **tomarse algo a c.** to take sth as a joke

cachondo, -a 1 ADJ (**a**) *Esp, Méx muy Fam (sexualmente)* **estar c.** to be randy; **ponerse c.** to get randy *o* turned on (**b**) *Esp Fam (divertido)* **ser c.** to be funny

cachorro, -a NM,F *(de perro)* pup, puppy; *(de gato)* kitten; *(de otros animales)* cub, baby

cacique NM *(jefe)* local boss

caco NM *Fam* thief

cacofonía NF cacophony

cacto NM, **cactus** NM INV *Bot* cactus

cada ADJ *(de dos)* each; *(de varios)* each, every; **c. día** every day; **c. dos días** every second day; **c. vez más** more and more; **¿c. cuánto?** how often?; **c. dos por tres** every other minute; **cuatro de c. diez** four out of (every) ten; **¡tienes c. cosa!** you come up with some fine ideas!

cadalso NM scaffold

cadáver NM *(de persona)* corpse, (dead) body; *(de animal)* body, carcass; **ingresar c.** to be dead on arrival

cadena NF (**a**) *(de eslabones, tiendas)* chain; *(correa de perro)* lead, leash; *Aut* **cadenas** tyre chains (**b**) *TV* channel (**c**) *(de proceso industrial)* line; **c. de montaje** assembly line; **trabajo en c.** assembly line work (**d**) *Geog* **c. montañosa** mountain range (**e**) *Der* **c. perpetua** life imprisonment

cadencia NF rhythm; *Mús* cadenza

cadera NF hip

cadete 1 NM *(en ejército)* cadet
2 NM,F *RP (chico de los recados)* office junior

caducar [44] VI to expire

caducidad NF expiry; **fecha de c.** *(en alimento, medicamento)* use-by date

caduco, -a ADJ (**a**) *Bot* deciduous (**b**) *(anticuado)* out-of-date

caer [39] **1** VI (**a**) *(hacia abajo)* to fall; **dejar c.** to drop; *Fig* **está al c.** *(llegar)* he'll arrive any minute now; *(ocurrir)* it's on the way (**b**) *(fecha)* to be; **su cumpleaños cae en sábado** his birthday falls on a Saturday (**c**) *(entender)* to understand, to see; **ya caigo** I get it; **no caí** I didn't twig (**d**) *Esp (estar, quedar)* **cae cerca de aquí** it's not far from here (**e**) **me cae bien/mal** I like/don't like her (**f**) **al c. el día** in the evening; **al c. la noche** at nightfall
2 caerse VPR to fall (down); **me caí de la moto** I fell off the motorbike; **se le cayó el pañuelo** he dropped his handkerchief

café NM (**a**) *(bebida)* coffee; **c. con leche** white coffee; *Esp, Andes, Ven* **c. tinto** black coffee (**b**) *(cafetería)* café

cafeína NF caffeine

cafetal NM coffee plantation

cafetera NF coffee-maker

cafetería NF snack bar, coffee bar; *Ferroc* buffet car

cafetero, -a ADJ (**a**) *(de café)* coffee (**b**) *Fam* **es muy c.** *(persona)* he loves coffee

cafiche NM *Andes Fam* pimp

cafre NMF savage, beast

cagado, -a ADJ *muy Fam (cobarde)* chicken, coward; **estar c. de miedo** to be shit-scared

cagar [42] *Fam* **1** VI to shit, to crap
2 cagarse VPR to crap oneself; **cagarse de miedo** to be shit-scared

caída NF (**a**) *(de persona, objeto)* fall; *(de pelo, diente)* loss (**b**) *(de precios)* drop (**c**) *(de tela, vestido)* drape (**d**) *Pol* downfall, collapse

caído, -a 1 ADJ fallen
2 NMPL **los caídos** the fallen

caigo INDIC PRES *de* **caer**

caimán NM alligator

Cairo N **El C.** Cairo

caja NF (**a**) *(recipiente)* box; *(de leche etc)* carton; *(de caudales)* safe; *Fam TV* **la c. tonta** the box, *Br* the telly, *US* the boob tube (**b**) *(de embalaje)* crate, case; **una c. de cerveza** a crate of beer (**c**) *Fin (en tienda)* cash desk; *(en banco)* cashier's desk (**d**) *Aut* **c. de cambios** gearbox (**e**) *Esp (entidad financiera)* **c. de ahorros** savings bank (**f**) *(féretro)* coffin

cajero, -a NM,F cashier; **c. automático** cash point, cash dispenser

cajetilla NF packet, pack

cajón NM (**a**) *(en un mueble)* drawer; *Fig* **c. de sastre** jumble; *Fam* **de c.** obvious, self-evident (**b**) *(caja grande)* crate, chest

cajuela NF *CAm, Méx (maletero) Br* boot, *US* trunk

cal¹ NF lime; *Fig* **a c. y canto** hermetically; *Fam* **una c. de y otra de arena** six of one and half a dozen of the other

cal² *(abr* **caloría)** cal

cala NF (**a**) *Geog* creek, cove (**b**) *Náut* hold

calabacín NM *Bot* (**a**) *(pequeño) Br* courgette, *US* zucchini (**b**) *(grande) Br* marrow, *US* squash

calabaza NF pumpkin, gourd

calabobos NM INV *Fam* drizzle

calabozo NM (**a**) *(prisión)* jail, prison (**b**) *(celda)* cell

calada NF *Esp Fam (de cigarrillo)* drag, puff

calado, -a 1 ADJ soaked
2 NM *Náut* draught

calamar NM squid *inv; Culin* **calamares a la romana** squid rings fried in batter

calambre NM (**a**) *Elec (descarga)* electric shock; **ese cable da c.** that wire is live (**b**) *(en músculo)* cramp

calamidad NF calamity

calaña NF *Pey* **de esa c.** of that ilk

calar 1 VT (**a**) *(mojar)* to soak, to drench (**b**) *(agujerear)* to pierce, to penetrate
2 VI (**a**) *(prenda)* to let in water (**b**) *Náut* to draw
3 calarse VPR (**a**) *(prenda, techo)* to let in

water; *(mojarse)* to get soaked (**b**) *(el sombrero)* to pull down (**c**) *Esp (motor)* to stall

calavera 1 NF (**a**) *(cráneo)* skull (**b**) *Méx Aut* **calaveras** tail lights
2 NM tearaway

calcar [44] VT (**a**) *(un dibujo)* to trace (**b**) *Fig (imitar)* to copy, to imitate

calceta NF **hacer c.** to knit

calcetín NM sock

calcinar VT to burn

calcio NM calcium

calco NM (**a**) *(reproducción)* tracing; **papel de c.** carbon paper (**b**) *(imitación)* carbon copy; **es un c. de** it's a carbon copy of (**c**) *Ling* calque, loan translation

calcomanía NF transfer

calculador, -a ADJ *también Fig* calculating

calculadora NF calculator

calcular VT (**a**) *Mat* to calculate (**b**) *(evaluar)* to (make an) estimate (**c**) *(suponer)* to figure, to guess

cálculo NM (**a**) *(operación)* calculation; **según mis cálculos** by my reckoning; **hacer cálculos mentales** to do mental arithmetic (**b**) *Med* gallstone (**c**) *Mat (ciencia)* calculus

caldear VT to heat up

caldera NF (**a**) *(industrial)* boiler; *(olla)* cauldron (**b**) *Urug (hervidor)* kettle

caldereta NF stew

calderilla NF small change

caldo NM stock, broth; **c. de cultivo** culture medium; *Fig* breeding ground

calé ADJ & NM gypsy

calefacción NF heating; **c. central** central heating

calefaccionar VT *CSur (calentar)* to heat (up), to warm (up)

calefactor NM heater

calefón NM *CSur (calentador)* water heater

caleidoscopio NM kaleidoscope

calendario NM calendar

calentador NM heater

calentamiento NM *Dep* warm-up; **c. global** global warming

calentar [1] **1** VT (**a**) *(agua, horno)* to heat; *(comida, habitación)* to warm up; *Fig* **no me calientes la cabeza** don't bug me (**b**) *Fam (pegar)* to smack (**c**) *Fam (excitar)* to arouse (sexually), to turn on
2 calentarse VPR (**a**) *(por calor) (persona)* to warm oneself, to get warm; *(cosa)* to heat up (**b**) *Fam (agitarse)* to get angry *o* annoyed (**c**) *Fig* **se calentaron los ánimos** people became very excited

calentura NF (**a**) *(fiebre)* fever, temperature (**b**) *(herida)* cold sore

calesita NF *RP* merry-go-round, *US* carousel

calibrar VT to gauge, to bore

calibre NM (**a**) *(de arma)* calibre (**b**) *Fig (importancia)* importance

calidad NF (**a**) quality; **de primera c.** first-class; **un vino de c.** a good-quality wine (**b**) **en c. de** as

cálido, -a ADJ warm; **una cálida acogida** a warm welcome

calidoscopio NM = **caleidoscopio**

caliente ADJ (**a**) *(a alta temperatura)* hot; *(templado)* warm (**b**) *Fig (debate)* heated; **en c.** in the heat of the moment (**c**) *Fam (cachondo)* hot, randy

calificación NF *Educ Br* mark, *US* grade

calificar [44] VT (**a**) *(llamar)* to describe (**de** as); **le calificó de inmoral** he called him immoral (**b**) *(examen) Br* to mark, *US* to grade

calificativo NM epithet

caligrafía NF calligraphy; *(modo de escribir)* handwriting

calima NF haze, mist

calimocho NM *Esp Fam* = drink made with wine and Coca-Cola®

calina NF = **calima**

cáliz NM chalice

caliza NF limestone

calizo, -a ADJ lime

callado, -a ADJ quiet; **te lo tenías muy c.** you were keeping that quiet

callar 1 VI (**a**) *(dejar de hablar)* to stop talking; **¡calla!** be quiet!, *Fam* shut up! (**b**) *(no hablar)* to keep quiet, to say nothing
2 VT *(noticia)* not to mention, to keep to oneself
3 callarse VPR to stop talking, to be quiet; **¡cállate!** shut up!

calle NF (**a**) *(en población)* street, road; **c. de dirección única** one-way street; **c. mayor** *Br* high street, *US* main street; **el hombre de la c.** the man in the street (**b**) *Esp Dep* lane

calleja NF narrow street

callejero, -a 1 NM *(mapa)* street directory
2 ADJ street; **gato c.** alley cat

callejón NM back alley o street; **c. sin salida** cul-de-sac, dead end

callejuela NF narrow street, lane

callista NMF chiropodist

callo NM (**a**) *Med* callus, corn; *Fam* **dar el c.** to slog (**b**) *Esp Culin* **callos** tripe

calma NF calm; **¡c.!** calm down!; **en c.** calm; **tómatelo con c.** take it easy

calmante NM painkiller

calmar 1 VT *(persona)* to calm (down); *(dolor)* to soothe, to relieve
2 calmarse VPR (**a**) *(persona)* to calm down (**b**) *(dolor, viento)* to ease off

caló NM *Esp* gypsy dialect

calor NM (**a**) *(temperatura)* heat; **hace c.** it's hot; **tengo c.** I'm hot; **entrar en c.** to warm up (**b**) *Fig (afecto)* warmth

caloría NF calorie

calote NM *RP Fam* swindle

calumnia NF *(oral)* slander; *(escrita)* libel

calumniar [43] VT *(de palabra)* to slander; *(por escrito)* to libel

calumnioso, -a ADJ *(de palabra)* slanderous; *(por escrito)* libellous

caluroso, -a ADJ hot; *(acogida etc)* warm

calva NF bald patch

calvario NM *(vía crucis)* Calvary, stations of the Cross; *Fig (sufrimiento)* ordeal

calvicie NF baldness

calvinismo NM Calvinism

calvo, -a 1 ADJ bald; **ni tanto ni tan c.** there's no need to go to extremes
2 NM bald man

calza NF (**a**) *(cuña)* wedge (**b**) *Col (en diente)* filling

calzada NF road (surface), *US* pavement

calzado NM shoes, footwear

calzador NM shoehorn

calzar [40] **1** VT (**a**) *(poner calzado)* to put shoes on; **¿qué número calzas?** what size shoe do you take? (**b**) *(mueble)* to wedge
2 calzarse VPR **calzarse los zapatos** to put on one's shoes

calzón NM (**a**) *Esp Dep* shorts (**b**) *Andes, Méx, RP (bragas)* panties, *Br* knickers; **un c., unos calzones** a pair of panties o *Br* knickers (**c**) *Bol, Méx* **calzones** *(calzoncillos) Br* underpants, *US* shorts

calzonazos NM INV *Fam* henpecked husband

calzoncillos NMPL *(slip)* briefs, *Br* (under)pants, *US* shorts; *(bóxer)* boxer shorts .

calzoneta NM *CAm* swimming trunks

cama NF bed; **estar en** o **guardar c.** to be confined to bed; **hacer la c.** to make the bed; **irse a la c.** to go to bed; **c. doble/individual** double/single bed; **c. turca** couch

camada NF litter

camafeo NM cameo

camaleón NM chameleon

cámara 1 NF (**a**) *(aparato)* camera; **a c. lenta** in slow motion; **c. de vídeo** video camera; **c. web** web camera, webcam (**b**) *Pol* Chamber, House; **C. Alta/Baja** Upper/Lower House (**c**) *Aut* inner tube (**d**) *(habitación)* room, chamber; **c. de gas** gas chamber; **c. frigorífica** cold-storage room; **música de c.** chamber music
2 NMF *(hombre)* cameraman; *(mujer)* camerawoman

camarada NMF comrade

camaradería NF camaraderie

camarera NF *(de hotel)* chambermaid

camarero, -a NM,F *(de restaurante) (hombre)* waiter; *(mujer)* waitress; *(tras la barra) (hombre)* barman; *(mujer)* barmaid

camarilla NF clique

camarón NM *Br* shrimp, *US* prawn

camarote NM cabin

camastro NM ramshackle bed

camba *Bol Fam* **1** ADJ of/from the forested lowland region of Bolivia
2 NMF person from the forested lowland region of Bolivia

cambalache NM *RP (tienda)* junk shop

cambiante ADJ changing; *(carácter)* changeable

cambiar [43] **1** VT (a) *(modificar, reemplazar)* to change; *(trasladar)* to move; **c. algo de sitio** to move sth (b) *(intercambiar)* to swap, to exchange (c) *(dinero)* to change
2 VI to change; **c. de casa** to move (house); **c. de idea** to change one's mind; **c. de trabajo** to get another job; **c. de velocidad** to change gear
3 cambiarse VPR (a) *(de ropa)* to change (clothes) (b) *(de casa)* to move (house)

cambiazo NM *Fam* switch

cambio **1** NM (a) *(modificación)* change; **c. de planes** change of plans; **un c. en la opinión pública** a shift in public opinion (b) *(dinero)* change; **¿tienes c. de cinco euros?** have you got change for five euros? (c) *Fin (de divisas)* exchange rate; *(de acciones)* price (d) *Aut* gear change; **c. automático** automatic transmission (e) *(reemplazo, trueque)* exchange; **a c. de** in exchange for
2 en cambio LOC ADV on the other hand

cambista NMF moneychanger

Camboya N Cambodia

camboyano, -a ADJ & NM,F Cambodian

cambur NM *Ven* banana

camelar VT *Fam* (a) *(convencer)* to cajole (b) *(galantear)* to win over

camelia NF camellia

camello, -a **1** NM,F camel
2 NM *Fam (traficante de drogas)* (drug) pusher

camellón NM *Col, Méx (en avenida) Br* central reservation, *US* median (strip)

camelo NM *Fam* (a) *(engaño)* hoax (b) *(trola)* cock-and-bull story

camembert ['kamember] *(pl* camemberts*)* NM camembert

camerino NM dressing room

Camerún N Cameroon

camilla NF *(con ruedas)* trolley; *(sin ruedas)* stretcher

camillero, -a NM,F stretcher-bearer

caminante NMF walker

caminar **1** VI to walk
2 VT to cover, to travel; **caminaron 10 km** they walked for 10 km

caminata NF long walk

camino NM (a) *(ruta)* route, way; **ir c. de** to be going to; **ponerse en c.** to set off; *Fig* **ir por buen/mal c.** to be on the right/wrong track; **abrirse c.** to break through; **a medio c.** halfway; **en el c. a** *o* **de c. a** on the way to; **estar**

en c. to be on the way; **nos coge** *o* **pilla de c.** it's on the way (b) *(vía)* path, track (c) *(modo)* way

camión NM (a) *(de mercancías)* truck, *Br* lorry; **c. de la basura** *Br* dustcart, *US* garbage truck; **c. cisterna** tanker; **c. frigorífico** refrigerated truck (b) *CAm, Méx (autobús)* bus

camionero, -a NM,F *Br* lorry driver, *US* trucker

camioneta NF van

camisa NF shirt; **en mangas de c.** in one's shirtsleeves; *Fig* **cambiar de c.** to change sides; **c. de fuerza** straitjacket

camisería NF *(tienda)* shirt shop, outfitter's

camiseta NF (a) *(ropa interior) Br* vest, *US* undershirt (b) *(de manga corta)* T-shirt (c) *Dep (de tirantes)* vest; *(con mangas)* shirt; **sudar la c.** to run oneself into the ground

camisola NF (a) *(prenda interior)* camisole (b) *Dep* sports shirt

camisón NM nightdress; *Fam* nightie

camomila NF camomile

camorra NF *Fam* trouble

camorrista **1** ADJ quarrelsome, rowdy
2 NMF troublemaker

camote NM (a) *Andes, CAm, Méx (batata)* sweet potato; *(bulbo)* tuber, bulb (b) *Méx Fam (complicación)* mess

campal ADJ **batalla c.** pitched battle

campamento NM camp

campana NF bell; **pantalones de campana** bell-bottom trousers

campanada NF (a) *(de campana)* peal (b) *(de reloj)* stroke (c) *Fig (suceso)* sensation; **dar la c.** to make a big splash, to cause a sensation

campanario NM belfry, bell tower

campanilla NF (a) *(de puerta)* (small) bell (b) *Anat* uvula (c) *Bot* bell flower

campante ADJ *Fam* **se quedó tan c.** he didn't bat an eyelid

campaña NF (a) *(acción organizada)* campaign; **c. electoral** election campaign; **c. publicitaria** advertising campaign (b) *Mil* campaign; **hospital/ambulancia de c.** field hospital/ambulance (c) *RP (campo)* countryside

campar VI *Fam* **c. por sus respetos** to do as one pleases

campechano, -a ADJ unpretentious

campeón, -ona NM,F champion; **c. mundial** world champion

campeonato NM championship; **un tonto de c.** a prize idiot

campera NF (a) *Esp* **camperas** *(botas)* cowboy boots (b) *RP (chaqueta)* jacket

campero, -a **1** ADJ *Esp* **botas camperas** cowboy boots
2 NM *Andes* Jeep®

campesino, -a NM,F *(hombre)* countryman; *(mujer)* countrywoman

campestre ADJ rural

cámping ['kampin] (*pl* **cámpings**) NM *(terreno)* campsite, *US* campground; **hacer** *o* **ir de c.** to go camping

campiña NF countryside

campista NMF camper

campo NM (**a**) *(no ciudad)* country, countryside; **a c. traviesa** *o* **través** cross-country; **trabaja (en) el c.** he works (on) the land; **trabajo de c.** fieldwork (**b**) *Fís, Fot & Inform* field; **c. magnético** magnetic field (**c**) *(ámbito)* field; **c. de acción** field of action; *Mil* **c. de batalla** battlefield (**d**) *(campamento)* camp; **c. de concentración** concentration camp; **c. de trabajo** work camp (**e**) *Esp Dep (de fútbol)* field, *Br* pitch; *(de tenis)* court; *(de golf)* course (**f**) *Andes (sitio)* room, space; **hazme c. para que me siente** make some room so I can sit down

camposanto NM cemetery

campus NM INV campus

camuflaje NM camouflage

camuflar VT to camouflage

cana NF *(gris)* grey hair; *(blanco)* white hair; **tener canas** to have grey hair; *Fam* **echar una c. al aire** to let one's hair down

Canadá N Canada

canadiense ADJ & NMF Canadian

canal NF (**a**) *(artificial)* canal; *(natural)* channel; **C. de la Mancha** English Channel (**b**) *TV, Elec & Inform* channel

canalizar [40] VT to channel

canalla 1 NM swine, rotter
2 NF riffraff, mob

canallesco, -a ADJ rotten, despicable

canalón NM *(de tejado)* gutter; *(en la pared)* drainpipe

canapé NM (**a**) *Culin* canapé (**b**) *(sofá)* couch, sofa

Canarias NFPL **las C.** the Canary Islands, the Canaries

canario, -a 1 ADJ & NM,F Canarian; **Islas Canarias** Canary Islands, Canaries
2 NM *(ave)* canary

canasta NF basket

canastilla NF small basket; *(de un bebé)* layette

canasto NM big basket, hamper

cancán NM frilly petticoat; *RP* **cancanes** *(leotardos)* *Br* tights, *US* pantyhose *(plural)*

cancela NF wrought-iron gate

cancelación NF cancellation

cancelar VT (**a**) *(acto etc)* to cancel (**b**) *(deuda)* to pay off (**c**) *Chile, Ven (compra)* to pay for

Cáncer NM Cancer

cáncer NM cancer; **c. de pulmón/mama** lung/ breast cancer

cancerbero, -a NM,F *Ftb* goalkeeper

cancerígeno, -a ADJ carcinogenic

canceroso, -a ADJ *(úlcera, tejido)* cancerous; *(enfermo)* suffering from cancer

cancha NF (**a**) *(de tenis, baloncesto, squash)* court; *Am (de fútbol)* field, *Br* pitch; *Am (de golf)* course; *Chile* **c. de aterrizaje** runway; *Am* **c. de carreras** racetrack (**b**) *Am (descampado)* open space, open ground; *(corral)* fenced yard (**c**) *Andes, PRico Fam (maíz)* toasted *Br* maize *o* *US* corn (**d**) *(expresiones)* **dar c. a algn** to give sb a chance; *RP* **tener c.** to be streetwise *o* savvy

canchero, -a ADJ *RP Fam* streetwise, savvy

canciller NM chancellor

cancillería NF *(de asuntos exteriores)* foreign ministry

canción NF song

cancionero NM songbook

candado NM padlock

candela NF fire

candelabro NM candelabrum

candelero NM candlestick; *Fig* **estar en c.** to be in the limelight

candente ADJ red-hot; *Fig* **tema c.** topical issue

candidato, -a NM,F candidate; *(a un puesto)* applicant

candidatura NF (**a**) *(lista)* list of candidates (**b**) **presentar su c.** to submit one's application

candidez NF candour

cándido, -a ADJ ingenuous, naive

> Observa que la palabra inglesa **candid** es un falso amigo y no es la traducción de la palabra española **cándido**. En inglés, **candid** significa "franco, sincero".

candil NM oil lamp; *Méx (candelabro)* chandelier

candilejas NFPL *Teatro* footlights

candor NM innocence, naivety

> Observa que la palabra inglesa **candour** es un falso amigo y no es la traducción de la palabra española **candor**. En inglés, **candour** significa "sinceridad, franqueza".

candoroso, -a ADJ innocent, pure

canela NF cinnamon

canelones NMPL *Culin* cannelloni

cangrejo NM *(de mar)* crab; *(de río)* freshwater crayfish

canguro 1 NM kangaroo
2 NMF *Esp Fam* baby-sitter

caníbal ADJ & NMF cannibal

canica NF marble

caniche NM poodle

canícula NF dog days, midsummer heat

canijo, -a ADJ *Fam* puny, weak

canilla NF (**a**) *Fam (espinilla)* shinbone (**b**) *RP (grifo)* *Br* tap, *US* faucet (**c**) *Méx (fuerza)* strength

canillera NF *Am (temblor de piernas)* **tenía c.** his legs were trembling *o* shaking

canillita NM *RP* newspaper vendor

canino, -a 1 ADJ canine; *Fam* **tener un hambre canina** to be starving
2 NM *(colmillo)* canine
canje NM exchange
canjeable ADJ exchangeable
canjear VT to exchange
cano, -a ADJ *(blanco)* white; *(gris)* grey
canoa NF canoe
canódromo NM dog *o* greyhound track
canon NM **(a)** *(norma)* canon, norm **(b)** *Mús & Rel* canon **(c)** *Com* royalty
canónico, -a ADJ canonical; *Der* **derecho c.** canon law
canónigo NM canon
canonizar [40] VT to canonize
canoso, -a ADJ *(de pelo blanco)* white-haired; *(de pelo gris)* grey-haired; *(pelo)* white, grey
cansado, -a ADJ **(a)** *(agotado)* tired, weary; **estar c.** to be tired **(b)** **ser c.** *(pesado)* to be boring *o* tiresome
cansador, -a ADJ *Andes, RP (que cansa)* tiring; *(que aburre)* boring
cansancio NM tiredness, weariness; *Fam* **estoy muerto de c.** I'm on my last legs
cansar 1 VT to tire
2 VI to be tiring
3 cansarse VPR to get tired; **se cansó de esperar** he got fed up (with) waiting
Cantabria N Cantabria
cantábrico, -a ADJ Cantabrian; **Mar C.** Bay of Biscay
cántabro, -a ADJ & NM,F Cantabrian
cantaleta NF *Am* **la misma c.** the same old story
cantante 1 NM,F singer
2 ADJ singing; **llevar la voz c.** to rule the roost
cantaor, -a NM,F flamenco singer
cantar¹ VT & VI **(a)** *Mús* to sing; *Fig* **en menos que canta un gallo** in a flash **(b)** *Fam (confesar)* to sing, to spill the beans **(c)** *Esp muy Fam (apestar)* to stink
cantar² NM *Literario* song; *Fam* **¡eso es otro c.!** that's a totally different thing!
cantarín, -ina ADJ *(voz)* singsong
cántaro NM pitcher; *Fig* **llover a cántaros** to rain cats and dogs
cantautor, -a NM,F singer-songwriter
cante NM **(a)** *(canto)* singing; **c. hondo, c. jondo** flamenco **(b)** *Esp Fam* **dar el c.** to attract attention
cantegril NM *Urug* shanty town
cantera NF **(a)** *(de piedra)* quarry **(b)** *Fig Ftb* young players
cantero NM **(a)** *(masón)* stonemason **(b)** *Cuba, RP (parterre)* flowerbed
cantidad 1 NF quantity; *(de dinero)* amount, sum; **en c.** a lot; *Fam* **c. de gente** thousands of people
2 ADV *Esp Fam* a lot; **me gusta c.** I really like it a lot

cantimplora NF water bottle
cantina NF *(de soldados)* mess; *(en fábrica)* canteen; *(en estación de tren)* buffet
canto¹ NM **(a)** *(arte)* singing **(b)** *(canción)* song
canto² NM *(borde)* edge; **de c.** on its side
canto³ NM *(guijarro)* pebble, stone; **c. rodado** *(grande)* boulder; *(pequeño)* pebble
cantor, -a 1 ADJ singing; **pájaro c.** songbird
2 NM,F singer
canturrear VI to hum, to croon
canutas NFPL *Esp Fam* **pasarlas c.** to have a hard time
canuto NM **(a)** *(tubo)* tube **(b)** *Fam (porro)* joint
caña NF **(a)** *Esp (de cerveza)* = small glass of beer **(b)** *Bot* reed; *(tallo)* cane, stem; **c. de azúcar** sugar cane **(c)** *(de pescar)* rod **(d)** *Fam* **darle c. al coche** to go at full speed **(e)** *Andes, Cuba, RP (aguardiente)* caña, = type of rum made using sugar cane spirit
cañada NF gully, ravine
cáñamo NM hemp
cañaveral NM reedbed
cañería NF (piece of) piping; **cañerías** plumbing
cañero, -a NM,F *Am (trabajador)* sugar plantation worker; *(propietario)* sugar plantation owner
cañí ADJ & NMF *Fam* gypsy
caño NM *(tubo)* tube; *(tubería)* pipe
cañón NM **(a)** *(arma)* gun; *Hist* cannon; *Fig* **estar siempre al pie del c.** to be always hard at work **(b)** *(de fusil)* barrel; *(de chimenea)* flue **(c)** *Geog* canyon
cañonazo NM gunshot
caoba NF mahogany
caos NM INV chaos
caótico, -a ADJ chaotic
cap. *(abr capítulo)* ch
capa NF **(a)** *(prenda)* cloak, cape; **de c. caída** low-spirited **(b)** *(de pintura)* layer, coat; *Culin* coating **(c)** *Geol* stratum, layer; **c. de ozono** ozone layer
capacidad NF **(a)** *(cabida)* capacity **(b)** *(aptitud)* capacity, ability .
capacitación NF training
capacitar VT *(habilitar)* to entitle; *(formar)* to train
capar VT to castrate
caparazón NM shell
capataz, -a NM,F *(hombre)* foreman; *(mujer)* forewoman
capaz 1 ADJ capable, able; **ser c. de hacer algo** *(tener la habilidad de)* to be able to do sth; *(atreverse a)* to dare to do sth; **si se entera es c. de despedirle** if he finds out he could quite easily sack him
2 ADV *Andes, RP Fam (tal vez)* maybe
capazo NM large wicker basket

capcioso, -a ADJ **pregunta capciosa** trick question

capea NF amateur bullfight

capear VT *(dificultad etc)* to dodge, to shirk; *Fig* **c. el temporal** to weather the storm

capellán NM chaplain

caperuza NF *(gorro)* hood; *(capuchón)* top, cap

capicúa ADJ **número c.** reversible number; **palabra c.** palindrome

capilar ADJ hair; **loción c.** hair lotion·

capilla NF chapel; **c. ardiente** chapel of rest

capirote NM *Fam* **tonto de c.** silly idiot

capital 1 NF capital
 2 NM *Fin* capital; **c. activo** *o* **social** working *o* share capital
 3 ADJ capital, main; **de importancia c.** of capital importance; **pena c.** capital punishment

capitalismo NM capitalism·

capitalista ADJ & NMF capitalist

capitalizar [40] VT to capitalize

capitán, -ana NM captain; **c. general** *Br* field marshal, *US* general of the army

capitanear VT *(a) Mil & Náut* to captain, to command *(b) (dirigir)* to lead; *Dep* to captain

capitanía NF *Mil (a) (empleo)* captaincy *(b) (oficina)* military headquarters; **c. general** Captaincy General

capitel NM *Arquit* capital

capitulación NF *Mil* capitulation; **capitulaciones matrimoniales** marriage settlement

capitular VI to capitulate, to surrender

capítulo NM *(a) (de libro)* chapter *(b) Fig* **dentro del c. de ...** *(tema)* under the heading of ...

capó NM *Aut Br* bonnet, *US* hood

capón NM rap on the head with the knuckles

capota NF *Aut Br* convertible roof, *US* convertible top

capote NM *(a) Taurom* cape *(b) Mil* greatcoat

capricho NM *(a) (antojo)* whim, caprice *(b) Mús* caprice, capriccio

caprichoso, -a ADJ whimsical

Capricornio NM Capricorn

cápsula NF capsule

captar VT *(a) (ondas)* to receive, to pick up *(b) (comprender)* to understand, to grasp *(c) (interés etc)* to attract

captura NF capture

capturar VT *(criminal)* to capture; *(cazar, pescar)* to catch; *Mil* to seize

capucha NF hood

capuchino NM *(café)* cappuccino

capullo 1 NM *(a) (de insecto)* cocoon *(b) (de flor)* bud *(c) Esp Vulg (glande)* head
 2 NM,F *Esp muy Fam (persona despreciable)* jerk, *Br* dickhead

caqui 1 ADJ *(color)* khaki
 2 NM *(fruto)* kaki

cara 1 NF *(a) (rostro)* face; **c. a c.** face to face; **c. a la pared** facing the wall; **poner mala c.** to pull a long face; **tener buena/mala c.** to look good/bad; *Fig* **c. de circunstancias** serious look; *Fig* **dar la c.** to face the consequences (of one's acts); *Fig* **dar la c. por algn** to stand up for sb; *Fig* **(de) c. a** with a view to; *Fig* **echarle a algn algo en c.** to reproach sb for sth; *Fig* **plantar c. a algn** to face up to sb *(b) (lado) (de moneda)* right side; **¿c. o cruz?** heads or tails?; **echar algo a c. o cruz** to toss (a coin) for sth, *US* to flip (a coin) for sth *(c) Fam (desfachatez)* cheek, nerve; **¡qué c. (más dura) tienes!** you've got a cheek!
 2 NMF *Fam (desvergonzado)* cheeky person

carabela NF caravel

carabina NF *(a) (arma)* carbine, rifle *(b) (persona)* chaperone

carabinero NM *(a) (marisco)* scarlet shrimp, = type of large red prawn *(b) Chile (policía)* military policeman

caracense 1 ADJ of/from Guadalajara
 2 NMF person from Guadalajara

caracol 1 NM *(a) (de tierra)* snail; *Am* shell *(b) (rizo)* kiss-curl
 2 INTERJ **¡caracoles!** good heavens!

caracola NF conch

caracolada NF *Culin* = stew made with snails

carácter *(pl* **caracteres)** NM *(a) (temperamento)* character; **de mucho c.** with a strong character; **tener buen/mal c.** to be good-natured/bad-tempered *(b) Fig (índole)* nature; **con c. de invitado** as a guest *(c) Impr* character

característica NF characteristic

característico, -a ADJ characteristic

caracterizar [40] VT to characterize

caradura NMF *Fam* cheeky devil; **¡qué c. eres!** you're so cheeky!

carajillo NM *Fam* = coffee with a dash of brandy

carajo INTERJ *Vulg* shit!; **¡vete al c.!** go to hell!

caramba INTERJ *Fam (sorpresa)* good heavens!, *Br* blimey!, *US* jeez!; *(enfado)* for heaven's sake!

carámbano NM icicle

carambola NF *Br* cannon, *US* carom

caramelo NM *(a) (dulce) Br* (boiled) sweet, *US* candy *(b) (azúcar quemado)* caramel; *Culin* **a punto de c.** syrupy

carantoña NF caress

caraota NF *Ven* bean

caraqueño, -a 1 ADJ of/from Caracas
 2 NM,F person from Caracas

carátula NF *(a) (cubierta)* cover *(b) (máscara)* mask

caravana NF *(a) (vehículo) Br* caravan, *US* trailer *(b) (de tráfico) Br* tailback, *US* backup *(c) Urug (aro, pendiente)* earring

caray INTERJ *(sorpresa)* good heavens!, *Br* blimey!, *US* jeez!; *(enfado)* for heaven's sake!

carbón NM coal; **c. vegetal** charcoal; **c. mineral** coal

carboncillo NM charcoal

carbonero NM coal merchant

carbónico, -a ADJ carbonic; **agua carbónica** mineral water

carbonilla NF coal dust

carbonizar [40] **1** VT to carbonize, to char; **morir carbonizado** to be burnt to death
2 carbonizarse VPR to carbonize, to char

carbono NM carbon

carburador NM carburettor

carburante NM fuel

carburar VI *Fam* to work properly

carca *Fam* **1** ADJ old fashioned; *Pol* reactionary
2 NMF old fogey; *Pol* reactionary

carcaj NM quiver

carcajada NF guffaw

carcamal, *Méx, RP* **carcamán** NM *Fam* old fogey

cárcel NF prison, jail

carcelario, -a ADJ prison, jail

carcelero, -a NM,F jailer, warder

carcoma NF woodworm

carcomer **1** VT to eat away
2 carcomerse VPR to be consumed (**de** with)

cardar VT *(lana)* to card; *(pelo)* to backcomb

cardenal NM (**a**) *Rel* cardinal (**b**) *Med* bruise

cárdeno, -a ADJ purple

cardiaco, -a, cardíaco, -a **1** ADJ cardiac, heart; **ataque c.** heart attack
2 NM,F person with a heart condition

cardinal ADJ cardinal; **punto/número c.** cardinal point/number

cardiólogo, -a NM,F cardiologist

cardo NM *(con espinas)* thistle

carear VT *Der* to bring face to face

carecer [33] VI **c. de** to lack

carencia NF lack (**de** of)

carente ADJ lacking; **c. de interés** lacking interest

careo NM *Der* confrontation

carestía NF **la c. de la vida** the high cost of living

careta NF mask; **c. antigás** gas mask

carey *(pl* **careys)** NM tortoiseshell

carezco INDIC PRES *de* **carecer**

carga NF (**a**) *(acción)* loading (**b**) *(cosa cargada)* load; *(de avión, barco)* cargo, freight; *Fig* **c. afectiva** emotional content (**c**) *Fin (gasto)* debit; **c. fiscal** tax charge (**d**) *Fig (obligación)* burden (**e**) *Mil & Elec* charge

cargado, -a ADJ (**a**) *(con peso)* loaded (**b**) *(bebida)* strong; **un café c.** a strong coffee (**c**) *(ambiente)* heavy; **atmósfera cargada** stuffy atmosphere (**d**) *Fig* burdened; **c. de deudas** up to one's eyes in debt (**e**) *Elec* charged

cargador NM (**a**) *(de arma)* chamber (**b**) *(persona)* loader; **c. de muelle** docker, stevedore (**c**) *(de baterías)* charger

cargamento NM (**a**) *(carga)* load (**b**) *(mercancías)* cargo, freight

cargante ADJ *Fam* annoying

cargar [42] **1** VT (**a**) *(con peso)* to load; *(mechero, pluma)* to fill; *(batería)* to charge; *Fig* **c. las culpas a algn** to put the blame on (**b**) *Com* to charge; **cárguelo a mi cuenta** charge it to my account; *Fam Educ* **me han cargado las matemáticas** I failed maths
2 VI (**a**) **c. con** *(llevar)* to carry; *Fig* **c. con la responsabilidad** to take the responsibility; *Fig* **c. con las consecuencias** to suffer the consequences (**b**) *Mil* **c. contra** to charge
3 cargarse VPR (**a**) *Esp Fam* **te la vas a cargar** you're asking for trouble and you're going to get it (**b**) *Fam (estropear)* to smash, to ruin (**c**) *Fam (matar)* to kill, to bump off

cargo NM (**a**) *(puesto)* post, position; **alto c.** *(puesto)* top job, high ranking position; *(persona)* top person (**b**) **estar al c. de** to be in charge of; **correr a c. de** *(gastos)* to be met by; **hacerse c. de** to take charge of; **hazte c. de mi situación** please try to understand my situation; **c. de conciencia** weight on one's conscience (**c**) *Fin* charge, debit; **con c. a mi cuenta** charged to my account (**d**) *Der* charge, accusation

cargosear VT *CSur* to annoy, to pester

cargoso, -a ADJ *CSur* annoying

carguero NM *(avión)* transport plane; *(barco)* freighter

cariado, -a ADJ decayed

cariarse VPR to decay

Caribe **1** ADJ **el mar C.** the Caribbean (Sea)
2 NM **el C.** *(mar)* the Caribbean (Sea); *(región)* the Caribbean

caribeño, -a **1** ADJ Caribbean
2 NM,F person from the Caribbean

caricatura NF caricature

caricaturizar [40] VT to caricature

caricia NF caress, stroke

caridad NF charity

caries NF INV decay, caries

cariño NM (**a**) *(amor)* affection; **coger/tener c. a algo/algn** to grow/to be fond of sth/sb; **con c.** *(en carta)* love (**b**) *(apelativo)* dear, love, *US* honey (**c**) *(abrazo)* cuddle

cariñoso, -a ADJ loving, affectionate

carisma NM charisma

carismático, -a ADJ charismatic

caritativo, -a ADJ charitable

cariz NM look

carmesí *(pl* **carmesíes)** ADJ & NM crimson

carmín NM *(de color)* **c.** carmine; **c. (de labios)** lipstick

carnal ADJ (**a**) *(de carne)* carnal (**b**) *(pariente)* first; **primo c.** first cousin

carnaval NM carnival

carne NF (**a**) *(de persona)* flesh; *Fam* **ser de c. y hueso** to be only human; *Fig* **c. de cañón**

cannon fodder; **c. de gallina** goosepimples; **c. viva** raw flesh (**b**) *(alimento)* meat; **c. de cerdo/cordero/ternera/vaca** pork/lamb/veal/beef (**c**) *(de fruta)* pulp

carné NM = **carnet**

carnear VT (**a**) *Andes, RP (sacrificar)* to slaughter, to butcher (**b**) *Chile (engañar)* to deceive, to take in

carnero NM ram; *Culin* mutton

carnet (*pl* carnets) NM card; **c. de conducir** *Br* driving licence, *US* driver's license; **c. de identidad** identity card

carnicería NF (**a**) *(tienda)* butcher's (shop) (**b**) *Fig (masacre)* slaughter

carnicero, -a NM,F butcher

cárnico, -a ADJ **productos cárnicos** meat products

carnitas NFPL *Méx* = small pieces of braised pork

carnívoro, -a 1 ADJ carnivorous
2 NM,F carnivore

carnoso, -a ADJ fleshy

caro, -a 1 ADJ expensive, dear
2 ADV **salir c.** to cost a lot; **te costará c.** *(amenaza)* you'll pay dearly for this

carozo NM *RP (de fruta, aceituna)* stone, *US* pit

carpa NF (**a**) *(pez)* carp (**b**) *(de circo)* big top; *(en parque, la calle)* marquee (**c**) *Am (de tienda de campaña)* tent

Cárpatos NMPL Carpathians

carpeta NF file, folder

> Observa que la palabra inglesa **carpet** es un falso amigo y no es la traducción de la palabra española **carpeta**. En inglés **carpet** significa "alfombra".

carpetazo NM **dar c. a un asunto** to shelve a matter

carpintería NF (**a**) *(oficio)* carpentry; **c. metálica** metalwork (**b**) *(taller)* carpenter's (shop)

carpintero, -a NM,F carpenter

carraca NF rattle

carraspear VI to clear one's throat

carraspeo NM clearing of the throat

carraspera NF **tener c.** to have a frog in one's throat

carrera NF (**a**) *(acción de correr)* run; **a la c.** in a hurry (**b**) *(competición)* race; **c. contra reloj** race against the clock; **c. de coches** rally, meeting; **echar una c. a algn** to race sb; **c. de armamentos** arms race (**c**) *(estudios)* university course; **hacer la c. de derecho/físicas** to study law/physics (at university) (**d**) *(profesión)* career, profession (**e**) *(en medias)* Br ladder, *US* run

carrerilla NF **tomar** *o* **Esp coger c.** to take a run; **decir algo de c.** to reel sth off

carreta NF cart

carrete NM *(de hilo)* reel; *(de película)* spool; *(de cable)* coil

carretera NF road; **c. de acceso** access road; *(en autopista)* slip road; **c. de circunvalación** *Br* ring road, *US* beltway; **c. comarcal** minor road; *Méx* **c. de cuota** toll road; **c. nacional** *Br* ≃ A road, *US* ≃ state highway

carretero, -a ADJ *Am* road; **un accidente c.** a road accident

carretilla NF wheelbarrow

carril NM (**a**) *Ferroc* rail (**b**) *Aut* lane

carrillo NM cheek; *Fam* **comer a dos carrillos** to devour, to gobble up

carriola NF *Méx (de bebé)* Br pram, *US* baby carriage

carrito NM trolley, *US* cart

carro NM (**a**) *(carreta)* cart; *Fam* **¡para el c.!** hang on a minute! (**b**) *Mil* **c. de combate** tank (**c**) *(de máquina de escribir)* carriage (**d**) *Am salvo RP (automóvil)* car (**e**) *Méx (vagón)* car; **c. comedor** dining car

carrocería NF *Aut* bodywork

carromato NM *(carro)* wagon

carroña NF carrion

carroza 1 NF (**a**) *(coche de caballos)* coach, carriage (**b**) *(de carnaval)* float
2 NMF *Fam* old fogey

carruaje NM carriage, coach

carrusel NM *(tiovivo)* merry-go-round, *US* carousel

carta NF (**a**) *(escrito)* letter; **c. certificada** *Br* recorded *o US* certified letter; **c. urgente** express letter (**b**) *(menú)* menu; **a la c.** à la carte; **c. de vinos** wine list (**c**) *Naipes* card; **echar las cartas a algn** to tell sb's fortune; *Fig* **poner las cartas sobre la mesa** to put *o* lay one's cards on the table, to come clean (**d**) *Geog (mapa)* chart (**e**) *(expresiones)* **adquirir c. de naturaleza** to become more widely accepted; **tomar cartas en un asunto** to intervene in an affair

cartabón NM set square

cartearse VPR to correspond (**con** with), to exchange letters (**con** with)

cartel NM poster; **pegar/fijar carteles** to put *o* stick up bills

cártel NM *Com* cartel

cartelera NF billboard, *Br* hoarding; *Prensa* **c. de espectáculos** entertainments section *o* page

cartera NF (**a**) *(de bolsillo)* wallet, *US* billfold (**b**) *(para documentos)* briefcase; *(de colegial)* satchel, schoolbag (**c**) *Pol (ministerio)* portfolio (**d**) *Com* portfolio; **c. de pedidos** order book (**e**) *Andes, RP (bolso)* Br handbag, *US* purse

carterista NM pickpocket

cartero, -a NM,F *(hombre)* Br postman, *US* mailman; *(mujer)* Br postwoman, *US* mailwoman

cartilla NF (a) *(libreta)* book; **c. de ahorros** savings book (b) *(libro)* first reader; *Fam* **leerle la c. a algn** to tell sb off

cartografía NF cartography

cartón NM (a) *(material)* card, cardboard; **c. piedra** papier mâché (b) *(de cigarrillos)* carton

cartucho NM (a) *(de balas)* cartridge (b) *(de papel)* cone

cartulina NF card

casa NF (a) *(edificio)* house; **c. de huéspedes** *Br* guesthouse, *US* rooming house; **c. de socorro** first-aid post (b) *(hogar)* home; **vete a c.** go home; **en c. de Daniel** at Daniel's; **de andar por c.** everyday (c) *(empresa)* company, firm; **c. matriz/principal** head/central office

casación NF *Der* annulment

casadero, -a ADJ of marrying age

casado, -a 1 ADJ married
2 NM,F married person; **los recién casados** the newlyweds

casamiento NM marriage; *(boda)* wedding

casar¹ 1 VT to marry
2 VI to match, to go o fit together
3 **casarse** VPR to marry, to get married; **casarse por la iglesia/por lo civil** to get married in church/in a registry office

casar² VT *Der* to annul, to quash

cascabel NM bell

cascada NF waterfall, cascade

cascado, -a ADJ (a) *Esp Fam (estropeado)* bust, *Br* clapped-out; *(persona, ropa)* worn-out (b) *(ronco)* rasping

cascanueces NM INV nutcracker

cascar [44] 1 VT (a) *(romper)* to crack (b) *Fam* **cascarla** to kick the bucket, to snuff it
2 VI *Esp Fam (hablar)* to witter on
3 **cascarse** VPR to crack

cáscara NF shell; *(de fruta)* skin, peel; *(de grano)* husk

cascarón NM eggshell

cascarrabias NMF INV *Fam* grouch, misery guts

casco NM (a) *(para la cabeza)* helmet (b) *(de caballo)* hoof (c) *Esp, Méx (envase)* empty bottle (d) **c. urbano** city centre (e) *(de barco)* hull (f) **cascos** *(auriculares)* headphones

cascote NM piece of rubble o debris

caserío NM country house

casero, -a 1 ADJ (a) *(hecho en casa)* home-made (b) *(persona)* home-loving
2 NM,F *(dueño)* *(hombre)* landlord; *(mujer)* landlady

caseta NF hut, booth; *(de feria, exposición)* stand, stall; *Méx* **c. de cobro** tollbooth; *Méx* **c. telefónica** *Br* phone box, *US* phone booth

casete 1 NM *(magnetófono)* cassette player o recorder
2 NF *(cinta)* cassette (tape)

casi ADV almost, nearly; **c. mil personas** almost one thousand people; **c. ni me acuerdo** I can hardly remember it; **c. nunca** hardly ever; **c. nadie** hardly anyone; **c. me caigo** I almost fell

casilla NF (a) *(de caja, armario)* compartment; *(para cartas)* pigeonhole; *Andes, RP* **c. de correos** PO Box; *CAm, Carib, Méx* **c. postal** PO Box (b) *(recuadro)* box (c) *Fig* **sacar a algn de sus casillas** to drive sb mad

casillero NM (set of) pigeonholes

casino NM casino

caso NM case; **el c. es que …** the fact o thing is that …; **el c. Mattei** the Mattei affair; **(en) c. contrario** otherwise; **en c. de necesidad** if need be; **en cualquier c.** in any case; **en el mejor/peor de los casos** at best/worst; **en ese c.** in that case; **en todo c.** in any case; **en un c. extremo, en último c.** as a last resort; **hacer c. a o de algn** to pay attention to sb; **hacer c. omiso de** to take no notice of; **no venir al c.** to be beside the point; **pongamos por c.** let's say

caspa NF dandruff

casposo, -a ADJ *Esp Fam (música, película)* cheesy; **los famosos casposos** C-list celebs

casquete NM (a) *(de bala)* case, shell (b) *Geog* **c. polar** polar icecap

> Observa que la palabra inglesa **casket** es un falso amigo y no es la traducción de la palabra española **casquete**. En inglés, **casket** significa "cofre, ataúd".

casquillo NM *(de bala)* case

cassette NM & NF = **casete**

casta NF (a) *(linaje)* lineage, descent (b) *(animales)* breed; **de c.** thoroughbred, pure-bred (c) *(división social)* caste

castaña NF chestnut; *Fig* **sacarle a algn las castañas del fuego** to save sb's bacon

castañetear VI *(dientes)* to chatter

castaño, -a 1 ADJ chestnut-brown; *(pelo, ojos)* brown, dark
2 NM *Bot* chestnut

castañuela NF castanet

castellano, -a 1 ADJ Castilian
2 NM,F *(persona)* Castilian
3 NM *(idioma)* Spanish, Castilian

castidad NF chastity

castigar [42] VT (a) *(imponer castigo)* to punish; *Dep* to penalize (b) *(dañar)* *(piel, salud)* to damage; *(por sol, viento, epidemia)* to devastate

castigo NM punishment; *Dep* **área de c.** penalty area

Castilla N Castile

castillo NM castle

castizo, -a ADJ pure, authentic

casto, -a ADJ chaste

castor NM beaver

castrar VT to castrate

castrense ADJ military

casual 1 ADJ accidental, chance
2 NM *Fam* chance
casualidad NF chance, coincidence; **de** *o* **por c.** by chance; **dio la c. que ...** it so happened that ...; **¿tienes un lápiz, por c.?** do you happen to have a pencil?; **¡que c.!** what a coincidence!

Observa que la palabra inglesa **casualty** es un falso amigo y no es la traducción de la palabra española **casualidad**. En inglés, **casualty** significa "víctima".

casualmente ADV by chance
cata NF tasting
cataclismo NM cataclysm
catacumbas NFPL catacombs
catador, -a NM,F taster
catalán, -ana 1 ADJ & NM,F Catalan
2 NM *(idioma)* Catalan
catalejo NM telescope
catalizador NM *Quím & Fig* catalyst; *Aut* catalytic converter
catalizar [40] VT to act as a catalyst for
catalogar [42] VT to catalogue; **c. a algn (de)** to class sb (as)
catálogo NM catalogue
Cataluña N Catalonia
catamarán NM catamaran
cataplasma NF **(a)** *Med* poultice **(b)** *Fam (pelmazo)* bore
catapulta NF catapult
catapultar VT to catapult
catar VT to taste
catarata NF **(a)** *(de agua)* waterfall **(b)** *Med* cataract
catarro NM (common) cold
catastral ADJ **valor c.** = value of a property recorded in the land register, *Br* ≃ rateable value, *US* ≃ assessed value
catastro NM land registry
catástrofe NF catastrophe
catastrófico, -a ADJ catastrophic
catear VT **(a)** *Esp Fam (suspender)* to fail, *US* to flunk **(b)** *Am (casa)* to search
catecismo NM catechism
cátedra NF (professorial) chair; **le han dado la c.** they have appointed him professor
catedral NF cathedral
catedrático, -a NM,F *Educ* **(a)** *Univ* professor **(b)** *(de instituto)* head of department
categoría NF category; *Fig* class; **de c.** *(persona)* important; *(vino etc)* quality
categórico, -a ADJ categorical
catequesis NF INV catechism lesson, ≃ Sunday school
cateto, -a NM,F *Pey* yokel, bumpkin
catire, -a ADJ *Carib (rubio)* blond, *f* blonde
catolicismo NM Catholicism
católico, -a ADJ & NM,F Catholic

catorce ADJ & NM INV fourteen
catre NM *Fam* camp bed, *US* cot
Cáucaso NM **el C.** the Caucasus
cauce NM **(a)** *(de un río)* bed **(b)** *Fig (canal)* channel; **cauces oficiales** official channels
caucho NM **(a)** *(sustancia)* rubber **(b)** *Ven (impermeable)* *Br* mac, *US* slicker **(c)** *Ven (neumático)* tyre
caudal NM **(a)** *(de un río)* flow **(b)** *(riqueza)* wealth, riches
caudaloso, -a ADJ *(río)* with a large flow
caudillo NM leader, head
causa NF **(a)** *(motivo)* cause; **a** *o* **por c. de** because of **(b)** *(ideal)* cause **(c)** *Der (caso)* case; *(juicio)* trial
causante 1 ADJ causal, causing
2 NMF **el c. del incendio** the person who caused the fire
causar VT to cause, to bring about; **me causa un gran placer** it gives me great pleasure; **c. buena/mala impresión** to make a good/bad impression
cáustico, -a ADJ caustic
cautela NF caution
cautivador, -a 1 ADJ captivating, enchanting
2 NM,F charmer
cautivar VT to captivate
cautiverio NM, **cautividad** NF captivity
cautivo, -a ADJ & NM,F captive
cauto, -a ADJ cautious, wary
cava 1 NF *(bodega)* wine cellar
2 NM *(vino espumoso)* cava, champagne
cavar VT to dig
caverna NF cave; **hombre de las cavernas** caveman
cavernícola NMF cave dweller
caviar NM caviar
cavidad NF cavity
cavilar VT to ponder
cayado NM *(de pastor)* crook; *(de obispo)* crosier, crozier
caza 1 NF **(a)** *(acción)* hunting; **ir de c.** to go hunting; **c. furtiva** poaching **(b)** *(animales)* game; **c. mayor/menor** big/small game **(c)** *Fig (persecución)* hunt; **c. de brujas** witch hunt
2 NM *Av* fighter, fighter plane
cazabe NM *Am* cassava bread
cazabombardero NM *Av* fighter bomber
cazador, -a NM,F hunter; **c. furtivo** poacher
cazadora NF (waist-length) jacket
cazar [40] VT to hunt; *Fam* **cazarlas al vuelo** to be quick on the uptake
cazatalentos NMF INV *(de artistas, deportistas)* talent scout; *(de ejecutivos)* headhunter
cazo NM **(a)** *(cacerola)* saucepan **(b)** *(cucharón)* ladle
cazuela NF saucepan; *(guiso)* casserole, stew; **a la c.** stewed

cazurro, -a ADJ (*bruto*) stupid
2 NM,F (*bruto*) idiot, fool

c/c (*abr* **cuenta corriente**) c/a

CC. OO. N (*abr* **Comisiones Obreras**) = Spanish left-wing trade union

CD (*pl* **CDs**) NM (*abr* **compact disc**) CD

CD-ROM ['θeðe'rrom] (*pl* **CD-ROMs**) NM CD-ROM

cebada NF barley

cebar 1 VT (**a**) (*animal*) to fatten; (*persona*) to feed up (**b**) (*anzuelo*) to bait (**c**) (*fuego, caldera*) to stoke, to fuel; (*máquina, arma*) to prime (**d**) *RP* (*mate*) to prepare, to brew
2 **cebarse** VPR **cebarse con** (*ensañarse*) to delight in tormenting

cebo NM bait

cebolla NF onion

cebolleta NF *Br* spring onion, *US* scallion

cebra NF zebra; **paso de c.** *Br* zebra crossing, *US* crosswalk

cecear VI to lisp

ceceo NM lisp

cedazo NM sieve

ceder 1 VT to give, to hand over; *Aut* **c. el paso** to give way
2 VI (**a**) (*cuerda, cable*) to give way (**b**) (*lluvia, calor*) to ease off *o* up (**c**) (*consentir*) to give in

cederrón NM CD-ROM

cedro NM cedar

cédula NF document, certificate; *Am* **c. de identidad** identity card

cegador, -a ADJ blinding

cegar [1] VT (**a**) (*persona*) to blind (**b**) (*puerta, ventana*) to wall up

cegato, -a *Fam* 1 ADJ short-sighted
2 NM,F short-sighted person

ceguera NF blindness

CEI (*abr* **Comunidad de Estados Independientes**) CIS

Ceilán N Ceylon

ceja NF eyebrow

cejar VI **c. en el empeño** to give up

celada NF trap, ambush

celador, -a NM,F (*de colegio*) *Br* caretaker; *US & Scot* janitor; (*de hospital*) porter, orderly; (*de prisión*) *Br* warder, *US* guard; (*de museo*) attendant

celda NF cell; **c. de castigo** punishment cell

celebración NF (**a**) (*festejo*) celebration (**b**) (*de juicio etc*) holding

celebrar 1 VT (**a**) (*fiesta, cumpleaños, victoria*) to celebrate (**b**) (*reunión, juicio, elecciones*) to hold (**c**) (*triunfo*) to laud (**d**) (*alegrarse de*) **celebro que todo saliera bien** I'm glad everything went well
2 **celebrarse** VPR (*llevarse a cabo*) to take place, to be held

célebre ADJ famous, well-known

celebridad NF (**a**) (*fama*) celebrity, fame (**b**) (*persona*) celebrity

celeste 1 ADJ (**a**) (*de cielo*) celestial (**b**) (*color*) sky-blue
2 NM sky blue

celestial ADJ celestial, heavenly

celibato NM celibacy

célibe ADJ & NMF celibate

celo NM (**a**) (*esmero*) zeal (**b**) **en c.** (*macho*) in rut; (*hembra*) *Br* on heat, *US* in heat (**c**) **celos** jealousy; **tener celos (de algn)** to be jealous (of sb)

celo® NM *Fam Br* Sellotape®, *US* Scotch tape®

celofán NM cellophane®

celosía NF lattice

celoso, -a ADJ (**a**) (*envidioso*) jealous (**b**) (*cumplidor*) conscientious

celta 1 ADJ Celtic
2 NMF Celt
3 NM (*idioma*) Celtic

célula NF cell

celular 1 ADJ (**a**) *Biol* cellular (**b**) **coche c.** police van (**c**) *Am* **teléfono c.** mobile phone, cellphone
2 NM *Am* mobile (phone), cellphone

celulitis NF INV cellulitis

celuloide NM celluloid

celulosa NF cellulose

cementerio NM cemetery, graveyard; **c. de coches** scrapyard

cemento NM cement; **c. armado** reinforced concrete

cena NF dinner, evening meal; (*antes de acostarse*) supper; **la Última C.** the Last Supper

cenagal NM marsh, swamp

cenar 1 VI to have supper/dinner
2 VT to have for supper/dinner

cencerro NM cowbell

cenefa NF (*de ropa*) edging, trimming; (*de suelo, techo*) ornamental border, frieze

cenetista 1 ADJ = of or related to the CNT
2 NMF member of the CNT

cenicero NM ashtray

cenit NM zenith

ceniza NF ash

cenizo NM *Fam* **ser un c.** to be jinxed

censar VT to take a census of

censo NM census; *Esp* **c. electoral** electoral roll

censor NM censor

censura NF (**a**) (*de libro, película*) censorship (**b**) *Pol* **moción de c.** vote of no confidence

censurar VT (**a**) (*libro, película*) to censor (**b**) (*criticar*) to censure, to criticize

centavo NM *Am Fin* cent, centavo

centella NF spark

centellear VI to flash, to sparkle

centelleo NM flashing, sparkling

centena NF, **centenar** NM hundred; **a centenares** in hundreds

centenar NM hundred; **un c. de** a hundred; **a centenares** by the hundred

centenario NM centenary, hundredth anniversary

centeno NM rye

centésimo, -a ADJ & NM,F hundredth

centígrado, -a ADJ centigrade

centilitro NM centilitre

centímetro NM centimetre

céntimo NM cent

centinela NM sentry

centollo NM spider crab

centrado, -a ADJ (**a**) (*situado en el centro*) centred (**b**) (*equilibrado*) stable, balanced

central 1 ADJ central
2 NF (**a**) *Elec* **c. nuclear/térmica** nuclear/coal-fired power station (**b**) (*oficina principal*) head office

centralismo NM centralism

centralita NF *Tel* switchboard

centralizar [40] VT to centralize

centrar 1 VT (**a**) (*colocar en el centro*) to centre (**b**) (*esfuerzos, atención*) to concentrate, to centre (**en** on)
2 centrarse VPR **centrarse en** (*concentrarse*) to concentrate on

céntrico, -a ADJ centrally situated; **una zona céntrica** an area in the centre of town, *US* a downtown area

centrifugar [42] VT to centrifuge; (*ropa*) to spin-dry

centrista *Pol* **1** ADJ centre; **partido c.** centre party
2 NM,F centrist

centro NM (**a**) (*punto, área*) centre (**b**) (*establecimiento*) centre; **c. comercial** shopping centre *o US* mall; **c. docente** educational institution (**c**) (*de ciudad*) city/town centre; **me voy al c.** I'm going to town

Centroamérica N Central America

centroamericano, -a ADJ & NM,F Central American

centrocampista NM,F *Ftb* midfielder

centuria NF century

ceñido, -a ADJ tight-fitting, clinging

ceñirse [6] VPR (**a**) (*atenerse, limitarse*) to limit oneself, to stick (**a** to); **c. al tema** to keep to the subject; **ciñéndonos a este caso en concreto** coming down to this particular case (**b**) **c. a** (*prenda*) to cling to

ceño NM scowl, frown; **con el c. fruncido** frowning

CEOE NF (*abr* **Confederación Española de Organizaciones Empresariales**) = Spanish employers' organization, *Br* ≃ CBI

cepa NF (**a**) (*de vid*) vine (**b**) *Fig* **vasco de pura c.** (*origen*) Basque through and through

cepillar 1 VT (**a**) (*con cepillo*) to brush (**b**) (*en carpintería*) to plane (down) (**c**) *Fam* (*robar*) to pinch
2 cepillarse VPR (**a**) (*con cepillo*) to brush (**b**) *Fam* (*matar*) to do in (**c**) *muy Fam* to lay

cepillo NM brush; (*en carpintería*) plane; **c. de dientes** toothbrush; **c. del pelo** hairbrush

cepo NM (**a**) (*para cazar*) trap (**b**) *Aut* clamp

CEPYME NF (*abr* **Confederación Española de la Pequeña y Mediana Empresa**) = Spanish confederation of small and medium-sized businesses

cera NF wax; (*de abeja*) beeswax

cerámica NF ceramics *sing*

ceramista NM,F potter

cerca¹ ADV (**a**) near, close; **ven más c.** come closer; **ya estamos c.** we are almost there (**b**) **c. de** (*al lado de*) near, close to; **el colegio está c. de mi casa** the school is near my house (**c**) **c. de** (*casi*) nearly, around; **c. de cien personas** about one hundred people (**d**) **de c.** closely; **lo vi muy de c.** I saw it close up

cerca² NF fence, wall

cercado NM (**a**) (*lugar cerrado*) enclosure (**b**) (*valla*) fence, wall

cercanía NF (**a**) (*cualidad*) proximity, nearness (**b**) **cercanías** (*lugar*) surrounding area; **tren de cercanías** local train

cercano, -a ADJ nearby; **el C. Oriente** the Near East

cercar [44] VT (**a**) (*tapiar*) to fence, to enclose (**b**) (*rodear*) to surround

cercenar VT to cut off, to amputate

cerciorarse VPR to make sure (**de** of)

cerco NM (**a**) (*marca*) circle, ring (**b**) *Mil* (*sitio*) siege; **poner c. a (una ciudad)** to besiege (a town)

cerda NF (**a**) *Zool* sow (**b**) (*pelo*) bristle; **cepillo de c.** bristle brush

Cerdeña N Sardinia

cerdo NM (**a**) (*animal*) pig (**b**) (*carne*) pork (**c**) *Fam* pig, *Br* arsehole, *US* asshole

cereal NM cereal

cerebral ADJ *Anat & Fig* cerebral

cerebro NM brain; *Fig* (*inteligencia*) brains

ceremonia NF ceremony

ceremonioso, -a ADJ ceremonious, formal; *Pey* pompous, stiff

cereza NF cherry

cerezo NM cherry tree

cerilla NF *Esp* match

cerillo NM *CAm, Ecuad, Méx* match

cernerse [3] VPR *Fig* to loom (**sobre** over)

cernícalo NM kestrel

cernirse [54] VPR = **cernerse**

cero NM zero; *Dep Br* nil, *US* zero; *Fig* **partir de c.** to start from scratch; *Fig* **ser un c. a la izquierda** to be useless *o* a good-for-nothing

cerquillo NM *Am Br* fringe, *US* bangs

cerrado, -a ADJ (**a**) closed, shut; **a puerta cerrada** behind closed doors (**b**) *(reservado)* reserved; *(intransigente)* uncompromising, unyielding; *Fam (torpe)* thick; *(acento)* broad; *(curva)* tight, sharp (**c**) *(barba)* bushy

cerradura NF lock

cerrajería NF (**a**) *(oficio)* locksmithery (**b**) *(local)* locksmith's (shop)

cerrajero, -a NM,F locksmith

cerrar [1] **1** VT to shut, to close; *(grifo, gas)* to turn off; *(luz)* to turn off, to switch off; *(cremallera)* to do up; *(negocio)* to close down; *(cuenta)* to close; *(carta)* to seal; *(puños)* to clench; **c. con llave** to lock; **c. el paso a algn** to block sb's way; *Fam* **c. el pico** to shut one's trap
  2 VI to close, to shut
  3 cerrarse VPR to close, to shut; *Fam* **cerrarse en banda** to stick to one's guns

cerro NM hill; *Esp Fig* **irse por los cerros de Ubeda** to go off at a tangent, to stray from the point

cerrojo NM bolt; **echar el c. de (una puerta)** to bolt (a door)

certamen NM competition, contest

certero, -a ADJ accurate

certeza NF certainty; **saber (algo) con c.** to be certain (of sth); **tener la c. de que ...** to be sure *o* certain that ...

certidumbre NF certainty

certificado, -a 1 ADJ *(documento)* certified; *(carta, paquete) Br* recorded, *US* certified
  2 NM certificate

certificar [44] VT *(constatar)* to certify

cervatillo NM fawn

cervecería NF (**a**) *(bar)* pub, bar (**b**) *(fábrica)* brewery

cerveza NF beer; **c. de barril** draught beer; **c. dorada** *o* **ligera** lager; **c. negra** stout

cervical 1 ADJ cervical
  2 cervicales NFPL neck vertebrae

cesante ADJ *(destituido)* dismissed, *Br* sacked; *CSur, Méx (parado)* unemployed

cesantear VT *Am* to make redundant

cesar 1 VI **c. (de)** to stop, to cease; **sin c.** incessantly
  2 VT *(empleado)* to dismiss, *Br* to sack

cesárea NF Caesarean (section)

cese NM (**a**) *(detención, paro)* stopping, ceasing cessation, suspension (**b**) *(despido)* dismissal

cesión NF cession, transfer; *Der* **c. de bienes** surrender of property

césped NM lawn, grass

cesta NF basket; **c. de Navidad** Christmas hamper

cesto NM basket

cetáceo NM cetacean, whale

cetrino, -a ADJ sallow

cetro NM sceptre

Ceuta N Ceuta

ceutí 1 ADJ of/from Ceuta
  2 NMF person from Ceuta

ceviche NM = raw fish marinated in lemon and garlic

chabacano, -a 1 ADJ cheap
  2 NM *Méx (fruto)* apricot; *(árbol)* apricot tree

chabola NF *Esp* shack; **barrio de chabolas** shanty town

chacal NM jackal

chacarero, -a NM,F *Andes, RP* farmer

chacha NF maid

cháchara NF *Fam* small talk, chinwag; **estar de c.** to have a yap

chachi ADJ *Esp Fam* cool, neat

chacinería NF pork butcher's (shop)

chacolí NM = light wine from the Basque Country

chacra NF *Andes, RP* farm

chafar VT (**a**) *Fam (plan etc)* to ruin, to spoil (**b**) *(aplastar)* to squash, to flatten

chal NM shawl

chalado, -a ADJ *Fam* crazy, nuts (**por** about)

chalé NM villa

chaleco NM *Br* waistcoat, *US* vest; *(de punto)* sleeveless pullover; **c. antibalas** bullet-proof vest; **c. salvavidas** life jacket

chalet *(pl* **chalets)** NM villa

chalupa NF (**a**) *(embarcación)* boat, launch (**b**) *Méx (torta)* = small tortilla with a raised rim to contain a filling

chamaco, -a NM,F *Méx Fam* (**a**) *(muchacho)* kid (**b**) *(novio)* boyfriend; *(novia)* girlfriend

chamarra NF sheepskin jacket

chamba NF *CAm, Méx, Perú, Ven Fam (trabajo)* job;

chambelán NM chamberlain

chambergo NM heavy coat

chambón, -ona NM,F *Am Fam* sloppy *o* shoddy worker

chamizo NM thatched hut

champa NF *CAm (tienda de campaña)* tent

champán NM, **champaña** NM *o* NF champagne

champiñón NM mushroom

champú *(pl* **champús** *o* **champúes)** NM shampoo

chamuscado, -a ADJ *(pelo, plumas)* singed; *(tela, papel)* scorched; *(tostada)* burnt

chamuscar [44] VT to singe, to scorch

chamusquina NF singeing, scorching; *Fam* **esto me huele a c.** there's something fishy going on here

chance 1 NM *o* NF *Am* opportunity, chance
  2 ADV *Méx* maybe

chanchada NF *Am* (**a**) *(porquería)* **¡no hagas chanchadas!** stop that, don't be digusting! (**b**) *Fam (jugarreta)* dirty trick

chancho, -a NM,F *Am* pig, *f* sow

chanchullo NM *Fam* fiddle, wangle

chancla, chancleta NF *Br* flip-flop, *US & Austr* thong

chanclo NM *(zueco)* clog; *(de goma)* overshoe, galosh

chándal (*pl* **chandals**) NM *Esp* tracksuit

changa NF *Bol, RP (trabajo temporal)* odd job

changador NM *RP (cargador)* porter

changarro NM *Méx (tienda)* small shop; *(puesto)* stand

chantaje NM blackmail; **hacer c. a algn** to blackmail sb

chantajear VT to blackmail

chantajista NMF blackmailer

chanza NF joke

chapa NF (**a**) *(de metal)* sheet; *(de madera)* panel-board (**b**) *(tapón)* bottle top, cap (**c**) *(de adorno)* badge (**d**) *RP (de matrícula) Br* numberplate, *US* license plate (**e**) *Col, Cuba, Méx (cerradura)* lock

chapado, -a ADJ *(metal)* plated; **c. en oro** gold-plated; *Fig* **c. a la antigua** old-fashioned

chapapote NM oil sludge

chapar 1 VT *(recubrir) (con metal)* to plate; *(con madera)* to veneer
2 VI *Esp muy Fam (cerrar)* to shut, to close

chaparro, -a 1 ADJ short and squat
2 NM *Bot* holm oak

chaparrón NM downpour, heavy shower

chapopote NM *Carib, Méx* bitumen, pitch

chapotear VI to splash about, to paddle

chapucería NF botch (job)

chapucero, -a ADJ *(trabajo)* slapdash, shoddy; *(persona)* bungling

chapulín NM *CAm, Méx (saltamontes)* grasshopper

chapurrear VT to speak badly o with difficulty; **sólo chapurreaba el francés** he spoke only a few words of French

chapuza 1 NF (**a**) *(trabajo mal hecho)* shoddy piece of work (**b**) *(trabajo ocasional)* odd job
2 chapuzas NMF INV *Fam (persona)* bungler

chapuzón NM dip; **darse un c.** to have a dip

chaqué NM morning coat

chaqueta NF jacket; *Pol* **cambiar de c.** to change sides

chaquetero, -a NM,F *Esp Fam* turncoat

chaquetilla NF short jacket

chaquetón NM heavy jacket, short coat

charanga NF *Mús* brass band

charca NF pond, pool

charco NM puddle

charcutería NF delicatessen

charla NF *(conversación)* talk, chat; *(conferencia)* informal lecture o address; *Inform* chat

charlar VI to talk, to chat; *Inform* to chat

charlatán, -ana 1 ADJ *(parlanchín)* talkative; *(chismoso)* gossipy
2 NM,F (**a**) *(parlanchín)* chatterbox; *(chismoso)*

gossip; *(bocazas)* bigmouth (**b**) *(embaucador)* trickster, charmer

charol NM (**a**) *(piel)* patent leather; **zapatos de c.** patent leather shoes (**b**) *Andes (bandeja)* tray

charola NF *Bol, CAm, Méx* tray

charque, charqui NM *Andes, RP* jerked o salted beef

charro, -a 1 ADJ (**a**) *Esp (salmantino)* Salamancan (**b**) *(recargado)* gaudy, showy (**c**) *Méx (líder sindical)* = in league with the bosses
2 NM,F (**a**) *Esp (salmantino)* Salamancan (**b**) *Méx (jinete)* horseman

chárter ADJ INV **(vuelo) c.** charter (flight)

chasca NF *Andes (greña)* mop of hair

chascar [44] VT = **chasquear**

chascarrillo NM funny story

chasco NM *Fam* disappointment; **llevarse un c.** to be disappointed

chasis NM INV chassis

chasquear VT *(lengua)* to click; *(dedos)* to snap; *(látigo)* to crack

chasqui NM = Inca messenger or courier

chasquido NM *(de la lengua)* click; *(de los dedos)* snap; *(de látigo, madera)* crack

chat (*pl* **chats**) NM *Inform (charla)* chat; *(sala)* chat room

chatarra NF scrap (metal), scrap iron; *Fam* junk

chatarrero, -a NM,F scrap (metal) dealer

chatear VI *Inform* to chat

chato, -a ADJ (**a**) *(nariz)* snub; *(persona)* snub-nosed (**b**) *(objeto)* flat, flattened (**c**) *PRico, RP Fam (sin ambiciones)* commonplace; **una vida chata** a humdrum existence
2 NM *Esp Fam* = small glass of wine

chau INTERJ *Bol, CSur, Perú Fam* bye!, see you!

chaucha 1 ADJ *RP Fam* dull, boring
2 NF (**a**) *Bol, RP* green bean (**b**) *Andes (patata)* early potato

chauvinista ADJ & NMF chauvinist

chaval, -a NM,F *Fam (chico)* boy, lad; *(chica)* girl

chaveta NF (**a**) *(clavija)* cotter pin (**b**) *Fam (cabeza)* nut, head; **perder la c.** *(volverse loco)* to go off one's rocker (**c**) *Andes (navaja)* penknife

chavo, -a *Fam* **1** NM,F *Méx* (**a**) *(chico)* guy; *(chica)* girl (**b**) *(novio)* boyfriend; *(novia)* girlfriend
2 NM *(dinero)* **no tener un c.** to be broke

che INTERJ *RP Fam* **¿qué hacés, c.?, ¿cómo andás, c.?** hey, how's it going, then?; **c., ¡vení para acá!** hey, over here, you!

checo, -a ADJ Czech

checoslovaco, -a 1 ADJ Czechoslovakian, Czech
2 NM,F *(persona)* Czechoslovakian, Czechoslovak, Czech

Checoslovaquia N Czechoslovakia

chef [tʃef] (*pl* **chefs**) NM chef

chele, -a *CAm* **1** ADJ *(rubio)* blond, *f* blonde; *(de piel blanca)* fair-skinned
2 NMF *(rubio)* blond, *f* blonde; *(de piel blanca)* fair-skinned person

chelín NM *Antes* shilling

chepa NF *Fam* hump

cheque NM *Br* cheque, *US* check; **c. al portador** cheque payable to bearer; **c. de viaje** *o* **(de) viajero** traveller's cheque

chequeo NM *Med* checkup; *Aut* service

chequera NF *Br* chequebook, *US* checkbook

chévere ADJ *Am salvo RP Fam* great, fantastic

chic ADJ INV chic, elegant

chicano, -a ADJ & NM,F chicano

chicha¹ NF (a) *Esp Fam (para comer)* meat (b) *Esp Fam (de persona)* flesh; **tiene pocas chichas** *(está flaco)* he's as thin as a rake (c) *(bebida alcohólica)* = alcoholic drink made from fermented maize (d) *(bebida refrescante)* = thick, sweet drink made from rice, condensed milk and vanilla

chicha² ADJ INV *Náut* **calma c.** dead calm

chícharo NM *CAm, Méx* pea

chicharra NF (a) *(insecto)* cicada (b) *Méx (timbre)* electric buzzer

chiche NM (a) *Andes, RP Fam (juguete)* toy (b) *Andes, RP (adorno)* delicate ornament (c) *CAm, Méx muy Fam (pecho)* tit

chichón NM bump, lump

chichonera NF *(para ciclistas)* hairnet

chicle NM chewing gum

chico, -a **1** NM,F *(muchacho)* boy, lad; *(muchacha)* girl
2 ADJ small, little

chicote NM *Am* whip

chiflado, -a ADJ *Fam* mad, crazy (**por** about)

chiflar VT (a) *(silbar)* to hiss (at), to boo (at) (b) *Fam* **le chiflan las motos** he's really into motorbikes

chiflido NM whistling

chigüín, -ina NM,F *CAm Fam* kid

chiita ADJ & NMF Shiite

chilango, -a *Méx Fam* **1** ADJ of/from Mexico City
2 NM,F person from Mexico City

Chile N Chile

chile NM *CAm, Méx* chilli

chileno, -a ADJ & NM,F Chilean

chillar VI *(persona)* to scream, to shriek; *(ratón)* to squeak; *(frenos)* to screech, to squeal; *(puerta)* to creak, to squeak

chillido NM *(de persona)* scream, shriek; *(de ratón)* squeak; *(de frenos)* screech, squeal; *(de puerta)* creaking, squeaking

chillón, -ona ADJ (a) *(voz)* shrill, high-pitched; *(sonido)* harsh, strident (b) *(color)* loud, gaudy

chilpotle NM *Méx* = smoked or pickled jalapeño chile

chimbo, -a ADJ *Col, Ven Fam* (a) *(de mala calidad)* lousy (b) *(complicado)* screwed-up

chimenea NF (a) *(hogar abierto)* fireplace, hearth (b) *(conducto)* chimney; *(de barco)* funnel, stack

chimichurri NM *RP* = barbecue sauce made from garlic, parsley, oregano and vinegar

chimpancé NM chimpanzee

China N China

china NF (a) *(piedra)* pebble, small stone; *Fam* **tocarle a uno la c.** to get the short straw (b) *Fam (droga)* deal

Observa que la palabra inglesa **china** es un falso amigo y no es la traducción de la palabra española **china**. En inglés, **china** significa "loza, porcelana".

chinampa NF *Méx* = man-made island for growing flowers, fruit and vegetables, in Xochimilco near Mexico City

chinche **1** NF bedbug; *Fam* **caer como chinches** to drop like flies
2 NMF *Fam* nuisance, pest

chincheta NF *Br* drawing pin, *US* thumbtack

chinchín INTERJ cheers!

chinchulín NM , **chinchulines** NMPL *Andes, RP (plato)* = piece of sheep. or cow intestine, plaited and then roasted

chinesco, -a ADJ **sombras chinescas** shadow theatre

chingado, -a ADJ *Esp, Méx muy Fam (estropeado)* bust, *Br* knackered

chingana NF *Andes Fam* = cheap bar or café

chingar [42] **1** VT (a) *Esp, Méx muy Fam (estropear)* to bust, *Br* to knacker (b) *Esp, Méx muy Fam (molestar)* **c. a algn** to piss sb off, to get up sb's nose (c) *Esp, Méx Vulg (copular)* to fuck; *Méx* **¡chinga tu madre!** fuck you!
2 VI *Esp, Méx Vulg (copular)* to screw, to fuck
3 **chingarse** VPR *Méx muy Fam (estropearse)* to pack in, to conk out

chino¹ NM *(piedrecita)* pebble, stone

chino², -a ADJ (a) *(de la China)* Chinese; *Fam* **eso me suena a c.** it's all Greek to me (b) *Am (mestizo)* of mixed ancestry (c) *(rizado)* curly

chip *(pl* **chips)** NM *Inform* chip

chipirón NM.baby squid

Chipre N Cyprus

chipriota ADJ & NMF Cypriot

chiqueo NM *Méx Fam* show of affection; **hacerle chiqueos a algn** to kiss and cuddle sb

chiquilín, -ina NM,F *RP (niño)* small boy; *(niña)* small girl

chiquillo, -a NM,F kid

chiquito, -a ADJ tiny

chirimiri NM *Esp* drizzle, fine misty rain

chirimoya NF custard apple

chiringuito NM *(en playa etc)* refreshment stall; *(en carretera)* roadside snack bar

chiripa NF fluke; *Fam Fig* **de** o **por c.** by a fluke, by chance; **cogió el tren por c.** it was sheer luck that he caught the train

chiripá (*pl* **chiripaes**) NM *CSur* = garment worn by gauchos over trousers

chirla NF small clam

chirona NF *Esp Fam* clink, *Br* nick

chirriar [29] VI (*puerta, madera*) to creak; (*frenos*) to screech, to squeal

chirrido NM (*de puerta, madera*) creak, creaking; (*de frenos*) screech, squeal

chisme NM (**a**) (*habladuría*) piece of gossip (**b**) *Fam* (*trasto*) knick-knack; (*cosa*) thing

chismorrear VI *Fam* to gossip

chismorreo NM *Fam* gossip, gossiping

chismoso, -a 1 ADJ gossipy
2 NM,F gossip

chispa NF (**a**) (*de fuego, electricidad*) spark; *Fam Fig* **echar chispas** to fume. (**b**) *Fam* (*un poco*) bit, tiny amount (**c**) *Fam* (*agudeza*) wit, sparkle; (*viveza*) liveliness

chispear V IMPERS (*lloviznar*) to spit

chiste NM joke; **contar un c.** to tell a joke; **c. verde** blue joke, dirty joke

chistera NF top hat

chistorra NF = type of cured pork sausage typical of Aragon and Navarre

chistoso, -a ADJ (*persona*) funny, witty; (*anécdota*) funny, amusing

chivarse VPR *Esp Fam* (*niños*) to tell, *Br* to split (**de** on); (*delincuentes*) to squeal, *Br* to grass (**de** on)

chivatazo NM *Esp Fam* tip-off; **dar el c.** to squeal, *Br* to grass

chivato, -a 1 NM,F *Esp Fam* (*delator*) *Br* grass, *US* rat; (*acusica*) telltale
2 NM (**a**) (*luz*) warning light (**b**) (*alarma*) alarm bell (**c**) *Ven Fam* (*pez gordo*) big cheese

chivito NM (**a**) *Arg* (*carne*) roast kid (**b**) *Urug* steak sandwich (*containing cheese and salad*)

chivo, -a NM,F *Zool* kid, young goat; *Fig* **c. expiatorio** scapegoat

chocante ADJ (*sorprendente*) surprising, startling; (*raro*) strange

chocar [44] **1** VI (**a**) (*topar*) to crash, to collide; **c. con** o **contra** to run into, to collide with (**b**) (*en discusión*) to clash (**c**) (*extrañar*) **me choca que ...** I'm surprised o puzzled that ...
2 VT (**a**) (*manos*) to shake; (*copas, vasos*) to clink; *Fam* **¡chócala!, ¡choca esos cinco!** shake (on it)!, put it there!

chochear VI (**a**) (*viejo*) to be senile o in one's dotage (**b**) *Fam* **c. con algn** to dote on sb

chocho, -a 1 ADJ (*senil*) senile; **viejo c.** old dodderer
2 NM (**a**) (*altramuz*) lupin (**b**) *Esp, Méx Vulg* (*vulva*) *Br* fanny, *US* beaver

choclo NM *Andes, RP* maize, *US* corn

chocolate NM (**a**) (*para comer*) chocolate; **c. con leche** milk chocolate (**b**) *Esp Fam* (*droga*) dope

chocolatería NF (**a**) (*fábrica*) chocolate factory (**b**) (*establecimiento*) = café where drinking chocolate is served

chocolatina NF bar of chocolate, chocolate bar

chofer (*pl* **choferes**) NM *Am* chauffeur

chófer (*pl* **chóferes**) NM *Esp* chauffeur

chollo NM *Esp Fam* (*ganga*) bargain

chomba NF (**a**) *Arg* polo shirt (**b**) *Chile, Perú* (*suéter*) sweater, pullover, *Br* jumper

chompa NF *Andes* sweater, pullover, *Br* jumper

chompipe NM *CAm, Méx* turkey

chongo NM *Méx* (**a**) (*moño*) bun (**b**) **chongos zamoranos** (*dulce*) = Mexican dessert made from milk curds, served in syrup

chonta NF *CAm, Perú* = type of palm tree

chop (*pl* **chops**) NM *CSur* (**a**) (*jarra*) beer mug (**b**) (*cerveza*) (mug of) beer

chopo NM poplar

chopp *CSur* (*pl* **chopps**) NM = **chop**

choque NM (**a**) (*impacto*) impact; (*de coches etc*) crash, collision; **c. frontal** head-on collision; **c. múltiple** pile-up (**b**) *Fig* (*contienda*) clash

choricear, chorizar VT *Esp Fam* to pinch

chorizo¹ NM (*embutido*) chorizo, = highly-seasoned pork sausage

chorizo² , -a NM,F *Esp Fam* (*ladrón*) thief

chorlito NM (*ave*) plover; *Fam Fig* **cabeza de c.** scatterbrain

choro NM *Andes* mussel

chorra *Esp Fam* **1** NMF (*tonto*) idiot, fool; **hacer el c.** to muck about
2 NF (*suerte*) luck

chorrada NF *Esp Fam* **decir una c.** to say something stupid; **chorradas** *Br* rubbish, *US* garbage

chorrear VI to drip, to trickle; *Fam* **c. de sudor** to pour with sweat; *Fam* **tengo el abrigo chorreando** my coat is dripping wet

chorro NM (**a**) (*de agua etc*) spurt; (*muy fino*) trickle; **salir a chorros** to gush forth (**b**) *Téc* jet (**c**) *Fig* stream, flood

choto NM,F (**a**) (*cabrito*) kid, young goat; *Fam* **estar como una chota** to be crazy, to be off one's rocker (**b**) (*ternero*) calf

chovinismo NM chauvinism

chovinista 1 ADJ chauvinistic
2 NMF chauvinist

choza NF hut, shack

christmas NM INV Christmas card

chubasco NM heavy shower, downpour

chubasquero NM raincoat, *Br* mac

chúcaro, -a ADJ *Andes, CAm, RP* (**a**) (*animal*) wild (**b**) *Fam* (*persona*) **ser c.** to be shy o withdrawn

chuchería NF *Fam Br* sweet, *US* candy

chucho NM *Fam* (**a**) *(perro)* mutt, dog (**b**) *RP* *(susto)* fright; **un c. de frío** a shiver

chueco, -a 1 ADJ *Am* *(torcido)* twisted; *(patizambo)* bowlegged; *Méx, Ven Fam (cojo)* lame
2 NM,F *Am (patizambo)* bowlegged person; *Méx, Ven Fam (cojo)* lame person

chufa NF groundnut

chulear VI *Fam* to strut around; **c. de** to go on about

chuleta NF (**a**) *(de carne)* chop; **c. de cerdo** pork chop (**b**) *Esp, Ven Fam (en exámenes)* crib note

chullo NM *Andes* woollen cap

chulo, -a *Fam* **1** NM,F *Esp* show-off
2 NM *(proxeneta)* pimp
3 ADJ *Esp, Méx Fam (bonito)* cool, *Br* top, *US* neat

chumbera NF prickly pear cactus

chungo, -a ADJ *Fam* dodgy

chuño NM *Andes, RP* potato starch

chupa NF *Esp Fam* coat

chupachups® NM INV *Esp* lollipop

chupacirios NM F INV *Fam Pey* holy Joe

chupado, -a ADJ (**a**) *(flaco)* skinny, thin (**b**) *Fam* **está c.** it's dead easy

chupamedias NMF *Andes, RP, Ven Fam* toady

chupar 1 VT (**a**) *(succionar)* to suck (**b**) *(lamer)* to lick (**c**) *(absorber)* to soak up, to absorb
2 VI to suck
3 chuparse VPR (**a**) **está para chuparse los dedos** it's really mouthwatering (**b**) *Esp Fam* **to** put up with; **nos chupamos toda la película** we sat through the whole film

chupatintas NM INV *Pey* penpusher

chupe NM (**a**) *Andes, Arg (comida)* stew (**b**) *Méx, RP Fam (bebida)* booze

chupete NM *Br* dummy, *US* pacifier

chupi ADJ *Esp Fam* great

chupito NM shot

chupón, -ona 1 NM,F *Fam (gorrón)* sponger, cadger
2 NM *Méx (chupete) Br* dummy, *US* pacifier

churrasco NM barbecued meat

churrería NF fritter shop

churrete NM dirty mark, grease spot

churro NM (**a**) *(para comer)* = dough formed into sticks or rings, fried in oil and covered in sugar (**b**) *Fam (chapuza)* mess

chusma NF rabble, mob

chutar 1 VI (**a**) *Dep (a gol)* to shoot (**b**) *Esp Fam (funcionar)* to work; **¡y vas que chutas!** and then you're well away!
2 chutarse VPR *Esp Fam (drogas)* to shoot up

chute NM (**a**) *Dep* shot (**b**) *Esp Fam (drogas)* fix

CI NM *(abr* **coeficiente intelectual)** IQ

Cía., cía *(abr* **compañía)** Co

cianuro NM cyanide

cibercafé, *Fam* **ciber** NM *Inform* Internet cafe, cybercafe

ciberespacio NM *Inform* cyberspace

cibernética NF cybernetics *sing*

cicatero, -a 1 ADJ stingy, mean
2 NM,F miser

cicatriz NF scar

cicatrizar [40] VT & VI *Med* to heal

cíclico, -a ADJ cyclical

ciclismo NM cycling

ciclista 1 ADJ cycling
2 NMF cyclist

ciclo NM cycle; *(de conferencias etc)* course, series

ciclocross NM cyclo-cross

ciclomotor NM moped

ciclón NM cyclone

ciego, -a 1 ADJ (**a**) *(invidente)* blind; **a ciegas** blindly (**b**) *Esp Fam (borracho)* blind drunk, *Br* pissed; *(de droga)* stoned
2 NM,F blind person; **los ciegos** the blind

cielo NM (**a**) *(atmósfera)* sky (**b**) *Rel* heaven; *Fig* **caído del c.** *(oportuno)* heaven-sent; *(inesperado)* out of the blue; **¡c. santo!** good heavens! (**c**) **c. del paladar** roof of the mouth (**d**) *(nombre cariñoso)* my love, my dear

ciempiés NM INV centipede

cien ADJ & NM INV hundred; **c. libras** a *o* one hundred pounds; **c. por c.** one hundred percent

ciénaga NF marsh, bog

ciencia NF science; *Fig* **saber algo a c. cierta** to know sth for certain; **c. ficción** science fiction; **c. infusa** intuition; **ciencias ocultas** the occult

cieno NM mud, mire

científico, -a 1 ADJ scientific
2 NM,F scientist

cientista NMF *CSur* **c. social** social scientist

ciento ADJ hundred; **c. tres** one hundred and three; **por c.** percent

ciernes NMPL **una campeona en c.** a budding champion; **tenemos un viaje en c.** we're planning a journey

cierre NM (**a**) *(acción)* closing, shutting; *(de fábrica)* closure; *TV* close-down; **c. patronal** lockout (**b**) *(de bolso)* clasp; *(de puerta)* catch; *(prenda)* fastener; **c. de seguridad** safety lock; **c. centralizado** central locking (**c**) *Andes, Méx, RP (cremallera) Br* zip (fastener), *US* zipper; **c.** *Andes, Méx* **relámpago** *o Chile* **eclair** *o Urug* **metálico** *Br* zip (fastener), *US* zipper

cierto, -a 1 ADJ (**a**) *(verdadero)* true; *(seguro)* certain; **estar en lo c.** to be right; **lo c. es que ...** the fact is that ...; **por c.** by the way (**b**) *(algún)* certain; **ciertas personas** certain *o* some people
2 ADV certainly

ciervo, -a NM,F deer; *(macho)* stag; *(hembra)* doe, hind

cifra NF (**a**) *(número)* figure, number; *Com* **c. de ventas** sales figures (**b**) *(código)* cipher, code

cifrar VT (**a**) *(codificar) (mensaje, texto)* to code (**b**) *(valorar) (pérdidas)* to estimate (**c**) *(reducir) (aspiraciones, esperanzas)* to pin, to place

cigala NF Dublin Bay prawn, scampi

cigarra NF cicada

cigarrillo NM cigarette

cigarro NM (a) *(puro)* cigar (b) *(cigarrillo)* cigarette

cigüeña NF (a) *(ave)* stork (b) *Téc* crank

cigüeñal NM crankshaft

cilindrada NF *Aut* cylinder capacity

cilíndrico, -a ADJ cylindrical

cilindro NM cylinder

cima NF summit

cimbrearse VPR to sway

cimentar VT to lay the foundations of; *Fig (amistad)* to strengthen

cimientos NMPL foundations; **echar** *o* **poner los c.** to lay the foundations

cinc NM zinc

cincel NM chisel

cincelar VT to chisel

cinco ADJ & NM INV five

cincuenta ADJ & NM INV fifty

cine NM (a) *(local)* cinema, *US* movie theater (b) *(arte)* cinema; **c. mudo** silent movies *o Br* films; **c. sonoro** talking pictures, talkies

cineasta NMF movie maker *o* director, *Br* film maker *o* director

cinéfilo, -a NM,F *(que va al cine)* (keen) moviegoer *o Br* filmgoer; *(que entiende de cine)* movie *o Br* film buff

cinematografía NF cinematography, *Br* film-making

cinematográfico, -a ADJ movie, *Br* film; **la industria cinematográfica** the movie *o Br* film industry

cíngaro, -a ADJ & NM,F gypsy.

cínico, -a 1 ADJ shameless

2 NM,F shameless person; **es un c.** he's shameless, he has no shame

> Observa que la palabra inglesa **cynic** es un falso amigo y no es la traducción de la palabra española **cínico.** En inglés **cynic** significa tanto "descreído, suspicaz" como "desaprensivo".

cinismo NM shamelessness

> Observa la palabra inglesa **cynicism** es un falso amigo y no es la traducción de la palabra española **cinismo.** En inglés **cynicism** significa "descreimiento, suspicacia".

cinta NF (a) *(tira)* band, strip; *(para adornar)* ribbon; *Cost* braid, edging (b) *Téc & Mús* tape; **c. adhesiva/aislante** adhesive/insulating tape; **c. de vídeo** video tape; **c. transportadora** conveyor belt (c) *Cin* movie, *Br* film

cinto NM belt

cintura NF waist

cinturón NM belt; *Fig* **apretarse el c.** to tighten one's belt; **c. de seguridad** safety belt; *Am* **c. de miseria** = slum or shanty town area round a large city

cipote ¹ NM (a) *Fam (bobo)* dimwit, moron (b) *Vulg (pene)* prick, cock

cipote², -a NM,F *CAm* kid

ciprés *(pl* **cipreses)** NM cypress

circense ADJ circus

circo NM circus

circuito NM circuit

circulación NF (a) *(de personas, sangre, dinero)* circulation (b) *(tráfico)* traffic

circular 1 ADJ & NF circular

2 VI *(moverse)* to circulate; *(líquido)* to flow; *(tren, autobús)* to run; *Fig (rumor)* to go round; **circule por la izquierda** *(en letrero)* keep to the left

circulatorio, -a ADJ circulatory; *Aut* **un caos c.** traffic chaos

círculo NM circle; *Fig* **c. vicioso** vicious circle

circuncisión NF circumcision

circundante ADJ surrounding

circundar VT to surround, to encircle

circunferencia NF circumference

circunloquio NM circumlocution

circunscribir *(pp* **circunscrito) 1** VT (a) *(limitar)* to restrict, to confine (b) *Geom* to circumscribe

2 circunscribirse VPR to confine *o* limit oneself (**a** to)

circunscripción NF district; **c. electoral** electoral district, *Br* constituency

circunscrito, -a 1 ADJ circumscribed

2 PP *de* circunscribir

circunspecto, -a ADJ circumspect

circunstancia NF circumstance; **en estas circunstancias ...** under the circumstances ...

circunstancial ADJ circumstantial

cirio NM wax candle

cirrosis NF INV cirrhosis

ciruela NF plum; **c. claudia** greengage; **c. pasa** prune

ciruelo NM plum tree

cirugía NF surgery; **c. estética** *o* **plástica** plastic surgery

cirujano, -a NM,F surgeon

cisma NM (a) *Rel* schism (b) *Pol* split

cisne NM swan

cisterna NF cistern, tank

cistitis NF INV cystitis

cita NF (a) *(profesional)* appointment; **darse c.** to arrange to meet (b) *(amorosa)* date (c) *(mención)* quotation

citación NF *Der* citation, summons *sing*

citado, -a ADJ aforementioned

citar 1 VT (a) *(dar cita)* to arrange to meet, to make an appointment with (b) *(mencionar)* to quote (c) *Der* to summons

2 citarse VPR **citarse (con algn)** to arrange to meet (sb)

citología NF *Med (análisis)* cervical smear, smear test

cítrico, -a 1 ADJ citric, citrus
 2 cítricos NMPL citrus fruits

ciudad NF town; *(capital)* city; *Méx* **c. perdida** shanty town

ciudadanía NF citizenship

ciudadano, -a 1 NM,F citizen; **el c. de a pie** the man in the street
 2 ADJ civic

cívico, -a ADJ civic

civil 1 ADJ civil; **matrimonio c.** civil marriage
 2 NMF **(a)** *(no militar)* civilian **(b)** *Fam (Guardia Civil)* member of the Guardia Civil

civilización NF civilization

civilizado, -a ADJ civilized

civilizar [40] VT to civilize

civismo NM **(a)** *(urbanidad)* public-spirited-ness **(b)** *(cortesía)* civility

cizaña NF *Bot* bearded darnel; *Fig* **sembrar c.** to sow discord

cl *(abr* **centilitro(s))** cl

clamar VT to cry out for, to clamour for

clamor NM clamour

clamoroso, -a ADJ resounding

clan NM clan

clandestinidad NF **en la c.** underground

clandestino, -a ADJ clandestine, under-ground; **aborto c.** backstreet abortion

clara NF **(a)** *(de huevo)* white **(b)** *Esp Fam (bebida)* shandy

claraboya NF skylight

clarear VI **(a)** *(amanecer)* to dawn **(b)** *(despejar)* to clear up **(c)** *(transparentar)* to wear thin, to become transparent

clarete 1 ADJ **vino c.** light red wine
 2 NM light red wine

claridad NF **(a)** *(luz)* light, brightness **(b)** *(inteligibilidad)* clarity; **con c.** clearly

clarificador, -a ADJ clarifying

clarificar [44] VT to clarify

clarín NM bugle

clarinete NM clarinet

clarividencia NF farsightedness, perception

clarividente 1 ADJ farsighted, perceptive
 2 NMF clairvoyant

claro, -a 1 ADJ **(a)** *(luminoso)* bright; *(color)* light; *(día)* clear **(b)** *(sonido)* clear **(c)** *(diluido)* *(té, café)* weak; *(salsa)* thin **(d)** *(poco tupido)* thin, sparse **(e)** *(explicación, ideas, libro)* clear **(f)** *(obvio, evidente)* clear; **está c. que ...** of course ...; **¿está c.?** is that clear?
 2 INTERJ of course!; **¡c. que no!** of course not!; **¡c. que sí!** certainly!
 3 NM **(a)** *(espacio)* gap, space; *(en un bosque)* clearing **(b)** *Met* bright spell
 4 ADV clearly

clase NF **(a)** *(grupo)* class; **c. alta/media** upper/middle class; **clases pasivas** pensioners; **primera/segunda c.** first/second class **(b)** *(tipo)* kind, sort; **toda c. de ...** all kinds of ... **(c)** *Educ (curso)* class; *(aula)* classroom; **c. particular** private class *o* lesson **(d)** *(estilo)* class; **tener c.** to have class

clásico, -a 1 ADJ classical; *(típico)* classic; *(en el vestir)* classic
 2 NM classic

clasificación NF classification; *Dep* league table

clasificador, -a 1 ADJ classifying
 2 NM *(mueble)* filing cabinet

clasificar [44] **1** VT to classify, to class
 2 clasificarse VPR *Dep* to qualify

claudicar [44] VI to give in

claustro NM **(a)** *Arquit* cloister **(b)** *(reunión)* ≃ staff meeting, *US* faculty meeting

claustrofobia NF claustrophobia

cláusula NF clause

clausura NF **(a)** *(cierre)* closure; **ceremonia de c.** closing ceremony **(b)** *Rel* enclosure

clausurar VT to close

clavadista NMF *CAm, Méx* diver

clavado, -a ADJ **(a)** *(con clavos)* nailed **(b)** *(a la medida)* just right **(c)** *(parecido)* almost identical; **ser c. a algn** to be the spitting image of sb

clavar 1 VT **(a)** *(con clavos)* to nail; *(clavo)* to bang *o* hammer in; *(estaca)* to drive in **(b)** *Fam (timar)* to sting, to fleece
 2 clavarse VPR **clavarse una astilla** to get a splinter

clave 1 NF key; **la palabra c.** the key word
 2 NM harpsichord

clavel NM carnation

clavícula NF collarbone

clavija NF *Téc* jack

clavo NM **(a)** *(pieza)* nail; *Fig* **dar en el c.** to hit the nail on the head **(b)** *(especia)* clove

claxon NM horn; **tocar el c.** to sound the horn

clemencia NF mercy, clemency

clementina NF clementine

cleptomanía NF kleptomania

cleptómano, -a ADJ & NM,F kleptomaniac

clerical ADJ clerical

clericó NM *RP* ≃ drink made of white wine and fruit

clérigo NM priest

clero NM clergy

clic *(pl* **clics),** **click** *(pl* **clicks)** NM *Inform* click; **hacer c.** to click; **hacer doble c.** to double-click

cliché NM **(a)** *Fig (tópico)* cliché **(b)** *Fot* negative **(c)** *Impr* plate

cliente NMF customer, client

clientela NF clientele

clima NM climate

climático, -a ADJ climatic
climatizado, -a ADJ air-conditioned
climatizar [40] VT to air-condition
climatología NF (a) *(tiempo)* climate (b) *(ciencia)* climatology
clímax NM INV climax
clínica NF clinic
clínico, -a ADJ clinical
clip *(pl* **clips)** NM clip
clítoris NM INV clitoris
cloaca NF sewer, drain
clorhídrico, -a ADJ hydrochloric
cloro NM chlorine
clorofila NF chlorophyll
cloroformo NM chloroform
cloruro NM chloride; **c. sódico** sodium chloride
clóset *(pl* **clósets)** NM *Am* fitted cupboard, *US* closet
club *(pl* **clubs** *o* **clubes)** NM club; **c. náutico** yacht club
cm *(abr* **centímetro(s))** cm
CNT NF *(abr* **Confederación Nacional del Trabajo)** = Spanish anarchist trade union federation
coacción NF coercion
coaccionar VT to coerce
coactivo, -a ADJ coercive
coagular **1** VT *(sangre)* to clot, to coagulate; *(líquido)* to coagulate
  2 coagularse VPR *(sangre)* to clot; *(líquido)* to coagulate
coágulo NM *Med* clot
coalición NF coalition
coartada NF alibi
coartar VT to restrict
coba NF *Esp, Méx Fam (halago)* flattery; **dar c. a algn** *(adular)* to suck up *o* crawl to sb; *(aplacar)* to soft-soap sb
cobalto NM cobalt
cobarde **1** ADJ cowardly
  2 NMF coward
cobardía NF cowardice
cobaya NF guinea pig
cobertizo NM shed, shack
cobertor NM bedspread
cobertura NF cover; *(de noticia)* coverage
cobija NF *Am (manta)* blanket
cobijar **1** VT to shelter
  2 cobijarse VPR to take shelter
cobijo NM shelter; *Fig (protección)* protection
cobra NF cobra
cobrador, -a NM,F (a) *(de autobús)* *(hombre)* conductor; *(mujer)* conductress (b) *(de luz, agua etc)* collector
cobrar **1** VT (a) *(dinero)* to charge; *(cheque)* to cash; *(salario)* to earn; **¿me cobra?** how much is that? (b) *Fig (fuerza)* to gain, to get; **c. ánimos** to take courage *o* heart; **c. impor-**

tancia to become important
  2 VI *Fam* to catch it
  3 cobrarse VPR **¿se cobra?** *(al pagar)* how much is that?
cobre NM copper
cobrizo, -a ADJ copper, copper-coloured
cobro NM *(pago)* collecting; *(de cheque)* cashing; *Tel* **llamada a c. revertido** *Br* reverse-charge call, *US* collect call
coca NF (a) *Bot* coca (b) *Fam (droga)* cocaine, coke
cocaína NF cocaine
cocainómano, -a NM,F cocaine addict
cocalero, -a *Bol, Perú* **1** ADJ **región cocalera** coca-producing area; **productor c.** coca farmer *o* producer
  2 NM,F coca farmer *o* producer
cocción NF cooking; *(en agua)* boiling; *(en horno)* baking
cocear VI to kick
cocer [41] **1** VT to cook; *(hervir)* to boil; *(hornear)* to bake
  2 VI *(hervir)* to boil
  3 cocerse VPR (a) *(comida)* to cook; *(hervir)* to boil; *(hornear)* to bake (b) *(tramarse)* to be going on
cochambroso, -a ADJ squalid
cochayuyo NM *Chile, Perú* seaweed
coche NM (a) *(automóvil)* car, *US* automobile; **en c.** by car; **c. de carreras** racing car; **c. de bomberos** fire engine, *US* fire truck; **c. fúnebre** hearse (b) *Ferroc* coach, *Br* carriage, *US* car; **c. cama** sleeping car, sleeper (c) *(de caballos)* carriage
cochecito NM *(de niño)* *Br* pram, *US* baby carriage
cochera NF (a) *(para coches)* garage (b) *(de autobuses)* depot
cochinillo NM suckling pig
cochino, -a **1** NM,F (a) *(macho)* pig; *(hembra)* sow (b) *Fam (persona)* filthy person, pig
  2 ADJ *(sucio)* filthy, disgusting
cocido NM stew
cociente NM quotient
cocina NF (a) *(habitación)* kitchen (b) *(aparato)* cooker, stove; **c. eléctrica/de gas** electric/gas cooker (c) *(arte)* cooking; **c. casera** home cooking; **c. española** Spanish cooking *o* cuisine
cocinar VT & VI to cook
cocinero, -a NM,F cook
cocktail NM = **cóctel**
coco¹ NM coconut; *Fam (cabeza)* nut; **comerle el c. a algn** to brainwash sb; **comerse el c.** to get obsessed
coco² NM *Fam (fantasma)* bogeyman
cocodrilo NM crocodile
cocoliche NM *RP Fam* = pidgin Spanish spoken by Italian immigrants
cocotero NM coconut palm

cóctel NM cocktail; **c. Molotov** Molotov cocktail

coctelera NF cocktail shaker

codazo NM (**a**) (*señal*) nudge with one's elbow (**b**) (*golpe*) blow with one's elbow

codearse VPR to rub shoulders (**con** with), to hobnob (**con** with)

codeína NF codeine

codicia NF greed

codiciar [43] VT to covet

codicioso, -a ADJ covetous, greedy

codificado, -a ADJ (*emisión de TV*) scrambled

codificar [44] VT (*ley*) to codify; (*mensajes*) to encode

código NM code; **c. de barras** bar code; **c. de circulación** highway code; **c. postal** *Br* postcode, postal code, *US* zip code

codo NM elbow; *Fig* **c. con c.** side by side; *Fam* **hablar por los codos** to talk nonstop

codorniz NF quail

coeficiente NM (*índice*) rate; *Mat & Fís* coefficient; **c. intelectual** intelligence quotient

coercitivo, -a ADJ coercive

coetáneo, -a ADJ & NM,F contemporary

coexistencia NF coexistence

coexistir VI to coexist

cofia NF bonnet

cofradía NF (*hermandad*) brotherhood; (*asociación*) association

cofre NM (*arca*) trunk, chest; (*para joyas*) box, casket

coger [53] *esp Esp* **1** VT (**a**) (*del suelo*) to take; (*del suelo*) to pick (up); (*fruta, flores*) to pick; (*asir*) to seize, to take hold of; (*bus, tren*) to take, to catch; (*pelota, ladrón, resfriado*) to catch; (*entender*) to grasp; (*costumbre*) to pick up; (*velocidad, fuerza*) to gather; (*atropellar*) to run over, to knock down (**b**) *Am Vulg* to screw, to fuck
2 VI *Fam* **cogió y se fue** he upped and left
3 cogerse VPR (*agarrarse*) to hold on

cogida NF goring

cognitivo, -a ADJ cognitive

cogollo NM (*de lechuga*) heart

cogote NM *Esp* nape *o* back of the neck

cohabitación NF cohabitation

cohabitar VI to live together, to cohabit

cohecho NM *Der* bribery

coherencia NF coherence

coherente ADJ coherent

cohesión NF cohesion

cohete NM rocket; **c. espacial** space rocket

cohibido, -a ADJ inhibited

cohibir **1** VT to inhibit
2 cohibirse VPR to feel inhibited

COI NM *Dep* (*abr* **Comité Olímpico Internacional**) IOC

coima NF *Andes, RP Fam* bribe, *Br* backhander

coincidencia NF coincidence

coincidir VI (**a**) (*versiones, gustos*) to coincide (**b**) (*concordar*) to agree; **todos coincidieron en señalar que ...** everyone agreed that ... (**c**) (*en un sitio*) to meet by chance (**d**) (*en el tiempo*) to coincide

coito NM intercourse, coitus

cojear VI (*persona*) to limp, to hobble; (*mueble*) to wobble

cojera NF limp

cojín NM cushion

cojinete NM *Téc* bearing; **c. de agujas/bolas** needle/ball bearing

cojo, -a **1** ADJ (*persona*) lame; (*mueble*) rickety
2 NM,F lame person

cojón NM *Esp Vulg* ball; **de cojones** (*estupendo*) *Br* bloody *o US* goddamn brilliant; (*pésimo*) *Br* bloody *o US* goddamn awful

cojonudo, -a ADJ *Esp muy Fam Br* bloody *o US* goddamn brilliant

cojudez NF *Andes muy Fam* **¡qué c.!** (*acto*) what a *Br* bloody *o US* goddamn stupid thing to do!; (*dicho*) what a *Br* bloody *o US* goddamn stupid thing to say!

cojudo, -a ADJ *Andes muy Fam Br* bloody *o US* goddamn stupid

col NF cabbage; **c. de Bruselas** Brussels sprout

cola NF (**a**) (*de animal*) tail; (*de vestido*) train; (*de pelo*) ponytail; (*en la parte de atrás*) rear; *Fam* **traer c.** to have consequences (**b**) (*fila*) *Br* queue, *US* line; **hacer c.** *Br* to queue (up), *US* to stand in line (**c**) (*pegamento*) glue

colaboración NF (**a**) (*cooperación*) collaboration (**b**) (*en prensa*) contribution

colaboracionismo NM *Pol* collaboration

colaborador, -a NM,F (*compañero*) associate, colleague; (*de prensa*) contributor, writer; **c. externo** freelancer

colaborar VI to collaborate, to co-operate

colación NF **sacar** *o* **traer (algo) a c.** to bring (sth) up

colada NF *Esp* wash, laundry; **hacer la c.** to do the washing *o* laundry

colado, -a ADJ (**a**) (*líquido*) strained (**b**) *Fam* (*enamorado*) **estar c. por algn** to have a crush on sb

colador NM colander, sieve; (*de té, café*) strainer

colapsar **1** VT to bring to a standstill
2 colapsarse VPR to come to a standstill

colapso NM (**a**) *Med* collapse (**b**) *Aut* **c. circulatorio** traffic jam, hold-up

colar [2] **1** VT (**a**) (*líquido*) to strain, to filter (**b**) (*por agujero*) to slip
2 VI *Fam* **esa mentira no cuela** that lie won't wash
3 colarse VPR (**a**) (*líquido*) **colarse por** to seep through (**b**) (*persona*) (*en un sitio*) to slip, to sneak; (*en una cola*) *Br* to jump the queue, *US* to cut in line (**c**) *Fam* (*equivocarse*) to slip up

colateral ADJ collateral

colcha NF bedspread

colchón NM mattress

colchoneta NF air bed

colear VI (a) *(animal)* to wag its tail; *Fam* **vivito y coleando** alive and kicking (b) *Fam* **el asunto aún colea** we haven't heard the last of it yet

colección NF collection

coleccionable ADJ & NM collectable

coleccionar VT to collect

coleccionista NMF collector

colecta NF collection

colectividad NF community

colectivo, -a 1 ADJ collective
2 NM (a) *(asociación)* association (b) *Andes (taxi)* collective taxi *(with a fixed rate and that travels a fixed route)* (c) *Arg, Bol (autobús)* bus

colega NMF (a) *(compañero profesional)* colleague, *US* co-worker (b) *Esp Fam (amigo)* pal, *Br* mate, *US* buddy

colegiado, -a N,M,F *Dep* referee

colegial, -a 1 ADJ *(escolar)* school
2 N,M,F *(alumno)* schoolboy; *(alumna)* schoolgirl; **los colegiales** the schoolchildren

colegio NM (a) *(escuela)* school; **c. privado** private school, *Br* public o independent school (b) *(profesional)* association, college; **c. de abogados** the Bar; *Pol* **c. electoral** electoral college (c) *Esp* **c. mayor** hall of residence

colegir [58] VT to infer, to deduce

cólera¹ NF anger, rage

cólera² NM *Med* cholera

colérico, -a ADJ furious

colesterol NM cholesterol

coleta NF pigtail, ponytail; *Fig* **cortarse la c.** to retire

coletazo NM **dar los últimos coletazos** to be on one's last legs

coletilla NF *(de discurso, escrito)* closing comment

colgado, -a ADJ (a) *Fam* **dejar (a algn) c.** to leave (sb) in the lurch (b) *Fam (atontado, loco)* crazy, daft; *(drogado)* high

colgador NM *(percha)* hanger, coathanger; *(gancho)* hook

colgante 1 NM *(joya)* pendant
2 ADJ hanging

colgar [2] **1** VT *(suspender, ahorcar)* to hang; *(colada)* to hang (out)
2 VI (a) *(pender)* to hang (**de** from); *Fig* **c. de un hilo** to hang by a thread (b) *Tel* to hang up
3 colgarse VPR *(ahorcarse)* to hang oneself

colibrí *(pl* colibrís o colibríes*)* NM hummingbird

cólico NM colic

coliflor NF cauliflower

colijo INDIC PRES *de* colegir

colilla NF (cigarette) end o butt

colimba NF *Arg Fam* military service

colina NF hill

colindante ADJ adjoining, adjacent

colindar VI to be adjacent (**con** to)

colirio NM eye-drops

colisión NF collision, crash

colisionar VI to collide, to crash

colitis NF INV colitis

colla *Bol* **1** ADJ of/from the altiplano
2 NMF = indigenous person from the altiplano

collage NM collage

collar NM (a) *(adorno)* necklace (b) *(de perro)* collar

collarín NM surgical collar

colmado, -a ADJ full, filled; *(cucharada)* heaped

colmar VT (a) *(vaso, copa)* to fill to the brim; **c. a algn de regalos/elogios** to shower gifts/praise on sb (b) *(ambiciones)* to fulfil, to satisfy

colmena NF beehive

colmillo NM eye o canine tooth; *Zool (de carnívoro)* fang; *(de jabalí, elefante)* tusk

colmo NM height; **el c. de** the height of; **¡eso es el c.!** that's the last straw!; **para c.** to top it all

colocación NF (a) *(acto)* positioning (b) *(disposición)* lay-out (c) *(empleo)* job, employment

colocado, -a ADJ (a) *(empleado)* employed (b) *Fam (drogado)* high

colocar [44] **1** VT (a) *(en una posición, un lugar)* to place, to put (b) *Fin (invertir)* to invest (c) *(emplear)* to find a job for (d) *Fam (drogar)* to give a high to
2 colocarse VPR (a) *(situarse)* to put oneself (b) *(emplearse)* to take a job (**de** as) (c) *Fam (drogarse)* to get high

colofón NM (a) *(remate, fin)* climax, culmination (b) *(apéndice)* colophon

Colombia N Colombia

colombiano, -a ADJ & N,M,F Colombian

Colón N Columbus

colón NM *Fin* colon, = standard monetary unit of Costa Rica and El Salvador

colonia¹ NF colony; *(campamento)* summer camp; *Méx (barrio)* district

colonia² NF *(perfume)* cologne

colonial ADJ colonial

colonialismo NM colonialism

colonización NF colonization

colonizar [40] VT to colonize

colono NM settler, colonist

coloquial ADJ colloquial

coloquio NM discussion, colloquium

color NM colour; *Cin & Fot* **en c.** in colour; **de colores** multicoloured; **de c.** *(persona)* coloured

colorado, -a 1 ADJ red; **ponerse c.** to blush
2 NM red

Observa que la palabra inglesa **coloured** es un falso amigo y no es la traducción de la palabra española **colorado**. En inglés, **coloured** significa "coloreado".

colorante NM colouring

colorear VT to colour

colorete NM rouge

colorido NM colour

colorín NM bright colour; **c. colorado, este cuento se ha acabado** and they all lived happily ever after

colosal ADJ colossal

columna NF column; *Anat* **c. vertebral** vertebral column, spinal column

columpiar [43] **1** VT to swing
  2 columpiarse VPR to swing

columpio NM swing

coma¹ NF (**a**) *Ling & Mús* comma (**b**) *Mat* point; **tres c. cinco** three point five

coma² NM *Med* coma

comadre NF (**a**) *(madrina)* = godmother of one's child, or mother of one's godchild (**b**) *Fam (amiga) Br* mate, *US* buddy

comadreja NF weasel

comadreo NM gossip, gossiping

comadrona NF midwife

comal NM *CAm, Méx* = flat clay or metal dish used for baking "tortillas"

comandancia NF (**a**) *(rango)* command (**b**) *(edificio)* command headquarters (**c**) *Méx (de policía)* police station

comandante NM (**a**) *Mil* commander, commanding officer (**b**) *Av* captain

comandar VT to command

comando NM (**a**) *Mil* commando (**b**) *Inform* command

comarca NF region

comarcal ADJ regional

comba NF *Esp* (**a**) *(juego)* skipping; **jugar a la c.** *Br* to skip, *US* to jump rope (**b**) *(cuerda) Br* skipping rope, *US* jump rope

combar VT to bend

combate NM combat; *(en boxeo)* fight; *Mil* battle; **fuera de c.** out for the count; *(eliminado)* out of action

combatiente 1 ADJ fighting
  2 NMF combatant

combatir 1 VT to combat
  2 VI **c. contra** to fight against

combativo, -a ADJ spirited, aggressive

combinación NF (**a**) *(acción)* combination (**b**) *(prenda)* slip

combinado, -a 1 ADJ combined
  2 NM (**a**) *(cóctel)* cocktail (**b**) *Dep* line-up

combinar 1 VT *(mezclar)* to combine; *(bebidas)* to mix; *(colores)* to match
  2 VI *(colores, ropa)* **c. con** to go with

combustible 1 NM fuel
  2 ADJ combustible

combustión NF combustion

comecocos NM INV (**a**) *Fam (para convencer)* **este panfleto es un c.** this pamphlet is designed to brainwash you (**b**) *Fam (cosa difícil de comprender)* mind-bending problem o puzzle (**c**) *(juego)* pac-man®

comedia NF comedy

comediante, -a NM,F actor, *f* actress

comedido, -a ADJ self-restrained, reserved

comedor NM dining room

comensal NMF companion at table

comentar VT **c. algo con algn** to talk sth over with sb; **me han comentado que ...** I've been told that ...

comentario NM (**a**) *(observación)* comment, remark; **sin c.** no comment (**b**) *(crítica)* commentary (**c**) **comentarios** *(cotilleos)* gossip

comentarista NMF commentator

comenzar [51] VT & VI to begin, to start; **comenzó a llover** it started raining o to rain; **comenzó diciendo que ...** he started by saying that ...

comer 1 VT (**a**) *(alimentos)* to eat (**b**) *(en juegos)* to take, to capture
  2 VI *(ingerir alimentos)* to eat; *Esp, Méx (al mediodía)* to have lunch; **dar de c. a algn** to feed sb
  3 comerse VPR (**a**) *(alimentos)* to eat (**b**) *(en los juegos de tablero)* to take, to capture

comercial ADJ commercial

comercialización NF marketing

comercializar [40] VT to market

comerciante NMF merchant

comerciar [43] VI to trade; **comercia con oro** he trades in gold

comercio NM (**a**) *(actividad)* commerce, trade; **c. exterior** foreign trade; *Inform* **c. electrónico** e-commerce; **c. justo** fair trade (**b**) *(tienda)* shop

comestible 1 ADJ edible
  2 comestibles NMPL food, foodstuff(s); **tienda de comestibles** grocer's shop, *US* grocery store

cometa 1 NM *Astron* comet
  2 NF *(juguete)* kite

cometer VT *(error, falta)* to make; *(delito, crimen)* to commit

cometido NM (**a**) *(tarea)* task, assignment (**b**) *(deber)* duty; **cumplir su c.** to do one's duty

comezón NM itch

cómic *(pl* **cómics)** NM comic

comicios NMPL elections

cómico, -a 1 ADJ (**a**) *(gracioso)* comic, comical (**b**) *(de la comedia)* comedy, comic; **actor c.** comedy actor
  2 NM,F *(humorista)* comedian, comic, *f* comedienne

comida NF (**a**) *(alimento)* food; **c. basura** junk food (**b**) *(almuerzo, cena)* meal; *Esp, Méx (al mediodía)* lunch

comidilla NF *Fam* **la c. del pueblo** the talk of the town

comienzo NM beginning, start; **a comienzos de** at the beginning of; **dar c. (a algo)** to begin *o* start (sth)

comillas NFPL inverted commas; **entre c.** in inverted commas

comilón, -ona 1 ADJ greedy, gluttonous
2 NM,F big eater, glutton

comilona NF *Fam* blow-out, *Br* slap-up meal

comino NM cumin, cummin; *Fam* **me importa un c.** I don't give a damn (about it)

comisaría NF police station, *US* precinct, *US* station house

comisario NM (**a**) *(de policía) Br* superintendent, *US* captain (**b**) *(delegado)* commissioner; **c. europeo** European Commissioner

comisión NF (**a**) *Com (retribución)* commission; **a** *o* **con c.** on a commission basis (**b**) *(comité)* committee; **la C. Europea** the European Commission

comisura NF corner *(of mouth, eyes)*

comité NM committee

comitiva NF suite, retinue

como 1 ADV (**a**) *(manera)* how; **me gusta c. cantas** I like the way you sing; **dilo c. quieras** say it however you like
(**b**) *(comparación)* as; **blanco c. la nieve** as white as snow; **habla c. su padre** he talks like his father
(**c**) *(según)* as; **c. decíamos ayer** as we were saying yesterday
(**d**) *(en calidad de)* as; **c. presidente** as president; **lo compré c. recuerdo** I bought it as a souvenir
(**e**) *(aproximadamente)* about; **c. a la mitad de camino** halfway; **c. unos diez** about ten
2 CONJ (**a**) *Esp (+ subj) (si)* if; **c. no estudies vas a suspender** if you don't study, you'll fail (**b**) *(porque)* as, since; **c. no venías me marché** as you didn't come, I left (**c**) **c. si** as if; **c. si nada** *o* **tal cosa** as if nothing had happened; *Fam* **c. si lo viera** I can imagine perfectly well

cómo 1 ADV (**a**) **¿c.?** *(¿perdón?)* what? (**b**) *(interrogativo)* how; **¿c. estás?** how are you?; **¿c. lo sabes?** how do you know?; **¿c. es de grande/ancho?** how big/wide is it?; *Esp* **¿a c. están los tomates?** how much are the tomatoes?; **¿c. es que no viniste a la fiesta?** *(por qué)* how come you didn't come to the party?; *Fam* **¿c. es eso?** how come? (**c**) *(exclamativo)* how; **¡c. has crecido!** you've really grown a lot!; **¡c. no!** but of course!
2 NM **el c. y el porqué** the whys and wherefores

cómoda NF chest of drawers

comodidad NF (**a**) *(estado, cualidad)* comfort (**b**) *(conveniencia)* convenience

Observa que la palabra inglesa **commodity** es un falso amigo y no es la traducción de la palabra española **comodidad**. En inglés, **commodity** significa "producto básico".

comodín NM *Naipes* joker

cómodo, -a ADJ (**a**) *(confortable)* comfortable; **ponerse c.** to make oneself comfortable (**b**) *(útil)* handy, convenient

comodón, -ona 1 ADJ *(amante de la comodidad)* comfort-loving; *(vago)* laid-back; **no seas c.** don't be so lazy
2 NM,F *(amante de la comodidad)* comfort-lover; *(vago)* laid-back person

comoquiera ADV **c. que** whichever way, however

compa NMF *Fam* pal, *Br* mate, *US* buddy

compact ['kompak] NM INV compact disc

compacto, -a ADJ compact; **disco c.** compact disc

compadecer [33] **1** VT to feel sorry for, to pity
2 compadecerse VPR to have *o* take pity (**de** on)

compadre NM (**a**) *(padrino)* = godfather of one's child, or father of one's godchild (**b**) *Fam (amigo) Br* mate, *US* buddy

compadrear VI *RP* to brag, to boast

compadreo NM *(amistad)* friendship

compaginar VT to combine

compañerismo NM companionship, comradeship

compañero, -a NM,F companion; **c. de colegio** school friend; *Esp* **c. de piso** *Br* flatmate, *US* roommate

compañía NF company; **hacer c. (a algn)** to keep (sb) company; **c. de seguros/de teatro** insurance/theatre company

comparable ADJ comparable

comparación NF comparison; **en c.** comparatively; **en c. con** compared to; **sin c.** beyond compare

comparar VT to compare (**con** with)

comparativo, -a ADJ & NM comparative

comparecencia NF appearance

comparecer [33] VI *Der* to appear (**ante** before)

comparsa NF band of revellers

compartimento, compartimiento NM compartment; **c. de primera/segunda clase** first-/second-class compartment

compartir VT to share

compás *(pl* **compases)** NM (**a**) *Téc* (pair of) compasses (**b**) *Náut* compass (**c**) *Mús (división)* time; *(intervalo)* beat; *(ritmo)* rhythm; **c. de espera** *Mús* bar rest; *Fig (pausa)* delay; **al c. de** in time to

compasión NF compassion, pity; **tener c. (de algn)** to feel sorry (for sb)

compasivo, -a ADJ compassionate

compatible ADJ compatible

compatriota NMF compatriot; *(hombre)* fellow countryman; *(mujer)* fellow countrywoman

compendiar [43] VT to abridge, to summarize

compendio NM compendium

compenetrarse VPR to understand each other o one another

compensación NF compensation

compensar 1 VT *(pérdida, error)* to make up for; *(indemnizar)* to compensate (for)
2 VI to be worthwhile; **este trabajo no compensa** this job's not worth my while

competencia NF **(a)** *(rivalidad, empresas rivales)* competition **(b)** *(capacidad)* competence **(c)** *(incumbencia)* field, province; **no es de mi c.** it's not up to me

competente ADJ competent

competición NF competition, contest

competido, -a ADJ hard-fought

competidor, -a 1 NM,F competitor
2 ADJ competing

competir [6] VI to compete (**con** with o against; **en** in; **por** for)

competitividad NF competitivity

competitivo, -a ADJ competitive

compilar VT to compile

compinche NMF **(a)** *(compañero)* chum, pal **(b)** *(cómplice)* accomplice

complacencia NF **(a)** *(satisfacción)* satisfaction **(b)** *(indulgencia)* indulgence

> Observa que la palabra inglesa **complacency** es un falso amigo y no es la traducción de la palabra española **complacencia**. En inglés, **complacency** significa "autocomplacencia".

complacer [60] **1** VT to please; *Fml* **me complace presentarles a …** it gives me great pleasure to introduce to you …
2 complacerse VPR to delight (**en** in), to take pleasure (**en** in)

complaciente ADJ obliging

complejidad NF complexity

complejo, -a ADJ & NM complex

complementar 1 VT to complement
2 complementarse VPR to complement (each other), to be complementary to (each other)

complementario, -a ADJ complementary

complemento NM complement; *Ling* object

completamente ADV completely

completar VT to complete

completo, -a ADJ **(a)** *(terminado)* complete; **por c.** completely **(b)** *(lleno)* full; **al c.** full up

complexión NF build; **de c. fuerte** well-built

> Observa que la palabra inglesa **complexion** es un falso amigo y no es la traducción de la palabra española **complexión**. En inglés **complexion** significa "tez".

complicación NF complication

complicado, -a ADJ **(a)** *(complejo)* complicated **(b)** *(implicado)* involved

complicar [44] **1** VT **(a)** *(dificultar)* to complicate **(b)** *(involucrar)* **c. a algn en** to involve sb in
2 complicarse VPR to get complicated; **complicarse la vida** to make life difficult for oneself

cómplice NMF accomplice

complot *(pl* **complots**) NM conspiracy, plot

componente 1 ADJ component
2 NM **(a)** *(pieza)* component; *(ingrediente)* ingredient **(b)** *(persona)* member

componer [19] *(pp* **compuesto**) **1** VT **(a)** *(formar)* to compose, to make up **(b)** *Mús & Lit* to compose **(c)** *(reparar)* to mend, to repair
2 componerse VPR **(a)** *(consistir)* **componerse de** to be made up of, to consist of **(b)** *(arreglarse)* to dress up **(c)** *Fam* **componérselas** to manage

comportamiento NM behaviour

comportar 1 VT to entail, to involve
2 comportarse VPR to behave; **comportarse mal** to misbehave

composición NF composition

compositor, -a NM,F composer

compostelano, -a ADJ of/from Santiago de Compostela

compostura NF composure

compota NF compote

compra NF *(acción)* buying; *(cosa comprada)* purchase, buy; **hace** *Esp* **la c.** o *Am* **las compras** to do the shopping; **ir de compras** to go shopping

comprador, -a NM,F purchaser, buyer

comprar VT **(a)** *(adquirir)* to buy **(b)** *(sobornar)* to bribe, to buy off

compraventa NF trading; **contrato de c.** contract of sale

comprender VT **(a)** *(entender)* to understand; **se comprende** it's understandable **(b)** *(contener)* to comprise, to include

comprensible ADJ understandable

comprensión NF understanding

comprensivo, -a ADJ understanding

> Observa que la palabra inglesa **comprehensive** es un falso amigo y no es la traducción de la palabra española **comprensivo**. En inglés **comprehensive** significa "amplio, detallado".

compresa NF **(a)** *(para mujer)* sanitary *Br* towel o *US* napkin **(b)** *Med* compress

compresor, -a 1 ADJ compressing
2 NM compressor

comprimido, -a 1 NM pill, tablet
2 ADJ compressed; **escopeta de aire c.** air rifle

comprimir VT to compress

comprobación NF checking

comprobante NM *(de compra etc)* voucher, receipt

comprobar [2] VT to check

comprometer 1 VT (**a**) *(arriesgar)* to compromise, to jeopardize (**b**) *(obligar)* to compel, to force

2 **comprometerse** VPR (**a**) **comprometerse a hacer algo** to undertake to do sth (**b**) *(novios)* to become engaged

comprometido, -a ADJ (**a**) *(situación)* difficult (**b**) *(para casarse)* engaged

compromiso NM (**a**) *(obligación)* obligation, commitment; **sin c.** without obligation; **por c.** out of a sense of duty (**b**) **poner (a algn) en un c.** to put (sb) in a difficult *o* embarrassing position (**c**) *(acuerdo)* agreement; *Fml* **c. matrimonial** engagement; **soltero y sin c.** single and unattached

> Observa que la palabra inglesa **compromise** es un falso amigo y no es la traducción de la palabra española **compromiso**. En inglés, **compromise** significa "solución negociada".

compuerta NF floodgate, sluicegate

compuesto, -a 1 ADJ (**a**) *(múltiple)* compound (**b**) **c. de** composed of

2 NM compound

3 PP *de* **componer**

compulsar VT to make a certified true copy of

compungido, -a ADJ *(arrepentido)* remorseful; *(triste)* sorrowful, sad

compuse PT INDEF *de* **componer**

computacional ADJ computational, computer

computadora NF, **computador** NM *esp Am* computer

cómputo NM calculation

comulgar [42] VI to receive Holy Communion; *Fig* **no comulgo con sus ideas** I don't share his ideas

común 1 ADJ (**a**) *(compartido) (amigo, interés, acuerdo)* mutual; *(bienes, pastos)* communal; **hacer algo en c.** to do sth together; **tener algo en c.** to have sth in common (**b**) *(habitual)* common; **poco c.** unusual; **por lo c.** generally

2 NM *Br Pol* **los Comunes** the Commons

comuna NF (**a**) *(colectividad)* commune (**b**) *Am (municipalidad)* municipality

comunal ADJ communal

comunero, -a NM,F *Perú, Méx (indígena)* = member of an indigenous village community

comunicación NF (**a**) *(contacto)* communication; **ponerse en c. (con algn)** to get in touch (with sb); **se nos cortó la c.** we were cut off (**b**) *(comunicado)* communication; **c. oficial** communiqué

comunicado, -a 1 ADJ **una zona bien comunicada** a well-served zone; **dos ciudades bien comunicadas** two towns with good connections (between them)

2 NM communiqué; **c. de prensa** press release

comunicador, -a NM,F communicator

comunicar [44] 1 VT (**a**) *(transmitir) (sentimientos, ideas)* to convey; *(movimiento, virus)* to transmit (**b**) *(información)* **c. algo a algn** to inform sb of sth, to tell sb sth (**c**) *(conectar)* to connect

2 VI (**a**) *(estar conectado)* **c. con** to lead to (**b**) *Esp (por teléfono) Br* to be engaged, *US* to be busy; **está comunicando** it's *Br* engaged *o US* busy

3 **comunicarse** VPR *(hablarse)* to communicate (with each other)

comunicativo, -a ADJ communicative

comunidad NF community; **C. Europea** European Community; **C. de Estados Independientes** Commonwealth of Independent States

comunión NF communion

comunismo NM communism

comunista ADJ & NMF communist

comunitario, -a ADJ (**a**) *(de la comunidad)* community (**b**) *(de UE)* Community, of the European Union

con PREP (**a**) *(modo, manera, instrumento)* with; **córtalo c. las tijeras** cut it with the scissors; **voy cómodo c. este jersey** I'm comfortable in this sweater (**b**) *(compañía)* with; **vine c. mi hermana** I came with my sister (**c**) *(estado)* **c. ese frío/niebla** in that cold/fog; **estar c. (la) gripe** to have the flu (**d**) *(contenido)* with; **una bolsa c. dinero** a bag (full) of money (**e**) *(a)* to; **habló c. todos** he spoke to everybody; **sé amable c. ella** be nice to her (**f**) *(con infinitivo)* **c. llamar será suficiente** it will be enough just to phone (**g**) (**+ que** + *subj*) **bastará c. que lo esboces** a general idea will do (**h**) **c. tal (de) que …** provided that …; **c. todo (y eso)** even so

conato NM attempt; **c. de asesinato** attempted murder

cóncavo, -a ADJ concave

concebible ADJ conceivable, imaginable

concebir [6] 1 VT (**a**) *(plan, hijo)* to conceive (**b**) *(entender)* to understand

2 VI *(mujer)* to become pregnant, to conceive

conceder VT to grant; *(premio)* to award

concejal, -a NM,F town councillor

concejo NM council

concentración NF concentration; *(de manifestantes)* gathering; *(de coches, motos)* rally; *(de equipo)* base

concentrado NM concentrate

concentrar 1 VT to concentrate

2 **concentrarse** VPR (**a**) *(mentalmente)* to concentrate (**en** on) (**b**) *(reunirse)* to gather

concepción NF conception

concepto NM (**a**) *(idea)* concept; **tener buen/mal c. de** to have a good/a bad opinion of; **bajo** *o* **por ningún c.** under no circumstances (**b**) **en c. de** under the heading of (**c**) *(en factura)* item

concerniente ADJ **c.** (**a**) concerning, regarding; *Fml* **en lo c. a** with regard to

concernir [54] V IMPERS (**a**) *(afectar)* to concern; **en lo que a mí concierne** as far as I am concerned; **en lo que concierne a** with regard o respect to (**b**) *(corresponder)* to be up to

concertación NF compromise, agreement

concertar [1] **1** VT (**a**) *(cita)* to arrange; *(precio)* to agree on; *(acuerdo)* to reach (**b**) *(una acción etc)* to plan, to co-ordinate
2 VI to agree, to tally

concesión NF (**a**) *(de préstamo, licencia)* granting; *(de premio)* awarding (**b**) *(cesión)* *(gen)* & *Com* concession; **sin hacer concesiones (a)** without making concessions (to)

concesionario, -a NM,F dealer

concha NF (**a**) *Zool (caparazón)* shell; *(carey)* tortoiseshell (**b**) *Andes, RP Vulg (vulva)* cunt (**c**) *Ven (de árbol)* bark; *(de fruta)* peel, rind; *(del pan)* crust; *(de huevo)* shell

conchabarse VPR *Fam* to gang up

concheto, -a *RP Fam* **1** ADJ posh
2 NM,F rich kid

conchudo, -a NM,F (**a**) *Andes, Méx, Ven Fam (desfachatado)* **ser un c.** to be shameless, *Br* to have a brass neck (**b**) *Andes, Méx, Ven Fam (cómodo)* lazybones, layabout (**c**) *Perú, RP muy Fam* jerk, *Br* dickhead

conciencia NF (**a**) *(moral)* conscience; **tener la c. tranquila** to have a clear conscience (**b**) *(conocimiento)* consciousness, awareness; **a c.** conscientiously; **tener/tomar c. (de algo)** to be/to become aware (of sth)

concienciar [43], *Am* **concientizar** [40] **1** VT to make aware (**de** of)
2 concienciarse, *Am* **concientizarse** VPR to become aware (**de** of)

concienzudo, -a ADJ conscientious

concierto NM (**a**) *Mús* concert; *(composición)* concerto (**b**) *(acuerdo)* agreement

conciliación NF *(en un litigio)* reconciliation; *(en un conflicto laboral)* conciliation

conciliar [43] VT to reconcile; **c. el sueño** to get to sleep

concilio NM council

concisión NF conciseness

conciso, -a ADJ concise

conciudadano, -a NM,F fellow citizen

concluir [37] VT to conclude

conclusión NF conclusion; **sacar una c.** to draw a conclusion

concluyente ADJ conclusive

concomerse VPR to be consumed; **c. de envidia** to be green with envy

concordancia NF *también Ling* agreement

concordar [2] **1** VI to agree; **esto no concuerda con lo que dijo ayer** this doesn't fit in with

what he said yesterday
2 VT to bring into agreement

concordia NF concord

concretamente ADV specifically

concretar VT *(precisar)* to specify, to state explicitly; *(fecha, hora)* to fix

concreto, -a 1 ADJ (**a**) *(preciso, real)* concrete (**b**) *(particular)* specific; **en c.** specifically; **en el caso c. de ...** in the specific case of ...
2 NM *Am* concrete

concubina NF concubine

concurrencia NF (**a**) *(de dos cosas)* concurrence (**b**) *(público)* audience

concurrente 1 ADJ concurrent
2 NMF person present

concurrido, -a ADJ crowded, busy

concurrir VI (**a**) *(gente)* to converge (**en** on), to meet (**en** in) (**b**) *(coincidir)* to concur, to coincide (**c**) *(participar)* to compete; *(en elecciones)* to be a candidate

concursante NMF (**a**) *(en competición)* contestant, competitor (**b**) *(para un empleo)* candidate

concursar VI to compete, to take part

concurso NM (**a**) *(competición)* competition; *(de belleza etc)* contest; *TV* quiz show; **presentar (una obra) a c.** to invite tenders (for a piece of work) (**b**) *Fml (ayuda)* help

Observa que la palabra inglesa **concourse** es un falso amigo y no es la traducción de la palabra española **concurso**. En inglés, **concourse** significa "vestíbulo".

condado NM *(territorio)* county

condal ADJ of o relating to a count; **la Ciudad C.** Barcelona

conde NM count

condecoración NF decoration

condecorar VT to decorate

condena NF (**a**) *Der* sentence (**b**) *(desaprobación)* condemnation, disapproval

condenado, -a 1 ADJ (**a**) *Der* convicted; **c. a muerte** condemned to death (**b**) *Rel & Fam* damned; **c. al fracaso** doomed to failure
2 NM,F (**a**) *Der* convicted person; *(a muerte)* condemned person (**b**) *Rel* damned person

condenar 1 VT (**a**) *Der* to convict, to find guilty; **c. a algn a muerte** to condemn sb to death (**b**) *(desaprobar)* to condemn
2 condenarse VPR *Rel* to be damned

condensación NF condensation

condensado, -a ADJ condensed; **leche condensada** condensed milk

condensador NM condenser

condensar VT to condense

condesa NF countess

condescender [3] VI **c. a** *(con amabilidad)* to consent to, to accede to; *(con desprecio)* to deign to, to condescend to

condescendiente ADJ obliging

condición NF (**a**) *(estado)* condition; **en buenas/malas condiciones** in good/bad condition; **condiciones de trabajo** working conditions (**b**) *(estipulación)* condition; **con la c. de que …** on the condition that … (**c**) *(manera de ser)* nature, character (**d**) *(calidad)* **en su c. de director** in his capacity as director

condicional ADJ conditional

condicionar VT **c. algo a algo** to make sth dependent on sth; **una cosa condiciona la otra** one thing determines the other

condimentar VT to season, to flavour

condimento NM seasoning, flavouring

condolerse [4] VPR **c. de** to sympathize with

condominio NM *Am (edificio) Br* block of flats, *US* condominium

condón NM condom

condonar VT *(ofensa)* to condone; *(deuda)* to cancel

cóndor NM condor

conducción NF (**a**) *Esp (de vehículo)* driving (**b**) *(por tubería)* piping; *(por cable)* wiring

conducir [10] **1** VT *(coche)* to drive; *(electricidad)* to conduct
2 VI (**a**) *Aut* to drive; **permiso de c.** *Br* driving licence, *US* driver's license (**b**) *(camino, actitud)* to lead; **eso no conduce a nada** this leads nowhere

conducta NF behaviour, conduct; **mala c.** misbehaviour, misconduct

conducto NM (**a**) *(tubería)* pipe; *Fig* **por conductos oficiales** through official channels (**b**) *Anat* duct, canal

conductor, -a 1 NM,F *Aut* driver
2 NM *Elec* conductor

conectar VT to connect; *Elec* to plug in, to switch on

coneja NF doe rabbit

conejera NF *(madriguera)* (rabbit) warren; *(para crianza)* rabbit hutch

conejillo NM **c. de Indias** guinea pig

conejo NM rabbit

conexión NF connection

confabularse VPR to conspire, to plot

confección NF (**a**) *Cost* dressmaking, tailoring; **el ramo de la c.** the clothing *o US* garment industry (**b**) *(de un plan etc)* making, making up

confeccionar VT to make (up)

confederación NF confederation

conferencia NF (**a**) *(charla)* lecture; **dar una c. (sobre algo)** to give a lecture (on sth) (**b**) **c. de prensa** press conference (**c**) *Tel* long-distance call

conferenciante NMF lecturer

conferir [5] VT *Fml (honor, privilegio)* to confer

confesar [1] **1** VT to confess, to admit; *(crimen)* to own up to; *Rel (pecados)* to confess
2 VI *Der* to own up

3 confesarse VPR to confess; **c. culpable** to admit one's guilt; *Rel* to go to confession

confesión NF confession, admission; *Rel* confession

confesionario NM *Rel* confessional

confesor NM confessor

confeti NM confetti

confiado, -a ADJ (**a**) *(seguro)* self-confident (**b**) *(crédulo)* gullible, unsuspecting

confianza NF (**a**) *(seguridad)* confidence; **tener c. en uno mismo** to be self-confident (**b**) **de c.** reliable (**c**) **tener c. con algn** to be on intimate terms with sb; **con toda c.** in all confidence; **tomarse (demasiadas) confianzas** to take liberties

confiar [29] **1** VT *(entregar)* to entrust; *(información, secreto)* to confide
2 VI **c. en** to trust; **confío en ella** I trust her; **no confíes en su ayuda** don't count on his help
3 confiarse VPR to confide (**en** *o* in); **confiarse demasiado** to be over-confident

confidencia NF confidence

confidencial ADJ confidential

confidente, -a NM,F (**a**) *(hombre)* confidant; *(mujer)* confidante (**b**) *(de la policía)* informer

configuración NF *también Inform* configuration

configurar VT to shape, to form

confín NM limit, boundary

confinar VT *Der* to confine

confirmación NF confirmation

confirmar VT to confirm; *Prov* **la excepción confirma la regla** the exception proves the rule

confiscar [44] VT to confiscate

confitado, -a ADJ candied; **frutas confitadas** crystallized fruit

confite NM *Br* sweet, *US* candy

confitería NF (**a**) *(tienda)* confectioner's (**b**) *RP (café)* café

confitura NF preserve, jam

conflagración NF **c. mundial** world war

conflictividad NF **c. laboral** industrial unrest

conflictivo, -a ADJ *(asunto)* controversial; *(época)* unsettled; **niño c.** problem child

conflicto NM conflict; **c. laboral** industrial dispute

confluencia NF confluence

confluir [37] VI to converge; *(caminos, ríos)* to meet, to come together

conformar VT to shape
2 conformarse VPR to resign oneself, to be content

conforme 1 ADJ (**a**) *(satisfecho)* satisfied; **c.** agreed, all right; **no estoy c.** I don't agree (**b**) **c. a** in accordance *o* keeping with
2 CONJ (**a**) *(según, como)* as; **c. lo vi/lo oí** as I saw/heard it (**b**) *(a medida que)* as; **la policía los detenía c. iban saliendo** the police were arresting them as they came out

conformidad NF (a) *(aprobación)* approval, consent (b) **en c. con** in conformity with

conformismo NM conformity

conformista ADJ & NMF conformist

confort *(pl* **conforts)** NM comfort; **todo c.** *(en anuncio)* all mod cons

confortable ADJ comfortable

confortar VT to comfort

confraternizar [40] VI to fraternize

confrontación NF (a) *(enfrentamiento)* confrontation (b) *(comparación)* comparison

confrontar VT (a) *(enfrentar)* to confront (b) *(comparar)* to compare

confundir 1 VT (a) *(trastocar)* to confuse (**con** with); **c. a una persona con otra** to mistake somebody for somebody else (b) *(liar)* to confuse (c) *(abrumar)* to confound
  2 confundirse VPR (a) *(equivocarse)* to be mistaken; *Tel* **se ha confundido** you've got the wrong number (b) *(mezclarse)* to mingle; **se confundió entre el gentío** he disappeared into the crowd

confusión NF confusion

confuso, -a ADJ (a) *(explicación)* confused; *(formas, recuerdo)* blurred, vague (b) *(turbado)* confused, bewildered

congelación NF (a) *(de alimentos)* freezing (b) *Fin* freeze; **c. salarial** wage freeze (c) *Med* frostbite

congelado, -a 1 ADJ frozen; *Med* frostbitten
  2 congelados NMPL frozen food

congelador NM freezer

congelar 1 VT to freeze
  2 congelarse VPR to freeze; *Med* to get o become frostbitten; *Fam* **me estoy congelando** I'm freezing

congeniar [43] VI to get on (**con** with)

congénito, -a ADJ congenital

congestión NF congestion; *Med* **c. cerebral** stroke

congestionar 1 VT to block
  2 congestionarse VPR (a) *(calle)* to become congested (b) *(cara)* to flush, to turn purple

conglomerado NM conglomerate

conglomerar VT *Téc* to conglomerate; *(intereses, tendencias)* to unite

congoja NF sorrow, grief

congraciarse [43] VPR to ingratiate oneself (**con** with)

congratular VT *Fml* to congratulate (**por** on)

congregación NF congregation

congregar [42] **1** VT to assemble, to bring together
  2 congregarse VPR to assemble, to gather

congresista NMF (a) *(en un congreso)* delegate (b) *(político)* *(hombre)* congressman; *(mujer)* congresswoman

congreso NM congress, conference; *Pol* **C. de los Diputados** = lower house of Spanish Parliament, *Br* ≃ House of Commons, *US* ≃ House of Representatives

congrio NM conger (eel)

congruente ADJ consistent, coherent

conjetura NF conjecture; **por c.** by guesswork

conjeturar VT to conjecture

conjugación NF conjugation

conjugar [42] VT to conjugate; *Fig (planes, opiniones)* to combine

conjunción NF conjunction

conjuntar VT to co-ordinate

conjuntivitis NF INV conjunctivitis

conjunto, -a 1 NM (a) *(grupo)* collection, group (b) *(todo)* whole; **de c.** overall; **en c.** on the whole (c) *Mús (pop)* group, band (d) *(prenda)* outfit, ensemble (e) *Mat* set (f) *Dep* team
  2 ADJ joint

conjurar 1 VT to exorcise; *(peligro)* to ward off
  2 conjurarse VPR to conspire, to plot

conjuro NM (a) *(exorcismo)* exorcism (b) *(encantamiento)* spell, incantation

conllevar VT to entail

conmemoración NF commemoration

conmemorar VT to commemorate

conmigo PRON PERS with me; **vino c.** he came with me; **él habló c.** he talked to me

conminar VT to threaten, to menace

conmoción NF commotion, shock; **c. cerebral** concussion

conmocionar VT to shock; *Med* to concuss

conmovedor, -a ADJ touching; **una película conmovedora** a moving film

conmover [4] VT to touch, to move

conmutador NM (a) *Elec* switch (b) *Am Tel* switchboard

conmutar VT to exchange; *Der* to commute; *Elec* to commutate

connivencia NF connivance, collusion

connotación NF connotation

cono NM cone; **C. Sur** = Chile, Argentina, Paraguay and Uruguay

conocedor, -a ADJ & NM,F expert; *(de vino, arte etc)* connoisseur

conocer [34] **1** VT (a) *(saber acerca de)* to know; **dar (algo/algn) a c.** to make (sth/sb) known; **no conozco Rusia** I've never been to Russia (b) *(a una persona)* *(por primera vez)* to meet; *(desde hace tiempo)* to know (c) *(reconocer)* to recognize; **te conocí por la voz** I recognized you by your voice
  2 conocerse VPR *(dos personas)* *(desde hace tiempo)* to know each other; *(por primera vez)* to meet

conocido, -a 1 ADJ known; *(famoso)* well-known
  2 NM,F acquaintance

conocimiento NM (a) *(saber)* knowledge; **con c. de causa** with full knowledge of the facts (**b**) *(conciencia)* consciousness; **perder/recobrar el c.** to lose/regain consciousness (**c**) **conocimientos** knowledge

conque CONJ so

conquense 1 ADJ of/from Cuenca
2 NMF person from Cuenca

conquista NF conquest

conquistador, -a NM,F conqueror

conquistar VT (**a**) *(país, ciudad)* to conquer; *Fig (puesto, título)* to win; *(a una persona)* to win over

consabido, -a ADJ (**a**) *(bien conocido)* well-known (**b**) *(usual)* familiar, usual

consagración NF (**a**) *Rel* consecration (**b**) *(de un artista)* recognition

consagrado, -a ADJ (**a**) *Rel* consecrated (**b**) *(dedicado)* dedicated (**c**) *(reconocido)* recognized, established

consagrar 1 VT (**a**) *Rel* to consecrate (**b**) *(artista)* to confirm (**c**) *(tiempo, vida)* to devote
2 consagrarse VPR (**a**) **consagrarse a** *(dedicarse)* to devote oneself to, to dedicate oneself to (**b**) *(lograr fama)* to establish oneself

consciente ADJ (**a**) *Med* conscious; **estar c.** to be conscious (**b**) **ser c. de algo** to be aware of sth

conscripto NM *Andes, Arg* conscript

consecución NF (**a**) *(de un objetivo)* achievement (**b**) *(obtención)* obtaining

consecuencia NF (**a**) *(resultado)* consequence; **a** o **como c. de** as a consequence o result of; **en c.** therefore; **tener** o **traer (malas) consecuencias** to have (ill) effects; **sacar como** o **en c.** to come to a·conclusion (**b**) *(coherencia)* **actuar en c.** to act accordingly

consecuente ADJ consistent

consecutivo, -a ADJ consecutive; **tres días consecutivos** three days in a row

conseguir [6] VT (**a**) *(obtener)* to get, to obtain; *(objetivo)* to achieve (**b**) **conseguí terminar** I managed to finish

consejero, -a NM,F (**a**) *(asesor)* adviser (**b**) *Pol* councillor (**c**) *Com* **c. delegado** managing director

consejo NM (**a**) *(recomendación)* advice; **un c.** a piece of advice (**b**) *(junta)* council; **c. de ministros** cabinet; *(reunión)* cabinet meeting; **c. de administración** board of directors; **c. de guerra** court martial

consenso NM consensus

consensuar [30] VT to approve by consensus

consentido, -a ADJ spoiled

consentimiento NM consent

consentir [5] **1** VT (**a**) *(tolerar)* to allow, to permit; **no consientas que haga eso** don't allow him to do that (**b**) *(mimar)* to spoil
2 VI to consent; **c. en** to agree to

conserje NM *(de colegio, ministerio)* doorman, *Br* porter; *(de bloque de viviendas) Br* caretaker, *US* superintendent, *US* supervisor

conserjería NF *(de colegio, ministerio)* porter's lodge; *(de bloque de viviendas) Br* caretaker's office, *US* superintendent's o supervisor's office

conserva NF canned food, *Br* tinned food

conservación NF (**a**) *(de alimentos)* preservation (**b**) *(mantenimiento)* maintenance, upkeep

conservador, -a 1 ADJ & NM,F conservative; *Pol* Conservative
2 NM *(de museo)* curator

conservadurismo NM conservatism

conservante NM preservative

conservar 1 VT (**a**) *(mantener) (alimento)* to preserve; *(amistad)* to sustain, to keep up; *(salud)* to look after; *(calor)* to retain (**b**) *(guardar) (libros, cartas, secreto)* to keep
2 conservarse VPR (**a**) *(tradición etc)* to survive (**b**) **conservarse bien** *(persona)* to age well

conservatorio NM conservatory

considerable ADJ considerable

consideración NF (**a**) *(reflexión)* consideration; **tomar algo en c.** to take sth into consideration o account (**b**) *(respeto)* regard (**c**) **de c.** important, considerable; **herido de c.** seriously injured

considerado, -a ADJ (**a**) *(atento)* considerate, thoughtful (**b**) **estar bien/mal c.** to be well/badly thought of

considerar VT to consider; **lo considero imposible** I think it's impossible

consigna NF (**a**) *(para maletas) Br* left-luggage office, *US* checkroom (**b**) *Mil* orders, instructions

consignar VT (**a**) *(puesto)* to allocate; *(cantidad)* to assign (**b**) *(mercancía)* to ship, to dispatch

consigo¹ PRON PERS (**a**) *(tercera persona) (hombre)* with him; *(mujer)* with her; *(cosa, animal)* with it; *(plural)* with them; *(usted)* with you (**b**) **hablar c. mismo** to speak to oneself

consigo² INDIC PRES de **conseguir**

consiguiente ADJ resulting, consequent; **por c.** therefore, consequently

consistencia NF (**a**) *(de masa)* consistency (**b**) *(de argumento)* soundness

consistente ADJ (**a**) *(firme)* firm, solid (**b**) *(teoría)* sound (**c**) **c. en** consisting of

> Observa que la palabra inglesa **consistent** es un falso amigo y no es la traducción de la palabra española **consistente**. En inglés, **consistent** significa "consequente".

consistir VI to consist (**en** of); **el secreto consiste en tener paciencia** the secret lies in being patient

consistorial ADJ **casa c.** town hall

consistorio NM town o US city council

consola NF console table; *Inform* console

consolación NF consolation; **premio de c.** consolation prize

consolador, -a 1 ADJ consoling, comforting
2 NM dildo

consolar [2] **1** VT to console, to comfort
2 consolarse VPR to console oneself, to take comfort (**con** from)

consolidación NF consolidation

consolidar VT to consolidate

consomé NM clear soup, consommé

consonancia NF **en c. con** in keeping with

consonante ADJ & NF consonant

consorcio NM consortium

consorte 1 ADJ **príncipe c.** prince consort
2 NMF *(cónyuge)* partner, spouse

conspicuo, -a ADJ conspicuous

conspiración NF conspiracy, plot

conspirar VI to conspire, to plot

constancia NF **(a)** *(perseverancia)* perseverance **(b)** *(testimonio)* record; **dejar c. de algo** to put sth on record

constante 1 ADJ **(a)** *(persona) (en una empresa)* persistent; *(en ideas, opiniones)* steadfast **(b)** *(acción)* constant
2 NF constant feature; *Mat* constant

constantemente ADV constantly

constar VI **(a)** *(figurar)* to figure, to be included (**en** in); **c. en acta** to be on record **(b) me consta que ...** I am absolutely certain that ... **(c) c. de** to be made up of, to consist of

constatar VT *(observar)* to confirm; *(comprobar)* to check

constelación NF constellation

consternación NF consternation, dismay

consternar VT to dismay

constipado, -a 1 ADJ **estar c.** to have a cold o a chill
2 NM cold, chill

Observa que la palabra inglesa **constipated** es un falso amigo y no es la traducción de la palabra española **constipado**. En inglés **constipated** significa "estreñido".

constiparse VPR to catch a cold o a chill

constitución NF constitution

constitucional ADJ constitutional

constituir [37] **1** VT **(a)** *(formar)* to constitute; **estar constituido por** to consist of **(b)** *(suponer)* to represent **(c)** *(fundar)* to constitute, to set up
2 constituirse VPR **constituirse en** to set oneself up as

constituyente ADJ & NMF constituent

constreñir [6] VT **(a)** *(forzar)* to compel, to force **(b)** *(oprimir)* to restrict **(c)** *Med* to constrict

construcción NF **(a)** *(acción)* construction; *(sector)* the building industry; **en c.** under construction **(b)** *(edificio)* building

constructivo, -a ADJ constructive

constructor, -a 1 NM,F builder
2 ADJ **empresa constructora** builders, construction company

construir [37] VT to build, to manufacture

Observa que el verbo inglés **to construe** es un falso amigo y no es la traducción del verbo español **construir**. En inglés **to construe** significa "interpretar".

consuelo NM consolation

cónsul NMF consul

consulado NM consulate

consulta NF **(a)** *(sobre un problema) (acción)* consultation; *(pregunta)* query, enquiry; **obra de c.** reference book **(b)** *(despacho de médico)* Br surgery, US office; **horas de c.** surgery hours

consultar VT to consult, to seek advice (**con** from); *(libro)* to look up

consultivo, -a ADJ consultative, advisory

consultorio NM **(a)** *(de un médico)* Br surgery, US office **(b)** *Prensa* problem page, advice column

consumado, -a ADJ **(a) hecho c.** fait accompli, accomplished fact **(b)** *(artista)* consummate

consumar VT *(realizar completamente)* to complete; *(crimen)* to commit; *(el matrimonio)* to consummate

consumición NF **(a)** *(acción)* consumption **(b)** *(bebida)* drink

consumidor, -a 1 NM,F consumer
2 ADJ consuming

consumir 1 VT to consume
2 consumirse VPR *(al hervir)* to boil away; *Fig (persona)* to waste away

consumismo NM consumerism

consumo NM consumption; **bienes de c.** consumer goods; **sociedad de c.** consumer society

contabilidad NF *Com* **(a)** *(profesión)* accountancy **(b)** *(de empresa, sociedad)* accounting, book-keeping

contabilizar [40] VT *Com* to enter in the books; *Dep* to score

contable NMF *Esp* accountant

contactar VI **c. con** to contact, to get in touch with

contacto NM contact; *Aut* ignition; **perder el c.** to lose touch; **ponerse en c.** to get in touch

contado, -a 1 ADJ few and far between; **contadas veces** very seldom; **tiene los días contados** his days are numbered
2 NM **pagar al c.** to pay cash

contador, -a 1 NM,F *Am (persona)* accountant; **c. público** *Br* chartered accountant, *US*

certified public accountant
2 NM *(aparato)* meter; **c. de agua** water meter

contagiar [43] **1** VT *Med* to pass on
2 **contagiarse** VPR (**a**) *(persona)* to get infected (**b**) *(enfermedad)* to be contagious

contagio NM contagion

contagioso, -a ADJ contagious; *Fam (risa)* infectious

container *(pl* **containers)** NM *(para mercancías)* container

contaminación NF contamination; *(del aire)* pollution

contaminado, -a ADJ *(alimento)* contaminated; *(medio ambiente)* polluted

contaminar VT to contaminate; *(aire, agua)* to pollute

contante ADJ **dinero c. (y sonante)** hard *o* ready cash

contar [2] **1** VT (**a**) *(sumar)* to count (**b**) *(narrar)* to tell
2 VI (**a**) *(hacer cálculos, importar)* to count (**b**) **c. con** *(confiar en)* to count on; *(tener)* to have
3 **contarse** VPR *Fam* **¿qué te cuentas?** how's it going?

contemplación NF (**a**) *(meditación)* contemplation (**b**) *(consideración)* **contemplaciones** consideration; **tratar a algn sin contemplaciones** not to take into account sb's feelings; **nos echaron sin contemplaciones** they threw us out unceremoniously

contemplar VT to contemplate; *(considerar)* to consider; *(estipular)* to stipulate

contemporáneo, -a ADJ & NM,F contemporary

contención NF **muro de c.** retaining wall; **c. salarial** wage restraint

contencioso, -a **1** ADJ *(tema, cuestión)* contentious; *Der* litigious
2 NM *Der* legal dispute

contendiente NMF *(en una competición)* contender; *(en una guerra)* warring faction

contenedor NM container; **c. de vidrio** bottle bank

contener [24] **1** VT (**a**) *(incluir)* to contain (**b**) *(pasiones etc)* to restrain, to hold back
2 **contenerse** VPR to control oneself, to hold (oneself) back

contenido NM content, contents

contentar **1** VT (**a**) *(satisfacer)* to please (**b**) *(alegrar)* to cheer up
2 **contentarse** VPR (**a**) *(conformarse)* to make do (**con** with), to be satisfied (**con** with) (**b**) *(alegrarse)* to cheer up

contento, -a ADJ happy, pleased (**con** with)

contestación NF answer; **dar c.** to answer

contestador NM **c. automático** answering machine

contestar VT *(a pregunta)* to answer; *Fam (replicar)* to answer back

contestatario, -a ADJ anti-establishment

contexto NM context

contienda NF *(competición, combate)* contest; *(guerra)* conflict, war

contigo PRON PERS with you

contiguo, -a ADJ contiguous (**a** to), adjoining

continental ADJ continental

continente NM (**a**) *Geog* continent (**b**) *(compostura)* countenance

contingencia NF contingency

contingente **1** ADJ *Fml* possible
2 NM contingent

continuación NF continuation; **a c.** next

continuamente ADV continuously

continuar [30] VT & VI to continue, to carry on (with); **continúa en Francia** he's still in France; **continuará** to be continued

continuidad NF continuity

continuo, -a **1** ADJ (**a**) *(ininterrumpido)* continuous; *Aut* **línea continua** solid white line (**b**) *(reiterado)* continual, constant
2 NM continuum

contonearse VPR to swing one's hips

contorno NM *Mat* contour; *(línea)* outline; **c. de cintura** waist (measurement)

contorsión NF contortion

contorsionarse VPR to contort *o* twist oneself

contra **1** PREP against; **en c. de** against
2 NM **los pros y los contras** the pros and cons

contraataque NM counterattack

contrabajo NM double bass

contrabandista NMF smuggler; **c. de armas** gunrunner

contrabando NM smuggling; **c. de armas** gunrunning; **pasar algo de c.** to smuggle sth in

contracción NF contraction

contracepción NF contraception

contrachapado NM plywood

contracorriente **1** NF crosscurrent
2 ADV **ir (a) c.** to go against the tide

contradecir [12] *(pp* **contradicho)** VT to contradict

contradicción NF contradiction

contradicho, -a PP *de* **constradecir**

contradictorio, -a ADJ contradictory

contraer [25] **1** VT to contract; **c. matrimonio con algn** to marry sb
2 **contraerse** VPR to contract

contraigo INDIC PRES *de* **contraer**

contraindicación NF contraindication

contraindicado, -a ADJ **está c. beber alcohol durante el embarazo** alcohol should be avoided during pregnancy

contraje PT INDEF *de* **contraer**

contralor NM *Am (en institución, empresa)* comptroller

contraloría NF *Am (oficina)* comptroller's office

contraluz NM view against the light; **a c.** against the light

contramaestre NM (**a**) *(en buque)* boatswain (**b**) *(capataz)* foreman

contramano: a contramano LOC ADV the wrong way

contrapartida NF **en c.** in return

contrapelo: a contrapelo LOC ADV *(acariciar)* the wrong way; **su intervención iba a c. del resto** his remarks went against the general opinion; **vivir a c.** to have an unconventional lifestyle

contrapeso NM counterweight

contraportada NF back page

contraposición NF contrast

contraproducente ADJ counterproductive

contraprogramación NF *TV* competitive scheduling

contrapunto NM counterpoint

contrariamente ADV **c. a …** contrary to …

contrariar [29] VT (**a**) *(oponerse a)* to oppose, to go against (**b**) *(disgustar)* to upset

contrariedad NF (**a**) *(dificultad)* obstacle, setback (**b**) *(disgusto)* annoyance

contrario, -a 1 ADJ (**a**) *(opuesto) (dirección, sentido, idea)* opposite; *(parte)* opposing; *(equipo)* opposing; **todo lo c.** quite the contrary (**b**) *(desfavorable)* **es c. a nuestros intereses** it goes against our interests (**c**) **ser c. a algo** to be opposed to sth
2 NM,F opponent, rival
3 NF **llevar la contraria** to be contrary

contrarrestar VT to offset, to counteract

contrasentido NM **es un c.** it doesn't make sense

contraseña NF password

contrastar VT to contrast (**con** with)

contraste NM contrast

contrata NF (fixed price) contract

contratar VT (**a**) *(personal)* to hire (**b**) *(servicio, obra, mercancía)* **c. algo a algn** to contract for sth with sb

contratiempo NM setback, hitch

contratista NM,F contractor

contrato NM contract; **c. de trabajo** work contract; **c. de alquiler** lease, leasing agreement; **c. basura** short-term contract with poor conditions

contravenir [27] VT to contravene, to infringe

contraventana NF shutter

contribución NF (**a**) *(aporte)* contribution (**b**) *(impuesto)* tax

contribuir [37] 1 VT to contribute (**a** to)
2 VI to contribute

contribuyente NM,F taxpayer

contrincante NM,F rival, opponent

control NM (**a**) *(dominio, mando)* control; **c. a distancia** remote control (**b**) *(inspección)* check; *(de policía)* checkpoint

controlador, -a NM,F **c. (aéreo)** air traffic controller

controlar 1 VT (**a**) *(dominar)* to control (**b**) *(comprobar)* to check (**c**) *(vigilar)* to watch, to keep an eye on
2 **controlarse** VPR to control oneself

controversia NF controversy

controvertido, -a ADJ controversial

contumaz ADJ obstinate

contundente ADJ (**a**) *(arma)* blunt (**b**) *(argumento)* forceful, convincing

contusión NF contusion, bruise

conuco NM *Carib (parcela)* small plot of land

convalecencia NF convalescence

convaleciente ADJ & NM,F convalescent

convalidar VT to validate; *(documento)* to ratify

convencer [49] VT to convince; **c. a algn de algo** to convince sb about sth

convencimiento NM conviction; **tener el c. de que …** to be convinced that …

convención NF convention

convencional ADJ conventional

convenido, -a ADJ agreed; **según lo c.** as agreed

conveniencia NF (**a**) *(provecho)* convenience (**b**) **conveniencias sociales** social proprieties

conveniente ADJ (**a**) *(oportuno)* convenient; *(aconsejable)* advisable (**b**) *(precio)* good, fair

convenio NM agreement; **c. laboral** agreement on salary and conditions

convenir [27] VT & VI (**a**) *(acordar)* to agree; **c. una fecha** to agree on a date; **sueldo a c.** salary negotiable; **c. en** to agree on (**b**) *(ser oportuno)* to suit, to be good for; **conviene recordar que …** it's as well to remember that …

convento NM *(de monjas)* convent; *(de monjes)* monastery

convergente ADJ convergent

converger [53] VI to converge

conversación NF conversation

conversada NF *Am Fam* chat

conversar VI to converse, to talk

conversión NF conversion

converso, -a NM,F convert

convertible ADJ convertible

convertir [54] 1 VT to change, to convert
2 **convertirse** VPR (**a**) **convertirse en** to turn into, to become (**b**) *Rel* to be converted (**a** to)

convexo, -a ADJ convex

convicción NF conviction; **tengo la c. de que …** I am convinced that …

convicto, -a ADJ convicted

convidado, -a ADJ & NM,F guest

convidar VT to invite

convincente ADJ convincing

convite NM reception

convivencia NF life together; *Fig* coexistence

convivir VI to live together; *Fig* to coexist (**con** with)

convocar [44] VT to summon; *(reunión, elecciones)* to call

convocatoria NF (**a**) *(a huelga etc)* call (**b**) *Educ* diet

convulsión NF *Med* convulsion; *(agitación social)* upheaval

convulsivo, -a ADJ convulsive

conyugal ADJ conjugal; **vida c.** married life

cónyuge NMF spouse; **cónyuges** married couple, husband and wife

coña NF *Esp muy Fam* **está de c.** he's just pissing around

coñac (*pl* **coñacs**) NM brandy, cognac

coñazo NM *Esp muy Fam* pain, drag; **dar el c.** to be a real pain

coño *esp Esp Vulg* **1** NM cunt, twat
2 INTERJ *(enfado)* for fuck's sake!

cooperación NF co-operation

cooperador, -a NM,F collaborator, co-operator

cooperante NMF (overseas) volunteer worker

cooperar VI to co-operate (**con** with)

cooperativa NF co-operative

coordenada NF co-ordinate

coordinación NF co-ordination

coordinador, -a NM,F co-ordinator

coordinadora NF co-ordinating committee; **c. general** joint committee

coordinar VT to co-ordinate

copa NF (**a**) *(para beber)* glass; **tomar una c.** to have a drink (**b**) *(de árbol)* top (**c**) *Dep* cup (**d**) *Naipes* **copas** = suit in Spanish deck of cards, with the symbol of a goblet

copar VT to monopolize

copartícipe NMF *(en empresa)* partner; *(en actividad)* participant

Copenhague N Copenhagen

copeo NM *Fam* drinking; **ir de c.** to go out drinking

copetín NM *RP (bebida)* aperitif; *(comida)* appetizer

copia NF copy; *Inform* **c. de seguridad** backup; *Inform* **hacer una c. de seguridad de algo** to back sth up

copiar [43] VT to copy

copiloto NM *Av* copilot; *Aut* co-driver

copioso, -a ADJ abundant, copious

copistería NF copy shop

copla NF verse, couplet

copo NM flake; *(de nieve)* snowflake; **copos de maíz** cornflakes

coproducción NF co-production, joint production

cópula NF (**a**) *(coito)* copulation, intercourse (**b**) *Ling* conjunction

copular VT to copulate (**con** with)

coqueta NF dressing table

coquetear VI to flirt (**con** with)

coqueto, -a 1 ADJ coquettish
2 NM,F flirt

coraje NM (**a**) *(valor)* courage (**b**) *(ira)* anger, annoyance; *Fig* **dar c. a algn** to infuriate sb; **¡qué c.!** how maddening!

coral¹ NM *Zool* coral

coral² NF *Mús* choral, chorale

Corán NM *Rel* **el C.** the Koran

coránico, -a ADJ *Rel* Koranic

coraza NF (**a**) *(de soldado)* cuirasse (**b**) *(de tortuga)* shell (**c**) *(protección)* shield

corazón NM (**a**) *(de persona, animal)* heart; *Fig* **de (todo) c.** in all sincerity; *Fig* **tener buen c.** to be kind-hearted (**b**) *(parte central)* heart; *(de fruta)* core (**c**) *Naipes* **corazones** hearts

corazonada NF hunch, feeling

corbata NF tie, *US* necktie; **con c.** wearing a tie

Córcega N Corsica

corchea NF *Mús Br* quaver, *US* eighth note

corchete NM (**a**) *Impr* square bracket (**b**) *Cost* hook and eye

corcho NM cork; *(de pesca)* float

cordel NM rope, cord

cordero, -a NM,F lamb

cordial ADJ cordial, warm

cordialidad NF cordiality, warmth

cordillera NF mountain chain *o* range

córdoba NM *Fin* cordoba, = monetary unit of Nicaragua

cordón NM (**a**) *(de zapatos)* lace; *(cable eléctrico)* flex; *Anat* **c. umbilical** umbilical cord; **c. policial** police cordon (**b**) *CSur, Cuba (de la vereda) Br* kerb, *US* curb

cordura NF common sense

Corea N Korea; **C. del Norte/Sur** North/South Korea

coreano, -a ADJ & NM,F Korean

corear VT *(exclamando)* to chorus; *(cantando)* to sing

coreografía NF choreography

corista 1 NMF *(en coro)* chorus singer
2 NF *(en cabaret)* chorus girl

cornada NF *Taurom* goring

cornamenta NF (**a**) *(de toro)* horns; *(de ciervo)* antlers (**b**) *Fam Fig (de marido engañado)* cuckold's horns

córnea NF cornea

corneja NF crow

córner (*pl* **córners**) NM *Dep* corner (kick); **sacar un c.** to take a corner

corneta NF bugle; **c. de llaves** cornet

cornete NM (**a**) *Anat* turbinate bone (**b**) *(helado)* cornet, cone

cornisa NF cornice

cornudo NM *Fam (marido)* cuckold

coro NM *Mús* choir; *Teatro* chorus; *Fig* **a c.** all together

corona NF (**a**) *(de rey)* crown (**b**) *(de flores etc)* wreath, garland; **c. funeraria** funeral wreath

coronación NF (**a**) *(de monarca)* coronation (**b**) *(remate, colmo)* culmination

coronar VT to crown

coronel NM colonel

coronilla NF crown of the head; *Fam* **estar hasta la c. (de)** to be fed up (with)

corpiño NM *(vestido)* bodice; *Arg (sostén)* bra

corporación NF corporation

corporal ADJ corporal; **castigo c.** corporal punishment; **olor c.** body odour, BO

corporativo, -a ADJ corporative

corpulento, -a ADJ corpulent, stout

corral NM farmyard, *US* corral; *(de casa)* courtyard

correa NF (**a**) *(tira)* strap; *(de reloj)* watchstrap; *(de pantalón)* belt; *(de perro)* lead, leash (**b**) *Téc* belt

corrección NF (**a**) *(rectificación)* correction (**b**) *(urbanidad)* courtesy, politeness

correcto, -a ADJ (**a**) *(sin errores)* correct (**b**) *(educado)* polite, courteous (**con** to); *(conducta)* proper

corredera NF **puerta/ventana de c.** sliding door/window

corredizo, -a ADJ sliding; **nudo c.** slipknot; **techo c.** sunroof

corredor, -a NM,F (**a**) *Dep* runner (**b**) *Fin* **c. de bolsa** stockbroker

corregir [58] **1** VT to correct
2 corregirse VPR to mend one's ways

correo NM (**a**) *Br* post, *US* mail; **echar algo al c.** to *Br* post o *US* mail sth; **por c.** by *Br* post o *US* mail; **c. aéreo** airmail; *Inform* **c. basura** spam; **c. certificado** registered *Br* post o *US* mail; *Inform* **c. electrónico** electronic mail, e-mail; *Inform* **me envió un c. (electrónico)** *(un mensaje)* she e-mailed me, she sent me an e-mail; **(tren) c.** mail train (**b**) *Esp* **Correos** *(institución)* the post office

correr 1 VI (**a**) to run; *(coche)* to go fast; *(conductor)* to drive fast; *(viento)* to blow; *Fig* **no corras, habla más despacio** don't rush, speak slower; **c. prisa** to be urgent (**b**) **c. con los gastos** to foot the bill; **corre a mi cargo** I'll take care of it
2 VT (**a**) *(cortina)* to draw; *(cerrojo)* to close; *(aventura etc)* to have; **c. el riesgo** o **peligro** to run the risk (**b**) *(mover)* to pull up, to draw up
3 correrse VPR (**a**) *(moverse)* to move over (**b**) *Fam* **correrse una juerga** to go on a spree (**c**) *Andes, Esp muy Fam (tener un orgasmo)* to come

correspondencia NF (**a**) *(relación, correo)* correspondence (**b**) *(de metro, tren)* connection

corresponder 1 VI (**a**) *(compensar)* **c. (con algo)** a algn/algo to repay sb/sth (with sth) (**b**) *(competer)* **c. a algn hacer algo** to be sb's responsibility to do sth (**c**) *(coincidir)* to correspond (**a/con** to/with) (**d**) *(pertenecer)*

me dieron lo que me correspondía they gave me my share
2 corresponderse VPR (**a**) *(ajustarse)* to correspond (**b**) *(dos cosas)* to tally; **no se corresponde con la descripción** it does not match the description (**c**) *(dos personas)* to love each other

correspondiente ADJ corresponding (**a** to)

corresponsal NMF correspondent

corrida NF **c. (de toros)** bullfight

corrido, -a ADJ (**a**) *(avergonzado)* abashed (**b**) **de c.** without stopping; **se lo sabe de c.** she knows it by heart

corriente 1 ADJ (**a**) *(común)* common (**b**) *(agua)* running (**c**) *(mes, año)* current, present; **el diez del c.** the tenth of this month (**d**) *Fin (cuenta)* current (**e**) **estar al c.** to be up to date
2 NF (**a**) *(de agua)* current, stream; *Fig* **ir** o **navegar contra c.** to go against the tide; *Fam* **seguirle** o **llevarle la c. a algn** to humour sb; *Elec* **c. eléctrica** (electric) current (**b**) *(de aire)* *Br* draught, *US* draft (**c**) *(tendencia)* trend, current

corrijo INDIC PRES *de* **corregir**

corrillo NM small group of people talking; *Fig* clique

corro NM (**a**) *(círculo)* circle, ring (**b**) *(juego)* ring-a-ring-a-roses

corroborar VT to corroborate

corroer [38] VT to corrode; *Fig* **la envidia le corroe** envy eats away at him

corromper 1 VT (**a**) *(pudrir)* to turn bad, to rot (**b**) *(pervertir)* to corrupt, to pervert
2 corromperse VPR (**a**) *(pudrirse)* to go bad, to rot (**b**) *(pervertirse)* to become corrupted

corrosivo, -a ADJ corrosive; *Fig (mordaz)* caustic

corrupción NF (**a**) *(delito, decadencia)* corruption; *Der* **c. de menores** corruption of minors (**b**) *(de sustancia)* decay

corrupto, -a ADJ corrupt

corsé NM corset

corsetería NF ladies' underwear shop

cortacésped NM o NF lawnmower

cortado, -a 1 ADJ (**a**) *(leche)* sour (**b**) *(labios)* chapped (**c**) *Fam (tímido)* shy
2 NM = small coffee with a dash of milk

cortafuego NM firebreak

cortante ADJ (**a**) *(afilado)* sharp (**b**) *Fig (tajante) (frase, estilo)* cutting; *(viento)* biting; *(frío)* bitter

cortapisa NF restriction, limitation

cortar 1 VT (**a**) to cut; *(carne)* to carve; *(árbol)* to cut down; *Fam* **c. por lo sano** to take drastic measures; *Fam* **cortó con su novio** she split up with her boyfriend (**b**) *(piel)* to chap, to crack (**c**) *(luz, teléfono)* to cut off (**d**) *(paso, carretera)* to block
2 cortarse VPR (**a**) *(herirse)* to cut oneself (**b**) **cortarse el pelo** to have one's hair cut (**c**)

(leche etc) to curdle (**d**) *Tel* **se cortó la comunicación** we were cut off (**e**) *Fam (aturdirse)* to become all shy

cortaúñas NM INV nail clippers

corte¹ NM (**a**) *(distancia, tiempo)* cut; **c. de pelo** haircut; **c. de mangas** ≃ V-sign; *TV* **c. publicitario** commercial break (**b**) *(sección)* section; **c. transversal** cross section (**c**) *Fam* rebuff; **dar un c. a algn** to cut sb dead

corte² NF (**a**) *(real)* court (**b**) *Esp* **las Cortes** (Spanish) Parliament

cortejar VT to court

cortejo NM (**a**) *(galanteo)* courting (**b**) *(comitiva)* entourage, retinue; **c. fúnebre** funeral cortège

cortés *(pl* **corteses**) ADJ courteous, polite

cortesía NF courtesy, politeness

corteza NF *(de árbol)* bark; *(de queso)* rind; *(de pan)* crust

cortijo NM Andalusian farm o farmhouse

cortina NF curtain; **c. de humo** smoke screen

corto, -a 1 ADJ (**a**) *(distancia, tiempo)* short; *Fam* **c. de luces** dim-witted; **c. de vista** short-sighted; *Aut* **luz corta** dipped headlights (**b**) *Fam* **quedarse c.** *(calcular mal)* to underestimate (**c**) *(apocado)* timid, shy
2 NM *Cin* short (movie o *Br* film)

cortocircuito NM short circuit

cortometraje NM short (movie o *Br* film)

corvo, -a ADJ curved, bent

cosa NF (**a**) thing; **no he visto c. igual** I've never seen anything like it; **no ser gran c.** not to be up to much (**b**) *(asunto)* matter, business; **eso es c. tuya** that's your business o affair; **eso es otra c.** that's different (**c**) **hace c. de una hora** about an hour ago

coscorrón NM knock o blow on the head

cosecha NF (**a**) *Agr* harvest, crop (**b**) *(año del vino)* vintage

cosechadora NF combine harvester

cosechar VT to harvest; to gather (in)

coser VT (**a**) *(tejido)* to sew; *Fam* **es c. y cantar** it's a piece of cake (**b**) *Med* to stitch up

cosmético, -a ADJ & NM cosmetic

cósmico, -a ADJ cosmic

cosmonauta NMF cosmonaut

cosmopolita ADJ & NMF cosmopolitan

cosmos NM INV cosmos

coso NM (**a**) *Taurom* bullring (**b**) *CSur Fam (objeto)* whatnot, thing; **¿para qué sirve ese c.?** *(en aparato)* what's this thing o thingumajig for?

cosquillas NFPL tickling; **hacer c. a algn** to tickle sb; **tener c.** to be ticklish

cosquilleo NM tickling

costa¹ NF coast; *(litoral)* coastline; *(playa)* beach, seaside

costa² NF **a c. de** at the expense of; **a toda c.** at all costs, at any price; **vive a c. mía** he lives off me

costado NM side; **de c.** sideways; **es catalana por los cuatro costados** she's Catalan through and through

costal NM sack

costanera NF *CSur* promenade

costar [2] VI (**a**) *(precio)* to cost; **¿cuánto cuesta?** how much is it?; **c. barato/caro** to be cheap/expensive (**b**) *Fig* **te va a c. caro** you'll pay dearly for this; **c. trabajo** o **mucho** to be hard; **me cuesta hablar francés** I find it difficult to speak French; **cueste lo que cueste** at any cost

Costa Rica N Costa Rica

costarricense ADJ & NMF, **costarriqueño, -a** ADJ & NMF Costa Rican

coste NM *Esp* cost; **a precio de c.** (at) cost price; **c. de la vida** cost of living

costear 1 VT to afford, to pay for; **c. los gastos** to foot the bill
2 costearse VPR to pay for

costero, -a 1 ADJ coastal; **ciudad costera** seaside town
2 NF *Méx* promenade

costilla NF (**a**) *Anat* rib (**b**) *Culin* cutlet

costo¹ NM cost

costo² NM *Esp Fam (hachís)* dope, shit, stuff

costoso, -a ADJ costly, expensive

costra NF crust; *Med* scab

costumbre NF (**a**) *(hábito)* habit; **como de c.** as usual; **tengo la c. de levantarme temprano** I usually get up early; **tenía la c. de …** he used to … (**b**) *(tradición)* custom

costura NF (**a**) *(acción)* sewing (**b**) *(confección)* dressmaking; **alta c.** haute couture (**c**) *(línea de puntadas)* seam

costurera NF seamstress

costurero NM sewing basket

cota NF *Geog* height above sea level; *Fig* rating

cotejar VT to compare

cotidiano, -a ADJ daily; **vida cotidiana** everyday life

cotilla NMF *Esp Fam* busybody, gossip

cotillear VI *Esp Fam* to gossip (**de** about)

cotilleo NM *Esp Fam* gossip

cotillón NM = party on New Year's Eve or 5th of January

cotización NF (**a**) *Fin* (market) price, quotation (**b**) *(cuota)* membership fees, subscription

cotizar [40] **1** VT *Fin* to quote
2 VI to pay national insurance
3 cotizarse VPR *Fin* **cotizarse a** to sell at

coto NM (**a**) *(lugar)* enclosure, reserve; **c. de caza** game reserve (**b**) **poner c. a** to put a stop to

cotorra NF parrot; *Fig (persona)* chatterbox

country (pl **countries**) NM *Arg* = luxury suburban housing development

coyote NM coyote, prairie wolf

coyuntura NF (a) *Anat* articulation, joint (b) *Fig (circunstancia)* juncture; **la c. económica** the economic situation

coz NF kick; **dar una c.** to kick

C.P. (*abr* **código postal**) *Br* postcode, *US* zip code

crac(k) NM (a) *Fin* crash (b) *(droga)* crack

cráneo NM cranium, skull

cráter NM crater

creación NF creation

creador, -a NM,F creator

crear VT to create

creatividad NF creativity

creativo, -a ADJ creative

crecer [33] VI to grow; **c. en importancia** to become more important

creces NFPL **con c.** fully, in full; **devolver con c.** to return with interest

crecido, -a ADJ *(persona)* grown-up

creciente ADJ growing, increasing; **cuarto c.** crescent

crecimiento NM growth

credencial ADJ credential; **(cartas) credenciales** credentials

credibilidad NF credibility

crédito NM (a) *Com & Fin* credit (b) *(confianza)* belief; **dar c. a** to believe

credo NM creed

crédulo, -a ADJ credulous, gullible

creencia NF belief

creer [36] **1** VT (a) *(estar convencido de)* to believe (b) *(pensar)* to think; **creo que no** I don't think so; **creo que sí** I think so; **ya lo creo** I should think so
2 VI to believe; **c. en** to believe in
3 creerse VPR (a) *(considerarse)* to consider oneself to be; **¿qué te has creído?** what *o* who do you think you are? (b) **no me lo creo** I can't believe it

creíble ADJ credible, believable

creído, -a 1 ADJ arrogant, vain
2 NM,F big head

crema NF cream

cremallera NF *Br* zip (fastener), *US* zipper

crematorio NM **(horno) c.** crematorium

cremoso, -a ADJ creamy

crepe NM crêpe, pancake

crepería NF creperie

crepitar VI to crackle

crepúsculo NM twilight

crespo, -a ADJ frizzy

crespón NM crepe

cresta NF (a) *(de gallo)* comb; *(de punk)* Mohican (b) *(de ola, montaña)* crest

Creta N Crete

cretino, -a 1 ADJ stupid, cretinous
2 NM,F cretin

creyente NMF believer

crezco INDIC PRES *de* **crecer**

cría NF (a) *(cachorro)* young (b) *(crianza)* breeding, raising

criada NF maid

criadero NM nursery

criadilla NF *Culin* bull's testicle

criado, -a 1 ADJ **mal c.** spoilt
2 NM,F servant

crianza NF *(de animales)* breeding; *Fig* **vinos de c.** vintage wines

criar [29] VT (a) *(animales)* to breed, to raise; *(niños)* to bring up, to rear (b) *(producir)* to have, to grow

criatura NF (a) *(ser)* (living) creature (b) *(crío)* baby, child

criba NF sieve

cribar VT to sieve, to sift

crimen NM murder; **c. de guerra** war crime

criminal NMF & ADJ criminal

crin NF, **crines** NFPL mane

crío, -a 1 NM *Fam* kid
2 ADJ babyish

criollo, -a ADJ & NM,F Creole

críquet NM cricket

crisantemo NM chrysanthemum

crisis NF INV crisis; **c. nerviosa** nervous breakdown

crispación NF tension

crispar VT to make tense; *Fig* **eso me crispa los nervios** that sets my nerves on edge

cristal NM (a) *(material)* crystal; **c. de roca** rock crystal (b) *Esp (vidrio)* glass; *(de gafas)* lens; *(de ventana)* (window) pane

cristalera NF *(puerta)* French window; *(ventana)* large window

cristalería NF (a) *(conjunto)* glassware (b) *(tienda)* glazier's (shop)

cristalino, -a ADJ crystal clear

cristalizar [40] VI to crystallize

cristiandad NF Christendom

cristianismo NM Christianity

cristiano, -a ADJ & NM,F Christian

Cristo NM Christ

criterio NM (a) *(pauta)* criterion (b) *(opinión)* opinion (c) *(discernimiento)* discretion; **lo dejo a tu c.** I'll leave it up to you

crítica NF (a) *(ataque)* criticism (b) *Prensa* review; **tener buena c.** to get good reviews (c) *(conjunto de críticos)* critics

criticar [44] **1** VT to criticize
2 VI *(murmurar)* to gossip

crítico, -a 1 ADJ critical
2 NM,F critic

criticón, -ona NM,F *Fam* fault-finder

Croacia N Croatia

croar VI to croak

croata 1 ADJ Croatian
2 NMF Croat, Croatian

croché NM crochet

croissant [krwa'san] (*pl* **croissants**) NM croissant

croissantería [krwasante'ria] NF = shop selling filled croissants

crol NM crawl

cromo NM (**a**) (*metal*) chromium, chrome (**b**) *Esp* (*estampa*) picture card

cromosoma NM chromosome

crónica NF (**a**) (*de la historia*) chronicle (**b**) *Prensa* feature, article

crónico, -a ADJ chronic

cronista NMF *Prensa* feature writer

cronología NF chronology

cronológico, -a ADJ chronological

cronometrar VT to time

cronómetro NM stopwatch

croqueta NF croquette

croquis NM INV sketch

cross NM INV *Dep* (*carrera*) cross-country race; (*deporte*) cross-country (running)

cruce NM (**a**) (*de líneas, paso*) crossing; (*de carreteras*) crossroads; (*de razas*) crossbreeding (**b**) *Tel* crossed line

crucero NM *Náut* cruise; (*barco*) cruiser

crucial ADJ crucial

crucificar [44] VT to crucify

crucifijo NM crucifix

crucigrama NM crossword (puzzle)

crudeza NF (**a**) (*de clima*) harshness (**b**) (*de descripción, imágenes*) brutality, harsh realism

crudo, -a 1 ADJ (**a**) (*natural*) raw; (*comida*) undercooked (**b**) (*clima*) harsh; *Fam Fig* **lo veo muy c.** it doesn't look too good (**c**) (*color*) cream
2 NM (*petróleo*) crude

cruel ADJ cruel

crueldad NF cruelty

cruento, -a ADJ bloody

crujido NM (*de madera*) creak, creaking

crujiente ADJ (*comida*) crunchy

crujir VI (*madera*) to creak; (*comida*) to crunch; (*dientes*) to grind

crustáceo NM crustacean

cruz NF (**a**) (*figura*) cross; **C. Roja** Red Cross; **c. gamada** swastika (**b**) **¿cara o c.?** ≃ heads or tails?

cruza NF *Am* cross, crossbreed

cruzada NF crusade

cruzado, -a 1 ADJ (**a**) (*cheque, piernas, brazos*) crossed (**b**) (*abrigo, chaqueta*) double-breasted (**c**) (*atravesado*) lying across (**d**) (*animal*) crossbred
2 NM *Hist* crusader

cruzar [40] **1** VT (**a**) (*lugar, piernas*) to cross (**b**) (*palabras, miradas*) to exchange (**c**) (*animal, planta*) to cross, to crossbreed
2 VI (*atravesar*) to cross
3 cruzarse VPR to cross; **cruzarse con algn** to pass sb

cta. *Com* (*abr* **cuenta**) a/c

cta. cte. *Com* (*abr* **cuenta corriente**) c/a

cte. (*abr* **corriente**) inst.

cuaderno NM notebook

cuadra NF (**a**) (*establo*) stable (**b**) *Am* (*en calle*) block (**c**) *Perú* (*recibidor*) reception room

cuadrado, -a 1 ADJ (**a**) *Geom* square (**b**) (*complexión física*) broad, stocky (**c**) *Fig* (*mente*) rigid
2 NM (**a**) *Geom* square (**b**) *Mat* square; **elevar (un número) al c.** to square (a number)

cuadrar 1 VT (**a**) *Mat* to square (**b**) *Andes* (*aparcar*) to park
2 VI (*coincidir*) to square, agree (**con** with); (*sumas, cifras*) to tally
3 cuadrarse VPR (*soldado*) to stand to attention

cuadriculado, -a ADJ **papel c.** square paper

cuadrilátero, -a 1 ADJ quadrilateral
2 NM (*en boxeo*) ring

cuadrilla NF (*equipo*) gang, team; *Mil* squad; *Taurom* bullfighter's team

cuadro NM (**a**) *Geom* square; **tela a cuadros** checked cloth (**b**) *Arte* painting, picture (**c**) *Teatro* scene (**d**) *Elec & Téc* panel; **c. de mandos** control panel (**e**) (*gráfico*) chart, graph

cuádruple ADJ quadruple, fourfold

cuajada NF curd

cuajar 1 VT (*leche*) to curdle; (*sangre*) to clot
2 VI (**a**) (*nieve*) to lie (**b**) (*moda*) to catch on; (*plan*) to get off the ground

cual 1 PRON REL (*precedido de artículo*) (**a**) (*persona*) (*sujeto*) who; (*objeto*) whom (**b**) (*cosa*) which
2 PRON (**a**) **tal c.** exactly as (**b**) *Literario* (*comparativo*) such as, like

cuál PRON (**a**) (*interrogativo*) which (one)?, what?; **¿c. quieres?** which one do you want? (**b**) (*en oraciones distributivas*) **a c. más tonto** each more stupid than the other

cualidad NF quality

cualificado, -a ADJ qualified

cualquier ADJ INDEF any; **c. cosa** anything; **en c. momento** at any moment *o* time

cualquiera (*pl* **cualesquiera**) **1** ADJ (**a**) (*indefinido*) any; **un profesor c.** any teacher (**b**) (*corriente*) ordinary

> Note that **cualquier** is used before singular nouns (e.g. **cualquier hombre** any man).

2 PRON INDEF (**a**) (*persona*) anybody; **c. te lo puede decir** anybody can tell you (**b**) (*cosa, animal*) any one (**c**) **c. que sea** whatever it is
3 NMF *Fig* **ser un c.** to be a nobody; **es una c.** she's a tart

cuando 1 ADV *(de tiempo)* when; **c. más** at the most; **c. menos** at least; **de c. en c., de vez en c.** from time to time
2 CONJ (**a**) *(temporal)* when; **c. quieras** whenever you want; **c. vengas** when you come (**b**) *(condicional) (si)* if (**c**) *(concesiva) (aunque)* (**aun**) c. even if
3 PREP during, at the time of; **c. la guerra** during the war; **c. niño** as a child
cuándo ADV INTERR when?; **¿desde c.?** since when?; **¿para c. lo quieres?** when do you want it for?
cuantía NF quantity, amount
cuantioso, -a ADJ substantial, considerable
cuanto, -a 1 ADJ all; **gasta c. dinero gana** he spends all the money *o* as much as he earns; **unas cuantas niñas** a few girls
2 PRON REL as much as; **coma c. quiera** eat as much as you want; **regala todo c. tiene** he gives away everything he's got
3 PRON INDEF PL **unos cuantos** a few
4 ADV (**a**) *(tiempo)* **c. antes** as soon as possible; **en c.** as soon as (**b**) *(cantidad)* **c. más … más** the more … the more; **c. más lo miro, más me gusta** the more I look at it, the more I like it; **cuantas más personas (haya) mejor** the more the merrier (**c**) **en c. a** with respect to, regarding; **en c. a Juan** as for Juan, as far as Juan is concerned
cuánto, -a 1 ADJ & PRON INTERR *(singular)* how much?; *(plural)* how many?; **¿cuántas veces?** how many times?; **¿c. es?** how much is it?
2 ADV how, how much; **¡cuánta gente hay!** what a lot of people there are!
cuarenta ADJ & NM INV forty; *Fam* **cantarle a algn las c.** to give sb a piece of one's mind
cuarentena NF *Med* quarantine
cuarentón, -ona NM,F forty-year-old
cuaresma NF Lent
cuartear 1 VT to cut *o* chop up
2 cuartearse VPR to crack
cuartel NM *Mil* barracks; **c. general** headquarters; *Fig* **no dar c.** to give no quarter
cuartelazo NM military uprising, revolt
cuartelillo NM *Mil* post, station
cuarteto NM quartet
cuartilla NF sheet of paper
cuarto, -a 1 NM (**a**) *(habitación)* room; **c. de baño** bathroom; **c. de estar** living room (**b**) *(cuarta parte)* quarter; **c. de hora** quarter of an hour; *Dep* **cuartos de final** quarter finals (**c**) *Fam* **cuartos** *(dinero)* dough, money
2 ADJ & NM,F fourth
cuarzo NM quartz
cuate NM,F *CAm, Ecuad, Méx* (**a**) *Fam (amigo)* pal, *US* buddy (**b**) *Fam (persona) (hombre)* guy, *Br* bloke; *(mujer)* woman
cuatro 1 ADJ & NM INV four
2 NM *Fam* a few; **cayeron c. gotas** it rained a little bit
cuatrocientos, -as ADJ & NM four hundred

Cuba N Cuba
cuba NF cask, barrel; *Fam* **como una c.** (as) drunk as a lord
cubalibre NM rum/gin and coke
cubano, -a ADJ & NM,F Cuban
cubata NM *Fam* = **cubalibre**
cubertería NF cutlery
cubeta NF *(cuba pequeña)* bucket, pail; *(de barómetro)* bulb; *Fot* tray
cúbico, -a ADJ cubic; *Mat* **raíz cúbica** cube root
cubierta NF (**a**) *(de libro, cama)* cover (**b**) *(de rueda)* tyre (**c**) *(de barco)* deck
cubierto, -a 1 ADJ (**a**) *(tapado)* covered; *(piscina)* indoors; *(cielo)* overcast (**b**) *(trabajo, plaza)* filled
2 NM (**a**) *(en la mesa)* place setting (**b**) **cubiertos** cutlery
3 PP *de* **cubrir**
cubil NM lair
cubismo NM cubism
cubito NM little cube; **c. de hielo** ice cube
cúbito NM *Anat* ulna
cubo NM (**a**) *(recipiente)* bucket; **c. de la basura** *Br* rubbish bin, *US* garbage can (**b**) *Mat* cube (**c**) *(de rueda)* hub
cubrecama NM bedspread
cubrir *(pp* **cubierto)** **1** VT to cover
2 cubrirse VPR *(cielo)* to become overcast
cucaracha NF cockroach
cuchara NF spoon
cucharada NF spoonful; **c. rasa/colmada** level/heaped spoonful
cucharilla NF teaspoon; **c. de café** coffee spoon
cucharón NM ladle
cuchichear VI to whisper
cuchicheo NM whispering
cuchilla NF blade; **c. de afeitar** razor blade
cuchillada NF, **cuchillazo** NM stab
cuchillo NM knife
cuchitril NM *Fam* hovel, hole
cuclillas NFPL **en c.** squatting; **ponerse en c.** to squat (down)
cuco, -a 1 NM cuckoo
2 ADJ *Fam (astuto)* shrewd, crafty
cucurucho NM (**a**) *(para helado)* cornet (**b**) *(de papel)* paper cone
cuello NM (**a**) *(de persona, animal, botella)* neck (**b**) *(de prendas)* collar
cuenca NF (**a**) *Geog* basin (**b**) *(del ojo)* socket
cuenco NM earthenware bowl
cuenta NF (**a**) *(factura)* bill; *(en restaurante) Br* bill, *US* check (**b**) *Fin (de banco)* account; **c. corriente** *Br* current account, *US* checking account (**c**) *(cálculo)* count; **hacer cuentas** to do sums; **c. atrás** countdown (**d**) *(de collar)* bead (**e**) *Inform* account; **c. de correo (electrónico)** e-mail account (**f**) *(locuciones)* **caer en la c., darse c.** to realize; **dar c. to**

report; **tener en c.** to take into account; **traer c.** to be worthwhile; **más sillas de la c.** too many chairs; **en resumidas cuentas** in short; **pedir cuentas** to ask for an explanation; **trabajar por c. propia** to be self-employed

cuentagotas NM INV dropper

cuentakilómetros NM INV *(distancia)* Br ≃ mileometer, US ≃ odometer; *(velocidad)* speedometer

cuento NM story; *Lit* short story; **contar un c.** to tell a story; **contar un c.** that's beside the point; **c. chino** tall story; **c. de hadas** fairy story

cuerda NF (**a**) *(cordel)* rope; *Fig* **bajo c.** dishonestly; **c. floja** tightrope; **cuerdas vocales** vocal cords (**b**) *(de instrumento)* string (**c**) *(del reloj)* spring; **dar c. al reloj** to wind up a watch

cuerdo, -a ADJ sane

cueriza NF *Andes Fam* beating, leathering

cuerno NM horn; *(de ciervo)* antler; *Fam* **¡vete al c.!** get lost!; *Fig* **ponerle cuernos a algn** to be unfaithful to sb

cuero NM (**a**) *(piel)* leather; **chaqueta de c.** leather jacket (**b**) **c. cabelludo** scalp; *Fam* **en cueros (vivos)** (stark) naked

cuerpo NM (**a**) *(cuerpo)* body; **de c. entero** full-length; *Fig* **tomar c.** to take shape (**b**) *(cadáver)* corpse; **de c. presente** lying in state (**c**) *(parte)* section, part (**d**) *(grupo)* corps, force; **c. de bomberos** Br fire brigade, US fire department; **c. diplomático** diplomatic corps

cuervo NM raven

cuesta 1 NF slope; **c. abajo** downhill; **c. arriba** uphill
2 **a cuestas** LOC ADV on one's back *o* shoulders

cuestión NF (**a**) *(asunto)* matter, question; **es c. de vida o muerte** it's a matter of life or death; **en c. de unas horas** in just a few hours (**b**) *(pregunta)* question

cuestionario NM questionnaire

cueva NF cave

cuezo INDIC PRES *de* cocer

cuico, -a NM,F *Méx Fam* cop

cuidado 1 NM care; **con c.** carefully; **tener c.** to be careful; **estar al c. de** *(cosa)* to be in charge of; *(persona)* to look after; **me trae sin c.** I couldn't care less; *Med* **cuidados intensivos** intensive care
2 INTERJ **¡c.!** look out!, watch out!; **¡c. con lo que dices!** watch what you say!; **¡c. con el escalón!** mind the step!

cuidadoso, -a ADJ careful

cuidar 1 VT to care for, to look after; **c. de que todo salga bien** to make sure that everything goes all right; **c. los detalles** to pay attention to details
2 **cuidarse** VPR **cuídate** look after yourself

cuitlacoche NM *CAm, Méx* corn smut, = edible fungus which grows on maize

culata NF (**a**) *(de arma)* butt (**b**) *Aut* cylinder head

culebra NF snake

culebrón NM *Esp Fam* soap opera

culinario, -a ADJ culinary

culminación NF culmination

culminante ADJ *(punto)* highest; *(momento)* culminating

culminar VI to culminate

culo NM (**a**) *Am Fam (nalgas)* Br bum, US butt; *Esp Vulg* **¡vete a tomar por c.!** fuck off! (**b**) *(de recipiente)* bottom

culpa NF (**a**) *(responsabilidad)* blame; **echar la c. a algn** to put the blame on sb; **fue c. mía** it was my fault; **por tu c.** because of you (**b**) *(sentimiento)* guilt

culpabilidad NF guilt, culpability

culpable 1 NM,F offender, culprit
2 ADJ guilty; *Der* **declararse c.** to plead guilty

culpar VT to blame; **c. a algn de un delito** to accuse sb of an offence

cultivado, -a ADJ cultivated

cultivar VT (**a**) *(tierra)* to farm, to cultivate; *(plantas)* to grow (**b**) *(amistad, inteligencia)* to cultivate (**c**) *(arte)* to practise (**d**) *(germen)* to culture

cultivo NM (**a**) *(de tierra)* farming; *(de plantas)* growing (**b**) *(plantación)* crop (**c**) *(de gérmenes)* culture

culto, -a 1 ADJ educated; *(palabra)* learned
2 NM cult; *Rel* worship

cultura NF culture

cultural ADJ cultural

culturismo NM body building

culturista NM,F body builder

cumbre NF (**a**) *(de montaña)* summit, top; **(conferencia) c.** summit conference (**b**) *Fig (culminación)* pinnacle

cumple NM *Fam* birthday

cumpleaños NM INV birthday; **¡feliz c.!** happy birthday!

cumplido, -a 1 ADJ (**a**) *(plazo)* expired; **misión cumplida** mission accomplished (**b**) *(cortés)* polite
2 NM compliment

cumplidor, -a ADJ reliable, dependable

cumplimiento NM *(de deber)* performance; *(de contrato, obligaciones)* fulfilment; *(de la ley)* observance; *(de órdenes)* carrying out; *(de promesa)* fulfilment

cumplir 1 VT (**a**) *(deber)* to do, to carry out, to perform; *(contrato, obligaciones)* to fulfil; *(ley)* to observe; *(orden)* to carry out; *(promesa)* to keep; *(sentencia)* to serve (**b**) *(años)* **ayer cumplí veinte años** I was twenty (years old) yesterday
2 VI (**a**) *(plazo)* to expire, to end (**b**) **c. con** *(normas)* to comply; **c. con su deber/trabajo** to do one's duty/job; **c. con algn** to do one's duty by sb

3 cumplirse VPR (**a**) *(deseo, sueño)* to be fulfilled, to come true (**b**) *(plazo)* to expire

cúmulo NM pile, load

cuna NF (**a**) *(de bebé)* cot, cradle (**b**) *(de movimiento, civilización)* cradle; *(de persona)* birthplace

cundir VI (**a**) *(propagarse)* to spread (**b**) *Esp (dar de sí) (comida, reservas)* to go a long way; *(trabajo, estudio)* to go well; **me cundió mucho el tiempo** I got a lot done

cuneta NF *(de la carretera)* gutter; **quedarse en la c.** to be left behind

cuña NF (**a**) *(pieza)* wedge; **c. publicitaria** commercial break (**b**) *Andes, RP Fam (enchufe)* **tener c.** to have friends in high places

cuñado, -a NM,F *(hombre)* brother-in-law; *(mujer)* sister-in-law

cuño NM **de nuevo c.** newly-coined

cuota NF (**a**) *(de club etc)* membership fees *pl*, dues *pl* (**b**) *Am (plazo)* instalment; **comprar en cuotas** to buy on *Br* hire purchase *o US* an installment plan (**c**) *(porción)* quota, share (**d**) *Méx (importe)* toll; **autopista de c.** toll motorway, *US* turnpike

cupe PT INDEF *de* **caber**

cupiera SUBJ IMPERF *de* **caber**

cuplé NM popular song

cupo NM ceiling; *Mil* **excedente de c.** exempt from military service

cupón NM coupon, voucher

cúpula NF dome, cupola; *(líderes)* leadership

cura 1 NM *Rel* priest

2 NF *Med* cure; *Fig* **no tiene c.** there's no remedy

curación NF cure, treatment

curandero, -a NM,F quack

curar 1 VT (**a**) *(sanar)* to cure; *(herida)* to dress; *(enfermedad)* to treat (**b**) *(carne, pescado)* to cure

2 VI *(sanar)* to recover, to get well; *(herida)* to heal up

3 curarse VPR to recover, to get well; *(herida)* to heal up; **c. en salud** to make sure

curcuncho, -a ADJ *Andes Fam* hunchbacked

curiosear VI to pry

curiosidad NF curiosity; **tener c. de** to be curious about

curioso, -a 1 ADJ (**a**) *(indiscreto)* curious, inquisitive (**b**) *(extraño)* strange, odd; **lo c. es que …** the strange thing is that … (**c**) *(limpio)* neat, tidy

2 NM,F (**a**) *(mirón)* onlooker (**b**) *(chismoso)* nosey-parker, busybody

curita NF *Am Br* (sticking-)plaster, *US* Band-aid®

currante *Esp Fam* **1** ADJ hard-working

2 NMF worker

currar VI *Esp Fam* to work

currículum (vitae) [ku'rrikulum ('bite)] *(pl* **currícula** *o* **currículums (vitae))** NM curriculum vitae, *Br* CV, *US* résumé

curro NM *Esp Fam* work

curry *(pl* **currys)** NM curry; **pollo al c.** chicken curry

cursar VT (**a**) *(estudiar)* to study (**b**) *(enviar)* to send

cursi ADJ *(vestido, canción)* tacky, *Br* naff; *(modales, persona)* affected

cursillo NM short course; **c. de reciclaje** refresher course

cursivo, -a ADJ **letra cursiva** italics

curso NM (**a**) *(año académico)* year; *(lecciones)* course (**b**) *(de acontecimientos, río)* course; **en el c. de** during; **año/mes en c.** current year/ month (**c**) *(circulación)* **moneda de c. legal** legal tender

cursor NM cursor

curtido, -a ADJ (**a**) *(piel)* weatherbeaten; *(cuero)* tanned (**b**) *Fig (persona)* hardened

curtiembre NF *Andes, RP* tannery

curtir VT (**a**) *(cuero)* to tan (**b**) *Fig (avezar)* to harden, to toughen

curva NF (**a**) *(línea, forma)* curve (**b**) *(en carretera)* bend; **c. cerrada** sharp bend

curvado, -a ADJ *(forma)* curved; *(espalda)* bent

curvilíneo, -a ADJ curvaceous

curvo, -a ADJ curved

cuscús NM INV couscous

cúspide NF summit, peak; *Fig* peak

custodia NF custody

custodiar [43] VT to watch over

cutáneo, -a ADJ cutaneous, skin; *Med* **erupción cutánea** rash

cutícula NF cuticle

cutis NM INV complexion

cutre ADJ *Esp Fam (sórdido)* shabby, dingy

cuyo, -a PRON REL & POS *(de persona)* whose; *(de cosa)* of which; **en c. caso** in which case

cv *(abr* **caballos de vapor)** hp

D, d [de] NF *(letra)* D, d

D. *(abr* **don)** Mr

Dª *(abr* **doña)** Mrs/Ms

dactilar ADJ **huella d.** fingerprint

dádiva NF *(regalo)* gift, present; *(donativo)* donation

dadivoso, -a ADJ generous

dado¹, -a ADJ **(a)** given; **en un momento d.** at a certain point; **ser d. a** to be given to **(b) d. que** since, given that

dado² NM die, dice

daga NF dagger

dalia NF dahlia

dálmata NM Dalmatian (dog)

daltónico, -a ADJ colour-blind

dama NF **(a)** *(señora)* lady **(b)** *(en damas)* king **(c) damas** *(juego)* Br draughts, US checkers

damasco NM **(a)** *(tela)* damask **(b)** Andes, RP *(albaricoque)* apricot

damnificado, -a NM,F victim

danés, -esa **1** ADJ Danish
2 NM,F *(persona)* Dane
3 NM **(a)** *(idioma)* Danish **(b) gran d.** *(perro)* Great Dane

Danubio NM **el D.** the Danube

danza NF dancing; *(baile)* dance

danzar [40] VT & VI to dance

dañar VT *(cosa)* to damage; *(persona)* to hurt, to harm

dañino, -a ADJ harmful, damaging (**para** to)

daño NM *(a cosa)* damage; *(a persona) (físico)* hurt; *(perjuicio)* harm; **se hizo d. en la pierna** he hurt his leg; Der **daños y perjuicios** (legal) damages

dar [11] **1** VT **(a)** to give; *(recado, recuerdos)* to pass on, to give; *(noticia)* to tell **(b)** *(mano de pintura, cera)* to apply, to put on **(c)** *(película)* to show, to screen; *(fiesta)* to throw, to give **(d)** *(cosecha)* to produce, to yield; *(fruto, flores)* to bear; *(beneficio, interés)* to give, to yield **(e)** *(bofetada etc)* to deal; **d. a algn en la cabeza** to hit sb on the head **(f) dale a la luz** switch the light on; **d. la mano a algn** to shake hands with sb; **d. los buenos días/las buenas noches a algn** to say good morning/good evening to sb; **me da lo mismo, me da igual** it's all the same to me; **¿qué más da?** what difference does it make? **(g)** *(hora)* to strike; **ya han dado las nueve** it's gone nine (o'clock) **(h) d. de comer a** to feed **(i) d. a conocer** *(noticia)* to release; **d. a entender a algn que ...** to give sb to understand that ... **(j) d. por** *(considerar)* to assume, to consider; **lo dieron por muerto** he was assumed dead, he was given up for dead; **d. por descontado** *o* **sabido** to take for granted, to assume

2 VI **(a) me dio un ataque de tos/risa** I had a coughing fit/an attack of the giggles **(b) d. a** *(ventana, habitación)* to look out onto, to overlook; *(puerta)* to open onto, to lead to **(c) d. con** *(persona)* to come across; **d. con la solución** to hit upon the solution **(d) d. de sí** *(ropa)* to stretch, to give **(e) d. en** to hit; **el sol me daba en los ojos** the sun was (shining) in my eyes **(f) d. para** to be enough *o* sufficient for; **el presupuesto no da para más** the budget will not stretch any further **(g) le dio por nadar** he took it into his head to go swimming **(h) d. que hablar** to set people talking; **el suceso dio que pensar** the incident gave people food for thought

3 darse VPR **(a) se dio un caso extraño** something strange happened **(b)** *(hallarse)* to be found, to exist **(c) darse a** to take to; **se dio a la bebida** he took to drink **(d) darse con** *o* **contra** to bump *o* crash into **(e) dárselas de** to consider oneself **(f) darse por satisfecho** to feel satisfied; **darse por vencido** to give in **(g) se le da bien/mal el francés** she's good/bad at French

dardo NM dart

dársena NF **(a)** *(en puerto)* dock **(b)** *(en estación de autobuses)* bay

datar **1** VI **d. de** to date back to *o* from
2 VT to date

dátil NM date

dato NM **(a)** *(hecho, cifra)* piece of information; **datos personales** personal details **(b)** Inform **datos** data

d.C. *(abr* **después de Cristo)** AD

dcha. *(abr* **derecha)** rt.

de PREP

> **de** combines with the article **el** to form the contraction **del** (e.g. **del hombre** of the man).

(a) *(pertenencia)* of; **el título de la novela** the title of the novel; **el coche/hermano de Sofía** Sofía's car/brother; **las bicicletas de los niños** the boys' bicycles (**b**) *(procedencia)* from; **de Madrid a Valencia** from Madrid to Valencia; **soy de Palencia** I'm from o I come from Palencia

(**c**) *(descripción)* **el niño de ojos azules** the boy with blue eyes; **el señor de la chaqueta** the man in the jacket; **el bobo del niño** the silly boy; **un reloj de oro** a gold watch; **un joven de veinte años** a young man of twenty

(**d**) *(contenido)* of; **un saco de patatas** a sack of potatoes

(**e**) **gafas de sol** sunglasses; **goma de borrar** eraser, *Br* rubber

(**f**) *(oficio)* by; as; **es arquitecto de profesión** he's an architect by profession; **trabaja de secretaria** she's working as a secretary

(**g**) *(acerca de)* about; **curso de informática** computer course

(**h**) *(tiempo)* **a las tres de la tarde** at three in the afternoon; **de día** by day; **de noche** at night; **de lunes a jueves** from Monday to Thursday; **de pequeño** as a child; **de año en año** year in year out

(**i**) *(precio)* at; **patatas de 30 céntimos el kilo** potatoes at 30 cents a kilo

(**j**) **una avenida de 15 km** an avenue 15 km long; **una botella de litro** a litre bottle

(**k**) *(con superlativo)* in; **el más largo de España** the longest in Spain

(**l**) *(causa)* with, because of; **llorar de alegría** to cry with joy; **morir de hambre** to die of hunger

(**m**) *(condicional)* **de haber llegado antes** if he had arrived before; **de no ser así** if that wasn't o weren't the case; **de ser cierto** if it was o were true

(**n**) **lo mismo de siempre** the usual thing

(**o**) **de cuatro en cuatro** in fours, four at a time

deambular VI to saunter, to stroll

debajo ADV underneath, below; **el mío es el de d.** mine is the one below; **está d. de la mesa** it's under the table; **por d. de lo normal** below normal; **salió por d. del coche** he came out from under the car

debate NM debate

debatir 1 VT to debate
2 debatirse VPR to struggle; **debatirse entre la vida y la muerte** to fight for one's life

debe NM *Com* debit, debit side

deber[1] NM (**a**) *(obligación)* duty; **cumplir con su d.** to do one's duty (**b**) *Educ* **deberes** homework

deber[2] **1** VT *(dinero, explicación)* to owe
2 VI (**a**) *(obligación)* must, to have to; **debe (de) comer** he must eat; **debe (de) irse ahora** she has to leave now; **la factura debe pagarse mañana** the bill must be paid tomorrow; **el tren debe llegar a las dos** the train is expected to arrive at two (**b**) *(consejo)* **deberías visitar a tus padres** you ought to visit your parents; **debería haber ido ayer** I should have gone yesterday; **no debiste hacerlo** you shouldn't have done it (**c**) *(suposición)* **deben de estar fuera** they must be out
3 deberse VPR **deberse a** to be due to; **esto se**

debe a la falta de agua this is due to lack of water

debidamente ADV duly, properly

debido, -a (**a**) *(justo, conveniente)* due; **a su d. tiempo** in due course; **con el d. respeto** with due respect (**b**) *(adecuado)* proper; **más de lo d.** too much; **tomaron las debidas precauciones** they took the proper precautions; **como es d.** properly (**c**) **d. a** because of, due to; **d. a que** because of the fact that

débil ADJ weak; *(luz)* dim; **punto d.** weak spot

debilidad NF weakness; *Fig* **tener d. por** *(persona)* to have a soft spot for; *(cosa)* to have a weakness for

debilitamiento NM weakening

debilitar 1 VT to weaken, to debilitate
2 debilitarse VPR to weaken, to grow weak

débito NM *(debe)* debit; *(deuda)* debt; *Am* **d. bancario** direct debit

debut *(pl* **debuts***)* NM début, debut

debutar VI to make one's début o debut

década NF decade; **en la d. de los noventa** during the nineties

decadencia NF decadence

decadente ADJ & NMF decadent

decaer [39] VI to deteriorate

decaído, -a ADJ down

decaimiento NM (**a**) *(debilidad)* weakness (**b**) *(desaliento)* low spirits

decano, -a NM,F *Univ* dean

decantarse VPR **d. por** to opt for

decapitar VT to behead, to decapitate

decena NF (about) ten; **una d. de veces** (about) ten times; **por decenas** in tens

decencia NF (**a**) *(decoro)* decency; *(en el vestir)* modesty (**b**) *(dignidad)* dignity

decenio NM decade

decente ADJ (**a**) *(digno)* decent; **un sueldo d.** a decent salary o wage (**b**) *(en el comportamiento)* proper; *(en el vestir)* modest (**c**) *(limpio)* clean

decepción NF disappointment

> Observa que la palabra inglesa **deception** es un falso amigo y no es la traducción de la palabra española **decepción**. En inglés **deception** significa "engaño".

decepcionante ADJ disappointing

decepcionar VT to disappoint

decididamente ADV (**a**) *(con decisión)* resolutely (**b**) *(sin duda)* definitely

decidido, -a ADJ determined, resolute

decidir 1 VT & VI to decide
2 decidirse VPR to make up one's mind; **decidirse a hacer algo** to make up one's mind to do sth; **decidirse por algo** to decide on sth

décima NF tenth

decimal ADJ & NM decimal; **el sistema métrico d.** the decimal system

décimo, -a 1 ADJ & NM,F tenth
2 NM (**a**) *(parte)* tenth (**b**) *(billete de lotería)* tenth part of a lottery ticket

decir¹ NM saying

decir² [12] *(pp dicho)* **1** VT (**a**) *(con palabras)* to say; **dice que no quiere venir** he says he doesn't want to come
(**b**) **d. una mentira/la verdad** to tell a lie/the truth
(**c**) *Esp* **¿diga?, ¿dígame?** *(al teléfono)* hello?
(**d**) **¿qué me dices del nuevo jefe?** what do you think of the new boss?
(**e**) *(mostrar)* to tell, to show; **su cara dice que está mintiendo** you can tell from his face that he's lying
(**f**) *(sugerir)* to mean; **esta película no me dice nada** this film doesn't appeal to me; **¿qué te dice el cuadro?** what does the picture mean to you?
(**g**) **querer d.** to mean
(**h**) *(locuciones)* **es d.** that is (to say); **por así decirlo** as it were, so to speak; **digamos** let's say; **digo yo** in my opinion; **el qué dirán** what people say; **ni que d. tiene** needless to say; **¡no me digas!** really!; *Esp* **¡y que lo digas!** you can say that again!
2 decirse VPR **¿cómo se dice "mesa" en inglés?** how do you say "mesa" in English?; **se dice que ...** they say that ...; **sé lo que me digo** I know what I am saying

decisión NF (**a**) *(acción)* decision; **tomar una d.** to take *o* make a decision (**b**) *(cualidad)* *(firmeza)* determination; *(resolución)* decisiveness; **con d.** decisively

decisivo, -a ADJ decisive

decisorio, -a ADJ decision-making

declamar VT & VI to declaim, to recite

declaración NF (**a**) *(afirmación)* declaration; **hacer declaraciones** to comment; **d. de (la) renta** tax return (**b**) *(ante la policía)* statement; *Der* **prestar d.** to give evidence

declarado, -a ADJ *(manifiesto)* open, professed; **es un homosexual d.** he is openly gay; **hay un odio d. entre ellos** there is open hostility between them

declarante NMF *Der* witness

declarar 1 VT (**a**) *(ante la autoridad)* to declare; **d. la guerra a** to declare war on (**b**) *(afirmar)* to state (**c**) *Der* **d. culpable/inocente a algn** to find sb guilty/not guilty
2 VI *Der* to testify
3 declararse VPR (**a**) **declararse a favor/en contra de** to declare oneself in favour of/against; **declararse en huelga** to go on strike; **declararse a algn** to declare one's love for sb (**b**) *(guerra, incendio)* to start, to break out (**c**) *Der* **declararse culpable** to plead guilty

declinar VT & VI to decline

declive NM (**a**) *(del terreno)* incline, slope (**b**) *(de imperio etc)* decline

decolaje NM *Am* take-off

decolar VI *Am* to take off

decolorante NM bleaching agent

decolorar 1 VT to bleach
2 decolorarse VPR to fade

decomisar VT to confiscate, to seize

decoración NF decoration

decorado NM scenery, set

decorador, -a NM,F interior designer; *Cin & Teatro* set designer

decorar VT to decorate

decorativo, -a ADJ decorative

decoro NM (**a**) *(pudor)* decency, decorum (**b**) *(dignidad)* dignity

decoroso, -a ADJ *(decente)* decent; *(correcto)* seemly, proper

decrecer [33] VI to decrease, to diminish

decrépito, -a ADJ decrepit

decretar VT to decree

decreto NM decree; **d.-ley** decree, *Br* order in council

dedal NM thimble

dedicación NF dedication

dedicar [44] **1** VT to dedicate; *(tiempo, esfuerzos)* to devote (**a** to)
2 dedicarse VPR **¿a qué se dedica Vd.?** what do you do for a living?; **los fines de semana ella se dedica a pescar** at weekends she spends her time fishing

dedicatoria NF dedication

dedillo NM **saber algo al d.** to know sth inside out

dedo NM *(de la mano)* finger; *(del pie)* toe; **d. anular/corazón/índice/meñique** ring/middle/index/little finger; **d. pulgar, d. gordo** thumb; **hacer d.** to hitchhike; *Fig* **elegir a algn a d.** to hand-pick sb

deducción NF deduction

deducir [10] VT (**a**) *(inferir)* to deduce; **de aquí se deduce que ...** from this it follows that ... (**b**) *(descontar)* to deduct

deductivo, -a ADJ deductive

defecar [44] VI to defecate

defecto NM defect, fault; **d. físico** physical defect

defectuoso, -a ADJ defective, faulty

defender [3] **1** VT to defend (**de** from); **d. del frío/viento** to shelter from the cold/wind
2 defenderse VPR (**a**) *(contra enemigo, peligro)* to defend oneself (**b**) *Fam* **se defiende en francés** he can get by in French

defendido, -a NM,F *Der* client *(of defence counsel)*

defensa 1 NF defence; **en d. propia, en legítima d.** in self-defence; **salir en d. de algn** to come out in defence of sb
2 NMF *Dep* defender

defensiva NF defensive; **estar/ponerse a la d.** to be/go on the defensive

defensivo, -a ADJ defensive

defensor, -a NM,F defender; **abogado d.** counsel for the defence; *Esp* **defensor del pueblo** ombudsman

deferencia NF deference; **en** *o* **por d. a** out of deference to

deficiencia NF deficiency, shortcoming; **d. mental** mental deficiency; **d. renal** kidney failure

deficiente 1 ADJ deficient
  2 NMF **d. (mental)** mentally handicapped person
  3 NM *Educ* fail

déficit (*pl* **déficits**) NM *Econ* deficit; *(carencia)* shortage

deficitario, -a ADJ *(empresa, operación)* loss-making; *(balance)* negative, showing a deficit

definición NF definition; **por d.** by definition

definido, -a ADJ **(a)** *(límite, idea)* (clearly) defined **(b)** *Ling* **artículo d.** definite article

definir VT to define

definitivamente ADV **(a)** *(para siempre)* for good, once and for all **(b)** *(con toda seguridad)* definitely

definitivo, -a ADJ definitive; **en definitiva** in short

deflación NF *Econ* deflation

deflacionista ADJ *Econ* deflationary

deformación NF deformation

deformar 1 VT to deform, to put out of shape; *(cara)* to disfigure; *Fig (la verdad, una imagen)* to distort
  2 deformarse VPR to go out of shape, to become distorted

deforme ADJ *(cuerpo)* deformed, disfigured; *(imagen)* distorted; *(objeto)* misshapen

defraudación NF *(fiscal)* tax evasion

defraudar VT **(a)** *(decepcionar)* to disappoint **(b)** *(estafar)* to defraud; **d. a Hacienda** to evade taxes

defunción NF *Fml* decease, demise

degeneración NF degeneration

degenerado, -a ADJ & NM,F degenerate

degenerar VI to degenerate

degollar [2] VT to behead

degradación NF degradation

degradante ADJ degrading

degradar VT to degrade

degustación NF tasting

degustar VT to taste, to sample

dehesa NF meadow

dejadez NF slovenliness

dejado, -a ADJ careless; *(aspecto)* slovenly

dejar 1 VT **(a)** *to leave;* **déjame en paz** leave me alone; **d. dicho** to leave word *o* a message **(b)** *Esp (prestar)* **d. algo a algn** to lend sb sth, to lend sth to sb **(c)** *(abandonar)* to give up; **d. algo por imposible** to give sth up; **dejé el tabaco y la bebida** I gave up smoking and drinking **(d)** *(permitir)* to let, to allow; **d. caer**

to drop; **d. entrar/salir** to let in/out **(e)** *(omitir)* to leave out, to omit **(f)** *(+ adj)* to make; **d. triste** to make sad; **d. preocupado/sorprendido** to worry/surprise **(g)** *(aplazar)* **dejaron el viaje para el verano** they put the trip off until the summer
  2 VAUX **d. de +** *infin* to stop, to give up; **dejó de fumar el año pasado** he gave up smoking last year; **no deja de llamarme** she's always phoning me up
  3 dejarse VPR **(a)** **me he dejado las llaves dentro** I've left the keys inside **(b)** *(locuciones)* **dejarse barba** to grow a beard; **dejarse caer** to flop down; **dejarse llevar por** to be influenced by

del *(contracción de* **de** *+ el) ver* **de**

delantal NM apron

delante ADV **(a)** *(en primer lugar, en la parte delantera)* in front; **la entrada de d.** the front entrance **(b)** **d. de** in front of; *(en serie)* ahead of **(c)** **por d.** in front; **se lo lleva todo por d.** he destroys everything in his path; **tiene toda la vida por d.** he has his whole life ahead of him

delantera NF lead; **tomar la d.** take the lead

delantero, -a 1 ADJ front
  2 NM *Ftb* forward; **d. centro** centre forward

delatar VT to inform against; *Fig* to give away

delator, -a NM,F informer

delegación NF **(a)** *(acto, delegados)* delegation **(b)** *(sucursal)* local office; *Esp* **D. del Gobierno** = office representing central government in each province; *Esp* **D. de Hacienda** = head tax office *(in each province)* **(c)** *Chile, Ecuad, Méx (distrito municipal)* municipal district

delegado, -a NM,F *(representante)* delegate; *(de curso)* reporesentative

delegar [42] VT to delegate **(en** to)

deleitar 1 VT to delight
  2 deleitarse VPR to delight in, to take delight in

deleite NM delight

deletrear VT to spell (out)

deleznable ADJ *(libro, actuación)* appalling; *(excusa, razón)* contemptible

delfín NM dolphin

delgadez NF slimness

delgado, -a ADJ slim; *(capa)* fine

deliberación NF deliberation

deliberado, -a ADJ deliberate

deliberar VI to deliberate (on), to consider

delicadeza NF **(a)** *(finura)* delicacy, daintiness **(b)** *(tacto)* tactfulness; **falta de d.** tactlessness

delicado, -a ADJ delicate

delicia NF delight; **hacer las delicias de algn** to delight sb

delicioso, -a ADJ *(comida)* delicious; *(agradable)* delightful

delictivo, -a ADJ criminal, punishable

delimitar VT *(terreno)* to set out the boundaries of; *(funciones)* to define

delincuencia NF delinquency

delincuente ADJ & NMF delinquent; **d. juvenil** juvenile delinquent

delineante NMF *(hombre)* draughtsman; *(mujer)* draughtswoman

delinear VT to delineate, to outline

delinquir [48] VI to commit a crime

delirante ADJ delirious

delirar VI to be delirious

delirio NM delirium; **delirios de grandeza** delusions of grandeur

delito NM crime, offence

delta NM delta; **ala d.** hang-glider

demacrado, -a ADJ emaciated

demagogia NF demagogy

demagogo, -a NM,F demagogue

demanda NF (a) *Der* lawsuit (b) *Com* demand

demandado, -a 1 NM,F defendant
2 ADJ in demand

demandante NMF claimant

demandar VT to sue

demarcar [44] VT to demarcate

demás 1 ADJ **los/las d.** the rest of; **la d. gente** the rest of the people
2 PRON **lo/los/las d.** the rest; **por lo d.** otherwise, apart from that; **y d.** etcetera

demasía NF **en d.** excessively

demasiado, -a 1 ADJ *(singular)* too much; *(plural)* too many; **hay demasiada comida** there is too much food; **quieres demasiadas cosas** you want too many things
2 ADV too (much); **es d. grande/caro** it is too big/dear; **fumas/trabajas d.** you smoke/work too much

demencia NF dementia, insanity

demente 1 ADJ insane, mad
2 NMF mental patient

democracia NF democracy

demócrata 1 ADJ democratic
2 NMF democrat

democrático, -a ADJ democratic

democratizar [40] VT to democratize

demografía NF demography

demográfico, -a ADJ demographic; **crecimiento d.** population growth

demoledor, -a ADJ *Fig* devastating

demoler [4] VT to demolish

demonio NM devil, demon; *Fam* **¿cómo/dónde demonios …?** how/where the hell …?; *Fam* **¡demonio(s)!** hell!, damn!; *Fam* **¡d. de niño!** you little devil!

demora NF delay

demorar 1 VT (a) *(retrasar)* to delay, hold up (b) *(tardar)* **demoraron 3 días en pintar la casa** it took them three days to paint the house
2 VI *Am (tardar)* **¡no demores!** don't be late!; **siempre demora en bañarse** he always takes

ages in the bathroom; **este quitamanchas demora en actuar** this stain remover takes a while to work
3 demorarse VPR (a) *(retrasarse)* to be delayed, be held up (b) *(detenerse)* to dally (c) *esp Am (tardar)* to be late; **no se demoren** don't be late

demostración NF demonstration; **una d. de fuerza/afecto** a show of strength

demostrar [2] VT (a) *(mostrar)* to show, to demonstrate (b) *(evidenciar)* to prove

demudado, -a ADJ pale

denegar [1] VT to turn down, to reject; *Der* **d. una demanda** to dismiss a claim

denigrante ADJ degrading

denigrar VT to denigrate, to vilify

denominación NF naming; **d. de origen** = guarantee of region of origin of a wine or other product

denominado, -a ADJ so-called

denominador NM denominator; *Mat & Fig* **d. común** common denominator

denominar VT to call

denotar VT to indicate, to show

densidad NF density; **d. de población** population density

denso, -a ADJ dense

dentadura NF teeth, set of teeth; **d. postiza** false teeth, dentures

dental ADJ dental

dentera NF **me da d.** it sets my teeth on edge

dentífrico, -a 1 ADJ **pasta/crema dentífrica** toothpaste
2 NM toothpaste

dentista NMF dentist

dentro ADV (a) *(en el interior)* inside; **aquí d.** in here; **por d.** (on the) inside; **por d. está triste** deep down (inside) he feels sad (b) **d. de** *(lugar)* inside (c) **d. de poco** shortly, soon; **d. de un mes** in a month's time; **d. de lo que cabe** all things considered

denuncia NF (a) *(a la policía)* complaint (b) *(condena)* denunciation

denunciante NMF = person who reports a crime

denunciar [43] VT (a) *(delito)* to report (**a** to) (b) *(criticar)* to denounce

deparar VT **no sabemos qué nos depara el destino** we don't know what fate has in store for us

departamento NM (a) *(en organización)* department (b) *(territorial)* province, district (c) *Arg (piso)* *Br* flat, *US* apartment

dependencia NF (a) *(de persona, drogas)* dependence (b) **dependencias** *(instalaciones)* outbuildings; **en dependencias policiales** on police premises

depender VI to depend (**de** on); *(económicamente)* to be dependent (**de** on)

dependienta NF *Br* shop *or* sales assistant, *US* salesclerk

dependiente 1 ADJ dependent (**de** on)
2 NM *Br* shop *or* sales assistant, *US* salesclerk

depilación NF hair removal; **d. a la cera** waxing

depilar VT *(piernas, axilas)* to remove the hair from; *(cejas)* to pluck; *(con cera)* to wax

depilatorio, -a 1 ADJ hair-removing
2 NM hair-remover

deplorable ADJ deplorable

deplorar VT to deplore

deponer [19] *(pp* **depuesto)** VT **(a)** *(destituir)* to remove from office; *(líder)* to depose **(b)** *(actitud)* to abandon; *(armas)* to lay down

deportado, -a NM,F deportee, deported person

deportar VT to deport

deporte NM sport; **hacer d.** to practise sports; **d. de aventura** adventure sport

deportista 1 NMF *(hombre)* sportsman; *(mujer)* sportswoman
2 ADJ sporty

deportividad NF sportsmanship

deportivo, -a 1 ADJ sports; **club/chaqueta d.** sports club/jacket
2 NM *Aut* sports car

deposición NF **(a)** *(de ministro, secretario)* removal from office; *(de líder, rey)* overthrow **(b)** *Med* **deposiciones** stools

depositar 1 VT **(a)** *Fin* to deposit **(b)** *(colocar)* to place, to put
2 depositarse VPR to settle

depósito NM **(a)** *Fin* deposit; **en d.** on deposit **(b)** *(de agua, gasolina)* tank **(c)** **d. de basuras** rubbish tip *o* dump; **d. de cadáveres** mortuary, morgue

depravación NF depravity

depravado, -a 1 ADJ depraved
2 NM,F **ser un d.** to be depraved *o* degenerate

depre *Fam* **1** ADJ **estar d.** to be feeling down
2 NF **tener la d.** to be feeling down

depreciación NF depreciation

depreciar [43] **1** VT to (cause to) depreciate
2 depreciarse VPR to depreciate

depredador, -a 1 ADJ predatory
2 NM,F predator

depresión NF depression; **d. nerviosa** nervous breakdown

depresivo, -a ADJ depressive

deprimente ADJ depressing

deprimido, -a ADJ depressed

deprimir 1 VT to depress
2 deprimirse VPR to get depressed

deprisa ADV quickly

depuesto, -a PP *de* **deponer**

depuración NF **(a)** *(del agua)* purification **(b)** *(purga)* purge

depurador, -a ADJ **planta depuradora** purification plant

depuradora NF purifier

depurar VT **(a)** *(agua)* to purify **(b)** *(partido)* to purge **(c)** *(estilo)* to refine

derecha NF **(a)** *(mano)* right hand **(b)** *(lugar)* right, right-hand side; **a la d.** to *o* on the right, on the right-hand side **(c)** *Pol* **la d.** the right; *Esp* **ser de derechas** to be right-wing

derechista NMF right-winger

derecho, -a 1 ADJ **(a)** *(de la derecha)* right **(b)** *(recto)* upright, straight
2 NM **(a)** *(privilegio)* right; **derechos civiles/ humanos** civil/human rights; **tener d. a** to be entitled to, to have the right to; **estar en su d.** to be within one's rights; **no hay d.** it's not fair; **d. de admisión** right to refuse admission **(b)** *Der* law; **d. penal/político** criminal/constitutional law **(c)** *Com* **derechos** duties; **derechos de autor** royalties; **derechos de matrícula** enrolment fees
3 ADV **siga todo d.** go straight ahead

deriva NF drift; **ir a la d.** to drift

derivada NF *Mat* derivative

derivado NM *(producto)* by-product

derivar 1 VT to divert; *(conversación)* to steer
2 VI **d. de** to derive from
3 derivarse VPR **(a)** **derivarse de** *(proceder)* to result *o* stem from **(b)** **derivarse de** *Ling* to be derived from

dermatitis NF INV dermatitis

dermatólogo, -a NM,F dermatologist

dermoprotector ADJ skin-protecting

derogar [42] VT to repeal

derramamiento NM spilling; **d. de sangre** bloodshed

derramar 1 VT to spill; *(lágrimas)* to shed
2 derramarse VPR to spill

derrame NM *Med* discharge; **d. cerebral** brain haemorrhage

derrapar VI to skid

derredor NM **en d. de** round, around

derretir [6] **1** VT to melt; *(hielo, nieve)* to thaw
2 derretirse VPR to melt; *(hielo, nieve)* to thaw

derribar VT **(a)** *(edificio)* to pull down, to knock down **(b)** *(avión)* to shoot down **(c)** *(gobierno)* to bring down

derrocar [44] VT *(gobierno)* to topple, to overthrow; *(rey)* to oust

derrochador, -a 1 ADJ wasteful
2 NM,F spendthrift

derrochar VT **(a)** *(malgastar)* to squander, to waste **(b)** *(rebosar de)* to ooze, to be full of

derroche NM **(a)** *(de dinero, energía)* waste, squandering **(b)** *(abundancia)* profusion, abundance

derrota NF defeat

derrotar VT to defeat, to beat

derrotero NM path, course *o* plan of action

derrotista ADJ & NMF defeatist

derruido, -a ADJ in ruins

derruir [37] VT to demolish

derrumbar 1 VT *(edificio)* to knock down, to pull down
2 derrumbarse VPR to collapse, to fall down; *(techo)* to fall in, to cave in

desaborido, -a ADJ dull

desabrido, -a ADJ *(tiempo)* unpleasant (**b**) *Esp (tono)* harsh; *(persona)* moody, irritable

desabrigarse [42] VPR (**a**) *(en la calle)* ¡no te desabrigues! make sure you wrap up warmly! (**b**) *(en la cama)* to throw off the covers

desabrochar 1 VT to undo
2 desabrocharse VPR (**a**) **desabróchate la camisa** undo your shirt (**b**) *(prenda)* to come undone

desacato NM lack of respect, disrespect (**a** for); *Der* **d. al tribunal** contempt of court

desacertado, -a ADJ unwise

desacierto NM mistake, error

desaconsejar VT to advise against

desacorde ADJ *(opiniones)* differing, conflicting

desacreditar VT (**a**) *(desprestigiar)* to discredit, to bring into discredit (**b**) *(criticar)* to disparage

desactivar VT *(bomba)* to defuse

desacuerdo NM disagreement

desafiante ADJ defiant

desafiar [29] VT to challenge

desafinado, -a ADJ out of tune

desafinar VI to sing out of tune; *(instrumento)* to play out of tune
2 desafinarse VPR to go out of tune

desafío NM challenge

desaforado, -a ADJ *(excesivo)* uncontrolled; *(furioso)* furious, wild

desafortunado, -a ADJ unlucky, unfortunate

desagradable ADJ unpleasant, disagreeable

desagradar VI to displease

desagradecido, -a 1 ADJ ungrateful
2 NM,F ungrateful person

desagrado NM displeasure

desagravio NM **en señal de d.** (in order) to make amends

desaguar [45] VT to drain

desagüe NM *(vaciado)* drain; *(cañería)* waste pipe, drainpipe

desaguisado NM *(destrozo)* mess; *(desorden)* shambles *sing*

desahogado, -a ADJ *(acomodado)* well-off, well-to-do; *(espacioso)* spacious, roomy

desahogarse [42] VPR to let off steam; **d. con algn** to pour out one's woes o to tell one's troubles to sb

desahogo NM *(económico)* ease; **vivir con d.** to be comfortably off

desahuciar [43] VT (**a**) *(inquilino)* to evict (**b**) *(enfermo)* to deprive of all hope

desahucio NM eviction

desairado, -a ADJ (**a**) *(humillado)* spurned (**b**) *(sin gracia)* awkward

desairar VT to slight, to snub

desaire NM slight, rebuff

desajustar 1 VT to upset
2 desajustarse VPR *(piezas)* to come apart

desajuste NM upset; **d. económico** economic imbalance; **un d. de horarios** clashing timetables

desalentador, -a ADJ discouraging, disheartening

desalentar [1] **1** VT to discourage, to dishearten
2 desalentarse VPR to get discouraged, to lose heart

desaliento NM discouragement

desaliñado, -a ADJ scruffy, untidy

desaliño NM scruffiness, untidiness

desalmado, -a ADJ cruel, heartless

desalojar VT (**a**) *(por emergencia)* *(edificio, personas)* to evacuate (**b**) *(por la fuerza)* *(ocupantes)* to eject, to remove; *(inquilinos)* to evict

desalojo NM (**a**) *(por emergencia)* *(de edificio, personas)* evacuation (**b**) *(por la fuerza)* *(de ocupantes)* ejection, removal; *(de inquilinos)* eviction

desamor NM lack of affection

desamortizar [40] VT to alienate, to disentail

desamparado, -a 1 ADJ helpless, unprotected
2 NM,F helpless o abandoned person

desamparo NM helplessness

desandar [8] VT **d. lo andado** to retrace one's steps

desangrarse VPR to lose (a lot of) blood

desanimado, -a ADJ downhearted, dejected

desanimar 1 VT to discourage, to dishearten
2 desanimarse VPR to lose heart, to get discouraged

desánimo NM discouragement, dejection

desapacible ADJ unpleasant

desaparecer [33] VI to disappear

desaparecido, -a 1 ADJ missing
2 NM,F missing person

desaparición NF disappearance

desapego NM indifference, lack of affection

desapercibido, -a ADJ (**a**) *(inadvertido)* unnoticed; **pasar d.** to go unnoticed (**b**) *(desprevenido)* unprepared

desaprensivo, -a 1 ADJ unscrupulous
2 NM,F unscrupulous person

desaprobar [2] VT *(no aprobar)* to disapprove of; *(propuesta, plan)* to reject

desaprovechar VT *(dinero, tiempo)* to waste; **d. una ocasión** to fail to make the most of an opportunity

desarmable ADJ *(mueble)* that can be dismantled

desarmador NM *Méx* screwdriver

desarmar VT (**a**) *(desmontar)* to dismantle, to take to pieces (**b**) *Mil* to disarm

desarme NM disarmament; **d. nuclear** nuclear disarmament

desarraigado, -a ADJ rootless, without roots

desarraigar [42] VT to uproot

desarraigo NM rootlessness

desarreglado, -a ADJ (**a**) *(lugar)* untidy (**b**) *(persona)* untidy, slovenly

desarreglar VT (**a**) *(desordenar)* to make untidy, to mess up (**b**) *(planes, horario)* to upset

desarreglo NM *(de vida)* disorder

desarrollado, -a ADJ developed; **país d.** developed country

desarrollar 1 VT to develop
  2 **desarrollarse** VPR (**a**) *(persona, enfermedad)* to develop (**b**) *(tener lugar)* to take place

desarrollo NM development; **países en vías de d.** developing countries

desarticular VT *(organización, banda)* to break up; *(plan)* to foil

desaseado, -a ADJ unkempt

desasirse [46] VPR to get loose; **d. de** to free o rid oneself of

desasosegar [1] VT to make restless o uneasy

desasosiego NM restlessness, uneasiness

desastrado, -a ADJ untidy, scruffy

desastre NM disaster; **eres un d.** you're just hopeless

desastroso, -a ADJ disastrous

desatar 1 VT to untie, to undo; *(provocar)* to unleash
  2 **desatarse** VPR (**a**) *(zapato, cordón)* to come undone (**b**) *(tormenta)* to break; *(pasión)* to run wild

desatascar [44] VT to unblock, to clear

desatender [3] VT to neglect, not to pay attention to

desatento, -a ADJ *(distraído)* inattentive; *(descortés)* impolite, discourteous

desatinado, -a ADJ unwise

desatino NM blunder

desatornillar VT to unscrew

desatrancar [44] VT to unblock; *(puerta)* to unbolt

desautorizar [40] VT (**a**) *(huelga, manifestación)* to ban, to forbid (**b**) *(noticia)* to deny (**c**) *(persona)* to discredit

desavenencia NF disagreement

desaventajado, -a ADJ at a disadvantage

desayunar 1 VI to have breakfast; *Fml* to breakfast
  2 VT to have for breakfast

desayuno NM breakfast

desazón NF unease

desazonar VT to cause unease to, to worry

desbancar [44] VT to oust

desbandada NF scattering; **hubo una d. general** everyone scattered

desbarajuste NM confusion, disorder

desbaratar VT to ruin, to wreck

desbloquear VT (**a**) *(negociaciones)* to end the deadlock in (**b**) *(cuenta)* to unfreeze

desbocado, -a ADJ *(caballo)* runaway

desbocarse [44] VPR *(caballo)* to bolt, to run away

desbolado, -a *RP Fam* 1 ADJ messy, untidy
  2 NM,F untidy person

desbolarse VPR *RP Fam* to undress, to strip

desbole NM *RP Fam* mess, chaos

desbordante ADJ overflowing, bursting

desbordar 1 VT to overflow; *Fig* to overwhelm
  2 VI to overflow (**de** with)
  3 **desbordarse** VPR to overflow, to flood

descabalgar [42] VI to dismount

descabellado, -a ADJ crazy, wild

descafeinado, -a ADJ (**a**) *(café)* decaffeinated (**b**) *Fig* watered-down, diluted

descalabrar VT (**a**) *(herir)* to wound in the head (**b**) *(perjudicar)* to do serious damage to

descalabro NM major setback, disaster

descalificar [44] VT to disqualify

descalzarse [40] VPR to take one's shoes off

descalzo, -a ADJ barefoot

descambiar [43] VT to exchange

descaminado, -a ADJ **ir d.** to be on the wrong track

descampado NM waste ground

descansado, -a ADJ (**a**) *(persona)* rested (**b**) *(vida, trabajo)* restful

descansar VI to rest, to have a rest; *(por corto tiempo)* to take a break; *Euf* **que en paz descanse** may he/she rest in peace

descansillo NM landing

descanso NM (**a**) *(del trabajo)* rest, break; **un día de d.** a day off (**b**) *(en cine)* intermission; *(en teatro)* *Br* interval, *US* intermission; *Dep* half-time, interval (**c**) *(alivio)* relief (**d**) *(rellano)* landing

descapotable ADJ & NM convertible

descarado, -a 1 ADJ (**a**) *(insolente)* cheeky, insolent; *(desvergonzado)* shameless (**b**) *Esp Fam* **d. que sí/no** *(por supuesto)* of course/course not
  2 NM,F cheeky person

descarga NF (**a**) *(de mercancías, peso)* unloading (**b**) *Elec & Mil* discharge

descargar [42] 1 VT (**a**) *(mercancías, peso)* to unload (**b**) *Elec* to discharge (**c**) *(disparar)* to fire; *(golpe)* to deal
  2 VI *(tormenta)* to burst
  3 **descargarse** VPR *(batería)* to go flat

descargo NM *Der* discharge; **testigo de d.** witness for the defence

descarnado, -a ADJ crude

descaro NM cheek, nerve; **¡qué d.!** what a cheek!

descarriarse [29] VPR *(ganado)* to stray; *(persona)* to lose one's way, to go astray

descarrilar VI to go off the rails, to be derailed

descartar 1 VT to rule out
2 descartarse VPR *Naipes* to discard cards; **me descarté de un cinco** I got rid of a five

descascarillarse VPR to chip, to peel

descendencia NF descendants; **morir sin d.** to die without issue

descendente ADJ *(número, temperatura)* falling; *(movimiento, dirección)* downward, descending

descender [3] **1** VI (**a**) *(temperatura, nivel)* to fall, to drop (**b**) **d. de** to descend from
2 VT to lower

descendiente NMF descendant

descenso NM (**a**) *(en el espacio)* descent; *(de temperatura)* fall, drop (**b**) *(en fútbol)* relegation

descentrado, -a ADJ off-centre

descentralizar [40] VT to decentralize

descifrar VT *(clave, mensaje)* to decipher; *(misterio)* to solve; *(motivos, causas)* to figure out

descojonarse VPR *muy Fam* to piss oneself laughing (**de** at)

descolgar [2] **1** VT *(el teléfono)* to pick up; *(cuadro, cortinas)* to take down
2 descolgarse VPR to let oneself down, to slide down

descolorido, -a ADJ faded

descombros NMPL rubble, debris

descompasado, -a ADJ excessive, uncontrollable

descomponer [19] *(pp* **descompuesto**) **1** VT (**a**) *(dividir)* to break down (**b**) *(corromper)* to rot, decompose
2 descomponerse VPR (**a**) *(corromperse)* to rot, decompose (**b**) *(ponerse nervioso)* to lose one's cool (**c**) *Am (el tiempo)* to turn nasty

descomposición NF (**a**) *(de carne)* decomposition, rotting; *(de país)* disintegration (**b**) *Quím* breakdown (**c**) *Esp (diarrea)* diarrhoea

descompostura NF (**a**) *Am (malestar)* unpleasant *o* nasty turn (**b**) *Méx, RP (avería)* breakdown

descompuesto, -a ADJ **1** (**a**) *(podrido)* rotten, decomposed (**b**) *(furioso)* furious
2 PP *de* **descomponer**

descompuse PT INDEF *de* **descomponer**

descomunal ADJ huge, massive

desconcertante ADJ disconcerting

desconcertar [1] **1** VT to disconcert
2 desconcertarse VPR to be bewildered, to be puzzled

desconchón NM bare patch

desconcierto NM chaos, confusion

desconectar VT to disconnect

desconexión NF disconnection

desconfiado, -a ADJ distrustful, wary

desconfianza NF distrust, mistrust

desconfiar [29] VI **d. (de)** to distrust, to mistrust

descongelar VT *(nevera)* to defrost; *(créditos)* to unfreeze

descongestionar VT to clear

desconocer [34] VT not to know, to be unaware of

desconocido, -a 1 ADJ unknown; *(irreconocible)* unrecognizable
2 NM **lo d.** the unknown
3 NM,F stranger

desconocimiento NM ignorance, lack of knowledge

desconsiderado, -a 1 ADJ inconsiderate, thoughtless
2 NM,F inconsiderate *o* thoughtless person

desconsolado, -a ADJ disconsolate, grief-stricken

desconsuelo NM grief, sorrow

descontado, -a ADJ **por d.** needless to say, of course; **dar por d.** to take for granted

descontar [2] VT (**a**) *(cantidad)* to deduct (**b**) *Dep (tiempo)* to add on

descontento, -a 1 ADJ unhappy
2 NM dissatisfaction

descontrol NM *Fam* lack of control; **había un d. total** it was absolute chaos

descontrolarse VPR to lose control

desconvocar [44] VT to call off

descorchar VT to uncork

descornarse [2] VPR *Fam (trabajar)* to slave (away)

descorrer VT to draw back

descortés ADJ impolite, discourteous

descortesía NF discourtesy, impoliteness

descoser VT to unstitch, to unpick

descosido NM *(en ropa)* open seam; *Fam* **como un d.** *(hablar)* endlessly, non-stop; *(beber, comer)* to excess; *(gritar)* wildly

descoyuntar VT to dislocate

descrédito NM disrepute, discredit

descremado, -a ADJ skimmed

describir *(pp* **descrito**) VT to describe

descripción NF description

descriptivo, -a ADJ descriptive

descrito, -a PP *de* **describir**

descuajaringar [42] VT *Fam* to pull *o* take to pieces

descuartizar [40] VT to cut up, to cut into pieces

descubierto, -a 1 ADJ open, uncovered; **a cielo d.** in the open
2 NM (**a**) *Fin* overdraft (**b**) **al d.** in the open; **poner al d.** to uncover, to bring out into the open
3 PP *de* **descubrir**

descubridor, -a NM,F discoverer

descubrimiento NM discovery

descubrir (*pp* **descubierto**) VT to discover; (*conspiración*) to uncover; (*placa*) to unveil

descuento NM discount

descuidado, -a ADJ (**a**) (*desaseado*) untidy, neglected (**b**) (*negligente*) careless, negligent (**c**) (*desprevenido*) off one's guard

descuidar 1 VT to neglect, to overlook
  2 VI **descuida, voy yo** don't worry, I'll go
  3 descuidarse VPR (*despistarse*) to be careless; **como te descuides, llegarás tarde** if you don't watch out, you'll be late

descuido NM (*olvido*) oversight; (*error*) slip; **por d.** inadvertently, by mistake

desde ADV (**a**) (*tiempo*) since; **d. ahora** from now on; **d. el lunes/entonces** since Monday/then; **espero d. hace media hora** I've been waiting for half an hour; **no lo he visto d. hace un año** I haven't seen him for a year; ¿**d. cuándo?** since when?; **d. siempre** always (**b**) (*lugar*) from; **d. aquí** from here; **d. arriba/abajo** from above/below (**c**) **d. luego** of course (**d**) **d. que** ever since; **d. lo que conozco** ever since I've known him

desdecir [12] (*pp* **desdicho**) **1** VI **d. de** not to live up to
  2 desdecirse VPR to go back on one's word

desdén NM disdain

desdentado, -a ADJ toothless

desdeñar VT to disdain

desdeñoso, -a ADJ disdainful

desdibujarse VPR to become blurred *o* faint

desdicha NF misfortune; **por d.** unfortunately

desdichado, -a 1 ADJ unfortunate
  2 NM,F poor devil, wretch

desdicho, -a PP *de* **desdecir**

desdigo INDIC PRES *de* **desdecir**

desdiré INDIC FUT *de* **desdecir**

desdoblar VT to unfold

deseable ADJ desirable

desear VT (*querer*) to want; (*felicidad*) to wish; (*sexualmente*) to desire; **deja mucho que d.** it leaves a lot to be desired; ¿**qué desea?** can I help you?; **estoy deseando que vengas** I'm looking forward to your coming; **te deseo buena suerte/feliz Navidad** I wish you good luck/a merry Christmas

desecar [44] VT to dry up

desechable ADJ disposable, throw-away

desechar VT (**a**) (*tirar*) to discard, to throw out *o* away (**b**) (*oferta*) to turn down, to refuse; (*idea, proyecto*) to drop, to discard

desecho NM (**a**) (*objeto usado*) unwanted object; **material de d.** (*residuos*) waste products (**b**) (*escoria*) dregs; **desechos** (*basura*) *Br* rubbish, *US* garbage, *US* trash; (*residuos*) waste products

desembalar VT to unpack

desembarcar [44] **1** VT (*mercancías*) to unload; (*personas*) to disembark
  2 VI to disembark

desembarco, desembarque NM (*de mercancías*) unloading; (*de personas*) disembarkation

desembocadura NF mouth

desembocar [44] VI **d. en** (*río*) to flow into; (*calle, situación*) to lead to

desembolsar VT to pay out

desembolso NM expenditure

desembragar [42] VT *Aut* to declutch

desembrollar VT *Fam* (**a**) (*aclarar*) to clarify, to clear up (**b**) (*desenredar*) to disentangle

desembuchar VI *Fam* to spit it out

desempañar VT (*con trapo*) to wipe the condensation from; (*electrónicamente*) to demist

desempaquetar VT (*paquete*) to unwrap; (*caja*) to unpack

desempatar VI *Dep* to break the deadlock

desempate NM play-off; **partido de d.** play-off, deciding match

desempeñar VT (**a**) (*cargo*) to hold, to occupy; (*función*) to fulfil; (*papel*) to play (**b**) (*recuperar*) to redeem

desempleado, -a 1 ADJ unemployed, out of work
  2 NM,F unemployed person; **los desempleados** the unemployed

desempleo NM unemployment; **cobrar el d.** to be on the dole

desempolvar VT (*pasado*) to revive; **voy a d. los libros de física** I'm going to dig out my physics books

desencadenar 1 VT (**a**) (*prisionero*) to unchain (**b**) (*suceso, polémica*) to give rise to, to spark off; (*pasión, furia*) to unleash
  2 desencadenarse VPR (**a**) (*pasión, conflicto*) to erupt (**b**) (*tormenta*) to burst

desencajar 1 VT (*pieza*) to knock out; (*hueso*) to dislocate
  2 desencajarse VPR (**a**) (*pieza*) to come out; (*hueso*) to become dislocated (**b**) (*cara*) to become distorted

desencaminado, -a ADJ = **descaminado**

desencanto NM disenchantment

desenchufar VT to unplug

desenfadado, -a ADJ carefree, free and easy

desenfado NM ease

desenfocado, -a ADJ out of focus

desenfrenado, -a ADJ (*ritmo*) frantic, frenzied; (*vicio, pasión*) unbridled

desenfreno NM (*descontrol*) lack of restraint; (*vicio*) debauchery

desenganchar VT (*vagón*) to uncouple; (*caballo*) to unhitch; (*pelo, jersey*) to free

desengañar 1 VT **d. a algn** to open sb's eyes
  2 desengañarse VPR to become disillusioned; **desengáñate** stop kidding yourself

desengaño NM disappointment; **llevarse** *o* **sufrir un d. con algo** to be disappointed in sth

desengrasar VT to degrease, to remove the grease from

desenlace NM ending, dénouement

desenmarañar VT (pelo) to untangle; (problema) to unravel; (asunto) to sort out

desenmascarar VT to unmask

desenredar VT to untangle, to disentangle

desenrollar VT (hilo, cinta) to unwind; (persiana) to roll down; (pergamino, papel) to unroll

desenroscar [44] VT to unscrew

desentenderse [3] VPR **se desentendió de mi problema** he didn't want to have anything to do with my problem

desenterrar [1] VT (a) (cadáver) to exhume, to disinter; (tesoro) to dig up (b) (recuerdo) to revive

desentonar VI (a) Mús (cantante) to sing out of tune; (instrumento) to be out of tune (b) (colores etc) not to match (c) (persona, comentario) to be out of place

desentrañar VT (misterio) to unravel, to get to the bottom of

desentrenado, -a ADJ out of training o shape

desentumecer [33] VT to put the feeling back into

desenvoltura NF ease

desenvolver [4] (pp **desenvuelto**) 1 VT to unwrap
2 **desenvolverse** VPR (a) (persona) to manage, to cope (b) (hecho) to develop

desenvuelto, -a 1 ADJ relaxed
2 PP de **desenvolver**

deseo NM wish; (sexual) desire; **formular un d.** to make a wish

deseoso, -a ADJ eager; **estar d. de** be eager to

desequilibrado, -a 1 ADJ unbalanced
2 NM,F unbalanced person

desequilibrar 1 VT to unbalance, to throw off balance
2 **desequilibrarse** VPR to become mentally disturbed

desequilibrio NM imbalance

deserción NF desertion

desertar VI to desert

desértico, -a ADJ desert

desertización NF desertification

desertor, -a NM,F deserter

desesperación NF (desesperanza) despair; (exasperación) desperation

desesperado, -a ADJ (a) (sin esperanza) desperate, hopeless (b) (exasperado) exasperated, infuriated

desesperante ADJ exasperating

desesperar 1 VT (a) (quitar la esperanza a) to drive to despair (b) (exasperar) to exasperate
2 **desesperarse** VPR to despair

desestabilizar [40] VT to destabilize

desestatización NF Am privatization, sell-off

desestatizar [40] VT Am to privatize, to sell off

desestimar VT to reject

desfachatez NF cheek, nerve

desfalco NM embezzlement

desfallecer [33] VI (a) (debilitarse) to feel faint; (desmayarse) to faint (b) (desanimarse) to lose heart

desfasado, -a ADJ (persona) out of touch; (libro, moda) out of date

desfase NM gap; **d. horario** time lag

desfavorable ADJ unfavourable

desfigurar VT (cara) to disfigure; (verdad) to distort

desfiladero NM narrow pass

desfilar VI to parade

desfile NM Mil parade, march past; (de carrozas) procession; **d. de modas** fashion show

desfogar [42] 1 VT to give vent to
2 **desfogarse** VPR to let off steam

desgajar 1 VT (naranja) to split into segments; (rama) to tear off
2 **desgajarse** VPR (rama) to break off; (hoja) to fall

desgana NF (a) (inapetencia) lack of appetite (b) (apatía) apathy, indifference; **con d.** reluctantly, unwillingly

desganado, -a ADJ (a) **estar d.** (inapetente) to have no appetite (b) (apático) apathetic

desgano NM Am = **desgana**

desgañitarse VPR Fam to shout oneself hoarse

desgarbado, -a ADJ ungraceful, ungainly

desgarrador, -a ADJ harrowing

desgarrar VT to tear

desgarrón NM big tear, rip

desgastar 1 VT to wear out
2 **desgastarse** VPR to become worn

desgaste NM wear; **d. del poder** wear and tear of power

desgracia NF (a) (mala suerte) misfortune; **por d.** unfortunately (b) (deshonor) disgrace (c) **desgracias personales** loss of life

desgraciadamente ADV unfortunately

desgraciado, -a 1 ADJ (a) (suceso) unfortunate (b) (persona) unhappy
2 NM,F (a) (infeliz) wretch; **un pobre d.** a poor wretch (b) (canalla) swine

desgravable ADJ tax-deductible

desgravación NF deduction; **d. fiscal** tax deduction

desgravar VI to be tax-deductible

desgreñado, -a ADJ dishevelled

desguazar [40] VT (barco) to break up; (vehículo) to scrap

deshabitado, -a ADJ uninhabited, unoccupied

deshabitar VT to abandon, to vacate

deshacer [15] (pp **deshecho**) 1 VT (a) (paquete) to undo; (maleta) to unpack (b) (disolver) to dissolve; (derretir) to melt (c)

(plan) to destroy, to ruin
  2 deshacerse VPR (**a**) *(nudo, trenza)* to come undone *o* untied (**b**) *(disolverse)* to dissolve; *(derretirse)* to melt (**c**) **deshacerse de algn/algo** to get rid of sb/sth (**d**) *(afligirse)* to go to pieces; **deshacerse en lágrimas** to cry one's eyes out

deshecho, -a 1 ADJ (**a**) *(cama)* unmade; *(maleta)* unpacked; *(paquete)* unwrapped (**b**) *(roto)* broken, smashed (**c**) *(disuelto)* dissolved; *(derretido)* melted (**d**) *(abatido)* devastated, shattered (**e**) *(cansado)* exhausted, tired out
  2 PP *de* **deshacer**

desheredar VT to disinherit

deshidratar VT to dehydrate

deshielo NM thaw

deshilachar VT to fray

deshilvanado, -a ADJ *(discurso)* disjointed

deshonesto, -a ADJ (**a**) *(sin honradez)* dishonest (**b**) *(sin pudor)* indecent, improper

deshonor NM, **deshonra** NF dishonour

deshonrar VT to dishonour; *(familia)* to bring disgrace on

deshora: a deshora LOC ADV *(en momento inoportuno)* at a bad time; *(en horas poco habituales)* at an unearthly hour; **comer a d.** to eat at odd times

deshuesar VT *(carne)* to bone; *(fruto)* Br to stone, US to pit

deshumanizar [40] VT to dehumanize

desidia NF apathy

desierto, -a 1 NM desert
  2 ADJ (**a**) *(deshabitado)* uninhabited (**b**) *(vacío)* empty, deserted (**c**) *(premio)* void

designación NF (**a**) *(nombre)* designation (**b**) *(nombramiento)* appointment

designar VT (**a**) *(nombrar)* to appoint (**b**) *(fecha, lugar)* to fix

designio NM intention, plan

desigual ADJ (**a**) *(terreno)* uneven (**b**) *(actuación)* inconsistent; *(lucha)* unequal (**c**) *(carácter)* changeable

desigualdad NF (**a**) *(económica, social, racial)* inequality (**b**) *(del terreno)* unevenness

desilusión NF *(chasco)* disappointment; *(estado de ánimo)* disillusionment

desilusionar 1 VT *(decepcionar)* to disappoint; *(dejar sin ilusiones)* to disillusion
  2 desilusionarse VPR *(decepcionarse)* to be disappointed; *(quedarse sin ilusiones)* to be disillusioned

desinfectante ADJ & NM disinfectant

desinfectar VT to disinfect

desinflar 1 VT to let down, to deflate
  2 desinflarse VPR *(balón)* to go down; *(neumático)* to go flat

desintegración NF disintegration

desintegrar 1 VT to disintegrate
  2 desintegrarse VPR to disintegrate

desinterés *(pl* **desintereses)** NM (**a**) *(indiferencia)* lack of interest, apathy (**b**) *(generosidad)* unselfishness

desinteresado, -a ADJ selfless, unselfish

desintoxicar [44] **1** VT to detoxify
  2 desintoxicarse VPR *(dejar de drogarse)* to come off drugs; *(dejar de beber)* to dry out

desistir VI to desist

deslavazado, -a ADJ disjointed

deslave NM landslide, Br landslip *(caused by flooding or rain)*

desleal ADJ disloyal; *(competencia)* unfair

deslealtad NF disloyalty

deslenguado, -a ADJ foul-mouthed

desliar [29] VT to unwrap

desligar [42] **1** VT (**a**) *(separar)* to separate (**b**) *(desatar)* to untie, to unfasten
  2 desligarse VPR **d. de** to disassociate oneself from

desliz NM mistake, slip; **cometer** *o* **tener un d.** to slip up

deslizar [40] **1** VI to slide
  2 deslizarse VPR (**a**) *(patinar)* to slide (**b**) *(fluir)* to flow

deslucido, -a ADJ (**a**) *(sin brillo)* faded; *(plata)* tarnished (**b**) *(sin gracia)* (acto, ceremonia) dull; *(actuación)* lacklustre, uninspired

deslucir [35] VT *(espectáculo)* to spoil

deslumbrante ADJ *(luz, belleza)* dazzling; **estaba d.** she looked stunning

deslumbrar VT to dazzle

desmadrarse VPR *Esp Fam* to go wild

desmadre NM *Fam (caos)* chaos, utter confusion; *(desenfreno)* rave-up

desmán NM (**a**) *(exceso)* excess (**b**) *(abuso de poder)* abuse (of power)

desmandarse VPR to get out of hand

desmano: a desmano LOC ADV out of the way; **me coge a d.** it is out of my way

desmantelar VT *(casa, fábrica)* to clear out, to strip; *(arsenal, instalaciones)* to dismantle; *(quiosco, andamios)* to take down; *(organización criminal)* to break up

desmaquillante, desmaquillador NM make-up remover

desmaquillarse VPR to remove one's make-up

desmarcarse [44] VPR (**a**) *Dep* to lose one's marker (**b**) *(apartarse)* **d. de** to distance oneself from

desmayado, -a ADJ unconscious; **caer d.** to faint

desmayarse VPR to faint

desmayo NM faint, fainting fit; **tener un d.** to faint

desmedido, -a ADJ disproportionate, out of all proportion; *(ambición)* unbounded

desmejorar VI to deteriorate, to go downhill

desmelenarse VPR *Fam* to let one's hair down

desmembración NF, **desmembramiento** NM dismemberment

desmemoriado, -a ADJ forgetful

desmentir [5] VT to deny

desmenuzar [40] VT (**a**) *(pan, pastel, roca)* to crumble; *(carne)* to chop up (**b**) *(asunto)* to examine in detail

desmerecer [33] VI **no desmerece en nada de** ... it easily bears comparison with ...

desmesura NF excess

desmesurado, -a ADJ excessive

desmilitarizar [40] VT to demilitarize

desmontable ADJ that can be taken to pieces

desmontar 1 VT (**a**) *(desarmar)* to take to pieces, to dismantle (**b**) *(allanar)* to level
2 VI **d. (de)** to dismount, to get off

desmoralizar [40] VT to demoralize

desmoronarse VPR to crumble, to fall to pieces

desnatado, -a ADJ *(leche)* skimmed

desnivel NM *(en el terreno)* drop, difference in height

desnivelar VT *(terreno)* to make uneven; *(situación)* to upset the balance of; *(encuentro)* to make unequal; *(balanza)* to tip

desnucarse [44] VPR to break one's neck

desnuclearizar VT to make nuclear-free

desnudar 1 VT to undress
2 desnudarse VPR to get undressed

desnudez NF nakedness, nudity

desnudo, -a 1 ADJ naked, nude
2 NM *Arte* nude

desnutrición NF malnutrition

desnutrido, -a ADJ undernourished

desobedecer [33] VT to disobey

desobediencia NF disobedience

desobediente 1 ADJ disobedient
2 NMF disobedient person

desocupado, -a ADJ (**a**) *(vacío)* empty, vacant (**b**) *(ocioso)* free, not busy (**c**) *(sin empleo)* unemployed

desocupar VT to empty, to vacate

desodorante ADJ & NM deodorant

desoír [17] VT not to listen to, to take no notice of; **d. los consejos de algn** to ignore sb's advice

desolación NF *(destrucción)* desolation; *(desconsuelo)* distress, grief

desolador, a ADJ *(imagen, espectáculo)* heart-rending; *(noticia)* devastating

desolar VT to devastate

desollar [2] VT to skin

desorbitado, -a ADJ *(precio)* exorbitant

desorden NM untidiness, mess; **¡qué d.!** what a mess!; **d. público** civil disorder

desordenado, -a ADJ messy, untidy

desordenar VT to make untidy, to mess up

desorganización NF disorganization

desorganizar [40] VT to disorganize, to disrupt

desorientación NF disorientation

desorientar 1 VT to disorientate
2 desorientarse VPR to lose one's sense of direction, to lose one's bearings; *Fig* to become disorientated

despabilado, -a ADJ (**a**) *(sin sueño)* wide awake (**b**) *(listo)* quick, smart

despachar VT (**a**) *(asunto)* to get through (**b**) *(correo)* to send, to dispatch (**c**) *(en tienda)* to serve (**d**) *Fam (despedir)* to send packing, to sack (**e**) *Am (facturar)* to check in

despacho NM (**a**) *(oficina)* office; *(en casa)* study (**b**) *(venta)* sale (**c**) *(comunicación)* dispatch

despachurrar VT *Fam* to squash, to flatten

despacio ADV (**a**) *(lentamente)* slowly (**b**) *esp Am (en voz baja)* quietly

despampanante ADJ *Fam* stunning

desparpajo NM self-assurance; **con d.** in a carefree manner

desparramar 1 VT *(líquido)* to spill; *(objetos)* to spread, to scatter
2 desparramarse VPR *(líquido)* to spill; *(objetos, personas)* to scatter, to spread out

despavorido, -a ADJ terrified

despecho NM spite; **por d.** out of spite

despectivo, -a ADJ derogatory, disparaging

despedazar [40] VT to cut o tear to pieces

despedida NF farewell, goodbye; **d. de soltera** hen party o night; **d. de soltero** stag party o night, *US* bachelor party

despedido, -a ADJ (**a**) *(por cierre, reducción de plantilla)* redundant; *(por razones disciplinarias)* sacked (**b**) **salir d.** to be off like a shot

despedir [6] **1** VT (**a**) *(decir adiós)* to see off, to say goodbye to (**b**) *(empleado) (por cierre, reducción de plantilla)* to make redundant, to lay off; *(por razones disciplinarias)* to fire, to sack (**c**) *(olor, humo)* to give off
2 despedirse VPR *(decir adiós)* to say goodbye (**de** to); **ya puedes despedirte del coche** you can say goodbye to the car

despegado, -a ADJ (**a**) *(objeto)* unstuck (**b**) *(persona)* cold, detached

despegar [42] **1** VT to take off, to detach
2 VI *Av* to take off
3 despegarse VPR to come unstuck

despego NM detachment

despegue NM take-off

despeinado, -a ADJ dishevelled, with untidy hair

despeinar 1 VT *(pelo)* to ruffle; **d. a algn** to mess up sb's hair
2 despeinarse VPR to get one's hair messed up

despejado, -a ADJ clear; *(cielo)* cloudless

despejar 1 VT to clear; *(misterio, dudas)* to clear up
2 despejarse VPR (**a**) *(cielo)* to clear (**b**) *(persona)* to clear one's head

despeje NM *Dep* clearance

despellejar VT to skin

despelotarse VPR *Esp Fam* (**a**) *(desnudarse)* to strip (**b**) **d. de risa** to laugh one's head off

despensa NF pantry, larder

despeñadero NM cliff, precipice

despeñarse VPR to go over a cliff

desperdiciar [43] VT to waste; *(oportunidad)* to throw away

desperdicio NM (**a**) *(acto)* waste (**b**) **desperdicios** *(basura)* rubbish; *(desechos)* scraps, leftovers

desperdigar [42] **1** VT to scatter, to disperse
2 desperdigarse VPR to scatter

desperezarse [40] VPR to stretch (oneself)

desperfecto NM (**a**) *(defecto)* flaw, imperfection (**b**) *(daño)* damage

despertador NM alarm clock

despertar [1] **1** VT to wake (up), to awaken; *Fig (sentimiento etc)* to arouse
2 despertarse VPR to wake (up)

despiadado, -a ADJ merciless

despido NM *(expulsión)* dismissal; *(por cierre, reducción de plantilla)* redundancy

despierto, -a ADJ (**a**) *(desvelado)* awake (**b**) *(vivo)* quick, sharp

despilfarrar VT to waste, to squander

despilfarro NM wasting, squandering

despiole NM *RP Fam* rumpus, shindy

despistado, -a ADJ (**a**) *(olvidadizo)* absent-minded (**b**) *(momentáneamente)* distracted (**c**) *(confuso)* confused

despistar **1** VT (**a**) *(perseguidor)* to shake off; *(perro)* to throw off the scent (**b**) *(confundir)* to mislead (**c**) *(distraer)* to distract
2 despistarse VPR (**a**) *(confundirse)* to get mixed up *o* confused (**b**) *(distraerse)* to get *o* be distracted

despiste NM (**a**) *(cualidad)* absent-mindedness (**b**) *(error)* slip-up

desplazamiento NM *(viaje)* trip, journey

desplazar [40] **1** VT (**a**) *(trasladar)* to move (**a** to) (**b**) *(tomar el lugar de)* to take the place of (**c**) *Náut* to displace
2 desplazarse VPR (**a**) *(viajar)* to travel (**b**) *(moverse)* to move

desplegar [1] **1** VT (**a**) *(tela, mapa)* to unfold; *(alas)* to spread, to open (**b**) *(cualidad)* to display (**c**) *Mil* to deploy
2 desplegarse VPR (**a**) *(abrirse)* to open (out), to spread (out) (**b**) *Mil* to deploy

despliegue NM (**a**) *Mil* deployment (**b**) *(de medios etc)* display

desplomarse VPR to collapse; *(precios)* to slump, to fall sharply

desplumar VT (**a**) *(ave)* to pluck (**b**) *Fam (estafar)* to fleece

despoblado, -a **1** ADJ unpopulated, deserted
2 NM deserted spot

despoblar [2] VT to depopulate

despojar VT to strip (**de** of)

despojos NMPL *(de animales)* offal; *(cadáver)* remains

desposado, -a NM,F *Fml (hombre)* groom; *(mujer)* bride; **los desposados** the newlyweds

desposar VT *Fml* to marry

desposeer [36] VT to dispossess (**de** of)

desposeído NM **los desposeídos** the have-nots

déspota NMF despot

despótico, -a ADJ despotic

despotismo NM despotism

despotricar [44] VI to rant and rave (**contra** about)

despreciable ADJ despicable, contemptible; *(cantidad)* negligible

despreciar [43] VT (**a**) *(desdeñar)* to scorn, to despise (**b**) *(rechazar)* to reject, to spurn

desprecio NM (**a**) *(desdén)* scorn, disdain (**b**) *(desaire)* slight, snub

desprender **1** VT (**a**) *(separar)* to remove, to detach (**b**) *(olor, humo etc)* to give off
2 desprenderse VPR (**a**) *(soltarse)* to come off *o* away (**b**) **desprenderse de** to rid oneself of, to free oneself from (**c**) **de aquí se desprende que …** it can be deduced from this that …

desprendido, -a ADJ generous

desprendimiento NM (**a**) *(separación)* detachment; **d. de tierras** landslide (**b**) *(generosidad)* generosity

despreocupado, -a ADJ (**a**) *(tranquilo)* unconcerned (**b**) *(descuidado)* careless; *(estilo)* casual

despreocuparse VPR (**a**) *(tranquilizarse)* to stop worrying (**b**) *(desentenderse)* to be unconcerned (**de** about), to be indifferent (**de** to)

desprestigiar [43] VT to discredit, to run down

desprestigio NM discredit, loss of reputation; **campaña de d.** smear campaign

desprevenido, -a ADJ unprepared; **coger** *o* **pillar a algn d.** to catch sb unawares

desprolijo, -a *RP* ADJ *(casa)* messy, untidy; *(cuaderno)* untidy; *(persona)* unkempt, dishevelled

desproporción NF disproportion, lack of proportion

desproporcionado, -a ADJ disproportionate

desprovisto, -a ADJ **d. (de)** lacking, without, devoid (of)

después ADV (**a**) *(más tarde)* later, afterwards; *(entonces)* then; *(seguidamente)* next; **una semana d.** a week later; **poco d.** soon after (**b**) *(lugar)* next (**c**) **d. de** after; **d. de la guerra** after the war; **mi calle está d. de la tuya** my street is the one after yours; **d. de cenar** after eating; **d. de todo** after all (**d**) **d. de que** after; **d. de que viniera** after he came

despuntar VI (**a**) *(día)* to dawn (**b**) *(destacar)* to excel, to stand out

desquiciar [43] **1** VT *(persona)* to unhinge
2 desquiciarse VPR *(persona)* to go crazy

desquitarse VPR to take revenge (**de** for)

desquite NM revenge

destacado, -a ADJ outstanding

destacamento NM detachment

destacar [44] **1** VT to emphasize, to stress
2 VI to stand out
3 destacarse VPR to stand out

destajo NM piecework; **trabajar a d.** to do piecework

destapador NM *Am* bottle opener

destapar 1 VT to take the lid off; *(botella)* to open; *Fig (asunto)* to uncover; *RP (caño)* to unblock
2 destaparse VPR to get uncovered

destartalado, -a ADJ rambling; *(desvencijado)* ramshackle

destello NM flash, sparkle

destemplado, -a ADJ (**a**) *(voz, gesto)* sharp, snappy; **con cajas destempladas** rudely, brusquely (**b**) *(tiempo)* unpleasant (**c**) *(enfermo)* indisposed, out of sorts (**d**) *Mús* out of tune, discordant

desteñir [6] **1** VT & VI to discolour
2 desteñirse VPR to lose colour, to fade

desternillarse VPR **d. (de risa)** to split one's sides laughing

desterrar [1] VT to exile

destiempo: a destiempo LOC ADV at the wrong time o moment

destierro NM exile

destilación NF distillation

destilado, -a ADJ distilled; **agua destilada** distilled water

destilar VT to distil

destilería NF distillery

destinado, -a ADJ destined, bound; *Fig* **d. al fracaso** doomed to failure

destinar VT (**a**) *(dinero etc)* to set aside, to assign (**b**) *(empleado)* to appoint

destinatario, -a NM,F (**a**) *(de carta)* addressee (**b**) *(de mercancías)* consignee

destino NM (**a**) *(rumbo)* destination; **el avión con d. a Bilbao** the plane to Bilbao (**b**) *(sino)* fate, fortune (**c**) *(de empleo)* post

destitución NF dismissal from office

destituir [37] VT to dismiss o remove from office

destornillador NM screwdriver

destornillar VT to unscrew

destreza NF skill

destrozado, -a ADJ (**a**) *(roto)* torn-up, smashed (**b**) *(cansado)* worn-out, exhausted (**c**) *(abatido)* shattered

destrozar [40] VT (**a**) *(destruir)* to destroy; *(rasgar)* to tear to shreds o pieces (**b**) *(persona)* to shatter; *(vida, reputación)* to ruin

destrozo NM damage

destrucción NF destruction

destructivo, -a ADJ destructive

destructor, -a 1 ADJ destructive
2 NM *Náut* destroyer

destruir [37] VT to destroy

desubicado, -a NM,F *Andes, RP* **es un d.** he has no idea of how to behave

desusado, -a ADJ old-fashioned, outdated

desuso NM disuse; **caer en d.** to fall into disuse; **en d.** obsolete, outdated

desvalido, -a ADJ defenceless

desvalijar VT *(robar)* to clean out, to rob; *(casa, tienda)* to burgle

desvalorizar [40] VT to devalue

desván NM attic, loft

desvanecerse [33] VPR (**a**) *(disiparse)* to vanish, to fade away (**b**) *(desmayarse)* to faint

desvanecimiento NM *(desmayo)* fainting fit

desvariar [29] VI to talk nonsense

desvarío NM (**a**) *(delirio)* raving, delirium (**b**) *(disparate)* nonsense

desvelado, -a ADJ awake, wide awake

desvelar 1 VT to keep awake
2 desvelarse VPR (**a**) *(despabilarse)* to stay awake (**b**) *(desvivirse)* to devote oneself (**por** to) (**c**) *CAm, Méx (quedarse despierto)* to stay up o awake

desvencijar 1 VT to take apart
2 desvencijarse VPR to fall apart

desventaja NF disadvantage; **estar en d.** to be at a disadvantage

desventura NF misfortune, bad luck

desvergonzado, -a 1 ADJ (**a**) *(indecente)* shameless (**b**) *(descarado)* insolent
2 NM,F (**a**) *(sinvergüenza)* shameless person (**b**) *(fresco)* insolent o cheeky person

desvergüenza NF (**a**) *(indecencia)* shamelessness (**b**) *(atrevimiento)* insolence; **tuvo la d. de negarlo** he had the cheek to deny it (**c**) *(impertinencia)* insolent o rude remark

desvestir [6] **1** VT to undress
2 desvestirse VPR to undress (oneself)

desviación NF *(de dirección, cauce, norma)* deviation; *(de carretera)* Br diversion, US detour; *Med* **d. de columna** slipped disc

desviar [29] **1** VT *(río, carretera)* to divert; *(golpe, conversación)* to deflect; **d. la mirada** to look away
2 desviarse VPR to go off course; *(vehículo)* to turn off; *Fig* **desviarse del tema** to digress

desvincular 1 VT to dissociate (**de** from)
2 desvincularse VPR to dissociate oneself (**de** from)

desvío NM *Br* diversion, *US* detour

desvirgar [42] VT to deflower

desvirtuar [30] VT to distort

desvivirse VPR **d. por algn** to do everything one can for sb; **d. por hacer algo** to bend over backwards to do sth

detalladamente ADV in (great) detail

detallado, -a ADJ detailed, thorough

detallar VT to give the details of

detalle NM (a) *(pormenor)* detail; **entrar en detalles** to go into details (b) *(delicadeza)* nice thought, nicety; **¡qué d.!** how nice!, how sweet! (c) *(toque decorativo)* touch, ornament

detallista 1 ADJ perfectionist
2 NMF *Com* retailer

detectar VT to detect

detective NMF detective; **d. privado** private detective o eye

detector NM detector; **d. de incendios** smoke detector

detención NF (a) *Der* arrest (b) **con d.** carefully, thoroughly

detener [24] 1 VT (a) *(parar)* to stop, to halt (b) *Der (arrestar)* to arrest
2 **detenerse** VPR to stop

detenidamente ADV carefully, thoroughly

detenido, -a 1 ADJ (a) *(parado)* standing still, stopped (b) *(arrestado)* detained (c) *(minucioso)* detailed, thorough
2 NM,F detainee, person under arrest

detenimiento NM **con d.** carefully, thoroughly

detentar VT to hold

detergente NM detergent; **d. (para la ropa)** washing powder

deteriorar 1 VT to spoil, to damage
2 **deteriorarse** VPR *(estropearse)* to deteriorate; *(empeorar)* to deteriorate, to get worse

deterioro NM *(empeoramiento)* deterioration, worsening; *(daño)* damage

determinación NF (a) *(resolución)* determination; **con d.** determinedly (b) *(decisión)* decision

determinado, -a ADJ (a) *(preciso)* definite, precise (b) *(resuelto)* decisive, resolute (c) *Ling* definite

determinante ADJ decisive

determinar 1 VT (a) *(fecha etc)* to fix, to set (b) *(decidir)* to decide on (c) *(condicionar)* to determine (d) *(ocasionar)* to bring about
2 **determinarse** VPR to make up one's mind to

detestable ADJ detestable, repulsive

detestar VT to detest, to hate

detonante NM detonator; *Fig* trigger

detonar VT to detonate

detractor, -a NM,F detractor

detrás ADV behind; **d. de** behind, on o at the back of

detrimento NM **en d. de** to the detriment of

detuve PT INDEF *de* **detener**

deuda NF debt; **estoy en d. contigo** *(monetaria)* I am in debt to you; *(moral)* I am indebted to you; **d. pública** *(concepto)* public debt; *(títulos)* government stock

deudor, -a 1 ADJ indebted
2 NM,F debtor

devaluación NF devaluation

devaluar [30] VT to devalue

devanar 1 VT *(hilo)* to wind; *(alambre)* to coil
2 **devanarse** VPR *Fam* **d. los sesos** to rack one's brains

devaneos NMPL *(amorosos)* flirtation; **tuvo sus d. con la ultraderecha** he flirted with the far right

devastador, -a ADJ devastating

devastar VT to devastate, to ravage

devengar [42] VT *Com* to earn, to accrue

devenir [27] VI to become

devoción NF (a) *Rel* devoutness (b) *(al trabajo etc)* devotion; *Fam* **Juan no es santo de mi d.** Juan isn't really my cup of tea

devolución NF *(de objeto)* return; *(de dinero)* refund

devolver [4] *(pp devuelto)* 1 VT to give back, return; *(dinero)* to refund
2 VI *(vomitar)* to vomit, throw o bring up
3 **devolverse** VPR *Am salvo RP* to come back

devorar VT to devour

devoto, -a 1 ADJ pious, devout
2 NM,F (a) *Rel* pious person (b) *(seguidor)* devotee

devuelto, -a PP *de* **devolver**

DF NM *(abr* **Distrito Federal)** *(en México)* Mexico City

DGI NF *RP (abr* **Dirección General Impositiva)** *Br* ≃ Inland Revenue, *US* ≃ IRS

DGT NF *(abr* **Dirección General de Tráfico)** = government department responsible for road transport

di (a) PT INDEF *de* **dar** (b) IMPERAT *de* **decir**

día NM day; **¿qué d. es hoy?** what's the date today?; **d. a d.** day by day; **de d.** by day; **durante el d.** during the daytime; **de un d. para otro** overnight; **un d. sí y otro no** every other day; **pan del d.** fresh bread; **hoy (en) d.** nowadays; **el d. de mañana** in the future; *Fig* **estar al d.** to be up to date; *Fig* **poner al d.** to bring up to date; **d. festivo** holiday; **d. laborable** working day; **d. libre** free day, day off; **es de d.** it is daylight; **hace buen/mal d.** it's a nice/bad day, the weather is nice/bad today

diabetes NF INV diabetes

diabético, -a ADJ & NM,F diabetic

diablo NM devil; *Fam* **¡al d. con …!** to hell with …!; *Fam* **vete al d.** get lost; *Fam* **¿qué/cómo diablos …?** what/how the hell …?

diablura NF mischief

diabólico, -a ADJ (a) *(del diablo)* diabolic (b) *(muy malo, difícil)* diabolical

diácono NM deacon

diadema NF tiara

diáfano, -a ADJ (a) *(claro)* *(luz, cielo, ojos)* clear; *(agua, explicación)* crystal-clear (b) *Esp (espacio)* open-plan

diafragma NM diaphragm

diagnosis NF INV diagnosis

diagnosticar [44] VT to diagnose

diagnóstico NM diagnosis

diagonal ADJ & NF diagonal; **en d.** diagonally

diagrama NM diagram; *Inform* **d. de flujo** flowchart

dial NM dial

dialecto NM dialect

dialogar [42] VI to have a conversation; *(para negociar)* to talk

diálogo NM dialogue

diamante NM diamond

diámetro NM diameter

diana NF (a) *Mil* reveille (b) *(blanco)* bull's eye

diapositiva NF slide

diariamente ADV daily, every day

diariero, -a NM,F *Andes, RP* newspaper seller

diario, -a 1 NM (a) *Prensa* (daily) newspaper (b) *(memorias)* diary; *Náut* **d. de a bordo, d. de navegación** logbook
  2 ADJ daily; **a d.** daily, every day

diarrea NF diarrhoea

diatriba NF diatribe

dibujante NMF (a) *(artista)* drawer; *(de cómic)* cartoonist (b) *Téc (hombre)* draughtsman; *(mujer)* draughtswoman

dibujar VT to draw

dibujo NM (a) *(técnica, obra)* drawing; **d. artístico** artistic drawing; **d. lineal** draughtsmanship; **dibujos animados** cartoons (b) *(en tela)* pattern

diccionario NM dictionary; **buscar** *o* **mirar una palabra en el d.** to look up a word in the dictionary

dicha NF happiness

dicharachero, -a ADJ talkative

dicho, -a 1 ADJ (a) said; **mejor d.** or rather; **d. de otro modo** to put it another way; **d. sea de paso** let it be said in passing; **d. y hecho** no sooner said than done (b) *(mencionado)* **dicha persona** the above-mentioned person
  2 PP *de* **decir**

dichoso, -a ADJ (a) *(feliz)* happy (b) *Fam* damned; **¡este d. trabajo!** this damned job!

diciembre NM December

dictado NM dictation; *Fig* **dictados** dictates

dictador, -a NM,F dictator

dictadura NF dictatorship

dictáfono® NM Dictaphone®

dictamen NM *(juicio)* ruling; *(informe)* report

dictaminar VI to rule (**sobre** on)

dictar VT (a) *(texto)* to dictate; *Am (clase)* to teach, to give (b) *(sentencia)* to pronounce, to pass; *(ley)* to enact; *(decreto)* to issue

dictatorial ADJ dictatorial

didáctico, -a ADJ didactic

diecinueve ADJ & NM INV nineteen

dieciocho ADJ & NM INV eighteen

dieciséis ADJ & NM INV sixteen

diecisiete ADJ & NM INV seventeen

diente NM tooth; *Téc* cog; *(de ajo)* clove; **d. de leche** milk tooth; **dientes postizos** false teeth; *Fig* **hablar entre dientes** to mumble; *Fig* **poner los dientes largos a algn** to make sb green with envy

diera SUBJ IMPERF *de* **dar**

diéresis NF INV diaeresis

diesel ADJ & NM diesel

diestra NF right hand

diestro, -a 1 ADJ (a) *(hábil)* skilful, clever (b) *Esp* **a d. y siniestro** right, left and centre
  2 NM *Taurom* bullfighter, matador

dieta NF (a) diet; **estar a d.** to be on a diet (b) **dietas** expense *o* subsistence allowance

dietética NF dietetics *sing*

dietista NMF dietician

diez ADJ & NM INV ten

difamación NF defamation, slander; *(escrita)* libel

difamar VT to defame, to slander; *(por escrito)* to libel

diferencia NF difference; **a d. de** unlike

diferencial 1 NM *Téc* differential
  2 NF *Mat* differential

diferenciar [43] **1** VT to differentiate, to distinguish (**entre** between)
  2 diferenciarse VPR to differ (**de** from), to be different (**de** from *o* US than)

diferente 1 ADJ different (**de** from *o* US than)
  2 ADV differently

diferido, -a ADJ *TV* **en d.** recorded

diferir [5] **1** VT *(posponer)* to postpone, to put off
  2 VI *(diferenciarse)* to differ, to be different; **d. de algn en algo** to differ from sb in sth

difícil ADJ difficult, hard; **d. de creer/hacer** difficult to believe/do; **es d. que venga** it is unlikely that she'll come

dificultad NF difficulty; *(aprieto)* trouble, problem

dificultar VT **d. algo** to make sth difficult

dificultoso, -a ADJ difficult, hard

difuminar VT to blur

difundir 1 VT *(noticia, doctrina, epidemia)* to spread; *(luz, calor)* to diffuse; *(emisión radiofónica)* to broadcast
  2 difundirse VPR *(noticia, doctrina, epidemia)* to spread; *(luz, calor)* to be diffused

difunto, -a 1 ADJ late, deceased
  2 NM,F deceased

difusión NF (a) *(de noticia)* spreading; **tener gran d.** to be widely broadcast (b) *Rad & TV* broadcasting

difuso, -a ADJ diffuse

digerir [5] VT to digest; *Fig* to assimilate

digestión NF digestion; **corte de d.** sudden indigestion

digestivo, -a ADJ digestive

digitador, -a NM,F *Am* keyboarder

digital ADJ digital; **huellas digitales** fingerprints; **tocadiscos d.** CD player

digitalizar VT to digitize

digitar VT *Am* to key, to type

dígito NM digit

dignarse VPR **d. (a)** to deign to, to condescend to

dignidad NF dignity

digno, -a ADJ (a) *(merecedor)* worthy; **d. de admiración** worthy of admiration; **d. de mención/verse** worth mentioning/seeing (b) *(decoroso)* decent, good

digo INDIC PRES *de* **decir**

dije PT INDEF *de* **decir**

dilación NF delay, hold-up; **sin d.** without delay

dilatado, -a ADJ (a) *(agrandado)* dilated (b) *(vasto)* vast, extensive

dilatar 1 VT (a) *(agrandar)* to expand (b) *(pupila)* to dilate
2 dilatarse VPR (a) *(agrandarse)* to expand (b) *(pupila)* to dilate

dilema NM dilemma

diligencia NF (a) *(prontitud)* **con d.** expeditiously (b) **diligencias** formalities; *Der* proceedings (c) *(vehículo)* stagecoach

diligente ADJ *(persona)* efficient, swift; *(respuesta)* prompt

dilucidar VT to elucidate

diluir [37] 1 VT to dilute
2 diluirse VPR to dilute

diluviar [43] V IMPERS to pour with rain

diluvio NM flood; **el D. (Universal)** the Flood

diluyo INDIC PRES *de* **diluir**

dimensión NF (a) *(en el espacio, tamaño)* dimension; **de grandes dimensiones** very large (b) *(magnitud)* scale

diminutivo, -a ADJ & NM diminutive

diminuto, -a ADJ minute, tiny

dimisión NF resignation; **presentar la d.** to hand in one's resignation

dimitir VI to resign (**de** from); **d. de un cargo** to give in *o* tender one's resignation

Dinamarca N Denmark

dinámica NF dynamics *sing*

dinámico, -a ADJ dynamic

dinamita NF dynamite

dinamitar VT to dynamite

dinamo, dínamo NF *Esp,* NM *Am* dynamo

dinar NM *Fin* dinar

dinastía NF dynasty

dineral NM *Fam* fortune

dinero NM money; **d. contante (y sonante)** cash; **d. efectivo** *o* **en metálico** cash; **gente de d.** wealthy people

dinosaurio NM dinosaur

diócesis NF INV diocese

dios NM god; **¡D. mío!** my God!; **¡por D.!** for goodness sake!; **a la buena de D.** any old

how; **hacer algo como D. manda** to do sth properly; *Fam* **ni d.** nobody; *Fam* **todo d.** everybody

diosa NF goddess

diploma NM diploma

diplomacia NF diplomacy

diplomado, -a 1 ADJ qualified
2 NM,F holder of a diploma

diplomarse VPR to graduate

diplomático, -a 1 ADJ diplomatic; **cuerpo d.** diplomatic corps
2 NM,F diplomat

diplomatura NF *Educ* ≃ diploma, = qualification obtained after three years of university study

diptongo NM diphthong

diputación NF *Esp* **d. provincial** = governing body of each province, ≃ county council

diputado, -a NM,F *Br* ≃ Member of Parliament, MP; *US* ≃ representative; **Congreso de Diputados** *Br* ≃ House of Commons, *US* ≃ Congress; **d. provincial** ≃ county councillor

dique NM dyke

diré FUT *de* **decir**

dirección NF (a) *(sentido, rumbo)* direction; *Aut (en letrero)* **d. prohibida** no entry; **calle de d. única** one-way street (b) *(señas)* address; *Inform* **d. de correo electrónico** e-mail address (c) *Cin & Teatro* direction (d) *(destino)* destination (e) *Aut & Téc* steering (f) *(mando)* *(de empresa, hospital)* management; *(de partido)* leadership; *(de colegio)* headship

direccional NM *o* NF *Col, Ecuad, Méx Br* indicator, *US* turn signal

directa NF *Aut* top gear

directamente ADV directly, straight away

directiva NF (a) *(junta)* board (of directors) (b) *(ley de la UE)* directive

directivo, -a ADJ directive; **junta directiva** board of directors

directo, -a ADJ direct; *TV & Rad* **en d.** live

director, -a NM,F *(de empresa)* director; *(de hotel, banco)* manager; *(de colegio)* *Br* headmaster, *f* headmistress, *US* principal; *(de periódico)* editor; **d. de cine** movie *o Br* film director; **d. de orquesta** conductor; **d. gerente** managing director

directorio NM *Inform* directory; *Am salvo RP* **d. telefónico** telephone directory

directriz NF (a) *(norma)* guideline (b) *Mat* directrix

dirigente 1 ADJ leading; **clase d.** ruling class
2 NMF leader

dirigir [57] 1 VT to direct; *(empresa)* to manage; *(negocio, colegio)* to run; *(orquesta)* to conduct; *(partido)* to lead; *(periódico)* to edit; *(coche, barco)* to steer; **d. la palabra a algn** to speak to sb
2 dirigirse VPR (a) **dirigirse a** *o* **hacia** to go to, to make one's way towards (b) *(escribir)* to

write; **diríjase al apartado de correos 42** write to PO Box 42 (**c**) (*hablar*) to speak

discapacidad NF disability

discapacitado, -a 1 ADJ disabled
2 NM,F disabled person

discar [44] VT *Andes, RP* to dial

discernir [54] VT to discern, to distinguish; **d. algo de algo** to distinguish sth from sth

disciplina NF discipline

disciplinado, -a ADJ disciplined

discípulo, -a NM,F disciple

disco NM (**a**) *Anat, Astron & Geom* disc; **d. de freno** brake disc (**b**) *Mús* record, album; **d. compacto** compact disc (**c**) *Inform* disk; **d. duro** hard disk (**d**) *Dep* discus (**e**) *Tel* dial

discográfico, -a ADJ **casa** *o* **compañía discográfica** record company

disconforme ADJ **estar d. con** to disagree with

discontinuo, -a ADJ *Aut* **línea discontinua** broken line

discordante ADJ discordant; **ser la nota d.** to be the odd man out

discordia NF discord; **la manzana de la d.** the bone of contention; **sembrar d.** to sow discord

discoteca NF (**a**) (*lugar*) nightclub (**b**) (*colección*) record collection

discreción NF (**a**) (*reserva*) discretion (**b**) **a d.** at will

discrecional ADJ (*cantidad*) according to taste; (*poderes*) discretionary; **parada d.** (*en autobús*) request stop

discrepancia NF (*desacuerdo*) disagreement; (*diferencia*) discrepancy

discrepar VI (*disentir*) to disagree (**de** with; **en** on); (*diferenciarse*) to be different (**de** from *o US* than)

discreto, -a ADJ (**a**) (*prudente, reservado*) discreet (**b**) (*mediocre*) average

discriminación NF discrimination

discriminar VT (**a**) (*marginar*) to discriminate against (**b**) *Fml* (*diferenciar*) to discriminate between, to distinguish

disculpa NF excuse; **dar disculpas** to make excuses; **pedir disculpas a algn** to apologize to sb

disculpar 1 VT to excuse
2 disculparse VPR to apologize (**por** for)

discurrir VI (**a**) (*reflexionar*) to think (**b**) *Fig* (*transcurrir*) to pass, to go by (**c**) *Fml* (*río*) to wander

discurso NM speech; **dar** *o* **pronunciar un d.** to make a speech

discusión NF argument

discutible ADJ debatable

discutir 1 VI to argue (**de** about)
2 VT to discuss, to talk about

disecar [44] VT (**a**) (*animal*) to stuff (**b**) (*planta*) to dry

diseminar VT to disseminate, to spread

disentir [54] VI to dissent, to disagree (**de** with)

diseñador, -a NM,F designer; **d. gráfico** graphic designer

diseñar VT to design

diseño NM design; **ropa de d.** designer clothes; **d. gráfico** graphic design; **d. industrial** industrial design

disertar VI to expound (**sobre** on *o* upon)

disfraz NM disguise; (*para fiesta*) fancy dress; **fiesta de disfraces** fancy dress party

disfrazar [40] **1** VT to disguise
2 disfrazarse VPR to disguise oneself; **disfrazarse de pirata** to dress up as a pirate

disfrutar 1 VI (**a**) (*gozar*) to enjoy oneself (**b**) (*poseer*) **d. (de)** to enjoy
2 VT to enjoy

disgregar [42] VT (**a**) (*multitud, manifestación*) to disperse, to break up (**b**) (*roca, imperio, Estado*) to break up; (*átomo*) to split

disgustado, -a ADJ upset

disgustar 1 VT (**a**) (*apenar*) to upset (**b**) (*desagradar*) **no me disgusta** it's not bad
2 disgustarse VPR (**a**) (*enojarse*) to get upset (**b**) (*enemistarse*) to fall out

> Observa que el verbo inglés **to disgust** es un falso amigo y no es la traducción del verbo español **disgustar**. En inglés **to disgust** significa "repugnar, indignar".

disgusto NM (**a**) (*pena*) **llevarse un d.** to get upset; **dar un d. a algn** to upset sb (**b**) (*desgracia*) trouble (**c**) (*pelea*) fall-out, disagreement (**d**) **estar a d.** to feel uncomfortable *o* uneasy; **hacer algo a d.** to do sth unwillingly *o* reluctantly

> Observa que la palabra inglesa **disgust** es un falso amigo y no es la traducción de la palabra española **disgusto**. En inglés **disgust** significa "repugnancia, asco".

disidente ADJ & NMF dissident

disimuladamente ADV quietly, discreetly

disimulado, -a ADJ (*oculto*) concealed

disimular 1 VT to conceal, to hide
2 VI to pretend

disimulo NM pretence

disipar 1 VT (**a**) (*dudas, sospechas*) to dispel (**b**) (*fortuna, herencia*) to squander, to throw away (**c**) (*niebla, humo, vapor*) to drive *o* blow away
2 disiparse VPR (**a**) (*dudas, sospechas*) to be dispelled (**b**) (*niebla, humo, vapor*) to vanish

dislexia NF dyslexia

dislocar [44] VT to dislocate

disminución NF decrease

disminuir [37] **1** VT to reduce
2 VI to diminish

disolución NF (*de empresa, partido, matrimonio*) dissolution; (*de manifestación*) breaking up

disolvente ADJ & NM solvent

disolver [4] *(pp* **disuelto)** 1 VT (**a**) *(en líquido)* to dissolve (**b**) *(reunión, manifestación)* to break up; *(empresa, partido, matrimonio)* to dissolve
2 **disolverse** VPR (**a**) *(en líquido)* to dissolve (**b**) *(reunión, manifestación)* to break up

disparar 1 VT *(pistola etc)* to fire; *(flecha, balón)* to shoot; **d. a algn** to shoot at sb
2 **dispararse** VPR (**a**) *(arma)* to go off, to fire (**b**) *(precios)* to rocket

disparatado, -a ADJ absurd

disparate NM (**a**) *(dicho)* nonsense; **decir disparates** to talk nonsense (**b**) *(acto)* foolish act

disparidad NF disparity

disparo NM shot; *Dep* **d. a puerta** shot (at goal)

dispensar VT (**a**) *(disculpar)* to pardon, to forgive (**b**) *(eximir)* to exempt

dispersar 1 VT to disperse; *(esparcir)* to scatter
2 **dispersarse** VPR to disperse

disperso, -a ADJ *(separado)* dispersed; *(esparcido)* scattered

displicencia NF condescension, disdain

displicente ADJ condescending, disdainful

disponer [19] *(pp* **dispuesto)** 1 VT (**a**) *(arreglar)* to arrange, to set out (**b**) *(ordenar)* to order
2 VI **d. de** to have at one's disposal
3 **disponerse** VPR to prepare, to get ready

disponible ADJ available

disposición NF (**a**) *(uso)* disposal; **a su d.** at your disposal o service (**b**) *(colocación)* arrangement, layout (**c**) **no estar en d. de** not to be prepared to (**d**) *(orden)* order, law

dispositivo NM device

dispuesto, -a 1 ADJ (**a**) *(ordenado)* arranged (**b**) *(a punto)* ready (**c**) *(decidido)* determined; **no estar d. a** not to be prepared to (**d**) **según lo d. por la ley** in accordance with what the law stipulates
2 PP *de* **disponer**

disputa NF *(discusión)* argument; *(contienda)* contest

disputar 1 VT (**a**) *(premio)* to compete for (**b**) *Dep (partido)* to play
2 **disputarse** VPR *(premio)* to compete for

disquete NM *Inform* diskette, floppy disk

disquetera NF *Inform* disk drive

distancia NF distance; **a d.** from a distance

distanciamiento NM distancing

distanciar [43] 1 VT to separate
2 **distanciarse** VPR to become separated; *(de otra persona)* to distance oneself

distante ADJ distant, far-off

distar VI to be distant o away; *Fig* **d. de** to be far from; **dista mucho de ser perfecto** it's far from (being) perfect

distender [3] VT to ease, to relax

distendido, -a ADJ relaxed, informal

distinción NF distinction; **a d. de** unlike; **sin d. de** irrespective of

distinguido, -a ADJ distinguished

distinguir [59] 1 VT (**a**) *(diferenciar)* to distinguish (**b**) *(reconocer)* to recognize (**c**) *(honrar)* to honour
2 VI *(diferenciar)* to discriminate
3 **distinguirse** VPR to distinguish oneself

distintivo, -a 1 ADJ distinctive, distinguishing
2 NM distinctive sign o mark

distinto, -a ADJ different

distorsión NF distortion

distracción NF (**a**) *(entretenimiento)* entertainment; *(pasatiempo)* pastime, hobby (**b**) *(descuido)* distraction, absent-mindedness

distraer [25] 1 VT (**a**) *(atención)* to distract (**b**) *(divertir)* to entertain, to amuse
2 **distraerse** VPR (**a**) *(divertirse)* to amuse oneself (**b**) *(abstraerse)* to let one's mind wander

distraído, -a ADJ (**a**) *(divertido)* entertaining (**b**) *(abstraido)* absent-minded

distribución NF (**a**) *(reparto, división)* distribution (**b**) *(de casa, habitaciones)* layout

distribuidor, -a 1 ADJ distributing
2 NM,F distributor

distribuir [37] VT to distribute; *(trabajo)* to share out

distrito NM district; **d. postal** postal district

disturbio NM riot, disturbance

disuadir VT to dissuade

disuasión NF deterrence

disuelto, -a PP *de* **disolver**

DIU NM *(abr* **dispositivo intrauterino)** IUD, coil

diurético, -a ADJ & NM diuretic

diurno, -a ADJ daytime

diva NF *Mús* diva, prima donna

divagar [42] VI to digress, to wander

diván NM divan, couch

divergencia NF *(de líneas)* divergence; *(de opiniones)* difference of opinion

divergente ADJ *(líneas)* divergent, diverging; *(opiniones)* different, differing

diversidad NF diversity

diversificar [44] 1 VT to diversify
2 **diversificarse** VPR to be diversified o varied; *(empresa)* to diversify

diversión NF fun

diverso, -a ADJ different; **diversos** several, various

divertido, -a ADJ amusing, funny

divertir [5] 1 VT to amuse, to entertain
2 **divertirse** VPR to enjoy oneself, to have a good time; **¡que te diviertas!** enjoy yourself!, have fun!

dividendo NM dividend

dividir 1 VT to divide (**en** into); *Mat* **15 dividido entre 3** 15 divided by 3
2 **dividirse** VPR to divide, to split up

divinidad NF divinity

divino, -a ADJ divine

divisa NF (**a**) (*emblema*) symbol, emblem (**b**) *Com* **divisas** foreign currency

divisar VT to make out, to discern

división NF division

divisorio, -a ADJ dividing

divorciado, -a 1 ADJ divorced
2 NM,F (*hombre*) divorcé; (*mujer*) divorcée

divorciar [43] **1** VT to divorce
2 divorciarse VPR to get divorced; **se divorció de él** she divorced him, she got a divorce from him

divorcio NM divorce

divulgación NF (*de noticia, secreto*) revelation; (*de cultura, ciencia*) popularization; **una obra de d. científica** a work of popular science

divulgar [42] VT (*noticia, secreto*) to reveal; (*cultura, ciencia*) to popularize

dizque ADV *Andes, Carib, Méx Fam* apparently

DNI NM (*abr* **Documento Nacional de Identidad**) Identity Card, ID card

do NM *Mús* (*de solfa*) doh, do; (*de escala diatónica*) C; **do de pecho** high C

dóberman NM Doberman (pinscher)

dobladillo NM (*de traje, vestido*) hem; (*de pantalón*) *Br* turn-up, *US* cuff

doblaje NM *Cin* dubbing

doblar 1 VT (**a**) (*duplicar*) to double; **me dobla la edad** he is twice as old as I am (**b**) (*plegar*) to fold *o* turn up (**c**) (*torcer*) to bend (**d**) (*la esquina*) to go round (**e**) (*película*) to dub
2 VI (**a**) (*girar*) to turn; **d. a la derecha/izquierda** to turn right/left (**b**) (*campanas*) to toll
3 doblarse VPR (**a**) (*plegarse*) to fold (**b**) (*torcerse*) to bend

doble 1 ADJ double; **arma de d. filo** double-edged weapon
2 NM (**a**) **el d.** twice as much; **gana el d. que tú** she earns twice as much as you do (**b**) (*persona parecida*) double; *Cin* stand-in

doblegar [42] **1** VT to bend
2 doblegarse VPR to give in

doblez 1 NM (*pliegue*) fold
2 NM *o* NF *Fig* two-facedness, hypocrisy

doce ADJ & NM INV twelve

docena NF dozen

docencia NF teaching

docente ADJ teaching; **centro d.** educational centre

dócil ADJ docile

doctor, -a NM,F doctor

doctorado NM *Univ* doctorate, PhD

doctorarse VPR to get one's doctorate (**en** in)

doctrina NF doctrine

documentación NF documentation; (*DNI, de conducir etc*) papers

documental ADJ & NM documentary

documentar 1 VT to document
2 documentarse VPR **d. (sobre)** to research (about *o* on)

documento NM document; **d. nacional de identidad** identity card

dogma NM dogma

dogmático, -a ADJ dogmatic

dogo NM bulldog

dólar NM dollar

dolarización NF *Econ* dollarization

dolencia NF ailment

doler [4] **1** VI to hurt, to ache; **me duele la cabeza** I've got a headache; **me duele la mano** my hand is sore
2 dolerse VPR to be sorry *o* sad

dolido, -a ADJ **estar d.** to be hurt

dolor NM (**a**) *Med* pain; **d. de cabeza** headache; **d. de muelas** toothache (**b**) (*pena*) grief, sorrow

dolorido, -a ADJ (**a**) (*dañado*) sore, aching (**b**) (*apenado*) hurt

doloroso, -a ADJ painful

domador, -a NM,F (*de animales salvajes*) tamer; (*de caballos*) breaker; **d. de leones** lion tamer

domar VT to tame; (*caballo*) to break in

domesticar [44] VT to domesticate; (*animal*) to tame

doméstico, -a ADJ domestic; **animal d.** pet

domiciliación NF *Esp* **pagar mediante d. (bancaria)** to pay by direct debit

domiciliar [43] VT **1** VT *Esp* (*pago*) to pay by direct debit
2 domiciliarse VPR (*persona*) to establish residence

domiciliario, -a ADJ **arresto d.** house arrest

domicilio NM home, residence; (*señas*) address; **sin d. fijo** of no fixed abode; **d. fiscal** registered office

dominación NF rule, dominion

dominante ADJ (**a**) (*prevaleciente*) dominant (**b**) (*déspota*) domineering

dominar 1 VT (**a**) (*país, territorio*) to dominate, to rule (**b**) (*situación*) to control; (*idioma*) to speak very well; (*técnica, tema*) to master; (*paisaje etc*) to overlook
2 dominarse VPR to control oneself

domingo NM INV Sunday; **D. de Resurrección** *o* **Pascua** Easter Sunday

dominguero, -a NM,F *Fam* (*excursionista*) weekend tripper; (*conductor*) weekend driver

dominical 1 ADJ Sunday
2 NM (*suplemento*) Sunday supplement

dominicano, -a ADJ & NM,F Dominican

dominio NM (**a**) (*poder*) control; (*de un idioma*) command; **d. de sí mismo** self-control (**b**) (*ámbito*) scope, sphere; **ser del d. público** to be public knowledge (**c**) (*territorio*) dominion (**d**) *Inform* domain

dominó NM dominoes

don¹ NM (**a**) *(habilidad)* gift, talent; **tener el d. de** to have a knack for; **tener d. de gentes** to get on well with people (**b**) *(regalo)* present, gift

don² NM (Señor) D. José García MrJosé Garcia; D. José Mr García; **un d. nadie** a nobody

donaire NM grace, elegance

donante NMF donor; *Med* **d. de sangre** blood donor

donar VT *Fml* to donate; *(sangre)* to give

donativo NM donation

doncella NF *Literario* maid, maiden

donde ADV REL where; **a** o **en d.** where; **de** o **desde d.** from where; **está d. lo dejaste** it is where you left it; *Fam* **está d. su tía** he's at his aunt's

> **donde** combines with the preposition **a** to form **adonde** when following a noun, a pronoun or an adverb expressing location (e.g. **el sitio adonde vamos** the place where we're going; **es allí adonde iban** that's where they were going).

dónde ADV INTERR where?; **¿de d. eres?** where are you from?; **¿por d. se va a la playa?** which way is it to the beach?

> **dónde** can combine with the preposition **a** to form **adónde** (e.g. **¿adónde vamos?** where are we going?).

dondequiera ADV **d. que** wherever; **d. que vaya** wherever I go

donostiarra *Esp* **1** ADJ of/from San Sebastián **2** NMF person from San Sebastián

dónut® *(pl* **dónuts)** NM doughnut

doña NF (Señora) D. Leonor Benítez Mrs Leonor Benítez; D. Leonor Mrs Benítez

dopaje NM *Dep* drug-taking

dopar **1** VT *(caballo etc)* to dope **2 doparse** VPR to take drugs

doping *(pl* **dopings)** NM *Dep* drug-taking

doquier ADV **por d.** everywhere

dorada NF *(pez)* gilthead bream

dorado, -a **1** ADJ golden **2** NM *Téc* gilding

dorar VT (**a**) *(con oro)* to gild (**b**) *Culin* to brown

dormido, -a ADJ (**a**) *(persona)* asleep; **quedarse d.** to fall asleep; *(no despertarse)* to oversleep, to sleep in (**b**) *(pierna, brazo)* numb

dormilón, -ona **1** ADJ *Fam* **ser d.** to be a sleepyhead **2** NM,F *Fam* sleepyhead **3** NF *Ven* nightdress

dormir [7] **1** VI to sleep; **tener ganas de d.** to feel sleepy **2** VT **d. la siesta** to have an afternoon nap **3 dormirse** VPR to fall asleep; **se me ha dormido el brazo** my arm has gone to sleep

dormitar VI to doze, to snooze

dormitorio NM (**a**) *(de una casa)* bedroom (**b**) *(de colegio, residencia)* dormitory; **ciudad d.** dormitory town

dorsal **1** ADJ **espina d.** spine **2** NM *Dep* number

dorso NM back; **instrucciones al d.** instructions over; **véase al d.** see overleaf

dos ADJ & NM INV two; **los d.** both; **nosotros/ vosotros d.** both of us/you; *Fam* **cada d. por tres** every other minute; *Fam* **en un d. por tres** in a flash

doscientos, -as ADJ & NM two hundred

dosel NM canopy

dosificación NF dosage

dosificar [44] VT (**a**) *(fármaco)* to dose (**b**) *(esfuerzos, energías)* to use sparingly

dosis NF INV dose

dossier NM dossier

dotación NF *(dinero)* amount granted; *(personal)* personnel, staff; *(de barco)* crew

dotado, -a ADJ (**a**) *(persona)* gifted (**b**) **d. de** *(persona)* blessed with; *(edificio, instalación, aparato)* equipped with

dotar VT **d. de** to provide with

dote NF (**a**) *(de novia)* dowry (**b**) **dotes** *(talento)* talent

doy INDIC PRES de **dar**

dpto. *(abr* **departamento)** Dept

Dr. *(abr* **doctor)** Dr

Dra. *(abr* **doctora)** Dr

dragar [42] VT to dredge

dragón NM dragon

drama NM drama

dramático, -a ADJ dramatic

dramatismo NM drama, dramatic quality

dramaturgo, -a NM,F playwright, dramatist

drástico, -a ADJ drastic

drenar VT to drain

driblar VI *Dep* to dribble

droga NF drug; **d. blanda/dura** soft/hard drug

drogadicción NF drug addiction

drogadicto, -a NM,F drug addict

drogar [42] **1** VT to drug **2 drogarse** VPR to take drugs

droguería NF *Esp* = shop selling paint, cleaning materials etc

dto. *(abr* **descuento)** discount

dual ADJ dual

dualidad NF duality

dubitativo, -a ADJ doubtful

Dublín N Dublin

dublinés, -esa **1** ADJ of/from Dublin **2** NM,F Dubliner

ducha NF shower; **darse/tomar una d.** to have o take a shower

ducharse VPR to shower, to have o take a shower

ducho, -a ADJ expert; **ser d. en** to be well versed in

duda NF doubt; **sin d.** without a doubt; **no cabe d.** (there is) no doubt; **poner algo en d.** to question sth; **sacar a algn de dudas** to dispel sb's doubts

dudar 1 VI (**a**) *(vacilar)* to hesitate (**en** to); **dudaba entre ir o quedarme** I hesitated whether to go or to stay (**b**) *(desconfiar)* **d. de algn** to suspect sb
2 VT to doubt

dudoso, -a ADJ (**a**) **ser d.** *(incierto)* to be uncertain o doubtful (**b**) **estar d.** *(indeciso)* to be undecided (**c**) *(poco honrado)* dubious

duelo¹ NM *(combate)* duel

duelo² NM *(luto)* mourning

duende NM (**a**) *(espíritu)* goblin, elf (**b**) *(encanto)* magic, charm

dueña NF owner; *(de pensión)* landlady

dueño NM owner; *(de casa etc)* landlord; *Fig* **ser d. de sí mismo** to be self-possessed

Duero N el **D.** the Douro

dulce 1 ADJ (**a**) *(sabor)* sweet (**b**) *(carácter, voz)* gentle (**c**) *(metal)* soft (**d**) **agua d.** fresh water
2 NM (**a**) *Culin (pastel)* cake (**b**) *(caramelo) Br* sweet, *US* candy

dulzura NF sweetness

duna NF dune

dúo NM duet

duodécimo, -a ADJ & NM,F twelfth

dúplex NM (**a**) *(vivienda)* duplex (**b**) *Elec* linkup

duplicado, -a 1 ADJ **por d.** in duplicate
2 NM duplicate, copy

duplicar [44] **1** VT to duplicate; *(cifras)* to double
2 duplicarse VPR to double

duplo NM double

duque NM duke

duquesa NF duchess

duración NF duration, length; **disco de larga d.** long-playing record

duradero, -a ADJ durable, lasting

durante PREP during; **d. el día** during the day; **d. todo el día** all day long; **viví en La Coruña d. un año** I lived in La Coruña for a year

durar VI to last; **¿cuánto dura la película?** how long is the film?

durazno NM *(fruto)* peach; *(árbol)* peach tree

Durex® NM *Méx (adhesivo) Br* Sellotape®, *US* Scotch® tape

dureza NF (**a**) *(de objeto, material)* hardness (**b**) *(de clima, persona)* harshness (**c**) *(callosidad)* callus, patch of hard skin

Observa que la palabra inglesa **duress** es un falso amigo y no es la traducción de la palabra española **dureza**. En inglés, **duress** significa "coacción".

duro, -a 1 ADJ (**a**) *(material, superficie)* hard; *(carne)* tough; *(pan)* stale (**b**) *(resistente)* tough; *(severo)* hard (**c**) *(clima)* harsh
2 NM *Esp Antes (moneda)* 5-peseta coin
3 ADV hard; **trabajar d.** to work hard

DVD NM *Inform (abr* **Disco Versátil Digital)** DVD

E

E, e [e] NF *(letra)* E, e

E *(abr* **Este)** E

e CONJ and

> **e** is used instead of **y** in front of words beginning with "i" or "hi" (e.g. **apoyo e interés** support and interest; **corazón e hígado** heart and liver)

ebanista NMF cabinet-maker

ébano NM ebony

ebrio, -a ADJ inebriated; **e. de dicha** drunk with joy

ebullición NF boiling; **punto de e.** boiling point

eccema NM eczema

echar 1 VT (**a**) *(lanzar)* to throw; *Fig* **e. una mano** to give a hand; *Fig* **e. una mirada/una ojeada** to have a look/a quick look *o* glance (**b**) *(carta)* to post, *US* to mail; *(vino, agua)* to pour; **e. sal al estofado** to put salt in the stew; **e. gasolina al coche** to put *Br* petrol *o US* gas in the car (**c**) *(expulsar)* to throw out; *(despedir)* to fire, *Br* to sack (**d**) *(humo, olor etc)* to give off (**e**) *Fam (película)* to show (**f**) **le echó 37 años** he reckoned she was about 37 (**g**) **e. de menos** *o* **en falta** to miss (**h**) **e. abajo** *(edificio)* to demolish

2 VI (+ **a** + *infin*) *(empezar)* to begin to; **echó a correr** he ran off

3 echarse VPR (**a**) *(tumbarse)* to lie down; *(lanzarse)* to throw oneself; *Fig* **la noche se nos echó encima** it was night before we knew it (**b**) **échate a un lado** stand aside; *Fig* **echarse atrás** to get cold feet (**c**) *Fam* **echarse novio/novia** to get a boyfriend/girlfriend (**d**) (+ **a** + *infin*) *(empezar)* to begin to; **echarse a llorar** to burst into tears; **echarse a reír** to burst out laughing; **echarse a perder** *(comida)* to go bad

ecléctico, -a ADJ & NM,F eclectic

eclesiástico, -a 1 ADJ ecclesiastical

2 NM clergyman

eclipsar VT to eclipse

eclipse NM eclipse

eco NM echo; *Fig* **hacerse e. de una noticia** to publish an item of news; **tener e.** to arouse interest

ecografía NF *(técnica)* ultrasound scanning; *(imagen)* ultrasound scan

ecología NF ecology

ecológico, -a ADJ *(medioambiental)* ecological; *(alimentos)* organic; *(detergente)* environmentally-friendly

ecologista 1 ADJ environmental, ecological

2 NMF environmentalist, ecologist

economía NF (**a**) *(actividad productiva)* economy; **e. de mercado** market economy (**b**) *(ciencia)* economics *sing* (**c**) *(ahorro)* **hacer economías** to save

económico, -a ADJ (**a**) *(de la economía)* *(asunto, doctrina, política)* economic (**b**) *(del dinero)* *(problemas, situación)* financial (**c**) *(barato)* cheap, low-cost (**d**) *(que gasta poco)* *(aparato)* economical

economista NMF economist

economizar [40] VT & VI to economize

ecopunto NM recycling bank

ecosistema NM ecosystem

ecotasa NF ecotax

ecoturismo NM ecotourism

ecuación NF equation

Ecuador N Ecuador

ecuador NM *Geog* equator

ecualizador NM **e. (gráfico)** graphic equalizer

ecuánime ADJ (**a**) *(temperamento)* equable, even-tempered (**b**) *(juicio)* impartial

ecuatorial ADJ equatorial

ecuatoriano, -a ADJ & NM,F Ecuadorian

ecuestre ADJ equestrian

ecuménico, -a ADJ ecumenical

eczema NM eczema

edad NF age; **¿qué e. tienes?** how old are you?; **la tercera e.** senior citizens; **E. Media** Middle Ages

edición NF (**a**) *(publicación)* publication; *(de sellos)* issue (**b**) *(conjunto de ejemplares)* edition

edicto NM edict, proclamation

edificante ADJ edifying

edificar [44] VT to build

edificio NM building

edil NMF town councillor

Edimburgo N Edinburgh

Edipo N Oedipus

editar VT (**a**) *(libro, periódico)* to publish; *(disco)* to release (**b**) *Inform* to edit

editor, -a 1 ADJ publishing

2 NM,F publisher

editorial 1 ADJ publishing
  2 NF publisher, publishing house
  3 NM *Prensa* editorial, leader article
edredón NM eiderdown, *Br* duvet
educación NF (**a**) *(enseñanza)* education; **e. física** physical education (**b**) *(modales)* **buena/mala e.** good/bad manners; **falta de e.** bad manners
educado, -a ADJ polite
educador, -a NM,F educator
educar [44] VT *(hijos)* to raise; *(alumnos)* to educate; *(la voz)* to train
educativo, -a ADJ educational; **sistema e.** education system
edulcorante NM sweetener
EE.UU. *(abr* **Estados Unidos**) USA
efectista ADJ designed for effect, dramatic
efectivamente ADV quite!, yes indeed!
efectividad NF effectiveness
efectivo, -a 1 ADJ effective; **hacer algo e.** to carry sth out; *Fin* **hacer e. un cheque** to cash a cheque
  2 NM (**a**) *Fin* **en e.** in cash (**b**) *Mil* **efectivos** forces
efecto NM (**a**) *(resultado)* effect; **efectos especiales/sonoros** special/sound effects; **efectos personales** personal belongings *o* effects; **a efectos de …** for the purposes of …; **en e.** indeed (**b**) *(impresión)* impression; **causar** *o* **hacer e.** to make an impression (**c**) *Dep* spin
efectuar [30] VT to carry out; *(viaje)* to make; *Com (pedido)* to place
efeméride NF event
efervescente ADJ effervescent; **aspirina e.** soluble aspirin
eficacia NF *(de persona)* efficiency; *(de remedio etc)* effectiveness
eficaz ADJ *(persona)* efficient; *(remedio, medida etc)* effective
eficiencia NF efficiency
eficiente ADJ efficient
efigie NF effigy
efímero, -a ADJ ephemeral
efusivo, -a ADJ effusive
Egeo N **el (Mar) E.** the Aegean Sea
egipcio, -a ADJ & NM,F Egyptian
Egipto N Egypt
egocéntrico, -a ADJ egocentric, self-centred
egoísmo NM selfishness, egotsm
egoísta 1 ADJ selfish, egotistic
  2 NMF selfish person, egotist
egregio, -a ADJ eminent, illustrious
egresar VI *Am (de escuela)* to leave school after completing one's studies, *US* to graduate; *(de universidad)* to graduate
egreso NM *Am (de universidad)* graduation
Eire N Eire, Republic of Ireland
ej. *(abr* **ejemplo**) example

eje NM (**a**) *Téc (de rueda)* axle; *(de máquina)* shaft (**b**) *Mat* axis (**c**) *Hist* **El E.** the Axis
ejecución NF (**a**) *(de orden)* carrying out (**b**) *(ajusticiamiento)* execution (**c**) *Mús* performance
ejecutar VT (**a**) *(orden)* to carry out (**b**) *(ajusticiar)* to execute (**c**) *Mús* to perform, to play (**d**) *Inform* to run
ejecutiva NF *Pol* executive
ejecutivo, -a 1 ADJ executive; *Pol* **el poder e.** the government
  2 NM executive
ejecutor, -a NM,F (**a**) *Der* executor (**b**) *(verdugo)* executioner
ejemplar 1 NM (**a**) *(de libro)* copy; *(de revista, periódico)* number, issue (**b**) *(espécimen)* specimen
  2 ADJ exemplary, model
ejemplificar [44] VT to exemplify
ejemplo NM example; **por e.** for example; **dar e.** to set an example
ejercer [49] **1** VT (**a**) *(profesión etc)* to practise (**b**) *(influencia)* to exert (**c**) **e. el derecho de** *o* **a …** to exercise one's right to …
  2 VI to practise (**de** as)
ejercicio NM (**a**) *(físico)* exercise; **hacer e.** to take *o* do exercise (**b**) *(de profesión)* practice (**c**) *Fin* tax year; **e. económico** financial *o* fiscal year
ejercitar VT to practise
ejército NM army
ejote NM *CAm, Méx* green bean
el *(f* **la,** *mpl* **los,** *fpl* **las)* **1** ART DEF (**a**) the (**b**) *(no se traduce)* **el Sr. García** Mr. García; **el hambre/ destino** hunger/fate (**c**) *(con partes del cuerpo, prendas de vestir)* **me he cortado el dedo** I've cut my finger; **métetelo en el bolsillo** put it in your pocket (**d**) *(con días de la semana)* **el lunes** on Monday

> **el** is used instead of **la** before feminine nouns which are stressed on the first syllable and begin with "a" or "ha" (e.g. **el agua, el hacha**). Note that **el** combines with the prepositions **a** and **de** to produce the contracted forms **al** and **del**.

  2 PRON (**a**) the one; **el de las once** the eleven o'clock one; **el que tienes en la mano** the one you've got in your hand; **el que quieras** whichever one you want (**b**) *(no se traduce)* **el de tu amigo** your friend's
él PRON PERS (**a**) *(sujeto) (persona)* he; *(animal, cosa)* it (**b**) *(complemento) (persona)* him; *(animal, cosa)* it

> Usually omitted in Spanish as a subject except for emphasis or contrast.

elaboración NF (**a**) *(de producto)* manufacture, production (**b**) *(de idea)* working out, development

elaborar VT (**a**) *(producto)* to manufacture, to produce (**b**) *(teoría)* to develop
elasticidad NF elasticity; *Fig* flexibility
elástico, -a ADJ & NM elastic
E/LE *(abr* **Español como Lengua Extranjera)** Spanish as a foreign language
elección NF choice; *Pol* **elecciones** election
elector, -a NM,F elector
electorado NM electorate
electoral ADJ electoral; **campaña e.** election campaign; **colegio e.** polling station
electoralismo NM electioneering
electricidad NF electricity
electricista NMF electrician
eléctrico, -a ADJ electric
electrificar [44] VT to electrify
electrizar [40] VT to electrify
electrochoque NM electric shock therapy
electrocutar VT to electrocute
electrodo NM electrode
electrodoméstico NM (domestic) electrical appliance
electroimán NM electromagnet
electromagnético, -a ADJ electromagnetic
electrón NM electron
electrónica NF electronics *sing*
electrónico, -a ADJ electronic
elefante NM elephant
elegancia NF elegance
elegante ADJ elegant
elegía NF elegy
elegir [58] VT (**a**) *(escoger)* to choose (**b**) *(por votación)* to elect
elemental ADJ (**a**) *(fundamental)* basic, fundamental (**b**) *(simple)* elementary
elemento NM (**a**) *(sustancia, medio, componente)* element (**b**) *(factor)* factor (**c**) *Esp Fam (persona)* Br chap, US guy; **un e. de cuidado** a bad lot (**d**) **elementos** *(atmosféricos)* elements; *(fundamentos)* rudiments
elepé NM LP (record)
elevación NF elevation; **e. de precios** rise in prices; **e. del terreno** rise in the ground
elevado, -a ADJ (**a**) *(alto)* high; *(edificio)* tall (**b**) *(pensamiento etc)* lofty, noble
elevador NM (**a**) *(montacargas)* hoist (**b**) *Méx (ascensor)* Br lift, US elevator
elevalunas NM INV *Aut* **e. eléctrico** electric windows
elevar 1 VT to raise
2 elevarse VPR (**a**) *(subir)* to rise; *(edificio)* to stand (**b**) **elevarse a** *(cantidad)* to amount *o* come to
elijo INDIC PRES *de* **elegir**
eliminación NF elimination
eliminar VT to eliminate
eliminatoria NF *Dep* heat, qualifying round
eliminatorio, -a ADJ qualifying, eliminatory

élite NF elite, élite
elitista ADJ elitist
elixir NM *(enjuague bucal)* mouthwash; *Literario* elixir
ella PRON PERS F (**a**) *(sujeto)* she; *(animal, cosa)* it, she (**b**) *(complemento)* her; *(animal, cosa)* it, her

> Usually omitted in Spanish as a subject except for emphasis or contrast.

ellas PRON PERS FPL *ver* **ellos**
ello PRON PERS NEUT it; **por e.** for that reason
ellos PRON PERS MPL (**a**) *(sujeto)* they (**b**) *(complemento)* them

> Usually omitted in Spanish as a subject except for emphasis or contrast.

elocuencia NF eloquence
elocuente ADJ eloquent; **los hechos son elocuentes** the facts speak for themselves
elogiar [43] VT to praise
elogio NM praise
elote NM *CAm, Méx (mazorca)* corncob, ear of maize *o US* corn; *(granos)* sweetcorn, *US* corn
El Salvador N El Salvador
elucidar VT to elucidate
eludir VT to avoid
e-mail ['imeil] *(pl* **e-mails)** NM e-mail
emanar VI to emanate (**de** from)
emancipar 1 VT to emancipate
2 emanciparse VPR to become emancipated
embadurnar VT to daub, to smear (**de** with)
embajada NF embassy
embajador, -a NM,F ambassador
embalaje NM packing, packaging
embalar 1 VT to pack
2 embalarse VPR to speed up; *Fig* **no te embales** hold your horses
embalsamar VT to embalm
embalsar 1 VT to dam
2 embalsarse VPR to form a pool
embalse NM reservoir
embarazada 1 ADJ pregnant; **dejar e.** to get pregnant
2 NF pregnant woman, expectant mother

> Observa que la palabra inglesa **embarrassed** es un falso amigo y no es la traducción de la palabra española **embarazada**. En inglés **embarrassed** significa "avergonzado".

embarazar [40] VT to hinder
embarazo NM (**a**) *(preñez)* pregnancy (**b**) *(obstáculo)* obstacle (**c**) *(turbación)* embarrassment
embarazoso, -a ADJ awkward, embarrassing
embarcación NF (**a**) *(nave)* boat, craft (**b**) *(embarco)* embarkation
embarcadero NM quay

embarcar [44] **1** VT to ship
2 VI to embark, to go on board
3 embarcarse VPR (**a**) **embarcarse (en)** *Náut* to go on board; *Av* to board (**b**) **embarcarse en un proyecto** to embark on a project

embarco NM embarkation

embargar [42] VT (**a**) *Der* to seize, to impound (**b**) *Fig* **le embarga la emoción** he's overwhelmed with joy

embargo 1 NM (**a**) *Der* seizure of property (**b**) *Com & Pol* embargo
2 sin embargo LOC ADV however, nevertheless

embarque NM (*de persona*) boarding; (*de mercancías*) loading; **tarjeta de e.** boarding card

embarrancar [44] **1** VI to run aground
2 embarrancarse VPR to run aground

embaucador, -a 1 ADJ deceitful
2 NM,F swindler, cheat

embaucar [44] VT to swindle, to cheat

embeber 1 VT to soak up
2 embeberse VPR to become absorbed *o* engrossed

embelesar VT to fascinate

embellecer [33] VT to embellish

embestida NF (*ataque*) attack; (*de toro*) charge

embestir [6] VT (*lanzarse contra*) to attack; (*sujeto: toro*) to charge

emblema NM emblem

embobado, -a ADJ fascinated

embobarse VPR to be fascinated *o* captivated (**con** by)

embolia NF embolism

émbolo NM piston

embolsarse VPR to pocket

emborrachar 1 VT (*sujeto: persona*) to get drunk; (*sujeto: bebida*) to make *o* get drunk
2 emborracharse VPR to get drunk

emboscada NF ambush; **tender una e.** to lay an ambush

embotar VT (*sentidos*) to dull; (*mente*) to befuddle

embotellamiento NM *Aut* traffic jam

embotellar VT (**a**) (*líquido*) to bottle (**b**) (*tráfico*) to block

embragar [42] VI *Aut* to engage the clutch

embrague NM clutch

embravecerse [33] VPR (*mar*) to become rough

embriagador, -a ADJ intoxicating

embriagar [42] **1** VT to intoxicate
2 embriagarse VPR to become intoxicated

embriaguez NF intoxication

embridar VT to bridle

embrión NM embryo

embrollar 1 VT to confuse, to muddle
2 embrollarse VPR to get muddled *o* confused

embrollo NM (**a**) (*lío*) muddle, confusion (**b**) (*aprieto*) fix, jam

embrujado, -a ADJ (*persona*) bewitched; (*sitio*) haunted

embrujar VT *también Fig* to bewitch

embrujo NM spell, charm; *Fig* attraction, fascination

embrutecer [33] VT to stultify

embuchar VT to stuff

embudo NM funnel

embuste NM lie, trick

embustero, -a NM,F cheater, liar

embutido NM sausage

embutir VT (**a**) (*rellenar*) to stuff (**de** with) (**b**) (*meter*) to stuff (**en** into)

emergencia NF emergency; **salida de e.** emergency exit; **en caso de e.** in an emergency

emergente ADJ emerging

emerger [53] VI to emerge

emigración NF emigration; (*de pájaros*) migration

emigrado, -a NM,F emigrant; *Pol* émigré

emigrante ADJ & NMF emigrant

emigrar VI to emigrate; (*pájaros*) to migrate

emilio NM *Fam* e-mail (message)

eminencia NF (*persona*) eminent figure, leading light; **e. gris** éminence grise; **Su E.** His Eminence

emirato NM emirate

emisario, -a NM,F emissary

emisión NF (**a**) (*de energía, rayos*) emission (**b**) (*de bonos, sellos*) issue (**c**) *Rad & TV* (*transmisión*) broadcasting; (*programa*) programme, broadcast

emisora NF (*de radio*) radio station

emitir VT (**a**) (*rayos, calor, sonidos*) to emit (**b**) (*opinión, juicio*) to express (**c**) *Rad & TV* to transmit (**d**) (*bonos, sellos*) to issue

emoción NF (**a**) (*sentimiento*) emotion (**b**) (*expectación*) excitement; **¡qué e.!** how exciting!

emocionado, -a ADJ deeply moved *o* touched

emocionante ADJ (**a**) (*conmovedor*) moving, touching (**b**) (*excitante*) exciting, thrilling

emocionar 1 VT (**a**) (*conmover*) to move, to touch (**b**) (*excitar*) to thrill
2 emocionarse VPR (**a**) (*conmoverse*) to be moved (**b**) (*excitarse*) to get excited

emoticón, emoticono NM *Inform* smiley, emoticon

emotivo, -a ADJ emotional

empacar [44] VT (**a**) (*mercancías*) to pack (**b**) *Am* to annoy

empachar VT to give indigestion to

empacho NM (*de comida*) indigestion, upset stomach; *Fig* surfeit

empadronarse VPR to register on the electoral roll

empalagar [42] VI los bombones me empalagan I find chocolates sickly; me empalaga con tanta cortesía I find his excessive politeness rather cloying

empalagoso, -a ADJ (a) (dulce) sickly sweet (b) (persona) smarmy

empalizada NF fence; Mil stockade

empalmar 1 VT (tubos, cables) to connect, to join
2 **empalmarse** VPR Esp Vulg to get a hard-on

empalme NM (a) (de cables, tubos) connection (b) (de líneas férreas, carreteras) junction

empanada NF pie

empanadilla NF pasty

empanado, -a ADJ (filete) breaded, in breadcrumbs

empantanarse VPR (a) (inundarse) to become flooded (b) Fig to be bogged down

empañar 1 VT (cristales) to steam up
2 **empañarse** VPR to mist up, to steam up

empapado, -a ADJ soaked

empapar 1 VT (a) (mojar) to soak (b) (absorber) to soak up
2 **empaparse** VPR (a) (persona) to get soaked (b) Fam Fig **empaparse (de)** to take in

empapelar VT to paper, to wallpaper

empaque NM bearing, presence

empaquetar VT to pack

emparedado NM sandwich

emparejar VT (cosas) to match; (personas) to pair off

empastar VT (diente) to fill

empaste NM (de diente) filling

empatado, -a ADJ (partido) drawn; (equipos) level; **estar** o **ir empatados** to be drawn

empatar 1 VI (en competición) to tie; (en partido) to draw
2 VT (a) Dep **e. el partido** to equalize (b) Andes, Ven (enlazar, empalmar) to join, to link

empate NM Dep draw, tie

empatía NF empathy

empecinarse VPR to dig one's heels in

empedernido, -a ADJ (fumador, bebedor) hardened

empedrado, -a 1 ADJ cobbled
2 NM (a) (adoquines) cobblestones (b) (acción) paving

empeine NM instep

empellón NM push, shove

empeñar 1 VT to pawn
2 **empeñarse** VPR (a) (insistir) to insist (en on), to be determined (en to) (b) (endeudarse) to get into debt

empeño NM (a) (insistencia) insistence; **poner e. en algo** to put a lot of effort into sth (b) (deuda) pledge; **casa de empeños** pawnshop

empeoramiento NM deterioration, worsening

empeorar 1 VI to deteriorate, to worsen
2 VT to make worse
3 **empeorarse** VPR to deteriorate, to worsen

empequeñecer [33] VT Fig to belittle

emperador NM emperor

emperatriz NF empress

emperifollarse VPR Fam to get dolled up

emperrarse VPR to insist (**en hacer algo** on doing sth)

empezar [51] VT & VI (a hacer algo) to begin; (algo) to start, to commence

empinado, -a ADJ (cuesta) steep

empinar 1 VT to raise; Fam **e. el codo** to drink
2 **empinarse** VPR (persona) to stand on tiptoe

empírico, -a ADJ empirical

emplasto NM poultice

emplazamiento NM (a) (lugar) location (b) Der summons sing

emplazar¹ [40] VT to locate

emplazar² [40] VT (citar) to summon; Der to summons

empleado, -a NM,F employee; (de oficina, banco) clerk; **empleada del hogar** maid

emplear VT (a) (usar) to use; (contratar) to employ (b) (dinero, tiempo) to spend

empleo NM (a) (oficio) job; Pol employment (b) (uso) use; **modo de e.** instructions for use

emplomar VT RP (diente) to fill

empobrecer [33] **1** VT to impoverish
2 **empobrecerse** VPR to become impoverished o poor

empobrecimiento NM impoverishment

empollar VT (a) (huevos) to sit on (b) Esp Fam (estudiar) to bone up on, Br to swot up

empollón, -ona NM,F Esp Fam Br swot, US grind

empolvarse VPR (la cara) to powder

emponzoñar VT to poison

emporio NM (a) Com emporium, trading o commercial centre (b) Am department store

empotrado, -a ADJ fitted

emprendedor, -a ADJ enterprising

emprender VT to undertake; Fam **emprenderla con algn** to pick on sb

empresa NF (a) Com & Ind firm, company; **e. punto com** dot com (company); **e. de trabajo temporal** temping agency (b) Pol **la libre e.** free enterprise (c) (tarea) undertaking

empresariado NM employers

empresarial 1 ADJ (estructura, crisis) business; **organización e.** employers' organization
2 **empresariales** NFPL Esp business studies

empresario, -a NM,F (a) (hombre) businessman; (mujer) businesswoman (b) (patrón) employer

empréstito NM Fin debenture loan

empujar VT to push, to shove

empuje NM (presión) pressure; (brío) verve, get-up-and-go

empujón NM push, shove; **dar empujones** to push and shove

empuñadura NF *(de espada)* hilt

empuñar VT to grasp, to seize

emular VT to emulate

emulsión NF emulsion

en PREP (a) *(posición)* in, on, at; **en Madrid/Bolivia** in Madrid/Bolivia; **en la mesa** on the table; **en el bolso** in the bag; **en casa/el trabajo** at home/work (b) *(movimiento)* into; **entró en el cuarto** he went into the room (c) *(tiempo)* in, on, at; **en 1940** in 1940; **en verano** in summer; *Am* **en la mañana/tarde** in the morning/afternoon; *Am* **en la noche** at night; **cae en martes** it falls on a Tuesday; **en ese momento** at that moment (d) *(transporte)* by, in; **en coche/tren** by car/train; **en avión** by air (e) *(modo)* **en español** in Spanish; **en broma** jokingly; **en serio** seriously (f) *(reducción, aumento)* by; **los precios aumentaron en un diez por ciento** the prices went up by ten percent (g) *(tema, materia)* at, in; **bueno en deportes** good at sports; **experto en política** expert in politics (h) *(división, separación)* in; **lo dividió en tres partes** he divided it in three (i) *(con infinitivo)* **fue rápido en responder** he was quick to answer; **la conocí en el andar** I recognized her by her walk; **ser sobrio en el vestir** to dress simply

enaguas NFPL underskirt, petticoat

enajenación NF, **enajenamiento** NM (a) **e. mental** mental derangement, insanity (b) *Der* alienation

enajenar VT (a) *Der* to alienate (b) *(turbar)* to drive insane

enaltecer [33] VT to praise, to extol

enamorado, -a 1 ADJ in love **2** NM,F person in love

enamorar 1 VT to win the heart of **2 enamorarse** VPR to fall in love (**de** with)

enano, -a ADJ & NM,F dwarf

enardecer [33] **1** VT *(sentimientos)* to rouse, to stir up; *(persona)* to fill with enthusiasm **2 enardecerse** VPR to become excited

encabezamiento NM *(de carta)* heading; *(de periódico)* headline; *(preámbulo)* foreword, preamble

encabezar [40] VT (a) *(carta, lista)* to head; *(periódico)* to lead (b) *(rebelión, carrera, movimiento)* to lead

encabritarse VPR (a) *(caballo)* to rear (up) (b) *(persona)* to get cross

encadenar VT to chain

encajar 1 VT (a) *(ajustar)* to insert; **e. la puerta** to push the door to (b) *Fam (asimilar)* to take (c) *(comentario)* to get in; **e. un golpe a algn** to land sb a blow

2 VI (a) *(ajustarse)* to fit (b) *Fig* **e. con** to fit (in) with, to square with

encaje NM lace

encalar VT to whitewash

encallar VI (a) *Náut* to run aground (b) *(proceso, proyecto)* to flounder, to fail

encaminado, -a ADJ **estar bien/mal e.** to be on the right/wrong track

encaminar 1 VT to direct **2 encaminarse** VPR to head (**a** for; **hacia** towards)

encamotarse VPR *Andes, CAm Fam* to fall in love

encandilar VT to dazzle

encantado, -a ADJ (a) *(contento)* delighted; **e. de conocerle** pleased to meet you (b) *(embrujado)* enchanted

encantador, -a 1 ADJ charming, delightful **2** NM,F magician

encantamiento NM spell

encantar VT *(hechizar)* to bewitch, to cast a spell on; *Fig* **me encanta nadar** I love swimming

encanto NM (a) *(atractivo)* charm; **ser un e.** to be charming (b) *(hechizo)* spell

encapotado, -a ADJ overcast

encapricharse VPR (a) *(obstinarse)* **e. con algo/hacer algo** to set one's mind on sth/doing sth (b) *Esp (sentirse atraído)* **e. de algn** to become infatuated with sb; **e. de algo** to take a real liking to sth

encapuchado, -a ADJ hooded

encaramarse VPR to climb up

encarar 1 VT to face, to confront **2 encararse** VPR **encararse con** to face up to

encarcelar VT to imprison, to jail

encarecer [33] **1** VT to put up the price of **2 encarecerse** VPR to go up (in price)

encarecidamente ADV earnestly, insistently; **le rogamos e. que ...** we would earnestly request you to ...

encarecimiento NM (a) *(de producto, coste)* increase in price (b) *(empeño)* **con e.** insistently

encargado, -a 1 NM,F *Com (hombre)* manager; *(mujer)* manager, manageress; *(responsable)* person in charge **2** ADJ in charge

encargar [42] **1** VT (a) *(poner al cargo)* **e. a algn de algo** to put sb in charge of sth; **e. a algn que haga algo** to tell sb to do sth (b) *(pedido)* to order; *(obra)* to commission **2 encargarse** VPR **encargarse de** to see to, to deal with

encargo NM (a) *(pedido)* order; *Esp* **hecho de e.** tailor-made (b) *(recado)* errand (c) *(tarea)* job, assignment

encariñarse VPR **e. con** to become fond of, to get attached to

encarnación NF incarnation, embodiment

encarnado, -a ADJ *(rojo)* red

encarnar VT to personify, to embody

encarnizado, -a ADJ fierce

encarrilar VT *(coche, tren)* to put on the road *o* rails; *Fig* to put on the right track

encasillar VT to pigeonhole

encausar VT to prosecute

encauzar [40] VT to channel

encendedor NM lighter

encender [3] **1** VT (**a**) *(luz, radio, tele)* to switch on, to put on; *(cigarro, vela, fuego)* to light; *(cerilla)* to strike, to light (**b**) *Fig* to inflame, to stir up
   2 encenderse VPR (**a**) *(fuego)* to catch; *(luz)* to go *o* come on (**b**) *(cara)* to blush, to go red

encendido NM ignition

encerado NM *(pizarra) Br* blackboard, *US* chalkboard

encerar VT to wax, polish

encerrar VT **1** VT (**a**) *(recluir)* to shut in; *(con llave)* to lock in (**b**) *Fig (contener)* to contain, to include
   2 encerrarse VPR to shut oneself up *o* in; *(con llave)* to lock oneself in

encestar VI *Dep* to score (a basket)

encharcar [44] **1** VT to flood, to swamp
   2 encharcarse VPR to get flooded

enchilada NF *Culin* enchilada, = stuffed corn tortilla seasoned with chilli

enchilarse VPR *Méx Fam* to get angry

enchinar VT *Méx* to curl

enchufado, -a *Fam* **1** ADJ **estar e.** to have good connections *o* contacts
   2 NM,F *(favorito)* pet

enchufar VT (**a**) *Elec* to plug in (**b**) *(unir)* to join, to connect (**c**) *Fam (para un trabajo)* to pull strings for

enchufe NM (**a**) *Elec (hembra)* socket; *(macho)* plug (**b**) *Fam* contact

encía NF gum

enciclopedia NF encyclopedia

encierro NM *Pol (protesta)* sit-in

encima ADV (**a**) *(arriba)* on top; **déjalo e.** put it on top; **¿llevas cambio e.?** do you have any change on you?; *Fig* **quitarse algo de e.** to get rid of sth; **ahí e.** up there (**b**) *(además)* besides (**c**) **e. de** *(sobre)* on; *(en el aire)* above; *Fig (además)* besides; **e. de la mesa** on the table (**d**) **por e.** above; *Fig* **por e. de sus posibilidades** beyond his abilities; **leer un libro por e.** to skip through a book

encimera NF *Esp (de cocina)* worktop

encina NF holm oak

encinta ADJ pregnant

enclaustrarse VPR to shut oneself up

enclave NM enclave

enclenque ADJ *(débil)* puny; *(enfermizo)* sickly

encoger [53] **1** VI *(contraerse)* to contract; *(prenda)* to shrink
   2 VT to contract; *(prenda)* to shrink

   3 encogerse VPR *(contraerse)* to contract; *(prenda)* to shrink; **encogerse de hombros** to shrug (one's shoulders)

encolar VT *(papel)* to paste; *(madera)* to glue

encolerizar [40] **1** VT to infuriate, to anger
   2 encolerizarse VPR to become furious

encomendar [1] **1** VT to entrust with, to put in charge of
   2 encomendarse VPR **e. a** to entrust oneself to

encomienda NF *Am (paquete)* parcel

encomio NM praise

enconado, -a ADJ (**a**) *(discusión)* bitter, fierce (**b**) *Med* inflamed, sore

encono NM spitefulness, ill feeling

encontrado, -a ADJ *(intereses, opiniones)* conflicting

encontrar [2] **1** VT (**a**) *(hallar)* to find; **no lo encuentro** I can't find it; **lo encuentro muy agradable** I find it very pleasant (**b**) *(dar con)* to meet; *(problema)* to run into, to come up against
   2 encontrarse VPR (**a**) *(persona)* to meet (**b**) *(sentirse)* to feel, to be; **encontrarse a gusto** to feel comfortable (**c**) *(estar)* to be

encontronazo NM *(choque)* collision, crash

encorvar **1** VT to bend
   2 encorvarse VPR to stoop *o* bend (over)

encrespar **1** VT (**a**) *(pelo)* to curl (**b**) *(mar)* to make choppy *o* rough (**c**) *(persona)* to infuriate
   2 encresparse VPR (**a**) *(mar)* to get rough (**b**) *(persona)* to get cross *o* irritated

encrucijada NF crossroads

encuadernación NF (**a**) *(oficio)* bookbinding (**b**) *(cubierta)* binding

encuadernador, -a NM,F bookbinder

encuadernar VT to bind

encuadrar VT *(imagen)* to frame

encuadre NM *Cin & TV* framing

encubierto, -a ADJ *(secreto)* hidden; *(operación)* covert

encubridor, -a NM,F *Der* accessory (after the fact), abettor

encubrir VT to conceal

encuentro NM (**a**) *(acción)* encounter, meeting (**b**) *Dep* meeting, match; **e. amistoso** friendly (match)

encuesta NF (**a**) *(sondeo)* (opinion) poll, survey (**b**) *(investigación)* investigation, inquiry

encuestador, -a NM,F pollster

encuestar VT to poll

encumbrar **1** VT to exalt
   2 encumbrarse VPR to rise to a high (social) position

ende: por ende LOC ADV therefore

endeble ADJ weak, feeble

endémico, -a ADJ *Med & Fig* endemic

endemoniado, -a ADJ (**a**) *(poseso)* possessed (**b**) *Fam (molesto) (niño)* wicked; *(trabajo)* very tricky

enderezar [40] **1** VT *(poner derecho)* to straighten out; *(poner vertical)* to set upright
  2 enderezarse VPR to straighten up

endeudarse VPR to get into debt

endiablado, -a ADJ (**a**) *(poseso)* possessed (**b**) *(travieso)* mischievous, devilish

endibia NF endive

endiñar VT *Esp Fam* **e. algo a algn** *(golpe)* to land o deal sb sth; *(tarea)* to lumber sb with sth

endiosarse VPR to become conceited

endivia NF endive

endocrino, -a *Med* **1** ADJ endocrine
  2 NM,F endocrinologist

endogamia NF endogamy

endomingado, -a ADJ *Fam* dressed-up, dolled-up

endorfina NF endorphin

endosar VT *Fam* **e. algo a algn** *(tarea)* to lumber sb with sthg

endoscopia NF *Med* endoscopy

endrina NF *Bot* sloe

endrogarse [42] VPR *Chile, Méx, Perú* to get into debt

endulzar [40] VT to sweeten

endurecer [33] **1** VT to harden
  2 endurecerse VPR to harden, to become hard

enebro NM juniper

enema NM enema

enemigo, -a 1 ADJ enemy; **soy e. de la bebida** I'm against drink
  2 NM,F enemy

enemistad NF hostility, enmity

enemistar 1 VT to set at odds, to cause a rift between
  2 enemistarse VPR to become enemies; **e. con algn** to fall out with sb

energético, -a ADJ energy

energía NF energy; **e. hidráulica/nuclear** hydro-electric/nuclear power; **e. vital** vitality

enérgico, -a ADJ energetic; *(decisión)* firm; *(tono)* emphatic

energúmeno, -a NM,F *Fam (hombre)* madman; *(mujer)* madwoman; **ponerse como un e.** to go up the wall

enero NM January

enervante ADJ exasperating

enervar VT to exasperate

enésimo, -a ADJ (**a**) *Mat* nth (**b**) *Fam* umpteenth; **por enésima vez** for the umpteenth time

enfadado, -a ADJ *esp Esp* (**a**) *(irritado)* angry; *(molesto)* annoyed (**b**) *(peleado)* **estamos enfadados** we've fallen out with each other

enfadar *esp Esp* **1** VT *(irritar)* to anger; *(molestar)* to annoy
  2 enfadarse VPR (**a**) *(irritarse)* to get angry (**con** with); *(molestarse)* to get annoyed (**con** with) (**b**) *(pelearse)* to fall out

enfado NM *esp Esp* (**a**) *(por irritarse)* anger; *(desavenencia)* fall-out (**b**)

enfangarse [42] VPR **e. en un asunto sucio** to get mixed up in a shady business

énfasis NM INV emphasis, stress; **poner e. en algo** to lay stress on sth

enfático, -a ADJ emphatic

enfatizar [40] VT to emphasize, to stress

enfermar VI to become o fall ill, to be taken ill

enfermedad NF illness; *(contagiosa)* disease

enfermería NF infirmary

enfermero, -a NM,F *(mujer)* nurse; *(hombre)* male nurse

enfermizo, -a ADJ unhealthy, sickly

enfermo, -a 1 ADJ ill; **caer e.** to be taken ill; *Fam* **esa gente me pone e.** those people make me sick
  2 NM,F ill person; *(paciente)* patient

enfervorizar [40] VT to enthuse

enfilar VI **e. hacia** to make for

enflaquecer [33] VT to make thin

enfocado, -a ADJ *Fot* **bien/mal enfocado** in/out of focus

enfocar [44] VT (**a**) *(imagen)* to focus; *(persona)* to focus on (**b**) *(tema)* to approach (**c**) *(con linterna)* to shine a light on

enfoque NM (**a**) *(de imagen)* focus (**b**) *(de tema)* approach

enfrentamiento NM clash

enfrentar 1 VT (**a**) *(situación, peligro)* to confront (**b**) *(enemistar)* to set at odds
  2 enfrentarse VPR (**a**) **enfrentarse con** o **a** to face up to, to confront (**b**) *Dep* **enfrentarse (a)** *(rival)* to meet

enfrente ADV (**a**) opposite; **la casa de e.** the house opposite o across the road (**b**) **e. de.** opposite (to), facing; **e. del colegio** opposite the school

enfriamiento NM (**a**) *(proceso)* cooling (**b**) *Med (catarro)* cold, chill

enfriar [29] **1** VT (**a**) *(quedarse frío)* to get o go cold (**b**) *(resfriarse)* to get o catch a cold (**c**) *Fig (pasión)* to cool down
  2 VI to cool down
  3 enfriarse VPR (**a**) *(quedarse frío)* to get o go cold (**b**) *(resfriarse)* to get o catch a cold (**c**) *Fig (pasión)* to cool down

enfurecer [33] **1** VT to enrage, to infuriate
  2 enfurecerse VPR to get furious, to lose one's temper

enfurruñarse VPR *Fam* to sulk

engalanar 1 VT to deck out, to adorn
  2 engalanarse VPR to dress up, to get dressed up

enganchado, -a ADJ *Fam* **estar e. (a la droga)** to be hooked (on drugs)

enganchar 1 VT (**a**) *(remolque, caballos)* to hitch up; *(vagones)* to couple (**b**) *Fam (atraer)* **e. a algn para que haga algo** to rope sb into doing sth
  2 VI *Fam (hacer adicto)* to be addictive

3 engancharse VPR *(a)* to get caught *o* hooked; *Fam (a la droga)* to get hooked

enganche NM *(gancho)* hook; *(de vagones)* coupling

engañabobos NM INV *(persona)* con man, confidence trickster; *(truco)* con trick

engañar 1 VT *(mentir)* to deceive; *(estafar)* to cheat, to trick; *(al esposo)* to be unfaithful to
2 engañarse VPR to deceive oneself

engañifa NF *Fam* swindle

engaño NM *(mentira, broma)* deceit; *(estafa)* swindle; *(ardid)* ploy, trick; **que nadie se llame a e.** let no one have any illusions about it

engañoso, -a ADJ *(palabras)* deceitful; *(apariencias)* deceptive; *(consejo)* misleading

engarzar [40] VT *(a)* *(abalorios)* to thread; *(perlas)* to string **(b)** *(diamante)* to set

engastar VT to set, to mount

engatusar VT *Fam* to coax; **e. a algn para que haga algo** to coax sb into doing sth

engendrar VT *(a)* *Biol* to engender **(b)** *Fig* to give rise to, to cause

engendro NM freak

englobar VT to include

engordar 1 VT to fatten (up), to make fat
2 VI *(a)* *(poner peso)* to put on weight, to get fat; **he engordado 3 kilos** I've put on 3 kilos **(b)** *(comida, bebida)* to be fattening

engorro NM bother, nuisance

engorroso, -a ADJ bothersome, tiresome

engranaje NM *(a)* *Téc* gearing **(b)** *Fig* machinery

engranar VT *Téc* to engage

engrandecer [33] VT to exalt

engrapadora NF *Am* stapler

engrapar VT *Am* to staple

engrasar VT *(a)* *(lubricar)* to lubricate, to oil **(b)** *(manchar)* to make greasy, to stain with grease

engrase NM lubrication

engreído, -a ADJ vain, conceited

engreírse [56] VPR to become vain *o* conceited

engrosar [2] VT *(incrementar)* to enlarge; *(cantidad)* to increase, to swell

engrudo NM paste

engullir VT to gobble up

enharinar VT to cover with flour

enhebrar VT to thread

enhorabuena NF congratulations; **dar la e. a algn** to congratulate sb

enigma NM enigma

enigmático, -a ADJ enigmatic

enjabonar VT to soap

enjalbegar [42] VT to whitewash

enjambre NM swarm

enjaular VT to cage

enjuagar [42] VT to rinse

enjuague NM rinse; **e. bucal** mouthwash

enjugar [42] VT *(lágrimas)* to wipe away

enjuiciamiento NM *Der (civil)* lawsuit; *(criminal)* trial, prosecution

enjuiciar [43] VT *Der* to indict, to prosecute

enjundia NF *(sustancia)* substance; *(importancia)* importance

enjuto, -a ADJ lean, skinny

enlace NM *(a)* *(unión)* link, connection; **e. químico** chemical bond **(b)** *Ferroc* connection **(c)** *(casamiento)* marriage **(d)** *(persona)* liaison officer; *Esp* **e. sindical** shop steward

enlatado, -a ADJ canned, tinned

enlatar VT to can, to tin

enlazar [40] VT & VI to link, to connect **(con** with)

enlodar VT *(a)* *(enfangar)* to muddy, to cover with mud **(b)** *(reputación)* to stain, to besmirch

enloquecedor, -a ADJ maddening

enloquecer [33] **1** VI to go mad
2 VT *(a)* *(volver loco)* to drive mad **(b)** *Fam* **me enloquecen las motos** I'm mad about motorbikes
3 enloquecerse VPR to go mad, to go out of one's mind

enlosar VT to tile

enlucir [35] VT *(pared)* to plaster; *(plata, oro)* to polish

enlutado, -a ADJ in mourning

enmarañar 1 VT *(a)* *(pelo)* to tangle **(b)** *(complicar)* to complicate, to confuse
2 enmarañarse VPR *(a)* *(pelo)* to get tangled **(b)** *(situación)* to get confused, to get into a mess *o* a muddle

enmarcar [44] VT to frame

enmascarado, -a NM,F *(hombre)* masked man; *(mujer)* masked woman

enmascarar VT *(a)* *(rostro)* to mask **(b)** *(problema, la verdad)* to mask, to disguise

enmendar [1] **1** VT *(corregir)* to correct, to put right; *Der* to amend
2 enmendarse VPR *(persona)* to reform, to mend one's ways

enmienda NF correction; *Der & Pol* amendment

enmohecerse [33] VPR *(metal)* to rust, to get rusty; *Bot* to go mouldy

enmoquetar VT *Esp, RP* to carpet

enmudecer [33] VI *(callar)* to fall silent; *Fig* to be dumbstruck

ennegrecer [33] **1** VT to blacken
2 ennegrecerse VPR to become blackened

ennoblecer [33] VT to ennoble

enojadizo, -a ADJ irritable, touchy

enojado, -a ADJ *(irritado)* angry; *(molesto)* annoyed

enojar *esp Am* **1** VT *(irritar)* to anger; *(molestar)* to annoy
2 enojarse VPR *(irritarse)* to get angry **(con** with); *(molestarse)* to get annoyed **(con** with)

enojo NM *esp Am (irritación)* anger; *(molestia)* annoyance

enorgullecer [33] **1** VT to fill with pride
2 enorgullecerse VPR to be *o* feel proud (**de** of)

enorme ADJ enormous

enormidad NF enormity; **me gustó una e.** I liked it enormously

enraizado, -a ADJ rooted

enraizarse [40] VPR *(persona)* to put down roots; *(planta, costumbre)* to take root

enrarecerse [33] VPR *(aire)* to become rarefied

enredadera NF climbing plant, creeper

enredar 1 VT (**a**) *(pelo)* to entangle, to tangle up (**b**) *Fig (asunto)* to confuse, to complicate (**c**) *Fig (implicar)* to involve (**en** in) (**d**) *(confundir)* to mix up
2 enredarse VPR (**a**) *(pelo)* to get entangled, to get tangled (up) *o* in a tangle (**b**) *Fig (asunto)* to get complicated *o* confused (**c**) *Fig* **enredarse con** *(involucrarse)* to get involved with (**d**) *(confundirse)* to get mixed up

enredo NM (**a**) *(maraña)* tangle (**b**) *Fig (lío)* muddle, mess

enrejado NM *(de ventana)* lattice

enrevesado, -a ADJ complicated, difficult

enriquecer [33] **1** VT to make rich; *Fig* to enrich
2 enriquecerse VPR to get *o* become rich, to prosper; *Fig* to become enriched

enrocar [44] VI *(en ajedrez)* to castle

enrojecer [33] **1** VT to redden, to turn red
2 VI *(ruborizarse)* to blush
3 enrojecerse VPR to blush

enrolarse VPR to enlist

enrollado, -a ADJ (**a**) *Esp (persona)* great (**b**) *Fam* **estar e. con algn** *(estar saliendo con)* to go out with sb

enrollar 1 VT to roll up; *(cable)* to coil; *(hilo)* to wind up
2 enrollarse VPR (**a**) *Fam (hablar)* to chatter, to go on and on (**b**) *Fam* **enrollarse con algn** *(tener relaciones)* to have an affair with sb

Observa que el verbo inglés **to enrol** es un falso amigo y no es la traducción del verbo español **enrollar**. En inglés, **to enrol** significa "matricular, inscribir".

enroscar [44] VT (**a**) *(tuerca)* to screw in; *(tapa)* to screw on (**b**) *(enrollar)* to roll up; *(cuerpo, cola)* to curl up

ensaimada NF = kind of spiral pastry from Majorca

ensalada NF salad

ensaladera NF salad bowl

ensaladilla NF *Esp* **e. rusa** Russian salad

ensalzar [40] VT to praise

ensamblador NM *Inform* assembler

ensamblar VT to assemble

ensanchar 1 VT *(orificio, calle)* to widen; *(ropa)* to let out; *(ciudad)* to expand
2 ensancharse VPR *(orificio, calle)* to widen, to open out

ensanche NM *(de calle)* widening; *(en la ciudad)* new suburb

ensangrentado, -a ADJ bloodstained, covered in blood

ensangrentar [1] VT to stain with blood, to cover in blood

ensañarse VPR **e. con** to torment, to treat cruelly

ensartar VT *(perlas)* to string together

ensayar VT to test, to try out; *Teatro* to rehearse; *Mús* to practise

ensayista NMF essayist

ensayo NM (**a**) *(prueba)* test, trial (**b**) *Teatro* rehearsal; **e. general** dress rehearsal (**c**) *(escrito)* essay

enseguida ADV *(inmediatamente)* immediately, straight away; *(pronto)* very soon; **e. voy** I'll be right there

ensenada NF inlet, cove

enseña NF ensign, standard

enseñanza NF (**a**) *(educación)* education (**b**) *(de idioma etc)* teaching (**c**) **enseñanzas** teachings

enseñar VT (**a**) *(instruir)* to teach; **e. a algn a hacer algo** to teach sb how to do sth (**b**) *(mostrar)* to show; *(señalar)* to point out

enseres NMPL *(bártulos)* belongings, goods; *(de trabajo)* tools

ensillar VT to saddle (up)

ensimismado, -a ADJ *(en la lectura)* engrossed; *(abstraído)* lost in thought

ensimismarse VPR *(en la lectura)* to become engrossed; *(abstraerse)* to be lost in thought

ensombrecer [33] **1** VT to cast a shadow over
2 ensombrecerse VPR to darken

ensopar VT *Andes, RP, Ven Fam* to soak

ensordecedor, -a ADJ deafening

ensordecer [33] **1** VT to deafen
2 VI to go deaf

ensortijado, -a ADJ curly

ensuciar [43] **1** VT (**a**) *(lugar, persona)* to get dirty (**b**) *Fig (reputación)* to harm, to damage
2 ensuciarse VPR to get dirty

ensueño NM dream; **una casa de e.** a dream house

entablar VT (**a**) *(conversación)* to open, to begin; *(amistad)* to strike up; *(negocios)* to start (**b**) *(pleito)* to initiate

entablillar VT *Med* to splint

entallado, -a ADJ *(vestido)* close-fitting; *(camisa)* fitted

entallar VT to take in at the waist

entarimado NM parquet floor

ente NM (**a**) *(institución)* organization, body; **e. público** public service organization (**b**) *(ser)* being

entendederas NFPL *Fam* brains; **ser duro de e.** to be slow on the uptake

entender [3] **1** VT *(comprender)* to understand; **a mi e.** to my way of thinking; **dar a algn a e. que ...** to give sb to understand that ...
2 VI (**a**) *(comprender)* to understand (**b**) **e. de** *(saber)* to know about
3 entenderse VPR (**a**) *(comprenderse)* to be understood, to be meant (**b**) *Fam* **entenderse (bien) con** to get on (well) with

entendido, -a 1 NM,F expert
2 ADJ **tengo e. que ...** I understand that ...

entendimiento NM understanding

enterado, -a 1 ADJ knowledgeable, well-informed; **estar e.** to be in the know; **estar e. de ...** to be aware of ...
2 NM,F *(listillo)* know-all

enteramente ADV entirely, completely

enterar 1 VT to inform (**de** about o of)
2 enterarse VPR to find out; **me he enterado de que ...** I understand ...; **ni me enteré** I didn't even realize it

entereza NF strength of character

enternecedor, -a ADJ moving, touching

enternecer [33] **1** VT to move, to touch
2 enternecerse VPR to be moved o touched

entero, -a 1 ADJ (**a**) *(completo)* entire, whole; **por e.** completely (**b**) *Fig (íntegro)* honest, upright (**c**) *Fig (firme)* strong
2 NM (**a**) *Mat* whole number (**b**) *Fin* point

enterrador, -a NM gravedigger

enterramiento NM burial

enterrar [1] VT to bury

entidad NF organization; **e. comercial** company, firm

entierro NM *(acción)* burial; *(ceremonia)* funeral

entlo. *(abr* **entresuelo***)* mezzanine

entomología NF entomology

entonación NF intonation

entonar 1 VT (**a**) *(canto)* to sing (**b**) *Med* to tone up
2 VI to be in harmony, to be in tune (**con** with)

entonces ADV then; **por aquel e.** at that time; **el e. ministro** the then minister

entornar VT *(ojos)* to half-close; *(puerta)* to leave ajar

entorno NM environment

entorpecer [33] VT *(obstaculizar)* to hinder, to impede

entrada NF (**a**) *(acción)* entry; *(lugar)* entrance (**b**) *(billete)* ticket; *(recaudación)* takings (**c**) *Culin* entrée (**d**) *Com* **anotar una e.** to enter up un item; **entradas** *(ingresos)* receipts, takings (**e**) *Esp (pago inicial)* down payment, deposit (**f**) *(en la frente)* receding hairline (**g**) *Inform* input (**h**) **de e.** for a start

entrado, -a ADJ **e. en años** advanced in years; **hasta bien entrada la noche** well into the night

entramado NM framework

entramparse VPR *Fam* to get into debt

entrante 1 ADJ coming; **el mes e.** next month; **el ministro e.** the incoming minister
2 NM *Esp* starter

entrañable ADJ (**a**) *(lugar)* intimate, close (**b**) *(persona)* affectionate, warm-hearted

entrañar VT to entail

entrañas NFPL bowels

entrar VI (**a**) *(introducirse) (viniendo)* to enter, to come in; *(yendo)* to enter, to go in; **el año que entra** next year, the coming year (**b**) *(encajar)* to fit; **no entra en la cerradura** it won't fit in the lock (**c**) *(incorporarse)* **e. en** *(colegio, empresa)* to start at; *(club, partido)* to join (**d**) *(estar incluido)* **e. en, e. dentro de** to be included in (**e**) **entrarle a algn: me entró dolor de cabeza** I got a headache; **me entraron ganas de reír** I felt like laughing; **no me entran las matemáticas** I can't get the hang of maths

entre PREP (**a**) *(dos)* between (**b**) *(más de dos)* among(st)

entreabierto, -a ADJ *(ojos etc)* half-open; *(puerta)* ajar

entreacto NM interval, intermission

entrecejo NM space between the eyebrows; **fruncir el e.** to frown, to knit one's brow

entrecortado, -a ADJ *(voz)* faltering, hesitant

entrecot *(pl* **entrecots** o **entrecotes***)* NM fillet steak

entrecruzarse [40] VPR to entwine

entredicho NM **estar en e.** to be suspect; **poner algo en e.** to bring sth into question

entrega NF (**a**) *(de productos)* delivery; *(de premios)* presentation (**b**) *(fascículo)* part, instalment (**c**) *(devoción)* selflessness

entregar [42] **1** VT to hand over; *(deberes etc)* to give in, to hand in; *Com* to deliver
2 entregarse VPR (**a**) *(rendirse)* to give in, to surrender (**b**) **entregarse a** to devote oneself to; *Pey* to indulge in

entrelazar [40] VT to entwine

entremedias ADV in between

entremeses NMPL *Culin* hors d'oeuvres

entremeterse VPR = entrometerse

entremezclarse VPR to mix, to mingle

entrenador, -a NM,F trainer, coach

entrenamiento NM training

entrenar 1 VT & VI to train
2 entrenarse VPR to train

entrepierna NF crotch, crutch

entresacar [44] VT to pick out, to select

entresijos NMPL nooks and crannies

entresuelo NM mezzanine

entretanto 1 ADV meanwhile
 2 NM **en el e.** in the meantime
entretejer VT to interweave
entretención NF *Chile* entertainment
entretener [24] **1** VT (**a**) *(divertir)* to entertain, to amuse (**b**) *(retrasar)* to delay; *(detener)* to hold up, to detain
 2 entretenerse VPR (**a**) *(distraerse)* to amuse oneself, to while away the time (**b**) *(retrasarse)* to be delayed, to be held up
entretenido, -a ADJ enjoyable, entertaining
entretenimiento NM entertainment, amusement
entretiempo 1 NM *CSur* half-time
 2 de entretiempo LOC ADJ **ropa de e.** spring/autumn clothes
entrever [28] VT to glimpse, to catch sight of; *Fig* **dejó e. que ...** she hinted that ...
entreverar *CSur* **1** VT to mix
 2 entreverarse VPR to get tangled
entrevero NM *CSur* tangle, mess
entrevista NF interview
entrevistador, -a NM,F interviewer
entrevistar 1 VT to interview
 2 entrevistarse VPR **entrevistarse con algn** to have an interview with sb
entristecer [33] **1** VT to sadden, to make sad
 2 entristecerse VPR to be sad (**por** about)
entrometerse VPR to meddle, to interfere (**en** in)
entrometido, -a 1 NM,F meddler, busybody
 2 ADJ interfering
entroncar [44] VI to connect
entumecer [33] **1** VT to numb
 2 entumecerse VPR to go numb
entumecido, -a ADJ numb
enturbiar [43] **1** VT (**a**) *(agua)* to make cloudy (**b**) *(asunto)* to cloud, to obscure
 2 enturbiarse VPR to become cloudy
entusiasmar 1 VT to fill with enthusiasm
 2 entusiasmarse VPR to get excited *o* enthusiastic (**con** about)
entusiasmo NM enthusiasm; **con e.** enthusiastically
entusiasta 1 ADJ enthusiastic, keen (**de** on)
 2 NMF enthusiast
enumerar VT to enumerate
enunciado NM *(de teoría, problema)* wording
envainar VT to sheathe
envanecer [33] **1** VT to make proud *o* vain
 2 envanecerse VPR to become conceited *o* proud, to give oneself airs
envasado, -a 1 NM *(en botella)* bottling; *(en paquete)* packing; *(en lata)* canning
 2 ADJ **e. al vacío** vacuum-packed
envasar VT *(embotellar)* to bottle; *(empaquetar)* to pack; *(enlatar)* to can, to tin
envase NM (**a**) *(acto)* packing; *(de botella)* bottling; *(de lata)* canning (**b**) *(recipiente)* container (**c**) *(botella vacía)* empty

envejecer [33] **1** VI to grow old
 2 VT to age
envejecimiento NM ageing
envenenamiento NM poisoning
envenenar VT to poison
envergadura NF (**a**) *(importancia)* importance, scope; **de gran e.** large-scale (**b**) *(de pájaro, avión)* span, wingspan; *Náut* breadth (of sail)
envés *(pl* **enveses)** NM other side
envestidura NF investiture
enviado, -a NM,F envoy; *Prensa* **e. especial** special correspondent
enviar [29] VT to send
enviciarse [43] VPR to become addicted (**con** to)
envidia NF envy; **tener e. de algn** to envy sb
envidiable ADJ enviable
envidiar [43] VT to envy; **no tener nada que e.** to be in no way inferior (**a** to)
envidioso, -a ADJ envious

Observa que la palabra inglesa **invidious** es un falso amigo y no es la traducción de la palabra española **envidioso**. En inglés, **invidious** significa "ingrato" o "injusto".

envilecer [33] VT to degrade, to debase
envío NM sending; *(remesa)* consignment; *(paquete)* parcel; **gastos de e.** postage and packing; **e. contra reembolso** cash on delivery
enviudar VI *(hombre)* to become a widower, to lose one's wife; *(mujer)* to become a widow, to lose one's husband
envoltorio NM wrapper, wrapping
envolver [4] *(pp* **envuelto)** **1** VT (**a**) *(con papel)* to wrap (**b**) *(cubrir)* to envelop (**c**) *(en complot etc)* to involve (**en** in)
 2 envolverse VPR (**a**) *(cubrirse)* to wrap oneself up (**en** in) (**b**) *(implicarse)* to become involved (**en** in)
enyesar VT to plaster; *Med* to put in plaster
enzima NF enzyme
épica NF epic poetry
epicentro NM epicentre
épico, -a ADJ epic
epidemia NF epidemic
epidermis NF INV *Anat* epidermis
epilepsia NF epilepsy
epílogo NM epilogue
episcopal ADJ episcopal
episodio NM episode
epístola NF epistle
epitafio NM epitaph
epíteto NM epithet
época NF time; *Hist* period, epoch; *Agr* season; **en esta é. del año** at this time of the year; **hacer é.** to be a landmark; **mueble de é.** period furniture

equidad NF equity

equilátero NM equilateral

equilibrado, -a ADJ (a) *(igualado)* balanced (b) *(sensato)* sensible

equilibrar VT to balance

equilibrio NM balance

equilibrismo NM balancing act

equilibrista NMF tightrope walker

equipaje NM *Br* luggage, *US* baggage; **hacer el e.** to pack, to do the packing

equipar VT to equip, to furnish (**con** *o* **de** with)

equiparable ADJ comparable (**a** to; **con** with)

equiparar VT to compare (**con** with), to liken (**con** to)

equipo NM (a) *(de expertos, jugadores)* team (b) *(aparatos)* equipment; **e. de alta fidelidad** hi-fi stereo system (c) *(ropas)* outfit

equis NF INV = name of the letter X

equitación NF horse *o US* horseback riding

equitativo, -a ADJ equitable, fair

equivalente ADJ equivalent

equivaler [26] VI to be equivalent (**a** to)

equivocación NF error, mistake

equivocado, -a ADJ mistaken, wrong

equivocar [44] **1** VT to mix up
2 equivocarse VPR to make a mistake; *Tel* **se equivocó de número** he dialled the wrong number; **se equivocó de fecha** he got the wrong date

equívoco, -a 1 ADJ equivocal, misleading
2 NM misunderstanding

era¹ NF *(época)* era, age

era² NF *Agr* threshing floor

era³ PT INDEF *de* **ser**

erario NM exchequer, treasury

eras PT INDEF *de* **ser**

erección NF erection

erecto, -a ADJ upright; *(pene)* erect

eres INDIC PRES *de* **ser**

erguido, -a ADJ upright

erguir [55] **1** VT to raise
2 erguirse VPR to rise up

erial NM uncultivated land

erigir [57] **1** VT to erect
2 erigirse VPR **e. en algo** to set oneself up in sth

erizado, -a ADJ bristly, prickly

erizarse [40] VPR to bristle, to stand on end

erizo NM hedgehog; **e. de mar** *o* **marino** sea urchin

ermita NF hermitage

> Observa que la palabra inglesa **hermit** es un falso amigo y no es la traducción de la palabra española **ermita**. En inglés, **hermit** significa "ermitaño".

ermitaño, -a NM,F hermit

erosión NF erosion

erosionar VT to erode

erótico, -a ADJ erotic

erotismo NM eroticism

erradicar [44] VT to eradicate

errante ADJ wandering

errar [50] **1** VT to miss, to get wrong
2 VI (a) *(vagar)* to wander, to roam (b) *(fallar)* to err

errata NF erratum, misprint

erre NF **e. que e.** stubbornly, pigheadedly

erróneo, -a ADJ erroneous, wrong

error NM error, mistake; *Inform* bug; **por e.** by mistake, in error; *Impr* **e. de imprenta** misprint; **caer en un e.** to make a mistake

Ertzaintza [er'tʃaintʃa] NF *Esp* = Basque police force

eructar VI to belch, to burp

eructo NM belch, burp

erudición NF erudition

erudito, -a 1 ADJ erudite, learned
2 NM,F scholar

erupción NF (a) *(de volcán)* eruption (b) *(en la piel)* rash

es INDIC PRES *de* **ser**

esa ADJ DEM *ver* **ese**

ésa PRON DEM *ver* **ése**

esbelto, -a ADJ slender

esbirro NM henchman

esbozar [40] VT to sketch, to outline

esbozo NM sketch, outline, rough draft

escabeche NM brine

escabechina NF *Fam (destrozo)* destruction

escabroso, -a ADJ *(tema)* unpleasant; *(detalles)* lurid; *(imágenes)* crude

escabullirse VPR to slip away, to scuttle *o* scurry off

escacharrar VT *Esp Fam* to bust

escafandra NF diving suit; **e. espacial** spacesuit

escala NF (a) *(para medir)* scale; *(de colores)* range; **e. musical** scale; **en gran e.** on a large scale (b) *(parada) Náut* port of call; *Av* stopover; **hacer e. en** to call in at, to stop over in (c) *Mús* scale

escalada NF (a) *(de montaña)* climb (b) *(de violencia, precios)* escalation, rise (**de** in)

escalador, -a NM,F climber, mountaineer

> Observa que la palabra inglesa **escalator** es un falso amigo y no es la traducción de la palabra española **escalador**. En inglés, **escalator** significa "escalera mecánica".

escalafón NM *(graduación)* rank; *(de salarios)* salary *o* wage scale

escalar VT to climb, to scale

escaldar VT to scald

escalera NF (a) *(en edificio)* stairs, staircase; *(de mano)* ladder; **e. de incendios** fire escape;

e. mecánica escalator; **e. de caracol** spiral staircase (**b**) *Naipes* run

escalerilla NF *(de piscina)* steps; *Náut* gangway; *Av* (boarding) ramp

escalfar VT to poach

escalinata NF stoop

escalofriante ADJ hair-raising, bloodcurdling

escalofrío NM shiver; **me dio un e.** it gave me the shivers

escalón NM step; **e. lateral** *(en letrero)* ramp

escalonar VT to place at intervals, to space out

escalope NM escalope

escalpelo NM scalpel

escama NF *Zool* scale; *(de jabón)* flake

escamarse VPR to smell a rat, to become suspicious

escamotear VT *Fam* to diddle out of, to do out of

escampar VI to stop raining, to clear up

escanciar [43] VT *(vino)* to pour out, to serve

escandalizar [40] **1** VT to scandalize, to shock
2 escandalizarse VPR to be shocked (**de** at *o* by)

escándalo NM (**a**) *(alboroto)* racket, din; **armar un e.** to kick up a fuss (**b**) *(desvergüenza)* scandal

escandaloso, -a ADJ (**a**) *(ruidoso)* noisy, rowdy (**b**) *(ofensivo)* scandalous

Escandinavia N Scandinavia

escandinavo, -a ADJ & NM,F Scandinavian

escanear VT *Inform & Med* to scan

escáner NM *Inform & Med (aparato)* scanner; *Med (imagen)* scan

escaño NM *(parlamentario)* seat

escapada NF (**a**) *(de prisión)* escape; *(en ciclismo)* breakaway (**b**) *(viaje rápido)* flying visit, quick trip

> Observa que la palabra inglesa **escapade** es un falso amigo y no es la traducción de la palabra española **escapada**. En inglés, **escapade** significa "aventura".

escapar 1 VI to escape, to run away
2 escaparse VPR (**a**) *(huir)* to escape, to run away (**b**) *(gas, agua)* to leak (**c**) *(dejar ir)* **se me escapó la risa** I let out a laugh; **se me escapó de las manos** it slipped out of my hands (**d**) *(pasar inadvertido)* **no se le escapa nada** he doesn't miss a thing

escaparate NM shop window

escaparatismo NM window dressing

escapatoria NF **no tener e.** to have no way out

escape NM (**a**) *(de gas)* leak (**b**) *(de coche)* exhaust; **tubo de e.** exhaust (pipe)

escaquearse VPR *Esp Fam* to duck out; **e. de hacer algo** to worm one's way out of doing sth

escarabajo NM beetle

escaramuza NF *Mil & Fig* skirmish

escarbar VT *(suelo)* to scratch; *(fuego)* to poke

escarceos NMPL forays; **e. amorosos** flirtations

escarcha NF hoarfrost, frost

escarchado, -a ADJ *(fruta)* crystallized, candied

escarlata ADJ & NM scarlet

escarlatina NF *Med* scarlet fever

escarmentar [1] VI to learn one's lesson

escarmiento NM punishment, lesson

escarnio NM derision, mockery

escarola NF curly endive

escarpado, -a ADJ *(paisaje)* craggy; *(pendiente)* steep

escasear VI to be scarce

escasez NF scarcity

escaso, -a ADJ scarce; *(dinero)* tight; *(conocimientos)* scant; **e. de dinero** short of money

escatimar VT to skimp on; **no escatimó esfuerzos para …** he spared no efforts to …

escayola NF *Constr* plaster of Paris; *Med* plaster; **una e.** a plaster cast

escayolar VT *Med* to put in plaster

escena NF (**a**) *(suceso, acto)* scene (**b**) *(escenario)* stage; **poner en e.** to stage

escenario NM (**a**) *Teatro* stage (**b**) *(entorno)* scenario; *(de crimen)* scene; *(de película)* setting

escénico, -a ADJ scenic

escenografía NF *Cin* set design; *Teatro* stage design

escepticismo NM scepticism

escéptico, -a ADJ & NM,F sceptic

escindirse VPR to split (off) (**en** into)

escisión NF split

esclarecer [33] VT to shed light on

esclava NF bangle

esclavitud NF slavery

esclavizar [40] VT to enslave

esclavo, -a ADJ & NM,F slave

esclusa NF lock, sluicegate

escoba NF brush, broom

escobilla NF brush

escocer [41] **1** VI to sting, to smart
2 escocerse VPR *(piel)* to chafe

escocés, -esa 1 ADJ Scottish, Scots; **falda escocesa** kilt
2 NM,F *(hombre)* Scotsman; *(mujer)* Scotswoman

Escocia N Scotland

escoger [53] VT to choose

escogido, -a ADJ chosen, selected; *(producto)* choice, select; *Lit* **obras escogidas** selected works

escolar 1 ADJ *(curso, año)* school
2 NM *(niño)* schoolboy; *(niña)* schoolgirl

escolaridad NF schooling

escollo NM reef; *Fig* pitfall

escolta NF escort

escoltar VT to escort

escombros NMPL rubbish, debris

esconder 1 VT to hide (**de** from), to conceal (**de** from)
 2 esconderse VPR to hide (**de** from)

escondidas ADV a **e.** secretly

escondite NM (**a**) (*lugar*) hiding place, hideout (**b**) (*juego*) hide-and-seek

escondrijo NM hiding place, hide-out

escopeta NF shotgun; **e. de aire comprimido** air gun; **e. de cañones recortados** *Br* sawnoff shotgun, *US* sawed-off shotgun

escorbuto NM *Med* scurvy

escoria NF scum, dregs

Escorpio NM Scorpio

escorpión NM scorpion

escotado, -a ADJ low-cut

escote NM low neckline

escotilla NF hatch, hatchway

escozor NM stinging, smarting

escribiente NMF clerk

escribir (*pp* **escrito**) **1** VT to write; **e. a mano** to write in longhand; **e. a máquina** to type
 2 escribirse VPR (**a**) (*dos personas*) to write to each other, to correspond (**b**) **se escribe con h** it is spelt with an h

escrito, -a 1 ADJ written; **e. a mano** handwritten, in longhand; **por e.** in writing
 2 NM writing
 3 PP *de* escribir

escritor, -a NM,F writer

escritorio NM (**a**) (*mueble*) writing desk, bureau; (*oficina*) office (**b**) *Inform* desktop

escritura NF (**a**) *Der* deed, document; **e. de propiedad** title deed (**b**) *Rel* **Sagradas Escrituras** Holy Scriptures

escrúpulo NM (**a**) (*duda, recelo*) scruple; **una persona sin escrúpulos** an unscrupulous person (**b**) (*esmero*) scrupulousness, great care (**c**) (*aprensión*) qualm; **le da e.** he has qualms about it

escrupuloso, -a ADJ (**a**) (*minucioso*) scrupulous (**b**) (*aprensivo*) particular, fussy

escrutar VT (**a**) (*con la mirada*) to scrutinize (**b**) (*votos*) to count

escrutinio NM (*de votos*) count

escuadra NF (**a**) (*instrumento*) square (**b**) *Mil* squad; *Náut* squadron; *Dep* team; (*de coches*) fleet

escuadrilla NF *Náut* squadron

escuadrón NM *Av* squadron

escuálido, -a ADJ emaciated

escucha NF listening; **escuchas telefónicas** phone tapping; **estar a la e. de** to be listening out for

escuchar 1 VT to listen to; (*oír*) to hear
 2 VI to listen; (*oír*) to hear

escudarse VPR **e. en algo** to hide behind sth

escudería NF motor racing team

escudilla NF bowl

escudo NM (**a**) (*arma defensiva*) shield (**b**) (*blasón*) coat of arms

escudriñar VT to scrutinize

escuela NF school; **e. de bellas artes** art school; **e. de conducir/de idiomas** driving/language school

escueto, -a ADJ plain, unadorned

escuezo INDIC PRES *de* escocer

esculcar [44] VT *Méx* to search

esculpir VT to sculpt; (*madera*) to carve; (*metal*) to engrave

escultor, -a NM,F (*hombre*) sculptor; (*mujer*) sculptress; (*de madera*) woodcarver; (*de metales*) engraver

escultura NF sculpture

escultural ADJ sculptural; (*persona*) statuesque

escupidera NF (*orinal*) chamberpot

escupir 1 VI to spit
 2 VT to spit out

escupitajo NM *Fam* spit

escurreplatos NM INV dish rack

escurridizo, -a ADJ (**a**) (*resbaladizo*) slippery (**b**) *Fig* (*huidizo*) elusive, slippery

escurridor NM colander

escurrir 1 VT (*plato, vaso*) to drain; (*ropa*) to wring out; **e. el bulto** to wriggle out
 2 escurrirse VPR (**a**) (*platos etc*) to drip (**b**) (*escaparse*) to run *o* slip away (**c**) (*resbalarse*) to slip

ese, -a (*pl* **esos, -as**) ADJ DEM (**a**) (*singular*) that (**b**) **esos, -as** those

ése, -a (*pl* **ésos, -as**) PRON DEM M,F (**a**) (*singular*) that one (**b**) **ésos, -as** those (ones); *Fam* **¡ni por ésas!** no way!; *Fam* **¡no me vengas con ésas!** come off it!

Note that **ése** and its various forms can be written without an accent when there is no risk of confusion with the adjective.

esencia NF essence

esencial ADJ essential; **lo e.** the main thing

esfera NF (**a**) (*figura*) sphere (**b**) (*de reloj*) face (**c**) (*social*) circle; **las altas esferas de la política** high political circles

esférico, -a 1 ADJ spherical
 2 NM (*balón*) ball

esfinge NF sphinx

esforzarse [2] VPR to make an effort (**por** to)

esfuerzo NM effort

esfumarse VPR *Fam* to beat it

esgrima NF *Dep* fencing

esgrimir VT to wield

esguince NM sprain

eslabón NM link

eslalon (*pl* **eslalons**) NM *Dep* slalom; **e. gigante** giant slalom

eslavo, -a 1 ADJ Slav, Slavonic
2 NM,F *(persona)* Slav
3 NM *(idioma)* Slavonic

eslip *(pl* **eslips)** NM men's briefs, underpants

eslogan NM slogan; **e. publicitario** advertising slogan

eslovaco, -a 1 ADJ & NM,F Slovak, Slovakian
2 NM *(idioma)* Slovak

Eslovaquia N Slovakia

Eslovenia N Slovenia

esloveno, -a 1 ADJ & NM,F Slovene
2 NM *(idioma)* Slovene

esmaltar VT to enamel

esmalte NM enamel; *(de uñas)* nail polish *o* varnish

esmerado, -a ADJ painstaking, careful

esmeralda NF emerald

esmerarse VPR to be careful; *(esforzarse)* to go to great lengths

esmero NM great care

esmoquin NM *Br* dinner jacket, *US* tuxedo

esnifar VT *Fam (drogas)* to sniff

esnob *(pl* **esnobs)** **1** ADJ *(persona)* snobbish; *(restaurante etc)* posh
2 NMF snob

esnobismo NM snobbery, snobbishness

ESO NF *(abr* **Enseñanza Secundaria Obligatoria)** = mainstream secondary education in Spain for pupils aged 12-16

eso PRON NEUT that; **¡e. es!** that's it!; **por e.** that's why; *Fam* **a e. de las diez** around ten; *Fam* **e. de las Navidades sale muy caro** this whole Christmas thing costs a fortune

esófago NM oesophagus

esos, -as ADJ DEM PL *ver* **ese**

ésos, -as PRON DEM M,F PL *ver* **ése**

esotérico, -a ADJ esoteric

espabilado, -a ADJ *(a) (despierto)* wide awake *(b) (niño)* bright

espabilar 1 VT to wake up
2 espabilarse VPR to wake up, to waken up

espachurrar VT to squash

espacial ADJ spatial; **nave e.** space ship

espaciar [43] VT to space out

espacio NM *(a) (lugar)* space; *(tiempo)* length; **a doble e.** double-spaced; **el e. (exterior)** (outer) space *(b) Rad & TV* programme

espacioso, -a ADJ spacious, roomy

espada 1 NF *(a) (arma)* sword; **estar entre la e. y la pared** to be between the devil and the deep blue sea; **pez e.** swordfish *(b) Naipes* **espadas** = suit in Spanish deck of cards, with the symbol of a sword
2 NM *Taurom* matador

Observa que la palabra inglesa **spade** es un falso amigo y no es la traducción de la palabra española **espada**. En inglés, **spade** significa "pala".

espadaña NF bullrush

espaguetis NMPL spaghetti

espalda NF **(a)** *Anat* back; **espaldas** back; **a espaldas de algn** behind sb's back; **por la e.** from behind; **volver la e. a algn** to turn one's back on sb; *Fam* **e. mojada** wetback **(b)** *(en natación)* backstroke

espaldilla NF shoulder blade

espantapájaros NM INV scarecrow

espantar 1 VT **(a)** *(asustar)* to frighten, to scare **(b)** *(ahuyentar)* to frighten away
2 espantarse VPR to get *o* feel frightened (**de** of), to get *o* feel scared (**de** of)

espanto NM fright; *Fam* **de e.** dreadful, shocking

espantoso, -a ADJ dreadful

España N Spain

español, -a 1 ADJ Spanish
2 NM,F Spaniard; **los españoles** the Spanish
3 NM *(idioma)* Spanish

esparadrapo NM *Br* (sticking-)plaster, *US* Band-aid®

esparcimiento NM relaxation

esparcir [52] **1** VT *(papeles, semillas)* to scatter; *Fig (rumor)* to spread
2 esparcirse VPR **(a)** *(papeles, semillas)* to be scattered **(b)** *(relajarse)* to relax

espárrago NM asparagus

espartano, -a ADJ spartan

espasmo NM spasm

espátula NF *Culin* spatula; *Arte* palette knife; *Téc* stripping knife; *(de albañil)* trowel

especia NF spice

especial ADJ special; **en e.** especially; **e. para ...** suitable for ...

especialidad NF speciality, *US* specialty; *Educ* main subject

especialista NMF specialist

especializarse [40] VPR to specialize (**en** in)

especialmente ADV *(exclusivamente)* specially; *(muy)* especially

especie NF **(a)** *Biol* species *inv* **(b)** *(clase)* kind; **una e. de salsa** a kind of sauce **(c)** *Com* **en e.** in kind

especificar [44] VT to specify

específico, -a ADJ specific; **peso e.** specific gravity

espécimen *(pl* **especímenes)** NM specimen

espectacular ADJ spectacular

espectáculo NM **(a)** *(escena)* spectacle, sight; *Fam* **dar un e.** to make a spectacle of oneself **(b)** *Teatro, Cin & TV* show; **montar un e.** to put on a show

espectador, -a NM,F *Dep* spectator; *(de accidente)* onlooker; *Teatro & Cin* member of the audience; **los espectadores** the audience; *TV* the viewers

espectro NM (**a**) *Fís* spectrum (**b**) *(fantasma)* spectre (**c**) *(gama)* range

especulación NF speculation; **e. del suelo** land speculation

especulador, -a NM,F *Fin* speculator

especular VI to speculate

especulativo, -a ADJ speculative

espejismo NM mirage

espejo NM mirror; *Aut* **e. retrovisor** rearview mirror

espeleología NF potholing, speleology

espeluznante ADJ hair-raising, horrifying

espera NF wait; **en e. de ...** waiting for ...; **a la e. de** expecting; **sala de e.** waiting room

esperanza NF hope; **tener la e. puesta en algo** to have one's hopes pinned on sth; **e. de vida** life expectancy; **en estado de buena e.** expecting, pregnant

esperanzador, -a ADJ encouraging

esperanzar [40] VT to give hope to

esperar 1 VI (**a**) *(aguardar)* to wait (**b**) *(tener esperanza de)* to hope
2 VT (**a**) *(aguardar)* to wait for; **espero a mi hermano** I'm waiting for my brother (**b**) *(tener esperanza de)* to hope for; **espero que sí** I hope so; **espero que vengas** I hope you'll come (**c**) *(estar a la espera de)* to expect; **te esperábamos ayer** we were expecting you yesterday (**d**) *Fig (bebé)* to be expecting

esperma NM sperm

espermatozoide NM spermatozoid

espermicida NM spermicide

esperpéntico, -a ADJ grotesque

espesar 1 VT to thicken
2 espesarse VPR to thicken, to get thicker

espeso, -a ADJ *(bosque, niebla)* dense; *(líquido)* thick; *(masa)* stiff

espesor NM thickness; **3 m de e.** 3 m thick

espesura NF denseness

espetar VT *(palabras)* to blurt out, to tell straight out

espía NMF spy

espiar [29] **1** VI to spy
2 VT to spy on

espichar VI *Fam* **espichar(la)** *(morir)* to kick the bucket

espiga NF (**a**) *(de trigo)* ear (**b**) *Téc* pin

espigado, -a ADJ slender

espina NF (**a**) *Bot* thorn (**b**) *(de pescado)* bone (**c**) *Anat* **e. dorsal** spinal column, spine (**d**) *Fig* **ése me da mala e.** there's something fishy about that one

espinaca NF spinach

espinal ADJ spinal; **médula e.** spinal marrow

espinazo NM spine, backbone

espinilla NF (**a**) *Anat* shin (**b**) *(en la piel)* spot

espinillera NF *Dep* shin pad

espino NM hawthorn; **alambre de e.** barbed wire

espionaje NM spying, espionage; **novela de e.** spy story

espiral ADJ & NF spiral

espirar VI to breathe out, to exhale

espiritismo NM spiritualism

espíritu NM (**a**) *(mente, actitud)* spirit; **e. deportivo** sportsmanship (**b**) *Rel (alma)* soul; **el E. Santo** the Holy Ghost

espiritual ADJ spiritual

espléndido, -a ADJ (**a**) *(magnífico)* splendid (**b**) *(generoso)* lavish, generous

esplendor NM splendour

esplendoroso, -a ADJ magnificent

espliego NM lavender

espolear VT to spur on

espolvorear VT to sprinkle (**de** with)

esponja NF sponge

esponjoso, -a ADJ spongy; *(bizcocho)* light

esponsales NMPL betrothal, engagement

espontaneidad NF spontaneity; **con e.** naturally

espontáneo, -a 1 ADJ spontaneous
2 NM *Taurom* = spectator who spontaneously joins in the bullfight

esporádico, -a ADJ sporadic

esposado, -a ADJ (**a**) *(recién casado)* newly married (**b**) *(con esposas)* handcuffed

esposar VT to handcuff

esposas NFPL handcuffs

esposo, -a NM,F spouse; *(hombre)* husband; *(mujer)* wife

espray *(pl* **esprays)** NM spray

esprint *(pl* **esprints)** NM sprint

esprintar VI to sprint

esprínter NMF sprinter

espuela NF spur

espuerta NF hod

espuma NF foam; *(de olas)* surf; *(de cerveza)* froth, head; *(de jabón)* lather; **e. de afeitar** shaving foam

espumoso, -a ADJ frothy; *(vino)* sparkling

esputo NM spit

esquela NF *Esp* funeral notice *(in newspaper)*

esquelético, -a ADJ (**a**) *Anat* skeletal (**b**) *(flaco)* skinny

esqueleto NM (**a**) *(huesos)* skeleton (**b**) *Constr* framework

esquema NM diagram

esquemático, -a ADJ *(escueto)* schematic; *(con diagramas)* diagrammatic

esquematizar [40] VT (**a**) *(en forma de gráfico)* to draw a diagram of (**b**) *(resumir)* to outline

esquí *(pl* **esquíes** *o* **esquís)** NM (**a**) *(objeto)* ski (**b**) *(deporte)* skiing; **e. acuático** waterskiing

esquiador, -a NM,F skier

esquiar [29] VI to ski

esquilar VT to shear

esquimal ADJ & NMF Eskimo

esquina NF corner; *Dep* **saque de e.** corner (kick)

esquinazo NM **dar e. a algn** to give sb the slip

esquirla NF splinter

esquirol NM *Ind* blackleg, scab

esquivar VT *(a una persona)* to avoid; *(un golpe)* to dodge

esquivo, -a ADJ cold, aloof

esquizofrenia NF schizophrenia

esquizofrénico, -a ADJ & NM,F schizophrenic

esta ADJ DEM *ver* **este²**

está INDIC PRES *de* **estar**

ésta PRON DEM F *ver* **éste**

estabilidad NF stability

estabilizar [40] VT to stabilize

estable ADJ stable

establecer [33] **1** VT to establish; *(fundar)* to set up, to found; *(récord)* to set
2 establecerse VPR to settle

establecimiento NM establishment

establo NM cow shed

estaca NF stake, post; *(de tienda de campaña)* peg

estacada NF fence; *Fig* **dejar a algn en la e.** to leave sb in the lurch

estación NF (**a**) *(edificio)* station; **e. de servicio** service station; **e. de esquí** ski resort (**b**) *(del año)* season

estacional ADJ seasonal

estacionamiento NM *Aut (acción)* parking; *(lugar) Br* car park, *US* parking lot

estacionar 1 VT to park
2 estacionarse VPR *Am* to park

estacionario, -a ADJ stationary

estadía NF *Am* stay

estadio NM (**a**) *Dep* stadium (**b**) *(fase)* stage

estadista NMF *Pol (hombre)* statesman; *(mujer)* stateswoman

estadística NF statistics *sing*; **una e.** a statistic

estado NM (**a**) *Pol* state (**b**) *(situación)* state, condition; **en buen e.** in good condition; **estar en e.** to be pregnant; **e. de ánimo** state of mind; **e. civil** marital status; *Com* **e. de cuentas** statement of accounts; **e. de excepción** state of emergency; **e. de salud** condition, state of health·(**c**) *Mil* **e. mayor** general staff (**d**) *(país, división territorial)* state; **Estados Unidos de América** United States of America

estadounidense 1 ADJ United States, American
2 NMF American

estafa NF swindle

estafador, -a NM,F swindler

estafar VT to swindle

estafeta NF **e. de Correos** sub-post office

estalactita NF stalactite

estalagmita NF stalagmite

estallar VI (**a**) *(bomba)* to explode, to go off; *(neumático)* to burst; *(guerra)* to break out (**b**) *Fig (de cólera etc)* to explode; **e. en sollozos** to burst into tears

estallido NM *(de bomba)* explosion; *(de guerra)* outbreak

estambre NM *Bot* stamen

Estambul N Istanbul

estamento NM *Hist* estate; *Fig (grupo)* group

estampa NF print, image

Observa que la palabra inglesa **stamp** es un falso amigo y no es la traducción de la palabra española **estampa**. En inglés, **stamp** significa "sello, tampón".

estampado, -a 1 ADJ *(tela)* printed
2 NM (**a**) *(tela)* print (**b**) *(proceso)* printing

estampar VT (**a**) *(tela)* to print (**b**) *(dejar impreso)* to imprint (**c**) *(bofetada, beso)* to plant, to place

estampida NF (**a**) *(estampido)* bang (**b**) *(carrera rápida)* stampede; **de e.** suddenly

estampido NM bang

estampilla NF *Am* (postage) stamp

estancado, -a ADJ *(agua)* stagnant; *Fig* static, at a standstill; **quedarse e.** to get bogged down o stuck

estancar [44] **1** VT (**a**) *(agua)* to hold back (**b**) *Fig (asunto)* to block; *(negociaciones)* to bring to a standstill
2 estancarse VPR to stagnate; *Fig* to get bogged down

estancia NF (**a**) *Esp, Méx (tiempo)* stay (**b**) *(habitación)* room (**c**) *CSur (hacienda)* ranch, farm

estanciero, -a NM,F *CSur* ranch owner, rancher

estanco, -a 1 NM *Esp* tobacconist's
2 ADJ watertight

estándar ADJ & NM standard

estandarizar [40] VT to standardize

estandarte NM standard, banner

estanque NM pool, pond

estanquero, -a NM,F tobacconist

estante NM shelf; *(para libros)* bookcase

estantería NF shelves, shelving

estaño NM tin

estar [13] **1** VI (**a**) to be; **está en la playa** he is at the beach; **e. en casa** to be in, to be at home; **estamos en Caracas** we are in Caracas; **¿está tu madre?** is your mother in?; **¿cómo estás?** how are you?; **los precios están bajos** prices are low; **el problema está en el dinero** the problem is money; **e. en lo cierto** to be right; **e. en todo** not to miss a trick
(**b**) *(+ adj)* to be; **está cansado/enfermo** he's tired/ill; **está vacío** it's empty
(**c**) *(+ adv)* to be; **está bien/mal** it's all right/ wrong; **e. mal de dinero** he's short of money; **estará enseguida** it'll be ready in a minute
(**d**) *(+ ger)* to be; **está escribiendo** she is

writing; **estaba comiendo** he was eating
(**e**) (+ a + fecha) to be; **¿a cuántos estamos?**
what's the date (today)?; **estamos a 2 de
Noviembre** it is the 2nd of November
(**f**) (+ precio) to be at; **están a dos euros el kilo**
they're two euros a kilo
(**g**) (locuciones) **e. al caer** to be just round the
corner; **¿estamos?** OK?
(**h**) (+ de) **e. de más** not to be needed; **e. de
paseo** to be out for a walk; **e. de vacaciones/
viaje** to be (away) on holiday/a trip; **estoy de
jefe hoy** I'm the boss today
(**i**) (+ para) **estará para las seis** it will be
finished by six; **hoy no estoy para bromas** I'm
in no mood for jokes today; **el tren está para
salir** the train is just about to leave
(**j**) (+ por) **está por hacer** it has still to be
done; **eso está por ver** it remains to be seen;
estoy por esperar (a favor de) I'm for waiting
(**k**) (+ con) to have; **e. con la gripe** to have the
flu, to be down with flu; **estoy con Jaime** (de
acuerdo con) I agree with Jaime
(**l**) (+ sin) to have no; **e. sin luz/agua** to have
no light/water
(**m**) (+ que) **está que se duerme** he is nearly
asleep; Fam **está que rabia** he's hopping mad
2 estarse VPR **¡estáte quieto!** keep still!, stop
fidgeting!

estárter (pl **estárters**) NM choke

estatal ADJ state; **enseñanza e.** state education

estático, -a ADJ static

estatua NF statue

estatura NF (**a**) (altura) height; **¿cuál es tu e.?**
how tall are you? (**b**) (renombre) stature

estatus NM INV status; **e. quo** status quo

estatutario, -a ADJ statutory

estatuto NM Der statute; (de ciudad) bylaw; (de
empresa etc) rules

este¹ 1 ADJ eastern; (dirección) easterly
2 NM east; **al e. de** to the east of

este², -a (pl **estos, -as**) ADJ DEM (**a**) (singular)
this (**b**) **estos, -as** these

esté SUBJ PRES de **estar**

éste, -a (pl **éstos, -as**) PRON DEM M,F (**a**)
(singular) this one; **aquél ... é.** the former ...
the latter (**b**) **éstos, -as** these (ones); **aquéllos ... é.** the former ... the latter

> Note that **éste** and its various forms can be
> written without an accent when there is no
> risk of confusion with the adjective.

estela NF (de barco) wake; (de avión) vapour
trail; (de cometa) tail

estelar ADJ (**a**) Astron stellar (**b**) Fig Cin &
Teatro star

estentóreo, -a ADJ stentorian, thundering

estepa NF steppe

estera NF rush mat

estercolero NM dunghill

estéreo NM & ADJ stereo

estereofónico, -a ADJ stereophonic, stereo

estereotipar VT to stereotype

estereotipo NM stereotype

estéril ADJ (**a**) (persona) sterile (**b**) Fig
(esfuerzo) futile

esterilidad NF sterility

esterilizar [40] VT to sterilize

esterilla NF small mat

esterlina ADJ sterling; **libra e.** pound (sterling)

esternón NM sternum, breastbone

estero NM (**a**) (pantano) Am marsh, swamp (**b**)
Ven (charca) puddle, pool (**c**) Chile (arroyo)
stream

estertor NM death rattle

estética NF aesthetics sing

esteticienne NF beautician

estético, -a ADJ aesthetic; **cirugía estética**
plastic surgery

estibador NM docker, stevedore

estiércol NM manure, dung

estigma NM stigma; Rel stigmata

estilarse VPR to be in vogue, to be fashionable

estilete NM (punzón) stylus; (puñal) stiletto

estilístico, -a ADJ stylistic

estilizar [40] VT to stylize

estilo NM (**a**) style; **algo por el e.** something
like that; **e. de vida** way of life (**b**) (en
natación) stroke (**c**) Ling **e. directo/indirecto**
direct/indirect speech

estilográfica NF (pluma) **e.** fountain pen

estima NF esteem, respect

estimación NF (**a**) (estima) esteem, respect (**b**)
(valoración) evaluation; (cálculo aproximado)
estimate

estimado, -a ADJ esteemed, respected; **E.
Señor** (en carta) Dear Sir

estimar VT (**a**) (apreciar) to esteem (**b**)
(considerar) to consider, to think; **lo estimo
conveniente** I think it appropriate (**c**)
(valorar) to value

estimativo, -a ADJ approximate, estimated

estimulante 1 ADJ stimulating
2 NM stimulant

estimular VT to stimulate; Fig to encourage

estímulo NM Biol & Fís stimulus; Fig encouragement

estío NM summer

estipendio NM stipend, fee

estipular VT to stipulate

estirado, -a ADJ Fig stiff

estirar 1 VT to stretch; Fig (dinero) to spin out;
Fig **e. la pata** to kick the bucket
2 estirarse VPR to stretch

estirón NM **dar** o **pegar un e.** to shoot up o grow
quickly

estirpe NF stock, pedigree

estival ADJ summer; **época e.** summertime

esto PRON NEUT this, this thing, this matter; *Fam* **e. de la fiesta** this business about the party

estocada NF *Taurom* stab

Estocolmo N Stockholm

estofado NM stew

estoicismo NM stoicism

estoico, -a 1 ADJ stoical
  2 NM,F stoic

estómago NM stomach; **dolor de e.** stomach ache

Estonia N Estonia

estonio, -a 1 ADJ & NM,F Estonian
  2 NM *(idioma)* Estonian

estoque NM *Taurom* sword

estorbar 1 VT **(a)** *(dificultar)* to hinder, to get in the way of **(b)** *(molestar)* to disturb
  2 VI to be in the way

estorbo NM **(a)** *(obstáculo)* obstruction, obstacle **(b)** *(molestia)* nuisance

estornino NM starling

estornudar VI to sneeze

estornudo NM sneeze

estos, -as ADJ DEM PL *ver* **este**

éstos, -as PRON DEM M,FPL *ver* **éste**

estoy INDIC PRES *de* **estar**

estrabismo NM squint

estrado NM platform; *Mús* bandstand; *Der* stand

estrafalario, -a ADJ *Fam* outlandish

estragos NMPL **hacer e. en** to wreak havoc with *o* on

estrambótico, -a ADJ *Fam* outlandish, eccentric

estrangulador, -a NM,F strangler

estrangular VT to strangle; *Med* to strangulate

estraperlo NM black market

Estrasburgo N Strasbourg

estratagema NF *Mil* stratagem; *Fam* trick, ruse

estratega NMF strategist

estrategia NF strategy

estratégico, -a ADJ strategic

estratificar [44] VT to stratify

estrato NM stratum

estraza NF **papel de e.** brown paper

estrechamente ADV *(íntimamente)* closely, intimately; **e. relacionados** closely related

estrechamiento NM **(a)** *(de calle, tubo)* narrowing **(b)** *(de relaciones entre países)* rapprochement

estrechar 1 VT **(a)** *(hacer estrecho)* to narrow; *(ropa)* to take in **(b)** *(mano)* to shake; *(lazos de amistad)* to tighten; **me estrechó entre sus brazos** he hugged me
  2 estrecharse VPR to narrow, to become narrower

> Observa que el verbo inglés **to stretch** es un falso amigo y no es la traducción del verbo español **estrechar**. En inglés, **to stretch** significa "estirar, desplegar".

estrechez NF **(a)** *(falta de anchura)* narrowness; **e. de miras** narrow-mindedness **(b)** *(dificultad económica)* **pasar estrecheces** to be hard up

estrecho, -a 1 ADJ **(a)** narrow; *(ropa, zapato)* tight; *(amistad, relación)* close, intimate **(b)** *Fig* **e. de miras** narrow-minded
  2 NM *Geog* strait, straits

estrella NF star; **e. de cine** movie *o* *Br* film star; *Zool* **e. de mar** starfish; **e. fugaz** shooting star

estrellado, -a ADJ **(a)** *(en forma de estrella)* star-shaped **(b)** *(cielo)* starry **(c)** *(huevos)* scrambled

estrellar 1 VT *Fam* to smash
  2 estrellarse VPR *(morir)* to die in a car crash; *Aut & Av* **estrellarse contra** *(chocar)* to crash into

estrellato NM stardom

estremecedor, -a ADJ bloodcurdling

estremecer [33] **1** VT to shake
  2 estremecerse VPR *(de horror, miedo)* to tremble, to shudder **(de** with); *(de frío)* to shiver **(de** with)

estrenar VT **(a)** *(objeto)* to use for the first time; *(ropa)* to wear for the first time **(b)** *Teatro & Cin* to premiere

estreno NM *Teatro* first performance; *Cin* premiere

estreñido, -a ADJ constipated

estreñimiento NM constipation

estrépito NM din, racket

estrepitoso, -a ADJ deafening; *Fig* *(fracaso)* spectacular

estrés NM INV stress

estresante ADJ stressful

estría NF **(a)** *(en la piel)* stretch mark **(b)** *Arquit* flute, fluting

estribar VI **e. en** to lie in, to be based on

estribillo NM *(en canción)* chorus; *(en poema)* refrain

estribo NM **(a)** *(de montura)* stirrup; *Fig* **perder los estribos** to lose one's temper, to lose one's head **(b)** *Arquit* buttress; *(de puente)* pier, support

estribor NM starboard

estricto, -a ADJ strict

estridente ADJ strident

estrofa NF verse

estropajo NM scourer

estropeado, -a ADJ **(a)** *(averiado)* broken **(b)** *(dañado)* damaged **(c)** *(echado a perder)* ruined, spoiled

estropear 1 VT *(averiar)* to break; *(dañar)* to damage; *(echar a perder)* to ruin, to spoil
  2 estropearse VPR *(máquina)* to break down; *(comida)* to go off, to spoil

estropicio NM **hacer** *o* **causar un e.** to wreak havoc

estructura NF structure; *(armazón)* frame, framework

estructurar VT to structure

estruendo NM roar

estrujar 1 VT (limón etc) to squeeze; (ropa) to wring; (apretar) to crush
2 estrujarse VPR Fam **e. los sesos** o **el cerebro** to rack one's brains

estuario NM estuary

estuche NM case; (para lápices) pencil case

estuco NM stucco

estudiante NMF student

estudiantil ADJ student

estudiar [43] VT & VI to study

estudio NM (a) (actividad) study; (encuesta) survey; Com **e. de mercado** market research (b) **estudios** (educación) studies (c) (de fotógrafo, pintor) studio; **e. cinematográfico/ de grabación** film/recording studio (d) (oficina) study; (apartamento) studio Br flat o US apartment

estudioso, -a 1 ADJ studious
2 NM,F specialist

estufa NF (calentador) heater, Br fire; Méx (cocina) stove

estupefaciente NM drug, narcotic

estupefacto, -a ADJ astounded, flabbergasted

estupendamente ADV wonderfully

estupendo, -a ADJ wonderful, marvellous; **¡e.!** great!

estupidez NF stupidity

estúpido, -a 1 ADJ stupid
2 NM,F idiot

estupor NM amazement, astonishment

estuve PT INDEF de **estar**

esvástica NF swastika

etapa NF stage; **por etapas** in stages

etarra NMF = member of ETA, terrorist Basque separatist organization

etc. (abr etcétera) etc

etcétera ADV etcetera

éter NM ether

etéreo, -a ADJ ethereal

eternidad NF eternity; Fam **una e.** ages

eterno, -a ADJ eternal

ética NF ethic; (ciencia) ethics sing

ético, -a ADJ ethical

etílico, -a ADJ ethylic; **alcohol e.** ethyl alcohol; **en estado e.** intoxicated; **intoxicación etílica** alcohol poisoning

etimología NF etymology

etimológico, -a ADJ etymological

etiope, etíope ADJ & NMF Ethiopian

Etiopía NF Ethiopia

etiqueta NF (a) (de producto) label (b) (ceremonia) etiquette; **de e.** formal

etiquetar VT to label

etnia NF ethnic group

étnico, -a ADJ ethnic

ETT NF (abr **Empresa de Trabajo Temporal**) temping agency

eucalipto NM eucalyptus

eucaristía NF eucharist

eufemismo NM euphemism

euforia NF euphoria

eufórico, -a ADJ euphoric

eureka INTERJ eureka!

euro NM (moneda) euro

Eurocámara NF European Parliament

eurodiputado, -a NM,F Euro MP

Europa N Europe

europeísmo NM Europeanism

europeizar [40] VT to europeanize

europeo, -a ADJ & NM,F European

Euskadi N the Basque Country

euskera ADJ & NM Basque

eutanasia NF euthanasia

evacuación NF evacuation

evacuar [47] VT to evacuate

evadir 1 VT (respuesta, peligro, impuestos) to avoid; (responsabilidad) to shirk
2 evadirse VPR to escape

evaluación NF evaluation; Educ assessment; **e. continua** continuous assessment

evaluar [30] VT to evaluate, to assess

evangélico, -a ADJ evangelical

evangelio NM gospel

evangelista NM evangelist

evangelización NF evangelization, evangelizing

evaporación NF evaporation

evaporar 1 VT to evaporate
2 evaporarse VPR to evaporate; Fig to vanish

evasión NF (fuga) escape; Fig evasion; **e. fiscal** o **de impuestos** tax evasion

evasiva NF evasive answer

evasivo, -a ADJ evasive

evento NM (a) (acontecimiento) event (b) (incidente) contingency, unforeseen event

eventual ADJ (a) (posible) possible; (gastos) incidental (b) (trabajo, obrero) casual, temporary

eventualidad NF contingency

eventualmente ADV by chance; **los problemas que e. surjan** such problems as may arise

Observa que las palabras inglesas **eventual** y **eventually** son falsos amigos y no son la traducción de las palabras españolas **eventual** y **eventualmente**. En inglés, **eventual** significa "final" o "consiguiente" y **eventually** "finalmente".

evidencia NF obviousness; **poner a algn en e.** to show sb up

evidenciar [43] VT to show, to demonstrate

evidente ADJ obvious

evidentemente ADV obviously

evitar VT to avoid; *(prevenir)* to prevent; *(desastre)* to avert

evocador, -a ADJ evocative

evocar [44] VT *(traer a la memoria)* to evoke; *(acordarse de)* to recall

evolución NF evolution; *(desarrollo)* development

evolucionar VI to develop; *Biol* to evolve; **el enfermo evoluciona favorablemente** the patient is improving

ex 1 PREF former, ex-; **ex alumno** former pupil, ex-student; **ex combatiente** *Br* ex-serviceman, *f* ex-servicewoman, *US* (war) veteran; **ex marido** ex-husband
 2 NMF *Fam* **mi ex** my ex

exabrupto NM sharp comment

exacerbar 1 VT **(a)** *(agravar)* to exacerbate, to aggravate **(b)** *(irritar)* to exasperate, to irritate
 2 exacerbarse VPR **(a)** *(agravarse)* to get worse **(b)** *(irritarse)* to feel exasperated

exactamente ADV exactly, precisely

exactitud NF accuracy; **con e.** precisely

exacto, -a ADJ exact; **¡e.!** precisely!; **para ser e.** to be precise

exageración NF exaggeration

exagerado, -a ADJ exaggerated; *(excesivo)* excessive

exagerar 1 VT to exaggerate
 2 VI to overdo it

exaltado, -a 1 ADJ excitable, hot-headed
 2 NM,F fanatic

exaltar 1 VT *(ensalzar)* to praise, to extol
 2 exaltarse VPR *(acalorarse)* to get overexcited, to get carried away

examen NM examination, exam; *Esp* **e. de conducir** driving test; *Am* **e. de manejar** driving test; *Med* **e. médico** checkup

examinador, -a NM,F examiner

examinar 1 VT to examine
 2 examinarse VPR *Esp* to take *o* sit an examination

exasperante ADJ exasperating

exasperar 1 VT to exasperate
 2 exasperarse VPR to become exasperated

Exc., Exca., Exc.ª *(abr* **Excelencia**) Excellency

excavación NF excavation; *(en arqueología)* dig

excavadora NF digger

excavar VT to excavate, to dig

excedencia NF *Esp* leave (of absence)

excedente ADJ & NM excess, surplus

exceder 1 VT to exceed, to surpass
 2 excederse VPR to go too far

excelencia NF **(a)** *(cualidad)* excellence; **por e.** par excellence **(b)** *(título)* **Su E.** His/Her Excellency

excelente ADJ excellent

excelso, -a ADJ sublime, lofty

excentricidad NF eccentricity

excéntrico, -a ADJ eccentric

excepción NF exception; **a e. de** with the exception of, except for; **de e.** exceptional; *Pol* **estado de e.** state of emergency

excepcional ADJ exceptional

excepto ADV except (for), apart from

exceptuar [30] VT to except, to exclude

excesivo, -a ADJ excessive

exceso NM excess; **en e.** in excess, excessively; **e. de equipaje** excess baggage; **e. de velocidad** speeding

excitable ADJ excitable

excitación NF *(sentimiento)* excitement

excitante 1 ADJ exciting; *Med* stimulating
 2 NM stimulant

excitar 1 VT to excite
 2 excitarse VPR to get excited

exclamación NF exclamation

exclamar VT & VI to exclaim, to cry out

excluir [37] VT *(dejar fuera)* to exclude **(de** from); *(opción)* to rule out; *(hacer imposible)* to preclude

exclusión NF exclusion

exclusiva NF *Prensa* exclusive; *Com* sole right

exclusive ADV *(en fechas)* exclusive

exclusivo, -a ADJ exclusive

Excma. *(abr* **Excelentísima**) Most Excellent

Excmo. *(abr* **Excelentísimo**) Most Excellent

excomulgar [42] VT to excommunicate

excomunión NF excommunication

excremento NM excrement

exculpar VT to exonerate

excursión NF excursion

excursionista NMF tripper; *(a pie)* hiker

excusa NF *(pretexto)* excuse; *(disculpa)* apology

excusado NM *(retrete)* toilet

excusar 1 VT **(a)** *(justificar)* to excuse **(b)** *(eximir)* to exempt **(de** from)
 2 excusarse VPR *(disculparse)* to apologize

execrar VT to execrate, to abhor

exención NF exemption; **e. de impuestos** tax exemption

exento, -a ADJ exempt, free **(de** from)

exequias NFPL funeral rites

exhalar VT to exhale, to breathe out; *(gas)* to give off, to emit; *(suspiro)* to heave

exhaustivo, -a ADJ exhaustive

exhausto, -a ADJ exhausted

exhibición NF exhibition

exhibicionista NMF exhibitionist

exhibir 1 VT **(a)** *(mostrar)* to exhibit, to display **(b)** *(lucir)* to show off
 2 exhibirse VPR to show off, to make an exhibition of oneself

exhortar VT to exhort

exhumar VT to exhume

exigencia NF **(a)** *(petición)* demand **(b)** *(requisito)* requirement

exigente ADJ demanding, exacting

exigir [57] VT to demand

exiguo, -a ADJ minute

exilado, -a 1 ADJ exiled, in exile
2 NM,F exile

exilar 1 VT to exile
2 **exilarse** VPR to go into exile

exiliado, -a ADJ & NM,F = **exilado**

exiliar [43] VT = **exilar**

exilio NM exile =

eximio, -a ADJ distinguished, eminent

eximir VT to exempt (**de** from)

existencia NF (**a**) (*vida*) existence (**b**) *Com* **existencias** stock, stocks

existente ADJ existing; *Com* in stock

existir VI to exist, to be (in existence)

éxito NM success; **con é.** successfully; **tener é.** to be successful

> Observa que la palabra inglesa **exit** es un falso amigo y no es la traducción de la palabra española **éxito**. En inglés, **exit** significa "salida".

exitoso, -a ADJ successful

éxodo NM exodus

exonerar VT to exonerate

exorbitante ADJ exorbitant, excessive

exorcista NMF exorcist

exorcizar [40] VT to exorcize

exótico, -a ADJ exotic

expandir 1 VT to expand
2 **expandirse** VPR to expand

expansión NF (**a**) (*de gas, empresa*) expansion (**b**) (*relajación*) relaxation; (*diversión*) recreation

expansionarse VPR (*divertirse*) to relax, to unwind; (*divertirse*) to have some fun *o* recreation

expatriado, -a ADJ & NM,F expatriate

expatriar [29] 1 VT to exile, to banish
2 **expatriarse** VPR to leave one's country

expectación NF expectancy, anticipation

expectativa NF **estar a la e. de** to be on the lookout for

expectorante NM expectorant

expedición NF expedition

expedientar VT to place under enquiry

expediente NM (**a**) (*informe*) dossier, record; (*ficha*) file; *Educ* **e. académico** academic record, *US* transcript; **abrirle e. a algn** to place sb under enquiry (**b**) *Der* proceedings, action

expedir [6] VT (**a**) (*carta*) to send, to dispatch (**b**) (*pasaporte etc*) to issue

expedito, -a ADJ free, clear

expendedor, -a 1 NM,F seller
2 NM **e. automático** vending machine

expendeduría NF *Br* tobacconist's, *US* cigar store

expensas NFPL **a e. de** at the expense of

experiencia NF (**a**) (*vivencia*) experience; **por e.** from experience (**b**) (*experimento*) experiment

experimentado, -a ADJ experienced

experimental ADJ experimental

experimentar 1 VI to experiment
2 VT to undergo; (*aumento*) to show; (*pérdida*) to suffer; (*sensación*) to experience, to feel; *Med* **e. una mejoría** to improve, to make progress

experimento NM experiment

experto, -a NM,F expert

expiar [29] VT to expiate, to atone for

expirar VI to expire

explanada NF esplanade

explayarse VPR to talk at length (about)

explicación NF explanation

explicar [44] 1 VT to explain
2 **explicarse** VPR (*persona*) to explain (oneself); **no me lo explico** I can't understand it

explicativo, -a ADJ explanatory

explícito, -a ADJ explicit

exploración NF exploration; *Med* (*interna*) exploration; (*externa*) examination; *Téc* scanning; *Mil* reconnaissance

explorador, -a NM,F explorer

explorar VT to explore; *Med* (*internamente*) to explore; (*externamente*) to examine; *Téc* to scan; *Mil* to reconnoitre

explosión NF explosion, blast; **hacer e.** to explode; **motor de e.** internal combustion engine; **e. demográfica** population explosion

explosionar VT & VI to explode, to blow up

explosivo, -a ADJ & NM explosive

explotación NF (**a**) (*abuso*) exploitation (**b**) (*uso*) exploitation, working; *Agr* cultivation (of land); (*granja*) farm

explotador, -a NM,F exploiter

explotar 1 VI (*bomba*) to explode, to go off
2 VT (**a**) (*aprovechar*) to exploit; (*recursos*) to tap; (*tierra*) to cultivate (**b**) (*abusar de*) to exploit

expoliar [43] VT to plunder, to pillage

exponente NMF exponent

exponer [19] (*pp* **expuesto**) 1 VT (**a**) (*mostrar*) to exhibit, to display (**b**) (*explicar*) to expound, to put forward (**c**) (*arriesgar*) to expose
2 **exponerse** VPR to expose oneself (**a** to); **te expones a perder el trabajo** you run the risk of losing your job

exportación NF export

exportador, -a 1 ADJ exporting
2 NM,F exporter

exportar VT to export

exposición NF (**a**) *Arte* exhibition; **e. universal** international exposition *o* exhibition, *US* world's fair; **sala de exposiciones** gallery (**b**) (*de hechos, ideas*) exposé (**c**) *Fot* exposure

expositor, -a 1 ADJ exponent
2 NM,F *(en feria)* exhibitor; *(de teoría)* exponent

exprés ADJ express; **(olla) e.** pressure cooker; **(café) e.** espresso (coffee)

expresamente ADV specifically, expressly

expresar 1 VT to express; *(manifestar)* to state
2 expresarse VPR to express oneself

expresión NF expression; **la mínima e.** the bare minimum

expresivo, -a ADJ expressive

expreso, -a 1 ADJ express; **con el fin e. de** with the express purpose of
2 NM *Ferroc* express (train)
3 ADV on purpose, deliberately

exprimidor NM squeezer, juicer

exprimir VT *(limón)* to squeeze; *(zumo)* to squeeze out; *Fig (persona)* to exploit, to bleed dry

expropiar [43] VT to expropriate

expuesto, -a 1 ADJ **(a)** *(sin protección)* exposed; **estar e. a** to be exposed to **(b)** *(peligroso)* risky, dangerous **(c)** *(exhibido)* on display, on show
2 PP *de* **exponer**

expulsar VT **(a)** *(de local, organización)* to throw out; *(de clase)* to send out; *(de colegio, organización)* to expel; *Dep (jugador)* to send off **(b)** *(humo)* to emit, to give off; *(objeto, sustancia)* to expel

expulsión NF expulsion; *Dep* sending off

expurgar [42] VT to expurgate; *Fig* to purge

expuse PT INDEF *de* **exponer**

exquisitez NF **(a)** *(cualidad)* exquisiteness **(b)** *(cosa)* exquisite thing; *(comida)* delicacy

exquisito, -a ADJ exquisite; *(comida)* delicious; *(gusto)* refined

extasiado, -a ADJ ecstatic; **quedarse e.** to go into ecstasies *o* raptures

extasiarse [29] VPR to go into ecstasies *o* raptures

éxtasis NM INV ecstasy

extender [3] **1** VT **(a)** *(ampliar)* to extend **(b)** *(mantel, mapa)* to spread (out), to open (out); *(mano, brazo)* to stretch (out) **(c)** *(crema, mantequilla)* to spread **(d)** *(cheque)* to make out; *(documento)* to draw up; *(certificado)* to issue
2 extenderse VPR **(a)** *(en el tiempo)* to extend, to last **(b)** *(en el espacio)* to spread out, to stretch **(c)** *(rumor, noticia)* to spread, to extend **(d)** *(hablar demasiado)* to go on

extendido, -a ADJ **(a)** *(mapa, plano)* spread out, open; *(mano, brazo)* outstretched **(b)** *(costumbre, rumor)* widespread

extensible ADJ extensible, extendible

extensión NF *(de libro etc)* length; *(de cuerpo)* size; *(de terreno)* area, expanse; *(edificio anexo)* extension; **en toda la e. de la palabra** in every sense of the word; **por e.** by extension

extensivo, -a ADJ **hacer e.** to extend; **ser e. a** to cover

extenso, -a ADJ *(terreno)* extensive; *(libro, película)* long

extenuar [30] **1** VT to exhaust
2 extenuarse VPR to exhaust oneself

exterior 1 ADJ **(a)** *(de fuera)* outer; *(puerta)* outside **(b)** *(política, deuda)* foreign; *Pol* **Ministerio de Asuntos Exteriores** Ministry of Foreign Affairs, *Br* ≃ Foreign Office, *US* ≃ State Department
2 NM **(a)** *(parte de fuera)* exterior, outside **(b)** *(extranjero)* abroad **(c) exteriores** *Cin* location

exteriorizar [40] VT to show

exteriormente ADV outwardly

exterminar VT to exterminate

exterminio NM extermination

externalización NF *Com* outsourcing

externalizar [40] VT *Com* to outsource

externo, -a 1 ADJ external; **de uso e.** *(medicamento)* for external use only
2 NM,F *Educ* day pupil

extinción NF extinction

extinguir [59] **1** VT *(fuego)* to extinguish, to put out; *(raza)* to wipe out
2 extinguirse VPR *(fuego)* to go out; *(especie)* to become extinct, to die out

extinto, -a ADJ extinct

extintor NM *Esp* fire extinguisher

extirpar VT **(a)** *Med* to remove **(b)** *Fig* to eradicate, to stamp out

extorsión NF extortion

extorsionar VT to extort

extra 1 ADJ **(a)** *(suplementario)* extra; **horas e.** overtime; **paga e.** bonus **(b)** *(superior)* top-quality
2 NM extra
3 NMF *Cin & Teatro* extra

extra- PREF extra-; **extramatrimonial** extra-marital

extracción NF extraction

extracto NM **(a)** *(resumen)* summary; *Fin* **e. de cuenta** statement of account **(b)** *(concentrado)* extract

extractor NM extractor

extradición NF extradition

extraer [25] VT to extract, to take out

extraescolar ADJ extracurricular

extrafino, -a ADJ superfine

extralimitarse VPR to overstep the mark

extranjería NF **ley de e.** law on aliens

extranjero, -a 1 ADJ foreign
2 NM,F foreigner
3 NM abroad; **en el e.** abroad

extrañar 1 VT **(a)** *(sorprender)* to surprise; **no es de e.** it's hardly surprising **(b)** *(echar de menos)* to miss

2 extrañarse VPR **extrañarse de** to be surprised at

extrañeza NF (**a**) *(sorpresa)* surprise, astonishment (**b**) *(singularidad)* strangeness

extraño, -a 1 ADJ strange; *Med* **cuerpo e.** foreign body
2 NM,F stranger

extraoficial ADJ unofficial

extraordinaria NF *(paga)* bonus

extraordinario, -a ADJ extraordinary; *Prensa* **edición extraordinaria** special edition

extrarradio NM outskirts, suburbs

extraterrestre NMF alien

extravagancia NF eccentricity

extravagante ADJ eccentric, outlandish

extravertido, -a ADJ & NM,F = extrovertido

extraviado, -a ADJ lost, missing

extraviar [29] **1** VT to mislay, to lose
2 extraviarse VPR to be missing, to get mislaid

extremadamente ADV extremely

extremado, -a ADJ extreme

Extremadura N Extremadura

extremar 1 VT **e. la prudencia** to be extremely careful
2 extremarse VPR to take great pains, to do one's utmost

extremaunción NF extreme unction

extremeño, -a 1 ADJ of/from Extremadura
2 NM,F person from Extremadura

extremidad NF (**a**) *(extremo)* end, tip (**b**) *Anat (miembro)* limb, extremity

extremista ADJ & NMF extremist

extremo, -a 1 NM *(de calle, cable)* end; *(máximo)* extreme; **en e.** very much; **en último e.** as a last resort
2 NM,F *(en fútbol)* winger; **e. derecha/izquierda** outside right/left
3 ADJ extreme; **E. Oriente** Far East

extrovertido, -a ADJ & NM,F extrovert

exuberante ADJ exuberant; *(vegetación)* lush, abundant

eyaculación NF ejaculation; **e. precoz** premature ejaculation

eyacular VI to ejaculate

eyectable ADJ **asiento e.** ejector seat

F

F, f ['efe] NF *(letra)* F, f

fa NM *Mús* F

fabada NF stew of beans, pork sausage and bacon

fábrica NF factory; **marca de f.** trademark; **precio de f.** factory *o* ex-works price

> Observa que la palabra inglesa **fabric** es un falso amigo y no es la traducción de la palabra española **fábrica**. En inglés **fabric** significa "tejido".

fabricación NF manufacture; **de f. casera** home-made; **de f. propia** our own make; **f. en cadena** mass production

fabricante NMF manufacturer

fabricar [44] VT (a) *Ind* to manufacture (b) *Fig (mentiras etc)* to fabricate

fabril ADJ manufacturing

fábula NF fable

fabuloso, -a ADJ fabulous

facción NF (a) *Pol* faction (b) **facciones** *(rasgos)* features

faceta NF facet

facha 1 NF (a) *(aspecto)* look (b) *(mamarracho)* mess; **vas hecho una f.** you look a mess
2 NMF *Esp Fam Pey (fascista)* fascist

fachada NF façade

facial ADJ facial

fácil ADJ (a) *(sencillo)* easy; **f. de comprender** easy to understand (b) *(probable)* likely, probable; **es f. que …** it's (quite) likely that …

facilidad NF (a) *(sencillez)* easiness (b) *(soltura)* ease (c) *(servicio)* facility; **dar facilidades** to make things easy; *Com* **facilidades de pago** easy terms (d) **f. para los idiomas** gift for languages

facilitar VT *(proporcionar)* to provide, to supply (a with)

fácilmente ADV easily

facsímil, facsímile NM facsimile

factible ADJ feasible

fáctico, -a ADJ **los poderes fácticos** the powers that be, the forces of the establishment

factor NM factor

factoría NF factory

factura NF (a) *Com* invoice (b) *Arg (repostería)* cakes and pastries

facturación NF (a) *Com* invoicing (b) *(de equipajes) (en aeropuerto)* check-in; *(en estación)* registration

facturar VT (a) *Com* to invoice (b) *(en aeropuerto)* to check in; *(en estación)* to register

facultad NF faculty; **facultades mentales** faculties

facultativo, -a 1 ADJ optional
2 NM,F doctor

faena NF (a) *(tarea)* task (b) *Fam (mala pasada)* dirty trick (c) *Taurom* performance

faenar VI to fish

fagot NM *Mús* bassoon

fainá NF *Urug (plato)* = baked dough made from chickpea flour, served with pizza

faisán NM pheasant

faja NF (a) *(corsé)* girdle, corset (b) *(banda)* sash (c) *(de terreno)* strip

fajo NM *(de ropa etc)* bundle; *(de billetes)* wad

falacia NF fallacy

falange NF (a) *Anat & Mil* phalanx (b) *Pol* **la F. (Española)** the Falange

falaz ADJ (a) *(erróneo)* fallacious (b) *(engañoso)* deceitful

falda NF (a) *(prenda)* skirt; **f. pantalón** culottes (b) *(de montaña)* slope, hillside (c) *(de mesa)* cover (d) *(regazo)* lap

faldero, -a ADJ **perro f.** lapdog

falencia NF (a) *Am Com (bancarrota)* bankruptcy (b) *CSur (error)* fault

falla NF (a) *(defecto)* defect, fault; **este cajón tiene una f.** there's something wrong with this drawer (b) *Am (error)* mistake; **un trabajo lleno de fallas** a piece of work full of mistakes (c) *Geol* fault

fallar¹ 1 VI *Der* to rule
2 VT *(premio)* to award

fallar² 1 VI to fail; **le falló la puntería** he missed his aim; *Fig* **no me falles** don't let me down
2 VT to miss

fallecer [33] VI *Fml* to pass away, to die

fallecido, -a ADJ deceased

fallecimiento NM demise

fallido, -a ADJ unsuccessful, vain

fallo¹ NM *Esp* (a) *(error)* mistake; **f. humano** human error (b) *(del corazón, de los frenos)* failure

fallo² NM (a) *Der* judgement, sentence (b) *(en concurso)* awarding

falluto, -a *RP Fam* **1** ADJ phoney, hypocritical
2 NM,F hypocrite

falo NM phallus

falsear VT *(hechos, la verdad)* to distort; *(informe etc)* to falsify

falsedad NF (**a**) *(falta de verdad, autenticidad)* falseness (**b**) *(mentira)* falsehood

falsete NM falsetto; **voz de f.** falsetto voice

falsificar [44] VT to falsify; *(cuadro, firma, moneda)* to forge

falso, -a ADJ (**a**) false; **dar un paso en f.** *(tropezar)* to trip, to stumble; *Fig* to make a blunder; **jurar en f.** to commit perjury (**b**) *(persona)* insincere

falta NF (**a**) *(carencia)* lack; **por f. de** for want o lack of; **sin f.** without fail; **f. de educación** bad manners (**b**) *(escasez)* shortage (**c**) *(ausencia)* absence; **echar algo/a algn en f.** to miss sth/sb (**d**) *(error)* mistake; *(defecto)* fault, defect; **f. de ortografía** spelling mistake; **sacar faltas a algo/a algn** to find fault with sth/sb (**e**) *Der* misdemeanour (**f**) *(en fútbol)* foul; *(en tenis)* fault (**g**) **hacer f.** to be necessary; **(nos) hace f. una escalera** we need a ladder; **harán f. dos personas para mover el piano** it'll take two people to move the piano; **no hace f. que ...** there is no need for ...

faltante NM *Am* deficit

faltar VI (**a**) *(no estar)* to be missing; **¿quién falta?** who is missing?

(**b**) *(escasear)* to be lacking o needed; **le falta confianza en sí mismo** he lacks confidence in himself; **¡lo que me faltaba!** that's all I needed!; **¡no faltaría o faltaba más!** *(por supuesto)* (but) of course!

(**c**) *(quedar)* to be left; **¿cuántos kilómetros faltan para Managua?** how many kilometres is it to Managua?; **ya falta poco para las vacaciones** it won't be long now till the holidays; **faltó poco para que me cayera** I very nearly fell

(**d**) **f. a la verdad** not to tell the truth; **f. al deber** to fail in one's duty; **f. a su palabra/promesa** to break one's word/promise; **f. al respeto a algn** to treat sb with disrespect

falto, -a ADJ **f. de** lacking in

fama NF (**a**) *(renombre)* fame; **tener f.** to be famous o well-known (**b**) *(reputación)* reputation; **buena/mala f.** good/bad reputation

famélico, -a ADJ starving, famished

familia NF family; **estar en f.** to be among friends; **f. numerosa** large family

familiar **1** ADJ (**a**) *(de la familia)* family; **empresa f.** family business (**b**) *(conocido)* familiar

2 NMF relation, relative

familiaridad NF familiarity

familiarizarse [40] VPR **f. con** to familiarize oneself with

famoso, -a **1** ADJ famous

2 NM,F famous person, celebrity

fan NMF fan

fanático, -a **1** ADJ fanatical

2 NM,F fanatic

fanatismo NM fanaticism

fandango NM *(baile)* fandango

fanfarrón, -ona *Fam* **1** ADJ boastful

2 NM,F show-off

fanfarronear VI *Fam* to brag, to boast (**de** about)

fango NM (**a**) *(barro)* mud (**b**) *Fig* degradation

fantasear VI to fantasize

fantasía NF fantasy; **joya de f.** imitation jewellery

fantasioso, -a ADJ imaginative

fantasma NM (**a**) *(espectro)* ghost (**b**) *Esp Fam (fanfarrón)* braggart, show-off

fantasmal ADJ ghostly

fantástico, -a ADJ fantastic

fantoche NM *Pey* nincompoop, ninny

faraón NM Pharaoh

fardar VI *Esp Fam* **f. de algo** to show (sth) off

fardo NM bundle

farfullar VT to jabber

faringe NF pharynx

faringitis NF INV pharyngitis

fariseo, -a NM,F *Hist* Pharisee; *(falso)* hypocrite

farmacéutico, -a **1** ADJ pharmaceutical

2 NM,F pharmacist, *Br* chemist, *US* druggist

farmacia NF (**a**) *(tienda)* pharmacy, *Br* chemist's (shop), *US* drugstore (**b**) *(ciencia)* pharmacology

fármaco NM medicine, medication

faro NM (**a**) *(torre)* lighthouse (**b**) *(de coche)* headlight, headlamp

farol NM (**a**) *(en la calle)* streetlight, streetlamp; *(lámpara)* lantern (**b**) *Fam (fanfarronada)* bragging; **tirarse un f.** to brag (**c**) *(en naipes)* bluff

farola NF streetlight, streetlamp

farolillo NM *Fig* **ser el f. rojo** to bring up the rear

farragoso, -a ADJ confused, rambling

farruco, -a ADJ cocky

farsa NF farce

farsante NM,F fake, impostor

fascículo NM instalment

fascinante ADJ fascinating

fascinar VT to fascinate

fascismo NM fascism

fascista ADJ & NMF fascist

fase NF (**a**) *(etapa)* phase, stage (**b**) *Elec & Fís* phase

fastidiado, -a ADJ *Esp Fam* (**a**) *(roto)* broken (**b**) *(enfermo)* sick; **tiene el estómago f.** he's got a bad stomach

fastidiar [43] **1** ·VT (**a**) *(molestar)* to annoy, to bother; *(dañar)* to hurt; *Fam* **¡no fastidies!** you're kidding! (**b**) *Esp Fam (estropear)* to damage, to ruin; *(planes)* to spoil

2 **fastidiarse** VPR *Esp* (**a**) *(aguantarse)* to put up with it, to resign oneself; **que se fastidie** that's his tough luck (**b**) *Fam (estropearse)* to get damaged, to break down (**c**) **me he fastidiado el tobillo** I've hurt my ankle

fastidio NM nuisance

fastuoso, -a ADJ *(acto)* splendid, lavish

fatal 1 ADJ (**a**) *Esp Fam (muy malo)* terrible, awful (**b**) *(mortal)* deadly, fatal (**c**) *(inexorable)* fateful, inevitable
   2 ADV *Esp Fam* awfully, terribly; **lo pasó f.** he had a rotten time

fatalidad NF (**a**) *(destino)* fate (**b**) *(desgracia)* misfortune

> Observa que la palabra inglesa **fatality** es un falso amigo y no es la traducción de la palabra española **fatalidad**. En inglés, **fatality** significa "víctima mortal".

fatalista 1 ADJ fatalistic
   2 NMF fatalist

fatiga NF (**a**) *(cansancio)* fatigue (**b**) **fatigas** *(dificultades)* troubles, difficulties

fatigar [42] **1** VT to tire, to weary
   2 fatigarse VPR to tire, to become tired

fatigoso, -a ADJ tiring, exhausting

fatuo, -a ADJ (**a**) *(envanecido)* conceited (**b**) *(necio)* fatuous, foolish

fauces NFPL jaws

fauna NF fauna

favor NM favour; **por f.** please; **¿puedes hacerme un f.?** can you do me a favour?; **estar a f. de** to be in favour of; **haga el f. de sentarse** please sit down

favorable ADJ favourable; **f. a** in favour of

favorecedor, -a ADJ flattering

favorecer [33] VT (**a**) *(beneficiar)* to favour (**b**) *(sentar bien)* to flatter

favoritismo NM favouritism

favorito, -a ADJ & NM,F favourite

fax NM (**a**) *(aparato)* fax (machine); **mandar algo por f.** to fax sth (**b**) *(documento)* fax

fayuca NF *Méx Fam* contraband

faz NF *Fml* face

fe NF (**a**) *(creencia)* faith; **de buena/mala fe** with good/dishonest intentions (**b**) *(certificado)* certificate; **fe de bautismo/matrimonio** baptism/marriage certificate (**c**) *Impr* **fe de erratas** errata

fealdad NF ugliness

febrero NM February

febril ADJ (**a**) *Med* feverish (**b**) *(actividad)* hectic

fecha NF date; **f. límite** o **tope** deadline; **f. de caducidad** sell-by date; **hasta la f.** so far; **en f. próxima** at an early date; **el año pasado por estas fechas** this time last year

fechar VT to date

fechoría NF bad deed, misdemeanour

fécula NF starch

fecundación NF fertilization; **f. in vitro** in vitro fertilization

fecundar VT to fertilize

fecundo, -a ADJ fertile

federación NF federation

federal ADJ & NMF federal

fehaciente ADJ irrefutable

felicidad NF happiness; **(muchas) felicidades** *(en cumpleaños)* many happy returns

felicitación NF **tarjeta de f.** greetings card

felicitar VT to congratulate (**por** on); **¡te felicito!** congratulations!

feligrés, -esa NM,F parishioner

felino, -a ADJ & NM feline

feliz ADJ (**a**) *(contento)* happy; **¡felices Navidades!** Happy o Merry Christmas! (**b**) *(decisión etc)* fortunate

felpa NF *Tex* plush

felpudo NM mat, doormat

femenino, -a ADJ (**a**) *(de mujer)* women's; *(sexo, órganos sexuales)* female; **un toque f.** a woman's touch (**b**) *(de la feminidad)* feminine

feminismo NM feminism

feminista ADJ & NMF feminist

fémur NM femur

fenecer [33] VI *Fml* to pass away, to die

fenomenal 1 ADJ (**a**) *(magnífico)* great, fantastic (**b**) *(enorme)* phenomenal
   2 ADV *Fam* wonderfully, marvellously; **lo pasámos f.** we had a fantastic time

fenómeno, -a 1 NM (**a**) *(suceso)* phenomenon (**b**) *(prodigio)* genius (**c**) *(monstruo)* freak
   2 ADJ *Fam* fantastic, terrific
   3 INTERJ fantastic!, terrific!

feo, -a 1 ADJ ugly; *(asunto etc)* nasty
   2 NM *Fam* **hacerle un f. a algn** to offend sb

féretro NM coffin

feria NF fair; **f. de muestras/del libro** trade/book fair

feriado, -a *Am* **1** ADJ **día f.** (public) holiday
   2 NM (public) holiday

ferial ADJ **recinto f.** *(de exposiciones)* exhibition centre; *(de fiestas)* fairground

fermentación NF fermentation

fermentar VI to ferment

fermento NM ferment

ferocidad NF ferocity, fierceness

feroz ADJ fierce, ferocious; **el lobo f.** the big bad wolf

férreo, -a ADJ iron

ferretería NF *Br* ironmonger's (shop), *US* hardware store

ferrocarril NM *Br* railway, *US* railroad

ferroviario, -a ADJ rail(way), *US* railroad

ferry (*pl* **ferrys** o **ferries**) NM ferry

fértil ADJ fertile

fertilidad NF fertility

fertilizante 1 ADJ fertilizing
   2 NM fertilizer

fertilizar [40] VT to fertilize

ferviente ADJ fervent

fervor NM fervour

fervoroso, -a ADJ fervent

festejar VT to celebrate

festejos NMPL festivities

festín NM feast, banquet

festival NM festival

festividad NF festivity

festivo, -a 1 ADJ (**a**) *(ambiente etc)* festive (**b**) **día f.** holiday
2 NM holiday

feta NF *RP* slice

fetal ADJ foetal

fetiche NM fetish

fétido, -a ADJ stinking, fetid

feto NM foetus

feudalismo NM feudalism

feudo NM fief; *Pol* stronghold

fiabilidad NF reliability, trustworthiness

fiable ADJ reliable, trustworthy

fiaca NF *CSur, Méx Fam (pereza)* laziness; **¡qué f. tener que ponerme a planchar!** what a pain *o Br* fag having to do the ironing!

fiador, -a NM,F guarantor; **salir** *o* **ser f. de algn** *(pagar fianza)* to stand bail for sb; *(avalar)* to vouch for sb

fiambre NM (**a**) *Culin Br* cold meat, *US* cold cut (**b**) *Fam (cadáver)* stiff, corpse

fiambrera NF lunch box

fianza NF *(depósito)* deposit; *Der* bail; **en libertad bajo f.** on bail

fiar [29] **1** VT (**a**) *(avalar)* to guarantee (**b**) *(vender sin cobrar)* to sell on credit
2 fiarse VPR **fiarse (de)** to trust

fiasco NM fiasco

fibra NF fibre; *(de madera)* grain; **f. óptica** optical fibre; **f. de vidrio** fibreglass

ficción NF fiction

ficha NF (**a**) *(tarjeta)* filing card; **f. técnica** specifications, technical data; *Cin* credits (**b**) *(en juegos)* counter; *(de ajedrez)* piece, man; *(de dominó)* domino

fichado, -a ADJ **está f. por la policía** he has a police record

fichaje NM *Dep* signing

fichar 1 VT (**a**) *(archivar)* to put on file (**b**) *Dep* to sign up
2 VI (**a**) *(en el trabajo) (al entrar)* to clock in *o* on, *US* to punch in; *(al salir)* to clock out *o* off, *US* to punch out (**b**) *Dep* to sign

fichero NM card index

ficticio, -a ADJ fictitious

fidedigno, -a ADJ reliable, trustworthy; **fuentes fidedignas** reliable sources

fidelidad NF faithfulness; **alta f.** high fidelity, hi-fi

fideo NM noodle

fiebre NF fever; **tener f.** to have a temperature

fiel 1 ADJ (**a**) *(leal)* faithful, loyal (**b**) *(exacto)* accurate, exact
2 NM (**a**) *(de balanza)* needle, pointer (**b**) *Rel* **los fieles** the congregation

fieltro NM felt

fiera NF wild animal; *Fam* **estaba hecho una f.** he was hopping mad

fiero, -a ADJ *(salvaje)* wild; *(feroz)* fierce, ferocious

fierro NM *Am (hierro)* iron

fiesta NF (**a**) *(entre amigos)* party (**b**) **día de f.** holiday (**c**) *Rel* feast; **f. de guardar** holiday of obligation (**d**) *(festividad)* celebration, festivity

figura NF figure

figurado, -a ADJ figurative; **en sentido f.** figuratively

figurar 1 VI *(en lista)* to figure
2 figurarse VPR to imagine, to suppose; **ya me lo figuraba** I thought as much; **¡figúrate!, ¡figúrese!** just imagine!

figurativo, -a ADJ *Arte* figurative

figurín NM fashion sketch; *Fig* **ir** *o* **estar hecho un f.** to be dressed up to the nines

figurinista NMF *Cin & Teatro* costume designer

fijador NM (**a**) *(gomina)* gel (**b**) *Fot* fixative

fijamente ADV **mirar f.** to stare

fijar 1 VT to fix; **prohibido f. carteles** *(en letrero)* post no bills
2 fijarse VPR (**a**) *(darse cuenta)* to notice (**b**) *(poner atención)* to pay attention, to watch

fijo, -a ADJ (**a**) *(no variable, inmóvil)* fixed; **sin domicilio f.** of no fixed abode (**b**) *(empleado, trabajo)* permanent

fila NF (**a**) *(hilera)* file; **en f. india** in single file; **poner en f.** to line up (**b**) *(de cine, teatro)* row (**c**) *Mil* **filas** ranks; **llamar a algn a filas** to call sb up; **¡rompan filas!** fall out!, dismiss!

filamento NM filament

filantropía NF philanthropy

filántropo, -a NM,F philanthropist

filarmónico, -a ADJ philharmonic

filatelia NF philately, stamp collecting

filete NM *(de carne, pescado)* fillet

filiación NF *Pol* affiliation

filial 1 ADJ (**a**) *(de hijos)* filial (**b**) *Com* subsidiary
2 NF *Com* subsidiary

filigrana NF (**a**) *(en orfebrería)* filigree (**b**) *Fig* **filigranas** intricacy, intricate work

Filipinas NPL **(las) F.** (the) Philippines

filipino, -a ADJ & NM,F Philippine, Filipino

film *(pl* **films)** NM film

filmar VT to film, to shoot

filme NM film

fílmico, -a ADJ film

filmoteca NF *(archivo)* film library; *(sala de cine)* film institute

filo NM (cutting) edge; **al f. de la medianoche** on the stroke of midnight; *Fig* **de doble f.** double-edged

filón NM (**a**) *Min* seam, vein (**b**) *Fig (buen negocio)* gold mine

filoso, -a ADJ *Am* sharp

filosofal ADJ **piedra f.** philosopher's stone

filosofar VI to philosophize

filosofía NF philosophy; *Fig* **con f.** philosophically

filosófico, -a ADJ philosophical

filósofo, -a NM,F philosopher

filtración NF *(de líquido)* filtration; *(de información)* leak

filtrar 1 VT (**a**) *(líquido)* to filter (**b**) *(información)* to leak
2 filtrarse VPR (**a**) *(líquido)* to seep (**b**) *(información)* to leak out

filtro NM filter

filudo, -a ADJ *Andes* sharp

fin NM (**a**) *(final)* end; **dar** *o* **poner f.** to put an end to; **llegar** *o* **tocar a su f.** to come to an end; **en f.** anyway; **¡por** *o* **al f.!** at last!; **f. de semana** weekend; **al f. y al cabo** when all's said and done; **noche de F. de Año** New Year's Eve (**b**) *(objetivo)* purpose, aim; **a f. de** in order to, so as to; **a f. de que** in order that, so that; **con el f. de** with the intention of

final 1 ADJ final
2 NM end; **al f.** in the end; **f. de línea** terminal; **f. feliz** happy ending; **a finales de octubre** at the end of October
3 NF *Dep* final

finalidad NF purpose, aim

finalista 1 NMF finalist
2 ADJ in the final

finalizar [40] VT & VI to end, to finish

finalmente ADV finally

financiación NF financing

financiar [43] VT to finance

financiero, -a 1 ADJ financial
2 NM,F financier

financista NMF *Am* financier

finanzas NFPL finances

finca NF *(inmueble)* property; *(de campo)* country house

fingido, -a ADJ feigned, false; **nombre f.** assumed name

fingir [57] **1** VT to feign
2 fingirse VPR to pretend to be

finlandés, -esa 1 ADJ Finnish
2 NM,F *(persona)* Finn
3 NM *(idioma)* Finnish

Finlandia N Finland

fino, -a 1 ADJ (**a**) *(hilo, capa)* fine (**b**) *(flaco)* thin (**c**) *(educado)* refined, polite (**d**) *(oído)* sharp, acute; *(olfato)* keen (**e**) *(humor, ironía)* subtle
2 NM *(vino)* = type of dry sherry

finura NF (**a**) *(refinamiento)* refinement, politeness (**b**) *(sutileza)* subtlety

fiordo NM *Geog* fiord

firma NF (**a**) *(rúbrica)* signature (**b**) *(empresa)* firm, company

firmamento NM firmament

firmante ADJ & NMF signatory; **el** *o* **la abajo f.** the undersigned

firmar VT to sign

firme 1 ADJ (**a**) *(fuerte, sólido)* firm; *Fig* **mantenerse f.** to hold one's ground; **tierra f.** terra firma (**b**) *Mil* **¡firmes!** attention!
2 NM *(de carretera)* road surface
3 ADV hard

firmemente ADV firmly

firmeza NF firmness

fiscal 1 ADJ fiscal
2 NMF *Der Br* ≃ public prosecutor, *US* ≃ district attorney

fiscalía NF *Der (cargo) Br* ≃ post of public prosecutor, *US* ≃ post of district attorney; *(oficina) Br* ≃ public prosecutor's office, *US* ≃ district attorney's office

fisco NM treasury, exchequer

fisgar [42] VI *Fam* to snoop, to pry

fisgón, -ona NM,F *Fam* snooper

fisgonear VI *Fam* to snoop, to pry

física NF physics *sing*

físico, -a 1 ADJ physical
2 NM,F *(profesión)* physicist
3 NM physique

fisión NF fission

fisioterapeuta NMF physiotherapist

fisioterapia NF physiotherapy

fisonomía NF physiognomy

fisonomista NMF *Fam* **ser buen/mal f.** to be good/no good at remembering faces

fisura NF fissure

flácido, -a ADJ flaccid, flabby

flaco, -a 1 ADJ (**a**) *(delgado)* skinny (**b**) *Fig* **punto f.** weak spot
2 NM,F *Am Fam (como apelativo)* **¿cómo estás, flaca?** hey, how are you doing?

flagelar VT to flagellate

flagelo NM *(látigo)* whip; *Fig* scourge

flagrante ADJ flagrant; **en f. delito** red-handed

flamante ADJ (**a**) *(nuevo)* brand-new (**b**) *(vistoso)* splendid

flamenco, -a 1 ADJ (**a**) *Mús* flamenco (**b**) *(de Flandes)* Flemish
2 NM (**a**) *Mús* flamenco (**b**) *(ave)* flamingo (**c**) *(idioma)* Flemish

flan NM crème caramel

Observa que la palabra inglesa **flan** es un falso amigo y no es la traducción de la palabra española **flan**. En inglés **flan** significa "tarta".

flanco NM flank, side

flanquear VT to flank

flaquear VI *(fuerzas, piernas)* to weaken, to give way

flaqueza NF weakness

flash [flaʃ, flas] NM *Fot* flash

flato NM *Esp* **tener f.** to have a stitch

flatulencia NF flatulence

flauta NF flute; **f. dulce** recorder

flautín NM *(instrumento)* piccolo

flautista NMF flute player, flautist, *US* flutist

flecha NF arrow

flechazo NM love at first sight

fleco NM fringe

flema NF phlegm

flemático, -a ADJ phlegmatic

flemón NM gumboil, abscess

flequillo NM *Br* fringe, *US* bangs

fletar VT to charter

flete NM (**a**) *(alquiler)* charter (**b**) *(carga)* freight

flexibilidad NF flexibility

flexible ADJ flexible

flexión NF (**a**) *Ling* inflection (**b**) **flexiones de brazo** push-ups, *Br* press-ups

flexionar VT to bend

flexo NM *Esp* adjustable table lamp *o* light, Anglepoise® lamp

flipante ADJ *Esp Fam* great, cool

flipar *Esp Fam* **1** VI *(asombrarse)* to be flabbergasted *o Br* gobsmacked
  2 VT **le flipan las motos** he's crazy about motorbikes

flirtear VI to flirt

flojear VI *(ventas etc)* to fall off, go down; *(piernas)* to weaken, grow weak; *(memoria)* to fail; *Andes Fam (holgazanear)* to laze about *o* around

flojedad NF weakness

flojera NF *Fam* weakness, faintness

flojo, -a ADJ (**a**) *(tornillo, cuerda etc)* loose, slack (**b**) *(perezoso)* lazy, idle; *(exámen, trabajo, resultado)* poor

flor NF (**a**) *(de planta)* flower; **en f.** in blossom; *Fig* **en la f. de la vida** in the prime of life; *Fig* **la f. y nata** the cream (of society) (**b**) **a f. de piel** skin-deep

flora NF flora

floreado, -a ADJ flowery

florecer [33] VI (**a**) *(plantas)* to flower (**b**) *(negocio)* to flourish, to thrive

floreciente ADJ flourishing, prosperous

florero NM vase

florido, -a ADJ (**a**) *(con flores)* flowery (**b**) *(estilo)* florid

floripondio NM *Pey (adorno)* heavy ornamentation

florista NMF florist

floristería NF florist's (shop)

flota NF fleet

flotador NM (**a**) *(de pesca)* float (**b**) *(para nadar)* rubber ring

flotar VI to float

flote NM floating; **a f.** afloat; **sacar a f. un negocio** to put a business on a sound footing

flotilla NF flotilla

fluctuación NF fluctuation

fluctuar [30] VI to fluctuate

fluidez NF fluency

fluido, -a 1 ADJ fluid; *(estilo etc)* fluent
  2 NM fluid; **f. eléctrico** current

fluir [37] VI to flow

flujo NM flow; *Fís* flux; *Med* discharge; **f. y reflujo** ebb and flow

flúor NM fluorine

fluorescente ADJ fluorescent

fluvial ADJ river

FM NF *(abr* **Frecuencia Modulada***)* FM

FMI NM *(abr* **Fondo Monetario Internacional***)* IMF

fobia NF phobia (**a** about)

foca NF seal

foco NM (**a**) *Elec* spotlight, floodlight (**b**) *(de ideas, revolución etc)* centre, focal point (**c**) *Am (de vehículo)* (car) headlight; *(farola)* streetlight (**d**) *Andes, Méx (bombilla)* light bulb

fofo, -a ADJ soft; *(persona)* flabby

fogata NF bonfire

fogón NM *(de cocina)* ring

fogonazo NM flash

fogosidad NF ardour, fire

fogoso, -a ADJ fiery, spirited

fogueo NM **cartucho de f.** blank cartridge

foie-gras [fwa'ɣras] NM INV (pâté de) foie-gras

folclore NM folklore

folclórico, -a 1 ADJ traditional, popular
  2 NM,F *Esp* = singer of traditional Spanish songs

fólder NM *Andes, CAm, Méx (carpeta)* folder

folio NM sheet of paper

folklore NM folklore

folklórico, -a ADJ = **folclórico**

follaje NM foliage

follar VI & VT *Esp muy Fam* to lay, *Br* to shag

folletín NM melodrama

folleto NM *(turístico, publicitario)* brochure; *(explicativo, de instrucciones)* leaflet

follón NM *Esp Fam* (**a**) *(discusión)* row (**b**) *(lío)* mess; **me hice un f. con las listas** I got into a real muddle *o* mess with the lists

follonero, -a NM,F *Esp Fam* troublemaker

fomentar VT to encourage, to promote

fomento NM encouragement, promotion; **Ministerio de F.** Ministry of Public Works

fonda NF inn

fondear VI to anchor

fondo¹ NM (**a**) *(parte más baja)* bottom; **a f.** thoroughly; **al f. de la calle** at the bottom of the street; **tocar f.** *Náut* to touch bottom; *Fig* to reach rock bottom; *Fig* **en el f. es bueno** deep down he's kind; **bajos fondos** dregs of society; **doble f.** false bottom (**b**) *(de habitación)* back; *(de pasillo)* end (**c**) *(segundo término)* background; **música de f.** background music (**d**) *Prensa* **artículo de f.** leading article (**e**) *Dep* **corredor de f.** long-distance runner; **esquí de f.** cross-country skiing (**f**) *RP (patio)* back patio (**g**) *Carib, Méx (prenda)* petticoat

fondo² NM *Fin* fund; **cheque sin fondos** bad cheque; *Fam* **f. común** kitty

fonendoscopio NM stethoscope

fonética NF phonetics *sing*

fonético, -a ADJ phonetic

fono NM *Am Fam* phone

fontanería NF plumbing

fontanero, -a NM,F plumber

footing NM jogging; **hacer f.** to go jogging

forajido, -a NM,F outlaw

foráneo, -a ADJ foreign

forastero, -a NM,F outsider, stranger

forcejear VI to wrestle, to struggle

forcejeo NM struggle

fórceps NM INV forceps

forense 1 ADJ forensic
  2 NMF **(médico) f.** forensic surgeon

forestal ADJ forest; **repoblación f.** reafforestation

forfait [for'fait, for'fe] *(pl* **forfaits**) NM (**a**) *(para esquiar)* ski pass (**b**) *Dep* default

forjado, -a ADJ *(hierro)* wrought

forjar VT *(metal)* to forge; *Fig* to create, to make

forma NF (**a**) *(figura)* form, shape; **en f. de L** L-shaped; **¿qué f. tiene?** what shape is it? (**b**) *(manera)* way; **de esta f.** in this way; **de f. que** so that; **de todas formas** anyway, in any case; **no hubo f. de convencerla** there was no way we could convince her; **f. de pago** method of payment (**c**) *Dep* form; **estar en f.** to be on form; **estar en baja f.** to be off form (**d**) *Rel* **Sagrada F.** Host (**e**) **formas** *(modales)* manners

formación NF (**a**) *(creación)* formation (**b**) *(educación)* upbringing; *(enseñanza)* training; **f. profesional** vocational training

formal ADJ (**a**) *(de la forma, legal)* formal (**b**) *(que se porta bien)* well-behaved, good (**c**) *(serio)* serious, serious-minded (**d**) *(fiable)* reliable, dependable

formalidad NF (**a**) *(requisito)* formality (**b**) *(seriedad)* seriousness (**c**) *(fiabilidad)* reliability (**d**) **formalidades** *(trámites)* formalities

formalizar [40] **1** VT to formalize
  2 formalizarse VPR to settle down

formar 1 VT (**a**) *(hacer)* to form; **f. parte de algo** to be a part of sth (**b**) *(educar)* to bring up; *(enseñar)* to educate, to train
  2 formarse VPR (**a**) *(hacerse, crearse)* to be formed, to form; **se formó un charco** a puddle

formed; **formarse una impresión de algo** to get an impression of sth (**b**) *(educarse)* to be educated *o* trained

formatear VT *Inform* to format

formato NM format

formica® NF Formica®

formidable ADJ (**a**) *(estupendo)* wonderful, terrific (**b**) *(espantoso)* formidable

fórmula NF formula; *Aut* **f. uno** formula one

formular VT *(queja, petición)* to make; *(deseo)* to express; *(pregunta)* to ask; *(teoría)* to formulate

formulario NM form

fornicar [44] VI to fornicate

fornido, -a ADJ strapping, hefty

foro NM (**a**) *(lugar de discusión)* forum; *Inform* **f. (de discusión)** discussion group (**b**) *Teatro* back (of the stage)

forofo, -a NM,F *Esp Fam* fan, supporter

forrado, -a ADJ lined; *Fam* **estar f.** to be well-heeled, to be well-off

forraje NM fodder

forrar 1 VT *(por dentro)* to line; *(por fuera)* to cover
  2 forrarse VPR *Fam (de dinero)* to make a packet

forro NM (**a**) *(por dentro)* lining; *(por fuera)* cover, case (**b**) *RP Fam (preservativo)* rubber, *Br* johnny

fortalecer [33] VT to fortify, to strengthen

fortaleza NF (**a**) *(fuerza) (física)* strength; *(de espíritu)* fortitude (**b**) *Mil* fortress, stronghold

fortificar [44] VT to fortify

fortísimo, -a ADJ very strong

fortuito, -a ADJ fortuitous

fortuna NF (**a**) *(destino)* fortune, fate (**b**) *(suerte)* luck; **por f.** fortunately (**c**) *(capital)* fortune

forzado, -a ADJ forced; **a marchas forzadas** at a brisk pace; **trabajos forzados** hard labour

forzar [2] VT (**a**) *(obligar)* to force; **f. a algn a hacer algo** to force sb to do sth (**b**) *(puerta, candado)* to force, to break open

forzosamente ADV necessarily

forzoso, -a ADJ obligatory, compulsory; *Av* **aterrizaje f.** forced landing

fosa NF (**a**) *(sepultura)* grave (**b**) *(hoyo)* pit; **f. séptica** septic tank (**c**) *Anat* **fosas nasales** nostrils

fosforescente ADJ phosphorescent

fósforo NM *(cerilla)* match

fósil ADJ & NM fossil

fosilizarse [40] VPR to fossilize, to become fossilized

foso NM (**a**) *(hoyo)* pit (**b**) *(de fortificación)* moat (**c**) *(en garaje)* inspection pit

foto NF *Fam* photo; **sacar/echar una f.** to take a photo

fotocopia NF photocopy

fotocopiadora NF photocopier

fotocopiar [43] VT to photocopy

fotogénico, -a ADJ photogenic

fotografía NF (a) *(imagen)* photograph; **echar** o **hacer** o **sacar fotografías** to take photographs (b) *(arte)* photography

fotografiar [29] VT to photograph, to take a photograph of

fotográfico, -a ADJ photographic

fotógrafo, -a NM,F photographer

fotograma NM *Cin* still

fotomatón NM passport photo machine

fotómetro NM light meter, exposure meter

FP NF *Educ (abr* **Formación Profesional)** vocational training

frac *(pl* **fracs** o **fraques)** NM dress coat, tails

fracasado, -a 1 ADJ unsuccessful
2 NM,F *(persona)* failure

fracasar VI to fail

fracaso NM failure; **el f. escolar** educational failure, poor performance at school

> Observa que la palabra inglesa **fracas** es un falso amigo y no es la traducción de la palabra española **fracaso**. En inglés, **fracas** significa "gresca, refriega".

fracción NF fraction

fraccionamiento NM *Méx* housing estate

fraccionar VT to divide, to break up; *(pago)* to split up into instalments

fraccionario, -a ADJ fractional; **moneda fraccionaria** small change

fractura NF fracture

fracturar 1 VT to fracture
2 fracturarse VPR to fracture

fragancia NF fragrance

fragata NF frigate

frágil ADJ (a) *(quebradizo)* fragile (b) *(débil)* frail

fragmentar 1 VT to fragment
2 fragmentarse VPR to break up

fragmento NM fragment; *(de novela etc)* passage

fragor NM din

fragua NF forge

fraguar [45] VT (a) *(metal)* to forge (b) *(plan)* to think up, to fabricate; *(conspiración)* to hatch

fraile NM friar, monk

frailecillo NM puffin

frambuesa NF raspberry

francamente ADV frankly

francés, -esa 1 ADJ French; *Culin* **tortilla francesa** plain omelette
2 NM,F *(hombre)* Frenchman; *(mujer)* Frenchwoman
3 NM *(idioma)* French

Fráncfort N Frankfurt; **salchicha de F.** frankfurter

Francia N France

francmasón, -ona NM,F freemason

franco¹, -a ADJ (a) *(persona)* frank (b) *Com* **f. a bordo** free on board; **f. fábrica** ex-works; **puerto f.** free port (c) *CSur, Méx (día)* **me dieron el día f.** they gave me the day off

franco² NM *Fin (moneda)* franc

francotirador, -a NM,F sniper

franela NF (a) *(tejido)* flannel (b) *Bol, Col, Ven (camiseta) (interior) Br* vest, *US* undershirt; *(exterior)* T-shirt (c) *Bol, Col, Ven (sudadera)* sweatshirt

franja NF *(de terreno)* strip; *(de bandera)* stripe; *Cost* fringe, border

franquear VT (a) *(atravesar)* to cross; *Fig (dificultad, obstáculo)* to overcome (b) *(carta)* to frank (c) *(camino, paso)* to free, to clear

franqueo NM postage

franqueza NF frankness

franquicia NF *Com* franchise

franquismo NM *Hist* (a) *(ideología)* Francoism (b) **el f.** *(régimen)* the Franco regime

franquista ADJ & NMF Francoist

frasco NM small bottle

frase NF *(oración)* sentence; *(expresión)* phrase; **f. hecha** set phrase o expression

fraternal ADJ brotherly, fraternal

fraternidad NF brotherhood, fraternity

fraternizar [40] VI to fraternize

fraterno, -a ADJ fraternal, brotherly

fraude NM fraud; **f. fiscal** tax evasion

fraudulento, -a ADJ fraudulent

fray NM *Rel* brother

frazada NF *Am* blanket

frecuencia NF frequency; **con f.** frequently, often

frecuentar VT to frequent

frecuente ADJ frequent

frecuentemente ADV frequently, often

fregadero NM *Esp, Méx* (kitchen) sink

fregado¹ NM (a) *(lavado)* washing (b) *Fam (follón)* racket

fregado², -a ADJ *Andes, Méx, Ven Fam* (a) *(persona) (ser)* annoying; **mi vecino es muy f.** my neighbour's a real pain (b) *(persona) (estar)* **perdí las llaves, ¡estoy fregada!** I've lost my keys, I've had it! (c) *(objeto) (roto)* bust

fregar [1] VT (a) *(lavar)* to wash; *(suelo)* to mop (b) *Andes, Méx, Ven Fam (molestar)* to annoy, irritate (c) *Andes, Méx, Ven Fam (estropear)* to bust, to break

fregón, -ona ADJ *Col, Ecuad, Méx (molesto)* annoying

fregona NF *Esp* mop

freidora NF (deep fat) fryer

freír [56] *(pp* **frito)** **1** VT to fry
2 freírse VPR to fry; *Fig* **freírse de calor** to be roasting

frenar VT to brake; *Fig (inflación etc)* to slow down; *(impulsos)* to restrain

frenazo NM sudden braking; **dar un f.** to jam on the brakes

frenesí (pl **frenesíes**) NM frenzy

frenético, -a ADJ frantic

freno NM (**a**) (de vehículo) brake; **pisar/soltar el f.** to press/release the brake; **f. de disco/tambor** disc/drum brake; **f. de mano** Br handbrake, US emergency brake (**b**) (de caballería) bit (**c**) Fig curb, check; **poner f. a algo** to curb sth

frente 1 NM front; **al f. de** at the head of; **chocar de f.** to crash head on; **hacer f. a algo** to face sth, to stand up to sth

2 NF Anat forehead; **f. a f.** face to face

3 ADV **f. a** in front of, opposite

fresa NF (**a**) Esp, CAm, Carib, Méx (planta, fruto) strawberry (**b**) Téc milling cutter

fresca NF Fam cheeky remark

fresco, -a 1 ADJ (**a**) (frío) cool (**b**) (comida, fruta) fresh (**c**) (reciente) fresh, new (**d**) (caradura) cheeky, forward, US fresh; **se quedó tan f.** he didn't bat an eyelid; **¡qué f.!** what a nerve!

2 NM (**a**) (frescor) fresh air, cool air; **al f.** in the cool; **hace f.** it's chilly (**b**) Arte fresco

frescor NM freshness

frescura NF (**a**) (frescor) freshness (**b**) (desvergüenza) cheek, nerve

fresno NM ash tree

fresón NM (large) strawberry

frialdad NF coldness

fríamente ADV coolly

fricción NF (**a**) (rozamiento, tensión) friction (**b**) (masaje) massage

friega NF rub

friegaplatos 1 NMF INV (persona) dishwasher

2 NM INF (aparato) dishwaser

frigider NM Andes refrigerator, Br fridge, US icebox

frígido, -a ADJ frigid

frigorífico, -a 1 NM Esp Br refrigerator, Br fridge, US icebox

2 ADJ **cámara frigorífica** cold store

frijol, fríjol NM Am salvo RP bean

frío, -a 1 ADJ (**a**) (a baja temperatura) cold (**b**) (indiferente) cold, cool; **su comentario me dejó f.** her remark left me cold

2 NM cold; **hace f.** it's cold

friolento, -a ADJ Am sensitive to the cold

friolera NF Fam **la f. de mil euros/dos horas** a mere thousand euros/two hours

friolero, -a ADJ sensitive to the cold

fritada NF fry-up, dish of fried food

fritanga NF (**a**) Esp (comida frita) fry-up (**b**) Am Pey (comida grasienta) greasy food

frito, -a 1 ADJ (**a**) Culin fried (**b**) Fam exasperated, fed up; **me tienes f.** I'm sick to death of you

2 NM **fritos** fried food

3 PP de **freír**

fritura NF fry-up, dish of fried food

frívolo, -a ADJ frivolous

frondoso, -a ADJ leafy, luxuriant

frontera NF frontier

fronterizo, -a ADJ frontier, border; **países fronterizos** neighbouring countries

frontón NM Dep pelota

frotar 1 VT to rub

2 frotarse VPR to rub; **frotarse las manos** to rub one's hands together

fructífero, -a ADJ fruitful

frugal ADJ frugal

fruncir [52] VT (**a**) Cost to gather (**b**) (labios) to purse, to pucker; **f. el ceño** to frown, to knit one's brow

frustración NF frustration

frustrado, -a ADJ (persona) frustrated; (plan) failed

frustrante ADJ frustrating

frustrar 1 VT to frustrate

2 frustrarse VPR (**a**) (esperanza) to fail, to go awry (**b**) (persona) to be frustrated

fruta NF fruit; **f. del tiempo** fresh fruit

frutal 1 ADJ fruit; **árbol f.** fruit tree

2 NM fruit tree

frutería NF fruit shop

frutero, -a 1 NM,F fruit seller, Br fruiterer

2 NM fruit dish o bowl

frutilla NF Bol, CSur, Ecuad strawberry

fruto NM fruit; **frutos secos** nuts; **dar f.** to bear fruit; Fig (dar buen resultado) to be fruitful; **sacar f. de algo** to profit from sth

fu INTERJ **ni fu ni fa** so-so

fucsia NF fuchsia

fuego NM (**a**) (llamas) fire; **fuegos artificiales** fireworks (**b**) (lumbre) light; **¿me da f., por favor?** have you got a light, please? (**c**) Culin **a f. lento** on a low flame; (al horno) in a slow oven

fuel NM fuel oil

fuelle NM (para soplar) bellows

fuente NF (**a**) (de agua) fountain; Chile, Col, Méx, Ven **f. de soda** (cafetería) = café or counter selling ice cream, soft drinks etc, US soda fountain (serving soft drinks and alcohol) (**b**) (recipiente) dish, serving dish (**c**) (de información) source

fuera¹ ADV (**a**) (en el exterior) outside, out; **quédate f.** stay outside; **sal f.** go out; **desde f.** from (the) outside; **por f.** on the outside; **la puerta de f.** the outer door (**b**) **f. de** out of; **f. de serie** extraordinary; Fig **estar f. de sí** to be beside oneself (**c**) Dep **el equipo de f.** the away team; **jugar f.** to play away; **f. de juego** offside

fuera² 1 SUBJ IMPERF de **ir**

2 SUBJ IMPERF de **ser**

fuero NM (**a**) Hist code of laws (**b**) Fig **en tu f. interno** deep down, in your heart of hearts

fuerte 1 ADJ strong; (dolor) severe; (sonido) loud; (comida) heavy; **el plato f.** the main

course; *Fig* the most important event
2 NM (**a**) *(fortaleza)* fort (**b**) *(punto fuerte)* forte, strong point
3 ADV ¡abrázame f.! hold me tight!; **comer f.** to eat a lot; ¡habla más f.! speak up!; ¡pégale f.! hit him hard!

fuerza NF (**a**) *(fortaleza)* strength; *Fig* **a f. de** by dint of (**b**) *(violencia)* force; **a la f.** *(por obligación)* of necessity; *(con violencia)* by force; **por f.** of necessity; **f. mayor** force majeure (**c**) *Fís* force (**d**) *(cuerpo)* force; **las fuerzas del orden** the forces of law and order; **f. aérea** air force; **fuerzas armadas** armed forces

fuese 1 SUBJ IMPERF *de* **ir**
2 SUBJ IMPERF *de* **ser**

fuete NM *Am salvo RP* whip

fuga NF (**a**) *(huida)* escape; **darse a la f.** to take flight (**b**) *(de gas etc)* leak

fugarse [42] VPR to escape; **f. de casa** to run away from home

fugaz ADJ fleeting, brief

fugitivo, -a NM,F fugitive

fui 1 PT INDEF *de* **ir**
2 PT INDEF *de* **ser**

fulana NF whore, tart

fulano, -a NM,F so-and-so; *(hombre)* what's-his-name; *(mujer)* what's-her-name; **Doña Fulana de tal** Mrs So-and-so

fular NM scarf

fulgor NM *Literario* brilliance, glow

fullero, -a *Fam* **1** ADJ cheating
2 NM,F cheat

fulminante ADJ *(cese)* summary; *(muerte, enfermedad)* sudden; *(mirada)* withering

fulminar VT to strike dead; **f. a algn con la mirada** to look daggers at sb

fumador, -a NM,F smoker; **los no fumadores** nonsmokers; **f. pasivo** passive smoker

fumar 1 VT & VI to smoke; **no f.** *(en letrero)* no smoking
2 fumarse VPR to smoke; **fumarse un cigarro** to smoke a cigarette

Observa que el verbo inglés **to fume** es un falso amigo y no es la traducción del verbo español **fumar**. En inglés, **to fume** significa "despedir humo".

fumigar [42] VT to fumigate

funambulista NMF, **funámbulo, -a** NM,F tightrope walker

función NF (**a**) *(papel)* function; **en f. de** depending on (**b**) *(cargo)* **entrar en funciones** to take up one's duties; **presidente en funciones** acting president (**c**) *Teatro* performance (**d**) *Ling & Mat* function

funcionamiento NM operation; **poner/entrar en f.** to put/come into operation

funcionar VI to work; **no funciona** *(en letrero)* out of order

funcionario, -a NM,F *(de la Administración central)* civil servant; *(profesor, bombero, enfermero)* public sector worker; **f. de prisiones** prison officer

funda NF cover; *(de gafas etc)* case; *(de espada)* sheath; **f. de almohada** pillowcase

fundación NF foundation

fundador, -a NM,F founder

fundamental ADJ fundamental

fundamentar VT to base (**en** on)

fundamento NM basis, grounds; **sin f.** unfounded

fundar 1 VT (**a**) *(empresa)* to found (**b**) *(teoría)* to base, to found
2 fundarse VPR (**a**) *(empresa)* to be founded (**b**) *(teoría)* to be based (**en** on)

Observa que el verbo inglés **to fund** es un falso amigo y no es la traducción del verbo español **fundar**. En inglés, **to fund** significa "financiar".

fundición NF (**a**) *(de metales)* smelting (**b**) *(fábrica)* foundry

fundir 1 VT (**a**) *(mantequilla, hielo)* to melt; *(hierro)* to smelt (**b**) *(bombilla, plomos)* to blow
2 fundirse VPR (**a**) *(derretirse)* to melt (**b**) *(bombilla, plomos)* to blow (**c**) *Com* to merge (**d**) *Am Fam (arruinarse)* to go bust

fúnebre ADJ (**a**) *(mortuorio)* funeral; **coche f.** hearse (**b**) *(lúgubre)* mournful, lugubrious

funeral NM funeral

funeraria NF undertaker's, *US* funeral home

funesto, -a ADJ ill-fated, fatal; *(consecuencias)* disastrous

fungir VI *Méx, Perú* to act, to serve (**de** o **como** as)

funicular NM funicular (railway)

furcia NF *Pey* whore, tart

furgón NM *Aut* van

furgoneta NF van

furia NF fury; **ponerse hecho una f.** to become furious, to fly into a rage

furibundo, -a ADJ furious, enraged

furioso, -a ADJ furious; **ponerse f.** to become furious

furor NM fury, rage; *Fig* **hacer f.** to be all the rage

furtivo, -a ADJ furtive, stealthy; **caza/pesca furtiva** poaching; **cazador/pescador f.** poacher

furúnculo NM *Med* boil

fuselaje NM fuselage

fusible NM fuse

fusil NM gun, rifle

fusilamiento NM shooting, execution

fusilar VT (**a**) *(ejecutar)* to shoot, to execute (**b**) *Fam (plagiar)* to plagiarize

fusión NF (**a**) *(de metales)* fusion; *(del hielo)* thawing, melting; **punto de f.** melting point (**b**) *Com* merger

fusionar 1 VT to merge
2 fusionarse VPR to merge

fustán NM *Am* petticoat

fútbol NM soccer, *Br* football; **f. sala** indoor five-a-side

futbolín NM *Esp Br* table football, *US* foosball

futbolista NMF soccer *o Br* football player, *Br* footballer

fútil ADJ futile, trivial

futilidad NF futility, triviality

futurista ADJ *(diseño, ropa)* futuristic; *Arte* futurist

futuro, -a 1 ADJ future
2 NM future; **en un f. próximo** in the near future; *CSur, Méx* **a f.** in the future

G

G, g [xe] NF *(letra)* G, g

g *(abr* **gramo***)* g

gabán NM overcoat

gabardina NF *(prenda)* raincoat

gabinete NM (**a**) *(despacho)* study; **g. de abogados** lawyers' office (**b**) *Pol* cabinet

gaceta NF gazette

gachas NFPL (corn) porridge

gacho, -a ADJ **con la cabeza gacha** hanging one's head

gaditano, -a 1 ADJ of/from Cadiz
2 NM,F person from Cadiz

gafar VT *Fam* to put a jinx on, to bring bad luck to

gafas NFPL glasses, spectacles; **g. de sol** sunglasses

gafe *Esp Fam* 1 ADJ jinxed; **ser g.** to be jinxed
2 NMF jinxed person

> Observa que la palabra inglesa **gaffe** es un falso amigo y no es la traducción de la palabra española **gafe**. En inglés, **gaffe** significa "metedura de pata, desliz".

gafete NM *Méx* badge

gaita NF bagpipes

gajes NMPL *Fam Irón* **g. del oficio** occupational hazards

gajo NM *(de fruta)* segment

gala NF (**a**) *(vestido)* full dress; **de g.** dressed up; *(ciudad)* decked out (**b**) *Esp (espectáculo)* gala; **hacer g. de** to glory in (**c**) **galas** finery

galán NM handsome young man; *Teatro* leading man

galante ADJ gallant

galantear VT to court

galanteo NM courtship

galantería NF gallantry

galápago NM turtle

galardón NM prize

galardonado, -a ADJ award-winning, prize-winning

galardonar VT to award a prize to

galaxia NF galaxy

galeón NM galleon

galera NF *Náut* galley

galería NF (**a**) *Arquit* covered balcony (**b**) *(museo)* art gallery (**c**) *Teatro* gallery

Gales N **(el país de) G.** Wales

galés, -esa 1 ADJ Welsh
2 NM,F *(hombre)* Welshman; *(mujer)* Welsh-woman; **los galeses** the Welsh
3 NM *(idioma)* Welsh

galgo NM greyhound

Galicia N Galicia

galimatías NM INV *Fam* gibberish

gallardo, -a ADJ (**a**) *(valiente)* brave, dashing (**b**) *(bien parecido)* fine-looking, striking

gallego, -a 1 ADJ & NM,F Galician; *CSur, Cuba Fam* Spanish
2 NM *(idioma)* Galician

galleta NF (**a**) *Culin Br* biscuit, *US* cookie (**b**) *Esp Fam (cachete)* slap

gallina 1 NF hen
2 NMF *Fam* coward, chicken

gallinero NM (**a**) *(de gallinas)* hen run (**b**) *Teatro* **el g.** the gods

gallito ADJ *Fam* cocky

gallo NM (**a**) *(ave)* cock, rooster; *Fam Fig* **en menos que canta un g.** before you could say Jack Robinson (**b**) *Fam Mús* off-key note

galón¹ NM *Mil* stripe

galón² NM *(medida)* gallon, *Br* = 4.55 l, *US* = 3.79 l

galopante ADJ *(inflación)* galloping

galopar VI to gallop

galope NM gallop; **a g. tendido** flat out

galpón NM *Andes, Carib, RP* shed

gama NF range; *Mús* scale

gamba NF *Br* prawn, *US* shrimp

gamberrismo NM *Esp* hooliganism

gamberro, -a *Esp* 1 NM,F hooligan, lout, *Br* yob
2 ADJ loutish

gamo NM fallow deer

gamonal NM *Andes, CAm, Ven* (**a**) *(cacique)* village chief (**b**) *(caudillo)* cacique, local political boss

gamuza NF (**a**) *Zool* chamois (**b**) *(trapo)* chamois o shammy leather

gana NF (**a**) *(deseo)* wish (**de** for); **de buena g.** willingly; **de mala g.** reluctantly; *Fam* **no me da la g.** I don't feel like it (**b**) **tener ganas de (hacer) algo** to feel like (doing) sth; **quedarse con las ganas** to not manage to (**c**) *(apetito)* appetite; **comer con ganas** to eat heartily

ganadería NF (**a**) *(crianza)* livestock farming (**b**) *(conjunto de ganado)* livestock

ganadero, -a NM,F livestock farmer

ganado NM livestock; **g. vacuno** cattle

ganador, -a ADJ winning
  2 NM,F winner

ganancia NF profit

ganar 1 VT (**a**) (*sueldo*) to earn (**b**) (*premio, competición*) to win (**c**) (*derrotar*) to beat (**d**) (*peso, tiempo*) to gain (**e**) (*alcanzar*) to reach
  2 VI (**a**) (*vencer*) to win (**b**) (*mejorar*) **g. en algo** to gain in sth
  3 ganarse VPR (**a**) (*obtener*) to earn; **ganarse el pan** to earn one's daily bread (**b**) (*merecer*) to deserve; **se lo ha ganado** he deserves it (**c**) (*conquistar*) (*simpatía, respeto*) to earn; (*persona*) to win over

ganchillo NM crochet work

gancho NM (**a**) (*garfio*) hook (**b**) *Fam Fig* (*gracia, atractivo*) charm (**c**) *Andes, CAm, Méx* (*horquilla*) hairpin (**d**) *Andes, CAm, Méx, Ven* (*percha*) hanger (**e**) *Col, Ven* (*pinza*) *Br* (clothes) peg, *US* clothespin

gandul, -a NM,F loafer

ganga NF bargain

gangoso, -a ADJ nasal

gangrena NF gangrene

gansada NF *Fam* silly thing to say/do

ganso, -a 1 NM,F (**a**) (*ave*) goose; (*macho*) gander (**b**) *Fam* dolt
  2 ADJ *Fam* ginormous; **pasta gansa** bread, dough

gánster (*pl* **gánsters** o **gánsteres**) NM gangster

ganzúa NF picklock

gañán NM (*obrero*) farmhand; (*hombre rudo*) lout, boor

garabatear VT & VI to scribble

garabato NM scrawl

garaje NM garage

garante NMF *Fin* guarantor

garantía NF (**a**) (*seguro, promesa*) guarantee; (*de producto*) guarantee, warranty (**b**) *Der* (*fianza*) security

garantizar [40] VT to guarantee

garbanzo NM chickpea

garbeo NM *Esp Fam* (*paseo*) stroll; **darse un g.** to go for a stroll

garbo NM grace

garfio NM hook, grappling iron

gargajo NM spit

garganta NF (**a**) *Anat* throat (**b**) (*desfiladero*) gorge

gargantilla NF short necklace

gárgaras NFPL gargling *sing*; *Fam* **¡vete a hacer g.!** get lost!

garita NF (*de centinela*) sentry box; (*de conserje*) porter's lodge

garito NM *Fam* joint

garra NF (**a**) *Zool* claw; (*de ave*) talon (**b**) *Fig* (*fuerza*) force; **tener g.** to be compelling

garrafa NF carafe

garrafal ADJ monumental

garrapata NF tick

garrote NM (**a**) (*porra*) club (**b**) *Der* garrotte

garrulo, -a ADJ *Fam* coarse, uncouth

garúa NF *Andes, RP, Ven* drizzle

garza NF heron

gas NM (**a**) (*fluido*) gas; *Esp* **g. ciudad** town gas; **gases (nocivos)** fumes; **g. de escape** exhaust fumes (**b**) (*en bebida*) fizz; **agua con g.** fizzy water (**c**) *Med* **gases** flatulence

gasa NF gauze

gaseosa NF (**a**) *Esp, Arg* (*bebida transparente*) pop, *Br* lemonade (**b**) *CAm, RP* (*refresco con gas*) fizzy drink, *US* soda

gaseoso, -a ADJ (*estado*) gaseous; (*bebida*) fizzy

gasfitería NF *Chile, Perú* plumber's (shop)

gasfitero, -a NM,F *Ecuad* plumber

gasoducto NM gas pipeline

gasóleo, gasoil NM diesel oil

gasolina NF *Br* petrol, *US* gas, *US* gasoline

gasolinera, *Méx* **gasolinería** NF *Br* petrol o *US* gas station

gastado, -a ADJ (*objeto*) worn out; *Fig* (*frase*) hackneyed

gastar 1 VT (**a**) (*consumir*) (*dinero, tiempo*) to spend; (*gasolina, electricidad*) to consume (**b**) (*malgastar*) to waste (**c**) *Esp* (*ropa*) to wear; **¿qué número gastas?** what size do you take? (**d**) **g. una broma a algn** to play a practical joke on sb
  2 gastarse VPR (**a**) (*deteriorarse*) to wear out (**b**) (*consumirse*) to run out

gasto NM expenditure; **gastos** expenses; **gastos de viaje** travelling expenses

gastritis NF INV *Med* gastritis

gastronomía NF gastronomy

gastronómico, -a ADJ gastronomic

gatas: a gatas LOC ADV on all fours

gatear VI to crawl

gatillo NM trigger; **apretar el g.** to pull the trigger

gato, -a 1 NM,F (*animal*) cat
  2 NM *Aut & Téc* jack

gauchada NF *CSur* favour

gaucho, -a 1 ADJ *RP Fam* (*servicial*) helpful, obliging
  2 NM,F gaucho

gaveta NF drawer

gavilán NM sparrowhawk

gaviota NF seagull

gay [gai, gei] (*pl* **gays**) ADJ INV & NM gay

gazapo NM (*error*) misprint

gaznate NM gullet

gazpacho NM gazpacho

gel NM gel; **g. (de ducha)** shower gel

gelatina NF (*de carne*) gelatine; (*de fruta*) *Br* jelly, *US* Jell-O®

gema NF gem

gemelo, -a 1 ADJ & NM,F (identical) twin
  2 gemelos NMPL (**a**) *(de camisa)* cufflinks (**b**) *(anteojos)* binoculars

gemido NM groan

Géminis NM Gemini

gemir [6] VI to groan

generación NF generation

generador NM *Elec* generator

general 1 ADJ general; **por lo** o **en g.** in general, generally
  2 NM *Mil & Rel* general

Generalitat NF Catalan/Valencian/Balearic parliament

generalización NF (**a**) *(comentario)* generalization (**b**) *(extensión)* spread

generalizar [40] **1** VT to spread, to make widespread
  2 VI to generalize
  3 generalizarse VPR to become widespread o common

generalmente ADV generally

generar VT to generate

género NM (**a**) *(clase)* kind, sort (**b**) *Arte & Lit* genre (**c**) *(mercancía)* article (**d**) *Ling* gender (**e**) *Biol* genus; **el g. humano** mankind

generosidad NF generosity

generoso, -a ADJ generous (**con** to)

Génesis NM *Rel* Genesis

genética NF genetics *sing*

genético, -a ADJ genetic

genial ADJ great, *Br* brilliant

> Observa que la palabra inglesa **genial** es un falso amigo y no es la traducción de la palabra española **genial**. En inglés **genial** significa "cordial, amable".

genio NM (**a**) *(carácter)* temperament; *(mal carácter)* temper; **estar de mal g.** to be in a bad mood (**b**) *(facultad)* genius

genital 1 ADJ genital
  2 genitales NMPL genitals

genocidio NM genocide

genoma NM genome

Génova N Genoa

gente NF (**a**) *(personas)* people (**b**) *(familia)* folks

gentil ADJ (**a**) *(amable)* kind (**b**) *(pagano)* pagan

> Observa que la palabra inglesa **genteel** es un falso amigo y no es la traducción de la palabra española **gentil**. En inglés **genteel** significa "fino, distinguido".

gentileza NF kindness; *Fml* **por g. de** by courtesy of

gentío NM crowd

gentuza NF *Pey* riffraff

genuino, -a ADJ *(puro)* genuine; *(verdadero)* authentic

geografía NF geography

geología NF geology

geometría NF geometry

geométrico, -a ADJ geometric

geranio NM geranium

gerencia NF management

gerente NMF manager

germano, -a 1 ADJ German, Germanic
  2 NM,F German

germen NM (**a**) *Biol* germ; **g. de trigo** wheat germ (**b**) *Fig (inicio)* germ; *(fuente)* origin

germinar VI to germinate

gerundio NM gerund

gesta NF heroic exploit

gestación NF gestation

gestar VT to gestate

gesticular VI *(con manos, brazos)* to gesticulate; *(con la cara)* to pull faces

gestión NF (**a**) *(administración)* management (**b**) **gestiones** *(negociaciones)* negotiations; *(trámites)* formalities

gestionar VT to take steps to acquire o obtain; *(negociar)* to negotiate

gesto NM (**a**) *(mueca)* face (**b**) *(con las manos)* gesture

gestor, -a NM,F = person who carries out dealings with public bodies on behalf of private customers or companies, combining the roles of solicitor and accountant

gestoría NF = office of a "gestor"

giba NF hump

Gibraltar N Gibraltar

gibraltareño, -a 1 ADJ of/from Gibraltar
  2 NM,F Gibraltarian

gigante, -a 1 NM,F giant
  2 ADJ giant, enormous

gigantesco, -a ADJ gigantic

gigoló NM gigolo

gil, -ila NM,F *CSur Fam* jerk, *Br* twit

gilipollas NMF INV *muy Fam Br* prat, *US* dork

gimnasia NF gymnastics *sing*

gimnasio NM gymnasium

gimnasta NMF gymnast

gimotear VI to whine

Ginebra N Geneva

ginebra NF *(bebida)* gin

ginecología NF gynaecology

ginecólogo, -a NM,F gynaecologist

gin-tonic [jin'tonik] *(pl* **gin-tonics***)* NM gin and tonic

gira NF *Mús & Teatro* tour

girar 1 VI (**a**) *(dar vueltas)* to spin (**b**) **g. a la derecha/izquierda** to turn right/left
  2 VT *Fin* (**a**) *(expedir)* to draw (**b**) *(dinero)* to transfer

girasol NM sunflower

giratorio, -a ADJ revolving

giro NM (**a**) *(vuelta)* turn (**b**) *(de aconteci-mientos)* direction (**c**) *(frase)* turn of phrase (**d**) *Fin* draft; **g. telegráfico** money order; **g. postal** postal o money order

gis NM *Méx* chalk

gitano, -a ADJ & NM,F gypsy, gipsy

glacial ADJ icy

glaciar NM glacier

glándula NF gland

glasear VT *Culin* to glaze

global ADJ comprehensive; **precio g.** all-inclusive price

globalización NF globalization

globalmente ADV as a whole

globo NM (**a**) *(de aire)* balloon (**b**) *(esfera)* globe (**c**) *(lámpara)* globe, glass lampshade

glóbulo NM *Med* blood cell, corpuscle

gloria NF (**a**) *(fama)* glory (**b**) *Rel* heaven; *Fam Fig* **estar en la g.** to be in seventh heaven (**c**) *Fam (delicia)* delight

glorieta NF (**a**) *(plazoleta)* small square (**b**) *Esp (rotonda)* Br roundabout, US traffic circle (**c**) *(en un jardín)* arbour

glorificar [44] VT to glorify

glorioso, -a ADJ glorious

glosa NF marginal note

glosar VT (**a**) *(explicar)* to gloss; *(texto)* to interpret (**b**) *(comentar)* to comment on

glosario NM glossary

glotón, -ona 1 ADJ greedy
2 NM,F glutton

glotonería NF gluttony, greed

glucosa NF glucose

gobernación NF (**a**) *Col (de provincia)* provincial government (**b**) *Méx* **G.** *(ministerio)* Br ≃ the Home Office, US ≃ the Department of the Interior

gobernador, -a NM,F governor

gobernante ADJ ruling

gobernar [1] **1** VT to govern; *(país)* to rule
2 VI *Náut* to steer

gobiernista *Andes, Méx* **1** ADJ government
2 NMF government supporter

gobierno NM (**a**) *Pol* government (**b**) *(mando)* running (**c**) *Náut* steering (**d**) *Náut (timón)* rudder

goce NM enjoyment

godo, -a 1 ADJ Gothic
2 NM,F *Hist* Goth

gofio NM *Andes, Carib, RP (harina)* roasted maize o US corn meal

gol NM goal

goleada NF **ganar por g.** to score a heavy victory

goleador, -a NM,F goal scorer

golear VT to hammer

golf NM golf; **palo de g.** golf club

golfista NMF golfer

golfo¹, -a 1 NM *(gamberro)* lout, *Br* yob; *(pillo)* rogue, wide boy
2 NF *Fam Pey* tart

golfo² NM *Geog* gulf; **el g. Pérsico** the Persian Gulf

golondrina NF swallow

golosina NF *Br* sweet, *US* candy

goloso, -a ADJ sweet-toothed

golpe NM (**a**) *(impacto)* blow; *(en puerta)* knock; *(puñetazo)* punch; **de g.** all of a sudden; **g. de estado** coup d'état; **g. de suerte** stroke of luck; **no dar ni g.** not to lift a finger (**b**) *Aut* bump (**c**) *(desgracia)* blow; **un duro g.** a great blow (**d**) *(de humor)* witticism

golpear VT to hit; *(con el puño)* to punch; *(puerta, cabeza)* to bang

golpiza NF *Am* beating

goma NF (**a**) *(material)* rubber; **g. de pegar** glue; **g. de borrar** eraser, *Br* rubber (**b**) *(elástica)* rubber o *Br* elastic band (**c**) *Cuba, CSur (neumático)* tyre (**d**) *Fam (preservativo)* rubber

gomaespuma NF foam rubber

gomal NM *Am Agr* rubber plantation

gomería NF *CSur* tyre centre

gomero NM *CSur (planta)* rubber plant

gomina NF hair cream

góndola NF (**a**) *(embarcación)* gondola (**b**) *Perú (autobús interurbano)* (intercity) bus (**c**) *Bol (autobús urbano)* city bus (**d**) *(en supermercado)* gondola

gordo, -a 1 ADJ (**a**) *(carnoso)* fat (**b**) *(grueso)* thick (**c**) *(importante)* big; **me cae g.** I can't stand him; **de g.** in a big way
2 NM,F (**a**) *(persona)* fat person; *Fam* fatty (**b**) *Am Fam (como apelativo)* **¿cómo estás, g.?** how's it going, big man?
3 NM **el g.** *(de lotería)* the jackpot

gordura NF fatness

gorgorito NM trill

gorila NM (**a**) *(animal)* gorilla (**b**) *Esp Fig (en discoteca etc)* bouncer

gorjear VI *(ave)* to chirp

gorjeo NM chirping

gorra NF cap; *(con visera)* peaked cap; *Esp, Méx Fam* **de g.** for free

gorrión NM sparrow

gorro NM *(de lana)* hat; **g. de baño** swimming cap; *Fam* **estar hasta el g. (de)** to be up to here (with)

gorrón, -ona NM,F *Esp, Méx* sponger

gota NF (**a**) *(de líquido)* drop; *(de sudor)* bead; **g. a g.** drop by drop; **ni g.** not a bit (**b**) *Med* gout

gotear V IMPERS to drip; **el techo gotea** there's a leak in the ceiling

gotera NF leak

gotero NM *(intravenous)* drip

gótico, -a ADJ Gothic

gozar [40] VI to enjoy oneself; **g. de algo** to enjoy sth

gozne NM hinge

gozo NM pleasure

grabación NF recording

grabado NM (**a**) (arte) engraving (**b**) (dibujo) drawing

grabadora NF tape recorder

grabar VT (**a**) (sonidos, imágenes) to record (**b**) Inform to save (**c**) Arte to engrave

gracia NF (**a**) (atractivo) grace (**b**) (chiste) joke; **hacer** o **tener g.** to be funny (**c**) (indulto) pardon

gracias NFPL (agradecimiento) thanks; **g. a** thanks to; **g. a Dios** thank God, thank goodness; **muchas** o **muchísimas g.** thank you very much

gracioso, -a 1 ADJ (**a**) (divertido) funny (**b**) (garboso) graceful
2 NM,F Teatro comic character

grada NF (**a**) (peldaño) step (**b**) **gradas** (en estadio) terraces

gradación NF scale

graderío NM Esp Teatro rows; Dep terraces

gradiente 1 NM gradient
2 NF CSur, Ecuad gradient, slope

grado NM (**a**) (unidad) degree (**b**) Mil rank (**c**) **de buen g.** willingly, gladly

graduable ADJ adjustable

graduación NF (**a**) (de la vista) eye-test; (de gafas) strength (**b**) Educ graduation (**c**) (de bebidas) strength, proof (**d**) Mil rank

graduado, -a NM,F graduate

gradual ADJ gradual

gradualmente ADV gradually

graduar [30] **1** VT (**a**) Educ to confer a degree on (**b**) Mil to confer a rank on (**c**) (regular) to regulate
2 graduarse VPR (**a**) Educ & Mil to graduate (**b**) **graduarse la vista** to have one's eyes tested

graffiti NM piece of graffiti

grafía NF written symbol

gráfico, -a 1 ADJ graphic; **diseño g.** graphic design
2 NM graph

grafista NMF graphic designer

gragea NF Med pill

grajo, -a 1 NM,F (ave) rook
2 NM Andes, Carib Fam (olor) BO, body odour

gramática NF grammar

gramatical ADJ grammatical

gramo NM gram, gramme

gran ADJ = **grande**

grana ADJ scarlet

granada NF (**a**) (fruto) pomegranate (**b**) Mil grenade

granate 1 ADJ INV (color) maroon
2 NM (color) maroon

grande ADJ (**a**) (tamaño) big, large; Fig (persona) great; **Gran Bretaña** Great Britain (**b**) (cantidad) large; **vivir a lo g.** to live in style; Fig **pasarlo en g.** to have a great time

> **gran** is used instead of **grande** before masculine singular nouns (e.g. **gran hombre** great man).

grandeza NF (**a**) (importancia) greatness (**b**) (grandiosidad) grandeur; **delirios de g.** delusions of grandeur

grandioso, -a ADJ grandiose

granel NM **a g.** (sin envase) loose; (en gran cantidad) in bulk; (en abundancia) in abundance; **vender/comprar vino a g.** to sell/buy wine from the barrel

granero NM Agr granary

granito NM granite

granizada NF hailstorm

granizado NM = drink of flavoured crushed ice

granizar [40] V IMPERS to hail

granizo NM hail

granja NF farm

granjear 1 VT to earn
2 granjearse VPR to gain, to earn

granjero, -a NM,F farmer

grano NM (**a**) (de cereal, arena) grain; (de café) bean; **ir al g.** to get to the point (**b**) (espinilla) spot

granuja NM (**a**) (pilluelo) ragamuffin (**b**) (estafador) con-man

grapa NF (para papeles) staple; (para heridas) stitch

grapadora NF stapler

grapar VT to staple

grasa NF grease

grasiento, -a ADJ greasy

graso, -a ADJ (pelo) greasy; (materia) fatty

gratificar [44] VT (**a**) (satisfacer) to gratify (**b**) (recompensar) to reward

gratinado ADJ Culin au gratin

gratinar VT Culin to cook au gratin

gratis ADJ INV & ADV free

gratitud NF gratitude

grato, -a ADJ pleasant

gratuito, -a ADJ (**a**) (de balde) free (of charge) (**b**) (arbitrario) gratuitous

grava NF gravel

gravamen NM tax

gravar VT (**a**) (cargar) to burden (**b**) (impuestos) to tax

grave ADJ (**a**) (importante) serious (**b**) (muy enfermo) seriously ill (**c**) (voz, nota) low

gravedad NF (**a**) (seriedad, importancia) seriousness (**b**) Fís gravity

gravilla NF chippings

gravitar VI (**a**) Fís to gravitate (**b**) **g. sobre** to rest on

gravoso, -a ADJ (a) *(costoso)* costly (b) *(molesto)* burdensome

graznar VI *(cuervo)* to caw; *(pato)* to quack; *(persona)* to squawk

graznido NM *(de cuervo)* caw; *(de pato)* quack; *(de persona)* squawk

Grecia N Greece

gregario, -a ADJ gregarious; **instinto g.** herd instinct

gremio NM (a) *Hist* guild (b) *(profesión)* profession, trade

greña NF lock of entangled hair; *Fam* **andar a la g.** to squabble

gres NM **artículos de g.** stoneware

gresca NF row

griego, -a ADJ & NM,F Greek

grieta NF crack; *(en la piel)* chap

grifero, -a NM,F *Perú (persona)* Br petrol pump attendant, *US* gas pump attendant

grifo NM (a) *Esp (llave)* Br tap, *US* faucet (b) *Perú (gasolinera)* Br petrol station, *US* gas station

grill [gril] *(pl* **grills)** NM grill

grillete NM shackle

grillo NM cricket

gringo, -a *Fam* **1** ADJ (a) *(estadounidense)* gringo, American (b) *Am (extranjero)* gringo, foreign

  2 NM,F (a) *(estadounidense)* gringo, American (b) *Am (extranjero)* gringo, foreigner *(from a non-Spanish speaking country)*

gripa NF *Col, Méx* flu

gripe NF flu

gris ADJ & NM grey

grisáceo, -a ADJ greyish

gritar VT & VI to shout

grito NM shout; **a voz en g.** at the top of one's voice

Groenlandia N Greenland

grosella NF *(fruto)* redcurrant; **g. negra** blackcurrant; **g. silvestre** gooseberry

grosería NF (a) *(ordinariez)* rude word o expression (b) *(rusticidad)* rudeness

grosero, -a ADJ *(tosco)* coarse; *(maleducado)* rude

grosor NM thickness

grotesco, -a ADJ grotesque

grúa NF (a) *Constr* crane (b) *Aut Br* breakdown van o truck, *US* tow truck

grueso, -a **1** ADJ thick; *(persona)* stout

  2 NM *(parte principal)* bulk

grulla NF *(ave)* crane

grumo NM lump; *(de leche)* curd

gruñido NM grunt

gruñir VI to grunt

gruñón, -ona ADJ grumpy

grupa NF hindquarters

grupo NM (a) *(conjunto)* group; *Inform* **g. de noticias** newsgroup (b) *Téc* unit, set

gruta NF cave

guaca NF (a) *Am (sepultura)* = pre-Columbian Indian tomb (b) *Am (tesoro)* hidden treasure (c) *CRica, Cuba (hucha)* moneybox

guacal NM (a) *CAm, Méx (calabaza)* gourd (b) *Carib, Col, Méx (jaula)* cage

guacamayo, -a NM,F macaw

guacamol, guacamole NM guacamole, avocado dip

guachafita NF *Col, Ven Fam* racket, uproar

guachimán NM *Am* night watchman

guacho, -a ADJ & NM,F *Andes, RP* (a) *muy Fam (persona huérfana)* orphan (b) *Fam (sinvergüenza)* bastard, swine

guaco NM *Am (cerámica)* = pottery object found in pre-Columbian Indian tomb

guadaña NF scythe

guagua NF (a) *Andes (niño)* baby (b) *Cuba, PRico, RDom* bus

guajiro, -a NM,F (a) *Cuba Fam (campesino)* peasant (b) *(de Guajira)* person from Guajira *(Colombia, Venezuela)*

guajolote NM *CAm, Méx* (a) *(pavo)* turkey (b) *(tonto)* fool, idiot

guampa NF *Bol, CSur* horn

guanajo NM *Carib* turkey

guantazo NM slap

guante NM glove

guantera NF *Aut* glove compartment

guapo, -a ADJ (a) *esp Esp (atractivo)* goodlooking; *(hombre)* handsome; *(mujer)* pretty (b) *Am (valiente)* gutsy; **ser g.** to have guts

guaraca NF *Am* sling

guarache NM *Méx (sandalia)* = crude sandal with a sole made from a tyre

guarangada NF *Bol, CSur* rude remark

guarango, -a ADJ rude

guarda NM,F guard; **g. jurado** security guard

guardabarros NM INV *Esp, Bol, RP (de automóvil, bicicleta) Br* mudguard, *US* fender

guardabosque NM,F gamekeeper

guardacoches NM,F INV parking attendant

guardacostas **1** NM,F INV *(persona)* coastguard

  2 NM INV *(barco)* coastguard boat

guardaespaldas NM,F INV bodyguard

guardafango NM INV *Andes, CAm, Carib (de vehículo) Br* mudguard, *US* fender

guardameta NM,F *Dep* goalkeeper

guardapolvo NM overalls

guardar **1** VT (a) *(conservar)* to keep (b) *(un secreto)* to keep; **g. silencio** to remain silent; **g. cama** to stay in bed (c) *(poner en un sitio)* to put away (d) *(reservar)* to keep (e) *Inform* to save

  2 guardarse VPR **guardarse de hacer algo** *(abstenerse)* to be careful not to do sth; **guardársela a algn** to have it in for sb

guardarropa NM (a) *(cuarto)* cloakroom (b) *(armario)* wardrobe

guardería NF g. infantil nursery (school)

guardia 1 NF (a) *(vigilancia)* watch (b) la G. Civil the Civil Guard (c) *(turno de servicio)* duty; *Mil* guard duty; de g. on duty; farmacia de g. duty chemist
  2 NMF policeman; *(mujer)* policewoman

guardián, -ana NM,F watchman

guarecer [33] **1** VT to shelter
  2 guarecerse VPR to take shelter o refuge (de from)

guarida NF *(de animal)* lair; *(refugio)* hide-out

guarismo NM digit

guarnecer [33] VT (a) *Culin* to garnish (b) *(adornar)* to decorate (c) *Mil* to garrison

guarnición NF (a) *Culin* garnish (b) *Mil* garrison

guarro, -a *Esp* **1** ADJ filthy
  2 NM,F pig

guarura NM *Méx Fam* bodyguard

guasa NF mockery

guasca NF *Chile, Perú* whip

guasearse VPR *Fam* to tease

guaso, -a ADJ (a) *Chile (campesino)* peasant (b) *Andes, RP* ser un g. *(grosero)* to be crude o coarse; *(maleducado)* to be rude

guasón, -ona **1** ADJ humorous
  2 NM,F joker

guata NF (a) *(relleno)* padding (b) *Andes Fam (barriga)* belly

Guatemala N (a) *(país)* Guatemala (b) *(ciudad)* Guatemala City

guatemalteco, -a ADJ & NM,F Guatemalan

guay ADJ INV *Esp Fam* cool, *US* neat

guayaba NF *(fruta)* guava

guayabera NF *CAm, Carib, Col* short jacket

guayabo NM (a) *(árbol)* guava tree (b) *Andes Fam (resaca)* hangover

guepardo NM cheetah

güero, -a ADJ *Méx Fam* blond, f blonde, fair-haired

guerra NF war; en g. at war; g. bacteriológica germ warfare; g. civil/fría/mundial/nuclear civil/cold/world/nuclear war; *Fam* dar g. to be a real nuisance

guerrero, -a **1** NM,F warrior
  2 ADJ warlike

guerrilla NF (a) *(partida armada)* guerrilla force o band (b) *(lucha)* guerrilla warfare

guerrillero, -a **1** ADJ guerrilla; ataque g. guerrilla attack
  2 NM,F guerrilla

güevón, -ona NM,F *Andes, Arg, Ven muy Fam (estúpido)* Br prat, *US* jerk

guía 1 NMF *(persona)* guide
  2 NF (a) *(norma)* guideline (b) *(libro)* guide; *(lista)* directory; *Esp, RP* g. telefónica o de teléfonos telephone directory

guiar [29] **1** VT (a) *(indicar el camino)* to guide (b) *Aut* to drive; *Náut* to steer; *(caballo, bici)* to ride
  2 guiarse VPR guiarse por to be guided by, to go by

guija NF pebble

guijarro NM pebble

guillotina NF guillotine

guinda NF *(fruto)* morello (cherry)

guindilla NF chilli

Guinea Ecuatorial N Equatorial Guinea

guineo NM *Andes, CAm* banana

guiñapo NM (a) *(andrajo)* rag (b) *Fig (persona)* wreck; poner a algn como un g. to tear sb to pieces

guiñar VT to wink

guiño NM wink

guiñol NM puppet theatre

guión NM (a) *Cin & TV* script (b) *Ling* hyphen, dash (c) *(esquema)* sketch

guionista NMF scriptwriter

guiri NMF *Esp Fam* foreigner

guirigay (pl guirigays o guirigáis) NM hubbub

guirnalda NF garland

guisa NF way, manner; a g. de as, by way of

guisado NM *Culin* stew

guisante NM *esp Esp* pea

guisar VT to cook

guiso NM dish; *(guisado)* stew

guita NF *Esp, RP Fam* dough

guitarra 1 NF guitar
  2 NMF guitarist

guitarreada NF *CSur* singalong *(to guitars)*

guitarrista NMF guitarist

gula NF gluttony

gurí, -isa NM,F *RP Fam (niño)* kid, child; *(chico)* lad, boy; *(chica)* lass, girl

gusano NM worm; *(oruga)* caterpillar; *Fam Pey (exiliado cubano)* = anti-Castro Cuban living in exile; g. de seda silkworm

gustar 1 VT (a) me gusta el vino I like wine; me gustaban los caramelos I used to like sweets; me gusta nadar I like swimming; me gustaría ir I would like to go (b) *Fml* ¿gustas? would you like some?; cuando gustes whenever you like
  2 VI g. de to enjoy

gusto NM (a) *(sentido)* taste (b) *(en fórmulas de cortesía)* pleasure; con (mucho) g. with (great) pleasure; tanto g. pleased to meet you (c) estar a g. to feel comfortable o at ease; por g. for the sake of it; ser de buen/mal g. to be in good/bad taste; tener buen/mal g. to have good/bad taste; tenemos el gusto de comunicarle que ... we are pleased to inform you that ...

gutural ADJ guttural

H, h [atʃe] NF *(letra)* H, h; **bomba H** H-bomb

ha INDIC PRES *de* **haber**

haba NF broad bean

> Takes the masculine articles **el** and **un**.

Habana NF **La H.** Havana

habano NM Havana cigar

haber [14] **1** V AUX **(a)** *(en tiempos compuestos)* to have; **lo he visto** I have seen it; **ya lo había hecho** he had already done it **(b) h. de** + *infin* *(obligación)* to have to; **has de ser bueno** you must be good

2 V IMPERS *(special form of present tense:* **hay)** **(a)** *(existir, estar) (singular used also with plural nouns)* **hay** there is/are; **había** there was/were; **había un gato en el tejado** there was a cat on the roof; **había muchos libros** there were a lot of books; **hay 500 km entre Madrid y Granada** it's 500 km from Madrid to Granada

(b) h. que + *infin* it is necessary to; **hay que trabajar** you've got to *o* you must work; **habrá que comprobarlo** I/you/we/*etc* will have to check it

(c) *(tener lugar)* **habrá una fiesta** there will be a party; **hoy hay partido** there's a match today; **los accidentes habidos en esta carretera** the accidents which have happened on this road

(d) había una vez … once upon a time …; **no hay de qué** you're welcome, don't mention it; **¿qué hay?** how are things?

3 NM **(a)** *Fin* credit; **haberes** assets **(b) en su h.** in his possession

habichuela NF *Esp, Carib, Col* bean

hábil ADJ **(a)** *(diestro)* skilful **(b)** *(astuto)* smart **(c) días hábiles** working days

habilidad NF **(a)** *(destreza)* skill **(b)** *(astucia)* cleverness

habilitar VT **(a)** *(espacio)* to fit out **(b)** *Der (autorizar)* to authorize **(c)** *(financiar)* to finance

habiloso, -a ADJ *Chile* shrewd, astute

habitación NF *(cuarto)* room; *(dormitorio)* bedroom; **h. individual/doble** single/double room

habitante NMF inhabitant

habitar 1 VT to live in, to inhabit
2 VI to live

hábitat *(pl* **hábitats)** NM habitat

hábito NM **(a)** *(costumbre)* habit **(b)** *Rel* habit

habitual ADJ usual, habitual; *(cliente, lector)* regular

habituar [30] **1** VT to accustom **(a** to)
2 habituarse VPR **habituarse a** to get used to, to become accustomed to

habla NF **(a)** *(idioma)* language; **países de h. española** Spanish-speaking countries **(b)** *(facultad de hablar)* speech; **quedarse sin h.** to be left speechless **(c)** *Tel* **¡al h.!** speaking!

> Takes the masculine articles **el** and **un**.

hablado, -a ADJ spoken; **el inglés h.** spoken English; **mal h.** coarse, foul-mouthed

hablador, -a ADJ *(parlanchín)* talkative; *(chismoso)* gossipy

habladuría NF *(rumor)* rumour; *(chisme)* piece of gossip

hablante NMF speaker

hablar 1 VI to speak, to talk; **h. con algn** to speak to sb; **¡ni h.!** certainly not!; *Fam* **¡quién fue a h.!** look who's talking!

2 VT **(a)** *(idioma)* to speak; **habla alemán** he speaks German **(b)** *(tratar un asunto)* to talk over, to discuss

3 hablarse VPR **(a)** *(dos personas)* to speak *o* talk to one another **(b) se habla español** *(en letrero)* Spanish spoken

habré INDIC FUT *de* **haber**

hacendado, -a NM,F **(a)** *(terrateniente)* landowner **(b)** *CSur (ganadero)* rancher

hacendoso, -a ADJ houseproud

hacer [15] **1** VT **(a)** *(crear, producir, fabricar)* to make; **h. una casa** to build a house **(b)** *(obrar, ejecutar)* to do; **eso no se hace** it isn't done; **hazme un favor** do me a favour; **¿qué haces?** *(en este momento)* what are you doing?; *(para vivir)* what do you do (for a living)?; **tengo mucho que h.** I have a lot to do; **h. deporte** to do sports; **h. una carrera/ medicina** to do a degree/medicine **(c)** *(conseguir) (amigos, dinero)* to make **(d)** *(obligar)* to make; **hazle callar/trabajar** make him shut up/work **(e)** *(arreglar)* to make; **h. la cama** to make the bed **(f)** *Mat (sumar)* to make; **y con éste hacen cien** and that makes a hundred **(g)** *(dar aspecto)* to make look; **el negro le hace más delgado** black makes him look slimmer **(h)** *(sustituyendo a otro verbo)* to do; **ya no puedo leer como solía hacerlo** I can't read as well as I used to **(i)** *(representar)* to play; **h. el bueno** to play

the (part of the) goody
(**j**) **¡bien hecho!** well done!
2 VI (**a**) *(actuar)* to play; **hizo de Desdémona** she played Desdemona (**b**) **h. por** *o* **para** + *infin* to try to; **hice por venir** I tried to come (**c**) *(fingir)* to pretend; **h. como si** to act as if (**d**) *(convenir)* to be suitable; **a las ocho si te hace** will eight o'clock be all right for you?
3 V IMPERS (**a**) **hace calor/frío** it's hot/cold (**b**) *(tiempo transcurrido)* ago; **hace mucho (tiempo)** a long time ago; **hace dos días que no le veo** I haven't seen him for two days; **hace dos años que vivo en Glasgow** I've been living in Glasgow for two years
4 hacerse VPR (**a**) *(volverse)* to become, to grow; **hacerse viejo** to grow old (**b**) *(simular)* to pretend; **hacerse el dormido** to pretend to be sleeping (**c**) *(apropiarse)* to get hold of (**d**) **hacerse a** *(habituarse)* to get used to; **enseguida me hago a todo** I soon get used to anything

hacha NF (**a**) *(herramienta)* axe (**b**) *Fam* **ser un h. en algo** to be an ace *o* a wizard at sth

> Takes the masculine articles **el** and **un**.

hachís NM hashish
hacia PREP (**a**) *(dirección)* towards, to; **h. abajo** down, downwards; **h. adelante** forwards; **h. arriba** up, upwards; **h. atrás** back, backwards (**b**) *(tiempo)* at about, at around; **h. las tres** at about three o'clock
hacienda NF (**a**) *(finca)* country estate *o* property (**b**) *Fin* **(el Ministerio de) H.** *Br* ≃ the Treasury, *US* ≃ the Department of the Treasury
hacinamiento NM *(de gente)* overcrowding
hacinarse VPR *(gente)* to be crowded together
hada NF fairy; **cuento de hadas** fairy tale; **h. madrina** fairy godmother

> Takes the masculine articles **el** and **un**.

hado NM destiny
hago INDIC PRES *de* **hacer**
Haití N Haiti
hala INTERJ *Esp* **¡h.!** *(para dar ánimo, prisa)* come on!; *(para expresar incredulidad)* no!, you're joking!; *(para expresar admiración, sorpresa)* wow!
halagar [42] VT to flatter
halago NM flattery
halagüeño, -a ADJ *(noticia, impresión)* promising
halcón NM falcon; **h. peregrino** peregrine (falcon)
hall [χol] *(pl* **halls**) NM entrance hall, foyer
hallar 1 VT *(encontrar)* to find; *(averiguar)* to find out; *(descubrir)* to discover
2 hallarse VPR *(estar)* to be, to find oneself; *(estar situado)* to be situated
hallazgo NM (**a**) *(descubrimiento)* discovery (**b**) *(cosa encontrada)* find

halógeno, -a ADJ *Quím* halogenous
halterofilia NF weightlifting
hamaca NF hammock; *(mecedora)* rocking chair
hambre NF *(apetito)* hunger; *(inanición)* starvation; *(catástrofe)* famine; **tener h.** to be hungry

> Takes the masculine articles **el** and **un**.

hambriento, -a ADJ starving
hamburguesa NF hamburger, *Br* beefburger
hampa NF underworld

> Takes the masculine articles **el** and **un**.

hámster ['χamster] *(pl* **hámsters**) NM hamster
han INDIC PRES *de* **haber**
hangar NM hangar
harapo NM rag; **hecho un h.** in tatters
hardware ['χarwer] NM *Inform* hardware
haré INDIC FUT *de* **hacer**
harén NM harem
harina NF flour
hartar 1 VT (**a**) *(cansar, fastidiar)* to annoy (**b**) *(atiborrar)* to satiate; **el dulce harta enseguida** sweet things soon fill you up
2 hartarse VPR (**a**) *(saciar el apetito)* to eat one's fill (**b**) *(cansarse)* to get fed up (**de** with), to grow tired (**de** of)
harto, -a 1 ADJ (**a**) *(de comida)* full (**b**) *(cansado)* fed up; **¡me tienes h.!** I'm fed up with you!; **estoy h. de trabajar** I'm fed up (with) working (**c**) *Am salvo RP (mucho)* lots of; **tiene h. dinero** he's got lots of money
2 ADV (**a**) *Esp Fml (muy)* very (**b**) *Am salvo RP (muy, mucho)* really
hartura NF **¡qué h.!** what a drag!
has INDIC PRES *de* **haber**
hasta 1 PREP (**a**) *(lugar)* up to, as far as, down to (**b**) *(tiempo)* until, till, up to; **h. el domingo** until Sunday; **h. el final** right to the end; **h. la fecha** up to now; **h. luego** see you later (**c**) *(con cantidad)* up to, as many as (**d**) *(incluso)* even (**e**) *CAm, Col, Ecuad, Méx (no antes de)* **pintaremos la casa h. fin de mes** we won't paint the house till the end of the month
2 CONJ **h. que** until
hastiado, -a ADJ sick, tired (**de** of)
hastiar [29] VT to sicken
hastío NM weariness
hato NM bundle
hay INDIC PRES *de* **haber**
haya¹ NF (**a**) *Bot (árbol)* beech (**b**) *(madera)* beech (wood)

> Takes the masculine articles **el** and **un**.

haya² SUBJ PRES *de* **haber**
haz¹ NM (**a**) *Agr* sheaf (**b**) *(de luz)* shaft
haz² NF *(de hoja)* top side
haz³ IMPERAT *de* **hacer**
hazaña NF deed, exploit

hazmerreír NM laughing stock

he¹ ADV **he ahí/aquí ...** there/here you have ...

he² INDIC PRES *de* **haber**

hebilla NF buckle

hebra NF thread; *(de carne)* sinew; *(de madera)* grain; *Esp* **pegar la h.** to chat

hebreo, -a 1 ADJ Hebrew
2 NM,F Hebrew

hecatombe NF disaster

hechicería NF witchcraft

hechicero, -a 1 ADJ bewitching
2 NM,F *(hombre)* wizard, sorcerer; *(mujer)* witch, sorceress

hechizar [40] VT (**a**) *(embrujar)* to cast a spell on (**b**) *Fig (fascinar)* to bewitch, to charm

hechizo NM (**a**) *(embrujo)* spell (**b**) *Fig (fascinación)* fascination, charm

hecho, -a 1 ADJ (**a**) *(carne)* done (**b**) *(persona)* mature (**c**) *(ropa)* ready-made
2 NM (**a**) *(realidad)* fact; **el h. es que ...** the fact is that ...; **de h.** in fact (**b**) *(suceso)* event, incident (**c**) *(acto)* act, deed

hechura NF *(forma)* shape; *Cost* cut

hectárea NF hectare

hectolitro NM hectolitre

heder [3] VI to stink, to smell foul

hediondo, -a ADJ foul-smelling

hedor NM stink, stench

hegemonía NF hegemony

helada NF frost

heladera NF *CSur (nevera)* refrigerator, *Br* fridge, *US* icebox

heladería NF ice-cream parlour

helado, -a 1 NM ice cream
2 ADJ (**a**) *(muy frío)* frozen, freezing cold; **estoy h. (de frío)** I'm frozen (**b**) *Fig* **quedarse h.** *(atónito)* to be flabbergasted

helar [1] **1** VT *(congelar)* to freeze
2 VIMPERS to freeze; **anoche heló** there was a frost last night
3 **helarse** VPR *(congelarse)* to freeze

helecho NM *Bot* fern

hélice NF (**a**) *Av & Náut* propeller (**b**) *Anat, Arquit & Mat* helix

helicóptero NM *Av* helicopter

helipuerto NM *Av* heliport

hematoma NM *Med* haematoma

hembra NF (**a**) *Bot & Zool* female (**b**) *(mujer)* woman (**c**) *Téc* female; *(de tornillo)* nut; *(de enchufe)* socket

hemiciclo NM *(en parlamento)* chamber

hemisferio NM hemisphere

hemorragia NF haemorrhage

hemos INDIC PRES *de* **haber**

henchir [6] VT to fill (up)

hender [3] VT to crack, to split

hendidura NF crack

hendir [5] VT = **hender**

heno NM hay

hepatitis NF INV hepatitis

heráldica NF heraldry

herbicida NM weedkiller, herbicide

herbívoro, -a 1 ADJ herbivorous, grass-eating
2 NM,F herbivore

herbolario NM herbalist's (shop)

herboristería NF herbalist's (shop)

hercio NM Hertz

heredad NF (**a**) *(finca)* country estate (**b**) *(conjunto de bienes)* private estate

heredar VT (**a**) *Der* to inherit (**b**) **ha heredado la sonrisa de su madre** she's got her mother's smile

heredero, -a NM,F *(hombre)* heir; *(mujer)* heiress; **príncipe h.** crown prince

hereditario, -a ADJ hereditary

hereje NMF *Rel* heretic

herejía NF *Rel* heresy

herencia NF (**a**) *Der* inheritance, legacy (**b**) *Biol* heredity

herida NF *(lesión)* injury; *(corte)* wound

herido, -a NM,F injured person; **no hubo heridos** there were no casualties

herir [5] **1** VT (**a**) *(físicamente) (lesionar)* to injure; *(cortar)* to wound (**b**) *(emocionalmente)* to hurt, to wound (**c**) *(vista)* to offend
2 **herirse** VPR to injure o hurt oneself

hermana NF (**a**) *(familiar)* sister; **h. política** sister-in-law; **prima h.** first cousin (**b**) *Rel (monja)* sister

hermanado, -a ADJ twinned; **ciudad hermanada** twin town

hermanar 1 VT (**a**) *(personas)* to unite spiritually (**b**) *(ciudades)* to twin (**c**) *(unir)* to unite, to combine
2 **hermanarse** VPR (**a**) *(ciudades)* to twin (**b**) *(combinar)* to combine

hermanastro, -a NM,F *(hombre)* stepbrother; *(mujer)* stepsister

hermandad NF (**a**) *(grupo)* fraternity, brotherhood, sisterhood (**b**) *(relación)* brotherhood, sisterhood

hermano NM (**a**) *(familiar)* brother; **h. político** brother-in-law; **primo h.** first cousin (**b**) *Rel (fraile)* brother (**c**) **hermanos** brothers and sisters

herméticamente ADV **h. cerrado** hermetically sealed

hermético, -a ADJ (**a**) *(cierre)* hermetic, airtight (**b**) *(persona)* uncommunicative

hermetismo NM uncommunicativeness

hermoso, -a ADJ (**a**) *(bello)* beautiful, lovely (**b**) *(grande)* fine

hermosura NF beauty

héroe NM hero

heroico, -a ADJ heroic

heroína NF (**a**) *(mujer)* heroine (**b**) *(droga)* heroin

heroinómano, -a NM,F heroin addict

heroísmo NM heroism

herradura NF horseshoe

herramienta NF *Téc* tool; **caja de herramientas** toolbox

herrar [1] VT (**a**) *(caballo)* to shoe (**b**) *(ganado)* to brand

herrería NF forge, smithy

herrero NM blacksmith, smith

herrumbre NF rust

hervidero NM *(lugar)* hotbed

hervir [5] **1** VT to boil
2 VI (**a**) *Culin* to boil; **romper a h.** to come to the boil (**b**) *(abundar)* to swarm, to seethe (**de** with)

heterodoxo, -a ADJ unorthodox

heterogéneo, -a ADJ heterogeneous

heterosexual ADJ & NMF heterosexual

hez NF (**a**) *(usu pl) (poso)* sediment, dregs (**b**) **heces** faeces

hiato NM *Ling* hiatus

híbrido, -a ADJ & NM hybrid

hice PT INDEF *de* **hacer**

hiciste PT INDEF *de* **hacer**

hidalgo NM *Hist* nobleman, gentleman

hidalguía NF nobility; *Fig* chivalry, gentlemanliness

hidratación NF *(de la piel)* moisturizing

hidratante ADJ moisturizing; **crema/leche h.** moisturizing cream/lotion

hidratar VT *(piel)* to moisturize; *Quím* to hydrate

hidráulico, -a ADJ hydraulic; **energía hidráulica** hydroelectric energy

hidroavión NM seaplane, *US* hydroplane

hidrófilo, -a ADJ **algodón h.** *Br* cotton wool, *Am* absorbent cotton

hidrógeno NM *Quím* hydrogen

hiedra NF ivy

hiel NF (**a**) *(bilis)* bile (**b**) *(mala intención)* spleen, bitterness

hielo NM ice; *Fig* **romper el h.** to break the ice

hiena NF hyena

hierba NF (**a**) *(césped)* grass; *Culin* herb; **mala h.** *Bot* weed; *Fig (persona)* bad lot; *Fam Hum* **y otras hierbas** among others; **h. luisa** lemon verbena (**b**) *Fam (marihuana)* grass

hierbabuena NF mint

hierro NM (**a**) *(metal)* iron; **h. forjado** wrought iron (**b**) *(punta de arma)* head, point (**c**) *(marca en el ganado)* brand

hígado NM (**a**) *Anat* liver (**b**) *Euf* guts

higiene NF hygiene

higiénico, -a ADJ hygienic; **papel h.** toilet paper

higo NM fig; *Fam Fig* **hecho un h.** wizened, crumpled

higuera NF *Bot* fig tree

hijastro, -a NM,F *(hombre)* stepson; *(mujer)* stepdaughter

hijo, -a NM,F (**a**) *(hombre)* son; *(mujer)* daughter; *Pey* **h. de papá** rich kid; *Vulg* **h. de puta** *o Méx* **de la chingada** bastard, *US* asshole (**b**) **hijos** children

hijoputa NM *Vulg* bastard, *US* asshole

hilandería NF mill; *(de algodón)* cotton mill

hilandero, -a NM,F spinner

hilar VT & VI to spin; *Fig* **h. muy fino** to split hairs

hilaridad NF hilarity, mirth

hilera NF line, row

hilo NM (**a**) *Cost* thread; *(grueso)* yarn; **h. dental** dental floss (**b**) *Fig (de historia, discurso)* thread; *(de pensamiento)* train; **perder el h.** to lose the thread; **h. musical** background music (**c**) *Tex* linen

hilvanar VT (**a**) *Cost Br* to tack, *US* to baste (**b**) *Fig (ideas etc)* to outline

himno NM hymn; **h. nacional** national anthem

hincapié NM **hacer h. en** *(insistir)* to insist on; *(subrayar)* to emphasize, to stress

hincar [44] **1** VT *(clavar)* to drive (in); **h. el diente a** to sink one's teeth into
2 hincarse VPR **hincarse de rodillas** to kneel (down)

hincha *Fam* **1** NMF *Ftb* fan, supporter
2 NF *(antipatía)* grudge, dislike; *Esp* **me tiene h.** he's got it in for me

hinchada NF *Fam Ftb* fans, supporters

hinchado, -a ADJ (**a**) *(inflado)* inflated, blown up (**b**) *Med (cara etc)* swollen, puffed up; *(estómago)* bloated (**c**) *Fig (estilo)* bombastic, pompous

hinchar 1 VT (**a**) *(inflar)* to inflate, to blow up (**b**) *Fig (exagerar)* to inflate, to exaggerate
2 hincharse VPR (**a**) *Med* to swell (up) (**b**) *Fam* **me hinché de comida** I stuffed myself; **me hinché de llorar** I cried for all I was worth

hinchazón NF *Med* swelling

hindú ADJ & NMF Hindu

hipermercado NM hypermarket

hipermetropía NF long-sightedness, *Espec* hypermetropia, *US* hypertropia

hipertensión NF high blood pressure

hipertexto NM *Inform* hypertext

hípica NF *(carreras de caballos)* horseracing; *(equitación)* showjumping

hípico, -a ADJ **concurso h.** *(de las carreras)* horseraces; *(de la equitación)* showjumping

hipnotizar [40] VT to hypnotize

hipo NM hiccups, hiccoughs; **me ha dado h.** it's given me the hiccups

hipocondríaco, -a ADJ & NM,F hypochondriac

hipocresía NF hypocrisy

hipócrita 1 ADJ hypocritical
2 NMF hypocrite

hipódromo NM racetrack, racecourse

hipopótamo NM hippopotamus

hipoteca NF *Fin* mortgage

hipotecar [44] VT (**a**) *Fin* to mortgage (**b**) *Fig* to jeopardize

hipótesis NF INV hypothesis

hipotético, -a ADJ hypothetical

hippy, hippie ['χipi] (*pl* **hippies**) ADJ & NMF hippy

hiriente ADJ offensive, wounding; (*palabras*) cutting

hirsuto, -a ADJ hirsute, hairy; (*cerdoso*) bristly

hispánico, -a ADJ Hispanic, Spanish

hispanidad NF **el Día de la H.** Columbus Day (*12 October*)

hispano, -a 1 ADJ (*español*) Spanish; (*español y sudamericano*) Hispanic; (*sudamericano*) Spanish American
2 NM,F (*hispanoamericano*) Spanish American; (*estadounidense*) Hispanic

Hispanoamérica NF Latin America

hispanoamericano, -a ADJ & NM,F Latin American

hispanohablante 1 ADJ Spanish-speaking
2 NMF Spanish speaker

histeria NF hysteria; **un ataque de h.** hysterics

histérico, -a ADJ hysterical; *Fam Fig* **me pones h.** you're driving me mad

historia NF (**a**) (*ciencia*) history; **esto pasará a la h.** this will go down in history (**b**) (*narración*) story, tale; *Fam* **¡déjate de historias!** don't give me that!

historiador, -a NM,F historian

historial NM (**a**) *Med* medical record, case history (**b**) (*antecedentes*) background

historiar [29] VT to recount

histórico, -a ADJ (**a**) (*novela, legado*) historical; (*centro*) historic (**b**) (*auténtico*) factual, true; **hechos históricos** true facts (**c**) (*de gran importancia*) historic; **máximo/mínimo h.** all-time high/low

historieta NF (**a**) (*cuento*) short story, tale (**b**) (*tira cómica*) comic strip

hito NM milestone

hizo PT INDEF *de* hacer

hnos. (*abr* **Hermanos**) Bros

hobby ['χoβi] (*pl* **hobbys**) NM hobby

hocico NM (**a**) (*de animal*) snout (**b**) (*de persona*) mug, snout; *Fam* **meter los hocicos en algo** to stick o poke one's nose into sth

hockey ['χokei] NM hockey; **h. sobre hielo** *Br* ice hockey, *US* hockey; **h. sobre hierba** *Br* hockey, *US* field hockey

hogar NM (**a**) (*casa*) home (**b**) (*de la chimenea*) hearth, fireplace (**c**) *Fig* **formar o crear un h.** (*familia*) to start a family

hogareño, -a ADJ (*vida*) home, family; (*persona*) home-loving, stay-at-home

hoguera NF bonfire

hoja NF (**a**) *Bot* leaf (**b**) (*pétalo*) petal (**c**) (*de papel*) sheet, leaf; **h. de cálculo** spreadsheet (**d**) (*de libro*) leaf, page (**e**) (*de metal*) sheet (**f**) (*de cuchillo, espada*) blade (**g**) (*impreso*) hand-out, printed sheet (**h**) (*de puerta, ventana*) leaf

hojalata NF tin, tin plate

hojaldre NM *Culin* puff pastry

hojarasca NF fallen o dead leaves

hojear VT to leaf through, to flick through

hola INTERJ hello!, hullo!, hi!

Holanda N Holland

holandés, -esa 1 ADJ Dutch
2 NM,F (*hombre*) Dutchman; (*mujer*) Dutchwoman
3 NM (*idioma*) Dutch

holding NM *Fin* holding company

holgado, -a ADJ (**a**) (*ropa*) loose, baggy (**b**) (*económicamente*) comfortable (**c**) (*espacio*) roomy; **andar h. de tiempo** to have plenty of time

holgar [2] VI (**a**) (*no trabajar*) to be idle (**b**) (*sobrar*) **huelga decir que …** it goes without saying that …

holgazán, -ana 1 ADJ lazy, idle
2 NM,F lazybones, layabout

holgura NF (**a**) (*de ropa*) looseness (**b**) (*espacio*) space, roominess; *Téc* play, give (**c**) (*económica*) affluence, comfort; **vivir con h.** to be comfortably off, to be well-off

hollar [2] VT to walk on; **terrenos jamás hollados** uncharted territory

hollín NM soot

hombre 1 NM (**a**) (*individuo*) man; **de h. a h.** man-to-man; **¡pobre h.!** poor *Br* chap o *US* guy!; **ser muy h.** to be every inch a man; **h. de estado** statesman; **h. de negocios** businessman (**b**) (*especie*) mankind, man
2 INTERJ *Esp* **¡h.! ¡qué alegría verte!** (hey,) how nice to see you!; **¡sí, h.!** sure!

hombrera NF shoulder pad

hombría NF manliness, virility

hombrillo NM *Ven* (*arcén*) (*de carretera*) verge; (*de autopista*) *Br* hard shoulder, *US* shoulder

hombro NM shoulder; **a hombros** on one's shoulders; **encogerse de hombros** to shrug one's shoulders; **mirar a algn por encima del h.** to look down one's nose at sb

hombruno, -a ADJ mannish, butch

homenaje NM homage, tribute; **rendir h. a algn** to pay homage o tribute to sb

homenajear VT to pay tribute to

homeopatía NF homeopathy

homeopático, -a ADJ homeopathic

homicida 1 NMF (*hombre*) murderer; (*mujer*) murderess
2 ADJ homicidal; **el arma h.** the murder weapon

homicidio NM homicide

homogéneo, -a ADJ homogeneous, uniform

homologable ADJ comparable (**con** to)

homologar [42] VT to give official approval o recognition to

homólogo, -a 1 ADJ *(semejante)* equivalent **2** NM,F *(persona)* counterpart

homosexual ADJ & NMF homosexual

homosexualidad NF homosexuality

honda NF sling

hondo, -a ADJ **(a)** *(profundo)* deep; **plato h.** soup dish **(b)** *Fig (pesar)* profound, deep

hondonada NF *Geog* hollow, depression

hondura NF depth; *Fig* **meterse en honduras** *(profundizar)* to go into too much detail

Honduras N Honduras

hondureño, -a ADJ & NM,F Honduran

honestidad NF **(a)** *(honradez)* honesty, uprightness **(b)** *(decencia)* modesty

honesto, -a ADJ **(a)** *(honrado)* honest, upright **(b)** *(decente)* modest

hongo NM **(a)** *Bot* fungus; **h. venenoso** toadstool **(b)** *(sombrero) Br* bowler (hat), *US* derby

honor NM **(a)** *(virtud)* honour; **palabra de h.** word of honour **(b)** **en h. a la verdad ...** to be fair ...; **es un h. para mí** it's an honour for me **(c)** **hacer h. a** to live up to

honorable ADJ honourable

honorario, -a 1 ADJ honorary **2 honorarios** NMPL fees, fee

honorífico, -a ADJ honorific

honra NF **(a)** *(dignidad)* dignity, self-esteem **(b)** *(fama)* reputation, good name **(c)** *(honor)* honour; **me cabe la h. de ...** I have the honour of ...; **¡a mucha h.!** and proud of it!

honradez NF honesty, integrity

honrado, -a ADJ **(a)** *(de fiar)* honest **(b)** *(decente)* upright, respectable

honrar VT **(a)** *(respetar)* to honour **(b)** *(enaltecer)* to be a credit to

honrilla NF self-respect, pride

honroso, -a ADJ honourable

hora NF **(a)** *(60 minutos)* hour; **media h.** half an hour; **a altas horas de la madrugada** in the small hours; **dar la h.** to strike the hour; **(trabajo) por horas** (work) paid by the hour; *Esp* **h. punta,** *Am* **h. pico** *(de mucho tráfico)* rush hour; *(de agua, electricidad)* peak times; **horas extra** overtime (hours) **(b)** *(en un reloj, momento)* time; **¿qué h. es?** what time is it?; **a su h.** at the proper time; **a última h.** at the last moment; *Esp, Andes, Carib, RP* **la h. de la verdad** the moment of truth **(c)** *(cita)* appointment; **pedir h.** *(al médico etc)* to ask for an appointment

horadar VT to drill o bore a hole in

horario, -a 1 NM *Br* timetable, *US* schedule **2** ADJ time; *Rad* **señal horaria** pips

horca NF gallows *sing*

horcajadas: a horcajadas LOC ADVastride

horchata NF *Culin* = cold drink made from ground tiger nuts, water and sugar

horda NF horde, mob

horizontal ADJ horizontal

horizonte NM horizon

horma NF *(de zapato)* last

hormiga NF ant

hormigón NM *Constr* concrete; **h. armado** reinforced concrete

hormigonera NF concrete mixer

hormiguear VI to itch, to tingle; **me hormigueaba la pierna** I had pins and needles in my leg

hormigueo NM pins and needles, tingling o itching sensation

hormiguero NM **(a)** *Zool* anthill **(b)** *Fig* **ser un h.** *(lugar)* to be swarming (with people)

hormona NF hormone

hornada NF batch

hornear VT to bake

hornillo NM *(de cocinar)* stove; *(placa)* hotplate

horno NM *(cocina)* oven; *Téc* furnace; *(para cerámica, ladrillos)* kiln; *Culin* **pescado al h.** baked fish; *Fam Fig* **esta habitación es un h.** this room is boiling hot

horóscopo NM horoscope

horquilla NF **(a)** *(del pelo)* hairpin, *Br* hairgrip **(b)** *(estadística)* chart **(c)** **h. de precios** price range

horrendo, -a ADJ horrifying, horrible

hórreo NM *Agr* granary

horrible ADJ horrible, dreadful, awful

horripilante ADJ hair-raising, scary

horror NM **(a)** *(miedo)* horror, terror; **¡qué h.!** how awful!; *Fam* **tengo h. a las motos** I hate motorbikes **(b)** *Fam* **Fig me gusta horrores** *(muchísimo)* I like it an awful lot

horrorizar [40] VT to horrify, to terrify

horroroso, -a ADJ **(a)** *(que da miedo)* horrifying, terrifying **(b)** *Fam (muy feo)* hideous, ghastly **(c)** *Fam (malísimo)* awful, dreadful

hortaliza NF vegetable

hortelano, -a NM,F *Br* market gardener, *US* truck farmer

hortensia NF *Bot* hydrangea

hortera ADJ *Esp Fam (decoración, ropa, canción)* tacky, *Br* naff; **es muy h.** he has really tacky o *Br* naff taste

horterada NF *Esp Fam* tacky thing o act

hosco, -a ADJ surly, sullen

hospedaje NM lodgings, *Br* accommodation, *US* accommodations

hospedar 1 VT to put up, to lodge **2 hospedarse** VPR to stay (**en** at)

hospicio NM orphanage

hospital NM hospital

hospitalario, -a ADJ **(a)** *(acogedor)* hospitable **(b)** *Med* hospital; **instalaciones hospitalarias** hospital facilities

hospitalidad NF hospitality

hospitalizar [40] VT to take o send into hospital, to hospitalize

hostal NM guesthouse

hostelería NF *(negocio)* catering business; *(estudios)* hotel management

hostelero, -a NM,F *(hombre)* landlord; *(mujer)* landlady

hostería NF *CSur (hotel)* country hotel

hostia 1 NF (**a**) *Rel* host (**b**) *Esp Vulg (golpe)* bash (**c**) *Esp Vulg* **estar de mala h.** to be in a foul mood; **ser la h.** *(fantástico)* to be *Br* bloody o *US* goddamn amazing; *(penoso)* to be *Br* bloody o *US* goddamn awful
2 INTERJ *Vulg* damn! *Br* bloody hell!

hostiar [29] VT *Vulg* to bash, to sock

hostigar [42] VT to harass

hostil ADJ hostile

hostilidad NF hostility

hotel NM hotel

hotelero, -a 1 ADJ hotel; **el sector h.** the hotel sector
2 NM,F hotel-keeper, hotelier

hoy ADV (**a**) *(día)* today (**b**) *Fig (presente)* now; **h. (en) día** nowadays; **h. por h.** at the present time

hoya NF *Geog* dale, valley

hoyo NM (**a**) *(agujero)* hole, pit (**b**) *(sepultura)* grave (**c**) *(de golf)* hole

hoyuelo NM dimple

hoz NF *Agr* sickle; **la h. y el martillo** the hammer and sickle

HR *(abr Hostal Residencia)* boarding house

huachafo, -a ADJ *Perú Fam* tacky

huacho, -a ADJ & NM,F *Andes, RP* = guacho

huasipungo NM *Andes* = small plot of land given by landowner to Indians in exchange for their labour

huaso, -a NM,F *Chile Fam* farmer, peasant

hube PT INDEF *de* **haber**

hubiera SUBJ IMPERF *de* **haber**

hucha NF *Esp* piggy bank

hueco, -a 1 ADJ (**a**) *(vacío)* empty, hollow (**b**) *(sonido)* resonant
2 NM (**a**) *(cavidad)* hollow, hole (**b**) *(sitio no ocupado)* empty space (**c**) *(rato libre)* free time

huele INDIC PRES *de* **oler**

huelga NF strike; **estar en o de h.** to be on strike; **h. de brazos caídos** go-slow; **h. de celo** *Br* work-to-rule, *US* job action

huelguista NMF striker

huella NF (**a**) *(del pie)* footprint; *(de coche)* track; **h. dactilar** fingerprint (**b**) *Fig (vestigio)* trace, sign; **dejar h.** to leave one's mark

huérfano, -a NM,F orphan

huero, -a ADJ empty

huerta NF *Agr* (**a**) *(parcela)* *Br* market garden, *US* truck farm (**b**) *(región)* = irrigated area used for cultivation

huerto NM *(de verduras)* vegetable garden, kitchen garden; *(de frutales)* orchard

hueso NM (**a**) *Anat* bone; **estar en los huesos** to be all skin and bone (**b**) *(de fruto)* *Br* stone, *US* pit (**c**) *Fig (difícil)* hard work; *(profesor)* hard nut (**d**) *Méx (enchufe)* contact; *(trabajo fácil)* cushy job

huésped, -a NM,F *(invitado)* guest; *(en hotel etc)* lodger, boarder; **casa de huéspedes** guesthouse

hueste NF *Mil* army, host

huesudo, -a ADJ bony

huevada NF *Andes, RP muy Fam (dicho)* crap; **lo que dijiste es una h.** what you said is a load of crap

huevo NM (**a**) *(de animal)* egg; **h. duro** hard-boiled egg; **h. escalfado** poached egg; **h. frito** fried egg; **h. pasado por agua**, *Andes* **h. a la copa**, *Méx* **h. tibio** soft-boiled egg; **huevos revueltos** scrambled eggs (**b**) *Vulg* **huevos** *(testículos)* balls; **hacer algo por huevos** to do sth even if it kills you; **tener huevos** to have guts

huevón, -ona NM,F *muy Fam* (**a**) *Cuba, Méx (vago)* **es un h.** *Br* he's a lazy sod o git, *US* he's so goddamn lazy (**b**) *Andes, Arg, Ven (tonto, torpe) Br* prat, *US* jerk

huida NF flight, escape

huidizo, -a ADJ elusive

huipil NM *CAm, Méx* = colourful embroidered dress or blouse traditionally worn by Indian women

huir [37] VI to run away (**de** from), to flee; **h. de la cárcel** to escape from prison; **h. de algn** to avoid sb

hule NM (**a**) *(tela impermeable)* oilcloth, oilskin (**b**) *(de mesa)* tablecloth (**c**) *CAm, Méx (caucho)* rubber

hulla NF soft coal

humanidad NF (**a**) *(género humano)* humanity, mankind (**b**) *(cualidad)* humanity, humaneness (**c**) *(bondad)* compassion, kindness

humanitario, -a ADJ humanitarian

humano, -a 1 ADJ (**a**) *(relativo al hombre)* human (**b**) *(compasivo)* humane
2 NM human (being); **ser h.** human being

humareda NF cloud of smoke; **¡qué h.!** what a lot of smoke!, it's so smoky!

humear VI *(echar humo)* to smoke; *(arrojar vapor)* to steam, to be steaming hot

humedad NF *(atmosférica)* humidity; *(de lugar)* dampness; **a prueba de h.** damp-proof

humedecer [33] **1** VT to moisten, to dampen
2 humedecerse VPR to become damp o wet o moist

húmedo, -a ADJ *(casa, ropa)* damp; *(clima)* humid, damp, moist

humildad NF humility

humilde ADJ humble

humillación NF humiliation

humillante ADJ humiliating, humbling

humillar 1 VT *(rebajar)* to humiliate, to humble **2 humillarse** VPR **humillarse ante algn** to humble oneself before sb

humita NF (**a**) *Chile (pajarita)* bow tie (**b**) *Andes, Arg (pasta de maíz)* = paste made of mashed *Br* maize *o US* corn kernels mixed with cheese, chilli, onion and other ingredients, wrapped in a *Br* maize *o US* corn husk and steamed

humo NM *(de combustión)* smoke; *(vapor)* steam; *(de vehículo)* fumes; *Fig* **¡qué humos tiene!** she thinks a lot of herself!

humor NM (**a**) *(genio)* mood; **estar de buen/ mal h.** to be in a good/bad mood (**b**) *(carácter)* temper; **es persona de mal h.** he's bad-tempered (**c**) *(gracia)* humour; **sentido del h.** sense of humour

humorismo NM humour

humorista NMF humorist; **h. gráfico** cartoonist

humorístico, -a ADJ humorous, funny

hundido, -a ADJ (**a**) *(barco)* sunken; *(ojos)* deep-set (**b**) *Fig (abatido)* down, demoralized

hundimiento NM (**a**) *(de barco)* sinking (**b**) *(de edificio)* collapse (**c**) *(de tierra)* subsidence (**d**) *Fin* crash, slump; *(ruina)* downfall

hundir 1 VT (**a**) *(barco)* to sink (**b**) *(edificio)* to bring *o* knock down (**c**) *Fig (desmoralizar)* to demoralize **2 hundirse** VPR (**a**) *(barco)* to sink (**b**) *(edificio)* to collapse (**c**) *Fig (empresa)* to collapse, to crash

húngaro, -a 1 ADJ Hungarian **2** NM,F *(persona)* Hungarian **3** NM *(idioma)* Hungarian

Hungría N Hungary

huracán NM hurricane

huraño, -a ADJ *Pey* unsociable

hurgar [42] **1** VI *(rebuscar)* to rummage around (**en** in); *(con dedo, palo)* to poke around (**en** in) **2 hurgarse** VPR **hurgarse la nariz** to pick one's nose

hurón, -ona NM *Zool* ferret

hurtadillas: a hurtadillas LOC ADV stealthily, on the sly

hurtar VT to steal, to pilfer

hurto NM petty theft, pilfering

husmear 1 VT *(olfatear)* to sniff out, to scent **2** VI *Fig (curiosear)* to snoop, to pry

huyo INDIC PRES *de* **huir**

I, i [i] NF *(letra)* I, i; **i griega** Y, y

ib. *(abr* **ibídem)** ibid.

ibérico, -a ADJ Iberian

Iberoamérica N Latin America

iberoamericano, -a ADJ & NM,F Latin American

iceberg *(pl* **icebergs)** NM iceberg

icono NM icon

iconoclasta 1 ADJ iconoclastic
2 NMF iconoclast

iconografía NF iconography

ictericia NF *Med* jaundice

I+D *(abr* **Investigación y Desarrollo)** R&D

íd. *(abr* **ídem)** id., idem.

ida NF *(billete de)* **i. y vuelta** *Br* return (ticket), *US* round-trip (ticket); **idas y venidas** comings and goings

idea NF **(a)** *(concepto, ocurrencia)* idea; **hacerse a la i. de** to get used to the idea of; *Fam* **ni i.** no idea, not a clue; **i. fija** fixed idea **(b)** *(opinión)* opinion; **cambiar de i.** to change one's mind **(c)** *(intención)* intention; **a mala i.** on purpose

ideal ADJ & NM ideal

idealismo NM idealism

idealista 1 ADJ idealistic
2 NMF idealist

idealizar [40] VT to idealize, to glorify

idear VT **(a)** *(inventar)* to devise, to invent **(b)** *(concebir)* to think up, to conceive

ídem ADV idem, ditto; *Fam* **í. de í.** exactly the same

idéntico, -a ADJ identical

identidad NF identity; **carnet de i.** identity card

identificación NF identification

identificar [44] **1** VT to identify
2 identificarse VPR to identify oneself; *Fig* **identificarse con** to identify with

ideología NF ideology

ideológico, -a ADJ ideological

idílico, -a ADJ idyllic

idilio NM **(a)** *Lit (romance)* idyll **(b)** *Fig (romance)* romance, love affair

idioma NM language

idiomático, -a ADJ idiomatic

idiosincrasia NF idiosyncrasy

idiota 1 ADJ idiotic, stupid
2 NMF idiot, fool

idiotez NF idiocy, stupidity

ido, -a ADJ **(a)** *(distraído)* absent-minded **(b)** *Fam (chiflado)* crazy, nuts

idólatra 1 ADJ idolatrous
2 NMF *(hombre)* idolater; *(mujer)* idolatress

idolatrar VT to worship; *Fig* to idolize

idolatría NF idolatry

ídolo NM idol

idóneo, -a ADJ suitable, fit

iglesia NF **(a)** *(edificio)* church **(b)** **la I.** *(institución)* the Church

ignominia NF ignominy

ignorancia NF ignorance

ignorante 1 ADJ **(a)** *(sin instrucción)* ignorant **(b)** *(no informado)* ignorant, unaware **(de** of)
2 NMF ignoramus

ignorar 1 VT **(a)** *(algo)* not to know **(b)** *(a algn)* to ignore
2 ignorarse VPR to be unknown

ignoto, -a ADJ unknown

igual 1 ADJ **(a)** *(idéntico)* the same, alike; **son todos iguales** they're all the same; **es i.** it doesn't matter; **i. que** the same as **(b)** *(equivalente)* equal; **a partes iguales** fifty-fifty **(c)** *Dep (empatados)* even; **treinta iguales** thirty all **(d)** *Mat* equal; **tres más tres i. a seis** three plus three equals six **(e)** **al i. que** just like **(f)** **por i.** equally
2 NMF equal; **de i. a i.** on an equal footing; **sin i.** unique, unrivalled
3 ADV **(a)** **lo haces i. que yo** you do it the same way I do **(b)** *Esp (posiblemente)* perhaps; **i. vengo** I'll probably come **(c)** *Andes, RP (aún así)* all the same; **estaba nublado pero i. fuimos a la playa** it was cloudy but we went to the beach all the same

igualar 1 VT **(a)** *(hacer igual)* to make equal **(b)** *(persona)* to be equal to; **nadie la iguala en generosidad** nobody is as generous as she is **(c)** *(nivelar)* to level **(d)** *Dep* **i. el partido** to equalize, to square the match
2 igualarse VPR **(a)** *(cosas diferentes)* to become equal **(b)** **igualarse con algn** to place oneself on an equal footing with sb

igualdad NF **(a)** *(equivalencia)* equality; **i. ante la ley** equality before the law **(b)** *(identidad)* sameness; **en i. de condiciones** on equal terms

igualitario, -a ADJ egalitarian

igualmente ADV equally; *(también)* also, likewise; *Fam* **encantado de conocerlo – ¡i.!** pleased to meet you – likewise!

ijada NF *Anat* flank

ikastola NF = primary school in the Basque Country where classes are given entirely in Basque

ikurriña NF = Basque national flag

ilegal ADJ illegal

ilegalidad NF illegality

ilegalmente ADV illegally

ilegible ADJ illegible, unreadable

ilegítimo, -a ADJ illegitimate

ileso, -a ADJ unhurt, unharmed

ilícito, -a ADJ illicit, unlawful

ilimitado, -a ADJ unlimited, limitless

Ilmo., -a *(abr* **Ilustrísimo)** His Excellence *o* Excellency

ilógico, -a ADJ illogical

iluminación NF *(alumbrado)* illumination, lighting

iluminar VT **(a)** *(dar luz a)* to illuminate, to light up; *(adornar con luces)* to light up **(b)** *(a persona)* to enlighten; *(tema)* to throw light upon

ilusión NF **(a)** *(esperanza)* hope; *(esperanza vana)* illusion, delusion; **hacerse ilusiones** to build up one's hopes **(b)** *(sueño)* dream **(c)** *Esp (emoción)* excitement, thrill; **me hace i. verla** I'm looking forward to seeing her; **¡qué i.!** how exciting!

ilusionar 1 VT **(a)** *(esperanzar)* to build up sb's hopes **(b)** *(entusiasmar)* to excite, to thrill
2 ilusionarse VPR **(a)** *(esperanzarse)* to build up one's hopes **(b)** *(entusiasmarse)* to be excited *o* thrilled **(con** about)

iluso, -a ADJ easily deceived, gullible

ilusorio, -a ADJ illusory, unreal

ilustración NF **(a)** *(grabado)* illustration, picture; *(ejemplo)* illustration **(b)** *(erudición)* learning, erudition; *Hist* **la I.** the Enlightenment

ilustrado, -a ADJ **(a)** *(con dibujos, ejemplos)* illustrated **(b)** *(erudito)* learned, erudite

ilustrar 1 VT **(a)** *(con dibujos, ejemplos)* to illustrate **(b)** *(aclarar)* to explain, to make clear
2 ilustrarse VPR to acquire knowledge **(sobre** of), to learn **(sobre** about)

ilustrativo, -a ADJ illustrative

ilustre ADJ illustrious, distinguished

imagen NF **(a)** *(figura, apariencia)* image; **ser la viva i. de algn** to be the spitting image of sb; **tener buena i.** to have a good image **(b)** *Rel* image, statue **(c)** *TV* picture; **imágenes de archivo** library pictures

imaginación NF imagination; **son imaginaciones tuyas** you're imagining things

imaginar 1 VT to imagine
2 imaginarse VPR to imagine; **me imagino que sí** I suppose so

imaginario, -a ADJ imaginary

imaginativo, -a ADJ imaginative

imán NM magnet

imbatible ADJ unbeatable

imbatido, -a ADJ unbeaten, undefeated

imbécil 1 ADJ stupid, silly
2 NM,F idiot, imbecile

imbecilidad NF stupidity, imbecility

imborrable ADJ indelible

imbuir [37] VT *Fml* to imbue

imitación NF imitation

imitar VT to imitate; *(gestos)* to mimic; **este collar imita al oro** this necklace is imitation gold

impaciencia NF impatience

impacientar 1 VT **i. a algn** to make sb lose patience, to exasperate sb
2 impacientarse VPR to get *o* grow impatient **(por** at)

impaciente ADJ *(deseoso)* impatient; *(intranquilo)* anxious

impactante ADJ **una noticia i.** a sensational piece of news

impactar VT to shock, to stun

impacto NM impact; *Mil* hit

impar ADJ *Mat* odd; **número i.** odd number

imparable ADJ *Dep* unstoppable

imparcial ADJ impartial, unbiased

imparcialidad NF impartiality

impartir VT *(clases)* to give

impasible ADJ impassive

impávido, -a ADJ fearless

impecable ADJ impeccable

impedido, -a 1 ADJ disabled, handicapped
2 NM,F disabled *o* handicapped person

impedimento NM impediment; *(obstáculo)* hindrance, obstacle

impedir [6] VT *(obstaculizar)* to impede, to hinder; *(imposibilitar)* to prevent, to stop; **i. el paso** to block the way

impeler VT *Téc* to drive, to propel; *Fig* to drive, to impel

impenetrable ADJ impenetrable

impenitente ADJ *Rel* impenitent, unrepentant

impensable ADJ unthinkable

impepinable ADJ *Esp Fam* dead sure, certain

imperante ADJ prevailing

imperar VI to prevail

imperativo, -a 1 ADJ imperative
2 NM *Ling* imperative

imperceptible ADJ imperceptible

imperdible NM safety pin

imperdonable ADJ unforgivable, inexcusable

imperecedero, -a ADJ imperishable; *Fig* enduring

imperfección NF **(a)** *(defecto)* defect, fault **(b)** *(cualidad)* imperfection

imperfecto, -a 1 ADJ (**a**) *(no perfecto)* imperfect; *(defectuoso)* faulty, defective (**b**) *Ling* imperfect
2 NM *Ling* imperfect

imperial ADJ imperial

imperialismo NM imperialism

impericia NF incompetence

imperio NM empire; **el i. de la ley** the rule of law

imperioso, -a ADJ (*necesidad*) pressing

impermeable 1 ADJ waterproof
2 NM raincoat, *Br* mac

impersonal ADJ impersonal

impertérrito, -a ADJ unperturbed, unmoved

impertinencia NF impertinence

impertinente 1 ADJ *(insolente)* impertinent; *(inoportuno)* irrelevant
2 impertinentes NMPL lorgnette

imperturbable ADJ imperturbable, unruffled

ímpetu NM (**a**) *(impulso)* impetus, momentum (**b**) *(violencia)* violence (**c**) *(energía)* energy

impetuoso, -a ADJ (**a**) *(olas, viento, ataque)* violent (**b**) *(persona)* impetuous, impulsive

implacable ADJ relentless, implacable

implantar VT *(costumbres)* to implant, to instil; *(reformas)* to introduce; *Med* to implant

implicación NF *(participación)* involvement; *(significado)* implication

implicancia NF *CSur* implication

implicar [44] VT (**a**) *(involucrar)* to involve, to implicate (**en** in) (**b**) *(conllevar)* to imply

implícito, -a ADJ implicit, implied

implorar VT to implore, to beg

impoluto, -a ADJ pure, spotless

imponente ADJ (**a**) *(impresionante)* imposing, impressive (**b**) *(sobrecogedor)* stunning (**c**) *Fam (atractivo)* terrific, tremendous, smashing

imponer [19] (*pp* **impuesto**) **1** VT **i. algo (a algn)** *(forzar a aceptar)* to impose sth (on sb); **i. respeto** to command respect
2 VI *(impresionar)* to be imposing
3 imponerse VPR (**a**) *(infundir respeto)* to command respect (**b**) *(prevalecer)* to prevail (**c**) *(ser necesario)* to be necessary

imponible ADJ *Fin* taxable

impopular ADJ unpopular, disliked

importación NF *(mercancía)* import; *(acción)* importing; **artículos de i.** imported goods

importancia NF importance, significance; **dar i. a** to attach importance to; **sin i.** unimportant

importante ADJ important, significant; **una suma i.** a considerable sum

importar¹ VI (**a**) *(atañer)* **eso no te importa a ti** that doesn't concern you, that's none of your business (**b**) *(tener importancia)* to be important; **no importa** it doesn't matter; *Fam* **me importa un bledo** o **una pito** I couldn't care less (**c**) *(molestar)* **¿te importaría repetirlo?** would you mind repeating it?; **¿te importa si fumo?** do you mind if I smoke?

2 VT *(valer)* to amount to; **los libros importan 15 euros** the books come to 15 euros

importar² VT to import

importe NM *Com & Fin* amount, total

importunar VT to bother, to pester

imposibilidad NF impossibility

imposibilitar VT (**a**) *(impedir)* to make impossible, to prevent (**b**) *(incapacitar)* to disable, to cripple

imposible ADJ impossible; **me es i. hacerlo** I can't (possibly) do it

imposición NF (**a**) *(disciplina, condiciones)* imposing (**b**) *Fin* deposit; *(impuesto)* taxation

impostor, -a NM,F *(farsante)* impostor

impotencia NF powerlessness, helplessness; *Med* impotence

impotente ADJ powerless, helpless; *Med* impotent

impracticable ADJ (**a**) *(inviable)* impracticable, unviable (**b**) *(camino)* impassable

imprecar [44] VT to imprecate, to curse

imprecisión NF imprecision, vagueness

impreciso, -a ADJ imprecise, vague

impregnar 1 VT to impregnate (**de** with)
2 impregnarse VPR to become impregnated

imprenta NF (**a**) *(taller)* printer's, print works (**b**) *(aparato)* printing press (**c**) **libertad de i.** freedom of the press

imprescindible ADJ essential, indispensable

impresentable 1 ADJ unpresentable
2 NMF **es un i.** he's a disgrace

impresión NF (**a**) *Fig (efecto)* impression; **causar i.** to make an impression (**b**) *Fig (opinión)* impression; **cambiar impresiones** to exchange impressions (**c**) *Impr (acto)* printing; *(edición)* edition (**d**) *(huella)* impression, imprint

impresionable ADJ impressionable

impresionante ADJ impressive, striking; *Fam* **un error i.** *(tremendo)* a terrible mistake

impresionar VT (**a**) *(causar admiración)* to impress; *(sorprender)* to stun, to shock (**b**) *Fot* to expose

impresionismo NM *Arte* impressionism

impresionista ADJ & NMF *Arte* impressionist

impreso, -a 1 ADJ printed
2 NM (**a**) *(papel, folleto)* printed matter (**b**) *(formulario)* form; **i. de solicitud** application form (**c**) **impresos** *(de correos)* printed matter
3 PP *de* **imprimir**

impresora NF *Inform* printer; **i. láser** laser printer; **i. de chorro de tinta** inkjet printer

imprevisible ADJ unforeseeable, unpredictable

imprevisión NF lack of foresight

imprevisto, -a 1 ADJ unforeseen, unexpected
2 NM *(incidente)* unforeseen event

imprimir (*pp* **impreso**) VT (**a**) *Impr & Inform* to print (**b**) *(marcar)* to stamp

improbable ADJ improbable, unlikely

ímprobo, -a ADJ Fml (trabajo, esfuerzo) Herculean, strenuous

improcedente ADJ (a) (inoportuno) inappropriate, unsuitable (b) Der inadmissible

improductivo, -a ADJ unproductive

improperio NM insult, offensive remark

impropio, -a ADJ inappropriate, unsuitable; i. de uncharacteristic of

improvisación NF improvisation; Mús extemporization

improvisado, -a ADJ (espontáneo) improvised, impromptu, ad lib; (provisional) makeshift; **discurso i.** impromptu speech

improvisar VT to improvise; Mús to extemporize

improviso ADJ de i. unexpectedly, suddenly; Fam pillar a algn de i. to catch sb unawares

imprudencia NF (a) (cualidad) (en los actos) carelessness, recklessness; (en los comentarios) indiscretion (b) (acción) careless o reckless act, indiscretion

imprudente ADJ (en los actos) careless, rash; (en los comentarios) indiscreet

impúdico, -a ADJ immodest, indecent

impuesto, -a 1 NM Fin tax; **i. sobre la renta** income tax; **libre de impuestos** tax-free; Esp **i. sobre el valor añadido**, Am **i. al valor agregado** value-added tax

2 ADJ imposed

3 PP de **imponer**

impugnar VT (teoría) to refute, to disprove; (decisión) to challenge, to contest

impulsar VT to impel, to drive

impulsivo, -a ADJ impulsive

impulso NM impulse, thrust; Dep **tomar i.** to take a run-up

impune ADJ unpunished

impunemente ADV with impunity

impunidad NF impunity

impureza NF impurity

impuro, -a ADJ impure

impuse PT INDEF de **imponer**

imputar VT **i. algo a algn** (delito) to accuse sb of sth; (fracaso, error) to attribute sth to sb

inabarcable ADJ unfathomable

inabordable ADJ unapproachable, inaccessible

inacabable ADJ interminable, endless

inaccesible ADJ inaccessible

inaceptable ADJ unacceptable

inactividad NF inactivity; Fin lull, stagnation

inactivo, -a ADJ inactive

inadaptación NF maladjustment

inadaptado, -a 1 ADJ maladjusted

2 NM,F misfit

inadecuado, -a ADJ unsuitable, inappropriate

inadmisible ADJ inadmissible

inadvertido, -a ADJ unnoticed; **pasar i.** to go unnoticed

inagotable ADJ (a) (recursos) inexhaustible (b) (persona) tireless, indefatigable

inaguantable ADJ unbearable, intolerable

inalámbrico, -a 1 ADJ cordless; Inform wireless

2 NM cordless phone

inalcanzable ADJ unattainable, unachievable

inalterable ADJ (a) **permanecer i.** to remain unchanged (b) (persona) impassive, imperturbable

inamovible ADJ immovable, fixed

inanición NF starvation

inanimado, -a ADJ inanimate

inapreciable ADJ (a) (valioso) invaluable, inestimable (b) (pequeño) imperceptible

inasequible ADJ (a) (producto) unaffordable (b) (meta) unattainable, unachievable (c) (persona) unapproachable, inaccessible

inaudito, -a ADJ (a) (sin precedente) unprecedented (b) (escandaloso) outrageous

inauguración NF inauguration, opening

inaugural ADJ inaugural, opening

inaugurar VT to inaugurate, to open

inca ADJ & NMF Inca

incalculable ADJ incalculable, indeterminate

incandescente ADJ white-hot, incandescent

incansable ADJ tireless, indefatigable

incapacidad NF (a) (imposibilidad) incapacity, inability; **i. física** physical disability; **i. laboral** industrial disability o Br disablement (b) (falta de aptitud) incompetence

incapacitado, -a ADJ (para trabajar) unfit; (para ejercer cargos, votar) disqualified (para from); (para testar, testificar) incapacitated

incapacitar VT (para ejercer cargos, votar) to disqualify (para from); (para trabajar) (sujeto: circunstancias) to render unfit; (sujeto: juez) to declare unfit

incapaz ADJ (a) (no capaz) incapable (de of); **soy i. de continuar** I can't go on (b) Der unfit

incautación NF Der seizure, confiscation

incautarse VPR Der **i. de** to seize, to confiscate

incauto, -a ADJ (a) (imprudente) incautious, unwary (b) (crédulo) gullible

incendiar [43] **1** VT to set fire to, to set alight

2 **incendiarse** VPR to catch fire

incendiario, -a 1 ADJ incendiary; Fig (discurso etc) inflammatory

2 NM,F (persona) arsonist, fire-raiser

incendio NM fire; **i. forestal** forest fire

incentivar VT to give an incentive to

incentivo NM incentive

incertidumbre NF uncertainty, doubt

incesante ADJ incessant, never-ending

incesto NM incest

incestuoso, -a ADJ incestuous

incidencia NF (**a**) *(repercusión)* impact, effect; **la huelga tuvo escasa i.** the strike had little effect (**b**) *(hecho)* incident (**c**) *Fís* incidence

incidente NM incident

incidir VI (**a**) *(incurrir)* to fall (**en** into) (**b**) **i. en** *(afectar)* to affect, to influence

incienso NM incense

incierto, -a ADJ uncertain

incineración NF *(de basuras)* incineration; *(de cadáveres)* cremation

incineradora NF *(de basura)* incinerator

incinerar VT *(basura)* to incinerate; *(cadáveres)* to cremate

incipiente ADJ incipient, budding

incisión NF incision, cut

incisivo, -a 1 ADJ *(mordaz)* incisive, cutting; *(cortante)* sharp
2 NM *Anat* incisor

inciso NM *(paréntesis)* digression; **a modo de i.** in passing, incidentally

incitación NF incitement

incitar VT to incite, to urge

inclemencia NF inclemency, harshness

inclemente ADJ inclement, harsh

inclinación NF (**a**) *(de terreno)* slope, incline; *(del cuerpo)* stoop (**b**) *(reverencia)* bow (**c**) *Fig (tendencia)* tendency, inclination, penchant

inclinado, -a ADJ inclined, slanting; *Fig* **me siento i. a creerle** I feel inclined to believe him

inclinar 1 VT *(doblar)* to incline, to bend; *(cabeza)* to nod; *(ladear)* to tilt
2 inclinarse VPR (**a**) *(doblarse)* to lean (**b**) *(al saludar)* to bow; **inclinarse ante** to bow down to (**c**) *(tender)* to be o feel inclined (**a** to); **me inclino a pensar que no** I'm rather inclined to think not (**d**) *(preferir)* **inclinarse por** to favour, to lean towards

incluido, -a ADJ (**a**) *(después del sustantivo)* included; *(antes del sustantivo)* including; **servicio no i.** service not included; **i. IVA** including VAT; **todos pagan, incluidos los niños** everyone has to pay, including children (**b**) *(adjunto)* enclosed

incluir [37] VT (**a**) *(comprender)* to include (**b**) *(adjuntar)* to enclose

inclusión NF inclusion

inclusive ADV (**a**) *(incluido)* inclusive; **de martes a viernes i.** from Tuesday to Friday inclusive; **hasta la lección ocho i.** up to and including lesson eight (**b**) *(incluso)* even

incluso ADV even; **i. mi madre** even my mother

incoar VT *Der* to initiate

incógnita NF (**a**) *Mat* unknown quantity, unknown (**b**) *(misterio)* mystery

incógnito NM **de i.** incognito

incoherencia NF *(cualidad)* incoherence; *(comentario)* nonsensical remark

incoherente ADJ *(inconexo)* incoherent; *(inconsecuente)* inconsistent

incoloro, -a ADJ colourless

incólume ADJ *Fml* unharmed; **salir i.** to escape unharmed

incombustible ADJ incombustible, fireproof

incomodar 1 VT (**a**) *(causar molestia)* to inconvenience, to put out (**b**) *(fastidiar)* to bother, to annoy
2 incomodarse VPR (**a**) *(tomarse molestias)* to put oneself out, to go out of one's way (**b**) *(disgustarse)* to get annoyed o angry

incomodidad NF *(falta de comodidad)* discomfort; *(molestia)* inconvenience

incómodo, -a ADJ uncomfortable; **sentirse i.** to feel uncomfortable o awkward

incomparable ADJ incomparable

incompatibilidad NF incompatibility; *Der* **i. de caracteres** mutual incompatibility

incompatible ADJ incompatible

incompetencia NF incompetence

incompetente ADJ & NMF incompetent

incompleto, -a ADJ incomplete; *(inacabado)* unfinished

incomprensible ADJ incomprehensible

incomprensión NF lack of understanding, failure to understand; *(indiferencia)* lack of sympathy

incomunicado, -a ADJ (**a**) *(aislado)* isolated; **el pueblo se quedó i.** the town was cut off (**b**) *(en la cárcel)* in solitary confinement

incomunicar [44] VT (**a**) *(ciudad)* to isolate, to cut off (**b**) *(recluso)* to place in solitary confinement

inconcebible ADJ inconceivable, unthinkable

inconcluso, -a ADJ unfinished

incondicional 1 ADJ unconditional; *(apoyo)* wholehearted; *(amigo)* faithful; *(partidario)* staunch
2 NM die-hard

inconexo, -a ADJ incoherent, confused

inconformismo NM nonconformity

inconformista ADJ & NMF nonconformist

inconfundible ADJ unmistakable, obvious

incongruencia NF *(cualidad)* inconsistency; **hacer/decir una i.** to do/say sth incongruous

incongruente ADJ *(fuera de lugar)* incongruous; *(desarticulado)* inconsistent; *(absurdo)* crazy, illogical

inconmensurable ADJ immeasurable, vast

inconsciencia NF *Med* unconsciousness; *Fig (irreflexión)* thoughtlessness; *(irresponsabilidad)* irresponsibility

inconsciente ADJ (**a**) *(con estar) (desmayado)* unconscious (**b**) *(con ser) (despreocupado)* unaware (**de** of); *Fig (irreflexivo)* thoughtless, irresponsible

inconsecuente ADJ inconsistent

inconsistente ADJ flimsy; *(argumento)* weak

inconstancia NF inconstancy, fickleness

inconstante ADJ inconstant, fickle

incontable ADJ countless, innumerable

incontenible ADJ uncontrollable, irrepressible

incontestable ADJ indisputable, unquestionable

incontinencia NF incontinence

incontrolable ADJ uncontrollable

incontrolado, -a 1 ADJ uncontrolled
2 NM,F troublemaker

inconveniencia NF inappropriateness

inconveniente 1 ADJ inappropriate
2 NM (a) (objeción) objection; **poner inconvenientes** to raise objections (b) (desventaja) disadvantage, drawback; (problema) difficulty; **¿tienes i. en acompañarme?** would you mind coming with me?

incordiar [43] VT *Esp Fam* to bother, to pester

incordio NM *Esp Fam* nuisance, pain

incorporación NF (unión, adición) addition; **su i. tendrá lugar el día 31** (a trabajo) he starts work on the 31st

incorporar 1 VT (a) (añadir) to incorporate (**en** into) (b) (levantar) to help to sit up
2 **incorporarse** VPR (a) **incorporarse a** (sociedad) to join; (trabajo) to start; *Mil* **incorporarse a filas** to join up (b) (en la cama) to sit up

incorrección NF (a) (falta) incorrectness, inaccuracy; (gramatical) mistake (b) (descortesía) discourtesy, impropriety

incorrecto, -a ADJ (a) (equivocado) incorrect, inaccurate (b) (grosero) impolite, discourteous

incorregible ADJ incorrigible

incrédulo, -a 1 ADJ sceptical, incredulous; *Rel* unbelieving
2 NM,F *Rel* unbeliever

increíble ADJ incredible, unbelievable

incrementar 1 VT to increase
2 **incrementarse** VPR to increase

incremento NM (aumento) increase; (crecimiento) growth; **i. de la temperatura** rise in temperature

increpar VT *Fml* to rebuke, to reprimand

incruento, -a ADJ bloodless

incrustar VT (a) (insertar) to encrust o incrust (b) (embutir) to inlay; **incrustado de perlas** inlaid with pearls

incubadora NF incubator

incubar VT to incubate

incuestionable ADJ unquestionable, indisputable

inculcar [44] VT (principios, ideas) to instil (**en** into)

inculpado, -a NM,F **el i.** the accused

inculpar VT to accuse (**de** of); *Der* to charge (**de** with)

inculto, -a 1 ADJ (ignorante) uneducated, uncouth
2 NM,F ignoramus

incultura NF lack of education

incumbencia NF **es/no es de nuestra i.** it is/isn't a matter for us, it falls/doesn't fall within our area of responsibility

incumbir VI **i. a algn** to be a matter for sb, to be within sb's area of responsibility

incumplimiento NM (de deber) non-fulfilment; (de orden) failure to execute; **i. de contrato** breach of contract

incumplir VT (deber) to fail to fulfil; (promesa, contrato) to break; (orden) to fail to carry out

incurable ADJ también Fig incurable

incurrir VI (cometer) to fall (**en** into); **i. en delito** to commit a crime; **i. en (un) error** to fall into error

incursión NF raid, incursion

incursionar VI (a) (territorio) to make an incursion (**en** into); (en ciudad) to make a raid (**en** into) (b) (en tema, asunto) to dabble

indagar [42] VT to investigate, to inquire into

indebido, -a ADJ (ilegal) unlawful; (incorrecto) improper

indecencia NF indecency, obscenity

indecente ADJ (a) (impúdico) indecent (b) (indigno) miserable, wretched

indecible ADJ unspeakable; (inefable) indescribable; **sufrir lo i.** to suffer agonies

indecisión NF indecision, hesitation

indeciso, -a ADJ (a) (vacilante) hesitant, irresolute (b) (resultados etc) inconclusive

indefenso, -a ADJ defenceless, helpless

indefinidamente ADV indefinitely

indefinido, -a ADJ (a) (indeterminado) indefinite; (impreciso) undefined, vague (b) *Ling* indefinite

indeleble ADJ indelible

indemne ADJ (persona) unharmed, unhurt; (cosa) undamaged

indemnización NF (a) (acto) indemnification (b) *Fin* (compensación) indemnity, compensation; **i. por despido** redundancy payment

indemnizar [40] VT to indemnify, to compensate (**por** for)

independencia NF independence

independiente ADJ (libre) independent; (individualista) self-reliant

independientemente ADV independently (**de** of); (aparte de) regardless, irrespective (**de** of)

independizar [40] 1 VT to make independent, to grant independence to
2 **independizarse** VPR to become independent

indescifrable ADJ indecipherable

indescriptible ADJ indescribable

indeseable ADJ & NMF undesirable

indeterminado, -a ADJ (a) (sin determinar) indefinite; (impreciso) vague (b) *Ling* indefinite

India N **la I.** India

indicación NF (**a**) *(señal)* indication, sign (**b**) *(instrucción)* instruction, direction; **por i. de algn** at sb's suggestion

indicado, -a ADJ right, suitable; **a la hora indicada** at the specified time; **en el momento menos i.** at the worst possible moment

indicador NM (**a**) *(signo)* indicator (**b**) *Téc* gauge, meter; *Aut* **i. del nivel de aceite** (oil) dipstick; *Aut* **i. de velocidad** speedometer

indicar [44] VT *(señalar)* to indicate; *(sujeto: flecha)* to point to; **¿me podría i. el camino?** could you show me the way?

indicativo, -a 1 ADJ indicative
2 NM *Ling* indicative

índice NM (**a**) *(de libro)* index, table of contents (**b**) *(relación)* rate; **í. de natalidad/mortalidad** birth/death rate; *Fin* **í. de precios** price index (**c**) *Anat* **(dedo) í.** index finger, forefinger

indicio NM (**a**) *(señal)* indication, sign, token (**de** of) (**b**) *Der* **indicios** *(prueba)* evidence

índico, -a ADJ Indian; **Océano Í.** Indian Ocean

indiferencia NF indifference, apathy

indiferente ADJ (**a**) *(no importante)* unimportant; **me es i.** it makes no difference to me (**b**) *(apático)* indifferent

indígena 1 ADJ indigenous, native (**de** to)
2 NMF native (**de** of)

indigencia NF *Fml* poverty, indigence

indigente ADJ *Fml* needy, poverty-stricken

indigestarse VPR (**a**) **se le indigestó la comida** the meal gave her indigestion (**b**) *(sufrir indigestión)* to get indigestion

indigestión NF indigestion

indigesto, -a ADJ *(comida)* indigestible, difficult to digest; **me siento i.** I've got indigestion

indignación NF indignation

indignado, -a ADJ indignant (**por** at o about)

indignante ADJ outrageous, infuriating

indignar 1 VT to infuriate, to make angry
2 **indignarse** VPR to be o feel indignant (**por** at o about)

indigno, -a ADJ (**a**) *(no merecedor)* unworthy (**de** of) (**b**) *(degradante)* shameful, appalling

indio, -a ADJ & NM,F Indian; **en fila india** in single file; *Esp Fam* **hacer el i.** to play the fool

indirecta NF *Fam (insinuación)* hint, insinuation; **tirar o lanzar una i.** to drop a hint; **coger la i.** to get the message

indirecto, -a ADJ indirect; *Ling* **estilo i.** indirect o reported speech

indisciplinado, -a ADJ undisciplined, unruly

indiscreción NF *(cualidad, hecho)* indiscretion; *(comentario)* tactless remark

indiscreto, -a ADJ indiscreet, tactless

indiscriminado, -a ADJ indiscriminate

indiscutible ADJ indisputable, unquestionable

indispensable ADJ indispensable, essential

indisponer [19] *(pp* **indispuesto)** 1 VT to upset, to make unwell
2 **indisponerse** VPR (**a**) *(enfermar)* to fall ill, to become unwell (**b**) **indisponerse con algn** to fall out with sb

indispuesto, -a ADJ indisposed, unwell

indispuse PT INDEF *de* **indisponer**

indistintamente ADV **utilizan i. el español y el inglés** they use Spanish and English interchangeably

indistinto, -a ADJ *(indiferente)* immaterial, inconsequential

individual 1 ADJ individual; **habitación i.** single room
2 **individuales** NMPL *Dep* singles

individualismo NM individualism

individualista 1 ADJ individualistic
2 NMF individualist

individuo NM individual

índole NF (**a**) *(carácter)* character, nature (**b**) *(clase, tipo)* kind, sort

indolencia NF indolence, laziness

indolente 1 ADJ indolent, lazy
2 NMF idler

indomable, indómito, -a ADJ (**a**) *(animal)* untamable (**b**) *(pueblo)* ungovernable, unruly; *(pasión)* indomitable

Indonesia N Indonesia

inducir [10] VT (**a**) *(incitar, mover)* to lead, to induce; **i. a error** to lead into error, to mislead (**b**) *Elec (corriente)* to induce

inductivo, -a ADJ inductive

indudable ADJ indubitable, unquestionable; **es i. que** there is no doubt that

induje PT INDEF *de* **inducir**

indulgencia NF indulgence, leniency

indulgente ADJ indulgent (**con** towards), lenient (**con** with)

indultar VT *Der* to pardon

indulto NM *Der* pardon, amnesty

indumentaria NF clothing, clothes

industria NF industry

industrial 1 ADJ industrial
2 NMF industrialist

industrialización NF industrialization

industrializado, -a ADJ industrialized

industrializar [40] VT to industrialize

induzco INDIC PRES *de* **inducir**

inédito, -a ADJ (**a**) *(libro, texto)* unpublished (**b**) *(nuevo)* completely new; *(desconocido)* unknown

inefable ADJ ineffable, indescribable

ineficacia NF *(ineptitud)* inefficiency; *(inutilidad)* ineffectiveness

ineficaz ADJ *(inepto)* inefficient; *(inefectivo)* ineffective

ineludible ADJ inescapable, unavoidable

ineptitud NF ineptitude, incompetence

inepto, -a 1 ADJ inept, incompetent
2 NM,F incompetent person

inequívoco, -a ADJ unmistakable, unequivocal

inercia NF (a) *Fís* inertia (b) *(pasividad)* inertia, passivity; **hacer algo por i.** to do sth out of habit

inerte ADJ *(inanimado)* inert; *(inmóvil)* motionless

inesperado, -a ADJ *(fortuito)* unexpected, unforeseen; *(imprevisto)* sudden

inestabilidad NF instability

inestable ADJ unstable, unsteady

inestimable ADJ inestimable, invaluable

inevitable ADJ inevitable, unavoidable

inexistente ADJ non-existent

inexorable ADJ inexorable

inexperiencia NF lack of experience

inexperto, -a ADJ *(sin habilidad)* inexpert; *(sin experiencia)* inexperienced

inexplicable ADJ inexplicable

inexpugnable ADJ *Mil* impregnable

infalible ADJ infallible

infame ADJ *(vil)* infamous, vile; *(despreciable)* dreadful, awful

infamia NF disgrace, infamy

infancia NF childhood, infancy

infante, -a 1 NM,F *(hijo del rey) (niño)* infante, prince; *(niña)* infanta, princess
2 NM *(soldado)* infantryman

infantería NF *Mil* infantry; **la i. de marina** the marines

infantil ADJ (a) **literatura i.** *(para niños)* children's literature (b) *(aniñado)* childlike; *Pey* childish, infantile

infarto NM *Med* infarction, infarct; **i. (de miocardio)** heart attack, coronary thrombosis; *Fam* **de i.** thrilling, stunning

infatigable ADJ indefatigable, tireless

infección NF infection

infeccioso, -a ADJ infectious

infectar 1 VT to infect
2 infectarse VPR to become infected *(de* with)

infeliz 1 ADJ unhappy; *(desdichado)* unfortunate
2 NMF *Fam* simpleton; **es un pobre i.** he is a poor devil

inferior 1 ADJ (a) *(más bajo)* lower (b) *(calidad)* inferior; **de calidad i.** of inferior quality (c) *(cantidad)* lower, less; **i. a la media** below average
2 NMF *(persona)* subordinate, inferior

inferioridad NF inferiority; **estar en i. de condiciones** to be at a disadvantage; **complejo de i.** inferiority complex

inferir [5] VT *Fml* to infer *(de* from)

infernal ADJ infernal, hellish; **había un ruido i.** there was a hell of a noise

infestar VT (a) **infestado de** *(parásitos)* infested with; *(plantas)* overgrown with (b) *Fig (llenar)* to overrun, to invade; **infestado de turistas** swarming with tourists (c) *(infectar)* to infect

inficción NF *Méx* pollution

infidelidad NF infidelity, unfaithfulness

infiel 1 ADJ *(desleal)* unfaithful
2 NMF *Rel* infidel

infierno NM (a) *Rel* hell (b) *Fig (tormento)* hell; **su vida es un i.** his life is sheer hell (c) *(horno)* inferno; **en verano esto es un i.** in summer it's like an inferno here; *Fam* **¡vete al i.!** go to hell!, get lost!

infiltración NF infiltration

infiltrado, -a NM,F infiltrator

infiltrar 1 VT to infiltrate
2 infiltrarse VPR to infiltrate *(en* into)

ínfimo, -a ADJ *(mínimo)* extremely low; **detalle í.** smallest detail; **ínfima calidad** very poor quality

infinidad NF **una i. de** an infinite number of; *(mucho)* masses of; **en i. de ocasiones** on countless occasions

infinitivo, -a ADJ & NM *Ling* infinitive

infinito, -a 1 ADJ infinite, endless
2 NM infinity
3 ADV *Fam (muchísimo)* infinitely, immensely

inflación NF *Econ* inflation

inflacionario, -a, inflacionista ADJ *Econ* inflationary

inflamable ADJ flammable

inflamación NF *Med* inflammation

inflamar 1 VT (a) *Med* to inflame (b) *(encender)* to set on fire, to ignite
2 inflamarse VPR (a) *Med* to become inflamed (b) *(incendiarse)* to catch fire

inflar 1 VT (a) *(hinchar)* to inflate, to blow up; *Náut (vela)* to swell (b) *Fig (exagerar)* to exaggerate
2 inflarse VPR (a) *(hincharse)* to inflate; *Náut (vela)* to swell (b) *Fam* **inflarse de** to overdo; **se inflaron de macarrones** they stuffed themselves with macaroni

inflexible ADJ inflexible

infligir [57] VT to inflict

influencia NF influence; **ejercer** *o* **tener i. sobre algn** to have an influence on *o* upon sb; **tener influencias** to be influential; **tráfico de influencias** influence peddling, *US* graft

influenciar [43] VT to influence

influir [37] **1** VT to influence
2 VI to have influence; **i. en** to influence, to have an influence on

influjo NM influence

influyente ADJ influential

información NF (a) *(conocimiento)* information; **para tu i.** for your information (b) *Prensa (noticias)* news *sing*; **i. deportiva** sports news (c) *Tel Br* directory enquiries, *US* information (**d**) *(oficina)* information office; *(mostrador)* information desk

informado, -a ADJ informed; **de fuentes bien informadas** from well-informed sources

informal ADJ (**a**) *(reunión, cena)* informal (**b**) *(comportamiento)* casual (**c**) *(persona)* unreliable, untrustworthy

informalidad NF *(incumplimiento)* unreliability; *(desenfado)* informality

informar 1 VT to inform (**de** of); *(dar informes)* to report
 2 informarse VPR *(procurarse noticias)* to find out (**de** about); *(enterarse)* to inquire (**de** about)

informática NF computing, information technology, IT

informático, -a 1 ADJ computer, computing
 2 NM,F *(computer)* technician

informativo, -a 1 ADJ (**a**) *Rad & TV* news; **boletín i.** news (broadcast) (**b**) *(explicativo)* informative, explanatory
 2 NM *Rad & TV* news bulletin

informe NM (**a**) *(documento)* report (**b**) **informes** references; **pedir informes sobre algn** to make inquiries about sb

infracción NF *(de ley)* infringement, breach (**de** of)

infractor, -a NM,F offender

infraestructura NF infrastructure

in fraganti LOC ADV in the act; **pillar a algn i.** to catch sb redhanded

infrahumano, -a ADJ subhuman

infranqueable ADJ impassable; *Fig* insurmountable

infrarrojo, -a ADJ infrared

infrautilizar VT to underuse

infringir [57] VT to infringe, to contravene; **i. una ley** to break a law

infructuoso, -a ADJ fruitless, unsuccessful

infundado, -a ADJ unfounded, groundless

infundir VT to infuse; *Fig* to instil; **i. dudas** to give rise to doubt; **i. respeto** to command respect

infusión NF infusion

infuso, -a ADJ *Fam Irón* **ciencia infusa** sheer genius

ingeniar [43] **1** VT to invent, to devise
 2 ingeniarse VPR **ingeniárselas para hacer algo** to manage to do sth

ingeniería NF engineering

ingeniero, -a NM,F engineer; **i. agrónomo** agricultural engineer; *Esp* **i. de caminos, canales y puertos** civil engineer; **i. de minas/montes** mining/forestry engineer; **i. de telecomunicaciones** telecommunications engineer; **i. técnico** technician

ingenio NM (**a**) *(talento)* talent; *(inventiva)* inventiveness, creativeness; *(agudeza)* wit (**b**) *(aparato)* device

ingenioso, -a ADJ ingenious, clever; *(vivaz)* witty

ingente ADJ huge, enormous

ingenuidad NF ingenuousness, naïveté

ingenuo, -a 1 ADJ ingenuous, naïve
 2 NM,F naïve person

ingerir [5] VT *(comida)* to ingest, to consume; *(líquidos, alcohol)* to drink, to consume

Inglaterra N England

ingle NF *Anat* groin

inglés, -esa 1 ADJ English
 2 NM *(hombre)* Englishman; *(mujer)* Englishwoman; **los ingleses** the English
 3 NM *(idioma)* English

ingratitud NF ingratitude, ungratefulness

ingrato, -a 1 ADJ (**a**) *(persona)* ungrateful (**b**) *(noticia)* unpleasant (**c**) *(trabajo)* thankless, unrewarding (**d**) *(tierra)* unproductive
 2 NM,F ungrateful person

ingrediente NM ingredient

ingresar 1 VT (**a**) *Esp (dinero)* to deposit, to pay in (**b**) *Med* to admit; **la ingresaron en el hospital** she was admitted to hospital
 2 VI to enter; **i. en el ejército** to enlist in the army, to join the army; **i. en un club** to join a club; *Esp* **i. cadáver** to be dead on arrival

ingreso NM (**a**) *(de dinero)* deposit; **hacer un i. en una cuenta** to pay money into an account (**b**) *(entrada)* entry (**en** into); *(admisión)* admission (**en** to) (**c**) **ingresos** *(sueldo, renta)* income; *(beneficios)* revenue

inhábil ADJ (**a**) *(incapaz)* unfit; **i. para el trabajo** unfit for work (**b**) **día i.** non-working day

inhabilitación NF (**a**) *Fml (incapacidad)* disablement (**b**) *Der* disqualification

inhabilitar VT (**a**) *Fml (incapacitar)* to disable; **inhabilitado para el trabajo** unfit for work (**b**) *Der* to disqualify

inhabitable ADJ uninhabitable

> Observa que la palabra inglesa **inhabitable** es un falso amigo y no es la traducción de la palabra española **inhabitable**. En inglés **inhabitable** significa "habitable".

inhalación NF inhalation

inhalador NM *Med* inhaler

inhalar VT to inhale

inherente ADJ inherent (**a** in)

inhibición NF inhibition

inhibir 1 VT to inhibit
 2 inhibirse VPR (**a**) *(cohibirse)* to be o feel inhibited (**b**) *(abstenerse)* to refrain (**de** from)

inhóspito, -a ADJ inhospitable

inhumación NF burial

inhumano, -a ADJ inhumane; *(cruel)* inhuman

inhumar VT to bury

iniciación NF (**a**) *(ceremonia)* initiation (**b**) *(principio)* start, beginning

inicial ADJ & NF initial; **punto i.** starting point

iniciar [43] **1** VT (**a**) *(empezar)* to begin, to start; *(discusión)* to initiate; *(una cosa nueva)* to pioneer (**b**) *(introducir)* to initiate
2 iniciarse VPR (**a**) **iniciarse en algo** *(aprender)* to start to study sth (**b**) *(empezar)* to begin, to start

iniciativa NF initiative; **i. privada** private enterprise; **por i. propia** on one's own initiative

inicio NM beginning, start; **a inicios de** at the beginning of

inimaginable ADJ unimaginable

inimitable ADJ inimitable

ininterrumpido, -a ADJ uninterrupted, continuous

injerencia NF interference, meddling (**en** in)

injerirse VPR to interfere, to meddle (**en** in)

injertar VT *Agr & Med* to graft

injerto NM graft

injuria NF *(insulto)* insult, affront; *(agravio)* outrage

injuriar [43] VT *(insultar)* to insult; *(ultrajar)* to outrage

injusticia NF injustice, unfairness

injustificado, -a ADJ unjustified

injusto, -a ADJ unjust, unfair

inmaculado, -a ADJ immaculate

inmadurez NF immaturity

inmaduro, -a ADJ immature

inmediaciones NFPL neighbourhood

inmediatamente ADV immediately, at once

inmediato, -a ADJ (**a**) *(en el tiempo)* immediate; **de i.** at once (**b**) *(en el espacio)* next (**a** to), adjoining

inmejorable ADJ *(trabajo)* excellent; *(precio)* unbeatable

inmemorial ADJ immemorial; **desde tiempos inmemoriales** since time immemorial

inmensidad NF immensity, enormity

inmenso, -a ADJ immense, vast

inmerecido, -a ADJ undeserved, unmerited

inmersión NF immersion; *(de submarino)* dive

inmerso, -a ADJ immersed (**en** in)

inmigración NF immigration

inmigrante ADJ & NMF immigrant

inmigrar VI to immigrate

inminente ADJ imminent, impending

inmiscuirse [37] VPR to interfere, to meddle (**en** in)

inmobiliaria NF *Br* estate agency *o* agent's, *US* real estate company

inmobiliario, -a ADJ property, *US* real estate; **agente i.** *Br* estate agent, *US* realtor

inmolar VT *Fml* to immolate, to sacrifice

inmoral ADJ immoral

inmoralidad NF immorality

inmortal ADJ & NMF immortal

inmortalidad NF immortality

inmortalizar [40] VT to immortalize

inmóvil ADJ motionless, immobile

inmovilista ADJ ultra-conservative

inmovilizar [40] VT (**a**) *(persona, cosa)* to immobilize (**b**) *Fin (capital)* to immobilize, to tie up

inmueble 1 ADJ **bienes inmuebles** real estate
2 NM building

inmundicia NF (**a**) *(suciedad)* dirt, filth; *Fig* dirtiness (**b**) *(basura)* rubbish, refuse

inmundo, -a ADJ dirty, filthy; *Fig* nasty

inmune ADJ immune (**a** to), exempt (**de** from)

inmunidad NF immunity (**contra** against); **i. diplomática/parlamentaria** diplomatic/parliamentary immunity

inmunizar [40] VT to immunize (**contra** against)

inmutarse VPR to change countenance; **ni se inmutó** he didn't turn a hair

innato, -a ADJ innate, inborn

innecesario, -a ADJ unnecessary

innegable ADJ undeniable

innovación NF innovation

innovar VT & VI to innovate

innumerable ADJ innumerable, countless

inocencia NF innocence

inocentada NF *Fam* ≃ April Fool's joke; **hacer una i. a algn** to play an April Fool's joke on sb

inocente 1 ADJ innocent
2 NMF innocent; **Día de los Inocentes** Holy Innocents' Day, 28 December, ≃ April Fools' Day

inocuo, -a ADJ innocuous

inodoro, -a 1 ADJ odourless
2 NM toilet, lavatory

inofensivo, -a ADJ harmless

inolvidable ADJ unforgettable

inoperante ADJ ineffective

inopia NF **estar en la i.** to be in the clouds, to be miles away

inopinado, -a ADJ unexpected

inoportuno, -a ADJ inappropriate; **llegó en un momento muy i.** he turned up at a very awkward moment

inorgánico, -a ADJ inorganic

inoxidable ADJ **acero i.** stainless steel

inquebrantable ADJ *(fe, amistad)* unshakeable; *(lealtad)* unswerving

inquietante ADJ worrying

inquietar 1 VT to worry
2 inquietarse VPR to worry (**por** about)

inquieto, -a ADJ (**a**) *(preocupado)* worried (**por** about) (**b**) *(intranquilo)* restless (**c**) *(emprendedor)* eager

inquietud NF (**a**) *(preocupación)* worry (**b**) *(agitación)* restlessness (**c**) *(anhelo)* eagerness

inquilino, -a NM,F tenant

inquirir [31] VT to investigate

inquisición NF (**a**) *(indagación)* inquiry, investigation (**b**) **la i.** *(tribunal)* the (Spanish) Inquisition

inquisitivo, -a ADJ inquisitive

inri NM *Fam* **para más** o **mayor i.** to make matters worse

insaciable ADJ insatiable

insalubre ADJ unhealthy

INSALUD NM *(abr* **Instituto Nacional de la Salud**) = Spanish national health service, *Br* ≃ NHS, *US* ≃ Medicaid

insano, -a ADJ (**a**) *(loco)* insane, mad (**b**) *(insalubre)* unhealthy

insatisfacción NF (**a**) *(disgusto, descontento)* dissatisfaction (**b**) *(falta, carencia)* lack of fulfilment

insatisfecho, -a ADJ dissatisfied

inscribir *(pp* **inscrito**) **1** VT (**a**) *(registrar)* to register; **i. a un niño en el registro civil** to register a child's birth (**b**) *(matricular)* to enrol (**c**) *(grabar)* to inscribe
  2 inscribirse VPR (**a**) *(registrarse)* to register; *(hacerse miembro)* to join (**b**) *(matricularse)* to enrol

inscripción NF (**a**) *(matriculación)* enrolment, registration (**b**) *(escrito etc)* inscription

inscrito PP *de* **inscribir**

insecticida NM insecticide

insecto NM insect

inseguridad NF (**a**) *(falta de confianza)* insecurity (**b**) *(duda)* uncertainty (**c**) *(peligro)* lack of safety; **la i. ciudadana** the breakdown of law and order

inseguro, -a ADJ (**a**) *(poco confiado)* insecure (**b**) *(dubitativo)* uncertain (**c**) *(peligroso)* unsafe

inseminación NF insemination; **i. artificial** artificial insemination

inseminar VT to inseminate

insensatez NF foolishness

insensato, -a 1 ADJ foolish
  2 NM,F fool

insensibilidad NF insensitivity

insensible ADJ (**a**) *(indiferente)* insensitive (**a** to) (**b**) *(imperceptible)* imperceptible (**c**) *Med* numb

inseparable ADJ inseparable

insertar VT to insert

inservible ADJ useless

insidia NF (**a**) *(trampa)* malicious ploy (**b**) *(malicia)* maliciousness

insidioso, -a ADJ insidious

insigne ADJ distinguished

insignia NF (**a**) *(emblema)* badge (**b**) *(bandera)* flag

insignificancia NF (**a**) *(intrascendencia)* insignificance (**b**) *(nadería)* trifle

insignificante ADJ insignificant

insinuación NF hint, insinuation; **insinua-ciones** *(amorosas)* innuendo

insinuante ADJ *(mirada, ropa)* suggestive; *(comentarios)* full of innuendo

insinuar [30] **1** VT to insinuate
  2 insinuarse VPR **insinuarse a algn** to make advances to sb

insípido, -a ADJ insipid; *Fig* dull, flat

insistencia NF insistence; **con i.** insistently

insistente ADJ insistent

insistir VI to insist (**en** on); **insistió en ese punto** he stressed that point

insociable ADJ unsociable

insolación NF *Med* sunstroke; **coger una i.** to get sunstroke

insolencia NF insolence

insolente ADJ insolent

insolidaridad NF unsupportive stance

insólito, -a ADJ *(poco usual)* unusual; *(extraño)* strange, odd

insoluble ADJ insoluble

insolvencia NF *Fin* insolvency

insolvente ADJ *Fin* insolvent

insomnio NM insomnia; **noche de i.** sleepless night

insondable ADJ unfathomable

insonorizado, -a ADJ soundproof

insonorizar [40] VT to soundproof

insoportable ADJ unbearable

insospechado, -a ADJ unsuspected

insostenible ADJ untenable

inspección NF inspection

inspeccionar VT to inspect

inspector, -a NM,F inspector; **i. de Hacienda** tax inspector

inspiración NF (**a**) *(mental)* inspiration (**b**) *(inhalación)* inhalation

inspirado, -a ADJ inspired

inspirar 1 VT (**a**) *(mentalmente)* to inspire (**b**) *(inhalar)* to inhale, to breathe in
  2 inspirarse VPR **inspirarse en** to be inspired by

instalación NF installation; **instalaciones deportivas** sports facilities

instalar 1 VT *(antena, aparato)* to install, to fit; *(local, puesto)* to set up
  2 instalarse VPR *(persona)* to settle (down)

instancia NF (**a**) *(solicitud)* request; **a instancia(s) de** at the request of (**b**) *(escrito)* application form (**c**) *Der* **tribunal de primera i.** court of first instance (**d**) **en primera i.** first of all; **en última i.** as a last resort

> Observa que la palabra inglesa **instance** es un falso amigo y no es la traducción de la palabra española **instancia**. En inglés, **instance** significa "caso, ejemplo".

instantánea NF snapshot

instantáneamente ADV instantly

instantáneo, -a ADJ instantaneous; **café i.** instant coffee

instante NM instant, moment; **a cada i.** constantly; **al i.** immediately, right away; **por instantes** with every second; **¡un i.!** just a moment!

instar VT to urge

instauración NF founding

instaurar VT to found

instigador, -a NM,F instigator

instigar [42] VT to instigate; **i. a la rebelión** to incite a rebellion

instintivo, -a ADJ instinctive

instinto NM instinct; **por i.** instinctively; **i. de conservación** survival instinct

institución NF institution

institucional ADJ institutional

instituir [37] VT to institute

instituto NM (a) *(corporación)* institute (b) *Esp (centro docente)* high school

institutriz NF governess

instituyo INDIC PRES *de* **instituir**

instrucción NF (a) *(educación)* education (b) *(indicación)* instruction; **instrucciones para el** *o* **de uso** directions for use (c) *Der* preliminary investigation; **la i. del sumario** proceedings; **juez de i.** examining magistrate (d) *Mil* drill

instructivo, -a ADJ instructive

instruido, -a ADJ educated, well-educated

instruir [37] VT (a) *(enseñar)* to instruct (b) *Der* to investigate (c) *Mil* to drill

instrumental ADJ instrumental

instrumento NM instrument

insubordinación NF insubordination

insubordinado, -a ADJ insubordinate

insubordinarse VPR to rebel (**contra** against)

insuficiencia NF *Med* failure, insufficiency; **i. cardiaca/renal** heart/kidney failure

insuficiente 1 ADJ insufficient
  2 NM *Educ (nota)* fail

insufrible ADJ insufferable

insular 1 ADJ insular, island
  2 NMF islander

insulso, -a ADJ insipid

insultante ADJ insulting

insultar VT to insult

insulto NM insult

insumisión NF = refusal to do military service

insumiso, -a 1 ADJ unsubmissive
  2 NM = person who refuses to do military service

insuperable ADJ (a) *(inmejorable)* unsurpassable (b) *(problema)* insurmountable

insurgente ADJ & NMF insurgent

insurrección NF insurrection

intachable ADJ irreproachable; **conducta i.** impeccable behaviour

intacto, -a ADJ intact

integración NF *también Mat* integration; **i. racial** racial integration

integral 1 ADJ (a) *(total)* total, complete (b) *(sin refinar) (pan, harina) Br* wholemeal, *US* wholewheat; *(arroz)* brown (c) *(constituyente)* integral; **ser parte i. de algo** to be an integral part of sth
  2 NF *Mat* integral

integrante 1 ADJ integral; **ser parte i. de** to be an integral part of
  2 NMF member

integrar 1 VT *(formar)* to compose, to make up; **el equipo lo integran once jugadores** there are eleven players in the team
  2 integrarse VPR to integrate (**en** with)

integridad NF integrity

íntegro, -a ADJ (a) *(entero)* whole, entire; *Cin & Lit* **versión íntegra** *(de libro)* unabridged edition; *(de película)* uncut version (b) *(honrado)* upright

intelecto NM intellect

intelectual ADJ & NMF intellectual

inteligencia NF *(intelecto)* intelligence; **co-ciente de i.** intelligence quotient, IQ

inteligente ADJ intelligent

inteligible ADJ intelligible

intemperie NF bad weather; **a la i.** in the open (air)

intempestivo, -a ADJ untimely

intención NF intention; **con i.** deliberately, on purpose; **con segunda** *o* **doble i.** with an ulterior motive; **tener la i. de hacer algo** to intend to do sth

intencionado, -a ADJ deliberate

intencional ADJ intentional

intendencia NF (a) *(militar) Br* ≃ Royal Army Service Corps, *US* ≃ Quartermaster Corps (b) *RP (corporación municipal) Br* town council, *US* city council (c) *Chile (gobernación)* regional government

intendente NM (a) *RP (alcalde)* mayor (b) *Chile (gobernador)* provincial governor

intensidad NF intensity; *(del viento)* force

intensificar [44] **1** VT to intensify
  2 intensificarse VPR to intensify

intensivo, -a ADJ intensive; *Agr* **cultivo i.** intensive farming; *Educ* **curso i.** crash course

intenso, -a ADJ intense

intentar VT to try, to attempt; *Fam* **¡inténtalo!** give it a go!

intento NM attempt; **i. de suicidio** attempted suicide

intentona NF *Pol* **i. (golpista)** attempted coup

intercalar VT to insert

intercambiar [43] VT to exchange

intercambio NM exchange; **i. comercial** trade

interceder VI to intercede

interceptar VT (**a**) *(detener)* to intercept (**b**) *(carretera)* to block; *(tráfico)* to hold up

intercesión NF intercession

intercontinental ADJ intercontinental

interdicto NM prohibition

interés (*pl* **intereses**) NM (**a**) *(provecho, curiosidad)* interest; **poner i. en** to take an interest in; **tener i. en** *o* **por** to be interested in (**b**) *(egoísmo)* self-interest; **hacer algo (sólo) por i.** to do sth (purely) out of self-interest; **intereses creados** vested interests (**c**) *Fin* interest; **con un i. del 11 por ciento** at an interest of 11 percent; **tipos de i.** interest rates

interesado, -a 1 ADJ (**a**) *(preocupado, curioso)* interested (**en** in); **las partes interesadas** the interested parties (**b**) *(egoísta)* selfish

2 NM,F interested person; **los interesados** those interested *o* concerned

interesante ADJ interesting

interesar 1 VT (**a**) *(tener interés)* to interest; **la poesía no me interesa nada** poetry doesn't interest me at all (**b**) *(concernir)* to concern

2 VI *(ser importante)* to be of interest, to be important; **interesaría llegar pronto** it is important to get there early

3 interesarse VPR **interesarse** *por o* **en** to be interested in; **se interesó por ti** he asked about *o* after you

interferencia NF interference; *Rad & TV* jamming

interferir [5] **1** VT (**a**) *(interponerse)* to interfere with (**b**) *Rad & TV* to jam

2 VI to interfere (**en** in)

interfono NM *Tel* intercom

interinidad NF temporariness

interino, -a 1 ADJ *(persona)* acting

2 NM,F *(suplente)* stand-in, deputy; *(médico, juez)* locum; *(profesor)* Br supply teacher, US substitute teacher

interior 1 ADJ (**a**) *(de dentro)* inside, inner; *(patio, jardín)* interior, inside; *(habitación, vida)* inner; **ropa i.** underwear (**b**) *Pol* domestic, internal (**c**) *Geog* inland

2 NM (**a**) *(parte de dentro)* interior; **en mi i.** deep down (**b**) *Geog* interior; *Pol* **Ministerio del I.** *Br* ≃ Home Office, *US* ≃ Department of the Interior

interiorizar [40] VT to internalize

interjección NF *Ling* interjection

interlocutor, -a NM,F speaker; *(negociador)* negotiator

intermediario NM *Com* middleman

intermedio, -a 1 ADJ intermediate

2 NM *TV (intervalo)* break

interminable ADJ endless

intermitente ADJ intermittent

2 NM *Esp, Col (en vehículo)* Br indicator, US turn signal

internacional ADJ international

internado, -a 1 NM,F inmate

2 NM *(colegio)* boarding school

internar 1 VT *(en hospital)* to confine

2 internarse VPR (**a**) *(penetrar)* to advance (**en** into) (**b**) *Dep* to break through

internauta NMF Net user

Internet NF *Inform* Internet; **está en I.** it's on the Internet

interno, -a 1 ADJ (**a**) *(de dentro)* internal; **por vía interna** internally (**b**) *Pol* domestic

2 NM,F *(alumno)* boarder; *Med (enfermo)* patient; *(preso)* inmate

3 NM *RP (extensión)* (telephone) extension; **i. 28, por favor** extension 28, please

interponer [19] (*pp* **interpuesto**) **1** VT to insert; *Der* **i. un recurso** to give notice of appeal

2 interponerse VPR to intervene

interpretación NF (**a**) *(de ideas, significado)* interpretation (**b**) *Mús & Teatro* performance (**c**) *(traducción)* interpreting

interpretar VT (**a**) *(entender, explicar, traducir)* to interpret (**b**) *Teatro (papel)* to play; *(obra)* to perform; *Mús (concierto)* to play, to perform; *(canción)* to sing

intérprete NMF (**a**) *(traductor)* interpreter (**b**) *Teatro* performer; *Mús (cantante)* singer; *(músico)* performer

interpuesto PP *de* interponer

interpuse PT INDEF *de* interponer

interrogación NF interrogation; *Ling* **(signo de) i.** question *o* interrogation mark

interrogante NF *Fig* question mark

interrogar [42] VT to question; *(testigo etc)* to interrogate

interrogatorio NM interrogation

interrumpir VT to interrupt; *(tráfico)* to block

interrupción NF interruption; **i. del embarazo** termination of pregnancy

interruptor NM *Elec* switch

intersección NF intersection

interurbano, -a ADJ intercity; *Tel* **conferencia interurbana** long-distance call

intervalo NM interval; **habrá intervalos de lluvia** there will be periods of rain

intervención NF (**a**) *(participación)* intervention, participation (**en** in); *(aportación)* contribution (**en** to) (**b**) *Med* intervention

intervenir [27] **1** VI *(mediar)* to intervene (**en** in); *(participar)* to take part (**en** in); *(contribuir)* to contribute (**en** to)

2 VT (**a**) *(confiscar)* to confiscate, to seize (**b**) *Tel (teléfono)* to tap (**c**) *Med* to operate on

interventor, -a NM,F *(supervisor)* inspector; *Fin* **i. (de cuentas)** auditor

interviú NF interview

intestino, -a 1 ADJ *(luchas)* internal

2 NM *Anat* intestine

intimar VI to become close (**con** to)

intimidad NF *(amistad)* intimacy; *(vida privada)* private life; *(privacidad)* privacy; **en la i.** privately, in private

intimidar VT to intimidate

íntimo, -a 1 ADJ *(vida, fiesta)* private; *(ambiente, restaurante)* intimate; *(relación, amistad)* close; *(sentimiento)* innermost
2 NM,F close friend, intimate

intocable ADJ *(persona, institución)* above criticism

intolerable ADJ intolerable

intolerancia NF intolerance

intolerante 1 ADJ intolerant
2 NMF intolerant person

intoxicación NF poisoning; **i. alimentaria** food poisoning

> Observa que la palabra inglesa **intoxication** es un falso amigo y no es la traducción de la palabra española **intoxicación**. En inglés **intoxication** significa "embriaguez".

intoxicar [44] VT to poison

> Observa que el verbo inglés **to intoxicate** es un falso amigo y no es la traducción del verbo español **intoxicar**. En inglés **to intoxicate** significa "embriagar, emborrachar".

intranet NF *Inform* intranet

intranquilidad NF worry

intranquilizarse VPR to get worried

intranquilo, -a ADJ *(preocupado)* worried; *(agitado)* restless

intransigente ADJ intransigent

intransitable ADJ impassable

intransitivo, -a ADJ *Ling* intransitive

intratable ADJ **(a)** *(problema)* intractable **(b)** *(persona)* unsociable

intrépido, -a ADJ intrepid

intriga NF intrigue; *Cin & Teatro* plot

intrigante 1 ADJ **(a)** *(interesante)* intriguing, interesting **(b)** *(maquinador)* scheming
2 NMF *(persona)* schemer

intrigar [42] **1** VT *(interesar)* to intrigue, to interest
2 VI *(maquinar)* to plot

intrincado, -a ADJ **(a)** *(cuestión, problema)* intricate **(b)** *(bosque)* dense

intrínseco, -a ADJ intrinsic

introducción NF introduction

introducir [10] VT **(a)** *(meter)* *(llave, carta)* to put in, to insert; *Inform (datos)* to input, to enter **(b)** *(mercancías)* to bring in, to introduce **(c)** *(dar a conocer)* **i. algo en** to introduce o bring sth to

intromisión NF *(injerencia)* meddling; **perdón por la i.** forgive the intrusion

introspectivo, -a ADJ introspective

introvertido, -a 1 ADJ introverted
2 NM,F introvert

intruso, -a 1 ADJ intrusive
2 NM,F intruder; *Der* trespasser

intuición NF intuition

intuir [37] VT to know by intuition, to sense

intuitivo, -a ADJ intuitive

inundación NF flood

inundar VT to flood; *Fig (de trabajo etc)* to swamp

inusitado, -a ADJ unusual

inusual ADJ unusual

inútil 1 ADJ **(a)** *(objeto)* useless; *(esfuerzo, intento)* vain, pointless **(b)** *Mil* unfit (for service)
2 NMF *Fam* good-for-nothing

inutilidad NF uselessness

inutilizar [40] VT to make o render useless; *(máquina etc)* to put out of action

invadir VT to invade; *Fig* **los estudiantes invadieron la calle** students poured out onto the street

invalidar VT to invalidate

invalidez NF **(a)** *Der (nulidad)* invalidity **(b)** *Med (minusvalía)* disability

inválido, -a 1 ADJ **(a)** *Der (nulo)* invalid **(b)** *Med (minusválido)* disabled, handicapped
2 NM,F *Med* disabled o handicapped person

invariable ADJ invariable

invasión NF invasion

invasor, -a 1 ADJ invading
2 NM,F invader

invencible ADJ **(a)** *(enemigo)* invincible **(b)** *(obstáculo)* insurmountable

invención NF *(invento)* invention; *(mentira)* fabrication

inventar VT to invent; *(excusa, mentira)* to make up, to concoct

inventario NM inventory

inventiva NF inventiveness; *(imaginación)* imagination

invento NM invention

inventor, -a NM,F inventor

invernadero NM greenhouse; **efecto i.** greenhouse effect

invernal ADJ winter, wintry

invernar [1] VI to hibernate

inverosímil ADJ unlikely, improbable

inversión NF **(a)** *(del orden)* inversion **(b)** *(de dinero, tiempo)* investment

inversionista NMF investor

inverso, -a ADJ opposite; **en sentido i.** in the opposite direction; **en orden i.** in reverse order

inversor, -a NM,F *Fin* investor

invertebrado, -a ADJ & NM *Zool* invertebrate

invertido, -a ADJ inverted, reversed

invertir [5] VT **(a)** *(orden)* to invert, to reverse **(b)** *(dinero)* to invest **(en** in); *(tiempo)* to spend **(en** on)

investidura NF investiture; *Pol* vote of confidence

investigación NF (a) *(policial etc)* investigation (b) *(científica)* research

investigador, -a NM,F (a) *(detective)* investigator (b) *(científico)* researcher, research worker

investigar [42] VT to research; *(indagar)* to investigate

investir [6] VT to invest

invidente 1 ADJ unsighted
2 NMF unsighted person

invierno NM winter

invisible ADJ invisible

invitación NF invitation

invitado, -a 1 ADJ invited; **artista i.** guest artist
2 NM,F guest

invitar VT to invite; **hoy invito yo** it's on me today; **me invitó a una copa** he treated me to a drink

invocar [44] VT to invoke

involucrar 1 VT to involve (**en** in)
2 involucrarse VPR to get involved (**en** in)

involuntario, -a ADJ involuntary; *(impremeditado)* unintentional

invulnerable ADJ invulnerable

inyección NF injection; **poner una i.** to give an injection

inyectar VT to inject (**en** into); **i. algo a algn** to inject sb with sth

IPC NM *(abr Esp* **Índice de Precios al Consumo** *o Am* **Índice de Precios al Consumidor)** RPI

ir [16] **1** VI(a) to go; **¡vamos!** let's go!; **voy a Lima** I'm going to Lima; **¡ya voy!** (I'm) coming!
(b) *(río, camino)* to lead; **esta carretera va a la frontera** this road leads to the border
(c) *(funcionar)* to work (properly); **el ascensor no va** the lift is out of order
(d) *(desenvolverse)* **¿cómo le va el nuevo trabajo?** how is he getting on in his new job?; **¿cómo va?** how are things?, how are you doing?
(e) *(sentar bien)* to suit; **el verde te va mucho** green really suits you
(f) *(combinar)* to match; **el rojo no va con el verde** red doesn't go with green
(g) *(vestir)* to wear; **ir con falda** to wear a skirt; **ir de blanco/de uniforme** to be dressed in white/in uniform
(h) *Fam (importar, concernir)* to concern; **eso va por ti también** and the same goes for you; **ni me va ni me viene** I don't care one way or the other
(i) *Fam (comportarse)* to act; **ir de guapo por la vida** to be a flash Harry
(j) **va para abogado** he's studying to be a lawyer
(k) *(ir + por)* **ir por la derecha** to keep (to the) right; *Esp (ir a buscar)* **ve (a) por agua** go and fetch some water; *(haber llegado)* **voy por la página 90** I've got as far as page 90
(l) *(locuciones)* **a eso iba** I was coming to that; **¡ahí va!** catch!; **en lo que va de año** so far this

year; **ir a parar** to end up; **¡qué va!** of course not!, nothing of the sort!; **va a lo suyo** he looks after his own interests; **¡vamos a ver!** let's see!; **¡vaya!** fancy that!; **¡vaya moto!** what a bike!
2 VAUX (a) *(ir + gerundio)* **ir andando** to go on foot; **va mejorando** she's improving (b) *(ir + pp)* **ya van rotos tres** three (of them) have already been broken (c) *(ir a + infin)* **iba a decir que** I was going to say that; **va a llover** it's going to rain; **vas a caerte** you'll fall
3 *irse* VPR (a) *(marcharse)* to go away, to leave; **me voy** I'm off; **¡vámonos!** let's go!; **¡vete!** go away!; **vete a casa** go home (b) *(líquido, gas) (escaparse)* to leak (c) *(direcciones)* **¿por dónde se va a ...?** which is the way to ...?; **por aquí se va al río** this is the way to the river

ira NF wrath, rage, anger

iracundo, -a ADJ (a) *(irascible)* irascible (b) *(enfadado)* irate, angry

Irak N Iraq

Irán N Iran

iraní *(pl* **iraníes)** ADJ & NMF Iranian

Iraq N = **Irak**

iraquí *(pl* **iraquíes)** ADJ & NMF Iraqi

irascible ADJ irascible, irritable

iris NM INV *Anat* iris; **arco i.** rainbow

Irlanda N Ireland; **I. del Norte** Northern Ireland

irlandés, -esa 1 ADJ Irish
2 NM,F *(hombre)* Irishman; *(mujer)* Irishwoman; **los irlandeses** the Irish
3 NM *(idioma)* Irish

ironía NF irony

irónico, -a ADJ ironic

IRPF NM *Econ (abr* **impuesto sobre la renta de las personas físicas)** income tax

irracional ADJ irrational

irradiar [43] VT (a) *(luz, calor)* to radiate (b) *(alimentos, enfermo)* to irradiate (c) *RP (emitir)* to broadcast

irreal ADJ unreal

irrealizable ADJ unattainable, unfeasible; *Fig* unreachable

irreconocible ADJ unrecognizable

irrecuperable ADJ irretrievable

irreemplazable ADJ = **irremplazable**

irregular ADJ irregular

irregularidad NF irregularity

irremediable ADJ irremediable, incurable

irremplazable ADJ irreplaceable

irreparable ADJ irreparable

irreprochable ADJ irreproachable, blameless

irresistible ADJ (a) *(impulso, persona)* irresistible (b) *(insoportable)* unbearable

irresoluto, -a ADJ irresolute

irresponsable ADJ irresponsible

irrestricto, -a ADJ *Am* unconditional, complete

irreverente ADJ irreverent

irreversible ADJ irreversible

irrigación NF irrigation

irrigar [42] VT to irrigate, to water

irrisorio, -a ADJ derisory, ridiculous

irritable ADJ irritable

irritación NF irritation

irritante ADJ irritating

irritar 1 VT (a) *(enfadar)* to irritate, to exasperate (b) *Med* to irritate
  2 **irritarse** VPR (a) *(enfadarse)* to lose one's temper, to get angry (b) *Med* to become irritated

irrompible ADJ unbreakable

irrumpir VI to burst (**en** into)

isla NF island, isle

islam NM *Rel* Islam

islámico, -a ADJ Islamic

islandés, -esa 1 ADJ Icelandic
  2 NM,F *(persona)* Icelander
  3 NM *(idioma)* Icelandic

Islandia N Iceland

isleño, -a 1 ADJ island
  2 NM,F islander

islote NM small island

ismo NM *Fam* ism

isotónico, -a ADJ isotonic

Israel N Israel

israelí *(pl* **israelíes)** ADJ & NMF Israeli

istmo NM *Geog* isthmus

itacate NM *Méx* packed lunch

Italia N Italy

italiano, -a 1 ADJ Italian
  2 NM,F *(persona)* Italian
  3 NM *(idioma)* Italian

itinerante ADJ itinerant, itinerating

itinerario NM itinerary, route

IVA NM *Econ (abr Esp* **impuesto sobre el valor añadido,** *Am* **impuesto al valor agregado)** *Br* VAT, *US* ≃ sales tax

izar [40] VT to hoist, to raise

izqda., izqdᵃ *(abr* **izquierda)** left

izqdo., izqdº *(abr* **izquierdo)** left

izquierda NF (a) *(lado)* left; **a la i.** on the left; **girar a la i.** to turn left (b) *(mano)* left hand (c) *Pol* **la i.** the left; *Esp* **de izquierdas** left-wing; *Am* **de i.** left-wing

izquierdista *Pol* 1 ADJ leftist, left-wing
  2 NMF leftist, left-winger

izquierdo, -a ADJ left; **brazo i.** left arm; **a mano izquierda** on the left-hand side

izquierdoso, -a ADJ *Fam* leftish

J, j ['xota] NF *(letra)* J, j

jabalí *(pl jabalíes)* NM wild boar

jabalina NF *Dep* javelin

jabato NM young wild boar

jabón NM soap; **j. de afeitar/tocador** shaving/toilet soap

jabonera NF soap dish

jaca NF *(caballo pequeño)* pony; *(yegua)* mare

jacal NM *Méx* hut

jacinto NM *Bot* hyacinth

jactancia NF boastfulness

jactancioso, -a 1 ADJ boastful
2 NM,F braggart

jactarse VPR to boast, to brag **(de** about)

jacuzzi® [ja'kusi] NM Jacuzzi®

jade NM jade

jadeante ADJ panting, breathless

jadear VI to pant, to gasp

jadeo NM panting, gasping

jaguar NM jaguar

jaiba NF *Am salvo RP* crayfish

jalar VT **(a)** *Esp Fam (comer)* to eat, *Br* to scoff **(b)** *Am salvo RP (tirar de)* to pull

jalbegar [42] VT to whitewash

jalea NF jelly; **j. real** royal jelly

jalear VT to cheer (on)

jaleo NM *(alboroto)* din, racket; *(riña)* row; *(confusión)* muddle; **armar j.** to make a racket

jalón NM *Am salvo RP* pull

Jamaica N Jamaica

jamaicano, -a ADJ & NM,F Jamaican

jamás ADV never; **j. he estado allí** I have never been there; **nunca j.** never again; **el mejor libro que j. se ha escrito** the best book ever written

jamba NF *Arquit* jamb

jamón NM ham; **j. de York/serrano** boiled/cured ham

jamona ADJ *Fam* buxom

Japón N **(el) J.** Japan

japonés, -esa 1 ADJ Japanese
2 NM,F *(persona)* Japanese; **los japoneses** the Japanese
3 NM *(idioma)* Japanese

japuta NF *(pez)* Ray's bream

jaque NM *(en ajedrez)* check; **dar j. a** to check; **j. mate** checkmate; **j. al rey** check

jaqueca NF migraine

jara NF *Bot* rock rose

jarabe NM syrup; **j. para la tos** cough mixture

jarana NF *Fam* **ir de j.** to go on a spree *o* a binge

jardín NM *Br* garden, *US* yard; **j. botánico** botanical garden; **j. de infancia** nursery school, kindergarten

jardinera NF planter

jardinería NF gardening

jardinero NM gardener

jarra NF pitcher; **j. de cerveza** beer mug; *Fig* **de** *o* **en jarras** (with) arms akimbo, hands on hips

jarro NM *(recipiente)* jug; *(contenido)* jugful; *Fig* **echar un j. de agua fría a** to pour cold water on

jarrón NM vase; *(en arqueología)* urn

jaspe NM jasper

Jauja NF promised land; **¡esto es J.!** this is the life!

jaula NF cage

jauría NF *(de perros, periodistas)* pack

jazmín NM *Bot* jasmine

jazz [jas] NM INV jazz

J.C. *(abr Jesucristo)* J.C.

jebo, -a NM,F *Ven Fam* = jevo

jeep [jip] NM *Aut* jeep

jefatura NF **(a)** *(cargo, dirección)* leadership **(b)** *(sede)* central office; **j. de policía** police headquarters

jefe, -a NM *(persona al mando)* boss; *(de empresa)* manager; *(de tribu, ejército)* chief; *(de departamento)* head; **J. de Estado** Head of State; **j. de estación** stationmaster; **j. de redacción** editor-in-chief; **j. de ventas** sales manager

Jehová NF Jehovah

jején NM *Am* gnat

jengibre NM *Bot* ginger

jeque NM sheik, sheikh

jerarquía NF hierarchy

jerárquico, -a ADJ hierarchical

jerez NM sherry

jerga NF *(argot)* *(técnica)* jargon; *(vulgar)* slang; **la j. legal** legal jargon

jerigonza NF gibberish

jeringa NF syringe

jeringar [42] VT *Fam* **(a)** *(molestar)* to pester, to annoy **(b)** *(romper)* to break

jeringuilla NF (hypodermic) syringe

jeroglífico, -a 1 ADJ hieroglyphic

2 NM (**a**) *Ling* hieroglyph, hieroglyphic (**b**) *(juego)* rebus

jersey *(pl* **jerseys** *o* **jerséis)** NM *Esp* sweater, *Br* jumper

Jerusalén N Jerusalem

Jesucristo NM Jesus Christ

jesuita ADJ & NMF Jesuit

Jesús 1 N Jesus

2 INTERJ (**a**) *(expresa sorpresa)* good heavens! (**b**) *Esp (al estornudar)* bless you!

jet NF *Esp* **la j.** the jet set

jeta NF *Fam* (**a**) *Esp (descaro)* cheek; **tener j.** to be cheeky, to have a nerve (**b**) *(cara)* mug, face (**c**) *(hocico)* snout

jet-set *Esp* NF, *Am* NM jet set

jeva NF *Carib Fam (mujer)* chick, *Br* bird

jevo, -a NF *Ven Fam (novio)* man, boyfriend; *(novia)* woman, girlfriend

jíbaro, -a NM,F (**a**) *(indio)* Jivaro (**b**) *Ven Fam (traficante)* pusher

jícama NF yam bean, jicama

jícara NF *CAm, Méx, Ven* (**a**) *(calabaza)* calabash, gourd (**b**) *(taza)* mug

jilguero NM goldfinch

jinete NM rider, horseman

jinetera NF *Cuba Fam* prostitute

jiñar VI *muy Fam* to shit

jirafa NF (**a**) *(animal)* giraffe (**b**) *(de micrófono)* boom

jirón NM (**a**) *(trozo desgarrado)* shred, strip; *(pedazo suelto)* bit, scrap; **hecho jirones** in shreds *o* tatters (**b**) *Perú (calle)* street

jitomate NM *Méx* tomato

JJOO NMPL *(abr* **Juegos Olímpicos)** Olympic Games

jocoso, -a ADJ funny, humorous

joda NF *RP, Ven muy Fam* (**a**) *(fastidio)* pain in the *Br* arse *o US* ass (**b**) *(broma)* piss-take; **¡no te enojes!, lo dije/hice en j.** don't be angry, I was just pissing around (**c**) *(fiesta)* **los espero el sábado en casa, va a haber j.** I'll see you at my place on Saturday, we're having a bash

joder *Vulg* **1** INTERJ shit!, *Br* bloody hell!

2 VT (**a**) *(fastidiar)* to piss off; **¡no me jodas!** come on, don't give me that! (**b**) *Esp (copular)* to fuck (**c**) *(echar a perder)* to screw up; **¡la jodiste!** you screwed it up! (**d**) *(romper)* to bust, *Br* bugger

3 joderse VPR (**a**) *(aguantarse)* to put up with it; **¡hay que joderse!** you'll just have to grin and bear it! (**b**) *(echarse a perder)* to get screwed up; **¡se jodió el invento!** that's really screwed things up!; **¡que se joda!** to hell with him! (**c**) *(romperse)* to go bust

jodido, -a ADJ *Vulg* (**a**) *(maldito)* damned, *Br* bloody (**b**) *(molesto)* annoying (**c**) *(enfermo)* in a bad way; *(cansado)* knackered, exhausted (**d**) *(estropeado, roto)* bust, *Br* knackered (**e**) *(difícil)* shitty

jodienda NF *Esp Vulg* (**a**) *(coito)* fuck (**b**) *(molestia)* pain in the *Br* arse *o US* ass

jofaina NF washbasin

jogging NM (**a**) *(deporte)* jogging; **hacer j.** to go jogging (**b**) *RP (ropa)* track *o* jogging suit

jolgorio NM *Fam (juerga)* binge; *(algazara)* fun

jolín, jolines INTERJ *Fam (enfado)* blast!, damn!; *(sorpresa)* gosh!, good grief!

Jordania N Jordan

jornada NF (**a**) **j.** *(laboral)* *(día de trabajo)* working day; **j. intensiva** continuous working day; **j. partida** working day with a lunch break; **trabajo de media j./j. completa** part-time/full-time work (**b**) **jornadas** conference

jornal NM *(paga)* day's wage; **trabajar a j.** to be paid by the day

> Observa que la palabra inglesa **journal** es un falso amigo y no es la traducción de la palabra española **jornal**. En inglés, **journal** significa "revista, diario".

jornalero, -a NM,F day labourer

joroba NF hump

jorobado, -a 1 ADJ hunchbacked

2 NM,F hunchback

jorobar *Fam* **1** VT (**a**) *(fastidiar)* to bug; **me joroba** it really gets up my nose; **¡no jorobes!** *(incredulidad)* pull the other one! (**b**) *(estropear)* to bust

2 jorobarse VPR (**a**) *(fastidiarse)* to grin and bear it (**b**) *(estropearse)* to bust

jorongo NM *Méx* (**a**) *(manta)* blanket (**b**) *(poncho)* poncho

jota¹ NF (**a**) *(letra)* = name of the letter J in Spanish (**b**) *(cantidad mínima)* **ni j.** not an iota; **no entiendo ni j.** I don't understand a thing

jota² NF *Mús* = Spanish dance and music

joven 1 ADJ young; **de aspecto j.** young-looking

2 NMF *(hombre)* youth, young man; *(mujer)* girl, young woman; **de j.** as a young man/woman; **los jóvenes** young people, youth

jovial ADJ jovial, good-humoured

joya NF jewel, piece of jewellery; **joyas de imitación** imitation jewellery; *Fig* **ser una j.** *(persona)* to be a real treasure *o* gem

joyería NF jewellery shop, jeweller's (shop)

joyero, -a 1 NM,F jeweller

2 NM jewel case *o* box

joystick ['joistik] *(pl* **joysticks)** NM joystick

juanete NM *(en el pie)* bunion

jubilación NF (**a**) *(acción)* retirement; **j. anticipada** early retirement (**b**) *(pensión)* pension

jubilado, -a 1 ADJ retired

2 NM,F *Br* pensioner, *US* retiree; **los jubilados** retired people

jubilar 1 VT *(retirar)* to retire, to pension off; *Fam Fig* to get rid of, to ditch

2 jubilarse VPR *(retirarse)* to retire, to go into retirement

júbilo NM jubilation, joy

judaísmo NM Judaism

judería NF *Hist* Jewish quarter

judía NF bean; *Esp* **j. verde** green bean

judicial ADJ judicial; **la vía j.** legal channels

judío, -a 1 ADJ Jewish
2 NM,F Jew

judo NM *Dep* judo

juego NM (**a**) *(acción)* play, playing; *Fig* **j. limpio/sucio** fair/foul play; **j. de palabras** play on words, pun (**b**) *(deporte, diversión)* game; **j. de azar** game of chance; **j. de cartas** card game; **j. de mesa** board game; **Juegos Olímpicos** Olympic Games; **j. de rol** fantasy role-playing game (**c**) *(apuestas)* gambling; *Fig* **poner algo en j.** to put sth at stake (**d**) *(conjunto de piezas)* set; **j. de café/té** coffee/ tea service; **ir a j. con** to match

juerga NF *Fam* binge, rave-up; **ir de j.** to go on a binge

juerguista 1 ADJ fun-loving
2 NMF fun-loving person, raver

jueves NM INV Thursday; **J. Santo** Maundy Thursday

juez NMF judge; **j. de instrucción** examining magistrate; **j. de paz** justice of the peace; *Dep* **j. de salida** starter; **j. de línea** *(hombre)* lines-man; *(mujer)* lineswoman

jugada NF (**a**) *(en deportes, juegos)* move; *(en billar)* shot (**b**) *Fam* dirty trick

jugador, -a NM,F player; *(apostador)* gambler

jugar [32] 1 VI (**a**) to play; **j. a(l) fútbol/tenis** to play football/tennis; *Fig* **j. sucio** to play dirty (**b**) **j. con** *(no tomar en serio)* to toy with
2 VT (**a**) to play (**b**) *(apostar)* to bet, to stake
3 jugarse VPR (**a**) *(arriesgar)* to risk; *Fam* **jugarse el pellejo** to risk one's neck (**b**) *(apostar)* to bet, to stake

jugarreta NF *Fam* dirty trick

jugo NM juice; *Fig* **sacar el j. a** *(aprovechar)* to make the most of; *(explotar)* to squeeze dry

jugoso, -a ADJ (**a**) *(alimento)* juicy; **un filete j.** a juicy steak (**b**) *Fig (sustancioso)* substantial, meaty; **un tema j.** a meaty topic

juguete NM toy; **pistola de j.** toy gun; *Fig* **ser el j. de algn** to be sb's plaything

juguetear VI to play

juguetería NF toy shop

juguetón, -ona ADJ playful

juicio NM (**a**) *(facultad mental)* judgement, discernment; *(opinión)* opinion, judgement; **a j. de** in the opinion of; **a mi j.** in my opinion (**b**) *(sensatez)* reason, common sense; **en su sano j.** in one's right mind; **perder el j.** to go mad (**c**) *Der* trial, lawsuit; **llevar a algn a j.** to take legal action against sb, to sue sb

juicioso, -a ADJ judicious, wise

julepe NM (**a**) *(juego de naipes)* = type of card game (**b**) *PRico, RP Fam (susto)* scare, fright; **dar un j. a algn** to give sb a scare

julio NM July

junco NM *Bot* rush

jungla NF jungle

junio NM June

júnior ADJ *Dep* junior; **campeonato j. de golf** junior golf championship

junta NF (**a**) *(reunión)* meeting, assembly; *Pol* **j. de gobierno** cabinet meeting (**b**) *(dirección)* board, committee; **j. directiva** board of directors (**c**) *Mil* junta; **j. militar** military junta (**d**) *(parlamento regional)* regional parliament (**e**) *Téc* joint

juntar 1 VT (**a**) *(unir)* to join, to put together; *(piezas)* to assemble (**b**) *(reunir) (sellos)* to collect; *(dinero)* to raise
2 juntarse VPR (**a**) *(unirse)* to join; *(ríos, caminos)* to meet; *(personas)* to gather (**b**) *(amancebarse)* to live together

junto, -a 1 ADJ together; **dos mesas juntas** two tables side by side; **todos juntos** all together
2 ADV **j. con** together with; **j. a** next to

juntura NF *Téc* joint, seam

jura NF *(acción)* oath; *(ceremonia)* swearing in; **j. de bandera** oath of allegiance to the flag

jurado NM (**a**) *(tribunal)* jury; *(en un concurso)* panel of judges, jury (**b**) *(miembro del tribunal)* juror, member of the jury

juramento NM (**a**) *Der* oath; **bajo j.** under oath (**b**) *(blasfemia)* swearword, curse

jurar 1 VI *Der & Rel* to swear, to take an oath
2 VT to swear; **j. el cargo** to take the oath of office; **j. por Dios** to swear to God
3 jurarse VPR *Fam* **tenérsela jurada a algn** to have it in for sb

jurel NM *(pez)* scad, horse mackerel

jurídico, -a ADJ legal

jurisdicción NF jurisdiction

jurisdiccional ADJ jurisdictional; **aguas juris-diccionales** territorial waters

jurista NMF jurist, lawyer

justamente ADV **¡j.!** precisely!; **j. detrás de** right behind

justicia NF justice; **tomarse la j. por su mano** to take the law into one's own hands

justicialismo NM *Pol* = Argentinian national-istic political movement founded by Juan Domingo Perón

justicialista ADJ *Pol* = belonging or related to "justicialismo"

justiciero, -a ADJ severe

justificable ADJ justifiable

justificación NF justification

justificado, -a ADJ justified, well-grounded

justificante NM written proof; **j. de pago** proof of payment

justificar [44] **1** VT to justify

2 justificarse VPR to clear oneself, to justify oneself

justo, -a 1 ADJ (**a**) *(equitativo)* fair; **un trato j.** a fair deal (**b**) *(apretado) (ropa)* tight; **estamos justos de tiempo** we're pressed for time (**c**) *(exacto)* right, accurate; **la palabra justa** the right word (**d**) *(preciso)* **llegamos en el momento j. en que salían** we arrived just as they were leaving (**e**) **lo j.** just enough

2 NM,F just *o* righteous person; **los justos** the just, the righteous

3 ADV *(exactamente)* exactly, precisely; **j. al lado** right beside

juvenil 1 ADJ *(aspecto)* youthful, young; **ropa j.** young people's clothes; **delincuencia j.** juvenile delinquency

2 NMF *Dep* **juveniles** ≃ youth team *(age 16-17)*

juventud NF (**a**) *(edad)* youth (**b**) *(jóvenes)* young people

juzgado NM court, tribunal; **j. de guardia** = court open during the night or at other times when ordinary courts are shut

juzgar [42] VT to judge; **a j. por ...** judging by ...

K, k [ka] NF *(letra)* K, k

karaoke NM karaoke

kárate NM *Dep* karate

karateka NMF *Dep* person who does karate

karting NM go-kart racing, karting

Kenia N Kenya

Kg, kg *(abr* **kilogramo(s)**) kg

kilo NM (**a**) *(medida)* kilo; *Fam* **pesa un k.** it weighs a ton (**b**) *Esp Antes Fam (millón)* a million (pesetas)

kilogramo NM kilogram, kilogramme

kilolitro NM kilolitre

kilometraje NM ≃ mileage

kilométrico, -a ADJ kilometric, kilometrical; **billete k.** multiple-journey ticket

kilómetro NM kilometre

kilovatio NM kilowatt; **k. hora** kilowatt-hour

kimono NM kimono

kínder NM *Andes, Méx* kindergarten, nursery school

kiosco NM = **quiosco**

kiwi NM (**a**) *(ave)* kiwi (**b**) *(fruto)* kiwi (fruit), Chinese gooseberry

kleenex® ['klines, 'klineks] NMINV paper hanky, (paper) tissue

km *(abr* **kilómetro(s)**) km

Kw, kw *(abr* **kilovatio(s)**) kW

L

L, l ['ele] NF *(letra)* L, l

l *(abr* **litro(s))** l

la¹ 1 ART DEF F the; **la mesa** the table
2 PRON DEM the one; **la del vestido azul** the one in the blue dress; **la que vino ayer** the one who came yesterday; *ver* **el**

la² PRON PERS F *(persona)* her; *(usted)* you; *(cosa)* it; **la invitaré** I'll invite her along; **no la dejes abierta** don't leave it open; **ya la avisaremos, señora** we'll let you know, madam; *ver* **le**

la³ NM *Mús* la, A

laberinto NM labyrinth

labia NF *Fam* loquacity; *Pey* glibness; **tener mucha l.** to have the gift of the gab

labio NM lip

labor NF (a) *(trabajo)* work; *(tarea)* task; **l. de equipo** teamwork; **profesión: sus labores** occupation: housewife (b) *Agr* farmwork (c) *(de costura)* needlework

laborable ADJ (a) **día l.** *(no festivo)* working day (b) *Agr* arable

laboral ADJ industrial; **accidente l.** industrial accident; **conflictividad l.** industrial unrest; **jornada l.** working day; **Universidad L.** technical training college

laboratorio NM laboratory

laborioso, -a ADJ (a) *(persona)* hardworking (b) *(tarea)* laborious

laborista *Pol* 1 ADJ Labour
2 NMF Labour (Party) member/supporter

labrador, -a NM,F *(granjero)* farmer; *(trabajador)* farm worker

labranza NF farming

labrar 1 VT (a) *Agr* to till (b) *(madera)* to carve; *(piedra)* to cut; *(metal)* to work
2 **labrarse** VPR *Fig* **labrarse un porvenir** to build a future for oneself

laburar VI *RP Fam* to work; **labura de vendedora** she works in a shop

laburo NM *RP Fam* job

laca NF (a) *(para el pelo)* hair lacquer, hairspray; **l. de uñas** nail polish o varnish (b) *Arte* lacquer

lacio, -a ADJ (a) *(pelo)* lank, limp (b) **qué l.!** *(soso)* what a weed!

lacónico, -a ADJ laconic; *(conciso)* terse

lacra NF evil, curse; **una l. social** a scourge of society

lacrar VT to seal with wax

lacre NM sealing wax

lacrimógeno, -a ADJ (a) **gas l.** tear gas (b) *Fig* **una película lacrimógena** a tear-jerker

lactancia NF lactation; **l. artificial** bottle feeding; **l. materna** breastfeeding

lactante NMF baby *(not yet eating solid food)*

lactar VI to breast-feed

lácteo, -a ADJ **productos lácteos** milk o dairy products

ladear 1 VT to tilt
2 **ladearse** VPR (a) *(inclinarse)* to lean, to tilt (b) *(desviarse)* to go off to one side

ladera NF slope

ladino, -a 1 ADJ *(astuto)* crafty
2 NM *CAm, Méx, Ven (no blanco)* = non-white Spanish-speaking person

lado NM (a) *(costado, parte)* side; **a un l.** aside; **al l.** close by, nearby; **al l. de** next to, beside; **ponte de l.** stand sideways (b) *(lugar)* place; **en otro l.** somewhere else; **por todos lados** everywhere, all around (c) *(expresiones)* **dar de l. a algn** to cold-shoulder sb; **por otro l.** *(además)* moreover; **por un l. ..., por otro l. ...** on the one hand ..., on the other hand ...

ladrar VI to bark

ladrido NM *también Fig* bark

ladrillo NM (a) *Constr* brick (b) *Fam (pesado)* bore, drag

ladrón, -ona 1 NM,F thief, robber; **¡al l.!** stop, thief!
2 NM *Elec* multiple socket

lagartija NF small lizard

lagarto NM lizard

lago NM lake

lágrima NF (a) *(en los ojos)* tear; **llorar a l. viva** to cry one's eyes out (b) *(en lámpara)* teardrop

lagrimoso, -a ADJ tearful

laguna NF (a) *(lago)* lagoon (b) *(en colección, memoria)* gap; *(en leyes, reglamento)* loophole

La Haya N The Hague

laico, -a 1 ADJ lay
2 NM,F lay person; *(hombre)* layman; *(mujer)* laywoman

lameculos NMF INV *muy Fam* bootlicker, *Br* arselicker, *US* ass-kisser

lamentable ADJ regrettable; *(malo)* lamentable

lamentar 1 VT to regret; **lo lamento** I'm sorry
2 **lamentarse** VPR to complain

lamento NM moan, wail

lamer VT to lick

lámina NF (**a**) *(plancha)* sheet; *(placa)* plate (**b**) *(rodaja)* slice (**c**) *(grabado)* engraving (**d**) *(dibujo)* plate

laminar VT (**a**) *(hacer láminas de)* to roll (**b**) *(cubrir con láminas)* to laminate

lámpara NF (**a**) *(aparato)* lamp; **l. de pie** *Br* standard lamp, *US* floor lamp (**b**) *(bombilla)* bulb (**c**) *Rad* valve (**d**) *Fam (mancha)* stain

lamparón NM *Fam* oil *o* grease stain

lana NF (**a**) *(de oveja)* wool; **pura l. virgen** pure new wool (**b**) *Andes, Méx Fam (dinero)* dough, cash

lanar ADJ **ganado l.** sheep

lance NM *Literario (episodio)* event, incident

> Observa que la palabra inglesa **lance** es un falso amigo y no es la traducción de la palabra española **lance**. En inglés, **lance** significa "lanza".

lanceta NF *Andes, Méx (aguijón)* sting

lancha NF motorboat, launch; **l. motora** speedboat; **l. neumática** rubber dinghy; **l. salvavidas** lifeboat

langosta NF (**a**) *(crustáceo)* lobster (**b**) *(insecto)* locust

langostino NM king prawn

languidecer [33] VI to languish

lánguido, -a ADJ languid; *(sin vigor)* listless

lanudo, -a ADJ woolly, fleecy; *(peludo)* furry

lanza NF spear, lance; **punta de l.** spearhead; *Fig* **romper una l. en favor de algn/algo** to defend sb/sth

lanzadera NF shuttle; **l. espacial** space shuttle

lanzado, -a ADJ *Fam* reckless; **ir l.** to tear along

lanzamiento NM (**a**) *(de objeto)* throwing, hurling (**b**) *Dep (de disco, jabalina)* throw; *(de peso)* put (**c**) *Mil (de cohete etc)* launching (**d**) *Com* launch; **precio de l.** launch price (**e**) *Náut* launch

lanzar [40] **1** VT (**a**) *(arrojar)* to throw, to fling (**b**) *(grito)* to let out (**c**) *Com, Mil & Náut* to launch

2 lanzarse VPR (**a**) *(arrojarse)* to throw *o* hurl oneself; **lanzarse al suelo** to throw oneself to the ground (**b**) *(emprender)* **lanzarse a** to embark on; **lanzarse a los negocios** to go into business

lapa NF (**a**) *Zool* limpet (**b**) **es una verdadera l.** he/she sticks to you like glue

lapicera NF *CSur* ballpoint (pen), Biro®; **l. fuente** fountain pen

lapicero NM (**a**) *Esp (lápiz)* pencil (**b**) *CAm, Perú (bolígrafo)* ballpoint (pen), Biro®

lápida NF headstone

lapidario, -a ADJ *(frase)* meaningful, oracular

lápiz NM pencil; **l. labial** *o* **de labios** lipstick; **l. de ojos** eyeliner

lapso NM (**a**) *(periodo de tiempo)* period (**b**) *(error)* lapse, slip

lapsus NM INV slip; **l. linguae** slip of the tongue

largar [42] **1** VT (**a**) *Fam (golpe, discurso, dinero)* to give (**b**) *Náut* **l. amarras** to cast off

2 largarse VPR *Fam* to clear off, to split; **¡lárgate!** beat it!

largas NFPL **dar l. a algo** to put sth off

largavistas NM INV *Bol, CSur* binoculars

largo, -a **1** ADJ (**a**) *(espacio)* long; *(tiempo)* long, lengthy; **pasamos un mes l. allí** we spent a good month there; **a lo l. de** *(espacio)* along; *(tiempo)* through; **a la larga** in the long run (**b**) *(excesivo)* too long; **se hizo l. el día** the day dragged on (**c**) **largos años** many years

2 NM (**a**) *(longitud)* length; **¿cuánto tiene de l.?** how long is it? (**b**) *Mús* largo

3 ADV **l. y tendido** at length; *Fam* **¡l. (de aquí)!** clear off!; **esto va para l.** this is going to last a long time

> Observa que la palabra inglesa **large** es un falso amigo y no es la traducción de la palabra española **largo**. En inglés **large** significa "grande".

largometraje NM feature film, full-length film

laringe NF larynx

laringitis NF INV laryngitis

las¹ 1 ART DEF FPL the; **l. sillas** the chairs; **lávate l. manos** wash your hands; *(no se traduce)* **me gustan l. flores** I like flowers

2 PRON **l. que** *(personas)* the ones who, those who; *(objetos)* the ones that, those that; **toma l. que quieras** take whichever ones you want; *ver* **la** *y* **los**

las² PRON PERS FPL *(ellas)* them; *(ustedes)* you; **l. llamaré mañana (a ustedes)** I'll call you tomorrow; **no l. rompas** don't break them; **Pepa es de l. mías** Pepa thinks the way I do; *ver* **los**

lasaña NF lasagna, lasagne

lascivo, -a ADJ lewd, lecherous

láser ADJ INV & NM INV laser

lástima NF pity; **¡qué l.!** what a pity!, what a shame!; **es una l. que ...** it's a pity that ...; **estar hecho una l.** to be a sorry sight; **tener l. a algn** to feel sorry for sb

lastimar VT to hurt, to injure

lastre NM (**a**) *(peso)* ballast (**b**) *Fig* dead weight

lata¹ NF (**a**) *(envase)* can, *esp Br* tin; **en l.** canned, *esp Br* tinned (**b**) *(hojalata)* tin(plate); **hecho de l.** made of tin

lata² NF *Esp Fam* nuisance, drag; **dar la l.** to be a nuisance *o* a pest

latente ADJ latent

lateral 1 ADJ side, lateral; **salió por la puerta l.** he went out by the side door; **escalón l.** *(en letrero)* ramp

2 NM side passage; *Aut* **(carril) l.** side lane

latido NM *(del corazón)* beat

latifundio NM large landed estate

latigazo NM lash

látigo NM whip

latín NM Latin

latino, -a 1 ADJ Latin; **América Latina** Latin America
2 NM,F Latin American

Latinoamérica NF Latin America

latinoamericano, -a ADJ & NM,F Latin American

latir VI to beat

latitud NF (a) *Geog* latitude (b) **latitudes** region, area

latón NM brass

latoso, -a ADJ *Fam* annoying

laucha NF *CSur* (a) *(ratón)* baby o small mouse (b) *Fam (persona)* **es una l.** he's a tiny little thing

laúd NM lute

laurel NM *Bot* laurel, (sweet) bay; *Culin* bay leaf; *Fig* **dormirse en los laureles** to rest on one's laurels

lava NF lava

lavable ADJ washable

lavabo NM (a) *(pila)* Br washbasin, US washbowl (b) *(retrete)* Br lavatory, US washroom

lavadero NM *(de coches)* carwash

lavado NM wash, washing; *Fig* **l. de cerebro** brainwashing; **l. en seco** dry-cleaning

lavadora NF washing machine

lavanda NF lavender

lavandería NF (a) *(automática)* launderette, US Laundromat® (b) *(atendida por personal)* laundry

lavaplatos NM INV dishwasher

lavar VT to wash; **l. en seco** to dry-clean

lavativa NF enema

lavatorio NM (a) *(en misa)* lavabo (b) *Andes, RP (lavabo)* Br washbasin, US washbowl

lavavajillas NM INV *(aparato)* dishwasher

laxante ADJ & NM laxative

laxitud NF laxity, laxness

lazada NF *(nudo)* bow

lazarillo NM **(perro) l.** guide dog, US seeing-eye dog

lazo NM (a) *(adorno)* bow (b) *(nudo)* knot; **l. corredizo** slipknot (c) *(para reses)* lasso (d) *Fig (usu pl) (vínculo)* tie, bond

le 1 PRON PERS MF *(objeto indirecto) (a él)* (to) him; *(a ella)* (to) her; *(a cosa)* (to) it; *(a usted)* (to) you; **lávale la cara** wash his face; **le compraré uno** I'll buy one for her; **¿qué le pasa (a usted)?** what's the matter with you?
2 PRON PERS M *Esp (objeto directo) (él)* him; *(usted)* you; **no le oigo** I can't hear him; **no quiero molestarle** I don't wish to disturb you

leal 1 ADJ loyal, faithful
2 NMF loyalist

lealtad NF loyalty, faithfulness

lebrel NM greyhound

lección NF lesson; *Fig* **dar una l. a algn** to teach sb a lesson; *Fig* **te servirá de l.** let that be a lesson to you

lechal 1 ADJ suckling, sucking
2 NM suckling lamb

lechazo NM suckling lamb

leche NF (a) *(líquido)* milk; **l. descremada** o **desnatada** Br skimmed milk, US skim milk (b) *muy Fam (humor)* **estar de mala l.** to be in a Br bloody o US goddamn awful mood (c) *Esp muy Fam (golpe)* knock; **dar** o **pegar una l. a algn** to clobber sb

lechera NF (a) *(vasija)* churn (b) *Fam* police car

lechería NF dairy, creamery

lechero, -a 1 ADJ milk, dairy; **central lechera** dairy co-operative; **vaca lechera** milk cow
2 NM milkman

lecho NM *Lit* bed; **l. del río** river-bed; **l. mortuorio** death-bed

lechón NM suckling-pig

lechosa NF *Carib* papaya

lechoso, -a ADJ milky

lechuga NF lettuce

lechuza NF owl

lectivo, -a ADJ school; **horas lectivas** teaching hours

lector, -a 1 NM,F (a) *(persona)* reader (b) *Esp Univ* lector, (language) assistant
2 NM reader; **l. de CD-ROM** CD-ROM drive; **l. de DVD** DVD player

lectura NF reading

leer [36] VT to read; **léenos el menú** read out the menu for us; *Fig* **l. entre líneas** to read between the lines

legado NM legacy

legajo NM bundle (of papers)

legal ADJ (a) *Der* legal, lawful; **requisitos legales** legal formalities (b) *Esp Fam (persona)* honest, decent

legalidad NF legality, lawfulness

legalizar [40] VT to legalize; *(documento)* to authenticate

legaña NF sleep

legar [42] VT *(propiedad)* to bequeath; *Fig (tradiciones)* to hand down, to pass on

legendario, -a ADJ legendary

legible ADJ legible

legión NF legion

legionella NF Legionnaire's Disease

legislación NF legislation

legislar VI to legislate

legislativo, -a ADJ legislative; **el poder l.** parliament

legislatura NF legislature

legitimar VT *(justificar)* to legitimize; *(autentificar)* to authenticate

legitimidad NF legitimacy

legítimo, -a ADJ (a) *Der* legitimate; **en legítima defensa** in self-defence (b) *(auténtico)* authentic, real; **oro l.** pure gold

lego, -a 1 ADJ *Rel* lay
2 NM (a) *(profano)* layman; **ser l. en la materia** to know nothing about the subject (b) *Rel* lay brother

legua NF *(medida)* league; *Fig* **se nota a la l.** it stands out a mile

legumbre NF pulse, pod vegetable; **legumbres secas** dried pulses; **legumbres verdes** green vegetables

lehendakari NMF = head of the Basque government

lejanía NF distance

lejano, -a ADJ distant, far-off; **parientes lejanos** distant relatives; **el L. Oriente** the Far East

lejía NF bleach

lejos ADV far (away); **a lo l.** in the distance; **de l.** from a distance; *Fig* **ir demasiado l.** to go too far; *Fig* **llegar l.** to go a long way; *Fig* **sin ir más l.** to take an obvious example

lelo, -a *Fam* **1** ADJ stupid, silly
2 NM,F ninny

lema NM (a) *(divisa)* motto, slogan (b) *(contraseña)* code name

lencería NF (a) *(prendas)* lingerie (b) *(ropa blanca)* linen (goods)

lengua NF (a) *Anat* tongue; *Fig* **malas lenguas** gossips; *Fam Fig* **irse de la l.** to spill the beans; *Fam Fig* **tirarle a algn de la l.** to draw sb out (b) *Ling* language; **l. materna** native *o* mother tongue

lenguado NM *(pez)* sole

lenguaje NM language; *Inform* language; **l. corporal** body language

lengüeta NF (a) *(de zapato)* tongue (b) *Mús* reed

lente 1 NF lens; **lentes de contacto** contact lenses
2 lentes NMPL *Am* glasses; **lentes de contacto** contact lenses

lenteja NF lentil

lentejuela NF sequin, spangle

lentilla NF *Esp* contact lens; **lentillas blandas/duras** soft/hard lenses

lentitud NF slowness; **con l.** slowly

lento, -a ADJ slow; **a fuego l.** on a low heat

leña NF (a) *(madera)* firewood; *Fig* **echar l. al fuego** to add fuel to the fire (b) *Fam (golpes)* knocks

leñador, -a NM,F woodcutter

leñazo NM *Fam (golpe)* blow, smash

leñe INTERJ *Esp Fam* damn it!

leño NM log

Leo NM Leo

león NM lion

leona NF lioness

leonera NF lion's den; *Fig (habitación)* den

leopardo NM leopard

leotardos NMPL *Esp* thick tights

lépero, -a *Fam* ADJ (a) *CAm, Méx (vulgar)* coarse, vulgar (b) *Cuba (ladino)* smart, crafty

lepra NF leprosy

leproso, -a 1 ADJ leprous
2 NM,F leper

les 1 PRON PERS MFPL *(objeto indirecto) (a ellos, -as)* them; *(a ustedes)* you; **dales el dinero** give them the money; **l. he comprado un regalo** I've bought you a present
2 PRON PERS MPL *Esp (objeto directo) (ellos)* them; *(ustedes)* you; **l. esperaré** I shall wait for you; **no quiero molestarles** I don't wish to disturb you

lesbiana NF lesbian

leseras NFPL *Chile Fam (tonterías)* nonsense, *Br* rubbish

lesión NF (a) *(corporal)* injury (b) *Der (perjuicio)* damage

lesionar VT to injure

leso, -a ADJ *Der* **crimen de lesa humanidad** crime against humanity

letal ADJ lethal, deadly

letanía NF litany

letargo NM lethargy

letón, -ona 1 ADJ Latvian
2 NM,F Latvian
3 NM *(idioma)* Latvian, Lettish

Letonia N Latvia

letra NF (a) *(signo)* letter; **l. de imprenta** block capitals; **l. mayúscula** capital letter; **l. minúscula** small letter; **l. pequeña** small print (b) *(escritura)* (hand)writing (c) *Mús (texto)* lyrics, words (d) *Fin* **l. (de cambio)** bill of exchange, draft (e) *Univ* **letras** arts

letrado, -a NM,F lawyer

letrero NM *(aviso)* notice, sign; *(cartel)* poster; **l. luminoso** neon sign

leucemia NF leukaemia

levadizo, -a ADJ **puente l.** drawbridge

levadura NF yeast; **l. en polvo** baking powder

levantamiento NM (a) *Dep* **l. de pesos** weightlifting (b) *(insurrección)* uprising

levantar 1 VT (a) *(alzar, elevar)* to raise, to lift; *(mano, voz)* to raise; *(edificio)* to erect; *Fig (ánimos)* to raise; **l. los ojos** to look up (b) *(castigo)* to suspend
2 levantarse VPR (a) *(ponerse de pie)* to stand up, to rise (b) *(salir de la cama)* to get up (c) *(concluir)* to finish; **se levanta la sesión** the meeting is closed (d) *Pol* to rise, to revolt; **levantarse en armas** to rise up in arms (e) *(viento)* to come up; *(tormenta)* to gather

levante NM (a) **(el) L.** Levante, = the regions of Valencia and Murcia (b) *(viento)* east wind, Levanter

levar VT **l. ancla** to weigh anchor

leve ADJ *(ligero)* light; *Fig (de poca importancia)* slight

levedad NF *(ligereza)* lightness; *Fig* slightness; **heridas de l.** minor injuries

levemente ADV slightly

levitar VI to levitate

léxico, -a *Ling* **1** NM *(diccionario)* lexicon; *(vocabulario)* vocabulary, word list
2 ADJ lexical

ley *(pl* **leyes)** NF *(a) (norma)* law; *(parlamentaria)* act; **leyes** *(derecho)* law *(b)* **oro de l.** pure gold; **plata de l.** sterling silver

leyenda NF *(a) (relato)* legend; *(en un mapa)* legend; *(en una moneda)* inscription; *(bajo ilustración)* caption

liar [29] **1** VT *(a) (envolver)* to wrap up; *(un cigarrillo)* to roll *(b) (enredar)* to muddle up; *(confundir)* to confuse
2 liarse VPR *(a) (embarullarse)* to get muddled up *(b) Esp Fam (salir)* to get involved (**con** with); *(besarse)* to neck *(c) Esp* **liarse a bofetadas** to come to blows

libanés, -esa ADJ & NM,F Lebanese

Líbano N **el L.** (the) Lebanon

libelo NM lampoon, satire

libélula NF dragonfly

liberación NF *(de país)* liberation; *(de prisionero)* release, freeing

liberal ADJ & NM,F liberal

liberalizar [40] VT to liberalize

liberar VT *(país)* to liberate; *(prisionero)* to free, to release

libertad NF freedom, liberty; **en l.** free; *Der* **(en) l. bajo palabra/fianza** (on) parole/bail; *Der* **(en) l. condicional** (on) parole; **l. de comercio** free trade; **l. de expresión** freedom of speech

libertador, -a NM,F liberator

libertar VT to set free, to release

libertinaje NM licentiousness

libertino, -a ADJ & NM,F libertine

Libia N Libya

libio, -a ADJ & NM,F Libyan

Libra NM Libra

libra NF *(unidad de peso, moneda)* pound; **l. esterlina** pound sterling

librar **1** VT *(a)* **l. a algn de algo** to free sb from sth *(b) Com (letra)* to draw *(c)* **l. batalla** to do *o* join battle
2 VI *Esp (no trabajar)* to be off work; **libro los martes** I have Tuesdays off
3 librarse VPR to escape; **librarse de algn** to get rid of sb

libre ADJ free; **entrada l.** *(gratis)* admission free; *(sin restricción)* open to the public; **l. cambio** free trade; **l. de impuestos** tax-free

librería NF *(a) (tienda)* bookshop, *US* bookstore *(b) Esp (mueble)* bookcase

Observa que la palabra inglesa **library** es un falso amigo y no es la traducción de la palabra española **librería**. En inglés **library** significa "biblioteca".

librero, -a **1** NM,F bookseller
2 NM *CAm, Col, Méx (mueble)* bookcase

Observa que la palabra inglesa **librarian** es un falso amigo y no es la traducción de la palabra española **librero**. En inglés **librarian** significa "bibliotecario".

libreta NF notebook; **l. (de ahorro)** savings book

libretista NMF *Am (guionista)* screenwriter, scriptwriter

libreto NM *Am (guión)* script

libro NM book; **l. de texto** textbook; *Com* **l. de caja** cashbook; *Fin* **l. mayor** ledger

liceal NMF *Urug Br* secondary school *o US* high school pupil

liceano, -a NM,F *Chile Br* secondary school *o US* high school pupil

liceísta NMF *Ven Br* secondary school *o US* high school pupil

licencia NF *(a) (permiso)* permission; *(documento)* permit, licence; **l. de armas/caza** gun/hunting licence; *Carib, Chile, Ecuad* **l. de conducir,** *Méx* **l. para conducir** *o* **de conductor** *Br* driving licence, *US* driver's license *(b) (libertad abusiva)* licence, licentiousness

licenciado, -a NM,F *(a) Univ* graduate; **l. en Ciencias** Bachelor of Science *(b) Am salvo RP (forma de tratamiento)* = form of address used to indicate respect; **el l.** Pérez Mr Pérez

licenciar [43] **1** VT *(a) Mil* to discharge *(b) Univ* to confer a degree on
2 licenciarse VPR *Univ* to graduate

licenciatura NF *Univ (título)* (bachelor's) degree (course); *(carrera)* degree (course)

liceo NM *(a) (sociedad literaria)* literary society *(b) (escuela) Br* secondary school, *US* high school

licitar VT *Com (pujar)* to bid for

lícito, -a ADJ *(permisible)* allowed; *Der* lawful

licor NM liquor, *US* spirits

licorería NF *(a) (fábrica)* distillery *(b) (tienda) Br* off-licence, *US* liquor store

licuadora NF *(a) Esp (para extraer zumo)* juice extractor, juicer *(b) Am (para batir)* blender, *Br* liquidizer

licuar [30] VT to liquidize

lid NF contest

líder NMF leader

liderar VT to lead, to head

liderato, liderazgo NM leadership; *Dep* top *o* first position

lidia NF bullfight, bullfighting

lidiador NM bullfighter

lidiar [43] **1** VT *Taurom* to fight
2 VI to fight; **l. con** to contend with, to fight against

liebre NF hare

liendre NF nit

lienzo NM (**a**) *Tex* linen (**b**) *Arte* canvas

lifting ['liftin] (*pl* **liftings**) NM face-lift

liga NF (**a**) *Dep & Pol* league; **hacer buena l.** to get on well together (**b**) *(para medias) (elástico)* garter; *(colgante)* Br suspender, US garter

ligamento NM ligament

ligar [42] **1** VT (*unir, aglutinar*) to bind; (*atar*) to tie (up); (*salsa*) to thicken
2 VI *Fam (encontrar pareja)* to score, *Br* to pull; **l. con algn** (*entablar relaciones*) *Br* to get off with sb, *US* to make out with sb
3 ligarse VPR *Esp Fam* **ligarse a algn** *Br* to get off with sb, *US* to make out with sb

ligazón NF bond, tie

ligeramente ADV (**a**) *(levemente)* lightly (**b**) *(un poco)* slightly

ligereza NF (**a**) *(levedad)* lightness (**b**) *(irreflexión)* rashness (**c**) *(rapidez)* speed

ligero, -a **1** ADJ (**a**) *(de poco peso)* light, lightweight; **l. de ropa** lightly clad (**b**) *(leve) (brisa, comida, roce)* light; *(dolor, diferencia)* slight (**c**) *(veloz)* swift, quick; *(ágil)* agile, nimble (**d**) **hacer algo a la ligera** to do sth without much thought; **tomarse algo a la ligera** not to take sth seriously
2 ADV *(rápido)* fast, swiftly

light [lait] ADJ INV *(tabaco)* mild; *Fig (persona)* lightweight

ligón, -ona ADJ *Esp Fam* **es muy l.** he's always *Br* getting off *o US* making out with somebody or other

ligue NM *Esp Fam (novio) Br* bloke, *US* squeeze; *(novia) Br* bird, *US* squeeze

liguero, -a **1** ADJ *Dep* league; **partido l.** league game *o Br* match
2 NM *Br* suspender belt, *US* garter belt

lija NF sandpaper; **papel de l.** sandpaper

lijar VT to sand *o* sandpaper (down)

lila¹ **1** NM *(color)* lilac
2 NF *(flor)* lilac
3 ADJ INV lilac

lila² *Fam* **1** ADJ *(tonto)* dumb, stupid
2 NMF *(tonto)* twit

lima¹ NF *(fruto)* lime

lima² NF *(herramienta)* file; **l. de uñas** nail-file

limar VT to file; *Fig* **l. asperezas** to smooth things over

limbo NM limbo

limitación NF limitation; **l. de velocidad** speed limit

limitar **1** VT to limit, to restrict
2 VI to border; **l. con** to border on

límite NM limit; *Geog & Pol* boundary, border; **caso l.** borderline case; **fecha l.** deadline; **velocidad l.** maximum speed

limítrofe ADJ neighbouring

limón NM lemon

limonada NF lemonade, = iced, sweetened lemon juice drink

limonero NM lemon tree

limosna NF alms; **pedir l.** to beg

limpiabotas NM INV shoeshine, *Br* bootblack

limpiacristales NM INV window cleaner

limpiador, -a **1** ADJ cleansing
2 NM,F *(persona)* cleaner
3 NM *(producto)* cleaner

limpiaparabrisas NM INV *Br* windscreen *o US* windshield wiper

limpiar [43] VT to clean; *(con trapo)* to wipe; *(zapatos)* to polish

limpieza NF *(calidad)* cleanliness; *(acción)* cleaning; **con l.** cleanly

limpio, -a **1** ADJ (**a**) *(aseado)* clean (**b**) *Dep* **juego l.** fair play (**c**) *Fin (neto)* net; **beneficios en l.** net profit (**d**) **pasar algo** *Esp* **a** *o Am* **en l.** to produce a fair copy of sth
2 ADV fairly; **jugar l.** to play fair

linaje NM lineage

linaza NF **aceite de l.** linseed oil

lince NM lynx; **tiene ojos de l.** he's eagle-eyed

linchar VT to lynch

lindante ADJ bordering

lindar VI **l. con** to border on

linde NM *o* NF boundary, limit

lindero, -a **1** ADJ bordering, adjoining
2 NM boundary, limit

lindo, -a **1** ADJ *esp Am (bonito)* pretty, lovely; **de lo l.** a great deal
2 ADV *Am (bien)* very well, beautifully; **dibuja muy l.** he draws very well *o* beautifully

línea NF (**a**) line; **l. aérea** airline; **en líneas generales** roughly speaking; *Inform* **en l.** on-line (**b**) **guardar la l.** to watch one's figure

lineal **1** ADJ linear; **dibujo l.** line drawing
2 NM *(en supermercado)* shelf

lingote NM ingot; *(de oro, plata)* bar

lingüista NMF linguist

lingüística NF linguistics *sing*

lingüístico, -a ADJ linguistic

lino NM (**a**) *Bot* flax (**b**) *Tex* linen

linterna NF *Br* torch, *US* flashlight

linyera NMF *RP (vagabundo)* tramp, *US* bum

lío NM (**a**) *(paquete)* bundle (**b**) *Fam (embrollo)* mess, muddle; **hacerse un l.** to get mixed up; **meterse en líos** to get into trouble; **armar un l.** to kick up a fuss (**c**) *Fam (relación amorosa)* affair

lioso, -a ADJ *Fam (asunto)* confusing

lipotimia NF fainting fit

liquidación NF (**a**) *Com (saldo)* clearance sale (**b**) *Fin* liquidation

liquidar **1** VT (**a**) *(deuda, cuenta)* to settle; *(mercancías)* to sell off (**b**) *Fam (matar)* to liquidate
2 liquidarse VPR *Fam (gastar)* to spend

liquidez NF *Fin* liquidity

líquido, -a 1 ADJ (**a**) liquid (**b**) *Fin* net
   2 NM (**a**) *(sustancia)* liquid; *Med* fluid (**b**) *Fin* liquid assets

lira NF (**a**) *Antes (moneda)* lira (**b**) *Mús* lyre

lírico, -a ADJ lyrical

lirio NM iris

lirismo NM lyricism.

lirón NM dormouse; *Fig* **dormir como un l.** to sleep like a log

Lisboa N Lisbon

lisiado, -a 1 ADJ crippled
   2 NM,F cripple

lisiar [43] VT to maim, to cripple

liso, -a 1 ADJ (**a**) *(superficie)* smooth, even; *Esp* **los cien metros lisos** the one hundred metres sprint (**b**) *(pelo, falda)* straight (**c**) *(tela)* self-coloured
   2 NM,F *Andes, CAm, Ven* cheeky; **es un l.** he's so cheeky

lisonjero, -a 1 ADJ flattering
   2 NM,F flatterer

lista NF (**a**) *(relación)* list; **l. de espera** waiting list; *(en avión)* standby; **pasar l.** to call the register o the roll; *Inform* **l. de correo** mailing list (**b**) *(franja)* stripe; **a listas** striped

listado, -a 1 ADJ striped
   2 NM list; *Inform* listing

listar VT (**a**) *Inform* to list (**b**) *Am (hacer una lista de)* to list

listín NM *Esp* **l. telefónico** telephone directory

listo, -a ADJ (**a**) **ser l.** *(inteligente)* to be clever o smart (**b**) **estar l.** *(a punto)* to be ready

listón NM *Dep* bar; *Fig* **subir el l.** to raise the requirements level

lisura NF (**a**) *Andes, CAm, Ven (atrevimiento)* cheek (**b**) *Andes, CAm, Ven (dicho grosero)* rude remark (**c**) *Perú (donaire)* grace

litera NF *(cama)* bunk bed; *(en tren)* couchette

literal ADJ literal

literario, -a ADJ literary

literato, -a NM,F writer, author

> Observa que la palabra inglesa **literate** es un falso amigo y no es la traducción de la palabra española **literato**. En inglés, **literate** significa "alfabetizado".

literatura NF literature

litigar [42] VI *Der* to litigate

litigio NM *Der* lawsuit; *Fig* dispute; **en l.** in dispute

litografía NF (**a**) *(técnica)* lithography (**b**) *(imagen)* lithograph

litoral 1 NM coast, seaboard
   2 ADJ coastal

litro NM litre

Lituania N Lithuania

lituano, -a 1 ADJ & NM,F Lithuanian
   2 NM *(idioma)* Lithuanian

liturgia NF liturgy

liviano, -a ADJ lightweight

lívido, -a ADJ livid

liza NF contest

llaga NF sore; *(herida)* wound

llama NF flame; **en llamas** in flames, ablaze

llamada NF call; *Tel* **l. interurbana** long-distance call; **señal de l.** ringing tone

llamado, -a 1 ADJ so-called
   2 NM *Am* (**a**) *(en general)* call; *(a la puerta)* knock; *(con timbre)* ring (**b**) *(telefónico)* call; **hacer un l.** to make a phone call (**c**) *(apelación)* appeal, call; **hacer un l. a algn para que haga algo** to call upon sb to do sth; **hacer un l. a la huelga** to call a strike

llamamiento NM appeal

llamar 1 VT (**a**) to call; **l. (por teléfono)** to call, to phone (**b**) *(atraer)* to draw, to attract; **l. la atención** to attract attention
   2 VI *(a la puerta)* to knock
   3 llamarse VPR to be called; **¿cómo te llamas?** what's your name?

llamarada NF blaze

llamativo, -a ADJ (**a**) *(color, ropa)* loud, flashy (**b**) *(persona)* striking

llaneza NF simplicity

llano, -a 1 ADJ (**a**) *(superficie)* flat, level (**b**) *(claro)* clear (**c**) *(sencillo)* simple; **el pueblo l.** the common people
   2 NM plain

llanta NF (**a**) *(aro metálico)* rim (**b**) *Am (neumático)* tyre

llanto NM crying, weeping

llanura NF plain

llave NF (**a**) *(de cerradura)* key; **bajo l.** under lock and key; **echar la l., cerrar con l.** to lock up; **l. en mano** *(vivienda)* ready for immediate occupation; **l. maestra** master key (**c**) *(grifo)* *Br* tap, *US* faucet; **l. de paso** stopcock; **cerrar la l. de paso** to turn the water/gas off at the *Br* mains o *US* main value (**c**) *(interruptor)* **l. de la luz** light switch (**d**) *(herramienta)* spanner; **l. allen** Allen key; **l. inglesa** monkey wrench, *Br* adjustable spanner (**e**) *(de judo)* hold, lock (**f**) *(signo ortográfico)* curly bracket

llavero NM key-ring

llegada NF arrival; *Dep* finish

llegar [42] **1** VI (**a**) *(a lugar)* to arrive; **l. a Madrid** to arrive in Madrid (**b**) *(ser bastante)* to be enough (**c**) *(alcanzar)* **l. a** to reach; **¿llegas al techo?** can you reach the ceiling?; *Fig* **l. a las manos** to come to blows; **l. a presidente** to become president (**d**) **l. a +** *infin* to go so far as to (**e**) **l. a ser** to become
   2 llegarse VPR to stop by

llenar 1 VT (**a**) *(recipiente)* to fill; *(superficie)* to cover; **l. a algn de** to fill sb with (**b**) *(satisfacer)* to satisfy
   2 VI *(comida)* to be filling
   3 llenarse VPR to fill (up), to become full

lleno, -a 1 ADJ full (up); *Fig* **de l.** fully
   2 NM *Teatro* full house

llevadero, -a ADJ bearable, tolerable

llevar 1 VT (**a**) *(de un lugar a otro)* to take; *(hacia el oyente)* to bring; **l. algo/a algn a** to take sth/sb to; **me llevó en coche** he drove me there (**b**) *(transportar)* to carry; **dejarse l.** to get carried away (**c**) *(prenda)* to wear; **llevaba una falda** she was wearing a skirt (**d**) *(soportar)* to bear; **¿cómo lleva lo de su enfermedad?** how's he bearing up? (**e**) *(tiempo)* **llevo dos años aquí** I've been here for two years; **esto lleva mucho tiempo** this takes a long time (**f**) *(ocuparse de) (problema, asunto)* to handle, to deal with; *(casa, negocio)* to look after, to run

2 VI (**a**) **l.** + *gerundio* to have been + *present participle*; **llevo dos años estudiando español** I've been studying Spanish for two years (**b**) **l.** + *participio* to have + *past participle*; **llevaba escritas seis cartas** I had written six letters

3 llevarse VPR (**a**) *(consigo)* to take; *(premio)* to win; *(recibir)* to get (**b**) *(arrastrar)* to carry away (**c**) *(estar de moda)* to be fashionable (**d**) **llevarse bien con algn** to get on well with sb

llorar VI to cry; *Lit* to weep

llorica NMF *Fam* crybaby

lloriquear VI to whimper, to snivel

llorón, -ona ADJ **un bebé l.** a baby which cries a lot

lloroso, -a ADJ tearful

llover [4] V IMPERS to rain

llovizna NF drizzle

lloviznar V IMPERS to drizzle

lluvia NF rain; **una l. de** lots of; **l. radiactiva** (nuclear) fallout; **l. ácida** acid rain

lluvioso, -a ADJ rainy

lo¹ ART NEUT the; **lo mejor** the best (part); **lo mismo** the same thing; **lo mío** mine; **lo tuyo** yours

lo² PRON PERS M & NEUT *(mpl* **los**, *fpl* **las)** (**a**) *(cosa)* it; **debes hacerlo** you must do it; **no lo creo** I don't think so; *(no se traduce)* **no se lo dije** I didn't tell her; *ver* **el** (**b**) **lo que ...** what ...; **no sé lo que pasa** I don't know what's going on (**c**) **lo cual ...** which ... (**d**) **lo de ...** the business of ...; **cuéntame lo del juicio** tell me about the trial

loable ADJ praiseworthy, laudable

loar VT to praise

lobo NM wolf; **como boca de l.** pitch-dark; *Fam* **¡menos lobos!** pull the other one!

lóbrego, -a ADJ gloomy

lóbulo NM lobe

local 1 ADJ local

2 NM *(recinto)* premises, site

localidad NF (**a**) *(pueblo)* locality; *(en impreso)* place of residence (**b**) *Cin & Teatro (asiento)* seat; *(entrada)* ticket

localización NF localization

localizar [40] VT (**a**) *(encontrar)* to find (**b**) *(restringir)* to localize

loción NF lotion

loco, -a 1 ADJ mad, crazy; **a lo l.** crazily; **l. por** crazy about; **volverse l.** to go mad; *Fam* **¡ni l.!** I'd sooner die!

2 NM,F madman, madwoman; **hacerse el l.** to act the fool

3 NM *Chile (molusco)* false abalone

locomotor, -triz ADJ locomotive

locomotora NF locomotive

locuaz ADJ loquacious, talkative

locución NF phrase

locura NF *(enfermedad)* madness, insanity; **con l.** madly; *Fam* **esto es una l.** this is crazy

locutor, -a NM,F *TV & Rad (de noticias) Br* newsreader, *US* news announcer; *(de programa de radio) Br* presenter, *US* host, *f* hostess

locutorio NM telephone booth

lodo NM mud

logaritmo NM logarithm

lógica NF logic; **no tiene l.** there's no logic to it

lógico, -a ADJ logical; **era l. que ocurriera** it was bound to happen

logística NF logistics *sing o pl*

logotipo NM logo

logrado, -a ADJ *(bien hecho)* accomplished

lograr VT (**a**) *(objetivo)* to achieve; *(puesto, beca, divorcio)* to get, to obtain; *(resultado)* to obtain, to achieve; *(premio)* to win (**b**) **l. hacer algo** to manage to do sth

logro NM achievement

loma NF hillock, rise

lombriz NF worm, earthworm

lomo NM (**a**) *(de animal)* back; **a lomo(s)** on the back (**b**) *Culin* loin (**c**) *(de libro)* spine

lona NF canvas

loncha NF slice; **l. de bacon** rasher of bacon

lonche NM (**a**) *Perú, Ven (merienda) (en escuela)* = snack eaten during break time; *(en casa)* (afternoon) tea (**b**) *Am (comida fría)* (packed) lunch (**c**) *Méx (torta)* filled roll

lonchería NF *Méx, Ven* = small fast food restaurant selling snacks, sandwiches etc

londinense 1 ADJ of/from London

2 NMF Londoner

Londres N London

longaniza NF spicy (pork) sausage

longevo, -a ADJ long-lived

longitud NF (**a**) *(dimensión)* length; **2 m de l.** 2 m long; **l. de onda** wavelength (**b**) *Geog* longitude

lonja¹ NF *(loncha)* slice

lonja² NF *Esp* **l. de pescado** fish market

loquería NF *Am* mental asylum, mental hospital

lord *(pl* **lores**) NM lord

loro NM parrot

los¹ 1 ART DEF MPL the; **l. libros** the books; **cierra l. ojos** close your eyes; **l. García** the Garcías; *ver* **el**, **las** y **los**

2 PRON **l. que** *(personas)* the ones who, those who; *(cosas)* the ones (that); **toma l. que quieras** take whichever ones you want; **esos son l. míos/tuyos** these are mine/yours; *ver* **les**

los² PRON PERS M PL them; **¿l. has visto?** have you seen them?

losa NF (stone) slab, flagstone

lote NM (**a**) *(para vender, subastar)* share (**b**) *(conjunto)* batch, lot (**c**) *Inform* batch (**d**) *Esp Fam* **darse el l. (con)** to neck (with), *Br* to snog (**e**) *Am (solar)* plot (of land)

loteamiento NM *Bol, Urug* parcelling out, division into plots

loteo NM *Andes, Méx, RP* parcelling out, division into plots

lotería NF lottery; **me tocó la l.** I won a prize in the lottery

lotización NF *Ecuad, Perú* parcelling out, division into plots

loto 1 NM *Bot* lotus

2 NF *Esp Fam* = weekly state-run lottery, *Br* ≃ National Lottery

loza NF (**a**) *(material)* earthenware (**b**) *(de cocina)* crockery

lozano, -a ADJ (**a**) *(persona)* healthy-looking (**b**) *(plantas)* lush, luxuriant

Ltda. *(abr* **Limitada)** Ltd

lubina NF sea bass

lubricante NM lubricant

lubricar [44] VT to lubricate

lucero NM (bright) star

lucha NF (**a**) *(combate, enfrentamiento)* fight, struggle; *(esfuerzo)* struggle; **l. de clases** class struggle (**b**) *Dep* wrestling; **l. libre** freestyle wrestling

luchador, -a NM,F (**a**) *(persona tenaz)* fighter (**b**) *Dep* wrestler

luchar VI (**a**) *(combatir)* to fight; *(esforzarse)* to struggle; **l. contra** to fight (against); **l. por** to fight for (**b**) *Dep* to wrestle

lucidez NF lucidity

lúcido, -a ADJ lucid, clear

luciérnaga NF glow-worm

lucir [35] **1** VI (**a**) *(brillar)* to shine (**b**) *Am (parecer)* to look; **luces cansada** you seem *o* look tired (**c**) *Fam (compensar)* **no le luce lo que estudia** his studies don't get him anywhere

2 VT *(ropas)* to sport; *(talento)* to display

3 **lucirse** VPR (**a**) *(hacer buen papel)* to do very well (**b**) *(pavonearse)* to show off

lucrativo, -a ADJ lucrative, profitable

lucro NM profit, gain; **afán de l.** greed for money

lúcuma NF *Andes* lucuma, = sweet, pear-shaped fruit

lúdico, -a ADJ relating to games, recreational

luego 1 ADV (**a**) *(después)* then, next, afterwards (**b**) *(más tarde)* later (on); **¡hasta l.!** so long!; **l. de** after (**c**) *desde l.* of course (**d**)

Chile, Ven (pronto) soon; **acaba l., te estoy esperando** hurry up and finish, I'm waiting for you; *Méx Fam* **l. l., l. lueguito** immediately, straight away

2 CONJ therefore

lugar NM (**a**) *(sitio)* place; **en primer l.** in the first place; **en l. de** instead of; **sin l. a dudas** without a doubt; **tener l.** to take place (**b**) **dar l. a** to cause, to give rise to

lugareño, -a NM,F local

lugarteniente NM,F lieutenant

lúgubre ADJ gloomy, lugubrious

lujo NM luxury; **productos de l.** luxury products; **no puedo permitirme ese l.** I can't afford that

lujoso, -a ADJ luxurious

lujuria NF lust

> Observa que la palabra inglesa **luxury** es un falso amigo y no es la traducción de la palabra española **lujuria.** En inglés, **luxury** significa "lujo".

lujurioso, -a ADJ lecherous, lustful

lumbago NM lumbago

lumbre NF fire

lumbrera NF luminary

luminoso, -a ADJ luminous; *Fig* bright

luna NF (**a**) *(astro)* moon; *Fig* **estar en la l.** to have one's head in the clouds; **l. creciente/ llena** crescent/full moon; **l. de miel** honeymoon (**b**) *(de escaparate)* pane; *(espejo)* mirror

lunar 1 ADJ lunar

2 NM *(redondel)* dot; *(en la piel)* mole, beauty spot; **vestido de lunares** spotted dress

lunático, -a NM,F lunatic

lunes NM INV Monday; **vendré el l.** I'll come on Monday

lupa NF magnifying glass

luso, -a ADJ & NM,F Portuguese

lustrabotas NM,F INV, **lustrador, -a** NM,F *Andes, RP* shoeshine, *Br* bootblack

lustradora NF *Andes, RP* floor polisher

lustrar VT to polish; *(zapatos)* to shine

lustre NM *(brillo)* shine, lustre; *Fig (esplendor)* splendour, glory; **dar** *o* **sacar l. a algo** to polish sth

lustro NM five-year period

lustroso, -a ADJ shiny, glossy

luto NM mourning

Luxemburgo N Luxembourg

luz NF (**a**) light; **apagar la l.** to put out the light; **a la l. de** in the light of; **a todas luces** obviously; *Fig* **dar a l. (a un niño)** to give birth (to a child) (**b**) *Aut* light; **luces de cruce** *Br* dipped headlights, *US* low beams; **luces de posición** sidelights (**c**) **luces** *(inteligencia)* intelligence; **corto de luces** dim-witted (**d**) **traje de luces** bullfighter's costume

luzco INDIC PRES *de* **lucir**

lycra® NF Lycra®

M

M, m ['eme] NF *(letra)* M, m

m (**a**) *(abr* **metro(s)**) m (**b**) *(abr* **minuto(s)**) min

macabro, -a ADJ macabre

macana NF (**a**) *Andes, Carib, Méx (garrote)* wooden *Br* truncheon *o US* billy club (**b**) *CSur, Perú, Ven Fam (fastidio)* pain, drag (**c**) *CAm, Cuba (azada)* hoe

macanear VT *CSur, Ven (hacer mal)* to botch, to do badly

macanudo, -a ADJ *Fam* great, terrific

macarra NM *Fam* lout, *Br* yob

macarrón NM (**a**) *(dulce)* macaroon (**b**) *Elec* sheath

macarrones NMPL macaroni

macedonia NF fruit salad

macerar VT to soak, to macerate

maceta NF *(tiesto)* plant-pot, flowerpot

machacar [44] **1** VT (**a**) *(aplastar)* to crush; *Dep* to smash (**b**) *Esp Fam (estudiar) Br* to swot up on, *US* to bone up on (**c**) *Fam (insistir en)* to harp on about, to go on about
2 VI (**a**) *Fam (insistir mucho)* to harp on, to go on (**b**) *Fam (estudiar con ahínco) Br* to swot, *US* to grind (**c**) *(en baloncesto)* to dunk

machacón, -ona *Fam* **1** ADJ *(repetitivo)* repetitious; *(pesado)* boring, tiresome
2 NM,F *(muy estudioso) Br* swot, *US* grind

machamartillo: a machamartillo LOC ADV *(con firmeza)* firmly; *(con obstinación)* obstinately

machete NM (**a**) *(arma)* machete (**b**) *Ven (amigo)* pal, *Br* mate, *US* buddy (**c**) *Arg Fam (chuleta)* crib note

machismo NM machismo, male chauvinism

machista ADJ & NM male chauvinist

macho 1 ADJ (**a**) *(animal, planta)* male (**b**) *Fam (viril)* manly, virile, macho
2 NM (**a**) *(animal, planta)* male (**b**) *Téc (pieza)* male piece *o* part; *(de enchufe)* (male) plug (**c**) *Fam (hombre viril)* macho man, he-man (**d**) *Esp Fam (como apelativo)* **¡oye, m.!** *Br* hey, mate!, *US* hey, buddy!

machote NM *CAm, Méx (borrador)* rough draft

macilento, -a ADJ wan

macizo, -a 1 ADJ (**a**) *(sólido)* solid; **de oro m.** of solid gold (**b**) *(robusto)* solid, robust; *Fam (atractivo)* well-built
2 NM *(masa sólida)* mass

macramé NM macramé

macro NF *Inform* macro

macro- PREF macro-

macroeconomía NF macroeconomics *sing*

macrofestival NM = large open-air music festival

macuto NM *(morral)* knapsack, haversack

madeja NF *(de lana etc)* hank, skein

madera NF (**a**) *(material)* wood; *(de construcción)* timber, *US* lumber; **de m.** wood, wooden (**b**) *Fig* **tiene m. de líder** he has all the makings of a leader (**c**) *Esp Fam (policía)* **la m.** the pigs

madero NM (**a**) *(de construcción)* timber, *US* lumber; *(leño)* log (**b**) *Fam (policía)* pig

madrastra NF stepmother

madre 1 NF (**a**) *(persona)* mother; **es m. de tres hijos** she is a mother of three (children); **m. adoptiva** adoptive mother; **m. de familia** mother, housewife; **m. política** mother-in-law; **m. soltera** unmarried mother; *Fig* **la m. patria** one's motherland; *Méx muy Fam* **me vale m.** I couldn't give a damn *o Br* a toss (**b**) *(de río)* bed
2 INTERJ **¡m. de Dios!, ¡m. mía!** good heavens!

madreperla NF *(nácar)* mother-of-pearl

madreselva NF honeysuckle

Madrid N Madrid

madriguera NF burrow, hole

madrileño, -a 1 ADJ of/from Madrid
2 NM,F person from Madrid

madrina NF (**a**) *(de bautizo)* godmother (**b**) *(de boda)* ≃ bridesmaid (**c**) *Fig (protectora)* protectress

madrugada NF (**a**) *(amanecer)* dawn; **de m.** at dawn (**b**) *(noche)* early morning; **las tres de la m.** three in the morning

madrugador, -a 1 ADJ early-rising
2 NM,F early riser

madrugar [42] VI to get up early

maduración NF *(de fruta)* ripening

madurar 1 VT *(plan)* to think out
2 VI (**a**) *(persona)* to mature (**b**) *(fruta)* to ripen

madurez NF (**a**) *(de la fruta)* ripeness (**b**) *(sensatez, juicio)* maturity (**c**) *(edad adulta)* adulthood

maduro, -a ADJ (**a**) *(persona)* mature; **de edad madura** middle-aged (**b**) *(fruta)* ripe

maestría NF (**a**) *(habilidad)* mastery, skill (**b**) *Am (título)* master's degree

maestro, -a 1 NM,F (**a**) *Educ* teacher; **m. de escuela** schoolteacher (**b**) *Méx (en universidad) Br* lecturer, *US* professor (**c**) *(especialista)* master; **m. de obras** foreman (**d**) *Mús* maestro **2** ADJ **obra maestra** masterpiece; **llave maestra** master key

mafia NF mafia

mafioso, -a 1 ADJ of/relating to the mafia **2** NM,F member of the mafia, mafioso

magdalena NF = small sponge cake

magia NF magic; **por arte de m.** as if by magic

mágico, -a ADJ (**a**) *(palabra, alfombra, varita)* magic (**b**) *(momento, situación)* magical

magisterio NM teaching

magistrado, -a NM,F judge

magistral ADJ *(excelente)* masterly; **una jugada m.** a master stroke

magistratura NF *(jueces)* magistrature; *(tribunal)* tribunal

magnánimo, -a ADJ magnanimous

magnate NM magnate, tycoon

magnesio NM magnesium

magnético, -a ADJ magnetic

magnetizar [40] VT (**a**) *(imantar)* to magnetize (**b**) *Fig (hipnotizar)* to hypnotize

magnetofónico, -a ADJ magnetic

magnetófono NM tape recorder

magnífico, -a ADJ magnificent, splendid

magnitud NF magnitude, dimension; **de primera m.** of the first order

magno, -a ADJ *Literario* great; **aula magna** main amphitheatre

magnolia NF magnolia

mago, -a NM,F wizard, magician; **los tres Reyes Magos** the Three Wise Men, the Three Kings

magrear VT *muy Fam* to fondle, to grope

magro, -a 1 NM *(de cerdo)* lean meat **2** ADJ *(sin grasa)* lean

magullar 1 VT to bruise, to damage **2 magullarse** VPR to get bruised, to get damaged

mahometano, -a ADJ & NM,F *Rel* Mohammedan, Muslim

mahonesa NF mayonnaise

maillot [ma'jot] *(pl* **maillots)** NM *(malla)* leotard; *Dep* shirt

maíz NM *(planta) Br* maize, *US* (Indian) corn; *(utilizado en cocina) Br* sweetcorn, *US* corn

maizal NM *Br* maize field, *US* cornfield

majadería NF silly thing, absurdity

majadero, -a NM,F fool, idiot

majareta, *Esp* **majara** ADJ *Fam* loony, nutty

majestad NF majesty

majestuosidad NF majesty

majestuoso, -a ADJ majestic, stately

majo, -a ADJ *Esp (bonito)* pretty, nice; *Fam (simpático)* nice; **tiene un hijo muy m.** she's

got a lovely little boy; *Fam* **ven aquí, m.** come here, dear

mal 1 NM (**a**) *(maldad)* evil; **el m.** evil (**b**) *(daño)* harm; **no le deseo ningún m.** I don't wish him any harm (**c**) *(enfermedad)* illness, disease; *Fam* **el m. de las vacas locas** mad cow disease **2** ADJ bad; **un m. año** a bad year; *ver* **malo 3** ADV badly, wrong; **lo hizo muy m.** he did it very badly; **menos m. que …** it's a good job (that) …; **no está (nada) m.** it is not bad (at all); **te oigo/veo (muy) m.** I can hardly hear/ see you; **tomar a m.** *(enfadarse)* to take badly

malabar ADJ **juegos malabares** juggling

malabarista NMF juggler

malaria NF malaria

malcriado, -a ADJ ill-mannered, ill-bred

malcriar [29] VT to spoil

maldad NF (**a**) *(cualidad)* badness, evil (**b**) *(acción)* evil *o* wicked thing

maldecir [12] **1** VT to curse **2** VI (**a**) *(blasfemar)* to curse (**b**) *(criticar)* to speak ill (**de** of)

maldición 1 NF curse **2** INTERJ damnation!

maldito, -a ADJ (**a**) *Fam (molesto)* damned, *Br* bloody (**b**) *(endemoniado)* damned, cursed; **¡maldita sea!** damn it!

maleable ADJ *también Fig* malleable

maleante NMF crook

malear VT to corrupt

malecón NM jetty

maleducado, -a 1 ADJ bad-mannered **2** NM,F bad-mannered person

maleficio NM curse, spell

maléfico, -a ADJ evil, harmful

malentendido NM misunderstanding

malestar NM (**a**) *(molestia)* discomfort (**b**) *(inquietud)* uneasiness; **tengo m.** I feel uneasy

maleta NF suitcase, case; **hacer la m.** to pack one's things *o* case

maletero NM *Esp, Cuba,* **maletera** NF *Am (de automóvil) Br* boot, *US* trunk

maletín NM briefcase

malévolo, -a ADJ malevolent

maleza NF (**a**) *(arbustos)* thicket, undergrowth (**b**) *(malas hierbas)* weeds

malformación NF malformation

malgastar VT to waste, to squander

malhablado, -a 1 ADJ foul-mouthed **2** NM,F foul-mouthed person

malhechor, -a NM,F wrongdoer, criminal

malhumor NM bad temper

malhumorado, -a ADJ *(de mal carácter)* bad-tempered; *(enfadado)* in a bad mood

malicia NF (**a**) *(mala intención)* malice, maliciousness (**b**) *(astucia)* cunning, slyness (**c**) *(maldad)* badness, evil

malicioso, -a 1 ADJ malicious, spiteful **2** NM,F malicious *o* spiteful person

maligno, -a ADJ malignant

malintencionado, -a ADJ ill-intentioned

malla NF (**a**) *Esp mallas (de gimnasia)* leotard; *(de ballet)* tights (**b**) *(red)* mesh (**c**) *Ecuad, Perú, RP (traje de baño)* swimsuit

Mallorca N Majorca

mallorquín, -ina ADJ & NM,F Majorcan

malo, -a 1 ADJ (**a**) bad; **un año m.** a bad year; **estar a malas** to be on bad terms; **por las malas** by force (**b**) *(persona) (malvado)* wicked, bad; *(travieso)* naughty (**c**) *(de poca calidad)* bad, poor; **una mala canción/comida** a poor song/meal (**d**) *(perjudicial)* harmful; **el tabaco es m.** tobacco is harmful (**e**) **lo m. es que …** the problem is that … (**f**) *(enfermo)* ill, sick

> **Mal** is used instead of **malo** before masculine singular nouns (e.g. **un mal ejemplo** a bad example). The comparative form of **malo** (= worse) is **peor**, the superlative forms (= the worst) are **el peor** (masculine) and **la peor** (feminine).

2 NM,F *Fam* **el m.** the baddy *o* villain

malograr 1 VT *Andes (estropear)* to make a mess of, to ruin

2 malograrse VPR (**a**) *(fracasar)* to fail, fall through (**b**) *Andes (estropearse) (máquina)* to break down; *(alimento)* to go off, to spoil; **se malogró el día** the day turned nasty

maloliente ADJ foul-smelling

malparado, -a ADJ **salir m.** to end up in a sorry state

malpensado, -a 1 ADJ nasty-minded
2 NM,F nasty-minded person

malsonante ADJ *(grosero)* rude, offensive; **palabras malsonantes** foul language

malta NF *(cebada)* malt

maltratado, -a ADJ battered

maltratar VT to ill-treat, to mistreat

maltrato NM ill-treatment; **m. psicológico** psychological abuse

maltrecho, -a ADJ in a sorry state, wrecked

malva 1 ADJ INV mauve
2 NM *(color)* mauve
3 NF *Bot* mallow

malvado, -a 1 ADJ evil, wicked
2 NM,F villain, evil person

malvender VT to sell at a loss

malversar VT to misappropriate, to embezzle

Malvinas NPL **las (Islas) M.** the Falkland Islands

malviviente NMF *CSur* criminal

malvivir VI to live very badly

mama NF (**a**) *(de mujer)* breast; *(de animal)* teat (**b**) *Fam (mamá) Br* mummy, *US* mommy

mamá NF *Fam Br* mum, *US* mom; *Col, Méx Fam* **m. grande** grandma

mamada NF (**a**) *(bebé)* (breast) feed (**b**) *Vulg (felatio)* blowjob

mamadera NF *RP* (baby's) bottle

mamar VT *(leche)* to suck; **lo mamó desde pequeño** *(lo aprendió)* he was immersed in it as a child

mamarracho, -a NM,F *Fam (persona)* ridiculous-looking person, mess, sight; *(cosa)* mess

mameluco NM (**a**) *Fam (torpe, necio)* idiot (**b**) *Méx (con mangas) Br* overalls, *US* coveralls; *CSur (de peto) Br* dungarees, *US* overalls

mamey NM (**a**) *(árbol)* mamey, mammee (**b**) *(fruto)* mamey, mammee (apple)

mamífero, -a NM,F mammal

mamón NM *muy Fam (insulto) Br* prat, *US* jerk

mampara NF screen

mamporro NM *Fam* wallop

mampostería NF masonry

mamut *(pl mamuts)* NM mammoth

manada NF (**a**) *Zool (de vacas, elefantes)* herd; *(de ovejas)* flock; *(de lobos, perros)* pack; *(de leones)* pride (**b**) *Fam (multitud)* crowd, mob; **en manada(s)** in crowds

manager ['manajer] *(pl managers)* NMF *Dep & Mús* manager

manantial NM spring

manar 1 VI to flow, to run *(de* from)
2 VT **la herida manaba sangre** blood flowed from his wound

manazas NMF INV *Fam* ham-fisted person.

mancebo NM *Literario* young man

Mancha N **el Canal de la M.** the English Channel

mancha NF stain, spot; **m. solar** sunspot; **m. de tinta/vino** ink/wine stain

manchado, -a ADJ dirty, stained; **leche manchada** milky coffee

manchar 1 VT to stain, to dirty; *Fig* to stain, to blemish
2 mancharse VPR to get dirty

manchego, -a 1 ADJ of/from La Mancha
2 NM,F person from La Mancha

manco, -a 1 ADJ (**a**) *(de un brazo)* one-armed; *(sin brazos)* armless (**b**) *(de una mano)* one-handed; *(sin manos)* handless
2 NM,F (**a**) *(de brazos)* one-armed/armless person (**b**) *(de manos)* one-handed/handless person

mancomunidad NF community, association

mancuerna NF (**a**) *(pesa)* dumbbell (**b**) *CAm, Chile, Col, Méx, Ven (gemelo)* cufflink

mandado NM order, errand

mandamás *(pl mandamases)* NMF *Fam Br* big boss, *US* head honcho

mandamiento NM (**a**) *(orden)* order, command (**b**) **los Diez Mandamientos** the Ten Commandments

mandar VT (**a**) *(ordenar)* to order; *Fam* **¿mande?** pardon? (**b**) *(grupo)* to lead, to be in charge *o* command of; *Mil* to command (**c**) *(enviar)* to send; **m. (a) por** to send for; **m.**

algo por correo to post sth, to send sth by post; **m. recuerdos** to send regards

mandarina NF mandarin (orange), tangerine

mandatario, -a NM,F *Pol* president

mandato NM (a) *(orden)* order, command (b) *Der* writ, warrant (c) *Pol (legislatura)* mandate, term of office

mandíbula NF jaw; *Fam* **reír a m. batiente** to laugh one's head off

mandil NM apron

Mandinga NM *Am* the devil

mando NM (a) *(autoridad)* command, control (b) **los altos mandos del ejército** high-ranking army officers (c) *Téc (control)* controls; *Aut* **cuadro** *o* **tablero de mandos** dashboard; **m. a distancia** remote control; **palanca de m.** *Téc* control lever; *(de avión, videojuego)* joystick

mandón, -ona 1 ADJ *Fam* bossy, domineering
2 NM,F *Fam* bossy *o* domineering person
3 NM *Chile (de mina)* foreman

manecilla NF *(de reloj)* hand

manejable ADJ manageable; *(herramienta)* easy-to-use; *(coche)* manoeuvrable

manejar 1 VT a (a) *(máquina)* to handle, to operate; *Fig (situación)* to handle (b) *(negocio)* to run, to manage (c) *(a otra persona)* to domineer, to boss about (d) *Am (conducir)* to drive
2 VI *Am (conducir)* to drive
3 **manejarse** VPR to manage

manejo NM (a) *(uso)* handling, use; **de fácil m.** easy-to-use (b) *(de un negocio)* management; *(de un coche)* driving

manera NF (a) *(forma)* way, manner; **a mi/tu m.** (in) my/your way; **de cualquier m.** *(mal)* carelessly, any old how; *(en cualquier caso)* in any case; **de esta m.** (in) this way; **de ninguna m.** in no way, certainly not; **de todas maneras** anyway, at any rate, in any case; **es mi m. de ser** that's the way I am; **no hay m.** it's impossible (b) **de m. que** so; **de tal m. que** in such a way that (c) **maneras** *(modales)* manners; **de buenas maneras** politely

manga NF (a) *(de ropa)* sleeve; **de m. corta/larga** short-/long-sleeved; **sin mangas** sleeveless; *Fig* **hacer un corte de mangas a algn** ≃ to give sb the finger; *Fig* **m. por hombro** messy and untidy; *Fig* **sacarse algo de la m.** to pull sth out of one's hat (b) *(de riego)* hose (c) *(del mar)* arm (d) *Dep* leg, round; *Ten* set

mangante NM,F *Fam* thief

mangar [42] VT *Fam* to pinch, *Br* to nick

mango NM (a) *(asa)* handle (b) *(fruta)* mango (c) *RP Fam (dinero)* **no tengo un m.** I haven't got a bean, I'm broke

mangonear VI *Fam* (a) *(entrometerse)* to meddle (b) *(dar órdenes)* to throw one's weight around

manguera NF hose

manguito NM (a) *(para las mangas)* oversleeve; *(para flotar)* armband (b) *Téc* sleeve

maní *(pl* **maníes)** NM *Andes, Carib, RP* peanut

manía NF (a) *(costumbre)* habit; **tiene la m. de morderse las uñas** he's always biting his fingernails (b) *(afición exagerada)* craze; **la m. de las motos** the motorbike craze (c) *Fam (ojeriza)* dislike; **me tiene m.** he has it in for me (d) *Med* mania

maniaco, -a, maníaco, -a 1 ADJ manic
2 NM,F maniac

maniatar VT to tie the hands of

maniático, -a 1 ADJ fussy
2 NM,F fusspot

manicomio NM *Br* mental *o* psychiatric hospital, *US* insane asylum

manicura NF manicure

manido, -a ADJ trite, hackneyed

manifestación NF (a) *(política)* demonstration (b) *(expresión)* manifestation, expression

manifestante NM,F demonstrator

manifestar [1] 1 VT (a) *(declarar)* to state, to declare (b) *(mostrar)* to show, to display
2 **manifestarse** VPR (a) *(por la calle)* to demonstrate (b) *(declararse)* to declare oneself; **se manifestó contrario a ...** he spoke out against ...

manifiesto, -a 1 ADJ clear, obvious; **poner de m.** *(revelar)* to reveal, to show; *(hacer patente)* to make clear
2 NM manifesto

manigua NF, **manigual** NM *Carib, Col (selva)* marshy tropical forest

manilla NF (a) *(de reloj)* hand (b) *esp Am (manivela)* crank

manillar NM handlebar

maniobra NF manoeuvre

maniobrar VI to manoeuvre

manipulación NF manipulation

manipular VT to manipulate; *(máquina)* to handle

maniquí *(pl* **maniquíes)** NM *(muñeco)* dummy

manitas NM,F INV *Esp Fam* (a) **ser un m.** to be handy, to be very good with one's hands (b) **hacer m.** to hold hands

manito NM *Méx Fam* pal, *Br* mate, *US* buddy

manivela NF *Téc* crank

manjar NM delicacy *(food)*

mano 1 NF (a) *(de persona)* hand; **a m.** *(sin máquina)* by hand; *(asequible)* at hand; **escrito a m.** hand-written; **hecho a m.** handmade; **a m. armada** armed; **estrechar la m. a algn** to shake hands with sb; **de segunda m.** second-hand; **echar una m. a algn** to give sb a hand; **¡manos a la obra!** shoulders to the wheel!; **meter m.** *(a problema)* to tackle; *Vulg (a persona)* to touch up; **traerse algo entre manos** to be up to sth; **equipaje de m.** hand luggage (**b**) *(lado)* side; **a m. derecha/izquierda** on the right/left(-hand side) (**c**) **m. de pintura** coat of paint (**d**) **m. de obra** labour (force) (**e**) *RP (dirección)* direction *(of traffic)*; **calle de una/doble m.** one-/two-way street

2 NM *Am salvo RP Fam* pal, *Br* mate, *US* buddy

3 manos libres NM INV *(teléfono)* hands-free set

manojo NM bunch; **ser un m. de nervios** to be a bundle of nerves

manopla NF mitten

manoseado, -a ADJ *(objeto)* worn(-out); *(tema)* hackneyed

manosear VT to touch repeatedly, to finger; *Fam* to paw

manotazo NM cuff, slap

mansalva: a mansalva LOC ADV *(en gran cantidad)* galore

mansedumbre NF (**a**) *(de persona)* meekness, gentleness (**b**) *(de animal)* tameness, docility

mansión NF mansion

manso, -a ADJ (**a**) *(persona)* gentle, meek (**b**) *(animal)* tame, docile (**c**) *Chile Fam (extraordinario)* tremendous; **tiene la mansa casa** he has a gigantic o massive house

manta 1 NF (**a**) *(de cama)* blanket; **m. eléctrica** electric blanket (**b**) *(zurra)* beating, hiding (**c**) *Méx (algodón)* = coarse cotton cloth (**d**) *Ven (vestido)* = traditional Indian woman's dress

2 NMF *Esp Fam* layabout

manteca NF (**a**) *Esp (de animal)* fat; **m. de cacao/cacahuete** cocoa/peanut butter; **m. de cerdo** lard (**b**) *RP, Ven (mantequilla)* butter

mantecado NM *Esp* = very crumbly shortbread biscuit

mantel NM tablecloth

> Observa que la palabra inglesa **mantle** es un falso amigo y no es la traducción de la palabra española **mantel**. En inglés, **mantle** significa "manto, capa".

mantelería NF set of table linen

mantener [24] **1** VT (**a**) *(conservar)* to keep; **mantén el fuego encendido** keep the fire burning; **m. la línea** to keep in trim (**b**) *(entrevista, reunión)* to have; **m. correspondencia con algn** to correspond with sb (**c**) *(ideas, opiniones)* to defend, to maintain (**d**) *(familia)* to support, to feed (**e**) *(peso)* to support, to hold up

2 mantenerse VPR (**a**) *(sostenerse)* to stand (**b**) **mantenerse firme** *(perseverar)* to hold one's ground (**c**) *(sustentarse)* to live (**de** on)

mantenimiento NM *Téc* maintenance, upkeep; **servicio de m.** maintenance service (**b**) *(alimento)* sustenance, support (**c**) **gimnasia de m.** keep fit

mantequilla NF butter

mantilla NF *(de mujer)* mantilla; *(de bebé)* shawl

manto NM cloak

mantón NM shawl

mantuve PT INDEF *de* **mantener**

manual 1 ADJ manual; **trabajo m.** manual labour; *Educ* **trabajos manuales** handicrafts

2 NM manual, handbook

manubrio NM *Am* handlebars

manufactura NF (**a**) *(fabricación)* manufacture (**b**) *(fábrica)* factory

manufacturar VT to manufacture

manuscrito NM manuscript

manutención NF maintenance

manzana NF (**a**) *(fruta)* apple (**b**) *(de edificios)* block

manzanilla NF (**a**) *Bot* camomile (**b**) *(infusión)* camomile tea (**c**) *(vino)* manzanilla

manzano NM apple tree

maña NF (**a**) *(astucia)* cunning (**b**) *(habilidad)* skill

mañana 1 NF morning; **a las dos de la m.** at two in the morning; **de m.** early in the morning; *Esp* **por la m.,** *Am* **en la m.** in the morning

2 NM **el m.** tomorrow, the future

3 ADV tomorrow; **¡hasta m.!** see you tomorrow!; **m. por la m.** tomorrow morning; **pasado m.** the day after tomorrow

mañanitas NFPL *Méx* birthday song

mañoco NM *Ven* tapioca

mañoso, -a ADJ *Esp* skilful

mapa NM map; **m. mudo** blank map; *Fam* **borrar del m.** to wipe out

maqueta NF (**a**) *(miniatura)* scale model, maquette (**b**) *Mús* demo (tape)

maquiavélico, -a ADJ Machiavellian

maquila NF *CAm, Méx (de artículos electrónicos)* assembly; *(de ropa)* making-up

maquiladora NF *CAm, Méx* = bonded assembly plant set up by a foreign firm near the US border, *US* maquiladora

maquillaje NM make-up

maquillar 1 VT to make up

2 maquillarse VPR (**a**) *(ponerse maquillaje)* to put one's make-up on, to make (oneself) up (**b**) *(usar maquillaje)* to wear make-up

máquina NF (**a**) machine; **escrito a m.** typewritten; **hecho a m.** machine-made; *Fam* **a toda m.** at full speed; **m. de afeitar (eléctrica)** (electric) razor o shaver; **m. de coser** sewing machine; **m. de escribir** typewriter; **m. fotográfica** o **de fotos** camera; **m.** *Esp* **tragaperras** o *Am* **tragamonedas** slot machine, *Br* fruit machine (**b**) *Cuba (automóvil)* car

maquinar VT to plot, to scheme

maquinaria NF (**a**) *(aparatos)* machinery (**b**) *(mecanismo)* (de reloj, aparato)* mechanism (**c**) *(de Estado, partido)* machinery

maquinilla NF **m. de afeitar** safety razor

maquinista NMF *Br* engine driver, *US* engineer

mar 1 NM o NF (**a**) sea; **en alta m.** on the high seas; **m. adentro** out to sea; **por m.** by sea; **m. gruesa** heavy sea; **m. picada** rough sea (**b**)

Fam **está la m. de guapa** she's looking really beautiful; **llover a mares** to rain cats and dogs

> Note that the feminine is used in literary language, by people such as fishermen with a close connection with the sea, and in some idiomatic expressions.

2 NM sea; **M. del Norte** North Sea; **M. Muerto/Negro** Dead/Black Sea

maraca NF maraca

maracuyá NF passion fruit

maraña NF tangle

maratón NM marathon

maratoniano, -a ADJ marathon

maravilla NF marvel, wonder; **de m.** wonderfully; **¡qué m. de película!** what a wonderful film!; *Fam* **a las mil maravillas** marvellously

maravillar 1 VT to amaze, to astonish
2 maravillarse VPR to marvel (**con** at), to wonder (**con** at)

maravilloso, -a ADJ wonderful, marvellous

marca NF (**a**) *(señal)* mark; *(de rueda, animal)* track (**b**) *Com (de tabaco, café)* brand; *(de vehículo, máquina)* make; **ropa de m.** designer clothes; **m. de fábrica** trademark; **m. registrada** registered trademark (**c**) *Dep (récord)* record; *(tiempo)* time

marcador NM (**a**) *Dep (tablero)* scoreboard; *(goleador)* scorer (**b**) *(para libros)* bookmark (**c**) *Am (rotulador)* felt-tip pen; *Méx (fluorescente)* highlighter pen

marcaje NM *Dep* marking

marcapasos NM INV *Med* pacemaker

marcar [44] **1** VT (**a**) *(poner o dejar marca en)* to mark (**b**) *Tel* to dial (**c**) *(indicar)* to indicate, to show; *(en termómetro, contador)* to read (**d**) *Dep (gol, puntos)* to score; *(jugador)* to mark (**e**) *(cabello)* to set
2 marcarse VPR *Esp Fam* **marcarse un detalle** to do something nice o kind

marcha NF (**a**) *Mil, Pol & Mús* march; **hacer algo sobre la m.** to do sth as one goes along; *Esp* **a marchas forzadas** against the clock (**b**) **estar en m.** *(vehículo)* to be in motion; *(máquina)* to be working; *(proyecto)* to be under way; **poner en m.** to start (**c**) *Aut* gear; **m. atrás** reverse (gear) (**d**) *Esp Fam (animación)* liveliness, life; **hay mucha m.** there's a great atmosphere (**e**) *(partida)* departure

marchante, -a NM,F (**a**) *(de arte)* dealer (**b**) *CAm, Méx, Ven Fam (cliente)* customer, patron

marchar 1 VI (**a**) *(ir)* to go, to walk; *Fam* **¡marchando!** on your way!; **¡una cerveza! – ¡marchando!** a beer, please! — coming right up! (**b**) *(aparato)* to be on; **m. bien** *(negocio)* to be going well (**c**) *Mil* to march
2 marcharse VPR *(irse)* to leave, to go away

marchitarse VPR to shrivel, to wither

marchito, -a ADJ shrivelled, withered

marchoso, -a *Esp Fam* **1** ADJ *(persona)* fun-loving, wild
2 NM,F raver, fun-lover

marcial ADJ martial; **artes marciales** martial arts

marciano, -a ADJ & NM,F Martian

marco NM (**a**) *(de cuadro, foto)* frame (**b**) *(ámbito)* framework; **acuerdo m.** framework agreement (**c**) *(moneda)* mark

marea NF (**a**) *(del mar)* tide; **m. alta/baja** high/low tide; **m. negra** oil slick (**b**) *(multitud)* crowd, mob

mareado, -a ADJ (**a**) *(con náuseas)* sick; *(en coche)* car-sick, travel-sick; *(en el mar)* seasick; *(en avión)* airsick (**b**) *(aturdido)* dizzy (**c**) *Euf (bebido)* tipsy

marear 1 VT (**a**) *(con náuseas)* to make sick; *(en coche)* to make car-sick o travel-sick; *(en el mar)* to make seasick; *(en avión)* to make airsick (**b**) *(aturdir)* to make dizzy (**c**) *Fam (fastidiar)* to annoy, to pester
2 marearse VPR (**a**) *(con náuseas)* to get sick/car-sick o travel-sick/seasick/airsick (**b**) *(quedar aturdido)* to get dizzy (**c**) *Euf (emborracharse)* to get tipsy

marejada NF heavy sea

maremoto NM tidal wave

mareo NM (**a**) *(náusea)* sickness; *(en el mar)* seasickness; *(en un avión)* airsickness; *(en un coche)* car-sickness, travel-sickness (**b**) *(aturdimiento)* dizziness, light-headedness

marfil NM ivory

margarina NF margarine

margarita NF daisy

margen 1 NM (**a**) *(de página)* margin (**b**) *(de camino)* side (**c**) *(límite)* margin; *Com* **m. de beneficio** profit margin (**d**) **dejar algn/algo al m.** to leave sb/sth out; **mantenerse al m.** not to get involved; **al m. de** leaving aside
2 NF *(de río)* bank

marginación NF exclusion

marginado, -a 1 ADJ excluded
2 NM,F socially excluded person

marginal ADJ (**a**) *(de fuera de la sociedad)* socially excluded (**b**) *Econ* marginal

marginar VT to exclude

maría NF *Fam* (**a**) *Esp, Ven (droga)* marijuana, pot (**b**) *Esp (asignatura fácil)* easy subject (**c**) *(mujer sencilla)* (typical) housewife

mariachi NM (**a**) *(música)* mariachi (music) (**b**) *(orquesta)* mariachi band; *(músico)* mariachi (musician)

marica NM *Fam Br* poof, *US* fag

maricón NM *muy Fam Br* poof, *US* fag

marido NM husband

marihuana NF marijuana

marimacho NM *Fam* mannish woman, butch woman

marimandón, -ona *Esp* NM,F *Fam* domineering person

marimorena NF *Fam* row, fuss; *Fam* **armar(se) la m.** to kick up a racket

marina NF (**a**) *Náut* seamanship (**b**) *Mil* navy; **m. de guerra** navy; **m. mercante** merchant navy

marinero, -a 1 NM sailor, seaman
2 ADJ seafaring

marino, -a 1 ADJ marine; **brisa marina** sea breeze
2 NM sailor

marioneta NF marionette, puppet

mariposa NF (**a**) *(insecto)* butterfly (**b**) *(lamparilla)* oil lamp (**c**) *(en natación)* butterfly

mariposear VI (**a**) *(flirtear)* to flirt (**b**) *(ser inconstante)* to be fickle

mariposón NM *Fam* fairy, pansy

mariquita 1 NF *(insecto)* Br ladybird, US ladybug
2 NM *Fam (marica)* fairy

mariscada NF seafood meal

mariscal NM *Mil* marshal; **m. de campo** *Br* field marshal, *US* general of the army

marisco(s) NM(PL) shellfish, seafood

marisma NF marsh

marisquería NF seafood restaurant, shellfish bar

marítimo, -a ADJ maritime, sea; **ciudad marítima** coastal town; **paseo m.** promenade

marketing ['marketin] *(pl* **marketings)** NM marketing

mármol NM marble

marmóreo, -a ADJ marble

maroma NF (**a**) *Náut* cable (**b**) *(cuerda)* thick rope

marqués *(pl* **marqueses)** NM marquis

marquesa NF marchioness

marquesina NF canopy; **m. (del autobús)** bus shelter

marquetería NF marquetry, inlaid work

marrano, -a 1 ADJ *(sucio)* filthy, dirty
2 NM,F (**a**) *Fam (persona)* dirty pig, slob (**b**) *(animal)* pig

marras: de marras LOC ADV **el individuo de m.** the man in question

marrón ADJ & NM brown

marroquí *(pl* **marroquíes)** ADJ & NMF Moroccan

marroquinería NF leather goods

Marruecos N Morocco

marrullero, -a 1 ADJ cajoling, wheedling
2 NM,F cajoler, wheedler

Marte N Mars

martes NM INV Tuesday; **m. y trece** ≃ Friday the thirteenth

martillero NM *CSur* auctioneer

martillo NM hammer

mártir NMF martyr

martirio NM (**a**) *Rel* martyrdom (**b**) *Fig (sufrimiento)* torment

martirizar [40] VT (**a**) *(torturar)* to martyr (**b**) *Fig (hacer sufrir)* to torture, to torment

marxista ADJ & NMF Marxist

marzo NM March

mas CONJ *Literario* but

más 1 ADV (**a**) *(adicional)* more; **no tengo m.** I haven't got any more
(**b**) *(comparativo)* more; **es m. alta/inteligente que yo** she's taller/more intelligent than me; **tengo m. dinero que tú** I've more money than you; **m. gente de la que esperas** more people than you're expecting; **m. de** *(con numerales, cantidad)* more than, over
(**c**) *(superlativo)* most; **es el m. bonito/caro** it's the prettiest/most expensive
(**d**) *(como interjección)* so …, what a …; **¡qué casa m. bonita!** what a lovely house!; **¡está m. guapa!** she looks so beautiful!
(**e**) *(después de pron interr e indef)* else; **¿algo m.?** anything else?; **no, nada m.** no, nothing else; **¿quién m.?** who else?; **nadie/alguien m.** nobody/somebody else
(**f**) *cada día o vez* **m.** more and more; **estar de m.** to be unnecessary; **traje uno de m.** I brought a spare one; **es m.** what's more, furthermore; **lo m. posible** as much as possible; **m. bien** rather; **m. o menos** more or less; **m. aún** even more; **¿qué m. da?** what's the difference?; **todo lo m.** at the most
(**g**) **por m.** (*+ adj/adv*) *+* **que** (*+ subjunctive)* however (much), no matter how (much); **por m. fuerte que sea** however strong he may be; **por m. que grites no te oirá nadie** no matter how much you shout nobody will hear you
2 NM INV **los m.** the majority, most people; **sus m. y sus menos** its pros and cons
3 PREP *Mat* plus; **dos m. dos** two plus *o* and two

masa NF (**a**) *(de materia)* mass; **m. salarial** total wage bill (**b**) *(multitud)* throng; **en m.** en masse; **las masas** the masses (**c**) *Culin* dough (**d**) *Elec (tierra)* Br earth, US ground (**e**) *RP (pastelito)* cake

masacrar VT to massacre

masacre NF massacre

masaje NM massage; **dar un masaje a algn** to give sb a massage

masajista NMF *(hombre)* masseur; *(mujer)* masseuse

mascar [44] VT & VI to chew, to masticate

máscara NF mask; **m. de gas** gas mask

> Observa que la palabra inglesa **mascara** es un falso amigo y no es la traducción de la palabra española **máscara**. En inglés **mascara** significa "rímel".

mascarilla NF (**a**) *(de protección)* mask; **m. de oxígeno** oxygen mask (**b**) *Med* face mask (**c**) *(cosmética)* face pack

mascota NF mascot

masculino, -a ADJ (**a**) *Zool & Bot* male (**b**) *(de hombre)* male, manly; **una voz masculina** a manly voice (**c**) *(para hombre)* men's; **ropa masculina** men's clothes, menswear (**d**) *Ling* masculine

mascullar VT to mumble

masía NF = traditional Catalan or Aragonese farmhouse

masificación NF overcrowding

masificado, -a ADJ overcrowded

masilla NF putty

masivo, -a ADJ massive

masón NM freemason, mason

masonería NF freemasonry, masonry

masoquista 1 ADJ masochistic
2 NM,F masochist

master *(pl* **masters**) NM Master's (degree)

masticar [44] VT to chew

mástil NM (**a**) *(asta)* mast, pole (**b**) *Náut* mast (**c**) *(de guitarra)* neck

mastín NM mastiff

masturbación NF masturbation

masturbar 1 VT to masturbate
2 masturbarse VPR to masturbate

mata NF (**a**) *(matorral)* bush, shrub; **m. de pelo** head of hair (**b**) *(ramita)* sprig

matadero NM slaughterhouse, abattoir

matador NM matador, bullfighter

matambre NM *Andes, RP* (**a**) *(carne)* flank o *Br* skirt steak (**b**) *(plato)* = flank steak rolled with boiled egg, olives and red pepper, which is cooked, then sliced and served cold

matanza NF slaughter

matar 1 VT to kill; *Fam* **m. el tiempo** to kill time; **comer algo para m. el hambre** to eat sth to keep one going
2 matarse VPR *(morir)* to die; *(suicidarse)* to kill oneself; **se mató en un accidente de coche** he was killed in a car accident

matarratas NM INV rat poison

matasellos NM INV postmark

matasuegras NM INV party blower

mate¹ ADJ *(sin brillo)* matt

mate² NM *(en ajedrez)* mate; **jaque m.** checkmate

mate³ NM *CSur (infusión)* maté

matemáticas NFPL mathematics *sing*

matemático, -a 1 ADJ mathematical
2 NM,F mathematician

materia NF (**a**) *(sustancia, asunto)* matter; **m. gris** grey matter (**b**) *(material)* material; **m. prima** raw material (**c**) *Educ (asignatura)* subject

material 1 ADJ material, physical; **daños materiales** damage to property
2 NM (**a**) *(sustancia)* material (**b**) *(equipo)* equipment; **m. escolar/de construcción** school/building materials; **m. de oficina** office stationery

materialista ADJ & NMF materialist

materialmente ADV physically

maternal ADJ maternal, motherly

maternidad NF *(estado)* motherhood; **permiso de/sala de m.** maternity leave/ward

materno, -a ADJ maternal; **abuelo m.** maternal grandfather; **lengua materna** native o mother tongue

matinal ADJ morning; **televisión m.** breakfast television

matiz NM (**a**) *(de color)* shade (**b**) *(de palabra)* shade of meaning, nuance; **un m. irónico** a touch of irony

matización NF clarification, explanation to add a rider

matizar [40] VT (**a**) *(puntualizar)* to clarify, to explain (**b**) *(teñir)* to tinge (**de** with) (**c**) *Arte* to blend

matón NM *Fam* thug, bully

matorral NM brushwood, thicket

matraca NF *(ruido)* rattle; *Fam* **dar la m. a algn** to pester o bother sb

matrero, -a NM,F *Andes, RP (fugitivo)* outlaw

matriarcado NM matriarchy

matriarcal ADJ matriarchal

matrícula NF (**a**) *(acción)* registration; **derechos de m.** registration fee; **m. de honor** distinction; **plazo de m.** registration period (**b**) *Aut Br* number plate, *US* license plate

matriculación NF registration

matricular 1 VT to register
2 matricularse VPR to register

matrimonial ADJ matrimonial; **agencia m.** marriage bureau; **enlace m.** wedding; **vida m.** married life

matrimonio NM (**a**) *(institución)* marriage; **contraer m.** to marry; **m. civil/religioso** registry office/church wedding; **cama de m.** double bed (**b**) *(pareja casada)* married couple; **el m. y los niños** the couple and their children; **el m. Romero** Mr and Mrs Romero, the Romeros

matriz 1 NF (**a**) *Anat* womb, uterus (**b**) *Mat* matrix (**c**) *(de documento) (original)* original, master copy (**d**) *Téc* mould
2 ADJ *(empresa)* parent; **casa m.** head office

matrona NF midwife

matutino, -a ADJ morning; **prensa matutina** morning papers

maullar VI to miaow

maullido NM miaowing, miaow

maxilar NM jaw, jawbone

máxima NF (**a**) *Met* maximum temperature (**b**) *(aforismo)* maxim

máxime ADV especially, all the more so

máximo, -a 1 ADJ maximum, highest; **la máxima puntuación** the highest score
2 NM maximum; **al m.** to the utmost; **como m.** *(como mucho)* at the most; *(lo más tarde)* at the latest

maya 1 ADJ Mayan
2 NMF Maya, Mayan
3 NM *(idioma)* Maya

mayo NM May

mayonesa NF mayonnaise

mayor 1 ADJ **(a)** *(comparativo) (tamaño)* larger, bigger (**que** than); *(edad)* older, elder; **m. que yo** older than me **(b)** *(superlativo) (tamaño)* largest, biggest; *(edad)* oldest, eldest; **la m. parte** the majority; **la m. parte de las veces** most often **(c)** *(adulto)* grown-up; **ser m. de edad** to be of age **(d)** *(maduro)* elderly, mature **(e)** *(principal)* major, main; *Educ* **colegio m.** *Br* hall of residence, *US* residence hall, *US* dormitory **(f)** *Mús* major **(g)** *Com* **al por m.** wholesale; *Fig (en abundancia)* by the score, galore
2 NM **(a)** *Mil* major **(b) mayores** *(adultos)* grown-ups, adults

mayordomo NM butler

mayoreo NM *Am* wholesale

mayoría NF majority; **en su m.** in the main; **la m. de los niños** most children; **m. absoluta** absolute majority; **m. relativa** *Br* relative majority, *US* plurality; **m. de edad** majority

mayorista 1 ADJ wholesale
2 NMF wholesaler; **precios de m.** wholesale prices

mayoritario, -a ADJ majority; **un gobierno m.** a majority government

mayúscula NF capital letter

mayúsculo, -a ADJ **(a)** *Ling (letra)* capital **(b)** *(error)* very big, enormous

mazacote NM **(a)** *Culin* solid mass, stodge **(b)** *(mezcla confusa)* hotchpotch

mazapán NM marzipan

mazmorra NF dungeon

mazo NM mallet

mazorca NF *Agr* cob

me PRON PERS **(a)** *(objeto directo)* me; **no me mires** don't look at me **(b)** *(objeto indirecto)* me, to me, for me; **¿me das un caramelo?** will you give me a sweet?; **me lo dio** he gave it to me; **me es difícil hacerlo** it is difficult for me to do it **(c)** *(pron reflexivo)* myself; **me he cortado** I've cut myself; **me voy/muero** *(no se traduce)* I'm off/dying

meada NF *Fam* piss; **echar una m.** to have a piss

meadero NM *Fam Br* bog, *US* john

meandro NM meander

mear *Fam* **1** VI to (have a) piss
2 mearse VPR to wet oneself; *Fig* **mearse de risa** to piss oneself (laughing)

mecachis INTERJ *Fam Br* sugar!, *US* shoot!

mecánica NF **(a)** *(ciencia)* mechanics *sing* **(b)** *(mecanismo)* mechanism, works

mecánico, -a 1 ADJ mechanical
2 NM,F mechanic

mecanismo NM mechanism

mecanizar [40] VT to mechanize

mecanografía NF typewriting, typing

mecanografiar [29] VT to type

mecanógrafo, -a NM,F typist

mecapal NM *CAm, Méx* = porter's leather harness

mecedora NF rocking-chair

mecenas NMF INV patron

mecer [49] **1** VT to rock
2 mecerse VPR to swing, to rock

mecha NF **(a)** *(de vela)* wick **(b)** *Mil & Min* fuse; *Fam* **aguantar m.** to grin and bear it **(c)** *(de pelo)* streak; **hacerse mechas** to have one's hair streaked

mechar VT *(carne)* to lard

mechero NM *Esp* (cigarette) lighter

mechón NM **(a)** *(de pelo)* lock **(b)** *(de lana)* tuft

medalla NF medal

medallón NM medallion

media NF **(a)** *(prenda interior)* **medias** *(hasta la cintura)* *Br* tights, *US* pantyhose; *(hasta medio muslo)* stockings **(b)** *(calcetín)* *(hasta la rodilla)* (knee-length) sock; *Am (de cualquier longitud)* sock **(c)** *(promedio)* average; *Mat* mean; **m. aritmética/geométrica** arithmetic/geometric mean **(d)** *(incompleto)* **a medias** unfinished; *(entre dos)* half and half; **ir a medias** to go halves

Observa que la palabra inglesa **media** es un falso amigo y no es la traducción de la palabra española **media**. En inglés, **media** significa "medios de comunicación".

mediación NF mediation, intervention; **por m. de un amigo** through a friend

mediado, -a 1 ADJ half-full, half-empty
2 a mediados de LOC PREP about the middle of

mediador, -a NM,F mediator

medialuna NF **(a)** *(símbolo musulmán)* crescent **(b)** *Am (bollo)* croissant

mediana NF **(a)** *(de autopista)* *Br* central reservation, *US* median (strip) **(b)** *Mat* median

mediano, -a ADJ **(a)** *(de tamaño)* medium; *(de calidad)* average **(b)** *(mediocre)* average, ordinary

medianoche NF midnight

mediante PREP by means of, with the help of, using; **Dios m.** God willing

mediar [43] VI **(a)** *(intervenir)* to mediate, to intervene; **m. en favor de** *o* **por algn** to intercede on behalf of sb **(b)** *(tiempo)* to pass; **mediaron tres semanas** three weeks passed

mediático, -a ADJ media

medicación NF medication

medicamento NM medicine

medicina NF medicine; **estudiante de m.** medical student

medicinal ADJ medicinal

médico, -a 1 NM,F doctor; **m. de cabecera** family doctor, general practitioner; **m. inter-**

no (residente) *Br* house officer, *US* intern
2 ADJ medical

medida 1 NF (**a**) *(dimensión)* measurement;
tomar las medidas a algn to take sb's meas-
urements; **a (la) m.** *(ropa)* made-to-measure;
m. de capacidad measure *(liquid or dry)* (**b**)
(grado) extent, degree; **en gran m.** to a great
extent (**c**) *(disposición)* measure; **adoptar** o
tomar medidas to take measures o steps
2 a medida LOC CONJ as; **a m. que**
avanzaba as he advanced

medidor NM *Am* meter

medieval ADJ medieval

medievo NM Middle Ages

medio, -a 1 ADJ (**a**) *(mitad)* half; **m. kilo** half a
kilo; **una hora y media** one and a half hours, an
hour and a half; **a m. camino** halfway; **a media
mañana/tarde** in the middle of the morning/
afternoon (**b**) *(intermedio)* *(estatura, tamaño)*
medium; *(posición, punto)* middle; **de clase
media** middle-class (**c**) *(normal)* average;
salario m. average wage
2 ADV half; **está m. muerta** she is half dead
3 NM (**a**) *(mitad)* half (**b**) *(centro)* middle; **en
m. (de)** *(en el centro)* in the middle (of); *(entre
dos)* in between (**c**) **medios de transporte**
means of transport; **por m. de ...** by means of
...; **medios económicos** means; **medios de
comunicación (de masas)** (mass) media (**d**)
m. ambiente environment (**e**) *Dep (jugador)*
half back

medioambiental ADJ environmental

mediocre ADJ mediocre

mediocridad NF mediocrity

mediodía NM (**a**) *(hora exacta)* midday, noon
(**b**) *(período aproximado)* early afternoon,
lunch-time

medir [6] **1** VT (**a**) *(distancia, superficie,
temperatura)* to measure (**b**) *(moderar)* to
weigh; **mide tus palabras** weigh your words
2 VI to measure, to be; **¿cuánto mides?** how
tall are you?; **mide 2 m** he is 2 m tall; **mide 2
m de alto/ancho/largo** it is 2 m high/wide/
long

meditar VT & VI to meditate, to ponder; **m.
sobre algo** to ponder over sth

mediterráneo, -a 1 ADJ Mediterranean
2 NM **el M.** the Mediterranean

médium NMF INV medium

medrar VI to climb the social ladder

médula NF (**a**) *Anat* (bone) marrow; **m. espinal**
spinal cord (**b**) *(lo más profundo)* marrow, pith;
hasta la m. to the marrow

medusa NF jellyfish

megabit (*pl* megabits) NM *Inform* megabit

megafonía NF public-address system, PA
system

megáfono NM megaphone

megalito NM megalith

megalómano, -a ADJ megalomaniac

mejicano, -a ADJ & NM,F Mexican

Méjico N Mexico; **ciudad de M.** Mexico City;
Nuevo M. New Mexico

mejilla NF cheek

mejillón NM mussel

mejor 1 ADJ (**a**) *(comparativo)* better (**que**
than); **es m. no decírselo** it's better not to tell
her; **es m. que vayas** you'd better go (**b**)
(superlativo) best; **tu m. amiga** your best
friend; **lo m.** the best thing
2 ADV (**a**) *(comparativo)* better (**que** than);
cada vez m. better and better; **ella conduce
m.** she drives better; **m. dicho** or rather;
¡mucho o **tanto m.!** so much the better! (**b**)
(superlativo) best; **es el que m. canta** he is the
one who sings the best; **a lo m.** *(quizás)*
perhaps; *(ojalá)* hopefully
3 NMF **el/la m.** the best; **el m. de los dos** the
better of the two; **el m. de los tres** the best of
the three

mejora NF improvement

mejorar 1 VT to improve; **m. la red vial** to
improve the road system; **m. una marca** o **un
récord** to break a record
2 VI to improve, to get better
3 mejorarse VPR to get better; **¡que te
mejores!** get well soon!

mejoría NF improvement

melancolía NF melancholy

melancólico, -a ADJ melancholic, melancholy

melé NF *Esp Dep* scrum

melena NF (head of) hair; *(de león)* mane

melindroso, -a 1 ADJ affected, fussy, finicky
2 NM,F affected o finicky person

mella NF (**a**) *(hendedura)* nick, notch; *(en plato,
taza etc)* chip (**b**) *(en dentadura)* gap (**c**) *Fig*
impression; **hacer m. en algn** to make an
impression on sb

mellado, -a ADJ *(sin dientes)* gap-toothed

mellizo, -a ADJ & NM,F twin

melocotón NM *esp Esp* peach

melocotonero NM *esp Esp* peach tree

melodía NF melody, tune; *(de teléfono)* ringtone

melodrama NM melodrama

melodramático, -a ADJ melodramatic

melón NM (**a**) *(fruto)* melon (**b**) *Fam (tonto)*
ninny (**c**) *muy Fam* **melones** *(tetas)* boobs

melopea NF *Esp Fam* **coger** o **agarrar/llevar
una m.** to get/be drunk o *Br* pissed

meloso, -a ADJ sweet, honeyed

membrana NF membrane

membresía NF *Am* membership

membrete NM letterhead

membrillo NM (**a**) *Bot (fruto)* quince; *(árbol)*
quince tree; *(dulce)* quince preserve o jelly
(**b**) *Fam (tonto)* dimwit

memela NF *Méx* = thick corn tortilla, oval in
shape

memo, -a *Fam* **1** ADJ silly, stupid
2 NM,F nincompoop, ninny

memorable ADJ memorable

memorándum (pl **memorándums**) NM memorandum

memoria NF (a) (capacidad de recordar) memory; **aprender/saber algo de m.** to learn/know sth by heart; **irse de la m.** to slip one's mind (b) (recuerdo) memory, recollection (c) (informe) report, statement; **m. anual** annual report (d) **memorias** (biografía) memoirs

memorístico, -a ADJ acquired by memory

memorizar [40] VT to memorize

menaje NM furniture and furnishing; **m. de cocina** kitchen equipment o utensils

mención NF mention; **m. honorífica** honourable mention

mencionar VT to mention

mendicidad NF begging

mendigar [42] VT & VI to beg

mendigo, -a NM,F beggar

mendrugo NM (a) (de pan) crust (of bread) (b) Esp Fam (idiota) fathead, idiot

mene NM Ven = deposit of oil at surface level

menear 1 VT (mover) to move; (cabeza) to shake; (cola) to wag
2 menearse VPR (moverse) to move (about); (agitarse) to shake

meneo NM shake; (de cola) wag, waggle

menester NM (a) **es m.** it is necessary (b) **menesteres** (deberes) jobs

menestra NF vegetable stew

mengano, -a NM,F Fam so-and-so, what's-his-o her-name

menguante ADJ waning, on the wane; **cuarto m.** last quarter

menguar [45] **1** VT (a) (disminuir) to diminish, to reduce (b) (en labor de punto) to decrease
2 VI (a) (disminuir) to diminish, to decrease (b) (luna) to wane

menopausia NF menopause

menor 1 ADJ (a) (comparativo) (de tamaño) smaller (**que** than); (de edad) younger (**que** than); **el mal m.** the lesser of two evils; **ser m. de edad** to be a minor o under age (b) (superlativo) (de tamaño) smallest; (de intensidad) least, slightest; (de edad) youngest; **al m. ruido** at the slightest noise (c) Mús minor (d) Com **al por m.** retail
2 NM,F (b) Der minor; **tribunal de menores** juvenile court (b) (superlativo) **el/la m.** (hijo, hermano) the youngest; **el m. de los dos** the smaller of the two; **el m. de los tres** the youngest of the three; **es la m.** she's the youngest child

Menorca N Minorca

menos 1 ADJ (a) (comparativo) (con singular) less; (con plural) fewer; **m. dinero/leche/tiempo que** less money/milk/time than; **m. libros/pisos que** fewer books/flats than; (con cláusula) **tiene m. años de lo que parece** he's younger than he looks (b) (superlativo) **fui el que perdí m. dinero** I lost the least money
2 ADV (a) **m. de** (con singular) less than; (con plural) fewer than, less than; **m. de media hora** less than half an hour (b) (superlativo) (con singular) least; (con plural) the fewest; (con cantidad) the least; **el m. inteligente de la clase** the least intelligent boy in the class; **ayer fue cuando vinieron m. personas** yesterday was when the fewest people came (c) Esp, RP (con las horas) to; **son las dos m. diez** it's ten to two, it's ten to
3 (locuciones) **a m. que** (+ subjunctive) unless; **al o por lo m.** at least; **echar de m. a algn** to miss sb; **eso es lo de m.** that's the least of it; **¡m. mal!** just as well!; **nada m. que** no less/no fewer than; **ni mucho m.** far from it
4 PREP (a) (excepto) but, except; **todo m. eso** anything but that (b) Mat minus; **tres m. uno** three minus one

menoscabar VT (a) (perjudicar) to damage (b) (desacreditar) to discredit

menoscabo NM (de fama, honra) damage; (de derechos, intereses, salud) harm; (de belleza, perfección) diminishing; **ir en m. de algo** to be to the detriment of sth

menospreciar [43] VT to scorn, to disdain

menosprecio NM contempt, scorn, disdain

mensáfono NM pager

mensaje NM message

mensajería NF (a) (de paquetes, cartas) courier service (b) (por teléfono) messaging

mensajero, -a NM,F messenger, courier

menso, -a ADJ Méx Fam foolish, stupid

menstruación NF menstruation

menstruar [30] VI to menstruate

mensual ADJ monthly; **dos visitas mensuales** two visits a month

mensualidad NF (pago) monthly payment; (sueldo) monthly salary o wage

menta NF (a) Bot mint (b) (licor) crème de menthe

mental ADJ mental

mentalidad NF mentality; **de m. abierta/cerrada** open-/narrow-minded

mentalizar [40] **1** VT to make aware
2 mentalizarse VPR to get into a frame of mind; **mentalizarse de que ...** to get used to the idea that ...

mentar [1] VT to mention, to name

mente NF mind; **se me quedó la m. en blanco** my mind went blank; **m. abierta/tolerante/cerrada** open/broad/closed mind

mentecato, -a NM,F fool, idiot

mentir [5] VI to lie, to tell lies

mentira NF lie; **aunque parezca m.** strange as it may seem; **parece m.** it is unbelievable

mentiroso, -a 1 ADJ lying
2 NM,F liar

mentís NM INV denial

mentón NM Anat chin

menú NM menu; **m. del día** set meal

menudeo NM Andes, Méx retailing

menudillos NMPL giblets

menudo, -a 1 ADJ minute, tiny; *(irónico)* tremendous; **la gente menuda** the little ones; **¡m. lío/susto!** what a mess/fright!
2 ADV **a m.** often

meñique ADJ & NM **(dedo) m.** little finger, *US & Scot* pinkie

meollo NM core, heart; **el m. de la cuestión** the nub of the question, the heart of the matter

mercadillo NM flea market

mercado NM market; *Antes* **M. Común** Common Market; **m. financiero** financial market; **m. negro** black market; **m. único** single market; **m. de valores** securities market; **sacar algo al m.** to put sth on the market

mercadotecnia NF marketing

mercancía NF merchandise, goods

mercante ADJ merchant; **barco/marina m.** merchant ship/navy

mercantil ADJ mercantile, commercial

merced NF *Fml* favour, grace; **a m. de** at the mercy of

mercenario, -a ADJ & NM,F mercenary

mercería NF *Br* haberdasher's (shop), *US* notions store

Mercosur NM *(abr* **Mercado Común del Sur)** MERCOSUR, = South American economic community consisting of Argentina, Brazil, Paraguay and Uruguay

mercurio NM *Quím* mercury, quicksilver

merecer [33] **1** VT (a) to deserve (b) **no merece la pena hacerlo** it's not worth (while) doing it
2 merecerse VPR to deserve

merecido, -a 1 ADJ deserved; **ella lo tiene m.** *(recompensa)* she deserves it; *(castigo)* it serves her right
2 NM just deserts

merendar [1] **1** VT to have as an afternoon snack, to have for tea
2 VI to have an afternoon snack, to have tea

merendero NM *(establecimiento)* tea room, snack-bar; *(en el campo)* picnic spot

merengue NM (a) *Culin* meringue (b) *(baile)* merengue

merezco INDIC PRES de **merecer**

meridiano NM meridian

meridional 1 ADJ southern
2 NMF southerner

merienda NF afternoon snack, tea

mérito NM merit, worth; **hacer méritos para algo** to strive to deserve sth

merluza NF hake

merma NF decrease, reduction

mermar 1 VT to cause to decrease o diminish
2 VI to decrease, to diminish

mermelada NF jam; *(de agrios)* marmalade; **m. de fresa** strawberry jam; **m. de naranja** orange marmalade

mero, -a ADJ (a) *(simple)* mere; **por el m. hecho de** through the mere fact of (b) *CAm, Méx Fam* **en el m. centro** right in the centre; *Méx* **el m. m.** the big shot

merodear VI to prowl

mes NM (a) *(tiempo)* month; **el m. pasado/que viene** last/next month (b) *(cobro)* monthly salary o wages; *(pago)* monthly payment (c) *Fam (menstruación)* period

mesa NF (a) *(mueble)* table; *(de despacho, oficina)* desk; **poner/recoger la m.** to set/ clear the table; **m. camilla** = small round table under which a heater is placed (b) *(comité)* board, committee; *(en un debate)* panel; **el presidente de la m.** the chairman; **m. electoral** electoral college; **m. redonda** *(coloquio)* round table

mesada NF (a) *Am (pago mensual)* monthly payment, monthly instalment (b) *RP (para adolescentes)* pocket money, *US* allowance (c) *RP (encimera)* worktop

mesero, -a NM,F *Col, Guat, Méx, Salv (hombre)* waiter; *(mujer)* waitress

meseta NF plateau, tableland, meseta; **la M.** the plateau of Castile

mesilla NF **m. de noche** bedside table

mesón NM = old-style tavern

mesonero, -a NM,F (a) *Esp (en mesón)* innkeeper (b) *Chile, Ven (camarero) (hombre)* waiter; *(mujer)* waitress

mestizo, -a 1 ADJ *(persona)* of mixed race, half-caste; *(animal, planta)* cross-bred
2 NM,F person of mixed race, half-caste

mesura NF *Fml* moderation, restraint

> Observa que la palabra inglesa **measure** es un falso amigo y no es la traducción de la palabra española **mesura**. En inglés, **measure** significa "medida".

meta NF (a) *(objetivo)* goal, aim, objective (b) *(de carrera)* finish, finishing line (c) *Ftb (portería)* goal

metabolismo NM metabolism

metadona NF methadone

metafísica NF metaphysics *sing*

metáfora NF metaphor

metal NM (a) *(material)* metal; **metales preciosos** precious metals (b) *Mús* brass

metálico, -a 1 ADJ metallic
2 NM cash; **pagar en m.** to pay (in) cash

metalizado, -a ADJ *(pintura)* metallic

metalúrgico, -a 1 ADJ metallurgical
2 NM,F metallurgist

metamorfosis NF INV *también Fig* metamorphosis

metate NM *Guat, Méx* grinding stone

metedura NF *Fam* **m. de pata** blunder, *Br* clanger

meteorito NM meteorite

meteoro NM meteor

meteorología NF meteorology

meteorológico, -a ADJ meteorological; **parte m.** weather report o forecast

meter 1 VT (**a**) *(poner)* to put (**en** in); *Fig* **m. las narices en algo** to poke one's nose into sth (**b**) *(comprometer)* to involve (**en** in), to get mixed up (**en** in) (**c**) *Fam Fig (dar)* to give; **m. un rollo** to go on and on; **m. prisa a algn** to hurry sb up (**d**) *(hacer)* to make; **m. ruido** to make a noise
2 meterse VPR (**a**) *(entrar)* to go/come in, to get in (**b**) *(estar)* to be; **¿dónde te habías metido?** where have you been (all this time)? (**c**) *(entrometerse)* to meddle (**d**) **meterse con algn** *(en broma)* to get at sb

metiche *Méx, Ven Fam* NMF busybody, *Br* nosey-parker

meticuloso, -a ADJ meticulous

metido, -a ADJ *Fam* **estar muy m. en algo** to be deeply involved in sth; **m. en años** getting on (in years)

metódico, -a ADJ methodical

método NM method

metodología NF methodology

metomentodo NMF INV *Fam* busybody, *Br* nosey-parker

metralla NF shrapnel

metralleta NF submachine-gun

métrico, -a ADJ metric; **sistema m.** metric system

metro NM (**a**) *(medida)* metre (**b**) *(tren) Br* underground, *US* subway (**c**) *(cinta métrica)* tape measure

metrópoli NF metropolis

metropolitano, -a 1 ADJ metropolitan
2 NM *Fml Br* underground, *US* subway

mexicano, -a ADJ & NM,F Mexican

México N Mexico

mezcla NF (**a**) *(acción)* mixing, blending; *Rad & Cin* mixing (**b**) *(producto)* mixture, blend

mezclar 1 VT (**a**) *(dos o más cosas)* to mix, to blend (**b**) *(desordenar)* to mix up (**c**) *(involucrar)* to involve, to mix up
2 mezclarse VPR (**a**) *(cosas)* to get mixed up; *(gente)* to mingle (**b**) *(relacionarse)* to get involved (**con** with)

mezcolanza NF *Fml* strange mixture, hotch-potch

mezquino, -a ADJ (**a**) *(persona)* mean, stingy (**b**) *(sueldo)* miserable

mezquita NF mosque

mg *(abr* **miligramo(s))** mg

mi¹ ADJ my; **mi casa/trabajo** my house/job; **mis cosas/libros** my things/books

mi² *(pl* **mis)** NM *Mús* E; **mi menor** E minor

mí PRON PERS me; **a mí me dio tres** he gave me three; **compra otro para mí** buy one for me too; **por mí mismo** just by myself

mía ADJ & PRON POS F *ver* **mío**

miaja NF crumb; *Fig* bit

miche NM *Ven* = cane spirit flavoured with herbs and spices

michelín NM *Fam* spare tyre

mico NM (**a**) *Zool* (long-tailed) monkey (**b**) *Fam (pequeño)* **es un m.** he's a midget o *Br* titch

micra NF micron

micro 1 NM *Fam* mike, microphone
2 NM o NF *Arg, Bol, Chile (autobús)* minibus

microbio NM microbe

microbús *(pl* **microbuses)** NM (**a**) *(autobús)* minibus (**b**) *Méx (taxi)* (collective) taxi

microchip *(pl* **microchips)** NM *Inform* micro-chip

microclima NM microclimate

microcrédito NM *Econ* microcredit

microficha NF microfiche

micrófono NM microphone

microondas NM INV **un (horno) m.** a microwave (oven)

microscopio NM microscope

miedica NMF *Esp Fam* scaredy-cat

miedo NM *(pavor)* fear; *(temor)* apprehension; **una película de m.** a horror movie o *Br* film; **tener m. de algn/algo** to be afraid of sb/sth; *Esp Fam* **de m.: lo pasamos de m.** we had a fantastic time; **un calor de m.** sizzling heat

miedoso, -a ADJ fearful

miel NF honey; **luna de m.** honeymoon

miembro NM (**a**) *(socio)* member; **estado m.** member state (**b**) *Anat* limb; **m. viril** penis

mientras 1 CONJ (**a**) *(al mismo tiempo que)* while (**b**) *(durante el tiempo que)* when, while; **m. viví en Barcelona** when I lived in Barcelona (**c**) **m. que** *(por el contrario)* whereas (**d**) *Fam (cuanto más)* **m. más/menos …** the more/less …
2 ADV **m. (tanto)** meanwhile, in the meantime

miércoles NM INV Wednesday; **M. de Ceniza** Ash Wednesday

mierda NF *Vulg* (**a**) *(excremento)* shit; *(suciedad)* crap; **ese libro es una m.** that book is crap; **¡vete a la m.!** piss off! (**b**) *Esp (borrachera)* bender

miga NF *(de pan etc)* crumb; *Fig* **hacer buenas migas con algn** to get on well with sb

migaja NF (**a**) *(trozo)* bit; *(de pan)* crumb (**b**) *(pizca)* scrap; **migajas** *(restos)* leftovers

migra NF *Méx Fam Pey* **la m.** = US police border patrol

migraña NF migraine

migrar VI to migrate

mijo NM millet

mil ADJ & NM thousand; **m. euros** a o one thousand euros

milagro NM miracle

milagroso, -a ADJ miraculous

milano NM kite

milenario, -a ADJ ancient

milenio NM millennium

milésima NF thousandth; **m. de segundo** lowest common multiple millisecond

milésimo, -a ADJ & NM thousandth; **la milésima parte** a thousandth

mili NF *Esp Antes Fam* military o national service

milicia NF *(grupo armado)* militia

milico NM *Andes, RP Fam Pey* soldier; **los milicos** the military

miligramo NM milligram

mililitro NM millilitre

milímetro NM millimetre

militante ADJ & NMF militant

militar 1 ADJ military

2 NM military man, soldier; **los militares** the military

3 VI *Pol (en partido)* to be a member

milla NF mile

millar NM thousand

millardo NM billion, thousand million

millón NM million; **dos millones** two million

millonario, -a ADJ & NM,F millionaire

millonésimo, -a ADJ & NM millionth

milpa NF *CAm, Méx* cornfield

mimado, -a ADJ spoilt

mimar VT to spoil, to pamper

> Observa que el verbo inglés **to mime** es un falso amigo y no es la traducción del verbo español **mimar**. En inglés, **to mime** significa "representar con gestos".

mimbre NM wicker

mímica NF mimicry

mimo NM (**a**) *(delicadeza)* care (**b**) *Fig (zalamería)* pampering (**c**) *Teatro (actor)* mime

mimosa NF *Bot* mimosa

mimoso, -a ADJ **está m.** he wants a cuddle

mina NF (**a**) *Geol & Mil* mine (**b**) *(de lápiz)* lead; (**c**) *Fig (cosa rentable)* goldmine (**d**) *CSur Fam (chica) Br* bird, *US* chick

minar VT (**a**) *Mil* to mine (**b**) *Fig (desgastar)* to undermine

mineral 1 ADJ mineral

2 NM (**a**) *Geol* mineral (**b**) *Min* ore; **m. de hierro** iron ore

minería NF *(técnica)* mining; *(sector)* mining industry

minero, -a 1 NM,F miner

2 ADJ mining

miniatura NF miniature

mini disk, mini disc NM INV mini disc

minifalda NF miniskirt

minifundio NM smallholding

minigolf (*pl* **minigolfs**) NM crazy golf

mínima NF minimum temperature

minimizar VT to minimize

mínimo, -a 1 ADJ (**a**) *(lo más bajo posible)* minimum (**b**) *(muy pequeño) (efecto, importancia)* minimal, very small; *(ruido, idea)* slightest; **como m.** at the very least

2 NM *(límite)* minimum; **m. común múltiplo** lowest common multiple

minipimer® (*pl* **minipímers**) NM o NF hand-held mixer

ministerio NM (**a**) *Pol Br* ministry, *US* department (**b**) *Rel* ministry

ministro, -a NM,F (**a**) *Pol Br* minister, *US* secretary; **primer m.** prime minister (**b**) *Rel* minister

minoría NF minority; *Der* **m. de edad** minority

minorista NMF retailer

minoritario, -a ADJ minority

minucioso, -a ADJ (**a**) *(persona)* meticulous (**b**) *(informe, trabajo)* minute, detailed

minúscula NF small letter, lower-case letter

minúsculo, -a ADJ minuscule, minute; **letra minúscula** lower-case o small letter

minusvalía NF (**a**) *Fin* capital loss (**b**) *(física)* disability, handicap

minusválido, -a 1 ADJ disabled, handicapped

2 NM,F disabled person, handicapped person

minuta NF *(factura)* fee

minutero NM minute hand

minuto NM minute

mío, -a 1 ADJ POS of mine; **un amigo m.** a friend of mine; **no es asunto m.** it is none of my business

2 PRON POS mine; **ese libro es m.** that book is mine; **lo m. es el tenis** tennis is my strong point; *Fam* **los míos** my people o folks

miope NMF short-sighted o *US* near-sighted person, *Espec* myopic person

miopía NF short-sightedness, *US* near-sightedness, *Espec* myopia

mira NF (**a**) *Téc* sight (**b**) *(objetivo)* aim, target; **con miras a** with a view to; **amplitud de miras** broad-mindedness

mirada NF look; **lanzar** o **echar una m. a** to glance at; **levantar la m.** to look up; **m. fija** stare

mirador NM (**a**) *(lugar con vista)* viewpoint (**b**) *(balcón)* bay window, windowed balcony

mirar 1 VT (**a**) *(observar)* to look at; *(fijamente)* to stare at; **mirándolo bien ...** if you think about it ...

2 VI (**a**) *(dirigir la vista)* to look; *(observar)* to watch; *(fijamente)* to stare; **¡mira!** look (at that!) (**b**) *(dar a)* to look, to face; **la casa mira al sur** the house faces south (**c**) **m. por algn/algo** *(cuidar)* to look after sb/sth

mirilla NF spyhole

mirlo NM blackbird

mirón, -ona *Fam* **1** ADJ *(curioso)* nosey; *(con lascivia)* peeping

2 NM,F *(espectador)* onlooker; *(curioso)* busy-body, *Br* nosy parker; *(voyeur)* peeping Tom

mirra NF myrrh

misántropo, -a 1 ADJ misanthropic

2 NM,F misanthrope, misanthropist

miscelánea NF (**a**) *(mezcla)* miscellany (**b**) *Méx (tienda)* = small general store

miserable 1 ADJ (**a**) *(mezquino) (persona)* despicable; *(sueldo etc)* miserable (**b**) *(pobre)* wretched, poor; **una vida m.** a wretched life
2 NMF (**a**) *(mezquino)* miser (**b**) *(canalla)* wretch

miseria NF (**a**) *(pobreza extrema)* extreme poverty (**b**) *(insignificancia)* pittance; **ganar una m.** to earn next to nothing (**c**) *(tacañería)* miserliness, meanness

misericordia NF mercy, compassion

mísero, -a ADJ miserable, wretched

misil NM missile

misión NF mission; **m. cumplida** mission accomplished

misionero, -a NM,F missionary

mismísimo, -a ADJ SUPERL *Fam (en persona)* in person

mismo, -a 1 ADJ (**a**) *(igual, no otro)* same (**b**) *(uso enfático)* **yo m.** I myself; **aquí m.** right here
2 PRON same; **es el m. de ayer** it's the same one as yesterday; **estamos en las mismas** we're back to square one; **lo m.** the same (thing); **dar** *o* **ser lo m.** to make no difference; **por eso m.** that is why; **por uno** *o* **sí m.** by oneself
3 ADV (**a**) *(por ejemplo)* for instance; **que venga alguien, Juan m.** ask one of them to come, Juan, for instance (**b**) **así m.** likewise

misógino, -a 1 ADJ misogynous
2 NM,F misogynist

miss NF beauty queen

misterio NM mystery

misterioso, -a ADJ mysterious

místico, -a 1 ADJ mystical
2 NM,F mystic

mitad NF (**a**) **la m.** half; **a m. de precio** half-price; **a m. de película** halfway through the movie *o Br* film (**b**) *(centro)* middle; **en m. de** in the middle of; **en m. del primer acto** halfway through the first act

mítico, -a ADJ mythical

mitigar [42] VT to mitigate; *(daño)* to reduce

mitin NM *Pol* meeting, rally

mito NM myth

mitología NF mythology

mitote NM *Méx Fam (alboroto)* racket

mixto, -a ADJ mixed

mm *(abr* **milímetro(s))** mm

mobiliario NM furniture

moca NM mocha

mocasín NM moccasin

mochila NF rucksack, backpack

mochuelo NM *Zool* little owl

moción NF motion; **m. de censura** vote of censure

moco NM snot; **sonarse los mocos** to blow one's nose; **tener mocos** to have a runny nose

mocoso, -a NM,F *Fam* brat

moda NF fashion; *(furor pasajero)* craze; **a la m., de m.** in fashion; **pasado de m.** old-fashioned

modales NMPL manners

modalidad NF form, type; *Com* **m. de pago** method of payment; *Dep* **m. deportiva** discipline

modelar VT to model, to shape; *Am (ropa)* to model

modélico, -a ADJ model

modelo 1 ADJ INV & NM model
2 NMF (fashion) model; **desfile de modelos** fashion show

módem *(pl* **modems)** NM *Inform* modem

moderación NF moderation

moderado, -a ADJ moderate; **un m. aumento de temperatura** a mild increase in temperature

moderador, -a NM,F chairperson; *(hombre)* chairman; *(mujer)* chairwoman

moderar 1 VT (**a**) *(atenuar)* to moderate; *(velocidad)* to reduce (**b**) *(debate)* to chair
2 **moderarse** VPR to be moderate

modernizar [40] 1 VT to modernize
2 **modernizarse** VPR to modernize

moderno, -a ADJ modern

modestia NF modesty; **m. aparte** without wishing to be immodest

modesto, -a ADJ modest

módico, -a ADJ moderate; **una módica suma** a modest *o* small sum

modificación NF alteration

modificar [44] VT to modify

modismo NM idiom

modisto, -a NM,F (**a**) *(diseñador)* fashion designer (**b**) *(sastre) (hombre)* couturier; *(mujer)* couturière

modo NM (**a**) *(manera)* way, manner; **de todos modos** in any case, anyway; **de m. que** *(así que)* so; **m. de empleo** instructions for use (**b**) **modos** manners (**c**) *Ling* mood

modorra NF drowsiness

modoso, -a ADJ *(recatado)* modest; *(educado)* well-behaved

modular VT to modulate

módulo NM module

mofa NF mockery; **en tono de m.** in a gibing tone

mofarse VPR to laugh (**de** at), to make fun (**de** of)

moflete NM chubby cheek

mogollón *Esp Fam* 1 NM (**a**) **m. de** loads of (**b**) *(confusión)* commotion
2 ADV loads, *Br* heaps; **me gusta m.** I like it loads

moho NM mould

mohoso, -a ADJ mouldy

moisés NM INV Moses basket

mojado, -a ADJ *(empapado)* wet; *(húmedo)* damp

mojar 1 VT to wet; *(humedecer)* to dampen; **m. pan en la leche** to dip *o* dunk bread in one's milk
2 mojarse VPR to get wet

mojigato, -a ADJ *(beato)* prudish; *(falsamente humilde)* sanctimonious

mojón NM **m. kilométrico** ≃ milestone

moka NM mocha

molar 1 VI *Esp Fam* **me mola cantidad** I really love it, it's brilliant
2 ADJ & NM *Anat* molar

molcajete NM *Méx* mortar

molde NM mould; **letras de m.** print; **pan de m.** ≃ sliced bread

moldeador NM *Esp (del pelo)* soft perm

moldear VT to mould

mole 1 NF mass, bulk
2 NM *Méx* = thick, cooked chilli sauce

molécula NF molecule

moler [4] VT (a) *(triturar)* to grind (b) **m. a algn a golpes** to beat sb up

molestar 1 VT (a) *(incomodar)* to disturb, to bother; **¿le molestaría esperar fuera?** would you mind waiting outside? (b) *(ofender)* to upset (c) *(doler)* **me molesta la pierna** my leg is giving me a bit of trouble
2 molestarse VPR (a) *(tomarse la molestia)* to bother (b) *(ofenderse)* to take offence, to get upset

molestia NF (a) *(incomodidad)* bother, trouble; **no es ninguna m.** it's no trouble at all; **perdone las molestias** forgive the inconvenience (b) *(dolor)* trouble, slight pain

molesto, -a ADJ (a) **ser m.** *(costumbre, ruido)* to be annoying; *(humo, sensación)* to be unpleasant (b) **estar m.** *(ofendido)* to be upset; *(con malestar)* to be in discomfort; *(incómodo)* to be uncomfortable

molestoso, -a *Am salvo RP Fam* **1** ADJ annoying
2 NM,F nuisance

molido, -a ADJ *Fam (cansado)* worn out

molinillo NM grinder

molino NM mill; **m. de viento** windmill

mollera NF *Fam* nut, *Br* bonce; **duro de m.** *(tonto)* dense, thick; *(testarudo)* pigheaded

molón, -ona ADJ *Esp Fam* (a) *(que gusta)* *Br* brilliant, *US* neat (b) *(elegante)* smart

molusco NM mollusc

momentáneo, -a ADJ momentary

momento NM (a) *(instante)* moment; **al m.** at once; **por momentos** by the minute (b) *(periodo)* time; **de m.** for the time being; **en cualquier m.** at any time

momia NF mummy

mona NF *Fam* **dormir la m.** to sleep it off

Mónaco N Monaco

monada NF *Fam* **¡qué m.!** how cute!

monaguillo NM *Rel* altar boy

monarca NMF monarch

monarquía NF monarchy

monasterio NM *Rel* monastery

monda NF (a) *(piel)* peel, skin (b) *Esp Fam* **ser la m.** *(divertido)* to be a scream

mondadientes NM INV toothpick

mondar 1 VT to peel
2 mondarse VPR *Esp Fam* **mondarse (de risa)** to laugh one's head off

moneda NF (a) *(pieza)* coin; **m. suelta** small change; **acuñar m.** to mint money (b) *Fin* currency; **m. única** single currency

monedero NM *Br* purse, *US* change purse

monería NF *Fam* = **monada**

monetario, -a ADJ monetary

mongol 1 ADJ & NMF Mongolian
2 NM *(idioma)* Mongolian

mongólico, -a *Med* **1** ADJ Down's syndrome
2 NM,F **ser m.** to have Down's syndrome

monigote NM (a) *Pey (persona)* wimp (b) *(dibujo)* rough drawing *o* sketch (of a person)

monitor, -a 1 NM,F *(persona)* instructor; **m. de esquí** skiing instructor
2 NM *Inform & Mec* monitor

monja NF nun

monje NM monk

mono, -a 1 NM (a) *(animal)* monkey (b) *(prenda)* *(con mangas)* *Br* overalls, *US* coveralls; *(con peto)* *Br* dungarees, *Br* boiler suit, *US* overalls; *Ven (de deporte)* tracksuit (c) *Esp Fam (síndrome de abstinencia)* cold turkey
2 ADJ *Fam (bonito)* pretty, cute

monobloque NM *Arg* tower block

monografía NF monograph

monográfico, -a 1 ADJ monographic
2 NM monograph

monolingüe ADJ monolingual

monólogo NM monologue

monoparental ADJ **familia m.** one-parent *o* single-parent family

monopatín NM *Esp* skateboard

monopolio NM monopoly

monopolizar [40] VT to monopolize

monótono, -a ADJ monotonous

monovolumen NM people carrier

monserga NF *Esp Fam* drivel

monstruo NM (a) *(ser fantástico)* monster (b) *(genio)* genius

monstruoso, -a ADJ (a) *(repugnante)* monstrous (b) *(enorme)* massive, huge

monta NF *Fig* **de poca m.** of little importance

montacargas NM INV *Br* goods lift, *US* freight elevator

montado, -a 1 ADJ *(nata)* whipped
2 NM *Esp (bocadillo)* = small piece of bread with a savoury topping

montador, -a NM,F (a) *(operario)* fitter (b) *Cin & TV* film editor

montaje NM (**a**) *Téc (instalación)* fitting; *(ensamblaje)* assembling; **cadena de m.** assembly line (**b**) *Cin* editing and mounting (**c**) *Teatro* staging (**d**) *Fot* montage (**e**) *Fam (farsa)* farce

montante NM *Fin* amount

montaña NF mountain; **m. rusa** big dipper

montañero, -a NM,F mountaineer

montañismo NM mountaineering

montañoso, -a ADJ mountainous

montar 1 VI (**a**) *(subirse)* to get on; *(en coche)* to get in; *(en bici, a caballo)* to ride (**b**) *Fin (ascender)* **m. a** to amount to, to come to
2 VT (**a**) *(colocar)* to put on (**b**) *(máquina etc)* to assemble; *(negocio)* to set up, to start (**c**) *Esp Culin (nata)* to whip (**d**) *Cin & Fot (película)* to edit, to mount; *(fotografía)* to mount (**e**) *Teatro (obra)* to stage, to mount (**f**) *Zool (cubrir)* to mount
3 montarse VPR (**a**) *(subirse)* to get on; *(en coche)* to get in (**en** to) (**b**) *Fam (organizarse)* **se montó un gran escándalo** there was a huge fuss (**c**) *Esp Fam* **montárselo bien** to have things (nicely) worked out o set up

monte NM (**a**) *(montaña)* mountain; *(con nombre propio)* mount; **de m.** wild (**b**) **el m.** *(zona)* the hills

montera NF bullfighter's hat

montés ADJ *(animal)* wild

montevideano, -a 1 ADJ of/from Montevideo
2 NM,F person from Montevideo

monto NM total

montón NM heap, pile; **un m. de** a load of; *Fam* **me gusta un m.** I really love it; *Fam* **del m.** run-of-the-mill, nothing special

montura NF (**a**) *(cabalgadura)* mount (**b**) *(de gafas)* frame

monumental ADJ (**a**) *(ciudad, lugar)* famous for its monuments (**b**) *(fracaso, éxito)* monumental

monumento NM monument

monzón NM monsoon

moño NM (**a**) *(de pelo)* bun (**b**) *Am (lazo)* bow (**c**) *Méx (pajarita)* bow tie

moquear VI to have a runny nose

moqueta NF *Esp* fitted carpet

mora NF blackberry

morado, -a 1 ADJ purple; *Esp Fam* **pasarlas moradas** to have a tough time; *Esp Fam* **ponerse m.** to stuff oneself
2 NM purple

moral 1 ADJ moral
2 NF (**a**) *(ética)* morals (**b**) *(ánimo)* morale, spirits; **levantar la m. a algn** to raise sb's spirits

moraleja NF moral

moralista 1 ADJ moralistic
2 NMF moralist

moratón NM bruise

moratoria NF moratorium

morbo NM *Fam* morbid curiosity

morboso, -a ADJ morbid, ghoulish

morcilla NF *Br* black pudding, *US* blood sausage; *Esp Fam* **que te/os den m.** you can stuff it, then!

mordaz ADJ biting

mordaza NF gag

mordedura NF bite

morder [4] VT to bite; **me ha mordido** it bit me; *Fig* **m. el anzuelo** to take the bait

mordida NF *CAm, Méx Fam* bribe, *Br* backhander

mordisco NM bite

mordisquear VT to nibble (at)

moreno, -a 1 ADJ (**a**) *(pelo, piel)* dark (**b**) *(bronceado)* tanned; **ponerse m.** to get a suntan; **pan/azúcar m.** brown bread/sugar
2 NM,F *(persona) (de pelo)* dark-haired person; *(de piel)* dark-skinned person

morera NF *Bot* white mulberry

moretón NM bruise

morfina NF morphine

morfinómano, -a 1 NM,F morphine addict
2 ADJ addicted to morphine

morgue NF morgue

moribundo, -a ADJ dying

morir [7] **1** VI to die; **m. de frío/hambre/cáncer** to die of cold/hunger/cancer; **m. de amor** o **pena** to die from a broken heart
2 morirse VPR to die; **morirse de hambre** to starve to death; *Fig* to be starving; **morirse de aburrimiento** to be bored to death; **morirse de ganas (de hacer algo)** to be dying (to do sth); **morirse de risa** to die laughing

mormón, -ona ADJ & NM,F Mormon

moro, -a NM,F (**a**) *Hist* Moor; *Fam* **no hay moros en la costa** the coast is clear (**b**) *Esp Fam Pey (árabe)* Arab, = pejorative term referring to a North African or Arab person

morocho, -a ADJ *Andes, RP (moreno)* dark-haired

moronga NF *CAm, Méx Br* black pudding, *US* blood sausage

moroso, -a NM,F bad debtor

> Observa que la palabra inglesa **morose** es un falso amigo y no es la traducción de la palabra española **moroso**. En inglés **morose** significa "hosco, huraño".

morral NM *(de cazador)* game bag

morralla NF *Pey (personas)* scum; *(cosas)* junk

morrear VI *Esp Fam* to smooch

morriña NF *Esp (por el país)* homesickness; *(por el pasado)* nostalgia

morro NM (**a**) *(de animal) (hocico)* snout (**b**) *Esp (de avión)* nose; *(de coche)* front (**c**) *Esp Fam* **morros** *(labios)* lips; *(boca)* mouth; **caerse de m.** to fall flat on one's face (**d**) *Esp Fam (caradura)* **¡qué m. tiene!** he's got a real nerve!

morrón ADJ **pimiento m.** *(fleshy)* red pepper

morsa NF walrus

morse NM Morse

mortadela NF mortadella

mortaja NF shroud

mortal 1 ADJ *(no inmortal)* mortal; *(caída, enfermedad)* fatal; *(aburrimiento, odio, enemigo)* deadly
2 NMF mortal

mortalidad NF mortality; **índice de m.** death rate

mortandad NF death toll

mortecino, -a ADJ colourless

mortero NM *Culin & Mil* mortar

mortífero, -a ADJ deadly, lethal

mortificar [44] VT to mortify

mortuorio, -a ADJ death; **lecho m.** death-bed

moruno, -a ADJ Moorish; *Esp Culin* **pincho m.** = kebab of marinated pork

mosaico NM mosaic

mosca NF fly; **peso m.** flyweight; *Esp Fam* **estar m.** to be suspicious; *Fam* **por si las moscas** just in case; *Fam* **¿qué m. te ha picado?** what's up with you?

moscada ADJ **nuez m.** nutmeg

moscardón NM **(a)** *(insecto)* blowfly **(b)** *Fam (pesado)* pest

moscatel NM Muscatel, = dessert wine made from muscat grapes; **uvas de m.** muscat grapes

moscovita ADJ & NMF Muscovite

Moscú N Moscow

mosquear 1 VT **(a)** *(enfadar)* **m. a algn** *Br* to get up sb's nose, *US* to tick sb off **(b)** *(hacer sospechar)* to make suspicious; **me mosquea que no haya llamado todavía** I'm a bit surprised he hasn't phoned yet
2 mosquearse VPR *(enfadarse)* to get in a huff

mosqueo NM *Fam* **tener un m.** *(enfado)* to be hacked off; *(sospechas)* to be suspicious

mosquetero NM *Hist* musketeer

mosquitero NM mosquito net

mosquito NM mosquito

mostaza NF *Bot & Culin* mustard

mosto NM *(bebida)* grape juice; *(residuo)* must

mostrador NM *(en tienda)* counter; *(en bar)* bar; *(en aeropuerto, de información)* desk

mostrar 1 VT to show; **muéstramelo** show it to me
2 mostrarse VPR to be; **se mostró muy comprensiva** she was very understanding

mota NF speck

mote¹ NM nickname

mote² NM *Andes* stewed *Br* maize o *US* corn

moteado, -a ADJ dotted

motel NM motel

motero, -a NM,F *Fam* biker

motín NM *(de tropas, en barco)* mutiny; *(en cárcel)* riot

motivación NF motivation

motivar VT *(impulsar)* to motivate; *(causar)* to cause

motivo NM **(a)** *(causa)* reason; *(usu pl)* grounds; **con este** o **tal m.** for this reason; **con m. de** on the occasion of; **sin m.** for no reason at all; **bajo ningún m.** under no circumstances **(b)** *Arte & Mús* motif, leitmotiv

moto NF motorbike, motorcycle; **m. náutica** o **acuática** jet ski

motocicleta NF motorbike, motorcycle

motociclismo NM motorcycling

motociclista NMF motorcyclist

motocross NM motocross

motoesquí *(pl* **motoesquís** o **motoesquíes)** NM snowbike

motoneta NF *Am* (motor) scooter

motonetista NMF *Am* scooter rider

motor, -a 1 NM *(grande)* engine; *(pequeño)* motor; **m. de reacción** jet engine; **m. de explosión** internal combustion engine; **m. eléctrico** electric motor; *Inform* **m. de búsqueda** search engine
2 ADJ *Téc* motive

motora NF motorboat

motorista NMF *Esp* motorcyclist

motorizar [40] **1** VT to motorize
2 motorizarse VPR *Fam* to get oneself a car/motorbike

motosierra NF power saw

motricidad NF motor function

motriz ADJ **fuerza m.** motive power

mouse [maus] NM INV *Am Inform* mouse

mousse [mus] NF, *Esp* NM mousse

movedizo, -a ADJ **arenas movedizas** quicksand

mover [4] **1** VT **(a)** *(desplazar)* to move; **m. algo de su sitio** to move sth out of its place **(b)** *(hacer funcionar)* to drive; **el motor mueve el coche** the engine drives the car **(c)** *(impulsar)* **m. a algn a hacer algo** to prompt sb to do sth
2 moverse VPR **(a)** *(desplazarse)* to move **(b)** *(darse prisa)* to hurry up; **¡muévete!** get a move on!

movida NF *Esp, RP Fam* **hay mucha m.** there's a lot going on

movido, -a ADJ **(a)** *Fot* blurred **(b)** *(jornada, viaje)* hectic

móvil 1 ADJ mobile; **teléfono m.** mobile phone; *TV & Rad* **unidad m.** outside broadcast unit
2 NM **(a)** *(de delito)* motive **(b)** *(teléfono)* mobile **(c)** *(juguete)* mobile

movilizar [40] VT to mobilize

movimiento NM **(a)** *(desplazamiento, corriente)* movement; *Fís & Téc* motion; **(poner algo) en m.** (to set sth) in motion; **m. sísmico** earth tremor **(b)** *(actividad)* activity **(c)** *Com & Fin (entradas y salidas)* operations

moviola NF editing projector

mozárabe 1 ADJ Mozarabic, = Christian in the time of Moorish Spain
2 NMF *(habitante)* Mozarab, = Christian of Moorish Spain
3 NM *(idioma)* Mozarabic

mozo, -a 1 NMF (**a**) *(niño)* young boy, young lad; *(niña)* young girl (**b**) *Andes, RP (camarero)* waiter; *(camarera)* waitress (**c**) *Col (novio)* boyfriend; *(novia)* girlfriend
2 NM (**a**) *(de estación)* porter; *(de hotel)* bellboy, *US* bellhop (**b**) *Esp (recluta)* conscript

mucamo, -a *Andes, RP* NM,F chamberperson; *(mujer)* chambermaid

muchacho, -a NM,F *(hombre)* boy; *(mujer)* girl

muchedumbre NF crowd

mucho, -a 1 ADJ (**a**) *(singular) (usu en frases afirmativas)* a lot of, lots of; *(usu en frases negativas)* much; **m. tiempo** a long time; **tengo m. sueño/mucha sed** I am very sleepy/thirsty; **hay m. tonto suelto** there are lots of idiots around; **¿bebes m. café? – no, no m.** do you drink a lot of coffee? – no, not much (**b**) *(demasiado)* **es m. coche para mí** this car is a bit too much for me (**c**) **muchos, -as** *(usu en frases afirmativas)* a lot of, lots of; *(usu en frases neg)* many; **tiene muchos años** he is very old
2 PRON (**a**) *(singular)* a lot, a great deal; **¿cuánta leche queda? – mucha** how much milk is there left? – a lot (**b**) **muchos, -as** a lot, lots, many; **¿cuántos libros tienes? – muchos** how many books have you got? – lots *o* a lot; **muchos creemos que ...** many of us believe that ...
3 ADV (**a**) *(singular)* a lot, very much; **lo siento m.** I'm very sorry; **como m.** at the most; **con m.** by far; **m. antes/después** long before/after; **¡ni m. menos!** no way!; **por m. (que)** (+ *subjunctive)* however much (**b**) *(tiempo)* **hace m. que no viene por aquí** he has not been to see us for a long time (**c**) *(a menudo)* often; **vamos m. al cine** we go to the cinema quite often

muda NF *(ropa)* change of underwear

mudanza NF move; **estar de m.** to be moving; **camión de m.** *Br* removal van, *US* moving van

mudar 1 VT (**a**) *(ropa)* to change (**b**) *(plumas, pelo)* to moult; *(piel)* to shed, to slough
2 mudarse VPR **mudarse de casa/ropa** to move house/to change one's clothes

mudéjar ADJ & NMF Mudejar

mudo, -a 1 ADJ (**a**) *(que no habla)* dumb; **cine m.** silent movies *o Br* films (**b**) *(callado)* speechless
2 NM,F mute

mueble 1 NM piece of furniture; **muebles** furniture; **con/sin muebles** furnished/unfurnished; **m. bar** cocktail cabinet
2 ADJ *Der* **bienes muebles** personal property

mueca NF *(gesto)* face, expression; *(de dolor)* grimace; **hacer muecas** to pull faces

muela NF (**a**) *Anat* molar; **dolor de muelas** toothache; **m. del juicio** wisdom tooth (**b**) *Téc (de molino)* millstone

muelle NM (**a**) *(resorte)* spring (**b**) *(en puerto)* dock, quay

muerdo NM *Esp Fam* bite

muermo NM *Esp Fam* **ser un m.** *(situación)* to be boring; *(persona)* to be a bore; **tener un m.** to be bored

muerte NF death; **m. natural** natural death; **dar m. a algn** to kill sb; **odiar a algn a m.** to loathe sb; *Esp* **de mala m.** badly; *Fam* **un susto de m.** the fright of one's life

muerto, -a 1 ADJ dead; **caer m.** to drop dead; **m. de hambre** starving; **m. de frío** frozen to death; **m. de miedo** scared stiff; **m. de risa** laughing one's head off; **horas muertas** spare time; *Aut* **(en) punto m.** (in) neutral
2 NM,F (**a**) *(difunto)* dead person; **hacerse el m.** to pretend to be dead; *Fam* **cargar con el m.** to do the dirty work (**b**) *(víctima)* fatality; **hubo dos muertos** two (people) died

muesca NF notch

muestra NF (**a**) *(espécimen)* sample, specimen (**b**) *(prueba, señal)* sign; **dar muestras de** to show signs of; **m. de cariño/respeto** token of affection/respect; **una m. más de ...** yet another example of ... (**c**) *(modelo a copiar)* model

muestreo NM sampling

mugido NM *(de vaca)* moo; *(de toro)* bellow

mugir [57] VI *(vaca)* to moo, to low; *(toro)* to bellow

mugre NF filth

mugriento, -a ADJ filthy

mujer NF (**a**) woman; **dos mujeres** two women; **m. de la limpieza** cleaner; **m. de su casa** houseproud woman (**b**) *(esposa)* wife; **su futura m.** his bride-to-be

mujeriego 1 ADJ woman-chasing
2 NM womanizer, woman chaser

mulato, -a ADJ & NM,F mulatto

muleta NF (**a**) *(prótesis)* crutch (**b**) *Taurom* muleta

muletilla NF *(frase)* pet phrase; *(palabra)* pet word

mullido, -a ADJ soft

mulo NM mule

multa NF fine; **poner una m. a algn** to fine sb

multar VT to fine

multicolor ADJ multicoloured

multilateral ADJ multilateral

multimedia ADJ INV *Inform* multimedia

multinacional ADJ & NF multinational

múltiple ADJ *(variado)* multiple; **múltiples** *(numerosos)* many, numerous

multiplicación NF multiplication

multiplicar [44] **1** VT & VI to multiply (**por** by)
2 multiplicarse VPR *(reproducirse, aumentar)* to multiply

múltiplo, -a ADJ & NM multiple

multipropiedad NF time-sharing

multirriesgo ADJ INV **póliza m.** multiple risk policy

multitud NF *(de personas)* crowd; **m. de cosas** a huge number of things

multiusuario ADJ INV multi-user

mundano, -a ADJ worldly

> Observa que la palabra inglesa **mundane** es un falso amigo y no es la traducción de la palabra española **mundano**. En inglés, **mundane** significa "prosaico".

mundial 1 ADJ *(política, economía, guerra)* world; *(tratado, organización, fama)* worldwide; **campeón m.** world champion; **de fama m.** world-famous
  2 NM World Championship(s); *(en fútbol)* World Cup

mundialmente ADV **m. famoso** world-famous, famous worldwide

mundo NM world; **todo el m.** everyone; **correr** *o* **ver m.** to travel widely; **nada del otro m.** nothing special; **el otro m.** the hereafter

munición NF ammunition

municipal 1 ADJ municipal
  2 NMF *Esp* (local) policeman, *f* (local) policewoman

municipio NM (**a**) *(corporación)* local council (**b**) *(territorio)* town, municipality

muñeca NF (**a**) *(del cuerpo)* wrist (**b**) *(juguete, muchacha)* doll (**c**) *Andes, RP Fam* **tener m.** *(enchufe)* to have friends in high places; *(habilidad)* to have the knack (**d**) *Méx (mazorca)* baby sweetcorn

muñeco NM *(juguete)* doll; **m. de trapo** rag doll; **m. de nieve** snowman

muñeira NF = popular Galician dance and music

muñequera NF wristband

muñón NM *Anat* stump

mural 1 ADJ *(pintura)* mural; *(mapa)* wall
  2 NM mural

muralla NF wall

Murcia N Murcia

murciélago NM *Zool* bat

murmullo NM murmur

murmuración NF gossip

murmurar VI (**a**) *(criticar)* to gossip (**b**) *(susurrar)* to whisper; *(refunfuñar)* to grumble (**c**) *Fig (río)* to murmur

muro NM wall

musa NF muse

musaraña NF *Fam* **estar pensando en las musarañas** to be daydreaming *o* in the clouds

musculación NF body-building

musculatura NF muscles

músculo NM muscle

musculoso, -a ADJ muscular

museo NM *(de ciencias, historia)* museum; *(de arte)* art gallery

musgo NM moss

música NF music; **m. clásica** classical music; **m. de fondo** background music

musical 1 ADJ musical
  2 NM musical

músico, -a 1 ADJ musical
  2 NM,F musician

muslo NM *(de persona)* thigh; *(de pollo, pavo)* *(entero)* leg; *(parte inferior)* drumstick

mustio, -a ADJ (**a**) *(plantas)* wilted, withered (**b**) *(persona)* sad, gloomy

musulmán, -ana ADJ & NM,F Muslim, Moslem

mutación NF *Biol* mutation

mutilación NF mutilation

mutilado, -a NM,F disabled person; **m. de guerra** disabled serviceman

mutilar VT to mutilate

mutis NM INV *Teatro* exit

mutismo NM silence

mutua NF *Br* friendly society, *US* mutual benefit society

mutual NF *CSur, Perú Br* friendly society, *US* mutual benefit society

mutualidad NF *Br* friendly society, *US* mutual benefit society

mutuo, -a ADJ mutual

muy ADV very; **m. bueno/malo** very good/bad; **¡m. bien!** very good!; **M. señor mío** Dear Sir; **m. de los andaluces** typically Andalusian; **m. de mañana/noche** very early/late

N, n ['ene] NF (*letra*) N, n

N (*abr* **Norte**) N

nabo NM (**a**) *Bot* turnip (**b**) *muy Fam* (*pene*) tool, *Br* knob

nácar NM mother-of-pearl

nacer [60] VI (**a**) (*persona*) to be born; **nací en Salamanca** I was born in Salamanca; **al n.** at birth (**b**) (*pájaro*) to hatch (out) (**c**) (*pelo*) to begin to grow (**d**) (*río*) to rise

nacido, -a ADJ born

naciente ADJ (*sol*) rising

nacimiento NM (**a**) (*de persona, animal*) birth; **sordo de n.** deaf from birth; **lugar de n.** birthplace, place of birth (**b**) *Fig* (*principio*) origin, beginning; (*de río*) source (**c**) (*belén*) Nativity scene, crib

nación NF nation; **las Naciones Unidas** the United Nations

nacional 1 ADJ (*equipo, moneda, monumento*) national; (*mercado, vuelo*) domestic

  2 NMF national; *Hist* **los nacionales** the Francoist forces

nacionalidad NF nationality

nacionalismo NM nationalism

nacionalista ADJ & NMF nationalist

nacionalizar [40] **1** VT (**a**) *Econ* (*banca, industria*) to nationalize (**b**) (*naturalizar*) to naturalize

  2 nacionalizarse VPR to become naturalized; **n. español** to take up Spanish citizenship

nada 1 PRON (**a**) (*como respuesta*) nothing; **¿qué quieres? – n.** what do you want? – nothing

  (**b**) (*con verbo*) not … anything; (*enfático*) nothing; **no sé n.** I don't know anything; **yo no digo n.** I'm saying nothing

  (**c**) (*con otro negativo*) anything; **no hace nunca n.** he never does anything; **nadie sabía n.** nobody knew anything

  (**d**) (*en ciertas construcciones*) anything; **más que n.** more than anything; **sin decir n.** without saying anything; **casi n.** hardly anything

  (**e**) **gracias – de n.** thanks – don't mention it; *Fam* **para n.** not at all; **casi n.** almost nothing; **como si n.** just like that; **un rasguño de n.** an insignificant little scratch; **n. de eso** nothing of the kind; **n. de n.** nothing at all; **n. más verla** as soon as he saw her

  2 ADV not at all; **no me gusta n.** I don't like it at all; **no lo encuentro n. interesante** I don't find it remotely interesting

  3 NF nothingness; **salir de la n.** to come out of nowhere

nadador, -a NM,F swimmer

nadar VI (**a**) *Dep* to swim; **n. a braza** to do the breaststroke (**b**) (*flotar*) to float

nadie 1 PRON (**a**) (*como respuesta*) no one, nobody; **¿quién vino? – n.** who came? – no one (**b**) (*con verbo*) not … anyone, not … anybody; (*enfático*) no one, nobody; **no conozco a n.** I don't know anyone *o* anybody; **no vi a n.** I didn't see anyone *o* anybody, I saw no one (**c**) (*con otro negativo*) anyone, anybody; **nunca habla con n.** he never speaks to anybody (**d**) (*en ciertas construcciones*) anybody, anyone; **más que n.** more than anyone; **sin decírselo a n.** without telling anyone; **casi n.** hardly anyone

  2 NM nobody; **ser un don n.** to be a nobody

nado: a nado LOC ADV swimming; **cruzar** *o* **pasar a n.** to swim across

NAFTA NM (*abr* **North American Free Trade Agreement**) NAFTA

nafta NF *RP* (*gasolina*) *Br* petrol, *US* gas, *US* gasoline

nahua, náhuatl 1 ADJ Nahuatl

  2 NMF (*individuo*) Nahuatl (Indian)

nailon NM nylon

naipe NM playing card

nalga NF buttock; **nalgas** bottom, buttocks

nana NF (**a**) (*canción*) lullaby (**b**) *Col, Méx* (*niñera*) nanny (**c**) *Col, Méx* (*nodriza*) wet nurse

napalm NM napalm

napias NFPL *Fam* snout

Nápoles N Naples

napolitano, -a ADJ & NM,F Neapolitan

naranja 1 NF orange; *Fig* **mi media n.** my better half

  2 ADJ & NM (*color*) orange

naranjada NF orangeade

naranjo NM orange tree

narciso NM (**a**) (*blanco*) narcissus; (*amarillo*) daffodil (**b**) *Fig* (*hombre*) narcissist

narcótico NM (*somnífero*) narcotic; (*droga*) drug

narcotizar [40] VT (*drogar*) to drug

narcotraficante NMF drug trafficker

narcotráfico NM drug trafficking

nariz NF (**a**) *Anat* nose; *Fam* **me da en la n. que …** I've got this feeling that … (**b**) *Fam* **narices**

nose; **en mis (propias) narices** right under my very nose; **estar hasta las narices de** to be fed up to the back teeth with; **meter las narices en algo** to poke one's nose into sth; *Esp* **tenemos que ir por narices** we have to go whether we like it or not; *Esp* **me estás hinchando las narices** you're beginning to get on my nerves

narración NF narration

narrador, -a NM,F narrator

narrar VT to narrate, to tell

narrativa NF narrative

narrativo, -a ADJ & NF narrative

nata NF (**a**) *Esp (crema de leche)* cream; **n. batida** o **montada** whipped cream (**b**) *(de leche hervida)* skin (**c**) *Fig* cream, best

natación NF *Dep* swimming

natal ADJ **mi país n.** my native country; **su pueblo n.** his home town

natalidad NF birth rate; **control de n.** birth control

natillas NFPL *Esp* custard

natividad NF Nativity

nativo, -a ADJ & NM,F native

nato, -a ADJ born

natura NF *Literario* nature; **contra n.** against nature

natural 1 ADJ natural; *(fruta, flor)* fresh; **de tamaño n.** life-size; **en estado n.** in its natural state; *Der* **hijo n.** illegitimate child
2 NMF native

naturaleza NF (**a**) nature; **en plena n.** in the wild, in unspoilt countryside; *Arte* **n. muerta** still life (**b**) *(complexión)* constitution

naturalidad NF *(sencillez)* naturalness; **con n.** naturally, straightforwardly

naturalismo NM naturalism

naturalista 1 ADJ naturalistic
2 NMF naturalist

naturalización NF naturalization

naturalizar [40] **1** VT to naturalize
2 naturalizarse VPR to become naturalized

naturalmente ADV naturally; **¡n.!** of course!

naturismo NM naturism

naturista NMF naturist

naufragar [42] VI *(barco)* to sink, to be wrecked; *(persona)* to be shipwrecked

naufragio NM *Náut* shipwreck

náufrago, -a NM,F shipwrecked person, castaway

náusea NF *(usu pl)* nausea, sickness; **me da n.** it makes me sick; **sentir náuseas** to feel sick

nauseabundo, -a ADJ nauseating, sickening

náutico, -a ADJ nautical

navaja NF (**a**) *(cuchillo)* penknife, pocketknife; **n. de afeitar** razor (**b**) *(molusco)* razor-shell

navajazo NM stab, gash

navajero NM *Fam* thug

naval ADJ naval

Navarra N Navarre

navarro, -a ADJ Navarrese, of/from Navarre
2 NM,F person from Navarre

nave NF (**a**) *(barco)* ship; **n. (espacial)** spaceship, spacecraft (**b**) *Ind* plant, building (**c**) *(de iglesia)* nave; **n. lateral** aisle

navegable ADJ navigable

navegación NF navigation; **n. costera** coastal shipping

navegador NM *Inform* browser

navegar [42] VI (**a**) *(en barco)* to navigate, to sail (**b**) *Av* to navigate, to fly (**c**) **n. por Internet** to surf the Net

Navidad NF Christmas; **árbol de N.** Christmas tree; **Feliz N., Felices Navidades** Merry Christmas

navideño, -a ADJ Christmas

navío NM ship

nazareno, -a 1 ADJ & NM,F Nazarene
2 NM = penitent in Holy Week processions; **el N.** Jesus of Nazareth

nazi ADJ & NMF Nazi

nazismo NM Nazism

n/c., n/cta. *(abr* **nuestra cuenta**) our account, our acct

neblina NF mist, thin fog

nebulosa NF *Astron* nebula

nebuloso, -a ADJ (**a**) *Met* cloudy, hazy (**b**) *Fig* nebulous, vague

necedad NF (**a**) *(estupidez)* stupidity, foolishness (**b**) *(tontería)* stupid thing to say/to do

necesario, -a ADJ necessary; **es n. hacerlo** it has to be done; **es n. que vayas** you must go; **no es n. que vayas** there is no need for you to go; **si fuera n.** if need be

neceser NM *(de aseo)* toilet bag; *(de maquillaje)* make-up bag

necesidad NF (**a**) need; **tener n. de** to need; **artículos de primera n.** essentials; **por n.** of necessity (**b**) *(pobreza)* poverty, hardship (**c**) **hacer sus necesidades** to relieve oneself

necesitado, -a 1 ADJ *(pobre)* needy, poor; **n. de** in need of
2 NM,F needy o poor person; **los necesitados** the poor

necesitar VT to need; **se necesita chico** *(en anuncios)* boy wanted

necio, -a 1 ADJ (**a**) *(tonto)* silly, stupid (**b**) *Am (terco)* stubborn, pigheaded (**c**) *Méx (susceptible)* touchy
2 NM,F (**a**) *(tonto)* fool, idiot (**b**) *Am (terco)* stubborn o pigheaded person (**c**) *Méx (susceptible)* touchy person; **es un n.** he's really touchy

nécora NF = small edible crab

necrológica NM,F obituary

necrológico, -a ADJ **nota necrológica** obituary

néctar NM nectar

nectarina NF nectarine

neerlandés, -esa 1 ADJ Dutch, of/from the Netherlands
  2 NM,F *(persona) (hombre)* Dutchman; *(mujer)* Dutchwoman; **los neerlandeses** the Dutch
  3 NM *(idioma)* Dutch

nefasto, -a ADJ (**a**) *(perjudicial)* harmful (**b**) *(funesto)* unlucky, ill-fated (**c**) *(inútil)* hopeless

negación NF (**a**) *(lo contrario)* negation (**b**) *(negativa)* denial; *(rechazo)* refusal (**c**) Ling negative

negado, -a 1 ADJ **ser n. para algo** to be hopeless *o* useless at sth
  2 NM,F no-hoper

negar [1] **1** VT (**a**) *(desmentir)* to deny; **negó haberlo robado** he denied stealing it (**b**) *(rechazar)* to refuse, to deny; **le negaron la beca** they refused him the grant
  2 negarse VPR to refuse (**a** to)

negativa NF denial

negativo, -a ADJ & NM negative

negligencia NF negligence

negociable ADJ negotiable

negociación NF negotiation

negociado NM *Andes, RP (chanchullo)* shady deal

negociador, -a ADJ negotiating; **comité n.** negotiating committee

negociante NMF dealer; *(hombre)* businessman; *(mujer)* businesswoman

negociar [43] **1** VT *Fin & Pol* to negotiate
  2 VI *(comerciar)* to do business, to deal

negocio NM *Com & Fin* business; *(transacción)* deal, transaction; *(asunto)* affair; **hombre de negocios** businessman; **mujer de negocios** businesswoman

negra NF (**a**) *Mús Br* crotchet, *US* quarter note (**b**) *(mala suerte)* **tener la n.** to be very unlucky

negrita ADJ & NF *Impr* bold (face)

negro, -a 1 ADJ (**a**) *(color)* black; **estar n.** *(bronceado)* to be suntanned (**b**) *Fig (suerte)* awful; *(porvenir)* black, gloomy; **verlo todo n.** to be very pessimistic; **vérselas negras para hacer algo** to have a tough time doing sth (**c**) *Fam (furioso)* furious, fuming; **me pone n.** it makes me mad
  2 NM *(hombre)* black; *(mujer)* black (woman)
  3 NM *(color)* black

nene, -a NM,F *(niño)* baby boy; *(niña)* baby girl

nenúfar NM *Bot* waterlily

neocelandés, -esa 1 ADJ of/from New Zealand
  2 NM,F New Zealander

neoclásico, -a ADJ *Arte & Lit* neoclassic, neoclassical

neologismo NM neologism

neón NM neon

neoyorquino, -a 1 ADJ of/from New York
  2 NM,F New Yorker

neozelandés, -esa ADJ & NM,F = neocelandés

nepotismo NM nepotism

Neptuno N Neptune

nervio NM (**a**) *Anat & Bot* nerve; *(de la carne)* sinew (**b**) *Fig (fuerza, vigor)* nerve, courage (**c**) **nervios** nerves; **ataque de nervios** fit of hysterics; **ser un manojo de nervios** to be a bundle of nerves; **tener los nervios de acero** to have nerves of steel

nerviosismo NM nerves

nervioso, -a ADJ nervous; **poner n. a algn** to get on sb's nerves

neto, -a ADJ (**a**) *(peso, cantidad)* net (**b**) *(nítido)* neat, clear

neumático, -a 1 ADJ pneumatic
  2 NM tyre; **n. de recambio** spare tyre

neumonía NF pneumonia

neurálgico, -a ADJ *Med* neuralgic; *Fig* **centro n.** nerve centre

neurólogo, -a NM,F neurologist

neurosis NF INV neurosis

neurótico, -a ADJ & NM,F neurotic

neutral ADJ neutral

neutralidad NF neutrality

neutralizar [40] VT to neutralize

neutro, -a ADJ (**a**) *(imparcial)* neutral (**b**) *Ling* neuter

neutrón NM *Fís* neutron

nevada NF snowfall

nevar [1] V IMPERS to snow

nevera NF (**a**) *(frigorífico)* refrigerator, *Br* fridge, *US* icebox (**b**) *(portátil)* cool box

nexo NM connection, link

ni CONJ (**a**) **no ... ni, ni ... ni** neither ... nor, not ... or; **no tengo tiempo ni dinero** I have got neither time nor money; **ni ha venido ni ha llamado** he hasn't come or phoned; **no vengas ni hoy ni mañana** don't come today or tomorrow (**b**) *(ni siquiera)* not even; **ni por dinero** not even for money; **ni se te ocurra** don't even think about it; **¡ni hablar!** no way!

Nicaragua N Nicaragua

nicaragüense ADJ & NMF Nicaraguan

nicho NM niche

nicotina NF nicotine

nido NM nest

niebla NF fog; **hay mucha n.** it is very foggy

nieto, -a NM,F *(niño)* grandson; *(niña)* granddaughter; **mis nietos** my grandchildren

nieve NF (**a**) *Met* snow; *Culin* **batir a punto de n.** to beat until stiff (**b**) *Fam (cocaína)* snow (**c**) *Carib, Méx (dulce)* sorbet

nigeriano, -a ADJ & NM,F Nigerian

Nilo N **el N.** the Nile

nilón NM *Tex* nylon

nimio, -a ADJ insignificant, petty

ninfómana NF nymphomaniac

ninguno, -a 1 ADJ (**a**) *(con verbo)* not ... any; **no leí ninguna revista** I didn't read any magazines; **no tiene ninguna gracia** it is not funny at all (**b**) **en ninguna parte** nowhere; **de ningún modo** no way

> **Ningún** is used instead of **ninguno** before masculine singular nouns (e.g. **ningún hombre** no man).

2 PRON (**a**) *(persona)* nobody, no one; **n. lo vio** no one saw it; **n. de los dos** neither of the two; **n. de ellos** none of them (**b**) *(cosa)* not ... any of them; *(enfático)* none of them; **no me gusta n.** I don't like any of them; **no vi n.** I saw none of them

niña NF *Anat* pupil; *Fig* **es la n. de sus ojos** she's the apple of his eye

niñera NF nursemaid, nanny

niñez NF infancy; *(a partir de los cuatro años)* childhood

niño, -a NM,F (**a**) *(crío) (varón)* child, boy; *(hembra)* child, girl; *(bebé)* baby; **de n.** as a child; **n. prodigio** child prodigy; *Pey* **n. bien** *o* **de papá** rich boy, rich kid; *Pey* **n. bonito** *o* **mimado** mummy's/daddy's boy (**b**) **niños** children; *Fig* **juego de niños** child's play

nipón, -ona ADJ & NM,F Japanese; **los nipones** the Japanese

níquel NM nickel

niqui NM *Esp* polo shirt

níspero NM *(fruto)* medlar; *(árbol)* medlar tree

nítido, -a ADJ *(claro)* clear; *(imagen)* sharp

nitrógeno NM nitrogen

nitroglicerina NF nitroglycerine

nivel NM (**a**) *(altura)* level; **a n. del mar** at sea level (**b**) *(categoría)* standard; **n. de vida** standard of living (**c**) *(instrumento)* level; **n. de aire** spirit level (**d**) *Ferroc* **paso a n.** *Br* level crossing, *US* grade crossing

nivelar VT (**a**) *(allanar)* to level out *o* off (**b**) *(equilibrar)* to even out

n° *(abr* **número)** no

no *(pl* **noes) 1** ADV (**a**) *(como respuesta)* no; **¿te gusta? – no** do you like it? – no (**b**) *(en otros contextos)* not; **no vi a nadie** I didn't see anyone; **aún no** not yet; **ya no** no longer, not any more; **no sin antes ...** not without first ...; **¿por qué no?** why not? (**c**) **no fumar/aparcar** *(en letrero)* no smoking/parking (**d**) **no sea que** (+ *subjunctive)* in case (**e**) **es rubia, ¿no?** she's blonde, isn't she?; **llegaron ayer, ¿no?** they arrived yesterday, didn't they? (**f**) *(como prefijo negativo)* non; **la no violencia** non-violence

2 NM no; **un no rotundo** a definite no

noble 1 ADJ noble

2 NMF *(hombre)* nobleman; *(mujer)* noblewoman; **los nobles** the nobility

nobleza NF nobility

noche NF evening; *(después de las diez)* night, night-time; **de n.,** *Esp* **por la n.,** *Am* **en la n.** at night; **esta n.** tonight; **mañana por la n.** tomorrow night/evening; **buenas noches** *(sa-*

ludo) good evening; *(despedida)* good night; **son las nueve de la n.** it's nine p.m.

nochebuena NF Christmas Eve

nochero NM (**a**) *CSur (vigilante)* night watchman (**b**) *Col (mesilla de noche)* bedside table

nochevieja NF New Year's Eve

noción NF (**a**) *(concepto)* notion, idea (**b**) **nociones** smattering, basic knowledge; **nociones de español** a smattering of Spanish

nocivo, -a ADJ noxious, harmful

noctámbulo, -a NM,F sleepwalker; *Fam* nightbird

nocturno, -a ADJ (**a**) night; **vida nocturna** night life; **clases nocturnas** evening classes (**b**) *Bot & Zool* nocturnal

nodriza 1 NF wet nurse

2 ADJ **buque/avión n.** refuelling ship/plane

nogal NM *Bot* walnut (tree)

nómada 1 ADJ nomadic

2 NMF nomad

nombrado, -a ADJ *(célebre)* famous, well-known

nombramiento NM appointment

nombrar VT (**a**) *(designar)* to name, to appoint; **n. a algn director** to appoint sb director (**b**) *(mencionar)* to name, to mention

nombre NM (**a**) *(apelativo)* name; **n. de pila** Christian name; **n. y apellidos** full name; **a n. de** *(carta)* addressed to; *(cheque)* made out to; **en n. de** on behalf of (**b**) *Ling* noun; **n. propio** proper noun

nomeolvides NM INV (**a**) *(flor)* forget-me-not (**b**) *(pulsera)* identity bracelet

nómina NF (**a**) *(de sueldo)* pay slip (**b**) *(plantilla)* payroll

nominar VT to nominate

nominativo, -a ADJ **cheque n. a** cheque made out to

non NM (**a**) *Mat* odd number; **pares y nones** odds and evens (**b**) *Fam* **nones** *(negación)* no; **decir (que) nones** to refuse

nono, -a ADJ = **noveno**

norcoreano, -a ADJ & NM,F North Korean

nordeste NM = **noreste**

nórdico, -a 1 ADJ (**a**) *(del norte)* northern (**b**) *(escandinavo)* Nordic

2 NM,F Nordic person

noreste NM northeast

noria NF (**a**) *Esp (de feria)* *Br* big wheel, *US* Ferris wheel (**b**) *(para agua)* water wheel

norirlandés, -esa 1 ADJ Northern Irish

2 NM,F *(persona) (hombre)* Northern Irishman; *(mujer)* Northern Irishwoman; **los norirlandeses** the Northern Irish

norma NF *(patrón, modelo)* standard; *(regla)* rule

normal ADJ normal, usual; **lo n.** the normal thing, what usually happens

normalidad NF normality; **volver a la n.** to return to normal

normalizar [40] **1** VT to normalize, to restore to normal
2 normalizarse VPR to return to normal

normativa NF rules

noroeste NM northwest

norte NM (**a**) *(geográfico)* north; **al n. de** to the north of (**b**) *(meta)* aim, goal

norteafricano, -a ADJ & NM,F North African

Norteamérica N North America

norteamericano, -a ADJ & NM,F (North) American

norteño, -a 1 ADJ northern
2 NM,F Northerner

Noruega N Norway

noruego, -a 1 ADJ Norwegian
2 NM,F Norwegian
3 NM *(idioma)* Norwegian

nos 1 PRON PERS *(directo)* us; *(indirecto)* (to) us; **n. ha visto** he has seen us; **n. trajo un regalo** he brought us a present; **n. lo dio** he gave it to us
2 PRON *(reflexivo)* ourselves; *(recíproco)* each other; **n. hemos divertido mucho** we enjoyed ourselves a lot; **n. queremos mucho** we love each other very much

nosotros, -as PRON PERS PL (**a**) *(sujeto)* we; **n. lo vimos** we saw it; **somos n.** it is us (**b**) *(complemento)* us; **con n.** with us

> Usually omitted in Spanish except for emphasis or contrast.

nostalgia NF nostalgia; *(morriña)* homesickness

nostálgico, -a ADJ nostalgic; *(con morriña)* homesick

nota NF (**a**) *(anotación)* note (**b**) *(calificación)* Br mark, US grade; **sacar** o **tener buenas notas** to get good Br marks o US grades (**c**) Fig *(detalle)* element, quality; **la n. dominante** the prevailing quality (**d**) Mús note; Fam **dar la n.** to make oneself noticed

notable 1 ADJ *(apreciable)* noticeable; *(destacado)* outstanding, remarkable
2 NM *(nota)* very good

notar 1 VT *(percibir)* to notice, to note
2 notarse VPR to be noticeable o evident, to show; **no se nota** it doesn't show; **se nota que …** one can see that …

notaría NF *(despacho)* notary's office

notarial ADJ notarial; **acta n.** affidavit

notario, -a NM,F notary (public), solicitor

noticia NF news *sing*; **una n.** a piece of news; **una buena n.** good news; **no tengo n. de esto** I don't know anything about it

> Observa que la palabra inglesa **notice** es un falso amigo y no es la traducción de la palabra española **noticia**. En inglés **notice** significa "aviso, anuncio".

noticiario, Am **noticiero** NM (**a**) Cin newsreel (**b**) Rad & TV television news

notificación NF notification; **sin n. previa** without (previous) notice; Der **n. judicial** summons *sing*

notificar [44] VT to notify

notorio, -a ADJ (**a**) *(evidente)* obvious, evident (**b**) *(famoso)* famous, well-known

> Observa que la palabra inglesa **notorious** es un falso amigo y no es la traducción de la palabra española **notorio**. En inglés, **notorious** significa "tristemente célebre".

novatada NF (**a**) *(broma)* rough joke, rag (**b**) **pagar la n.** to learn the hard way

novato, -a 1 ADJ *(persona)* inexperienced; Fam green
2 NM,F (**a**) *(principiante)* novice, beginner (**b**) Univ fresher

novecientos, -as ADJ & NM nine hundred

novedad NF (**a**) *(cosa nueva)* novelty; **últimas novedades** latest arrivals (**b**) *(cambio)* change, development (**c**) *(cualidad)* newness

novedoso, -a ADJ (**a**) *(nuevo)* new, full of novelties (**b**) *(innovador)* innovative

novel 1 ADJ new, inexperienced
2 NMF beginner, novice

novela NF Lit novel; **n. corta** short story; **n. policíaca** detective story

novelero, -a ADJ fond of new things

novelesco, -a ADJ (**a**) *(de novela)* novelistic, fictional (**b**) *(extraordinario)* bizarre, fantastic

novelista NMF novelist

noveno, -a ADJ & NM ninth; **novena parte** ninth

noventa ADJ & NM INV ninety

novia NF (**a**) *(amiga)* girlfriend (**b**) *(prometida)* fiancée (**c**) *(en boda)* bride

noviar VI CSur, Méx Fam **n. con algn** to go out with sb, US to date sb; **novian hace tiempo** they've been going out together o US dating for a while

noviazgo NM engagement

noviembre NM November

novillada NF Taurom = bullfight with young bulls

novillero, -a NM,F Taurom apprentice matador

novillo, -a NM,F (**a**) *(toro)* young bull; *(vaca)* young cow (**b**) Esp Fam **hacer novillos** to play Br truant o US hookey

novio NM (**a**) *(amigo)* boyfriend (**b**) *(prometido)* fiancé (**c**) *(en boda)* bridegroom; **los novios** the bride and groom

nubarrón NM Fam storm cloud

nube NF cloud; Fig **vivir en las nubes** to have one's head in the clouds; Fig **poner a algn por las nubes** to praise sb to the skies

nublado, -a ADJ cloudy, overcast

nublarse VPR to become cloudy, to cloud over; Fig **se le nubló la vista** his eyes clouded over

nubosidad NF cloudiness, clouds

nuboso, -a ADJ cloudy

nuca NF nape, back of the neck

nuclear ADJ nuclear; **central n.** nuclear power station

núcleo NM nucleus; *(parte central)* core; **n. urbano** city centre

nudillo NM *(usu pl)* knuckle

nudismo NM nudism

nudista ADJ & NMF nudist

nudo NM (**a**) *(lazo)* knot; **hacer un n.** to tie a knot; *Fig* **se me hizo un n. en la garganta** I got a lump in my throat (**b**) *(de comunicaciones)* centre

nuera NF daughter-in-law

nuestro, -a 1 ADJ POS (**a**) *(antes del sustantivo)* our; **nuestra familia** our family (**b**) *(después del sustantivo)* of ours; **un amigo n.** a friend of ours

2 PRON POS ours; **este libro es n.** this book is ours

nuevamente ADV again

Nueva Zelanda N New Zealand

nueve ADJ & NM INV nine

nuevo, -a 1 ADJ (**a**) new; *Fam* **¿qué hay de n.?** what's new?; **de n.** again; **Nueva York** New York; **Nueva Zelanda** New Zealand (**b**) *(adicional)* further

2 NM,F newcomer; *(principiante)* beginner

nuez NF (**a**) *(fruto)* walnut; **n. moscada** nutmeg (**b**) *Anat* **n. (de Adán)** Adam's apple

nulidad NF (**a**) *(ineptitud)* incompetence (**b**) *Der* nullity

nulo, -a ADJ (**a**) *(inepto)* useless, totally incapable (**b**) *(sin valor)* null and void, invalid; **voto n.** invalid vote (**c**) **crecimiento n.** zero growth

núm. *(abr* **número)** no

numeral ADJ & NM numeral

numerar VT to number

numerario, -a 1 ADJ **profesor no n.** teacher on a temporary contract

2 NM *(miembro)* full member

numérico, -a ADJ numerical

número NM (**a**) *(signo)* number; **n. de matrícula** *Br* registration number, *US* license number; **n. de serie** serial number; *Fig* **sin n.** countless (**b**) *(de zapatos)* size (**c**) *Prensa* number, issue; **n. atrasado** back number (**d**) *(en espectáculo)* sketch, act; *Fam* **montar un n.** to make a scene

numeroso, -a ADJ numerous

numismática NF *(estudio)* numismatics *sing*

nunca ADV (**a**) *(como respuesta)* never; **¿cuándo volverás? – n.** when will you come back? – never (**b**) *(con verbo)* never; *(enfático)* not … ever; **no he estado n. en España** I've never been to Spain; **yo no haría n. eso** I wouldn't ever do that (**c**) *(en ciertas construcciones)* ever; **casi n.** hardly ever; **más que n.** more than ever (**d**) **n. jamás** never ever; *(futuro)* never again

nupcial ADJ wedding, nuptial; **marcha n.** wedding march

nupcias NFPL *Fml* wedding, nuptials; **casarse en segundas n.** to marry again

nutria NF otter

nutrición NF nutrition

nutricionista NMF nutritionist

nutrir 1 VT to nourish, to feed

2 nutrirse VPR to feed *(de o con* on)

nutritivo, -a ADJ nutritious, nourishing; **valor n.** nutritional value

ñandutí NM *Par* fine lace

ñapa *Ven Fam* NF bonus, extra; **ni de ñ.** no way

ñato, -a ADJ *Andes, RP* snub-nosed

ñoñería, ñoñez NF inanity

ñoño, -a ADJ (**a**) *(remilgado)* squeamish; *(quejica)* whining (**b**) *(soso)* dull, insipid

ñoqui NM *Culin* gnocchi

O

O, o [o] NF *(letra)* O, o

O. *(abr* **Oeste)** W

o CONJ or; **jueves o viernes** Thursday or Friday; **o ... o** either ... or; **o sea** that is (to say), in other words

> **u** is used instead of **o** in front of words beginning with "o" or "ho" (e.g. **mujer u hombre** woman or man). Note that **ó** (with acute accent) is used between figures.

oasis NM INV oasis

obcecado, -a ADJ stubborn

obcecar [44] **1** VT to blind; **la ira lo obceca** he is blinded by anger
   2 obcecarse VPR to become stubborn; **obcecarse en hacer algo** to stubbornly insist on doing sth

obedecer [33] **1** VT to obey
   2 VI **o. a** *(provenir)* to be due to; **¿a qué obedece esa actitud?** what's the reason behind this attitude?

obediencia NF obedience

obediente ADJ obedient

obertura NF overture

obesidad NF obesity

obeso, -a ADJ obese

óbice NM obstacle; **eso no es ó. para que yo no lo haga** it won't prevent me from doing it

obispo NM bishop

objeción NF objection; **poner una o.** to raise an objection, to object

objetar VT to object to

objetividad NF objectivity

objetivo, -a 1 NM **(a)** *(fin, meta)* objective, aim **(b)** *Mil* target **(c)** *Cin & Fot* lens; **o. zoom** zoom lens
   2 ADJ objective

objeto NM **(a)** *(cosa)* object; **objetos perdidos** lost property, *US* lost and found; **mujer o.** sex object **(b)** *(fin)* aim, purpose; **con o. de ...** in order to ...; **tiene por o. ...** it is designed to ... **(c)** *Ling* object

objetor, -a NM,F objector; **o. de conciencia** conscientious objector

obligación NF **(a)** *(deber)* obligation; **por o.** out of a sense of duty; **tengo o. de ...** I have to ... **(b)** *Fin* bond, security

obligado, -a ADJ obliged; **verse** *o* **estar o. a** to be obliged to

obligar [42] VT to compel, to force

obligatorio, -a ADJ compulsory, obligatory

obra NF **(a)** *(trabajo)* (piece of) work; **por o. de** thanks to **(b)** *Arte* work; **o. maestra** masterpiece **(c)** *(acto)* deed **(d)** *Constr* building site **(e)** **obras** *(arreglos)* repairs; **carretera en obras** *(en letrero)* roadworks; **cerrado por obras** *(en letrero)* closed for repairs

obrar 1 VI **(a)** *(proceder)* to act, to behave; **o. bien/mal** to do the right/wrong thing **(b)** *Fml* **obra en nuestro poder ...** we are in receipt of
...
   2 VT *(milagro)* to work

obrero, -a 1 NM,F worker, labourer
   2 ADJ working; **clase obrera** working class; **movimiento o.** labour movement

obscenidad NF obscenity

obsceno, -a ADJ obscene

obscurecer [33] V IMPERS, VT & VPR = **oscurecer**

obscuridad NF = **oscuridad**

obscuro, -a ADJ = **oscuro**

obsequiar [43] VT *Esp* **o. a algn con algo,** *Am* **o. algo a algn** to present sb with sth

obsequio NM gift, present

observación NF observation

observador, -a 1 NM,F observer
   2 ADJ observant

observancia NF observance

observar VT **(a)** *(mirar)* to observe, to watch **(b)** *(notar)* to notice **(c)** *(cumplir)* to observe

observatorio NM observatory

obsesión NF obsession

obsesionar 1 VT to obsess; **estoy obsesionado con eso** I can't get it out of my mind
   2 obsesionarse VPR to get obsessed

obsesivo, -a ADJ obsessive

obseso, -a NM,F obsessed person; **un o. sexual** a sex maniac

obsoleto, -a ADJ obsolete

obstaculizar [40] VT to obstruct, to get in the way of

obstáculo NM obstacle

obstante ADV **no o.** nevertheless, however

obstetricia NF obstetrics *sing*

obstinación NF obstinacy

obstinado, -a ADJ obstinate

obstinarse VPR to persist **(en** in)

obstrucción NF obstruction; *Med* blockage

obstruir [37] **1** VT (**a**) *(salida, paso)* to block, to obstruct (**b**) *(progreso)* to impede, to block
2 obstruirse VPR to get blocked up

obtención NF obtaining

obtener [24] **1** VT *(alcanzar)* to obtain, to get
2 obtenerse VPR **obtenerse de** *(provenir)* to come from

obturador NM *Fot* shutter

obtuso, -a ADJ obtuse

obús NM shell

obviar [43] VT *(problema)* to get round

obvio, -a ADJ obvious

oca NF goose

ocasión NF (**a**) *(momento)* occasion; **con o. de ...** on the occasion of ...; **en cierta o.** once (**b**) *(oportunidad)* opportunity, chance; **aprovechar una o.** to make the most of an opportunity (**c**) *Com* bargain; **de o.** cheap; **precios de o.** bargain prices

ocasional ADJ (**a**) *(eventual)* occasional; **trabajo o.** casual work; **de forma o.** occasionally (**b**) *(fortuito)* accidental, chance

ocasionar VT to cause, to bring about

ocaso NM *(anochecer)* sunset; *Fig (declive)* fall, decline

occidental ADJ western, occidental

occidente NM west; **el O.** the West

OCDE NF *(abr* **Organización para la Cooperación y el Desarrollo Económico)** OECD

Oceanía N Oceania

oceánico, -a ADJ oceanic

océano NM ocean

ochenta ADJ & NM INV eighty

ocho ADJ & NM INV eight

ochocientos, -as ADJ & NM eight hundred

ocio NM leisure; **en mis ratos de o.** in my spare o leisure time

ocioso, -a ADJ (**a**) *(inactivo)* idle (**b**) *(inútil)* pointless

ocre NM ochre

octavilla NF *(panfleto)* handout, leaflet

octavo, -a ADJ & NM,F eighth

octogenario, -a ADJ & NM,F octogenarian

octogésimo, -a ADJ & NM,F eightieth

octubre NM October

ocular ADJ **testigo o.** eye witness

oculista NMF ophthalmologist

ocultar **1** VT to conceal, to hide; **o. algo a algn** to hide sth from sb
2 ocultarse VPR to hide

oculto, -a ADJ concealed, hidden

ocupación NF occupation

ocupado, -a ADJ *(persona)* busy; *(asiento)* taken; *(teléfono) Br* engaged, *US* busy; *(lavabo)* engaged; *(puesto de trabajo)* filled

ocupante NMF *(de casa)* occupant, occupier; *(ilegal)* squatter; *(de vehículo)* occupant

ocupar **1** VT (**a**) *(invadir)* *(territorio, edificio)* to occupy (**b**) *(espacio, tiempo)* to take up; *(cargo)* to hold, fill (**c**) *CAm, Méx (usar, emplear)* to use
2 ocuparse VPR **ocuparse de** *(cuidar)* to look after; *(encargarse)* to see to

ocurrencia NF *(agudeza)* witty remark, wisecrack; *(idea)* bright idea

> Observa que la palabra inglesa **occurrence** es un falso amigo y no es la traducción de la palabra española **ocurrencia**. En inglés, **occurrence** significa "suceso, incidencia".

ocurrente ADJ witty

ocurrir **1** V IMPERS to happen, to occur; **¿qué ocurre?** what's going on?; **¿qué te ocurre?** what's the matter with you?
2 ocurrirse VPR **no se me ocurre nada** I can't think of anything; **se me ocurre que ...** it occurs to me that ...

odiar [43] VT to detest, to hate; **odio tener que ...** I hate having to ...

odio NM hatred, loathing; **mirada de o.** hateful look

odioso, -a ADJ hateful

odontología NF dentistry, odontology

odontólogo, -a NM,F dental surgeon, odontologist

odre NM wineskin

OEA NF *(abr* **Organización de Estados Americanos)** OAS

oeste NM west

ofender **1** VT to offend
2 ofenderse VPR to be offended (**por** by), to take offence (**por** at)

ofensa NF offence

ofensiva NF offensive

ofensivo, -a ADJ offensive

oferta NF offer; *Fin & Ind* bid, tender, proposal; *Com* **de** o **en o.** on (special) offer; **o. y demanda** supply and demand

ofertar VT to offer

off ADJ **voz en o.** *Cin & TV* voice-over; *Teatro* voice offstage

offset NM *Impr* offset

oficial **1** ADJ official
2 NMF (**a**) *Mil & Náut* officer (**b**) *(empleado)* clerk (**c**) *(obrero)* skilled worker

oficialismo NM *Am* (**a**) **el o.** *(gobierno)* the Government (**b**) **el o.** *(partidarios del gobierno)* government supporters

oficialista *Am* **1** ADJ pro-government
2 NM,F government supporter

oficina NF office; **o. de empleo** *Br* job centre, *US* job office; **o. de turismo** tourist office; **o. de correos** post office; **horas/horario de o.** office hours

oficinista NMF office worker, clerk

oficio NM (**a**) *(ocupación)* job, occupation; *(profesión)* trade; **ser del o.** to be in the trade (**b**) *(comunicación oficial)* official letter *o* note; **de o.** ex-officio; **abogado de o.** state-appointed lawyer (**c**) *Rel* service

oficioso, -a ADJ *(noticia, fuente)* unofficial

Observa que la palabra inglesa **officious** es un falso amigo y no es la traducción de la palabra española **oficioso**. En inglés, **officious** significa "excesivamente celoso o diligente".

ofimática NF office automation

ofrecer [33] **1** VT (**a**) *(dar)* to offer (**b**) *(tener)* *(aspecto, dificultades)* to present
2 ofrecerse VPR (**a**) *(prestarse)* to offer, to volunteer (**b**) *(situación)* to present itself (**c**) *Fml* **¿qué se le ofrece?** what can I do for you?

ofrecimiento NM offering

ofrendar VT *Rel* to offer up

ofrezco INDIC PRES *de* **ofrecer**

oftalmología NF ophthalmology

oftalmólogo, -a NM,F ophthalmologist

ofuscación NF, **ofuscamiento** NM blindness

ofuscar [44] VT (**a**) *(confundir)* to blind (**b**) *(deslumbrar)* to dazzle

ogro NM *también Fig* ogre

oídas: de oídas LOC ADV by hearsay

oído NM (**a**) *(sentido)* hearing (**b**) *(órgano)* ear; **aprender de o.** to learn by ear; *Fig* **hacer oídos sordos** to turn a deaf ear

oír [17] VT to hear; **¡oye!** hey!; **¡oiga!** excuse me!; *Fam* **como lo oyes** believe it or not

ojal NM buttonhole

ojalá 1 INTERJ let's hope so!, I hope so!
2 CONJ *(+ subjunctive)* **¡o. sea cierto!** I hope it's true!

ojeada NF **echar una o.** to have a quick look

ojeras NFPL rings *o* bags under the eyes

ojeriza NF dislike

ojo 1 NM (**a**) *(para ver)* eye; **o. morado** black eye; **ojos saltones** bulging eyes; *Fig* **a ojos vista** clearly, openly; *Fig* **calcular a o.** to guess; *Fam* **no pegué o.** I didn't sleep a wink (**b**) *(de aguja)* eye; *(de cerradura)* keyhole (**c**) *(de un puente)* span
2 INTERJ careful!, look out!

ojota NF (**a**) *Andes (zapatilla)* sandal (**b**) *RP (chancleta)* Br flip-flop, *US, Austr* thong

okupa NMF *Esp Fam* squatter

ola NF wave; **o. de calor** heat wave

ole, olé INTERJ bravo!

oleada NF wave; *Fig* **o. de turistas** influx of tourists

oleaje NM swell

óleo NM *Arte* oil; **pintura** *o* **cuadro al ó.** oil painting

oleoducto NM (oil) pipeline

oler [65] **1** VT (**a**) *(percibir olor)* to smell (**b**) *Fig (adivinar)* to smell, to feel
2 VI (**a**) *(exhalar)* to smell; **o. a** to smell of; **o.**

bien/mal to smell good/bad (**b**) *Fig (parecer)* to smack (**a** of)
3 olerse VPR *Fig (adivinar)* to feel, to sense; **me lo olía** I thought as much

olfatear VT (**a**) *(oler)* to sniff (**b**) *Fig (indagar)* to pry into

olfato NM sense of smell; *Fig* good nose, instinct

oligarquía NF oligarchy

olimpiada NF *Dep* Olympiad, Olympic Games; **las olimpiadas** the Olympic Games

olímpicamente ADV *Fam* **paso o. de estudiar** I couldn't give a damn about studying

olímpico, -a ADJ Olympic; **Juegos Olímpicos** Olympic Games

oliva NF olive; **aceite de o.** olive oil

olivar NM olive grove

olivo NM olive (tree)

olla NF saucepan, pot; **o. exprés** *o* **a presión** pressure cooker

olmo NM smooth-leaved elm

olor NM smell; **o. corporal** body odour

oloroso, -a ADJ fragrant, sweet-smelling

OLP NF *(abr* **Organización para la Liberación de Palestina)** PLO

olvidadizo, -a ADJ forgetful

olvidar 1 VT (**a**) *(hecho, dato, persona)* to forget; *Fam* **¡olvídame!** leave me alone! (**b**) *(dejarse)* to leave; **olvidé el paraguas allí** I left my umbrella there
2 olvidarse VPR to forget; **se me ha olvidado hacerlo** I forgot to do it

olvido NM (**a**) *(desmemoria)* oblivion (**b**) *(lapsus)* oversight

ombligo NM navel

ominoso, -a ADJ abominable

omisión NF omission

omiso, -a ADJ **hacer caso o. de** to take no notice of

omitir VT to omit, to leave out

ómnibus *(pl* **ómnibus** *o* **omnibuses)** NM *Cuba, Urug (urbano)* bus; *Andes, Cuba, Urug (interurbano, internacional)* Br coach, *US* bus

omnipotente ADJ omnipotent, almighty

omnipresente ADJ omnipresent

omnisciente ADJ omniscient, all-knowing

omnívoro, -a 1 ADJ omnivorous
2 NM,F omnivore

omoplato NM shoulder blade

OMS NF *(abr* **Organización Mundial de la Salud)** WHO

ONCE NF *(abr* **Organización Nacional de Ciegos Españoles)** ≃ RNIB

once ADJ & NM INV eleven

onda NF (**a**) *Fís* wave; *Fam Fig* **estar en la o.** to be with it; **o. expansiva** shock wave; *Rad* **o. larga/media/corta** long/medium/short wave (**b**) *(en el agua)* ripple (**c**) *(de pelo)* wave (**d**) *Méx, RP* **¿qué o.?** *(¿qué tal?)* how's it going?, how are things?; *Méx, RP* **captar** *o* **agarrar la onda** *(entender)* to catch the drift

ondear VI *(bandera)* to flutter

ondulación NF *(onda)* ripple; *(del pelo)* wave

ondulado, -a ADJ *(pelo)* wavy; *(paisaje)* rolling

ondulante ADJ undulating

ondular 1 VT *(pelo)* to wave
2 VI *(moverse)* to undulate

oneroso, -a ADJ *(impuesto)* heavy

ONG NF INV *(abr* **Organización no Guberna-mental)** NGO

onomástica NF saint's day

onomatopeya NF onomatopoeia

ONU NF *(abr* **Organización de las Naciones Unidas)** UN

onubense 1 ADJ of/from Huelva
2 NMF person from Huelva

onza NF *(medida)* ounce

OPA NF *(abr* **Oferta Pública de Adquisición)** takeover bid

opaco, -a ADJ opaque

ópalo NM opal

opción NF *(a)* *(elección)* option, choice; *(alternativa)* alternative *(b)* *(posibilidad)* opportunity, chance

opcional ADJ optional

open NM *Dep* open

OPEP NF *(abr* **Organización de los Países Exportadores de Petróleo)** OPEC

ópera NF *Mús* opera

operación NF *(a)* *Med* operation; **o. quirúrgica** surgical operation *(b)* *Fin* transaction, deal; **operaciones bursátiles** stock exchange transactions *(c)* *Mat* operation

operador, -a NM,F *(a)* *(técnico)* operator *(b)* *Cin (de cámara) (hombre)* cameraman; *(mujer)* camerawoman; *(del proyector)* projectionist *(c)* *Tel* operator

operante ADJ operative

operar 1 VT *(a)* *Med* **o. a algn (de algo)** to operate on sb (for sth) *(b)* *(cambio etc)* to bring about
2 VI *Fin* to deal, to do business *(con* with)
3 operarse VPR *(a)* *Med* to have an operation *(de* for) *(b)* *(producirse)* to occur, to come about

operario, -a NM,F operator; *(obrero)* worker

operativo, -a 1 ADJ operative
2 NM operation

opereta NF operetta

opinar 1 VT *(pensar)* to think
2 VI *(declarar)* to give one's opinion

opinión NF *(juicio)* opinion; **cambiar de o.** to change one's mind

opio NM opium

oponente NMF opponent

oponer [19] *(pp* **opuesto) 1** VT *(resistencia)* to offer
2 oponerse VPR *(estar en contra)* to be

opposed; **se opone a aceptarlo** he refuses to accept it

oporto NM *(vino)* port

oportunidad NF opportunity, chance

oportunista ADJ & NMF opportunist

oportuno, -a ADJ *(a)* *(adecuado)* timely; **¡qué o.!** what good timing! *(b)* *(conveniente)* appropriate; **si te parece o.** if you think it appropriate

oposición NF *(a)* *(resistencia)* opposition *(b)* *(examen)* = competitive examination for public sector jobs *(c)* *Pol* **la o.** the opposition

opositar VI = to sit a competitive public examination

opositor, -a NM,F *(a)* *(candidato)* = candidate in a competitive public examination *(b)* *Am Pol* opponent

opresión NF oppression; **o. en el pecho** tightness of the chest

opresivo, -a ADJ oppressive

opresor, -a 1 NM,F oppressor
2 ADJ oppressive, oppressing

oprimir VT *(a)* *(pulsar)* to press *(b)* *(subyugar)* to oppress

oprobio NM ignominy, opprobrium

optar VI *(a)* *(elegir)* to choose *(entre* between); **opté por ir yo mismo** I decided to go myself *(b)* *(aspirar)* to apply *(a* for); **puede o. a medalla** he's in with a chance of winning a medal

optativo, -a ADJ optional, *US* elective

óptica NF *(a)* *(tienda)* optician's (shop) *(b)* *(punto de vista)* angle

óptico, -a 1 ADJ optical
2 NM,F optician

optimismo NM optimism

optimista 1 ADJ optimistic
2 NMF optimist

óptimo, -a ADJ optimum, excellent

opuesto, -a 1 ADJ *(a)* *(contrario)* contrary; **en direcciones opuestas** in opposite directions; **gustos opuestos** conflicting tastes *(b)* *(de enfrente)* opposite; **el extremo o.** the other end
2 PP *de* **oponer**

opulencia NF opulence

opulento, -a ADJ opulent

opuse PT INDEF *de* **oponer**

oración NF *(a)* *Rel* prayer *(b)* *Ling* clause, sentence

oráculo NM oracle

orador, -a NM,F speaker, orator

oral ADJ oral; *Med* **por vía o.** to be taken orally

órale INTERJ *Méx Fam (a)* *(venga)* come on! *(b)* *(de acuerdo)* right!, OK!

orangután NM orang-outang, orang-utan

orar VI *Rel* to pray

oratoria NF oratory

órbita NF *(a)* *(de planeta)* orbit *(b)* *Anat* eye socket

orca NF killer whale

orden 1 NM order; **o. público** law and order; **por o. alfabético** in alphabetical order; **de primer o.** first-rate; **o. del día** agenda; **del o. de** approximately
2 NF (**a**) *(mandato)* order; *Mil* **¡a la o.!** sir! (**b**) *Der* warrant, order; **o. de registro** search warrant; **o. judicial** court order

ordenado, -a ADJ tidy

ordenador NM *Esp* computer; **o. personal** personal computer

ordenamiento NM ordering

ordenanza 1 NM *(empleado)* office boy
2 NF regulations; **o. municipal** bylaw

ordenar 1 VT (**a**) *(organizar)* to put in order; *(habitación)* to tidy up (**b**) *(mandar)* to order (**c**) *Am (pedir)* to order
2 ordenarse VPR *Rel* to be ordained (**de** as), take holy orders

ordeñar VT to milk

ordinario, -a ADJ (**a**) *(corriente)* ordinary, common (**b**) *(grosero)* vulgar, common

orégano NM oregano, marjoram

oreja NF ear; *(de sillón)* wing

orfanato NM orphanage

orfebre NMF *(del oro)* goldsmith; *(de la plata)* silversmith

orfebrería NF gold/silver work

orfelinato NM orphanage

orgánico, -a ADJ organic

organigrama NM organization chart; *Inform* flow chart

organillo NM barrel organ

organismo NM (**a**) *(ser vivo)* organism (**b**) *(institución)* organization, body

organización NF organization

organizado, -a ADJ organized; **viaje o.** package tour

organizador, -a 1 ADJ organizing
2 NM,F organizer

organizar [40] **1** VT to organize
2 organizarse VPR *(persona)* to organize oneself

órgano NM organ

orgasmo NM orgasm

orgía NF orgy

orgullo NM (**a**) *(propia estima)* pride (**b**) *(arrogancia)* arrogance

orgulloso, -a ADJ (**a**) **estar o.** *(satisfecho)* to be proud (**b**) **ser o.** *(arrogante)* to be arrogant *o* haughty

orientación NF (**a**) *(dirección)* orientation, direction (**b**) *(guía)* guidance; **curso de o.** induction course

oriental 1 ADJ (**a**) *(del este)* eastern, oriental; *(del Lejano Oriente)* oriental (**b**) *Am (uruguayo)* Uruguayan
2 NMF (**a**) *(del Lejano Oriente)* oriental (**b**) *Am (uruguayo)* Uruguayan

orientar 1 VT (**a**) *(enfocar)* to aim (**a** at), to intend (**a** for); **orientado al consumo** intended for consumption (**b**) *(indicar camino)* to give directions to; *Fig (aconsejar)* to advise (**c**) **una casa orientada al sur** a house facing south (**d**) *(esfuerzo)* to direct
2 orientarse VPR *(encontrar el camino)* to get one's bearings, to find one's way about

oriente NM East, Orient; **el Extremo** *o* **Lejano/Medio/Próximo O.** the Far/Middle/Near East

orificio NM hole, opening; *Anat & Téc* orifice; **o. de entrada** inlet; **o. de salida** outlet

origen NM origin; **país de o.** country of origin; **dar o. a** to give rise to

original ADJ & NM original

originalidad NF originality

originar 1 VT to cause, to give rise to
2 originarse VPR to originate

originariamente ADV originally

originario, -a ADJ native

orilla NF *(borde)* edge; *(del río)* bank; *(del mar)* shore

orillero, -a ADJ *RP, Ven* common, low-class

orín¹ NM *(herrumbre)* rust

orín² NM orines *(orina)* urine

orina NF urine

orinal NM chamberpot; *Fam* potty

orinar 1 VI to urinate
2 orinarse VPR to wet oneself

oriundo, -a ADJ **ser o. de** to come from

orla NF *Univ* graduation photograph

ornamento NM ornament

ornar VT to adorn, to embellish

ornato NM *(atavío)* finery; *(adorno)* decoration

ornitología NF ornithology

ornitólogo, -a NM,F ornithologist

oro NM (**a**) *(metal)* gold; **de o.** gold, golden; **o. de ley** pure *o* real gold, standard gold (**b**) *Naipes* **oros** = suit in Spanish deck of cards, with the symbol of a gold coin

orquesta NF orchestra; *(de verbena)* dance band

orquestar VT to orchestrate

orquídea NF orchid

ortiga NF *(stinging)* nettle

ortodoxia NF orthodoxy

ortodoxo, -a ADJ orthodox

ortografía NF spelling, orthography; **faltas de o.** spelling mistakes

ortográfico, -a ADJ spelling; **signos ortográficos** punctuation

ortopédico, -a ADJ orthopaedic; **pierna ortopédica** artificial leg

oruga NF caterpillar

orzuelo NM *Med* sty, stye

os PRON PERS PL (**a**) *(complemento directo)* you; **os veo mañana** I'll see you tomorrow (**b**) *(complemento indirecto)* you, to you; **os daré**

el dinero I'll give you the money; **os escribiré** I'll write to you (**c**) *(con verbo reflexivo)* yourselves (**d**) *(con verbo recíproco)* each other; **os queréis mucho** you love each other very much

osa NF **O. Mayor** *Br* Great Bear, *US* Big Dipper; **O. Menor** *Br* Little Bear, *US* Little Dipper

osadía NF (**a**) *(audacia)* daring (**b**) *(desvergüenza)* impudence

osado, -a ADJ (**a**) *(audaz)* daring (**b**) *(desvergonzado)* shameless

osar VI to dare

osario NM ossuary

Óscar NM *Cin* Oscar

oscilación NF (**a**) *Fís* oscillation (**b**) *(de precios)* fluctuation

oscilar VI (**a**) *Fís* to oscillate (**b**) *(variar)* to vary, to fluctuate

oscuras: a oscuras LOC ADV in the dark; **nos quedamos a o.** we were left in darkness

oscurecer [33] **1** V IMPERS to get dark
   2 VT to darken
   3 oscurecerse VPR to darken

oscuridad NF darkness; *Fig* obscurity

oscuro, -a ADJ (**a**) *(sin luz)* dark (**b**) *(origen, idea)* obscure; *(asunto)* shady; *(nublado)* overcast

óseo, -a ADJ osseous, bony; **tejido ó.** bone tissue

osito NM *Fam* **o. (de peluche)** teddy bear

ósmosis, osmosis NF INV osmosis

oso NM bear; **o. polar** polar bear; **o. hormiguero** anteater; **o. marino** fur seal; *Fam Fig* **hacer el o.** to play the fool

osobuco NM *Culin* osso bucco

ostensible ADJ ostensible

ostentación NF ostentation; **hacer o. de algo** to show sth off

ostentar VT (**a**) *(lucir)* to flaunt (**b**) *(cargo)* to hold

ostentoso, -a ADJ ostentatious

osteópata NMF osteopath

osteopatía NF osteopathy

ostión NM (**a**) *Méx (ostra)* Portuguese oyster, Pacific oyser (**b**) *Chile (vieira)* scallop

ostra NF oyster; *Fig* **aburrirse como una o.** to be bored stiff; *Esp Fam* **¡ostras!** *Br* crikey!, *US* gee!

ostracismo NM ostracism

OTAN NF *(abr* **Organización del Tratado del Atlántico Norte**) NATO

otear VT *(horizonte)* to scan, to search

OTI NF *(abr* **Organización de Televisiones Iberoamericanas**) = association of all Spanish-speaking television networks

otitis NF INV infection and inflammation of the ear, *Espec* otitis

otoñal ADJ autumn, autumnal, *US* fall

otoño NM autumn, *US* fall

otorgamiento NM *(concesión)* granting; *(de un premio)* awarding

otorgar [42] VT (**a**) *(premio)* to award (**a** to); **o. un indulto** to grant pardon (**b**) *(permiso)* to grant (**a** to)

otorrino, -a NM,F *Fam* ear, nose and throat specialist

otorrinolaringólogo, -a NM,F ear, nose and throat specialist

otro, -a 1 ADJ INDEF (**a**) *(sin artículo) (singular)* another; *(plural)* other; **o. coche** another car; **otras personas** other people (**b**) *(con artículo definido)* other; **el o. coche** the other car (**c**) **otra cosa** something else; **otra vez** again
   2 PRON INDEF (**a**) *(sin artículo) (sing)* another (one); *(pl) (personas)* others; *(cosas)* other ones; **dame o.** give me another (one); **no es mío, es de o.** it's not mine, it's somebody else's (**b**) *(con artículo definido) (sing)* **el o./la otra** the other (one); *(pl) (personas)* **los otros/las otras** the others; *(cosas)* the other ones (**c**) **hacer o. tanto** to do likewise

ovación NF ovation

ovacionar VT to give an ovation to, to applaud

oval, ovalado, -a ADJ oval

óvalo NM oval

ovario NM ovary

oveja NF sheep; *(hembra)* ewe; *Fig* **la o. negra** the black sheep

overol NM *Am (de peto) Br* dungarees, *US* overalls; *(completo)* overalls, *Br* boilersuit

ovillo NM ball (of wool); *Fig* **hacerse un o.** to curl up into a ball

ovino, -a ADJ ovine; **ganado o.** sheep *pl*

OVNI NM *(abr* **objeto volador no identificado**) UFO

ovular 1 ADJ ovular
   2 VI to ovulate

óvulo NM ovule

oxidación NF *Quím* oxidation; *(de metal)* rusting

oxidado, -a ADJ rusty

oxidar 1 VT *Quím* to oxidize; *(metal)* to rust
   2 oxidarse VPR *Quím* to oxidize; *(metal)* to rust, to go rusty

óxido NM (**a**) *Quím* oxide; **ó. de carbono** carbon monoxide (**b**) *(herrumbre)* rust

oxigenado, -a ADJ oxygenated; **agua oxigenada** (hydrogen) peroxide

oxígeno NM oxygen; **bomba de o.** oxygen cylinder *o* tank

oye INDIC PRES & IMPERAT *de* **oír**

oyente NMF (**a**) *Rad* listener (**b**) *Univ Br* occasional student, *US* auditing student

ozono NM ozone; **capa de o.** ozone layer

P, p [pe] NF *(letra)* P, p

pabellón NM (**a**) **p. de deportes** sports centre (**b**) *(en feria)* stand (**c**) *(bloque)* wing (**d**) *(bandera)* flag

pábulo NM *Fml* **dar p. a** to encourage

pacer [60] VT & VI to graze, to pasture

pachá NM *Fam* **vivir como un p.** to live like a king

pachanguero, -a ADJ *Fam Pey (música)* catchy

pacharán NM = liqueur made from brandy and sloes

pachorra NF *Fam* **tener p.** to be phlegmatic

paciencia NF patience; **armarse de p.** to grin and bear it

paciente ADJ & NMF patient

pacificación NF pacification

pacificador, -a 1 ADJ pacifying
2 NM,F peacemaker

pacificar [44] **1** VT to pacify; *Fig (apaciguar)* to appease, to calm
2 pacificarse VPR to calm down

Pacífico NM **el (océano) P.** the Pacific (Ocean)

pacífico, -a ADJ peaceful

pacifismo NM pacifism

pacifista ADJ & NMF pacifist

pack [pak] *(pl* **packs)** NM pack; **un p. de seis** a six-pack

paco, -a NM,F *Andes, Pan Fam (policía)* cop

pacotilla NF *Fam* **de p.** second-rate

pactar VT to agree to

pacto NM pact; **el P. de Varsovia** the Warsaw Pact; **p. de caballeros** gentlemen's agreement

padecer [33] VT & VI to suffer; **padece del corazón** he suffers from heart trouble

padecimiento NM suffering

padrastro NM (**a**) *(hombre)* stepfather (**b**) *(pellejo)* hangnail

padrazo NM easy-going *o* indulgent father

padre 1 NM (**a**) *(hombre)* father; **p. de familia** family man (**b**) **padres** parents
2 ADJ *Fam* (**a**) *Esp (tremendo)* huge; **fue el cachondeo p.** it was a great laugh (**b**) *Méx (genial)* great, fantastic

padrenuestro NM Lord's Prayer

padrino NM (**a**) *(de bautizo)* godfather; *(de boda)* best man; **padrinos** godparents (**b**) *(espónsor)* sponsor

padrísimo, -a ADJ *Méx Fam* fantastic, great

padrón NM census

padrote NM (**a**) *Méx Fam (proxeneta)* pimp (**b**) *CAm, Ven (caballo)* stallion

paella NF paella, = rice dish made with vegetables, meat and/or seafood

paellera NF paella pan

pág. *(abr* **página)** p

paga NF *(salario)* wage; *(de niños)* pocket money, *US* allowance; **p. extra** bonus

pagadero, -a ADJ payable; *Fin* **cheque p. al portador** cheque payable to bearer

pagado, -a ADJ paid

pagano, -a ADJ & NM,F pagan, heathen

pagar [42] VT *(persona, factura)* to pay; *(gastos, delito)* to pay for; *(deuda)* to pay off, to settle; *(ayuda, favor)* to repay; **p. en metálico** *o* **al contado** to pay cash; **p. por** *(producto, mala acción)* to pay for; *Fig* **lo ha pagado caro** he's paid dearly for it

pagaré NM *Fin* promissory note, IOU; **p. del tesoro** treasury note

página NF page; **en la p. 3** on page 3; *Fig* **una p. importante de la historia** an important chapter in history; *Inform* **p. personal** home page; *Inform* **p. de inicio** home page; *Inform* **p. web** web page

pago NM payment; **p. adelantado** *o* **anticipado** advance payment; **p. contra reembolso** cash on delivery; **p. inicial** down payment; **p. por visión** pay-per-view

paila NF *Andes, CAm, Carib (sartén)* frying pan

paipái *(pl* **paipáis), paipay** *(pl* **paipays)** NM = large palm fan

país NM country, land; **vino del p.** local wine; **los Países Bajos** the Netherlands; **P. Vasco** Basque Country; **P. Valenciano** Valencia

paisaje NM landscape, scenery

paisano, -a 1 ADJ of the same country
2 NM,F *(compatriota)* fellow countryman/countrywoman, compatriot; **en traje de p.** in plain clothes

paja NF (**a**) *(hierba, caña)* straw (**b**) *Fig (relleno)* padding, waffle (**c**) *Vulg* **hacerse una** *o Am* **la p.** to jerk off, *Br* to have a wank

pajar NM hayloft

pajarita NF (**a**) *Esp (corbata)* bow tie (**b**) *(de papel)* paper bird

pájaro NM bird; **Madrid a vista de p.** a bird's-eye view of Madrid; **p. carpintero** woodpecker

paje NM page

pajita NF (drinking) straw

Pakistán N Pakistan

pakistaní ADJ & NMF Pakistani

pala NF (a) *(herramienta)* spade; *(para recoger)* shovel; *(de cocina)* slice (b) *Dep (de ping-pong, frontón)* bat, *US* paddle; *(de remo)* blade

palabra NF (a) *(vocablo)* word; **de p.** by word of mouth; **dirigir la p. a algn** to address sb; **juego de palabras** pun (b) *(promesa)* word; **p. de honor** word of honour (c) *(turno para hablar)* right to speak; **tener la p.** to have the floor

palabrería NF *Fam* hot air, talk

palabrota NF swearword

palacio NM *(grande)* palace; *(pequeño)* mansion; **P. de Justicia** Law Courts

paladar NM (a) *(en la boca)* palate (b) *(sabor)* taste

paladear VT to savour, to relish

palanca NF (a) *(barra, mando)* lever; *Aut* **p. de cambio** *Br* gear lever, gearstick, *US* gearshift, stick shift; **p. de mando** joystick (b) *(trampolín)* diving board

palangana NF *Br* washbasin, *US* washbowl

palco NM box

paleolítico, -a ADJ palaeolithic, paleolithic

paleontología NF palaeontology, paleontology

Palestina N Palestine

palestino, -a ADJ & NM,F Palestinian

palestra NF arena; *Fig* **salir** o **saltar a la p.** to enter the fray, to take the field

paleta NF (a) *(espátula)* slice (b) *(de pintor)* palette; *(de albañil)* trowel (c) *Dep (de ping-pong)* bat, *US* paddle (d) *Andes, CAm, Méx (pirulí)* lollipop; *Bol, Col, Perú (polo) Br* ice lolly, *US* Popsicle®

paletilla NF *Culin* shoulder

paleto, -a *Esp Fam Pey* **1** ADJ unsophisticated, boorish

2 NM,F country bumpkin, yokel

paliar [43] VT to alleviate, to palliate

paliativo, -a ADJ & NM palliative

palidecer [33] VI (a) *(persona)* to turn pale (b) *Fig (perder importancia)* to pale, to fade

palidez NF paleness, pallor

pálido, -a ADJ pale

palillero NM toothpick case

palillo NM (a) *(mondadientes)* toothpick; **palillos chinos** chopsticks (b) *Mús* drumstick

palio NM canopy

palique NM *Fam* chat, small talk

paliza NF (a) *(zurra)* thrashing, beating; **darle a algn una p.** to beat sb up (b) *(derrota)* beating (c) *Fam (pesadez)* bore, pain (in the neck)

palma NF (a) *Anat* palm (b) *Bot* palm tree (c) **hacer palmas** to applaud

palmada NF (a) *(golpe)* slap (b) **palmadas** applause, clapping

palmar VI *Fam* to kick the bucket, to snuff it

palmarés *(pl* **palmareses)** NM (a) *(historial)* record (b) *(vencedores)* list of winners

palmatoria NF candlestick

palmera NF palm tree

palmo NM *(medida)* span; *Fig* **p. a p.** inch by inch

palo NM (a) *(de madera)* stick; *(vara)* rod; *(de escoba)* broomstick; *Fig* **a p. seco** on its own (b) *(golpe)* blow; *Fig* **dar un p. a algn** to let sb down (c) **de p.** wooden (d) *Dep (de portería)* woodwork (e) *(de golf)* club (f) *Naipes* suit

paloma NF pigeon; *Lit* dove; **p. mensajera** homing o carrier pigeon

palomar NM pigeon house, dovecot

palomilla NF wing o butterfly nut

palomitas NFPL **p. (de maíz)** popcorn

palpable ADJ palpable

palpar VT to touch, to feel; *Med* to palpate

palpitación NF beating; *(con fuerza)* throbbing; *Med* **palpitaciones** palpitations

palpitante ADJ (a) *(corazón)* beating; *(con fuerza)* throbbing (b) *(cuestión)* burning

palpitar VI to beat; *(con fuerza)* to throb

palta NF *Andes, RP (fruto)* avocado

palúdico, -a ADJ malarial

paludismo NM malaria

palurdo, -a ADJ uncouth, boorish

pamela NF broad-brimmed hat

pampa NF pampa, pampas

pamplinas NFPL *Fam* nonsense

pan NM bread; **p. de molde** packaged sliced bread; **p. integral** *Br* wholemeal o *US* wholewheat bread; **p. rallado** breadcrumbs pl; **p. dulce** *Méx (bollo)* bun; *RP (panetone)* panettone; *Arg* **p. lactal** sliced bread; *Fam Fig* **más bueno que el p.** as good as gold; *Fam Fig* **es p. comido** it's a piece of cake

pana NF corduroy

panacea NF panacea

panadería NF baker's (shop), bakery

panadero, -a NM,F baker

panal NM honeycomb

Panamá N Panama

panamá NM *(sombrero)* Panama hat

panameño, -a ADJ & NM,F Panamanian

pancarta NF placard; *(en manifestación)* banner

pancho NM *RP* hot dog

páncreas NM INV pancreas

panda 1 ADJ **oso p.** panda

2 NM panda

3 NF *Esp (de amigos)* crowd, gang; *(de gamberros, delincuentes)* gang

pandereta NF tambourine

pandilla NF *Fam* gang

panecillo NM bread roll

panel NM panel

panera NF *(para guardar) Br* bread bin, *US* bread box; *(para servir)* bread basket

pánfilo, -a ADJ *Fam (bobo)* silly, stupid; *(crédulo)* gullible

panfleto NM lampoon, political pamphlet

pánico NM panic; **sembrar el p.** to cause panic

panocha NF *(de maíz)* ear, cob

panorama NM *(vista)* panorama, view; *(situación)* overall state; *(perspectiva)* outlook

panorámica NF panorama

panorámico, -a ADJ panoramic

panqueque NM *Am* pancake

pantaleta NF, **pantaletas** NFPL *CAm, Carib, Méx (bragas)* panties, *Br* knickers

pantalla NF **(a)** *Cin, TV & Inform* screen **(b)** *(de lámpara)* shade **(c)** *Fig* **servir de p.** to act as a decoy

pantalón NM *(usu pl)* trousers, *US* pants; **p. vaquero** jeans

pantano NM *Geog* **(a)** *(natural)* marsh, bog **(b)** *(artificial)* reservoir

panteón NM pantheon, mausoleum; **p. familiar** family vault

pantera NF panther

pantimedias NFPL *Méx Br* tights, *US* pantyhose

pantomima NF *Teatro* pantomime, mime; *Pey (farsa)* farce

pantorrilla NF *Anat* calf

pants NMPL *Méx (traje)* tracksuit, jogging suit; *(pantalón)* tracksuit bottoms o *US* pants

pantufla NF slipper

panty *(pl* **pantis)** NM *Br* tights, *US* pantyhose

> Observa que la palabra inglesa **panties** es un falso amigo y no es la traducción de la palabra española **panty**. En inglés **panties** significa "bragas".

panza NF *Fam* belly, paunch

panzada NF *Fam* bellyful

pañal NM *Br* nappy, *US* diaper; *Fam Fig* **estar en pañales** to be in its infancy

paño NM *(tela)* cloth, material; *(de lana)* woollen cloth; *(para polvo)* duster, rag; *(de cocina) Br* tea towel, *US* dish towel; *Fig* **paños calientes** half-measures; **en paños menores** in one's underclothes

pañoleta NF shawl

pañuelo NM *(de nariz)* handkerchief; *(para el cuello)* scarf; *(para la cabeza)* headscarf; **p. de papel** tissue, paper handkerchief

Papa NM **el P.** the Pope

papa NF *esp Am* potato; *Fam* **no saber ni p. (de algo)** not to have the faintest idea (about sth)

papá NM *Fam* dad, daddy, *US* pop

papachar VT *Méx* to cuddle, to pamper

papada NF double chin

papagayo NM **(a)** *(animal)* parrot **(b)** *Carib, Méx (cometa)* kite

papalote NM *CAm, Méx* kite

papamoscas NM INV flycatcher

papanatas NMF INV sucker, twit

paparrucha NF *(piece of)* nonsense

papaya NF papaya o pawpaw fruit

papear VT & VI *Esp, Ven Fam* to eat, to scoff

papel NM **(a)** *(material)* paper; *(hoja)* piece o sheet of paper; **p. higiénico** toilet paper; **p. carbón** o *RP* **carbónico** carbon paper; **p. de carta** writing paper, stationery; *Chile* **p. confort** toilet paper; **p. de alumimio/de estraza** aluminium foil/brown paper; **p. de fumar** cigarette paper; **p. lija** sandpaper; *Fin* **p. moneda** paper money, banknotes *pl*; **p. pintado** wallpaper; *Cuba* **p. sanitario** toilet paper; **p. secante** blotting paper; *Guat, Ven* **p. toilette** o **tualé** toilet paper **(b)** *Cin & Teatro* role, part **(c)** **papeles** *(documentos)* documents, identification papers; **los sin papeles** undocumented immigrants

papeleo NM *Fam* paperwork

papelera NF **(a)** *(en despacho)* wastepaper basket o *Br* bin; *(en calle) Br* litter bin, *US* garbage can **(b)** *Inform (en Windows)* recycle bin; *(en Macintosh) Br* wastebasket, *US* trash can

papelería NF *(tienda)* stationer's (shop)

papeleta NF **(a)** *(de rifa)* ticket; *(de votación)* ballot paper; *(de resultados)* report **(b)** *Fam (dificultad)* tricky problem, difficult job

papeo NM *Fam* grub

paperas NFPL *Med* mumps *sing*

papilla NF *(de niños)* baby food, *US* formula

papista ADJ & NMF papist

Papúa Nueva Guinea N Papua New Guinea

paquete NM **(a)** *(de cigarrillos etc)* pack, packet; *(postal)* parcel, package **(b)** *(conjunto)* set, package; *Fin* **p. de acciones** share package **(c)** *Inform* software package **(d)** *Fam (castigo)* punishment **(e)** *Esp muy Fam (genitales)* packet, bulge

Paquistán N Pakistan

paquistaní *(pl* **paquistaníes)** ADJ & NMF Pakistani

par 1 ADJ *Mat* even

2 NM **(a)** *(pareja)* pair; *(dos)* couple **(b)** *Mat* even number; **pares y nones** odds and evens **(c)** *(noble)* peer **(d)** *(locuciones)* **a la p.** *(a la vez)* at the same time; **de p. en p.** wide open; *Fig* **sin p.** matchless

para PREP **(a)** *(finalidad)* for; **bueno p. la salud** good for your health; **¿p. qué?** what for?; **p. que lo disfrutes** for you to enjoy **(b)** *(con infinitivo)* to, in order to; **p. terminar antes** to o in order to finish earlier **(c)** *(tiempo)* by; **p. entonces** by then **(d)** *(comparación)* for; **p. ser inglés habla muy bien español** for an Englishman he speaks very good Spanish **(e)** *(expresiones)* **decir p. sí** to say to oneself; **ir p. viejo** to be getting old; **no es p. tanto** it's not as bad as all that; **p. mí** in my opinion

parábola NF (**a**) *Geom* parabola (**b**) *Rel* parable

parabólica NF satellite dish

parabólico, -a ADJ parabolic; *TV* **antena parabólica** satellite dish

parabrisas NM INV *Br* windscreen, *US* windshield

paracaídas NM INV parachute

paracaidista NMF *Dep* parachutist; *Mil* paratrooper

parachoques NM INV bumper, *US* fender

parada NF (**a**) *(detención)* stop; **p. de autobús** bus stop; **p. de taxis** taxi stand *o* rank (**b**) *Ftb* save, stop

paradero NM (**a**) *(lugar)* whereabouts *sing* (**b**) *Chile, Col, Méx, Perú (de autobús)* stop

parado, -a 1 ADJ (**a**) *(inmóvil) (vehículo)* stationary, standing; *(persona)* still, motionless; *(fábrica)* at a standstill (**b**) *Esp (desempleado)* unemployed, out of work (**c**) *Esp (pasivo)* **ser muy p.** to lack initiative (**d**) *Am (en pie)* standing (**e**) *Chile, PRico (orgulloso)* vain, conceited (**f**) **salir bien/mal p.** to come off well/badly

2 NM,F *Esp* unemployed person

paradoja NF paradox

paradójico, -a ADJ paradoxical

parador NM roadside inn; **p. (nacional)** = state-owned luxury hotel, usually a building of historic or artistic importance

parafernalia NF paraphernalia *pl*

parafrasear VT to paraphrase

paráfrasis NF INV paraphrase

paragolpes NM PL INV *RP* bumper, *US* fender

paraguas NM INV umbrella

Paraguay N Paraguay

paraguayo, -a 1 ADJ & NM,F Paraguayan
2 NM *(fruta)* = fruit similar to peach

paragüero NM umbrella stand

paraíso NM (**a**) *(lugar perfecto)* paradise; **p. terrenal** heaven on earth; *Fin* **p. fiscal** tax haven (**b**) *Teatro* gods, gallery

paraje NM spot, place

paralelo, -a ADJ & NM parallel

parálisis NF INV paralysis; **p. infantil** poliomyelitis

paralítico, -a ADJ & NM,F paralytic

paralización NF (**a**) *Med* paralysis (**b**) *(detención)* halting, stopping

paralizar [40] **1** VT to paralyse
2 paralizarse VPR *(producción, proyecto)* to come to a standstill

parámetro NM parameter

paramilitar ADJ paramilitary

páramo NM bleak plain *o* plateau, moor

parangón NM *Fml* comparison; **sin p.** incomparable

paranoia NF paranoia

paranoico, -a ADJ & NM,F paranoiac, paranoid

parapente NM *(desde montaña)* paragliding, parapenting

parapeto NM parapet

parapléjico, -a ADJ & NM,F paraplegic

parar 1 VT (**a**) *(detener)* to stop (**b**) *Dep* to save (**c**) *Am (levantar)* to raise
2 VI (**a**) to stop; **p. de hacer algo** to stop doing sth; **sin p.** nonstop, without stopping; *Fam* **no p.** to be always on the go (**b**) *(acabar)* **fue a p. a la cárcel** he ended up in jail
3 pararse VPR (**a**) to stop; **p. a pensar** to stop to think (**b**) *Am (ponerse en pie)* to stand up

pararrayos NM INV lightning rod *o* conductor

parásito, -a ADJ parasitic
2 NM parasite

parasol NM sunshade, parasol

parcela NF plot

parche NM (**a**) *(de tela, goma)* patch (**b**) *(para salir del paso)* makeshift solution

parchís (*pl* **parchises**) NM *Br* ≃ ludo, *US* ≃ Parcheesi®

parcial 1 ADJ (**a**) *(partidario)* biased (**b**) *(no completo)* partial; **a tiempo p.** part-time
2 NM **(examen) p.** class examination

parcialmente ADV partially, partly

parco, -a ADJ (**a**) *(moderado)* sparing (**en** in) (**b**) *(escaso)* meagre; *(cena)* frugal; *(explicación)* brief, concise

pardillo, -a 1 NM,F *Esp Fam* (**a**) *(ingenuo)* naive person (**b**) *(palurdo) Br* bumpkin, *US* hick
2 NM *(ave)* linnet

pardo, -a ADJ *(marrón)* brown; *(gris)* dark grey

parecer¹ NM (**a**) *(opinión)* opinion (**b**) *(aspecto)* appearance

parecer² [33] **1** VI to seem, to look (like); **parece difícil** it seems *o* looks difficult; **parecía (de) cera** it looked like wax; *(uso impers)* **parece que no arranca** it looks as if it won't start; **como te parezca** whatever you like; **¿te parece?** is that okay with you?; **parece que sí/no** I think/don't think so; **¿qué te parece?** what do you think of it?
2 parecerse VPR (**a**) to be alike; **no se parecen** they're not alike (**b**) **parecerse a** to look like, to resemble; **se parecen a su madre** they look like their mother

parecido, -a 1 ADJ (**a**) *(similar)* alike, similar (**b**) **bien p.** good-looking
2 NM likeness, resemblance; **tener p. con algn** to bear a resemblance to sb

pared NF wall

paredón NM **le llevaron al p.** he was executed by firing squad

pareja NF (**a**) *(de cosas, personas)* pair; **por parejas** in pairs (**b**) *(hombre y mujer)* couple; *(hijo e hija)* boy and girl; **hacen buena p.** they make a nice couple, they're well matched; **p. de hecho** ≃ common-law heterosexual *or* homosexual relationship (**c**) *(en naipes)* pair; **doble p.** two pairs (**d**) *(de baile, juego)* partner

parejo, -a ADJ (**a**) *(parecido)* similar, alike (**b**) **ir parejos** to be neck and neck

parentela NF *Fam* relations, relatives

parentesco NM relationship, kinship

paréntesis NM INV (**a**) *(signo)* bracket, parenthesis; **entre p.** in brackets *o* parentheses (**b**) *(descanso)* break; *(digresión)* digression

pareo NM wraparound skirt

parezco INDIC PRES *de* **parecer**

paria NMF pariah

parida NF *Esp Fam* **decir paridas** to talk *Br* rubbish *o US* garbage

pariente NMF relative, relation

> Observa que la palabra inglesa **parent** es un falso amigo y no es la traducción de la palabra española **pariente**. En inglés **parent** significa tanto "padre" como "madre".

parir 1 VI to give birth; *Esp Fam* **poner algo/a algn a p.** *Br* to slag sth/sb off, *US* to badmouth sth/sb
  2 VT to give birth to

París N Paris

parking (*pl* **parkings**) NM *Br* car park, *US* parking lot

parlamentario, -a 1 ADJ parliamentary
  2 NM,F member of parliament

parlamento NM parliament

parlanchín, -ina ADJ *Fam* talkative, chatty

paro NM (**a**) *(huelga)* strike, stoppage (**b**) *Esp (desempleo)* unemployment; **estar en p.** to be unemployed; **cobrar el p.** to receive unemployment benefit, *Br* to be on the dole

parodia NF parody

parodiar [43] VT to parody

parpadear VI *(ojos)* to blink; *Fig (luz)* to flicker

parpadeo NM *(de ojos)* blinking; *Fig (de luz)* flickering

párpado NM eyelid

parque NM (**a**) *(zona)* park; **p. de atracciones** funfair; **p. eólico** wind farm; **p. infantil** playground; **p. nacional/natural** national park/ nature reserve; **p. temático** theme park (**b**) *(de niños)* playpen (**c**) *(vehículos)* fleet; **p. móvil** fleet

parqué NM parquet

parqueadero NM *Col, Ecuad, Pan, Ven Br* car park, *US* parking lot

parquear VT *Bol, Carib, Col* to park

parquet [par'ke] (*pl* **parquets**) NM *(suelo)* parquet (floor)

parquímetro NM *Aut* parking meter

parra NF grapevine

párrafo NM paragraph

parranda NF *Fam* spree

parricidio NM parricide

parrilla NF (**a**) *Culin* grill; **pescado a la p.** grilled fish (**b**) *Téc* grate (**c**) *Aut & Dep* starting grid

parrillada NF mixed grill

párroco NM parish priest

parronal NM *Chile* vineyard

parroquia NF parish; *(iglesia)* parish church

parroquiano, -a NM,F *(regular)* customer

parsimonia NF phlegm, calmness

parte 1 NF (**a**) *(sección)* part (**b**) *(en una repartición)* share (**c**) *(lugar)* place, spot; **en** *o* **por todas partes** everywhere; **se fue por otra p.** he went another way (**d**) *Der* party (**e**) *(bando)* side; **estoy de tu p.** I'm on your side (**f**) *Euf* **partes** *(genitales)* private parts (**g**) *(locuciones)* **por mi p.** as far as I am concerned; **de p. de …** on behalf of …; *Tel* **¿de p. de quién?** who's calling?; **en gran p.** to a large extent; **en p.** partly; **la mayor p.** the majority; **por otra p.** on the other hand; **tomar p. en** to take part in
  2 NM *(informe)* report

partición NF *(reparto)* division; *(de herencia, territorio)* partitioning

participación NF (**a**) *(colaboración, intervención)* participation (**b**) *Fin (acción)* share; **p. en los beneficios** profit-sharing (**c**) *(en lotería)* part of a lottery ticket (**d**) *(notificación)* notice, notification

participante 1 ADJ participating
  2 NMF participant

participar 1 VI (**a**) *(colaborar, intervenir)* to take part, to participate (**en** in) (**b**) *Fin* to have a share (**en** in) (**c**) *(compartir)* **p. de** to share
  2 VT *(notificar)* to notify

partícipe NMF **hacer p. de algo a algn** *(notificar)* to notify sb of sth; *(compartir)* to share sth with sb

participio NM *Ling* participle

partícula NF particle

particular 1 ADJ (**a**) *(concreto)* particular (**b**) *(privado)* private, personal (**c**) *(raro)* peculiar
  2 NMF *(individuo)* private individual
  3 NM *(asunto)* subject, matter

particularidad NF special feature

partida NF (**a**) *(salida)* departure (**b**) *Com (remesa)* batch, consignment (**c**) *(juego)* game (**d**) *Fin (entrada)* item (**e**) *Der (certificado)* certificate; **p. de nacimiento** birth certificate

partidario, -a 1 ADJ **ser/no ser p. de algo** to be for/against sth
  2 NM,F supporter, follower; **es p. del aborto** he is in favour of abortion

partidista ADJ biased, partisan

partido NM (**a**) *Pol* party (**b**) *Dep* game, *Br* match; **p. amistoso** friendly; **p. de vuelta** return game *o Br* match (**c**) *(provecho)* advantage; **sacar p. de** to profit from (**d**) *Der (distrito)* district (**e**) **tomar p. por** to side with (**f**) **ser un buen p.** to be a good catch

partir 1 VT to break; *(dividir)* to split, to divide; *(cortar)* to cut; **p. a algn por la mitad** to mess things up for sb

2 VI (**a**) *(marcharse)* to leave, to set out o off (**b**) **a p. de** from
3 partirse VPR to split (up), to break (up); *Fam* **partirse de risa** to split one's sides laughing

partisano, -a NM,F partisan

partitura NF *Mús* score

parto NM childbirth, labour; **estar de p.** to be in labour

parvulario NM nursery school, kindergarten

párvulo, -a NM,F *Br* infant, *US* preschooler

pasa NF raisin; **p. de Corinto** currant

pasable ADJ passable, tolerable

pasaboca NM *Col* snack, appetizer

pasacalle NM (**a**) *(procesión)* street procession *(during town festival)* (**b**) *(banderola)* Col, Urug banner *(hung across street)*

pasada NF (**a**) **de p.** in passing (**b**) *(jugarreta)* dirty trick (**c**) *Esp Fam* **es una p.** *(una barbaridad)* it's way over the top

pasadizo NM passage

pasado, -a 1 ADJ (**a**) *(último)* last; **el año/lunes p.** last year/Monday (**b**) *(anticuado)* dated, old-fashioned; **p. (de moda)** out of date o fashion (**c**) *(alimento)* bad (**d**) *Culin* cooked; **lo quiero muy p.** I want it well done (**e**) **p. mañana** the day after tomorrow
2 NM past

pasador NM (**a**) *(para el pelo) Br* (hair) slide, *US* barrette (**b**) *(pestillo)* bolt

pasaje NM (**a**) *(calle)* passage (**b**) *(pasajeros)* passengers (**c**) *(billete)* ticket

pasajero, -a 1 ADJ passing, temporary; **aventura pasajera** fling
2 NM,F passenger

pasamanos NM INV *(barra)* handrail; *(de escalera)* banister, bannister

pasamontañas NM INV balaclava

pasapalo NM *Ven* snack, appetizer

pasaporte NM passport

pasapurés NM INV *Culin* potato masher

pasar 1 VT (**a**) *(dar, transmitir)* to pass; *(noticia, aviso)* to pass on; *(página)* to turn; **p. algo** *Esp* **a** o *Am* **en limpio** to make a fair copy of sth (**b**) *(tiempo)* to spend, to pass; **p. el rato** to kill time (**c**) *(experimentar)* to go through, to experience; **p. hambre** to go hungry; **pasarlo bien** to enjoy oneself, to have a good time; **pasarlo mal** to have a hard time of it (**d**) *(cruzar)* (río, calle) to cross; *(barrera)* to pass through o over; *(límite)* to go beyond (**e**) *(trasladar)* **p. algo a** to move sth to (**f**) *(consentir)* **p. algo a algn** to let sb get away with sth (**g**) *(examen)* to pass (**h**) *Cin* to run, to show
2 VI (**a**) *(ir, moverse)* to pass; **¿ha pasado el autobús?** has the bus gone by?; **ha pasado un hombre corriendo** a man has ran past; **p. de largo** to go by (without stopping); **el tren pasa por Burgos** the train goes via Burgos; **pasa por casa mañana** come round to my house tomorrow

(**b**) **p. a** *(continuar)* to go on to; **p. a ser** to become
(**c**) *(entrar)* to come in
(**d**) *(tiempo)* to pass, to go by
(**e**) *(suceder)* to happen; **¿qué pasa aquí?** what's going on here?; **¿qué te pasa?** what's the matter?; **pase lo que pase** whatever happens, come what may; *Fam* **¿qué pasa?** *(saludo)* how are you?
(**f**) **p. sin** to do without; *Fam* **paso de tí** I couldn't care less about you; *Fam* **yo paso** count me out
3 pasarse VPR (**a**) **se me pasó la ocasión** I missed my chance; **se le pasó llamarme** he forgot to phone me (**b**) *(gastar)* (tiempo) to spend, to pass; **pasárselo bien/mal** to have a good/bad time (**c**) *(comida)* to go off (**d**) *Fam (excederse)* to go too far; **no te pases** don't overdo it (**e**) **pásate por mi casa** call round at my place

pasarela NF *(puente)* footbridge; *(de barco)* gangway; *(de moda) Br* catwalk, *US* runway

pasatiempo NM pastime, hobby

pascua NF (**a**) *(de los cristianos)* Easter; *(de los judíos)* Passover (**b**) **Pascuas** *(Navidad)* Christmas; **¡felices Pascuas!** Merry Christmas!

pascualina NF *RP, Ven* = tart with spinach and hard-boiled egg

pase NM (**a**) *(permiso)* pass, permit (**b**) *Esp (proyección)* showing

pasear 1 VI to go for a walk, to take a walk
2 VT (**a**) *(persona)* to take for a walk; *(perro)* to walk (**b**) *Fig (exhibir)* to show off
3 pasearse VPR to go for a walk

paseíllo NM *Taurom* opening parade

paseo NM (**a**) *(a pie)* walk; *(en bicicleta, caballo)* ride; *(en coche)* drive; **dar un p.** to go for a walk/ a ride (**b**) *(avenida)* avenue

pasillo NM corridor; *Av* **p. aéreo** air corridor

pasión NF passion

pasional ADJ passionate; **crimen p.** crime of passion

pasividad NF passivity, passiveness

pasivo, -a 1 ADJ passive; *(inactivo)* inactive
2 NM *Com* liabilities

pasmado, -a ADJ *(asombrado)* astounded, amazed; *(atontado)* flabbergasted; **dejar p.** to astonish; **quedarse p.** to be amazed

pasmo NM astonishment, amazement

paso¹, -a ADJ **ciruela pasa** prune; **uva pasa** raisin

paso² NM (**a**) *(con el pie)* step; *(modo de andar)* gait, walk; *(ruido al andar)* footstep; *Mil* **llevar el p.** to keep in step; *Fig* **a dos pasos** a short distance away; *Fig* **seguir los pasos de algn** to follow in sb's footsteps (**b**) *(camino)* passage, way; **abrirse p.** to force one's way through; *Aut* **ceda el p.** *(en letrero) Br* give way, *US* yield; **prohibido el p.** *(en letrero)* no entry; **p. de cebra** *Br* zebra crossing, = pedestrian crossing marked with black and white lines;

p. elevado *Br* flyover, *US* overpass; **p. a nivel** *Br* level crossing, *US* grade crossing; **p. peatonal** *o* **de peatones** *Br* pedestrian crossing, *US* crosswalk; **p. subterráneo** *(para peatones)* *Br* subway, *US* underpass; *(para coches)* underpass (**c**) *(acción)* passing; **a su p. por la ciudad** when he was in town; **el p. del tiempo** the passage of time; **estar de p.** to be just passing through

pasodoble NM paso doble

pasota ADJ *Esp Fam* apathetic

pasta NF (**a**) *(masa)* paste; **p. de dientes** *o* **dentífrica** toothpaste (**b**) *(de pasteles)* dough; *(italiana)* pasta (**c**) *(pastelito)* shortcake *Br* biscuit *o US* cookie (**d**) *Esp Fam (dinero)* dough

pastar VI to graze, to pasture

pastel NM (**a**) *(dulce)* cake; *(de carne, fruta)* pie (**b**) *Arte* pastel (**c**) *Fam* **descubrir el p.** to spill the beans

pastelería NF (**a**) *(tienda)* cake shop, patisserie (**b**) *(repostería)* pastries

pastelero, -a NM,F pastry cook, confectioner

pastiche NM pastiche

pastilla NF (**a**) *Med* tablet, pill; **pastillas para la tos** cough drops (**b**) *(de jabón)* bar (**c**) *Esp Fam* **a toda p.** at top speed, *Br* like the clappers

pastizal NM grazing land, pasture

pasto NM (**a**) *(hierba)* grass (**b**) *(alimento)* fodder; **ser p. de** to fall prey to (**c**) *Am (césped)* lawn, grass

pastor, -a NM,F shepherd; *(mujer)* shepherdess; **perro p.** sheepdog
2 NM (**a**) *Rel* pastor, minister (**b**) *(perro)* **p. alemán** Alsatian

pastoreo NM shepherding

pastoso, -a ADJ *(blando)* pasty; *(arroz)* sticky; **tener la boca pastosa** to have a furry tongue

pata 1 NF leg; *Fig* **patas arriba** upside down; **estirar la p.** to kick the bucket; **mala p.** bad luck; **meter la p.** to put one's foot in it; **p. de gallo** crow's foot
2 NM *Perú Fam (amigo)* pal, *Br* mate, *US* buddy; *(tipo)* guy, *Br* bloke

patada NF *(puntapié)* kick, stamp

patalear VI *(en el aire)* to kick about; *(en el suelo)* to stamp one's feet

pataleo NM *(en el aire)* kicking; *(de rabia)* stamping

patán NM bumpkin, yokel

patata NF *Esp* potato; **patatas fritas** *(de sartén)* *Br* chips, *US* (French) fries; *(de bolsa)* *Br* crisps, *US* (potato) chips

patatús NM INV *Fam* dizzy spell, queer turn

paté NM pâté

patear 1 VT *(pisotear)* to stamp on
2 VI *(patalear)* to stamp one's feet
3 **patearse** VPR *Fam (recorrer)* to tramp; **se pateó toda la ciudad** he tramped *o* traipsed all over town

patena NF paten; *Esp* **limpio** *o* **blanco como una p.** as clean as a new pin

patentar VT to patent

patente 1 NF (**a**) *(autorización)* licence; *(de invención)* patent (**b**) *CSur (matrícula)* *Br* number plate, *US* license plate
2 ADJ *(evidente)* patent, obvious

paternal ADJ paternal, fatherly

paternalista ADJ paternalistic

paternidad NF *(estado)* fatherhood; *Der* paternity

paterno, -a ADJ paternal

patético, -a ADJ (**a**) *(emotivo)* pathetic, moving (**b**) *(ridículo)* pathetic

patíbulo NM scaffold, gallows *sing*

patidifuso, -a ADJ *Fam* dumbfounded, flabbergasted

patilla NF (**a**) *(de gafas)* leg (**b**) **patillas** *(pelo)* sideburns

patín NM (**a**) *(para el pie)* skate; **p. de ruedas/ de hielo** roller-/ice-skate; **p. en línea** rollerblade (**b**) *(patinete)* scooter (**c**) *Esp (embarcación)* pedal boat

patinaje NM skating; **p. artístico** figure skating; **p. sobre hielo/ruedas** ice-/roller-skating

patinar VI (**a**) *(sobre hielo)* to skate; *(sobre ruedas)* to roller-skate; *(con patines en línea)* to roller-blade (**b**) *(deslizarse)* to slide; *(resbalar)* to slip; *(vehículo)* to skid (**c**) *Fam (equivocarse)* to put one's foot in it, to slip up

patinazo NM (**a**) *(de vehículo)* skid (**b**) *Fam (equivocación)* blunder, boob

patinete NM scooter

patio NM (**a**) *(de una casa)* yard, patio; *(de recreo)* playground (**b**) *Esp Teatro & Cin* **p. de butacas** stalls

pato NM duck; *Fam* **pagar el p.** *Br* to carry the can, *US* to pick up the tab

patógeno, -a ADJ pathogenic

patología NF pathology

patológico, -a ADJ pathological

patoso, -a ADJ *Esp* clumsy

patota NF *Perú, RP (de gamberros)* street gang

patraña NF absurd story

patria NF fatherland, native country; **madre p.** motherland; **p. chica** one's home town/region

patriarca NM patriarch

patrimonio NM *(de empresa)* assets; *(propios)* estate, assets; *(herencia)* inheritance

patriota NMF patriot

patriótico, -a ADJ patriotic

patriotismo NM patriotism

patrocinador, -a 1 ADJ sponsoring
2 NM,F sponsor

patrocinar VT to sponsor

patrocinio NM sponsorship, patronage

patrón, -ona 1 NM,F (**a**) *(jefe)* boss (**b**) *Esp (de pensión)* *(hombre)* landlord; *(mujer)* landlady (**c**) *Rel* patron saint

2 NM (a) (modelo) pattern (b) (medida) standard

patronal 1 ADJ employers'; **cierre p.** lockout; **clase p.** managerial class
2 NF (dirección) management

patronato NM trust

patronazgo NM patronage

patrono, -a NM,F (a) (de empresa) (encargado) boss; (empresario) employer (b) Rel patron saint

patrulla NF patrol; **estar de p.** to be on patrol; **coche p.** patrol car

patrullar 1 VT to patrol
2 VI to be on patrol

patrullero NM (a) (barco) patrol boat (b) CSur (auto) police (patrol) car, US cruiser

paulatino, -a ADJ gradual

paupérrimo, -a ADJ extremely poor, poverty-stricken

pausa NF pause, break; Mús rest

pausado, -a ADJ unhurried, calm

pauta NF guidelines

pava NF (a) CAm (flequillo) Br fringe, US bangs (b) Chile, Perú (broma) coarse o tasteless joke (c) Arg (hervidor) kettle

pavada NF RP (a) Fam (estupidez) **decir una pavada** to say something stupid; **decir pavadas** to talk nonsense (b) (cosa sin importancia) silly little thing

pavesa NF ash

pavimentar VT (carretera) to surface; (acera) to pave; (suelo) to floor

pavimento NM (de carretera) road (surface), US pavement; (de acera) paving; (de habitación) flooring

pavo NM (a) (ave) turkey; Fam **no ser moco de p.** to be nothing to scoff at; Fam **estar en la edad del p.** to be growing up (b) Fam (tonto) twit

pavonearse VPR Fam to show off, to strut

pavoneo NM Fam showing off, strutting

pavor NM terror, dread

pay (pl **pays**) NM Chile, Méx, Ven pie

payaso NM clown; **hacer el p.** to act the clown

payés, -esa NM,F = Catalan or Balearic peasant

payo, -a NM,F non-gipsy person

paz NF peace; (sosiego) peacefulness; Fam **¡déjame en p.!** leave me alone!; **hacer las paces** to make (it) up

pazguato, -a ADJ (a) (estúpido) silly, stupid (b) (mojigato) prudish

pazo NM = Galician mansion, belonging to noble family

PC NM (abr **personal computer**) PC

pe NF Fam **de pe a pa** from A to Z

peaje NM toll; **autopista de p.** Br toll motorway, US turnpike

peatón NM pedestrian

peatonal ADJ pedestrian; **calle p.** pedestrian street

peca NF freckle

pecado NM Rel sin; **p. capital** o **mortal** deadly sin

pecador, -a NM,F sinner

pecaminoso, -a ADJ sinful

pecar [44] VI to sin; Fig **p. por defecto** to fall short of the mark

pecera NF fish bowl, fish tank

pecho NM (a) Anat chest; (de mujer) breast, bust; (de animal) breast; **dar el p. (a un bebé)** to breast-feed (a baby); Fig **tomar(se) algo a p.** to take sth to heart (b) Am (en natación) breaststroke; **nadar p.** to do the breaststroke

pechuga NF (a) (de ave) breast (b) Fam (de mujer) bust

pecoso, -a ADJ freckly

pectoral ADJ pectoral, chest

peculiar ADJ (raro) peculiar; (característico) characteristic

peculiaridad NF (a) (cualidad) uniqueness (b) (detalle) particular feature o characteristic

pedagogía NF pedagogy

pedagógico, -a ADJ pedagogical

pedagogo, -a NM,F (especialista) educationalist; (profesor) teacher, educator

pedal NM pedal

pedalear VI to pedal

pedante 1 ADJ pretentious
2 NMF pretentious person

pedantería NF (cualidad) pretentiousness; (dicho, hecho) piece of pretentiousness

pedazo NM piece, bit; **a pedazos** in pieces; **caerse a pedazos** to fall apart o to pieces; **hacer pedazos** to break o tear to pieces, to smash (up); Fam **¡qué p. de coche!** what a terrific car!

pederasta NM pederast

pedernal NM flint

pedestal NM pedestal

pediatra NMF paediatrician

pediatría NF paediatrics sing

pedicura NF pedicure

pedido NM (a) Com order; **hacer un p. a** to place an order with (b) (petición) request

pedigrí NM pedigree

pedir [6] **1** VT (a) (solicitar) to ask for; **p. algo a algn** to ask sb for sth; **p. a algn que haga algo** to ask sb to do sth; **p. prestado** to borrow; Fig **p. cuentas** to ask for an explanation (b) (en bares, restaurantes) to order
2 VI (a) (mendigar) to beg (b) (rezar) **p. por ...** to pray for ...

pedo NM (a) (ventosidad) fart; **tirarse un p.** to fart (b) Fam (borrachera) bender

pedrada NF **a pedradas** by stoning; **rompió la ventana de una p.** he smashed the window with a stone

pedrea NF *Esp (en lotería)* small prizes

pedregoso, -a ADJ stony, rocky

pedrería NF precious stones, gems

pedrisco NM hailstorm

pega NF (a) *Fam (obstáculo)* difficulty, hitch; **poner pegas (a)** to find problems (with) (b) **de p.** *(falso)* false, fake

pegadizo, -a ADJ catchy

pegado, -a ADJ (a) *(adherido)* stuck (b) *(quemado)* burnt

pegajoso, -a ADJ *(pegadizo)* sticky; *Fig (persona)* tiresome, hard to get rid of

pegamento NM glue

pegar [42] **1** VT (a) *(adherir)* to stick; *(con pegamento)* to glue; *(coser)* to sew on; *Fam* **no pegó ojo** he didn't sleep a wink; **p. fuego a** to set fire to (b) *(golpear)* to hit (c) **p. un grito** to shout; **p. un salto** to jump (d) *Fam (contagiar)* to give; **me ha pegado sus manías** I've caught his bad habits (e) *(arrimar)* **p. algo a** o **contra algo** to put o place sth against sth
2 VI (a) *(adherirse)* to stick (b) *(armonizar)* to match, to go; **el azul no pega con el verde** blue and green don't go together o don't match; *Fig* **ella no pegaría aquí** she wouldn't fit in here (c) *(sol)* to beat down
3 **pegarse** VPR (a) *(adherirse)* to stick; *(pelearse)* to fight (b) *Fam (darse)* to have, to get; **pegarse un tiro** to shoot oneself (c) *(comida)* to get burnt; **se me ha pegado el sol** I've got a touch of the sun (d) *Esp Fam* **pegársela a algn** to trick o deceive sb (e) *(arrimarse)* to get close (f) *Fam Fig* to stick (g) *Med (enfermedad)* to be catching o contagious; *Fig (melodía)* to be catchy

pegatina NF *Esp* sticker

peinado NM hairstyle; *Fam* hairdo

peinar 1 VT (a) *(pelo)* to comb (b) *(registrar)* to comb
2 **peinarse** VPR to comb one's hair

peine NM comb

peineta NF = ornamental comb worn in hair

p.ej. *(abr por ejemplo)* e.g

peladilla NF sugared almond

pelado, -a 1 ADJ (a) *(cabeza)* shorn; *(piel, fruta)* peeled; *(terreno)* bare (b) *Fam* **saqué un cinco p.** *(en escuela)* I just scraped a pass; **a grito p.** shouting and bawling (c) *Fam (arruinado)* broke, *Br* skint (d) *(desvergonzado)* impudent, insolent
2 NM *Fam* haircut
3 NM,F (a) *Andes Fam (niño, adolescente)* kid (b) *CAm, Méx Fam (persona humilde)* common person, *Br* pleb, *Br* oik

pelagatos NMF INV *Fam Pey* poor devil, nobody

pelaje NM *(de gato, oso, conejo)* fur; *(de perro, caballo)* coat

pelambrera NF *Fam* long thick hair

pelapatatas NM INV potato peeler

pelar 1 VT (a) *Fam (cortar el pelo a)* to cut the hair of (b) *(fruta, patata)* to peel; *Fam* **hace un**

frío que pela it's brass monkey weather
2 VI *(despellejar)* to peel
3 **pelarse** VPR *Fam* (a) *(cortarse el pelo)* to get one's hair cut (b) **corre que se las pela** she runs like the wind

peldaño NM step; *(de escalera de mano)* rung

pelea NF fight; *(riña)* row, quarrel; **buscar p.** to look for trouble

peleado, -a ADJ **estar p. (con algn)** not to be on speaking terms (with sb)

pelear 1 VI to fight; *(reñir)* to quarrel
2 **pelearse** VPR (a) *(luchar)* to fight; *(reñir)* to quarrel (b) *(enemistarse)* to fall out

pelele NM (a) *Fam Pey (persona)* puppet (b) *(muñeco)* guy, straw doll

peleón, -ona ADJ (a) *(persona)* quarrelsome, aggressive (b) *(vino)* cheap

peletería NF furrier's; *(tienda)* fur shop

peletero, -a NM,F furrier

peliagudo, -a ADJ difficult, tricky

pelícano NM pelican

película NF (a) *Cin* movie, *Br* film; **p. de miedo** o **terror** horror movie o *Br* film; **p. del Oeste** Western; *Fam* **de p.** fabulous (b) *Fot* film

peligrar VI to be in danger, to be threatened; **hacer p.** to endanger, to jeopardize

peligro NM danger; *(riesgo)* risk; **con p. de ...** at the risk of ...; **correr (el) p. de ...** to run the risk of ...; **poner en p.** to endanger

peligroso, -a ADJ dangerous, risky

pelirrojo, -a 1 ADJ red-haired; *(anaranjado)* ginger-haired
2 NM,F redhead

pellejo NM (a) *(piel)* skin (b) *(odre)* wineskin (c) *Fam* **arriesgar** o **jugarse el p.** to risk one's neck

pelliza NF fur jacket

pellizcar [44] VT to pinch, to nip

pellizco NM pinch, nip

pelma NMF, **pelmazo, -a** NM,F *Esp (persona)* bore, drag

pelo NM (a) *(de persona)* hair; **cortarse el p.** *(uno mismo)* to cut one's hair; *(en la peluquería)* to have one's hair cut; *Fig* **no tiene ni un p. de tonto** he's no fool; *Fig* **no tener pelos en la lengua** to be very outspoken; *Fig* **tomar el p. a algn** to pull sb's leg, *Br* to take the mickey out of sb; *Fam* **con pelos y señales** in full detail; *Fam* **por los pelos** by the skin of one's teeth; *Fam* **me puso el p. de punta** it gave me the creeps (b) *(de animal)* fur, coat, hair (c) *Tex (de una tela)* nap, pile (d) *(cerda)* bristle

pelón, -ona ADJ *(sin pelo)* bald

pelota 1 NF (a) *(para jugar)* ball; **cortarse el p.** to give tit for tat; **p. vasca** pelota (b) *Fam (cabeza)* nut (c) *Esp* **hacer la p. a algn** to toady to sb, to butter sb up (d) *muy Fam* **pelotas** *(testículos)* balls; **en pelotas** *Br* starkers, *US* butt-naked
2 NMF *Esp Fam (persona)* crawler

pelotari NM pelota player

peloteo NM *Ten* knock-up

pelotilla NF *Esp Fam* **hacer la p. (a algn)** to fawn (on sb)

pelotillero, -a NM,F *Esp Fam* crawler

pelotón NM (a) *Mil* squad (b) *Fam (grupo)* small crowd, bunch; *(en ciclismo)* pack (c) *(amasijo)* bundle

pelotudo, -a ADJ *RP Fam* (a) *(estúpido)* damn stupid (b) *(grande)* massive

peluca NF wig

peluche NM **(osito de) p.** teddy bear

peludo, -a ADJ hairy, furry

peluquería NF hairdresser's (shop)

peluquero, -a NM,F hairdresser

peluquín NM toupee

pelusa NF *(de tela)* fluff; *(de polvo)* ball of fluff

pelvis NF INV pelvis

pena NF (a) *(tristeza)* grief, sorrow; *Fig* **me da p. de ella** I feel sorry for her; **¡qué p.!** what a pity! (b) *(dificultad)* hardships *pl,* trouble; **no merece** o **vale la p. (ir)** it's not worth while (going); **a duras penas** with great difficulty (c) *(castigo)* punishment, penalty; **p. de muerte** o **capital** death penalty (d) *CAm, Carib, Col, Méx (vergüenza)* embarrassment; **me da p.** I'm embarrassed about it

penacho NM (a) *(de ave)* crest, tuft (b) *Mil (de plumas)* plume

penal 1 ADJ penal; *Der* **código p.** penal code
2 NM prison, jail

penalidades NFPL hardships, troubles

penalización NF penalization; *Dep* penalty

penalizar [40] VT to penalize

penalti NM *Dep* penalty; *Esp Fam* **casarse de p.** to have a shotgun wedding

penar VI to be in torment, to suffer

pendejo, -a NM,F (a) *Am muy Fam (tonto)* jerk, *Br* tosser (b) *RP Fam Pey (adolescente)* spotty teenager

pendenciero, -a ADJ quarrelsome, argumentative

pendiente 1 ADJ (a) *(por resolver)* pending; *Educ* **asignatura p.** failed subject; *Com* **p. de pago** unpaid (b) **estar p. de** *(esperar)* to be waiting for; *(vigilar)* to be on the lookout for (c) *(colgante)* hanging **(de** from)
2 NM *Esp* earring
3 NF slope; *(de tejado)* pitch

pendón NM (a) *(bandera)* banner (b) *Pey (mujer)* floozy; *(hombre)* layabout, good-for-nothing

péndulo NM pendulum

pene NM penis

penetración NF (a) *(introducción)* penetration (b) *(perspicacia)* insight, perception

penetrante ADJ penetrating; *(frío, voz)* piercing

penetrar 1 VT to penetrate; **p. un misterio** to get to the bottom of a mystery
2 VI *(entrar)* to go o get **(en** in)

penicilina NF penicillin

península NF peninsula

peninsular ADJ peninsular

penique NM penny; **peniques** pence

penitencia NF penance

penitenciaría NF prison

penitenciario, -a ADJ penitentiary, prison

penitente NMF penitent

penoso, -a ADJ (a) *(lamentable)* sorry, distressing (b) *(laborioso)* laborious, difficult (c) *CAm, Carib, Col, Méx (embarazoso)* embarrassing (d) *CAm, Carib, Col, Méx (persona)* shy

pensado, -a ADJ **bien p., ...** on reflection, ...; **en el momento menos p.** when least expected; **mal p.** twisted; **tener algo p.** to have sth planned, to have sth in mind; **tengo p. ir** I intend to go

pensador, -a NM,F thinker

pensamiento NM (a) *(facultad, idea)* thought (b) *(máxima)* saying, motto (c) *Bot* pansy

pensar [1] 1 VI to think **(en** o about; **sobre** about o over); *Fig* **sin p.** *(con precipitación)* without thinking; *(involuntariamente)* involuntarily
2 VT (a) *(opinar, creer)* to think **(de** of); *(considerar)* to think over o about; **piénsalo bien** think it over; *Fam* **¡ni pensarlo!** not on your life! (b) *(proponerse)* to intend; **pienso quedarme** I plan to stay (c) *(idear)* to think up

pensativo, -a ADJ pensive, thoughtful

pensión NF (a) *(residencia)* boarding house; *(hotel)* guesthouse; **media p.** half board; **p. completa** full board (b) *(paga)* pension, allowance; **p. vitalicia** life annuity

pensionista NMF *(jubilado)* pensioner

pentágono NM pentagon

pentagrama NM staff, stave

penthouse NM *CSur, Ven* penthouse

penúltimo, -a ADJ & NM,F next to the last, penultimate

penumbra NF penumbra, half-light

penuria NF scarcity, shortage

peña NF (a) *(roca)* rock, crag (b) *(de amigos)* club (c) *Esp Fam (gente)* people

peñasco NM rock, crag

peñón NM rock; **el P. de Gibraltar** the Rock of Gibraltar

peón NM (a) *(obrero)* unskilled labourer; **p. agrícola** farmhand (b) *(en ajedrez)* pawn

peonada NF day's work

peonza NF (spinning) top

peor 1 ADJ (a) *(comparativo)* worse (b) *(superlativo)* worst; **en el p. de los casos** if the worst comes to the worst; **lo p. es que** the worst of it is that
2 ADV (a) *(comparativo)* worse; **¡p. para mí/ti/** *etc.***!** too bad! (b) *(superlativo)* worst

pepa NF (**a**) *Am salvo RP (pepita)* pip; *(hueso)* stone (**b**) *Méx, RP, Ven muy Fam (vulva)* pussy (**c**) *Ven (en la piel)* blackhead

pepenador, -a *CAm, Méx* NM,F scavenger *(on rubbish tip)*

pepián NM *Andes, CAm, Méx* = **pipián**

pepinillo NM gherkin

pepino NM cucumber; *Fam* **me importa un p.** I don't give a hoot

pepita NF *(de fruta)* pip, seed; *(de metal)* nugget

pepito NM *Esp (de carne)* grilled meat sandwich

pepitoria NF fricassee; **pollo en p.** fricassee of chicken

peque NMF *Fam (niño)* kid

pequeño, -a 1 ADJ small, little; *(bajo)* short
  2 NM,F child; **de p.** as a child

Pequín N Peking

pera NF (**a**) *Bot* pear; **p. de agua** juicy pear (**b**) *CSur Fam (mentón)* chin

peral NM pear tree

percance NM mishap, setback

percatarse VPR **p. de** to realize

percebe NM (**a**) *(marisco)* goose barnacle (**b**) *Fam (persona)* twit

percepción NF perception

perceptible ADJ perceptible

percha NF *(colgador)* (coat) hanger; *(de gallina)* perch

perchero NM coat rack

percibir VT (**a**) *(notar)* to perceive, to notice (**b**) *(cobrar)* to receive

percusión NF percussion

percutor NM hammer, firing pin

perdedor, -a 1 ADJ losing
  2 NM,F loser

perder [3] 1 VT (**a**) *(dinero, objeto, amigo)* to lose (**b**) *(tren, vuelo)* to miss; *(tiempo)* to waste; *(oportunidad)* to miss (**c**) *(pervertir)* to be the ruin o downfall of
  2 VI to lose; **echar (algo) a p.** to spoil (sth); **echarse a p.** to be spoilt; **salir perdiendo** to come off worst
  3 **perderse** VPR (**a**) *(extraviarse) (persona)* to get lost; **se me ha perdido la llave** I've lost my key; **no te lo pierdas** don't miss it (**b**) *(pervertirse)* to go to rack and ruin

perdición NF undoing, downfall

pérdida NF (**a**) *(de objeto, persona, peso)* loss; *Esp* **no tiene p.** you can't miss it (**b**) *(de tiempo, esfuerzos)* waste (**c**) *Mil* **pérdidas** losses

perdido, -a ADJ (**a**) *(extraviado)* lost (**b**) *Fam (sucio)* filthy (**c**) *Fam* **loco p.** mad as a hatter (**d**) **estar p. por algn** *(enamorado)* to be crazy about sb (**e**) *(acabado)* finished; **¡estoy p.!** I'm a goner!

perdigón NM pellet

perdiguero, -a ADJ partridge-hunting; **perro p.** setter

perdiz NF partridge

perdón NM pardon, forgiveness; **¡p.!** sorry!; **pedir p.** to apologize

perdonar VT (**a**) *(remitir)* to forgive (**b**) **¡perdone!** sorry!; **perdone que le moleste** sorry to bother you (**c**) *(eximir)* to pardon; **perdonarle la vida a algn** to spare sb's life; **p. una deuda** to write off a debt

perdurable ADJ (**a**) *(eterno)* everlasting (**b**) *(duradero)* durable, long-lasting

perdurar VI (**a**) *(durar)* to endure, to last (**b**) *(persistir)* to persist, to continue to exist

perecedero, -a ADJ perishable; **artículos perecederos** perishables

perecer [33] VI to perish, to die

peregrinación NF, **peregrinaje** NM pilgrimage

peregrino, -a 1 NM,F pilgrim
  2 ADJ **ideas peregrinas** crazy ideas

perejil NM parsley

perenne ADJ perennial, everlasting

perentorio, -a ADJ peremptory, urgent

pereza NF laziness, idleness

perezoso, -a ADJ *(vago)* lazy, idle

perfección NF perfection; **a la p.** to perfection

perfeccionamiento NM (**a**) *(acción)* perfecting (**b**) *(mejora)* improvement

perfeccionar VT to perfect; *(mejorar)* to improve, to make better

perfeccionista ADJ & NMF perfectionist

perfectamente ADV perfectly; **¡p.!** *(de acuerdo)* agreed!, all right!

perfecto, -a ADJ perfect

perfidia NF perfidy, treachery

perfil NM (**a**) *(físico, psicológico)* profile; *(contorno)* outline, contour; **de p.** in profile (**b**) *Geom* cross-section

perfilar 1 VT *(dar forma a)* to shape, to outline
  2 **perfilarse** VPR *(tomar forma)* to take shape

perforación NF perforation; *Min* drilling, boring; *Inform (de tarjetas)* punching

perforadora NF *(para papel)* punch; *(herramienta)* drill

perforar VT to perforate; *(con taladro)* to drill, to bore

perfumar 1 VT to perfume
  2 **perfumarse** VPR to put on perfume

perfume NM perfume, scent

perfumería NF *(tienda, arte)* perfumery

pergamino NM parchment

pérgola NF pergola

pericia NF expertise, skill

periferia NF periphery; *(alrededores)* outskirts

periférico, -a 1 ADJ peripheral
  2 NM (**a**) *Inform* peripheral (**b**) *CAm, Méx (carretera) Br* ring road, *US* beltway

perífrasis NF INV *Ling* **p. verbal** compound verb

perilla NF *(barba)* goatee; *Fam* **venir de p.** o **perillas** to be just the right thing

perímetro NM perimeter

periódico, -a 1 NM newspaper
2 ADJ periodic(al); *Quím* **tabla periódica** periodic table

periodismo NM journalism

periodista NMF journalist, reporter

periodo, período NM period

peripecia NF incident, adventure

periplo NM voyage, tour

periquete NM *Fam* **en un p.** in a jiffy

periquito NM budgerigar; *Fam* budgie

periscopio NM periscope

peritaje NM *(estudios)* technical studies

perito, -a NM,F technician, expert; **p. industrial/agrónomo** ≃ industrial/agricultural expert

peritonitis NF INV *Med* peritonitis

perjudicar [44] VT to harm, to injure; *(intereses)* to prejudice

perjudicial ADJ prejudicial, harmful

perjuicio NM harm, damage; **en p.** de to the detriment of; **sin p.** de without prejudice to

perjurar VI to commit perjury

perjurio NM perjury

perla NF pearl; *Fig (persona)* gem, jewel; *Fam* **me viene de perlas** it's just the ticket

permanecer [33] VI to remain, to stay

permanencia NF (a) *(inmutabilidad)* permanence (b) *(estancia)* stay

permanente 1 ADJ permanent
2 NF *(de pelo)* permanent wave, perm; **hacerse la p.** to have one's hair permed

permisivo, -a ADJ permissive

permiso NM (a) *(autorización)* permission (b) *(licencia)* licence, permit; **p. de conducción** o **de conducir** *Br* driving licence, *US* driver's license; **p. de residencia/trabajo** residence/work permit (c) *Mil* leave; **estar de p.** to be on leave

permitir 1 VT to permit, to allow; **¿me permite?** may I?
2 **permitirse** VPR (a) *(uno mismo)* to allow oneself; **me permito recordarle que** let me remind you that (b) *(económicamente)* **no puedo permitírmelo** I can't afford it

permutar VT to exchange

pernicioso, -a ADJ pernicious

pernil NM *(de pantalón)* leg; *(jamón)* leg of pork

pernocta NF *Mil (pase de)* **p.** overnight pass

pernoctar VI to stay overnight

pero 1 CONJ but; **p., ¿qué pasa aquí?** now, what's going on here?
2 NM objection

perogrullada NF truism, platitude

perol NM large saucepan, pot

perorata NF boring speech

perpendicular ADJ & NF perpendicular

perpetrar VT to perpetrate, to commit

perpetuar [30] VT to perpetuate

perpetuo, -a ADJ perpetual, everlasting; *Der* **cadena perpetua** life imprisonment

perplejidad NF perplexity, bewilderment

perplejo, -a ADJ perplexed, bewildered

perra NF (a) *(animal)* bitch (b) *Esp Fam (dinero)* penny; **estar sin una p.** to be broke

perrera NF kennel, kennels

perrería NF *Fam* dirty trick

perro, -a 1 NM dog; *Fam* **un día de perros** a lousy day; *Fam* **vida de perros** dog's life; *Culin* **p. caliente** hot dog
2 ADJ *Fam (vago)* lazy

persa 1 ADJ & NMF Persian
2 NM *(idioma)* Persian, Farsi

persecución NF (a) *(seguimiento)* pursuit (b) *(acoso)* persecution

perseguir [6] VT (a) *(seguir)* to pursue, to chase; *(correr trás)* to run after, to follow (b) *(acosar)* to persecute (c) *(tratar de obtener)* to pursue

perseverante ADJ persevering

perseverar VI to persevere, to persist

persiana NF blind

pérsico, -a ADJ Persian; **golfo P.** Persian Gulf

persignarse VPR to cross oneself

persistencia NF persistence

persistente ADJ persistent

persistir VI to persist

persona NF person; **algunas personas** some people; *Fam* **p. mayor** grown-up

personaje NM (a) *Cin, Lit & Teatro* character (b) *(celebridad)* celebrity, important person

personal 1 ADJ personal, private
2 NM (a) *(plantilla)* staff, personnel (b) *Esp Fam (gente)* people

personalidad NF personality

personarse VPR to present oneself, to appear in person

personero, -a NM,F *Am* (a) *(representante)* representative (b) *(portavoz)* spokesperson

personificar [44] VT to personify

perspectiva NF (a) *(en dibujo, punto de vista)* perspective (b) *(futuro, posibilidad)* prospect

perspicacia NF insight, perspicacity

perspicaz ADJ sharp, perspicacious

persuadir VT to persuade; **estar persuadido de que** to be convinced that

persuasión NF persuasion

persuasivo, -a ADJ persuasive, convincing

pertenecer [33] VI to belong (**a** to)

perteneciente ADJ belonging

pertenencia 1 NF *(a un partido etc)* affiliation, membership
2 **pertenencias** NFPL belongings

pértiga NF pole; *Dep* **salto con p.** pole vault

pertinaz ADJ (a) *(persistente)* persistent (b) *(obstinado)* obstinate, stubborn

pertinente ADJ *(adecuado)* appropriate; *(relevante)* pertinent, relevant

perturbación NF disturbance; **p. del orden público** breach of the peace; *Med* **p. mental** mental disorder

perturbado, -a ADJ (mentally) deranged o unbalanced

perturbador, -a 1 ADJ disturbing
2 NM,F unruly person

perturbar VT *(el orden)* to disturb

Perú N Peru

peruano, -a ADJ & NM,F Peruvian

perversión NF perversion

perverso, -a ADJ perverse, evil

pervertir [5] VT to pervert, to corrupt

pervivir VI to survive

pesa NF weight; **levantamiento de pesas** weightlifting

pesadez NF **(a)** *(sensación)* heaviness; *(de estómago)* fullness **(b)** *Fam (fastidio)* drag, pain

pesadilla NF nightmare; **de p.** nightmarish

pesado, -a 1 ADJ **(a)** *(que pesa)* heavy **(b)** *(sueño)* deep **(c)** *(aburrido)* tedious, dull **(d)** *(molesto)* annoying; **ponerse p.** to be a pain
2 NM,F bore

pesadumbre NF grief, affliction

pésame NM condolences, sympathy; **dar el p.** to offer one's condolences; **mi más sentido p.** my deepest sympathy

pesar 1 VT to weigh
2 VI **(a)** *(tener peso)* to weigh; **¿cuánto pesas?** how much do you weigh? **(b)** *(ser pesado)* to be heavy; **pesa mucho** it's very heavy **(c)** *(tener importancia)* **este factor pesa mucho** this is a very important factor **(d)** *(entristecer)* **me pesa tener que hacerlo** I regret having to do it
3 NM **(a)** *(pena)* sorrow, grief **(b)** *(arrepentimiento)* regret; **a su p.** to his regret
4 **a pesar de** LOC PREP in spite of

pesaroso, -a ADJ **(a)** *(triste)* sorrowful, sad **(b)** *(arrepentido)* regretful, sorry

pesca NF fishing; *Fam* **y toda la p.** and all that

pescadería NF fish shop, fishmonger's (shop)

pescadero, -a NM,F fishmonger

pescadilla NF whiting

pescado NM fish

pescador, -a 1 ADJ fishing
2 NM,F *(hombre)* fisherman; *(mujer)* fisherwoman

pescar [44] **1** VI to fish
2 VT **(a)** *(peces)* to fish **(b)** *Fam (coger)* to catch

pescozón NM slap on the neck/head

pescuezo NM *Fam* neck

pese: pese a que LOC ADV in spite of (the fact that)

pesebre NM manger, stall

pesero NM *Méx (vehículo)* collective taxi *(with a fixed rate and that travels a fixed route)* **(b)** *(persona)* collective taxi driver

peseta NF *Antes* peseta

pesetero, -a NM,F *Esp Fam Pey* skinflint

pesimismo NM pessimism

pesimista 1 ADJ pessimistic
2 NMF pessimist

pésimo, -a ADJ very bad, awful, terrible

peso NM **(a)** weight; **al p.** by weight; **p. bruto/ neto** gross/net weight; *Fig* **me quité un p. de encima** it took a load off my mind; **p. mosca/ pesado** *(en boxeo)* flyweight/heavyweight **(b)** *(importancia)* importance; **de p.** *(persona)* influential; *(razón)* convincing **(c)** *(moneda)* peso

pespunte NM backstitch

pesquero, -a 1 ADJ fishing
2 NM fishing boat

pesquisa NF inquiry

pestaña NF **(a)** *(del ojo)* eyelash, lash **(b)** *(en página Web)* tab

pestañear VI to blink; **sin p.** without batting an eyelid

peste NF **(a)** *(hedor)* stench, stink **(b)** *Med* plague; *Hist* **la p. negra** the Black Death **(c)** **decir** o **echar pestes de algn** *Br* to slag sb off, *US* to badmouth sb

pesticida NM pesticide

pestilencia NF stench, stink

pestilente ADJ stinking, foul

pestillo NM bolt, latch

petaca NF **(a)** *(para cigarrillos)* cigarette case; *(para bebidas)* flask **(b)** *Méx (maleta)* suitcase **(c)** *Méx Fam* **petacas** *(nalgas)* buttocks

pétalo NM petal

petanca NF petanque

petardo NM **(a)** *(cohete)* firecracker, *Br* banger; *Mil* petard **(b)** *Fam (persona aburrida)* bore **(c)** *Esp Fam (porro)* joint

petate NM *Mil* luggage

petenera NF *Esp Fam* **salir por peteneras** to go off at a tangent

petición NF request; *Der* petition, plea

petiso, -a ADJ *Andes, RP Fam* short

peto NM **pantalón de p.** dungarees

petrificar [44] VT to petrify

petróleo NM petroleum, oil

> Observa que en el inglés británico **petrol** es un falso amigo y no es la traducción de la palabra española **petróleo**. En inglés británico **petrol** significa "gasolina".

petrolero NM oil tanker

petrolífero, -a ADJ oil; **pozo p.** oil well

petulancia NF arrogance

petulante ADJ arrogant, vain

> Observa que la palabra inglesa **petulant** es un falso amigo y no es la traducción de la palabra española **petulante**. En inglés **petulant** significa "caprichoso".

petunia NF petunia

peúco NM bootee

peyorativo, -a ADJ pejorative, derogatory

pez¹ NM fish; **ella está como p. en el agua** she's in her element; **p. gordo** big shot

pez² NF pitch, tar

pezón NM nipple

pezuña NF hoof

piadoso, -a ADJ (**a**) (*devoto*) pious (**b**) (*compasivo*) compassionate; **mentira piadosa** white lie

pianista NMF pianist, piano player

piano NM piano

piar [29] VI to chirp, to tweet

piara NF herd of pigs

PIB NM *Fin* (*abr* **producto** *Esp* **interior** *o Am* **bruto**) GDP

pibe, -a NM,F *Fam* (**a**) *Esp* (*hombre*) guy; (*mujer*) girl (**b**) *Arg* (*niño*) kid, boy; (*niña*) kid, girl

pica NF (**a**) (*lanza*) pike (**b**) **picas** (*palo de baraja*) spades

picada NF (**a**) *RP* (*tapas*) appetizers, snacks (**b**) *RP Br* mince, *US* ground beef (**c**) *Am* (*de avión*) nose dive; **hacer una p.** to dive

picadero NM riding school

picadillo NM (**a**) (*de carne*) minced meat; (*de verduras*) vegetable salad (**b**) *Chile* (*tapas*) appetizers, snacks

picado, -a 1 ADJ (**a**) *Esp, RP* (*carne*) *Br* minced, *US* ground (**b**) (*fruta*) bad; (*diente*) decayed (**c**) (*mar*) choppy (**d**) **estar p. con** (*en competición*) to be at loggerheads with
2 NM *Esp Av* dive; **caer en p.** to plummet

picador NM *Taurom* mounted bullfighter, picador

picadora NF *Esp, RP* mincer

picadura NF (**a**) (*mordedura*) bite; (*de avispa, abeja*) sting (**b**) (*en fruta*) spot; *Med* (*de viruela*) pockmark; (*en diente*) decay, caries *sing*; (*en metalurgia*) pitting

picajoso, -a ADJ touchy

picante ADJ (**a**) *Culin* hot, spicy (**b**) (*chiste etc*) risqué, spicy

picantería NF *Andes* (*restaurante*) cheap restaurant

picapica NM (**polvos de**) **p.** itching powder

picaporte NM (*aldaba*) door knocker; (*pomo*) door handle

picar [44] 1 VT (**a**) (*de insecto, serpiente*) to bite; (*de avispas, abejas*) to sting; (*barba*) to prick (**b**) (*comer*) (*de aves*) to peck (at); (*de persona*) to nibble, to pick at (**c**) (*de pez*) to bite (*d*) (*perforar*) to prick, to puncture (**e**) *Culin Esp, RP* (*carne*) *Br* to mince, *US* to grind (**f**) (*incitar*) to incite, to goad; **p. la curiosidad (de algn)** to arouse (sb's) curiosity
2 VI (**a**) (*escocer*) to itch; (*herida*) to smart; (*el sol*) to burn (**b**) *Culin* to be hot (**c**) (*pez*) to bite (**d**) *Fig* (*dejarse engañar*) to swallow it
3 **picarse** VPR (**a**) (*hacerse rivales*) to be at loggerheads (**b**) (*fruta*) to spot, to rot; (*ropa*)

to become moth-eaten; (*dientes*) to decay (**c**) (*enfadarse*) to get cross (**d**) (*drogadicto*) to shoot up

picardía 1 NF (**a**) (*astucia*) craftiness (**b**) (*de niño*) mischief
2 **picardías** NM INV (*prenda femenina*) negligee

pícaro, -a 1 ADJ (**a**) (*travieso*) naughty, mischievous; (*astuto*) sly, crafty (**b**) (*procaz*) risqué
2 NM,F rascal, rogue

picatoste NM crouton

pichi NM *Br* pinafore dress, *US* jumper

pichincha NF *RP Fam* snip, bargain

pichón NM young pigeon; **tiro al** *o* **de p.** pigeon shooting

pickles NMPL *RP* pickles

picnic (*pl* **picnics**) NM picnic

pico NM (**a**) (*de ave*) beak, bill; *Fam* (*boca*) mouth, *esp Br* gob; **tener un p. de oro** to have the gift of the gab (**b**) (*punta*) corner (**c**) *Geog* peak (**d**) (*herramienta*) pick, pickaxe (**e**) (*cantidad*) odd amount; **cincuenta y p.** fifty odd; **las dos y p.** just after two (**f**) (*drogas*) fix

picor NM itch, tingling

picoso, -a ADJ *Méx* spicy, hot

picotazo NM peck

picotear VT & VI (**a**) (*pájaro*) to peck (**b**) (*comer*) to nibble

pictórico, -a ADJ pictorial

pie NM (**a**) (*de persona*) foot; **pies** feet; **a p.** on foot; **de p.** standing up; **de pies a cabeza** from head to foot; **en p.** standing; **el acuerdo sigue en p.** the agreement still stands; **hacer p.** to touch the bottom; **perder p.** to get out of one's depth; *Fig* **a pies juntillas** blindly; *Fig* **al p. de la letra** to the letter, word for word; *Fig* **con buen/mal p.** on the right/wrong footing; *Fig* **con pies de plomo** gingerly, cautiously; *Fig* **dar p. a** to give cause for (**b**) (*de instrumento*) stand; (*de copa*) stem (**c**) (*de página*) foot; (*de ilustración*) caption (**d**) (*medida*) foot (**e**) *Teatro* cue (**f**) *Lit* foot

piedad NF (**a**) (*religiosidad*) piety (**b**) (*compasión*) pity

piedra NF stone; (*de mechero*) flint; **poner la primera p.** to lay the foundation stone; *Fam Fig* **me dejó** *o* **me quedé de p.** I was flabbergasted

piel NF (**a**) (*de persona*) skin; **p. de gallina** goose pimples (**b**) (*de fruta, de patata*) skin, peel (**c**) *Esp, Méx* (*cuero*) leather (**d**) (*pelo*) fur

pienso NM fodder, feed; **piensos compuestos** mixed feed

pierna NF leg

pieza NF (**a**) (*pedazo, parte*) piece; **p. de recambio** spare part, *US* extra; *Fig* **me dejó** *o* **me quedé de una p.** I was speechless *o* dumbfounded *o* flabbergasted (**b**) (*habitación*) room (**c**) *Teatro* play

pigmento NM pigment

pigmeo, -a NM,F pygmy, pigmy

pijama NM pyjamas

pijo, -a *Esp* **1** ADJ *Fam* posh; **un barrio p.** a posh area
  2 NM,F *Fam* rich kid
  3 NM *muy Fam (pene)* prick, cock

pila NF **(a)** *Elec* battery **(b)** *(montón)* pile, heap; *Fig* **una p. de** *(muchos)* piles o heaps o loads of **(c)** *(lavadero)* basin **(d)** *Fig* **nombre de p.** Christian name

pilar NM **(a)** *Arquit* pillar **(b)** *(fuente)* waterhole

píldora NF pill; **p. abortiva** morning-after pill; *Fig* **dorar la p. a algn** to butter sb up

pileta NF *RP* **(a)** *(en baño)* wasbasin; *(en cocina)* sink **(b)** *(piscina)* swimming pool

pilila NF *Fam Br* willy, *US* peter

pillaje NM looting, pillage

pillar 1 VT **(a)** *(robar)* to plunder, to loot **(b)** *(coger)* to catch; *(alcanzar)* to catch up with; **lo pilló un coche** he was run over by a car **(c)** *Fam* to be; **me pilla un poco lejos** it's a bit far for o from me
  2 pillarse VPR to catch; **pillarse un dedo/una mano** to catch one's finger/hand

pillo, -a 1 ADJ **(a)** *(travieso)* naughty **(b)** *(astuto)* sly, cunning
  2 NM,F rogue

pilotar VT *Av* to pilot, to fly; *Aut* to drive; *Náut* to pilot, to steer

piloto NM **(a)** *Av & Náut* pilot; *Aut* driver; **piso p.** show flat; **programa p.** pilot programme **(b)** *(luz)* pilot lamp o light

piltrafa NF *Fam* **estar hecho una p.** to be on one's last legs

pimentón NM paprika, red pepper

pimienta NF pepper

pimiento NM *(fruto)* pepper; *(planta)* pimiento; **p. morrón** sweet pepper; *Fam* **me importa un p.** I don't give a damn, I couldn't care less

pimpollo NM **(a)** *Bot* shoot **(b)** *Fam (hombre)* hunk; *(mujer)* babe

pin *(pl* **pins)** NM pin, (lapel) badge

pinacoteca NF art gallery

pináculo NM pinnacle

pinar NM pine grove, pine wood

pincel NM brush, paintbrush

pincelada NF brushstroke, stroke of a brush

pinchadiscos NMF INV disc jockey, DJ

pinchar 1 VT **(a)** *(punzar)* to prick; *(balón, globo)* to burst; *(rueda)* to puncture **(b)** *Fam (incitar)* to prod; *(molestar)* to get at, to nag **(c)** *Med* to give an injection to **(d)** *Tel* to bug
  2 VI **(a)** *Aut* to get a puncture **(b)** *Fam* **ni pincha ni corta** his opinion doesn't count for anything

Observa que el verbo inglés **to pinch** es un falso amigo y no es la traducción del verbo español **pinchar**. En inglés, **to pinch** significa "pellizcar".

pinchazo NM **(a)** *(punzadura)* prick; *Aut* puncture, blowout **(b)** *(de dolor)* sudden o sharp pain

pinche[1] NMF **(a)** *(de cocina)* *(hombre)* kitchen boy; *(mujer)* maid **(b)** *RP Fam (en oficina)* office junior

pinche[2] ADJ *Méx Fam* damn, *Br* bloody; **¡ese p. perro!** that damn o *Br* bloody dog!

pincho NM **(a)** *(púa)* barb **(b)** *Esp (tapa)* bar snack, aperitif; **p. moruno** $\simeq$ shish kebab; **p. de tortilla** = small portion of omelette

pinga NF *Andes, Méx, Ven Vulg* prick, cock

ping-pong [pim'pon] NM ping-pong, table-tennis

pingüe ADJ abundant, plentiful; **pingües beneficios** fat profits

pingüino NM penguin

pino NM pine; *Esp Fig* **hacer el p.** to do a handstand; *Esp Fam* **en el quinto p.** in the back of beyond

pinol, pinole NM *CAm, Méx Br* maize flour, *US* corn flour

pinta 1 NF **(a)** *Fam (aspecto)* look; **tiene p. de ser interesante** it looks interesting **(b)** *(mota)* dot; *(lunar)* spot **(c)** *(medida)* pint
  2 NMF *Fam* shameless person

pintada NF graffiti

pintado, -a ADJ **recién p.** *(en letrero)* wet paint; *Fam Fig* **nos viene que ni p.** it is just the ticket; *Fam Fig* **te está que ni p.** it suits you to a T

pintalabios NM INV lipstick

pintar 1 VT **(a)** *(dar color)* to paint **(b)** *(dibujar)* to draw, to sketch
  2 VI *(importar)* to count; *Fig* **yo aquí no pinto nada** I am out of place here
  3 pintarse VPR **(a)** *(maquillarse)* to put make-up on **(b)** *Fam* **pintárselas** to manage

pintarrajear VT to daub

pintor, -a NM,F painter

pintoresco, -a ADJ **(a)** *(lugar)* picturesque **(b)** *(raro)* eccentric, bizarre

pintura NF **(a)** *(técnica, cuadro)* painting; **p. rupestre** cave painting; *Fam Fig* **no la puedo ver ni en p.** I can't stand the sight of her **(b)** *(materia)* paint **(c)** *(lápiz)* colour pencil; *(de cera)* crayon

pinza NF *(para tender)* *Br* clothes peg, *US* clothespin; *(de animal)* pincer, claw; **pinzas** *(para depilar)* tweezers; *(para hielo)* tongs

piña NF **(a)** *(de pino)* pine cone; *(ananás)* pineapple **(b)** *Fig (grupo)* clan, clique **(c)** *Fam (golpe)* thump

piñón NM **(a)** *(del pino)* pine seed o nut **(b)** *Téc* pinion

pío[1] NM **¡p., p.!** cheep, cheep!; *Fam* **no dijo ni p.** there wasn't a cheep out of him

pío[2], **-a** ADJ pious

piojo NM louse

piola ADJ *RP Fam* **(a)** *(simpático)* fun **(b)** *Irón (listo)* smart, clever **(c)** *(lugar)* cosy

piolín NM *Andes, RP* cord

pionero, -a NM,F pioneer

pipa NF (**a**) *(de fumar)* pipe; **fumar en p.** to smoke a pipe (**b**) *(de fruta)* pip; *(de girasol)* sunflower seed

pipí NM *Fam* pee, *Br* wee-wee; **hacer p.** to have a pee

pipián NM *Andes, CAm, Méx* (**a**) *(salsa)* = sauce thickened with ground nuts or seeds (**b**) *(guiso)* = type of stew in which the sauce is thickened with ground nuts or seeds

pique NM (**a**) *(enfado)* grudge (**b**) *(rivalidad)* needle (**c**) **a p. de** on the point of (**d**) **irse a p.** *Náut* to sink; *(un plan)* to fall through; *(un negocio)* to go bust

piqueta NF pickaxe

piquete NM (**a**) *(de huelga)* picket (**b**) *Mil* **p. de ejecución** firing squad

pira NF pyre

pirado, -a *Fam* **1** ADJ crazy
2 NM,F loony, *Br* nutter

piragua NF canoe

piragüismo NM canoeing

piragüista NMF canoeist

pirámide NF pyramid

piraña NF piranha

pirarse VPR *Esp, RP Fam* to clear off, to hop it

pirata ADJ & NMF pirate

piratear VT *Fig* to pirate

Pirineo(s) NM(PL) Pyrenees

pirita NF pyrite

pirómano, -a NM,F *Med* pyromaniac; *Der* arsonist

piropo NM **echar un p.** to pay a compliment

pirueta NF pirouette; *Fig Pol* **hacer una p.** to do a U-turn

piruja NF *Col, Méx muy Fam* whore, *US* hooker

pirulí NM lollipop

pis NM *Fam* pee; **hacer p.** to have a pee

pisada NF step, footstep; *(huella)* footprint

pisapapeles NMINV paperweight

pisar VT to tread on, to step on

piscifactoría NF fish farm

piscina NF swimming pool

Piscis NMINV Pisces

pisco NM pisco, = Andean grape brandy

piscolabis NMINV *Esp Fam* snack

piso NM (**a**) *Esp (vivienda)* apartment, *Br* flat; *Pol* **p. franco** safe house (**b**) *(planta)* floor; *(de carretera)* surface

pisotear VT *(aplastar)* to stamp on; *(pisar)* to trample on

pisotón NM **me dio un p.** he stood on my foot

pista NF (**a**) *(de atletismo, forestal)* track; **p. de baile** dance floor; *Dep* **p. de esquí** ski run o slope; *Dep* **p. de patinaje** ice rink; *Dep* **p. de tenis** tennis court; **p. de aterrizaje** landing strip; **p. de despegue** runway (**b**) *(rastro)* trail, track (**c**) *(indicio)* clue; **dame una p.** give me a clue

pistacho NM pistachio nut

pisto NM *Culin* ≃ ratatouille

pistola NF (**a**) *(arma)* gun, pistol (**b**) *(para pintar)* spray gun

pistolero NM gunman, gangster

pistón NM (**a**) *Téc (émbolo)* piston (**b**) *Mús* key

pita NF agave

pitada NF (**a**) *(silbidos de protesta)* booing, whistling (**b**) *Am Fam (calada)* drag, puff

pitar **1** VT (**a**) *(silbato)* to blow (**b**) *Dep* **el árbitro pitó un penalti** the referee awarded a penalty
2 VI (**a**) *(con silbato)* to whistle (**b**) *Aut* to toot one's horn (**c**) *Dep* to referee (**d**) *Esp Fam* **salir pitando** to fly off

pitido NM whistle

pitillera NF cigarette case

pitillo NM (**a**) *(cigarrillo)* cigarette (**b**) *Col (paja)* drinking straw

pito NM (**a**) *(silbato)* whistle; *Aut* horn; *Fam* **me importa un p.** I don't give a hoot (**b**) *Fam (cigarrillo)* fag (**c**) *Fam (pene) Br* willy, *US* peter

pitón NM (**a**) *(serpiente)* python (**b**) *(de toro)* horn

pitorreo NM *Esp Fam* scoffing, teasing; **hacer algo de p.** to do sth for a laugh

pivote NMF (**a**) *(eje)* pivot (**b**) *Dep* pivot

pizarra NF (**a**) *(encerado) Br* blackboard, *US* chalkboard (**b**) *(roca, material)* slate

pizarrón NM *Am Br* blackboard, *US* chalkboard

pizca NF little bit, tiny piece; **ni p.** not a bit; **una p. de sal** a pinch of salt

pizza ['pitsa] NF pizza

pizzería [pitse'ria] NF pizzeria, pizza parlour

placa NF (**a**) *(lámina)* plate; **p. solar** solar panel (**b**) *(conmemorativa)* plaque (**c**) *Med* **p. dental** dental plaque

placaje NM *Dep* tackle

placentero, -a ADJ pleasant, agreeable

placer [33] **1** VT to please
2 NM pleasure; **ha sido un p. (conocerle)** it's been a pleasure (meeting you); *Fml* **tengo el p. de** it gives me great pleasure to; **un viaje de p.** a holiday trip

placidez NF placidity

plácido, -a ADJ placid, easy-going

plaga NF (**a**) *(de insectos)* plague (**b**) *Agr* pest, blight

plagar [42] VT to cover, to fill

plagiar [43] VT (**a**) *(copiar)* to plagiarize (**b**) *CAm, Col, Perú, Méx (secuestrar)* to kidnap

plagiario, -a NM,F *CAm, Col, Perú, Méx* kidnapper

plagio NM (**a**) *(copia)* plagiarism (**b**) *CAm, Col, Perú, Ven (secuestro)* kidnapping

plan NM (**a**) *(proyecto)* plan (**b**) *(programa)* scheme, programme; *Educ* **p. de estudios**

syllabus; **estar a p.** to be on a diet (**c**) *Fam* **en p. de broma** for a laugh; **si te pones en ese p.** if you're going to be like that (about it); **en p. barato** cheaply (**d**) *Fam (cita)* date

plana NF (**a**) *(página)* page; **a toda p.** full page; **primera p.** front page (**b**) *Mil* **p. mayor** staff

plancha NF (**a**) *(para la ropa)* iron; *(de metal)* plate (**b**) *Culin* hotplate; **sardinas a la p.** grilled sardines (**c**) *Impr* plate

planchado NM ironing

planchar VT to iron

planchazo NM *Fam* blunder, boob

planeador NM glider

planear 1 VT to plan
2 VI to glide

planeta NM planet

planetario, -a 1 ADJ planetary
2 NM planetarium

planicie NF plain

planificación NF planning; **p. familiar** family planning

planificar [44] VT to plan

planilla NF (**a**) *Am (formulario)* form (**b**) *Am (nómina)* payroll

plano, -a 1 NM (**a**) *(de ciudad)* map; *Arquit* plan, draft (**b**) *Cin* shot; **un primer p.** a close-up; *Fig* **estar en primer/segundo p.** to be in the limelight/in the background (**c**) *Mat* plane
2 ADJ flat, even

planta NF (**a**) *(vegetal)* plant (**b**) *(del pie)* sole (**c**) *(piso)* floor, storey; **p. baja** *Br* ground floor, *US* first floor (**d**) *(fábrica)* plant

plantación NF (**a**) *(terreno)* plantation (**b**) *(acción)* planting

plantado, -a ADJ *Fam* **dejar a algn p.** to stand sb up

plantar 1 VT (**a**) *(árboles, campo)* to plant (**b**) *(poner)* to put, to place; **p. cara a algn** to stand up to sb (**c**) *Fam* **p. a algn en la calle** to throw sb out; **le ha plantado su novia** his girlfriend has ditched him
2 plantarse VPR (**a**) *(ponerse)* to plant oneself (**b**) *(en un sitio con rapidez)* **plantarse en** to get to, to make it to

planteamiento NM *(enfoque)* approach

plantear 1 VT (**a**) *(problema)* to pose, to raise (**b**) *(planear)* to plan (**c**) *(proponer)* to put forward (**d**) *(exponer)* to present
2 plantearse VPR (**a**) *(considerar)* to consider (**b**) *(problema)* to arise

plantel NM team

plantilla NF (**a**) *(personal)* staff, personnel (**b**) *(de zapato)* insole (**c**) *(patrón)* model, pattern

plantón NM *Fam* **dar un p. a algn** to stand sb up

plañir VI to mourn

plasmar 1 VT (**a**) *(reproducir)* to capture (**b**) *(expresar)* to express
2 plasmarse VPR **p. en** to take the shape of

plasta NMF *Esp Fam* bore

plástico, -a ADJ & NM plastic

plastificar [44] VT to coat o cover with plastic

plastilina® NF Plasticine®

plata NF (**a**) *(metal)* silver; *(objetos de plata)* silverware; *Fam* **hablar en p.** to lay (it) on the line; **p. de ley** sterling silver (**b**) *Am Fam (dinero)* money

plataforma NF platform

plátano NM (**a**) *(fruta)* banana (**b**) *(árbol)* plane tree; **falso p.** sycamore

platea NF *Br* stalls, *US* orchestra

plateado, -a ADJ (**a**) *(con plata)* silver-plated (**b**) *(color)* silvery

platense 1 ADJ of/from the River Plate
2 NMF person from the River Plate

plateresco NM plateresque, = 16th century Spanish architectural style

plática NF *CAm, Méx (charla)* talk, chat

platicar [44] VI *CAm, Méx* to chat, to talk

platillo NM (**a**) *(para taza)* saucer; **p. volador,** *Esp* **p. volante** flying saucer (**b**) *Mús* cymbal

platina NF deck; **doble p.** double deck

platino NM (**a**) *(metal)* platinum (**b**) *Aut* **platinos** contact breaker, points

plato NM (**a**) *(recipiente)* plate, dish (**b**) *(parte de una comida)* course; **de primer p.** for starters; **p. fuerte** main course; **p. combinado** one-course meal (**c**) *(guiso)* dish (**d**) *(de balanza)* pan, tray (**e**) *(de tocadiscos)* turntable

plató NM *Cin & TV (film)* set

platudo, -a ADJ *Am Fam* loaded, rolling in it

plausible ADJ (**a**) *(admisible)* plausible, acceptable (**b**) *(loable)* commendable

playa NF (**a**) *(junto al mar)* beach (**b**) *Am* **p. de estacionamiento** *Br* car park, *US* parking lot

play-back ['pleiβak] *(pl* **play-backs)** NM **hacer p.** to mime (the lyrics)

playera NF (**a**) *(zapatilla)* *Br* sandshoe, *US* sneaker (**b**) *Méx (camiseta)* teeshirt

plaza NF (**a**) *(en población)* square (**b**) *(sitio)* place; **tenemos plazas limitadas** there are a limited number of places available; **p. de aparcamiento** parking space (**c**) *(mercado)* market, marketplace (**d**) *Aut (asiento)* seat (**e**) *(laboral)* post, position (**f**) **p. de toros** bullring

plazo NM (**a**) *(periodo)* time, period; *(término)* deadline; **a corto/largo p.** in the short term/ in the long run; **el p. termina el viernes** Friday is the deadline (**b**) *Fin* **comprar a plazos** to buy on *Br* hire purchase o *US* an installment plan; **en seis plazos** in six instalments

pleamar NF high tide

plebe NF masses, plebs

plebeyo, -a 1 ADJ plebeian
2 NM,F plebeian, pleb

plebiscito NM plebiscite

plegable ADJ folding, collapsible

plegar [1] **1** VT to fold
2 plegarse VPR to give way, to bow

plegaria NF prayer

pleitear VI to conduct a lawsuit, to plead

pleito NM (**a**) *Der* lawsuit, litigation; **poner un p. (a algn)** to sue (sb) (**b**) *Am (discusión)* argument

plenilunio NM full moon

plenitud NF plenitude, fullness; **en la p. de la vida** in the prime of life

pleno, -a 1 ADJ full; **en plena noche** in the middle of the night; **los empleados en p.** the entire staff
2 NM plenary meeting

pletórico, -a ADJ abundant

plexiglás® NM Perspex®, *US* Plexiglass®

pliego NM (*hoja*) sheet *o* piece of paper; **p. de condiciones** bidding specifications

pliegue NM (**a**) *(doblez)* fold (**b**) *(en plisado)* pleat

plinto NM *Dep* vaulting box

plisar VT to pleat

plomería NF *Méx, RP, Ven* (**a**) *(negocio)* plumber's (**b**) *(instalación)* plumbing

plomero NM *Méx, RP, Ven* plumber

plomizo, -a ADJ *(color, cielo)* leaden

plomo NM (**a**) *(en metalurgia)* lead (**b**) *Elec (fusible)* fuse (**c**) *(bala)* slug, pellet

pluma NF (**a**) *(de ave)* feather (**b**) *(estilográfica)* fountain pen (**c**) *Carib, Méx (bolígrafo)* (ballpoint) pen (**d**) *Carib, Col, Méx (grifo)* Br tap, *US* faucet

plumaje NM plumage

plumazo NM **de un p.** at a stroke

plumero NM (**a**) *(para el polvo)* feather duster (**b**) *Fam* **se te ve el p.** I can see through you

plumier (*pl* **plumiers**) NM pencil box

plumón NM *(de ave)* down

plural ADJ & NM plural

pluralidad NF diversity

pluralismo NM pluralism

pluriempleo NM **hacer p.** to have more than one job

plus NM bonus

plusmarca NF record

plusmarquista NMF record breaker

plusvalía NF *(tras venta)* capital gain; *Econ* surplus value

Plza. *(abr* **Plaza)** Sq

PM NF *(abr* **policía militar)** MP

p.m. *(abr* **post meridiem)** p.m.

población NF (**a**) *(ciudad)* town; *(pueblo)* village (**b**) *(habitantes)* population (**c**) *Chile (barrio)* **p. (callampa)** shanty town

poblado, -a ADJ (**a**) *(zona)* populated; *Fig* **p. de** full of (**b**) *(barba)* bushy, thick

poblador, -a NM,F settler

poblar [2] VT (**a**) *(con gente)* to settle, to people; *(con plantas)* to plant (**b**) *(vivir en)* to inhabit

pobre 1 ADJ poor; **¡p.!** poor thing!; **un hombre p.** a poor man; **un p. hombre** a poor devil
2 NMF poor person; **los pobres** the poor

pobreza NF poverty; *Fig (de medios, recursos)* lack

pocho, -a ADJ (**a**) *(fruta)* bad, overripe (**b**) *Fig (persona) (débil)* off-colour; *(triste)* depressed, down (**c**) *Méx Fam (americanizado)* Americanized

pochoclo NM *Arg* popcorn

pocilga NF pigsty

pocillo NM (**a**) *RP (pequeño)* small cup (**b**) *Méx, Ven (grande)* enamel mug

pócima NF potion; *Pey* concoction, brew

poción NF potion

poco, -a 1 NM (**a**) *(con adj o adv)* a little; **un p. tarde/frío** a little late/cold (**b**) **un p.** *(con sustantivo)* a little; **un p. de azúcar** a little sugar
2 ADJ (**a**) *(en singular)* not much, little; **p. sitio/tiempo** not much *o* little space/time; **poca cosa** not much (**b**) **pocos, -as** not many, few; **pocas personas** not many *o* few people
3 PRON (**a**) *(escasa cantidad)* not much; **queda p.** there isn't much left (**b**) *(breve tiempo)* **p. antes/después** shortly *o* a little before/ afterwards; **a p. de** shortly *o* a little after; **dentro de p.** soon (**c**) **pocos, -as** *(cosas)* few, not many; **tengo muy pocos** I have very few, I don't have very many (**d**) **pocos, -as** *(personas)* few people, not many people; **vinieron pocos** few people came, not many people came; **unos pocos** a few
4 ADV (**a**) *(con verbo)* not (very) much, little; **ella come p.** she doesn't eat much, she eats little (**b**) *(con adj)* not very; **es p. probable** it's not very likely (**c**) *(en frases)* **p. a p.** little by little, gradually; **por p.** almost

podadera, *Am* **podadora** NF garden shears

podar VT to prune

poder[1] NM power; *Econ* **p. adquisitivo** purchasing power

poder[2] [18] **1** VI (**a**) *(capacidad)* to be able to; **no puede hablar** she can't speak; **no podré llamarte** I won't be able to phone; **no puedo más** I can't take any more; **guapa a más no p.** unbelievably pretty
(**b**) *(permiso)* can, may; **¿puedo pasar?** can *o* may I come in?; **¿se puede (entrar)?** may I (come in)?; **aquí no se puede fumar** you can't smoke here
(**c**) *(uso impers) (posibilidad)* may, might; **puede que no lo sepan** they may *o* might not know; **no puede ser** that's impossible; **puede (ser) (que sí)** maybe, perhaps
(**d**) *(deber)* **no podemos portarnos así con él** we can't treat him like that
(**e**) **p. con** *(enfermedad, rival)* to be able to overcome; *(tarea, problema)* to be able to cope with
2 VT *(batir)* to be stronger than; **les puede a todos** he can take on anybody

poderoso, -a ADJ powerful

podio, pódium NM *Dep* podium

podré INDIC FUT *de* **poder**[2]

podrido, -a ADJ (**a**) *(putrefacto)* rotten, putrid (**b**) *(corrupto)* rotten; *Fam* **estar p. de dinero** *o Am* **en plata** to be filthy rich (**c**) *RP Fam (harto)* fed up, sick

poema NM poem

poesía NF (**a**) *(género)* poetry (**b**) *(poema)* poem

poeta NMF poet

poético, -a ADJ poetic

póker NM poker

polaco, -a 1 ADJ Polish
2 NM,F Pole
3 NM *(idioma)* Polish

polar ADJ polar

polaridad NF polarity

polarizar [40] VT (**a**) *Fís* to polarize (**b**) *Fig (ánimo, atención)* to concentrate

polea NF pulley

polémica NF controversy

polémico, -a ADJ controversial

polemizar [40] VI to argue, to debate

polen NM pollen

polera NF (**a**) *Arg, Chile (polo)* polo shirt (**b**) *Urug (de cuello alto)* turtleneck *o Br* polo neck sweater

poli *Fam* **1** NMF cop
2 NF **la p.** the fuzz *pl*

polichinela NM (**a**) *(personaje)* Punchinello (**b**) *(títere)* puppet, marionette

policía 1 NF police (force)
2 NMF *(hombre)* policeman; *(mujer)* police-woman

policíaco, -a, policiaco, -a, policial ADJ police; **novela/película policíaca** detective story/movie *o Br* film

polideportivo NM sports centre

poliéster NM polyester

polietileno NM *Br* polythene, *US* polyethylene

polifacético, -a ADJ versatile, many-sided; **es un hombre muy p.** he's a man of many talents

poligamia NF polygamy

políglota ADJ & NMF polyglot

polígono NM polygon; **p. industrial** *Br* industrial estate, *US* industrial area

polilla NF moth

polio NF polio

politécnico, -a ADJ & NM polytechnic

política NF (**a**) *(ciencia, actividad)* politics *sing* (**b**) *(medidas)* policy

políticamente ADV **p. correcto** politically correct

político, -a 1 ADJ (**a**) *(de gobierno)* political (**b**) *(pariente)* in-law; **hermano p.** brother-in-law; **su familia política** her in-laws
2 NM,F politician

póliza NF (**a**) *(sello)* stamp (**b**) **p. de seguros** insurance policy

polizón NM stowaway

polla NF *Vulg* prick

pollera NF (**a**) *CSur (occidental)* skirt (**b**) *Andes (indígena)* = long skirt worn in layers by Indian women

pollo NM (**a**) *(ave)* chicken (**b**) *Fam (joven)* lad

polo NM (**a**) *Elec & Geog* pole; **P. Norte/Sur** North/South Pole (**b**) *(helado)* Br ice lolly, *US* Popsicle® (**c**) *(prenda)* polo shirt (**d**) *Dep* polo

pololear VI *Chile Fam* to go out (together)

pololo, -a NM,F *Chile Fam (hombre)* boyfriend; *(mujer)* girlfriend

Polonia N Poland

poltrona NF easy chair

polución NF pollution

polvareda NF cloud of dust

polvera NF powder compact

polvo NM (**a**) *(en el aire)* dust; **limpiar** *o* **quitar el p.** to dust (**b**) *(de producto)* powder; **en p.** powdered; **polvo(s) de talco** talcum powder (**c**) *Fam* **estar hecho p.** *(cansado)* to be *Br* knackered *o US* bushed; *(deprimido)* to be depressed (**d**) *muy Fam* **echar un p.** to have a screw *o Br* a shag

pólvora NF gunpowder

polvoriento, -a ADJ dusty

polvorín NM gunpowder arsenal; *Fig* powder keg

polvorón NM sweet pastry

pomada NF ointment

pomelo NM *(fruto)* grapefruit; *(árbol)* grape-fruit tree

pómez ADJ INV **piedra p.** pumice (stone)

pomo NM *(de puerta)* knob

pompa NF (**a**) **p. (de jabón)** (soap) bubble (**b**) *(suntuosidad)* pomp (**c**) *Méx Fam* **pompas** behind, bottom

pompis NM INV *Fam* botty

pomposo, -a ADJ pompous

pómulo NM cheekbone

ponchar 1 VT (**a**) *CAm, Carib, Méx (rueda)* to puncture (**b**) *Am (en béisbol)* to strike out
2 poncharse VPR (**a**) *CAm, Carib, Méx (rueda)* to blow (**b**) *Am (en béisbol)* to strike out

ponche NM punch

poncho NM poncho

ponderar VT (**a**) *(asunto)* to weigh up *o* consider (**b**) *(alabar)* to praise

pondré INDIC FUT *de* **poner**

ponencia NF paper

poner [19] *(pp* **puesto) 1** VT (**a**) *(colocar, meter)* to put; *(mesa, huevo)* to lay; *(gesto)* to make; *(multa)* to impose; *(telegrama)* to send; *(negocio)* to set up
(**b**) *(tele, radio etc)* to turn *o* switch on
(**c**) *(+ adj)* to make; **p. triste a algn** to make sb sad; **p. colorado a algn** to make sb blush
(**d**) **¿qué llevaba puesto?** what was he wearing?
(**e**) *Esp (decir)* **¿qué pone aquí?** what does it say here?
(**f**) *(suponer)* to suppose; **pongamos que Ana**

no viene supposing Ana doesn't turn up (**g**) *TV & Cin* to put on, to show; **¿qué ponen en la tele?** what's on the telly? (**h**) *Esp Tel* **ponme con Manuel** put me through to Manuel (**i**) *(nombrar)* **le pondremos (de nombre) Pilar** we are going to call her Pilar **2** V IMPERS *Am Fam (parecer)* **se me pone que … ** it seems to me that …
3 ponerse VPR (**a**) *(colocarse)* to put oneself; **ponte en mi lugar** put yourself in my place; **ponte más cerca** come closer (**b**) *(vestirse)* to put on; **ella se puso el jersey** she put her sweater on (**c**) *(+ adj)* to become; **ponerse furioso/malo** to become furious/ill (**d**) *(sol)* to set (**e**) *Tel* **ponerse al teléfono** to answer the phone (**f**) **ponerse a** to start to; **ponerse a trabajar** to get down to work

poney *(pl* **poneys)** NM pony

pongo INDIC PRES *de* **poner**

poniente NM (**a**) *(occidente)* West (**b**) *(viento)* westerly (wind)

ponqué NM *Col, Ven* = fruit or custard-filled cake

pontífice NM Pontiff; **el Sumo P.** His Holiness the Pope

ponzoña NF venom, poison

ponzoñoso, -a ADJ venomous, poisonous

popa NF stern; *Fig* **ir viento en p.** to go full speed ahead

popote NM *Méx* (drinking) straw

populacho NM *Pey* plebs, masses

popular ADJ (**a**) *(creencia, movimiento, revuelta)* popular; *(arte, música)* folk; *(lenguaje)* colloquial (**b**) *(famoso, aceptado)* popular

popularidad NF popularity

popularizar [40] VT to popularize

populoso, -a ADJ densely populated

popurrí NM *Mús* medley

póquer NM poker

por PREP (**a**) *(agente)* by; **pintado p. Picasso** painted by Picasso
(**b**) **p. qué** why
(**c**) *(causa)* because of; **p. sus ideas** because of her ideas; **p. necesidad/amor** out of need/love; **suspendió p. no estudiar** he failed because he didn't study
(**d**) *(tiempo)* **p. la mañana/noche** in the morning/at night; **p. ahora** for the time being; **p. entonces** at that time
(**e**) *(en favor de)* for; **lo hago p. mi hermano** I'm doing it for my brother('s sake)
(**f**) *(lugar)* **pasamos p. Córdoba** we went through Córdoba; **p. ahí** over there; **¿p. dónde vamos?** which way are we taking *o* going?; **p. la calle** in the street; **mirar p. la ventana** to look out the window; **entrar p. la ventana** to get in through the window
(**g**) *(medio)* by; **p. avión/correo** by plane/post
(**h**) *(a cambio de)* for; **cambiar algo p. otra cosa** to exchange sth for something else
(**i**) *(distributivo)* **p. cabeza** a head, per person;

p. hora/mes per hour/month
(**j**) *Mat* **dos p. tres, seis** two times three is six; **un 10 p. ciento** 10 percent
(**k**) *(con infinitivo)* in order to, so as to; **hablar p. hablar** to talk for the sake of it
(**l**) *(locuciones)* **p. así decirlo** so to speak; **p. más o muy … que sea** no matter how … he/she is; **p. mí** as far as I'm concerned

porcelana NF porcelain

porcentaje NM percentage

porche NM porch

porcino, -a ADJ **ganado p.** pigs

porción NF portion, part

pordiosero, -a NM,F tramp, *US* bum

porfiado, -a ADJ *(insistente)* persistent; *(tozudo)* stubborn

pormenor NM detail; **venta al p.** retail

porno ADJ INV *Fam* porn

pornografía NF pornography

pornográfico, -a ADJ pornographic

poro NM pore

poroso, -a ADJ porous

poroto NM *Andes, RP (judía)* kidney bean

porque CONJ (**a**) *(causal)* because; **¡p. no!** just because! (**b**) *(final) (+ subj)* so that, in order that

porqué NM reason

porquería NF (**a**) *(suciedad)* dirt, filth (**b**) *(cosa de mala calidad) Br* rubbish, *US* garbage (**c**) **porquerías** *(comida) Br* rubbish, *US* garbage

porra NF (**a**) *(de policía)* truncheon, baton (**b**) *Fam (locuciones)* **¡una p.!** *Br* rubbish!, *US* garbage!; **¡vete a la p.!** get lost!

porrazo NM thump

porro NM (**a**) *Fam (de droga)* joint (**b**) *Am (puerro)* leek

porrón NM = glass wine vessel used for drinking wine from its long spout

portaaviones NM INV aircraft carrier

portada NF (**a**) *(de libro etc)* cover; *(de periódico)* front page; *(de disco)* sleeve (**b**) *(fachada)* front, facade

portador, -a NM,F *Com* bearer; *Med* carrier

portaequipajes NM INV (**a**) *Aut (maletero) Br* boot, *US* trunk; *(baca)* roof *o* luggage rack (**b**) *(carrito)* luggage trolley

portafolios NM INV briefcase

portal NM (**a**) *(zaguán)* porch, entrance hall (**b**) *(puerta de la calle)* main door (**c**) **p. de Belén** Nativity scene (**d**) *Inform* portal

portamaletas NM INV = **portaequipajes**

portaminas NM INV propelling pencil

portamonedas NM INV purse

portarse VPR to behave; **p. mal** to misbehave

portátil ADJ portable

portaviones NM INV = **portaaviones**

portavoz NMF spokesperson; *(hombre)* spokesman; *(mujer)* spokeswoman

portazo NM **oímos un p.** we heard a slam o bang; **dar un p.** to slam the door

porte NM (**a**) *(aspecto)* bearing (**b**) *(transporte)* carriage

portento NM (**a**) *(cosa)* wonder, marvel (**b**) *(persona)* genius

portentoso, -a ADJ extraordinary, prodigious

porteño, -a 1 ADJ of/from Buenos Aires
2 NM,F person from Buenos Aires

portería NF (**a**) *(de casa, colegio)* Br caretaker's office, US super(intendent)'s office; *(de hotel, ministerio)* porter's office (**b**) Dep goal, goalmouth

portero, -a 1 NM,F (**a**) *(de casa, colegio)* Br caretaker, US super(intendent); *(de hotel, ministerio)* *(en recepción)* porter; *(a la puerta)* doorman (**b**) Dep goalkeeper
2 NM **p. automático** entryphone

pórtico NM (**a**) *(portal)* portico, porch (**b**) *(con arcadas)* arcade

portorriqueño, -a ADJ & NM,F Puerto Rican

portuario, -a ADJ harbour, port

Portugal N Portugal

portugués, -esa 1 ADJ & NM,F Portuguese
2 NM *(idioma)* Portuguese

porvenir NM future; **sin p.** with no prospects

pos ADV **en p. de** after

posada NF inn

posaderas NFPL *Fam* buttocks

posadero, -a NM,F innkeeper

posar 1 VI *(para retrato etc)* to pose
2 VT to put o lay down
3 posarse VPR to settle, to alight

posavasos NM INV coaster

posdata NF postscript

pose NF (**a**) *(postura)* pose (**b**) *(afectación)* posing

poseedor, -a NM,F possessor

poseer [36] VT to possess, to own

poseído, -a ADJ possessed

posesión NF possession; **estar en p. de** to have; **tomar p. (de un cargo)** to take up (a post)

posesivo, -a ADJ possessive

poseso, -a ADJ & NM,F possessed

posguerra NF postwar period

posibilidad NF possibility; *(oportunidad)* chance

posibilitar VT to make possible

posible ADJ possible; **de ser p.** if possible; **en (la medida de) lo p.** as far as possible; **haré todo lo p.** I'll do everything I can; **lo antes p.** as soon as possible; **es p. que venga** he might come

posición NF position

positivo, -a ADJ positive

posmoderno, -a ADJ postmodern

poso NM dregs, sediment

posponer [19] VT (*pp* **pospuesto**) (**a**) *(aplazar)* to postpone, to put off (**b**) *(relegar)* to put in second place o behind, to relegate

posta NF **a p.** on purpose

postal 1 ADJ postal
2 NF postcard

poste NM pole; Dep *(de portería)* post

póster (*pl* **pósters** o **posters**) NM poster

postergar [42] VT (**a**) *(relegar)* to relegate (**b**) *(retrasar)* to delay; *(aplazar)* to postpone

posteridad NF posterity; **pasar a la p.** to go down in history

posterior ADJ (**a**) *(lugar)* posterior, rear (**b**) *(tiempo)* later (**a** than), subsequent (**a** to)

posterioridad NF posteriority; **con p.** later

posteriormente ADV subsequently, later

postgrado NM postgraduate; **estudios de p.** postgraduate studies

postgraduado, -a ADJ & NM,F postgraduate

postigo NM *(de puerta)* wicket; *(de ventana)* shutter

postín NM *Fam* boasting, showing off; **darse p.** to show off, to swank; **de p.** posh, swanky

postizo, -a 1 ADJ false; **dentadura postiza** false teeth, dentures
2 NM hairpiece

postor NM bidder

postrarse VPR to prostrate oneself, to kneel down

postre NM dessert, Br pudding

postrero, -a ADJ last

> **Postrer** is used instead of **postrero** before masculine singular nouns (e.g. **el postrer día** the last day).

postrimerías NFPL final stages

postular 1 VT (**a**) *(defender)* to call for (**b**) *Am (candidatar)* to nominate
2 VI *(en colecta)* to collect
3 postularse VPR *Am* (**a**) *Pol (para cargo)* to stand, to run (**b**) *CSur (para trabajo)* to apply (**para** for)

póstumo, -a ADJ posthumous

postura NF (**a**) *(física)* position, posture (**b**) *(actitud)* attitude

posventa, postventa ADJ INV **servicio p.** after-sales service

potable ADJ drinkable; **agua p./no p.** drinking water/not drinking water

potaje NM hotpot, stew

pote NM pot

potencia NF power; **en p.** potential

potencial 1 ADJ potential
2 NM potential; **p. eléctrico** voltage; **p. humano** manpower

potenciar [43] VT to promote, to strengthen

potente ADJ powerful, strong

potestad NF power, authority

potingue NM *Fam (cosmético)* potion

potra NF *Fam* luck

potrero NM *Am* field, pasture

potro NM *Zool* colt; *(de gimnasia)* horse

poyo NM stone bench

pozo NM well; *Min* shaft, pit

pozole NM *CAm, Carib, Méx (guiso)* = stew made with maize kernels, pork or chicken and vegetables

PP NM *(abr* **Partido Popular)** = Spanish political party to the right of the political spectrum

práctica NF **(a)** *(ejercicio, destreza)* practice; **en la p.** in practice **(b)** *(clase no teórica)* practical **(c) prácticas** *(laborales)* training

practicante 1 ADJ *Rel* practising
2 NMF *Med* medical assistant

practicar [44] **1** VT to practise; *(operación)* to carry out
2 VI to practise

práctico, -a ADJ practical; *(útil)* handy, useful

pradera NF meadow

prado NM meadow, field

Praga N Prague

pragmático, -a 1 ADJ pragmatic
2 NM,F pragmatist

preámbulo NM **(a)** *(introducción)* preamble **(b)** *(rodeo)* circumlocution

preaviso NM previous warning, notice

precalentamiento NM warm-up

precalentar [1] VT to preheat

precario, -a ADJ precarious

precaución NF **(a)** *(cautela)* caution; **con p.** cautiously **(b)** *(medida)* precaution

precaver 1 VT to guard against
2 precaverse VPR to take precautions **(de** *o* **contra** against)

precavido, -a ADJ cautious, prudent

precedencia NF precedence, priority

precedente 1 ADJ preceding
2 NMF predecessor
3 NM precedent; **sin p.** unprecedented

preceder VT to precede

precepto NM precept

preciarse [43] VPR to have self-respect; **p. de** to pride oneself on

precintar VT to seal

precinto NM seal

> Observa que la palabra inglesa **precinct** es un falso amigo y no es la traducción de la palabra española **precinto**. En inglés, **precinct** significa "recinto" o "distrito".

precio NM price; **p. de costo** cost price; **a cualquier p.** at any price

preciosidad NF **(a)** *(hermosura) (cosa)* lovely thing; *(persona)* darling **(b)** *Fml (cualidad)* preciousness

precioso, -a ADJ **(a)** *(hermoso)* lovely, beautiful **(b)** *(valioso)* precious, valuable

precipicio NM precipice

precipitación NF **(a)** *(prisa)* haste **(b)** *(lluvia)* rainfall

precipitado, -a ADJ *(apresurado)* hasty, hurried; *(irreflexivo)* rash

precipitar 1 VT **(a)** *(acelerar)* to hurry, to rush **(b)** *(arrojar)* to throw, to hurl down
2 precipitarse VPR **(a)** *(persona)* to hurl oneself; *(acontecimientos)* to gather speed **(b)** *(actuar irreflexivamente)* to hurry, to rush

precisamente ADV *(con precisión)* precisely; *(exactamente)* exactly; **p. por eso** for that very reason

precisar VT **(a)** *(determinar)* to determine, to give full details of; *(especificar)* to specify **(b)** *(necesitar)* to require, to need

precisión NF **(a)** *(exactitud)* precision, accuracy; **con p.** precisely, accurately **(b)** *(aclaración)* clarification

preciso, -a ADJ **(a)** *(necesario)* necessary, essential **(b)** *(exacto)* accurate, exact; **en este p. momento** at this very moment **(c)** *(claro)* concise, clear

preconizar [40] VT to advocate

precoz ADJ **(a)** *(persona)* precocious **(b)** *(fruta)* early

precursor, -a NM,F precursor

predecesor, -a NM,F predecessor

predecir [12] *(pp* **predicho)** VT to foretell, to predict

predestinado, -a ADJ predestined

predeterminar VT to predetermine

predicado NM *Ling* predicate

predicador, -a NM,F preacher

predicar [44] VT to preach

predicción NF prediction, forecast

predice INDIC PRES *de* predecir

predicho, -a PP *de* predecir

predije PT INDEF *de* predecir

predilección NF predilection

predilecto, -a ADJ favourite, preferred

predisponer [19] *(pp* **predispuesto)** VT to predispose

predisposición NF predisposition

predispuesto, -a PP *de* predisponer

predominante ADJ predominant

predominar VI to predominate

predominio NM predominance

preeminente ADJ preeminent

preescolar ADJ preschool; **en p.** in nursery school

prefabricado, -a ADJ prefabricated

prefacio NM preface

preferencia NF preference

preferente, preferencial ADJ preferential

preferible ADJ preferable; **es p. que no vengas** you'd better not come

preferido, -a NM,F favourite

preferir [5] VT to prefer

prefijo NM (a) *Tel Br* dialling code, *US* area code (b) *Ling* prefix

pregón NM (a) *(bando)* proclamation, announcement (b) *(discurso)* speech

pregonar VT *(anunciar)* to announce publicly; *Fig (divulgar)* to reveal, to disclose

pregonero, -a NM,F *(de pueblo)* town crier; *Fig (bocazas)* blabbermouth

pregunta NF question; **hacer una p.** to ask a question

preguntar 1 VT to ask; **p. algo a algn** to ask sb sth; **p. por algn** to ask after o about sb
2 preguntarse VPR to wonder; **me pregunto si ...** I wonder whether ...

preguntón, -ona NM,F *Fam* nosey person, *Br* nosey parker

prehistoria NF prehistory

prehistórico, -a ADJ prehistoric

prejubilación NF = voluntary redundancy before entitlement to early retirement

prejuicio NM prejudice; **tener prejuicios** to be prejudiced, to be biased

preliminar ADJ & NM preliminary

preludio NM prelude

prematrimonial ADJ premarital

prematuro, -a ADJ premature

premeditación NF premeditation; **con p.** deliberately

premeditado, -a ADJ premeditated, deliberate

premiado, -a ADJ prize-winning

premiar [43] VT (a) *(en competición, sorteo)* to award a prize to (b) *(recompensar)* to reward

premio NM (a) *(en competición, sorteo)* prize, award (b) *(recompensa)* reward

premisa NF premise

premonición NF premonition

premura NF urgency; **p. de tiempo** haste

prenatal ADJ antenatal, prenatal

prenda NF (a) *(prenda)* garment (b) *(garantía)* token, pledge

prendar 1 VT to captivate, to delight
2 prendarse VPR to fall in love (**de** with)

prendedor NM brooch, pin

prender 1 VT (a) *(arrestar)* to arrest, to apprehend (b) *(sujetar)* to fasten (c) *(encender)* esp *Am (luz, interruptor)* to light; **p. fuego a algo** to set fire to sth, to set sth on fire
2 VI (a) *(arder)* to catch (fire) (b) *(planta)* to take root
3 prenderse VPR to catch fire

prensa NF press; *Fig* **tener buena/mala p.** to have a good/bad press

prensar VT to press

preñado, -a ADJ (a) *(hembra)* pregnant (b) *Fig (lleno)* pregnant (**de** with), full (**de** of)

preñar VT to make pregnant

preocupación NF worry, concern

preocupado, -a ADJ worried, concerned

preocupar 1 VT to worry; **me preocupa que llegue tan tarde** I'm worried about him arriving so late
2 preocuparse VPR to worry, to get worried (**por** about); **no te preocupes** don't worry; **preocuparse de algn** to look after sb; **preocuparse de algo** to see to sth

prepago NM *Tel* pay-as-you-go

preparación NF preparation; *(formación)* training

preparado, -a 1 ADJ (a) *(dispuesto)* ready, prepared; **comidas preparadas** ready-cooked meals (b) *(capacitado)* trained, qualified
2 NM *(medicamento)* preparation

preparador, -a NM,F coach, trainer

preparar 1 VT (a) *(disponer, elaborar)* to prepare, to get ready; **p. un examen** to prepare for an exam (b) *Dep (entrenar)* to train, to coach
2 prepararse VPR (a) *(disponerse)* to prepare oneself, to get ready (b) *Dep (entrenarse)* to train

preparativo NM preparation

preparatorio, -a ADJ preparatory

preponderante ADJ preponderant

preposición NF *Ling* preposition

prepotente ADJ domineering; *(arrogante)* overbearing

prerrogativa NF prerogative

presa NF (a) *(de animal)* prey; *Fig* **ser p. de** to be a victim of; **p. del pánico** panic-stricken (b) *(embalse)* dam

presagiar [43] VT to predict, to foretell

presagio NM (a) *(señal)* omen; **buen/mal p.** good/bad omen (b) *(premonición)* premonition

presbiteriano, -a ADJ & NM,F Presbyterian

presbítero NM priest

prescindir VI **p. de** to do without

prescribir *(pp prescrito)* VT to prescribe

prescripción NF prescription; **p. facultativa** medical prescription

prescrito, -a PP de **prescribir**

presencia NF presence; **hacer acto de p.** to put in an appearance; **p. de ánimo** presence of mind

presencial ADJ **testigo p.** eyewitness

presenciar [43] VT *(ver)* to witness

presentable ADJ presentable; **no estoy p.** I'm not dressed for the occasion

presentación NF presentation; *(aspecto)* appearance; *(de personas)* introduction

presentador, -a NM,F *Rad & TV* presenter

presentar 1 VT (a) *(mostrar, anunciar)* to present (b) *(una persona a otra)* to introduce; **le presento al doctor Ruiz** may I introduce you to Dr Ruiz (c) *(ofrecer) (disculpas, excusas)* to make; *(respetos)* to pay (d) *(tener) (aspecto)* to have, to show
2 presentarse VPR (a) *(comparecer)* to

present oneself; *(inesperadamente)* to turn o come up (**b**) *(ocasión, oportunidad)* to present itself, to arise (**c**) *(candidato)* to stand; **presentarse a unas elecciones** to stand for election, *US* to run for office; **presentarse a un examen** to sit an examination (**d**) *(darse a conocer)* to introduce oneself (**a** to)

presente 1 ADJ present; **la p.** *(carta)* this letter; **hacer p.** to declare, to state; **tener p.** *(tener en cuenta)* to bear in mind; *(recordar)* to remember
  2 NM present

presentimiento NM presentiment, premonition; **tengo el p. de que …** I have the feeling that …

presentir [5] VT to have a presentiment o premonition of

preservación NF preservation, protection

preservar VT to preserve, to protect (**de** from; **contra** against)

preservativo NM sheath, condom

presidencia NF (**a**) *Pol* presidency (**b**) *(de una reunión)* (hombre) chairmanship; *(mujer)* chairwomanship

presidenciable NMF *esp Am* potential presidential candidate

presidencial ADJ presidential

presidente, -a NM,F (**a**) *Pol (de nación)* president; **p. (del gobierno)** prime minister (**b**) *(de una reunión)* chairperson

presidiario, -a NM,F prisoner, convict

presidio NM prison, penitentiary

presidir VT (**a**) *Pol* to rule, to head (**b**) *(reunión)* to chair, to preside over

presión NF pressure; **a** o **bajo p.** under pressure; **grupo de p.** pressure group, lobby; **p. arterial** o **sanguínea** blood pressure; **p. atmosférica** atmospheric pressure

presionar VT to press; *Fig* to pressurize, to put pressure on

preso, -a 1 ADJ imprisoned
  2 NM,F prisoner

prestación NF (**a**) *(de servicio)* (acción) provision; *(resultado)* service (**b**) *(subsidio)* benefit (**c**) **prestaciones** *(de vehículo)* performance

prestado, -a ADJ **dejar p.** to lend; **pedir p.** to borrow; **vivir de p.** to scrounge

prestamista NMF moneylender

préstamo NM loan

prestar 1 VT (**a**) *(dejar)* (dinero, cosa) to lend, to loan; **¿me prestas tu pluma?** can I borrow your pen? (**b**) *(atención)* to pay; *(ayuda)* to give; *(servicio)* to do
  2 prestarse VPR (**a**) *(ofrecerse)* to offer oneself (**a** to) (**b**) **prestarse a** *(dar motivo)* to cause; **se presta a (crear) malentendidos** it makes for misunderstandings

presteza NF promptness; **con p.** promptly

prestidigitador, -a NM,F conjuror, magician

prestigiar [43] VT to give prestige to

prestigio NM prestige

prestigioso, -a ADJ prestigious

presto, -a ADJ *Fml* (**a**) *(dispuesto)* ready, prepared (**b**) *(rápido)* swift, prompt

presumible ADJ probable, likely

presumido, -a 1 ADJ vain, conceited
  2 NM,F vain person

presumir 1 VT *(suponer)* to presume, to suppose
  2 VI (**a**) *(ser vanidoso)* to show off (**b**) **presume de guapo** he thinks he's good-looking

presunción NF (**a**) *(suposición)* presumption, supposition (**b**) *(vanidad)* vanity, conceit

presunto, -a ADJ supposed; *Der* alleged

presuntuoso, -a ADJ (**a**) *(vanidoso)* vain, conceited (**b**) *(pretencioso)* pretentious, showy

Observa que la palabra inglesa **presumptuous** es un falso amigo y no es la traducción de la palabra española **presuntuoso**. En inglés **presumptuous** significa "impertinente".

presuponer [19] (pp **presupuesto**) VT to presuppose

presupuestar VT to budget

presupuestario, -a ADJ budgetary

presupuesto, -a 1 NM (**a**) *Fin* budget; *(cálculo)* estimate (**b**) *(supuesto)* supposition, assumption
  2 PP *de* **presuponer**

presuroso, -a ADJ *(rápido)* quick; *(con prisa)* in a hurry

pretencioso, -a ADJ pretentious

pretender VT (**a**) *(intentar)* to try; **¿qué pretendes insinuar?** what are you getting at? (**b**) *(afirmar)* to claim (**c**) *(aspirar a)* to try for (**d**) *(cortejar)* to court, to woo

pretendiente, -a NM,F (**a**) *(al trono)* pretender (**b**) *(a un cargo)* applicant, candidate (**c**) *(amante)* suitor

pretensión NF (**a**) *(aspiración)* aim, aspiration (**b**) *(presunción)* pretentiousness

pretérito, -a 1 ADJ past, former
  2 NM *Ling* preterite, simple past tense

pretextar VT to plead, to allege

pretexto NM pretext, excuse

pretil NM parapet

prevalecer [33] VI to prevail

prevención NF (**a**) *(precaución)* prevention; **en p. de** as a prevention against (**b**) *(medida)* precaution

prevenir [27] VT (**a**) *(preparar)* to prepare, to get ready (**b**) *(prever)* to prevent, to forestall; *(evitar)* to avoid; **para p. la gripe** to prevent flu; *Prov* **más vale p. que curar** prevention is better than cure (**c**) *(advertir)* to warn

preventivo, -a ADJ preventive; *(medidas)* precautionary; *Der* **detención** o **prisión preventiva** remand in custody

prever [28] *(pp previsto)* VT (**a**) *(prevenir)* to foresee, to forecast (**b**) *(preparar de antemano)* to cater for

previo, -a ADJ previous, prior; **p. pago de su importe** only on payment; **sin p. aviso** without prior notice

previsible ADJ predictable

previsión NF (**a**) *(predicción)* forecast; **p. del tiempo** weather forecast (**b**) *(precaución)* precaution; **en p. de** as a precaution against (**c**) *Andes, RP* **p. social** social security

previsor, -a ADJ careful, far-sighted

previsto, -a 1 ADJ foreseen, forecast; **según lo p.** as expected
2 PP *de* **prever**

prieto, -a ADJ (**a**) *(ceñido)* tight; **íbamos muy prietos en el coche** we were really squashed together in the car (**b**) *Méx (oscuro)* dark

prima NF *(gratificación)* bonus; **p. de seguro** insurance premium

primacía NF primacy

primar 1 VI to have priority, to prevail
2 VT to give a bonus to

primaria NF *(enseñanza)* primary education

primario, -a ADJ primary

primavera NF spring

primer ADJ *(delante de nm)* ver **primero**

primera NF (**a**) *(en tren)* first class (**b**) *Aut (marcha)* first gear (**c**) **a la p.** at the first attempt; *Fam* **de p.** great, first-class

primero, -a 1 ADJ first; **a primera hora de la mañana** first thing in the morning; **primera página** o **plana** front page; **de primera necesidad** basic

> **Primer** is used instead of **primero** before masculine singular nouns (e.g. **el primer hombre** the first man).

2 NM,F first; **a primero(s) de mes** at the beginning of the month
3 ADV (**a**) *(en primer lugar)* first (**b**) *(más bien)* rather, sooner

primicia NF scoop, exclusive

primitivo, -a ADJ primitive

primo, -a 1 NM,F (**a**) *(familiar)* cousin; **p. hermano** first cousin (**b**) *Fam (tonto)* fool, drip, dunce
2 ADJ (**a**) **materia prima** raw material (**b**) *(número)* prime

primogénito, -a ADJ & NM,F first-born

primor NM (**a**) *(delicadeza)* delicacy (**b**) *(belleza)* beauty

primordial ADJ essential, fundamental

primoroso, -a ADJ delicate, exquisite

princesa NF princess

principado NM principality

principal ADJ main, principal; **lo p. es que …** the main thing is that …; **puerta p.** front door

príncipe NM prince

principiante 1 ADJ novice
2 NMF beginner, novice

principio NM (**a**) *(comienzo)* beginning, start; **a principio(s) de** at the beginning of; **al p., en un p.** at first, in the beginning (**b**) *(fundamento)* principle; **en p.** in principle (**c**) **principios** rudiments, basics

pringar [42] **1** VT *(ensuciar)* to make greasy/dirty
2 VI *Fam (trabajar)* to work hard
3 **pringarse** VPR (**a**) *(ensuciarse)* to get greasy/dirty (**b**) *Fam (meterse de lleno)* to get involved

pringoso, -a ADJ *(grasiento)* greasy; *(sucio)* dirty

pringue NM *(grasa)* grease

prior, -a NM,F *(hombre)* prior; *(mujer)* prioress

priori: a priori LOC ADV a priori

prioridad NF priority

prioritario, -a ADJ priority

prisa NF (**a**) *(rapidez)* hurry; **date p.** hurry up; **tener p.** to be in a hurry; **de/a p.** in a hurry (**b**) **correr p.** to be urgent; **me corre mucha p.** I need it right away

prisión NF prison, jail

prisionero, -a NM,F prisoner

prisma NM prism

prismáticos NMPL binoculars, field glasses

priva NF *Esp Fam* booze

privación NF deprivation

privado, -a ADJ private

privar 1 VT *(despojar)* to deprive (**de** of)
2 VI (**a**) *Fam (gustar)* to like; *(estar de moda)* to be fashionable o popular (**b**) *Fam (beber)* to booze
3 **privarse** VPR *(abstenerse)* to deprive oneself (**de** of), to go without

privativo, -a ADJ exclusive (**de** of)

privilegiado, -a 1 ADJ privileged
2 NM,F privileged person

privilegio NM privilege

pro 1 NM advantage; **los pros y los contras** the pros and cons; **en p. de** in favour of
2 PREP in favour of; **campaña p. desarme** campaign for disarmament, disarmament campaign

proa NF prow, bows

probabilidad NF probability, likelihood; **tiene pocas probabilidades** he stands little chance

probable ADJ probable, likely; **es p. que llueva** it'll probably rain

probador NM fitting room

probar [2] **1** VT (**a**) *(comida, bebida)* to try (**b**) *(comprobar)* to test, to check (**c**) *(intentar)* to try (**d**) *(demostrar)* to prove, to show
2 VI to try; **p. a** to attempt o try to
3 **probarse** VPR *(ropa)* to try on

probeta NF test tube; **niño p.** test-tube baby

problema NM problem

problemático, -a ADJ problematic

procedencia NF origin, source

procedente ADJ (a) *(originario)* coming (**de** from) (b) *(adecuado)* appropriate; *Der* proper

proceder 1 VI (a) **p. de** *(provenir)* to come from (b) *(actuar)* to act (c) *(ser oportuno)* to be advisable o appropriate; *Der* **la protesta no procede** objection overruled (d) **p. a** *(continuar)* to go on to
2 NM *(comportamiento)* behaviour

procedimiento NM (a) *(método)* procedure (b) *Der (trámites)* proceedings

procesado, -a 1 NM,F accused
2 NM *Inform* processing

procesador NM processor; **p. de textos** word processor

procesamiento NM (a) *Der* prosecution (b) *Inform* **p. de datos/textos** data/word processing

procesar VT (a) *Der* to prosecute (b) *(elaborar, transformar)* to process; *Inform* to process

procesión NF procession

proceso NM (a) *(operación)* process; *Inform* **p. de datos** data processing (b) *Der* trial

proclamación NF proclamation

proclamar VT to proclaim

proclive ADJ prone, inclined

procreación NF procreation

procrear VT to procreate

procurador, -a NM,F *Der* attorney

procuraduría NF *Méx* **p. general de justicia** Ministry of Justice

procurar VT (a) *(intentar)* to try, to attempt; **procura que no te vean** make sure they don't see you (b) *(proporcionar)* (to manage) to get

prodigar [42] *Fml* 1 VT *(dar generosamente)* to lavish
2 **prodigarse** VPR **prodigarse en** to be lavish in

prodigio NM prodigy, miracle; **hacer prodigios** to work wonders; **niño p.** child prodigy

prodigioso, -a ADJ *(sobrenatural)* prodigious; *(maravilloso)* wonderful, marvellous

pródigo, -a ADJ generous, lavish; **es p. en regalos** he's very generous with presents

producción NF (a) *(acción)* production; *(producto)* product; **p. en cadena/serie** assembly-line/mass production (b) *Cin & TV* production

producir [10] 1 VT (a) *(producto, sonido)* to produce; *(fruto, cosecha)* to yield, to bear; *(ganancias)* to yield (b) *Fig (originar)* to cause, to bring about (c) *Cine & TV* to produce
2 **producirse** VPR to take place, to happen

productividad NF productivity

productivo, -a ADJ productive; *(beneficioso)* profitable

producto NM product; *Agr (producción)* produce

productor, -a 1 ADJ producing
2 NM,F producer

proeza NF heroic deed, exploit

profanación NF desecration, profanation

profanar VT to desecrate, to profane

profano, -a 1 ADJ profane, secular
2 NM,F *(hombre)* layman; *(mujer)* laywoman

profecía NF prophecy

proferir [31] VT to utter; **p. insultos** to hurl insults

profesar VT to profess

profesión NF profession; **de p.** by profession

profesional ADJ & NMF professional

profesionista ADJ & NMF *Méx* professional

profeso: ex profeso LOC ADV intentionally

profesor, -a NM,F teacher; *Univ Br* lecturer, *US* professor

profesorado NM *(profesión)* teaching; *(grupo de profesores)* staff

profeta NM prophet

profetizar [40] VT to prophesy, to foretell

profiláctico, -a 1 ADJ prophylactic
2 NM condom

prófugo, -a 1 ADJ & NM,F fugitive
2 NM *Mil* deserter

profundidad NF depth; *Fig (de ideas etc)* profundity, depth; **un metro de p.** one metre deep o in depth

profundizar [40] 1 VT *(hoyo, conocimientos)* to deepen
2 VI *(en excavación)* to dig deeper; *(en estudio, conocimientos)* to go into depth; **p. en** *(tema)* to study in depth

profundo, -a ADJ deep; *Fig (idea, sentimiento)* profound

profusión NF profusion

progenitor, -a NM,F *(antepasado)* ancestor, progenitor; **progenitores** *(padres)* parents

programa NM programme; *Inform* program; *Educ* syllabus

programación NF *Rad & TV* programme planning

programador, -a NM,F *Inform* programmer

programar VT to programme; *Inform* to program

progre ADJ & NMF *Fam* lefty

progresar VI to progress, to make progress

progresista ADJ & NMF progressive

progresivo, -a ADJ progressive

progreso NM progress; **hace grandes progresos** he's making great progress

prohibición NF prohibition, ban

prohibido, -a ADJ forbidden, prohibited; **prohibida la entrada** *(en letrero)* no admittance; **p. aparcar/fumar** *(en letrero)* no parking/smoking

prohibir VT to forbid, to prohibit; **se prohíbe pasar** *(en letrero)* no admittance o entry

prohibitivo, -a ADJ prohibitive

prójimo, -a NM,F one's fellow man, one's neighbour

proletariado NM proletariat

proletario, -a ADJ & NM,F proletarian

proliferación NF proliferation; **p. nuclear** proliferation (of nuclear arms)

proliferar VI to proliferate

prolífico, -a ADJ prolific

prolijo, -a ADJ verbose, long-winded

prólogo NM prologue

prolongación NF prolonging, extension, prolongation

prolongado, -a ADJ long

prolongar [42] **1** VT (*alargar*) to prolong, to extend
2 prolongarse VPR (*continuar*) to carry on

promedio NM average; **como p.** on average

promesa NF promise; *Fig* **la joven p. de la música** the promising young musician

prometedor, -a ADJ promising

prometer 1 VT to promise; **te lo prometo** I promise
2 VI to be promising
3 prometerse VPR (*pareja*) to get engaged

prometido, -a 1 ADJ promised
2 NM,F (*hombre*) fiancé; (*mujer*) fiancée

prominente ADJ (*elevado*) protruding, projecting; (*importante*) prominent

promiscuo, -a ADJ promiscuous

promoción NF promotion; *Educ* **p. universitaria** class, year

promocionar VT (*cosas*) to promote; (*personas*) to promote

promotor, -a 1 ADJ promoting
2 NM,F promoter

promover [4] VT (**a**) (*cosas, personas*) to promote; (*juicio, querella*) to initiate (**b**) (*causar*) to cause, to give rise to

promulgar [42] VT to promulgate

pronombre NM pronoun

pronosticar [44] VT to predict, to forecast; *Med* to make a prognosis of

pronóstico NM (*del tiempo*) forecast; *Med* prognosis

pronto, -a 1 ADJ quick, prompt; *Fml* (*dispuesto*) prepared
2 NM (*impulso*) sudden impulse
3 ADV (**a**) (*deprisa*) quickly, rapidly; **al p.** at first; **de p.** suddenly; **por de** *o* **lo p.** (*para empezar*) to start with (**b**) (*dentro de poco*) soon; **¡hasta p.!** see you soon! (**c**) *Esp* (*temprano*) early; **salimos p.** we left early

pronunciación NF pronunciation

pronunciamiento NM (**a**) *Mil* uprising, insurrection (**b**) *Der* pronouncement

pronunciar [43] **1** VT to pronounce; (*discurso*) to deliver
2 pronunciarse VPR (**a**) (*opinar*) to declare oneself (**b**) (*sublevarse*) to rise up

propagación NF propagation, spreading

propagador, -a NM,F propagator

propaganda NF (*política*) propaganda; (*comercial*) advertising, publicity

propagar [42] **1** VT to propagate, to spread
2 propagarse VPR to spread

propano NM propane

propasarse VPR to go too far

propensión NF tendency, inclination

propenso, -a ADJ (**a**) (*inclinado*) prone, inclined (**b**) *Med* susceptible

propiamente ADV **p. dicho** strictly speaking

propiciar [43] VT (*causar*) to cause

propicio, -a ADJ propitious, suitable; **ser p. a** to be inclined to

propiedad NF (**a**) (*posesión*) ownership; (*cosa poseída*) property (**b**) (*cualidad*) property, quality; *Fig* **con p.** properly, appropriately

propietario, -a NM,F owner

propina NF tip; **dar p. (a algn)** to tip (sb)

propinar VT to give

propio, -a ADJ (**a**) (*de uno*) own; **en su propia casa** in his own house (**b**) (*correcto*) suitable, appropriate; **juegos propios para su edad** games suitable for their age (**c**) (*característico*) typical, peculiar (**d**) (*mismo*) (*hombre*) himself; (*mujer*) herself; (*animal, cosa*) itself; **el p. autor** the author himself (**e**) **propios, -as** themselves; **los propios inquilinos** the tenants themselves (**f**) *Ling* proper

proponer [19] (*pp* **propuesto**) **1** VT to propose, to suggest
2 proponerse VPR to intend

proporción NF (**a**) (*relación*) proportion; **en p. con** in proportion to (**b**) **proporciones** (*tamaño*) size

proporcionado, -a ADJ (*mesurado*) proportionate, in proportion

proporcional ADJ proportional

proporcionar VT (*dar*) to give, to supply, to provide

proposición NF (**a**) (*propuesta*) proposal (**b**) (*oración*) clause

propósito NM (**a**) (*intención*) intention (**b**) **a p.** (*por cierto*) by the way; (*adrede*) on purpose, intentionally …; **a p. de viajes …** speaking of travelling …

propuesta NF suggestion, proposal

propuesto, -a PP *de* **proponer**

propugnar VT to advocate

propulsar VT (*vehículo*) to drive; *Fig* (*idea*) to promote

propulsión NF propulsion

propulsor, -a NM,F promoter

propuse PT INDEF *de* **proponer**

prórroga NF (**a**) (*prolongación*) extension; *Dep Br* extra time, *US* overtime (**b**) (*aplazamiento*) postponement; *Mil* deferment

prorrogar [42] VT (**a**) *(prolongar)* to extend (**b**) *(aplazar)* to postpone; *Mil* to defer

prorrumpir VI to burst (**en** into)

prosa NF prose

proscrito, -a 1 ADJ *(persona)* exiled, banished; *(cosa)* banned
2 NM,F exile, outlaw

proseguir [6] VT & VI to carry on, to continue

prospección NF (**a**) *Min* prospect (**b**) *Com* survey

prospecto NM leaflet, prospectus

prosperar VI *(negocio, país)* to prosper, to thrive; *(propuesta)* to be accepted

prosperidad NF prosperity

próspero, -a ADJ prosperous, thriving; **¡p. año nuevo!** Happy New Year!

prostíbulo NM brothel

prostitución NF prostitution

prostituir [37] **1** VT to prostitute
2 prostituirse VPR to prostitute oneself

prostituta NF prostitute

protagonista NMF (**a**) *(de obra, película)* main character, leading role; **¿quién es el p.?** who plays the lead? (**b**) *Fig* **ser p. de** *(acontecimiento histórico)* to play a leading part in; *(accidente)* to be one of the main people involved in

protagonizar [40] VT (**a**) *(obra, película)* to play the lead in, to star in (**b**) *(acontecimiento histórico)* to play a leading part in; *(accidente)* to be one of the main people involved in

protección NF protection

proteccionismo NM protectionism

protector, -a 1 ADJ protecting, protective
2 NM,F protector

proteger [53] VT to protect, to defend

protegido, -a NM,F *(hombre)* protégé; *(mujer)* protégée

proteína NF protein

prótesis NF INV prosthesis

protesta NF protest; *Der* objection

protestante ADJ & NMF *Rel* Protestant

protestar VI (**a**) *(quejarse)* to complain (**por** about); *Der* to object (**b**) *Pol* to protest

protestón, -ona NM,F *Fam* moaner

protocolo NM protocol

protón NM proton

prototipo NM prototype

protuberancia NF protuberance

protuberante ADJ protuberant, bulging

prov. *(abr* **provincia)** prov

provecho NM profit, benefit; **¡buen p.!** enjoy your meal!; **sacar p. de algo** to benefit from sth

provechoso, -a ADJ beneficial

proveedor, -a NM,F supplier, purveyor; *Inform* **p. de acceso (a Internet)** Internet access provider

proveer [36] *(pp* **provisto)** VT to supply, to provide

proveniente ADJ *(procedente)* coming; *(resultante)* arising, resulting

provenir [27] VI **p. de** to come from

proverbio NM proverb

providencia NF providence

provincia NF province

provincial ADJ provincial

provinciano, -a ADJ & NM,F *Pey* provincial

provisión NF provision

provisional, *Am* **provisorio, -a** ADJ provisional

provisto, -a 1 ADJ **p. de** equipped with
2 PP *de* **proveer**

provocación NF provocation

provocado, -a ADJ provoked, caused; **incendio p.** arson

provocador, -a 1 NM,F instigator, agent provocateur
2 ADJ provocative

provocar [44] VT (**a**) *(causar)* to cause; **p. un incendio** to start a fire (**b**) *(instigar)* to provoke (**c**) *Carib, Col, Méx Fam (apetecer)* **¿te provoca ir al cine?** would you like to go to the movies?, *Br* do you fancy going to the cinema?

provocativo, -a ADJ provocative

proxeneta NMF procurer, pimp

próximamente ADV *(pronto)* soon; *Cin & Teatro (en letrero)* coming soon

proximidad NF proximity, closeness; **en las proximidades de** close to, in the vicinity of

próximo, -a ADJ (**a**) *(cercano)* near, close (**b**) *(siguiente)* next

proyección NF (**a**) *(de mapa)* projection (**b**) *Cin* screening, showing

proyectar VT (**a**) *(luz)* to project (**b**) *(planear)* to plan (**c**) *Cin* to project, to screen

proyectil NM projectile

proyecto NM *(plan)* project, plan; **tener algo en p.** to be planning sth; **p. de ley** bill

proyector NM *Cin* projector

prudencia NF prudence, discretion; *(moderación)* care

prudente ADJ prudent, sensible; *(conductor)* careful; **a una hora p.** at a reasonable time

prueba NF (**a**) *(demostración)* piece of evidence; *(concluyente)* proof; **en p. de** as a sign of (**b**) *(examen etc)* test; **a p.** on trial; **a p. de agua/balas** waterproof/bullet-proof; **haz la p.** try it (**c**) *Dep* event

psicoanálisis NM INV psychoanalysis

psicodélico, -a ADJ psychedelic

psicología NF psychology

psicológico, -a ADJ psychological

psicólogo, -a NM,F psychologist

psicópata NMF psychopath

psicosis NF INV psychosis

psicotécnico, -a ADJ psychometric

psicoterapeuta NMF psychotherapist

psicoterapia NF psychotherapy

psicótico, -a ADJ & NM,F psychotic

psique NF psyche

psiquiatra NMF psychiatrist

psiquiatría NF psychiatry

psiquiátrico, -a 1 ADJ psychiatric; **hospital p.** psychiatric hospital
　2 NM psychiatric hospital

psíquico, -a ADJ psychic

PSOE NM *Pol* (*abr* **Partido Socialista Obrero Español**) = Spanish political party to the centre-left of the political spectrum

pta. (*pl* **ptas.**) *Antes* (*abr* **peseta**) peseta

púa NF (**a**) (*de planta*) thorn; (*de animal*) quill, spine; (*de peine*) tooth; **alambre de púas** barbed wire (**b**) *Mús* plectrum

pub [paβ, paf] (*pl* **pubs**) NM pub

pubertad NF puberty

pubis NM INV pubes

publicación NF publication

publicar [44] VT (**a**) (*libro etc*) to publish (**b**) (*secreto*) to publicize

publicidad NF (**a**) *Com* advertising (**b**) (*conocimiento público*) publicity

publicitario, -a ADJ advertising

público, -a 1 ADJ public
　2 NM public; *Teatro* audience; *Dep* spectators

pucha INTERJ *Andes, RP Fam Euf* (**a**) (*lamento, enojo*) *Br* sugar!, *US* shoot! (**b**) (*sorpresa*) wow!

pucherazo NM rigging of an election

puchero NM (**a**) (*olla*) cooking pot; (*cocido*) stew (**b**) **hacer pucheros** to pout

pucho NM *Fam* (**a**) *Andes, RP* (*cigarrillo*) cigarette, *Br* fag (**b**) *Andes, RP* (*colilla*) cigarette butt (**c**) *Chile, Ecuad* (*hijo menor*) youngest child

pude PT INDEF *de* **poder**

pudendo, -a ADJ **partes pudendas** private parts

púdico, -a ADJ modest

pudiente ADJ rich, wealthy

pudor NM modesty

pudoroso, -a ADJ modest

pudrir 1 VT to rot
　2 pudrirse VPR to rot

pueblerino, -a ADJ *Pey* countrified, provincial

pueblo NM (**a**) (*población*) (*pequeña*) village; (*grande*) town (**b**) (*gente*) people; **el p. español** the Spanish people

puente NM (**a**) (*construcción*) bridge; *Av* **p. aéreo** (*civil*) air shuttle service; *Mil* airlift; **p. colgante** suspension bridge; **p. levadizo** drawbridge (**b**) (*vacaciones*) ≃ long weekend (**c**) (*en dientes*) bridge

puerco, -a 1 ADJ filthy
　2 NM,F pig
　3 NM **p. espín** porcupine

puericultura NF paediatrics *sing*

pueril ADJ childish, puerile

puerro NM leek

puerta NF door; (*verja, en aeropuerto*) gate; *Dep* goal; **p. corredera/giratoria** sliding/revolving door; *Fig* **a las puertas, en puertas** imminent; *Fig* **a p. cerrada** behind closed doors

puerto NM (**a**) (*de mar*) port, harbour; **p. deportivo** marina (**b**) (*de montaña*) (mountain) pass

Puerto Rico N Puerto Rico

puertorriqueño, -a ADJ & NM,F Puerto Rican

pues CONJ (**a**) (*puesto que*) as, since (**b**) (*por lo tanto*) therefore (**c**) (*entonces*) so (**d**) (*para reforzar*) **¡p. claro que sí!** but of course!; **p. como iba diciendo** well, as I was saying; **¡p. mejor!** so much the better!; **¡p. no!** certainly not! (**e**) (*como pregunta*) **¿p.?** why?

puesta NF (**a**) **p. de sol** sunset (**b**) *Fig* **p. a punto** tuning, adjusting; *Fig* **p. al día** updating; *Teatro* **p. en escena** staging; **p. en marcha** starting-up, start-up

puestero, -a NM,F *Am* stallholder

puesto, -a 1 CONJ *p. que* since, as
　2 NM (**a**) (*lugar*) place; (*asiento*) seat (**b**) (*empleo*) position, post, job; **p. de trabajo** job, post (**c**) (*tienda*) stall (**d**) *Mil* post
　3 ADJ (**a**) (*colocado*) set, put (**b**) **llevar p.** (*ropa*) to have on; *Fam* **ir muy p.** to be all dressed up (**c**) *Fam* (*borracho*) drunk (**d**) *Fam* **estar p. en una materia** to be well up in a subject
　4 PP *de* **poner**

púgil NM boxer

pugna NF battle, fight

pugnar VI to fight, to struggle (**por** for)

puja NF (*acción*) bidding; (*cantidad*) bid

pujante ADJ thriving, prosperous

pujanza NF strength, vigour

pujar VI (**a**) (*pugnar*) to struggle (**b**) (*en subasta*) to bid higher

pulcro, -a ADJ (extremely) neat

pulga NF flea; *Fam* **tener malas pulgas** to be bad-tempered, *Br* to be stroppy

pulgada NF inch

pulgar NM thumb

pulidora NF polisher

pulimentar VT to polish

pulir VT (**a**) (*metal, madera*) to polish (**b**) (*mejorar*) to polish up

pulla NF dig

pulmón NM lung

pulmonía NF pneumonia

pulpa NF pulp

pulpería NF *Am* general store

púlpito NM pulpit

pulpo NM octopus

pulque NM *CAm, Méx* pulque, = fermented agave cactus juice

pulquería NF *CAm, Méx* "pulque" bar

pulsación NF keystroke

pulsar VT *(timbre, botón)* to press; *(tecla)* to hit, to strike

pulsera NF *(aro)* bracelet; *(de reloj)* watchstrap; **reloj de p.** wristwatch

pulso NM **(a)** *(latido)* pulse; *Fig* **tomar el p. a la opinión pública** to sound out opinion **(b)** *(firmeza)* **tener buen p.** to have a steady hand; **a p.** freehand **(c)** *(lucha)* **echar un p. (con algn)** to arm-wrestle (with sb) **(d)** *(situación conflictiva)* battle of wills

pulverizador NM spray, atomizer

pulverizar [40] VT *(sólidos)* to pulverize; *(líquidos)* to spray; *(récord)* to smash

puma NM puma

puna NF *Andes* **(a)** *(llanura)* Andean plateau **(b)** *(mal de altura)* altitude sickness

pundonor NM self-respect, self-esteem

punk [pank] *(pl* **punks)** ADJ NM & NMF punk

punki ['panki] ADJ & NMF punk

punta NF **(a)** *(extremo)* tip; *(extremo afilado)* point; *(de cabello)* end; **sacar p. a un lápiz** to sharpen a pencil; **tecnología p.** state-of-the-art technology; **me pone los nervios de p.** he makes me very nervous **(b)** *(periodo)* peak; **hora p.** rush hour **(c)** *(pequeña cantidad)* bit; **una p. de sal** a pinch of salt **(d)** *(clavo)* nail

puntada NF **(a)** *(pespunte)* stitch **(b)** *RP (dolor)* stabbing pain **(c)** *Méx (broma)* witticism

puntaje NF *Am (calificación)* mark, *US* grade; *(en concursos, competiciones)* score

puntal NM *(madero)* prop; *Fig (soporte)* pillar, support

puntapié NM kick

puntear VT **(a)** *(dibujar)* to dot **(b)** *Mús (guitarra)* to pluck

punteo NM plucking

puntera NF *(de zapato)* toecap; *(de calcetín)* toe

puntería NF aim; **tener buena/mala p.** to be a good/bad shot

puntero, -a **1** ADJ leading **2** NM,F *CSur Dep* winger

puntiagudo, -a ADJ pointed, sharp

puntilla NF **(a)** *(encaje)* lace **(b)** **dar la p.** *Taurom* to finish (the bull) off; *Fig (liquidar)* to finish off **(c)** **de puntillas** on tiptoe

puntilloso, -a ADJ touchy

punto NM **(a)** *(unidad, tanto)* point; **p. muerto** *Aut* neutral; *Fig (impase)* deadlock; **p. de vista** point of view **(b)** *(marca)* dot; **línea de puntos** dotted line **(c)** *(lugar)* place, point **(d)** *(signo ortográfico)* **p. y aparte** *Br* full stop *o US* period, new paragraph; **p. y coma** semicolon; **p. y seguido** *Br* full stop, *US* period *(no new paragraph)*; **dos puntos** colon **(e)** *Cost & Med* stitch; **hacer p.** to knit **(f)** *(expresiones)* **a p.** ready; *Culin* **en su p.** just right; **a p. de** on the point of; **hasta cierto p.** to a certain *o* some extent; **en p.** *(tiempo)* sharp, on the dot

puntocom NF *(empresa)* dotcom

puntuable ADJ *Dep* **una prueba p. para** a race counting towards

puntuación NF **(a)** *Ling* punctuation **(b)** *Dep* score **(c)** *Educ* mark

puntual **1** ADJ **(a)** *(en el tiempo)* punctual **(b)** *(exacto)* accurate, precise **(c)** *(aislado)* specific **2** ADV punctually

puntualidad NF punctuality

puntualización NF clarification

puntualizar [40] VT to specify, to clarify

puntuar [30] **1** VT *(al escribir)* to punctuate **2** VI **(a)** *(marcar)* to score **(b)** *(ser puntuable)* to count

punzada NF *(de dolor)* sudden sharp pain

punzante ADJ *(objeto)* sharp; *(dolor)* acute, piercing

punzar [40] VT *Téc* to punch

punzón NM *(herramienta)* punch

puñado NM handful; *Fam* **a puñados** by the score, galore

puñal NM dagger

puñalada NF stab; *Fig* **p. trapera** stab in the back

puñeta NF *Fam* **hacer la p. a algn** to pester sb, to annoy sb; **¡puñetas!** damn!; **¡vete a hacer puñetas!** go to hell!

puñetazo NM punch

puñetero, -a *Esp Fam* **1** ADJ **(a)** *(persona)* damn **(b)** *(cosa)* tricky, awkward **2** NM,F pain

puño NM **(a)** *(mano cerrada)* fist **(b)** *(de camisa etc)* cuff **(c)** *(de herramienta)* handle

pupa NF **(a)** *(herida)* cold sore **(b)** *Fam (daño)* pain

pupila NF *(de ojo)* pupil

pupilo, -a NM,F pupil

pupitre NM desk

purasangre ADJ & NM thoroughbred

puré NM purée; **p. de patatas** mashed potatoes; **p. de verduras** thick vegetable soup

pureta NMF *Fam* old fogey

pureza NF purity

purga NF *Med* purgative; *Fig* purge

purgante ADJ & NM purgative

purgar [42] VT *Med & Fig* to purge

purgatorio NM purgatory

purificación NF purification

purificar [44] VT to purify

purista NMF purist

puritano, -a **1** ADJ puritanical **2** NM,F puritan, Puritan

puro, -a **1** ADJ **(a)** *(sin mezclas)* pure; **aire p.** fresh air; **la pura verdad** the plain truth; *Pol* **y duro** hardline **(b)** *(mero)* sheer, mere; **por pura curiosidad** out of sheer curiosity **(c)** *(casto)* chaste, pure **2** NM *(cigarro)* cigar

púrpura ADJ INV purple

purpúreo, -a ADJ purple

pus NM pus

puse PT INDEF *de* **poner**

pusilánime ADJ faint-hearted

pústula NF sore, pustule

puta NF *Vulg* whore; **de p. madre** great, terrific; **de p. pena** *Br* bloody *o US* goddamn awful; **no tengo ni p. idea** I haven't (got) a *Br* bloody *o US* goddamn clue; **pasarlas putas** to go through hell, to have a rotten time

putada NF *muy Fam* dirty trick; **¡qué p.!** what a bugger!

puteada NF *RP muy Fam (insulto)* swear word

putear VT *muy Fam* (**a**) *(fastidiar)* **p. a algn** to screw *o* bugger sb around (**b**) *Am (insultar)* **p. a algn** to call sb for everything, to call sb every name under the sun

puticlub NM *Fam* brothel

puto, -a 1 ADJ *Vulg* fucking
2 NM male prostitute, stud

putrefacto, -a, pútrido, -a ADJ putrefied, rotten

puzzle NM jigsaw puzzle

PVC NM *(abr* **cloruro de polivinilo**) PVC

PVP NM *(abr* **precio de venta al público**) RRP

PYME NF *(abr* **Pequeña y Mediana Empresa**) SME

Pza. *(abr* **Plaza**) Sq

Q

Q, q [ku] NF *(letra)* Q, q

que¹ PRON REL (**a**) *(sujeto)* *(persona)* who; *(cosa)* that, which; **el hombre q. vino** the man who came; **la bomba q. estalló** the bomb that o which went off (**b**) *(complemento)* *(persona)* no se traduce o that o who o *Fml* whom; *(cosa)* no se traduce o that o which; **la chica q. conocí** the girl (that o who o whom) I met; **el coche q. compré** the car (that o which) I bought (**c**) **lo q.** what; **lo q. más me gusta** what I like best o which; *(con infinitivo)* no se traduce **hay mucho q. hacer** there's a lot to do

que² CONJ (**a**) *no se traduce o* that; **dijo q. llamaría** he said (that) he would call; **quiero q. vengas** I want you to come

(**b**) *(consecutivo)* no se traduce o that; *(en comparativas)* than; **habla tan bajo q. no se le oye** he speaks so quietly (that) he can't be heard; **más alto q. yo** taller than me

(**c**) *(causal)* no se traduce **date deprisa q. no tenemos mucho tiempo** hurry up, we haven't got much time

(**d**) *(enfático)* no se traduce **¡q. no!** no!; **¡q. te calles!** I said be quiet!

(**e**) *(deseo, mandato)* (+ *subjunctive*) *no se traduce;* **¡q. te diviertas!** enjoy yourself!

(**f**) *(final)* so that; **ven q. te dé un beso** come and let me give you a kiss

(**g**) *(disyuntivo)* whether; **me da igual q. suba o no** it doesn't matter to me whether he comes up or not

(**h**) *(locuciones)* **¿a q. no …?** I bet you can't …!; **q. yo sepa** as far as I know; **yo q. tú** if I were you

qué 1 PRON (**a**) what; **¿q. quieres?** what do you want?; *Fam* **¿y q.?** so what? (**b**) *(exclamativo)* (+ *adj*) how; (+ *n*) what a; **¡q. bonito!** how pretty!; **¡q. lástima!** what a pity!; *Fam* **¡q. de …!** what a lot of …!

2 ADJ which; **¿q. libro quieres?** which book do you want?

quebrada NF *Am (arroyo)* stream

quebradero NM **q. de cabeza** headache

quebradizo, -a ADJ *(débil)* fragile; *(cabello, hielo)* brittle

quebrado NM *Mat* fraction

quebrantamiento NM *(de ley)* violation, infringement

quebrantar VT (**a**) *(promesa, ley)* to break (**b**) *(moral, resistencia)* to break

quebrar [1] **1** VT *(romper)* to break
2 VI *Fin* to go bankrupt

3 quebrarse VPR to break; *Med* to rupture oneself

queda NF **toque de q.** curfew

quedar 1 VI (**a**) *(restar)* to be left, to remain; **quedan dos** there are two left (**b**) *(en un lugar)* to arrange to meet; **quedamos en el bar** I'll meet you in the bar (**c**) **me queda corta** *(ropa)* it is too short for me; **quedaría muy bien allí** *(objeto)* it would look very nice there (**d**) *(acordar)* to agree (**en** to); **¿en qué quedamos?** so what's it to be? (**e**) *(estar situado)* to be; **¿dónde queda la estación?** where's the station? (**f**) **q. bien/mal** to make a good/bad impression

2 quedarse VPR (**a**) *(permanecer)* to stay; **se quedó en casa** she stayed (at) home; **quedarse sin dinero/pan** to run out of money/bread; **quedarse con hambre** to still be hungry (**b**) **quedarse (con)** *(retener)* to keep; **quédese (con) el cambio** keep the change (**c**) *Esp Fam* **quedarse con algn** to make a fool of sb

quedo ADV softly, quietly

quehacer NM task, chore

queja NF complaint; *(de dolor)* groan, moan

quejarse VPR to complain (**de** about)

quejica *Fam* **1** ADJ grumpy
2 NMF moaner

quejido NM groan, cry

quemado, -a ADJ (**a**) *(por el fuego)* burnt, burned; *(por el sol)* sunburnt (**b**) *Fig (agotado)* burnt-out

quemador NM *(de cocina)* burner

quemadura NF burn

quemar 1 VT *(amar)* to love; *Fig (agotar)* to burn out
2 VI to be burning hot; **este café quema** this coffee's boiling hot
3 quemarse VPR *Fig* to burn out

quemarropa: a quemarropa LOC ADV point-blank

quemazón NF smarting

quena NF Andean flute

quepa *etc ver* caber

quepo INDIC PRES *de* caber

queque NM *Andes, CAm, Méx* sponge (cake)

querella NF *Der* lawsuit

querer [20] **1** VT (**a**) *(amar)* to love (**b**) *(desear)* to want; **¿cuánto quiere por la casa?** how much does he want for the house?; **sin q.** without meaning to; **queriendo** on purpose; **¡por lo que más quieras!** for heaven's sake!;

¿quiere pasarme el pan? would you pass me the bread? (**c**) **q. decir** to mean (**d**) **no quiso darme permiso** he refused me permission
2 quererse VPR to love each other
3 NM love, affection

querido, -a 1 ADJ dear, beloved; **q. amigo** (*en carta*) dear friend
2 NM,F (*amante*) lover; (*mujer*) mistress

queroseno, *Am* **querosén** NM kerosene, kerosine

querré INDIC FUT *de* **querer**

quesadilla NF (**a**) *CAm, Méx* (*salada*) = filled fried tortilla (**b**) *Ecuad* (*dulce*) = sweet, cheese-filled pasty

queso NM cheese; **q. rallado** grated cheese; **q. de cerdo** *Br* brawn, *US* headcheese

quetzal NM quetzal, = standard monetary unit of Guatemala

quicio NM (*de puerta*) doorpost; *Fig* **sacar de q.** (*persona*) to infuriate; (*cosa*) to take too far

quid NM crux; **has dado en el q.** you've hit the nail on the head

quiebra NF *Fin* (*bancarrota*) bankruptcy; (*crack*) crash

quiebro NM (*con el cuerpo*) dodge; *Ftb* dribbling

quien PRON REL (**a**) (*con prep*) *no se traduce o Fml* whom; **el hombre con q. vino** the man she came with; *Fml* the man with whom she came (**b**) (*indefinido*) whoever, anyone who; **q. quiera venir que venga** whoever wants to can come; **hay q. dice lo contrario** some people say the opposite; *Fig* **q. más q. menos** everybody

quién PRON INTERR (**a**) (*sujeto*) who?; **¿q. es?** who is it? (**b**) (*complemento*) who, *Fml* whom; **¿para q. es?** who is it for?; **¿de q. es esa bici?** whose bike is that?

quienquiera (*pl* **quienesquiera**) PRON whoever; **q. que venga** whoever comes

quieto, -a ADJ still; (*mar*) calm; **¡estáte q.!** keep still!, don't move!

quietud NF (*inmovilidad*) stillness; (*calma*) calm

quijada NF jawbone

quilate NM carat

quilla NF keel

quillango NM *Arg, Chile* fur blanket

quilo NM = **kilo**

quilombo NM *RP muy Fam* (**a**) (*burdel*) whorehouse (**b**) (*lío, desorden*) **se armó un gran q.** all hell broke loose

quimera NF fantasy, pipe dream

química NF chemistry

químico, -a 1 ADJ chemical
2 NM,F chemist

quimioterapia NF chemotherapy

quimono NM kimono

quincallería NF trinkets

quince ADJ & NM INV fifteen

quinceañero, -a ADJ & NM,F fifteen-year-old

quincena NF fortnight, two weeks

quincenal ADJ fortnightly

quincho NM (**a**) *Andes, RP* (*techo*) thatched roof (**b**) *Andes, RP* (*refugio*) thatched shelter

quinielas NFPL *Esp Br* (football) pools, *US* sports lottery

quinientos, -as ADJ & NM five hundred

quinina NF quinine

quinqué NM oil lamp

quinquenal ADJ quinquennial, five-year

quinta NF (**a**) (*casa*) country house (**b**) *Mil* call-up year

quintaesencia NF quintessence

quintal NM (*medida*) = 46 kg; **q. métrico** ≃ 100 kg

quinteto NM quintet

quinto, -a 1 ADJ & NM,F fifth
2 NM *Mil* conscript, recruit

quiosco NM kiosk; **q. de periódicos** newspaper stand

quipos, quipus NMPL *Andes* quipus, = knotted cords used for record keeping by the Incas

quirófano NM operating *Br* theatre *o US* room

quiromancia NF palmistry

quirúrgico, -a ADJ surgical

quise INDIC FUT *de* **querer**

quisque, quisqui PRON *Fam* **todo** *o* **cada q.** everyone, everybody

quisquilloso, -a 1 ADJ fussy, finicky
2 NM,F fusspot

quiste NM cyst

quitaesmalte NM INV nail varnish *o* polish remover

quitamanchas NM INV stain remover

quitanieves NM INV snow plough

quitar 1 VT (**a**) to remove; (*ropa*) to take off; (*la mesa*) to clear; (*mancha*) to remove; (*dolor*) to relieve; (*hipo*) to stop; (*sed*) to quench; (*hambre*) to take away (**b**) (*apartar*) to take away, to take off; **q. importancia a algo** to play sth down; **q. las ganas a algn** to put sb off (**c**) (*robar*) to steal, to take; (*tiempo*) to take up; (*sitio*) to take (**d**) (*descontar*) to take off (**e**) *Fam* (*apagar*) to turn off (**f**) **eso no quita para que ...** that's no reason not to be ... (**g**) **¡quita!** go away!
2 quitarse VPR (**a**) (*apartarse*) to move away (**b**) (*mancha*) to come out; (*dolor*) to go away; **se me han quitado las ganas** I don't feel like it any more (**c**) (*ropa, gafas*) to take off (**d**) **quitarse de beber/fumar** to give up drinking/smoking (**e**) **quitarse a algn de encima** to get rid of sb

Observa que el verbo inglés **to quit** es un falso amigo y no es la traducción del verbo español **quitar**. En inglés, **to quit** significa "dejar, abandonar".

quizá(s) ADV perhaps, maybe

R, r ['erre] NF (letra) R, r

rábano NM radish; Fam **me importa un r.** I couldn't care less

rabia NF (a) Fig (ira) fury, rage; **¡qué r.!** how annoying!; **me da r.** it gets up my nose; **me tiene r.** he's got it in for me (b) Med rabies sing

rabiar [43] VI (enfadar) to rage; **hacer r. a algn** to make sb see red

rabieta NF Fam tantrum; **coger una r.** to throw a tantrum

rabillo NM (del ojo) corner

rabino NM rabbi

rabioso, -a ADJ (a) Med rabid; **perro r.** rabid dog (b) Fig (enfadado) furious (c) **de rabiosa actualidad** up-to-the-minute

rabo NM tail; (de fruta etc) stalk

racanear VI Fam to be stingy

rácano, -a ADJ Fam stingy, mean

racha NF (de viento) gust, squall; Fam (período) spell, patch; **a rachas** in fits and starts

racial ADJ **discriminación r.** racial discrimination; **disturbios raciales** race riots

racimo NM bunch, cluster

raciocinio NM reason

ración NF portion

racional ADJ rational

racionalizar [40] VT to rationalize

racionamiento NM rationing; **cartilla de r.** ration book

racionar VT (limitar) to ration; (repartir) to ration out

racismo NM racism

racista ADJ & NMF racist

radar NM Téc radar

radiación NF radiation

radiactividad NF radioactivity

radiactivo, -a ADJ radioactive

radiador NM radiator

radial ADJ (a) (en forma de estrella) radial (b) Am (de la radio) radio

radiante ADJ radiant (de with)

radiar [43] VT to broadcast, to transmit

radical ADJ radical

radicalizar [40] **1** VT to harden, to make more radical
2 radicalizarse VPR to become more radical o extreme

radicar [44] VI (estar) to be (situated) (en in), to be rooted (en in)

radio 1 NF (medio) radio; Esp, CSur (aparato) radio (set)
2 NM (a) Anat & Geom radius; **r. de acción** field of action, scope (b) (de rueda) spoke (c) Quím radium (d) Am salvo CSur (transistor) radio

radioactividad NF radioactivity

radioactivo, -a ADJ radioactive

radioaficionado, -a NM,F radio ham

radiocasete NM radio cassette

radiodespertador NM clock radio

radiodifusión NF broadcasting

radioescucha NMF listener

radiograbador NM, **radiograbadora** NF CSur radio cassette

radiografía NF (imagen) X-ray

radiólogo, -a NM,F radiologist

radionovela NF radio soap opera

radiotaxi NM (aparato de radio) = taxi-driver's two-way radio; (taxi) taxi (fitted with two-way radio)

radioyente NMF listener

ráfaga NF (de viento) gust, squall; (de disparos) burst

rafting NM Dep rafting

raído, -a ADJ worn

raigambre NF roots

raíl NM rail

raíz NF root; **r. cuadrada** square root; Fig **a r. de** as a result of

raja NF (corte) cut, slit; (hendidura) crack, split

rajar 1 VT (hender) to crack, split; Fam (acuchillar) to cut up
2 VI Esp Fam to natter on, to witter on
3 rajarse VPR (a) (partirse) to crack (b) Esp Fam (echarse atrás) to back o pull out

rajatabla: a rajatabla LOC ADV to the letter, strictly

ralea NF Pey type, sort

ralentí NM neutral; **estar al r.** to be ticking over

ralentizar VT to slow down

rallado, -a ADJ **queso r.** grated cheese; **pan r.** breadcrumbs

rallador NM grater

ralladura NF gratings

rallar VT to grate

rally ['rrali] (pl rallys) NM rally

ralo, -a ADJ sparse, thin

rama NF branch; Fam **andarse o irse por las ramas** to beat about the bush

ramaje NM branches

ramalazo NM *Fam* **cuando le da el r.** when the mood takes him

rambla NF *(avenida)* boulevard, avenue

ramera NF prostitute, whore

ramificación NF ramification

ramificarse [44] VPR to ramify, to branch (out)

ramillete NM *(de flores)* posy

ramo NM (a) *(de flores)* bunch, bouquet (b) *(sector)* branch

rampa NF ramp; **r. de lanzamiento** launch pad

ramplón, -ona ADJ coarse, vulgar

rana NF frog; *Fam* **salir r.** to be a disappointment

ranchera NF (a) *Mús* = popular Mexican song (b) *(automóvil) Br* estate (car), *US* station wagon

ranchero, -a NM,F rancher, farmer

rancho NM (a) *(granja)* ranch (b) *Mil (comida)* mess (c) *RP (en la playa)* = thatched beachside building (d) *CSur, Ven (en la ciudad)* shack, shanty (e) *Méx (pequeña finca)* = small farmhouse and outbuildings

rancio, -a ADJ (a) *(comida)* stale (b) *(antiguo)* ancient

rango NM rank; *(jerarquía elevada)* high social standing

ranura NF slot

rapar VT *(afeitar)* to shave; *(pelo)* to crop

rapaz¹ ADJ predatory; **ave r.** bird of prey

rapaz², -aza NM,F youngster; *(muchacho)* lad; *(muchacha)* lass

rape NM (a) *(pez)* angler fish (b) *Fam* **cortado al r.** close-cropped

rapero, -a NM,F *Mús* rapper

rápidamente ADV quickly

rapidez NF speed, rapidity

rápido, -a 1 ADJ quick, fast, rapid
2 ADV quickly
3 NM (a) *(tren)* fast train (b) **rápidos** *(de un río)* rapids

rapiña NF robbery, theft; **ave de r.** bird of prey

raptar VT to kidnap, to abduct

rapto NM (a) *(secuestro)* kidnapping, abduction (b) *Fig (arrebato)* outburst, fit

raqueta NF (a) *(de tenis)* racquet; *(de pingpong) Br* bat, *US* paddle (b) *(de nieve)* snowshoe

raquítico, -a ADJ *Fam (escaso)* small, meagre; *(delgado)* emaciated

raquitismo NM rickets *sing*

rareza NF (a) *(de persona, cosa)* rarity (b) *(extravagancia)* eccentricity

raro, -a ADJ (a) *(extraño)* odd, strange (b) *(excepcional)* rare; **rara vez** seldom

ras NM level; **a r. de** (on a) level with; **a r. de tierra** at ground level

rasante 1 NF *Aut* **cambio de r.** brow of a hill
2 ADJ *(vuelo)* low

rasar VT *(nivelar)* to level

rasca NF *Esp Fam (frío)* cold

rascacielos NM INV skyscraper

rascador NM *(herramienta)* scraper

rascar [44] **1** VT *(con las uñas)* to scratch; *(guitarra)* to strum
2 VI to chafe

rasero NM *Fig* **medir con el mismo r.** to treat impartially

rasgado, -a ADJ *(ojos)* slit, almond-shaped

rasgar [42] VT to tear, to rip

rasgo NM *(característica)* characteristic, feature; *(de la cara)* feature; *Fig* **a grandes rasgos** broadly speaking

rasgón NM tear, rip

rasguñar VT to scratch, to scrape

rasguño NM scratch, scrape

raso, -a 1 ADJ *(llano)* flat, level; *(vuelo)* low; *(cielo)* clear, cloudless; **soldado r.** private
2 NM satin

raspa NF *(de pescado)* bone, backbone

raspador NM scraper

raspadura NF scraping, scrapings

raspar 1 VT to scrape (off)
2 VI *(ropa etc)* to chafe

rastra NF **a la r., a rastras** dragging; *Fig (de mal grado)* grudgingly

rastreador NM tracker

rastrear VT to search, to comb

rastreo NM searching, combing

rastrero, -a ADJ despicable

rastrillo NM (a) *(herramienta)* rake (b) *(mercado)* flea market (c) *Méx (para afeitarse)* razor

rastro NM (a) *(pista)* trace; *(en el suelo)* trail (b) *(mercado)* flea market

rastrojo NM stubble

rasurar VT to shave

rata 1 NF rat
2 NM *Fam (tacaño)* mean o stingy person

ratero, -a NM,F pickpocket

ratificar [44] VT to ratify

rato NM (a) *(momento)* while, time; **a ratos** at times; **al poco r.** shortly after; **hay para r.** it'll take a while; **pasar un buen/mal r.** to have a good/bad time; **ratos libres** free time (b) *Esp Fam* **un r.** *(mucho)* very, a lot

ratón NM mouse; *Esp Inform* mouse

ratonera NF mousetrap

raudal NM torrent, flood; *Fig* **a raudales** in abundance

raya NF (a) *(línea)* line; *(del pantalón)* crease; *Esp, Andes, RP (del pelo) Br* parting, *US* part; **camisa a rayas** striped shirt (b) *Fig* **tener a r.** to keep at bay; **pasarse de la r.** to go over the score (c) *(de droga)* fix, dose

rayano, -a ADJ bordering *(en* on)

rayar 1 VT *(arañar)* to scratch
2 VI **r. en** o **con** to border on

rayo NM (**a**) *(de luz)* ray; *Fís* ray, beam; **rayos X** X-rays (**b**) *(relámpago)* (flash of) lightning; **¡mal r. la parta!** to hell with her!

rayón NM rayon

rayuela NF hopscotch

raza NF (**a**) *(humana)* race (**b**) *(de animal)* breed (**c**) *Méx Pey (populacho)* **la r.** the masses (**d**) *Perú (descaro)* cheek, nerve

razón NF (**a**) *(facultad)* reason; **uso de r.** power of reasoning (**b**) *(motivo)* reason; **r. de más para** all the more reason to (**c**) *(justicia)* rightness, justice; **dar la r. a algn** to say that sb is right; **tienes r.** you're right (**d**) *(proporción)* ratio, rate; **a r. de** at the rate of (**e**) **r. aquí** *(en letrero)* enquire within, apply within

razonable ADJ reasonable

razonado, -a ADJ reasoned, well-reasoned

razonamiento NM reasoning

razonar 1 VT *(argumentar)* to reason out
2 VI *(discurrir)* to reason

reacción NF reaction; **avión de r.** jet (plane); **r. en cadena** chain reaction

reaccionar VI to react

reaccionario, -a ADJ & NM,F reactionary

reacio, -a ADJ reluctant, unwilling

reactor NM reactor; *(avión)* jet (plane)

readaptación NF readjustment

reafirmar VT to reaffirm, to reassert

reagrupar VT to regroup

reajuste NM readjustment; *Com* **r. de plantillas** downsizing; **r. ministerial** cabinet reshuffle

real¹ ADJ *(efectivo, verdadero)* real; **en la vida r.** in real life

real² ADJ *(regio)* royal

realce NM *(relieve)* relief; *Fig (esplendor)* splendour

realeza NF royalty

realidad NF reality; **en r.** in fact, actually; **la r. es que ...** the fact of the matter is that ...

realismo NM realism

realista 1 ADJ realistic
2 NM,F realist

realizable ADJ feasible

realización NF *(ejecución)* carrying out; *Cin & TV* production

realizador, -a NM,F *Cin & TV* producer

realizar [40] 1 VT (**a**) *(hacer)* to carry out; *(ambición)* to achieve, to fulfil (**b**) *Cin & TV* to produce (**c**) *Fin* to realize
2 **realizarse** VPR *(persona)* to fulfil oneself; *(sueño)* to come true

realmente ADV really; *(en realidad)* actually, in fact

realzar [40] VT *(belleza, importancia)* to enhance, to heighten

reanimación NF (**a**) *(física, moral)* recovery (**b**) *Med* resuscitation

reanimar 1 VT (**a**) *(físicamente)* to revive (**b**) *(moralmente)* to cheer up (**c**) *Med* to resuscitate
2 **reanimarse** VPR to revive

reanudación NF renewal, resumption; **r. de las clases** return to school

reanudar 1 VT to renew, to resume; **r. el paso** o **la marcha** to set off again; **r. las clases** to go back to school
2 **reanudarse** VPR to start again, to resume

reaparición NF reappearance, recurrence; *(de artista etc)* comeback

reapertura NF reopening

rearme NM rearmament

reaseguro NM reinsurance

reavivar VT to revive

rebaja NF *(descuento)* reduction, discount; **rebajas** sales; **precio de r.** sale price

rebajado, -a ADJ (**a**) *(precio)* reduced (**b**) *(diluido)* diluted (**con** with)

rebajar 1 VT (**a**) *(precio)* to cut, to reduce; *(cantidad)* to take off (**b**) *(color)* to tone down, to soften; *(intensidad)* to diminish (**c**) *(trabajador)* to excuse, to exempt (**de** from) (**d**) *(humillar)* to humiliate
2 **rebajarse** VPR *(humillarse)* to humble oneself

rebanada NF slice

rebanar VT to slice, to cut into slices

rebañar VT to scrape clean

rebaño NM *(de ovejas)* flock; *(de otros animales)* herd

rebasar VT (**a**) *(exceder)* to exceed, to go beyond (**b**) *Aut* to overtake

rebatir VT to refute

> Observa que la palabra inglesa **rebate** es un falso amigo y no es la traducción del verbo español **rebatir**. En inglés, **rebate** significa "devolución".

rebeca NF cardigan

rebelarse VPR to rebel, to revolt

rebelde 1 NM,F rebel
2 ADJ rebellious; *Fig* **una tos r.** a persistent cough

rebeldía NF (**a**) *(cualidad)* rebelliousness (**b**) *Der* default

rebelión NF rebellion, revolt

rebenque NM *RP (fusta)* (riding) crop, whip

reblandecer [33] VT to soften

rebobinar VT to rewind

rebosante ADJ overflowing (**de** with), brimming (**de** with)

rebosar 1 VI to overflow, to brim over; *Fig* **r. de** to be overflowing o brimming with
2 VT *(irradiar)* to radiate

rebotar VI to bounce (**en** off), to rebound (**en** off)

rebote NM (**a**) *(bote)* bounce, bouncing; *Fig* **de r.** by chance, indirectly (**b**) *Dep* rebound; **de r.** on the rebound

rebozado, -a ADJ *Culin* coated in batter/breadcrumbs; *Fig* **r. de** o **en** *(barro)* covered in

rebozar [40] VT to coat in batter/breadcrumbs

rebozo NM *Am* wrap, shawl; **sin r.** *(con franqueza)* frankly

rebullirse VPR to stir

rebuscado, -a ADJ recherché

rebuznar VI to bray

recabar VT *(información)* to obtain, to manage to get

recado NM *(mandado)* errand; *(mensaje)* message; **dejar un r.** to leave a message

recaer [39] VI (a) *Med* to relapse (b) *(culpa, responsabilidad)* to fall (**sobre** on)

recaída NF relapse

recalcar [44] VT to stress, to emphasize

recalcitrante ADJ recalcitrant

recalentar [1] VT *(comida)* to reheat, to warm up; *(calentar demasiado)* to overheat

recámara NF (a) *(de rueda)* tube (b) *(habitación)* dressing room (c) *CAm, Col, Méx (dormitorio)* bedroom

recamarera NF *CAm, Col, Méx* chambermaid

recambiar [43] VT to change (over)

recambio NM (a) *(repuesto)* spare (part); **rueda de r.** spare wheel (b) *(de pluma etc)* refill

recapacitar VI to think

recarga NF *(de móvil)* top-up

recargable ADJ *(pluma)* refillable; *(mechero)* rechargeable

recargado, -a ADJ overloaded; *Fig (estilo)* overelaborate, affected

recargar [42] 1 VT (a) *Elec* to recharge (b) *(sobrecargar)* to overload; *(adornar mucho)* to overelaborate (c) *Fin* to increase
2 **recargarse** VPR *Méx (apoyarse)* to lean (**contra** against)

recargo NM extra charge, surcharge

recatado, -a ADJ *(modesto)* modest, decent

recato NM *(pudor)* modesty; **sin r.** openly, without reserve

recaudación NF *(cobro)* collection; *(cantidad recaudada)* takings; *Dep* gate

recaudador, -a NM,F tax collector

recaudar VT to collect

recaudo NM **estar a buen r.** to be in safekeeping

recelar VI **r. de** to distrust

recelo NM suspicion, distrust

receloso, -a ADJ suspicious, distrustful

recepción NF reception; *(en hotel)* reception (desk)

recepcionista NMF receptionist

receptivo, -a ADJ receptive

receptor, -a 1 NM,F *(persona)* recipient
2 NM *Rad & TV* receiver

recesión NF recession

receta NF recipe; *Med* prescription

recetar VT *Med* to prescribe

rechazar [40] VT to reject, to turn down; *Mil* to repel, to drive back

rechazo NM rejection

rechiflar VT (a) *(silbar)* to hiss, to boo (b) *(mofarse)* to mock, to jeer at

rechinar VI *(dientes)* to grind; *(madera)* to creak; *(metal)* to squeak, to screech

rechistar VI **sin r.** without a word of protest

rechoncho, -a ADJ *Fam* chubby, tubby

rechupete: de rechupete LOC *Fam* **estaba de r.** it was mouthwateringly good

recibidor NM entrance hall

recibimiento NM reception, welcome

recibir 1 VT to receive; *(en casa)* to welcome; *(en la estación etc)* to meet
2 **recibirse** VPR *Am (graduarse)* to graduate, to qualify (**de** as)

recibo NM (a) *(factura)* invoice, bill; *(resguardo)* receipt; **r. de la luz** electricity bill (b) **acusar r. de** to acknowledge receipt of

reciclado, -a 1 ADJ recycled
2 NM *(reciclaje)* recycling

reciclaje NM *(de residuos)* recycling; *Fig (renovación)* retraining; **curso de r.** refresher course

reciclar VT *(residuos)* to recycle; *Fig (profesores etc)* to retrain

recién ADV (a) *(recientemente) (antes de pp)* recently, newly; **café r. hecho** freshly-made coffee; **r. casados** newlyweds; **r. nacido** newborn baby (b) *Am (apenas)* just now, recently; **regresó r. ayer** she only o just got back yesterday (c) *Am (ahora mismo)* (only) just; **r. me entero** I've (only) just heard (d) *Am (sólo)* only; **r. el martes sabremos el resultado** we'll only know the result on Tuesday, we won't know the result until Tuesday

reciente ADJ recent

recientemente ADV recently, lately

recinto NM *(cercado)* enclosure; **r. comercial** shopping precinct

recio, -a 1 ADJ *(robusto)* strong, sturdy; *(grueso)* thick; *(voz)* loud
2 ADV hard

recipiente NM receptacle, container

Observa que la palabra inglesa **recipient** es un falso amigo y no es la traducción de la palabra española **recipiente**. En inglés **recipient** significa "receptor, destinatario".

recíproco, -a ADJ reciprocal

recital NM *Mús* recital; *Lit* reading

recitar VT to recite

reclamación NF (a) *(demanda)* claim, demand (b) *(queja)* complaint

reclamar 1 VT to demand, to ask for
2 VI (a) *(quejarse)* to complain (**contra** about) (b) *Der* to appeal

reclamo NM (**a**) *(publicitario)* appeal (**b**) *(en caza)* decoy bird, lure; *Fig* inducement (**c**) *Am (queja)* complaint (**d**) *Am (reivindicación)* claim

reclinar 1 VT to lean (**sobre** on)
2 reclinarse VPR to lean back, to recline

recluir [37] VT to shut away, to lock away; *(encarcelar)* to imprison, to intern

reclusión NF seclusion; *(encarcelamiento)* imprisonment, internment

recluso, -a NM,F prisoner

> Observa que la palabra inglesa **recluse** es un falso amigo y no es la traducción de la palabra española **recluso**. En inglés, **recluse** significa "solitario".

recluta NMF recruit

reclutamiento NM *(voluntario)* recruitment; *(obligatorio)* conscription

recobrar 1 VT to recover, to retrieve; *(conocimiento)* to regain; **r. el aliento** to get one's breath back
2 recobrarse VPR to recover, to recuperate

recochineo NM *Fam* mockery

recodo NM *(de río)* twist, turn; *(de camino)* bend

recogedor NM dustpan

recoger [53] **1** VT (**a**) *(del suelo etc)* to pick up (**b**) *(datos etc)* to gather, to collect (**c**) *(ordenar, limpiar)* to clean; **r. la mesa** to clear the table (**d**) *(ir a buscar)* to pick up, to fetch (**e**) *(cosecha)* to gather, to pick
2 recogerse VPR (**a**) *(irse a casa)* to go home (**b**) *(pelo)* to lift up

recogida NF collection; *Agr (cosecha)* harvest, harvesting

recolección NF *Agr* harvest, harvesting; *(recogida)* collection, gathering

> Observa que la palabra inglesa **recollection** es un falso amigo y no es la traducción de la palabra española **recolección**. En inglés, **recollection** significa "recuerdo".

recomendable ADJ recommendable

recomendación NF recommendation, reference

recomendado, -a ADJ *Am (carta, paquete)* registered

recomendar [1] VT to recommend

recompensa NF reward

recompensar VT to reward

recomponer [19] *(pp* **recompuesto)** VT to repair, to mend

reconciliación NF reconciliation

reconciliar [43] **1** VT to reconcile
2 reconciliarse VPR to be reconciled

recóndito, -a ADJ hidden, secret

reconfortante ADJ comforting

reconfortar VT to comfort

reconocer [34] VT (**a**) *(identificar)* to recognize (**b**) *(admitir)* to admit (**c**) *Med (paciente)* to examine

reconocimiento NM (**a**) *(identificación, admisión)* recognition (**b**) *Med* examination, checkup (**c**) *(agradecimiento)* gratitude

reconquista NF reconquest

reconstruir [37] VT to reconstruct

reconversión NF restructuring; **r. industrial** rationalization of industry

reconvertir [5] VT *(reestructurar)* to restructure; *(industria)* to rationalize

recopilación NF compilation, collection

recopilar VT to compile, to collect

récord *(pl* **récords)** NM record

recordar [2] **1** VT (**a**) *(rememorar)* to remember (**b**) **r. algo a algn** to remind sb of sth
2 VI to remember

recordatorio NM *(aviso)* reminder; *(de defunción)* notice of death

recorrer VT *(distancia)* to cover, to travel; *(país)* to tour, to travel through *o* round; *(ciudad)* to visit, to walk round

recorrido NM, *Am* **recorrida** NF *(distancia)* distance travelled; *(trayecto)* trip, journey; *(itinerario)* itinerary, route

recortable ADJ & NM cutout

recortar VT to cut out

recorte NM *(acción, de periódico)* cutting; *(de salarios etc)* cut

recostado, -a ADJ reclining, leaning

recostar [2] **1** VT to lean
2 recostarse VPR *(tumbarse)* to lie down

recoveco NM nook, corner

recrear 1 VT to recreate
2 recrearse VPR **r. con** to take pleasure *o* delight in

recreativo, -a ADJ recreational

recreo NM *(en el colegio)* break, recreation

recriminar VT to reproach

recrudecerse [33] VPR to worsen

recrudecimiento NM worsening

recta NF *Geom* straight line; *(de carretera)* straight stretch; *Dep* **la r. final** the home straight

rectangular ADJ rectangular

rectángulo NM rectangle

rectificación NF *(de error)* rectification; *(en periódico)* correction

rectificar [44] VT *(error)* to rectify; *(conducta, actitud)* to improve

rectilíneo, -a ADJ straight

rectitud NF straightness; *Fig* uprightness, rectitude

recto, -a 1 ADJ (**a**) *(derecho)* straight (**b**) *(honesto)* upright, honest (**c**) *Geom* right
2 NM *Anat* rectum
3 ADV straight (on)

rector, -a 1 ADJ *(principio)* guiding, ruling
2 NM *Rel* rector

recua NF string, series

recuadro NM box

recubrir *(pp recubierto)* VT to cover

recuento NM count; **hacer (el) r. de** to count

recuerdo NM **(a)** *(memoria)* memory **(b)** *(regalo etc)* souvenir **(c) recuerdos** regards

recuperación NF recovery; *(examen)* resit

recuperar 1 VT *(salud)* to recover; *(conocimiento)* to regain; *(tiempo, clases)* to make up
2 recuperarse VPR to recover

recurrir VI **(a)** *Der* to appeal **(b) r. a** *(a algn)* to turn to; *(a algo)* to make use of, to resort to

Observa que el verbo inglés **to recur** es un falso amigo y no es la traducción del verbo español **recurrir**. En inglés, **to recur** significa "repetirse".

recurso NM **(a)** *(bien, riqueza)* resource; **recursos humanos** human resources; **recursos naturales** natural resources; **como último r.** as a last resort **(b)** *Der* appeal

red NF net; *(sistema)* network; *Com (cadena)* chain of supermarkets; *Fig (trampa)* trap; **la R.** *(Internet)* the Net

redacción NF *(escrito)* composition, essay; *(acción)* writing; *Prensa* editing; *(redactores)* editorial staff

redactar VT to draft; *Prensa* to edit

redactor, -a NM,F *Prensa* editor

redada NF **r. policial** *(en un solo sitio)* raid; *(en varios lugares a la vez)* round-up

redentor, -a NM,F redeemer

redil NM fold, sheepfold

redimir VT to redeem

redoblar 1 VT to redouble
2 VI *(tambor)* to roll

redoble NM roll; *(de campanas)* peal

redomado, -a ADJ utter, out-and-out

redonda NF **a la r.** around

redondeado, -a ADJ rounded

redondear VT *(objeto)* to round, to make round; *(cantidad)* to round up

redondel NM *Fam (círculo)* circle, ring; *Taurom* ring, arena

redondo, -a ADJ **(a)** *(circular)* round; *Fig* **caer r.** to collapse **(b)** *(rotundo)* categorical; *(perfecto)* perfect

reducción NF reduction

reducido, -a ADJ *(disminuido)* reduced, decreased; *(pequeño)* limited, small

reducir [10] **1** VT *(disminuir)* to reduce
2 reducirse VPR **(a)** *(disminuirse)* to be reduced, to diminish **(b)** *(limitarse)* to confine oneself

redundancia NF redundancy, superfluousness; **valga la r.** if I might say so again

redundante ADJ redundant

redundar VI **r. en** to result in, to lead to

reembolsar VT to reimburse; *(deuda)* to repay; *(importe)* to refund

reembolso NM reimbursement; *(de deuda)* repayment; *(devolución)* refund; **contra r.** cash on delivery

reemplazar [40] VT to replace **(con** with)

reemplazo NM replacement; *Mil* call-up

reestrenar VT *Cin* to rerun; *Teatro* to revive

reestreno NM **(a)** *Cin* rerun, re-release; **cine de r.** second-run cinema **(b)** *Teatro* revival

reestructuración NF restructuring

reestructurar VT to restructure

refacción NF **(a)** *Andes, CAm, RP, Ven (reforma)* refurbishment; *(reparación)* restoration **(b)** *Méx (recambio)* spare part

refaccionar VT *Andes, CAm, Ven (reformar)* to refurbish; *(reparar)* to restore

referencia NF reference; **con r. a** with reference to

referéndum *(pl referéndums)* NM referendum

referente ADJ **r. a** concerning, regarding

referir [5] **1** VT to tell, to relate
2 referirse VPR *(aludir)* to refer **(a** to); **¿a qué te refieres?** what do you mean?

refilón: de refilón LOC ADV *(de pasada)* briefly; **mirar algo de r.** to look at sth out of the corner of one's eye

refinado, -a ADJ refined

refinamiento NM refinement

refinar VT to refine

refinería NF refinery

reflector, -a 1 ADJ reflecting
2 NM *Elec* spotlight, searchlight

reflejar 1 VT to reflect
2 reflejarse VPR to be reflected **(en** in)

reflejo, -a 1 NM **(a)** *(imagen)* reflection **(b)** *(destello)* gleam, glint **(c)** *Anat* reflex **(d)** **reflejos** *(en el cabello)* streaks, highlights
2 ADJ *(movimiento)* reflex

reflexión NF reflection

reflexionar VI to reflect **(sobre** on), to think **(sobre** about)

reflexivo, -a ADJ **(a)** *(persona)* thoughtful **(b)** *Ling* reflexive

reflujo NM ebb (tide)

reforma NF **(a)** *(modificación)* reform; **r. fiscal** tax reform **(b)** *(en local, casa)* alterations

reformar 1 VT to reform; *(edificio)* to renovate
2 reformarse VPR to reform

reformatorio NM reformatory, reform school

reforzar [2] VT to reinforce, to strengthen

refractario, -a ADJ *Téc* heat-resistant

refrán NM proverb, saying

refregar [1] VT to rub vigorously; *Fig* **no me lo refriegues** don't rub it in

refrenar 1 VT to restrain, to curb
2 refrenarse VPR to restrain oneself

refrendar VT *(firmar)* to endorse, to counter-sign; *(aprobar)* to approve

refrescante ADJ refreshing

refrescar [44] **1** VT to refresh
2 VI *(a)* *(tiempo)* to turn cool *(b)* *(bebida)* to be refreshing
3 refrescarse VPR to cool down

refresco NM soft drink, refreshments

refriega NF *(lucha)* scuffle, brawl; *(escaramuza)* skirmish

refrigeración NF refrigeration

refrigerado, -a ADJ air-conditioned

refrigerador NM refrigerator, *Br* fridge, *US* icebox

refrigerar VT to refrigerate

refrigerio NM refreshments

refuerzo NM reinforcement

refugiado, -a ADJ & NM,F refugee

refugiarse [43] VPR to shelter, to take refuge

refugio NM refuge

refulgir [57] VI *(brillar)* to shine; *(resplandecer)* to glitter, to sparkle

refunfuñar VI to grumble, to moan

refutar VT to refute

regadera NF *(a)* *(para regar)* watering can; *Esp Fam* **estar como una r.** to be as mad as a hatter *(b)* *Col, Méx, Ven (ducha)* shower

regadío NM *(tierra)* irrigated land

regalado, -a ADJ *(a)* *(gratis)* free; *(muy barato)* dirt-cheap *(b)* **una vida regalada** an easy life

regalar VT *(a)* *(dar)* to give (as a present); *(en ofertas etc)* to give away *(b)* **r. el oído a algn** to flatter sb

regaliz NM liquorice

regalo NM present, gift; **de r.** as a present

regalón, -ona ADJ *CSur Fam (niño)* spoilt

regañadientes: a regañadientes LOC ADV reluctantly, unwillingly

regañar VT to tell off

regañina NF telling-off

regar [1] VT to water

regata NF boat race

regatear **1** VI *(a)* *(al comprar)* to haggle *(b)* *Dep* to dribble
2 VT **no r. esfuerzos** to spare no effort

regateo NM *(a)* *(de precios)* haggling *(b)* *Dep* dribbling

regazo NM lap

regeneración NF regeneration

regenerar VT to regenerate

regentar VT to rule, to govern; *(cargo)* to hold

regente **1** NMF *Pol* regent
2 NMF *(a)* *(director)* manager *(b)* *Méx (alcalde)* mayor, *f* mayoress

régimen *(pl* **regímenes)** NM *(a)* *Pol* regime *(b)* *Med* diet; **estar a r.** to be on a diet

regimiento NM regiment

regio, -a ADJ *(a)* *(real)* royal, regal *(b)* *Andes, RP (genial)* great, fabulous

región NF region

regional ADJ regional

regir [58] **1** VT to govern
2 VI to be in force
3 regirse VPR to be guided, to go *(por* by)

registrado, -a ADJ *(a)* *(patentado, inscrito)* registered; **marca registrada** registered trademark *(b)* *Am (certificado)* registered

registrador, -a ADJ **caja registradora** cash register

registradora NF *Am* cash register

registrar **1** VT *(a)* *(examinar)* to search *(b)* *(inscribir)* to register *(c)* *(grabar)* to record
2 registrarse VPR *(a)* *(inscribirse)* to register, to enrol *(b)* *(detectarse)* to be recorded

registro NM *(a)* *(inspección)* inspection *(b)* *(inscripción)* registration; *(oficina)* registry office; *(libro)* register *(c)* *Ling & Mús* register

regla NF *(a)* *(norma)* rule; **en r.** in order; **por r. general** as a (general) rule; **r. de oro** golden rule *(b)* *(instrumento)* ruler *(c)* *Mat* rule *(d)* *Med (periodo)* period

reglamentación NF regulation

reglamentar VT to regulate

reglamentario, -a ADJ statutory; *Mil* **arma reglamentaria** regulation gun

reglamento NM regulations, rules

reglar VT to regulate

regocijar **1** VT to delight, to amuse
2 regocijarse VPR to be delighted, to rejoice

regocijo NM *(placer)* delight, joy; *(alborozo)* rejoicing, merriment

regodearse VPR *Fam* to delight *(con* in)

regodeo NM *Fam* delight

regordete, -a ADJ *Fam* plump, chubby

regresar **1** VI to return
2 VT *Am salvo RP (devolver)* to give back
3 regresarse VPR *Am salvo RP (yendo)* to go back, to return; *(viniendo)* to come back, to return

regresión NF regression

regreso NM return

reguero NM *(de líquido)* trickle; *(de humo, arena)* trail

regulable ADJ adjustable

regular **1** VT *(a)* *(actividad, economía, tráfico)* to regulate, to control *(b)* *(mecanismo)* to adjust
2 ADJ *(a)* *(uniforme)* regular; **vuelo r.** sched-uled flight; **por lo r.** as a rule *(b)* *(mediano)* average, so-so
3 ADV so-so

regularidad NF regularity; **con r.** regularly

regularizar [40] VT to regularize

regusto NM aftertaste

rehabilitar VT to rehabilitate; *(edificio)* to convert

rehacer [15] (*pp* **rehecho**) **1** VT to redo
2 rehacerse VPR to recover, to recuperate

rehén NM hostage

rehogar [42] VT to brown

rehuir [37] VT to shun, to avoid

rehusar VT to refuse

reina NF queen

reinado NM reign

reinante ADJ (*que reina*) reigning, ruling; (*prevaleciente*) prevailing

reinar VI to reign

reincidente NMF *Der* recidivist

reincidir VI to relapse, to fall back (**en** into)

reincorporarse VPR **r. al trabajo** to return to work

reino NM kingdom; **el R. Unido** the United Kingdom

reinserción NF (*social*) reintegration, rehabilitation

reinsertar VT (*en sociedad*) to reintegrate, to rehabilitate

reintegrar VT (**a**) (*trabajador*) to reinstate (**b**) (*dinero*) to reimburse, to refund

reintegro NM (*en lotería*) winning of one's stake

reír [56] **1** VI to laugh
2 reírse VPR to laugh (**de** at)

reiterar VT to reiterate, to repeat

reivindicación NF claim, demand

reivindicar [44] VT to claim, to demand; **el atentado fue reivindicado por los terroristas** the terrorists claimed responsibility for the attack

reivindicativo, -a ADJ protest

reja NF (**a**) (*de ventana*) grill, grating; *Fam* **estar entre rejas** to be behind bars (**b**) *Agr* ploughshare

rejilla NF (*de ventana, ventilador, radiador*) grill; (*de horno*) gridiron; (*para equipaje*) luggage rack

rejoneador, -a NM,F *Taurom* = bullfighter on horseback

rejonear VT *Taurom* to fight on horseback

rejuvenecer [33] VT to rejuvenate

relación NF (**a**) (*conexión*) relation, connection; **con** *o* **en r.** with regard to (**b**) (*entre personas*) relationship; **relaciones públicas** public relations; **relaciones sexuales** sexual relations (**c**) (*lista*) list; (*relato*) account (**d**) *Mat & Téc* ratio

relacionado, -a ADJ related (**con** to), connected (**con** with)

relacionar 1 VT to relate (**con** to), to connect (**con** with)
2 relacionarse VPR (*alternar*) to mix (**con** with)

relajación NF relaxation

relajante ADJ relaxing

relajar 1 VT to relax
2 relajarse VPR to relax; (*moral*) to deteriorate

relajo NM (**a**) *Am Fam* (*alboroto*) **se armó un r.** there was an almighty row; **esta mesa es un r.** this table is a complete mess (**b**) *Méx, RP* (*complicación*) nuisance, hassle (**c**) *CAm, Carib, Méx* (*broma*) joke

relamerse VPR to lick one's lips

relamido, -a ADJ (*afectado*) affected; (*pulcro*) prim and proper

relámpago NM flash of lightning; *Fig* **pasó como un r.** he flashed past; *Fig* **visita r.** flying visit

relampaguear V IMPERS to flash

relanzar VT to relaunch

relatar VT to narrate, to relate

relatividad NF relativity

relativo, -a ADJ relative (**a** to); **en lo r. a** with regard to, concerning

relato NM (*cuento*) tale, story

relax NM *Fam* relaxation

relegar [42] VT to relegate

relevancia NF importance

> Observa que la palabra inglesa **relevance** es un falso amigo y no es la traducción de la palabra española **relevancia**. En inglés, **relevance** significa "pertinencia".

relevante ADJ important

relevar 1 VT to relieve, to take over from; **fue relevado del cargo** he was relieved of his duties
2 relevarse VPR (*turnarse*) to relieve one another

relevo NM relief; *Dep* relay

relieve NM *Arte* relief; *Fig* **poner de r.** to emphasize

religión NF religion

religioso, -a 1 ADJ religious
2 NM,F (*hombre*) monk; (*mujer*) nun

relinchar VI to neigh, to whinny

relincho NM neigh, whinny

reliquia NF relic

rellamada NF *Tel* redial

rellano NM landing

rellenar VT (**a**) (*impreso etc*) to fill in (**b**) (*un ave*) to stuff; (*un pastel*) to fill

relleno, -a 1 NM (*de aves*) stuffing; (*de pasteles*) filling
2 ADJ stuffed

reloj NM clock; (*de pulsera*) watch; **r. de arena** hourglass; **r. de sol** sundial; **r. despertador** alarm clock

relojería NF (*tienda*) watchmaker's, clockmaker's; **bomba de r.** time bomb

relojero, -a NM,F watchmaker, clockmaker

reluciente ADJ shining, gleaming

relucir [35] VI to shine, to gleam; **sacar a r. un tema** to bring up a subject

relumbrar VI to shine, to gleam

reluzco INDIC PRES *de* **relucir**

remachar VT to drive home, to hammer home

remache NM rivet

remanente NM *(restos)* remainder; *(extra)* surplus

remangar [42] **1** VT to roll up
2 remangarse VPR *(mangas, camisa)* to roll up one's sleeves; **remangarse los pantalones** to roll up one's trouser legs

remanso NM still pool; **r. de paz** oasis of peace

remar VI to row

remarcar [44] VT to stress, to underline

Observa que el verbo inglés **to remark** es un falso amigo y no es la traducción del verbo español **remarcar**. En inglés, **to remark** significa "comentar, observar".

rematadamente ADV **r. loco** as mad as a hatter

rematar VT (**a**) *(acabar)* to finish off, to put the finishing touches to (**b**) *Com* to sell off cheaply

remate NM (**a**) *(final)* end, finish; **para r.** to crown it all (**b**) *Dep* shot at goal (**c**) **de r.** utter, utterly

rembolsar VT = **reembolsar**

rembolso NM = **reembolso**

remedar VT to imitate, to copy

remediar [43] VT (**a**) *(daño)* to remedy; *(problema)* to solve; *(crisis, situación)* to resolve (**b**) *(evitar)* to avoid, to prevent; **no pude remediarlo** I couldn't help it

remedio NM *(cura)* remedy, cure; *(solución)* solution; **¡qué r.!** what else can I do?; **no hay más r.** there's no choice; **sin r.** without fail; *Fam* **¡no tienes r.!** you're hopeless!

remedo NM *(imitación)* imitation, copy; *(parodia)* parody

rememorar VT to remember, to recall

remendar [1] VT *(ropa)* to patch

remera NF *RP (prenda)* T-shirt

remero, -a NM,F rower

remesa NF *(de mercancías)* consignment, shipment; *(de dinero)* remittance

remiendo NM *(parche)* patch

remilgado, -a ADJ *(afectado)* affected; *(melindroso)* fussy, finicky; *(gazmoño)* prudish

remilgo NM affectation; *(gazmoñería)* prudishness

reminiscencia NF reminiscence

remise NM *RP* taxi *(in private car without meter)*

remisero, -a NM,F *RP* taxi driver *(of private car without meter)*

remiso, -a ADJ reluctant

remite NM *(en carta)* = sender's name and address

remitente NMF sender

remitir 1 VT (**a**) *(enviar)* to send (**b**) *(referir)* to refer
2 VI *(fiebre, temporal)* to subside
3 remitirse VPR **si nos remitimos a los hechos** if we look at the facts; **remítase a la página 10** see page 10

remítase a la página 10 see page 10

remo NM oar; *(deporte)* rowing

remoción NF *Andes, RP (de escombros)* removal; *(de heridos)* transport

remodelación NF reshaping; *(reorganización)* reorganization; *Pol* **r. ministerial** *o* **del gobierno** cabinet reshuffle

remodelar VT to reshape; *(reorganizar)* to reorganize

remojar VT to soak (**en** in)

remojo NM **dejar** *o* **poner en r.** to soak, to leave to soak

remojón NM *Fam* **darse un r.** to go for a dip

remolacha NF *(planta)* Br beetroot, US beet

remolcador NM (**a**) *Náut* tug, tugboat (**b**) *Aut Br* breakdown van *o* truck, *US* tow truck

remolcar [44] VT to tow

remolino NM *(de agua)* whirlpool, eddy; *(de aire)* whirlwind

remolón, -ona 1 ADJ lazy
2 NM,F **hacerse el r.** to shirk, to slack

remolonear VI to shirk, to slack

remolque NM *(acción)* towing; *(vehículo)* trailer; *Fig* **ir a r. de algn** to trundle along behind sb

remontar 1 VT (**a**) *(subir)* to go up (**b**) *(superar)* to overcome
2 remontarse VPR (**a**) *(pájaros, aviones)* to soar (**b**) *(datar)* to go back, to date back (**a** to)

remorder [4] VT **me remuerde la conciencia por …** I've got a bad conscience about …

remordimiento NM remorse

remoto, -a ADJ remote, faraway; **no tengo la más remota idea** I haven't got the faintest idea

remover [4] VT (**a**) *(trasladar)* to move over (**b**) *(tierra)* to turn over; *(líquido)* to shake up; *(comida etc)* to stir; *(asunto)* to stir up

Observa que el verbo inglés **to remove** es un falso amigo y no es la traducción del verbo español **remover**. En inglés, **to remove** significa "quitar, despedir".

remozar [40] VT to modernize

remplazar [40] VT = **reemplazar**

remplazo NM = **reemplazo**

remuneración NF remuneration

remunerar VT to remunerate

renacentista ADJ Renaissance

renacer [60] VI (**a**) *(flores, hojas)* to grow again (**b**) *(sentimiento, interés)* to return, to revive; **sentirse r.** to feel reborn, to feel one has a new lease of life

Renacimiento NM Renaissance

renacuajo NM tadpole; *Fam (niño pequeño)* shrimp

renal ADJ kidney; **insuficiencia r.** kidney failure

rencilla NF quarrel

rencor NM rancour; *(resentimiento)* resentment; **guardar r. a algn** to have a grudge against sb

rencoroso, -a ADJ *(hostil)* rancorous; *(resentido)* resentful

rendición NF surrender

rendido, -a ADJ exhausted, worn out

rendija NF crack, split

rendimiento NM *(producción)* yield, output; *(de máquina, motor)* efficiency, performance

rendir [6] **1** VT (a) *(fruto, beneficios)* to yield, to produce (b) *(cansar)* to exhaust, to wear out (c) **r. culto a** to worship; **r. homenaje a** to pay homage to

2 VI *(dar beneficios)* to pay, to be profitable

3 rendirse VPR (a) *(entregarse)* to give oneself up, to surrender; *(ceder, abandonar)* to give in; **¡me rindo!** I give in *o* up! (b) *(cansarse)* to wear oneself out

renegado, -a ADJ & NM,F renegade

renegar [1] VT **r. de** to renounce, to disown

renegrido, -a ADJ blackened

RENFE NF *(abr* Red Nacional de los Ferrocarriles Españoles*)* = Spanish state railway company

renglón NM line; **a r. seguido** immediately afterwards

rengo, -a ADJ *Andes, RP* lame

renguear VI *Andes, RP* to limp, to hobble

reno NM reindeer

renombrado, -a ADJ renowned, famous

renombre NM renown, fame

renovable ADJ renewable

renovación NF *(de contrato, pasaporte)* renewal; *(de una casa)* renovation

renovar [2] VT to renew; *(edificio)* to renovate

renta NF (a) *Fin (ingresos)* income; *(beneficio)* interest, return; **r. per cápita** per capita income; **r. fija** fixed-interest security (b) *(alquiler)* rent

rentable ADJ profitable

rentar **1** VT (a) *(rendir)* to produce, yield (b) *Méx (alquilar)* to rent; *(vehículo)* to hire

2 VI to be profitable

renuncia NF (a) *(abandono)* giving up (b) *(dimisión)* resignation

renunciar [43] VI (a) **r. a** to renounce, to give up; *(no aceptar)* to decline (b) *(dimitir)* to resign

reñido, -a ADJ *(disputado)* tough, hard-fought

reñir [6] **1** VT *(regañar)* to scold, to tell off

2 VI *(discutir)* to quarrel, to argue; *(pelear)* to fight; **r. con algn** to fall out with sb

reo NMF *(acusado)* defendant, accused; *(culpable)* culprit

reojo NM **de reojo** LOC ADV **mirar algo de r.** to look at sth out of the corner of one's eye

reparación NF repair; *(compensación)* reparation, amends

reparar **1** VT to repair; *(ofensa, injuria)* to make amends for; *(daño)* to make good

2 VI **r. en** *(darse cuenta de)* to notice; *(reflexionar sobre)* to think about

reparo NM **no tener reparos en** not to hesitate to; **me da r.** I feel embarrassed

repartidor, -a NM,F distributor

repartir VT (a) *(dividir)* to distribute, to share out (b) *(regalo, premio)* to give out, to hand out; *(correo)* to deliver; *Naipes* to deal

reparto NM (a) *(división)* distribution, sharing out (b) *(distribución)* handing out; *(de mercancías)* delivery (c) *Cin & Teatro* cast

repasador NM *RP (trapo)* tea towel

repasar VT (a) *(revisar)* to revise, to go over; *(estudiar)* to revise (b) *(ropa)* to mend

repaso NM revision

repatear VT *Fam* to annoy

repatriar [29] VT to repatriate

repecho NM steep slope

repelente ADJ repulsive, repellent; *Fam* **niño r.** little know-all

repeler VT *(rechazar)* to repel, to repulse; *(repugnar)* to disgust

repente **1** NM *(arrebato)* fit

2 de repente LOC ADV suddenly

repentino, -a ADJ sudden

repercusión NF repercussion

repercutir VI **r. en** to have repercussions on, to affect

repertorio NM repertoire, repertory

repesca NF *Fam (examen)* resit

repetición NF repetition; **r. de la jugada** action replay

repetido, -a ADJ **repetidas veces** repeatedly

repetidor, -a **1** ADJ repeating

2 NM,F *Fam Educ* = student who is repeating a year

repetir [6] **1** VT to repeat; *(plato)* to have a second helping of

2 VI *Educ* to repeat a year

3 repetirse VPR (a) *(persona)* to repeat oneself (b) *(hecho)* to recur (c) **el pepino se repite** cucumber repeats (on me/you/him/*etc*)

repicar [44] VT & VI to ring

repipi ADJ *Fam* **niño r.** precocious brat

repique NM ringing

repiquetear VT & VI *(campanas)* to ring; *(tambor)* to beat

repisa NF shelf, ledge

replantear **1** VT (a) *(situación, problema)* to restate (b) *(cuestión)* *(de nuevo)* to raise again

2 replantearse VPR to reconsider

replegarse [1] VPR to fall back, to retreat

repleto, -a ADJ full (up), jam-packed; **r. de** packed with, crammed with

réplica NF (a) *(respuesta)* reply (b) *(copia)* replica

replicar [44] **1** VT (**a**) *(responder)* to answer back (**b**) *(objetar)* to answer back, to retort
2 VI *(objetar)* to answer back

repliegue NM *Mil* withdrawal, retreat

repoblación NF repopulation; **r. forestal** reafforestation

repoblar [2] VT to repopulate; *(bosque)* to reafforest

repollo NM cabbage

reponer [19] (PP **repuesto**) **1** VT (**a**) *(existencias)* to replace (**b**) *Cine & Teatro* to re-run; *TV (programa)* to repeat
2 reponerse VPR to recover (**de** from)

reportaje NM *Prensa & Rad* report; *(noticias)* article, news item

reportar 1 VT (**a**) *(beneficios etc)* to bring (**b**) *Andes, CAm, Méx, Ven (informar)* to report (**c**) *CAm, Méx (denunciar)* to report (to the police)
2 reportarse VPR *CAm, Méx, Ven (presentarse)* to report (**a** to)

reporte NM *Andes, CAm, Méx, Ven (informe)* report; *(noticia)* news item *o* report; **recibí reportes de mi hermano** I was sent news by my brother; **el r. del tiempo** weather report *o* forecast

reportero, -a NM,F reporter

reposacabezas NM INV *Aut* headrest

reposar 1 VT to rest (**en** on)
2 VI *(descansar)* to rest, to take a rest; *(té)* to infuse; *(comida)* to stand

reposera NF *RP (silla) Br* sun-lounger, *US* beach recliner

reposición NF *TV* repeat; *Cin* rerun, reshowing

reposo NM rest; **en r.** at rest

repostar VT *(provisiones)* to stock up with; *(gasolina)* to fill up with

repostería NF confectionery; *(tienda)* confectioner's (shop)

repostero, -a NM,F confectioner

reprender VT to reprimand, to scold

represalia NF reprisal

representación NF (**a**) *(gen)* & *Com* representation; **en r. de** on behalf of (**b**) *Teatro* performance

representante NMF representative

representar VT (**a**) *(simbolizar, sustituir)* to represent (**b**) *(significar)* to mean, to represent (**c**) *Teatro (obra)* to perform

representativo, -a ADJ representative

represión NF repression

represivo, -a ADJ repressive

reprimenda NF reprimand

reprimir VT to repress

reprobar [2] VT (**a**) *(cosa)* to condemn; *(persona)* to reproach, reprove (**b**) *Am (estudiante, examen)* to fail

réprobo, -a ADJ & NM,F reprobate

reprochar VT to reproach; **r. algo a algn** to reproach sb for sth

reproche NM reproach

reproducción NF reproduction

reproducir [10] **1** VT to reproduce
2 reproducirse VPR (**a**) *(procrear)* to reproduce, to breed (**b**) *(repetirse)* to recur, to happen again

reproductor, -a ADJ reproductive

reptar VI to slither

reptil NM reptile

república NF republic; **la R. Checa** the Czech Republic; **la R. Dominicana** the Dominican Republic

republicano, -a ADJ & NM,F republican

repudiar [43] VT to repudiate

repuesto 1 NM *(recambio)* spare part, spare; *Aut* **rueda de r.** spare wheel
2 PP *de* **reponer**

repugnancia NF loathing, disgust

repugnante ADJ disgusting, revolting

repugnar VT to disgust, to revolt

repujar VT to emboss

repulsa NF rebuff

repulsión NF repulsion, repugnance

repulsivo, -a ADJ repulsive, revolting

repuntar VI *Am (mejorar)* to improve

repunte NM *(aumento)* rise, increase; **un r. en las ventas** an improvement *o* increase in sales

repuse PT INDEF *de* **reponer**

reputación NF reputation

reputado, -a ADJ highly reputed

requemar VT to scorch

requerimiento NM (**a**) *(súplica)* request (**b**) *Der (aviso)* summons *sing*

> Observa que la palabra inglesa **requirement** es un falso amigo y no es la traducción de la palabra española **requerimiento**. En inglés, **requirement** significa "requisito".

requerir [5] VT (**a**) *(necesitar)* to require (**b**) *(solicitar)* to request (**c**) *Der (avisar)* to summon

requesón NM cottage cheese

requete- PREF *Fam* really, very, incredibly; **requetebueno** brilliant

réquiem *(pl* **réquiems***)* NM requiem

requisa NF (**a**) *(inspección)* inspection (**b**) *Mil* requisition

requisar VT to requisition

requisito NM requirement, requisite

res NF animal

resabiado, -a ADJ *Pey* pedantic

resabio NM (**a**) *(mal sabor)* unpleasant *o* bad aftertaste (**b**) *(vicio)* bad habit

resaca NF (**a**) *(de alcohol)* hangover (**b**) *Náut* undertow, undercurrent

resaltar VI to stand out

resarcir [52] VT to compensate

resbalada NF *Am Fam* slip; **dar** *o* **pegar una r.** to slip

resbaladizo, -a ADJ slippery

resbalar 1 VI (**a**) *(caer)* to slip (**con** *o* **en** on) (**b**) *(estar resbaladizo)* to be slippery
2 resbalarse VPR to slip (over)

resbalón NM slip

rescatar VT *(persona)* to rescue; *(objeto)* to recover

rescate NM (**a**) *(salvamento)* rescue; *(recuperación)* recovery (**b**) *(suma)* ransom

rescindir VT to rescind, to cancel

rescisión NF cancellation

rescoldo NM embers

resecarse [44] VPR to dry up, to become parched

reseco, -a ADJ very dry, parched

resentido, -a ADJ resentful

resentimiento NM resentment

resentirse [5] VPR (**a**) **r. de** to suffer from, to feel the effects of (**b**) *(ofenderse)* to feel offended; **r. por algo** to take offence at sth, to feel bitter about sth

reseña NF review; *Prensa* write-up

reserva 1 NF (**a**) *(de entradas etc)* reservation, booking (**b**) *(provisión)* reserve, stock; **un vino de r.** a vintage wine (**c**) *Mil* reserve, reserves (**d**) *(duda)* reservation
2 NMF *Dep* reserve, substitute

reservación NF *Méx* reservation

reservado, -a 1 ADJ *(persona)* reserved, quiet
2 NM private room

reservar 1 VT (**a**) *(billetes etc)* to reserve, to book (**b**) *(dinero, tiempo etc)* to keep, to save
2 reservarse VPR (**a**) *(uno mismo)* to save oneself (**para** for) (**b**) *(sentimientos)* to keep to oneself (**c**) **reservarse el derecho de** to reserve the right to

resfriado, -a 1 NM *(catarro)* cold; **coger un r.** to catch (a) cold
2 ADJ **estar r.** to have a cold

resfriarse VPR to catch (a) cold

resfrío NM *Andes, RP* cold

resguardar VT *(proteger)* to protect, to shelter (**de** from)

resguardo NM (**a**) *(recibo)* receipt (**b**) *(protección)* protection, shelter

residencia NF residence; **r. de ancianos** old people's home

residencial ADJ residential

residente ADJ & NMF resident

residir VI to reside, to live (**en** in); *Fig* to lie (**en** in)

residuo NM (**a**) *Quím* residue (**b**) **residuos** waste

resignación NF resignation

resignado, -a ADJ resigned

resignarse VPR to resign oneself (**a** to)

resina NF resin

resistencia NF (**a**) *(oposición)* resistance (**b**) *(aguante)* stamina (**c**) *Elec* resistance

resistente ADJ *(fuerte)* tough, strong; **r. al calor** heat-resistant

resistir 1 VT *(peso, dolor, ataque)* to withstand; *(tentación)* to resist; *(situación, persona)* to put up with
2 VI (**a**) *(ejército, ciudad)* to resist (**b**) *(persona)* to keep going
3 resistirse VPR **resistirse (a algo)** to resist (sth); **resistirse a hacer algo** to refuse to do sth

resollar [2] VI to breathe heavily; *(con silbido)* to wheeze

resolución NF (**a**) *(solución)* solution (**b**) *(decisión)* resolution

resolver [4] *(pp* **resuelto)** **1** VT *(problema)* to solve; *(asunto)* to settle
2 VI *(decidir)* to resolve, to decide
3 resolverse VPR (**a**) *(solucionarse)* to be solved (**b**) *(decidirse)* to resolve, to make up one's mind (**a** to)

resonancia NF (**a**) *(sonora)* resonance (**b**) *(repercusión)* repercussions

resonar [2] VI to resound; *(tener eco)* to echo

resoplar VI *(respirar)* to breathe heavily; *(de cansancio)* to puff and pant; *(de enfado)* to huff and puff

resoplido NM *(silbido)* wheezing; *(de cansancio)* panting; *(de enfado)* snort

resorte NM spring

> Observa que la palabra inglesa **resort** es un falso amigo y no es la traducción de la palabra española **resorte**. En inglés, **resort** significa "recurso" o "lugar de vacaciones;".

respaldar VT to support, to back (up)

respaldo NM *(de asiento)* back; *Fig (apoyo)* support, backing

respectar VT to concern, to regard; **por lo que a mí respecta** as far as I'm concerned

respectivo, -a ADJ respective; **en lo r. a** with regard to, regarding

respecto NM **al r., a este r.** in this respect; **con r. a, r. a, r. de** with regard to; **r. a mí** as for me, as far as I am concerned

respetable 1 ADJ respectable
2 NM *Fam* **el r.** the audience

respetar VT to respect; **hacerse r. de todos** to command everyone's respect

respeto NM respect; **por r.** out of consideration

respetuoso, -a ADJ respectful

respingo NM start, jump

respingón, -ona ADJ *(nariz)* snub, upturned

respiración NF *(acción)* breathing, respiration; *(aliento)* breath; **r. artificial** artificial resuscitation

respirar VI to breathe; **¡por fin respiro!** well, that's a relief!

respiratorio, -a ADJ respiratory

respiro NM *(descanso)* breather, break; *(alivio)* relief, respite

resplandecer [33] VI to shine

resplandeciente ADJ *(brillante)* shining; *(esplendoroso)* resplendent, radiant

resplandor NM *(brillo)* brightness; *(muy intenso)* brilliance; *(de fuego)* glow, blaze

responder 1 VT to answer
2 VI (**a**) *(una carta)* to reply (**b**) *(reaccionar)* to respond (**c**) *(protestar)* to answer back (**d**) **r. de algn** to be responsible for sb; **r. por algn** to vouch for sb

respondón, -ona ADJ *Fam* argumentative, cheeky

responsabilidad NF responsibility

responsabilizar [40] **1** VT to make *o* hold responsible (**de** for)
2 responsabilizarse VPR to assume *o* claim responsibility (**de** for)

responsable 1 ADJ responsible
2 NMF *el/la* **r.** *(encargado)* the person in charge; *(de robo etc)* the perpetrator

respuesta NF answer, reply; *(reacción)* response

resquebrajarse VPR to crack

resquemor NM resentment, ill feeling

resquicio NM crack, chink

resta NF subtraction

restablecer [33] **1** VT to re-establish; *(el orden)* to restore
2 restablecerse VPR *Med* to recover

restablecimiento NM re-establishment; *(del orden etc)* restoration; *Med* recovery

restante ADJ remaining; **lo r.** the rest, the remainder

restar 1 VT (**a**) *Mat* to subtract, to take away (**b**) **r. importancia a algo** to play sth down
2 VI *(quedar)* to be left, to remain

restauración NF restoration

restaurador, -a 1 NM,F restorer
2 ADJ restoring

restaurante NM restaurant

restaurar VT to restore

restitución NF restitution

restituir [37] VT *(restablecer)* to restore; *(devolver)* to return, to give back

resto NM (**a**) **el r.** the rest; *Mat* the remainder (**b**) **restos** remains; *(de comida)* leftovers

restregar [1] VT to rub hard, to scrub

restricción NF restriction

restrictivo, -a ADJ restrictive

restringir [57] VT to restrict, to limit

resucitar VT & VI to resuscitate

resuello NM breath, gasp

resuelto, -a 1 ADJ *(decidido)* resolute, determined
2 PP *de* **resolver**

resultado NM result; *(consecuencia)* outcome; **dar buen r.** to work, to give results

resultante ADJ resulting

resultar VI (**a**) *(ser)* to turn *o* work out; **así resulta más barato** it works out cheaper this way; **me resultó fácil** it turned out to be easy for me (**b**) *(ocurrir)* **resulta que ...** the thing is ...; **y ahora resulta que no puede venir** and now it turns out that she can't come (**c**) *(tener éxito)* to be successful; **la fiesta no resultó** the party wasn't a success

resultas NFPL **a r. de** as a result of

resumen NM summary; **en r.** in short, to sum up

resumir 1 VT to sum up; *(recapitular)* to summarize
2 resumirse VPR (**a**) *(abreviarse)* **se resume en pocas palabras** it can be summed up in a few words (**b**) **resumirse en** *(saldarse con)* to result in

> Observa que la palabra inglesa **resume** es un falso amigo y no es la traducción de la palabra española **resumir**. En inglés **resume** significa "reanudar".

resurgir [57] VI to reappear

resurrección NF resurrection

retablo NM altarpiece

retaguardia NF rearguard

retahíla NF series *sing*, string

retal NM remnant

retar VT to challenge

retardo NM delay

retazo NM *(pedazo)* scrap; *(fragmento)* fragment, piece

retén NM (**a**) **r. (de bomberos)** squad (of firefighters) (**b**) *Am (de menores)* reformatory, reform school

retención NF retention; *Fin* deduction; **r. de tráfico** (traffic) hold-up, traffic jam

retener [24] VT (**a**) *(conservar)* to retain (**b**) *Fin (descontar)* to deduct (**c**) *(detener)* to detain

reticencia NF reticence, reserve

reticente ADJ reticent, reserved

retina NF retina

retintín NM innuendo, sarcastic tone

retirada NF retreat, withdrawal

retirado, -a 1 ADJ (**a**) *(alejado)* remote (**b**) *(jubilado)* retired
2 NM,F retired person, *US* retiree

retirar 1 VT to take away, to remove; *(dinero)* to withdraw; *(ofensa)* to take back
2 retirarse VPR (**a**) *(apartarse)* to withdraw, to draw back; *(irse)* to retire (**b**) *(jubilarse)* to retire (**c**) *Mil* to retreat, to withdraw

retiro NM (**a**) *(jubilación)* retirement; *(pensión)* pension (**b**) *(lugar tranquilo)* retreat (**c**) *Rel* retreat

reto NM challenge

retocar [44] VT to touch up

retoño NM *(rebrote)* shoot, sprout; *(niño)* kid

retoque NM retouching, touching up; **los últimos retoques** the finishing touches

retorcer [41] **1** VT *(cuerda, hilo)* to twist; *(ropa)* to wring (out)
   2 retorcerse VPR to twist, to become twisted; **retorcerse de dolor** to writhe in pain
retorcido, -a ADJ *(malintencionado)* twisted
retórica NF rhetoric
retórico, -a ADJ rhetorical
retornable ADJ returnable; **envase no r.** non-deposit bottle
retornar 1 VT to return, to give back
   2 VI to return, to come back, to go back
retorno NM return
retortijón NM stomach cramp
retozar [40] VI to frolic, to romp
retracción NF retraction
retractar 1 VT to retract
   2 retractarse VPR **r. (de)** to retract, to take back
retraerse VPR *(retirarse)* to withdraw; *(por miedo)* to shy away
retraído, -a ADJ shy, reserved
retraimiento NM shyness
retransmisión NF broadcast, transmission
retransmitir VT to broadcast
retrasado, -a 1 ADJ **(a)** *(tren)* late; *(reloj)* slow; **voy r.** I'm behind schedule **(b)** *(país)* backward, underdeveloped **(c)** *(mental)* retarded, backward
   2 NM,F **r. (mental)** mentally retarded person
retrasar 1 VT **(a)** *(retardar)* to slow down **(b)** *(atrasar)* to delay, to postpone **(c)** *(reloj)* to put back
   2 retrasarse VPR to be late, to be delayed; *(reloj)* to be slow
retraso NM delay; **con r.** late; **una hora de r.** an hour behind schedule; **r. mental** mental deficiency
retratar 1 VT *(pintar)* to paint a portrait of; *Fot* to take a photograph of; *Fig (describir)* to describe, to depict
   2 retratarse VPR *Fot* to have one's photograph taken
retrato NM *(pintura)* portrait; *Fot* photograph; **r. robot** Identikit® picture, *Br* Photofit® picture; **ser el vivo r. de** to be the spitting image of
retreta NF retreat
retrete NM toilet, *Br* bathroom
retribución NF *(pago)* payment; *(recompensa)* reward

Observa que la palabra inglesa **retribution** es un falso amigo y no es la traducción de la palabra española **retribución**. En inglés, **retribution** significa "represalias".

retribuir VT *(pagar)* to pay; *(recompensar)* to reward
retro ADJ INV *(estilo, moda)* retro
retroactivo, -a ADJ retroactive; **con efecto r.** retrospectively
retroceder VI to move back, to back away

retroceso NM **(a)** *(movimiento)* backward movement **(b)** *(en enfermedad)* deterioration, worsening
retrógrado, -a ADJ & NM,F *(en política)* reactionary
retropropulsión NF *Av* jet propulsion
retrospectivo, -a ADJ & NF retrospective
retrovisor NM *Aut* rear-view mirror
retumbar VI *(resonar)* to resound; *(tronar)* to thunder, to boom
retuve PT INDEF *de* retener
reúma NM rheumatism
reumático, -a ADJ & NM,F rheumatic
reumatismo NM rheumatism
reunión NF meeting; *(reencuentro)* reunion
reunir 1 VT to gather together; *(dinero)* to raise; *(cualidades)* to have, to possess; *(requisitos)* to fulfil
   2 reunirse VPR to meet, to gather; **reunirse con algn** to meet sb
revalidar VT to ratify, to confirm; *Dep (título)* to retain
revalorizar [40] **1** VT *(aumentar el valor de)* to increase the value of; *(moneda)* to revalue
   2 revalorizarse VPR *(aumentar de valor)* to appreciate; *(moneda)* to be revalued
revancha NF revenge; *Dep* return match
revanchista ADJ vengeful, vindictive
revelación NF revelation
revelado NM *Fot* developing
revelar VT **(a)** *(descubrir)* to reveal, to disclose **(b)** *Fot (película)* to develop
revender VT to tout
reventa NF *(de entradas)* touting
reventado, -a ADJ *Fam (cansado)* knackered
reventar [1] **1** VT **(a)** *(explotar)* to burst **(b)** *(romper)* to break, to smash **(c)** *Fam (fastidiar)* to annoy, to bother
   2 VI *(explotar)* to burst; **r. de** *(estar lleno)* to be bursting with; **r. de ganas de hacer algo** to be dying to do sth
   3 reventarse VPR *(explotar)* to burst, to explode
reventón NM *(de neumático)* blowout, *Br* puncture, *US* flat
reverberación NF reverberation
reverberar VI to reverberate
reverencia NF **(a)** *(respeto)* reverence **(b)** *(inclinación) (de hombre)* bow; *(de mujer)* curtsy
reverenciar [43] VT to revere, to venerate
reverendo, -a ADJ & NM,F reverend
reversa NF *Méx* reverse
reversible ADJ reversible
reverso NM reverse, back
revertido, -a ADJ *ver* cobro
revertir [5] VI to result *(en* in)
revés *(pl reveses)* NM **(a)** *(reverso)* reverse; **al** *o* **del r.** *(al contrario)* the other way round; *(la*

parte interior en el exterior) inside out; *(boca abajo)* upside down; *(la parte de detrás delante)* back to front; **al r. de lo que dicen** contrary to what they say (**b**) *(bofetada)* slap; **Ten** backhand (stroke) (**c**) *Fig (contrariedad)* setback, reverse; **los reveses de la vida** life's misfortunes; **reveses de fortuna** setbacks, blows of fate

revestimiento NM *Téc* covering, coating

revestir [6] VT *(recubrir)* to cover (**de** with); *(con pintura)* to coat (**de** with); **la herida no reviste importancia** the wound is not serious

revisar VT to check; *(coche)* to service

revisión NF checking; *(de coche)* service, overhaul; **r. médica** checkup

revisor, -a NM,F ticket inspector

revista NF (**a**) *(publicación)* magazine; *(académica)* journal (**b**) **pasar r. a** to inspect, to review (**c**) *Teatro* revue

revistero NM *(mueble)* magazine rack

revitalizar [40] VT to revitalize

revivir VT & VI to revive

revocar [44] VT to revoke, to repeal

revolcar [2] **1** VT *Fam (oponente)* to floor, to crush
  2 revolcarse VPR to roll about

revolcón NM fall, tumble; *Fam (sexual)* romp

revolotear VI to fly about, to flutter about

revoltijo, revoltillo NM jumble

revoltoso, -a ADJ *(travieso)* mischievous, naughty

revolución NF revolution

revolucionar VT to revolutionize

revolucionario, -a ADJ & NM,F revolutionary

revolver [4] **1** VT *(mezclar)* to stir, to mix; *(desordenar)* to mess up; **me revuelve el estómago** it turns my stomach
  2 revolverse VPR (**a**) *(agitarse)* to roll (**b**) *Fig* **revolverse contra algn** to turn against sb (**c**) *(el tiempo)* to turn stormy; *(el mar)* to become rough

Observa que el verbo inglés **to revolve** es un falso amigo y no es la traducción del verbo español **revolver**. En inglés, **to revolve** significa "girar".

revólver NM revolver

revuelo NM stir, commotion

revuelta NF (**a**) *(insurrección)* revolt (**b**) *(curva)* bend, turn

revuelto, -a 1 ADJ (**a**) *(desordenado)* jumbled, in a mess (**b**) *(tiempo)* stormy, unsettled; *(mar)* rough (**c**) *(agitado)* excited
  2 PP *de* **revolver**

revulsivo NM (**a**) *(fármaco)* counter-irritant, *Espec* revulsive (**b**) *(estímulo)* kick-start, stimulus

rey *(pl* **reyes)** NM king; *Rel* **(el día de) Reyes** (the) Epiphany, 6 January

reyerta NF quarrel, dispute

rezagado, -a NM,F straggler, latecomer

rezagarse [42] VPR to lag o fall behind

rezar [40] **1** VI (**a**) *(orar)* to pray (**b**) *(decir)* to say, to read
  2 VT *(oración)* to say

rezo NM prayer

rezumar VT to ooze; *Fig* to exude

ría NF estuary

riachuelo NM brook, stream

riada NF flood

ribera NF *(de río)* bank; *(zona)* riverside, waterfront

ribete NM edging, border

ribetear VT to edge, to border

ricamente ADV *Fam* **tan r.** quite happily

rico, -a 1 ADJ (**a**) **ser r.** *(adinerado)* to be rich o wealthy; *(abundante)* to be rich; *(bonito)* to be lovely o adorable; *(fértil)* to be rich o fertile (**b**) **estar r.** *(delicioso)* to be delicious
  2 NM,F rich person

rictus NM INV *(de dolor)* wince; **un r. de amargura** a bitter expression

ridiculez NF ridiculous thing; *(cualidad)* ridiculousness

ridiculizar [40] VT to ridicule

ridículo, -a 1 ADJ ridiculous
  2 NM ridicule; **hacer el r., quedar en r.** to make a fool of oneself; **poner a algn en r.** to make a fool of sb

riego NM watering, irrigation; **r. sanguíneo** blood circulation

riel NM rail

rienda NF rein; *Fig* **dar r. suelta a** to give free rein to; *Fig* **llevar las riendas** to hold the reins, to be in control

riesgo NM risk; **correr el r. de** to run the risk of; **seguro a todo r.** fully comprehensive insurance

riesgoso, -a ADJ *Am* risky

rifa NF raffle

rifar VT to raffle (off)

rifle NM rifle

rigidez NF rigidity, stiffness; *Fig (severidad)* strictness, inflexibility

rígido, -a ADJ rigid, stiff; *Fig (severo)* strict, inflexible

rigor NM rigour; *(severidad)* severity; **con r.** rigorously; **de r.** indispensable

rigurosamente ADV *(severamente)* strictly; **r. cierto** absolutely true

riguroso, -a ADJ (**a**) *(severo)* strict (**b**) *(exacto)* rigorous, disciplined (**c**) *(inclemente)* harsh

rijo INDIC PRES *de* **regir**

rima NF rhyme

rimar VT & VI to rhyme (**con** with)

rimbombante ADJ *(lenguaje)* pompous, pretentious

rímel NM mascara

rincón NM corner; *Fam (lugar remoto)* nook

ring [rriŋ] (*pl* **rings**) NM (boxing) ring

rinoceronte NM rhinoceros

riña NF *(pelea)* fight; *(discusión)* row, quarrel

riñón NM kidney; *Fam* **costar un r.** to cost an arm and a leg; *Med* **r. artificial** kidney machine

riñonera NF *(pequeño bolso)* *Br* bum bag, *US* fanny pack

río NM river; **r. abajo** downstream; **r. arriba** upstream

rioja NM Rioja (wine)

rioplatense ADJ of/from the River Plate region

RIP *(abr* **requiescat in pace)** RIP

ripio NM *Lit* = word or phrase included to complete a rhyme; *Fam* **no perder r.** not to miss a trick

riqueza NF **(a)** *(fortuna)* wealth **(b)** *(cualidad)* wealthiness

risa NF laugh; *(carcajadas)* laughter; **es (cosa) de r.** it's laughable; **me da r.** it makes me laugh; **tomarse algo a r.** to laugh sth off; *Fig* **morirse** *o* **mondarse de r.** to die *o* fall about laughing; *Fam* **mi hermano es una r.** my brother is a laugh; *Fam Fig* **tener algo muerto de r.** to leave sth lying around

risco NM crag, cliff

risible ADJ laughable

risilla, risita NF giggle, titter; *(risa falsa)* false laugh

risotada NF guffaw

ristra NF string

ristre NM **en r.** at the ready

risueño, -a ADJ smiling

rítmico, -a ADJ rhythmic

ritmo NM **(a)** *(compás, repetición)* rhythm, beat; *(cardíaco)* beat **(b)** *(velocidad)* rate; **llevar un buen r. de trabajo** to work at a good pace

rito NM **(a)** *Rel* rite **(b)** *(costumbre)* ritual

ritual ADJ & NM ritual

rival ADJ & NMF rival

rivalidad NF rivalry

rivalizar [40] VI to rival **(en in)**

rizado, -a ADJ **(a)** *(pelo)* curly **(b)** *(mar)* choppy

rizar [40] **1** VT *(pelo)* to curl; *(tela, papel)* to crease; *Fig* **r. el rizo** to make things even more complicated
2 rizarse VPR *(pelo)* to curl, to go curly

rizo NM **(a)** *(de pelo)* curl **(b)** *(en el agua)* ripple

RNE NF *(abr* **Radio Nacional de España)** = Spanish state radio station

robar VT **(a)** *(objeto)* to steal; *(banco, persona)* to rob; *(casa)* to burgle; *Fig* **en aquel supermercado te roban** they really rip you off in that supermarket **(b)** *Naipes* to draw

roble NM oak (tree)

robo NM robbery, theft; *(en casa)* burglary; *Fam (timo)* rip-off

robot *(pl* **robots)** NM robot; **r. de cocina** food processor

robustecer [33] VT to strengthen

robusto, -a ADJ robust, sturdy

roca NF rock

rocambolesco, -a ADJ incredible, far-fetched

roce NM **(a)** *(fricción)* rubbing; *(en la piel)* chafing **(b)** *(marca)* *(en la pared etc)* scuff mark; *(en la piel)* chafing mark, graze **(c)** *(contacto ligero)* brush, light touch **(d)** *Fam (trato entre personas)* contact **(e)** *Fam (discusión)* brush

rociar [29] VT *(salpicar)* to spray, to sprinkle

rocín NM nag, hack

rocío NM dew

rock NM INV rock; **r. duro** hard rock; **r. and roll** rock and roll

Rocosas NFPL **las R.** the Rockies

rocoso, -a ADJ rocky, stony

rodaballo NM *(pez)* turbot

rodado, -a ADJ **(a)** **canto r.** boulder **(b)** **tráfico r.** road traffic, vehicular traffic

rodaja NF slice; **en rodajas** sliced

rodaje NM **(a)** *(filmación)* filming, shooting **(b)** *Aut* running in

rodante ADJ rolling

rodar [2] **1** VT *(película etc)* to film, to shoot
2 VI to roll, to turn

rodear 1 VT to surround, to encircle
2 rodearse VPR to surround oneself **(de with)**

rodeo NM **(a)** *(desvío)* detour **(b)** *(al hablar)* evasiveness; **andarse con rodeos** to beat about the bush; **no andarse con rodeos** to get straight to the point **(c)** *(espectáculo)* rodeo

rodilla NF knee; **de rodillas** *(arrodillado)* kneeling; **hincarse** *o* **ponerse de rodillas** to kneel down, to go down on one's knees

rodillera NF *(de pantalón)* knee patch; *Dep* knee pad

rodillo NM roller; **r. de cocina** rolling pin

rododendro NM rhododendron

roedor NM rodent

roer [38] VT *(hueso)* to gnaw; *(galleta)* to nibble at; *Fig (conciencia)* to gnaw at, to nag at; *Fig* **un hueso duro de r.** a hard nut to crack

rogar [2] VT *(pedir)* to request, to ask; *(implorar)* to beg; **hacerse de r.** to play hard to get; **se ruega silencio** *(en letrero)* silence please; **rogamos disculpen la molestia** please forgive the inconvenience

roído, -a ADJ gnawed, eaten away

rojizo, -a ADJ reddish

rojo, -a 1 ADJ **(a)** *(color)* red; *Fin* **estar en números rojos** to be in the red **(b)** *Pol (comunista)* red
2 NM *(color)* red; **al r. vivo** *(caliente)* red-hot; *Fig (tenso)* very tense
3 NM,F *Pol (comunista)* red

rol NM role

rollizo, -a ADJ chubby, plump

rollo NM **(a)** *(de papel etc)* roll **(b)** *Fam (pesadez)* drag, bore; **es el mismo r. de**

siempre it's the same old story; **un r. de libro** a boring book (**c**) *Esp Fam (amorío)* affair

Roma N Rome

romance NM (**a**) *(aventura amorosa)* romance (**b**) *(idioma)* Romance (**c**) *Lit* narrative poem, ballad

románico, -a ADJ & NM Romanesque

romano, -a ADJ & NM,F Roman

romanticismo NM romanticism

romántico, -a ADJ & NM,F romantic

rombo NM rhombus

romería NF *Rel* pilgrimage

romero NM *Bot* rosemary

romo, -a ADJ (**a**) *(sin filo)* blunt (**b**) *(nariz)* snub

rompecabezas NM INV *(juego)* (jigsaw) puzzle; *Fig (problema)* riddle, puzzle

rompeolas NM INV breakwater, jetty

romper (*pp* roto) **1** VT (**a**) *(partir, estropear) (papel, tela)* to tear; *(vajilla, cristal)* to smash, to shatter (**b**) *(relaciones)* to break off
2 VI (**a**) *(olas, día)* to break (**con** with); **rompió con su novio** she broke it off with her boyfriend (**c**) **r. a llorar** to burst out crying; **r. en llanto** to burst into tears
3 romperse VPR to break; *(papel, tela)* to tear; **se rompió por la mitad** *o* split in half; *Fig* **romperse la cabeza** to rack one's brains

rompevientos NM INV *RP (jersey) Br* polo neck, *US* turtleneck; *(anorak)* windcheater

rompimiento NM *Am* break

ron NM rum

roncar [44] VI to snore

roncha NF *(en la piel)* swelling, lump

ronco, -a ADJ hoarse; **quedarse r.** to lose one's voice

ronda NF (**a**) *(de vigilancia)* patrol (**b**) *(en el juego, de conversaciones, bebidas)* round (**c**) *(carretera) Br* ring road, *US* beltway; *(avenida)* avenue

rondar 1 VT (**a**) *(vigilar)* to patrol, to do the rounds of (**b**) *Pey (merodear)* to prowl around, to hang about (**c**) *(estar cerca de)* to be about *o* approximately; **ronda los cuarenta** he is about forty
2 VI (**a**) *(vigilar)* to patrol (**b**) *(merodear)* to prowl around, to roam around

rondín NM *Andes* (**a**) *(vigilante)* watchman, guard (**b**) *(armónica)* mouth organ

ronquera NF hoarseness

ronquido NM snore

ronronear VI to purr

ronroneo NM purring

roña NF (**a**) *(mugre)* filth, dirt (**b**) *(sarna)* mange

roñica *Fam* **1** ADJ mean, stingy
2 NMF scrooge, miser

roñoso, -a ADJ (**a**) *(mugriento)* filthy, dirty (**b**) *(sarnoso)* mangy (**c**) *Fam (tacaño)* mean, stingy

ropa NF clothes, clothing; *Fig* **a quema r.** point-blank; **r. blanca** (household) linen; **r. interior** underwear

> Observa que la palabra inglesa **rope** es un falso amigo y no es la traducción de la palabra española **ropa**. En inglés, **rope** significa "cuerda, soga".

ropaje NM clothes

ropero NM **(armario) r.** wardrobe

roque ADJ *Fam* **quedarse r.** to fall fast asleep

roquefort [rroke'for] NM Roquefort (cheese)

rosa 1 ADJ INV *(color)* pink; **novela r.** romantic novel
2 NF *Bot* rose; *(en la piel)* birthmark; **r. de los vientos** compass (rose)
3 NM *(color)* pink

rosáceo, -a ADJ rose-coloured, rosy

rosado, -a 1 ADJ *(color)* pink, rosy; *(vino)* rosé
2 NM *(vino)* rosé

rosal NM rosebush

rosaleda NF rose garden

rosario NM *Rel* rosary; *(sarta)* string, series *sing*

rosbif NM roast beef

rosca NF (**a**) *(de tornillo)* thread; **tapón de r.** screw top; *Fig* **pasarse de r.** to go too far (**b**) *(espiral)* spiral, coil

rosco NM = ring-shaped bread roll; *Esp Fam* **nunca se come un r.** he never gets off with anyone

roscón NM = ring-shaped bread roll; **r. de Reyes** = ring-shaped pastry eaten on 6th January

rosetón NM rose window

rosquilla NF ring-shaped pastry; *Fam Fig* **venderse como rosquillas** to sell like hot cakes

rosticería NF *Chile, Méx* = shop selling roast chicken

rostro NM face; *Fam* **tener mucho r.** to have a lot of nerve; *Fam* **¡vaya r.!** what a cheek!

> Observa que la palabra inglesa **rostrum** es un falso amigo y no es la traducción de la palabra española **rostro**. En inglés, **rostrum** significa "estrado".

rotación NF rotation

rotativo, -a 1 ADJ rotary, revolving
2 NM newspaper

roto, -a 1 ADJ broken; *(papel)* torn; *(ropa)* in tatters, tattered
2 NM *(agujero)* hole, tear
3 NM,F *Chile Fam* (**a**) *(tipo)* guy; *(mujer)* woman (**b**) *Pey (trabajador)* worker
4 PP *de* **romper**

rotonda NF (**a**) *(glorieta)* roundabout (**b**) *(plaza)* circus

rotoso, -a *Andes, RP* ADJ ragged, in tatters

rótula NF (**a**) *Anat* kneecap (**b**) *Téc* ball-and-socket joint

rotulador NM felt-tip pen

rotular VT to letter, to label

rótulo NM *(letrero)* sign, notice; *(titular)* title, heading

rotundo, -a ADJ categorical; **éxito r.** resounding success; **un no r.** a flat refusal

rotura NF *(ruptura)* breaking; *Med* fracture

roturar VT to plough

roulotte NF Br caravan, US trailer

rozadura NF scratch, abrasion

rozamiento NM rubbing, friction

rozar [40] **1** VT to touch, to rub against, to brush against
2 VI to rub
3 rozarse VPR to rub, to brush (**con** against)

Rte. *(abr* **remite, remitente)** sender

ruana NF *Andes (cerrada)* poncho; *RP (abierta)* wrap-around poncho

rubeola NF German measles *sing*, rubella

rubí *(pl* **rubís** o **rubíes)** NM ruby

rubicundo, -a ADJ rosy, reddish

rubio, -a 1 ADJ *(pelo, persona)* fair, blond, *f* blonde; **r. de bote** peroxide blonde; **tabaco r.** Virginia tobacco
2 NM,F blond, *f* blonde

rublo NM rouble

rubor NM blush, flush

ruborizarse [40] VPR to blush, to go red

ruboroso, -a ADJ blushing, bashful

rúbrica NF **(a)** *(de firma)* = flourish added to a signature **(b)** *(título)* title, heading

rudeza NF roughness, coarseness

rudimentario, -a ADJ rudimentary

rudimento NM rudiment

rudo, -a ADJ rough, coarse

rueda NF **(a)** *(pieza)* wheel; *Aut* **r. de recambio** spare wheel; *Aut* **r. delantera/trasera** front/rear wheel; **r. de prensa** press conference; *Fam* **ir sobre ruedas** to go very smoothly **(b)** *(rodaja)* round slice

ruedo NM **(a)** *Taurom* bullring, arena **(b)** *(de falda)* hem

ruego NM request

rufián NM villain, scoundrel

rugby NM rugby

rugido NM *(de animal)* roar; *(del viento)* howl; *(de tripas)* rumbling

rugir [57] VI to roar; *(viento)* to howl

rugoso, -a ADJ rough .

ruibarbo NM rhubarb

ruido NM noise; *(sonido)* sound; *(jaleo)* din, row; *Fig* stir, commotion; **hacer r.** to make a noise

ruidoso, -a ADJ noisy, loud

ruin ADJ **(a)** *(vil)* vile, despicable **(b)** *(tacaño)* mean, stingy

ruina NF ruin; *(derrumbamiento)* collapse; *(de persona)* downfall

ruindad NF *(cualidad)* vileness, meanness; *(acto)* mean act, low trick

ruinoso, -a ADJ dilapidated, tumbledown

ruiseñor NM nightingale

ruleta NF roulette

ruletear VI *CAm, Méx Fam (en taxi)* to drive a taxi

ruletero NM *CAm, Méx Fam (de taxi)* taxi driver

rulo NM **(a)** *(para el pelo)* curler, roller **(b)** *Culin* rolling pin

rulot *(pl* **rulots)** NF Br caravan, US trailer

ruma NF *Andes, Ven* heap, pile

Rumanía N Romania

rumano, -a 1 ADJ & NM,F Romanian
2 NM *(idioma)* Romanian

rumba NF rhumba, rumba

rumbo NM direction, course; **(con) r. a** bound for, heading for

rumiante NM ruminant

rumiar [43] **1** VT **(a)** *(mascar)* to chew **(b)** *Fig (pensar)* to ruminate, to reflect on, to chew over
2 VI to ruminate, to chew the cud

rumor NM **(a)** *(chisme)* rumour **(b)** *(ruido sordo)* murmur

rumorearse V IMPERS to be rumoured

runrún, runruneo NM buzz, noise

rupestre ADJ **pintura r.** cave painting

ruptura NF breaking; *(de relaciones)* breaking off

rural ADJ rural, country

Rusia N Russia

ruso, -a 1 ADJ & NM,F Russian
2 NM *(idioma)* Russian

rústico, -a ADJ rustic, rural

ruta NF route, road

rutilante ADJ sparkling

rutina NF routine; **por r.** as a matter of course

rutinario, -a ADJ routine

S, s ['ese] NF *(letra)* S, s

S *(abr* **Sur)** S

S. *(abr* **San, Santo)** St

s. *(abr* **siglo)** c

S.A. *(abr* **Sociedad Anónima)** *Br* ≃ PLC, *US* ≃ Inc

sábado NM Saturday

sabana NF savannah

sábana NF sheet; *Fam* **se me pegaron las sábanas** I overslept

sabandija NF *(insecto)* creepy-crawly; *(persona)* creep

sabañón NM chilblain

sabático, -a ADJ sabbatical

sabelotodo NMF INV know-all

saber¹ NM knowledge

saber² [21] **1** VT (**a**) *(conocer)* to know; **hacer s.** to inform; **para que lo sepas** for your information; **que yo sepa** as far as I know; **vete tú a s.** goodness knows; **¡y yo qué sé!** how should I know!; *Fig* **a s.** namely (**b**) *(tener habilidad)* to be able to; **¿sabes cocinar?** can you cook?; **¿sabes hablar inglés?** can you speak English? (**c**) *(enterarse)* to learn, to find out; **lo supe ayer** I found this out yesterday

2 VI (**a**) *(tener sabor a)* to taste (**a** of); **sabe a fresa** it tastes of strawberries; *Fig* **me sabe mal** I feel guilty *o* bad about that (**b**) *Am (soler)* **s. hacer algo** to be in the habit of doing sth

sabido, -a ADJ known; **como es s.** as everyone knows

sabiduría NF wisdom

sabiendas: a sabiendas LOC ADV **lo hizo a s.** he did it in the full knowledge of what he was doing; **a s. de que …** knowing full well that …

sabihondo, -a NM,F *Fam* know-all

sabio, -a 1 ADJ *(prudente)* wise

2 NM,F scholar

sabiondo, -a NM,F *Fam* = sabihondo

sable NM sabre

sabor NM *(gusto)* taste, flavour; **con s. a limón** lemon-flavoured; **sin s.** tasteless; **me deja mal s. de boca** it leaves a bad taste in my mouth

saborear VT *(degustar)* to taste; *Fig (apreciar)* to savour

sabotaje NM sabotage

saboteador, -a NM,F saboteur

sabotear VT to sabotage

sabré INDIC FUT *de* saber²

sabroso, -a ADJ (**a**) *(gustoso)* tasty (**b**) *Carib, Col, Méx (grato)* pleasant, nice; *(entretenido)* entertaining (**c**) *Carib, Col, Méx (contagioso) (ritmo)* catchy; *(risa)* contagious

sabueso NM bloodhound

sacacorchos NM INV corkscrew

sacapuntas NM INV pencil sharpener

sacar [44] VT (**a**) *(extraer)* to take out; *(con más fuerza)* to pull out; **s. dinero del banco** to withdraw money from the bank; **s. la lengua** to stick one's tongue out; *Fig* **s. faltas a algo** to find fault with sth; *Fig* **s. adelante** to help to get on; **s. provecho de algo** to benefit from sth; **s. algo en claro** *o* **en limpio** to make sense of sth (**b**) *(obtener)* to get; *(dinero)* to get, to make; *(conclusiones)* to draw, to reach; *(entrada)* to get, to buy (**c**) *(producto, libro, disco)* to bring out; *(nueva moda)* to bring in (**d**) *(fotografía)* to take; *(fotocopia)* to make (**e**) *Ten* to serve; *Ftb* to kick off

sacarina NF saccharin

sacerdotal ADJ priestly

sacerdote NM priest; **sumo s.** high priest

saciar [43] VT to satiate; *(sed)* to quench; *(deseos, hambre)* to satisfy; *(ambiciones)* to fulfil

saciedad NF satiety; **repetir algo hasta la s.** to repeat sth ad nauseam

saco NM (**a**) *(bolsa)* sack; **s. de dormir** sleeping bag (**b**) *Mil* **entrar a s. en una ciudad** to pillage a town (**c**) *Am (abrigo)* jacket; *(de tela)* jacket; *(de punto)* cardigan

sacralizar [40] VT to consecrate

sacramento NM sacrament

sacrificar [44] **1** VT to sacrifice

2 sacrificarse VPR to make a sacrifice *o* sacrifices

sacrificio NM sacrifice

sacrilegio NM sacrilege

sacrílego, -a ADJ sacrilegious

sacristán NM verger, sexton

sacristía NF vestry, sacristy

sacro, -a ADJ sacred

sacudida NF (**a**) *(movimiento)* shake; *(espasmo)* jolt, jerk; **s. eléctrica** electric shock (**b**) *(de terremoto)* tremor

sacudir VT (**a**) *(agitar)* to shake; *(alfombra, sábana)* to shake out; *(arena, polvo)* to shake off (**b**) *(golpear)* to beat (**c**) *(conmover)* to shock, to stun

sádico, -a 1 ADJ sadistic
2 NM,F sadist
sadismo NM sadism
sadomasoquista 1 ADJ sadomasochistic
2 NMF sadomasochist
saeta NF (a) (dardo) dart (b) (canción) = flamenco-style song sung on religious occasions
safari NM (cacería) safari; (parque) safari park
sagacidad NF (del listo) cleverness; (del astuto) astuteness, shrewdness
sagaz ADJ (listo) clever; (astuto) astute, shrewd
Sagitario NM Sagittarius
sagrado, -a ADJ sacred
sagrario NM tabernacle
Sáhara ['saɣara], **Sahara** [sa'ara] N Sahara
saharaui [saɣa'rawi] ADJ & NMF Saharan
sahariana [saa'rjana] NF safari jacket
sainete NM Teatro comic sketch, one-act farce
sajón, -ona ADJ & NM,F Saxon
sal[1] NF (a) Culin & Quím s. fina table salt; s. gema salt crystals; Esp s. gorda cooking salt (b) Fig (gracia) wit
sal[2] IMPERAT de salir
sala NF room; (en un hospital) ward; Der courtroom; s. de estar lounge, living room; s. de espera waiting room; s. de exposiciones exhibition hall; s. de fiestas nightclub, discotheque; s. de lectura reading room
saladito NM RP savoury snack o appetizer
salado, -a ADJ (a) (con sal) salted; (con exceso de sal) salty; agua salada salt water (b) Esp (gracioso, simpático) amusing; (encantador) charming (c) CAm, Carib, Méx (desgraciado) unlucky
salamandra NF salamander
salamanquesa NF gecko
salame NM CSur salami
salar VT to salt, to add salt to
salarial ADJ salary, wage
salario NM salary, wages; s. mínimo minimum wage
salazones NFPL salted meat/fish
salchicha NF sausage
salchichón NM = salami-type sausage
salchichonería NF Méx delicatessen
saldar VT (a) Fin (cuenta) to settle; (deuda) to pay off (b) Com (vender barato) to sell off (c) Fig (diferencias) to settle, to resolve
saldo NM (a) saldos sales; a precio de s. at bargain prices (b) Fin balance (c) (de una deuda) liquidation, settlement (d) (resto de mercancía) remainder, leftover
saldré INDIC FUT de salir
salero NM (a) (recipiente) saltcellar, US salt-shaker (b) Fig (gracia) charm
salgo INDIC PRES de salir
salida NF (a) (partida) departure; (puerta etc) exit, way out; callejón sin s. dead end; s. de

emergencia emergency exit (b) Dep start; línea de s. starting line; s. nula false start (c) te vi a la s. del cine I saw you leaving the cinema (d) (de un astro) rising; s. del sol sunrise (e) (profesional) opening; Com outlet (f) (recurso) solution, way out; no tengo otra s. I have no other option (g) Fam (ocurrencia) witty remark, witticism (h) Inform output
salido, -a ADJ muy Fam (persona) horny
saliente ADJ (a) (destacable) salient (b) (cesante) outgoing
salina NF salt mine
salino, -a ADJ saline
salir [22] **1** VI (a) (de un sitio) to go out, to leave; (venir de dentro) to come out; salió de la habitación she left the room; s. de la carretera to turn off the road (b) (tren etc) to depart (c) (novios) to go out (con with) (d) (aparecer) to appear; (revista, disco) to come out; (ley) to come in; (trabajo, vacante) to come up (e) (resultar) to turn out, to turn out to be; el pequeño les ha salido muy listo their son has turned out to be very clever; ¿cómo te salió el examen? how did your exam go?; s. ganando to come out ahead o on top; salió presidente he was elected president (f) s. a (precio) to come to, to work out at; s. barato/caro to work out cheap/expensive (g) ha salido al abuelo she takes after her grandfather (h) (problema) to work out; esta cuenta no me sale I can't work this sum out (i) ¡con qué cosas sales! the things you come out with!
2 salirse VPR (a) (líquido, gas) to leak (out); Fig salirse de lo normal to be out of the ordinary; se salió de la carretera he went off the road (b) Fam salirse con la suya to get one's own way
saliva NF saliva
salivar VI to salivate
salivazo NM spit
salmantino, -a 1 ADJ of/from Salamanca
2 NM,F person from Salamanca
salmo NM psalm
salmón 1 NM (pescado) salmon
2 ADJ INV (color) salmon pink, salmon
salmonete NM (pescado) red mullet
salmorejo NM (salsa) = sauce made from vinegar, water, pepper and salt
salmuera NF brine
salobre ADJ (agua) brackish; (gusto) salty, briny
salón NM (a) (en una casa) lounge, sitting room (b) s. de actos assembly hall; s. de baile dance hall (c) s. de belleza beauty salon; s. de té tearoom, teashop (d) s. del automóvil motor show
salpicadera NF Méx Br mudguard, US fender
salpicadero NM Esp dashboard

salpicadura NF splashing

salpicar [44] VT (a) *(rociar)* to splash; **me salpicó el abrigo de barro** he splashed mud on my coat (b) *Fig (esparcir)* to sprinkle

salpicón NM *Culin* = cold dish of chopped fish or meat, seasoned with pepper, salt, vinegar and onion

salpimentar [1] VT to season

salpullido NM rash

salsa NF sauce; *(de carne)* gravy; *Fig* **en su (propia) s.** in one's element

salsera NF gravy boat

saltamontes NM INV grasshopper

saltar 1 VT *(obstáculo, valla)* to jump (over)
  2 VI (a) *(moverse)* to jump; *Fig* **s. a la vista** to be obvious (b) *(cristal etc)* to break, to shatter; *(plomos)* to go, to blow (c) *(desprenderse)* to come off (d) *(encolerizarse)* to explode, to blow up; **por menos de nada salta** the smallest thing makes him explode
  3 saltarse VPR (a) *(omitir)* to skip, to miss out; **saltarse el semáforo/turno** to jump the lights/the queue (b) *(botón)* to come off; **se me saltaron las lágrimas** tears came to my eyes

salteado, -a ADJ (a) *(espaciado)* spaced out (b) *Culin* sauté, sautéed

saltear VT *Culin* to sauté

saltimbanqui NMF acrobat, tumbler

salto NM (a) *(acción)* jump, leap; *Fig (paso adelante)* leap forward; **a saltos** in leaps and bounds; **dar** *o* **pegar un s.** to jump, to leap; **de un s.** in a flash; *Fig* **a s. de mata** every now and then; **s. de agua** waterfall; **s. de cama** negligée (b) *Dep* jump; **s. de altura** high jump; **s. de longitud** long jump; **s. mortal** somersault

saltón, -ona ADJ **ojos saltones** bulging eyes

salubre ADJ salubrious

salubridad NF healthiness; **por razones de s.** for health reasons

salud NF health; **beber a la s. de algn** to drink to sb's health; *Fam* **¡s.!** cheers!

saludable ADJ (a) *(sano)* healthy, wholesome (b) *(beneficioso)* good, beneficial

saludar VT (a) *(decir hola a)* to say hello to, to greet; **saluda de mi parte a** give my regards to; **le saluda atentamente** *(en una carta)* yours faithfully (b) *Mil* to salute

saludo NM greeting; *Mil* salute; **un s. de** best wishes from

salva NF *Mil* salvo, volley

salvación NF salvation

salvado NM bran

Salvador NM (a) *Rel* **el S.** the Saviour (b) *Geog* **El S.** El Salvador

salvador, -a NM,F saviour

salvadoreño, -a ADJ & NM,F Salvadoran, Salvadorian

salvaguarda NF *(defensa)* protection

salvaguardar VT to safeguard (**de** from), to protect (**de** from)

salvaguardia NF = **salvaguarda**

salvajada NF brutal act

salvaje ADJ (a) *Bot* wild, uncultivated; *Zool* wild; *(pueblo, tribu)* savage, uncivilized (b) *Fam (violento)* savage, wild

salvajismo NM savagery

salvamanteles NM INV *(plano)* table mat; *(con pies)* trivet

salvamento NM rescue

salvar 1 VT (a) *(de peligro)* to save, to rescue (**de** from) (b) *(obstáculo)* to clear; *(dificultad)* to get round, to overcome (c) *(exceptuar)* to exclude, to except; **salvando ciertos errores** except for a few mistakes
  2 salvarse VPR (a) *(sobrevivir)* to survive, to come out alive; *Fam (escaparse)* to escape (**de** from); **¡sálvese quien pueda!** every man for himself!; *Fam* **salvarse por los pelos** to have a narrow escape (b) *Rel* to be saved, to save one's soul

salvavidas NM INV life belt

salvedad NF exception

salvia NF *Bot* sage

salvo, -a 1 ADJ unharmed, safe; **a s.** safe
  2 ADV *(exceptuando)* except (for); **s. que** unless

salvoconducto NM safe-conduct

San ADJ Saint

sanar 1 VT *(curar)* to cure, to heal
  2 VI (a) *(persona)* to recover, to get better (b) *(herida)* to heal

sanatorio NM sanatorium

sanción NF (a) *(castigo)* penalty; *Econ* sanction (b) *(aprobación)* approval, sanction

sancionar VT (a) *(castigar)* to penalize (b) *(aprobar)* to sanction

sancocho NM *Andes (comida)* = stew of beef, chicken or fish, vegetables and green bananas

sandalia NF sandal

sándalo NM sandalwood

sandez NF piece of nonsense

sandía NF watermelon

sándwich ['sanwitʃ, 'sanwis] *(pl* **sándwiches)** NM sandwich

sandwichera NF toasted sandwich maker

saneamiento NM *(de terreno)* drainage, draining; *(de una empresa)* reorganization

sanear VT *(terrenos)* to drain; *(empresa)* to reorganize

sangrar 1 VT (a) *(sacar sangre)* to bleed (b) *Fam (sacar dinero)* to bleed dry
  2 VI to bleed

sangre NF blood; **donar s.** to give blood; **s. fría** sangfroid; **a s. fría** in cold blood

sangría NF (a) *Med* bleeding, bloodletting; *Fig* drain (b) *(timo)* rip-off (c) *(bebida)* sangria

sangriento, -a ADJ *(guerra etc)* bloody

sanguijuela NF leech, bloodsucker

sanguinario, -a ADJ bloodthirsty

sanguíneo, -a ADJ blood; **grupo s.** blood group

sanidad NF health; **Ministerio de S.** Department of Health

> Observa que la palabra inglesa **sanity** es un falso amigo y no es la traducción de la palabra española **sanidad**. En inglés **sanity** significa "cordura, sensatez".

sanitario, -a 1 ADJ health
2 NM toilet, *US* bathroom

sano, -a ADJ (a) *(bien de salud)* healthy; **s. y salvo** safe and sound (b) *(comida)* healthy, wholesome (c) **en su s. juicio** in one's right mind

> Observa que la palabra inglesa **sane** es un falso amigo y no es la traducción de la palabra española **sano**. En inglés, **sane** significa "cuerdo, sensato".

Santa Claus, *Méx, Ven* **Santa Clos** N Santa Claus

santería NF (a) *(religión)* santería, = form of religion common in the Caribbean in which people allegedly have contact with the spirit world (b) *Am (tienda)* = shop selling religious mementoes such as statues of saints

santero, -a NM,F *(curandero)* = faith healer who calls on the saints to assist with the healing process

santiamén NM *Fam* **en un s.** in a flash, in no time at all

santidad NF saintliness, holiness

santificar [44] VT to sanctify

santiguarse [45] VPR to cross oneself

santo, -a 1 ADJ (a) *(sagrado)* holy (b) *(bueno)* saintly; **un s. varón** a saint
2 NM,F *Rel & Fig* saint; *Fam* **¡por todos los santos!** for heaven's sake!; *Fig* **se me fue el s. al cielo** I clean forgot
3 NM *(onomástica)* saint's day; *Fig* **¿a s. de qué?** why on earth?

santuario NM sanctuary, shrine

saña NF fury; **con s.** furiously

sapo NM toad; *Fam* **echar sapos y culebras** to rant and rave

saque NM (a) *Ftb* **s. inicial** kick-off; **s. de banda** throw-in; **s. de esquina** corner kick (b) *Ten* service

saquear VT *(ciudad)* to sack, to plunder; *(casas, tiendas)* to loot

saqueo NM *(de ciudad)* sacking, plundering; *(de casas, tiendas)* looting

S.A.R. *(abr* **Su Alteza Real)** H.R.H.

sarampión NM measles *sing*

sarao NM knees-up

sarcasmo NM sarcasm

sarcástico, -a ADJ sarcastic

sarcófago NM sarcophagus

sardana NF sardana, = Catalan dance and music

sardina NF sardine

sardónico, -a ADJ sardonic

sargento NM sergeant

sarmiento NM vine shoot

sarna NF *Med* scabies *sing; Zool* mange

sarpullido NM rash

sarro NM *(sedimento)* deposit; *(en los dientes)* tartar; *(en la lengua)* fur

sarta NF string

sartén NF frying pan; *US* fry-pan; *Fam Fig* **tener la s. por el mango** to call the shots

sastre NM tailor

sastrería NF *(oficio)* tailoring; *(taller)* tailor's (shop); *Cin & Teatro* wardrobe (department)

Satanás N Satan

satánico, -a ADJ satanic

satélite NM satellite; *Fig* **país s.** satellite state; **televisión vía s.** satellite TV

satén NM satin

satinar VT to gloss, to make glossy

sátira NF satire

satírico, -a ADJ satirical

satirizar [40] VT to satirize

satisfacción NF satisfaction; **s. de un deseo** fulfilment of a desire

satisfacer [15] VT (a) *(deseos, necesidades)* to satisfy (b) *(requisitos)* to meet, to satisfy (c) *(deuda)* to pay

satisfactorio, -a ADJ satisfactory

satisfecho, -a 1 ADJ satisfied; **me doy por s.** that's good enough for me; **s. de sí mismo** self-satisfied, smug
2 PP *de* **satisfacer**

saturar VT to saturate

Saturno N Saturn

sauce NM willow; **s. llorón** weeping willow

saudí, saudita ADJ & NMF Saudi; **Arabia Saudita** Saudi Arabia

sauna NF sauna

savia NF sap

saxo NM *Fam Mús* sax

saxofón NM saxophone

saxofonista NMF saxophonist

sayo NM cassock, smock

sazonar VT to season, to flavour

s/c. *(abr* **su cuenta)** your account

Sdad. *(abr* **sociedad)** Soc.

se[1] PRON (a) *(reflexivo) (objeto directo) (a él mismo)* himself; *(animal)* itself; *(a ella misma)* herself; *(animal)* itself; *(a usted mismo)* yourself; *(a ellos mismos)* themselves; *(a ustedes mismos)* yourselves
(b) *(objeto indirecto) (a él mismo)* (to/for) himself; *(animal)* (to/for) itself; *(a ella misma)* (to/for) herself; *(animal)* (to/for) itself; *(a usted mismo)* (to/for) yourself; *(a ellos mismos)*

(to/for) themselves; *(a ustedes mismos)* (to/for) yourselves; **se compró un nuevo coche** he bought himself a new car; **todos los días se lava el pelo** she washes her hair every day (**c**) *(recíproco)* one another, each other (**d**) *(voz pasiva)* **el vino se guarda en cubas** wine is kept in casks (**e**) *(uso impers)* **nunca se sabe** you never know; **se habla inglés** *(en letrero)* English spoken here; **se dice que ...** it is said that ...

se² PRON PERS *(a él)* (to/for) him; *(a ella)* (to/for) her; *(a usted o ustedes)* (to/for) you; *(a ellos)* (to/for) them; **se lo diré en cuanto les vea** I'll tell them as soon as I see them; **¿se lo explico?** shall I explain it to you?; **¿se lo has dado ya?** have you given it to him yet?

sé¹ INDIC PRES *de* saber

sé² IMPERAT *de* ser

sea SUBJ PRES *de* ser

sebo NM fat

secado NM drying

secador NM dryer; **s. de pelo** hairdryer

secadora NF tumble dryer

secano NM dry land

secante ADJ **papel s.** blotting paper

secar [44] **1** VT to dry
2 secarse VPR (**a**) *(objeto, suelo)* to dry; **sécate** dry yourself; **secarse las manos** to dry one's hands (**b**) *(planta, pozo)* to dry up

sección NF section

seco, -a ADJ (**a**) *(sin humedad)* dry; *(higos, pasas)* dried; **limpieza en s.** dry-cleaning; *Fig* **a secas** just, only (**b**) *(tono)* curt, sharp; *(golpe, ruido)* sharp; *Fig* **frenar en s.** to pull up sharply; *Fig* **parar en s.** to stop dead (**c**) *(delgado)* skinny

secreción NF secretion

secretaría NF *(oficina)* secretary's office; **S. de Estado** *(en España)* = government department under the control of *Br* a junior minister *o US* an under-secretary; *(en Latinoamérica)* ministry; *(en Estados Unidos)* State Department

secretariado NM (**a**) *(oficina)* secretariat (**b**) *Educ* secretarial course

secretario, -a NM,F secretary; **s. de dirección** secretary to the director; **s. de Estado** *(en España)* *Br* junior minister, *US* under-secretary; *(en Latinoamérica)* *Br* minister, *US* secretary; *(en Estados Unidos)* Secretary of State

secreto, -a 1 ADJ secret; **en s.** in secret, secretly
2 NM secret; **guardar un s.** to keep a secret; **con mucho s.** in great secrecy

secta NF sect

sectario, -a ADJ sectarian

sector NM (**a**) *(división)* section; *Econ* industry, sector (**b**) *(zona)* area; **un s. de la ciudad** an area of the city

sectorial ADJ sectoral

secuela NF consequence

secuencia NF sequence

secuestrador, -a NM,F (**a**) *(de persona)* kidnapper; *(de un avión)* hijacker (**b**) *Der* sequestrator

secuestrar VT (**a**) *(persona)* to kidnap; *(aviones)* to hijack (**b**) *Der* to confiscate

secuestro NM (**a**) *(de persona)* kidnapping; *(de un avión)* hijacking (**b**) *Der* confiscation

secular ADJ (**a**) *Rel* secular, lay (**b**) *(antiquísimo)* ancient, age-old

secundar VT to back

secundario, -a ADJ secondary

secuoya NF *Bot* redwood, sequoia; **s. gigante** giant sequoia

sed NF thirst; **tener s.** to be thirsty

seda NF silk

sedal NM fishing line

sedante ADJ & NM sedative

sede NF (**a**) *(de organización, empresa)* headquarters; *(de gobierno)* seat; *(de acontecimiento)* venue; **s. social** head office (**b**) **la Santa S.** the Holy See

sedentario, -a ADJ sedentary

sedición NF sedition

sedicioso, -a 1 ADJ rebellious
2 NM,F rebel

sediento, -a ADJ thirsty; *Fig* **s. de poder** hungry for power

sedimentario, -a ADJ sedimentary

sedimentarse VPR to settle

sedimento NM sediment, deposit

sedoso, -a ADJ silky, silken

seducción NF seduction

seducir [10] VT to seduce; *(persuadir)* to tempt

seductor, -a 1 ADJ seductive; *(persuasivo)* tempting
2 NM,F seducer

segador, -a NM,F *(agricultor)* reaper

segadora NF *(máquina)* reaper, harvester

segar [1] VT to reap, to cut

seglar 1 ADJ secular, lay
2 NMF lay person; *(hombre)* layman; *(mujer)* laywoman

segmento NM segment

segregación NF (**a**) *(separación)* segregation (**b**) *(secreción)* secretion

segregar [42] VT (**a**) *(separar)* to segregate (**b**) *(secretar)* to secrete

seguida: en seguida LOC ADV = enseguida

seguido, -a 1 ADJ (**a**) *(continuo)* continuous (**b**) *(consecutivo)* consecutive, successive; **tres veces seguidas** on three consecutive occasions; **tres lunes seguidos** three Mondays in a row
2 ADV (**a**) *(en línea recta)* straight on; **todo s.** straight on *o* ahead (**b**) *Am (a menudo)* often

seguidor, -a NM,F follower

seguimiento NM *(de elecciones, enfermedad)* monitoring; *(por radio, radar)* tracking; *(de persona, noticia)* following

seguir [6] **1** VT **(a)** *(ir detrás de)* to follow **(b)** *(camino)* to continue **(c)** *(perseguir)* to chase **2** VI **(a)** *(sucederse)* **s. a algo** to follow sth **(b)** *(continuar)* to continue, to go on; **siguió hablando** he continued o went on o kept on speaking; **sigo resfriado** I've still got a cold; **sigue con vida** he's still alive **3 seguirse** VPR to follow, to ensue

según 1 PREP **(a)** *(de acuerdo con)* according to; **s. la Biblia** according to the Bible **(b)** *(en función de)* depending on; **varía s. el tiempo (que haga)** it varies depending on the weather **2** ADV **(a)** *(en función de cómo)* depending on; **s. estén las cosas** depending on how things stand; **¿vendrás mañana? – s.** will you come tomorrow? – it depends **(b)** *(tal como)* just as; **estaba s. lo dejé** it was just as I had left it **(c)** *(a medida que)* as; **s. iba leyendo ...** as I read on ...

segunda NF **(a)** *Aut* second (gear); **meter (la) s.** to go into second (gear) **(b)** *Av & Ferroc* second class; **viajar en s.** to travel second class

segundero NM second hand

segundo¹, -a 1 ADJ second; *Fig* **decir algo con segundas (intenciones)** to say sth with a double meaning **2** NM,F *(de una serie)* second (one)

segundo² NM *(tiempo)* second; **sesenta segundos** sixty seconds

seguramente ADV **(a)** *(seguro)* surely **(b)** *(probablemente)* most probably; **s. no lloverá** it isn't likely to rain

seguridad NF **(a)** *(física)* safety; **s. en carretera** road safety; **para mayor s.** to be on the safe side **(b)** *(protección)* security; **cerradura de s.** security lock **(c)** *(confianza)* confidence; **s. en sí mismo** self-confidence **(d)** *(certeza)* certainty; **con toda s.** most probably; **tener la s. de que ...** to be certain that ... **(e)** **S. Social** ≃ Social Security, *Br* ≃ National Health Service

seguro, -a 1 ADJ **(a)** *(sin peligro)* safe; *Fig* **ir sobre s.** to play safe **(b)** *(protegido, estable)* secure **(c)** *(cierto)* definite, certain; **tener por s. que ...** to be sure that ... **(d)** *(confiado)* sure; **estoy s. de que ...** I am sure that ... **2** NM **(a)** *(contrato)* insurance; **s. a todo riesgo** fully comprehensive insurance; **s. contra terceros** third party insurance; **s. de vida** life insurance **(b)** *(dispositivo)* safety catch o device **(c)** *CAm, Méx (imperdible)* safety pin **3** ADV for sure, definitely

seis ADJ & NM INV six

seiscientos, -as ADJ & NM six hundred

seísmo NM *(terremoto)* earthquake; *(temblor de tierra)* earth tremor

selección NF **(a)** *(acción)* selection **(b)** *Dep* team

seleccionador, -a NM,F *Dep* manager

seleccionar VT to select

selectividad NF selectivity; *Esp (examen)* **(prueba de) s.** entrance examination

selectivo, -a ADJ selective

selecto, -a ADJ select; **ambiente s.** exclusive atmosphere

selector, -a 1 ADJ selecting **2** NM selector (button)

self-service NM self-service cafeteria

sellar VT *(documento)* to seal; *(carta)* to stamp

sello NM **(a)** *(de correos)* stamp; *(para documentos)* seal **(b)** *(precinto)* seal

selva NF jungle

semáforo NM traffic lights

semana NF week; **entre s.** during the week; **S. Santa** Holy Week

semanada NF *Am* (weekly) pocket money

semanal ADJ & NM weekly

semanario NM weekly magazine

semblante NM *Literario (cara)* face; *Fig (aspecto)* look

sembrado NM sown field

sembrar [1] VT **(a)** *Agr* to sow **(b)** *Fig* **s. el pánico** to spread panic

semejante 1 ADJ **(a)** *(parecido)* similar; **nunca he visto nada s.** I've never seen anything like it **(b)** *Pey (comparativo)* such; **s. desvergüenza** such insolence **2** NM *(prójimo)* fellow being

semejanza NF similarity, likeness

semen NM semen

semental NM stud

semestral ADJ half-yearly

semestre NM six-month period, *US* semester

semicírculo NM semicircle

semidesnatado, -a ADJ semi-skimmed

semidirecto, -a 1 ADJ express **2** NM *(tren)* = through train, a section of which becomes a stopping train

semifinal NF semifinal

semifinalista NM,F semifinalist

semilla NF seed

semillero NM seedbed

seminario NM **(a)** *Educ* seminar **(b)** *Rel* seminary

sémola NF semolina

Sena N el S. the Seine

senado NM senate

senador, -a NM,F senator

sencillez NF simplicity

sencillo, -a 1 ADJ **(a)** *(fácil)* simple, easy **(b)** *(natural)* natural, unaffected **(c)** *(billete) Br* single, *US* one-way **(d)** *(sin adornos)* simple, plain **2** NM *Andes, CAm, Méx Fam (cambio)* loose change

senda NF, **sendero** NM path

sendos, -as ADJ PL **con sendas carteras** each carrying a briefcase

senil ADJ senile

seno NM (a) *(pecho)* breast (b) *Fig* bosom, heart; **en el s. de** within (c) *Mat* sine

sensación NF (a) *(percepción)* sensation, feeling; **tengo la s. de que …** I have a feeling that … (b) *(efecto)* sensation; **causar s.** to cause a sensation

sensacional ADJ sensational

sensacionalismo NM sensationalism

sensacionalista ADJ sensationalist; **prensa s.** gutter press

sensato, -a ADJ sensible

sensibilidad NF (a) *(percepción)* feeling; **no tiene s. en los brazos** she has no feeling in her arms (b) *(emotividad)* sensitivity; **tener la s. a flor de piel** to be easily hurt, to be very sensitive

sensibilizar [40] VT to make aware; **s. a la opinión pública** to increase public awareness

sensible ADJ (a) *(gen)* sensitive (b) *(evidente)* noticeable; *(importante)* significant

sensiblemente ADV noticeably, considerably

Observa que la palabra inglesa **sensible** es un falso amigo y no es la traducción de la palabra española **sensible**. En inglés, **sensible** significa tanto "sensato" como "práctico".

sensiblero, -a ADJ over-sentimental, mawkish

sensitivo, -a ADJ (a) *(de los sentidos)* sensory (b) *(receptible)* sensitive

sensorial ADJ sensory

sensual ADJ sensual

sensualidad NF sensuality

sentada NF (a) *(protesta)* sit-in (b) *Fam* **de una s.** at one sitting, in one go

sentado, -a ADJ *(establecido)* established; settled; **dar algo por s.** to take sth for granted; **dejar s. que …** to make it clear that …

sentar [1] **1** VT (a) *(en asiento)* to seat, to sit (b) *(establecer)* to establish; **s. las bases** to lay the foundations

2 VI (a) *(color, ropa etc)* to suit; **el pelo corto te sienta mal** short hair doesn't suit you (b) **s. bien/mal a** *(comida)* to agree/disagree with; **la sopa se sentará bien** the soup will do you good (c) **le sentó mal la broma** she didn't like the joke

3 sentarse VPR to sit, to sit down

sentencia NF (a) *Der* sentence; **visto para s.** ready for judgement (b) *(aforismo)* maxim, saying

sentenciar [43] VT *Der* to sentence (**a** to)

sentido, -a 1 NM (a) *(capacidad)* sense; **los cinco sentidos** the five senses; **s. común** common sense; **s. del humor** sense of humour *(significado)* meaning; **doble s.** double meaning; **no tiene s.** it doesn't make sense (c) *(dirección)* direction; **(de) s. único** one-way (d) *(conciencia)* consciousness; **perder el s.** to faint

2 ADJ deeply felt; *Fml* **mi más s. pésame** my deepest sympathy

sentimental 1 ADJ sentimental; **vida s.** love life

2 NMF sentimental person

sentimiento NM feeling; *Fml* **le acompaño en el s.** my deepest sympathy

sentir¹ NM (a) *(sentimiento)* feeling (b) *(opinión)* opinion, view

sentir² [5] **1** VT (a) *(notar)* to feel; **s. hambre/calor** to feel hungry/hot (b) *(lamentar)* to regret, to be sorry about; **lo siento (mucho)** I'm (very) sorry; **siento molestarle** I'm sorry to bother you

2 sentirse VPR to feel; **me siento mal** I feel ill; **sentirse con ánimos de hacer algo** to feel like doing sth

seña NF (a) *(gesto, indicio)* sign, signal; **hacer señas a algn** to signal to sb (b) **señas** *(dirección)* address

señal NF (a) *(indicio)* sign, indication; **en s. de** as a sign of, as a token of (b) *(placa)* sign; **s. de tráfico** road sign (c) *(gesto etc)* signal, sign (d) *(marca)* mark; *(vestigio)* trace (e) *Tel* tone; **s. de llamada** *Br* dialling tone, *US* dial tone (f) *Com* deposit

señalado, -a ADJ *(importante)* important; **un día s.** a red-letter day

señalar VT (a) *(indicar)* to mark, to indicate; **s. con el dedo** to point at (b) *(resaltar)* to point out (c) *(precio, fecha)* to fix, to arrange

señalero NM *Urug Br* indicator, *US* turn signal

señor NM (a) *(hombre)* man; *(caballero)* gentleman (b) *Rel* **El S.** the Lord (c) *(con apellido)* Mr; *(tratamiento de respeto)* sir; **el Sr. Gutiérrez** Mr Gutiérrez; **muy s. mío** *(en carta)* Dear Sir (d) *(con título)* *(no se traduce)* **el s. ministro** the Minister

señora NF (a) *(mujer)* woman, *Fml* lady; **¡señoras y señores!** ladies and gentlemen! (b) *Rel* **Nuestra S.** Our Lady (c) *(con apellido)* Mrs; *(tratamiento de respeto)* madam; **la Sra. Salinas** Mrs Salinas; **muy s. mía** *(en carta)* Dear Madam (d) *(con título)* *(no se traduce)* **la s. ministra** the Minister (e) *(esposa)* wife

señoría NF (a) *Der (hombre)* lordship; *(mujer)* ladyship (b) *Pol* **sus señorías** the honourable gentlemen

señorita NF (a) *(joven)* young woman, *Fml* young lady (b) *(tratamiento de respeto)* Miss; **S. Padilla** Miss Padilla (c) *Educ* **la s.** the teacher, Miss

señorito, -a 1 ADJ *Fam Pey (refinado)* lordly

2 NM (a) *Anticuado (hijo del amo)* master (b) *Fam Pey (niñato)* rich kid

señuelo NM decoy

sepa SUBJ PRES *de* **saber**

separación NF (a) *(acción)* separation; *Der* **s. conyugal** legal separation (b) *(espacio)* space, distance

separado, -a ADJ (**a**) *(apartado)* separate; **por s.** separately, individually (**b**) *(divorciado)* separated

separar 1 VT (**a**) *(desunir, alejar)* to separate (**de** from) (**b**) *(apartar)* to move away
2 separarse VPR (**a**) *(ir por distinto lugar)* to separate, to part company (**b**) *(matrimonio)* to separate (**c**) *(apartarse)* to move away (**de** from)

separata NF offprint

separatismo NM separatism

separatista ADJ & NMF separatist

separo NM *Méx* cell

sepia 1 NF *(pez)* cuttlefish
2 ADJ & NM *(color)* sepia

septentrional ADJ northern

septiembre NM September; **el 5 de s.** the 5th of September; **en s.** in September

séptimo, -a ADJ & NM,F seventh; **la** *o* **una séptima parte** a seventh

sepulcral ADJ *(silencio)* deathly

sepulcro NM tomb

sepultura NF grave

sepulturero, -a NM,F gravedigger

sequía NF drought

séquito NM entourage, retinue

ser¹ NM being; **s. humano** human being; **s. vivo** living being

ser² [23] VI (**a**) *(+ adj)* to be; **es alto y rubio** he is tall and fair; **el edificio es gris** the building is grey
(**b**) *(+ profesión)* to be a(n); **Rafael es músico** Rafael is a musician
(**c**) **s. de** *(procedencia)* to be *o* come from; **¿de dónde eres?** where are you from?, where do you come from?
(**d**) **s. de** *(+ material)* to be made of
(**e**) **s. de** *(+ poseedor)* to belong to; **el perro es de Miguel** the dog belongs to Miguel; **¿de quién es este abrigo?** whose coat is this?
(**f**) **s. para** *(finalidad)* to be for; **esta agua es para lavar** this water is for washing
(**g**) *(+ día, hora)* to be; **hoy es 2 de noviembre** today is the 2nd of November; **son las cinco de la tarde** it's five o'clock (in the afternoon), its five p.m.
(**h**) *(+ cantidad)* **¿cuántos estaremos en la fiesta?** how many of us will there be at the party?
(**i**) *(costar)* to be, to cost; **¿cuánto es?** how much is it?
(**j**) *(tener lugar)* to be; **el estreno será mañana** tomorrow is the opening night
(**k**) **¿qué es de Gonzalo?** what has become of Gonzalo?
(**l**) *(auxiliar en pasiva)* to be; **fue asesinado** he was murdered
(**m**) *(locuciones)* **¿cómo es eso?, ¿cómo puede s.?** how can that be?; **es más** furthermore; **es que ...** it's just that ...; **como sea** anyhow; **lo que sea** whatever; **o sea** that

is (to say); **por si fuera poco** to top it all; **sea como sea** in any case, be that as it may; **a no s. que** unless; **de no s. por ...** had it not been for ...; **eso era de esperar** it was to be expected

> The auxiliary verb **ser** is used with the past participle of a verb to form the passive (e.g. **la película fue criticada** the film was criticized).

serenar 1 VT *(calmar)* to calm
2 serenarse VPR *(calmarse)* to calm down

serenidad NF serenity

sereno¹ NM *(vigilante)* nightwatchman

sereno², -a ADJ (**a**) *(en calma)* calm (**b**) *Fam (sobrio)* sober

serial NM *Rad & TV* serial

serie NF (**a**) *(sucesión, conjunto)* series *sing*; **fabricación en s.** mass production; **lleva ABS de s.** it has ABS fitted as standard; **fuera de s.** out of the ordinary (**b**) *Rad & TV* series *sing*

seriedad NF (**a**) *(gravedad)* seriousness (**b**) *(formalidad)* reliability, dependability; **falta de s.** irresponsibility

serio, -a 1 ADJ (**a**) *(grave)* serious (**b**) *(formal)* reliable, responsible
2 en serio LOC ADV seriously

sermón NM sermon

sermonear VT & VI *Fam* to lecture

seropositivo, -a ADJ HIV-positive

serpentear VI to wind one's way, to meander

serpentina NF *(de papel)* streamer

serpiente NF snake; **s. de cascabel** rattlesnake; **s. pitón** python

serranía NF mountainous area/country

serrar [1] VT to saw

serrín NM sawdust

serrucho NM handsaw

servicial ADJ helpful, obliging

servicio NM (**a**) *(asistencia)* service; **s. a domicilio** home delivery service; **s. público** public service (**b**) *(funcionamiento)* service; **estar fuera de s.** *(máquina)* to be out of order (**c**) *Mil* service; **s. militar** military service; **estar de s.** to be on duty (**d**) *Esp (WC)* toilet, *US* bathroom (**e**) *Econ* **servicios** *(sector terciario)* services (**f**) *Dep* serve, service

servidor, -a 1 NM,F servant; *Fam* **un s.** yours truly
2 NM *Inform* server

servidumbre NF (**a**) *(criados)* servants (**b**) *(dependencia)* servitude

servil ADJ servile

servilleta NF napkin, *Br* serviette

servilletero NM serviette ring, napkin ring

servir [6] **1** VT to serve; **¿en qué puedo servirle?** what can I do for you?, may I help you?; **¿te sirvo una copa?** will I pour you a drink?
2 VI (**a**) *(prestar servicio)* to serve (**b**) *(valer)* to

be useful, to be suitable; **no sirve de nada
llorar** it's no use crying; **ya no sirve** it's no
use; **¿para qué sirve esto?** what is this
(used) for?; **s. de** to serve as, to act as
3 servirse VPR (**a**) *(comida)* to help oneself
(**b**) *Fml* **sírvase comunicarnos su decisión**
please inform us of your decision

sésamo NM sesame

sesenta ADJ & NM INV sixty

sesgar [42] VT (**a**) *(cortar)* to cut diagonally (**b**)
(torcer) to slant

sesgo NM *Fig* slant, turn; **tomar un s. favorable**
to take a turn for the better

sesión NF (**a**) *(reunión)* meeting, session; *Der*
session, sitting (**b**) *Cin* showing

seso NM brain

set NM *Ten* set

seta NF *Esp (comestible)* mushroom; **s. venenosa** toadstool

setecientos, -as ADJ & NM seven hundred

setenta ADJ & NM INV seventy

setiembre NM = **septiembre**

seto NM hedge

seudónimo NM pseudonym; *(de escritores)* pen
name

severidad NF severity

severo, -a ADJ severe

Sevilla N Seville

sevillana NF = Andalusian dance and song

sexismo NM sexism

sexista ADJ sexist

sexo NM (**a**) *(género, actividad)* sex (**b**)
(órgano) genitals

sexólogo, -a NM,F sexologist

sexto, -a ADJ & NM,F sixth

sexual ADJ sexual; **vida s.** sex life

sexualidad NF sexuality

sexy ADJ sexy

shock NM shock

shorts [ʃorts] NMPL, *Am* **short** [ʃor, ʃort] (*pl*
shores) NM shorts

show [ʃou, tʃou] (*pl* **shows**) NM show

si¹ CONJ (**a**) *(condicional)* if; **como si** as if; **si no** if
not; **si quieres** if you like, if you wish (**b**)
(pregunta indirecta) whether, if; **me preguntó
si me gustaba** he asked me if I liked it; **no sé
si ir o no** *(disyuntivo)* I don't know whether to
go or not (**c**) *(sorpresa)* **¡si está llorando!** but
she's crying!

si² *(pl* **síes)** 1 ADV (**a**) *(afirmación)* yes; **dije que
sí** I said yes, I accepted, I agreed; **porque sí** just
because; **¡que sí!** yes, I tell you!; **un día sí y**

otro no every other day (**b**) *(uso enfático) (no
se traduce)* **sí que me gusta** of course I like it;
¡eso sí que no! certainly not!

2 NM yes; **los síes** *(en parlamento)* the ayes

siamés, -esa NM,F Siamese twin

sibarita NM,F sybarite

sicario NM hired gunman; *Fam* hitman

Sicilia N Sicily

sico- = **psico-**

sicómoro NM sycamore

sida NM *(abr* **síndrome de inmunodeficiencia
adquirida)** AIDS

sidecar NM sidecar

siderurgia NF iron and steel industry

siderúrgico, -a ADJ iron and steel; **la industria
siderúrgica** the iron and steel industry

sidra NF *Br* cider, *US* hard cider

siega 1 *ver* **segar**

2 NF (**a**) *(acción)* reaping, harvesting (**b**)
(época) harvest (time)

siembra 1 *ver* **sembrar**

2 NF (**a**) *(acción)* sowing (**b**) *(época)* sowing
time

siempre ADV (**a**) *(todo el tiempo)* always; **s.
pasa lo mismo** it's always the same; **como s.**
as usual; **a la hora de s.** at the usual time; **eso
es así desde s.** it has always been like that;
para s. for ever; **s. que** *(cada vez que)* whenever; *(a condición de que)* provided, as long
as; **s. y cuando** provided, as long as (**b**) *Am
(todavía)* still; **s. viven allí** they still live there
(**c**) *Méx Fam (enfático)* **s. sí quiero ir** I do still
want to go; **s. no me marcho** I'm still not
leaving

sien NF temple

sierra NF (**a**) *(herramienta)* saw; **s. mecánica**
power saw (**b**) *Geog* mountain range, sierra

siervo, -a NM,F slave

siesta NF siesta, nap; **dormir la s.** to have a
siesta o an afternoon nap

siete 1 ADJ seven

2 NM INV seven

3 NM *RP Fam Euf* **¡la gran s.!** *Br* sugar!, *US* shoot!

sietemesino, -a NM,F seven-month baby,
premature baby

sífilis NF INV syphilis

sifón NM siphon; **whisky con s.** whisky and
soda

sig. *(abr* **siguiente)** following

sigilo NM secrecy; **entrar con mucho s.** to
tiptoe in

sigilosamente ADV *(secretamente)* secretly;
entró s. en la habitación she crept o slipped
into the room

sigiloso, -a ADJ secretive

sigla NF acronym

siglo NM century; **el s. veintiuno** the twenty-
first century; *Fam* **hace siglos que no le veo** I
haven't seen him for ages

signatario, -a ADJ & NM,F signatory

si² NM *Mús* B; *(en solfeo)* ti

sí¹ PRON PERS (**a**) *(singular) (él)* himself; *(ella)*
herself; *(cosa)* itself; *(plural)* themselves; **de
por sí, en sí** in itself; **hablaban entre sí** they
were talking among themselves o to each
other; **por sí mismo** by himself (**b**) *(uno
mismo)* oneself; **decir para sí** to say to oneself

significación NF (**a**) *(sentido)* meaning (**b**) *(importancia)* significance

significado NM meaning

significar [44] VT to mean

significativo, -a ADJ significant; *(expresivo)* meaningful

signo NM (**a**) *(señal)* sign (**b**) *Ling* mark; **s. de interrogación** question mark (**c**) *(del zodiaco)* (star) sign

sigo INDIC PRES *de* **seguir**

siguiente ADJ following, next; **¡el s.!** next, please!; **al día s.** the following day

sílaba NF syllable

silbar VI to whistle; *(abuchear)* to hiss, to boo

silbato NM whistle

silbido NM whistle, whistling; *(agudo)* hiss

silenciador NM *(de arma)* silencer; *(de coche, moto)* Br silencer, US muffler

silenciar [43] VT (**a**) *(sonido)* to muffle (**b**) *(noticia)* to hush up

silencio NM silence; **imponer s. a algn** to make sb be quiet

silencioso, -a ADJ quiet, silent

silicio NM silicon

silicona NF silicone

silla NF (**a**) *(mueble)* chair; **s. de ruedas** wheelchair; **s. giratoria** swivel chair (**b**) *(de montura)* saddle

sillín NM saddle

sillón NM armchair

silo NM silo

silueta NF silhouette; *(de cuerpo)* figure

silvestre ADJ wild

simbólico, -a ADJ symbolic; **precio s.** token price

simbolizar [40] VT to symbolize

símbolo NM symbol

simetría NF symmetry

simétrico, -a ADJ symmetrical

simiente NF seed

similar ADJ similar

similitud NF similarity

simio NM monkey

simpatía NF liking, affection; **le tengo mucha s.** I am very fond of him

> Observa que la palabra inglesa **sympathy** es un falso amigo y no es la traducción de la palabra española **simpatía**. En inglés **sympathy** significa tanto "compasión" como "comprensión".

simpático, -a ADJ *(amable)* nice, likeable; **me cae s.** I like him

> Observa que la palabra inglesa **sympathetic** es un falso amigo y no es la traducción de la palabra española **simpático**. En inglés **sympathetic** significa tanto "comprensivo" como "compasivo".

simpatizante NMF sympathizer

simpatizar [40] VI (**a**) *(persona)* to hit it off (**con** with) (**b**) *(idea)* to sympathize (**con** with)

simple 1 ADJ (**a**) *(sencillo)* simple (**b**) *(fácil)* simple, easy (**c**) *(mero)* mere (**d**) *(persona)* simple, simple-minded
    2 NM *(persona)* simpleton

simpleza NF *(de persona)* simple-mindedness

simplicidad NF simplicity

simplificar [44] VT to simplify

simposio NM symposium

simulacro NM sham, pretence; **un s. de ataque** a mock attack

simular VT to simulate

simultanear VT to combine; **simultanea el trabajo y los estudios** he's working and studying at the same time

simultáneo, -a ADJ simultaneous

sin PREP (**a**) without; **s. dinero/tí** without money/you; **estamos s. pan** we're out of bread; **s. hacer nada** without doing anything; **cerveza s.** alcohol-free beer; **s. más ni más** without further ado (**b**) *(+ infin)* **está s. secar** it hasn't been dried

sinagoga NF synagogue

sincerarse VPR to open one's heart (**con** to)

sinceridad NF sincerity; **con toda s.** in all sincerity

sincero, -a ADJ sincere

sincronizar [40] VT to synchronize

sindical ADJ *(Br trade o US labor)* union

sindicalista NMF union member, *Br* trade unionist

sindicar [44] VT *Andes, RP, Ven* to accuse; **s. a algn de algo** to accuse sb of sth

sindicato NM *(Br trade o US labor)* union

síndrome NM syndrome

sinfín NM endless number; **un s. de** lots of

sinfonía NF symphony

sinfónico, -a ADJ symphonic

singani NM *Bol* grape brandy

singular 1 ADJ (**a**) *(excepcional)* exceptional, unique (**b**) *(raro)* peculiar, odd (**c**) *Ling* singular
    2 NM *Ling* singular; **en s.** in the singular

siniestrado, -a ADJ stricken

siniestro, -a 1 ADJ sinister, ominous
    2 NM disaster, catastrophe

sinnúmero NM **un s. de** countless

sino¹ NM *Fml* fate, destiny

sino² CONJ (**a**) but; **no fui a Madrid, s. a Barcelona** I didn't go to Madrid but to Barcelona (**b**) *(excepto)* **nadie s. él** no one but him; **no quiero s. que me oigan** I only want them to listen (to me)

sinónimo, -a 1 ADJ synonymous
    2 NM synonym

sinóptico, -a ADJ **cuadro s.** diagram, chart

sinsabor NM *(usu pl)* trouble, worry

síntesis NF INV synthesis; **en s.** in short

sintético, -a ADJ synthetic

sintetizador NM synthesizer

sintetizar [40] VT to synthesize

síntoma NM symptom

sintonía NF (**a**) *Elec & Rad* tuning (**b**) *Mús & Rad (de programa)* theme tune, *Br* signature tune (**c**) *Fig* harmony

sintonizador NM *Rad* tuning knob

sintonizar [40] VT (**a**) *Rad* to tune in to (**b**) *(simpatizar)* **sintonizaron muy bien** they clicked straight away

sinuoso, -a ADJ *(camino)* winding

sinvergüenza 1 ADJ *(desvergonzado)* shameless; *(descarado)* cheeky

2 NMF *(desvergonzado)* rogue; *(caradura)* cheeky devil

sionismo NM Zionism

siquiera 1 ADV *(por lo menos)* at least; **ni s.** not even

2 CONJ *Fml (aunque)* although, even though

sirena NF (**a**) *(mujer)* mermaid, siren (**b**) *(señal acústica)* siren

Siria N Syria

sirimiri NM fine drizzle

sirio, -a ADJ & NM,F Syrian

sirviente, -a NM,F servant

sisa NF (**a**) *(de manga)* armhole (**b**) *(de dinero)* pilfering

sisar VT to pilfer, to filch

sisear VI to hiss

sísmico, -a ADJ seismic

sismógrafo NM seismograph

sistema NM system; **por s.** as a rule; **s. nervioso** nervous system; **s. montañoso** mountain chain

sistemático, -a ADJ systematic

sitiar [43] VT to besiege

sitio¹ NM (**a**) *(lugar)* place; **en cualquier s.** anywhere; **en todos los sitios** everywhere; *Fig* **quedarse en el s.** to die (**b**) *(espacio)* room; **hacer s.** to make room (**c**) *Méx (parada de taxis)* taxi *Br* rank o *US* stand (**d**) *Inform* site; **s. web** website

sitio² NM siege; **estado de s.** state of emergency

sito, -a ADJ *Fml* situated, located

situación NF (**a**) *(circunstancias)* situation; *(legal, social)* status; **su s. económica es buena** his financial position is good; **estar en s. de hacer algo** to be in a position to do sth (**b**) *(ubicación)* location, situation

situado, -a ADJ situated; *Fig* **estar bien s.** to have a good position

situar [30] **1** VT to locate

2 **situarse** VPR to be situated o located

sketch *(pl* **sketches)** NM *Cin & Teatro* sketch

skin [es'kin] *(pl* **skin** o **skins), skinhead** [es'kinχeð] *(pl* **skinheads)** NMF skinhead

S.L. *(abr* **Sociedad Limitada)** *Br* ≃ Ltd, *US* ≃ Inc

slip *(pl* **slips)** NM briefs

slogan NM slogan

S.M. *(abr* **Su Majestad)** *(rey)* His Majesty; *(reina)* Her Majesty

SMS NM INV *Tel (abr* **short message service)** SMS; **un S.** an SMS

s/n. *(abr* **sin número)** = abbreviation used in addresses after the street name, where the building has no number

snob ADJ & NMF = esnob

snobismo NM = esnobismo

so¹ PREP *(bajo)* under; **so pena de** under penalty of

so² NM *Fam* **¡so imbécil!** you damned idiot!

sobaco NM armpit

sobar VT *(tocar)* to finger, to paw; *Fam (persona)* to touch up, to fondle

soberanía NF sovereignty

soberano, -a 1 ADJ (**a**) *(independiente)* sovereign (**b**) *Fam (grande)* massive

2 NM,F *(monarca)* sovereign

soberbia NF pride

soberbio, -a ADJ (**a**) *(arrogante)* proud (**b**) *(magnífico)* splendid, magnificent

sobornar VT to bribe

soborno NM *(acción)* bribery; *(dinero etc)* bribe

sobra NF (**a**) **de s.** *(no necesario)* superfluous; **tener de s.** to have plenty; **estar de s.** not to be needed; **saber algo de s.** to know sth only too well (**b**) **sobras** *(restos)* leftovers

sobradamente ADV only too well

sobrado, -a ADJ *(que sobra)* abundant, more than enough; **sobradas veces** repeatedly; **andar s. de tiempo/dinero** to have plenty of time/money

sobrante 1 ADJ remaining, spare

2 NM surplus, excess

sobrar VI (**a**) *(haber de más)* to be more than enough, *(singular)* to be too much, *(plural)* to be too many; **sobran tres sillas** there are three chairs too many; **sobran comentarios** I've nothing further to add; *Fam* **tú sobras aquí** you are not wanted here (**b**) *(quedar)* to be left over; **ha sobrado carne** there's still some meat left

sobrasada NF sausage spread

sobre¹ NM (**a**) *(para carta)* envelope (**b**) *(de sopa etc)* packet

sobre² PREP (**a**) *(encima de)* on, upon, on top of (**b**) *(por encima)* over, above (**c**) *(acerca de)* about, on (**d**) *(aproximadamente)* about; **vendré s. las ocho** I'll come at about eight o'clock (**e**) **s. todo** especially, above all

sobre- PREF super-, over-

sobrealimentado, -a ADJ overfed

sobrecarga NF overload

sobrecargar [42] VT to overload

sobrecogedor, -a ADJ dramatic, awesome

sobrecoger [53] VT *(impresionar)* to shock; *(asustar)* to frighten, to startle

sobredosis NF INV overdose

sobreentenderse VPR se sobreentiende that goes without saying

sobrehumano, -a ADJ superhuman

sobreimpresión NF *Fot & Cin* superimposing

sobrellevar VT to endure, to bear

sobremesa¹ NF afternoon

sobremesa² NF ordenador de s. desktop computer

sobrenatural ADJ supernatural

sobrenombre NM nickname

sobrepasar 1 VT to exceed, to surpass; *(rival)* to beat
2 **sobrepasarse** VPR to go too far

sobrepeso NM *(de carga)* overload, excess weight; *(de persona)* excess weight

sobreponer [19] (PP **sobrepuesto**) 1 VT (a) *(poner encima)* to put on top (b) *Fig (anteponer)* s. algo a algo to put sth before sth
2 **sobreponerse** VPR **sobreponerse a algo** to overcome sth

sobreproducción NF overproduction

sobrepuesto, -a PP *de* sobreponer

sobresaliente 1 NM *(nota)* ≃ A
2 ADJ *(que destaca)* outstanding, excellent

sobresalir [22] VI to stick out, to protrude; *Fig (destacar)* to stand out, to excel

sobresaltar 1 VT to startle
2 **sobresaltarse** VPR to be startled, to start

sobresalto NM *(movimiento)* start; *(susto)* fright

sobreseer [36] VT *Der* to stay; s. una causa to stay proceedings

sobretiempo NM *Andes* (a) *(en trabajo)* overtime (b) *(en deporte)* Br extra time, US overtime

sobrevalorar VT to overestimate

sobrevenir [27] VI to happen unexpectedly

sobreviviente 1 ADJ surviving
2 NMF survivor

sobrevivir VI to survive

sobrevolar [2] VT to fly over

sobriedad NF sobriety; *(en la bebida)* soberness

sobrino, -a NM *(hombre)* nephew; *(mujer)* niece; mis sobrinos my nieces and nephews

sobrio, -a ADJ sober

socarrón, -ona ADJ sarcastic

socavar VT to undermine

socavón NM *(hoyo)* hollow; *(en la carretera)* pothole

sociable ADJ sociable, friendly

social ADJ social

socialdemócrata 1 ADJ social democratic
2 NMF social democrat

socialismo NM socialism

socialista ADJ & NMF socialist

socializar [40] VT to socialize

sociedad NF (a) *(de seres vivos)* society; s. de consumo consumer society (b) *(asociación)* association, society (c) *Com (empresa)* company; s. anónima Br public (limited) company, US incorporated company; s. limitada private limited company

socio, -a NM,F (a) *(miembro)* member; hacerse s. de un club to become a member of a club, to join a club (b) *Com (asociado)* partner

sociología NF sociology

sociológico, -a ADJ sociological

sociólogo, -a NM,F sociologist

socorrer VT to help, to assist

socorrido, -a ADJ handy, useful

socorrismo NM first aid; *(en la playa)* lifesaving

socorrista NMF life-saver, lifeguard

socorro NM help, assistance; ¡s.! help!; puesto de s. first-aid post

soda NF soda water

soez ADJ vulgar, crude

sofá NM sofa, settee; s. cama sofa bed, studio couch

sofisticado, -a ADJ sophisticated

sofocado, -a ADJ suffocated

sofocante ADJ suffocating, stifling; hacía un calor s. it was unbearably hot

sofocar [44] 1 VT (a) *(ahogar)* to suffocate, to smother (b) *(incendio)* to extinguish, to put out
2 **sofocarse** VPR (a) *(ahogarse)* to suffocate, to stifle (b) *Fam (irritarse)* to get upset

sofoco NM *Fig (vergüenza)* embarrassment; le dio un s. *(disgusto)* it gave her quite a turn

sofocón NM *Fam* shock; llevarse un s. to get upset

sofreír [56] VT to fry lightly, to brown

sofrito NM = fried tomato and onion sauce

software ['sofwer] NM software

soga NF rope; *Fig* estar con la s. al cuello to be in dire straits

soja NF (a) *(planta, fruto)* Br soya bean, US soy bean (b) *(proteína)* soya

sojuzgar [42] VT to subjugate

sol¹ NM (a) *(astro)* sun (b) *(luz)* sunlight; *(luz y calor)* sunshine; hace s. it's sunny, the sun is shining; tomar el s. to sunbathe; al *o* bajo el s. in the sun; de s. a s. from sunrise to sunset (c) *Fin* = standard monetary unit of Peru

sol² NM *Mús* G; *(solfeo)* so

solamente ADV only; no s. not only; s. con mirarte lo sé I know just by looking at you; s. que ... except that ...

solapa NF *(de chaqueta)* lapel; *(de sobre, bolsillo, libro)* flap

solapadamente ADV stealthily, in an underhand way

solapado, -a ADJ *(persona)* sly

solapamiento NM overlap

solapar VT to cover up

solar¹ ADJ solar; **luz s.** sunlight

solar² NM *(terreno)* plot; *(en obras)* building site

solario, solárium *(pl* **solariums)** NM solarium

solaz NM *Fml (descanso)* rest, relaxation; *(esparcimiento)* recreation, entertainment

solazarse [40] VPR *(relajar)* to relax; *(divertir)* to entertain oneself, to amuse oneself

soldado NM soldier; **s. raso** private

soldador, -a 1 NM,F welder
2 NM soldering iron

soldar [2] VT *(cable)* to solder; *(chapa)* to weld

soleado, -a ADJ sunny

soledad NF *(estado)* solitude; *(sentimiento)* loneliness

solemne ADJ **(a)** *(majestuoso)* solemn **(b)** Pey downright

solemnidad NF solemnity

soler [4] VI **(a)** *(en presente)* to be in the habit of; **solemos ir en coche** we usually go by car; **sueles equivocarte** you are usually wrong **(b)** *(en pasado)* **solía pasear por aquí** he used to walk round here

solera NF **de s.** old-established; **vino de s.** vintage wine

solfa NF *Mús* solfa; *Fam* **poner en s.** to ridicule

solicitar VT *(información etc)* to request, to ask for; *(trabajo)* to apply for

solícito, -a ADJ obliging, attentive

solicitud NF *(petición)* request; *(de trabajo)* application

solidaridad NF solidarity

solidario, -a ADJ *(actitud)* supportive; *(con* of); **ser s. con algn** to show solidarity with sb

solidarizarse VPR to show one's solidarity *(con* with)

solidez NF solidity, strength

sólido, -a ADJ solid, strong

soliloquio NM soliloquy

solista NMF soloist

solitario, -a 1 ADJ *(que está solo)* solitary, lone; *(que se siente solo)* lonely
2 NM **(a)** *(diamante)* solitaire **(b)** *Naipes Br* patience, *US* solitaire

soliviantar VT *(incitar)* to stir up; *(indignar)* to exasperate

sollozar [40] VI to sob

sollozo NM sob

solo, -a 1 ADJ **(a)** *(sin nadie)* alone; *(único)* single; **ni un s. día** not a single day; **una sola vez** only once, just once **(b)** *(solitario)* lonely **(c)** **hablar s.** to talk to oneself; **se enciende s.** it switches itself on automatically; **a solas** alone, by oneself
2 NM *Mús* solo

sólo ADV only; **tan s.** only; **no s. ... sino (también)** not only ... but (also); **con s., (tan) s. con** just by

Note that the adverb **sólo** can be written without an accent when there is no risk of confusion with the adjective.

solomillo NM sirloin

soltar [2] **1** VT **(a)** *(desasir)* to let go of; **¡suéltame!** let me go! **(b)** *(prisionero)* to release **(c)** *(humo, olor)* to give off **(d)** *(bofetada)* to deal; *(carcajada)* to let out; **me soltó un rollo** he bored me to tears
2 soltarse VPR **(a)** *(desatarse)* to come loose **(b)** *(perro etc)* to get loose, to break loose **(c)** *(desprenderse)* to come off

soltero, -a 1 ADJ single, unmarried
2 NM *(hombre)* bachelor, single man
3 NF **soltera** *(mujer)* single woman, spinster

solterón, -ona NM,F old bachelor, *f* old maid

soltura NF *(agilidad)* agility; *(seguridad)* confidence, assurance; **habla italiano con s.** he speaks Italian fluently

soluble ADJ soluble; **café s.** instant coffee

solución NF solution

solucionar VT to solve; *(arreglar)* to settle

solvencia NF **(a)** *Fin* solvency **(b)** *(fiabilidad)* reliability; **fuentes de toda s.** completely reliable sources

solventar VT *(problema)* to solve, to resolve; *(deuda, asunto)* to settle

solvente ADJ **(a)** *Fin* solvent **(b)** *(fiable)* reliable

sombra NF **(a)** *(silueta proyectada)* shadow; **s. de ojos** eyeshadow; *Fam Fig* **tener mala s.** to be nasty *o* a swine **(b)** *(zona)* shade; **a la s.** in the shade

sombrero NM hat; **s. de copa** top hat; **s. hongo** *Br* bowler hat, *US* derby

sombrilla NF parasol, sunshade

sombrío, -a ADJ *(oscuro)* dark; *(tenebroso)* sombre, gloomy; *Fig (persona)* gloomy, sullen

somero, -a ADJ superficial, shallow

someter 1 VT **(a)** **s. algn a algo** to subject sb to sth; **s. a prueba** to put to the test; **s. algo a votación** to put sth to the vote **(b)** *(rebeldes)* to subdue, to put down
2 someterse VPR **(a)** *(subordinarse)* to submit **(b)** *(rendirse)* to surrender, to yield **(c)** **someterse a un tratamiento** to undergo treatment

somier NM spring mattress

somnífero NM sleeping pill

somnoliento, -a ADJ sleepy, drowsy

son NM sound; **al s. del tambor** to the sound of the drum; **venir en s. de paz** to come in peace

sonado, -a ADJ **(a)** *(renombrado)* much talked of **(b)** *Fam (trastocado)* mad, crazy

sonajero NM rattle

sonámbulo, -a NM,F somnambulist, sleepwalker

sonar [2] **1** VI **(a)** *(producir sonido)* to sound; **sonaba una sirena** you could hear (the sound of) a siren; **s. a** to sound like; **suena bien** it sounds good (**b**) *(timbre, teléfono)* to ring; **sonaron las cinco** the clock struck five (**c**) *(ser familiar)* **tu nombre/cara me suena** your name/face rings a bell

  2 sonarse VPR **sonarse (la nariz)** to blow one's nose

sonda NF (**a**) *Med* sound, probe (**b**) **s. espacial** space probe

sondear VT (**a**) *(opinión)* to test, to sound out (**b**) *Med* to sound, to probe (**c**) *Náut* to sound

sondeo NM (**a**) *(encuesta)* poll (**b**) *Med* sounding, probing (**c**) *Náut* sounding

soneto NM *Lit* sonnet

sonido NM sound

sonoro, -a ADJ (**a**) *Cin* sound; **banda sonora** soundtrack (**b**) *(resonante)* loud, resounding (**c**) *Ling* voiced

sonreír [56] **1** VI to smile; **me sonrió** she smiled at me

  2 sonreírse VPR to smile

sonriente ADJ smiling

sonrisa NF smile

sonrojarse VPR to blush

sonsacar [44] VT **s. algo a algn** to extract sth from sb

sonso, -a ADJ *Am* foolish, silly

soñador, -a NM,F dreamer

soñar [2] VT & VI to dream; **s. con** to dream of o about; *Fig* **¡ni soñarlo!** not on your life!; **s. despierto** to daydream

soñoliento, -a ADJ sleepy, drowsy

sopa NF soup; **s. juliana** spring vegetable soup; *Fig* **quedar hecho una s.** to get soaked to the skin

sope NM *Méx* = fried corn tortilla, with beans and cheese or other toppings

sopera NF soup tureen

sopero, -a ADJ **cuchara sopera** soup spoon

sopesar VT to weigh up

sopetón NM *Fam* **de s.** all of a sudden

soplagaitas NMF INV *Fam* jerk, *Br* prat

soplar 1 VI *(viento)* to blow

  2 VT (**a**) *(polvo etc)* to blow away (**b**) *(para enfriar)* to blow on (**c**) *(para apagar)* to blow out (**d**) *(para inflar)* to blow up (**e**) *(en examen etc)* **me sopló las respuestas** he whispered the answers to me

soplete NM blowlamp, blowtorch

soplido NM blow, puff

soplillo NM *Fam* **orejas de s.** sticky-out ears

soplo NM (**a**) *(acción)* blow, puff; *(de viento)* gust (**b**) *Med* murmur

soplón, -ona NM,F *Fam (niño)* telltale, sneak; *(delator) Br* grass, *US* rat

soporífero, -a ADJ (**a**) *(que adormece)* soporific, sleep-inducing (**b**) *(aburrido)* boring, dull

soportable ADJ bearable

soportal NM porch; **soportales** arcade

soportar VT (**a**) *(peso)* to support, to bear (**b**) *Fig (calor, ruido)* to bear, to endure; *(situación)* to put up with, to bear; **no te soporto** I can't stand you

soporte NM support; **s. publicitario** advertising medium

soprano NMF soprano

sorber VT (**a**) *(beber)* to sip (**b**) *(absorber)* to soak up, to absorb

sorbete NM sorbet, sherbet

sorbo NM sip; *(trago)* gulp; **de un s.** in one gulp

sordera NF deafness

sórdido, -a ADJ squalid, sordid

sordo, -a 1 ADJ (**a**) *(persona)* deaf; **s. como una tapia** stone-deaf (**b**) *(golpe, ruido, dolor)* dull

  2 NM,F deaf person; **los sordos** the deaf *pl*; *Fam Fig* **hacerse el s.** to turn a deaf ear

sordomudo, -a 1 ADJ deaf and dumb, deaf-mute

  2 NM,F deaf and dumb person, deaf-mute

soroche NM (**a**) *Andes, Arg (mal de altura)* altitude sickness (**b**) *Chile (rubor)* blush, flush

sorprendente ADJ surprising

sorprender VT (**a**) *(extrañar)* to surprise (**b**) *(coger desprevenido)* to catch unawares, to take by surprise

sorpresa NF surprise; **coger de** o **por s.** to take by surprise

sorpresivo, -a ADJ unexpected, surprising

sortear VT (**a**) *(echar a suertes)* to draw lots for; *(rifar)* to raffle (off) (**b**) *(evitar)* to avoid, to get round

sorteo NM draw; *(rifa)* raffle

sortija NF ring

sortilegio NM spell

SOS NM SOS

sosa NF soda; **s. cáustica** caustic soda

sosegado, -a ADJ calm, quiet

sosegar [1] **1** VT to calm, to quieten

  2 sosegarse VPR to calm down

sosiego NM *(calma)* calmness; *(paz)* peace, tranquillity

soslayo: de soslayo LOC ADV **mirar de s.** to look sideways (at)

soso, -a ADJ lacking in salt; *Fig (persona)* insipid, dull

sospecha NF suspicion

sospechar 1 VI to suspect; **s. de algn** to suspect sb

  2 VT to suspect

sospechoso, -a 1 ADJ suspicious; **s. de** suspected of

  2 NM,F suspect

sostén NM (**a**) *(apoyo)* support (**b**) *(sustento)* sustenance (**c**) *(prenda)* bra, brassière

sostener [24] **1** VT (**a**) *(sujetar)* to support, to hold up (**b**) *(con la mano)* to hold (**c**) *Fig (teoría etc)* to defend, to uphold; **s. que ...** to maintain that ... (**d**) *(conversación)* to hold, to sustain (**e**) *(familia)* to support

2 sostenerse VPR (**a**) *(mantenerse)* to support oneself (**b**) *(permanecer)* to stay, to remain

sostenible ADJ *(desarrollo)* sustainable

sostenido, -a ADJ (**a**) *(continuado)* sustained (**b**) *Mús* sharp

sostuve PT INDEF *de* sostener

sota NF *Naipes* jack, knave

sotana NF cassock, soutane

sótano NM basement, cellar

soto NM grove

soviético, -a ADJ & NM,F Soviet; *Hist* **la Unión Soviética** the Soviet Union

soy INDIC PRES *de* ser

sport: de sport LOC ADJ casual, sports; **chaqueta de s.** sports jacket

spot *(pl* spots*)* NM *TV* commercial, advert, ad

spray *(pl* sprays*)* NM spray

sprint *(pl* sprints*)* NM sprint

squash NM INV *Dep* squash

Sr. *(abr* Señor*)* Mr

Sra. *(abr* Señora*)* Mrs

S.R.C., s.r.c. *(abr* se ruega contestación*)* please reply, R.S.V.P.

Sres. *(abr* señores*)* Messrs

Srta. *(abr* Señorita*)* Miss

SS.AA. *(abr* Sus Altezas*)* Their Royal Highnesses

SS.MM. *(abr* Sus Majestades*)* their Royal Highnesses

Sta. *(abr* Santa*)* St

stand *(pl* stands*)* NM *Com* stand

standard ADJ & NM standard

standing *(pl* standings*)* NM standing, social status; **un apartamento de alto s.** a luxury flat

status NM INV status

Sto. *(abr* Santo*)* St

stock *(pl* stocks*)* NM *Com* stock

stop *(pl* stops*)* NM *(señal)* stop sign

su *(pl* sus*)* ADJ POS *(de él)* his; *(de ella)* her; *(de usted, ustedes)* your; *(de animales o cosas)* its; *(impersonal)* one's; *(de ellos)* their; **su coche** his/her/your/their car; **su pata** its leg; **sus libros** his/her/your/their books; **sus patas** its legs

suave ADJ *(piel, color, voz)* soft; *(jabón, sabor, clima)* mild; *(movimiento)* smooth; *(cuesta, brisa, carácter)* gentle

> Observa que la palabra inglesa **suave** es un falso amigo y no es la traducción de la palabra española **suave**. En inglés **suave** significa «fino, cortés».

suavidad NF *(de piel, color, voz)* softness; *(de jabón, sabor, clima)* mildness; *(de movimiento)* smoothness; *(de cuesta, brisa, carácter)* gentleness

suavizante NM *(para el pelo)* (hair) conditioner; *(para la ropa)* fabric softener

suavizar [40] **1** VT *(poner blando)* to soften; *(hacer liso)* to smooth; *(ropa, cabello)* to condition

2 suavizarse VPR *(temperatura)* to get milder; *(persona)* to calm down

subacuático, -a ADJ underwater

subalimentado, -a ADJ undernourished, underfed

subalterno, -a ADJ & NM,F subordinate, subaltern

subarrendar [1] VT to sublet, to sublease

subasta NF (**a**) *(venta)* auction (**b**) *(contrata)* tender

subastar VT to auction (off), to sell at auction

subcampeón, -ona NM,F *Dep* runner-up

subconsciente ADJ & NM subconscious

subcontratación NF *Com* outsourcing

subdesarrollado, -a ADJ underdeveloped

subdesarrollo NM underdevelopment

subdirector, -a NM,F assistant manager

subdirectorio NM *Inform* subdirectory

súbdito, -a NM,F subject, citizen; **s. francés** French citizen

subdividir VT to subdivide

subestimar VT to underestimate

subida NF (**a**) *(de temperatura)* rise; *(de precios, salarios)* rise, increase (**b**) *(ascenso)* ascent, climb (**c**) *(pendiente)* slope, hill (**d**) *Fam (drogas)* high

subido, -a ADJ **s. de tono** daring, risqué

subir 1 VT (**a**) *(calle, escaleras, montaña)* to go up (**b**) *(llevar arriba)* to take/bring up; *(poner arriba)* to lift up (**c**) *(precio, salario)* to raise, to put up; *(volumen)* to turn up; *(voz)* to raise

2 VI (**a**) *(ir arriba)* to go/come up (**b**) **s. a** *(coche)* to get into; *(autobús)* to get on; *(barco, avión, tren)* to board, to get on (**c**) *(precio, temperatura)* to rise, to go up

3 subirse VPR (**a**) **subirse a** *(árbol)* to climb up; *(mesa)* to climb onto; *Fig* **el vino se le subió a la cabeza** the wine went to his head (**b**) **subirse a** *(coche)* to get into; *(autobús, avión, tren)* to get on, to board; *(caballo, bici)* to get on (**c**) *(cremallera)* to do up; *(mangas)* to roll up

súbitamente ADV suddenly

súbito, -a ADJ sudden

subjetivo, -a ADJ subjective

subjuntivo, -a ADJ & NM subjunctive

sublevación NF rising, rebellion

sublevar 1 VT *Fig (indignar)* to infuriate, to enrage

2 sublevarse VPR to rebel, to revolt

sublime ADJ sublime

submarinismo NM skin-diving

submarinista NMF scuba diver

submarino, -a 1 ADJ submarine, underwater

2 NM submarine

subnormal 1 ADJ *(retrasado)* mentally retarded; *(insulto)* moronic
  2 NMF *(retrasado)* mentally retarded person; *(insulto)* moron, cretin

suboficial NMF *Mil* noncommissioned officer

subordinado, -a ADJ & NM,F subordinate

subordinar VT to subordinate

subproducto NM by-product

subrayar VT to underline

subrepticio, -a ADJ surreptitious

subrutina NF subroutine

subsanar VT *(error)* to rectify, to put right; *(daño)* to make up for

subscribir *(pp* subscrito*)* VT = **suscribir**

subscripción NF subscription

subscrito, -a PP *de* **subscribir**

subsecretario, -a NM,F undersecretary

subsidiario, -a ADJ subsidiary

subsidio NM allowance, benefit; **s. de desempleo** unemployment benefit

subsistencia NF subsistence

subsistir VI to subsist, to remain; *(vivir)* to live on, to survive

subsuelo NM subsoil

subte NM *RP* metro, *Br* underground, *US* subway

subterráneo, -a 1 ADJ underground
  2 NM *(túnel)* tunnel, underground passage

subtítulo NM subtitle

suburbano, -a 1 ADJ suburban
  2 NM *(tren)* suburban train

suburbio NM poor suburb

subvención NF subsidy

subvencionar VT to subsidize

subversión NF subversion

subversivo, -a ADJ subversive

subyacente ADJ underlying

subyugar [42] VT to subjugate

succionar VT to suck (in)

sucedáneo, -a ADJ & NM substitute

suceder 1 VI (a) *(ocurrir)* (uso impers) to happen, to occur; **¿qué sucede?** what's going on?, what's the matter? (b) *(seguir)* to follow, to succeed
  2 sucederse VPR to follow one another, to come one after the other

sucesión NF (a) *(serie)* series *sing*, succession (b) *(al trono)* succession (c) *(descendencia)* issue, heirs

sucesivamente ADV **y así s.** and so on

sucesivo, -a ADJ following, successive; **en lo s.** from now on

suceso NM *(hecho)* event, occurrence; *(incidente)* incident; *Prensa* **sección de sucesos** accident and crime reports

Observa que la palabra inglesa **success** es un falso amigo y no es la traducción de la palabra española **suceso**. En inglés, **success** significa "éxito".

sucesor, -a NM,F successor

suciedad NF (a) *(porquería)* dirt (b) *(calidad)* dirtiness

sucinto, -a ADJ concise, succinct

sucio, -a 1 ADJ dirty; **en s.** in rough; *Fig* **juego s.** foul play; *Fig* **negocio s.** shady business
  2 ADV **jugar s.** to play dirty

sucre NM *Fin* sucre, = standard monetary unit of Ecuador

suculento, -a ADJ succulent, juicy

sucumbir VI to succumb, to yield

sucursal NF *Com & Fin* branch, branch office

sudaca NMF *Fam Pey* South American

sudadera NF sweatshirt

Sudáfrica N South Africa

sudafricano, -a ADJ & NM,F South African

Sudamérica N South America

sudamericano, -a ADJ & NM,F South American

sudar VT & VI to sweat; *Fam Fig* **s. la gota gorda** to sweat blood

sudeste NM southeast

sudoeste NM southwest

sudor NM sweat; *Fig* **con el s. de mi frente** by the sweat of my brow

sudoroso, -a ADJ sweaty

Suecia N Sweden

sueco, -a 1 ADJ Swedish
  2 NM,F *(persona)* Swede
  3 NM *(idioma)* Swedish

suegro, -a NM *(hombre)* father-in-law; *(mujer)* mother-in-law; **mis suegros** my in-laws

suela NF *(de zapato)* sole

sueldo NM salary, wages; **sueldo mínimo** minimum wage

suelo NM (a) *(superficie)* ground; *(de interior)* floor; *Fig* **estar por los suelos** *(precios)* to be rock-bottom (b) *(territorio)* soil, land (c) *(campo, terreno)* land; **s. cultivable** arable land (d) *(de carretera)* surface

suelto, -a 1 ADJ (a) *(animal, criminal, tornillo)* loose (b) *(no envasado, separado)* loose; **hojas sueltas** loose sheets (of paper); **se venden sueltos** they are sold singly o separately o loose; **dinero s.** loose change
  2 NM *(dinero)* (loose) change

sueño NM (a) *(estado)* sleep; *(ganas de dormir)* sleepiness; **tener s.** to feel o be sleepy (b) *(cosa soñada)* dream

suero NM *Med* serum; *(de la leche)* whey

suerte NF (a) *(fortuna)* luck; **por s.** fortunately; **probar s.** to try one's luck; **tener s.** to be lucky; **¡que tengas s.!** good luck! (b) **echar algo** *Esp* **a suertes** o *Am* **a la s.** to draw lots for sth (c) *(destino)* fate, destiny (d) *Fml (género)* kind, sort, type

suéter NM sweater

suficiente 1 ADJ *(bastante)* sufficient, enough
  2 NM *Educ* pass

suficientemente ADV sufficiently; **no es lo s. rico como para ...** he isn't rich enough to ...

sufijo NM suffix

sufragar [42] **1** VT *(gastos)* to pay, defray
2 VI *Am* to vote

sufragio NM *Pol* suffrage; *(voto)* vote

sufrido, -a ADJ *(persona)* long-suffering

sufrimiento NM suffering

sufrir 1 VI to suffer; **s. del corazón** to have a heart condition
2 VT (**a**) *(accidente)* to have; *(operación)* to undergo; *(dificultades, cambios)* to experience; **s. dolores de cabeza** to suffer from headaches (**b**) *(aguantar)* to bear, to put up with

sugerencia NF suggestion

sugerente ADJ suggestive

sugerir [5] VT to suggest

sugestión NF suggestion

sugestionar 1 VT to influence
2 sugestionarse VPR to become obsessed

sugestivo, -a ADJ suggestive; *(atractivo)* alluring

suiche NM *Col, Ven* switch

suicida 1 NMF *(persona)* suicide
2 ADJ suicidal

suicidarse VPR to commit suicide, to kill oneself

suicidio NM suicide

suite NF suite

Suiza N Switzerland

suizo, -a 1 ADJ Swiss
2 NM,F *(persona)* Swiss
3 NM *Esp (bollo)* = type of sugared bun

sujetador NM *Esp* bra, brassière

sujetar 1 VT (**a**) *(agarrar)* to hold (**b**) *(fijar)* to hold down, to hold in place (**c**) *Fig (someter)* to restrain
2 sujetarse VPR *(agarrarse)* to hold on

sujeto, -a 1 NM subject; *(individuo)* fellow, individual
2 ADJ *(atado)* fastened, secure; **s. a** *(sometido)* subject to, liable to

sulfato NM sulphate

sulfurar 1 VT *Fam (exasperar)* to exasperate, to infuriate
2 sulfurarse VPR *Fam* to lose one's temper, to blow one's top

sultán NM sultan

suma NF (**a**) *(cantidad)* sum, amount (**b**) *Mat* sum, addition; **s. total** sum total (**c**) **en s.** in short

sumamente ADV extremely, highly

sumar 1 VT *Mat* to add, to add up
2 sumarse VPR **sumarse a** *(huelga)* to join; *(propuesta)* to support

sumario, -a 1 ADJ summary, brief; *Der* **juicio s.** summary proceedings
2 NM *Der* summary

sumarísimo, -a ADJ *Der* swift, expeditious

sumergible ADJ & NM submersible

sumergir [57] **1** VT to submerge, to submerse; *(hundir)* to sink, to plunge
2 sumergirse VPR to submerge, to go underwater; *(hundirse)* to sink

sumidero NM drain, sewer

suministrar VT to supply, to provide; **s. algo a algn** to supply sb with sth

suministro NM supply

sumir VT **s. a algn en** to plunge sb into

sumiso, -a ADJ submissive, obedient

sumo, -a ADJ *(supremo)* supreme; **con s. cuidado** with extreme care; **a lo s.** at (the) most

suntuoso, -a ADJ sumptuous, magnificent

supe PT INDEF *de* **saber²**

supeditar VT to subject (**a** to)

súper *Fam* **1** ADJ super, great
2 NM (**a**) *(supermercado)* supermarket (**b**) *(gasolina) Br* four-star (petrol), *US* regular

superación NF overcoming; **afán de s.** drive to improve

superado, -a ADJ outdated, obsolete

superar 1 VT (**a**) *(obstáculo etc)* to overcome, to surmount; *(prueba)* to pass (**b**) *(aventajar)* to surpass, to excel
2 superarse VPR to improve o better oneself

superávit NM surplus

superdotado, -a 1 ADJ exceptionally gifted
2 NM,F genius

superficial ADJ superficial

superficialidad NF superficiality

superficie NF surface; *(área)* area; *Com* **grandes superficies** hypermarkets

superfluo, -a ADJ superfluous

superhombre NM superman

superior 1 ADJ (**a**) *(posición)* top, upper (**b**) *(cantidad)* greater, higher, larger (**a** than) (**c**) *(calidad)* superior; **calidad s.** top quality (**d**) *Educ* higher
2 NM *(jefe)* superior

superioridad NF superiority

supermán NM superman

supermercado NM supermarket

superpoblación NF overpopulation

superponer [19] (PP **superpuesto**) VT to superimpose

superpotencia NF superpower

superproducción NF (**a**) *Ind* overproduction (**b**) *Cin* mammoth production

superpuesto, -a 1 ADJ superimposed
2 PP *de* **superponer**

supersónico, -a ADJ supersonic

superstición NF superstition

supersticioso, -a ADJ superstitious

supervisar VT to supervise

supervisor, -a NM,F supervisor

supervivencia NF survival

superviviente 1 ADJ surviving
2 NMF survivor

supino, -a ADJ (**a**) *(boca arriba)* supine, face up (**b**) *(absoluto)* total, absolute

suplantar VT to supplant, to take the place of

suplementario, -a ADJ supplementary, additional

suplemento NM supplement; **sin s.** without extra charge

suplente ADJ & NMF *(sustituto)* substitute, stand-in; *Dep* substitute

supletorio, -a ADJ supplementary, additional; **cama supletoria** extra bed; **teléfono s.** extension

súplica NF entreaty, plea

suplicar [44] VT to beseech, to beg

suplicio NM *(tortura)* torture; *Fig (tormento)* torment

suplir VT (**a**) *(reemplazar)* to replace, to substitute (**b**) *(compensar)* to make up for

suponer [19] *(pp* **supuesto***)* VT (**a**) *(significar)* to mean (**b**) *(implicar)* to entail (**c**) *(representar)* to account for (**d**) *(pensar)* to suppose; **supongo que sí** I suppose so; **supongamos que …** let's assume that … (**e**) *(adivinar)* to guess; **(me) lo suponía** I guessed as much

suposición NF supposition

supositorio NM suppository

supremacía NF supremacy

supremo, -a ADJ supreme

supresión NF *(de ley)* abolition; *(de restricción)* lifting; *(de palabra)* deletion; *(de rebelión)* suppression

suprimir VT (**a**) *(ley, impuesto)* to abolish; *(restricción)* to lift; *(palabra)* to delete, to take/leave out; *(rebelión)* to suppress (**b**) *(omitir)* to omit

supuesto, -a 1 ADJ (**a**) *(asumido)* supposed, assumed; **¡por s.!** of course!; **dar algo por s.** to take sth for granted (**b**) *(presunto)* alleged
2 NM assumption; **en el s. de que** on the assumption that
3 PP *de* **suponer**

supurar VI to suppurate, to fester

supuse PT INDEF *de* **suponer**

sur NM south

Suramérica N South America

suramericano, -a ADJ & NM,F South American

surcar [44] VT *Agr* to plough; *Fig (olas)* to cut through

surco NM *Agr* furrow; *(en un disco)* groove

sureño, -a 1 ADJ southern
2 NM,F southerner

sureste NM = **sudeste**

surf, surfing NM surfing

surfista NMF surfer

surgir [57] VI *(aparecer)* to arise, to emerge, to appear; *(problema, dificultad)* to crop up

suroeste NM = **sudoeste**

surrealista ADJ & NMF surrealist

surtido, -a 1 ADJ (**a**) *(variado)* assorted (**b**) **bien s.** well-stocked
2 NM selection, assortment

surtidor NM spout; **s. de gasolina** *Br* petrol pump, *US* gas pump

surtir VT (**a**) *(proveer)* to supply (**de** with) (**b**) **s. efecto** to have the desired effect

susceptible ADJ (**a**) *(sensible)* oversensitive (**b**) *(posible)* **s. de** liable to

suscitar VT *(provocar)* to cause, to provoke; *(rebelión)* to stir up, to arouse; *(interés etc)* to arouse

suscribir *(pp* **suscrito***)* **1** VT (**a**) *(ratificar)* to subscribe to, to endorse (**b**) *(firmar)* to sign
2 suscribirse VPR to subscribe (**a** to)

suscripción NF subscription

suscrito, -a PP *de* **suscribir**

susodicho, -a ADJ above-mentioned, aforesaid

suspender 1 VT (**a**) *(interrumpir)* to suspend; *(reunión)* to adjourn (**b**) *Esp (estudiante, examen)* to fail (**c**) *(colgar)* to hang, to suspend
2 VI *(alumno)* to fail

suspense NM suspense; **novela/película de s.** thriller

suspensión NF (**a**) *(de servicio)* suspension; *Fin & Der* **s. de pagos** suspension of payments (**b**) *Aut* suspension

suspensivo, -a ADJ **puntos suspensivos** suspension points

suspenso NM (**a**) *Esp (nota)* **sacar un s.** to fail (**b**) **en s.** *(asunto, trabajo)* pending; **estar en s.** to be pending

suspicacia NF suspicion

suspicaz ADJ suspicious

suspirar VI to sigh

suspiro NM sigh

sustancia NF substance

sustancial ADJ substantial

sustantivo, -a 1 ADJ substantive
2 NM *Ling* noun

sustentar VT (**a**) *(familia)* to support (**b**) *(teoría)* to support, to defend

sustento NM (**a**) *(alimento)* sustenance, food (**b**) *(apoyo)* support

sustitución NF replacement

sustituir [37] VT to replace (**por** with); *(temporalmente)* to substitute for

sustituto, -a NM,F substitute, replacement

susto NM fright, scare; **llevarse** *o* **darse un s.** to get a fright

sustracción NF (**a**) *(robo)* theft (**b**) *Mat* subtraction

sustraer [25] VT (**a**) *Mat* to subtract (**b**) *(robar)* to steal, to remove

sustrato NM substratum

susurrar VT to whisper

susurro NM whisper

sutil ADJ (**a**) *(diferencia, pregunta)* subtle (**b**) *(aroma)* delicate

sutileza NF *(dicho)* subtlety

suyo, -a ADJ & PRON POS *(de él)* his; *(de ella)* hers; *(de usted, ustedes)* yours; *(de animal o cosa)* its; *(de ellos, ellas)* theirs; **los zapatos no son suyos** the shoes aren't hers; **varios amigos suyos** several friends of his/hers/yours/theirs; *Fam* **es muy s.** he's very aloof; *Fam* **hacer de las suyas** to be up to one's tricks; *Fam* **ir (cada uno) a lo s.** to mind one's own business; *Fam* **salirse con la suya** to get one's (own) way

T, t [te] NF (letra) T, t

t (abr **tonelada(s)**) t

tabaco NM (**a**) (planta, hoja) tobacco; **t. rubio** Virginia tobacco (**b**) (cigarrillos) cigarettes

tábano NM horsefly

tabaquismo NM smoking; **t. pasivo** passive smoking

tabarra NF Fam **dar la t.** to go on and on

tabasco® NM Tabasco® (sauce)

taberna NF pub, bar; (antiguamente) tavern

tabernero, -a NM,F publican; (hombre) land-lord; (mujer) landlady

tabique NM (**a**) (pared) partition (wall) (**b**) Anat **t. nasal** nasal wall

tabla NF (**a**) (de madera) plank; Dep (de surf, vela, trampolín) board; **t. de planchar** ironing board; **t. de quesos** cheeseboard (**b**) (lista, gráfico) table; **t. de multiplicación** multipli-cation table (**c**) (de vestido) pleat (**d**) **tablas** (en ajedrez) stalemate, draw; **quedar en ta-blas** (juego) to end in a draw (**e**) Fig **tener (mu-chas) tablas** to be an old hand

tablado NM (de teatro) stage; (de baile) dance-floor; (plataforma) platform

tablao NM Fam = flamenco bar or show

tablero NM (**a**) (tablón) panel, board; **t. de mandos** (de coche) dash(board) (**b**) (en jue-gos) board; **t. de ajedrez** chessboard

tableta NF (de chocolate) bar

tablón NM plank; (en construcción) beam; **t. de anuncios** Br noticeboard, US bulletin board

tabú (pl **tabúes**) ADJ & NM taboo

tabular VT to tabulate

taburete NM stool

tacaño, -a 1 ADJ mean, stingy
2 NM,F miser

tacatá, tacataca NM baby-walker

tacha NF **sin t.** flawless, without blemish

tachar VT (**a**) (lo escrito) to cross out (**b**) (acusar) **t. de** to accuse of

tachero NM RP Fam (de taxi) taxi driver

tacho NM Andes, RP (metálico, de hojalata) tin; (de plástico) container; (papelera) Br waste-paper bin o basket, US waste basket

tachón NM (borrón) crossing out

tachuela NF tack, stud

tácito, -a ADJ tacit

taciturno, -a ADJ (**a**) (callado) taciturn (**b**) (triste) sullen

taco NM (**a**) (tarugo) plug; (de billetes) wad; (de bota de fútbol) stud; (en billar) cue (**b**) (cubo) (de jamón, queso) cube, piece (**c**) Culin (tortilla de maíz) taco, = rolled-up tortilla pancake (**d**) Esp Fam (palabrota) swearword (**e**) Esp Fam (lío) mess, muddle; **armarse** o **hacerse un t.** to get all mixed up (**f**) **me gusta hacerse un t.** I like it a lot (**g**) Esp Fam **tacos** (años) years

tacón NM heel; **zapatos de t.** high-heeled shoes

taconeo NM (pisada) heel-tapping; (golpe) stamping with the heels

táctica NF tactics

táctico, -a ADJ tactical

táctil ADJ tactile; **pantalla t.** touch screen

tacto NM (**a**) (sentido) touch (**b**) Fig (delicadeza) tact; **tener t.** to be tactful

taekwondo NM tae kwon do

tafetán NM taffeta

tai-chi NM tai chi

tailandés, -esa 1 ADJ & NM,F Thai
2 NM (idioma) Thai

Tailandia N Thailand

taimado, -a ADJ sly, crafty

Taiwán [tai'wan] N Taiwan

tajada NF (**a**) (de comida) slice; Fig **sacar** o **llevarse t.** to take one's share (**b**) Esp Fam (borrachera) drunkenness

tajante ADJ incisive

Tajo N el T. the Tagus

tajo NM (**a**) (corte) deep cut (**b**) Esp (trabajo) workplace, work

tal 1 ADJ (**a**) (semejante) such; (más sustantivo singular contable) such a; **en tales condicio-nes** in such conditions; **nunca dije t. cosa** I never said such a thing (**b**) (indeterminado) such and such; **t. día y a t. hora** such and such a day and at such and such a time (**c**) (persona) person called …; **te llamó una t. Amelia** someone called Amelia phoned you (**d**) (locuciones) **t. vez** perhaps, maybe; **como si t. cosa** as if nothing had happened

2 ADV (**a**) (así) just; **t. cual** just as it is; **t. (y) como** just as (**b**) ¿**qué t.?** how are things?; ¿**qué t. ese vino?** how do you find this wine?

3 CONJ as; **con t. (de) que** (+ subjunctive) so long as, provided

4 PRON (cosa) something; (persona) someone, somebody; **t. para cual** two of a kind; **y t. y cual** and so on

tala NF felling

taladradora NF drill

taladrar VT to drill; *(pared)* to bore through; *(papeles)* to punch

taladro NM (**a**) *(herramienta)* drill (**b**) *(agujero)* hole

talante NM (**a**) *(carácter)* character, disposition (**b**) *(voluntad)* **de buen t.** willingly; **de mal t.** unwillingly, reluctantly

talar VT *(árboles)* to fell, to cut down

talco NM talc; **polvos de t.** talcum powder

talego NM *Esp Fam (cárcel)* clink, hole

talento NM talent

Talgo NM = fast passenger train

talibán ADJ & NMF Taliban

talismán NM talisman, lucky charm

talla NF (**a**) *(de prenda)* size; **¿qué t. usas?** what size are you? (**b**) *(estatura)* height; *Fig* stature; *Fig* **dar la t.** to make the grade (**c**) *(escultura)* carving, sculpture (**d**) *(tallado)* cutting, carving

tallado NM *(de madera)* carving; *(de piedras preciosas)* cutting; *(de metales)* engraving

tallar VT *(madera, piedra)* to carve; *(piedras preciosas)* to cut; *(metales)* to engrave

tallarines NMPL tagliatelle

talle NM (**a**) *(cintura)* waist (**b**) *(cuerpo) (de hombre)* build, physique; *(de mujer)* figure, shape

taller NM (**a**) *(obrador)* workshop; *Aut* **t. de reparaciones** garage (**b**) *Ind* factory, mill

tallo NM stem, stalk

talón NM (**a**) *(del pie)* heel (**b**) *(cheque)* cheque

> Observa que la palabra inglesa **talon** es un falso amigo y no es la traducción de la palabra española **talón**. En inglés, **talon** significa "garra".

talonario NM *(de cheques)* cheque book; *(de billetes)* book of tickets

tamal NM *(comida)* tamale, = steamed maize dumpling with savoury or sweet filling, wrapped in maize husks or a banana leaf

tamaño, -a 1 ADJ such a big, so big a
2 NM size; **de gran t.** large; **del t. de** as large as, as big as

tamarindo NM tamarind

tambalearse VPR *(persona)* to stagger; *(mesa)* to wobble; *Fig* to teeter

tambero NM (**a**) *RP (granjero)* dairy farmer (**b**) *(dueño) (de una tienda)* shopkeeper; *(de un tenderete)* stall holder

también ADV *(igualmente)* too, also, as well; **tú t. puedes venir** you can come too; **¿lo harás? yo t.** are you going to do it? so am I

tambo NM (**a**) *Andes (posada)* wayside inn (**b**) *Andes (tienda)* shop; *(tenderete)* stall (**c**) *RP (granja)* dairy farm (**d**) *Méx (recipiente)* drum

tambor NM (**a**) *(musical, de lavadora)* drum (**b**) *Anat* eardrum

Támesis N el T. the Thames

tamiz NM sieve

tamizar [40] VT to sieve

tampoco ADV (**a**) *(en afirmativas)* nor, neither; **Juan no vendrá y María t.** Juan won't come and neither will Maria; **no lo sé – yo t.** I don't know – neither do I (**b**) *(en negativas)* either, not ... either; **la Bolsa no sube, pero t. baja** the stock market isn't going up, but it's not going down either

tampón NM tampon

tan ADV (**a**) *(con adjetivo)* so; *(con sustantivo singular)* such a; **no me gusta t. dulce** I don't like it so sweet; **t. grande/deprisa que ...** so big/quickly that ...; **nunca había visto una casa t. grande** I had never seen such a big house; **¡qué vestido t. bonito!** what a beautiful dress! (**b**) *(comparativo)* **t. ... como** as ... as; **t. alto como tú** as tall as you (are) (**c**) **t. siquiera** at least; **t. sólo** only

tanda NF *(conjunto)* batch, lot; *(serie)* series sing; **por tandas** in groups

tándem NM tandem

tanga NM tanga

tangente NF tangent; *Fig* **salirse o escaparse por la t.** to go off at a tangent

tangible ADJ tangible

tango NM tango

tanguero, -a 1 ADJ **ser muy t.** to love the tango
2 NMF *(aficionado)* tango enthusiast

tanque NM tank

tantear 1 VT (**a**) **t. a algn** to sound sb out; **t. el terreno** to see how the land lies (**b**) *(calcular)* to estimate, to guess
2 VI *Dep* to (keep) score

tanteo NM (**a**) *(cálculo)* estimate, guess (**b**) *Dep* score

tanto, -a 1 NM (**a**) *(punto)* point (**b**) *(cantidad imprecisa)* so much, a certain amount; **t. por ciento** percentage (**c**) **un t.** a bit; **la casa es un t. pequeña** the house is rather *o* somewhat small (**d**) **estar al t.** *(informado)* to be informed; *(pendiente)* to be on the lookout
2 ADJ (**a**) *(+ singular)* so much; *(+ plural)* so many; **no le des t. dinero** don't give him so much money; **¡ha pasado t. tiempo!** it's been so long!; **no comas tantas manzanas** don't eat so many apples (**b**) **cincuenta y tantas personas** fifty-odd people; **en el año sesenta y tantos** in nineteen sixty-something (**c**) **t. como** as much as; **tantos como** as many as
3 PRON (**a**) *(+ singular)* so much; **otro t.** as much again, the same again; **no es** *o* **hay para t.** it's not that bad (**b**) *(+ plural)* so many; **otros tantos** as many again; **uno de tantos** run-of-the-mill; *Fam* **a las tantas** very late, at an unearthly hour
4 ADV (**a**) *(cantidad)* so much; **t. mejor/peor** so much the better/worse; **t. más cuanto que** all the more so because (**b**) *(tiempo)* so long (**c**) *(frecuencia)* so often (**d**) **t. ... como** both ... and; **t. tú como yo** both you and I; **t. si vienes como si no** whether you come or not

(e) *(locuciones)* **por lo t.** therefore; **¡y t.!** oh yes!, and how!

tañer VT to play

tapa NF **(a)** *(cubierta)* lid; *Andes, RP (de botella)* top; *(de libro)* cover; *(de zapato)* heelplate; *Aut (de cilindro)* head **(b)** *(aperitivo)* appetizer, snack

tapabarros NM INV **(a)** *(de hombre primitivo)* loincloth **(b)** *(tanga)* tanga briefs

tapadera NF *(tapa)* cover, lid; *Fig* cover, front

tapadillo: de tapadillo LOC ADV on the sly

tapado NM *CSur (abrigo)* overcoat

tapar 1 VT **(a)** *(cerrar) (recipiente)* to put the lid/top on; *(con ropa o manta)* to wrap up **(b)** *(ocultar)* to cover; *(vista)* to block **(c)** *(encubrir)* to cover up
2 taparse VPR *(cubrirse)* to cover oneself; *(abrigarse)* to wrap up

taparrabos NM INV loincloth

tapeo NM *Esp* **ir de t.** to go out for some tapas

tapete NM *(table)* cover; *Fig* **poner algo sobre el t.** to table sth

tapia NF garden wall

tapiar [43] VT **(a)** *(área)* to wall off **(b)** *(puerta, ventana)* to wall, to close up

tapicería NF **(a)** *(de muebles, coche)* upholstery **(b)** *(tienda)* upholsterer's shop/workshop **(c)** *(arte)* tapestry

tapioca NF tapioca

tapiz NM tapestry

tapizar [40] VT to upholster

tapón NM **(a)** *(de lavabo etc)* stopper, plug; *(de botella)* cap, cork; **t. de rosca** screw-on cap **(b)** *(de oídos)* earplug **(c)** *(en baloncesto)* block **(d)** *Aut (de tráfico)* traffic jam **(e)** *Am (plomo)* fuse

taponar 1 VT **(a)** *(tubería, hueco)* to plug **(b)** *Med (herida)* to tampon
2 taponarse VPR **se me han taponado los oídos** my ears are blocked up

taquería NF *Méx (quiosco)* taco stall; *(restaurante)* taco restaurant

taquigrafía NF shorthand

taquígrafo, -a NM,F shorthand writer

taquilla NF **(a)** *(ventanilla)* ticket office, booking office; *Cin & Teatro* box-office; **un éxito de t.** a box-office success **(b)** *(recaudación)* takings **(c)** *(armario)* locker

taquillero, -a 1 ADJ popular; **película taquillera** box-office hit
2 NM,F booking *o* ticket clerk

tara NF **(a)** *(peso)* tare **(b)** *(defecto)* defect, fault

tarántula NF tarantula

tararear VT & VI to hum

tardanza NF delay

tardar 1 VT *(llevar tiempo)* to take; **¿cuánto va a t.?** how long will it take?; **tardé dos horas en venir** it took me two hours to get here
2 VI *(demorar)* to take long; **si tarda mucho, me voy** if it takes much longer, I'm going; **no tardes** don't be long; **a más t.** at the latest

3 tardarse VPR **¿cuánto se tarda en llegar?** how long does it take to get there?

tarde 1 NF **(a)** *(hasta las cinco)* afternoon **(b)** *(después de las cinco)* evening **(c)** **la t. noche** late evening
2 ADV late; **siento llegar t.** sorry I'm late; **de t. en t.** very rarely, not very often; **(más) t. o (más) temprano** sooner or later

tardío, -a ADJ late, belated

tarea NF job, task; **tareas** *(de ama de casa)* housework; *(de estudiante)* homework

tarifa NF **(a)** *(precio)* tariff, rate; *(en transportes)* fare **(b)** *(lista de precios)* price list

tarima NF platform, dais

tarjeta NF card; **t. de crédito** credit card; **t. postal** postcard; **t. telefónica** phonecard; **t. de visita** visiting card, *US* calling card

tarraconense 1 ADJ of/from Tarragona
2 NMF person from Tarragona

tarro NM **(a)** *(vasija)* jar, pot **(b)** *Esp Fam (cabeza)* nut, *Br* bonce

tarta NF tart, pie

tartamudear VI to stutter, to stammer

tartamudo, -a 1 ADJ stuttering, stammering
2 NM,F stutterer, stammerer

tartana NF *Fam (coche viejo)* banger, heap

tártaro, -a ADJ & NM,F Tartar

tartera NF lunch box

tarugo NM **(a)** *(de madera)* lump of wood **(b)** *Fam (persona)* blockhead

tarumba ADJ *Fam* crazy, mad; **estar t.** to be bonkers

tasa NF **(a)** *(precio)* fee; **tasas académicas** course fees **(b)** *(impuesto)* tax; **tasas de aeropuerto** airport tax **(c)** *(índice)* rate; **t. de natalidad/mortalidad** birth/death rate **(d)** *(valoración)* valuation, appraisal

tasación NF valuation

tasador, -a NM,F valuer

tasar VT **(a)** *(valorar)* to value; **t. una casa en 10 millones de euros** to value a house at 10 million euros **(b)** *(poner precio)* to set *o* fix the price of

tasca NF cheap bar

tata 1 NF *Esp (niñera)* nanny
2 NM *Am Fam (papá)* dad, *US* pop

tatarabuelo, -a NM,F *(hombre)* great-great-grandfather; *(mujer)* great-great-grandmother; **tatarabuelos** great-great-grandparents

tataranieto, -a NM,F *(hombre)* great-great-grandson; *(mujer)* great-great-granddaughter; **tataranietos** great-great-grandchildren

tatuaje NM tattoo

tatuar [30] VT to tattoo

taurino, -a ADJ bullfighting

Tauro NM Taurus

tauromaquia NF tauromachy, (art of) bullfighting

taxativo, -a ADJ categorical

taxi NM taxi

taxímetro NM taximeter, clock

taxista NMF taxi driver

taza NF (**a**) *(para líquido)* cup; **una t. de café** *(recipiente)* coffee cup; *(contenido)* a cup of coffee (**b**) *(de retrete)* bowl

tazón NM bowl

te PRON PERS (**a**) *(complemento directo)* you; *(complemento indirecto)* (to/for) you; **no quiero verte** I don't want to see you; **te compraré uno** I'll buy one for you, I'll buy you one; **te lo dije** I told you so (**b**) *(reflexivo)* yourself; **lávate** wash yourself; *(sin traducción)* **bébetelo todo** drink it up; **no te vayas** don't go

té NM tea; **té con limón** lemon tea

tea NF torch

teatral ADJ (**a**) **grupo t.** theatre company; **obra t.** play (**b**) *Fig (teatrero)* theatrical

teatrero, -a ADJ theatrical

teatro NM (**a**) *(espectáculo, edificio)* theatre; **obra de t.** play; **autor de t.** playwright (**b**) *(fingimiento)* play-acting

tebeo NM *Esp* (children's) comic

techar VT to roof

techo NM *(de habitación)* ceiling; *(tejado)* roof; *Aut* **t. corredizo** sun roof

tecla NF key; *Fig* **dar en la t.** to get it right

teclado NM keyboard; *Inform* **t. expandido** expanded keyboard

teclear **1** VT to key in
2 VI to drum with one's fingers

técnica NF (**a**) *(tecnología)* technology (**b**) *(método)* technique (**c**) *(habilidad)* skill

técnico, -a **1** ADJ technical
2 NM,F technician, technical expert

tecnócrata NMF technocrat

tecnología NF technology

tecnológico, -a ADJ technological

tecolote NM *CAm, Méx* owl

tedio NM tedium, boredom

tedioso, -a ADJ tedious, boring

teja NF tile; *Fam Fig* **a toca t.** on the nail

tejado NM roof

tejanos NMPL jeans

tejemaneje NM *Fam* intrigue, scheming

tejer VT *(en el telar)* to weave; *(hacer punto)* to knit; *(telaraña)* to spin; *Fig (plan)* to plot, to scheme

tejido NM (**a**) *(material)* fabric; **t. de punto** knitted fabric (**b**) *Anat* tissue

tejo NM *Esp Fam* **tirar los tejos a algn** to make a play for sb

tejón NM badger

tel. *(abr* **teléfono)** tel.

tela NF (**a**) *Tex* material, fabric, cloth; *(de la leche)* skin; **t. de araña** cobweb; **t. metálica** gauze (**b**) *Fam (dinero)* dough (**c**) *Arte* canvas

(**d**) *Fig* **poner en t. de juicio** to question; *Fig* **tiene mucha t.** it's not an easy thing

telar NM loom

telaraña NF cobweb, spider's web

tele NF *Fam* TV, *Br* telly

telearrastre NM ski lift

telebanca NF telephone banking, home banking

telebasura NF *Fam* junk TV

telecabina NF cable car

telecomunicaciones NFPL telecommunications

telediario NM television news

teledirigido, -a ADJ remote-controlled

telefax NM telefax, fax

teleférico NM cable car

telefilm, telefilme NM TV film

telefonazo NM **dar un t. (a algn)** to give (sb) a buzz *o Br* ring

telefonear VT & VI to phone, *Br* to ring

telefonía NF **t. móvil** mobile phones

telefónica NF **Compañía T.** ≃ British Telecom

telefónico, -a ADJ telephone; **llamada telefónica** telephone call

telefonista NMF (telephone) operator

teléfono NM telephone, phone; **t. móvil** *or Am* **celular** *Br* mobile phone, *US* cellphone; **t. fijo** land line (phone); **t. inalámbrico** cordless telephone; **está hablando por t.** she's on the phone; **te llamó por t.** she phoned you

telegrafiar [29] VT to telegraph, to wire

telegráfico, -a ADJ telegraphic; **giro t.** giro, money order

telégrafo NM (**a**) *(medio, aparato)* telegraph (**b**) **telégrafos** telegraph office

telegrama NM telegram, cable

teleimpresora NF teleprinter

telele NM *Fam* **darle a uno un t.** to have a fit

telemando NM remote control (unit)

telemarketing NM telemarketing

telenovela NF television serial

teleobjetivo NM telephoto lens *sing*

telepatía NF telepathy

telepático, -a ADJ telepathic

telescopio NM telescope

teleserie NF television series *sing*

telesilla NM chair lift

telespectador, -a NM,F TV viewer

telesquí *(pl* **telesquíes** *o* **telesquís)** NM ski lift

teletexto NM teletext

teletienda NF home shopping programme

teletipo NM teleprinter

teletrabajador, -a NM,F teleworker

teletrabajo NM teleworking

televenta NF *(por teléfono)* telesales

televidente NMF TV viewer

televisar VT to televise

televisión NF (**a**) *(sistema)* television (**b**) *Fam (aparato)* television set; **t. en color/en blanco y negro** colour/black-and-white television; **t. digital** digital television; **t. por cable** cable television; **ver la t.** to watch television

televisivo, -a ADJ television; **espacio t.** television programme

televisor NM television set

télex NM INV telex

telón NM *Teatro* curtain; *Pol & Hist* **t. de acero** Iron Curtain; **t. de fondo** *Teatro* backdrop; *Fig* background

telonero, -a NM,F *(grupo)* support (band); *(cantante)* supporting artist

tema NM (**a**) *(asunto)* topic, subject; *(de examen)* subject; **temas de actualidad** current affairs (**b**) *Mús* theme

temario NM *(de examen)* programme

temática NF subject matter

temático, -a ADJ thematic

temblar [1] VI *(de frío)* to shiver; *(de miedo, por nervios)* to tremble, to shake (**de** with); *(voz)* to quiver

tembleque NM *Fam* shaking fit

temblón, -ona ADJ *Fam* trembling, shaky

temblor NM tremor, shudder; **t. de tierra** earth tremor

tembloroso, -a ADJ shaking; *(voz)* quivering; *(de frío)* shivering; *(de miedo)* trembling; **manos temblorosas** shaky hands

temer 1 VT to fear, to be afraid of; **temo que esté muerto** I fear he's dead; **temo que no podrá recibirle** I'm afraid (that) he won't be able to see you
2 VI to be afraid
3 temerse VPR to fear, to be afraid; **¡me lo temía!** I was afraid this would happen!

temerario, -a ADJ reckless, rash

temeridad NF (**a**) *(actitud)* temerity, rashness (**b**) *(acto temerario)* reckless act

temeroso, -a ADJ fearful, timid

temible ADJ fearful, frightful

temor NM (**a**) *(miedo)* fear (**b**) *(recelo)* worry, apprehension

témpano NM ice floe

temperamental ADJ temperamental

temperamento NM temperament; **tener t.** to have a strong character

temperatura NF temperature

tempestad NF storm; *Fig* turmoil, uproar

tempestuoso, -a ADJ stormy, tempestuous

templado, -a ADJ (**a**) *(agua)* lukewarm; *(clima)* mild, temperate (**b**) *Mús (afinado)* tuned

templanza NF moderation, restraint

templar VT (**a**) *(algo frío)* to warm up; *(algo caliente)* to cool down (**b**) *(calmar) (nervios, ánimos)* to calm; *(ira, pasiones)* to restrain; *(voz)* to soften (**c**) *Mús (instrumento)* to tune (**d**) *Téc (metal)* to temper

temple NM (**a**) *(fortaleza)* boldness, courage (**b**) *Arte* tempera

templete NM bandstand

templo NM temple

temporada NF (**a**) *(periodo concreto)* season; **t. alta** high o peak season; **t. baja** low o off season (**b**) *(periodo indefinido)* (period of) time; **por temporadas** on and off

temporal 1 ADJ temporary, provisional
2 NM storm

temporario, -a ADJ *Am* temporary

temporero, -a NM,F seasonal o temporary worker

tempranero, -a ADJ (**a**) *(persona)* early-rising (**b**) *(cosecha)* early

temprano, -a ADJ & ADV early

tenacidad NF tenacity, perseverance

tenacillas NFPL *(para pelo)* curling tongs

tenaz ADJ tenacious

tenaza NF, **tenazas** NFPL *(herramienta)* pliers, pincers; *(para el fuego)* tongs

tendedero NM clothes line, drying place

tendencia NF tendency

tendencioso, -a ADJ tendentious, biased

tender [3] **1** VT (**a**) *(mantel etc)* to spread out; *(para secar)* to hang out (**b**) *Am (cama)* to make; *(mesa)* to set, to lay (**c**) *(red)* to cast; *(puente)* to build; *(vía, cable)* to lay; *(trampa)* to lay, to set (**d**) *(mano)* to stretch o hold out (**e**) *(tumbar)* to lay
2 VI to tend (**a** to), have a tendency (**a** to)
3 tenderse VPR to lie down, stretch out

tenderete NM *(puesto)* market stall

tendero, -a NM,F shopkeeper

tendido NM (**a**) *(de vía, cable)* laying; *(de puente)* construction; **t. eléctrico** electrical installation (**b**) *Taurom (asientos)* = front tiers of seats

tendón NM tendon, sinew

tenebroso, -a ADJ *(sombrío)* dark, gloomy; *(siniestro)* sinister, shady

tenedor NM fork

teneduría NF **t. de libros** bookkeeping

tenencia NF *Der* **t. ilícita de armas** illegal possession of arms

tener [24] **1** VT (**a**) *(haber)* to have, have got; **tenemos un examen** we've got o we have an exam; **va a t. un niño** she's going to have a baby, she's expecting; **¡ahí (lo) tienes!** there you are!
(**b**) *(poseer)* to own, possess
(**c**) *(sostener)* to hold; **tenme el bolso un momento** hold my bag a minute; **ten, es para ti** take this o here you are, it's for you
(**d**) **t. calor/frío** to be hot/cold; **t. cariño a algn** to be fond of sb; **t. miedo** to be frightened
(**e**) *(edad)* to be; **tiene dieciocho (años)** he's eighteen (years old)
(**f**) *Am (llevar)* **tengo tres años aquí** I've been here for three years
(**g**) *(medida)* **la casa tiene 100 metros**

cuadrados the house is 100 square metres (**h**) *(contener)* to hold, to contain (**i**) *(mantener)* to keep; **me tuvo despierto toda la noche** he kept me up all night (**j**) **t. por** *(considerar)* to consider, to think; **me tienen por estúpido** they think I'm a fool; **ten por seguro que lloverá** you can be sure it'll rain (**k**) **t. que** to have (got) to; **tengo que irme** I must leave; **tienes/tendrías que verlo** you must/should see it

2 tenerse VPR (**a**) **tenerse en pie** to stand (up) (**b**) **tenerse por** *(considerarse)* to think o consider oneself; **se tiene por muy inteligente** he thinks he's very intelligent

tenga SUBJ PRES *de* **tener**

tengo INDIC PRES *de* **tener**

teniente NM (**a**) *Mil* lieutenant (**b**) **t. (de) alcalde** deputy mayor

tenis NM tennis

tenista NMF tennis player

tenor¹ NM *Mús* tenor

tenor² NM **a t. de** according to

tensar VT *(cable etc)* to tighten; *(arco)* to draw

tensión NF (**a**) *(estado emocional)* tension; **en t.** tense; **t. nerviosa** nervous tension (**b**) *(de la sangre)* **t. (arterial)** blood pressure (**c**) *Elec* voltage (**d**) *Téc* stress

tenso, -a ADJ (**a**) *(cuerda, cable)* tense, taut (**b**) *(persona)* tense; *(relaciones)* strained

tentación NF temptation

tentáculo NM tentacle

tentador, -a ADJ tempting

tentar [1] VT (**a**) *(palpar)* to feel, to touch (**b**) *(incitar)* to tempt

tentativa NF attempt; *Der* **t. de asesinato** attempted murder

tentempié NM *Fam* (**a**) *(comida)* snack, bite (**b**) *(juguete)* tumbler

tenue ADJ (**a**) *(luz, sonido)* subdued, faint (**b**) *(delgado)* thin, light

teñir [6] **1** VT (**a**) *(pelo etc)* to dye (**b**) *Fig* to tinge with

2 teñirse VPR **teñirse el pelo** to dye one's hair

teología NF theology

teorema NM theorem

teoría NF theory; **en t.** theoretically

teórico, -a ADJ theoretical

teorizar [40] VI to theorize (**sobre** on)

tepache NM = non-alcoholic Mexican drink made from fermented pineapple peelings and unrefined sugar

tequila NF tequila

terapeuta NMF therapist

terapia NF therapy

tercer ADJ third; **el t. mundo** the third world

tercera NF *Aut* third (gear)

tercerización NF *Am Com* outsourcing

tercermundista ADJ third-world

tercero, -a 1 ADJ third

> **Tercer** is used instead of **tercero** before masculine singular nouns (e.g. **el tercer piso** the third floor).

2 NM,F *(de una serie)* third; *Esp* **a la tercera va la vencida** third time lucky **3** *(mediador)* mediator; *Der* third party

terceto NM *Mús* trio

terciar [43] **1** VI (**a**) *(mediar)* to mediate, to arbitrate (**b**) *(participar)* to take part, to participate

2 terciarse VPR **si se tercia** should the occasion arise

terciario, -a ADJ tertiary

tercio NM (**a**) *(parte)* (one) third (**b**) *(de cerveza)* = medium-sized bottle of beer (**c**) *Taurom* stage, part *(of a bullfight)*

terciopelo NM velvet

terco, -a ADJ stubborn, obstinate

tereré NM *Arg, Par (mate)* cold maté

tergal® NM = type of synthetic fibre containing polyester

tergiversar VT *(verdad)* to distort; *(palabras)* to twist

termal ADJ thermal

termas NFPL *(baños)* spa, hot baths o springs

térmico, -a ADJ thermal; **central térmica** coal-fired power station

terminación NF completion

terminal 1 ADJ terminal

2 NF *(de aeropuerto)* terminal; *(de autobús)* terminus

3 NM *Elec & Inform* terminal

terminante ADJ (**a**) *(categórico)* categorical, final (**b**) *(dato, resultado)* conclusive

terminantemente ADV categorically; **t. prohibido** strictly forbidden

terminar 1 VT *(acabar)* to finish, to complete; *(completamente)* to finish off

2 VI (**a**) *(acabarse)* to finish, to end; **termina en seis** it ends with a six; **no termina de convencerse** he still isn't quite convinced (**b**) *(ir a parar)* to end up (**en** in); **terminó por comprarlo** he ended up buying it (**c**) **t. con** *(eliminar)* to put an end to

3 terminarse VPR (**a**) *(finalizar)* to finish, to end, to be over (**b**) *(vino, dinero etc)* to run out

término NM (**a**) *(final)* end, finish (**b**) *(palabra)* term, word; **en otros términos** in other words; **en términos generales** generally speaking (**c**) **t. municipal** district (**d**) **por t. medio** on average (**e**) *Fig* **en último t.** as a last resort

terminología NF terminology

termita NF termite

termo NM Thermos® (flask), flask

termodinámico, -a ADJ thermodynamic

termómetro NM thermometer

termonuclear ADJ thermonuclear

termostato NM thermostat

ternera NF *(carne)* veal

ternero, -a NM,F *(animal)* calf

terno NM (**a**) *(trío)* trio (**b**) *(traje)* three-piece suit

ternura NF tenderness

terquedad NF stubbornness, obstinacy

terracota NF terracotta

terraja ADJ *RP Fam (persona)* flashy, tacky; *(decoración, ropa, canción)* tacky, *Br* naff

terrajada NF *RP Fam* **esos zapatos son una t.** those shoes are tacky

terral NM *Am (polvareda)* dust cloud

Terranova N Newfoundland

terraplén NM embankment

terráqueo, -a ADJ **globo t.** *(tierra)* (the) earth; *(esfera)* globe

terrateniente NMF landowner

terraza NF (**a**) *(balcón)* balcony (**b**) *(de café)* terrace, patio (**c**) *(azotea)* terrace roof

terremoto NM earthquake

terrenal ADJ **un paraíso t.** a heaven on earth

terreno NM (**a**) *(tierra)* (piece of) land; ground; *(por su relieve)* terrain; *(campo)* field; **ganar/perder t.** to gain/lose ground (**b**) *Dep* **t. de juego** *Ten* court; *Ftb* field (**c**) *Fig* field, sphere

terrestre ADJ (**a**) *(de la tierra)* terrestrial, earthly (**b**) *(por tierra)* by land; **por vía t.** by land

terrible ADJ terrible, awful

terrícola NMF *(en ciencia ficción)* earthling

terrier NM terrier

territorio NM territory

terrón NM *(de azúcar)* lump; *(de tierra)* clod

terror NM terror; *Cin* horror

terrorífico, -a ADJ terrifying, frightening

terrorismo NM terrorism

terrorista ADJ & NMF terrorist

terroso, -a ADJ *(color)* earth-coloured

terruño NM *(terreno)* piece of land; *(patria chica)* homeland, native land

terso, -a ADJ smooth

tersura NF smoothness

tertulia NF get-together; **t. literaria** literary gathering

tesina NF (undergraduate) dissertation

tesis NF INV thesis; *(opinión)* view, theory

tesón NM tenacity, firmness

tesorero, -a NM,F treasurer

tesoro NM *también Fig* treasure

test *(pl* **tests***)* NM test

testaferro NM front man

testamentario, -a *Der* **1** ADJ testamentary **2** NM,F executor

testamento NM (**a**) *Der* will; **hacer** *o* **otorgar t.** to make *o* draw up one's will (**b**) *Rel* Testament

testar VI to make *o* draw up one's will

testarudo, -a ADJ stubborn, obstinate

testear VT *CSur* to test

testículo NM testicle

testificar [44] VT to testify

testigo 1 NMF witness; *Der* **t. de cargo/descargo** witness for the prosecution/defence; *Der* **t. ocular/presencial** eyewitness; *Rel* **Testigos de Jehová** Jehovah's Witnesses **2** NM *Dep* baton

testimoniar [43] VT to testify to, to attest to

testimonio NM *Der* testimony; *(prueba)* proof

teta NF *Fam* (**a**) *(de mujer)* tit, boob; **niño de t.** breastfeeding baby (**b**) *(de animal)* teat

tétanos NM INV tetanus

tetera NF teapot

tetero NM *Col, Ven (biberón)* baby's bottle

tetilla NF (**a**) *(de hombre, animal)* nipple (**b**) *(de biberón)* teat

tetina NF teat

tetrabrik® *(pl* **tetrabriks***)* NM **un t. de leche** a carton of milk

tétrico, -a ADJ gloomy, dull

textil ADJ & NM textile

texto NM text; **libro de t.** textbook

textual ADJ textual; *(exacto)* literal; **en palabras textuales** literally

textura NF texture

tez NF complexion

ti PRON PERS you; **es para ti** it's for you; **hazlo por ti** do it for your own sake; **piensas demasiado en ti mismo** you think too much about yourself

tianguis NM INV *CAm, Méx* open-air market

tibia NF shinbone, tibia

tibieza NF tepidity

tibio, -a ADJ tepid, lukewarm; *Fam* **ponerse t. de cerveza** to down bucketfuls of beer

tiburón NM shark

tic *(pl* **tics***)* NM tic, twitch; **t. nervioso** nervous tic *o* twitch

ticket *(pl* **tickets***)* NM *(billete)* ticket; *(recibo)* receipt

tictac NM tick-tock, ticking

tiempo NM (**a**) time; **a t.** in time; **a su (debido) t.** in due course; **a un t., al mismo t.** at the same time; **al poco t.** soon afterwards; **antes de t.** (too) early *o* soon; **con el t.** in the course of time, with time; **con t.** in advance; **¿cuánto t.?** how long?; **¿cuánto t. hace?** how long ago?; **demasiado t.** too long; **estar a t. de** to still have time to; **hacer t.** to kill time; **¿nos da t. de llegar?** have we got (enough) time to get there?; **t. libre** free time; *Fig* **dar t. al t.** to let matters take their course

(**b**) *(meteorológico)* weather; **¿qué t. hace?** what's the weather like?; **hace buen/mal t.** the weather is good/bad

(**c**) *(edad)* age; **¿cuánto** *o* **qué t. tiene tu niño?** how old is your baby/child?

(**d**) *Mús* movement

(**e**) *Dep* half

(**f**) *Ling* tense

tienda NF (a) *(establecimiento)* shop, store; **ir de tiendas** to go shopping (b) **t. (de campaña)** tent

tientas: a tientas LOC ADV **andar a t.** to feel one's way; **buscar (algo) a t.** to grope (for sth)

tiento NM tact; **con t.** tactfully

tierno, -a ADJ (a) *(blando)* tender, soft (b) *(reciente)* fresh

tierra NF (a) *(planeta)* earth (b) *Agr* land, soil (c) *(continente)* land; **tocar t.** to land (d) *(país)* country; **t. de nadie** no-man's-land (e) *(suelo)* ground; *Fig* **echar o tirar por t.** to spoil (f) *Elec* **(toma de) t.** *Br* earth, *US* ground

tierral NM *Am (polvareda)* dust cloud

tieso, -a ADJ *(rígido)* stiff, rigid; *(erguido)* up-right, erect

tiesto NM flowerpot

tifoideo, -a ADJ typhoid

tifón NM typhoon

tifus NM INV typhus (fever)

tigre NM tiger; *Am (jaguar)* jaguar

tijeras NFPL (pair of) scissors

tijereta NF (a) *(insecto)* earwig (b) *Dep* scissors kick

tila NF *(flor)* lime o linden blossom; *(infusión)* lime o linden blossom tea

tildar VT to call, to brand; **me tildó de ladrón** he called me a thief

tilde NF written accent

tilín NM *(sonido)* ting-a-ling; *Fam Fig* **Raúl le hace t.** she fancies Raúl

tilma NF *Méx* woollen blanket

tilo NM lime tree

timar VT to swindle; **me han timado** they did me

timbal NM kettledrum

timbrar VT *(carta)* to stamp; *(documento)* to seal

timbre NM (a) *(de puerta)* bell (b) *(sello)* stamp, seal; *Fin* fiscal o revenue stamp (c) *Mús (sonido)* timbre

timidez NF shyness

tímido, -a ADJ shy; *Fig (mejoría)* light; *(intento)* cautious

timo NM swindle, fiddle; **es un t.** it's a rip-off

timón NM (a) *(de barco) (palanca)* tiller, helm; *(rueda)* wheel, helm; *(pieza articulada)* rud-der; **estar al t.** to be at the helm (b) *Andes, Cuba (steering wheel)* steering wheel

timonel NM helmsman

tímpano NM *Anat* eardrum

tina NF (a) *(tinaja)* pitcher (b) *(gran cuba)* vat (c) *CAm, Col, Méx (bañera)* bathtub

tinaja NF large earthenware jar

tinerfeño, -a 1 ADJ of/from Tenerife
2 NM,F person from Tenerife

tinglado NM *Fam* (a) **todo el t.** the whole caboodle (b) *(desorden)* chaos

tinieblas NFPL darkness

tino NM (a) *(puntería)* (good) aim; **tener buen t.** to be a good shot (b) *(tacto)* (common) sense, good judgement

tinta NF ink; **t. china** Indian ink; **t. simpática** invisible ink; *Fig* **medias tintas** ambiguities, half measures

tinte NM (a) *(color)* dye (b) *Fig (matiz)* shade, overtone

tintero NM inkpot, inkwell; *Fig* **se quedó en el t.** it wasn't said

tintinear VI *(vidrio)* to clink; *(campana)* to jingle, to tinkle

tintineo NM *(de vidrio)* clinking; *(de campana)* jingling

tinto 1 ADJ *(vino)* red
2 NM (a) *(vino)* red wine (b) *Col, Ven (café)* black coffee

tintorería NF dry-cleaner's

tintura NF *Quím* tincture; **t. de yodo** iodine

tío, -a NM,F (a) *(pariente) (hombre)* uncle; *(mujer)* aunt; **mis tíos** my uncle and aunt (b) *Esp Fam (persona) (hombre)* guy, *Br* bloke; *(mujer)* girl, woman

tiovivo NM merry-go-round, *US* carousel

tipazo NM *Fam* good figure

tipear VT & VI *Am* to type

típico, -a ADJ (a) *(característico)* typical; **eso es t. de Antonio** that's just like Antonio (b) *(baile, traje)* traditional

tipificar [44] VT to classify

tipismo NM local colour

tipo NM (a) *(clase)* type, kind (b) *Fam (persona)* guy, *Br* bloke; **t. raro** weirdo (c) *Anat (de hombre)* build, physique; *(de mujer)* figure (d) *Fin* rate; **t. de cambio/interés** rate of ex-change/interest (e) **el político t. de la iz-quierda** the typical left-wing politician

tipografía NF typography

tipográfico, -a ADJ typographic; **error t.** printing error

tipógrafo, -a NM,F typographer

tiquismiquis NMF INV *Fam* fusspot

tira 1 NF (a) *(banda, cinta)* strip (b) *(de dibujos)* comic strip (c) *Fam* **la t. de gente** a lot o loads of people (d) *Méx Fam* **la t.** *(la policía)* the law, *US* the heat
2 tira y afloja NM tug of war

tirabuzón NM ringlet

tirachinas NM INV *Br* catapult, *US* slingshot

tirada NF (a) *(lanzamiento)* throw (b) *(impre-sión)* print run

tirado, -a ADJ *Fam* (a) *(barato)* dirt-cheap (b) *(fácil)* dead easy (c) *Fam* **dejar t. (a algn)** to let (sb) down

tirador NM (a) *(persona)* marksman (b) *(pomo)* knob, handle; *(cordón)* bell pull (c) *(tirachinas)* *Br* catapult, *US* slingshot

tiraje NM *Am* print run

tiralíneas NM INV tracer, drawing o ruling pen

tiranía NF tyranny

tiránico, -a ADJ tyrannical

tiranizar [40] VT to tyrannize

tirano, -a NM,F tyrant

tirante 1 ADJ *(cable etc)* tight, taut; *(situación, relación)* tense
2 NM (**a**) *(de vestido etc)* strap; **tirantes** *Br* braces, *US* suspenders (**b**) *Téc* brace, stay

tirar 1 VT (**a**) *(echar)* to throw (**b**) *(dejar caer)* to drop (**c**) *(desechar)* to throw away; *Fig (dinero)* to squander (**d**) *(derribar)* to knock down; **t. la puerta (abajo)** to smash the door in (**e**) *(foto)* to take (**f**) *Impr* to print (**g**) *(beso)* to blow
2 VI (**a**) **t. de** *(cuerda, puerta)* to pull (**b**) *(chimenea, estufa)* to draw (**c**) *(funcionar)* to work, to run (**d**) **ir tirando** to get by (**e**) **t. a** to tend towards; **tira a rojo** it's reddish (**f**) **tira a la izquierda** turn left; **¡venga, tira ya!** come on, get going! (**g**) *(disparar)* to shoot, to fire; *Ftb* **t. a puerta** to shoot at goal
3 tirarse VPR (**a**) *(lanzarse)* to throw *o* hurl oneself; **tirarse de cabeza al agua** to dive into the water (**b**) *(tumbarse)* to lie down (**c**) *Fam (tiempo)* to spend; **me tiré una hora esperando** I waited (for) a good hour (**d**) *Vulg* **tirarse a algn** to lay sb

tirita NF *Br* (sticking) plaster, *US* Band-aid®

tiritar VI to shiver, to shake

tiro NM (**a**) *(lanzamiento)* throw (**b**) *(disparo, ruido)* shot; *Ftb* **a gol** shot at goal; **t. al blanco** target shooting; **t. al plato** clay pigeon shooting; **t. con arco** archery (**c**) *(de vestido)* shoulder width (**d**) *(de chimenea)* draught; **animal de t.** draught animal

tirón NM pull, tug; *(de bolso)* snatch; *Fam* **de un t.** in one go

tirotear VT to shoot at, to snipe at

tiroteo NM shooting, firing to and fro

tirria NF *Fam* **le tengo t.** I can't stand him

tísico, -a ADJ tubercular, consumptive

tisis NF INV tuberculosis, consumption

tisú NM tissue, paper hankie

títere NM *(marioneta)* puppet; **no dejar t. con cabeza** to spare no one

titilar VI *(luz)* to flicker; *(estrella)* to twinkle

titiritero, -a NM,F puppeteer

titubeante ADJ *(actitud)* hesitant; *(voz)* hesitant, faltering

titubear VI *(dudar)* to hesitate; *(al hablar)* to falter, to hesitate

titubeo NM hesitation, hesitancy

titulación NF qualifications

titulado, -a ADJ *(licenciado)* graduate; *(diplomado)* qualified

titular¹ 1 NM,F *(persona)* holder
2 NM *Prensa* headline
3 ADJ appointed, official

titular² 1 VT *(poner título)* to call
2 titularse VPR (**a**) *(película etc)* to be called; **¿cómo se titula?** what is it called? (**b**) *Educ* to graduate (**en** in)

titularidad NF *Educ* tenure

título NM (**a**) *(de obra)* title (**b**) *Educ* degree; *(diploma)* diploma (**c**) *Prensa (titular)* headline (**d**) **a t. de ejemplo** by way of example

tiza NF chalk; **una t.** a piece of chalk

tiznar VT to blacken (with soot)

tizón NM half-burnt stick, brand

tlapalería NF *Méx* ironmonger's (shop)

toalla NF towel; **tirar la t.** to throw in the towel

toallero NM towel *Br* rail *o US* bar

tobillo NM ankle

tobogán NM slide, chute

toca NF *(sombrero)* headdress; *(de monja)* wimple

tocadiscos NM INV record player; **t. digital** *o* **compacto** CD player

tocado¹ NM (**a**) *(peinado)* coiffure, hairdo (**b**) *(prenda)* headdress

tocado², -a ADJ *Fam* crazy, touched

tocador NM (**a**) *(mueble)* dressing table (**b**) *(habitación)* dressing room; **t. de señoras** powder room

tocante ADJ **en lo t. a …** with reference to …

tocar [44] **1** VT (**a**) *(entrar en contacto con)* to touch; *Fam Fig* **toca madera** touch wood (**b**) *(instrumento, canción)* to play; *(timbre, campana)* to ring; *(bocina)* to blow (**c**) *(tema, asunto)* to touch on (**d**) *(afectar)* to concern; **por lo que a mí me toca** as far as I am concerned
2 VI (**a**) **¿a quién le toca?** *(en juegos)* whose turn is it? (**b**) **me tocó el gordo** *(en rifa)* I won the jackpot (**c**) **t. con** to be next to; *Fig* **t. a su fin** to be coming to an end (**d**) *(llamar)* **t. a la puerta** to knock on the door
3 tocarse VPR (**a**) *(una cosa con otra)* to touch each other (**b**) **¿os tocáis algo?** *(ser parientes)* are you related? (**c**) *(cubrirse la cabeza)* to cover one's head

tocata 1 NF *Mús* toccata
2 NM *Fam* record player

tocateja: a tocateja LOC ADV **pagar a t.** to pay on the nail

tocayo, -a NM,F namesake

tocho NM *Fam (libro grande)* tome

tocino NM pork *o* bacon fat; **t. de cielo** = sweet made with egg yolk

tocólogo, -a NM,F obstetrician

tocuyo NM *Andes, Arg* coarse cotton cloth

todavía ADV (**a**) *(aún)* still; *(en negativas)* yet; **t. la quiere** he still loves her; **t. no** not yet; **no mires t.** don't look yet (**b**) *(para reforzar)* even, still; **t. más/menos** even more/less

todo, -a 1 ADJ (**a**) *(el total de)* all; **t. el pan** all the bread; **t. el mundo** (absolutely) everybody; **t. el día** all day, the whole *o* entire day; **todas las manzanas** all the apples; *Fam* **t. quisqui** every Tom, Dick and Harry (**b**) *(cada)* every; **t. ciudadano de más de dieciocho años** every citizen over eighteen years of age (**c**) *(entero)* complete, thorough; **es toda una mujer** she is every inch a woman (**d**) *(con expresiones de tiempo)* every; **todos los niños** all the children; **todos los martes** every Tuesday

2 NM *(totalidad)* whole

3 PRON (**a**) *(sin excluir nada)* all, everything; **ante t.** first of all; **con t.** in spite of everything; **del t.** completely; **después de t.** after all; **eso es t.** that's all, that's it; **estar en t.** to be really with it; **hay de t.** there are all sorts; **lo sé t.** I know all about it; **t. lo contrario** quite the contrary *o* opposite; **t. lo más** at the most (**b**) *(cualquiera)* anybody; **t. aquél** *o* **el que quiera** anybody who wants (to) (**c**) *(cada uno)* **todos aprobamos** we all passed; **todos fueron** they all went

4 ADV completely, totally; **volvió t. sucio** he was all dirty when he got back

todopoderoso, -a ADJ all-powerful, almighty

todoterreno NM four-wheel drive, all-terrain vehicle

toga NF (**a**) *(de académico)* gown; *(de magistrado)* robes (**b**) *Hist* toga

Tokio N Tokyo

toldo NM *(cubierta)* awning

tolerancia NF tolerance

tolerante ADJ tolerant

tolerar VT to tolerate; *(situación)* to stand; *(gente)* to put up with

toma NF (**a**) *(acción)* taking; *Elec* **t. de corriente** power point, socket (**b**) *Med* dose (**c**) *Mil* capture (**d**) *Cin* take, shot (**e**) **t. de posesión** swearing in (**f**) *Fam Fig* **t. y daca** give and take

tomado, -a ADJ (**a**) *(voz)* hoarse (**b**) *Am Fam (persona)* tight, tanked up (**c**) **tenerla tomada con algn** to have it in for sb

tomadura NF *Fam* **t. de pelo** leg-pull; *(timo)* rip-off

tomar 1 VT (**a**) *(coger)* to take; *(autobús, tren)* to catch; *(decisión)* to make, to take; **toma** here (you are); **t. el sol** to sunbathe; *Av* **t. tierra** to land; *Fam* **tomarla con algn** to have it in for sb (**b**) *(comer, beber)* to have (**c**) **t. algo a mal** to take sth badly; **t. en serio/broma** to take seriously/as a joke (**d**) *(confundir)* to take (**por** for) (**e**) *Mil* to take

2 VI *Am (beber alcohol)* to drink

3 tomarse VPR (**a**) *(comer)* to eat; *(beber)* to drink (**b**) *Fam* **no te lo tomes así** don't take it like that

tomate NM tomato; **salsa de t.** *(de lata)* tomato sauce; *(de botella)* ketchup

tomavistas NM INV *cine o* movie camera

tómbola NF tombola

tomillo NM thyme

tomo NM volume; *Fam* **de t. y lomo** utter, out-and-out

ton NM **sin t. ni son** without rhyme or reason

tonada NF (**a**) *Mús* tune, song (**b**) *Am (acento)* (regional) accent

tonalidad NF tonality

tonel NM barrel, cask

tonelada NF ton; **t. métrica** tonne

tonelaje NM tonnage

tonelero, -a NM,F cooper

tongo NM fix

tónico, -a 1 NM *Med* tonic; *(cosmético)* skin tonic

2 tónica NF (**a**) *(tendencia)* tendency, trend; **tónica general** overall trend (**b**) *(bebida)* tonic (water) (**c**) *Mús* tonic

3 ADJ *Ling* tonic, stressed (**b**) *Med & Mús* tonic

tonificante ADJ invigorating

tonificar [44] VT to tone up, to invigorate

tono NM tone; **a t. con** in tune *o* harmony with; **subir de t.** *o* **el t.** to speak louder; **un t. alto/bajo** a high/low pitch; **dar el t.** to set the tone; *Fig* **darse t.** to put on airs; *Fig* **fuera de t.** inappropriate, out of place

tontear VI to flirt

tontería NF (**a**) *(dicho, hecho)* silly *o* stupid thing (**b**) *(insignificancia)* trifle

tonto, -a 1 ADJ silly, dumb

2 NM,F fool, idiot; **t. de remate** *o* **de capirote** prize idiot

topacio NM topaz

topadora NF *RP* bulldozer

toparse VPR **t. con** to bump into; *(dificultades)* to run up against, to encounter; **t. con algo** to come across sth

tope 1 NM (**a**) *(límite)* limit, end; *Fam* **a t.** *(al máximo)* flat out; *Fig* **estar hasta los topes** to be full up; **fecha t.** deadline (**b**) *Téc* stop, check (**c**) *Ferroc* buffer

2 ADV *Fam* incredibly; **t. difícil** really difficult

tópico, -a 1 NM cliché

2 ADJ *Med* for external use

Observa que la palabra inglesa **topic** es un falso amigo y no es la traducción de la palabra española **tópico**. En inglés **topic** significa "tema".

topo NM mole

topografía NF topography

topónimo NM place name

toque NM (**a**) *(detalle, retoque)* touch (**b**) *(de campanas)* peal; **t. de queda** curfew (**c**) *Fam* **dar un t. a algn** *(avisar)* to let sb know; *(advertir)* to warn sb

toquetear VT to fiddle with, to finger

toquilla NF (knitted) shawl

tórax NM thorax

torbellino NM (**a**) *(de viento)* whirlwind (**b**) *Fig (confusión)* whirl, turmoil

torcedura NF *(acción)* twist, twisting; *Med* sprain

torcer [41] **1** vt (**a**) *(metal)* to bend; *(cuerda, hilo)* to twist; *Med* to sprain; *Fig (esquina)* to turn (**b**) *(inclinar)* to slant
2 vi to turn (left *o* right)
3 torcerse vpr (**a**) *(doblarse)* to twist, to bend (**b**) *Med* **se me torció el tobillo** I sprained my ankle (**c**) *(plan)* to fall through (**d**) *(desviarse)* to go off to the side

torcido, -a ADJ twisted; *(ladeado)* slanted, lopsided; *(corbata)* crooked

tordo, -a 1 ADJ dapple-grey
2 NM *(ave)* thrush

torear 1 vt to fight; *Fam* **t. a algn** to tease *o* confuse sb; *Fam* **t. un asunto** to tackle a matter skilfully
2 vi to fight

toreo NM bullfighting

torera NF *(prenda)* bolero (jacket)

torero, -a NM,F bullfighter

tormenta NF storm

tormento NM *(tortura)* torture; *(padecimiento)* torment

tormentoso, -a ADJ stormy

tornado NM tornado

tornar *Fml* **1** vt *(convertir)* to transform, to turn (**en** into)
2 vi *(regresar)* to return, to go back; **t. en sí** to regain consciousness
3 tornarse vpr to become, to turn

tornasolado, -a ADJ iridescent

torneo NM (**a**) *Dep* tournament, *US* tourney (**b**) *Hist* tourney, joust

tornillo NM screw

torniquete NM (**a**) *(en entrada)* turnstile (**b**) *Med* tourniquet

torno 1 NM *(de carpintero)* lathe; *(de alfarero)* wheel
2 en torno a LOC PREP *(alrededor de)* around, round; *(aproximadamente)* around, about

toro NM bull; **¿te gustan los toros?** do you like bullfighting?

toronja NF grapefruit

torpe ADJ (**a**) *(sin habilidad)* clumsy (**b**) *(tonto)* dim, thick (**c**) *(movimiento)* slow, awkward

torpedear vt to torpedo

torpedo NM torpedo

torpeza NF (**a**) *(física)* clumsiness; *(mental)* dimness, stupidity (**b**) *(lentitud)* slowness, heaviness (**c**) *(error)* blunder

torre NF (**a**) *(construcción)* tower (**b**) *Mil* turret (**c**) *(en ajedrez)* rook, castle

torrefacto, -a ADJ roasted; **café t.** high roast coffee

torrencial ADJ torrential

torrente NM (**a**) *(de agua)* torrent (**b**) *Fig* **t. de voz** strong *o* powerful voice

torrezno NM = rasher of fried bacon

tórrido, -a ADJ torrid

torrija NF ≃ French toast *(sweetened)*

torsión NF (**a**) *(torcedura)* twist, twisting (**b**) *Téc* torsion

torso NM (**a**) *Anat* torso (**b**) *Arte* bust

torta NF (**a**) *Culin Esp (de harina)* = flat, round plain cake; *CSur, Ven (dulce)* cake; *Andes, CAm, Carib, RP (salada)* pie; *Méx (sandwich)* filled roll (**b**) *Fam (golpe)* slap, punch

tortazo NM *Fam* (**a**) *(bofetada)* slap, punch (**b**) *(golpe)* whack, thump

tortícolis NF INV crick in the neck

tortilla NF (**a**) *(egg)* omelette; **t. española** Spanish *o* potato omelette; **t. francesa** French *o* plain omelette (**b**) *(de maíz)* tortilla, = thin maize pancake

tortillera NF *muy Fam* dyke, lesbian

tórtola NF dove

tortuga NF *(de tierra)* tortoise, *US* turtle; *(de mar)* turtle

tortuoso, -a ADJ tortuous

tortura NF torture

torturar vt to torture

tos NF cough; **t. ferina** whooping cough

tosco, -a ADJ *(basto)* rustic, rough; *(persona)* uncouth

toser vi to cough

tosquedad NF roughness

tostada NF (slice of) toast

tostado, -a ADJ (**a**) *(pan)* toasted (**b**) *(moreno)* tanned, brown

tostador NM toaster

tostar [2] vt *(pan)* to toast; *(café)* to roast; *(carne, pescado)* to brown; *Fig (la piel)* to tan

tostón NM (**a**) *(cochinillo)* roast sucking pig (**b**) *(de pan)* crouton (**c**) *Fam (tabarra)* bore, drag

total 1 ADJ *(completo)* total
2 NM (**a**) *(todo)* whole; **en t.** in all (**b**) *Mat* total
3 ADV so, in short; **¿t. para qué?** what's the point anyhow?; *Fam* **t. que ...** so ...; **t., tampoco te hará caso** he won't listen to you anyway

totalidad NF whole, totality; **la t. de** all of; **en su t.** as a whole

totalitario, -a ADJ totalitarian

totalizar [40] **1** vt to total
2 vi to amount to

tóxico, -a 1 ADJ toxic, poisonous
2 NM poison

toxicomanía NF drug addiction

toxicómano, -a *Med* **1** ADJ addicted to drugs
2 NM,F drug addict

tozudo, -a ADJ obstinate, stubborn

traba NF (**a**) *(de rueda)* chock; *(enlace)* bond, tie (**b**) *Fig (obstáculo)* hindrance, obstacle

trabajador, -a 1 NM,F worker, labourer
2 ADJ hard-working

trabajar 1 vi to work; **trabaja mucho** he works hard; **t. de camarera** to work as a waitress
2 vt (**a**) *(hierro, barro, tierra)* to work; *(masa)* to knead (**b**) *(vender) (producto, género,*

marca) to sell, to stock (**c**) *(mejorar)* to work on *o* at

trabajo NM (**a**) *(ocupación)* work; **t. a destajo** piecework; **t. eventual** casual labour; **trabajos manuales** arts and crafts (**b**) *(empleo)* employment, job (**c**) *(tarea)* task, job (**d**) *Educ (redacción)* report, paper (**e**) *(esfuerzo)* effort; **cuesta t. creerlo** it's hard to believe

trabajoso, -a ADJ *(laborioso)* hard, laborious; *(difícil)* difficult

trabalenguas NM INV tongue twister

trabar 1 VT (**a**) *(sujetar)* to lock, to fasten; *(plan)* to obstruct (**b**) *(conversación, amistad)* to start, to strike up (**c**) *(salsa)* to thicken
2 **trabarse** VPR (**a**) *(cuerdas)* to get tangled up (**b**) *Fig* **se le trabó la lengua** he got tongue-tied

trabazón NF *(de ideas)* link

trabilla NF *(de pantalón)* belt loop

traca NF string of firecrackers

tracción NF traction; *Aut* **t. delantera/trasera** front-/rear-wheel drive; *Aut* **t. en las cuatro ruedas** four-wheel drive

tractor NM tractor

tradición NF tradition

tradicional ADJ traditional

traducción NF translation; **t. directa/inversa** translation from/into a foreign language

traducir [10] 1 VT to translate (**a** into)
2 **traducirse** VPR *Fig* to result (**en** in)

traductor, -a NM,F translator

traer [25] 1 VT (**a**) *(de un lugar a otro)* to bring; **trae** give it to me (**b**) *(llevar encima, consigo)* to carry (**c**) *(llevar puesto)* to wear (**d**) *(problemas)* to cause; **traerá como consecuencia …** it will result in …
2 **traerse** VPR *(llevar consigo)* to bring along; *Fig* **¿qué se trae entre manos?** what is he up to?

traficante NMF *(de drogas etc)* trafficker, pusher

traficar [44] VI *(ilegalmente)* to traffic (**con** in)

tráfico NM (**a**) *Aut* traffic; **t. rodado** road traffic (**b**) *Com* traffic, trade; **t. de drogas** drug traffic

tragaluz NM skylight

tragaperras, *Am* **tragamonedas** NF INV *Fam* **(máquina) t.** slot machine

tragar [42] 1 VT (**a**) *(ingerir)* to swallow (**b**) *Fam (engullir)* to gobble up, to tuck away (**c**) *Fig (soportar) (persona)* to stand, to stomach (**d**) *Fig (creer)* to believe, to swallow
2 **tragarse** VPR (**a**) *(ingerir)* to swallow (**b**) *Fig (creer)* to believe, to swallow

tragedia NF tragedy

trágico, -a ADJ tragic

tragicomedia NF tragicomedy

trago NM (**a**) *(bebida)* swig; **de un t.** in one go (**b**) *Fig* **pasar un mal t.** to have a bad time of it

tragón, -ona NM,F big eater

traición NF treason, betrayal; **a t.** treacherously; **alta t.** high treason

traicionar VT *(amigo, ideal, país)* to betray; *(descubrir)* to give away

traicionero, -a ADJ treacherous

traidor, -a 1 ADJ treacherous
2 NM,F traitor

traigo INDIC PRES *de* **traer**

tráiler *(pl* **tráilers)** NM (**a**) *Cin* trailer, *US* preview (**b**) *Aut Br* articulated lorry, *US* semitrailer (**c**) *Méx (casa rodante) Br* caravan, *US* trailer

traje[1] NM (**a**) *(de hombre)* suit; **t. de baño** swimming costume, bathing suit *o Br* costume; **t. de luces** bullfighter's costume; **t. de paisano** civilian clothes (**b**) *(de mujer)* dress; **t. de chaqueta** two-piece suit; **t. de novia** wedding dress

traje[2] PT INDEF *de* **traer**

trajeado, -a ADJ *Fam* sharp, dapper

trajín NM *Fam* comings and goings, hustle and bustle

trajinar VI to run *o* bustle about

trama NF (**a**) *Tex* weft, woof (**b**) *Lit* plot

tramar VT to plot, to cook up; **¿qué tramas?** what are you up to?

tramitar VT (**a**) *(gestionar)* to take the necessary (legal) steps to obtain (**b**) *Fml (despachar)* to convey, to transmit (**c**) *Com, Der & Fin* to carry out, to process

trámite NM *(paso)* step; *(formalidad)* formality; *Com, Der & Fin* **trámites** procedures, proceedings

tramo NM *(de carretera)* section, stretch; *(de escalera)* flight

tramontana NF north wind

tramoya NF *(maquinaria)* stage machinery; *(trama)* plot, scheme

trampa NF (**a**) *(de caza)* trap, snare (**b**) *(puerta)* trapdoor (**c**) *(engaño)* fiddle; **hacer trampa(s)** to cheat (**d**) *(truco)* trick

> Observa que la palabra inglesa **tramp** es un falso amigo y no es la traducción de la palabra española **trampa**. En inglés, **tramp** significa "vagabundo".

trampilla NF trapdoor, hatch

trampolín NM (**a**) *(de piscina)* diving board (**b**) *(de esquí)* ski jump

> Observa que la palabra inglesa **trampoline** es un falso amigo y no es la traducción de la palabra española **trampolín**. En inglés, **trampoline** significa "cama elástica".

tramposo, -a 1 ADJ cheating
2 NM,F cheat

tranca NF *(en puerta, ventana)* bar; *Fam* **a trancas y barrancas** with great difficulty

trancar 1 VT *(asegurar) (con cerrojo)* to bolt; *(con tranca)* to bar
2 **trancarse** VPR *Am (atascarse)* to get stuck; **la**

llave se trancó en la cerradura the key got stuck in the lock

trance NM (**a**) *(coyuntura)* (critical) moment; **estar en t. de ...** to be on the point of ... (**b**) *(éxtasis)* trance

tranquilidad NF calmness, tranquillity; **con t.** calmly; **pídemelo con toda t.** don't hesitate to ask me

tranquilizante NM tranquillizer

tranquilizar [40] **1** VT to calm down; **lo dijo para tranquilizarme** he said it to reassure me
2 tranquilizarse VPR to calm down

tranquillo NM knack; **coger el t. a algo** to get the knack of sth

tranquilo, -a ADJ (**a**) *(persona, lugar)* calm; *(agua)* still; *(conciencia)* clear; *Fam* **tú t.** don't you worry (**b**) *(despreocupado)* placid, easy-going

transacción NF transaction, deal

transar VI *Fam* (**a**) *Am (transigir)* to compromise, to give in (**b**) *Am (negociar)* to come to an arrangement, to reach a compromise (**c**) *RP (droga)* to deal

transatlántico, -a 1 ADJ transatlantic
2 NM *Náut* (ocean) liner

transbordador NM (car) ferry; **t. espacial** space shuttle

transbordar 1 VT to transfer; *Náut (mercancías)* to tranship
2 VI *Ferroc* to change trains, *US* to transfer

transbordo NM (**a**) *Ferroc* change, *US* transfer; **hacer t.** to change, *US* to transfer (**b**) *Náut* transhipment

transcurrir VI (**a**) *(tiempo)* to pass, to go by (**b**) *(acontecer)* to take place

transcurso NM course *o* passing (of time); **en el t. de** in the course of, during

transeúnte NMF passer-by

transferencia NF transfer

transferible ADJ transferable

transferir [5] VT to transfer

transformación NF transformation

transformador NM *Elec* transformer

transformar 1 VT to transform, to change
2 transformarse VPR to change, to turn (**en** into); *(algo plegable)* to convert

tránsfuga NMF (**a**) *Mil* deserter (**b**) *Pol* turn-coat

transfusión NF transfusion

transgénico, -a 1 ADJ transgenic
2 transgénicos NMPL GM foods

transgredir VT to transgress, to break

transgresor, -a NM,F transgressor, lawbreaker

transición NF transition

transido, -a ADJ *Fml* **t. de dolor** racked with pain

transigente ADJ tolerant

transigir [57] VI to compromise

transistor NM transistor

transitable ADJ passable

transitado, -a ADJ busy

transitar VI to pass

transitivo, -a ADJ *Ling* transitive

tránsito NM (**a**) *Aut* traffic (**b**) *(movimiento)* movement, passage; **pasajeros en t.** passengers in transit

transitorio, -a ADJ transitory

translúcido, -a ADJ translucent

translucirse [35] VPR = **traslucirse**

transmisión NF (**a**) *(de sonido, datos, virus)* transmission (**b**) *Rad & TV (programa)* broadcast; *(servicio)* broadcasting (**c**) *Téc* drive; **t. delantera/trasera** front-/rear-wheel drive

transmisor NM transmitter

transmitir VT (**a**) *(sonido, datos, virus)* to transmit (**b**) *Rad & TV* to broadcast

transparencia NF transparency

transparentarse VPR *(tela)* to be see-through; *(cristal, líquido)* to be transparent; **esta tela se transparenta** this is see-through material; **se le transparentaban las bragas** you could see her panties

transparente ADJ transparent

transpiración NF perspiration

transpirar VI to perspire

transplantar VT = **trasplantar**

transplante NM = **trasplante**

transponer [19] (PP **transpuesto**) **1** VT to transpose, to move about
2 transponerse VPR *(desmayarse)* to faint

transportar VT to transport; *(pasajeros)* to carry; *(mercancías)* to ship

transporte NM transport, *US* transportation; **t. de mercancías** freight transport; **t. marítimo** shipment

transportista NMF carrier

transpuesto PP *de* **transponer**

transvase NM (**a**) *(de líquidos)* decanting (**b**) *(de ríos)* transfer

transversal ADJ transverse, cross

tranvía NM *Br* tram, *US* streetcar

trapecio NM trapeze

trapecista NMF trapeze artist

trapero, -a 1 NM *Br* rag-and-bone man, *US* junkman
2 ADJ **puñalada trapera** stab in the back

trapichear VI *Fam* to be on the fiddle

trapicheo NM *Fam* (**a**) *(negocio sucio)* fiddle (**b**) *(tejemaneje)* scheme

trapo NM (**a**) *(viejo, roto)* rag (**b**) *(bayeta)* cloth; *Fam* **poner a algn como un t.** to tear sb to pieces; **t. de cocina** *Br* tea towel, *US* dish towel; **t. del polvo** dust cloth, *Br* duster

tráquea NF trachea, windpipe

traqueteo NM rattle, clatter

tras PREP (**a**) *(después de)* after; **uno t. otro** one after the other (**b**) *(detrás)* behind; **sentados uno t. otro** sitting one behind the other (**c**)

andar/ir t. to be after; **la policía iba t. ella** the police were after her

trasatlántico, -a ADJ & NM = transatlántico

trasbordador NM = transbordador

trasbordar VT & VI = transbordar

trasbordo NM = transbordo

trascendencia NF (a) *(importancia)* importance, significance (b) *(en filosofía)* transcendence

trascendental, trascendente ADJ (a) *(importante)* momentous (b) *(en filosofía)* transcendental

trascender [3] VI (a) *(noticia)* to become known, to leak out (b) *(tener consecuencias)* to have far-reaching consequences (c) **t. de** to go beyond

trascurrir VI = transcurrir

trascurso NM = transcurso

trasero, -a 1 ADJ back, rear; **en la parte trasera** at the back

    2 NM *Euf* backside

transferencia NF = transferencia

trasferible ADJ = transferible

trasferir [5] VT = transferir

trasfondo NM background

trasformación NF = transformación

trasformador NM = transformador

trasformar VT = transformar

tránsfuga NMF = tránsfuga

trasfusión NF = transfusión

trasgredir VT = transgredir

trasgresor, -a NM,F = transgresor

trashumancia NF = seasonal movement of livestock

trasiego NM comings and goings, hustle and bustle

trasladar 1 VT *(cosa)* to move; *(persona)* to move, to transfer

    2 **trasladarse** VPR to go, to move

traslado NM *(de casa)* move, removal; *(de personal)* transfer; *Educ* **t. de expediente** transfer of student record

traslucirse [35] VPR to show through

trasluz NM **mirar algo al t.** to hold sth against the light

trasmano: a trasmano LOC ADV out of reach; **(me) coge a t.** it's out of my way

trasmisión NF = transmisión

trasmisor NM = transmisor

trasmitir VT = transmitir

trasnochado, -a ADJ old, hackneyed

trasnochador, -a 1 ADJ given to staying up late

    2 NM,F night owl

trasnochar VI to stay up (very) late

traspapelar 1 VT to mislay, to misplace

    2 **traspapelarse** VPR to get mislaid o misplaced

trasparencia NF = transparencia

trasparentarse VPR = transparentarse

trasparente ADJ = transparente

traspasar VT (a) *(atravesar)* to go through (b) *(negocio, jugador)* to transfer; **se traspasa** *(en letrero)* (business) for sale

> Observa que el verbo inglés **to trespass** es un falso amigo y no es la traducción del verbo español **traspasar**. En inglés, **to trespass** significa "entrar sin autorización".

traspaso NM *(de propiedad, jugador)* transfer; *(de negocio)* sale (as a going concern); **t. de competencias** devolution

traspié NM stumble, trip; **dar un t.** to trip; *Fig* to slip up

traspiración NF = transpiración

traspirar VI = transpirar

trasplantar VT to transplant

trasplante NM transplant; **t. de corazón** heart transplant

trasponer [19] VT = transponer

trasportar VT = transportar

trasporte NM = transporte

traspuesto, -a ADJ **quedarse t.** to doze off

trasquilar VT *(oveja)* to shear; *(pelo)* to crop

trastabillar VI to stagger, to totter

trastada NF *Fam* **hacer trastadas** to be up to mischief

trastazo NM *Fam* wallop, thump

traste¹ NM *Mús* fret

traste² NM (a) *Am salvo RP (utensilio de cocina)* cooking utensil; **fregar los trastes** to wash the dishes (b) *CSur Fam (trasero)* bottom, *US* tush (c) *Fig* **dar al t. (con un plan)** to spoil (a plan); **irse al t.** to fall through

trastear VI to rummage about

trastero NM **(cuarto) t.** junk room

trastienda NF back shop

trasto NM *(objeto cualquiera)* thing; *(cosa inservible)* piece of junk

trastocar [44] VT = trastornar

trastornado, -a ADJ *(loco)* mad, unhinged

trastornar 1 VT (a) *(planes)* to disrupt (b) *Fig (persona)* to unhinge

    2 **trastornarse** VPR *(enloquecer)* to go out of one's mind, to go mad

trastorno NM *(molestia)* trouble, inconvenience; **t. mental** mental disorder o disturbance

trasvase NM = transvase

trasversal ADJ = transversal

trata NF slave trade o traffic; **t. de blancas** white slave trade

tratado NM (a) *(pacto)* treaty (b) *(estudio)* treatise

tratamiento NM (a) *(hacia persona)* treatment; *(título)* title, form of address (b) *(de enfermo, sustancia, tema)* treatment (c) *Inform* processing; **t. de textos** word processing

tratar 1 VT (**a**) *(comportarse con)* to treat; **t. bien/mal** to treat well/badly (**b**) *(enfermo, sustancia, tema)* to treat (**c**) *Inform* to process (**d**) **la traté muy poco** I didn't have much to do with her; **me trata de tú** he addresses me as "tú"

2 VI (**a**) **t. de** *(intentar)* to try (**b**) **t. de** o **sobre** o **acerca de** to be about; **¿de qué trata?** what is it about? (**c**) **t. con** *(tener tratos)* to deal with; *(negociar)* to negotiate with; *(relacionarse)* to move among (**d**) *Com* **t. en** to deal in

3 tratarse VPR (**a**) *(relacionarse)* to be on speaking terms (**b**) **se trata de** *(es cuestión de)* it's a question of; **se trata de un caso excepcional** it's an exceptional case

tratativas NFPL *CSur* negotiation

trato NM (**a**) *(de personas)* manner; *(contacto)* contact; **malos tratos** ill-treatment (**b**) *(acuerdo)* agreement; **¡t. hecho!** it's a deal! (**c**) *Com* deal

trauma NM trauma

traumático, -a ADJ traumatic

traumatizar VT *Med* to traumatize; *Fam* to shock

través 1 PREP (**a**) **a t. de** *(superficie)* across, over; *(agujero etc)* through; **a t. del río** across the river; **a t. del agujero** through the hole (**b**) *Fig* **a t. de** through; **a t. del periódico** through the newspaper

2 ADV **de t.** *(en diagonal)* crosswise; *(de lado)* sideways

3 NM *(pl* **traveses)** *Fig (desgracia)* misfortune

travesaño NM *Ftb* crossbar

travesía NF *(viaje)* crossing

travestí *(pl* **travestíes** o **travestís), travesti** NMF *(que se viste de mujer)* transvestite, cross-dresser; *(artista)* drag artist

> Observa que la palabra inglesa **travesty** es un falso amigo y no es la traducción de la palabra española **travestí**. En inglés, **travesty** significa "parodia burda".

travesura NF mischief, childish prank

travieso, -a ADJ mischievous

trayecto NM (**a**) *(distancia)* distance; *(recorrido)* route; *(trecho)* stretch (**b**) *(viaje)* journey

trayectoria NF (**a**) *(de proyectil, geométrica)* trajectory (**b**) *Fig (orientación)* line, course

traza NF *(apariencia)* looks, appearance; **no lleva trazas de curarse** it doesn't look as if he's going to get better

trazado NM (**a**) *(plano)* layout, plan (**b**) *(de carretera, ferrocarril)* route

trazar [40] VT *(línea)* to draw; *(plano)* to design; *Fig (plan)* to sketch out

trazo NM (**a**) *(línea)* line (**b**) *(de letra)* stroke

trébol NM (**a**) *(planta)* clover (**b**) *Naipes* club

trece 1 ADJ INV thirteen

2 NM INV thirteen; *Fig* **estar** o **mantenerse** o **seguir en sus t.** to stick to one's guns

trecho NM distance, way; *(tramo)* stretch; **de t. en t.** from time to time

tregua NF *Mil* truce; *Fig* respite

treinta ADJ & NM INV thirty

treintavo, -a ADJ & NM thirtieth

treintena NF **una t. de** *(about)* thirty

tremendista ADJ over the top

tremendo, -a ADJ (**a**) *(terrible)* terrible, dreadful (**b**) *(muy grande)* enormous; *Fig* tremendous

trementina NF turpentine

trémulo, -a ADJ *Literario (vacilante)* quivering, tremulous; *(luz)* flickering

tren NM (**a**) *(ferrocarril)* train (**b**) *Av* **t. de aterrizaje** undercarriage; **t. de lavado** car wash (**c**) **t. de vida** lifestyle

trenca NF duffle coat

trenza NF *(de pelo)* plait, *esp US* braid

trepador, -a ADJ climbing

trepar VT & VI to climb

trepidante ADJ vibrating, shaking; *Fig* **lleva un ritmo de vida t.** he leads a hectic o frantic life

trepidar VI to vibrate, to shake

tres 1 ADJ INV *(cardinal)* three; *(ordinal)* third; *Fam* **de t. al cuarto** cheap, of little value

2 NM three; **t. en raya** *Br* noughts and crosses, *US* tick-tack-toe

trescientos, -as ADJ & NM three hundred

tresillo NM (**a**) *(mueble)* (three-piece) suite (**b**) *Mús* triplet

treta NF trick, ruse

trial NM *Dep* trial

triangular ADJ triangular

triángulo NM triangle; *Fig* **t. amoroso** eternal triangle

tribal ADJ tribal

tribu NF tribe

tribuna NF (**a**) *(plataforma)* rostrum, dais; **t. de (la) prensa** press box (**b**) *Dep* stand

tribunal NM (**a**) *Der* court; **t. de apelación** court of appeal; **el T. Supremo** *Br* ≃ the High Court, *US* ≃ the Supreme Court (**b**) *(de examen)* board of examiners

tributar VT to pay

tributario, -a ADJ **sistema t.** tax system

tributo NM (**a**) *Com* tax (**b**) *(homenaje)* tribute

triciclo NM tricycle

tricornio NM three-cornered hat

tricotar VT & VI to knit

tridimensional ADJ three-dimensional

trienio NM three-year period

trifásico, -a 1 ADJ *Elec* three-phase

2 NM adapter

trigésimo, -a ADJ & NM,F thirtieth; **t. primero** thirty-first

trigo NM wheat

trigueño, -a ADJ *Am (pelo)* light brown, corn-coloured; *(persona)* light brown-skinned

trilla NF threshing

trillado, -a ADJ Fig well-worn

trilladora NF threshing machine; **t. segadora** combine harvester

trillar VT to thresh

trillizo, -a NM,F triplet

trilogía NF trilogy

trimestral ADJ quarterly, three-monthly

trimestre NM quarter; Educ term

trinar VI (a) (pájaro) to warble (b) Fam **está que trina** he's really fuming

trincar¹ [44] VT Fam (capturar) to catch

trincar² VT Fam to drink

trinchar VT (carne) to carve, to slice (up)

trinchera NF trench

trineo NM sledge, sleigh

Trinidad NF **la Santísima T.** the HolyTrinity

trino NM warble, trill

trío NM trio

tripa NF (a) (intestino) gut, intestine; Esp Fam tummy; **dolor de t.** stomach ache (b) **tripas** innards

triple ADJ & NM triple

triplicado, -a ADJ triplicate; **por t.** in triplicate

triplicar [44] VT to triple, to treble

trípode NM tripod

tríptico NM (a) (cuadro) triptych (b) (folleto) leaflet (folded twice to form three parts)

tripulación NF crew

tripulante NMF crew member

tripular VT to man

triquiñuela NF Fam trick, dodge

tris NM **estar en un t. de** to be on the verge of

triste ADJ (a) (persona, situación) sad (b) (lugar) gloomy

tristeza NF sadness

triturar VT (machacar) to grind (up)

triunfador, -a 1 ADJ winning
2 NM,F winner

triunfal ADJ triumphant

triunfar VI to triumph

triunfo NM (a) (victoria) triumph, victory; Dep win (b) (éxito) success

trivial ADJ trivial

trivialidad NF triviality

trivializar VT to trivialize, to minimize

triza NF bit, fragment; **hacer trizas** to tear to shreds

trocar [64] VT (a) (transformar) **t. algo (en algo)** to change sth (into sth) (b) (intercambiar) to swap, to exchange

trocear VT to cut up (into bits o pieces)

trocha NF Am path

trofeo NM trophy

trola NF Fam fib

tromba NF **t. de agua** violent downpour

trombón NM trombone

trombosis NF INV thrombosis

trompa NF (a) Mús horn (b) (de elefante) trunk (c) Anat tube (d) Fam **estar t.** to be sloshed o plastered

trompazo NM Fam bump; **darse o pegarse un t.** to have a bump

trompeta NF trumpet

trompetista NMF trumpet player, trumpeter

trompicón NM trip, stumble; **hacer algo a trompicones** to do sth in fits and starts

trompo NM spinning top

trona NF high chair

tronar [2] **1** VI to thunder
2 VT Méx Fam (a) (destruir, acabar con) to get rid of (b) (suspender) to fail

tronchar 1 VT (partir) to snap
2 troncharse VPR Fam **troncharse de risa** to split one's sides laughing

tronco NM (a) Anat trunk, torso (b) Bot (de árbol) trunk; (leño) log; Fam Fig **dormir como un t.** to sleep like a log

tronera NF (a) (de billar) pocket (b) (ventana) small window; (de fortificación) loophole; Náut porthole

trono NM throne

tropa NF (no oficiales) rank and file; (ejército) troops

tropel NM throng, mob; **en t.** in a mad rush

tropezar [1] VI (a) (con los pies) to trip, to stumble (**con** on) (b) (por casualidad) **t. con algo** to come across sth; **t. con algn/ dificultades** to run into sb/difficulties

tropezón NM (a) (con los pies) trip, stumble; **dar un t.** to trip (b) (error) slip-up, faux pas (c) (de comida) chunk of meat

tropical ADJ tropical

trópico NM tropic

tropiezo 1 NM (a) (con los pies) trip, stumble (b) Fig (error) blunder, faux pas
2 INDIC PRES de **tropezar**

trotamundos NMF INV globetrotter

trotar VI to trot

trote NM (a) (de caballo) trot; **al t.** at a trot (b) Fam **ya no está para esos trotes** he cannot keep up the pace any more

trovador NM troubadour

trozar VT Am (carne) to cut up; (res, tronco) to butcher, to cut up

trozo NM piece

trucar [44] VT to doctor, to alter

trucha NF trout

truco NM (a) (ardid) trick; **aquí hay t.** there's something fishy going on here (b) **coger el t. (a algo)** to get the knack o hang (of sth)

truculento, -a ADJ horrifying, terrifying

Observa que la palabra inglesa **truculent** es un falso amigo y no es la traducción de la palabra española **truculento**. En inglés, **truculent** significa "agresivo, airado".

trueno NM thunder; **un t.** a thunderclap

trueque NM barter

trufa NF truffle

truhán, -ana NM,F rogue, crook

truncar [44] VT *(vida, carrera)* to cut short; *(esperanzas)* to shatter

trusa NF (**a**) *Carib (traje de baño)* swimsuit (**b**) *Perú (short)* briefs (**c**) *RP (faja)* girdle

trust [trus(t)] *(pl* **trusts**) NM trust, cartel

tu *(pl* **tus**) ADJ POS your; **tu libro** your book; **tus libros** your books

tú PRON you; **de tú a tú** on equal terms

> Usually omitted in Spanish except for emphasis or contrast.

tuba NF tuba

tubérculo NM (**a**) *Bot* tuber (**b**) *Med* tubercle

tuberculosis NF INV tuberculosis

tubería NF (**a**) *(de agua)* piping, pipes (**b**) *(de gas)* pipeline

tubo NM (**a**) *(cilindro, recipiente)* tube; **t. de ensayo** test tube (**b**) *(tubería)* pipe; *Aut* **t. de escape** exhaust (pipe)

tucán NM toucan

tuerca NF nut

tuerto, -a 1 ADJ one-eyed, blind in one eye **2** NM,F one-eyed person

tuerzo INDIC PRES *de* **torcer**

tuétano NM marrow; *Fig* **hasta el t.** to one's fingertips

tufo NM *Fam* stench, foul smell

tugurio NM *Fam* hovel

tul NM tulle

tulipa NF *(de lámpara)* tulip-shaped lampshade

tulipán NM tulip

tullido, -a ADJ crippled, disabled

tullir VT to cripple

tumba NF grave, tomb

tumbar 1 VT to knock down *o* over **2 tumbarse** VPR *(acostarse)* to lie down, to stretch out

tumbo NM **dar tumbos** to reel

tumbona NF *Br* sun-lounger, *US* (beach) recliner

tumor NM tumour

tumulto NM tumult, commotion

tumultuoso, -a ADJ tumultuous, riotous

tuna NF (**a**) *(agrupación musical)* = group of student minstrels (**b**) *Am (higo chumbo)* prickly pear

> Observa que la palabra inglesa **tuna** es un falso amigo y no es la traducción de la palabra española **tuna**. En inglés, **tuna** significa "atún, bonito".

tunante, -a NM,F rogue, crook

túnel NM tunnel; **el T. del Canal de la Mancha** the Channel Tunnel

Túnez N (**a**) *(país)* Tunisia (**b**) *(ciudad)* Tunis

túnica NF tunic

tuno, -a 1 NM,F *(bribón)* rogue, crook **2** NM = member of a "tuna"

tuntún: al tuntún LOC ADV haphazardly, any old how

tupé NM quiff

tupido, -a ADJ thick, dense

turba[1] NF *(combustible)* peat

turba[2] NF *(muchedumbre)* mob, crowd

turbado, -a ADJ (**a**) *(alterado)* disturbed (**b**) *(preocupado)* worried, anxious (**c**) *(desconcertado)* confused

turbante NM turban

turbar 1 VT (**a**) *(alterar)* to unsettle (**b**) *(preocupar)* to upset *o* worry (**c**) *(desconcertar)* to baffle, to put off **2 turbarse** VPR (**a**) *(preocuparse)* to be *o* become upset (**b**) *(desconcertarse)* to be *o* become confused *o* baffled

turbina NF turbine

turbio, -a ADJ *(agua)* cloudy; *(negocio etc)* shady, dubious

turbulencia NF turbulence

turbulento, -a ADJ turbulent

turco, -a 1 ADJ Turkish **2** NM,F *(persona)* Turk **3** NM *(idioma)* Turkish

turismo NM (**a**) *(actividad)* tourism; **hacer t. (por)** to go touring (round); **t. rural** country holidays, rural tourism (**b**) *Aut* private car

turista NMF tourist

turístico, -a ADJ tourist; **de interés t.** of interest to tourists

túrmix® NF INV blender, liquidizer

turnarse VPR to take turns

turno NM (**a**) *(en juegos etc)* turn, go (**b**) *(de trabajo)* shift; **estar de t.** to be on duty; **t. de día/noche** day/night shift

turquesa ADJ INV & NF turquoise

Turquía N Turkey

turrón NM nougat

tute NM *Fam* **darse un t. de algo** to go to town doing sth

tutear 1 VT = to address as "tú" **2 tutearse** VPR = to address each other as "tú"

tutela NF (**a**) *Der* guardianship, tutelage (**b**) *Fig (protección)* protection, guidance

tuteo NM = use of the "tú" form of address

tutor NM (**a**) *Der* guardian (**b**) *Educ* tutor

tuve PT INDEF *de* **tener**

tuyo, -a 1 ADJ POS *(con personas)* of yours; *(con objetos)* one of your; **¿es amigo t.?** is he a friend of yours?; **unas amigas tuyas** some friends of yours; **un libro t.** one of your books **2** PRON POS yours; **éste es t.** this one is yours; *Fam* **los tuyos** *(familiares)* your family

U

U, u [u] NF *(letra)* U, u

u CONJ *(delante de palabras que empiecen por o o ho)* or; **siete u ocho** seven or eight; **ayer u hoy** yesterday or today

ubicación NF location, position

ubicar [44] **1** VT (**a**) *(situar) (edificio, fábrica)* to locate (**b**) *(colocar)* to put (**c**) *Am (encontrar)* to find, to locate; **no veo su ficha por acá, pero en cuanto la ubique le aviso** I can't see your card here, but as soon as I find it I'll let you know
2 ubicarse VPR (**a**) *(edificio)* to be situated o located (**b**) *Am (persona)* to get one's bearings; **¿ya te ubicas en la ciudad?** are you finding your way around the city all right?

ubicuo, -a ADJ ubiquitous

ubre NF udder

UCI NF *(abr* **unidad de cuidados intensivos)** ICU

Ucrania N Ukraine

ucraniano, -a ADJ & NM,F Ukrainian

Ud., Uds. *(abr* **usted, ustedes)** you

UE NF *(abr* **Unión Europea)** EU

ufanarse VPR to boast (**de** of)

ufano, -a ADJ conceited

UGT NF *(abr* **Unión General de Trabajadores)** = major socialist trade union in Spain

ujier NM usher

úlcera NF ulcer

ulcerarse VPR to ulcerate

ulterior ADJ subsequent

últimamente ADV lately, recently

ultimar VT (**a**) *(terminar)* to finalize (**b**) *Am (asesinar)* to kill

ultimátum *(pl* **ultimátums)** NM ultimatum

último, -a 1 ADJ (**a**) *(en una serie, en el tiempo)* last; **el ú. día** the last day; **por ú.** finally (**b**) *(más reciente)* latest; **últimas noticias** latest news (**c**) *(más alto)* top; *(más bajo)* bottom; **el ú. piso** the top floor; **la última fila** the back row (**d**) *(definitivo)* final
2 NM,F **llegar el ú.** to arrive last; **a últimos de mes** at the end of the month; **en las últimas** on one's last legs; *Fam* **a la última** up to the minute; **el ú. de la lista** the lowest in the list

ultra NMF *Pol* extreme right-winger

ultraderecha NF *Pol* extreme right

ultrajar VT to outrage, to offend

ultraje NM outrage, offence

ultramarinos NM INV *(tienda)* grocer's (shop)

ultranza: a ultranza 1 LOC ADJ die-hard, hardline
2 LOC ADV to the last, at any price

ultratumba NF afterlife

ultravioleta ADJ INV ultraviolet

ulular VI *(viento)* to howl; *(búho)* to hoot

umbral NM threshold

umbrío, -a, umbroso, -a ADJ shady

un, una 1 ART INDEF (**a**) *(singular)* a; *(antes de vocal)* an; **un coche** a car; **un huevo** an egg; **una flor** a flower (**b**) *(plural)* some; **unas flores** some flowers
2 ADJ *(delante de nm sing)* one; **un chico y dos chicas** one boy and two girls; *ver también* **uno**

unánime ADJ unanimous

unanimidad NF unanimity; **por u.** unanimously

unción NF unction

undécimo, -a ADJ eleventh

UNED NF *(abr* **Universidad Nacional de Educación a Distancia)** = Spanish open university

ungir [57] VT *Rel* to anoint

ungüento NM ointment

únicamente ADV only, solely

único, -a ADJ (**a**) *(solo)* only; **es el ú. que tengo** it's the only one I've got; **hijo ú.** only child; **lo ú. que quiero** the only thing I want; **el Mercado Ú.** the Single Market; **el Acta Única** the Single European Act (**b**) *(extraordinario)* unique

unidad NF (**a**) *(elemento, medida, sección)* unit; **u. de cuidados intensivos** intensive care unit (**b**) *(cohesión)* unity

unido, -a ADJ united; **están muy unidos** they are very attached to one another; **una familia muy unida** a very close family

unifamiliar ADJ **vivienda u.** detached house

unificación NF unification

unificar [44] VT to unify

uniformar VT (**a**) *(igualar)* to make uniform, to standardize (**b**) *(poner un uniforme a)* to put into uniform, to give a uniform to

uniforme 1 NM *(prenda)* uniform
2 ADJ (**a**) *(igual)* uniform (**b**) *(superficie)* even

uniformidad NF (**a**) *(igualdad)* uniformity (**b**) *(de superficie)* evenness

unilateral ADJ unilateral

unión NF union

Unión Soviética N *Hist* Soviet Union

unir 1 VT *(juntar)* to unite, to join (together); **esta carretera une las dos comarcas** this road links both districts

2 unirse VPR *(juntarse)* to unite, to join

unisex ADJ INV unisex

unísono NM unison; **al u.** in unison

unitario, -a ADJ unitary; **precio u.** unit price

universal ADJ universal; **historia u.** world history

universidad NF university; **u. a distancia** = distance learning university; ≃ Open University; **u. laboral** technical college

universitario, -a 1 ADJ university

2 NM,F university student

universo NM universe

uno, -a 1 NM INV one; **el u.** (number) one; **el u. de mayo** the first of May

2 NF **es la una** *(hora)* it's one o'clock

3 ADJ **unos, -as** some; **unas cajas** some boxes; **habrá unos** o **unas veinte** there must be around twenty

4 PRON (**a**) *(indefinido, numeral)* one; **u. (de ellos), una (de ellas)** one of them; **unos cuantos** a few; **se miraron el u. al otro** they looked at each other; **de u. en u.** one by one; **un tras otro** one after the other; **una de dos** one of the two (**b**) *(persona)* someone, somebody; **u. que pasaba por allí** some passer-by; **vive con u.** she's living with some man; **unos ... otros** some people ... others (**c**) *(impersonal)* you, one; **u. tiene que ...** you have to ...

untar VT to grease, to smear; *(mantequilla)* to spread

uña NF (**a**) *(de mano)* nail, fingernail; *(de pie)* toenail; **morderse** o **comerse las uñas** to bite one's fingernails; *Fig* **ser u. y carne** to be hand in glove (**b**) *Zool (garra)* claw; *(pezuña)* hoof

uperizado, -a ADJ **leche uperizada** UHT milk

uralita® NF = material made of asbestos and cement, usually corrugated and used mainly for roofing

uranio NM uranium

Urano NM Uranus

urbanidad NF urbanity, politeness

urbanismo NM town planning

urbanístico, -a ADJ town-planning

urbanización NF (**a**) *(barrio)* housing development o estate (**b**) *(proceso)* urbanization

urbanizar VT to build up

urbano, -a ADJ urban, city; **guardia u.** (traffic) policeman

urbe NF large city

urdimbre NF (**a**) *Tex* warp (**b**) *(trama)* intrigue

urdir VT (**a**) *Tex* to warp (**b**) *(tramar)* to plot, to scheme

urgencia NF (**a**) *(cualidad)* urgency; **con u.** urgently (**b**) *(en hospital) (caso)* emergency (case); **urgencias** *Br* casualty (department),

accident and emergency (department), *US* emergency room

urgente ADJ urgent; **correo u.** express mail

urgir [57] VI to be urgent o pressing; **me urge (tenerlo)** I need it urgently

urinario NM urinal, *US* comfort station

urna NF (**a**) *Pol* ballot box (**b**) *(vasija)* urn

urólogo, -a NM,F *Med* urologist

urraca NF magpie

URSS NF *Hist (abr* **Unión de Repúblicas Socialistas Soviéticas)** USSR

urticaria NF *Med* hives

Uruguay N (**el**) **U.** Uruguay

uruguayo, -a ADJ & NM,F Uruguayan

usado, -a ADJ *(ropa)* second-hand, used

usanza NF *Literario* **a la antigua u.** in the old style

usar 1 VT (**a**) *(aparato, término)* to use (**b**) *(prenda)* to wear

2 usarse VPR to be used o in fashion

usina NF *Andes, RP* plant; **u. eléctrica** power station, power plant; **u. nuclear** nuclear power station, nuclear power plant

uso NM (**a**) use; **hacer u. de** *(utilizar)* to make use of, to use; *(de prerrogativa, derecho)* to exercise; **de u. externo** *(medicamento)* for external use only (**b**) *(de prenda)* wearing; **haga u. del casco** wear a helmet (**c**) *(costumbre)* usage, custom; **al u.** conventional

usted *(pl* **ustedes)** PRON PERS *Fml* you; **¿quién es u.?, ¿quiénes son ustedes?** who are you?

> Usually omitted in Spanish except for emphasis or contrast. Although formal in peninsular Spanish, it is not necessarily so in Latin American Spanish.

usual ADJ usual, common

usuario, -a NM,F user

usura NF usury

usurero, -a NM,F usurer

usurpar VT to usurp

utensilio NM utensil; *(herramienta)* tool

útero NM uterus, womb

útil 1 ADJ useful; *(día)* working

2 NM *(herramienta)* tool, instrument

utilidad NF usefulness, utility; *(beneficio)* profit

utilitario, -a 1 ADJ utilitarian

2 NM *(coche)* utility vehicle

utilización NF use, utilization

utilizar [40] VT to use, to utilize

utopía NF utopia

utópico, -a ADJ & NM,F utopian

uva NF grape; **u. blanca** green grape

UVI NF *(abr* **unidad de vigilancia intensiva)** ICU

V

V, v ['uβe] NF *(letra)* V, v

V *Elec (abr voltio(s))* V

vaca NF (a) *(animal)* cow (b) *(carne)* beef

vacaciones NFPL holiday, *Br* holidays, *US* vacation; **durante las v.** during the holidays; **estar/irse de v.** to be/go on *Br* holiday *o US* vacation

vacacionista NMF *Am Br* holidaymaker, *US* vacationer

vacante 1 ADJ vacant
  2 NF vacancy

vaciar [29] **1** VT (a) *(recipiente)* to empty; *(contenido)* to empty out (b) *(terreno)* to hollow out (c) *Arte* to cast, to mould
  2 vaciarse VPR to empty

vacilación NF hesitation

vacilante ADJ (a) *(persona)* hesitant, irresolute (b) *(voz)* hesitant, faltering (c) *(luz)* flickering

vacilar VI (a) *(dudar)* to hesitate; **sin v.** without hesitation (b) *(voz)* to falter (c) *(luz)* to flicker (d) *Fam (jactarse)* to show off

vacilón, -ona *Fam* **1** ADJ (a) *(fanfarrón)* swanky (b) *Esp, Carib, Méx (bromista)* jokey, teasing
  2 NM,F (a) *(fanfarrón)* show-off (b) *Esp, Carib, Méx (bromista)* tease
  3 NM *CAm, Carib, Méx (fiesta)* party

vacío, -a 1 ADJ (a) *(recipiente, palabras, vida)* empty (b) *(sin ocupar)* vacant, unoccupied
  2 NM (a) *(abismo, carencia)* void (b) *Fís* vacuum; **envasado al v.** vacuum-packed (c) *(hueco)* gap; *(espacio)* (empty) space

vacuna NF vaccine

vacunación NF vaccination

vacunar 1 VT to vaccinate (**contra** against); *Fig* to inure
  2 vacunarse VPR to get oneself vaccinated

vacuno, -a ADJ bovine; **ganado v.** cattle

vacuo, -a ADJ vacuous, empty

vadear VT *(río)* to ford; *Fig (dificultad)* to overcome

vado NM (a) *(de río)* ford (b) *Aut* **v. permanente** *(en letrero)* keep clear

vagabundear VI to wander, to roam

vagabundo, -a 1 ADJ *(persona)* vagrant; **perro v.** stray dog
  2 NM,F *(sin casa)* tramp, vagrant, *US* bum

vagancia NF idleness, laziness

vagar [42] VI to wander about, to roam about

vagina NF vagina

vago, -a 1 ADJ (a) *(perezoso)* lazy (b) *(indefinido)* vague
  2 NM,F (a) *(holgazán)* layabout (b) *Der* vagrant

vagón NM *(para pasajeros)* carriage, coach, *US* car; *(para mercancías)* truck, wagon, *US* freight car, *US* boxcar

vagoneta NF wagon

vaguedad NF vagueness

vaho NM *(de aliento)* breath; *(vapor)* vapour

vaina NF (a) *(de espada)* sheath, scabbard (b) *Bot* pod (c) *Col, Perú, Ven muy Fam (cosa molesta)* pain (in the neck)
  2 NMF *Col, Perú, Ven muy Fam* **ése es un v.** he's a pain

vainilla NF vanilla

vaivén NM (a) *(oscilación)* swinging, to-and-fro movement (b) *(de gente)* coming and going, bustle; *Fig* **vaivenes** ups and downs

vajilla NF crockery, dishes; **una v.** a set of dishes, a dinner service

valdré INDIC FUT *de* **valer**

vale¹ INTERJ *Esp* all right!, O.K.!

vale² NM (a) *(comprobante)* voucher (b) *(pagaré)* promissory note, IOU (I owe you) (c) *Méx, Ven Fam (amigo)* pal, *Br* mate, *US* buddy

valedero, -a ADJ valid

valenciano, -a 1 ADJ & NM,F Valencian
  2 NM *(idioma)* Valencian

valentía NF courage, bravery

valentón, -ona *Pey* **1** ADJ bragging, boastful
  2 NM,F braggart

valer [26] **1** VT (a) *(tener un valor de)* to be worth; **no vale nada** it is worthless; **vale una fortuna** it is worth a fortune; **no vale la pena (ir)** it's not worth while (going) (b) *(costar)* to cost; **¿cuánto vale?** how much is it? (c) *(proporcionar)* to earn
  2 VI (a) *(servir)* to be useful, to be of use (b) *(ser válido)* to be valid, to count; **no vale hacer trampa** cheating isn't on (c) **más vale** it is better; **más vale que te vayas ya** you had better leave now
  3 valerse VPR **valerse de** to use, to make use of; **valerse por sí mismo** to be able to manage on one's own

valeriana NF valerian, allheal

valeroso, -a ADJ brave, courageous

valgo INDIC PRES *de* **valer**

valía NF value, worth

validez NF validity

válido, -a ADJ valid

valiente ADJ (a) *(valeroso)* brave, courageous (b) *Irón* **¡v. amigo eres tú!** a fine friend you are!

valija NF (a) *(maleta)* case, suitcase; **v. diplomática** diplomatic bag (b) *(de correos)* mailbag

valioso, -a ADJ valuable

valla NF (a) *(cerca)* fence; *(muro)* wall; **v. publicitaria** billboard, *Br* hoarding (b) *Dep* hurdle; **los 100 metros vallas** the 100 metres hurdle race

vallado NM fence

vallar VT to fence (in)

valle NM valley

vallisoletano, -a 1 ADJ of/from Valladolid **2** NM,F person from Valladolid

valor NM (a) *(precio, utilidad, mérito)* value; **objetos de v.** valuables; **sin v.** worthless; **v. alimenticio** food value (b) *(valentía)* courage (c) *(desvergüenza)* cheek, nerve (d) **valores** *(principios)* values; *Fin* securities

valoración NF *(de propiedad, obra)* valuation; *(de pérdidas, daños)* assessment, estimation

valorar VT (a) *(tasar) (propiedad, obra)* to value; *(pérdidas, daños)* to assess, to estimate (b) *(apreciar)* to value

valorizar [40] VT to raise the value of

vals NM waltz

válvula NF valve; **v. de seguridad** safety valve

vampiro NM vampire

vanagloriarse [43] VPR to boast (**de** of)

vandalismo NM vandalism

vándalo, -a NM,F vandal

vanguardia NF (a) *(cultural)* avant-garde, vanguard; **ir a la v. de** to be at the forefront of (b) *Mil* vanguard

vanguardista 1 ADJ avant-garde **2** NMF avant-gardist

vanidad NF vanity

vanidoso, -a ADJ vain, conceited

vano, -a ADJ (a) *(vanidoso)* vain, conceited (b) *(esfuerzo, esperanza)* vain, futile; **en v.** in vain

vapor NM (a) *(de agua hirviendo)* steam; *Culin* **al v.** steamed (b) *(gas)* vapour; **v. de agua** water vapour

vaporizador NM vaporizer, spray

vaporizar [40] **1** VT to vaporize **2 vaporizarse** VPR to vaporize, to evaporate

vaporoso, -a ADJ vaporous

vapulear VT *(físicamente)* to shake; *(con palabras)* to slate

vaquero, -a 1 NM cowboy **2** ADJ **pantalón v.** jeans, pair of jeans **3 vaqueros** NMPL *(prenda)* jeans, pair of jeans

vara NF pole, rod

varar 1 VT to beach, to dock **2** VI to run aground

variable ADJ & NF variable

variación NF variation

variado, -a ADJ varied; **galletas variadas** assorted *Br* biscuits o *US* cookies

variante NF variant

variar [29] **1** VT to vary, to change **2** VI to vary, to change; *Irón* **para v.** as usual, just for a change

varicela NF chickenpox

variedad NF (a) *(cualidad)* variety (b) *Teatro* **variedades** variety, *Br* music hall, *US* vaudeville

varilla NF *(vara)* rod, stick; *(de abanico, paraguas)* rib

variopinto, -a ADJ diverse, assorted; **un público v.** a varied audience

varios, -as ADJ several

varita NF **v. mágica** magic wand

variz NF varicose vein

varón NM *(hombre)* man; *(chico)* boy; **hijo v.** male child; **sexo v.** male sex

varonil ADJ manly, virile

Varsovia N Warsaw

vas INDIC PRES de **ir**

vasallo, -a NM,F *Hist* vassal

vasco, -a 1 ADJ Basque; **el País V.** the Basque Country **2** NM,F Basque **3** NM *(idioma)* Basque

vascuence NM *(idioma)* Basque

vasectomía NF vasectomy

vaselina NF Vaseline®

vasija NF pot

vaso NM (a) *(para beber)* glass (b) *Anat* vessel

Observa que la palabra inglesa **vase** es un falso amigo y no es la traducción de la palabra española **vaso**. En inglés, **vase** significa "jarrón".

vástago NM *(descendiente)* offspring

vasto, -a ADJ vast

váter NM toilet

Vaticano NM **el V.** the Vatican

vaticinar VT to prophesy, to predict

vaticinio NM prophecy, prediction

vatio NM watt

vaya¹ INTERJ **¡v. lío!** what a mess!

vaya² SUBJ PRES de **ir**

Vd., Vds. *(abr usted, ustedes)* you

ve 1 IMPERAT de **ir** **2** INDIC PRES de **ver**

vecinal ADJ local

vecindad NF (a) *(barrio)* neighbourhood (b) *(alrededores)* vicinity

vecindario NM neighbourhood

vecino, -a 1 NM,F (a) *(persona)* neighbour; **el v. de al lado** the next-door neighbour (b) *(residente)* resident **2** ADJ neighbouring, nearby

veda NF *(de caza)* closed season; **levantar la v.** to open the season

vedado, -a ADJ **coto v. de caza** private hunting ground

vedar VT to forbid, to prohibit

vega NF fertile plain o lowland

vegetación NF **(a)** *Bot* vegetation **(b)** *Med* **vegetaciones** adenoids

vegetal NM vegetable

vegetar VI to vegetate

vegetariano, -a ADJ & NM,F vegetarian

vehemencia NF vehemence

vehemente ADJ vehement

vehículo NM vehicle

veinte ADJ & NM INV twenty

veintena NF *(veinte)* twenty; **una v. de** about twenty

vejación NF humiliation

vejar VT to humiliate

vejatorio, -a ADJ humiliating

vejez NF old age

vejiga NF bladder

vela¹ NF **(a)** *(de cera)* candle; *Fam* **quedarse a dos velas** to be in the dark **(b)** *(vigilia)* **pasar la noche en v.** to have a sleepless night

vela² NF *Náut* sail

velada NF evening (party)

velado, -a ADJ veiled, hidden

velador NM **(a)** *(mesa)* table **(b)** *Andes, Méx (mesilla)* bedside table **(c)** *Méx, RP (lámpara)* bedside lamp

velar 1 VI **v. por** to watch over
2 VT *(muerto)* to keep a vigil over; *(enfermo)* to sit up with

velatorio NM vigil, wake

velcro® NM Velcro®

veleidad NF fickleness

veleidoso, -a ADJ fickle

velero NM sailing boat o ship

veleta 1 NF weather vane, weathercock
2 NMF *Fam* fickle o changeable person

veliz NF *Méx* suitcase

vello NM hair

vellón NM fleece

velloso, -a, velludo, -a ADJ downy

velo NM veil

velocidad NF **(a)** *(rapidez)* speed; *(de proyectil etc)* velocity; *Aut* **v. máxima** speed limit; *Inform* **v. de transmisión** bit rate; *Inform* **v. operativa** operating speed **(b)** *Aut (marcha)* gear

velocímetro NM speedometer

velocista NMF sprinter

velódromo NM cycle track, velodrome

velomotor NM moped

velorio NM wake

veloz 1 ADJ swift, rapid
2 ADV quickly, fast

vena NF vein

venado NM deer, stag; *Culin* venison

vencedor, -a 1 NM,F winner
2 ADJ winning

vencejo NM swift

vencer [49] **1** VT **(a)** *(al enemigo)* to defeat; *(al contrincante)* to beat **(b)** *(dificultad)* to overcome, to surmount
2 VI **(a)** *(pago, deuda)* to fall due, to be payable **(b)** *(plazo)* to expire
3 vencerse VPR *(torcerse)* to warp

vencido, -a ADJ **(a)** *Mil (derrotado)* defeated; *Dep* beaten; *Fig* **darse por v.** to give up, to accept defeat **(b)** *(pago, deuda)* due, payable **(c)** *(plazo)* expired **(d)** *Fam* **a la tercera va la vencida** third time lucky

vencimiento NM **(a)** *Com* maturity **(b)** *(de un plazo)* expiry

venda NF bandage

vendaje NM bandaging, dressing

vendar VT to bandage; *Fig* **v. los ojos a algn** to blindfold sb

vendaval NM gale

vendedor, -a NM,F seller; *(hombre)* salesman; *(mujer)* saleswoman

vender 1 VT to sell; **v. a plazos/al contado** to sell on credit/for cash; **v. al por mayor/menor** to (sell) wholesale/retail
2 venderse VPR **(a)** *(producto)* to sell; **este disco se vende bien** this record is selling well; **se vende** *(en letrero)* for sale **(b)** *(claudicar)* to sell out

vendimia NF grape harvest

vendimiador, -a NM,F grape picker

vendimiar [43] **1** VT to harvest *(grapes)*
2 VI to pick grapes

vendré INDIC FUT *de* **venir**

Venecia N Venice

veneno NM poison; *(de serpiente)* venom

venenoso, -a ADJ poisonous

venerable ADJ venerable

veneración NF veneration

venerar VT to venerate, to revere

venéreo, -a ADJ venereal

venezolano, -a ADJ & NM,F Venezuelan

Venezuela N Venezuela

venga SUBJ PRES *de* **venir**

venganza NF vengeance, revenge

vengar [42] **1** VT to avenge
2 vengarse VPR to avenge oneself; **vengarse de algn** to take revenge on sb

vengativo, -a ADJ vengeful, vindictive

vengo INDIC PRES *de* **venir**

venia NF **(a)** *Fml (permiso)* permission **(b)** *(perdón)* pardon

venial ADJ venial

venida NF coming, arrival

venidero, -a ADJ future, coming

venir [27] **1** VI **(a)** to come; *Fig* **v. a menos** to come down in the world; *Fig* **v. al mundo** to be

born; **el año que viene** next year; *Fig* **me viene a la memoria** I remember; *Fam* **¡venga ya!** *(vamos)* come on!; *(expresa incredulidad)* come off it! (**b**) **v. grande/pequeño** *(ropa)* to be too big/small; **v. mal/bien** to be inconvenient/convenient; **el metro me viene muy bien** I find the *Br* underground o *US* subway very handy (**c**) *(en pasivas)* **esto vino provocado por ...** this was brought about by ... (**d**) **esto viene ocurriendo desde hace mucho tiempo** this has been going on for a long time now
  2 venirse VPR **venirse abajo** to collapse

venta NF (**a**) *(acción)* sale; **en v.** for sale; **a la v.** on sale; **v. al contado** cash sale; **v. al por mayor/menor** wholesale/retail; **v. a plazos** sale by instalments, *Br* hire purchase (**b**) *(posada)* country inn

ventaja NF advantage; **llevar v. a** to have the advantage over; **le sacó 2 m de v.** he beat him by 2 m

ventajoso, -a ADJ advantageous

ventana NF (**a**) *(en edificio)* window (**b**) *(de la nariz)* nostril

ventanal NM large window

ventanilla NF (**a**) *(de vehículo, sobre)* window (**b**) *(taquilla)* counter

ventanuco NM small window

ventilación NF ventilation; **sin v.** unventilated

ventilador NM ventilator; *(de coche)* fan

ventilar 1 VT *(habitación)* to ventilate, to air
  2 ventilarse VPR *Fam (terminar)* to finish off

ventisca NF blizzard; *(de nieve)* snowstorm

ventosa NF sucker; *Med* cupping glass

ventosear VI to break wind

ventoso, -a ADJ windy

ventrílocuo, -a NM,F ventriloquist

ventura NF (**a**) *(felicidad)* happiness (**b**) *(suerte)* luck; *(casualidad)* chance

venturoso, -a ADJ lucky, fortunate

Venus NM Venus

veo-veo NM *Fam* **el (juego del) v.** I-spy

ver¹ NM **de buen v.** good-looking

ver² [28] **1** VT to see; *(televisión)* to watch; **a v.** let me see, let's see; **a v. si escribes** I hope you'll write; **(ya) veremos** we'll see; **no tener nada que v. con** to have nothing to do with
  2 a ver LOC ADV *(veamos)* let's see; *(al empezar algo)* right!; **¿a ver?** let me see, let's have a look
  3 verse VPR *(imagen etc)* to be seen (**b**) *(encontrarse con algn)* to meet, see each other; **¡nos vemos!** see you later!

vera NF edge, border; **a la v. de** beside, next to

veracidad NF veracity, truthfulness

veraneante NMF *Br* holidaymaker, *US* (summer) vacationer

veranear VI **v. en** to spend one's summer *Br* holidays o *US* vacation in

veraneo NM summer *Br* holidays o *US* vacation

veraniego, -a ADJ summer

veranillo NM Indian summer

verano NM summer

veras NFPL **de v.** really, seriously

veraz ADJ veracious, truthful

verbal ADJ verbal

verbena NF street party

verbo NM verb

verborrea NF *Fam* verbosity, verbal diarrhoea

verdad NF (**a**) **la v.** the truth; **es v.** it is true; **a decir v.** to tell the truth; **¡de v!.** really!, truly!; **un amigo de v.** a real friend (**b**) *(buscando confirmación)* **está muy bien, ¿(no es) v.?** it is very good, isn't it?; **no te gusta, ¿v.?** you don't like it, do you?

verdaderamente ADV truly, really

verdadero, -a ADJ true, real

verde 1 ADJ (**a**) *(color)* green (**b**) *(poco maduro) (fruta)* unripe, green; *(proyecto, plan)* in its early stages (**c**) *(ecologista)* Green, green (**d**) *Fam (obsceno)* blue, dirty; **viejo v.** dirty old man (**e**) *Fam Fig* **poner v. a algn** to call sb every name under the sun
  2 NM (**a**) *(color)* green (**b**) *Pol* **los Verdes** the Greens

verdear VI to turn green

verdor NM greenness

verdoso, -a ADJ greenish

verdugo NM (**a**) *(de preso)* executioner; *(que ahorca)* hangman (**b**) *(pasamontañas)* balaclava

verdulería NF greengrocer's (shop)

verdulero, -a NM,F greengrocer

verdura(s) NF(PL) vegetables, greens

vereda NF (**a**) *(camino)* path, lane (**b**) *CSur, Perú (acera) Br* pavement, *US* sidewalk (**c**) *Col (distrito)* area, district

veredicto NM verdict

verga NF penis

vergonzoso, -a ADJ (**a**) *(penoso)* shameful, disgraceful (**b**) *(tímido)* shy, bashful

vergüenza NF (**a**) *(deshonra)* shame; **¿no te da v.?** aren't you ashamed?, have you no shame?; **¡es una v.!** it's a disgrace! (**b**) *(bochorno)* embarrassment; **me da v.** I'm too embarrassed; **sentir v. ajena** to feel embarrassed for 'sb (**c**) *(timidez)* shyness, bashfulness

vericueto NM winding path; *Fig* **los vericuetos** the ins and outs

verídico, -a ADJ truthful, true

verificar [44] **1** VT *(comprobar)* to check
  2 verificarse VPR to take place, to occur

verja NF *(reja)* grating; *(cerca)* railing, railings; *(puerta)* iron gate

vermut *(pl* vermuts), **vermú 1** NM (**a**) *(licor)* vermouth (**b**) *(aperitivo)* aperitif
  2 NF *esp Andes, RP (en cine)* early-evening showing; *(en teatro)* early-evening performance

verosímil ADJ probable, likely; *(creíble)* credible

verruga NF wart

versado, -a ADJ well-versed (**en** in)

versar VI **v. sobre** to be about, to deal with

versátil ADJ (**a**) (*polifacético*) versatile (**b**) (*voluble*) changeable, inconstant

versículo NM verse

versión NF version; **película en v. original** movie *o* Br film in the original language

verso NM (**a**) (*poesía*) verse (**b**) (*línea*) line

vértebra NF vertebra

vertebrado, -a ADJ & NM vertebrate

vertedero NM (*de basura*) Br rubbish tip *o* dump, US garbage dump

verter [3] **1** VT (**a**) (*líquido*) to pour (out) (**b**) (*basura*) to dump
2 VI (*río*) to flow, to run (**a** into)

vertical ADJ vertical

vértice NM vertex

vertidos NMPL (*residuo*) waste; **vertidos radiactivos** radioactive waste

vertiente NF (**a**) (*de una montaña, un tejado*) slope; *Fig* aspect (**b**) *CSur* (*manantial*) spring

vertiginoso, -a ADJ (*aumento, desarrollo*) dramatic, spectacular; (*velocidad*) dizzying; (*ritmo*) frenetic

vértigo NM vertigo; **me da v.** it makes me dizzy

vesícula NF vesicle; **v. biliar** gall bladder

vespa® NF (motor) scooter

vespertino, -a 1 ADJ evening
2 NM *Prensa* evening newspaper

vespino® NM moped

vestíbulo NM (*de casa*) hall; (*de edificio público*) foyer

vestido, -a 1 NM (*ropa*) clothes; (*de mujer*) dress
2 ADJ dressed; **policía v. de paisano** plainclothes policeman

vestiduras NFPL (*ropa*) clothes; (*sacerdotales*) vestments

vestigio NM vestige, trace

vestimenta NF clothes, garments

vestir [6] **1** VT (**a**) (*a algn*) to dress (**b**) (*llevar puesto*) to wear
2 VI (**a**) (*llevar ropa*) to dress (**b**) (*ser elegante*) **ropa de (mucho) v.** formal dress; *Fam* **la seda viste mucho** silk always looks very elegant
3 vestirse VPR (*ponerse ropa*) to get dressed, to dress; **vestirse de** to wear, to dress in; (*disfrazarse*) to dress up as

vestuario NM (**a**) (*conjunto de vestidos*) clothes, wardrobe; *Teatro* wardrobe, costumes (**b**) (*camerino*) dressing room (**c**) *Dep* changing room, US locker room

veta NF *Min* vein, seam; (*de carne*) streak

vetar VT to veto

veterano, -a ADJ & NM,F veteran

veterinaria NF (*ciencia*) veterinary medicine *o* science

veterinario, -a NM,F (*persona*) vet, Br veterinary surgeon, US veterinarian

veto NM veto; **derecho a v.** power *o* right of veto

vetusto, -a ADJ *Fml* ancient

vez NF (**a**) (*ocasión*) time; **una v.** once; **dos veces** twice; **cinco veces** five times; **a** *o* **algunas veces** sometimes; **cada v.** each *o* every time; **cada v. más** more and more; **de v. en cuando** now and again, every now and then; **¿le has visto alguna v.?** have you ever seen him?; **otra v.** again; **a la v.** at the same time; **tal v.** perhaps, maybe; **de una v.** in one go; **de una v. para siempre** once and for all; **en v. de** instead of; **érase** *o* **había una v.** (*en cuentos etc*) once upon a time (**b**) (*turno*) turn (**c**) **hacer las veces de** to do duty as

v.g(r). (*abr* verbigracia) eg

vía 1 NF (**a**) *Ferroc* track, line (**b**) (*camino*) road; **v. pública** public thoroughfare; **V. Láctea** Milky Way (**c**) *Anat* passage, tract; **(por) v. oral** to be taken orally (**d**) *Fig* **por v. oficial** through official channels; **por v. aérea/marítima** by air/sea (**e**) **en vías de** in the process of; **países en vías de desarrollo** developing countries
2 PREP (*a través de*) via, through; **v. París** via Paris; **transmisión v. satélite** satellite transmission

viable ADJ viable

viaducto NM viaduct

viajante NMF (*hombre*) travelling salesman; (*mujer*) travelling saleswoman

viajar VI to travel

viaje NM (*recorrido*) journey, trip; (*largo, en barco*) voyage; **¡buen v.!** bon voyage!, have a good trip!; **estar de v.** to be away (on a trip); **irse** *o* **marcharse de v.** to go on a journey *o* trip; **v. de negocios** business trip; **v. de novios** honeymoon

viajero, -a NM,F traveller; (*en transporte público*) passenger

vianda NF *Méx*, *RP* (*tentempié*) packed lunch; (*fiambrera*) lunchbox

viandante NMF passer-by

viario, -a ADJ road, highway; **red viaria** road network

víbora NF viper

vibración NF vibration

vibrador NM vibrator

vibrar VT & VI to vibrate

vicario, -a NM,F vicar

vicepresidente, -a NM,F (**a**) *Pol* vice-president (**b**) (*de compañía, comité*) vice-chairperson, US vice-president; (*hombre*) vice-chairman; (*mujer*) vice-chairwoman

vicesecretario, -a NM,F assistant secretary

viceversa ADV vice versa

viciado, -a ADJ (**a**) (*corrompido*) corrupt (**b**) (*aire*) stuffy

viciar [43] **1** VT (**a**) (*corromper*) to corrupt (**b**) (*estropear*) to ruin
2 viciarse VPR (**a**) (*deformarse*) to go out of

shape (**b**) *(corromperse)* to become corrupted; *(enviciarse)* to get into a bad habit

vicio NM (**a**) *(libertinaje, actividad inmoral)* vice (**b**) *(mala costumbre)* bad habit (**c**) *(defecto, error)* defect

vicioso, -a 1 ADJ (**a**) *(persona)* depraved, perverted (**b**) **círculo v.** vicious circle
2 NM,F depraved person; **v. del trabajo** workaholic

vicisitud NF *(usu pl)* vicissitude

víctima NF victim

victimar VT *Am* to kill, to murder

victimario, -a NM,F *Am* killer, murderer

victoria NF victory

victorioso, -a ADJ victorious

vicuña NF vicuña

vid NF vine, grapevine

vida NF life; *(período)* lifetime; **de toda la v.** lifelong; **en mi v.** never in my life; **de por v.** for life; **ganarse la v.** to earn one's living; **¿qué es de tu v.?** how's life?; **estar con/sin v.** to be alive/dead

vidente NMF clairvoyant

vídeo, *Am* **video** NM video; **grabar en v.** to videotape

videocámara NF video camera

videocasete NM video, video cassette

videoclub NM video club

videoconferencia NF *(concepto)* videoconferencing; *(sesión)* videoconference

videoconsola NF game console

videojuego NM video game

vidriera NF (**a**) *(ventana)* glass window; *(en catedrales)* stained-glass window (**b**) *Am (escaparate)* shop window

vidrio NM glass

vieira NF scallop

viejo, -a 1 ADJ old; **hacerse v.** to grow old; **un v. amigo** an old friend
2 NM,F (**a**) *(hombre, padre)* old man; *(mujer, madre)* old woman; *Fam* **los viejos** old people; *Fam* **mis viejos** my parents (**b**) *Am Fam (amigo)* pal, *Br* mate, *US* buddy; *(amiga)* girl, *US* girlfriend (**c**) *Chile* **el V. de Pascua** o **Pascuero** Father Christmas

Viena N Vienna

vienés, -esa ADJ & NM,F Viennese

viento NM wind; **hace** o **sopla mucho v.** it is very windy; *Fam Fig* **¡vete a tomar v.!** get lost!

vientre NM stomach, belly; **hacer de v.** to have a bowel movement

viernes NM INV Friday; **V. Santo** Good Friday

Vietnam N Vietnam

vietnamita ADJ & NMF Vietnamese

viga NF *(de madera)* beam; *(de hierro)* girder

vigencia NF validity; **entrar en v.** to come into force o effect

vigente ADJ in force

vigésimo, -a ADJ & NM,F twentieth

vigía 1 NF watchtower, lookout post
2 NMF lookout; *(hombre)* watchman; *(mujer)* watchwoman

vigilancia NF (**a**) *(cuidado)* vigilance; *Med* **v. intensiva** intensive care (**b**) *(control)* surveillance

vigilante NMF guard; **v. nocturno** night watchman

vigilar 1 VT *(lugar)* to guard; *(espiar)* to watch; **vigila que no entren** make sure they don't get in
2 VI to keep watch

vigilia NF (**a**) *(vela)* wakefulness (**b**) *(víspera)* eve (**c**) *Rel (abstinencia)* abstinence

vigor NM (**a**) *(fuerza)* vigour (**b**) **en v.** *(ley)* in force; *(contrato, tarifa)* current

vigoroso, -a ADJ vigorous

VIH NM *(abr* **virus de la inmunodeficiencia humana)** HIV

vikingo, -a ADJ & NM,F Viking

vil ADJ vile, base

vileza NF (**a**) *(cualidad)* vileness, baseness (**b**) *(acto)* vile act, despicable deed

vilipendiar [43] VT *Fml* to vilify, to revile

villa NF (**a**) *(población)* town (**b**) *(casa)* villa, country house (**c**) *Arg, Bol* **v. miseria** shanty town

villancico NM (Christmas) carol

vilo: en vilo LOC ADV on tenterhooks

vinagre NM vinegar

vinagrera NF **vinagreras** oil and vinegar cruets, cruet (stand)

vinagreta NF vinaigrette sauce

vinajeras NFPL cruets

vincha NF *Andes, RP* headband

vinculación NF link, connection

vinculante ADJ binding

vincular VT to link, to bind; *(relacionar)* to relate, to connect

vínculo NM link

vine PT INDEF *de* venir

vinícola ADJ wine-producing

vinicultor, -a NM,F wine producer

vinicultura NF wine production o growing

vinilo NM vinyl

vino NM wine; **tomar un v.** to have a glass of wine; **v. blanco/tinto** white/red wine; **v. dulce/seco** sweet/dry wine; **v. rosado** rosé

viña NF vineyard

viñedo NM vineyard

viñeta NF illustration

viola NF viola

violación NF (**a**) *(de una persona)* rape (**b**) *(de ley, derecho)* violation, infringement

violador NM rapist

violar VT (**a**) *(persona)* to rape (**b**) *(ley, derecho)* to violate, to infringe

violencia NF (a) *(agresividad)* violence; **v. doméstica** domestic violence (b) *(incomodidad)* awkwardness

violentar VT (a) *(forzar)* to force, to break open; *(sitio)* to break into, to enter by force (b) *(enojar)* to infuriate

violento, -a ADJ (a) *(agresivo)* violent (b) *(incómodo)* *(situación)* embarrassing, awkward; **sentirse v.** to feel embarrassed *o* awkward

violeta 1 ADJ & NM *(color)* violet
   2 NF *(flor)* violet

violín NM violin; *Fam* fiddle

violinista NMF violinist

violón NM double bass

violoncelista, violonchelista NMF cellist

violoncelo, violonchelo NM violoncello, cello

VIP NMF *(abr* **very important person**) VIP

viraje NM *(en coche)* swerve; *(en barco)* tack

virar VI *(girar)* to turn round *o* around

virgen 1 ADJ (a) *(persona, selva)* virgin (b) *(aceite, lana)* pure; *(cinta)* blank
   2 NMF virgin; *Fam* **ser un viva la v.** to be a devil-may-care person

virginidad NF virginity

Virgo NM Virgo

virgo NM hymen

virguería NF *Fam* **hacer virguerías** to work wonders, to be a dab hand

vírico, -a ADJ viral

viril ADJ virile, manly; **miembro v.** penis

virilidad NF virility

virtual ADJ virtual

virtud NF (a) *(moral)* virtue (b) *(facultad)* power; **tener la v. de** to have the power *o* ability to (c) **en v. de** by virtue of

virtuoso, -a 1 ADJ virtuous
   2 NM,F *(músico)* virtuoso

viruela NF smallpox; **viruelas** pockmarks

virulé: a la virulé LOC ADJ *Fam* (a) *(torcido)* crooked, twisted (b) **un ojo a la v.** a black eye

virulencia NF virulence

virulento, -a ADJ virulent

virus NM INV virus

viruta NF shaving

visado NM, *Am* **visa** NF visa

víscera NF internal organ; **vísceras** *(órganos)* entrails; *(comida)* offal

visceral ADJ profound, deep-rooted

viscosa NF *(tejido)* viscose

viscoso, -a ADJ viscous

visera NF *(de gorra)* peak; *(de casco)* visor

visibilidad NF visibility; **curva con mala v.** blind corner

visible ADJ visible; *(evidente)* evident

visillo NM net curtain, lace curtain

visión NF (a) *(capacidad)* vision, sight (b) *(interpretación)* view; **v. de conjunto** overall view; **con v. de futuro** forward-looking (c) *(aparición)* vision

visionario, -a ADJ & NM,F visionary

visita NF (a) *(acción)* visit; **hacer una v.** to pay a visit; **estar de v.** to be visiting (b) *(invitado)* visitor, guest

visitante 1 NMF visitor
   2 ADJ *(equipo)* away

visitar VT to visit

vislumbrar VT to glimpse

viso NM (a) *(reflejo)* sheen (b) *Fig* **tener visos de** to seem, to appear

visón NM mink

visor NM *Fot* viewfinder

> Observa que la palabra inglesa **visor** es un falso amigo y no es la traducción de la palabra española **visor**. En inglés, **visor** significa "visera".

víspera NF *(día anterior)* day before; *(de festivo)* eve; **en vísperas de** in the period leading up to

vista NF (a) *(sentido)* sight; **a la v.** visible; **a primera** *o* **simple v.** at first sight, on the face of it; **corto de v.** short-sighted; **conocer a algn de v.** to know sb by sight; **perder de v. a** to lose sight of; **quítalo de mi v.** take it away; *Fig* **tener mucha v. para** to have a good eye for; *Fig* **volver la v. atrás** to look back; *Fam* **¡hasta la v.!** goodbye!, see you!; *Fam* **hacer la v. gorda** to turn a blind eye (b) *(panorama)* view; **con vista(s) al mar** overlooking the sea (c) *Der* trial, hearing (d) *(locuciones)* **con vistas a** with a view to; **en v. de** in view of, considering

vistazo NM glance; **echar un v. a algo** *(ojear)* to have a (quick) look at sth; *(tener cuidado de)* to keep an eye on sth

visto, -a 1 ADJ (a) **está v. que ...** it is obvious that ...; **por lo v.** evidently, apparently; **v. que** in view of the fact that, seeing *o* given that (b) **estar bien v.** to be well looked upon, to be considered acceptable; **estar mal v.** to be frowned upon (c) **estar muy v.** to be old hat
   2 NM **v. bueno** approval, O.K.

vistoso, -a ADJ eye-catching

visual ADJ visual; **campo v.** field of vision

visualizar [40] VT to visualize; *(película)* to view

vital ADJ (a) *(órgano, energía)* vital; **es v.** it is vital (b) *(persona)* full of vitality

vitalicio, -a ADJ life, for life; **cargo v.** position held for life; **pensión v.** life pension

vitalidad NF vitality

vitamina NF vitamin

vitamínico, -a ADJ vitamin; **complejo v.** multi-vitamins

viticultor, -a NM,F wine grower

viticultura NF wine growing

vitorear VT to cheer

vítreo, -a ADJ vitreous

vitrina NF *(aparador)* glass o display cabinet; *(de exposición)* glass case, showcase; *Am (escaparate)* shop window

vituallas NFPL provisions

vituperar VT to condemn

vituperio NM condemnation

viudo, -a NM,F *(hombre)* widower; *(mujer)* widow

viva INTERJ ¡v.! hurrah!

vivacidad NF vivacity

vivaracho, -a ADJ lively, sprightly

vivaz ADJ alert, lively

vivencias NFPL personal experience

víveres NMPL provisions, supplies

vivero NM *(de plantas)* nursery; *(de peces)* fish farm o hatchery; **v. (de empresas)** business incubator

viveza NF **(a)** *(de colorido, descripción)* vividness **(b)** *(de persona, discusión, ojos)* liveliness; *(de ingenio, inteligencia)* sharpness

vividor, -a NM,F *Pey* sponger, scrounger

vivienda NF *(casa)* home; *(alojamiento)* housing

vivir 1 VI to live; **vive de sus ahorros** she lives off her savings; **viven de la pesca** they make their living by fishing
  2 VT to live through
  3 NM life

vivito, -a ADJ *Fam* **v. y coleando** alive and kicking

vivo, -a 1 ADJ **(a)** *(ser, lengua)* living; **un animal v.** a live animal; **estar v.** to be alive; **de viva voz** verbally, by word of mouth; **en v.** *(programa)* live **(b)** *(gestos, ojos, descripción)* lively, vivid; *(dolor, deseo)* intense; *(luz, color)* bright; *(ingenio)* quick, sharp
  2 NM,F **los vivos** the living

Vizcaya N **el golfo de V.** the Bay of Biscay

V.° B.° *(abr* **visto bueno)** *(en documento)* approved

vocablo NM word, term

vocabulario NM vocabulary

vocación NF vocation, calling; **con v. europea** with leanings towards Europe

vocacional ADJ vocational

vocal 1 NF *Ling* vowel
  2 NMF member

vocalista NMF *Mús* vocalist, singer

vocalizar [40] VT & VI to vocalize

voceador, -a NM,F *Col, Ecuad, Méx* newspaper seller

vocerío NM shouting

vocero, -a NM,F *esp Am (hombre)* spokesperson, spokesman; *(mujer)* spokesperson, spokeswoman

vociferante ADJ vociferous

vociferar VT & VI to vociferate

vodka NM vodka

vol. *(abr* **volumen)** vol

volado, -a ADJ *Fam* **estar v.** to have a screw loose

volador, -a ADJ flying

volandas: en volandas LOC ADV in the air, flying through the air

volante 1 NM **(a)** *Aut* steering wheel; **ir al v.** to be driving; **un as del v.** a motor-racing champion **(b)** *Cost* frill, ruffle **(c)** *Esp (del médico)* (referral) note
  2 ADJ flying; **platillo v.** flying saucer

volantín NM *Carib, Chile* kite

volar [2] **1** VI **(a)** *(en el aire)* to fly; *Fig* **lo hizo volando** he did it in a flash **(b)** *Fam (desaparecer)* to disappear, to vanish
  2 VT *(edificio)* to blow up; *(caja fuerte)* to blow open; *Min* to blast
  3 **volarse** VPR *(papel etc)* to be blown away

volátil ADJ volatile

volcán NM volcano

volcánico, -a ADJ volcanic

volcar [2] **1** VT **(a)** *(cubo etc)* to knock over; *(barco, bote)* to capsize **(b)** *(vaciar)* to empty out **(c)** *(tiempo)* to invest
  2 VI *(coche)* to turn over; *(barco)* to capsize
  3 **volcarse** VPR **(a)** *(vaso, jarra)* to fall over, to tip over; *(coche)* to turn over; *(barco)* to capsize **(b)** *Fig* **volcarse con** to do one's utmost for

voleibol NM volleyball

voleo NM **a v.** at random, haphazardly

volquete NM dumper truck, *US* dump truck

voltaje NM voltage

voltear 1 VT **(a)** *Am (derribar) (objeto)* to knock over; *(gobierno)* to overthrow, to bring down **(b)** *Am salvo RP (poner del revés) (boca abajo)* to turn upside down; *(lo de dentro fuera)* to turn inside out; *(lo de detrás delante)* to turn back to front **(c)** *Am salvo RP (cabeza, espalda)* to turn
  2 VI *Méx (doblar la esquina)* to turn
  3 **voltearse** VPR **(a)** *Am salvo RP (volverse)* to turn round o around **(b)** *Méx (vehículo)* to overturn

voltereta NF somersault

voltio NM volt

voluble ADJ fickle, changeable

> Observa que la palabra inglesa **voluble** es un falso amigo y no es la traducción de la palabra española **voluble**. En inglés, **voluble** significa "locuaz".

volumen NM volume

voluminoso, -a ADJ voluminous; *(enorme)* massive, bulky

voluntad NF will; **fuerza de v.** willpower; **tiene mucha v.** he is very strong-willed; **a v.** at will

voluntario, -a 1 ADJ voluntary
  2 NM,F volunteer; **ofrecerse v.** to volunteer

voluntarioso, -a ADJ willing

voluptuoso, -a ADJ voluptuous

volver [4] (*pp* vuelto) **1** VI (**a**) (*ir*) to go back, to return; (*venir*) to come back, to return; **v. en sí** to come round, to recover consciousness (**b**) **v. a hacer algo** to do sth again

2 VT (**a**) (*convertir*) to turn, to make; **me vas a v. loco** you are driving me mad (**b**) (*dar la vuelta a*) to turn over; (*boca abajo*) to turn upside down; (*de fuera adentro*) to turn inside out; (*de atrás adelante*) to turn back to front; **volverle la espalda a algn** to turn one's back on sb; *Fig* **v. la vista atrás** to look back; **al v. la esquina** on turning the corner

3 volverse VPR (**a**) (*girar*) to turn (**b**) (*regresar*) (*venir*) to come back; (*ir*) to go back (**c**) (*convertirse*) to become; **volverse loco(a)** to go mad

vomitar 1 VI to vomit, to be sick; **tengo ganas de v.** I feel sick, I want to be sick

2 VT to vomit, to bring up

vómito NM (*lo vomitado*) vomit; (*acción*) vomiting

vomitona NF *Fam* vomit

voracidad NF voracity, voraciousness

vorágine NF confusion, whirl

voraz ADJ voracious

vórtice NM vortex

vos PRON PERS *Am* (*tú*) you

> The **vos** form is used alongside **tú** in many Latin American countries, and in some countries (Argentina, Paraguay and Uruguay) is the preferred form.

V.O.S.E. NF (*abr* **versión original subtitulada en español**) = original language version subtitled in Spanish

vosotros, -as PRON PERS PL *Esp* (**a**) (*sujeto*) you (**b**) (*con prep*) your; **entre v.** among yourselves; **sin vosotras** without you

> Usually omitted in Spanish except for emphasis or contrast. In Latin America, **vosotros** is not used. Instead, **ustedes** is used as the second person plural in all contexts, without necessarily suggesting formality.

votación NF (**a**) (*voto*) vote, ballot (**b**) (*acción*) voting

votante NMF voter

votar VI to vote; **v. a algn** to vote for sb

voto NM (**a**) (*en elección*) vote; **tener v.** to have a vote; **v. secreto** secret ballot (**b**) *Rel* vow

vox NF **v. populi** common knowledge

voy INDIC PRES *de* **ir**

voz NF (**a**) (*sonido, tono*) voice; **en v. alta** aloud; **en v. baja** in a low voice; **a media v.** in a low voice, softly; **de viva v.** verbally (**b**) (*grito*) shout; **a voces** shouting; **dar voces** to shout; *Fig* **estar pidiendo algo a voces** to be crying out for sth; *Fig* **secreto a voces** open secret; **a v. en grito** at the top of one's voice (**c**) **no tener ni v. ni voto** to have no say in the matter; *Fig* **llevar la v. cantante** to rule the roost (**d**) *Ling* **v. pasiva** passive voice

vudú (*pl* **vudús** *o* **vudúes**) NM voodoo

vuelco NM upset, tumble; **dar un v.** (*coche*) to overturn; *Fig* **me dio un v. el corazón** my heart missed a beat

vuelo NM (**a**) flight; **v. chárter/regular** charter/scheduled flight; **v. sin motor** gliding; *Fig* **cazarlas** *o* **cogerlas al v.** to be quick on the uptake (**b**) *Cost* **una falda de v.** a full skirt

vuelta NF (**a**) (*regreso*) return; (*viaje*) return journey; **a v. de correo** by return of post; **estar de v.** to be back; *Dep* **partido de v.** return match (**b**) (*giro*) turn; (*en carreras*) lap; *Dep* (*ciclista*) tour; **dar media v.** to turn round *o* around; *Fig* **la cabeza me da vueltas** my head is spinning; *Fig* **no le des más vueltas** stop worrying about it; **v. de campana** somersault (**c**) (*dinero*) change (**d**) **dar una v.** (*a pie*) to go for a walk *o* stroll; (*en coche*) to go for a drive *o* a spin (in the car) (**e**) *Fig* **no tiene v. de hoja** there's no doubt about it

vuelto, -a 1 ADJ **jersey de cuello v.** rollneck sweater

2 NM *Am* change

3 PP *de* **volver**

vuestro, -a *Esp* **1** ADJ POS (*antes del sustantivo*) your; (*después del sustantivo*) of yours; **v. libro** your book; **un amigo v.** a friend of yours

2 PRON POS yours; **éstos son los vuestros** these are yours; **lo v.** what is yours, what belongs to you

vulgar ADJ (**a**) (*no refinado*) vulgar (**b**) (*no técnico*) **el término v.** the everyday term

vulgaridad NF vulgarity

vulgarizar [40] VT to popularize

vulgarmente ADV **v. llamado** commonly known as

vulgo NM **el v.** the common people; *Pey* the masses

vulnerable ADJ vulnerable

vulnerar VT (*ley, acuerdo*) to violate

vulva NF vulva

W X

W, w [uβe'ðoβle] NF *(letra)* W, w

W *Elec (abr* **vatio(s)***)* W

walkie-talkie [*Esp* 'walki'talki, *Am* 'woki'toki] NM walkie-talkie

walkman® ['walman] *(pl* **walkmans***)* NM Walkman®

WAP [wæp] NM *(abr* **Wireless Application Protocol***)* WAP

wáter [*Esp* 'bater, *Am* 'water] NM toilet

waterpolo [water'polo] NM water polo

WC [*Esp* uβe'θe, *Am* doβleβe'se] NM *(abr* **water closet***)* WC

Web, web [web] *Inform* **1** NF *(World Wide Web)* la W. the Web
2 NM O NF *(página web)* web site

whisky ['wiski] *(pl* **whiskys***)* NM *(escocés)* whisky; *(irlandés, US)* whiskey

windsurf ['winsurf], **windsurfing** ['winsurfin] NM windsurfing

windsurfista [winsur'fista] NMF windsurfer

wireless ['waiales] ADJ *Inform (tecnología, red)* wireless

xenofobia NF xenophobia

xenófobo, -a 1 ADJ xenophobic
2 NM,F xenophobe

xilofón, xilófono NM xylophone

Y

Y, y [iɣri'eɣa] NF *(letra)* Y, y

y CONJ (**a**) and; **una chica alta y morena** a tall, dark-haired girl; **son las tres y cuarto** it's a quarter past three (**b**) **¿y qué?** so what?; **¿y si no llega a tiempo?** what if he doesn't arrive in time?; **¿y tú?** what about you?; **¿y eso?** how come?; **y eso que** although, even though; **¡y tanto!** you bet!, and how!; *ver* **e**

ya 1 ADV (**a**) *(en el pasado)* already; **ya lo sabía** I already knew; **ya en la Edad Media** as far back as the Middle Ages (**b**) *(ahora mismo)* now; **es preciso actuar ya** it is vital that we act now; **¡hazlo ya!** do it at once!; **ya mismo** right away (**c**) *(en el futuro)* **ya hablaremos luego** we'll talk about it later; **ya nos veremos** see you!; **ya verás** you'll see (**d**) **ya no** no longer; **ya no viene por aquí** he doesn't come round here any more (**e**) *(refuerza el verbo)* **ya era hora** about time too; **ya lo creo** of course, I should think so; **¡ya voy!** coming!; **¡ya está!** that's it!

2 CONJ **ya que** since

yacer [61] VI (**a**) *(estar tumbado, enterrado)* to lie; **aquí yace ...** here lies ... (**b**) *(tener relaciones sexuales)* to lie together

yacimiento NM bed, deposit; **yacimientos petrolíferos** oilfields

yaguar NM jaguar

yanqui Pey **1** ADJ Yankee
2 NMF Yankee, Yank

yarará NF *Am* = large poisonous snake

yaraví *(pl yaravíes o yaravís)* NM *Am* = type of melancholy Indian song

yarda NF yard

yate NM yacht

yaya NF (**a**) *Perú (insecto)* mite (**b**) *Cuba, PRico (árbol)* lancewood

yayo, -a NM,F *Fam (hombre)* grandad; *(mujer)* grandma

yegua NF mare

yema NF (**a**) *(de huevo)* yolk (**b**) *Bot* bud (**c**) **y. del dedo** fingertip (**d**) *Culin* = sweet made from sugar and egg yolk

Yemen N **(el) Y.** Yemen

yen NM *(moneda)* yen

yendo GERUNDIO *de* **ir**

yerba NF (**a**) = **hierba** (**b**) *RP* maté; **y. mate** (yerba) maté leaves

yerbatero, -a 1 NM,F *Andes, Carib (curandero)* witch doctor who uses herbs; *(vendedor de hierbas)* herbalist
2 ADJ *RP* maté

yermo, -a ADJ barren, uncultivated

yerno NM son-in-law

yerro INDIC PRES *de* **errar**

yeso NM (**a**) *Geol* gypsum (**b**) *Constr* plaster

Yibuti N Djibouti

yiu-yitsu NM ju-jitsu

yo PRON PERS I; **entre tú y yo** between you and me; **¿quién es? – soy yo** who is it? – it's me; **yo no** not me; **yo que tú** if I were you; **yo mismo** I myself

> Usually omitted as a personal pronoun in Spanish except for emphasis or contrast.

yodo NM iodine

yoga NM yoga

yogur *(pl yogures)*, **yogurt** *(pl yogurts)* NM yogurt, yoghurt

yogurtera NF yoghurt maker

yonqui NMF *Fam* junkie, drug addict

yoyó NM yo-yo

yuca NF yucca

yudo NM judo

yudoka NMF judoka

yugo NM yoke

Yugoslavia N Yugoslavia

yugoslavo, -a ADJ & NM,F Yugoslav, Yugoslavian

yugular NF jugular

yunque NM anvil

yunta NF yoke *o* team of oxen

yuxtaponer [19] *(pp yuxtapuesto)* VT to juxtapose

yuxtaposición NF juxtaposition

yuxtapuesto, -a PP *de* **yuxtaponer**

yuyo NM (**a**) *CSur (mala hierba)* weed; *(hierba medicinal)* medicinal herb (**b**) *Andes (hierba silvestre)* wild herb

Z

Z, z ['θeta] NF *(letra)* Z, z

zacate NM *CAm, Méx* fodder

zafarse VPR *(librarse)* to get away, to escape (**de** from)

zafio, -a ADJ uncouth

zafiro NM sapphire

zaga NF **a la z.** behind, at the rear

zaguán NM hall, hallway

zaherir VT to hurt

Zaire N Zaire

zalamero, -a 1 NM,F flatterer, fawner
2 ADJ flattering, fawning

zamarra NF sheepskin jacket

Zambia N Zambia

zambo, -a 1 ADJ *(piernas, persona)* knock-kneed
2 NM,F *Am* = person who has one Black and one Indian parent

zambomba NF = kind of primitive drum

zambullida NF plunge

zambullirse VPR to plunge

zamparse VPR *Fam* to gobble down

zanahoria NF carrot

zancada NF stride

zancadilla NF **ponerle la z. a algn** to trip sb up

zanco NM stilt

zancudo, -a 1 ADJ (a) *(ave)* wading (b) *(persona)* long-legged
2 NM *Am* mosquito

zángano, -a 1 NM *(insecto)* drone
2 NM,F *Fam (persona)* idler, lazybones *inv*

zanja NF ditch, trench

zanjar VT *(asunto)* to settle

zapallito NM *CSur Br* courgette, *US* zucchini

zapallo NM (a) *Andes, RP* **z. (italiano)** *Br* courgette, *US* zucchini (b) *Andes, RP (calabaza)* pumpkin (c) *RP Fam (bobo)* mug, *Br* wally

zapata NF (a) *(cuña)* wedge (b) *Téc* shoe

zapateado NM = type of flamenco dance where the dancers stamp their feet rhythmically

zapatear VI to tap one's feet

zapatería NF shoe shop

zapatero, -a NM,F *(vendedor)* shoe dealer; *(fabricante)* shoemaker, cobbler

zapatilla NF slipper; **zapatillas de deporte** *Br* trainers, *US* sneakers

zapato NM shoe; **zapatos de tacón** high-heeled shoes

zapping ['θapin] NM INV *Fam* channel-hopping, *US* channel surfing; **hacer z.** to channel-hop

zar NM czar, tsar

Zaragoza N Saragossa

zaragozano, -a 1 ADJ of/from Saragossa
2 NM,F person from Saragossa

zarandear VT to shake

zarandeo NM shaking

zarina NF czarina, tsarina

zarpa NF *(uña)* claw; *(mano)* paw

zarpar VI to weigh anchor, to set sail

zarpazo NM clawing; **dar** *o* **pegar un z. a** to claw

zarza NF bramble, blackberry bush

zarzal NM bramble patch

zarzamora NF *(zarza)* blackberry bush; *(fruto)* blackberry

zarzuela NF (a) *Mús* = Spanish operetta (b) **la Z.** = royal residence in Madrid (c) *Culin* = fish stew

zenit NM zenith

zigzag *(pl* **zigzags** *o* **zigzagues)** NM zigzag

zigzaguear VI to zigzag

Zimbabwe N Zimbabwe

zinc NM zinc

zíper NM *CAm, Méx Br* zip, *US* zipper

zipizape NM *Fam* squabble, set-to

zócalo NM (a) *(de pared)* skirting board (b) *(pedestal)* plinth

zodiaco, zodíaco NM zodiac

zona NF zone; *(región)* region; **z. euro** euro zone; **z. verde** park, green area

zoo NM zoo

zoología NF zoology

zoológico, -a 1 ADJ zoological; **parque z.** zoo
2 NM zoo

zoom NM *Cin & Fot* zoom

zopenco, -a NM,F *Fam* dope, halfwit

zopilote NM *CAm, Méx* black vulture

zoquete 1 NMF *Fam* blockhead
2 NM *CSur (calcetín)* ankle sock

zorra NF (a) *(animal)* vixen (b) *Esp Fam* slut

zorro, -a 1 NM fox
2 ADJ (a) *(astuto)* cunning, sly (b) *Esp muy Fam* **no tengo ni zorra (idea)** I haven't got a *Br* bloody *o US* goddamn clue

zorzal NM *(ave)* thrush

zozobrar VI to be in danger of going under

zueco NM clog

zumbado, -a ADJ *Fam* crazy, mad

zumbar 1 VI to buzz, to hum; **me zumban los oídos** my ears are buzzing; *Fam* **salir zumbando** to zoom off

  2 VT *Fam* to thrash

zumbido NM buzzing, humming

zumo NM *Esp* juice

zurcir [52] VT *Cost* to darn; *Fam* **¡que te zurzan!** go to hell!

zurda NF *(mano)* left hand

zurdo, -a 1 NM,F *(persona)* left-handed person

  2 ADJ left-handed

zurrar VT *(pegar)* to beat, to flog

zutano, -a NM,F *Fam* so-and-so; *(hombre)* what's-his-name; *(mujer)* what's-her-name

Spanish Verbs

Regular Spelling Changes

The rules of spelling in Spanish cause a number of verbs to have regular spelling changes. These are listed below.

Spanish verbs fall into three groups depending on whether their infinitive ends in **-ar, -er** or **-ir.** The stem of the verb is the part which is left when the **-ar, -er** or **-ir** is removed from the infinitive. For example, the stem of **tomar** is **tom**, the stem of **beber** is **beb**, and the stem of **salir** is **sal**.

In the lists given below, the following indicators are used:

     (**1**) first person singular present indicative
     (**2**) present subjunctive, all persons
     (**3**) first person singular preterite

Verbs ending in -ar

i) Verbs with a stem ending in **c**, for example **buscar**

The **c** changes to **qu** in:

     (**2**) busque, busques, busque, busquemos, busquéis, busquen
     (**3**) busqué

ii) Verbs with a stem ending in **g**, for example **cargar**

The **g** changes to **gu** in:

     (**2**) cargue, cargues, cargue, carguemos, carguéis, carguen
     (**3**) cargué

iii) Verbs with a stem ending in **gu**, for example **averiguar**

The **gu** changes to **gü** in:

     (**2**) averigüe, averigües, averigüe, averigüemos, averigüéis, averigüen
     (**3**) averigüé

iv) Verbs with a stem ending in **z**, for example **realizar**

The **z** changes to **c** in:

     (**2**) realice, realices, realice, realicemos, realicéis, realicen
     (**3**) realicé

Verbs ending in -er *or* -ir

i) Verbs with a stem ending in **c**, for example **esparcir**

The **c** changes to **z** in:

> (**1**) esparzo
> (**2**) esparza, esparzas, esparza, esparzamos, esparzáis, esparzan

ii) Verbs with a stem ending in **g**, for example **coger**

The **g** changes to **j** in:

> (**1**) cojo
> (**2**) coja, cojas, coja, cojamos, cojáis, cojan

iii) Verbs with a stem ending in **qu**, for example **delinquir**

The **qu** changes to **c** in:

> (**1**) delinco
> (**2**) delinca, delincas, delinca, delincamos, delincáis, delincan

iv) Verbs with a stem ending in **gu**, for example **distinguir**

The **gu** changes to **g** in:

> (**1**) distingo
> (**2**) distinga, distingas, distinga, distingamos, distingáis, distingan

Models for regular conjugation

TOMAR to take

INDICATIVE

PRESENT	FUTURE	CONDITIONAL
1. tomo	tomaré	tomaría
2. tomas	tomarás	tomarías
3. toma	tomará	tomaría
1. tomamos	tomaremos	tomaríamos
2. tomáis	tomaréis	tomaríais
3. toman	tomarán	tomarían

IMPERFECT	PRETERITE	PERFECT
1. tomaba	tomé	he tomado
2. tomabas	tomaste	has tomado
3. tomaba	tomó	ha tomado
1. tomábamos	tomamos	hemos tomado
2. tomabais	tomasteis	habéis tomado
3. tomaban	tomaron	han tomado

FUTURE PERFECT	CONDITIONAL PERFECT	PLUPERFECT
1. habré tomado	habría tomado	había tomado
2. habrás tomado	habrías tomado	habías tomado
3. habrá tomado	habría tomado	había tomado
1. habremos tomado	habríamos tomado	habíamos tomado
2. habréis tomado	habríais tomado	habíais tomado
3. habrán tomado	habrían tomado	habían tomado

SUBJUNCTIVE

PRESENT	IMPERFECT	PERFECT/PLUPERFECT
1. tome	tom-ara/ase	haya/hubiera* tomado
2. tomes	tom-aras/ases	hayas/hubieras tomado
3. tome	tom-ara/ase	haya/hubiera tomado

* the alternative form 'hubiese' etc is also possible.

1. tomemos	tom-áramos/ásemos	hayamos/hubiéramos tomado
2. toméis	tom-arais/aseis	hayáis/hubierais tomado
3. tomen	tom-aran/asen	hayan/hubieran tomado

IMPERATIVE

(tú) toma
(Vd) tome
(nosotros) tomemos
(vosotros) tomad
(Vds) tomen

INFINITIVE

PRESENT
tomar

PERFECT
haber tomado

PARTICIPLE

PRESENT
tomando

PAST
tomado

COMER to eat

PRESENT	FUTURE	CONDITIONAL
1. como	comeré	comería
2. comes	comerás	comerías
3. come	comerá	comería
1. comemos	comeremos	comeríamos
2. coméis	comeréis	comeríais
3. comen	comerán	comerían

IMPERFECT	PRETERITE	PERFECT
1. comía	comí	he comido
2. comías	comiste	has comido
3. comía	comió	ha comido
1. comíamos	comimos	hemos comido
2. comíais	comisteis	habéis comido
3. comían	comieron	han comido

FUTURE PERFECT	CONDITIONAL PERFECT	PLUPERFECT
1. habré comido	habría comido	había comido
2. habrás comido	habrías comido	habías comido
3. habrá comido	habría comido	había comido
1. habremos comido	habríamos comido	habíamos comido
2. habréis comido	habríais comido	habíais comido
3. habrán comido	habrían comido	habían comido

PRESENT	IMPERFECT	PERFECT/PLUPERFECT
1. coma	com-iera/iese	haya/hubiera* comido
2. comas	com-ieras/ieses	hayas/hubieras comido
3. coma	com-iera/iese	haya/hubiera comido
1. comamos	com-iéramos/iésemos	hayamos/hubiéramos comido
2. comáis	com-ierais/ieseis	hayáis/hubierais comido
3. coman	com-ieran/iesen	hayan/hubieran comido

* the alternative form 'hubiese' etc is also possible

| |

IMPERATIVE	INFINITIVE	PARTICIPLE
(tú) come	**PRESENT**	**PRESENT**
(Vd) coma	comer	comiendo
(nosotros) comamos		
(vosotros) comed	**PERFECT**	**PAST**
(Vds) coman	haber comido	comido

PARTIR to leave

INDICATIVE

PRESENT	FUTURE	CONDITIONAL
1. parto	partiré	partiría
2. partes	partirás	partirías
3. parte	partirá	partiría
1. partimos	partiremos	partiríamos
2. partís	partiréis	partiríais
3. parten	partirán	partirían

IMPERFECT	PRETERITE	PERFECT
1. partía	partí	he partido
2. partías	partiste	has partido
3. partía	partió	ha partido
1. partíamos	partimos	hemos partido
2. partíais	partisteis	habéis partido
3. partían	partieron	han partido

FUTURE PERFECT	CONDITIONAL PERFECT	PLUPERFECT
1. habré partido	habría partido	había partido
2. habrás partido	habrías partido	habías partido
3. habrá partido	habría partido	había partido
1. habremos partido	habríamos partido	habíamos partido
2. habréis partido	habríais partido	habíais partido
3. habrán partido	habrían partido	habían partido

SUBJUNCTIVE

PRESENT	IMPERFECT	PERFECT/PLUPERFECT
parta	parti-era/ese	haya/hubiera* partido
partas	parti-eras/eses	hayas/hubieras partido
parta	parti-era/ese	haya/hubiera partido
partamos	parti-éramos/ésemos	hayamos/hubiéramos partido
partáis	parti-erais/eseis	hayáis/hubierais partido
partan	parti-eran/esen	hayan/hubieran partido

* the alternative form 'hubiese' etc is also possible

IMPERATIVE	INFINITIVE	PARTICIPLE
(tú) parte	PRESENT	PRESENT
(Vd) parta	partir	partiendo
(nosotros) partamos	PERFECT	PAST
(vosotros) partid	haber partido	partido
(Vds) partan		

Models for irregular conjugation

[1] pensar PRES pienso, piensas, piensa, pensamos, pensáis, piensan; PRES SUBJ piense, pienses, piense, pensemos, penséis, piensen; IMPERAT piensa, piense, pensemos, pensad, piensen

[2] contar PRES cuento, cuentas, cuenta, contamos, contáis, cuentan; PRES SUBJ cuente, cuentes, cuente, contemos, contéis, cuenten; IMPERAT cuenta, cuente, contemos, contad, cuenten

[3] perder PRES pierdo, pierdes, pierde, perdemos, perdéis, pierden; PRES SUBJ pierda, pierdas, pierda, perdamos, perdáis, pierdan; IMPERAT pierde, pierda, perdamos, perded, pierdan

[4] morder PRES muerdo, muerdes, muerde, mordemos, mordéis, muerden; PRES SUBJ muerda, muerdas, muerda, mordamos, mordáis, muerdan; IMPERAT muerde, muerda, mordamos, morded, muerdan

[5] sentir PRES siento, sientes, siente, sentimos, sentís, sienten; PRES SUBJ sienta, sientas, sienta, sintamos, sintáis, sientan; PRES P sintiendo; IMPERAT siente, sienta, sintamos, sentid, sientan

[6] vestir PRES visto, vistes, viste, vestimos, vestís, visten; PRES SUBJ vista, vistas, vista, vistamos, vistáis, vistan; PRES P vistiendo; IMPERAT viste, vista, vistamos, vestid, vistan

[7] dormir PRES duermo, duermes, duerme, dormimos, dormís, duermen; PRES SUBJ duerma, duermas, duerma, durmamos, durmáis, duerman; PRES P durmiendo; IMPERAT duerme, duerma, durmamos, dormid, duerman

[8] andar PRET anduve, anduviste, anduvo, anduvimos, anduvisteis, anduvieron; IMPERF SUBJ anduviera/anduviese

[9] caber PRES quepo, cabes, cabe, cabemos, cabéis, caben; PRES SUBJ quepa, quepas, quepa, quepamos, quepáis, quepan; FUT cabré; COND cabría; PRET cupe, cupiste, cupo, cupimos, cupisteis, cupieron; IMPERF SUBJ cupiera/cupiese; IMPERAT cabe, quepa, quepamos, cabed, quepan

[10] conducir PRES conduzco, conduces, conduce, conducimos, conducís, conducen; PRES SUBJ conduzca, conduzcas, conduzca, conduzcamos, conduzcáis, conduzcan; PRET conduje, condujiste, condujo, condujimos, condujisteis, condujeron; IMPERF SUBJ condujera/condujese; IMPERAT conduce, conduzca, conduzcamos, conducid, conduzcan

[11] dar PRES doy, das, da, damos, dais, dan; PRES SUBJ dé, des, dé, demos, deis, den; PRET di, diste, dio, dimos, disteis, dieron; IMPERF SUBJ diera/diese; IMPERAT da, dé, demos, dad, den

[12] decir PRES digo, dices, dice, decimos, decís, dicen; PRES SUBJ diga, digas, diga, digamos, digáis, digan; FUT diré; COND diría; PRET dije, dijiste, dijo, dijimos, dijisteis, dijeron; IMPERF SUBJ dijera/dijese; PRES P diciendo; PP dicho; IMPERAT di, diga, digamos, decid, digan

[13] ESTAR to be

PRESENT	FUTURE	CONDITIONAL
1. estoy	estaré	estaría
2. estás	estarás	estarías
3. está	estará	estaría
1. estamos	estaremos	estaríamos
2. estáis	estaréis	estaríais
3. están	estarán	estarían

IMPERFECT	PRETERITE	PERFECT
1. estaba	estuve	he estado
2. estabas	estuviste	has estado
3. estaba	estuvo	ha estado
1. estábamos	estuvimos	hemos estado
2. estabais	estuvisteis	habéis estado
3. estaban	estuvieron	han estado

FUTURE PERFECT	CONDITIONAL PERFECT	PLUPERFECT
1. habré estado	habría estado	había estado
2. habrás estado	habrías estado	habías estado
3. habrá estado	habría estado	había estado
1. habremos estado	habríamos estado	habíamos estado
2. habréis estado	habríais estado	habíais estado
3. habrán estado	habrían estado	habían estado

SUBJUNCTIVE

PRESENT	IMPERFECT	PERFECT/PLUPERFECT
1. esté	estuv-iera/iese	haya/hubiera* estado
2. estés	estuv-ieras/ieses	hayas/hubieras estado
3. esté	estuv-iera/iese	haya/hubiera estado
1. estemos	estuv-iéramos/iésemos	hayamos/hubiéramos estado
2. estéis	estuv-ierais/ieseis	hayáis/hubierais estado
3. estén	estuv-ieran/iesen	hayan/hubieran estado

IMPERATIVE

	INFINITIVE	PARTICIPLE
(tú) está	**PRESENT**	**PRESENT**
(Vd) esté	estar	estando
(nosotros) estemos		
(vosotros) estad	**PERFECT**	**PAST**
(Vds) estén	haber estado	estado

* the alternative form 'hubiese' etc is also possible

[14] HABER to have (*auxiliary*)

INDICATIVE

PRESENT	FUTURE	CONDITIONAL
1. he	habré	habría
2. has	habrás	habrías
3. ha/hay*	habrá	habría
1. hemos	habremos	habríamos
2. habéis	habréis	habríais
3. han	habrán	habrían

IMPERFECT	PRETERITE	PERFECT
1. había	hube	
2. habías	hubiste	
3. había	hubo	ha habido*
1. habíamos	hubimos	
2. habíais	hubisteis	
3. habían	hubieron	

FUTURE PERFECT	CONDITIONAL PERFECT	PLUPERFECT
1.		
2.		
3. habrá habido*	habría habido*	había habido*
1.		
2.		
3.		

SUBJUNCTIVE

PRESENT	IMPERFECT	PERFECT/PLUPERFECT
1. haya	hub-iera/iese	
2. hayas	hub-ieras/ieses	
3. haya	hub-iera/iese	haya/hubiera** habido*
1. hayamos	hub-iéramos/iésemos	
2. hayáis	hub-ierais/ieseis	
3. hayan	hub-ieran/iesen	

INFINITIVE

PRESENT
haber
PERFECT
haber habido*

PARTICIPLE

PRESENT
habiendo
PAST
habido

* 'haber' is an auxiliary verb used with the participle of another verb to form compound tenses (eg he bebido – I have drunk). 'hay' means 'there is/are' and all third person singular forms in their respective tenses have this meaning. The forms highlighted with an asterisk are used only for this latter construction.

** the alternative form 'hubiese' is also possible.

[15] hacer PRES hago, haces, hace, hacemos, hacéis, hacen; **PRES SUBJ** haga, hagas, haga, hagamos, hagáis, hagan; **FUT** haré; **COND** haría; **PRET** hice, hiciste, hizo, hicimos, hicisteis, hicieron; **IMPERF SUBJ** hiciera/hiciese; **PP** hecho; **IMPERAT** haz, haga, hagamos, haced, hagan

[16] ir PRES voy, vas, va, vamos, vais, van; **PRES SUBJ** vaya, vayas, vaya, vayamos, vayáis, vayan; **IMPERF** iba, ibas, iba, íbamos, ibais, iban; **PRET** fui, fuiste, fue, fuimos, fuisteis, fueron; **IMPERF SUBJ** fuera/fuese; **PRES P** yendo; **IMPERAT** ve, vaya, vamos, id, vayan

[17] oír PRES oigo, oyes, oye, oímos, oís, oyen; **PRES SUBJ** oiga, oigas, oiga, oigamos, oigáis, oigan; **PRET** oí, oíste, oyó, oímos, oísteis, oyeron; **IMPERF SUBJ** oyera/oyese; **PRES P** oyendo; **PP** oído; **IMPERAT** oye, oiga, oigamos, oíd, oigan

[18] poder PRES puedo, puedes, puede, podemos, podéis, pueden; **PRES SUBJ** pueda, puedas, pueda, podamos, podáis, puedan; **FUT** podré; **COND** podría; **PRET** pude, pudiste, pudo, pudimos, pudisteis, pudieron; **IMPERF SUBJ** pudiera/pudiese; **PRES P** pudiendo; **IMPERAT** puede, pueda, podamos, poded, puedan

[19] poner PRES pongo, pones, pone, ponemos, ponéis, ponen; **PRES SUBJ** ponga, pongas, ponga, pongamos, pongáis, pongan; **FUT** pondré; **PRET** puse, pusiste, puso, pusimos, pusisteis, pusieron; **IMPERF SUBJ** pusiera/pusiese; **PP** puesto; **IMPERAT** pon, ponga, pongamos, poned, pongan

[20] querer PRES quiero, quieres, quiere, queremos, queréis, quieren; **PRES SUBJ** quiera, quieras, quiera, queramos, queráis, quieran; **FUT** querré; **COND** querría; **PRET** quise, quisiste, quiso, quisimos, quisisteis, quisieron; **IMPERF SUBJ** quisiera/quisiese; **IMPERAT** quiere, quiera, queramos, quered, quieran

[21] saber PRES sé, sabes, sabe, sabemos, sabéis, saben; **PRES SUBJ** sepa, sepas, sepa, sepamos, sepáis, sepan; **FUT** sabré; **COND** sabría; **PRET** supe, supiste, supo, supimos, supisteis, supieron; **IMPERF SUBJ** supiera/supiese; **IMPERAT** sabe, sepa, sepamos, sabed, sepan

[22] salir PRES salgo, sales, sale, salimos, salís, salen; **PRES SUBJ** salga, salgas, salga, salgamos, salgáis, salgan; **FUT** saldré; **COND** saldría; **IMPERAT** sal, salga, salgamos, salid, salgan

[23] ser PRES soy, eres, es, somos, sois, son; **PRES SUBJ** sea, seas, sea, seamos, seáis, sean; **IMPERF** era, eras, era, éramos, erais, eran; **PRET** fui, fuiste, fue, fuimos, fuisteis, fueron; **IMPERF SUBJ** fuera/fuese; **IMPERAT** sé, sea, seamos, sed, sean

[24] tener PRES tengo, tienes, tiene, tenemos, tenéis, tienen; **PRES SUBJ** tenga, tengas, tenga, tengamos, tengáis, tengan; **FUT** tendré; **COND** tendría; **PRET** tuve, tuviste, tuvo, tuvimos, tuvisteis, tuvieron; **IMPERF SUBJ** tuviera/tuviese; **IMPERAT** ten, tenga, tengamos, tened, tengan

[25] traer PRES traigo, traes, trae, traemos, traéis, traen; **PRES SUBJ** traiga, traigas, traiga, traigamos, traigáis, traigan; **PRET** traje, trajiste, trajo, trajimos, trajisteis, trajeron; **IMPERF SUBJ** trajera/trajese; **IMPERAT** trae, traiga, traigamos, traed, traigan

[26] valer PRES valgo, vales, vale, valemos, valéis, valen; **PRES SUBJ** valga, valgas, valga, valgamos, valgáis, valgan; **FUT** valdré; **COND** valdría; **IMPERAT** vale, valga, valemos, valed, valgan

[27] venir PRES vengo, vienes, viene, venimos, venís, vienen; **PRES SUBJ** venga, vengas, venga, vengamos, vengáis, vengan; **FUT** vendré; **COND** vendría; **PRET** vine, viniste, vino, vinimos, vinisteis, vinieron; **IMPERF SUBJ** viniera/viniese; **PRES P** viniendo; **IMPERAT** ven, venga, vengamos, venid, vengan

[28] ver PRES veo, ves, ve, vemos, veis, ven; PRES SUBJ vea, veas, vea, veamos, veáis, vean; IMPERF veía, veías, veía, veíamos, veíais, veían; PRET vi, viste, vio, vimos, visteis, vieron; IMPERF SUBJ viera/viese; IMPERAT ve, vea, veamos, ved, vean

[29] desviar PRES desvío, desvías, desvía, desviamos, desviáis, desvían; PRES SUBJ desvíe, desvíes, desvíe, desviemos, desviéis, desvíen; IMPERAT desvía, desvíe, desviemos, desviéis, desvíen

[30] continuar PRES continúo, continúas, continúa, continuamos, continuáis, continúan; PRES SUBJ continúe, continúes, continúe, continuemos, continuéis, continúen; IMPERAT continúa, continúe, continuemos, continuad, continúen

[31] adquirir PRES adquiero, adquieres, adquiere, adquirimos, adquirís, adquieren; PRES SUBJ adquiera, adquieras, adquiera, adquiramos, adquiráis, adquieran; IMPERAT adquiere, adquiera, adquiramos, adquirid, adquieran

[32] jugar PRES juego, juegas, juega, jugamos, jugáis, juegan; PRES SUBJ juegue, juegues, juegue, juguemos, juguéis, jueguen; IMPERAT juega, juegue, juguemos, jugad, jueguen

[33] agradecer PRES agradezco, agradeces, agradece, agradecemos, agradecéis, agradecen; PRES SUBJ agradezca, agradezcas, agradezca, agradezcamos, agradezcáis, agradezcan; IMPERAT agradece, agradezca, agradezcamos, agradeced, agradezcan

[34] conocer PRES conozco, conoces, conoce, conocemos, conocéis, conocen; PRES SUBJ conozca, conozcas, conozca, conozcamos, conozcáis, conozcan; IMPERAT conoce, conozca, conozcamos, conoced, conozcan

[35] lucir PRES luzco, luces, luce, lucimos, lucís, lucen; PRES SUBJ luzca, luzcas, luzca, luzcamos, luzcáis, luzcan; IMPERAT luce, luzca, luzcamos, lucid, luzcan

[36] leer PRET leí, leíste, leyó, leímos, leísteis, leyeron; IMPERF SUBJ leyera/leyese; PRES P leyendo; PP leído; IMPERAT lee, lea, leamos, leed, lean

[37] huir PRES huyo, huyes, huye, huimos, huís, huyen; PRES SUBJ huya, huyas, huya, huyamos, huyáis, huyan; PRET huí, huiste, huyó, huimos, huisteis, huyeron; IMPERF SUBJ huyera/huyese; PRES P huyendo; PP huido; IMPERAT huye, huya, huyamos, huid, huyan

[38] roer PRES roo/roigo/royo, roes, roe, roemos, roéis, roen; PRES SUBJ roa/roiga/roya, roas, roa, roamos, roáis, roan; PRET roí, roíste, royó, roímos, roísteis, royeron; IMPERF SUBJ royera/royese; PRES P royendo; PP roído; IMPERAT roe, roa, roamos, roed, roan

[39] caer PRES caigo, caes, cae, caemos, caéis, caen; PRES SUBJ caiga, caigas, caiga, caigamos, caigáis, caigan; PRES P cayendo; PP caído; IMPERAT cae, caiga, caigamos, caed, caigan

[40] cazar PRET cacé, cazaste, cazó, cazamos, cazasteis, cazaron; PRES SUBJ cace, caces, cace, cacemos, cacéis, cacen

[41] cocer PRES cuezo, cueces, cuece, cocemos, cocéis, cuecen; PRES SUBJ cueza, cuezas, cueza, cozamos, cozáis, cuezan; IMPERAT cuece, cueza, cozamos, coced, cuezan

[42] llegar PRET llegué, llegaste, llegó, llegamos, llegasteis, llegaron; PRES SUBJ llegue, llegues, llegue, lleguemos, lleguéis, lleguen

[43] cambiar PRES cambio, cambias, cambia, cambiamos, cambiáis, cambian; **PRES SUBJ** cambie, cambies, cambie, cambiemos, cambiéis, cambien; **IMPERAT** cambia, cambie, cambiemos, cambiad, cambien

[44] sacar PRET saqué, sacaste, sacó, sacamos, sacasteis, sacaron; **PRES SUBJ** saque, saques, saque, saquemos, saquéis, saquen; **IMPERAT** saca, saque, saquemos, sacad, saquen

[45] averiguar PRET averigüé, averiguaste, averiguó, averiguamos, averiguasteis, averiguaron; **PRES SUBJ** averigüe, averigües, averigüe, averigüemos, averigüéis, averigüen; **IMPERAT** averigua, averigüe, averigüemos, averiguad, averigüen

[46] asir PRES asgo, ases, ase, asimos, asís, asen; **PRES SUBJ** asga, asgas, asga, asgamos, asgáis, asgan; **IMPERAT** ase, asga, asgamos, asid, asgan

[47] adecuar PRES adecuo/adecúo, adecuas/adecúas, adecua/adecúa, adecuamos, adecuáis, adecuan/adecúan; **PRES SUBJ** adecue/adecúe, adecues/adecúes, adecue/adecúe, adecuemos, adecuéis, adecuen/adecúen; **IMPERAT** adecua/adecúa, adecue/adecúe, adecuemos, adecuad, adecuen/adecúen

[48] delinquir PRES delinco, delinques, delinque, delinquimos, delinquís, delinquen; **PRES SUBJ** delinca, delincas, delinca, delincamos, delincáis, delincan; **IMPERAT** delinque, delinca, delincamos, delinquid, delincan

[49] mecer PRES mezo, meces, mece, mecemos, mecéis, mecen; **PRES SUBJ** meza, mezas, meza, mezamos, mezáis, mezan; **IMPERAT** mece, meza, mezamos, meced, mezan

[50] errar PRES yerro, yerras, yerra, erramos, erráis, yerran; **PRES SUBJ** yerre, yerres, yerre, erremos, erréis, yerren; **IMPERAT** yerra, yerre, erremos, errad, yerren

[51] comenzar PRES comienzo, comienzas, comienza, comenzamos, comenzáis, comienzan; **PRES SUBJ** comience, comiences, comience, comencemos, comencéis, comiencen; **IMPERAT** comienza, comience, comencemos, comenzad, comiencen

[52] zurcir PRES zurzo, zurces, zurce, zurcimos, zurcís, zurcen; **PRES SUBJ** zurza, zurzas, zurza, zurzamos, zurzáis, zurzan; **IMPERAT** zurce, zurza, zurzamos, zurcid, zurzan

[53] proteger PRES protejo, proteges, protege, protegemos, protegéis, protegen; **PRES SUBJ** proteja, protejas, proteja, protejamos, protejáis, protejan; **IMPERAT** protege, proteja, protejamos, proteged, protejan

[54] discernir PRES discierno, disciernes, discierne, discernimos, discernís, disciernen; **PRES SUBJ** discierna, disciernas, discierna, discernamos, discernáis, disciernan; **IMPERAT** discierne, discierna, discernamos, discernid, disciernan

[55] erguir PRES irgo/yergo, irgues/yergues, irgue/yergue, erguimos, erguís, irguen/yerguen; **PRET** erguí, erguiste, irguió, erguimos, erguisteis, irguieron; **PRES SUBJ** irga/yerga, irgas/yergas, irga/yerga, irgamos/yergamos, irgáis/yergáis, irgan/yergan; **IMPERF SUBJ** irguiera/irguiese; **IMPERAT** irgue/yergue, irga/yerga, irgamos/yergamos, erguid, irgan/yergan

[56] reír PRES río, ríes, ríe, reímos, reís, ríen; **PRET** reí, reíste, rió, reímos, reísteis, rieron; **PRES SUBJ** ría, rías, ría, riamos, riáis, rían; **IMPERF SUBJ** riera/riese; **IMPERAT** ríe, ría, riamos, reíd, rían

[57] dirigir PRES dirijo, diriges, dirige, dirigimos, dirigís, dirigen; **PRES SUBJ** dirija, dirijas, dirija, dirijamos, dirijáis, dirijan; **IMPERAT** dirige, dirija, dirijamos, dirigid, dirijan

[58] regir PRES rijo, riges, rige, regimos, regís, rigen; **PRES SUBJ** rija, rijas, rija, rijamos, rijáis, rijan; **IMPERAT** rige, rija, rijamos, regid, rijan

[59] distinguir PRES distingo, distingues, distingue, distinguimos, distinguís, distinguen; PRES SUBJ distinga, distingas, distinga, distingamos, distingáis, distingan; IMPERAT distingue, distinga, distingamos, distinguid, distingan

[60] nacer PRES nazco, naces, nace, nacemos, nacéis, nacen; PRES SUBJ nazca, nazcas, nazca, nazcamos, nazcáis, nazcan; IMPERAT nace, nazca, nazcamos, naced, nazcan

[61] yacer PRES yazco/yazgo/yago, yaces, yace, yacemos, yacéis, yacen; PRES SUBJ yazca/yazga/yaga; IMPERAT yace/yaz, yazca/yazga/yaga, yazcamos/yazgamos/yagamos, yaced, yazcan/yazgan/yagan

[62] argüir PRES arguyo, arguyes, arguye, argüimos, argüís, arguyen; PRET argüí, argüiste, arguyó, argüimos, argüisteis, arguyeron; PRES SUBJ arguya, arguyas, arguya, arguyamos, arguyáis, arguyan; IMPERF SUBJ arguyera/arguyese; IMPERAT arguye, arguya, arguyamos, argüid, arguyan

[63] avergonzar PRES avergüenzo, avergüenzas, avergüenza, avergonzamos, avergonzáis, avergüenzan; PRET avergoncé, avergonzaste, avergonzó, avergonzamos, avergonzasteis, avergonzaron; PRES SUBJ avergüence, avergüences, avergüence, avergoncemos, avergoncéis, avergüencen; IMPERAT avergüenza, avergüence, avergoncemos, avergonzad, avergüencen

[64] trocar PRES trueco, truecas, trueca, trocamos, trocáis, truecan; PRET troqué, trocaste, trocó, trocamos, trocasteis, trocaron; PRES SUBJ trueque, trueques, trueque, troquemos, troquéis, truequen; IMPERAT trueca, trueque, troquemos, trocad, truequen

[65] oler PRES huelo, hueles, huele, olemos, oléis, huelen; PRES SUBJ huela, huelas, huela, olamos, oláis, huelan; IMPERAT huele, huela, olamos, oled, huelan

Verbos irregulares ingleses

INFINITIVE	PAST SIMPLE	PAST PARTICIPLE
arise	arose	arisen
awake	awoke	awoken
be	was, were	been
bear	bore	borne
beat	beat	beaten
become	became	become
begin	began	begun
bend	bent	bent
bet	bet, betted	bet, betted
bid *(offer)*	bid	bid
bind	bound	bound
bite	bit	bitten
bleed	bled	bled
blow	blew	blown
break	broke	broken
breed	bred	bred
bring	brought	brought
broadcast	broadcast	broadcast
build	built	built
burn	burnt, burned	burnt, burned
burst	burst	burst
buy	bought	bought
cast	cast	cast
catch	caught	caught
choose	chose	chosen
cling	clung	clung
come	came	come
cost	cost	cost
creep	crept	crept
cut	cut	cut
deal	dealt	dealt
dig	dug	dug
dive	dove	dived
do	did	done
draw	drew	drawn
dream	dreamt, dreamed	dreamt, dreamed
drink	drank	drunk
drive	drove	driven
eat	ate	eaten
fall	fell	fallen
feed	fed	fed
feel	felt	felt
fight	fought	fought
find	found	found
flee	fled	fled

INFINITIVE	PAST SIMPLE	PAST PARTICIPLE
fling	flung	flung
fly	flew	flown
forbid	forbad(e)	forbidden
forecast	forecast	forecast
foresee	foresaw	foreseen
forget	forgot	forgotten
forgive	forgave	forgiven
freeze	froze	frozen
get	got	gotten
give	gave	given
go	went	gone
grind	ground	ground
grow	grew	grown
hang	hung, hanged	hung, hanged
have	had	had
hear	heard	heard
hide	hid	hidden
hit	hit	hit
hold	held	held
hurt	hurt	hurt
keep	kept	kept
kneel	knelt, kneeled	knelt, kneeled
know	knew	known
lay	laid	laid
lead	led	led
lean	leant, leaned	leant, leaned
leap	leapt, leaped	leapt, leaped
learn	learnt, learned	learnt, learned
leave	left	left
lend	lent	lent
let	let	let
lie	lay	lain
light	lit, lighted	lit, lighted
lose	lost	lost
make	made	made
mean	meant	meant
meet	met	met
mislay	mislaid	mislaid
mislead	misled	misled
mistake	mistook	mistaken
misunderstand	misunderstood	misunderstood
mow	mowed	mown, mowed
outdo	outdid	outdone
overcome	overcame	overcome
overdo	overdid	overdone
overtake	overtook	overtaken
pay	paid	paid
put	put	put
quit	quit	quit
read	read	read
redo	redid	redone

INFINITIVE	PAST SIMPLE	PAST PARTICIPLE
rend	rent	rent
rewind	rewound	rewound
ride	rode	ridden
ring	rang	rung
rise	rose	risen
run	ran	run
saw	sawed	sawn, sawed
say	said	said
see	saw	seen
seek	sought	sought
sell	sold	sold
send	sent	sent
set	set	set
sew	sewed	sewn, sewed
shake	shook	shaken
shear	sheared	shorn, sheared
shed	shed	shed
shine	shone	shone
shoot	shot	shot
show	showed	shown, showed
shrink	shrank, shrunk	shrunk
shut	shut	shut
sing	sang	sung
sink	sank	sunk
sit	sat	sat
sleep	slept	slept
slide	slid	slid
sling	slung	slung
slink	slunk	slunk
slit	slit	slit
smell	smelt, smelled	smelt, smelled
sneak	sneaked, snuck	sneaked, snuck
sow	sowed	sown, sowed
speak	spoke	spoken
speed	sped, speeded	sped, speeded
spell	spelt, spelled	spelt, spelled
spend	spent	spent
spill	spilt, spilled	spilt, spilled
spin	spun	spun
spit	spat	spat
split	split	split
spoil	spoilt, spoiled	spoilt, spoiled
spread	spread	spread
spring	sprang	sprung
stand	stood	stood
steal	stole	stolen
stick	stuck	stuck
sting	stung	stung
stink	stank	stunk
stride	strode	stridden
strike	struck	struck, stricken

INFINITIVE	PAST SIMPLE	PAST PARTICIPLE
string	strung	strung
strive	strove	striven
swear	swore	sworn
sweep	swept	swept
swell	swelled	swollen, swelled
swim	swam	swum
swing	swung	swung
take	took	taken
teach	taught	taught
tear	tore	torn
tell	told	told
think	thought	thought
thrive	thrived, throve	thrived
throw	threw	thrown
thrust	thrust	thrust
tread	trod	trodden
undergo	underwent	undergone
understand	understood	understood
undertake	undertook	undertaken
undo	undid	undone
upset	upset	upset
wake	woke	woken
wear	wore	worn
weave	wove	woven
weep	wept	wept
wet	wet, wetted	wet, wetted
win	won	won
wind	wound	wound
withdraw	withdrew	withdrawn
withhold	withheld	withheld
wring	wrung	wrung
write	wrote	written

Countries and Regions
Países y regiones

Africa *(African)*	África *f (africano, -a)*
Albania *(Albanian)*	Albania *f (albanés, -esa)*
Algeria *(Algerian)*	Argelia *f (argelino, -a)*
America *(American)*	América *f (americano, -a)*
Antarctica, the Antarctic *(Antarctic)*	la Antártida *f*, el Antártico *m (antártico, -a)*
Arabia *(Arab, Arabic)*	Arabia *f (árabe)*
the Arctic *(Arctic)*	el Ártico *m (ártico, -a)*
Argentina *(Argentinian, Argentine)*	Argentina *f (argentino, -a)*
Asia *(Asian)*	Asia *f (asiático, -a)*
Australia *(Australian)*	Australia *f (australiano, -a)*
Austria *(Austrian)*	Austria *f (austriaco, -a)*
Belgium *(Belgian)*	Bélgica *f (belga)*
Bolivia *(Bolivian)*	Bolivia *f (boliviano, -a)*
Brazil *(Brazilian)*	Brasil *m (brasileño, -a, brasilero, -a)*
Bulgaria *(Bulgarian)*	Bulgaria *f (búlgaro, -a)*
Burma *(Burmese)*	Birmania *f (birmano, -a)*
Canada *(Canadian)*	Canadá *m (canadiense)*
Central America *(Central American)*	Centroamérica *f (centroamericano, -a)*
Chile *(Chilean)*	Chile *m (chileno, -a)*
China *(Chinese)*	China *f (chino, -a)*
Colombia *(Colombian)*	Colombia *f (colombiano, -a)*
Costa Rica *(Costa Rican)*	Costa Rica *f (costarricense, costarriqueño, -a)*
Crete *(Cretan)*	Creta *f (cretense)*
Cuba *(Cuban)*	Cuba *f (cubano, -a)*
Cyprus *(Cypriot)*	Chipre *m (chipriota)*
Czech Republic *(Czech)*	República Checa *f (checo, -a)*
Denmark *(Danish)*	Dinamarca *f (danés, -esa)*
Dominican Republic *(Dominican)*	República Dominicana *f (dominicano, -a)*
Ecuador *(Ecuadorian)*	Ecuador *m (ecuatoriano, -a)*
Egypt *(Egyptian)*	Egipto *m (egipcio, -a)*
El Salvador *(Salvadoran, Salvadorian)*	El Salvador *m (salvadoreño, -a)*
England *(English)*	Inglaterra *f (inglés, -esa)*
Ethiopia *(Ethiopian)*	Etiopía *f (etíope)*
Europe *(European)*	Europa *f (europeo, -a)*
Finland *(Finnish)*	Finlandia *f (finlandés, -a)*
France *(French)*	Francia *f (francés, -esa)*
Germany *(German)*	Alemania *f (alemán, -ana)*
Gibraltar *(Gibraltarian)*	Gibraltar *m (gibraltareño, -a)*
Great Britain *(British)*	Gran Bretaña *f (británico, -a)*
Greece *(Greek)*	Grecia *f (griego, -a)*
Holland *(Dutch)*	Holanda *f (holandés, -esa)*

Honduras *(Honduran)*	Honduras *f (hondureño, -a)*
Hungary *(Hungarian)*	Hungría *f (húngaro, -a)*
Iceland *(Icelandic)*	Islandia *f (islandés, -esa)*
India *(Indian)*	India *f (indio, -a)*
Indonesia *(Indonesian)*	Indonesia *f (indonesio, -a)*
Iran *(Iranian)*	Irán *m (iraní)*
Iraq *(Iraqi)*	Irak, Iraq *m (iraquí)*
Ireland *(Irish)*	Irlanda *f (irlandés, -esa)*
Israel *(Israeli)*	Israel *m (israelí)*
Italy *(Italian)*	Italia *f (italiano, -a)*
Jamaica *(Jamaican)*	Jamaica *f (jamaicano, -a)*
Japan *(Japanese)*	Japón *m (japonés, -esa)*
Kenya *(Kenyan)*	Kenia *f (keniano, -a)*
Korea *(Korean)*	Corea *f (coreano, -a)*
Latin America *(Latin American)*	Latinoamérica *f (latinoamericano, -a);* Hispanoamérica *f (hispanoamericano, -a);* Iberoamérica *f (iberoamericano, -a)*
Latvia *(Latvian)*	Letonia *f (letón, -ona)*
the Lebanon *(Lebanese)*	Líbano *m (libanés, -esa)*
Libya *(Libyan)*	Libia *f (libio, -a)*
Lithuania *(Lithuanian)*	Lituania *f (lituano, -a)*
Luxembourg *(Luxembourger)*	Luxemburgo *m (luxemburgués)*
Malaysia *(Malay)*	Malasia *f (malasio, -a)*
Mexico *(Mexican)*	México, Méjico *m (mexicano, -a, mejicano, -a)*
Mongolia *(Mongolian)*	Mongolia *f (mongol, -a)*
Morocco *(Moroccan)*	Marruecos *m (marroquí)*
the Netherlands, the Low Countries *(Dutch)*	Países Bajos *mpl (neerlandés, -esa)*
Nicaragua *(Nicaraguan)*	Nicaragua *f (nicaragüense, nicaragüeño, -a)*
North Africa *(North African)*	África *f* del Norte *(norteafricano, -a)*
North America *(North American)*	Norteamérica *f (norteamericano, -a)*
Northern Ireland *(Northern Irish)*	Irlanda del Norte *f*
Norway *(Norwegian)*	Noruega *f (noruego, -a)*
Pakistan *(Pakistani)*	Pakistán, Paquistán *m (paquistaní)*
Palestine *(Palestinian)*	Palestina *f (palestino, -a)*
Panama *(Panamanian)*	Panamá *m (panameño, -a)*
Paraguay *(Paraguayan)*	Paraguay *m (paraguayo, -a)*
Peru *(Peruvian)*	Perú *m (peruano, -a)*
(the) Philippines *(Philippine, Filipino)*	Filipinas *fpl (filipino, -a)*
Poland *(Polish)*	Polonia *f (polaco, -a)*
Portugal *(Portuguese)*	Portugal *m (portugués, -esa)*
Puerto Rico *(Puerto Rican)*	Puerto Rico *m (portorriqueño, -a, puertorriqueño, -a)*
Romania *(Romanian)*	Rumanía *f (rumano, -a)*
Russia *(Russian)*	Rusia *f (ruso, -a)*
Saudi Arabia *(Saudi Arabian, Saudi)*	Arabia Saudí *f (saudí)*
Scandinavia *(Scandinavian)*	Escandinavia *f (escandinavo, -a)*
Scotland *(Scottish, Scots)*	Escocia *f (escocés, -esa)*

Slovakia *(Slovak)*	Eslovaquia f *(eslovaco, -a)*
South Africa *(South African)*	Sudáfrica f *(sudafricano, -a)*
South America *(South American)*	Sudamérica f *(sudamericano, -a)*; Suramérica f *(suramericano, -a)*
Spain *(Spanish)*	España f *(español, -a)*
Sweden *(Swedish)*	Suecia f *(sueco, -a)*
Switzerland *(Swiss)*	Suiza f *(suizo, -a)*
Syria *(Syrian)*	Siria f *(sirio, -a)*
Thailand *(Thai)*	Tailandia f *(tailandés, -esa)*
Tunisia *(Tunisian)*	Túnez m *(tunecino, -a)*
Turkey *(Turkish)*	Turquía f *(turco, -a)*
Ukraine *(Ukrainian)*	Ucrania f *(ucraniano, -a)*
the United States *(United States, American)*	Estados Unidos mpl *(estadounidense)*
Uruguay *(Uruguayan)*	Uruguay m *(uruguayo, -a)*
Venezuela *(Venezuelan)*	Venezuela f *(venezolano, -a)*
Vietnam *(Vietnamese)*	Vietnam m *(vietnamita)*
Wales *(Welsh)*	Gales m (el país m de) *(galés, -esa)*
the West Indies *(West Indian)*	Antillas f *(antillano, -a)*

Numbers
Los números

zero	0	cero
one	1	uno/una
two	2	dos
three	3	tres
four	4	cuatro
five	5	cinco
six	6	seis
seven	7	siete
eight	8	ocho
nine	9	nueve
ten	10	diez
eleven	11	once
twelve	12	doce
thirteen	13	trece
fourteen	14	catorce
fifteen	15	quince
sixteen	16	dieciséis
seventeen	17	diecisiete
eighteen	18	dieciocho
nineteen	19	diecinueve
twenty	20	veinte
twenty-one	21	veintiuno
twenty-two	22	veintidós
thirty	30	treinta
thirty-one	31	treinta y uno
thirty-two	32	treinta y dos
forty	40	cuarenta
fifty	50	cincuenta
sixty	60	sesenta
seventy	70	setenta
eighty	80	ochenta
ninety	90	noventa
a *or* one hundred	100	cien
a *or* one hundred and one	101	ciento uno
a *or* one hundred and ten	110	ciento diez
two hundred	200	doscientos/doscientas
five hundred	500	quinientos/quinientas
seven hundred	700	setecientos/setecientas
a *or* one thousand	1,000/1.000	mil
two hundred thousand	200,000/200.000	doscientos/ doscientas mil
a *or* one million	1,000,000/1.000.000	un millón

English – Spanish
Inglés – Español

A, a [eɪ] N (**a**) *(the letter)* A, a *f* (**b**) *Mus* **A** la *m* (**c**) *Br* **A road** ≃ carretera *f* nacional

a [eɪ, *unstressed* ə] INDEF ART *(before vowel or silent h* **an**) (**a**) *(in general)* un, una; **a woman** una mujer; **a man/a woman** un hombre/una mujer; **he has a big nose** tiene la nariz grande (**b**) *(omitted in Spanish)* **half a litre/an hour** medio litro/ media hora; **a hundred/thousand people** cien/mil personas; **let's have a drink** vamos a beber algo; **he's a teacher** es profesor; **what a pity** qué pena (**c**) *(each)* **60 pence a kilo** 60 peniques el kilo; **to eat grapes two at a time** comer las uvas de dos en dos; **three times a week** tres veces a la semana (**d**) *(a certain)* **a Mr Rees phoned** llamó un tal Sr. Rees

AA [eɪ'eɪ] N (**a**) *(abbr* **Alcoholics Anonymous**) AA, alcohólicos *mpl* anónimos (**b**) *(abbr* **Automobile Association**) = asociación automovilística británica, *Esp* ≃ RACE *m*, *Arg* ≃ ACA *m*

AAA [eɪeɪ'eɪ] N (**a**) *Br* (*abbr* **Amateur Athletic Association**) = federación británica de atletismo aficionado (**b**) *US* (*abbr* **American Automobile Association**) = asociación automovilística estadounidense, *Esp* ≃ RACE *m*, *Arg* ≃ ACA *m*

aback [ə'bæk] ADV **to be taken a.** quedarse de una pieza (**by** por)

abandon [ə'bændən] **1** N desenfreno *m*; **with reckless a.** desenfrenadamente
2 VT *(child)* abandonar; *(job)* dejar; *(project)* renunciar a

abase [ə'beɪs] VT **to a. oneself** humillarse

abashed [ə'bæʃt] ADJ avergonzado(a), abochornado(a), *Am salvo RP* apenado(a)

abate [ə'beɪt] VI *(anger)* apaciguarse; *(storm)* amainar

abattoir ['æbətwɑː(r)] N matadero *m*

abbey ['æbɪ] N abadía *f*

abbot ['æbət] N abad *m*

abbreviate [ə'briːvɪeɪt] VT abreviar

abbreviation [əbriːvɪ'eɪʃən] N abreviatura *f*

abdicate ['æbdɪkeɪt] VT & VI abdicar

abdication [æbdɪ'keɪʃən] N abdicación *f*

abdomen ['æbdəmən] N abdomen *m*

abduct [æb'dʌkt] VT raptar, secuestrar

abduction [əb'dʌkʃən] N rapto *m*, secuestro *m*

aberration [æbə'reɪʃən] N aberración *f*

abet [ə'bet] VT **to aid and a. sb** ser cómplice de algn

abeyance [ə'beɪəns] N **to be in a.** estar en desuso

abhor [əb'hɔː(r)] VT aborrecer

abhorrent [əb'hɒrənt] ADJ aborrecible

abide [ə'baɪd] VT aguantar; **I can't a. it** no lo aguanto
▶ **abide by** VT INSEP *(promise)* cumplir con; *(rules)* atenerse a

ability [ə'bɪlɪtɪ] N *(capability)* capacidad *f*, aptitud *f*; *(talent)* talento *m*

abject ['æbdʒekt] ADJ *(state)* miserable; *(apology)* rastrero(a)

ablaze [ə'bleɪz] ADJ & ADV en llamas, ardiendo

able ['eɪbəl] ADJ *(capable)* capaz; **will you be a. to come on Tuesday?** ¿podrás venir el martes?

able-bodied [eɪbəl'bɒdɪd] ADJ sano(a); **a. seaman** marinero *m* de primera

abnormal [æb'nɔːməl] ADJ anormal

abnormally [æb'nɔːməlɪ] ADV anormalmente; *(large, quiet)* excepcionalmente

aboard [ə'bɔːd] **1** ADV a bordo; **to go a.** *(ship)* embarcarse; *(train)* subir
2 PREP a bordo de

abode [ə'bəʊd] N *Jur* **of no fixed a.** sin domicilio fijo

abolish [ə'bɒlɪʃ] VT abolir

abolition [æbə'lɪʃən] N abolición *f*

abominable [ə'bɒmɪnəbəl] ADJ deplorable, abominable; **her handwriting is a.** tiene una letra malísima *or* lamentable

aborigine [æbə'rɪdʒɪnɪ] N aborigen *mf* australiano(a)

abort [ə'bɔːt] **1** VT *Med* hacer abortar; *Fig (plan etc)* archivar
2 VI *Med* abortar

abortion [ə'bɔːʃən] N *Med* aborto *m*; **a. law** ley *f* del aborto; **to have an a.** abortar

abortive [ə'bɔːtɪv] ADJ *(plan)* fracasado(a); *(attempt)* frustrado(a)

abound [ə'baʊnd] VI **to a. in** *or* **with** abundar en

about [ə'baʊt] ADV & PREP (**a**) *(concerning)* acerca de, sobre; **a programme a. Paris** un programa sobre París; **to be worried a. sth** estar preocupado(a) por algo; **to speak a. sth** hablar de algo; **what's it all a.?** *(what's happening?)* ¿qué pasa?; *(story etc)* ¿de qué se trata?; *Fam* **how a. a game of tennis?** ¿qué te parece un partido de tenis?
(**b**) *(around)* por todas partes; **don't leave things lying a.** no dejes las cosas por medio;

there's nobody a. no hay nadie; **to look a.** mirar alrededor; **to rush a.** correr de un lado para otro; **we went for a walk a. the town** dimos una vuelta por el pueblo **(c)** *(approximately)* más o menos; **it's a. three o'clock** son más o menos las tres; **it's a. time you got up** ya es hora de que te levantes; **it's just a. finished** está casi terminado; **she's a. forty** tiene unos cuarenta años **(d) it's a. to start** está a punto de empezar; **not to be a. to do sth** no estar dispuesto(a) a hacer algo

about-face [əbaʊtˈfeɪs], *Br* **about-turn** [əbaʊtˈtɜːn] N media vuelta *f*; **to do an a.** dar media vuelta; *Fig* cambiar de idea por completo

above [əˈbʌv] ADV & PREP **(a)** *(higher than)* encima de, sobre, arriba; **100 m a. sea level** 100 m sobre el nivel del mar; **it's a. the door** está encima de la puerta; **the flat a.** el piso de arriba **(b)** *(greater than)* superior (a); **amounts a. £10** cantidades superiores a las 10 libras; *Fig* **a policy imposed from a.** una política impuesta desde arriba **(c) a. all** sobre todo; **he's not a. stealing** es capaz incluso de robar **(d)** *(in book etc)* más arriba

above-board [əˈbʌvˈbɔːd] ADJ *(scheme)* legítimo(a)

above-mentioned [əˈbʌvmenʃənd] ADJ susodicho(a)

abrasive [əˈbreɪsɪv] **1** ADJ *(substance)* abrasivo(a); *Fig (voice, wit etc)* cáustico(a) **2** N abrasivo *m*

abreast [əˈbrest] ADV **to walk three a.** ir de tres en fondo; *Fig* **to keep a. of things** mantenerse al día

abridged [əˈbrɪdʒd] ADJ *(book)* abreviado(a)

abroad [əˈbrɔːd] ADV **to be a.** estar en el extranjero; **to go a.** irse al extranjero

abrupt [əˈbrʌpt] ADJ *(manner)* brusco(a); *(tone)* áspero(a); *(change)* súbito(a)

abruptly [əˈbrʌptlɪ] ADV *(act)* bruscamente; *(speak)* con aspereza; *(change)* repentinamente

abscess [ˈæbses] N absceso *m*; *(on gum)* flemón *m*

abscond [əbˈskɒnd] VI huir

absence [ˈæbsəns] N *(of person)* ausencia *f*; *(of thing)* falta *f*

absent [ˈæbsənt] ADJ ausente; *Fig* **an a. look** una mirada distraída

absentee [æbsənˈtiː] N ausente *mf*; **a. landlord** (propietario(a) *m,f*) ausentista *mf or Esp* absentista *mf*

absenteeism [æbsənˈtiːɪzəm] N ausentismo *m*, *Esp* absentismo *m*

absently [ˈæbsəntlɪ] ADV distraídamente

absent-minded [æbsəntˈmaɪndɪd] ADJ distraído(a)

absolute [ˈæbsəluːt] ADJ *(complete, total)* absoluto(a); *(for emphasis)* absoluto(a), auténti-

co(a); **it's an a. disgrace** es una auténtica vergüenza

absolutely [æbsəˈluːtlɪ] **1** ADV *(completely)* completamente; **a. wrong** totalmente equivocado(a); **a. not** en absoluto; **you're a. right** tienes toda la razón **2** INTERJ **a.!** ¡desde luego!

absolve [əbˈzɒlv] VT absolver **(from** de)

absorb [əbˈzɔːb] VT *(liquid)* absorber; *(sound, blow)* amortiguar; *Fig* **to be absorbed in sth** estar absorto(a) en algo

absorbing [əbˈzɔːbɪŋ] ADJ *(book, work)* absorbente

abstain [əbˈsteɪn] VI *(not vote)* abstenerse **(from** de); *(not drink alcohol)* no beber alcohol, *Am* no tomar

abstemious [əbˈstiːmɪəs] ADJ abstemio(a)

abstention [əbˈstenʃən] N abstención *f*

abstinence [ˈæbstɪnəns] N abstinencia *f*

abstract [ˈæbstrækt] **1** ADJ abstracto(a) **2** N *(of thesis etc)* resumen *m*

abstruse [əbˈstruːs] ADJ abstruso(a)

absurd [əbˈsɜːd] ADJ absurdo(a)

abundance [əˈbʌndəns] N abundancia *f*

abundant [əˈbʌndənt] ADJ abundante, rico(a) **(in** en)

abuse 1 N [əˈbjuːs] **(a)** *(ill-treatment)* malos tratos; *(misuse)* abuso *m* **(b)** *(insults)* injurias *fpl* **2** VT [əˈbjuːz] **(a)** *(ill-treat)* maltratar; *(misuse)* abusar de **(b)** *(insult)* injuriar

abusive [əˈbjuːsɪv] ADJ *(insulting)* insultante

abysmal [əˈbɪzməl] ADJ *(conditions)* extremo(a); *Fam (very bad)* fatal, pésimo(a)

abyss [əˈbɪs] N abismo *m*; *Fig* extremo *m*

AC [eɪˈsiː] *(abbr* **alternating current)** CA

academic [ækəˈdemɪk] **1** ADJ *(of school, university)* académico(a); *(intellectual)* académico(a), intelectual; **a. year** año *m* escolar **2** N *(university teacher)* profesor(a) *m,f* de universidad

academy [əˈkædəmɪ] N *(society)* academia *f*; *Educ* instituto *m* de enseñanza media; **a. of music** conservatorio *m*

accede [ækˈsiːd] VI acceder **(to** a)

accelerate [ækˈseləreɪt] **1** VT *(engine)* acelerar; *(step)* aligerar **2** VI *(car, engine)* acelerar

acceleration [ækseləˈreɪʃən] N aceleración *f*

accelerator [ækˈseləreɪtə(r)] N acelerador *m*

accent [ˈæksənt] N acento *m*

accentuate [ækˈsentʃʊeɪt] VT subrayar

accept [əkˈsept] **1** VT *(in general)* aceptar; *(reasons)* aceptar, admitir; *(blame)* admitir, reconocer; **do you a. that ...?** ¿estás de acuerdo en que ...? **2** VI aceptar

acceptable [əkˈseptəbəl] ADJ *(satisfactory)* aceptable; *(tolerable)* admisible

acceptance [ək'septəns] N *(act of accepting)* aceptación f; *(good reception)* aprobación f

access ['ækses] N acceso m; *Comput* a. **provider** proveedor m de acceso (a Internet); a. **road** carretera f de acceso; **to have a. to sth** tener libre acceso a algo

accessible [ək'sesəbəl] ADJ accesible

accession [ək'seʃən] N subida f (al trono)

accessory [ək'sesərɪ] N (a) *Jur* cómplice mf (b) **accessories** accesorios mpl; *(for outfit)* complementos mpl

accident ['æksɪdənt] N accidente m; *(coincidence)* casualidad f; **it was an a. on my part** lo hice sin querer; **car a.** accidente m de carretera; **by a.** por casualidad

accidental [æksɪ'dentəl] ADJ accidental, casual

accidentally [æksɪ'dentəlɪ] ADV *(by chance)* por casualidad; **he did it a.** lo hizo sin querer

accident-prone ['æksɪdəntprəʊn] ADJ propenso(a) a los accidentes

acclaim [ə'kleɪm] **1** N aclamación f
  2 VT aclamar

acclimatization [əklaɪmətaɪ'zeɪʃən], *US* **acclimation** [æklɪ'meɪʃən] N aclimatación f

acclimatize [ə'klaɪmətaɪz], *US* **acclimate** ['æklɪmeɪt] VT aclimatar

acclimatized [ə'klaɪmətaɪzd] ADJ aclimatado(a); **to become a.** aclimatarse

accolade ['ækəleɪd] N elogio m

accommodate [ə'kɒmədeɪt] VT (a) *(guests)* alojar (b) **to a. sb's wishes** complacer a algn

accommodating [ə'kɒmədeɪtɪŋ] ADJ *(obliging)* complaciente; *(understanding)* comprensivo(a)

accommodation [əkɒmə'deɪʃən] N *(US also* **accommodations***) (lodgings)* alojamiento m

accompany [ə'kʌmpənɪ] VT acompañar

accomplice [ə'kʌmplɪs] N cómplice mf

accomplish [ə'kʌmplɪʃ] VT *(aim)* conseguir; *(task, mission)* llevar a cabo

accomplished [ə'kʌmplɪʃt] ADJ dotado(a), experto(a)

accomplishment [ə'kʌmplɪʃmənt] N (a) *(of task)* realización f; *(of duty)* cumplimiento m (b) **accomplishments** *(talents)* dotes fpl

accord [ə'kɔːd] **1** N *(agreement)* acuerdo m; **of her/his own a.** espontáneamente
  2 VT *(honour etc)* conceder

accordance [ə'kɔːdəns] N **in a. with** de acuerdo con

according [ə'kɔːdɪŋ] PREP **a. to** según; **everything went a. to plan** todo salió conforme a los planes

accordingly [ə'kɔːdɪŋlɪ] ADV (a) **to act a.** *(appropriately)* obrar según y conforme (b) *(therefore)* así pues

accordion [ə'kɔːdɪən] N acordeón m

account [ə'kaʊnt] N (a) *(report)* informe m; **by all accounts** al decir de todos (b) **I was fearful on her a.** sufría por ella; **it's of no a.**

no tiene importancia; **on a. of** a causa de; **on no a.** bajo ningún concepto; **to take a. of, to take into a.** tener en cuenta (c) *Com* cuenta f; **to keep the accounts** llevar las cuentas; **accounts department** servicio m de contabilidad; **to open/close an a.** abrir/cancelar una cuenta; **current a.** cuenta corriente; **a. number** número m de cuenta

▸ **account for** VT INSEP *(explain)* explicar

accountable [ə'kaʊntəbəl] ADJ **to be a. to sb for sth** ser responsable ante algn de algo

accountancy [ə'kaʊntənsɪ] N contabilidad f

accountant [ə'kaʊntənt] N *Esp* contable mf, *Am* contador(a) m,f

accounting [ə'kaʊntɪŋ] N contabilidad f

accredited [ə'kredɪtɪd] ADJ acreditado(a)

accrue [ə'kruː] VI *(interest)* acumularse

accumulate [ə'kjuːmjʊleɪt] **1** VT acumular
  2 VI acumularse

accuracy ['ækjʊrəsɪ] N *(of number etc)* exactitud f; *(of shot, criticism)* certeza f

accurate ['ækjʊrət] ADJ *(number)* exacto(a); *(shot, criticism)* certero(a); *(answer)* correcto(a); *(observation)* acertado(a); *(instrument)* de precisión; *(translation)* fiel

accusation [ækjʊ'zeɪʃən] N acusación f

accuse [ə'kjuːz] VT acusar

accused [ə'kjuːzd] N **the a.** el/la acusado(a)

accustom [ə'kʌstəm] VT acostumbrar; **to be accustomed to doing sth** estar acostumbrado(a) a hacer algo

ace [eɪs] N (a) *Cards & Fig* as m (b) *(in tennis)* ace m

acetate ['æsɪteɪt] N acetato m

acetone ['æsɪtəʊn] N acetona f

ache [eɪk] **1** N dolor m; **aches and pains** achaques mpl
  2 VI doler; **my back aches** me duele la espalda

achieve [ə'tʃiːv] VT *(attain)* conseguir, alcanzar; *(accomplish)* llevar a cabo, realizar

achievement [ə'tʃiːvmənt] N *(attainment)* logro m; *(completion)* realización f; *(feat)* hazaña f

acid ['æsɪd] **1** ADJ *(chemical, taste)* ácido(a); *(remark)* sarcástico(a); **a. rain** lluvia ácida; *Fig* **a. test** prueba f de fuego
  2 N ácido m

acknowledge [ək'nɒlɪdʒ] VT (a) *(recognize)* reconocer; *(claim, defeat)* admitir; *(present)* agradecer; *(letter)* acusar recibo de (b) *(greet)* saludar

acknowledgement [ək'nɒlɪdʒmənt] N (a) *(recognition)* reconocimiento m; *(of letter)* acuse m de recibo (b) **acknowledgements** *(in preface)* menciones fpl

acne ['æknɪ] N acné m

acorn ['eɪkɔːn] N bellota f

acoustic [ə'kuːstɪk] **1** ADJ acústico(a)
  2 NPL **acoustics** acústica f

acquaint [ə'kweɪnt] VT **to a. sb with the facts** informar a algn de los detalles; **to be**

acquainted with the procedure estar al corriente de como se procede; **to be acquainted with sb** conocer a algn

acquaintance [ə'kweɪntəns] N (**a**) *(familiarity)* *(with person)* relación *f*; *(with facts)* conocimiento *m*; **to make sb's a.** conocer a algn (**b**) *(person)* conocido(a) *m,f*

acquiesce [ækwɪ'es] VI consentir (**in** en)

acquiescent [ækwɪ'esənt] ADJ conforme

acquire [ə'kwaɪə(r)] VT adquirir

acquisition [ækwɪ'zɪʃən] N adquisición *f*

acquisitive [ə'kwɪzɪtɪv] ADJ codicioso(a)

acquit [ə'kwɪt] VT (**a**) *Jur* **to a. sb of sth** absolver a algn de algo (**b**) **to a. oneself well** defenderse bien

acquittal [ə'kwɪtəl] N absolución *f*

acre ['eɪkə(r)] N acre *m* (= 4.047*m*²)

acrid ['ækrɪd] ADJ *(smell, taste)* acre

acrimonious [ækrɪ'məʊnɪəs] ADJ *(remark)* cáustico(a); *(dispute)* enconado(a)

acrobat ['ækrəbæt] N acróbata *mf*

acrobatic [ækrə'bætɪk] ADJ acrobático(a)

acronym ['ækrənɪm] N siglas *fpl*, acrónimo *m*

across [ə'krɒs] **1** ADV a través; **the river is 30 m a.** el río mide 30 m de ancho; **to go a.** atravesar; **to run a.** atravesar corriendo

2 PREP (**a**) *(from one side to the other of)* a través de; **to go a. the street** cruzar la calle (**b**) *(on the other side of)* al otro lado de; **they live a. the road** viven enfrente

acrylic [ə'krɪlɪk] ADJ acrílico(a)

act [ækt] **1** N (**a**) *(action)* acto *m*, acción *f*; **a. of God** caso *m* de fuerza mayor (**b**) *(law)* **a.** (*Br* **of parliament** *or US* **of Congress**) ley *f* (**c**) *Th* acto *m*; *(turn in show)* número *m*

2 VT *Th (part)* interpretar; *(character)* representar; *Fig* **to a. the fool** hacer el tonto

3 VI (**a**) *Th* hacer teatro; *Cin* hacer cine; *Fig (pretend)* fingir (**b**) *(behave)* comportarse (**c**) *(take action)* actuar, obrar; **to a. on sb's advice** seguir el consejo de algn (**d**) *(work)* funcionar; *(drug etc)* actuar; **to a. as a deterrent** servir de disuasivo (**e**) **to a. as director** hacer de director

▸ **act out** VT SEP exteriorizar

▸ **act up** VI *Fam (machine)* funcionar mal; *(child)* dar guerra

acting ['æktɪŋ] **1** ADJ interino(a)

2 N *(profession)* teatro *m*; **he's done some a.** ha hecho algo de teatro

action ['ækʃən] N (**a**) *(deed)* acción *f*; *Mil* acción de combate; **to be out of a.** *(person)* estar fuera de servicio; *(machine)* estar estropeado(a); **to take a.** tomar medidas (**b**) *Jur* demanda *f* (**c**) *Br* TV **a. replay** repetición *f*

activate ['æktɪveɪt] VT activar

active ['æktɪv] ADJ *(person, imagination, life)* activo(a); *(interest, dislike)* profundo(a); *Gram* **a. voice** voz activa; *Comput* **a. window** ventana activa

activist ['æktɪvɪst] N activista *mf*

activity [æk'tɪvɪtɪ] N *(of person)* actividad *f*; *(on street etc)* bullicio *m*

actor ['æktə(r)] N actor *m*

actress ['æktrɪs] N actriz *f*

actual ['æktʃʊəl] ADJ real, verdadero(a)

> Note that the Spanish word **actual** is a false friend and is never a translation for the English word **actual**. In Spanish **actual** means "current, up-to-date, topical".

actually ['æktʃʊəlɪ] ADV *(really)* en efecto, realmente; *(even)* incluso, hasta; *(in fact)* de hecho

> Note that the Spanish word **actualmente** is a false friend and is never a translation for the English word **actually**. In Spanish **actualmente** means "nowadays, at the moment".

actuary ['æktʃʊərɪ] N actuario(a) *m,f* de seguros

acumen ['ækjʊmən] N perspicacia *f*

acupuncture ['ækjʊpʌŋktʃə(r)] N acupuntura *f*

acute [ə'kjuːt] ADJ *(pain, mind, eyesight)* agudo(a); *(hearing, sense of smell)* muy fino(a); *(problem, shortage)* acuciante; *(embarrassment)* intenso(a); *(person)* perspicaz

AD [eɪ'diː] *(abbr* **Anno Domini)** d.J.C., d.C.

ad [æd] N *Fam* anuncio *m*

adamant ['ædəmənt] ADJ firme, inflexible

adapt [ə'dæpt] **1** VT adaptar (**to** a); **to a. oneself to sth** adaptarse a algo

2 VI adaptarse

adaptable [ə'dæptəbəl] ADJ *(instrument)* ajustable; **he's very a.** se amolda fácilmente a las circunstancias

adaptation [ædəp'teɪʃən] N adaptación *f*

adapter, adaptor [ə'dæptə(r)] N *Elec* ladrón *m*

add [æd] **1** VT *(numbers)* sumar; *(one thing to another)* añadir

2 VI *(count)* sumar

▸ **add to** VT INSEP aumentar

▸ **add up** **1** VT SEP sumar

2 VI *(numbers)* sumar; *Fig* **it doesn't a. up** no tiene sentido; **it doesn't a. up to much** no es gran cosa

added ['ædɪd] ADJ adicional

adder ['ædə(r)] N víbora *f*

addict ['ædɪkt] N adicto(a) *m,f*; *Fam* **television a.** teleadicto(a) *m,f*

addicted [ə'dɪktɪd] ADJ adicto(a); **to become a. to sth** enviciarse con algo

addiction [ə'dɪkʃən] N *(to gambling etc)* vicio *m*; *(to drugs)* adicción *f*

addictive [ə'dɪktɪv] ADJ que crea adicción

addition [ə'dɪʃən] N *Math* adición *f*; *(increase)* aumento *m*; **an a. to the family** un nuevo miembro de la familia; **in a. to** además de

additional [ə'dɪʃənəl] ADJ adicional

additive ['ædɪtɪv] N aditivo *m*

address [ə'dres] **1** N (**a**) *(on letter)* dirección *f*, señas *fpl* (**b**) *(speech)* discurso *m*
2 VT (**a**) *(letter)* dirigir (**to** a) (**b**) *(speak to)* dirigirse a; **to a. the floor** tomar la palabra (**c**) *(use form of address to)* tratar (**as** de)

adenoids ['ædɪnɔɪdz] NPL vegetaciones *fpl* (adenoideas)

adept 1 [ə'dept] ADJ experto(a) (**at** en)
2 ['ædept] N experto(a) *m,f*

> Note that the Spanish word **adepto** is a false friend and is never a translation for the English word **adept**. In Spanish **adepto** means "follower, supporter".

adequate ['ædɪkwɪt] ADJ *(enough)* suficiente; *(satisfactory)* adecuado(a)

adhere [əd'hɪə(r)] VI *(stick)* pegarse (**to** a)
▶ **adhere to** VT INSEP *(policy)* adherirse a; *(contract)* cumplir con

adherent [əd'hɪərənt] N partidario(a) *m,f*

adhesive [əd'hi:sɪv] **1** ADJ adhesivo(a), adherente; **a. tape** cinta adhesiva
2 N adhesivo *m*

ad hoc [æd'hɒk] ADJ *(remark)* improvisado(a); **an a. committee** un comité especial

ad infinitum [ædɪnfɪ'naɪtəm] ADV hasta el infinito

adjacent [ə'dʒeɪsənt] ADJ *(building)* contiguo(a); *(land)* colindante; **a. to** contiguo(a) a

adjective ['ædʒɪktɪv] N adjetivo *m*

adjoining [ə'dʒɔɪnɪŋ] ADJ *(building, room)* contiguo(a)

adjourn [ə'dʒɜːn] **1** VT *(postpone)* aplazar; *(court)* levantar
2 VI **the meeting adjourned** se levantó la sesión

adjudicate [ə'dʒuːdɪkeɪt] VT juzgar

adjudicator [ə'dʒuːdɪkeɪtə(r)] N juez(a) *m,f*

adjust [ə'dʒʌst] **1** VT *(machine etc)* ajustar; *Fig (methods)* variar
2 VI *(person)* adaptarse (**to** a)

adjustable [ə'dʒʌstəbəl] ADJ ajustable; **a.** *Br* **spanner** or *US* **wrench** llave *f* inglesa

adjustment [ə'dʒʌstmənt] N *(to machine etc)* ajuste *m*; *(by person)* adaptación *f* (**b**) *(change)* modificación *f*

ad lib [æd'lɪb] **1** ADV *(speak)* sin preparación; *(continue)* a voluntad
2 ADJ *(speech)* improvisado(a)
3 ad-lib VI improvisar

administer [əd'mɪnɪstə(r)] VT *(country)* gobernar; *(justice)* administrar

administration [ədmɪnɪ'streɪʃən] N *(management)* *(of justice)* administración *f*; *(governing body)* dirección *f*; *US (government)* gobierno *m*, administración *f*

administrative [əd'mɪnɪstrətɪv] ADJ administrativo(a)

administrator [əd'mɪnɪstreɪtə(r)] N administrador(a) *m,f*

admirable ['ædmərəbəl] ADJ admirable

admiral ['ædmərəl] N almirante *m*

admiration [ædmə'reɪʃən] N admiración *f*

admire [əd'maɪə(r)] VT admirar

admirer [əd'maɪərə(r)] N admirador(a) *m,f*

admissible [əd'mɪsəbəl] ADJ admisible

admission [əd'mɪʃən] N (**a**) *(to school etc)* ingreso *m*; *(price)* entrada *f* (**b**) *(of fact)* reconocimiento *m*; *(confession)* confesión *f*

admit [əd'mɪt] VT (**a**) *(person)* dejar entrar; **to be admitted to hospital** ser ingresado(a) en el hospital (**b**) *(acknowledge)* reconocer; *(crime, guilt)* confesar

admittance [əd'mɪtəns] N *(entry)* entrada *f*

admittedly [əd'mɪtɪdlɪ] ADV la verdad es que …

admonish [əd'mɒnɪʃ] VT amonestar

ad nauseam [æd'nɔːzɪæm] ADV hasta la saciedad

ado [ə'duː] N **without further a.** sin más

adolescence [ædə'lesəns] N adolescencia *f*

adolescent [ædə'lesənt] N adolescente *mf*

adopt [ə'dɒpt] VT *(child, approach, measure)* adoptar; *(candidate)* nombrar

adopted [ə'dɒptɪd] ADJ **a. child** hijo(a) adoptivo(a)

adoption [ə'dɒpʃən] N adopción *f*; **country of a.** país adoptivo

adorable [ə'dɔːrəbəl] ADJ encantador(a)

adore [ə'dɔː(r)] VT adorar

adorn [ə'dɔːn] VT adornar

adornment [ə'dɔːnmənt] N adorno *m*

adrenalin [ə'drenəlɪn] N adrenalina *f*

Adriatic [eɪdrɪ'ætɪk] ADJ **the A. (Sea)** el (mar) Adriático

adrift [ə'drɪft] ADV **to come a.** *(boat)* irse a la deriva; *(rope)* soltarse; *Fig* **to go a.** *(plans)* ir a la deriva

ADSL [eɪdiːes'el] N *Comput* (ABBR **asymmetrical digital subscriber line**) ADSL *m*

adult ['ædʌlt] **1** ADJ *(person)* adulto(a), mayor; *(film)* para adultos; *(education)* de adultos
2 N adulto(a) *m,f*

adulterate [ə'dʌltəreɪt] VT adulterar

adulterer [ə'dʌltərə(r)] N adúltero *m*

adulteress [ə'dʌltrɪs] N adúltera *f*

adultery [ə'dʌltərɪ] N adulterio *m*

advance [əd'vɑːns] **1** N (**a**) *(movement)* avance *m*; *Fig (progress)* progreso *m*; **to have sth ready in a.** tener algo preparado de antemano; **to make advances (to)** *(person)* insinuarse (a) (**b**) *(loan)* anticipo *m*
2 ADJ *(before time)* adelantado(a); *Cin & Th* **a. bookings** reservas *fpl* por adelantado
3 VT (**a**) *(troops)* avanzar; *(time, date)* adelantar (**b**) *(idea)* proponer; *(opinion)* adelantar
4 VI *(move forward)* avanzar, adelantarse; *(make progress)* hacer progresos; *(gain promotion)* ascender

advanced [əd'vɑːnst] ADJ *(developed)* avanzado(a); *(student)* adelantado(a); *(course)* superior; *Br* **A. level** = examen final o diploma en una asignatura de los estudios preuniversitarios

advancement [əd'vɑːnsmənt] N *(progress)* adelanto *m*; *(promotion)* ascenso *m*

advantage [əd'vɑːntɪdʒ] N ventaja *f*; *(in tennis)* **a. Velasco** ventaja para Velasco; **to take a.** of *(person)* aprovecharse de; *(opportunity)* aprovechar

advantageous [ædvən'teɪdʒəs] ADJ ventajoso(a)

advent ['ædvent] N *(arrival)* llegada *f*; *(of Christ)* advenimiento *m*; **A.** Adviento *m*

adventure [əd'ventʃə(r)] N aventura *f*; **a. sport** deporte *m* de aventura

adventurous [əd'ventʃərəs] ADJ aventurero(a)

adverb ['ædvɜːb] N adverbio *m*

adversary ['ædvəsərɪ] N adversario(a) *m,f*

adverse ['ædvɜːs] ADJ *(effect)* desfavorable; *(conditions)* adverso(a); *(winds)* contrario(a)

adversity [əd'vɜːsɪtɪ] N adversidad *f*

advert ['ædvɜːt] N *Br Fam* anuncio *m*

advertise [əd'vɜːtaɪz] **1** VT anunciar
  2 VI poner un anuncio (**for** sth/sb pidiendo algo/a alguien)

advertisement [əd'vɜːtɪsmənt] N anuncio *m*; **advertisements** publicidad *f*

advertiser ['ædvətaɪzə(r)] N anunciante *mf*

advertising ['ædvətaɪzɪŋ] **1** N publicidad *f*, propaganda *f*; *(in newspaper)* anuncios *mpl*
  2 ADJ publicitario(a); **a. agency** agencia *f* de publicidad

advice [əd'vaɪs] N consejos *mpl*; **a piece of a.** un consejo; **to take legal a. on a matter** consultar un caso con un abogado; **to take sb's a.** seguir los consejos de algn

advisable [əd'vaɪzəbəl] ADJ aconsejable

advise [əd'vaɪz] VT *(give advice to)* aconsejar; *(give professional guidance)* asesorar (**on** sobre); **I a. you to do it** te aconsejo que lo hagas

adviser [əd'vaɪzə(r)] N consejero(a) *m,f*; *(professional)* asesor(a) *m,f*

advisory [əd'vaɪzərɪ] ADJ asesor(a)

advocate **1** N ['ædvəkɪt] *Scot Jur* abogado(a) *m,f*, *(supporter)* defensor(a) *m,f*
  2 VT ['ædvəkeɪt] *(reform)* abogar por; *(plan)* apoyar

aerial ['eərɪəl] **1** ADJ aéreo(a)
  2 N antena *f*

aerobics [eə'rəʊbɪks] N SING aerobic *m*

aerodrome ['eərədrəʊm] N *Br* aeródromo *m*

aerodynamics [eərəʊdaɪ'næmɪks] N SING aerodinámica *f*

aeroplane ['eərəpleɪn] N *Br* avión *m*

aerosol ['eərəsɒl] N aerosol *m*

aerospace ['eərəʊspeɪs] ADJ aeroespacial

aesthetic [iːs'θetɪk] ADJ estético(a)

afar [ə'fɑː(r)] ADV lejos; **from a.** desde lejos

affair [ə'feə(r)] N *(matter)* asunto *m*; *(event)* acontecimiento *m*; **that's my a.** eso es asunto mío; **business affairs** negocios *mpl*; **foreign affairs** asuntos exteriores; **love a.** aventura amorosa

affect [ə'fekt] VT *(person, health)* afectar; *(prices, future)* influir en; *(touch emotionally)* conmover

affected [ə'fektɪd] ADJ (**a**) *(unnatural)* afectado(a) (**b**) *(influenced)* influido(a) (**c**) *(touched emotionally)* conmovido(a) (**d**) *(pretended)* fingido(a)

affection [ə'fekʃən] N afecto *m*, cariño *m*

affectionate [ə'fekʃənɪt] ADJ cariñoso(a)

affidavit [æfɪ'deɪvɪt] N declaración escrita y jurada

affiliated [ə'fɪlɪeɪtɪd] ADJ afiliado(a); **to be/become a.** (**to** *or* **with**) afiliarse (a)

affinity [ə'fɪnɪtɪ] N afinidad *f*; *(liking)* simpatía *f*

affirm [ə'fɜːm] VT afirmar, sostener

affirmation [æfə'meɪʃən] N afirmación *f*

affirmative [ə'fɜːmətɪv] **1** ADJ *(answer)* afirmativo(a); *US* **a. action** discriminación positiva
  2 N **he answered in the a.** contestó que sí

affix [ə'fɪks] VT *(stamp)* pegar

afflict [ə'flɪkt] VT afligir

affluence ['æfluəns] N opulencia *f*

affluent ['æfluənt] ADJ *(society)* opulento(a); *(person)* rico(a)

afford [ə'fɔːd] VT (**a**) *(be able to buy)* permitirse el lujo de; **I can't a. a new car** no puedo pagar un coche nuevo (**b**) *(be able to do)* permitirse; **you can't a. to miss the opportunity** no puedes perderte la ocasión

affordable [ə'fɔːdəbəl] ADJ *(price, purchase)* asequible

affront [ə'frʌnt] **1** N afrenta *f*
  2 VT afrentar

Afghanistan [æf'gænɪstɑːn] N Afganistán

afield [ə'fiːld] ADV **far a.** muy lejos

afloat [ə'fləʊt] ADV **to keep a.** mantenerse a flote

afoot [ə'fʊt] ADV **there's a plan a.** hay un proyecto en marcha; **there's something strange a.** se está tramando algo

aforementioned [ə'fɔːmenʃənd], **aforesaid** [ə'fɔːsed] ADJ susodicho(a)

afraid [ə'freɪd] ADJ (**a**) **to be a.** tener miedo (**of** sb/of sth a algn/de algo); **I'm a. of it** me da miedo (**b**) **I'm a. not** me temo que no; **I'm a. so** me temo que sí; **I'm a. you're wrong** me temo que estás equivocado(a)

afresh [ə'freʃ] ADV de nuevo

Africa ['æfrɪkə] N Africa

African ['æfrɪkən] ADJ & N africano(a) *(m,f)*

Afro ['æfrəʊ] ADJ & N *Fam (hairstyle)* afro *(m)*

aft [ɑːft] ADV en popa; **to go a.** ir en popa

after ['ɑːftə(r)] **1** ADV después; **soon a.** poco después; **the day a.** el día siguiente

2 PREP (**a**) (later) después de; US **it's ten a. five** son las cinco y diez; **soon a. arriving** al poco rato de llegar; **the day a. tomorrow** pasado mañana (**b**) (behind) detrás de, tras; **a. you!** ¡pase usted!; **they went in one a. the other** entraron uno tras otro; **the police are a. them** la policía anda tras ellos (**c**) (about) por; **they asked a. you** preguntaron por ti; **what's he a.?** ¿qué pretende?

3 CONJ después (de) que; **a. it happened** después de que ocurriera

after-effect ['ɑːftərɪfekt] N efecto secundario

afterlife ['ɑːftəlaɪf] N vida f después de la muerte

aftermath ['ɑːftəmæθ] N secuelas fpl

afternoon [ɑːftə'nuːn] N tarde f; **good a.!** ¡buenas tardes!; **in the a.** por la tarde

afternoons [ɑːftə'nuːnz] ADV US por las tardes

afters ['ɑːftəz] NPL Fam postre m

after-sales service [ɑːftəseɪlz'sɜːvɪs] N Com servicio m posventa

aftershave ['ɑːftəʃeɪv] N (as perfume) colonia f; **a.** (balm or lotion) loción f para después del afeitado or Méx rasurado

afterthought ['ɑːftəθɔːt] N ocurrencia f tardía

afterward(s) ['ɑːftəwəd(z)] ADV después, más tarde

again [ə'gen] ADV (**a**) (in general) de nuevo, otra vez; **I tried a. and a.** lo intenté una y otra vez; **to do sth a.** volver a hacer algo; **never a.!** ¡nunca más!; **now and a.** de vez en cuando; **once a.** otra vez (**b**) (besides) además; **then a.** por otra parte

against [ə'genst] PREP (**a**) (touching) contra (**b**) (opposing) contra, en contra (de); **a. the grain** a contrapelo; **it's a. the law** es ilegal (**c**) **as a.** en contraste con, comparado con

age [eɪdʒ] **1** N (**a**) (of person, object) edad f; **she's eighteen years of a.** tiene dieciocho años; **to be under a.** ser menor de edad; **to come of a.** llegar a la mayoría de edad; **a. limit** límite m de edad; **old a.** vejez f (**b**) (period) época f; **the Iron A.** la Edad de Hierro (**c**) Fam (long time) eternidad f; **it's ages since I last saw her** hace siglos que no la veo

2 VT & VI envejecer

aged¹ [eɪdʒd] ADJ de or a la edad de

aged² ['eɪdʒɪd] NPL **the a.** los ancianos

agency ['eɪdʒənsɪ] N (**a**) Com agencia f (**b**) **by the a. of** por medio de

agenda [ə'dʒendə] N orden m del día

agent ['eɪdʒənt] N agente mf; (representative) representante mf

aggravate ['ægrəveɪt] VT (worsen) agravar; (annoy) fastidiar, molestar, RP hinchar

aggregate ['ægrɪgɪt] N conjunto m; **on a.** en conjunto

aggression [ə'greʃən] N agresión f

aggressive [ə'gresɪv] ADJ (violent) agresivo(a), violento(a); (dynamic) dinámico(a)

aggrieved [ə'griːvd] ADJ apenado(a)

aghast [ə'gɑːst] ADJ espantado(a)

agile [Br 'ædʒaɪl, US 'ædʒəl] ADJ ágil

agitate ['ædʒɪteɪt] **1** VT (shake) agitar; Fig (worry) perturbar

2 VI Pol **to a. against sth** hacer campaña en contra de algo

agitated [ædʒɪteɪtɪd] ADJ inquieto(a), agitado(a); **to be a.** estar inquieto(a) or agitado(a)

agitator ['ædʒɪteɪtə(r)] N Pol agitador(a) m,f

AGM [eɪdʒiː'em] N Br (abbr **annual general meeting**) junta f general anual

agnostic [æg'nɒstɪk] N agnóstico(a) m,f

ago [ə'gəʊ] ADV **a long time a.** hace mucho tiempo; **as long a. as 1910** en 1910; **a week a.** hace una semana; **how long a.?** ¿hace cuánto tiempo?

agog [ə'gɒg] ADJ ansioso(a)

agonizing ['ægənaɪzɪŋ] ADJ (pain) atroz; (decision) desesperante

agony ['ægənɪ] N dolor m muy fuerte; (anguish) angustia f; **he was in a. with his back** tenía un dolor insoportable de espalda

agree [ə'griː] **1** VI (**a**) (be in agreement) estar de acuerdo; (reach agreement) ponerse de acuerdo; (consent) consentir; **to a. to do sth** consentir en hacer algo; **to a. with sb** estar de acuerdo con algn (**b**) (harmonize) (things) concordar; (people) congeniar; **onions don't a. with me** la cebolla no me sienta bien

2 VT acordar

agreeable [ə'griːəbəl] ADJ (pleasant) agradable; (person) simpático(a); (in agreement) de acuerdo

agreement [ə'griːmənt] N (arrangement) acuerdo m; Com contrato m; **to reach an a.** llegar a un acuerdo

agricultural [ægrɪ'kʌltʃərəl] ADJ agrícola; **a. college** escuela f de agricultura

agriculture ['ægrɪkʌltʃə(r)] N agricultura f

aground [ə'graʊnd] ADV **to run a.** encallar, varar

ahead [ə'hed] ADV (forwards) adelante; (in front) delante, Am adelante; (early) antes; **go a.!** ¡adelante!; **to be a.** llevar la ventaja; **to go a.** ir adelante; Fig **to go a. with sth** llevar algo adelante; (start) comenzar algo; **to get a.** triunfar; **to look a.** pensar en el futuro

aid [eɪd] **1** N ayuda f; (rescue) auxilio m; **in a. of** a beneficio de; **to come to the a. of sb** acudir en ayuda de algn; **a. worker** cooperante mf

2 VT ayudar; **to a. and abet sb** ser cómplice de algn

aide [eɪd] N ayudante mf

AIDS [eɪdz] N (abbr **Acquired Immune Deficiency Syndrome**) sida m

ailing ['eɪlɪŋ] ADJ achacoso(a)

ailment ['eɪlmənt] N enfermedad f (leve), achaque m

aim [eɪm] 1 N *(with weapon)* puntería f; *(target)* propósito m
2 VT *(gun)* apuntar (**at** a *or* hacia); *(attack, action)* dirigir (**at** a *or* hacia)
▸ **aim at** VT INSEP *(target)* tirar para; **to a. at doing sth** tener pensado hacer algo
▸ **aim to** VT INSEP **to a. to do sth** tener la intención de hacer algo

aimless ['eɪmlɪs] ADJ sin objeto, sin propósito

aimlessly ['eɪmlɪslɪ] ADV *(wander)* sin rumbo fijo

air [eə(r)] 1 N (**a**) *(atmosphere, sky)* aire m; **to throw sth up in the a.** lanzar algo al aire; *Fig* **it's still in the a.** todavía queda por resolver; *Aut* **a. bag** airbag m; **a. bed** colchón m hinchable; **a. conditioning** aire acondicionado; **a. freshener** ambientador m; **a. gun** pistola f de aire comprimido; **a. pocket** bache m; **a. pressure** presión atmosférica (**b**) *(relating to air travel)* **to travel by a.** viajar en avión; **a. base** base aérea; **a. fare** (precio m del) *Esp* billete m or Am boleto m or Am pasaje m; **A. Force** Fuerzas Aéreas; **a. hostess** azafata f de vuelo, Am aeromoza f; **a. raid** ataque aéreo; **a. terminal** terminal aérea; **a. traffic control** control m de tráfico aéreo; **a. traffic controller** controlador(a) aéreo(a) (**c**) *Rad & TV* **to be on the a.** *(programme)* estar emitiendo; *(person)* estar transmitiendo (**d**) *(melody)* melodía f, aire m (**e**) *(look, manner)* aire m
2 VT *(bed, clothes)* airear; *(room)* ventilar; *Fig (grievance)* airear; *(knowledge)* hacer alarde de

airborne ['eəbɔːn] ADJ *(aircraft)* en vuelo; *(troops)* aerotransportado(a)

air-conditioned ['eəkɒndɪʃənd] ADJ climatizado(a)

aircraft ['eəkrɑːft] N *(pl* **aircraft**) avión m; **a. carrier** portaviones m inv

airfield ['eəfiːld] N campo m de aviación

airlift ['eəlɪft] N puente aéreo

airline ['eəlaɪn] N línea aérea

airlock ['eəlɒk] N *(in pipe)* bolsa f de aire; *(in spacecraft)* esclusa f de aire

airmail ['eəmeɪl] N correo aéreo; **by a.** por avión

airplane ['eəpleɪn] N *US* avión m

airport ['eəpɔːt] N aeropuerto m; **a. tax** tasas fpl de aeropuerto

airsick ['eəsɪk] ADJ **to be a.** marearse en avión

airstrip ['eəstrɪp] N pista f de aterrizaje

airtight ['eətaɪt] ADJ hermético(a)

airy ['eərɪ] ADJ (**airier, airiest**) *(well-ventilated)* bien ventilado(a); *(vague, carefree)* ligero(a)

aisle [aɪl] N *(in church)* nave f; *(in theatre)* pasillo m

ajar [ə'dʒɑː(r)] ADJ & ADV entreabierto(a)

akin [ə'kɪn] ADJ semejante

alacrity [ə'lækrɪtɪ] N *Fml* **with a.** con presteza

à la mode [ælə'məʊd] ADJ *US (dessert)* con helado

alarm [ə'lɑːm] 1 N (**a**) *(warning, alert)* alarma f; **a. clock** despertador m (**b**) *(anxiety)* inquietud f; **to cause a.** provocar temor
2 VT alarmar

alas [ə'læs] INTERJ ¡ay!, ¡ay de mí!

Albania [æl'beɪnɪə] N Albania

Albanian [æl'beɪnɪən] 1 N (**a**) *(person)* albanés(esa) m,f (**b**) *(language)* albanés m
2 ADJ albanés(esa)

albatross ['ælbətrɒs] N albatros m

albeit [ɔːl'biːɪt] CONJ aunque, no obstante

album ['ælbəm] N álbum m

alcohol ['ælkəhɒl] N alcohol m

alcoholic [ælkə'hɒlɪk] ADJ & N alcohólico(a) *(m,f)*

alcopop ['ælkəʊpɒp] N *Br* = combinado alcohólico con aspecto de refresco que se comercializa envasado

alcove ['ælkəʊv] N hueco m

Note that the Spanish word **alcoba** is a false friend and is never a translation for the English word **alcove**. In Spanish **alcoba** means "bedroom".

ale [eɪl] N cerveza f; **brown/pale a.** cerveza negra/rubia

alert [ə'lɜːt] 1 ADJ *(watchful)* alerta; *(lively)* despabilado(a)
2 N alerta m; **to be on the a.** estar alerta
3 VT **to a. sb to sth** avisar a algn de algo

A-level ['eɪlevəl] N *Br Educ (abbr* **Advanced level**) = examen final o diploma en una asignatura de los estudios preuniversitarios

algae ['ældʒiː] NPL algas fpl

algebra ['ældʒɪbrə] N álgebra f

Algeria [æl'dʒɪərɪə] N Argelia

Algerian [æl'dʒɪərɪən] ADJ & N argelino(a) *(m,f)*

Algiers [æl'dʒɪəz] N Argel

alias ['eɪlɪəs] 1 N alias m
2 ADV alias

alibi ['ælɪbaɪ] N coartada f

alien ['eɪlɪən] 1 ADJ *(foreign)* extranjero(a); *(from space)* extraterrestre; **a. to** ajeno(a) a
2 N *(foreigner)* extranjero(a) m,f; *(from space)* extraterrestre mf

alienate ['eɪlɪəneɪt] VT (**a**) **to a. sb** ofender a algn; **to a. oneself from sb** alejarse de algn (**b**) *Jur* enajenar

alight¹ [ə'laɪt] ADJ *(burning)* **to be a.** estar ardiendo *or* en llamas

alight² [ə'laɪt] VI *(get off)* apearse (**from** de)

align [ə'laɪn] VT alinear

alike [ə'laɪk] 1 ADJ *(similar)* parecidos(as); *(the same)* iguales
2 ADV *(in the same way)* de la misma manera, igualmente; **dressed a.** vestidos(as) iguales

alimony ['ælɪmənɪ] N *Jur* pensión alimenticia

alive [ə'laɪv] ADJ vivo(a); **to be a.** estar vivo(a); *Fig* **to be a. with** *(teeming)* ser un hervidero de

alkaline ['ælkəlaɪn] ADJ alcalino(a)

all [ɔːl] **1** ADJ todo(a), todos(as); **a. year** *(durante)* todo el año; **a. kinds of things** todo tipo de cosas; **at a. hours** a todas horas; **at a. times** siempre; **she works a. the time** siempre está trabajando; **a. six of us were there** los seis estábamos allí

2 PRON todo(a), todos(as); **after a.** al fin y al cabo; **a. of his work** toda su obra; **a. of us** todos(as) nosotros(as); **a. who saw it** todos los que lo vieron; **a. you can do is wait** lo único que puedes hacer es esperar; **I don't like it at a.** no me gusta en absoluto; **is that a.?** ¿eso es todo?; **most of** *or* **above a.** sobre todo; **once and for a.** de una vez por todas; **thanks – not at a.** gracias – de nada; **a. in a.** en conjunto; **that's a.** ya está; **the score was one a.** empataron a uno

3 ADV **a. by myself** completamente solo(a); **a. at once** *(suddenly)* de repente; *(altogether)* de una vez; **a. the better** tanto mejor; **he knew a. along** lo sabía desde el principio; **it's a. but impossible** es casi imposible; **I'm not a. that tired** no estoy tan cansado(a) como eso

Allah ['ælə] N Alá *m*

all-around ['ɔːlərəʊnd] ADJ *US* = **all-round**

allay [ə'leɪ] VT *(fears, doubts)* apaciguar

allegation [ælɪ'geɪʃən] N alegato *m*

allege [ə'ledʒ] VT sostener, pretender (**that** que); **it is alleged that she accepted a bribe** supuestamente aceptó un soborno

allegedly [ə'ledʒɪdlɪ] ADV supuestamente

allegiance [ə'liːdʒəns] N lealtad *f*

allergic [ə'lɜːdʒɪk] ADJ alérgico(a) (**to** a)

allergy ['ælədʒɪ] N alergia *f*

alleviate [ə'liːvɪeɪt] VT *(pain)* aliviar

alley ['ælɪ] N callejón *m*

alliance [ə'laɪəns] N alianza *f*

allied ['ælaɪd] ADJ aliado(a)

alligator ['ælɪgeɪtə(r)] N caimán *m*

all-in ['ɔːlɪn] ADJ *(price)* todo incluido; *Sport* **a. wrestling** lucha *f* libre

alliteration [əlɪtə'reɪʃən] N aliteración *f*

all-night ['ɔːlnaɪt] ADJ *(café etc)* abierto(a) toda la noche; *(vigil)* que dura toda la noche

allocate ['æləkeɪt] VT destinar (**to** para)

allocation [ælə'keɪʃən] N (**a**) *(distribution)* asignación *f* (**b**) *(amount allocated)* cuota *f*

allot [ə'lɒt] VT asignar

allotment [ə'lɒtmənt] N (**a**) *(of time, money)* asignación *f* (**b**) *Br (plot of land)* huerto *m* de ocio, parcela *f (arrendada por el ayuntamiento para cultivo)*

all-out ['ɔːlaʊt] **1** ADJ *(effort)* supremo(a); *(attack)* concentrado(a)
2 all out ADV **to go all out to do sth** emplearse a fondo para hacer algo

allow [ə'laʊ] VT (**a**) *(permit)* permitir; *(a request)* acceder a; **to a. sb to do sth** permitir que algn haga algo (**b**) *(allot)* *(time)* dejar; *(money)* destinar

▸ **allow for** VT INSEP tener en cuenta

allowance [ə'laʊəns] N *(money given)* asignación *f*; *US (pocket money)* paga *f*; **to make allowances for sb/sth** disculpar a algn/tener algo en cuenta; **tax a.** desgravación *f* fiscal; **travel a.** dietas *fpl* de viaje

alloy ['ælɔɪ] N aleación *f*

all-purpose ['ɔːl'pɜːpəs] ADJ *(cleaner, adhesive)* multiuso

all right [ɔːl'raɪt] **1** ADJ *(okay)* bien; **thank you very much – that's a.** muchas gracias – de nada
2 ADV (**a**) *(well)* bien (**b**) *(definitely)* sin duda (**c**) *(okay)* de acuerdo, vale

all-round ['ɔːlraʊnd] ADJ *(athlete)* completo(a)

all-terrain [ɔːltə'reɪn] ADJ **a. vehicle** todoterreno *m*

all-time ['ɔːltaɪm] ADJ **an a. low** una baja sin antecedente; **the a. greats** los grandes de siempre

allude [ə'luːd] VI **to a. to** aludir a

alluring [ə'ljʊərɪŋ] ADJ atractivo(a)

allusion [ə'luːʒən] N alusión *f*

ally ['ælaɪ] **1** N aliado(a) *m,f*
2 VT **to a. oneself to/with sb** aliarse a/con algn

almighty [ɔːl'maɪtɪ] **1** ADJ *(all-powerful)* todopoderoso(a)
2 N **the A.** El Todopoderoso

almond ['ɑːmənd] N almendra *f*

almost ['ɔːlməʊst] ADV casi

alms [ɑːmz] NPL limosna *f*

aloft [ə'lɒft] ADV arriba

alone [ə'ləʊn] **1** ADJ solo(a); **can I speak to you a.?** ¿puedo hablar contigo a solas?; **let a.** ni mucho menos; **leave it a.!** ¡no lo toques!; **leave me a.** déjame en paz; **to be a.** estar solo(a)
2 ADV solamente, sólo

along [ə'lɒŋ] **1** ADV **come a.!** ¡anda, ven!; **he'll be a. in ten minutes** llegará dentro de diez minutos; **a. with** junto con
2 PREP *(the length of)* a lo largo de; **to walk a. the street** andar por la calle; **it's just a. the street** está un poco más abajo

alongside [ə'lɒŋsaɪd] **1** ADV *Naut* de costado
2 PREP al lado de

aloof [ə'luːf] **1** ADJ *(person)* distante
2 ADV **to keep oneself a. (from)** mantenerse a distancia (de)

aloud [ə'laʊd] ADV en voz alta

alphabet ['ælfəbet] N alfabeto *m*

alphabetical [ælfə'betɪkəl] ADJ alfabético(a)

alphabetically [ælfə'betɪkəlɪ] ADV por orden alfabético

alpine ['ælpaɪn] ADJ alpino(a)

Alps [ælps] NPL **the A.** los Alpes
already [ɔːlˈredɪ] ADV ya
alright [ɔːlˈraɪt] ADJ & ADV = **all right**
Alsatian [ælˈseɪʃən] N pastor *m* alemán
also [ˈɔːlsəʊ] ADV también, además
also-ran [ˈɔːlsəʊræn] N *Fam (person)* segundón(ona) *m,f*
altar [ˈɔːltə(r)] N altar *m*
alter [ˈɔːltə(r)] **1** VT *(plan)* cambiar, retocar; *(project)* modificar; *(clothing)* arreglar; *(timetable)* revisar
　2 VI cambiar, cambiarse
alteration [ɔːltəˈreɪʃən] N *(to plan)* cambio *m*; *(to project)* modificación *f*; *(to clothing)* arreglo *m*; *(to timetable)* revisión *f*; **alterations** *(to building)* reformas *fpl*
alternate 1 ADJ [ɔːlˈtɜːnɪt] alterno(a); **on a. days** cada dos días
　2 VT [ˈɔːltəneɪt] alternar
alternately [ɔːlˈtɜːnɪtlɪ] ADV **a. hot and cold** ahora caliente, ahora frío
alternative [ɔːlˈtɜːnətɪv] **1** ADJ alternativo(a)
　2 N alternativa *f*; **I have no a. but to accept** no tengo más remedio que aceptar
alternatively [ɔːlˈtɜːnətɪvlɪ] ADV o bien; **a., you could walk** o bien podrías ir andando
alternator [ˈɔːltəneɪtə(r)] N *Aut* alternador *m*
although [ɔːlˈðəʊ] CONJ aunque
altitude [ˈæltɪtjuːd] N altitud *f*
alto [ˈæltəʊ] ADJ & N *(male singer, instrument)* alto *(m)*; *(female singer)* contralto *(f)*
altogether [ɔːltəˈgeðə(r)] ADV *(in total)* en conjunto, en total; *(completely)* completamente, del todo
altruism [ˈæltruːɪzəm] N altruismo *m*
aluminium [æljʊˈmɪnɪəm], *US* **aluminum** [əˈluːmɪnəm] N aluminio *m*
alumnus [əˈlʌmnəs] N *(pl* **alumni** [əˈlʌmnaɪ]*) US* antiguo alumno
always [ˈɔːlweɪz] ADV siempre
AM [eɪˈem] *Rad (abbr* **amplitude modulation***)* AM
am [æm] 1ST PERSON SING PRES *of* **be**
a.m. [eɪˈem] *(abbr* **ante meridiem***)* a.m., de la mañana
amalgamate [əˈmælgəmeɪt] **1** VT *(metals)* amalgamar
　2 VI *(metals)* amalgamarse; *(companies)* fusionarse
amalgamation [əmælgəˈmeɪʃən] N fusión *f*
amass [əˈmæs] VT *(money)* amontonar; *(information)* acumular
amateur [ˈæmətə(r)] **1** N amateur *mf*, aficionado(a) *m,f*
　2 ADJ *(painter, musician)* aficionado(a); *Pej (work etc)* chapucero(a), de aficionado
amateurish [ˈæmətərɪʃ] ADJ chapucero(a)
amaze [əˈmeɪz] VT asombrar, pasmar; **to be amazed at sth** quedarse pasmado(a) de algo

amazement [əˈmeɪzmənt] N asombro *m*, sorpresa *f*
amazing [əˈmeɪzɪŋ] ADJ asombroso(a), increíble
ambassador [æmˈbæsədə(r)] N embajador(a) *m,f*
amber [ˈæmbə(r)] **1** N ámbar *m*
　2 ADJ ambarino(a); *Br* **a. light** semáforo *m* en ámbar
ambiguity [æmbɪˈgjuːɪtɪ] N ambigüedad *f*
ambiguous [æmˈbɪgjʊəs] ADJ ambiguo(a)
ambition [æmˈbɪʃən] N ambición *f*
ambitious [æmˈbɪʃəs] ADJ ambicioso(a)
ambivalent [æmˈbɪvələnt] ADJ ambivalente
amble [ˈæmbəl] VI deambular
ambulance [ˈæmbjʊləns] N ambulancia *f*; **a. man** ambulanciero *m*
ambush [ˈæmbʊʃ] **1** N *also Fig* emboscada *f*
　2 VT *also Fig* tender una emboscada a
amen [ɑːˈmen] INTERJ amén
amenable [əˈmiːnəbəl] ADJ **I'd be quite a. to doing that** no me importaría nada hacer eso; **a. to reason** razonable
amend [əˈmend] VT *(law)* enmendar; *(error)* subsanar
amendment [əˈmendmənt] N enmienda *f*
amends [əˈmendz] NPL **to make a. to sb for sth** compensar a algn por algo
amenities [əˈmiːnɪtɪz] NPL comodidades *fpl*
America [əˈmerɪkə] N *(continent)* América *f*; *(USA)* (los) Estados Unidos; **South A.** América del Sur, Sudamérica *f*
American [əˈmerɪkən] ADJ & N americano(a) *(m,f)*; *(of USA)* norteamericano(a) *(m,f)*, estadounidense *(mf)*
amiable [ˈeɪmɪəbəl] ADJ amable, afable
amicable [ˈæmɪkəbəl] ADJ amistoso(a)
amid(st) [əˈmɪd(st)] PREP entre, en medio de
amiss [əˈmɪs] ADJ & ADV mal; **there's sth a.** algo anda mal; **to take sth a.** tomar algo a mal
ammonia [əˈməʊnɪə] N amoníaco *m*
ammunition [æmjʊˈnɪʃən] N municiones *fpl*
amnesia [æmˈniːzjə] N amnesia *f*
amnesty [ˈæmnɪstɪ] N amnistía *f*
amok [əˈmɒk] ADV *Fig* **to run a.** *(child)* desmadrarse; *(inflation etc)* dispararse
among(st) [əˈmʌŋ(st)] PREP entre
amoral [eɪˈmɒrəl] ADJ amoral
amorous [ˈæmərəs] ADJ cariñoso(a)
amorphous [əˈmɔːfəs] ADJ amorfo(a)
amount [əˈmaʊnt] N cantidad *f*; *(of money)* suma *f*; *(of bill)* importe *m*
▸ **amount to** VT INSEP *(add up to)* ascender a; *Fig (mean)* equivaler a
amp [æmp], **ampère** [ˈæmpeə(r)] N amperio *m*
amphetamine [æmˈfetəmiːn] N anfetamina *f*
amphibian [æmˈfɪbɪən] ADJ & N anfibio(a) *(m)*
amphibious [æmˈfɪbɪəs] ADJ anfibio(a)

amphitheatre, *US* **amphitheater** ['æmfɪ-θɪətə(r)] N anfiteatro *m*

ample ['æmpəl] ADJ *(enough)* bastante; *(more than enough)* abundante; *(large)* amplio(a)

amplifier ['æmplɪfaɪə(r)] N amplificador *m*

amplify ['æmplɪfaɪ] VT *(essay, remarks)* ampliar; *(current, volume)* amplificar

amputate ['æmpjʊteɪt] VT amputar

Amtrak ['æmtræk] N = compañía ferroviaria estadounidense

amuck [ə'mʌk] ADV = **amok**

amuse [ə'mjuːz] VT divertir, entretener

amusement [ə'mjuːzmənt] N *(enjoyment)* diversión *f*; *(laughter)* risa *f*; *(pastime)* pasatiempo *m*; **a. arcade** salón *m* de juegos; **a. park** parque *m* de atracciones

amusing [ə'mjuːzɪŋ] ADJ divertido(a)

an [æn, *unstressed* ən] *see* **a**

anabolic steroid [ænəbɒlɪk'stɪərɔɪd] N esteroide *m* anabolizante

anaemia [ə'niːmɪə] N anemia *f*

anaemic [ə'niːmɪk] ADJ *Med* anémico(a); *Fig (weak)* pobre

anaesthetic [ænɪs'θetɪk] N anestesia *f*

anaesthetist [ə'niːsθətɪst] N anestesista *mf*

analog(ue) ['ænəlɒg] N análogo *m*; **a. computer** ordenador analógico, *Am* computadora analógica; **a. watch** reloj *m* de agujas

analogy [ə'nælədʒɪ] N analogía *f*

analyse ['ænəlaɪz] VT analizar

analysis [ə'nælɪsɪs] N *(pl* **analyses** [ə'nælɪsiːz]) análisis *m inv*

analyst ['ænəlɪst] N analista *mf*; *(psychoanalyst)* psicoanalista *mf*

analytic(al) [ænə'lɪtɪk(əl)] ADJ analítico(a)

analyze ['ænəlaɪz] VT *US* = **analyse**

anarchist ['ænəkɪst] N anarquista *mf*

anarchy ['ænəkɪ] N anarquía *f*

anathema [ə'næθəmə] N **the very idea was a. to him** le repugnaba sólo de pensarlo

anatomy [ə'nætəmɪ] N anatomía *f*

ancestor ['ænsestə(r)] N antepasado *m*

anchor ['æŋkə(r)] **1** N *Naut* ancla *f*; *Fig* áncora *f* **2** VT *Naut* anclar; *Fig (fix securely)* sujetar **3** VI anclar

anchovy [*Br* 'æntʃəvɪ, *Am* æn'tʃəʊvɪ] N anchoa *f*

ancient ['eɪnʃənt] ADJ antiguo(a)

ancillary [æn'sɪlərɪ] ADJ & N auxiliar *(mf)*

and [ænd, *unstressed* ənd, ən] CONJ y; *(before* **i**, **hi**) e; **a hundred a. one** ciento uno; **a. so on** etcétera; **Bill a. Pat** Bill y Pat; **Chinese a. Indian** chino e indio; **come a. see us** ven a vernos; **four a. a half** cuatro y medio; **she cried a. cried** no paró de llorar; **try a. help me** trata de ayudarme; **wait a. see** espera a ver; **worse a. worse** cada vez peor

Andalusia [ændə'luːzɪə] N Andalucía

Andalusian [ændə'luːzɪən] ADJ andaluz(a)

Andes ['ændiːz] NPL **the A.** los Andes

Andorra [æn'dɔːrə] N Andorra

anecdote ['ænɪkdəʊt] N anécdota *f*

anemia [ə'niːmɪə] N *US* = **anaemia**

anemic [ə'niːmɪk] N *US* = **anaemic**

anesthetic [ænɪs'θetɪk] N *US* = **anaesthetic**

anesthetist [ə'niːsθətɪst] N *US* = **anaesthetist**

angel ['eɪndʒəl] N ángel *m*

anger ['æŋgə(r)] **1** N ira *f*, *esp Esp* enfado *m*, *esp Am* enojo *m* **2** VT *esp Esp* enfadar, *esp Am* enojar

angina [æn'dʒaɪnə] N angina *f* (de pecho)

angle ['æŋgəl] N ángulo *m*; *Fig* punto *m* de vista

angler ['æŋglə(r)] N pescador(a) *m,f* de caña

Anglican ['æŋglɪkən] ADJ & N anglicano(a) *(m,f)*

Anglo-Saxon [æŋgləʊ'sæksən] ADJ & N anglosajón(ona) *(m,f)*

Angola [æŋ'gəʊlə] N Angola

angrily ['æŋgrɪlɪ] ADV airadamente, con *esp Esp* enfado *or esp Am* enojo

angry ['æŋgrɪ] ADJ (**angrier**, **angriest**) *(person)* *esp Esp* enfadado(a), *esp Am* enojado(a); *(voice, letter)* airado(a); **to get a.** estar *esp Esp* enfadado(a) *or esp Am* enojado(a)

anguish ['æŋgwɪʃ] N angustia *f*

angular ['æŋgjʊlə(r)] ADJ *(shape)* angular; *(face)* anguloso(a)

animal ['ænɪməl] **1** ADJ animal **2** N animal *m*; *Fig* bestia *f*

animate 1 ADJ ['ænɪmɪt] vivo(a) **2** VT ['ænɪmeɪt] animar

animated ['ænɪmeɪtɪd] ADJ *(lively)* animado(a)

animation [ænɪ'meɪʃən] N animación *f*

animosity [ænɪ'mɒsɪtɪ] N animosidad *f*

aniseed ['ænɪsiːd] N anís *m*

ankle ['æŋkəl] N tobillo *m*; **a. boots** botines *mpl*; **a. socks** calcetines cortos, *CSur* zoquetes *mpl*, *Col* medias tobilleras

annex [ə'neks] VT *(territory)* anexionar

annexe, *US* **annex** ['æneks] N *(building)* (edificio *m*) anexo *m*

annihilate [ə'naɪəleɪt] VT aniquilar

anniversary [ænɪ'vɜːsərɪ] N aniversario *m*; **wedding a.** aniversario de bodas

announce [ə'naʊns] VT anunciar

announcement [ə'naʊnsmənt] N anuncio *m*; *(news)* comunicación *f*; *(statement)* declaración *f*

announcer [ə'naʊnsə(r)] N *Rad & TV* locutor(a) *m,f*

annoy [ə'nɔɪ] VT fastidiar, molestar, *esp Am* enojar; **to get annoyed** molestarse, *esp Esp* enfadarse, *esp Am* enojarse

annoyance [ə'nɔɪəns] N *(feeling) esp Esp* enfado *m*, *esp Am* enojo *m*; *(thing)* molestia *f*, fastidio *m*

annoying [ə'nɔɪɪŋ] ADJ molesto(a), fastidioso(a)

annual ['ænjʊəl] **1** ADJ anual **2** N *(book)* anuario *m*; *(plant)* anual *m*

annually ['ænjʊəlɪ] ADV anualmente

annuity [ə'njuːɪtɪ] N *Fin* anualidad *f*

annul [ə'nʌl] VT anular

annulment [ə'nʌlmənt] N anulación *f*

anomaly [ə'nɒmǝlɪ] N anomalía *f*

anonymity [ænə'nɪmɪtɪ] N anonimato *m*

anonymous [ə'nɒnɪməs] ADJ anónimo(a)

anorak ['ænəræk] N anorak *m*

anorexia [ænə'reksɪə] N anorexia *f*

another [ə'nʌðə(r)] **1** ADJ otro(a); **a. one** otro(a); **without a. word** sin más
2 PRON otro(a); **have a.** toma otro(a); **to love one a.** quererse el uno al otro

Ansaphone® ['ɑːnsəfəʊn] N mensáfono *m*

answer ['ɑːnsə(r)] **1** N *(to question, letter)* respuesta *f*, contestación *f*; *(to problem)* solución *f*; **in a. to your letter** contestando a su carta; **there's no a.** *(on telephone)* no contestan; *(at door)* no abren
2 VT *(person, question, letter)* responder a, contestar; *(problem)* solucionar; *(door)* abrir; *(phone)* contestar, *Esp* coger
3 VI contestar, responder

▸ **answer back** VI replicar; **don't a. back!** ¡no seas respondón!

▸ **answer for** VT INSEP responder de; **he's got a lot to a. for** es responsable de muchas cosas

▸ **answer to** VT INSEP *(name)* responder a; *(description)* corresponder a; **to a. to sb (for sth)** ser responsable ante algn (de algo)

answerable ['ɑːnsərəbəl] ADJ **to be a. to sb for sth** ser responsable ante algn de algo

answering machine ['ɑːnsərɪŋməʃiːn] N contestador automático

ant [ænt] N hormiga *f*; **a. hill** hormiguero *m*

antagonism [æn'tægənɪzəm] N antagonismo *m* *(between* entre), hostilidad *f (towards* hacia)

antagonize [æn'tægənaɪz] VT enemistar, malquistar

Antarctic [æn'tɑːktɪk] **1** ADJ antártico(a); **A. Ocean** océano Antártico
2 N **the A.** la Antártida

Antarctica [æn'tɑːktɪkə] N Antártida *f*

antecedent [æntɪ'siːdənt] N antecedente *m*

antelope ['æntɪləʊp] N antílope *m*

antenatal [æntɪ'neɪtəl] ADJ prenatal; **a. clinic** clínica *f* de obstetricia *or* de preparación al parto

antenna [æn'tenə] N **(a)** *(pl* **antennae** [æn'teniː]) *(of animal, insect)* antena *f* **(b)** *(pl* **antennas)** *Rad & TV* antena *f*

anthem ['ænθəm] N motete *m*; **national a.** himno *m* nacional

anthology [æn'θɒlədʒɪ] N antología *f*

anthracite ['ænθrəsaɪt] N antracita *f*

anthropology [ænθrə'pɒlədʒɪ] N antropología *f*

anti-aircraft [æntɪ'eəkrɑːft] ADJ antiaéreo(a)

antibiotic [æntɪbaɪ'ɒtɪk] N antibiótico *m*

antibody ['æntɪbɒdɪ] N anticuerpo *m*

anticipate [æn'tɪsɪpeɪt] VT **(a)** *(expect)* esperar **(b)** *(predict)* prever; *(get ahead of)* anticiparse a, adelantarse a

anticipation [æntɪsɪ'peɪʃən] N *(expectation)* esperanza *f*; *(expectancy)* ilusión *f*

anticlimax [æntɪ'klaɪmæks] N *(disappointment)* decepción *f*

anticlockwise [æntɪ'klɒkwaɪz] ADV *Br* en sentido opuesto al de las agujas del reloj

antics ['æntɪks] NPL payasadas *fpl*; *(naughtiness)* travesuras *fpl*

anticyclone [æntɪ'saɪkləʊn] N anticiclón *m*

antidote ['æntɪdəʊt] N antídoto *m*

antifreeze ['æntɪfriːz] N anticongelante *m*

antihistamine [æntɪ'hɪstəmɪn] N antihistamínico *m*

antinuclear [æntɪ'njuːklɪə(r)] ADJ antinuclear

antipathy [æn'tɪpəθɪ] N antipatía *f (to* a)

antiperspirant [æntɪ'pɜːspɪrənt] N antitranspirante *m*

antiquated ['æntɪkweɪtɪd] ADJ anticuado(a)

antique [æn'tiːk] **1** ADJ antiguo(a)
2 N antigüedad *f*; **a. dealer** anticuario(a) *m,f*; **a. shop** tienda *f* de antigüedades

antiquity [æn'tɪkwɪtɪ] N antigüedad *f*

antisemitic [æntɪsɪ'mɪtɪk] ADJ *(person)* antisemita; *(beliefs, remarks)* antisemítico(a)

anti-Semitism [æntɪ'semɪtɪzəm] N antisemitismo *m*

antiseptic [æntɪ'septɪk] ADJ & N antiséptico(a) *(m)*

antisocial [æntɪ'səʊʃəl] ADJ *(delinquent)* antisocial; *(unsociable)* insociable

antithesis [æn'tɪθɪsɪs] N antítesis *f*

antivirus ['æntɪ'vaɪrəs] ADJ *Comput (program, software)* antivirus

antler ['æntlə(r)] N cuerna *f*; **antlers** cornamenta *f*

Antwerp ['æntwɜːp] N Amberes

anus ['eɪnəs] N ano *m*

anvil ['ænvɪl] N yunque *m*

anxiety [æŋ'zaɪɪtɪ] N *(concern)* inquietud *f*; *(worry)* preocupación *f*; *(fear)* angustia *f*; *(eagerness)* ansia *f*

anxious ['æŋkʃəs] ADJ *(concerned)* inquieto(a); *(worried)* preocupado(a); *(fearful)* angustiado(a); *(eager)* ansioso(a); **to be a. about sth** estar preocupado(a) por algo

any ['enɪ] **1** ADJ **(a)** *(in questions, conditionals)* algún(una); **are there a. seats left?** ¿quedan plazas?; **have you a. apples?** ¿tienes manzanas?; **have you a. money?** ¿tienes (algo de) dinero? **(b)** *(in negative clauses)* ningún(una); **I don't have a. time** no tengo tiempo **(c)** *(no matter which)* cualquier(a); **a. doctor will say the same** cualquier médico te dirá lo mismo; **at a. moment** en cualquier momento **(d)** *(every)* todo(a); **in a. case** de todas formas
2 PRON **(a)** *(in questions)* alguno(a); **do they have a.?** ¿tienen alguno?; **I need some paper,**

have you a.? necesito papel, ¿tienes? (**b**) *(in negative clauses)* ninguno(a); **I don't want a.** no quiero ninguno (**c**) *(no matter which)* cualquiera; **you can have a. (one)** coge el/la que quieras

3 ADV **is there a. more?** ¿hay más?; **I used to like it, but not a. more/longer** antes me gustaba pero ya no; **is he a. better?** ¿está mejor?

anybody ['enɪbɒdɪ] PRON *(in questions, conditionals)* alguien, alguno(a); *(in negative clauses)* nadie, ninguno(a); *(no matter who)* cualquiera; **a. but me** cualquiera menos yo; **bring a. you like** trae a quien quieras; **do you see a. over there?** ¿ves a alguien allí?; **I can't find a.** no encuentro a nadie

anyhow ['enɪhaʊ] ADV (**a**) *(in spite of that)* en todo caso, de todas formas; *(changing the subject)* bueno, pues (**b**) *(carelessly)* desordenadamente, de cualquier modo o forma

anyone ['enɪwʌn] PRON = **anybody**

anyplace ['enɪpleɪs] ADV *US* = **anywhere**

anything ['enɪθɪŋ] **1** PRON *(in questions, conditionals)* algo, alguna cosa; *(in negative clauses)* nada; *(no matter what)* cualquier cosa; **a. but that** cualquier cosa menos eso; **a. else?** ¿algo más?; **can I do a. for you?** ¿puedo ayudarte en algo?; **hardly a.** casi nada; **if a., I'd buy the big one** de comprar uno compraría el grande; **to run/work like a.** correr/trabajar a más no poder

2 ADV **is this a. like what you wanted?** ¿viene a ser éste lo que querías?

anyway ['enɪweɪ] ADV = **anyhow (a)**

anywhere ['enɪweə(r)] ADV (**a**) *(in questions, conditionals)* *(situation)* en alguna parte; *(movement)* a alguna parte; **could it be a. else?** ¿podría estar en otro sitio? (**b**) *(in negative clauses)* *(situation)* en ninguna parte; *(movement)* a ninguna parte; *(no matter where)* dondequiera, en cualquier parte; **go a. you like** ve a donde quieras; **we aren't a. near finished** no hemos terminado ni mucho menos

apart [ə'pɑːt] ADV (**a**) *(at a distance)* alejado(a), separado(a); **to be poles a.** ser polos opuestos; **you can't tell the twins a.** no se puede distinguir los mellizos el uno del otro (**b**) *(to pieces)* **to fall a.** deshacerse; **to take sth a.** desmontar algo (**c**) **a. from** *(excepting)* aparte de

apartheid [ə'pɑːtheɪt] N apartheid *m*

apartment [ə'pɑːtmənt] N *US* apartamento *m Esp* piso *m, Arg* departamento *m*; **a. block** edificio *m* or bloque *m* de apartamentos or *Esp* pisos or *Arg* departamentos

apathetic [æpə'θetɪk] ADJ apático(a)

apathy ['æpəθɪ] N apatía *f*

ape [eɪp] **1** N mono *m*
2 VT imitar, copiar

apéritif [ə'perɪtiːf] N aperitivo *m*

aperture ['æpətʃə(r)] N *(hole, crack)* resquicio *m*, rendija *f*; *Phot* abertura *f*

APEX ['eɪpeks] ADJ **A. ticket** billete *m* or *Am* boleto *m* or *Am* pasaje *m* (con tarifa) APEX

apex ['eɪpeks] N *(of triangle)* vértice *m*; *Fig* cumbre *f*

aphrodisiac [æfrə'dɪzɪæk] N afrodisíaco *m*

apiece [ə'piːs] ADV cada uno(a)

aplomb [ə'plɒm] N aplomo *m*

apocalypse [ə'pɒkəlɪps] N apocalipsis *m inv*

apolitical [eɪpə'lɪtɪkəl] ADJ apolítico(a)

apologetic [əpɒlə'dʒetɪk] ADJ *(remorseful)* de disculpa; **he was very a.** pidió mil perdones

apologetically [əpɒlə'dʒetɪklɪ] ADV disculpándose, pidiendo perdón

apologize [ə'pɒlədʒaɪz] VI *(say sorry)* disculparse; **they apologized to us for the delay** se disculparon con nosotros por el retraso

apology [ə'pɒlədʒɪ] N disculpa *f*, excusa *f*; *Fam* **what an a. for a meal!** ¡vaya birria de comida!

apoplectic [æpə'plektɪk] ADJ *Med* apopléctico(a); *Fam* **to be a. with rage** estar furioso(a)

apostle [ə'pɒsəl] N apóstol *m*

apostrophe [ə'pɒstrəfɪ] N apóstrofo *m*

appal, *US* **appall** [ə'pɔːl] VT horrorizar

appalling [ə'pɔːlɪŋ] ADJ *(horrifying)* horroroso(a); *Fam (very bad)* pésimo(a), fatal

apparatus [æpə'reɪtəs] N aparato *m*; *(equipment)* equipo *m*

apparel [ə'pærəl] N *US* indumentaria *f*, ropa *f*

apparent [ə'pærənt] ADJ *(obvious)* evidente; *(seeming)* aparente; **to become a.** ponerse de manifiesto

apparently [ə'pærəntlɪ] ADV *(seemingly)* por lo visto

apparition [æpə'rɪʃən] N aparición *f*

appeal [ə'piːl] **1** N (**a**) *(request)* solicitud *f*; *(plea)* súplica *f* (**b**) *(attraction)* atractivo *m*; *(interest)* interés *m* (**c**) *Jur* apelación *f*
2 VI (**a**) *(plead)* rogar, suplicar (**to** a); **to a. for help** solicitar ayuda (**b**) *(attract)* atraer; *(interest)* interesar; **it doesn't a. to me** no me dice nada (**c**) *Jur* apelar

appealing [ə'piːlɪŋ] ADJ *(moving)* conmovedor(a); *(attractive)* atractivo(a); *(tempting)* atrayente

appear [ə'pɪə(r)] VI (**a**) *(become visible)* aparecer; *(publicly)* presentarse; *(on stage)* actuar; **to a. before a court** comparecer ante un tribunal; **to a. on television** salir en la televisión (**b**) *(seem)* parecer; **he appears relaxed** parece relajado; **so it appears** según parece

appearance [ə'pɪərəns] N (**a**) *(becoming visible)* aparición *f*; *(publicly)* presentación *f*; *(on stage)* actuación *f*; *(before court)* comparecencia *f*; *(of book etc)* publicación *f*; **to put in an a.** hacer acto de presencia (**b**) *(look)* apariencia *f*, aspecto *m*; **to all appearances** al parecer

appease [ə'pi:z] VT *(anger)* aplacar, apaciguar; *(person)* calmar, apaciguar; *Pol* contemporizar con

appeasement [ə'pi:zmənt] N *Pol* contemporización *f*

appendices [ə'pendɪsi:z] PL *of* **appendix**

appendicitis [əpendɪ'saɪtɪs] N apendicitis *f*

appendix [ə'pendɪks] N *(pl* **appendices)** apéndice *m*

appetite ['æpɪtaɪt] N apetito *m*; *Fig* deseo *m*

appetizer ['æpɪtaɪzə(r)] N *(drink)* aperitivo *m*; *(snack)* tapa *f*, pincho *m*

appetizing ['æpɪtaɪzɪŋ] ADJ apetitoso(a)

applaud [ə'plɔ:d] VT & VI aplaudir

applause [ə'plɔ:z] N aplausos *mpl*

apple ['æpəl] N manzana *f*; **a. tree** manzano *m*

appliance [ə'plaɪəns] N dispositivo *m*

applicable [ə'plɪkəbəl] ADJ aplicable

applicant ['æplɪkənt] N *(for post)* candidato(a) *m,f*; *(to court, for tickets)* solicitante *mf*

application [æplɪ'keɪʃən] N **(a)** *(of cream)* aplicación *f* **(b)** *(for post etc)* solicitud *f*; **a. form** solicitud; **job a.** solicitud de empleo **(c)** *(effort)* aplicación *f*; **she lacks a.** no se aplica

applied [ə'plaɪd] ADJ aplicado(a)

apply [ə'plaɪ] **1** VT aplicar; *(brake)* emplear; *(law)* recurrir a; *(pressure)* ejercer; **to a. oneself** to dedicarse a
 2 VI **(a)** *(law, rule)* aplicarse; **that applies to you too!** ¡esto es válido *or* vale para tí también! **(b)** to apply (to sb) for sth *(job, grant)* solicitar algo (a algn)
 ▸ **apply for** VT INSEP *(post, information)* solicitar; *(tickets)* pedir

appoint [ə'pɔɪnt] VT *(person)* nombrar; *(time, place etc)* fijar, señalar

appointment [ə'pɔɪntmənt] N **(a)** *(to post)* nombramiento *m*; *(post)* cargo *m* **(b)** *(meeting)* cita *f*; **to make an a. with** citarse con; *(at doctor's)* pedir hora a

apportion [ə'pɔːʃən] VT *Fig (blame)* echar

appraisal [ə'preɪzəl] N evaluación *f*

appreciable [ə'pri:ʃəbəl] ADJ *(difference)* apreciable; *(sum)* importante

appreciate [ə'pri:ʃɪeɪt] **1** VT **(a)** *(be thankful for)* agradecer **(b)** *(understand)* entender **(c)** *(value)* apreciar, valorar
 2 VI *(increase in value)* apreciarse

appreciation [əpri:ʃɪ'eɪʃən] N **(a)** *(of help, advice)* agradecimiento *m*; *(of difficulty)* comprensión *f*; *(of wine etc)* aprecio *m*; *(appraisal)* evaluación *f* **(b)** *(increase in value)* apreciación *f*

appreciative [ə'pri:ʃɪətɪv] ADJ *(thankful)* agradecido(a); *(responsive)* apreciativo(a)

apprehend [æprɪ'hend] VT *(arrest)* detener

apprehension [æprɪ'henʃən] N **(a)** *(arrest)* detención *f* **(b)** *(fear)* aprensión *f*

apprehensive [æprɪ'hensɪv] ADJ *(fearful)* aprensivo(a)

apprentice [ə'prentɪs] N aprendiz(a) *m,f*

apprenticeship [ə'prentɪsʃɪp] N aprendizaje *m*

approach [ə'prəʊtʃ] **1** N **(a)** *(coming near)* acercamiento *m*; *(to town)* acceso *m*; **a. road** vía *f* de acceso **(b)** *(to problem)* enfoque *m*
 2 VT *(come near to)* acercarse a; *(be similar to)* aproximarse a; *Fig (problem)* abordar; *(person)* dirigirse a; **to a. sb about sth** dirigirse a algn a propósito de algo
 3 VI acercarse

approachable [ə'prəʊtʃəbəl] ADJ *(person)* accesible

appropriate[1] [ə'prəʊprɪət] ADJ *(suitable)* apropiado(a), adecuado(a); *(convenient)* oportuno(a)

appropriate[2] [ə'prəʊprɪeɪt] VT *(allocate)* asignar; *(steal)* apropiarse de

approval [ə'pru:vəl] N aprobación *f*, visto bueno; *Com* **to get sth on a.** adquirir algo sin compromiso de compra

approve [ə'pru:v] VT aprobar; *Br Formerly* **approved school** reformatorio *m*, correccional *m*
 ▸ **approve of** VT INSEP aprobar

approving [ə'pru:vɪŋ] ADJ *(look etc)* aprobatorio(a)

approx [ə'prɒks] *(abbr* **approximately)** aprox.

approximate 1 ADJ [ə'prɒksɪmɪt] aproximado(a)
 2 VT [ə'prɒksɪmeɪt] aproximarse a

approximately [ə'prɒksɪmɪtlɪ] ADV aproximadamente

apricot ['eɪprɪkɒt] N *(fruit) Esp* albaricoque *m*, *Andes, RP* damasco *m*, *Méx* chabacano *m*; **a. tree** *Esp* albaricoquero *m*, *Andes, RP* damasco *m*, *Méx* chabacano *m*

April ['eɪprəl] N abril *m*; **A. Fools' Day** día *m* uno de abril, ≃ día de los Inocentes (28 de diciembre)

apron ['eɪprən] N delantal *m*; *(for workman)* mandil *m*

apt [æpt] ADJ **(a)** *(suitable)* apropiado(a); *(remark)* acertado(a), oportuno(a); *(name)* justo(a); *(description)* exacto(a) **(b)** **to be a. to do sth** ser propenso(a) a hacer algo

aptitude ['æptɪtju:d] N capacidad *f*; **a. test** prueba *f* de aptitud

aptly ['æptlɪ] ADV acertadamente

aqualung ['ækwəlʌŋ] N botella *f* de oxígeno

aquamarine [ækwəmə'ri:n] **1** N *(gem)* aguamarina *f*
 2 ADJ de color de aguamarina

aquarium [ə'kweərɪəm] N acuario *m*

Aquarius [ə'kweərɪəs] N Acuario *m*

aquatic [ə'kwætɪk] ADJ acuático(a)

aqueduct ['ækwɪdʌkt] N acueducto *m*

Arab ['ærəb] ADJ & N árabe *(mf)*

Arabian [ə'reɪbɪən] ADJ árabe

Arabic ['ærəbɪk] **1** ADJ árabe, arábigo(a); **A. numerals** numeración arábiga
2 N *(language)* árabe *m*

arable ['ærəbəl] ADJ cultivable

Aragon ['ærəgən] N Aragón

arbitrary ['ɑ:bɪtrərɪ] ADJ arbitrario(a)

arbitrate ['ɑ:bɪtreɪt] VT & VI arbitrar

arbitration [ɑ:bɪ'treɪʃən] N arbitraje *m*

arc [ɑ:k] N arco *m*; **a. lamp** arco voltaico

arcade [ɑ:'keɪd] N arcada *f*; *(passageway)* pasaje *m*; **shopping a.** galerías *fpl* (comerciales)

arch [ɑ:tʃ] **1** N (**a**) *Archit* arco *m*; *(vault)* bóveda *f* (**b**) *Anat* empeine *m*
2 VT *(back)* arquear

archaeologist [ɑ:kɪ'ɒlədʒɪst] N arqueólogo(a) *m,f*

archaeology [ɑ:kɪ'ɒlədʒɪ] N arqueología *f*

archaic [ɑ:'keɪɪk] ADJ arcaico(a)

archbishop [ɑ:tʃ'bɪʃəp] N arzobispo *m*

arched [ɑ:tʃt] ADJ arqueado(a)

archeologist [ɑ:kɪ'ɒlədʒɪst] N *US* = archaeologist

archeology [ɑ:kɪ'ɒlədʒɪ] N *US* = archaeology

archer ['ɑ:tʃə(r)] N arquero(a) *m,f*

archery ['ɑ:tʃərɪ] N tiro *m* con arco

archetypal ['ɑ:kɪtaɪpəl] ADJ arquetípico(a)

archipelago [ɑ:kɪ'peligəʊ] N archipiélago *m*

architect ['ɑ:kɪtekt] N arquitecto(a) *m,f*

architectural [ɑ:kɪ'tektʃərəl] ADJ arquitectónico(a)

architecture ['ɑ:kɪtektʃə(r)] N arquitectura *f*

archives ['ɑ:kaɪvz] NPL archivos *mpl*

archway ['ɑ:tʃweɪ] N *(arch)* arco *m*; *(vault)* bóveda *f*; *(in church)* atrio *m*; *(passage)* pasaje *m*

arctic ['ɑ:ktɪk] **1** ADJ ártico(a); **A. Circle** círculo polar Ártico
2 N **the A.** el Ártico

ardent ['ɑ:dənt] ADJ *(supporter etc)* apasionado(a); *(desire)* ardiente

ardour, *US* **ardor** ['ɑ:də(r)] N pasión *f*, ardor *m*

arduous ['ɑ:djʊəs] ADJ arduo(a), penoso(a)

are [ɑ:(r)] 2ND PERSON SING PRES, 1ST, 2ND, 3RD PERSON PL PRES *of* **be**

area ['eərɪə] N *(surface)* área *f*, superficie *f*; *(space)* extensión *f*; *(region)* región *f*; *(of town)* zona *f*; *Fig (field)* campo *m*; *US Tel* **a. code** prefijo *m* local

arena [ə'ri:nə] N *(stadium)* estadio *m*; *(bullring)* plaza *f*; *(circus)* pista *f*; *Fig (stage)* campo *m* de batalla

Argentina [ɑ:dʒən'ti:nə] N Argentina

Argentinian [ɑ:dʒən'tɪnɪən] ADJ & N argentino(a) *(m,f)*

arguable ['ɑ:gjʊəbəl] ADJ discutible

arguably ['ɑ:gjʊəblɪ] ADV **it's a. the best** hay quienes dicen que es el mejor

argue ['ɑ:gju:] **1** VT *(reason)* discutir; *(point of view)* mantener
2 VI *(quarrel)* discutir; *(reason)* argumentar, razonar; **to a. for** abogar por; **to a. against sth** ponerse en contra de algo

argument ['ɑ:gjʊmənt] N *(reason)* argumento *m* (**for** a favor de; **against** en contra de); *(quarrel)* discusión *f*, disputa *f*; **for the sake of a.** por decir algo

argumentative [ɑ:gjʊ'mentətɪv] ADJ **she's very a.** le gusta discutir por todo

aria ['ɑ:rɪə] N aria *f*

arid ['ærɪd] ADJ árido(a)

Aries ['eəri:z] N Aries *m*

arise [ə'raɪz] VI (pt **arose**; pp **arisen** [ə'rɪzən]) *(get up)* levantarse; *(happen)* surgir; **should the occasion a.** si se presenta la ocasión

aristocracy [ærɪ'stɒkrəsɪ] N aristocracia *f*

aristocrat [*Br* 'ærɪstəkræt, *US* ə'rɪstəkræt] N aristócrata *mf*

arithmetic [ə'rɪθmətɪk] N aritmética *f*

ark [ɑ:k] N arca *f*; **Noah's A.** el arca de Noé

arm [ɑ:m] **1** N (**a**) *(of person, chair)* brazo *m*; *(of garment)* manga *f*; **to walk a. in a.** ir cogidos(as) del brazo (**b**) *Mil* **arms** armas *fpl*; **arms race** carrera armamentística; **coat of arms** escudo *m*
2 VT armar; **to a. oneself against sth** armarse contra algo

armaments ['ɑ:məmənts] NPL armamentos *mpl*

armband ['ɑ:mbænd] N *(at funeral, for swimming)* brazalete *m*

armchair ['ɑ:mtʃeə(r)] N sillón *m*

armed ['ɑ:md] ADJ armado(a); **a. forces** fuerzas armadas; **a. robbery** robo *m* a mano armada

Armenia [ɑ:'mi:nɪə] N Armenia

armistice ['ɑ:mɪstɪs] N armisticio *m*

armour, *US* **armor** ['ɑ:mə(r)] N *(on vehicle)* blindaje *m*; *(suit of)* **a.** armadura *f*

armoured car, *US* **armored car** ['ɑ:məd'kɑ:(r)] N coche blindado

armour-plated, *US* **armor-plated** ['ɑ:mə'pleɪtɪd] ADJ acorazado(a)

armoury, *US* **armory** ['ɑ:mərɪ] N arsenal *m*

armpit ['ɑ:mpɪt] N axila *f*, sobaco *m*

army ['ɑ:mɪ] N ejército *m*

aroma [ə'rəʊmə] N aroma *m*

aromatic [ærəʊ'mætɪk] ADJ aromático(a)

arose [ə'rəʊz] PT *of* **arise**

around [ə'raʊnd] **1** ADV alrededor; **all a.** por todos los lados; **are the children a.?** ¿están los niños por aquí?; **he looked a.** miró (a su) alrededor
2 PREP (**a**) *(indicating position)* alrededor de; **a. the corner** a la vuelta de la esquina; **a. here** por aquí (**b**) *(approximately)* aproximadamente

arouse [ə'raʊz] VT *(sleeper, emotion)* despertar; *(sexually)* excitar

arrange [ə'reɪndʒ] **1** VT **(a)** *(order)* ordenar; *(hair, flowers)* arreglar; *Mus* adaptar **(b)** *(plan)* organizar; *(agree on)* quedar en; **to a. a time** fijar una hora; **arranged marriage** boda arreglada
2 VI **I shall a. for him to be there** lo arreglaré para que pueda asistir

arrangement [ə'reɪndʒmənt] N **(a)** *(display)* colocación *f*; *Mus* adaptación *f* **(b)** *(agreement)* acuerdo *m* **(c) arrangements** *(plans)* planes *mpl*; *(preparations)* preparativos *mpl*

array [ə'reɪ] N colección *f*; **a great a. of goods** un gran surtido de productos

arrears [ə'rɪəz] NPL atrasos *mpl*; **to be in a. with the rent** estar atrasado(a) en el pago del alquiler *or* Méx de la renta; **to be paid in a.** cobrar con retraso

arrest [ə'rest] **1** N detención *f*; **to be under a.** estar detenido(a)
2 VT *(criminal)* detener; *Fig (progress)* frenar

arresting [ə'restɪŋ] ADJ llamativo(a)

arrival [ə'raɪvəl] N llegada *f*; **a new a.** un(a) recién llegado(a)

arrive [ə'raɪv] VI llegar **(at/in** a**)**

arrogance ['ærəgəns] N arrogancia *f*

arrogant ['ærəgənt] ADJ arrogante

arrow ['ærəʊ] N flecha *f*

arse [ɑːs] N *BrVulg (buttocks)* culo *m*

arsenal ['ɑːsənəl] N arsenal *m*

arsenic ['ɑːsnɪk] N arsénico *m*

arson ['ɑːsən] N incendio provocado

art [ɑːt] N **(a)** *(in general)* arte *m*; **the arts** las bellas artes; **arts and crafts** artes *fpl* y oficios *mpl*; **a. gallery** galería *f* de arte **(b) arts** *(branch of knowledge)* letras *fpl*

artefact ['ɑːtɪfækt] N artefacto *m*; *(in archaeology)* objeto *m* de arte

artery ['ɑːtərɪ] N arteria *f*

artful ['ɑːtfʊl] ADJ *(cunning)* ladino(a)

arthritis [ɑː'θraɪtɪs] N artritis *f*

artichoke ['ɑːtɪtʃəʊk] N alcachofa *f*, *Am* alcaucil *m*

article ['ɑːtɪkəl] **1** N artículo *m*; **a. of clothing** prenda *f* de vestir
2 VT **to be articled to a firm of solicitors** trabajar en prácticas *or* hacer una pasantía en un bufete de abogados

articulate[1] [ɑː'tɪkjʊlɪt] ADJ *(speech)* claro(a); *(person)* elocuente

articulate[2] [ɑː'tɪkjʊleɪt] VT *(word)* articular; *(idea, feeling)* formular, expresar

articulated lorry [ɑː'tɪkjʊleɪtɪd'lɒrɪ] N *Br* camión articulado

artificial [ɑːtɪ'fɪʃəl] ADJ artificial; *(limb)* postizo(a); **a. intelligence** inteligencia *f* artificial

artillery [ɑː'tɪlərɪ] N artillería *f*

artisan ['ɑːtɪzæn] N artesano(a) *m,f*

artist ['ɑːtɪst] N artista *mf*; *(painter)* pintor(a) *m,f*

artistic [ɑː'tɪstɪk] ADJ artístico(a)

artistry ['ɑːtɪstrɪ] N arte *m*, talento artístico

arty ['ɑːtɪ] ADJ **(artier, artiest)** *Fam (person)* = que se interesa por las artes

as [æz, *unstressed* əz] **1** ADV & CONJ **(a)** *(comparison)* **as ... as ...** tan ... como ...; **as far as** hasta; *Fig* **as far as I'm concerned** por lo que a mí respecta; **as many as** tantos(as) como; **as much as** tanto(a) como; **as tall as me** tan alto(a) como yo; **as opposed to** a diferencia de; **as little as £5** tan sólo 5 libras; **as soon as they arrive** en cuanto lleguen; **I'll stay as long as I can** quedaré todo el tiempo que pueda; **just as big** igual de grande; **three times as fast** tres veces más rápido; **the same as** igual que
(b) *(manner)* como; **as a rule** por regla general; **as you know** como ya sabéis; **as you like** como quieras; **do as I say** haz lo que yo te digo; **he's working as a doctor** está trabajando de médico; **I thought as much** ya me lo suponía; **it serves as a table** sirve de mesa; **leave it as it is** déjalo tal como está; **he was dressed as a pirate** iba vestido de pirata
(c) *(while, when)* mientras (que); **as a child** de niño(a); **as I was eating** mientras comía; **as we were leaving, we saw Pat** al salir vimos a Pat
(d) *(though)* aunque; **be that as it may** por mucho que así sea; **young as he is** aunque es joven
(e) *(because)* como, ya que
(f) *(and so)* igual que; **as do I** igual que yo; **as well** también
(g) *(purpose)* para; **so as to do sth** para hacer algo
(h) as for my brother en cuanto a mi hermano
(i) as from, as of a partir de
(j) to act as if actuar como si (+ *subj*); **it looks as if the concert is off** parece ser que no habrá concierto
(k) it's late enough as it is ya es muy tarde; **as it were** por así decirlo
(l) as long as *(only if)* siempre que, con tal de que
(m) as regards en cuanto a, por lo que se refiere a; **as usual** como siempre; **as yet** aún, todavía
2 REL PRON **such as** tal(es) como

asap [eɪeseɪ'piː] ADV *(abbr* **as soon as possible***)* cuanto antes, lo antes posible

asbestos [æz'bestəs] N amianto *m*, asbesto *m*

ascend [ə'send] VI subir, ascender

ascendancy [ə'sendənsɪ] N dominio *m*, influencia *f*

ascendant [ə'sendənt] N **to be in the a.** estar en auge

ascent [ə'sent] N subida *f*

ascertain [æsə'teɪn] VT averiguar, enterarse de

ascribe [ə'skraɪb] VT **to a. sth to sth/sb** imputar algo a algo/algn

aseptic [ə'septɪk] ADJ aséptico(a)

ash[1] [æʃ] N *Bot* fresno *m*

ash² [æʃ] N ceniza f; **a. bin**, US **a. can** cubo m de la basura; Rel **A. Wednesday** miércoles m inv de ceniza

ashamed [ə'ʃeɪmd] ADJ avergonzado(a), Am salvo RP apenado(a); **you ought to be a. of yourself!** ¡debería darte vergüenza or Am salvo RP pena!

ashen ['æʃən] ADJ (face) pálido(a)

ashore [ə'ʃɔː(r)] ADV (position) en tierra; **to go a.** desembarcar; **to swim a.** nadar hacia tierra

ashtray ['æʃtreɪ] N cenicero m

Asia ['eɪʒə] N Asia; **A. Minor** Asia Menor

Asian ['eɪʒən] **1** N asiático(a) m,f; Br (person from Indian subcontinent) = persona de la India, Paquistán o Bangladesh
2 ADJ asiático(a); Br (from Indian subcontinent) = de la India, Paquistán o Bangladesh

aside [ə'saɪd] **1** ADV al lado, aparte; **to cast a.** echar a un lado; **to stand a.** apartarse
2 PREP **a. from** (apart from) aparte de; (as well as) además de
3 N Th aparte m

ask [ɑːsk] **1** VT **(a)** (enquire about) preguntar; **to a. sb a question** hacer una pregunta a algn **(b)** (request) pedir, solicitar; **she asked me to post it** me pidió que lo echara al buzón **(c)** (invite) invitar
2 VI (enquire) preguntar; (request) pedir
▶ **ask after** VT INSEP **to a. after sb** preguntar por algn
▶ **ask for** VT INSEP (help) pedir, solicitar; (person) preguntar por
▶ **ask out** VT SEP **to a. sb out** invitar a algn a salir

askance [ə'skæns] ADV **to look a. at sb** mirar a algn con recelo

askew [ə'skjuː] **1** ADJ ladeado(a)
2 ADV de lado

asleep [ə'sliːp] ADJ (person) dormido(a); (limb) adormecido(a); **to fall a.** quedarse dormido(a)

asparagus [ə'spærəgəs] N INV espárragos mpl

aspect ['æspekt] N **(a)** (of question) aspecto m **(b)** (of building) orientación f

aspersions [ə'spɜːʃənz] NPL **to cast a. on sb** difamar a algn

asphalt ['æsfælt] N asfalto m

asphyxiate [æs'fɪksɪeɪt] **1** VT asfixiar
2 VI asfixiarse

asphyxiation [æsfɪksɪ'eɪʃən] N asfixia f

aspiration [æspə'reɪʃən] N aspiración f

aspire [ə'spaɪə(r)] VI **to a. to** aspirar a

aspirin ['æsprɪn] N aspirina f

ass¹ [æs] N asno(a) m,f, burro(a) m,f

ass² [æs] N US Vulg culo m

assailant [ə'seɪlənt] N agresor(a) m,f, atacante mf

assassin [ə'sæsɪn] N asesino(a) m,f

assassinate [ə'sæsɪneɪt] VT asesinar

assassination [əsæsɪ'neɪʃən] N asesinato m

assault [ə'sɔːlt] **1** N Mil ataque m (**on** a); Jur agresión f
2 VT Mil asaltar, atacar; Jur agredir; (sexually) violar

assemble [ə'sembəl] **1** VT (people) reunir, juntar; (furniture) montar
2 VI (people) reunirse, juntarse

assembly [ə'semblɪ] N reunión f, asamblea f; Tech montaje m; Br Sch = reunión de todos los profesores y los alumnos al principio de la jornada escolar; Ind **a. line** cadena f de montaje

assent [ə'sent] **1** N (agreement) asentimiento m; (consent) consentimiento m; (approval) aprobación f
2 VI asentir, consentir (**to** en)

assert [ə'sɜːt] VT afirmar; **to a. oneself** imponerse; **to a. one's rights** hacer valer sus derechos

assertion [ə'sɜːʃən] N afirmación f

assertive [ə'sɜːtɪv] ADJ enérgico(a)

assess [ə'ses] VT (estimate value of) valorar; (damages, price) calcular; (tax) gravar; Fig (effect) evaluar

assessment [ə'sesmənt] N (of value) valoración f; (of damages etc) cálculo m; (of taxes) gravamen m; Fig juicio m

assessor [ə'sesə(r)] N asesor(a) m,f

asset ['æset] N **(a)** (benefit) ventaja f; **to be an a.** (person) ser de gran valor **(b)** Fin **assets** bienes mpl; **fixed assets** bienes raíces

asshole ['æshəʊl] N US Vulg (unpleasant person) hijo(a) m,f de puta, cabrón(ona) m,f

assiduous [ə'sɪdjʊəs] ADJ asiduo(a)

assign [ə'saɪn] VT (task) asignar; (property etc) ceder; **to a. sb to a job** designar a algn para un trabajo

assignment [ə'saɪnmənt] N (allocation) asignación f; (task) tarea f; (mission) misión f; (appointment) cita f

assimilate [ə'sɪmɪleɪt] VT asimilar

assist [ə'sɪst] VT & VI ayudar

assistance [ə'sɪstəns] N ayuda f, auxilio m

assistant [ə'sɪstənt] N ayudante mf; **a. manager** subdirector(a) m,f; **shop a.** dependiente(a) m,f; Br (language) **a.** (in school) auxiliar mf de conversación; (in university) lector(a) m,f de lengua extranjera

associate¹ [ə'səʊʃɪeɪt] **1** VT (ideas) relacionar; (companies) asociar; **to be associated with sth** estar relacionado(a) con algo
2 VI **to a. with** tratar con

associate² [ə'səʊʃɪt] **1** ADJ asociado(a)
2 N (colleague) colega mf; (partner) socio(a) m,f; (accomplice) cómplice mf

association [əsəʊsɪ'eɪʃən] N asociación f; (company) sociedad f

assorted [ə'sɔːtɪd] ADJ surtido(a), variado(a)

assortment [ə'sɔːtmənt] N surtido m, variedad f

assume [ə'sjuːm] **1** VT *(power)* asumir; *(attitude, name)* adoptar; **an assumed name** un nombre falso
2 VI *(suppose)* suponer

assumption [ə'sʌmpʃən] N **(a)** *(of power)* toma f; **a. of office** toma de posesión **(b)** *(supposition)* suposición f

assurance [ə'ʃʊərəns] N **(a)** *(guarantee)* garantía f **(b)** *(confidence)* confianza f **(c)** Br *(insurance)* seguro m

assure [ə'ʃʊə(r)] VT asegurar

asterisk ['æstərɪsk] N asterisco m

astern [ə'stɜːn] ADV a popa

asthma ['æsmə] N asma f

astonish [ə'stɒnɪʃ] VT asombrar, pasmar; **I was astonished** me quedé pasmado(a)

astonishing [ə'stɒnɪʃɪŋ] ADJ asombroso(a), pasmoso(a)

astonishment [ə'stɒnɪʃmənt] N asombro m; **to my a.** para gran sorpresa mía

astound [ə'staʊnd] VT asombrar, pasmar

astounding [ə'staʊndɪŋ] ADJ pasmoso(a), asombroso(a)

astray [ə'streɪ] ADV **to go a.** extraviarse; Fig equivocarse; **to lead sb a.** llevar a algn por mal camino

astride [ə'straɪd] PREP a horcajadas sobre

astrology [ə'strɒlədʒɪ] N astrología f

astronaut ['æstrənɔːt] N astronauta mf

astronomer [ə'strɒnəmə(r)] N astrónomo(a) m,f

astronomical [æstrə'nɒmɪkəl] ADJ astronómico(a)

astronomy [ə'strɒnəmɪ] N astronomía f

Asturias [æ'stʊəriːæs] N Asturias

astute [ə'stjuːt] ADJ astuto(a)

asylum [ə'saɪləm] N **(a)** *(protection)* asilo m; **to seek political a.** pedir asilo político **(b)** **mental a.** manicomio m

at [æt, *unstressed* ət] PREP **(a)** *(position)* a, en; **at school/work** en el colegio/trabajo; **at the window** a la ventana; **at the top** en lo alto **(b)** *(direction)* a; **to be angry at sb** estar *esp Esp* enfadado(a) *or esp Am* enojado(a) con algn; **to laugh at sb** reírse de algn; **to look at sth/sb** mirar algo/a algn; **to shout at sb** gritarle a algn **(c)** *(time)*: **at Easter/Christmas** en Semana Santa/Navidad; **at six o'clock** a las seis; **at night** *Esp* por la noche, *Am* en la noche; **at first** al principio; **at last** por fin; **at once** enseguida; **at that time** entonces; **at the moment** ahora **(d)** *(manner)* a, en; **at best/worst** en el mejor/peor de los casos; **at hand** a mano; **at least** por lo menos; **not at all** en absoluto; *(don't mention it)* de nada **(e)** *(rate)* a; **they retail at 100 euros each** se venden a 100 euros la unidad; **two at a time** de dos en dos

ate [et, eɪt] PT *of* **eat**

atheist ['eɪθɪɪst] N ateo(a) m,f

Athens ['æθɪnz] N Atenas

athlete ['æθliːt] N atleta mf

athletic [æθ'letɪk] **1** ADJ atlético(a)
2 NPL **athletics** Br *(track and field)* atletismo m; US deportes mpl

Atlantic [ət'læntɪk] ADJ **the A. (Ocean)** el (océano) Atlántico

atlas ['ætləs] N atlas m

ATM [eɪtiː'em] N Fin *(abbr* **automated teller machine***)* cajero automático

atmosphere ['ætməsfɪə(r)] N atmósfera f; Fig *(ambience)* ambiente m

atmospheric [ætməs'ferɪk] ADJ atmosférico(a)

atom ['ætəm] N átomo m; **a. bomb** bomba atómica

atomic [ə'tɒmɪk] ADJ atómico(a)

atone [ə'təʊn] VI **to a. for** expiar

atrocious [ə'trəʊʃəs] ADJ atroz

atrocity [ə'trɒsɪtɪ] N atrocidad f

attach [ə'tætʃ] VT *(stick)* pegar; *(fasten)* sujetar; *(document)* adjuntar; **to a. importance to sth** dar importancia a algo; Fig **to be attached to** *(be fond of)* tener cariño a

attaché [ə'tæʃeɪ] N agregado(a) m,f; **a. case** maletín m

attachment [ə'tætʃmənt] N **(a)** Tech accesorio m; *(action)* acoplamiento m **(b)** *(fondness)* apego m **(to** por) **(c)** Comput *(to e-mail)* archivo adjunto, anexo m

attack [ə'tæk] **1** N **(a)** *(assault)* ataque m, asalto m; **an a. on sb's life** un atentado contra la vida de algn **(b)** Med ataque m
2 VT *(assault)* atacar, asaltar; Fig *(problem)* abordar; *(job)* emprender; Fig *(criticize)* atacar

attacker [ə'tækə(r)] N asaltante mf, agresor(a) m,f

attain [ə'teɪn] VT *(aim)* lograr; *(rank, age)* llegar a

attainment [ə'teɪnmənt] N *(achievement)* logro m; *(skill)* talento m

attempt [ə'tempt] **1** N intento m, tentativa f; **at the second a.** a la segunda; **an a. on sb's life** un atentado contra la vida de algn
2 VT intentar; **to a. to do sth** tratar de *or* intentar hacer algo; Jur **attempted murder/rape** intento m de asesinato/violación

attend [ə'tend] **1** VT *(be present at)* asistir a; *(care for, wait on)* atender
2 VI *(be present)* asistir; *(pay attention)* prestar atención
▸ **attend to** VT INSEP *(business)* ocuparse de; *(in shop)* atender a

attendance [ə'tendəns] N asistencia f

attendant [ə'tendənt] N *(in cinema etc)* acomodador(a) m,f; *(in museum)* guía mf; *(in car park)* vigilante(a) m,f

attention [ə'tenʃən] N **(a)** *(in general)* atención f; **for the a. of Miss Jones** a la atención de la Srta. Jones; **pay a.!** ¡atiende!; **to pay a. to sth/**

sb prestar atención a algo/algn (**b**) *Mil* **a.!** ¡firmes!; **to stand to a.** estar firmes

attentive [əˈtentɪv] ADJ *(listener)* atento(a); *(helpful)* solícito(a)

attest [əˈtest] VI **to a. to** dar testimonio de

attic [ˈætɪk] N ático *m*

attire [əˈtaɪə(r)] N *Fml* traje *m*

attitude [ˈætɪtjuːd] N actitud *f*; *(position of body)* postura *f*; **an a. of mind** un estado de ánimo

attorney [əˈtɜːnɪ] N (**a**) *US (lawyer)* abogado(a) *m,f*; **A. General** ≃ Ministro(a) *m,f* de Justicia; **district a.** fiscal *mf* (**b**) *Jur* **power of a.** poderes *mpl*

attract [əˈtrækt] VT atraer; **to a. attention** llamar la atención; **to a. a waiter's attention** llamar a un camarero

attraction [əˈtrækʃən] N (**a**) *(power)* atracción *f* (**b**) *(attractive thing)* atractivo *m*; *(charm)* encanto *m*; *(incentive)* aliciente *m*; **the main a.** el número fuerte

attractive [əˈtræktɪv] ADJ atractivo(a)

attribute¹ [ˈætrɪbjuːt] N *(quality)* atributo *m*

attribute² [əˈtrɪbjuːt] VT atribuir

attrition [əˈtrɪʃən] N **war of a.** guerra *f* de desgaste

aubergine [ˈəʊbəʒiːn] N *Br* berenjena *f*

auburn [ˈɔːbən] ADJ castaño rojizo *inv*

auction [ˈɔːkʃən] **1** N subasta *f*
 2 VT subastar

auctioneer [ɔːkʃəˈnɪə(r)] N subastador(a) *m,f*

audacious [ɔːˈdeɪʃəs] ADJ *(daring)* audaz; *(bold)* atrevido(a); *(impudent)* descarado(a)

audacity [ɔːˈdæsɪtɪ] N audacia *f*

audible [ˈɔːdɪbəl] ADJ audible

audience [ˈɔːdɪəns] N (**a**) *(spectators)* público *m*; *(at concert, conference)* auditorio *m*; *(television)* telespectadores *mpl* (**b**) *(meeting)* audiencia *f*

audiobook [ˈɔːdɪəʊbʊk] N audiolibro *m*

audio-visual [ɔːdɪəʊˈvɪzjʊəl] ADJ audiovisual; **a. aids** apoyo *m* audiovisual

audit [ˈɔːdɪt] **1** N revisión *f* de cuentas
 2 VT revisar, intervenir

audition [ɔːˈdɪʃən] **1** N prueba *f*
 2 VT **to a. sb for a part** probar a algn para un papel

auditor [ˈɔːdɪtə(r)] N revisor(a) *m,f* de cuentas

auditorium [ɔːdɪˈtɔːrɪəm] N auditorio *m*

augment [ɔːgˈment] VT aumentar

augur [ˈɔːgə(r)] VI **to a. well** ser de buen agüero

August [ˈɔːgəst] N agosto *m*

aunt [ɑːnt] N *(also Fam* **auntie, aunty** [ˈɑːntɪ]) tía *f*

au pair [əʊˈpeə(r)] N **au pair (girl)** au pair *f*

aura [ˈɔːrə] N aura *f*; *Rel* aureola *f*

aural [ˈɔːrəl] ADJ auditivo(a), del oído

auspices [ˈɔːspɪsɪz] NPL **under the a. of** bajo los auspicios de

auspicious [ɔːˈspɪʃəs] ADJ de buen augurio

austere [ɒˈstɪə(r)] ADJ austero(a)

austerity [ɒˈsterɪtɪ] N austeridad *f*

Australia [ɒˈstreɪlɪə] N Australia

Australian [ɒˈstreɪlɪən] ADJ & N australiano(a) *(m,f)*

Austria [ˈɒstrɪə] N Austria

Austrian [ˈɒstrɪən] ADJ & N austríaco(a) *(m,f)*

authentic [ɔːˈθentɪk] ADJ auténtico(a)

author [ˈɔːθə(r)] N autor(a) *m,f*

authoritarian [ɔːθɒrɪˈteərɪən] ADJ autoritario(a)

authoritative [ɔːˈθɒrɪtətɪv] ADJ *(reliable)* autorizado(a); *(authoritarian)* autoritario(a)

authority [ɔːˈθɒrɪtɪ] N autoridad *f*; **local a.** ayuntamiento *m*

authorization [ɔːθəraɪˈzeɪʃən] N autorización *f*

authorize [ˈɔːθəraɪz] VT autorizar; **to a. sb to do sth** autorizar a algn a hacer algo

autistic [ɔːˈtɪstɪk] ADJ autista

auto [ˈɔːtəʊ] N *US* automóvil *m*, *Esp* coche *m*, *Am* carro *m*, *RP* auto *m*

autobiography [ɔːtəʊbaɪˈɒgrəfɪ] N autobiografía *f*

autograph [ˈɔːtəgrɑːf] **1** N autógrafo *m*
 2 VT *(sign)* firmar; *(book, photo)* dedicar

automata [ɔːˈtɒmətə] PL *of* automaton

automatic [ɔːtəˈmætɪk] **1** ADJ automático(a)
 2 N *(car) Esp* coche *or Am* carro *or RP* auto *m* (con cambio) automático; *(gun)* pistola automática

automatically [ɔːtəˈmætɪklɪ] ADV automáticamente

automation [ɔːtəˈmeɪʃən] N automatización *f*; **office a.** ofimática *f*

automaton [ɔːˈtɒmətən] N *(pl* **automata**) autómata *m*

automobile [ˈɔːtəməbiːl] N *US* automóvil *m*, *Esp* coche *m*, *Am* carro *m*, *RP* auto *m*

autonomous [ɔːˈtɒnəməs] ADJ autónomo(a)

autonomy [ɔːˈtɒnəmɪ] N autonomía *f*

autopsy [ˈɔːtɒpsɪ] N autopsia *f*

autumn [ˈɔːtəm] N otoño *m*

auxiliary [ɔːgˈzɪljərɪ] ADJ auxiliar

Av., av. *(abbr* **Avenue)** Av., Avda.

avail [əˈveɪl] **1** N **to no a.** en vano
 2 VT **a. oneself of sth** aprovecharse de algo

availability [əveɪləˈbɪlɪtɪ] N disponibilidad *f*

available [əˈveɪləbəl] ADJ *(thing)* disponible; *(person)* libre

avalanche [ˈævəlɑːnʃ] N avalancha *f*

avarice [ˈævərɪs] N avaricia *f*

Ave *(abbr* **Avenue)** Av., Avda.

avenge [əˈvendʒ] VT vengar

avenue [ˈævɪnjuː] N avenida *f*; *Fig* vía *f*

average [ˈævərɪdʒ] **1** N promedio *m*, media *f*; **on a.** por término medio
 2 ADJ *(mean, typical)* medio(a); *(unexceptional)* regular
 3 VT sacar la media de; **he averages eight**

hours' work a day trabaja una media de ocho horas al día

▸ **average out at** VT INSEP salir a una media de

averse [ə'vɜːs] ADJ **to be a. to sth** ser reacio(a) a algo

aversion [ə'vɜːʃən] N *(feeling)* aversión f; *(thing)* bestia negra

avert [ə'vɜːt] VT *(eyes, thoughts)* apartar (**from** de); *(accident)* impedir; *(danger)* evitar

aviation [eɪvɪ'eɪʃən] N aviación f

avid ['ævɪd] ADJ *(reader)* voraz

avidly ['ævɪdlɪ] ADV vorazmente

avocado [ævə'kɑːdəʊ] N **a. (pear)** aguacate m, Andes, CSur palta f

avoid [ə'vɔɪd] VT *(person, thing)* evitar; *(punishment, danger, question)* evitar, eludir

avoidable [ə'vɔɪdəbəl] ADJ evitable

await [ə'weɪt] VT esperar, Esp aguardar

awake [ə'weɪk] **1** ADJ despierto(a); **to be a.** estar despierto(a)

2 *(pt* **awoke, awaked**; *pp* **awoken, awaked)** despertar

awaken [ə'weɪkən] VT & VI *(pt* **awakened**; *pp* **awoken**) = **awake 2**

awakening [ə'weɪkənɪŋ] N despertar m

award [ə'wɔːd] **1** N *(prize)* premio m; *(medal)* condecoración f; Jur indemnización f; *(grant)* beca f

2 VT *(prize)* conceder, otorgar; *(medal)* dar; *(damages)* adjudicar

aware [ə'weə(r)] ADJ *(informed)* enterado(a); **not that I'm a. of** que yo sepa no; **to be a. of sth** ser consciente de algo; **to become a. of sth** darse cuenta de algo

awareness [ə'weənɪs] N conciencia f (**of** de)

awash [ə'wɒʃ] ADJ inundado(a) (**with** de)

away [ə'weɪ] ADV **far a.** lejos; **go a.!** ¡lárgate!; **it's 3 miles a.** está a 3 millas (de distancia); **keep a. from the fire!** ¡no te acerques al fuego!; **right a.** en seguida; **to be a.** *(absent)* estar ausente; *(out)* estar fuera; **to die a.** desvanecerse; **to give sth a.** regalar algo; *(secret)* revelar algo; **to go a.** irse; Sport **to play a.** jugar fuera; **to turn a.** volver la cara; **to work a.** trabajar

awe [ɔː] N *(fear)* temor m; *(amazement)* asombro m; **he was in a. of his father** le intimidaba su padre

awe-inspiring ['ɔːɪnspaɪərɪŋ] ADJ impresionante, imponente

awesome ['ɔːsəm] ADJ impresionante

awful ['ɔːfʊl] ADJ Fam espantoso(a); **an a. lot of people** un montón de gente, Am salvo RP harta gente

awfully ['ɔːfʊlɪ] ADV Fam terriblemente

awkward ['ɔːkwəd] ADJ *(clumsy)* torpe; *(difficult)* pesado(a); *(object)* incómodo(a); *(moment)* inoportuno(a); *(situation)* embarazoso(a); *(problem)* difícil

awning ['ɔːnɪŋ] N *(on ship)* toldo m; *(on shop)* marquesina f

awoke [ə'wəʊk] PT of **awake**

awoken [ə'wəʊkən] PP of **awake, awaken**

axe, US **ax** [æks] **1** N hacha f

2 VT Fig *(jobs)* eliminar; *(costs)* reducir; *(plan)* cancelar; *(person)* despedir

axis ['æksɪs] N *(pl* **axes** ['æksiːz]) eje m

axle ['æksəl] N eje m; Tech árbol m

ayatollah [aɪə'tɒlə] N ayatolá m

Aztec ['æztek] ADJ & N azteca *(mf)*

B

B, b [biː] N (**a**) *(the letter)* B, b f; *Br Aut* **B road**
carretera secundaria (**b**) *Mus* B si m; **B flat** si
bemol

BA [biːˈeɪ] N *(abbr Bachelor of Arts)* *(person)*
licenciado(a) m,f en Filosofía y Letras

babble [ˈbæbəl] VI *(baby)* balbucear; *(brook)*
murmurar

babe [beɪb] N (**a**) *(baby)* bebé m, *Andes* guagua
mf, *RP* nene(a) m,f (**b**) *Fam* nena f, bombón m

baboon [bəˈbuːn] N zambo m

baby [ˈbeɪbɪ] N (**a**) *(infant)* bebé m, *Andes*
guagua mf, *RP* nene(a) m,f; *Br* **B. Buggy**®
sillita f de paseo *or* de niño; *US* **b. buggy** *or*
carriage cochecito m de niño; **b. face** cara f
de niño (**b**) *Fam (darling)* querido(a) m,f

baby-sit [ˈbeɪbɪsɪt] VI cuidar a niños, hacer de
Esp canguro *or* Am babysitter

baby-sitter [ˈbeɪbɪsɪtə(r)] N *Esp* canguro mf, Am
babysitter mf

baby-walker [ˈbeɪbɪwɔːkə(r)] N *Br* tacataca m

bachelor [ˈbætʃələ(r)] N soltero m; *Univ* **B. of
Arts/Science** licenciado(a) m,f en Filosofía y
Letras/Ciencias

back [bæk] **1** N (**a**) *(of person)* espalda f; *(of
animal)* lomo m; **b. to front** al revés; *Fig* **to
get sb's b. up** poner negro a algn; *Fig* **to have
one's b. to the wall** estar en un aprieto (**b**) *(of
book)* lomo m; *(of chair)* respaldo m; *(of coin)*
reverso m; *(of hand)* dorso m; *(of house, car)*
parte f de atrás (**c**) *(of stage, cupboard)* fondo
m (**d**) *Ftb* defensa mf (**e**) *US* **in b. (of)** *(behind)*
en la parte de atrás (de), detrás (de); *(to the rear
of)* al fondo (de)
   2 ADJ (**a**) *(in space)* trasero(a), de atrás; **b.
door** puerta f de atrás; **b. seat** asiento m de
detrás (**b**) *(in time)* **b. rent** alquiler m *or* Am
renta f pendiente de pago; **b. pay** atrasos mpl
   3 ADV (**c**) *(to the rear)* atrás; *(towards the rear)*
hacia atrás; **b. and forth** de acá para allá (**d**)
some years b. hace unos años
   4 VT (**a**) *(support)* apoyar, respaldar (**b**) *Fin*
financiar (**c**) *(bet on)* apostar por (**d**) *(car etc)*
dar marcha atrás a
   5 VI (**a**) *(move backwards)* retroceder (**b**) *(car
etc)* dar marcha atrás

▸ **back away** VI retirarse

▸ **back down** VI echarse atrás

▸ **back off** VI desistir

▸ **back out** VI *(withdraw)* retractarse, volverse
atrás

▸ **back up 1** VT SEP (**a**) *(support)* apoyar (**b**)
Comput (file) hacer una copia de seguridad de
2 VI *Aut* ir marcha atrás

backache [ˈbækeɪk] N dolor m de espalda

backbencher [bækˈbentʃə(r)] N *Br* diputado(a)
m,f ordinario(a) *(sin cargo en el Gobierno o la
oposición)*

backbiting [ˈbækbaɪtɪŋ] N *Fam* chismorreo m,
murmuración f, *RP* chusmerío m

backbone [ˈbækbəʊn] N *Anat* columna f

backcloth [ˈbækklɒθ] N telón m de fondo

backdate [bækˈdeɪt] VT antedatar

backdated [bækˈdeɪtɪd] ADJ con efecto retroactivo

backdrop [ˈbækdrɒp] N telón m de fondo

backer [ˈbækə(r)] N (**a**) *Fin* promotor(a) m,f (**b**)
Pol partidario(a) m,f (**c**) *(person who bets)*
apostante mf

backfire [bækˈfaɪə(r)] VI (**a**) *Aut* petardear (**b**)
Fig **our plan backfired** nos salió el tiro por la
culata

background [ˈbækgraʊnd] N (**a**) *(in scene,
painting, view)* fondo m; **to stay in the b.**
quedarse en segundo plano; **b. music** música
f de fondo (**b**) *(of person)* *(social)* origen m;
(past) pasado m; *(education)* formación f (**c**)
(circumstances) antecedentes mpl

backhand [ˈbækhænd] N *Sport* revés m

backhanded [ˈbækhændɪd] ADJ equívoco(a),
ambiguo(a)

backhander [ˈbækhændə(r)] N *Br Fam (bribe)*
soborno m, *Andes, RP* coima f, *CAm, Méx*
mordida f

backing [ˈbækɪŋ] N (**a**) *(support)* apoyo m; *Com
& Fin* respaldo financiero (**b**) *Mus* acompañamiento m

backlash [ˈbæklæʃ] N reacción violenta y
repentina

backlog [ˈbæklɒg] N **to have a b. of work** tener
un montón de trabajo atrasado

backpack [ˈbækpæk] N mochila f

backpedal [bækˈpedəl] VI *Fam* dar marcha
atrás

backside [bækˈsaɪd] N *Fam* trasero m, culo m

backstage [bækˈsteɪdʒ] ADV entre bastidores

backstroke [ˈbækstrəʊk] N espalda f

backtrack [ˈbæktræk] VI *Fig* volverse atrás

backup [ˈbækʌp] N (**a**) *(support)* apoyo m,
respaldo m; *Comput* **b. (file)** fichero m de
apoyo (**b**) *US (of traffic)* caravana f

backward ['bækwəd] **1** ADJ (**a**) *(movement)* hacia atrás (**b**) *(country)* subdesarrollado(a); *(child)* retrasado(a)
2 ADV *esp US* hacia atrás

backwards ['bækwəds] ADV hacia atrás; **to walk b.** andar de espaldas

backyard [bæk'jɑ:d] N patio trasero; *US* jardín trasero

bacon ['beɪkən] N panceta *f*, *Méx* tocino *m*, *Esp* bacon, *Esp* beicon *m*

bacteria [bæk'tɪərɪə] NPL bacterias *fpl*

bad [bæd] ADJ (**worse, worst**) (**a**) *(poor)* malo(a); **to go from b. to worse** ir de mal en peor (**b**) *(decayed)* podrido(a); **to go b.** echarse a perder (**c**) **that's too b.!** ¡qué pena! (**d**) *(wicked)* malo(a); **to use b. language** ser mal hablado(a) (**e**) *(accident)* grave; *(headache)* fuerte (**f**) *(ill)* enfermo(a) (**g**) **b. debt** deuda *f* incobrable

bade [bæd, beɪd] PT *of* **bid**

badge [bædʒ] N insignia *f*; *(metal disc)* chapa *f*

badger ['bædʒə(r)] **1** N tejón *m*
2 VT acosar

badly ['bædlɪ] ADV (**a**) *(not well)* mal; **he did b. in the exam** le salió mal el examen; **to be b. off** andar mal de dinero (**b**) *(seriously)* gravemente (**c**) *(very much)* mucho; **to miss sb b.** echar mucho de menos a algn; **we need it b.** nos hace mucha falta

bad-mannered [bæd'mænəd] ADJ maleducado(a)

badminton ['bædmɪntən] N bádminton *m*

bad-tempered [bæd'tempəd] ADJ **to be b.** *(temperament)* tener mal genio; *(temporarily)* estar de mal humor

baffle ['bæfəl] **1** VT desconcertar
2 N *Tech* pantalla acústica

baffling ['bæflɪŋ] ADJ incomprensible, enigmático(a)

bag [bæg] N (**a**) *(large)* bolsa *f*; *(handbag)* bolso *m*, *Andes, RP* cartera *f*, *Méx* bolsa; *Fam* **bags of** montones de; **travel b.** bolsa de viaje (**b**) *(hunting)* caza *f*; *Fam* **it's in the b.** es cosa hecha (**c**) *Br very Fam Pej* **old b.** *(woman)* bruja *f* (**d**) **to have bags under one's eyes** tener ojeras

baggage ['bægɪdʒ] N equipaje *m*; **b. handler** mozo *m*, *f* de equipajes

baggy ['bægɪ] ADJ (**baggier, baggiest**) holgado(a); **b. trousers** pantalones anchos

bagpipes ['bægpaɪps] NPL gaita *f*

Bahamas [bə'hɑ:məz] NPL **the B.** las Bahamas

bail[1] [beɪl] N *Jur* fianza *f*; **on b.** bajo fianza; **to stand** *or US* **post b. for sb** salir fiador por algn
▶ **bail out** VT SEP *Fig (person)* sacar de apuros a

bail[2] [beɪl] VI *Naut* to be. (**out**) achicar

bailiff ['beɪlɪf] N (**a**) *Jur* alguacil *m* (**b**) *(steward)* administrador *m*

bait [beɪt] **1** N cebo *m*; **to rise to the b.** tragar el anzuelo, picar
2 VT (**a**) *(for fishing)* cebar (**b**) *(torment)* hostigar

baize [beɪz] N bayeta *f*; **green b.** tapete *m* verde

bake [beɪk] **1** VT (**a**) *(bread, cake)* cocer al horno; *(potatoes)* asar (**b**) *(dry, harden)* resecar
2 VI *Fam* hacer mucho calor

baked [beɪkt] ADJ al horno; **b. potato** patata *f or Am* papa *f* al horno

baker ['beɪkə(r)] N panadero(a) *m,f*

bakery ['beɪkərɪ] N panadería *f*

baking ['beɪkɪŋ] N cocción *f*; **b. dish** fuente *f* para horno; **b. powder** levadura *f* en polvo; **b. tin** molde *m*

balaclava [bælə'klɑ:və] N pasamontañas *m inv*

balance ['bæləns] **1** N (**a**) *(scales)* balanza *f*; *Fig* **to hang in the b.** estar en juego (**b**) *(equilibrium)* equilibrio *m*; *Pol* **b. of power** equilibrio de fuerzas (**c**) *Fin* saldo *m*; **b. of payments** balanza *f* de pagos; **b. sheet** balance *m*; **credit b.** saldo acreedor (**d**) *(remainder)* resto *m*
2 VT (**a**) *(object)* poner en equilibrio (**on** en) (**b**) *(budget)* ajustar; **to b. the books** hacer que cuadren las cuentas (**c**) *(consider)* sopesar
3 VI guardar el equilibrio
▶ **balance out** VI *(figures)* corresponderse

balanced ['bælənst] ADJ equilibrado(a)

balcony ['bælkənɪ] N balcón *m*; *Th* anfiteatro *m*

bald [bɔːld] ADJ (**a**) *(person)* calvo(a) (**b**) *(tyre)* desgastado(a) (**c**) *(style)* escueto(a)

baldness ['bɔːldnɪs] N (**a**) *(of person)* calvicie *f* (**b**) *(of tyre)* desgaste *m* (**c**) *(of style)* sencillez *f*

bale[1] [beɪl] **1** N *(of cloth)* fardo *m*
2 VT embalar

bale[2] [beɪl] VT = **bail**[2]
▶ **bale out 1** VI *Av* saltar en paracaídas de un avión
2 VT SEP *Fig (person)* sacar de apuros a

Balearic [bælɪ'ærɪk] ADJ **the B. Islands** las Islas Baleares

baleful ['beɪlfʊl] ADJ funesto(a), siniestro(a)

Balkans ['bɔːlkənz] NPL **the B.** los Balcanes

ball[1] [bɔːl] N (**a**) *(in cricket, tennis etc)* pelota *f*; *Ftb* balón *m*; *(in billiards, golf etc)* bola *f*; *Fig* **the b. is in your court** ahora te toca a tí; *Fig* **to play b. with sb** cooperar con algn; *Fam* **to be on the b.** ser un(a) espabilado(a); *Tech* **b. bearing** rodamiento *m* de bolas; **b. game** *(in general)* juego *m* de pelota; *US (baseball match)* partido *m* de béisbol *m*; *Fig* **it's a whole new b. game** es otra historia (**b**) *(of paper)* bola *f*; *(of wool)* ovillo *m*

ball[2] [bɔːl] N *(dance)* baile *m*

ballad ['bæləd] N balada *f*

ballast ['bæləst] N *Naut* lastre *m*

ballerina [bælə'riːnə] N bailarina *f*

ballet ['bæleɪ] N ballet *m*; **b. dancer** bailarín(ina) *m,f*

ballistic [bə'lɪstɪk] ADJ balístico(a)

ballistics [bəˈlɪstɪks] N SING balística f

balloon [bəˈluːn] 1 N (a) *(for party, travel)* globo m (b) *(in cartoon)* bocadillo m
2 VI *(swell)* hincharse como un globo; *(grow dramatically)* dispararse

ballot [ˈbælət] 1 N votación f; **b. box** urna f; **b. paper** papeleta f (de voto), *Chile, Méx* voto m, *Col* tarjetón m, *RP* boleta f
2 VT *(membership)* consultar por votación

ballpark [ˈbɔːlpɑːk] N *US* campo m de béisbol

ballpoint [ˈbɔːlpɔɪnt] N **b. (pen)** bolígrafo m, *Carib, Méx* pluma f, *Col, Ecuad* esterográfico m, *CSur* lapicera f

ballroom [ˈbɔːlruːm] N salón m de baile

ballyhoo [bælɪˈhuː] N *Fam (fuss)* alboroto m, *Esp* escandalera f, *RP* batifondo m

balm [bɑːm] N bálsamo m

balmy [ˈbɑːmɪ] ADJ *(balmier, balmiest) (weather)* suave

Baltic [ˈbɔːltɪk] ADJ báltico(a); **the B. (Sea)** el (mar) Báltico

balustrade [ˈbæləstreɪd] N barandilla f

bamboo [bæmˈbuː] N bambú m

bamboozle [bæmˈbuːzəl] VT *Fam* (a) *(puzzle)* dejar perplejo(a) (b) *(trick)* engañar, embaucar

ban [bæn] 1 N prohibición f
2 VT (a) *(prohibit)* prohibir (b) *(exclude)* excluir

banal [bəˈnɑːl] ADJ banal, trivial

banana [bəˈnɑːnə] N plátano m, *CAm, Col* banano m, *Ven* cambur m, *RP* banana f; *Fam* **to be bananas** *(mad)* estar como una cabra or *Méx* destrompado(a) or *RP* de la nuca

band [bænd] 1 N (a) *(strip)* tira f; *(ribbon)* cinta f (b) *(stripe)* raya f (c) *(group)* grupo m; *(of youths)* pandilla f; *(of thieves)* banda f (d) *Mus* banda f
2 VI **to b. together** unirse, juntarse

bandage [ˈbændɪdʒ] 1 N venda f
2 VT vendar

Band-Aid® [ˈbændeɪd] N *US Esp* tirita® f, *Am* curita f

bandit [ˈbændɪt] N bandido m

bandstand [ˈbændstænd] N quiosco m de música

bandwagon [ˈbændwægən] N *Fig* **to jump on the b.** subirse al tren

bandwidth [ˈbændwɪdθ] N *Comput* ancho m de banda

bandy [ˈbændɪ] 1 VT *(words, ideas)* intercambiar
2 ADJ *(bandier, bandiest)* torcido(a) hacia fuera
▶ **bandy about** VT SEP *(ideas)* propagar, difundir

bandy-legged [ˈbændɪˈleg(ɪ)d] ADJ patizambo(a)

bang [bæŋ] 1 N (a) *(blow)* golpe m (b) *(noise)* ruido m; *(explosion)* estallido m; *(of gun)* estampido m
2 NPL *US* **bangs** flequillo m, *Am* cerquillo m *(corto)*
3 VT golpear; **to b. sth shut** cerrar algo de golpe
4 VI golpear; **to b. shut** cerrarse de golpe
5 INTERJ *(blow)* ¡zas!; **b., b.!** *(of gun)* ¡pum, pum!
6 ADV *Fam* justo

banger [ˈbæŋə(r)] N (a) *(firework)* petardo m (b) *Fam (sausage)* salchicha f (c) *Fam* **old b.** *(car)* tartana f

bangle [ˈbæŋgəl] N brazalete m

banish [ˈbænɪʃ] VT desterrar

banister [ˈbænɪstə(r)] N pasamanos m inv

banjo [ˈbændʒəʊ] N *(pl banjos)* banjo m

bank¹ [bæŋk] 1 N (a) *(financial institution)* banco m; **b. account** cuenta bancaria; **b. card** tarjeta bancaria; **b. clerk** empleado(a) m,f de banca; **b. draft** letra bancaria; *Br* **b. holiday** fiesta f nacional; **b. statement** extracto m de cuenta (b) *(in gambling)* banca f (c) *(store)* banco m
2 VT *(money, cheque)* depositar, *Esp* ingresar
3 VI **to b. with** tener una cuenta en
▶ **bank on** VT INSEP contar con

bank² [bæŋk] 1 N (a) *(mound)* loma f; *(embankment)* terraplén m (b) *(of river)* ribera f; *(edge)* orilla f
2 VT *Av* ladear
3 VI *Av* ladearse

bankbook [ˈbæŋkbʊk] N libreta f de ahorros

banker [ˈbæŋkə(r)] N banquero(a) m,f

banking [ˈbæŋkɪŋ] N banca f

banknote [ˈbæŋknəʊt] N billete m de banco

bankrupt [ˈbæŋkrʌpt] 1 ADJ en quiebra; **to go b.** quebrar
2 VT llevar a la bancarrota

bankruptcy [ˈbæŋkrʌptsɪ] N quiebra f, bancarrota f

banner [ˈbænə(r)] N *(in demonstration)* pancarta f; *(flag)* bandera f

banns [bænz] NPL amonestaciones f pl

banquet [ˈbæŋkwɪt] N banquete m

banter [ˈbæntə(r)] 1 N bromas f pl
2 VI bromear

bap [bæp] N *Br* = panecillo blando redondo

baptism [ˈbæptɪzəm] N bautismo m

Baptist [ˈbæptɪst] N baptista mf, bautista mf

baptize [bæpˈtaɪz, *US* ˈbæptaɪz] VT bautizar

bar [bɑː(r)] 1 N (a) *(of gold)* barra f; *(of chocolate)* tableta f; *(of soap)* pastilla f; *Com* **b. code** código m de barras (b) *(of cage)* barrote m; *Fam* **to be behind bars** estar en la cárcel (c) *(obstacle)* obstáculo m (d) *Jur (dock)* banquillo m; *(court)* tribunal m (e) *Jur* **the B.** *Br (barristers)* = conjunto de los abogados que ejercen en tribunales superiores; *US (lawyers in general)* la abogacía f (f) *(pub)* bar m; *(counter)* barra f (g) *Mus* compás m
2 VT (a) *(door)* atrancar; *(road)* cortar (b)

(exclude) excluir (**from** de) (**c**) *(prohibit)* prohibir

3 PREP salvo; **b. none** sin excepción

barbarian [baː'beərɪən] ADJ & N bárbaro(a) *(m,f)*

barbaric [baː'bærɪk] ADJ bárbaro(a)

barbecue ['baːbɪkjuː] **1** N barbacoa *f, Andes, RP* asado *m*

2 VT asar en la barbacoa

barbed [baːbd] ADJ (**a**) **b. wire** alambre *m* de púas (**b**) *Fig (remark)* mordaz

barber ['baːbə(r)] N barbero(a) *m,f*, **b.'s (shop)** barbería *f*

barbiturate [baː'bɪtjʊrɪt] N barbitúrico *m*

bare [beə(r)] **1** ADJ (**a**) *(not covered)* desnudo(a); *(head)* descubierto(a); *(foot)* descalzo(a); *(room)* vacío(a); **to lay b.** poner al descubierto; **with his b. hands** sólo con las manos (**b**) *(basic)* mero(a); **the b. minimum** lo mínimo

2 VT descubrir

bareback(ed) ['beə'bæk(t)] ADV **to ride b.** montar un caballo a pelo

barefaced ['beəfeɪst] ADJ desvergonzado(a)

barefoot ['beə'fʊt] ADJ & ADV descalzo(a)

barely ['beəlɪ] ADV apenas

bargain ['baːgɪn] **1** N (**a**) *(agreement)* pacto *m*; *(deal)* negocio *m*; **into the b.** por añadidura, además; **to drive a hard b.** imponer condiciones duras; **to strike a b.** cerrar un trato (**b**) *(cheap purchase)* ganga *f*; **b. price** precio *m* de oferta

2 VI (**a**) *(negotiate)* negociar (**b**) *(haggle)* regatear

▸ **bargain for** VT INSEP esperar, contar con

barge [baːdʒ] **1** N gabarra *f*

2 VI *Fam* **to b. into** *(room)* irrumpir en; *(person)* tropezar con

▸ **barge in** VI *Fam* (**a**) *(go in)* entrar sin permiso (**b**) *(interfere)* entrometerse

baritone ['bærɪtəʊn] ADJ & N barítono *(m)*

bark¹ [baːk] **1** N ladrido *m*

2 VI *(dog)* ladrar

bark² [baːk] N *Bot* corteza *f*

barley ['baːlɪ] N cebada *f*; **b. sugar** azúcar *m* cande

barmaid ['baːmeɪd] N *esp Br* camarera *f*, *Am* mesera *f*, *RP* moza *f*

barman ['baːmən] N camarero *m*, *Am* mesero *m*, *RP* mozo *m*

barn [baːn] N granero *m*; **b. dance** baile *m* popular

barnacle ['baːnəkəl] N percebe *m*

barnyard ['baːnjaːd] N corral *m*

barometer [bə'rɒmɪtə(r)] N barómetro *m*

baron ['bærən] N barón *m*

baroness ['bærənɪs] N baronesa *f*

baroque [bə'rɒk] ADJ barroco(a)

barrack ['bærək] VT *Br (heckle)* abuchear

barracks ['bærəks] N *Mil* cuartel *m*

barrage ['bæraːdʒ] N (**a**) *(dam)* presa *f* (**b**) *Mil* barrera *f* de fuego (**c**) *Fig (of questions)* lluvia *f*

barrel ['bærəl] N (**a**) *(of wine)* tonel *m*; *(of beer, oil)* barril *m* (**b**) *(of firearm)* cañón *m*

barren ['bærən] ADJ *(land, woman)* yermo(a); *(landscape)* árido(a)

barricade [bærɪ'keɪd] **1** N barricada *f*

2 VT poner barricadas en; **to b. oneself in** parapetarse

barrier ['bærɪə(r)] N barrera *f*

barring ['bærɪŋ] PREP salvo, excepto; **b. a miracle** a menos que ocurra un milagro

barrister ['bærɪstə(r)] N *Br* abogado(a) *m,f (que ejerce en tribunales superiores)*

barrow ['bærəʊ] N carretilla *f*

bartender ['baːtendə(r)] N *US* camarero *m*, *Am* mesero *m*, *RP* barman *m*

barter ['baːtə(r)] VT trocar (**for** por)

base [beɪs] **1** N base *f*; *(of company)* sede *f* central; **air/naval b.** base aérea/naval

2 VT (**a**) *(found)* basar (**on** en) (**b**) *(troops)* estacionar

3 ADJ (**a**) *Fml (despicable)* bajo(a), despreciable (**b**) *(metal)* común

baseball ['beɪsbɔːl] N béisbol *m*

baseline ['beɪslaɪn] N *(in tennis)* línea *f* de saque

basement ['beɪsmənt] N sótano *m*

bases ['beɪsiːz] PL *of* basis

bash [bæʃ] **1** N *(heavy blow)* golpetazo *m*; *(dent)* bollo *m*; *Fam (attempt)* intento *m*

2 VT golpear

bashful ['bæʃfʊl] ADJ tímido(a)

basic ['beɪsɪk] **1** ADJ básico(a); **b. pay** sueldo *m* base

2 NPL **the basics** lo fundamental

basically ['beɪsɪklɪ] ADV fundamentalmente

basil [*Br* 'bæzəl, *US* 'beɪzəl] N albahaca *f*

basin ['beɪsən] N (**a**) *(for cooking)* recipiente *m*, bol *m*; *(for washing hands)* lavabo *m*, *Am* lavamanos *m inv*; *(plastic, for washing up)* palangana *f*, *Esp* barreño *m* (**b**) *(of river)* cuenca *f*

basis ['beɪsɪs] N *(pl* **bases**) base *f*; **on the b. of** en base a

bask [baːsk] VI tostarse; **to b. in the sun** tomar el sol

basket ['baːskɪt] N cesta *f*; *(in basketball)* canasta *f*

basketball ['baːskɪtbɔːl] N baloncesto *m*

Basque [bæsk, baːsk] **1** ADJ vasco(a); **B. Country** País Vasco, Euskadi; **B. flag** ikurriña *f*; **B. nationalist** abertzale *mf*

2 N (**a**) *(person)* vasco(a) *m,f* (**b**) *(language)* vasco *m*, euskera *m*

bass¹ [bæs] N INV *(seawater)* lubina *f*; *(freshwater)* perca *f*

bass² [beɪs] **1** N (**a**) *(singer)* bajo *m* (**b**) *(notes)* graves *mpl*; **b. drum** bombo *m*; **b. guitar** bajo *m*

2 ADJ bajo(a)

bassoon [bə'suːn] N fagot *m*

bastard ['bɑːstəd, 'bæstəd] **1** N (**a**) *(illegitimate child)* hijo(a) ilegítimo(a), (hijo(a) bastardo(a) m,f (**b**) *very Fam (unpleasant person)* cabrón m, hijo m de puta; **poor b.!** ¡el pobre!
2 ADJ bastardo(a)

baste [beɪst] VT *Culin* regar con grasa

bastion ['bæstɪən] N baluarte m, bastión m

bat¹ [bæt] **1** N *(in cricket, baseball)* bate m; *(in table tennis)* pala f; *Br Fam* **to do sth off one's own b.** hacer algo por cuenta propia
2 VI *(in cricket, baseball)* batear

bat² [bæt] N *Zool* murciélago m

bat³ [bæt] VT *Fam* **without batting an eyelid** sin pestañear

batch [bætʃ] N *(of bread)* hornada f; *(of goods)* lote m; *Comput* **b. processing** procesamiento m por lotes

bated ['beɪtɪd] ADJ **with b. breath** sin respirar

bath [bɑːθ] **1** N (**a**) *(action)* baño m; **to have a b.** bañarse; **b. towel** toalla f de baño (**b**) *(tub)* bañera f, *Am* tina f (**c**) *Br* **(swimming) baths** piscina f, *Méx* alberca f, *RP* pileta f
2 VT bañar

bathe [beɪð] **1** VI bañarse
2 VT (**a**) *(wound)* lavar (**b**) **he was bathed in sweat** *(covered)* estaba empapado de sudor

bather ['beɪðə(r)] N bañista mf

bathing ['beɪðɪŋ] N baño m; **b. cap** gorro m de baño; **b. costume** bañador m, traje m de baño, *Col* vestido m de baño; *RP* malla f; **b. trunks** bañador m (de hombre)

bathrobe ['bɑːθrəʊb] N albornoz m

bathroom ['bɑːθruːm] N *(with bath)* cuarto m de baño; *(toilet)* baño m, servicio m, *CSur* toilette m

bathtub ['bɑːθtʌb] N bañera f, *Am* tina f

baton ['bætən, 'bætɒn] N (**a**) *Mus* batuta f (**b**) *(of policeman)* porra f (**c**) *Sport* testigo m

battalion [bə'tæljən] N batallón m

batter¹ ['bætə(r)] VT aporrear, apalear

batter² ['bætə(r)] N *(in cricket, baseball)* bateador(a) m,f

batter³ ['bætə(r)] *Culin* **1** N pasta f (para rebozar); **fish in b.** pescado rebozado
2 VT rebozar

battered ['bætəd] ADJ *(car)* abollado(a); *(person)* maltratado(a)

battering ['bætərɪŋ] N paliza f; **to take a b.** recibir una paliza; *Mil* **b. ram** ariete m

battery ['bætərɪ] N (**a**) *(for torch, radio)* pila f; *Aut* batería f (**b**) *Jur* **assault and b.** lesiones fpl

battle ['bætəl] **1** N batalla f; *Fig* lucha f; **to do b.** librar batalla; *Fig* **b. cry** lema m
2 VI luchar

battlefield ['bætəlfiːld] N campo m de batalla

battleship ['bætəlʃɪp] N acorazado m

bauble ['bɔːbəl] N chuchería f

baulk [bɔːk] **1** VT *(frustrate, defeat)* frustrar, hacer fracasar

2 VI **to b. at sth** *(of person)* mostrarse reticente *or* echarse atrás ante algo

bawdy ['bɔːdɪ] ADJ (**bawdier, bawdiest**) *(joke etc)* verde

bawl [bɔːl] VI gritar, chillar

bay¹ [beɪ] N *Geog* bahía f; *(large)* golfo m; **B. of Biscay** golfo de Vizcaya; **B. of Bengal** golfo de Bengala

bay² [beɪ] N (**a**) *(recess)* hueco m; **b. window** ventana f salediza (**b**) *(in factory)* nave f; **cargo b.** bodega f de carga

bay³ [beɪ] N *Bot* laurel m

bay⁴ [beɪ] **1** VI *(dog)* aullar
2 N ladrido m; *Fig* **at b.** acorralado(a); *Fig* **to keep sb at b.** mantener a algn a raya

bayonet ['beɪənɪt] N bayoneta f

bazaar [bə'zɑː(r)] N (**a**) *(market)* bazar m (**b**) *(church)* **(charity bazaar)** rastrillo benéfico

B & B [biːən'biː] N *Br (abbr* **bed and breakfast)** *(hotel)* = hostal familiar en el que el desayuno está incluido en el precio de la habitación

BBC [biːbiː'siː] N *(abbr* **British Broadcasting Corporation)** BBC f

BC [biː'siː] *(abbr* **before Christ)** a.d.C.

be [biː, *unstressed* bɪ]

En el inglés hablado, y en el escrito en estilo coloquial, el verbo **be** se contrae de forma que **I am** se transforma en **I'm**, **he/she/it is** se transforman en **he's/she's/it's** y **you/we/they are** se transforman en **you're/we're/they're**. Las formas negativas **is not**, **are not, was not** y **were not** se transforman en **isn't, aren't, wasn't** y **weren't**.

1 VI *(pres 1st person sing* **am**; *3rd person sing* **is**; *2nd person sing & all persons pl* **are**; *pt 1st & 3rd persons sing* **was**; *2nd person sing & all persons pl* **were**; *pp* **been**) (**a**) *(indicating permanent quality, condition)* ser; **he is very tall** es muy alto; **Madrid is the capital** Madrid es la capital; **sugar is sweet** el azúcar es dulce
(**b**) *(nationality, occupation)* ser; **he's Italian** es italiano
(**c**) *(origin, ownership)* ser; **the car is Domingo's** el coche es de Domingo
(**d**) *(price)* costar; *(total)* ser; **a return ticket is £24** un billete de ida y vuelta cuesta £24; **how much is it?** ¿cuánto es?
(**e**) *(temporary state)* estar; **how are you? – I'm very well** ¿cómo estás? – estoy muy bien; **this soup is cold** esta sopa está fría; **to be cold/afraid/hungry** *(person)* tener frío/miedo/hambre
(**f**) *(location)* estar; **Birmingham is 120 miles from London** Birmingham está a 120 millas de Londres
(**g**) *(age)* tener; **she is thirty (years old)** tiene treinta años
2 V AUX (**a**) *(with pres p)* estar; **he is writing a letter** está escribiendo una carta; **she was singing** estaba cantando; **they are leaving next week** se van la semana que viene; **we**

have been waiting for a long time hace mucho que estamos esperando; **he is coming** *(emphatic)* es seguro que viene (**b**) *(passive)* ser; **he was murdered** fue asesinado; **she is allowed to smoke** se le permite fumar (**c**) *(obligation)* **I am to see him this afternoon** debo verle esta tarde; **you are not to smoke here** no se puede fumar aquí

3 V IMPERS (**a**) *(with there)* haber; **there is, there are** hay; **there was, there were** había; **there will be** habrá; **there would be** habría; **there have been a lot of complaints** ha habido muchas quejas; **there were ten of us** éramos diez (**b**) *(with it)* **it's late** es tarde; **it is said that ...** se dice que ...; **who is it? – it's me** ¿quién es? – soy yo; **what is it?** ¿qué pasa? (**c**) *(weather)* **it's foggy** hay niebla; **it's cold/ hot** hace frío/calor (**d**) *(time)* ser; **it's one o'clock** es la una; **it's four o'clock** son las cuatro (**e**) *(date)* **it's the 11th/Tuesday today** hoy es 11/martes (**f**) *(in tag questions)* **it's lovely, isn't it?** es bonito, ¿no?; **you're happy, aren't you?** estás contento, ¿verdad?; **he's not very clever, is he?** no es muy listo, ¿verdad? (**g**) *(unreal conditions)* **if I was/were you ...** yo en tu lugar ...; **if you were a millionaire ...** si fueras millonario ... (**h**) *(as past participle of go)* **I've been to Paris** he estado en París

beach [biːtʃ] **1** N playa *f* **2** VT varar

beacon ['biːkən] N (**a**) *Av & Naut* baliza *f* (**b**) *(lighthouse)* faro *m*

bead [biːd] N (**a**) *(of necklace etc)* cuenta *f*; **glass b.** abalorio *m* (**b**) *(of liquid)* gota *f*

beady ['biːdɪ] ADJ (**beadier, beadiest**) *(eyes)* pequeños y brillantes

beagle ['biːgəl] N beagle *m*

beak [biːk] N (**a**) *(of bird)* pico *m* (**b**) *Fam (nose)* nariz ganchuda

beaker ['biːkə(r)] N *(tumbler)* taza alta, jarra *f*

beam [biːm] **1** N (**a**) *(in building)* viga *f* (**b**) *(of light)* rayo *m*; *Phys* haz *m* **2** VI (**a**) *(sun)* brillar (**b**) *(smile)* sonreír **3** VT *(broadcast)* difundir, emitir

beaming ['biːmɪŋ] ADJ *(smiling)* radiante

bean [biːn] N *(vegetable)* *Esp* alubia *f*, *Esp* judía *f*, *Am salvo RP* frijol *m*, *Andes, RP* poroto *m*; *(of coffee)* grano *m*; **to be full of beans** estar lleno(a) de vitalidad

beansprout ['biːnspraʊt] N brote *m* de soja

bear[1] [beə(r)] *(pt* **bore**; *pp* **borne**) **1** VT (**a**) *(carry)* llevar; **to b. in mind** tener presente (**b**) *(support)* sostener (**c**) *(endure)* soportar, aguantar; **I can't b. him** no lo soporto (**d**) *(give birth to)* dar a luz a; **he was born in Wakefield** nació en Wakefield

2 VI *(turn)* girar, torcer; **to b. left** girar a la izquierda

▸ **bear down** VI *(approach)* correr (**on** sobre)

▸ **bear out** VT SEP *(confirm)* confirmar

▸ **bear up** VI *(endure)* resistir

▸ **bear with** VT INSEP tener paciencia con

bear[2] [beə(r)] N *(animal)* oso *m*; **b. cub** osezno *m*

bearable ['beərəbəl] ADJ soportable

beard [bɪəd] N barba *f*

bearer ['beərə(r)] N portador(a) *m,f*; *(of passport, office)* titular *mf*

bearing ['beərɪŋ] N (**a**) *(posture)* porte *m* (**b**) *(relevance)* relación *f*; **to have a b. on** estar relacionado(a) con (**c**) *Tech* cojinete *m* (**d**) *Naut* **bearings** posición *f*, orientación *f*; **to get one's bearings** orientarse

beast [biːst] N (**a**) *(animal)* bestia *f*; **b. of burden** bestia de carga (**b**) *Fam (unpleasant person)* bestia *f*, bruto *m*

beastly ['biːstlɪ] ADJ (**beastlier, beastliest**) *Fam* asqueroso(a)

beat [biːt] **1** VT (*pt* **beat**; *pp* **beaten** ['biːtən]) (**a**) *(hit)* pegar, golpear; *(drum)* tocar; *Fam* **b. it!** ¡largo!, ¡esfúmate!, *RP* ¡bórrate! (**b**) *Culin* batir (**c**) *(defeat)* batir, vencer; **we b. them 5-2** les ganamos 5 a 2; *Fam* **it beats me** *(puzzle)* no lo entiendo (**d**) *Mus (time)* marcar

2 VI (**a**) *(heart)* latir (**b**) *(strike)* dar golpes; *Fam* **to b. about the bush** andarse por las ramas

3 N (**a**) *(of heart)* latido *m* (**b**) *Mus* ritmo *m*, compás *m* (**c**) *Br (of policeman)* ronda *f*

▸ **beat down** VI *(sun)* apretar

▸ **beat off** VT SEP rechazar

▸ **beat up** VT SEP *Fam* dar una paliza a

beater ['biːtə(r)] N (**a**) *(in hunting)* ojeador(a) *m,f* (**b**) *(in cookery)* batidora *f*, batidor *m*

beating ['biːtɪŋ] N (**a**) *(thrashing)* paliza *f* (**b**) *(defeat)* derrota *f* (**c**) *(of drum)* toque *m* (**d**) *(of heart)* latido *m*

beautician [bjuːˈtɪʃən] N esteticista *mf*

beautiful ['bjuːtɪfʊl] ADJ *(woman)* bonita, *esp Esp* guapa; *(child, animal)* bonito(a), precioso(a); *(music, dress, landscape)* hermoso(a), precioso(a); *(smell, taste)* delicioso(a)

beauty ['bjuːtɪ] N belleza *f*, hermosura *f*; **b. contest** concurso *m* de belleza; **b. parlour** salón *m* de belleza; **b. queen** miss *f*; **b. salon** salón de belleza; **b. spot** *(on face)* lunar *m*; *(place)* lugar pintoresco

beaver ['biːvə(r)] **1** N castor *m* **2** VI **to b. away at sth** meterse de lleno en algo

became [bɪˈkeɪm] PT of **become**

because [bɪˈkɒz] **1** CONJ porque **2** PREP **b. of** a causa de, debido a

beckon ['bekən] VT & VI llamar (con la mano); **to b. to sb** llamar a algn con señas

become [bɪˈkʌm] **1** VI (*pt* **became**; *pp* **become**) *(a teacher, doctor)* hacerse; *(boring, jealous,* *suspicious)* volverse; *(old, difficult, stronger)* hacerse; *(happy, sad, thin)* ponerse; **to b. angry** *esp Esp* enfadarse, *esp Am* enojarse; **to b. interested** interesarse; **what will b. of him?** ¿qué va a ser de él?

2 VT *Fml (of clothes, colour)* sentar bien a

becoming [bɪ'kʌmɪŋ] ADJ **(a)** *(dress)* favorecedor(a) **(b)** *(behaviour)* conveniente, apropiado(a)

bed [bed] N **(a)** *(for sleeping)* cama *f*; **to get out of b.** levantarse de la cama; **to go to b.** acostarse; **to make the b.** hacer la cama; *Br* **b. and breakfast** *(service)* cama y desayuno *m*, *(sign)* pensión *f*; **b. linen** ropa *f* de cama **(b)** *(of river)* lecho *m*; *(of sea)* fondo *m* **(c)** *Geol* estrato *m* **(d)** **(flower) b.** arriate *m*

bedbug ['bedbʌg] N chinche *f* or *m*

bedclothes ['bedkləʊðz] NPL, **bedding** ['bedɪŋ] N ropa *f* de cama

bedlam ['bedləm] N algarabía *f*, alboroto *m*

bedraggled [bɪ'drægəld] ADJ *(wet)* mojado(a); *(dirty)* ensuciado(a)

bedridden ['bedrɪdən] ADJ postrado(a) en cama

bedroom ['bedruːm] N *(in house)* dormitorio *m*, habitación *f*, cuarto *m*, *CAm, Col, Méx* recámara *f*; *(in hotel)* habitación *f*, *Am* cuarto *m*, *CAm, Col, Méx* recámara *f*

bedside ['bedsaɪd] N **at sb's b.** al lado de la cama de algn; **b. table** mesilla *f* or mesita *f* (de noche), *Andes* velador *m*, *Méx* buró *m*, *RP* mesa *f* de luz

bedsit ['bedsɪt], *Fam* **bedsitter** [bed'sɪtə(r)] N *Br* estudio *m*

bedspread ['bedspred] N colcha *f*

bedtime ['bedtaɪm] N hora *f* de acostarse

bee [biː] N abeja *f*

beech [biːtʃ] N haya *f*

beef [biːf] N carne *f* de vaca, *Am* carne de res; **roast b.** rosbif *m*

▸ **beef up** VT SEP *Fam* reforzar

beefburger ['biːfbɜːgə(r)] N hamburguesa *f*

beefsteak ['biːfsteɪk] N filete *m*, bistec *m*, *RP* bife *m*

beehive ['biːhaɪv] N colmena *f*

beeline ['biːlaɪn] N *Fam* **to make a b. for sth** ir directo hacia algo

been [biːn, bɪn] PP *of* **be**

beep [biːp] N *(of apparatus)* pitido *m*; *(of horn)* pito *m*

beer [bɪə(r)] N cerveza *f*; **a glass of b.** una caña

beet [biːt] N *US* remolacha *f*, *Méx* betabel *m*

beetle ['biːtəl] N escarabajo *m*

beetroot ['biːtruːt] N *Br* remolacha *f*, *Méx* betabel *m*

befit [bɪ'fɪt] VT convenir a, corresponder a

before [bɪ'fɔː(r)] **1** CONJ **(a)** *(earlier than)* antes de que *(+ subj)*, antes de *(+ infin)*; **b. she goes** antes de que se vaya; **b. leaving** antes de salir

(b) *(rather than)* antes que *(+ infin)*

2 PREP **(a)** *(place)* delante de; *(in the presence of)* ante **(b)** *(order, time)* antes de; **b. Christ** antes de Cristo; **b. long** dentro de poco; **b. 1950** antes de 1950; **I saw it b. you** lo vi antes que tú

3 ADV **(a)** *(time)* antes; **I have met him b.** ya lo conozco; **not long b.** poco antes; **the night b.** la noche anterior **(b)** *(place)* delante, por delante

beforehand [bɪ'fɔːhænd] ADV **(a)** *(earlier)* antes **(b)** *(in advance)* de antemano, con anticipación

befriend [bɪ'frend] VT trabar amistad con

beg [beg] **1** VT **(a)** *(money etc)* pedir **(b)** *(beseech)* rogar, suplicar; **I b. your pardon!** ¡perdone usted!; **I b. your pardon?** ¿cómo ha dicho usted?

2 VI **(a)** *(solicit)* mendigar; *(dog)* pedir; **to b. for money** pedir limosna **(b)** **to b. for help/ mercy** *(beseech)* implorar ayuda/compasión

began [bɪ'gæn] PT *of* **begin**

beggar ['begə(r)] N mendigo(a) *m,f*; *Br Fam* **poor b.!** ¡pobre diablo!

begin [bɪ'gɪn] VT & VI *(pt* **began**; *pp* **begun**) empezar, comenzar; **to b. again** volver a empezar; **to b. at the beginning** empezar por el principio; **to b. doing** *or* **to do sth** empezar a hacer algo; **to b. with ...** *(initially)* para empezar ...

beginner [bɪ'gɪnə(r)] N principiante *mf*

beginning [bɪ'gɪnɪŋ] N principio *m*, comienzo *m*; **at the b. of May** a principios de mayo; **from the b.** desde el principio; **in the b.** al principio; **the beginnings of civilization** los orígenes de la civilización

begonia [bɪ'gəʊnɪə] N begonia *f*

begrudge [bɪ'grʌdʒ] VT *(resent)* dar de mala gana; *(envy)* envidiar

beguile [bɪ'gaɪl] VT *(charm)* seducir

begun [bɪ'gʌn] PP *of* **begin**

behalf [bɪ'hɑːf] N **on b. of**, *US* **in b. of** en nombre de, de parte de; **don't worry on my b.** no te preocupes por mí

behave [bɪ'heɪv] VI **(a)** *(person)* portarse, comportarse; **b. yourself!** ¡pórtate bien!; **to b. well/badly** portarse bien/mal **(b)** *(machine)* funcionar

behaviour, *US* **behavior** [bɪ'heɪvjə(r)] N **(a)** *(of person)* comportamiento *m*, conducta *f* **(b)** *(of machine)* funcionamiento *m*

behead [bɪ'hed] VT decapitar

beheld [bɪ'held] PT & PP *of* **behold**

behind [bɪ'haɪnd] **1** PREP detrás de; **b. sb's back** a espaldas de algn; **b. the scenes** entre bastidores; **b. the times** *(less advanced than)* anticuado(a); **to be b. sb** *(support)* apoyar a algn; **what was there b. the crime?** ¿cuál fue el móvil del crimen?

2 ADV **(a)** *(in the rear)* detrás, atrás; **I've left my umbrella b.** se me ha olvidado el paraguas **(b)**

to be b. with one's payments *(late)* estar atrasado(a) en los pagos
  3 N *Fam* trasero *m*

behold [bɪ'həʊld] VT *(pt & pp* **beheld***) Literary* contemplar

beige [beɪʒ] ADJ & N beige *(m inv)*, *Esp* beis *(m inv)*

Beijing [beɪ'ʒɪŋ] N Pekín

being ['biːɪŋ] N (**a**) *(creature)* ser *m* (**b**) *(existence)* existencia *f*; **to come into b.** nacer

Belarus [belə'ruːs] N Bielorrusia

belated [bɪ'leɪtɪd] ADJ tardío(a)

belch [beltʃ] **1** VI *(person)* eructar
  2 VT *(smoke, flames)* vomitar, arrojar
  3 N eructo *m*

beleaguered [bɪ'liːgəd] ADJ asediado(a)

belfry ['belfrɪ] N campanario *m*

Belgian ['beldʒən] ADJ & N belga *(mf)*

Belgium ['beldʒəm] N Bélgica

Belgrade [bel'greɪd] N Belgrado

belie [bɪ'laɪ] VT desmentir

belief [bɪ'liːf] N (**a**) *(conviction)* creencia *f*; **it is my b. that ...** estoy convencido(a) de que ...; **beyond b.** increíble (**b**) *(religious faith)* creencias *fpl*, fe *f* (**c**) *(confidence)* confianza *f* (**in** en)

believable [bɪ'liːvəbəl] ADJ verosímil

believe [bɪ'liːv] **1** VI (**a**) *(have faith)* creer (**b**) **to b. in** *(be in favour of)* ser partidario(a) de (**c**) *(think)* creer; **I b. so** creo que sí
  2 VT creer

believer [bɪ'liːvə(r)] N (**a**) *Rel* creyente *mf* (**b**) *(supporter)* partidario(a) *m,f* (**in** de)

belittle [bɪ'lɪtəl] VT *(person)* menospreciar; *(problem)* minimizar

bell [bel] N *(of church)* campana *f*; *(small)* campanilla *f*; *(of school, door, bicycle etc)* timbre *m*; *(on cat)* cascabel *m*; *(on cow)* cencerro *m*; *Fig* **that rings a b.** eso me suena; **b. jar** campana de vidrio *or Esp* cristal; **b. tower** campanario *m*

bell-bottoms ['belbɒtəmz] NPL pantalones *mpl* de campana

bellboy ['belbɔɪ], **bellhop** ['belhɒp] N *US* botones *m inv*

belligerent [bɪ'lɪdʒərənt] ADJ agresivo(a)

bellow ['beləʊ] VI *(bull)* bramar; *(person)* rugir

bellows ['beləʊz] NPL **(pair of) b.** fuelle *m*

belly ['belɪ] N (**a**) *(of person)* vientre *m*, barriga *f*; **b. flop** panzazo *m* (**b**) *(of animal)* panza *f*

bellyache ['belɪeɪk] N *Fam* dolor *m* de barriga

belong [bɪ'lɒŋ] VI (**a**) **to b. to** *(be property of)* pertenecer a (**b**) *(be a member)* ser socio(a) (**to** de); *Pol* **to b. to a party** ser miembro de un partido (**c**) *(have a proper place)* corresponder; **this chair belongs here** esta silla va aquí

belongings [bɪ'lɒŋɪŋz] NPL efectos *mpl* personales

beloved [bɪ'lʌvɪd, bɪ'lʌvd] **1** ADJ amado(a), querido(a)
  2 N amado(a) *m,f*

below [bɪ'ləʊ] **1** PREP debajo de, bajo, *Am* abajo de; **b. average** por debajo de la media; **10 degrees b. zero** 10 grados bajo cero
  2 ADV abajo; **above and b.** arriba y abajo; **see b.** véase más abajo

belt [belt] **1** N (**a**) *(for trousers)* cinturón *m*, correa *f*; **blow below the b.** golpe bajo (**b**) *(of machine)* correa *f* (**c**) *(of land)* franja *f*, cinturón *m*
  2 VT *Fam* pegar una paliza a

▸ **belt along** VI *Fam* ir a todo gas

▸ **belt out** VT SEP *Fam (song)* cantar a voz en grito

▸ **belt up** VI *Br Fam* callarse

beltway ['beltweɪ] N *US* carretera *f* de circunvalación

bemused [bɪ'mjuːzd] ADJ perplejo(a)

bench [bentʃ] N (**a**) *(seat)* banco *m* (**b**) *(in parliament)* escaño *m* (**c**) *Br* **the B.** *(judges)* la magistratura (**d**) *Sport* banquillo *m*

bend [bend] **1** VT *(pt & pp* **bent***)* doblar; *Fam* **to b. the rules** hacer una excepción
  2 VI (**a**) *(road, river)* hacer una curva, girar; *(tree)* doblarse (**b**) **to b. to. (over)** inclinarse; *Fam* **he bends over backwards to please her** hace lo imposible por complacerla
  3 N *(of river, road)* curva *f*; *(of pipe, arm)* codo *m*; *Br Fam* **to be round the b.** estar *Esp* majara *or Am* zafado(a) *or RP* piantado(a)

▸ **bend down** VI inclinarse

beneath [bɪ'niːθ] **1** PREP *(below)* bajo, debajo de; *Fig* **it's b. him** es indigno de él
  2 ADV debajo

benefactor ['benɪfæktə(r)] N bienhechor(a) *m,f*

beneficial [benɪ'fɪʃəl] ADJ (**a**) *(doing good)* benéfico(a) (**b**) *(advantageous)* beneficioso(a)

beneficiary [benɪ'fɪʃərɪ] N beneficiario(a) *m,f*

benefit ['benɪfɪt] **1** VT beneficiar
  2 VI sacar provecho (**from** *or* **by** de)
  3 N (**a**) *(advantage)* beneficio *m*, provecho *m*; **for the b. of** en beneficio de; **I did it for your b.** lo hice por tu bien (**b**) *(allowance)* subsidio *m*; **unemployment b.** subsidio de desempleo (**c**) *(event)* función benéfica

benevolent [bɪ'nevələnt] ADJ benévolo(a)

Bengal [beŋ'gɔːl] N Bengala

benign [bɪ'naɪn] ADJ benigno(a)

bent [bent] **1** ADJ (**a**) *(curved)* curvado(a) (**b**) **to be b. on doing sth** *(determined)* estar empeñado(a) en hacer algo (**c**) *Br Fam (dishonest)* deshonesto(a)
  2 N *(inclination)* inclinación *f* (**towards** hacia)
  3 PT & PP *of* bend

benzine ['benziːn] N *Chem* bencina *f*

bequeath [bɪ'kwiːð] VT *Jur* legar

bequest [bɪ'kwest] N *Jur* legado *m*

bereaved [bɪˈriːvd] NPL **the b.** los familiares del/de un difunto

bereavement [bɪˈriːvmənt] N *(mourning)* duelo *m*

bereft [bɪˈreft] ADJ **b. of** privado(a) de

beret [ˈbereɪ] N boina *f*

Berlin [bɜːˈlɪn] N Berlín

Bermuda [bəˈmjuːdə] N las (Islas) Bermudas; **B. shorts** bermudas *fpl*

Bern [bɜːn] N Berna

berry [ˈberɪ] N baya *f*

berserk [bəˈsɜːk, bəˈzɜːk] ADJ **to go b.** volverse loco(a)

berth [bɜːθ] *Naut* **1** N (a) *(mooring)* amarradero *m; Fig* **to give sb a wide b.** evitar a algn (b) *(bed)* litera *f*
2 VT atracar

beseech [bɪˈsiːtʃ] VT *(pt & pp* **besought** *or* **beseeched)** suplicar, implorar

beset [bɪˈset] VT *(pt & pp* **beset)** acosar; **it is b. with dangers** está plagado de peligros

beside [bɪˈsaɪd] PREP (a) *(next to)* al lado de, junto a (b) *(compared with)* comparado con (c) **he was b. himself with joy** estaba loco de alegría; **that's b. the point** eso no viene al caso; **to be b. oneself** estar fuera de sí

besides [bɪˈsaɪdz] **1** PREP (a) *(in addition to)* además de (b) *(except)* excepto, menos; **no one b. me** nadie más que yo
2 ADV además

besiege [bɪˈsiːdʒ] VT *(city)* sitiar; *Fig* asediar

besought [bɪˈsɔːt] PT & PP *of* **beseech**

best [best] **1** ADJ *(superl of* **good)** mejor; **b. man** ≃ padrino *m* de boda; **her b. friend** su mejor amiga; **the b. thing would be to phone them** lo mejor sería llamarles; **we had to wait the b. part of a year** tuvimos que esperar casi un año; **with b. wishes from Mary** *(in letter)* con mis mejores deseos, Mary
2 ADV *(superl of* **well)** mejor; **as b. I can** lo mejor que pueda; **I like this one b.** éste es el que más me gusta; **the world's b. dressed man** el hombre mejor vestido del mundo
3 N **the b.** el/la/lo mejor; **all the b.!** *(at the end of letter)* ¡un saludo!, *RP* cariños; **at b.** a lo más; **to be at one's b.** estar en plena forma; **to do one's b.** hacer todo lo posible; **to make the b. of sth** sacar el mejor partido de algo; **to the b. of my knowledge** que yo sepa

bestiality [bestɪˈælɪtɪ] N bestialidad *f*

bestow [bɪˈstəʊ] VT *(favour etc)* conceder; *(honours, power)* otorgar (**on** a); *(title etc)* conferir (**on** a)

best-seller [bestˈselə(r)] N best-seller *m*

best-selling [ˈbestselɪŋ] ADJ **a b. author** un autor de superventas

bet [bet] **1** N apuesta *f*
2 VT *(pt* **bet** *or* **betted)** apostar
3 VI apostar (**on** por); *Fam* **you b.!** ¡y tanto!

Bethlehem [ˈbeθlɪhem] N Belén

betray [bɪˈtreɪ] VT (a) *(person, country)* traicionar; *(spouse)* engañar (b) *(secret, fact)* revelar

betrayal [bɪˈtreɪəl] N traición *f*

better [ˈbetə(r)] **1** ADJ (a) *(comp of* **good)** mejor; **that's b.!** ¡así está mejor!; **the weather is b. than last week** hace mejor tiempo que la semana pasada; **to be no b. than ...** no ser más que ...; **to get b.** mejorar (b) *(healthier)* mejor (de salud) (c) **b. off** *(better)* mejor; *(richer)* más rico(a); **you'd be b. off going home** lo mejor es que te vayas a casa (d) **the b. part of the day** la mayor parte del día
2 ADV *(comp of* **well)** mejor; **we had b. leave** más vale que nos vayamos; **to think b. of** *(plan)* cambiar de; **all the b., so much the b.** tanto mejor; **b. and b.** cada vez mejor; *Prov* **late than never** más vale tarde que nunca
3 N mejor; **a change for the b.** una mejora; **to get the b. of sb** vencer a algn
4 VT (a) *(improve)* mejorar (b) *(surpass)* superar

betting [ˈbetɪŋ] N apuestas *fpl;* **b. shop** quiosco *m* de apuestas

between [bɪˈtwiːn] **1** PREP entre; **b. you and me** entre nosotros; **closed b. one and two** cerrado de una a dos
2 ADV **in b.** *(position)* en medio; *(time)* entretanto, mientras (tanto)

beverage [ˈbevərɪdʒ] N bebida *f*

bevy [ˈbevɪ] N bandada *f*

beware [bɪˈweə(r)] VI tener cuidado (**of** con); **b.!** ¡cuidado!; **b. of the dog** *(sign)* cuidado con el perro

bewildered [bɪˈwɪldəd] ADJ desconcertado(a)

bewilderment [bɪˈwɪldəmənt] N desconcierto *m*

bewitching [bɪˈwɪtʃɪŋ] ADJ fascinador(a)

beyond [bɪˈjɒnd] **1** PREP más allá de; **b. belief** increíble; **b. doubt** sin lugar a dudas; **it is b. me why ...** no comprendo por qué ...; **it's b. a joke** eso ya no tiene gracia; **she is b. caring** ya no le importa; **this task is b. me** no puedo con esta tarea
2 ADV más allá, más lejos

bias [ˈbaɪəs] N *(tendency)* tendencia *f* (**towards** hacia); *(prejudice)* prejuicio *m*

bias(s)ed [ˈbaɪəst] ADJ parcial; **to be b. against sth/sb** tener prejuicio en contra de algo/algn

bib [bɪb] N *(for baby)* babero *m; (of apron)* peto *m*

Bible [ˈbaɪbəl] N Biblia *f; Fam Pej* **B. thumper** *or Br* **basher** evangelista *mf*

biblical [ˈbɪblɪkəl] ADJ bíblico(a)

bibliography [bɪblɪˈɒɡrəfɪ] N bibliografía *f*

bicarbonate [baɪˈkɑːbənɪt] N bicarbonato *m;* **b. of soda** bicarbonato sódico

bicentenary [baɪsenˈtiːnərɪ], *US* **bicentennial** [baɪsenˈtenɪəl] N bicentenario *m*

biceps [ˈbaɪseps] N bíceps *m*

bicker [ˈbɪkə(r)] VI reñir

bicycle ['baısıkəl] N bicicleta *f*; **b. pump** bomba *f* (de aire); **to go by b.** ir en bicicleta

bid [bıd] **1** VT (*pt* **bid** *or* **bade**; *pp* **bid** *or* **bidden** ['bıdən]) (**a**) *Literary (say)* decir; *(command)* mandar, ordenar; **to b. sb farewell** despedirse de algn (**b**) *(at auction) (pt & pp* **bid**) pujar
  2 VI *(pt & pp* **bid**) *(at auction)* pujar (**for** por)
  3 N (**a**) *(offer)* oferta *f* (**b**) *(at auction)* puja *f* (**c**) *(attempt)* intento *m*, tentativa *f*

bidder ['bıdə(r)] N **the highest b.** el mejor postor

bidding ['bıdıŋ] N (**a**) *(at auction)* puja *f* (**b**) *(order)* orden *f*; **to do sb's b.** cumplir la orden de algn

bide [baıd] VT *(pt* **bided** *or* **bode**; *pp* **bided**) esperar; **to b. one's time** esperar el momento oportuno

bidet ['bi:deı] N bidé *m*

bifocal [baı'fəʊkəl] **1** ADJ bifocal
  2 NPL **bifocals** gafas *fpl or Am* anteojos *fpl* (con lentes) bifocales

big [bıg] **1** ADJ grande (**gran** *before singular noun)*; **a b. clock** un reloj grande; **a b. surprise** una gran sorpresa; **my b. brother** mi hermano mayor; *Fam Ironic* **b. deal!** ¿y qué?; **b. business** los grandes negocios; **b. dipper** montaña rusa; *US Astron* **B. Dipper** Osa *f* Mayor; *Fam* **b. gun, b. shot** pez gordo; *Fam* **to make the b. time** tener éxito; **b. toe** dedo gordo del pie; *Fam* **b. top** carpa *f*
  2 ADV (**a**) *(on a grand scale)* a lo grande (**b**) *(well)* de manera excepcional

bigamy ['bıgəmı] N bigamia *f*

bighead ['bıghed] N *Fam* creído(a) *m,f*, engreído(a) *m,f*

bigheaded [bıg'hedıd] ADJ creído(a), engreído(a)

bigot ['bıgət] N intolerante *mf*

> Note that the Spanish word **bigote** is a false friend and is never a translation for the English word **bigot**. In Spanish **bigote** means "moustache".

bigoted ['bıgətıd] ADJ intolerante

bigotry ['bıgətrı] N intolerancia *f*

bigwig ['bıgwıg] N *Fam* pez gordo

bike [baık] N *Fam (abbr* **bicycle** *or* **motorbike)** *(bicycle)* bici *f*; *(motorcycle)* moto *f*; *Br* **on your b.!** *(go away)* ¡largo!, ¡piérdete!; *(don't talk nonsense)* ¡no digas *Esp* chorradas *or Am* pendejadas *or RP* pavadas!

bikini [bı'ki:nı] N bikini *m*

bilateral [baı'lætərəl] ADJ bilateral

bile [baıl] N bilis *f*

bilingual [baı'lıŋgwəl] ADJ bilingüe

Bill [bıl] N *Br Fam* **the Old B.** *Esp* la pasma, *Andes* los pacos, *Méx* los cuicos, *RP* la cana

bill¹ [bıl] **1** N (**a**) *(for gas etc)* factura *f*, recibo *m* (**b**) *(in restaurant)* cuenta *f* (**c**) *Pol* proyecto *m* de ley; **B. of Rights** = las diez primeras enmiendas a la constitución esta-

dounidense, relacionadas con la garantía de las libertades individuales (**d**) *US (banknote)* billete *m* de banco (**e**) *(poster)* cartel *m* (**f**) *Fin* **b. of exchange** letra *f* de cambio
  2 VT (**a**) *(send bill to)* facturar (**b**) *Th* programar

bill² [bıl] N *(of bird)* pico *m*

billboard ['bılbɔ:d] N *(hoarding)* cartelera *f*

billet ['bılıt] **1** N alojamiento *m*
  2 VT alojar

billfold ['bılfəʊld] N *US* cartera *f*, billetero *m*

billiards ['bıljədz] N SING billar *m*

billion ['bıljən] N mil millones *mpl*, millardo *m*; *Br Old-fashioned* billón *m*

billionaire [bıljə'neə(r)] N multimillonario(a) *m,f*

billow ['bıləʊ] **1** N *(of water)* ola *f*; *(of smoke)* nube *f*
  2 VI *(sea)* ondear; *(sail)* hincharse

billy goat ['bılıgəʊt] N macho cabrío

bin [bın] N *(for storage)* cajón *m*; *Br* **bread b.** panera *f*; *Br* **(rubbish) b.** cubo *m or Am* bote *m* de la basura

binary ['baınərı] ADJ **b. number** número binario

bind [baınd] VT *(pt & pp* **bound**) (**a**) *(tie up)* atar (**b**) *Med (bandage)* vendar (**c**) *(book)* encuadernar (**d**) *(require)* obligar (**e**) *(join etc)* unir

▸ **bind over** VT SEP *Jur* obligar legalmente

binder ['baındə(r)] N *(file)* carpeta *f*

binding ['baındıŋ] ADJ *(promise)* comprometedor(a); *(contract)* vinculante

binge [bındʒ] N *Fam* borrachera *f*; **to go on a b.** irse de juerga

bingo ['bıŋgəʊ] N bingo *m*

binoculars [bı'nɒkjʊləz] NPL prismáticos *mpl*, gemelos *mpl*

biochemistry [baıəʊ'kemıstrı] N bioquímica *f*

biodegradable [baıəʊdı'greıdəbəl] ADJ biodegradable

biodiversity [baıəʊdaı'vɜ:sıtı] N biodiversidad *f*

biography [baı'ɒgrəfı] N biografía *f*

biological [baıə'lɒdʒıkəl] ADJ biológico(a); **b. warfare** guerra biológica

biologist [baı'ɒlədʒıst] N biólogo(a) *m,f*

biology [baı'ɒlədʒı] N biología *f*

biorhythm ['baıəʊrıðəm] N biorritmo *m*

biosphere ['baıəsfıə(r)] N biosfera *f*

birch [bɜ:tʃ] **1** N (**a**) *Bot* abedul *m* (**b**) *Br (rod for whipping)* vara *f*
  2 VT azotar

bird [bɜ:d] N (**a**) *(in general)* pájaro *m*, *(as opposed to mammals, reptiles etc)* ave *f*; *Fig* **to kill two birds with one stone** matar dos pájaros de un tiro; **they're birds of a feather** son tal para cual; **b. of prey** ave de rapiña (**b**) *Br Fam (woman)* nena *f*, *Arg* piba *f*

birdcage ['bɜ:dkeıdʒ] N jaula *f*

birdie ['bɜ:dı] N *(in golf)* birdie *m*

bird's-eye view [bɜːdzaɪˈvjuː] N vista f de pájaro

bird-watcher [ˈbɜːdwɒtʃə(r)] N ornitólogo(a) m,f

Biro® [ˈbaɪrəʊ] N (pl **Biros**) Br bolígrafo m, Carib, Méx pluma f, Col, Ecuad esferográfico m, CSur lapicera f

birth [bɜːθ] N also Fig nacimiento m; (childbirth) parto m; **by b.** de nacimiento; **of noble b.** (parentage) de noble linaje; **to give b. to a child** dar a luz a un niño; **b. certificate** partida f de nacimiento; **b. control** (family planning) control m de la natalidad; (contraception) métodos anticonceptivos; **b. rate** índice m de natalidad

birthday [ˈbɜːθdeɪ] N cumpleaños m inv

birthmark [ˈbɜːθmɑːk] N antojo m

birthplace [ˈbɜːθpleɪs] N lugar m de nacimiento

Biscay [ˈbɪskeɪ] N Vizcaya; **the Bay of B.** el golfo de Vizcaya

biscuit [ˈbɪskɪt] N (a) Br (sweet, salted) galleta f; Fam **that really takes the b.!** ¡eso ya es el colmo! (b) US (muffin) tortita f, bollo m

bisect [baɪˈsekt] VT Geom bisecar; (town, area) dividir por la mitad

bisexual [baɪˈseksjʊəl] ADJ bisexual

bishop [ˈbɪʃəp] N (a) Rel obispo m (b) (in chess) alfil m

bison [ˈbaɪsən] N INV bisonte m

bit¹ [bɪt] N (a) (small piece) trozo m, pedazo m; **to smash sth to bits** hacer añicos algo (b) (small quantity) poco m; **a b. of advice** un consejo; **bits and pieces** trastos mpl; Fig **b. by b.** poco a poco (c) **a b.** (slightly) un poco; **a b. longer** un ratito más; **a b. worried** un poco preocupado(a) (d) (coin) moneda f

bit² [bɪt] N (of tool) broca f

bit³ [bɪt] N Comput bit m

bit⁴ [bɪt] PT of **bite**

bitch [bɪtʃ] 1 N (a) Zool (female) hembra f; (dog) perra f (b) Fam (spiteful woman) bruja f
2 VI Fam (complain) quejarse, Esp dar la tabarra

bitchy [ˈbɪtʃɪ] ADJ (**bitchier, bitchiest**) Fam malicioso(a), Esp puñetero(a)

bite [baɪt] 1 N (a) (of person, dog) mordisco m; (of insect) picadura f; (of snake) mordedura f, picadura f (b) (mouthful) bocado m (c) Fam (snack) bocado m
2 VT (pt **bit**; pp **bitten**) (of person, dog) morder; (of insect, snake) picar; **to b. one's nails** morderse las uñas; Fam **to b. sb's head off** echarle una bronca a algn
3 VI (person, dog) morder; (insect, snake) picar

biting [ˈbaɪtɪŋ] ADJ (wind) cortante; Fig (criticism) mordaz

bitten [ˈbɪtən] PP of **bite**

bitter [ˈbɪtə(r)] 1 ADJ (a) (taste) amargo(a) (b) (wind, cold, weather) recio(a) (c) (person) amargado(a), resentido(a) (d) (struggle) encarnizado(a); (hatred) implacable
2 N Br (beer) = cerveza sin burbujas y de tono castaño

bitterly [ˈbɪtəlɪ] ADV **she was b. disappointed** sufrió una terrible decepción

bitterness [ˈbɪtənɪs] N (a) (taste) amargor m (b) (of wind, cold, weather) crudeza f (c) (of person) amargura f, amargor m

bittersweet [bɪtəˈswiːt] ADJ agridulce

bitumen [ˈbɪtjʊmɪn] N betún m

bizarre [bɪˈzɑː(r)] ADJ (odd) extraño(a); (eccentric) estrafalario(a)

blab [blæb] VI Fam parlotear; Esp largar, Méx platicar; (let out a secret) chivarse

black [blæk] 1 ADJ (a) (colour) negro(a); **a b. and white television** un televisor en blanco y negro; Fig **b. and blue** amoratado(a); **to put sth down in b. and white** poner algo por escrito; Av **b. box** caja negra; **b. coffee** café solo; **the B. Country** = la región industrial de los Midlands; **b. eye** ojo morado; **b. hole** agujero negro; **b. humour** humor negro; **b. magic** magia negra; **b. market** mercado negro; esp Br **b. pudding** morcilla f; **the B. Sea** el Mar Negro; Fig **b. sheep** oveja negra (b) (gloomy) negro(a); Fig **a b. day** un día aciago; Aut **b. spot** punto negro
2 N (a) (colour) negro m (b) (person) negro(a) m,f
3 VT (a) (make black) ennegrecer (b) (polish) lustrar (c) Br (boycott) boicotear

▶ **black out** VT SEP (a) (extinguish lights in) apagar las luces de (b) (censor) censurar
2 VI (faint) desmayarse

blackberry [ˈblækbərɪ] N zarzamora f

blackbird [ˈblækbɜːd] N mirlo m

blackboard [ˈblækbɔːd] N pizarra f, encerado m, Am pizarrón m

blackcurrant [blækˈkʌrənt] N grosella negra

blacken [ˈblækən] VT (a) (make black) ennegrecer (b) Fig (defame) manchar

blackhead [ˈblækhed] N espinilla f

blackjack [ˈblækdʒæk] N (a) US (truncheon) porra f (b) (card game) veintiuna f

blackleg [ˈblækleg] N esquirol m

blacklist [ˈblæklɪst] N lista negra

blackmail [ˈblækmeɪl] 1 N chantaje m
2 VT chantajear

blackout [ˈblækaʊt] N (a) (of lights) apagón m (b) Rad & TV censura f (c) (fainting) pérdida f de conocimiento

blacksmith [ˈblæksmɪθ] N herrero m

bladder [ˈblædə(r)] N vejiga f; **gall b.** vesícula f biliar

blade [bleɪd] N (a) (of grass) brizna f (b) (of knife etc) hoja f (c) (of propeller, oar) pala f

blame [bleɪm] 1 N culpa f; **to take the b. for sth** asumir la responsabilidad de algo
2 VT echar la culpa a; **he is to b.** él tiene la culpa

blameless ['bleɪmlɪs] ADJ *(person)* inocente; *(conduct)* intachable

blanch [blɑːntʃ] **1** VT *Culin* escaldar
2 VI *(go pale)* palidecer, ponerse pálido(a)

blancmange [blə'mɒnʒ] N = tipo de budín dulce

bland [blænd] ADJ *(food)* soso(a)

> Note that the Spanish word **blando** is a false friend and is never a translation for the English word **bland**. In Spanish **blando** means "soft".

blank [blæŋk] **1** ADJ (**a**) *(without writing)* en blanco; *Fin* **b. cheque** cheque *m* en blanco (**b**) *(empty)* vacío(a); **a. b. look** una mirada inexpresiva (**c**) **a b. refusal** *(absolute)* una negativa rotunda
2 N (**a**) *(space)* espacio *m* en blanco; **to draw a b.** no tener éxito (**b**) *Mil* cartucho *m* de fogueo (**c**) *US (form)* impreso *m*

blanket ['blæŋkɪt] **1** N manta *f*, *Am* cobija *f*, *Am* frazada *f*; *Fig* capa *f*
2 ADJ general

blare [bleə(r)] VI resonar
▶ **blare out** VT SEP pregonar

blasé [*Br* 'blɑːzeɪ, *US* blɑː'zeɪ] ADJ de vuelta (de todo)

blasphemous ['blæsfəməs] ADJ blasfemo(a)

blasphemy ['blæsfəmɪ] N blasfemia *f*

blast [blɑːst] **1** N (**a**) *(of wind)* ráfaga *f* (**b**) *(of horn etc)* toque *m*; **at full b.** a toda marcha (**c**) *(explosion)* explosión *f* (**d**) *(shock wave)* onda *f* de choque
2 VT (**a**) *(blow up)* volar; *Br Fam* **b. (it)!** ¡maldito sea! (**b**) *Fig (destroy)* arruinar (**c**) *Fig (criticize)* criticar

blasted ['blɑːstɪd] ADJ maldito(a)

blast-off ['blɑːstɒf] N despegue *m*

blatant ['bleɪtənt] ADJ *(very obvious)* evidente; *(shameless)* descarado(a); **a b. lie** una mentira patente

blaze[1] [bleɪz] **1** N (**a**) *(burst of flame)* llamarada *f* (**b**) *(fierce fire)* incendio *m* (**c**) *(of sun)* resplandor *m* (**d**) *Fig (of anger)* arranque *m*
2 VI (**a**) *(fire)* arder (**b**) *(sun etc)* brillar

blaze[2] [bleɪz] VT **to b. a trail** abrir un camino

blazer ['bleɪzə(r)] N chaqueta *f* sport

blazing ['bleɪzɪŋ] ADJ *(building)* en llamas; *Fig* **a b. row** una discusión violenta

bleach [bliːtʃ] **1** N *(household)* lejía *f*, *Arg* lavandina *f*, *CAm, Chile, Méx, Ven* cloro *m*, *Col* decol *m*, *Urug* jane *f*
2 VT (**a**) *(whiten)* blanquear; *(fade)* descolorir (**b**) *(hair)* decolorar

bleachers ['bliːtʃəz] NPL *US Sport (seats)* gradas *fpl*

bleak [bliːk] ADJ (**a**) *(countryside)* desolado(a) (**b**) *(weather)* desapacible (**c**) *(future)* poco prometedor(a)

bleary ['blɪərɪ] ADJ (**blearier, bleariest**) *(eyes)* *(due to tears)* lloroso(a); *(due to tiredness)* cansado(a)

bleary-eyed [blɪərɪ'aɪd] ADJ con los ojos llorosos/cansados

bleat [bliːt] **1** N balido *m*
2 VI *(animal)* balar

bleed [bliːd] **1** VI (*pt & pp* **bled** [bled]) sangrar
2 VT *Med* sangrar; *Fam* **to b. sb dry** sacarle a algn hasta el último céntimo

bleeding ['bliːdɪŋ] **1** N hemorragia *f*
2 ADJ (**a**) *(wound)* sangrante (**b**) *Br Fam (for emphasis)* **you b. liar!** ¡pedazo de *or Méx* pinche mentiroso!

bleep [bliːp] N bip *m*, pitido *m*
2 VI pitar

bleeper ['bliːpə(r)] N *Br* buscapersonas *m inv*, *Esp* busca *m*, *Méx* localizador *m*, *RP* radiomensaje *m*

blemish ['blemɪʃ] N *(flaw)* defecto *m*; *(on fruit)* maca *f*; *Fig* mancha *f*; *Fig* **without b.** sin tacha

blend [blend] **1** N mezcla *f*
2 VT *(mix)* mezclar; *(colours)* armonizar
3 VI *(mix)* mezclarse; *(colours)* armonizar

blender ['blendə(r)] N *Esp* batidora *f*, *Am* licuadora *f*

bless [bles] VT (*pt & pp* **blessed** *or* **blest**) *(say blessing for)* bendecir; **b. you!** *(when someone sneezes)* ¡salud! *Esp* ¡jesús!; **blessed with good eyesight** dotado(a) de buena vista

blessed ['blesɪd] ADJ (**a**) *(holy)* sagrado(a), santo(a) (**b**) *Fam (for emphasis)* dichoso(a)

blessing ['blesɪŋ] N bendición *f*; *(advantage)* ventaja *f*; **a mixed b.** una ventaja relativa

blest [blest] PT & PP *of* **bless**

blew [bluː] PT *of* **blow**

blight [blaɪt] **1** N plaga *f*
2 VT *Fig (spoil)* arruinar; *(frustrate)* frustrar

blimey ['blaɪmɪ] INTERJ *Br Fam* ¡miércoles!, ¡caramba!, *Méx* ¡ay güey!

blind [blaɪnd] **1** ADJ ciego(a); **a b. man** un ciego; **a b. woman** una ciega; *Fig* **b. faith** fe ciega; *Fig* **to turn a b. eye** hacer la vista gorda; **b. alley** callejón *m* sin salida; **b. spot** ángulo muerto; *Fam* **b. date** cita *f* a ciegas
2 ADV a ciegas; *Fam* **to get b. drunk** agarrar una curda
3 N (**a**) *Br (on window)* persiana *f* (**b**) PL **the b.** los ciegos
4 VT *(deprive of sight, dazzle)* cegar, dejar ciego

blinders ['blaɪndəz] NPL *US* anteojeras *fpl*

blindfold ['blaɪndfəʊld] **1** N venda *f*
2 VT vendar los ojos a

blinding ['blaɪndɪŋ] ADJ cegador(a), deslumbrante

blindly ['blaɪndlɪ] ADV a ciegas, ciegamente

blindness ['blaɪndnɪs] N ceguera *f*

blink [blɪŋk] VI *(eyes)* pestañear; *(lights)* parpadear

blinkered ['blɪŋkəd] ADJ *Fig* de miras estrechas

blinkers ['blɪŋkəz] NPL *(on horse)* anteojeras *fpl*

bliss [blɪs] N felicidad *f*; **it was b.!** ¡fue maravilloso!

blissful ['blɪsfʊl] ADJ *(happy)* feliz; *(marvellous)* maravilloso(a)

blister ['blɪstə(r)] 1 N *(on skin)* ampolla *f*; *(on paint)* burbuja *f*
2 VI ampollarse

blithe [blaɪð] ADJ alegre

blithely ['blaɪðlɪ] ADV alegremente

blitz [blɪts] 1 N bombardeo aéreo
2 VT bombardear

blizzard ['blɪzəd] N ventisca *f*

bloated ['bləʊtɪd] ADJ hinchado(a)

blob [blɒb] N *(drop)* gota *f*; *(spot)* mancha *f*

bloc [blɒk] N *Pol* bloque *m*

block [blɒk] 1 N (**a**) *(of ice, wood, stone)* bloque *m*; *(of butcher, for execution)* tajo *m*; **in b. capitals** en mayúsculas (**b**) *Br* **a b. of flats** un bloque de pisos (**c**) *(group of buildings)* manzana *f*, *Am* cuadra *f* (**d**) *(obstruction)* bloqueo *m*
2 VT *(obstruct)* obstruir; **to b. the way** cerrar el paso

▸ **block up** VT SEP bloquear, obstruir; **to get blocked up** *(pipe)* obstruirse

blockade [blɒ'keɪd] N bloqueo *m*

blockage ['blɒkɪdʒ] N bloqueo *m*, obstrucción *f*

blockbuster ['blɒkbʌstə(r)] N *Fam* exitazo *m*; *Cin & TV* gran éxito *m* de taquilla; *(book)* éxito de ventas

blog [blɒg] N *Comput (abbr* **weblog**) blog *m*, bitácora *f*

bloke [bləʊk] N *Br Fam* tipo *m*, *Esp* tío *m*

blond [blɒnd] 1 N *(man)* rubio *m*, *Méx* güero *m*, *CAm* chele *m*, *Carib* catire *m*, *Col* mono *m*
2 ADJ rubio(a), *Méx* güero(a), *CAm* chele(a), *Carib* catire(a), *Col* mono(a)

blonde [blɒnd] 1 N *(man, woman)* rubio(a) *m,f*, *Méx* güero(a) *m,f*, *CAm* chele(a) *m,f*, *Carib* catire(a) *m,f*, *Col* mono(a) *m,f*
2 ADJ rubio(a), *Méx* güero(a), *CAm* chele(a), *Carib* catire(a), *Col* mono(a)

blood [blʌd] N (**a**) *(body fluid)* sangre *f*; **b. bank** banco *m* de sangre; **b. cell** glóbulo *m*; **b. donor** donante *mf* de sangre; **b. group** grupo sanguíneo; **b. pressure** tensión *f* arterial; *US* **b. sausage** morcilla *f*; **b. test** análisis *m* de sangre; **b. transfusion** transfusión *f* de sangre; **b. vessel** vaso sanguíneo; **blue b.** sangre azul; **high/low b. pressure** hipertensión *f*/hipotensión *f* (**b**) *(breeding, kinship)* **of noble/ Italian b.** de sangre noble/italiana

bloodbath ['blʌdbɑːθ] N *Fig* baño *m* de sangre

bloodhound ['blʌdhaʊnd] N sabueso *m*

bloodshed ['blʌdʃed] N derramamiento *m* de sangre

bloodshot ['blʌdʃɒt] ADJ inyectado(a) de sangre

bloodstream ['blʌdstriːm] N corriente sanguínea

bloodthirsty ['blʌdθɜːstɪ] ADJ sanguinario(a)

bloody ['blʌdɪ] 1 ADJ (**bloodier, bloodiest**) (**a**) *(bleeding)* sanguinolento(a), sangriento(a); *(bloodstained)* ensangrentado(a); *(battle, revolution)* sangriento(a); *Fig* **to give sb a b. nose** poner a algn en su sitio (**b**) *Br, Austr very Fam (for emphasis)* maldito(a), *Esp* puñetero(a), *Méx* pinche; **a b. liar** un(a) mentiroso(a) de mierda; **b. hell!** ¡me cago en la mar!, ¡mierda!, *Méx* ¡en la madre!
2 ADV *Br, Austr very Fam* **it's b. hot!** hace un calor del carajo *or Esp* de la leche *or RP* de mierda; **he can b. well do it himself!** ¡que lo haga él, carajo *or Esp* joder!

bloody-minded [blʌdɪ'maɪndɪd] ADJ *Br Fam* terco(a)

bloom [bluːm] 1 N (**a**) *(flower)* flor *f*; **in full b.** en flor (**b**) *(on fruit)* vello *m*
2 VI *(blossom)* florecer

blooming ['bluːmɪŋ] ADJ (**a**) *(blossoming)* floreciente (**b**) *Br Fam (for emphasis)* condenado(a)

blossom ['blɒsəm] 1 N *(flower)* flor *f*
2 VI florecer; *Fig* **to b. out** alcanzar la plenitud

blot [blɒt] 1 N *(of ink)* borrón *m*; *Fig* mancha *f*
2 VT (**a**) *(with ink)* emborronar (**b**) *(dry)* secar
3 VI *(ink)* correrse

▸ **blot out** VT SEP *(memories)* borrar; *(view)* ocultar

blotch [blɒtʃ] N *(on skin)* mancha *f*, enrojecimiento *m*

blotchy ['blɒtʃɪ] ADJ (**blotchier, blotchiest**) *(skin etc)* enrojecido(a); *(paint etc)* cubierto(a) de manchas

blotting-paper ['blɒtɪŋpeɪpə(r)] N papel *m* secante

blouse [blaʊz] N blusa *f*

blow¹ [bləʊ] N golpe *m*; **to come to blows** llegar a las manos; **it came as a terrible b.** fue un duro golpe

blow² [bləʊ] 1 VI *(pt* **blew***; pp* **blown**) (**a**) *(wind)* soplar (**b**) *(fuse)* fundirse (**c**) *(tyre)* reventar
2 VT (**a**) *(kiss)* mandar (**b**) *(trumpet etc)* tocar (**c**) *(one's nose)* sonarse (**d**) *(fuse)* fundir (**e**) *Br Fam (money)* fundir, *RP* fumar

▸ **blow away** VT SEP & VI = **blow off**

▸ **blow down** VT SEP derribar

▸ **blow off** VT SEP *(by wind)* llevarse
2 VI *(hat)* salir volando

▸ **blow out** 1 VT SEP apagar
2 VI apagarse

▸ **blow over** VI *(storm)* calmarse; *(scandal)* olvidarse

▸ **blow up** 1 VT SEP (**a**) *(building)* volar (**b**) *(inflate)* inflar (**c**) *Phot* ampliar
2 VI *(explode)* explotar

blowlamp ['bləʊlæmp] N *Br* soplete *m*

blown [bləʊn] PP *of* **blow**

blowout ['bləʊaʊt] N (**a**) *(of tyre)* reventón *m*, *Am* ponchadura *f* (**b**) *Fam (big meal)* comilona *f*, *Esp* cuchipanda *f*

blowtorch ['bləʊtɔːtʃ] N *US* soplete *m*

blow-up ['bləʊʌp] N *Phot* ampliación *f*

blubber ['blʌbə(r)] **1** N grasa *f* de ballena
2 VI *Fam* llorar a moco tendido

bludgeon ['blʌdʒən] VT aporrear; *Fig* **to b. sb into doing sth** forzar a algn a hacer algo

blue [bluː] **1** ADJ (**a**) *(colour)* azul; *Fig* **once in a b. moon** de uvas a peras, *RP* cada muerte de obispo; *Fam* **to scream b. murder** gritar como un loco; **b. jeans** vaqueros *mpl*, tejanos *mpl* (**b**) *(sad)* triste; **to feel b.** sentirse deprimido(a) (**c**) *(obscene)* verde; **b. joke** chiste *m* verde
2 N (**a**) *(colour)* azul *m*; *Fam* **the boys in b.** los maderos (**b**) **out of the b.** *(suddenly)* de repente; *(unexpectedly)* como llovido del cielo

bluebell ['bluːbel] N campanilla *f*

blueberry ['bluːbərɪ] N arándano *m*

bluebottle ['bluːbɒtəl] N moscarda *f*, mosca *f* azul

blue-collar ['bluːkɒlə(r)] ADJ **b. worker** obrero(a) *m,f*

blueprint ['bluːprɪnt] N anteproyecto *m*

blues [bluːz] N (**a**) *Mus* **the b.** el blues (**b**) *Fam (sadness)* tristeza *f*, melancolía *f*; **to have the b.** estar muy depre

bluetit ['bluːtɪt] N herrerillo *m* común

bluff [blʌf] **1** N *(trick)* farol *m*; **to call sb's b.** hacer que algn ponga sus cartas encima de la mesa
2 ADJ *(abrupt)* brusco(a); *(forthright)* francote(a)
3 VI tirarse un farol; **to b. one's way through sth** hacer colar algo

blunder ['blʌndə(r)] **1** N metedura *f* o *Am* metida *f* de pata; *Fam* patinazo *m*
2 VI meter la pata, pegar un patinazo

blunt [blʌnt] **1** ADJ (**a**) *(knife)* desafilado(a); *(pencil)* despuntado(a); **b. instrument** instrumento *m* contundente (**b**) *(frank)* directo(a), francote(a); *(statement)* tajante
2 VT *(pencil)* despuntar; *(knife)* desafilar

bluntly ['blʌntlɪ] ADV francamente

blur [blɜː(r)] **1** N aspecto borroso
2 VT *(windows)* empañar; *(shape)* desdibujar; *(memory)* enturbiar

blurb [blɜːb] N *(in book)* resumen *m*

blurred [blɜːd] ADJ borroso(a)

blurt [blɜːt] VT **to b. out** dejar escapar

blush [blʌʃ] **1** N rubor *m*
2 VI ruborizarse

blusher ['blʌʃə(r)] N colorete *m*

blustery ['blʌstərɪ] ADJ borrascoso(a)

BO [biː'əʊ] N *Fam (abbr* **body odour)** sobaquina *f*, olor *m* a sudor

boar [bɔː(r)] N verraco *m*; **wild b.** jabalí *m*

board [bɔːd] **1** N (**a**) *(plank)* tabla *f* (**b**) *(work surface)* mesa *f*; *(blackboard)* pizarra *f*, *Am* pizarrón *m*; *(for games)* tablero *m* (**c**) *(meals)* pensión *f*; **full b.** pensión completa; **b. and lodging** *or US* **room** casa *f* y comida (**d**) *(committee)* junta *f*, consejo *m*; **b. of directors** consejo de administración; **b. room** sala *f* del consejo (**e**) *Naut* **on b.** a bordo (**f**) *Fig* **above b.** en regla; **across-the-b.** general; **to let sth go by the b.** abandonar algo
2 VT *(ship, plane etc)* embarcarse en, subir a
3 VI (**a**) *(lodge)* alojarse (**b**) *(at school)* estar interno(a)
▸ **board up** VT SEP tapar

boarder ['bɔːdə(r)] N (**a**) *(in boarding house)* huésped *mf* (**b**) *(at school)* interno(a) *m,f*

boarding ['bɔːdɪŋ] N (**a**) *(embarkation)* embarque *m*; **b. card, b. pass** tarjeta *f* de embarque (**b**) *(lodging)* alojamiento *m*, pensión *f*; **b. house** pensión; **b. school** internado *m*

boardwalk ['bɔːdwɔːk] N *US* paseo marítimo entarimado

boast [bəʊst] **1** N jactancia *f*, alarde *m*
2 VI jactarse, alardear (**about** de)
3 VT presumir de, alardear de; **the town boasts an Olympic swimming pool** la ciudad disfruta de una piscina olímpica

boastful ['bəʊstfʊl] ADJ jactancioso(a), presuntuoso(a)

boat [bəʊt] N barco *m*; *(small)* barca *f*, bote *m*; *(launch)* lancha *f*; *(large)* buque *m*; *Fig* **we're all in the same b.** todos estamos en el mismo barco; **fishing b.** barco de pesca

boater ['bəʊtə(r)] N canotié *m*, canotier *m*

boatswain ['bəʊsən] N contramaestre *m*

boatyard ['bəʊtjɑːd] N astillero *m*

bob [bɒb] **1** N (**a**) *(haircut)* pelo *m* a lo chico (**b**) *Fam (pl* **bob)** *Br Formerly (shilling)* chelín *m*
2 VI **to b. up and down** subir y bajar

bobbin ['bɒbɪn] N *(of sewing machine)* canilla *f*; *(for lace-making)* bolillo *m*

bobby ['bɒbɪ] N *Br Fam (policeman)* poli *m*

bobby-pin ['bɒbɪpɪn] N *US (hairgrip)* horquilla *f*

bobsleigh ['bɒbsleɪ] N bobsleigh *m*

bode¹ [bəʊd] PT *of* **bide**

bode² [bəʊd] **1** VT presagiar
2 VI **to b. well/ill** ser de buen/mal agüero

bodice ['bɒdɪs] N (**a**) *(sleeveless undergarment)* corpiño *m* (**b**) *(of dress)* cuerpo *m*

bodily ['bɒdɪlɪ] **1** ADJ físico(a); **b. harm** daños *mpl* corporales
2 ADV **to carry sb b.** llevar a algn en brazos

body ['bɒdɪ] N (**a**) *(of person, animal)* cuerpo *m*; **b. odour** olor *m* corporal (**b**) *(corpse)* cadáver *m* (**c**) *(main part)* parte *f* principal (**d**) *Aut* carrocería *f* (**e**) *(organization)* entidad *f* (**f**) *(group of people)* conjunto *m*, grupo *m*

body-blow ['bɒdɪbləʊ] N *Fig* duro golpe

body-builder ['bɒdɪbɪldə(r)] N culturista *mf*

body-building ['bɒdɪbɪldɪŋ] N culturismo *m*

bodyguard ['bɒdɪgɑːd] N guardaespaldas *mf inv*

bodywork ['bɒdɪwɜːk] N *Aut* carrocería *f*

Boer ['bəʊə(r)] ADJ **the B. War** la guerra del Transvaal

bog [bɒg] N (**a**) *(marsh)* ciénaga *f* (**b**) *Br Fam (lavatory)* baño *m*, *Esp* tiger *m*
► **bog down** VT SEP **to get bogged down** atascarse

bogey ['bəʊgɪ] N (**a**) *(spectre)* espectro *m*, fantasma *m* (**b**) *(bugbear)* pesadilla *f* (**c**) *(in golf)* bogey *m* (**d**) *Br Fam (mucus)* moco *m*

boggle ['bɒgəl] VI *Fam* **the mind boggles!** ¡es alucinante!

bogus ['bəʊgəs] ADJ falso(a); **b. company** compañía *f* fantasma

boil¹ [bɔɪl] **1** N **to come to the b.** empezar a hervir
2 VT *(water)* hervir; *(food)* cocer; *(egg)* cocer, pasar por agua
3 VI hervir; *Fig* **to b. with rage** estar furioso(a)
► **boil down** VI reducirse (**to** a)
► **boil over** VI *(milk)* salirse

boil² [bɔɪl] N *Med* furúnculo *m*

boiled [bɔɪld] ADJ **b. egg** huevo cocido *or* pasado por agua

boiler ['bɔɪlə(r)] N caldera *f*; *Br* **b. suit** mono *m* (de trabajo), *Am* overol *m*, *CSur, Cuba* mameluco *m*

boiling ['bɔɪlɪŋ] ADJ **b. water** agua *f* hirviendo; **it's b. hot** *(food)* quema; *(weather)* hace un calor agobiante; **b. point** punto *m* de ebullición

boisterous ['bɔɪstərəs] ADJ (**a**) *(person, party)* bullicioso(a) (**b**) *(weather)* borrascoso(a)

bold [bəʊld] ADJ (**a**) *(brave)* valiente (**b**) *(daring)* audaz (**c**) *Typ* **b. type** negrita *f*

Bolivia [bə'lɪvɪə] N Bolivia

Bolivian [bə'lɪvɪən] ADJ & N boliviano(a) *(m,f)*

bollard ['bɒlɑːd] N *Br (traffic barrier)* hito *m*

bollocks ['bɒləks] NPL *Br very Fam* cojones *mpl*; **b.!** *(disagreement)* ¡y un huevo!

Bolshevik ['bɒlʃəvɪk] ADJ & N bolchevique *(mf)*

bolster ['bəʊlstə(r)] **1** N *(pillow)* cabezal *m*, travesaño *m*
2 VT *(strengthen)* reforzar; *(support)* apoyar

bolt [bəʊlt] **1** N (**a**) *(on door)* cerrojo *m*; *(small)* pestillo *m* (**b**) *Tech* perno *m*, tornillo *m* (**c**) *(of lightning)* rayo *m*
2 VT (**a**) *(lock)* cerrar con cerrojo (**b**) *Tech* sujetar con pernos (**c**) *Fam (food)* engullir
3 VI *(person)* largarse; *(horse)* desbocarse
4 ADV **b. upright** derecho(a)

bomb [bɒm] **1** N bomba *f*; *Br Fam* **to cost a b.** costar un ojo de la cara; **car b.** coche-bomba *m*; **letter b.** carta-bomba *f*; **b. disposal squad** brigada *f* de artificieros; **b. scare** amenaza *f* de bomba
2 VT *(city etc)* bombardear; *(by terrorists)* volar
3 VI *Br Fam* **to b. (along)** *(car)* ir a toda pastilla

bombard [bɒm'bɑːd] VT bombardear

bombardment [bɒm'bɑːdmənt] N bombardeo *m*

bombastic [bɒm'bæstɪk] ADJ rimbombante

bomber ['bɒmə(r)] N (**a**) *Av* bombardero *m*; **b. jacket** cazadora *f or CSur* campera *f or Méx* chamarra *f* de aviador (**b**) *(person)* terrorista *mf (que coloca bombas)*

bombshell ['bɒmʃel] N (**a**) *Mil* obús *m* (**b**) *Fig (surprise)* bomba *f* (**c**) *Fam* **a blonde b.** una rubia explosiva

bona fide [bəʊnə'faɪdɪ] ADJ (**a**) *(genuine)* auténtico(a) (**b**) *(in good faith)* bienintencionado(a)

bond [bɒnd] **1** N (**a**) *(link)* lazo *m*, vínculo *m* (**b**) *Fin* bono *m* (**c**) *(binding agreement)* acuerdo *m*
2 VT *(stick)* pegar
3 VI *(form attachment)* unirse (**with** a)

bondage ['bɒndɪdʒ] N esclavitud *f*

bone [bəʊn] **1** N (**a**) *(of person, animal)* hueso *m*; *(in fish)* espina *f*; *Fig* **b. of contention** manzana *f* de la discordia; *Fig* **he made no bones about it** no trató de disimularlo; **b. china** porcelana fina (**b**) **bones** *(remains)* restos *mpl*; **the bare bones** lo esencial
2 VT *(meat)* deshuesar; *(fish)* quitar las espinas a
► **bone up on** VT INSEP *Fam* empollar

bone-dry ['bəʊn'draɪ] ADJ completamente seco(a)

bone-idle ['bəʊn'aɪdəl] ADJ gandul(a)

bonfire ['bɒnfaɪə(r)] N hoguera *f*, fogata *f*; *Br* **B. Night** = fiesta del 5 de noviembre en que de noche se hacen hogueras y hay fuegos artificiales

bonkers ['bɒŋkəz] ADJ *Br Fam* **to be b.** estar chiflado(a) *or Esp* majareta

bonnet ['bɒnɪt] N (**a**) *(child's)* gorra *f* (**b**) *Br (of car)* capó *m*, *CAm, Méx* cofre *m*

bonus ['bəʊnəs] N (**a**) *(on wages)* prima *f* (**b**) *Fin (on shares)* dividendo *m* extraordinario (**c**) *Br Ins* beneficio *m*

bony ['bəʊnɪ] ADJ (**bonier, boniest**) *(person)* huesudo(a); *(fish)* lleno(a) de espinas

boo [buː] **1** INTERJ ¡bu!
2 N abucheo *m*
3 VT abuchear

boob [buːb] N *Br Fam* (**a**) *(silly mistake)* metedura *f or Am* metida *f* de pata (**b**) **boobs** *(breasts)* tetas *fpl*

booby ['buːbɪ] N **b. prize** premio *m* de consolación; **b. trap** *(trick)* trampa *f*; *(explosive device)* trampa explosiva, bomba trampa *or* camuflada

booby-trap ['buːbɪtræp] VT *(pt & pp* **booby-trapped**) colocar una bomba trampa en

boogie ['buːgɪ] VI *Fam* bailar

book [bʊk] **1** N (**a**) *(printed volume)* libro *m*; *Fig* **by the b.** según las reglas; **b. end** sujetalibros *m inv* (**b**) *(of stamps)* carpeta *f*; *(of matches)* cajetilla *f* (**c**) *Com* **books** cuentas *fpl*

2 VT (**a**) *(reserve)* reservar; *(return flight)* cerrar (**b**) *(engage)* contratar (**c**) *(by police)* poner una multa a

▸ **book into** VT INSEP *(hotel)* reservar una habitación en

▸ **book out** VI *(of hotel)* marcharse

▸ **book up** VT SEP **booked up** *(sign)* completo

bookcase ['bʊkkeɪs] N librería *f*, estantería *f*

booking ['bʊkɪŋ] N *esp Br (reservation)* reserva *f*; **b. office** taquilla *f*, *Am* boletería *f*

bookkeeping ['bʊkki:pɪŋ] N *Fin* contabilidad *f*

booklet ['bʊklɪt] N folleto *m*

bookmaker ['bʊkmeɪkə(r)] N corredor(a) *m,f* de apuestas

bookmark ['bʊkmɑːk] N marcador *m*

bookseller ['bʊkselə(r)] N librero(a) *m,f*

bookshelf ['bʊkʃelf] N **bookshelves** estantería *f*

bookshop ['bʊkʃɒp] N librería *f*

bookstall ['bʊkstɔːl] N *(in street)* puesto *m* de libros; *Br (in railway station)* quiosco *m* de prensa

bookstore ['bʊkstɔː(r)] N *US* librería *f*

bookworm ['bʊkwɜːm] N *Fam* ratón *m* de biblioteca

boom¹ [buːm] **1** N (**a**) *(noise)* estampido *m*, trueno *m* (**b**) *(sudden prosperity)* boom *m*, auge *m*

2 VI (**a**) *(thunder)* retumbar; *(cannon)* tronar (**b**) *(prosper)* estar en auge

boom² [buːm] N *(of microphone)* jirafa *f*

boomerang ['buːməræŋ] N bumerang *m*, bumerán *m*

booming ['buːmɪŋ] ADJ (**a**) *(voice, thunder)* que retumba (**b**) *(prosperous)* en auge

boon [buːn] N *(blessing)* bendición *f*

boor ['bʊə(r)] N grosero(a) *m,f*, cafre *mf*

boost [buːst] **1** N estímulo *m*, empujón *m*

2 VT (**a**) *(increase)* aumentar (**b**) **to b. sb's confidence** subirle la moral a algn (**c**) *(tourism, exports)* fomentar (**d**) *(voltage)* elevar

booster ['buːstə(r)] N (**a**) *Elec* elevador *m* de voltaje (**b**) *Rad & TV (amplifier)* amplificador *m* (**c**) *Med* **b. (shot)** revacunación *f*

boot¹ [buːt] **1** N (**a**) *(footwear)* bota *f*; *(ankle-length)* botín *m*; *Fig* **he's too big for his boots** es muy creído; *Br Fam* **to put the b. in** pisotear; *Fam* **she got the b.** la echaron (del trabajo); **b. polish** betún *m* (**b**) *Br (of car)* maletero *m*, *CAm, Méx* cajuela *f*, *CSur* baúl *m*

2 VT *Fam (ball)* chutar (**b**) **to b. (out)** echar a patadas (**c**) *Comput* arrancar

3 VI *Comput* **to b. (up)** arrancar

boot² [buːt] N **to b.** además

bootblack ['buːtblæk] N *esp US* limpiabotas *mf inv*

booth [buːð, buːθ] N (**a**) *(in language lab etc)* cabina *f*; **telephone b.** cabina telefónica (**b**) *(at fair)* puesto *m*

bootleg ['buːtleg] ADJ de contrabando

bootlegger ['buːtlegə(r)] N contrabandista *mf*

booty ['buːtɪ] N botín *m*

booze [buːz] *Fam* **1** N bebida *f*, *Esp* priva *f*, *RP* chupi *m*

2 VI empinar el codo, *Esp* privar, *RP* chupar

bop [bɒp] *Br Fam* **1** N *(dance)* baile *m*

2 VI *Fam (dance)* bailar

Bordeaux [bɔːˈdəʊ] N (**a**) *(city)* Burdeos (**b**) *(wine)* burdeos *m*

border ['bɔːdə(r)] N (**a**) *(edge)* borde *m*; *(on clothes)* ribete *m* (**b**) *(frontier)* frontera *f* (**c**) *(flowerbed)* arriate *m*

▸ **border on** VT INSEP (**a**) *Geog* lindar con (**b**) *Fig* rayar en

borderline ['bɔːdəlaɪn] **1** N (**a**) *(border)* frontera *f* (**b**) *(dividing line)* línea divisoria

2 ADJ *(case etc)* dudoso(a)

bore¹ [bɔː(r)] **1** VT *Tech* taladrar, perforar

2 N (**a**) *Tech (hole)* taladro *m* (**b**) *(of gun)* calibre *m*

bore² [bɔː(r)] **1** VT aburrir

2 N *(person)* pesado(a) *m,f*, pelma *mf*; *(thing)* lata *f*, rollo *m*; **what a b.!** ¡qué rollo!

bore³ [bɔː(r)] PT *of* bear

bored [bɔːd] ADJ aburrido(a); **to be b. stiff** *or* **to tears** estar aburrido(a) como una ostra *or* *RP* un perro

boredom ['bɔːdəm] N aburrimiento *m*

boring ['bɔːrɪŋ] ADJ *(uninteresting)* aburrido(a); *(tedious)* pesado(a), latoso(a)

born [bɔːn] **1** PP *of* bear; **to be b.** nacer; **I wasn't b. yesterday** no nací ayer

2 ADJ *(having natural ability)* nato(a); **b. poet** poeta nato

born-again ['bɔːnəgen] ADJ *Rel* converso(a)

borne [bɔːn] PP *of* bear

borough ['bʌrə] N (**a**) *(town)* ciudad *f*; *US (municipality)* municipio *m* (**b**) *Br (constituency)* = división administrativa y electoral que comprende un municipio o un distrito urbano

borrow ['bɒrəʊ] **1** VT (**a**) *(take on loan)* tomar prestado(a); **can I b. your pen?** ¿me prestas *or* dejas tu bolígrafo? (**b**) *(ideas etc)* apropiarse

2 VI **she's always borrowing from other people** siempre está pidiendo cosas prestadas a los demás

borstal ['bɔːstal] N *Br Formerly* correccional *m*, reformatorio *m*

Bosnia ['bɒznɪə] N Bosnia

Bosnia-Herzegovina ['bɒznɪəhɜːtsəgəˈviːnə] N Bosnia y Hercegóvina

Bosnian ['bɒznɪən] ADJ & N bosnio(a) *(m,f)*

bosom ['bʊzəm] N (**a**) *(breast)* pecho *m*; *(breasts)* pechos *mpl*; **b. friend** amigo(a) *m,f* del alma (**b**) *Fig* seno *m*

boss [bɒs] **1** N (**a**) *(head)* jefe(a) *m,f*; *(factory owner etc)* patrón(ona) *m,f* (**b**) *esp US Pol* jefe *m*; *Pej* cacique *m*

2 VT **to b. sb about** *or* **around** mandar sobre algn

bossy ['bɒsɪ] ADJ (**bossier, bossiest**) *Fam* mandón(ona)

bosun ['bəʊsən] N contramaestre *m*

botanic(al) [bə'tænɪk(əl)] ADJ botánico(a); **b. garden** jardín botánico

botany ['bɒtənɪ] N botánica *f*

botch [bɒtʃ] 1 VT chapucear; **a botched job** una chapuza
2 N chapuza *f*

both [bəʊθ] 1 ADJ ambos(as), los dos/las dos; **b. men are teachers** ambos son profesores; **hold it with b. hands** sujétalo con las dos manos
2 PRON **b. (of them)** ambos(as), los dos/las dos; **b. of you** vosotros dos
3 CONJ a la vez; **b. England and Spain are in Europe** tanto Inglaterra como España están en Europa

bother ['bɒðə(r)] 1 VT (**a**) *(disturb)* molestar; *(be a nuisance to)* dar la lata a (**b**) *(worry)* preocupar; *Fam* **I can't be bothered** no tengo ganas
2 VI molestarse; **don't b. about me** no te preocupes por mí; **he didn't b. shaving** no se molestó en afeitarse
3 N (**a**) *(disturbance)* molestia *f*; *(nuisance)* lata *f* (**b**) *(trouble)* problemas *mpl*
4 INTERJ *Br* ¡maldito sea!

bothersome ['bɒðəsəm] ADJ molesto(a)

bottle ['bɒtəl] 1 N botella *f*; *(of perfume, ink)* frasco *m*; **baby's b.** biberón *m*; **b. bank** contenedor *m* de vidrio; **b. opener** abrebotellas *m inv*
2 VT *(wine)* embotellar; *(fruit)* enfrascar
▸ **bottle out** VI *Br Fam* rajarse
▸ **bottle up** VT SEP reprimir

bottled ['bɒtəld] ADJ *(beer, wine)* en botella, embotellado(a); *(fruit)* envasado(a)

bottle-green ['bɒtəlgriːn] ADJ verde botella

bottleneck ['bɒtəlnek] N *Aut* embotellamiento *m*, atasco *m*

bottom ['bɒtəm] 1 ADJ (**a**) *(lowest)* más bajo(a); *(drawer, shelf)* de abajo; *Aut* **b. gear** primera *f* (**b**) *(last)* último(a); **b. line** *Fin* saldo *m* final; *Fig* resultado *m* final
2 N (**a**) *(lowest part)* *(of well, sea)* fondo *m*; *(of stairs, mountain, page)* pie *m*; *(of list)* final *m*; *Educ* **to be (at) the b. of the class** ser el último/la última de la clase; **to touch b.** tocar fondo; *Fam* **bottoms up!** ¡salud! (**b**) *(fundamental part, source)* **to get to the b. of a matter** llegar al meollo de una cuestión; **who is at the b. of all this?** ¿quién está detrás de todo esto? (**c**) *Fam (buttocks)* trasero *m*
▸ **bottom out** VI *Fin* tocar fondo

bottomless ['bɒtəmlɪs] ADJ *(abyss)* sin fondo; *(reserve)* inagotable

boudoir ['buːdwɑː(r)] N tocador *m*

bough [baʊ] N rama *f*

bought [bɔːt] PT & PP *of* buy

bouillon ['buːjɒn] N caldo *m*; *US* **b. cube** pastilla *f or* cubito *m* de caldo (concentrado)

boulder ['bəʊldə(r)] N canto rodado

boulevard ['buːlvɑː(r)] N bulevar *m*

bounce [baʊns] 1 VI (**a**) *(ball)* rebotar (**b**) *(jump)* saltar (**c**) *Fam (cheque)* ser rechazado (por el banco)
2 VT *(ball)* botar
3 N (**a**) *(of ball)* bote *m* (**b**) *(jump)* salto *m* (**c**) *(energy)* vitalidad *f*
▸ **bounce back** VI *(recover health)* recuperarse, recobrarse

bouncer ['baʊnsə(r)] N *Fam* gorila *m*

bound¹ [baʊnd] ADJ (**a**) *(tied up)* atado(a) (**b**) *(obliged)* obligado(a) (**c**) **b. (up)** *(linked)* vinculado(a) (**with**) (**d**) **it's b. to happen** sucederá con toda seguridad; **it was b. to fail** estaba destinado al fracaso

bound² [baʊnd] 1 VI saltar
2 N salto *m*

bound³ [baʊnd] PT & PP *of* bind

bound⁴ [baʊnd] ADJ **b. for** con destino a, rumbo a; **to be b. for** dirigirse a

boundary ['baʊndərɪ] N límite *m*

boundless ['baʊndlɪs] ADJ ilimitado(a), sin límites

bounds [baʊndz] NPL **beyond the b. of reality** más allá de la realidad; **her ambition knows no b.** su ambición no conoce límites; **the river is out of b.** está prohibido bajar al río

bounty ['baʊntɪ] N prima *f*, gratificación *f*

bouquet [buː'keɪ] N (**a**) *(of flowers)* ramillete *m* (**b**) *(of wine)* aroma *m*, buqué *m*

bourbon ['bɜːbən] N *US (whiskey)* whisky americano, bourbon *m*

bourgeois ['bʊəʒwɑː] ADJ & N burgués(esa) *(m,f)*

bourgeoisie [bʊəʒwɑː'ziː] N burguesía *f*

bout [baʊt] N (**a**) *(of work)* turno *m*; *(of illness)* ataque *m* (**b**) *(in boxing)* combate *m*

boutique [buː'tiːk] N boutique *f*, tienda *f*

bow¹ [baʊ] 1 VI (**a**) *(as greeting, sign of respect)* inclinar la cabeza (**b**) *(give in)* ceder
2 N *(with head, body)* reverencia *f*
▸ **bow out** VI retirarse (**of** de)

bow² [bəʊ] N *Sport & Mus* arco *m*; *Fig* **to have more than one string to one's b.** ser una persona de recursos (**b**) *(knot)* lazo *m*; **b. tie** *Esp* pajarita *f*, *CAm, Carib, Col* corbatín *m*, *Méx* corbata *f* de moño

bow³ [baʊ] N *(of ship)* proa *f*

bowel ['baʊəl] N intestino *m*; **bowels** entrañas *fpl*

bowl¹ [bəʊl] N (**a**) *(dish)* cuenco *m*; *(for soup)* tazón *m*; *(for washing hands)* palangana *f*; *(for washing clothes, dishes)* barreño *m*; *(of toilet)* taza *f* (**b**) *Geol* cuenca *f*

bowl² [bəʊl] 1 N bola *f*
2 VT *(in cricket)* lanzar
3 VI (**a**) *(play bowls)* jugar a los bolos (**b**) *(in cricket)* lanzar la pelota
▸ **bowl along** VI *Fam (car)* ir volando

▸ **bowl out** VT SEP *(in cricket)* eliminar

▸ **bowl over** VT SEP (**a**) *(knock down)* derribar (**b**) *Fig (astonish)* desconcertar

bow-legged ['bəʊleg(ɪ)d] ADJ patizambo(a)

bowler¹ ['bəʊlə(r)] N *(in cricket)* lanzador(a) *m,f*

bowler² ['bəʊlə(r)] N *(hat)* bombín *m*

bowling ['bəʊlɪŋ] N *(game)* bolos *mpl*; **b. alley** bolera *f*; **b. ball** bola *f* (de jugar a los bolos)

bowls [bəʊlz] NPL *Sport* bolos *mpl*

box¹ [bɒks] N (**a**) *(container)* caja *f*; *(of matches)* cajetilla *f*; *Cin & Th* **b. office** taquilla *f* (**b**) *Th* palco *m* (**c**) *Br Fam (television)* **the b.** la tele
2 VT *(pack)* embalar

box² [bɒks] *Sport* 1 VI boxear
2 VT *(hit)* pegar; **to b. sb's ears** dar un cachete a algn

boxcar ['bɒkskɑː(r)] N *US* vagón *m* de mercancías, furgón *m* (de mercancías)

boxer ['bɒksə(r)] N (**a**) *(fighter)* boxeador *m* (**b**) *(dog)* bóxer *m*

boxing ['bɒksɪŋ] N boxeo *m*, *CAm, Méx* box *m*; **b. ring** cuadrilátero *m*

Boxing Day ['bɒksɪŋdeɪ] N *Br* = el día de San Esteban *(26 de diciembre)*

boxroom ['bɒksruːm] N *Br* = en una vivienda, cuarto pequeño sin ventana que se suele usar como trastero

boy [bɔɪ] N (**a**) *(child)* niño *m*, chico *m*; *(youth)* joven *m*; **b. band** = grupo musical juvenil compuesto por adolescentes varones; *Fam* **oh b.!** ¡vaya! (**b**) *(son)* hijo *m*

boycott ['bɔɪkɒt] 1 N boicot *m*
2 VT boicotear

boyfriend ['bɔɪfrend] N novio *m*; *(live-in)* compañero *m*

boyhood ['bɔɪhʊd] N niñez *f*, juventud *f*

boyish ['bɔɪʃ] ADJ juvenil, de muchacho

bra [brɑː] N sostén *m*, *Esp* sujetador *m*, *Carib, Col, Méx* brasier *m*, *RP* corpiño *m*

brace [breɪs] 1 N (**a**) *(clamp)* abrazadera *f*; *(of drill)* berbiquí *m*; *(for teeth)* aparato *m* (**b**) *Br* **braces** *(for trousers)* tirantes *mpl*
2 VT (**a**) *(reinforce)* reforzar (**b**) **to b. oneself (for)** prepararse *or Chile, Méx, Ven* alistarse (para)

▸ **brace up** VI cobrar ánimo

bracelet ['breɪslɪt] N pulsera *f*

bracing ['breɪsɪŋ] ADJ *(wind)* fresco(a); *(stimulating)* tonificante

bracken ['brækən] N helecho *m*

bracket ['brækɪt] 1 N (**a**) *Typ (round)* paréntesis *m*; *(square)* corchete *m*; *(curly)* llave *f*; **in brackets** entre paréntesis (**b**) *(support)* soporte *m*; *(for lamp)* brazo *m*; *(shelf)* repisa *f* (**c**) *(for tax)* sector *m*
2 VT (**a**) *(phrase etc)* poner entre paréntesis (**b**) *(group together)* agrupar, juntar

brag [bræg] VI jactarse (**about** de)

braggart ['brægət] N fanfarrón(ona) *m,f*

braid [breɪd] 1 VT trenzar
2 N (**a**) *Sewing* galón *m* (**b**) *esp US (plait)* trenza *f*

Braille [breɪl] N braille *m*

brain [breɪn] N (**a**) *(organ)* cerebro *m*; **she's got cars on the b.** está obsesionada por los coches; *Med* **b. death** muerte *f* cerebral; *Fig* **b. drain** fuga *f* de cerebros; **b. wave** idea *f* genial (**b**) *Fam* **brains** inteligencia *f*; **to have brains** ser inteligente; *Br* **brains** *or US* **b. trust** grupo *m* de expertos (**c**) *Culin* **brains** sesos *mpl*

brainchild ['breɪntʃaɪld] N invento *m*, idea *f* genial

brainpower ['breɪnpaʊə(r)] N capacidad *f* intelectual

brainstorm ['breɪnstɔːm] N (**a**) *(outburst)* arranque *m* (**b**) *(brainwave)* genialidad *f*, lluvia *f* de ideas

brainwash ['breɪnwɒʃ] VT lavar el cerebro a

brainy ['breɪnɪ] ADJ (**brainier, brainiest**) *Fam* listo(a)

braise [breɪz] VT estofar, *Andes, Méx* ahogar

brake [breɪk] 1 N *Aut (also pl)* freno *m*; **b. drum** tambor *m* del freno; **b. fluid** líquido *m* de frenos; **b. light** luz *f* de freno
2 VI frenar, echar el freno

bramble ['bræmbəl] N zarza *f*, zarzamora *f*

bran [bræn] N salvado *m*

branch [brɑːntʃ] 1 N *(of tree)* rama *f*; *(of road)* bifurcación *f*; *(of science etc)* ramo *m*; *Com* **b. (office)** sucursal *f*
2 VI *(road)* bifurcarse

▸ **branch off** VI desviarse

▸ **branch out** VI diversificarse

brand [brænd] 1 N (**a**) *Com* marca *f*; **b. name** marca de fábrica (**b**) *(type)* clase *f* (**c**) *(on cattle)* hierro *m*
2 VT (**a**) *(animal)* marcar con hierro candente (**b**) *(label)* tildar

brandish ['brændɪʃ] VT blandir

brand-new ['brænd'njuː] ADJ flamante

brandy ['brændɪ] N brandy *m*, coñac *m*, *RP* cognac *m*

brash [bræʃ] ADJ (**a**) *(impudent)* descarado(a) (**b**) *(reckless)* temerario(a) (**c**) *(loud, showy)* chillón(ona)

brass [brɑːs] N (**a**) *(metal)* latón *m* (**b**) *Br Fam (money)* *Esp* pasta *f*, *Esp, RP* guita *f*, *Am* plata *f*, *Méx* lana *f* (**c**) *Mus* instrumentos *mpl* de metal; **b. band** banda *f* de metal

brassiere ['bræzɪə(r)] N sostén *m*, *Esp* sujetador *m*, *Carib, Col, Méx* brasier *m*, *RP* corpiño *m*

brat [bræt] N *Fam* mocoso(a) *m,f*

bravado [brə'vɑːdəʊ] N bravuconería *f*

brave [breɪv] 1 ADJ valiente, valeroso(a)
2 N *US* **(Indian) b.** guerrero indio
3 VT (**a**) *(face)* hacer frente a (**b**) *(defy)* desafiar

bravely ['breɪvlɪ] ADV valientemente

bravery ['breɪvərɪ] N valentía *f*, valor *m*

bravo [brɑːˈvəʊ] INTERJ ¡bravo!

brawl [brɔːl] 1 N reyerta f
2 VI pelearse

brawn [brɔːn] N (a) *(strength)* fuerza física (b) *Br Culin* queso m de cerdo

bray [breɪ] 1 N *(of donkey)* rebuzno m
2 VI rebuznar

brazen [ˈbreɪzən] ADJ descarado(a)

Brazil [brəˈzɪl] N (el) Brasil

brazil [brəˈzɪl] N **b. nut** nuez f del Brasil

Brazilian [brəˈzɪlɪən] ADJ & N brasileño(a) *(m,f)*

breach [briːtʃ] 1 N (a) *(in wall)* brecha f (b) *(violation)* incumplimiento m; **b. of confidence** abuso m de confianza; **b. of contract** incumplimiento de contrato; **b. of the law** violación f de la ley; **b. of the peace** alteración f del orden público (c) *(in relations)* ruptura f
2 VT violar

bread [bred] N (a) *(food)* pan m; **b. and butter** pan con mantequilla, *Am* pan con manteca; *Fig* **our daily b.** el pan nuestro de cada día (b) *Fam (money)* Esp pasta f, Esp, RP guita f, Am plata f, Méx lana f

breadboard [ˈbredbɔːd] N tabla f (para cortar el pan)

breadcrumb [ˈbredkrʌm] N miga f de pan; **breadcrumbs** pan rallado

breadline [ˈbredlaɪn] N *Fam* miseria f; **to be on the b.** vivir en la miseria

breadth [bredθ] N (a) *(width)* anchura f; **it is 2 m in b.** tiene 2 m de ancho (b) *(extent)* amplitud f

breadwinner [ˈbredwɪnə(r)] N cabeza mf de familia

break [breɪk] 1 VT *(pt* broke; *pp* broken) (a) *(in general)* romper; **to b. a leg** romperse la pierna; **to b. a record** batir un récord; *Fig* **to b. sb's heart** partirle el corazón a algn (b) *(fail to keep)* faltar a; **to b. a contract** romper un contrato; **to b. the law** violar la ley (c) *(destroy)* Fin arruinar (d) *(interrupt)* interrumpir (e) *(soften) (fall)* amortiguar (f) **she broke the news to him** le comunicó la noticia
2 VI (a) *(glass, machine, bone)* romperse; *(waves)* romper (b) *(storm)* estallar (c) *(voice)* cambiar (d) *(health)* resentirse (e) **when day breaks** al rayar el alba (f) *(story)* divulgarse
3 N (a) *(fracture)* rotura f; *(crack)* grieta f; *(opening)* abertura f (b) *(in relationship)* ruptura f (c) *(pause)* pausa f, descanso m; *(at school)* recreo m; **to take a b.** descansar un rato; *(holiday)* tomar unos días libres (d) *Fam (chance)* oportunidad f

► **break away** VI (a) *(become separate)* desprenderse **(from** de) (b) *(escape)* escaparse

► **break down** 1 VT SEP (a) *(door)* derribar (b) *(resistance)* acabar con (c) *(costs)* desglosar
2 VI (a) *Aut* tener una avería (b) *(resistance)*

ceder (c) *(health)* debilitarse (d) *(weep)* ponerse a llorar

► **break in** 1 VT SEP acostumbrar; **to b. in a pair of shoes** cogerle la forma a los zapatos
2 VI *(burglar)* entrar por la fuerza

► **break into** VT INSEP (a) *(burgle) (house)* allanar; *(safe)* forzar (b) **to b. into song** empezar a cantar

► **break off** 1 VT SEP partir
2 VI (a) *(become detached)* desprenderse (b) *(talks)* interrumpirse (c) *(stop)* pararse

► **break out** VI (a) *(prisoners)* escaparse (b) *(war etc)* estallar; **she broke out in a rash** le salió un sarpullido

► **break through** 1 VT INSEP (a) *(crowd)* abrirse paso por; *(cordon)* romper (b) *(clouds)* atravesar
2 VI (a) *(crowd)* abrirse paso (b) *(sun)* salir

► **break up** 1 VT SEP *(object)* romper; *(car)* desguazar; *(crowd)* disolver
2 VI (a) *(object)* romperse (b) *(crowd)* disolverse; *(meeting)* levantarse (c) *(relationship)* fracasar; *(couple)* separarse (d) *Educ* terminar

► **break with** VT INSEP *(past)* romper con

breakable [ˈbreɪkəbəl] ADJ frágil

breakage [ˈbreɪkɪdʒ] N *(breaking)* rotura f

breakaway [ˈbreɪkəweɪ] ADJ disidente

breakdown [ˈbreɪkdaʊn] N (a) *Aut* avería f; *Br* **b. truck** grúa f (b) *(nervous)* **b.** crisis nerviosa (c) *(in communications)* Esp fallo m, Am falla f (d) *(analysis)* análisis m; Fin desglose m

breaker [ˈbreɪkə(r)] N (a) *(wave)* ola f grande (b) *Tech* trituradora f (c) *(switch)* interruptor automático

breakfast [ˈbrekfəst] 1 N desayuno m; **to have b.** desayunar
2 VI desayunar

break-in [ˈbreɪkɪn] N robo m *(con allanamiento de morada)*

breaking [ˈbreɪkɪŋ] N (a) **b. point** *(of person, patience)* límite m (b) *Jur* **b. and entering** allanamiento m de morada

breakthrough [ˈbreɪkθruː] N paso m adelante, avance m

breakwater [ˈbreɪkwɔːtə(r)] N rompeolas m inv

breast [brest] N *(chest)* pecho m; *(of woman)* pecho, seno m; *(of chicken etc)* pechuga f; *Fig* **to make a clean b. of it** dar la cara

breast-feed [ˈbrestfiːd] VT dar el pecho a, amamantar a

breaststroke [ˈbreststrəʊk] N braza f

breath [breθ] N respiración f; **in the same b.** al mismo tiempo; **out of b.** sin aliento; **to catch one's b.** recobrar el aliento; **to draw b.** respirar; **under one's b.** en voz baja; *Fig* **to take sb's b. away** dejar pasmado(a) a algn; **to go out for a b. of fresh air** salir a tomar el aire; *Aut* **b. test** alcoholemia f

Breathalyser®, *US* **Breathalyzer®** [ˈbreθəlaɪzə(r)] N *Br* alcoholímetro m

breathe [bri:ð] **1** VT respirar; **to b. a sigh of relief** dar un suspiro de alivio
2 VI respirar; **to b. in** aspirar; **to b. out** espirar; **to b. heavily** resoplar

breather ['bri:ðə(r)] N *Fam (rest)* descanso *m*

breathing ['bri:ðɪŋ] N respiración *f*; **b. space** pausa *f*, respiro *m*

breathless ['breθlɪs] ADJ sin aliento, jadeante

breathtaking ['breθteɪkɪŋ] ADJ impresionante

bred [bred] PT & PP of **breed**

breeches ['brɪtʃɪz, 'brɪ:tʃɪz] NPL bombachos *mpl*; **knee b., riding b.** pantalones *mpl* de montar

breed [bri:d] **1** N *(of animal)* raza *f*; *Fig (class)* clase *f*
2 VT *(pt & pp* **bred)** *(animals)* criar; *Fig (ideas)* engendrar
3 VI *(animals)* reproducirse

breeder ['bri:də(r)] N **(a)** *(person)* criador(a) *m,f* **(b)** *(fast)* **b. reactor** reactor *m* generador

breeding ['bri:dɪŋ] N **(a)** *(of animals)* cría *f*; *Fig* **b. ground** caldo *m* de cultivo **(b)** *(of person)* educación *f*

breeze [bri:z] **1** N brisa *f*; *Br Constr* **b. block** bloque *m* de cemento
2 VI **to b. in/out** entrar/salir despreocupadamente

breezy ['bri:zɪ] ADJ **(breezier, breeziest)** **(a)** *(weather)* ventoso(a) **(b)** *(person)* despreocupado(a)

brevity ['brevɪtɪ] N brevedad *f*

brew [bru:] **1** VT *(beer)* elaborar; *(hot drink)* preparar
2 VI *(tea)* reposar; *Fig* **a storm is brewing** se prepara una tormenta; *Fam* **something's brewing** algo se está cociendo
3 N **(a)** *(of tea)* infusión *f*; *Fam (of beer)* birra *f* **(b)** *(magic potion)* brebaje *m*

brewer ['bru:ə(r)] N cervecero(a) *m,f*

brewery ['bru:ərɪ] N cervecería *f*

brewing ['bru:ɪŋ] **1** ADJ cervecero(a)
2 N *(of beer)* elaboración *f* de la cerveza

briar ['braɪə(r)] N brezo *m*

bribe [braɪb] **1** VT sobornar
2 N soborno *m*, *Andes, CSur* coima *f*, *CAm, Méx* mordida *f*

bribery ['braɪbərɪ] N soborno *m*

bric-a-brac ['brɪkəbræk] N baratijas *fpl*

brick [brɪk] N ladrillo *m*; *Br Fam Old-fashioned* **he's a b.** es un gran tipo

bricklayer ['brɪkleɪə(r)] N albañil *m*

brickwork ['brɪkwɜ:k] N ladrillos *mpl*

bridal ['braɪdəl] ADJ nupcial

bride [braɪd] N novia *f*; **the b. and groom** los novios

bridegroom ['braɪdgru:m] N novio *m*

bridesmaid ['braɪdzmeɪd] N dama *f* de honor

bridge¹ [brɪdʒ] **1** N puente *m*; *(of nose)* caballete *m*; *(of ship)* puente de mando
2 VT **(a)** *(river)* tender un puente sobre **(b)**

(gap) llenar; *Br Fin* **bridging loan** crédito *m* a corto plazo

bridge² [brɪdʒ] N *Cards* bridge *m*

bridle ['braɪdəl] **1** N brida *f*; *(bit)* freno *m*; **b. path** camino *m* de herradura
2 VT *(horse)* embridar

brief [bri:f] **1** ADJ **(a)** *(short)* breve **(b)** *(concise)* conciso(a)
2 N **(a)** *(report)* informe *m*; **in b.** en resumen **(b)** *Jur* expediente *m* **(c)** *Mil* instrucciones *fpl* **(d)** **briefs** *(for men)* calzoncillos *mpl*, *Chile* fundillos *mpl*, *Méx* calzones *mpl*; *(for women)* *Esp* bragas *fpl*, *Chile, Col, Méx* calzones *mpl*, *RP* bombacha *f*
3 VT **(a)** *(inform)* informar **(b)** *(instruct)* dar instrucciones a

briefcase ['bri:fkeɪs] N cartera *f*, portafolios *m inv*

briefing ['bri:fɪŋ] N *(meeting)* reunión informativa

briefly ['bri:flɪ] ADV brevemente; **as b. as possible** con la mayor brevedad (posible)

brigade [brɪ'geɪd] N brigada *f*

brigadier [brɪgə'dɪə(r)] N *Br* general *m* de brigada; *US* **b. general** general de brigada

bright [braɪt] ADJ **(a)** *(light, sun, eyes)* brillante; *(colour)* vivo(a); *(day)* claro(a) **(b)** *(cheerful)* alegre **(c)** *(clever)* listo(a), espabilado(a) **(d)** *(promising)* prometedor(a)

brighten ['braɪtən] VI *(prospects)* mejorarse; *(face)* iluminarse
▶ **brighten up 1** VT SEP *(room etc)* alegrar
2 VI *(weather)* despejarse; *(person)* animarse

brightly ['braɪtlɪ] ADV brillantemente

brightness ['braɪtnɪs] N **(a)** *(of sun)* resplandor *m*; *(of day)* claridad *f*; *(of colour)* viveza *f* **(b)** *(cleverness)* inteligencia *f*

brilliance ['brɪljəns] N **(a)** *(of light)* brillo *m*; *(of colour)* viveza *f* **(b)** *(of person)* brillantez *f*

brilliant ['brɪljənt] **1** ADJ **(a)** *(bright, intense)* radiante, resplandeciente; *(colour)* brillante **(b)** *(person, idea)* genial **(c)** *Br (excellent)* genial, *Am salvo RP* chévere, *Andes, CSur* macanudo(a), *Méx* padre, *RP* bárbaro(a)
2 N brillante *m*

brim [brɪm] **1** N borde *m*; *(of hat)* ala *f*; **full to the b.** lleno(a) hasta el borde
2 VI rebosar (**with** de)
▶ **brim over** VI rebosar

brine [braɪn] N salmuera *f*

bring [brɪŋ] VT *(pt & pp* **brought)** **(a)** *(carry, take)* traer; *(lead)* llevar **(b)** *(cause)* provocar; **he brought it upon himself** se lo buscó **(c)** *(persuade)* convencer; **how did they b. themselves to do it?** ¿cómo llegaron a hacerlo?
▶ **bring about** VT SEP provocar
▶ **bring along** VT SEP traer
▶ **bring back** VT SEP **(a)** *(return)* devolver **(b)** *(reintroduce)* volver a introducir **(c)** *(make one remember)* traerle a la memoria

▶ **bring down** VT SEP (**a**) (*from upstairs*) bajar (**b**) (*government*) derribar; *Th* **to b. the house down** echar el teatro abajo con los aplausos (**c**) (*reduce*) rebajar

▶ **bring forward** VT SEP (**a**) (*meeting etc*) adelantar (**b**) (*present*) presentar (**c**) *Fin* **brought forward** suma y sigue

▶ **bring in** VT SEP (**a**) (*yield*) dar (**b**) (*show in*) hacer entrar (**c**) (*law etc*) introducir; (*fashion*) lanzar

▶ **bring off** VT SEP lograr, conseguir

▶ **bring on** VT SEP provocar

▶ **bring out** VT SEP (**a**) (*publish*) publicar (**b**) (*reveal*) recalcar; **he brings out the worst in me** despierta lo peor que hay en mí

▶ **bring round** VT SEP (**a**) (*revive*) hacer volver en sí (**b**) (*persuade*) convencer

▶ **bring to** VT SEP reanimar

▶ **bring up** VT SEP (**a**) (*educate*) criar, educar (**b**) (*subject*) plantear (**c**) (*vomit*) devolver

brink [brɪŋk] N (*edge*) borde *m*; *Fig* **on the b. of ruin** al borde de la ruina; **on the b. of tears** a punto de llorar

brisk [brɪsk] ADJ (*person, manner*) enérgico(a); (*pace*) rápido(a); (*trade*) activo(a); (*weather, wind*) fresco(a)

bristle ['brɪsəl] 1 N cerda *f*
2 VI (**a**) (*animal's fur*) erizarse (**b**) (*show anger*) enfurecerse (**at** con)

▶ **bristle with** VT INSEP (*be full of*) estar lleno(a) de

Brit [brɪt] N *Fam* británico(a) *m,f*

Britain ['brɪtən] N (**Great**) **B.** Gran Bretaña

British ['brɪtɪʃ] 1 ADJ británico(a); **the B. Isles** las Islas Británicas
2 NPL **the B.** los británicos

Brittany ['brɪtənɪ] N Bretaña

brittle ['brɪtəl] ADJ quebradizo(a), frágil

broach [brəʊtʃ] VT (*subject*) abordar

broad [brɔːd] ADJ (**a**) (*wide*) ancho(a); (*large*) extenso(a) (**b**) **a b. hint** (*clear*) una indirecta clara (**c**) (*daylight*) pleno(a) (**d**) (*not detailed*) general (**e**) (*accent*) marcado(a), cerrado(a)

broadband ['brɔːdbænd] 1 N *Tel* banda *f* ancha
2 ADJ *Comput* de banda ancha

broadcast ['brɔːdkɑːst] *Rad & TV* 1 N emisión *f*
2 VT (*pt & pp* **broadcast**) emitir, transmitir

broadcaster ['brɔːdkɑːstə(r)] N locutor(a) *m,f*

broadcasting ['brɔːdkɑːstɪŋ] N *Rad* radiodifusión *f*; *TV* transmisión *f*; *Rad* **b. station** emisora *f*

broaden ['brɔːdən] VT ensanchar

broadly ['brɔːdlɪ] ADV en términos generales

broad-minded [brɔːd'maɪndɪd] ADJ liberal, tolerante

broadsheet ['brɔːdʃiːt] N folleto *m*

broccoli ['brɒkəlɪ] N brécol *m*

brochure ['brəʊʃə(r), 'brəʊʃjʊə(r)] N folleto *m*

broil [brɔɪl] VT *US* (*grill*) asar a la parrilla

broiler ['brɔɪlə(r)] N (**a**) (*chicken*) pollo (tomatero) (**b**) *US* (*grill*) parrilla *f*

broke [brəʊk] 1 ADJ *Fam* **to be b.** estar sin un centavo *or Méx* sin un peso *or Esp* sin blanca
2 PT of **break**

broken ['brəʊkən] 1 ADJ (**a**) (*object, bone, promise*) roto(a); (*machinery*) estropeado(a); (**b**) (*home*) deshecho(a); (*person*) destrozado(a); (*ground*) accidentado(a); **to speak b. English** chapurrear el inglés
2 PP of **break**

broken-hearted [brəʊkən'hɑːtɪd] ADJ *Fig* con el corazón destrozado

broker ['brəʊkə(r)] N corredor *m*, agente *mf* de Bolsa

brolly ['brɒlɪ] N *Br Fam* paraguas *m inv*

bronchitis [brɒŋ'kaɪtɪs] N bronquitis *f*

bronze [brɒnz] 1 N bronce *m*
2 ADJ (*material*) de bronce; (*colour*) bronceado(a)

bronzed [brɒnzd] ADJ (*suntanned*) bronceado(a)

brooch [brəʊtʃ] N broche *m*

brood [bruːd] 1 N (*birds*) cría *f*; *Hum* (*children*) prole *m*
2 VI (*hen*) empollar; *Fig* **to b. over a problem** darle vueltas a un problema

broody ['bruːdɪ] ADJ (**broodier, broodiest**) (**a**) (*pensive*) pensativo(a) (**b**) (*moody*) melancólico(a) (**c**) *Br Fam* (*woman*) con ganas de tener hijos

brook[1] [brʊk] N arroyo *m*

brook[2] [brʊk] VT *Fml* (*tolerate*) soportar, consentir

broom [bruːm] N (**a**) (*for cleaning*) escoba *f* (**b**) *Bot* retama *f*

broomstick ['bruːmstɪk] N palo *m* de escoba

Bros *Com* (*abbr* **Brothers**) Hnos

broth [brɒθ] N caldo *m*

brothel ['brɒθəl] N burdel *m*

brother ['brʌðə(r)] N hermano *m*; **brothers and sisters** hermanos

brotherhood ['brʌðəhʊd] N hermandad *f*

brother-in-law ['brʌðərɪnlɔː] N (*pl* **brothers-in-law**) cuñado *m*

brotherly ['brʌðəlɪ] ADJ fraternal

brought [brɔːt] PT & PP of **bring**

brow [braʊ] N (**a**) (*forehead*) frente *f* (**b**) (*eyebrow*) ceja *f* (**c**) (*of hill*) cima *f*

brown [braʊn] 1 ADJ marrón, *Am* café; (*hair, eyes*) castaño(a); (*skin*) moreno(a); **b. bread** pan *m* integral; **b. paper** papel *m* de estraza; **b. sugar** azúcar moreno
2 N marrón *m*, *Am* color *m* café
3 VT *Culin* dorar; (*tan*) broncear

Brownie ['braʊnɪ] N escultista *f*

brownish ['braʊnɪʃ] ADJ pardusco(a)

browse [braʊz] 1 VI (*in shop*) mirar; (*through book*) hojear

2 VT *Comput* **to b. the Web** navegar por la Web
3 N **to have a b. (in)** dar un vistazo (a)

browser ['braʊzə(r)] N *Comput* navegador *m*

bruise [bruːz] **1** N morado *m*, cardenal *m*
2 VT *(body)* contusionar; *(fruit)* estropear
3 VI *(body)* magullarse; *(fruit)* estropearse

brunch [brʌntʃ] N *Fam* desayuno-comida *m*, *RP* brunch *m*

brunette [bruːˈnet] ADJ & N morena *(f)*

brunt [brʌnt] N **the b.** lo peor; **to bear the b.** llevar el peso

brush¹ [brʌʃ] **1** N **(a)** *(for hair, teeth)* cepillo *m*; *Art* pincel *m*; *(for house-painting)* brocha *f* **(b)** *(with the law)* roce *m*
2 VT **(a)** *(clean)* cepillar; **to b. one's hair** cepillarse el pelo; **to b. one's teeth** cepillarse los dientes **(b)** *(touch lightly)* rozar
3 VI **to b. against** rozar al pasar
▸ **brush aside** VT SEP dejar de lado
▸ **brush off** VT SEP *Fam* no hacer caso a, *Esp* pasar de
▸ **brush up** VT SEP repasar

brush² [brʌʃ] N *(undergrowth)* broza *f*, maleza *f*

brush-off ['brʌʃɒf] N *Fam* **to give sb the b.** no hacer ni caso a algn

brushwood ['brʌʃwʊd] N maleza *f*

brusque [bruːsk, brʊsk] ADJ brusco(a)

Brussels ['brʌsəlz] N Bruselas

brutal ['bruːtəl] ADJ brutal, cruel

brute [bruːt] **1** ADJ bruto(a); **b. force** fuerza bruta
2 N *(animal)* bruto *m*; *(person)* bestia *f*

BSc [biːesˈsiː] N *(abbr* **Bachelor of Science***)* *(person)* licenciado(a) *m,f* en Ciencias

BSE [biːesˈiː] N *(abbr* **bovine spongiform encephalopathy***)* encefalopatía *f* espongiforme bovina *(enfermedad de las vacas locas)*

bubble ['bʌbəl] **1** N burbuja *f*; **b. bath** espuma *f* de baño; **b. gum** chicle *m*; **soap b.** pompa *f* de jabón
2 VI *(form bubbles)* burbujear, borbotear

bubbly ['bʌblɪ] **1** ADJ **(bubblier, bubbliest)** efervescente
2 N *Fam* champán *m*, cava *m*

buck¹ [bʌk] **1** N *(male deer)* ciervo *m*; *(male goat)* macho cabrío; *Fam* **to pass the b. to sb** echarle el muerto a algn
2 VI *(horse)* corcovear
▸ **buck up 1** VT SEP *Fam* **b. your ideas up!** ¡espabílate!
2 VI *(cheer up)* animarse

buck² [bʌk] N *US, Austr Fam* dólar *m*

bucket ['bʌkɪt] **1** N balde *m*, *Esp* cubo *m*; *Br Fam* **it's raining buckets** llueve a cántaros or *RP* a baldes
2 VI *Fam* **it's bucketing (down)** llueve a cántaros or *RP* a baldes

buckle ['bʌkəl] **1** N hebilla *f*
2 VT abrochar *(con hebilla)*

3 VI **(a)** *(wall, metal)* combarse **(b)** *(knees)* doblarse

bud [bʌd] **1** N *(shoot)* brote *m*; *(flower)* capullo *m*
2 VI *(plant)* brotar, salir; *Fig (talent)* brotar, nacer

Buddhism ['bʊdɪzəm] N budismo *m*

Buddhist ['bʊdɪst] ADJ & N budista *(mf)*

budding ['bʌdɪŋ] ADJ en ciernes

buddy ['bʌdɪ] N *US Fam Esp* colega *mf*, *Am* compadre *m*, *Am* hermano(a) *m,f*, *Méx* cuate *m*

budge [bʌdʒ] VI **(a)** *(move)* moverse **(b)** *(yield)* ceder

budgerigar ['bʌdʒərɪgɑː(r)] N periquito *(australiano)*

budget ['bʌdʒɪt] **1** N presupuesto *m*; *Br Pol* **the B.** ≃ los Presupuestos Generales del Estado
2 VI hacer un presupuesto **(for** para)

budgie ['bʌdʒɪ] N *Br Fam* = **budgerigar**

buff¹ [bʌf] **1** ADJ & N *(colour)* color *(m)* de ante
2 VT dar brillo a

buff² [bʌf] N *Fam (enthusiast)* aficionado(a) *m,f*

buffalo ['bʌfələʊ] N *(pl* **buffaloes** or **buffalo***)* búfalo *m*

buffer ['bʌfə(r)] **1** N **(a)** *(device)* amortiguador *m*; *Rail* tope *m*; **b. zone** zona *f* de seguridad **(b)** *Comput* memoria intermedia
2 VT amortiguar

buffet¹ ['bʊfeɪ] N **(a)** *(snack bar)* bar *m*; *(at railway station)* cantina *f*; *Rail* **b. car** coche *m* restaurante **(b)** *(self-service meal)* bufet *m* libre **(c)** *(item of furniture)* aparador *m*

buffet² ['bʌfɪt] VT golpear

buffoon [bəˈfuːn] N bufón *m*, payaso *m*

bug [bʌg] **1** N **(a)** *(insect)* bicho *m* **(b)** *Fam (microbe)* microbio *m*; **the flu b.** el virus de la gripe **(c)** *(hidden microphone)* micrófono oculto **(d)** *Comput* error *m*
2 VT *Fam* **(a) to b. a room** ocultar micrófonos en una habitación **(b)** *(annoy)* fastidiar, molestar

bugger ['bʌgə(r)] **1** N *Br very Fam (unpleasant person)* cabrón(ona) *m,f*; **you silly b.** ¡qué tonto(a) eres!; **the poor b.!** ¡pobre desgraciado!; **b. all** nada de nada
2 VT **(a)** *(sodomize)* sodomizar **(b)** *Br very Fam* **b. (it)!** ¡carajo!, *Esp* ¡joder!, *RP* ¡la puta (digo)!
▸ **bugger about** *very Fam* **1** VI hacer chorradas
2 VT SEP **they really buggered him about** se las hicieron pasar canutas
▸ **bugger off** VI *very Fam Pej* pirarse; **b. off!** ¡vete a la mierda!
▸ **bugger up** VT SEP *very Fam* jorobar

buggy ['bʌgɪ] N **(a)** *Br (baby's pushchair)* sillita *f* de niño **(b)** *US (pram)* cochecito *m* (de niño)

bugle ['bjuːgəl] N bugle *m*

build [bɪld] **1** VT *(pt & pp* **built***)* construir
2 N *(physique)* tipo *m*, físico *m*

▶ **build up** VT SEP *(accumulate)* acumular; **to b. up a reputation** labrarse una buena reputación

builder ['bɪldə(r)] N constructor(a) *m,f*; *(contractor)* contratista *mf*

building ['bɪldɪŋ] N edificio *m*, construcción *f*; **b. site** obra *f*; *Br* **b. society** sociedad hipotecaria

build-up ['bɪldʌp] N (a) *(accumulation)* aumento *m*; *(of gas)* acumulación *f* (b) *(publicity)* propaganda *f*

built [bɪlt] PT & PP *of* **build**

built-in ['bɪlt'ɪn] ADJ (a) *(cupboard)* empotrado(a) (b) *(incorporated)* incorporado(a)

built-up ['bɪlt'ʌp] ADJ urbanizado(a)

bulb [bʌlb] N (a) *Bot* bulbo *m* (b) *(light bulb)* *Esp* bombilla *f*, *Andes, Méx* foco *m*, *CAm, Carib* bombillo *m*, *RP* lamparita *f*

Bulgaria [bʌl'geərɪə] N Bulgaria

Bulgarian [bʌl'geərɪən] 1 ADJ búlgaro(a)
2 N (a) *(person)* búlgaro(a) *m,f* (b) *(language)* búlgaro *m*

bulge [bʌldʒ] 1 N protuberancia *f*; *(in pocket)* bulto *m*
2 VI *(swell)* hincharse; *(be full)* estar repleto(a)

bulimia [buːˈlɪmɪə] N *Med* bulimia *f*

bulk [bʌlk] N (a) *(mass)* masa *f*, volumen *m*; *Com* **in b.** a granel; **to buy sth in b.** comprar algo al por mayor (b) *(greater part)* mayor parte *f*

bulky ['bʌlkɪ] ADJ (**bulkier, bulkiest**) (a) *(large)* voluminoso(a) (b) **this crate is rather b.** esta caja es un armatoste

bull [bʊl] N (a) *(animal)* toro *m*; *Fig* **to take the b. by the horns** agarrar *or Esp* coger el toro por los cuernos (b) *Fin* **b. market** mercado *m* al alza

bulldog ['bʊldɒg] N buldog *m*

bulldoze ['bʊldəʊz] VT *(land)* nivelar; *(building)* derribar

bulldozer ['bʊldəʊzə(r)] N bulldozer *m*

bullet ['bʊlɪt] N bala *f*; **b. wound** balazo *m*

bulletin ['bʊlɪtɪn] N boletín *m*; *Rad & TV* **news b.** boletín de noticias; *US* **b. board** tablón *m* de anuncios

bullet-proof ['bʊlɪtpruːf] ADJ a prueba de balas; **b. vest** chaleco *m* antibalas

bullfight ['bʊlfaɪt] N corrida *f* de toros

bullfighter ['bʊlfaɪtə(r)] N torero(a) *m,f*

bullfighting ['bʊlfaɪtɪŋ] N los toros *mpl*; *(art)* tauromaquia *f*

bullion ['bʊljən] N **gold/silver b.** oro/plata en lingotes

bullish ['bʊlɪʃ] ADJ *Fin (market)* en alza

bullock ['bʊlək] N buey *m*

bullring ['bʊlrɪŋ] N plaza *f* de toros

bull's-eye ['bʊlzaɪ] N *(of target)* blanco *m*

bully ['bʊlɪ] 1 N matón *m*; *(at school)* *Esp* abusón(ona) *m,f*, *Am* abusador(a) *m,f*

2 VT *(terrorize)* intimidar; *(bulldoze)* tiranizar
3 INTERJ *Ironic* **b. for you!** ¡bravo!

bulwark ['bʊlwək] N baluarte *m*

bum[1] [bʌm] N *Br Fam (bottom)* culo *m*, *Am* cola *f*

bum[2] [bʌm] *Fam* 1 N (a) *US (tramp)* vagabundo *m* (b) *(idler)* holgazán(ana) *m,f*
2 VI gorronear

▶ **bum around** VI *Fam* vaguear

bumblebee ['bʌmblbiː] N abejorro *m*

bumbling ['bʌmblɪŋ] ADJ torpe

bump [bʌmp] 1 N (a) *(swelling)* chichón *m*; *(lump)* abolladura *f*; *(on road)* bache *m* (b) *(blow)* choque *m*, golpe *m* (c) *(jolt)* sacudida *f*
2 VT golpear; **to b. one's head** darse un golpe en la cabeza
3 VI chocar (**into** contra)

▶ **bump into** VT INSEP *(meet)* tropezar con

▶ **bump off** VT SEP *Fam* liquidar

bumper ['bʌmpə(r)] 1 ADJ abundante; *Br* **b. issue** número *m* especial
2 N *Br (of car)* parachoques *m inv*, *Méx* defensas *fpl*, *RP* paragolpes *m inv*

bumptious ['bʌmpʃəs] ADJ presuntuoso(a), engreído(a)

bumpy ['bʌmpɪ] ADJ (**bumpier, bumpiest**) con muchos baches

bun [bʌn] N (a) *(bread)* panecillo *m*; *(sweet)* bollo *m*; *Fig Euph* **she's got a b. in the oven** está preñada (b) *(of hair)* moño *m*

bunch [bʌntʃ] 1 N *(of keys)* manojo *m*; *(of flowers)* ramo *m*; *(of grapes)* racimo *m*; *(of people)* grupo *m*; *(gang)* pandilla *f*
2 VI **to b. together** juntarse, agruparse

bundle ['bʌndəl] 1 N *(of clothes)* bulto *m*, fardo *m*; *(of papers)* fajo *m*; *(of wood)* haz *m*
2 VT (a) *(make a bundle of)* liar, atar (b) *(push)* empujar

bung [bʌŋ] 1 N tapón *m*
2 VT *Fam (put, throw)* echar, *Am* botar

▶ **bung up** VT SEP *Fam* atascar

bungalow ['bʌŋgələʊ] N chalé *m*, bungalow *m*

bungle ['bʌŋgəl] VT chapucear

bunion ['bʌnjən] N juanete *m*

bunk [bʌŋk] N *(bed)* litera *f*

bunker ['bʌŋkə(r)] N (a) *(coal)* carbonera *f* (b) *Mil* búnker *m* (c) *Br (on golf course)* búnker *m*

bunny ['bʌnɪ] N *Fam (baby talk)* **b. (rabbit)** conejito *m*

bunting ['bʌntɪŋ] N *(material)* lanilla *f*; *(flags)* banderines *mpl*; *Naut* empavesada *f*

buoy [bɔɪ] N boya *f*

▶ **buoy up** VT SEP (a) *(keep afloat)* mantener a flote (b) *(person, spirits)* alentar, animar

buoyancy ['bɔɪənsɪ] N (a) *(of object)* flotabilidad *f* (b) *Fin* tendencia *f* alcista (c) *(optimism)* optimismo *m*

buoyant ['bɔɪənt] ADJ (a) *(object)* flotante (b) *Fin* con tendencia alcista (c) *(optimistic)* optimista

burble ['bɜːbəl] VI (**a**) *(stream)* murmurar; *(baby)* balbucear (**b**) *(talk quickly)* farfullar

burden ['bɜːdən] **1** N carga f; *Fig* **to be a b. to sb** ser una carga para algn
2 VT cargar (**with** con)

bureau ['bjʊərəʊ] N (*pl* **bureaux**) (**a**) *(office)* agencia f, oficina f (**b**) *Br (desk)* escritorio m (**c**) *US (chest of drawers)* cómoda f

bureaucracy [bjʊə'rɒkrəsɪ] N burocracia f

bureaucrat ['bjʊərəkræt] N burócrata mf

bureaucratic [bjʊərə'krætɪk] ADJ burocrático(a)

burgeon ['bɜːdʒən] VI florecer

burger ['bɜːgə(r)] N *Fam (hamburger)* hamburguesa f

burglar ['bɜːglə(r)] N ladrón(ona) m,f; **b. alarm** alarma f antirrobo

burglarize ['bɜːgləraɪz] VT *US* robar, desvalijar

burglary ['bɜːglərɪ] N robo m con allanamiento de morada

burgle ['bɜːgəl] VT robar, desvalijar

burial ['berɪəl] N entierro m

burly ['bɜːlɪ] ADJ (**burlier**, **burliest**) fornido(a), fuerte

Burma ['bɜːmə] N Birmania f

Burmese [bɜː'miːz] **1** ADJ birmano(a)
2 N (**a**) *(person)* birmano(a) m,f (**b**) *(language)* birmano m

burn [bɜːn] **1** N quemadura f
2 VT (*pt & pp* **burnt** *or* **burned**) quemar
3 VI (**a**) *(fire)* arder; *(building, food)* quemarse (**b**) *(lamp)* estar encendido(a) (**c**) *(sore)* escocer
▶ **burn down** **1** VT SEP incendiar
2 VI incendiarse
▶ **burn out** VI *(person)* quemarse
▶ **burn up** VT SEP *(energy, calories)* quemar

burner ['bɜːnə(r)] N quemador m

burning ['bɜːnɪŋ] ADJ (**a**) *(on fire)* incendiado(a); *(hot)* abrasador(a) (**b**) *(passionate)* ardiente (**c**) **a b. question** una cuestión candente

burnt [bɜːnt] **1** ADJ quemado(a); **b. almonds** almendras tostadas
2 PT & PP *of* **burn**

burp [bɜːp] **1** N eructo m
2 VI eructar

burrow ['bʌrəʊ] **1** N *(animal)* madriguera f
2 VI (**a**) *(dig) (person, animal)* excavar (**b**) *(search)* rebuscar

bursar ['bɜːsə(r)] N tesorero(a) m,f

bursary ['bɜːsərɪ] N *Br (scholarship)* beca f

burst [bɜːst] **1** N (**a**) *(explosion)* estallido m; *(of tyre)* reventón m (**b**) *(of applause)* arranque m; *(of rage)* arrebato m; **b. of gunfire** ráfaga f de tiros; **b. of laughter** carcajadas fpl
2 VT (*pt & pp* **burst**) *(balloon)* reventar; *Fig* **the river b. its banks** el río se salió de madre
3 VI *(balloon, tyre, pipe)* reventarse; *(shell)* estallar

▶ **burst into** VT INSEP (**a**) *(enter)* irrumpir en (**b**) *(suddenly start)* **to b. into laughter/tears** echarse a reír/llorar
▶ **burst open** VI abrirse violentamente
▶ **burst out** VI **to b. out laughing** echarse a reír

bursting ['bɜːstɪŋ] ADJ **the bar was b. with people** el bar estaba atestado de gente; *Fam* **to be b. to do sth** reventar por hacer algo

bury ['berɪ] VT (**a**) *(body, treasure)* enterrar; **to be buried in thought** estar absorto(a) en pensamientos (**b**) *(hide)* ocultar

bus [bʌs] N (*pl* **buses**, *US* **busses**) autobús m, *Andes* buseta f, *Bol, RP* colectivo m, *CAm, Carib* guagua f, *CAm, Méx* camión m, *Urug* ómnibus m, *Ven* microbusete m; **b. conductor** cobrador(a) m,f de autobús; **b. driver** conductor(a) m,f de autobús; **b. stop** parada f de autobús

bush [bʊʃ] N (**a**) *(shrub)* arbusto m (**b**) *Austr* **the b.** el monte; *Fam* **b. telegraph** *Esp* radio f macuto, *Cuba, CRica, Pan* radio f bemba

bushy ['bʊʃɪ] ADJ (**bushier**, **bushiest**) espeso(a), tupido(a)

business ['bɪznɪs] N (**a**) *(commerce)* negocios mpl; **how's b.?** ¿cómo andan los negocios?; **to be away on b.** estar en viaje de negocios; **b. deal** negocio m; **b. hours** horas fpl de oficina; **b. trip** viaje m de negocios (**b**) *(firm)* empresa f (**c**) *(matter)* asunto m; **I mean b.** estoy hablando en serio; **it's no b. of mine** no es asunto mío; **to make it one's b. to …** encargarse de …; **to get down to b.** ir al grano; **to go about one's b.** ocuparse de sus asuntos

businesslike ['bɪznɪslaɪk] ADJ *(practical)* eficiente; *(methodical)* metódico(a); *(serious)* serio(a)

businessman ['bɪznɪsmən] N hombre m de negocios

businesswoman ['bɪznɪswʊmən] N mujer f de negocios

busker ['bʌskə(r)] N *Br Fam* músico(a) m,f callejero(a)

bust¹ [bʌst] N (**a**) *(of woman)* pecho m (**b**) *Art* busto m

bust² [bʌst] *Fam* **1** VT (**a**) *(break)* estropear, *Esp* escacharrar (**b**) *(person)* trincar; *(place)* hacer una redada en
2 ADJ (**a**) *(broken)* **to be b.** estar estropeado(a) *or Esp* escacharrado(a) (**b**) **to go b.** *(bankrupt)* quebrar

bustle ['bʌsəl] **1** N *(activity, noise)* bullicio m
2 VI **to b. about** ir y venir

bustling ['bʌslɪŋ] ADJ bullicioso(a)

bust-up ['bʌstʌp] N *Br Fam* bronca f

busy ['bɪzɪ] **1** ADJ (**busier**, **busiest**) (**a**) *(person)* ocupado(a); *(day, office)* ajetreado(a); *(street)* transitado(a) (**b**) *US Tel* ocupado(a); **b. signal** señal f de comunicando
2 VT **to b. oneself doing sth** ocuparse haciendo algo

busybody ['bɪzɪbɒdɪ] N entrometido(a) m,f

but [bʌt] **1** CONJ (**a**) *(in general)* pero; **b. yet** a pesar de todo (**b**) *(after negative)* sino; **not two b. three** no dos sino tres

2 ADV **b. for her we would have drowned** si no hubiera sido por ella, nos habríamos ahogado

3 PREP salvo, menos; **everyone b. her** todos menos ella

butane ['bjuːteɪn] N butano *m*; **b. gas** gas butano

butcher ['bʊtʃə(r)] **1** N carnicero(a) *m,f*; **b.'s (shop)** carnicería *f*

2 VT *(animals)* matar; *(people)* masacrar

butler ['bʌtlə(r)] N mayordomo *m*

butt¹ [bʌt] N (**a**) *(of rifle)* culata *f*; *(of cigarette)* colilla *f* (**b**) *US Fam (bottom)* culo *m*

butt² [bʌt] N *(with head)* cabezazo *m*

2 VT *(strike with head)* dar un cabezazo a

▸ **butt in** VI entrar en la conversación

butter ['bʌtə(r)] **1** N mantequilla *f*, *RP* manteca *f*; **b. dish** mantequera *f*

2 VT untar con mantequilla *or RP* manteca

buttercup ['bʌtəkʌp] N ranúnculo *m*, botón *m* de oro

butterfingers ['bʌtəfɪŋgəz] N SING *Fam* manazas *mf inv*

butterfly ['bʌtəflaɪ] N mariposa *f*

buttock ['bʌtək] N nalga *f*; **buttocks** nalgas *fpl*

button ['bʌtən] **1** N (**a**) *(on clothes, machine)* botón *m* (**b**) *US (badge)* chapa *f*

2 VT **to b. (up)** abrochar(se), abotonar(se)

buttonhole ['bʌtənhəʊl] N ojal *m*

buttress ['bʌtrɪs] **1** N (**a**) *Archit* contrafuerte *m* (**b**) *(support)* apoyo *m*

2 VT *(support)* *(argument, system)* respaldar

buxom ['bʌksəm] ADJ *(woman)* pechugona

buy [baɪ] **1** N compra *f*; **a good b.** una ganga

2 VT *(pt & pp **bought**)* (**a**) *(purchase)* comprar; **she bought that car from a neighbour** compró ese coche a un vecino (**b**) *Fam (believe)* tragar

▸ **buy off** VT SEP sobornar

▸ **buy out** VT SEP adquirir la parte de

▸ **buy up** VT SEP comprar en grandes cantidades

buyer ['baɪə(r)] N comprador(a) *m,f*

buzz [bʌz] **1** N (**a**) *(of bee)* zumbido *m*; *(of conversation)* rumor *m* (**b**) *Fam (telephone call)* telefonazo *m*

2 VI zumbar

buzzer ['bʌzə(r)] N timbre *m*

by [baɪ] **1** PREP (**a**) *(indicating agent)* por; **composed by Bach** compuesto(a) por Bach; **a film by Almodóvar** una película de Almodóvar (**b**) *(via)* por; **he left by the back door** salió por la puerta trasera

(**c**) *(manner)* por; **by car/train** en coche/tren; **by credit card** con tarjeta de crédito; **by day/ night** de día/noche; **by chance** por casualidad; **by oneself** solo(a); **made by hand** hecho(a) a mano

(**d**) *(amount)* por; **little by little** poco a poco; **they are sold by the dozen** se venden por docenas; **to be paid by the hour** cobrar por horas; **by far** con mucho

(**e**) *(beside)* al lado de, junto a; **side by side** juntos(as)

(**f**) **to walk by a building** *(pass)* pasar por delante de un edificio

(**g**) *(time)* para; **by now** ya; **by then** para entonces; **we have to be there by nine** tenemos que estar allí para las nueve

(**h**) *Math* por

(**i**) *(according to)* según; **is that O.K. by you?**

(**j**) *(phrases)* **bit by bit** poco a poco; **day by day** día a día; **what do you mean by that?** ¿qué quieres decir con eso?; **by the way** a propósito; **by and large** en conjunto

2 ADV (**a**) **to go by** *(past)* pasar; **she just walked by** pasó de largo (**b**) **by and by** con el tiempo; **by and large** en conjunto

bye [baɪ] **1** N **by the b.** por cierto

2 INTERJ *Fam* ¡adiós!, ¡hasta luego!, *Am* ¡bye!, *Am* ¡chau!

bye-bye ['baɪ'baɪ] INTERJ *Fam* ¡adiós!, ¡hasta luego!, *Am* ¡bye!, *Am* ¡chau!

by-election ['baɪɪlekʃən] N *Br* elección *f* parcial

bygone ['baɪgɒn] **1** ADJ pasado(a)

2 NPL **let bygones be bygones** lo pasado pasado está, *Am* lo pasado, pisado

by-law ['baɪlɔː] N ley *f* municipal

bypass ['baɪpɑːs] **1** N (**a**) *(road)* carretera *f* de circunvalación (**b**) *Med* **b. surgery** cirugía *f* de bypass

2 VT evitar

by-product ['baɪprɒdʌkt] N *Chem & Ind* derivado *m*, subproducto *m*; *Fig* consecuencia *f*

byroad ['baɪrəʊd] N carretera secundaria

bystander ['baɪstændə(r)] N testigo *mf*

byte [baɪt] N *Comput* byte *m*, octeto *m*

byword ['baɪwɜːd] N **it became a b. for modernity** se convirtió en sinónimo de modernidad

C

C, c [siː] N (**a**) *(letter)* C, c (**b**) *Mus* do *m* (**c**) *Sch (grade)* aprobado *m*; **to get a C** *(in exam, essay)* sacar un aprobado

C [siː] (**a**) *(abbr* **celsius** *or* **centigrade)** C, centígrado (**b**) *(abbr* **century)** s., siglo; **C. 16** s. XVI

cab [kæb] N taxi *m*; **c. driver** taxista *mf*

cabaret ['kæbəreɪ] N cabaret *m*

cabbage ['kæbɪdʒ] N col *f*, berza *f*; **red c.** (col) lombarda *f*

cabin ['kæbɪn] N (**a**) *(hut)* choza *f*; **log c.** cabaña *f* (**b**) *Naut* camarote *m* (**c**) *(of lorry, plane)* cabina *f*

cabinet ['kæbɪnɪt] N (**a**) *(item of furniture)* armario *m*; *(glass-fronted)* vitrina *f*; **c. maker** ebanista *mf* (**b**) *Pol* gabinete *m*, consejo *m* de ministros

cable ['keɪbəl] **1** N cable *m*; **c. car** teleférico *m*; **c. company** cableoperador(a) *m,f*; **c. TV** televisión *f* por cable
2 VT & VI cablegrafiar, telegrafiar

caboose [kə'buːs] N *US (on train)* furgón *m* de cola

cache [kæʃ] N (**a**) *(place)* alijo *m* (**b**) *Comput* caché *f*

cackle ['kækəl] VI cacarear

cactus ['kæktəs] N *(pl* **cacti** ['kæktaɪ]*)* cactus *m*

CAD [kæd] N *(abbr* **computer-aided** *or* **-assisted design)** CAD *m*, diseño asistido por *Esp* ordenador *or Am* computadora

cad [kæd] N *Br Fam Old-fashioned* canalla *m*

caddie ['kædɪ] N *(in golf)* cadi *m*

cadet [kə'det] N *Mil* cadete *m*

cadge [kædʒ] VT & VI *Fam* gorrear, *Esp, Méx* gorronear, *RP* garronear (**from** *or* **off** a)

Caesarean [siː'zeərɪən] N *Med* **she had a C.** le hicieron una cesárea; **C. section** operación *f* cesárea

café ['kæfeɪ], **cafeteria** [kæfɪ'tɪərɪə] N cafetería *f*

cafetiere [kæfə'tjɜː(r)] N *Br* cafetera *f* (de émbolo)

caffeine ['kæfiːn] N cafeína *f*

cage [keɪdʒ] **1** N jaula *f*
2 VT enjaular

cagey ['keɪdʒɪ] ADJ (**cagier, cagiest**) **to be c. (about sth)** *(cautious)* ir *or Esp* andar con tiento (con algo); *(evasive)* salirse por la tangente (en cuanto a algo)

cagoule [kə'guːl] N *Br (garment)* chubasquero *m*

Cairo ['kaɪrəʊ] N (el) Cairo

cajole [kə'dʒəʊl] VT engatusar

cake [keɪk] N pastel *m*, tarta *f*

calamity [kə'læmɪtɪ] N calamidad *f*

calcium ['kælsɪəm] N calcio *m*

calculate ['kælkjʊleɪt] VT calcular

calculated ['kælkjʊleɪtɪd] ADJ intencionado(a)

calculating ['kælkjʊleɪtɪŋ] ADJ (**a**) **c. machine** calculadora *f* (**b**) *Pej (person)* calculador(a)

calculation [kælkjʊ'leɪʃən] N cálculo *m*

calculator ['kælkjʊleɪtə(r)] N calculadora *f*

calendar ['kælɪndə(r)] N calendario *m*; **c. year** año *m* natural, *Am* año calendario

calf¹ [kɑːf] N *(pl* **calves)** *(of cattle)* becerro(a) *m,f*, ternero(a) *m,f*, *(of other animals)* cría *f*

calf² [kɑːf] N *(pl* **calves)** *Anat* pantorrilla *f*

calfskin ['kɑːfskɪn] N piel *f* de becerro

calibre, *US* **caliber** ['kælɪbə(r)] N calibre *m*

call [kɔːl] **1** VT (**a**) *(on phone)* llamar, telefonear, *Am* hablar; **to c. sb names** poner verde a algn; **what's he called?** ¿cómo se llama? (**b**) *(meeting etc)* convocar; **to c. sth to mind** traer algo a la memoria
2 VI (**a**) *(on phone)* llamar, *Am* hablar; *Tel* **who's calling?** ¿de parte de quién? (**b**) **to c. at sb's (house)** pasar por casa de algn; **to c. for sth/sb** pasar a recoger algo/a algn (**c**) *(trains)* parar (**d**) **to c. for** *(require)* exigir; **that wasn't called for** eso no estaba justificado
3 N (**a**) *(shout) (of person)* llamada *f*, grito *m*, *Am* llamado *m* (**b**) *(visit)* visita *f*; **to pay a c. on sb** visitar a algn (**c**) *Tel (phone)* **c.** llamada *f*, *Am* llamado *m*; **c. box** *Br* cabina telefónica; *US* teléfono *m* de emergencia; **c. centre** centro *m* de atención telefónica

▸ **call away** VT SEP **to be called away on business** tener que ausentarse por motivos de trabajo

▸ **call back** VI *(phone again)* volver a llamar *or Am* hablar; *(visit again)* volver

▸ **call in** VT SEP *(doctor)* llamar
2 VI (**a**) **I'll c. in tomorrow** *(visit)* mañana me paso (**b**) *Naut* hacer escala (**at** en)

▸ **call off** VT SEP suspender

▸ **call on** VT INSEP (**a**) *(visit)* visitar (**b**) **to c. on sb for support** recurrir a algn en busca de apoyo

▸ **call out 1** VT SEP (a) (shout) gritar (b) (doctor) hacer venir; (workers) convocar a la huelga
2 VI gritar

▸ **call up** VT SEP (a) Tel llamar, Am hablar (b) Mil llamar a filas, reclutar

caller ['kɔːlə(r)] N visita mf; Tel persona f que llama

calling ['kɔːlɪŋ] N esp Rel vocación f; US **c. card** tarjeta f de visita

callous ['kæləs] ADJ insensible, duro(a)

call-up ['kɔːlʌp] N Mil llamada f or Am llamado m a filas, reclutamiento m

calm [kɑːm] **1** ADJ (a) (weather, sea) en calma (b) (relaxed) tranquilo(a); **keep c.!** ¡tranquilo(a)!
2 N (a) (of weather, sea) calma f (b) (tranquillity) tranquilidad f
3 VT calmar, tranquilizar
4 VI to **c. (down)** calmarse, tranquilizarse

Calor Gas® ['kælagæs] N Br butano m

calorie, calory ['kælərɪ] N caloría f

calve [kɑːv] VI (cow) parir (un becerro)

calves [kɑːvz] PL of **calf¹, calf²**

Cambodia [kæm'bəʊdɪə] N Camboya

camcorder ['kæmkɔːdə(r)] N videocámara f (portátil)

came [keɪm] PT of **come**

camel ['kæməl] N camello(a) m,f

cameo ['kæmɪəʊ] N camafeo m

camera ['kæmərə] N (a) (photographic) cámara (fotográfica); Cin & TV cámara (b) Jur **in c.** a puerta cerrada

cameraman ['kæmərəmən] N cámara m

Cameroon [kæmə'ruːn] N Camerún

camomile ['kæməmaɪl] N camomila f; **c. tea** (infusión f de) manzanilla f

camouflage ['kæməflɑːʒ] **1** N camuflaje m
2 VT camuflar

camp¹ [kæmp] **1** N campamento m; **c. bed** cama f plegable; **c. site** camping m
2 VI **to go camping** ir de camping

camp² [kæmp] ADJ Fam afeminado(a); (affected) amanerado(a)

campaign [kæm'peɪn] **1** N campaña f
2 VI **to c. for/against** hacer campaña a favor de/en contra de

campaigner [kæm'peɪnə(r)] N defensor(a) m,f (for de)

camper ['kæmpə(r)] N (a) (person) campista mf (b) US (vehicle) caravana f

camping ['kæmpɪŋ] N **c. ground, c. site** camping m

campus ['kæmpəs] N campus m, ciudad universitaria

can¹ [kæn, unstressed kən] V AUX (pt could)

El verbo **can** carece de infinitivo, de gerundio y de participio. En infinitivo o en participio, se empleará la forma correspondiente de **be able to**, por ejemplo: **he wanted to be able**

to speak English; she has always been able to swim. En el inglés hablado, la forma negativa **cannot** se transforma en **can't** y la forma negativa **could not** se transforma en **couldn't**.

(a) (be able to) poder; **he could have come** podría haber venido; **I'll phone you as soon as I c.** te llamaré en cuanto pueda; **she can't do it** no puede hacerlo; **I can't understand why** no entiendo por qué (b) (know how to) saber; **c. you ski?** ¿sabes esquiar?; **I can't speak English** no sé hablar inglés (c) (be permitted to) poder; **he can't go out tonight** no le dejan salir esta noche (d) (be possible) poder; **she could have forgotten** puede (ser) que lo haya olvidado; **they can't be very poor** no deben ser muy pobres; **what c. it be?** ¿qué será?

can² [kæn] **1** N (a) (of oil) bidón m (b) (container) lata f, Am tarro m; **c. opener** abrelatas m inv
2 VT (fish, fruit) enlatar

Canada ['kænədə] N Canadá

Canadian [kə'neɪdɪən] ADJ & N canadiense (mf)

canal [kə'næl] N canal m

canary [kə'neərɪ] N canario m

Canary Islands [kə'neərɪaɪləndz] NPL (Islas fpl) Canarias fpl

cancel ['kænsəl] VT (train, contract) cancelar; Com anular; (permission) retirar; (decree) revocar

cancellation [kænsɪ'leɪʃən] N cancelación f; Com anulación f

cancer ['kænsə(r)] N (a) Med cáncer m; **breast c.** cáncer de mama; **c. research** cancerología f (b) **C.** (in astrology) Cáncer m

candelabra [kændɪ'lɑːbrə] N candelabro m

candid ['kændɪd] ADJ franco(a), sincero(a)

> Note that the Spanish word **cándido** is a false friend and is never a translation for the English word **candid**. In Spanish **cándido** means "ingenuous, naive".

candidate ['kændɪdeɪt, 'kændɪdɪt] N candidato(a) m,f; (in exam) opositor(a) m,f

candle ['kændəl] N vela f; (in church) cirio m

candlelight ['kændəllaɪt] N luz f de vela; **by c.** a la luz de las velas

candlestick ['kændəlstɪk] N candelero m, palmatoria f; (in church) cirial m

candour, US **candor** ['kændə(r)] N sinceridad f, franqueza f

> Note that the Spanish word **candor** is a false friend and is never a translation for the English word **candour**. In Spanish, **candor** means "innocence, naïvety".

candy ['kændɪ] N US (sweet) caramelo m; (sweets) dulces mpl; **c. store** confitería f

candyfloss ['kændɪflɒs] N Br algodón m dulce

cane [keɪn] **1** N (**a**) *Bot* caña *f*; **c. sugar** azúcar *m* de caña (**b**) *(wicker)* mimbre *m* (**c**) *(walking stick)* bastón *m*; *(for punishment)* palmeta *f*
2 VT castigar con la palmeta

canine ['keɪnaɪn] ADJ *Zool* canino(a); **c. tooth** colmillo *m*

canister ['kænɪstə(r)] N bote *m*

cannabis ['kænəbɪs] N hachís *m*, cannabis *m*

canned [kænd] ADJ enlatado(a); **c. foods** conservas *fpl*

cannelloni [kænə'ləʊnɪ] N canelones *mpl*

cannibal ['kænɪbəl] ADJ & N caníbal *(mf)*

cannon ['kænən] **1** N (**a**) *(pl* **cannons** *or* **cannon**) cañón *m*; *Fig* **c. fodder** carne *f* de cañón (**b**) *Br (in billiards, snooker)* carambola *f*
2 VI chocar (**into** contra)

cannonball ['kænənbɔːl] N bala *f* de cañón

cannot ['kænɒt, kæ'nɒt] = **can not**

canoe [kə'nuː] N canoa *f*; *Sport* piragua *f*

canoeing [kə'nuːɪŋ] N piragüismo *m*; **to go c.** ir a hacer piragüismo

canon ['kænən] N *Rel* canon *m*

canopy ['kænəpɪ] N (**a**) *(on throne)* dosel *m* (**b**) *(awning)* toldo *m*

can't [kɑːnt] = **can not**

Cantabria [kæn'tæbrɪə] N Cantabria

cantankerous [kæn'tæŋkərəs] ADJ intratable

canteen [kæn'tiːn] N (**a**) *(restaurant)* cantina *f* (**b**) *Br (set of cutlery)* juego *m* de cubiertos (**c**) *(flask)* cantimplora *f*

canter ['kæntə(r)] **1** N medio galope
2 VI ir a medio galope

canvas ['kænvəs] N (**a**) *Tex* lona *f* (**b**) *(painting)* lienzo *m*

canvass ['kænvəs] VI (**a**) *Pol* hacer propaganda electoral (**b**) *Com* hacer promoción, buscar clientes

canvasser ['kænvəsə(r)] N *Pol* = persona que hace propaganda electoral de puerta en puerta

canyon ['kænjən] N cañón *m*; **the Grand C.** el Gran Cañón

canyoning ['kænjənɪŋ] N *Sport* barranquismo *m*

CAP [siːeɪ'piː] N *(abbr* **Common Agricultural Policy)** PAC *f*

cap [kæp] **1** N (**a**) *(headgear) (without peak)* gorro *m*; *(with peak)* gorra *f* (**b**) *Br Sport* **to win a c. for England** ser seleccionado(a) para el equipo de Inglaterra (**c**) *(of pen)* capuchón *m*; *(of bottle)* chapa *f*
2 VT (**a**) *(bottle)* poner la chapa a; *Fig* **to c. it all** para colmo (**b**) *Br Sport* seleccionar

capability [keɪpə'bɪlɪtɪ] N habilidad *f*

capable ['keɪpəbəl] ADJ (**a**) *(skilful)* hábil (**b**) *(able)* capaz (**of** de)

capacity [kə'pæsɪtɪ] N (**a**) *(of container, theatre)* capacidad *f* (**b**) *(aptitude)* **to have a c. for sth** tener capacidad para algo (**c**) *(role)* **in her c. as manageress** en calidad de gerente

cape¹ [keɪp] N *(garment)* capa *f*

cape² [keɪp] N *Geog* cabo *m*, promontorio *m*; **C. Horn** Cabo de Hornos; **C. Town** Ciudad del Cabo; **C. Verde** Cabo Verde

caper ['keɪpə(r)] N *(prank)* travesura *f*

capital ['kæpɪtəl] **1** N (**a**) *(town)* capital *f* (**b**) *(letter)* mayúscula *f* (**c**) *Fin* capital *m*
2 ADJ (**a**) *(city)* capital (**b**) **c. punishment** pena *f* capital (**c**) **c. letter** mayúscula *f*

capitalism ['kæpɪtəlɪzəm] N capitalismo *m*

capitalist ['kæpɪtəlɪst] ADJ & N capitalista *(mf)*

capitalize ['kæpɪtəlaɪz] **2** VT *Fin* capitalizar
2 VI **to c. on sth** sacar provecho *or* beneficio de algo

capitulate [kə'pɪtjʊleɪt] VI capitular

cappuccino [kæpə'tʃiːnəʊ] N *(café m)* capuchino *m*

Capricorn ['kæprɪkɔːn] N Capricornio *m*

capsicum ['kæpsɪkəm] N pimiento *m*

capsize [kæp'saɪz] **1** VT hacer zozobrar
2 VI zozobrar

capsule ['kæpsjuːl] N cápsula *f*

captain ['kæptɪn] **1** N capitán *m*
2 VT capitanear

caption ['kæpʃən] N *(under picture)* pie *m* de foto; *Cin* subtítulo *m*

captivating ['kæptɪveɪtɪŋ] ADJ seductor(a)

captive ['kæptɪv] **1** N cautivo(a) *m,f*
2 ADJ cautivo(a)

captivity [kæp'tɪvɪtɪ] N cautiverio *m*

capture ['kæptʃə(r)] **1** VT (**a**) *(person)* capturar; *Mil (town)* tomar; *(in chess, draughts)* comer (**b**) *(market)* acaparar (**c**) *Fig (mood)* reflejar
2 N *(of fugitive)* captura *f*; *(of town)* toma *f*

car [kɑː(r)] N (**a**) *(automobile)* coche *m*, *Am* carro *m*, *CSur* auto *m*; *Br* **c. park** parking *m*, *Esp* aparcamiento *m*; **c. wash** túnel *m* de lavado (**b**) *US Rail* coche *m*

carafe [kə'ræf, kə'rɑːf] N jarra *f*

caramel ['kærəmel] N azúcar quemado; *(sweet)* caramelo *m*

carat ['kærət] N quilate *m*

caravan ['kærəvæn] N (**a**) *Br (vehicle)* caravana *f* (**b**) *(in desert)* caravana *f*

carbohydrate [kɑːbəʊ'haɪdreɪt] N hidrato *m* de carbono, carbohidrato *m*

carbon ['kɑːbən] N carbono *m*; **c. copy** copia *f* al papel carbón; *Fig* copia exacta; **c. dioxide** dióxido *m* de carbono; **c. paper** papel *m* carbón

carburettor [kɑːbjʊ'retə(r)], *US* **carburetor** ['kɑːbəreɪtər] N carburador *m*

carcass ['kɑːkəs] N res muerta

card [kɑːd] N (**a**) *(thin cardboard)* cartulina *f* (**b**) *(with printed information)* tarjeta *f*; *(postcard)* (tarjeta) postal *f*; **birthday/Christmas c.** tarjeta de cumpleaños/de Navidad (**c**) *(in file)* ficha *f*; *(for identification)* carné *m*, *CSur, Méx* credencial *m*; **c. index** fichero *m* (**d**) **(playing) c.** naipe *m*, carta *f*; **pack of cards** baraja *f*, cartas *fpl*; *Fig Br* **on** *or US* **in the cards** previsto(a)

cardboard ['kɑːdbɔːd] N cartón *m*; **c. box** caja *f* de carton; **c. cutout** recortable *m*

cardiac ['kɑːdiæk] ADJ cardíaco(a); **c. arrest** paro cardíaco

cardigan ['kɑːdɪgən] N rebeca *f*

cardinal ['kɑːdɪnəl] **1** N *Rel* cardenal *m*
2 ADJ cardinal; **c. numbers** números *mpl* cardinales

care [keə(r)] **1** VI *(be concerned)* preocuparse (**about** por); **I don't c.** no me importa; *Fam* **for all I c.** me trae sin cuidado; *Fam* **he couldn't c. less** le importa un bledo
2 N (**a**) *(attention, protection)* cuidado *m*, atención *f*; **c. of ...** *(on letter)* al cuidado de ...; **medical c.** asistencia médica; **to take c. of** cuidar; *(business)* ocuparse de (**b**) *(carefulness)* cuidado *m*; **take c.** *(be careful)* ten cuidado; *(as farewell)* ¡cuídate! (**c**) *(worry)* preocupación *f*
► **care for** VT INSEP (**a**) *(look after)* cuidar (**b**) *Fml (like)* **would you c. for a coffee?** ¿te apetece *or Carib, Col, Méx* provoca un café?

career [kə'rɪə(r)] **1** N carrera *f*
2 VI correr a toda velocidad

carefree ['keəfriː] ADJ despreocupado(a)

careful ['keəful] ADJ *(taking care, thorough)* cuidadoso(a); *(prudent)* cauto(a), precavido(a); **be c.!** ¡ojo!; **to be c.** tener cuidado

carefully ['keəfulɪ] ADV *(painstakingly)* cuidadosamente; *(cautiously)* con cuidado

careless ['keəlɪs] ADJ *(negligent)* descuidado(a); **c. driving** conducción temeraria; **a c. mistake** un descuido

carelessly ['keəlɪslɪ] ADV descuidadamente, a la ligera

carelessness ['keəlɪsnɪs] N descuido *m*

carer ['keərə(r)] N = persona que cuida de un familiar enfermo o anciano, sin que necesariamente reciba compensación económica por ello

caress [kə'res] **1** N caricia *f*
2 VT acariciar

caretaker ['keəteɪkə(r)] N *Br (of building)* conserje *m*, portero(a) *m,f*; *(of school)* conserje *m*

carfare ['kɑːfeə(r)] N *US (precio m del)* billete *m* *or Am* boleto *m*

cargo ['kɑːgəʊ] N *(pl cargoes or US cargos)* carga *f*, cargamento *m*; *Naut* **c. boat** buque *m* de carga, carguero *m*

Caribbean [kærɪ'biən, *US* kə'rɪbiən] ADJ caribe, caribeño(a); **the C. (Sea)** el (mar) Caribe

caricature ['kærɪkətjʊə(r)] N caricatura *f*

caring ['keərɪŋ] ADJ solidario(a)

carnage ['kɑːnɪdʒ] N *Fig* carnicería *f*

carnal ['kɑːnəl] ADJ carnal

carnation [kɑː'neɪʃən] N clavel *m*

carnival ['kɑːnɪvəl] N carnaval *m*

carnivorous [kɑː'nɪvərəs] ADJ carnívoro(a)

carol ['kærəl] N villancico *m*

carom ['kærəm] N *US (in billiards, pool)* carambola *f*

carousel [kærə'sel] N (**a**) *US (at fair)* tiovivo *m* (**b**) *(at airport)* cinta transportadora de equipajes

carp¹ [kɑːp] N *(fish)* carpa *f*

carp² [kɑːp] VI refunfuñar

carpenter ['kɑːpɪntə(r)] N carpintero(a) *m,f*

carpentry ['kɑːpɪntrɪ] N carpintería *f*

carpet ['kɑːpɪt] **1** N alfombra *f*
2 VT *(floor) Esp* enmoquetar, *Am* alfombrar

> Note that the Spanish word **carpeta** is a false friend and is never a translation for the English word **carpet**. In Spanish **carpeta** means "file, folder".

carriage ['kærɪdʒ] N (**a**) *(horse-drawn)* carruaje *m* (**b**) *Br (of train)* vagón *m*, coche *m* (**c**) *(of gun)* cureña *f* (**d**) *(of typewriter)* carro *m* (**e**) *(of goods)* porte *m*, transporte *m*

carriageway ['kærɪdʒweɪ] N *Br* calzada *f*; **dual c.** autovía *f*

carrier ['kærɪə(r)] N (**a**) *(company)* transportista *mf*; *Br* **c. bag** bolsa *f* de plástico; **c. pigeon** paloma mensajera; *Med* portador(a) *m,f*

carrot ['kærət] N zanahoria *f*

carry ['kærɪ] **1** VT (**a**) *(transport, convey)* llevar; *(goods, passengers)* transportar (**b**) *(stock)* tener; *(responsibility, penalty)* conllevar, implicar (**c**) *(disease)* ser portador(a) de
2 VI *(sound)* oírse
► **carry away** VT SEP llevarse; **to get carried away** entusiasmarse
► **carry forward** VT SEP *Fin* **carried forward** suma y sigue
► **carry off** VT SEP *(prize)* llevarse; *Fam* **to c. it off** salir airoso(a)
► **carry on** **1** VT SEP *(business)* dirigir, gestionar; *(conversation)* mantener
2 VI (**a**) *(continue)* continuar, seguir; **c. on!** ¡sigue!, ¡adelante! (**b**) *Fam (make a fuss)* hacer una escena; **don't c. on about it!** ¡no te enrolles! (**c**) *Fam* **to c. on with sb** tener un lío *or Méx* una movida *or RP* un asunto con algn
► **carry out** VT SEP *(plan)* llevar a cabo, realizar; *(test)* verificar

carryall ['kærɪɔːl] N *US* bolsa *f (de viaje o de deporte)*

carrycot ['kærɪkɒt] N *Br* moisés *m*, capazo *m*

car-sick ['kɑːsɪk] ADJ mareado(a) *(en el coche)*

cart [kɑːt] **1** N *(horse-drawn)* carro *m*; *(handcart)* carretilla *f*; *US (in supermarket)* carrito *m*
2 VT carretear

cartel [kɑː'tel] N cártel *m*

cartilage ['kɑːtɪlɪdʒ] N cartílago *m*

carton ['kɑːtən] N *(of cream etc)* caja *f*

cartoon [kɑːˈtuːn] N *(strip)* tira cómica, historieta *f*; *Art* cartón *m*; *(animated)* dibujos animados

cartoonist [kɑːˈtuːnɪst] N caricaturista *mf*

cartridge [ˈkɑːtrɪdʒ] N (**a**) *(for firearm, of film)* cartucho *m* (**b**) *(for pen)* recambio *m*; **c. paper** papel guarro

carve [kɑːv] VT (**a**) *(wood)* tallar; *(stone, metal)* cincelar, esculpir (**b**) *(meat)* trinchar

carving [ˈkɑːvɪŋ] N (**a**) *Art* talla *f* (**b**) **c. knife** *(for meat)* cuchillo *m* de trinchar

cascade [kæˈskeɪd] N cascada *f*

case¹ [keɪs] N (**a**) *(instance, situation)* caso *m*; **a c. in point** un buen ejemplo; **in any c.** en cualquier caso, de todas formas; **in c. of doubt** en caso de duda; **just in c.** por si acaso (**b**) *Med* caso *m*; **c. history** historial clínico (**c**) *Jur* causa *f*

case² [keɪs] N (**a**) *(suitcase)* maleta *f*, *RP* valija *f*; *(small)* estuche *m*; *(soft)* funda *f* (**b**) **a c. of wine** una caja de botellas de vino (**c**) *Typ* **lower c.** minúscula *f*; **upper c.** mayúscula *f*

cash [kæʃ] **1** N dinero efectivo; **to pay c.** pagar al contado *or* en efectivo; *Br* **c. desk** caja *f*; **c. on delivery** entrega *f* contra reembolso; **c. dispenser** cajero automático; **c. register** caja registradora
2 VT *(cheque)* cobrar
▸ **cash in** VI *Fam Fig* **to c. in on sth** sacar provecho de algo
2 VT SEP hacer efectivo(a)

cash-and-carry [kæʃənˈkærɪ] ADJ & ADV = de venta al por mayor y pago al contado

cashew [ˈkæʃuː] N **c.** *(nut)* anacardo *m*

cashier [kæˈʃɪə(r)] N cajero(a) *m,f*

cashmere [ˈkæʃmɪə(r)] N cachemira *f*

casino [kəˈsiːnəʊ] N casino *m*

cask [kɑːsk] N tonel *m*, barril *m*

casket [ˈkɑːskɪt] N *(box)* cofre *m*; *US (coffin)* ataúd *m*

> Note that the Spanish word **casquete** is a false friend and is never a translation for the English word **casket**. In Spanish **casquete** means "shell case".

casserole [ˈkæsərəʊl] N (**a**) *(container)* cacerola *f* (**b**) *Culin* guisado *m*

cassette [kəˈset] N cinta *f*, casete *f*; **c. recorder** casete *m*

cast [kɑːst] **1** VT *(pt & pp cast)* (**a**) *(net, fishing line)* echar, arrojar; *(light)* proyectar; *(glance)* lanzar; *(vote)* emitir (**b**) *Fig* **to c. doubt on sth** poner algo en duda; **to c. suspicion on sb** levantar sospechas sobre algn (**c**) *(metal)* moldear; **c. iron** hierro fundido (**d**) *Th (play)* hacer el reparto de
2 N (**a**) *(mould)* molde *m*; *(product)* pieza *f* (**b**) *Med (plaster)* **c.** escayola *f*, *esp Am* yeso *m* (**c**) *Th* reparto *m*
▸ **cast off** VI *Naut* soltar (las) amarras

castanets [kæstəˈnets] NPL castañuelas *fpl*

castaway [ˈkɑːstəweɪ] N náufrago(a) *m,f*

caste [kɑːst] N casta *f*

caster sugar [ˈkɑːstə(r)ˈʃʊgə(r)] N *Br* azúcar extrafino(a)

Castile [kæˈstiːl] N Castilla

Castilian [kæˈstɪlɪən] **1** ADJ castellano(a)
2 N **C. (Spanish)** *(language)* castellano *m*

casting [ˈkɑːstɪŋ] N **c. vote** voto *m* de calidad

cast-iron [ˈkɑːstaɪən] ADJ de hierro fundido

castle [ˈkɑːsəl] **1** N (**a**) *(building)* castillo *m* (**b**) *(in chess)* torre *f*
2 VI *(in chess)* enrocar

castor¹ [ˈkɑːstə(r)] N **c. oil** aceite *m* de ricino

castor² [ˈkɑːstə(r)] N *(on furniture)* ruedecilla *f*

castrate [kæˈstreɪt] VT castrar

casual [ˈkæʒʊəl] ADJ (**a**) *(meeting etc)* fortuito(a) (**b**) *(worker)* eventual (**c**) *(clothes)* (de) sport (**d**) *(visit)* de paso (**e**) *(person, attitude)* despreocupado(a), informal

casualty [ˈkæʒʊəltɪ] N (**a**) *Mil* baja *f*; **casualties** pérdidas *fpl* (**b**) *(injured)* herido(a) *m,f*

> Note that the Spanish word **casualidad** is a false friend and is never a translation for the English word **casualty**. In Spanish **casualidad** means "chance, coincidence".

cat [kæt] N gato(a) *m,f*; *Fig* **to let the c. out of the bag** revelar el secreto, *Esp* descubrir el pastel

Catalan [ˈkætəlæn] **1** ADJ catalán(ana)
2 N (**a**) *(person)* catalán(ana) *m,f* (**b**) *(language)* catalán *m*

catalogue, *US* **catalog** [ˈkætəlɒg] **1** N catálogo *m*
2 VT catalogar

Catalonia [kætəˈləʊnɪə] N Cataluña

catalyst [ˈkætəlɪst] N catalizador *m*

catapult [ˈkætəpʌlt] N *Br* tirachinas *m inv*

cataract [ˈkætərækt] N *(in river)* & *Med* catarata *f*

catarrh [kəˈtɑː(r)] N catarro *m*

catastrophe [kəˈtæstrəfɪ] N catástrofe *f*

catastrophic [kætəˈstrɒfɪk] ADJ catastrófico(a)

catch [kætʃ] **1** VT *(pt & pp caught)* (**a**) *(thrown object, falling object)* atrapar, *Esp* coger, *Am* agarrar; *(fish)* pescar; *(prey, mouse, thief)* atrapar, capturar; **c. (it)!** *(when throwing something)* ¡agárralo!, *Esp* ¡cógelo!; *(train, bus)* tomar, *Esp* coger, *Am* agarrar; **to c. a cold** *Esp* coger *or Am* agarrar un resfriado; **to c. fire** *(log)* prenderse; *(building)* incendiarse; **to c. hold of** agarrar; **to c. sb's eye** captar la atención de algn; **to c. sight of** entrever (**b**) *(surprise)* pillar, sorprender (**c**) *(hear)* alcanzar a) oír (**d**) **to c. one's breath** *(hold)* sostener la respiración; *(recover)* recuperar el aliento
2 VI *(sleeve etc)* engancharse (**on** en); *(fire)* encenderse

3 N (**a**) *(of ball)* parada *f*; *(of fish)* presa *f* (**b**) *(on door)* pestillo *m* (**c**) *(disadvantage)* trampa *f*

► **catch on** VI *Fam* (**a**) *(become popular)* ganar popularidad (**b**) *(understand)* caer en la cuenta

► **catch out** VT SEP *Fam* **to c. sb out** *(discover, trick) Esp* pillar *or Am* agarrar a algn

► **catch up** VI (**a**) **to c. up with sb** *(reach)* alcanzar a algn (**b**) *(with news)* ponerse al corriente (**on** de); **to c. up on sleep** recuperar el sueño perdido; **to c. up with work** ponerse al día de trabajo

catching ['kætʃɪŋ] ADJ *(disease)* contagioso(a)

catchment ['kætʃmənt] N **c. area** zona *f* de captación

catchword ['kætʃwɜːd] N lema *m*

catchy ['kætʃɪ] ADJ (**catchier, catchiest**) *Fam (tune)* pegadizo(a)

categoric(al) [kætɪ'gɒrɪk(əl)] ADJ categórico(a)

categorize ['kætɪgəraɪz] VT clasificar

category ['kætɪgərɪ] N categoría *f*

cater ['keɪtə(r)] VI (**a**) **to c. for** *(wedding etc)* proveer comida para (**b**) **to c. for** *(taste)* atender a

caterer ['keɪtərə(r)] N proveedor(a) *m,f*

catering ['keɪtərɪŋ] N abastecimiento *m* (de comidas por encargo)

caterpillar ['kætəpɪlə(r)] N oruga *f*; **c. (tractor)** tractor *m* de oruga

cathedral [kə'θiːdrəl] N catedral *f*

Catholic ['kæθəlɪk] ADJ & N católico(a) *(m,f)*

catholic ['kæθəlɪk] ADJ católico(a)

Catholicism [kə'θɒlɪsɪzəm] N catolicismo *m*

cat's-eye® ['kætsaɪ] N *Br* captafaro *m*, = baliza reflectante en la calzada

cattle ['kætəl] NPL ganado (vacuno)

catty ['kætɪ] ADJ (**cattier, cattiest**) *Fam (remark)* malintencionado(a); *(person)* malicioso(a)

catwalk ['kætwɔːk] N pasarela *f*

Caucasian [kɔː'keɪzɪən] ADJ & N caucásico(a) *(m,f)*, blanco(a) *(m,f)*

caucus ['kɔːkəs] N comité *m* central, ejecutiva *f*

caught [kɔːt] PT & PP *of* **catch**

cauliflower ['kɒlɪflaʊə(r)] N coliflor *f*

cause [kɔːz] **1** N (**a**) *(origin)* causa *f* (**b**) *(reason)* motivo *m* (**c**) **for a good c.** por una buena causa

2 VT causar; **to c. sb to do sth** hacer que algn haga algo

caustic ['kɔːstɪk] ADJ *Chem* cáustico(a); *Fig (sarcastic)* cáustico(a), mordaz

caution ['kɔːʃən] **1** N (**a**) *(care)* cautela *f*, prudencia *f* (**b**) *(warning)* aviso *m*, advertencia *f* (**c**) *Br Jur* represión *f*

2 VT advertir, amonestar

cautious ['kɔːʃəs] ADJ cauteloso(a), prudente

cavalcade [kævəl'keɪd] N cabalgata *f*

cavalier [kævə'lɪə(r)] **1** ADJ arrogante

2 N caballero *m*

cavalry ['kævəlrɪ] N caballería *f*

cave [keɪv] N cueva *f*

► **cave in** VI *(roof etc)* derrumbarse, hundirse

caveman ['keɪvmæn] N hombre *m* de las cavernas

cavern ['kævən] N caverna *f*

caviar(e) ['kævɪɑː(r)] N caviar *m*

cavity ['kævɪtɪ] N (**a**) *(hole)* cavidad *f* (**b**) *(in tooth)* caries *f inv*

cavort [kə'vɔːt] VI retozar, brincar

CB [siː'biː] *(abbr* **Citizens' Band**) banda ciudadana

CBI [siːbiː'aɪ] N *Br (abbr* **Confederation of British Industry**) = organización empresarial británica, ≃ CEOE *f*

cc [siː'siː] *(abbr* **cubic centimetre(s)**) cc

CCTV [siːsiːtiː'viː] N *(abbr* **closed-circuit television**) circuito cerrado de televisión

CD [siː'diː] N *(abbr* **compact disc**) CD *m*; **CD player** (lector *m or* reproductor *m* de) CD *m*

CD-ROM [siːdiː'rɒm] N *Comput (abbr* **compact disc read-only memory**) CD-ROM *m*

cease [siːs] **1** VT cesar; **to c. doing** *or* **to do sth** dejar de hacer algo

2 VI terminar

cease-fire [siːs'faɪə(r)] N alto *m* el fuego

ceaseless ['siːslɪs] ADJ incesante

cedar ['siːdə(r)] N cedro *m*

cede [siːd] VT ceder

ceiling ['siːlɪŋ] N techo *m*

celebrate ['selɪbreɪt] **1** VT *(occasion)* celebrar

2 VI divertirse

celebrated ['selɪbreɪtɪd] ADJ célebre

celebration [selɪ'breɪʃən] N celebración *f*; **celebrations** festividades *fpl*

celebrity [sɪ'lebrɪtɪ] N celebridad *f*

celery ['selərɪ] N apio *m*

celibate ['selɪbɪt] ADJ & N célibe *(mf)*

cell [sel] N (**a**) *(in prison)* celda *f* (**b**) *Biol & Pol* célula *f* (**c**) *Elec* pila *f*

cellar ['selə(r)] N sótano *m*; *(for wine)* bodega *f*

cello ['tʃeləʊ] N violoncelo *m*

Cellophane® ['seləfeɪn] N *Br* celofán *m*

cellphone ['selfəʊn] N teléfono *m* móvil *or Am* celular

cellular ['seljʊlə(r)] ADJ celular; **c. phone** teléfono *m* móvil *or Am* celular

celluloid ['seljʊlɔɪd] N celuloide *m*

cellulose ['seljʊləʊs] N celulosa *f*

Celsius ['selsɪəs] ADJ Celsio

Celt [kelt, selt] N celta *mf*

Celtic ['keltɪk, 'seltɪk] **1** N *(language)* celta *m*

2 ADJ celta

cement [sɪ'ment] **1** N cemento *m*; **c. mixer** hormigonera *f*

2 VT *Constr* unir con cemento; *Fig (friendship)* cimentar

cemetery ['semitri] N cementerio *m*

censor ['sensə(r)] **1** N censor(a) *m,f*
2 VT censurar

censorship ['sensəʃip] N censura *f*

censure ['senʃə(r)] **1** N censura *f*
2 VT censurar

census ['sensəs] N censo *m*

cent [sent] N centavo *m*, céntimo *m*

centenary [sen'ti:nəri] N centenario *m*

center ['sentər] N & VT *US* = **centre**

centigrade ['sentigreid] ADJ centígrado(a)

centilitre, *US* **centiliter** ['sentili:tə(r)] N centilitro *m*

centimetre, *US* **centimeter** ['sentimi:tə(r)] N centímetro *m*

centipede ['sentipi:d] N ciempiés *m inv*

central ['sentrəl] ADJ central; **c. heating** calefacción *f* central; **C. America** Centroamérica; **C. American** centroamericano(a) *m,f*; *Br* **c. reservation** *(on motorway)* mediana *f*, *Col, Méx* camellón *m*

centralize ['sentrəlaiz] VT centralizar

centrally ['sentrəli] ADV **c. heated** con calefacción central; **c. situated** céntrico(a)

centre, *US* **center** ['sentə(r)] **1** N centro *m*; **town c.** centro de la ciudad; *Ftb* **c. forward** delantero centro; *Ftb* **c. half** medio centro; *Pol* **c. party** partido *m* centrista; **sports c.** centro deportivo
2 VT *(attention etc)* centrar (**on** en)

century ['sentʃəri] N siglo *m*; **the nineteenth c.** el siglo diecinueve

ceramic [si'ræmik] **1** N cerámica *f*
2 ADJ de cerámica

ceramics [si'ræmiks] N SING cerámica *f*

cereal ['siəriəl] N cereal *m*

cerebral ['seribrəl, si'ri:brəl] ADJ cerebral; **c. palsy** parálisis *f* cerebral

ceremony ['seriməni] N ceremonia *f*

certain ['sɜ:tən] ADJ (a) *(sure)* seguro(a); **to be c.** estar seguro(a); **to make c. of sth** asegurarse de algo; **for c.** a ciencia cierta (b) **to a c. extent** hasta cierto punto (c) *(not known)* cierto(a); **a c. Miss Ward** una tal señorita Ward (d) *(true)* cierto(a)

certainly ['sɜ:tənli] ADV desde luego; **c. not** de ninguna manera

certainty ['sɜ:tənti] N certeza *f*; *(assurance)* seguridad *f*

certificate [sə'tifikit] N certificado *m*; *Educ* diploma *m*

certified ['sɜ:tifaid] ADJ *(qualified)* diplomado(a); *(document)* certificado(a); *US* **c. public accountant** censor(a) jurado(a) de cuentas, auditor(a) *m,f*, *Am* contador(a) público(a)

certify ['sɜ:tifai] VT certificar

cervical ['sɜ:vikəl, sə'vaikəl] ADJ **c. cancer** cáncer *m* del útero; **c. smear** frotis *m* cervical

cervix ['sɜ:viks] N (a) *(uterus)* cuello *m* del útero (b) *(neck)* cerviz *f*, cuello *m*

cessation [se'seiʃən] N cese *m*

cesspit ['sespit] N pozo negro

Ceylon [si'lɒn] N Ceilán

cf [si:'ef] *(abbr* **confer, compare)** cf., cfr.

chador ['tʃʌdə(r)] N chador *m*

chafe [tʃeif] **1** VT *(make sore)* rozar
2 VI *(skin)* irritarse; *(item of clothing)* rozar

chaffinch ['tʃæfintʃ] N pinzón *m* vulgar

chagrin ['ʃægrin] N disgusto *m*, desilusión *f*

chain [tʃein] **1** N cadena *f*; *Fig (of events)* serie *f*; **c. of mountains** cordillera *f*; **c. reaction** reacción *f* en cadena; **c. saw** sierra mecánica
2 VT **to c. (up)** encadenar

chain-smoke ['tʃeinsməʊk] VI fumar un pitillo tras otro

chair [tʃeə(r)] **1** N (a) *(seat)* silla *f*; *(armchair)* sillón *m*; **c. lift** telesilla *m* (b) *(of meeting)* presidente(a) *m,f* (c) *Univ (of professor)* cátedra *f*
2 VT *(meeting)* presidir

chairman ['tʃeəmən] N presidente *m*

chairperson ['tʃeəpɜ:sən] N presidente(a) *m,f*

chalet ['ʃælei] N chalet *m*, chalé *m*

chalk [tʃɔ:k] N *(for writing)* tiza *f*, *Méx* gis *m*
► **chalk up** VT SEP *Fam (victory etc)* apuntarse

challenge ['tʃælindʒ] **1** VT (a) *(to a contest, fight)* retar, desafiar; **to c. sb to do sth** retar a algn a que haga algo (b) *(authority, statement)* cuestionar, poner en duda (c) *Mil* dar el alto a
2 N (a) *(exacting task, to duel)* reto *m*, desafío *m* (b) *Mil* quién vive *m*

challenger ['tʃælindʒə(r)] N aspirante *mf*

challenging ['tʃælindʒiŋ] ADJ *(idea)* desafiante; *(task)* que presenta un desafío

chamber ['tʃeimbə(r)] N (a) *(hall)* cámara *f*; **C. of Commerce** Cámara de Comercio (b) *Mus* **c. music** música *f* de cámara (c) *Br Jur* **chambers** gabinete *m*

chambermaid ['tʃeimbəmeid] N camarera *f*

chameleon [kə'mi:liən] N camaleón *m*

champagne [ʃæm'pein] N *(French)* champán *m*; *(from Catalonia)* cava *m*

champion ['tʃæmpiən] N campeón(ona) *m,f*; *Fig* **c. of human rights** defensor(a) *m,f* de los derechos humanos

championship ['tʃæmpiənʃip] N campeonato *m*

chance [tʃɑ:ns] **1** N (a) *(fortune)* casualidad *f*, azar *m*; **by c.** por casualidad; **to take a c.** arriesgarse; **c. meeting** encuentro *m* casual (b) *(likelihood)* posibilidad *f*; **(the) chances are that …** lo más posible es que … (c) *(opportunity)* oportunidad *f*, *Am* chance *f*
2 VT arriesgar
► **chance upon** VT INSEP encontrar por casualidad

chancellor ['tʃɑːnsələ(r)] N (**a**) *(head of state, in embassy)* canciller *m* (**b**) *Univ Br* rector(a) honorario(a); *US* rector(a) *m,f* (**c**) *Br* **C. of the Exchequer** ≃ ministro(a) *m,f* de Hacienda

chandelier [ʃændɪˈlɪə(r)] N araña *f* (de luces)

change [tʃeɪndʒ] **1** VT cambiar; **to c. gear** cambiar de marcha; **to c. one's mind/the subject** cambiar de opinión/de tema; **to c. trains** hacer transbordo; **to get changed** cambiarse de ropa; *Fig* **to c. hands** cambiar de dueño(a)
2 VI cambiar, cambiarse; **to c. for the better/worse** mejorar/empeorar; **to c. into** convertirse en
3 N (**a**) *(alteration)* cambio *m*; **for a c.** para variar; **c. of heart** cambio de parecer; **c. of scene** cambio de aires (**b**) *(money)* cambio *m*, *Andes, CAm, Méx* sencillo *m*, *RP* vuelto *m*; **small c.** suelto *m*
▸ **change over** VI cambiarse

changeable ['tʃeɪndʒəbəl] ADJ *(weather)* variable; *(person)* inconstante

changeover ['tʃeɪndʒəʊvə(r)] N conversión *f*

changing ['tʃeɪndʒɪŋ] **1** N (**a**) **c. room** vestuario *m* (**b**) *Mil* relevo *m* (de la guardia)
2 ADJ cambiante

channel ['tʃænəl] **1** N (**a**) *Geog* canal *m*; *(of river)* cauce *m*; **the C. Islands** las Islas Anglonormandas; **the English C.** el Canal de la Mancha (**b**) *(administrative)* vía *f* (**c**) *Rad & TV* canal *m*, cadena *f*
2 VT *Fig (ideas etc)* canalizar, encauzar

chant [tʃɑːnt] **1** N *Rel* cántico *m*; *(of demonstrators)* slogan *m*
2 VT & VI *Rel* cantar; *(demonstrators)* corear

chaos ['keɪɒs] N caos *m*

chaotic [keɪˈɒtɪk] ADJ caótico(a)

chap [tʃæp] N *Fam (man)* tipo *m*, *Esp* tío *m*; **a good c.** un buen tipo

chapel ['tʃæpəl] N capilla *f*

chaperon(e) [ˈʃæpərəʊn] N señora *f* de compañía, *Esp* carabina *f*, *Am* chaperona *f*

chaplain ['tʃæplɪn] N capellán *m*

chapter ['tʃæptə(r)] N (**a**) *(of book)* capítulo *m* (**b**) *Rel* cabildo *m*

char [tʃɑː(r)] VT chamuscar, carbonizar

character ['kærɪktə(r)] N (**a**) *(nature, personality)* carácter *m* (**b**) *(unusual person)* personaje *m*; *Pej* **some c. in a uniform** un tipo de uniforme (**c**) *(in novel, play)* personaje *m* (**d**) *Typ & Comput* carácter *m*

characteristic [kærɪktəˈrɪstɪk] **1** N característica *f*
2 ADJ característico(a)

characterize ['kærɪktəraɪz] VT caracterizar

charcoal ['tʃɑːkəʊl] N carbón *m* vegetal; *Art* **c. drawing** carboncillo *m*; **c. grey** gris marengo *or* oscuro

charge [tʃɑːdʒ] **1** VT (**a**) *(price)* cobrar; **c. it to my account** cárguelo en mi cuenta (**b**) **to c. sb with a crime** acusar a algn de un delito (**c**)

Mil cargar contra (**d**) *Elec* cargar
2 VI *Elec & Mil* cargar; **to c. about** andar a lo loco
3 N (**a**) *(cost)* precio *m*; **free of c.** gratis (**b**) **to be in c. of** estar a cargo de; **to take c. of** hacerse cargo de (**c**) *Jur* cargo *m*, acusación *f* (**d**) *(explosive)* carga explosiva (**e**) *Mil* carga *f* (**f**) *Elec* carga *f*

charged [tʃɑːdʒd] ADJ *Fig* emotivo(a)

charismatic [kærɪzˈmætɪk] ADJ carismático(a)

charitable ['tʃærɪtəbəl] ADJ *(person, action)* caritativo(a); *(organization)* benéfico(a)

charity ['tʃærɪtɪ] N caridad *f*; *(organization)* institución benéfica

charlady ['tʃɑːleɪdɪ] N *Br* señora *f* de la limpieza

charlatan ['ʃɑːlətən] N *(doctor)* curandero(a) *m,f*

charm [tʃɑːm] **1** N (**a**) *(quality)* encanto *m* (**b**) *(spell)* hechizo *m*; **lucky c.** amuleto *m*
2 VT encantar

charming ['tʃɑːmɪŋ] ADJ encantador(a)

chart [tʃɑːt] **1** N (**a**) *(giving information)* tabla *f*; *(graph)* gráfico *m* (**b**) *(map)* carta *f* de navegación (**c**) *Mus* **the charts** la lista de éxitos
2 VT *Av & Naut (on map)* trazar

charter ['tʃɑːtə(r)] **1** N (**a**) *(of institution)* estatutos *mpl*; *(of rights)* carta *f* (**b**) **c. flight** vuelo *m* chárter
2 VT *(plane, boat)* fletar

chartered accountant [tʃɑːtədəˈkaʊntənt] N *Br* censor(a) *m,f* jurado(a) de cuentas, *Am* contador(a) *m,f* público(a)

chase [tʃeɪs] **1** VT *(pursue)* perseguir
2 N *(pursuit)* persecución *f*

chasm ['kæzəm] N *Geog* sima *f*; *Fig* abismo *m*

chassis ['ʃæsɪ] N chasis *m inv*

chaste [tʃeɪst] ADJ casto(a)

chastise [tʃæsˈtaɪz] VT castigar

chastity ['tʃæstɪtɪ] N castidad *f*

chat [tʃæt] **1** N (**a**) *(informal conversation)* charla *f* *CAm, Méx* plática *f*; *Br* **c. show** coloquio *m* (**b**) *Comput* chat *m*; **c. room** sala *f* de conversación
2 VI (**a**) *(talk informally)* charlar, *CAm, Méx* platicar (**b**) *Comput* chatear (**to** *or* **with** con)
▸ **chat up** VT SEP *Br Fam* **to chat sb up** intentar ligar con algn, *RP* intentar levantar a algn

chatter ['tʃætə(r)] **1** VI *(person)* parlotear; *(bird)* piar; *(teeth)* castañetear
2 N *(of person)* parloteo *m*; *(of birds)* gorjeo *m*; *(of teeth)* castañeteo *m*

chatterbox ['tʃætəbɒks] N *Fam* parlanchín(ina) *m,f*

chatty ['tʃætɪ] ADJ (**chattier, chattiest**) hablador(a)

chauffeur ['ʃəʊfə(r), ʃəʊˈfɜ:(r)] N *Esp* chófer *m*, *Am* chofer *m*

chauvinism ['ʃəʊvɪnɪzəm] N chovinismo *m*; **male c.** machismo *m*

chauvinist ['ʃəʊvɪnɪst] ADJ & N chovinista (mf); **male c.** machista m

cheap [tʃiːp] 1 ADJ (inexpensive) barato(a); (fare, rate) económico(a), reducido(a); (joke) de mal gusto; (contemptible) bajo(a)
2 N Br Fam **on the c.** en plan barato
3 ADV barato

cheapen ['tʃiːpən] VT Fig degradar

cheaply ['tʃiːplɪ] ADV barato, en plan económico

cheat [tʃiːt] 1 VT engañar; **to c. sb out of sth** estafar algo a algn
2 VI (a) (at games) hacer trampa; (in exam etc) copiar(se) (b) Fam (husband, wife) poner cuernos (on a)
3 N (trickster) tramposo(a) m,f

check [tʃek] 1 VT (a) (verify, examine) (information) comprobar, Guat, Méx checar; (passport, ticket) revisar (b) (restrain) (inflation, enemy advance) frenar; (emotion, impulse) contener, reprimir
2 VI comprobar, Guat, Méx checar
3 N (a) (inspection) control m, inspección f (b) (in chess) jaque m (c) (pattern) cuadro m (d) **to keep in c.** (feelings) contener; (enemy) mantener a raya (e) US = **cheque**
▶ **check in** VI (at airport) facturar; (at hotel) registrarse (at en)
▶ **check out 1** VI (of hotel) dejar el hotel
2 VT SEP (facts) verificar
▶ **check up** VI **to c. up on sb** hacer averiguaciones sobre algn; **to c. up on sth** comprobar algo

checked [tʃekt] ADJ a cuadros

checker ['tʃekər] N US (cashier) cajero(a) m,f

checkered ['tʃekəd] ADJ US = **chequered**

checkers ['tʃekəz] N SING US (game) damas fpl

check-in ['tʃekɪn] N **c. desk** (at airport) mostrador m de facturación

checking account ['tʃekɪŋ ə'kaʊnt] N US cuenta f corriente

checkmate ['tʃekmeɪt] 1 N (in chess) jaque mate m
2 VT (in chess) dar jaque mate a; Fig (opponent) frustrar

checkout ['tʃekaʊt] N (counter) caja f

checkpoint ['tʃekpɔɪnt] N control m

checkroom ['tʃekruːm] N US (for coats, hats) guardarropa m; (for luggage) consigna f

checkup ['tʃekʌp] N Med chequeo m, examen médico

cheek [tʃiːk] N (a) (of face) mejilla f (b) Fam (nerve) cara f; **he's got a c.!** ¡qué caradura!, Esp ¡vaya morro!

cheekbone ['tʃiːkbəʊn] N pómulo m

cheeky ['tʃiːkɪ] ADJ (cheekier, cheekiest) Fam fresco(a), descarado(a)

cheep [tʃiːp] 1 N (of bird) pío m
2 VI piar

cheer [tʃɪə(r)] 1 VI aplaudir, aclamar
2 VT (a) (applaud) vitorear, aclamar (b) (make hopeful) animar
3 N viva m; **cheers** aplausos mpl; Br Fam **cheers!** (thank you) ¡gracias!; (before drinking) ¡salud!
▶ **cheer up 1** VI animarse
2 VT SEP **to c. sb up** alegrar or animar a algn

cheerful ['tʃɪəfʊl] ADJ alegre

cheerio [tʃɪərɪ'əʊ] INTERJ Br Fam ¡chao!, Am ¡chau!

cheese [tʃiːz] N queso m

cheesecake ['tʃiːzkeɪk] N tarta f de queso

cheetah ['tʃiːtə] N guepardo m

chef [ʃef] N chef m

chemical ['kemɪkəl] 1 N sustancia química, producto químico
2 ADJ químico(a)

chemist ['kemɪst] N (a) (scientist) químico(a) m,f (b) Br (pharmacist) farmacéutico(a) m,f; **c.'s (shop)** farmacia f

chemistry ['kemɪstrɪ] N química f

chemotherapy ['kiːməʊ'θerəpɪ] N Med quimioterapia f

cheque [tʃek] N cheque m; **to pay by c.** pagar con (un) cheque; **c. book** talonario m (de cheques); Br **c. card** = tarjeta que avala los cheques

chequered ['tʃekəd] ADJ a cuadros; Fig **a c. career** una carrera con altibajos

cherish ['tʃerɪʃ] VT (a) (person) tenerle mucho cariño a (b) Fig (hopes etc) abrigar

cherry ['tʃerɪ] N cereza f

chess [tʃes] N ajedrez m

chessboard ['tʃesbɔːd] N tablero m de ajedrez

chesspiece ['tʃespiːs] N pieza f de ajedrez

chest [tʃest] N (a) Anat pecho m (b) (for linen) arca f; (for valuables) cofre m; **c. of drawers** cómoda f

chestnut ['tʃesnʌt] N (tree, colour) castaño m; (nut) castaña f

chew [tʃuː] VT masticar, mascar

chewing gum ['tʃuːɪŋgʌm] N chicle m

chewy ['tʃuːɪ] ADJ (chewier, chewiest) (meat, bread) correoso(a); (confectionery) gomoso(a), correoso(a)

chic [ʃiːk] ADJ elegante

chick [tʃɪk] N (a) (young chicken) pollito m (b) Fam (woman) nena f, Arg piba f, Méx chava f

chicken ['tʃɪkɪn] 1 N (a) (bird) gallina f; (meat) pollo m (b) Fam (coward) gallina mf, Esp miedica mf
2 VI Fam **to c. out** acobardarse, Méx ciscarse, RP achicarse

chickenpox ['tʃɪkɪnpɒks] N varicela f

chickpea ['tʃɪkpiː] N garbanzo m

chicory ['tʃɪkərɪ] N achicoria f

chief [tʃiːf] 1 N jefe m
2 ADJ principal

chiefly ['tʃiːflɪ] ADV *(above all)* sobre todo; *(mainly)* principalmente

chiffon ['ʃɪfɒn] N gasa *f*

chilblain ['tʃɪlbleɪn] N sabañón *m*

child [tʃaɪld] N *(pl* **children)** niño(a) *m,f*; *(son)* hijo *m*; *(daughter)* hija *f*; **c. minder** = persona que cuida niños en su propia casa

childbirth ['tʃaɪldbɜːθ] N parto *m*

childhood ['tʃaɪldhʊd] N infancia *f*, niñez *f*

childish ['tʃaɪldɪʃ] ADJ pueril, aniñado(a)

childlike ['tʃaɪldlaɪk] ADJ infantil

children ['tʃɪldrən] PL *of* **child**

Chile ['tʃɪlɪ] N Chile

Chilean ['tʃɪlɪən] ADJ & N chileno(a) *(m,f)*

chili ['tʃɪlɪ] N = **chilli**

chill [tʃɪl] 1 N (a) *Med* resfriado *m* (b) *(coldness)* fresco *m*
2 ADJ frío(a)
3 VT *(meat)* refrigerar; *(wine)* enfriar
▸ **chill out** VI *Fam* relajarse, estar tranqui

chilli ['tʃɪlɪ] N **c. (pepper)** chile *m*, *Esp* guindilla *f*, *Andes*, *RP* ají *m*

chilly ['tʃɪlɪ] ADJ *(***chillier, chilliest)** frío(a)

chime [tʃaɪm] 1 N *(peal)* campanada *f*
2 VT **to c. five o'clock** *(of clock)* dar las cinco
3 VI sonar
▸ **chime in** VI *Fam* meter baza *or Méx, RP* la cuchara

chimney ['tʃɪmnɪ] N chimenea *f*; **c. sweep** deshollinador *m*

chimpanzee [tʃɪmpæn'ziː] N chimpancé *m*

chin [tʃɪn] N barbilla *f*, mentón *m*; **double c.** papada *f*

China ['tʃaɪnə] N China

china ['tʃaɪnə] N loza *f*, porcelana *f*

> Note that the Spanish word **china** is a false friend and is never a translation for the English word **china**. In Spanish **china** means "pebble, small stone".

Chinese [tʃaɪ'niːz] 1 ADJ chino(a)
2 N (a) *(person)* chino,f *m,f* (b) *(language)* chino *m*

chink[1] [tʃɪŋk] N *(opening)* resquicio *m*; *(crack)* grieta *f*

chink[2] [tʃɪŋk] 1 VI tintinear
2 N tintineo *m*

chip [tʃɪp] 1 N (a) *(of wood)* astilla *f*; *(of stone)* lasca *f*; *(in cup)* mella *f* (b) *Br Culin* **chips** *Esp* patatas *or Am* papas fritas; *US* **(potato) chips** *(crisps)* *Esp* patatas *or Am* papas fritas *(de bolsa)* (c) *Comput* chip *m* (d) *(in gambling)* ficha *f*
2 VT *(wood)* astillar; *(stone)* resquebrajar; *(china, glass)* mellar
3 VI *(wood)* astillarse; *(china, glass)* mellarse; *(paint)* desconcharse
▸ **chip in** VI *Fam* (a) *(in discussion)* meter baza *or Méx, RP* la cuchara, terciar (b) *(with money)* poner algo *(de dinero)*

chiropodist [kɪ'rɒpədɪst] N podólogo(a) *m,f*, *Am* podiatra *mf*

chirp [tʃɜːp] VI *(birds)* gorjear

chisel ['tʃɪzəl] N cincel *m*

chit [tʃɪt] N nota *f*; *(small invoice)* vale *m*

chitchat ['tʃɪttʃæt] N *Fam* charla *f*, cháchara *f*, *CAm, Méx* plática *f*

chivalry ['ʃɪvəlrɪ] N caballerosidad *f*

chives [tʃaɪvz] NPL cebolleta *f*

chlorine ['klɔːriːn] N cloro *m*

chock-a-block [tʃɒkə'blɒk], **chock-full** [tʃɒk'fʊl] ADJ *Fam* (lleno(a)) hasta los topes

chocolate ['tʃɒkəlɪt] 1 N chocolate *m*; **chocolates** bombones *mpl*
2 ADJ de chocolate

choice [tʃɔɪs] 1 N elección *f*; **a wide c.** un gran surtido; **by c.** por gusto
2 ADJ selecto(a)

choir ['kwaɪə(r)] N coro *m*, coral *f*

choirboy ['kwaɪəbɔɪ] N niño *m* de coro

choke [tʃəʊk] 1 VT (a) *(person)* ahogar (b) *(obstruct)* obstruir
2 VI ahogarse; **to c. on food** atragantarse con la comida
3 N *Aut* estárter *m*
▸ **choke back** VT SEP *(emotions)* tragarse

cholera ['kɒlərə] N cólera *m*

cholesterol [kə'lestərɒl] N colesterol *m*

choose [tʃuːz] 1 VT *(pt* **chose***; pp* **chosen)** elegir, escoger; **to c. to do sth** decidir hacer algo
2 VI elegir, escoger

choos(e)y ['tʃuːzɪ] ADJ *(***choosier, choosiest)** *Fam* exigente

chop [tʃɒp] 1 VT (a) *(wood)* cortar; *(tree)* talar (b) *Culin* cortar a pedacitos
2 N (a) *(blow)* tajo *m*; *(with axe)* hachazo *m* (b) *Culin* chuleta *f*

chopper ['tʃɒpə(r)] N *Fam* helicóptero *m*

choppy ['tʃɒpɪ] ADJ *(***choppier, choppiest)** *(sea)* picado(a)

chopsticks ['tʃɒpstɪks] NPL palillos *mpl*

choral ['kɔːrəl] ADJ coral

chord [kɔːd] N *Mus* acorde *m*; *Fig* **it strikes a c.** (me) suena

chore [tʃɔː(r)] N quehacer *m*, tarea *f*

chortle ['tʃɔːtəl] VI reír con ganas

chorus ['kɔːrəs] N *Mus & Th* coro *m*; *(in a song)* estribillo *m*; **c. girl** corista *f*

chose [tʃəʊz] PT *of* **choose**

chosen ['tʃəʊzən] PP *of* **choose**

Christ [kraɪst] N Cristo *m*, Jesucristo *m*

christen ['krɪsən] VT bautizar

christening ['krɪsənɪŋ] N bautizo *m*

Christian ['krɪstʃən] 1 ADJ cristiano(a); **c. name** nombre *m* de pila
2 N cristiano(a) *m,f*

Christianity [krɪstɪ'ænɪtɪ] N cristianismo *m*

Christmas ['krısməs] N Navidad *f*; **merry C.!** ¡feliz Navidad!; **C. carol** villancico *m*; **C. Day** día *m* de Navidad; **C. Eve** Nochebuena *f*

chrome [krəum] N cromo *m*

chromium ['krəumıəm] N cromo *m*; **c. plating** cromado *m*

chromosome ['krəuməsəum] N cromosoma *m*

chronic ['krɒnık] ADJ crónico(a)

chronicle ['krɒnıkəl] **1** N crónica *f*
2 VT hacer la crónica de

chronological [krɒnə'lɒdʒıkəl] ADJ cronológico(a)

chrysanthemum [krı'sænθəməm] N crisantemo *m*

chubby ['tʃʌbı] ADJ (**chubbier, chubbiest**) rellenito(a)

chuck [tʃʌk] VT *Fam* tirar, *Am* botar **to c. one's job in** *or* **up** dejar el trabajo; **to c. sb out** echar a algn; **to c. sth away** *or* **out** tirar *or Am* botar algo

chuckle ['tʃʌkəl] **1** VI reír entre dientes
2 N sonrisita *f*

chug [tʃʌg] VI traquetear

chum [tʃʌm] N compinche *mf*, compañero(a) *m,f*

chunk [tʃʌŋk] N *Fam* cacho *m*, pedazo *m*

church [tʃɜːtʃ] N iglesia *f*; **to go to c.** ir a misa; **C. of England** Iglesia Anglicana

churchyard ['tʃɜːtʃjɑːd] N cementerio *m*, campo santo

churlish ['tʃɜːlıʃ] ADJ grosero(a)

churn [tʃɜːn] **1** N (*for butter*) mantequera *f*; *Br* (*for milk*) lechera *f*
2 VT (*butter*) hacer
3 VI revolverse, agitarse
► **churn out** VT SEP *Fam* producir en serie

chute [ʃuːt] N (*channel*) conducto *m*; (*slide*) tobogán *m*

chutney ['tʃʌtnı] N conserva *f* (de frutas) picante

CIA [siːaı'eı] N *US* (*abbr* **Central Intelligence Agency**) CIA *f*

CID [siːaı'diː] N *Br* (*abbr* **Criminal Investigation Department**) = policía judicial británica

cider ['saıdə(r)] N sidra *f*

cigar [sı'gɑː(r)] N puro *m*

cigarette [sıgə'ret] N cigarrillo *m*; **c. case** pitillera *f*; **c. end** colilla *f*, *Am* pucho *m*; **c. holder** boquilla *f*; **c. lighter** encendedor *m*, *Esp* mechero *m*

cinder ['sındə(r)] N **cinders** cenizas *fpl*; **burnt to a c.** completamente carbonizado(a)

Cinderella [sındə'relə] N Cenicienta *f*

cine camera ['sınıkæmərə] N *Br* cámara *f* de cine

cinema ['sınımə] N (**a**) *Br* (*building*) cine *m* (**b**) (*art*) cine *m*

cinnamon ['sınəmən] N canela *f*

cipher ['saıfə(r)] N (*numeral*) cifra *f*

circle ['sɜːkəl] **1** N (**a**) (*shape, group*) círculo *m*; **in business circles** en el mundo de los negocios (**b**) *Th* anfiteatro *m*
2 VT (*surround*) rodear; (*move round*) dar la vuelta a
3 VI dar vueltas

circuit ['sɜːkıt] N (**a**) (*journey*) recorrido *m* (**b**) *Elec* circuito *m* (**c**) *Br* (*motor-racing track*) circuito *m*

circular ['sɜːkjulə(r)] ADJ & N circular (*f*)

circulate ['sɜːkjuleıt] **1** VT (*news*) hacer circular
2 VI circular

circulation [sɜːkju'leıʃən] N (**a**) (*of blood*) circulación *f* (**b**) (*of newspaper*) tirada *f*

circumcise ['sɜːkəmsaız] VT circuncidar

circumference [sə'kʌmfərəns] N circunferencia *f*

circumspect ['sɜːkəmspekt] ADJ circunspecto(a), *Esp* comedido(a)

circumstance ['sɜːkəmstəns] N (*situation*) circunstancia *f*; **under no circumstances** en ningún caso; **economic circumstances** situación económica

circumvent [sɜːkəm'vent] VT *Fig* burlar

circus ['sɜːkəs] N circo *m*

cirrhosis [sı'rəusıs] N cirrosis *f*

CIS [siːaı'es] N (*abbr* **Commonwealth of Independent States**) CEI *f*

cistern ['sıstən] N cisterna *f*

cite [saıt] VT (*quote*) citar

citizen ['sıtızən] N ciudadano(a) *m,f*

citizenship ['sıtızənʃıp] N ciudadanía *f*

citrus ['sıtrəs] ADJ **c. fruits** agrios *mpl*

city ['sıtı] N ciudad *f*; *Br* **the C.** la City (de Londres), = el barrio financiero y bursátil de Londres; *US* **c. council** ayuntamiento *m*; *US* **c. hall** ayuntamiento

civic ['sıvık] ADJ cívico(a); *Br* **c. centre** centro cívico; **c. duties** obligaciones cívicas

civics ['sıvıks] N SING (*subject*) educación *f* cívica

civil ['sıvəl] ADJ (**a**) (*of society*) civil; **c. defence** defensa *f* civil; **c. engineer** ingeniero(a) *m,f* de caminos; **c. rights** derechos *mpl* civiles; **c. servant** funcionario(a) *m,f*; *Pol* **c. service** administración pública (**b**) (*polite*) cortés

civilian [sı'vıljən] ADJ & N civil (*mf*); **c. clothing** traje *m* de paisano

civilization [sıvılaı'zeıʃən] N civilización *f*

civilized ['sıvılaızd] ADJ civilizado(a)

clad [klæd] **1** ADJ *Literary* vestido(a)
2 PT & PP of **clothe**

claim [kleım] **1** VT (**a**) (*benefits, rights*) reclamar; *Jur* (*compensation*) exigir (**b**) (*assert*) afirmar
2 N (**a**) (*demand*) reclamación *f*; *Jur* demanda *f*; **to put in a c.** reclamar una indemnización (**b**) (*right*) derecho *m* (**c**) (*assertion*) pretensión *f*

claimant ['kleımənt] N *Jur* demandante *mf*

clairvoyant [kleə'vɔɪənt] N clarividente *mf*

clam [klæm] N almeja *f*

► **clam up** VI *Fam* callarse

clamber ['klæmbə(r)] VI trepar (**over** por)

clammy ['klæmɪ] ADJ (**clammier, clammiest**) *(weather)* bochornoso(a); *(hand)* pegajoso(a)

clamour, *US* **clamor** ['klæmə(r)] 1 N clamor *m*
2 VI clamar; **to c. for** pedir a gritos

clamp [klæmp] 1 N *(for carpentry)* tornillo *m* de banco; *Tech* abrazadera *f*; **wheel c.** cepo *m*
2 VT sujetar con abrazaderas

► **clamp down on** VT INSEP aumentar los esfuerzos contra

clan [klæn] N clan *m*

clandestine [klæn'destɪn] ADJ clandestino(a)

clang [klæŋ] 1 VI sonar
2 N sonido metálico

clap [klæp] 1 VI aplaudir
2 N (a) *(with hands)* **to give sb a c.** aplaudir a algn (b) *(noise)* **a c. of thunder** un trueno

clapping ['klæpɪŋ] N aplausos *mpl*

claret ['klærət] N *Br (wine)* clarete *m*; *(colour)* burdeos *m*

clarification [klærɪfɪ'keɪʃən] N aclaración *f*

clarify ['klærɪfaɪ] VT aclarar

clarinet [klærɪ'net] N clarinete *m*

clarity ['klærɪtɪ] N claridad *f*

clash [klæʃ] 1 VI (a) *(cymbals)* sonar; *(swords)* chocar; *Fig (disagree)* estar en desacuerdo (b) *(colours)* desentonar (c) *(dates)* coincidir
2 N (a) *(sound)* sonido *m* (b) *(fight)* choque *m*; *Fig (conflict)* conflicto *m*

clasp [klɑːsp] 1 N (a) *(on belt)* cierre *m*; *(on necklace)* broche *m* (b) *(grasp)* apretón *m*; **c. knife** navaja *f*
2 VT *(object)* agarrar; **to c. hands** juntar las manos

class [klɑːs] 1 N clase *f*; **c. struggle** lucha *f* de clases; *US Educ* **c. of 2004** promoción *f* de 2004
2 VT clasificar

classic ['klæsɪk] 1 ADJ clásico(a)
2 N (a) *(author)* autor clásico; *(work)* obra clásica (b) **the classics** *(literature)* las obras clásicas; **classics** *(languages)* clásicas *fpl*

classical ['klæsɪkəl] ADJ clásico(a)

classification [klæsɪfɪ'keɪʃən] N clasificación *f*

classified ['klæsɪfaɪd] ADJ *(information)* secreto(a); **c. advertisements** anuncios *mpl* por palabras

classify ['klæsɪfaɪ] VT clasificar

classless ['klɑːslɪs] ADJ sin clases

classmate ['klɑːsmeɪt] N compañero(a) *m,f* de clase

classroom ['klɑːsruːm] N aula *f*, clase *f*

classy ['klɑːsɪ] ADJ (**classier, classiest**) *Fam* con clase, elegante

clatter ['klætə(r)] 1 VI **he clattered up the stairs** subió las escaleras con estrépito
2 N ruido *m*, estrépito *m*

clause [klɔːz] N (a) *Jur* cláusula *f* (b) *Gram* oración *f*

claustrophobic [klɔːstrə'fəʊbɪk] ADJ claustrofóbico(a)

claw [klɔː] 1 N *(of bird, animal)* garra *f*; *(of crab, lobster)* pinza *f*
2 VT *(scratch)* arañar

► **claw at** VT INSEP agarrar, arañar

clay [kleɪ] N arcilla *f*; **c. pigeon shooting** tiro *m* al plato

clean [kliːn] 1 ADJ (a) *(not dirty)* limpio(a) (b) *(unmarked, pure)* sin defecto; **to have a c. record** no tener antecedentes (penales) (c) *(not obscene)* decente
2 ADV (a) **to play c.** jugar limpio; *Fam* **to come c.** confesarlo todo (b) *Fam* por completo; **it went c. through the middle** pasó justo por el medio
3 VT *(room)* limpiar; **to c. one's teeth** lavarse los dientes

► **clean out** VT SEP *(room)* limpiar a fondo

► **clean up** VT SEP & VI limpiar

clean-cut ['kliːn'kʌt] ADJ *(person)* limpio(a), pulcro(a)

cleaner ['kliːnə(r)] N limpiador(a) *m,f*

cleaning ['kliːnɪŋ] N limpieza *f*

cleanliness ['klenlɪnɪs] N limpieza *f*

cleanse [klenz] VT limpiar

clean-shaven ['kliːn'ʃeɪvən] ADJ *(man, face)* (bien) afeitado(a)

cleansing ['klenzɪŋ] N **c. lotion** loción limpiadora

clear [klɪə(r)] 1 ADJ (a) *(liquid, explanation)* claro(a); *(road, day)* despejado(a); **c. conscience** conciencia tranquila (b) *(obvious)* claro(a); **to make sth c.** aclarar algo (c) *(majority)* absoluto(a); *(profit)* neto(a) (d) *(free)* libre
2 ADV (a) *Fig* **loud and c.** claramente (b) **stand c.!** ¡apártese!; **to stay c. of** evitar
3 VT (a) *(room)* vaciar; *Com* liquidar; **to c. one's throat** aclararse la garganta; **to c. the table** quitar la mesa (b) *(authorize)* autorizar (c) *(hurdle)* salvar (d) **to c. sb of a charge** exculpar a algn de un delito
4 VI *(sky)* despejarse

► **clear away** VT SEP quitar

► **clear off** VI *Br Fam* largarse; **c. off!** ¡largo!

► **clear out** VT SEP *(room)* limpiar a fondo; *(cupboard)* vaciar

► **clear up** VT SEP (a) *(tidy)* recoger; *(arrange)* ordenar (b) *(mystery)* resolver; *(misunderstanding)* aclarar
2 VI *(weather)* despejarse; *(problem)* desaparecer

clearance ['klɪərəns] N (a) *(of area)* despeje *m*; *Com* **c. sale** liquidación *f* (de existencias) (b) *(space)* espacio *m* libre (**c**) *(authorization)* autorización *f*

clear-cut [klɪə'kʌt] ADJ claro(a)

clearing ['klɪərɪŋ] N (**a**) *(in wood)* claro *m* (**b**) *(of rubbish)* limpieza *f* (**c**) *(of cheque)* compensación *f*

clearly ['klɪəlɪ] ADV claramente

clearway ['klɪəweɪ] N *Br* = carretera donde está prohibido parar

cleaver ['kli:və(r)] N cuchillo *m* de carnicero

clef [klef] N clave *f*; **bass/treble c.** clave de fa/ de sol

cleft [kleft] N hendidura *f*, grieta *f*

clementine ['kleməntaɪn] N *Br* clementina *f*

clench [klentʃ] VT *(teeth, fist)* apretar

clergy ['klɜːdʒɪ] N clero *m*

clergyman ['klɜːdʒɪmən] N clérigo *m*

cleric ['klerɪk] N *Rel* clérigo *m*

clerical ['klerɪkəl] ADJ (**a**) *Rel* clerical (**b**) *(staff, work)* de oficina

clerk [klɑːk, *US* klɜːrk] N (**a**) *(office worker)* oficinista *mf*; *(civil servant)* funcionario(a) *m,f* (**b**) *US Com* dependiente(a) *m,f*, vendedor(a) *m,f*

clever ['klevə(r)] ADJ (**a**) *(person)* inteligente, listo(a); **to be c. at sth** tener aptitud para algo; *Br Fam Pej* **c. clogs** *or* **dick** sabelotodo *mf*, *Esp* listillo(a) *m,f* (**b**) *(argument)* ingenioso(a)

cliché ['kli:ʃeɪ] N cliché *m*

click [klɪk] **1** N *(sound)* clic *m*
 2 VT *(tongue)* chasquear
 3 VI **it didn't c.** *(I didn't realize)* no me di cuenta

client ['klaɪənt] N cliente *mf*

clientele [kli:ɒn'tel] N clientela *f*

cliff [klɪf] N acantilado *m*

climate ['klaɪmɪt] N clima *m*

climax ['klaɪmæks] N (**a**) *(peak)* clímax *m*, punto *m* culminante (**b**) *(sexual)* orgasmo *m*

climb [klaɪm] **1** VT *(ladder)* subir a; *(mountain)* escalar; *(tree)* trepar a
 2 VI *(plants)* trepar; *Av* subir; *Fig (socially)* ascender
 3 N subida *f*, ascensión *f*

▸ **climb down** VI *(descend)* bajar; *Fig (in argument)* echarse atrás

climber ['klaɪmə(r)] N alpinista *mf*, *Am* andinista *mf*

climbing ['klaɪmɪŋ] N *Sport* montañismo *m*, alpinismo *m*, *Am* andinismo *m*

clinch [klɪntʃ] **1** VT *(deal)* cerrar; *(argument)* zanjar
 2 N *(of lovers, fighters)* abrazo *m*

cling [klɪŋ] VI *(pt & pp* **clung***)* *(hang on)* agarrarse; *(clothes)* ajustarse; *(smell)* pegarse; **to c. together** unirse

clingfilm ['klɪŋfɪlm] N *Br* plástico *m* transparente *(para envolver alimentos)*

clinic ['klɪnɪk] N *(in state hospital)* ambulatorio *m*; *(specialized)* clínica *f*

clinical ['klɪnɪkəl] ADJ (**a**) *Med* clínico(a) (**b**) *(detached)* frío(a)

clink [klɪŋk] **1** VI tintinear
 2 N tintineo *m*

clip¹ [klɪp] **1** VT *(cut)* cortar; *(ticket)* picar
 2 N (**a**) *(of film)* extracto *m* (**b**) *(with scissors)* tijeretada *f*

clip² [klɪp] **1** N *(for hair)* pasador *m*; *(for paper)* clip *m*, sujetapapeles *m inv*; *(brooch)* clip
 2 VT sujetar

clippers ['klɪpəz] NPL *(for hair)* maquinilla *f* para rapar; *(for nails)* cortauñas *m inv*; *(for hedge)* tijeras *fpl* de podar

clipping ['klɪpɪŋ] N recorte *m*

clique [kli:k] N *Pej* camarilla *f*

cloak [kləʊk] **1** N *(garment)* capa *f*
 2 VT encubrir

cloakroom ['kləʊkru:m] N guardarropa *m*; *Br Euph (toilets)* servicios *mpl*

clock [klɒk] **1** N reloj *m*
 2 VT *(race)* cronometrar

▸ **clock in, clock on** VI fichar (a la entrada), *Am* marcar tarjeta (a la entrada)

▸ **clock off, clock out** VI fichar (a la salida), *Am* marcar tarjeta (a la salida)

▸ **clock up** VT SEP *(mileage)* hacer

clockwise ['klɒkwaɪz] ADJ & ADV en el sentido de las agujas del reloj

clockwork ['klɒkwɜːk] N mecanismo *m*; **c. toy** juguete *m* de cuerda

clog [klɒg] **1** VT obstruir, atascar; **to get clogged up** atascarse
 2 N *(footwear)* zueco *m*

cloister ['klɔɪstə(r)] N claustro *m*

clone [kləʊn] **1** N clon *m*
 2 VT *Biol* clonar

close¹ [kləʊs] **1** ADJ (**a**) *(in space, time)* cercano(a); *(contact)* directo(a); **c. to** cerca de; **c. together** juntos(as) (**b**) *(relationship)* estrecho(a); *(friend)* íntimo(a) (**c**) *(inspection)* detallado(a); *(watch)* atento(a) (**d**) *(contest)* reñido(a); **a c. resemblance** un gran parecido (**e**) *(air)* cargado(a); *(weather)* bochornoso(a)
 2 ADV cerca; **they live c. by** *or* **c. at hand** viven cerca; **to stand c. together** estar apretados(as)

close² [kləʊz] **1** VT (**a**) *(door, eyes, shop)* cerrar; **closing time** hora *f* de cierre (**b**) *(meeting, debate)* terminar; *(conference)* clausurar
 2 VI (**a**) *(shut)* cerrar, cerrarse (**b**) *(end)* concluirse, terminarse
 3 N fin *m*, final *m*

▸ **close down** VI *(business)* cerrar para siempre; *Br Rad & TV* finalizar la emisión

▸ **close in** VI **to c. in on sb** rodear a algn

closed [kləʊzd] ADJ cerrado(a); *Ind* **c. shop** = empresa que emplea solamente a miembros de un sindicato

close-knit [kləʊs'nɪt] ADJ *Fig* unido(a)

closely ['kləʊslɪ] ADV (**a**) *(tightly)* estrechamente, muy; **c. contested** muy reñido(a); **they are c. related** *(people)* son parientes próximos (**b**) *(attentively)* con atención; **to follow (events) c.** seguir de cerca (los acontecimientos)

closet ['klɒzɪt] N *US* armario *m*

close-up ['kləʊsʌp] N primer plano *m*

closure ['kləʊʒə(r)] N cierre *m*

clot [klɒt] **1** N (**a**) *(of blood)* coágulo *m*; *Med* **c. on the brain** embolia *f* cerebral (**b**) *Br Fam* lelo(a) *m,f*, *Esp* memo(a) *m,f*
2 VI coagularse

cloth [klɒθ] N tela *f*, paño *m*; *(rag)* trapo *m*; *(tablecloth)* mantel *m*

clothe [kləʊð] VT *(pt & pp clothed or clad)* vestir (**in** or **with** de); *Fig* revestir, cubrir (**in** or **with** de)

clothes [kləʊðz] NPL ropa *f*, vestidos *mpl*; **c. brush** cepillo *m* de la ropa; **c. hanger** percha *f*; **c. horse** tendedero *m* plegable; **c. line** tendedero *m*; **c.** *Br* **peg** or *US* **pin** pinza *f*

clothing ['kləʊðɪŋ] N ropa *f*

cloud [klaʊd] **1** N nube *f*
2 VT nublar; *Fig* **to c. the issue** complicar el asunto
3 VI **to c. over** nublarse

cloudy ['klaʊdɪ] ADJ (**cloudier, cloudiest**) (**a**) *(sky)* nublado(a) (**b**) *(liquid)* turbio(a)

clout [klaʊt] *Fam* **1** N (**a**) *(blow)* tortazo *m* (**b**) *(influence)* influencia *f*
2 VT *(hit)* sacudir, *Esp* atizar, *RP* mandar

clove[1] [kləʊv] N *(spice)* clavo *m*

clove[2] [kləʊv] N *(of garlic)* diente *m*

clover ['kləʊvə(r)] N trébol *m*

clown [klaʊn] **1** N payaso *m*
2 VI **to c. (about** or **around)** hacer el payaso

cloying ['klɔɪɪŋ] ADJ empalagoso(a)

club [klʌb] **1** N (**a**) *(society)* club *m*; **sports c.** club deportivo (**b**) *(nightclub)* discoteca *f*, sala *f* (de fiestas) (**c**) *(heavy stick)* garrote *m*, porra *f*; *(in golf)* palo *m* (**d**) *Cards* trébol *m*
2 VT aporrear
3 VI **to c. together** pagar entre varios

clubhouse ['klʌbhaʊs] N sede *f* de un club

cluck [klʌk] **1** N cloqueo *m*
2 VI cloquear

clue [klu:] N *(sign)* indicio *m*; *(to mystery)* pista *f*; *(in crossword)* clave *f*; *Fam* **I haven't a c.** no tengo ni idea

clump [klʌmp] N *(of trees)* grupo *m*; *(of plants)* mata *f*

clumsy ['klʌmzɪ] ADJ (**clumsier, clumsiest**) *(person, movement)* torpe

clung [klʌŋ] PT & PP *of* **cling**

cluster ['klʌstə(r)] **1** N grupo *m*; *(of grapes)* racimo *m*
2 VI agruparse

clutch [klʌtʃ] **1** VT agarrar
2 VI *Fig* **to c. at straws** aferrarse a cualquier cosa
3 N (**a**) *Aut* embrague *m* (**b**) *Fig* **to fall into sb's clutches** caer en las garras de algn

clutter ['klʌtə(r)] VT **to c. (up)** llenar, atestar

cm *(abbr* **centimetre(s))** cm

CND [si:en'di:] N *Br (abbr* **Campaign for Nuclear Disarmament)** = organización británica en favor del desarme nuclear

Co (**a**) *Com (abbr* **Company)** Cía. (**b**) *(abbr* **County)** condado

c/o [si:'əʊ] *(abbr* **care of)** en el domicilio de

coach [kəʊtʃ] **1** N (**a**) *esp Br (bus)* autobús *m*, *Esp* autocar *m*; *(carriage)* carruaje *m*; **c. tour** excursión *f* en autocar (**b**) *Rail* coche *m*, vagón *m* (**c**) *Sport* entrenador(a) *m,f*
2 VT *Sport* entrenar; *Educ* dar clases particulares a

coagulate [kəʊ'ægjʊleɪt] VI coagularse

coal [kəʊl] N carbón *m*, hulla *f*; **c. bunker** carbonera *f*; **c. merchant** carbonero *m*; **c. mine** mina *f* de carbón

coalfield ['kəʊlfi:ld] N yacimiento *m* de carbón

coalition [kəʊə'lɪʃən] N coalición *f*

coarse [kɔ:s] ADJ *(material)* basto(a); *(skin)* áspero(a); *(language)* grosero(a), ordinario(a)

coast [kəʊst] N costa *f*, litoral *m*

coastal ['kəʊstəl] ADJ costero(a)

coaster ['kəʊstə(r)] N *(mat)* salvamanteles *m inv*

coastguard ['kəʊstgɑ:d] N *esp Br (person)* guardacostas *mf inv*

coastline ['kəʊstlaɪn] N litoral *m*, costa *f*

coat [kəʊt] **1** N (**a**) *(overcoat)* abrigo *m*; *(jacket)* chaqueta *f*, *Méx* chamarra *f*, *RP* campera *f*; **c. hanger** percha *f* (**b**) *(of animal)* pelo *m* (**c**) *(of paint)* mano *f*, capa *f*
2 VT cubrir (**with** de); *(with liquid)* bañar (**with** en)

coating ['kəʊtɪŋ] N capa *f*, baño *m*

coax [kəʊks] VT engatusar

cob [kɒb] N mazorca *f*

cobble ['kɒbəl] N adoquín *m*

cobbled ['kɒbəld] ADJ *(path, street)* adoquinado(a)

cobbler ['kɒblə(r)] N zapatero *m*

cobweb ['kɒbweb] N telaraña *f*

cocaine [kə'keɪn] N cocaína *f*

cock [kɒk] **1** N (**a**) *(male fowl)* gallo *m*; *(male bird)* macho *m* (**b**) *(on gun)* percutor *m* (**c**) *Vulg (penis)* *Esp* polla *f*, *Am* verga *f*, *Chile* pico *m*, *Méx* pito *m*, *RP* pija *f*
2 VT *(gun)* amartillar; *(ears)* erguir
► **cock up** VT SEP *Br very Fam* **to c. sth up** cagar or *Esp* joder or *Méx* madrear algo

cocker ['kɒkə(r)] N **c. spaniel** cocker *m*

cockerel ['kɒkərəl] N gallo *m* joven

cockeyed ['kɒkaɪd] ADJ *Fam (lopsided)* torcido(a); *(scheme)* disparatado(a)

cockle ['kɒkəl] N berberecho *m*

cockney ['kɒknɪ] **1** ADJ = del East End londinense
2 N = persona del East End londinense

cockpit ['kɒkpɪt] N cabina *f* del piloto

cockroach ['kɒkrəʊtʃ] N cucaracha *f*

cocktail ['kɒkteɪl] N cóctel *m*; **c. lounge** bar *m*; **c. party** cóctel; **prawn c.** cóctel de gambas; **Molotov c.** cóctel Molotov

cocky ['kɒkɪ] ADJ **(cockier, cockiest)** *Fam* gallito(a), engreído(a), *Esp* chulo(a)

cocoa ['kəʊkəʊ] N cacao *m*

coconut ['kəʊkənʌt] N coco *m*

cocoon [kə'kuːn] N capullo *m*

COD [siːəʊ'diː] *Br (abbr* **cash on delivery)** CAE

cod [kɒd] N bacalao *m*; **c. liver oil** aceite *m* de hígado de bacalao

code [kəʊd] **1** N código *m*; *(symbol)* clave *f*; *Tel* prefijo *m*.
2 VT *(message)* cifrar, poner en clave

co-ed [kəʊ'ed] *Fam* **1** ADJ mixto(a)
2 N colegio mixto

coeducational ['kəʊedjʊ'keɪʃənəl] ADJ mixto(a)

coerce [kəʊ'ɜːs] VT coaccionar

coercion [kəʊ'ɜːʃən] N coacción *f*

coexist [kəʊɪg'zɪst] VI coexistir

coffee ['kɒfɪ] N café *m*; **c. bar/shop** cafetería *f*; **c. break** descanso *m*; **c. table** mesita *f* de café

coffeepot ['kɒfɪpɒt] N cafetera *f*

coffer ['kɒfə(r)] N arca *f*

coffin ['kɒfɪn] N ataúd *m*

cog [kɒg] N diente *m*

cognac ['kɒnjæk] N coñac *m*

cognitive ['kɒgnɪtɪv] ADJ cognitivo(a)

cohabit [kəʊ'hæbɪt] VI cohabitar, convivir

coherent [kəʊ'hɪərənt] ADJ coherente

coil [kɔɪl] **1** VT **to c. (up)** enrollar
2 VI enroscarse
3 N **(a)** *(loop)* vuelta *f*; *(of rope)* rollo *m*; *(of hair)* rizo *m* **(b)** *Br (contraceptive)* espiral *f* **(c)** *Elec* carrete *m*, bobina *f*

coin [kɔɪn] **1** N moneda *f*
2 VT **(a)** *(money)* acuñar **(b)** *Fig* **to c. a phrase** por así decirlo

coinage ['kɔɪnɪdʒ] N moneda *f*, sistema monetario

coincide [kəʊɪn'saɪd] VI coincidir **(with** con)

coincidence [kəʊ'ɪnsɪdəns] N coincidencia *f*

coincidental [kəʊɪnsɪ'dentəl] ADJ casual

coincidentally [kəʊɪnsɪ'dentəlɪ] ADV por casualidad *or* coincidencia

Coke® [kəʊk] N *Fam* Coca-Cola® *f*

coke [kəʊk] N *(coal)* coque *m*

colander ['kɒləndə(r)] N colador *m*

cold [kəʊld] **1** ADJ frío(a); **I'm c.** tengo frío; **it's c.** *(weather)* hace frío; *(thing)* está frío(a); *Fig* **to get c. feet (about doing sth)** entrarle miedo a algn (de hacer algo); **c. cream** crema *f* hidratante; *Fig* **it leaves me c.** ni me va ni me viene, *Esp* me deja frío(a); **c. sore** herpes *m inv* labial, *Esp* calentura *f*, *Méx* fuego *m*; **c. war** guerra fría
2 N **(a)** *(low temperature)* frío *m* **(b)** *(illness)* catarro *m*, *Esp, Méx* resfriado *m*, *Andes, RP* resfrío *m*; **to have a c.** estar acatarrado(a), tener un *Esp, Méx* resfriado *orAndes, RP* resfrío

cold-blooded [kəʊld'blʌdɪd] ADJ **(a)** *(animal)* de sangre fría **(b)** *Fig (person)* frío(a); *(crime)* a sangre fría

coldness ['kəʊldnɪs] N *(of weather, manner)* frialdad *f*

coleslaw ['kəʊlslɔː] N ensalada *f* de col

collaborate [kə'læbəreɪt] VI colaborar **(with** con)

collaboration [kəlæbə'reɪʃən] N *also Pej* colaboración *f*

collaborator [kə'læbəreɪtə(r)] N *Pol* colaboracionista *mf*

collapse [kə'læps] **1** VI *(break down)* derrumbarse; *(cave in)* hundirse; *Fig (prices)* caer en picado; *Med* sufrir un colapso
2 VT *(table)* plegar
3 N *(breaking down)* derrumbamiento *m*; *(caving in)* hundimiento *m*; *Med* colapso *m*

collapsible [kə'læpsəbəl] ADJ plegable

collar ['kɒlə(r)] **1** N *(of garment)* cuello *m*; *(for dog)* collar *m*
2 VT *Fam* pescar, agarrar

collarbone ['kɒləbəʊn] N clavícula *f*

collateral [kɒ'lætərəl] **1** N *Fin* garantía subsidiaria
2 ADJ colateral

colleague ['kɒliːg] N colega *mf*

collect [kə'lekt] **1** VT **(a)** *(gather)* recoger **(b)** *(stamps etc)* coleccionar **(c)** *(taxes)* recaudar
2 VI **(a)** *(people)* reunirse **(b)** *(for charity)* hacer una colecta **(for** para)
3 ADV *US* **to call sb c.** llamar *or Am* hablar a algn a cobro revertido

collection [kə'lekʃən] N **(a)** *(of mail)* recogida *f*; *(of money)* colecta *f* **(b)** *(of stamps)* colección *f*

collective [kə'lektɪv] **1** ADJ colectivo(a); **c. bargaining** negociación colectiva
2 N colectivo *m*

collector [kə'lektə(r)] N *(of stamps)* coleccionista *mf*

college ['kɒlɪdʒ] N colegio *m*; *Br (of university)* colegio universitario; *US (university)* universidad *f*

collide [kə'laɪd] VI chocar, colisionar

collie ['kɒlɪ] N perro *m* pastor escocés

colliery ['kɒljərɪ] N *Br* mina *f* de carbón

collision [kə'lɪʒən] N choque *m*

colloquial [kə'ləʊkwɪəl] ADJ coloquial

collusion [kə'luːʒən] N conspiración *f*

cologne [kə'ləʊn] N (agua *f* de) colonia *f*

Colombia [kə'lɒmbɪə] N Colombia

Colombian [kə'lɒmbɪən] ADJ & N colombiano(a) (m,f)

colon¹ ['kəʊlən] N *Typ* dos puntos *mpl*

colon² ['kəʊlən] N *Anat* colon *m*

colonel ['kɜːnəl] N coronel *m*

colonial [kə'ləʊnɪəl] ADJ colonial

colonize ['kɒlənaɪz] VT colonizar

colony ['kɒlənɪ] N colonia *f*

color ['kʌlər] N, VT & VI *US* = **colour**

colossal [kə'lɒsəl] ADJ colosal

colour ['kʌlə(r)] **1** N (**a**) *(hue)* color *m*; **what c. is it?** ¿de qué color es?; **c. film/television** película *f*/televisión *f* en color; **c. scheme** combinación *f* de colores (**b**) *(skin colour)* color *m* de la piel; **c. bar** discriminación *f* racial (**c**) **colours** *Br Sport* colores *mpl*; *Mil (flag)* bandera *f*
2 VT colorear
3 VI to **c. (up)** ruborizarse

colour-blind ['kʌləblaɪnd] ADJ daltónico(a)

coloured ['kʌləd] ADJ *(clothes)* de color; *(photograph)* en color

> Note that the Spanish word **colorado** is a false friend and is never a translation for the English word **coloured**. In Spanish **colorado** means "red".

colourful ['kʌləfʊl] ADJ (**a**) *(having bright colours)* de colores vivos (**b**) *(interesting, exciting)* lleno(a) de colorido; *(person)* pintoresco(a)

colouring ['kʌlərɪŋ] N *(colour)* colorido *m*

colourless ['kʌləlɪs] ADJ *(clear)* incoloro(a); *Fig (dull)* insulso(a)

colt [kəʊlt] N potro *m*

column ['kɒləm] N columna *f*

columnist ['kɒləmnɪst] N columnista *mf*

coma ['kəʊmə] N coma *m*; **to go into a c.** entrar en coma

comb [kəʊm] **1** N peine *m*
2 VT peinar; **to c. one's hair** peinarse

combat ['kɒmbæt] **1** N combate *m*
2 VT *(enemy, disease)* combatir
3 VI combatir (**against** contra)

combination [kɒmbɪ'neɪʃən] N combinación *f*

combine [kəm'baɪn] **1** VT combinar
2 VI *(merge)* unirse, combinarse; *(people)* unirse
3 N ['kɒmbaɪn] (**a**) *Com* asociación *f* (**b**) **c. harvester** cosechadora *f*

combustion [kəm'bʌstʃən] N combustión *f*

come [kʌm] VI *(pt* **came**; *pp* **come**) (**a**) *(in general)* venir (**from** de); *(arrive)* venir, llegar; **coming!** ¡voy!; **to c. and go** ir y venir; *Fig* **in years to c.** en el futuro (**b**) *(happen)* suceder; **c. what may** pase lo que pase (**c**) **I came to believe that …** llegué a creer que …

▶ **come about** VI ocurrir, suceder

▶ **come across 1** VT INSEP *(thing)* encontrar por casualidad; **to c. across sb** tropezar con algn
2 VI *Fig* **to c. across well** causar buena impresión

▶ **come along** VI (**a**) *(arrive)* venir; **c. along!** ¡vamos!, *Esp* ¡venga! (**b**) *(make progress)* progresar

▶ **come away** VI *(leave)* salir; *(part)* desprenderse (**from** de)

▶ **come back** VI *(return)* volver, *Col, Méx* regresarse

▶ **come before** VT INSEP (**a**) *(in time)* preceder (**b**) *(court)* comparecer ante

▶ **come by** VT INSEP adquirir

▶ **come down** VI *(descend)* bajar; *(rain)* caer; *(building)* ser derribado(a); **to c. down with the flu** *Esp* pillar un resfriado, *Am* agarrarse un resfrío

▶ **come forward** VI *(advance)* avanzar; *(volunteer)* ofrecerse

▶ **come in** VI (**a**) *(enter)* entrar; **c. in!** ¡pase! (**b**) *(arrive)* *(train)* llegar; *(tide)* subir; *Fam Fig* **where do I c. in?** y yo ¿qué pinto? (**c**) **to c. in handy** venir bien (**d**) **to c. in for** ser objeto de

▶ **come into** VT INSEP (**a**) *(enter)* entrar en (**b**) *(inherit)* heredar

▶ **come off 1** VT INSEP *(fall from)* caerse de; *Fam* **c. off it!** ¡venga ya!
2 VI (**a**) *(fall)* caerse; *(stain)* quitarse; *(button)* caerse (**b**) *Fam (take place)* pasar; *(succeed)* salir bien; **to c. off badly** salir mal

▶ **come on** VI (**a**) **c. on!** *(hurry)* ¡vamos!, *Esp* ¡venga! (**b**) *(make progress)* progresar (**c**) *(rain, illness)* comenzar

▶ **come out** VI (**a**) *(person, sun, book)* salir; *(product)* estrenarse; *(facts)* revelarse (**b**) *(stain)* quitarse; *(colour)* desteñir (**c**) **to c. out against/in favour of sth** declararse en contra/a favor de algo; *Br Ind* **to c. out (on strike)** declararse en huelga (**d**) *(turn out)* salir

▶ **come over 1** VI venir
2 VT INSEP (**a**) *(hill)* aparecer en lo alto de (**b**) *Fam* **what's c. over you?** ¿qué te pasa?

▶ **come round 1** VT INSEP *(corner)* dar la vuelta a
2 VI (**a**) *(visit)* venir (**b**) *(regain consciousness)* volver en sí (**c**) **to c. round to sb's way of thinking** dejarse convencer por algn

▶ **come through 1** VT INSEP (**a**) *(cross)* cruzar (**b**) *(illness)* recuperarse de; *(accident)* sobrevivir
2 VI *(message)* llegar

▶ **come to 1** VI *(regain consciousness)* volver en sí
2 VT INSEP (**a**) *Fig* **to c. to one's senses** recobrar la razón (**b**) *(amount to)* costar (**c**) *(arrive at)* llegar a; **to c. to an end** terminar; *Fam* **c. to that** a propósito

▶ **come under** VT INSEP *Fig* **to c. under fire from sb** ser criticado(a) por algn

▶ **come up** VI (**a**) *(rise)* subir; *(approach)* acercarse (**to** a) (**b**) *(difficulty, question)* surgir; **to**

c. up with a solution encontrar una solución; to c. up against problems encontrarse con problemas (c) (sun) salir (d) to c. up to igualar; to c. up to sb's expectations satisfacer a algn (e) Br Fam three chips, coming up! ¡van tres de patatas fritas!

▸ **come upon** VT INSEP = **come across 1**

comeback ['kʌmbæk] N Fam (a) (of person) reaparición f; to make a c. reaparecer (b) (answer) réplica f

comedian [kə'mi:dɪən] N cómico m

comedienne [kəmi:di'en] N cómica f

comedown ['kʌmdaʊn] N Fam desilusión f, revés m

comedy ['kɒmɪdɪ] N comedia f

comet ['kɒmɪt] N cometa m

comeuppance [kʌm'ʌpəns] N Fam to get one's c. llevarse su merecido

comfort ['kʌmfət] 1 N (a) (ease) comodidad f; US c. station servicios mpl, Esp aseos mpl, Am baños mpl (b) (consolation) consuelo m; to take c. in or from sth consolarse con algo
2 VT consolar

comfortable ['kʌmfətəbəl] ADJ (chair, person, margin) cómodo(a); (temperature) agradable

comfortably ['kʌmfətəblɪ] ADV (win) con facilidad; to be c. off vivir cómodamente

comforter ['kʌmfətə(r)] N (a) Br (scarf) bufanda f (b) (for baby) chupete m (c) US (quilt) edredón m

comforting ['kʌmfətɪŋ] ADJ consolador(a)

comic ['kɒmɪk] 1 ADJ cómico(a); c. strip tira cómica, historieta f
2 N (a) (person) cómico(a) m,f (b) c. (book) (for children) Esp tebeo m, Am revista f de historietas; (for adults) cómic m

coming ['kʌmɪŋ] 1 ADJ (year) próximo(a); (generation) futuro(a)
2 N venida f, llegada f; comings and goings idas fpl y venidas; Fig c. and going ajetreo m

comma ['kɒmə] N coma f

command [kə'mɑːnd] 1 VT (a) (order) mandar (b) (respect) infundir; (attention) obtener (c) (have at one's disposal) disponer de
2 N (a) (order) orden f; (authority) mando m; to be at sb's c. estar a las órdenes de algn (b) (of language) dominio m (c) (disposal) disposición f (d) Comput comando m, instrucción f

commandeer [kɒmən'dɪə(r)] VT requisar

commander [kə'mɑːndə(r)] N comandante m

commanding [kə'mɑːndɪŋ] ADJ dominante; Mil c. officer comandante m

commandment [kə'mɑːndmənt] N mandamiento m

commando [kə'mɑːndəʊ] N comando m

commemorate [kə'meməreɪt] VT conmemorar

commemoration [kəmemə'reɪʃən] N conmemoración f; in c. of en conmemoración de

commence [kə'mens] VT & VI Fml comenzar

commend [kə'mend] VT (a) (praise) alabar, elogiar (b) (entrust) encomendar (c) (recommend) recomendar

commendable [kə'mendəbəl] ADJ encomiable

commensurate [kə'menʃərɪt] ADJ proporcional; c. to or with en proporción con

comment ['kɒment] 1 N comentario m; no c. sin comentario
2 VI hacer comentarios

commentary ['kɒməntərɪ] N comentario m

commentator ['kɒmənteɪtə(r)] N comentarista mf

commerce ['kɒmɜːs] N comercio m

commercial [kə'mɜːʃəl] 1 ADJ comercial; TV c. break corte publicitario
2 N TV anuncio m

commercialize [kə'mɜːʃəlaɪz] VT explotar

commiserate [kə'mɪzəreɪt] VI compadecerse (with de)

commission [kə'mɪʃən] 1 N (a) Mil despacho m (de oficial); out of c. fuera de servicio (b) (of inquiry) comisión f; (job) encargo m (c) (payment) comisión f
2 VT (a) Mil nombrar (b) (order) encargar (c) Naut poner en servicio

commissionaire [kəmɪʃə'neə(r)] N Br (at hotel, cinema) portero m de librea

commissioner [kə'mɪʃənə(r)] N (official) comisario m; c. of police comisario de policía

commit [kə'mɪt] VT (a) (crime) cometer; to c. suicide suicidarse (b) to c. oneself (to do sth) comprometerse a hacer algo) (c) to c. sth to sb's care confiar algo a algn

commitment [kə'mɪtmənt] N compromiso m

committee [kə'mɪtɪ] N comisión f, comité m

commode [kə'məʊd] N (chair) silla f con orinal; (chest of drawers) cómoda f

commodity [kə'mɒdɪtɪ] N producto básico

Note that the Spanish word **comodidad** is a false friend and is never a translation for the English word **commodity**. In Spanish **comodidad** means "comfort, convenience".

common ['kɒmən] 1 ADJ (a) (frequent) común, frecuente (b) (shared) común; that's c. knowledge eso lo sabe todo el mundo; c. law derecho consuetudinario; C. Market Mercado m Común; c. room (for students) sala f de estudiantes; (for teachers) sala f de profesores (c) (ordinary) corriente (d) (vulgar) ordinario(a), maleducado(a)
2 N (land) campo m or terreno m comunal

commonly ['kɒmənlɪ] ADV comúnmente

commonplace ['kɒmənpleɪs] ADJ corriente

Commons ['kɒmənz] NPL Br, Can the (House of) C. la Cámara de los Comunes

Commonwealth ['kɒmənwelθ] N Br the C. la Commonwealth; C. of Independent States Comunidad f de Estados Independientes

commotion [kə'məʊʃən] N alboroto m

communal ['komjunəl] ADJ comunal

commune¹ [kə'mju:n] VI *(converse)* conversar íntimamente; *(with nature)* estar en comunión (**with** con)

commune² ['komju:n] N comuna f

communicate [kə'mju:nɪkeɪt] **1** VI comunicarse (**with** con)
2 VT comunicar

communication [kəmju:nɪ'keɪʃən] N comunicación f; *Br Rail* **c. cord** timbre m de alarma

communicator [kə'mju:nɪkeɪtə(r)] N comunicador(a) m,f

communion [kə'mju:nɪən] N comunión f; **to take c.** comulgar

communiqué [kə'mju:nɪkeɪ] N comunicado m oficial

communism ['komjunɪzəm] N comunismo m

communist ['komjunɪst] ADJ & N comunista *(mf)*

community [kə'mju:nɪtɪ] N comunidad f; *(people)* colectividad f; **c. centre** centro m social

commute [kə'mju:t] **1** VI = viajar diariamente al lugar de trabajo
2 VT *Jur* conmutar

commuter [kə'mju:tə(r)] N = persona que viaja diariamente al lugar de trabajo

compact¹ **1** ADJ [kəm'pækt] compacto(a)
2 N ['kompækt] *(for powder)* polvera f

compact² ['kompækt] N *Pol* pacto m

compact disc ['kompækt'dɪsk] N disco compacto

companion [kəm'pænjən] N compañero(a) m,f

companionship [kəm'pænjənʃɪp] N compañerismo m

company ['kʌmpənɪ] N **(a)** *(companionship)* compañía f; **to keep sb c.** hacer compañía a algn **(b)** *Com* empresa f, compañía f

comparable ['kompərəbəl] ADJ comparable (**to** *or* **with** con)

comparative [kəm'pærətɪv] **1** ADJ *(comfort, wealth)* relativo(a); *(study, research)* comparado(a)
2 N *Gram* comparativo m

comparatively [kəm'pærətɪvlɪ] ADV relativamente

compare [kəm'peə(r)] **1** VT comparar (**to** *or* **with** con); **(as) compared with** en comparación con
2 VI compararse

comparison [kəm'pærɪsən] N comparación f; **by c.** en comparación; **there's no c.** no se puede comparar

compartment [kəm'pɑ:tmənt] N *(section)* compartimiento m; *Rail* departamento m

compass ['kʌmpəs] N **(a)** *(for finding direction)* brújula f **(b)** *(pair of)* **compasses** compás m **(c)** *Fig (range)* límites mpl

compassion [kəm'pæʃən] N compasión f

compassionate [kəm'pæʃənət] ADJ compasivo(a)

compatible [kəm'pætəbəl] ADJ compatible

compatriot [kəm'pætrɪət] N compatriota mf

compel [kəm'pel] VT **(a)** *(oblige)* obligar; **to c. sb to do sth** obligar a algn a hacer algo **(b)** *(admiration)* despertar

compelling [kəm'pelɪŋ] ADJ irresistible

compensate ['kompənseɪt] **1** VT compensar; **to c. sb for sth** indemnizar a algn de algo
2 VI compensar

compensation [kompən'seɪʃən] N compensación f; *(for loss)* indemnización f

compere ['kompeə(r)] N *Br* animador(a) m,f

compete [kəm'pi:t] VI competir

competence ['kompɪtəns] N **(a)** *(ability)* aptitud f **(b)** *(of court etc)* competencia f

competent ['kompɪtənt] ADJ competente

competition [kompɪ'tɪʃən] N **(a)** *(contest)* concurso m **(b)** *Com* competencia f

competitive [kəm'petɪtɪv] ADJ competitivo(a)

competitor [kəm'petɪtə(r)] N competidor(a) m,f

compilation [kompɪ'leɪʃən] N recopilación f

compile [kəm'paɪl] VT compilar, recopilar

complacency [kəm'pleɪsənsɪ] N autocomplacencia f

> Note that the Spanish word **complacencia** is a false friend and is never a translation for the English word **complacency**. In Spanish, **complacencia** means "satisfaction, indulgence".

complacent [kəm'pleɪsənt] ADJ autocomplaciente

complain [kəm'pleɪn] VI quejarse (**of/about** de)

complaint [kəm'pleɪnt] N **(a)** *(grievance)* queja f; *Com (formal protest)* queja f, reclamación f, *Am* reclamo m **(b)** *Med* afección f, problema m

complement ['komplɪmənt] **1** N **(a)** *Ling* complemento m **(b)** *Naut* dotación f
2 VT complementar

complementary [komplɪ'mentərɪ] ADJ complementario(a)

complete [kəm'pli:t] **1** ADJ **(a)** *(entire)* completo(a) **(b)** *(absolute)* total
2 VT completar; **to c. a form** rellenar un formulario

completely [kəm'pli:tlɪ] ADV completamente, por completo

completion [kəm'pli:ʃən] N terminación f; **near c.** casi terminado(a); **on c.** en cuanto se termine

complex ['kompleks] **1** ADJ complejo(a)
2 N complejo m; **inferiority c.** complejo de inferioridad

complexion [kəm'plekʃən] N tez f; *Fig* aspecto m

> Note that the Spanish word **complexión** is a false friend and is never a translation for the English word **complexion**. In Spanish **complexión** means "build".

compliance [kəm'plaɪəns] N conformidad *f*; **in c. with** de acuerdo con

complicate ['kɒmplɪkeɪt] VT complicar

complicated ['kɒmplɪkeɪtɪd] ADJ complicado(a)

complication [kɒmplɪ'keɪʃən] N complicación *f*

complicity [kəm'plɪsɪtɪ] N complicidad *f*

compliment 1 N ['kɒmplɪmənt] cumplido *m*; **to pay sb a c.** hacerle un cumplido a algn; **with compliments** con mis mejores deseos
2 VT ['kɒmplɪment] felicitar; **to c. sb on sth** felicitar a algn por algo

complimentary [kɒmplɪ'mentərɪ] ADJ **(a)** *(praising)* elogioso(a) **(b)** *(free)* gratis

comply [kəm'plaɪ] VI obedecer; **to c. with** *(order)* cumplir con; *(request)* acceder a

component [kəm'pəʊnənt] **1** N componente *m*
2 ADJ componente; **c. part** parte *f*

compose [kəm'pəʊz] **1** VT **(a)** *(music, poetry)* componer **(b)** *(constitute)* **to be composed of** estar compuesto(a) de **(c)** *(calm)* **to c. oneself** calmarse
2 VI *(create music)* componer

composed [kəm'pəʊzd] ADJ *(calm)* sereno(a)

composer [kəm'pəʊzə(r)] N compositor(a) *m,f*

composite ['kɒmpəzɪt] ADJ compuesto(a)

composition [kɒmpə'zɪʃən] N composición *f*; *(essay)* redacción *f*

compost ['kɒmpɒst] N abono *m*

composure [kəm'pəʊʒə(r)] N calma *f*, serenidad *f*

compound[1] ['kɒmpaʊnd] **1** N compuesto *m*
2 ADJ compuesto(a); **c. fracture** fractura abierta
3 VT [kəm'paʊnd] *(problem)* agravar

compound[2] ['kɒmpaʊnd] N *(enclosure)* recinto *m*

comprehend [kɒmprɪ'hend] VT comprender

comprehensible [kɒmprɪ'hensəbəl] ADJ comprensible

comprehension [kɒmprɪ'henʃən] N comprensión *f*

comprehensive [kɒmprɪ'hensɪv] ADJ **(a)** *(knowledge)* amplio(a); *(study)* detallado(a) **(b)** *Ins* a todo riesgo **(c)** *Br* **c. school** ≃ instituto *m* de segunda enseñanza

Note that the Spanish word **comprensivo** is a false friend and is never a translation for the English word **comprehensive**. In Spanish **comprensivo** means "understanding".

compress 1 VT [kəm'pres] comprimir
2 N ['kɒmpres] compresa *f*

comprise [kəm'praɪz] VT *(include)* comprender; **to be comprised of** constar de

compromise ['kɒmprəmaɪz] **1** N solución negociada; **to reach a c.** llegar a un acuerdo
2 VI *(two people)* llegar a un acuerdo; *(individual)* transigir
3 VT *(person)* comprometer

Note that the Spanish word **compromiso** is a false friend and is never a translation for the English word **compromise**. In Spanish **compromiso** means "obligation, commitment, agreement".

compulsion [kəm'pʌlʃən] N obligación *f*

compulsive [kəm'pʌlsɪv] ADJ compulsivo(a)

compulsory [kəm'pʌlsərɪ] ADJ obligatorio(a)

computational [kɒmpjuː'teɪʃənəl] ADJ computacional

computer [kəm'pjuːtə(r)] N *Esp* ordenador *m*, *Am* computadora *f*; **personal c.** ordenador personal, *Am* computadora personal; **c. programmer** programador(a) *m,f*; **c. science** informática *f*

computerize [kəm'pjuːtəraɪz] VT informatizar, *Am* computarizar, *Am* computadorizar

computing [kəm'pjuːtɪŋ] N informática *f*, *Am* computación *f*

comrade ['kɒmreɪd] N **(a)** *(companion)* compañero(a) *m,f* **(b)** *Pol* camarada *mf*

comradeship ['kɒmreɪdʃɪp] N camaradería *f*

con [kɒn] *Fam* **1** VT timar, *RP* cagar
2 N timo *m*, *Andes*, *RP* truchada *f*; **c. man** timador *m*, *Andes*, *RP* cagador *m*

concave ['kɒnkeɪv] ADJ cóncavo(a)

conceal [kən'siːl] VT *(object)* ocultar, esconder **(from** de); *(fact)* ocultar **(from** de)

concede [kən'siːd] VT conceder

conceit [kən'siːt] N presunción *f*, vanidad *f*

conceited [kən'siːtɪd] ADJ presuntuoso(a)

conceivable [kən'siːvəbəl] ADJ concebible

conceive [kən'siːv] VT & VI concebir

concentrate [kən'sentreɪt] **1** VT concentrar
2 VI **to c. on sth** concentrarse en algo

concentration [kɒnsən'treɪʃən] N concentración *f*; **c. camp** campo *m* de concentración

concept ['kɒnsept] N concepto *m*

conception [kən'sepʃən] N *Med* concepción *f*; *(understanding)* concepto *m*, idea *f*

concern [kən'sɜːn] **1** VT **(a)** *(affect)* concernir, incumbir; **as far as I'm concerned** por lo que a mí se refiere **(b)** *(worry)* preocupar
2 N **(a)** **it's no c. of mine** no es asunto mío **(b)** *(worry)* preocupación *f* **(c)** *Com* negocio *m*

concerned [kən'sɜːnd] ADJ **(a)** *(affected)* afectado(a) **(b)** *(worried)* preocupado(a) **(about** por)

concerning [kən'sɜːnɪŋ] PREP con respecto a, en cuanto a

concert ['kɒnsət] N *Mus* concierto *m*; **c. hall** sala *f* de conciertos

concerted [kən'sɜːtɪd] ADJ concertado(a)

concertina [kɒnsə'tiːnə] N concertina *f*

concerto [kən'tʃɜːtəʊ] N concierto *m*

concession [kən'seʃən] N **(a)** *(compromise)* concesión *f* **(b)** *Br (discount)* descuento *m*

conciliatory [kən'sɪlɪətərɪ] ADJ conciliador(a)

concise [kənˈsaɪs] ADJ conciso(a)

conclude [kənˈkluːd] VT & VI concluir

conclusion [kənˈkluːʒən] N conclusión *f*; **to reach a c.** llegar a una conclusión

conclusive [kənˈkluːsɪv] ADJ concluyente

concoct [kənˈkɒkt] VT *(dish)* confeccionar; *Fig (plan)* fraguar; *(excuse)* inventar

concoction [kənˈkɒkʃən] N *(mixture)* mezcolanza *f*; *Pej (brew)* brebaje *m*

concourse [ˈkɒŋkɔːs] N explanada *f*

Note that the Spanish word **concurso** is a false friend and is never a translation for the English word **concourse**. In Spanish **concurso** means "competition, contest".

concrete [ˈkɒŋkriːt] **1** N hormigón *m*, *Am* concreto *m*; **c. mixer** hormigonera *f*
2 ADJ **(a)** *(definite)* concreto(a) **(b)** *(made of concrete)* de hormigón

concur [kənˈkɜː(r)] VI **(a)** **to c. with** *(agree)* estar de acuerdo con **(b)** *(coincide)* coincidir

concurrent [kənˈkʌrənt] ADJ simultáneo(a)

concussion [kənˈkʌʃən] N conmoción *f* cerebral

condemn [kənˈdem] VT condenar

condemnation [kɒndemˈneɪʃən] N condena *f*

condensation [kɒndenˈseɪʃən] N condensación *f*

condense [kənˈdens] **1** VT condensar
2 VI condensarse

condensed [kənˈdenst] ADJ **c. milk** leche condensada

condescending [kɒndɪˈsendɪŋ] ADJ condescendiente

condition [kənˈdɪʃən] **1** N condición *f*; **to be in good c.** estar en buen estado; **on c. that …** a condición de que …; **on one c.** con una condición; **heart c.** enfermedad cardíaca; **conditions** *(circumstances)* circunstancias *fpl*
2 VT condicionar

conditional [kənˈdɪʃənəl] ADJ condicional

conditioner [kənˈdɪʃənə(r)] N acondicionador *m*

condo [ˈkɒndəʊ] N *US Fam* = **condominium**

condolences [kənˈdəʊlənsɪz] NPL pésame *m*; **please accept my c.** le acompaño en el sentimiento

condom [ˈkɒndəm] N preservativo *m*

condominium [kɒndəˈmɪnɪəm] N *US (building)* = bloque de apartamentos poseídos por diferentes propietarios; *(apartment)* apartamento *m*, *Esp* piso *m*, *Arg* departamento *m* (en propiedad)

condone [kənˈdəʊn] VT perdonar, consentir

condor [ˈkɒndɔː(r)] N cóndor *m*

conducive [kənˈdjuːsɪv] ADJ conducente

conduct 1 N [ˈkɒndʌkt] *(behaviour)* conducta *f*, comportamiento *m*
2 VT [kənˈdʌkt] *(lead)* guiar; *(business, orchestra)* dirigir; **conducted tour** visita acom-

pañada; **to c. oneself** comportarse
3 VI *Mus* dirigir

conductor [kənˈdʌktə(r)] N **(a)** *Br (on bus)* cobrador(a) *m,f*, *RP* guarda *mf* **(b)** *US Rail* revisor(a) *m,f* **(c)** *Mus* director(a) *m,f* **(d)** *Phys* conductor *m*

conductress [kənˈdʌktrɪs] N *Br (on bus)* cobradora *f*, *RP* guarda *f*

cone [kəʊn] N **(a)** *(shape)* cono *m*; **ice-cream c.** cucurucho *m*; *(for traffic)* cono *m* *(de tráfico)* **(b)** *Bot* piña *f*

confectioner [kənˈfekʃənə(r)] N confitero(a) *m,f*; **c.'s (shop)** *(sweet shop)* confitería *f*

confectionery [kənˈfekʃənərɪ] N dulces *mpl*

confederate [kənˈfedərɪt] **1** ADJ confederado(a)
2 N confederado(a) *m,f*; *Jur* cómplice *mf*

confederation [kənfedəˈreɪʃən] N confederación *f*

confer [kənˈfɜː(r)] **1** VT **to c. a title on sb** conferir un título a algn
2 VI consultar

conference [ˈkɒnfərəns] N conferencia *f*

confess [kənˈfes] **1** VI confesar; *Rel* confesarse
2 VT confesar, admitir; *Rel* confesar

confession [kənˈfeʃən] N confesión *f*

confessional [kənˈfeʃənəl] N confesionario *m*

confetti [kənˈfetɪ] N confeti *m*

confide [kənˈfaɪd] VI **to c. in sb** confiar en algn

confidence [ˈkɒnfɪdəns] N **(a)** *(trust)* confianza *f*; *(self-assurance)* confianza *f* (en uno mismo); **vote of c./no c.** voto *m* de confianza/de censura; **c. trick** camelo *m* **(b)** *(secret)* confidencia *f*; **in c.** en confianza

confident [ˈkɒnfɪdənt] ADJ seguro(a)

confidential [kɒnfɪˈdenʃəl] ADJ *(secret)* confidencial; *(entrusted)* de confianza

confidently [ˈkɒnfɪdəntlɪ] ADV con seguridad

confine [kənˈfaɪn] VT confinar, recluir; **to c. oneself to sth** *(limit)* limitarse a algo

confinement [kənˈfaɪnmənt] N **(a)** *(prison)* reclusión *f*, encierro *m*; **to be in solitary c.** estar incomunicado(a) **(b)** *Old-fashioned Med* parto *m*

confirm [kənˈfɜːm] VT confirmar

confirmation [kɒnfəˈmeɪʃən] N confirmación *f*

confirmed [kənˈfɜːmd] ADJ empedernido(a)

confiscate [ˈkɒnfɪskeɪt] VT confiscar

conflict 1 N [ˈkɒnflɪkt] conflicto *m*
2 VI [kənˈflɪkt] chocar (**with** con)

conflicting [kənˈflɪktɪŋ] ADJ contradictorio(a)

conform [kənˈfɔːm] VI conformarse; **to c. to** *or* **with** *(customs)* amoldarse a; *(rules)* someterse a

confound [kənˈfaʊnd] VT confundir, desconcertar

confront [kənˈfrʌnt] VT hacer frente a

confrontation [kɒnfrʌnˈteɪʃən] N confrontación *f*

confuse [kən'fju:z] VT *(person)* despistar; *(thing)* confundir (**with** con); **to get confused** confundirse

confused [kən'fju:zd] ADJ *(person)* confundido(a); *(mind, ideas)* confuso(a)

confusing [kən'fju:zɪŋ] ADJ confuso(a)

confusion [kən'fju:ʒən] N confusión *f*

congeal [kən'dʒi:l] VI coagularse

congenial [kən'dʒi:nɪəl] ADJ agradable

congenital [kən'dʒenɪtəl] ADJ congénito(a)

congested [kən'dʒestɪd] ADJ **(a)** *(street)* repleto(a) de gente; *(city)* superpoblado(a) (**b**) *Med* congestionado(a)

congestion [kən'dʒestʃən] N congestión *f*

conglomeration [kənglɒmə'reɪʃən] N conglomeración *f*

congratulate [kən'grætjʊleɪt] VT felicitar

congratulations [kəngrætjʊ'leɪʃənz] NPL felicitaciones *fpl*; **c.!** ¡enhorabuena!

congregate ['kɒŋgrɪgeɪt] VI congregarse

congregation [kɒŋgrɪ'geɪʃən] N *(group)* congregación *f*; *Rel* fieles *mpl*

congress ['kɒŋgres] N **(a)** *(conference)* congreso *m* (**b**) *US Pol* **C.** el Congreso *(de los Estados Unidos)*

Congressman ['kɒŋgresmən] N *US Pol* congresista *m*, *Am* congresal *m*

Congresswoman ['kɒŋgreswʊmən] N *US Pol* congresista *f*, *Am* congresal *f*

conifer ['kɒnɪfə(r)] N conífera *f*

conjecture [kən'dʒektʃə(r)] **1** N conjetura *f*
2 VT conjeturar
3 VI hacer conjeturas

conjugal ['kɒndʒʊgəl] ADJ conyugal

conjugate ['kɒndʒʊgeɪt] VT conjugar

conjunction [kən'dʒʌŋkʃən] N conjunción *f*; *Fig* **in c. with** conjuntamente con

conjunctivitis [kəndʒʌŋktɪ'vaɪtɪs] N conjuntivitis *f*

conjure ['kʌndʒə(r)] **1** VT **to c. (up)** *(of magician)* hacer aparecer; *(memories)* evocar
2 VI hacer juegos de manos

conjurer ['kʌndʒərə(r)] N prestidigitador(a) *m,f*

conker ['kɒŋkə(r)] N *Fam* castaña *f*

connect [kə'nekt] **1** VT **(a)** *(pipes, wires, gas)* conectar, empalmar (**to** con or a) (**b**) *(link)* conectar; *Fig* **to be connected by marriage** estar emparentado(a) por matrimonio (**c**) *Tel (person)* pasar, *Esp* poner (**d**) *(associate) (person, problem)* relacionar (**with** con)
2 VI *(wires, roads, pipes)* conectarse, empalmarse; *(train, flight)* enlazar (**with** con)

connected [kə'nektɪd] ADJ *(events)* relacionado(a); *Fig* **to be well c.** *(person) (socially)* estar bien relacionado(a)

connection [kə'nekʃən] N **(a)** *(joint)* juntura *f*, unión *f*; *Elec* conexión *f*; *Tel* instalación *f* (**b**) *Rail* correspondencia *f* (**c**) *Fig (of ideas)* relación *f*; **in c. with** *(regarding)* con respecto a (**d**) *(person)* contacto *m*

connive [kə'naɪv] VI **to c. at** hacer la vista gorda con

connoisseur [kɒnɪ'sɜ:(r)] N conocedor(a) *m,f*

connotation [kɒnə'teɪʃən] N connotación *f*

conquer ['kɒŋkə(r)] VT *(enemy, bad habit)* vencer; *(country)* conquistar

conqueror ['kɒŋkərə(r)] N conquistador *m*

conquest ['kɒŋkwest] N conquista *f*

conscience ['kɒnʃəns] N conciencia *f*; **to have a clear c.** tener la conciencia tranquila; **to have a guilty c.** sentirse culpable

conscientious [kɒnʃɪ'enʃəs] ADJ concienzudo(a); **c. objector** objetor(a) *m,f* de conciencia

conscious ['kɒnʃəs] ADJ *(aware)* consciente; *(choice etc)* deliberado(a)

consciousness ['kɒnʃəsnɪs] N *Med* conocimiento *m*; *(awareness)* consciencia *f*

conscript ['kɒnskrɪpt] N recluta *m*

conscription [kən'skrɪpʃən] N servicio militar obligatorio

consecrate ['kɒnsɪkreɪt] VT consagrar

consecutive [kən'sekjʊtɪv] ADJ consecutivo(a)

consensus [kən'sensəs] N consenso *m*

consent [kən'sent] **1** N consentimiento *m*; **by common c.** de común acuerdo
2 VI consentir (**to** en)

consequence ['kɒnsɪkwəns] N consecuencia *f*

consequent ['kɒnsɪkwənt] ADJ consiguiente

consequently ['kɒnsɪkwəntlɪ] ADV por consiguiente

conservation [kɒnsə'veɪʃən] N conservación *f*.

conservative [kən'sɜ:vətɪv] **1** ADJ cauteloso(a)
2 ADJ & N *Br Pol* **C.** conservador(a) *(m,f)*

conservatory [kən'sɜ:vətrɪ] N **(a)** *(greenhouse)* invernadero *m* (**b**) *Mus* conservatorio *m*

conserve 1 VT [kən'sɜ:v] conservar
2 N ['kɒnsɜ:v] conserva *f*

consider [kən'sɪdə(r)] VT **(a)** *(ponder on, regard)* considerar; **to c. doing sth** pensar hacer algo (**b**) *(keep in mind)* tener en cuenta

considerable [kən'sɪdərəbəl] ADJ considerable

considerably [kən'sɪdərəblɪ] ADV bastante

considerate [kən'sɪdərɪt] ADJ considerado(a)

consideration [kənsɪdə'reɪʃən] N consideración *f*; **without due c.** sin reflexión

considering [kən'sɪdərɪŋ] PREP teniendo en cuenta

consign [kən'saɪn] VT *Com* consignar; *Fig* entregar

consignment [kən'saɪnmənt] N envío *m*

consist [kən'sɪst] VI **to c. of** consistir en

consistency [kən'sɪstənsɪ] N **(a)** *(of actions)* consecuencia *f* (**b**) *(of mixture)* consistencia *f*

consistent [kən'sɪstənt] ADJ consecuente; **c. with** de acuerdo con

Note that the Spanish word **consistente** is a false friend and is never a translation for the English word **consistent**. In Spanish **consistente** means "firm, solid, sound".

consolation [kɒnsə'leɪʃən] N consuelo *m*; **c. prize** premio *m* de consolación

console[1] [kən'səʊl] VT consolar

console[2] ['kɒnsəʊl] N consola *f*; **(game)** c. videoconsola *f*

consolidate [kən'sɒlɪdeɪt] **1** VT consolidar
2 VI consolidarse

consonant ['kɒnsənənt] N consonante *f*

consortium [kən'sɔːtɪəm] N consorcio *m*

conspicuous [kən'spɪkjʊəs] ADJ *(striking)* llamativo(a); *(easily seen)* visible; *(mistake)* evidente

conspiracy [kən'spɪrəsɪ] N conjura *f*

conspire [kən'spaɪə(r)] VI conspirar

constable ['kʌnstəbəl] N *Br* policía *mf*; **chief c.** jefe *m* de policía

constabulary [kən'stæbjʊlərɪ] N *Br* (cuerpo *m* de) policía *f*

constant ['kɒnstənt] **1** ADJ *(price, temperature)* constante; *(continuous)* continuo(a), constante
2 N constante *f*

constellation [kɒnstɪ'leɪʃən] N constelación *f*

consternation [kɒnstə'neɪʃən] N consternación *f*

constipated ['kɒnstɪpeɪtɪd] ADJ **to be c.** estar estreñido(a)

Note that the Spanish word **constipado** is a false friend and is never a translation for the English word **constipated**. In Spanish **constipado** means both "cold, chill" and "suffering from a cold".

constipation [kɒnstɪ'peɪʃən] N estreñimiento *m*

constituency [kən'stɪtjʊənsɪ] N circunscripción *f* electoral

constituent [kən'stɪtjʊənt] **1** ADJ *(component)* constituyente
2 N **(a)** *(part)* componente *m* **(b)** *Pol* votante *mf*

constitute ['kɒnstɪtjuːt] VT constituir

constitution [kɒnstɪ'tjuːʃən] N constitución *f*

constitutional [kɒnstɪ'tjuːʃənəl] ADJ constitucional

constrained [kən'streɪnd] ADJ **to feel c. to do sth** sentirse obligado(a) a hacer algo

constraint [kən'streɪnt] N coacción *f*; **to feel c. in sb's presence** sentirse cohibido(a) ante algn

construct [kən'strʌkt] VT construir

construction [kən'strʌkʃən] N construcción *f*

constructive [kən'strʌktɪv] ADJ constructivo(a)

construe [kən'struː] VT interpretar

Note that the Spanish verb **construir** is a false friend and is never a translation for the English verb **to construe**. In Spanish, **construir** means "to build, to manufacture".

consul ['kɒnsəl] N cónsul *mf*

consulate ['kɒnsjʊlɪt] N consulado *m*

consult [kən'sʌlt] VT & VI consultar (**about** sobre)

consultancy [kən'sʌltənsɪ] N *Com* asesoría *f*, consultoría *f*

consultant [kən'sʌltənt] N *Med* especialista *mf*; *Com & Ind* asesor(a) *m,f*

consultation [kɒnsəl'teɪʃən] N consulta *f*

consulting [kən'sʌltɪŋ] ADJ **c. room** consulta *f*

consume [kən'sjuːm] VT consumir

consumer [kən'sjuːmə(r)] N consumidor(a) *m,f*; **c. goods** bienes *mpl* de consumo

consummate 1 VT ['kɒnsəmeɪt] consumar
2 ADJ ['kɒnsəmɪt] consumado(a)

consumption [kən'sʌmpʃən] N **(a)** *(of food)* consumo *m*; **fit for c.** apto(a) para el consumo **(b)** *Med* tisis *f*

cont. *(abbr* **continued)** sigue

contact ['kɒntækt] **1** N contacto *m*; **c. lens** lente *f* de contacto, *Esp* lentilla *f*, *Méx* pupilente *f*
2 VT ponerse en contacto con

contagious [kən'teɪdʒəs] ADJ contagioso(a)

contain [kən'teɪn] VT contener; **to c. oneself** contenerse

container [kən'teɪnə(r)] N **(a)** *(box, package)* recipiente *m*; *(bottle)* envase *m* **(b)** *Naut* contenedor *m*

contaminate [kən'tæmɪneɪt] VT contaminar

contamination [kəntæmɪ'neɪʃən] N contaminación *f*

contd. *(abbr* **continued)** sigue

contemplate ['kɒntempleɪt] VT **(a)** *(consider)* considerar, pensar en **(b)** *(look at)* contemplar

contemporary [kən'temprərɪ] ADJ & N contemporáneo(a) *(m,f)*

contempt [kən'tempt] N desprecio *m*; **to hold in c.** despreciar; **c. of court** desacato *m* a los tribunales

contemptible [kən'temptəbəl] ADJ despreciable

contemptuous [kən'temptjʊəs] ADJ despectivo(a)

contend [kən'tend] **1** VI competir; *Fig* **there are many problems to c. with** se han planteado muchos problemas
2 VT afirmar

contender [kən'tendə(r)] N contendiente *mf*

content[1] ['kɒntent] N contenido *m*; **table of contents** índice *m* de materias

content[2] [kən'tent] **1** ADJ cóntento(a)
2 VT contentar
3 N contento *m*; **to one's heart's c.** todo lo que uno quiera

contented [kən'tentɪd] ADJ contento(a), satisfecho(a)

contention [kən'tenʃən] N **(a)** *(dispute)* controversia *f* **(b)** *(point)* punto *m* de vista

contentment [kən'tentmənt] N contento *m*

contest 1 N ['kɒntest] concurso *m*; *Sport* prueba *f*
    2 VT [kən'test] **(a)** *(matter)* rebatir; *(verdict)* impugnar; *Fig (will)* disputar **(b)** *Pol (seat)* luchar por

contestant [kən'testənt] N concursante *mf*

context ['kɒntekst] N contexto *m*

continent ['kɒntɪnənt] N continente *m*; *Br* **(on) the C.** (en) Europa

continental [kɒntɪ'nentəl] ADJ **(a)** *(in geography)* continental; **c. shelf** plataforma *f* continental **(b)** *Br* de la Europa continental; **c. quilt** edredón *m*

contingency [kən'tɪndʒənsɪ] N contingencia *f*; **c. plans** planes *mpl* para casos de emergencia

contingent [kən'tɪndʒənt] ADJ & N contingente *(m)*

continual [kən'tɪnjʊəl] ADJ continuo(a), constante

continuation [kəntɪnjʊ'eɪʃən] N *(sequel etc)* continuación *f*; *(extension)* prolongación *f*

continue [kən'tɪnjuː] VT & VI continuar, seguir; **to c. to do sth** seguir *or* continuar haciendo algo

continuous [kən'tɪnjʊəs] ADJ continuo(a)

contort [kən'tɔːt] VT retorcer

contortion [kən'tɔːʃən] N contorsión *f*

contour ['kɒntʊə(r)] N contorno *m*; **c. line** línea *f* de nivel

contraband ['kɒntrəbænd] N contrabando *m*

contraception [kɒntrə'sepʃən] N anticoncepción *f*

contraceptive [kɒntrə'septɪv] ADJ & N anticonceptivo *(m)*

contract 1 VI [kən'trækt] *(shrink)* contraerse
    2 VT **(a)** *(illness, debt)* contraer **(b) to c. to do sth** *(make agreement)* firmar un contrato para hacer algo
    3 N ['kɒntrækt] contrato *m*; **to enter into a c.** hacer un contrato

contraction [kən'trækʃən] N contracción *f*

contractor [kən'træktə(r)] N contratista *mf*

contradict [kɒntrə'dɪkt] VT contradecir

contradiction [kɒntrə'dɪkʃən] N contradicción *f*; **it's a c. in terms** no tiene lógica

contradictory [kɒntrə'dɪktərɪ] ADJ contradictorio(a)

contraption [kən'træpʃən] N *Fam* cacharro *m*

contrary ['kɒntrərɪ] **1** ADJ **(a)** *(opposite)* contrario(a) **(b)** [kən'treərɪ] *(awkward)* terco(a)
    2 N **on the c.** todo lo contrario; **unless I tell you to the c.** a menos que te diga lo contrario
    3 ADV **c. to** en contra de

contrast 1 VI [kən'trɑːst] contrastar
    2 N ['kɒntrɑːst] contraste *m*

contrasting [kən'trɑːstɪŋ] ADJ opuesto(a)

contravene [kɒntrə'viːn] VT contravenir

contribute [kən'trɪbjuːt] **1** VT contribuir con, aportar

2 VI contribuir; **to c. to a newspaper** escribir para un periódico

contribution [kɒntrɪ'bjuːʃən] N **(a)** *(of money)* contribución *f*; *(of ideas etc)* aportación *f* **(b)** *Press* colaboración *f*

contributor [kən'trɪbjʊtə(r)] N *(to newspaper)* colaborador(a) *m,f*

contrive [kən'traɪv] VT inventar, idear; **to c. to do sth** buscar la forma de hacer algo

contrived [kən'traɪvd] ADJ artificial, forzado(a)

control [kən'trəʊl] **1** VT *(company, country)* controlar, regular; *(child, pupils, animal)* controlar, dominar; *(vehicle)* manejar, controlar; **to c. one's temper** controlarse
    2 N **(a)** *(power)* control *m*, dominio *m*; *(authority)* autoridad *f*; **out of c.** fuera de control; **to be in c.** estar al mando; **to be under c.** *(situation)* estar bajo control; **to go out of c.** descontrolarse; **to lose/regain c.** perder/recuperar el control **(b)** *Aut & Av (device)* mando *m*; *Rad & TV* botón *m* de control; **c. panel** tablero *m* de instrumentos; **c. room** sala *f* de control; *Av* **c. tower** torre *f* de control

controversial [kɒntrə'vɜːʃəl] ADJ controvertido(a), polémico(a)

controversy ['kɒntrəvɜːsɪ, kən'trɒvəsɪ] N polémica *f*

conurbation [kɒnɜː'beɪʃən] N conurbación *f*

convalesce [kɒnvə'les] VI convalecer

convalescence [kɒnvə'lesəns] N convalecencia *f*

convalescent [kɒnvə'lesənt] ADJ convaleciente; **c. home** clínica *f* de reposo

convene [kən'viːn] **1** VT convocar
    2 VI reunirse

convenience [kən'viːnɪəns] N conveniencia *f*, comodidad *f*; **all modern conveniences** todas las comodidades; **at your c.** cuando le convenga; **c. food** comida precocinada; *Br* **public conveniences** *(toilets)* servicio *m* público, *Esp* aseos *mpl*, *Am* baños *mpl* públicos

convenient [kən'viːnɪənt] ADJ *(time, arrangement)* conveniente, oportuno(a); *(place)* bien situado(a)

convent ['kɒnvənt] N convento *m*

convention [kən'venʃən] N convención *f*

conventional [kən'venʃənəl] ADJ convencional

converge [kən'vɜːdʒ] VI convergir

conversant [kən'vɜːsənt] ADJ *Fml* **to be c. with a subject** ser versado(a) en una materia

conversation [kɒnvə'seɪʃən] N conversación *f*, *CAm, Méx* plática *f*

conversational [kɒnvə'seɪʃənəl] ADJ coloquial

converse¹ [kən'vɜːs] VI conversar

converse² ['kɒnvɜːs] N **the c.** lo opuesto

conversely ['kɒnvɜːslɪ] ADV a la inversa

conversion [kən'vɜːʃən] N *Math & Rel* conversión *f* *(to* a; *into* en)

convert 1 VT [kən'vɜːt] convertir
2 N ['kɒnvɜːt] converso(a) m,f

convertible [kən'vɜːtəbəl] **1** ADJ convertible
2 N (car) descapotable m, Am convertible m

convex ['kɒnveks, kɒn'veks] ADJ convexo(a)

convey [kən'veɪ] VT (**a**) (carry) transportar (**b**) (sound) transmitir; (idea) comunicar

conveyor [kən'veɪə(r)] N **c. belt** cinta transportadora

convict 1 VT [kən'vɪkt] declarar culpable a, condenar
2 N ['kɒnvɪkt] presidiario(a) m,f

conviction [kən'vɪkʃən] N (**a**) (belief) creencia f, convicción f (**b**) Jur condena f

convince [kən'vɪns] VT convencer

convincing [kən'vɪnsɪŋ] ADJ convincente

convoluted ['kɒnvəluːtɪd] ADJ intrincado(a)

convoy ['kɒnvɔɪ] N convoy m

convulse [kən'vʌls] VT convulsionar; Fam **to be convulsed with laughter** troncharse de risa

convulsion [kən'vʌlʃən] N convulsión f

coo [kuː] VI (pigeon) arrullar

cook [kʊk] **1** VT (boil, bake, fry) guisar, cocinar; (dinner) preparar; Fam **to c. the books** falsificar las cuentas
2 VI (person) cocinar, guisar; (food) cocerse
3 N cocinero(a) m,f

cookbook ['kʊkbʊk] N US libro m de cocina

cooker ['kʊkə(r)] N cocina f, Col, Méx, Ven estufa f

cookery ['kʊkərɪ] N cocina f; **c. book** libro m de cocina

cookie ['kʊkɪ] N US galleta f

cooking ['kʊkɪŋ] N cocina f

cool [kuːl] **1** ADJ (**a**) (cold) fresco(a); **it's c.** hace fresco (**b**) (person) (calm) tranquilo(a); (reserved) frío(a)
2 N (**a**) (coldness) fresco m (**b**) (calm) **to lose one's c.** perder la calma
3 VT (air) refrescar; (drink) enfriar
4 ADV Fam **to play it c.** aparentar calma

▸ **cool down, cool off** VI Fig calmarse; (feelings) enfriarse

coolness ['kuːlnɪs] N (**a**) Fig (calmness) calma f; (composure) aplomo m (**b**) Fam (nerve, cheek) frescura f

coop [kuːp] N gallinero m
2 VT **to c. (up)** encerrar

co-op ['kəʊɒp] N cooperativa f

co-operate [kəʊ'ɒpəreɪt] VI cooperar

co-operation [kəʊɒpə'reɪʃən] N cooperación f

co-operative [kəʊ'ɒpərətɪv] **1** ADJ (helpful) cooperador(a)
2 N cooperativa f

co-ordinate 1 VT [kəʊ'ɔːdɪneɪt] coordinar
2 N [kəʊ'ɔːdɪnɪt] (**a**) Math coordenada f (**b**) **co-ordinates** (clothes) conjunto m

co-ordination [kəʊɔːdɪ'neɪʃən] N coordinación f

cop [kɒp] Fam **1** N (policeman) poli m
2 VT Br you'll c. it te vas a ganar una buena

▸ **cop out** VI Fam zafarse, Esp escaquearse, RP zafar

cope [kəʊp] VI arreglárselas; **to c. with** (person, work) poder con; (problem) hacer frente a

Copenhagen [kəʊpən'heɪgən] N Copenhague

copier ['kɒpɪə(r)] N (photocopying machine) fotocopiadora f

copious ['kəʊpɪəs] ADJ copioso(a), abundante

copper¹ ['kɒpə(r)] **1** N (metal) cobre m
2 ADJ (colour) cobrizo(a)

copper² ['kɒpə(r)] N Fam poli mf

coppice ['kɒpɪs], **copse** [kɒps] N arboleda f, bosquecillo m

copulate ['kɒpjʊleɪt] VI copular

copy ['kɒpɪ] **1** N (**a**) (in general) copia f (**b**) (of book) ejemplar m
2 VT & VI copiar

copycat ['kɒpɪkæt] N Fam copión(ona) m,f

copyright ['kɒpɪraɪt] N derechos mpl de autor

coral ['kɒrəl] N coral m; **c. reef** arrecife m de coral

cord [kɔːd] N (**a**) (string) cuerda f; Elec cordón m (**b**) Tex (corduroy) pana f; **cords** pantalones mpl de pana

cordial ['kɔːdɪəl] **1** ADJ cordial
2 N licor m

cordless ['kɔːdlɪs] ADJ **c. phone** teléfono inalámbrico

cordon ['kɔːdən] **1** N cordón m
2 VT **to c. off a street** acordonar una calle

corduroy ['kɔːdərɔɪ] N pana f

core [kɔː(r)] **1** N (of fruit) corazón m; Elec núcleo m; Fig **the hard c.** los incondicionales
2 VT quitarle el corazón a

coriander [kɒrɪ'ændə(r)] N culantro m

cork [kɔːk] N corcho m; **c. oak** alcornoque m

corkscrew ['kɔːkskruː] N sacacorchos m inv

corn¹ [kɔːn] N (**a**) Br (wheat) trigo m; (**b**) (maize) maíz m, Andes, RP cochlo m; **c. bread** pan m de maíz or Andes, RP choclo; **c. on the cob** mazorca f de maíz or Andes, RP choclo, Méx elote m

corn² [kɔːn] N Med callo m

corncob ['kɔːnkɒb] N mazorca f

cornea ['kɔːnɪə] N córnea f

corner ['kɔːnə(r)] **1** N (**a**) (of street) esquina f; (bend in road) curva f; **round the c.** a la vuelta de la esquina; Ftb **c. kick** córner m; Br **c. shop** or US **store** tienda pequeña de barrio (**b**) (of room) rincón m
2 VT (enemy) arrinconar (**b**) Com acaparar
3 VI Aut tomar una curva

cornerstone ['kɔːnəstəʊn] N piedra f angular

cornet [Br 'kɔːnɪt, US kɔː'net] N (**a**) Mus corneta f (**b**) Br (for ice cream) cucurucho m

cornflakes ['kɔːnfleɪks] NPL copos mpl de maíz, cornflakes mpl

cornflour ['kɔ:nflaʊə(r)], *US* **cornstarch** ['kɔ:rnstɑ:rtʃ] N harina *f* de maíz *or Andes, RP* choclo, maicena® *f*

Cornwall ['kɔ:nwəl] N Cornualles

corny ['kɔ:nɪ] ADJ (**cornier, corniest**) *Fam* gastado(a)

corollary [kə'rɒlərɪ] N corolario *m*

coronary ['kɒrənərɪ] ADJ coronario(a); **c. thrombosis** trombosis coronaria

coronation [kɒrə'neɪʃən] N coronación *f*

coroner ['kɒrənə(r)] N juez *mf* de instrucción

corporal[1] ['kɔ:pərəl] ADJ corporal; **c. punishment** castigo *m* corporal

corporal[2] ['kɔ:pərəl] N *Mil* cabo *m*

corporate ['kɔ:pərɪt] ADJ corporativo(a)

corporation [kɔ:pə'reɪʃən] N (**a**) *(business)* sociedad anónima (**b**) *(of city)* ayuntamiento *m*

corps [kɔ:(r)] N *(pl corps* [kɔ:z]) cuerpo *m*

corpse [kɔ:ps] N cadáver *m*

corpulent ['kɔ:pjʊlənt] ADJ corpulento(a)

corpuscle ['kɔ:pʌsəl] N corpúsculo *m*

corral [kə'rɑ:l] N *US* corral *m*

correct [kə'rekt] **1** VT corregir
2 ADJ (**a**) *(amount, figure)* exacto(a); *(information, use, spelling)* correcto(a) (**b**) *(person, behaviour)* correcto(a)

correction [kə'rekʃən] N corrección *f*

correlation [kɒrə'leɪʃən] N correlación *f*

correspond [kɒrɪ'spɒnd] VI (**a**) *(be in accordance, be equivalent)* corresponder (**with** *or* **to** con *or* a), corresponderse (**with** *or* **to** con) (**b**) *(by letter)* mantener correspondencia (**with** con)

correspondence [kɒrɪ'spɒndəns] N correspondencia *f*; **c. course** curso *m* por correspondencia

correspondent [kɒrɪ'spɒndənt] N *Press* corresponsal *mf*; **special c.** enviado(a) *m,f* especial

corresponding [kɒrɪ'spɒndɪŋ] ADJ correspondiente

corridor ['kɒrɪdɔ:(r)] N pasillo *m*

corroborate [kə'rɒbəreɪt] VT corroborar

corrode [kə'rəʊd] **1** VT corroer
2 VI corroerse

corrosion [kə'rəʊʒən] N corrosión *f*

corrugated ['kɒrʊgeɪtɪd] ADJ **c. iron** hierro ondulado

corrupt [kə'rʌpt] **1** ADJ *(person)* corrompido(a), corrupto(a); *(actions)* deshonesto(a)
2 VT & VI corromper

corruption [kə'rʌpʃən] N corrupción *f*

corset ['kɔ:sɪt] N *(garment)* faja *f*

Corsica ['kɔ:sɪkə] N Córcega

cortège [kɔ:'teɪʒ] N cortejo *m*, comitiva *f*

cosh [kɒʃ] N *Br* porra *f*

cosmetic [kɒz'metɪk] **1** N cosmético *m*
2 ADJ cosmético(a); **c. surgery** cirugía plástica

cosmic ['kɒzmɪk] ADJ cósmico(a)

cosmonaut ['kɒzmənɔ:t] N cosmonauta *mf*

cosmopolitan [kɒzmə'pɒlɪtən] ADJ cosmopolita

cosset ['kɒsɪt] VT mimar

cost [kɒst] **1** N *(price)* costo *m*, *Esp* coste *m*; **c. of living** costo *or Esp* coste de la vida; **to count the c.** considerar las desventajas; **at all costs** a toda costa
2 VT & VI *(pt & pp cost)* costar, valer; **how much does it c.?** ¿cuánto cuesta?; **whatever it costs** cueste lo que cueste
3 VT *(pt & pp costed)* *Com & Ind* calcular el costo *or Esp* coste de

co-star ['kəʊstɑ:(r)] N *Cin & Th* coprotagonista *mf*

Costa Rica [kɒstə'ri:kə] N Costa Rica

Costa Rican [kɒstə'ri:kən] ADJ & N costarricense *(mf)*

cost-effective [kɒstɪ'fektɪv] ADJ rentable

costly ['kɒstlɪ] ADJ (**costlier, costliest**) costoso(a)

costume ['kɒstju:m] N traje *m*; **(swimming) c.** traje *m* de baño, *Esp* bañador *m*, *RP* malla *f*; **c. jewellery** bisutería *f*

cosy ['kəʊzɪ] ADJ (**cosier, cosiest**) *(atmosphere)* acogedor(a); *(bed)* calentito(a); **it's c. in here** aquí se está bien

cot [kɒt] N (**a**) *Br (for child)* cuna *f* (**b**) *US (folding bed)* catre *m*, cama *f* plegable

cottage ['kɒtɪdʒ] N casa *f* de campo; **c. cheese** queso fresco; **c. industry** industria casera; *Br* **c. pie** = pastel de carne picada y puré de *Esp* patata *or Am* papa

cotton ['kɒtən] N algodón *m*, *Am* cotón *m*; **a c. shirt** una camisa de algodón; **c. bud** bastoncillo *m* (de algodón); *US* **c. candy** algodón dulce; *Br* **c. wool** algodón (hidrófilo)

▶ **cotton on** VI *Fam* enterarse, *Esp* coscarse, *RP* captar

couch [kaʊtʃ] N sofá *m*; *(in surgery)* camilla *f*

couchette [ku:'ʃet] N *Rail* litera *f*

cough [kɒf] **1** VI toser
2 N tos *f*; **c. drop** pastilla *f* para la tos; **c. mixture** jarabe *m* para la tos

▶ **cough up** VT SEP *Fam (money)* poner, *Esp* apoquinar, *RP* garpar

could [kʊd] VAUX *see* **can**[1]

council ['kaʊnsəl] N *(body)* consejo *m*; *Br* **c. house** vivienda *f* de protección oficial; **town c.** consejo municipal, ayuntamiento *m*

councillor, *US* **councilor** ['kaʊnsələ(r)] N concejal *mf*

counsel ['kaʊnsəl] **1** N (**a**) *(advice)* consejo *m* (**b**) *Jur* abogado(a) *m,f*
2 VT aconsejar

counselling ['kaʊnsəlɪŋ] N apoyo m psicológico, orientación f psicológica

counsellor, US **counselor** ['kaʊnsələ(r)] N (**a**) (adviser) asesor(a) m,f (**b**) US Jur abogado(a) m,f

count¹ [kaʊnt] **1** VT (**a**) (enumerate) contar (**b**) Fig to c. oneself lucky considerarse afortunado(a)
2 VI contar; that doesn't c. eso no vale; to c. to ten contar hasta diez
3 N (**a**) (calculation) cuenta f; (of votes) recuento m (**b**) Jur cargo m
► **count on** VT INSEP contar con

count² [kaʊnt] N (nobleman) conde m

countdown ['kaʊntdaʊn] N cuenta f atrás

countenance ['kaʊntɪnəns] **1** N semblante m, rostro m
2 VT aprobar

counter¹ ['kaʊntə(r)] N (**a**) (in shop) mostrador m; (in bank) ventanilla f (**b**) (in board games) ficha f

counter² ['kaʊntə(r)] N contador m

counter³ ['kaʊntə(r)] **1** ADV c. to en contra de
2 VT (attack) contestar a; (trend) contrarrestar
3 VI contestar

counteract [kaʊntər'ækt] VT contrarrestar

counterattack ['kaʊntərətæk] N contraataque m

counter-clockwise ['kaʊntə'klɒkwaɪz] ADV US en sentido opuesto al de las agujas del reloj

counterfeit ['kaʊntəfɪt] **1** ADJ falsificado(a); c. coin moneda falsa
2 N falsificación f
3 VT falsificar

counterfoil ['kaʊntəfɔɪl] N Br (of cheque) matriz f

countermand [kaʊntə'mɑːnd] VT (command) revocar; Com (order) anular

counterpart ['kaʊntəpɑːt] N homólogo(a) m,f

counterproductive [kaʊntəprə'dʌktɪv] ADJ contraproducente

countersign ['kaʊntəsaɪn] VT refrendar

countess ['kaʊntɪs] N condesa f

countless ['kaʊntlɪs] ADJ innumerable, incontable

country ['kʌntrɪ] N (**a**) (state) país m; native c. patria f (**b**) (rural area) campo m; c. dancing baile m popular

countryman ['kʌntrɪmən] N (**a**) (rural) hombre m del campo (**b**) (compatriot) compatriota m

countryside ['kʌntrɪsaɪd] N (area) campo m; (scenery) paisaje m

county ['kaʊntɪ] N condado m

coup [kuː] N (pl coups [kuːz]) golpe m; c. d'état golpe de estado

couple ['kʌpəl] **1** N (**a**) (of people) pareja f; a married c. un matrimonio (**b**) (of things) par m; Fam a c. of times un par de veces
2 VT (wagons) enganchar

coupling ['kʌplɪŋ] N Rail enganche m

coupon ['kuːpɒn] N (**a**) (for discount, rationing) cupón m (**b**) Br football or pools c. boleto m (de las quinielas)

courage ['kʌrɪdʒ] N coraje m, valentía f

courageous [kə'reɪdʒəs] ADJ valeroso(a), valiente

courgette [kʊə'ʒet] N Br calabacín m, CSur zapallito m, Méx calabacita f

courier ['kʊrɪə(r)] N (**a**) (messenger) mensajero(a) m,f; c. service mensajería f (**b**) (guide) guía mf turístico(a)

course [kɔːs] N (**a**) (of river) curso m; Naut & Av rumbo m (**b**) Fig desarrollo m; in the c. of construction en vías de construcción; in the c. of time con el tiempo (**c**) (series) ciclo m; a c. of treatment un tratamiento (**d**) Educ curso m; Univ asignatura f (**e**) (for golf) Esp campo m, Am cancha f; (for horse-racing) hipódromo m (**f**) Culin plato m (**g**) of c. claro, por supuesto; of c. not! ¡claro que no!

court [kɔːt] **1** N (**a**) Jur tribunal m; c. martial consejo m de guerra; c. order orden f judicial (**b**) (royal) corte f (**c**) Sport pista f, cancha f
2 VT (woman) hacer la corte a; Fig to c. danger buscar el peligro; Fig to c. disaster exponerse al desastre
3 VI (couple) tener relaciones

courteous ['kɜːtɪəs] ADJ cortés

courtesy ['kɜːtɪsɪ] N cortesía f; by c. of por cortesía de

courthouse ['kɔːthaʊs] N US palacio m de justicia

courtier ['kɔːtɪə(r)] N cortesano(a) m,f

court-martial [kɔːt'mɑːʃəl] VT hacer un consejo de guerra a

courtroom ['kɔːtruːm] N sala f de justicia

courtyard ['kɔːtjɑːd] N patio m

cousin ['kʌzən] N primo(a) m,f; first c. primo(a) hermano(a)

cove [kəʊv] N cala f, ensenada f

covenant ['kʌvənənt] N convenio m, pacto m

cover ['kʌvə(r)] **1** VT (**a**) (person, object) cubrir (with de); (with lid) tapar; (book) forrar (**b**) (hide) disimular (**c**) (protect) abrigar (**d**) (distance) recorrer (**e**) Press (story) cubrir (**f**) (deal with) abarcar (**g**) (include) incluir
2 VI to c. for sb sustituir a algn
3 N (**a**) (lid) tapa f; (on bed) manta f, Am frazada f, cobija f; (of chair etc) funda f (**b**) (of book) tapa f; (of magazine) portada f (**c**) (in restaurant) cubierto m (**d**) (protection) abrigo m; to take c. abrigarse; under c. al abrigo; (indoors) bajo techo
► **cover up** VT SEP (**a**) (person, object) cubrir; (with a lid) tapar (**b**) (conceal) ocultar
2 VI (**a**) (person) abrigarse (**b**) to c. up for sb encubrir a algn

coverage ['kʌvərɪdʒ] N cobertura f

coveralls ['kʌvərɔːlz] NPL US mono m (de trabajo), Am overol m

covering [ˈkʌvərɪŋ] **1** N *(on furniture)* funda *f*; *(of snow, dust, chocolate)* capa *f*
  2 ADJ *(letter)* explicatorio(a)

covert [ˈkʌvət] ADJ disimulado(a), secreto(a)

cover-up [ˈkʌvərʌp] N encubrimiento *m*

covet [ˈkʌvɪt] VT codiciar

cow¹ [kaʊ] N vaca *f*; *Pej (woman)* arpía *f*, bruja *f*

cow² [kaʊ] VT intimidar

coward [ˈkaʊəd] N cobarde *mf*

cowardice [ˈkaʊədɪs] N cobardía *f*

cowardly [ˈkaʊədlɪ] ADJ cobarde

cowboy [ˈkaʊbɔɪ] N vaquero *m*

cower [ˈkaʊə(r)] VI *(with fear)* encogerse

cox [kɒks] N timonel *m*

coy [kɔɪ] ADJ **(coyer, coyest)** *(shy)* tímido(a); *(demure)* coquetón(ona)

cozy [ˈkəʊzɪ] ADJ *US* = **cosy**

CPA [siːpiːˈeɪ] N *US (abbr* **certified public accountant)** *Esp* censor(a) *m,f* jurado(a) de cuentas, *Am* contador(a) *m,f* público(a)

crab [kræb] N **(a)** *(crustacean)* cangrejo *m*, *Am* jaiba *f* **(b) c. apple** manzana *f* silvestre

crack [kræk] **1** VT **(a)** *(cup)* partir; *(bone)* fracturar; *(nut)* cascar; *(safe)* forzar **(b)** *(whip)* hacer restallar **(c)** *Fig (problem)* dar con la solución de; *(joke)* contar
  2 VI **(a)** *(glass)* partirse; *(wall)* agrietarse **(b)** *(whip)* restallar **(c)** *Fam* **to get cracking on sth** ponerse a hacer algo
  3 N **(a)** *(in cup)* raja *f*; *(in wall, ground)* grieta *f* **(b)** *(of whip)* restallido *m*; *(of gun)* detonación *f* **(c)** *Fam (drug)* crack *m*
  4 ADJ *Fam* de primera
  ▸ **crack down on** VT INSEP atajar con mano dura
  ▸ **crack up** VI *Fam Fig (go mad)* desquiciarse; *(with laughter)* partirse de risa, *Méx* atacarse de risa

cracker [ˈkrækə(r)] N **(a)** *(biscuit)* galleta salada **(b)** *(firework)* petardo *m*

crackle [ˈkrækəl] VI *(twigs)* crujir; *(fire)* crepitar

cradle [ˈkreɪdəl] N *(baby's)* cuna *f*

craft [krɑːft] N **(a)** *(occupation)* oficio *m*; *(art)* arte *m*; *(skill)* destreza *f* **(b)** *(cunning)* maña *f* **(c)** *Naut* embarcación *f*

craftsman [ˈkrɑːftsmən] N artesano *m*

craftsmanship [ˈkrɑːftsmənʃɪp] N arte *f*

crafty [ˈkrɑːftɪ] ADJ **(craftier, craftiest)** astuto(a)

crag [kræg] N peña *f*, peñasco *m*

cram [kræm] **1** VT atiborrar; **crammed with** atestado(a) de
  2 VI *Fam Educ* matarse estudiando, *Esp* empollar, *RP* tragar

cramp¹ [kræmp] N *Med* calambre *m*; **cramps** retortijones *mpl*

cramp² [kræmp] VT *(development etc)* poner trabas a

cramped [kræmpt] ADJ *(room)* estrecho(a); *(writing)* apretado(a)

cranberry [ˈkrænbərɪ] N arándano *m*

crane [kreɪn] **1** N **(a)** *Zool* grulla *f* común **(b)** *(device)* grúa *f*
  2 VT estirar

crank [kræŋk] N **(a)** *Tech* manivela *f* **(b)** *Fam (eccentric)* rarito(a) *m,f*

crankshaft [ˈkræŋkʃɑːft] N árbol *m* del cigüeñal

cranny [ˈkrænɪ] N *Fig* **in every nook and c.** en todos los rincones

crap [kræp] N *very Fam* **(a)** *(excrement)* mierda *f* **(b)** *(worthless things)* mierdas *fpl*, porquerías *fpl*; *(nonsense) Esp* gilipolleces *fpl*, *Esp* paridas *fpl*, *Col, Méx* pendejadas *fpl*, *RP* pelotudeces *fpl*

crash [kræʃ] **1** VT **to c. one's car** tener un accidente con el coche *orAm* carro *or CSur* auto
  2 VI **(a)** *(car, plane)* estrellarse; *(collide)* chocar; **to c. into** estrellarse contra **(b)** *(business, economy)* quebrar **(c)** *Comput* bloquearse, colgarse
  3 N **(a)** *(noise)* estrépito *m* **(b)** *(collision)* choque *m*; **car/plane c.** accidente *m* de coche *orAm* carro *or CSur* auto/de avión; *Fig* **c. course** curso *m* intensivo; **c. helmet** casco *m* (protector) **(c)** *(financial)* quiebra financiera), crac *m*

crash-land [kræʃˈlænd] VI hacer un aterrizaje forzoso

crass [kræs] ADJ *(person)* grosero(a); *(error)* garrafal

crate [kreɪt] N caja *f*, cajón *m (para embalaje)*

crater [ˈkreɪtə(r)] N cráter *m*

cravat [krəˈvæt] N pañuelo *m (de hombre)*

crave [kreɪv] VI **to c. for sth** ansiar algo

craving [ˈkreɪvɪŋ] N ansia *f*; *(in pregnancy)* antojo *m*

crawfish [ˈkrɔːfɪʃ] N langosta *f*

crawl [krɔːl] **1** VI *(baby)* gatear; *(vehicle)* avanzar lentamente; *Fig* **to c. to sb** arrastrarse a los pies de algn
  2 N *(swimming)* crol *m*

crayfish [ˈkreɪfɪʃ] N cangrejo *m* de río

crayon [ˈkreɪɒn] N cera *f*

craze [kreɪz] N manía *f*; *(fashion)* moda *f*; **it's the latest c.** es el último grito

crazy [ˈkreɪzɪ] ADJ **(crazier, craziest)** *Fam* loco(a), chalado(a)

creak [kriːk] VI *(floor)* crujir; *(hinge)* chirriar

cream [kriːm] **1** N **(a)** *(of milk) Esp* nata *f*, *Am* crema *f* (de leche); **c.-coloured** color crema; *Fig* **the c.** la flor y nata; **c. cheese** queso blanco para untar **(b)** *(cosmetic)* crema *f*
  2 VT **(a)** *(milk)* desnatar **(b)** *Culin* batir; **creamed potatoes** puré *m* de patatas *or Am* papas

creamy [ˈkriːmɪ] ADJ **(creamier, creamiest)** cremoso(a)

crease [kriːs] **1** N *(wrinkle)* arruga *f*; *(fold)* pliegue *m*; *(on trousers)* raya *f*
  2 VT *(clothes)* arrugar
  3 VI arrugarse

create [kri:'eɪt] VT crear

creation [kri:'eɪʃən] N creación f

creative [kri:'eɪtɪv] ADJ (person) creativo(a)

creativity [kri:eɪ'tɪvɪtɪ] N creatividad f

creator [kri:'eɪtə(r)] N creador(a) m,f

creature ['kri:tʃə(r)] N (animal) criatura f

crèche [kreɪʃ, kreʃ] N Br guardería f (infantil)

credence ['kri:dəns] N **to give c. to** dar crédito a

credentials [krɪ'denʃəlz] NPL credenciales fpl

credibility [kredɪ'bɪlɪtɪ] N credibilidad f

credible ['kredɪbəl] ADJ creíble

credit ['kredɪt] **1** N (a) Fin crédito m; **on c.** a crédito; **c. card** tarjeta f de crédito (**b**) **to give c. to sb for sth** reconocer algo a algn (**c**) (benefit) honor m; **to be a c. to** hacer honor a (**d**) Cin & TV **credits** créditos mpl

2 VT (**a**) Fin abonar (**b**) (believe) creer (**c**) Fig atribuir; **he is credited with having ...** se le atribuye haber ...

creditor ['kredɪtə(r)] N acreedor(a) m,f

creed [kri:d] N credo m

creek [kri:k] N (**a**) Br cala f (**b**) US, Austr riachuelo m

creep [kri:p] **1** VI (pt & pp **crept**) (animal, person) andar silenciosamente; (plant) trepar; **to c. up on sb** sorprender a algn

2 N Fam (unpleasant person) asqueroso(a) m,f; Br (obsequious person) pelota mf, Am arrastrado(a) m,f, Méx lambiscón(ona) m,f, RP chupamedias mf inv

creeper ['kri:pə(r)] N Bot trepadora f

creepy ['kri:pɪ] ADJ (**creepier, creepiest**) Fam espeluznante

cremate [krɪ'meɪt] VT incinerar

cremation [krɪ'meɪʃən] N incineración f, cremación f

crematorium [kremə'tɔ:rɪəm] N crematorio m

crêpe [kreɪp] N (**a**) Tex crepé m (**b**) **c. paper** papel m crespón

crept [krept] PT & PP of **creep**

crescendo [krɪ'ʃendəʊ] N crescendo m

crescent ['kresənt] **1** N (shape) medialuna f; Br (street) calle f en medialuna

2 ADJ creciente

cress [kres] N berro m

crest [krest] N (**a**) (of cock, wave) cresta f; (on helmet) penacho m; (of hill) cima f (**b**) (heraldic) blasón m

crestfallen ['krestfɔ:lən] ADJ abatido(a)

Crete [kri:t] N Creta

cretin ['kretɪn] N cretino(a) m,f

crevasse [krɪ'væs] N grieta f, fisura f

crevice ['krevɪs] N grieta f, hendedura f

crew [kru:] N Av & Naut tripulación f; **c. cut** corte m al rape; **c.-neck sweater** jersey m con cuello redondo

crib [krɪb] **1** N (**a**) (manger) pesebre m (**b**) (for baby) cuna f (**c**) Fam (in exam) Esp, Ven chuleta f,

Arg machete m, Col, Méx acordeón m

2 VT Fam (**a**) (copy) copiar (**b**) (steal) quitar

crick [krɪk] N Fam **a c. in the neck** una tortícolis

cricket¹ ['krɪkɪt] N (insect) grillo m

cricket² ['krɪkɪt] N Sport cricket m

crikey ['kraɪkɪ] INTERJ Fam Old-fashioned ¡caramba!

crime [kraɪm] N delincuencia f; (offence) delito m

criminal ['krɪmɪnəl] ADJ & N criminal (mf); **c. law** derecho m penal; **c. record** antecedentes mpl penales

crimson ['krɪmzən] ADJ & N carmesí (m)

cringe [krɪndʒ] VI abatirse, encogerse

crinkle ['krɪŋkəl] VT fruncir, arrugar

cripple ['krɪpəl] **1** N lisiado(a) m,f, mutilado(a) m,f

2 VT (person) dejar inválido(a), lisiar; Fig (industry, system) deteriorar, arruinar

crisis ['kraɪsɪs] N (pl **crises** ['kraɪsi:z]) crisis f inv

crisp [krɪsp] **1** ADJ (**a**) (pastry, bacon) crujiente; (apple, lettuce) fresco(a) (**b**) (clothing, linen) fresco(a); (banknote) nuevo(a) (**c**) (air, breeze) fresco(a) (**d**) (style) conciso(a)

2 N Br **crisps** patatas or Am papas fritas (de bolsa)

crisscross ['krɪskrɒs] N líneas entrecruzadas

criterion [kraɪ'tɪərɪən] N (pl **criteria** [kraɪ'tɪərɪə]) criterio m

critic ['krɪtɪk] N Art & Th crítico(a) m,f

critical ['krɪtɪkəl] ADJ crítico(a)

critically ['krɪtɪkəlɪ] ADV críticamente; **c. ill** gravemente enfermo(a)

criticism ['krɪtɪsɪzəm] N crítica f

criticize ['krɪtɪsaɪz] VT criticar

croak [krəʊk] VI (frog) croar; (raven) graznar; (person) hablar con voz ronca

Croat ['krəʊæt] **1** ADJ croata

2 N (**a**) (person) croata mf (**b**) (language) croata m

Croatia [krəʊ'eɪʃə] N Croacia

Croatian [krəʊ'eɪʃən] ADJ & N = **Croat**

crochet ['krəʊʃeɪ] N ganchillo m, Col, CSur crochet m, Méx gancho m

crockery ['krɒkərɪ] N loza f

crocodile ['krɒkədaɪl] N cocodrilo m

crocus ['krəʊkəs] N azafrán m

crony ['krəʊnɪ] N compinche mf

crook [krʊk] **1** N (**a**) (of shepherd) cayado m (**b**) Fam caco m

2 VT (arm) doblar

crooked ['krʊkɪd] ADJ (**a**) (stick, picture) torcido(a); (path) tortuoso(a) (**b**) Fam (dishonest) deshonesto(a)

crop [krɒp] **1** N (**a**) (variety) cultivo m; (harvest) cosecha f (**b**) (whip) fusta f

2 VT (hair) rapar; (grass) cortar

▸ **crop up** VI Fam surgir, presentarse

croquet ['krəʊkeɪ] N croquet m

croquette ['krɒ'ket] N *Culin* croqueta *f*

cross [krɒs] 1 N (a) *(religious symbol)* cruz *f* (b) *(breeds)* cruce *m, Am* cruza *f*
2 VT (a) *(go across)* cruzar (b) *Rel* to c. oneself hacer la señal de la cruz; *Fam* c. my heart! ¡te lo juro!
3 VI *(pass over)* cruzar; *(roads)* cruzarse; to c. over cruzar
4 ADJ *(annoyed)* esp *Esp* enfadado(a), esp *Am* enojado(a)
► **cross off, cross out** VT SEP tachar, rayar

crossbar ['krɒsbɑː(r)] N travesaño *m*

cross-country 1 ADJ ['krɒskʌntrɪ] c. race cros *m*
2 ADV [krɒs'kʌntrɪ] campo través

cross-examine [krɒsɪg'zæmɪn] VT interrogar

cross-eyed ['krɒsaɪd] ADJ bizco(a)

crossfire ['krɒsfaɪə(r)] N *also Fig* fuego cruzado

crossing ['krɒsɪŋ] N cruce *m; pedestrian c.* paso *m* de peatones; **sea c.** travesía *f*

cross-legged [krɒs'leg(ɪ)d] ADJ con las piernas cruzadas

cross-reference [krɒs'refərəns] N remisión *f*

crossroads ['krɒsrəʊdz] N cruce *m; Fig* encrucijada *f*

cross-section ['krɒs'sekʃən] N sección *f* transversal

crosswalk ['krɒswɔːk] N *US* paso *m* de peatones

crosswind ['krɒswɪnd] N viento *m* lateral

crossword ['krɒswɜːd] N c. (puzzle) crucigrama *m*

crotch [krɒtʃ] N entrepierna *f*

crotchet ['krɒtʃɪt] N *Br Mus* negra *f*

crotchety ['krɒtʃɪtɪ] ADJ *Fam* gruñón(ona)

crouch [kraʊtʃ] VI to c. (down) agacharse

crow[1] [krəʊ] N cuervo *m; Fig* as the c. flies en línea recta; **c.'s-feet** patas *fpl* de gallo

crow[2] [krəʊ] 1 VI (a) *(cock)* cantar; *Fig* to c. over sth jactarse de algo (b) *(baby)* balbucir
2 N *(of cock)* canto *m*

crowbar ['krəʊbɑː(r)] N palanca *f*

crowd [kraʊd] 1 N muchedumbre *f; Fam (gang)* pandilla *f, Méx* bola *f, RP* barra *f*; **the c.** el populacho
2 VT *(streets)* llenar
3 VI apiñarse; to c. in/out entrar/salir en tropel

crowded ['kraʊdɪd] ADJ atestado(a), lleno(a)

crown [kraʊn] 1 N (a) *(of king)* corona *f;* **the c. jewels** las joyas de la corona (b) *(of head)* coronilla *f*
2 VT coronar

crucial ['kruːʃəl] ADJ decisivo(a)

crucifix ['kruːsɪfɪks] N crucifijo *m*

crucifixion [kruːsɪ'fɪkʃən] N crucifixión *f*

crucify ['kruːsɪfaɪ] VT crucificar

crude [kruːd] ADJ (a) *(manners, style)* tosco(a), grosero(a); *(tool)* primitivo(a) (b) **c. oil** crudo *m*

cruel [kruːəl] ADJ cruel (**to** con)

cruelty ['kruːəltɪ] N crueldad *f* (**to** hacia)

cruet ['kruːɪt] N **c. set** vinagreras *fpl*

cruise [kruːz] 1 VI (a) *Naut* hacer un crucero (b) *Aut* viajar a velocidad constante; *Av* viajar a velocidad de crucero
2 N (a) *Naut* crucero *m* (b) **c. missile** misil teledirigido

cruiser ['kruːzə(r)] N *(barco m)* crucero *m*

crumb [krʌm] N miga *f*, migaja *f*

crumble ['krʌmbəl] 1 VT desmigar
2 VI *(wall)* desmoronarse; *Fig (hopes)* desvanecerse

crumbly ['krʌmblɪ] ADJ (**crumblier, crumbliest**) que se desmigaja

crumpet ['krʌmpɪt] N = torta pequeña que se come con mantequilla

crumple ['krʌmpəl] VT arrugar

crunch [krʌntʃ] 1 VT *(food)* ronchar; *(with feet)*
2 N *Fam* when it comes to the c. a la hora de la verdad

crunchy ['krʌntʃɪ] ADJ (**crunchier, crunchiest**) crujiente

crusade [kruː'seɪd] N cruzada *f*

crush [krʌʃ] 1 VT (a) *(squash) (person, thing)* estrujar, aplastar; *(grapes, garlic)* prensar, aplastar (b) *(squeeze, press)* apretujar (c) *(wrinkle)* arrugar (d) *(opponent, revolt)* aplastar, destrozar
2 N (a) *(of people)* gentío *m* (b) **orange c.** naranjada *f*

crushing ['krʌʃɪŋ] ADJ *Fig (defeat, reply)* aplastante

crust [krʌst] N corteza *f*

crutch [krʌtʃ] N *Med* muleta *f; Fig* apoyo *m*

crux [krʌks] N **the c. of the matter** el quid de la cuestión

cry [kraɪ] 1 VI *(pt & pp* **cried**) (a) *(shout, call)* gritar (b) *(weep)* llorar
2 VT gritar; *Fig* to c. wolf dar una falsa alarma
3 N (a) *(call)* grito *m* (b) *(weep)* llanto *m*
► **cry off** VI *Fam* rajarse
► **cry out** VI gritar; to c. out for sth pedir algo a gritos

crying ['kraɪɪŋ] ADJ it's a c. shame es una vergüenza

crypt [krɪpt] N cripta *f*

cryptic ['krɪptɪk] ADJ enigmático(a)

crystal ['krɪstəl] N cristal *m*

crystal-clear [krɪstəl'klɪə(r)] ADJ claro(a) como el agua

crystallize ['krɪstəlaɪz] 1 VT cristalizar
2 VI cristalizar

cub [kʌb] N (a) *(animal)* cachorro *m* (b) *(junior scout)* niño *m* explorador

Cuba ['kjuːbə] N Cuba

Cuban ['kjuːbən] ADJ & N cubano(a) *(m,f)*

cubbyhole ['kʌbɪhəʊl] N cuchitril *m*

cube [kju:b] 1 N cubo m; *(of sugar)* terrón m; **c. root** raíz f cúbica
2 VT *Math* elevar al cubo

cubic ['kju:bɪk] ADJ cúbico(a)

cubicle ['kju:bɪkəl] N cubículo m; *(at swimming pool)* caseta f

cuckoo ['kuku:] 1 N cuco m; **c. clock** reloj m de cuco, *RP* reloj m cucú
2 ADJ *Fam (mad)* **to be c.** estar pirado(a), *Méx* estar zafado(a)

cucumber ['kju:kʌmbə(r)] N pepino m

cuddle ['kʌdəl] 1 VT abrazar
2 VI abrazarse

cuddly ['kʌdlɪ] ADJ **(cuddlier, cuddliest) c. toy** muñeco m de peluche

cue¹ [kju:] N *Th* pie m

cue² [kju:] N *(in billiards)* taco m; **c. ball** bola blanca

cuff¹ [kʌf] N *(of sleeve)* puño m; *US (of trousers)* dobladillo m; *Fig* **to do sth off the c.** improvisar algo

cuff² [kʌf] 1 VT *(hit)* dar un sopapo *or Am* una cachetada a
2 N *(blow)* cachete m, cate m

cufflinks ['kʌflɪŋks] NPL gemelos mpl

cul-de-sac ['kʌldəsæk] N callejón m sin salida

culinary ['kʌlɪnərɪ] ADJ culinario(a)

cull [kʌl] VT **(a)** *(choose)* escoger **(b)** *(animals)* eliminar

culminate ['kʌlmɪneɪt] VI **to c. in** terminar en

culmination [kʌlmɪ'neɪʃən] N culminación f, punto m culminante

culottes [kju:'lɒts] NPL falda f *or Am* pollera f pantalón

culprit ['kʌlprɪt] N culpable mf

cult [kʌlt] N culto m; **c. figure** ídolo m

cultivate ['kʌltɪveɪt] VT cultivar

cultivated ['kʌltɪveɪtɪd] ADJ *(person)* culto(a)

cultivation [kʌltɪ'veɪʃən] N cultivo m (de la tierra)

cultural ['kʌltʃərəl] ADJ cultural

culture ['kʌltʃə(r)] N cultura f

cultured ['kʌltʃəd] ADJ = **cultivated**

cumbersome ['kʌmbəsəm] ADJ *(awkward)* incómodo(a); *(bulky)* voluminoso(a)

cum(m)in ['kʌmɪn] N comino m

cumulative ['kju:mjʊlətɪv] ADJ acumulativo(a)

cunning ['kʌnɪŋ] 1 ADJ astuto(a)
2 N astucia f

cup [kʌp] 1 N taza f; *Sport* copa f; **C. Final** final f de copa; **c. tie** partido m de copa
2 VT *(hands)* ahuecar

cupboard ['kʌbəd] N armario m; *(on wall)* alacena f

cupcake ['kʌpkeɪk] N *(cake)* ≃ magdalena f

curable ['kjʊərəbəl] ADJ curable

curate ['kjʊərɪt] N cura m coadjutor

curator [kjʊə'reɪtə(r)] N conservador(a) m,f

curb [kɜ:b] 1 N **(a)** *(limit)* freno m **(b)** *US (kerb)* bordillo m (de la acera), *Chile* solera f, *Col, Perú* sardinel m, *CSur* cordón m (de la vereda), *Méx* borde m (de la banqueta)
2 VT *(horse)* refrenar; *Fig (public spending)* contener

curd [kɜ:d] N cuajada f

curdle ['kɜ:dəl] VI cuajarse

cure [kjʊə(r)] 1 VT curar
2 N *(remedy)* cura f, remedio m

curfew ['kɜ:fju:] N toque m de queda

curiosity [kjʊərɪ'ɒsɪtɪ] N curiosidad f

curious ['kjʊərɪəs] ADJ **(a)** *(inquisitive)* curioso(a) **(b)** *(odd)* extraño(a)

curl [kɜ:l] 1 VT *(hair)* rizar; *(lip)* fruncir
2 VI rizarse
3 N *(of hair)* rizo m, *Andes, RP* rulo m; *(of smoke)* espiral f
▶ **curl up** VI enroscarse

curler ['kɜ:lə(r)] N *(for hair)* rulo m, *Chile* tubo m, *RP* rulero m, *Ven* rollo m

curly ['kɜ:lɪ] ADJ **(curlier, curliest)** rizado(a), *Chile, Col* crespo(a), *Méx* quebrado(a), *RP* enrulado(a)

currant ['kʌrənt] N pasa f (de Corinto)

currency ['kʌrənsɪ] N **(a)** *Fin* moneda f; **foreign c.** divisa f **(b)** *(acceptance)* **to gain c.** cobrar fuerza

current ['kʌrənt] 1 ADJ **(a)** *(opinion)* general; *(word)* en uso; *(year)* en curso; *Br* **c. account** cuenta f corriente; **c. affairs** actualidad (política); *Fin* **c. assets** activo m disponible **(b) the c. issue** *(of magazine, newspaper)* el último número
2 N corriente f

currently ['kʌrəntlɪ] ADV actualmente

curriculum [kə'rɪkjʊləm] N *(pl* **curricula** [kə'rɪkjʊlə]*)* plan m de estudios; *esp Br* **c. vitae** currículum m (vitae)

curry¹ ['kʌrɪ] N curry m; **chicken c.** pollo m al curry

curry² ['kʌrɪ] VT **to c. favour with** congraciarse con

curse [kɜ:s] 1 N maldición f; *(oath)* palabrota f; *Fig* azote m
2 VT maldecir
3 VI blasfemar

cursor ['kɜ:sə(r)] N cursor m

cursory ['kɜ:sərɪ] ADJ rápido(a)

curt [kɜ:t] ADJ brusco(a), seco(a)

curtail [kɜ:'teɪl] VT *(expenses)* reducir; *(text)* acortar

curtain ['kɜ:tən] N cortina f; *Th* telón m; *Fig* velo m

curts(e)y ['kɜ:tsɪ] 1 N reverencia f
2 VI hacer una reverencia **(to** a)

curve [kɜ:v] 1 N curva f
2 VT encorvar
3 VI torcerse, describir una curva

cushion ['kʊʃən] **1** N cojín m; *(large)* almohadón m; *(of billiard table)* banda f
2 VT *Fig* amortiguar; *(person)* proteger

cushy ['kʊʃɪ] ADJ (**cushier, cushiest**) *Fam* fácil; **a c. number** una ganga, *Esp* un chollo, *Méx* pan m comido

custard ['kʌstəd] N natillas *fpl*; **c. powder** polvos *mpl* para hacer natillas

custodian [kʌ'stəʊdɪən] N conserje *mf*, guarda *mf*

custody ['kʌstədɪ] N custodia f; **to take into c.** detener

custom ['kʌstəm] N (**a**) *(habit)* costumbre f (**b**) *Com* clientela f

customary ['kʌstəmərɪ] ADJ habitual

customer ['kʌstəmə(r)] N cliente *mf*; **c. care** or **services** atención f al cliente

customize ['kʌstəmaɪz] VT hacer por encargo

custom-made [kʌstəm'meɪd] ADJ hecho(a) a la medida

customs ['kʌstəmz] NPL aduana f; **c. duty** derechos *mpl* de aduana; **c. officer** agente *mf* de aduana

cut [kʌt] **1** N (**a**) *(in flesh, wood, cloth)* corte m (**b**) *(of meat)* clase f de carne (**c**) *(in wages, prices)* recorte m (**d**) *(style) (of clothes, hair)* corte m
2 VT *(pt & pp* **cut**) (**a**) *(in general)* cortar; *(stone)* tallar; *(in slices)* rebanar; **to c. one's finger** cortarse el dedo; *Fig* **to c. a long story short** en resumidas cuentas; *Fig* **to c. corners** recortar presupuestos (**b**) *(wages, prices)* recortar (**c**) *(divide up)* dividir (**into** en)
3 VI *(of knife, scissors)* cortar

▸ **cut back** VT SEP *(expenses)* reducir; *(production)* disminuir

▸ **cut down 1** VT SEP *(tree)* talar
2 VT INSEP **to c. down on** reducir

▸ **cut in** VI *(driver)* adelantar bruscamente

▸ **cut off** VT SEP *(water etc)* cortar; *(place)* aislar; *(heir)* excluir; *Tel* **I've been c. off** me han cortado (la comunicación)

▸ **cut out 1** VT SEP (**a**) *(from newspaper)* recortar; *(person)* **to be c. out for sth** estar hecho(a) para algo (**b**) *(delete)* suprimir
2 VI *(engine)* calarse

▸ **cut up** VT SEP cortar en pedazos

cutback ['kʌtbæk] N reducción f (**in** de)

cute [kjuːt] ADJ (**a**) *(sweet)* bonito(a), mono(a) (**b**) *US Fam Pej (clever)* listo(a)

cuticle ['kjuːtɪkəl] N cutícula f

cutlery ['kʌtlərɪ] N cubiertos *mpl*

cutlet ['kʌtlɪt] N chuleta f

cut-price [kʌt'praɪs] ADJ *(article)* a precio rebajado

cutthroat ['kʌtθrəʊt] **1** N asesino(a) *m,f*, matón m
2 ADJ *(cruel)* cruel; *(competition)* feroz

cutting ['kʌtɪŋ] **1** N *(of plant)* esqueje m; *(from newspaper)* recorte m; *Rail* desmonte m
2 ADJ *(wind)* cortante; *(remark)* hiriente, cortante

CV, cv [siː'viː] N *(abbr* **curriculum vitae**) CV m

cwt. *(abbr* **hundredweight)** *(metric)* 50 kg; *Br (112 lb)* = 50,8 kg; *US (100 lb)* = 45,36 kg

cyanide ['saɪənaɪd] N cianuro m

cybercafe ['saɪbəkæfeɪ] N *Comput* cibercafé m

cybernetics [saɪbə'netɪks] N *Comput* cibernética f

cyberspace ['saɪbəspeɪs] N *Comput* ciberespacio m

cycle ['saɪkəl] **1** N (**a**) *(pattern)* ciclo m (**b**) *(bicycle)* bicicleta f; *(motorcycle)* moto f
2 VI ir en bicicleta

cycling ['saɪklɪŋ] N ciclismo m

cyclist ['saɪklɪst] N ciclista *mf*

cyclone ['saɪkləʊn] N ciclón m

cygnet ['sɪgnɪt] N pollo m de cisne

cylinder ['sɪlɪndə(r)] N (**a**) *(shape, in engine)* cilindro m (**b**) *(for gas)* bombona f

cymbal ['sɪmbəl] N címbalo m, platillo m

cynic ['sɪnɪk] N descreído(a) *m,f*, suspicaz *mf*

> Note that the Spanish word **cínico** is a false friend and is never a translation for the English word **cynic**. In Spanish, **cínico** means "shameless person".

cynical ['sɪnɪkəl] ADJ (**a**) *(sceptical)* descreído(a), suspicaz (**b**) *(unscrupulous)* desaprensivo(a), sin escrúpulos

> Note that the Spanish word **cínico** is a false friend and is never a translation for the English word **cynical**. In Spanish **cínico** means "shameless".

cynicism ['sɪnɪsɪzəm] N descreimiento m, suspicacia f

> Note that the Spanish word **cinismo** is a false friend and is never a translation for the English word **cynicism**. In Spanish, **cinismo** means "shamelessness".

cypress ['saɪprəs] N ciprés m

Cypriot ['sɪprɪət] ADJ & N chipriota *(mf)*

Cyprus ['saɪprəs] N Chipre

cyst [sɪst] N quiste m

cystitis [sɪ'staɪtɪs] N cistitis f

czar [zɑː(r)] N zar m

Czech [tʃek] **1** ADJ checo(a); **the C. Republic** la República Checa
2 N (**a**) *(person)* checo(a) *m,f* (**b**) *(language)* checo m

Czechoslovakia [tʃekəʊsləˈvækɪə] N *Hist* Checoslovaquia

D, d [diː] N (**a**) *(the letter)* D, d *f* (**b**) *Mus* D re *m*

DA [diːˈeɪ] N *US (abbr* **district attorney)** fiscal *mf* (del distrito)

dab [dæb] **1** N *(small quantity)* toque *m*
   2 VT (**a**) *(apply)* aplicar (**b**) *(touch lightly)* tocar ligeramente

dabble [ˈdæbəl] VI **to d. in politics** meterse en política

dachshund [ˈdækshʊnd] N perro *m* salchicha

dad [dæd], **daddy** [ˈdædɪ] N *Fam* papá *m*

daddy-longlegs [dædɪˈlɒŋlegz] N INV *Fam* (**a**) *Br (cranefly)* típula *f* (**b**) *US (harvestman)* segador *m*

daffodil [ˈdæfədɪl] N narciso *m*

daft [dɑːft] ADJ *Br Fam (persona, idea)* tonto(a), *Am* sonso(a), *Am* zonzo(a)

dagger [ˈdægə(r)] N puñal *m*, daga *f*

dahlia [ˈdeɪlɪə] N dalia *f*

daily [ˈdeɪlɪ] **1** ADJ diario(a), cotidiano(a)
   2 ADV diariamente; **three times d.** tres veces al día
   3 N (**a**) *(newspaper)* diario *m* (**b**) *Br Fam (cleaning lady)* asistenta *f*

dainty [ˈdeɪntɪ] ADJ (**daintier, daintiest**) *(movement)* grácil; *(features, lace)* delicado(a), fino(a)

dairy [ˈdeərɪ] N *(on farm)* vaquería *f*; *(shop)* lechería *f*; **d. farming** industria lechera; **d. produce** productos lácteos

dais [ˈdeɪs] N *(in hall)* tarima *f*; *(in ceremony)* estrado *m*

daisy [ˈdeɪzɪ] N margarita *f*

daisywheel [ˈdeɪzɪwiːl] N *(printer)* margarita *f*

dale [deɪl] N valle *m*, hondonada *f*

Dalmatian [dælˈmeɪʃən] N *(perro m)* dálmata *m*

dam [dæm] **1** N *(barrier)* dique *m*; *(lake)* presa *f*
   2 VT *(water)* represar
   ▸ **dam up** VT SEP *Fig (emotion)* contener

damage [ˈdæmɪdʒ] **1** N (**a**) *(to machine, building)* daños *mpl*; *(to health, reputation)* perjuicio *m* (**b**) *Jur* **damages** daños *mpl* y perjuicios *mpl*
   2 VT *(machine, building)* dañar; *(health, reputation)* perjudicar

damaging [ˈdæmɪdʒɪŋ] ADJ perjudicial

damn [dæm] **1** VT condenar
   2 INTERJ *Fam* **d. (it)!** ¡maldito(a) sea!; **well, I'll be damned!** ¡vaya por Dios!
   3 N *Fam* **I don't give a d.** me importa un bledo

4 ADJ *Fam* maldito(a)
   5 ADV *Fam* muy, sumamente

damned [dæmd] ADJ & ADV = **damn**

damnedest [ˈdæmdɪst] N *Fam* **to do one's d. to ...** hacer todo lo posible para ...

damning [ˈdæmɪŋ] ADJ *(evidence)* irrefutable; *(criticism)* mordaz

damp [dæmp] **1** ADJ húmedo(a)
   2 N humedad *f*
   3 VT (**a**) *(for ironing)* humedecer (**b**) **to d. (down)** *(fire)* sofocar; *Fig (violence)* frenar

dampen [ˈdæmpən] VT humedecer; *Fig* frenar

damper [ˈdæmpə(r)] N *Fig* **to put a d. on sth** poner freno a algo

damsel [ˈdæmzəl] N *Literary* doncella *f*

damson [ˈdæmzən] N ciruela damascena

dance [dɑːns] **1** N baile *m*; *(classical, tribal)* danza *f*; **d. band** orquesta *f* de baile; **d. floor** pista *f* de baile; **d. hall** salón *m* de baile
   2 VI & VT bailar

dancer [ˈdɑːnsə(r)] N *(by profession)* bailarín(ina) *m,f*

dancing [ˈdɑːnsɪŋ] N baile *m*

dandelion [ˈdændɪlaɪən] N diente *m* de león

dandruff [ˈdændrəf] N caspa *f*

Dane [deɪn] N danés(esa) *m,f*

danger [ˈdeɪndʒə(r)] N (**a**) *(risk)* riesgo *m*; *(of war etc)* amenaza *f* (**b**) *(peril)* peligro *m*; **d. (sign)** peligro; **out of d.** fuera de peligro

dangerous [ˈdeɪndʒərəs] ADJ peligroso(a); **d. driving** conducción temeraria

dangerously [ˈdeɪndʒərəslɪ] ADV peligrosamente

dangle [ˈdæŋgəl] **1** VI *(hang)* colgar; *(swing)* balancearse
   2 VT *(legs)* colgar; *(bait)* dejar colgado(a); *(swing)* balancear en el aire

Danish [ˈdeɪnɪʃ] **1** ADJ danés(esa); **D. pastry** pastel *m* de hojaldre
   2 N *(language)* danés *m*

dapper [ˈdæpə(r)] ADJ pulcro(a)

dappled [ˈdæpəld] ADJ *(shade)* moteado(a)

dare [deə(r)] **1** VI atreverse, osar; **he doesn't d. be late** no se atreve a llegar tarde; **how d. you!** ¿cómo te atreves?; *esp Br* **I d. say** quizás; *Ironic* ya (lo creo)
   2 VT *(challenge)* desafiar
   3 N desafío *m*

daredevil [ˈdeədevəl] ADJ & N atrevido(a) *(m,f)*, temerario(a) *(m,f)*

daring ['deərɪŋ] **1** ADJ (**a**) (*bold*) audaz, osado(a) (**b**) (*clothes*) atrevido(a)
2 N atrevimiento *m*, osadía *f*

dark [dɑ:k] **1** ADJ (**a**) (*room, colour*) oscuro(a); (*hair, complexion*) moreno(a); (*eyes, future*) negro(a) (**b**) Fig (*gloomy*) triste (**c**) Fig (*sinister*) siniestro(a)
2 N (**a**) (*darkness*) oscuridad *f*, tinieblas *fpl*; **after d.** después del anochecer (**b**) Fig **to be in the d.** (**about sth**) *Esp* estar in albis (sobre algo), *Am* no tener ni idea (sobre algo)

darken ['dɑ:kən] **1** VT (*sky, colour*) oscurecer
2 VI (*sky, colour*) oscurecerse; Fig (*thoughts, mood*) ensombrecerse

darkness ['dɑ:knɪs] N oscuridad *f*, tinieblas *fpl*

darkroom ['dɑ:kru:m] N cuarto *m* oscuro

darling ['dɑ:lɪŋ] ADJ & N querido(a) (*m,f*)

darn [dɑ:n] **1** VT zurcir
2 N zurcido *m*

dart [dɑ:t] **1** N (**a**) (*missile*) dardo *m* (**b**) **darts** (*game*) dardos *mpl*
2 VI (*fly about*) revolotear; **to d. in/out** entrar/salir corriendo

dartboard ['dɑ:tbɔ:d] N diana *f*

dash [dæʃ] **1** N (**a**) (*rush*) carrera *f* (**b**) *esp US* (*race*) sprint *m* (**c**) (*small amount*) poquito *m*; (*of salt*) pizca *f*; (*of liquid*) gota *f* (**d**) *Typ* guión largo; (*hyphen*) guión
2 VT (*throw*) arrojar
3 VI (*rush*) correr; **to d. around** correr de un lado a otro; **to d. out** salir corriendo
▸ **dash off** VI salir corriendo

dashboard ['dæʃbɔ:d] N tablero *m* de mandos, *Esp* salpicadero *m*

dashing ['dæʃɪŋ] ADJ (*appearance*) garboso(a)

data ['deɪtə, 'dɑ:tə] NPL datos *mpl*; **d. bank** *or* **base** banco *m* de datos; **d. processing** (*act*) proceso *m* de datos; (*science*) informática *f*; **d. protection act** ley *f* de informática

date[1] [deɪt] **1** N (**a**) (*day*) fecha *f*; **what's the d. today?** ¿a qué (fecha) estamos hoy?, ¿qué fecha es hoy?, *Am* ¿a cómo estamos?; **out of d.** (*ideas*) anticuado(a); (*expression*) desusado(a); (*invalid*) caducado(a); **to d.** hasta la fecha; Fig **to be up to d.** estar al día; **d. of birth** fecha de nacimiento (**b**) (*social event*) compromiso *m*; *Fam* (*with girl, boy*) cita *f* (**c**) *US Fam* (*person dated*) ligue *m*
2 VT (*ruins*) datar
3 VT (*ideas*) quedar anticuado(a)
▸ **date back to, date from** VT INSEP remontar a, datar de

date[2] [deɪt] N (*fruit*) dátil *m*; **d. palm** datilera *f*

dated ['deɪtɪd] ADJ (*idea*) anticuado(a); (*fashion*) pasado(a) de moda; (*expression*) desusado(a)

daub [dɔ:b] VT embadurnar (**with** de)

daughter ['dɔ:tə(r)] N hija *f*

daughter-in-law ['dɔ:tərɪnlɔ:] N nuera *f*, hija política

daunting ['dɔ:ntɪŋ] ADJ desalentador(a)

dawdle ['dɔ:dəl] VI *Fam* (*walk slowly*) andar despacio; (*waste time*) perder el tiempo

dawn [dɔ:n] **1** N alba *f*, amanecer *m*
2 VI (**a**) (*day*) amanecer (**b**) Fig (*age, hope*) comenzar (**c**) Fig **suddenly it dawned on him that ...** de repente cayó en la cuenta de que ...

day [deɪ] N (**a**) (*period of 24 hours*) día *m*; **one of these days** un día de éstos; (**on**) **the next** *or* **following** **d.** el *or* al día siguiente; **the d. after tomorrow** pasado mañana; **the d. before yesterday** anteayer; **the other d.** el otro día (**b**) (*daylight*) día *m*; **by d.** de día (**c**) (*era*) **in those days** en aquellos tiempos; **these days** hoy (en) día

daybreak ['deɪbreɪk] N amanecer *m*

daydream ['deɪdri:m] **1** N fantasía *f*
2 VI fantasear, soñar despierto(a)

daylight ['deɪlaɪt] N luz *f* del día; **in broad d.** en pleno día; **to scare the (living) daylights out of sb** pegarle a algn un susto de muerte

daytime ['deɪtaɪm] N día *m*; **in the d.** de día

day-to-day ['deɪtədeɪ] ADJ cotidiano(a), diario(a)

daze [deɪz] N aturdimiento *m*; **in a d.** aturdido(a)

dazed [deɪzd] ADJ aturdido(a), atontado(a)

dazzle ['dæzəl] VT deslumbrar

D-day ['di:deɪ] N día *m* D

deacon ['di:kən] N diácono *m*

dead [ded] **1** ADJ (**a**) (*not alive*) muerto(a); **to be d.** estar muerto(a); **a d. man** un muerto (**b**) (*battery*) gastado(a), agotado(a); **the phone is d.** no hay línea (**c**) (*numb*) dormido(a); **my leg went d.** se me durmió la pierna (**d**) (*silence, secrecy*) total; **d. end** callejón *m* sin salida
2 ADV (*very*) muy; *Fam* **you're d. right** tienes toda la razón; **to stop d.** pararse en seco
3 NPL **the d.** los muertos

deaden ['dedən] VT (*impact, noise*) amortiguar; Fig (*pain, feeling*) calmar, aliviar

deadline ['dedlaɪn] N (*date*) fecha *f* tope; (*time*) hora *f* tope; **we have to meet the d.** tenemos que hacerlo dentro del plazo

deadlock ['dedlɒk] N punto muerto

deadly ['dedlɪ] **1** ADJ (**deadlier, deadliest**) (*poison, blow, enemy*) mortal; (*weapon*) mortífero(a); (*aim*) certero(a)
2 ADV (*extremely*) terriblemente, sumamente

deadpan ['dedpæn] ADJ *Fam* (*face*) sin expresión; (*humour*) guasón(ona)

deaf [def] **1** ADJ sordo(a); Fig **to turn a d. ear** hacerse el sordo; **d. mute** sordomudo(a) *m,f*
2 NPL **the d.** los sordos; **the d. and dumb** los sordomudos

deafen ['defən] VT ensordecer

deafening ['defənɪŋ] ADJ ensordecedor(a)

deafness ['defnɪs] N sordera *f*

deal [di:l] **1** N (**a**) *Com & Pol* trato *m*, pacto *m*; **business d.** negocio *m*, transacción *f*; **to do a d. with sb** (*transaction*) cerrar un trato con algn; *(agreement)* pactar algo con algn; *Fam* **it's a d.!** ¡trato hecho! **(b)** *(amount)* cantidad *f*; **a good d. of criticism** muchas críticas; **a good d. slower** mucho más despacio **(c)** *Cards* reparto *m*

2 VT *(pt & pp dealt)* **(a)** *Cards* dar **(to** a) **(b) to d. sb a blow** asestarle un golpe a algn

▶ **deal in** VT INSEP *(goods)* comerciar en, tratar en; *(drugs)* traficar con

▶ **deal out** VT SEP repartir

▶ **deal with** VT INSEP *(firm, person)* tratar con; *(subject, problem)* abordar, ocuparse de; *(in book etc)* tratar de

dealer ['diːlə(r)] N **(a)** *Com (in goods)* comerciante *mf*; *(in drugs)* traficante *mf* **(b)** *Cards* repartidor(a) *m,f*

dealings ['diːlɪŋz] NPL **(a)** *(relations)* trato *m* **(b)** *Com* negocios *mpl*

dealt [delt] PT & PP of **deal**

dean [diːn] N **(a)** *Rel* deán *m* **(b)** *Univ* decano *m*

dear [dɪə(r)] **1** ADJ **(a)** *(loved)* querido(a); **D. Andrew** *(in letter)* Querido Andrew; *Fml* **D. Madam** Estimada señora; *Fml* **D. Sir(s)** Muy señor(es) mío(s) **(b)** *(expensive)* caro(a)

2 N querido(a) *m,f*; **my d.** mi vida

3 INTERJ **oh d.!, d. me!** *(surprise)* ¡caramba!; *(disappointment)* ¡qué pena!

dearly ['dɪəlɪ] ADV muchísimo; *Fig* **he paid d. for his mistake** su error le costó caro

dearth [dɜːθ] N *Fml* escasez *f*

death [deθ] N muerte *f*; *Fml* fallecimiento *m*; *Fam* **to be bored to d.** aburrirse como una ostra; *Fam* **to be scared to d.** estar muerto(a) de miedo; *Fam Fig* **to be sick to d. of** estar hasta la coronilla de; **d. certificate** certificado *m* de defunción; **d. penalty, d. sentence** pena *f* de muerte

deathbed ['deθbed] N **to be on one's d.** estar en el lecho de muerte

deathly ['deθlɪ] ADJ **(deathlier, deathliest)** *(silence)* sepulcral; **d. pale** pálido(a) como un muerto

debacle [deɪ'bɑːkəl] N debacle *f*

debar [dɪ'bɑː(r)] VT *Fml* excluir, prohibir

debase [dɪ'beɪs] VT *Fig* envilecer; **to d. oneself** humillarse

debatable [dɪ'beɪtəbəl] ADJ discutible

debate [dɪ'beɪt] **1** N debate *m*; **a heated d.** una discusión acalorada

2 VT **(a)** *(discuss)* discutir **(b)** *(wonder about)* dar vueltas a

3 VI discutir

debateable [dɪ'beɪtəbəl] ADJ = **debatable**

debauchery [dɪ'bɔːtʃərɪ] N libertinaje *m*

debilitating [dɪ'bɪlɪteɪtɪŋ] ADJ debilitador(a), debilitante

debit ['debɪt] **1** N débito *m*; **d. balance** saldo negativo

2 VT **d. Mr Jones with £20** cargar la suma de 20 libras en la cuenta del Sr. Jones

debris ['debriː, 'deɪbriː] N SING escombros *mpl*

debt [det] N deuda *f*; **to be deeply in d.** estar cargado(a) de deudas; *Fig* **to be in sb's d.** estar en deuda con algn

debtor ['detə(r)] N deudor(a) *m,f*

debug [diː'bʌg] VT *Comput* eliminar fallos de

debunk [diː'bʌŋk] VT *Fam* desacreditar, desprestigiar

debut ['debjuː, 'deɪbjuː] N debut *m*; **to make one's d.** debutar

debutante ['debjʊtɑːnt] N debutante *f*

decade [de'keɪd, 'dekeɪd] N decenio *m*, década *f*

decadence ['dekədəns] N decadencia *f*

decadent ['dekədənt] ADJ decadente

decaffeinated [diː'kæfɪneɪtɪd] ADJ descafeinado(a)

decanter [dɪ'kæntə(r)] N jarra *f*, jarro *m*

decapitate [dɪ'kæpɪteɪt] VT decapitar

decay [dɪ'keɪ] **1** N *(of food, body)* putrefacción *f*, descomposición *f*; *(of teeth)* caries *f inv*; *(of building)* ruina *f*; *(of civilization)* decadencia *f*

2 VI *(food, body)* pudrirse, descomponerse; *(teeth)* cariarse; *(decline)* declinarse

deceased [dɪ'siːst] ADJ *Fml* difunto(a), fallecido(a)

deceit [dɪ'siːt] N **(a)** *(dishonesty)* falta *f* de honradez, falsedad *f* **(b)** *(trick)* engaño *m*, mentira *f*

deceitful [dɪ'siːtfʊl] ADJ falso(a)

deceive [dɪ'siːv] VT *(mislead)* engañar; *(lie to)* mentir

December [dɪ'sembə(r)] N diciembre *m*

decency ['diːsənsɪ] N decencia *f*; *(modesty)* pudor *m*; *(morality)* moralidad *f*

decent ['diːsənt] ADJ **(a)** *(respectable)* decente, decoroso(a); **a d. wage** un sueldo decente **(b)** *Fam (kind)* **a d. chap** un buen tipo

decentralize [diː'sentrəlaɪz] VT descentralizar

deception [dɪ'sepʃən] N engaño *m*

> Note that the Spanish word **decepción** is a false friend and is never a translation for the English word **deception**. In Spanish **decepción** means "disappointment".

deceptive [dɪ'septɪv] ADJ engañoso(a)

deceptively [dɪ'septɪvlɪ] ADV **it looks d. simple** parece engañosamente sencillo(a)

decibel ['desɪbel] N decibelio *m*

decide [dɪ'saɪd] **1** VT **(a)** *(choose, resolve)* decidir; **to d. to do sth** decidir hacer algo **(b)** *(matter, question)* resolver, determinar

2 VI *(reach decision)* decidirse; **to d. against sth** decidirse en contra de algo

▶ **decide on** VT INSEP *(choose)* optar por

decided [dɪ'saɪdɪd] ADJ **(a)** *(noticeable)* marcado(a) **(b)** *(resolute)* decidido(a); *(views)* categórico(a)

decidedly [dɪ'saɪdɪdlɪ] ADV *Fml* **(a)** *(clearly)* indudablemente **(b)** *(resolutely)* decididamente

deciding [dɪ'saɪdɪŋ] ADJ decisivo(a)

deciduous [dɪ'sɪdjʊəs] ADJ de hoja caduca

decimal ['desɪməl] **1** ADJ decimal; **d. point** coma *f* (de fracción decimal)
2 N decimal *m*

decimate ['desɪmeɪt] VT diezmar

decipher [dɪ'saɪfə(r)] VT descifrar

decision [dɪ'sɪʒən] N (**a**) *(choice, judgement)* decisión *f*; **to come to a d.** llegar a una decisión; **to make** *or* **take a d.** tomar una decisión (**b**) *Fml (decisiveness)* **to act with d.** actuar con decisión

decisive [dɪ'saɪsɪv] ADJ (**a**) *(resolute)* decidido(a), resuelto(a) (**b**) *(conclusive)* decisivo(a)

deck [dek] **1** N (**a**) *(of ship)* cubierta *f*; **d. chair** tumbona *f* (**b**) *(of bus)* piso *m*; **top d.** piso de arriba (**c**) *esp US (of cards)* baraja *f* (**d**) *(of record player)* plato *m*
2 VT **to d. out** adornar

declaration [deklə'reɪʃən] N declaración *f*

declare [dɪ'kleə(r)] VT declarar; **to d. war (on)** declarar la guerra (a); **to d. sb guilty/innocent** declarar a algn culpable/inocente

declared [dɪ'kleəd] ADJ *(opponent)* declarado(a); *(intention)* manifiesto(a)

decline [dɪ'klaɪn] **1** N (**a**) *(decrease)* disminución *f* (**b**) *(deterioration)* deterioro *m*; *(of health)* empeoramiento *m*; **to fall into d.** empezar a decaer
2 VI (**a**) *(decrease)* disminuir; *(amount)* bajar; *(business)* decaer (**b**) *(deteriorate)* deteriorarse; *(health)* empeorar (**c**) *(refuse)* negarse
3 VT (**a**) *(refuse)* rechazar (**b**) *Gram* declinar

declutch [dɪ'klʌtʃ] VI soltar el embrague

decode [diː'kəʊd] VT descifrar

decompose [diːkəm'pəʊz] VI descomponerse

décor ['deɪkɔː(r)] N decoración *f*; *Th* decorado *m*

decorate ['dekəreɪt] VT (**a**) *(adorn)* decorar, adornar (**with** con) (**b**) *(paint)* pintar; *(wallpaper)* empapelar (**c**) *(honour)* condecorar

decoration [dekə'reɪʃən] N (**a**) *(decor)* decoración *f*; **Christmas decorations** adornos navideños (**b**) *(medal)* condecoración *f*

decorative ['dekərətɪv] ADJ decorativo(a)

decorator ['dekəreɪtə(r)] N decorador(a) *m,f*; *(painter)* pintor(a) *m,f*; *(paperhanger)* empapelador(a) *m,f*

decorum [dɪ'kɔːrəm] N decoro *m*

decoy ['diːkɔɪ] N *Fig* señuelo *m*

decrease 1 N ['diːkriːs] reducción *f*, disminución *f* (**in** en)
2 VI [dɪ'kriːs] disminuir, reducirse
3 VT disminuir, reducir

decree [dɪ'kriː] **1** N (**a**) *Pol & Rel* decreto *m* (**b**) *esp US Jur* sentencia *f*; **d. absolute** sentencia definitiva de divorcio; **d. nisi** sentencia provisional de divorcio
2 VT *Pol & Rel* decretar, pronunciar

decrepit [dɪ'krepɪt] ADJ decrépito(a)

dedicate ['dedɪkeɪt] VT consagrar, dedicar

dedicated ['dedɪkeɪtɪd] ADJ ardiente; **d. to** entregado(a) a

dedication [dedɪ'keɪʃən] N *(act)* dedicación *f*; *(commitment)* entrega *f*; *(in book)* dedicatoria *f*

deduce [dɪ'djuːs] VT deducir (**from** de)

deduct [dɪ'dʌkt] VT descontar (**from** de)

deduction [dɪ'dʌkʃən] N (**a**) *(conclusion)* conclusión *f* (**b**) *(subtraction)* descuento *m*

deed [diːd] N (**a**) *(act)* acto *m*; *(feat)* hazaña *f* (**b**) *Jur* escritura *f*; **title deeds** título *m* de propiedad

deem [diːm] VT *Fml* estimar

deep [diːp] **1** ADJ (**a**) *(water, sleep, thinker)* profundo(a); *(breath, sigh)* hondo(a); **it's 10 m d.** tiene 10 m de profundidad (**b**) *(voice)* grave (**c**) *(colour)* intenso(a)
2 ADV **to be d. in thought** estar absorto(a); **to look d. into sb's eyes** penetrar a algn con la mirada

deepen ['diːpən] **1** VT *(well)* profundizar, ahondar; *Fig (knowledge)* aumentar
2 VI *(river etc)* hacerse más hondo *or* profundo; *Fig (knowledge)* aumentar; *(colour, emotion)* intensificarse; *(sound, voice)* hacerse más grave

deep-freeze [diːp'friːz] **1** N congelador *m*
2 VT congelar

deep-fry [diːp'fraɪ] VT freír en mucho aceite

deeply ['diːplɪ] ADV profundamente; **to care d. about** preocuparse profundamente por

deep-rooted [diːp'ruːtɪd], **deep-seated** [diːp'siːtɪd] ADJ *(fear, prejudice)* arraigado(a)

deep-set [diːp'set] ADJ *(eyes)* hundido(a)

deer [dɪə(r)] N INV ciervo *m*

deface [dɪ'feɪs] VT *(book, poster)* garabatear

de facto [deɪ'fæktəʊ] ADJ & ADV *Fml* de hecho

defamation [defə'meɪʃən] N difamación *f*

default [dɪ'fɔːlt] **1** VI (**a**) *(not act)* faltar a sus compromisos (**b**) *Jur* estar en rebeldía (**c**) *(not pay)* suspender pagos
2 N (**a**) *(failure to act)* omisión *f* (**b**) *(failure to pay)* incumplimiento *m* de pago (**c**) *Jur* rebeldía *f*; **in d. of** a falta de; **to win by d.** ganar por incomparecencia del adversario

defaulter [dɪ'fɔːltə(r)] N *(on loan)* moroso(a) *m,f*; *Jur & Mil* rebelde *mf*

defeat [dɪ'fiːt] **1** VT *(opponent)* derrotar, vencer; *(proposal, bill)* rechazar
2 N *(of opponent)* derrota *f*; *(of proposal, bill)* rechazo *m*

defeatist [dɪ'fiːtɪst] ADJ & N derrotista *(mf)*

defect 1 N ['diːfekt] defecto *m*; *(flaw)* desperfecto *m*
2 VI [dɪ'fekt] desertar (**from** de); *(from country)* huir

defective [dɪ'fektɪv] ADJ *(faulty)* defectuoso(a); *(flawed)* con desperfectos; *(lacking)* incompleto(a)

defector [dɪ'fektə(r)] N *Pol* tránsfuga *mf*, trásfuga *mf*

defence [dɪ'fens] N (**a**) *(of country)* defensa *f; Br* **the Ministry of D.,** *US* **the Department of Defense** el Ministerio de Defensa; **to come to sb's d.** salir en defensa de algn (**b**) *Jur* defensa *f* (**c**) *Sport* [*Br* dɪ'fens, *US* 'diːfens] **the d.** la defensa

defenceless [dɪ'fenslɪs] ADJ indefenso(a)

defend [dɪ'fend] VT defender

defendant [dɪ'fendənt] N *Jur* acusado(a) *m,f*

defender [dɪ'fendə(r)] N defensor(a) *m,f; Sport* defensa *mf*

defending [dɪ'fendɪŋ] ADJ *Sport* defensor(a); **d. champion** campeón(ona) *m,f* titular

defense [dɪ'fens, 'diːfens] N *US* = **defence**

defensive [dɪ'fensɪv] **1** ADJ defensivo(a)
2 N **to be on the d.** estar a la defensiva

defer[1] [dɪ'fɜː(r)] VT aplazar, retrasar

defer[2] [dɪ'fɜː(r)] VI **to d. to** deferir a

deference ['defərəns] N *Fml* deferencia *f*, respeto *m*; **out of** *or* **in d. to** por respeto *or* por deferencia a

defiance [dɪ'faɪəns] N (**a**) *(challenge)* desafío *m*; **in d. of** a despecho de (**b**) *(resistance)* resistencia *f*

defiant [dɪ'faɪənt] ADJ *(challenging)* desafiante; *(bold)* insolente

deficiency [dɪ'fɪʃənsɪ] N (**a**) *(lack)* falta *f*, carencia *f* (**b**) *(shortcoming)* defecto *m*

deficient [dɪ'fɪʃənt] ADJ deficiente; **to be d. in sth** carecer de algo

deficit ['defɪsɪt] N déficit *m*

defile [dɪ'faɪl] VT *Fml* (**a**) *(mind)* corromper; *(honour)* manchar; *(woman)* deshonrar (**b**) *(desecrate)* profanar

define [dɪ'faɪn] VT *(term, word)* definir; *(duties, powers)* delimitar

definite ['defɪnɪt] ADJ (**a**) *(clear)* claro(a); *(progress)* notable (**b**) *(date, place)* determinado(a)

definitely ['defɪnɪtlɪ] **1** ADV sin duda; **he was d. drunk** no cabe duda de que estaba borracho
2 INTERJ ¡desde luego!

definition [defɪ'nɪʃən] N definición *f*; **by d.** por definición

definitive [dɪ'fɪnɪtɪv] ADJ definitivo(a)

deflate [dɪ'fleɪt] VT (**a**) *(tyre etc)* desinflar (**b**) *Fig* rebajar; **to d. sb** hacer bajar los humos a algn (**c**) **to d. the economy** tomar medidas deflacionistas

deflationary [dɪ'fleɪʃənərɪ] ADJ *Econ* deflacionista

deflect [dɪ'flekt] VT desviar

deflection [dɪ'flekʃən] N desviación *f*

deforestation [diːfɒrɪ'steɪʃən] N deforestación *f*

deformed [dɪ'fɔːmd] ADJ deforme

deformity [dɪ'fɔːmɪtɪ] N deformidad *f*

defraud [dɪ'frɔːd] VT estafar

defrost [diː'frɒst] VT (**a**) *(freezer, food)* descongelar (**b**) *US (windscreen)* desempañar

deft [deft] ADJ hábil, diestro(a)

defunct [dɪ'fʌŋkt] ADJ *(person)* difunto(a); *(thing)* en desuso

defuse [diː'fjuːz] VT *(bomb)* desactivar; *Fig* **to d. a situation** reducir la tensión de una situación

defy [dɪ'faɪ] VT (**a**) *(person)* desafiar; *(law, order)* contravenir (**b**) *(challenge)* retar, desafiar

degenerate 1 VI [dɪ'dʒenəreɪt] degenerar (**into** en)
2 ADJ & N [dɪ'dʒenərɪt] degenerado(a) *(m,f)*

degrading [dɪ'greɪdɪŋ] ADJ degradante

degree [dɪ'griː] N (**a**) *(extent, level)* & *Geom & Phys* grado *m*; **to some d.** hasta cierto punto; **by degrees** poco a poco (**b**) *(qualification)* título *m*; *(doctorate)* doctorado *m*; **to have a d. in science** ser licenciado(a) en ciencias

dehydrated [diːhaɪ'dreɪtɪd] ADJ *(person)* deshidratado(a); *(vegetables)* seco(a)

de-ice [diː'aɪs] VT quitar el hielo a, deshelar

de-icer [diː'aɪsə(r)] N anticongelante *m*

deign [deɪn] VI dignarse

deity ['deɪtɪ] N deidad *f*

dejected [dɪ'dʒektɪd] ADJ desalentado(a), abatido(a)

delay [dɪ'leɪ] **1** VT (**a**) *(flight, train)* retrasar; *(person)* entretener; **delayed action** acción retardada (**b**) *(postpone)* aplazar
2 VI **don't d.** no lo deje para más tarde
3 N retraso *m*, *Am* demora *f*

delectable [dɪ'lektəbəl] ADJ delicioso(a)

delegate 1 N ['delɪgɪt] delegado(a) *m,f*
2 VT ['delɪgeɪt] delegar (**to** en); **to d. sb to do sth** encargar a algn que haga algo

delegation [delɪ'geɪʃən] N delegación *f*

delete [dɪ'liːt] VT tachar, suprimir

deliberate 1 ADJ [dɪ'lɪbərɪt] *(intentional)* deliberado(a), intencionado(a); *(studied)* premeditado(a); *(careful)* prudente; *(unhurried)* pausado(a)
2 VT [dɪ'lɪbəreɪt] deliberar
3 VI deliberar (**on** *or* **about** sobre)

deliberately [dɪ'lɪbərɪtlɪ] ADV *(intentionally)* a propósito; *(unhurriedly)* pausadamente

deliberation [dɪlɪbə'reɪʃən] N (**a**) *(consideration)* deliberación *f* (**b**) *(care)* cuidado *m*; *(unhurriedness)* pausa *f*

delicacy ['delɪkəsɪ] N (**a**) *(fineness)* delicadeza *f* (**b**) *(food)* manjar (exquisito)

delicate ['delɪkɪt] ADJ *(glass, situation)* delicado(a); *(health)* frágil, delicado(a); *(flavour, colour)* suave

delicatessen [delɪkə'tesən] N *(shop)* = tienda de ultramarinos *or Am* enlatados de calidad

delicious [dɪ'lɪʃəs] ADJ delicioso(a)

delight [dɪ'laɪt] **1** N (**a**) *(pleasure)* placer *m*; **he took d. in it** le encantó (**b**) *(source of pleasure)* encanto *m*, delicia *f*
2 VT encantar

delighted [dɪ'laɪtɪd] ADJ encantado(a); **I'm d. to see you** me alegro mucho de verte

delightful [dɪ'laɪtfʊl] ADJ *(person, smile)* encantador(a); *(meal, evening)* delicioso(a)

delinquency [dɪ'lɪŋkwənsɪ] N delincuencia *f*; **juvenile d.** delincuencia juvenil

delinquent [dɪ'lɪŋkwənt] ADJ & N delincuente *(mf)*

delirious [dɪ'lɪrɪəs] ADJ delirante

deliver [dɪ'lɪvə(r)] VT **(a)** *(goods)* repartir, entregar; *(message)* dar; *(order)* despachar **(b)** *(blow)* asestar; *(speech, verdict)* pronunciar **(c)** *Med* ayudar en el nacimiento de **(d)** *Fml (rescue)* liberar

delivery [dɪ'lɪvərɪ] N **(a)** *(of goods)* reparto *m*, entrega *f* **(b)** *(of speech)* declamación *f* **(c)** *(of baby)* parto *m*

delta ['deltə] N *Geog* delta *m*

delude [dɪ'luːd] VT engañar; **don't d. yourself** no te hagas ilusiones

deluge ['deljuːdʒ] **1** N *(flood)* inundación *f*; *(rain)* diluvio *m*; *Fig (of letters etc)* avalancha *f* **2** VT *Fml* inundar

delusion [dɪ'luːʒən] N **(a)** *(state, act)* engaño *m* **(b)** *(false belief)* ilusión (vana); **delusions of grandeur** delirios *mpl* de grandeza

de luxe [də'lʌks, də'lʊks] ADJ de lujo *inv*

delve [delv] VI **to d. into** *(pocket)* hurgar en; *(subject)* profundizar en

demagogue ['deməgɒg] N demagogo(a) *m,f*

demand [dɪ'mɑːnd] **1** N **(a)** *(request)* exigencia *f*; **on d.** a petición **(b)** *(for goods)* demanda *f* **(for** de); **to be in d.** estar muy solicitado(a) **(c)** *Econ* demanda *f* **2** VT **(a)** *(request)* exigir; **to d. that ...** insistir en que ... *(+ subj)* **(b)** *(require)* requerir

demanding [dɪ'mɑːndɪŋ] ADJ **(a)** *(person)* exigente **(b)** *(job)* agotador(a)

demean [dɪ'miːn] VT *Fml* **to d. oneself** rebajarse

demeaning [dɪ'miːnɪŋ] ADJ *Fml* humillante

demeanour, *US* **demeanor** [dɪ'miːnə(r)] N *Fml* **(a)** *(behaviour)* comportamiento *m*, conducta *f* **(b)** *(bearing)* porte *m*

demented [dɪ'mentɪd] ADJ *Med* demente; *Fam* loco(a)

demise [dɪ'maɪz] N *Fml (death)* fallecimiento *m*; *Fig (of institution)* desaparición *f*; *(of ambition etc)* fracaso *m*

demister [diː'mɪstə(r)] N *Br Aut* luneta *f* térmica, dispositivo *m* antivaho

demo ['deməʊ] N *Fam* manifestación *f*; **d. tape** maqueta *f*

demobilize [diː'məʊbɪlaɪz] VT desmovilizar

democracy [dɪ'mɒkrəsɪ] N democracia *f*

democrat ['deməkræt] N demócrata *mf*; *Pol* **Christian D.** democratacristiano(a) *m,f*; **Social D.** socialdemócrata *mf*

democratic [demə'krætɪk] ADJ democrático(a); *US Pol* **D. party** partido *m* demócrata

demographic [demə'græfɪk] ADJ demográfico(a)

demolish [dɪ'mɒlɪʃ] VT *(building)* derribar, demoler; *Fig (theory, proposal)* echar por tierra

demolition [demə'lɪʃən] N demolición *f*

demon ['diːmən] N demonio *m*

demonstrate ['demənstreɪt] **1** VT demostrar **2** VI *Pol* manifestarse

demonstration [demən'streɪʃən] N **(a)** *(proof)* demostración *f*, prueba *f* **(b)** *(explanation)* explicación *f* **(c)** *Pol* manifestación *f*

demonstrative [dɪ'mɒnstrətɪv] ADJ expresivo(a)

demonstrator ['demənstreɪtə(r)] N manifestante *mf*

demoralize [dɪ'mɒrəlaɪz] VT desmoralizar

demoralizing [dɪ'mɒrəlaɪzɪŋ] ADJ desmoralizador(a), desmoralizante

demote [dɪ'məʊt] VT rebajar de graduación a

demure [dɪ'mjʊə(r)] ADJ *(person)* recatado(a)

den [den] N **(a)** *(of animal)* guarida *f* **(b)** *Fam (study)* estudio *m*

denial [dɪ'naɪəl] N **(a)** *(of charge)* desmentido *m* **(b)** *(of rights)* denegación *f*; *(of request)* negativa *f*

denim ['denɪm] N tela *f* vaquera; **denims** *(jeans)* vaqueros *mpl*, *Andes, Ven* bluyíns *nmpl*, *Méx* pantalones *mpl* de mezclilla; **d. skirt/shirt** falda *f*/camisa *f* vaquera

Denmark ['denmɑːk] N Dinamarca

denomination [dɪnɒmɪ'neɪʃən] N **(a)** *Rel* confesión *f* **(b)** *Fin (of coins)* valor *m*

denominator [dɪ'nɒmɪneɪtə(r)] N denominador *m*

denote [dɪ'nəʊt] VT *(show)* indicar; *(mean)* significar

denounce [dɪ'naʊns] VT denunciar; *(criticize)* censurar

dense [dens] ADJ **(a)** *(smoke, fog)* denso(a); *(crowd)* nutrido(a) **(b)** *Fam (stupid)* corto(a)

densely ['denslɪ] ADV densamente

density ['densɪtɪ] N densidad *f*

dent [dent] **1** N abolladura *f* **2** VT *(car)* abollar

dental ['dentəl] ADJ dental; **d. floss** hilo *m* dental; **d. surgeon** odontólogo(a) *m,f*; **d. surgery** *(place)* clínica *f* dental; *(treatment)* cirugía *f* dental

dentist ['dentɪst] N dentista *mf*

dentistry ['dentɪstrɪ] N odontología *f*

dentures ['dentʃəz] N (set of) **d.** dentadura postiza

denunciation [dɪnʌnsɪ'eɪʃən] N denuncia *f*, condena *f*

deny [dɪ'naɪ] VT **(a)** *(repudiate)* negar; *(rumour, report)* desmentir; *(charge)* rechazar **(b)** *(refuse)* negar

deodorant [diː'əʊdərənt] N desodorante *m*

depart [dɪ'pɑːt] VI marcharse, irse; *Fig (from subject)* desviarse (**from** de)

department [dɪ'pɑːtmənt] N sección *f*; *(in university)* departamento *m*; *(in government)* ministerio *m*; **d. store** grandes almacenes *mpl*; *US* **D. of the Interior** Ministerio *m* del Interior

departure [dɪ'pɑːtʃə(r)] N partida *f*; *Av & Rail* salida *f*; *Av* **d. lounge** sala *f* de embarque

depend [dɪ'pend] **1** VI *(rely)* fiarse (**on** or **upon** de)
2 V IMPERS *(be determined by)* depender (**on** or **upon** de); **it depends on the weather** según el tiempo que haga; **that depends** según

dependable [dɪ'pendəbəl] ADJ *(person)* formal; *(friend)* leal; *(car)* fiable, *Am* confiable

dependant [dɪ'pendənt] N dependiente *mf*

dependence [dɪ'pendəns] N dependencia *f*

dependent [dɪ'pendənt] **1** ADJ dependiente; **to be d. on sth** depender de algo
2 N *US* = **dependant**

depict [dɪ'pɪkt] VT *Art* representar; *Fig* describir

deplete [dɪ'pliːt] VT reducir

deplorable [dɪ'plɔːrəbəl] ADJ lamentable

deplore [dɪ'plɔː(r)] VT deplorar

deploy [dɪ'plɔɪ] VT *Mil* desplegar; *Fig* utilizar

depopulate [diː'pɒpjʊleɪt] VT despoblar

deport [dɪ'pɔːt] VT expulsar (**from** de; **to** a)

deportation [diːpɔː'teɪʃən] N expulsión *f*

deportment [dɪ'pɔːtmənt] N *Fml* porte *m*

depose [dɪ'pəʊz] VT deponer

deposit [dɪ'pɒzɪt] **1** N **(a)** *(in bank)* depósito *m*; *Br* **d. account** cuenta *f* de ahorros **(b)** *(returnable)* señal *f*, fianza *f*; *(first payment)* entrega *f* inicial, *Esp* entrada *f* **(c)** *(of minerals)* yacimiento *m*; *(in wine)* poso *m*
2 VT depositar; *(in bank account) Esp* ingresar, *Am* depositar

deposition [depə'zɪʃən] N **(a)** *(of leader)* destitución *f* **(b)** *Jur (of witness)* declaración *f*

depositor [dɪ'pɒzɪtə(r)] N depositante *mf*

depot [*Br* 'depəʊ, *US* 'diːpəʊ] N almacén *m*; *Mil* depósito *m*; *Br (for keeping and repairing buses)* cochera *f*; *US (bus station)* estación *f* de autobuses, *CAm, Méx* central *f* camionera

depraved [dɪ'preɪvd] ADJ *(person)* depravado(a)

deprecate ['deprɪkeɪt] VT desaprobar, censurar

depreciate [dɪ'priːʃɪeɪt] VI depreciarse

depreciation [dɪpriːʃɪ'eɪʃən] N depreciación *f*

depress [dɪ'pres] VT **(a)** *(person)* deprimir **(b)** *Econ (profits)* reducir; *(trade)* dificultar **(c)** *Fml (switch, lever etc)* presionar; *(clutch, piano pedal)* pisar

depressed [dɪ'prest] ADJ **(a)** *(person)* deprimido(a); **to get d.** deprimirse **(b)** *(market)* en crisis **(c)** *(surface)* hundido(a)

depressing [dɪ'presɪŋ] ADJ deprimente

depression [dɪ'preʃən] N depresión *f*

deprivation [deprɪ'veɪʃən] N *(hardship)* privación *f*; *(loss)* pérdida *f*

deprive [dɪ'praɪv] VT privar (**of** de)

deprived [dɪ'praɪvd] ADJ necesitado(a)

dept *(abbr* **department)** dpt, dpto

depth [depθ] N profundidad *f*; **to be in the depths of despair** estar completamente desesperado(a); **in d.** *(investigate, discuss)* a fondo, en profundidad

deputation [depjʊ'teɪʃən] N delegación *f*

deputy ['depjʊti] N **(a)** *(substitute)* suplente *mf*; **d. chairman** vicepresidente *m*; **d. head** subdirector(a) *m,f* **(b)** *Pol* diputado(a) *m,f*

derail [dɪ'reɪl] VT hacer descarrilar

deranged [dɪ'reɪndʒd] ADJ trastornado(a)

derby [*Br* 'dɑːbɪ, *US* dɜːrbɪ] N **(a)** *Sport* derby *m* **(b)** *US* bombín *m*, sombrero hongo

derelict ['derɪlɪkt] ADJ abandonado(a), en ruinas

deride [dɪ'raɪd] VT ridiculizar, burlarse de

derisive [dɪ'raɪsɪv] ADJ burlón(ona)

derisory [dɪ'raɪsərɪ] ADJ irrisorio(a)

derivative [dɪ'rɪvətɪv] **1** ADJ *(art, writing)* sin originalidad
2 N *(of word, substance)* derivado *m*

derive [dɪ'raɪv] **1** VT sacar
2 VI *(word)* derivarse (**from** de); *(skill)* provenir (**from** de)

derogatory [dɪ'rɒgətərɪ] ADJ *(remark, article)* despectivo(a); *(meaning)* peyorativo(a)

derrick ['derɪk] N torre *f* de perforación

descend [dɪ'send] **1** VI descender; **to d. from** *(be related to)* descender de
2 VT *(stairs)* bajar

descendant [dɪ'sendənt] N descendiente *mf*

descent [dɪ'sent] N **(a)** *(downward movement)* descenso *m* **(b)** *(ancestry)* ascendencia *f*

describe [dɪ'skraɪb] VT **(a)** *(depict verbally)* describir; *(characterize)* definir **(b)** *Fml (draw) (circle)* trazar

description [dɪ'skrɪpʃən] N descripción *f*; **to defy d.** superar la descripción

desecrate ['desɪkreɪt] VT profanar

desert[1] ['dezət] N desierto *m*

desert[2] [dɪ'zɜːt] **1** VT *(place, family)* abandonar
2 VI *Mil* desertar (**from** de)

deserted [dɪ'zɜːtɪd] ADJ desierto(a)

deserter [dɪ'zɜːtə(r)] N desertor(a) *m,f*

desertion [dɪ'zɜːʃən] N abandono *m*; *Pol* defección *f*; *Mil* deserción *f*

deserts [dɪ'zɜːts] NPL **to get one's just d.** llevarse su merecido

deserve [dɪ'zɜːv] VT merecer, merecerse, *Am* ameritar

deservedly [dɪ'zɜːvɪdlɪ] ADV con (toda) razón

deserving [dɪ'zɜːvɪŋ] ADJ *(person)* de valía; *(cause)* meritorio(a)

design [dɪ'zaɪn] **1** N **(a)** *(of car, furniture, clothes)* diseño *m* **(b)** *(drawing, blueprint)*

plano *m* (**c**) *(layout)* disposición *f* (**d**) *(pattern)* dibujo *m* (**e**) *Fig (scheme)* intención *f*; **by d.** a propósito; *Fam* **to have designs on** tener puestas las miras en
2 VT diseñar

designate 1 VT ['dezɪgneɪt] (**a**) *(appoint)* designar, nombrar (**b**) *Fml (boundary)* señalar
2 ADJ ['dezɪgnɪt] designado(a)

designer [dɪ'zaɪnə(r)] N *Art* diseñador(a) *m,f*; **d. jeans** pantalones *mpl* de marca

desirable [dɪ'zaɪərəbəl] ADJ deseable; *(asset, offer)* atractivo(a)

desire [dɪ'zaɪə(r)] **1** N deseo *m*; **I feel no d. to go** no me *Esp* apetece *or Carib, Col, Méx* provoca nada ir, no tengo nada de ganas de ir
2 VT desear

desist [dɪ'zɪst] VI *Fml* desistir (**from** de)

desk [desk] N *(in school)* pupitre *m*; *(in office)* escritorio *m*; *US* **d. clerk** recepcionista *mf*; **d. job** trabajo *m* de oficina; **news d.** redacción *f*; **reception d.** recepción *f*

desktop ['desktɒp] N *Comput* escritorio *m*; **d. computer** *Esp* ordenador *or Am* computadora *f* de sobremesa; **d. publishing** autoedición *f*

desolate ['desəlɪt] ADJ (**a**) *(uninhabited)* desierto(a); *(barren)* yermo(a) (**b**) *(person)* desconsolado(a)

desolation [desə'leɪʃən] N (**a**) *(of place)* desolación *f*; *(by destruction)* asolamiento *m* (**b**) *(of person)* desconsuelo *m*

despair [dɪ'speə(r)] **1** N desesperación *f*; **to drive sb to d.** desesperar a algn
2 VI desesperar(se) (**of** de)

despairing [dɪ'speərɪŋ] ADJ desesperado(a)

despatch [dɪ'spætʃ] N & VT = **dispatch**

desperate ['despərɪt] ADJ *(person, situation)* desesperado(a); *(struggle)* encarnizado(a)

desperately ['despərɪtlɪ] ADV *(fight, plead)* desesperadamente; *(struggle)* encarnizadamente; *(ill)* gravísimamente; *(in love)* locamente

desperation [despə'reɪʃən] N desesperación *f*; **in d.** a la desesperada

despicable [dɪ'spɪkəbəl] ADJ despreciable; *(behaviour)* indigno(a)

despise [dɪ'spaɪz] VT despreciar, menospreciar

despite [dɪ'spaɪt] PREP *Fml* a pesar de

despondent [dɪ'spɒndənt] ADJ abatido(a)

despot ['despɒt] N déspota *mf*

dessert [dɪ'zɜːt] N postre *m*; **d. wine** vino *m* dulce

dessertspoon [dɪ'zɜːtspuːn] N cuchara *f or Ven* cucharilla *f* de postre; *(as measurement)* cucharada *f* de las de postre

destination [destɪ'neɪʃən] N destino *m*

destined ['destɪnd] ADJ (**a**) **d. to fail** condenado(a) al fracaso (**b**) *(bound)* con destino (**for** a)

destiny ['destɪnɪ] N destino *m*

destitute ['destɪtjuːt] ADJ indigente

destroy [dɪ'strɔɪ] VT destruir; *(vehicle, old furniture)* destrozar

destroyer [dɪ'strɔɪə(r)] N *Naut* destructor *m*

destruction [dɪ'strʌkʃən] N destrucción *f*; *Fig* ruina *f*

destructive [dɪ'strʌktɪv] ADJ *(gale etc)* destructor(a); *(tendency, criticism)* destructivo(a)

detach [dɪ'tætʃ] VT *(remove)* separar

detachable [dɪ'tætʃəbəl] ADJ separable (**from** de)

detached [dɪ'tætʃt] ADJ (**a**) *(separated)* separado(a); *esp Br* **d. house** casa *f* independiente (**b**) *(impartial)* objetivo(a)

detachment [dɪ'tætʃmənt] N (**a**) *(impartiality)* objetividad *f*; *(aloofness)* desapego *m* (**b**) *Mil* destacamento *m*

detail [*Br* 'diːteɪl, *US* dɪ'teɪl] **1** N (**a**) *(item of information)* detalle *m*; **without going into detail(s)** sin entrar en detalles; **details** *(information)* detalles *mpl*; *(address and phone number)* datos *mpl* (**b**) *Mil* destacamento *m*
2 VT (**a**) *(list)* detallar, enumerar (**b**) *Mil (appoint)* destacar

detailed ['diːteɪld] ADJ detallado(a), minucioso(a)

detain [dɪ'teɪn] VT (**a**) *Jur* detener (**b**) *(delay)* retener

detainee [diːteɪ'niː] N *Pol* preso(a) *m,f*

detect [dɪ'tekt] VT *(of person)* percibir; *(of machine)* detectar; *(source of a problem)* identificar, hallar

detection [dɪ'tekʃən] N *(of mines, plane)* detección *f*; *(by detective)* investigación *f*

detective [dɪ'tektɪv] N detective *mf*; **d. story** novela policíaca

detector [dɪ'tektə(r)] N aparato *m* detector

detention [dɪ'tenʃən] N *(of suspect etc)* detención *f*, arresto *m*; *Educ* **to get d.** quedarse castigado(a)

deter [dɪ'tɜː(r)] VT *(dissuade)* disuadir (**from** de); *(stop)* impedir

detergent [dɪ'tɜːdʒənt] N detergente *m*

deteriorate [dɪ'tɪərɪəreɪt] VI deteriorarse

deterioration [dɪtɪərɪə'reɪʃən] N empeoramiento *m*; *(of substance, friendship)* deterioro *m*

determination [dɪtɜːmɪ'neɪʃən] N *(resolution)* resolución *f*

determine [dɪ'tɜːmɪn] VT determinar

determined [dɪ'tɜːmɪnd] ADJ *(person)* decidido(a); *(effort)* enérgico(a)

deterrent [dɪ'terənt] **1** ADJ disuasivo(a)
2 N fuerza disuasoria

detest [dɪ'test] VT detestar, odiar

detonate ['detəneɪt] VT & VI detonar

detonation [detə'neɪʃən] N detonación *f*

detour ['diːtʊə(r)] N desvío *m*

detract [dɪ'trækt] VI quitar mérito (**from** a)

detractor [dɪ'træktə(r)] N detractor(a) m,f

detriment ['detrɪmənt] N perjuicio m (**to** de)

detrimental [detrɪ'mentəl] ADJ perjudicial (**to** para)

deuce [dju:s] N (in tennis) cuarenta iguales mpl

devaluation [di:vælju:'eɪʃən] N devaluación f

devastate ['devəsteɪt] VT (city, area) asolar; Fig (person) desolar

devastating ['devəsteɪtɪŋ] ADJ (fire) devastador(a); (wind, flood) arrollador(a)

devastation [devə'steɪʃən] N asolación f

develop [dɪ'veləp] 1 VT (a) (theory, argument, design) desarrollar; (skills) perfeccionar (b) (natural resources) aprovechar; (site, land) urbanizar (c) (habit) adquirir; (interest) mostrar (d) Phot revelar
2 VI (a) (body, industry) desarrollarse; (system) perfeccionarse; (interest) crecer (b) (appear) crearse; (evolve) evolucionar

developer [dɪ'veləpə(r)] N (**property) d.** inmobiliaria f

development [dɪ'veləpmənt] N (a) (of theory, argument, design) desarrollo m; (of trade) fomento m; (of skill) perfección f; (of character) formación f (b) (progress, change) cambio m, variación f; **there are no new developments** no hay ninguna novedad (c) (exploitation) explotación f (d) (housing project) urbanización f

deviate ['di:vɪeɪt] VI desviarse (**from** de)

deviation [di:vɪ'eɪʃən] N (from norm, route) desviación f (**from** de); (from truth) alejamiento m

device [dɪ'vaɪs] N (a) (for measuring, processing, cutting) aparato m; (for safety, security) dispositivo m (b) (method, scheme) estratagema f

devil ['devəl] N diablo m, demonio m; **d.'s advocate** abogado(a) m,f del diablo; Fam **where the d. did you put it?** ¿dónde demonios lo pusiste?; **you lucky d.!** ¡vaya suerte que tienes!

devious ['di:vɪəs] ADJ (a) (winding) tortuoso(a) (b) (person, mind) retorcido(a)

devise [dɪ'vaɪz] VT idear, concebir

devoid [dɪ'vɔɪd] ADJ desprovisto(a) (**of** de)

devolution [di:və'lu:ʃən] N Pol = transmisión de poderes a las regiones

devote [dɪ'vəʊt] VT dedicar; **she devoted her life to helping the poor** consagró su vida a la ayuda de los pobres

devoted [dɪ'vəʊtɪd] ADJ fiel, leal (**to** a)

devotee [devə'ti:] N (of religion) devoto(a) m,f; (of theatre, sport) aficionado(a) m,f; Pol partidario(a) m,f

devotion [dɪ'vəʊʃən] N devoción f; (to cause) dedicación f

devour [dɪ'vaʊə(r)] VT devorar

devout [dɪ'vaʊt] ADJ devoto(a)

dew [dju:] N rocío m

dexterity [dek'sterɪtɪ] N destreza f

dext(e)rous ['dekstrəs] ADJ diestro(a)

diabetes [daɪə'bi:ti:z, daɪə'bi:tɪs] N diabetes f

diabetic [daɪə'betɪk] ADJ & N diabético(a) (m,f)

diabolical [daɪə'bɒlɪkəl] ADJ (a) (evil) diabólico(a) (b) Br Fam (very bad) espantoso(a)

diagnose ['daɪəgnəʊz] VT diagnosticar

diagnosis [daɪəg'nəʊsɪs] N (pl **diagnoses** [daɪəg'nəʊsi:z]) diagnóstico m

diagonal [daɪ'ægənəl] ADJ & N diagonal (f)

diagonally [daɪ'ægənəlɪ] ADV en diagonal, diagonalmente

diagram ['daɪəgræm] N diagrama m; (of process, system) esquema m; (of workings) gráfico m

dial ['daɪəl, daɪl] 1 N (of clock) esfera f; (of radio) cuadrante m; (of telephone) disco m; (of machine) botón m selector
2 VT & VI Tel marcar, Andes, CSur discar; Br **dialling** or US **d. code** prefijo m; Br **dialling** or US **d. tone** señal f de marcar or Andes, CSur discar

dialect ['daɪəlekt] N dialecto m

dialogue, US **dialog** ['daɪəlɒg] N diálogo m

dialysis [daɪ'ælɪsɪs] N Med diálisis f inv

diameter [daɪ'æmɪtə(r)] N diámetro m

diametrically [daɪə'metrɪkəlɪ] ADV diametralmente

diamond ['daɪəmənd] N (a) (gem) diamante m (b) (shape) rombo m

diaper ['daɪəpə(r)] N US pañal m

diaphragm ['daɪəfræm] N diafragma m

diarrhoea, US **diarrhea** [daɪə'rɪə] N diarrea f

diary ['daɪərɪ] N (a) (as record) diario m; **to keep a d.** llevar un diario (b) (for appointments) agenda f

dice [daɪs] 1 N (pl **dice**) dado m
2 VT Culin cortar en cuadritos

dichotomy [daɪ'kɒtəmɪ] N dicotomía f

dictate 1 VT [dɪk'teɪt] (letter, order) dictar
2 VI **to d. to sb** dar órdenes a algn
3 N ['dɪkteɪt] Fig **the dictates of conscience** los dictados de la conciencia

dictation [dɪk'teɪʃən] N dictado m

dictator [dɪk'teɪtə(r)] N dictador(a) m,f

dictatorship [dɪk'teɪtəʃɪp] N dictadura f

diction ['dɪkʃən] N dicción f

dictionary ['dɪkʃənərɪ] N diccionario m

did [dɪd] PT of do

die [daɪ] VI morir, morirse; Fam Fig **to be dying for sth/to do sth** morirse por algo/de ganas de hacer algo
▶ **die away** VI desvanecerse
▶ **die down** VI (fire) extinguirse; (wind) amainar; (noise, excitement) disminuir
▶ **die off** VI morir uno por uno
▶ **die out** VI extinguirse

die-hard ['daɪhɑ:d] N reaccionario(a) m,f

diesel ['di:zəl] N (**a**) *(oil)* gasoil *m*; **d. engine** motor *m* diesel (**b**) *Fam (vehicle)* vehículo *m* diesel

diet ['daɪət] **1** N *(normal food)* dieta *f*; *(selected food)* régimen *m*; **to be on a d.** estar a régimen **2** VI estar a régimen

dietician [daɪə'tɪʃən] N especialista *mf* en dietética, *Am* dietista *mf*

differ ['dɪfə(r)] VI *(be unlike)* ser distinto(a); *(disagree)* discrepar

difference ['dɪfərəns] N (**a**) *(dissimilarity)* diferencia *f*; **it makes no d. (to me)** (me) da igual; **what d. does it make?** ¿qué más da? (**b**) *(disagreement)* desacuerdo *m*

different ['dɪfərənt] ADJ diferente, distinto(a); **you look d.** pareces otro(a)

differentiate ['dɪfə'renʃɪeɪt] **1** VT distinguir, diferenciar (**from** de) **2** VI distinguir (**between** entre)

differently ['dɪfərəntlɪ] ADV de otra manera

difficult ['dɪfɪkəlt] ADJ difícil

difficulty ['dɪfɪkəltɪ] N dificultad *f*; *(problem)* problema *m*; **to be in difficulties** estar en un apuro

diffident ['dɪfɪdənt] ADJ tímido(a)

diffuse 1 ADJ [dɪ'fju:s] *(light)* difuso(a); *Fig* vago(a) **2** VT [dɪ'fju:z] difundir; *(heat)* desprender

dig [dɪg] **1** N (**a**) *(poke)* codazo *m* (**b**) *Fam (gibe)* pulla *f* **2** VT *(pt & pp dug)* (**a**) *(earth)* cavar; *(tunnel)* excavar (**b**) *Fam Fig* **to d. one's heels in** mantenerse en sus trece **3** VI *(person)* cavar; *(animal)* escarbar
▸ **dig in** VI *Mil* atrincherarse
▸ **dig out** VT SEP *Fig (old suit)* sacar; *(information)* descubrir
▸ **dig up** VT SEP *(weeds)* arrancar; *(buried object)* desenterrar; *(road)* levantar; *Fig* sacar a relucir

digest 1 N ['daɪdʒest] *(summary)* resumen *m* **2** VT [dɪ'dʒest] *(food)* digerir; *Fig (facts)* asimilar

digestion [dɪ'dʒestʃən] N digestión *f*

digestive [dɪ'dʒestɪv] ADJ digestivo(a); *Br* **d. biscuit** galleta *f* integral

digger ['dɪgə(r)] N excavadora *f*

digit ['dɪdʒɪt] N (**a**) *Math* dígito *m* (**b**) *Fml Anat* dedo *m*

digital ['dɪdʒɪtəl] ADJ digital; **d. television** televisión *f* digital

dignified ['dɪgnɪfaɪd] ADJ *(manner)* solemne, serio(a); *(appearance)* majestuoso(a)

dignitary ['dɪgnɪtərɪ] N dignatario *m*

dignity ['dɪgnɪtɪ] N dignidad *f*

digress [daɪ'gres] VI apartarse del tema

dike [daɪk] N *US* = **dyke**

dilapidated [dɪ'læpɪdeɪtɪd] ADJ en mal estado

dilemma [dɪ'lemə, daɪ'lemə] N dilema *m*

diligent ['dɪlɪdʒənt] ADJ *(worker)* diligente; *(inquiries, search)* esmerado(a)

dilute [daɪ'lu:t] **1** VT diluir; *(wine, milk)* aguar; *Fig (effect, influence)* atenuar **2** VI diluirse

dim [dɪm] **1** ADJ (**dimmer, dimmest**) (**a**) *(light)* débil, tenue; *(room)* oscuro(a); *(outline)* borroso(a); *(eyesight)* defectuoso(a); *Fig (memory)* vago(a); *Fig (future)* sombrío(a) (**b**) *Fam (stupid)* tonto(a), corto(a) de alcances, *Am* sonso(a) **2** VT *(light)* bajar **3** VI *(light)* bajarse; *(sight)* nublarse; *Fig (joy)* extinguirse

dime [daɪm] N *US* moneda *f* de diez centavos

dimension [daɪ'menʃən] N dimensión *f*

diminish [dɪ'mɪnɪʃ] VT & VI disminuir

diminutive [dɪ'mɪnjutɪv] **1** ADJ diminuto(a) **2** N *Gram* diminutivo *m*

dimly ['dɪmlɪ] ADV vagamente

dimmer ['dɪmə(r)] N **d. (switch)** regulador *m* de voltaje

dimple ['dɪmpəl] N hoyuelo *m*

din [dɪn] N *(of crowd)* alboroto *m*; *(of machinery)* estruendo *m*

dine [daɪn] VI *Fml* cenar; **to d. out** cenar fuera

diner ['daɪnə(r)] N (**a**) *(person)* comensal *mf* (**b**) *US (restaurant)* restaurante barato

dinghy ['dɪŋɪ] N bote *m*; **(rubber) d.** bote neumático

dingy ['dɪndʒɪ] ADJ (**dingier, dingiest**) (**a**) *(dark)* oscuro(a) (**b**) *(dirty)* sucio(a) (**c**) *(colour)* desteñido(a)

dining car ['daɪnɪŋkɑ:(r)] N vagón *m* restaurante

dining room ['daɪnɪŋru:m] N comedor *m*

dinner ['dɪnə(r)] N *(at midday)* comida *f*; *(in evening)* cena *f*; **d. jacket** smoking *m*; **d. service** vajilla *f*; **d. table** mesa *f* de comedor

dinosaur ['daɪnəsɔ:(r)] N dinosaurio *m*

dint [dɪnt] N **by d. of** a fuerza de

diocese ['daɪəsɪs] N diócesis *f inv*

dioxide [daɪ'ɒksaɪd] N bióxido *m*

dip [dɪp] **1** N (**a**) *Fam (bathe)* chapuzón *m* (**b**) *(of road)* pendiente *f*; *(in ground)* depresión *f* (**c**) *Culin* salsa *f (para mojar aperitivos)* **2** VT (**a**) *(immerse)* meter (**in(to)** en); *(food)* mojar (**in(to)** en) (**b**) *Br Aut* **to d. one's headlights** poner las luces de cruce **3** VI *(road)* bajar
▸ **dip into** VT INSEP (**a**) *(savings)* echar mano de (**b**) *(book)* hojear

diphthong ['dɪfθɒŋ] N diptongo *m*

diploma [dɪ'pləʊmə] N diploma *m*

diplomacy [dɪ'pləʊməsɪ] N diplomacia *f*

diplomat ['dɪpləmæt] N diplomático(a) *m,f*

diplomatic [dɪplə'mætɪk] ADJ diplomático(a)

dipstick ['dɪpstɪk] N indicador *m* de nivel del aceite

dire ['daɪə(r)] ADJ *(urgent)* extremo(a); *(serious)* grave

direct [dɪ'rekt, 'daɪrekt] 1 ADJ directo(a); **the d. opposite** todo lo contrario; *Elec* **d. current** corriente continua
2 ADV directamente
3 VT **(a)** *(remark, gaze, effort)* dirigir (**at** a); **can you d. me to a bank?** ¿me puede indicar dónde hay un banco? **(b)** *(instruct)* mandar

direction [dɪ'rekʃən, daɪ'rekʃən] N **(a)** *(way)* dirección f; **sense of d.** sentido m de la orientación **(b)** **directions** *(to place)* señas fpl; **directions for use** modo m de empleo **(c)** *(of play, film)* dirección f

directive [dɪ'rektɪv, daɪ'rektɪv] N directiva f

directly [dɪ'rektlɪ, daɪ'rektlɪ] 1 ADV **(a)** *(above etc)* exactamente, justo **(b)** *(speak)* francamente **(c)** *(descend)* directamente **(d)** *(come)* en seguida
2 CONJ *Fam* en cuanto

director [dɪ'rektə(r), daɪ'rektə(r)] N director(a) m,f

directory [dɪ'rektərɪ, daɪ'rektərɪ] N *Tel* guía telefónica, *Am* directorio m de teléfonos; **d. enquiries** *(servicio m de)* información f

dirt [dɜːt] N suciedad f

dirt-cheap [dɜːt'tʃiːp] ADV & ADJ *Fam* tirado(a)

dirty ['dɜːtɪ] 1 ADJ **(dirtier, dirtiest)** **(a)** *(unclean)* sucio(a) **(b)** **to give sb a d. look** fulminar a algn con la mirada **(c)** *(joke)* verde; *(mind)* pervertido(a); **d. word** palabrota f; **d. old man** viejo m verde
2 VT ensuciar

disability [dɪsə'bɪlɪtɪ] N incapacidad f, discapacidad f; **d. pension** pensión f por invalidez

disabled [dɪ'seɪbəld] 1 ADJ minusválido(a)
2 NPL **the d.** los minusválidos

disadvantage [dɪsəd'vɑːntɪdʒ] N desventaja f; *(obstacle)* inconveniente m

disaffection [dɪsə'fekʃən] N descontento m

disagree [dɪsə'griː] VI **(a)** *(differ)* no estar de acuerdo (**with** con); **to d. on** or **over sth** reñir por algo **(b)** *(not match)* discrepar (**with** de or con) **(c)** **garlic disagrees with me** el ajo no me sienta bien

disagreeable [dɪsə'griːəbəl] ADJ desagradable

disagreement [dɪsə'griːmənt] N **(a)** *(failure to agree)* desacuerdo m; *(argument)* discusión f **(b)** *(discrepancy)* discrepancia f

disallow [dɪsə'laʊ] VT *(goal)* anular; *(objection)* rechazar

disappear [dɪsə'pɪə(r)] VI desaparecer

disappearance [dɪsə'pɪərəns] N desaparición f

disappoint [dɪsə'pɔɪnt] VT *(person)* decepcionar, defraudar; *(hope, ambition)* frustrar

disappointed [dɪsə'pɔɪntɪd] ADJ decepcionado(a)

disappointing [dɪsə'pɔɪntɪŋ] ADJ decepcionante

disappointment [dɪsə'pɔɪntmənt] N decepción f

disapproval [dɪsə'pruːvəl] N desaprobación f

disapprove [dɪsə'pruːv] VI **to d. of** desaprobar

disarm [dɪs'ɑːm] 1 VT desarmar
2 VI desarmarse

disarmament [dɪs'ɑːməmənt] N desarme m

disarray [dɪsə'reɪ] N *Fml* **in d.** *(room, papers)* en desorden; *(hair)* desarreglado(a); *(thoughts)* confuso(a)

disaster [dɪ'zɑːstə(r)] N desastre m

disastrous [dɪ'zɑːstrəs] ADJ desastroso(a)

disband [dɪs'bænd] 1 VT disolver
2 VI disolverse

disbelief [dɪsbɪ'liːf] N incredulidad f

disc [dɪsk] N disco m; *Comput* disquete m; **d. jockey** disc-jockey mf, pinchadiscos mf inv

discard [dɪs'kɑːd] VT *(old things)* deshacerse de; *(plan)* descartar

discern [dɪ'sɜːn] VT *(shape, difference)* percibir; *(truth)* darse cuenta de

discerning [dɪ'sɜːnɪŋ] ADJ *(person)* perspicaz; *(taste)* refinado(a)

discharge *Fml* 1 VT [dɪs'tʃɑːdʒ] *(prisoner)* soltar; *(patient)* dar de alta a; *(soldier)* licenciar; *(employee)* despedir; *(gun)* descargar
2 N ['dɪstʃɑːdʒ] **(a)** *(of current, load, gun)* descarga f; *(of gases)* escape m **(b)** *(of prisoner)* liberación f; *(of patient)* alta f; *(of soldier)* licencia f

disciple [dɪ'saɪpəl] N discípulo(a) m,f

discipline ['dɪsɪplɪn] 1 N disciplina f
2 VT *(child)* castigar; *(worker)* sancionar; *(official)* expedientar

disclaim [dɪs'kleɪm] VT *Fml* negar tener

disclose [dɪs'kləʊz] VT revelar

disclosure [dɪs'kləʊʒə(r)] N revelación f

disco ['dɪskəʊ] N *Fam (abbr* **discotheque)** disco f

discolour, *US* **discolor** [dɪs'kʌlə(r)] VT descolorir

discomfort [dɪs'kʌmfət] N **(a)** *(lack of comfort)* incomodidad f **(b)** *(pain)* malestar m **(c)** *(unease)* inquietud f

disconcert [dɪskən'sɜːt] VT desconcertar

disconcerting [dɪskən'sɜːtɪŋ] ADJ desconcertante

disconnect [dɪskə'nekt] VT desconectar (**from** de); *(gas, electricity)* cortar

disconnected [dɪskə'nektɪd] ADJ inconexo(a)

disconsolate [dɪs'kɒnsəlɪt] ADJ desconsolado(a)

discontent [dɪskən'tent] N descontento m

discontented [dɪskən'tentɪd] ADJ descontento(a)

discontinue [dɪskən'tɪnjuː] VT *Fml* abandonar; *(work)* interrumpir

discord ['dɪskɔːd] N (**a**) *Fml* discordia *f* (**b**) *Mus* disonancia *f*

discordant [dɪs'kɔːdənt] ADJ discordante

discotheque ['dɪskətek] N discoteca *f*

discount 1 N ['dɪskaʊnt] descuento *m*
2 VT [dɪs'kaʊnt] (**a**) *(price)* rebajar (**b**) *(view, suggestion)* descartar

discourage [dɪs'kʌrɪdʒ] VT *(dishearten)* desanimar; *(advances)* rechazar

discouraging [dɪs'kʌrɪdʒɪŋ] ADJ desalentador(a)

discover [dɪ'skʌvə(r)] VT descubrir; *(missing person, object)* encontrar

discovery [dɪ'skʌvərɪ] N descubrimiento *m*

discredit [dɪs'kredɪt] **1** N descrédito *m*
2 VT *(person, régime)* desacreditar; *(theory)* poner en duda

discreet [dɪ'skriːt] ADJ discreto(a); *(distance, silence)* prudente; *(hat, house)* modesto(a)

discrepancy [dɪ'skrepənsɪ] N diferencia *f*

discretion [dɪ'skreʃən] N discreción *f*; *(prudence)* prudencia *f*; **at the d. of ...** a juicio de ...

discriminate [dɪ'skrɪmɪneɪt] VI discriminar (**between** entre); **to d. against sth/sb** discriminar algo/a algn

discriminating [dɪ'skrɪmɪneɪtɪŋ] ADJ *(person)* entendido(a); *(taste)* refinado(a)

discrimination [dɪskrɪmɪ'neɪʃən] N (**a**) *(bias)* discriminación *f* (**b**) *(distinction)* diferenciación *f*

discus ['dɪskəs] N disco *m (para lanzamientos)*

discuss [dɪ'skʌs] VT discutir; *(in writing)* tratar de

discussion [dɪ'skʌʃən] N discusión *f*; *Comput* **d. group** foro *m* (de discusión)

disdain [dɪs'deɪn] *Fml* **1** N desdén *m*
2 VT desdeñar

disdainful [dɪs'deɪnfʊl] ADJ *Fml* desdeñoso(a)

disease [dɪ'ziːz] N enfermedad *f*; *Fig* mal *m*

disembark [dɪsɪm'bɑːk] VT & VI desembarcar

disenchanted [dɪsɪn'tʃɑːntɪd] ADJ desencantado(a), desilusionado(a)

disengage [dɪsɪn'geɪdʒ] VT soltar; *Aut* **to d. the clutch** soltar el embrague, desembragar

disentangle [dɪsɪn'tæŋɡəl] VT desenredar

disfigure [dɪs'fɪɡə(r)] VT desfigurar

disgrace [dɪs'greɪs] **1** N (**a**) *(disfavour)* desgracia *f*; **to be in d.** estar desacreditado(a); **to fall into d.** caer en desgracia (**b**) *(shame)* vergüenza *f*, escándalo *m*
2 VT deshonrar, desacreditar

disgraceful [dɪs'greɪsfʊl] ADJ vergonzoso(a)

disgruntled [dɪs'ɡrʌntəld] ADJ contrariado(a), disgustado(a)

disguise [dɪs'ɡaɪz] **1** N disfraz *m*; **in d.** disfrazado(a)
2 VT (**a**) *(person)* disfrazar (**as** de) (**b**) *(feelings)* disimular

disgust [dɪs'ɡʌst] **1** N (**a**) *(loathing)* repugnancia *f*, asco *m* (**b**) *(strong disapproval)* indignación *f*
2 VT (**a**) *(revolt)* repugnar, dar asco a (**b**) *(offend)* indignar

> Note that the Spanish words **disgusto** and **disgustar** are false friends and are never a translation for the English word **disgust**. In Spanish **disgusto** means "annoyance, trouble" and **disgustar** means "to upset".

disgusting [dɪs'ɡʌstɪŋ] ADJ asqueroso(a), repugnante; *(behaviour, state of affairs)* intolerable

dish [dɪʃ] N *(for serving)* fuente *f*; *(course)* plato *m*; **to wash** *or* **do the dishes** fregar los platos
▸ **dish out** VT SEP *Fam (food)* servir; *(books, advice)* repartir; **to d. it out (to sb)** *(criticize)* criticar (a algn)
▸ **dish up** VT SEP *(meal)* servir

dishcloth ['dɪʃklɒθ] N *(for washing)* bayeta *f*; *(for drying)* paño *m* (de cocina), *CAm* secador *m*, *Méx* trapón *m*, *RP* repasador *m*

dishearten [dɪs'hɑːtən] VT desanimar

dishevelled, *US* **disheveled** [dɪ'ʃevəld] ADJ *(hair)* despeinado(a); *(appearance)* desaliñado(a)

dishonest [dɪs'ɒnɪst] ADJ *(person)* poco honrado(a); *(means)* fraudulento(a)

dishonesty [dɪs'ɒnɪstɪ] N *(of person)* falta *f* de honradez

dishonour, *US* **dishonor** [dɪs'ɒnə(r)] **1** N *Fml* deshonra *f*
2 VT *(name)* deshonrar

dishonourable, *US* **dishonorable** [dɪs'ɒnərəbəl] ADJ deshonroso(a)

dishtowel ['dɪʃtaʊəl] N paño *m* (de cocina), *CAm* secador *m*, *Méx* trapón *m*, *RP* repasador *m*

dishwasher ['dɪʃwɒʃə(r)] N lavaplatos *m inv*; *(person)* lavaplatos *mf inv*

disillusion [dɪsɪ'luːʒən] VT desilusionar

disincentive [dɪsɪn'sentɪv] N freno *m*

disinfect [dɪsɪn'fekt] VT desinfectar

disinfectant [dɪsɪn'fektənt] N desinfectante *m*

disinherit [dɪsɪn'herɪt] VT desheredar

disintegrate [dɪs'ɪntɪɡreɪt] VI desintegrarse

disintegration [dɪsɪntɪ'ɡreɪʃən] N desintegración *f*

disinterested [dɪs'ɪntrɪstɪd] ADJ desinteresado(a)

disjointed [dɪs'dʒɔɪntɪd] ADJ inconexo(a)

disk [dɪsk] N *US* disco *m*; *Comput* disquete *m*; **on d.** en disco; **d. drive** disquetera *f*, disketera *f*

diskette [dɪs'ket] N *Comput* disquete *m*

dislike [dɪs'laɪk] **1** N antipatía *f*, aversión *f* (**of a** *or* hacia)
2 VT tener antipatía *or* aversión a *or* hacia

dislocate ['dɪsləkeɪt] VT *(joint)* dislocar

dislodge [dɪs'lɒdʒ] VT sacar

disloyal [dɪs'lɔɪəl] ADJ desleal

dismal ['dɪzməl] ADJ (**a**) *(prospect)* sombrío(a); *(place, weather)* deprimente; *(person)* triste (**b**) *(failure)* horroroso(a)

dismantle [dɪs'mæntəl] VT desmontar

dismay [dɪs'meɪ] **1** N consternación *f*
2 VT consternar

dismiss [dɪs'mɪs] VT (**a**) *(idea)* descartar (**b**) *(employee)* despedir; *(official)* destituir (**c**) **to d. sb** *(from room, presence)* dar permiso a algn para retirarse (**d**) *Jur (case)* sobreseer

dismissal [dɪs'mɪsəl] N (**a**) *(of employee)* despido *m*; *(of official)* destitución *f* (**b**) *Jur (of case)* sobreseimiento *m*

dismount [dɪs'maʊnt] VI *Fml* apearse (**from** de)

disobedience [dɪsə'bi:dɪəns] N desobediencia *f*

disobedient [dɪsə'bi:dɪənt] ADJ desobediente

disobey [dɪsə'beɪ] VT & VI desobedecer; *(law)* violar

disorder [dɪs'ɔːdə(r)] N (**a**) *(untidiness)* desorden *m* (**b**) *(riot)* disturbio *m* (**c**) *(of organ, mind)* trastorno *m*; *(of speech)* defecto *m*

disorderly [dɪs'ɔːdəlɪ] ADJ (**a**) *(untidy)* desordenado(a) (**b**) *(meeting)* alborotado(a); *(conduct)* escandaloso(a)

disorganized [dɪs'ɔːgənaɪzd] ADJ desorganizado(a)

disorient [dɪs'ɔːrɪənt], **disorientate** [dɪs'ɔːrɪənteɪt] VT desorientar

disown [dɪs'əʊn] VT desconocer

disparaging [dɪ'spærɪdʒɪŋ] ADJ despectivo(a)

disparity [dɪ'spærɪtɪ] N *Fml* disparidad *f*

dispassionate [dɪs'pæʃənɪt] ADJ desapasionado(a)

dispatch [dɪ'spætʃ] **1** N (**a**) *(official message)* despacho *m*; *(journalist's report)* reportaje *m*; *(military message)* parte *m* (**b**) *(of mail)* envío *m*; *(of goods)* consignación *f*
2 VT (**a**) *(mail)* enviar; *(goods)* expedir (**b**) *Fam (food)* zamparse; *(job)* despachar

dispel [dɪ'spel] VT disipar

dispensary [dɪ'spensərɪ] N dispensario *m*

dispense [dɪ'spens] VT *(supplies)* repartir; *(justice)* administrar
▶ **dispense with** VT INSEP *(do without)* prescindir de

dispenser [dɪ'spensə(r)] N máquina expendedora; **cash d.** cajero automático; **soap d.** dosificador *m* de jabón

dispensing chemist [dɪspensɪŋ'kemɪst] N *Br* farmacéutico(a) *m,f*

dispersal [dɪ'spɜːsəl] N dispersión *f*

disperse [dɪ'spɜːs] **1** VT dispersar
2 VI dispersarse; *(fog)* disiparse

dispirited [dɪ'spɪrɪtɪd] ADJ abatido(a)

displace [dɪs'pleɪs] VT (**a**) *(shift)* desplazar; **displaced person** desplazado(a) *m,f* (**b**) *(supplant)* sustituir

display [dɪ'spleɪ] **1** N *(exhibition)* exposición *f*; *Comput* visualización *f*; *(of feelings, skills)* demostración *f*; *(of force)* despliegue *m*; **d. window** escaparate *m*, *Am* vidriera *f*, *Chile, Col, Méx* vitrina *f*; **military d.** desfile *m* militar
2 VT (**a**) *(on sign, screen)* mostrar; *(goods)* exponer; *Comput* visualizar (**b**) *(feelings)* manifestar

displease [dɪs'pli:z] VT disgustar; *(offend)* ofender

displeasure [dɪs'pleʒə(r)] N disgusto *m*

disposable [dɪ'spəʊzəbəl] ADJ (**a**) *(throwaway)* desechable (**b**) *(available)* disponible

disposal [dɪ'spəʊzəl] N (**a**) *(of rubbish)* eliminación *f* (**b**) **at my d.** *(available)* a mi disposición

dispose [dɪ'spəʊz] **1** VI **to d. of** *(remove)* eliminar; *(rubbish)* tirar; *(unwanted object)* deshacerse de; *(matter)* resolver; *(sell)* vender; *(property)* traspasar
2 VT *Fml (arrange)* disponer

disposed [dɪ'spəʊzd] ADJ *(inclined)* dispuesto(a)

disposition [dɪspə'zɪʃən] N (**a**) *(temperament)* genio *m* (**b**) *Fml (arrangement)* disposición *f*

dispossess [dɪspə'zes] VT desposeer (**of** de)

disproportionate [dɪsprə'pɔːʃənɪt] ADJ desproporcionado(a) (**to** a)

disprove [dɪs'pru:v] VT refutar

dispute 1 N ['dɪspjuːt] *(disagreement)* discusión *f*; *(quarrel)* disputa *f*; **industrial d.** conflicto *m* laboral
2 VT [dɪ'spjuːt] *(claim)* refutar; *(territory)* disputar; *(matter)* discutir
3 VI discutir (**about** *or* **over** de *or* sobre)

disqualify [dɪs'kwɒlɪfaɪ] VT (**a**) *Sport* descalificar (**b**) *(make ineligible)* incapacitar

disquiet [dɪs'kwaɪət] N preocupación *f*, inquietud *f*

disregard [dɪsrɪ'gɑːd] **1** N indiferencia *f*; *(for safety)* despreocupación *f*
2 VT descuidar; *(ignore)* ignorar

disrepair [dɪsrɪ'peə(r)] N mal estado *m*; **in a state of) d.** en mal estado; **to fall into d.** deteriorarse

disreputable [dɪs'repjʊtəbəl] ADJ *(person, area)* de mala fama; *(behaviour)* vergonzoso(a)

disrepute [dɪsrɪ'pjuːt] N mala fama, oprobio *m*

disrespectful [dɪsrɪ'spektfʊl] ADJ irrespetuoso(a)

disrupt [dɪs'rʌpt] VT *(meeting, traffic)* interrumpir; *(schedule etc)* desbaratar

disruption [dɪs'rʌpʃən] N *(of meeting, traffic)* interrupción *f*; *(of schedule etc)* desbaratamiento *m*

disruptive [dɪs'rʌptɪv] ADJ **to be d.** ocasionar trastornos

dissatisfaction [dɪssætɪs'fækʃən] N descontento *m*, insatisfacción *f*

dissatisfied [dɪs'sætɪsfaɪd] ADJ descontento(a)

dissect [dɪ'sekt, daɪ'sekt] VT disecar

disseminate [dɪˈsemɪneɪt] VT *Fml* diseminar, difundir

dissent [dɪˈsent] **1** N disentimiento *m*
2 VI disentir

dissertation [dɪsəˈteɪʃən] N *Univ Br (for higher degree)* tesina *f*; *US (doctoral)* tesis *f*

disservice [dɪsˈsɜːvɪs] N perjuicio *m*; **to do sth/ sb a d.** perjudicar algo/a algn

dissident [ˈdɪsɪdənt] ADJ & N disidente *(mf)*

dissimilar [dɪˈsɪmɪlə(r)] ADJ distinto(a)

dissipate [ˈdɪsɪpeɪt] **1** VT *(fears, doubts)* disipar; *(fortune, one's energy)* derrochar
2 VI *(mist, doubts)* disiparse

dissociate [dɪˈsəʊʃɪeɪt] VT **to d. oneself (from)** desmarcarse (de)

dissolute [ˈdɪsəluːt] ADJ disoluto(a)

dissolution [dɪsəˈluːʃən] N disolución *f*; *(of agreement)* rescisión *f*

dissolve [dɪˈzɒlv] **1** VT disolver
2 VI disolverse

dissuade [dɪˈsweɪd] VT disuadir (**from** de)

distance [ˈdɪstəns] **1** N distancia *f*; **in the d.** a lo lejos; *Fam* **to stay the d.** completar la prueba
2 VT **to d. oneself (from)** distanciarse (de)

distant [ˈdɪstənt] ADJ (**a**) *(place, time)* lejano(a); *(look)* distraído(a) (**b**) *(aloof)* distante, frío(a)

distaste [dɪsˈteɪst] N aversión *f*

distasteful [dɪsˈteɪstfʊl] ADJ desagradable

distend [dɪˈstend] *Fml* **1** VT dilatar
2 VI dilatarse

distil, *US* **distill** [dɪˈstɪl] VT destilar

distillery [dɪˈstɪlərɪ] N destilería *f*

distinct [dɪˈstɪŋkt] ADJ (**a**) *(different)* diferente; **as d. from** a diferencia de (**b**) *(smell, change)* marcado(a); *(idea, intention)* claro(a)

distinction [dɪˈstɪŋkʃən] N (**a**) *(difference)* diferencia *f* (**b**) *(excellence)* distinción *f* (**c**) *Educ* sobresaliente *m*

distinctive [dɪˈstɪŋktɪv] ADJ distintivo(a)

distinctly [dɪsˈtɪŋktlɪ] ADV (**a**) *(clearly) (speak, hear)* claramente, con claridad (**b**) *(decidedly) (better, easier)* claramente; *(ill-mannered, stupid)* verdaderamente

distinguish [dɪˈstɪŋgwɪʃ] VT distinguir

distinguished [dɪˈstɪŋgwɪʃt] ADJ distinguido(a)

distinguishing [dɪˈstɪŋgwɪʃɪŋ] ADJ distintivo(a), característico(a)

distort [dɪˈstɔːt] VT *(misrepresent)* deformar; *(words)* tergiversar

distortion [dɪˈstɔːʃən] N deformación *f*; *(of sound, image)* distorsión *f*

distract [dɪˈstrækt] VT distraer

distracted [dɪˈstræktɪd] ADJ distraído(a)

distraction [dɪˈstrækʃən] N *(interruption)* distracción *f*; *(confusion)* confusión *f*; **to drive sb to d.** sacar a algn de quicio

distraught [dɪˈstrɔːt] ADJ *(anguished)* afligido(a)

distress [dɪˈstres] **1** N *(mental)* angustia *f*; *(physical)* dolor *m*; **d. signal** señal *f* de socorro
2 VT *(upset)* apenar

distressing [dɪˈstresɪŋ] ADJ penoso(a)

distribute [dɪˈstrɪbjuːt] VT distribuir, repartir

distribution [dɪstrɪˈbjuːʃən] N distribución *f*

distributor [dɪˈstrɪbjʊtə(r)] N (**a**) *Com* distribuidor(a) *m,f* (**b**) *Aut* distribuidor *m*, *Esp* delco® *m*

district [ˈdɪstrɪkt] N *(of country)* región *f*; *(of town)* barrio *m*; *US* **d. attorney** fiscal *m*; **d. council** corporación *f* local; *Br* **d. nurse** practicante *mf*

distrust [dɪsˈtrʌst] **1** N recelo *m*
2 VT desconfiar de

disturb [dɪˈstɜːb] VT (**a**) *(inconvenience)* molestar (**b**) *(silence)* romper; *(sleep)* interrumpir (**c**) *(worry)* perturbar (**d**) *(papers)* desordenar

disturbance [dɪˈstɜːbəns] N (**a**) *(of routine)* alteración *f* (**b**) *(commotion)* disturbio *m*, alboroto *m*

disturbed [dɪˈstɜːbd] ADJ *(mentally)* inestable

disturbing [dɪˈstɜːbɪŋ] ADJ inquietante

disuse [dɪsˈjuːs] N desuso *m*

disused [dɪsˈjuːzd] ADJ abandonado(a)

ditch [dɪtʃ] **1** N zanja *f*; *(at roadside)* cuneta *f*; *(for irrigation)* acequia *f*
2 VT *Fam (plan, friend)* abandonar

dither [ˈdɪðə(r)] VI *Br Fam* vacilar, titubear

ditto [ˈdɪtəʊ] ADV ídem, lo mismo

dive [daɪv] **1** N (**a**) *(into water)* salto *m* de cabeza; *(of submarine)* inmersión *f*; *(of plane)* *Esp* picado *m*, *Am* picada *f*; *Sport* salto (**b**) *Fam (bar)* antro *m*
2 VI (**a**) *(from poolside, diving board)* tirarse de cabeza; *(submarine)* sumergirse; *(plane)* lanzarse en *Esp* picado *or Am* picada; *Sport* saltar (**b**) *(move quickly)* **he dived for the phone** se precipitó hacia el teléfono

diver [ˈdaɪvə(r)] N *(person)* buceador(a) *m,f*; *(professional)* buzo *m*; *Sport* saltador(a) *m,f*

diverge [daɪˈvɜːdʒ] VI divergir

diverse [daɪˈvɜːs] ADJ *(varied)* diverso(a), variado(a); *(different)* distinto(a), diferente

diversify [daɪˈvɜːsɪfaɪ] **1** VT diversificar
2 VI *(of company)* diversificarse

diversion [daɪˈvɜːʃən] N (**a**) *(distraction)* distracción *f* (**b**) *Br (detour)* desvío *m*

diversity [daɪˈvɜːsɪtɪ] N diversidad *f*

divert [daɪˈvɜːt] VT desviar

divide [dɪˈvaɪd] **1** VT dividir
2 VI *(road, stream)* bifurcarse
3 N división *f*, diferencia *f*

dividend [ˈdɪvɪdend] N *Fin* dividendo *m*; *Fig* beneficio *m*

divine [dɪˈvaɪn] ADJ divino(a)

diving board [ˈdaɪvɪŋbɔːd] N trampolín *m*

divinity [dɪˈvɪnɪtɪ] N (**a**) *(divine nature, god)* divinidad *f* (**b**) *(subject)* teología *f*

division [dɪ'vɪʒən] N (**a**) (separation, in maths) división f (**b**) (distribution) reparto m (**c**) (of organization) división f

divorce [dɪ'vɔːs] **1** N divorcio m
2 VT **she divorced him, she got divorced from him** se divorció de él
3 VI divorciarse

divorcee [dɪvɔː'siː] N divorciado(a) m,f

divorcée [dɪvɔː'seɪ] N divorciada f

divulge [daɪ'vʌldʒ] VT Fml divulgar, revelar

DIY [diːaɪ'waɪ] N Br (abbr **do-it-yourself**) bricolaje m

dizziness ['dɪzɪnɪs] N vértigo m

dizzy ['dɪzɪ] ADJ (**dizzier, dizziest**) (**a**) (person) (unwell) mareado(a) (**b**) (height, pace) vertiginoso(a)

DJ ['diːdʒeɪ] N Fam (abbr **disc jockey**) pinchadiscos mf inv, disc-jockey mf

DNA [diːen'eɪ] N (abbr **deoxyribonucleic acid**) ADN m

do [duː, unstressed dʊ, də] **1** V AUX

En el inglés hablado, y en el escrito en estilo coloquial, las formas negativas **do not**, **does not** y **did not** se transforman en **don't**, **doesn't** y **didn't**.

(3rd person sing pres **does**; pt **did**; pp **done**) (**a**) (in negatives and questions) (not translated in Spanish) **do you want some coffee?** ¿quieres café?; **do you drive?** ¿tienes carnet de conducir?; **don't you want to come?** ¿no quieres venir?; **he doesn't smoke** no fuma (**b**) (emphatic) (not translated in Spanish) **DO come with us!** ¡ánimo, vente con nosotros!; **DO like your bag** me encanta tu bolso (**c**) (substituting main verb in sentence) (not translated in Spanish) **neither/so do I** yo tampoco/también; **I'll go if you do** si vas tú, voy yo; **I think it's dear, but he doesn't** a mí me parece caro pero a él no; **who went? – I did** ¿quién asistió? – yo (**d**) (in question tags) **he refused, didn't he?** dijo que no, ¿verdad?; **I don't like it, do you?** a mí no me gusta, ¿y a ti?
2 VT hacer; (task) realizar; (duty) cumplir con; **to do one's best** hacer todo lo posible; **to do sth again** volver a hacer algo; **to do sth for sb** hacer algo por algn; **to do the cooking/cleaning** cocinar/limpiar; **what can I do for you?** ¿en qué puedo servirle?; **what do you do (for a living)?** ¿a qué te dedicas?; Fam **he's done it!** ¡lo ha conseguido!

Do, unido a muchos nombres, expresa actividades, como **to do the gardening**, **to do the ironing**, etc. En este diccionario, estas estructuras se encuentran bajo los nombres respectivos.

3 VI (**a**) (act) hacer; **do as I tell you** haz lo que te digo; **you did right** hiciste bien (**b**) **he did badly in the exams** los exámenes le salieron mal; **how are you doing?** ¿qué tal?; **how do you do?** (greeting) ¿cómo está usted?; (answer) mucho gusto; **to do well** (person) tener éxito; (business) ir bien (**c**) **£5 will do** (suffice) con 5 libras será suficiente; Fam **that will do!** ¡basta ya! (**d**) **this cushion will do as a pillow** (be suitable) este cojín servirá de almohada; **this won't do** esto no puede ser
4 N Br Fam (party) fiesta f; (event) ceremonia f

▸ **do away with** VT INSEP (**a**) (abolish) abolir; (discard) deshacerse de (**b**) (kill) asesinar

▸ **do down** VT SEP Br (criticize) desacreditar, menospreciar

▸ **do for** VT INSEP Fam (destroy, ruin) arruinar; Fig **I'm done for if I don't finish this** estoy perdido(a) si no acabo esto

▸ **do in** VT SEP Fam (**a**) (kill) cargarse (**b**) esp Br **I'm done in** (exhausted) estoy hecho(a) polvo

▸ **do over** VT SEP Fam (**a**) US (repeat) repetir (**b**) Br (thrash) dar una paliza a

▸ **do up** VT SEP (**a**) (wrap) envolver (**b**) (belt etc) abrochar; (laces) atar (**c**) (dress up) arreglar (**d**) Fam (redecorate) renovar

▸ **do with** VT INSEP (**a**) **I could do with a rest** (need) un descanso no me vendría nada mal (**b**) **to have** or **be to do with** (concern) tener que ver con

▸ **do without** VT INSEP pasar sin, prescindir de

docile ['dəʊsaɪl] ADJ dócil; (animal) manso(a)

dock[1] [dɒk] **1** N Naut **the docks** el muelle
2 VI (**a**) (ship) atracar (**b**) (spacecraft) acoplarse

dock[2] [dɒk] VT (reduce) descontar

dock[3] [dɒk] N Jur banquillo m (de los acusados)

docker ['dɒkə(r)] N estibador m

dockland ['dɒklænd] N zona f del puerto

dockyard ['dɒkjɑːd] N astillero m

doctor ['dɒktə(r)] **1** N (**a**) Med médico(a) m,f (**b**) Univ doctor(a) m,f; **D. of Law** doctor(a) en derecho
2 VT Pej (figures) falsificar; (text) arreglar; (drink etc) adulterar

doctorate ['dɒktərɪt] N doctorado m

doctrine ['dɒktrɪn] N doctrina f

document ['dɒkjʊmənt] **1** N documento m; **documents** (of vehicle, cargo) documentación f
2 VT ['dɒkjʊment] documentar

documentary [dɒkjʊ'mentərɪ] ADJ & N documental (m)

dodge [dɒdʒ] **1** VT (**a**) (blow) esquivar; (pursuer) despistar; Fig eludir (**b**) Fam **to d. one's taxes** engañar a Hacienda
2 VI (move aside) echarse a un lado
3 N (**a**) (movement) regate m (**b**) Fam (trick) truco m

Dodgems® ['dɒdʒəmz] NPL Br autos mpl or coches mpl de choque, Méx carritos mpl chocones, CSur autitos mpl chocadores

dodgy ['dɒdʒɪ] ADJ (**dodgier, dodgiest**) Br Fam (risky) peligroso(a), Esp chungo(a); (untrust-

worthy) dudoso; **a d. business deal** un chanchullo; **the engine sounds a bit d.** el motor no suena nada bien

doe [dəʊ] N *(of deer)* gama f; *(of rabbit)* coneja f

does [dʌz] 3RD PERSON SING PRES *of* **do**

doesn't ['dʌzənt] = **does not**

dog [dɒg] 1 N perro(a) m,f
2 VT acosar; **to d. sb's footsteps** seguir los pasos de algn

dog-eared ['dɒgɪəd] ADJ *(book)* con los bordes de las páginas doblados; *(shabby)* sobado(a)

dogged ['dɒgɪd] ADJ obstinado(a), tenaz

doghouse ['dɒghaʊs] N *US Fam* perrera f; *Fig* **to be in the d.** estar castigado(a)

dogma ['dɒgmə] N dogma m

dogmatic [dɒg'mætɪk] ADJ dogmático(a)

dogsbody ['dɒgzbɒdɪ] N *Br Fam (drudge)* burro m de carga

doh [dəʊ] N *Mus* do m

doing ['du:ɪŋ] N *(a) (action)* obra f; **it was none of my d.** yo no tuve nada que ver; *Fig* **it took some d.** costó trabajo hacerlo *(b)* **doings** *(activities)* actividades fpl

do-it-yourself [du:ɪtjə'self] N bricolaje m

doldrums ['dɒldrəmz] NPL *Fam Fig* **to be in the d.** *(person)* estar con la moral baja, *Am* estar con el ánimo por el piso; *(trade)* estar estancado(a)

dole [dəʊl] *Fam* 1 N *Br Fam* subsidio m de desempleo, *Esp* paro m; **to be on the d.** cobrar el subsidio de desempleo *or Esp* el paro; **to go on the d.** apuntarse para cobrar el desempleo, *Esp* apuntarse al paro
2 VT **to d. (out)** repartir

doleful ['dəʊlfʊl] ADJ triste, afligido(a)

doll [dɒl] 1 N *(a) (toy)* muñeca f *(b) US Fam (girl)* muñeca f
2 VT *Fam* **to d. oneself up** ponerse guapa

dollar ['dɒlə(r)] N dólar m

dolphin ['dɒlfɪn] N delfín m

domain [də'meɪn] N *(a) (sphere)* campo m, esfera f; **that's not my d.** no es de mi competencia *(b) (territory)* dominio m *(c) Comput* dominio m; **d. name** nombre m de dominio

dome [dəʊm] N *(roof)* cúpula f; *(ceiling)* bóveda f

domestic [də'mestɪk] ADJ *(a) (appliance, pet)* doméstico(a); *Br* **d. science** economía doméstica; **d. violence** violencia doméstica *(b) (home-loving)* casero(a) *(c) (flight, news)* nacional; *(trade, policy)* interior

domesticate [də'mestɪkeɪt] VT *(make home-loving)* volver hogareño(a) *or* casero(a)

domicile ['dɒmɪsaɪl] N domicilio m

dominant ['dɒmɪnənt] ADJ dominante

dominate ['dɒmɪneɪt] VT & VI dominar

domineering [dɒmɪ'nɪərɪŋ] ADJ dominante

Dominican [də'mɪnɪkən] ADJ & N *(of Dominica)* dominicano(a) *(m,f)*; **D. Republic** República Dominicana

dominion [də'mɪnjən] N dominio m

domino ['dɒmɪnəʊ] N *(pl* **dominoes)** *(piece)* ficha f de dominó; **dominoes** *(game)* dominó m

don [dɒn] N *Br Univ* profesor(a) m,f

donate [dəʊ'neɪt] VT donar

donation [dəʊ'neɪʃən] N donativo m

done [dʌn] 1 ADJ *(a) (finished)* terminado(a); **it's over and d. with** se acabó *(b) Fam (tired)* rendido(a) *(c) (meat)* hecho(a); *(vegetables)* cocido(a)
2 PP *of* **do**

donkey ['dɒŋkɪ] N burro(a) m,f

donor ['dəʊnə(r)] N donante m

don't [dəʊnt] = **do not**

donut ['dəʊnʌt] N *US* dónut m

doodle ['du:dəl] VI *Fam (write)* garabatear; *(draw)* hacer dibujos

doom [du:m] 1 N *(fate)* destino (funesto); *(ruin)* perdición f; *(death)* muerte f
2 **to be doomed** *(about to die)* ir hacia una muerte segura; *(plan, marriage)* estar condenado(a) al fracaso

doomsday ['du:mzdeɪ] N día m del juicio final

door [dɔː(r)] N puerta f; **front/back d.** puerta principal/trasera; **Fig behind closed doors** a puerta cerrada; **d. handle** manilla f (de la puerta); **d. knocker** picaporte m; **next d. (to)** (en) la casa de al lado (de)

doorbell ['dɔːbel] N timbre m (de la puerta)

doorknob ['dɔːnɒb] N pomo m

doorman ['dɔːmən] N portero m

doormat ['dɔːmæt] N felpudo m, esterilla f

doorstep ['dɔːstep] N peldaño m; *Fig* **on one's d.** a la vuelta de la esquina

door-to-door ['dɔːtə'dɔː(r)] ADJ a domicilio

doorway ['dɔːweɪ] N portal m, entrada f

dope [dəʊp] 1 N *(a) Fam (drug)* chocolate m *(b) Fam (person)* tonto(a) mf, *Am* zonzo(a) m,f
2 VT *(food, drink)* adulterar con drogas; *Sport* dopar

dop(e)y ['dəʊpɪ] ADJ *(*dopier, dopiest*) Fam (stupid)* tonto(a), bobo(a), *Am* sonso(a), *Am* zonzo(a)

dork [dɔːk] N *US Fam* petardo(a) m,f

dormant ['dɔːmənt] ADJ inactivo(a); *Fig (rivalry)* latente

dormitory ['dɔːmɪtərɪ] N *(a) (in school)* dormitorio m *(b) US (in university)* colegio m mayor

dosage ['dəʊsɪdʒ] N *Fml (amount)* dosis f inv

dose [dəʊs] 1 N dosis f inv
2 VT *(patient)* medicar

doss [dɒs] VI *Br Fam* sobar

dosshouse ['dɒshaʊs] N *Br Fam* pensión f de mala muerte

dossier ['dɒsɪeɪ] N expediente m

dot [dɒt] 1 N punto m; **on the d.** en punto; *Comput* **d. matrix printer** impresora f matricial *or* de agujas
2 VT *(a) Fam* **to d. one's i's and cross one's t's**

poner los puntos sobre las íes (**b**) *(scatter)* esparcir, salpicar

dotcom ['dɒtkɒm] N *(company)* puntocom f

dote [dəʊt] VI to d. on sb chochear con algn

double ['dʌbəl] 1 ADJ doble; **it's d. the price** cuesta dos veces más; **d. bass** contrabajo m; **d. bed** cama f de matrimonio; *Br* **d. cream** *Esp* nata f para montar, *Am* crema líquida enriquecida, *RP* crema f doble
2 ADV doble; **folded d.** doblado(a) por la mitad; **to earn d.** ganar el doble
3 N vivo retrato m; *Cin & Th* doble m
4 VT doblar; *Fig (efforts)* redoblar
5 VI (**a**) *(increase)* doblarse (**b**) **to d. as** *(serve)* hacer las veces de

▶ **double back** VI to d. back on one's tracks volver sobre sus pasos

▶ **double up** 1 VT SEP *(bend)* doblar
2 VI (**a**) *(bend)* doblarse (**b**) *(share room)* compartir la habitación (**with** con)

double-barrelled ['dʌbəlbærəld] ADJ (**a**) *(gun)* de dos cañones (**b**) *Br (surname)* compuesto(a)

double-breasted ['dʌbəlbrestɪd] ADJ cruzado(a)

double-check [dʌbəl'tʃek] VT & VI repasar dos veces

double-cross [dʌbəl'krɒs] *Fam* 1 VT engañar, traicionar
2 N engaño m, traición f

double-decker [dʌbəl'dekə(r)] N *Br* **d. (bus)** autobús m de dos pisos

double-edged ['dʌbəledʒd] ADJ de doble filo

double-glazing ['dʌbəl'gleɪzɪŋ] N doble acristalamiento m

doubt [daʊt] 1 N duda f; **beyond (all) d.** sin duda alguna; **no d.** sin duda; **there's no d. about it** no cabe la menor duda; **to be in d. about sth** dudar algo; **to be open to d.** *(fact)* ser dudoso(a); *(outcome)* ser incierto(a)
2 VT (**a**) *(distrust)* desconfiar de (**b**) *(not be sure of)* dudar; **I d. if** *or* **whether he'll come** dudo que venga

doubtful ['daʊtfʊl] ADJ (**a**) *(future)* dudoso(a), *(look)* dubitativo(a); **I'm a bit d. about it** no me convence del todo; **it's d. whether …** no se sabe seguro si … (**b**) *(questionable)* sospechoso(a)

doubtless ['daʊtlɪs] ADV sin duda, seguramente

dough [dəʊ] N (**a**) *(for bread)* masa f (**b**) *Fam (money) Esp* pasta f, *Esp, RP* guita f, *Am* plata f, *Méx* lana f

doughnut ['dəʊnʌt] N rosquilla f, dónut® m

douse [daʊs] VT (**a**) *(soak)* mojar (**b**) *(extinguish)* apagar

dove [dʌv] N paloma f

dovetail ['dʌvteɪl] VT *Fig (plans)* sincronizar

dowdy ['daʊdɪ] ADJ (**dowdier, dowdiest**) poco elegante

down [daʊn] 1 PREP (**a**) *(to or at a lower level)* **d. the river** río abajo; **to go d. the road** bajar la calle (**b**) *(along)* por
2 ADV (**a**) *(to lower level)* (hacia) abajo; *(to floor)* al suelo; *(to ground)* a tierra; **sales are d. by 5 percent** las ventas han bajado un 5 por ciento; **to fall d.** caerse (**b**) *(at lower level)* abajo; **d. there** allí abajo; *Fam Fig* **to feel d.** estar deprimido(a); *Br Fam* **d. under** en/a Australia y Nueva Zelanda
3 ADJ *(payment)* al contado; *(on property)* de entrada
4 VT *Fam (drink)* tomarse de un trago; *(food)* zamparse

down-and-out ['daʊnən'aʊt] 1 ADJ en las últimas
2 N vagabundo(a) m,f

downbeat ['daʊnbiːt] ADJ *Fam (gloomy)* deprimido(a)

downcast ['daʊnkɑːst] ADJ abatido(a)

downfall ['daʊnfɔːl] N *(of regime)* caída f; *(of person)* perdición f

downgrade ['daʊngreɪd] VT degradar

downhearted [daʊn'hɑːtɪd] ADJ desalentado(a)

downhill [daʊn'hɪl] 1 ADJ *(skiing)* de descenso; *Fam* **after the first exam, the rest were all d.** después del primer examen, los demás le fueron sobre ruedas
2 ADV **to go d.** ir cuesta abajo; *Fig (standards)* deteriorarse

download ['daʊnləʊd] VT *Comput* bajar, descargar

down-market [daʊn'mɑːkɪt] 1 ADJ barato(a)
2 ADV **to move d.** *(of company)* producir artículos más asequibles

downpour ['daʊnpɔː(r)] N chaparrón m

downright ['daʊnraɪt] *Fam* 1 ADJ *(blunt)* tajante; *(categorical)* categórico(a); **it's a d. lie** es una mentira y gorda
2 ADV *(totally)* completamente

downsizing ['daʊnsaɪzɪŋ] N *Com* reajuste m de plantillas

downstairs 1 ADV [daʊn'steəz] abajo; *(to ground floor)* a la planta baja; **to go d.** bajar la escalera
2 ADJ ['daʊnsteəz] *(on ground floor)* de la planta baja

downstream [daʊn'striːm] ADV río abajo

down-to-earth [daʊntʊ'ɜːθ] ADJ realista

downtown [daʊn'taʊn] ADV *US* en el centro (de la ciudad)

downturn ['daʊntɜːn] N baja f

downward ['daʊnwəd] 1 ADJ *(slope)* descendente; *(look)* hacia abajo; *Fin (tendency)* a la baja
2 ADV = **downwards**

downwards ['daʊnwədz] ADV hacia abajo

dowry ['daʊərɪ] N dote f

doz *(abbr* **dozen**) docena f

doze [dəʊz] **1** VI dormitar
2 N cabezada f; **to have a d.** echar una cabezada
▶ **doze off** VI quedarse dormido(a)

dozen ['dʌzən] N docena f; **half a d./a d. eggs** media docena/una docena de huevos; *Fam* **dozens of** un montón de

Dr (*abbr* **Doctor**) Dr., Dra.

drab [dræb] ADJ (**drabber, drabbest**) (**a**) (*ugly*) feo(a); (*dreary*) monótono(a), gris (**b**) (*colour*) pardo(a)

draft [drɑːft] **1** N (**a**) (*of letter, text*) borrador m (**b**) *US* servicio militar obligatorio (**c**) *US* = **draught**
2 VT (**a**) (*of letter, text*) hacer un borrador de (**b**) *US Mil* reclutar

draftsman ['drɑːftsmən] N *US* = **draughtsman**

drag [dræg] **1** VT (*pull*) arrastrar
2 VI (*trail*) arrastrarse
3 N *Fam* (*nuisance*) lata f
▶ **drag off** VT SEP llevarse arrastrando
▶ **drag on** VI (*war, strike*) hacerse interminable
▶ **drag out** VT SEP (*speech etc*) alargar

dragon ['drægən] N dragón m

dragonfly ['drægənflaɪ] N libélula f

drain [dreɪn] **1** N (**a**) (*for water*) desagüe m; (*for sewage*) alcantarilla f (**b**) (*grating*) sumidero m (**c**) *Fig* **the boys are a d. on her strength** los niños la dejan agotada
2 VT (**a**) (*marsh etc*) avenar; (*reservoir*) desecar (**b**) (*crockery*) escurrir (**c**) (*empty*) (*glass*) apurar; *Fig* (*capital etc*) agotar
3 VI (**a**) (*crockery*) escurrirse (**b**) **to d. (away)** (*liquid*) irse

drainage ['dreɪnɪdʒ] N (*of marsh*) drenaje m; (*of reservoir, building*) desagüe m; (*of town*) alcantarillado m

drainpipe ['dreɪnpaɪp] N tubo m de desagüe

dram [dræm] N *Fam* trago m (*de whisky*)

drama ['drɑːmə] N (**a**) (*play*) obra f de teatro; *Fig* drama m (**b**) (*subject*) teatro m

dramatic [drə'mætɪk] ADJ (**a**) (*change*) impresionante; (*moment*) emocionante (**b**) *Th* dramático(a), teatral

dramatist ['dræmətɪst] N dramaturgo(a) m,f

dramatization [dræmətaɪ'zeɪʃən] N adaptación f teatral

dramatize ['dræmətaɪz] VT (**a**) (*adapt*) hacer una adaptación teatral de (**b**) (*exaggerate*) dramatizar

drank [dræŋk] PT *of* **drink**

drape [dreɪp] **1** VT **to d. sth over sth** colgar algo sobre algo; **draped with** cubierto(a) de
2 N (**a**) (*of fabric*) caída f (**b**) *US* cortina f

draper ['dreɪpə(r)] N *Br* pañero(a) m,f

drastic ['dræstɪk] ADJ (**a**) (*measures*) drástico(a), severo(a) (**b**) (*change*) radical

draught [drɑːft] N (**a**) (*of cold air*) corriente f (de aire) (**b**) (*of liquid*) trago m; **d. (beer)** cerveza f de barril (**c**) *Br* **draughts** (*game*) damas fpl

draughtboard ['drɑːftbɔːd] N *Br* tablero m de damas

draughtsman ['drɑːftsmən] N delineante mf

draw [drɔː] **1** VT (*pt* **drew**; *pp* **drawn**) (**a**) (*picture*) dibujar; (*line*) trazar (**b**) (*pull*) tirar de; (*train, carriage*) arrastrar; (*curtains*) (*open*) descorrer; (*close*) correr; (*blinds*) bajar (**c**) (*extract*) sacar; (*salary*) cobrar; (*cheque*) librar (**d**) (*attract*) atraer; (*attention*) llamar (**e**) *Fig* (*strength*) sacar (**f**) (*comparison*) hacer; (*conclusion*) sacar
2 VI (**a**) (*sketch*) dibujar (**b**) (*move*) **the train drew into/out of the station** el tren entró en/ salió de la estación; **to d. apart (from)** separarse (de) (**c**) *Sport* **they drew two all** empataron a dos
3 N (**a**) (*raffle*) sorteo m (**b**) *Sport* empate m (**c**) (*attraction*) atracción f
▶ **draw in** VI (*days*) acortarse
▶ **draw on** VT INSEP (*savings*) recurrir a; (*experience*) aprovecharse de
▶ **draw out** VT SEP (**a**) (*make long*) alargar (**b**) (*encourage to speak*) desatar la lengua a (**c**) (*from pocket, drawer etc*) sacar
▶ **draw up** VT SEP (*contract*) preparar; (*plan*) esbozar

drawback ['drɔːbæk] N desventaja f, inconveniente m

drawbridge ['drɔːbrɪdʒ] N puente levadizo

drawer ['drɔːə(r)] N cajón m

drawing ['drɔːɪŋ] N dibujo m; *Br* **d. pin** *Esp* chincheta f, *Am* chinche m; *Fml* **d. room** sala f de estar

drawl [drɔːl] **1** VI hablar arrastrando las palabras
2 N voz cansina; *US* **a Southern d.** un acento sureño

drawn [drɔːn] **1** ADJ (*tired*) ojeroso(a)
2 PP *of* **draw**

dread [dred] **1** VT temer a, tener pavor a
2 N temor m

dreadful ['dredful] ADJ (**a**) (*shocking*) espantoso(a) (**b**) *Fam* (*awful*) fatal; **how d.!** ¡qué horror!

dreadfully ['dredfulɪ] ADV *Fam* terriblemente

dreadlocks ['dredlɒks] NPL trenzas fpl rastafari

dream [driːm] **1** N sueño m; **it worked like a d.** salió a la perfección
2 VT (*pt & pp* **dreamed** *or* **dreamt**) soñar
3 VI soñar (*of* or **about** con)

dreamer ['driːmə(r)] N soñador(a) m,f

dreamt [dremt] PT & PP *of* **dream**

dreamy ['driːmɪ] ADJ (**dreamier, dreamiest**) (*absent-minded*) distraído(a); (*wonderful*) de ensueño

dreary ['drɪərɪ] ADJ (**drearier, dreariest**) (**a**) (*gloomy*) triste (**b**) *Fam* (*boring*) aburrido(a), pesado(a)

dredge [dredʒ] VT & VI dragar, rastrear

▸ **dredge up** VT SEP (**a**) *(body)* sacar del agua (**b**) *Fam Fig* sacar a relucir

dregs [dregz] NPL poso *m*

drench [drentʃ] VT empapar

dress [dres] **1** N (**a**) *(frock)* vestido *m* (**b**) *(clothing)* ropa *f*; **d. rehearsal** ensayo *m* general; **d. shirt** camisa *f* de etiqueta
2 VT (**a**) *(person)* vestir; **he was dressed in a grey suit** llevaba (puesto) un traje gris (**b**) *(salad)* aderezar, *Esp* aliñar (**c**) *(wound)* vendar
3 VI vestirse

▸ **dress up 1** VI (**a**) *(in disguise)* disfrazarse (**as** de) (**b**) *(in best clothes)* vestirse elegante
2 VT SEP *Fig* disfrazar

dresser ['dresə(r)] N (**a**) *Br (in kitchen)* aparador *m* (**b**) *US (in bedroom)* cómoda *f* (**c**) *Th* ayudante *mf* de camerino

dressing ['dresɪŋ] N (**a**) *(bandage)* vendaje *m* (**b**) *(salad)* aliño *m* (**c**) **d. gown** bata *f*; **d. room** *Th* camerino *m*; *Sport* vestuario *m*; **d. table** tocador *m*

dressmaker ['dresmeɪkə(r)] N modista *mf*

dressy ['dresɪ] ADJ (**dressier, dressiest**) vistoso(a)

drew [dru:] PT of **draw**

dribble ['drɪbəl] **1** VI (**a**) *(baby)* babear (**b**) *(liquid)* gotear
2 VT *Sport (ball)* driblar
3 N *(saliva)* saliva *f*; *(of water, blood)* gotas *fpl*

dried [draɪd] ADJ *(fruit)* seco(a); *(milk)* en polvo

drier ['draɪə(r)] N = **dryer**

drift [drɪft] **1** VI (**a**) *(boat)* ir a la deriva; *Fig (person)* ir sin rumbo, vagar; **they drifted away** se marcharon poco a poco (**b**) *(snow)* amontonarse
2 N (**a**) *(flow)* flujo *m* (**b**) *(of snow)* ventisquero *m*; *(of sand)* montón *m* (**c**) *Fig (meaning)* idea *f*

driftwood ['drɪftwʊd] N madera *f* flotante

drill [drɪl] **1** N (**a**) *(hand tool)* taladro *m*; *Min* barrena *f*; **dentist's d.** fresa *f*; **pneumatic d.** martillo neumático (**b**) *esp Mil* instrucción *f*
2 VT (**a**) *(wood etc)* taladrar (**b**) *(soldiers, children)* instruir
3 VI *(by hand)* taladrar; *(for oil, coal)* perforar, sondar

drink [drɪŋk] **1** VT (*pt* **drank**; *pp* **drunk**) beber
2 VI beber; **to have sth to d.** tomarse algo; **to d. to sth/sb** brindar por algo/algn
3 N bebida *f*; *(alcoholic)* copa *f*

drinker [drɪŋkə(r)] N bebedor(a) *m,f*

drinking ['drɪŋkɪŋ] N **d. water** agua *f* potable

drip [drɪp] **1** N (**a**) *(drop)* gota *f*; *(sound)* goteo *m* (**b**) *Med* gota a gota *m inv* (**c**) *Fam (weak person)* sosaina *mf*
2 VI gotear; **he was dripping with sweat** el sudor le caía a gotas

drip-dry ['drɪp'draɪ] ADJ que no necesita planchado

dripping ['drɪpɪŋ] N *Culin* pringue *f*

drive [draɪv] **1** VT (*pt* **drove**; *pp* **driven**) (**a**) *(vehicle)* conducir, *Am* manejar; *(person)* llevar (**b**) *(power)* impulsar (**c**) *(compel)* forzar, obligar; **to d. sb mad** volver loco(a) a algn; **to d. off** rechazar
2 VI *Aut* conducir, *Am* manejar
3 N (**a**) *(trip)* paseo *m* en coche *or Am* carro *or CSur* auto; **to go for a d.** dar una vuelta en coche *or Am* carro *or CSur* carro (**b**) *(to house)* camino *m* de entrada (**c**) *(campaign)* campaña *f* (**d**) *(energy)* energía *f*, vigor *m* (**e**) *Comput* unidad *f* de disco

drive-in ['draɪvɪn] N *US (cinema)* autocine *m*

drivel ['drɪvəl] N *Fam Esp* chorradas *fpl*, *CAm, Méx* babosadas *fpl*, *Chile* leseras *fpl*, *CSur, Perú, Ven* macanas *fpl*;

driven ['drɪvən] PP of **drive**

driver ['draɪvə(r)] N *(of car, bus)* conductor(a) *m,f*; *(of train)* maquinista *mf*, *Am* chofer *mf*; *(of lorry)* camionero(a) *m,f*; *(of racing car)* piloto *mf*; *US* **d.'s license** *Esp* carné *m* or permiso *m* de conducir, *Bol, Ecuad, Perú* brevet *m*, *Carib* licencia *f* de conducir, *Méx* licencia *f* de manejar or para conducir, *RP* permiso *m* de conductor

driveway ['draɪvweɪ] N *(to house)* camino *m* de entrada

driving ['draɪvɪŋ] **1** N conducción *f*, *Am* manejo *m*; *Br* **d. licence** *Esp* carné *m* or permiso *m* de conducir, *Bol, Ecuad, Perú* brevet *m*, *Carib* licencia *f* de conducir, *Méx* licencia *f* de manejar or para conducir, *RP* permiso *m* de conductor; **d. school** autoescuela *f*; **d. test** examen *m* de conducir
2 ADJ **d. force** fuerza *f* motriz

drizzle ['drɪzəl] **1** N llovizna *f*, *Andes, RP* garúa *f*
2 VI lloviznar, chispear, *Andes, RP* garuar

droll [drəʊl] ADJ gracioso(a)

dromedary ['drɒmədərɪ] N dromedario *m*

drone [drəʊn] N *(bee etc)* zumbar

droop [dru:p] VI *(flower)* marchitarse; *(eyelids)* caerse

drop [drɒp] **1** N (**a**) *(of liquid)* gota *f*; **eye drops** colirio *m* (**b**) *(descent)* desnivel *m* (**c**) *(in price)* bajada *f*; *(in temperature)* descenso *m*
2 VT (**a**) *(let fall)* dejar caer; *(lower)* bajar; *(reduce)* disminuir; **to d. a hint** soltar una indirecta (**b**) *(abandon) (subject, charge etc)* abandonar, dejar; *Sport* **he was dropped from the team** le echaron del equipo
3 VI *(object)* caerse; *(person)* tirarse; *(voice, price, temperature)* bajar; *(wind)* amainar; *(speed)* disminuir

▸ **drop by, drop in** VI *Fam (visit)* pasarse (**at** por)

▸ **drop off 1** VI *Fam (fall asleep)* quedarse dormido(a)
2 VT SEP *(deliver)* dejar

▸ **drop out** VI *(from college)* dejar los estudios; *(from society)* marginarse; *(from competition)* retirarse

► **drop round** vɪ *Fam* = **drop by**

dropout ['drɒpaʊt] N *Fam Pej* automarginado(a) *m,f*

dropper ['drɒpə(r)] N cuentagotas *m inv*

droppings ['drɒpɪŋz] NPL excrementos *mpl*

drought [draʊt] N sequía *f*

drove [drəʊv] 1 N *(of cattle)* manada *f*
2 PT *of* **drive**

drown [draʊn] 1 VT (**a**) *(kill by drowning)* ahogar (**b**) *(flood)* inundar (**c**) *(make inaudible)* ahogar
2 VI ahogarse; **he (was) drowned** murió ahogado

drowsy ['draʊzɪ] ADJ (**drowsier, drowsiest**) soñoliento(a); **to feel d.** tener sueño

drudgery ['drʌdʒərɪ] N trabajo duro y pesado

drug [drʌg] 1 N (**a**) *(medicine)* medicamento *m* (**b**) *(narcotic)* droga *f*, estupefaciente *m*; **to be on drugs** drogarse; **d. addict** drogadicto(a) *m,f*; **d. addiction** drogadicción *f*; **d. squad** brigada *f* antidroga
2 VT *(person)* drogar; *(food, drink)* adulterar con drogas

druggist ['drʌgɪst] N *US* farmacéutico(a) *m,f*

drugstore ['drʌgstɔːr] N *US* = establecimiento donde se compran medicamentos, periódicos, etc

drum [drʌm] 1 N (**a**) *(musical instrument)* tambor *m*; **to play the drums** tocar la batería (**b**) *(container)* barril *m*; *(for oil)* bidón *m*
2 VI *Fig (with fingers)* tabalear
3 VT *Fig* **to d. sth into sb** enseñar algo a algn a machamartillo

► **drum up** VT SEP *Fam* solicitar

drummer ['drʌmə(r)] N *(in band)* tambor *mf*; *(in pop group)* batería *mf*, *Am* baterista *mf*

drumstick ['drʌmstɪk] N (**a**) *Mus* baqueta *f* (**b**) *(chicken leg)* muslo *m*

drunk [drʌŋk] 1 ADJ borracho(a); **to get d.** emborracharse
2 N borracho(a) *m,f*
3 PP *of* **drink**

drunkard ['drʌŋkəd] N borracho(a) *m,f*

drunken ['drʌŋkən] ADJ *(person)* borracho(a); **d. brawl** trifulca *f* de borrachos

dry [draɪ] 1 ADJ (**drier, driest** *or* **dryer, dryest**) (**a**) *(weather, clothing, wine)* seco(a); *US* **d. goods store** mercería *f*, tienda *f* de confección (**b**) *(wry)* socarrón(ona)
2 VT *(pt & pp dried)* secar
3 VI **to d. (off)** secarse

dry-clean [draɪ'kliːn] VT limpiar *or* lavar en seco

dryer ['draɪə(r)] N secadora *f*

DTP [diːtiː'piː] N *Comput (abbr desktop publishing)* autoedición *f*

dual ['djʊəl] ADJ doble; *Br* **d. carriageway** *(road)* (tramo *m* de) autovía *f*

dub¹ [dʌb] VT *(subtitle)* doblar (**into** a)

dub² [dʌb] VT (**a**) *(give nickname to)* apodar (**b**) *(knight)* armar

dubious ['djuːbɪəs] ADJ (**a**) *(morals etc)* dudoso(a); *(compliment)* equívoco(a) (**b**) *(doubting)* indeciso(a)

Dublin ['dʌblɪn] N Dublín

duchess ['dʌtʃɪs] N duquesa *f*

duck¹ [dʌk] N pato(a) *m,f*; *Culin* pato *m*

duck² [dʌk] 1 VT (**a**) *(submerge)* dar una ahogadilla a (**b**) *(evade)* esquivar
2 VI (**a**) *(evade blow)* esquivar (**b**) *Fam* **to d. (out)** rajarse

duckling ['dʌklɪŋ] N patito *m*

duct [dʌkt] N *(for fuel etc)* conducto *m*; *Anat* canal *m*

dud [dʌd] *Fam* 1 ADJ (**a**) *(useless)* inútil; *(defective)* estropeado(a) (**b**) *(banknote)* falso(a); *(cheque)* sin fondos
2 N *(useless thing)* engañifa *f*; *(person)* desastre *m*

dude [duːd] N *US Fam (man)* tipo *m*, *Esp* tío *m*

due [djuː] ADJ (**a**) *(expected)* esperado(a); **the train is d. (to arrive) at ten** el tren debe llegar a las diez (**b**) *Fml (proper)* debido(a); **in d. course** a su debido tiempo (**c**) *(owing)* pagadero(a); **how much are you d.?** *(owed)* ¿cuánto te deben? (**d**) **to be d. to** *(caused by)* deberse a; **d. to** *(because of)* debido de

duel ['djuːəl] N duelo *m*

duet [djuː'et] N dúo *m*

duffel ['dʌfəl] N **d. bag** petate *m*; **d. coat** trenca *f*

dug [dʌg] PT & PP *of* **dig**

duke [djuːk] N duque *m*

dull [dʌl] 1 ADJ (**a**) *(boring)* pesado(a); *(place)* sin interés (**b**) *(light)* apagado(a); *(weather)* gris (**c**) *(sound, ache)* sordo(a) (**d**) *(not intelligent)* tonto(a), torpe, *Am* sonso(a)
2 VT *(pain)* aliviar

duly ['djuːlɪ] ADV *Fml (properly)* debidamente; *(as expected)* como era de esperar; *(in due course)* a su debido tiempo

dumb [dʌm] 1 ADJ (**a**) *Med* mudo(a) (**b**) *Fam (stupid)* tonto(a)
2 NPL **the d.** los mudos

dumbbell ['dʌmbel] N *Sport* pesa *f*

dumbfounded [dʌm'faʊndɪd] ADJ pasmado(a)

dumbstruck ['dʌmstrʌk] ADJ pasmado(a)

dummy ['dʌmɪ] N (**a**) *(sham)* imitación *f* (**b**) *(in shop window)* maniquí *m*; *(of ventriloquist)* muñeco *m* (**c**) *Br (for baby)* chupete *m*

dump [dʌmp] 1 N (**a**) *(tip)* vertedero *m*; *(for old cars)* cementerio *m* (de coches) (**b**) *Fam Pej (place)* estercolero *m*; *(town)* poblacho *m*; *(dwelling)* tugurio *m* (**c**) *Mil* depósito *m*
2 VT (**a**) *(rubbish)* verter; *(truck contents)* descargar (**b**) *(person)* dejar; *Com* inundar el mercado con (**c**) *Comput (transfer)* copiar de memoria interna

dumping ['dʌmpɪŋ] N vertido *m*

dumpling ['dʌmplɪŋ] N *Culin* = bola de masa hervida

Dumpster® ['dʌmpstə(r)] N contenedor *m* (de escombros)

dumpy ['dʌmpɪ] ADJ (**dumpier, dumpiest**) *Fam* rechoncho(a)

dunce [dʌns] N *Fam* tonto(a) *m,f*

dune [djuːn] N (**sand**) **d.** duna *f*

dung [dʌŋ] N estiércol *m*

dungarees [dʌŋgə'riːz] NPL mono *m*

dungeon ['dʌndʒən] N calabozo *m*, mazmorra *f*

duo ['djuːəʊ] N *Mus* dúo *m*; *Fam* pareja *f*

dupe [djuːp] **1** VT engañar
2 N ingenuo(a) *m,f*

duplex ['djuːpleks] N *US* (**house**) casa adosada; **d. apartment** dúplex *m inv*

duplicate 1 VT ['djuːplɪkeɪt] (**a**) (*copy*) duplicar; (*film, tape*) reproducir (**b**) (*repeat*) repetir
2 N ['djuːplɪkɪt] duplicado *m*; **in d.** por duplicado

durable ['djʊərəbəl] ADJ duradero(a)

duration [djʊ'reɪʃən] N *Fml* duración *f*

duress [djʊ'res] N *Fml* coacción *f*

> Note that the Spanish word **dureza** is a false friend and is never a translation for the English word **duress**. In Spanish, **dureza** means "hardness, harshness".

during ['djʊərɪŋ] PREP durante

dusk [dʌsk] N *Fml* crepúsculo *m*; **at d.** al anochecer

dust [dʌst] **1** N polvo *m*; **d. cloud** polvareda *f*; **d. jacket** sobrecubierta *f*
2 VT (**a**) (*furniture*) quitar el polvo a (**b**) (*cake*) espolvorear

dustbin ['dʌstbɪn] N *Br* cubo *m* or *Am* bote *m* de la basura

dustcart ['dʌstkɑːt] N *Br* camión *m* de la basura

duster ['dʌstə(r)] N *Br* (*cloth*) trapo *m* or bayeta *f* (del polvo); **feather d.** plumero *m*

dustman ['dʌstmən] N *Br* basurero *m*

dustpan ['dʌstpæn] N recogedor *m*

dusty ['dʌstɪ] ADJ (**dustier, dustiest**) polvoriento(a)

Dutch [dʌtʃ] **1** ADJ holandés(esa); *Fig* **D. cap** diafragma *m*
2 N (**a**) PL **the D.** los holandeses (**b**) (*language*) holandés *m*; **it's double D. to me** me suena a chino
3 ADV *Fam* **to go D.** pagar cada uno lo suyo, *Esp* pagar a escote

Dutchman ['dʌtʃmən] N holandés *m*

Dutchwoman ['dʌtʃwʊmən] N holandesa *f*

duty ['djuːtɪ] N (**a**) (*obligation*) deber *m*; **to do one's d.** cumplir con su deber (**b**) (*task*) **duties** tareas *fpl* (**c**) **to be on d.** estar de servicio; *Med & Mil* estar de guardia (**d**) (*tax*) impuesto *m*

duty-free [djuːtɪ'friː] ADJ libre de impuestos

duvet ['duːveɪ] N *Br* edredón *m*

DVD [diːviː'diː] N *Comput* (*abbr* **Digital Versatile Disk, Digital Video Disk**) DVD *m*

dwarf [dwɔːf] **1** N (*pl* **dwarves** [dwɔːvz]) (*person*) enano(a) *m,f*
2 VT hacer parecer pequeño(a) a

dwell [dwel] VI (*pt & pp* **dwelt**) *Fml* morar
► **dwell on** VT INSEP hablar extensamente de; **let's not d. on it** olvidémoslo

dwelling ['dwelɪŋ] N *Fml & Hum* morada *f*, vivienda *f*

dwelt [dwelt] PT & PP *of* **dwell**

dwindle ['dwɪndəl] VI menguar, disminuir

dye [daɪ] **1** N tinte *m*
2 VT (*pres p* **dyeing**; *pt & pp* **dyed**) teñir; **to d. one's hair black** teñirse el pelo de negro

dying ['daɪɪŋ] ADJ (*person*) moribundo(a), agonizante; *Fig* (*custom*) en vías de desaparición

dyke [daɪk] N (**a**) (*bank*) dique *m*; (*causeway*) terraplén *m* (**b**) *very Fam Pej* tortillera *f*

dynamic [daɪ'næmɪk] ADJ dinámico(a)

dynamics [daɪ'næmɪks] N SING dinámica *f*

dynamism ['daɪnəmɪzəm] N dinamismo *m*

dynamite ['daɪnəmaɪt] N dinamita *f*

dynamo ['daɪnəməʊ] N dínamo *f*

dynasty ['dɪnəstɪ] N dinastía *f*

dysentery ['dɪsəntrɪ] N disentería *f*

dyslexia [dɪs'leksɪə] N dislexia *f*

E, e [i:] N (**a**) *(the letter)* E, e f (**b**) *Mus* E mi m

E [i:] N (**a**) *(abbr* **East**) E (**b**) *Fam (abbr* **ecstasy**) *(drug)* éxtasis m inv

each [i:tʃ] **1** ADJ cada; **e. day/month** todos los días/meses; **e. person** cada cual; **e. time I see him** cada vez que lo veo

2 PRON (**a**) *(both, all)* cada uno(a); **£2 e.** 2 libras cada uno; **we bought one e.** nos compramos uno cada uno (**b**) *(reciprocal)* **e. other** el uno al otro; **they hate e. other** se odian

eager ['i:gə(r)] ADJ *(anxious)* impaciente; *(desirous)* deseoso(a); **e. to begin** impaciente por empezar; **to be e. for success** codiciar el éxito

eagerly ['i:gəlɪ] ADV *(anxiously)* con impaciencia; *(keenly)* con ilusión

eagle ['i:gəl] N águila f

ear [ɪə(r)] N (**a**) *(external part)* oreja f; *(internal part, sense of hearing)* oído m (**b**) *(of wheat)* espiga f

earache ['ɪəreɪk] N dolor m de oídos

eardrum ['ɪədrʌm] N tímpano m

earl [ɜːl] N conde m

earlobe ['ɪələʊb] N lóbulo m

early ['ɜːlɪ] *(earlier, earliest)* **1** ADJ (**a**) *(before the usual time)* temprano(a); **to have an e. night** acostarse pronto; **you're e.!** ¡qué pronto has venido! (**b**) *(at first stage, period)* **at an e. age** siendo joven; **in e. July** a principios de julio; **e. work** obra de juventud; **in her e. forties** a los cuarenta y pocos

2 ADV (**a**) *(before the expected time)* temprano, *Esp* pronto; **earlier on** antes; **five minutes e.** con cinco minutos de adelanto (**b**) *(near the beginning)* **as e. as 1914** ya en 1914; **as e. as possible** tan pronto como sea posible; **to book e.** reservar con tiempo; **e. on** temprano

earmark ['ɪəmɑːk] VT destinar (**for** para *or* a)

earn [ɜːn] VT (**a**) *(money)* ganar; **to e. one's living** ganarse la vida (**b**) *(reputation)* ganarse (**c**) **to e. interest** cobrar interés *or* intereses

earnest ['ɜːnɪst] **1** ADJ serio(a), formal

2 N **in e.** de veras, en serio

earnings ['ɜːnɪŋz] NPL ingresos mpl

earphones ['ɪəfəʊnz] NPL auriculares mpl

earring ['ɪərɪŋ] N pendiente m, *Am* arete m

earshot ['ɪəʃɒt] N **out of e.** fuera del alcance del oído; **within e.** al alcance del oído

earth [ɜːθ] **1** N (**a**) *(soil)* tierra f; **the E.** la Tierra; *Fig* **to be down to e.** ser práctico; *Fam* **where/**

why on e. …? ¿pero dónde/por qué demonios …? (**b**) *Br Elec* toma f de tierra

2 VT *Br Elec* conectar a tierra

earthenware ['ɜːθənweə(r)] **1** N loza f

2 ADJ de barro

earthquake ['ɜːkweɪk] N terremoto m

earthshattering ['ɜːθʃætərɪŋ] ADJ trascendental; **e. news** noticia bomba

earthworm ['ɜːwɜːm] N lombriz f de tierra

earthy ['ɜːθɪ] ADJ *(earthier, earthiest)* (**a**) *(taste)* terroso(a) (**b**) *(bawdy)* tosco(a)

earwig ['ɪəwɪg] N tijereta f

ease [i:z] **1** N (**a**) *(freedom from discomfort)* tranquilidad f; **at e.** relajado(a) (**b**) *(lack of difficulty)* facilidad f

2 VT *(pain)* aliviar

▸ **ease off, ease up** VI (**a**) *(decrease)* disminuir (**b**) *(slow down)* ir más despacio

easel ['i:zəl] N caballete m

easily ['i:zɪlɪ] ADV fácilmente; **e. the best** con mucho el mejor

east [i:st] **1** N este m; **the Middle E.** el Oriente Medio

2 ADJ del este, oriental; **E. Germany** Alemania Oriental

3 ADV al *or* hacia el este

Easter ['i:stə(r)] N Semana Santa, Pascua f; **E. egg** huevo m de Pascua; **E. Sunday** Domingo m de Resurrección

easterly ['i:stəlɪ] ADJ *(from the east)* del este; *(to the east)* hacia al este

eastern ['i:stən] ADJ oriental, del este

eastward(s) ['i:stwəd(z)] ADV hacia el este

easy ['i:zɪ] *(easier, easiest)* **1** ADJ (**a**) *(simple)* fácil, sencillo(a) (**b**) *(unworried, comfortable)* cómodo(a), tranquilo(a); *Fam* **I'm e.!** ¡me da lo mismo!; **e. chair** butacón m

2 ADV **go e. on the wine** no te pases con el vino; *Fam* **to take things e.** tomarse las cosas con calma; *Fam* **take it e.!** ¡tranquilo!

easy-going [i:zɪ'gəʊɪŋ] ADJ *(calm)* tranquilo(a); *(lax)* despreocupado(a); *(undemanding)* poco exigente

eat [i:t] VT *(pt* **ate**; *pp* **eaten**) comer

▸ **eat away** VT SEP desgastar; *(metal)* corroer

▸ **eat into** VT INSEP (**a**) *(wood)* roer (**b**) *Fig (savings)* consumir

▸ **eat out** VI comer fuera

▶ **eat up** VT SEP (**a**) *(meal)* terminar (**b**) *Fig (petrol)* consumir; *(miles)* recorrer rápidamente

eatable [ˈiːtəbəl] ADJ comestible

eaten [ˈiːtən] PP of **eat**

eau de Cologne [əʊdəkəˈləʊn] N colonia *f*

eaves [iːvz] NPL alero *m*

eavesdrop [ˈiːvzdrɒp] VI escuchar disimuladamente

ebb [eb] **1** N reflujo *m*; *Fig* **the e. and flow** *(of events)* los vaivenes; *Fig* **to be at a low e.** estar decaído
  2 VI (**a**) *(tide)* bajar; **to e. and flow** subir y bajar (**b**) *Fig* **to e. away** decaer

ebony [ˈebənɪ] **1** N ébano *m*
  2 ADJ de ébano

eccentric [ɪkˈsentrɪk] ADJ & N excéntrico(a) *(m,f)*

ecclesiastic [ɪkliːzɪˈæstɪk] ADJ & N eclesiástico(a) *(m,f)*

echelon [ˈeʃəlɒn] N escalafón *m*

echo [ˈekəʊ] **1** N *(pl echoes)* eco *m*
  2 VT *(repeat)* repetir
  3 VI resonar, hacer eco

eclectic [ɪˈklektɪk] ADJ ecléctico(a)

eclipse [ɪˈklɪps] **1** N eclipse *m*
  2 VT eclipsar

ecological [iːkəˈlɒdʒɪkəl] ADJ ecológico(a)

ecology [ɪˈkɒlədʒɪ] N ecología *f*

e-commerce [iːˈkɒmaːs] N comercio electrónico

economic [iːkəˈnɒmɪk] ADJ económico(a); *(profitable)* rentable

economical [iːkəˈnɒmɪkəl] ADJ económico(a)

economics [iːkəˈnɒmɪks] N SING *(science)* economía *f*; *Educ* (ciencias *fpl*) económicas *fpl*

economist [ɪˈkɒnəmɪst] N economista *mf*

economize [ɪˈkɒnəmaɪz] VI economizar

economy [ɪˈkɒnəmɪ] N (**a**) *Pol* **the e.** la economía (**b**) *(saving)* ahorro *m*; **e. class** clase *f* turista

ecosystem [ˈiːkəʊsɪstəm] N ecosistema *m*

ecotax [ˈiːkəʊtæks] N ecotasa *f*

ecotourism [ˈiːkəʊtɔːrɪzəm] N ecoturismo *m*

ecstasy [ˈekstəsɪ] N éxtasis *m inv*

ecstatic [ekˈstætɪk] ADJ extático(a)

Ecuador [ˈekwədɔː(r)] N Ecuador

eczema [ˈeksɪmə] N eczema *m*

eddy [ˈedɪ] **1** N remolino *m*
  2 VI arremolinarse

edge [edʒ] **1** N borde *m*; *(of knife)* filo *m*; *(of coin)* canto *m*; *(of water)* orilla *f*; **on the e. of town** en las afueras de la ciudad
  2 VT *Sewing* ribetear
  3 VI **to e. forward** avanzar poco a poco

edgeways [ˈedʒweɪz], **edgewise** [ˈedʒwaɪz] ADV de lado; *Fig* **I couldn't get a word in e.** no pude decir ni pío

edging [ˈedʒɪŋ] N borde *m*; *Sewing* ribete *m*

edgy [ˈedʒɪ] ADJ (**edgier, edgiest**) nervioso(a)

edible [ˈedɪbəl] ADJ comestible

edict [ˈiːdɪkt] N *Hist* edicto *m*; *Jur* decreto *m*

Edinburgh [ˈedɪnbrə] N Edimburgo

edit [ˈedɪt] VT (**a**) *(prepare for printing)* preparar para la imprenta (**b**) *(rewrite)* corregir (**c**) *Press* ser redactor(a) de (**d**) *Cin, Rad & TV* montar; *(cut)* cortar

edition [ɪˈdɪʃən] N edición *f*

editor [ˈedɪtə(r)] N *(of book)* editor(a) *m,f*; *Press* redactor(a) *m,f*; *Cin & TV* montador(a) *m,f*

editorial [edɪˈtɔːrɪəl] **1** ADJ editorial; **e. staff** redacción *f*
  2 N editorial *m*

educate [ˈedjʊkeɪt] VT educar

educated [ˈedjʊkeɪtɪd] ADJ culto(a)

education [edjʊˈkeɪʃən] N (**a**) *(schooling)* enseñanza *f*; **Ministry of E.** Ministerio *m* de Educación (**b**) *(training)* formación *f* (**c**) *(studies)* estudios *mpl* (**d**) *(culture)* cultura *f*

educational [edjʊˈkeɪʃənəl] ADJ educativo(a), educacional

eel [iːl] N anguila *f*

eerie [ˈɪərɪ] ADJ (**eerier, eeriest**) siniestro(a)

efface [ɪˈfeɪs] VT borrar

effect [ɪˈfekt] **1** N (**a**) *(result)* efecto *m*; **in e.** efectivamente; **to come into e.** entrar en vigor; **to have an e. on** afectar a; **to take e.** *(drug)* surtir efecto; *(law)* entrar en vigor (**b**) *(impression)* impresión *f*
  2 VT *Fml* provocar

effective [ɪˈfektɪv] ADJ (**a**) *(successful)* eficaz (**b**) *(real)* efectivo(a) (**c**) *(impressive)* impresionante

effectively [ɪˈfektɪvlɪ] ADV (**a**) *(successfully)* eficazmente (**b**) *(in fact)* en efecto

effeminate [ɪˈfemɪnɪt] ADJ afeminado(a)

effervescent [efəˈvesənt] ADJ efervescente

efficiency [ɪˈfɪʃənsɪ] N *(of person)* eficacia *f*; *(of machine)* rendimiento *m*

efficient [ɪˈfɪʃənt] ADJ eficaz, eficiente; *(machine)* de buen rendimiento

effigy [ˈefɪdʒɪ] N efigie *f*

effluent [ˈefluənt] N vertidos *mpl*

effort [ˈefət] N (**a**) *(exertion)* esfuerzo *m*; **to make an e.** hacer un esfuerzo, esforzarse (**b**) *(attempt)* intento *m*

effortless [ˈefətlɪs] ADJ sin esfuerzo

effrontery [ɪˈfrʌntərɪ] N desfachatez *f*

effusive [ɪˈfjuːsɪv] ADJ efusivo(a)

eg [iːˈdʒiː] *(abbr exempli gratia)* p. ej.

egalitarian [ɪgælɪˈteərɪən] ADJ igualitario(a)

egg [eg] **1** N huevo *m*, *CAm, Méx* blanquillo *m*; **e. cup** huevera *f*; **e. timer** reloj *m* de arena; **e. white** clara *f* de huevo
  2 VT **to e. sb on (to do sth)** empujar a algn (a hacer algo)

eggplant [ˈegplɑːnt] N *US* berenjena *f*

eggshell [ˈegʃel] N cáscara *f* de huevo

ego ['iːgəʊ, 'egəʊ] N (a) *Psy* ego *m*; *Fam* **e. trip** autobombo *m* (b) *(self-esteem)* amor *m* propio

egocentric(al) [iːgəʊ'sentrɪk(əl)] ADJ egocéntrico(a)

egotism ['iːgəʊɪzəm] N egoísmo *m*

egotist ['iːgəʊɪst] N egoísta *mf*

egotistic(al) [iːgəʊ'tɪstɪk(əl)] ADJ egotista

Egypt ['iːdʒɪpt] N Egipto

Egyptian [ɪ'dʒɪpʃən] ADJ & N egipcio(a) *(m,f)*

eiderdown ['aɪdədaʊn] N edredón *m*

eight [eɪt] ADJ & N ocho *(m inv)*

eighteen [eɪ'tiːn] ADJ & N dieciocho *(m inv)*

eighteenth [eɪ'tiːnθ] 1 ADJ & N decimoctavo *(m,f)*
2 N *(fraction)* decimoctavo *m*

eighth [eɪtθ] 1 ADJ & N octavo(a) *(m,f)*
2 N *(fraction)* octavo *m*

eighty ['eɪtɪ] ADJ & N ochenta *(m inv)*

Eire ['eərə] N Eire

either ['aɪðə(r), 'iːðə(r)] 1 PRON (a) *(affirmative)* cualquiera; **e. of them** cualquiera de los dos; **e. of us** cualquiera de nosotros dos (b) *(negative)* ninguno/ninguna, ni el uno ni el otro/ni la una ni la otra; **I don't want e. of them** no quiero ninguno de los dos
2 ADJ *(both)* cada, los dos/las dos; **on e. side** en ambos lados; **in e. case** en cualquier de los dos casos
3 CONJ o; **e. ... or ...** o ... o ...; **e. Friday or Saturday** o (bien) el viernes o el sábado
4 ADV *(after negative)* tampoco; **I don't want to do it e.** yo tampoco quiero hacerlo

ejaculate [ɪ'dʒækjʊleɪt] VI *(man)* eyacular

eject [ɪ'dʒekt] 1 VT expulsar
2 VI *Av* eyectarse

eke [iːk] VT **to e. out a living** ganarse la vida a duras penas

elaborate 1 VT [ɪ'læbəreɪt] (a) *(devise)* elaborar (b) *(explain)* explicar detalladamente
2 VI explicarse; **to e. on sth** explicar algo con más detalles
3 ADJ [ɪ'læbərɪt] (a) *(complicated)* complicado(a) (b) *(detailed)* detallado(a); *(style)* esmerado(a)

elapse [ɪ'læps] VI transcurrir, pasar

elastic [ɪ'læstɪk] 1 ADJ elástico(a); *Fig* flexible; **e. band** goma elástica
2 N elástico *m*

Elastoplast® [ɪ'lɑːstəplɑːst] N *Br Esp* tirita *f*, *Am* curita *f*

elated [ɪ'leɪtɪd] ADJ eufórico(a)

elation [ɪ'leɪʃən] N regocijo *m*

elbow ['elbəʊ] 1 N codo *m*; *Fig* **e. room** espacio *m*
2 VT **to e. sb** dar un codazo a algn

elder¹ ['eldə(r)] 1 ADJ mayor
2 N **the elders** los ancianos

elder² ['eldə(r)] N *Bot* saúco *m*

elderly ['eldəlɪ] 1 ADJ anciano(a)
2 NPL **the e.** los ancianos

eldest ['eldɪst] 1 ADJ mayor
2 N **the e.** el/la mayor

elect [ɪ'lekt] 1 VT (a) *Pol* elegir (b) **to e. to do sth** *(choose)* decidir hacer algo
2 ADJ **the president e.** el presidente electo

election [ɪ'lekʃən] 1 N elección *f*; **general e.** elecciones *fpl* generales
2 ADJ electoral

electioneering [ɪlekʃə'nɪərɪŋ] N electoralismo *m*

elective [ɪ'lektɪv] ADJ *Univ (course)* optativo(a), opcional

elector [ɪ'lektə(r)] N elector(a) *m,f*

electoral [ɪ'lektərəl] ADJ electoral

electorate [ɪ'lektərɪt] N electorado *m*

electric [ɪ'lektrɪk] ADJ eléctrico(a); *Fig (atmosphere)* electrizado(a); **e. blanket** manta eléctrica, *Am* frazada eléctrica; **e. chair** silla eléctrica; **e. shock** electrochoque *m*

electrical [ɪ'lektrɪkəl] ADJ eléctrico(a)

electrician [ɪlek'trɪʃən] N electricista *mf*

electricity [ɪlek'trɪsɪtɪ] N electricidad *f*; **e. bill** recibo *m* de la luz

electrify [ɪ'lektrɪfaɪ] VT (a) *(railway line)* electrificar (b) *Fig (excite)* electrizar

electrocute [ɪ'lektrəkjuːt] VT electrocutar

electron [ɪ'lektrɒn] N electrón *m*

electronic [ɪlek'trɒnɪk] ADJ electrónico(a); **e. banking** banca electrónica, telebanca *f*

electronics [ɪlek'trɒnɪks] 1 N SING *(science)* electrónica *f*
2 NPL *(of machine)* componentes *mpl* electrónicos

elegant ['elɪgənt] ADJ elegante

element ['elɪmənt] N (a) *(constituent part)* elemento *m* (b) *(factor)* componente *m*, elemento *m* (c) *(electrical)* resistencia *f* (d) *Fam Fig* **to be in one's e.** estar en su salsa

elementary [elɪ'mentərɪ] ADJ *(basic)* elemental; *(not developed)* rudimentario(a); *(easy)* fácil; *US* **e. school** escuela primaria

elephant ['elɪfənt] N elefante *m*

elevate ['elɪveɪt] VT elevar; *(in rank)* ascender

elevation [elɪ'veɪʃən] N (a) *(above sea level)* altitud *f* (b) *Archit* alzado *m*

elevator ['elɪveɪtər] N *US* ascensor *m*

eleven [ɪ'levən] ADJ & N once *(m inv)*

elevenses [ɪ'levənzɪz] NPL *Br Fam* tentempié *m* (de la mañana), *Am* onces *fpl*

eleventh [ɪ'levənθ] 1 ADJ & N undécimo(a) *(m,f)*
2 N *(fraction)* undécimo *m*

elicit [ɪ'lɪsɪt] VT obtener

eligible ['elɪdʒəbəl] ADJ apto(a); **he isn't e. to vote** no tiene derecho al voto

eliminate [ɪ'lɪmɪneɪt] VT eliminar

elite [ɪ'liːt] N elite *f*

elitist [ɪ'liːtɪst] ADJ elitista

elm [elm] N olmo *m*

elocution [elə'kjuːʃən] N elocución *f*

elongate ['iːlɒŋgeɪt] VT alargar

elope [ɪ'ləʊp] VI fugarse para casarse

eloquent ['eləkwənt] ADJ elocuente

else [els] ADV (**a**) **anyone e.** alguien más; **anything e.?** ¿algo más?; **everything e.** todo lo demás; **no one e.** nadie más; **someone e.** otro(a); **something e.** otra cosa, algo más; **somewhere e.** en otra parte; **what e.?** ¿qué más?; **where e.?** ¿en qué otro sitio? (**b**) **or e.** (*otherwise*) si no

elsewhere [els'weə(r)] ADV en otra parte

elucidate [ɪ'luːsɪdeɪt] VT aclarar

elude [ɪ'luːd] VT (**a**) (*escape*) eludir; **his name eludes me** no consigo acordarme de su nombre (**b**) (*avoid*) esquivar

elusive [ɪ'luːsɪv] ADJ esquivo(a); (*evasive*) evasivo(a)

emaciated [ɪ'meɪsɪeɪtɪd] ADJ demacrado(a)

e-mail ['iːmeɪl] *Comput* **1** N (*system*) correo *m* electrónico; (*message*) (mensaje *m* por) correo electrónico; **e. address** dirección *f* de correo electrónico
  2 VT (*person*) enviar un correo electrónico a; (*file*) enviar por correo electrónico

emanate ['eməneɪt] VI provenir (**from** de)

emancipate [ɪ'mænsɪpeɪt] VT emancipar

emancipation [ɪmænsɪ'peɪʃən] N emancipación *f*

embankment [ɪm'bæŋkmənt] N (**a**) (*made of earth*) terraplén *m* (**b**) (*of river*) dique *m*

embargo [em'bɑːgəʊ] N (*pl* **embargoes**) embargo *m*

embark [em'bɑːk] **1** VT (*merchandise*) embarcar
  2 VI embarcar, embarcarse; *Fig* **to e. upon** emprender; (*sth difficult*) embarcarse en

embarkation [embɑː'keɪʃən] N embarque *m*

embarrass [ɪm'bærəs] VT avergonzar, *Am salvo RP* apenar

embarrassed [ɪm'bærəst] ADJ (*ashamed*) avergonzado(a), *Am salvo RP* apenado(a); (*uncomfortable*) azorado(a), violento(a)

> Note that the Spanish word **embarazado** is a false friend and is never a translation for the English word **embarrassed**. In Spanish, **embarazado** means "pregnant".

embarrassing [ɪm'bærəsɪŋ] ADJ embarazoso(a), *Am salvo RP* penoso(a)

embarrassment [ɪm'bærəsmənt] N (*shame*) vergüenza *f*, *Am salvo RP* pena *f*; (*discomfort*) apuro *m*, embarazo *m*

embassy ['embəsɪ] N embajada *f*

embed [ɪm'bed] VT (*jewels*) incrustar; *Fig* grabar

embellish [ɪm'belɪʃ] VT embellecer; (*story*) exagerar

ember ['embə(r)] N ascua *f*, rescoldo *m*

embezzle [ɪm'bezəl] VT desfalcar, malversar

embezzlement [ɪm'bezəlmənt] N malversación *f*

embitter [ɪm'bɪtə(r)] VT amargar

embittered [ɪm'bɪtəd] ADJ amargado(a), resentido(a)

emblem ['embləm] N emblema *m*

embody [ɪm'bɒdɪ] VT (**a**) (*include*) abarcar (**b**) (*personify*) encarnar

embossed [ɪm'bɒst] ADJ en relieve

embrace [ɪm'breɪs] **1** VT (*person, belief*) abrazar; (*include*) abarcar
  2 VI abrazarse
  3 N abrazo *m*

embroider [ɪm'brɔɪdə(r)] VT (**a**) *Sewing* bordar (**b**) *Fig* (*story, truth*) adornar, embellecer

embroidery [ɪm'brɔɪdərɪ] N bordado *m*

embryo ['embrɪəʊ] N embrión *m*

emerald ['emərəld] N esmeralda *f*

emerge [ɪ'mɜːdʒ] VI salir; (*problem*) surgir; **it emerged that ...** resultó que ...

emergence [ɪ'mɜːdʒəns] N aparición *f*

emergency [ɪ'mɜːdʒənsɪ] N emergencia *f*; *Med* urgencia *f*; **in an e.** en caso de emergencia; **e. exit** salida *f* de emergencia; **e. landing** aterrizaje forzoso; **e. measures** medidas *fpl* de urgencia; *US* **e. room** sala *f* de urgencias; *Aut* **e. stop** frenazo *m* en seco; *Pol* **state of e.** estado *m* de excepción

emery ['emərɪ] N **e. board** lima *f* de uñas

emigrant ['emɪgrənt] N emigrante *mf*

emigrate ['emɪgreɪt] VI emigrar

emigration [emɪ'greɪʃən] N emigración *f*

eminent ['emɪnənt] ADJ eminente

emission [ɪ'mɪʃən] N emisión *f*

emit [ɪ'mɪt] VT (*signals*) emitir; (*smells*) despedir; (*sound*) producir

emoticon [ɪ'mɒtɪkɒn] N *Comput* emoticono *m*

emotion [ɪ'məʊʃən] N emoción *f*

emotional [ɪ'məʊʃənəl] ADJ (*problem, reaction*) emocional; (*film, farewell*) conmovedor(a)

emotive [ɪ'məʊtɪv] ADJ emotivo(a)

empathy ['empəθɪ] N empatía *f*

emperor ['empərə(r)] N emperador *m*

emphasis ['emfəsɪs] N (*pl* **emphases** ['emfəsiːz]) énfasis *m*; **to place e. on sth** hacer hincapié en algo

emphasize ['emfəsaɪz] VT subrayar, hacer hincapié en; (*insist*) insistir; (*highlight*) hacer resaltar

emphatic [em'fætɪk] ADJ (*forceful*) enfático(a); (*convinced*) categórico(a)

emphatically [em'fætɪklɪ] ADV categóricamente

empire ['empaɪə(r)] N imperio *m*

employ [ɪm'plɔɪ] VT emplear; (*time*) ocupar

employee [em'plɔiː, emplɔɪ'iː] N empleado(a) *m,f*

employer [ɪm'plɔɪə(r)] N patrón(ona) *m,f*

employment [ɪm'plɔɪmənt] N empleo *m*; **e. agency** agencia *f* de colocaciones; **full e.** pleno empleo

empower [ɪm'pauə(r)] VT autorizar

empress ['emprɪs] N emperatriz *f*

emptiness ['emptɪnɪs] N vacío *m*

empty ['emptɪ] **1** ADJ (**emptier, emptiest**) vacío(a); **an e. house** una casa deshabitada; **e. promises** promesas *fpl* vanas
2 VT vaciar
3 VI vaciarse
4 NPL **empties** *(bottles)* cascos *mpl*

empty-handed [emptɪ'hændɪd] ADJ con las manos vacías

emulate ['emjʊleɪt] VT emular

emulsion [ɪ'mʌlʃən] N emulsión *f*; **e. paint** pintura *f* mate

enable [ɪn'eɪbəl] VT permitir

enact [ɪn'ækt] VT *(play)* representar; *(law)* promulgar

enamel [ɪ'næməl] N esmalte *m*

enamoured, *US* **enamored** [ɪn'æməd] ADJ **to be e. of** estar enamorado(a) de; **I'm not greatly e. of the idea** no me entusiasma la idea

encase [ɪn'keɪs] VT **encased in** revestido(a) de

enchant [ɪn'tʃɑːnt] VT encantar

enchanting [ɪn'tʃɑːntɪŋ] ADJ encantador(a)

encircle [ɪn'sɜːkəl] VT rodear

enclave ['enkleɪv] N enclave *m*

enclose [ɪn'kləʊz] VT (**a**) *(surround)* rodear (**b**) *(fence in)* cercar (**c**) *(in envelope)* adjuntar; **please find enclosed** le enviamos adjunto

enclosure [ɪn'kləʊʒə(r)] N (**a**) *(fenced area)* cercado *m* (**b**) *(in envelope)* documento adjunto (**c**) *(of racecourse)* recinto *m*

encompass [ɪn'kʌmpəs] VT abarcar

encore ['ɒŋkɔː(r)] **1** INTERJ ¡otra!, ¡bis!
2 N repetición *f*, bis *m*

encounter [ɪn'kauntə(r)] **1** N *(meeting)* encuentro *m*
2 VT encontrar, encontrarse con; *(problems)* tropezar con

encourage [ɪn'kʌrɪdʒ] VT (**a**) *(person)* animar (**b**) *(tourism, trade)* fomentar

encouragement [ɪn'kʌrɪdʒmənt] N estímulo *m*

encroach [ɪn'krəʊtʃ] VI **to e. on** *(territory)* invadir; *(rights)* usurpar; *(time, freedom)* quitar

encrusted [ɪn'krʌstɪd] ADJ incrustado(a) (**with** de)

encumber [ɪn'kʌmbə(r)] VT estorbar; *(with debts)* gravar

encyclop(a)edia [ensaɪkləʊ'piːdɪə] N enciclopedia *f*

end [end] **1** N (**a**) *(of stick)* punta *f*; *(of street)* final *m*; *(of table)* extremo *m*; *Fig* **to make ends meet** llegar a final de mes (**b**) *(conclusion)* fin *m*, final *m*; **in the e.** al final; **for hours on e.** hora tras hora; **to bring an e. to sth** poner fin a algo; **to put an e. to** acabar con (**c**) *(aim)* objetivo *m*, fin *m*
2 VT acabar, terminar
3 VI acabarse, terminarse

▶ **end up** VI terminar; **it ended up in the dustbin** fue a parar al cubo de la basura; **to e. up doing sth** terminar por hacer algo

endanger [ɪn'deɪndʒə(r)] VT poner en peligro

endangered [ɪn'deɪndʒəd] ADJ en peligro

endearing [ɪn'dɪərɪŋ] ADJ simpático(a)

endeavour, *US* **endeavor** [ɪn'devə(r)] **1** N esfuerzo *m*
2 VT intentar, procurar

ending ['endɪŋ] N final *m*

endive ['endaɪv] N *Bot* (**a**) *(curly)* escarola *f* (**b**) *esp US (chicory)* endibia *f*, achicoria *f*

endless ['endlɪs] ADJ interminable

endorse [ɪn'dɔːs] VT (**a**) *(document, cheque)* endosar (**b**) *(approve) (opinion, action)* apoyar, respaldar

endorsement [ɪn'dɔːsmənt] N (**a**) *(on document, cheque)* endoso *m* (**b**) *Br (on driving licence)* infracción *f* anotada (**c**) *(approval)* aprobación *f*

endow [ɪn'dau] VT dotar; **to be endowed with** estar dotado(a) de

endurance [ɪn'djʊərəns] N resistencia *f*

endure [ɪn'djʊə(r)] **1** VT *(bear)* aguantar, soportar
2 VI perdurar

enemy ['enəmɪ] ADJ & N enemigo(a) *(m,f)*

energetic [enə'dʒetɪk] ADJ enérgico(a)

energy ['enədʒɪ] N energía *f*

enforce [ɪn'fɔːs] VT *(law)* hacer cumplir

enforcement [ɪn'fɔːsmənt] N aplicación *f*

engage [ɪn'geɪdʒ] VT (**a**) *(hire)* contratar (**b**) *(attention)* llamar (**c**) *(in conversation)* entablar

engaged [ɪn'geɪdʒd] ADJ (**a**) *(betrothed)* prometido(a); **to get e.** prometerse (**b**) *(busy)* ocupado(a); *Br Tel* **it's e.** está comunicando

engagement [ɪn'geɪdʒmənt] N (**a**) *(betrothal)* petición *f* de mano; *(period)* noviazgo *m*; **e. ring** anillo *m* de compromiso (**b**) *(appointment)* cita *f* (**c**) *Mil* combate *m*

engaging [ɪn'geɪdʒɪŋ] ADJ simpático(a), agradable

engender [ɪn'dʒendə(r)] VT engendrar

engine ['endʒɪn] N motor *m*; *Rail* locomotora *f*; **e. room** sala *f* de máquinas; **e. driver** maquinista *mf*

engineer [endʒɪ'nɪə(r)] **1** N ingeniero(a) *m,f*; *Naut & US Rail* maquinista *mf*
2 VT *(cause, bring about)* urdir

engineering [endʒɪ'nɪərɪŋ] N ingeniería *f*; **electrical e.** electrotecnia *f*; **civil e.** ingeniería civil

England ['ɪŋglənd] N Inglaterra *f*

English ['ɪŋglɪʃ] **1** ADJ inglés(esa)
2 N (**a**) *(language)* inglés *m* (**b**) PL **the E.** los ingleses

Englishman ['ɪŋglɪʃmən] N inglés *m*

English-speaking ['ɪŋglɪʃspiːkɪŋ] ADJ de habla inglesa

Englishwoman ['ɪŋglɪʃwʊmən] N inglesa *f*

engraving [ɪn'greɪvɪŋ] N grabado *m*

engrossed [ɪn'grəʊst] ADJ absorto(a) (**in** en)

engulf [ɪn'gʌlf] VT tragarse

enhance [ɪn'hɑːns] VT *(beauty)* realzar; *(power, chances)* aumentar

enigma [ɪ'nɪgmə] N enigma *m*

enjoy [ɪn'dʒɔɪ] VT (**a**) *(take pleasure from)* disfrutar de; **to e. oneself** pasarlo bien (**b**) *(benefit from)* gozar de

enjoyable [ɪn'dʒɔɪəbəl] ADJ agradable; *(amusing)* divertido(a)

enjoyment [ɪn'dʒɔɪmənt] N placer *m*, gusto *m*

enlarge [ɪn'lɑːdʒ] **1** VT extender, ampliar; *Phot* ampliar

2 VI **to e. upon a subject** extenderse sobre un tema

enlargement [ɪn'lɑːdʒmənt] N *Phot* ampliación *f*

enlighten [ɪn'laɪtən] VT iluminar

enlightened [ɪn'laɪtənd] ADJ (**a**) *(learned)* culto(a); *(informed)* bien informado(a) (**b**) *Hist* ilustrado(a)

enlightenment [ɪn'laɪtənmənt] N **the Age of E.** el Siglo de las Luces

enlist [ɪn'lɪst] **1** VT *Mil* reclutar; **to e. sb's help** conseguir ayuda de algn

2 VI *Mil* alistarse

enmity ['enmɪtɪ] N enemistad *f*, hostilidad *f*

enormous [ɪ'nɔːməs] ADJ enorme

enormously [ɪ'nɔːməslɪ] ADV enormemente; **I enjoyed myself e.** lo pasé genial

enough [ɪ'nʌf] **1** ADJ bastante, suficiente; **e. books** bastantes libros; **e. money** bastante dinero; **have we got e. petrol?** ¿tenemos suficiente gasolina?

2 ADV bastante; **oddly e. ...** lo curioso es que ...; **sure e.** en efecto

3 PRON lo bastante, lo suficiente; **e. to live on** lo suficiente para vivir; **it isn't e.** no basta; **more than e.** más que suficiente; *Fam* **I've had e.!** ¡estoy harto!

enquire [ɪn'kwaɪə(r)] VI preguntar

enquiry [ɪn'kwaɪərɪ] N (**a**) *(question)* pregunta *f*; **to make an e.** preguntar; **enquiries** información *f* (**b**) *(investigation)* investigación *f*

enrage [ɪn'reɪdʒ] VT enfurecer

enrich [ɪn'rɪtʃ] VT enriquecer

enrol, *US* **enroll** [ɪn'rəʊl] **1** VT matricular, inscribir

2 VI matricularse, inscribirse

> Note that the Spanish verb **enrollar** is a false friend and is never a translation for the English verb **enrol**. In Spanish **enrollar** means "to roll up".

enrolment, *US* **enrollment** [ɪn'rəʊlmənt] N matrícula *f*

en route [ɒn'ruːt] ADV en *or* por el camino

ensign ['ensaɪn] N (**a**) *(flag)* bandera *f*, enseña *f* (**b**) *US (naval officer)* alférez *m* de fragata

enslave [ɪn'sleɪv] VT esclavizar

ensue [ɪn'sjuː] VI (**a**) *(follow)* seguir (**b**) *(result)* resultar (**from** de)

ensure [ɪn'ʃʊə(r)] VT asegurar

entail [ɪn'teɪl] VT *(involve)* suponer

entangle [ɪn'tæŋgəl] VT enredar

enter ['entə(r)] **1** VT (**a**) *(go into)* entrar en; *Fig (join)* ingresar en (**b**) *(write down)* apuntar, anotar (**c**) *Comput* dar entrada a

2 VI entrar

▶ **enter into** VT INSEP (**a**) *(agreement)* firmar; *(negotiations)* iniciar; *(bargain)* cerrar (**b**) *(relations)* establecer; *(conversation)* entablar

enterprise ['entəpraɪz] N empresa *f*; **free e.** libre empresa; **private e.** iniciativa privada; *(as a whole)* el sector privado; **public e.** el sector público

enterprising ['entəpraɪzɪŋ] ADJ emprendedor(a)

entertain [entə'teɪn] **1** VT (**a**) *(amuse)* divertir (**b**) *(consider)* considerar; **to e. an idea** abrigar una idea

2 VI tener invitados

entertainer [entə'teɪnə(r)] N artista *mf*

entertaining [entə'teɪnɪŋ] ADJ divertido(a)

entertainment [entə'teɪnmənt] N (**a**) *(amusement)* entretenimiento *m*, diversión *f* (**b**) *Th* espectáculo *m*

enthralling [ɪn'θrɔːlɪŋ] ADJ fascinante

enthuse [ɪn'θjuːz] VI entusiasmarse (**over** por)

enthusiasm [ɪn'θjuːzɪæzəm] N entusiasmo *m*

enthusiast [ɪn'θjuːzɪæst] N entusiasta *mf*

enthusiastic [ɪnθjuːzɪ'æstɪk] ADJ entusiasta; *(praise)* caluroso(a); **to be e. about sth** entusiasmarse por algo

entice [ɪn'taɪs] VT seducir, atraer

enticing [ɪn'taɪsɪŋ] ADJ atractivo(a), tentador(a)

entire [ɪn'taɪə(r)] ADJ entero(a), todo(a)

entirely [ɪn'taɪəlɪ] ADV (**a**) *(completely)* totalmente (**b**) *(solely)* exclusivamente

entirety [ɪn'taɪərɪtɪ] N **in its e.** en su totalidad

entitle [ɪn'taɪtl] VT (**a**) *(allow)* dar derecho a; **to be entitled to** tener derecho a (**b**) *(book etc)* titular

entity ['entɪtɪ] N entidad *f*

entourage [ɒntʊ'rɑːʒ] N séquito *m*

entrails ['entreɪlz] NPL tripas *fpl*; *Fig* entrañas *fpl*

entrance¹ ['entrəns] N (**a**) *(way in, act of entering)* entrada *f*; **e. fee** *(to museum etc)* entrada; *(to organization)* cuota *f* (**b**) *(admission)* entrada *f*, ingreso *m*; **e. examination** examen *m* de ingreso

entrance² [ɪn'trɑːns] VT encantar

entrant ['entrənt] N *(in competition)* participante *mf*; *(applicant)* aspirante *mf*

entreat [ɪnˈtriːt] VT *Fml* suplicar, rogar

entrée [ˈɒntreɪ] N *Br (first course)* entrada *f*, primer plato *m*; *US (main course)* plato *m* principal

entrenched [ɪnˈtrentʃt] ADJ firmemente enraizado(a)

entrepreneur [ɒntrəprəˈnɜː(r)] N empresario(a) *m,f*

entrust [ɪnˈtrʌst] VT encargar (**with** de); **to e. sth to sb** dejar algo al cuidado de algn

entry [ˈentrɪ] N (**a**) *(entrance)* entrada *f*; **no e.** *(sign)* dirección prohibida (**b**) *(in competition)* participante *mf*

enumerate [ɪˈnjuːməreɪt] VT enumerar

enunciate [ɪˈnʌnsɪeɪt] VT *(words)* articular; *(ideas)* formular

envelop [ɪnˈveləp] VT envolver

envelope [ˈenvələʊp] N sobre *m*

envious [ˈenvɪəs] ADJ envidioso(a); **to feel e.** tener envidia

environment [ɪnˈvaɪərənmənt] N medio ambiente

environmental [ɪnvaɪərənˈmentəl] ADJ medioambiental

environmentally [ɪnvaɪərənˈmentəlɪ] ADV ecológicamente; **e. friendly** ecológico(a), que no daña el medio ambiente

envisage [ɪnˈvɪzɪdʒ] VT *(imagine)* imaginarse; *(foresee)* prever

envoy [ˈenvɔɪ] N enviado(a) *m,f*

envy [ˈenvɪ] **1** N envidia *f*
2 VT envidiar, tener envidia de

enzyme [ˈenzaɪm] N enzima *m*

ephemeral [ɪˈfemərəl] ADJ efímero(a)

epic [ˈepɪk] **1** N epopeya *f*
2 ADJ épico(a)

epidemic [epɪˈdemɪk] N epidemia *f*; *Fig (of crime etc)* ola *f*

epilepsy [ˈepɪlepsɪ] N epilepsia *f*

epilogue, *US* **epilog** [ˈepɪlɒg] N epílogo *m*

episode [ˈepɪsəʊd] N episodio *m*

epistle [ɪˈpɪsəl] N epístola *f*

epitaph [ˈepɪtɑːf] N epitafio *m*

epitome [ɪˈpɪtəmɪ] N *Fml* personificación *f*

epitomize [ɪˈpɪtəmaɪz] VT *Fml* personificar

epoch [ˈiːpɒk] N época *f*

equable [ˈekwəbəl] ADJ (**a**) *(person)* ecuánime (**b**) *(climate)* uniforme

equal [ˈiːkwəl] **1** ADJ igual; **to be e. to the occasion** estar a la altura de las circunstancias; **e. pay** igualdad *f* de salarios
2 N igual *mf*; **to treat sb as an e.** tratar a algn de igual a igual
3 VT *(pt & pp* **equalled,** *US* **equaled)** (**a**) *Math* equivaler a (**b**) *(match)* igualar

equality [iːˈkwɒlɪtɪ] N igualdad *f*

equalize [ˈiːkwəlaɪz] **1** VI *Ftb* empatar
2 VT igualar

equalizer [ˈiːkwəlaɪzə(r)] N *Ftb* gol *m* del empate; *(of sound)* ecualizador *m*

equally [ˈiːkwəlɪ] ADV igualmente; **e. pretty** igual de bonito(a); **to share sth e.** dividir algo en partes iguales

equanimity [ekwəˈnɪmɪtɪ] N ecuanimidad *f*

equate [ɪˈkweɪt] VT equiparar, comparar (**to con**)

equation [ɪˈkweɪʒən, ɪˈkweɪʃən] N *Math* ecuación *f*

equator [ɪˈkweɪtə(r)] N ecuador *m*

equatorial [ekwəˈtɔːrɪəl] ADJ ecuatorial

equestrian [ɪˈkwestrɪən] ADJ ecuestre

equilibrium [iːkwɪˈlɪbrɪəm] N equilibrio *m*

equinox [ˈiːkwɪnɒks] N equinoccio *m*

equip [ɪˈkwɪp] VT *(with tools, machines)* equipar; *(with food)* proveer

equipment [ɪˈkwɪpmənt] N *(materials)* equipo *m*; **office e.** material *m* de oficina

equipped [ɪˈkwɪpt] ADJ *(with tools, machines)* equipado(a); *(with skills)* dotado(a)

equitable [ˈekwɪtəbəl] ADJ equitativo(a)

equities [ˈekwɪtɪz] NPL acciones ordinarias

equivalent [ɪˈkwɪvələnt] ADJ & N equivalente *(m)*; **to be e. to** equivaler a, ser equivalente a

equivocal [ɪˈkwɪvəkəl] ADJ equívoco(a)

era [ˈɪərə] N era *f*

eradicate [ɪˈrædɪkeɪt] VT erradicar

erase [ɪˈreɪz] VT borrar

eraser [*Br* ɪˈreɪzə(r), *US* ɪˈreɪsər] N goma *f* de borrar

erect [ɪˈrekt] **1** ADJ (**a**) *(upright)* erguido(a) (**b**) *(penis)* erecto(a)
2 VT *(monument)* levantar, erigir

erection [ɪˈrekʃən] N (**a**) *(of building)* construcción *f* (**b**) *(penis)* erección *f*

ermine [ˈɜːmɪn] N armiño *m*

erode [ɪˈrəʊd] VT (**a**) *(rock, soil)* erosionar (**b**) *(metal)* corroer, desgastar; *Fig (power, confidence)* hacer perder

erosion [ɪˈrəʊʒən] N *Geol* erosión *f*

erotic [ɪˈrɒtɪk] ADJ erótico(a)

err [ɜː(r)] VI errar; **to e. on the side of caution** pecar de prudente

errand [ˈerənd] N recado *m*; **e. boy** recadero *m*

erratic [ɪˈrætɪk] ADJ *(performance, behaviour)* irregular; *(weather)* muy variable; *(person)* caprichoso(a)

erroneous [ɪˈrəʊnɪəs] ADJ erróneo(a)

error [ˈerə(r)] N error *m*, equivocación *f*

erupt [ɪˈrʌpt] VI (**a**) *(volcano)* entrar en erupción; *(violence)* estallar (**b**) **his skin erupted in a rash** le salió una erupción

eruption [ɪˈrʌpʃən] N erupción *f*

escalate [ˈeskəleɪt] VI *(war)* intensificarse; *(prices)* aumentar; *(change)* convertirse (**into** en)

escalation [eskəˈleɪʃən] N *(of war)* intensificación *f*, escalada *f*; *(of prices)* subida *f*

escalator [ˈeskəleɪtə(r)] N escalera mecánica

Note that the Spanish word **escalador** is a false friend and is never a translation for the English word **escalator**. In Spanish **escalador** means "climber, mountaineer".

escalope [ˈeskəlɒp] N escalope m

escapade [ˈeskəpeɪd] N aventura f

Note that the Spanish word **escapada** is a false friend and is never a translation for the English word **escapade**. In Spanish **escapada** means both "escape" and "quick trip".

escape [ɪˈskeɪp] 1 N huída f, fuga f; (of gas) escape m; **e. route** vía f de escape
2 VI escaparse
3 VT (a) (avoid) evitar, huir de; **to e. punishment** librarse del castigo (b) Fig **his name escapes me** no recuerdo su nombre

escapism [ɪˈskeɪpɪzəm] N evasión f

escort 1 N [ˈeskɔːt] (a) (companion) acompañante mf (b) Mil escolta f
2 VT [ɪˈskɔːt] (a) (accompany) acompañar (b) (protect) escoltar

Eskimo [ˈeskɪməʊ] ADJ & N esquimal (mf)

esoteric [esəʊˈterɪk] ADJ esotérico(a)

especial [ɪˈspeʃəl] ADJ especial

especially [ɪˈspeʃəlɪ] ADV especialmente, sobre todo

espionage [ˈespɪənɑːʒ] N espionaje m

esplanade [espləˈneɪd] N paseo marítimo

espouse [ɪˈspaʊz] VT Fml (cause) abrazar, adoptar

espresso [eˈspresəʊ] **e. (coffee)** café m exprés or Esp solo or Am negro

esquire [ɪˈskwaɪə(r)] N Br señor m; **Timothy Whiteman E.** Sr. Don Timothy Whiteman

essay [ˈeseɪ] N Educ redacción f

essence [ˈesəns] N esencia f; **in e.** esencialmente

essential [ɪˈsenʃəl] 1 ADJ esencial, imprescindible
2 N necesidad básica; **the essentials** lo fundamental

essentially [ɪˈsenʃəlɪ] ADV esencialmente

establish [ɪˈstæblɪʃ] VT (a) (found) establecer; (business) montar (b) Jur **to e. a fact** probar un hecho; **to e. the truth** demostrar la verdad

established [ɪˈstæblɪʃt] ADJ (person) establecido(a); (fact) conocido(a)

establishment [ɪˈstæblɪʃmənt] N establecimiento m; **the E.** el sistema

estate [ɪˈsteɪt] N (a) (land) finca f; Br **e. agent** agente mf inmobiliario(a); Br **e. (car)** ranchera f, Esp coche m modelo familiar (b) Br (housing) **e.** urbanización f (c) Jur (of deceased person) herencia f

esteem [ɪˈstiːm] 1 N **to hold sb in great e.** apreciar mucho a algn
2 VT estimar

esthetic [esˈθetɪk] ADJ US = **aesthetic**

estimate 1 N [ˈestɪmɪt] (calculation) cálculo m; (likely cost of work) presupuesto m; **rough e.** cálculo aproximado
2 VT [ˈestɪmeɪt] calcular; Fig pensar, creer

estimation [estɪˈmeɪʃən] N (a) (opinion) juicio m, opinión f (b) (esteem) estima f

Estonia [eˈstəʊnɪə] N Estonia

Estonian [eˈstəʊnɪən] 1 ADJ estonio(a)
2 N (a) (person) estonio(a) m,f (b) (language) estonio m

estrange [ɪˈstreɪndʒ] VT **to become estranged (from)** alejarse (de)

estuary [ˈestjʊərɪ] N estuario m

etc [etˈsetrə] ADV (et cetera) etc., etcétera

etching [ˈetʃɪŋ] N aguafuerte m

eternal [ɪˈtɜːnəl] ADJ eterno(a), incesante; **e. triangle** triángulo amoroso

eternity [ɪˈtɜːnɪtɪ] N eternidad f

ether [ˈiːθə(r)] N éter m

ethereal [ɪˈθɪərɪəl] ADJ etéreo(a)

ethical [ˈeθɪkəl] ADJ ético(a)

ethics [ˈeθɪks] N ética f

Ethiopia [iːθɪˈəʊpɪə] N Etiopía

ethnic [ˈeθnɪk] ADJ étnico(a)

ethos [ˈiːθɒs] N carácter distintivo

e-ticket [ˈiːˈtɪkɪt] N Esp billete m or Am boleto m or Am pasaje m electrónico

etiquette [ˈetɪket] N protocolo m, etiqueta f

etymology [etɪˈmɒlədʒɪ] N etimología f

EU [iːˈjuː] N (abbr European Union) UE f

eucalyptus [juːkəˈlɪptəs] N eucalipto m

euphemism [ˈjuːfɪmɪzəm] N eufemismo m

euphoria [juːˈfɔːrɪə] N euforia f

euro [ˈjʊərəʊ] N (pl **euros**) (European currency) euro m

Eurocrat [ˈjʊərəʊkræt] N eurócrata mf

Euro-MP [ˈjʊərəʊempiː] N eurodiputado(a) m,f

Europe [ˈjʊərəp] N Europa

European [jʊərəˈpiːən] ADJ & N europeo(a) (m,f); **E. Union** Unión Europea

Eurosceptic [ˈjʊərəʊskeptɪk] N Br euroescéptico(a) m,f

euthanasia [juːθəˈneɪzɪə] N eutanasia f

evacuate [ɪˈvækjʊeɪt] VT evacuar

evacuation [ɪvækjʊˈeɪʃən] N evacuación f

evade [ɪˈveɪd] VT evadir

evaluate [ɪˈvæljʊeɪt] VT evaluar

evaluation [ɪvæljʊˈeɪʃən] N evaluación f

evangelical [iːvænˈdʒelɪkəl] ADJ evangélico(a)

evangelist [ɪˈvændʒɪlɪst] N evangelista mf

evaporate [ɪˈvæpəreɪt] 1 VT evaporar; **evaporated milk** leche condensada sin endulzar
2 VI evaporarse; Fig desvanecerse

evasion [ɪˈveɪʒən] N (**a**) (*of pursuer, question*) evasión f (**b**) (*evasive answer*) evasiva f

evasive [ɪˈveɪsɪv] ADJ evasivo(a)

eve [iːv] N víspera f; **on the e. of** en vísperas de

even [ˈiːvən] **1** ADJ (**a**) (*smooth*) liso(a); (*level*) llano(a) (**b**) (*regular*) uniforme (**c**) (*equally balanced*) igual; **to get e. with sb** desquitarse con algn (**d**) (*number*) par (**e**) (*at the same level*) a nivel (**f**) (*quantity*) exacto(a)
2 ADV (**a**) (*for emphasis*) incluso, aun; **e. now** incluso ahora; **e. so** aun así; **e. the children knew** hasta los niños lo sabían (**b**) (*negative*) **not e.** ni siquiera; **she can't e. write her name** ni siquiera sabe escribir su nombre (**c**) (*before comparative*) aun, todavía; **e. worse** aun peor (**d**) **e. if** incluso si; **e. though** aunque
3 VT igualar

evening [ˈiːvnɪŋ] N (**a**) (*early*) tarde f; (*late*) noche f; **in the e.** por la tarde; **tomorrow e.** mañana por la tarde; **e. class** clase nocturna; **e. dress** (*for man*) traje m de etiqueta; (*for woman*) traje de noche; **e. paper** periódico vespertino (**b**) (*greeting*) **good e.!** (*early*) ¡buenas tardes!; (*late*) ¡buenas noches!

evenly [ˈiːvənlɪ] ADV (*uniformly*) uniformemente; (*fairly*) equitativamente

event [ɪˈvent] N (**a**) (*happening*) suceso m, acontecimiento m (**b**) (*case*) caso m; **in the e. of fire** en caso de incendio (**c**) *Sport* prueba f

eventful [ɪˈventfʊl] ADJ **an e. day** (*busy*) un día agitado; (*memorable*) un día memorable

eventual [ɪˈventʃʊəl] ADJ (*ultimate*) final; (*resulting*) consiguiente

> Note that the Spanish word **eventual** is a false friend and is never a translation for the English word **eventual**. In Spanish **eventual** means both "possible" and "temporary".

eventuality [ɪventʃʊˈælɪtɪ] N eventualidad f

eventually [ɪˈventʃʊəlɪ] ADV finalmente

> Note that the Spanish word **eventualmente** is a false friend and is never a translation for the English word **eventually**. In Spanish **eventualmente** means both "by chance" and "possibly".

ever [ˈevə(r)] ADV (**a**) (*always, at any time*) siempre; **for e.** para siempre; **stronger than e.** más fuerte que nunca (**b**) (*with negative sense*) **not e.** nunca (**c**) (*in questions*) alguna vez; **have you e. been there?** ¿has estado allí alguna vez? (**d**) (*emphasis*) **how e. did you manage it?** ¿cómo diablos lo conseguiste?; **thank you e. so much** muchísimas gracias

evergreen [ˈevəɡriːn] **1** ADJ de hoja perenne
2 N árbol m de hoja perenne

everlasting [evəˈlɑːstɪŋ] ADJ eterno(a)

evermore [evəˈmɔː(r)] ADV **for e.** para siempre jamás

every [ˈevrɪ] ADJ (**a**) (*each*) cada; **e. now and then** de vez en cuando; **e. day** todos los días; **e. other day** cada dos días; **e. one of you**

todos(as) vosotros(as); **e. citizen** todo ciudadano (**b**) **you had e. right to be angry** tenías toda la razón para estar *esp Esp* enfadado *or esp Am* enojado

everybody [ˈevrɪbɒdɪ] PRON todo el mundo, todos(as)

everyday [ˈevrɪdeɪ] ADJ diario(a), de todos los días; **an e. occurrence** un suceso cotidiano

everyone [ˈevrɪwʌn] PRON todo el mundo, todos(as)

everyplace [ˈevrɪpleɪs] ADV *US* = **everywhere**

everything [ˈevrɪθɪŋ] PRON todo; **he eats e.** come de todo; **she means e. to me** ella lo es todo para mí

everywhere [ˈevrɪweə(r)] ADV en todas partes, por todas partes

evict [ɪˈvɪkt] VT desahuciar

evidence [ˈevɪdəns] N (**a**) (*proof*) evidencia f (**b**) *Jur* testimonio m; **to give e.** prestar declaración (**c**) (*sign*) indicio m, señal f; **to be in e.** dejarse notar

evident [ˈevɪdənt] ADJ evidente, manifiesto(a)

evidently [ˈevɪdəntlɪ] ADV evidentemente, al parecer

evil [ˈiːvəl] **1** ADJ (*wicked*) malo(a), malvado(a); (*harmful*) nocivo(a); (*unfortunate*) aciago(a)
2 N mal m

evocative [ɪˈvɒkətɪv] ADJ evocador(a)

evoke [ɪˈvəʊk] VT evocar

evolution [iːvəˈluːʃən] N evolución f; *Biol* desarrollo m

evolve [ɪˈvɒlv] **1** VI (*species*) evolucionar; (*ideas*) desarrollarse
2 VT desarrollar

ewe [juː] N oveja f

ex [eks] N **her ex** su ex marido; **his ex** su ex mujer

ex- [eks] PREF ex, antiguo(a); **ex-minister** ex ministro

exacerbate [ɪɡˈzæsəbeɪt] VT exacerbar

exact [ɪɡˈzækt] **1** ADJ (*accurate*) exacto(a); (*definition*) preciso(a); **this e. spot** ese mismo lugar
2 VT exigir

exacting [ɪɡˈzæktɪŋ] ADJ exigente

exactly [ɪɡˈzæktlɪ] ADV exactamente; precisamente; **e.!** ¡exacto!

exaggerate [ɪɡˈzædʒəreɪt] VI & VT exagerar

exaggeration [ɪɡzædʒəˈreɪʃən] N exageración f

exalt [ɪɡˈzɔːlt] VT *Fml* exaltar

exam [ɪɡˈzæm] N *Fam* examen m

examination [ɪɡzæmɪˈneɪʃən] N (**a**) *Educ* examen m; **to sit an e.** hacer un examen (**b**) *Med* reconocimiento m (**c**) *Jur* interrogatorio m

examine [ɪɡˈzæmɪn] VT *Educ* examinar; (*customs*) registrar; *Med* hacer un reconocimiento médico a; *Jur* interrogar

examiner [ɪɡˈzæmɪnə(r)] N examinador(a) m,f

example 107 **exhibition**

example [ɪg'zɑ:mpəl] N ejemplo m; *(specimen)* ejemplar m; **for e.** por ejemplo

exasperate [ɪg'zɑ:spəreɪt] VT exasperar

exasperation [ɪgzɑ:spə'reɪʃən] N exasperación f

excavate ['ekskəveɪt] VT excavar

excavation [ekskə'veɪʃən] N excavación f

exceed [ek'si:d] VT exceder, sobrepasar

exceedingly [ek'si:dɪŋlɪ] ADV extremadamente, sumamente

excel [ɪk'sel] 1 VI sobresalir
2 VT superar

excellency ['eksələnsɪ] N **His E.** Su Excelencia

excellent ['eksələnt] ADJ excelente

except [ɪk'sept] 1 PREP excepto, salvo; **e. for the little ones** excepto los pequeños; **e. that ...** salvo que ...
2 VT exceptuar

exception [ɪk'sepʃən] N excepción f; **with the e. of** a excepción de; **without e.** sin excepción; **to take e. to sth** *(be offended)* ofenderse por algo

exceptional [ɪk'sepʃənəl] ADJ excepcional

excerpt ['eksɜ:pt] N extracto m

excess 1 N [ɪk'ses] exceso m
2 ADJ ['ekses] excedente; **e. baggage** exceso m de equipaje; **e. fare** suplemento m

excessive [ɪk'sesɪv] ADJ excesivo(a)

excessively [ɪk'sesɪvlɪ] ADV excesivamente, en exceso

exchange [ɪks'tʃeɪndʒ] 1 N (a) *(of prisoners, ideas)* intercambio m; **e. of ideas** intercambio m de ideas; **in e. for** a cambio de (b) *Fin* **e. rate** tipo m de cambio (c) **(telephone) e.** central telefónica
2 VT (a) *(insults, gifts, information)* intercambiar; **to e. blows** golpearse (b) *Fin (currency)* cambiar

exchequer [ɪks'tʃekə(r)] N *Br* **the E.** Hacienda f; **Chancellor of the E.** Ministro m de Hacienda

excise ['eksaɪz] N impuesto m sobre el consumo; **e. duty** derechos mpl de aduana

excitable [ɪk'saɪtəbəl] ADJ excitable

excite [ɪk'saɪt] VT *(person)* entusiasmar, emocionar; *(stimulate)* excitar

excited [ɪk'saɪtɪd] ADJ entusiasmado(a), emocionado(a)

excitement [ɪk'saɪtmənt] N *(stimulation)* excitación f; *(emotion)* emoción f; *(commotion)* agitación f

exciting [ɪk'saɪtɪŋ] ADJ apasionante, emocionante

exclaim [ɪk'skleɪm] 1 VI exclamar
2 VT gritar

exclamation [eksklə'meɪʃən] N exclamación f; **e.** *Br* **mark** or *US* **point** signo m de admiración

exclude [ɪk'sklu:d] VT excluir; *(from club)* no admitir

excluding [ɪk'sklu:dɪŋ] PREP excepto

exclusion [ɪk'sklu:ʒən] N exclusión f

exclusive [ɪk'sklu:sɪv] 1 ADJ exclusivo(a); *(neighbourhood)* selecto(a); *(club)* cerrado(a)
2 N *Press* exclusiva f

exclusively [ɪk'sklu:sɪvlɪ] ADV exclusivamente

excommunicate [ekskə'mju:nɪkeɪt] VT excomulgar

excrement ['ekskrɪmənt] N excremento m

excruciating [ɪk'skru:ʃɪeɪtɪŋ] ADJ insoportable

excruciatingly [ɪk'skru:ʃɪeɪtɪŋlɪ] ADV horriblemente

excursion [ɪk'skɜ:ʃən] N excursión f

excusable [ɪk'skju:zəbəl] ADJ perdonable

excuse 1 VT [ɪk'skju:z] (a) *(forgive)* disculpar, excusar; **e. me!** *(to attract attention)* ¡perdón!, ¡oiga (por favor)!; *(when trying to get past)* con permiso; **may I be excused for a moment?** ¿puedo salir un momento? (b) *(exempt)* dispensar (c) *(justify)* justificar
2 N [ɪk'skju:s] excusa f; **to make an e.** dar excusas

ex-directory [eksdɪ'rektərɪ] ADJ *Br* **e. (telephone) number** = número de teléfono que no figura en la guía or *Am* en el directorio

execute ['eksɪkju:t] VT (a) *(order)* cumplir; *(task)* realizar (b) *Jur* cumplir (c) *(person)* ejecutar

execution [eksɪ'kju:ʃən] N (a) *(of order)* cumplimiento m; *(of task)* realización f (b) *Jur* cumplimiento m (c) *(of person)* ejecución f

executioner [eksɪ'kju:ʃənə(r)] N verdugo m

executive [ɪg'zekjʊtɪv] 1 ADJ ejecutivo(a)
2 N ejecutivo(a) m,f

executor [ɪg'zekjʊtə(r)] N albacea m

exemplary [ɪg'zemplərɪ] ADJ ejemplar

exemplify [ɪg'zemplɪfaɪ] VT ejemplificar

exempt [ɪg'zempt] 1 VT eximir (**from** de)
2 ADJ exento(a); **e. from tax** libre de impuesto

exemption [ɪg'zempʃən] N exención f

exercise ['eksəsaɪz] 1 N ejercicio m; **e. book** cuaderno m
2 VT (a) *(rights, duties)* ejercer (b) *(dog)* sacar de paseo
3 VI hacer ejercicio

exert [ɪg'zɜ:t] VT *(influence)* ejercer; **to e. oneself** esforzarse

exertion [ɪg'zɜ:ʃən] N esfuerzo m

exhale [eks'heɪl] 1 VT *(breathe)* exhalar
2 VI espirar

exhaust [ɪg'zɔ:st] 1 VT agotar
2 N *(gas)* gases mpl de combustión; **e. pipe** tubo m de escape

exhausted [ɪg'zɔ:stɪd] ADJ agotado(a)

exhausting [ɪg'zɔ:stɪŋ] ADJ agotador(a)

exhaustion [ɪg'zɔ:stʃən] N agotamiento m

exhaustive [ɪg'zɔ:stɪv] ADJ exhaustivo(a)

exhibit [ɪg'zɪbɪt] 1 N *Art* objeto expuesto; *Jur* prueba f instrumental
2 VT *Art* exponer; *(surprise etc)* mostrar

exhibition [eksɪ'bɪʃən] N exposición f

exhibitionist [eksɪˈbɪʃənɪst] ADJ & N exhibicionista (mf)

exhilarating [ɪgˈzɪləreɪtɪŋ] ADJ estimulante

exhilaration [ɪgzɪləˈreɪʃən] N regocijo m

exhume [eksˈhjuːm] VT exhumar

exile [ˈeksaɪl] 1 N (a) (banishment) exilio m (b) (person) exiliado(a) m,f
2 VT exiliar

exist [ɪgˈzɪst] VI existir; (have little money) malvivir

existence [ɪgˈzɪstəns] N existencia f

existing [ɪgˈzɪstɪŋ] ADJ existente, actual

exit [ˈeksɪt] 1 N salida f; to make an e. salir
2 VI (leave) & Comput salir

Note that the Spanish word **éxito** is a false friend and is never a translation for the English word **exit**. In Spanish **éxito** means "success".

exodus [ˈeksədəs] N éxodo m

exonerate [ɪgˈzɒnəreɪt] VT Fml exonerar (from de)

exorbitant [ɪgˈzɔːbɪtənt] ADJ exorbitante, desorbitado(a)

exotic [ɪgˈzɒtɪk] ADJ exótico(a)

expand [ɪkˈspænd] 1 VT (enlarge) ampliar; (gas, metal) dilatar
2 VI (grow) ampliarse; (metal) dilatarse; (become more friendly) abrirse
▶ expand on VT INSEP ampliar

expanse [ɪkˈspæns] N extensión f

expansion [ɪkˈspænʃən] N (in size) expansión f; (of gas, metal) dilatación f

expatriate 1 ADJ & N [eksˈpætrɪt] expatriado(a) (m,f)
2 VT [eksˈpætrɪeɪt] expatriar

expect [ɪkˈspekt] 1 VT (a) (anticipate) esperar; I half expected that to happen suponía que iba a ocurrir (b) (demand) contar con (c) (suppose) suponer
2 VI Fam to be expecting estar embarazada

expectancy [ɪkˈspektənsɪ] N expectación f

expectant [ɪkˈspektənt] ADJ ilusionado(a); e. mother mujer embarazada

expectation [ekspekˈteɪʃən] N esperanza f, contrary to e. contrariamente a lo que se esperaba

expedient [ɪkˈspiːdɪənt] 1 ADJ conveniente, oportuno(a)
2 N expediente m, recurso m

expedition [ekspɪˈdɪʃən] N expedición f

expel [ɪkˈspel] VT expulsar

expend [ɪkˈspend] VT gastar

expendable [ɪkˈspendəbəl] ADJ prescindible

expenditure [ɪkˈspendɪtʃə(r)] N desembolso m

expense [ɪkˈspens] N gasto m; all expenses paid con todos los gastos pagados; to spare no e. no escatimar gastos; Fig at the e. of a costa de; e. account cuenta f de gastos de representación

expensive [ɪkˈspensɪv] ADJ caro(a), costoso(a)

experience [ɪkˈspɪərɪəns] 1 N experiencia f
2 VT (sensation) experimentar; (difficulty, loss) sufrir

experienced [ɪkˈspɪərɪənst] ADJ experimentado(a)

experiment [ɪkˈsperɪmənt] 1 N experimento m
2 VI experimentar, hacer experimentos (on or with con)

experimental [ɪksperɪˈmentəl] ADJ experimental

expert [ˈekspɜːt] 1 ADJ experto(a)
2 N experto(a) m,f, especialista mf

expertise [ekspɜːˈtiːz] N pericia f

expire [ɪkˈspaɪə(r)] VI (a) (die) expirar; (mandate) terminar (b) Com & Ins vencer; (ticket) caducar

expiry [ɪkˈspaɪərɪ] N vencimiento m; e. date fecha f de caducidad

explain [ɪkˈspleɪn] 1 VT explicar; (clarify) aclarar; to e. oneself justificarse
2 VI explicarse

explanation [ekspləˈneɪʃən] N explicación f; (clarification) aclaración f

explanatory [ɪkˈsplænətərɪ] ADJ explicativo(a), aclaratorio(a)

expletive [ɪkˈspliːtɪv] N palabrota f, Esp taco m

explicit [ɪkˈsplɪsɪt] ADJ explícito(a)

explode [ɪkˈspləʊd] 1 VT (a) (bomb) hacer explotar (b) Fig (theory) echar por tierra
2 VI (bomb) estallar, explotar; Fig to e. with or in anger montar en cólera

exploit 1 N [ˈeksplɔɪt] proeza f, hazaña f
2 VT [ek·splɔɪt] explotar

exploitation [eksplɔɪˈteɪʃən] N explotación f

exploratory [ekˈsplɒrətərɪ] ADJ exploratorio(a)

explore [ɪkˈsplɔː(r)] VT explorar

explorer [ɪkˈsplɔːrə(r)] N explorador(a) m,f

explosion [ɪkˈspləʊʒən] N explosión f

explosive [ɪkˈspləʊsɪv] 1 ADJ explosivo(a); e. issue asunto delicado
2 N explosivo m

exponent [ɪkˈspəʊnənt] N exponente m; (supporter) defensor(a) m,f

export 1 VT [ɪkˈspɔːt] exportar
2 N [ˈekspɔːt] (a) (trade) exportación f (b) (commodity) artículo m de exportación

exporter [ɪkˈspɔːtə(r)] N exportador(a) m,f

expose [ɪkˈspəʊz] VT (uncover) exponer; (secret) revelar; (plot) descubrir; to e. oneself exhibirse desnudo

exposed [ɪkˈspəʊzd] ADJ expuesto(a)

exposure [ɪkˈspəʊʒə(r)] N (a) (to light, cold, heat) exposición f; to die of e. morir de frío (b) Phot fotografía f; e. meter fotómetro m (c) (of criminal) descubrimiento m

expound [ɪkˈspaʊnd] VT exponer

express [ɪkˈspres] 1 ADJ (a) (explicit) expreso(a) (b) Br (letter) urgente; e. train expreso m

2 N *Rail* expreso *m*
3 VT expresar
4 ADV **send it e.** mándalo urgente
expression [ɪk'spreʃən] N expresión *f*
expressive [ɪk'spresɪv] ADJ expresivo(a)
expressly [ɪk'spreslɪ] ADV *Fml* expresamente
expressway [ɪk'spreswei] N *US* autopista *f*
expulsion [ɪk'spʌlʃən] N expulsión *f*
exquisite [ɪk'skwɪzɪt] ADJ exquisito(a)
extend [ɪk'stend] 1 VT **(a)** *(enlarge)* ampliar;
(lengthen) alargar; *(increase)* aumentar; *Fig*
**the prohibition was extended to cover
cigarettes** extendieron la prohibición a los
cigarrillos **(b)** *(give)* rendir, dar; **to e. a
welcome to sb** recibir a algn **(c)** *(prolong)*
prolongar
2 VI **(a)** *(stretch)* extenderse **(b)** *(last)*
prolongarse
extension [ɪk'stenʃən] N **(a)** *(on building)*
ampliación *f*; *(of time)* prórroga *f* **(b)** *(for
telephone)* extensión *f*, *RP* interno *m*
extensive [ɪk'stensɪv] ADJ extenso(a)
extent [ɪk'stent] N **(a)** *(area)* extensión *f* **(b)** **to
some e.** hasta cierto punto; **to a large e.** en
gran parte; **to a lesser e.** en menor grado; **to
such an e.** hasta tal punto
extenuating [ɪk'stenjʊeitɪŋ] ADJ atenuante
exterior [ɪk'stiərɪə(r)] 1 ADJ exterior, externo(a)
2 N exterior *m*
exterminate [ɪk'stɜ:mɪneɪt] VT exterminar
extermination [ɪkstɜ:mɪ'neɪʃən] N extermina-
ción *f*, exterminio *m*
external [ɪk'stɜ:nəl] ADJ externo(a), exterior
extinct [ɪk'stɪŋkt] ADJ extinguido(a)
extinction [ɪk'stɪŋkʃən] N extinción *f*
extinguish [ɪk'stɪŋgwɪʃ] VT extinguir, apagar
extinguisher [ɪk'stɪŋgwɪʃə(r)] N extintor *m*
extol, *US* **extoll** [ɪk'stəʊl] VT ensalzar
extort [ɪk'stɔ:t] VT arrancar; *(money)* sacar
extortion [ɪk'stɔ:ʃən] N extorsión *f*
extortionate [ɪk'stɔ:ʃənɪt] ADJ desorbitado(a)
extra ['ekstrə] 1 ADJ extra; *(spare)* de sobra; **e.
time** *(in soccer match)* prórroga *f*
2 ADV extra; **e. fine** extra fino
3 N *(additional charge)* suplemento *m*; *Cin*
extra *mf*; *(newspaper)* edición *f* especial
extract 1 N ['ekstrækt] extracto *m*
2 VT [ɪk'strækt] *(tooth, information)* extraer;
(confession) arrancar
extraction [ɪk'strækʃən] N extracción *f*
extracurricular [ekstrəkə'rɪkjʊlə(r)] ADJ extracurricular
extradite ['ekstrədait] VT extraditar
extramarital [ekstrə'mærɪtəl] ADJ extramatrimonial
extramural [ekstrə'mjʊərəl] ADJ **e. course =**
curso para estudiantes libres

extraordinary [ɪk'strɔ:dənərɪ] ADJ *(meeting)*
extraordinario(a); *(behaviour etc)* extraño(a)
extravagance [ɪk'strævəgəns] N *(with money)*
derroche *m*; *(of behaviour)* extravagancia *f*
extravagant [ɪk'strævəgənt] ADJ *(wasteful)*
derrochador(a); *(excessive)* exagerado(a);
(luxurious) lujoso(a)
Extremadura [ekstrəmə'djuːrə] N Extremadura
extreme [ɪk'striːm] 1 ADJ extremo(a); **an e.
case** un caso excepcional; **to hold e. views**
tener opiniones radicales
2 N extremo *m*; **in the e.** en sumo grado
extremely [ɪk'striːmlɪ] ADV extremadamente;
I'm e. sorry lo siento de veras
extremist [ɪk'striːmɪst] N extremista *mf*
extremity [ɪk'stremɪtɪ] N extremidad *f*
extricate ['ekstrɪkeit] VT sacar; **to e. oneself
(from)** lograr salir (de)
extrovert ['ekstrəvɜːt] ADJ & N extrovertido(a)
(m,f)
exuberant [ɪg'zjuːbərənt] ADJ exuberante
exude [ɪg'zjuːd] VT & VI *(moisture, sap)* exudar;
Fig rebosar
exultant [ɪg'zʌltənt] ADJ jubiloso(a)
eye [ai] 1 N ojo *m*; *Fig* **I couldn't believe my
eyes** no podía creerlo; *Fig* **in the eyes of** de
según; *Fig* **not to take one's eyes off sb/sth**
no quitar la vista de encima a algo/algn; *Fig*
to catch sb's e. llamar la atención a algn; *Fig*
to have an e. for tener buen ojo para; *Fig* **to
make eyes at sb** echar miraditas a algn; *Fig*
to see e. to e. with sb estar de acuerdo con
algn; *Fig* **to turn a blind e. (to)** hacer la vista
gorda (a); *Fig* **with an e. to** con miras a; **to
keep an e. on sb/sth** vigilar a algo/algn; **to
keep an e. out for** estar pendiente de; **black
e.** ojo morado; *US* **e. doctor** óptico(a) *m,f*
2 VT observar
eyeball ['aibɔːl] N globo *m* ocular
eyebrow ['aibrau] N ceja *f*
eyecatching ['aikætʃɪŋ] ADJ llamativo(a)
eye-drops ['aidrops] NPL *(medicine)* colirio *m*
eyeglasses ['aiɡlɑːsɪz] NPL *US (spectacles)* gafas
fpl, *Am* lentes *mpl*, anteojos *mpl*
eyelash ['ailæʃ] N pestaña *f*
eyelid ['ailɪd] N párpado *m*
eyeliner ['ailainə(r)] N lápiz *m* de ojos
eye-opener ['aiəʊpənə(r)] N revelación *f*, gran
sorpresa *f*
eyeshadow ['aiʃædəʊ] N sombra *f* de ojos
eyesight ['aisait] N vista *f*
eyesore ['aisɔː(r)] N monstruosidad *f*
eyestrain ['aistrein] N vista cansada
eyewash ['aiwɒʃ] N colirio *m*; *Fig* **it's all e.** eso
son disparates
eyewitness ['aiwitnis] N testigo *mf* ocular

F

F, f [ef] N (**a**) *(the letter)* F, f *f* (**b**) *Mus* **F** fa *m*

F *(abbr* **Fahrenheit)** F

fable ['feɪbəl] N fábula *f*

fabric ['fæbrɪk] N (**a**) *Tex* tejido *m* (**b**) *Constr* estructura *f*

> Note that the Spanish word **fábrica** is a false friend and is never a translation for the English word **fabric**. In Spanish **fábrica** means "factory".

fabricate ['fæbrɪkeɪt] VT fabricar

fabrication [fæbrɪ'keɪʃən] N *Fig* fabricación *f*

fabulous ['fæbjʊləs] ADJ fabuloso(a)

façade [fə'saːd, fæ'saːd] N fachada *f*

face [feɪs] **1** N (**a**) *(of person)* cara *f*, rostro *m*; **f. to f.** cara a cara; **f. cloth** paño *m* (**b**) *(expression)* cara *f*, expresión *f*; **to pull faces** hacer muecas (**c**) *(surface)* superficie *f*; *(of card, coin)* cara *f*; *(of watch)* esfera *f*; **f. down/up** boca abajo/arriba (**d**) *(appearance)* aspecto *m*; **to take sth at f. value** entender algo sólo en su sentido literal; **to lose f.** desprestigiarse; **to save f.** salvar las apariencias
2 VT (**a**) *(look on to)* dar a; *(be opposite)* estar enfrente de (**b**) **to f. the wall/window** *(of person)* estar de cara a la pared/ventana (**c**) *(problem)* hacer frente a; **to f. up to** hacer cara a
3 VI **to f. on to** dar a; **to f. towards** mirar hacia; **f. this way** vuélvase de este lado

faceless ['feɪslɪs] ADJ anónimo(a)

facelift ['feɪslɪft] N *Med* lifting *m*; *Fig* renovación *f*

facet ['fæsɪt] N faceta *f*

facetious [fə'siːʃəs] ADJ bromista

facial ['feɪʃəl] ADJ facial

facile ['fæsaɪl] ADJ superficial

facilitate [fə'sɪlɪteɪt] VT facilitar

facility [fə'sɪlɪtɪ] N (**a**) *(ease)* facilidad *f* (**b**) **facilities** *(means)* facilidades *fpl*; **credit facilities** facilidades de crédito (**c**) **facilities** *(rooms, equipment)* instalaciones *fpl*; **cooking facilities** derecho *m* a cocina

facing ['feɪsɪŋ] ADJ de enfrente

facsimile [fæk'sɪmɪlɪ] N (**a**) *(copy)* facsímil *m* (**b**) *(message)* telefax *m* (**c**) *(machine)* facsímil *m*

fact [fækt] N hecho *m*; **as a matter of f.** de hecho; **the f. that he confessed** el hecho de que confesara; **in f.** en realidad

fact-finding ['fæktfaɪndɪŋ] ADJ investigador(a)

faction ['fækʃən] N *(group)* facción *f*

factor ['fæktə(r)] N factor *m*

factory ['fæktərɪ] N fábrica *f*

factual ['fæktʃʊəl] ADJ **a f. error** un error de hecho

faculty ['fækəltɪ] N (**a**) *(of mind, section of university)* facultad *f* (**b**) *US Univ* cuerpo *m* docente

fad [fæd] N *Fam (craze)* moda pasajera; *(whim)* capricho *m*

fade [feɪd] VI *(colour)* desteñirse; *(flower)* marchitarse; *(light)* apagarse
▶ **fade away** VI desvanecerse
▶ **fade in, fade out** VT SEP *Cin & TV* fundir

faded ['feɪdɪd] ADJ *(colour)* desteñido(a); *(flower)* marchito(a)

fag [fæg] N (**a**) *Br Fam (cigarette)* pitillo *m* (**b**) *US very Fam (homosexual)* maricón *m*, *Méx* tortillón *m*, *RP* trolo *m*

faggot ['fægət] N (**a**) *Br (meatball)* albóndiga *f* (**b**) *US very Fam (homosexual)* maricón *m*, *Méx* tortillón *m*, *RP* trolo *m*

fail [feɪl] **1** N (**a**) *(in exam)* *Esp* suspenso *m*, *Am* reprobado *m* (**b**) **without f.** sin falta
2 VT (**a**) **don't f. me** no me falles (**b**) *(exam)* suspender (**c**) *(be unable)* no lograr (**d**) *(neglect)* dejar de
3 VI (**a**) *(show, film)* fracasar; *(in exam)* *Esp* suspender, *Am* reprobar; *(brakes)* fallar (**b**) *(business)* quebrar (**c**) *(of health)* deteriorarse

failing ['feɪlɪŋ] **1** N (**a**) *(shortcoming)* defecto *m* (**b**) *(weakness)* punto *m* débil
2 PREP a falta de

failure ['feɪljə(r)] N (**a**) *(lack of success)* fracaso *m* (**b**) *(of company)* quiebra *f* (**c**) *(in exam, course)* *Esp* suspenso *m*, *Am* reprobado *m* (**d**) *(person)* fracasado(a) *m,f*

faint [feɪnt] **1** ADJ (**a**) *(sound)* débil; *(colour)* pálido(a); *(outline)* borroso(a); *(recollection)* vago(a) (**b**) *(giddy)* mareado(a)
2 N desmayo *m*
3 VI desmayarse

faint-hearted [feɪnt'hɑːtɪd] ADJ temeroso(a)

fair¹ [feə(r)] **1** ADJ (**a**) *(impartial)* imparcial; *(just)* justo(a); **it's not f.** no hay derecho; *Fam* **f. enough!** de acuerdo *or Esp* vale (**b**) *(hair)* rubio(a), *Méx* güero(a); *(skin)* claro(a) (**c**) *(weather)* bueno(a) (**d**) *(beautiful)* bello(a) (**e**) **a f. number** un buen número; **he has a f.**

chance tiene bastantes probabilidades
2 ADV **to play f.** jugar limpio

fair² [feə(r)] N (**a**) Br (funfair) feria f (**b**) **trade f.** feria de muestras

fairground ['feəgraʊnd] N real m de la feria

fairly ['feəlɪ] ADV (**a**) (justly) justamente (**b**) (moderately) bastante

fairness ['feənɪs] N justicia f, equidad f; **in all f.** para ser justo(a)

fairy ['feərɪ] N (**a**) (in folklore) hada f; **f. godmother** hada madrina; **f. tale** cuento m de hadas (**b**) Fam Pej (homosexual) mariquita m

fait accompli [feɪtə'kɒmpliː] N Fml hecho consumado

faith [feɪθ] N (**a**) Rel fe f (**b**) (trust) confianza f; **in good f.** de buena fe

faithful ['feɪθfʊl] **1** ADJ fiel
2 NPL **the f.** los fieles

faithfully ['feɪθfʊlɪ] ADV fielmente; **yours f.** (in letter) le saluda atentamente

fake [feɪk] **1** ADJ falso(a)
2 N (**a**) (object) falsificación f (**b**) (person) impostor(a) m,f
3 VT (**a**) (forge) falsificar (**b**) (feign) fingir
4 VI (pretend) fingir

falcon ['fɔːlkən] N halcón m

Falklands ['fɔːlkləndz] NPL **the F.** las (Islas) Malvinas

fall [fɔːl] **1** N (**a**) (of person, prices, besieged city) caída f; **f. of snow** nevada f (**b**) (decrease) baja f (**c**) US (autumn) otoño m (**d**) **falls** (waterfall) cascada f; **Niagara Falls** las cataratas del Niágara
2 VI (pt **fell**; pp **fallen**) (**a**) (drop) caer; (trip, tumble) caerse; **they f. into two categories** se dividen en dos categorías; Fig **night was falling** anochecía; Fig **to f. short of** (**a**) no alcanzar (**b**) (in battle) caer (**c**) (temperature, prices) bajar (**d**) (become) **to f. asleep** dormirse; **to f. ill** caer enfermo(a), enfermar, RP,Ven enfermarse; **to f. in love** enamorarse

▸ **fall back** VI replegarse

▸ **fall back on** VT INSEP echar mano a, recurrir a

▸ **fall behind** VI (in race) quedarse atrás; **to f. behind with one's work** retrasarse en el trabajo

▸ **fall down** VI (**a**) (picture etc) caerse (**b**) (building) derrumbarse

▸ **fall for** VT INSEP (**a**) (person) enamorarse de (**b**) (trick) dejarse engañar por

▸ **fall in** VI (**a**) (roof) desplomarse (**b**) Mil formar filas

▸ **fall off 1** VI (**a**) (drop off) caerse (**b**) (part) desprenderse (**c**) (diminish) disminuir
2 VT INSEP **to f. off sth** caerse de algo

▸ **fall out** VI (**a**) (hair) caerse (**b**) Mil romper filas (**c**) (quarrel) pelearse

▸ **fall over** VI caerse

▸ **fall through** VI (plan) fracasar

fallacy ['fæləsɪ] N falacia f

fallen ['fɔːlən] PP of **fall**

fallible ['fælɪbəl] ADJ falible

fall-out ['fɔːlaʊt] N (**radioactive**) **f.** lluvia radioactiva; **f. shelter** refugio antiatómico

fallow ['fæləʊ] ADJ Agr en barbecho

false [fɔːls] ADJ falso(a); **f. teeth** dentadura postiza; **f. alarm** falsa alarma

falsehood ['fɔːlshʊd] N falsedad f

falsify ['fɔːlsɪfaɪ] VT (records, accounts) falsificar; (story) falsear

falter ['fɔːltə(r)] VI vacilar; (voice) fallar

faltering ['fɔːltərɪŋ] ADJ vacilante

fame [feɪm] N fama f

familiar [fə'mɪlɪə(r)] ADJ (**a**) (common) familiar, conocido(a); **his face is f.** su cara me suena (**b**) (aware, knowledgeable) enterado(a), al corriente (**with** de) (**c**) **to be on f. terms with sb** (know well) tener confianza con algn

familiarity [fəmɪlɪ'ærɪtɪ] N (**a**) (awareness, knowledge) familiaridad f (**with** con) (**b**) (intimacy) confianza f

familiarize [fə'mɪljəraɪz] VT (**a**) (become acquainted) familiarizar (**with** con); **to f. oneself with sth** familiarizarse con algo (**b**) (make widely known) popularizar

family ['fæmɪlɪ] N familia f; **f. allowance** subsidio m familiar; **f. doctor** médico m de cabecera; **f. man** hombre hogareño; **f. planning** planificación f familiar; **f. tree** árbol m genealógico

famine ['fæmɪn] N hambre f, escasez f de alimentos

famished ['fæmɪʃt] ADJ Fam muerto(a) de hambre

famous ['feɪməs] ADJ célebre, famoso(a) (**for** por)

famously ['feɪməslɪ] ADV Fam estupendamente

fan [fæn] **1** N (**a**) (cooling device) (hand-held) abanico m; (mechanical) ventilador m (**b**) (person) aficionado(a) m,f; (of pop star etc) fan mf; **f. club** club m de fans; **football f.** hincha mf
2 VT (**a**) (with fan) abanicar (**b**) (fire, passions) avivar

▸ **fan out** VI (troops) desplegarse en abanico

fanatic [fə'nætɪk] ADJ & N fanático(a) (m,f)

fanatical [fə'nætɪkəl] ADJ fanático(a)

fanciful ['fænsɪfʊl] ADJ (**a**) (person) caprichoso(a) (**b**) (idea) fantástico(a)

fancy ['fænsɪ] **1** ADJ (**fancier, fanciest**) de fantasía; **f. dress** disfraz m
2 N (**a**) (imagination) fantasía f (**b**) (whim) capricho m, antojo m; **to take a f. to sb** cogerle cariño a algn; **to take a f. to sth** encapricharse con algo
3 VT (**a**) (imagine) imaginarse; Fam **f. seeing you here!** ¡qué casualidad verte por aquí! (**b**) (like, want) apetecer; **do you f. a drink?** ¿te apetece una copa?; Br Fam **I f. her** ella me gusta

fanfare ['fænfeə(r)] N fanfarria f

fang [fæŋ] N colmillo m

fanny ['fænɪ] N (**a**) *US Fam (buttocks)* culo *m* (**b**) *BrVulg (vagina) Esp* coño *m*, *Andes, RP* concha *f*; *Méx* paloma *f*

fantasize ['fæntəsaɪz] VI fantasear

fantastic [fæn'tæstɪk] ADJ fantástico(a)

fantasy ['fæntəsɪ] N fantasía *f*

FAQ [fæk] (*abbr* **frequently asked questions**) N *Comput* preguntas *fpl* más frecuentes

far [fɑː(r)] (*farther or* **further**, *farthest or* **furthest**) 1 ADJ (**a**) *(distant)* lejano(a); **the F. East** el Lejano Oriente (**b**) **at the f. end** en el otro extremo (**c**) *Pol* **the f. left/right** la extrema izquierda/derecha
2 ADV (**a**) *(distant)* lejos; **f. off** a lo lejos; **farther back/north** más atrás/al norte; **how f. is it to Cardiff?** ¿cuánto hay de aquí a Cardiff?; **as f. as I know** que yo sepa; **as f. as possible** en lo posible; *Fig* **f. from complaining, he seemed pleased** lejos de quejarse, parecía contento; *Fig* **I'm f. from satisfied** no estoy satisfecho(a) ni mucho menos; *Fam* **to go too f.** pasarse de la raya (**b**) *(in time)* **as f. back as the fifties** ya en los años cincuenta; **so f.** hasta ahora (**c**) *(much)* mucho; **by f.** con diferencia *or* mucho, *RP* por lejos; **f. cleverer** mucho más listo(a); **f. too much** demasiado

faraway ['fɑːrəweɪ] ADJ lejano(a), remoto(a)

farce [fɑːs] N farsa *f*

farcical ['fɑːsɪkəl] ADJ absurdo(a)

fare [feə(r)] 1 N (**a**) *(ticket price)* tarifa *f*, precio *m* del billete; *(for boat)* pasaje *m*; **half f.** media tarifa (**b**) *(passenger)* pasajero(a) *m,f* (**c**) *(food)* comida *f*
2 VI **how did you f.?** ¿qué tal te fue?

farewell [feə'wel] 1 INTERJ *Literary* ¡adiós!
2 N despedida *f*

far-fetched [fɑː'fetʃt] ADJ rebuscado(a)

farm [fɑːm] 1 N *(small)* granja *f*; *(large)* hacienda *f*, *CSur* estancia *f*
2 VT cultivar, labrar
▸ **farm out** VT SEP encargar fuera

farmer ['fɑːmə(r)] N granjero(a) *m,f*, *Am* hacendado(a) *m,f*

farmhand ['fɑːmhænd] N peón *m*, labriego(a) *m,f*

farmhouse ['fɑːmhaʊs] N granja *f*, *Am* hacienda *f*

farming ['fɑːmɪŋ] 1 N (**a**) *(agriculture)* agricultura *f* (**b**) *(of land)* cultivo *m*, labranza *f*
2 ADJ agrícola

farmyard ['fɑːmjɑːd] N corral *m*

far-reaching [fɑː'riːtʃɪŋ] ADJ de gran alcance

far-sighted [fɑː'saɪtɪd] ADJ (**a**) *(person)* con visión de futuro (**b**) *(plan)* con miras al futuro

fart [fɑːt] *Fam* 1 N pedo *m*
2 VI echarse un pedo

farther ['fɑːðə(r)] ADJ & ADV COMP *of* **far**

farthest ['fɑːðɪst] ADJ & ADV SUPERL *of* **far**

fascinate ['fæsɪneɪt] VT fascinar

fascinating ['fæsɪneɪtɪŋ] ADJ fascinante

fascination [fæsɪ'neɪʃən] N fascinación *f*

fascism ['fæʃɪzəm] N fascismo *m*

fascist ['fæʃɪst] ADJ & N fascista *(mf)*

fashion ['fæʃən] 1 N (**a**) *(manner)* manera *f*, modo *m*; **after a f.** más o menos (**b**) *(latest style)* moda *f*; **to go/be out of f.** pasar/no estar de moda; **f. designer** diseñador(a) *m,f* de modas; **f. parade** desfile *m* de modelos
2 VT *(metal)* labrar; *(clay)* formar

fashionable ['fæʃənəbəl] ADJ de moda

fast[1] [fɑːst] 1 ADJ (**a**) *(quick)* rápido(a) (**b**) **hard and f. rules** reglas estrictas (**c**) *(clock)* adelantado(a)
2 ADV (**a**) *(rapidly)* rápido, deprisa; **how f.?** ¿a qué velocidad? (**b**) *(securely)* firmemente; **f. asleep** profundamente dormido(a)

fast[2] [fɑːst] 1 N ayuno *m*
2 VI ayunar

fasten ['fɑːsən] 1 VT (**a**) *(attach)* sujetar; *(fix)* fijar (**b**) *(belt)* abrochar; *(bag)* asegurar; *(shoelaces)* atar
2 VI *(dress)* abrocharse

fastener ['fɑːsənə(r)] N cierre *m*

fastidious [fæ'stɪdɪəs] ADJ quisquilloso(a)

fat [fæt] 1 ADJ (**fatter**, **fattest**) (**a**) *(person)* gordo(a) (**b**) *(book, file)* grueso(a) (**c**) *(meat)* que tiene mucha grasa
2 N grasa *f*; **cooking f.** manteca *f* de cerdo

fatal ['feɪtəl] ADJ (**a**) *(accident, illness)* mortal (**b**) *(ill-fated)* fatal, funesto(a) (**c**) *(fateful)* fatídico(a)

fatalistic [feɪtə'lɪstɪk] ADJ fatalista

fatality [fə'tælɪtɪ] N víctima *f* mortal

> Note that the Spanish word **fatalidad** is a false friend and is never a translation for the English word **fatality**. In Spanish **fatalidad** means both "fate" and "misfortune".

fatally ['feɪtəlɪ] ADV **f. wounded** mortalmente herido(a)

fate [feɪt] N destino *m*, suerte *f*

fateful ['feɪtfʊl] ADJ fatídico(a), aciago(a)

father ['fɑːðə(r)] N (**a**) *(parent)* padre *m*; **my f. and mother** mis padres; **F. Christmas** Papá *m* Noel (**b**) *Rel* padre *m*

fatherhood ['fɑːðəhʊd] N paternidad *f*

father-in-law ['fɑːðərɪnlɔː] N suegro *m*

fatherland ['fɑːðəlænd] N patria *f*

fatherly ['fɑːðəlɪ] ADJ paternal

fathom ['fæðəm] 1 N *Naut* braza *f*
2 VT comprender
▸ **fathom out** VT SEP comprobar; **I can't f. it out** no me lo explico

fatigue [fə'tiːg] N (**a**) *(tiredness)* fatiga *f* (**b**) *Mil* faena *f*; **f. dress** traje *m* de faena

fatten ['fætən] VT engordar

fattening ['fætənɪŋ] ADJ que engorda

fatty ['fætɪ] 1 ADJ (**fattier**, **fattiest**) *(food)* graso(a); *Anat (tissue)* adiposo(a)
2 N *Fam (person)* gordinflón(ona) *m,f*

fatuous ['fætjʊəs] ADJ necio(a)

faucet ['fɔːsɪt] N *US Esp* grifo *m*, *Chile, Col, Méx* llave *f*, *RP* canilla *f*

fault [fɔːlt] 1 N (a) *(defect)* defecto *m*; *(in merchandise)* desperfecto *m* (b) *(blame)* culpa *f*; **to be at f.** tener la culpa (c) *(mistake)* error *m* (d) *Geol* falla *f*
2 VT criticar

faultless ['fɔːltlɪs] ADJ intachable

faulty ['fɔːltɪ] ADJ (**faultier, faultiest**) defectuoso(a)

fauna ['fɔːnə] N fauna *f*

faux pas [fəʊ'pɑː] N *(pl* **faux pas**) *Fml (mistake)* paso *m* en falso; *(blunder)* metedura *f* de pata

favour, *US* **favor** ['feɪvə(r)] 1 N favor *m*; **in f.** of a favor de; **to be in f. with sb** gozar del favor de algn; **to ask sb a f.** pedirle un favor a algn; **1-0 in our f.** *(advantage)* 1-0 a favor nuestro
2 VT (a) *(person)* favorecer a (b) *(approve)* estar a favor de

favourable, *US* **favorable** ['feɪvərəbəl] ADJ favorable

favourite, *US* **favorite** ['feɪvərɪt] ADJ & N favorito(a) *(m,f)*

favouritism, *US* **favoritism** ['feɪvərɪtɪzəm] N favoritismo *m*

fawn¹ [fɔːn] 1 ADJ beige, *Esp* beis
2 N (a) *Zool* cervatillo *m* (b) *(colour)* beige *m*, *Esp* beis *m*

fawn² [fɔːn] VI adular (**on** a)

fax [fæks] 1 N *(machine, message)* fax *m*; **f. modem** modem *m* fax
2 VT mandar por fax

fear [fɪə(r)] 1 N miedo *m*, temor *m*; **for f. of** por temor a; *Fam* **no f.!** ¡ni pensarlo!
2 VT temer; **I f. it's too late** me temo que ya es tarde
3 VI temer (**for** por)

fearful ['fɪəfʊl] ADJ (a) *(person)* temeroso(a) (b) *(frightening)* espantoso(a)

fearless ['fɪəlɪs] ADJ intrépido(a)

feasibility [fiːzə'bɪlɪtɪ] N viabilidad *f*

feasible ['fiːzəbəl] ADJ *(practicable)* factible; *(possible)* viable

feast [fiːst] N banquete *m*; *Rel* **f. day** fiesta *f* de guardar

feat [fiːt] N hazaña *f*

feather ['feðə(r)] 1 N pluma *f*; **f. duster** plumero *m*
2 VT *Fam* **to f. one's nest** hacer su agosto

feature ['fiːtʃə(r)] 1 N (a) *(of face)* rasgo *m*, facción *f* (b) *(characteristic)* característica *f* (c) **f. film** largometraje *m* (d) *Press* crónica *f* especial
2 VT (a) *(of car, appliance, house)* contar or estar equipado(a) con (b) *Cin* tener como protagonista a
3 VI figurar

February ['febrʊərɪ] N febrero *m*

fed [fed] 1 ADJ *Fam* **f. up (with)** harto(a) (de)
2 PT & PP *of* **feed**

federal ['fedərəl] ADJ federal

federation [fedə'reɪʃən] N federación *f*

fee [fiː] N *(of lawyer, doctor)* honorarios *mpl*; *Ftb* **transfer f.** prima *f* de traslado; *Univ* **tuition fees** derechos *mpl* de matrícula

feeble ['fiːbəl] ADJ débil

feed [fiːd] 1 VT *(pt & pp* **fed***)* (a) *(give food to)* dar de comer a; *Fig (fire)* alimentar; **to f. a baby** *(breast-feed)* amamantar a un bebé; *(with bottle)* dar el biberón a un bebé (b) *Elec* alimentar (c) *(insert)* introducir
2 VI *(cows, sheep)* pacer; **to f. on sth** *(person)* comer algo
3 N (a) *(food)* comida *f*; **cattle f.** pienso *m* (b) *Tech* alimentación *f*
► **feed up** VT SEP cebar

feedback ['fiːdbæk] N (a) *Tech* feedback *m* (b) *Fig* reacción *f*

feeder ['fiːdə(r)] N *Tech* alimentador *m*

feeding ['fiːdɪŋ] N **f. bottle** biberón *m*

feel [fiːl] 1 VI *(pt & pp* **felt***)* (a) *(emotion, sensation)* sentir; **how do you f.?** ¿qué tal te encuentras?; **I f. bad about it** me da pena; **to f. happy/uncomfortable** sentirse feliz/incómodo; **to f. cold/sleepy** tener frío/sueño (b) *(seem)* **your hand feels cold** tienes la mano fría; **it feels like summer** parece verano (c) *(opinion)* opinar; **I f. sure that ...** estoy seguro(a) de que ... (d) **I f. like an ice cream** me tomaría *or Esp* me apetece un helado, *Carib, Col, Méx* me provoca un sorbete; **to f. like doing sth** tener ganas de hacer algo
2 VT (a) *(touch)* tocar (b) **she feels a failure** se siente inútil (c) *(notice, be aware of)* notar
3 N (a) *(touch, sensation)* tacto *m*; *Fig* **to get the f. for sth** *Esp* cogerle el truco a algo, *Am* agarrar la onda a algo (b) *(atmosphere)* ambiente *m*
► **feel for** VT INSEP (a) *(search for)* buscar (b) *(have sympathy for)* compadecer

feeler ['fiːlə(r)] N *(of insect)* antena *f*; *Fig* **to put one's feelers out** tantear el terreno

feeling ['fiːlɪŋ] 1 N (a) *(emotion)* sentimiento *m*; **ill f.** rencor *m* (b) *(compassion)* compasión *f* (c) **I had the f. that ...** *(impression)* tuve la impresión de que ... (d) *(sensitivity)* sensibilidad *f* (e) *(opinion)* opinión *f*; **to express one's feelings** expresar sus opiniones
2 ADJ sensible, compasivo(a)

feet [fiːt] PL *of* **foot**

feign [feɪn] VT fingir

feint [feɪnt] *Sport* 1 N finta *f*
2 VI fintar

feline ['fiːlaɪn] 1 N felino *m*, félido *m*
2 ADJ felino(a)

fell¹ [fel] PT *of* **fall**

fell² [fel] VT *(trees)* talar; *Fig (enemy)* derribar

fellow ['feləʊ] N (a) *(companion)* compañero(a) *m,f*; **f. citizen** conciudadano(a) *m,f*; **f. country-**

man/countrywoman compatriota *mf*; **f. men** prójimos *mpl*; **f. passenger/student** compañero(a) *m,f* de viaje/estudios (**b**) *Fam (chap)* tipo *m*, tío *m* (**c**) *(of society)* socio(a) *m,f*

fellowship ['feləʊʃɪp] N (**a**) *(comradeship)* camaradería *f* (**b**) *Univ* beca *f* de investigación

felony ['felənɪ] N *US Jur* crimen *m*, delito *m* grave

felt¹ [felt] PT & PP of **feel**

felt² [felt] N *Tex* fieltro *m*

felt-tip(ped) ['felttɪp(t)] ADJ **f. pen** rotulador *m*

female ['fiːmeɪl] 1 ADJ (**a**) *Zool* hembra (**b**) *(person)* femenino(a)
2 N (**a**) *Zool* hembra *f* (**b**) *(woman)* mujer *f*; *(girl)* chica *f*

feminine ['femɪnɪn] ADJ femenino(a)

feminism ['femɪnɪzəm] N feminismo *m*

feminist ['femɪnɪst] ADJ & N feminista *(mf)*

fence [fens] 1 N cerca *f*, valla *f*; *Fig* **to sit on the f.** ver los toros desde la barrera
2 VI *Sport* practicar la esgrima
▸ **fence in** VT SEP meter en un cercado

fencing ['fensɪŋ] N *Sport* esgrima *f*

fend [fend] VI **to f. for oneself** valerse por sí mismo
▸ **fend off** VT SEP *(blow)* parar; *(question)* rehuir; *(attack)* rechazar

fender ['fendə(r)] N (**a**) *(fireplace)* pantalla *f* (**b**) *US Aut Esp, Bol, RP* guardabarros *mpl*, *Andes, CAm, Carib* guardafango *m*, *Méx* salpicadera *f* (**c**) *Naut* defensa *f*

ferment VT & VI [fə'ment] fermentar

fern [fɜːn] N helecho *m*

ferocious [fə'rəʊʃəs] ADJ feroz

ferocity [fə'rɒsɪtɪ] N ferocidad *f*

ferret ['ferɪt] 1 N hurón *m*
2 VI huronear, husmear
▸ **ferret out** VT SEP descubrir

ferry ['ferɪ] 1 N (**a**) *(small)* barca *f* de pasaje (**b**) *(large, for cars)* transbordador *m*, ferry *m*
2 VT transportar

fertile ['fɜːtaɪl] ADJ fértil

fertility [fə'tɪlɪtɪ] N *(of soil)* fertilidad *f*

fertilize ['fɜːtɪlaɪz] VT (**a**) *(soil)* abonar (**b**) *(egg)* fecundar

fertilizer ['fɜːtɪlaɪzə(r)] N abono *m*

fervent ['fɜːvənt] ADJ ferviente

fervour, *US* **fervor** ['fɜːvə(r)] N fervor *m*

fester ['festə(r)] VI supurar

festival ['festɪvəl] N *(event)* festival *m*; *(celebration)* fiesta *f*

festive ['festɪv] ADJ festivo(a); **the f. season** las fiestas de Navidad

festivity [fe'stɪvɪtɪ] N **the festivities** las fiestas

festoon [fe'stuːn] VT adornar

fetch [fetʃ] VT (**a**) *(go for)* ir a buscar (**b**) *(bring)* traer (**c**) **how much did it f.?** *(sell for)* ¿por cuánto se vendió?

fetching ['fetʃɪŋ] ADJ atractivo(a)

fete [feɪt] 1 N fiesta *f*
2 VT festejar

fetish ['fetɪʃ, 'fiːtɪʃ] N fetiche *m*

fetus ['fiːtəs] N *US* = **foetus**

feud [fjuːd] 1 N enemistad duradera
2 VI pelear

feudal ['fjuːdəl] ADJ feudal

fever ['fiːvə(r)] N fiebre *f*

feverish ['fiːvərɪʃ] ADJ febril

few [fjuː] 1 ADJ (**a**) *(not many)* pocos(as); **as f. as** solamente (**b**) *(some)* algunos(as), unos(as) cuantos(as); **a f. books** unos *or* algunos libros; **she has fewer books than I thought** tiene menos libros de lo que pensaba; **for the past f. years** durante estos últimos años; **in the next f. days** dentro de unos días; **quite a f.** bastantes
2 PRON (**a**) *(not many)* pocos(as); **there are too f.** no hay suficientes (**b**) *(some)* algunos(as), unos(as) cuantos(as); **who has the fewest?** ¿quién tiene menos?

fiancé [fɪ'ɒnseɪ] N prometido *m*

fiancée [fɪ'ɒnseɪ] N prometida *f*

fiasco [fɪ'æskəʊ] N *(pl Br* fiascos, *US* fiascoes*)* fiasco *m*

fib [fɪb] *Fam* 1 N trola *f*
2 VI contar trolas

fibre, *US* **fiber** ['faɪbə(r)] N fibra *f*

fibreglass, *US* **fiberglass** ['faɪbəɡlɑːs] N fibra *f* de vidrio

fickle ['fɪkəl] ADJ inconstante, voluble

fiction ['fɪkʃən] N ficción *f*

fictional ['fɪkʃənəl] ADJ (**a**) *Lit* novelesco(a) (**b**) *(imaginative)* ficticio(a)

fictitious [fɪk'tɪʃəs] ADJ ficticio(a)

fiddle ['fɪdəl] 1 N (**a**) *(violin)* violín *m* *(en música folk)* (**b**) *esp Br Fam (swindle)* timo *m*
2 VT *Br Fam* amañar
3 VI juguetear (**with** con)
▸ **fiddle about** VI perder tiempo

fiddly ['fɪdlɪ] ADJ (**fiddlier, fiddliest**) *Fam* laborioso(a)

fidelity [fɪ'delɪtɪ] N fidelidad *f*

fidget ['fɪdʒɪt] VI enredar, trastear; **stop fidgeting!** ¡estáte quieto!

field [fiːld] 1 N (**a**) *(of crops)* & *Comput* campo *m*; **f. glasses** gemelos *mpl*; **f. marshal** mariscal *m* de campo (**b**) *Geol & Min* yacimiento *m* (**c**) **f. trip** viaje *m* de estudios; **f. work** trabajo *m* de campo
2 VT *Sport* (**a**) *(ball)* parar y devolver (**b**) *(team)* presentar

fiend [fiːnd] N demonio *m*; *Fam (fanatic)* fanático(a) *m,f*

fiendish ['fiːndɪʃ] ADJ *Fam* diabólico(a)

fierce [fɪəs] ADJ *(animal)* feroz; *(argument)* acalorado(a); *(heat, competition)* intenso(a); *(wind)* violento(a)

fiery ['faɪərɪ] ADJ (**fierier, fieriest**) *(temper)* fogoso(a); *(speech)* acalorado(a); *(colour)* encendido(a)

fifteen [fɪf'ti:n] ADJ & N quince *(m inv)*

fifteenth [fɪf'ti:nθ] **1** ADJ & N decimoquinto(a) *(m,f)*
2 N *(fraction)* quinzavo *m*

fifth [fɪfθ] **1** ADJ & N quinto(a) *(m,f)*
2 N *(fraction)* quinto *m*

fifty ['fɪftɪ] ADJ & N cincuenta *(m inv)*

fifty-fifty ['fɪftɪ'fɪftɪ] *Fam* **1** ADJ **a f. chance** una probabilidad del cincuenta por ciento
2 ADV **to go f.** ir a medias

fig¹ [fɪg] N *(fruit)* higo *m*

fig² [fɪg] *(abbr* **figure***)* fig

fight [faɪt] **1** VT *(pt & pp* **fought***)* (a) *(enemy, rivals)* luchar contra; *(of boxer)* pelear contra; *Fig (corruption)* combatir (b) *(war, battle)* librar (c) *(decision)* recurrir contra
2 VI (a) *(physically)* luchar (**about/with** por/contra) (b) *(quarrel)* reñir; **to f. over sth** disputarse la posesión de algo (c) *Fig (struggle)* luchar (**for/against** por/contra)
3 N (a) *(physical, verbal)* pelea *f*; *(in boxing)* combate *m* (b) *(quarrel)* riña *f* (c) *Fig (struggle)* lucha *f*

▸ **fight back 1** VT SEP *(tears)* contener
2 VI contraatacar

▸ **fight off** VT SEP (a) *(attack)* rechazar (b) *(illness)* cortar

▸ **fight out** VT SEP discutir

fighter ['faɪtə(r)] N (a) *(person)* combatiente *mf*; *(in boxing)* púgil *m* (b) *Fig* luchador(a) *m,f*; **f. (plane)** *(avión m de)* caza *m*; **f. bomber** cazabombardero *m*

fighting ['faɪtɪŋ] **1** ADJ **he's got a f. chance** tiene verdaderas posibilidades
2 N lucha *f*

figment ['fɪgmənt] N **it's a f. of your imagination** es un producto de tu imaginación

figurative ['fɪgərətɪv] ADJ figurado(a)

figure ['fɪgə(r), *US* 'fɪgjər] **1** N (a) *(form, outline)* forma *f*, silueta *f* (b) *(shape, statue, character)* figura *f*; **she has a good f.** tiene buen tipo (c) *(in book)* dibujo *m* (d) **f. of speech** figura retórica (e) *Math* cifra *f*
2 VT *US Fam* pensar, figurarse
3 VI (a) *(appear) (in list, book)* figurar (b) *Fam (make sense)* **that figures!** (es) normal or lógico

▸ **figure out** VT SEP *Fam* comprender; **I can't f. it out** no me lo explico

figurehead ['fɪgəhed] N *Fig* figura decorativa

filament ['fɪləmənt] N filamento *m*

filch [fɪltʃ] VT *Fam* afanar, *Esp* mangar

file [faɪl] **1** N (a) *(tool)* lima *f* (b) *(folder)* carpeta *f* (c) *(archive, of computer)* archivo *m*; **on f.** archivado(a); **f. manager** administrador *m* de archivos (d) *(line)* fila *f*; **in single f.** en fila india
2 VT (a) *(smooth)* limar (b) *(put away)* archivar
3 VI **to f. past** desfilar

filing ['faɪlɪŋ] N clasificación *f*; **f. cabinet** archivador *m*; *(for cards)* fichero *m*

Filipino [fɪlɪ'pi:nəʊ] N filipino(a) *m,f*

fill [fɪl] **1** VT (a) *(space, time)* llenar (**with** de) (b) *(post, requirements)* cubrir (c) *Culin* rellenar
2 VI llenarse (**with** de)
3 N **to eat one's f.** comer hasta hartarse

▸ **fill in 1** VT SEP (a) *(space, form)* rellenar (b) *Fam (inform)* poner al corriente (**on** de) (c) *(time)* pasar
2 VI **to f. in for sb** sustituir a algn

▸ **fill out 1** VT SEP *US (form)* llenar
2 VI *Fam* engordar

▸ **fill up 1** VT SEP llenar hasta arriba; *Fam Aut* **f. her up!** ¡llénelo!
2 VI llenarse

fillet ['fɪlɪt] N filete *m*; **f. steak** filete

filling ['fɪlɪŋ] **1** ADJ que llena mucho
2 N (a) *(stuffing)* relleno *m* (b) *(in tooth)* empaste *m* (c) *Br* **f. station** gasolinera *f*, estación *f* de servicio, *Andes, Ven* bomba *f*, *Méx* gasolinería *f*, *Perú* grifo *m*

fillip ['fɪlɪp] N *Fam* estímulo *m*

film [fɪlm] **1** N (a) *esp Br (at cinema)* película *f*; **f. star** estrella *f* de cine (b) *(layer)* capa *f* (c) *(photographic)* **a (roll of) f.** un rollo *or* carrete
2 VT *Cin* filmar
3 VI *Cin* rodar

film-strip ['fɪlmstrɪp] N cortometraje *m*

filter ['fɪltə(r)] **1** N filtro *m*; *Aut* **f. lane** carril *m* de acceso
2 VT filtrar

▸ **filter through** VI *Fig* filtrarse (**to** a)

filter-tip ['fɪltətɪp] N *(cigarette)* cigarrillo *m* con filtro

filth [fɪlθ] N *(dirt)* porquería *f*; *Fig* porquerías *fpl*

filthy ['fɪlθɪ] ADJ (**filthier, filthiest**) (a) *(dirty)* asqueroso(a) (b) *(obscene)* obsceno(a)

fin [fɪn] N *Zool & Av* aleta *f*

final ['faɪnəl] **1** ADJ (a) *(last)* último(a), final (b) *(definitive)* definitivo(a)
2 N (a) *Sport* final *f* (b) *Univ* **finals** *Br* exámenes *mpl* de fin de carrera; *US* exámenes *mpl* finales

finale [fɪ'nɑ:lɪ] N final *m*

finalist ['faɪnəlɪst] N finalista *mf*

finalize ['faɪnəlaɪz] VT ultimar; *(date)* fijar

finally ['faɪnəlɪ] ADV *(lastly)* por último; *(at last)* por fin

finance ['faɪnæns, fɪ'næns] **1** N (a) *(business, funding)* finanzas *fpl* (b) **finances** *(funds)* finanzas *fpl*
2 VT financiar

financial [faɪ'nænʃəl, fɪ'nænʃəl] ADJ financiero(a); **f. crisis** crisis económica; *Br* **f. year** *(for budget)* ejercicio (económico); *(for tax)* año *m* fiscal

financier [faɪ'nænsɪə(r), fɪ'nænsɪə(r)] N financiero(a) *m,f*

finch [fɪntʃ] N pinzón *m*

find [faɪnd] **1** VT (*pt & pp* **found**) (**a**) (*locate*) encontrar (**b**) (*think*) encontrar (**c**) (*discover*) descubrir (**d**) *Jur* **to f. sb guilty/not guilty** declarar culpable/inocente a algn (**e**) **I can't f. the courage to tell him** no tengo valor para decírselo; **I found it impossible to get away** me resultó imposible irme
2 N hallazgo *m*

▸ **find out 1** VT SEP (**a**) (*inquire*) averiguar (**b**) (*discover*) descubrir
2 VI (**a**) **to f. out about sth** informarse sobre algo (**b**) (*discover*) enterarse

findings ['faɪndɪŋz] NPL conclusiones *fpl*

fine¹ [faɪn] **1** N multa *f*
2 VT multar

fine² [faɪn] **1** ADJ (**a**) (*delicate etc*) fino(a) (**b**) (*subtle*) sutil (**c**) (*excellent*) excelente (**d**) (*weather*) bueno(a) (**e**) (*all right*) bien
2 ADV *Fam* muy bien
3 INTERJ ¡vale!

finely ['faɪnlɪ] ADV (**a**) (*skilfully*) acertadamente, hábilmente (**b**) (*chopped, sliced*) muy fino (**c**) **f. tuned** a punto

finery ['faɪnərɪ] N galas *fpl*

finesse [fɪ'nes] N (*delicacy*) finura *f*; (*cunning*) astucia *f*; (*tact*) sutileza *f*

finger ['fɪŋgə(r)] **1** N dedo *m* (de la mano)
2 VT tocar; *Pej* manosear

fingernail ['fɪŋgəneɪl] N uña *f*

fingerprint ['fɪŋgəprɪnt] N huella *f* dactilar

fingertip ['fɪŋgətɪp] N punta *f* or yema *f* del dedo

finicky ['fɪnɪkɪ] ADJ (*person*) quisquilloso(a)

finish ['fɪnɪʃ] **1** N (**a**) (*of day, meeting*) final *m*; (*of race*) llegada *f* (**b**) (*surface*) acabado *m*
2 VT (**a**) (*complete*) acabar, terminar; **to f. doing sth** terminar de hacer algo (**b**) (*use up*) agotar
3 VI acabar, terminar; **to f. second** quedar el segundo

▸ **finish off** VT SEP (**a**) (*complete*) terminar completamente (**b**) *Fam* (*kill*) rematar

▸ **finish up 1** VT SEP acabar, agotar
2 VI **to f. up in jail** ir a parar a la cárcel

finished ['fɪnɪʃt] ADJ (**a**) (*product*) acabado(a) (**b**) *Fam* (*exhausted*) rendido(a)

finishing ['fɪnɪʃɪŋ] ADJ **to put the f. touch(es) to sth** darle los últimos toques a algo; **f. line** (línea *f* de) meta *f*; **f. school** = escuela privada de modales para señoritas

finite ['faɪnaɪt] ADJ finito(a); (*verb*) conjugable

Finland ['fɪnlənd] N Finlandia

Finn [fɪn] N finlandés(esa) *m,f*

Finnish ['fɪnɪʃ] **1** ADJ finlandés(esa)
2 N (*language*) finlandés *m*

fir [fɜː(r)] N abeto *m*

fire ['faɪə(r)] **1** N (**a**) (*element, in hearth*) fuego *m* (**b**) (*accident etc*) incendio *m*; **to be on f.** estar en llamas; **to catch f.** incendiarse; **f. alarm** alarma *f* de incendios; *Br* **f. brigade,** *US* **f.**

department (cuerpo *m* de) bomberos *mpl*; **f. engine** coche *m* de bomberos; **f. escape** escalera *f* de incendios; **f. exit** salida *f* de emergencia; **f. extinguisher** extintor *m*; **f. fighter** bombero(a) *m,f*; **f. station** parque *m* de bomberos (**c**) (*heater*) estufa *f* (**d**) *Mil* fuego *m*; **to open f.** abrir fuego
2 VT (**a**) (*gun*) disparar (**at** a); (*rocket*) lanzar; *Fig* **to f. questions at sb** bombardear a algn a preguntas (**b**) *Fam* (*dismiss*) despedir
3 VI (*shoot*) disparar (**at** sobre)

firearm ['faɪərɑːm] N arma *f* de fuego

fireman ['faɪəmən] N bombero *m*

fireplace ['faɪəpleɪs] N chimenea *f*; (*hearth*) hogar *m*

fireside ['faɪəsaɪd] N hogar *m*; **by the f.** al calor de la lumbre

firewood ['faɪəwʊd] N leña *f*

fireworks ['faɪəwɜːks] NPL fuegos *mpl* artificiales

firing ['faɪərɪŋ] N *Mil* tiroteo *m*; **f. line** línea *f* de fuego; **f. squad** pelotón *m* de fusilamiento

firm [fɜːm] **1** ADJ firme; **to be f. with sb** (*strict*) tratar a algn con firmeza
2 N *Com* empresa *f*, firma *f*

firmly ['fɜːmlɪ] ADV firmemente

firmness ['fɜːmnɪs] N firmeza *f*

first [fɜːst] **1** ADJ primero(a); (*before masculine singular noun*) primer; **Charles the F.** Carlos Primero; **for the f. time** por primera vez; **in the f. place** en primer lugar; **f. aid** primeros auxilios; **f. floor** *Br* primer piso, *US* planta baja; **f. name** nombre *m* de pila
2 ADV (*before anything else*) primero; **f. of all** en primer lugar
3 N (**a**) **the f.** el primero/la primera; **the f. of April** el primero *or Esp* el uno de abril (**b**) **at f.** al principio; **from the (very) f.** desde el principio (**c**) *Aut* primera *f*

first-class ['fɜːst'klɑːs] **1** ADJ de primera clase
2 ADV **to travel f.** viajar en primera

first-hand ['fɜːst'hænd] ADV & ADJ de primera mano

firstly ['fɜːstlɪ] ADV en primer lugar

first-rate ['fɜːstreɪt] ADJ de primera

fiscal ['fɪskəl] ADJ fiscal

fish [fɪʃ] **1** N (*pl* **fish**) (*animal*) pez *m*; (*food*) pescado *m*; **f. shop** pescadería *f*; *Br* **f. and chips** = pescado frito con patatas *or Am* papas fritas; **f.** *Br* **finger** *or US* **stick** palito *m* de pescado
2 VI pescar; *Fig* **to f. in one's pocket for sth** buscar algo en el bolsillo

fishbone ['fɪʃbəʊn] N espina *f*, raspa *f*

fisherman ['fɪʃəmən] N pescador *m*

fishing ['fɪʃɪŋ] N pesca *f*; **to go f.** ir de pesca; **f. net** red *f* de pesca; **f. rod** caña *f* de pescar; **f. tackle** aparejo *m* de pescar

fishmonger ['fɪʃmʌŋgə(r)] N *Br* pescadero(a) *m,f*; **f.'s (shop)** pescadería *f*

fishy ['fɪʃɪ] ADJ (**fishier, fishiest**) de pescado; *Fam (suspicious)* sospechoso(a)

fist [fɪst] N puño *m*

fit¹ [fɪt] **1** VT (**a**) *(match)* ajustarse a, adecuarse a; **that suit doesn't f. you** ese traje no te entalla; **the key doesn't f. the lock** la llave no es de esta cerradura; *Fig* **she doesn't f. the description** no responde a la descripción (**b**) *(install)* colocar; **a car fitted with a radio** un coche provisto de radio
2 VI (**a**) *(be of right size)* caber (**b**) *(facts etc)* cuadrar
3 ADJ (**a**) *(suitable)* apto(a), adecuado(a) (**for** para); **are you f. to drive?** ¿estás en condiciones de conducir? (**b**) *(healthy)* en (plena) forma; **to keep f.** mantenerse en forma
4 N ajuste *m*; **to be a good f.** encajar bien
▸ **fit in 1** VI (**a**) he didn't f. in with his colleagues no encajó con sus compañeros de trabajo (**b**) *(tally)* cuadrar (**with** con)
2 VT SEP *(find time for)* encontrar un hueco para
▸ **fit out** VT SEP equipar

fit² [fɪt] N (**a**) *Med* ataque *m* (**b**) *Fig* arrebato *m*; **f. of anger** arranque *m* de cólera; *Fig* **by fits and starts** a trompicones

fitful ['fɪtful] ADJ discontinuo(a)

fitness ['fɪtnɪs] N (**a**) *(aptitude)* aptitud *f*, capacidad *f* (**b**) *(health)* (buen) estado físico

fitted ['fɪtɪd] ADJ empotrado(a); **f. carpet** moqueta *f*; **f. cupboard** armario empotrado

fitter ['fɪtə(r)] N ajustador(a) *m,f*

fitting ['fɪtɪŋ] **1** ADJ apropiado(a)
2 N (**a**) *(of dress)* prueba *f*; **f. room** probador *m* (**b**) *(of office)* equipamiento *m*; **fittings** *(of bathroom)* accesorios *mpl*

five [faɪv] ADJ & N cinco (*m inv*)

fiver ['faɪvə(r)] N *Fam Br* cinco libras *fpl*; *US* cinco dólares *mpl*

fix [fɪks] **1** N (**a**) *Fam* **to be in a f.** estar en un apuro (**b**) *Fam (drugs)* chute *m*
2 VT (**a**) *(fasten)* fijar, asegurar (**b**) *(date, price)* fijar; *(limit)* señalar (**c**) *(repair)* arreglar (**d**) *US (food, drink)* preparar
▸ **fix up** VT SEP *(arrange)* arreglar; **to f. sb up with sth** proveer a algn de algo

fixation [fɪk'seɪʃən] N idea fija

fixed [fɪkst] ADJ (**a**) *(unchanging)* fijo(a) (**b**) *Fam (match etc)* amañado(a)

fixture ['fɪkstʃə(r)] N (**a**) *Br (in football)* encuentro *m* (**b**) **fixtures** *(in building)* accesorios *mpl*

fizz [fɪz] **1** N burbujeo *m*
2 VI burbujear
▸ **fizzle out** ['fɪzəl] VI *Fam (plan)* quedarse en nada *or Esp* en agua de borrajas

fizzy ['fɪzɪ] ADJ (**fizzier, fizziest**) *(water)* con gas

flabbergasted ['flæbəgɑːstɪd] ADJ pasmado(a)

flabby ['flæbɪ] ADJ (**flabbier, flabbiest**) fofo(a)

flag [flæg] **1** N bandera *f*; *Naut* pabellón *m*
2 VT *Fig* **to f. down a car** hacer señales a un coche para que pare
3 VI *(interest)* decaer; *(conversation)* languidecer

flagpole ['flægpəʊl] N asta *f* de bandera

flagrant ['fleɪɡrənt] ADJ flagrante

flagship ['flægʃɪp] N buque *m* insignia

flagstone ['flægstəʊn] N losa *f*

flair [fleə(r)] N facilidad *f*

flak [flæk] N (**a**) *Mil* fuego antiaéreo (**b**) *Fam* críticas *fpl*

flake [fleɪk] **1** N *(of snow)* copo *m*; *(of skin, soap)* escama *f*; *(of paint)* desconchón *m*
2 VI *(skin)* descamarse; *(paint)* desconcharse

flamboyant [flæm'bɔɪənt] ADJ extravagante

flame [fleɪm] N (**a**) *(of fire)* llama *f*; **to go up in flames** incendiarse (**b**) *Comput* llamada *f*, = mensaje ofensivo

flameproof ['fleɪmpruːf] ADJ ininflamable

flamingo [flə'mɪŋɡəʊ] N flamenco *m*

flammable ['flæməbəl] ADJ inflamable

flan [flæn] N tarta *f*; **fruit f.** tarta de fruta

> Note that the Spanish word **flan** is a false friend and is never a translation for the English word **flan**. In Spanish **flan** means "crème caramel".

flank [flæŋk] **1** N (**a**) *(of animal)* ijada *f* (**b**) *Mil* flanco *m*
2 VT flanquear

flannel ['flænəl] N (**a**) *Tex* franela *f* (**b**) *Br (facecloth)* toallita *f*

flap [flæp] **1** VT *(wings, arms)* batir
2 VI *(wings)* aletear; *(flag)* ondear
3 N (**a**) *(of envelope, pocket)* solapa *f*; *(of tent)* faldón *m* (**b**) *(of wing)* aletazo *m* (**c**) *Fam* **to get into a f.** ponerse nervioso(a)

flare [fleə(r)] **1** N (**a**) *(flame)* llamarada *f* (**b**) *Mil & Naut* bengala *f*
2 VI **to f. (up)** *(fire)* llamear; *Fig (person)* encolerizarse; *(trouble)* estallar

flared [fleəd] ADJ *(trousers etc)* acampanado(a)

flash [flæʃ] **1** N (**a**) *(of light)* destello *m*; *(of lightning)* relámpago *m*; *Fig* **in a f.** en un santiamén (**b**) **news f.** noticia *f* de última hora (**c**) *Phot* flash *m*
2 ADJ *Br Fam (showy)* llamativo(a), ostentoso(a)
3 VT (**a**) *(torch)* dirigir (**b**) *Rad & TV* transmitir
4 VI (**a**) *(light)* destellar (**b**) **a car flashed past** un coche pasó como un rayo

flashback ['flæʃbæk] N flashback *m*

flashcube ['flæʃkjuːb] N cubo *m* flash

flashlight ['flæʃlaɪt] N *US* linterna *f*

flashy ['flæʃɪ] ADJ (**flashier, flashiest**) *Fam* chillón(ona)

flask [flɑːsk] N frasco *m*; **(Thermos®) f.** termo *m*

flat [flæt] **1** ADJ (**flatter, flattest**) (**a**) *(surface)* llano(a) (**b**) *(beer)* sin gas (**c**) *(battery)* descargado(a); *(tyre)* desinflado(a) (**d**) *(rate)* fijo(a) (**e**) *(dull)* soso(a) (**f**) *Mus* **B f.** si *m* bemol

2 ADV (**a**) **to fall f. on one's face** caerse de bruces (**b**) **in ten seconds f.** en diez segundos justos (**c**) *Fam* **to go f. out** ir a todo gas

3 N (**a**) *Br (apartment)* apartamento *m*, *Esp* piso *m*, *Arg* departamento *m* (**b**) *US Aut* pinchazo *m*

flatly ['flætlɪ] ADV rotundamente

flatmate ['flætmeɪt] N *Br* compañero(a) *m,f* de apartamento *or Esp* piso *or Arg* departamento

flatten ['flætən] VT (**a**) *(make level)* allanar (**b**) *(crush)* aplastar

flatter ['flætə(r)] VT (**a**) *(of person)* adular, halagar (**b**) *(of clothes, portrait)* favorecer (**c**) **to f. oneself** hacerse ilusiones

flattering ['flætərɪŋ] ADJ (**a**) *(words)* halagador(a) (**b**) *(dress, portrait)* favorecedor(a)

flattery ['flætərɪ] N adulación *f*, halago *m*

flaunt [flɔːnt] VT hacer alarde de

flavour, *US* **flavor** ['fleɪvə(r)] **1** N sabor *m*
2 VT *Culin* sazonar (**with** con)

flavoured, *US* **flavored** ['fleɪvəd] ADJ **strawberry f.** con sabor a fresa *or Bol, CSur, Ecuad* frutilla

flavouring, *US* **flavoring** ['fleɪvərɪŋ] N condimento *m*; **artificial f.** aroma *m* artificial

flaw [flɔː] N *(failing)* defecto *m*; *(fault)* desperfecto *m*

flawed [flɔːd] ADJ defectuoso(a)

flawless ['flɔːlɪs] ADJ perfecto(a)

flax [flæks] N lino *m*

flaxen ['flæksən] ADJ *(hair)* rubio(a) pajizo(a)

flea [fliː] N pulga *f*; **f. market** rastro *m*

fleck [flek] N *(speck)* mota *f*, punto *m*

fled [fled] PT & PP of **flee**

fledg(e)ling ['fledʒlɪŋ] ADJ *Fig* novato(a)

flee [fliː] **1** VT *(pt & pp* **fled***)* huir de
2 VI huir (**from** de)

fleece [fliːs] **1** N (**a**) *(sheep's coat)* lana *f* (**b**) *(sheared)* vellón *m*
2 VT *Fam (cheat)* sangrar

fleet [fliːt] N flota *f*

fleeting ['fliːtɪŋ] ADJ fugaz

Flemish ['flemɪʃ] **1** ADJ flamenco(a)
2 N *(language)* flamenco *m*

flesh [fleʃ] N (**a**) *(of person, animal)* carne *f*; *Fig* **in the f.** en persona; *Fig* **to be of f. and blood** ser de carne y hueso; **f. wound** herida *f* superficial (**b**) *(of fruit)* pulpa *f*

flew [fluː] PT of **fly**[1]

flex [fleks] **1** N *Br Elec* cable *m*
2 VT *(muscles)* flexionar

flexibility [fleksɪ'bɪlɪtɪ] N flexibilidad *f*

flexible ['fleksɪbəl] ADJ flexible

flexitime ['fleksɪtaɪm] N horario *m* flexible

flick [flɪk] **1** N movimiento rápido; *(of finger)* capirotazo *m*
2 VT *(with finger)* dar un capirotazo a
▸ **flick through** VT INSEP *(book)* hojear

flicker ['flɪkə(r)] **1** N parpadeo *m*; *Fig* **a f. of hope** un destello de esperanza
2 VI *(flame)* parpadear

flier ['flaɪə(r)] N aviador(a) *m,f*

flight [flaɪt] N (**a**) *(act of flying)* vuelo *m*; **f. attendant** auxiliar *mf* de vuelo; **f. path** trayectoria *f* de vuelo (**b**) *(of ball)* trayectoria *f* (**c**) *(escape)* huida *f*, fuga *f*; **to take f.** darse a la fuga (**d**) *(of stairs)* tramo *m*

flight-deck ['flaɪtdek] N *(cockpit)* cabina *f* del piloto

flimsy ['flɪmzɪ] ADJ (**flimsier, flimsiest**) *(cloth)* ligero(a); *(paper)* fino(a); *(structure)* poco sólido(a); *(excuse)* poco convincente

flinch [flɪntʃ] VI *(wince)* estremecerse

fling [flɪŋ] **1** VT *(pt & pp* **flung***)* arrojar
2 N *Fam* **to have a f.** echar una cana al aire

flint [flɪnt] N (**a**) *(stone)* pedernal *m* (**b**) *(in lighter)* piedra *f* de mechero

flip [flɪp] **1** N *(flick)* capirotazo *m*; **f. chart** flip chart *m*, pizarra *f* de conferencia *(con bloc)*
2 VT *(toss)* tirar (al aire); **to f. a coin** echar a cara o cruz

flip-flop ['flɪpflɒp] N (**a**) *Comput* báscula *f* biestable (**b**) *Br (footwear)* chancla *f*

flippant ['flɪpənt] ADJ frívolo(a)

flipper ['flɪpə(r)] N aleta *f*

flirt [flɜːt] **1** N coqueto(a) *m,f*
2 VI flirtear, coquetear; **to f. with death** jugar con la muerte

flirtation [flɜː'teɪʃən] N flirteo *m*, coqueteo *m*

flit [flɪt] VI **to f. about** *(bird)* revolotear; *Fig* **to f. from one thing to another** saltar de una cosa a otra

float [fləʊt] **1** N (**a**) *(on fishing line, as swimming aid)* flotador *m* (**b**) *(in procession)* carroza *f*
2 VT (**a**) *(ship)* flotar (**b**) *(shares)* emitir; *(currency, business)* hacer flotar
3 VI flotar

floating ['fləʊtɪŋ] ADJ flotante; *(voter)* indeciso(a)

flock [flɒk] **1** N *Zool* rebaño *m*; *(of birds)* bandada *f*; *Rel* grey *f*; *(crowd)* multitud *f*
2 VI acudir en masa

flog [flɒg] VT (**a**) *(beat)* azotar; *Fam* **to f. a subject to death** agotar completamente un tema (**b**) *Br Fam (sell)* enchufar, vender

flood [flʌd] **1** N inundación *f*; *(of river)* riada *f*; *Fig* torrente *m*
2 VT inundar
3 VI *(river)* desbordarse; *Fig* **to f. in** entrar a raudales

flooding ['flʌdɪŋ] N inundaciones *fpl*

floodlight ['flʌdlaɪt] N foco *m*

floor [flɔː(r)] **1** N (**a**) *(of room)* suelo *m*; **dance f.** pista *f* de baile (**b**) *(of ocean, forest)* fondo *m* (**c**) *(storey)* piso *m*; **first f.** *Br* primer piso, *US* planta baja; *Br* **ground f.** planta baja

2 VT *Fig* dejar perplejo(a)

floorboard ['flɔːbɔːd] N tabla *f* (del suelo)

flop [flɒp] **1** N *Fam* fracaso *m*
2 VI (**a**) **to f. down on the bed** tumbarse en la cama (**b**) *Fam* fracasar

floppy ['flɒpɪ] ADJ (**floppier, floppiest**) flojo(a); *Comput* **f. disk** disco *m* flexible

flora ['flɔːrə] N flora *f.*

florid ['flɒrɪd] ADJ *(style)* florido(a)

florist ['flɒrɪst] N florista *mf*; **f.'s shop** floristería *f*

flounce¹ [flaʊns] VI **to f. in/out** entrar/salir airadamente

flounce² [flaʊns] N *Sewing* volante *m*, *Chile* vuelo *m*, *RP, Ven* volado *m*

flounder¹ ['flaʊndə(r)] N *(fish)* platija *f*

flounder² ['flaʊndə(r)] VI (**a**) *(struggle)* forcejear; *Fig* enredarse (**b**) *(be at a loss)* no saber qué decir/hacer

flour ['flaʊə(r)] N harina *f*

flourish ['flʌrɪʃ] **1** N (**a**) *(gesture)* ademán *m* (teatral) (**b**) *(under signature)* rúbrica *f*
2 VT *(brandish)* agitar
3 VI *(thrive)* florecer; *(plant)* crecer

flourishing ['flʌrɪʃɪŋ] ADJ floreciente

flout [flaʊt] VT *Jur* desacatar

flow [fləʊ] **1** N flujo *m*; *(of river)* corriente *f*; *(of traffic)* circulación *f*; *(of capital)* movimiento *m*; *(of people, goods)* afluencia *f*; **f. chart** diagrama *m* de flujo; *Comput* organigrama *m*
2 VI *(blood, river)* fluir; *(sea)* subir; *(traffic)* circular

flower ['flaʊə(r)] **1** N flor *f*; **f. bed** arriate *m*
2 VI florecer

flowerpot ['flaʊəpɒt] N maceta *f*

flowery ['flaʊərɪ] ADJ *Fig* florido(a)

flowing ['fləʊɪŋ] ADJ *(hair)* suelto(a); *(dress)* de mucho vuelo; *(style)* fluido(a); *(shape, movement)* natural

flown [fləʊn] PP *of* **fly¹**

flu [fluː] N *(abbr* **influenza***)* gripe *f*, *Am* gripa *f*

fluctuate ['flʌktjʊeɪt] VI fluctuar

fluctuation [flʌktjʊ'eɪʃən] N fluctuación *f*

flue [fluː] N conducto *m* de humos; *(chimney)* cañón *m*

fluent ['fluːənt] ADJ (**a**) **he speaks f. German** habla el alemán con soltura (**b**) *(eloquent)* fluido(a)

fluff [flʌf] **1** N *(down)* pelusa *f*
2 VT *Fam* **to f. sth** hacer algo mal

fluffy ['flʌfɪ] ADJ (**fluffier, fluffiest**) *(pillow)* mullido(a); *(toy)* de peluche; *(cake)* esponjoso(a)

fluid ['fluːɪd] **1** ADJ *(movement)* natural; *(style, prose)* fluido(a); *(situation)* incierto(a)
2 N fluido *m*, líquido *m*

fluke [fluːk] N *Fam* chiripa *f*; **by a f.** por chiripa

flummox ['flʌməks] VT *Fam* desconcertar

flung [flʌŋ] PT & PP *of* **fling**

flunk [flʌŋk] VT & VI *US Fam Esp* catear, *Am* reprobar, *Méx* tronar

fluorescent [flʊə'resənt] ADJ fluorescente

fluoride ['flʊəraɪd] N fluoruro *m*

flurry ['flʌrɪ] N (**a**) *(of wind)* ráfaga *f*; *(of snow)* nevasca *f* (**b**) *Fig (bustle)* agitación *f*

flush [flʌʃ] **1** ADJ **f. with** *(level)* a ras de
2 N *(blush)* rubor *m*
3 VT **to f. the lavatory** tirar de la cadena
4 VI *(blush)* ruborizarse

flushed [flʌʃt] ADJ *(cheeks)* rojo(a), encendido(a); *Fig* **f. with success** emocionado(a) ante el éxito

fluster ['flʌstə(r)] VT **to get flustered** ponerse nervioso(a)

flute [fluːt] N flauta *f*

flutist ['fluːtɪst] N *US Mus* flautista *mf*

flutter ['flʌtə(r)] **1** VI *(leaves, birds)* revolotear; *(flag)* ondear
2 N *Br Fam (bet)* apuesta *f*

flux [flʌks] N *(flow)* flujo *m*; *(instability)* inestabilidad *f*; *Fig* **to be in a state of f.** estar cambiando constantemente

fly¹ [flaɪ] **1** VT *(pt* **flew***; pp* **flown***)* (**a**) *Av* pilotar (**b**) *(merchandise, troops)* transportar (**c**) *(distance)* recorrer (**d**) *(kite)* hacer volar
2 VI (**a**) *(bird, plane)* volar (**b**) *(go by plane)* ir en avión (**c**) *(flag)* ondear (**d**) **to f. into a rage** montar en cólera (**e**) *Fam* **to go flying** *(fall)* caerse
3 N **f., flies** bragueta *f*

fly² [flaɪ] N *(insect)* mosca *f*; **f. spray** spray *m* matamoscas

flying ['flaɪɪŋ] **1** ADJ volador(a); *(rapid)* rápido(a); **a f. visit** una visita relámpago; *Fig* **to come out of an affair with f. colours** salir airoso(a) de un asunto; *Fig* **to get off to a f. start** empezar con buen pie; **f. saucer** platillo *m* volante
2 N (**a**) *(action)* vuelo *m* (**b**) *(aviation)* aviación *f*

flyleaf ['flaɪliːf] N *(of book)* guarda *f*

flyover ['flaɪəʊvə(r)] N *Br* paso elevado

flypast ['flaɪpɑːst] N *BrAv* desfile aéreo

flyweight ['flaɪweɪt] N *(in boxing)* peso *m* mosca

FM [ef'em] N *Rad (abbr* **frequency modulation***)* FM *f*, frecuencia *f* modulada

foal [fəʊl] N potro *m*,*f*

foam [fəʊm] **1** N espuma *f*; **f. bath** espuma de baño; **f. rubber** goma espuma
2 VI hacer espuma

fob [fɒb] N *(chain)* cadena *f* (de reloj)
► **fob off** VT SEP *Fam* **he fobbed off his old radio on a stranger** le colocó su radio vieja a un desconocido; **to f. sb off with excuses** darle largas a algn

focus ['fəʊkəs] **1** VT centrarse (**on** en)
2 VI enfocar; **to f. on sth** Phot enfocar algo; Fig centrarse en algo
3 N (pl **focuses**) foco m; **to be in f./out of f.** estar enfocado(a)/desenfocado(a)

fodder ['fɒdə(r)] N pienso m

foe [fəʊ] N Fml enemigo(a) m,f

foetus ['fiːtəs] N feto m

fog [fɒg] N niebla f; (at sea) bruma f

fogey ['fəʊgɪ] N Fam **old f.** cascarrabias mf inv

foggy ['fɒgɪ] ADJ (**foggier, foggiest**) **it is f.** hay niebla; Fam **I haven't the foggiest (idea)** no tengo la más mínima idea

foghorn ['fɒghɔːn] N sirena f (de niebla)

foglamp ['fɒglæmp], US **foglight** ['fɒglaɪt] N faro m antiniebla

foil [fɔɪl] **1** N (**a**) aluminium **f.** papel m de aluminio (**b**) (in fencing) florete m
2 VT (plot) desbaratar

fold [fəʊld] **1** N (crease) pliegue m
2 VT plegar, doblar; **to f. one's arms** cruzar los brazos
3 VI **to f. (up)** (chair etc) plegarse; Com quebrar

folder ['fəʊldə(r)] N carpeta f

folding ['fəʊldɪŋ] ADJ (chair etc) plegable

foliage ['fəʊlɪdʒ] N follaje m

folk [fəʊk] **1** NPL Fam (**a**) (people) gente f (**b**) **my/your folks** mi/tu familia; US (parents) mis/tus padres
2 ADJ popular; **f. music** música f folk; **f. song** canción f popular

folklore ['fəʊklɔː(r)] N folklore m

follow ['fɒləʊ] **1** VT seguir; (pursue) perseguir; (understand) comprender; (way of life) llevar
2 VI (**a**) (come after) seguir; **as follows** como sigue (**b**) (result) resultar; **that doesn't f.** eso no es lógico (**c**) (understand) entender
▸ **follow through, follow up** VT SEP (idea) llevar a cabo; (clue) investigar

follower ['fɒləʊə(r)] N seguidor(a) m,f

following ['fɒləʊɪŋ] **1** ADJ siguiente
2 N seguidores mpl

folly ['fɒlɪ] N locura f, desatino m

fond [fɒnd] ADJ (loving) cariñoso(a); **to be f. of sb** tenerle mucho cariño a algn; **to be f. of doing sth** ser aficionado(a) a hacer algo

fondle ['fɒndəl] VT acariciar

fondly ['fɒndlɪ] ADV (**a**) (lovingly) cariñosamente (**b**) (naively) **to f. imagine that ...** creer ingenuamente que ...

fondness ['fɒndnɪs] N (love) cariño m (**for** a); (liking) afición f (**for** a)

font [fɒnt] N Rel pila f

food [fuːd] N comida f; **f. chain** cadena trófica; **f. poisoning** intoxicación alimenticia

foodstuffs ['fuːdstʌfs] NPL productos alimenticios

fool [fuːl] **1** N (**a**) (stupid person) idiota mf; **to make a f. of sb** poner a algn en ridículo (**b**) Culin ≃ mousse f de fruta
2 VT (deceive) engañar
3 VI (joke) bromear; **to f. about** or **around** hacer el tonto

foolhardy ['fuːlhɑːdɪ] ADJ (**foolhardier, foolhardiest**) temerario(a); (person) intrépido(a)

foolish ['fuːlɪʃ] ADJ estúpido(a)

foolproof ['fuːlpruːf] ADJ infalible

foot [fʊt] **1** N (pl **feet**) pie m; Zool pata f; **on f.** a pie, Esp andando
2 VT (bill) pagar

footage ['fʊtɪdʒ] N Cin metraje m

football ['fʊtbɔːl] N (**a**) (soccer) fútbol m; **bar f.** futbolín m; **f. ground** campo m de fútbol; **f. match** partido m de fútbol; Br **f. pools** quinielas fpl (**b**) (ball) balón m

footballer ['fʊtbɔːlə(r)] N futbolista mf

footbridge ['fʊtbrɪdʒ] N puente m para peatones

foothills ['fʊthɪlz] NPL estribaciones fpl

foothold ['fʊthəʊld] N Fig **to gain a f.** afianzarse en una posición

footing ['fʊtɪŋ] N **to lose one's f.** perder el equilibrio; **on a friendly f.** en plan amistoso; **on an equal f.** en pie de igualdad

footlights ['fʊtlaɪts] NPL candilejas fpl

footman ['fʊtmən] N lacayo m

footnote ['fʊtnəʊt] N nota f a pie de página

footpath ['fʊtpɑːθ] N (track) sendero m

footprint ['fʊtprɪnt] N pisada f

footsore ['fʊtsɔː(r)] ADJ con los pies doloridos

footstep ['fʊtstep] N paso m

footwear ['fʊtweə(r)] N calzado m

for [fɔː(r), unstressed fə(r)] **1** PREP (**a**) (intended) para; **curtains f. the bedroom** cortinas para el dormitorio
(**b**) (representing) por; **a cheque f. £10** un cheque de 10 libras; **what's the Spanish f. "rivet"?** ¿cómo se dice "rivet" en español?
(**c**) (purpose) para; **what's this f.?** ¿para qué sirve esto?
(**d**) (because of) por; **famous f. its cuisine** famoso(a) por su cocina
(**e**) (on behalf of) por; **will you do it f. me?** ¿lo harás por mí?
(**f**) (during) por, durante; **I shall stay f. two weeks** me quedaré dos semanas; **I've been here f. three months** hace tres meses que estoy aquí
(**g**) (distance) **I walked f. 10 km** caminé 10 km
(**h**) (at a point in time) para; **I can do it f. next Monday** puedo hacerlo para el lunes que viene; **f. the last time** por última vez
(**i**) (destination) para
(**j**) (in exchange) por; **I got the car f. £500** conseguí el coche por 500 libras; **how much did you sell it f.?** ¿por cuánto lo vendiste?
(**k**) (in favour of) a favor de; **are you f. or against?** ¿estás a favor o en contra?; **to vote f. sb** votar a algn
(**l**) (to obtain) para; **to run f. the bus** correr para alcanzar al autobús; **to send sb f. water**

mandar a algn a por agua
(**m**) *(with respect to)* en cuanto a; **as f. him** en cuanto a él; **f. all I know** que yo sepa
(**n**) *(despite)* a pesar de; **he's tall f. his age** está muy alto para su edad
(**o**) *(towards)* hacia, por; **his love f. you** su amor por ti
(**p**) *(as)* por; **what do you use f. fuel?** ¿qué utilizan como combustible?
(**q**) *(+ object + infin)* es hora de que; **it's time f. you to go** es hora de que os marchéis; **it's easy f. him to say that** le es fácil decir eso
2 CONJ *(since, as)* ya que, puesto que

forage ['fɒrɪdʒ] 1 N forraje *m*
2 VI hurgar

foray ['fɒreɪ] N incursión *f*

forbade [fə'beɪd] PT of **forbid**

forbearance [fɔː'beərəns] N paciencia *f*

forbid [fə'bɪd] VT *(pt* **forbade**; *pp* **forbidden** [fə'bɪdən])* prohibir; **to f. sb to do sth** prohibirle a algn hacer algo

forbidding [fə'bɪdɪŋ] ADJ *(stern)* severo(a); *(bleak)* inhóspito(a)

force [fɔːs] 1 N (**a**) *(strength, violence, influence)* fuerza *f*; **by f.** por la fuerza; **to come into f.** entrar en vigor (**b**) *Mil* fuerza *f*; **the (armed) forces** las fuerzas armadas; **the police f.** la policía
2 VT forzar; **to f. sb to do sth** forzar a algn a hacer algo

forced [fɔːst] ADJ forzado(a); **f. landing** aterrizaje forzoso

force-feed ['fɔːsfiːd] VT alimentar a la fuerza

forceful ['fɔːsfʊl] ADJ (**a**) *(person)* enérgico(a) (**b**) *(argument)* convincente

forceps ['fɔːseps] NPL fórceps *m*

forcible ['fɔːsəbəl] ADJ *Jur* **f. entry** allanamiento *m* de morada, *Am* invasión *f* de domicilio

forcibly ['fɔːsəblɪ] ADV a *or* por la fuerza

ford [fɔːd] 1 N vado *m*
2 VT vadear

fore [fɔː(r)] N *Fig* **to come to the f.** empezar a destacar

forearm ['fɔːrɑːm] N antebrazo *m*

foreboding [fɔː'bəʊdɪŋ] N presentimiento *m*

forecast ['fɔːkɑːst] 1 N pronóstico *m*
2 VT *(pt & pp* **forecast** *or* **forecasted)** pronosticar

forecourt ['fɔːkɔːt] N *(of garage)* área *f* de servicio

forefathers ['fɔːfɑːðəz] NPL antepasados *mpl*

forefinger ['fɔːfɪŋɡə(r)] N (dedo *m*) índice *m*

forefront ['fɔːfrʌnt] N **in the f.** a la vanguardia

forego [fɔː'ɡəʊ] VT *(pt* **forewent**; *pp* **foregone** [fɔː'ɡɒn])* *Fml* renunciar a

foregone ['fɔːɡɒn] ADJ **a f. conclusion** un resultado inevitable

foreground ['fɔːɡraʊnd] N primer plano *m*

forehead ['fɒrɪd, 'fɔːhed] N frente *f*

foreign ['fɒrɪn] ADJ extranjero(a); *(trade, policy)* exterior; **f. exchange** divisas *fpl*; *Br* **the F. Office** el Ministerio de Asuntos Exteriores; **f. body** cuerpo extraño

foreigner ['fɒrɪnə(r)] N extranjero(a) *m,f*

foreman ['fɔːmən] N (**a**) *Ind* capataz *m* (**b**) *Jur* presidente *m* del jurado

foremost ['fɔːməʊst] ADJ principal; **first and f.** ante todo

forename ['fɔːneɪm] N nombre *m* de pila

forensic [fə'rensɪk] ADJ forense

forerunner ['fɔːrʌnə(r)] N precursor(a) *m,f*

foresee [fɔː'siː] VT *(pt* **foresaw** [fɔː'sɔː]; *pp* **foreseen**)* prever

foreseeable [fɔː'siːəbəl] ADJ previsible; **in the f. future** en un futuro próximo

foreseen [fɔː'siːn] PP of **foresee**

foreshadow [fɔː'ʃædəʊ] VT presagiar

foresight ['fɔːsaɪt] N previsión *f*

forest ['fɒrɪst] N bosque *m*

forestall [fɔː'stɔːl] VT *(plan)* anticiparse a; *(danger)* prevenir

forestry ['fɒrɪstrɪ] N silvicultura *f*

foretaste ['fɔːteɪst] N anticipo *m* (**of** de)

foretell [fɔː'tel] VT *(pt & pp* **foretold** [fɔː'təʊld])* presagiar

forever [fə'revə(r)] ADV (**a**) *(eternally)* siempre (**b**) *(for good)* para siempre (**c**) *Fam* *(ages)* siglos *mpl*

forewent [fɔː'went] PT of **forego**

foreword ['fɔːwɜːd] N prefacio *m*

forfeit ['fɔːfɪt] 1 N *(penalty)* pena *f*; *(in games)* prenda *f*
2 VT perder

forgave [fə'ɡeɪv] PT of **forgive**

forge [fɔːdʒ] 1 N (**a**) *(furnace)* fragua *f* (**b**) *(blacksmith's)* herrería *f*
2 VT (**a**) *(counterfeit)* falsificar (**b**) *(metal)* forjar
3 VI **to f. ahead** hacer grandes progresos

forged [fɔːdʒd] ADJ *(banknote, letter)* falso(a), falsificado(a)

forger ['fɔːdʒə(r)] N falsificador(a) *m,f*

forgery ['fɔːdʒərɪ] N falsificación *f*

forget [fə'ɡet] 1 VT *(pt* **forgot**; *pp* **forgotten**)* olvidar, olvidarse de; **I've forgotten my key** he olvidado la llave
2 VI olvidarse

forgetful [fə'ɡetfʊl] ADJ olvidadizo(a)

forget-me-not [fə'ɡetmɪnɒt] N nomeolvides *f inv*

forgive [fə'ɡɪv] VT *(pt* **forgave**; *pp* **forgiven** [fə'ɡɪvən])* perdonar; **to f. sb for sth** perdonarle algo a algn

forgiveness [fə'ɡɪvnɪs] N perdón *m*

forgo [fɔː'ɡəʊ] VT *Fml* = **forego**

forgot [fə'ɡɒt] PT of **forget**

forgotten [fə'ɡɒtən] PP of **forget**

fork [fɔːk] **1** N (**a**) *Agr* horca *f* (**b**) *(cutlery)* tenedor *m* (**c**) *(in road)* bifurcación *f* **2** VI *(roads)* bifurcarse

▸ **fork out** VT SEP *Fam (money)* aflojar, *Esp* apoquinar, *RP* garpar

fork-lift truck [fɔːklɪft'trʌk] N carretilla *f* elevadora de horquilla

forlorn [fə'lɔːn] ADJ *(forsaken)* abandonado(a); *(desolate)* triste; *(without hope)* desesperado(a)

form [fɔːm] **1** N (**a**) *(shape)* forma *f* (**b**) *(type)* clase *f* (**c**) *(document)* formulario *m* (**d**) **on/on top/off f.** en/en plena/en baja forma (**e**) *Br Educ* clase *f*; **the first f.** el primer curso **2** VT formar; **to f. an impression** formarse una impresión **3** VI formarse

formal ['fɔːməl] ADJ (**a**) *(official)* oficial; **a f. application** una solicitud en forma (**b**) *(party, dress)* de etiqueta (**c**) *(ordered)* formal (**d**) *(person)* formalista

formality [fɔː'mælɪtɪ] N formalidad *f*

formally ['fɔːməlɪ] ADV oficialmente

format ['fɔːmæt] **1** N formato *m* **2** VT *Comput* formatear

formation [fɔː'meɪʃən] N formación *f*

formative ['fɔːmətɪv] ADJ formativo(a)

former ['fɔːmə(r)] ADJ (**a**) *(time)* anterior (**b**) *(one-time)* antiguo(a); *(person)* ex; **the f. champion** el excampeón (**c**) *(first)* aquél/ aquélla; **Peter and Lisa came, the f. wearing a hat** vinieron Peter y Lisa, aquél llevaba sombrero

formerly ['fɔːməlɪ] ADV antiguamente

formidable ['fɔːmɪdəbəl] ADJ *(prodigious)* formidable; *(daunting)* terrible

formula ['fɔːmjʊlə] N fórmula *f*

formulate ['fɔːmjʊleɪt] VT formular

forsake [fə'seɪk] VT *(pt forsook* [fə'sʊk]; *pp forsaken* [fə'seɪkən]) *Literary* (**a**) *(abandon, desert)* abandonar (**b**) *(give up)* renunciar a

fort [fɔːt] N fortaleza *f*

forte ['fɔːteɪ] N fuerte *m*

forth [fɔːθ] ADV *Fml* **and so f.** y así sucesivamente; **to go back and f.** ir de acá para allá

forthcoming [fɔːθ'kʌmɪŋ] ADJ (**a**) *(event)* próximo(a) (**b**) **no money was f.** no hubo oferta de dinero (**c**) *(communicative)* comunicativo(a)

forthright ['fɔːθraɪt] ADJ franco(a)

fortieth ['fɔːtɪəθ] ADJ & N cuadragésimo(a) *(m,f)*

fortification [fɔːtɪfɪ'keɪʃən] N fortificación *f*

fortify ['fɔːtɪfaɪ] VT fortificar

fortitude ['fɔːtɪtjuːd] N fortaleza *f*, fuerza *f*

fortnight ['fɔːtnaɪt] N *Br* quincena *f*

fortnightly ['fɔːtnaɪtlɪ] *Br* **1** ADJ quincenal **2** ADV cada quince días

fortress ['fɔːtrɪs] N fortaleza *f*

fortunate ['fɔːtʃənɪt] ADJ afortunado(a); **it was f. that he came** fue una suerte que viniera

fortunately ['fɔːtʃənɪtlɪ] ADV afortunadamente

fortune ['fɔːtʃən] N (**a**) *(luck, fate)* suerte *f*; **to tell sb's f.** echar la buenaventura a algn (**b**) *(money)* fortuna *f*

fortune-teller ['fɔːtʃəntelə(r)] N adivino(a) *m,f*

forty ['fɔːtɪ] ADJ & N cuarenta *(m inv)*

forum ['fɔːrəm] N foro *m*

forward ['fɔːwəd] **1** ADV (**a**) *(also* **forwards**) *(direction and movement)* hacia adelante (**b**) *Fig* **to come f.** ofrecerse (**c**) **from this day f.** de ahora en adelante **2** ADJ (**a**) *(movement)* hacia adelante; *(position)* delantero(a) (**b**) *(person)* fresco(a) **3** N *Sport* delantero(a) *m,f* **4** VT (**a**) *(send on)* remitir (**b**) *Fml (send goods)* expedir (**c**) *Fml (further)* fomentar

fossil ['fɒsəl] N fósil *m*; **f. fuel** combustible *m* fósil

foster ['fɒstə(r)] **1** VT (**a**) *(child)* adoptar (temporalmente), acoger (**b**) *Fml (hopes)* abrigar; *(relations)* fomentar **2** ADJ **f. child** niño(a) *m,f* en régimen de acogida; **f. parents** familia *f* de acogida

fostering ['fɒstərɪŋ] N acogida *f* familiar *(de un niño)*

fought [fɔːt] PT & PP of **fight**

foul [faʊl] **1** ADJ (**a**) *(smell)* fétido(a); *(taste)* asqueroso(a) (**b**) *(deed)* atroz; *(weather)* de perros (**c**) *(language)* grosero(a) (**d**) *Sport* **f. play** juego sucio **2** N *Sport* falta *f* **3** VT (**a**) *(dirty)* ensuciar; *(air)* contaminar (**b**) *Sport* cometer una falta contra

found¹ [faʊnd] PT & PP of **find**

found² [faʊnd] VT *(establish)* fundar

foundation [faʊn'deɪʃən] N (**a**) *(establishment)* fundación *f* (**b**) *(basis)* fundamento *m* (**c**) *Constr* **foundations** cimientos *mpl*

founder¹ ['faʊndə(r)] N fundador(a) *m,f*

founder² ['faʊndə(r)] VI (**a**) *Fml (sink)* hundirse (**b**) *Fig (plan, hopes)* fracasar

foundry ['faʊndrɪ] N fundición *f*

fountain ['faʊntɪn] N *(structure)* fuente *f*; *(jet)* surtidor *m*; **f. pen** pluma estilográfica, *CSur* lapicera *f* fuente, *Perú* lapicero *m*

four [fɔː(r)] ADJ & N cuatro *(m inv)*; **on all fours** a gatas

four-door ['fɔːdɔː(r)] ADJ *Aut* de cuatro puertas

four-poster [fɔː'pəʊstə(r)] ADJ & N **f. (bed)** cama *f* con dosel

foursome ['fɔːsəm] N grupo *m* de cuatro personas

fourteen [fɔː'tiːn] ADJ & N catorce *(m inv)*

fourteenth [fɔː'tiːnθ] **1** ADJ & N decimocuarto(a) *(m,f)* **2** N *(fraction)* catorceavo *m*

fourth [fɔːθ] **1** ADJ & N cuarto(a) *(m,f)* **2** N (**a**) *(fraction)* cuarto *m* (**b**) *Aut* cuarta *f* *(velocidad)*

fowl [faʊl] N *(pl* **fowl**) ave *f* de corral

fox [fɒks] 1 N zorro(a) m,f
2 VT (a) (perplex) dejar perplejo(a) (b) (deceive) engañar

foyer ['fɔɪeɪ,'fɔɪə(r)] N vestíbulo m

fracas ['fræka:] N gresca f, refriega f

> Note that the Spanish word **fracaso** is a false friend and is never a translation for the English word **fracas**. In Spanish, **fracaso** means "failure".

fraction ['frækʃən] N fracción f

fracture ['fræktʃə(r)] 1 N fractura f
2 VT fracturar

fragile ['frædʒaɪl] ADJ frágil

fragment ['frægmənt] N fragmento m

fragrance ['freɪgrəns] N fragancia f, perfume m

fragrant ['freɪgrənt] ADJ fragante, aromático(a)

frail [freɪl] ADJ frágil, delicado(a)

frame [freɪm] 1 N (a) (of window, door, picture) marco m; (of machine) armazón m; (of bicycle) cuadro m; (of spectacles) montura f; Fig f. of mind estado m de ánimo (b) Cin & TV fotograma m
2 VT (a) (picture) enmarcar (b) (question) formular (c) Fam (innocent person) incriminar

framework ['freɪmwɜːk] N Fig within the f. of ... dentro del marco de ...

franc [fræŋk] N franco m

France [frɑːns] N Francia f

franchise ['fræntʃaɪz] N (a) Pol derecho m al voto (b) Com concesión f, licencia f

frank [fræŋk] 1 ADJ franco(a)
2 VT (mail) franquear

frankly ['fræŋklɪ] ADV francamente

frankness ['fræŋknɪs] N franqueza f

frantic ['fræntɪk] ADJ (anxious) desesperado(a); (hectic) frenético(a)

fraternal [frə'tɜːnəl] ADJ fraterno(a)

fraternity [frə'tɜːnɪtɪ] N (society) asociación f; Rel hermandad f, cofradía f; US Univ = asociación de estudiantes que suele funcionar como club social

fraternize ['frætənaɪz] VI confraternizar (with con)

fraud [frɔːd] N (a) (deception) fraude m (b) (person) impostor(a) m,f

fraught [frɔːt] ADJ (a) (full) cargado(a) (with de) (b) (tense) nervioso(a)

fray[1] [freɪ] VI (a) (cloth) deshilacharse (b) (nerves) crisparse; his temper frequently frayed se irritaba a menudo

fray[2] [freɪ] N combate m

freak [friːk] 1 N (a) (monster) monstruo m (b) Fam (eccentric) estrafalario(a) m,f (c) Fam (fan) fanático(a) m,f
2 ADJ (a) (unexpected) inesperado(a) (b) (unusual) insólito(a)

freckle ['frekəl] N peca f

free [friː] 1 ADJ (a) (unrestricted, unoccupied) libre; to set sb f. poner en libertad a algn; f.

kick tiro m libre; **f. speech** libertad f de expresión; **f. will** libre albedrío m (b) **f. (of charge)** (gratis) gratuito(a); **f. gift** obsequio m
2 ADV (a) (for) f. gratis (b) (loose) suelto(a)
3 VT (a) (liberate) poner en libertad (b) (let loose, work loose) soltar (c) (untie) desatar (d) (exempt) eximir (**from** de)

freebie ['friːbɪ] N Fam regalito m

freedom ['friːdəm] N (a) (liberty) libertad f; **f. of the press** libertad de prensa (b) (exemption) exención f

free-for-all ['friːfərɔːl] N Fam (fight, discussion) bronca f, gresca f, Méx agarrón m

freehold ['friːhəʊld] N propiedad absoluta

freelance ['friːlɑːns] ADJ independiente

freely ['friːlɪ] ADV libremente; **to be f. available** encontrarse fácilmente

freemason ['friːmeɪsən] N francmasón m

free-range ['friːreɪndʒ] ADJ Br de granja

free-style ['friːstaɪl] N estilo m libre

freeway ['friːweɪ] N US autopista f

freewheel [friː'wiːl] VI ir en punto muerto

freeze [friːz] 1 VT (pt froze; pp frozen) congelar
2 N Met helada f; **price f.** congelación f de precios; TV & Cin **f. frame** imagen congelada
3 VI (liquid) helarse; (food) congelarse

freeze-dried ['friːzdraɪd] ADJ liofilizado(a)

freezer ['friːzə(r)] N congelador m

freezing ['friːzɪŋ] ADJ (a) (rain, wind) helado(a); (weather, temperature) muy frío(a) (b) **f. point** punto m de congelación; **above/below f. point** sobre/bajo cero

freight [freɪt] N (a) (transport) transporte m (b) (goods, price) flete m; US **f. car** vagón m; US **f. elevator** montacargas m inv; **f. train** tren m de mercancías

French [frentʃ] 1 ADJ francés(esa); **F. bean** judía f verde, Bol, RP chaucha f, CAm ejote m, Col, Cuba habichuela f, Chile poroto m verde, Ven vainita f; **F. dressing** vinagreta f; US **F. fries** patatas fpl or Am papas fpl fritas; **F. window** puerta f vidriera
2 N (a) (language) francés m (b) PL the F. los franceses

Frenchman ['frentʃmən] N francés m

Frenchwoman ['frentʃwʊmən] N francesa f

frenetic [frɪ'netɪk] ADJ frenético(a)

frenzy ['frenzɪ] N frenesí m

frequency ['friːkwənsɪ] N frecuencia f

frequent 1 ADJ ['friːkwənt] frecuente
2 VT [frɪ'kwent] frecuentar

frequently ['friːkwəntlɪ] ADV frecuentemente, a menudo

fresh [freʃ] ADJ (a) (food, air) fresco(a); **f. water** agua f dulce; **f. bread** pan m del día (b) (page, attempt) nuevo(a) (c) (original) novedoso(a), original (d) US Fam (cheeky) fresco(a)

freshen ['freʃən] VI (wind) refrescar
▸ **freshen up** VI asearse

fresher ['freʃə(r)] N Br Univ novato(a) m,f

freshly ['freʃlɪ] ADV recién, recientemente

freshman ['freʃmən] N *US* = fresher

freshness ['freʃnɪs] N frescura *f*

freshwater ['freʃwɔːtə(r)] ADJ de agua dulce

fret [fret] VI preocuparse (**about** por)

FRG [efɑːˈdʒiː] N (*abbr* **Federal Republic of Germany**) RFA *f*

friar ['fraɪə(r)] N fraile *m*

friction ['frɪkʃən] N fricción *f*

Friday ['fraɪdɪ] N viernes *m*

fridge [frɪdʒ] N *esp Br* nevera *f*, frigorífico *m*, *Andes* frigider *m*, *RP* heladera *f*

fried [fraɪd] ADJ frito(a)

friend [frend] N amigo(a) *m,f*; **a f. of mine** un(a) amigo(a) mío(a); **to make friends with sb** hacerse amigo(a) de algn; **to make friends again** hacer las paces

friendliness ['frendlɪnɪs] N amabilidad *f*, simpatía *f*

friendly ['frendlɪ] ADJ (**friendlier, friendliest**) (*person*) simpático(a); (*atmosphere*) acogedor(a); **f. advice** consejo *m* de amigo; **f. nation** nación amiga

friendship ['frendʃɪp] N amistad *f*

frieze [friːz] N friso *m*

frigate ['frɪgɪt] N fragata *f*

fright [fraɪt] N (**a**) (*fear*) miedo *m*; **to take f.** asustarse (**b**) (*shock*) susto *m*; **to get a f.** pegarse un susto

frighten ['fraɪtən] VT asustar

▸ **frighten away, frighten off** VT SEP ahuyentar

frightened ['fraɪtənd] ADJ asustado(a); **to be f. of sb** tenerle miedo a algn

frightening ['fraɪtənɪŋ] ADJ espantoso(a)

frightful ['fraɪtfʊl] ADJ espantoso(a), horroroso(a)

frightfully ['fraɪtfʊlɪ] ADV tremendamente, terriblemente

frigid ['frɪdʒɪd] ADJ frígido(a)

frill [frɪl] N (*on dress*) volante *m*; *Fig* **frills** (*decorations*) adornos *mpl*

fringe [frɪndʒ] N (**a**) *Br* (*of hair*) flequillo *m*, *Am* cerquillo *m* (**b**) (*edge*) borde *m*; *Fig* **on the f. of society** al margen de la sociedad; **f. theatre** teatro *m* experimental; **f. benefits** extras *mpl*

Frisbee® ['frɪzbɪ] N platillo *m*

frisk [frɪsk] VT *Fam* (*search*) registrar

frisky ['frɪskɪ] ADJ (**friskier, friskiest**) (**a**) (*children, animals*) juguetón(ona) (**b**) (*adult*) vivo(a)

fritter ['frɪtə(r)] N buñuelo *m*

▸ **fritter away** VT SEP malgastar

frivolous ['frɪvələs] ADJ frívolo(a)

frizzy ['frɪzɪ] ADJ (**frizzier, frizziest**) crespo(a)

frock [frɒk] N vestido *m*; **f. coat** levita *f*

frog [frɒg] N rana *f*

frogman ['frɒgmən] N hombre *m* rana

frolic ['frɒlɪk] VI retozar, juguetear

from [from, *unstressed* frəm] PREP (**a**) (*time*) desde, a partir de; **f. now on** a partir de ahora; **f. Monday to Friday** de lunes a viernes; **f. the 8th to the 17th** desde el 8 hasta el 17 (**b**) (*price, number*) desde, de; **a number f. one to ten** un número del uno a diez (**c**) (*origin*) de; **a letter f. her father** una carta de su padre; **f. English into Spanish** del inglés al español; **he's f. Malaga** es de Málaga; **the train f. Bilbao** el tren procedente de Bilbao (**d**) (*distance*) de; **the town is 4 miles f. the coast** el pueblo está a 4 millas de la costa (**e**) (*out of*) de; **bread is made of flour** el pan se hace con harina (**f**) (*remove, subtract*) a; **he took the book f. the child** le quitó el libro al niño; **take three f. five** restar tres a cinco (**g**) (*according to*) según, por; **f. what the author said** según lo que dijo el autor (**h**) (*position*) desde, de; **f. here** desde aquí (**i**) **can you tell margarine f. butter?** ¿puedes distinguir entre la margarina y la mantequilla?

front [frʌnt] **1** N (**a**) (*not back*) parte delantera; **in f. (of)** delante (de) (**b**) (*of building*) fachada *f* (**c**) *Mil, Pol & Met* frente *m* (**d**) (*seaside*) paseo marítimo (**e**) *Fig* **she put on a brave f.** hizo de tripas corazón

2 ADJ delantero(a), de delante; **f. door** puerta *f* principal; **f. seat** asiento *m* de delante

frontier ['frʌntɪə(r)] N frontera *f*

front-page ['frʌntpeɪdʒ] ADJ de primera página

frost [frɒst] **1** N (**a**) (*covering*) escarcha *f* (**b**) (*freezing*) helada *f*

2 VT *US Culin* recubrir con azúcar glas

▸ **frost over** VI escarchar

frostbite ['frɒstbaɪt] N congelación *f*

frosted ['frɒstɪd] ADJ (**a**) (*glass*) esmerilado(a) (**b**) *US Culin* recubierto(a) de azúcar glas

frosty ['frɒstɪ] ADJ (**frostier, frostiest**) (**a**) **it will be a f. night tonight** esta noche habrá helada (**b**) *Fig* glacial

froth [frɒθ] **1** N espuma *f*; (*from mouth*) espumarajos *mpl*

2 VI espumar

frothy ['frɒθɪ] ADJ (**frothier, frothiest**) espumoso(a)

frown [fraʊn] VI fruncir el ceño

▸ **frown upon** VT INSEP desaprobar

froze [frəʊz] PT *of* **freeze**

frozen ['frəʊzən] **1** ADJ (*liquid, feet etc*) helado(a); (*food*) congelado(a)

2 PP *of* **freeze**

frugal ['fruːgəl] ADJ frugal

fruit [fruːt] N (**a**) *Bot* fruto *m* (**b**) (*apple, orange etc*) fruta *f*; **f. cake** pastel *m* con fruto seco; **f. machine** (máquina *f*) tragaperras *f inv*; **f. salad** macedonia *f* de frutas (**c**) **fruits** (*rewards*) frutos *mpl*

fruitful ['fruːtfʊl] ADJ *Fig* provechoso(a)

fruition [fru:'ɪʃən] N *Fml* **to come to f.** realizarse

fruitless ['fru:tlɪs] ADJ infructuoso(a)

frustrate [frʌ'streɪt] VT frustrar

frustrated [frʌ'streɪtɪd] ADJ frustrado(a)

frustrating [frʌ'streɪtɪŋ] ADJ frustrante

frustration [frʌ'streɪʃən] N frustración *f*

fry¹ [fraɪ] 1 VT (*pt & pp* **fried**) freír
　2 VI *Fig* asarse

fry² [fraɪ] NPL **small f.** gente *f* de poca monta

frying pan ['fraɪŋpæn], *US* **fry-pan** ['fraɪpæn] N sartén *f*

ft (*abbr* **foot**) pie *m*; (*abbr* **feet**) pies *mpl*

fuck [fʌk] *Vulg* 1 VT (**a**) (*have sex with*) *Esp* follar, *Am* coger, *Méx* chingar (**b**) (*expressing surprise, irritation*) **f. (it)!** ¡carajo!, *Esp* ¡joder!
　2 VI *Esp* follar, *Am* coger, *Méx* chingar

▸ **fuck off** VI *Vulg* **f. off!** *Esp* ¡vete a tomar por (el) culo!, *Méx* ¡vete a la chingada!, *RP* ¡ándate a la puta que te parió!

▸ **fuck up** VT SEP *Vulg* joder

fucking ['fʌkɪŋ] *Vulg* 1 ADJ **f. idiot!** *Esp* ¡gilipollas!, *Am* ¡pendejo!, *Méx* ¡boludo!; **where's the f. key?** ¿dónde está la puta llave?
　2 ADV **a f. good film** una película de puta madre

fuddy-duddy ['fʌdɪdʌdɪ] N *Fam* **an old f.** un carcamal *or Am* carcamán

fudge [fʌdʒ] 1 N *Culin* = dulce hecho con azúcar, leche y mantequilla
　2 VT (*figures*) amañar

fuel ['fjʊəl] 1 N combustible *m*; (*for engines*) carburante *m*; **f. tank** depósito *m* de combustible
　2 VT *Fig* (*ambition*) estimular; (*difficult situation*) empeorar

fugitive ['fju:dʒɪtɪv] N *Fml* fugitivo(a) *m,f*

fulfil, *US* **fulfill** [fʊl'fɪl] VT (**a**) (*task, ambition*) realizar; (*promise*) cumplir; (*role*) desempeñar (**b**) (*wishes*) satisfacer

fulfilment, *US* **fulfillment** [fʊl'fɪlmənt] N (**a**) (*of ambition*) realización *f* (**b**) (*of duty, promise*) cumplimiento *m*

full [fʊl] 1 ADJ (**a**) (*container, room*) lleno(a); **f. of** lleno(a) de; **I'm f. (up)** no puedo más (**b**) (*complete*) (*amount, support*) total; (*explanation, recovery*) completo(a); **at f. speed** a toda velocidad; **f. employment** pleno empleo; **f. moon** luna llena; **f. stop** punto *m*
　2 N **in f.** en su totalidad; **name in f.** nombre y apellidos completos
　3 ADV **f. well** perfectamente

full-blown ['fʊlbləʊn] ADJ auténtico(a)

full-fledged ['fʊlfledʒd] ADJ *US* = **fully-fledged**

fullness ['fʊlnɪs] N **in the f. of time** con el tiempo

full-scale ['fʊlskeɪl] ADJ (**a**) (*model*) de tamaño natural (**b**) **f. search** registro *m* a fondo; **f. war** guerra generalizada *or* total

full-time ['fʊl'taɪm] 1 ADJ de jornada completa
　2 ADV **to work f.** trabajar a tiempo completo

fully ['fʊlɪ] ADV completamente

fully-fledged ['fʊlɪfledʒd] ADJ *Br Fig* hecho(a) y derecho(a)

fulsome ['fʊlsəm] ADJ excesivo(a), exagerado(a)

fumble ['fʌmbəl] VI hurgar; **to f. for sth** buscar algo a tientas; **to f. with sth** manejar algo con torpeza

fume [fju:m] 1 N **fumes** humos *mpl*
　2 VI despedir humo

> Note that the Spanish verb **fumar** is a false friend and is never a translation for the English verb **to fume**. In Spanish **fumar** means "to smoke".

fun [fʌn] 1 N (*amusement*) diversión *f*; **in** or **for f.** en broma; **to have f.** divertirse, pasarlo bien; **to make f. of sb** reírse de algn
　2 ADJ divertido(a)

function ['fʌŋkʃən] 1 N (**a**) (*of machine, person, institution*) función *f* (**b**) (*ceremony*) acto *m*; (*party*) recepción *f*
　2 VI funcionar

functional ['fʌŋkʃənəl] ADJ funcional

fund [fʌnd] 1 N (**a**) *Fin* fondo *m* (**b**) **funds** (*available money*) fondos *mpl*
　2 VT (*finance*) financiar

> Note that the Spanish verb **fundar** is a false friend and is never a translation for the English verb **to fund**. In Spanish **fundar** means "to found".

fundamental [fʌndə'mentəl] 1 ADJ fundamental
　2 NPL **fundamentals** principios básicos

funeral ['fju:nərəl] N funeral *m*; *US* **f. home** funeraria *f*; **f. march** marcha *f* fúnebre; *Br* **f. parlour** funeraria *f*; **f. service** misa *f* de cuerpo presente

funfair ['fʌnfeə(r)] N *Br* parque *m* de atracciones

fungus ['fʌŋɡəs] N (*pl* **fungi** ['fʌŋɡaɪ]) (**a**) *Bot* hongo *m* (**b**) *Med* fungo *m*

funnel ['fʌnəl] 1 N (**a**) (*for liquids*) embudo *m* (**b**) *Naut* chimenea *f*
　2 VT (*pt & pp* **funnelled,** *US* **funneled**) *Fig* (*funds, energy*) encauzar

funnily ['fʌnɪlɪ] ADV *Fam* **f. enough** aunque parezca extraño

funny ['fʌnɪ] ADJ (**funnier, funniest**) (**a**) (*peculiar*) raro(a), extraño(a); **that's f.!** ¡qué raro! (**b**) (*amusing*) divertido(a), gracioso(a); **I found it very f.** me hizo mucha gracia (**c**) *Fam* (*ill*) mal

fur [fɜ:(r)] 1 N (**a**) (*of living animal*) pelo *m* (**b**) (*of dead animal*) piel *f* (**c**) (*in kettle, on tongue*) sarro *m*
　2 ADJ de piel; **f. coat** abrigo *m* de pieles

furious ['fjʊərɪəs] ADJ (**a**) (*angry*) furioso(a) (**b**) (*vigorous*) violento(a)

furlong ['fɜːlɒŋ] N *(measurement)* = aprox 201 m

furnace ['fɜːnɪs] N horno *m*

furnish ['fɜːnɪʃ] VT (**a**) *(house)* amueblar (**b**) *Fml (food)* suministrar; *(details)* facilitar.

furnishings ['fɜːnɪʃɪŋz] NPL *(furniture, fittings)* mobiliario *m*, muebles *mpl*

furniture ['fɜːnɪtʃə(r)] N muebles *mpl*; **a piece of f.** un mueble

furrow ['fʌrəʊ] N *Agr* surco *m*; *(on forehead)* arruga *f*

furry ['fɜːrɪ] ADJ (**furrier, furriest**) (**a**) *(hairy)* peludo(a) (**b**) *(tongue, kettle)* sarroso(a)

further ['fɜːðə(r)] *(comp of far)* **1** ADJ (**a**) *(new)* nuevo(a); **until f. notice** hasta nuevo aviso (**b**) *(additional)* otro(a), adicional (**c**) *(later)* posterior; *Br* **f. education** estudios *mpl* superiores

2 ADV (**a**) *(more)* más; **f. back** más atrás; **f. along** más adelante (**b**) *Fml (besides)* además

3 VT fomentar

furthermore [fɜːðə'mɔː(r)] ADV *Fml* además

furthest ['fɜːðɪst] ADJ *(superl of far)* más lejano(a)

furtive ['fɜːtɪv] ADJ furtivo(a)

fury ['fjʊərɪ] N furia *f*, furor *m*

fuse [fjuːz] **1** N (**a**) *Elec* fusible *m*; **f. box** caja *f* de fusibles (**b**) *(of bomb)* mecha *f*

2 VI (**a**) *Br Elec* **the lights fused** se fundieron

los plomos (**b**) *Fig (merge)* fusionarse (**c**) *(melt)* fundirse

3 VT (**a**) *Br Elec* **a surge of power fused the lights** se fundieron los plomos y se fue la luz por una subida de corriente (**b**) *Fig (merge)* fusionar (**c**) *(melt)* fundir

fuselage ['fjuːzɪlɑːʒ] N fuselaje *m*

fusion ['fjuːʒən] N fusión *f*

fuss [fʌs] **1** N *(commotion)* jaleo *m*; **to kick up a f.** armar un escándalo; **stop making a f.** *(complaining)* deja ya de quejarte; **to make a f. of** *(pay attention to)* mimar a

2 VI preocuparse (**about** por)

fussy ['fʌsɪ] ADJ (**fussier, fussiest**) exigente; *(nitpicking)* quisquilloso(a)

futile ['fjuːtaɪl] ADJ inútil, vano(a)

futility [fjuː'tɪlɪtɪ] N inutilidad *f*

futon ['fuːtɒn] N futón *m*

future ['fjuːtʃə(r)] **1** N futuro *m*, porvenir *m*; **in the near f.** en un futuro próximo; **in f.** de aquí en adelante

2 ADJ futuro(a)

futuristic [fjuːtʃə'rɪstɪk] ADJ futurista

fuze [fjuːz] N, VI & VT *US* = **fuse**

fuzzy ['fʌzɪ] ADJ (**fuzzier, fuzziest**) (**a**) *(hair)* muy rizado(a) (**b**) *(blurred)* borroso(a)

FYI *(abbr for your information)* para tu información

G

G, g [dʒiː] N (**a**) *(the letter)* G, g f (**b**) *Mus* G sol m

G [dʒiː] ADJ *US Cin* ≃ (apta) para todos los públicos

g *(abbr* **gramme)** g

gabble ['gæbəl] **1** N chapurreo m
2 VI hablar atropelladamente

gable ['geɪbəl] N aguilón m

gadget ['gædʒɪt] N artilugio m, aparato m

Gaelic ['geɪlɪk] **1** ADJ gaélico(a)
2 N *(language)* gaélico m

gaffe [gæf] N metedura f de pata, desliz m; **to make a g.** meter la pata, patinar

> Note that the Spanish word **gafe** is a false friend and is never a translation for the English word **gaffe**. In Spanish **gafe** means "jinxed person".

gag [gæg] **1** N (**a**) *(on mouth)* mordaza f (**b**) *Fam (joke)* chiste m
2 VT amordazar

gage [geɪdʒ] N & VT *US* = **gauge**

gaiety ['geɪətɪ] N regocijo m

gaily ['geɪlɪ] ADV alegremente

gain [geɪn] **1** N ganancia f, beneficio m; *(increase)* aumento m
2 VT ganar; *Fig* **to g. ground** ganar terreno; **to g. speed** ganar velocidad, acelerar; **to g. weight** aumentar de peso

gait [geɪt] N paso m, manera f de caminar *or Esp* andar m

gal *(abbr* **gallon)** galón m

gala ['gɑːlə, 'geɪlə] N gala f, fiesta f

galaxy ['gæləksɪ] N galaxia f

gale [geɪl] N vendaval m

Galicia [gə'lɪʃə] N Galicia

Galician [gə'lɪʃɪən, gə'lɪʃən] **1** ADJ gallego(a)
2 N (**a**) *(person)* gallego(a) m,f (**b**) *(language)* gallego m

gall [gɔːl] **1** N *Fam* descaro m
2 VT molestar, irritar

gallant ['gælənt] ADJ *(brave)* valiente; *(also* [gə'lænt]) *(chivalrous)* galante

gallantry ['gæləntrɪ] N *(bravery)* gallardía f; *(politeness)* galantería f

galleon ['gælɪən] N galeón m

gallery ['gælərɪ] N (**a**) *(art)* **g.** *(for sale)* galería f de arte; *(for exhibition)* museo m (de arte) (**b**) *Th* galería f

galley ['gælɪ] N (**a**) *(ship)* galera f; **g. slave** galeote m (**b**) *(kitchen)* cocina f

Gallicism ['gælɪsɪzəm] N galicismo m

gallivant ['gælɪvænt] VI *Fam* callejear

gallon ['gælən] N galón m (*Br* = 4,55 l; *US* = 3,79 l)

gallop ['gæləp] **1** N galope m
2 VI galopar

gallows ['gæləʊz] N SING horca f, patíbulo m

gallstone ['gɔːlstəʊn] N cálculo m biliar

galore [gə'lɔː(r)] ADV *Fam* en cantidad, en abundancia

galvanize ['gælvənaɪz] VT *(metal)* galvanizar; *Fig* **to g. sb into action** galvanizar a algn

galvanized ['gælvənaɪzd] ADJ galvanizado(a)

gambit ['gæmbɪt] N *(in chess)* gambito m; *Fig* táctica f

gamble ['gæmbəl] **1** N *(risk)* riesgo m; *(risky undertaking)* empresa arriesgada; *(bet)* apuesta f
2 VI *(bet)* jugar; *(take a risk)* arriesgarse

gambler ['gæmblə(r)] N jugador(a) m,f

gambling ['gæmblɪŋ] N juego m

gambol ['gæmbəl] VI brincar

game [geɪm] **1** N (**a**) *(activity, sport)* juego m; **g. of chance** juego de azar (**b**) *(match)* partido m; *(of bridge)* partida f (**c**) **games** *(sporting event)* juegos mpl; *Br (school subject)* deportes mpl (**d**) *(hunting)* caza f; *Fig* presa f
2 ADJ **g. for anything** dispuesto(a) a todo

gamekeeper ['geɪmkiːpə(r)] N guardabosque mf

gamely ['geɪmlɪ] ADV resueltamente

gammon ['gæmən] N *Br* jamón ahumado *or* curado

gamut ['gæmət] N gama f; **to run the g. of ...** experimentar todas las posibilidades de ...

gang [gæŋ] N *(of criminals)* banda f; *(of youths)* pandilla f; *(of workers)* cuadrilla f
▶ **gang up** VI *Fam* confabularse (**on** contra)

gangplank ['gæŋplæŋk] N plancha f

gangrene ['gæŋɡriːn] N gangrena f

gangster ['gæŋstə(r)] N gángster m

gangway ['gæŋweɪ] N *Naut* pasarela f; *Th* pasillo m

gantry ['gæntrɪ] N puente m transversal

gaol [dʒeɪl] N & VT *Br* = **jail**

gap [gæp] N (**a**) *(physical opening)* hueco m; *(blank space)* espacio m en blanco (**b**) *(in time)* intervalo m; *(in age, ability)* diferencia f; *(in knowledge)* laguna f

gape [geɪp] VI *(person)* quedarse boquiabierto(a), mirar boquiabierto(a); *(thing)* estar abierto(a)

gaping ['geɪpɪŋ] ADJ *Fig* profundo(a)

garage ['gærɑːʒ, 'gærɪdʒ, *US* gə'rɑːʒ] N garaje *m*; *(for repairs)* taller mecánico; *(filling station)* gasolinera *f*, estación *f* de servicio, *Andes, Ven* bomba *f*, *Méx* gasolinería *f*, *Perú* grifo *m*

garbage ['gɑːbɪdʒ] N *US* basura *f*, *Méx* cochera *f*; *Fig* tonterías *fpl*

garbanzo [gaːˈbɑːnzəʊ] N *(pl* **garbanzos***) US* g. **(bean)** garbanzo *m*

garbled ['gɑːbəld] ADJ embrollado(a); **g. account** relato confuso

garden ['gɑːdən] N jardín *m*; **g. centre** centro *m* de jardinería; **g. party** recepción *f* al aire libre

gardener ['gɑːdənə(r)] N jardinero(a) *m,f*

gardenia [gaːˈdiːnɪə] N gardenia *f*

gardening ['gɑːdənɪŋ] N jardinería *f*; **his mother does the g.** su madre es la que cuida el jardín

gargle ['gɑːgəl] VI hacer gárgaras

gargoyle ['gɑːgoɪl] N gárgola *f*

garish ['geərɪʃ] ADJ chillón(ona)

garland ['gɑːlənd] N guirnalda *f*

garlic ['gɑːlɪk] N ajo *m*

garment ['gɑːmənt] N prenda *f*

garnish ['gɑːnɪʃ] VT guarnecer

garrison ['gærɪsən] N guarnición *f*

garrulous ['gærʊləs] ADJ locuaz

garter ['gɑːtə(r)] N liga *f*

gas [gæs] **1** N **(a)** *(for cooking, heating)* gas *m*; **g. cooker** cocina *f* de gas; **g. fire** estufa *f* de gas; **g. mask** careta *f* antigás; **g. ring** hornillo *m* de gas **(b)** *US* gasolina *f*, *RP* nafta *f*; **g. pump** surtidor *m* de gasolina; **g. station** gasolinera *f*, estación *f* de servicio, *Andes, Ven* bomba *f*, *Méx* gasolinería *f*, *Perú* grifo *m*; **g. tank** depósito *m* de la gasolina
2 VT *(asphyxiate)* asfixiar con gas
3 VI *Fam (talk)* charlotear

gash [gæʃ] **1** N herida profunda
2 VT hacer un corte en; **he gashed his forehead** se hizo una herida en la frente

gasket ['gæskɪt] N junta *f*

gasoline ['gæsəliːn] N *US* gasolina *f*, *RP* nafta *f*

gasp [gɑːsp] **1** N *(cry)* grito sordo; *(breath)* bocanada *f*; *Fig* **to be at one's last g.** estar en las últimas
2 VI *(in surprise)* quedar boquiabierto(a); *(breathe)* jadear

gassy ['gæsɪ] ADJ **(gassier, gassiest)** gaseoso(a)

gastric ['gæstrɪk] ADJ gástrico(a)

gastronomic [gæstrə'nɒmɪk] ADJ gastronómico(a)

gate [geɪt] N **(a)** *(entrance)* puerta *f* **(b)** *Sport (spectators)* entrada *f*; **g. (money)** taquilla *f*

gateau ['gætəʊ] N *(pl* **gateaux** ['gætəʊz]) pastel *m* con nata

gatecrash ['geɪtkræʃ] **1** VT colarse en
2 VI colarse

gateway ['geɪtweɪ] N puerta *f*; *Fig* pasaporte *m*

gather ['gæðə(r)] **1** VT **(a)** *(collect)* reunir; *(fruit, flowers)* recoger **(b)** *(bring together)* reunir **(c)** *(harvest)* cosechar **(d)** **to g. speed** ir ganando velocidad; **to g. strength** cobrar fuerzas **(e)** *(understand)* suponer; **I g. that …** tengo entendido que …
2 VI **(a)** *(come together)* reunirse **(b)** *(form)* formarse

▶ **gather round** VI agruparse

gathering ['gæðərɪŋ] **1** ADJ creciente
2 N reunión *f*

gauche [gəʊʃ] ADJ *(clumsy)* torpe; *(tactless)* sin tacto

gaudy ['gɔːdɪ] ADJ **(gaudier, gaudiest)** chillón(ona)

gauge [geɪdʒ] **1** N **(a)** *(of gun, screw, wire)* calibre *m*; *(of railway track)* ancho *m* de vía **(b)** *(instrument)* calibrador *m* **(c)** *Fig (indicator)* indicador *m*
2 VT **(a)** *(measure)* medir, calibrar **(b)** *Fig (judge)* juzgar

gaunt [gɔːnt] ADJ *(lean)* demacrado(a); *(desolate)* lúgubre

gauntlet ['gɔːntlɪt] N guantelete *m*; *Fig* **to run the g. of …** estar sometido(a) a …; *Fig* **to throw down the g.** arrojar el guante, *Am* desafiar a algn

gauze [gɔːz] N gasa *f*

gave [geɪv] PT *of* give

gawky ['gɔːkɪ] ADJ **(gawkier, gawkiest)** desgarbado(a)

gay [geɪ] ADJ **(a)** *(homosexual)* gay **(b)** *(happy)* alegre

gaze [geɪz] **1** N mirada fija
2 VI mirar fijamente

gazelle [gə'zel] N gacela *f*

gazette [gə'zet] N gaceta *f*; *US* periódico *m*

gazump [gə'zʌmp] VI *Br Fam* = romper un compromiso de venta para vender a un precio más alto

GB [dʒiː'biː] *(abbr* **Great Britain)** GB

GCSE [dʒiːsiːes'iː] N *Br (abbr* **General Certificate of Secondary Education)** = certificado de enseñanza secundaria

GDP [dʒiːdiː'piː] N *(abbr* **gross domestic product)** PIB *m*

GDR [dʒiːdiː'ɑː(r)] N *Hist (abbr* **German Democratic Republic)** RDA *f*

gear [gɪə(r)] **1** N **(a)** *(equipment)* equipo *m* **(b)** *Fam (belongings)* bártulos *mpl* **(c)** *Fam (clothing)* ropa *f* **(d)** *Tech* engranaje *m* **(e)** *Aut* velocidad *f*, marcha *f*; **first g.** primera *f* *(velocidad f)*; **g. lever** *or US* **shift** palanca *f* de cambio
2 VT ajustar, adaptar

gearbox ['gɪəbɒks] N caja *f* de cambios

gearstick ['gɪəstɪk], *US* **gearshift** ['gɪəʃɪft] N palanca *f* de cambio

gee [dʒiː] INTERJ *US* **g. (whizz)!** ¡anda!, ¡caramba!

geek [giːk] *Fam* lelo(a) *m,f*, tontaina *mf*

geese [giːs] PL *of* **goose**

gel [dʒel] **1** N gel *m*; *(for hair)* gomina *f*
2 VI *Fig (ideas etc)* cuajar
3 VT *(hair)* engominar

gelatin ['dʒelətɪn] N gelatina *f*

gelignite ['dʒelɪgnaɪt] N gelignita *f*

gem [dʒem] N piedra preciosa; *Fig (person)* joya *f*

Gemini [dʒemɪnaɪ] N Géminis *m inv*

gen [dʒen] N *Br Fam (information)* información *f*, datos *mpl*

gender ['dʒendə(r)] N género *m*

gene [dʒiːn] N gene *m*, gen *m*

general ['dʒenərəl] **1** ADJ general; **g. knowledge** conocimientos *mpl* generales; **in g.** en general; **the g. public** el público; **g. practitioner** médico *m* de cabecera
2 N *Mil* general *m*; *US* **g. of the army** mariscal *m* de campo

generalization [dʒenərəlaɪ'zeɪʃən] N generalización *f*

generalize ['dʒenərəlaɪz] VT & VI generalizar

generally ['dʒenərəlɪ] ADV generalmente, en general

generate ['dʒenəreɪt] VT generar

generation [dʒenə'reɪʃən] N generación *f*; **g. gap** abismo *m* or conflicto *m* generacional

generator ['dʒenəreɪtə(r)] N generador *m*

generosity [dʒenə'rɒsɪtɪ] N generosidad *f*

generous ['dʒenərəs] ADJ generoso(a); *(plentiful)* copioso(a)

genetic [dʒɪ'netɪk] ADJ genético(a); **g. engineering** ingeniería genética

genetically [dʒɪ'netɪklɪ] ADV **g. modified** *(plant, food)* modificado(a) genéticamente

genetics [dʒɪ'netɪks] N SING genética *f*

Geneva [dʒɪ'niːvə] N Ginebra

genial ['dʒiːnɪəl, 'dʒiːnjəl] ADJ cordial, amable

Note that the Spanish word **genial** is a false friend and is never a translation for the English word **genial**. In Spanish, **genial** means both "brilliant" and "terrific".

genie ['dʒiːnɪ] N duende *m*, genio *m*

genitals ['dʒenɪtəlz] NPL órganos *mpl* genitales

genius ['dʒiːnjəs, 'dʒiːnɪəs] N (**a**) *(person)* genio *m* (**b**) *(gift)* don *m*

genome ['dʒiːnəʊm] N *Biol* genoma *m*

genre ['ʒɑːnrə] N género *m*

gent [dʒent] N *Br Fam (abbr* **gentleman)** señor *m*, caballero *m*; **the gents** *(toilets)* el baño *or Esp* el servicio *or CSur* la toilette de caballeros

genteel [dʒen'tiːl] ADJ fino(a), distinguido(a)

Note that the Spanish word **gentil** is a false friend and is never a translation for the English word **genteel**. In Spanish, **gentil** means both "kind" and "pagan".

gentle ['dʒentəl] ADJ dulce, tierno(a); *(breeze)* suave

gentleman ['dʒentəlmən] N caballero *m*; **g.'s agreement** pacto *m* de caballeros

gently ['dʒentlɪ] ADV con cuidado

gentry ['dʒentrɪ] N pequeña nobleza, alta burguesía

genuine ['dʒenjʊɪn] ADJ auténtico(a), genuino(a); *(sincere)* sincero(a)

genuinely ['dʒenjʊɪnlɪ] ADV auténticamente

geographic(al) [dʒɪə'græfɪk(əl)] ADJ geográfico(a)

geography [dʒɪ'ɒgrəfɪ] N geografía *f*

geologic(al) [dʒɪə'lɒdʒɪk(əl)] ADJ geológico(a)

geology [dʒɪ'ɒlədʒɪ] N geología *f*

geometric(al) [dʒɪə'metrɪk(əl)] ADJ geométrico(a)

geometry [dʒɪ'ɒmɪtrɪ] N geometría *f*

geopolitical [dʒiːəʊpə'lɪtɪkəl] ADJ geopolítico(a)

geranium [dʒɪ'reɪnɪəm] N geranio *m*

geriatric [dʒerɪ'ætrɪk] ADJ geriátrico(a)

germ [dʒɜːm] N (**a**) *Biol & Fig* germen *m* (**b**) *Med* microbio *m*

German ['dʒɜːmən] **1** ADJ alemán(ana); **G. measles** rubeola *f*
2 N (**a**) *(person)* alemán(ana) *m,f* (**b**) *(language)* alemán *m*

Germany ['dʒɜːmənɪ] N Alemania

germinate ['dʒɜːmɪneɪt] VI germinar

gestation [dʒe'steɪʃən] N gestación *f*

gesticulate [dʒe'stɪkjʊleɪt] VI gesticular

gesture ['dʒestʃə(r)] **1** N gesto *m*, ademán *m*; **it's an empty g.** es pura formalidad
2 VI gesticular, hacer gestos

get [get] **1** VT *(pt & pp* **got**, *US pp* **gotten)** (**a**) *(obtain)* obtener, conseguir; *(receive)* recibir; *(earn)* ganar (**b**) *(fetch) (something)* traer; *(somebody)* ir a por; **can I g. you something to eat?** ¿quieres comer algo?; **g. the police!** ¡llama a la policía! (**c**) *(bus, train)* tomar, *Esp* coger, *Am* agarrar (**d**) *(have done)* **g. him to call me** dile que me llame; **to g. sb to agree to sth** conseguir que algn acepte algo; **to g. one's hair cut** cortarse el pelo (**e**) **have got, have got to** *see* **have** (**f**) *Fam (understand)* entender

2 VI (**a**) *(become)* ponerse; **to g. dressed** vestirse; **to g. drunk** emborracharse; **to g. married** casarse; **to g. paid** cobrar (**b**) **to g. to** *(arrive, come to)* llegar a; **to g. to know sb** llegar a conocer a algn

▸ **get about** VI *(person)* salir; *(news)* difundirse

▸ **get across** VT SEP *(idea etc)* hacer comprender

▶ **get ahead** VI progresar

▶ **get along** VI (**a**) *(leave)* marcharse (**b**) *(manage)* arreglárselas (**c**) *(two people)* llevarse bien

▶ **get around** VI *(person)* salir; *(travel)* viajar; *(news)* difundirse

▶ **get at** VT INSEP (**a**) *(reach)* alcanzar (**b**) *(insinuate)* insinuar; **what are you getting at?** ¿a dónde quieres llegar?

▶ **get away** VI escaparse

▶ **get away with** VT INSEP salir impune de

▶ **get back** 1 VI (**a**) *(return)* regresar, volver (**b**) **g. back!** *(move backwards)* ¡atrás!
2 VT SEP *(recover)* recuperar; *Fam* **to g. one's own back on sb** vengarse de algn

▶ **get by** VI *(manage)* arreglárselas; **she can g. by in French** sabe defenderse en francés

▶ **get down** 1 VT SEP *(depress)* deprimir
2 VI *(descend)* bajar

▶ **get down to** VT INSEP ponerse a; **to g. down to the facts** ir al grano

▶ **get in** 1 VI (**a**) *(arrive)* llegar (**b**) *Pol* ser elegido(a)
2 VT SEP (**a**) *(buy)* comprar (**b**) *(collect)* recoger

▶ **get into** VT INSEP *Fig* **to g. into bad habits** adquirir malas costumbres; **to g. into trouble** meterse en un lío

▶ **get off** 1 VT INSEP *(bus etc)* bajarse de
2 VT SEP *(remove)* quitar, *Andes, RP* sacar
3 VI (**a**) *(descend from vehicle)* bajarse; *Fam* **g. off!** ¡fuera! (**b**) **to g. off to a good start** *(begin)* empezar bien (**c**) *(go unpunished)* librarse

▶ **get off with** VT INSEP *Fam* ligar

▶ **get on** 1 VT INSEP *(board)* subir a
2 VT SEP (**a**) *(board)* subirse (**b**) *(make progress)* hacer progresos; **how are you getting on?** ¿cómo te van las cosas? (**c**) **to g. on well (with sb)** llevarse bien (con algn) (**d**) *(continue)* seguir; **to g. on with one's work** seguir trabajando

▶ **get on to** VT INSEP (**a**) *(find a person)* localizar; *(find out)* descubrir (**b**) *(continue)* pasar a

▶ **get out** 1 VT SEP *(object)* sacar
2 VI (**a**) *(room etc)* salir (**of** de); *(train)* bajar (**of** de) (**b**) *(escape)* escaparse (**of** de); **to g. out of an obligation** librarse de un compromiso (**c**) *(news)* difundirse; *(secret)* hacerse público

▶ **get over** 1 VT INSEP (**a**) *(illness)* recuperarse de (**b**) *(difficulty)* vencer
2 VT SEP *(convey)* hacer comprender

▶ **get round** VT INSEP (**a**) *(problem)* salvar; *(difficulty)* vencer (**b**) *(rule)* soslayar

▶ **get round to** VT INSEP **if I g. round to it** si tengo tiempo

▶ **get through** 1 VI (**a**) *(message)* llegar (**b**) *Educ* aprobar (**c**) *Tel* **to g. through to sb** conseguir comunicar con algn
2 VT INSEP (**a**) **to g. through a lot of work** trabajar mucho (**b**) *(consume)* consumir

▶ **get together** 1 VI *(people)* juntarse, reunirse
2 VT SEP *(people)* juntar, reunir

▶ **get up** 1 VI *(rise)* levantarse, *Am* pararse
2 VT SEP *(wake)* despertar

▶ **get up to** VT INSEP hacer; **to g. up to mischief** hacer de las suyas

getaway ['getəweɪ] N fuga *f*; **to make one's g.** fugarse

get-together ['gettəgeðə(r)] N reunión *f*

geyser ['giːzə(r), *US* 'gaɪzər] N (**a**) *Geog* géiser *m* (**b**) *(water heater)* calentador *m* de agua

ghastly ['gɑːstlɪ] ADJ (**ghastlier, ghastliest**) horrible, espantoso(a)

gherkin ['gɜːkɪn] N pepinillo *m*

ghetto ['getəʊ] N gueto *m*

ghost [gəʊst] N fantasma *m*; **g. story** cuento *m* de fantasmas; **g. town** pueblo *m* fantasma

ghost-writer ['gəʊstraɪtə(r)] N negro(a) *m,f*

ghoulish ['guːlɪʃ] ADJ macabro(a)

giant ['dʒaɪənt] ADJ & N gigante *(m)*

gibberish ['dʒɪbərɪʃ] N galimatías *m inv*

gibe [dʒaɪb] 1 N mofa *f*
2 VI mofarse (**at** de)

giblets ['dʒɪblɪts] NPL menudillos *mpl*

Gibraltar [dʒɪˈbrɔːltə(r)] N Gibraltar

Gibraltarian [dʒɪbrɔːlˈteərɪən] ADJ & N gibraltareño(a) *(m,f)*

giddiness ['gɪdɪnɪs] N mareo *m*; *(vertigo)* vértigo *m*

giddy ['gɪdɪ] ADJ (**giddier, giddiest**) mareado(a); **it makes me g.** me da vértigo; **to feel g.** sentirse mareado(a)

gift [gɪft] N (**a**) *(present)* regalo *m*, obsequio *m*; **g. token** vale *m* (**b**) *(talent)* don *m*; **to have a g. for music** estar muy dotado(a) para la música

gifted ['gɪftɪd] ADJ dotado(a)

gig [gɪg] N *Fam Mus* actuación *f*

gigabyte ['dʒɪgəbaɪt] N *Comput* gigabyte *m*

gigantic [dʒaɪˈgæntɪk] ADJ gigantesco(a)

giggle ['gɪgəl] 1 N risita *f*; *esp Br Fam* **to do sth for a g.** hacer algo de broma
2 VI soltar risitas

gild [gɪld] VT dorar

gill¹ [dʒɪl] N *(liquid measure)* = 0,142 l

gill² [gɪl] N *(of fish)* branquia *f*, agalla *f*

gilt [gɪlt] 1 ADJ dorado(a)
2 N *(colour)* dorado *m*

gilt-edged ['gɪltedʒd] ADJ **g. securities** *or* **stock** *Br* títulos *mpl* de deuda pública, valores *mpl* del Estado; *US* títulos *mpl* *or* valores *mpl* de máxima garantía

gimmick ['gɪmɪk] N truco *m*; *(in advertising)* reclamo *m*

gin [dʒɪn] N ginebra *f*; **g. and tonic** gin tonic *m*

ginger ['dʒɪndʒə(r)] 1 N jengibre *m*; **g. ale** ginger ale *m*
2 ADJ *(hair)* pelirrojo(a)

gingerbread ['dʒɪndʒəbred] N pan *m* de jengibre

gingerly ['dʒɪndʒəlɪ] ADV cautelosamente

gipsy ['dʒɪpsɪ] ADJ & N gitano(a) (m,f)

giraffe [dʒɪ'rɑːf] N jirafa f

girder ['gɜːdə(r)] N viga f

girdle ['gɜːdəl] N faja f

girl [gɜːl] N (a) (young woman) chica f; (child, baby) niña f; Br g. guide, US g. scout exploradora f (b) (daughter) hija f (c) (sweetheart) novia f

girlfriend ['gɜːlfrend] N (a) (lover) novia f (b) (female friend) amiga f

girlhood ['gɜːlhʊd] N niñez f

girlish ['gɜːlɪʃ] ADJ (a) (of girl, young woman) de niña (b) (effeminate) afeminado(a)

giro ['dʒaɪrəʊ] N Br Fam (unemployment cheque) cheque m del desempleo or Esp paro

gist [dʒɪst] N esencia f; did you get the g. of what he was saying? ¿cogiste la idea de lo que decía?

give [gɪv] 1 N (elasticity) elasticidad f
2 VT (pt gave; pp given) (a) (in general) dar; (as present) regalar; to g. sth to sb dar algo a algn; to g. sb sth to eat dar de comer a algn (b) (pay) pagar (c) (speech) pronunciar (d) (grant) otorgar; to g. sb one's attention prestar atención a algn (e) (yield) ceder; to g. way Aut ceder el paso; Fig ceder; (of legs) flaquear
3 VI (yield) ceder; (fabric) dar de sí
▶ **give away** VT SEP (a) (prize) repartir; (present) regalar (b) (reveal) revelar; to g. the game away descubrir el pastel (c) (betray) traicionar
▶ **give back** VT SEP devolver
▶ **give in** 1 VI (a) (admit defeat) darse por vencido(a); (surrender) rendirse (b) to g. in to ceder ante
2 VT SEP (hand in) entregar
▶ **give off** VT SEP (smell etc) despedir
▶ **give out** VT SEP distribuir, repartir
▶ **give over** VT SEP (hand over) entregar; (devote) dedicar
▶ **give up** 1 VT SEP (a) (idea) abandonar; to g. up smoking dejar de fumar (b) (hand over) entregar; to g. oneself up entregarse
2 VI (admit defeat) darse por vencido(a), rendirse
▶ **give up on** VT INSEP darse por vencido con

given ['gɪvən] 1 ADJ (a) (particular) dado(a); at a g. time en un momento dado (b) g. to dado(a) a
2 CONJ (considering) dado(a)
3 PP of give

glacial ['gleɪsɪəl] ADJ (a) Geol glaciar (b) (icy) glacial; Fig g. look mirada f glacial

glacier ['glæsɪə(r)] N glaciar m

glad [glæd] ADJ (gladder, gladdest) contento(a); (happy) alegre; he'll be only too g. to help you tendrá mucho gusto en ayudarle; to be g. alegrarse

gladiator ['glædɪeɪtə(r)] N Hist gladiador m

gladly ['glædlɪ] ADV con mucho gusto

glamor ['glæmər] N US = glamour

glamorous ['glæmərəs] ADJ atractivo(a), encantador(a)

glamour ['glæmə(r)] N atractivo m; (charm) encanto m; Fam g. girl bombón m, Am muñequita f

glance [glɑːns] 1 N mirada f, vistazo m; at a g. de un vistazo; at first g. a primera vista
2 VI echar un vistazo (at a)
▶ **glance off** VT INSEP (of ball etc) rebotar de

glancing ['glɑːnsɪŋ] ADJ (blow) oblicuo(a)

gland [glænd] N glándula f

glandular ['glændjʊlə(r)] ADJ glandular; g. fever mononucleosis infecciosa

glare [gleə(r)] 1 N (light) luz f deslumbrante; (dazzle) deslumbramiento m; (look) mirada f feroz
2 VI (dazzle) deslumbrar; (look) lanzar una mirada furiosa (at a)

glaring ['gleərɪŋ] ADJ (light) deslumbrante; (colour) chillón(ona); (obvious) evidente

glass [glɑːs] N (a) (material) vidrio m; pane of g. cristal m (b) (drinking vessel) vaso m; wine g. copa f (para vino) (c) glasses (spectacles) gafas fpl, Am lentes mpl, anteojos mpl; to wear glasses llevar gafas or Am lentes or anteojos

glasshouse ['glɑːshaʊs] N Br invernadero m

glassware ['glɑːsweə(r)] N cristalería f

glassy ['glɑːsɪ] ADJ (glassier, glassiest) (water) cristalino(a); (eyes) vidrioso(a)

glaze [gleɪz] 1 N (varnish) barniz m; (for pottery) vidriado m
2 VT (a) (windows) acristalar; (b) (varnish) barnizar; (ceramics) vidriar (c) Culin glasear

glazed [gleɪzd] ADJ (eyes) de mirada ausente

glazier ['gleɪzɪə(r)] N vidriero(a) m,f

gleam [gliːm] 1 N (of light) destello m
2 VI resplandecer, relucir

gleaming ['gliːmɪŋ] ADJ brillante, reluciente

glean [gliːn] VT Fig recoger, cosechar

glee [gliː] N gozo m

gleeful ['gliːfʊl] ADJ gozoso(a)

glen [glen] N cañada f

glib [glɪb] ADJ (glibber, glibbest) Pej (person) con mucha labia, CAm, Ecuad, Méx labioso(a); (excuse, answer) fácil

glide [glaɪd] VI (a) (slip, slide) deslizarse (b) Av planear

glider ['glaɪdə(r)] N planeador m

gliding ['glaɪdɪŋ] N vuelo m sin motor

glimmer ['glɪmə(r)] N (a) (light) luz f tenue (b) Fig (trace) destello m

glimpse [glɪmps] 1 N atisbo m
2 VT atisbar

glint [glɪnt] 1 N destello m, centelleo m; he had a g. in his eye le brillaban los ojos
2 VI destellar, centellear

glisten ['glɪsən] VI relucir, brillar

glitter ['glɪtə(r)] **1** N brillo *m*
2 VI relucir

gloat [gləʊt] VI jactarse; **to g. over another's misfortune** recrearse con la desgracia de otro

global ['gləʊbəl] ADJ (**a**) (*of the world*) mundial; **g. warming** calentamiento *m* global (**b**) (*overall*) global

globalization [gləʊbəlaɪ'zeɪʃən] N mundialización *f*, globalización *f*

globe [gləʊb] N globo *m*, esfera *f*

gloom [glu:m] N (*obscurity*) penumbra *f*; (*melancholy*) melancolía *f*; (*despair*) desolación *f*

gloomy ['glu:mɪ] ADJ (**gloomier, gloomiest**) (*dark*) oscuro(a); (*weather*) gris; (*dismal*) deprimente; (*despairing*) pesimista; (*sad*) triste

glorify ['glɔ:rɪfaɪ] VT glorificar

glorious ['glɔ:rɪəs] ADJ (*momentous*) glorioso(a); (*splendid*) magnífico(a), espléndido(a)

glory ['glɔ:rɪ] N (*honour, praise*) gloria *f*; (*splendour*) esplendor *m*; (*triumph*) triunfo *m*

gloss [glɒs] **1** N (**a**) (*explanation*) glosa *f* (**b**) (*sheen*) brillo *m*; **g. (paint)** pintura *f* brillante
2 VI glosar

▸ **gloss over** VT INSEP *Fig* encubrir

glossary ['glɒsərɪ] N glosario *m*

glossy ['glɒsɪ] ADJ (**glossier, glossiest**) lustroso(a); **g. magazine** revista *f* de lujo

glove [glʌv] N guante *m*; *Aut* **g. compartment** guantera *f*

glow [gləʊ] **1** N brillo *m*; (*of fire*) incandescencia *f*; (*of sun*) arrebol *m*; (*heat*) calor *m*; (*light*) luz *f*; (*in cheeks*) rubor *m*
2 VI brillar; (*fire*) arder; *Fig* rebosar de

glower ['glaʊə(r)] VI poner cara de enfadado(a)

glowing ['gləʊɪŋ] ADJ (**a**) (*fire*) incandescente; (*colour*) vivo(a); (*light*) brillante (**b**) (*cheeks*) encendido(a) (**c**) *Fig* (*report*) entusiasta

glucose ['glu:kəʊz] N glucosa *f*

glue [glu:] **1** N pegamento *m*, cola *f*
2 VT pegar (**to** a)

glum [glʌm] ADJ (**glummer, glummest**) alicaído(a)

glut [glʌt] N superabundancia *f*, exceso *m*

glutton ['glʌtən] N glotón(ona) *m,f*

GM [dʒi:'em] ADJ (*abbr* **genetically modified**) transgénico(a), modificado(a) genéticamente; **GM food** (alimentos) transgénicos

GMO [dʒi:em'əʊ] N (*abbr* **genetically modified organism**) OMG *m*

GMT [dʒi:em'ti:] N (*abbr* **Greenwich Mean Time**) hora *f* del meridiano de Greenwich

gnarled [nɑ:ld] ADJ nudoso(a)

gnash [næʃ] VT rechinar

gnat [næt] N mosquito *m*

gnaw [nɔ:] VT & VI (*chew*) roer

gnome [nəʊm] N gnomo *m*

GNP [dʒi:en'pi:] N (*abbr* **gross national product**) PNB *m*

go [gəʊ] **1** VI (*3rd person sing pres* **goes**; *pt* **went**; *pp* **gone**) (**a**) (*in general*) ir; **to go for a walk** (ir a) dar un paseo
(**b**) (*depart*) irse, marcharse
(**c**) (*function*) funcionar
(**d**) (*be sold*) venderse
(**e**) (*become*) quedarse, volverse; **to go blind** quedarse ciego(a); **to go mad** volverse loco(a)
(**f**) (*progress*) ir, marchar; **everything went well** todo salió bien; **how's it going?** ¿qué tal (te van las cosas)?
(**g**) **to be going to** (*in the future*) ir a; (*on the point of*) estar a punto de
(**h**) (*fit*) caber
(**i**) (*be available*) quedar; **I'll take whatever's going** me conformo con lo que hay
(**j**) (*be acceptable*) valer; **anything goes** todo vale
(**k**) (*time*) pasar; **there are only two weeks to go** sólo quedan dos semanas
(**l**) (*say*) decir; **as the saying goes** según el dicho
(**m**) **to let sth go** soltar algo
2 VT (**a**) (*travel*) hacer, recorrer (**b**) **to go it alone** apañárselas solo
3 N (**a**) (*energy*) energía *f*, dinamismo *m* (**b**) (*try*) intento *m*; **to have a go at sth** probar suerte con algo; **to have a go at sb** criticar a algn (**c**) (*turn*) turno *m*; **it's your go** te toca a ti (**d**) **to make a go of sth** tener éxito en algo

▸ **go about 1** VT INSEP (**a**) (*task*) emprender; **how do you go about it?** ¿cómo hay que hacerlo? (**b**) **to go about one's business** ocuparse de sus asuntos
2 VI (*rumour*) correr

▸ **go after** VT INSEP (*pursue*) ir tras

▸ **go against** VT INSEP (*oppose*) ir en contra de; (*verdict*) ser desfavorable a

▸ **go ahead** (**a**) (*proceed*) proceder (**b**) **we'll go on ahead** iremos delante

▸ **go along 1** VT INSEP (*street*) pasar por
2 VI (*progress*) progresar

▸ **go along with** VT INSEP (**a**) (*agree with*) estar de acuerdo con (**b**) (*accompany*) acompañar

▸ **go around** VI (**a**) (*rumour*) correr (**b**) **there's enough to go around** hay para todos

▸ **go away** VI marcharse

▸ **go back** VI (**a**) (*return*) volver, regresar (**b**) *Fig* **to go back to** (*date from*) datar de

▸ **go back on** VT INSEP **to go back on one's word** faltar a su palabra

▸ **go back to** VT INSEP volver a

▸ **go by** VI pasar; **as time goes by** con el tiempo

▸ **go down** VI (**a**) (*descend*) bajar; (*sun*) ponerse; (*ship*) hundirse (**b**) (*diminish*) disminuir; (*temperature*) bajar (**c**) (*be received*) ser acogido(a)

▸ **go down with** VT INSEP (*contract*) agarrar, *Esp* coger

▸ **go for** VT INSEP (**a**) (*attack*) lanzarse sobre (**b**) (*fetch*) ir por

▶ **go in** VI entrar

▶ **go in for** VT INSEP *(exam)* presentarse a; *(hobby)* dedicarse a

▶ **go into** VT INSEP (a) *(enter)* entrar en; **to go into journalism** dedicarse al periodismo (b) *(study)* examinar; *(matter)* investigar

▶ **go off** 1 VI (a) *(leave)* irse, marcharse (b) *(bomb)* explotar; *(gun)* dispararse; *(alarm)* sonar (c) *(food)* pasarse

2 VT INSEP *Fam* **to go off sth** perder el gusto *or* el interés por algo

▶ **go on** VI (a) *(continue)* seguir, continuar; **to go on talking** seguir hablando; *Fam* **to go on and on about sth** no parar de hablar sobre algo; *(complain)* quejarse constantemente de algo (b) *(time)* transcurrir, pasar (c) *(light)* encenderse, *Am* prenderse

▶ **go out** VI (a) *(leave)* salir; **to go out for a meal** comer *or* cenar fuera (b) *(boy and girl)* salir juntos (c) *(fire, light)* apagarse (d) *(tide)* bajar

▶ **go over** VT INSEP *(revise)* repasar

▶ **go over to** VT INSEP (a) *(approach)* acercarse a (b) *(switch to)* **to go over to a different system** cambiar de sistema; **to go over to the enemy** pasarse al enemigo

▶ **go round** VI (a) *(revolve)* dar vueltas (b) **to go round to sb's house** pasar por casa de algn

▶ **go through** 1 VI *(bill)* ser aprobado(a)

2 VT INSEP (a) *(examine)* examinar; *(search)* registrar (b) *(rehearse)* ensayar (c) *(spend)* gastar (d) *(list etc)* explicar (e) *(endure)* sufrir

▶ **go through with** VT INSEP llevar a cabo

▶ **go under** VI (a) *(ship)* hundirse (b) *(business)* fracasar

▶ **go up** VI (a) *(price etc)* subir (b) **to go up to sb** acercarse a algn (c) *(in a lift)* subir

▶ **go with** VT INSEP (a) *(accompany)* ir con (b) *(colours)* hacer juego con

▶ **go without** VT INSEP pasarse sin, prescindir de

goad [gəʊd] VT aguijonear

go-ahead ['gəʊəhed] N *Fam* **to give sb the g.** dar luz verde a algn

goal [gəʊl] N (a) *Sport* gol m; **g. post** poste m (b) *(aim, objective)* meta f, objetivo m

goalkeeper ['gəʊlkiːpə(r)] N portero(a) m,f

goat [gəʊt] N *(female)* cabra f; *(male)* macho cabrío

gob [gɒb] N *esp Br very Fam* pico m

gobble ['gɒbl] VT engullir

go-between ['gəʊbɪtwiːn] N intermediario(a) m,f

goblet ['gɒblɪt] N copa f

god [gɒd] N dios m; **G.** Dios; **(my) G.!** ¡Dios mío!

godchild ['gɒdtʃaɪld] N ahijado(a) m,f

goddam(n) [gɒdæm] US *Fam* 1 ADJ maldito(a), dichoso(a), *Méx* pinche

2 ADV **that was g. stupid!** ¡eso fue una auténtica estupidez!

goddaughter ['gɒddɔːtə(r)] N ahijada f

goddess ['gɒdɪs] N diosa f

godfather ['gɒdfɑːðə(r)] N padrino m

godforsaken ['gɒdfəseɪkən] ADJ *(place)* remoto(a)

godmother ['gɒdmʌðə(r)] N madrina f

godparents ['gɒdpeərənts] NPL padrinos mpl

godsend ['gɒdsend] N regalo inesperado

godson ['gɒdsʌn] N ahijado m

goggles ['gɒglz] NPL gafas fpl protectoras, *CSur* antiparras fpl

going ['gəʊɪŋ] 1 ADJ (a) *(price)* corriente; **the g. rate** el precio medio (b) **a g. concern** un negocio que marcha bien (c) **to get or be g.** marcharse (d) **to keep g.** resistir

2 N **to get out while the g. is good** retirarse antes que sea demasiado tarde

goings-on [gəʊɪŋz'ɒn] NPL *Fam* tejemanejes mpl

go-kart ['gəʊkɑːt] N *Sport* kart m

gold [gəʊld] 1 N oro m; **g. leaf** pan m de oro; **g. medal** medalla f de oro; **g. mine** mina f de oro

2 ADJ de oro; *(colour)* oro, dorado(a)

golden ['gəʊldən] ADJ de oro; *(colour)* dorado(a); *Fig* **a g. opportunity** una excelente oportunidad; **g. eagle** águila f real; *Fig* **g. handshake** indemnización f por despido; **g. wedding** bodas fpl de oro

goldfish ['gəʊldfɪʃ] N pez m de colores

gold-plated [gəʊld'pleɪtɪd] ADJ chapado(a) en oro

goldsmith ['gəʊldsmɪθ] N orfebre m

golf [gɒlf] N golf m; **g. ball** pelota f de golf; **g. club** *(stick)* palo m de golf; *(place)* club m de golf; **g. course** campo m de golf

golfer ['gɒlfə(r)] N golfista mf

golly ['gɒlɪ] INTERJ ¡vaya!

gone [gɒn] 1 ADJ desaparecido(a)

2 PP *of* **go**

gong [gɒŋ] N gong m

good [gʊd] 1 ADJ (**better, best**) (a) *(before noun)* buen(a); *(after noun)* bueno(a); **a g. book** un buen libro; **g. afternoon/evening** buenas tardes; **g. morning** buenos días; **g. night** buenas noches; **it looks g.** tiene buena pinta; **to feel g.** sentirse bien; **to smell g.** oler bien; **to have a g. time** pasarlo bien (b) *(kind)* amable (c) *(morally correct)* correcto(a); **be g.!** ¡pórtate bien! (d) **he's g. at languages** tiene facilidad para los idiomas (e) *(attractive)* bonito(a); **g. looks** atractivo m, belleza f (f) *(propitious)* propicio(a); (g) *(character)* agradable; **he's in a g. mood** está de buen humor

2 N (a) *(in general)* bien m; **g. and evil** el bien y el mal; **to do g.** hacer el bien (b) *(advantage)* bien m, provecho m; **for your own g.** para tu propio bien; **it's no g. waiting** no sirve de nada esperar; **it will do you g.** te hará bien (c) *Com* **goods** artículos mpl, géneros mpl; **goods train** m de mercancías

3 **for good** ADV **she's gone for g.** se ha ido para siempre

4 INTERJ ¡muy bien!

goodbye [gʊd'baɪ] **1** INTERJ ¡adiós!
2 N adiós *m*, despedida *f*; **to say g. to sb** despedirse de algn
good-for-nothing ['gʊdfənʌθɪŋ] ADJ & N inútil *(mf)*
good-hearted [gʊd'hɑːtɪd] ADJ de buen corazón
good-looking [gʊd'lʊkɪŋ] ADJ guapo(a)
good-natured [gʊd'neɪtʃəd] ADJ amable, bondadoso(a)
goodness ['gʊdnɪs] N bondad *f*; **my g.!** ¡Dios mío!; **thank g.!** ¡gracias a Dios!; **for g. sake!** ¡por Dios!
good-tempered [gʊd'tempəd] ADJ apacible
goodwill [gʊd'wɪl] N (**a**) *(benevolence)* buena voluntad (**b**) *Com* fondo *m* de comercio
goof [guːf] *US Fam* **1** N metedura *f or Am* metida *f* de pata
2 VI meter la pata
goose [guːs] N *(pl* **geese**) ganso *m*, oca *f*
gooseberry ['gʊzbərɪ, 'guːsbərɪ] N uva espina, grosella espinosa; *Br Fam* **to play g.** *Esp* hacer de carabina *or* de sujetavelas, *Méx* hacer mal tercio, *RP* estar de paleta
gooseflesh ['guːsfleʃ] N, **goosepimples** ['guːspɪmpəlz] NPL carne *f* de gallina
goose-step ['guːsstep] VI ir a paso de la oca
gore¹ [gɔː(r)] N sangre derramada
gore² [gɔː(r)] VT *(of bull)* cornear, dar cornadas a
gorge [gɔːdʒ] **1** N desfiladero *m*
2 VT & VI **to g. (oneself) (on)** atiborrarse (de)
gorgeous ['gɔːdʒəs] ADJ magnífico(a), estupendo(a); *(person)* atractivo(a), guapo(a)
gorilla [gə'rɪlə] N gorila *m*
gorse [gɔːs] N aulaga *f*
gory ['gɔːrɪ] ADJ (**gorier, goriest**) sangriento(a)
gosh [gɒʃ] INTERJ *Fam* ¡cielos!, ¡caray!
go-slow [gəʊ'sləʊ] N *Br* huelga *f* de celo
gospel ['gɒspəl] N **the G.** el Evangelio; *Fam* **it's the g. truth** es la pura verdad
gossip ['gɒsɪp] **1** N (**a**) *(rumour)* cotilleo *m*; **g. column** ecos *mpl* de sociedad (**b**) *(person)* chismoso(a) *m,f*, cotilla *mf*
2 VI *(natter)* cotillear, chismorrear
got [gɒt] PT & PP *of* **get**
Gothic ['gɒθɪk] ADJ gótico(a)
gotten ['gɒtən] *US* PP *of* **get**
gourmet ['gʊəmeɪ] N gourmet *mf*
gout [gaʊt] N gota *f*
govern ['gʌvən] VT (**a**) *(state, country)* gobernar; *(emotions)* dominar (**b**) *(of scientific law)* regir, determinar
governess ['gʌvənɪs] N institutriz *f*
governing ['gʌvənɪŋ] ADJ gobernante; **g. body** consejo *m* de administración
government ['gʌvənmənt] N gobierno *m*
governmental [gʌvən'mentəl] ADJ gubernamental

governor ['gʌvənə(r)] N *(ruler)* gobernador(a) *m,f*; *(of prison)* director(a) *m,f*; *(of school)* administrador(a) *m,f*
gown [gaʊn] N *(dress)* vestido largo; *Jur & Univ* toga *f*
GP [dʒiː'piː] N *Br (abbr* **general practitioner**) médico(a) *m,f* de familia *or* de cabecera
GPO [dʒiːpiː'əʊ] N *Br Formerly (abbr* **General Post Office**) ≃ (Administración *f* Central de) Correos *mpl*
grab [græb] **1** N agarrón *m*; *Fam* **to be up for grabs** estar disponible
2 VT (**a**) *(snatch)* agarrar; **to g. hold of sb** agarrarse a algn (**b**) *Fam (take hurriedly)* **to g. a bite to eat** comer algo en cualquier parte (**c**) *Fam (attract, interest)* **how does that g. you?** ¿qué te parece?
grace [greɪs] **1** N (**a**) *(of movement, language)* gracia *f*, elegancia *f* (**b**) *Rel* gracia *f* (**c**) **to say g.** bendecir la mesa (**d**) **five days' g.** *(reprieve)* un plazo de cinco días
2 VT (**a**) *(adorn)* adornar (**b**) *(honour)* honrar
graceful ['greɪsfʊl] ADJ elegante; *(movement)* garboso(a)
gracefully ['greɪsfʊlɪ] ADV (**a**) *(beautifully)* con gracia, con elegancia (**b**) *(accept)* con cortesía
gracious ['greɪʃəs] **1** ADJ (**a**) *(elegant)* elegante (**b**) *(courteous)* cortés (**c**) *(kind)* amable
2 INTERJ **good g. (me)!, goodness g.!** ¡santo cielo!
grade [greɪd] **1** N (**a**) *(quality)* grado *m*; *(rank)* categoría *f*; *Mil* rango *m* (**b**) *US Educ (mark)* nota *f* (**c**) *US Educ (class)* clase *f*; **g. school** escuela primaria (**d**) *(level)* nivel *m* (**e**) *US* **g. crossing** paso *m* a nivel
2 VT clasificar
gradient ['greɪdɪənt] N *(graph)* declive *m*; *(hill)* cuesta *f*, pendiente *f*
gradual ['grædjʊəl] ADJ gradual, progresivo(a)
gradually ['grædjʊəlɪ] ADV poco a poco
graduate 1 N ['grædjʊɪt] *Univ* licenciado(a) *m,f*; *US (from high school)* ≃ bachiller *mf*
2 VI ['grædjʊeɪt] (**a**) *Univ* licenciarse (**in** en) (**b**) *US (from high school)* ≃ sacar el bachillerato
graduation [grædjʊ'eɪʃən] N graduación *f*; *Univ* **g. ceremony** ceremonia *f* de entrega de los títulos
graffiti [grə'fiːtɪ] NPL grafiti *mpl*
graft [grɑːft] **1** N (**a**) *Med* injerto *m* (**b**) *Br Fam (work)* trabajo *m* (**c**) *US (bribery)* corruptelas *fpl*
2 VT *Med* injertar (**on to** en)
3 VI *Br Fam* trabajar mucho, *Esp* currar a tope, *Méx* chambear duro, *RP* laburar como loco
grain [greɪn] N (**a**) *(cereals)* cereales *mpl* (**b**) *(particle)* grano *m*; *Fig* **there's not a g. of truth in it** no tiene ni pizca de verdad (**c**) *(in wood)* fibra *f*; *(in stone)* veta *f*; *(in leather)* flor *f*; *Fig* **to go against the g.** ir a contrapelo
gram [græm] N gramo *m*

grammar ['græmə(r)] N gramática *f*; **g. (book)** libro *m* de gramática; *Br* **g. school** instituto *m* de enseñanza secundaria *(al que sólo se accede después de superar un examen de ingreso)*

grammatical [grə'mætɪkəl] ADJ gramatical

gramme [græm] N gramo *m*

gramophone ['græməfəʊn] N gramófono *m*

granary ['grænərɪ] N granero *m*

grand [grænd] **1** ADJ (**a**) *(imposing)* grandioso(a), imponente; *(plan, scheme)* ambicioso(a); **g. piano** piano *m* de cola (**b**) *(overall)* global; **g. total** total *m* (**c**) *Fam (excellent)* genial, *Am salvo RP* chévere, *Méx* padre, *RP* bárbaro(a)
2 N *Fam* mil libras *fpl*; *US* mil dólares *mpl*

grandchild ['græntʃaɪld] N nieto(a) *m,f*

granddad ['grændæd] N *Fam* abuelo *m*

granddaughter ['grændɔːtə(r)] N nieta *f*

grandeur ['grændʒə(r)] N grandeza *f*, grandiosidad *f*

grandfather ['grænfɑːðə(r)] N abuelo *m*; **g. clock** reloj *m* de caja

grandiose ['grændɪəʊs] ADJ grandioso(a)

grandma ['grænmɑː] N *Fam* abuelita *f*

grandmother ['grænmʌðə(r)] N abuela *f*

grandpa ['grænpɑː] N *Fam* abuelito *m*

grandparents ['grænpeərənts] NPL abuelos *mpl*

grandson ['grænsʌn] N nieto *m*

grandstand ['grænstænd] N tribuna *f*

granite ['grænɪt] N granito *m*

granny ['grænɪ] N *Fam* abuelita *f*

grant [grɑːnt] **1** VT (**a**) *(allow)* conceder, otorgar (**b**) *(admit)* admitir; **to take sb for granted** no apreciar a algn en lo que vale; **to take sth for granted** dar algo por sentado
2 N *Educ* beca *f*; *(subsidy)* subvención *f*

granulated ['grænjʊleɪtɪd] ADJ granulado(a)

granule ['grænjuːl] N gránulo *m*

grape [greɪp] N uva *f*; **g. juice** mosto *m*

grapefruit ['greɪpfruːt] N pomelo *m*, *Am* toronja *f*

grapevine ['greɪpvaɪn] N *Bot* vid *f*; *(against wall)* parra *f*; *Fam* **I heard it on** *or* **through the g.** me enteré por ahí

graph [grɑːf, græf] N gráfica *f*

graphic ['græfɪk] ADJ gráfico(a); **g. arts** artes gráficas; **g. designer** grafista *mf*

graphics ['græfɪks] **1** N *(study)* grafismo *m*
2 NPL *Comput* gráficas *fpl*

grapple ['græpəl] **1** VI *(struggle)* luchar cuerpo a cuerpo (**with** con); *Fig* **to g. with a problem** intentar resolver un problema
2 N *(hook)* garfio *m*

grasp [grɑːsp] **1** VT (**a**) *(hold firmly)* agarrar, asir (**b**) *(understand)* comprender
2 N (**a**) *(grip)* agarrón *f* (**b**) *(understanding)* comprensión *f*; **within sb's g.** al alcance de algn

grasping ['grɑːspɪŋ] ADJ avaro(a)

grass [grɑːs] N hierba *f*; *(lawn)* césped *m*; *Fig* **g. roots** base *f*
▸ **grass over** VI cubrirse de hierba

grasshopper ['grɑːshɒpə(r)] N saltamontes *m inv*

grassland ['grɑːslænd] N pradera *f*

grass-roots ['grɑːsruːts] ADJ de base; **at g. level** a nivel popular

grassy ['grɑːsɪ] ADJ (**grassier, grassiest**) cubierto(a) de hierba

grate¹ [greɪt] **1** VT *Culin* rallar
2 VI chirriar

grate² [greɪt] N (**a**) *(in fireplace)* rejilla *f* (**b**) *(fireplace)* chimenea *f* (**c**) *Constr* rejilla *f*, reja *f*

grateful ['greɪtfʊl] ADJ agradecido(a); **to be g. for** agradecer

grater ['greɪtə(r)] N *Culin* rallador *m*

gratification [grætɪfɪ'keɪʃən] N *(pleasure)* placer *m*, satisfacción *f*

gratify ['grætɪfaɪ] VT (**a**) *(please)* complacer (**b**) *(yield to)* sucumbir a

gratifying ['grætɪfaɪɪŋ] ADJ grato(a)

grating¹ ['greɪtɪŋ] N rejilla *f*, reja *f*

grating² ['greɪtɪŋ] ADJ chirriante; *(tone)* áspero(a)

gratis ['greɪtɪs, 'grætɪs] ADV gratis

gratitude ['grætɪtjuːd] N agradecimiento *m*

gratuitous [grə'tjuːɪtəs] ADJ gratuito(a)

gratuity [grə'tjuːɪtɪ] N gratificación *f*

grave¹ [greɪv] N sepultura *f*, tumba *f*

grave² [greɪv] ADJ *(look etc)* serio(a); *(situation)* grave

gravel ['grævəl] N grava *f*, gravilla *f*

gravestone ['greɪvstəʊn] N lápida *f* sepulcral

graveyard ['greɪvjɑːd] N cementerio *m*

gravity ['grævɪtɪ] N gravedad *f*

gravy ['greɪvɪ] N salsa *f*, jugo *m* (de la carne)

gray [greɪ] ADJ & N *US* = **grey**

graze¹ [greɪz] VI pacer, pastar

graze² [greɪz] **1** VT *(scratch)* rasguñar; *(brush against)* rozar
2 N rasguño *m*

grease [griːs, griːz] **1** N grasa *f*
2 VT engrasar

greaseproof ['griːspruːf] ADJ *Br* **g. paper** papel graso

greasy ['griːsɪ, 'griːzɪ] ADJ (**greasier, greasiest**) (**a**) *(oily)* grasiento(a); *(hair, food)* graso(a) (**b**) *(slippery)* resbaladizo(a) (**c**) *Fam (manner)* adulador(a), *Méx, RP* arrastrado(a)

great [greɪt] **1** ADJ (**a**) *(large, important)* grande; *(before singular noun)* gran; *(pain, heat)* fuerte; **a g. many** muchos(as); **G. Britain** Gran Bretaña; *Br* **G. Bear** Osa *f* Mayor (**b**) *Fam (excellent)* genial, *Am salvo RP* chévere, *Méx* padre, *RP* bárbaro(a); **to have a g. time** pasarlo muy bien
2 ADV *Fam* muy bien, estupendamente

great-aunt [greɪt'ɑːnt] N tía abuela

great-grandchild [greɪt'grænt∫aɪld] N bisnieto(a) m,f

great-grandfather [greɪt'grænfɑːðə(r)] N bisabuelo m

great-grandmother [greɪt'grænmʌðə(r)] N bisabuela f

greatly ['greɪtlɪ] ADV muy, mucho

greatness ['greɪtnɪs] N grandeza f

great-uncle [greɪt'ʌŋkəl] N tío abuelo

Greece [griːs] N Grecia

greed [griːd], **greediness** ['griːdɪnɪs] N (for food) gula f; (for money) codicia f, avaricia f

greedy ['griːdɪ] ADJ (**greedier, greediest**) (for food) glotón(ona); (for money) codicioso(a) (for de)

Greek [griːk] 1 ADJ griego(a)
2 N (**a**) (person) griego(a) m,f (**b**) (language) griego m

green [griːn] 1 N (**a**) (colour) verde m (**b**) (in golf) campo m; **village g.** plaza f (del pueblo) (**c**) **greens** (vegetables) verdura(s) f(pl)
2 ADJ (**a**) (colour) verde; **g. bean** judía f verde, Bol, RP chaucha f, CAm ejote m, Col, Cuba habichuela f, Chile poroto m verde, Ven vainita f; **g. belt** zona f verde; US **g. card** (work permit) permiso m de trabajo; **she was g. with envy** se la comía la envidia (**b**) (inexperienced) verde, novato(a); (gullible) crédulo(a) (**c**) Pol **G. Party** Partido m Verde

greenery ['griːnərɪ] N follaje m

greenfly ['griːnflaɪ] N pulgón m

greengage ['griːngeɪdʒ] N ciruela claudia

greengrocer ['griːngrəʊsə(r)] N Br verdulero(a) m,f

greenhouse ['griːnhaʊs] N invernadero m; **effect** efecto invernadero

greenish ['griːnɪ∫] ADJ verdoso(a)

Greenland ['griːnlənd] N Groenlandia

greet [griːt] VT (wave at) saludar; (receive) recibir; (welcome) dar la bienvenida a

greeting ['griːtɪŋ] N saludo m; **New Year/ birthday greetings** felicitaciones fpl de Año Nuevo/cumpleaños; Br **greetings** or US **g. card** tarjeta f de felicitación

gregarious [grɪ'geərɪəs] ADJ gregario(a), sociable

Grenada [gre'neɪdə] N Granada

grenade [grɪ'neɪd] N granada f

grew [gruː] PT of **grow**

grey [greɪ] 1 ADJ (colour) gris; (hair) cano(a); (sky) nublado(a); **g. matter** materia f gris
2 N (**a**) (colour) gris m (**b**) (horse) caballo m tordo

grey-haired ['greɪheəd] ADJ canoso(a)

greyhound ['greɪhaʊnd] N galgo m

greyish ['greɪɪ∫] ADJ grisáceo(a)

grid [grɪd] N (**a**) (on map) cuadrícula f (**b**) (of electricity etc) red f nacional (**c**) (for cooking) parrilla f

griddle ['grɪdəl] N (for cooking) plancha f

gridiron ['grɪdaɪən] N Culin parrilla f

grief [griːf] N dolor m, pena f; Fam **to come to g.** (car, driver) sufrir un accidente; (plans) irse al traste

grievance ['griːvəns] N (wrong) agravio m; (resentment) queja f

grieve [griːv] 1 VT apenar, dar pena a
2 VI apenarse, afligirse; **to g. for sb** llorar la muerte de algn

grievous ['griːvəs] ADJ (offence) grave; Br Jur **g. bodily harm** lesiones fpl corporales graves

grill [grɪl] 1 VT (**a**) Culin asar (a la parrilla) (**b**) Fam (interrogate) interrogar duramente
2 N Br (on cooker) grill m; (for open fire) parrilla f; (dish) parrillada f

grill(e) [grɪl] N (grating) reja f

grim [grɪm] ADJ (**grimmer, grimmest**) (**a**) (sinister) macabro(a); (landscape) lúgubre (**b**) (person) ceñudo(a) (**c**) Fam (unpleasant) desagradable

grimace [grɪ'meɪs] 1 N mueca f
2 VI hacer una mueca

grime [graɪm] N mugre f, porquería f

grimy ['graɪmɪ] ADJ (**grimier, grimiest**) mugriento(a)

grin [grɪn] 1 VI sonreír abiertamente
2 N sonrisa abierta

grind [graɪnd] 1 VT (pt & pp **ground**) (mill) moler; (crush) triturar; (sharpen) afilar; US (meat) picar
2 VI (**a**) (wheels, gears) chirriar; **to g. to a halt** (vehicle) pararse lentamente; (production etc) pararse poco a poco (**b**) US Fam empollar
3 N (**a**) Fam **the daily g.** la rutina cotidiana (**b**) US Fam (studious pupil) empollón(ona) m,f
▸ **grind down** VT SEP Fig **to g. down the opposition** acabar con la oposición

grinder ['graɪndə(r)] N (for coffee, pepper) molinillo m; (crusher) trituradora f; (for sharpening) afilador m

grip [grɪp] 1 N (**a**) (hold) agarrón m; (handshake) apretón m; **to get to grips with a problem** superar un problema (**b**) (handle) (of oar, handlebars, racket) empuñadura f (**c**) US (bag) bolsa f de viaje
2 VT (**a**) (seize) agarrar, asir; (hand) apretar (**b**) Fig (of film, story) captar la atención de; **to be gripped by fear** ser presa del miedo

gripe [graɪp] 1 VI Fam (complain) quejarse
2 N (**a**) Med (pain) retortijón m (**b**) Fam (complaint) queja f

gripping ['grɪpɪŋ] ADJ (film, story) apasionante

grisly ['grɪzlɪ] ADJ (**grislier, grisliest**) espeluznante

gristle ['grɪsəl] N cartílago m, ternilla f

grit [grɪt] **1** N (**a**) *(gravel)* grava *f* (**b**) *Fam (courage)* valor *m*
2 VT *Fig* **to g. one's teeth** apretar los dientes

gritty ['grɪtɪ] ADJ (**grittier, grittiest**) valiente

grizzly ['grɪzlɪ] ADJ **g. bear** oso pardo

groan [grəʊn] **1** N (**a**) *(of pain)* gemido *m* (**b**) *Fam (of disapproval)* gruñido *m*
2 VI (**a**) *(in pain)* gemir (**b**) *Fam (complain)* quejarse (**about** de)

grocer ['grəʊsə(r)] N tendero(a) *m,f; Br* **g.'s (shop)** tienda *f* de comestibles *or* de ultramarinos, *Andes, CSur* bodega *f, CAm, Méx* (tienda *f* de) abarrotes *mpl*

groceries ['grəʊsərɪz] NPL comestibles *mpl*

grocery ['grəʊsərɪ] N *esp US* **g. (store)** tienda *f* de comestibles *or* de ultramarinos, *Andes, CSur* bodega *f, CAm, Méx* (tienda *f* de) abarrotes *mpl*

groggy ['grɒgɪ] ADJ (**groggier, groggiest**) *Fam (boxer)* grogui; *Fig (unsteady)* atontado(a); *(weak)* débil

groin [grɔɪn] N ingle *f*

groom [gruːm] **1** N (**a**) *(of horse)* mozo *m* de cuadra (**b**) *(bridegroom)* novio *m*
2 VT *(horse)* almohazar; *(clothes, appearance)* cuidar

groove [gruːv] N *(furrow etc)* ranura *f;* *(of record)* surco *m*

grope [grəʊp] VI (**a**) *(search about)* andar a tientas; **to g. for sth** buscar algo a tientas (**b**) *Fam (fondle)* meter mano

gross [grəʊs] **1** ADJ (**a**) *(fat)* muy gordo(a) (**b**) *(vulgar) (joke, person)* basto(a), grosero(a) (**c**) *(blatant) (indecency, incompetence)* tremendo(a); *(error, ignorance)* craso(a) (**d**) *(profit, income)* bruto(a); *Econ* **g. national product** producto nacional bruto
2 VT *(earn)* ganar en bruto

grossly ['grəʊslɪ] ADV enormemente

grotesque [grəʊˈtesk] ADJ grotesco(a)

grotto ['grɒtəʊ] N gruta *f*

ground¹ [graʊnd] **1** N (**a**) *(earth)* suelo *m*, tierra *f;* **at g. level** al nivel del suelo; *Br* **g. floor** planta baja (**b**) *(land)* terreno *m* (**c**) *US Elec* toma *f* de tierra (**d**) **grounds** *(gardens)* jardines *mpl* (**e**) **grounds** *(reason)* motivo *m* (**f**) **grounds** *(sediment)* poso *m*
2 VT (**a**) *Av* obligar a quedarse en tierra; *Naut* varar (**b**) *US Elec* conectar con tierra

ground² [graʊnd] **1** ADJ *(coffee)* molido(a); *US (meat) Esp, RP* picado(a); *Am* molido(a)
2 PT & PP *of* **grind**

grounding ['graʊndɪŋ] N base *f;* **to have a good g. in** tener buenos conocimientos de

groundless ['graʊndlɪs] ADJ infundado(a)

groundsheet ['graʊndʃiːt] N *Br (of tent)* suelo *m*

groundsman ['graʊndzmən] N *Br* encargado(a) *m,f* del mantenimiento del campo de juego

groundwork ['graʊndwɜːk] N trabajo preparatorio

group [gruːp] **1** N grupo *m*, conjunto *m*
2 VT agrupar, juntar (**into** en)
3 VI **to g. (together)** agruparse, juntarse

grouse¹ [graʊs] N *(bird)* urogallo *m*

grouse² [graʊs] *Fam* **1** VI quejarse (**about** de)
2 N queja *f*

grove [grəʊv] N arboleda *f*

grovel ['grɒvəl] VI *(pt & pp* **grovelled**, *US* **groveled**) humillarse (**to** ante); *(crawl)* arrastrarse (**to** ante)

grow [grəʊ] **1** VT *(pt* **grew**; *pp* **grown**) *(cultivate)* cultivar; **to g. a beard** dejarse (crecer) la barba
2 VI (**a**) *(increase in size)* crecer (**b**) *(become)* hacerse, volverse; **to g. accustomed to** acostumbrarse a; **to g. dark** oscurecer; **to g. old** envejecer
▸ **grow out of** VT INSEP (**a**) **he's grown out of his shirt** se le ha quedado pequeña la camisa (**b**) *Fig (phase etc)* superar
▸ **grow up** VI crecer, hacerse mayor

grower ['grəʊə(r)] N cultivador(a) *m,f*

growing ['grəʊɪŋ] ADJ *(child)* que crece; *(problem etc)* creciente; **he's a g. boy** está dando el estirón

growl [graʊl] **1** VI gruñir
2 N gruñido *m*

grown [grəʊn] **1** ADJ crecido(a), adulto(a)
2 PP *of* **grow**

grown-up ['grəʊnʌp] ADJ & N adulto(a) *(m,f);* **the grown-ups** los mayores

growth [grəʊθ] N (**a**) *(increase in size)* crecimiento *m;* *(development)* desarrollo *m* (**b**) *(lump)* bulto *m*

grub [grʌb] N (**a**) *(larva)* gusano *m* (**b**) *Fam (food)* papeo *m*

grubby ['grʌbɪ] ADJ (**grubbier, grubbiest**) sucio(a)

grudge [grʌdʒ] **1** N rencor *m;* **to bear sb a g.** guardar rencor a algn
2 VT *(give unwillingly)* dar a regañadientes; **he grudges me my success** me envidia el éxito

grudgingly ['grʌdʒɪŋlɪ] ADV a regañadientes

gruelling, *US* **grueling** ['gruːəlɪŋ] ADJ penoso(a)

gruesome ['gruːsəm] ADJ espantoso(a), horrible

gruff [grʌf] ADJ *(manner)* brusco(a); *(voice)* áspero(a)

grumble ['grʌmbəl] **1** VI refunfuñar
2 N queja *f*

grumpy ['grʌmpɪ] ADJ (**grumpier, grumpiest**) gruñón(ona)

grunt [grʌnt] **1** VI gruñir
2 N gruñido *m*

guarantee [gærənˈtiː] **1** N garantía *f;* *(certificate)* certificado *m* de garantía
2 VT garantizar; *(assure)* asegurar

guard [gɑːd] **1** VT (**a**) *(protect)* defender, proteger; *(keep watch over)* vigilar (**b**) *(control)* guardar

2 VI protegerse (**against** de or contra)

3 N (**a**) to be on one's **g.** estar en guardia; **to catch sb off his g.** pillar or Esp coger or Am agarrar desprevenido a algn (**b**) (sentry) guardia mf; **g. dog** perro m guardián (**c**) Br Rail jefe m de tren; **g.'s van** furgón m de cola (**d**) (on machine) dispositivo m de seguridad; **fire g.** pantalla f

guarded ['gɑːdɪd] ADJ cauteloso(a), precavido(a)

guardhouse ['gɑːdhaʊs] N Mil (**a**) (headquarters) cuerpo m de guardia (**b**) (prison) prisión f militar

guardian ['gɑːdɪən] N (**a**) (of standards) guardián(ana) m,f; **g. angel** ángel m de la guarda (**b**) Jur (of minor) tutor(a) m,f

Guatemala [gwɑːtə'mɑːlə] N Guatemala

Guatemalan [gwɑːtə'mɑːlən] ADJ & N guatemalteco(a) (m,f)

guava ['gwɑːvə] N Bot guayaba f; **g. tree** guayabo m

guer(r)illa [gə'rɪlə] N guerrillero(a) m,f; **g. warfare** guerra f de guerrillas

guess [ges] **1** VT & VI (**a**) (estimate) adivinar; **I guessed as much** me lo imaginaba; **to g. right/wrong** acertar/no acertar (**b**) (suppose) suponer; **I g. so** supongo que sí
2 N conjetura f; (estimate) cálculo m; **at a rough g.** a ojo de buen cubero; **to have** or **make a g.** intentar adivinar

guesswork ['geswɜːk] N conjetura f

guest [gest] N (at home) invitado(a) m,f; (in hotel) cliente(a) m,f, huésped(a) m,f; **g. artist** artista mf invitado(a); **g. room** cuarto m de los invitados

guesthouse ['gesthaʊs] N casa f de huéspedes

guffaw [gʌ'fɔː] VI reírse a carcajadas

guidance ['gaɪdəns] N orientación f, consejos mpl; **for your g.** a título de información

guide [gaɪd] **1** VT guiar, dirigir
2 N (**a**) (person) guía mf; Br **girl g.** exploradora f; **g. dog** perro m lazarillo (**b**) (guidebook) guía f

guidebook ['gaɪdbʊk] N guía f

guided ['gaɪdɪd] ADJ dirigido(a); **g. tour** visita con guía; **g. missile** misil m teledirigido

guideline ['gaɪdlaɪn] N pauta f

guild [gɪld] N gremio m

guile [gaɪl] N astucia f

guillotine ['gɪlətiːn] N guillotina f

guilt [gɪlt] N (**a**) (blame) culpa f (**b**) (emotion) culpabilidad f

guilty ['gɪltɪ] ADJ (**guiltier, guiltiest**) culpable (**of** de); **to have a g. conscience** remorderle a uno la conciencia

guinea¹ ['gɪnɪ] N **g. pig** conejillo m de Indias, cobayo m; Fig **to act as a g. pig** servir de conejillo de Indias

guinea² ['gɪnɪ] N Br (coin) guinea f (= 21 chelines)

guise [gaɪz] N **under the g. of** so pretexto de

guitar [gɪ'tɑː(r)] N guitarra f

guitarist [gɪ'tɑːrɪst] N guitarrista mf

gulf [gʌlf] N (**a**) (bay) golfo m; **G. of Mexico** Golfo de Méjico; **G. Stream** corriente f del Golfo de Méjico; **the G. War** la guerra del Golfo (**b**) Fig abismo m

gull [gʌl] N gaviota f

gulley ['gʌlɪ] N = gully

gullible ['gʌləbəl] ADJ crédulo(a)

gully ['gʌlɪ] N barranco m, hondonada f

gulp [gʌlp] **1** N trago m
2 VT tragar; **to g. sth down** (drink) tomarse algo de un trago; (food) engullir algo
3 VI (**a**) (swallow air) tragar aire (**b**) Fig (with fear) tragar saliva

gum¹ [gʌm] **1** N (**a**) (adhesive) goma f (**b**) Br (sweet) chicle m
2 VT pegar con goma

gum² [gʌm] N Anat encía f

gumboot ['gʌmbuːt] N bota f de agua or goma or Méx, Ven caucho

gun [gʌn] N arma f de fuego; (handgun) pistola f, revólver m; (rifle) fusil m, escopeta f; (cannon) cañón m; Fam **the big guns** los peces gordos
▶ **gun down** VT SEP matar a tiros

gunboat ['gʌnbəʊt] N cañonera f

gunfire ['gʌnfaɪə(r)] N tiros mpl

gunman ['gʌnmən] N pistolero m, gángster m

gunpoint ['gʌnpɔɪnt] N **at g.** a punta de pistola

gunpowder ['gʌnpaʊdə(r)] N pólvora f

gunrunner ['gʌnrʌnə(r)] N traficante mf de armas

gunshot ['gʌnʃɒt] N disparo m, tiro m

gunsmith ['gʌnsmɪθ] N armero m

gurgle ['gɜːgəl] VI (baby) gorjear; (liquid) gorgotear; (stream) murmurar

guru ['gʊruː, 'gʊːruː] N gurú m

gush [gʌʃ] **1** VI (**a**) (spurt, pour) manar, correr (**b**) Fig **to g. about sth** hablar con excesiva entusiasmo de algo
2 N (of water) chorro m; (of words) torrente m

gushing ['gʌʃɪŋ] ADJ Fig (person) efusivo(a)

gusset ['gʌsɪt] N escudete m

gust [gʌst] N (of wind) ráfaga f, racha f

gusto ['gʌstəʊ] N entusiasmo m

gut [gʌt] **1** N (**a**) Anat intestino m (**b**) guts (entrails) tripas fpl; Fam **to have guts** tener agallas
2 VT (**a**) (fish) destripar (**b**) (destroy) destruir por dentro
3 ADJ Fam **g. reaction** reacción f visceral

gutter ['gʌtə(r)] N (in street) arroyo m; (on roof) canalón m; Fig **g. press** prensa amarilla

guttural ['gʌtərəl] ADJ gutural

guy¹ [gaɪ] N Fam (man) tipo m, Esp tío m

guy² [gaɪ] N (rope) viento m, cuerda f

guzzle ['gʌzəl] VT & VI *Fam (food etc)* zamparse; *(car)* tragar mucho

gym [dʒɪm] N *Fam* (**a**) *(gymnasium)* gimnasio *m* (**b**) *(gymnastics)* gimnasia *f*; **g. shoes** zapatillas *fpl* de deporte

gymnasium [dʒɪm'neɪzɪəm] N gimnasio *m*

gymnast ['dʒɪmnæst] N gimnasta *mf*

gymnastics [dʒɪm'næstɪks] N SING gimnasia *f*

gynaecologist, *US* **gynecologist** [gaɪnɪ'kɒlədʒɪst] N ginecólogo(a) *m,f*

gypsy ['dʒɪpsɪ] ADJ & N gitano(a) *(m,f)*

gyrate [dʒaɪ'reɪt] VI girar

H, h [eɪtʃ] N (*the letter*) H, h f

haberdashery [ˈhæbəˈdæʃərɪ] N (**a**) *Br* (*sewing items, shop*) mercería f de caballero (**b**) *US* (*men's clothes*) ropa f de caballero; (*shop*) tienda f de confección de caballero

habit [ˈhæbɪt] N (**a**) (*custom*) hábito m, costumbre f (**b**) (*garment*) hábito m

habitable [ˈhæbɪtəbəl] ADJ habitable

habitat [ˈhæbɪtæt] N hábitat m

habitual [həˈbɪtjʊəl] ADJ habitual; (*drinker, liar*) empedernido(a)

habitually [həˈbɪtjʊəlɪ] ADV por costumbre

hack¹ [hæk] **1** N (*cut*) corte m; (*with axe*) hachazo m
2 VT (*with knife, axe*) cortar; (*kick*) dar un puntapié a

hack² [hæk] N *Fam* (*writer*) escritorzuelo(a) m,f; (*journalist*) gacetillero(a) m,f

hacker [ˈhækə(r)] N *Comput* pirata mf informático(a), hacker mf

hackneyed [ˈhæknɪd] ADJ trillado(a)

hacksaw [ˈhæksɔː] N sierra f para metales

had [hæd] PT & PP *of* have

haddock [ˈhædək] N abadejo m

haemophilia [hiːməʊˈfɪlɪə] N hemofilia f

haemophiliac [hiːməʊˈfɪlɪæk] ADJ & N hemofílico(a) (*m,f*)

haemorrhage [ˈhemərɪdʒ] N hemorragia f

haemorrhoids [ˈhemərɔɪdz] NPL hemorroides fpl

hag [hæg] N *Pej* bruja f, arpía f

haggard [ˈhægəd] ADJ ojeroso(a)

haggle [ˈhægəl] VI regatear

Hague [heɪg] N **The H.** La Haya

hail¹ [heɪl] **1** N granizo m; *Fig* **a h. of bullets/insults** una lluvia de balas/insultos
2 VI granizar

hail² [heɪl] **1** VT (**a**) (*taxi etc*) parar (**b**) (*acclaim*) aclamar
2 VI **to h. from** (*originate*) ser nativo(a) de

hailstone [ˈheɪlstəʊn] N granizo m

hailstorm [ˈheɪlstɔːm] N granizada f

hair [heə(r)] N (*strand*) pelo m, cabello m; (*mass*) pelo, cabellos mpl; (*on arm, leg*) vello m; **to have long h.** tener el pelo largo

hairbrush [ˈheəbrʌʃ] N cepillo m (para el pelo)

haircut [ˈheəkʌt] N corte m de pelo; **to have a h.** cortarse el pelo

hairdo [ˈheəduː] N *Fam* peinado m

hairdresser [ˈheədresə(r)] N peluquero(a) m,f; **h.'s (shop)** peluquería f

hairdryer, hairdrier [ˈheədraɪə(r)] N secador m (de pelo)

hairgrip [ˈheəɡrɪp] N *Br* horquilla f

hairline [ˈheəlaɪn] **1** ADJ muy fino(a)
2 N nacimiento m del pelo; **receding h.** entradas fpl

hairnet [ˈheənet] N redecilla f

hairpiece [ˈheəpiːs] N postizo m

hairpin [ˈheəpɪn] N horquilla f; **h. bend** curva muy cerrada

hair-raising [ˈheəreɪzɪŋ] ADJ espeluznante

hair-remover [ˈheərɪmuːvə(r)] N depilatorio m

hairspray [ˈheəspreɪ] N laca f (para el pelo)

hairstyle [ˈheəstaɪl] N peinado m, corte m de pelo

hairy [ˈheərɪ] ADJ (**hairier, hairiest**) (**a**) (*with hair*) peludo(a) (**b**) *Fig* (*frightening*) enervante, espantoso(a)

hake [heɪk] N merluza f; (*young*) pescadilla f

half [hɑːf] **1** N (*pl* halves) mitad f; *Sport* (*period*) tiempo m; **he's four and a h.** tiene cuatro años y medio; **to cut in h.** cortar por la mitad
2 ADJ medio(a); **h. a dozen/an hour** media docena/hora; **h. board** media pensión; **h. fare** media tarifa; **h. term** medio trimestre
3 ADV medio, a medias; **h. asleep** medio dormido(a)

half-caste [ˈhɑːfkɑːst] ADJ & N mestizo(a) (*m,f*)

half-day [hɑːfˈdeɪ] N media jornada

half-hearted [hɑːfˈhɑːtɪd] ADJ ppco entusiasta

half-hour [hɑːfˈaʊə(r)] N media hora

half-life [ˈhɑːflaɪf] N media vida

half-mast [hɑːfˈmɑːst] N *Br* **at h.** a media asta

half-price [hɑːfˈpraɪs] ADV a mitad de precio

half-time [hɑːfˈtaɪm] N descanso m

half-way [hɑːfˈweɪ] **1** ADJ intermedio(a)
2 ADV **halfway** [hɑːfˈweɪ] ADV a medio camino, a mitad de camino

half-yearly [ˈhɑːfjɪəlɪ] ADJ semestral

halibut [ˈhælɪbət] N mero m

hall [hɔːl] N (**a**) (*lobby*) vestíbulo m (**b**) (*building*) sala f; *Br Univ* **h. of residence** residencia f de estudiantes, *Esp* colegio m mayor

hallmark [ˈhɔːlmɑːk] N (**a**) (*on gold, silver*) contraste m (**b**) *Fig* sello m

hallo [həˈləʊ] INTERJ ¡hola!

hallowed ['hæləʊd] ADJ santificado(a)

Hallowe(')en [hæləʊ'iːn] N víspera f de Todos los Santos

hallucinate [hə'luːsɪneɪt] VI alucinar

hallucination [həluːsɪ'neɪʃən] N alucinación f

hallucinogenic [həluːsɪnəʊ'dʒenɪk] ADJ alucinógeno(a)

hallway ['hɔːlweɪ] N vestíbulo m

halo ['heɪləʊ] N (a) Rel aureola f (b) Astron halo m

halt [hɔːlt] 1 N (stop) alto m, parada f; **to call a h. to sth** poner fin a algo
2 VT parar
3 VI pararse

halting ['hɔːltɪŋ] ADJ vacilante

halve [hɑːv] VT (a) (divide in two) dividir (en dos); (cake, fruit) partir por la mitad (b) (reduce by half) reducir a la mitad

halves [hɑːvz] PL of **half**

ham [hæm] N jamón m; **boiled h.** jamón de York; **Parma** or **cured h.** jamón serrano

hamburger ['hæmbɜːgə(r)] N hamburguesa f

hamlet ['hæmlɪt] N aldea f

hammer ['hæmə(r)] 1 N (a) (tool) & Sport martillo m; (b) (of gun) percutor m
2 VT (a) (hit with hammer) martillear; Fig **to h. home** insistir sobre (b) Fam (defeat) dar una paliza a
3 VI martillar, dar golpes

hammering ['hæmərɪŋ] N Fam paliza f

hammock ['hæmək] N hamaca f; Naut coy m

hamper¹ ['hæmpə(r)] N cesta f

hamper² ['hæmpə(r)] VT estorbar, dificultar

hamster ['hæmstə(r)] N hámster m

hamstring ['hæmstrɪŋ] N tendón m de la corva

hand [hænd] 1 N (a) (part of body) mano f; **by h.** a mano; **(close) at h.** a mano; **hands up!** ¡manos arriba!; **on the one/other h.** por una/otra parte; Fig **to get out of h.** descontrolarse; Fig **to wash one's hands of sth** lavarse las manos de algo; Fig **to give sb a h.** echarle una mano a algn; **h. grenade** granada f de mano (b) (worker) trabajador(a) m,f; Naut tripulante m (c) (of clock) manecilla f (d) (handwriting) letra f
2 VT (give) dar, entregar
▶ **hand back** VT SEP devolver
▶ **hand down** VT SEP dejar en herencia
▶ **hand in** VT SEP (homework) entregar; (resignation) presentar
▶ **hand out** VT SEP repartir
▶ **hand over** VT SEP entregar
▶ **hand round** VT SEP repartir

handbag ['hændbæg] N Br (woman's) Esp bolso m, Col, CSur cartera f, Méx bolsa f

handball ['hændbɔːl] N Sport balonmano m

handbook ['hændbʊk] N manual m

handbrake ['hændbreɪk] N freno m de mano

handcuff ['hændkʌf] 1 VT esposar
2 NPL **handcuffs** esposas fpl

handful ['hændfʊl] N puñado m

handicap ['hændɪkæp] 1 N (a) Med minusvalía f (b) Sport hándicap m, desventaja f
2 VT impedir

handicapped ['hændɪkæpt] ADJ (a) (physically) minusválido(a); (mentally) retrasado(a) (b) Sport en desventaja (c) Fig desfavorecido(a)

handicraft ['hændɪkrɑːft] N artesanía f

handiwork ['hændɪwɜːk] N (work) obra f; (craft) artesanía f

handkerchief ['hæŋkətʃiːf] N pañuelo m

handle ['hændəl] 1 N (of knife) mango m; (of cup) asa f; (of door) pomo m; (of drawer) tirador m
2 VT (a) (touch, hold) manejar; **h. with care** (sign) frágil (b) (problem) encargarse de; (people) tratar; Fam (put up with) soportar

handlebars ['hændəlbɑːz] N (of bicycle, motorbike) manillar m, Am manubrio m

handmade [hænd'meɪd] ADJ hecho(a) a mano

hand-out ['hændaʊt] N (a) (leaflet) folleto m; Press nota f de prensa (b) (charity) limosna f

hand-picked [hænd'pɪkt] ADJ selecto(a)

handrail ['hændreɪl] N pasamanos m inv, baranda f, Esp barandilla f

hands-free ['hænzfriː] ADJ (telephone) de manos libres

handshake ['hændʃeɪk] N apretón m de manos

handsome ['hænsəm] ADJ (a) (person) guapo(a) (b) (substantial) considerable

handwriting ['hændraɪtɪŋ] N letra f

handwritten ['hændrɪtən] ADJ manuscrito(a), escrito(a) a mano

handy ['hændɪ] ADJ (handier, handiest) (a) (useful) útil, práctico(a); (nearby) a mano (b) (dextrous) diestro(a)

handyman ['hændɪmæn] N (person good at odd jobs) persona f habilidosa, Esp manitas mf inv

hang [hæŋ] 1 VT (pt & pp hung) (a) (suspend) colgar (b) (head) bajar (c) (pt hanged) ahorcar
2 VI (a) (be suspended) colgar (from de); (in air) flotar (b) (criminal) ser ahorcado(a); **to h. oneself** ahorcarse
▶ **hang about, hang around** VI Fam (wait) esperar
▶ **hang on** VI (a) (hold) agarrarse (b) (wait) esperar
▶ **hang out** 1 VT SEP (washing) tender
2 VI Fam (frequent) frecuentar
▶ **hang round** VI Fam = **hang about**
▶ **hang together** VI (ideas) ser coherente
▶ **hang up** VT SEP (picture, telephone) colgar

hangar ['hæŋə(r)] N hangar m

hanger ['hæŋə(r)] N percha f

hang-glider ['hæŋglaɪdə(r)] N ala delta

hang-gliding ['hæŋglaɪdɪŋ] N vuelo m libre

hangman ['hæŋmən] N verdugo m

hangover ['hæŋəʊvə(r)] N resaca f

hang-up ['hæŋʌp] N *Fam (complex)* complejo m

hanker ['hæŋkə(r)] VI **to h. after sth** anhelar algo

hankie, hanky ['hæŋkɪ] N *Fam* pañuelo m

haphazard [hæp'hæzəd] ADJ caótico(a), desordenado(a)

happen ['hæpən] VI suceder, ocurrir; **it so happens that** lo que pasa es que; **if you h. to see my friend** si por casualidad ves a mi amigo

happening ['hæpənɪŋ] N acontecimiento m

happily ['hæpɪlɪ] ADV *(with pleasure)* felizmente; *(fortunately)* afortunadamente

happiness ['hæpɪnɪs] N felicidad f

happy ['hæpɪ] ADJ *(happier, happiest) (cheerful)* feliz, contento(a); *(fortunate)* afortunado(a); **h. birthday!** ¡feliz cumpleaños!

happy-go-lucky [hæpɪgəʊ'lʌkɪ] ADJ despreocupado(a); **a h. fellow** un viva la virgen

harangue [hə'ræŋ] **1** VT arengar
2 N arenga f

harass ['hærəs] VT acosar

harassment ['hærəsmənt, hə'ræsmənt] N hostigamiento m, acoso m

harbour, US harbor ['hɑːbə(r)] **1** N puerto m
2 VT **(a)** *(criminal)* encubrir **(b)** *(doubts)* abrigar

hard [hɑːd] **1** ADJ **(a)** *(substance)* duro(a); *Comput* **h. disk** disco duro f; *BrUS* **h. shoulder** *Esp* arcén m, *Andes* berma f, *Méx* acotamiento m, *RP* banquina f **(b)** *(difficult)* difícil; **h. of hearing** duro(a) de oído; *Fam Fig* **to be h. up** estar sin blanca **(c)** *(harsh)* severo(a); *(strict)* estricto(a); **h. drugs** drogas duras; *Pol* **h. left** extrema izquierda; **h. sell** promoción f de venta agresiva **(d)** **a h. worker** un trabajador concienzudo **(e)** **h. luck!** ¡mala suerte! **(f)** **h. evidence** pruebas definitivas; **h. currency** divisa f fuerte
2 ADV **(a)** *(hit)* fuerte **(b)** *(work)* mucho, concienzudamente

hardback ['hɑːdbæk] N edición f de tapas duras

hardball ['hɑːdbɔːl] N *US (baseball)* béisbol m

hard-boiled ['hɑːdbɔɪld] ADJ duro(a)

hard-core ['hɑːdkɔː(r)] ADJ irreductible

harden ['hɑːdən] **1** VT endurecer
2 VI endurecerse

hardened ['hɑːdənd] ADJ *Fig* habitual

hard-headed ['hɑːd'hedɪd] ADJ realista

hard-hearted [hɑːd'hɑːtɪd] ADJ insensible

hardliner [hɑːd'laɪnə(r)] N duro(a) m,f

hardly ['hɑːdlɪ] ADV apenas; **h. anyone/ever** casi nadie/nunca; **he had h. begun when …** apenas había comenzado cuando …; **I can h. believe it** apenas lo puedo creer

hardship ['hɑːdʃɪp] N privación f, apuro m

hardware ['hɑːdweə(r)] N **(a)** *(goods)* ferretería f; *US* **h. store** *(ironmonger's)* ferretería **(b)** *Comput* hardware m

hardwearing [hɑːd'weərɪŋ] ADJ duradero(a)

hardworking ['hɑːdwɜːkɪŋ] ADJ muy trabajador(a)

hardy ['hɑːdɪ] ADJ *(hardier, hardiest) (person)* robusto(a), fuerte; *(plant)* resistente

hare [heə(r)] **1** N liebre f
2 VI correr muy de prisa

haricot ['hærɪkəʊ] N **h. (bean)** alubia f blanca, *Esp* judía f blanca, *Am salvo RP* frijol m blanco, *Andes, RP* poroto m blanco

harm [hɑːm] **1** N daño m, perjuicio m; **to be out of h.'s way** estar a salvo
2 VT hacer daño a, perjudicar

harmful ['hɑːmfʊl] ADJ perjudicial **(to** para)

harmless ['hɑːmlɪs] ADJ inofensivo(a)

harmonica [hɑː'mɒnɪkə] N armónica f

harmonious [hɑː'məʊnɪəs] ADJ armonioso(a)

harmonize ['hɑːmənaɪz] VT & VI armonizar

harmony ['hɑːmənɪ] N armonía f

harness ['hɑːnɪs] **1** N *(for horse)* arreos mpl
2 VT **(a)** *(horse)* enjaezar **(b)** *Fig (resources etc)* aprovechar

harp [hɑːp] N arpa f

▶ **harp on** VI *Fam* hablar sin parar

harpoon [hɑː'puːn] **1** N arpón m
2 VT arponear

harrowing ['hærəʊɪŋ] ADJ angustioso(a)

harsh [hɑːʃ] ADJ severo(a); *(voice)* áspero(a); *(sound)* discordante

harvest ['hɑːvɪst] **1** N cosecha f; *(of grapes)* vendimia f
2 VT cosechar, recoger

harvester ['hɑːvɪstə(r)] N **(a)** *(person)* segador(a) m,f **(b)** *(machine)* cosechadora f

has [hæz] 3RD PERSON SING PRES of **have**

has-been ['hæzbiːn] N *Fam Pej* vieja gloria f

hash¹ [hæʃ] N *Culin* guiso m de carne con *Esp* patatas or *Am* papas, *Andes, Méx* ahogado m de carne con papas; *Fam Fig* **to make a h. of sth** hacer algo muy mal; **h. browns** = fritura de *Esp* patata or *Am* papa y cebolla

hash² [hæʃ] N *Fam* chocolate m, *Esp* costo m

hashish ['hæʃiːʃ] N hachís m

hassle ['hæsəl] *Fam* **1** N **(a)** *(trouble, inconvenience)* lío m, *Esp* follón m; **to give sb h.** dar la lata a algn **(b)** *(wrangle)* trifulca f
2 VT fastidiar

haste [heɪst] N *Fml* prisa f; **to make h.** darse prisa

hasten ['heɪsən] VI apresurarse

hastily ['heɪstɪlɪ] ADV *(quickly)* de prisa

hasty ['heɪstɪ] ADJ *(hastier, hastiest)* apresurado(a); *(rash)* precipitado(a)

hat [hæt] N sombrero m

hatch¹ [hætʃ] N escotilla f; **serving h.** ventanilla f

hatch² [hætʃ] **1** VT **(a)** *(eggs)* empollar **(b)** *Fig (plan)* tramar
2 VI **to h. (out)** salirse del huevo

hatchback ['hætʃbæk] N coche *m* de 3/5 puertas

hatchet ['hætʃɪt] N hacha *f*; *Fam* **h. man** matón *m*

hate [heɪt] **1** N odio *m*
2 VT odiar

hateful ['heɪtfʊl] ADJ odioso(a)

hatred ['heɪtrɪd] N odio *m*

haughty ['hɔːtɪ] ADJ (**haughtier**, **haughtiest**) altanero(a), arrogante

haul [hɔːl] **1** N (**a**) *(journey)* trayecto *m* (**b**) *(of fish)* redada *f* (**c**) *(loot)* botín *m*
2 VT (**a**) *(pull)* arrastrar (**b**) *(transport)* acarrear
▸ **haul up** VT SEP *Fam (to court)* llevar

haulage ['hɔːlɪdʒ] N transporte *m*

haulier ['hɔːljə(r)], *US* **hauler** ['hɔːlə(r)] N *(company)* empresa *f* de transportes, transportista *mf*

haunch [hɔːntʃ] N *(of person)* cadera *f*; **to sit or squat on one's haunches** ponerse en cuclillas

haunt [hɔːnt] **1** N guarida *f*
2 VT (**a**) *(of ghost)* aparecerse en (**b**) *Fig* atormentar (**c**) *(frequent)* frecuentar

haunted ['hɔːntɪd] ADJ encantado(a), embrujado(a)

Havana [hə'vænə] N La Habana; **H. cigar** habano *m*

have [hæv] *(3rd person sing pres* **has***; pt & pp* **had***)*

> En el inglés hablado, y en el escrito en estilo coloquial, el verbo auxiliar **have** se contrae de forma que **I have** se transforma en **I've**, **he/she/it has** se transforman en **he's/she's/it's** y **you/we/they have** se transforman en **you've/we've/they've**. Las formas de pasado **I/you/he** *etc* **had** se transforman en **I'd**, **you'd**, **he'd** *etc*. Las formas negativas **has not**, **have not** y **had not** se transforman en **hasn't**, **haven't** y **hadn't**.

1 VT (**a**) *(possess)* tener; **h. you got** or **do you h. a car?** ¿tienes coche?
(**b**) *(get, experience, suffer)* tener; **to h. a holiday** tomarse unas vacaciones
(**c**) *(partake of) (drink)* tomar; **to h. breakfast/dinner/lunch/tea** desayunar/cenar/comer/merendar; **to h. a bath/shave** bañarse/afeitarse
(**d**) *(+ to) (obligation)* tener que, deber
(**e**) *(make happen)* hacer que; **I'll h. someone come round** haré que venga alguien
(**f**) *(receive)* recibir; **to h. people round** invitar a gente
(**g**) *(party, meeting)* hacer, celebrar
(**h**) **to h. a baby** tener un niño
(**i**) **we won't h. it** *(allow)* no lo consentiremos
(**j**) *(hold)* tener; *Fig* **to h. sth against sb** tener algo en contra de algn
(**k**) *Fam (deceive)* engañar
(**l**) **you'd better stay** más vale que te quedes

2 VAUX (**a**) *(compound)* haber; **I had been waiting for half an hour** hacía media hora que esperaba; **he hasn't eaten yet** no ha comido aún; **she had broken the window** había roto el cristal; **we h. lived here for ten years** hace diez años que vivimos aquí; **so I h.!** *(emphatic)* ¡ay, sí!, es verdad; **yes I h.!** ¡que sí! (**b**) *(tag questions)* **you haven't seen my book, h. you?** no has visto mi libro, ¿verdad?; **he's been to France, hasn't he?** ha estado en Francia, ¿verdad? or ¿no? (**c**) *(have + just)* **to h. just done sth** acabar de hacer algo
▸ **have on** VT SEP (**a**) *(wear)* vestir (**b**) *Fam* **to h. sb on** tomarle el pelo or *Esp, Carib, Méx* vacilar a algn
▸ **have out** VT SEP *Fam* **to h. it out with sb** ajustar cuentas con algn
▸ **have over** VT SEP *(invite)* recibir

haven ['heɪvən] N puerto *m*; *Fig* refugio *m*

haversack ['hævəsæk] N mochila *f*

havoc ['hævək] N **to play h. with** hacer estragos en

hawk [hɔːk] N *(bird) & Pol* halcón *m*

hawker ['hɔːkə(r)] N vendedor(a) *m,f* ambulante

hawthorn ['hɔːθɔːn] N espino *m* albar

hay [heɪ] N heno *m*; **h. fever** fiebre *f* del heno

haystack ['heɪstæk] N almiar *m*

haywire ['heɪwaɪə(r)] ADJ *Fam* en desorden; **to go h.** *(machine etc)* estropearse; *(person)* volverse loco(a)

hazard ['hæzəd] **1** N peligro *m*, riesgo *m*; *(in golf)* obstáculo *m*
2 VT *Fml* arriesgar; **to h. a guess** intentar adivinar

hazardous ['hæzədəs] ADJ arriesgado(a), peligroso(a)

haze [heɪz] N *(mist)* neblina *f*; *Fig (blur)* confusión *f*

hazel ['heɪzəl] ADJ *(de color)* avellana

hazelnut ['heɪzəlnʌt] N avellana *f*

hazy ['heɪzɪ] ADJ (**hazier**, **haziest**) nebuloso(a)

he [hiː] PERS PRON él *(usually omitted in Spanish, except for contrast)*; **HE did it** ha sido él; **he who** el que el que

head [hed] **1** N (**a**) *(of person)* cabeza *f*; *(mind)* mente *f*; **£3 a h.** *(each)* 3 libras por cabeza; *Fig* **to lose one's h.** perder la cabeza; **success went to his h.** se le subió el éxito a cabeza (**b**) *(of nail)* cabeza *f*; *(of beer)* espuma *f* (**c**) *(boss)* cabeza *m*; *(of company)* director(a) *m,f*, *Br* **h. (teacher)** director(a) *m,f* (**d**) *(of coin)* cara *f*; **heads or tails** cara o cruz
2 ADJ principal; **h. office** oficina *f* central
3 VT (**a**) *(list etc)* encabezar (**b**) *Ftb* cabecear
▸ **head for** VT INSEP dirigirse hacia
▸ **head off 1** VI irse
2 VT SEP *(avert)* evitar

headache ['hedeɪk] N dolor *m* de cabeza; *Fig* quebradero *m* de cabeza

headband ['hedbænd] N cinta f para la cabeza

headcheese ['hedtʃiːz] N US queso m de cerdo

header ['hedə(r)] N *Ftb* cabezazo m

head-first [hed'fɜːst] ADV de cabeza

head-hunter ['hedhʌntə(r)] N *Fig* cazatalentos mf inv

heading ['hedɪŋ] N título m; (of letter) membrete m

headlamp ['hedlæmp] N faro m

headland ['hedlənd] N punta f, cabo m

headlight ['hedlaɪt] N faro m

headline ['hedlaɪn] N titular m; **the headlines** (on radio, TV) los titulares

headlong ['hedlɒŋ] ADJ & ADV de cabeza; **to rush h. into sth** lanzarse a hacer algo sin pensar

headmaster [hed'mɑːstə(r)] N director m

headmistress [hed'mɪstrɪs] N directora f

head-on ['hedɒn] ADJ **a h. collision** un choque frontal

headphones ['hedfəʊnz] NPL auriculares mpl

headquarters ['hedkwɔːtəz] NPL (a) (of organization) central f, sede f (b) *Mil* cuartel m general

headrest ['hedrest] N *Aut* apoyacabezas m inv

headroom ['hedruːm] N altura f libre

headscarf ['hedskɑːf] N pañuelo m

headstrong ['hedstrɒŋ] ADJ testarudo(a)

headway ['hedweɪ] N **to make h.** avanzar, progresar

headwind ['hedwɪnd] N viento m de proa

heady ['hedɪ] ADJ (**headier, headiest**) embriagador(a)

heal [hiːl] 1 VT (wound) curar
2 VI cicatrizar

health [helθ] N salud f; *Fig* prosperidad f; **to be in good/bad h.** estar bien/mal de salud; **your good h.!** ¡salud!; **h. foods** alimentos mpl naturales; **h. food shop** tienda f de alimentos naturales; *Br* **the H. Service** el sistema de sanidad pública británico

healthy ['helθɪ] ADJ (**healthier, healthiest**) sano(a); (good for health) saludable; (thriving) próspero(a)

heap [hiːp] 1 N montón m
2 VT amontonar; *Fig* **to h. praise on sb** colmar a algn de alabanzas; **a heaped spoonful** una cucharada colmada

hear [hɪə(r)] 1 VT (pt & pp **heard** [hɜːd]) (a) (perceive) oír (b) (listen to) escuchar (c) (find out) enterarse (d) *Jur* ver; (evidence) oír
2 VI **to h. from sb** tener noticias de algn

hearing ['hɪərɪŋ] N (a) (sense) oído m; **h. aid** audífono m (b) *Jur* audiencia f

hearsay ['hɪəseɪ] N rumores mpl

hearse [hɜːs] N coche m fúnebre

heart [hɑːt] N (a) (organ, seat of emotions) corazón m; **h. attack** infarto m de miocardio; *Med* **h. failure** insuficiencia cardíaca; **h. transplant** trasplante m de corazón; **a broken h.** un corazón roto; **at h.** en el fondo; **to take sth to h.** tomarse algo a pecho; **to have a good h.** (be kind) tener buen corazón (b) (courage, enthusiasm) valor m; **his h. wasn't in it** no ponía interés en ello; **to lose h.** desanimarse (c) (core) meollo m; (of lettuce) cogollo m

heartache ['hɑːteɪk] N dolor m, tristeza f

heartbeat ['hɑːtbiːt] N latido m del corazón

heart-breaking ['hɑːtbreɪkɪŋ] ADJ desgarrador(a)

heart-broken ['hɑːtbrəʊkən] ADJ hundido(a); **he's h.** tiene el corazón destrozado

heartburn ['hɑːtbɜːn] N acedía f

heartening ['hɑːtənɪŋ] ADJ alentador(a)

heartfelt ['hɑːtfelt] ADJ sincero(a)

hearth [hɑːθ] N (a) (fireplace) chimenea f (b) *Fml* (home) hogar m

heartless ['hɑːtlɪs] ADJ cruel, insensible

heart-throb ['hɑːtθrɒb] N ídolo m

hearty ['hɑːtɪ] ADJ (**heartier, heartiest**) (person) francote, (meal) abundante; (welcome) cordial; **to have a h. appetite** ser de buen comer

heat [hiːt] 1 N (a) (high temperature) calor m (b) *Sport* eliminatoria f (c) *Zool* **in** or *Br* **on h.** en celo
2 VT calentar
▶ **heat up** VI (a) (warm up) calentarse (b) (increase excitement) acalorarse

heated ['hiːtɪd] ADJ *Fig* (argument) acalorado(a)

heater ['hiːtə(r)] N calentador m

heath [hiːθ] N (land) brezal m

heathen ['hiːðən] ADJ & N pagano(a) (m,f)

heather ['heðə(r)] N brezo m

heating ['hiːtɪŋ] N calefacción f

heatwave ['hiːtweɪv] N ola f de calor

heave [hiːv] 1 N (pull) tirón m; (push) empujón m
2 VT (a) (lift) levantar; (haul) tirar; (push) empujar (b) (throw) arrojar
3 VI subir y bajar

heaven ['hevən] 1 N cielo m; **the heavens** (sky) cielo m; **for h.'s sake!** ¡por Dios!; **h. on earth** un paraíso en la tierra
2 INTERJ (**good**) **heavens!** ¡por Dios!

heavenly ['hevənlɪ] ADJ celestial

heavily ['hevɪlɪ] ADV **it rained h.** llovió mucho; **to sleep h.** dormir profundamente

heavy ['hevɪ] 1 ADJ (**heavier, heaviest**) pesado(a); (rain, meal) fuerte; (traffic) denso(a); (loss) grande; **h. going** duro(a); **is it h.?** ¿pesa mucho?; **a h. drinker/smoker** un(a) bebedor(a)/fumador(a) empedernido(a); *Mus* **h. metal** heavy metal m
2 N *Fam* gorila m

heavyweight ['hevɪweɪt] N peso pesado

Hebrew ['hi:bru:] **1** ADJ hebreo(a)
2 N *(person)* hebreo(a) *m,f*; *(language)* hebreo *m*

Hebrides ['hebrɪdi:z] NPL **the H.** las (Islas) Hébridas

heckle ['hekəl] VT interrumpir

heckler ['heklə(r)] N altercador(a) *m,f*

hectare ['hektɑ:(r)] N hectárea *f*

hectic ['hektɪk] ADJ agitado(a)

hedge [hedʒ] **1** N seto *m*
2 VT cercar con un seto; *Fig* **to h. one's bets** cubrirse

hedgehog ['hedʒhɒg] N erizo *m*

hedgerow ['hedʒrəʊ] N seto vivo

heed [hi:d] N **to take h. of** hacer caso de

heedless ['hi:dlɪs] ADJ desatento(a)

heel [hi:l] N *(of foot)* talón *m*; *(of shoe)* tacón *m*; *(of palm)* pulpejo *m*; *Fig* **to be on sb's heels** pisarle los talones a algn; **high heels** zapatos *mpl* de tacón alto

hefty ['heftɪ] ADJ (**heftier, heftiest**) (**a**) *(person)* fornido(a); *(package)* pesado(a) (**b**) *(large)* grande

height [haɪt] N *(of building, mountain, tree)* altura *f*; *(of person)* estatura *f*; **to gain/lose h.** subir/bajar; **what h. are you?** ¿cuánto mides?; *Fig* **the h. of ignorance** el colmo de la ignorancia

heighten ['haɪtən] VT *(intensify)* realzar; *(increase)* aumentar

heir [eə(r)] N heredero *m*

heiress ['eərɪs] N heredera *f*

heirloom ['eəlu:m] N reliquia *f*/joya *f* de familia

held [held] PT & PP of **hold**

helicopter ['helɪkɒptə(r)] N helicóptero *m*

helium ['hi:lɪəm] N helio *m*

hell [hel] N infierno *m*; *Fam* **what the h. are you doing?** ¿qué diablos estás haciendo?; *Fam Pej* **go to h.!** ¡vete a hacer puñetas!; *Fam* **a h. of a party** una fiesta estupenda; *Fam* **she's had a h. of a day** ha tenido un día fatal

hellish ['helɪʃ] ADJ *Fam* infernal

hello [hə'ləʊ, he'ləʊ] INTERJ ¡hola!; *(on phone)* *(when answering)* ¿sí?, ¿diga?, *Am* ¿aló?, *Méx* ¿bueno?; *(showing surprise)* ¡hala!

helm [helm] N timón *m*; **to be at the h.** llevar el timón

helmet ['helmɪt] N casco *m*

help [help] **1** N (**a**) *(aid)* ayuda *f*; **h.!** ¡socorro! (**b**) *(person)* (**daily**) **h.** asistenta *f*
2 VT (**a**) *(aid)* ayudar; **can I h. you?** *(in shop)* ¿qué desea? (**b**) *(alleviate)* aliviar (**c**) **h. yourself!** *(to food etc)* ¡sírvete! (**d**) *(avoid)* evitar; **I can't h. it** no lo puedo remediar

► **help out** VT SEP **to h. sb out** echarle una mano a algn

helper ['helpə(r)] N ayudante(a) *m,f*

helpful ['helpfʊl] ADJ *(person)* amable; *(thing)* útil

helping ['helpɪŋ] N ración *f*; **who wants a second h.?** ¿quién quiere repetir?

helpless ['helplɪs] ADJ *(defenceless)* desamparado(a); *(powerless)* incapaz

helplessly ['helplɪslɪ] ADV inútilmente, en vano

helpline ['helplaɪn] N teléfono *m* de asistencia *or* ayuda

helter-skelter [heltə'skeltə(r)] **1** N *Br (at fairground)* tobogán *m*
2 ADJ atropellado(a)
3 ADV atropelladamente

hem [hem] **1** N *Sewing* dobladillo *m*
2 VT *Sewing* hacer un dobladillo a

► **hem in** VT SEP cercar, rodear

hemisphere ['hemɪsfɪə(r)] N hemisferio *m*

hemophilia [hi:məʊ'fɪlɪə] N *US* = **haemophilia**

hemophiliac [hi:məʊ'fɪlɪæk] ADJ & N *US* = **haemophiliac**

hemorrhage ['hemərɪdʒ] N *US* = **haemorrhage**

hemorrhoids ['hemərɔɪdz] NPL *US* = **haemorrhoids**

hen [hen] N gallina *f*; *Fam* **h. party** reunión *f* de mujeres

hence [hens] ADV *Fml* (**a**) **six months h.** *(from now)* de aquí a seis meses (**b**) *(consequently)* por lo tanto

henceforth [hens'fɔ:θ] ADV *Fml* de ahora en adelante

henchman ['hentʃmən] N *Pej* secuaz *m*

henna ['henə] N *Bot* alheña *f*; *(dye)* henna *f*

henpecked ['henpekt] ADJ *Fam* **a h. husband** un calzonazos

hepatitis [hepə'taɪtɪs] N hepatitis *f*

her [hɜ:(r), *unstressed* hə(r)] **1** POSS ADJ *(one thing)* su; *(more than one)* sus; *(to distinguish)* de ella; **are they h. books or his?** ¿los libros son de ella o de él?; **she has cut h. finger** se ha cortado el dedo
2 PRON (**a**) *(direct object)* la; **I saw h. recently** la vi hace poco (**b**) *(indirect object)* le; *(with other third person pronouns)* se; **he gave h. money** le dio dinero; **they handed it to h.** se lo entregaron (**c**) *(after prep)* ella; **for h.** para ella (**d**) *(as subject)* *Fam* ella; **look, it's h.!** ¡mira, es ella!

herald ['herəld] **1** N heraldo *m*
2 VT anunciar

heraldry ['herəldrɪ] N heráldica *f*

herb [hɜ:b, *US* ɜ:rb] N hierba *f*; **h. tea** infusión *f*

herbal ['hɜ:bəl] ADJ herbario(a); **h. remedies** curas *fpl* de hierbas

herd [hɜ:d] N *(of cattle)* manada *f*; *(of goats)* rebaño *m*; *Fig (large group)* multitud *f*

here [hɪə(r)] ADV aquí; **come h.** ven aquí; **h.!** ¡presente!; **h. goes!** ¡vamos a ver!; **h.'s to success!** ¡brindemos por el éxito!; **h. you are!** ¡toma!; **look h., you can't do that!** ¡oiga, que no se permite hacer eso!

hereafter [hɪər'ɑːftə(r)] *Fml* **1** ADV de ahora en adelante
2 N **the h.** la otra vida, el más allá
hereby [hɪə'baɪ] ADV *Fml* por la presente .
hereditary [hɪ'redɪtərɪ] ADJ hereditario(a)
heresy ['herəsɪ] N herejía *f*
heretic ['herətɪk] N hereje *mf*
heritage ['herɪtɪdʒ] N patrimonio *m*; *Jur* herencia *f*
hermetically [hɜː'metɪklɪ] ADV **h. sealed** herméticamente cerrado(a)
hermit ['hɜːmɪt] N ermitaño(a) *m,f*

> Note that the Spanish word **ermita** is a false friend and is never a translation for the English word **hermit**. In Spanish, **ermita** means "hermitage".

hermitage ['hɜːmɪtɪdʒ] N ermita *f*
hernia ['hɜːnɪə] N hernia *f*
hero ['hɪərəʊ] N *(pl* **heroes***)* héroe *m*; *(in novel)* protagonista *m*; **h. worship** idolatría *f*
heroic [hɪ'rəʊɪk] ADJ heroico(a)
heroin ['herəʊɪn] N heroína *f*
heroine ['herəʊɪn] N heroína *f*; *(in novel)* protagonista *f*
heron ['herən] N garza *f*
herring ['herɪŋ] N arenque *m*
hers [hɜːz] POSS PRON **(a)** *(attribute) (one thing)* suyo(a); *(more than one)* suyos(as); *(to distinguish)* de ella; **they are h., not his** son de ella, no de él **(b)** *(noun reference) (one thing)* el suyo/la suya; *(more than one)* los suyos/las suyas; **my car is blue and h. is red** mi coche es azul y el suyo es rojo
herself [hɜː'self] PERS PRON **(a)** *(reflexive)* se; **she dressed h.** se vistió **(b)** *(alone)* ella misma; **she was by h.** estaba sola **(c)** *(emphatic)* **she told me so h.** eso me dijo ella
hesitant ['hezɪtənt] ADJ vacilante
hesitate ['hezɪteɪt] VI vacilar
hesitation [hezɪ'teɪʃən] N indecisión *f*
heterogeneous [hetərəʊ'dʒiːnɪəs] ADJ heterogéneo(a)
heterosexual [hetərəʊ'seksjʊəl] ADJ & N heterosexual *(mf)*
hexagon ['heksəgən] N hexágono *m*
hey [heɪ] INTERJ ¡oye!, ¡oiga!
heyday ['heɪdeɪ] N auge *m*, apogeo *m*
HGV [eɪtʃdʒiː'viː] N *Br (abbr* **heavy goods vehicle)** vehículo *m* de carga pesada
hi [haɪ] INTERJ *Fam* ¡hola!
hiatus [haɪ'eɪtəs] N *Fml* laguna *f*
hibernate ['haɪbəneɪt] VI hibernar
hibernation [haɪbə'neɪʃən] N hibernación *f*
hibiscus [haɪ'bɪskəs] N hibisco *m*
hiccup, hiccough ['hɪkʌp] N hipo *m*; *Fam (minor problem)* problemilla *m*; **to have hiccups** tener hipo

hide¹ [haɪd] **1** VT *(pt* **hid** [hɪd]; *pp* **hidden** ['hɪdən]) *(conceal)* esconder; *(obscure)* ocultar
2 VI esconderse, ocultarse
3 N puesto *m*
hide² [haɪd] N *(of animal)* piel *f*
hide-and-seek [haɪdən'siːk] N escondite *m*
hideous ['hɪdɪəs] ADJ *(horrific)* horroroso(a); *(extremely ugly)* espantoso(a)
hide-out ['haɪdaʊt] N escondrijo *m*, guarida *f*
hiding¹ ['haɪdɪŋ] N **to go into h.** esconderse
hiding² ['haɪdɪŋ] N *Fam* paliza *f*
hierarchy ['haɪərɑːkɪ] N jerarquía *f*
hi-fi ['haɪfaɪ] N hifi *m*; **h. equipment** equipo *m* de alta fidelidad
high [haɪ] **1** ADJ **(a)** *(mountain, building)* alto(a); **how h. is that wall?** ¿qué altura tiene esa pared?; **it's 3 feet h.** tiene 3 pies de alto; **h. chair** silla alta para niños; **h. jump** salto *m* de altura **(b)** *(price, speed, standards)* alto(a), elevado(a); **to have a h. opinion of sb** tener muy buena opinión de algn; **h. blood pressure** tensión alta **(c)** *(rank, position)* elevado(a), alto(a); **h. wind** viento *m* fuerte; **h. school** instituto *m* de enseñanza media; **Br the H. Street** la Calle Mayor **(d)** *Fam (drugged)* colocado(a)
2 ADV alto; **to fly h.** volar a gran altura
3 N *(high point)* punto máximo
highbrow ['haɪbraʊ] ADJ & N intelectual *(mf)*
high-class ['haɪklɑːs] ADJ de alta categoría
higher ['haɪə(r)] **1** ADJ superior; **h. education** enseñanza *f* superior
2 N *Scot Educ* **H.** = examen final de los estudios preuniversitarios
high-five ['haɪfaɪv] N *US Fam* palmada *f* en el aire *(saludo entre dos)*
high-flier, high-flyer [haɪ'flaɪə(r)] N *Fig* = persona dotada y ambiciosa
high-handed [haɪ'hændɪd] ADJ despótico(a)
high-heeled ['haɪhiːld] ADJ de tacón, *Am* de taco alto
highlands ['haɪləndz] NPL tierras altas
highlight ['haɪlaɪt] **1** N **(a)** *(in hair)* reflejo *m* **(b)** *(of event)* atracción *f* principal
2 VT **(a)** *(problem, difference)* destacar **(b)** *(text)* resaltar *(con rotulador fluorescente)*
highly ['haɪlɪ] ADV *(very)* sumamente; **to speak h. of sb** hablar muy bien de algn
highly-strung [haɪlɪ'strʌŋ] ADJ muy nervioso(a)
Highness ['haɪnɪs] N **Your H.** Su Alteza
high-pitched ['haɪpɪtʃt] ADJ estridente
high-powered ['haɪpaʊəd] ADJ *(person)* dinámico(a)
high-ranking ['haɪrænkɪŋ] ADJ **h. official** alto funcionario
high-rise ['haɪraɪz] ADJ **h. building** rascacielos *m inv*
high-speed ['haɪspiːd] ADJ **h. lens** objetivo ultrarrápido; **h. train** tren *m* de alta velocidad

high-tech ['haɪ'tek] ADJ de alta tecnología

highway ['haɪweɪ] N *US* carretera *f*, autopista *f*; *Br* **H. Code** código *m* de la circulación

highwayman ['haɪweɪmən] N salteador *m* de caminos

hijack ['haɪdʒæk] **1** VT secuestrar
2 N secuestro *m*

hijacker ['haɪdʒækə(r)] N secuestrador(a) *m,f*; *(of planes)* pirata *mf* del aire

hike [haɪk] **1** N (**a**) *(walk)* excursión *f* (**b**) **price h.** aumento *m* de precio
2 VI ir de excursión

hiker ['haɪkə(r)] N excursionista *mf*

hilarious [hɪ'leərɪəs] ADJ graciosísimo(a)

hill [hɪl] N colina *f*; *(slope)* cuesta *f*

hillside ['hɪlsaɪd] N ladera *f*

hilltop ['hɪltɒp] N cima *f* de una colina

hilly ['hɪlɪ] ADJ (**hillier, hilliest**) accidentado(a)

hilt [hɪlt] N puño *m*, empuñadura *f*; **I'll support you up to the h.** te daré mi apoyo total

him [hɪm] PRON (**a**) *(direct object)* lo, le; **hit h.!** ¡pégale!; **she loves h.** lo quiere (**b**) *(indirect object)* le; *(with other third person pronouns)* se; **give h. the money** dale el dinero; **give it to h.** dáselo (**c**) *(after prep)* él; **it's not like h. to say that** no es propio de él decir eso (**d**) *Fam (as subject)* él; **it's h.** es él

himself [hɪm'self] PERS PRON (**a**) *(reflexive)* se; **he hurt h.** se hizo daño (**b**) *(alone)* solo, por sí mismo; **by h.** solo (**c**) *(emphatic)* él mismo

hind¹ [haɪnd] ADJ trasero(a); **h. legs** patas traseras

hind² [haɪnd] N *Zool* cierva *f*

hinder ['hɪndə(r)] VT dificultar, estorbar; **to h. sb from doing sth** impedir a algn hacer algo

hindrance ['hɪndrəns] N estorbo *m*

hindsight ['haɪndsaɪt] N retrospectiva *f*

Hindu [hɪn'duː, 'hɪnduː] ADJ & N hindú *(mf)*

Hinduism ['hɪnduɪzəm] N hinduismo *m*

hinge [hɪndʒ] **1** N bisagra *f*; *Fig* eje *m*
2 VT engoznar

▸ **hinge on** VT INSEP depender de

hint [hɪnt] **1** N (**a**) *(allusion)* indirecta *f*; **to take the h.** pillar *or Esp* coger la indirecta (**b**) *(clue)* pista *f* (**c**) *(trace)* pizca *f* (**d**) *(advice)* consejo *m*
2 VT to the h. that ... insinuar que ...

hip¹ [hɪp] N cadera *f*; **h. flask** petaca *f*

hip² [hɪp] ADJ *Fam (trendy)* moderno(a), a la última, *Am* de onda

hip-hop ['hɪphɒp] N hip-hop *m*

hippie ['hɪpɪ] ADJ & N *Fam* hippy *(mf)*

hippopotamus [hɪpə'pɒtəməs] N *(pl* **hippopotami** [hɪpə'pɒtəmaɪ]*)* hipopótamo *m*

hire ['haɪə(r)] **1** N *Br (of car, room, suit)* alquiler *m*, *Méx* renta *f*; **bicycles for h.** se alquilan bicicletas; **for h.** *(taxi)* libre; **h. purchase** compra *f* a plazos
2 VT (**a**) *Br (rent)* alquilar, *Méx* rentar (**b**) *(employ)* contratar

▸ **hire out** VT SEP *Br (car)* alquilar, *Méx* rentar; *(one's services)* ofrecer

his [hɪz] **1** POSS ADJ *(one thing)* su; *(more than one)* sus; *(to distinguish)* de él; **he washed h. face** se lavó la cara; **is it h. dog or hers?** ¿el perro es de él o de ella?
2 POSS PRON (**a**) *(attribute) (one thing)* suyo(a); *(more than one)* suyos(as); *(to distinguish)* de él (**b**) *(noun reference) (one thing)* el suyo/la suya; *(more than one)* los suyos/las suyas; **my car is blue and h. is red** mi coche es azul y el suyo rojo

Hispanic [hɪ'spænɪk] **1** ADJ hispánico(a)
2 N *US* hispano(a) *m,f*, latino(a) *m,f*

hiss [hɪs] **1** N siseo *m*; *Th* silbido *m*
2 VT & VI silbar

historian [hɪ'stɔːrɪən] N historiador(a) *m,f*

historic [hɪ'stɒrɪk] ADJ histórico(a)

historical [hɪ'stɒrɪkəl] ADJ histórico(a); **h. novel** novela histórica

history ['hɪstərɪ] N historia *f*

hit [hɪt] **1** N (**a**) *(blow)* golpe *m*; **direct h.** impacto directo; *Fam* **h. list** lista negra; *Fam* **h. man** asesino *m* a sueldo (**b**) *(success)* éxito *m*; **h. parade** lista *f* de éxitos (**c**) *Comput (visit to web site)* acceso *m*, visita *f*
2 VT *(pt & pp* hit*)* (**a**) *(strike)* golpear, pegar; **he was h. in the leg** le dieron en la pierna; **the car h. the kerb** el coche chocó contra el bordillo (**b**) *(affect)* afectar (**c**) **to h. the headlines** ser noticia

▸ **hit back** VI *(reply to criticism)* replicar

▸ **hit on** VT INSEP dar con; **we h. on the idea of ...** se nos ocurrió la idea de ...

▸ **hit out** VI **to h. out at sb** atacar a algn

▸ **hit upon** VT INSEP = **hit on**

hit-and-run [hɪtən'rʌn] ADJ **h. driver** = conductor que atropella a algn y no para

hitch [hɪtʃ] **1** N dificultad *f*
2 VT *(fasten)* atar
3 VI *Fam (hitch-hike)* hacer autostop

▸ **hitch up** VT SEP remangarse

hitch-hike ['hɪtʃhaɪk] VI hacer autostop *or* dedo

hitch-hiker ['hɪtʃhaɪkə(r)] N autostopista *mf*

hitherto [hɪðə'tuː] ADV *Fml* hasta la fecha

HIV [eɪtʃaɪ'viː] N *(abbr* **human immunodeficiency virus***)* VIH *m*; **to be diagnosed HIV positive/negative** dar seropositivo(a)/seronegativo(a) en la prueba del SIDA

hive [haɪv] N colmena *f*; *Fig* lugar muy activo

HM *(abbr* **His/Her Majesty***)* SM

hoard [hɔːd] **1** N *(provisions)* reservas *fpl*; *(money etc)* tesoro *m*
2 VT *(objects)* acumular; *(money)* atesorar

hoarding ['hɔːdɪŋ] N *(temporary fence)* valla *f*; *Br (billboard)* valla publicitaria

hoarfrost ['hɔːfrɒst] N escarcha *f*

hoarse [hɔːs] ADJ ronco(a); **to be h.** tener la voz ronca

hoax [həʊks] N *(joke)* broma pesada; *(trick)* engaño m

hob [hɒb] N *(of cooker)* fuego m, Esp, Andes, Méx hornilla f, RP hornalla f

hobble [ˈhɒbəl] VI cojear, Andes, RP renguear

hobby [ˈhɒbɪ] N pasatiempo m, afición f

hobbyhorse [ˈhɒbɪhɔːs] N *(toy)* caballito m de juguete; Fig *(fixed idea)* idea fija, manía f

hobo [ˈhəʊbəʊ] N US vagabundo(a) m,f

hockey [ˈhɒkɪ] N Br *(on grass)* hockey m (sobre hierba or Am césped); US *(on ice)* hockey (sobre hielo)

hog [hɒg] **1** N cerdo m, puerco m; Fam **to go the whole h.** liarse la manta a la cabeza
2 VT Fam acaparar

hoist [hɔɪst] **1** N *(crane)* grúa f; *(lift)* montacargas m inv
2 VT levantar, subir

hold [həʊld] **1** VT *(pt & pp held)* **(a)** *(keep in hand)* aguantar, tener (en la mano); *(grip)* agarrar; *(support) (weight)* soportar; *(opinion)* sostener; **to h. sb** abrazar a algn; **to h. sb's hand** cogerle la mano a algn **(b)** *(contain)* dar cabida a; **the jug holds a litre** en la jarra cabe un litro **(c)** *(meeting)* celebrar; *(conversation)* mantener **(d)** **to h. office** ocupar un puesto **(e)** **he was held for two hours at the police station** estuvo detenido durante dos horas en la comisaría; **to h. one's breath** contener la respiración; **to h. sb hostage** retener a algn como rehén **(f)** Tel **to h. the line** no colgar
2 VI *(rope)* aguantar
3 N **(a)** **to get h. of** *(grip)* agarrar, Esp coger; Fig localizar **(b)** Naut bodega f **(c)** *(in wrestling)* llave f

▸ **hold back 1** VT SEP *(crowd)* contener; *(feelings)* reprimir; *(truth)* ocultar; **I don't want to h. you back** *(delay)* no quiero entretenerte
2 VI *(hesitate)* vacilar

▸ **hold down** VT SEP **(a)** *(control)* dominar **(b)** Fam *(job)* desempeñar

▸ **hold off** VT SEP mantener a distancia

▸ **hold on** VI **(a)** *(keep a firm grasp)* agarrarse bien **(b)** *(wait)* esperar; Tel **h. on!** ¡no cuelgue!

▸ **hold out 1** VT SEP *(hand)* tender
2 VI *(last) (things)* durar; *(person)* resistir

▸ **hold up** VT SEP **(a)** *(rob) (train)* asaltar; *(bank)* atracar **(b)** *(delay)* retrasar **(c)** *(raise)* levantar **(d)** *(support)* apuntalar

holdall [ˈhəʊldɔːl] N esp Br bolsa f *(de viaje o de deporte)*

holder [ˈhəʊldə(r)] N **(a)** *(receptacle)* recipiente m **(b)** *(owner)* poseedor(a) m,f; *(of passport)* titular mf; **record h.** plusmarquista mf

holding [ˈhəʊldɪŋ] N **(a)** *(property)* propiedad f **(b)** Fin valor m en cartera; **h. company** holding m

hold-up [ˈhəʊldʌp] N **(a)** *(robbery)* atraco m **(b)** *(delay)* retraso m; *(in traffic)* atasco m

hole [həʊl] N **(a)** *(in roof, clothing)* agujero m; *(in ground)* hoyo m; *(in the road)* bache m **(b)** *(in golf)* hoyo m **(c)** Fam *(of place)* antro m

holiday [ˈhɒlɪdeɪ] **1** N *(one day)* Esp *(día m de)* fiesta, Am feriado m; Br *(several days)* vacaciones fpl; **to be/go on h.** estar/irse de vacaciones; **h. resort** lugar turístico
2 VI Br pasar las vacaciones; *(in summer)* veranear

holidaymaker [ˈhɒlɪdeɪmeɪkə(r)] N esp Br turista mf; *(in summer)* veraneante mf

holiness [ˈhəʊlɪnɪs] N santidad f

Holland [ˈhɒlənd] N Holanda

hollow [ˈhɒləʊ] **1** ADJ **(a)** *(container, log)* hueco(a) **(b)** *(cheeks, eyes)* hundido(a) **(c)** Fig *(insincere)* falso(a); *(empty)* vacío(a)
2 N hueco m; Geog hondonada f
3 VT **to h. (out)** hacer un hueco en

holly [ˈhɒlɪ] N acebo m

holocaust [ˈhɒləkɔːst] N holocausto m

hologram [ˈhɒləgræm] N holograma m

holster [ˈhəʊlstə(r)] N pistolera f

holy [ˈhəʊlɪ] ADJ *(**holier, holiest**)* sagrado(a), santo(a); *(blessed)* bendito(a); **H. Ghost** Espíritu Santo; **H. Land** Tierra Santa; **H. See** Santa Sede

homage [ˈhɒmɪdʒ] N homenaje m; **to pay h. to sb** rendir homenaje a algn

home [həʊm] **1** N **(a)** *(house)* casa f; *(family)* hogar m; **at h.** en casa; Fig **make yourself at h.!** ¡estás en tu casa!; Fig **to feel at h.** estar a gusto; **h. banking** telebanco m; Comput **h. page** *(initial page)* portada f, página f inicial or de inicio; *(personal page)* página personal; **h. shopping** telecompra f **(b)** *(institution)* residencia f; **old people's h.** asilo de ancianos **(c)** Sport **to play at h.** jugar en casa; **h. run** carrera completa
2 ADJ **(a)** *(domestic)* del hogar; Br **h. help** asistenta f **(b)** Pol interior; Br **H. Office** Ministerio m del Interior; Br **H. Secretary** Ministro(a) m,f del Interior **(c)** *(native)* natal
3 ADV en casa; **to go h.** irse a casa; **to leave h.** irse de casa

homeland [ˈhəʊmlænd] N patria f; *(birthplace)* tierra f natal

homeless [ˈhəʊmlɪs] **1** ADJ sin techo
2 NPL **the h.** los sin techo

homely [ˈhəʊmlɪ] ADJ *(**homelier, homeliest**)* **(a)** Br *(person)* casero(a); *(atmosphere)* familiar **(b)** US *(ugly)* feúcho(a)

home-made [ˈhəʊmmeɪd] ADJ casero(a)

homeopathy [həʊmɪˈɒpəθɪ] N US = **homoeopathy**

homesick [ˈhəʊmsɪk] ADJ **to be h.** tener morriña

homeward(s) [ˈhəʊmwəd(z)] ADV hacia casa

homework [ˈhəʊmwɜːk] N deberes mpl

homey [ˈhəʊmɪ] ADJ US Fam hogareño(a)

homicide [ˈhɒmɪsaɪd] N homicidio m

homing ['həʊmɪŋ] ADJ (**a**) **h. device** cabeza buscadora (**b**) **h. pigeon** paloma mensajera

homoeopathy [həʊmɪ'ɒpəθɪ] N homeopatía *f*

homogeneous [həmə'dʒiːnɪəs] ADJ homogéneo(a)

homosexual [həʊməʊ'seksjʊəl] ADJ & N homosexual *(mf)*

Honduran [hɒn'djʊərən] ADJ & N hondureño(a) *(m,f)*

Honduras [hɒn'djʊərəs] N Honduras

honest ['ɒnɪst] ADJ honrado(a); *(sincere)* sincero(a), franco(a); *(fair)* justo(a); **the h. truth** la pura verdad

honestly ['ɒnɪstlɪ] ADV honradamente; *(question)* ¿de verdad?; *(exclamation)* ¡hay que ver!; **h., it doesn't matter** de verdad, no tiene importancia

honesty ['ɒnɪstɪ] N honradez *f*

honey ['hʌnɪ] N miel *f*; *esp US Fam (endearment)* cariño *m*

honeycomb ['hʌnɪkəʊm] N panal *m*

honeymoon ['hʌnɪmuːn] N luna *f* de miel

honeysuckle ['hʌnɪsʌkəl] N madreselva *f*

honk [hɒŋk] VI *Aut* tocar la bocina

honor ['ɒnə(r)] N & VT *US* = **honour**

honorable ['ɒnərəbəl] ADJ *US* = **honourable**

honorary ['ɒnərərɪ] ADJ *(member)* honorario(a); *(duties)* honorífico(a)

honour ['ɒnə(r)] **1** N (**a**) *(respect)* honor *m* (**b**) *US Jur* **Her H./His H./Your H.** Su Señoría *f* (**c**) *Mil* **honours** honores *mpl* (**d**) **Honours degree** licenciatura *f* superior
2 VT (**a**) *(respect)* honrar (**b**) *(obligation)* cumplir con

honourable ['ɒnərəbəl] ADJ *(person)* honrado(a); *(action)* honroso(a)

hood [hʊd] N (**a**) *(of garment)* capucha *f* (**b**) *Br (of car, pram)* capota *f*; *US (car bonnet)* capó *m* (**c**) *US Fam (gangster)* matón(ona) *m,f*

hoodlum ['huːdləm] N matón(ona) *m,f*

hoodwink ['hʊdwɪŋk] VT *Fam* engañar, *Esp* timar

hoof [huːf] N (*pl* **hoofs** *or* **hooves**) *(of horse)* casco *m*; *(of cow, sheep)* pezuña *f*

hook [hʊk] **1** N (**a**) *(in general)* gancho *m*; *(in fishing)* anzuelo *m*; *Sewing* **hooks and eyes** corchetes *mpl*; **to take the phone off the h.** descolgar el teléfono (**b**) *(in boxing)* gancho *m*
2 VT enganchar

▸ **hook up** VT SEP & VI *Rad, TV & Comput* conectar (**with** con)

hooked [hʊkt] ADJ (**a**) *(nose)* aguileño(a) (**b**) *Fam (addicted)* enganchado(a) (**on** a); **to get h.** engancharse

hooker ['hʊkə(r)] N *US Fam (prostitute)* fulana *f*, puta *f*

hookey ['hʊkɪ] N *US Fam* **to play h.** faltar a clase, *Esp* hacer novillos, *Col* capar clase, *Méx* irse de pinta, *RP* hacer la rabona

hook-up ['hʊkʌp] N (**a**) *Comput* conexión *f* (**b**) *Rad & TV* emisión *f* múltiple

hooky ['hʊkɪ] N *US Fam* = **hookey**

hooligan ['huːlɪgən] N *Fam* gamberro(a) *m,f*

hoop [huːp] N aro *m*; *(of barrel)* fleje *m*

hooray [huː'reɪ] INTERJ ¡hurra!

hoot [huːt] **1** N (**a**) *(of owl)* ululato *m*; *Fam* **hoots of laughter** carcajadas *fpl*; *Fam* **I don't care a h.** me importa un pepino (**b**) *(of car horn)* bocinazo *m*
2 VI (**a**) *(owl)* ulular (**b**) *(car)* dar un bocinazo; *(train)* silbar; *(siren)* pitar

hooter ['huːtə(r)] N *Br (of car)* bocina *f*; *(of ship, factory)* sirena *f*

Hoover® ['huːvə(r)] *Br* **1** N aspiradora *f*
2 VT **to h.** pasar la aspiradora por

hooves [huːvz] PL *of* **hoof**

hop¹ [hɒp] **1** VI saltar; **to h. on one leg** andar a la pata coja
2 N *(small jump)* brinco *m*

hop² [hɒp] N *Bot* lúpulo *m*

hope [həʊp] **1** N esperanza *f*; *(false)* ilusión *f*; **to have little h. of doing sth** tener pocas posibilidades de hacer algo
2 VT & VI esperar; **I h. so/not** espero que sí/no; **we h. you're well** esperamos que estés bien

hopeful ['həʊpfʊl] ADJ *(confident)* optimista; *(promising)* prometedor(a)

hopefully ['həʊpfʊlɪ] ADV (**a**) *(confidently)* con optimismo (**b**) **h. the weather will be fine** *(it is hoped)* esperemos que haga buen tiempo

hopeless ['həʊplɪs] ADJ desesperado(a); *Fam* **to be h. at sports** ser negado(a) para los deportes

hopelessly ['həʊplɪslɪ] ADV desesperadamente; **h. lost** completamente perdido(a)

horde [hɔːd] N multitud *f*

horizon [hə'raɪzən] N horizonte *m*

horizontal [hɒrɪ'zɒntəl] ADJ horizontal

hormone ['hɔːməʊn] N hormona *f*

horn [hɔːn] N (**a**) *(of animal)* cuerno *m* (**b**) *Fam Mus* trompeta *f*; **French h.** trompa *f*; **hunting h.** cuerno *m* de caza (**c**) *Aut* bocina *f*

hornet ['hɔːnɪt] N avispón *m*

horny ['hɔːnɪ] ADJ (**hornier, horniest**) (**a**) *(hands)* calloso(a) (**b**) *very Fam (sexually aroused) Esp, Méx* cachondo(a), *CAm, Col, Méx, Ven* arrecho(a), *RP* caliente

horoscope ['hɒrəskəʊp] N horóscopo *m*

horrendous [hɒ'rendəs] ADJ horrendo(a)

horrible ['hɒrəbəl] ADJ horrible

horrid ['hɒrɪd] ADJ horrible

horrific [hə'rɪfɪk] ADJ horrendo(a)

horrify ['hɒrɪfaɪ] VT horrorizar

horror ['hɒrə(r)] N horror *m*; *Fam* **a little h.** un diablillo; **h. film** película *f* de miedo *or* de terror

hors d'oeuvre [ɔː'dɜːvr] N (*pl* **hors d'oeuvres**) entremés *m*

horse [hɔːs] N (**a**) *(animal)* caballo *m*; **h. race** carrera *f* de caballos (**b**) **h. chestnut** *(tree)* castaño *m* de Indias

horseback ['hɔːsbæk] N **on h.** a caballo; *US* **h. riding** equitación *f*

horseman ['hɔːsmən] N jinete *m*

horseplay ['hɔːspleɪ] N payasadas *fpl*

horsepower ['hɔːspaʊə(r)] N caballo *m* (de vapor)

horseradish ['hɔːsrædɪʃ] N rábano rusticano

horseshoe ['hɔːsʃuː] N herradura *f*

horsewoman ['hɔːswʊmən] N amazona *f*

horticulture ['hɔːtɪkʌltʃə(r)] N horticultura *f*

hose [həʊz] N *(pipe)* manguera *f*

hosepipe ['həʊzpaɪp] N manguera *f*

hosiery ['həʊzɪərɪ] N medias *fpl* y calcetines *mpl*

hospice ['hɒspɪs] N residencia *f* para enfermos terminales

hospitable ['hɒspɪtəbəl, hɒ'spɪtəbəl] ADJ hospitalario(a); **h. atmosphere** ambiente acogedor

hospital ['hɒspɪtəl] N hospital *m*

hospitality [hɒspɪ'tælɪtɪ] N hospitalidad *f*

host¹ [həʊst] N (**a**) *(at home, party)* anfitrión *m* (**b**) *Th & TV* presentador *m* (**c**) *Biol* huésped *m* **2** VT *Th & TV* presentar

host² [həʊst] N *(large number)* montón *m*

host³ [həʊst] N *Rel* hostia *f*

hostage ['hɒstɪdʒ] N rehén *m*

hostel ['hɒstəl] N hostal *m*

hostess ['həʊstɪs] N (**a**) *(at home, party)* anfitriona *f* (**b**) *Th & TV* presentadora *f* (**c**) **(air) h.** azafata *f*

hostile ['hɒstaɪl, *US* 'hɒstəl] ADJ hostil

hostility [hɒ'stɪlɪtɪ] N hostilidad *f*

hot [hɒt] ADJ *(hotter, hottest)* (**a**) *(high in temperature)* caliente; *Fig* **h. line** teléfono rojo (**b**) *(day, weather)* caluroso(a); **it's very h.** hace mucho calor; **to feel h.** tener calor (**c**) *(spicy)* picante; **h. dog** perrito *m* caliente, *Col, Méx* perro *m* caliente, *RP* pancho *m* (**d**) *(temper)* fuerte (**e**) *Fam (good)* bueno(a); **it's not so h.** no es nada del otro mundo (**f**) *(popular)* popular

► **hot up** VI *Fam (situation, contest) Esp* calentarse, *Am* ponerse bravo(a)

hotbed ['hɒtbed] N *Fig* hervidero *m*

hotcake ['hɒtkeɪk] N *US* crepe *f*, panqueque *m*, *Esp* tortita *f*

hotel [həʊ'tel] N hotel *m*

hotelier [həʊ'teljeɪ] N hotelero(a) *m,f*

hot-headed [hɒt'hedɪd] ADJ impetuoso(a)

hothouse ['hɒthaʊs] N invernadero *m*

hotplate ['hɒtpleɪt] N *(cooker)* placa *f* de cocina; *(to keep food warm)* calientaplatos *m inv*

hotshot ['hɒtʃɒt] N *Fam* as *m*, *Esp* hacha *f*

hot-water [hɒt'wɔːtə(r)] ADJ **h. bottle** bolsa *f* de agua caliente

hound [haʊnd] **1** N perro *m* de caza **2** VT acosar

hour ['aʊə(r)] N hora *f*; **60 miles an h.** 60 millas por hora; **by the h.** por horas; **h. hand** manecilla *f*

hourly ['aʊəlɪ] **1** ADJ cada hora **2** ADV por horas

house 1 N [haʊs] (**a**) *(dwelling)* casa *f*; **at my h.** en mi casa; *Fig* **on the h.** cortesía de la casa; **h. plant** planta *f* de interior (**b**) *Pol* **H. of Commons** Cámara *f* de los Comunes; **H. of Lords** Cámara *f* de los Lores; *US* **H. of Representatives** Cámara de Representantes; **Houses of Parliament** Parlamento *m* (**c**) *(company)* empresa *f*; **publishing h.** editorial *f* (**d**) *Th* sala *f* **2** VT [haʊz] alojar; *(store)* guardar

houseboat ['haʊsbəʊt] N casa *f* flotante

housebound ['haʊsbaʊnd] ADJ **to be h.** estar confinado(a) en casa

housebreaking ['haʊsbreɪkɪŋ] N robos *mpl* de casas, *RP* escruche *m*

housebroken ['haʊsbrəʊkən] ADJ *US (pet)* = que ya ha aprendido a no hacer sus necesidades en casa

housecoat ['haʊskəʊt] N bata *f*

household ['haʊshəʊld] N hogar *m*, *Esp* unidad *f* familiar; **h. products** productos domésticos

housekeeper ['haʊskiːpə(r)] N ama *f* de llaves

housekeeping ['haʊskiːpɪŋ] N administración doméstica; **h. money** dinero *m* para los gastos domésticos

house-train ['haʊstreɪn] VT *(pet)* educar

house-warming ['haʊswɔːmɪŋ] N **h. (party)** = fiesta que se da al estrenar casa

housewife ['haʊswaɪf] N ama *f* de casa

housework ['haʊswɜːk] N trabajo doméstico

housing ['haʊzɪŋ] N vivienda *f*; *Br* **h. estate** *(public housing)* ≃ viviendas *fpl* de protección oficial; *(private housing)* urbanización *f*, *Am* condominio *m*

hovel ['hʌvəl, 'hɒvəl] N casucha *f*

hover ['hɒvə(r)] VI *(bird)* cernerse; *(aircraft)* permanecer inmóvil (en el aire)

hovercraft ['hɒvəkrɑːft] N aerodeslizador *m*

how [haʊ] ADV (**a**) *(direct question)* ¿cómo?; **h. are you?** ¿cómo estás?; *Fam* **h. come?** ¿por qué? (**b**) *(indirect question)* cómo (**c**) *(very)* qué; **h. funny!** ¡qué divertido! (**d**) *(suggestion)* **h. about going to the cinema?** ¿te apetece ir al cine? (**e**) *(quantity)* cuánto; **h. old is she?** ¿cuántos años tiene?; **h. tall are you?** ¿cuánto mides? (**f**) **h. many?** ¿cuántos(as)?; **h. much?** ¿cuánto(a)?

however [haʊ'evə(r)] ADV (**a**) *(nevertheless)* no obstante, sin embargo (**b**) *(with adjective)* **h. difficult it may be** por difícil que sea; **h. much** por mucho que (+ *subj*)

howl [haʊl] **1** N aullido *m* **2** VI aullar

howler ['haʊlə(r)] N *Fam* error *m* grave *or Esp* de bulto

HP, hp [eɪtʃ'piː] N (**a**) *Br* (*abbr* **hire purchase**) compra *f* a plazos (**b**) (*abbr* **horsepower**) cv *mpl*

HQ [eɪtʃ'kjuː] N (*abbr* **headquarters**) sede *f*, central *f*

hub [hʌb] N *Aut* cubo *m*; *Fig* eje *m*

hubbub ['hʌbʌb] N alboroto *m*

hubcap ['hʌbkæp] N *Aut* tapacubos *m inv*

huddle ['hʌdəl] 1 N grupo *m*
  2 VI **to h. (up** *or* **together)** acurrucarse

hue¹ [hjuː] N (*colour*) tinte *m*; (*shade*) matiz *m*

hue² [hjuː] N **h. and cry** fuerte protesta *f*

huff [hʌf] N **to be in a h.** estar mosqueado(a) *or Esp* enfurruñado(a)

hug [hʌg] 1 VT abrazar
  2 N abrazo *m*

huge [hjuːdʒ] ADJ enorme

hugely ['hjuːdʒlɪ] ADV enormemente

hulk [hʌlk] N (**a**) *Naut* casco *m* (**b**) (*thing, person*) armatoste *m*

hull [hʌl] N *Naut* casco *m*

hullabal(l)oo [hʌləbə'luː] N *Fam* follón *m*

hullo [hʌ'ləʊ] INTERJ *Br* ¡hola!

hum [hʌm] 1 VT (*tune*) tararear
  2 VI (*bees, engine*) zumbar; (*sing*) tararear
  3 N (*of bees*) zumbido *m*

human ['hjuːmən] 1 ADJ humano(a); **h. race** raza humana; **h. being** ser humano
  2 N ser humano

humane [hjuː'meɪn] ADJ humano(a)

humanitarian [hjuːmænɪ'teərɪən] ADJ humanitario(a)

humanity [hjuː'mænɪtɪ] N humanidad *f*; *Univ* **the humanities** las humanidades

humble ['hʌmbəl] 1 ADJ humilde
  2 VT humillar

humbug ['hʌmbʌg] N (**a**) *Fam* tonterías *fpl* (**b**) *Br* (*mint*) **h.** caramelo *m* de menta

humdrum ['hʌmdrʌm] ADJ monótono(a), aburrido(a)

humid ['hjuːmɪd] ADJ húmedo(a)

humidity [hjuː'mɪdɪtɪ] N humedad *f*

humiliate [hjuː'mɪlɪeɪt] VT humillar

humiliation [hjuːmɪlɪ'eɪʃən] N humillación *f*

humility [hjuː'mɪlɪtɪ] N humildad *f*

humor ['hjuːmə(r)] N & VT *US* = **humour**

humorous ['hjuːmərəs] ADJ (*writer*) humorístico(a); (*person, story*) gracioso(a), divertido(a)

humour ['hjuːmə(r)] 1 N humor *m*
  2 VT seguir la corriente a

hump [hʌmp] 1 N (**a**) (*on back*) joroba *f* (**b**) (*small hill*) montículo *m*
  2 VT *esp Br Fam* (*carry*) acarrear

humus ['hjuːməs] N mantillo *m*, humus *m*

hunch [hʌntʃ] N *Fam* corazonada *f*

hunchback ['hʌntʃbæk] N jorobado(a) *m,f*

hundred ['hʌndrəd] 1 N cien *m*, ciento *m*; (*rough number*) centenar *m*; **a h. and twenty-five** ciento veinticinco; **five h.** quinientos
  2 ADJ cien; **a h. people** cien personas; **a h. percent** cien por cien; **two h. chairs** doscientas sillas

hundredth ['hʌndrədθ] ADJ & N centésimo(a) (*m,f*)

hundredweight ['hʌndrədweɪt] N *Br* = 50,8 kg; *US* = 45,36 kg

hung [hʌŋ] 1 ADJ *Fam* (**a**) **h. over** con resaca (**b**) **h. up** acomplejado(a)
  2 PT & PP *of* **hang**

Hungarian [hʌŋ'geərɪən] ADJ & N húngaro(a) (*m,f*)

Hungary ['hʌŋgərɪ] N Hungría

hunger ['hʌŋgə(r)] 1 N hambre *f*; **h. strike** huelga *f* de hambre
  2 VI *Fig* tener hambre (**for** de)

hungry ['hʌŋgrɪ] ADJ (**hungrier, hungriest**) hambriento(a); **to be h.** tener hambre; **to go h.** pasar hambre

hunk [hʌŋk] N (**a**) (*piece*) buen pedazo *m* (**b**) *Fam* (*man*) machote *m*

hunt [hʌnt] 1 VT cazar
  2 VI (*for game*) cazar; (*search*) buscar
  3 N caza *f*; (*search*) búsqueda *f*
  ▸ **hunt down** VT SEP perseguir

hunter ['hʌntə(r)] N cazador(a) *m,f*

hunting ['hʌntɪŋ] N caza *f*; (*expedition*) cacería *f*

hurdle ['hɜːdəl] N *Sport* valla *f*; *Fig* obstáculo *m*

hurl [hɜːl] VT arrojar, lanzar

hurrah [hʊ'rɑː], **hurray** [hʊ'reɪ] INTERJ ¡hurra!; **h. for John!** ¡viva John!

hurricane ['hʌrɪkən, *US* 'hʌrɪkeɪn] N huracán *m*

hurried ['hʌrɪd] ADJ apresurado(a); (*action etc*) hecho(a) de prisa

hurriedly ['hʌrɪdlɪ] ADV deprisa, apresuradamente

hurry ['hʌrɪ] 1 VT meter prisa a
  2 VI darse prisa, apresurarse, *Am* apurarse
  3 N **to be in a h.** tener prisa *or Am* apuro

hurt [hɜːt] 1 VT (*pt & pp* **hurt**) hacer daño a; (*wound*) herir; (*feelings*) ofender
  2 VI doler; **my arm hurts** me duele el brazo
  3 ADJ (*physically*) herido(a); (*mentally*) dolido(a)

hurtful ['hɜːtfʊl] ADJ hiriente

hurtle ['hɜːtəl] VI lanzarse; **to h. down** desplomarse

husband ['hʌzbənd] N marido *m*, esposo *m*

hush [hʌʃ] 1 VT callar; **to h. sth up** echar tierra a un asunto
  2 N silencio *m*
  3 INTERJ ¡silencio!

hush-hush [hʌʃ'hʌʃ] ADJ *Fam* confidencial

husky¹ ['hʌskɪ] ADJ (**huskier, huskiest**) ronco(a)

husky² ['hʌskɪ] N (*dog*) perro *m* esquimal

hustings ['hʌstɪŋz] NPL *Pol* (**a**) *(platform)* tribuna *f* electoral (**b**) *(election)* elecciones *fpl*

hustle ['hʌsəl] **1** VT (**a**) *(jostle)* empujar (**b**) *Fam* meter prisa a
2 N bullicio *m*; **h. and bustle** ajetreo *m*

hut [hʌt] N cabaña *f*; *(shed)* cobertizo *m*; *Mil* barraca *f*

hutch [hʌtʃ] N jaula *f*; **rabbit h.** conejera *f*

hyacinth ['haɪəsɪnθ] N jacinto *m*

hybrid ['haɪbrɪd] ADJ & N híbrido(a) *(m,f)*

hydrant ['haɪdrənt] N **fire h.** boca *f* de incendio

hydraulic [haɪ'drɒlɪk] ADJ hidráulico(a)

hydrocarbon [haɪdrəʊ'kɑːbən] N hidrocarburo *m*

hydrochloric [haɪdrəʊ'klɒrɪk] ADJ **h. acid** ácido clorhídrico

hydroelectric [haɪdrəʊɪ'lektrɪk] ADJ hidroeléctrico(a)

hydrofoil ['haɪdrəfɔɪl] N hidroala *f*, *RP* alíscafo *m*

hydrogen ['haɪdrədʒən] N hidrógeno *m*

hydroplane ['haɪdrəpleɪn] N *US (seaplane)* hidroavión *m*

hyena [haɪ'iːnə] N hiena *f*

hygiene ['haɪdʒiːn] N higiene *f*

hygienic [haɪ'dʒiːnɪk] ADJ higiénico(a)

hymn [hɪm] N himno *m*; **h. book** cantoral *m*

hype [haɪp] N *Fam* campaña publicitaria, movida *f*

hyper- ['haɪpə(r)] PREF hiper-; **hyperactive** hiperactivo(a)

hypermarket ['haɪpəmɑːkɪt] N *Br* hipermercado *m*

hypersensitive [haɪpə'sensɪtɪv] ADJ hipersensible

hypertext ['haɪpətekst] N *Comput* hipertexto *m*

hyphen ['haɪfən] N guión *m*

hypnosis [hɪp'nəʊsɪs] N hipnosis *f*

hypnotist ['hɪpnətɪst] N hipnotizador(a) *m,f*

hypnotize ['hɪpnətaɪz] VT hipnotizar

hypoallergenic [haɪpəʊælə'dʒenɪk] ADJ hipoalergénico(a)

hypochondriac [haɪpə'kɒndrɪæk] ADJ & N hipocondríaco(a) *(m,f)*

hypocrisy [hɪ'pɒkrəsɪ] N hipocresía *f*

hypocrite ['hɪpəkrɪt] N hipócrita *mf*

hypocritical [hɪpə'krɪtɪkəl] ADJ hipócrita

hypodermic [haɪpə'dɜːmɪk] ADJ *Med* hipodérmico(a); **h. needle** aguja hipodérmica

hypothesis [haɪ'pɒθɪsɪs] N *(pl* **hypotheses** [haɪ'pɒθɪsiːz]) hipótesis *f*

hypothetic(al) [haɪpə'θetɪk(əl)] ADJ hipotético(a)

hysteria [hɪ'stɪərɪə] N histeria *f*

hysterical [hɪ'sterɪkəl] ADJ histérico(a)

hysterics [hɪ'sterɪks] NPL (**a**) *(panic)* ataque *m* de histeria (**b**) *Fam (of laughter)* ataque *m* de risa

I, i [aɪ] N (the letter) I, i f

I [aɪ] PERS PRON yo (usually omitted in Spanish, except for contrast); **I know her** (yo) la conozco

IAEA [aɪeɪiː'eɪ] N (abbr **International Atomic Energy Agency**) AIEA f

ICBM [aɪsiː.biː'em] N (abbr **intercontinental ballistic missile**) misil m balístico intercontinental

ice [aɪs] **1** N hielo m; **i. axe** pico m (de alpinista); **i. cream** helado m, Am sorbete; **i. cube** cubito m de hielo; **i. hockey** hockey m sobre hielo; Br **i. lolly** polo m; **i. rink** pista f de patinaje; **i. skate** patín m de cuchilla
2 VT (cake) alcorzar

▸ **ice over, ice up** VI (pond etc) helarse; (windscreen, plane wings) cubrirse de hielo

iceberg ['aɪsbɜːg] N iceberg m

icebox ['aɪsbɒks] N (**a**) Br (compartment of fridge) congelador m (**b**) US (fridge) nevera f, Méx refrigerador m, RP heladera f

icecap ['aɪskæp] N casquete m glaciar

Iceland ['aɪslənd] N Islandia

ice-skating ['aɪsskeɪtɪŋ] N patinaje m sobre hielo

icicle ['aɪsɪkəl] N carámbano m

icing ['aɪsɪŋ] N alcorza f; Br **i. sugar** azúcar m Esp, Méx glas or Esp de lustre or Chile flor or RP impalpable

icon ['aɪkɒn] N icono m

icy ['aɪsɪ] ADJ (**icier, iciest**) (road etc) helado(a); Fig (smile) glacial

ID [aɪ'diː] N US documentación f; **ID card** DNI m

I'd [aɪd] = **I would**; **I had**

idea [aɪ'dɪə] N idea f; (**I've**) **no idea** (no tengo) ni idea; Fam **what's the big i.?** ¿a qué viene esto?

ideal [aɪ'dɪəl] ADJ & N ideal (m)

idealist [aɪ'dɪəlɪst] N idealista mf

idealistic [aɪdɪə'lɪstɪk] ADJ idealista

idealize [aɪ'dɪəlaɪz] VT idealizar

ideally [aɪ'dɪəlɪ] ADV (**a**) (perfectly) perfectamente (**b**) (in the best conditions) de ser posible

identical [aɪ'dentɪkəl] ADJ idéntico(a)

identification [aɪdentɪfɪ'keɪʃən] N (**a**) (of body, criminal) identificación f (**b**) (papers) documentación f

identify [aɪ'dentɪfaɪ] **1** VT (body) identificar; (cause) descubrir
2 VI identificarse (**with** con)

Identikit® [aɪ'dentɪkɪt] N **I. picture** retrato m robot

identity [aɪ'dentɪtɪ] N identidad f; **i. card** carné m de identidad; **proof of i.** prueba f de identidad

ideological [aɪdɪə'lɒdʒɪkəl] ADJ ideológico(a)

ideology [aɪdɪ'ɒlədʒɪ] N ideología f

idiom ['ɪdɪəm] N modismo m; Fig (style) lenguaje m

idiomatic [ɪdɪə'mætɪk] ADJ idiomático(a)

idiosyncrasy [ɪdɪəʊ'sɪŋkrəsɪ] N idiosincrasia f

idiot ['ɪdɪət] N idiota mf, tonto(a) m,f

idiotic [ɪdɪ'ɒtɪk] ADJ (behaviour) idiota, tonto(a); (joke, plan) estúpido(a)

idle ['aɪdəl] ADJ holgazán(ana); (not working) (person) desempleado(a); (machinery) parado(a); (gossip) frívolo(a); (threat) vano(a)
2 VI (engine) funcionar en vacío

▸ **idle away** VT SEP (time) desperdiciar

idleness ['aɪdəlnɪs] N (laziness) holgazanería f; (unemployment) desempleo m; (stoppage) paro m

idol ['aɪdəl] N ídolo m

idolize ['aɪdəlaɪz] VT idolatrar

idyllic [ɪ'dɪlɪk] ADJ idílico(a)

i.e. [aɪ'iː] (abbr **id est**) i.e., es decir

if [ɪf] **1** CONJ (**a**) (conditional) si; **if not** si no; **if so** de ser así; **if I were you** yo en tu lugar; **if only she were here!** ¡ojalá estuviera aquí! (**b**) (whenever) si; **if you need help, ask** siempre que necesites ayuda, pídela
2 N **ifs and buts** pegas fpl

igloo ['ɪgluː] N iglú m

ignite [ɪg'naɪt] **1** VT encender
2 VI encenderse

ignition [ɪg'nɪʃən] N ignición f; Aut encendido m; **i. key** llave f de contacto

ignorance ['ɪgnərəns] N ignorancia f

ignorant ['ɪgnərənt] ADJ ignorante (**of** de); **to be i. of the facts** ignorar or desconocer los hechos

ignore [ɪg'nɔː(r)] VT (warning, remark) no hacer caso de; (behaviour, fact) pasar por alto

ill [ɪl] **1** ADJ (**a**) (unwell) enfermo(a); **to feel i.** encontrarse mal (**b**) (bad) malo(a); **i. feeling** resentimiento m; **i. will** mala voluntad
2 N mal m
3 ADV difícilmente

I'll [aɪl] = **I shall**; **I will**

ill-advised [ɪləd'vaɪzd] ADJ *(person)* imprudente; *(act)* desatinado(a); **you'd be i. to go** harías mal en ir

ill-disposed [ɪldɪ'spəʊzd] ADJ poco dispuesto(a)

illegal [ɪ'li:gəl] ADJ ilegal

illegible [ɪ'ledʒɪbəl] ADJ ilegible

illegitimate [ɪlɪ'dʒɪtɪmɪt] ADJ ilegítimo(a)

ill-fated [ɪl'feɪtɪd] ADJ abocado(a) al fracaso

ill-founded [ɪl'faʊndɪd] ADJ infundado(a)

illicit [ɪ'lɪsɪt] ADJ ilícito(a)

illiteracy [ɪ'lɪtərəsɪ] N analfabetismo *m*

illiterate [ɪ'lɪtərɪt] ADJ *(person)* analfabeto(a); *Fam (uneducated)* inculto(a)

illness ['ɪlnɪs] N enfermedad *f*

illogical [ɪ'lɒdʒɪkəl] ADJ ilógico(a)

ill-treat [ɪl'tri:t] VT maltratar

illuminate [ɪ'lu:mɪneɪt] VT (**a**) *(light up)* iluminar, alumbrar; *Fig (clarify)* aclarar (**b**) *(manuscript)* iluminar

illuminating [ɪ'lu:mɪneɪtɪŋ] ADJ *(experience, book)* instructivo(a); *(remark)* revelador(a)

illumination [ɪlu:mɪ'neɪʃən] N (**a**) *(lighting)* iluminación *f*; *Fig (clarification)* aclaración *f* (**b**) **illuminations** *(decorative lights)* iluminación *f*

illusion [i'lu:ʒən] N ilusión *f*; **to be under the i. that ...** engañarse pensando que ...

illusory [ɪ'lu:sərɪ] ADJ ilusorio(a)

illustrate ['ɪləstreɪt] VT ilustrar

illustration [ɪlə'streɪʃən] N ilustración *f*; *(example)* ejemplo *m*

illustrious [ɪ'lʌstrɪəs] ADJ ilustre

I'm [aɪm] = **I am**

image ['ɪmɪdʒ] N imagen *f*

imagery ['ɪmɪdʒərɪ] N *Lit* imágenes *fpl*

imaginary [ɪ'mædʒɪnərɪ] ADJ imaginario(a)

imagination [ɪmædʒɪ'neɪʃən] N imaginación *f*; *(inventiveness)* inventiva *f*

imaginative [ɪ'mædʒɪnətɪv] ADJ imaginativo(a)

imagine [ɪ'mædʒɪn] VT *(visualize)* imaginar; *(think)* suponer, imaginarse; **just i.!** ¡imagínate!

imbalance [ɪm'bæləns] N desequilibrio *m*

imbecile ['ɪmbɪsi:l] N imbécil *mf*

IMF [aɪe'mef] N *(abbr* **International Monetary Fund)** FMI *m*

imitate ['ɪmɪteɪt] VT imitar

imitation [ɪmɪ'teɪʃən] **1** N imitación *f*, copia *f*; *Pej* remedo *m*
2 ADJ de imitación

immaculate [ɪ'mækjʊlɪt] ADJ *(clean)* inmaculado(a); *(tidy)* perfectamente ordenado(a); *(clothes)* impecable; *(work)* perfecto(a); **the I. Conception** la Inmaculada Concepción

immaterial [ɪmə'tɪərɪəl] ADJ irrelevante; **it's i. to me whether ...** me trae sin cuidado si ...

immature [ɪmə'tjʊə(r)] ADJ inmaduro(a)

immediate [ɪ'mi:dɪət] ADJ inmediato(a); **in the i. future** en un futuro inmediato; **the i. family** la familia más cercana

immediately [ɪ'mi:dɪətlɪ] **1** ADV inmediatamente
2 CONJ en cuanto

immense [ɪ'mens] ADJ inmenso(a), enorme

immensely [ɪ'menslɪ] ADV *(rich)* enormemente; *(interesting, difficult)* sumamente

immerse [ɪ'mɜːs] VT sumergir (**in** en); *Fig* **to be immersed in sth** estar absorto(a) en algo

immersion [ɪ'mɜːʃən] N inmersión *f*; *Br* **i. heater** calentador *m* de inmersión; **i. course** cursillo intensivo

immigrant ['ɪmɪgrənt] ADJ & N inmigrante *(mf)*

immigrate ['ɪmɪgreɪt] VI inmigrar

immigration [ɪmɪ'greɪʃən] N inmigración *f*

imminent ['ɪmɪnənt] ADJ inminente

immobile [ɪ'məʊbaɪl] ADJ inmóvil

immobilize [ɪ'məʊbɪlaɪz] VT inmovilizar

immodest [ɪ'mɒdɪst] ADJ indecente

immoral [ɪ'mɒrəl] ADJ inmoral

immortal [ɪ'mɔːtəl] ADJ inmortal

immortality [ɪmɔː'tælɪtɪ] N inmortalidad *f*

immortalize [ɪ'mɔːtəlaɪz] VT inmortalizar

immune [ɪ'mju:n] ADJ inmune; *(exempt)* exento(a)

immunity [ɪ'mju:nɪtɪ] N inmunidad *f*

immunize ['ɪmjʊnaɪz] VT inmunizar (**against** contra)

impact ['ɪmpækt] N impacto *m*; *(crash)* choque *m*

impair [ɪm'peə(r)] VT perjudicar; *(sight etc)* dañar

impart [ɪm'pɑːt] VT *Fml (news)* comunicar; *(knowledge)* transmitir

impartial [ɪm'pɑːʃəl] ADJ imparcial

impassable [ɪm'pɑːsəbəl] ADJ *(road, ground)* intransitable; *(barrier)* infranqueable

impasse [æm'pɑːs] N punto muerto

impassive [ɪm'pæsɪv] ADJ impasible

impatience [ɪm'peɪʃəns] N impaciencia *f*

impatient [ɪm'peɪʃənt] ADJ impaciente; *(fretful)* irritable; **to get i.** perder la paciencia

impeccable [ɪm'pekəbəl] ADJ impecable

impede [ɪm'pi:d] VT *(prevent)* impedir; *(hinder)* estorbar; *(obstruct)* poner trabas a

impediment [ɪm'pedɪmənt] N impedimento *m*; *(obstacle)* estorbo *m*; **speech i.** defecto *m* del habla

impending [ɪm'pendɪŋ] ADJ *Fml* inminente

impenetrable [ɪm'penɪtrəbəl] ADJ impenetrable; *Fig (mystery, thoughts)* insondable

imperative [ɪm'perətɪv] **1** ADJ *Fml* imperativo(a); *(tone)* imperioso(a); *(urgent)* urgente
2 N *Gram* imperativo *m*

imperceptible [ɪmpə'septəbəl] ADJ imperceptible

imperfect [ɪm'pɜ:fɪkt] **1** ADJ imperfecto(a); *(goods)* defectuoso(a)
2 N *Gram* imperfecto *m*

imperfection [ɪmpə'fekʃən] N defecto *m*

imperial [ɪm'pɪərɪəl] ADJ (**a**) *(of empire)* imperial (**b**) *(measure)* **i. gallon** galón británico *(aprox 4,546 l)*

imperialism [ɪm'pɪərɪəlɪzəm] N imperialismo *m*

imperialist [ɪm'pɪərɪəlɪst] ADJ & N imperialista *(mf)*

imperious [ɪm'pɪərɪəs] ADJ imperioso(a)

impersonal [ɪm'pɜ:sənəl] ADJ impersonal

impersonate [ɪm'pɜ:səneɪt] VT hacerse pasar por; *(famous people)* imitar

impersonation [ɪmpɜ:sə'neɪʃən] N imitación *f*

impertinent [ɪm'pɜ:tɪnənt] ADJ impertinente

impervious [ɪm'pɜ:vɪəs] ADJ *(rock)* impermeable; *Fig* **to be i. to reason** no atender a razones

impetuous [ɪm'petjʊəs] ADJ impetuoso(a)

impetus ['ɪmpɪtəs] N ímpetu *m*; *Fig* impulso *m*

impinge [ɪm'pɪndʒ] VI *Fml* afectar (**on** a)

implant *Med* **1** VT [ɪm'plɑ:nt] implantar
2 N ['ɪmplɑ:nt] implantación *f*

implement 1 N ['ɪmplɪmənt] *(tool)* herramienta *f*; *(instrument)* instrumento *m*; **farm implements** *mpl* de labranza
2 VT ['ɪmplɪment] *(decision, plan)* llevar a cabo; *(law, policy)* aplicar

implicate ['ɪmplɪkeɪt] VT implicar (**in** en)

implication [ɪmplɪ'keɪʃən] N implicación *f*; *(consequence)* consecuencia *f*

implicit [ɪm'plɪsɪt] ADJ *(implied)* implícito(a); *(trust)* absoluto(a); *(faith)* incondicional

implore [ɪm'plɔ:(r)] VT implorar, suplicar

imply [ɪm'plaɪ] VT (**a**) *(involve)* implicar (**b**) *(hint)* dar a entender; *(mean)* significar

impolite [ɪmpə'laɪt] ADJ maleducado(a)

import 1 N ['ɪmpɔ:t] (**a**) *Com* importación *f*; **i. duty** derechos *mpl* de importación (**b**) *Fml (meaning)* sentido *m*
2 VT [ɪm'pɔ:t] *Com* importar

importance [ɪm'pɔ:təns] N importancia *f*; *(standing)* envergadura *f*; **of little i.** de poca monta

important [ɪm'pɔ:tənt] ADJ importante; **it's not i.** no importa

importer [ɪm'pɔ:tə(r)] N *Com* importador(a) *m,f*

impose [ɪm'pəʊz] **1** VT imponer (**on** *or* **upon** a)
2 VI **to i. on** *or* **upon** *(take advantage of)* abusar de

imposing [ɪm'pəʊzɪŋ] ADJ imponente, impresionante

imposition [ɪmpə'zɪʃən] N *(of tax etc)* imposición *f*; *(unfair demand)* abuso *m*; **would it be an i. if ...?** ¿le molestaría si ...?

impossibility [ɪmpɒsə'bɪlɪtɪ] N imposibilidad *f*

impossible [ɪm'pɒsəbəl] **1** ADJ imposible; *(person)* insoportable
2 N **to do the i.** hacer lo imposible

impossibly [ɪm'pɒsəblɪ] ADV de manera insoportable; **i. difficult** de una dificultad insuperable

impostor [ɪm'pɒstə(r)] N impostor(a) *m,f*

impotent ['ɪmpətənt] ADJ impotente

impound [ɪm'paʊnd] VT incautarse de

impoverished [ɪm'pɒvərɪʃt] ADJ *(person, country)* empobrecido(a); *(soil)* agotado(a)

impracticable [ɪm'præktɪkəbəl] ADJ impracticable, irrealizable

impractical [ɪm'præktɪkəl] ADJ *(person)* poco práctico(a); *(project, solution etc)* poco viable

imprecise [ɪmprɪ'saɪs] ADJ impreciso(a)

impregnable [ɪm'pregnəbəl] ADJ inexpugnable

impregnate ['ɪmpregneɪt] VT (**a**) *(soak)* impregnar (**with** de) (**b**) *Fml (fertilize)* fecundar

impress [ɪm'pres] VT (**a**) *(make an impression on)* impresionar; **to i. sb favourably/unfavourably** dar a algn buena/mala impresión (**b**) *(mark)* imprimir (**on** en); *(pattern)* estampar (**on** en); *Fig* **to i. sth on sb** convencer a algn de la importancia de algo

impression [ɪm'preʃən] N (**a**) *(effect)* impresión *f*; **to be under the i. that ...** tener la impresión de que ...; **to give the i. of ...** dar la impresión de ... (**b**) *(imprint)* marca *f*; *(in snow)* huella *f* (**c**) *(imitation)* imitación *f*

impressionist [ɪm'preʃənɪst] ADJ & N impresionista *(mf)*

impressive [ɪm'presɪv] ADJ impresionante

imprint 1 VT [ɪm'prɪnt] *(mark)* dejar huella (**on** en)
2 N ['ɪmprɪnt] (**a**) *(mark)* marca *f*; *(left by foot etc)* huella *f* (**b**) *(publisher's name)* pie *m* de imprenta

imprison [ɪm'prɪzən] VT encarcelar

imprisonment [ɪm'prɪzənmənt] N encarcelamiento *m*

improbable [ɪm'prɒbəbəl] ADJ *(event)* improbable; *(story)* inverosímil

impromptu [ɪm'prɒmptju:] **1** ADJ *(speech)* improvisado(a); *(visit)* imprevisto(a)
2 ADV de improviso

improper [ɪm'prɒpə(r)] ADJ (**a**) *(use, purpose)* impropio(a), incorrecto(a); *(suggestion, behaviour)* indecoroso(a) (**b**) *(dishonest)* impropio(a), irregular

improve [ɪm'pru:v] **1** VT mejorar; *(knowledge)* perfeccionar; *(mind)* cultivar; *(increase)* aumentar
2 VI mejorarse; *(increase)* aumentar

▶ **improve on** VT INSEP superar; *(offer, bid)* sobrepujar

improvement [ɪm'pru:vmənt] N mejora *f*; *(in skill)* perfeccionamiento *m*; *(increase)* aumento *m*

improvise ['ɪmprəvaɪz] VT & VI improvisar

imprudent [ɪm'pru:dənt] ADJ imprudente

impudence ['ɪmpjʊdəns] N insolencia *f*

impudent ['ɪmpjʊdənt] ADJ insolente

impulse ['ımpʌls] N impulso *m*; **to act on (an) i.** dejarse llevar por un impulso

impulsive [ım'pʌlsɪv] ADJ irreflexivo(a)

impunity [ım'pju:nɪtɪ] N impunidad *f*

impure [ım'pjʊə(r)] ADJ (**a**) *(act)* impuro(a); *(thought)* impúdico(a) (**b**) *(air)* contaminado(a)

impurity [ım'pjʊərɪtɪ] N (**a**) *(of act)* deshonestidad *f* (**b**) *(in air, substance)* impureza *f*

in [ın] **1** PREP (**a**) *(place)* en; *(within)* dentro de; **in bed** en la cama; **in Brazil** en Brasil; **in prison** en la cárcel
(**b**) *(motion)* en; **she arrived in Paris** llegó a París
(**c**) *(time) (during)* en, durante; **I haven't seen her in years** hace años que no la veo; **in May/ 1945** en mayo/1945; **in spring** en primavera; **in the daytime** durante el día; **in the morning** por la mañana; **at ten in the morning** a las diez de la mañana
(**d**) *(time) (within)* dentro de; **I arrived in time** llegué a tiempo
(**e**) *(time) (after)* al cabo de
(**f**) *(manner)* en; **in a loud/quiet voice** en voz alta/baja; **in fashion** de moda; **in French** en francés; **in writing** por escrito; **write in pencil** escribe con lápiz
(**g**) *(wearing)* **dressed in blue** vestido(a) de azul; **in uniform** de uniforme
(**h**) *(weather etc)* a, en; **in the rain** bajo la lluvia; **in the sun** al sol; en la oscuridad; **in daylight** a la luz del día
(**i**) *(state, emotion)* en; **in danger/public/ silence** en peligro/público/silencio; **in love** enamorado(a); **in tears** llorando
(**j**) *(ratio, numbers)* de; **in threes** de tres en tres; **one in six** uno de cada seis; **2 m in length** 2 m de largo
(**k**) *(after superlative)* de; **the smallest car in the world** el coche más pequeño del mundo
(**l**) *(phrases)* **in all** en total; **in itself/himself/ herself** en sí; **in that ...** dado que ...
2 ADV **in here/there** aquí/allí dentro; **let's go in** vamos adentro; **to be in** *(at home)* estar (en casa); *(at work)* estar; *(tide)* estar alta; *Fam (in fashion)* estar de moda; **the bus is in** el autobús ha llegado; *Fam* **to be in on sth** estar enterado(a) de algo
3 ADJ *Fam* (**a**) *(fashionable) (place)* de moda; *(clothes)* del último grito (**b**) **an in joke** una broma privada
4 N *Fam* **ins and outs** detalles *mpl*

inability [ınə'bılıtı] N incapacidad *f*

inaccessible [ınæk'sesəbəl] ADJ inaccesible

inaccurate [ın'ækjʊrɪt] ADJ inexacto(a); *(statement)* erróneo(a); *(figures, total)* incorrecto(a)

inactivity [ınæk'tɪvɪtɪ] N inactividad *f*

inadequate [ın'ædɪkwɪt] ADJ (**a**) *(lacking)* insuficiente (**b**) *(not capable)* incapaz; *(unsuitable)* inadecuado(a) (**c**) *(defective)* defectuoso(a)

inadvertent [ınəd'vɜ:tənt] ADJ involuntario(a)

inadvertently [ınəd'vɜ:təntlı] ADV involuntariamente

inadvisable [ınəd'vaızəbəl] ADJ imprudente

inane [ı'neın] ADJ necio(a), fatuo(a)

inanimate [ın'ænımıt] ADJ inanimado(a)

inappropriate [ınə'prəʊprııt] ADJ inoportuno(a); *(behaviour)* poco apropiado(a)

inarticulate [ına:'tɪkjʊlıt] ADJ *(cry, sound)* inarticulado(a); **to be i.** *(person)* expresarse mal

inasmuch as [ınəz'mʌtʃəz] CONJ *Fml* (**a**) *(since)* puesto que, ya que (**b**) *(insofar as)* en la medida en que

inattentive [ınə'tentıv] ADJ desatento(a)

inaudible [ın'ɔ:dəbəl] ADJ inaudible

inaugural [ın'ɔ:gjʊrəl] ADJ inaugural

inaugurate [ın'ɔ:gjʊreıt] VT *(building)* inaugurar; *(president)* investir

inauguration [ınɔ:gjʊ'reıʃən] N *(of building)* inauguración *f*; *(of president)* investidura *f*

inauspicious [ınɔ:'spıʃəs] ADJ *(start)* poco prometedor(a); *(circumstances)* desfavorable

inborn ['ınbɔ:n] ADJ innato(a)

inbred ['ınbred] ADJ (**a**) *(quality)* innato(a) (**b**) *(family)* endogámico(a)

Inc, inc *US Com (abbr* **Incorporated**) ≃ S.A.

incalculable [ın'kælkjʊləbəl] ADJ incalculable

incapable [ın'keıpəbəl] ADJ incapaz

incapacitate [ınkə'pæsıteıt] VT *Fml* incapacitar

incapacity [ınkə'pæsıtı] N incapacidad *f*

incarcerate [ın'ka:səreıt] VT *Fml* encarcelar

incarnation [ınka:'neıʃən] N encarnación *f*

incendiary [ın'sendıərı] **1** ADJ incendiario(a) **2** N bomba incendiaria

incense[1] ['ınsens] N incienso *m*

incense[2] [ın'sens] VT enfurecer, sacar de quicio

incentive [ın'sentıv] N incentivo *m*

incessant [ın'sesənt] ADJ incesante; *(demands)* constante

incessantly [ın'sesəntlı] ADV sin cesar

incest ['ınsest] N incesto *m*

inch [ıntʃ] N pulgada *f (aprox 2,54 cm); Fig* **i. by i.** poco a poco; *Fig* **she wouldn't give an i.** no quería ceder ni un ápice
▸ **inch forward** VT SEP & VI avanzar poco a poco

incidence ['ınsıdəns] N frecuencia *f*

incident ['ınsıdənt] N incidente *m*

incidental [ınsı'dentəl] ADJ *(accessory)* incidental, accesorio(a); *(risk)* inherente (**to** a); **i. music** música *f* de fondo

incidentally [ınsı'dentəlı] ADV a propósito

incinerator [ın'sınəreıtə(r)] N incinerador *m*

incipient [ın'sıpıənt] ADJ *Fml* incipiente

incision [ın'sıʒən] N incisión *f*

incisive [ın'saısıv] ADJ *(comment)* incisivo(a); *(reply)* tajante; *(mind)* penetrante

incite [ın'saıt] VT incitar; **to i. sb to do sth** incitar a algn a hacer algo

inclination [ɪnklɪ'neɪʃən] N inclinación *f*; **my i. is to stay** yo prefiero quedarme

incline [ɪn'klaɪn] **1** VT (**a**) **I'm inclined to believe him** me inclino a creerlo; **she's inclined to be aggressive** tiende a ser agresiva (**b**) *(head etc)* inclinar **2** VI *(slope)* inclinarse **3** N ['ɪnklaɪn] *(slope)* pendiente *f*

include [ɪn'kluːd] VT incluir (**in** en); *(in price)* comprender (**in** en); *(in list)* figurar (**in** en)

including [ɪn'kluːdɪŋ] PREP incluso, inclusive

inclusion [ɪn'kluːʒən] N inclusión *f*

inclusive [ɪn'kluːsɪv] ADJ inclusivo(a); **pages 6 to 10 i.** de la página 6 a la 10, ambas inclusive; **the rent is i. of bills** el alquiler incluye las facturas

incognito [ɪnkɒg'niːtəʊ] ADV de incógnito

incoherent [ɪnkəʊ'hɪərənt] ADJ incoherente

income ['ɪnkʌm] N ingresos *mpl*; *(from investment)* réditos *mpl*; **i. tax** impuesto *m* sobre la renta; **i. tax return** declaración *f* de la renta

incoming ['ɪnkʌmɪŋ] ADJ *(flight)* de llegada; *(president)* entrante; *(tide)* ascendente; *(mail)* recibido(a); *(phone call)* de fuera

incomparable [ɪn'kɒmpərəbəl] ADJ incomparable, sin par

incompatible [ɪnkəm'pætəbəl] ADJ incompatible (**with** con)

incompetence [ɪn'kɒmpɪtəns] N incompetencia *f*

incompetent [ɪn'kɒmpɪtənt] ADJ incompetente

incomplete [ɪnkəm'pliːt] ADJ incompleto(a)

incomprehensible [ɪnkɒmprɪ'hensəbəl] ADJ incomprensible

inconceivable [ɪnkən'siːvəbəl] ADJ inconcebible

inconclusive [ɪnkən'kluːsɪv] ADJ *(vote)* no decisivo(a); *(proof)* no concluyente

incongruous [ɪn'kɒŋgrʊəs] ADJ incongruente

inconsiderate [ɪnkən'sɪdərɪt] ADJ desconsiderado(a); **how i. of you!** ¡qué falta de consideración por tu parte!

inconsistency [ɪnkən'sɪstənsɪ] N inconsecuencia *f*; *(contradiction)* contradicción *f*

inconsistent [ɪnkən'sɪstənt] ADJ inconsecuente; *(contradictory)* contradictorio(a); **your evidence is i. with the facts** su testimonio no concuerda con los hechos

inconspicuous [ɪnkən'spɪkjʊəs] ADJ que pasa desapercibido(a); *(discreet)* discreto(a)

incontrovertible [ɪnkɒntrə'vɜːtəbəl] ADJ *Fml* incontrovertible

inconvenience [ɪnkən'viːnɪəns] **1** N inconveniente *f*; *(annoyance)* molestia *f* **2** VT *(annoy)* molestar; *(cause difficulty to)* incomodar

inconvenient [ɪnkən'viːnɪənt] ADJ molesto(a); *(time)* inoportuno(a); *(design)* poco práctico(a)

incorporate [ɪn'kɔːpəreɪt] VT incorporar (**in** or **into** a); *(include)* incluir; *(contain)* contener

incorporated [ɪn'kɔːpəreɪtɪd] ADJ *US Com* **i. company** sociedad anónima

incorrect [ɪnkə'rekt] ADJ incorrecto(a)

incorrigible [ɪn'kɒrɪdʒəbəl] ADJ incorregible

increase 1 N ['ɪnkriːs] aumento *m*; *(in number)* incremento *m*; *(in price etc)* subida *f* **2** VT [ɪn'kriːs] aumentar; *(price etc)* subir **3** VI aumentar

increasing [ɪn'kriːsɪŋ] ADJ creciente

increasingly [ɪn'kriːsɪŋlɪ] ADV cada vez más

incredible [ɪn'kredəbəl] ADJ increíble

incredulous [ɪn'kredjʊləs] ADJ incrédulo(a)

increment ['ɪnkrɪmənt] N incremento *m*

incriminate [ɪn'krɪmɪneɪt] VT incriminar

incriminating [ɪn'krɪmɪneɪtɪŋ] ADJ incriminatorio(a)

incubation [ɪnkjʊ'beɪʃən] N incubación *f*

incubator ['ɪnkjʊbeɪtə(r)] N incubadora *f*

incumbent [ɪn'kʌmbənt] **1** N titular *mf* **2** ADJ *Fml* **to be i. on sb to do sth** ser la obligación de algn hacer algo

incur [ɪn'kɜː(r)] VT *(blame)* incurrir en; *(risk)* correr; *(debt)* contraer; *(loss)* sufrir

incurable [ɪn'kjʊərəbəl] ADJ incurable

indebted [ɪn'detɪd] ADJ endeudado(a); *Fig (grateful)* agradecido(a); *Fig* **to be i. to sb** estar en deuda con algn

indecent [ɪn'diːsənt] ADJ indecente; **i. assault** atentado *m* contra el pudor; **i. exposure** exhibicionismo *m*

indecision [ɪndɪ'sɪʒən] N indecisión *f*

indecisive [ɪndɪ'saɪsɪv] ADJ *(person)* indeciso(a); *(evidence)* poco concluyente; *(victory)* no decisivo(a)

indeed [ɪn'diːd] ADV (**a**) *Fml (in fact)* efectivamente, en realidad (**b**) **I'm very sorry i.** lo siento de veras; **it's very hard i.** es verdaderamente difícil; **thank you very much i.** muchísimas gracias

indefinite [ɪn'defɪnɪt] ADJ indefinido(a)

indefinitely [ɪn'defɪnɪtlɪ] ADV indefinidamente

indelible [ɪn'deləbəl] ADJ indeleble

indemnify [ɪn'demnɪfaɪ] VT indemnizar (**for** por)

indemnity [ɪn'demnɪtɪ] N (**a**) *(insurance)* indemnidad *f* (**b**) *(compensation)* indemnización *f*

indentation [ɪnden'teɪʃən] N (**a**) *Typ* sangría *f* (**b**) *(of edge)* muesca *f*; *(of surface)* depresión *f*

independence [ɪndɪ'pendəns] N independencia *f*; *US* **I. Day** Día *m* de la Independencia *(4 julio)*

independent [ɪndɪ'pendənt] ADJ independiente; *Br* **i. school** colegio *m* privado; **to become i.** independizarse

in-depth ['ɪndepθ] ADJ minucioso(a), exhaustivo(a)

indescribable [ɪndɪs'kraɪbəbəl] ADJ *(pain, beauty)* indescriptible

indestructible [ɪndɪ'strʌktəbəl] ADJ indestructible

indeterminate [ɪndɪ'tɜ:mɪnɪt] ADJ indeterminado(a)

index ['ɪndeks] **1** N (*pl* **indexes** *or* **indices**) (**a**) *(in book)* índice *m; (in library)* catálogo *m;* **i. card** ficha *f* (**b**) *Math* exponente *m; Econ* índice *m* (**c**) **i. finger** dedo *m* índice
2 VT catalogar

index-linked ['ɪndekslɪŋkt] ADJ sujeto(a) al aumento de la inflación

India ['ɪndɪə] N (la) India

Indian ['ɪndɪən] ADJ & N *(of America)* indio(a) *(m,f)*, *Am* indígena *(mf); (of India)* indio(a), hindú *(mf);* **I. Ocean** Océano Índico; **I. summer** veranillo *m* de San Martín

indicate ['ɪndɪkeɪt] **1** VT indicar
2 VI *BrAut* poner el intermitente

indication [ɪndɪ'keɪʃən] N indicio *m*

indicative [ɪn'dɪkətɪv] **1** ADJ indicativo(a)
2 N *Gram* indicativo *m*

indicator ['ɪndɪkeɪtə(r)] N indicador *m; Br Aut* intermitente *m*

indices ['ɪndɪsi:z] PL *of* **index**

indict [ɪn'daɪt] VT acusar (**for** de)

indictment [ɪn'daɪtmənt] N *Jur* acusación *f; Fig* **a damning i. of his books** una crítica feroz de sus libros

indifference [ɪn'dɪfərəns] N indiferencia *f*

indifferent [ɪn'dɪfərənt] ADJ (**a**) *(uninterested)* indiferente (**b**) *(mediocre)* regular

indigenous [ɪn'dɪdʒɪnəs] ADJ indígena

indigestion [ɪndɪ'dʒestʃən] N indigestión *f;* **to suffer from i.** tener un empacho

indignant [ɪn'dɪgnənt] ADJ indignado(a); *(look)* de indignación; **to get i. about sth** indignarse por algo

indignity [ɪn'dɪgnɪtɪ] N indignidad *f*

indigo ['ɪndɪgəʊ] **1** N añil *m*
2 ADJ (de color) añil

indirect [ɪndɪ'rekt, ɪndaɪ'rekt] ADJ indirecto(a)

indiscreet [ɪndɪ'skri:t] ADJ indiscreto(a)

indiscretion [ɪndɪ'skreʃən] N indiscreción *f*

indiscriminate [ɪndɪs'krɪmɪnɪt] ADJ indiscriminado(a)

indispensable [ɪndɪ'spensəbəl] ADJ indispensable, imprescindible

indisposed [ɪndɪ'spəʊzd] ADJ *Fml* indispuesto(a)

indisputable [ɪndɪ'spju:təbəl] ADJ indiscutible, incontestable

indistinct [ɪndɪ'stɪŋkt] ADJ indistinto(a); *(memory)* confuso(a), vago(a); *(shape etc)* borroso(a)

indistinguishable [ɪndɪ'stɪŋgwɪʃəbəl] ADJ indistinguible

individual [ɪndɪ'vɪdjʊəl] **1** ADJ (**a**) *(separate)* individual; *(for one)* particular; *(personal)* personal (**b**) *(characteristic)* particular; *(original)* original

2 N *(person)* individuo *m;* **private i.** particular *m*

individualist [ɪndɪ'vɪdjʊəlɪst] N individualista *mf*

indoctrinate [ɪn'dɒktrɪneɪt] VT adoctrinar

indoctrination [ɪndɒktrɪ'neɪʃən] N adoctrinamiento *m*

indolent ['ɪndələnt] ADJ *Fml* indolente

Indonesia [ɪndəʊ'ni:zɪə] N Indonesia

Indonesian [ɪndəʊ'ni:zɪən] **1** ADJ indonesio(a)
2 N (**a**) *(person)* indonesio(a) *m,f* (**b**) *(language)* indonesio *m*

indoor ['ɪndɔ:(r)] ADJ *(plant)* de interior; **i. football** fútbol *m* sala; **i. pool** piscina cubierta

indoors [ɪn'dɔ:z] ADV *(inside)* dentro (de casa); *(at home)* en casa; **let's go i.** vamos adentro

induce [ɪn'dju:s] VT (**a**) *(persuade)* inducir, persuadir (**b**) *(cause)* producir; *Med (labour)* provocar

inducement [ɪn'dju:smənt] N incentivo *m*, aliciente *m*

induction [ɪn'dʌkʃən] N (**a**) *Med (of labour)* inducción *f* (**b**) *(into new job, group)* iniciación *f* (**c**) *Elec* inducción *f*

indulge [ɪn'dʌldʒ] **1** VT (**a**) *(child)* consentir; *(person)* complacer; **to i. oneself** darse gusto (**b**) *(whim)* ceder a, satisfacer
2 VI darse el gusto (**in** de)

indulgence [ɪn'dʌldʒəns] N (**a**) *(of child)* mimo *m; (of attitude)* indulgencia *f* (**b**) *(of whim)* satisfacción *f*

indulgent [ɪn'dʌldʒənt] ADJ indulgente

industrial [ɪn'dʌstrɪəl] ADJ industrial; **to take i. action** declararse en huelga; *Br* **i. estate**, *US* **i. park** polígono *m* industrial

industrialist [ɪn'dʌstrɪəlɪst] N industrial *mf*

industrialize [ɪn'dʌstrɪəlaɪz] VT industrializar; **to become industrialized** industrializarse

industrious [ɪn'dʌstrɪəs] ADJ trabajador(a)

industry ['ɪndəstrɪ] N (**a**) *(economic)* industria *f* (**b**) *(hard work)* aplicación *f*

inebriated [ɪn'i:brieɪtɪd] ADJ embriagado(a)

inedible [ɪn'edəbəl] ADJ incomible

ineffective [ɪnɪ'fektɪv] ADJ ineficaz

ineffectual [ɪnɪ'fektʃʊəl] ADJ *(aim, protest)* ineficaz; *(person)* incompetente

inefficiency [ɪnɪ'fɪʃənsɪ] N ineficacia *f; (of person)* incompetencia *f*

inefficient [ɪnɪ'fɪʃənt] ADJ ineficaz; *(person)* inepto(a)

ineligible [ɪn'elɪdʒəbəl] ADJ no apto(a) (**for** para)

inept [ɪn'ept] ADJ *(person)* inepto(a); *(remark)* estúpido(a)

inequality [ɪnɪ'kwɒlɪtɪ] N desigualdad *f*

inert [ɪn'ɜ:t] ADJ inerte

inertia [ɪn'ɜ:ʃə] N inercia *f*

inescapable [ɪnɪ'skeɪpəbəl] ADJ ineludible

inevitability [ɪnevɪtə'bɪlɪtɪ] N inevitabilidad *f*

inevitable [ɪn'evɪtəbəl] ADJ inevitable

inexcusable [ɪnɪk'skjuːzəbəl] ADJ inexcusable, imperdonable

inexhaustible [ɪnɪg'zɔːstəbəl] ADJ inagotable

inexorable [ɪn'eksərəbəl] ADJ *Fml* inexorable

inexpensive [ɪnɪk'spensɪv] ADJ económico(a)

inexperience [ɪnɪk'spɪərɪəns] N inexperiencia *f*

inexperienced [ɪnɪk'spɪərɪənst] ADJ inexperto(a)

inexplicable [ɪnɪk'splɪkəbəl] ADJ inexplicable

infallible [ɪn'fæləbəl] ADJ infalible

infamous ['ɪnfəməs] ADJ infame

infancy ['ɪnfənsɪ] N infancia *f*

infant ['ɪnfənt] N niño(a) *m,f*; *Br* **i. school** parvulario *m*

infantile ['ɪnfəntaɪl] ADJ infantil

infantry ['ɪnfəntrɪ] N infantería *f*

infatuated [ɪn'fætjʊeɪtɪd] ADJ encaprichado(a)

infatuation [ɪnfætjʊ'eɪʃən] N encaprichamiento *m*

infect [ɪn'fekt] VT *(cut)* infectar; *(water)* contaminar; *(person)* contagiar

infection [ɪn'fekʃən] N *(of cut)* infección *f*; *(of water)* contaminación *f*; *(with illness)* contagio *m*

infectious [ɪn'fekʃəs] ADJ *(disease)* infeccioso(a); *Fig* contagioso(a)

infer [ɪn'fɜː(r)] VT inferir (**from** de)

inference ['ɪnfərəns] N inferencia *f*

inferior [ɪn'fɪərɪə(r)] **1** ADJ inferior (**to** a)
  2 N *Pej* inferior *mf*

inferiority [ɪnfɪərɪ'ɒrɪtɪ] N inferioridad *f*

inferno [ɪn'fɜːnəʊ] N *Literary* infierno *m*; *Fig* **the house was a raging i.** la casa ardía en llamas

infertile [ɪn'fɜːtaɪl] ADJ estéril

infertility [ɪnfə'tɪlɪtɪ] N esterilidad *f*

infest [ɪn'fest] VT infestar, plagar (**with** de)

infidelity [ɪnfɪ'delɪtɪ] N infidelidad *f*

infighting ['ɪnfaɪtɪŋ] N *Fig* luchas internas

infiltrate ['ɪnfɪltreɪt] VT infiltrarse (**into** en)

infinite ['ɪnfɪnɪt] ADJ infinito(a)

infinitive [ɪn'fɪnɪtɪv] N infinitivo *m*

infinity [ɪn'fɪnɪtɪ] N infinidad *f*; *Math* infinito *m*

infirm [ɪn'fɜːm] **1** ADJ *(ailing)* enfermizo(a); *(weak)* débil
  2 NPL **the i.** los inválidos

infirmary [ɪn'fɜːmərɪ] N hospital *m*

infirmity [ɪn'fɜːmɪtɪ] N *Fml (ailment)* enfermedad *f*; *(weakness)* debilidad *f*

inflame [ɪn'fleɪm] VT *(passion)* encender; *(curiosity)* avivar; *(crowd)* enardecer

inflamed [ɪn'fleɪmd] ADJ inflamado(a); **to become i.** inflamarse

inflammable [ɪn'flæməbəl] ADJ *(material)* inflamable; *Fig (situation)* explosivo(a)

inflammation [ɪnflə'meɪʃən] N inflamación *f*

inflatable [ɪn'fleɪtəbəl] ADJ inflable

inflate [ɪn'fleɪt] **1** VT inflar
  2 VI inflarse

inflated [ɪn'fleɪtɪd] ADJ (**a**) *Fig (prices)* inflacionista (**b**) *Pej (view, idea)* exagerado(a)

inflation [ɪn'fleɪʃən] N inflación *f*

inflexible [ɪn'fleksəbəl] ADJ inflexible

inflict [ɪn'flɪkt] VT *(blow)* asestar (**on** a); *(damage)* causar (**on** a); *(defeat)* infligir (**on** a)

in-flight ['ɪnflaɪt] ADJ durante el vuelo

influence ['ɪnflʊəns] **1** N influencia *f*; *Fam* **to be under the i.** llevar una copa de más
  2 VT influir en

influential [ɪnflʊ'enʃəl] ADJ influyente

influenza [ɪnflʊ'enzə] N gripe *f*

influx ['ɪnflʌks] N afluencia *f*

info ['ɪnfəʊ] N *Fam* información *f*

inform [ɪn'fɔːm] **1** VT informar *or CAm, Méx* reportar (**of/about** de/sobre); *(police)* avisar (**of/about** de)
  2 VI **to i. against** *or* **on** denunciar

informal [ɪn'fɔːməl] ADJ (**a**) *(occasion, behaviour)* informal; *(language, treatment)* familiar (**b**) *(unofficial)* no oficial

informality [ɪnfɔː'mælɪtɪ] N *(of occasion, behaviour)* sencillez *f*; *(of treatment)* familiaridad *f*

informant [ɪn'fɔːmənt] N informante *mf*

information [ɪnfə'meɪʃən] N (**a**) *(news, facts)* información *f*; *(details)* detalles *mpl*; *(knowledge)* conocimientos *mpl*; **a piece of i.** un dato; **i. bureau** centro *m* de información; **i. (super)highway** autopista *f* de la información; **i. technology** informática *f* (**b**) *US Tel* información *f*, *Am* informaciones *fpl*

informative [ɪn'fɔːmətɪv] ADJ informativo(a)

informed [ɪn'fɔːmd] ADJ enterado(a); **keep me i.** téngame al corriente

informer [ɪn'fɔːmə(r)] N delator(a) *m,f*, *(to the police)* soplón(ona) *m,f*

infrared [ɪnfrə'red] ADJ infrarrojo(a)

infrastructure ['ɪnfrəstrʌktʃə(r)] N infraestructura *f*

infrequent [ɪn'friːkwənt] ADJ infrecuente

infringe [ɪn'frɪndʒ] **1** VT *(law, rule)* infringir; *(copyright)* no respetar
  2 VT **to i. on** *or* **upon** *(rights)* violar; *(privacy)* invadir

infringement [ɪn'frɪndʒmənt] N *(of law, rule)* infracción *f*; *(of rights)* violación *f*

infuriate [ɪn'fjʊərɪeɪt] VT poner furioso(a)

infuriating [ɪn'fjʊərɪeɪtɪŋ] ADJ exasperante

infusion [ɪn'fjuːʒən] N infusión *f*

ingenious [ɪn'dʒiːnɪəs] ADJ ingenioso(a)

ingenuity [ɪndʒɪ'njuːɪtɪ] N ingenio *m*

ingenuous [ɪn'dʒenjʊəs] ADJ ingenuo(a)

ingot ['ɪŋgət] N lingote *m*

ingrained [ɪn'greɪnd] ADJ *Fig* arraigado(a)

ingratiate [ɪn'greɪʃɪeɪt] VT *Pej* **to i. oneself with sb** congraciarse con algn

ingratiating [ɪn'greɪʃɪeɪtɪŋ] ADJ zalamero(a)

ingratitude [ɪnˈɡrætɪtjuːd] N ingratitud f
ingredient [ɪnˈɡriːdɪənt] N ingrediente m
inhabit [ɪnˈhæbɪt] VT vivir en, ocupar
inhabitable [ɪnˈhæbɪtəbəl] ADJ habitable

Note that the Spanish word **inhabitable** is a false friend and is never a translation for the English word **inhabitable**. In Spanish, **inhabitable** means "uninhabitable".

inhabitant [ɪnˈhæbɪtənt] N habitante mf
inhale [ɪnˈheɪl] 1 VT (gas) inhalar; (air) aspirar
  2 VI aspirar; (smoker) tragar el humo
inherent [ɪnˈhɪərənt] ADJ inherente
inherit [ɪnˈherɪt] VT heredar (**from** de)
inheritance [ɪnˈherɪtəns] N herencia f
inhibit [ɪnˈhɪbɪt] VT (freedom) limitar; (person) cohibir; **to i. sb from doing sth** impedir a algn hacer algo
inhibited [ɪnˈhɪbɪtɪd] ADJ cohibido(a)
inhibition [ɪnhɪˈbɪʃən] N cohibición f
inhospitable [ɪnhɒˈspɪtəbəl] ADJ inhospitalario(a); (climate, place) inhóspito(a)
inhuman [ɪnˈhjuːmən] ADJ inhumano(a)
inhumane [ɪnhjuːˈmeɪn] ADJ inhumano(a)
iniquity [ɪˈnɪkwɪtɪ] N Fml iniquidad f
initial [ɪˈnɪʃəl] 1 ADJ inicial, primero(a)
  2 N inicial f; **initials** iniciales fpl
  3 VT (pt & pp **initialled**, US **initialed**) firmar con las iniciales
initially [ɪˈnɪʃəlɪ] ADV al principio
initiate [ɪˈnɪʃɪeɪt] VT (a) Fml (begin) iniciar; (legal proceedings) emprender (b) (into secret society) admitir (into a algn
initiation [ɪnɪʃɪˈeɪʃən] N (a) (start) principio m (b) (admission) iniciación f
initiative [ɪˈnɪʃɪətɪv] N iniciativa f
inject [ɪnˈdʒekt] VT (a) (drug etc) inyectar (b) Fig (capital) invertir; (life, hope) infundir
injection [ɪnˈdʒekʃən] N inyección f; **to give sb an i.** poner una inyección a algn
injunction [ɪnˈdʒʌŋkʃən] N interdicto m
injure [ˈɪndʒə(r)] VT herir; **to i. oneself** hacerse daño; Fig (health, reputation) perjudicar
injured [ˈɪndʒəd] 1 ADJ herido(a); Fig (look, tone) ofendido(a)
  2 NPL **the i.** los heridos
injury [ˈɪndʒərɪ] N (hurt) herida f; Fig (harm) daño m; Sport **i. time** (tiempo m de) descuento m
injustice [ɪnˈdʒʌstɪs] N injusticia f
ink [ɪŋk] N tinta f; **invisible i.** tinta simpática
inkjet printer [ˈɪŋkdʒetˈprɪntə(r)] N Comput impresora f de chorro de tinta
inkling [ˈɪŋklɪŋ] N (idea) idea f; (suspicion) sospecha f; (sign) señal f
inkwell [ˈɪŋkwel] N tintero m
inlaid [ɪnˈleɪd] ADJ (wood) taraceado(a); (ivory, gems) incrustado(a)

inland 1 ADJ [ˈɪnlənd] (del) interior; Br **I. Revenue** ≃ Hacienda f
  2 ADV [ɪnˈlænd] (travel) tierra adentro
in-laws [ˈɪnlɔːz] NPL Fam familia f política
inlet [ˈɪnlet] N (a) (in coastline) ensenada f, cala f (b) (in pipe, machine) entrada f, admisión f
inline [ˈɪnlaɪn] ADJ **i. skates** patines mpl en línea
inmate [ˈɪnmeɪt] N (of prison) preso(a) m,f; (of hospital) enfermo(a) m,f; (of asylum, camp) internado(a) m,f
inn [ɪn] N (with lodging) posada f, mesón m
innate [ɪˈneɪt] ADJ innato(a)
inner [ˈɪnə(r)] ADJ (a) (region) interior; (structure) interno(a); **i. city** zona urbana desfavorecida; **i. tube** cámara f de aire (b) Fig (thoughts) íntimo(a); (peace etc) interior
innermost [ˈɪnəməʊst] ADJ (room) más interior; Fig (thoughts) más íntimo(a)
innings [ˈɪnɪŋz] NPL (in cricket) turno m para batear, Am inning m
innocence [ˈɪnəsəns] N inocencia f
innocent [ˈɪnəsənt] ADJ & N inocente (mf)
innocuous [ɪˈnɒkjuəs] ADJ inocuo(a)
innovation [ɪnəˈveɪʃən] N novedad f
innuendo [ɪnjuˈendəʊ] N indirecta f
innumerable [ɪˈnjuːmərəbəl] ADJ innumerable
inoculate [ɪˈnɒkjʊleɪt] VT inocular
inoculation [ɪnɒkjʊˈleɪʃən] N inoculación f
inoffensive [ɪnəˈfensɪv] ADJ inofensivo(a)
inopportune [ɪnˈɒpətjuːn, ɪnɒpəˈtjuːn] ADJ inoportuno(a)
inordinate [ɪˈnɔːdɪnɪt] ADJ desmesurado(a)
inpatient [ˈɪnpeɪʃənt] N interno(a) m,f
input [ˈɪnpʊt] N (of resources) inversión f; (of power) entrada f; Comput (of data) input m, entrada
inquest [ˈɪnkwest] N investigación f judicial
inquire [ɪnˈkwaɪə(r)] 1 VT preguntar; (find out) averiguar
  2 VI preguntar (**about** por); (find out) informarse (**about** de)
▸ **inquire after** VT INSEP preguntar por
▸ **inquire into** VT INSEP investigar, indagar
inquiry [ɪnˈkwaɪərɪ] N (a) (request for information) consulta f; **inquiries** (sign) información (b) (investigation) investigación f (oficial)
inquisitive [ɪnˈkwɪzɪtɪv] ADJ (curious) curioso(a); (questioning) preguntón(ona)
inroads [ˈɪnrəʊdz] NPL **the firm is making i. into the market** la empresa está ganando terreno en el mercado; **to make i. into one's capital** reducir su capital
insane [ɪnˈseɪn] ADJ loco(a); (act) insensato(a); Fig **to drive sb i.** volver loco(a) a algn
insanity [ɪnˈsænɪtɪ] N demencia f, locura f
insatiable [ɪnˈseɪʃəbəl] ADJ insaciable
inscribe [ɪnˈskraɪb] VT Fml inscribir; (book) dedicar

inscription [ɪn'skrɪpʃən] N *(on stone, coin)* inscripción *f*; *(in book, on photo)* dedicatoria *f*

inscrutable [ɪn'skruːtəbəl] ADJ inescrutable, insondable

insect ['ɪnsekt] N insecto *m*; **i. bite** picadura *f*

insecticide [ɪn'sektɪsaɪd] N insecticida *m*

insecure [ɪnsɪ'kjʊə(r)] ADJ inseguro(a)

insecurity [ɪnsɪ'kjʊərɪtɪ] N inseguridad *f*

insemination [ɪnsemɪ'neɪʃən] N inseminación *f*

insensible [ɪn'sensəbəl] ADJ *Fml* inconsciente

insensitive [ɪn'sensɪtɪv] ADJ insensible

inseparable [ɪn'sepərəbəl] ADJ inseparable

insert 1 N ['ɪnsɜːt] encarte *m*
2 VT [ɪn'sɜːt] introducir

insertion [ɪn'sɜːʃən] N introducción *f*; *(of clause, text)* inserción *f*

inshore 1 ADJ ['ɪnʃɔː(r)] *(fishing)* de bajura
2 ADV [ɪn'ʃɔː(r)] cerca de la costa

inside [ɪn'saɪd] **1** N **(a)** *(of house)* interior *m*; **on the i.** por dentro; **to turn sth i. out** volver algo al revés **(b)** *Fam* **insides** tripas *fpl*
2 ADJ ['ɪnsaɪd] interior; *Aut* **i. lane** carril *m* interior
3 ADV *(be)* dentro, adentro; *(run etc)* (hacia) adentro; **to come i.** entrar
4 PREP **(a)** *(place)* dentro de **(b)** *Fam* **i. (of)** *(time)* en menos de

insider [ɪn'saɪdə(r)] N **i. dealing** = uso indebido de información privilegiada y confidencial para operaciones comerciales

insidious [ɪn'sɪdɪəs] ADJ insidioso(a)

insight ['ɪnsaɪt] N perspicacia *f*

insignia [ɪn'sɪgnɪə] N INV insignia *f*

insignificant [ɪnsɪg'nɪfɪkənt] ADJ insignificante

insincere [ɪnsɪn'sɪə(r)] ADJ poco sincero(a)

insinuate [ɪn'sɪnjʊeɪt] VT insinuar

insipid [ɪn'sɪpɪd] ADJ soso(a), insulso(a)

insist [ɪn'sɪst] **1** VI insistir (**on** en); *(argue)* obstinarse (**on** en)
2 VT **to i. that …** insistir en que …

insistence [ɪn'sɪstəns] N insistencia *f*

insistent [ɪn'sɪstənt] ADJ insistente

insofar as [ɪnsəʊ'fɑːrəz] ADV en tanto que

insole ['ɪnsəʊl] N *(of shoe)* plantilla *f*

insolent ['ɪnsələnt] ADJ insolente

insoluble [ɪn'sɒljʊbəl] ADJ insoluble

insolvent [ɪn'sɒlvənt] ADJ *Fin* insolvente

insomnia [ɪn'sɒmnɪə] N insomnio *m*

insomniac [ɪn'sɒmnɪæk] N insomne *mf*

inspect [ɪn'spekt] VT inspeccionar, examinar; *(troops)* pasar revista a

inspection [ɪn'spekʃən] N inspección *f*; *(of troops)* revista *f*

inspector [ɪn'spektə(r)] N inspector(a) *m,f*; *Br (on bus, train)* revisor(a) *m,f*

inspiration [ɪnspɪ'reɪʃən] N inspiración *f*; **to get i. from sth/sb** inspirarse en algo/algn

inspire [ɪn'spaɪə(r)] VT inspirar; **to i. respect in sb** infundir respeto a algn; **to i. sb to do sth** animar a algn a hacer algo

inspired [ɪn'spaɪəd] ADJ inspirado(a)

instability [ɪnstə'bɪlɪtɪ] N inestabilidad *f*

install, *US* **instal** [ɪn'stɔːl] VT instalar

installation [ɪnstə'leɪʃən] N instalación *f*

instalment, *US* **installment** [ɪn'stɔːlmənt] N **(a)** *(of payment)* plazo *m*; **to pay by instalments** pagar a plazos; *US* **i. plan** venta *f*/compra *f* a plazos **(b)** *(of novel, programme)* entrega *f*; *(of journal)* fascículo *m*

instance ['ɪnstəns] N caso *m*, ejemplo *m*; **for i.** por ejemplo; **in the first i.** en primer lugar

> Note that the Spanish word **instancia** is a false friend and is never a translation for the English word **instance**. In Spanish **instancia** means "request".

instant ['ɪnstənt] **1** N *(moment)* instante *m*, momento *m*; **in an i.** en un instante
2 ADJ inmediato(a); *(coffee, meal)* instantáneo(a)

instantaneous [ɪnstən'teɪnɪəs] ADJ instantáneo(a)

instantly ['ɪnstəntlɪ] ADV inmediatamente

instead [ɪn'sted] **1** ADV en cambio
2 PREP **i. of** en vez de, en lugar de

instep ['ɪnstep] N empeine *m*

instigate ['ɪnstɪgeɪt] VT *(strike, violence)* instigar; *(inquiry, changes)* iniciar

instigation [ɪnstɪ'geɪʃən] N instigación *f*

instil, *US* **instill** [ɪn'stɪl] VT *(idea, habit)* inculcar (**in** a or en); *(courage, respect)* infundir (**in** a)

instinct ['ɪnstɪŋkt] N instinto *m*

instinctive [ɪn'stɪŋktɪv] ADJ instintivo(a)

institute ['ɪnstɪtjuːt] **1** N instituto *m*; *(centre)* centro *m*; *(professional body)* colegio *m*
2 VT *Fml* **(a)** *(system)* establecer **(b)** *(start)* iniciar; *(proceedings)* entablar

institution [ɪnstɪ'tjuːʃən] N **(a)** *(organization)* institución *f* **(b)** *(home)* asilo *m*; *(asylum)* manicomio *m*

instruct [ɪn'strʌkt] VT instruir; *(order)* mandar; **I am instructed to say that …** me han encargado decir que …

instruction [ɪn'strʌkʃən] N **(a)** *(training)* instrucción *f* **(b)** **instructions** instrucciones *fpl*; **instructions for use** modo de empleo

instructive [ɪn'strʌktɪv] ADJ instructivo(a)

instructor [ɪn'strʌktə(r)] N instructor(a) *m,f*; *(of driving)* profesor(a) *m,f*

instrument ['ɪnstrəmənt] N instrumento *m*; **i. panel** tablero *m* de mandos

instrumental [ɪnstrə'mentəl] ADJ **(a)** *Mus* instrumental **(b)** **to be i. in sth** contribuir decisivamente a algo

insubordinate [ɪnsə'bɔːdɪnɪt] ADJ insubordinado(a)

insubstantial [ɪnsəb'stænʃəl] ADJ insubstancial; *(structure)* poco sólido(a)

insufferable [ɪn'sʌfərəbəl] ADJ insoportable

insufficient [ɪnsə'fɪʃənt] ADJ insuficiente

insular ['ɪnsjʊlə(r)] ADJ (a) *Geog* insular (b) *Fig Pej* estrecho(a) de miras

insulate ['ɪnsjʊleɪt] VT aislar (**against** *or* **from** de)

insulating tape ['ɪnsjʊleɪtɪŋteɪp] N *Br* cinta *f* aislante

insulation [ɪnsjʊ'leɪʃən] N aislamiento *m*

insulin ['ɪnsjʊlɪn] N insulina *f*

insult 1 N ['ɪnsʌlt] *(words)* insulto *m*; *(action)* afrenta *f*, ofensa *f*
2 VT [ɪn'sʌlt] insultar, ofender

insulting [ɪn'sʌltɪŋ] ADJ insultante, ofensivo(a)

insuperable [ɪn'suːpərəbəl] ADJ insuperable

insurance [ɪn'ʃʊərəns] N seguro *m*; **fire i.** seguro contra incendios; **i. broker** agente *mf* de seguros; **i. company** compañía *f* de seguros; **i. policy** póliza *f* (de seguros); **private health i.** seguro médico privado

insure [ɪn'ʃʊə(r)] VT asegurar (**against** contra)

insurgent [ɪn'sɜːdʒənt] ADJ & N insurrecto(a) *(m,f)*

insurmountable [ɪnsə'maʊntəbəl] ADJ *(problem etc)* insuperable; *(barrier)* infranqueable

intact [ɪn'tækt] ADJ intacto(a)

intake ['ɪnteɪk] N (a) *(of air, water)* entrada *f*; *(of electricity etc)* toma *f* (b) *(of food, calories)* consumo *m* (c) *(of students, recruits)* número *m* de admitidos

integral ['ɪntɪgrəl] **1** ADJ (a) *(intrinsic)* integrante (b) *(whole)* íntegro(a) (c) *Math* integral
2 N *Math* integral *f*

integrate ['ɪntɪgreɪt] **1** VT integrar
2 VI integrarse

integration [ɪntɪ'greɪʃən] N integración *f*

integrity [ɪn'tegrɪtɪ] N integridad *f*, honradez *f*

intellect ['ɪntɪlekt] N intelecto *m*

intellectual [ɪntɪ'lektʃʊəl] ADJ & N intelectual *(mf)*

intelligence [ɪn'telɪdʒəns] N (a) *(faculty)* inteligencia *f* (b) *(information)* información *f*

intelligent [ɪn'telɪdʒənt] ADJ inteligente

intelligentsia [ɪntelɪ'dʒentsɪə] N intelectualidad *f*

intelligible [ɪn'telɪdʒəbəl] ADJ inteligible

intend [ɪn'tend] VT (a) *(mean)* tener la intención de (b) **to i. sth for sb** destinar algo a algn

intended [ɪn'tendɪd] ADJ *(planned)* previsto(a)

intense [ɪn'tens] ADJ intenso(a); *(person)* muy serio(a)

intensely [ɪn'tenslɪ] ADV *(extremely)* enormemente, sumamente

intensify [ɪn'tensɪfaɪ] VT *(search)* intensificar; *(effort)* redoblar; *(production, pollution)* aumentar

intensity [ɪn'tensɪtɪ] N intensidad *f*

intensive [ɪn'tensɪv] ADJ intensivo(a); *Med* **i. care unit** unidad *f* de vigilancia intensiva

intent [ɪn'tent] **1** ADJ *(absorbed)* absorto(a); *(gaze etc)* atento(a); **to be i. on doing sth** estar resuelto(a) a hacer algo
2 N *Fml* intención *f*, propósito *m*; **to all intents and purposes** a todos los efectos

intention [ɪn'tenʃən] N intención *f*

intentional [ɪn'tenʃənəl] ADJ deliberado(a)

intentionally [ɪn'tenʃənəlɪ] ADV a propósito

interact [ɪntər'ækt] VI *(people)* interrelacionarse

interaction [ɪntər'ækʃən] N interacción *f*

interactive [ɪntər'æktɪv] ADJ interactivo(a)

intercede [ɪntə'siːd] VI interceder (**with** ante)

intercept [ɪntə'sept] VT interceptar

interchange 1 N ['ɪntətʃeɪndʒ] (a) *(exchange)* intercambio *m* (b) *(on motorway)* cruce *m*
2 VT [ɪntə'tʃeɪndʒ] intercambiar (**with** con)

interchangeable [ɪntə'tʃeɪndʒəbəl] ADJ intercambiable

intercity [ɪntə'sɪtɪ] N *Rail Esp* intercity *m*, *Am* interurbano *m*

intercom ['ɪntəkɒm] N portero automático

intercontinental [ɪntəkɒntɪ'nentəl] ADJ **i. ballistic missile** misil balístico intercontinental

intercourse ['ɪntəkɔːs] N (a) *(dealings)* trato *m* (b) *(sexual)* relaciones *fpl* sexuales

interest ['ɪntrɪst] **1** N (a) *(curiosity)* interés *m*; *(hobby)* afición *f* (b) *(benefit)* **in the i. of** en pro de (c) *(financial stake)* participación *f* (d) *Fin* interés *m*; **i. rate** tipo *m* de interés
2 VT interesar; **he's interested in politics** le interesa la política

interesting ['ɪntrɪstɪŋ] ADJ interesante

interface ['ɪntəfeɪs] N *Comput* interface *f*

interfere [ɪntə'fɪə(r)] VI (a) *(meddle)* entrometerse (**in** en); **to i. with** *(hinder)* dificultar; *(spoil)* estropear; *(prevent)* impedir (b) *Rad & TV* interferir (**with** con)

interference [ɪntə'fɪərəns] N *(meddling)* intromisión *f*; *(hindrance)* estorbo *m*; *Rad & TV* interferencia *f*

interim ['ɪntərɪm] **1** N *Fml* **in the i.** en el ínterin
2 ADJ interino(a), provisional

interior [ɪn'tɪərɪə(r)] **1** ADJ interior
2 N interior *m*; **i. design** diseño *m* de interiores

interlock [ɪntə'lɒk] VI encajarse; *(fingers)* entrelazarse; *(cogs)* engranarse

interloper ['ɪntələʊpə(r)] N intruso(a) *m,f*

interlude ['ɪntəluːd] N *(break)* intervalo *m*; *Cin & Th* intermedio *m*; *Mus* interludio *m*

intermediary [ɪntə'miːdɪərɪ] N intermediario(a) *m,f*

intermediate [ɪntə'miːdɪət] ADJ intermedio(a)

interminable [ɪn'tɜːmɪnəbəl] ADJ interminable

intermission [ɪntə'mɪʃən] N *Cin & Th* intermedio *m*

intermittent [ɪntə'mɪtənt] ADJ intermitente

intern 1 VT [ɪn'tɜ:n] recluir
2 N ['ɪntɜ:n] (**a**) US Med médico(a) m,f interno(a) residente (**b**) Com (on work placement) becario(a) m,f

internal [ɪn'tɜ:nəl] ADJ interior; (dispute, injury) interno(a); US **I. Revenue Service** ≃ Hacienda f

internally [ɪn'tɜ:nəlɪ] ADV interiormente; **not to be taken i.** (on medicine) uso externo

international [ɪntə'næʃənəl] **1** ADJ internacional
2 N Sport (player) internacional mf; (match) partido m internacional

Internet ['ɪntənet] N Comput **the I.** Internet f; **it's on the I.** está en Internet; **I. access provider** proveedor m de acceso a Internet; **I. service provider** proveedor m de (acceso a) Internet

interplay ['ɪntəpleɪ] N interacción f

interpret [ɪn'tɜ:prɪt] **1** VT interpretar
2 VI actuar de intérprete

interpretation [ɪntɜ:prɪ'teɪʃən] N interpretación f

interpreter [ɪn'tɜ:prɪtə(r)] N intérprete mf

interrelated [ɪntərɪ'leɪtɪd] ADJ estrechamente relacionado(a)

interrogate [ɪn'terəgeɪt] VT interrogar

interrogation [ɪntərə'geɪʃən] N interrogatorio m

interrogative [ɪntə'rɒgətɪv] Gram **1** ADJ interrogativo(a)
2 N (word) palabra interrogativa

interrupt [ɪntə'rʌpt] VT & VI interrumpir

interruption [ɪntə'rʌpʃən] N interrupción f

intersect [ɪntə'sekt] **1** VT cruzar
2 VI cruzarse

intersection [ɪntə'sekʃən] N (**a**) (crossroads) cruce m (**b**) (of two lines) intersección f

intersperse [ɪntə'spɜ:s] VT esparcir

interstate ['ɪntəsteɪt] N US autopista f interestatal

intertwine [ɪntə'twaɪn] **1** VT entrelazar (**with** con)
2 VI entrelazarse (**with** con)

interval ['ɪntəvəl] N (**a**) (of time, space) intervalo m; **at intervals** (time, space) a intervalos; (time) de vez en cuando (**b**) Br Cin & Th intermedio m

intervene [ɪntə'vi:n] VI (**a**) (person) intervenir (**in** en) (**b**) (event) sobrevenir (**c**) (time) transcurrir

intervention [ɪntə'venʃən] N intervención f

interview ['ɪntəvju:] **1** N entrevista f; **to give an i.** conceder una entrevista
2 VT entrevistar

interviewer ['ɪntəvju:ə(r)] N entrevistador(a) m,f

intestine [ɪn'testɪn] N intestino m; **large/small i.** intestino grueso/delgado

intimacy ['ɪntɪməsɪ] N (closeness) intimidad f; Euph (sex) relación íntima; **intimacies** intimidades fpl

intimate¹ ['ɪntɪmɪt] ADJ íntimo(a); (knowledge) profundo(a)

intimate² ['ɪntɪmeɪt] VT Fml dar a entender

intimidate [ɪn'tɪmɪdeɪt] VT intimidar

intimidating [ɪn'tɪmɪdeɪtɪŋ] ADJ atemorizante

into ['ɪntu:, unstressed 'ɪntə] PREP (**a**) (motion) en, a, con; **he fell i. the water** se cayó al agua; **to get i. a car** subir a un coche; **to go i. a house** entrar en una casa (**b**) (state) en, a; **to change pounds i. euros** cambiar libras en or por euros; **to translate sth i. French** traducir algo al francés (**c**) **to divide sth i. three** dividir algo en tres (**d**) Fam **to be i. sth** ser aficionado(a) a algo

intolerable [ɪn'tɒlərəbəl] ADJ intolerable

intolerance [ɪn'tɒlərəns] N intolerancia f

intolerant [ɪn'tɒlərənt] ADJ intolerante

intonation [ɪntə'neɪʃən] N entonación f

intoxicated [ɪn'tɒksɪkeɪtɪd] ADJ borracho(a)

> Note that the Spanish word **intoxicado** is a false friend and is never a translation for the English word **intoxicated**. In Spanish **intoxicado** means "poisoned".

intoxicating [ɪn'tɒksɪkeɪtɪŋ] ADJ embriagador(a); **i. liquor** bebida alcohólica

intoxication [ɪntɒksɪ'keɪʃən] N embriaguez f

> Note that the Spanish word **intoxicación** is a false friend and is never a translation for the English word **intoxication**. In Spanish, **intoxicación** means "poisoning".

intractable [ɪn'træktəbəl] ADJ Fml (person) intratable; (problem) insoluble

intranet ['ɪntrənet] N Comput intranet f

intransigent [ɪn'trænsɪdʒənt] ADJ Fml intransigente, intolerante

intransitive [ɪn'trænsɪtɪv] ADJ intransitivo(a)

intravenous [ɪntrə'vi:nəs] ADJ intravenoso(a)

in-tray ['ɪntreɪ] N bandeja f de asuntos pendientes

intrepid [ɪn'trepɪd] ADJ intrépido(a), audaz

intricate ['ɪntrɪkɪt] ADJ intrincado(a)

intrigue 1 N [ɪn'tri:g, 'ɪntri:g] intriga f
2 VT [ɪn'tri:g] intrigar
3 VI intrigar, conspirar

intriguing [ɪn'tri:gɪŋ] ADJ intrigante

intrinsic [ɪn'trɪnsɪk] ADJ Fml intrínseco(a)

introduce [ɪntrə'dju:s] VT (**a**) (person, programme) presentar (**to** a) (**b**) (bring in) introducir (**into** or **to** en); Com (product) lanzar (**into** or **to** a); (topic) proponer

introduction [ɪntrə'dʌkʃən] N (**a**) (of person, programme) presentación f; (in book) introducción f (**b**) (bringing in) introducción f; Com (of product) lanzamiento m

introductory [ɪntrə'dʌktəri] ADJ introductorio(a); *(remarks)* preliminar; *Com* de lanzamiento

introspective [ɪntrə'spektɪv] ADJ introspectivo(a)

introvert ['ɪntrəvɜːt] N introvertido(a) *m,f*

intrude [ɪn'truːd] VI entrometerse *(into or on* en); *(disturb)* molestar

intruder [ɪn'truːdə(r)] N intruso(a) *m,f*

intrusion [ɪn'truːʒən] N incursión *f*

intuition [ɪntjʊ'ɪʃən] N intuición *f*

inundate ['ɪnʌndeɪt] VT inundar *(with* de)

invade [ɪn'veɪd] VT invadir

invader [ɪn'veɪdə(r)] N invasor(a) *m,f*

invalid¹ ['ɪnvəlɪd] N *(disabled person)* minusválido(a) *m,f; (sick person)* enfermo(a) *m,f*

invalid² [ɪn'vælɪd] ADJ inválido(a), nulo(a)

invalidate [ɪn'vælɪdeɪt] VT invalidar

invaluable [ɪn'væljʊəbəl] ADJ inestimable

invariable [ɪn'veərɪəbəl] ADJ invariable

invariably [ɪn'veərɪəblɪ] ADV invariablemente

invasion [ɪn'veɪʒən] N invasión *f*

invent [ɪn'vent] VT inventar

invention [ɪn'venʃən] N invento *m; (creativity)* inventiva *f; (lie)* mentira *f*

inventive [ɪn'ventɪv] ADJ inventivo(a)

inventor [ɪn'ventə(r)] N inventor(a) *m,f*

inventory ['ɪnvəntəri] N inventario *m*

invert [ɪn'vɜːt] VT invertir

invertebrate [ɪn'vɜːtɪbrɪt] **1** ADJ invertebrado(a)
 2 N invertebrado *m*

inverted [ɪn'vɜːtɪd] ADJ **(in) i. commas** (entre) comillas *fpl*

invest [ɪn'vest] **1** VT invertir *(in* en); **to i. sb with sth** conferir algo a algn
 2 VI invertir *(in* en)

investigate [ɪn'vestɪgeɪt] VT *(crime, subject)* investigar; *(cause, possibility)* estudiar

investigation [ɪnvestɪ'geɪʃən] N *(of crime)* investigación *f; (of cause)* examen *m*

investigator [ɪn'vestɪgeɪtə(r)] N investigador(a) *m,f;* **private i.** detective privado

investment [ɪn'vestmənt] N inversión *f*

investor [ɪn'vestə(r)] N inversor(a) *m,f*

inveterate [ɪn'vetərɪt] ADJ empedernido(a)

invidious [ɪn'vɪdɪəs] ADJ *(task)* ingrato(a); *(comparison)* injusto(a)

Note that the Spanish word **envidioso** is a false friend and is never a translation for the English word **invidious**. In Spanish, **envidioso** means "envious".

invigilator [ɪn'vɪdʒɪleɪtə(r)] N *Br (in exam)* vigilante *mf*

invigorating [ɪn'vɪgəreɪtɪŋ] ADJ vigorizante

invincible [ɪn'vɪnsəbəl] ADJ invencible

invisible [ɪn'vɪzəbəl] ADJ invisible

invitation [ɪnvɪ'teɪʃən] N invitación *f*

invite [ɪn'vaɪt] VT *(a) (guest)* invitar *(to* a) *(b) (comments etc)* solicitar; *(criticism)* provocar; **to i. trouble** buscarse problemas

inviting [ɪn'vaɪtɪŋ] ADJ *(attractive)* atractivo(a); *(food)* apetitoso(a)

invoice ['ɪnvɔɪs] **1** N factura *f*
 2 VT facturar

invoke [ɪn'vəʊk] VT *Fml* invocar

involuntary [ɪn'vɒləntəri] ADJ involuntario(a)

involve [ɪn'vɒlv] VT *(a) (concern)* implicar *(in* en); **the issues involved** las cuestiones en juego; **to be involved in an accident** sufrir un accidente *(b) (entail)* suponer, implicar; *(trouble, risk)* acarrear

involved [ɪn'vɒlvd] ADJ *(complicated)* complicado(a); *Fam (romantically attached)* enredado(a), liado(a)

involvement [ɪn'vɒlvmənt] N *(participation)* participación *f; (in crime)* implicación *f*

invulnerable [ɪn'vʌlnərəbəl] ADJ invulnerable

inward ['ɪnwəd] **1** ADJ interior
 2 ADV = **inwards**

inwardly ['ɪnwədlɪ] ADV interiormente, por dentro

inwards ['ɪnwədz] ADV hacia dentro

in-your-face ['ɪnjə'feɪs] ADJ *(style)* descarado(a); *(movie, advert)* impactante, fuerte

iodine ['aɪədiːn] N yodo *m*

iota [aɪ'əʊtə] N pizca *f,* ápice *m*

IOU [aɪəʊ'juː] N *(abbr* **I owe you)** pagaré *m*

IQ [aɪ'kjuː] N *(abbr* **intelligence quotient)** CI *m*

IRA [aɪɑː'reɪ] N *(a) (abbr* **Irish Republican Army)** IRA *m (b) US (abbr* **individual retirement account)** cuenta *f* de retiro *or* jubilación individual

Iran [ɪ'rɑːn] N Irán

Iranian [ɪ'reɪnɪən] ADJ & N iraní *(mf)*

Iraq [ɪ'rɑːk] N Irak

Iraqi [ɪ'rɑːkɪ] ADJ & N iraquí *(mf)*

irascible [ɪ'ræsɪbəl] ADJ *Fml* irascible

irate [aɪ'reɪt] ADJ airado(a), furioso(a)

Ireland ['aɪələnd] N Irlanda; **Republic of I.** República de Irlanda

iris ['aɪərɪs] N *(a) Anat* iris *m inv (b) Bot* lirio *m*

Irish ['aɪrɪʃ] **1** ADJ irlandés(esa); **I. coffee** café *m* irlandés; **I. Sea** Mar *m* de Irlanda
 2 N *(a) (language)* irlandés *m (b)* PL **the I.** los irlandeses

Irishman ['aɪrɪʃmən] N irlandés *m*

Irishwoman ['aɪrɪʃwʊmən] N irlandesa *f*

irksome ['ɜːksəm] ADJ fastidioso(a)

iron ['aɪən] **1** N *(a) (metal)* hierro *m;* **the i. and steel industry** la industria siderúrgica *(b) (for clothes)* plancha *f*
 2 VT *(clothes)* planchar
 ▶ **iron out** VT SEP *(a) (crease)* planchar *(b) Fam Fig (problem)* resolver

ironic(al) [aɪ'rɒnɪk(əl)] ADJ irónico(a)

ironing ['aɪənɪŋ] N (**a**) **to do the i.** planchar; **i. board** mesa *f* de la plancha (**b**) *(clothes to be ironed)* ropa *f* para planchar; *(clothes ironed)* ropa planchada

ironmonger ['aɪənmʌŋgə(r)] N *Br* ferretero(a) *m,f*; **i.'s (shop)** ferretería *f*

irony ['aɪrənɪ] N ironía *f*

irradiate [ɪ'reɪdɪeɪt] VT irradiar

irrational [ɪ'ræʃənəl] ADJ irracional

irreconcilable [ɪrekən'saɪləbəl] ADJ irreconciliable

irrefutable [ɪrɪ'fju:təbəl] ADJ *Fml* irrefutable

irregular [ɪ'regjʊlə(r)] ADJ irregular

irrelevant [ɪ'reləvənt] ADJ no pertinente

irreparable [ɪ'repərəbəl] ADJ irreparable

irreplaceable [ɪrɪ'pleɪsəbəl] ADJ irremplazable

irrepressible [ɪrɪ'presəbəl] ADJ incontenible

irresistible [ɪrɪ'zɪstəbəl] ADJ irresistible

irresolute [ɪ'rezəlu:t] ADJ *Fml* indeciso(a)

irrespective [ɪrɪ'spektɪv] ADJ **i. of** sin tener en cuenta

irresponsible [ɪrɪ'spɒnsəbəl] ADJ irresponsable

irreverent [ɪ'revərənt] ADJ irreverente

irrevocable [ɪ'revəkəbəl] ADJ irrevocable

irrigate ['ɪrɪgeɪt] VT regar

irrigation [ɪrɪ'geɪʃən] N riego *m*; **i. channel** .acequia *f*; **i. system** sistema *m* de regadío

irritable ['ɪrɪtəbəl] ADJ irritable

irritate ['ɪrɪteɪt] VT *(annoy)* fastidiar; *Med* irritar

irritating ['ɪrɪteɪtɪŋ] ADJ irritante

irritation [ɪrɪ'teɪʃən] N (**a**) *(annoyance)* fastidio *m*; *(ill humour)* mal humor *m* (**b**) *Med* irritación *f*

IRS [aɪɑ:'res] N *US (abbr* **Internal Revenue Service**) **the I.** Hacienda, *Esp* ≃ la Agencia Tributaria, *Méx* ≃ el Servicio de Administración Tributaria

is [ɪz] 3RD PERSON SING PRES *of* **be**

Islam ['ɪzlɑ:m] N islam *m*

Islamic [ɪz'læmɪk] ADJ islámico(a)

island ['aɪlənd] N isla *f*; **(traffic) i.** isleta *f*

islander ['aɪləndə(r)] N isleño(a) *m,f*

isle [aɪl] N isla *f*

isn't ['ɪzənt] = **is not**

isolate ['aɪsəleɪt] VT aislar (**from** de)

isolated ['aɪsəleɪtɪd] ADJ aislado(a)

isolation [aɪsə'leɪʃən] N aislamiento *m*

ISP [aɪes'pi:] N *Comput (abbr* **Internet Service Provider**) PSI *m*

Israel ['ɪzreɪəl] N Israel

Israeli [ɪz'reɪlɪ] ADJ & N israelí *(mf)*

issue ['ɪʃu:] **1** N (**a**) *(matter)* cuestión *f*; **to take i. with sb (over sth)** manifestar su desacuerdo con algn (en algo) (**b**) *(of magazine)* ejemplar

m (**c**) *Fml (outcome)* resultado *m* (**d**) *Jur (offspring)* descendencia *f*
2 VT (**a**) *(book)* publicar; *(banknotes etc)* emitir; *(passport)* expedir (**b**) *(supplies)* repartir (**c**) *(order, instructions)* dar; *(warrant)* dictar

isthmus ['ɪsməs] N istmo *m*

IT [aɪ'ti:] N *Comput (abbr* **information technology**) informática *f*

it [ɪt] PERS PRON (**a**) *(subject)* él/ella/ello *(usually omitted in Spanish, except for contrast);* **it's here** está aquí (**b**) *(direct object)* lo/la; **I don't believe it** no me lo creo; **I liked the house and bought it** me gustó la casa y la compré (**c**) *(indirect object)* le; **give it a kick** dale una patada (**d**) *(after prep)* él/ella/ello; **I saw the beach and ran towards it** vi la playa y fui corriendo hacia ella; **we'll talk about it later** ya hablaremos de ello (**e**) *(abstract)* ello; **let's get down to it!** ¡vamos a ello! (**f**) *(impersonal)* **it's late** es tarde; **it's me** soy yo; **it's raining** está lloviendo; **it's 2 miles to town** hay 2 millas de aquí al pueblo; **who is it?** ¿quién es?

Italian [ɪ'tæljən] **1** ADJ italiano(a)
2 N (**a**) *(person)* italiano(a) *m,f* (**b**) *(language)* italiano *m*

italic [ɪ'tælɪk] N **i., italics** cursiva *f*

Italy ['ɪtəlɪ] N Italia

itch [ɪtʃ] **1** N picor *m*; *Fig* **an i. to travel** unas ganas locas de viajar
2 VI (**a**) *(skin)* picar (**b**) *Fig* anhelar; *Fam* **to be itching to do sth** tener muchas ganas de hacer algo

itchy ['ɪtʃɪ] ADJ (**itchier, itchiest**) que pica

item ['aɪtəm] N (**a**) *(in list)* artículo *m*; *(in collection)* pieza *f*; **i. of clothing** prenda *f* de vestir (**b**) *(on agenda)* asunto *m*; *(in show)* número *m*; **news i.** noticia *f*

itemize ['aɪtəmaɪz] VT detallar

itinerant [ɪ'tɪnərənt] ADJ *Fml* itinerante

itinerary [aɪ'tɪnərərɪ] N itinerario *m*

it'll ['ɪtəl] = **it will**

its [ɪts] POSS ADJ *(one thing)* su; *(more than one)* sus

itself [ɪt'self] PERS PRON (**a**) *(reflexive)* se; **the cat scratched i.** el gato se arañó (**b**) *(emphatic)* él mismo/ella misma/ello mismo; *(after prep)* sí (mismo(a)); **in i.** en sí

ITV [aɪti:'vi:] N *Br (abbr* **Independent Television**) = canal privado de televisión británico

IUD [aɪju:'di:] N *(abbr* **intrauterine (contraceptive) device**) DIU *m*

IVF [aɪvi:'ef] N *Med (abbr* **in vitro fertilization**) fertilización *f* in vitro

ivory ['aɪvərɪ] N marfil *m*

ivy ['aɪvɪ] N hiedra *f*

J, j [dʒeɪ] N *(the letter)* J, j f

jab [dʒæb] **1** N pinchazo m; *(poke)* golpe seco **2** VT pinchar; *(with fist)* dar un puñetazo a

jabber ['dʒæbə(r)] VI *Fam (chatter)* charlotear; *(speak quickly)* hablar atropelladamente

jack [dʒæk] N **(a)** *Aut* gato m **(b)** *Cards* sota f **(c)** *(bowls)* boliche m

► **jack in** VT SEP *Br Fam (job)* dejar

► **jack up** VT SEP *Fam (price, salaries)* subir

jackal ['dʒækɔːl] N chacal m

jackdaw ['dʒækdɔː] N grajilla f

jacket ['dʒækɪt] N **(a)** *(coat) (formal)* chaqueta f, americana f, *Am* saco m; *(casual)* cazadora f; *(bomber jacket)* cazadora f **(b)** *(of book)* sobrecubierta f; *US (of record)* funda f **(c)** **j. potatoes** patatas fpl or *Am* papas fpl al horno

jack-knife ['dʒæknaɪf] **1** N navaja f **2** VI colear

jack-of-all-trades [dʒækəvˈɔːltreɪdz] N persona f mañosa or de muchos oficios

jackpot ['dʒækpɒt] N (premio m) gordo m

Jacuzzi® [dʒəˈkuːzɪ] N jacuzzi® m

jade [dʒeɪd] N jade m

jaded ['dʒeɪdɪd] ADJ *(tired)* agotado(a); *(palate)* hastiado(a)

jagged ['dʒægɪd] ADJ dentado(a)

jaguar [*Br* 'dʒægjʊə(r), *US* 'dʒægwɑː(r)] N jaguar m

jail [dʒeɪl] **1** N cárcel f, prisión f **2** VT encarcelar

jailbreak ['dʒeɪlbreɪk] N fuga f, evasión f

jailer ['dʒeɪlə(r)] N carcelero(a) m,f

jam¹ [dʒæm] N *Culin* mermelada f

jam² [dʒæm] **1** N *(blockage)* atasco m; *Fam (fix)* apuro m **2** VT **(a)** *(cram)* meter a la fuerza **(b)** *(block)* atascar; *Rad* interferir **3** VI *(door)* atrancarse; *(brakes)* agarrotarse

Jamaica [dʒəˈmeɪkə] N Jamaica

jam-packed [dʒæmˈpækt] ADJ *Fam (with people)* atestado(a); *(with things)* atiborrado(a)

jangle ['dʒæŋgəl] VI tintinear

janitor ['dʒænɪtə(r)] N *US, Scot (caretaker)* conserje m, bedel m

January ['dʒænjʊərɪ] N enero m

Japan [dʒəˈpæn] N (el) Japón

Japanese [dʒæpəˈniːz] **1** ADJ japonés(esa) **2** N *(person)* japonés(esa) m,f; *(language)* japonés m

jar¹ [dʒɑː(r)] N *(container)* tarro m; *Br Fam* **to have a j.** tomar una copa

jar² [dʒɑː(r)] VI *(sounds)* chirriar; *(appearance)* chocar; *(colours)* desentonar; *Fig* **to j. on one's nerves** ponerle a uno los nervios de punta

jargon ['dʒɑːgən] N jerga f, argot m

jasmin(e) ['dʒæzmɪn] N jazmín m

jaundice ['dʒɔːndɪs] N icteria f

jaundiced ['dʒɔːndɪst] ADJ *Med* ictérico(a); *Fig (bitter)* amargado(a)

jaunt [dʒɔːnt] N *(walk)* paseo m; *(trip)* excursión f

jaunty ['dʒɔːntɪ] ADJ **(jauntier, jauntiest)** *(sprightly)* garboso(a); *(lively)* vivaz

javelin ['dʒævəlɪn] N jabalina f

jaw [dʒɔː] **1** N mandíbula f **2** VI *Fam* estar de palique

jay [dʒeɪ] N arrendajo m (común)

jaywalker ['dʒeɪwɔːkə(r)] N peatón m imprudente

jaywalking ['dʒeɪwɔːkɪŋ] N imprudencia f peatonal

jazz [dʒæz] N jazz m

► **jazz up** VT SEP alegrar; *(premises)* arreglar

jazzy ['dʒæzɪ] ADJ **(jazzier, jazziest)** *Fam (showy)* llamativo(a); *(brightly coloured)* de colores chillones

jealous ['dʒeləs] ADJ celoso(a); *(envious)* envidioso(a); **to be j. of ...** tener celos de ...

jealousy ['dʒeləsɪ] N celos mpl; *(envy)* envidia f

jeans [dʒiːnz] NPL vaqueros mpl, tejanos mpl

Jeep® [dʒiːp] N jeep m, todo terreno m inv

jeer [dʒɪə(r)] **1** N *(boo)* abucheo m; *(mocking)* mofa f **2** VI *(boo)* abuchear; *(mock)* burlarse

jeering ['dʒɪərɪŋ] ADJ burlón(ona)

Jehovah [dʒɪˈhəʊvə] N **J.'s Witness** testigo mf de Jehová

Jell-O®, jello ['dʒeləʊ] N *US* gelatina f

jelly ['dʒelɪ] N *Br (dessert)* gelatina f, *esp US (jam)* mermelada f, confitura f

jellyfish ['dʒelɪfɪʃ] N medusa f

jeopardize ['dʒepədaɪz] VT poner en peligro; *(agreement etc)* comprometer

jeopardy ['dʒepədɪ] N riesgo m, peligro m

jerk [dʒɜːk] **1** N **(a)** *(jolt)* sacudida f; *(pull)* tirón m **(b)** *Pej (idiot)* imbécil mf **2** VT *(shake)* sacudir; *(pull)* dar un tirón a **3** VI *(move suddenly)* dar una sacudida

jerkin ['dʒɜːkɪn] N chaleco m

jersey ['dʒɜːzɪ] N suéter m, Esp jersey m, RP pulóver m

jest [dʒest] **1** N broma f
2 VI bromear

Jesuit ['dʒezjʊɪt] ADJ & N jesuita (m)

Jesus ['dʒiːzəs] N Jesús m; **J. Christ** Jesucristo m

jet¹ [dʒet] **1** N (**a**) (stream of water) chorro m (**b**) (spout) surtidor m (**c**) Av reactor m; **j. engine** reactor; **j. lag** = cansancio debido al desfase horario; **j. ski** moto náutica or acuática; **the j. set** Esp la jet(-set), Am el jet-set
2 VI Fam volar

jet² [dʒet] N **j. black** negro(a) como el azabache

jettison ['dʒetɪsən] VT also Fig tirar or echar or Am salvo RP botar por la borda

jetty ['dʒetɪ] N muelle m, malecón m

Jew [dʒuː] N judío(a) m,f

jewel ['dʒuːəl] N joya f; (stone) piedra preciosa; (in watch) rubí m; Fig (person) joya

jeweller, US jeweler ['dʒuːələ(r)] N joyero(a) m,f; **j.'s (shop)** joyería f

jewellery, US jewelry ['dʒuːəlrɪ] N joyas fpl, alhajas fpl

Jewess ['dʒuːɪs] N judía f

Jewish ['dʒuːɪʃ] ADJ judío(a)

jibe [dʒaɪb] N & VI = gibe

jiffy ['dʒɪfɪ] N Fam momento m; **in a j.** en un santiamén; **just a j.!** ¡un momento!

jig [dʒɪg] N Mus giga f

jigsaw ['dʒɪgsɔː] N (puzzle) rompecabezas m inv

jilt [dʒɪlt] VT Fam dejar plantado(a)

jingle ['dʒɪŋgəl] **1** N Rad & TV = canción que acompaña un anuncio
2 VI tintinear

jingoistic [dʒɪŋgəʊ'ɪstɪk] ADJ patriotero(a)

jinx [dʒɪŋks] **1** N (person) gafe mf
2 VT gafar

jitters ['dʒɪtəz] NPL Fam **to get the j.** tener canguelo

jive [dʒaɪv] **1** N swing m
2 VI bailar el swing

job [dʒɒb] N (**a**) (task) tarea f (**b**) (post) (puesto m de) trabajo m, empleo m; US **j. office** oficina f de empleo; **j. sharing** trabajo compartido a tiempo parcial (**c**) Fam **we had a j. to ...** nos costó (trabajo) ... (**d**) Br Fam **it's a good j. that ...** menos mal que ...

Jobcentre ['dʒɒbsentə(r)] N Br oficina f de empleo

jobless ['dʒɒblɪs] ADJ parado(a)

jockey ['dʒɒkɪ] **1** N jinete m, jockey m
2 VI **to j. for position** luchar para conseguir una posición aventajada

jocular ['dʒɒkjʊlə(r)] ADJ jocoso(a)

jog [dʒɒg] **1** N trote m
2 VT empujar; Fig (memory) refrescar
3 VI Sport hacer footing

jogging ['dʒɒgɪŋ] N footing m

john [dʒɒn] N US Fam **the j.** (lavatory) el váter m

join [dʒɔɪn] **1** VT (**a**) (unite, connect) unir; **to j. forces with sb** unir fuerzas con algn (**b**) (road) empalmar con; (river) desembocar en (**c**) (meet) reunirse con (**d**) (institution) entrar; (army) alistarse a; (discussion, game) unirse a (**e**) (party, union) afiliarse a; (club) ingresar en
2 VI (**a**) (pipes, roads, rivers) juntarse, unirse (**b**) (in party, union) afiliarse; (in club) ingresar
3 N juntura f
▸ **join in 1** VI participar, tomar parte; (debate) intervenir
2 VT INSEP participar en, tomar parte en
▸ **join up 1** VT SEP juntar
2 VI (of roads) unirse; Mil alistarse

joiner ['dʒɔɪnə(r)] N carpintero(a) m,f

joinery ['dʒɔɪnərɪ] N carpintería f

joint [dʒɔɪnt] **1** N (**a**) Anat & Tech articulación f (**b**) (in woodwork) junta f, juntura f (**c**) (of meat) (raw) pieza f; (roasted) asado m (**d**) Fam (nightclub etc) garito m (**e**) Fam (drug) porro m
2 ADJ colectivo(a); **j. account** cuenta conjunta; **j. venture** empresa conjunta

jointly ['dʒɔɪntlɪ] ADV conjuntamente, en común

joist [dʒɔɪst] N vigueta f

joke [dʒəʊk] **1** N (**a**) (funny story) chiste m; (prank) broma f; **to play a j. on sb** gastarle una broma a algn; **to tell a j.** contar un chiste (**b**) Fam (person) hazmerreír m, payaso(a) m,f; **to be a j.** (of thing) ser de chiste
2 VI estar de broma; **you must be joking!** ¡no hablarás en serio!

joker ['dʒəʊkə(r)] N (**a**) (clown) bromista mf (**b**) Cards comodín m

jolly ['dʒɒlɪ] **1** ADJ (jollier, jolliest) alegre
2 ADV Br Fam (very) bien; **she played j. well** jugó muy bien

jolt [dʒəʊlt] **1** N (shake) sacudida f; (shock, surprise) susto m
2 VT (shake) sacudir
3 VI (shake) dar sacudidas

Jordan ['dʒɔːdən] N (**a**) (river) Jordán m (**b**) (country) Jordania

joss-stick ['dʒɒsstɪk] N varita f de incienso

jostle ['dʒɒsəl] **1** VT dar empujones a
2 VI dar empujones

jot [dʒɒt] N jota f, pizca f; **not a j.** ni jota
▸ **jot down** VT SEP apuntar

jotter ['dʒɒtə(r)] N Br bloc m

journal ['dʒɜːnəl] N (**a**) (publication) revista f (especializada) (**b**) (diary) diario m

Note that the Spanish word **jornal** is a false friend and is never a translation for the English word **journal**. In Spanish **jornal** means "day's wage".

journalism ['dʒɜːnəlɪzəm] N periodismo m

journalist ['dʒɜːnəlɪst] N periodista mf

journey ['dʒɜːnɪ] **1** N viaje m; *(distance)* trayecto m
2 VI *Fml* viajar

jovial ['dʒəʊvɪəl] ADJ jovial

jowl [dʒaʊl] N quijada f

joy [dʒɔɪ] N alegría f; *(pleasure)* placer m

joyful ['dʒɔɪfʊl] ADJ alegre, contento(a)

joyous ['dʒɔɪəs] ADJ *Literary* alegre

joyride ['dʒɔɪraɪd] N *Fam* paseo m en un coche robado

joystick ['dʒɔɪstɪk] N *Av* palanca f de mando; *(of video game)* joystick m

JP [dʒeɪ'piː] N *BrJur (abbr* **Justice of the Peace)** juez mf de paz

Jr *(abbr* **Junior)** Neil Smith, Jr Neil Smith, hijo

jubilant ['dʒuːbɪlənt] ADJ jubiloso(a)

jubilation [dʒuːbɪ'leɪʃən] N júbilo m

jubilee ['dʒuːbɪliː] N festejos mpl; **golden j.** quincuagésimo aniversario

judge [dʒʌdʒ] **1** N juez mf, jueza f; *(in competition)* jurado m
2 VT (**a**) *Jur* juzgar (**b**) *(estimate)* considerar (**c**) *(competition)* actuar de juez de (**d**) *(assess)* juzgar
3 VI juzgar; **judging from what you say** a juzgar por lo que dices

judg(e)ment ['dʒʌdʒmənt] N (**a**) *Jur* sentencia f, fallo m (**b**) *(opinion)* juicio m (**c**) *(ability)* buen juicio m

judicial [dʒuː'dɪʃəl] ADJ judicial

judiciary [dʒuː'dɪʃərɪ] N magistratura f

judicious [dʒuː'dɪʃəs] ADJ *Fml* juicioso(a)

judo ['dʒuːdəʊ] N judo m

jug [dʒʌg] N *Br* jarra f; **milk j.** jarra de leche

juggernaut ['dʒʌgənɔːt] N *Br* camión m grande, tráiler m

juggle ['dʒʌgəl] VI *(perform)* hacer juegos malabares (**with** con); *Fig (responsibilities)* ajustar

juggler ['dʒʌglə(r)] N malabarista mf

juice [dʒuːs] N *(of fruit)* zumo m, *Am* jugo m; *(of meat)* jugo m

juicy ['dʒuːsɪ] ADJ (**juicier, juiciest**) *also Fig* jugoso(a)

jukebox ['dʒuːkbɒks] N rocola f

July [dʒuː'laɪ, dʒə'laɪ] N julio m

jumble ['dʒʌmbəl] **1** N revoltijo m; *Br* **j. sale** rastrillo benéfico
2 VT revolver

jumbo ['dʒʌmbəʊ] ADJ **j. (jet)** jumbo m

jump [dʒʌmp] **1** N *(leap)* salto m; *(sudden increase)* subida repentina; **j. suit** mono m
2 VI (**a**) *(leap) (person, animal)* saltar, brincar; *Fig* **to j. to conclusions** sacar conclusiones precipitadas (**b**) *Fig (start)* sobresaltarse (**c**) *(increase)* aumentar de golpe
3 VT saltar; *Br* **to j. the queue** colarse; *US* **to j. rope** saltar a la comba
► **jump at** VT INSEP aceptar sin pensarlo

jumper ['dʒʌmpə(r)] N (**a**) *Br (sweater)* suéter m, *Esp* jersey m, *RP* pulóver m (**b**) *US (dress) Esp* pichi m, *CSur, Méx* jumper m (**c**) *US Aut* **j. cables** cables mpl de emergencia

jumpy ['dʒʌmpɪ] ADJ (**jumpier, jumpiest**) *Fam* nervioso(a)

junction ['dʒʌŋkʃən] N *(of roads)* cruce m; *Elec & Rail* empalme m

juncture ['dʒʌŋktʃə(r)] N *Fml* **at this j.** en esta coyuntura

June [dʒuːn] N junio m

jungle ['dʒʌŋgəl] N jungla f, selva f; *Fig* laberinto m; **the concrete j.** la jungla de asfalto

junior ['dʒuːnjə(r)] **1** ADJ (**a**) *(son of)* hijo; **David Hughes J.** David Hughes hijo (**b**) *US* **j. high (school)** *(between 11 and 15)* escuela secundaria; *Br* **j. school** *(between 7 and 11)* escuela primaria; **j. team** equipo m juvenil (**c**) *(lower in rank)* subalterno(a)
2 N (**a**) *(person of lower rank)* subalterno(a) m,f (**b**) *(younger person)* menor mf

junk [dʒʌŋk] N (**a**) *Fam* trastos mpl; **j. food** comida basura; **j. mail** propaganda f (por correo); **j. shop** tienda f de segunda mano (**b**) *(boat)* junco m

junkie ['dʒʌŋkɪ] N *Fam* yonqui mf

junkman ['dʒʌŋkmæn] N *US* trapero m

junta ['dʒʌntə, *US* 'hʊntə] N junta f militar

jurisdiction [dʒʊərɪs'dɪkʃən] N *Fml* jurisdicción f

juror ['dʒʊərə(r)] N jurado(a) m,f

jury ['dʒʊərɪ] N jurado m

just [dʒʌst] **1** ADJ *(fair)* justo(a); *Fml (well-founded)* justificado(a)
2 ADV (**a**) **he had j. arrived** acababa de llegar (**b**) *(at this very moment)* ahora mismo, en este momento; **he was j. leaving when ...** estaba a punto de salir cuando ...; **I'm j. coming!** ¡ya voy!; (**c**) *(only)* solamente; **j. in case** por si acaso; **j. a minute!** ¡un momento! (**d**) *(barely)* por poco; **j. about** casi; **j. enough** justo lo suficiente (**e**) *(emphatic)* **it's j. fantastic!** ¡es sencillamente fantástico! (**f**) *(exactly)* exactamente, justo; **as I thought** me lo figuraba; **j. as fast as** tan rápido como

justice ['dʒʌstɪs] N (**a**) *(power of law, fairness)* justicia f; **you didn't do yourself j.** no diste lo mejor de ti (**b**) *Jur (judge)* juez mf; **J. of the Peace** juez de paz

justifiable ['dʒʌstɪfaɪəbəl] ADJ justificable

justification [dʒʌstɪfɪ'keɪʃən] N justificación f

justified ['dʒʌstɪfaɪd] ADJ **to be j. in doing sth** tener razón en hacer algo

justify ['dʒʌstɪfaɪ] VT justificar

jut [dʒʌt] VI sobresalir; **to j. out over** proyectarse sobre

juvenile ['dʒuːvənaɪl] **1** ADJ (**a**) *(for young people)* juvenil; **j. court** tribunal m de menores; **j. delinquent** delincuente mf juvenil (**b**) *(immature)* infantil
2 N menor mf, joven mf

juxtapose [dʒʌkstə'pəʊz] VT yuxtaponer

K

K, k [keɪ] N *(the letter)* K, k *f*

kaleidoscope [kə'laɪdəskəʊp] N caleidoscopio *m*

Kampuchea [kæmpʊ'tʃɪə] N Kampuchea

kangaroo [kæŋgə'ru:] N canguro *m*

karaoke [kærɪ'əʊkɪ] N karaoke *m*

karat ['kærət] N *US* quilate *m*

karate [kə'rɑːtɪ] N kárate *m*

kebab [kə'bæb] N Culin pincho moruno, brocheta *f*

keel [kiːl] N quilla *f*; *Fig* **to be on an even k.** estar en calma

▸ **keel over** VI *Fam* desmayarse

keen [kiːn] ADJ **(a)** *(eager)* entusiasta **(b)** *(intense)* profundo(a) **(c)** *(mind, senses)* agudo(a); *(look)* penetrante; *(blade)* afilado(a); *(competition)* fuerte

keep [kiːp] **1** N **(a) to earn one's k.** ganarse el pan **(b)** *Fam* **for keeps** para siempre
   2 VT *(pt & pp* **kept**) **(a)** *(retain)* quedarse con, guardar; *(store)* guardar **(b)** *(maintain) (diary, accounts)* llevar; *(a promise)* cumplir; *(a secret)* guardar **(c)** *(maintain in a certain state)* mantener; **to k. one's room tidy** mantener su cuarto limpio; **to k. sb waiting** hacer esperar a algn **(d)** *(look after) (animals)* tener; *(shop, hotel)* llevar **(e)** *(detain)* entretener **(f)** *(prevent)* **to k. sb from doing sth** impedir a algn hacer algo
   3 VI **(a)** *(remain)* seguir; **k. still!** ¡estáte quieto(a)!; **to k. fit** mantenerse en forma; **to k. going** seguir adelante **(b)** *(do frequently)* no dejar de; **she keeps forgetting her keys** siempre se olvida las llaves **(c)** *(food)* conservarse

▸ **keep at** VT INSEP perseverar en

▸ **keep away 1** VT SEP mantener a distancia
   2 VI mantenerse a distancia

▸ **keep back** VT SEP *(information)* ocultar, callar; *(money etc)* retener

▸ **keep down** VT SEP **to k. prices down** mantener los precios bajos

▸ **keep off** VT INSEP **k. off the grass** *(sign)* prohibido pisar la hierba

▸ **keep on 1** VT SEP **(a)** *(clothes etc)* no quitarse; **to k. an eye on sth/sb** vigilar algo/a algn **(b)** *(continue to employ)* no despedir a
   2 VI *(continue to do)* seguir

▸ **keep out 1** VT SEP no dejar pasar
   2 VI no entrar; **k. out!** *(sign)* ¡prohibida la entrada!

▸ **keep to** VT INSEP *(subject)* limitarse a; **to k. to one's room** quedarse en el cuatro; **k. to the point!** ¡cíñete a la cuestión!; **to k. to the left** circular por la izquierda

▸ **keep up** VT SEP **(a)** *(custom)* mantener; **to k. up appearances** guardar las apariencias **(b)** **k. it up!** ¡sigue así! **(c)** *(prevent from sleeping)* mantener despierto(a)

▸ **keep up with** VT INSEP **to k. up with the times** estar al día

keeper ['kiːpə(r)] N *(in zoo)* guarda *mf*; *(in record office)* archivero(a) *m,f*; *(in museum)* conservador(a) *m,f*

keeping ['kiːpɪŋ] N **(a)** *(care)* cuidado *m* **(b)** **in k. with** en armonía con; **out of k. with** en desacuerdo con

keepsake ['kiːpseɪk] N recuerdo *m*

keg [keg] N barril *m*

kennel ['kenəl] N caseta *f* para perros; **kennels** hotel *m* de perros

Kenya ['kenjə, 'kiːnjə] N Kenia

Kenyan ['kenjən, 'kiːnjən] ADJ & N keniano(a) *(m,f)*

kept [kept] PT & PP *of* **keep**

kerb [kɜːb] N *Br* bordillo *m* (de la acera), *Chile* solera *f*, *Col, Perú* sardinel *m*, *CSur* cordón *m* (de la vereda), *Méx* borde *m* (de la banqueta)

kernel ['kɜːnəl] N *(of fruit, nut)* pepita *f*; *(of wheat)* grano *m*; *Fig* meollo *m*

kerosene, kerosine ['kerəsiːn] N *US* queroseno *m*

ketchup ['ketʃəp] N ketchup *m*, salsa *f* de tomate

kettle ['ketəl] N hervidor *m*; **that's a different k. of fish** eso es harina de otro costal

key [kiː] **1** N **(a)** *(for lock)* llave *f*; **k. ring** llavero *m* **(b)** *(of piano, typewriter)* tecla *f* **(c)** *Mus* tono *m*
   2 ADJ clave
   3 VT *Comput* teclear

▸ **key in** VT SEP *Comput* introducir

keyboard ['kiːbɔːd] N teclado *m*

keyed up [kiːd'ʌp] ADJ nervioso(a)

keyhole ['kiːhəʊl] N ojo *m* de la cerradura

keynote ['kiːnəʊt] N *Mus* tónica *f*; *Fig* nota *f* dominante

kg *(abbr* **kilogram(s))** kg

khaki ['kɑːkɪ] ADJ & N caqui *(m)*

kick [kɪk] **1** N *(from person)* patada *f*, puntapié *m*; *(from horse etc)* coz *f*

2 VT dar un puntapié a

3 VI (animal) cocear; (person) dar patadas

► **kick off** VI Fam empezar; Ftb sacar

► **kick out** VT SEP echar a patadas

► **kick up** VT INSEP Fam **to k. up a fuss** armar or Esp montar un alboroto

kick-off ['kɪkɒf] N Ftb saque m inicial

kid¹ [kɪd] N (a) Zool cabrito m; Fig **to handle sb with k. gloves** tratar a algn con guante blanco (b) Fam niño(a) m,f, CAm chavalo(a) m,f, Méx chavo(a) mf; **the kids** los críos

kid² [kɪd] **1** VT tomar el pelo a; **to k. oneself** (fool) hacerse ilusiones

2 VI Fam tomar el pelo; **no kidding!** ¡va en serio!

kidnap ['kɪdnæp] VT secuestrar

kidnapper ['kɪdnæpə(r)] N secuestrador(a) m,f

kidnapping ['kɪdnæpɪŋ] N secuestro m

kidney ['kɪdnɪ] N riñón m

kill [kɪl] VT matar; Fig **to k. time** pasar el rato; Fam **my feet are killing me!** ¡cómo me duelen los pies!

► **kill off** VT SEP exterminar

killer ['kɪlə(r)] N asesino(a) m,f; **k. whale** orca f

killing ['kɪlɪŋ] N asesinato m; Fig **to make a k.** forrarse de dinero

killjoy ['kɪldʒɔɪ] N aguafiestas mf inv

kiln [kɪln] N horno m

kilo ['kiːləʊ] N kilo m

kilobyte ['kɪləbaɪt] N Comput kilobyte m

kilogram(me) ['kɪləʊgræm] N kilogramo m

kilometre, US **kilometer** [kɪ'lɒmɪtə(r)] N kilómetro m

kilowatt ['kɪləʊwɒt] N kilovatio m

kilt [kɪlt] N falda escocesa, kilt m

kin [kɪn] N familiares mpl, parientes mpl

kind¹ [kaɪnd] **1** N tipo m, clase f; **they are two of a k.** son tal para cual; **in k.** (payment) en especie; (treatment) con la misma moneda

2 ADV Fam **k. of** en cierta manera

kind² [kaɪnd] ADJ amable, simpático(a); Fml **would you be so k. as to …?** ¿me haría usted el favor de …?

kindergarten ['kɪndəgɑːtən] N jardín m de infancia

kind-hearted [kaɪnd'hɑːtɪd] ADJ bondadoso(a)

kindle ['kɪndəl] VT encender, Am prender

kindly ['kaɪndlɪ] **1** ADJ (**kindlier, kindliest**) amable, bondadoso(a)

2 ADV Fml (please) por favor; **k. remit a cheque** sírvase enviar cheque; **to look k. on** aprobar

kindness ['kaɪndnɪs] N bondad f, amabilidad f

kindred ['kɪndrɪd] ADJ **k. spirits** almas gemelas

kinetic [kɪ'netɪk] ADJ cinético(a)

king [kɪŋ] N rey m; (draughts) dama f

kingdom ['kɪŋdəm] N reino m

kingfisher ['kɪŋfɪʃə(r)] N martín m pescador

king-size ['kɪŋsaɪz] ADJ extralargo(a)

kink [kɪŋk] N (in rope) coca f; (in hair) rizo m

kinky ['kɪŋkɪ] ADJ (**kinkier, kinkiest**) Fam (person) aberrante, pervertido(a); (erotic, pornographic) erótico(a)

kiosk ['kiːɒsk] N quiosco m

kip [kɪp] Br Fam

1 N **to have a k.** echar un sueño

2 VI (pt & pp **kipped**) dormir

kipper ['kɪpə(r)] N arenque m ahumado

kiss [kɪs] **1** N beso m

2 VT besar

3 VI besarse

kit [kɪt] N (a) (gear) equipo m; Mil avíos mpl (b) (clothing) ropa f (c) (toy model) maqueta f

► **kit out** VT SEP equipar

kitchen ['kɪtʃɪn] N cocina f; **k. sink** fregadero m

kite [kaɪt] N (a) (toy) cometa f (b) (bird) milano m

kitten ['kɪtən] N gatito(a) m,f

kitty ['kɪtɪ] N (money) fondo m común; Cards bote m

kiwi ['kiːwiː] N (a) (bird) kiwi m (b) **k. (fruit)** kiwi m

klutz [klʌts] N US Fam (stupid person) bobo(a) m,f, Esp chorra mf; (clumsy person) torpe, Esp patoso(a) m,f

km (pl **km** or **kms**) (abbr **kilometre(s)**) km

knack [næk] N **to get the k. of doing sth** cogerle el truquillo a algo

knackered ['nækəd] ADJ Br Fam **to be k.** (tired) estar hecho(a) polvo or reventado(a); (broken, damaged) estar hecho(a) polvo

knapsack ['næpsæk] N mochila f

knead [niːd] VT dar masaje a; (bread etc) amasar

knee [niː] **1** N rodilla f

2 VT dar un rodillazo a

kneecap ['niːkæp] **1** N rótula f

2 VT romper la rótula a

kneel [niːl] VI (pt & pp **knelt**) **to k. (down)** arrodillarse

knell [nel] N Literary toque m de difuntos

knelt [nelt] PT & PP of **kneel**

knew [njuː] PT of **know**

knickers ['nɪkəz] NPL Br bragas fpl, Chile, Col, Méx calzones mpl, RP bombacha f

knick-knack ['nɪknæk] N Fam chuchería f, baratija f

knife [naɪf] **1** N (pl **knives**) cuchillo m

2 VT apuñalar, dar una puñalada a

knight [naɪt] **1** N Hist caballero m; (in chess) caballo m

2 VT armar caballero

knighthood ['naɪthʊd] N (rank) título m de caballero

knit [nɪt] **1** VT (pt & pp **knitted** or **knit**) (a) (sweater) tejer (b) **to k. (together)** (join) juntar; Fig **to k. one's brow** fruncir el ceño

2 VI (**a**) *(with wool)* tejer, hacer punto (**b**) *(bone)* soldarse

knitting ['nɪtɪŋ] N punto *m*; **k. machine** máquina *f* de tejer; **k. needle** aguja *f* de tejer

knitwear ['nɪtweə(r)] N prendas *fpl* de punto *or Am* tejidas

knives [naɪvz] PL *of* **knife**

knob [nɒb] N (**a**) *(of stick)* puño *m*; *(of drawer)* tirador *m*; *(button)* botón *m* (**b**) *(small portion)* trozo *m*

knock [nɒk] **1** N golpe *m*; *Fig* revés *m*

2 VT (**a**) *(hit)* golpear (**b**) *Fam (criticize)* criticar

3 VI chocar (**against** *or* **into** contra); *(at door)* llamar (**at** a)

► **knock down** VT SEP (**a**) *(demolish)* derribar (**b**) *Aut* atropellar (**c**) *(price)* rebajar

► **knock off 1** VT SEP (**a**) *(cause to fall off)* tirar (**b**) *Fam (steal) Esp* mangar, *Am* volar (**c**) *Fam (kill)* asesinar a, *Esp* cepillarse a

2 VI *Fam* **they k. off at five** se piran a las cinco

► **knock out** VT SEP (**a**) *(make unconscious)* dejar sin conocimiento; *(in boxing)* poner fuera de combate, derrotar por K.O. (**b**) *(surprise)* dejar pasmado(a)

► **knock over** VT SEP *(cup)* volcar; *(with car)* atropellar

knocker ['nɒkə(r)] N *(on door)* aldaba *f*

knock-kneed [nɒk'niːd] ADJ patizambo(a), *Am* chueco(a)

knockout ['nɒkaʊt] N (**a**) *(in boxing)* K.O. *m*, knock-out *m* (**b**) *Fam* maravilla *f*

knot [nɒt] **1** N nudo *m*; *(group of people)* corro *m*

2 VT anudar

knotty ['nɒtɪ] ADJ (**knottier, knottiest**) nudoso(a); *Fig* **a k. problem** un problema espinoso

know [nəʊ] **1** VT *(pt* **knew**; *pp* **known**) (**a**) *(have knowledge of)* saber; **she knows how to ski** sabe esquiar; **to get to k. sth** enterarse de algo (**b**) *(be acquainted with)* conocer; **we got to k. each other at the party** nos conocimos en la fiesta

2 VI saber; **as far as I k.** que yo sepa; **to let sb k.** avisar a algn

know-all ['nəʊɔːl] N *Fam* sabelotodo *mf*

know-how ['nəʊhaʊ] N *Fam* conocimiento práctico

knowing ['nəʊɪŋ] ADJ *(deliberate)* delibera-do(a); **a k. smile** una sonrisa de complicidad

knowingly ['nəʊɪŋlɪ] ADV *(shrewdly)* a sabien-das; *(deliberately)* deliberadamente

know-it-all ['nəʊɪtɔːl] N *Fam* sabihondo(a) *m,f*, sabelotodo *mf*

knowledge ['nɒlɪdʒ] N (**a**) *(awareness)* cono-cimiento *m*; **without my k.** sin saberlo yo (**b**) *(learning)* conocimientos *mpl*

knowledgeable ['nɒlɪdʒəbəl] ADJ erudito(a); **k. about** muy entendido(a) en

known [nəʊn] **1** ADJ conocido(a)

2 PP *of* **know**

knuckle ['nʌkəl] N *Anat* nudillo *m*; *Culin* hueso *m*

► **knuckle down** VI *Fam* ponerse a trabajar en serio

KO [keɪ'əʊ] N *Fam (abbr* **knockout**) K.O. *m*

Koran [kɔː'rɑːn] N Corán *m*

Koranic [kə'rænɪk] ADJ coránico(a)

Korea [kə'riːə] N Corea

Korean [kə'riːən] ADJ & N coreano(a) *(m,f)*

Kurd [kɜːd] N curdo(a) *m,f*

Kuwait [kʊ'weɪt] N Kuwait

L, l [el] N *(the letter)* L, l f

lab [læb] N *Fam (abbr laboratory)* laboratorio m

label ['leɪbəl] 1 N etiqueta f; **record l.** ≃ casa discográfica
   2 VT *(pt & pp labelled, US labeled)* poner etiqueta a

labor ['leɪbə(r)] N, ADJ, VT & VI *US* = **labour**

laboratory [lə'bɒrətərɪ, *US* 'læbrətɔːrɪ] N laboratorio m

labored ['leɪbəd] ADJ *US* = **laboured**

laborer ['leɪbərə(r)] N *US* = **labourer**

laborious [lə'bɔːrɪəs] ADJ penoso(a)

labour ['leɪbə(r)] 1 N **(a)** *(work)* trabajo m **(b)** *(workforce)* mano f de obra **(c)** **labours** esfuerzos mpl **(d)** **the L. Party** el Partido Laborista **(e)** *(childbirth)* **to be in l.** estar de parto
   2 ADJ laboral
   3 VT *(stress, linger on)* machacar; *(a point)* insistir en
   4 VI *(work)* trabajar (duro)

laboured ['leɪbəd] ADJ *(breathing)* fatigoso(a); *(style)* forzado(a)

labourer ['leɪbərə(r)] N peón m; **farm l.** peón m agrícola

labour-saving ['leɪbəseɪvɪŋ] ADJ **l. devices** electrodomésticos mpl

labyrinth ['læbərɪnθ] N laberinto m

lace [leɪs] 1 N **(a)** *(fabric)* encaje m **(b)** **laces** cordones mpl
   2 VT **(a)** *(shoes)* atar (los cordones de) **(b)** *(add spirits to)* echar licor a
▶ **lace up** VT SEP atar con cordones

lacerate ['læsəreɪt] VT lacerar

lack [læk] 1 N falta f, escasez f; **for l. of** por falta de
   2 VT carecer de
   3 VI carecer (**in** de)

lackadaisical [lækə'deɪzɪkəl] ADJ *(lazy)* perezoso(a); *(indifferent)* indiferente

lacklustre, *US* **lackluster** ['læklʌstə(r)] ADJ *(eyes)* apagado(a); *(performance)* anodino(a)

laconic [lə'kɒnɪk] ADJ lacónico(a)

lacquer ['lækə(r)] 1 N laca f
   2 VT *(hair)* poner laca en

lad [læd] N *Fam* chaval m, muchacho m; **(stable) l.** mozo m de cuadra

ladder ['lædə(r)] 1 N **(a)** *(for climbing)* escalera f; *Fig* escala f **(b)** *(in stocking)* carrera f

   2 VT **I've laddered my stocking** me he hecho una carrera en las medias

laden ['leɪdən] ADJ cargado(a) (**with** de)

ladle ['leɪdəl] N cucharón m

lady ['leɪdɪ] N señora f; *Pol* **First L.** primera dama; *Ladies (sign on WC)* Señoras; **ladies and gentlemen!** ¡señoras y señores!; **L. Brown** Lady Brown

ladybird ['leɪdɪbɜːd], *US* **ladybug** ['leɪdɪbʌg] N mariquita f

lady-in-waiting [leɪdɪɪn'weɪtɪŋ] N dama f de honor

ladylike ['leɪdɪlaɪk] ADJ elegante

ladyship ['leɪdɪʃɪp] N **Her/Your L.** su señoría

lag [læg] 1 N **time l.** demora f
   2 VT revestir
   3 VI **to l. (behind)** quedarse atrás, retrasarse

lager ['lɑːgə(r)] N cerveza rubia

lagoon [lə'guːn] N laguna f

laid [leɪd] PT & PP *of* **lay**

laid-back [leɪd'bæk] ADJ *Fam* tranquilo(a), *Esp* cachazudo(a)

lain [leɪn] PP *of* **lie²**

lair [leə(r)] N guarida f

lake [leɪk] N lago m

lamb [læm] N cordero m; *(meat)* carne f de cordero; **l. chop** chuleta f de cordero; **l.'s wool** lana f de cordero

lame [leɪm] ADJ **(a)** *(person, animal)* cojo(a) **(b)** *(excuse, argument)* endeble, pobre

lament [lə'ment] 1 N *Mus* elegía f
   2 VT *(death)* llorar, lamentar
   3 VI llorar (**for** a), lamentarse (**over** de)

lamentable ['læməntəbəl] ADJ lamentable

laminated ['læmɪneɪtɪd] ADJ *(metal)* laminado(a); *(glass)* inastillable; *(paper)* plastificado(a)

lamp [læmp] N lámpara f; *Aut* faro m

lampoon [læm'puːn] 1 N sátira f
   2 VT satirizar

lamp-post ['læmppəʊst] N farola f

lampshade ['læmpʃeɪd] N pantalla f

lance [lɑːns] 1 N lanza f; *Br Mil* **l. corporal** cabo interino
   2 VT *Med* abrir con lanceta

Note that the Spanish word **lance** is a false friend and is never a translation for the English word **lance**. In Spanish **lance** means "event, incident".

land [lænd] **1** N (**a**) *(not sea)* tierra *f*; **by l.** por tierra (**b**) *Literary (country)* país *m* (**c**) *(property)* tierras *fpl*; **piece of l.** terreno *m*
2 VT (**a**) *(plane)* hacer aterrizar (**b**) *(disembark)* desembarcar (**c**) *Fam (obtain)* conseguir; *(contract)* ganar (**d**) *Fam* **she got landed with the responsibility** tuvo que cargar con la responsabilidad (**e**) *Fam (blow)* asestar
3 VI (**a**) *(plane)* aterrizar (**b**) *(disembark)* desembarcar
▶ **land up** VI *Fam* ir a parar

landing ['lændɪŋ] N (**a**) *(of staircase)* rellano *m* (**b**) *(of plane)* aterrizaje *m*; **l. strip** pista *f* de aterrizaje (**c**) *(of passengers)* desembarco *m*; **l. stage** desembarcadero *m*

landlady ['lændleɪdɪ] N *(of flat)* dueña *f*, propietaria *f*; *(of boarding house)* patrona *f*; *(of pub)* dueña

landlord ['lændlɔːd] N *(of flat)* dueño *m*, propietario *m*; *(of pub)* patrón *m*, dueño

landmark ['lændmɑːk] N (**a**) *(distinctive feature)* punto *m* de referencia (**b**) *Fig (in history)* hito *m*

landowner ['lændəʊnə(r)] N terrateniente *mf*

landscape ['lændskeɪp] **1** N paisaje *m*
2 VT ajardinar

landslide ['lændslaɪd] N desprendimiento *m* de tierras; **l. victory** victoria arrolladora

lane [leɪn] N *(in country)* camino *m*; *(in town)* callejón *m*; *(of motorway)* carril *m*; *Sport* calle *f*; *Naut* ruta *f*

language ['læŋgwɪdʒ] N (**a**) *(of a people)* idioma *m*, lengua *f*; **l. laboratory** laboratorio *m* de idiomas; **l. school** academia *f* de idiomas (**b**) *(style of speech or writing)* lenguaje *m*; **bad l.** palabrotas *fpl*

languid ['læŋgwɪd] ADJ lánguido(a)

languish ['læŋgwɪʃ] VI languidecer; *(project, plan etc)* quedar abandonado(a); *(in prison)* pudrirse

lank [læŋk] ADJ *(hair)* lacio(a)

lanky ['læŋkɪ] ADJ (**lankier, lankiest**) larguirucho(a)

lantern ['læntən] N farol *m*

lap¹ [læp] N *Anat* regazo *m*

lap² [læp] **1** N *(circuit)* vuelta *f*; *Fig* etapa *f*
2 VT *(overtake)* doblar

lap³ [læp] **1** VT *(pt & pp lapped)* *(of cat)* beber a lengüetadas
2 VI *(waves)* lamer, besar
▶ **lap up** VT SEP (**a**) *(of cat)* beber a lengüetadas (**b**) *Fig (wallow in)* disfrutar con; *(flattery)* recibir con entusiasmo (**c**) *Fig (believe)* tragar

lapel [lə'pel] N solapa *f*

Lapland ['læplænd] N Laponia

lapse [læps] **1** N (**a**) *(of time)* lapso *m* (**b**) *(error)* error *m*, desliz *m*; *(of memory)* fallo *m*
2 VI (**a**) *(time)* pasar, transcurrir (**b**) *(expire)* caducar (**c**) *(err)* cometer un error; *(fall back)* caer (**into** en)

laptop ['læptɒp] N *Comput* **l. (computer)** *Esp* ordenador *m* or *Am* computadora *f* portátil

larceny ['lɑːsənɪ] N *Jur* (delito *m* de) robo *m* or latrocinio *m*

larch [lɑːtʃ] N alerce *m*

lard [lɑːd] N manteca *f* de cerdo

larder ['lɑːdə(r)] N despensa *f*

large [lɑːdʒ] **1** ADJ grande; *(amount)* importante; *(extensive)* amplio(a); **by and l.** por lo general
2 N **to be at l.** andar suelto(a); **the public at l.** el público en general

> Note that the Spanish word **largo** is a false friend and is never a translation for the English word **large**. In Spanish **largo** means "long".

largely ['lɑːdʒlɪ] ADV *(mainly)* en gran parte; *(chiefly)* principalmente

large-scale ['lɑːdʒskeɪl] ADJ *(project, problem etc)* de gran envergadura; *(map)* a gran escala

lark¹ [lɑːk] N *(bird)* alondra *f*

lark² [lɑːk] N *Fam (joke)* broma *f*; **what a l.!** ¡qué risa!
▶ **lark about, lark around** VI *Fam* hacer el tonto

larva ['lɑːvə] N larva *f*

laryngitis [lærɪn'dʒaɪtɪs] N laringitis *f*

larynx ['lærɪŋks] N *Anat* laringe *f*

laser ['leɪzə(r)] N láser *m*; **l. printer** impresora *f* láser

lash [læʃ] **1** N (**a**) *(eyelash)* pestaña *f* (**b**) *(blow with whip)* latigazo *m*
2 VT (**a**) *(beat)* azotar (**b**) *(rain)* azotar (**c**) *(tie)* atar
▶ **lash out** VI (**a**) *(with fists)* repartir golpes a diestro y siniestro; *(verbally)* criticar (**at** a) (**b**) *Fam (spend money)* tirar or *Am* salvo *RP* botar la casa por la ventana

lass [læs] N *Fam* chavala *f*, muchacha *f*

lasso [læ'suː] **1** N lazo *m (para ganado)*
2 VT capturar con lazo, *CSur* lacear

last [lɑːst] **1** ADJ (**a**) *(final)* último(a), final; *Fam* **the l. straw** el colmo (**b**) *(most recent)* último(a) (**c**) *(past)* pasado(a); *(previous)* anterior; **l. but one** penúltimo(a); **l. month** el mes pasado; **l. night** anoche
2 ADV (**a**) **when I l. saw her** la última vez que la vi (**b**) *(at the end)* en último lugar; *(in race etc)* último; **at (long) l.** por fin; **l. but not least** el último en orden pero no en importancia
3 N **the l.** el último/la última
4 VI (**a**) *(time)* durar; *(hold out)* aguantar (**b**) *(be enough for)* llegar, alcanzar

last-ditch ['lɑːstdɪtʃ] ADJ *(effort, attempt)* último(a) y desesperado(a)

lasting ['lɑːstɪŋ] ADJ duradero(a)

lastly ['lɑːstlɪ] ADV por último, finalmente

last-minute ['lɑːstmɪnɪt] ADJ de última hora

latch [lætʃ] N picaporte *m*, pestillo *m*

late [leɪt] **1** ADJ (**a**) *(not on time)* tardío(a); *(hour)* avanzado(a); **to be five minutes l.** llegar con cinco minutos de retraso (**b**) *(far on in time)* tarde; **in l. autumn** a finales del otoño; **in the l. afternoon** a última hora de la tarde; **she's in her l. twenties** ronda los treinta (**c**) *(dead)* difunto(a)
2 ADV (**a**) *(not on time)* tarde; **to arrive l.** llegar tarde (**b**) *(far on in time)* tarde; **l. at night** a altas horas de la noche; **l. in life** a una edad avanzada (**c**) **as l. as 1950** todavía en 1950; **of l.** últimamente

latecomer [ˈleɪtkʌmə(r)] N tardón(ona) *m,f*

lately [ˈleɪtlɪ] ADV últimamente, recientemente

latent [ˈleɪtənt] ADJ latente

later [ˈleɪtə(r)] **1** ADJ (**a**) *(subsequent)* posterior; **in her l. novels** en sus novelas posteriores (**b**) *(more recent)* más reciente
2 ADV más tarde, después; **l. on** más adelante, más tarde

lateral [ˈlætərəl] ADJ lateral

latest [ˈleɪtɪst] **1** ADJ *(superl of* **late**) *(most recent)* último(a), más reciente
2 N **the l.** lo último; **have you heard the l.?** ¿te enteraste de lo último?; **Friday at the l.** el viernes a más tardar

lathe [leɪð] N *Tech* torno *m*

lather [ˈlɑːðə(r)] **1** N *(of soap)* espuma *f*; *(horse's sweat)* sudor *m*
2 VT *(with soap)* enjabonar

Latin [ˈlætɪn] **1** ADJ & N latino(a) *(m,f)*; **L. America** América Latina, Latinoamérica *f*; **L. American** latinoamericano(a) *(m,f)*
2 N *(language)* latín *m*

latitude [ˈlætɪtjuːd] N latitud *f*

latrine [ləˈtriːn] N letrina *f*

latter [ˈlætə(r)] **1** ADJ (**a**) *(last)* último(a) (**b**) *(second of two)* segundo(a)
2 PRON éste(a); **the former ... the l.** aquél ... éste/aquélla ... ésta

lattice [ˈlætɪs] N enrejado *m*, rejilla *f*

laudable [ˈlɔːdəbəl] ADJ loable

laugh [lɑːf] **1** N risa *f*; *(guffaw)* carcajada *f*; **for a l.** para divertirse
2 VI reír, reírse
► **laugh about** VT INSEP **to l. about sth/sb** reírse de algo/algn
► **laugh at** VT INSEP **to l. at sth/sb** reírse de algo/algn
► **laugh off** VT SEP tomar a risa

laughable [ˈlɑːfəbəl] ADJ *(situation, suggestion)* ridículo(a); *(amount, offer)* irrisorio(a)

laughing-stock [ˈlɑːfɪŋstɒk] N hazmerreír *m inv*

laughter [ˈlɑːftə(r)] N risa *f*

launch [lɔːntʃ] **1** N (**a**) *(vessel)* lancha *f* (**b**) *(of product)* lanzamiento *m*
2 VT (**a**) *(attack, rocket, new product)* lanzar; *(ship)* botar (**b**) *(company)* fundar; *(scheme)* iniciar

launching [ˈlɔːntʃɪŋ] N (**a**) *(of rocket, new product)* lanzamiento *m* (**b**) *(of ship)* botadura *f* (**c**) *(of film, play)* estreno *m* (**d**) *(of new company)* fundación *f*

launchpad [ˈlɔːntʃpæd] N plataforma *f* de lanzamiento

launder [ˈlɔːndə(r)] VT lavar y planchar; *Fig (money)* blanquear

laund(e)rette [lɔːndəˈret], US **Laundromat**® [ˈlɔːndrəmæt] N lavandería *f*

laundry [ˈlɔːndrɪ] N (**a**) *(place)* lavandería *f* (**b**) *(dirty clothes)* ropa sucia; **to do the l.** lavar la ropa

laurel [ˈlɒrəl] N laurel *m*; *Fam Fig* **to rest on one's laurels** dormirse en los laureles

lava [ˈlɑːvə] N lava *f*

lavatory [ˈlævətərɪ] N (**a**) *(receptacle)* váter *m*, retrete *m* (**b**) *(room)* (cuarto *m* de) baño *m*; **public l.** servicios *mpl, Esp* aseos *mpl*

lavender [ˈlævəndə(r)] N lavanda *f*

lavish [ˈlævɪʃ] **1** ADJ (**a**) *(generous)* pródigo(a) (**b**) *(abundant)* abundante (**c**) *(luxurious)* lujoso(a)
2 VT **to l. praise on sb** colmar de alabanzas a algn; **to l. attention on sb** prodigarse en atenciones con algn

law [lɔː] N (**a**) *(rule, set of rules)* ley *f*; **by l.** según la ley; **l. and order** el orden público; **to lay down the l.** dictar la ley (**b**) *(as subject)* derecho *m*; **l. court** tribunal *m* de justicia (**c**) *Fam* **the l.** *(police)* la poli

law-abiding [ˈlɔːəbaɪdɪŋ] ADJ respetuoso(a) de la ley

lawful [ˈlɔːfʊl] ADJ legal; *(permitted by law)* lícito(a); *(legitimate)* legítimo(a)

lawn [lɔːn] N césped *m*; **l. tennis** tenis *m* sobre hierba

lawnmower [ˈlɔːnməʊə(r)] N cortacésped *m*

lawsuit [ˈlɔːsjuːt] N pleito *m*

lawyer [ˈlɔːjə(r)] N abogado(a) *m,f*; **l.'s office** bufete *m* de abogados

lax [læks] ADJ *(morals, discipline)* relajado(a), laxo(a); *(person)* negligente, poco riguroso(a); *(security, standards)* descuidado(a), poco riguroso(a)

laxative [ˈlæksətɪv] ADJ & N laxante *(m)*

laxity [ˈlæksɪtɪ] N *(of morals, discipline)* laxitud *f, Esp* relajo *m*; *(of person)* negligencia *f* (**in doing sth** al hacer algo); *(of security, standards)* falta *f* de rigor

lay¹ [leɪ] ADJ (**a**) *Rel* laico(a) (**b**) *(non-specialist)* lego(a)

lay² [leɪ] VT *(pt & pp* **laid**)
1 (**a**) *(place)* poner, colocar; *(cable, trap)* tender; *(foundations)* echar (**b**) *(fire)* preparar; *(table)* poner (**c**) *(eggs)* poner
2 PT *of* **lie²**
► **lay aside** VT SEP dejar a un lado
► **lay by** VT SEP *(save)* guardar; *(money)* ahorrar

▶ **lay down** VT SEP (**a**) *(put down)* poner; *(let go)* dejar; **to l. down one's arms** rendir las armas (**b**) *(establish)* fijar, imponer; *(principles)* sentar

▶ **lay into** VT INSEP *Fam (physically)* dar una paliza a; *(verbally)* arremeter contra

▶ **lay off 1** VT SEP *(dismiss)* despedir
2 VT INSEP *Fam* dejar en paz

▶ **lay on** VT SEP *(provide)* proveer de; *(food)* preparar

▶ **lay out** VT SEP (**a**) *(open out)* extender (**b**) *(arrange)* disponer (**c**) *(ideas)* exponer (**d**) *(plan)* trazar (**e**) *Fam (spend)* gastar

▶ **lay up** VT SEP (**a**) *(store)* guardar (**b**) *(accumulate)* almacenar (**c**) *Fam* **to be laid up** tener que guardar cama

layabout ['leɪəbaʊt] N *Fam* vago(a) *m,f*

lay-by ['leɪbaɪ] N *Br* área *f* de descanso

layer ['leɪə(r)] N capa *f*

layman ['leɪmən] N lego(a) *m,f*

layout ['leɪaʊt] N *(arrangement)* disposición *f*; *(presentation)* presentación *f*; *Typ* composición *f*; *(plan)* diseño *m*, trazado *m*

laze [leɪz] VI **to l.** *(about/around)* holgazanear, gandulear

laziness ['leɪzɪnɪs] N pereza *f*, holgazanería *f*

lazy ['leɪzɪ] ADJ (**lazier, laziest**) perezoso(a), holgazán(ana); **at a l. pace** a paso lento

lb *(abbr* **pound)** libra *f*

lead¹ [led] N (**a**) *(metal)* plomo *m* (**b**) *(in pencil)* mina *f*

lead² [li:d] **1** N (**a**) *(front position)* delantera *f*; *(advantage)* ventaja *f*; **to take the l.** *(in race)* tomar la delantera (**b**) *(clue)* pista *f* (**c**) *Th* primer papel *m* (**d**) *(leash)* correa *f* (**e**) *Elec* cable *m*
2 VT *(pt & pp* **led***)* (**a**) *(conduct)* llevar, conducir (**b**) *(be the leader of)* dirigir, encabezar (**c**) *(influence)* llevar a; **this leads me to believe that** esto me lleva a creer que (**d**) *(life)* llevar
3 VI (**a**) *(road)* llevar, conducir *(to* a) (**b**) *(go first)* ir delante; *(in race)* llevar la delantera (**c**) **to l. to** llevar a

▶ **lead away** VT SEP llevar

▶ **lead on 1** VT SEP *(deceive)* engañar, timar
2 VI *(go ahead)* ir adelante

▶ **lead up to** VT INSEP llevar a

leaden ['ledən] ADJ *(sky)* plomizo(a); *(food)* pesado(a)

leader ['li:də(r)] N (**a**) *(of group, in race)* líder (**b**) *Press* editorial *m*

leadership ['li:dəʃɪp] N (**a**) *(command)* dirección *f*, mando *m*; *Pol* liderazgo *m* (**b**) *(leaders)* dirigentes *mpl*, cúpula *f*

lead-free ['ledfri:] ADJ sin plomo

leading ['li:dɪŋ] ADJ (**a**) *(main)* principal (**b**) *(outstanding)* destacado(a)

leaf [li:f] N *(pl* **leaves***)* hoja *f*; **to turn over a new l.** hacer borrón y cuenta nueva

▶ **leaf through** VT INSEP hojear

leaflet ['li:flɪt] N folleto *m*

league [li:g] N (**a**) *(alliance)* alianza *f*; *(association)* sociedad *f*; *Fam* **to be in l. with sb** estar conchabado(a) con algn (**b**) *Sport* liga *f*

leak [li:k] **1** N (**a**) *(hole)* agujero *m*; *(in roof)* gotera *f* (**b**) *(of gas, liquid)* fuga *f*, escape *m*; *(of information)* filtración *f*
2 VT *(information)* filtrar *(to* a)
3 VI (**a**) *(container)* tener un agujero; *(pipe)* tener un escape; *(roof)* gotear; *(boat)* hacer agua (**b**) *(gas, liquid)* escaparse; *(information)* filtrarse; *(news)* trascender

leaky ['li:kɪ] ADJ (**leakier, leakiest**) *(container)* agujereado(a); *(roof)* que tiene goteras; *(ship)* que hace agua

lean¹ [li:n] ADJ *(meat)* magro(a); *(person)* flaco(a); *(harvest)* escaso(a)

lean² [li:n] **1** VT apoyar *(on* en)
2 VI *(pt & pp* **leaned** *or* **leant***)* (**a**) *(building, tree)* inclinarse (**b**) *(for support)* **to l. on/ against** apoyarse en/contra; *Fig* **to l. on sb** *(pressurize)* presionar a algn; *(depend)* depender de algn

▶ **lean back** VI reclinarse

▶ **lean forward** VI inclinarse hacia delante

▶ **lean out** VI asomarse

▶ **lean over** VI inclinarse

leaning ['li:nɪŋ] **1** ADJ inclinado(a)
2 N *Fig (tendency)* inclinación *f*, tendencia *f*

leant [lent] *Br* PT & PP of **lean**

lean-to ['li:ntu:] N *(hut)* cobertizo *m*

leap [li:p] **1** N *(jump)* salto *m*; *Fig* paso *m*; **l. year** año bisiesto
2 VI *(pt & pp* **leaped** *or* **leapt***)* saltar; *Fig* **her heart leapt** su corazón dio un vuelco

▶ **leap at** VT INSEP *Fig (chance)* no dejar escapar

leapfrog ['li:pfrɒg] N pídola *f*

leapt [lept] PT & PP of **leap**

learn [lɜ:n] **1** VT *(pt & pp* **learned** *or* **learnt***)* (**a**) *(language, skill)* aprender; **to l. (how) to ski** aprender a esquiar (**b**) *(find out about)* **to l. that** enterarse de que
2 VI (**a**) *(acquire knowledge)* aprender (**b**) *(find out)* **to l. about** *or* **of** enterarse de

learned ['lɜ:nɪd] ADJ erudito(a)

learner ['lɜ:nə(r)] N *(beginner)* principiante *mf*; **l. driver** aprendiz(a) *m,f* de conductor

learning ['lɜ:nɪŋ] N *(knowledge)* conocimientos *mpl*; *(erudition)* saber *m*

learnt [lɜ:nt] *Br* PT & PP of **learn**

lease [li:s] **1** N contrato *m* de arrendamiento; *Fig* **to give sb a new l.** *Br* **of** *or* *US* **on life** dar nueva vida a algn
2 VT arrendar

leasehold ['li:shəʊld] **1** N derechos *mpl* de arrendamiento
2 ADJ *(property)* arrendado(a)

leash [li:ʃ] N correa *f*

least [li:st] *(superl of little)* **1** ADJ menor, mínimo(a); **he has the l. time** él es quien menos tiempo tiene

2 ADV menos; **l. of all him** él menos que nadie

3 N **the l.** lo menos; **at l.** por lo menos, al menos; **to say the l.** por no decir más

leather ['leðə(r)] **1** N piel *f*, cuero *m*

2 ADJ de piel

leave¹ [li:v] **1** VT *(pt & pp left)* **(a)** *(depart from)* *(place)* irse de, marcharse de; *(room)* salir de; *(person)* dejar **(b)** *(allow to remain)* dejar; **l. him alone!** ¡déjale en paz!; *Fam* **l. it to me** yo me encargo **(c)** *(put, deposit)* **to l. sth somewhere** *(deliberately)* dejar algo en algún sitio; *(by mistake)* dejarse algo en algún sitio **(d)** *(bequeath)* legar **(e)** *(remain)* **to be left** quedar

2 VI *(go away)* irse, marcharse; *(go out)* salir; **the train leaves in five minutes** el tren sale dentro de cinco minutos

▸ **leave behind** VT SEP **to l. sth behind** dejarse algo

▸ **leave on** VT SEP **(a)** *(clothes)* dejar puesto(a) **(b)** *(lights, radio)* dejar encendido(a) *or Am* prendido(a)

▸ **leave out** VT SEP *(omit)* omitir; *Fig* **to feel left out** sentirse excluido(a)

▸ **leave over** VT SEP **to be left over** *(food, money)* sobrar

leave² [li:v] N **(a)** *(permission)* permiso *m* **(b)** *(time off)* vacaciones *fpl*; *Mil* **on l.** de permiso; **l. of absence** excedencia *f* **(c)** **to take one's l. of sb** despedirse de algn

leaves [li:vz] PL *of* leaf

Lebanon ['lebənən] N **(the) L.** (el) Líbano

lecherous ['letʃərəs] ADJ lascivo(a)

lecture ['lektʃə(r)] **1** N **(a)** *(public speech)* conferencia *f*; *Univ* clase *f*; **to give a l. (on)** dar una conferencia (sobre); **l. theatre** sala *f* de conferencias; *Univ* aula *f* **(b)** *(rebuke)* sermón *m*

2 VT *(reproach)* sermonear

3 VI dar una conferencia; *Univ* dar clases

lecturer ['lektʃərə(r)] N conferenciante *mf*; *Br Univ* profesor(a) *m,f* de universidad

led [led] PT & PP *of* lead

ledge [ledʒ] N **(a)** *(shelf)* repisa *f*; *(of window)* alféizar *m* **(b)** *(on mountain)* saliente *m*

ledger ['ledʒə(r)] N libro *m* mayor

lee [li:] N **(a)** *Naut* sotavento *m* **(b)** *Fig* abrigo *m*

leech [li:tʃ] N sanguijuela *f*

leek [li:k] N puerro *m*

leer [lɪə(r)] VI mirar con lascivia

leeway ['li:weɪ] N libertad *f*; **this gives me a certain amount of l.** esto me da cierto margen de libertad

left¹ [left] **1** ADJ izquierdo(a); *Pol* **l. wing** izquierda *f*

2 ADV a la izquierda

3 N izquierda *f*; **on the l.** a mano izquierda; *Pol* **to be on the l.** ser de izquierdas

left² [left] PT & PP *of* leave

left-hand ['lefthænd] ADJ **l. drive** con el volante a la izquierda; **on the l. side** a mano izquierda

left-handed [left'hændɪd] ADJ zurdo(a)

left-luggage [left'lʌgɪdʒ] N *Br* **l. office** consigna *f*

leftovers ['leftəʊvəz] NPL sobras *fpl*

left-wing ['leftwɪŋ] ADJ de izquierdas, izquierdista

leg [leg] N **(a)** *(of person)* pierna *f*; *(of animal, table)* pata *f*; *Culin (of lamb)* pierna; *(of trousers)* pernera *f* **(b)** *(stage)* etapa *f*

legacy ['legəsɪ] N herencia *f*, legado *m*

legal ['li:gəl] ADJ **(a)** *(lawful, legitimate)* legal; **l. tender** moneda *f* de curso legal **(b)** *(relating to the law)* legal, jurídico(a); **l. aid** asesoramiento jurídico gratuito; **l. dispute** contencioso *m*; *US* **l. holiday** fiesta *f* nacional

legalize ['li:gəlaɪz] VT legalizar

legally ['li:gəlɪ] ADV legalmente

legend ['ledʒənd] N leyenda *f*

legendary ['ledʒəndərɪ] ADJ legendario(a)

leggings ['legɪŋz] NPL polainas *fpl*

legible ['ledʒəbəl] ADJ legible

legion ['li:dʒən] N legión *f*

legislation [ledʒɪs'leɪʃən] N legislación *f*

legislative ['ledʒɪslətɪv] ADJ legislativo(a)

legislator ['ledʒɪsleɪtə(r)] N legislador(a) *m,f*

legislature ['ledʒɪsleɪtʃə(r)] N asamblea legislativa

legitimate [lɪ'dʒɪtɪmɪt] ADJ legítimo(a)

legroom ['legru:m] N espacio *m* para las piernas

leisure ['leʒə(r), *US* 'li:ʒər] N ocio *m*, tiempo *m* libre; **at l.** con calma; **do it at your l.** hazlo cuando tengas tiempo; **l. activities** pasatiempos *mpl*; **l. centre** centro recreativo

leisurely ['leʒəlɪ, *US* 'li:ʒərlɪ] ADJ *(unhurried)* tranquilo(a); *(slow)* lento(a)

lemon ['lemən] N limón *m*; **l. curd** crema *f* de limón; **l. juice** zumo *m* de limón; **l. tea** té *m* con limón

lemonade [lemə'neɪd] N *(still)* limonada *f*; *Br (fizzy) Esp, Arg* gaseosa *f*, *Am* gaseosa *f* de lima *or* limón

lend [lend] VT *(pt & pp lent)* prestar; **to l. oneself/itself to sth** prestarse a *or* para algo

lender ['lendə(r)] N *Fin* prestamista *mf*

lending ['lendɪŋ] N **l. library** biblioteca *f* de préstamo

length [leŋkθ, leŋθ] N **(a)** *(in space)* longitud *f*; **it is 5 m in l.** tiene 5 m de largo; *Fig* **to go to any lengths to achieve sth** hacer lo que sea para conseguir algo **(b)** *(duration)* duración *f* **(c)** *(of string)* trozo *m*; *(of cloth)* retal *m* **(d)** **at l.** *(finally)* finalmente; *(in depth)* a fondo

lengthen ['leŋkθən, 'leŋθən] **1** VT alargar; *(lifetime)* prolongar

2 VI alargarse; *(lifetime)* prolongarse

lengthways ['leŋθweɪz] ADV a lo largo

lengthy ['leŋθɪ, 'leŋθi] ADJ (**lengthier, lengthiest**) largo(a); *(film, illness)* de larga duración; *(meeting, discussion)* prolongado(a)

lenient ['li:nɪənt] ADJ indulgente

lens [lenz] N *(of eye)* cristalino m; *(of spectacles)* lente f; *Phot* objetivo m

Lent [lent] N Cuaresma f

lent [lent] PT & PP of **lend**

lentil ['lentɪl] N lenteja f

Leo ['li:əʊ] N Leo m

leopard ['lepəd] N leopardo m

leotard ['li:ətɑ:d] N leotardo m

leper ['lepə(r)] N leproso(a) m,f

leprosy ['leprəsɪ] N lepra f

lesbian ['lezbɪən] ADJ & N lesbiana (f)

less [les] **1** ADJ *(comp of little)* menos
2 PRON menos; **the l. said about it, the better** cuanto menos se hable de eso mejor
3 ADV menos; **l. and l.** cada vez menos
4 PREP menos

lessen ['lesən] VT & VI disminuir

lesser ['lesə(r)] ADJ menor; **to a l. extent** en menor grado

lesson ['lesən] N (**a**) *(session)* clase f; *(in book)* lección f; **Spanish lessons** clases de español (**b**) *Rel* lectura f

lest [lest] CONJ *Fml (in case)* para que no; **l. we forget** para que no olvidemos

let [let] **1** VT *(pt & pp let)* (**a**) *(allow)* dejar, permitir; **to l. go of sth** soltar algo; **to l. sb know** avisar a algn; *Fig* **to l. oneself go** dejarse ir (**b**) *(rent out)* alquilar, *Méx* rentar; **to l.** *(sign)* se alquila (**c**) **l. alone** ni mucho menos
2 V AUX **l. him wait** que espere; **l. me go!** ¡suéltame!; **l.'s go!** ¡vamos!, ¡vámonos!; **l.'s see** a ver
▶ **let down** VT SEP (**a**) *(lower)* bajar; *(lengthen)* alargar (**b**) *(deflate)* desinflar (**c**) *(fail)* fallar, defraudar
▶ **let in** VT SEP (**a**) *(admit)* dejar entrar (**b**) **to l. oneself in for** meterse en
▶ **let off** VT SEP (**a**) *(bomb)* hacer explotar; *(fireworks)* hacer estallar (**b**) *(liquid, air)* soltar (**c**) *Fam* **to l. sb off** *(pardon)* perdonar
▶ **let on** VI *Fam* **don't l. on** *(reveal information)* no se lo digas
▶ **let out** VT SEP (**a**) *(release)* soltar; *(news)* divulgar; *(secret)* revelar (**b**) *(air, water)* dejar salir (**c**) *(cry)* soltar (**d**) *Sewing* ensanchar
▶ **let up** VI cesar, parar

letdown ['letdaʊn] N decepción f

lethal ['li:θəl] ADJ letal

lethargic [lɪ'θɑ:dʒɪk] ADJ aletargado(a)

letter ['letə(r)] N (**a**) *(of alphabet)* letra f; *Fig* **to the l.** al pie de la letra (**b**) *(written message)* carta f; *Br* **l. box** buzón m; *Com* **l. of credit** carta de crédito

letterhead ['letəhed] N membrete m

lettering ['letərɪŋ] N rótulo m

lettuce ['letɪs] N lechuga f

let-up ['letʌp] N *Fam* descanso m, respiro m

leukaemia, *US* **leukemia** [lu:'ki:mɪə] N leucemia f

level ['levəl] **1** ADJ (**a**) *(flat)* llano(a); *(even)* nivelado(a); *(equal)* igual, parejo(a); **a l. spoonful of** una cucharada rasa de; **to be l. with** estar a nivel de; *Br* **l. crossing** paso m a nivel (**b**) *(steady)* estable; *(tone)* uniforme
2 VT *(pt & pp* **levelled,** *US* **leveled**) (**a**) *(make level)* nivelar (**b**) *(building)* arrasar (**c**) *(stare, criticism)* dirigir
3 N nivel m; **to be on a l. with** estar al mismo nivel que
▶ **level off, level out** VI estabilizarse
▶ **level with** VT INSEP *Fam* ser franco(a) con

level-headed [levəl'hedɪd] ADJ sensato(a)

lever ['li:və(r), *US* 'levə(r)] **1** N palanca f
2 VT apalancar; **to l. sth out** sacar algo con palanca

leverage ['li:vərɪdʒ] *Fig* influencia f

levy ['levɪ] **1** VT *(tax)* recaudar; *(fine)* imponer
2 N *(of tax)* recaudación f; *(of fine)* imposición f

lewd [lu:d] ADJ *(person)* lascivo(a); *(story)* obsceno(a)

liability [laɪə'bɪlɪtɪ] N (**a**) *Jur* responsabilidad f (**b**) *(handicap)* estorbo m (**c**) *Fin* **liabilities** pasivo m

liable ['laɪəbəl] ADJ (**a**) *Jur* responsable; *(susceptible)* sujeto(a); **to be l. for** ser responsable de (**b**) **to be l. to do sth** ser propenso(a) a hacer algo; **it's l. to happen** es muy probable que (así) suceda

liaise [lɪ'eɪz] VI comunicarse (**with** con)

liaison [lɪ'eɪzɒn] N (**a**) *(cooperation)* coordinación f; **l. officer** oficial mf de enlace (**b**) *(love affair)* amorío m

liar ['laɪə(r)] N mentiroso(a) m,f, embustero(a) m,f

libel ['laɪbəl] **1** N libelo m
2 VT *(pt & pp* **libelled,** *US* **libeled**) difamar, calumniar

liberal ['lɪbərəl] **1** ADJ (**a**) *(tolerant)* liberal; **L. Party** Partido m Liberal (**b**) *(abundant)* abundante
2 N *Pol* **L.** liberal mf

liberate ['lɪbəreɪt] VT liberar; *(prisoner etc)* poner en libertad; **liberated woman** mujer liberada

liberation [lɪbə'reɪʃən] N liberación f

liberty ['lɪbətɪ] N libertad f; **to be at l. to say sth** ser libre de decir algo; **to take liberties** tomarse libertades

Libra ['li:brə] N Libra m

librarian [laɪ'breərɪən] N bibliotecario(a) m,f

Note that the Spanish word **librero** is a false friend and is never a translation for the English word **librarian**. In Spanish **librero** means "bookseller".

library ['laɪbrərɪ] N biblioteca f

> Note that the Spanish word **librería** is a false friend and is never a translation for the English word **library**. In Spanish **librería** means "bookshop".

Libya ['lɪbɪə] N Libia f

Libyan ['lɪbɪən] ADJ & N libio(a) *(m,f)*

lice [laɪs] PL of **louse**

licence, *US* **license** ['laɪsəns] N (a) *(permit)* licencia f, permiso m; *Aut* **l. number** matrícula f; *US* **l. plate** (placa f de la) matrícula (b) *(freedom)* libertad f, *(excessive freedom)* libertinaje m

license ['laɪsəns] **1** VT dar licencia a, autorizar
2 N *US* = **licence**

licensed ['laɪsənst] ADJ *Br* **l. premises** = local autorizado para la venta de bebidas alcohólicas; **l. restaurant** = restaurante con licencia para vender bebidas alcohólicas

licentious [laɪˈsenʃəs] ADJ licencioso(a)

lichen ['laɪkən, 'lɪtʃən] N liquen m

lick [lɪk] **1** VT lamer; **to l. one's lips** relamerse
2 N lamedura f; *Fam* **a l. of paint** una mano de pintura

licorice ['lɪkərɪs] N *US* = **liquorice**

lid [lɪd] N (a) *(cover)* tapa f (b) *(of eye)* párpado m

lie¹ [laɪ] **1** VI mentir
2 N mentira f

lie² [laɪ] **1** VI *(pt lay; pp lain)* (a) *(act)* echarse, acostarse; *(state)* estar echado(a), estar acostado(a); *(be buried)* yacer (b) *(be situated)* encontrarse, hallarse; **the valley lay before us** el valle se extendía ante nosotros (c) *(remain)* quedarse
2 N *(position)* situación f; *(direction)* orientación f

▸ **lie about, lie around** VI *(person)* estar tumbado(a); *(things)* estar tirado(a)

▸ **lie down** VI acostarse, echarse

lie-in ['laɪɪn] N *Fam* **to have a l.** levantarse tarde

lieu [ljuː, luː] N **in l. of** en lugar de

lieutenant [*Br* lefˈtenənt, *US* luːˈtenənt] N (a) *Mil* teniente m (b) *(deputy, assistant)* lugarteniente m

life [laɪf] N *(pl lives)* (a) *(in general)* vida f; **to come to l.** cobrar vida; **to take one's own l.** suicidarse; *Fam* **how's l.?** ¿qué tal?; **l. belt** cinturón m salvavidas; **l. imprisonment** cadena perpetua; **l. insurance** seguro m de vida; **l. jacket** chaleco m salvavidas; **l. style** estilo m de vida; **l. story** biografía f (b) *(liveliness)* vitalidad f

lifeboat ['laɪfbəʊt] N *(on ship)* bote m salvavidas; *(on shore)* lancha f de socorro

lifeguard ['laɪfgɑːd] N socorrista mf

lifeless ['laɪflɪs] ADJ sin vida

lifelike ['laɪflaɪk] ADJ natural; *(portrait)* fiel

lifeline ['laɪflaɪn] N *Fig* cordón m umbilical

lifelong ['laɪflɒŋ] ADJ de toda la vida

life-size(d) ['laɪfsaɪz(d)] ADJ (de) tamaño natural

lifetime ['laɪftaɪm] N vida f; **in his l.** durante su vida; **it's the chance of a l.** es una ocasión única

lift [lɪft] **1** VT (a) *(raise, move)* levantar (b) *(troops)* transportar (c) *Fam (steal)* birlar
2 VI *(clouds, mist)* disiparse
3 N (a) *Br (elevator)* ascensor m (b) **to give sb a l.** llevar a algn en coche (c) *Fig (boost)* estímulo m

▸ **lift up** VT SEP levantar, alzar

lift-off ['lɪftɒf] N despegue m

ligament ['lɪgəmənt] N ligamento m

light¹ [laɪt] **1** N (a) *(illumination)* luz f; *Fig* **in the l. of** en vista de; *Fig* **to bring sth to l.** sacar algo a la luz; *Fig* **to come to l.** salir a la luz; **l. bulb** bombilla f; **l. switch** interruptor m de la luz; **l. year** año m luz (b) *(lamp)* luz f, lámpara f; *(traffic light)* semáforo m; *(headlight)* faro m (c) *(flame)* lumbre f; **to set l. to sth** prender fuego a algo; *Fam* **have you got a l.?** ¿tiene fuego?
2 VT *(pt & pp lighted or lit)* (a) *(illuminate)* iluminar, alumbrar (b) *(ignite)* encender
3 ADJ claro(a); *(hair)* rubio(a)

▸ **light up 1** VT SEP iluminar, alumbrar
2 VI (a) *(sky)* iluminarse (b) *Fam* encender un cigarrillo

light² [laɪt] **1** ADJ ligero(a); *(rain)* fino(a); *(breeze)* suave; *Fig (sentence etc)* leve; *Fig* **to make l. of sth** dar poca importancia a algo
2 ADV **to travel l.** ir ligero(a) de equipaje

lighten¹ ['laɪtən] **1** VT (a) *(colour)* aclarar (b) *(illuminate)* iluminar
2 VI aclararse

lighten² ['laɪtən] VT (a) *(weight)* aligerar (b) *Fig (mitigate)* aliviar; *(heart)* alegrar

lighter ['laɪtə(r)] N *(cigarette)* **l.** encendedor m, mechero m

light-headed [laɪtˈhedɪd] ADJ (a) *(dizzy)* mareado(a) (b) *(frivolous)* frívolo(a)

light-hearted ['laɪthɑːtɪd] ADJ alegre

lighthouse ['laɪthaʊs] N faro m

lighting ['laɪtɪŋ] N (a) *(act)* iluminación f (b) *(system)* alumbrado m

lightly ['laɪtlɪ] ADV ligeramente; **to get off l.** salir casi indemne

lightness¹ ['laɪtnɪs] N luminosidad f, claridad f

lightness² ['laɪtnɪs] N *(of weight)* ligereza f

lightning ['laɪtnɪŋ] N (a) *(flash)* relámpago m; *(stroke)* rayo m; **l. conductor** or **rod** pararrayos m inv; **l. strike** huelga f relámpago

lightweight ['laɪtweɪt] ADJ *(suit etc)* ligero(a); *(boxer)* de peso ligero; *Fig (person)* light

like¹ [laɪk] **1** ADJ *(similar)* parecido(a), similar
2 ADV **(as) l. as not** a lo mejor
3 PREP (a) *(similar to)* como, parecido(a) a; *(the same as)* igual que; **it's not l. her to do that** no es propio de ella hacer eso; **I've never**

seen anything l. it nunca he visto cosa igual; **l. that** así; **people l. that** ese tipo de gente; **what's he l.?** ¿cómo es? (**b**) **to feel l.** *(want)* tener ganas de; **I feel l. a change** me apetece un cambio

4 N brushes, combs and the l. cepillos, peines y cosas por el estilo

like² [laɪk] **1** VT (**a**) **do you l. chocolate?** ¿te gusta el chocolate?; **he likes dancing** le gusta bailar; **she likes children** le gustan los niños (**b**) *(want)* querer; **whether you l. it or not** quieras o no (quieras); **would you l. a drink?** ¿te apetece tomar algo?

2 VI querer, gustar; **as you l.** como quieras

3 N gusto *m*

likeable ['laɪkəbəl] ADJ simpático(a)

likelihood ['laɪklɪhʊd] N probabilidad *f*

likely ['laɪklɪ] **1** ADJ (**likelier, likeliest**) probable; **he's l. to cause trouble** es probable que cause problemas; **where are you l. to be this afternoon?** ¿dónde piensas estar esta tarde?

2 ADV probablemente; **not l.!** ¡ni hablar!

liken ['laɪkən] VT comparar (**to** a *or* con)

likeness ['laɪknɪs] N (**a**) *(similarity)* parecido *m* (**b**) *(portrait)* retrato *m*

likewise ['laɪkwaɪz] ADV (**a**) *(also)* también, asimismo (**b**) *(the same)* lo mismo, igual

liking ['laɪkɪŋ] N *(for thing)* afición *f*; *(for person)* simpatía *f*; *(for friend)* cariño *m*; **to take a l. to sth** cogerle el gusto a algo; **to take a l. to sb** tomar *or Esp* coger cariño a algn

lilac ['laɪlək] **1** N (**a**) *Bot* lila *f* (**b**) *(colour)* lila *m*

2 ADJ lila, de color lila

lilt [lɪlt] N melodía *f*

lily ['lɪlɪ] N lirio *m*, azucena *f*; **l. of the valley** lirio de los valles

limb [lɪm] N miembro *m*; *Fig* **to be out on a l.** *(in danger)* estar en peligro; *Br (isolated)* estar aislado(a)

▸ **limber up** ['lɪmbə(r)] VI *Sport* entrar en calor; *Fig* prepararse (**for** para)

limbo ['lɪmbəʊ] N limbo *m*; *Fig* olvido *m*; **to be in l.** caer en el olvido

lime¹ [laɪm] N *Chem* cal *f*

lime² [laɪm] N *(fruit)* lima *f*; *(tree)* limero *m*

limelight ['laɪmlaɪt] N *Fig* **to be in the l.** estar en el candelero

limerick ['lɪmərɪk] N quintilla humorística

limestone ['laɪmstəʊn] N piedra caliza

limit ['lɪmɪt] **1** N límite *m*; *(maximum)* máximo *m*; *(minimum)* mínimo *m*

2 VT *(restrict)* limitar

limitation [lɪmɪ'teɪʃən] N limitación *f*

limited ['lɪmɪtɪd] ADJ limitado(a); *US (train)* semidirecto(a); **l. company** sociedad (de responsabilidad) limitada; **l. edition** edición limitada; **l. liability** responsabilidad limitada

limitless ['lɪmɪtlɪs] ADJ ilimitado(a)

limousine ['lɪməzɪːn, lɪmə'zɪːn] N limusina *f*

limp¹ [lɪmp] **1** VI cojear

2 N cojera *f*

limp² [lɪmp] ADJ (**a**) *(floppy)* flojo(a) (**b**) *(weak)* débil

limpet ['lɪmpɪt] N lapa *f*

linchpin ['lɪntʃpɪn] N *Tech* pezonera *f*; *Fig* eje *m*

line¹ [laɪn] N (**a**) *(in general)* línea *f*; *(straight)* raya *f* (**b**) *(of writing)* renglón *m*; *(of poetry)* verso *m*; *Th* **to learn one's lines** aprenderse el papel (**c**) *(row)* fila *f*; *(of trees)* hilera *f*; *US (queue)* cola *f*; *Fig* **to be in l. (with)** coincidir (con); *US* **to stand in l.** *(queue)* hacer cola; *Fig* **sth along these lines** algo por el estilo; **l. dancing** baile *m* en línea, = baile al ritmo de música country en el que los participantes se colocan en hileras y dan los mismos pasos (**d**) *(rope)* cuerda *f*; *(wire)* cable *m* (**e**) *Tel* línea *f*; **hold the l.!** ¡no cuelgue! (**f**) *Br Rail* vía *f* (**g**) *(range of goods)* surtido *m*; **a new l.** una nueva línea

▸ **line up 1** VT SEP *(arrange in rows)* poner en fila

2 VI *(people)* ponerse en fila; *(troops)* formar; *(in queue)* hacer cola

line² [laɪn] VT *(pipe etc)* revestir; *Sewing* forrar; *Fam* **to l. one's pockets** forrarse

linear ['lɪnɪə(r)] ADJ lineal

lined [laɪnd] ADJ (**a**) *(paper)* rayado(a); *(face)* arrugado(a) (**b**) *(garment)* forrado(a)

linen ['lɪnɪn] N (**a**) *(cloth)* lino *m* (**b**) *(clothes)* ropa *f*; *(sheets etc)* ropa blanca

liner ['laɪnə(r)] N transatlántico *m*

linesman ['laɪnzmən] N *Sport* juez *m* de línea

line-up ['laɪnʌp] N *Sport* alineación *f*

linger ['lɪŋgə(r)] VI tardar; *(dawdle)* rezagarse; *(smell, doubt)* persistir; *Fig (memory)* perdurar

lingerie ['lænʒərɪː] N *Fml* ropa *f* interior (de mujer)

lingering ['lɪŋgərɪŋ] ADJ *(doubt)* persistente; *(look)* fijo(a)

lingo ['lɪŋgəʊ] N *(pl* **lingoes**) *Fam* (**a**) *(language)* lengua *f*, idioma *m* (**b**) *(jargon)* jerga *f*

linguist ['lɪŋgwɪst] N lingüista *mf*; **he's a good l.** se le dan bien los idiomas

linguistic [lɪŋ'gwɪstɪk] ADJ lingüístico(a)

linguistics [lɪŋ'gwɪstɪks] N SING lingüística *f*

lining ['laɪnɪŋ] N forro *m*

link [lɪŋk] **1** N (**a**) *(of chain)* eslabón *m* (**b**) *(connection)* conexión *f*; *Fig* vínculo *m*; **rail l.** enlace ferroviario (**c**) **links** campo *m* de golf

2 VT unir

▸ **link up** VI unirse; *(meet)* encontrarse; *(spaceships)* acoplarse

link-up ['lɪŋkʌp] N *Tel & TV* conexión *f*; *(meeting)* encuentro *m*; *(of spaceships)* acoplamiento *m*

lino ['laɪnəʊ] N *Fam* linóleo *m*

linoleum [lɪ'nəʊlɪəm] N linóleo *m*, linóleum *m*

lint [lɪnt] N *(for wounds)* hilas *fpl*

lion ['laɪən] N león *m*

lioness ['laɪənɪs] N leona *f*

lip [lɪp] N (**a**) *(of mouth)* labio *m* (**b**) *(of jug)* pico *m*

lip-read ['lɪpriːd] VT & VI leer en los labios

lip-service ['lɪpsɜːvɪs] N palabrería *f*

lipstick ['lɪpstɪk] N lápiz *m* de labios

liqueur [lɪ'kjʊə(r)] N licor *m*

liquid ['lɪkwɪd] ADJ & N líquido(a) *(m)*

liquidate ['lɪkwɪdeɪt] VT liquidar

liquidation [lɪkwɪ'deɪʃən] N liquidación *f*; **to go into l.** entrar en liquidación

liquidize ['lɪkwɪdaɪz] VT licuar

liquidizer ['lɪkwɪdaɪzə(r)] N *Br Esp* batidora *f*, *Am* licuadora *f*

liquor ['lɪkər] N *US* alcohol *m*, bebidas alcohólicas; **l. store** tienda *f* de bebidas alcohólicas

liquorice ['lɪkərɪs] N regaliz *m*

Lisbon ['lɪzbən] N Lisboa

lisp [lɪsp] 1 N ceceo *m*
2 VI cecear

list¹ [lɪst] 1 N lista *f*; *(catalogue)* catálogo *m*
2 VT *(make a list of)* hacer una lista de; *(put on a list)* poner en una lista; **it is not listed** no figura en la lista

list² [lɪst] *Naut* 1 N escora *f*
2 VI escorar

listen ['lɪsən] VI escuchar; *(pay attention)* prestar atención
▸ **listen out for** VT INSEP estar atento(a) a

listener ['lɪsənə(r)] N oyente *mf*

listless ['lɪstlɪs] ADJ apático(a)

lit [lɪt] PT & PP *of* light

liter ['liːtə(r)] N *US* = litre

literacy ['lɪtərəsɪ] N alfabetización *f*

literal ['lɪtərəl] ADJ literal

literally ['lɪtərəlɪ] ADV literalmente

literary ['lɪtərərɪ] ADJ literario(a)

literate ['lɪtərɪt] ADJ alfabetizado(a)

Note that the Spanish word **literato** is a false friend and is never a translation for the English word **literate**. In Spanish **literato** means "writer, author".

literature ['lɪtərətʃə(r)] N (**a**) *(fiction, poetry)* literatura *f* (**b**) *Fam (documentation)* folleto informativo

lithe [laɪð] ADJ *Fml* ágil

Lithuania [lɪθjʊ'eɪnɪə] N Lituania

Lithuanian [lɪθjʊ'eɪnɪən] 1 ADJ lituano(a)
2 N *(person)* lituano(a) *m,f*; *(language)* lituano *m*

litigation [lɪtɪ'geɪʃən] N litigio *m*

litmus ['lɪtməs] N *Fig* **l. test** prueba *f* contundente

litre ['liːtə(r)] N litro *m*

litter ['lɪtə(r)] 1 N (**a**) *(rubbish)* basura *f*; *(papers)* papeles *mpl*; **l. bin** papelera *f* (**b**) *(offspring)* camada *f*
2 VT ensuciar

littered ['lɪtəd] ADJ cubierto(a) (**with** de)

little ['lɪtəl] 1 ADJ (**a**) *(small)* pequeño(a); **a l. dog** un perrito; **a l. house** una casita; **l. finger** *(dedo m)* meñique *m* (**b**) *(not much)* poco(a); **a l. cheese** un poco de queso
2 PRON poco *m*; **save me a l.** guárdame un poco
3 ADV poco; **l. by l.** poco a poco; **as l. as possible** lo menos posible

live¹ [lɪv] 1 VT vivir; **to l. an interesting life** vivir una vida interesante
2 VI vivir; **long l. the King!** ¡viva el Rey!
▸ **live down** VT SEP conseguir que se olvide
▸ **live for** VT INSEP vivir para
▸ **live off** VT INSEP vivir de
▸ **live on** 1 VT INSEP *(food, money)* vivir de
2 VI *(memory)* persistir
▸ **live through** VT INSEP vivir durante
▸ **live together** VI vivir juntos
▸ **live up** VT SEP *Fam* **to l. it up** pegarse la gran vida
▸ **live up to** VT INSEP *(promises)* cumplir con; **it didn't l. up to expectations** no fue lo que se esperaba
▸ **live with** VT INSEP (**a**) *(cohabit with)* vivir con (**b**) *(accept)* aceptar

live² [laɪv] ADJ (**a**) *(living)* vivo(a) (**b**) *Rad & TV* en directo, en vivo (**c**) *(ammunition)* real; *(bomb)* sin explotar; *Elec* con corriente; *Fam* **he's a real l. wire!** ¡éste no para nunca!

livelihood ['laɪvlɪhʊd] N sustento *m*

lively ['laɪvlɪ] ADJ (**livelier, liveliest**) *(person)* vivo(a); *(place)* animado(a); *Fig (interest)* entusiástico(a)

liven ['laɪvən] VT **to l. (up)** animar

liver ['lɪvə(r)] N hígado *m*

livery ['lɪvərɪ] N librea *f*

lives [laɪvz] PL *of* life

livestock ['laɪvstɒk] N ganado *m*

livid ['lɪvɪd] ADJ lívido(a); *Fam (angry)* furioso(a)

living ['lɪvɪŋ] 1 ADJ vivo(a)
2 N vida *f*; **l. conditions** condiciones *fpl* de vida; **l. expenses** dietas *fpl*; **to earn** *or* **make one's l.** ganarse la vida; **l. room** sala *f* de estar; **l. standards** nivel *m* de vida; **l. wage** sueldo mínimo

lizard ['lɪzəd] N *(large)* lagarto *m*; *(small)* lagartija *f*

llama ['lɑːmə] N llama *f*

load [ləʊd] 1 N *(cargo)* carga *f*; *(weight)* peso *m*; *Elec & Tech* carga; *Fam* **loads (of)** montones de; *Fam* **that's a l. of rubbish!** ¡no son más que tonterías!
2 VT cargar
▸ **load up** VT SEP & VI cargar

loaded ['ləʊdɪd] ADJ (**a**) *(lorry, gun)* cargado(a) (**with** de); *Fig* **a l. question** una pregunta intencionada (**b**) *Fam* **to be l.** *(rich)* estar forrado(a)

loading ['ləʊdɪŋ] N carga *f*; **l. bay** cargadero *m*

loaf¹ [ləʊf] N (*pl* **loaves**) pan *m*; (*French stick*) barra *f* de pan; (*sliced*) pan de molde

loaf² [ləʊf] VI **to l. (about** *or* **around)** holgazanear

loan [ləʊn] **1** N préstamo *m*; *Fin* empréstito *m*; **on l.** prestado(a); (*footballer*) cedido(a)
2 VT prestar

loath [ləʊθ] ADJ **to be l. to do sth** ser reacio(a) a hacer algo

loathe [ləʊð] VT aborrecer, odiar

loathing ['ləʊðɪŋ] N aborrecimiento *m*, odio *m*

loathsome ['ləʊðsəm] ADJ odioso(a), repugnante

loaves [ləʊvz] PL *of* **loaf**

lobby ['lɒbɪ] **1** N (**a**) (*hall*) vestíbulo *m* (**b**) (*pressure group*) grupo *m* de presión, lobby *m*
2 VT presionar
3 VI ejercer presiones

lobe [ləʊb] N lóbulo *m*

lobster ['lɒbstə(r)] N langosta *f*

local ['ləʊkəl] **1** ADJ local; (*person*) del pueblo; *Med* **l. anaesthetic** anestesia *f* local; *Tel* **l. call** llamada urbana; **l. government** gobierno *m* municipal
2 N *Fam* **the locals** los vecinos (**b**) *Br* (*pub*) bar *m* del barrio

locality [ləʊ'kælɪtɪ] N localidad *f*

localize ['ləʊkəlaɪz] VT (*restrict*) localizar

locally ['ləʊkəlɪ] ADV en *or* de la localidad

locate [ləʊ'keɪt] VT (*situate*) situar, ubicar; (*find*) localizar

location [ləʊ'keɪʃən] N (**a**) (*place*) emplazamiento *m*, ubicación *f* (**b**) *Cin* **l. shots** exteriores *mpl*; **they're on l. in Australia** están rodando en Australia

loch [lɒx, lɒk] N *Scot* (*lake*) lago *m*; (*inlet*) ría *f*

lock¹ [lɒk] **1** N (**a**) (*on door etc*) cerradura *f*; (*bolt*) cerrojo *m*; (*padlock*) candado *m* (**b**) (*on canal*) esclusa *f*
2 VT cerrar con llave/cerrojo/candado
3 VI (*door etc*) cerrarse; (*wheels*) trabarse

▶ **lock up** VT SEP (*house*) cerrar; (*jail*) meter en la cárcel

lock² [lɒk] Ñ *Literary* (*of hair*) mechón *m*

locker ['lɒkə(r)] N (*cupboard*) armario ropero; *US* **l. room** vestuarios *mpl*

locket ['lɒkɪt] N medallón *m*

lockout ['lɒkaʊt] N cierre *m* patronal

locksmith ['lɒksmɪθ] N cerrajero *m*

lockup ['lɒkʌp] N (**a**) *Br* (*for storage*) garaje *m*, *Am* cochera *f* (**b**) *Fam* (*police cells*) calabozo *m*

loco ['ləʊkəʊ] ADJ *US Fam* pirado(a)

locomotive [ləʊkə'məʊtɪv] N locomotora *f*

locust ['ləʊkəst] N langosta *f*

lodge [lɒdʒ] **1** N (*gamekeeper's*) casa *f* del guarda; (*porter's*) portería *f*; (*hunter's*) refugio *m*
2 VT (**a**) (*accommodate*) alojar (**b**) (*complaint*) presentar

3 VI (**a**) (*live*) alojarse (**b**) (*get stuck*) meterse (**in** en)

lodger ['lɒdʒə(r)] N huésped(a) *m,f*

lodging ['lɒdʒɪŋ] N alojamiento *m*; **l. house** casa *f* de huéspedes

loft [lɒft] N desván *m*

lofty ['lɒftɪ] ADJ (**loftier, loftiest**) *Literary* (*high*) alto(a); *Pej* (*haughty*) altivo(a)

log [lɒg] **1** N (**a**) (*tree-trunk*) tronco *m*; (*for fuel*) leño *m*; **l. cabin** cabaña *f* de troncos (**b**) *Naut* diario *m* de a bordo
2 VT (*record*) registrar

▶ **log in, log on** VI *Comput* entrar (en sistema)

▶ **log out, log off** VI *Comput* salir (del sistema)

logarithm ['lɒgərɪðəm] N logaritmo *m*

log-book ['lɒgbʊk] N *Naut* diario *m* de a bordo; *Av* diario de vuelo; *Aut* documentación *f* (del coche)

loggerheads ['lɒgəhedz] NPL *Fam* **to be at l. with sb** estar peleado(a) *or Esp* andar a la greña con algn

logic ['lɒdʒɪk] N lógica *f*

logical ['lɒdʒɪkəl] ADJ lógico(a)

logistics [lə'dʒɪstɪks] NPL logística *f*

logo ['ləʊgəʊ] N logotipo *m*

loin [lɔɪn] N (*of animal*) ijada *f*; *Culin* (*of pork*) lomo *m*; (*of beef*) solomillo *m*

loiter ['lɔɪtə(r)] VI (*hang about*) holgazanear; (*lag behind*) rezagarse; (*prowl*) merodear

loll [lɒl] VI (*tongue, head*) colgar

▶ **loll about, loll around** VI repantigarse

lollipop ['lɒlɪpɒp] N pirulí *m*, chupachup® *m*; *Br Fam* **l. lady/man** = persona encargada de ayudar a cruzar la calle a los colegiales

lolly ['lɒlɪ] N *Fam* (**a**) (*sweet*) pirulí *m*, chupachup® *m*; **ice(d) l.** polo *m* (**b**) *Br Fam* (*money*) *Esp* pasta *f*, *Am* plata *f*

London ['lʌndən] N Londres

Londoner ['lʌndənə(r)] N londinense *mf*

lone [ləʊn] ADJ (*solitary*) solitario(a); (*single*) solo(a)

loneliness ['ləʊnlɪnɪs] N soledad *f*

lonely ['ləʊnlɪ] ADJ (**lonelier, loneliest**) solo(a), solitario(a)

long¹ [lɒŋ] **1** ADJ (**a**) (*size*) largo(a); **how l. is the table?** ¿cuánto tiene de largo la mesa?; **it's 3 m l.** tiene 3 m de largo; **l. jump** salto *m* de longitud (**b**) (*time*) mucho(a); **at l. last** por fin; **how l. is the film?** ¿cuánto tiempo dura la película?
2 ADV mucho, mucho tiempo; **all day l.** todo el día; **as l. as the exhibition lasts** mientras dure la exposición; **as l. as** *or* **so l. as you don't mind** con tal de que no te importe; **before l.** dentro de poco; **how l. have you been here?** ¿cuánto tiempo llevas aquí?

long² [lɒŋ] VI añorar; **to l. for** anhelar

long-distance ['lɒŋdɪstəns] ADJ de larga distancia; **l. call** conferencia interurbana; **l. runner** corredor(a) *m,f* de fondo

longhand ['lɒŋhænd] N escritura f a mano

longing ['lɒŋɪŋ] N *(desire)* anhelo m; *(nostalgia)* nostalgia f

longitude ['lɒndʒɪtjuːd] N longitud f

long-playing ['lɒŋpleɪɪŋ] ADJ de larga duración; **l. record** elepé m

long-range ['lɒŋreɪndʒ] ADJ *(missile etc)* de largo alcance; *(weather forecast)* de largo plazo

long-sighted [lɒŋ'saɪtɪd] ADJ **(a)** Med présbita **(b)** Fig previsor(a)

long-standing ['lɒŋstændɪŋ] ADJ antiguo(a), de mucho tiempo

long-suffering ['lɒŋsʌfərɪŋ] ADJ sufrido(a)

long-term ['lɒŋtɜːm] ADJ a largo plazo

long-winded [lɒŋ'wɪndɪd] ADJ prolijo(a)

loo [luː] N Br Fam baño m, wáter m

look [lʊk] **1** N **(a)** *(glance)* mirada f; **to take a l. at** *(peep)* echar un vistazo a; *(examine)* examinar **(b)** *(appearance)* aspecto m, apariencia f; **I don't like the l. of it** me da mala espina **(c)** *(fashion)* moda f **(d)** *(good)* **looks** belleza f
  2 VI **(a)** *(in general)* mirar, Am ver **(b)** *(seem)* parecer; **it looks delicious** tiene un aspecto buenísimo; **she looks like her father** *(resembles)* se parece a su padre
  3 VT mirar
  ▸ **look after** VT INSEP cuidar a, ocuparse de
  ▸ **look at** VT INSEP mirar; Fig **whichever way you l. at it** se mire desde cualquier punto de vista
  ▸ **look away** VI apartar la mirada
  ▸ **look back** VI **(a)** *(in space)* mirar atrás; Fig **since then he has never looked back** desde entonces ha ido prosperando **(b)** *(remember)* recordar
  ▸ **look down** VI Fig **to l. down on sth/sb** despreciar algo/a algn
  ▸ **look for** VT INSEP buscar
  ▸ **look forward to** VT INSEP esperar con ansia; **I l. forward to hearing from you** *(in letter)* espero noticias suyas
  ▸ **look into** VT INSEP examinar, investigar
  ▸ **look on 1** VT INSEP *(consider)* considerar
  2 VI quedarse mirando
  ▸ **look onto** VT INSEP dar a
  ▸ **look out** VI **(a)** **the bedroom looks out onto the garden** el dormitorio da al jardín **(b)** **l. out!** *(take care)* ¡cuidado!, ¡ojo!
  ▸ **look over** VT SEP *(examine)* revisar; *(place)* inspeccionar
  ▸ **look round 1** VT INSEP *(house, shop)* ver
  2 VI mirar alrededor; *(turn head)* volver la cabeza
  ▸ **look through** VT INSEP **(a)** *(window)* mirar por **(b)** *(leaf through)* hojear; *(examine, check)* registrar
  ▸ **look to** VT INSEP **(a)** *(take care of)* velar por **(b)** *(turn to)* recurrir a
  ▸ **look up 1** VT SEP **(a)** *(look for)* buscar **(b)** *(visit)* ir a visitar
  2 VI **(a)** *(glance upwards)* alzar la vista **(b)** Fam *(improve)* mejorar
  ▸ **look upon** VT INSEP considerar
  ▸ **look up to** VT INSEP *(person)* respetar

lookout ['lʊkaʊt] N *(person)* centinela mf; *(place)* mirador m; **to be on the l. for** estar al acecho de; Fam **that's his l.!** ¡eso es asunto suyo!

loom¹ [luːm] N telar m

loom² [luːm] VI alzarse; Fig *(threaten)* amenazar

loony ['luːnɪ] ADJ (**loonier, looniest**) Fam loco(a)

loop [luːp] **1** N **(a)** *(of rope, ribbon)* lazo m **(b)** Comput bucle m
  2 VT **(a)** *(string)* enrollar **(b)** Av **to l. the l.** rizar el rizo

loophole ['luːphəʊl] N Fig escapatoria f

loose [luːs] ADJ **(a)** *(not secure)* flojo(a); *(papers, hair, clothes)* suelto(a); *(tongue)* desatado(a); *(baggy)* holgado(a); **to set sb l.** soltar a algn **(b)** *(not packaged)* a granel; **l. change** suelto m **(c)** *(not exact)* vago(a); *(translation)* libre **(d)** *(lax)* relajado(a); **a l. woman** una mujer fácil

loosely ['luːslɪ] ADV **(a)** *(approximately)* aproximadamente **(b)** *(vaguely)* vagamente

loosen ['luːsən] **1** VT aflojar; *(belt)* desabrochar; Fig *(restrictions)* flexibilizar
  2 VI *(slacken)* aflojarse

loot [luːt] **1** N botín m
  2 VT saquear

looting ['luːtɪŋ] N saqueo m, pillaje m

lop [lɒp] VT podar
  ▸ **lop off** VT SEP cortar

lope [ləʊp] VI andar a zancadas

lopsided [lɒp'saɪdɪd] ADJ ladeado(a)

lord [lɔːd] N **(a)** *(aristocrat)* señor m, lord m; Br **the (House of) Lords** la cámara de los lores; **the L. Mayor** el señor alcalde **(b)** Rel **the L.** El Señor; **good L.!** ¡Dios mío!; **the L.'s Prayer** el Padrenuestro **(c)** *(judge)* señoría mf

lordship ['lɔːdʃɪp] N Br **His/Your L.** su señoría

lorry ['lɒrɪ] N Br camión m; **l. driver** camionero(a) m,f; **l. load** carga f

lose [luːz] **1** VT *(pt & pp* **lost**) perder; **to l. time** *(of clock)* atrasarse
  2 VI perder; **to l. to sb** perder contra algn; **to l. out** salir perdiendo

loser ['luːzə(r)] N perdedor(a) m,f

loss [lɒs] N pérdida f; **to make a l.** perder; Fig **to be at a l. for words** quedarse de una pieza; **to be at a l. what to do** no saber qué hacer

lost [lɒst] **1** ADJ **(a)** *(missing)* perdido(a); **to get l.** perderse; Fam **get l.!** ¡vete a la porra!; **l. property office**, US **l. and found department** oficina f de objetos perdidos **(b)** *(disoriented)* desorientado(a); *(distracted)* distraído(a); **l. in thought** ensimismado(a)
  2 PT & PP of **lose**

lot [lɒt] N (**a**) (fate) suerte f (**b**) US (plot of land) parcela f (**c**) (in an auction) lote m (**d**) (everything) todo m; **he ate the l.** se lo comió todo (**e**) **a l. of** (much) mucho(a); (many) muchos(as); **he feels a l. better** se encuentra mucho mejor; Fam **lots of** montones de, cantidad de

lotion ['ləʊʃən] N loción f

lottery ['lɒtərɪ] N lotería f; **l. ticket** ≃ décimo m de lotería

loud [laʊd] **1** ADJ (**a**) (voice) alto(a); (noise) fuerte; (laugh) estrepitoso(a); (applause) clamoroso(a); (protests, party) ruidoso(a) (**b**) (flashy) chillón(ona) (**c**) (vulgar) hortera
2 ADV **to read/think out l.** leer/pensar en voz alta

loudhailer [laʊd'heɪlə(r)] N Br megáfono m

loudspeaker [laʊd'spiːkə(r)] N altavoz m

lounge [laʊndʒ] **1** N Br salón m, sala f de estar
2 VI hacer el vago

louse [laʊs] N (pl lice) piojo m

lousy ['laʊzɪ] ADJ (lousier, lousiest) Fam fatal; **a l. trick** una cochinada

lout [laʊt] N gamberro m

lovable ['lʌvəbəl] ADJ adorable

love [lʌv] **1** N (**a**) (between lovers or members of a family) amor m (**for** por); (affection) cariño m; **to be in l. with** sb estar enamorado(a) de algn; **to fall in l.** enamorarse; **to make l.** hacer el amor; (**with**) **l.** (**from**) **Mary** (in letter) un abrazo, Mary; **l. affair** amorío m; **l. letter/story** carta f/historia f de amor; **l. life** vida f sentimental (**b**) (person) amor m, cariño m; Fam chato(a) m,f; **my l.** mi amor (**c**) (in tennis) **forty l.** cuarenta a cero
2 VT (person) querer a, amar a; **he loves cooking/football** le encanta cocinar/el fútbol

lovely ['lʌvlɪ] ADJ (lovelier, loveliest) (charming) encantador(a); (beautiful) precioso(a), Am lindo(a); (delicious) riquísimo(a)

lover ['lʌvə(r)] N (**a**) (sexual partner) amante mf (**b**) (enthusiast) aficionado(a) m,f, amigo(a) m,f

loving ['lʌvɪŋ] ADJ cariñoso(a)

low¹ [ləʊ] **1** ADJ (**a**) (not high, not loud) bajo(a); (neckline) escotado(a) (**b**) (small in quantity) bajo(a) (**c**) (poor) pobre (**d**) (battery) gastado(a); **l. frequency** baja frecuencia (**e**) **to feel l.** sentirse deprimido(a) (**f**) (reprehensible) malo(a)
2 ADV bajo
3 N (**a**) Met área f de baja presión (**b**) (low point) punto más bajo; **to reach an all-time l.** tocar fondo

low² [ləʊ] VI (cow) mugir

lowdown ['ləʊdaʊn] N Fam pormenores mpl

lower ['ləʊə(r)] **1** ADJ (comp of low) inferior; Typ **l. case** minúscula f; **l. class** clase baja
2 ADV COMP OF low
3 VT bajar; (flag) arriar; (reduce) reducir; (price) rebajar

lower-class ['ləʊəklɑːs] ADJ de clase baja

lowest ['ləʊɪst] **1** ADJ (superl of low) más bajo(a); (price, speed) mínimo(a)
2 N **at the l.** como mínimo

low-key [ləʊ'kiː] ADJ sin ceremonia

lowlands ['ləʊləndz] NPL tierras bajas

lowly ['ləʊlɪ] ADJ (lowlier, lowliest) humilde

low-necked ['ləʊnekt] ADJ escotado(a)

loyal ['lɔɪəl] ADJ leal, fiel

loyalty ['lɔɪəltɪ] N lealtad f, fidelidad f

lozenge ['lɒzɪndʒ] N pastilla f

LP [el'piː] N (abbr **long-playing record**) LP m

L-plate ['elpleɪt] N Br placa f de la "L"

LSD [eles'diː] N (abbr **lysergic acid diethylamide**) LSD m

Ltd Br Com (abbr **limited**) S.L.

lubricant ['luːbrɪkənt] N lubricante m

lubricate ['luːbrɪkeɪt] VT lubricar; (engine) engrasar

lubrication [luːbrɪ'keɪʃən] N engrase m

lucid ['luːsɪd] ADJ lúcido(a)

luck [lʌk] N suerte f; **bad l.!** ¡mala suerte!; **good l.!** ¡(buena) suerte!; **to be in l.** estar de suerte; **to be out of l.** no tener suerte; Fig **to push one's l.** tentar la suerte; Fig **to try one's l.** probar fortuna

luckily ['lʌkɪlɪ] ADV por suerte, afortunadamente

lucky ['lʌkɪ] ADJ (luckier, luckiest) (person) afortunado(a); (day) de suerte; (move) oportuno(a); (charm) de la suerte; **to be lucky** tener suerte; **a l. break** una oportunidad

lucrative ['luːkrətɪv] ADJ lucrativo(a)

ludicrous ['luːdɪkrəs] ADJ absurdo(a), ridículo(a)

lug [lʌg] VT Fam arrastrar

luggage ['lʌgɪdʒ] N equipaje m; **l. rack** Aut baca f; Rail portaequipajes m inv

lukewarm ['luːkwɔːm] ADJ (water etc) tibio(a); Fig (reception etc) poco entusiasta

lull [lʌl] **1** N (in storm) calma chicha; (in fighting) tregua f
2 VT (cause to sleep) adormecer; **to l. sb into a false sense of security** infundir una falsa seguridad a algn

lullaby ['lʌləbaɪ] N canción f de cuna, nana f

lumbago [lʌm'beɪgəʊ] N lumbago m

lumber ['lʌmbə(r)] **1** N (**a**) Br (junk) trastos viejos (**b**) US (wood) maderos mpl
2 VT Fam cargar (**with** de)

lumberjack ['lʌmbədʒæk] N leñador m

lumberyard ['lʌmbəjɑːd] N US almacén m maderero, maderería f, RP barraca f maderera

luminous ['luːmɪnəs] ADJ luminoso(a)

lump [lʌmp] **1** N (of coal etc) trozo m; (of sugar, earth) terrón m; (in sauce) grumo m; (swelling) bulto m; Fam Fig (in throat) nudo m; **l. sum** cantidad f global
2 VT Fam (endure) aguantar

▸ **lump together** VT SEP apelotonar

lumpy ['lʌmpɪ] ADJ (**lumpier, lumpiest**) *(bed)* lleno(a) de bultos; *(sauce)* grumoso(a)

lunacy ['luːnəsɪ] N locura *f*

lunar ['luːnə(r)] ADJ lunar

lunatic ['luːnətɪk] ADJ & N loco(a) *(m,f)*; **l. asylum** manicomio *m*

lunch [lʌntʃ] **1** N comida *f*, almuerzo *m*; **l. box** tartera *f*, fiambrera *f*; **l. hour** hora *f* de comer
2 VI comer, almorzar

luncheon ['lʌntʃən] N *Old-fashioned Fml* almuerzo *m*; **l. voucher** vale *m* de comida; **(pork) l. meat** carne *f* de cerdo troceada, chopped *m*

lunchtime ['lʌntʃtaɪm] N hora *f* de comer

lung [lʌŋ] N pulmón *m*

lunge [lʌndʒ] **1** N arremetida *f*
2 VI **to l. (forward)** arremeter; **to l. (out) at sb** arremeter contra algn

lurch [lɜːtʃ] **1** N (**a**) *(of vehicle)* sacudida *f*; *(of person)* tambaleo *m* (**b**) *Fam* **to leave sb in the l.** dejar a algn en la cuneta
2 VI *(vehicle)* dar sacudidas; *(person)* tambalearse

lure [lʊə(r)] **1** N *(decoy)* señuelo *m*; *(bait)* cebo *m*; *Fig (charm)* aliciente *m*
2 VT atraer con engaños

lurid ['lʊərɪd] ADJ (**a**) *(gruesome)* espeluznante; *(sensational)* sensacionalista (**b**) *(gaudy)* chillón(ona)

lurk [lɜːk] VI *(lie in wait)* estar al acecho; *(hide)* esconderse

luscious ['lʌʃəs] ADJ *(food)* delicioso(a)

lush [lʌʃ] ADJ *(vegetation)* exuberante

lust [lʌst] **1** N *(sexual desire)* lujuria *f*; *(craving)* ansia *f*; *(greed)* codicia *f*
2 VI **to l. after sth/sb** codiciar algo/desear a algn

lustre, *US* **luster** ['lʌstə(r)] N lustre *m*

lusty ['lʌstɪ] ADJ (**lustier, lustiest**) robusto(a)

lute [luːt] N laúd *m*

Luxembourg ['lʌksəmbɜːg] N Luxemburgo

luxuriant [lʌg'zjʊərɪənt] ADJ *(plants)* exuberante; *(hair etc)* abundante

luxurious [lʌg'zjʊərɪəs] ADJ lujoso(a)

luxury ['lʌkʃərɪ] N lujo *m*; **l. flat** piso *m* de lujo

Note that the Spanish word **lujuria** is a false friend and is never a translation for the English word **luxury**. In Spanish **lujuria** means "lust".

lychee ['laɪtʃiː] N lichi *m*

lying ['laɪɪŋ] **1** ADJ mentiroso(a)
2 N mentiras *fpl*

lynch [lɪntʃ] VT linchar

lyre [laɪə(r)] N *Mus* lira *f*

lyric ['lɪrɪk] **1** ADJ lírico(a)
2 N (**a**) *(poem)* poema lírico (**b**) **lyrics** *(words of song)* letra *f*

lyrical ['lɪrɪkəl] ADJ lírico(a)

M

M, m [em] N *(the letter)* M, m *f*

m (**a**) *(abbr* **metre(s))** m (**b**) *(abbr* **million(s))** m

MA [em'eɪ] N *Univ (abbr* **Master of Arts)** máster *m or Am* maestría *f* (en Humanidades)

mac [mæk] N *Br Fam (raincoat)* impermeable *m*, gabardina *f*

macabre [mə'kɑːbrə] ADJ macabro(a)

mac(c)aroni [mækə'rəʊnɪ] N macarrones *mpl*

mace¹ [meɪs] N *(club, ceremonial staff)* maza *f*

mace² [meɪs] N *(spice)* macis *f inv*

Macedonia [mæsə'dəʊnɪə] N Macedonia

Macedonian [mæsə'dəʊnɪən] ADJ & N macedonio(a) *(m,f)*

machine [mə'ʃiːn] **1** N máquina *f*; **m. gun** ametralladora *f*
   2 VT trabajar a máquina

machine-gun [mə'ʃiːngʌn] VT ametrallar

machine-readable [mə'ʃiːn'riːdəbəl] ADJ *Comput* legible para *Esp* el ordenador *or Am* la computadora

machinery [mə'ʃiːnərɪ] N *(machines)* maquinaria *f; (workings of machine)* mecanismo *m*

macho ['mætʃəʊ] ADJ *(remark, attitude)* muy de macho

macintosh 'mækɪntɒʃ] N = **mackintosh**

mackerel ['mækrəl] N *(pl* **mackerel)** caballa *f*

mackintosh ['mækɪntɒʃ] N impermeable *m*

macro ['mækrəʊ] N *(pl* **macros)** *Comput* macro *m or f*

macrobiotic [mækrəʊbaɪ'ɒtɪk] ADJ macrobiótico(a)

macroeconomics [mækrəʊiːkə'nɒmɪks] N SING macroeconomía *f*

mad [mæd] ADJ *(* **madder, maddest)** (**a**) *(insane) (person)* loco(a); *(dog)* rabioso(a); **to be/go m.** estar/volverse loco(a); *Fam* **to run/work like m.** correr/trabajar como (un(a)) loco(a); *Fam* **m. cow disease** el mal de las vacas locas (**b**) *(idea, plan)* disparatado(a) (**c**) *Fam* **to be m. about sth/sb** estar loco(a) por algo/algn (**d**) *esp US Fam (angry) esp Esp* enfadado(a), *esp Am* enojado(a); **to be m. with** *or* **at sb** estar muy *esp Esp* enfadado(a) *or esp Am* enojado(a) con algn

madam ['mædəm] N señora *f*; **Dear M.** *(in letter)* Muy señora mía, Estimada señora

madden ['mædən] VT volver loco(a)

maddening ['mædənɪŋ] ADJ exasperante

made [meɪd] PT & PP *of* **make**

Madeira [mə'dɪərə] N (**a**) *(island)* Madeira (**b**) *(wine)* madeira *m*; **M. cake** bizcocho *m*

made-to-measure ['meɪdtə'meʒə(r)] ADJ hecho(a) a (la) medida

made-up ['meɪdʌp] ADJ (**a**) *(face, person)* maquillado(a); *(eyes, lips)* pintado(a) (**b**) *(story, excuse)* inventado(a)

madly ['mædlɪ] ADV (**a**) *(desperately) (rush, struggle)* como loco(a) (**b**) *Fam (extremely)* terriblemente; **to be m. in love with sb** estar locamente enamorado(a) de algn

madman ['mædmən] N loco *m*

madness ['mædnɪs] N locura *f*

Madrid [mə'drɪd] N Madrid

Mafia ['mæfɪə] N mafia *f*

magazine [mægə'ziːn] N (**a**) *(periodical)* revista *f* (**b**) *(in rifle)* recámara *f* (**c**) *Mil (storehouse)* almacén *m; (for explosives)* polvorín *m*

maggot ['mægət] N larva *f*, gusano *m*

magic ['mædʒɪk] **1** N magia *f*
   2 ADJ (**a**) *(spell, trick)* mágico(a); **m. wand** varita mágica (**b**) *Fam (excellent)* genial, *Esp* guay, *Am salvo RP* chévere, *Méx* padrísimo(a), *RP* bárbaro(a)

magical ['mædʒɪkəl] ADJ mágico(a)

magician [mə'dʒɪʃən] N (**a**) *(wizard)* mago *m,f* (**b**) *(conjurer)* prestidigitador(a) *m,f*

magistrate ['mædʒɪstreɪt] N *Br* juez *mf* de primera instancia; **magistrates' court** juzgado *m* de primera instancia

magnanimous [mæg'nænɪməs] ADJ magnánimo(a)

magnesium [mæg'niːzɪəm] N *Chem* magnesio *m*

magnet ['mægnɪt] N imán *m*

magnetic [mæg'netɪk] ADJ magnético(a); *Fig (personality)* carismático(a); **m. tape** cinta magnetofónica

magnetism ['mægnɪtɪzəm] N magnetismo *m*

magnificence [mæg'nɪfɪsəns] N magnificencia *f*

magnificent [mæg'nɪfɪsənt] ADJ magnífico(a)

magnify ['mægnɪfaɪ] VT (**a**) *(enlarge)* aumentar (**b**) *Fig (exaggerate)* exagerar

magnifying glass ['mægnɪfaɪŋglɑːs] N lupa *f*

magnitude ['mægnɪtjuːd] N magnitud *f*

magpie ['mægpaɪ] N urraca *f*

mahogany [mə'hɒgənɪ] **1** N caoba *f*
   2 ADJ de caoba

maid [meɪd] N (**a**) *(servant)* criada *f*, *Andes, RP* mucama *f* (**b**) *Pej* **old m.** solterona *f*

maiden ['meɪdən] ADJ (**a**) *(unmarried)* soltera; **m. name** apellido *m* de soltera (**b**) *(voyage, flight)* inaugural

mail [meɪl] **1** N correo *m*; **by m.** por correo; **m. order** venta *f* por correo
2 VT *esp US* enviar *or* mandar (por correo)

mailbox ['meɪlbɒks] N *US* buzón *m*

mailing list ['meɪlɪŋlɪst] N lista *f* de direcciones *(para envío de publicidad)*

mailman ['meɪlmæn] N *US* cartero *m*

maim [meɪm] VT lisiar

main [meɪn] **1** ADJ *(problem, door etc)* principal; *(square, mast, sail)* mayor; *(office)* central; *Culin* **m. course** plato *m* principal; **m. road** carretera *f* principal; *US* **M. Street** la Calle Mayor
2 N (**a**) *(pipe, wire)* conducto *m* principal; **the mains** *(water or gas system)* la cañería maestra; *Elec* la red eléctrica (**b**) **in the m.** por regla general

mainframe ['meɪnfreɪm] N **m. (computer)** *Esp* ordenador *m or Am* computadora *f* central

mainland ['meɪnlənd] N continente *m*

mainly ['meɪnlɪ] ADV principalmente, sobre todo; *(for the most part)* en su mayoría

mainstay ['meɪnsteɪ] N *Fig* sustento *m*, sostén *m*

mainstream ['meɪnstriːm] N corriente *f* principal

maintain [meɪn'teɪn] VT mantener; *(conversation)* sostener; *(silence, appearances)* guardar; *(road, machine)* conservar en buen estado

maintenance ['meɪntənəns] N (**a**) *(of car, equipment, roads)* mantenimiento *m* (**b**) *(divorce allowance)* pensión *f*

maisonette [meɪzə'net] N dúplex *m*

maître d' ['meɪtrə'diː] N *US* maître *mf* (d'hôtel)

maize [meɪz] N maíz *m*, *Andes, RP* choclo *m*

majestic [mə'dʒestɪk] ADJ majestuoso(a)

majesty ['mædʒɪstɪ] N majestad *f*

major ['meɪdʒə(r)] **1** ADJ (**a**) *(important)* importante, de primer orden (**b**) *Mus* mayor
2 N (**a**) *Mil* comandante *m* (**b**) *US Univ* especialidad *f*
3 VI *US Univ* **to m. in** especializarse en

Majorca [mə'jɔːkə] N Mallorca

Majorcan [mə'jɔːkən] ADJ & N mallorquín(ina) (*m,f*)

majority [mə'dʒɒrɪtɪ] N mayoría *f*; **to be in the m.** ser (la) mayoría

make [meɪk] *(pt & pp* **made**) **1** VT (**a**) *(produce, prepare, perform)* hacer; *(manufacture)* hacer, fabricar; *(clothes, curtains)* confeccionar; *(meal)* preparar; *(payment)* efectuar; *(speech)* pronunciar; *(decision)* tomar; *(mistake)* cometer; **to be made of** ser de; **to m. a noise** hacer ruido
(**b**) *(cause to be)* hacer; **to m. sb happy** hacer feliz a algn; **to m. sb sad** entristecer a algn; **he made it clear that ...** dejó claro que ...

(**c**) *(convert)* convertir (**into** en); *(appoint)* nombrar
(**d**) *(force, compel)* obligar; **to m. sb do sth** hacer que algn haga algo
(**e**) *(earn)* ganar; **to m. a living** ganarse la vida
(**f**) **7 and 5 m. 12** 7 y 5 son 12
(**g**) **to m. do with sth** arreglárselas con algo
(**h**) *(calculate, reckon)* calcular; **I don't know what to m. of it** no sé qué pensar de eso; **what time do you m. it?** ¿qué hora tienes?
(**i**) *(reach)* *Fam* **to m. it** *(arrive in time)* llegar (a tiempo); *(finish in time)* terminar a tiempo; **to m. the charts** *(record)* llegar a las listas de éxitos
(**j**) *(become, be)* ser; **he'll m. a good doctor/singer** será un buen médico/cantante
2 VI (**a**) **to m. sure** *or* **certain (of sth)** asegurarse (de algo) (**b**) **she made as if** *or* **as though to leave** hizo como si quisiera marcharse
3 N *(brand)* marca *f*

▶ **make for** VT INSEP *(move towards)* dirigirse hacia

▶ **make out 1** VT SEP (**a**) *(list, receipt)* hacer; *(cheque)* extender (**b**) *(perceive)* distinguir; *(writing)* descifrar (**c**) *(understand)* entender (**d**) *Fam (claim)* **to m. out (that) ...** decir *or* pretender que ...
2 VI (**a**) *(get on)* **how did you m. out?** ¿qué tal te fue? (**b**) *US Fam (sexually) (neck)* meterse mano, *Esp* darse el lote; *(have sex)* enrollarse

▶ **make up 1** VT SEP (**a**) *(parcel, list)* hacer; *(prescription)* preparar; *(assemble)* montar (**b**) *(story)* inventar (**c**) *(apply cosmetics to)* maquillar; *(one's face)* maquillarse (**d**) *(loss)* compensar; *(lost time)* recuperar (**e**) *(constitute)* componer (**f**) **to m. it up (with sb)** hacer las paces (con algn)
2 VI maquillarse

▶ **make up for** VT INSEP *(losses)* compensar; *(lost time)* recuperar

▶ **make up to** VT SEP **to m. it up to sb for sth** compensar a algn por algo

make-believe ['meɪkbɪliːv] N *(fantasy)* fantasía *f*; *(pretence)* fingimiento *m*; **to live in a world of m.** vivir en un mundo de ensueño

makeover ['meɪkəʊvə(r)] N renovación *f or* cambio *m* de imagen

maker ['meɪkə(r)] N fabricante *mf*

makeshift ['meɪkʃɪft] ADJ *(improvised)* improvisado(a); *(temporary)* provisional

make-up ['meɪkʌp] N (**a**) *(cosmetics)* maquillaje *m*; **m. remover** desmaquillador *m* (**b**) *(composition)* composición *f*; *(character)* carácter *m*

making ['meɪkɪŋ] N (**a**) *(manufacture)* fabricación *f*; *(preparation)* preparación *f* (**b**) **he has the makings of a politician** tiene madera de político

maladjusted [mælə'dʒʌstɪd] ADJ inadaptado(a)

malaise [mæ'leɪz] N malestar *m*

malaria [mə'leərɪə] N malaria *f*

Malay [mə'leɪ] **1** ADJ malayo(a)
 2 N (**a**) (person) malayo(a) m,f (**b**) (language) malayo m

Malaysia [mə'leɪzɪə] N Malasia

male [meɪl] **1** ADJ (animal, plant) macho; (person) varón; (sex) masculino; Pej **m. chauvinism** machismo m
 2 N (person) varón m; (animal, plant) macho m

malevolent [mə'levələnt] ADJ malévolo(a)

malfunction [mæl'fʌŋkʃən] **1** N Esp fallo m, Am falla f
 2 VI funcionar mal

malice ['mælɪs] N malicia f; Jur **with m. aforethought** con premeditación

malicious [mə'lɪʃəs] ADJ malévolo(a)

malign [mə'laɪn] **1** ADJ perjudicial, pernicioso(a)
 2 VT difamar

malignant [mə'lɪgnənt] ADJ (**a**) (person) malvado(a) (**b**) Med maligno(a)

malingerer [mə'lɪŋgərə(r)] N = persona que se finge enferma (para no ir a trabajar)

mall [mɔːl] N US centro m comercial

malleable ['mælɪəbəl] ADJ maleable

mallet ['mælɪt] N mazo m

malnutrition [mælnjuː'trɪʃən] N desnutrición f

malpractice [mæl'præktɪs] N negligencia f (profesional); esp US Jur **m. suit** demanda f por negligencia (profesional)

malt [mɔːlt] N malta f

Malta ['mɔːltə] N Malta

mammal ['mæməl] N mamífero m

mammary ['mæmərɪ] ADJ **m. gland** mama f

mammoth ['mæməθ] **1** N Zool mamut m
 2 ADJ gigantesco(a)

man [mæn] **1** N (pl **men**) (**a**) (adult male) hombre m; **old m.** viejo m; **young m.** joven m; Fig **the m. in the street** el hombre de la calle (**b**) (humanity) el hombre (**c**) (husband) marido m; (partner) pareja f (**d**) (in chess) pieza f; (in draughts) ficha f
 2 VT (boat, plane) tripular; (post) servir; **manned flight** vuelo tripulado

manacles ['mænəkəlz] NPL (for hands) esposas fpl; (for feet) grilletes mpl

manage ['mænɪdʒ] **1** VT (**a**) (company, household) llevar; (money, affairs, person) manejar (**b**) (succeed) conseguir; **to m. to do sth** lograr hacer algo
 2 VI (cope physically) poder; (esp financially) arreglárselas; **we're managing** vamos tirando

manageable ['mænɪdʒəbəl] ADJ manejable

management ['mænɪdʒmənt] N dirección f

manager ['mænɪdʒə(r)] N (**a**) (of company, bank) director(a) m,f; (head of department) jefe(a) m,f (**b**) (of pop group etc) mánager m (**c**) Sport entrenador(a) m,f

manageress [mænɪdʒə'res] N (of shop, restaurant) encargada f; (of company) directora f

managerial [mænɪ'dʒɪərɪəl] ADJ directivo(a)

managing ['mænɪdʒɪŋ] ADJ esp Br **m. director** director(a) m,f gerente

mandarin ['mændərɪn] N **m. (orange)** mandarina f

mandate ['mændeɪt] N mandato m

mandatory ['mændətərɪ] ADJ Fml obligatorio(a)

mane [meɪn] N (of horse) crin f; (of lion) melena f

maneuver [mə'nuːvər] N, VT & VI US = **manoeuvre**

manfully ['mænfʊlɪ] ADV con hombría, valientemente

manger ['meɪndʒə(r)] N pesebre m

mangle¹ ['mæŋgəl] N (for wringing) rodillo m

mangle² ['mæŋgəl] VT (crush) aplastar; (destroy by cutting) despedazar

mango ['mæŋgəʊ] N (pl **mangoes**) mango m

mangy ['meɪndʒɪ] ADJ (**mangier, mangiest**) (animal) sarnoso(a); Fam (carpet) raído(a)

manhandle ['mænhændəl] VT **they manhandled him into the car** lo metieron en el coche orAm carro orCSur auto a empujones

manhole ['mænhəʊl] N (boca f de) alcantarilla f

manhood ['mænhʊd] N (**a**) (age) madurez f; **to reach m.** alcanzar la madurez (**b**) (masculinity) hombría f

mania ['meɪnɪə] N manía f

maniac ['meɪnɪæk] N maníaco(a) m,f; **to drive like a m.** Esp conducir orAm manejar como un loco

manic ['mænɪk] ADJ maníaco(a)

manic-depressive ['mænɪkdɪ'presɪv] ADJ & N maníaco(a) depresivo(a)

manicure ['mænɪkjʊə(r)] **1** N manicura f
 2 VT **to m. one's nails** hacerse la manicura

manifest ['mænɪfest] Fml **1** ADJ manifiesto(a)
 2 VT manifestar

manifesto [mænɪ'festəʊ] N programa m electoral

manifold ['mænɪfəʊld] ADJ Fml (numerous) múltiple; (varied) diverso(a)

manipulate [mə'nɪpjʊleɪt] VT (controls, people, statistics) manipular

mankind [mæn'kaɪnd] N la humanidad, el género humano

manly ['mænlɪ] ADJ (**manlier, manliest**) varonil, viril

man-made ['mænmeɪd] ADJ (lake) artificial; (fibres, fabric) sintético(a)

manner ['mænə(r)] N (**a**) (way, method) manera f, modo m; **in this m.** de esta manera (**b**) (attitude, behaviour) actitud f (**c**) (type) **all m. of ...** toda clase de ... (**d**) (etiquette) (**good**) **manners** buenos modales; **bad manners** falta f de educación

mannerism ['mænərɪzəm] N (gesture) gesto m; (affectation) amaneramiento m

manoeuvre [mə'nuːvə(r)] **1** N maniobra f
 2 VT maniobrar; (person) manejar
 3 VI maniobrar

manor ['mænə(r)] N **m. (house)** casa solariega

manpower ['mænpaʊə(r)] N mano f de obra

mansion ['mænʃən] N casa f grande; *(in country)* casa solariega

manslaughter ['mænslɔːtə(r)] N homicidio involuntario

mantelpiece ['mæntəlpiːs] N *(shelf)* repisa f de chimenea; *(fireplace)* chimenea f

mantle ['mæntəl] N *Fig (of lava, snow)* manto m, capa f

> Note that the Spanish word **mantel** is a false friend and is never a translation for the English word **mantle**. In Spanish, **mantel** means "tablecloth".

manual ['mænjʊəl] ADJ & N manual *(m)*

manufacture [mænjʊ'fæktʃə(r)] **1** VT fabricar
2 N fabricación f

manufacturer [mænjʊ'fæktʃərə(r)] N fabricante m

manure [mə'njʊə(r)] N abono m, estiércol m

manuscript ['mænjʊskrɪpt] N manuscrito m

many ['menɪ] **1** ADJ **(more, most)** mucho(a)/ muchos(as); **a great m.** muchísimos(as); **as m. ... as ...** tantos(as) ... como ...; **how m. days?** ¿cuántos días?; **too m.** demasiados(as)
2 PRON muchos(as)

map [mæp] **1** N *(of country)* mapa m; *(of town, bus route)* plano m
2 VT trazar un mapa de
► **map out** VT SEP *(route)* trazar en un mapa; *Fig (future etc)* planear

maple ['meɪpəl] N arce m

mar [mɑː(r)] VT estropear; **to m. sb's enjoyment** aguarle la fiesta a algn

marathon ['mærəθən] N maratón m

marble ['mɑːbəl] **1** N **(a)** *(stone)* mármol m **(b)** *(glass ball)* canica f
2 ADJ de mármol

March [mɑːtʃ] N marzo m

march [mɑːtʃ] **1** N **(a)** *(of soldiers)* marcha f **(b)** *(demonstration)* manifestación f
2 VI **(a)** *(soldiers)* marchar; *(at ceremony, on parade)* desfilar **(b)** *(demonstrate)* manifestarse
3 VT *Mil* hacer marchar

mare [meə(r)] N yegua f

margarine [mɑːdʒə'riːn] N margarina f

margin ['mɑːdʒɪn] N margen m; *Fig* **to win by a narrow m.** ganar por escaso margen

marginal ['mɑːdʒɪnəl] ADJ **(a)** *(improvement, increase)* marginal **(b)** *Br Pol (seat, constituency)* muy reñido(a)

marginally ['mɑːdʒɪnəlɪ] ADV ligeramente

marigold ['mærɪɡəʊld] N caléndula f

marijuana, marihuana [mærɪ'hwɑːnə] N marihuana f, marijuana f

marina [mə'riːnə] N puerto deportivo

marinade [mærɪ'neɪd] *Culin* **1** N adobo m
2 VT = **marinate**

marinate ['mærɪneɪt] VT *Culin* adobar

marine [mə'riːn] **1** ADJ marino(a)
2 N marine mf, infante mf de marina, *Am* fusilero m naval

marital ['mærɪtəl] ADJ matrimonial; **m. status** estado m civil

maritime ['mærɪtaɪm] ADJ marítimo(a)

marjoram ['mɑːdʒərəm] N mejorana f

mark¹ [mɑːk] **1** N **(a)** *(left by blow etc)* señal f; *(stain)* mancha f **(b)** *(sign, token)* señal f **(c)** *(in exam etc)* nota f
2 VT **(a)** *(stain)* manchar **(b)** *(with tick, cross)* señalar **(c)** *(exam)* corregir; *(student)* dar notas a **(d)** **m. my words** fíjate en lo que te digo
► **mark out** VT SEP **(a)** *(area)* delimitar **(b)** **to m. sb out for** destinar a algn a

mark² [mɑːk] N *(unit of currency)* marco m

marked [mɑːkt] ADJ *(noticeable)* marcado(a), acusado(a)

marker ['mɑːkə(r)] N **(a)** *(of essay, exam)* examinador(a) m,f, corrector(a) m,f de exámenes **(b)** *Sport* marcador(a) m,f **(c)** *(indicator)* señal f **(d)** *(pen)* **m. (pen)** rotulador m, *Col* marcador m, *Méx* plumón m

market ['mɑːkɪt] **1** N mercado m, *CSur* feria f, *CAm, Méx* tianguis m; **on the m.** en venta; **m. forces** tendencias fpl del mercado; **m. price** precio m de mercado; **m. research** estudio m de mercado
2 VT *(sell)* poner en venta; *(promote)* promocionar

marketable ['mɑːkɪtəbəl] ADJ comerciable

marketing ['mɑːkɪtɪŋ] N marketing m, mercadotecnia f

marketplace ['mɑːkɪtpleɪs] N mercado m

marking ['mɑːkɪŋ] N **(a)** **markings** *(on animal)* marcas fpl, manchas fpl; *(on plane)* distintivo m **(b)** *(of essay, exam)* corrección f

marksman ['mɑːksmən] N tirador m

marmalade ['mɑːməleɪd] N mermelada f *(de cítricos)*

maroon [mə'ruːn] ADJ *(de color)* granate

marooned [mə'ruːnd] ADJ bloqueado(a)

marquee [mɑː'kiː] N **(a)** *Br (tent)* carpa f **(b)** *US (of building)* marquesina f

marquess, marquis ['mɑːkwɪs] N marqués m

marriage ['mærɪdʒ] N **(a)** *(wedding)* boda f, *Andes* matrimonio m, *RP* casamiento m; *(institution, period, relationship)* matrimonio m; **m. bureau** agencia f matrimonial; **m. certificate** certificado m de matrimonio

married ['mærɪd] ADJ casado(a); **to be m.** estar or *Am* ser casado(a)

marrow ['mærəʊ] N **(a)** *(bone)* **m.** médula f **(b)** *Br* **(vegetable) m.** calabacín m

marry ['mærɪ] VT *(take in marriage)* casarse con; *(give in marriage)* casar **(to** con); *(unite in marriage)* casar; **to get married** casarse

Mars [mɑːz] N Marte m

marsh [mɑːʃ] N pantano m; **salt m.** marisma f

marshal ['mɑ:ʃəl] 1 N *(army officer)* mariscal *m*; *US (police chief)* jefe(a) *m,f* de policía; *(fire chief)* jefe(a) *m,f* de bomberos; *(police officer)* policía *mf*
2 VT *(pt & pp* **marshalled**, *US* **marshaled**) **(a)** *(people, troops)* dirigir **(b)** *(arguments, thoughts)* poner en orden

marshy ['mɑ:ʃɪ] ADJ **(marshier, marshiest)** pantanoso(a)

martial ['mɑ:ʃəl] ADJ marcial; **m. arts** artes *fpl* marciales

Martian ['mɑ:ʃən] ADJ & N marciano(a) *(m,f)*

martyr ['mɑ:tə(r)] 1 N mártir *mf*
2 VT martirizar

martyrdom ['mɑ:tədəm] N martirio *m*

marvel ['mɑ:vəl] 1 N maravilla *f*
2 VI to m. at maravillarse de

marvellous, *US* **marvelous** ['mɑ:vələs] ADJ maravilloso(a)

Marxism ['mɑ:ksɪzəm] N marxismo *m*

Marxist ['mɑ:ksɪst] ADJ & N marxista *(mf)*

marzipan ['mɑ:zɪpæn] N mazapán *m*

mascara [mæ'skɑ:rə] N rímel *m*

> Note that the Spanish word **máscara** is a false friend and is never a translation for the English word **mascara**. In Spanish **máscara** means "mask".

mascot ['mæskət] N mascota *f*

masculine ['mæskjʊlɪn] ADJ masculino(a); *(woman)* hombruna

mash [mæʃ] 1 N *(for animals)* afrecho *m*
2 VT to m. (up) machacar; **mashed potatoes** puré *m* de *Esp* patatas or *Am* papas

mask [mɑ:sk] 1 N máscara *f*; *(of doctor, dentist etc)* mascarilla *f*
2 VT enmascarar; *Fig (conceal)* ocultar (**from** de)

masochism ['mæsəkɪzəm] N masoquismo *m*

masochist ['mæsəkɪst] ADJ & N masoquista *(mf)*

mason ['meɪsən] N **(a)** *(builder)* albañil *m* **(b)** *(freemason)* masón *m*, francmasón *m*

masonic [mə'sɒnɪk] ADJ masónico(a)

masonry ['meɪsənrɪ] N *(stonework)* albañilería *f*

masquerade [mæskə'reɪd] 1 N *(pretence)* farsa *f*
2 VI to m. as hacerse pasar por

mass¹ [mæs] N *Rel* misa *f*; **to say m.** decir misa

mass² [mæs] 1 N **(a)** *(shapeless substance) & Phys* masa *f* **(b)** *(large number)* sinnúmero *m*; *(of people)* multitud *f* **(c)** *Pol* **the masses** las masas
2 ADJ masivo(a); **m. media** medios *mpl* de comunicación (de masas); **m. production** fabricación *f* en serie
3 VI *(troops, people)* congregarse, concentrarse

massacre ['mæsəkə(r)] 1 N masacre *f*
2 VT masacrar

massage ['mæsɑ:ʒ, mə'sɑ:dʒ] 1 N masaje *m*
2 VT **(a)** *(body, scalp)* dar un masaje a **(b)** *Fig (figures)* maquillar

masseur [mæ'sɜ:(r)] N masajista *m*

masseuse [mæ'sɜ:z] N masajista *f*

massive ['mæsɪv] ADJ enorme; *(heart attack)* grave

mast [mɑ:st] N **(a)** *Naut* mástil *m* **(b)** *Rad & TV* torre *f*

master ['mɑ:stə(r)] 1 N **(a)** *(of servants)* señor *m*; *(of ship)* patrón *m*; *(of slave, dog)* amo *m* **(b)** *Br (teacher)* profesor *m* **(c)** *Univ* **m.'s degree** ≃ máster *m* **(d)** *(expert)* maestro *m*
2 ADJ **(a)** **m. copy** original *m*; **m. key** llave maestra **(b)** *(expert)* maestro(a)
3 VT **(a)** *(person, situation)* dominar **(b)** *(subject, skill)* llegar a dominar

masterful ['mɑ:stəfʊl] ADJ autoritario(a); *(imperious)* imperioso(a); *(personality)* dominante

masterly ['mɑ:stəlɪ] ADJ magistral

mastermind ['mɑ:stəmaɪnd] 1 N *(person)* cerebro *m*
2 VT ser el cerebro de

masterpiece ['mɑ:stəpi:s] N obra maestra

mastery ['mɑ:stərɪ] N **(a)** *(control)* dominio *m* (**of** de) **(b)** *(skill, expertise)* maestría *f*

masturbate ['mæstəbeɪt] VI masturbarse

mat¹ [mæt] N *(rug)* alfombrilla *f*; *(doormat)* felpudo *m*; *(rush mat)* estera *f*; *Sport* colchoneta *f*

mat² [mæt] ADJ mate

match¹ [mætʃ] N fósforo *m*, *Esp* cerilla *f*, *Am* cerillo *m*

match² [mætʃ] 1 N **(a)** *Sport* partido *m*; *(in boxing)* combate *m* **(b)** *Fig* **to meet one's m.** *(equal)* encontrar uno la horma de su zapato
2 VT **(a)** *(equal, be the equal of)* igualar **(b)** *(be in harmony with)* armonizar; **they are well matched** *(teams)* van iguales; *(couple)* hacen buena pareja **(c)** *(colours, clothes)* hacer juego con; *(pair of socks, gloves)* ser el compañero de
3 VI *(harmonize)* hacer juego

matchbox ['mætʃbɒks] N caja *f* de fósforos or *Esp* cerillas or *Am* cerillos

matching ['mætʃɪŋ] ADJ que hace juego

matchstick ['mætʃstɪk] N fósforo *m*, *Esp* cerilla *f*, *Am* cerillo *m*

mate [meɪt] 1 N **(a)** *Br, Austr Fam (friend)* amigo(a) *m,f*, *Esp* colega *mf*, *Méx* cuate *mf* **(b)** *Zool (male)* macho *m*; *(female)* hembra *f* **(c)** *(assistant)* ayudante *mf* **(d)** *(on ship)* oficial *m*; **(first) m.** primer oficial
2 VI *Zool* aparearse

material [mə'tɪərɪəl] 1 N **(a)** *(substance)* materia *f* **(b)** *(cloth)* tejido *m*, tela *f* **(c)** **materials** *(ingredients, equipment)* materiales *mpl*
2 ADJ **(a)** *(important)* substancial **(b)** *(physical)* material

materialistic [mətɪərɪə'lɪstɪk] ADJ materialista

materialize [mə'tɪərɪəlaɪz] vɪ (a) *(hopes)* realizarse; *(plan, idea)* concretarse (b) *(show up)* presentarse

maternal [mə'tɜːnəl] ADJ maternal; *(uncle etc)* materno(a)

maternity [mə'tɜːnɪtɪ] N maternidad *f*; **m. dress** vestido *m* premamá; **m. hospital** maternidad

math [mæθ] N *US* = **maths**

mathematical [mæθə'mætɪkəl] ADJ matemático(a)

mathematician [mæθəmə'tɪʃən] N matemático(a) *m,f*

mathematics [mæθə'mætɪks] N SING matemáticas *fpl*

maths [mæθs] N SING *Br Fam* matemáticas *fpl*

matinée ['mætɪneɪ] N *Cin* sesión *f* de tarde; *Th* función *f* de tarde

mating ['meɪtɪŋ] N apareamiento *m*; **m. call** reclamo *m*; **m. season** época *f* de celo

matrices ['meɪtrɪsiːz] PL of **matrix**

matriculate [mə'trɪkjuleɪt] vɪ *Univ* matricularse

matriculation [mətrɪkju'leɪʃən] N *Univ* matriculación *f*

matrimonial [mætrɪ'məunɪəl] ADJ matrimonial

matrimony ['mætrɪmənɪ] N matrimonio *m*; *(married life)* vida *f* conyugal

matrix ['meɪtrɪks] N *(pl* matrices*)* matriz *f*

matron ['meɪtrən] N *(in hospital)* enfermera *f* jefe

matronly ['meɪtrənlɪ] ADJ madura y recia

matt [mæt] ADJ mate

matted ['mætɪd] ADJ enmarañado(a)

matter ['mætə(r)] 1 N (a) *(affair, question)* asunto *m*; **a m. of opinion/taste** una cuestión de opinión/gustos; **as a m. of fact** en realidad (b) *(problem)* **what's the m.?** ¿qué pasa? (c) **no m. what he does** haga lo que haga; **no m. where you go** dondequiera que vayas; **no m. how** como sea (d) *(substance)* materia *f*, sustancia *f* (e) *(content)* contenido *m*; *(subject)* tema *m*
2 vɪ importar; **it doesn't m.** no importa, da igual

matter-of-fact ['mætərəv'fækt] ADJ *(person)* práctico(a); *(account)* realista; *(style)* prosaico(a)

mattress ['mætrɪs] N colchón *f*

mature [mə'tʃuə(r)] 1 ADJ maduro(a); *Fin* vencido(a)
2 vɪ madurar; *Fin* vencer
3 vᴛ madurar

maturity [mə'tʃuərɪtɪ] N madurez *f*

maul [mɔːl] vᴛ (a) *(wound)* agredir (b) *(handle roughly)* maltratar (c) *(touch in unpleasant way)* sobar

mausoleum [mɔːsə'liːəm] N *(pl* mausoleums *or* mausolea* [mɔːsə'liːə]*)* mausoleo *m*

mauve [məuv] ADJ & N malva *(m)*

maverick ['mævərɪk] ADJ & N inconformista *(mf)*, disidente *(mf)*

mawkish ['mɔːkɪʃ] ADJ *Pej* empalagoso(a)

max [mæks] N *(abbr* maximum*)* máx

maxim ['mæksɪm] N máxima *f*

maxima ['mæksɪmə] PL of **maximum**

maximize ['mæksɪmaɪz] vᴛ maximizar

maximum ['mæksɪməm] 1 N *(pl* maxima*)* máximo *m*
2 ADJ máximo(a)

May [meɪ] N mayo *m*; **M. Day** el Primero *or* el Uno de Mayo

may [meɪ] v AUX *(pt* might*)*

En el inglés hablado, y en el escrito en estilo coloquial, la forma negativa **might not** se transforma en **mightn't**. La forma **might have** se transforma en **might've**.

(a) *(expressing possibility)* poder, ser posible; **come what m.** pase lo que pase; **he m.** *or* **might come** puede que venga; **you m.** *or* **might as well stay** más vale que te quedes (b) *(permission)* poder; **m. I?** ¿me permite?; **you m. smoke** puede fumar (c) *(wish)* **m. you always be happy!** ¡ojalá seas siempre feliz!

maybe ['meɪbiː] ADV quizá(s), tal vez

mayhem ['meɪhem] N *(disturbance)* alboroto *m*; *(havoc)* estragos *mpl*

mayonnaise [meɪə'neɪz] N mayonesa *f*, mahonesa *f*

mayor [meə(r)] N *(man)* alcalde *m*; *(woman)* alcaldesa *f*

mayoress ['meərɪs] N alcaldesa *f*

maze [meɪz] N laberinto *m*

MB *Comput (abbr* megabyte*)* MB

MBA [embiː'eɪ] N *Univ (abbr* Master of Business Administration*)* MBA *m*, máster *m* en administración de empresas

MD [em'diː] N (a) *(abbr* Doctor of Medicine*)* Doctor(a) *m,f* en Medicina (b) *Fam (abbr* Managing Director*)* director(a) *m,f* gerente

me [miː, *unstressed* mɪ] PRON (a) *(as object)* me; **he gave it to me** me lo dio; **listen to me** escúchame; **she knows me** me conoce (b) *(after prep)* mí; **it's for me** es para mí; **with me** conmigo (c) *(emphatic)* yo; **it's me** soy yo; **what about ME?** ¿y yo, qué?

meadow ['medəu] N prado *m*, pradera *f*

meagre, *US* **meager** ['miːgə(r)] ADJ exiguo(a)

meal¹ [miːl] N *(flour)* harina *f*

meal² [miːl] N *(food)* comida *f*

mealtime ['miːltaɪm] N hora *f* de comer

mealy-mouthed [miːlɪ'mauðd] ADJ *Pej* evasivo(a); **to be m.** andarse con rodeos

mean¹ [miːn] vᴛ *(pt & pp* meant*)* (a) *(signify) (of word, event)* significar; *(of person)* querer decir; **what do you m. by that?** ¿qué quieres decir con eso?; **it means a lot to me** significa mucho para mí (b) *(intend)* pensar, tener la intención de; **I m. it** (te) lo digo en serio; **she didn't m. to do it** lo hizo sin querer (c) *(entail)* suponer; **it would m. having to give up smoking** significaría tener que dejar de fumar (**d**) *(refer to)* referirse a (**e**) *(destine)* destinar (**for** a *or* para)

mean² [mi:n] ADJ (**a**) *(miserly)* tacaño(a) (**b**) *(unkind)* malo(a); *(petty)* mezquino(a); *US (bad-tempered)* malhumorado(a); **to be m. to sb** tratar mal a algn (**c**) *(skilful)* **it was no m. feat** fue toda una hazaña (**d**) *US Fam (good)* genial, *Esp* guay, *Am salvo RP* chévere, *Méx* padre, *RP* macanudo(a)

mean³ [mi:n] **1** ADJ *(average)* medio(a)
2 N *(average)* promedio *m*; *Math* media *f*

meander [mi'ændə(r)] VI *(river)* serpentear; *(person)* vagar; *Fig (digress)* divagar

meaning ['mi:nɪŋ] N sentido *m*, significado *m*

meaningful ['mi:nɪŋfʊl] ADJ significativo(a)

meaningless ['mi:nɪŋlɪs] ADJ sin sentido

meanness ['mi:nnɪs] N (**a**) *(miserliness)* tacañería *f* (**b**) *(nastiness)* maldad *f*

means [mi:nz] N (**a**) SING OR PL *(method)* medio *m*, manera *f*; **by m. of** por medio de, mediante (**b**) PL *(resources, wealth)* medios *mpl* (de vida), recursos (económicos) (**c**) **by all m.!** ¡por supuesto!

meant [ment] PT & PP *of* **mean**

meantime ['mi:ntaɪm] **1** ADV mientras tanto
2 N **in the m.** mientras tanto

meanwhile ['mi:nwaɪl] ADV mientras tanto

measles ['mi:zəlz] N SING sarampión *m*

measly ['mi:zlɪ] ADJ (**measlier, measliest**) *Fam* ridículo(a), irrisorio(a)

measure ['meʒə(r)] **1** N (**a**) *(action, step)* medida *f* (**b**) *(measurement, quantity)* medida *f*; *(means of estimating)* indicador *m*, índice *m*; *(ruler)* regla *f* (**c**) **in some m.** hasta cierto punto (**d**) *Mus* compás *m*
2 VT *(object, area)* medir; *(person)* tomar las medidas de

Note that the Spanish word **mesura** is a false friend and is never a translation for the English word **measure**. In Spanish **mesura** means "moderation, restraint". measure up vi to m. (up) (to sth) estar a la altura (de algo)

▸ **measure up** VI **to m. up (to sth)** estar a la altura (de algo)

measurement ['meʒəmənt] N medida *f*

meat [mi:t] N carne *f*; *Culin* **m. pie** empanada *f* de carne

meatball ['mi:tbɔ:l] N albóndiga *f*

meaty ['mi:tɪ] ADJ (**meatier, meatiest**) (**a**) *(fleshy)* carnoso(a) (**b**) *Fig (story)* jugoso(a)

Mecca ['mekə] N la Meca

mechanic [mɪ'kænɪk] N *(person)* mecánico(a) *m,f*

mechanical [mɪ'kænɪkəl] ADJ mecánico(a)

mechanics [mɪ'kænɪks] **1** N SING *(science)* mecánica *f*
2 NPL *(technical aspects)* mecanismo *m*

mechanism ['mekənɪzəm] N mecanismo *m*

medal ['medəl] N medalla *f*

medalist ['medəlɪst] *US* = **medallist**

medallion [mɪ'dæljən] N medallón *m*

medallist ['medəlɪst] N medallista *mf*

meddle ['medəl] VI entrometerse (**in** en); **to m. with sth** manosear algo

media ['mi:dɪə] NPL **medios** *mpl* de comunicación; **m. coverage** cobertura periodística

Note that the Spanish word **media** is a false friend and is never a translation for the English word **media**. In Spanish **media** means both "stocking, sock" and "average".

median ['mi:dɪən] **1** ADJ mediano(a); *US Aut* **m. (strip)** mediana *f*, *Col, Méx* camellón *m*
2 N *Geom* mediana *f*; *Math* valor mediano

mediate ['mi:dɪeɪt] VI mediar

mediator ['mi:dɪeɪtə(r)] N mediador(a) *m,f*

Medicaid ['medɪkeɪd] N *(in US)* = seguro médico estatal para personas con renta baja

medical ['medɪkəl] **1** ADJ *(treatment)* médico(a); *(book)* de medicina
2 N *Fam* reconocimiento médico

Medicare ['medɪkeə(r)] N *(in US)* = seguro médico para ancianos y algunos discapacitados

medicated ['medɪkeɪtɪd] ADJ medicinal

medication [medɪ'keɪʃən] N medicamento *m*, medicina *f*

medicine ['medsɪn] N *(science)* medicina *f*; *(drugs etc)* medicamento *m*

medieval [medɪ'i:vəl] ADJ medieval

mediocre [mi:dɪ'əʊkə(r)] ADJ mediocre

meditate ['medɪteɪt] VI meditar (**on** sobre)

meditation [medɪ'teɪʃən] N meditación *f*

Mediterranean [medɪtə'reɪnɪən] **1** ADJ mediterráneo(a)
2 N **the M.** el Mediterráneo

medium ['mi:dɪəm] **1** ADJ *(average)* mediano(a); *Br Rad* **m. wave** onda media
2 N (**a**) *(pl* **media**) *(means)* medio *m* (**b**) *(pl* **mediums**) *(spiritualist)* médium *mf*

medley ['medlɪ] N *(mixture)* mezcla *f*; *Mus* popurrí *m*

meek [mi:k] ADJ manso(a), sumiso(a); *(humble)* humilde

meet [mi:t] **1** VT *(pt & pp* **met**) (**a**) *(encounter) (by chance)* encontrar, encontrarse con; *(by arrangement)* reunirse con; *(in formal meeting)* entrevistarse con (**b**) *(become acquainted with)* conocer; **I'd like you to m. my mother** quiero presentarte a mi madre; **the first time I met him** cuando lo conocí (**c**) *(join with)* unirse con, juntarse con; **where East meets West** donde se encuentran el Oriente y el Occidente (**d**) *(encounter) (danger)* encontrar; *(opponent)* enfrentarse con (**e**) *(satisfy) (demand, need, condition)* satisfacer; *(objection, criticism)* responder a

2 VI (**a**) *(by chance)* encontrarse; *(by arrangement)* reunirse; *(for formal meeting)* entrevistarse (**b**) *(become acquainted)* conocerse (**c**) *Sport* enfrentarse (**d**) *(rivers, roads)* encontrarse, unirse
3 N *(sports event)* encuentro *m*; *(in athletics)* reunión *f* atlética
▸ **meet up** VI encontrarse, quedar (**with** con)
▸ **meet with** VT INSEP *(difficulty)* tropezar con; *(loss)* sufrir; *(success)* tener; *esp US (person)* reunirse con

meeting ['mi:tɪŋ] N *(chance encounter)* encuentro *m*; *(prearranged)* cita *f*; *(formal)* entrevista *f*; *(of committee etc)* reunión *f*; *(of assembly)* sesión *f*; *(of shareholders)* junta *f*; *(rally)* mitin *m*; *Sport* encuentro *m*; *(of rivers)* confluencia *f*

mega ['megə] ADJ *Fam (excellent)* genial, guay, *Andes, CAm, Carib, Méx* chévere, *RP* bárbaro(a)

megabyte ['megəbaɪt] N *Comput* megabyte *m*

megalomania [megələʊ'meɪnɪə] N megalomanía *f*

megaphone ['megəfəʊn] N megáfono *m*

melancholy ['melənkəlɪ] **1** N melancolía *f*
2 ADJ melancólico(a)

Melilla [me'liːjə] N Melilla

mellow ['meləʊ] **1** ADJ maduro(a); *(wine)* añejo(a); *(colour, voice)* suave; *(person)* apacible
2 VI *(fruit)* madurar; *(colour, voice)* suavizarse

melodrama ['melədrɑːmə] N melodrama *m*

melodramatic [melədrə'mætɪk] ADJ melodramático(a)

melody ['melədɪ] N melodía *f*

melon ['melən] N melón *m*

melt [melt] **1** VT *(metal)* fundir; *Fig (sb's heart)* ablandar
2 VI *(snow)* derretirse; *(metal)* fundirse; *Fig* ablandarse
▸ **melt away** VI *(snow)* derretirse; *Fig (money)* desaparecer; *Fig (confidence)* desvanecerse
▸ **melt down** VT SEP *(metal)* fundir

melting ['meltɪŋ] N fundición *f*; **m. point** punto *m* de fusión; **m. pot** crisol *m*

member ['membə(r)] N miembro *mf*; *(of a society)* socio(a) *m,f*; *(of party, union)* afiliado(a) *m,f*; *US* **M. of Congress** congresista *mf*; *Br* **M. of Parliament** diputado(a) *m,f*

membership ['membəʃɪp] N *(state)* calidad *f* de socio; *(entry)* ingreso *m*; *Pol* afiliación *f*; *(number of members)* número *m* de socios; **m. card** carnet *m* de socio

memento [mə'mentəʊ] N recuerdo *m*

memo ['meməʊ] N *(official note)* memorándum *m*; *(personal note)* nota *f*, apunte *m*

memoirs ['memwɑːz] NPL memorias *fpl*

memorabilia [memərə'bɪlɪə] NPL *wartime* m. objetos *mpl* de la época de la guerra

memorable ['memərəbəl] ADJ memorable

memorandum [memə'rændəm] N *(pl* **memoranda**) *(official note)* memorándum *m*; *(personal note)* nota *f*, apunte *m*

memorial [mɪ'mɔːrɪəl] **1** ADJ *(plaque etc)* conmemorativo(a)
2 N monumento conmemorativo

memorize ['meməraɪz] VT memorizar, aprender de memoria

memory ['memərɪ] N memoria *f*; *(recollection)* recuerdo *m*

men [men] PL *of* **man**

menace ['menɪs] **1** N *(threat)* amenaza *f*; *(danger)* peligro *m*; *Fam (person)* pesado(a) *m,f*
2 VT amenazar

menacing ['menɪsɪŋ] ADJ amenazador(a)

menagerie [mɪ'nædʒərɪ] N casa *f* de fieras

mend [mend] **1** VT reparar, arreglar; *(clothes)* remendar; *(socks etc)* zurcir
2 VI *(ill person)* reponerse
3 N *(patch)* remiendo *m*; *(darn)* zurcido *m*

mending ['mendɪŋ] N *(repair)* reparación *f*; *(darning)* zurcido *m*; *(clothes for mending)* ropa *f* para remendar

menial ['miːnɪəl] ADJ *(task)* servil, bajo(a)

meningitis [menɪn'dʒaɪtɪs] N meningitis *f inv*

menopause ['menəpɔːz] N menopausia *f*

menstrual ['menstrʊəl] ADJ menstrual

menstruation [menstru'eɪʃən] N menstruación *f*

menswear ['menzweə(r)] N ropa *f* de caballero *or* hombre

mental ['mentəl] ADJ (**a**) *(state, age)* mental; **m. hospital** hospital psiquiátrico; **m. illness** enfermedad *f* mental (**b**) *Br Fam (mad)* pirado(a), *CSur* rayado(a)

mentality [men'tælɪtɪ] N mentalidad *f*

mentally ['mentəlɪ] ADV **m. ill** enfermo(a) mental; **to be m. handicapped** ser un/una disminuido(a) psíquico(a)

mention ['menʃən] **1** N mención *f*
2 VT mencionar; **don't m. it!** ¡de nada!

mentor ['mentɔː(r)] N mentor *m*

menu [menjuː] N (**a**) *(card)* carta *f*; *(fixed meal)* menú *m*; **today's m.** el menú del día (**b**) *Comput* menú *m*

MEP [emiː'piː] N *Br (abbr* **Member of the European Parliament**) eurodiputado(a) *m,f*

mercenary ['mɜːsɪnərɪ] ADJ & N mercenario(a) *(m,f)*

merchandise ['mɜːtʃəndaɪz] N mercancías *fpl*, géneros *mpl*

merchant ['mɜːtʃənt] N *Com & Fin* comerciante *mf*; *(retailer)* detallista *mf*; **m. bank** banco *m* comercial

merciful ['mɜːsɪfʊl] ADJ clemente, compasivo(a) *(towards con)*

merciless ['mɜːsɪlɪs] ADJ despiadado(a)

Mercury ['mɜːkjʊrɪ] N Mercurio *m*

mercury ['mɜːkjʊrɪ] N mercurio *m*

mercy ['mɜːsɪ] N misericordia f, compasión f; **at the m. of** a la merced de; **to have m. on** tener compasión de

mere [mɪə(r)] ADJ mero(a), simple

merely ['mɪəlɪ] ADV simplemente

merge [mɜːdʒ] **1** VT (blend) unir (**with** con); Com fusionar
2 VI unirse; (roads) empalmar; Com fusionarse

merger ['mɜːdʒə(r)] N Com fusión f

meridian [mə'rɪdɪən] N Geog & Astron meridiano m

meringue [mə'ræŋ] N merengue m

merit ['merɪt] **1** N (of person) mérito m; (of plan etc) ventaja f
2 VT merecer, Am ameritar

mermaid ['mɜːmeɪd] N sirena f

merry ['merɪ] ADJ (**merrier, merriest**) (happy) alegre; Fam (slightly drunk) alegre, Esp piripi; **m. Christmas!** ¡felices Navidades!

merry-go-round ['merɪgəʊraʊnd] N tiovivo m, carrusel m, RP calesita f

mesh [meʃ] **1** N Tex malla f; Tech engranaje m; Fig red f
2 VT Tech engranar

mesmerize ['mezməraɪz] VT hipnotizar

mess [mes] N (**a**) (confusion) confusión f; (disorder) desorden m; **to be in a m.** (of room etc) estar desordenado(a) (**b**) (in life, affairs) lío m; **to get into a m.** meterse en un lío (**c**) (dirt) suciedad f (**d**) Mil (room) comedor m
▶ **mess about, mess around** Fam **1** VT SEP fastidiar
2 VI (act the fool) hacer el primo; (idle) gandulear; (kill time) pasar el rato
▶ **mess about with** VT INSEP Fam (fiddle with) manosear; **to m. about with sb** tener un lío con algn
▶ **mess up** VT SEP Fam (make untidy) desordenar; (dirty) ensuciar; (spoil) estropear

message ['mesɪdʒ] N (communication) recado m; (of story etc) mensaje m; Fam **to get the m.** comprender

messaging ['mesɪdʒɪŋ] N mensajería f

messenger ['mesɪndʒə(r)] N mensajero(a) m,f

Messiah [mɪ'saɪə] N Rel Mesías m inv

Messrs ['mesəz] NPL (abbr **Messieurs**) Sres.

messy ['mesɪ] ADJ (**messier, messiest**) (**a**) (untidy) (room) desordenado(a); (person) desaliñado(a) (**b**) (dirty) sucio(a) (**c**) (confused) enredado(a)

met [met] PT & PP of **meet**

metabolism [me'tæbəlɪzəm] N metabolismo m

metal ['metəl] **1** N metal m
2 ADJ metálico(a)

metallic [mɪ'tælɪk] ADJ metálico(a); **m. blue** azul metalizado

metallurgy [me'tælədʒɪ] N metalurgia f

metalwork ['metəlwɜːk] N (craft) metalistería f; (objects) objetos mpl de metal

metamorphosis [metə'mɔːfəsɪs] N (pl meta-morphoses [metə'mɔːfəsiːz]) metamorfosis f inv

metaphor ['metəfə(r)] N metáfora f

mete [miːt] VT **to m. out** imponer

meteor ['miːtɪə(r)] N bólido m

meteoric [miːtɪ'ɒrɪk] ADJ meteórico(a)

meteorite ['miːtɪəraɪt] N meteorito m

meteorology [miːtɪə'rɒlədʒɪ] N meteorología f

meter¹ ['miːtə(r)] N contador m

meter² ['miːtər] N US = **metre**

method ['meθəd] N método m

methodical [mɪ'θɒdɪkəl] ADJ metódico(a)

Methodist ['meθədɪst] ADJ & N metodista (mf)

methylated spirits ['meθɪleɪtɪd'spɪrɪts], Br Fam **meths** [meθs] N alcohol desnaturalizado (con metanol), alcohol m de quemar

meticulous [mə'tɪkjʊləs] ADJ meticuloso(a)

metre ['miːtə(r)] N metro m

metric ['metrɪk] ADJ métrico(a)

metropolis [mɪ'trɒpəlɪs] N metrópoli f

metropolitan [metrə'pɒlɪtən] ADJ metropolitano(a)

mettle ['metəl] N valor m

mew [mjuː] VI (cat) maullar

mews [mjuːz] N SING Br (street) callejuela f; **m. flat** = apartamento de lujo en unas caballerizas reconvertidas

Mexican ['meksɪkən] ADJ & N mejicano(a) (m,f), mexicano(a) (m,f)

Mexico ['meksɪkəʊ] N México, Méjico

mezzanine ['metsəniːn] N **m. (floor)** entreplanta f

miaow [miː'aʊ] **1** VI maullar
2 N maullido m

mice [maɪs] PL of **mouse**

mickey ['mɪkɪ] N Fam **to take the m. (out of sb)** tomar el pelo (a algn)

microbe ['maɪkrəʊb] N microbio m

microchip ['maɪkrəʊtʃɪp] N microplaqueta f, microchip m

microcomputer ['maɪkrəʊkəm'pjuːtə(r)] N Esp microordenador m, Am microcomputadora f

microcosm ['maɪkrəʊkɒzəm] N microcosmo m

microfiche ['maɪkrəʊfiːʃ] N microficha f

microfilm ['maɪkrəʊfɪlm] N microfilm m

microphone ['maɪkrəfəʊn] N micrófono m

microprocessor [maɪkrəʊ'prəʊsesə(r)] N microprocesador m

microscope ['maɪkrəskəʊp] N microscopio m

microwave ['maɪkrəʊweɪv] N microonda f; **m. (oven)** (horno m) microondas m inv

mid [mɪd] ADJ (**in**) **m. afternoon** a media tarde; (**in**) **m. April** a mediados de abril; **to be in one's m. thirties** tener unos treinta y cinco años

midair 1 ADJ ['mɪdeə(r)] (collision, explosion) en el aire

2 N [mɪdˈeə(r)] *Fig* **to leave sth in m.** dejar algo en el aire

midday 1 N [mɪdˈdeɪ] mediodía *m*
2 ADJ [ˈmɪddeɪ] de mediodía

middle [ˈmɪdəl] **1** ADJ (a) de en medio; **m. age** mediana edad; **the M. Ages** la Edad Media; **the m. class** la clase media
2 N (a) *(in general)* medio *m*; **in the m. of** en medio de; **in the m. of winter** en pleno invierno; *Fam* **in the m. of nowhere** en el quinto pino (b) *(waist)* cintura *f*

middle-aged [mɪdəlˈeɪdʒd] ADJ de mediana edad

middle-class [mɪdəlˈklɑːs] ADJ de clase media
middleman [ˈmɪdəlmæn] N intermediario *m*
middleweight [ˈmɪdəlweɪt] N peso medio
middling [ˈmɪdlɪŋ] ADJ mediano(a)
midfielder [mɪdˈfiːldə(r)] N *Sport* centrocampista *mf*
midge [mɪdʒ] N mosca enana
midget [ˈmɪdʒɪt] N enano(a) *m,f*
Midlands [ˈmɪdləndz] NPL **the M.** = la región central de Inglaterra
midnight [ˈmɪdnaɪt] N medianoche *f*
midriff [ˈmɪdrɪf] N diafragma *m*
midst [mɪdst] N **in the m. of** en medio de
midsummer [mɪdˈsʌmə(r)] N pleno verano; **M.'s Day** Día *m* de San Juan *(24 de junio)*
midterm [ˈmɪdˈtɜːm] ADJ (a) *Pol Br* **m. by-election** = elecciones parciales a mitad de legislatura; *US* **m. elections** = elecciones a mitad del mandato presidencial (b) *Sch Univ* de mitad de trimestre
midway [ˈmɪdweɪ] ADV a medio camino
midweek [mɪdˈwiːk] **1** ADV [mɪdˈwiːk] entre semana
2 ADJ [ˈmɪdwiːk] de entre semana
Mid-West [ˈmɪdˈwest] N Medio Oeste *m* (de Estados Unidos)
midwife [ˈmɪdwaɪf] N comadrona *f*, partera *f*
midwifery [ˈmɪdwɪfərɪ] N obstetricia *f*
midwinter [mɪdˈwɪntə(r)] N pleno invierno *m*
might¹ [maɪt] V AUX *see* **may**
might² [maɪt] N *Fml* fuerza *f*, poder *m*
mighty [ˈmaɪtɪ] **1** ADJ (**mightier, mightiest**) *(strong)* fuerte; *(powerful)* poderoso(a); *(great)* enorme
2 ADV *US Fam* un montón, *Esp* cantidad
migraine [ˈmiːgreɪn, ˈmaɪgreɪn] N jaqueca *f*
migrant [ˈmaɪgrənt] **1** ADJ migratorio(a)
2 N *(person)* emigrante *mf*; *(bird)* ave migratoria
migrate [maɪˈgreɪt] VI emigrar
migration [maɪˈgreɪʃən] N migración *f*
mike [maɪk] N *Fam* micro *m*
mild [maɪld] ADJ *(person, character)* apacible; *(climate)* templado(a); *(punishment)* leve; *(tobacco, taste)* suave
mildew [ˈmɪldjuː] N moho *m*; *(on plants)* añublo *m*

mildly [ˈmaɪldlɪ] ADV *(softly, gently)* suavemente; *(slightly)* ligeramente; **and that's putting it m.** y esto es decir poco
mildness [ˈmaɪldnɪs] N *(of character)* apacibilidad *f*; *(of climate, taste)* suavidad *f*; *(of punishment)* levedad *f*
mile [maɪl] N milla *f*; *Fam* **miles better** muchísimo mejor
mileage [ˈmaɪlɪdʒ] N kilometraje *m*
milestone [ˈmaɪlstəʊn] N hito *m*
milieu [ˈmiːljɜː] N medio *m* ambiente
militant [ˈmɪlɪtənt] ADJ & N militante *(mf)*
military [ˈmɪlɪtərɪ] ADJ militar; **to do one's m. service** hacer el servicio militar
militia [mɪˈlɪʃə] N milicia *f*
milk [mɪlk] **1** N *(for drinking)* leche *f*; **m. chocolate** chocolate *m* con leche; **m. shake** batido *m*, *Am* licuado *m*
2 VT (a) *(cow, goat)* ordeñar (b) *Fam* **they milked him of all his money** le sangraron hasta el último centavo
milkman [ˈmɪlkmən] N lechero *m*
milky [ˈmɪlkɪ] ADJ (**milkier, milkiest**) lechoso(a); *(colour)* pálido(a); **M.Way** Vía Láctea
mill [mɪl] **1** N *(grinder)* molino *m*; *(for coffee)* molinillo *m*; *(factory)* fábrica *f*; **cotton m.** hilandería *f*
2 VT moler
▶ **mill about, mill around** VI arremolinarse
millennium [mɪˈlenɪəm] N *(pl millenniums or millennia* [mɪˈlenɪə]*)* milenio *m*
miller [ˈmɪlə(r)] N molinero(a) *m,f*
millet [ˈmɪlɪt] N mijo *m*
milligram(me) [ˈmɪlɪgræm] N miligramo *m*
millilitre, *US* **milliliter** [ˈmɪlɪliːtə(r)] N mililitro *m*
millimetre, *US* **millimeter** [ˈmɪlɪmiːtə(r)] N milímetro *m*
milliner [ˈmɪlɪnə(r)] N sombrerero(a) *m,f*
millinery [ˈmɪlɪnərɪ] N sombreros *mpl* de señora
million [ˈmɪljən] N millón *m*
millionaire [mɪljəˈneə(r)] N millonario(a) *m,f*
millstone [ˈmɪlstəʊn] N muela *f*; *Fig* carga *f*
mime [maɪm] **1** N *(art)* mímica *f*; *(play)* pantomima *f*
2 VT representar con gestos

Note that the Spanish verb **mimar** is a false friend and is never a translation for the English verb **to mime**. In Spanish **mimar** means "to spoil, to pamper".

mimic [ˈmɪmɪk] **1** ADJ & N mímico(a) *(m,f)*
2 VT imitar
mimicry [ˈmɪmɪkrɪ] N imitación *f*
minaret [ˈmɪnəret] N alminar *m*, minarete *m*
mince [mɪns] **1** N *Br (meat)* carne *Esp, RP* picada *or Am* molida; **m. pie** *(containing meat)* = empanada de carne picada; *(containing fruit)* = pastel navideño relleno de "mincemeat"
2 VT picar

mincemeat ['mɪnsmiːt] N *(meat)* carne *Esp, RP* picada *or Am* molida; *(fruit)* = relleno a base de fruta escarchada, frutos secos y especias

mincer ['mɪnsə(r)] N picadora *f* de carne

mind [maɪnd] **1** N **(a)** *(thoughts, intellect)* mente *f*; **to bear** *or* **keep sth in m.** tener algo en cuenta; **what kind of car do you have in m.?** ¿en qué clase de coche estás pensando?; **to lose one's m.** perder el juicio; **I'm sure if you put your m. to it you could do it** estoy seguro de que podrías hacerlo si pusieses tus cinco sentidos (en ello); **it slipped my m.** lo olvidé por completo **(b)** *(opinion)* **to be in two minds (about sth)** estar indeciso(a) (acerca de algo); **to have a m. of one's own** ser capaz de pensar *or* decidir por sí mismo(a); **to my m.** a mi parecer; *Fam* **I gave him a piece of my m.** le canté las cuarenta

2 VT **(a)** *(child)* cuidar; *(house)* vigilar; *(be careful of)* tener cuidado con; **m. the step!** ¡ojo con el escalón!; **m. your own business!** ¡no te metas donde no te llaman!; **m. you, he is fifty** ten en cuenta que tiene cincuenta años **(b)** *(object to)* **I don't m. the cold** el frío no me importa *or* no me molesta; **I wouldn't m. a cup of coffee** me vendría bien un café; **would you m. not doing that?** ¿te importaría no hacer eso?

3 VI **(a) (b)** *(object)* importar; **do you m. if I open the window?** ¿le importa que abra la ventana?; **never m.!** ¡es igual!

mind-boggling ['maɪndbɒglɪŋ], **mind-blowing** ['maɪndbləʊɪŋ] ADJ *Fam* alucinante

minder ['maɪndə(r)] N **(a)** *Br Fam (bodyguard)* gorila *m*, *Méx* guarura *m* **(b) (child** *or* **baby) m.** *Esp* canguro *mf*, *Am* baby-sitter *f*, *Méx* nana *f*

mindful ['maɪndfʊl] ADJ consciente

mindless ['maɪndlɪs] ADJ *(task)* de autómata; *(violence)* injustificable

mine¹ [maɪn] POSS PRON (el) mío/(la) mía, (los) míos/(las) mías, lo mío; **a friend of m.** un amigo mío; **these gloves are m.** estos guantes son míos; **which is m.?** ¿cuál es el mío?

mine² [maɪn] **1** N mina *f*; *Fig* **a m. of information** un pozo de información

2 VT *(coal etc)* extraer; *Mil* minar

minefield ['maɪnfiːld] N campo *m* de minas

miner ['maɪnə(r)] N minero(a) *m,f*

mineral ['mɪnərəl] **1** ADJ mineral; **m. water** agua *f* mineral

2 N mineral *m*

minesweeper ['maɪnswiːpə(r)] N dragaminas *m inv*

mingle ['mɪŋgəl] VI mezclarse

miniature ['mɪnɪtʃə(r)] **1** N miniatura *f*

2 ADJ *(railway)* en miniatura; *(camera, garden)* diminuto(a)

minibus ['mɪnɪbʌs] N microbús *m*

minicab ['mɪnɪkæb] N *Br* taxi *m* (que sólo se puede pedir por teléfono)

minim ['mɪnɪm] N *Br Mus* blanca *f*

minimal ['mɪnɪməl] ADJ mínimo(a)

minimize ['mɪnɪmaɪz] VT minimizar, reducir al mínimo

minimum ['mɪnɪməm] **1** ADJ mínimo(a); **m. wage** salario mínimo

2 N mínimo *m*

mining ['maɪnɪŋ] **1** N minería *f*, explotación *f* de minas; *Mil & Naut* minado *m*

2 ADJ minero(a)

miniskirt ['mɪnɪskɜːt] N minifalda *f*

minister ['mɪnɪstə(r)] **1** N *Pol* ministro(a) *m,f*; *Rel* pastor(a) *m,f*

2 VI **to m. to sb** atender a algn

ministerial [mɪnɪ'stɪərɪəl] ADJ *Pol* ministerial

ministry ['mɪnɪstrɪ] N *Pol* ministerio *m*; *Rel* sacerdocio *m*

mink [mɪŋk] N visón *m*; **m. coat** abrigo *m* de visón

minnow ['mɪnəʊ] N alevín *m*

minor ['maɪnə(r)] **1** ADJ *(lesser)* menor; *(unimportant)* sin importancia; *(role)* secundario(a); *Mus* menor

2 N *Jur* menor *mf* de edad

Minorca [mɪ'nɔːkə] N Menorca *f*

minority [maɪ'nɒrɪtɪ] N minoría *f*; **to be in the m.** ser (la) minoría; *Pol* **m. party** partido minoritario

mint¹ [mɪnt] **1** N *Fin* **the (Royal) M.** ≃ la Casa de la Moneda, *Esp* ≃ la Fábrica Nacional de Moneda y Timbre

2 VT *(coin, words)* acuñar

mint² [mɪnt] N *Bot* menta *f*; *(sweet)* pastilla *f* de menta

minus ['maɪnəs] **1** PREP **5 m. 3** 5 menos 3; **m. 10 degrees** 10 grados bajo cero

2 ADJ negativo(a)

3 N **m. (sign)** signo *m* (de) menos

minute¹ ['mɪnɪt] N **(a)** *(of time)* minuto *m*; **at the last m.** a última hora; **just a m.** (espera) un momento; **this very m.** ahora mismo **(b) the minutes** *(notes)* el acta

minute² [maɪ'njuːt] ADJ *(tiny)* diminuto(a); *(examination)* minucioso(a)

miracle ['mɪrəkəl] N milagro *m*

miraculous [mɪ'rækjʊləs] ADJ milagroso(a)

mirage [mɪ'rɑːʒ] N espejismo *m*

mire [maɪə(r)] N fango *m*, lodo *m*; *(muddy place)* lodazal *m*

mirror ['mɪrə(r)] **1** N espejo *m*; *Fig* reflejo *m*; **rear-view m.** retrovisor *m*

2 VT reflejar

mirth [mɜːθ] N alegría *f*, *(laughter)* risas *fpl*

misadventure [mɪsəd'ventʃə(r)] N desgracia *f*; **death by m.** muerte *f* accidental

misanthropist [mɪ'zænθrəpɪst] N misántropo(a) *m,f*

misapprehension [mɪsæprɪ'henʃən] N malentendido *m*

misbehave [mɪsbɪ'heɪv] VI portarse mal

miscalculate [mɪs'kælkjʊleɪt] VT & VI calcular mal

miscarriage ['mɪskærɪdʒ] N Med aborto (espontáneo); **m. of justice** error m judicial

miscellaneous [mɪsɪ'leɪnɪəs] ADJ variado(a); **m. expenses** gastos diversos

mischief ['mɪstʃɪf] N (naughtiness) travesura f; Fml (evil) malicia f; **to get up to m.** hacer travesuras; Br Fam Hum (injury) **to do oneself a m.** hacerse daño

mischievous ['mɪstʃɪvəs] ADJ (naughty) travieso(a); (playful) juguetón(ona); Fml (wicked) malicioso(a)

misconception [mɪskən'sepʃən] N concepto erróneo

misconduct [mɪs'kɒndʌkt] N mala conducta

misconstrue [mɪskən'struː] VT interpretar mal

miscount [mɪs'kaʊnt] VT (votes etc) contar mal

misdeed [mɪs'diːd] N fechoría f

misdemeanour, US **misdemeanor** [mɪsdɪ'miːnə(r)] N (misdeed) fechoría f; Jur falta m

miser ['maɪzə(r)] N avaro(a) m,f

miserable ['mɪzərəbəl] ADJ (a) (sad) triste (b) (unpleasant) lamentable; (weather) horroroso(a) (c) (wretched) miserable

miserly ['maɪzəlɪ] ADJ avaro(a), tacaño(a)

misery ['mɪzərɪ] N (sadness) tristeza f; (wretchedness) desgracia f; (suffering) sufrimiento m; (poverty) miseria f; Fam (person) aguafiestas mf

misfire [mɪs'faɪə(r)] VI (engine, plan etc) fallar

misfit ['mɪsfɪt] N (person) inadaptado(a) m,f

misfortune [mɪs'fɔːtʃən] N desgracia f

misgiving [mɪs'gɪvɪŋ] N (doubt) recelo m; (fear) temor m

misguided [mɪs'gaɪdɪd] ADJ equivocado(a)

mishandle [mɪs'hændəl] VT llevar or manejar mal

mishap ['mɪshæp] N contratiempo m

misinform [mɪsɪn'fɔːm] VT informar mal

misinterpret [mɪsɪn'tɜːprɪt] VT interpretar mal

misjudge [mɪs'dʒʌdʒ] VT juzgar mal

mislay [mɪs'leɪ] VT extraviar

mislead [mɪs'liːd] VT despistar; (deliberately) engañar

misleading [mɪs'liːdɪŋ] ADJ (erroneous) erróneo(a); (deliberately) engañoso(a)

mismanagement [mɪs'mænɪdʒmənt] N mala administración

misnomer [mɪs'nəʊmə(r)] N nombre equivocado

misogynist [mɪ'sɒdʒɪnɪst] N misógino(a) m,f

misplace [mɪs'pleɪs] VT (trust) encauzar mal; (book, spectacles etc) extraviar

misprint ['mɪsprɪnt] N errata f, error m de imprenta

misquote [mɪs'kwəʊt] VT (a) (accidentally) citar equivocadamente (b) (deliberately) (person) tergiversar las palabras de; (words) tergiversar

misrepresent [mɪsreprɪ'zent] VT (facts) desvirtuar; (words) tergiversar

miss¹ [mɪs] N señorita f

▸ **miss out 1** VT SEP (omit) saltarse; (on purpose) pasar por alto
2 VT INSEP **to m. out on** perderse

miss² [mɪs] **1** N (throw etc) Esp fallo m, Am falla f; Fam **to give sth a m.** pasar de algo
2 VT (a) (target) no acertar en; (shot, penalty) Esp fallar, Am errar; **the car just missed me** el coche or Am carro or CSur auto no me atropelló por poco (b) (train etc) perder; (opportunity) dejar pasar; **you have missed the point** no has captado la idea (c) (feel lack of) echar de menos, esp Am extrañar; **I m. you** te echo de menos, esp Am te extraño
3 VI (a) (miss target) (when throwing) fallar; (when shooting) errar (b) (be absent) **to be missing** faltar

misshapen [mɪs'ʃeɪpən] ADJ deforme

missile ['mɪsaɪl, US 'mɪsəl] N Mil misil m; (object thrown) proyectil m

missing ['mɪsɪŋ] ADJ (object) perdido(a); (person) desaparecido(a); (from meeting etc) ausente; **m. person** desaparecido(a) m,f; **three cups are m.** faltan tres tazas

mission ['mɪʃən] N misión f; **m. (station)** misión f; Com **m. statement** declaración f de (la) misión, misión f

missionary ['mɪʃənərɪ] N misionero(a) m,f

misspell ['mɪs'spel] (pt & pp **misspelt** ['mɪs'spelt]) VT escribir incorrectamente

misspent ['mɪsspent] ADJ (youth) malgastado(a)

mist [mɪst] **1** N neblina f; (thick) niebla f; (at sea) bruma f
2 VI **to m. over** or **up** (countryside) cubrirse de neblina; (window etc) empañarse

mistake [mɪ'steɪk] **1** N error m; **by m.** por equivocación; **I hurt him by m.** le golpeé sin querer; **to make a m.** equivocarse, cometer un error
2 VT (pt mistook; pp mistaken) (meaning) malentender; **to m. Jack for Bill** confundir a Jack con Bill

mistaken [mɪ'steɪkən] ADJ equivocado(a), erróneo(a); **you are m.** estás equivocado(a)

mister ['mɪstə(r)] N señor m

mistletoe ['mɪsəltəʊ] N muérdago m

mistook [mɪ'stʊk] PT of **mistake**

mistreat [mɪs'triːt] VT tratar mal

mistress ['mɪstrɪs] N (a) (of servant, house) señora f, ama f (b) (lover) amante f (c) Educ (primary school) maestra f; (secondary school) profesora f

mistrust [mɪs'trʌst] **1** N recelo m
2 VT desconfiar de

misty ['mɪstɪ] ADJ (**mistier**, **mistiest**) (day) de niebla; (window etc) empañado(a)

misunderstand [mɪsʌndə'stænd] VT & VI
malentender

misunderstanding [mɪsʌndə'stændɪŋ] N malentendido m; (disagreement) desavenencia f

misuse 1 N [mɪs'juːs] mal uso m; (of funds) malversación f; (of power) abuso m
2 VT [mɪs'juːz] emplear mal; (funds) malversar; (power) abusar de

miter ['maɪtər] N US = mitre

mitigate ['mɪtɪgeɪt] VT atenuar

mitigating ['mɪtɪgeɪtɪŋ] ADJ **m. circumstances**
circunstancias fpl atenuantes

mitre ['maɪtə(r)] N mitra f

mitten ['mɪtən] N manopla f; (fingerless) mitón m

mix [mɪks] **1** N mezcla f
2 VT mezclar
3 VI (blend) mezclarse (**with** con); (go well
together) ir bien juntos(as)
► **mix up** VT SEP (confuse) confundir (**with** con);
(papers) revolver; **to be mixed up in sth** estar
involucrado/a en algo

mixed [mɪkst] ADJ (assorted) surtido(a); (varied)
variado(a); (school) mixto(a); (feelings) contra-
dictorio(a)

mixed-up [mɪkst'ʌp] ADJ (objects, papers etc)
revuelto(a); (person) confuso(a)

mixer ['mɪksə(r)] N (**a**) (for cooking) batidora f
(**b**) **to be a good m.** (person) tener don de
gentes

mixture ['mɪkstʃə(r)] N mezcla f

mix-up ['mɪksʌp] N Fam confusión f, lío m

mm (abbr **millimetre(s)**) mm

moan [məʊn] **1** N (groan) gemido m, quejido m
2 VI (groan) gemir; (complain) quejarse
(**about** de)

moat [məʊt] N foso m

mob [mɒb] **1** N multitud f; (riff-raff) gentuza f;
the m. el populacho
2 VT acosar

mobile ['məʊbaɪl, US 'məʊbəl] **1** ADJ móvil; **m.
home** caravana f; **m. phone** teléfono m móvil,
Am teléfono m celular
2 N (**a**) (hanging ornament) móvil m (**b**) Fam
(mobile phone) móvil m, Am celular m

mobility [məʊ'bɪlɪtɪ] N movilidad f

mobilize ['məʊbɪlaɪz] VT movilizar

moccasin ['mɒkəsɪn] N mocasín m

mock [mɒk] **1** ADJ (sympathy etc) fingido(a);
(objects) de imitación
2 VT (make fun of) burlarse de
3 VI burlarse (**at** de)

mockery ['mɒkərɪ] N burla f

mod cons ['mɒd'kɒnz] NPL Br Fam **with all m.**
con todas las comodidades

mode [məʊd] N (manner) modo m, estilo m;
(fashion) moda f

model ['mɒdəl] **1** N (person, example) modelo
m; (scale) maqueta f
2 ADJ (railway) en miniatura; (pupil) ejemplar;
(school) modelo

3 VT (clay etc) modelar; (clothes) presentar;
Comput simular por Esp ordenador or Am
computadora
4 VI (make models) modelar; (work as model)
trabajar de modelo

modem ['məʊdem] N Comput modem m

moderate[1] ['mɒdərɪt] **1** ADJ moderado(a);
(reasonable) razonable; (average) regular;
(ability) mediocre
2 N Pol moderado(a) m,f

moderate[2] ['mɒdəreɪt] **1** VT moderar
2 VI moderarse; (wind) calmarse; (in debate)
arbitrar

moderately ['mɒdərɪtlɪ] ADV medianamente

moderation [mɒdə'reɪʃən] N moderación f; **in
m.** con moderación

modern ['mɒdən] ADJ moderno(a); (history)
contemporáneo(a); **m. languages** lenguas
modernas

modernize ['mɒdənaɪz] VT modernizar

modest ['mɒdɪst] ADJ modesto(a); (chaste)
púdico(a); (price) módico(a); (success) discre-
to(a)

modesty ['mɒdɪstɪ] N (humility) modestia f;
(chastity) pudor m

modification [mɒdɪfɪ'keɪʃən] N modificación f

modify ['mɒdɪfaɪ] VT modificar

module ['mɒdjuːl] N módulo m

mogul ['məʊgʌl] N magnate m

mohair ['məʊheə(r)] **1** N mohair m
2 ADJ de mohair

moist [mɔɪst] ADJ húmedo(a)

moisten ['mɔɪsən] VT humedecer

moisture ['mɔɪstʃə(r)] N humedad f

moisturizer ['mɔɪstʃəraɪzə(r)] N crema f or
leche f hidratante

molar ['məʊlə(r)] N muela f

molasses [mə'læsɪz] N SING melaza f

mold[1] [məʊld] N US = **mould**[1]

mold[2] [məʊld] N & VT US = **mould**[2]

molder ['məʊldər] VI US = **moulder**

molding ['məʊldɪŋ] N US = **moulding**

moldy ['məʊldɪ] ADJ US = **mouldy**

mole[1] [məʊl] N (beauty spot) lunar m

mole[2] [məʊl] N (animal) topo m

molecule ['mɒlɪkjuːl] N molécula f

molest [mə'lest] VT importunar; (sexually
assault) acosar (sexualmente)

mollycoddle ['mɒlɪkɒdəl] VT Fam mimar,
consentir

molt [məʊlt] VI US = **moult**

molten ['məʊltən] ADJ fundido(a); (lava) lí-
quido(a)

mom [mɒm] N US Fam mamá f

moment ['məʊmənt] N momento m; **at the m.**
en este momento; **for the m.** de momento; **in
a m.** dentro de un momento; **at any m.** de un
momento a otro

momentarily ['məʊməntərɪlɪ] ADV momentáneamente; *US (soon)* dentro de poco

momentary ['məʊməntərɪ] ADJ momentáneo(a)

momentous [məʊ'mentəs] ADJ trascendental

momentum [məʊ'mentəm] N *Phys* momento *m; (speed)* velocidad *f; Fig* **to gather m.** cobrar velocidad

mommy ['mɒmɪ] N *US Fam* mamá *f*

Monaco ['mɒnəkəʊ] N Mónaco

monarch ['mɒnək] N monarca *m*

monarchy ['mɒnəkɪ] N monarquía *f*

monastery ['mɒnəstərɪ] N monasterio *m*

Monday ['mʌndɪ] N lunes *m*

monetarism ['mʌnɪtərɪzəm] N monetarismo *m*

monetary ['mʌnɪtərɪ] ADJ monetario(a)

money ['mʌnɪ] N dinero *m; (currency)* moneda *f;* **to make m.** ganar dinero

moneylender ['mʌnɪlendə(r)] N prestamista *mf*

money-spinner ['mʌnɪspɪnə(r)] N *Fam* negocio *m* rentable

Mongolia [mɒŋ'gəʊlɪə] N Mongolia

mongolism ['mɒŋgəlɪzəm] N mongolismo *m*

mongrel ['mʌŋgrəl] N perro mestizo

monitor ['mɒnɪtə(r)] **1** N *(screen)* monitor *m; Educ* delegado(a) *m,f*
2 VT *(check)* controlar; *(progress, events)* seguir de cerca

monk [mʌŋk] N monje *m*

monkey ['mʌŋkɪ] N mono *m; Br* **m. nut** *Esp* cacahuete *m, Am* maní *m, CAm, Méx* cacahuate *m*

monochrome ['mɒnəkrəʊm] ADJ monocromo(a); *(television, photo)* en blanco y negro

monocle ['mɒnəkəl] N monóculo *m*

monogamous [mɒ'nɒgəməs] ADJ monógamo(a)

monolingual [mɒnəʊ'lɪŋgwəl] ADJ monolingüe

monologue, *US* **monolog** ['mɒnəlɒg] N monólogo *m*

monopolize [mə'nɒpəlaɪz] VT *Fin* monopolizar; *(attention etc)* acaparar

monopoly [mə'nɒpəlɪ] N monopolio *m*

monosyllable [mɒnəʊ'sɪləbəl] N monosílabo *m*

monotone ['mɒnətəʊn] N **in a m.** con una voz monótona

monotonous [mə'nɒtənəs] ADJ monótono(a)

monotony [mə'nɒtənɪ] N monotonía *f*

monsoon [mɒn'suːn] N monzón *m*

monster ['mɒnstə(r)] N monstruo *m*

monstrosity [mɒn'strɒsɪtɪ] N monstruosidad *f*

monstrous ['mɒnstrəs] ADJ *(huge)* enorme; *(hideous)* monstruoso(a); *(outrageous)* escandaloso(a)

montage ['mɒntɑːʒ] N montaje *m*

month [mʌnθ] N mes *m*

monthly ['mʌnθlɪ] **1** ADJ mensual; **m. instalment** mensualidad *f*

2 N *(periodical)* revista *f* mensual
3 ADV mensualmente, cada mes

monument ['mɒnjʊmənt] N monumento *m*

monumental [mɒnjʊ'mentəl] ADJ monumental; *Fam (huge)* enorme

moo [muː] **1** N mugido *m*
2 VI mugir

mooch [muːtʃ] *Fam* **1** VI **to m. around** vagar, dar vueltas
2 VT **to m. sth off sb** *(cadge)* gorronearle algo a algn

mood [muːd] N humor *m;* **to be in a good/bad m.** estar de buen/mal humor; **to be in the m. for (doing) sth** estar de humor para (hacer) algo

moody ['muːdɪ] ADJ **(moodier, moodiest)** *(changeable)* de humor variable; *(badtempered)* malhumorado(a)

moon [muːn] N luna *f; Fam* **over the m.** en el séptimo cielo

moonlight ['muːnlaɪt] N luz *f* de la luna

moonlighting ['muːnlaɪtɪŋ] N *Fam* pluriempleo *m*

moonlit ['muːnlɪt] ADJ iluminado(a) por la luna

Moor [mʊə(r)] N moro(a) *m,f*

moor[1] [mʊə(r)] N *(heath)* páramo *m*

moor[2] [mʊə(r)] VT *Naut* amarrar

Moorish ['mʊərɪʃ] ADJ moro(a)

moorland ['mʊələnd] N páramo *m*

moose [muːs] N *(pl* **moose)** alce *m*

moot [muːt] ADJ **it's a m. point** es discutible

mop [mɒp] **1** N *(for floor)* fregona *f*
2 VT fregar

▶ **mop up** VT SEP *(liquids)* enjugar; *(enemy forces)* acabar con

▶ **mope about, mope around** VI andar abatido(a)

mope [məʊp] VI estar alicaído(a)

moped ['məʊped] N ciclomotor *m,* vespa *f*

moral ['mɒrəl] **1** ADJ moral
2 N moraleja *f;* **morals** moral *f,* moralidad *f*

morale [mə'rɑːl] N moral *f,* estado *m* de ánimo

morality [mə'rælɪtɪ] N moralidad *f*

morass [mə'ræs] N pantano *m; Fig* lío *m*

moratorium [mɒrə'tɔːrɪəm] N *(pl* **moratoriums** or **moratoria** [mɒrə'tɔːrɪə]) moratoria *f* **(on** sth)

morbid ['mɔːbid] ADJ *Med* mórbido(a); *(mind)* morboso(a)

more [mɔː(r)] **1** ADJ más; **is there any m. tea?** ¿queda más té?; **I've no m. money** no me queda más dinero; **m. tourists** más turistas
2 PRON más; **how many m.?** ¿cuántos más?; **many/much m.** muchos(as)/mucho más; **m. than a hundred** más de cien; **the m. he has, the m. he wants** cuanto más tiene más quiere; **and what is m.** y lo que es más
3 ADV más; **I won't do it any m.** no lo volveré a hacer; **she doesn't live here any m.** ya no vive aquí; **m. and m. difficult** cada vez más difícil; **m. or less** más o menos

moreish ['mɔːrɪʃ] ADJ *Fam (food)* irresistible, adictivo(a)

moreover [mɔː'rəʊvə(r)] ADV además

morgue [mɔːg] N depósito *m* de cadáveres

morning ['mɔːnɪŋ] 1 N mañana *f*; *(before dawn)* madrugada *f*; **in the m.** por la mañana; **on Monday mornings** los lunes por la mañana; **tomorrow m.** mañana por la mañana
2 ADJ matutino(a)

Moroccan [mə'rɒkən] ADJ & N marroquí *(mf)*

Morocco [mə'rɒkəʊ] N Marruecos

moron ['mɔːrɒn] N *Fam* subnormal *mf*, *Am* zonzo(a) *m,f*

morose [mə'rəʊs] ADJ hosco(a), huraño(a)

> Note that the Spanish word **moroso** is a false friend and is never a translation for the English word **morose**. In Spanish, **moroso** means "bad debtor".

morphine ['mɔːfiːn] N morfina *f*

Morse [mɔːs] N **M. (code)** (alfabeto *m*) Morse *m*

morsel ['mɔːsəl] N *(of food)* bocado *m*; *Fig* trozo *m*

mortal ['mɔːtəl] 1 ADJ mortal
2 N mortal *mf*

mortality [mɔː'tælɪtɪ] N mortalidad *f*

mortally ['mɔːtəlɪ] ADV mortalmente; **m. wounded** herido(a) de muerte

mortar ['mɔːtə(r)] N mortero *m*

mortgage ['mɔːgɪdʒ] 1 N hipoteca *f*
2 VT hipotecar

mortician [mɔː'tɪʃən] N *US (undertaker)* encargado(a) *m,f* de funeraria

mortify ['mɔːtɪfaɪ] VT mortificar; *Fam* **I was mortified** me sentí avergonzado(a)

mortuary ['mɔːtʃʊərɪ] N depósito *m* de cadáveres

mosaic [mə'zeɪk] N mosaico *m*

Moscow ['mɒskəʊ, *US* 'mɒskaʊ] N Moscú

Moslem ['mɒzləm] ADJ & N musulmán(ana) *(m,f)*

mosque [mɒsk] N mezquita *f*

mosquito [mɒs'kiːtəʊ] N *(pl* **mosquitoes)** mosquito *m*, *Am* zancudo *m*; **m. net** mosquitero *m*

moss [mɒs] N musgo *m*

most [məʊst] 1 ADJ *(superl of* **much, many)** **(a)** *(greatest in quantity etc)* más; **this house suffered (the) m. damage** esta casa fue la más afectada; **who made (the) m. mistakes?** ¿quién cometió más errores? **(b)** *(the majority of)* la mayoría de, la mayor parte de; **m. people** la mayoría de la gente
2 PRON *(greatest part)* la mayor parte; *(greatest number)* lo máximo, lo más; *(the majority of people)* la mayoría; **at the (very) m.** como máximo; **to make the m. of sth** aprovechar algo al máximo
3 ADJ *(superl of* **much) (a)** *(to form superlative)* **the most** el/la más; **the m. intelligent student** el estudiante más inteligente **(b)** *(with verbs)*

más; **what I like m.** lo que más me gusta **(c)** *(very)* muy; **m. of all** sobre todo

mostly ['məʊstlɪ] ADV *(chiefly)* en su mayor parte; *(generally)* generalmente; *(usually)* normalmente

MOT [eməʊ'tiː] N *Br (abbr* **Ministry of Transport)** **M. test** inspección técnica de vehículos, *Esp* ≃ ITV; *Esp* ≃ VTV *f*

motel [məʊ'tel] N motel *m*

moth [mɒθ] N mariposa nocturna; **clothes m.** polilla *f*

mother ['mʌðə(r)] 1 N madre *f*; **M.'s Day** Día *m* de la Madre; **m. tongue** lengua materna
2 VT cuidar maternalmente

motherhood ['mʌðəhʊd] N maternidad *f*

mother-in-law ['mʌðərɪnlɔː] N *(pl* **mothers-in-law)** suegra *f*

motherly ['mʌðəlɪ] ADJ maternal

mother-of-pearl [mʌðərəv'pɜːl] N madreperla *f*, nácar *m*

mother-to-be [mʌðətə'biː] N *(pl* **mothers-to-be)** futura madre

motif [məʊ'tiːf] N *Art & Mus* motivo *m*; *(embroidered etc)* adorno *m*; *Fig (main subject)* tema *m*

motion ['məʊʃən] 1 N *(movement)* movimiento *m*; *(gesture)* ademán *m*; *(proposal)* moción *f*
2 VT & VI **to m. (to) sb to do sth** hacer señas a algn para que haga algo

motionless ['məʊʃənlɪs] ADJ inmóvil

motivate ['məʊtɪveɪt] VT motivar

motivation [məʊtɪ'veɪʃən] N motivación *f*

motive ['məʊtɪv] 1 ADJ *(force)* motriz
2 N *(reason)* motivo *m*; *Jur* móvil *m*

motley ['mɒtlɪ] ADJ **(motlier, motliest)** *(multicoloured)* abigarrado(a); *(varied)* variado(a)

motor ['məʊtə(r)] N *(engine)* motor *m*; *Br Fam (car)* coche *m*, *Am* carro *m*, *CSur* auto *m*; **m. racing** carreras *fpl* de coches *or Am* carros *or CSur* autos

motorbike ['məʊtəbaɪk] N *Fam* motocicleta *f*, moto *f*

motorboat ['məʊtəbəʊt] N (lancha) motora *f*

motorcar ['məʊtəkɑː(r)] N *Br* coche *m*, automóvil *m*

motorcycle ['məʊtəsaɪkəl] N motocicleta *f*

motorcyclist ['məʊtəsaɪklɪst] N motociclista *mf*

motoring ['məʊtərɪŋ] N automovilismo *m*

motorist ['məʊtərɪst] N automovilista *mf*

motorway ['məʊtəweɪ] N *Br* autopista *f*

mottled ['mɒtəld] ADJ *(skin, animal)* con manchas; *(surface)* moteado(a)

motto ['mɒtəʊ] N lema *m*

mould¹ [məʊld] N *(fungus)* moho *m*

mould² [məʊld] 1 N molde *m*
2 VT moldear; *(clay)* modelar

moulder ['məʊldə(r)] VI **to m. (away)** desmoronarse

moulding ['məʊldɪŋ] N moldura *f*

mouldy ['məʊldɪ] ADJ (**mouldier, mouldiest**) mohoso(a); **to go m.** enmohecerse

moult [məʊlt] VI mudar

mound [maʊnd] N montón m; (small hill) montículo m

mount¹ [maʊnt] N monte m; **M. Everest** (Monte) Everest m

► **mount up** VI (accumulate) acumularse

mount² [maʊnt] **1** N (horse) montura f; (support) soporte m, base f; (for photograph) marco m; (for jewel) engaste m

2 VT (horse) subirse or montar a; (campaign) organizar; (photograph) enmarcar; (jewel) engastar

3 VI (go up) subir; (get on horse, bike) montar; (increase) subir

mountain ['maʊntɪn] **1** N montaña f; Fig (pile) montón m

2 ADJ de montaña, montañés(esa); **m. range** sierra f, cordillera f

mountaineer [maʊntɪ'nɪə(r)] N montañero(a) m,f, alpinista mf, Am andinista mf

mountaineering [maʊntɪ'nɪərɪŋ] N montañismo m, alpinismo m, Am andinismo m

mountainous ['maʊntɪnəs] ADJ montañoso(a)

mourn [mɔːn] **1** VT llorar la muerte de

2 VI **to m. for sb** llorar la muerte de algn

mourner ['mɔːnə(r)] N doliente mf

mournful ['mɔːnfʊl] ADJ triste; (voice) lúgubre

mourning ['mɔːnɪŋ] N luto m; **in m.** de luto

mouse [maʊs] N (pl mice) (**a**) (animal) ratón m (**b**) Comput Esp ratón m, Am mouse m

mousetrap ['maʊstræp] N ratonera f

mousse [muːs] N Culin mousse f; (for hair) (styling) espuma f, moldeadora)

moustache [mə'stɑːʃ] N bigote m

mousy ['maʊsɪ] ADJ (**mousier, mousiest**) (colour) pardusco(a); (hair) castaño claro; (shy) tímido(a)

mouth [maʊθ] **1** N (pl mouths [maʊðz]) (**a**) (of person, animal, tunnel) boca f (**b**) (of river) desembocadura f

2 VT [maʊð] (without sincerity) decir mecánicamente; (silently) decir moviendo sólo los labios

mouthful ['maʊθfʊl] N (of food) bocado m; (of drink) trago m

mouth organ ['maʊθɔːgən] N armónica f

mouthpiece ['maʊθpiːs] N Mus boquilla f; (of telephone) micrófono m; Fig (spokesman) portavoz m

mouthwash ['maʊθwɒʃ] N elixir m, enjuague m bucal

mouthwatering ['maʊθwɔːtərɪŋ] ADJ muy apetitoso(a), que le hace a uno la boca agua

movable ['muːvəbəl] ADJ movible, móvil

move [muːv] **1** N (**a**) (movement) movimiento m; **to be on the m.** estar en marcha; **we must make a m.** debemos irnos ya; Fam **get a m. on!** ¡date prisa!, Am ¡apúrate! (**b**) (action, step)

paso m; **to make the first m.** dar el primer paso (**c**) (in game) jugada f; (turn) turno m (**d**) (to new home) mudanza f; (to new job) traslado m

2 VT (**a**) (shift) mover; (furniture etc) cambiar de sitio; (transfer) trasladar; **to m. house** mudarse (de casa) (**b**) (in game) mover (**c**) (motivate) inducir; (persuade) persuadir; **I won't be moved** no me harán cambiar de parecer (**d**) (affect emotionally) conmover

3 VI (**a**) (change position) moverse, desplazarse; (change house) mudarse (de casa); (change post) trasladarse (**b**) (train etc) estar en marcha; **to start moving** ponerse en marcha (**c**) (leave) irse, marcharse (**d**) (in game) hacer una jugada

► **move about 1** VT SEP cambiar de sitio

2 VI (be restless) ir y venir; (travel) viajar de un lugar a otro

► **move along 1** VT SEP (move forward) hacer avanzar; (keep moving) hacer circular

2 VI (move forward) avanzar; (keep moving) circular; **m. along!** (to person on bench) ¡haz sitio!

► **move around** VT SEP & VI = **move about**

► **move away 1** VT SEP alejar, apartar (**from** de)

2 VI (move aside) alejarse, apartarse; (leave) irse; (change house) mudarse (de casa)

► **move back 1** VT SEP (to original place) volver

2 VI (withdraw) retirarse; (to original place) volver

► **move forward 1** VT SEP avanzar

2 VI avanzar, adelantarse

► **move in** VI (into new home) instalarse

► **move off** VI (go away) irse, marcharse; (train) salir

► **move on** VI (keep moving) circular; (go forward) avanzar; (time) transcurrir

► **move out** VI (leave) irse, marcharse; (leave house) mudarse

► **move over** VI correrse

► **move up** VI (go up) subir; Fig (be promoted) ser ascendido(a), ascender; (move along) correrse, hacer sitio

movement ['muːvmənt] N (**a**) (change of position, location) movimiento m; (gesture) gesto m, ademán m (**b**) (of goods) transporte m; (of employees) traslado m (**c**) (of goods, capital) circulación f

movie ['muːvɪ] N película f; **to go to the movies** ir al cine; **m. star** estrella f de cine; US **m. theater** cine m

moving ['muːvɪŋ] ADJ (that moves) móvil; (car etc) en marcha; Fig (touching) conmovedor(a)

mow [məʊ] VT (pt mowed; pp mown or mowed) (lawn) cortar; (corn, wheat) segar; Fig **to m. down** segar

mower ['məʊə(r)] N cortacésped m

mown [məʊn] PP of **mow**

MP [em'piː] N Br Pol (abbr **Member of Parliament**) diputado(a) m,f

mph [empiː'eɪtʃ] (*abbr* **miles per hour**) millas *fpl* por hora

MPhil [em'fɪl] N (*abbr* **Master of Philosophy**) = curso de posgrado de dos años de duración, superior a un máster e inferior a un doctorado

Mr ['mɪstə(r)] (*abbr* **Mister**) Sr

Mrs ['mɪsɪz] (*abbr* **Missus**) Sra

Ms [məz] N Sra/Srta

> **Ms** es el equivalente femenino de **Mr**, y se utiliza para dirigirse a una mujer sin precisar su estado civil.

MSc [emes'siː] N (*abbr* **Master of Science**) máster *m or Am* maestría *f* en Ciencias

much [mʌtʃ] **1** ADJ mucho(a); **as m. ... as** tanto(a) ... como; **how m. chocolate?** ¿cuánto chocolate?; **so m.** tanto(a)
2 ADV mucho; **as m. as** tanto como; **as m. as possible** todo lo posible; **how m.?** ¿cuánto?; **how m. is it?** ¿cuánto es?, ¿cuánto vale?; **m. better** mucho mejor; **m. more** mucho más; **thank you very m.** muchísimas gracias; **too m.** demasiado
3 PRON mucho; **I thought as m.** lo suponía; **m. of the town was destroyed** gran parte de la ciudad quedó destruida; **m. remains to be done** queda mucho por hacer

muck [mʌk] N (*dirt*) suciedad *f*; (*mud*) lodo *m*; *Fig* porquería *f*

▸ **muck about, muck around** *Br Fam* **1** VI (*idle*) perder el tiempo; (*play the fool*) hacer el tonto
2 VT SEP **to m. sb about** fastidiar a algn

▸ **muck up** VT SEP (*dirty*) ensuciar; *Fig* (*spoil*) echar a perder

mucky ['mʌkɪ] ADJ (**muckier, muckiest**) sucio(a)

mucus ['mjuːkəs] N moco *m*, mucosidad *f*

mud [mʌd] N lodo *m*, barro *m*; (*thick*) fango *m*; *Fig* **to sling m. at sb** poner a algn por los suelos; **m. flat** marisma *f*

muddle ['mʌdəl] **1** N desorden *m*; *Fig* (*mix-up*) embrollo *m*, lío *m*; **to get into a m.** hacerse un lío
2 VT confundir

▸ **muddle through** VI arreglárselas, ingeniárselas

▸ **muddle up** VT SEP confundir

muddy ['mʌdɪ] ADJ (**muddier, muddiest**) (*lane*) fangoso(a); (*hands*) cubierto(a) de lodo; (*liquid*) turbio(a)

mudguard ['mʌdɡɑːd] N *Br Esp, RP* guardabarros *m inv*, *Andes, CAm, Carib* guardafango *m*, *Méx* salpicadera *f*

muff¹ [mʌf] N manguito *m*; **ear muffs** orejeras *fpl*

muff² [mʌf] VT *Fam* pifiar; **to m. it (up)** estropearlo

muffin ['mʌfɪn] N *Br* (*teacake*) tortita *f*; *US* ≃ magdalena *f*

muffle ['mʌfəl] VT (*sound*) amortiguar; **to m. (up)** (*person*) abrigar

muffler ['mʌflə(r)] N *US Aut* silenciador *m*

mug¹ [mʌɡ] N (*large cup*) tazón *m*; (*beer tankard*) jarra *f*

mug² [mʌɡ] **1** N *Br Fam* (*gullible person*) bobo(a) *m,f*, primo(a) *m,f*, *Am* zonzo(a) *m,f*; (*face*) jeta *f*
2 VT atracar, asaltar

mugger ['mʌɡə(r)] N atracador(a) *m,f*

mugging ['mʌɡɪŋ] N asalto *m*

muggy ['mʌɡɪ] ADJ (**muggier, muggiest**) bochornoso(a)

mule [mjuːl] N mulo(a) *m,f*

mull [mʌl] VT **mulled wine** = vino caliente con especias

▸ **mull over** VT SEP **to m. sth over** darle vueltas a algo

multicoloured, *US* **multicolored** ['mʌltɪkʌləd] ADJ multicolor

multicultural [mʌltɪ'kʌltʃərəl] ADJ multicultural

multilingual [mʌltɪ'lɪŋɡwəl] ADJ (*person*) polígloto(a); (*dictionary, document*) multilingüe

multimedia [mʌltɪ'miːdɪə] **1** N multimedia *f*
2 ADJ multimedia *inv*

multimillionaire [mʌltɪmɪljə'neə(r)] N multimillonario(a) *m,f*

multinational [mʌltɪ'næʃənəl] ADJ & N multinacional (*f*)

multiple ['mʌltɪpəl] **1** ADJ múltiple; **m. sclerosis** esclerosis *f* múltiple
2 N múltiplo *m*

multiplex ['mʌltɪpleks] N multicine *m*

multiplication [mʌltɪplɪ'keɪʃən] N multiplicación *f*; **m. sign** signo *m* de multiplicar

multiply ['mʌltɪplaɪ] **1** VT multiplicar (**by** por)
2 VI multiplicarse

multipurpose [mʌltɪ'pɜːpəs] ADJ multiuso *inv*

multiracial [mʌltɪ'reɪʃəl] ADJ multirracial

multistorey, *US* **multistory** [mʌltɪ'stɔːrɪ] ADJ (*building*) de varios pisos; **m. car park** estacionamiento *m or Esp* aparcamiento *m or Col* parqueadero *m* de varias plantas

multitude ['mʌltɪtjuːd] N multitud *f*, muchedumbre *f*

mum¹ [mʌm] N *Br Fam* mamá *f*

mum² [mʌm] ADJ **to keep m.** no decir ni pío

mumble ['mʌmbəl] **1** VI hablar entre dientes
2 VT decir entre dientes

mumbo-jumbo ['mʌmbəʊ'dʒʌmbəʊ] N (*nonsense*) palabrería *f*, monsergas *fpl*

mummy¹ ['mʌmɪ] N *Br Fam* (*mother*) mamá *f*

mummy² ['mʌmɪ] N (*body*) momia *f*

mumps [mʌmps] N SING paperas *fpl*

munch [mʌntʃ] VT & VI mascar

mundane [mʌn'deɪn] ADJ *Pej* (*ordinary*) prosaico(a); (*job, life*) rutinario(a)

Note that the Spanish word **mundano** is a false friend and is never a translation for the English word **mundane**. In Spanish, **mundano** means "worldly".

municipal [mjuːˈnɪsɪpəl] ADJ municipal

municipality [mjuːnɪsɪˈpælɪtɪ] N municipio *m*

munitions [mjuːˈnɪʃənz] NPL municiones *fpl*, armamento *m*

mural [ˈmjʊərəl] ADJ & N mural *(m)*

murder [ˈmɜːdə(r)] **1** N asesinato *m*, homicidio *m*
2 VT asesinar

murderer [ˈmɜːdərə(r)] N asesino(a) *m,f*

murderess [ˈmɜːdərɪs] N asesina *f*

murderous [ˈmɜːdərəs] ADJ homicida

murky [ˈmɜːkɪ] ADJ (**murkier, murkiest**) oscuro(a); *(water)* turbio(a)

murmur [ˈmɜːmə(r)] **1** N murmullo *m*; *(of traffic)* ruido *m*; *(complaint)* queja *f*
2 VT & VI murmurar

muscle [ˈmʌsəl] **1** N músculo *m*
2 VI *Fam* **to m. in on sth** entrometerse en algo

muscular [ˈmʌskjʊlə(r)] ADJ *(pain, tissue)* muscular; *(person)* musculoso(a)

Muse [mjuːz] N *(in mythology)* musa *f*

muse [mjuːz] VI **to m. on** *or* **about sth** meditar algo

museum [mjuːˈzɪəm] N museo *m*

mushroom [ˈmʌʃruːm] **1** N hongo *m*, *Esp* seta *f*; *(button mushroom)* champiñón *m*
2 VI *Fig* crecer de la noche a la mañana

music [ˈmjuːzɪk] N música *f*; **m. hall** teatro *m* de variedades; **m. library** fonoteca *f*

musical [ˈmjuːzɪkəl] **1** ADJ musical; **to be m.** estar dotado(a) para la música
2 N musical *m*

musician [mjuːˈzɪʃən] N músico(a) *m,f*

musk [mʌsk] N almizcle *m*

Muslim [ˈmʊzlɪm] ADJ & N musulmán(ana) *(m,f)*

muslin [ˈmʌzlɪn] N muselina *f*

mussel [ˈmʌsəl] N mejillón *m*

must [mʌst] **1** VAUX (**a**) *(obligation)* deber, tener que; **you m. arrive on time** tienes que *or* debes llegar a la hora (**b**) *(probability)* deber de; **he m. be ill** debe de estar enfermo
2 N *Fam* **to be a m.** ser imprescindible

mustache [ˈmʌstæʃ] N *US* bigote *m*

mustard [ˈmʌstəd] N mostaza *f*

muster [ˈmʌstə(r)] **1** VT *Fig* **to m. (up) courage** cobrar fuerzas
2 VI reunirse, juntarse

mustn't [ˈmʌsənt] = **must not**

musty [ˈmʌstɪ] ADJ (**mustier, mustiest**) que huele a cerrado *or* a humedad

mutant [ˈmjuːtənt] ADJ & N mutante *(mf)*

mute [mjuːt] **1** ADJ mudo(a)
2 N *(person)* mudo(a) *m,f*; *Mus* sordina *f*

muted [ˈmjuːtɪd] ADJ *(sound)* sordo(a); *(colour)* suave

mutilate [ˈmjuːtɪleɪt] VT mutilar

mutiny [ˈmjuːtɪnɪ] **1** N motín *m*
2 VI amotinarse

mutter [ˈmʌtə(r)] **1** N *(mumble)* murmullo *m*
2 VT murmurar, decir entre dientes
3 VI *(angrily)* refunfuñar

mutton [ˈmʌtən] N (carne *f* de) cordero *m*

mutual [ˈmjuːtʃʊəl] ADJ mutuo(a); *(shared)* común

mutually [ˈmjuːtʃʊəlɪ] ADV mutuamente

Muzak® [ˈmjuːzæk] N música *f* de supermercado

muzzle [ˈmʌzəl] **1** N *(snout)* hocico *m*; *(for dog)* bozal *m*; *(of gun)* boca *f*
2 VT *(dog)* abozalar; *Fig* amordazar

my [maɪ] POSS ADJ mi; **my cousins** mis primos; **my father** mi padre; **one of my friends** un amigo mío; **I washed my hair** me lavé el pelo; **I twisted my ankle** me torcí el tobillo

myriad [ˈmɪrɪəd] N *Literary* miríada *f*

myself [maɪˈself] PERS PRON (**a**) *(emphatic)* yo mismo(a); **my husband and m.** mi marido y yo (**b**) *(reflexive)* me; **I hurt m.** me hice daño (**c**) *(after prep)* mí (mismo(a))

mysterious [mɪˈstɪərɪəs] ADJ misterioso(a)

mystery [ˈmɪstərɪ] N misterio *m*

mystical [ˈmɪstɪkəl] ADJ místico(a)

mystify [ˈmɪstɪfaɪ] VT dejar perplejo(a)

mystique [mɪˈstiːk] N aureola *f* de misterio

myth [mɪθ] N mito *m*; **it's a complete m.** es pura fantasía

mythology [mɪˈθɒlədʒɪ] N mitología *f*

N, n [en] N *(the letter)* N, n *f*

N *(abbr* **North)** N

nab [næb] VT *Fam (catch)* pescar, *Esp* trincar

naff [næf] ADJ *Br Fam (tasteless)* ordinario(a), *Esp* hortera, *Esp* cutre, *Chile* cuico(a), *RP* terraja; *(comment, behaviour)* de mal gusto; **a n. remark** una bordería

NAFTA ['næftə] N *(abbr* **North American Free Trade Agreement)** NAFTA *f*, TLC *m*

nag [næg] **1** VT fastidiar, dar la lata a; **to n. sb to do sth** fastidiar *or* dar la lata a algn para que haga algo
2 VI quejarse

nagging ['nægɪŋ] ADJ *(persistent)* continuo(a); **the n. truth** la pura verdad

nail [neɪl] **1** N (**a**) *(of finger, toe)* uña *f*; **n. clippers** cortaúñas *m inv*; **n. polish** *or* **varnish** esmalte *m or* laca *f* de uñas (**b**) *(metal)* clavo *m*
2 VT (**a**) *(in carpentry)* clavar (**b**) *Fam (catch, trap)* pillar, pescar

nailbrush ['neɪlbrʌʃ] N cepillo *m* de uñas

nailfile ['neɪlfaɪl] N lima *f* de uñas

nail-scissors ['neɪlsɪzəz] NPL tijeras *fpl* de uñas

naïve [naɪ'iːv] ADJ ingenuo(a)

naked ['neɪkɪd] ADJ desnudo(a); *(flame)* sin protección; **the n. truth** la pura verdad

name [neɪm] **1** N (**a**) *(of person)* nombre *m*; *(surname)* apellido *m*; **what's your n.?** ¿cómo te llamas?; **to call sb names** poner verde a algn (**b**) *(reputation)* reputación *f*; **to make a n. for oneself** hacerse famoso(a)
2 VT (**a**) *(give name to)* poner nombre a, bautizar; **to n. sb after** *or US* **for sb** poner a algn el nombre de algn (**b**) *(appoint)* nombrar (**c**) *(refer to)* mencionar

nameless ['neɪmlɪs] ADJ anónimo(a); **to remain n.** permanecer en el anonimato

namely ['neɪmlɪ] ADV a saber

namesake ['neɪmseɪk] N tocayo(a) *m,f*

nanny ['nænɪ] N niñera *f*

nap [næp] **1** N *(sleep)* siesta *f*; **to have a n.** echar la *or* una siesta
2 VI *Fig* **to catch sb napping** pillar *or Esp* coger *or Am* agarrar a algn desprevenido(a)

napalm ['neɪpɑːm] N napalm *m*

nape [neɪp] N nuca *f*, cogote *m*

napkin ['næpkɪn] N *(table)* **n.** servilleta *f*

Naples ['neɪpəlz] N Nápoles

nappy ['næpɪ] N *Br* pañal *m*

narcissus [nɑː'sɪsəs] N *Bot* narciso *m*

narcotic [nɑː'kɒtɪk] **1** ADJ narcótico(a)
2 N narcótico *m*

narrate [nə'reɪt] VT narrar, relatar

narration [nə'reɪʃən] N narración *f*, relato *m*

narrative ['nærətɪv] **1** N *Lit* narrativa *f*; *(story)* narración *f*
2 ADJ narrativo(a)

narrator [nə'reɪtə(r)] N narrador(a) *m,f*

narrow ['nærəʊ] **1** ADJ (**a**) *(passage, road etc)* estrecho(a), angosto(a) (**b**) *(restricted)* reducido(a); *(sense)* estricto(a); **to have a n. escape** librarse por los pelos
2 VI estrecharse

▸ **narrow down 1** VT SEP reducir, limitar
2 VI **to n. down to** reducirse a

narrowly ['nærəʊlɪ] ADV (**a**) *(closely)* de cerca (**b**) *(by a small margin)* por poco

narrow-minded ['nærəʊ'maɪndɪd] ADJ de miras estrechas

nasal ['neɪzəl] ADJ nasal; *(voice)* gangoso(a)

nastiness ['nɑːstɪnɪs] N (**a**) *(unpleasantness)* carácter *m* desagradable (**b**) *(maliciousness)* mala intención

nasty ['nɑːstɪ] ADJ (**nastier, nastiest**) (**a**) *(person)* desagradable; **to turn n.** *(of weather, situation)* ponerse feo(a) (**b**) *(unfriendly)* antipático(a); *(malicious)* mal intencionado(a); *Br Fam* **he's a n. piece of work** es un asco de tío (**c**) *(illness, accident)* grave

nation ['neɪʃən] N nación *f*

national ['næʃnəl] **1** ADJ nacional; **n. anthem** himno *m* nacional; **n. insurance** seguridad *f* social; *Mil* **n. service** servicio *m* militar
2 N súbdito(a) *m,f*

nationalism ['næʃnəlɪzəm] N nacionalismo *m*

nationalist ['næʃnəlɪst] ADJ & N nacionalista *(mf)*

nationality [næʃə'nælɪtɪ] N nacionalidad *f*

nationalization [næʃnəlaɪ'zeɪʃən] N nacionalización *f*

nationalize ['næʃnəlaɪz] VT nacionalizar

nationwide ['neɪʃənwaɪd] ADJ de ámbito nacional

native ['neɪtɪv] **1** ADJ (**a**) *(place)* natal; **n. land** patria *f*; **n. language** lengua materna (**b**) *(plant, animal)* originario(a) (**to** de)
2 N nativo(a) *m,f*, natural *mf*; *(original inhabitant)* indígena *mf*

NATO, Nato ['neɪtəʊ] N *(abbr* **North Atlantic Treaty Organization)** OTAN *f*

natter ['nætə(r)] *Fam* **1** VI charlar, darle a la lengua, *CAm, Méx* platicar
2 N charla *f*, *CAm, Méx* plática *f*

natural ['nætʃərəl] **1** ADJ (**a**) *(colour, taste)* natural (**b**) *(normal)* normal; **it's only n. that ...** es lógico que ... (**c**) *(born)* nato(a)
2 N (**a**) **she's a n. for the job** es la persona ideal para el trabajo (**b**) *Mus* becuadro *m*

naturalize ['nætʃərəlaɪz] VT **to become naturalized** naturalizarse

naturally ['nætʃərəlɪ] ADV (**a**) *(of course)* naturalmente (**b**) *(by nature)* por naturaleza (**c**) *(in a relaxed manner)* con naturalidad

nature ['neɪtʃə(r)] N (**a**) *(the natural world)* naturaleza *f* (**b**) *(character)* naturaleza *f*, carácter *m*; **by n.** por naturaleza; **human n.** la naturaleza humana (**c**) *(sort, kind)* índole *f*, clase *f*

naught [nɔ:t] *US* = **nought**

naughtily ['nɔ:tɪlɪ] ADV **to behave n.** portarse mal

naughty ['nɔ:tɪ] ADJ (**naughtier, naughtiest**) (**a**) *(child)* travieso(a) (**b**) *(joke, story)* atrevido(a), picante

nausea ['nɔ:zɪə] N *Med (sickness)* náusea *f*

nauseate ['nɔ:zɪeɪt] VT *(disgust)* dar asco a

nauseating ['nɔ:zɪeɪtɪŋ] ADJ nauseabundo(a)

nautical ['nɔ:tɪkəl] ADJ náutico(a); **n. mile** milla marítima

naval ['neɪvəl] ADJ naval; **n. officer** oficial *mf* de marina; **n. power** potencia marítima *or* naval

Navarre [nə'vɑ:(r)] N Navarra

nave [neɪv] N *Archit* nave *f*

navel ['neɪvəl] N *Anat* ombligo *m*

navigate ['nævɪgeɪt] **1** VT *(river)* navegar por; *Naut (ship)* gobernar
2 VI navegar; *(in driving)* indicar la dirección

navigation [nævɪ'geɪʃən] N *Naut* navegación *f*

navigator ['nævɪgeɪtə(r)] N (**a**) *Naut* navegante *mf*, oficial *mf* de derrota (**b**) *Aut & Av* copiloto *mf*

navvy ['nævɪ] N *Br Fam* peón *m*

navy ['neɪvɪ] N marina *f*; **n. blue** azul marino

Nazi ['nɑ:tsɪ] ADJ & N nazi *(mf)*

Nazism ['nɑ:tsɪzəm] N nazismo *m*

NB, nb [en'bi:] *(abbr* **nota bene)** N.B.

neap [ni:p] N **n. (tide)** marea muerta

near [nɪə(r)] **1** ADJ *(in space)* cercano(a); *(in time)* próximo(a); **in the n. future** en un futuro próximo
2 ADV *(in space)* cerca; **that's n. enough** (ya) vale, está bien
3 PREP cerca de; **n. the end of the film** hacia el final de la película
4 VT acercarse a

nearby 1 ADJ ['nɪəbaɪ] cercano(a)
2 ADV [nɪə'baɪ] cerca

nearly ['nɪəlɪ] ADV casi; **we haven't n. enough** no alcanza ni con mucho

nearside ['nɪəsaɪd] N *Br Aut* lado *m* del copiloto

near-sighted [nɪə'saɪtɪd] ADJ miope

neat [ni:t] ADJ (**a**) *(room, habits etc)* ordenado(a); *(handwriting)* claro(a); *(appearance)* pulcro(a) (**b**) *(idea)* ingenioso(a) (**c**) *(whisky etc)* solo(a) (**d**) *US Fam (fine)* genial, fenomenal

neatly ['ni:tlɪ] ADV (**a**) *(carefully)* cuidadosamente (**b**) *(cleverly)* hábilmente

necessarily [nesɪ'serəlɪ] ADV necesariamente, por fuerza

necessary ['nesɪsərɪ] **1** ADJ (**a**) *(essential)* necesario(a); **if n.** si es preciso (**b**) *(unavoidable)* inevitable
2 N **the n.** lo necesario

necessitate [nɪ'sesɪteɪt] VT necesitar, exigir

necessity [nɪ'sesɪtɪ] N (**a**) *(need)* necesidad *f*; **out of n.** por necesidad (**b**) **necessities** *(articles)* necesidades *fpl*

neck [nek] N cuello *m*; *(of animal)* pescuezo *m*; **to stick one's n. out** arriesgarse

necklace ['neklɪs] N collar *m*

neckline ['neklaɪn] N *(of dress)* escote *m*

necktie ['nektaɪ] N *US* corbata *f*

nectar ['nektə(r)] N néctar *m*

nectarine ['nektəri:n] N nectarina *f*

née [neɪ] ADJ **n. Brown** de soltera Brown

need [ni:d] **1** N (**a**) *(necessity, requirement)* necesidad *f*; **there's no n. for you to do that** no hace falta que hagas eso (**b**) *(poverty)* indigencia *f*; **to be in n.** estar necesitado(a)
2 VT *(of person)* necesitar; **I n. to see him** tengo que verle; **you'll n. to take more money** te hará falta más dinero; **this work needs a lot of patience** este trabajo requiere mucha paciencia; *Ironic* **that's all I n.** sólo me faltaba eso
3 VAUX tener que, deber; **n. he go?** ¿tiene que ir?; **you needn't wait** no hace falta que esperes

> Cuando se emplea como verbo modal sólo existe una forma, y los auxiliares **do/does** no se usan: **he need only worry about himself**; **need she go?**; **it needn't matter**.

needle ['ni:dəl] N (**a**) *(for sewing, knitting)* aguja *f* (**b**) *Bot* hoja *f*

needless ['ni:dlɪs] ADJ innecesario(a); **n. to say** huelga decir

needlessly ['ni:dlɪslɪ] ADV innecesariamente

needlework ['ni:dəlwɜ:k] N *(sewing)* costura *f*; *(embroidery)* bordado *m*

needy ['ni:dɪ] ADJ (**needier, neediest**) necesitado(a)

negate [nɪ'geɪt] VT (**a**) *(deny)* negar (**b**) *(nullify)* anular

negative ['negətɪv] **1** ADJ negativo(a)
2 N (**a**) *Ling* negación *f* (**b**) *Phot* negativo *m*

neglect [nɪ'glekt] **1** VT (**a**) *(child, duty etc)* descuidar, desatender (**b**) **to n. to do sth** *(omit to do)* no hacer algo
2 N dejadez *f*

neglectful [nɪ'glektfʊl] ADJ descuidado(a), negligente

negligée ['neglɪʒeɪ] N salto m de cama

negligence ['neglɪdʒəns] N negligencia f, descuido m

negligent ['neglɪdʒənt] ADJ negligente, descuidado(a)

negligible ['neglɪdʒɪbəl] ADJ insignificante

negotiate [nɪ'gəʊʃɪeɪt] **1** VT (**a**) (contract) negociar (**b**) Fig (obstacle) salvar, franquear
2 VI negociar

negotiation [nɪgəʊʃɪ'eɪʃən] N negociación f

negro ['niːgrəʊ] N (pl negroes) negro(a) m,f

neigh [neɪ] **1** N relincho m
2 VI relinchar

neighbour, US **neighbor** ['neɪbə(r)] N vecino(a) m,f; Rel prójimo m

neighbourhood, US **neighborhood** ['neɪbəhʊd] N (district) vecindad f, barrio m; (people) vecindario m

neighbouring, US **neighboring** ['neɪbərɪŋ] ADJ vecino(a)

neither ['naɪðə(r), 'niːðə(r)] **1** ADJ & PRON ninguno de los dos/ninguna de las dos
2 ADV **n. ... nor** ni ... ni
3 CONJ tampoco; **she was not there and n. was her sister** ella no estaba, ni su hermana tampoco

neon ['niːɒn] N neón m; **n. light** luz f de neón

nephew ['nefjuː] N sobrino m

nerd [nɜːd] N Fam (**a**) (boring person) petardo(a) m,f, RP nerd mf (**b**) (as insult) bobo(a) m,f

nerve [nɜːv] N (**a**) Anat nervio m; **to get on sb's nerves** poner los nervios de punta a algn (**b**) (courage) valor m (**c**) Fam (cheek) cara f, descaro m; **what a n.!** ¡qué cara!

nerve-racking ['nɜːvrækɪŋ] ADJ crispante, exasperante

nervous ['nɜːvəs] ADJ (**a**) (of the nerve system) nervioso(a); **n. breakdown** depresión nerviosa (**b**) (apprehensive) nervioso(a), inquieto(a)

nest [nest] **1** N (of bird) nido m; (hen's) nidal m; (animal's) madriguera f; Fig **n. egg** ahorros mpl
2 VI (birds) anidar

nestle ['nesəl] **1** VT recostar
2 VI (settle comfortably) acomodarse

Net [net] N Fam Comput **the N.** (Internet) la Red; **N. user** internauta mf

net¹ [net] N red f; Br **n. curtains** visillos mpl

net² [net] **1** ADJ neto(a); **n. weight** peso neto
2 VT (earn) ganar neto

netball ['netbɔːl] N Sport baloncesto femenino

Netherlands ['neðələndz] NPL **the N.** los Países Bajos

netiquette ['netɪket] N Comput netiqueta f

netting ['netɪŋ] N redes fpl, malla f

nettle ['netəl] **1** N Bot ortiga f
2 VT Fam irritar

network ['netwɜːk] **1** N red f
2 VI (establish contacts) establecer contactos

neurosis [njʊ'rəʊsɪs] N neurosis f

neurotic [njʊ'rɒtɪk] ADJ & N neurótico(a) (m,f)

neuter ['njuːtə(r)] **1** ADJ neutro(a)
2 N Ling neutro m
3 VT (geld) castrar

neutral ['njuːtrəl] **1** ADJ neutro(a); Pol **to remain n.** permanecer neutral
2 N Aut punto muerto

neutrality [njuː'trælɪtɪ] N neutralidad f

neutralize ['njuːtrəlaɪz] VT neutralizar

neutron ['njuːtrɒn] N Phys neutrón m; **n. bomb** bomba f de neutrones

never ['nevə(r)] ADV nunca, jamás; **n. again** nunca (ja)más; Fam **n. mind** da igual, no importa

never-ending ['nevər'endɪŋ] ADJ sin fin, interminable

nevertheless [nevəðə'les] ADV sin embargo, no obstante

new [njuː] ADJ nuevo(a); **as good as n.** como nuevo; **n. moon** luna nueva; **N. Year** Año nuevo; **N. Year's Eve** Nochevieja f

newborn ['njuːbɔːn] ADJ recién nacido(a)

newcomer ['njuːkʌmə(r)] N recién llegado(a) m,f; (to job etc) nuevo(a) m,f

newfangled ['njuːfæŋgəld] ADJ novedoso(a)

newly ['njuːlɪ] ADV recién, recientemente

newlywed ['njuːlɪwed] N recién casado(a) m,f

news [njuːz] N SING noticias fpl; (TV programme) telediario m, Am noticiero m, Andes, RP noticioso m; **a piece of n.** una noticia; **n. agency** agencia f de información; US **n. in brief** avance informativo; **n. bulletin** boletín informativo; **n. summary** avance informativo

newsagent ['njuːzeɪdʒənt] N Br vendedor(a) m,f de periódicos

newsflash ['njuːzflæʃ] N noticia f de última hora

newsgroup ['njuːzgruːp] N Comput grupo m de noticias

newsletter ['njuːzletə(r)] N hoja informativa

newspaper ['njuːzpeɪpə(r)] N periódico m, diario m

newsprint ['njuːzprɪnt] N papel m de periódico

newsreader ['njuːzriːdə(r)] N Rad & TV presentador(a) m,f de los informativos

newsreel ['njuːzriːl] N noticiario m

news-stand ['njuːzstænd] N quiosco m de periódicos

newt [njuːt] N Zool tritón m

next [nekst] **1** ADJ (**a**) (in place) de al lado (**b**) (in time) próximo(a); **the n. day** el día siguiente; **n. Friday** el viernes que viene; **n. time** la próxima vez; **the week after n.** dentro de dos semanas (**c**) (in order) siguiente, próximo(a); **n. of kin** pariente m más cercano
2 ADV después, luego; **what shall we do n.?** ¿qué hacemos ahora?
3 PREP **n. to** al lado de, junto a; **n. to nothing** casi nada

next-door 1 ADJ ['neksdɔ:(r)] de al lado; **our n. neighbour** el vecino/la vecina de al lado
2 ADV [neks'dɔ:(r)] al lado

NGO [endʒi:'əʊ] N (*pl* **NGOs**) (*abbr* **non-governmental organization**) ONG *f*

NHS [eneɪtʃ'es] N *Br* (*abbr* **National Health Service**) = la sanidad pública británica

nib [nɪb] N plumilla *f*

nibble ['nɪbəl] VT & VI mordisquear

nice [naɪs] ADJ (**a**) (*person*) simpático(a), *Esp* majo(a), *RP* dulce; (*thing*) agradable; **n. and cool** fresquito(a); **to smell/taste n.** oler/saber bien (**b**) (*nice-looking*) bonito(a), *Am* lindo(a) (**c**) *Ironic* menudo(a)

nicely ['naɪslɪ] ADV muy bien

niche [ni:ʃ] N (**a**) *Archit* hornacina *f*, nicho *m* (**b**) *Fig* hueco *m*

nick [nɪk] **1** N (**a**) (*notch*) muesca *f*; (*cut*) herida pequeña; *Fam* **in the n. of time** en el momento preciso (**b**) *Br Fam* (*prison*) cárcel *f*, *Esp* trullo *m*, *Andes*, *RP* cana *f*, *Méx* bote *m*
2 VT *Br Fam* (**a**) (*steal*) afanar, *Esp* mangar (**b**) (*arrest*) detener, *Esp* trincar

nickel ['nɪkəl] N (**a**) (*metal*) níquel *m* (**b**) *US* moneda *f* de 5 centavos

nickname ['nɪkneɪm] **1** N apodo *m*
2 VT apodar

nicotine ['nɪkəti:n] N nicotina *f*

niece [ni:s] N sobrina *f*

nifty ['nɪftɪ] ADJ (**niftier, niftiest**) (**a**) (*quick*) rápido(a); (*agile*) ágil (**b**) (*ingenious*) ingenioso(a)

Nigeria [naɪ'dʒɪərɪə] N Nigeria

nigger ['nɪgə(r)] N *Fam Pej* = término generalmente ofensivo para referirse a un negro, *RP* grone *m*

niggling ['nɪgəlɪŋ] ADJ (*trifling*) insignificante; (*irritating*) molesto(a)

night [naɪt] N noche *f*; **at n.** de noche; **at twelve o'clock at n.** a las doce de la noche; **last n.** anoche; **n. life** vida nocturna; **n. school** escuela nocturna; **n. shift** turno *m* de noche; *US* **n. stand** *or* **table** mesita *f or* mesilla *f* de noche

nightclub ['naɪtklʌb] N sala *f* de fiestas; (*disco*) discoteca *f*

nightdress ['naɪtdres] N camisón *m*

nightfall ['naɪtfɔ:l] N anochecer *m*

nightgown ['naɪtgaʊn] N camisón *m*

nightie ['naɪtɪ] N *Fam* camisón *m*

nightingale ['naɪtɪŋgeɪl] N ruiseñor *m*

nightly ['naɪtlɪ] **1** ADJ de cada noche
2 ADV todas las noches

nightmare ['naɪtmeə(r)] N pesadilla *f*

nightshade ['naɪtʃeɪd] N *Bot* **deadly n.** belladona *f*

night-time ['naɪttaɪm] N noche *f*; **at n.** por la noche

nil [nɪl] N nada *f*; *Sport* cero *m*; *Br* **two n.** dos a cero

Nile [naɪl] N **the N.** el Nilo

nimble ['nɪmbəl] ADJ ágil, rápido(a)

nine [naɪn] ADJ & N nueve (*m inv*)

nineteen [naɪn'ti:n] ADJ & N diecinueve (*m inv*)

nineteenth [naɪn'ti:nθ] ADJ decimonoveno(a)

ninety ['naɪntɪ] ADJ & N noventa (*m inv*)

ninth [naɪnθ] **1** ADJ & N noveno(a) (*m,f*)
2 N (*fraction*) noveno *m*

nip [nɪp] **1** VT (**a**) (*pinch*) pellizcar (**b**) (*bite*) morder; **to n. sth in the bud** cortar algo de raíz
2 N (**a**) (*pinch*) pellizco *m* (**b**) (*bite*) mordisco *m*

nipple ['nɪpəl] N (**a**) *Anat* (*female*) pezón *m*; (*male*) tetilla *f* (**b**) *US* (*on baby's bottle*) tetilla *f*, tetina *f*

nippy ['nɪpɪ] ADJ (**nippier, nippiest**) *Fam* (**a**) *Br* (*quick*) rápido(a) (**b**) (*cold*) fresquito(a)

nit [nɪt] N (*insect*) piojo *m*; (*insect's egg*) liendre *f*

nitrogen ['naɪtrədʒən] N *Chem* nitrógeno *m*

nitroglycerin(e) [naɪtrəʊ'glɪsəri:n] N *Chem* nitroglicerina *f*

nitty-gritty [nɪtɪ'grɪtɪ] N *Fam* **to get down to the n.** ir al grano

nitwit ['nɪtwɪt] N *Fam* imbécil *mf*

no [nəʊ] **1** ADV no; **come here! – no!** ¡ven aquí! – ¡no!; **no longer** ya no; **no less than** no menos de
2 ADJ ninguno(a); **she has no children** no tiene hijos; **I have no idea** no tengo (ni) idea; **it's no good** *or* **use** no vale la pena; *Aut* **no parking** (*sign*) prohibido aparcar; *Fam* **no way!** ¡ni hablar!
3 N no *m*; **to say no** decir que no

no. (*pl* **nos.**) (*abbr* **number**) nº, núm.

nobility [nəʊ'bɪlɪtɪ] N nobleza *f*

noble ['nəʊbəl] ADJ noble

nobleman ['nəʊbəlmən] N noble *m*

noblewoman ['nəʊbəlwʊmən] N noble *f*

nobody ['nəʊbədɪ] **1** PRON nadie; **there was n. there** no había nadie; **n. else** nadie más
2 N nadie *m*; **he's a n.** es un don nadie

no-brainer ['nəʊ'breɪnə(r)] N *Fam* **it's a n.** está tirado

nocturnal [nɒk'tɜ:nəl] ADJ nocturno(a)

nod [nɒd] **1** N (*of greeting*) saludo *m* (con la cabeza); (*of agreement*) señal *f* de asentimiento
2 VI (*greet*) saludar con la cabeza; (*agree*) asentir con la cabeza
3 VT **to n. one's head** inclinar la cabeza
▸ **nod off** VI dormirse

no-go ['nəʊ'gəʊ] ADJ **n. area** zona prohibida

noise [nɔɪz] N ruido *m*; **to make a n.** hacer ruido

noiseless ['nɔɪzlɪs] ADJ silencioso(a), sin ruido

noisy ['nɔɪzɪ] ADJ (**noisier, noisiest**) ruidoso(a)

nomad ['nəʊmæd] N nómada *mf*

no-man's-land ['nəʊmænzlænd] N tierra *f* de nadie

nominal ['nɒmɪnəl] ADJ nominal; (*payment, rent*) simbólico(a)

nominate ['nɒmɪneɪt] VT (**a**) *(propose)* designar, proponer (**b**) *(appoint)* nombrar

nomination [nɒmɪ'neɪʃən] N (**a**) *(proposal)* propuesta *f* (**b**) *(appointment)* nombramiento *m*

nominative ['nɒmɪnətɪv] N nominativo *m*

nominee [nɒmɪ'ni:] N persona propuesta

non- [nɒn] PREF no

non-aggression [nɒnə'greʃən] N *Pol* no agresión *f*; **n. pact** pacto *m* de no agresión

non-alcoholic [nɒnælkə'hɒlɪk] ADJ sin alcohol

non-aligned [nɒnə'laɪnd] ADJ *Pol* no alineado(a)

nonchalant ['nɒnʃələnt] ADJ *(indifferent)* indiferente; *(calm)* imperturbable, impasible

noncommittal [nɒnkə'mɪtəl] ADJ *(person)* evasivo(a); *(answer)* que no compromete (a nada)

nonconformist [nɒnkən'fɔ:mɪst] N inconformista *mf*

nondescript [*Br* 'nɒndɪskrɪpt, *US* nɒndɪ'skrɪpt] ADJ indescriptible; *(uninteresting)* soso(a)

none [nʌn] 1 PRON ninguno(a); **I know n. of them** no conozco a ninguno de ellos; **n. at all** nada en absoluto; **n. other than ...** nada menos que ...
2 ADV de ningún modo; **she's n. the worse for it** no se ha visto afectada *or* perjudicada por ello; **n. too soon** a buena hora

nonentity [nɒ'nentɪtɪ] N *(person)* cero *m* a la izquierda

nonetheless [nʌnðə'les] ADV no obstante, sin embargo

nonevent [nɒnɪ'vent] N fracaso *m*

nonexistent [nɒnɪg'zɪstənt] ADJ inexistente

nonfiction [nɒn'fɪkʃən] N no ficción *f*

no-nonsense ['nəʊ'nɒnsəns] ADJ *(person)* recto(a), serio(a)

nonplussed [nɒn'plʌst] ADJ perplejo(a)

non-profit(-making) [nɒn'prɒfɪt(meɪkɪŋ)] ADJ sin fines lucrativos

nonreturnable [nɒnrɪ'tɜ:nəbəl] ADJ no retornable

nonsense ['nɒnsəns] N tonterías *fpl*, disparates *mpl*; **that's n.** eso es absurdo

nonsmoker [nɒn'sməʊkə(r)] N no fumador(a) *m,f*, persona *f* que no fuma

nonstarter [nɒn'stɑ:tə(r)] N *Fig* **to be a n.** *(plan)* ser irrealizable

nonstick [nɒn'stɪk] ADJ antiadherente

nonstop [nɒn'stɒp] 1 ADJ sin parar; *(train)* directo(a)
2 ADV sin parar

noodles ['nu:dəlz] NPL *Culin* tallarines *mpl* *(chinos)*

nook [nʊk] N recoveco *m*, rincón *m*

noon [nu:n] N mediodía *m*; **at n.** a mediodía

no one ['nəʊwʌn] PRON nadie; **n. came** no vino nadie

noose [nu:s] N lazo *m*; *(hangman's)* soga *f*

nor [nɔ:(r)] CONJ ni, ni tampoco; **neither ... n.** ni ... ni; **neither you n. I** ni tú ni yo; **n. do I** (ni) yo tampoco

norm [nɔ:m] N norma *f*

normal ['nɔ:məl] ADJ normal

normality [nɔ:'mælɪtɪ], *US* **normalcy** ['nɔ:məlsɪ] N normalidad *f*

normally ['nɔ:məlɪ] ADV normalmente

Normandy ['nɔ:məndɪ] N Normandía

north [nɔ:θ] 1 N norte *m*; **the N.** el norte; **N. America** América del Norte, Norteamérica; **N. Korea** Corea del Norte; **N. Pole** Polo *m* Norte
2 ADV hacia el norte, al norte
3 ADJ del norte; **n. wind** viento *m* del norte

northeast [nɔ:θ'i:st] N nor(d)este *m*

northerly ['nɔ:ðəlɪ] ADJ norte, del norte

northern ['nɔ:ðən] ADJ del norte, septentrional; **n. hemisphere** hemisferio *m* norte; **N. Ireland** Irlanda del Norte

northerner ['nɔ:ðənə(r)] N norteño(a) *m,f*

northward ['nɔ:θwəd] ADJ & ADV hacia el norte

northwest [nɔ:θ'west] N noroeste *m*

Norway ['nɔ:weɪ] N Noruega

Norwegian [nɔ:'wi:dʒən] 1 ADJ noruego(a)
2 N (**a**) *(person)* noruego(a) *m,f* (**b**) *(language)* noruego *m*

nose [nəʊz] N (**a**) *(of person)* nariz *f*; *(of animal)* hocico *m* (**b**) *(sense of smell)* olfato *m* (**c**) *(of car, plane)* morro *m*

▶ **nose about, nose around** VI curiosear

nosebleed ['nəʊzbli:d] N hemorragia *f* nasal

nosedive ['nəʊzdaɪv] *Av* 1 N *Esp* picado *m*, *Am* picada *f*
2 VI hacer *Esp* un picado *or Am* una picada

no-smoking [nəʊ'sməʊkɪŋ] ADJ *(carriage, area)* de *or* para no fumadores

nostalgia [nɒ'stældʒɪə] N nostalgia *f*

nostalgic [nɒ'stældʒɪk] ADJ nostálgico(a)

nostril ['nɒstrɪl] N *Anat* orificio *m* nasal

nosy ['nəʊzɪ] ADJ (**nosier, nosiest**) *Fam* entrometido(a)

not [nɒt] ADV no; **he's n. in today** hoy no está; **n. at all** en absoluto; **thank you – n. at all** gracias – no hay de qué; **n. too well** bastante mal; *Fam* **n. likely!** ¡ni hablar!

> En el inglés hablado, y en el escrito en estilo coloquial, **not** se contrae después de verbos modales y auxiliares.

notable ['nəʊtəbəl] ADJ notable

notably ['nəʊtəblɪ] ADV notablemente

notary ['nəʊtərɪ] N *Jur* **n. (public)** notario(a) *m,f*, *Am* escribano(a) *m,f*

notch [nɒtʃ] N muesca *f*; *(cut)* corte *m*

▶ **notch up** VT SEP *Fig* **to n. up a victory** apuntarse una victoria

note [nəʊt] 1 N (**a**) *Mus* nota *f* (**b**) *(on paper)* nota *f* (**c**) **to take n. of** *(notice)* prestar atención a (**d**) *esp Br (banknote)* billete *m* (de banco) (**e**) **notes** apuntes *mpl*; **to take n.** tomar apuntes

2 VT (**a**) *(write down)* apuntar, anotar (**b**) *(notice)* notar, fijarse en

notebook ['nəʊtbʊk] N (**a**) cuaderno *m*, libreta *f* (**b**) *Comput Esp* ordenador *m* or *Am* computadora *f* portátil

noted ['nəʊtɪd] ADJ notable, célebre

notepad ['nəʊtpæd] N bloc *m* de notas

notepaper ['nəʊtpeɪpə(r)] N papel *m* de carta

noteworthy ['nəʊtwɜːðɪ] ADJ digno(a) de mención

nothing ['nʌθɪŋ] **1** N nada; **I saw n.** no vi nada; **for n.** *(free of charge)* gratis; **it's n.** no es nada; **it's n. to do with you** no tiene nada que ver contigo; **n. else** nada más; *Fam* **n. much** poca cosa

2 ADV **she looks n. like her sister** no se parece en nada a su hermana

notice ['nəʊtɪs] **1** N (**a**) *(warning)* aviso *m*; **he gave a month's n.** presentó la dimisión con un mes de antelación; **at short n.** con poca antelación; **until further n.** hasta nuevo aviso; **without n.** sin previo aviso (**b**) *(attention)* atención *f*; **to take no n. of sth** no hacer caso de algo; **to take n. of sth** prestar atención a algo; **to come to one's n.** llegar al conocimiento de uno (**c**) *(in newspaper etc)* anuncio *m* (**d**) *(sign)* letrero *m*, aviso *m*

2 VT darse cuenta de, notar

> Note that the Spanish word **noticia** is a false friend and is never a translation for the English word **notice**. In Spanish **noticia** means "(piece of) news".

noticeable ['nəʊtɪsəbəl] ADJ que se nota, evidente

noticeboard ['nəʊtɪsbɔːd] N *Br* tablón *m* de anuncios

notification [nəʊtɪfɪ'keɪʃən] N aviso *m*

notify ['nəʊtɪfaɪ] VT avisar

notion ['nəʊʃən] N (**a**) *(idea, concept)* idea *f*, noción *f* (**b**) *(whim)* capricho *m*

notorious [nəʊ'tɔːrɪəs] ADJ *Pej* tristemente célebre

> Note that the Spanish word **notorio** is a false friend and is never a translation for the English word **notorious**. In Spanish **notorio** means both "obvious" and "famous, well-known".

notwithstanding [nɒtwɪθ'stændɪŋ] **1** PREP a pesar de

2 ADV sin embargo, no obstante

nougat ['nuːgɑː] N turrón blando

nought [nɔːt] N cero *m*

noun [naʊn] N nombre *m*, sustantivo *m*

nourish ['nʌrɪʃ] VT nutrir; *Fig (hopes)* abrigar

nourishing ['nʌrɪʃɪŋ] ADJ nutritivo(a)

nourishment ['nʌrɪʃmənt] N alimentación *f*, nutrición *f*

novel¹ ['nɒvəl] N novela *f*

novel² ['nɒvəl] ADJ original, novedoso(a)

novelist ['nɒvəlɪst] N novelista *mf*

novelty ['nɒvəltɪ] N novedad *f*

November [nəʊ'vembə(r)] N noviembre *m*

novice ['nɒvɪs] N (**a**) *(beginner)* novato(a) *m,f*, principiante *mf* (**b**) *Rel* novicio(a) *m,f*

now [naʊ] **1** ADV (**a**) *(at this moment)* ahora; **just n., right n.** ahora mismo; **from n. on** de ahora en adelante; **n. and then, n. and again** de vez en cuando (**b**) *(for events in past)* entonces (**c**) *(at present, these days)* actualmente, hoy (en) día (**d**) *(not related to time)* **n. (then)** ahora bien; **n., n.!** ¡vamos!, ¡ya está bien!

2 CONJ **n. (that)** ahora que, ya que

3 N until **n.** hasta ahora; **he'll be home by n.** ya habrá llegado a casa

nowadays ['naʊədeɪz] ADV hoy (en) día, actualmente

nowhere ['nəʊweə(r)] ADV en ninguna parte; **that will get you n.** eso no te servirá de nada; **it's n. near ready** no está preparado, ni mucho menos

noxious ['nɒkʃəs] ADJ nocivo(a)

nozzle ['nɒzəl] N boca *f*, boquilla *f*

nuance ['njuːɑːns] N matiz *m*

nub [nʌb] N **the n. of the matter** el quid de la cuestión

nuclear ['njuːklɪə(r)] ADJ nuclear; **n. arms** *fpl* nucleares; **n. power** energía *f* nuclear; **n. power station** central *f* nuclear

nucleus ['njuːklɪəs] N núcleo *m*

nude [njuːd] **1** ADJ desnudo(a)

2 N *Art & Phot* desnudo *m*; **in the n.** al desnudo

nudge [nʌdʒ] **1** VT dar un codazo a

2 N codazo *m*

nudist ['njuːdɪst] ADJ & N nudista *(mf)*

nudity ['njuːdɪtɪ] N desnudez *f*

nugget ['nʌgɪt] N *Min* pepita *f*; **gold n.** pepita de oro

nuisance ['njuːsəns] N (**a**) *(annoying thing)* molestia *f*, pesadez *f*; **what a n.!** ¡qué lata! (**b**) *(person)* pesado(a) *m,f*

nuke [njuːk] *Fam* **1** N *(bomb)* bomba *f* nuclear or atómica

2 VT atacar con armas nucleares

null [nʌl] ADJ nulo(a); **n. and void** nulo(a) y sin valor

nullify ['nʌlɪfaɪ] VT anular

numb [nʌm] **1** ADJ *(without feeling)* entumecido(a); *Fig* paralizado(a); **n. with fear** paralizado(a) de miedo

2 VT *(with cold)* entumecer (de frío); *(with anaesthetic)* adormecer

number ['nʌmbə(r)] **1** N (**a**) *(figure)* número *m*; *Tel* **have you got my n.?** ¿tienes mi (número de) teléfono? (**b**) *(quantity)* **a n. of people** varias personas (**c**) *Br (of car)* matrícula *f*; **n. plate** (placa *f* de la) matrícula *f*

2 VT (**a**) *(put a number on)* numerar (**b**) *(count)* contar

numeral ['njuːmərəl] N número *m*, cifra *f*

numerate ['njuːmərət] ADJ **to be n.** tener un conocimiento básico de matemáticas

numerical [njuːˈmerɪkəl] ADJ numérico(a)

numerically [njuːˈmerɪkəlɪ] ADV numéricamente

numerous ['njuːmərəs] ADJ numeroso(a)

numismatics [njuːmɪzˈmætɪks] N SING numismática *f*

nun [nʌn] N monja *f*

nuptial ['nʌpʃəl] ADJ nupcial

nurse [nɜːs] **1** N enfermera *f*; *(male)* enfermero *m*
2 VT (**a**) *(look after)* cuidar, atender (**b**) *(baby)* acunar (**c**) *(suckle)* amamantar (**d**) *Fig (grudge etc)* guardar

nursery ['nɜːsərɪ] N (**a**) *(institution)* guardería *f*; **n. school** jardín *m* de infancia (**b**) *(in house)* cuarto *m* de los niños; **n. rhyme** poema *m* infantil (**c**) *(garden centre)* vivero *m*

nursing ['nɜːsɪŋ] N **n. home** *Br (where children are born)* maternidad *f*; *(for old people, war veterans)* residencia *f*

nurture ['nɜːtʃə(r)] VT *(animal)* alimentar; *(feelings)* abrigar

nut [nʌt] N (**a**) *(fruit)* fruto seco (**b**) *Fam (head)* coco *m* (**c**) *Fam (mad person)* chiflado(a) *m,f*, chalado(a) *m,f* (**d**) *Tech* tuerca *f*

nutcase ['nʌtkeɪs] N *Fam* chalado(a) *m,f*

nutcracker ['nʌtkrækə(r)] N cascanueces *m inv*

nutmeg ['nʌtmeg] N nuez moscada

nutrition [njuːˈtrɪʃən] N nutrición *f*

nutritious [njuːˈtrɪʃəs] ADJ nutritivo(a), alimenticio(a)

nuts [nʌts] ADJ *Fam* chiflado(a), *Esp* majara; **to be n.** estar chiflado(a) *or Esp* majara

nutshell ['nʌtʃel] N cáscara *f*; *Fig* **in a n.** en pocas palabras

nylon ['naɪlɒn] **1** N (**a**) *(textile)* nilón *m*, nailon *m* (**b**) **nylons** medias *fpl* de nilón
2 ADJ de nilón

nymph [nɪmf] N ninfa *f*

nymphomaniac [nɪmfəˈmeɪnɪæk] N ninfómana *f*

O

O, o [əʊ] N (**a**) *(the letter)* O, o f (**b**) *Math & Tel* cero m

oaf [əʊf] N tarugo m, zote m

oak [əʊk] N roble m

OAP [əʊeɪˈpiː] N *Br* (*abbr* **old-age pensioner**) pensionista mf, jubilado(a) m,f

oar [ɔː(r)] N remo m

oarsman [ˈɔːzmən] N remero m

oasis [əʊˈeɪsɪs] N (*pl* **oases** [əʊˈeɪsiːz]) oasis m inv

oat [əʊt] N avena f; **rolled oats** copos mpl de avena

oath [əʊθ] N (*pl* **oaths** [əʊðz]) (**a**) *Jur* juramento m; **to take an o.** prestar juramento (**b**) *(swearword)* palabrota f

oatmeal [ˈəʊtmiːl] N harina f de avena

obedience [əˈbiːdɪəns] N obediencia f

obedient [əˈbiːdɪənt] ADJ obediente

obese [əʊˈbiːs] ADJ obeso(a)

obey [əˈbeɪ] VT obedecer; *(law)* cumplir con

obituary [əˈbɪtjʊərɪ] N necrología f

object¹ [ˈɒbdʒɪkt] N (**a**) *(thing)* objeto m (**b**) *(aim, purpose)* fin m, objetivo m (**c**) *(obstacle)* inconveniente m (**d**) *Ling* complemento m

object² [əbˈdʒekt] VI oponerse (**to** a); **do you o. to my smoking?** ¿le molesta que fume?

objection [əbˈdʒekʃən] N (**a**) *(protest)* objeción f (**b**) *(drawback)* inconveniente m; **provided there's no o.** si no hay inconveniente

objectionable [əbˈdʒekʃənəbəl] ADJ *(unacceptable)* inaceptable; *(unpleasant)* ofensivo(a)

objective [əbˈdʒektɪv] **1** ADJ objetivo(a) **2** N objetivo m

objector [əbˈdʒektə(r)] N objetor(a) m,f

obligation [ɒblɪˈgeɪʃən] N obligación f; **to be under an o. to sb** estarle muy agradecido(a) a algn

obligatory [ɒˈblɪgətərɪ] ADJ obligatorio(a)

oblige [əˈblaɪdʒ] VT (**a**) *(compel)* obligar; **I'm obliged to do it** me veo obligado(a) a hacerlo (**b**) *(do a favour for)* hacer un favor a (**c**) **to be obliged** *(grateful)* estar agradecido(a)

obliging [əˈblaɪdʒɪŋ] ADJ solícito(a)

oblique [əˈbliːk] ADJ oblicuo(a), inclinado(a); *Fig* **an o. reference** una alusión indirecta

obliterate [əˈblɪtəreɪt] VT (**a**) *(memory)* borrar (**b**) *(species, race)* eliminar; *(village)* arrasar

oblivion [əˈblɪvɪən] N olvido m; **to sink into o.** caer en el olvido

oblivious [əˈblɪvɪəs] ADJ inconsciente

oblong [ˈɒblɒŋ] **1** ADJ oblongo(a) **2** N rectángulo m

obnoxious [əbˈnɒkʃəs] ADJ repugnante

oboe [ˈəʊbəʊ] N oboe m

obscene [əbˈsiːn] ADJ obsceno(a)

obscenity [əbˈsenɪtɪ] N obscenidad f

obscure [əbˈskjʊə(r)] **1** ADJ (**a**) *(not clear)* oscuro(a); *(vague)* vago(a) (**b**) *(little-known) (author, poet etc)* desconocido(a) **2** VT *(truth)* ocultar

obsequious [əbˈsiːkwɪəs] ADJ servil

observance [əbˈzɜːvəns] N (**a**) *(of law, custom)* observancia f (**b**) *Rel* **observances** prácticas religiosas

observant [əbˈzɜːvənt] ADJ observador(a)

observation [ɒbzəˈveɪʃən] N observación f; *(surveillance)* vigilancia f

observatory [əbˈzɜːvətərɪ] N observatorio m

observe [əbˈzɜːv] VT (**a**) *(watch)* observar; *(in surveillance)* vigilar (**b**) *(remark)* advertir (**c**) *(law, customs)* observar, acatar

observer [əbˈzɜːvə(r)] N observador(a) m,f

obsess [əbˈses] VT obsesionar; **to be obsessed (with** *or* **by)** estar obsesionado(a) (con)

obsession [əbˈseʃən] N obsesión f

obsessive [əbˈsesɪv] ADJ obsesivo(a)

obsolete [ˈɒbsəliːt, ɒbsəˈliːt] ADJ obsoleto(a)

obstacle [ˈɒbstəkəl] N obstáculo m; *Fig* impedimento m; **o. race** carrera f de obstáculos

obstinate [ˈɒbstɪnɪt] ADJ (**a**) *(person)* obstinado(a), terco(a) (**b**) *(pain)* persistente

obstruct [əbˈstrʌkt] VT (**a**) *(block) (road, pipe)* obstruir, bloquear; *(view)* impedir (**b**) *(hinder)* estorbar; *(progress)* dificultar

obstruction [əbˈstrʌkʃən] N (**a**) *(action)* obstrucción f (**b**) *(hindrance)* obstáculo m

obtain [əbˈteɪn] VT obtener, conseguir

obtainable [əbˈteɪnəbəl] ADJ obtenible

obtrusive [əbˈtruːsɪv] ADJ (**a**) *(interfering)* entrometido(a) (**b**) *(noticeable)* llamativo(a)

obtuse [əbˈtjuːs] ADJ obtuso(a)

obviate [ˈɒbvɪeɪt] VT *Fml* obviar

obvious [ˈɒbvɪəs] ADJ obvio(a), evidente

obviously [ˈɒbvɪəslɪ] ADV evidentemente; **o.!** ¡claro!, ¡por supuesto!

occasion [əˈkeɪʒən] **1** N (**a**) *(time)* ocasión f; **on o.** de vez en cuando (**b**) *(event)* acontecí-

miento *m*; **on the o. of** con ocasión de (**c**) *Fml (cause)* motivo *m*
  2 VT *Fml* ocasionar

occasional [ə'keɪʒənəl] ADJ esporádico(a), eventual

occasionally [ə'keɪʒənəlɪ] ADV de vez en cuando

occupant ['ɒkjʊpənt] N ocupante *mf*; *(tenant)* inquilino(a) *m,f*

occupation [ɒkjʊ'peɪʃən] N (**a**) *(job, profession)* profesión *f*, ocupación *f* (**b**) *(pastime)* pasatiempo *m* (**c**) *(of building, house, country)* ocupación *f*

occupational [ɒkjʊ'peɪʃənəl] ADJ profesional, laboral; **o. hazard** gaje *m* del oficio

occupied ['ɒkjʊpaɪd] ADJ ocupado(a)

occupier ['ɒkjʊpaɪə(r)] N *Br* ocupante *mf*; *(tenant)* inquilino(a) *m,f*

occupy ['ɒkjʊpaɪ] VT (**a**) *(live in)* ocupar, habitar (**b**) *(time)* pasar; **to o. one's time in doing sth** dedicar su tiempo a hacer algo (**c**) *(building, factory etc in protest)* tomar posesión de

occur [ə'kɜː(r)] VI (**a**) *(event)* suceder, acaecer; *(change)* producirse (**b**) *(be found)* encontrarse (**c**) **it occurred to me that ...** se me ocurrió que ...

occurrence [ə'kʌrəns] N suceso *m*, incidencia *f*

> Note that the Spanish word **ocurrencia** is a false friend and is never a translation for the English word **occurrence**. In Spanish **ocurrencia** means "witty remark" and "bright idea".

ocean ['əʊʃən] N océano *m*

ocean-going ['əʊʃəngəʊɪŋ] ADJ de alta mar

ochre, *US* **ocher** ['əʊkə(r)] **1** N ocre *m*; **red o.** almagre *m*; **yellow o.** ocre amarillo
  2 ADJ (de color) ocre

o'clock [ə'klɒk] ADV **(it's) one o.** (es) la una; **(it's) two o.** (son) las dos

octave ['ɒktɪv] N octava *f*

October [ɒk'təʊbə(r)] N octubre *m*

octogenarian [ɒktəʊdʒɪ'neərɪən] ADJ & N octogenario(a) *(m,f)*

octopus ['ɒktəpəs] N pulpo *m*

OD [əʊ'diː] *(pt & pp* **OD'd** *or* **OD'ed)** VI *Fam* meterse una sobredosis

odd [ɒd] **1** ADJ (**a**) *(strange)* raro(a), extraño(a) (**b**) *(occasional)* esporádico(a); **o. job** trabajillo *m* (**c**) **an o. number** *(not even)* un impar (**d**) *(unpaired)* desparejado(a); **an o. sock** un calcetín suelto
  2 ADV y pico; **twenty o. people** veinte y pico *or* y tantas personas

oddity ['ɒdɪtɪ] N (**a**) *(thing)* curiosidad *f*; *(person)* estrafalario(a) *m,f* (**b**) *(quality)* rareza *f*

oddly ['ɒdlɪ] ADV extrañamente; **o. enough** por extraño que parezca

odds [ɒdz] NPL (**a**) *(chances)* probabilidades *fpl*; **the o. are that ...** lo más probable es que ... *(+ subj)* (**b**) *(in betting)* puntos *mpl* de ventaja; **the o. are five to one** las apuestas están cinco a uno (**c**) *Br* **it makes no o.** da lo mismo (**d**) **at o. with sb** *(in disagreement)* reñido(a) con algn (**e**) **o. and ends** *(small things)* cositas *fpl*; *(trinkets)* chucherías *fpl*

odds-on ['ɒdzɒn] ADJ seguro(a); **o. favourite** *(horse)* caballo favorito

ode [əʊd] N oda *f*

odious ['əʊdɪəs] ADJ repugnante

odour, *US* **odor** ['əʊdə(r)] N olor *m*; *(fragrance)* perfume *m*

OECD [əʊiːsiː'diː] N *(abbr* **Organization for Economic Co-operation and Development)** OCDE *f*

of [ɒv, *unstressed* əv] PREP de; **a friend of mine** un amigo mío; **a bottle of wine** una botella de vino; **a dress (made) of silk** un vestido de seda; **that's very kind of you** es usted muy amable; **there are four of us** somos cuatro; **two of them** dos de ellos; **south of** al sur de; **the 7th of November** el 7 de noviembre

off [ɒf] **1** PREP de; **she fell o. her horse** se cayó del caballo; **a few kilometres o. the coast** a unos kilómetros de la costa; **I'm o. wine** he perdido el gusto al vino
  2 ADV (**a**) **he turned o. the radio** apagó la radio (**b**) *(absent)* fuera; **I have a day o.** tengo un día libre; **to be o. sick** estar de baja por enfermedad (**c**) *(distant)* **6 miles o.** a 6 millas (**d**) **I'm o. to London** me voy a Londres (**e**) **10 percent o.** un descuento del 10 por ciento (**f**) **o. and on** de vez en cuando
  3 ADJ (**a**) *(gas etc)* apagado(a); *(water)* cortado(a) (**b**) *(cancelled)* cancelado(a) (**c**) *(low)* bajo(a); *(unsatisfactory)* malo(a); **on the o. chance** por si acaso; **the o. season** la temporada baja (**d**) *(gone bad) (meat, fish)* malo(a), pasado(a); *(milk)* agrio(a)

offal ['ɒfəl] N *(of chicken etc)* menudillos *mpl*; *(of cattle, pigs)* asaduras *fpl*

off-colour, *US* **off-color** ['ɒf'kʌlə(r)] ADJ (**a**) *Br (ill)* indispuesto(a) (**b**) *(joke, story)* indecente

offence [ə'fens] N (**a**) *Jur* delito *m* (**b**) *(insult)* ofensa *f*; **to give o.** ofender; **to take o. at sth** ofenderse por algo (**c**) *Mil (attack)* ofensiva *f*

offend [ə'fend] VT ofender

offender [ə'fendə(r)] N *(criminal)* delincuente *mf*

offense [ə'fens] N *US* = **offence**

offensive [ə'fensɪv] **1** ADJ (**a**) *(insulting)* ofensivo(a) (**b**) *(repulsive)* repugnante
  2 N *Mil* ofensiva *f*; **to be on the o.** estar a la ofensiva

offer ['ɒfə(r)] **1** VT ofrecer; **to o. to do a job** ofrecerse para hacer un trabajo
  2 N oferta *f*; **on o.** *(reduced)* de oferta; *(available)* disponible; **o. of marriage** proposición *f* de matrimonio

offering ['ɒfərɪŋ] N (**a**) *(thing presented)* entrega *f* (**b**) *Rel* ofrenda *f*

offhand 1 ADJ ['ɒfhænd] *(abrupt)* brusco(a); *(inconsiderate)* descortés

2 ADV [ɒf'hænd] **I don't know o.** así sin pensarlo, no lo sé

office ['ɒfɪs] N (**a**) *(room)* despacho *m*; *(building)* oficina *f*; *(of lawyer)* despacho, bufete *m*; *US (of doctor, dentist)* consulta *f*; **o. hours** horas *fpl* de oficina (**b**) *Br Pol* ministerio *m* (**c**) *US (federal agency)* agencia *f* gubernamental (**d**) *(position)* cargo *m* (**e**) *Pol* **to be in o.** estar en el poder

officer ['ɒfɪsə(r)] N (**a**) *Mil* oficial *mf* (**b**) *(police)* **o.** agente *mf* de policía (**c**) *(government official)* funcionario(a) *m,f* (**d**) *(of company, society)* director(a) *m,f*

official [ə'fɪʃəl] **1** ADJ oficial

2 N funcionario(a) *m,f*

officially [ə'fɪʃəlɪ] ADV oficialmente

officiate [ə'fɪʃɪeɪt] VI (**a**) *(act in official capacity)* oficiar; **to o. as** ejercer funciones de (**b**) *Rel* oficiar

officious [ə'fɪʃəs] ADJ *Pej* excesivamente celoso(a) *or* diligente

> Note that the Spanish word **oficioso** is a false friend and is never a translation for the English word **officious**. In Spanish, **oficioso** means "unofficial".

off-licence ['ɒflaɪsəns] N *Br* tienda *f* de bebidas alcohólicas

off-line ['ɒflaɪn] ADJ *Comput* desconectado(a)

off-peak [ɒf'piːk] ADJ *(flight)* de temporada baja; *(rate)* de fuera de las horas punta

off-putting ['ɒfpʊtɪŋ] ADJ *Br Fam* desconcertante

offset [ɒf'set] VT *(pt & pp offset)* *(balance out)* compensar

offshoot ['ɒfʃuːt] N (**a**) *Bot* renuevo *m* (**b**) *Fig (of organization)* ramificación *f*

offshore ['ɒf'ʃɔː(r)] ADJ (**a**) *(breeze etc)* terral (**b**) *(oil rig)* costa afuera (**c**) *(overseas)* en el extranjero; **o. investment** inversión *f* en el extranjero

offside 1 ADV [ɒf'saɪd] *Ftb* fuera de juego

2 N ['ɒfsaɪd] *Aut (with left-hand drive)* lado derecho; *(with right-hand drive)* lado izquierdo

offspring ['ɒfsprɪŋ] N *(pl offspring)* *(child)* vástago *m*; *(children)* progenitura *f*

offstage 1 ADV [ɒf'steɪdʒ] fuera del escenario

2 ADJ ['ɒfsteɪdʒ] de fuera del escenario

often ['ɒfən, 'ɒftən] ADV a menudo, con frecuencia; **every so o.** de vez en cuando

ogle ['əʊgəl] VT & VI **to o. (at) sb** comerse a algn con los ojos

oh [əʊ] INTERJ ¡oh!, ¡ay!; **oh, my God!** ¡Dios mío!

oil [ɔɪl] **1** N (**a**) *(for cooking, lubricating)* aceite *m*; **o. lamp** lámpara *f* de aceite, quinqué *m*; **o. slick** mancha *f* de aceite (**b**) *(petroleum)* petróleo *m*; **o. rig** plataforma petrolera; **o.**

tanker petrolero *m* (**c**) *(paint)* **o. paint** pintura *f* al óleo

2 VT engrasar

oilcan ['ɔɪlkæn] N aceitera *f*

oilfield ['ɔɪlfiːld] N yacimiento petrolífero

oilskin ['ɔɪlskɪn] N (**a**) *(fabric)* hule *m* (**b**) **oilskins** chubasquero *m*, impermeable *m* de hule

oily ['ɔɪlɪ] ADJ *(oilier, oiliest)* aceitoso(a), grasiento(a); *(hair, skin)* graso(a)

ointment ['ɔɪntmənt] N ungüento *m*, pomada *f*

O.K., okay [əʊ'keɪ] *Fam* **1** INTERJ de acuerdo, *Esp* vale, *Am* ok, *Méx* ándale

2 ADJ bien; **is it O.K. if ...?** ¿está bien si ...?

3 VT dar el visto bueno a

old [əʊld] **1** ADJ (**a**) *(not young, not new)* viejo(a); **an o. man** un anciano; **o. age** vejez *f*; *Br* **o. age pensioner** pensionista *mf*; *Br* **o. boy** *(addressing sb)* muchacho; **o. hand** veterano(a) *m,f*; **good o. John!** ¡el bueno de John! (**b**) **how o. are you?** ¿cuántos años tienes?; **she's five years o.** tiene cinco años (**c**) *(previous)* antiguo(a); **o. boy** antiguo alumno

2 N of **o.** de antaño

old-fashioned [əʊld'fæʃənd] ADJ *(outdated)* a la antigua; *(unfashionable)* anticuado(a), pasado(a) de moda

olive ['ɒlɪv] N (**a**) *(tree)* olivo *m* (**b**) *(fruit)* aceituna *f*, oliva *f*; **o. oil** aceite *m* de oliva

Olympic [ə'lɪmpɪk] **1** ADJ olímpico(a); **O. Games** Juegos Olímpicos

2 NPL **the Olympics** las Olimpiadas

omelette, *US* **omelet** ['ɒmlɪt] N tortilla *f*; **Spanish o.** tortilla española *or* de patatas *or* *Am* de papas

omen ['əʊmen] N presagio *m*

ominous ['ɒmɪnəs] ADJ de mal agüero

omission [əʊ'mɪʃən] N omisión *f*; *Fig* olvido *m*

omit [əʊ'mɪt] VT omitir; *(accidentally)* pasar por alto; *(forget)* olvidarse (**to** de)

omnipotent [ɒm'nɪpətənt] **1** ADJ omnipotente

2 N **the O.** el Todopoderoso

on [ɒn] **1** PREP (**a**) *(location)* sobre, encima de, en; **I hit him on the head** le di un golpe en la cabeza; **it's on the desk** está encima de *or* sobre el escritorio; **hanging on the wall** colgado de la pared; **on page 4** en la página 4 (**b**) *(alongside)* en; **a town on the coast** un pueblo en la costa

(**c**) *(direction)* en, a; **on the right** a la derecha; **on the way** en el camino

(**d**) *(time)* **on 3 April** el 3 de abril; **on a sunny day** un día de sol; **on Monday** el lunes; **on Mondays** los lunes; **on time** a tiempo

(**e**) *(indicating medium)* **on TV/the radio** en la tele/radio; **on the phone** al teléfono

(**f**) *(at the time of)* a; **on his arrival** a su llegada; **on learning of this** al conocer esto

(**g**) *(transport)* en, a; **on foot** a pie

(**h**) *(state, process)* en, de; **on holiday/ business** de vacaciones/negocios

(i) *(regarding)* sobre; **a lecture on numismatics** una conferencia sobre numismática

(j) *(against)* contra; **an attack on** un ataque contra

2 ADV (**a**) *(covering)* encima, puesto; **she had a coat on** llevaba puesto un abrigo (**b**) *Fam* **have you anything on tonight?** ¿tienes algún plan para esta noche? (**c**) **and so on** y así sucesivamente; **he talks on and on** habla sin parar; **to work on** seguir trabajando (**d**) **from that day on** a partir de aquel día; **later on** más tarde

3 ADJ *Fam* (**a**) **to be on** *(TV, radio, light)* estar encendido(a) *or Am* prendido(a); *(film, play)* estar en cartelera (**b**) *(definitely planned)* previsto(a); **you're on!** ¡trato hecho! (**c**) *Br Fam (acceptable)* **that isn't on** eso no está bien

once [wʌns] **1** ADV (**a**) *(one time)* una vez; **o. a week** una vez por semana; **o. more** una vez más; **o. or twice** un par de veces; *Fig* **o. and for all** de una vez por todas (**b**) *(formerly)* en otro tiempo; **o. (upon a time) there was ...** érase una vez ... (**c**) **at o.** en seguida, inmediatamente

2 CONJ una vez que *(+ subj)*, en cuanto (+ *subj)*

oncoming ['ɒnkʌmɪŋ] ADJ *(car, traffic)* que viene en dirección contraria

one [wʌn] **1** ADJ (**a**) *(number)* un(a); **for o. thing** primero; **you're the o. person who knows** tú eres el único que lo sabe (**b**) *(indefinite)* un(a); **he'll come back o. day** un día volverá

2 PRON (**a**) *(identifying)* **that o.** ése/ésa; **this o.** éste/ésta; *(distant)* aquél/aquélla; **any o.** cualquiera; **the blue ones** los azules/las azules; **the o. on the table** el/la que está encima de la mesa; **the ones that, the ones who** los/las que (**b**) *(indefinite)* uno(a) *m,f*; **o. at a time** de uno en uno; **o. by o.** uno tras otro (**c**) *(impersonal)* uno(a) *m,f*; **o. has to fight** hay que luchar; **o. hopes that will never happen** esperemos que no ocurra (**d**) *(reciprocal)* **o. another** el uno al otro; **they love o. another** se aman

3 N *(digit)* uno *m*; **o. hundred/thousand** cien/mil

one-armed ['wʌnɑːmd] ADJ *(person)* manco(a); *Br Fam* **o. bandit** *(máquina f)* tragaperras *f inv*, *RP* tragamonedas *f inv*

one-man ['wʌnmæn] ADJ **a o. show** un espectáculo con un solo artista

one-man band [wʌnmæn'bænd] N hombre *m* orquesta

one-off ['wʌnɒf] ADJ *Br Fam* único(a), fuera de serie

oneself [wʌn'self] PRON (**a**) *(reflexive)* uno(a) mismo(a) *m,f*, sí mismo(a) *m,f*; **to talk to o.** hablar para sí (**b**) *(alone)* uno(a) mismo(a) *m,f*; **by o.** solo(a)

one-sided [wʌn'saɪdɪd] ADJ *(bargain)* desigual; *(judgement)* parcial; *(decision)* unilateral

one-to-one ['wʌntə'wʌn] ADJ **o. tuition** clases *fpl* individuales

one-way ['wʌnweɪ] ADJ (**a**) *US (ticket)* de ida (**b**) *(street)* de dirección única

ongoing ['ɒngəʊɪŋ] ADJ (**a**) *(in progress)* en curso, actual (**b**) *(developing)* en desarrollo

onion ['ʌnjən] N cebolla *f*

on-line ['ɒnlaɪn] ADJ *Comput* conectado(a)

onlooker ['ɒnlʊkə(r)] N espectador(a) *m,f*

only ['əʊnlɪ] **1** ADJ único(a); **o. son** hijo único

2 ADV solamente, sólo; **staff o.** *(sign)* reservado al personal; **he has o. just left** acaba de marcharse hace un momento; **o. yesterday** ayer mismo

3 CONJ pero

onset ['ɒnset] N *(start)* comienzo *m*

onslaught ['ɒnslɔːt] N embestida *f*

onto ['ɒntʊ, *unstressed* 'ɒntə] PREP sobre, encima de

onus ['əʊnəs] N responsabilidad *f*

onward ['ɒnwəd] ADJ hacia adelante

onward(s) ['ɒnwəd(z)] ADV a partir de, en adelante; **from this time o.** de ahora en adelante

ooze [uːz] **1** VI rezumar

2 VT rebosar

opaque [əʊ'peɪk] ADJ opaco(a)

OPEC ['əʊpek] N *(abbr* **Organization of Petroleum-Exporting Countries)** OPEP *f*

open ['əʊpən] **1** ADJ (**a**) *(in general)* abierto(a); **in the o. air** al aire libre; **to be o. with sb** ser sincero(a) con algn; **to keep an o. mind** no tener prejuicios; **I am o. to suggestions** acepto cualquier sugerencia; **o. to criticism** susceptible a la crítica; **an o. question** una cuestión sin resolver; **o. season** *(in hunting)* temporada *f* de caza; *Av & Rail* **o. ticket** billete *or Am* boleto abierto; **o. verdict** veredicto inconcluso (**b**) *(opposition)* manifiesto(a)

2 VT *(in general)* abrir; *(exhibition etc)* inaugurar; *(negotiations, conversation)* entablar; **to o. fire** abrir fuego

3 VI (**a**) *(door, window, flower)* abrirse; *(shop, bank)* abrir; **to o. onto** *(of door, window)* dar a (**b**) *(start)* empezar; *Th & Cin* estrenarse

4 N **in the o.** al aire libre

▸ **open out 1** VT SEP abrir, desplegar

2 VI *(flowers)* abrirse; *(view)* extenderse

▸ **open up 1** VT SEP *(market etc)* abrir; *(possibilities)* crear

2 VI *(shopkeeper, new shop)* abrir; *(flower, new market)* abrirse; *Fam* **o. up!** ¡abre la puerta!

opener ['əʊpənə(r)] N tin *or US* **can o.** abrelatas *m inv*

opening ['əʊpənɪŋ] N (**a**) *(act)* apertura *f*; **o. night** noche *f* de estreno (**b**) *(beginning)* comienzo *m* (**c**) *(aperture)* abertura *f*; *(gap)* brecha *f* (**d**) *Com* oportunidad *f* (**e**) *(vacancy)* vacante *f*

openly ['əʊpənlɪ] ADV abiertamente

open-minded [əupən'maɪndɪd] ADJ sin pre-juicios

openness ['əupənnɪs] N franqueza f

open-plan ['əupənplæn] ADJ *(office)* abierto(a)

opera ['ɒpərə] N ópera f; **o. house** ópera, teatro m de la ópera

operate ['ɒpəreɪt] **1** VI (a) *(function)* funcionar (b) *Med* operar; **to o. on sb for appendicitis** operar a algn de apendicitis
2 VT (a) *(control)* manejar (b) *(business)* dirigir

operatic [ɒpə'rætɪk] ADJ de ópera

operating ['ɒpəreɪtɪŋ] N (a) **o. costs** gastos mpl or Esp costes mpl de explotación; Comput **o. system** sistema operativo (b) Med **o. table** mesa f de operaciones; **o. theatre** or US **room** quirófano m

operation [ɒpə'reɪʃən] N (a) *(of machine)* funcionamiento m; *(by person)* manejo m (b) Mil maniobra f (c) Med operación f, intervención quirúrgica; **to undergo an o. for** ser operado(a) de

operational [ɒpə'reɪʃənəl] ADJ (a) *(ready for use)* operativo(a) (b) Mil operacional

operative ['ɒpərətɪv] ADJ (a) Jur *(in force)* vigente; **to become o.** entrar en vigor (b) *(significant)* clave, significativo(a); **the o. word** la palabra clave

operator ['ɒpəreɪtə(r)] N (a) Ind operario(a) m,f (b) Tel operador(a) m,f (c) *(dealer)* negociante mf, agente mf; **tour o.** agente de viajes

opinion [ə'pɪnjən] N opinión f; **in my o.** en mi opinión, a mi juicio; **it's a matter of o.** es cuestión de opiniones; **to have a high o. of sb** tener buen concepto de algn; **o. poll** encuesta f, sondeo m

opinionated [ə'pɪnjəneɪtɪd] ADJ dogmático(a)

opium ['əupɪəm] N opio m

opponent [ə'pəunənt] N adversario(a) m,f

opportune ['ɒpətjuːn] ADJ oportuno(a)

opportunist [ɒpə'tjuːnɪst] ADJ & N oportunista *(mf)*

opportunity [ɒpə'tjuːnɪtɪ] N oportunidad f, ocasión f; **a job with opportunities** un trabajo con buenas perspectivas

oppose [ə'pəuz] VT oponerse a

opposed [ə'pəuzd] ADJ opuesto(a); **to be o. to sth** estar en contra de algo; **as o. to** comparado(a) con

opposing [ə'pəuzɪŋ] ADJ adversario(a)

opposite ['ɒpəzɪt] **1** ADJ (a) *(facing)* de enfrente; *(page)* contiguo(a) (b) *(contrary)* opuesto(a), contrario(a); **in the o. direction** en dirección contraria
2 N **the o.** lo contrario; **quite the o.!** ¡al contrario!
3 PREP enfrente de, frente a
4 ADV enfrente

opposition [ɒpə'zɪʃən] N (a) *(resistance)* oposición f; **in o. to** en contra de (b) Br Pol **the O.** la oposición

oppress [ə'pres] VT oprimir

oppression [ə'preʃən] N opresión f

oppressive [ə'presɪv] ADJ opresivo(a); *(atmosphere)* agobiante; *(heat)* sofocante

opt [ɒpt] VI optar; **to o. for** optar por; **to o. to do sth** optar por hacer algo
▸ **opt out** VI retirarse; **to o. out of doing sth** decidir no hacer algo

optical ['ɒptɪkəl] ADJ óptico(a)

optician [ɒp'tɪʃən] N óptico(a) m,f

optics ['ɒptɪks] N SING óptica f

optimism ['ɒptɪmɪzəm] N optimismo m

optimist ['ɒptɪmɪst] N optimista mf

optimistic [ɒptɪ'mɪstɪk] ADJ optimista

optimistically [ɒptɪ'mɪstɪkəlɪ] ADV con optimismo

optimum ['ɒptɪməm] **1** N grado óptimo
2 ADJ óptimo(a)

option ['ɒpʃən] N opción f; **I have no o.** no tengo más remedio; **to keep one's options open** no comprometerse; **with the o. of** con opción a

optional ['ɒpʃənəl] ADJ optativo(a), facultativo(a); Educ **o. subject** (asignatura) optativa

opulence ['ɒpjuləns] N opulencia f

or [ɔː(r), unstressed ə(r)] CONJ (a) *(in general)* o; *(before a word beginning with* o *or* ho) u; **or else** si no, o bien; **whether you like it or not** tanto si te gusta como si no; **either a bun or a piece of cake** (o) una magdalena o un trozo de pastel (b) *(with negative)* ni; **he can't read or write** no sabe leer ni escribir; *see* **nor**

oral ['ɔːrəl, 'ɒrəl] **1** ADJ oral
2 N examen m oral

orally ['ɔːrəlɪ, 'ɒrəlɪ] ADV **to be taken o.** *(on medicine)* por vía oral

orange ['ɒrɪndʒ] **1** N naranja f; **o. juice** Esp zumo m or Am jugo m de naranja
2 ADJ de color naranja

orator ['ɒrətə(r)] N orador(a) m,f

oratory ['ɒrətərɪ] N oratoria f

orbit ['ɔːbɪt] **1** N Astron órbita f
2 VT girar alrededor de
3 VI girar

orchard ['ɔːtʃəd] N huerto m

orchestra ['ɔːkɪstrə] N orquesta f; US *(in theatre)* platea f, patio m de butacas

orchestral [ɔː'kestrəl] ADJ orquestal

orchid ['ɔːkɪd] N orquídea f

ordain [ɔː'deɪn] VT (a) Rel ordenar; **to be ordained** ordenarse (b) *(decree)* decretar

ordeal [ɔː'diːl] N mala experiencia

order ['ɔːdə(r)] **1** N (a) *(sequence)* orden m; **to put in o.** ordenar (b) *(condition)* estado m; **out of o.** *(sign)* averiado(a) (c) *(peace)* orden m; **to restore o.** reestablecer el orden público (d) *(command)* orden f (e) Com pedido m, encargo m; **o. form** hoja f de pedido (f) Rel orden f (g) **in o. that** para que *(+ subj)*, a fin de que *(+ subj)*; **in o. to** *(+ infin)* para *(+ infin)*, a fin de *(+ infin)*

2 vt (**a**) (command) ordenar, mandar; **to o. sb to do sth** mandar a algn hacer algo (**b**) Com pedir, encargar

orderly ['ɔːdəlɪ] ADJ (tidy etc) ordenado(a)

ordinal ['ɔːdɪnəl] ADJ & N ordinal (m)

ordinance ['ɔːdɪnəns] N Fml (decree) ordenanza f, decreto m

ordinary ['ɔːdɪnrɪ] **1** ADJ usual, normal; (average) corriente, común; **the o. citizen** el ciudadano de a pie
2 N **the o.** lo corriente, lo normal; **out of the o.** fuera de lo común

ordnance ['ɔːdnəns] N Br **O. Survey** = instituto británico de cartografía

ore [ɔː(r)] N mineral m

organ ['ɔːgən] N Mus & Anat órgano m

organic [ɔːˈgænɪk] ADJ orgánico(a); (farming, food) biológico(a), ecológico(a)

organism ['ɔːgənɪzəm] N organismo m

organization [ɔːgənaɪˈzeɪʃən] N organización f

organize ['ɔːgənaɪz] VT organizar

organizer ['ɔːgənaɪzə(r)] N organizador(a) m,f

orgasm ['ɔːgæzəm] N orgasmo m

orgy ['ɔːdʒɪ] N orgía f

Orient ['ɔːrɪənt] N **the O.** el Oriente

Oriental [ɔːrɪˈentəl] ADJ & N oriental (mf)

orientate ['ɔːrɪənteɪt] VT orientar

origin ['ɒrɪdʒɪn] N origen m; **country of o.** país m natal or de origen

original [əˈrɪdʒɪnəl] **1** ADJ (first, innovative) original; Rel **o. sin** pecado m original
2 N original m

originality [ərɪdʒɪˈnælɪtɪ] N originalidad f

originally [əˈrɪdʒɪnəlɪ] ADV (**a**) (at first) en un principio (**b**) (with imagination) con originalidad

originate [əˈrɪdʒɪneɪt] **1** VT originar
2 VI **to o. from** or **in** tener su origen en

Orkneys ['ɔːknɪz] NPL **the O.** las (Islas) Orcadas

ornament ['ɔːnəmənt] N ornamento m, adorno m

ornamental [ɔːnəˈmentəl] ADJ decorativo(a)

ornate [ɔːˈneɪt] ADJ vistoso(a)

ornithology [ɔːnɪˈθɒlədʒɪ] N ornitología f

orphan ['ɔːfən] **1** N huérfano(a) m,f
2 VT **she was orphaned** quedó huérfana

orphanage ['ɔːfənɪdʒ] N orfanato m

orthodox ['ɔːθədɒks] ADJ ortodoxo(a)

orthodoxy ['ɔːθədɒksɪ] N ortodoxia f

orthopaedic, US **orthopedic** [ɔːθəʊˈpiːdɪk] ADJ ortopédico(a)

Oscar ['ɒskə(r)] N Óscar m

oscillate ['ɒsɪleɪt] VI oscilar

ostensible [ɒˈstensɪbəl] ADJ (**a**) (apparent) ostensible (**b**) (pretended) aparente

ostentatious [ɒstenˈteɪʃəs] ADJ ostentoso(a)

osteopath ['ɒstɪəpæθ] N osteópata mf

ostracize ['ɒstrəsaɪz] VT (from society) condenar al ostracismo; (from group) aislar, excluir

ostrich ['ɒstrɪtʃ] N avestruz f

other ['ʌðə(r)] **1** ADJ otro(a); **every o. day** cada dos días; **on the o. hand** por otra parte; **o. people have seen it** otros lo han visto; **the o. four** los otros cuatro; **the o. one** el otro/la otra; **the o. thing** lo otro
2 PRON otro(a) m,f; **many others** otros muchos; **the others** los otros, los demás; **we see each o. quite often** nos vemos con bastante frecuencia; **he must be somewhere or o.** debe de estar en alguna parte

otherwise ['ʌðəwaɪz] **1** ADV (**a**) (if not) si no (**b**) (differently) de otra manera (**c**) (in other respects) por lo demás
2 ADJ distinto(a)

OTT [əʊtiːˈtiː] ADJ Br Fam (abbr **over the top**) exagerado(a)

otter ['ɒtə(r)] N nutria f

ouch [aʊtʃ] INTERJ (expressing pain) ¡ay!

ought [ɔːt] V AUX

En el inglés hablado, y en el escrito en estilo coloquial, la forma negativa **ought not** se transforma en **oughtn't**.

(**a**) (obligation) deber; **I thought I o.** to tell you creí que debía decírtelo; **she o.** to do it debería hacerlo (**b**) (vague desirability) tener que, deber; **you o.** to see the exhibition deberías ver la exposición (**c**) (expectation) **he o.** to pass the exam seguramente aprobará el examen; **that o.** to do con eso bastará

ounce [aʊns] N onza f

our [aʊə(r)] POSS ADJ nuestro(a)

ours [aʊəz] POSS PRON (**a**) (singular) el nuestro m, la nuestra f; (plural) los nuestros mpl, las nuestras fpl (**b**) **of o.** nuestro(a); **a friend of o.** un amigo nuestro

ourselves [aʊəˈselvz] PERS PRON PL (**a**) (reflexive) nos (**b**) (emphatic) nosotros mismos/nosotras mismas (**c**) **by o.** a solas

oust [aʊst] VT (**a**) (from a post) desbancar (**b**) (from property etc) desalojar

out [aʊt] **1** ADV (outside, away) fuera; **to go o.** salir
2 ADJ (**a**) **the sun is o.** ha salido el sol (**b**) (unfashionable) pasado(a) de moda (**c**) (fire) apagado(a) (**d**) **she's o.** (not in) ha salido, no está (**e**) (inaccurate) equivocado(a); **to be o. in one's calculations** equivocarse en los cálculos (**f**) **before the week is o.** antes de que acabe la semana
3 PREP Fam (out of) por; **he jumped o. the window** saltó por la ventana
4 out of ADV (**a**) (place, control, danger) fuera de; **to go o. of the room** salir de la habitación (**b**) (cause, motive) por; **o. of love** por amor (**c**) (made from) de; **made o. of wood** hecho de madera (**d**) (short of, without) sin; **I'm o. of**

cash me he quedado sin dinero (**e**) *(in proportions)* de; **three days o. of four** tres días de cada cuatro

out-and-out ['autənaut] ADJ redomado(a)

outboard ['autbɔ:d] ADJ **o. motor** fueraborda *m*

outbreak ['autbreɪk] N *(of war)* comienzo *m*; *(of disease)* brote *m*; *(of violence)* ola *f*; **at the o. of war** cuando estalló la guerra

outbuilding ['autbɪldɪŋ] N dependencia *f*

outburst ['autbɜ:st] N *(of anger)* arrebato *m*; *(of generosity)* arranque *m*

outcast ['autkɑ:st] N marginado(a) *m,f*

outcome ['autkʌm] N resultado *m*

outcrop ['autkrɒp] N *Geol* afloramiento *m*

outcry ['autkraɪ] N **there was an o.** hubo fuertes protestas

outdated [aut'deɪtɪd] ADJ anticuado(a), obsoleto(a)

outdo [aut'du:] VT *(pt* **outdid** [aut'dɪd]; *pp* **outdone** [aut'dʌn]) **to o. sb** superar a algn

outdoor ['autdɔ:(r)] ADJ (**a**) *(games, sports, work)* al aire libre (**b**) *(clothes)* de calle

outdoors [aut'dɔ:z] ADV fuera, al aire libre

outer ['autə(r)] ADJ exterior, externo(a)

outfit ['autfɪt] N (**a**) *(kit, equipment)* equipo *m* (**b**) *(set of clothes)* conjunto *m* (**c**) *Fam (group)* grupo *m*

outgoing ['autgəʊɪŋ] **1** ADJ (**a**) *(departing)* saliente (**b**) *(sociable)* extrovertido(a)
2 NPL *Br* **outgoings** gastos *mpl*

outgrow [aut'grəʊ] VT *(pt* **outgrew** [aut'gru:]; *pp* **outgrown** [aut'grəʊn]) **he's outgrowing all his clothes** toda la ropa se le está quedando pequeña; **she'll o. it** se le pasará con la edad

outhouse ['authaʊs] N = **outbuilding**

outing ['autɪŋ] N excursión *f*

outlandish [aut'lændɪʃ] ADJ estrafalario(a), extravagante

outlast [aut'lɑ:st] VT *(person)* sobrevivir a; *(thing)* durar más que

outlaw ['autlɔ:] **1** N proscrito(a) *m,f*
2 VT prohibir

outlay ['autleɪ] N *(expense)* desembolso *m*

outlet ['autlet] N (**a**) *(opening)* salida *f* (**b**) *(for emotions)* válvula *f* de escape (**c**) *Com* mercado *m*

outline ['autlaɪn] **1** N (**a**) *(draft)* bosquejo *m* (**b**) *(outer line)* contorno *m*; *(silhouette)* perfil *m*
2 VT (**a**) *(draw lines of)* perfilar (**b**) *(summarize)* resumir (**c**) *(describe roughly)* trazar las líneas generales de

outlive [aut'lɪv] VT sobrevivir a

outlook ['autluk] N (**a**) *(point of view)* punto *m* de vista (**b**) *(prospect)* perspectiva *f*; *Met* previsión *f*

outlying ['autlaɪɪŋ] ADJ *(remote)* periférico(a)

outmoded [aut'məʊdɪd] ADJ anticuado(a)

outnumber [aut'nʌmbə(r)] VT exceder en número

out-of-the-way ['autəvðə'weɪ] ADJ (**a**) *(distant)* apartado(a), remoto(a) (**b**) *(uncommon)* fuera de lo común

outpatient ['autpeɪʃənt] N paciente externo(a); **outpatients' department** clínica ambulatoria

outpost ['autpəʊst] N enclave *m*

output ['autput] N (**a**) *(of goods, of author)* producción *f*; *(of machine)* rendimiento *m* (**b**) *Elec* potencia *f* (**c**) *Comput* salida *f*

outrage ['autreɪdʒ] **1** N ultraje *m*; **it's an o.!** ¡es un escándalo!
2 VT **to be outraged by sth** indignarse por algo

outrageous [aut'reɪdʒəs] ADJ *(behaviour)* escandaloso(a); *(clothes)* extravagante; *(price)* exorbitante

outright 1 ADJ ['autraɪt] *(absolute)* absoluto(a)
2 ADV [aut'raɪt] (**a**) *(completely)* por completo (**b**) *(directly)* directamente, sin reserva (**c**) *(immediately)* en el acto

outset ['autset] N comienzo *m*, principio *m*

outside 1 PREP [aut'saɪd, 'autsaɪd] (**a**) *(physically)* fuera de (**b**) *(beyond)* más allá de (**c**) *(other than)* aparte de
2 ADJ ['autsaɪd] (**a**) *(exterior)* exterior, externo(a) (**b**) *(remote)* remoto(a)
3 ADV [aut'saɪd] fuera, afuera
4 N [aut'saɪd, 'autsaɪd] exterior *m*; **on the o.** por fuera; *Fam* **at the o.** como mucho

outsider [aut'saɪdə(r)] N (**a**) *(stranger)* extraño(a) *m,f*, forastero(a) *m,f* (**b**) *Pol* = candidato(a) con pocas posibilidades de ganar

outsize(d) ['autsaɪz(d)] ADJ *(clothes)* de talla especial; *(appetite, ego)* desmedido(a)

outskirts ['autskɜ:ts] NPL afueras *fpl*

outsourcing ['autsɔ:sɪŋ] N *Com* externalización *f*, subcontratación *f*, *Am* tercerización *f*; *Am* terciarización *f*

outspoken [aut'spəʊkən] ADJ directo(a), abierto(a)

outstanding [aut'stændɪŋ] ADJ (**a**) *(exceptional)* destacado(a) (**b**) *(unpaid, unresolved)* pendiente

outstretched [aut'stretʃt] ADJ extendido(a)

outward ['autwəd] **1** ADJ (**a**) *(external)* exterior, externo(a) (**b**) **the o. journey** el viaje de ida
2 ADV = **outwards**

outwardly ['autwədlɪ] ADV aparentemente, en apariencia

outwards ['autwədz] ADV hacia (a)fuera

outweigh [aut'weɪ] VT (**a**) *(be more important than)* tener más peso que (**b**) *(weigh more than)* pesar más que

oval ['əʊvəl] **1** ADJ oval, ovalado(a)
2 N óvalo *m*

ovary ['əʊvərɪ] N ovario *m*

ovation [əʊ'veɪʃən] N ovación *f*

oven ['ʌvən] N horno *m*

ovenproof ['ʌvənpru:f] ADJ refractario(a)

over ['əʊvə(r)] **1** PREP (**a**) *(above, on top of)* sobre, encima de, *Am* arriba de (**b**) *(across)* al otro lado de; **the bridge o. the river** el puente que cruza el río (**c**) *(during)* durante (**d**) *(throughout)* por (**e**) *(by the agency of)* por; **o. the phone** por teléfono (**f**) *(more than)* más de; **men o. twenty-five** hombres mayores de veinticinco años; **o. and above** además de (**g**) *(recovered from)* recuperado(a) de

2 ADV (**a**) **o. here/there** aquí/allí, *Am* acá/allá (**b**) *(throughout)* por; **all o.** por todas partes (**c**) *(more)* más (**d**) *(again)* otra vez; **o. and o.** *(again)* una y otra vez (**e**) *(in excess)* de más

3 ADJ *(finished)* acabado(a); **it's (all) o.** se acabó

overall ['əʊvərɔːl] **1** ADJ total, global

2 N *Br* **overalls** *(boiler suit)* mono *m* (de trabajo), *Am* overol *m*

3 ADV [əʊvər'ɔːl] *(on the whole)* por lo general, en conjunto

overawe [əʊvər'ɔː] VT **to be overawed by sth/sb** quedarse anonadado(a) por algo/algn

overbearing [əʊvə'beərɪŋ] ADJ *(domineering)* dominante; *(important)* significativo(a)

overboard ['əʊvəbɔːd] ADV por la borda; **man o.!** ¡hombre al agua!; *Fam* **to go o.** pasarse

overbook ['əʊvə'bʊk] VT *(flight, holiday)* **they've overbooked this flight** este vuelo tiene overbooking

overcast ['əʊvəkɑːst] ADJ nublado(a)

overcharge [əʊvə'tʃɑːdʒ] VT (**a**) *(charge too much)* cobrar demasiado a (**b**) *(overload)* sobrecargar

overcoat ['əʊvəkəʊt] N abrigo *m*

overcome [əʊvə'kʌm] VT (**a**) *(conquer)* vencer; **o. by grief** deshecho(a) por el dolor (**b**) *(obstacle)* superar

overconfident [əʊvə'kɒnfɪdənt] ADJ demasiado confiado(a)

overcrowded [əʊvə'kraʊdɪd] ADJ *(room)* atestado(a) (de gente); *(country)* superpoblado(a)

overcrowding [əʊvə'kraʊdɪŋ] N *(of slums, prisons)* hacinamiento *m*; *(of classrooms)* masificación *f*; *(of country)* superpoblación *f*

overdo [əʊvə'duː] VT *(pt* **overdid** [əʊvə'dɪd]*; pp* **overdone** [əʊvə'dʌn]*)* (**a**) *(carry too far)* exagerar; **don't o. it** no te pases (**b**) *Culin* cocer *or* asar demasiado

overdose ['əʊvədəʊs] N sobredosis *f*

overdraft ['əʊvədrɑːft] N giro *m* en descubierto; *(amount)* saldo *m* deudor

overdrawn [əʊvə'drɔːn] VT **to be o.** tener la cuenta en descubierto

overdue [əʊvə'djuː] ADJ **to be o.** *(person, train)* retrasarse, venir con retraso *or Am* demora; *(bill)* estar sin pagar

overestimate [əʊvər'estɪmeɪt] VT sobreestimar

overflow 1 VI [əʊvə'fləʊ] *(river)* desbordarse; *(cup etc)* derramarse

2 N ['əʊvəfləʊ] *(of river etc)* desbordamiento *m*; **o. pipe** cañería *f* de desagüe

overgrown [əʊvə'grəʊn] ADJ (**a**) *(with grass)* cubierto(a) (de hierba) (**b**) *(in size)* demasiado grande

overhaul 1 VT [əʊvə'hɔːl] revisar

2 N ['əʊvəhɔːl] revisión *f* y reparación *f*

overhead 1 ADJ ['əʊvəhed] *(por)* encima de la cabeza; **o. cable** cable aéreo

2 ADV [əʊvə'hed] arriba, por encima de la cabeza

3 N ['əʊvəhed] *US* = **overheads**

overheads ['əʊvəhedz] NPL *Br* gastos *mpl* generales

overhear [əʊvə'hɪə(r)] VT *(pt & pp* **overheard** [əʊvə'hɜːd]*)* oír por casualidad

overheat [əʊvə'hiːt] VI recalentarse

overjoyed [əʊvə'dʒɔɪd] ADJ rebosante de alegría

overlap [əʊvə'læp] VI superponerse; *Fig* **our plans o.** nuestros planes coinciden parcialmente

overleaf [əʊvə'liːf] ADV al dorso

overload 1 VT [əʊvə'ləʊd] sobrecargar

2 N ['əʊvələʊd] sobrecarga *f*

overlook [əʊvə'lʊk] VT (**a**) *(fail to notice)* saltarse (**b**) *(ignore)* no hacer caso de; **we'll o. it this time** esta vez lo pasaremos por alto (**c**) *(have a view of)* dar a, tener vista a

overmanning [əʊvə'mænɪŋ] N *Ind* exceso *m* de empleados

overnight 1 ADV [əʊvə'naɪt] (**a**) *(during the night)* por la noche; **we stayed there o.** pasamos la noche allí (**b**) *(suddenly)* de la noche a la mañana

2 ADJ ['əʊvənaɪt] *(sudden)* repentino(a); **o. stay** *Esp, Méx* estancia *f or Am* estadia *f* de una noche

overpass ['əʊvəpɑːs] N *US* paso elevado

overpay [əʊvə'peɪ] VT *(pt & pp* **overpaid** [əʊvə'peɪd]*)* pagar demasiado a

overpower [əʊvə'paʊə(r)] VT (**a**) *(subdue)* dominar (**b**) *(affect strongly)* abrumar

overpowering [əʊvə'paʊərɪŋ] ADJ *(emotion, heat)* tremendo(a), desmesurado(a); *(smell, taste)* fortísimo(a), intensísimo(a)

overpriced [əʊvə'praɪst] ADJ excesivamente caro(a)

overrate [əʊvə'reɪt] VT sobreestimar, supervalorar

overreact [əʊvərɪ'ækt] VI reaccionar exageradamente

override [əʊvə'raɪd] VT *(pt* **overrode**; *pp* **overridden** [əʊvə'rɪdən]*)* (**a**) *(disregard)* hacer caso omiso de (**b**) *(annul, cancel out)* anular (**c**) *(be more important than)* contar más que

overriding [əʊvə'raɪdɪŋ] ADJ principal; *(importance)* primordial; *(need)* imperioso(a)

overrode [əʊvə'rəʊd] PT *of* **override**

overrule [əʊvə'ruːl] VT invalidar; *Jur* denegar

overrun [əʊvə'rʌn] VT (**a**) *(country)* invadir (**b**) *(allotted time)* rebasar, excederse de

oversaw [əʊvə'sɔː] PT*of* oversee

overseas 1 ADV [əʊvə'siːz] en ultramar; **to live o.** vivir en el extranjero
2 ADJ ['əʊvəsiːz] de ultramar; *(visitor)* extranjero(a); *(trade)* exterior

oversee [əʊvə'siː] VT *(pt* **oversaw;** *pp* **overseen** [əʊvə'siːn]) supervisar

overseer ['əʊvəsiːə(r)] N supervisor(a) *m,f*; *(foreman)* capataz *m*

overshadow [əʊvə'ʃædəʊ] VT *Fig* eclipsar

overshoot [əʊvə'ʃuːt] VT *(pt & pp* **overshot** [əʊvə'ʃɒt]) **to o. a turning** pasarse un cruce; *Fig* **to o. the mark** pasarse de la raya

oversight ['əʊvəsaɪt] N descuido *m*

oversleep [əʊvə'sliːp] VI *(pt & pp* **overslept** [əʊvə'slept]) quedarse dormido(a)

overspill ['əʊvəspɪl] N *esp Br* exceso *m* de población

overstate [əʊvə'steɪt] VT exagerar

overstep [əʊvə'step] VT *Fig* **to o. the mark** pasarse de la raya

overt [əʊ'vɜːt] ADJ patente

overtake [əʊvə'teɪk] VT *(pt* **overtook;** *pp* **overtaken** [əʊvə'teɪkən]) (**a**) *Br Aut* adelantar (**b**) *(surpass)* superar a (**c**) *(of night)* sorprender

overthrow [əʊvə'θrəʊ] VT *(pt* **overthrew** [əʊvə-'θruː];* *pp* **overthrown** [əʊvə'θrəʊn]) *(government)* derribar

overtime ['əʊvətaɪm] N (**a**) *(work)* horas *fpl* extra (**b**) *US* prórroga *f*

overtone ['əʊvətəʊn] N matiz *m*

overtook [əʊvə'tʊk] PT*of* overtake

overture ['əʊvətjʊə(r)] N (**a**) *Mus* obertura *f*; *Fig (introduction)* introducción *f* (**b**) *(proposal)* propuesta *f*

overturn [əʊvə'tɜːn] VT & VI volcar

overweight [əʊvə'weɪt] ADJ demasiado pesado(a)

overwhelm [əʊvə'welm] VT (**a**) *(defeat)* aplastar; *(overpower)* abrumar; **I'm overwhelmed** estoy abrumado (**b**) *(with letters, work etc)* inundar

overwhelming [əʊvə'welmɪŋ] ADJ *(defeat)* aplastante; *(desire etc)* irresistible

overwork [əʊvə'wɜːk] **1** VI trabajar demasiado **2** VT *(person)* forzar; *(excuse etc)* abusar de

overwrought [əʊvə'rɔːt] ADJ (**a**) *(tense)* muy nervioso(a) (**b**) *Literary (too elaborate)* forzado(a)

owe [əʊ] VT deber

owing ['əʊɪŋ] ADJ **o. to** debido a, a causa de

owl [aʊl] N (**short-eared**) **o.** búho *m*, *CAm, Méx* tecolote *m*; (**barn**) **o.** lechuza *f*

own [əʊn] **1** ADJ propio(a); **it's his o. fault** es culpa suya
2 PRON (**a**) **my o./your o./his o.***/etc* lo mío/lo tuyo/lo suyo*/etc*; *Fam* **to get one's o. back** tomarse la revancha (**b**) **on one's o.** *(without help)* uno(a) mismo(a); *(alone)* solo(a)
3 VT poseer, ser dueño(a) de
▸ **own up** VI **to o. up (to sth)** confesar (algo)

own-brand ['əʊn'brænd] ADJ *Br Com* de marca blanca

owner ['əʊnə(r)] N propietario(a) *m,f*, dueño(a) *m,f*

ownership ['əʊnəʃɪp] N propiedad *f*, posesión *f*

ox [ɒks] N *(pl* **oxen** ['ɒksən]) buey *m*

oxide ['ɒksaɪd] N *Chem* óxido *m*

oxtail ['ɒksteɪl] N rabo *m* de buey

oxygen ['ɒksɪdʒən] N oxígeno *m*; **o. mask** máscara *f* de oxígeno

oyster ['ɔɪstə(r)] N ostra *f*

Oz [ɒz] N *Fam* Australia

oz *(abbr* **ounce(s)**) onza(s) *f(pl)*

ozone ['əʊzəʊn] N ozono *m*; **o. layer** capa *f* de ozono

P

P, p [piː] N *(the letter)* P, p f

p (a) *(pl* **pp)** *(abbr* **page)** pág., p (b) [piː] *Br Fam* *(abbr* **penny, pence)** penique(s) *m(pl)*

PA [piːˈeɪ] N *Fam* (a) *(abbr* **personal assistant)** ayudante *mf* personal (b) *(abbr* **public-address (system))** megafonía f

pa [pɑː] N *US Fam (dad)* papá m

p.a. *(abbr* **per annum)** al año

pace [peɪs] 1 N *(step)* paso m; *(speed)* ritmo m; **to keep p. with** seguir a; *Fig* avanzar al mismo ritmo que; **to set the p.** marcar el paso; *Fig* marcar la pauta

2 VI **to p. up and down** ir de un lado a otro

pacemaker ['peɪsmeɪkə(r)] N *Sport* liebre f; *Med* marcapasos *m inv*

Pacific [pə'sɪfɪk] ADJ **the P. (Ocean)** el (océano) Pacífico

pacifier ['pæsɪfaɪə(r)] N *US (for baby)* chupete m

pacifist ['pæsɪfɪst] ADJ & N pacifista *(mf)*

pacify ['pæsɪfaɪ] VT *(person)* calmar; *(country)* pacificar

pack¹ [pæk] 1 N *(parcel)* paquete m; *(bundle)* bulto m; *US (of cigarettes)* paquete; *Br (of playing cards)* baraja f; *(of hounds)* jauría f

2 VT (a) *(goods)* embalar, envasar; *(in suitcase)* poner; **to p. one's suitcase** hacer la maleta *or Am* valija; *Fig* **to p. one's bags** marcharse (b) *(fill)* atestar (c) *(press down) (snow)* apretar

3 VI (a) *(prepare luggage)* hacer las maletas; *Fam* **to send sb packing** mandar a paseo a algn (b) *(of people)* apiñarse (**into** en)

▸ **pack in** VT SEP *Fam (give up)* dejar

▸ **pack off** VT SEP *Fam* mandar

▸ **pack up** *Fam* 1 VT SEP *(give up)* dejar

2 VI *(stop working)* dejarlo, parar de trabajar; *(machine etc)* estropearse

pack² [pæk] VT *(meeting)* llenar de partidarios

package ['pækɪdʒ] 1 N (a) *(parcel)* paquete m; *(bundle)* bulto m (b) *(of proposals etc)* paquete m; *(agreement)* acuerdo m; **p. deal** convenio m general; **p. tour** viaje m todo incluido

2 VT *(goods)* envasar, embalar

packaging ['pækɪdʒɪŋ] N *(for transport, freight)* embalaje m; *(of product)* envasado m

packed [pækt] ADJ (a) *(crowded)* abarrotado(a) (b) **p. lunch** comida preparada de casa *(para excursión, trabajo, colegio)*

packet ['pækɪt] N (a) *(of tea, cigarettes)* paquete m; *(bag)* bolsa f (b) *Fam (lot of money)* **to make**

or **earn a p.** ganar una millonada *or Méx* un chorro de lana *or RP* una ponchada de guita

packing ['pækɪŋ] N embalaje m; **p. case** caja f de embalar; **to do one's p.** hacer las maletas

pact [pækt] N pacto m

pad¹ [pæd] 1 N (a) *(for protection)* almohadilla f; *(of paper)* bloc m, taco m (b) **launch p.** plataforma f de lanzamiento (c) *Fam (flat)* casa f, *Esp* choza f

2 VT *(chair)* acolchar

▸ **pad out** VT SEP *Fig* meter paja en

pad² [pæd] VI **to p. about** *or* **around** andar silenciosamente

padded ['pædɪd] ADJ *(envelope, jacket)* acolchado(a); **p. cell** celda acolchada

padding ['pædɪŋ] N *(material)* relleno m; *Fig (in speech etc)* paja f

paddle¹ ['pædəl] 1 N (a) *(oar)* pala f; **p. boat** *or* **steamer** vapor m de ruedas (b) *US (for table tennis)* pala f

2 VT *(boat)* remar con pala en

3 VI *(in boat)* remar con pala

paddle² ['pædəl] VI chapotear

paddling pool ['pædlɪŋpuːl] N *(inflatable)* piscina f *or Méx* alberca f *or RP* pileta f hinchable; *(in park)* piscina f *or Méx* alberca f *or RP* pileta f para niños

paddock ['pædək] N potrero m; *(in race course)* paddock m

paddy ['pædɪ] N arrozal m

padlock ['pædlɒk] 1 N candado m

2 VT cerrar con candado

paediatrician [piːdɪə'trɪʃən] N pediatra *mf*

paedophile ['piːdəʊfaɪl] N pedófilo(a) *m,f*

pagan ['peɪgən] ADJ & N pagano(a) *(m,f)*

page¹ [peɪdʒ] N página f

page² [peɪdʒ] 1 N *(servant)* paje m; *(of knight)* escudero m; *(at club)* botones *m inv*

2 VT *(call)* avisar por megafonía

pageant ['pædʒənt] N *(show)* espectáculo m; *(procession)* desfile m; *(on horses)* cabalgata f

pageantry ['pædʒəntrɪ] N pompa f, boato m

pager ['peɪdʒə(r)] N buscapersonas *m inv, Esp* busca m, *Méx* localizador m, *RP* radiomensaje m

paid [peɪd] 1 ADJ pagado(a); *Fig* **to put p. to sth** acabar con algo

2 PT & PP *of* **pay**

pail [peɪl] N cubo m; *(child's)* cubito m

pain [peɪn] 1 N (**a**) (*physical*) dolor *m*; (*grief*) sufrimiento *m*; *Fam* **he's a p. (in the neck)** es un plomazo *or* pelmazo *or Méx* sangrón; **on p. of death** so pena de muerte (**b**) **to take pains over sth** esmerarse en algo
2 VT (*grieve*) dar pena a

pained [peɪnd] ADJ de reproche

painful ['peɪnful] ADJ doloroso(a); *Fam (very bad)* malísimo(a)

painfully ['peɪnfʊlɪ] ADV (**a**) **p. shy** lastimosamente tímido(a) (**b**) *Fam* terriblemente

painkiller ['peɪnkɪlə(r)] N analgésico *m*

painless ['peɪnlɪs] ADJ sin dolor; *Fig* sin dificultades

painstaking ['peɪnzteɪkɪŋ] ADJ (*person*) concienzudo(a); (*care, research*) esmerado(a)

paint [peɪnt] 1 N pintura *f*
2 VT pintar; **to p. sth white** pintar algo de blanco
3 VI pintar

paintbrush ['peɪntbrʌʃ] N *Art* pincel *m*; (*for walls*) brocha *f*

painter ['peɪntə(r)] N pintor(a) *m,f*

painting ['peɪntɪŋ] N cuadro *m*; (*activity*) pintura *f*

paintwork ['peɪntwɜːk] N pintura *f*

pair [peə(r)] N (*of gloves, shoes*) par *m*; (*of people, cards*) pareja *f*; **a p. of scissors** unas tijeras; **a p. of trousers** un pantalón, unos pantalones

pajamas [pə'dʒæməz] NPL *US* = **pyjamas**

Pakistan [pɑːkɪ'stɑːn] N Paquistán

Pakistani [pɑːkɪ'stɑːnɪ] ADJ & N paquistaní (*mf*)

pal [pæl] N *Fam* amigote(a) *m,f*, *Esp* colega *mf*

palace ['pælɪs] N palacio *m*

palatable ['pælətəbəl] ADJ (*tasty*) sabroso(a); *Fig* aceptable

palate ['pælɪt] N paladar *m*

palatial [pə'leɪʃəl] ADJ suntuoso(a), señorial

palaver [pə'lɑːvə(r)] N *Br Fam* lío *m*, *Esp* follón *m*

pale[1] [peɪl] 1 ADJ (*skin*) pálido(a); (*colour*) claro(a); (*light*) tenue; **to turn p.** palidecer
2 VI palidecer

pale[2] [peɪl] N *Fig* **to be beyond the p.** ser inaceptable

Palestine ['pælɪstaɪn] N Palestina

Palestinian [pælɪ'stɪnɪən] ADJ & N palestino(a) (*m,f*)

palette ['pælɪt] N paleta *f*; **p. knife** espátula *f*

paling ['peɪlɪŋ] N valla *f*

palisade [pælɪ'seɪd] N palizada *f*, estacada *f*

pall[1] [pɔːl] N *Fig* manto *m*; (*of smoke*) cortina *f*

pall[2] [pɔːl] VI aburrir; **it never palls** nunca cansa

pallet ['pælɪt] N plataforma *f* de carga

pallid ['pælɪd] ADJ pálido(a)

pallor ['pælə(r)] N palidez *f*

palm[1] [pɑːm] N (*tree*) palmera *f*; (*leaf*) palma *f*; **date p.** palma datilera; **P. Sunday** domingo *m* de Ramos
▸ **palm off** VT SEP **to p. sth off on sb** colocar *or* endosar algo a algn

palm[2] [pɑːm] N *Anat* palma *f*

palmistry ['pɑːmɪstrɪ] N quiromancia *f*

palpable ['pælpəbəl] ADJ palpable

palpitate ['pælpɪteɪt] VI palpitar

palpitation [pælpɪ'teɪʃən] N palpitación *f*

paltry ['pɔːltrɪ] ADJ (**paltrier, paltriest**) insignificante

pamper ['pæmpə(r)] VT mimar, consentir

pamphlet ['pæmflɪt] N folleto *m*

pan[1] [pæn] 1 N (**a**) (*saucepan*) cazuela *f*, cacerola *f* (**b**) (*of scales*) platillo *m* (**c**) *Br* (*of lavatory*) taza *f*
2 VT *Fam (criticize)* vapulear, *Esp* poner por los suelos

pan[2] [pæn] VI *Cin* tomar vistas panorámicas

panacea [pænə'sɪə] N panacea *f*

panache [pə'næʃ] N garbo *m*, salero *m*

Panama ['pænəmɑː] N Panamá; **P. Canal** Canal *m* de Panamá

pancake ['pænkeɪk] N crepe *f*

panda ['pændə] N panda *m*; *Br* **p. car** coche *m or Am* carro *m or CSur* auto *m* patrulla

pandemonium [pændɪ'məʊnɪəm] N alboroto *m*

pander ['pændə(r)] VI **to p. to** (*person*) complacer a; (*wishes*) acceder a

pane [peɪn] N **p. (of glass)** hoja *f* de vidrio *or Esp* cristal

panel ['pænəl] N (**a**) (*of wall*) panel *m*; (*flat surface*) tabla *f*; (*of instruments*) tablero *m*; (*of ceiling*) artesón *m* (**b**) (*jury*) jurado *m*; *Rad & TV* concursantes *mpl*

panelling, *US* **paneling** ['pænəlɪŋ] N paneles *mpl*

pang [pæŋ] N (*of pain, hunger*) punzada *f*; *Fig* (*of conscience*) remordimiento *m*; **birth pangs** dolores *mpl* del parto

panic ['pænɪk] 1 N pánico *m*; **to get into a p.** ponerse histérico(a)
2 VI aterrarse

panicky ['pænɪkɪ] ADJ asustadizo(a)

panic-stricken ['pænɪkstrɪkən] ADJ aterrado(a)

panorama [pænə'rɑːmə] N panorama *m*

pansy ['pænzɪ] N *Bot* pensamiento *m*; *Fam Pej* mariquita *f*

pant [pænt] 1 N jadeo *m*
2 VI jadear

panther ['pænθə(r)] N pantera *f*

panties ['pæntɪz] NPL *esp US Esp* bragas *fpl*, *Chile, Col, Méx* calzones *mpl*, *Ecuad* follones *mpl*, *RP* bombacha *f*

> Note that the Spanish word **panty** is a false friend and is never a translation for the English word **panties**. In Spanish, **panty** means "(pair of) tights".

pantomime ['pæntəmaɪm] N *Br Th* = obra de teatro musical para niños basada en un cuento de hadas y representada en Navidad

pantry ['pæntrɪ] N despensa *f*

pants [pænts] NPL (**a**) *Br (men's underwear)* calzoncillos *mpl*, *Chile* fundillos *mpl*, *Col* pantaloncillos *mpl*, *Méx* calzones *mpl*, *Méx* chones *mpl*; *(women's underwear) Esp* bragas *fpl*, *Chile*, *Col*, *Méx* calzones *mpl*, *RP* bombacha *f* (**b**) *US (trousers)* pantalones *mpl*

pantyhose ['pæntɪhəʊz] N *US* medias *fpl*, pantis *mpl*

papal ['peɪpəl] ADJ papal

paparazzo [pæpə'rætsəʊ] N *(pl* **paparazzi** [pæpə'rætsiː]) paparazzi *mf*

paper ['peɪpə(r)] 1 N (**a**) *(material)* papel *m*; *Fig* **on p.** en teoría; **writing p.** papel de escribir (**b**) *(exam)* examen *m*; *(essay)* trabajo (escrito) (**c**) *Pol* libro *m* (**d**) *(newspaper)* periódico *m*; **the papers** la prensa (**e**) **papers** *(documents)* documentos *mpl*
2 VT empapelar

paperback ['peɪpəbæk] N libro *m* en rústica

paperclip ['peɪpəklɪp] N clip *m*, sujetapapeles *m inv*

paperweight ['peɪpəweɪt] N pisapapeles *m inv*

paperwork ['peɪpəwɜːk] N papeleo *m*

papier-mâché [pæpjer'mæʃeɪ] N cartón *m* piedra

paprika ['pæprɪkə] N pimentón molido

par [pɑː(r)] N *(parity)* igualdad *f*; *(in golf)* par *m*; *Fig* **it's p. for the course** es lo normal en estos casos; *Fig* **to feel below p.** estar en baja forma

parable ['pærəbəl] N parábola *f*

paracetamol [pærə'siːtəmɒl] N paracetamol *m*

parachute ['pærəʃuːt] 1 N paracaídas *m inv*
2 VI **to p. (down)** saltar *or* lanzarse en paracaídas

parade [pə'reɪd] 1 N desfile *m*; *Mil* **to be on p.** pasar revista
2 VT *Mil* hacer desfilar; *Fig (flaunt)* hacer alarde de
3 VI *(troops)* pasar revista; *(procession)* desfilar

paradise ['pærədaɪs] N paraíso *m*

paradox ['pærədɒks] N paradoja *f*

paradoxical [pærə'dɒksɪkəl] ADJ paradójico(a)

paraffin ['pærəfɪn] N parafina *f*; **liquid p.** aceite *m* de parafina; **p. lamp** lámpara *f* de petróleo

paragliding ['pærəglaɪdɪŋ] N parapente *m*

paragon ['pærəgən] N modelo *m*

paragraph ['pærəgrɑːf] N párrafo *m*

Paraguay ['pærəgwaɪ] N Paraguay

Paraguayan [pærə'gwaɪən] ADJ & N paraguayo(a) *(m,f)*

paralegal [pærə'liːgəl] N *US* ayudante *mf* de un abogado, *RP* procurador(a) *m,f*

parallel ['pærəlel] 1 ADJ paralelo(a) (**to** *or* **with** a); *Fig* comparable (**to** *or* **with** a)
2 N *Geog* paralelo *m*; *Geom* paralela *f*; *Fig* paralelo
3 VT *Fig* ser paralelo(a) a

paralyse ['pærəlaɪz] VT paralizar

paralysis [pə'rælɪsɪs] N parálisis *f*

paralyze ['pærəlaɪz] VT *US* = **paralyse**

paramedic [pærə'medɪk] N auxiliar *mf* sanitario(a)

parameter [pə'ræmɪtə(r)] N parámetro *m*

paramilitary [pærə'mɪlɪtərɪ] ADJ paramilitar

paramount ['pærəmaʊnt] ADJ **of p. importance** de suma importancia

paranoid ['pærənɔɪd] ADJ & N paranoico(a) *(m,f)*

paraphernalia [pærəfə'neɪlɪə] N parafernalia *f*

paraphrase ['pærəfreɪz] VT parafrasear

parasite ['pærəsaɪt] N parásito *m*

parasol ['pærəsɒl] N sombrilla *f*

paratrooper ['pærətruːpə(r)] N paracaidista *mf*

parcel ['pɑːsəl] 1 N paquete *m*; **p. bomb** paquete bomba
2 VT **to p. up** envolver, empaquetar

parched [pɑːtʃt] ADJ *(land)* reseco(a); *(lips, mouth)* seco(a); *Fig* **to be p.** estar muerto(a) de sed

parchment ['pɑːtʃmənt] N pergamino *m*

pardon ['pɑːdən] 1 N perdón *m*; *Jur* indulto *m*; **I beg your p.** (Usted) perdone; **(I beg your) p.?** ¿cómo (dice)?
2 VT perdonar; *Jur* indultar; **p. me!** ¡(Usted) perdone!

parent ['peərənt] N **parents** padres *mpl*

> Note that the Spanish word **pariente** is a false friend and is never a translation for the English word **parent**. In Spanish **pariente** means "relative, relation".

parental [pə'rentəl] ADJ paternal; **p. guidance** consejos *mpl* paternales

parenthesis [pə'renθɪsɪs] N *(pl* **parentheses** [pə'renθɪsiːz]) paréntesis *m inv*; **in p.** entre paréntesis

pariah [pə'raɪə] N paria *mf*

Paris ['pærɪs] N París

parish ['pærɪʃ] N parroquia *f*

Parisian [pə'rɪzɪən] ADJ & N parisino(a) *(m,f)*

parity ['pærɪtɪ] N igualdad *f*; *(of shares)* paridad *f*

park [pɑːk] 1 N parque *m*
2 VT estacionar, *Esp* aparcar

parking ['pɑːkɪŋ] N estacionamiento *m*, *Esp* aparcamiento *m*; **no p.** *(sign)* prohibido estacionar *or Esp* aparcar, estacionamiento prohibido; *US* **p. lot** *Esp* aparcamiento *m*, *RP* playa *f* de estacionamiento, *Col* parqueadero *m*; **p. meter** parquímetro *m*; **p. space** estacionamiento *m*, sitio *m or* hueco *m* para estacionar

parliament ['pɑːləmənt] N parlamento *m*

parliamentary [pɑːlə'mentərɪ] ADJ parlamentario(a)

parlour, US **parlor** ['pɑːlə(r)] N salón m

parochial [pə'rəʊkɪəl] ADJ parroquial; Pej (narrow-minded) de miras estrechas

parody ['pærədɪ] N parodia f

parole [pə'rəʊl] N Jur libertad f condicional; **on p.** en libertad bajo palabra

parquet ['pɑːkeɪ] N **p. floor** suelo m de parqué

parrot ['pærət] N loro m, papagayo m

parry ['pærɪ] VT parar

parsimonious [pɑːsɪ'məʊnɪəs] ADJ tacaño(a)

parsley ['pɑːslɪ] N perejil m

parsnip ['pɑːsnɪp] N chirivía f

parson ['pɑːsən] N cura m

part [pɑːt] **1** N (**a**) (portion, element) parte f; (episode) capítulo m; Tech pieza f; **for the most p.** en la mayor parte (**b**) Cin & Th papel m; **to take p. in sth** participar en algo (**c**) (place) lugar m; **in these parts** por estos lugares (**d**) **for my p.** por mi parte; **to take sb's p.** tomar partido por algn (**e**) US (in hair) raya f, Col, Méx, Ven carrera f
2 ADJ (partial) parcial
3 ADV (partly) en parte
4 VT (separate) separar; **to p. one's hair** hacerse raya or Col, Méx, Ven carrera (en el pelo)
5 VI separarse; (say goodbye) despedirse
▸ **part with** VT INSEP separarse de

partial ['pɑːʃəl] ADJ parcial; **to be p. to sth** ser aficionado(a) a algo

participant [pɑː'tɪsɪpənt] N participante mf; (in competition) concursante mf

participate [pɑː'tɪsɪpeɪt] VI participar (**in** en)

participation [pɑːtɪsɪ'peɪʃən] N participación f

participle ['pɑːtɪsɪpəl] N participio m

particle ['pɑːtɪkəl] N partícula f

particular [pə'tɪkjʊlə(r)] **1** ADJ (**a**) (special) particular, especial; **in this p. case** en este caso concreto; **that p. person** esa persona en particular (**b**) (fussy) exigente
2 NPL **particulars** pormenores mpl; **to take down sb's particulars** anotar los datos personales de algn

particularly [pə'tɪkjʊlɪlɪ] ADV particularmente, especialmente

parting ['pɑːtɪŋ] **1** N (separation) separación f; (farewell) despedida f; Br (in hair) raya f, Col, Méx, Ven carrera f
2 ADJ de despedida

partisan [pɑːtɪ'zæn, 'pɑːtɪzæn] **1** N Mil guerrillero(a) m,f; (supporter) partidario(a) m,f
2 ADJ (supporter) a ultranza; (of party) partidista

partition [pɑː'tɪʃən] **1** N (wall) tabique m; (of country) partición f
2 VT dividir

partly ['pɑːtlɪ] ADV en parte

partner ['pɑːtnə(r)] **1** N compañero(a) m,f; (in dancing, tennis) pareja f; (husband) marido m; (wife) mujer f; Com socio(a) m,f
2 VT acompañar

partnership ['pɑːtnəʃɪp] N (relationship) vida f en común; Com sociedad f

partridge ['pɑːtrɪdʒ] N perdiz pardilla

part-time ['pɑːt'taɪm] **1** ADJ (work etc) de tiempo parcial
2 ADV a tiempo parcial

party ['pɑːtɪ] **1** N (**a**) (celebration) fiesta f (**b**) (group) grupo m (**c**) Pol partido m; **p. political broadcast** espacio m electoral
2 ADJ de fiesta

pass [pɑːs] **1** N (**a**) (of mountain) desfiladero m (**b**) (permit) permiso m; **bus p.** abono m de autobús (**c**) Sport pase m
2 VT (**a**) (go past) (person, place) pasar junto a; (frontier) pasar; (overtake) adelantar (**b**) (exam, law) aprobar; Jur **to p. sentence** dictar sentencia
3 VI (**a**) (go past) pasar; (procession) desfilar; (car) adelantar; Sport hacer un pase; **we passed on the stairs** nos cruzamos en la escalera (**b**) (in exam) aprobar
▸ **pass away** VI Euph pasar a mejor vida
▸ **pass by 1** VT SEP pasar de largo
2 VI pasar
▸ **pass for** VT INSEP pasar por
▸ **pass off 1** VT SEP hacer pasar; **to p. oneself off as sth** hacerse pasar por algo
2 VI (happen) transcurrir
▸ **pass on 1** VT SEP (hand on) transmitir
2 VI Euph pasar a mejor vida
▸ **pass out** VI (faint) desmayarse; Mil graduarse
▸ **pass over** VT INSEP (**a**) (aircraft) volar por (**b**) (disregard) pasar por alto
▸ **pass up** VT SEP Fam (opportunity) dejar pasar; (offer) rechazar

passable ['pɑːsəbəl] ADJ (road) transitable; (acceptable) pasable

passage ['pæsɪdʒ] N (**a**) (alleyway) callejón m; (hallway) pasillo m (**b**) (movement) tránsito m; Naut travesía f (**c**) Mus & Lit pasaje m

passageway ['pæsɪdʒweɪ] N (interior) pasillo m; (exterior) pasaje m

passbook ['pɑːsbʊk] N libreta f de banco

passenger ['pæsɪndʒə(r)] N pasajero(a) m,f

passer-by [pɑːsə'baɪ] N (pl passers-by [pɑːsəz'baɪ]) transeúnte mf

passing ['pɑːsɪŋ] **1** N (**a**) (of time) transcurso m; **in p.** de pasada (**b**) (of law) aprobación f
2 ADJ que pasa; (glance) rápido(a); (thought) pasajero(a)

passion ['pæʃən] N pasión f; **p. fruit** granadilla f

passionate ['pæʃənɪt] ADJ apasionado(a)

passive ['pæsɪv] ADJ pasivo(a); **p. smoker** fumador(a) pasivo(a)

Passover ['pɑːsəʊvə(r)] N Pascua f de los judíos

passport ['pɑːspɔːt] N pasaporte m

password ['pɑːswɜːd] N contraseña f

past [pɑːst] **1** N pasado m; **in the p.** en el pasado; **to have a p.** tener antecedentes
2 ADJ pasado(a); (former) anterior; **in the p.**

weeks en las últimas semanas
3 ADV por delante; **to run p.** pasar corriendo
4 PREP *(beyond)* más allá de; *(more than)* más de; **he's p. forty** pasa de los cuarenta (años); *Br* **it's five p. ten** son las diez y cinco; *Fam* **to be p. it** estar muy carroza

pasta ['pæstə] N pasta *f*, pastas *fpl*

paste [peɪst] **1** N pasta *f*; *(glue)* engrudo *m*
2 VT *(stick)* pegar; *(put paste on)* engomar

pastel ['pæstəl] ADJ & N pastel *(m)*

pasteurized ['pæstʃəraɪzd] ADJ pasteurizado(a)

pastille ['pæstɪl] N pastilla *f*

pastime ['pɑːstaɪm] N pasatiempo *m*

pastor ['pɑːstə(r)] N pastor *m*

pastoral ['pɑːstərəl] ADJ pastoral

pastry ['peɪstrɪ] N *(dough)* pasta *f*; *(cake)* pastel *m*, *Col, CSur* torta *f*

pasture ['pɑːstʃə(r)] N pasto *m*

pasty¹ ['pæstɪ] N *Culin* empanada *f*, pastel *m* de carne

pasty² ['peɪstɪ] ADJ (**pastier, pastiest**) *(complexion)* pálido(a)

pat [pæt] **1** N *(caress)* caricia *f*; *(tap)* palmadita *f*; *Fig* **to give sb a p. on the back** felicitar a algn
2 VT acariciar; **to p. sb on the back** dar a algn una palmadita en la espalda

patch [pætʃ] N *(of material)* parche *m*; *Br (of land)* terreno *m*; *(of colour, light)* mancha *f*; *Br Fam* **to be going through a bad p.** estar pasando por una mala racha

► **patch up** VT SEP *(wounded person)* hacer una cura *or Méx* curación de urgencia a; **to p. things up** *(after argument)* limar asperezas

patchwork ['pætʃwɜːk] **1** N labor *f* de retales
2 ADJ *(quilt etc)* hecho(a) con retales distintos

patchy ['pætʃɪ] ADJ (**patchier, patchiest**) *(colour, performance)* desigual; *(knowledge)* incompleto(a)

pâté ['pæteɪ] N paté *m*

patent ['pætənt, *Br* 'peɪtənt] **1** N *Com* patente *f*
2 ADJ *(obvious)* patente, evidente
3 VT *Com* patentar

patently [*Br* 'peɪtəntlɪ *US* 'pætəntlɪ] ADV **it is p. obvious** está clarísimo

paternal [pə'tɜːnəl] ADJ paternal; *(grandmother etc)* paterno(a)

paternity [pə'tɜːnɪtɪ] N paternidad *f*

path [pɑːθ] N camino *m*, sendero *m*; *(route)* ruta *f*; *(of missile)* trayectoria *f*

pathetic [pə'θetɪk] ADJ *(pitiful)* patético(a); *Fam (hopeless)* malísimo(a); **she was a p. sight** daba lástima verla

pathological [pæθə'lɒdʒɪkəl] ADJ patológico(a)

pathologist [pə'θɒlədʒɪst] N patólogo(a) *m,f*

pathology [pə'θɒlədʒɪ] N patología *f*

pathos ['peɪθɒs] N patetismo *m*

pathway ['pɑːθweɪ] N camino *m*, sendero *m*

patience ['peɪʃəns] N **(a)** *(quality)* paciencia *f*; **to lose one's p. with sb** perder la paciencia con algn **(b)** *Br Cards* solitario *m*

patient ['peɪʃənt] **1** ADJ paciente; **to be p. with sb** tener paciencia con algn
2 N *Med* paciente *mf*

patio ['pætɪəʊ] N patio *m*

patriot ['pætrɪət, 'peɪtrɪət] N patriota *mf*

patriotic [pætrɪ'ɒtɪk] ADJ *(person)* patriota; *(speech, act)* patriótico(a)

patrol [pə'trəʊl] **1** N patrulla *f*; **p. car** coche *m or Am* carro *m or CSur* auto *m* patrulla
2 VT patrullar por

patrolman [pə'trəʊlmən] N *US* policía *m*

patron ['peɪtrən] N **(a)** *(of charity)* patrocinador(a) *m,f*; *(of arts)* mecenas *m inv*; **p. saint** (santo(a)) patrón(ona) **(b)** *(customer)* cliente(a) *m,f* habitual

patronize ['pætrənaɪz] VT **(a)** *(arts)* fomentar; *(shop)* ser cliente(a) *m,f* habitual de; *(club etc)* frecuentar **(b)** *Pej (person)* tratar con condescendencia

patronizing ['pætrənaɪzɪŋ] ADJ *Pej* condescendiente

patter¹ ['pætə(r)] **1** N *(of rain)* repiqueteo *m*; *(of feet)* pasito *m*
2 VI *(rain)* repiquetear; *(feet)* hacer ruido sordo

patter² ['pætə(r)] N *Fam* labia *f*; *(of salesman)* discursillo preparado

pattern ['pætən] N *Sewing* patrón *m*; *(design)* dibujo *m*; *(on material)* estampado *m*; *Fig (of behaviour)* modelo *m*

paunch [pɔːntʃ] N barriga *f*, panza *f*, *Chile* guata *f*

pauper ['pɔːpə(r)] N pobre *mf*

pause [pɔːz] **1** N pausa *f*; *(silence)* silencio *m*
2 VI hacer una pausa; *(be silent)* callarse

pave [peɪv] VT pavimentar; *(with stones)* empedrar; *Fig* **to p. the way for sth/sb** preparar el terreno para algo/algn

pavement ['peɪvmənt] N **(a)** *Br (beside road)* acera *f*, *CSur* vereda *f*, *CAm, Méx* banqueta *f* **(b)** *US (roadway)* calzada *f*

pavilion [pə'vɪljən] N pabellón *m*; *Br Sport (changing rooms)* vestuarios *mpl*

paving ['peɪvɪŋ] N *(on road)* pavimento *m*; *(on floor)* enlosado *m*; *(with stones)* empedrado *m*; **p. stone** losa *f*

paw [pɔː] **1** N *(foot)* pata *f*; *(of cat)* garra *f*; *(of lion)* zarpa *f*
2 VT *(of lion)* dar zarpazos a; *Pej (of person)* manosear, sobar

pawn¹ [pɔːn] N *(in chess)* peón *m*; *Fig* **to be sb's p.** ser el juguete de algn

pawn² [pɔːn] VT empeñar

pawnbroker ['pɔːnbrəʊkə(r)] N prestamista *mf*

pawnshop ['pɔːnʃɒp] N casa *f* de empeños

pay [peɪ] **1** N *(wages)* paga *f*, sueldo *m*; **p.** *Br* **packet** *or US* **envelope** sobre *m* de la paga; **p.** *Br* **rise** *or US* **raise** aumento *m* del sueldo; **p. slip** nómina *f*

2 VT (*pt & pp* **paid**) (**a**) (*person, money, bill*) pagar; **to be** *or* **get paid** cobrar (**b**) (*attention*) prestar; (*homage*) rendir; (*visit*) hacer; **to p. sb a compliment** halagar a algn (**c**) (*be profitable for*) compensar

3 VI (**a**) (*give payment*) pagar; **to p. for sth** pagar (por) algo (**b**) (*be profitable*) ser rentable
▸ **pay back** VT SEP reembolsar; *Fig* **to p. sb back** vengarse de algn
▸ **pay in** VT SEP (*money*) *Esp* ingresar, *Am* depositar
▸ **pay off** **1** VT SEP (*debt*) liquidar; (*mortgage*) cancelar
   2 VI (*be successful*) dar resultado
▸ **pay out** VT SEP (*spend*) gastar (**on** en)
▸ **pay up** VI pagar

payable ['peɪəbəl] ADJ pagadero(a)
pay-as-you-go ['peɪəzjuː'gəʊ] N (*with mobile phone*) prepago *m*
payday ['peɪdeɪ] N día *m* de pago
PAYE [piːeɪwaɪ'iː] N *Br* (*abbr* **pay-as-you-earn**) retención *f* del impuesto sobre la renta
payee [peɪ'iː] N portador(a) *m,f*
payment ['peɪmənt] N pago *m*; (*of cheque*) cobro *m*; **advance p.** anticipo *m*; **down p.** entrada *f*; **monthly p.** mensualidad *f*
payoff ['peɪɒf] N *Fam* (*reward*) compensación *f*; (*bribe*) soborno *m*, *Méx* mordida *f*, *RP* coima *f*
pay-per-view ['peɪpə'vjuː] N pago *m* por visión
payroll ['peɪrəʊl] N nómina *f*
PC ['piː'siː] **1** N (**a**) *Br* (*abbr* **Police Constable**) agente *mf* de policía (**b**) (*abbr* **personal computer**) PC *m*
   2 ADJ (*abbr* **politically correct**) políticamente correcto(a)
pc (*abbr* **per cent**) p.c.
PE ['piː'iː] N *Sch* (*abbr* **physical education**) educación física
pea [piː] N guisante *m*, *Am* arveja *f*, *Carib, Méx* chícharo *m*
peace [piːs] N paz *f*; (*calm*) tranquilidad *f*; **at** *or* **in p.** en paz; **p. and quiet** tranquilidad; **to make p.** hacer las paces; (*of countries*) firmar la paz
peaceable ['piːsəbəl] ADJ pacífico(a)
peaceful ['piːsfʊl] ADJ (*demonstration*) pacífico(a); (*place*) tranquilo(a)
peace-keeping ['piːskiːpɪŋ] ADJ pacificador(a); **p. forces** fuerzas *fpl* de pacificación
peach [piːtʃ] N melocotón *m*, *Am* durazno *m*
peacock ['piːkɒk] N pavo *m* real
peak [piːk] N (*of cap*) visera *f*; (*of mountain*) pico *m*; (*summit*) cima *f*; *Fig* cumbre *f*; **p. hours** horas *fpl* punta; **p. period** horas de mayor consumo; **p. season** temporada alta
peal [piːl] N (*of bells*) repique *m*; **p. of thunder** trueno *m*; **peals of laughter** carcajadas *fpl*
peanut ['piːnʌt] N cacahuete *m*, *Andes, Carib, RP* maní *m*, *CAm, Méx* cacahuate *m*; **p. butter**

mantequilla *f* *or* crema *f* de cacahuete *or* *Andes, Carib, RP* maní *or* *CAm, Méx* cacahuate
pear [peə(r)] N pera *f*
pearl [pɜːl] N perla *f*
peasant ['pezənt] ADJ & N campesino(a) (*m,f*)
peat [piːt] N turba *f*; **p. bog** turbera *f*
pebble ['pebəl] N guijarro *m*; (*small*) china *f*
pecan [*Br* 'piːkən, *US* pɪ'kæn] N pacana *f*
peck [pek] **1** N (*of bird*) picotazo *m*; *Fam* (*kiss*) besito *m*
   2 VT (*of bird*) picotear; *Fam* (*kiss*) dar un besito a
   3 VI **to p. at one's food** picar la comida
pecking order ['pekɪŋɔːdə(r)] N *Fig* jerarquía *f*
peckish ['pekɪʃ] ADJ *Br Fam* **to be p.** tener un poco de hambre *or Esp* gusa
peculiar [pɪ'kjuːlɪə(r)] ADJ (*odd*) extraño(a); (*particular*) característico(a)
peculiarity [pɪkjuːlɪ'ærɪtɪ] N (*oddity*) rareza *f*; (*characteristic*) característica *f*, peculiaridad *f*
pedal ['pedəl] **1** N pedal *m*
   2 VI pedalear
pedantic [pɪ'dæntɪk] ADJ pedante
peddle ['pedəl] VT & VI *Com* vender de puerta en puerta; **to p. drugs** traficar con drogas
peddler ['pedlə(r)] N (*of drugs*) traficante *mf*
pedestal ['pedɪstəl] N pedestal *m*; *Fig* **to put sb on a p.** poner a algn sobre un pedestal
pedestrian [pɪ'destrɪən] **1** N peatón(ona) *m,f*; **p. crossing** paso *m* de peatones
   2 ADJ *Pej* prosaico(a)
pediatrician [piːdɪə'trɪʃən] N *US* = **paediatrician**
pedigree ['pedɪgriː] **1** N linaje *m*; (*family tree*) árbol genealógico; (*of animal*) pedigrí *m*
   2 ADJ (*animal*) de raza
pedophile ['piːdəʊfaɪl] N *US* = **paedophile**
pee [piː] *Fam* **1** N pis *m*
   2 VI hacer pis
peek [piːk] **1** N ojeada *f*
   2 VI **to p. at sth** mirar algo a hurtadillas
peel [piːl] **1** N piel *f*; (*of orange, lemon*) cáscara *f*
   2 VT (*fruit*) pelar
   3 VI (*paint*) desconcharse; (*wallpaper*) despegarse; (*skin*) pelarse
peeler ['piːlə(r)] N **potato p.** pelapatatas *m inv*
peelings ['piːlɪŋz] NPL peladuras *fpl*, mondaduras *fpl*
peep¹ [piːp] N (*sound*) pío *m*
peep² [piːp] **1** N (*glance*) ojeada *f*; (*furtive look*) mirada furtiva
   2 VI **to p. at sth** echar una ojeada a algo; **to p. out from behind sth** dejarse ver detrás de algo
peephole ['piːphəʊl] N mirilla *f*
peer¹ [pɪə(r)] N (*equal*) igual *mf*; *Br* (*noble*) par *m*; **p. group** grupo parejo
peer² [pɪə(r)] VI mirar detenidamente; (*short-sightedly*) mirar con ojos de miope
peerage ['pɪərɪdʒ] N título *m* de nobleza

peeved [pi:vd] ADJ *Fam* fastidiado(a), de mal humor

peevish ['pi:vɪʃ] ADJ malhumorado(a)

peg [peg] **1** N clavija *f*; *(for coat, hat)* percha *f*
2 VT *(clothes)* tender; *(prices)* fijar

pejorative [prɪˈdʒɒrətɪv] ADJ peyorativo(a)

Pekinese [pi:kəˈni:z] ADJ & N pequinés(esa) *(m,f)*

Peking [pi:ˈkɪŋ] N Pekín

pelican ['pelɪkən] N pelícano *m*; *Br* **p. crossing** paso *m* de peatones

pellet ['pelɪt] N bolita *f*; *(for gun)* perdigón *m*

pelt¹ [pelt] N *(skin)* pellejo *m*

pelt² [pelt] **1** VT **to p. sb with sth** tirar algo a algn
2 VI *Fam* **(a) it was pelting (down)** *(raining)* diluviaba, *Esp* caían chuzos de punta **(b) to p. along** *(rush)* correr a toda prisa

pelvis ['pelvɪs] N pelvis *f*

pen¹ [pen] **1** N *(for writing)* pluma (estilográfica); *(ballpoint)* bolígrafo *m*, *Chile* lápiz *m* (de pasta), *Col*, *Ecuad*, *Ven* esferográfica *f*, *Méx* pluma *f*, *RP* birome *f*
2 VT escribir

pen² [pen] **1** N *(enclosure)* corral *m*; *(for sheep)* redil *m*; *(for children)* corralito *m*
2 VT **to p. in** acorralar

penal ['pi:nəl] ADJ penal

penalize ['pi:nəlaɪz] VT castigar; *Sport* penalizar

penalty ['penəltɪ] N *(punishment)* pena *f*; *Sport* castigo *m*, *Ftb* penalti *m*, *Am* penal; **to pay the p. for sth** cargar con las consecuencias de algo; **p. area** área *f* de castigo

penance ['penəns] N penitencia *f*

pence [pens] PL of **penny**

pencil ['pensəl] N lápiz *m*; **p. case** estuche *m* de lápices; **p. sharpener** sacapuntas *m inv*

pendant ['pendənt] N colgante *m*

pending ['pendɪŋ] **1** ADJ pendiente
2 PREP a la espera de; **p. a decision** *(until)* hasta que se tome una decisión

pendulum ['pendjʊləm] N péndulo *m*

penetrate ['penɪtreɪt] **1** VT penetrar; *Fig* adentrarse en
2 VI penetrar

penetrating ['penɪtreɪtɪŋ] ADJ *(look)* penetrante; *(mind)* perspicaz; *(sound)* agudo(a)

penfriend ['penfrend] N amigo(a) *m,f* por carta

penguin ['peŋgwɪn] N pingüino *m*

penicillin [penɪˈsɪlɪn] N penicilina *f*

peninsula [prˈnɪnsjʊlə] N península *f*

penis ['pi:nɪs] N pene *m*

penitent ['penɪtənt] ADJ *Rel* penitente; *(repentant)* arrepentido(a)

penitentiary [penɪˈtenʃərɪ] N *US* cárcel *f*, penal *m*

penknife ['pennaɪf] N navaja *f*, cortaplumas *m inv*

penniless ['penɪlɪs] ADJ **to be p.** estar sin un centavo *or Esp* duro

penny ['penɪ] N *(pl* **pennies, pence***) Br* penique *m*; *US* centavo *m*

penpal ['penpæl] N *US* = **penfriend**

pension ['penʃən] N pensión *f*; **retirement p.** jubilación *f*

pensioner ['penʃənə(r)] N jubilado(a) *m,f*

pensive ['pensɪv] ADJ pensativo(a)

pentagon ['pentəgɒn] N *US Pol* **the P.** el Pentágono

Pentecost ['pentɪkɒst] N Pentecostés *m*

penthouse ['penthaʊs] N ático *m*

pent-up ['pentʌp] ADJ reprimido(a)

penultimate [prˈnʌltɪmɪt] ADJ penúltimo(a)

people ['pi:pəl] NPL **(a)** *(as group)* gente *f*; *(individuals)* personas *fpl*; **many p.** mucha gente; **old p.'s home** asilo *m* de ancianos; **p. say that …** se dice que …; **some p.** algunas personas **(b)** *(citizens)* ciudadanos *mpl*; *(inhabitants)* habitantes *mpl*; **the p.** el pueblo **(c)** *(nation)* pueblo *m*, nación *f*

pep [pep] N *Fam* ánimo *m*, energía *f*; **p. talk** discurso *m* enardecedor

▶ **pep up** VT SEP *Fam* animar

pepper ['pepə(r)] **1** N *(spice)* pimienta *f*; *(vegetable)* pimiento *m*, *Méx* chile *m*, *RP* ají *m*, *Col*, *Ven* pimentón *m*; **black p.** pimienta negra; *Br* **p. pot** pimentero *m*; **red/green p.** pimiento rojo/verde; **p. mill** molinillo *m* de pimienta
2 VT *Fig* **peppered with** salpicado(a) de

peppermint ['pepəmɪnt] N menta *f*; *(sweet)* pastilla *f* de menta

per [pɜ:(r)] PREP por; **five times p. week** cinco veces a la semana; **p. cent** por ciento; **p. day/ annum** al *or* por día/año; **p. capita** per cápita

perceive [pəˈsi:v] VT *(see)* percibir

percentage [pəˈsentɪdʒ] N porcentaje *m*

perceptible [pəˈseptəbəl] ADJ *(visible)* perceptible; *(sound)* audible; *(improvement)* sensible

perception [pəˈsepʃən] N percepción *f*

perceptive [pəˈseptɪv] ADJ perspicaz

perch¹ [pɜ:tʃ] N *(fish)* perca *f*

perch² [pɜ:tʃ] **1** N *(for bird)* percha *f*
2 VI *(bird)* posarse **(on** en)

percolate ['pɜ:kəleɪt] **1** VT filtrar; **percolated coffee** café *m* de cafetera
2 VI filtrarse

percolator ['pɜ:kəleɪtə(r)] N cafetera *f*

percussion [pəˈkʌʃən] N percusión *f*

perennial [pəˈreniəl] ADJ *Bot* perenne

perfect 1 ADJ ['pɜ:fɪkt] perfecto(a); **he's a p. stranger to us** nos es totalmente desconocido; **p. tense** tiempo perfecto
2 VT [pəˈfekt] perfeccionar

perfection [pəˈfekʃən] N perfección *f*

perfectly ['pɜ:fɪktlɪ] ADV perfectamente; *(absolutely)* completamente

perforate ['pɜ:fəreɪt] VT perforar

perforation [pɜːfə'reɪʃən] N perforación f; *(on stamps etc)* perforado m

perform [pə'fɔːm] 1 VT *(task)* ejecutar, realizar; *(piece of music)* interpretar; Th representar
  2 VI *(machine)* funcionar; Mus tocar, interpretar; Th actuar

performance [pə'fɔːməns] N *(of task)* ejecución f, realización f; Mus interpretación f; Th representación f; Sport actuación f; *(of machine etc)* rendimiento m

performer [pə'fɔːmə(r)] N Mus intérprete mf; Th actor m, actriz f

perfume ['pɜːfjuːm] N perfume m

perfunctory [pə'fʌŋktərɪ] ADJ superficial

perhaps [pə'hæps, præps] ADV tal vez, quizá(s), Am talvez

peril ['perɪl] N *(risk)* riesgo m; *(danger)* peligro m

perilous ['perɪləs] ADJ *(risky)* arriesgado(a); *(dangerous)* peligroso(a)

perilously ['perɪləslɪ] ADV peligrosamente

perimeter [pə'rɪmɪtə(r)] N perímetro m

period ['pɪərɪəd] 1 N **(a)** *(stretch of time)* período m; *(stage)* etapa f **(b)** Educ clase f **(c)** US *(full stop)* punto m **(d)** *(menstruation)* regla f
  2 ADJ *(dress, furniture)* de época

periodic [pɪərɪ'ɒdɪk] ADJ periódico(a)

periodical [pɪərɪ'ɒdɪkəl] 1 ADJ periódico(a)
  2 N revista f

periodically [pɪərɪ'ɒdɪklɪ] ADV de vez en cuando

peripheral [pə'rɪfərəl] 1 ADJ periférico(a)
  2 N Comput unidad periférica

perish ['perɪʃ] VI perecer; *(material)* echarse a perder

perishable ['perɪʃəbəl] ADJ perecedero(a)

perjury ['pɜːdʒərɪ] N perjurio m

perk [pɜːk] N Br Fam extra m

▶ **perk up** VI *(person)* animarse; *(after illness)* reponerse

perky ['pɜːkɪ] ADJ (**perkier, perkiest**) animado(a), alegre

perm [pɜːm] 1 N permanente f
  2 VT **to have one's hair permed** hacerse la permanente

permanent ['pɜːmənənt] ADJ permanente; *(address, job)* fijo(a)

permeate ['pɜːmɪeɪt] 1 VT impregnar
  2 VI **to p. through sth** *(liquid)* filtrarse a través de algo; *(fear, suspicion)* extenderse por algo

permissible [pə'mɪsəbəl] ADJ admisible

permission [pə'mɪʃən] N permiso m

permissive [pə'mɪsɪv] ADJ permisivo(a)

permit 1 N ['pɜːmɪt] permiso m; Com licencia f
  2 VT [pə'mɪt] **to p. sb to do sth** permitir a algn hacer algo

pernicious [pə'nɪʃəs] ADJ pernicioso(a)

perpendicular [pɜːpən'dɪkjʊlə(r)] 1 ADJ perpendicular; *(cliff)* vertical
  2 N perpendicular f

perpetrate ['pɜːpɪtreɪt] VT cometer

perpetrator ['pɜːpɪtreɪtə(r)] N autor(a) m,f

perpetual [pə'petʃʊəl] ADJ *(noise)* continuo(a); *(arguing)* interminable; *(snow)* perpetuo(a)

perplex [pə'pleks] VT dejar perplejo(a)

perplexing [pə'pleksɪŋ] ADJ desconcertante

persecute ['pɜːsɪkjuːt] VT perseguir; *(harass)* acosar

persecution [pɜːsɪ'kjuːʃən] N persecución f; *(harassment)* acoso m

perseverance [pɜːsɪ'vɪərəns] N perseverancia f

persevere [pɜːsɪ'vɪə(r)] VI perseverar

Persian ['pɜːʒən] ADJ persa; **P. Gulf** golfo Pérsico

persist [pə'sɪst] VI empeñarse (**in** en)

persistence [pə'sɪstəns] N empeño m

persistent [pə'sɪstənt] ADJ *(person)* perseverante; *(smell etc)* persistente; *(continual)* constante

person ['pɜːsən] N *(pl* **people**) persona f; *(individual)* individuo m; **in p.** en persona

personable ['pɜːsənəbəl] ADJ *(handsome)* bien parecido(a); *(pleasant)* amable

personal ['pɜːsənəl] ADJ **(a)** *(private)* personal; *(friend)* íntimo(a); **p. computer** ordenador m personal, Am computadora f personal; **p. column** anuncios mpl personales; **p. pronoun** pronombre m personal **(b)** *(in person)* en persona; **he will make a p. appearance** estará aquí en persona **(c)** Pej *(comment etc)* indiscreto(a)

personality [pɜːsə'nælɪtɪ] N personalidad f

personally ['pɜːsənəlɪ] ADV *(for my part)* personalmente; *(in person)* en persona

personify [pɜː'sɒnɪfaɪ] VT personificar, encarnar

personnel [pɜːsə'nel] N personal m

perspective [pə'spektɪv] N perspectiva f

Perspex® ['pɜːspeks] N plexiglás® m

perspiration [pɜːspə'reɪʃən] N transpiración f

perspire [pə'spaɪə(r)] VI transpirar

persuade [pə'sweɪd] VT persuadir; **to p. sb to do sth** persuadir a algn para que haga algo

persuasion [pə'sweɪʒən] N persuasión f; *(opinion, belief)* credo m

persuasive [pə'sweɪsɪv] ADJ persuasivo(a)

pert [pɜːt] ADJ pizpireta, coqueto(a)

pertain [pə'teɪn] VI estar relacionado(a) (**to** con)

pertinent ['pɜːtɪnənt] ADJ *(relevant)* pertinente; **p. to** relacionado(a) con, a propósito de

perturbing [pə'tɜːbɪŋ] ADJ inquietante

Peru [pə'ruː] N Perú

peruse [pə'ruːz] VT Fml leer

Peruvian [pə'ruːvɪən] ADJ & N peruano(a) *(m,f)*

pervade [pɜː'veɪd] VT *(of smell)* penetrar; *(of light)* difundirse por; Fig *(of influence)* extenderse por

pervasive [pɜː'veɪsɪv] ADJ *(smell)* penetrante; *(influence)* extendido(a)

perverse [pə'vɜ:s] ADJ (wicked) perverso(a); (contrary) contrario(a) a todo

perversion [Br pə'vɜ:ʃən, US pə'vɜ:rʒən] N Med & Psy perversión f; (of justice, truth) desvirtuación f

pervert 1 N ['pɜ:vɜ:t] Med pervertido(a) m,f (sexual)
2 VT [pə'vɜ:t] pervertir; (justice, truth) desvirtuar

pessimism ['pesɪmɪzəm] N pesimismo m

pessimist ['pesɪmɪst] N pesimista mf

pessimistic [pesɪ'mɪstɪk] ADJ pesimista

pest [pest] N (a) Zool animal nocivo; Bot planta nociva (b) Fam (person) pelma mf; (thing) lata f

pester ['pestə(r)] VT molestar, Esp incordiar

pesticide ['pestɪsaɪd] N pesticida m

pet [pet] **1** N (a) (animal) animal doméstico (b) (favourite) preferido(a) m,f; Fam (addressing sb) cariño m
2 ADJ (favourite) preferido(a)
3 VT acariciar
4 VI Fam (sexually) Esp darse or pegarse el lote, Am manosearse

petal ['petəl] N pétalo m

peter ['pi:tə(r)] **1** N US Fam (penis) pilila f, pito m
2 VI to p. out agotarse

petite [pə'ti:t] ADJ menuda, chiquita

petition [pɪ'tɪʃən] N petición f

petrify ['petrɪfaɪ] VT Literary petrificar; Fig they were petrified se quedaron de piedra

petrol ['petrəl] N Br gasolina f, RP nafta f; **p. can** bidón m de gasolina or RP nafta; **p. pump** surtidor m de gasolina or RP nafta; **p. station** gasolinera f, estación f de servicio, Andes grifo m; **p. tank** depósito m de gasolina, RP tanque m de nafta

> Note that the Spanish word **petróleo** is a false friend and is never a translation for the English word **petrol**. In Spanish **petróleo** means "oil, petroleum".

petroleum [pə'trəʊlɪəm] N petróleo m

petticoat ['petɪkəʊt] N enaguas fpl

petty ['petɪ] ADJ (pettier, pettiest) (trivial) insignificante; (small-minded) mezquino(a); **p. cash** dinero m para gastos pequeños; Naut **p. officer** sargento m de marina

petulant ['petjʊlənt] ADJ malhumorado(a)

> Note that the Spanish word **petulante** is a false friend and is never a translation for the English word **petulant**. In Spanish, **petulante** means "opinionated, arrogant".

pew [pju:] N banco m de iglesia; Br Fam take a p.! ¡siéntate!

pewter ['pju:tə(r)] N peltre m

phantom ['fæntəm] ADJ & N fantasma (m)

pharmaceutical [fɑ:mə'sju:tɪkəl] ADJ farmacéutico(a)

pharmacist ['fɑ:məsɪst] N farmacéutico(a) m,f

pharmacy ['fɑ:məsɪ] N farmacia f

phase [feɪz] **1** N fase f
2 VT to p. sth in/out introducir/retirar algo progresivamente

PhD [pi:eɪtʃ'di:] N (abbr Doctor of Philosophy) (person) Doctor(a) m,f en Filosofía

pheasant ['fezənt] N faisán m (vulgar)

phenomena [fɪ'nɒmɪnə] PL of phenomenon

phenomenal [fɪ'nɒmɪnəl] ADJ fenomenal

phenomenon [fɪ'nɒmɪnən] N (pl phenomena) fenómeno m

phial ['faɪəl] N frasco m

philanthropist [fɪ'lænθrəpɪst] N filántropo(a) m,f

philately [fɪ'lætəlɪ] N filatelia f

Philippines ['fɪlɪpi:nz] NPL the P. las (Islas) Filipinas

philosopher [fɪ'lɒsəfə(r)] N filósofo(a) m,f

philosophical [fɪlə'sɒfɪkəl] ADJ filosófico(a)

philosophy [fɪ'lɒsəfɪ] N filosofía f

phlegm [flem] N flema f

phlegmatic [fleg'mætɪk] ADJ flemático(a)

phobia ['fəʊbɪə] N fobia f

phone [fəʊn] N = **telephone**

phonecard ['fəʊnkɑ:d] N tarjeta telefónica

phone-in ['fəʊnɪn] N Fam = programa de radio o televisión con línea telefónica abierta

phonetic [fə'netɪk] **1** ADJ fonético(a)
2 N phonetics fonética f

phoney ['fəʊnɪ] **1** ADJ (phonier, phoniest) (thing) falso(a); (person) farsante
2 N (person) farsante mf

phosphate ['fɒsfeɪt] N fosfato m

photo ['fəʊtəʊ] N foto f

photocopier ['fəʊtəʊkɒpɪə(r)] N fotocopiadora f

photocopy ['fəʊtəʊkɒpɪ] **1** N fotocopia f
2 VT fotocopiar

photogenic [fəʊtəʊ'dʒenɪk] ADJ fotogénico(a)

photograph ['fəʊtəgræf, 'fəʊtəgrɑ:f] **1** N fotografía f; **black and white/colour p.** fotografía en blanco y negro/en color
2 VT fotografiar

photographer [fə'tɒgrəfə(r)] N fotógrafo(a) m,f

photography [fə'tɒgrəfɪ] N fotografía f

phrase [freɪz] **1** N frase f; **p. book** libro m de frases
2 VT expresar

physical ['fɪzɪkəl] ADJ físico(a); **p. education** educación física

physically ['fɪzɪkəlɪ] ADV físicamente; **p. handicapped** minusválido(a); **to be p. fit** estar en forma

physician [fɪ'zɪʃən] N médico(a) m,f

physicist ['fɪzɪsɪst] N físico(a) m,f

physics ['fɪzɪks] N SING física f

physiological [fɪzɪə'lɒdʒɪkəl] ADJ fisiológico(a)

physiology [fɪzɪ'ɒlədʒɪ] N fisiología f

physiotherapist [fɪzɪəʊ'θerəpɪst] N fisiotera-peuta *mf*

physique [fɪ'ziːk] N físico *m*

pianist ['pɪənɪst] N pianista *mf*

piano [pɪ'ænəʊ] N piano *m*

piccolo ['pɪkələʊ] N flautín *m*

pick [pɪk] **1** N (**a**) *(tool)* pico *m*, piqueta *f* (**b**) **take your p.** *(choice)* elige el que quieras

2 VT (**a**) *(choose)* escoger; *(team)* seleccionar (**b**) *(flowers, fruit)* recoger, *Esp* coger (**c**) *(scratch)* hurgar; **to p. one's nose** hurgarse la nariz (**d**) *(lock)* forzar

3 VI **to p. at one's food** comer sin ganas

▸ **pick off** VT SEP (**a**) *(remove)* quitar (**b**) *(shoot)* matar uno a uno

▸ **pick on** VT INSEP *(persecute)* meterse con

▸ **pick out** VT SEP *(choose)* elegir; *(distinguish)* distinguir; *(identify)* identificar

▸ **pick up 1** VT SEP (**a**) *(object on floor)* recoger, *Esp* coger; *(telephone)* descolgar; **to p. oneself up** levantarse; *Fig* reponerse (**b**) *(collect)* recoger; *(shopping, person)* buscar; **to p. up speed** ganar velocidad (**c**) *(acquire)* conse-guir; *(learn)* aprender

2 VI *(improve)* mejorarse, ir mejorando; *(prices)* subir

pickaxe, *US* **pickax** ['pɪkæks] N piqueta *f*

picket ['pɪkɪt] **1** N piquete *m*; **p. line** piquete

2 VT piquetear

3 VI hacer piquete

pickle ['pɪkəl] **1** N (**a**) *Br (sauce)* = salsa agridulce a base de trocitos de fruta y verduras (**b**) *Fam (mess)* lío *m*, apuro *m*

2 VT *Culin* conservar en adobo *or* escabeche; **pickled onions** cebollas *fpl* en vinagre

pick-me-up ['pɪkmɪʌp] N *Fam* reconstituyente *m*, tónico *m*

pickpocket ['pɪkpɒkɪt] N carterista *mf*

pick-up ['pɪkʌp] N *Br* **p. (arm)** *(on record player)* brazo *m*; **p. (truck)** furgoneta *f*

picnic ['pɪknɪk] **1** N comida *f* de campo, picnic *m*

2 VI hacer una comida de campo

pictorial [pɪk'tɔːrɪəl] ADJ ilustrado(a)

picture ['pɪktʃə(r)] **1** N (**a**) *(painting)* cuadro *m*; *(drawing)* dibujo *m*; *(portrait)* retrato *m*; *(photo)* foto *f*; *(illustration)* ilustración *f*; **p. book** libro ilustrado; **p. postcard** tarjeta *f* postal (**b**) *TV* imagen *f*; *Cin* película *f*; *Br* **to go to the pictures** ir al cine

2 VT *(imagine)* imaginarse

picturesque [pɪktʃə'resk] ADJ pintoresco(a)

pie [paɪ] N *(of fruit)* tarta *f*, pastel *m*; *(of meat, fish)* empanada *f*, pastel, *Col, CSur* torta *f*; *(pasty)* empanadilla *f*

piece [piːs] N (**a**) *(of food)* pedazo *m*, trozo *m*; *(of paper)* trozo; *(part)* pieza *f*; **a p. of advice** un consejo; **a p. of news** una noticia; **to break sth into pieces** hacer algo pedazos; *Fig* **to go to pieces** perder el control (de sí mismo(a)) (**b**) *Lit & Mus* obra *f*, pieza *f* (**c**)

(coin) moneda *f* (**d**) *(in chess)* pieza *f*; *(in draughts)* ficha *f*

▸ **piece together** VT SEP *(facts)* reconstruir; *(jigsaw)* hacer

piecemeal ['piːsmiːl] ADV *(by degrees)* poco a poco, a etapas; *(unsystematically)* desordena-damente

piecework ['piːswɜːk] N trabajo *m* a destajo; **to be on p.** trabajar a destajo

pier [pɪə(r)] N embarcadero *m*, muelle *m*; *(promenade)* = paseo de madera que entra en el mar

pierce [pɪəs] VT perforar; *(penetrate)* penetrar en

piercing ['pɪəsɪŋ] ADJ *(sound etc)* penetrante

piety ['paɪɪtɪ] N piedad *f*

pig [pɪg] N (**a**) *(animal)* cerdo *m* (**b**) *Fam (greedy person)* comilón(ona) *m,f*, glotón(ona) *m,f*, *Am* chancho *m*; *(unpleasant person)* cerdo(a) *m,f*, asqueroso(a) *m,f*, *Am* chancho *m* (**c**) *Fam Pej (policeman)* *Esp* madero *m*, *Andes* paco *m*, *Méx* tamarindo *m*, *RP* cana *m*

pigeon ['pɪdʒɪn] N paloma *f*; *Culin & Sport* pichón *m*

pigeonhole ['pɪdʒɪnhəʊl] N casilla *f*

piggy ['pɪgɪ] N **p. bank** hucha *f*, *Am* alcancía *f* (en forma de cerdito)

pigheaded [pɪg'hedɪd] ADJ terco(a), cabezota

piglet ['pɪglɪt] N cerdito *m*, lechón *m*

pigment ['pɪgmənt] N pigmento *m*

pigskin ['pɪgskɪn] N piel *f* de cerdo

pigsty ['pɪgstaɪ] N pocilga *f*

pigtail ['pɪgteɪl] N trenza *f*; *(bullfighter's)* coleta *f*

pike [paɪk] N *(fish)* lucio *m*

pilchard ['pɪltʃəd] N sardina *f*

pile¹ [paɪl] **1** N montón *m*

2 VT amontonar

3 VI *Fam* **to p. into** meterse atropelladamente en

▸ **pile up 1** VT SEP *(things)* amontonar; *(riches, debts)* acumular

2 VI amontonarse

pile² [paɪl] N *(on carpet)* pelo *m*; **thick p.** pelo largo

piles [paɪlz] NPL *Med* almorranas *fpl*, hemo-rroides *fpl*

pile-up ['paɪlʌp] N *Aut* choque *m* en cadena

pilfer ['pɪlfə(r)] VT & VI hurtar, *Esp* sisar

pilgrim ['pɪlgrɪm] N peregrino(a) *m,f*

pilgrimage ['pɪlgrɪmɪdʒ] N peregrinación *f*

pill [pɪl] N píldora *f*, pastilla *f*; **to be on the p.** estar tomando la píldora (anticonceptiva)

pillage ['pɪlɪdʒ] VT & VI pillar, saquear

pillar ['pɪlə(r)] N pilar *m*, columna *f*; *Br* **p. box** buzón *m*

pillion ['pɪljən] N asiento trasero *(de una moto)*

pillow ['pɪləʊ] N almohada *f*

pillowcase ['pɪləʊkeɪs] N funda *f* de almohada

pilot ['paɪlət] 1 N piloto m
2 ADJ (trial) piloto inv; **p. light** piloto m; **p. scheme** proyecto piloto
3 VT pilotar

pimp [pɪmp] N proxeneta m, Esp chulo m, RP cafiolo m

pimple ['pɪmpəl] N grano m, espinilla f

PIN [pɪn] N (abbr **personal identification number**) **P. (number)** PIN m

pin [pɪn] 1 N (for sewing) alfiler m; (bolt) clavija f; Br (of electric plug) clavija f; (in bowling) bolo m; (brooch, badge) pin m; **pins and needles** hormigueo m
2 VT (on board) clavar con chinchetas; (garment etc) sujetar con alfileres; **to p. sb against a wall** tener a algn contra una pared; Fig **to p. one's hopes on sth** poner sus esperanzas en algo; Fam **to p. a crime on sb** endosar un delito a algn
▸ **pin down** VT SEP Fig **to p. sb down** hacer que algn se comprometa

pinafore ['pɪnəfɔː(r)] N (apron) delantal m; **p. dress** Esp pichi m, CSur, Méx jumper m

pinball ['pɪnbɔːl] N flipper m, máquina f de petacos

pincers ['pɪnsəz] NPL (on crab) pinzas fpl; (tool) tenazas fpl

pinch [pɪntʃ] 1 N (nip) pellizco m; Fig Br **at** or US **in a p.** en caso de apuro; **a p. of salt** una pizca de sal
2 VT pellizcar; Br Fam (steal) afanar, Esp levantar
3 VI (shoes) apretar

> Note that the Spanish verb **pinchar** is a false friend and is never a translation for the English verb **to pinch**. In Spanish **pinchar** means "to prick, to puncture".

pincushion ['pɪnkʊʃən] N acerico m

pine¹ [paɪn] N (tree) pino m; **p. cone** piña f

pine² [paɪn] VI **to p. (away)** consumirse, morirse de pena; **to p. for sth/sb** echar de menos or añorar algo/a algn, Am extrañar algo/a algn

pineapple ['paɪnæpəl] N piña f, RP ananá m

ping [pɪŋ] N sonido metálico; (of bullet) silbido m

Ping-Pong® ['pɪŋpɒŋ] N ping-pong® m

pink [pɪŋk] 1 N (colour) rosa m; Bot clavel m
2 ADJ (colour) rosa inv; Pol Fam rojillo(a)

pinnacle ['pɪnəkəl] N (of building) pináculo m; (of mountain) cima f, pico m; Fig (of success) cumbre f

pinpoint ['pɪnpɔɪnt] VT señalar

pinstripe ['pɪnstraɪp] ADJ a rayas

pint [paɪnt] N pinta f; Br Fam **a p. (of beer)** una pinta (de cerveza)

pioneer [paɪə'nɪə(r)] 1 N (settler) pionero(a) m,f; (forerunner) precursor(a) m,f
2 VT ser pionero(a) en

pious ['paɪəs] ADJ piadoso(a), devoto(a); Pej beato(a)

pip¹ [pɪp] N (seed) pepita f

pip² [pɪp] N (sound) señal (corta); (on dice) punto m

pipe [paɪp] 1 N (**a**) (tube) conducto m, tubería f; (of organ) caramillo m; Fam **the pipes** (bagpipes) la gaita (**b**) (for smoking) pipa f; **p. cleaner** limpiapipas m inv; Fig **p. dream** sueño m imposible
2 VT (water) llevar por tubería; (oil) transportar por oleoducto; **piped music** hilo m musical
▸ **pipe down** VI Fam callarse
▸ **pipe up** VI Fam hacerse oír

pipeline ['paɪplaɪn] N tubería f, cañería f; (for gas) gasoducto m; (for oil) oleoducto m

piper ['paɪpə(r)] N gaitero(a) m,f

piping ['paɪpɪŋ] 1 N (for water, gas etc) tubería f, cañería f
2 ADJ **p. hot** bien caliente

piquant ['piːkənt] ADJ picante; (fig) intrigante

pique [piːk] 1 N enojo m
2 VT herir

pirate ['paɪrɪt] N pirata m; **p. edition** edición f pirata; **p. radio** emisora f pirata; **p. ship** barco m pirata

pirouette [pɪrʊ'et] 1 N pirueta f
2 VI hacer piruetas

Pisces ['paɪsiːz] N Piscis m inv

piss [pɪs] very Fam 1 VI mear
2 N meada f

pissed [pɪst] ADJ very Fam (**a**) Br (drunk) Esp, Méx pedo inv, Col caído(a), RP en pedo (**b**) US (angry) cabreado(a)

pistachio [pɪs'taːʃɪəʊ] N (nut) pistacho m

pistol ['pɪstəl] N pistola f

piston ['pɪstən] N pistón m

pit¹ [pɪt] 1 N hoyo m; (large) hoya f; (coal mine) mina f de carbón; Th platea f; **the pits** (in motor racing) los boxes
2 VT **to p. one's wits against sb** medirse con algn

pit² [pɪt] N (of cherry) hueso m, pipo m, RP carozo m; US (of peach, plum) hueso m, RP carozo m

pitch [pɪtʃ] 1 VT (**a**) (throw) lanzar, arrojar (**b**) (tent) armar
2 N (**a**) Mus (of sound) tono m (**b**) esp Br Sport campo m, cancha f

pitch-black [pɪtʃ'blæk], **pitch-dark** [pɪtʃ'daːk] ADJ negro(a) como la boca del lobo

pitched [pɪtʃt] ADJ **p. battle** batalla f campal

pitcher ['pɪtʃə(r)] N (container) cántaro m, jarro m

pitchfork ['pɪtʃfɔːk] N horca f

piteous ['pɪtɪəs] ADJ lastimoso(a)

pitfall ['pɪtfɔːl] N dificultad f, obstáculo m

pith [pɪθ] N (of orange) piel blanca; Fig meollo m

pithy ['pɪθɪ] ADJ (**pithier, pithiest**) *Fig* contundente

pitiful ['pɪtɪfʊl] ADJ *(producing pity)* lastimoso(a); *(terrible)* lamentable

pitiless ['pɪtɪlɪs] ADJ despiadado(a), implacable

pittance ['pɪtəns] N miseria *f*

pity ['pɪtɪ] **1** N (**a**) *(compassion)* compasión *f*, piedad *f*; **to take p. on sb** compadecerse de algn (**b**) *(shame)* lástima *f*, pena *f*; **what a p.!** ¡qué pena!, ¡qué lástima!
2 VT compadecerse de; **I p. them** me dan pena

pivot ['pɪvət] **1** N pivote *m*
2 VI girar sobre su eje

pizza ['piːtsə] N pizza *f*; **p. parlour** pizzería *f*

placard ['plækɑːd] N pancarta *f*

placate [plə'keɪt] VT aplacar, apaciguar

place [pleɪs] **1** N (**a**) *(location)* sitio *m*, lugar *m*; **to be in/out of p.** estar en/fuera de su sitio; **to take p.** tener lugar (**b**) *(seat)* sitio *m*; *(on bus)* asiento *m*; *(at university)* plaza *m*; **to change places with sb** intercambiar el sitio con algn; **to take sb's p.** sustituir a algn (**c**) *(position on scale)* posición *f*; *(social position)* rango *m*; **in the first p.** en primer lugar (**d**) *(house)* casa *f*; *(building)* lugar *m*; **we're going to his p.** vamos a su casa
2 VT (**a**) *(put)* poner, colocar; **to p. an order with sb** hacer un pedido a algn (**b**) *(face, person)* recordar; *(in job)* colocar en un empleo

placid ['plæsɪd] ADJ apacible

plagiarize ['pleɪdʒəraɪz] VT plagiar

plague [pleɪg] **1** N *(of insects)* plaga *f*; *Med* peste *f*
2 VT **to p. sb with requests** acosar a algn a peticiones

plaice [pleɪs] N *(pl plaice)* *(fish)* platija *f*

plaid [plæd, pleɪd] N *(cloth)* tejido *m* escocés

plain [pleɪn] **1** ADJ (**a**) *(clear)* claro(a), evidente; *Fig* **he likes p. speaking** le gusta hablar con franqueza (**b**) *(simple)* sencillo(a); *(chocolate)* amargo(a); *(flour)* sin levadura; **in p. clothes** vestido(a) de paisano; **the p. truth** la verdad lisa y llana (**c**) *(unattractive)* poco atractivo(a)
2 N *Geog* llanura *f*, llano *m*

plainly ['pleɪnlɪ] ADV claramente; *(simply)* sencillamente; **to speak p.** hablar con franqueza

plaintiff ['pleɪntɪf] N demandante *mf*

plaintive ['pleɪntɪv] ADJ lastimero(a)

plait [plæt] **1** N trenza *f*
2 VT trenzar

plan [plæn] **1** N *(scheme)* plan *m*, proyecto *m*; *(drawing)* plano *m*
2 (**a**) *(for future)* planear, proyectar; *(economy)* planificar (**b**) *(intend)* pensar, tener la intención de; **it wasn't planned** no estaba previsto
3 VI hacer planes; **to p. on doing sth** tener la intención de hacer algo

plane¹ [pleɪn] **1** N (**a**) *Math* plano *m*; *Fig* nivel *m* (**b**) *Fam* Av avión *m*
2 ADJ *Geom* plano(a)
3 VI *(glide)* planear

plane² [pleɪn] **1** N *(tool)* cepillo *m*
2 VT cepillar

plane³ [pleɪn] N *Bot* **p. (tree)** plátano *m*

planet ['plænɪt] N planeta *m*

plank [plæŋk] N tabla *f*, tablón *m*

planner ['plænə(r)] N planificador(a) *m,f*

planning ['plænɪŋ] N planificación *f*; **family p.** planificación familiar; *Br* **p. permission** licencia *f* de obras

plant¹ [plɑːnt] **1** N planta *f*
2 VT *(flowers)* plantar; *(seeds)* sembrar; *(bomb)* colocar

plant² [plɑːnt] N *(factory)* planta *f*, fábrica *f*; *(machinery)* maquinaria *f*

plantation [plæn'teɪʃən] N plantación *f*

plaque [plæk] N placa *f*; *(on teeth)* sarro *m*

plasma ['plæzmə] N plasma *m*; *Comput* **p. screen** pantalla *f* de plasma

plaster ['plɑːstə(r)] **1** N *Constr* yeso *m*; *Med* escayola *f*; *Br* **(sticking) p.** tirita® *f*, *Am* curita *f*; **p. of Paris** yeso mate
2 VT *Constr* enyesar; *Fig* *(cover)* cubrir (**with** de)

plastered ['plɑːstəd] ADJ *Fam* borracho(a), trompa

plasterer ['plɑːstərə(r)] N yesero(a) *m,f*

plastic ['plæstɪk] **1** N plástico *m*
2 ADJ *(cup, bag)* de plástico; **p. surgery** cirugía plástica

Plasticine® ['plæstɪsiːn] N plastilina® *f*

plate [pleɪt] **1** N (**a**) *(for food)* plato *m* (**b**) *(sheet)* placa *f*; **gold p.** chapa *f* de oro; **p. glass** vidrio cilindrado (**c**) *(in book)* grabado *m*, lámina *f*
2 VT chapar

plateau ['plætəʊ] N meseta *f*

platform ['plætfɔːm] N (**a**) *(raised flat surface)* plataforma *f*; *(stage)* estrado *m*; *(at meeting)* tribuna *f* (**b**) *Rail* andén *m*; **p. ticket** billete *m* de andén (**c**) *Pol* *(programme)* programa *m*

platinum ['plætɪnəm] N platino *m*

platitude ['plætɪtjuːd] N lugar *m* común, tópico *m*

platoon [plə'tuːn] N *Mil* pelotón *m*

platter ['plætə(r)] N fuente *f*

plausible ['plɔːzəbəl] ADJ plausible

play [pleɪ] **1** VT (**a**) *(game)* jugar a; *(team)* jugar contra (**b**) *(instrument, tune)* tocar; **to p. a CD** poner un CD (**c**) *(in play, film)* interpretar; *Fig* **to p. a part in sth** participar en algo
2 VI (**a**) *(children)* jugar (**with** con); *(animals)* juguetear (**b**) *Sport* jugar; *Fig* **to p. for time** tratar de ganar tiempo (**c**) *(joke)* bromear (**d**) *Mus* tocar; *(instrument)* sonar
3 N (**a**) *Th* obra *f* de teatro (**b**) *Sport* juego *m* (**c**) *Tech & Fig* *(movement)* juego *m*; **a p. on words** un juego de palabras

▸ **play around** VI (*waste time*) gandulear; (*be unfaithful*) tener líos

▸ **play down** VT SEP minimizar, quitar importancia a

▸ **play on** VT INSEP (*take advantage of*) aprovecharse de; (*nerves etc*) exacerbar

▸ **play up 1** VT SEP (*annoy*) dar la lata a, fastidiar
2 VI Br (*child, injury etc*) dar guerra

playboy ['pleɪbɔɪ] N playboy m

player ['pleɪə(r)] N Sport jugador(a) m,f; Mus músico(a) m,f; Th (*man*) actor m; (*woman*) actriz f

playful ['pleɪfʊl] ADJ juguetón(ona)

playground ['pleɪgraʊnd] N patio m de recreo

playgroup ['pleɪgruːp] N jardín m de infancia

playing ['pleɪɪŋ] N juego m; **p. card** carta f, naipe m; **p. field** campo m de deportes

playmate ['pleɪmeɪt] N compañero(a) m,f de juego

play-off ['pleɪɒf] N Sport partido m de desempate

playpen ['pleɪpen] N corralito m or parque m (de niños)

playschool ['pleɪskuːl] N escuela f infantil, guardería f

plaything ['pleɪθɪŋ] N juguete m

playtime ['pleɪtaɪm] N (*at school*) recreo m

playwright ['pleɪraɪt] N dramaturgo(a) m,f

PLC, plc [piːel'siː] N Br (*abbr public limited company*) ≃ S.A.

plea [pliː] N (a) (*request*) petición f, súplica f, Am pedido m; (*excuse*) pretexto m, disculpa f (b) Jur alegato m

plead [pliːd] **1** VT (a) Jur & Fig **to p. sb's cause** defender la causa de algn (b) **to p. ignorance** (*give as excuse*) alegar ignorancia
2 VI (a) (*beg*) rogar, suplicar; **to p. with sb to do sth** suplicar a algn que haga algo (b) Jur **to p. guilty/not guilty** declararse culpable/inocente

pleasant ['plezənt] ADJ agradable

pleasantry ['plezəntrɪ] N cumplido m

please [pliːz] **1** VT (*give pleasure to*) agradar, complacer; (*satisfy*) satisfacer; Fam **p. yourself** como quieras; **easy/hard to p.** poco/muy exigente
2 VI (*give pleasure*) complacer, agradar
3 ADV por favor; **may I? – p. do** ¿me permite? – desde luego; **p. do not smoke** (*sign*) se ruega no fumar; **yes, p.** sí, por favor

pleased [pliːzd] ADJ (*happy*) contento(a); (*satisfied*) satisfecho(a); **p. to meet you!** ¡encantado(a)!, ¡mucho gusto!; **to be p. about sth** alegrarse de algo

pleasing ['pliːzɪŋ] ADJ (*pleasant*) agradable, grato(a); (*satisfactory*) satisfactorio(a)

pleasure ['pleʒə(r)] N placer m; **it's a p. to talk to him** da gusto hablar con él; **to take great p. in doing sth** disfrutar mucho haciendo algo; **with p.** con mucho gusto

pleat [pliːt] **1** N pliegue m
2 VT hacer pliegues en

pledge [pledʒ] **1** N promesa f; (*token of love etc*) señal f; (*guarantee*) prenda f
2 VT (*promise*) prometer; (*pawn*) empeñar

plentiful ['plentɪfʊl] ADJ abundante

plenty ['plentɪ] N abundancia f; **p. of books** muchos libros; **p. of time** tiempo de sobra; **we've got p.** tenemos de sobra

Plexiglas® ['pleksɪglɑːs] N US plexiglás® m

pliable ['plaɪəbəl] ADJ flexible

pliers ['plaɪəz] NPL alicates mpl, tenazas fpl

plight [plaɪt] N situación f grave

plimsolls ['plɪmsɒlz] NPL Br zapatos mpl de tenis

plinth [plɪnθ] N plinto m

plod [plɒd] VI andar con paso pesado; Fig **to p. on** perseverar; Fig **to p. through a report** estudiar laboriosamente un informe

plodder ['plɒdə(r)] N trabajador(a) m,f/estudiante mf tenaz

plonk¹ [plɒŋk] VT esp Br Fam dejar caer

plonk² [plɒŋk] N Br Fam (*cheap wine*) vino m peleón

plot¹ [plɒt] **1** N (a) (*conspiracy*) complot m (b) Th & Lit (*story*) argumento m, trama f
2 VT (a) (*course, route*) trazar (b) (*scheme*) fraguar
3 VI conspirar, tramar

plot² [plɒt] N Agr terreno m; (*for building*) solar m; **vegetable p.** campo m de hortalizas

plough [plaʊ] **1** N arado m
2 VT arar
3 VI **to p. into sth** chocar contra algo

▸ **plough back** VT SEP (*profits*) reinvertir

plow [plaʊ] N, VT & VI US = **plough**

ploy [plɔɪ] N estratagema f

pluck [plʌk] **1** VT (a) (*hair, feathers*) arrancar (**out of** de) (b) (*flower*) arrancar (c) (*chicken*) desplumar (d) (*guitar*) puntear
2 N (*courage*) valor m, ánimo m

▸ **pluck up** VT SEP **to p. up courage** armarse de valor

plucky ['plʌkɪ] ADJ (**pluckier, pluckiest**) valiente

plug [plʌg] **1** N (a) (*in bath etc*) tapón m (b) Elec enchufe m, clavija f; **two-/three-pin p.** clavija bipolar/tripolar
2 VT (a) (*hole*) tapar (b) Fam (*publicize*) dar publicidad a; (*idea etc*) hacer hincapié en

▸ **plug in** VT SEP enchufar

plughole ['plʌghəʊl] N desagüe m

plum [plʌm] **1** N (*fruit*) ciruela f
2 ADJ **a p. job** Esp un chollo or Méx churro (de trabajo), RP un laburazo

plumage ['pluːmɪdʒ] N plumaje m

plumb [plʌm] **1** ADV Fam **p. in the middle** justo en medio; US **he's p. crazy** está completamente loco
2 VT Fig **to p. the depths** tocar fondo

plumber ['plʌmə(r)] N fontanero(a) m,f, Méx, RP, Ven plomero(a) m,f

plumbing ['plʌmɪŋ] N (occupation) fontanería f, Méx, RP, Ven plomería f; (system) tuberías fpl, cañerías fpl

plume [pluːm] N penacho m

plummet ['plʌmɪt] VI (bird, plane) desplomarse, caer en picado or Am picada; Fig (prices) bajar vertiginosamente; (morale) caer a plomo

plump¹ [plʌmp] ADJ (person) relleno(a); (baby) rechoncho(a)
▸ **plump down** VT SEP dejar caer
▸ **plump up** VT SEP (cushions) ahuecar

plump² [plʌmp] VI to p. for sth optar por algo

plunder ['plʌndə(r)] 1 VT saquear
2 N (action) saqueo m, pillaje m; (loot) botín m

plunge [plʌndʒ] 1 VT (immerse) sumergir; (thrust) arrojar
2 VI (dive) lanzarse, zambullirse; Fig (fall) caer, hundirse; (prices) desplomarse
3 N (dive) zambullida f; Fig (fall) desplome m; to take the p. dar el paso decisivo

plunger ['plʌndʒə(r)] N Tech émbolo m; (for pipes) desatascador m

pluperfect [pluː'pɜːfɪkt] N pluscuamperfecto m

plural ['plʊərəl] ADJ & N plural (m)

plus [plʌs] 1 PREP más; three p. four makes seven tres más cuatro hacen siete
2 N Math signo m más; Fig (advantage) ventaja f

plush [plʌʃ] 1 N felpa f
2 ADJ Fam lujoso(a), Esp muy puesto(a)

plutonium [pluː'təʊnɪəm] N plutonio m

ply [plaɪ] 1 VT to p. one's trade ejercer su oficio; to p. sb with drinks no parar de ofrecer copas a algn
2 VI (ship) ir y venir; to p. for hire ir en busca de clientes

plywood ['plaɪwʊd] N madera contrachapada

PM [piː'em] N Br (abbr Prime Minister) primer(a) ministro(a) m,f

p.m. [piː'em] (abbr post meridiem) después del mediodía; at 2 p.m. a las dos de la tarde

PMT [piːem'tiː] N (abbr premenstrual tension) tensión f premenstrual

pneumatic [njuː'mætɪk] ADJ neumático(a)

pneumonia [njuː'məʊnɪə] N pulmonía f

PO [piː'əʊ] N (abbr Post Office) oficina f de correos; PO Box apartado m de correos, CAm, Carib, Méx casilla f postal, Andes, RP casilla de correos

poach¹ [pəʊtʃ] VT (a) to p. fish/game pescar/cazar furtivamente (b) Fam Fig (steal) birlar

poach² [pəʊtʃ] VT Culin (egg) escalfar; (fish) hervir

poacher ['pəʊtʃə(r)] N pescador/cazador furtivo

pocket ['pɒkɪt] 1 N (a) (in trousers, jacket) bolsillo m, CAm, Méx, Perú bolsa f; Fig to be £10 in/out of p. salir ganando/perdiendo 10 libras; p. money dinero m para gastos (b) (of air) bolsa f (c) (of resistance) foco m
2 VT (money) embolsarse

pocketbook ['pɒkɪtbʊk] N US (wallet) cartera f; (handbag) Esp bolso m, Col, CSur cartera f, Méx bolsa f

pocketknife ['pɒkɪtnaɪf] N navaja f

pod [pɒd] N vaina f

podgy ['pɒdʒɪ] ADJ (podgier, podgiest) Br gordinflón(ona), regordete

podiatrist [pə'daɪətrɪst] N US pedicuro(a) m,f

podium ['pəʊdɪəm] N podio m

poem ['pəʊɪm] N poema m

poet ['pəʊɪt] N poeta mf

poetic [pəʊ'etɪk] ADJ poético(a)

poetry ['pəʊɪtrɪ] N poesía f

poignant ['pɔɪnjənt] ADJ conmovedor(a)

point [pɔɪnt] 1 N (a) (sharp end) punta f (b) (place) punto m; Fig p. of no return punto sin retorno (c) (quality) good/bad p. cualidad buena/mala (d) (moment) at that p. en aquel momento; to be on the p. of doing sth estar a punto de hacer algo (e) (score) punto m, tanto m (f) (in argument) punto m; I take your p. entiendo lo que quieres decir (g) (purpose) propósito m; I don't see the p. no veo el sentido; there's no p. in going no merece la pena ir; to come to the p. llegar al meollo de la cuestión (h) (on scale) punto m; (in share index) entero m; six p. three seis coma tres (i) Geog punta f (j) points Aut platinos mpl; Br Rail agujas fpl
2 VT (way etc) señalar, indicar; to p. a gun at sb apuntar a algn con una pistola
3 VI señalar, indicar; to p. at sth/sb señalar algo/a algn con el dedo
▸ **point out** VT SEP indicar, señalar; (mention) hacer resaltar

point-blank ['pɔɪnt'blæŋk] 1 ADJ a quemarropa; (refusal) rotundo(a)
2 ADV (shoot) a quemarropa; (refuse) rotundamente

pointed ['pɔɪntɪd] ADJ (sharp) puntiagudo(a); Fig (comment) intencionado(a); (cutting) mordaz

pointedly ['pɔɪntɪdlɪ] ADV Fig (significantly) con intención; (cuttingly) con mordacidad

pointer ['pɔɪntə(r)] N (a) (indicator) indicador m, aguja f; (for map) puntero m (b) (dog) perro m de muestra

pointless ['pɔɪntlɪs] ADJ sin sentido

poise [pɔɪz] 1 N (bearing) porte m; (self-assurance) aplomo m

2 VT *Fig* **to be poised to do sth** estar listo(a) para hacer algo

poison ['pɔɪzən] **1** N veneno *m*
2 VT envenenar

poisoning ['pɔɪzənɪŋ] N envenenamiento *m*; *(by food etc)* intoxicación *f*

poisonous ['pɔɪzənəs] ADJ *(plant, snake)* venenoso(a); *(gas)* tóxico(a); *Fig (rumour)* pernicioso(a)

poke [pəʊk] VT *(with finger or stick)* dar con la punta del dedo/del bastón a; **to p. one's head out** asomar la cabeza; **to p. the fire** atizar el fuego

▸ **poke about, poke around** VI fisgonear, hurgar

▸ **poke out** VT SEP *(eye)* sacar

poker¹ ['pəʊkə(r)] N *(for fire)* atizador *m*

poker² ['pəʊkə(r)] N *Cards* póquer *m*

poker-faced ['pəʊkəfeɪst] ADJ *Fam* de cara impasible

poky ['pəʊkɪ] ADJ **(pokier, pokiest)** *Fam Pej* minúsculo(a); **a p. little room** un cuartucho

Poland ['pəʊlənd] N Polonia

polar ['pəʊlə(r)] ADJ polar; **p. bear** oso *m* polar

Pole [pəʊl] N polaco(a) *m,f*

pole¹ [pəʊl] N palo *m*; **p. vault** salto *m* con pértiga

pole² [pəʊl] N *Geog* polo *m*; *Fig* **to be poles apart** ser polos opuestos

police [pə'liːs] **1** NPL policía *f*; **p. car** coche *m* or *Am* carro *m* or *CSur* auto *m* de policía; *Br* **p. constable** policía *m*; **p. force** cuerpo *m* de policía; **p. record** antecedentes *mpl* penales; **p. state** estado *m* policial; **p. station** comisaría *f*
2 VT vigilar

policeman [pə'liːsmən] N policía *m*

policewoman [pə'liːswʊmən] N (mujer *f*) policía *f*

policy ['pɒlɪsɪ] N *Pol* política *f*; *(of company)* norma *f*, principio *m*; *Ins* póliza *f* (de seguros)

polio ['pəʊlɪəʊ] N poliomielitis *f*

Polish ['pəʊlɪʃ] **1** ADJ polaco(a)
2 N **(a) the P.** los polacos **(b)** *(language)* polaco *m*

polish ['pɒlɪʃ] **1** VT pulir; *(furniture)* encerar; *(shoes)* limpiar; *(silver)* sacar brillo a
2 N **(a)** *(for furniture)* cera *f*; *(for shoes)* betún *m*; *(for nails)* esmalte *m* **(b)** *(shine)* brillo *m*; *Fig (refinement)* refinamiento *m*

▸ **polish off** VT SEP *Fam (work)* despachar; *(food)* zamparse

▸ **polish up** VT SEP *Fig* perfeccionar

polished ['pɒlɪʃt] ADJ *Fig (manners)* refinado(a); *(style)* pulido(a); *(performance)* impecable

polite [pə'laɪt] ADJ educado(a)

politeness [pə'laɪtnɪs] N educación *f*

politic ['pɒlɪtɪk] ADJ prudente

political [pə'lɪtɪkəl] ADJ político(a)

politically [pə'lɪtɪklɪ] ADV políticamente; **p. correct** políticamente correcto(a)

politician [pɒlɪ'tɪʃən] N político(a) *m,f*

politics ['pɒlɪtɪks] N SING política *f*

polka ['pɒlkə] N *(dance)* polca *f*; **p. dot** lunar *m*

poll [pəʊl] **1** N **(a)** *(voting)* votación *f*; **the polls** las elecciones; **to go to the polls** acudir a las urnas **(b)** *(survey)* encuesta *f*
2 VT *(votes)* obtener

pollen ['pɒlən] N polen *m*

polling ['pəʊlɪŋ] N votación *f*; **p. booth** cabina *f* electoral; **p. station** colegio *m* electoral

pollute [pə'luːt] VT contaminar

pollution [pə'luːʃən] N contaminación *f*, polución *f*; **environmental p.** contaminación ambiental

polo ['pəʊləʊ] N *Sport* polo *m*; *Br* **p. neck (sweater)** suéter *m* or *Esp* jersey *m* or *Col* saco *m* or *RP* pulóver *m* de cuello alto or de cisne

polyester [pɒlɪ'estə(r)] N poliéster *m*

polyethylene [pɒlɪ'eθəliːn] N *US* polietileno *m*

polymer ['pɒlɪmə(r)] N *Chem* polímero *m*

Polynesia [pɒlɪ'niːʒɪə] N Polinesia

polystyrene [pɒlɪ'staɪriːn] N poliestireno *m*

polythene ['pɒlɪθiːn] N *Br* polietileno *m*

polyunsaturated [pɒlʌn'sætʃʊreɪtɪd] ADJ poliinsaturado(a)

pomegranate ['pɒmɪgrænɪt] N granada *f*

pomp [pɒmp] N pompa *f*

pompom ['pɒmpɒm], **pompon** ['pɒmpɒn] N borla *f*, pompón *m*

pompous ['pɒmpəs] ADJ *(person)* presumido(a); *(speech)* rimbombante

pond [pɒnd] N estanque *m*

ponder ['pɒndə(r)] **1** VT considerar
2 VI **to p. over sth** meditar sobre algo

ponderous ['pɒndərəs] ADJ pesado(a)

pong [pɒŋ] N *Br Fam* tufo *m*

pontoon¹ [pɒn'tuːn] N *Constr* pontón *m*

pontoon² [pɒn'tuːn] N *Br Cards* veintiuna *f*

pony ['pəʊnɪ] N poney *m*

ponytail ['pəʊnɪteɪl] N cola *f* de caballo

poo [puː] N *Fam* caca *f*

poodle ['puːdəl] N caniche *m*

poof [pʊf] N *Br Fam Pej* maricón *m*, marica *m*

pool¹ [puːl] N *(of water, oil etc)* charco *m*; *(pond)* estanque *m*; *(in river)* pozo *m*; **(swimming) p.** piscina *f*, *Méx* alberca *f*, *RP* pileta *f*

pool² [puːl] **1** N **(a)** *(common fund)* fondo *m* común **(b)** *(typing p.)* servicio *m* de mecanografía **(c)** *US (snooker)* billar americano **(d)** *Br* **the pools** las quinielas *fpl*, *Arg* el Prode, *Col*, *CRica* el totogol
2 VT *(funds)* reunir; *(ideas, resources)* juntar

poor [pʊə(r)] **1** ADJ pobre; *(quality)* malo(a); *Fam* **you p. thing!** ¡pobrecito!
2 NPL **the p.** los pobres

poorly ['pʊəlɪ] **1** ADV *(badly)* mal
2 ADJ **(poorlier, poorliest)** *(ill)* mal, malo(a)

pop [pɒp] **1** VT *(burst)* hacer reventar; *(cork)* hacer saltar
2 VI **(a)** *(burst)* reventar; *(cork)* saltar **(b)** *Fam* **I'm just popping over to Ian's** voy un momento a casa de Ian
3 N **(a)** *(noise)* pequeña explosión **(b)** *Fam (drink)* gaseosa f **(c)** *US Fam (father)* papá m **(d)** *Fam Mus (music)* música f pop; **p. singer** cantante mf pop
► **pop in** VI *Fam* entrar un momento, pasar

popcorn ['pɒpkɔːn] N palomitas fpl de maíz, *RP* pochoclo m

Pope [pəʊp] N **the P.** el Papa

poplar ['pɒplə(r)] N álamo m

poppy ['pɒpɪ] N amapola f

Popsicle® ['pɒpsɪkəl] N *US* polo m

populace ['pɒpjʊləs] N *(people)* pueblo m

popular ['pɒpjʊlə(r)] ADJ popular; *(fashionable)* de moda; *(common)* corriente

popularity [pɒpjʊ'lærɪtɪ] N popularidad f

popularize ['pɒpjʊləraɪz] VT popularizar

populate ['pɒpjʊleɪt] VT poblar

population [pɒpjʊ'leɪʃən] N población f; **the p. explosion** la explosión demográfica

pop-up menu ['pɒpʌp'menjuː] N *Comput* menú m desplegable

porcelain ['pɔːsəlɪn] N porcelana f

porch [pɔːtʃ] N *Br (entrance)* zaguán m; *US (veranda)* terraza f

porcupine ['pɔːkjʊpaɪn] N puerco m espín

pore¹ [pɔː(r)] VI **to p. over sth** leer or estudiar algo detenidamente

pore² [pɔː(r)] N *Anat* poro m

pork [pɔːk] N *(carne f de)* cerdo m or *Am* chancho m

pornography [pɔː'nɒgrəfɪ] N pornografía f

porous ['pɔːrəs] ADJ poroso(a)

porpoise ['pɔːpəs] N marsopa f

porridge ['pɒrɪdʒ] N gachas fpl de avena

port¹ [pɔːt] N *(harbour)* puerto m; **p. of call** puerto de escala

port² [pɔːt] N *Naut & Av* babor m

port³ [pɔːt] N *(wine)* vino m de Oporto, oporto m

portable ['pɔːtəbəl] ADJ portátil

portal ['pɔːtəl] N *Comput (web page)* portal m

portent ['pɔːtent] N *Fml* augurio m

porter ['pɔːtə(r)] N *(at station)* mozo m de equipaje; *esp Br (at hotel)* portero(a) m,f, conserje mf; *US (on train)* mozo m

portfolio [pɔːt'fəʊliəʊ] N *(file)* carpeta f; *(of artist, politician)* cartera f

porthole ['pɔːthəʊl] N portilla f

portion ['pɔːʃən] N *(part, piece)* parte f, porción f; *(of food)* ración f
► **portion out** VT SEP repartir

portly ['pɔːtlɪ] ADJ *(* **portlier, portliest**) corpulento(a)

portrait ['pɔːtreɪt] N retrato m

portray [pɔː'treɪ] VT *(paint portrait of)* retratar; *(describe)* describir; *Th* representar

Portugal ['pɔːtjʊgəl] N Portugal

Portuguese [pɔːtjʊ'giːz] **1** ADJ portugués(esa)
2 N *(person)* portugués(esa) m,f; *(language)* portugués m

pose [pəʊz] **1** VT *(problem)* plantear; *(threat)* representar
2 VI *(for painting)* posar; *Pej (behave affectedly)* hacer pose; **to p. as** hacerse pasar por
3 N *(stance)* postura f; *Pej (affectation)* pose f

posh [pɒʃ] ADJ *Br Fam* elegante, de lujo; *(person, accent) Esp* pijo(a), *Méx* fresa, *RP* (con)cheto(a)

position [pə'zɪʃən] **1** N **(a)** *(physical posture)* posición f; *(location)* situación f; *(rank)* rango m; **to be in a p. to do sth** estar en condiciones de hacer algo **(b)** *(opinion)* postura f **(c)** *(job)* puesto m
2 VT colocar

positive ['pɒzɪtɪv] ADJ positivo(a); *(sign)* favorable; *(proof)* incontrovertible; *(sure)* seguro(a); *Fam (absolute)* auténtico(a)

possess [pə'zes] VT poseer; *(of fear)* apoderarse de

possessed [pə'zest] ADJ poseído(a)

possession [pə'zeʃən] N posesión f; **possessions** bienes mpl

possessive [pə'zesɪv] ADJ posesivo(a)

possibility [pɒsɪ'bɪlɪtɪ] N posibilidad f; **possibilities** *(potential)* potencial m

possible ['pɒsɪbəl] ADJ posible; **as much as p.** todo lo posible; **as often as p.** cuanto más mejor; **as soon as p.** cuanto antes

possibly ['pɒsɪblɪ] ADV posiblemente; *(perhaps)* tal vez, quizás; **I can't p. come** no puedo venir de ninguna manera

post¹ [pəʊst] **1** N *(of wood)* poste m
2 VT *(affix)* poner, pegar

post² [pəʊst] **1** N *(job)* puesto m; *US* **trading p.** factoría f
2 VT *Br (assign)* destinar

post³ [pəʊst] *esp Br* **1** N *(mail)* correo m; **by p.** por correo; **p. office** oficina f de correos; **P. Office Box** apartado m de correos, *CAm, Carib, Méx* casilla f postal, *Andes, RP* casilla de correos
2 VT *(letter)* echar al correo; **to p. sth to sb** mandar algo por correo a algn

postage ['pəʊstɪdʒ] N franqueo m

postal ['pəʊstəl] ADJ postal, de correos; *Br* **p. code** código m postal; *Br* **p. order** giro m postal; **p. vote** voto m por correo

postbox ['pəʊstbɒks] N *Br* buzón m (de correos)

postcard ['pəʊstkɑːd] N *(tarjeta f)* postal f

postcode ['pəʊstkəʊd] N *Br* código m postal

postdate [pəʊst'deɪt] VT *(cheque)* extender con fecha posterior

poster ['pəʊstə(r)] N póster m; *(advertising)* cartel m

posterior [pɒˈstɪərɪə(r)] **1** N *Hum* trasero *m*, pompis *m*
2 ADJ posterior

posterity [pɒˈsterɪtɪ] N posteridad *f*

postgraduate [pəʊstˈgrædjʊɪt] **1** N posgraduado(a) *m,f*
2 ADJ de posgraduado

posthumous [ˈpɒstjʊməs] ADJ póstumo(a)

postman [ˈpəʊstmən] N *Br* cartero *m*

postmark [ˈpəʊstmɑːk] N matasellos *m inv*

postmaster [ˈpəʊstmɑːstə(r)] N administrador *m* de correos; **p. general** director *m* general de correos

postmortem [pəʊstˈmɔːtəm] N autopsia *f*

postpone [pəsˈpəʊn] VT aplazar

postscript [ˈpəʊsskrɪpt] N posdata *f*

posture [ˈpɒstʃə(r)] **1** N postura *f*; *(affected)* pose *f*
2 VI adoptar una pose

postwar [ˈpəʊstwɔː(r)] ADJ de la posguerra

posy [ˈpəʊzɪ] N ramillete *m*

pot [pɒt] **1** N *(container)* tarro *m*, pote *m*; *(for cooking)* olla *f*; *(for flowers)* maceta *f*; *Fam* **to go to p.** irse al garete *or Am* al diablo
2 VT *(plant)* poner en una maceta

potassium [pəˈtæsɪəm] N potasio *m*

potato [pəˈteɪtəʊ] N *(pl* **potatoes)** patata *f*, *Am* papa *f*

potent [ˈpəʊtənt] ADJ potente

potential [pəˈtenʃəl] **1** ADJ potencial, posible
2 N potencial *m*

potentially [pəˈtenʃəlɪ] ADV en potencia

pothole [ˈpɒthəʊl] N *Geol* cueva *f*; *(in road)* bache *m*

potholing [ˈpɒthəʊlɪŋ] N *Br* espeleología *f*

potion [ˈpəʊʃən] N poción *f*, pócima *f*

potluck [pɒtˈlʌk] N *Fam* **to take p.** conformarse con lo que haya

potted [ˈpɒtɪd] ADJ *(food)* en conserva; *(plant)* en maceta *or* tiesto

potter¹ [ˈpɒtə(r)] N alfarero(a) *m,f*

potter² [ˈpɒtə(r)] VI *Br* **to p. about** *or* **around** entretenerse

pottery [ˈpɒtərɪ] N *(craft, place)* alfarería *f*; *(objects)* cerámica *f*

potty¹ [ˈpɒtɪ] ADJ (**pottier, pottiest**) *Br Fam* pirado(a), *Col* corrido(a), *CSur* rayado(a), *Méx* zafado(a)

potty² [ˈpɒtɪ] N *Fam* orinal *m*

pouch [paʊtʃ] N *(a) (for money)* saquito *m*; *(for ammunition)* morral *m*; *(for tobacco)* petaca *f* (**b**) *Zool* bolsa *f* abdominal

poultry [ˈpəʊltrɪ] N *(live)* aves *fpl* de corral; *(food)* pollos *mpl*

pounce [paʊns] VI **to p. on** abalanzarse encima de

pound¹ [paʊnd] **1** VT *(strike)* aporrear
2 VI *(heart)* palpitar; *(walk heavily)* andar con paso pesado

pound² [paʊnd] N *(money, weight)* libra *f*

pound³ [paʊnd] N *(for dogs)* perrera *f*; *(for cars)* depósito *m* de coches

pour [pɔː(r)] **1** VT echar, verter; **to p. sb a drink** servirle una copa a algn
2 VI correr, fluir; **it's pouring with rain** está lloviendo a cántaros

▸ **pour out** VT SEP echar, verter; *Fig* **to p. one's heart out to sb** desahogarse con algn

pouring [ˈpɔːrɪŋ] ADJ *(rain)* torrencial

pout [paʊt] **1** VI hacer pucheros
2 N puchero *m*

poverty [ˈpɒvətɪ] N pobreza *f*

poverty-stricken [ˈpɒvətɪstrɪkən] ADJ necesitado(a); **to be p.** vivir en la miseria

powder [ˈpaʊdə(r)] **1** N polvo *m*; **p. compact** polvera *f*; **p. keg** polvorín *m*; **p. puff** borla *f*; **p. room** baño *m or Esp* servicios *mpl or CSur* toilette *m* de señoras
2 VT **to p. one's nose** ponerse polvos en la cara; *Euph* ir a los servicios *or* al tocador

powdered [ˈpaʊdəd] ADJ *(milk)* en polvo

power [ˈpaʊə(r)] **1** N (**a**) *(physical strength)* fuerza *f*; *(energy)* energía *f* (**b**) *Elec* **to cut off the p.** cortar la corriente; *esp Br* **p. point** enchufe *m*; **p. station** central *or Andes, RP* usina eléctrica (**c**) *(capacity)* capacidad *f*, facultad *f* (**d**) *(authority)* poder *m*; *(nation)* potencia *f*; *(influence)* influencia *f*; **to be in p.** estar en el poder (**e**) *Tech* potencia *f*; *(output)* rendimiento *m*
2 VT propulsar, impulsar

powerboat [ˈpaʊəbəʊt] N lancha (motora)

powerful [ˈpaʊəfʊl] ADJ *(strong)* fuerte; *(influential)* poderoso(a); *(remedy)* eficaz; *(engine, machine)* potente; *(emotion)* fuerte; *(speech)* conmovedor(a)

powerless [ˈpaʊəlɪs] ADJ impotente, ineficaz

pp *(abbr* **pages)** págs., pp

PR [piːˈɑː(r)] *(abbr* **public relations**) N relaciones públicas

practicable [ˈpræktɪkəbəl] ADJ factible

practical [ˈpræktɪkəl] ADJ práctico(a); *(useful)* útil; *(sensible)* adecuado(a)

practicality [præktɪˈkælɪtɪ] N *(of suggestion, plan)* factibilidad *f*; **practicalities** detalles prácticos

practically [ˈpræktɪkəlɪ] ADV *(almost)* casi

practice [ˈpræktɪs] **1** N (**a**) *(habit)* costumbre *f* (**b**) *(exercise)* práctica *f*; *Sport* entrenamiento *m*; *Mus* ensayo *m*; **to be out of p.** no estar en forma (**c**) *(way of doing sth)* práctica *f*; **in p.** en la práctica; **to put sth into p.** poner algo en práctica (**d**) *(of profession)* ejercicio *m* (**e**) *(place) (of doctors)* consultorio *m*; *(of lawyers)* bufete *m* (**f**) *(clients) (of doctors)* pacientes *mpl*; *(of lawyers)* clientela *f*
2 VT & VI *US* = **practise**

practicing [ˈpræktɪsɪŋ] ADJ *US* = **practising**

practise [ˈpræktɪs] **1** VT practicar; *(method)* seguir; *(principle)* poner en práctica; *Mus* ensayar; *(profession)* ejercer

  2 VI practicar; *Sport* entrenar; *Mus* ensayar; *(doctor)* practicar; *(lawyer)* ejercer

practising ['præktɪsɪŋ] ADJ *(doctor etc)* en ejercicio; *(Christian etc)* practicante

practitioner [præk'tɪʃənə(r)] N *Br Med* **general p.** médico(a) *m,f* de cabecera

pragmatic [præg'mætɪk] ADJ pragmático(a)

prairie ['preərɪ] N *Br* pradera *f*; *US* llanura *f*

praise [preɪz] **1** N alabanza *f*

  2 VT alabar, elogiar

praiseworthy ['preɪzwɜ:ðɪ] ADJ loable

pram [præm] N *Br* cochecito *m* de niño

prance [prɑ:ns] VI *(horse)* encabritarse; **to p. about** *(person)* pegar brincos

prank [præŋk] N *(of child)* travesura *f*

prat [præt] N *Br Fam* soplagaitas *mf inv, Am* pendejo(a) *m,f*

prawn [prɔ:n] N gamba *f, Am* camarón *m*

pray [preɪ] VI rezar, orar

prayer [preə(r)] N rezo *m*, oración *f*; *(entreaty)* súplica *f*; **p. book** misal *m*

preach [pri:tʃ] VI predicar

preacher ['pri:tʃə(r)] N predicador(a) *m,f*

precarious [prɪ'keərɪəs] ADJ precario(a)

precaution [prɪ'kɔ:ʃən] N precaución *f*

precede [prɪ'si:d] VT preceder

precedence ['presɪdəns] N preferencia *f*, prioridad *f*; **to take p. over sth/sb** tener prioridad sobre algo/algn

precedent ['presɪdənt] N precedente *m*

preceding [prɪ'si:dɪŋ] ADJ precedente

precinct ['pri:sɪŋkt] N **(a)** *Br (area)* **pedestrian/ shopping p.** zona *f* peatonal/comercial **(b)** *US (administrative, police division)* distrito *m*; *(police station)* comisaría *f* (de policía)

> Note that the Spanish word **precinto** is a false friend and is never a translation for the English word **precinct**. In Spanish **precinto** means "seal".

precious ['preʃəs] **1** ADJ precioso(a); **p. stones** piedras preciosas

  2 ADV *Fam* **p. little/few** muy poco/pocos

precipice ['presɪpɪs] N precipicio *m*

precipitate 1 VT [prɪ'sɪpɪteɪt] precipitar; *Fig* arrojar

  2 ADJ [prɪ'sɪpɪtət] precipitado(a)

precise [prɪ'saɪs] ADJ preciso(a), exacto(a); *(meticulous)* meticuloso(a)

precisely [prɪ'saɪslɪ] ADV *(exactly)* precisamente, exactamente; **p.!** ¡eso es!, ¡exacto!

precision [prɪ'sɪʒən] N precisión *f*

preclude [prɪ'klu:d] VT excluir; *(misunderstanding)* evitar

precocious [prɪ'kəʊʃəs] ADJ precoz

preconceived [pri:kən'si:vd] ADJ preconcebido(a)

precondition [pri:kən'dɪʃən] N condición previa

precursor [prɪ'kɜ:sə(r)] N precursor(a) *m,f*

predator ['predətə(r)] N depredador *m*

predecessor ['pri:dɪsesə(r)] N antecesor(a) *m,f*

predetermine [pri:dɪ'tɜ:mɪn] VT predeterminar

predicament [prɪ'dɪkəmənt] N apuro *m*, aprieto *m*

predict [prɪ'dɪkt] VT predecir, pronosticar

predictable [prɪ'dɪktəbəl] ADJ previsible

prediction [prɪ'dɪkʃən] N pronóstico *m*

predispose [pri:dɪ'spəʊz] VT **to be predisposed to do sth** estar predispuesto(a) a hacer algo

predominant [prɪ'dɒmɪnənt] ADJ predominante

predominantly [prɪ'dɒmɪnəntlɪ] ADV en su mayoría

predominate [prɪ'dɒmɪneɪt] VI predominar

pre-empt [prɪ'empt] VT adelantarse a

preen [pri:n] VT **to p. oneself** *(of bird)* arreglarse las plumas; *Fig (of person)* pavonearse

prefab ['pri:fæb] N *Br Fam (house)* casa prefabricada

prefabricated [pri:'fæbrɪkeɪtɪd] ADJ prefabricado(a)

preface ['prefɪs] **1** N prefacio *m*

  2 VT prologar

prefect ['pri:fekt] N *Br Educ* monitor(a) *m,f*

prefer [prɪ'fɜ:(r)] VT preferir; **I p. coffee to tea** prefiero el café al té

preferable ['prefərəbəl] ADJ preferible (**to** a)

preferably ['prefərəblɪ] ADV preferentemente

preference ['prefərəns] N preferencia *f*; *(priority)* prioridad *f*; **to give p. to sth** dar prioridad a algo

preferential [prefə'renʃəl] ADJ preferente

prefix ['pri:fɪks] N prefijo *m*

pregnancy ['pregnənsɪ] N embarazo *m*

pregnant ['pregnənt] ADJ *(woman)* embarazada; *(animal)* preñada; *Fig* **a p. pause** una pausa cargada de significado

prehistoric(al) [pri:hɪ'stɒrɪk(əl)] ADJ prehistórico(a)

prejudge [pri:'dʒʌdʒ] VT prejuzgar

prejudice ['predʒʊdɪs] **1** N *(bias)* prejuicio *m*; *(harm)* perjuicio *m*

  2 VT *(bias)* predisponer; *(harm)* perjudicar

prejudiced ['predʒʊdɪst] ADJ parcial; **to be p. against/in favour of** estar predispuesto(a) en contra/a favor de

preliminary [prɪ'lɪmɪnərɪ] **1** ADJ preliminar; *Sport (round)* eliminatorio(a)

  2 N **preliminaries** preliminares *mpl*

prelude ['prelju:d] N preludio *m*

premarital [pri:'mærɪtəl] ADJ prematrimonial

premature [premə'tjʊə(r), 'premətjʊə(r)] ADJ prematuro(a)

prematurely [premə'tjʊəlɪ, 'premətjʊəlɪ] ADV antes de tiempo

premeditate [prɪ'medɪteɪt] VT *(crime)* premeditar

premenstrual [priː'menstrʊəl] ADJ **p. tension** tensión *f* premenstrual

premier ['premjə(r)] **1** N *Pol* primer(a) ministro(a) *m,f*
2 ADJ primer, primero(a)

premiere ['premɪeə(r)] N *Cin* estreno *m*

premise ['premɪs] N premisa *f*

premises ['premɪsɪz] NPL local *m*; **on the p.** en el local

premium ['priːmɪəm] N *Com, Fin & Ind* prima *f*; **to be at a p.** tener sobreprecio; *Fig* estar muy solicitado(a); *Br* **p. bonds** = bonos numerados emitidos por el Gobierno británico, cuyo comprador entra en un sorteo mensual de premios en metálico

premonition [premə'nɪʃən] N presentimiento *m*

preoccupied [priː'ɒkjʊpaɪd] ADJ preocupado(a); **to be p. with sth** preocuparse por algo

prep [prep] N *Br Fam* deberes *mpl*; **p. school** = colegio privado para alumnos de entre 7 y 13 años

prepacked [priː'pækt] ADJ empaquetado(a)

prepaid [priː'peɪd] ADJ con el porte pagado

preparation [prepə'reɪʃən] N preparación *f*; *(plan)* preparativo *m*

preparatory [prɪ'pærətərɪ] ADJ preparatorio(a), preliminar; **p. school** *Br* = colegio privado para alumnos de entre 7 y 13 años; *US* = escuela secundaria privada

prepare [prɪ'peə(r)] **1** VT preparar; **to p. to do sth** prepararse *or Am* alistarse para hacer algo
2 VI prepararse, *Am* alistarse **(for** para)

prepared [prɪ'peəd] ADJ *(ready)* preparado(a); **to be p. to do sth** *(willing)* estar dispuesto(a) a hacer algo

preponderance [prɪ'pɒndərəns] N preponderancia *f*

preposition [prepə'zɪʃən] N preposición *f*

preposterous [prɪ'pɒstərəs] ADJ absurdo(a), ridículo(a)

prerequisite [priː'rekwɪzɪt] N condición *f* previa

prerogative [prɪ'rɒgətɪv] N prerrogativa *f*

preschool [priː'skuːl] ADJ preescolar

prescribe [prɪ'skraɪb] VT *(set down)* prescribir; *Med* recetar; *Fig (recommend)* recomendar

prescription [prɪ'skrɪpʃən] N *Med* receta *f*

presence ['prezəns] N presencia *f*; *(attendance)* asistencia *f*; *Fig* **p. of mind** presencia de ánimo

present¹ ['prezənt] **1** ADJ **(a)** *(in attendance)* presente; *Ling* **p. tense** (tiempo *m*) presente *m*; **to be p. at** estar presente en **(b)** *(current)* actual
2 N *(time)* presente *m*, actualidad *f*; **at p.**

actualmente; **for the p.** de momento; **up to the p.** hasta ahora

present² **1** VT [prɪ'zent] **(a)** *(give as gift)* regalar; *(medal, prize etc)* entregar; **to p. sb with sth** obsequiar a algn con algo **(b)** *(report etc)* presentar; *(opportunity)* ofrecer; *(problem)* plantear **(c)** *(introduce) (person, programme)* presentar
2 N ['prezənt] *(gift)* regalo *m*; *(formal)* obsequio *m*

presentable [prɪ'zentəbəl] ADJ presentable; **to make oneself p.** arreglarse

presentation [prezən'teɪʃən] N **(a)** *(of person)* presentación *f*; **p. ceremony** ceremonia *f* de entrega **(b)** *(formal talk)* exposición *f*, charla *f* *(con la ayuda de gráficos, diapositivas, etc)*

present-day ['prezəntdeɪ] ADJ actual, de hoy en día

presenter [prɪ'zentə(r)] N *Br Rad* locutor(a) *m,f*; *TV* presentador(a) *m,f*

presently ['prezəntlɪ] ADV *(soon)* dentro de poco; *US (now)* ahora

preservation [prezə'veɪʃən] N conservación *f*

preservative [prɪ'zɜːvətɪv] N conservante *m*

preserve [prɪ'zɜːv] **1** VT **(a)** *(keep)* mantener **(b)** *Culin* conservar
2 N **(a)** *(hunting)* coto *m* **(b)** *Culin* conserva *f*

preside [prɪ'zaɪd] VI presidir

presidency ['prezɪdənsɪ] N presidencia *f*

president ['prezɪdənt] N *Pol* presidente(a) *m,f*; *US Com* director(a) *m,f*, gerente *mf*

presidential [prezɪ'denʃəl] ADJ presidencial

press [pres] **1** VT **(a)** *(push, squeeze)* apretar; *(grapes)* prensar; *(trousers etc)* planchar **(b)** *(pressurize)* presionar; **to p. sb to do sth** acosar a algn para que haga algo
2 VI **(a)** *(push)* apretar; **to p. against sth/sb** apretarse contra algo/algn; **to p. (down) on sth** hacer presión sobre algo **(b)** *(be urgent)* **time is pressing** el tiempo apremia
3 N **(a)** *(machine)* prensa *f*; **to go to p.** *(of newspaper)* entrar en prensa **(b)** *Press* **the p.** la prensa; **p. agency** agencia *f* de prensa; **p. conference** rueda *f* de prensa

▶ **press on** VI seguir adelante

pressed [prest] ADJ **to be (hard) p. for** andar escaso(a) de; **I'd be hard p. to do it** me costaría mucho hacerlo

pressing ['presɪŋ] ADJ apremiante, urgente

press-up ['presʌp] N *Br* flexión *f* (de brazos)

pressure ['preʃə(r)] N presión *f*; *Med & Met* **high/low p.** altas/bajas presiones; **p. cooker** olla *f* a presión; **p. gauge** manómetro *m*; *Fig* **to bring p. (to bear) on sb** ejercer presión sobre algn

pressurize ['preʃəraɪz] VT *Fig* presionar; **pressurized cabin** cabina presurizada

prestige [pre'stiːʒ] N prestigio *m*

prestigious [pres'tɪdʒəs] ADJ prestigioso(a)

presumably [prɪ'zju:məblɪ] ADV es de suponer que

presume [prɪ'zju:m] **1** VT suponer, presumir; **we p. so/not** suponemos que sí/no **2** VI (*suppose*) suponer

presumption [prɪ'zʌmpʃən] N (**a**) (*supposition*) suposición f (**b**) (*boldness*) osadía f; (*conceit*) presunción f

presumptuous [prɪ'zʌmptjʊəs] ADJ impertinente

Note that the Spanish word **presuntuoso** is a false friend and is never a translation for the English word **presumptuous**. In Spanish, **presuntuoso** means "vain" and "pretentious".

presuppose [pri:sə'pəʊz] VT presuponer

pretence [prɪ'tens] N (**a**) (*deception*) fingimiento m; **false pretences** estafa f; **under the p. of** so pretexto de (**b**) (*claim*) pretensión f

pretend [prɪ'tend] **1** VT (*feign*) fingir, aparentar; (*claim*) pretender **2** VI (*feign*) fingir

pretense [prɪ'tens] N *US* = **pretence**

pretention [prɪ'tenʃən] N pretensión f

pretentious [prɪ'tenʃəs] ADJ presuntuoso(a), pretencioso(a)

pretext ['pri:tekst] N pretexto m; **on the p. of** so pretexto de

pretty ['prɪtɪ] **1** ADJ (**prettier, prettiest**) bonito(a), Am lindo(a) **2** ADV *Fam* bastante; **p. much the same** más o menos lo mismo

prevail [prɪ'veɪl] VI (**a**) (*predominate*) predominar (**b**) (*be successful*) prevalecer (**c**) **to p. upon** *or* **on sb to do sth** (*persuade*) persuadir *or* convencer a algn para que haga algo

prevailing [prɪ'veɪlɪŋ] ADJ (*wind*) predominante; (*opinion*) general; (*condition, fashion*) actual

prevalent ['prevələnt] ADJ predominante; (*illness*) extendido(a)

prevaricate [prɪ'værɪkeɪt] VI andar con ambages

prevent [prɪ'vent] VT impedir; (*accident*) evitar; (*illness*) prevenir; **to p. sb from doing sth** impedir a algn hacer algo; **to p. sth from happening** evitar que pase algo

prevention [prɪ'venʃən] N prevención f

preventive [prɪ'ventɪv] ADJ preventivo(a)

preview ['pri:vju:] N (*of film etc*) preestreno m

previous ['pri:vɪəs] **1** ADJ anterior, previo(a); **p. conviction** antecedente m penal **2** ADV **p. to going** antes de ir

previously ['pri:vɪəslɪ] ADV anteriormente, previamente

prewar ['pri:wɔ:(r)] ADJ de antes de la guerra

prey [preɪ] **1** N presa f; *Fig* víctima f **2** VI **to p. on** alimentarse de

price [praɪs] **1** N precio m; **what p. is that coat?** ¿cuánto cuesta el abrigo?; **p. list** lista f de precios; **p. tag** etiqueta f **2** VT (*put price on*) poner un precio a; (*value*) valorar

priceless ['praɪslɪs] ADJ que no tiene precio

pricey ['praɪsɪ] ADJ (**pricier, priciest**) *Fam* carillo(a)

prick [prɪk] **1** VT picar; **to p. one's finger** pincharse el dedo; *Fig* **to p. up one's ears** aguzar el oído **2** N (**a**) (*with pin*) pinchazo m (**b**) *Vulg* (*penis*) *Esp* polla f, *Am* verga f, *Méx* pito m, *RP* pija f (**c**) *Vulg* (*person*) *Esp* gilipollas mf inv, *Am* pendejo(a) m,f, *RP* forro m

prickle ['prɪkəl] **1** N espina f; (*spike*) pincho m; (*sensation*) picor m **2** VT & VI pinchar, picar

prickly ['prɪklɪ] ADJ (**pricklier, prickliest**) espinoso(a); *Fig* (*touchy*) enojadizo(a); **p. heat** = sarpullido por causa del calor; **p. pear** higo chumbo, *Am* tuna f

pride [praɪd] **1** N orgullo m; (*arrogance*) soberbia f; **to take p. in sth** enorgullecerse de algo **2** VT **to p. oneself on** enorgullecerse de

priest [pri:st] N sacerdote m, cura m

priestess ['pri:stɪs] N sacerdotisa f

priesthood ['pri:sthʊd] N (*clergy*) clero m; (*office*) sacerdocio m

prig [prɪg] N gazmoño(a) m,f, mojigato(a) m,f

prim [prɪm] ADJ (**primmer, primmest**) **p. (and proper)** remilgado(a)

primaeval [praɪ'mi:vəl] ADJ primitivo(a)

primarily ['praɪmərɪlɪ] ADV ante todo

primary ['praɪmərɪ] **1** ADJ fundamental, principal; **of p. importance** primordial; **p. colour** color primario; **p. education/school** enseñanza/escuela primaria **2** N *US Pol* (elección) primaria

primate¹ ['praɪmeɪt] N *Rel* primado m

primate² ['praɪmeɪt] N *Zool* primate m

prime [praɪm] **1** ADJ (*principal*) principal, primordial; **P. Minister** primer(a) ministro(a) (**b**) (*first-rate*) de primera; **p. number** número primo **2** N **in the p. of life** en la flor de la vida **3** VT (*pump, engine*) cebar; (*surface*) imprimar; *Fig* (*prepare*) preparar

primer¹ ['praɪmə(r)] N (*textbook*) cartilla f

primer² ['praɪmə(r)] N (*paint*) imprimación f

primeval [praɪ'mi:vəl] ADJ = **primaeval**

primitive ['prɪmɪtɪv] ADJ primitivo(a); (*method, tool*) rudimentario(a)

primrose ['prɪmrəʊz] N primavera f

Primus® ['praɪməs] N infiernillo m, camping-gas m inv, *Am* primus m inv

prince [prɪns] N príncipe m; **P. Charming** Príncipe Azul

princess [prɪn'ses] N princesa f

principal ['prɪnsɪpəl] 1 ADJ principal
2 N *Educ* director(a) *m,f*; *Th (in play)* protagonista *mf* principal

principle ['prɪnsɪpəl] N principio *m*; **in p.** en principio; **on p.** por principio

print [prɪnt] 1 VT (**a**) *(book)* imprimir; *(newspaper)* publicar; *Fig* grabar; **printed matter** impresos *mpl* (**b**) *(write)* escribir con letra de imprenta
2 N (**a**) *(of hand, foot)* huella *f* (**b**) *(written text)* letra *f*; **out of p.** agotado(a) (**c**) *Tex* estampado *m* (**d**) *Art* grabado *m*; *Phot* copia *f*
▸ **print out** VT SEP *Comput* imprimir

printer ['prɪntə(r)] N *(person)* impresor(a) *m,f*; *(machine)* impresora *f*

printing ['prɪntɪŋ] N *(industry)* imprenta *f*; *(process)* impresión *f*; *(print run)* tirada *f*; **p. press** prensa *f*

print-out ['prɪntaʊt] N *Comput* impresión *f*; *(copy)* copia impresa

prior ['praɪə(r)] ADJ previo(a), anterior; **p. to leaving** antes de salir

priority [praɪ'ɒrɪtɪ] N prioridad *f*

prise [praɪz] VT **to p. sth open** abrir algo con palanca; **to p. sth off** arrancar algo

prism ['prɪzəm] N prisma *f*

prison ['prɪzən] N cárcel *f*, prisión *f*

prisoner ['prɪzənə(r)] N preso(a) *m,f*; **to hold sb p.** detener a algn; **p. of war** prisionero(a) *m,f* de guerra

privacy ['praɪvəsɪ, 'prɪvəsɪ] N intimidad *f*

private ['praɪvɪt] 1 ADJ privado(a); *(secretary)* particular; *(matter)* personal; *(letter)* confidencial; **one's p. life** la vida privada de uno; **p.** *(notice) (on road)* carretera privada; *(on gate)* propiedad privada; *(on envelope)* confidencial; **p. detective**, *Fam* **p. eye** detective privado(a); **p. school** escuela privada
2 N *Mil* soldado raso

privately ['praɪvɪtlɪ] ADV en privado; *(personally)* personalmente

privatize ['praɪvɪtaɪz] VT privatizar

privet ['prɪvɪt] N alheña *f*

privilege ['prɪvɪlɪdʒ] N privilegio *m*

privileged ['prɪvɪlɪdʒd] ADJ privilegiado(a)

privy ['prɪvɪ] 1 ADJ *Br* **P. Council** Consejo Privado; **to be p. to sth** estar enterado(a) de algo
2 N *(lavatory)* retrete *m*

prize [praɪz] 1 N premio *m*
2 ADJ *(first-class)* de primera (categoría *or* clase)
3 VT *(value)* apreciar, valorar

prize-giving ['praɪzgɪvɪŋ] N distribución *f* de premios

prizewinner ['praɪzwɪnə(r)] N premiado(a) *m,f*

pro¹ [prəʊ] N pro *m*; **the pros and cons of an issue** los pros y los contras de una cuestión

pro² [prəʊ] N *Fam* profesional *mf*, *Méx* profesionista *mf*

pro- [prəʊ] PREF *(in favour of)* pro-

proactive [prəʊ'æktɪv] ADJ **to be p.** tomar la iniciativa

probability [prɒbə'bɪlɪtɪ] N probabilidad *f*

probable ['prɒbəbəl] ADJ probable

probably ['prɒbəblɪ] ADV probablemente

probation [prə'beɪʃən] N *Jur* **to be on p.** estar en libertad condicional; **to be on two months' p.** *(at work)* trabajar dos meses de prueba

probe [prəʊb] 1 N *Med* & *(in outer space)* sonda *f*; *(investigation)* sondeo *m*
2 VT *Med* sondar; *(investigate)* investigar
▸ **probe into** VT INSEP investigar

problem ['prɒbləm] N problema *m*

problematic(al) [prɒblə'mætɪk(əl)] ADJ problemático(a); **it's p.** tiene sus problemas

procedure [prə'siːdʒə(r)] N procedimiento *m*; *(legal, business)* gestión *f*, trámite *m*

proceed [prə'siːd] VI seguir, proceder; **to p. to do sth** ponerse a hacer algo; **to p. to the next matter** pasar a la siguiente cuestión

proceedings [prə'siːdɪŋz] NPL *(of meeting)* actas *fpl*; *(measures)* medidas *fpl*; *Jur* proceso *m*

proceeds ['prəʊsiːdz] NPL ganancias *fpl*

process ['prəʊses] 1 N proceso *m*; *(method)* método *m*, sistema *m*; **in the p. of** en vías de
2 VT *(information)* tramitar; *(food)* tratar; *Comput* procesar

processing ['prəʊsesɪŋ] N *(of information)* evaluación *f*; *Comput* tratamiento *m*

procession [prə'seʃən] N desfile *m*; *Rel* procesión *f*

processor ['prəʊsesə(r)] N *Comput* procesador *m*

proclaim [prə'kleɪm] VT proclamar, declarar

proclamation [prɒklə'meɪʃən] N proclamación *f*

procrastinate [prəʊ'kræstɪneɪt] VI dejar las cosas para después

procure [prə'kjʊə(r)] VT conseguir, procurarse

prod [prɒd] VT *(with stick etc)* golpear; *(push)* empujar

prodigal ['prɒdɪgəl] ADJ pródigo(a)

prodigious [prə'dɪdʒəs] ADJ prodigioso(a)

prodigy ['prɒdɪdʒɪ] N prodigio *m*

produce 1 VT [prə'djuːs] (**a**) *(create) (food, goods)* producir (**b**) *Th* dirigir; *Rad* & *TV* realizar; *Cin* producir (**c**) *(give birth to)* dar a luz a (**d**) *(document)* enseñar; *(bring out)* sacar
2 N ['prɒdjuːs] productos *mpl*; **p. of Spain** producto *m* de España

producer [prə'djuːsə(r)] N (**a**) *(of crops, goods)* productor(a) *m,f* (**b**) *(of film, play, radio or TV programme)* productor(a) *m,f*

product ['prɒdʌkt] N producto *m*

production [prə'dʌkʃən] N (**a**) *(manufacture)* producción *f*; **p. line** cadena *f* de producción (**b**) *(play)* montaje *m*; *(film, radio or TV programme)* producción *f*

productive [prə'dʌktɪv] ADJ productivo(a)

productivity [prɒdʌk'tɪvɪtɪ] N productividad *f*

profane [prə'feɪn] ADJ *(secular)* profano(a); *(language)* blasfemo(a)

profess [prə'fes] VT *(faith)* profesar; *(opinion)* expresar; *(claim)* pretender

profession [prə'feʃən] N profesión *f*

professional [prə'feʃənəl] **1** ADJ profesional; *(soldier)* de profesión; *(polished)* de gran calidad
   2 N profesional *mf*

professor [prə'fesə(r)] N *Univ Br* catedrático(a) *m*,*f*; *US* profesor(a) *m*,*f*

proficiency [prə'fɪʃənsɪ] N *(in language)* capacidad *f*; *(in skill)* pericia *f*

proficient [prə'fɪʃənt] ADJ *(in language)* experto(a); *(in skill)* hábil

profile ['prəʊfaɪl] N perfil *m*; **in p.** de perfil

profit ['prɒfɪt] **1** N (**a**) *(of company, on deal)* beneficio *m*; **to make a p. on** sacar beneficios de (**b**) *(advantage)* provecho *m*
   2 VI *Fig* sacar provecho; **to p. from** aprovecharse de

profitability [prɒfɪtə'bɪlɪtɪ] N rentabilidad *f*

profitable ['prɒfɪtəbəl] ADJ *Com* rentable; *Fig (worthwhile)* provechoso(a)

profiteer [prɒfɪ'tɪə(r)] **1** N especulador(a) *m*,*f*
   2 VI obtener beneficios excesivos

profound [prə'faʊnd] ADJ profundo(a)

profuse [prə'fjuːs] ADJ profuso(a), abundante

profusely [prə'fjuːslɪ] ADV con profusión; **to sweat p.** sudar mucho

profusion [prə'fjuːʒən] N profusión *f*, abundancia *f*

prognosis [prɒg'nəʊsɪs] N *Med* pronóstico *m*; *Fig (prediction)* augurio *m*

program ['prəʊgræm] *Comput* **1** N programa *m*
   2 VI & VT programar
   3 *US* = **programme**

programer ['prəʊgræmə(r)] N *US* = **programmer**

programme ['prəʊgræm] **1** N programa *m*; *(plan)* plan *m*
   2 VT (**a**) *(plan)* planear, planificar (**b**) *(computer)* programar

programmer ['prəʊgræmə(r)] N programador(a) *m*,*f*

progress 1 N ['prəʊgres] progreso *m*; *(development)* desarrollo *m*; *Med* mejora *f*; **to make p.** hacer progresos; **in p.** en curso
   2 VI [prəʊ'gres] avanzar; *(develop)* desarrollar; *(improve)* hacer progresos; *Med* mejorar

progressive [prə'gresɪv] ADJ *(increasing)* progresivo(a); *Pol* progresista

progressively [prə'gresɪvlɪ] ADV progresivamente

prohibit [prə'hɪbɪt] VT prohibir; **to p. sb from doing sth** prohibir a algn hacer algo

prohibitive [prə'hɪbɪtɪv] ADJ prohibitivo(a)

project 1 N ['prɒdʒekt] proyecto *m*; *(plan)* plan *m*; *Educ* trabajo *m*; *US* **(housing) p.** = urbanización con viviendas de protección oficial
   2 VT [prə'dʒekt] proyectar, planear
   3 VI *(stick out)* sobresalir

projectile [prə'dʒektaɪl] N *Fml* proyectil *m*

projection [prə'dʒekʃən] N (**a**) *(overhang)* saliente *m* (**b**) *Cin* proyección *f* (**c**) *(forecast)* proyección *f*

projector [prə'dʒektə(r)] N *Cin* proyector *m*

proletariat [prəʊlɪ'teərɪət] N proletariado *m*

prolific [prə'lɪfɪk] ADJ prolífico(a)

prologue ['prəʊlɒg] N prólogo *m*

prolong [prə'lɒŋ] VT prolongar

prom [prɒm] N *Br Fam (seafront)* paseo marítimo; *Br (concert)* = concierto sinfónico en que parte del público está de pie; *US (school dance)* = baile de fin de curso

promenade [prɒmə'nɑːd] **1** N *Br (at seaside)* paseo marítimo
   2 VI pasearse

prominence ['prɒmɪnəns] N prominencia *f*; *Fig (importance)* importancia *f*

prominent ['prɒmɪnənt] ADJ *(standing out)* saliente; *Fig (important)* importante; *(famous)* eminente

promiscuous [prə'mɪskjʊəs] ADJ promiscuo(a)

promise ['prɒmɪs] **1** N promesa *f*; **to show p.** ser prometedor(a)
   2 VT & VI prometer

promising ['prɒmɪsɪŋ] ADJ prometedor(a)

promontory ['prɒməntərɪ] N promontorio *m*

promote [prə'məʊt] VT ascender; *(product)* promocionar; *(ideas)* fomentar; *Ftb* **they've been promoted** han subido

promoter [prə'məʊtə(r)] N promotor(a) *m*,*f*

promotion [prə'məʊʃən] N *(in rank)* promoción *f*, ascenso *m*; *(of product)* promoción; *(of arts etc)* fomento *m*

prompt ['prɒmpt] **1** ADJ *(quick)* rápido(a); *(punctual)* puntual
   2 ADV **at two o'clock p.** a las dos en punto
   3 VT (**a**) *(motivate)* incitar; **to p. sb to do sth** instar a algn a hacer algo (**b**) *(actor)* apuntar

promptly [prɒmptlɪ] ADV *(quickly)* rápidamente; *(punctually)* puntualmente

prone [prəʊn] ADJ (**a**) **to be p. to do sth** ser propenso(a) a hacer algo (**b**) *Fml (face down)* boca abajo

prong [prɒŋ] N punta *f*, diente *m*

pronoun ['prəʊnaʊn] N pronombre *m*

pronounce [prə'naʊns] **1** VT pronunciar; *Fml (declare)* declarar
   2 VI *Fml* **to p. on sth** opinar sobre algo

pronounced [prə'naʊnst] ADJ pronunciado(a)

pronouncement [prə'naʊnsmənt] N *Fml* declaración *f*

pronunciation [prənʌnsɪ'eɪʃən] N pronunciación *f*

proof [pru:f] **1** N prueba f
2 ADJ (**a**) *(secure)* a prueba de (**b**) **this rum is 70 percent p.** este ron tiene 70 grados
3 VT impermeabilizar

prop¹ [prɒp] **1** N *(support)* puntal m; *Fig* sostén m
2 VT *(support)* apoyar; *Fig* sostener
▸ **prop up** VT SEP apoyar

prop² [prɒp] N *Fam Th* accesorio m

propaganda [prɒpə'gændə] N propaganda f

propel [prə'pel] VT propulsar

propeller [prə'pelə(r)] N hélice f

propelling pencil [prə'pelɪŋ'pensəl] N *Br* portaminas m inv

propensity [prə'pensɪtɪ] N *Fml* propensión f

proper ['prɒpə(r)] ADJ (**a**) *(correct)* correcto(a); *(real)* verdadero(a); **he isn't a p. doctor** no es médico de verdad (**b**) *(appropriate, place)* adecuado(a), apropiado(a) (**c**) *(characteristic)* propio(a); *Ling* **p. noun** nombre propio

properly ['prɒpəlɪ] ADV *(suitably, correctly, decently)* correctamente; **it wasn't p. closed** no estaba bien cerrado; **she refused, quite p.** se negó, y con razón

property ['prɒpətɪ] N (**a**) *(quality)* propiedad f (**b**) *(possession)* propiedad f, posesión f; **personal p.** bienes mpl; **public p.** dominio público (**c**) *(estate)* finca f

prophecy ['prɒfɪsɪ] N profecía f

prophesy ['prɒfɪsaɪ] VT *(predict)* predecir; *Rel* profetizar

prophet ['prɒfɪt] N profeta mf

proportion [prə'pɔ:ʃən] N proporción f; *(part, quantity)* parte f; **in p. to** or **with** en proporción a

proportional [prə'pɔ:ʃənəl] ADJ proporcional (**to** a); *Pol* **p. representation** representación f proporcional

proportionate [prə'pɔ:ʃənɪt] ADJ proporcional

proposal [prə'pəʊzəl] N propuesta f, *(suggestion)* sugerencia f; **p. of marriage** propuesta de matrimonio

propose [prə'pəʊz] **1** VT proponer; *(suggest)* sugerir; *Fml (intend)* tener la intención de
2 VI declararse

proposition [prɒpə'zɪʃən] N propuesta f; *Math* proposición f

proprietor [prə'praɪətə(r)] N propietario(a) m,f

propriety [prə'praɪətɪ] N *(decency)* decoro m

propulsion [prə'pʌlʃən] N propulsión f

prosaic [prəʊ'zeɪɪk] ADJ prosaico(a)

prose [prəʊz] N *Lit* prosa f; *Educ* texto m para traducir

prosecute ['prɒsɪkju:t] VT procesar

prosecution [prɒsɪ'kju:ʃən] N *(action)* proceso m, juicio m; **the p.** la acusación

prosecutor ['prɒsɪkju:tə(r)] N acusador(a) m,f

prospect 1 N ['prɒspekt] *(outlook)* perspectiva f; *(hope)* esperanza f; **the job has prospects** es un trabajo con porvenir

2 VT [prə'spekt] explorar
3 VI **to p. for gold/oil** buscar oro/petróleo

prospective [prə'spektɪv] ADJ *(future)* futuro(a); *(possible)* eventual, probable

prospector [prə'spektə(r)] N **gold p.** buscador(a) m,f del oro

prospectus [prə'spektəs] N prospecto m

prosper ['prɒspə(r)] VI prosperar

prosperity [prɒ'sperɪtɪ] N prosperidad f

prosperous ['prɒspərəs] ADJ próspero(a)

prostate ['prɒsteɪt] N *Anat* **p. (gland)** próstata f

prostitute ['prɒstɪtju:t] N prostituta f

prostitution [prɒstɪ'tju:ʃən] N prostitución f

prostrate ['prɒstreɪt] ADJ *(face down)* boca abajo; **p. with grief** deshecho(a) de dolor

protagonist [prəʊ'tægənɪst] N protagonista mf

protect [prə'tekt] VT proteger; *(interests etc)* salvaguardar; **to p. sb from sth** proteger a algn de algo

protection [prə'tekʃən] N protección f

protective [prə'tektɪv] ADJ protector(a)

protégé ['prəʊtəʒeɪ] N protegido m

protégée ['prəʊtəʒeɪ] N protegida f

protein ['prəʊti:n] N proteína f

protest 1 N ['prəʊtest] protesta f; *(complaint)* queja f
2 VT [prə'test] *US* protestar en contra de
3 VI *Br* protestar

Protestant ['prɒtɪstənt] ADJ & N protestante *(mf)*

protester [prə'testə(r)] N manifestante m

protocol ['prəʊtəkɒl] N protocolo m

prototype ['prəʊtətaɪp] N prototipo m

protracted [prə'træktɪd] ADJ prolongado(a)

protrude [prə'tru:d] VI *Fml* sobresalir

protuberance [prə'tju:bərəns] N *Fml* protuberancia f

proud [praʊd] ADJ orgulloso(a); *(arrogant)* soberbio(a)

prove [pru:v] **1** VT *(demonstrate)* probar, demostrar; *Math* comprobar; **to p. oneself** dar pruebas de valor
2 VI *(turn out)* **it proved to be disastrous** resultó ser desastroso(a)

proverb ['prɒvɜ:b] N refrán m, proverbio m

provide [prə'vaɪd] **1** VT proporcionar; *(supplies)* suministrar, proveer
2 VI proveer; **to p. for sb** mantener a algn

provided [prə'vaɪdɪd] CONJ **p. (that)** con tal de que

providing [prə'vaɪdɪŋ] CONJ = **provided**

province ['prɒvɪns] N provincia f; *Fig (field of knowledge)* campo m

provincial [prə'vɪnʃəl] **1** ADJ provincial; *Pej* provinciano(a)
2 N *Pej (person)* provinciano(a) m,f

provision [prə'vɪʒən] N provisión f; *(supply)* suministro m; **provisions** *(food)* provisiones fpl, víveres mpl

provisional [prə'vɪʒənəl] ADJ provisional

proviso [prə'vaɪzəʊ] N (pl **provisos**, US **provisoes**) **with the p. that** a condición de que

provocation [prɒvə'keɪʃən] N provocación f

provocative [prə'vɒkətɪv] ADJ provocador(a); (flirtatious) provocativo(a)

provoke [prə'vəʊk] VT provocar

prow [praʊ] N proa f

prowess ['praʊɪs] N destreza f

prowl [praʊl] 1 N merodeo m; **to be on the p.** merodear, rondar
2 VI merodear; Fam **to p. about** or **around** rondar

prowler ['praʊlə(r)] N Fam merodeador m

proximity [prɒk'sɪmɪtɪ] N proximidad f; **in p. to**, **in the p. of** cerca de

proxy ['prɒksɪ] N Jur (power) poderes mpl; (person) apoderado(a) m,f; **by p.** por poderes

prudence ['pruːdəns] N prudencia f

prudent ['pruːdənt] ADJ prudente

prudish ['pruːdɪʃ] ADJ remilgado(a)

prune¹ [pruːn] N ciruela pasa

prune² [pruːn] VT (roses etc) podar; Fig acortar

pry [praɪ] VI curiosear, husmear; **to p. into sth** entrometerse en algo

PS, ps [piː'es] (abbr **postscript**) P.S., P.D.

psalm [sɑːm] N salmo m

pseudo- ['sjuːdəʊ] PREF pseudo-, seudo-

pseudonym ['sjuːdənɪm] N (p)seudónimo m

psyche ['saɪkɪ] N psique f

psychiatric [saɪkɪ'ætrɪk] ADJ psiquiátrico(a)

psychiatrist [saɪ'kaɪətrɪst] N psiquiatra mf

psychiatry [saɪ'kaɪətrɪ] N psiquiatría f

psychic ['saɪkɪk] 1 ADJ psíquico(a)
2 N médium m

psychoanalysis [saɪkəʊə'nælɪsɪs] N psicoanálisis f

psychoanalyst [saɪkəʊ'ænəlɪst] N psicoanalista mf

psychological [saɪkə'lɒdʒɪkəl] ADJ psicológico(a)

psychologist [saɪ'kɒlədʒɪst] N psicólogo(a) m,f

psychology [saɪ'kɒlədʒɪ] N psicología f

psychopath ['saɪkəʊpæθ] N psicópata mf

psychosomatic [saɪkəʊsə'mætɪk] ADJ psicosomático(a)

psychotherapist ['saɪkəʊ'θerəpɪst] N psicoterapeuta mf

psychotherapy ['saɪkəʊ'θerəpɪ] N psicoterapia f

psychotic [saɪ'kɒtɪk] ADJ & N psicótico(a) (m,f)

PT [piː'tiː] N (abbr **physical training**) educación física

PTA [piːtiː'eɪ] N (abbr **Parent-Teacher Association**) = asociación de padres de alumnos y profesores, ≃ APA f

PTO, pto [piːtiː'əʊ] (abbr **please turn over**) sigue

pub [pʌb] N Br Fam bar m, pub m

puberty ['pjuːbətɪ] N pubertad f

pubic ['pjuːbɪk] ADJ púbico(a)

public ['pʌblɪk] 1 ADJ público(a); **to make sth p.** hacer público(a) algo; Com **to go p.** (of company) pasar a cotizar en Bolsa; **p. address system** (sistema m de) megafonía f; **p. company** empresa pública; Br **p. convenience** servicios o Esp aseos públicos; **p. holiday** día festivo o Am feriado; Br **p. house** pub m, taberna f; Br **p. limited company** sociedad anónima; **p. opinion** opinión pública; Br **p. prosecutor** fiscal m; **p. relations** relaciones públicas; **p. school** Br colegio privado; US colegio público; **p. transport** transporte público
2 N **the p.** el público; **in p.** en público

publican ['pʌblɪkən] N Br dueño(a) m,f de un "pub"

publication [pʌblɪ'keɪʃən] N publicación f

publicity [pʌ'blɪsɪtɪ] N publicidad f

publicize ['pʌblɪsaɪz] VT (make public) hacer público(a); (advertise) hacer publicidad a

public-spirited [pʌblɪk'spɪrɪtɪd] ADJ de espíritu cívico

publish ['pʌblɪʃ] VT publicar, editar

publisher ['pʌblɪʃə(r)] N (person) editor(a) m,f; (firm) (casa f) editorial f

publishing ['pʌblɪʃɪŋ] N (business) industria f editorial; **p. company** or **house** casa f editorial

pucker ['pʌkə(r)] VT (lips, brow) fruncir, arrugar

pudding ['pʊdɪŋ] N Culin pudín m; Br (dessert) postre m; **Christmas p.** = pudín a base de frutos secos típico de Navidad; **p. basin** cuenco m; **steamed p.** budín f

puddle ['pʌdəl] N charco m

Puerto Rican ['pweətəʊ'riːkən] ADJ & N portorriqueño(a) (m,f), puertorriqueño(a) (m,f)

Puerto Rico ['pweətəʊ'riːkəʊ] N Puerto Rico

puff [pʌf] 1 N (of wind) racha f; (of smoke) nube f; **p. pastry** pasta f de hojaldre
2 VI (person) jadear, resoplar; (train) echar humo; **to p. on a cigarette** dar chupadas or Esp caladas or Am pitadas a un cigarrillo
3 VT (cigarette) dar una calada a
▶ **puff up** VI hincharse

puffy ['pʌfɪ] ADJ (**puffier**, **puffiest**) hinchado(a)

pugnacious [pʌg'neɪʃəs] ADJ belicoso(a)

puke [pjuːk] VI Fam echar la papa, devolver

pull [pʊl] 1 N (a) (act of pulling) tirón m, Am salvo RP jalón m; **to give sth a p.** dar un tirón or Am salvo RP jalón a algo (b) (attraction) atracción f; (influence) enchufe m
2 VT (a) (tug) dar un tirón or Am salvo RP jalón a; **to p. the trigger** apretar el gatillo; **to p. to pieces** hacer pedazos; Fig poner por los suelos; Fig **to p. sb's leg** tomar el pelo a algn (b) (draw) tirar, arrastrar (c) (draw out) sacar (d) Fam (people) atraer
3 VI (drag) tirar, Am salvo RP jalar

► **pull apart** VT SEP desmontar; *Fig (criticize)* poner por los suelos

► **pull down** VT SEP *(building)* derribar

► **pull in 1** VT SEP *(crowds)* atraer
2 VI *(train)* entrar en la estación; *(stop)* parar

► **pull off 1** VT SEP *Fam (carry out)* llevar a cabo
2 VI *(vehicle)* arrancar

► **pull out 1** VT SEP *(withdraw)* retirar
2 VI *Aut* **to p. out to overtake** salir para adelantar

► **pull over** VI *(driver)* parar en *Esp* el arcén *or Méx* el acotamiento

► **pull through** VI reponerse, restablecerse

► **pull together** VT SEP **to p. oneself together** calmarse

► **pull up 1** VT SEP **(a)** *(uproot)* desarraigar **(b)** *(chair)* acercar
2 VI *(stop)* pararse

pulley ['pʊlɪ] N polea *f*

pullover ['pʊləʊvə(r)] N suéter *m*, *Esp* jersey *m*, *RP* pulóver *m*

pulp [pʌlp] N *(of paper, wood)* pasta *f*; *(of fruit)* pulpa *f*

pulpit ['pʊlpɪt] N púlpito *m*

pulsate [pʌl'seɪt] VI vibrar, palpitar

pulse¹ [pʌls] N *Anat* pulso *m*

pulse² [pʌls] N *Bot & Culin* legumbre *f*

pumice ['pʌmɪs] N **p. (stone)** piedra *f* pómez

pummel ['pʌməl] VT aporrear

pump¹ [pʌmp] **1** N bomba *f*
2 VT bombear; **to p. sth in/out** meter/sacar algo con una bomba

► **pump out** VT SEP *(empty)* vaciar

► **pump up** VT SEP *(tyre)* inflar

pump² [pʌmp] N *Br (shoe)* zapatilla *f*

pumpkin ['pʌmpkɪn] N calabaza *f*, *Andes, RP* zapallo *m*, *Col, Carib* ahuyama *f*

pun [pʌn] N juego *m* de palabras

punch¹ [pʌntʃ] **1** N *(for making holes)* perforadora *f*, *(for tickets)* taladradora *f*; *(for leather etc)* punzón *m*
2 VT *(make hole in)* perforar; *(ticket)* picar; *(leather)* punzar

punch² [pʌntʃ] **1** N *(blow)* puñetazo *m*; *(in boxing)* pegada *f*; *Fig* **it lacks p.** le falta fuerza; **p. line** remate *m (de un chiste)*
2 VT *(with fist)* dar un puñetazo a

punch³ [pʌntʃ] N *(drink)* ponche *m*

punch-up ['pʌntʃʌp] N *Fam* pelea *f*

punctual ['pʌŋktjʊəl] ADJ puntual

punctuate ['pʌŋktjʊeɪt] VT puntuar; *Fig* salpicar

punctuation [pʌŋktjʊ'eɪʃən] N puntuación *f*

puncture ['pʌŋktʃə(r)] **1** N pinchazo *m*, *Guat, Méx* ponchadura *f*
2 VT *(tyre)* pinchar, *Guat, Méx* ponchar

pundit ['pʌndɪt] N *Fam* experto(a) *m,f*

pungent ['pʌndʒənt] ADJ *(smell)* acre; *(taste)* fuerte

punish ['pʌnɪʃ] VT castigar

punishable ['pʌnɪʃəbəl] ADJ castigable, punible

punishment ['pʌnɪʃmənt] N castigo *m*

punk [pʌŋk] N *Fam* **(a)** *(person)* punk *mf*; **p. (music)** *(música f)* punk *m* **(b)** *US (contemptible person)* desgraciado(a) *m,f*

punt [pʌnt] **1** VT *(boat)* batea *f*
2 VI ir en batea

punter ['pʌntə(r)] N *(gambler)* jugador(a) *m,f*; *(customer)* cliente(a) *m,f*

puny ['pjuːnɪ] ADJ **(punier, puniest)** enclenque, endeble

pup [pʌp] N cachorro(a) *m,f*

pupil¹ ['pjuːpəl] N *Educ* alumno(a) *m,f*

pupil² ['pjuːpəl] N *Anat* pupila *f*

puppet ['pʌpɪt] N títere *m*

puppy ['pʌpɪ] N cachorro(a) *m,f*, perrito *m*

purchase ['pɜːtʃɪs] **1** N compra *f*
2 VT comprar; **purchasing power** poder adquisitivo

purchaser ['pɜːtʃɪsə(r)] N comprador(a) *m,f*

pure [pjʊə(r)] ADJ puro(a)

purée ['pjʊəreɪ] N puré *m*

purely ['pjʊəlɪ] ADV simplemente

purge [pɜːdʒ] **1** N purga *f*
2 VT purgar

purify ['pjʊərɪfaɪ] VT purificar

puritanical [pjʊərɪ'tænɪkəl] ADJ puritano(a)

purity ['pjʊərɪtɪ] N pureza *f*

purl [pɜːl] VI *(in knitting)* hacer punto del revés

purple ['pɜːpəl] ADJ morado(a), purpúreo(a); **to go p. (in the face)** ponerse morado(a)

purport [pɜː'pɔːt] VI *Fml* pretender; **to p. to be sth** pretender ser algo

purpose ['pɜːpəs] N **(a)** *(object, aim)* propósito *m*, objeto *m*; **on p.** a propósito **(b)** *(use)* finalidad *f*

purposeful ['pɜːpəsfʊl] ADJ *(resolute)* decidido(a), resoluto(a)

purr [pɜː(r)] VI *(cat)* ronronear; *(engine)* zumbar

purse [pɜːs] N **(a)** *Br (for coins)* monedero *m*; *US (bag)* *Esp* bolso *m*, *Col, CSur* cartera *f*, *Méx* bolsa *f*; *(prize money)* premio *m* en metálico
2 VT **to p. one's lips** apretarse los labios

purser ['pɜːsə(r)] N contador(a) *m,f*

pursue [pə'sjuː] VT *(criminal)* perseguir; *(person)* seguir; *(pleasure)* buscar; *(career)* ejercer

pursuer [pə'sjuːə(r)] N *Fml* perseguidor(a) *m,f*

pursuit [pə'sjuːt] N *(of criminal)* persecución *f*; *(of animal)* caza *f*; *(of pleasure)* búsqueda *f*; *(pastime)* pasatiempo *m*

purveyor [pə'veɪə(r)] N *Fml* proveedor(a) *m,f*

pus [pʌs] N pus *m*

push [pʊʃ] **1** N empujón *m*, *CAm, Méx* aventón *m*; *Fig (drive)* brío *m*, dinamismo *m*
2 VT **(a)** *(in general)* empujar; *(button)* pulsar, apretar; **to p. one's finger into a hole** meter el dedo en un agujero **(b)** *Fig (pressurize)* instar; *(harass)* acosar; *Fam* **to be (hard) pushed for**

time estar apurado(a) *or RP* corto(a) de tiempo (**c**) *Fam (product)* promover; **to p. drugs** pasar droga
3 VI empujar
▸ **push aside** VT SEP *(object)* apartar
▸ **push in** VI colarse
▸ **push off** VI *(in boat)* desatracar; *Fam* **p. off!** ¡lárgate!
▸ **push on** VI *(continue)* seguir adelante
▸ **push through** VT SEP abrirse paso entre
pushchair ['pʊtʃeə(r)] N *Br* sillita *f* (de ruedas)
pusher ['pʊʃə(r)] N *Fam (of drugs)* camello *m*, *Am* dealer *m*
pushover ['pʊʃəʊvə(r)] N *Fam* **it's a p.** está chupado; **she's a p.** es un ligue fácil
push-up ['pʊʃʌp] N flexión *f* (de brazos)
pushy ['pʊʃɪ] ADJ (**pushier, pushiest**) *Fam* agresivo(a)
puss [pʊs], **pussy** ['pʊsɪ] N *Fam* minino *m*
put [pʊt] **1** VT (*pt & pp* **put**) (**a**) *(place)* poner; *(carefully)* colocar; *(insert)* meter; **to p. sb to bed** acostar a algn; **to p. a picture up on the wall** colgar un cuadro en la pared (**b**) *(present)* presentar, exponer; **to p. a question to sb** hacer una pregunta a algn (**c**) *(express)* expresar, decir; **to p. sth simply** explicar algo de manera sencilla (**d**) *(estimate)* calcular (**e**) *(money)* ingresar; *(invest)* invertir
2 VI *Naut* **to p. to sea** zarpar
3 ADV **to stay p.** quedarse quieto(a)
▸ **put about** VT SEP *(rumour)* hacer correr
▸ **put across** VT SEP *(idea etc)* comunicar
▸ **put aside** VT SEP *(money)* ahorrar; *(time)* reservar
▸ **put away** VT SEP *(tidy away)* recoger; *Fam (eat)* zamparse; *(save) (money)* ahorrar
▸ **put back** VT SEP *(postpone)* aplazar; **to p. the clock back** retrasar la hora
▸ **put by** VT SEP *(money)* ahorrar
▸ **put down** VT SEP *(set down)* dejar; *(suppress)* sofocar; *(humiliate)* humillar; *(criticize)* criticar; *(animal)* provocar la muerte de; *(write down)* apuntar
▸ **put down to** VT SEP achacar a
▸ **put forward** VT SEP *(theory)* exponer; *(proposal)* hacer; **to p. one's name forward for sth** presentarse como candidato(a) para algo
▸ **put in** **1** VT SEP *(install)* instalar; *(complaint, request)* presentar; *(time)* pasar
2 VI *Naut* hacer escala (**at** en)
▸ **put off** VT SEP *(postpone)* aplazar; **to p. sb off doing sth** quitarle *or Am* sacarle a algn las ganas de hacer algo

▸ **put on** VT SEP *(clothes)* poner, ponerse; *(show)* montar; *(concert)* dar; *(switch on) (radio)* poner; *(light)* encender; *Am* prender; *(water, gas)* abrir; **to p. on weight** aumentar de peso; **to p. on the brakes** frenar; *Fig* **to p. on a straight face** poner cara de serio(a)
▸ **put out** VT SEP (**a**) *(light, fire)* apagar (**b**) *(place outside)* sacar (**c**) *(extend) (arm)* extender; *(tongue)* sacar; *(hand)* tender (**d**) *(spread) (rumour)* hacer correr (**e**) *(annoy)* molestar; *(inconvenience)* incordiar (**f**) *(anger)* **to be p. out by sth** *Esp* enfadarse *or Am* enojarse por algo
▸ **put through** VT SEP *Tel* **p. me through to Pat, please** póngame con Pat, por favor
▸ **put together** VT SEP *(join)* unir, reunir; *(assemble)* armar, montar
▸ **put up** VT SEP *(raise)* levantar, subir; *(picture)* colocar; *(curtains)* colgar; *(building)* construir; *(tent)* armar; *(prices)* subir, aumentar; *(accommodate)* alojar, hospedar; **to p. up a fight** ofrecer resistencia
▸ **put up to** VT SEP **to p. sb up to sth** incitar a algn a hacer algo
▸ **put up with** VT INSEP aguantar, soportar
putrid ['pjuːtrɪd] ADJ *Fml* putrefacto(a)
putt [pʌt] **1** N tiro *m* al hoyo
2 VT & VI tirar al hoyo
putting ['pʌtɪŋ] N **p. green** minigolf *m*
putty ['pʌtɪ] N masilla *f*
puzzle ['pʌzəl] **1** N rompecabezas *m inv*; *(crossword)* crucigrama *m*; *Fig (mystery)* misterio *m*
2 VT dejar perplejo(a); **to be puzzled about sth** no entender algo
▸ **puzzle over** VT INSEP **to p. over sth** dar vueltas a algo (en la cabeza)
puzzling ['pʌzlɪŋ] ADJ extraño(a), curioso(a)
PVC [piːviːˈsiː] N (*abbr* **polyvinyl chloride**) PVC *m*
pygmy ['pɪgmɪ] N pigmeo(a) *m,f*; *Fig* enano(a) *m,f*
pyjamas [pəˈdʒɑːməz] NPL pijama *m*, *Am* piyama *m or f*
pylon ['paɪlən] N torre *f* (de conducción eléctrica)
pyramid ['pɪrəmɪd] N pirámide *f*
Pyrenees [pɪrəˈniːz] NPL **the P.** los Pirineos
Pyrex® ['paɪreks] N pírex® *m*
python ['paɪθən] N pitón *m*

Q, q [kju:] N *(the letter)* Q, q *f*

quack [kwæk] N **1** (**a**) *(of duck)* graznido *m* (**b**) *Br Fam Pej or Hum (doctor)* matasanos *m inv*
2 VI graznar

quad [kwɒd] N *Fam* (**a**) *Br (of school, university)* patio *m* interior (**b**) *(quadruplet)* cuatrillizo(a) *m,f*

quadrangle ['kwɒdræŋgəl] N (**a**) *Geom* cuadrángulo *m* (**b**) *(courtyard)* patio *m* interior

quadruple ['kwɒdrʊpəl, kwɒ'dru:pəl] **1** cuádruplo *m*
2 ADJ cuádruple
3 VT cuadruplicar
4 VI cuadruplicarse

quadruplet ['kwɒdrʊplɪt, kwɒ'dru:plɪt] N cuatrillizo(a) *m,f*

quagmire ['kwægmaɪə(r), 'kwɒgmaɪə(r)] N *(land)* cenagal *m*

quail[1] [kweɪl] N *(bird)* codorniz *f*

quail[2] [kweɪl] VI *Fig* encogerse

quaint [kweɪnt] ADJ *(picturesque)* pintoresco(a); *(original)* singular

quake [kweɪk] **1** VI temblar
2 N *Fam* temblor *m* de tierra

Quaker ['kweɪkə(r)] N cuáquero(a) *m,f*

qualification [kwɒlɪfɪ'keɪʃən] N (**a**) *(ability)* aptitud *f* (**b**) *(requirement)* requisito *m* (**c**) *(diploma etc)* título *m* (**d**) *(reservation)* reserva *f*

qualified ['kwɒlɪfaɪd] ADJ (**a**) *(having diploma)* titulado(a); *(competent)* capacitado(a); **q. teacher** profesor(a) titulado(a) (**b**) *(modified)* aprobación *f* condicional

qualify ['kwɒlɪfaɪ] **1** VT (**a**) *(entitle)* capacitar (**b**) *(modify)* modificar; *(statement)* matizar; *Ling* calificar
2 VI (**a**) **to q. as** *(doctor etc)* sacar el título de; **when did you q.?** ¿cúando terminaste la carrera? (**b**) *(in competition)* quedar clasificado(a)

qualifying ['kwɒlɪfaɪɪŋ] ADJ *(round, exam)* eliminatorio(a)

quality ['kwɒlɪtɪ] N (**a**) *(excellence)* calidad *f*; **q. control** control *m* de calidad; *Br* **q. newspapers** prensa *f* no sensacionalista (**b**) *(attribute)* cualidad *f*

qualm [kwɑ:m] N (**a**) *(scruple)* escrúpulo *m* (**b**) *(doubt)* duda *f*

quandary ['kwɒndərɪ, 'kwɒndrɪ] N **to be in a q.** estar en un dilema

quango ['kwæŋgəʊ] *(abbr quasi-autonomous non-governmental organization)* N *Br* = organismo público semiindependiente

quantity ['kwɒntɪtɪ] N cantidad *f*

quarantine ['kwɒrəntiːn] N cuarentena *f*

quarrel ['kwɒrəl] **1** N *(argument)* riña *f*, pelea *f*; *(disagreement)* desacuerdo *m*
2 VI *(argue)* pelearse, reñir; **to q. with sth** discrepar de algo

quarrelsome ['kwɒrəlsəm] ADJ camorrista

quarry[1] ['kwɒrɪ] *Min* **1** N cantera *f*
2 VT extraer

quarry[2] ['kwɒrɪ] N presa *f*

quart [kwɔːt] N *(measurement)* = cuarto de galón *(Br = 1,13 l; US = 0,94 l)*

quarter ['kwɔːtə(r)] **1** N (**a**) *(fraction, of orange, of moon)* cuarto *m*; **a q. of an hour** un cuarto de hora (**b**) *(in telling time) Br* **it's a q. to three**, *US* **it's a q. of three** son las tres menos cuarto; **it's a q.** *Br* **past** *or US* **after six** son las seis y cuarto (**c**) *US (coin)* cuarto *m* (de dólar) (**d**) *(district)* barrio *m* (**e**) **quarters** *(lodgings)* alojamiento *m* (**f**) *US Mus* **q. note** negra *f*
2 VT (**a**) *(cut into quarters)* dividir en cuartos (**b**) *(accommodate)* alojar

quarterback ['kwɔːtəbæk] N *US* quarterback *m Méx* mariscal *m* de campo

quarterfinal ['kwɔːtə'faɪnəl] N *Sport* cuarto *m* de final

quarterly ['kwɔːtəlɪ] **1** ADJ trimestral
2 N publicación *f* trimestral
3 ADV trimestralmente

quartermaster ['kwɔːtəmɑːstə(r)] N *Mil* oficial *m* de intendencia

quartet(te) [kwɔː'tet] N cuarteto *m*

quartz [kwɔːts] N cuarzo *m*; **q. watch** reloj *m* de cuarzo

quash [kwɒʃ] VT *Jur* anular; *(uprising)* aplastar

quasi ['kwɑːzɪ, 'kweɪzaɪ] PREF cuasi

quaver ['kweɪvə(r)] **1** N (**a**) *Br Mus* corchea *f* (**b**) *(in voice)* temblor *m*
2 VI *(voice)* temblar

quay(side) ['kiː(saɪd)] N muelle *m*

queasy ['kwiːzɪ] ADJ (**queasier, queasiest**) **to feel q.** *(ill)* tener náuseas

queen [kwiːn] N (**a**) *(of country)* reina *f* (**b**) *Fam Pej* loca *f*, marica *m*

queer [kwɪə(r)] **1** ADJ *(strange)* extraño(a), raro(a)
2 N *Fam Pej* marica *m*, maricón *m*

quell [kwel] VT reprimir

quench [kwentʃ] VT apagar

querulous ['kwerʊləs, 'kwerjʊləs] ADJ *Fml* quejumbroso(a)

query ['kwɪərɪ] **1** N *(question)* pregunta *f*
  2 VT *(ask questions about)* preguntar acerca de; *(have doubts about)* poner en duda

quest [kwest] N *Literary* búsqueda *f*

question ['kwestʃən] **1** N pregunta *f*; **to ask sb a q.** hacer una pregunta a algn; **he did it without q.** lo hizo sin rechistar; **to call sth into q.** poner algo en duda; **that's out of the q.!** ¡ni hablar!; **q. mark** signo *m* de interrogación; *Fig* interrogante *m*
  2 VT *(ask questions of)* hacer preguntas a; *(interrogate)* interrogar; *(query)* poner en duda

questionable ['kwestʃənəbəl] ADJ *(doubtful)* dudoso(a); *(debatable)* discutible

questionnaire [kwestʃə'neə(r)] N cuestionario *m*

queue [kjuː] **1** N cola *f*
  2 VI **to q. (up)** hacer cola

quibble ['kwɪbəl] **1** N pega *f*
  2 VI poner pegas (**with** a); *Fam* buscarle tres pies al gato

quiche [kiːʃ] N quiche *m* or *f*

quick [kwɪk] ADJ *(a)* *(fast)* rápido(a); **a q. look** un vistazo; **a q. snack** un bocado; **be q.!** ¡date prisa!, *Am* ¡apúrate! *(b)* *(clever)* espabilado(a); *(wit)* agudo(a) *(c)* **she has a q. temper** *Esp* se enfada *or Am* se enoja con nada

quicken ['kwɪkən] **1** VT acelerar; **to q. one's pace** acelerar el paso
  2 VI *(speed up)* acelerarse

quickly ['kwɪklɪ] ADV rápidamente, de prisa

quickness ['kwɪknɪs] N *(a)* *(speed)* rapidez *f* *(b)* *(of wit)* agudeza *f*, viveza *f*

quicksand ['kwɪksænd] N arenas movedizas

quicksilver ['kwɪksɪlvə(r)] N mercurio *m*

quick-witted [kwɪk'wɪtɪd] ADJ agudo(a)

quid [kwɪd] N *(pl* quid*)* *Br Fam (pound)* libra *f*

quiet ['kwaɪət] **1** N *(a)* *(silence)* silencio *m* *(b)* *(calm)* tranquilidad *f*
  2 ADJ *(a)* *(silent)* silencioso(a); *(street)* tranquilo(a); **keep q.!** ¡silencio! *(b)* *(calm)* tranquilo(a) *(c)* *(person)* reservado(a) *(d)* *(not showy)* *(clothes)* sobrio(a); *(colours)* apagado(a)
  3 VT *US* calmar
  4 VI *US* calmarse

quieten ['kwaɪətən] **1** VT *(silence)* callar; *(calm)* calmar
  2 VI *(silence)* callarse; *(calm)* calmarse
  ▶ **quieten down** *Br* **1** VT SEP calmar
  2 VI calmarse

quietly ['kwaɪətlɪ] ADV *(a)* *(silently)* silenciosamente; **he spoke q.** habló en voz baja *(b)* *(calmly)* tranquilamente *(c)* *(discreetly)* discretamente

quietness ['kwaɪətnɪs] N *(a)* *(silence)* silencio *m* *(b)* *(calm)* tranquilidad *f*

quill [kwɪl] N *(feather, pen)* pluma *f*; *(of porcupine)* púa *f*

quilt [kwɪlt] **1** N edredón *m*
  2 VT acolchar

quin [kwɪn] N *Fam* quintillizo(a) *m,f*

quinine ['kwɪniːn, *US* 'kwaɪnaɪn] N quinina *f*

quint [kwɪnt] N *US Fam* = **quin**

quintessential [kwɪntɪ'senʃəl] ADJ fundamental

quintet(te) [kwɪn'tet] N quinteto *m*

quintuple ['kwɪntjʊpəl, kwɪn'tjuːpəl] **1** N quíntuplo *m*
  2 ADJ quíntuplo(a)
  3 VT quintuplicar
  4 VI quintuplicarse

quintuplet ['kwɪntjʊplɪt, kwɪn'tjuːplɪt] N quintillizo(a) *m,f*

quip [kwɪp] **1** N salida *f*; *(joke)* chiste *m*
  2 VI bromear

quirk [kwɜːk] N *(a)* *(peculiarity)* manía *f* *(b)* *(of fate)* arbitrariedad *f*

quit [kwɪt] **1** VT *(pt & pp* quitted *or* quit*)* *(a)* *(leave)* dejar, abandonar *(b)* **q. making that noise!** ¡deja de hacer ese ruido!
  2 VI *(a)* *(go)* irse; *(give up)* abandonar *(b)* *(resign)* dimitir
  3 ADJ **let's call it quits** dejémoslo estar

> Note that the Spanish verb **quitar** is a false friend and is never a translation for the English verb **to quit**. In Spanish **quitar** means both "to remove" and "to take away".

quite [kwaɪt] ADV *(a)* *(entirely)* totalmente; **she's q. right** tiene toda la razón *(b)* *(rather)* bastante; **q. a while** un buen rato; **that's q. enough!** ¡ya está bien!; **it's q. something** es increíble *(c)* *(exactly)* exactamente; **q. (so)!** ¡en efecto!, ¡exacto!

quiver¹ ['kwɪvə(r)] VI temblar

quiver² ['kwɪvə(r)] N *(for arrows)* aljaba *f*, carcaj *m*

quiz [kwɪz] **1** N *Rad & TV* **q. show** concurso *m*
  2 VT hacer preguntas a

quizzical ['kwɪzɪkəl] ADJ *(a)* *(bemused)* burlón(ona) *(b)* *(enquiring)* curioso(a)

quorum ['kwɔːrəm] N quórum *m inv*

quota ['kwəʊtə] N *(a)* *(proportional share)* cuota *f*, parte *f* *(b)* *(prescribed amount, number)* cupo *m*

quotation [kwəʊ'teɪʃən] N *(a)* *Lit* cita *f*; **q. marks** comillas *fpl* *(b)* *Fin* cotización *f*

quote [kwəʊt] **1** VT *(a)* *(cite)* citar *(b)* *Com* **to q. a price** dar un presupuesto *(c)* *Fin* cotizar
  2 N *(a)* *Lit* cita *f* *(b)* *Com* presupuesto *m*

quotient ['kwəʊʃənt] N cociente *m*

R

R, r [ɑː(r)] N *(the letter)* R, r f

rabbi ['ræbaɪ] N rabí m, rabino m

rabbit ['ræbɪt] **1** N conejo(a) m,f; **r. hutch** conejera f
2 VI *Fam* **to r. (on)** enrollarse

rabble ['ræbəl] N *Pej* **the r.** el populacho

rabies ['reɪbiːz] N rabia f

RAC [ɑːreɪ'siː] N *Br (abbr Royal Automobile Club)* = organización británica de ayuda al automovilista, *Esp* ≃ RACE m, *Arg* ≃ ACA m

raccoon [rə'kuːn] N mapache m

race¹ [reɪs] **1** N **(a)** *Sport* carrera f **(b)** *Br* **the races** las carreras (de caballos)
2 VT **(a) I'll r. you!** ¡te echo una carrera! **(b)** *(car, horse)* hacer correr **(c)** *(engine)* acelerar
3 VI *(go quickly)* correr; *(pulse)* acelerarse

race² [reɪs] N *(people)* raza f

racecourse ['reɪskɔːs] N hipódromo m

racehorse ['reɪshɔːs] N caballo m de carreras

racer ['reɪsə(r)] N *Sport* **(a)** *(person)* corredor(a) m,f **(b)** *(bicycle)* bicicleta f de carreras; *(car)* coche m or *Am* carro m or *Csur* auto m de carreras

racetrack ['reɪstræk] N *(for cars, people, bikes)* pista f; *US (for horses)* hipódromo m

racial ['reɪʃəl] ADJ racial

racing ['reɪsɪŋ] **1** N carreras fpl
2 ADJ de carreras; **r. bicycle** bicicleta f de carreras; **r. car** coche m or *Am* carro m or *CSur* auto m de carreras

racism ['reɪsɪzəm] N racismo m

racist ['reɪsɪst] ADJ & N racista *(mf)*

rack [ræk] **1** N **(a)** *(shelf)* estante m; *(for clothes)* percha f; **luggage r.** portaequipajes m inv; **roof r.** baca f **(b)** *(for torture)* potro m
2 VT *Literary (torment)* atormentar; *Fam Fig* **to r. one's brains** devanarse los sesos

racket¹ ['rækɪt] N **(a)** *(din)* estruendo m, *Esp* jaleo m **(b)** *(swindle)* timo m; *(shady business)* chanchullo m

racket² ['rækɪt] N *Sport* raqueta f

racquet ['rækɪt] N = **racket²**

racy ['reɪsɪ] ADJ *(racier, raciest)* *(lively)* vivo(a); *(risqué)* atrevido(a)

radar ['reɪdɑː(r)] N radar m

radiance ['reɪdɪəns] N resplandor m

radiant ['reɪdɪənt] ADJ radiante, resplandeciente

radiate ['reɪdɪeɪt] VT irradiar; *Fig* **she radiated happiness** rebosaba de alegría

radiation [reɪdɪ'eɪʃən] N radiación f

radiator ['reɪdɪeɪtə(r)] N radiador m

radical ['rædɪkəl] ADJ radical

radii ['reɪdɪaɪ] PL of **radius**

radio ['reɪdɪəʊ] N radio f; **on the r.** en or por la radio; **r. station** emisora f (de radio)

radioactive [reɪdɪəʊ'æktɪv] ADJ radiactivo(a)

radio-controlled [reɪdɪəʊkən'trəʊld] ADJ teledirigido(a)

radiography [reɪdɪ'ɒgrəfɪ] N radiografía f

radiology [reɪdɪ'ɒlədʒɪ] N radiología f

radiotherapy [reɪdɪəʊ'θerəpɪ] N radioterapia f

radish ['rædɪʃ] N rábano m

radius ['reɪdɪəs] N *(pl radii)* radio m; **within a r. of** en un radio de

RAF [ɑːreɪ'ef] N *Br (abbr Royal Air Force)* = fuerzas aéreas británicas

raffle ['ræfəl] **1** N rifa f
2 VT rifar

raft [rɑːft] N balsa f

rafter ['rɑːftə(r)] N viga f de madera

rag [ræg] N **(a)** *(torn piece)* harapo m **(b)** *(for cleaning)* trapo m **(c)** *Fam* **rags** *(clothes)* trapos mpl **(d)** *Pej Press* periodicucho m

rag-and-bone ['rægən'bəʊn] ADJ *Br* **r. man** trapero m

rage [reɪdʒ] **1** N **(a)** *(fury)* cólera f **(b)** *Fam* **it's all the r.** hace furor
2 VI **(a)** *(person)* rabiar, estar furioso(a) **(b)** *Fig (storm, sea)* rugir; *(wind)* bramar

ragged ['rægɪd] ADJ **(a)** *(clothes)* hecho(a) jirones **(b)** *(person)* harapiento(a) **(c)** *(edge)* mellado(a) **(d)** *Fig (uneven)* desigual

raging ['reɪdʒɪŋ] ADJ **(a)** *(angry)* furioso(a) **(b)** *Fig (sea)* embravecido(a) **(c)** *(intense)* feroz; *(storm)* violento(a)

raid [reɪd] **1** N *Mil* incursión f; *(by police)* redada f; *(robbery etc)* atraco m
2 VT *Mil* hacer una incursión en; *(of police)* hacer una redada en; *(rob)* asaltar; *Fam* **to r. the larder** vaciar la despensa

raider ['reɪdə(r)] N *(invader)* invasor(a) m,f

rail [reɪl] N **(a)** *(railing)* baranda f, *Esp* barandilla f **(b)** *Rail* carril m; **by r. (send sth)** por ferrocarril; *(travel)* en tren

railcard ['reɪlkɑːd] N *Br* **family/young person's r.** = tarjeta familiar/juvenil para obtener billetes de tren con descuento

railing ['reɪlɪŋ] N *(metal post)* reja f; **railings** *(fence)* verja f

railroad ['reɪlrəʊd] N *US* ferrocarril *m*

railway ['reɪlweɪ] N *Br* ferrocarril *m*; **r. line, r. track** vía férrea; **r. station** estación *f* de ferrocarril

railwayman ['reɪlweɪmən] N *Br* ferroviario *m*

rain [reɪn] **1** N lluvia *f*; **in the r.** bajo la lluvia
2 VI llover; **it's raining** llueve

rainbow ['reɪnbəʊ] N arco *m* iris

raincoat ['reɪnkəʊt] N impermeable *m*

raindrop ['reɪndrɒp] N gota *f* de lluvia

rainfall ['reɪnfɔːl] N *(falling of rain)* precipitación *f*; *(amount)* pluviosidad *f*

rainforest ['reɪnfɒrɪst] N selva *f* tropical

rainy ['reɪnɪ] ADJ *(rainier, rainiest)* lluvioso(a)

raise [reɪz] **1** N *US* aumento *m* (de sueldo)
2 VT **(a)** *(lift)* levantar; *(voice)* alzar, levantar **(b)** *(prices)* aumentar **(c)** *(money)* reunir **(d)** *(issue)* plantear **(e)** *(crops, children)* criar **(f)** *(standards)* mejorar

raisin ['reɪzən] N pasa *f*

rake¹ [reɪk] **1** N *(garden tool)* rastrillo *m*; *(for fire)* hurgón *m*
2 VT *(leaves)* rastrillar; *(fire)* hurgar; *(with machine gun)* barrer

rake² [reɪk] N *(dissolute man)* calavera *m*, libertino *m*

rally ['rælɪ] **1** N **(a)** *(gathering)* reunión *f*; *Pol* mitin *m* **(b)** *Aut* rallye *m* **(c)** *(in tennis)* jugada *f*
2 VT *(support)* reunir
3 VI recuperarse

▶ **rally round** VI **her family rallied round** su familia la arropó

RAM [ræm] N *Comput (abbr* **random access memory)** RAM *f*

ram [ræm] **1** N **(a)** *Zool* carnero *m* **(b)** *Tech* maza *f*
2 VT **(a)** *(drive into place)* hincar; *(cram)* embutir; *Fam* **to r. sth home** hacer algo patente **(b)** *(crash into)* chocar con

ramble ['ræmbəl] **1** N *(walk)* caminata *f*
2 VI **(a)** *(walk)* hacer una excursión a pie **(b)** *Fig (digress)* divagar

rambler ['ræmblə(r)] N **(a)** *(person)* excursionista *mf* **(b)** *Bot* rosal *m* trepador

rambling ['ræmblɪŋ] ADJ **(a)** *(incoherent)* incoherente **(b)** *(house)* laberíntico(a) **(c)** *Bot* trepador(a)

ramp [ræmp] N **(a)** *(to ease access)* rampa *f* **(b)** *(to plane)* escalerilla *f*

rampage 1 N ['ræmpeɪdʒ] **to be on the r.** desmandarse
2 VI [ræm'peɪdʒ] **to r. about** comportarse como un/una loco(a)

rampant ['ræmpənt] ADJ incontrolado(a); **corruption is r.** la corrupción está muy extendida

rampart ['ræmpɑːt] N muralla *f*

ramshackle ['ræmʃækəl] ADJ destartalado(a)

ran [ræn] PT of **run**

ranch [rɑːntʃ] N *US* rancho *m*, hacienda *f*

rancher ['rɑːntʃə(r)] N *US* ranchero(a) *m,f*

rancid ['rænsɪd] ADJ rancio(a)

rancour, *US* **rancor** ['ræŋkə(r)] N *Fml* rencor *m*

random ['rændəm] **1** N **at r.** al azar
2 ADJ fortuito(a); **r. selection** selección hecha al azar

randy ['rændɪ] ADJ *(randier, randiest) Br Fam* caliente, *Esp, Méx* cachondo(a)

rang [ræŋ] PT of **ring**

range [reɪndʒ] **1** N **(a)** *(of mountains)* cordillera *f*, sierra *f* **(b)** *US (open land)* pradera *f* **(c)** *(choice)* surtido *m*; *(of products)* gama *f* **(d)** **firing r.** campo *m* de tiro **(e)** *(of missile)* alcance *m*; **at close r.** de cerca **(f)** *(cooker)* fogón *m*, cocina *f* or *Col, Méx, Ven* estufa *f* de carbón
2 VI *(extend)* extenderse *(to* hasta*)*; **prices r. from £5 to £20** los precios oscilan entre 5 y 20 libras

ranger ['reɪndʒə(r)] N **(a)** **(forest) r.** guardabosques *mf inv* **(b)** *US Mil* comando *m*

rank¹ [ræŋk] **1** N **(a)** *Mil (row)* fila *f*; **the ranks** los soldados rasos **(b)** *(position in army)* graduación *f*; *(in society)* rango *m* **(c)** *Br* **(taxi) r.** parada *f* de taxis
2 VT *(classify)* clasificar
3 VI *(figure)* figurar; **to r. above/below sb** figurar por encima/debajo de algn; **to r. with** estar al mismo nivel que

rank² [ræŋk] ADJ *Fml (foul-smelling)* fétido(a)

ransack ['rænsæk] VT *(plunder)* saquear; *(rummage in)* registrar

ransom ['rænsəm] N rescate *m*; **to hold sb to r.** pedir rescate por algn; *Fig* poner a algn entre la espada y la pared

rant [rænt] VI vociferar; *Fam* **to r. and rave** pegar gritos

rap [ræp] **1** N **(a)** *(blow)* golpe seco; *(on door)* golpecito *m* **(b)** *Mus* rap *m*
2 VT & VI *(knock)* golpear

rape¹ [reɪp] *Jur* **1** N violación *f*
2 VT violar

rape² [reɪp] N *Bot* colza *f*

rapeseed ['reɪpsiːd] N **r. oil** aceite *m* de colza

rapid ['ræpɪd] **1** ADJ rápido(a)
2 N **rapids** *(in river)* rápidos *mpl*

rapidity [rə'pɪdɪtɪ] N rapidez *f*

rapist ['reɪpɪst] N violador(a) *m,f*

rapper ['ræpə(r)] N rapero(a) *m,f*

rapport [ræ'pɔː(r)] N compenetración *f*

rapture ['ræptʃə(r)] N éxtasis *m*

rapturous ['ræptʃərəs] ADJ muy entusiasta

rare¹ [reə(r)] ADJ raro(a), poco común

rare² [reə(r)] ADJ *(steak)* poco hecho(a)

rarefied ['reərɪfaɪd] ADJ enrarecido(a)

rarely ['reəlɪ] ADV raras veces

raring ['reərɪŋ] ADJ *Fam* **to be r. to do sth** morirse de ganas de hacer algo

rarity ['reərɪtɪ] N rareza *f*

rascal ['rɑːskəl] N granuja *mf*

rash¹ [ræʃ] N (**a**) *Med* erupción *f*, sarpullido *m* (**b**) *Fig (of robberies etc)* racha *f*

rash² [ræʃ] ADJ *(reckless)* impetuoso(a); *(words, actions)* precipitado(a), imprudente

rasher ['ræʃə(r)] N *Br* **r. (of bacon)** loncha *f* de tocino *or Esp* beicon

raspberry ['rɑːzbərɪ] N frambuesa *f*

rasping ['rɑːspɪŋ] ADJ áspero(a)

rat [ræt] N (**a**) *(animal)* rata *f*; **r. poison** raticida *m* (**b**) *US Fam (informer)* soplón(ona) *m,f*, chivato(a) *m,f*

rate [reɪt] 1 N (**a**) *(ratio)* índice *m*, tasa *f*; **at any r.** *(at least)* al menos; *(anyway)* en cualquier caso (**b**) *(cost)* precio *m*; *Fin (of interest, exchange)* tipo *m*, tasa *f* (**c**) **at the r. of** *(of speed)* a la velocidad de; *(quantity)* a razón de (**d**) *Br* **(business) rates** impuestos *mpl* municipales *(para empresas)*

2 VT (**a**) *(estimate)* estimar (**b**) *(evaluate)* tasar (**c**) *(consider)* considerar

rateable ['reɪtəbəl] ADJ *Br* **r. value** valor *m* catastral

ratepayer ['reɪtpeɪə(r)] N *Br* contribuyente *mf*

rather ['rɑːðə(r)] ADV (**a**) *(quite)* más bien, bastante; *(very much so)* muy (**b**) *(more accurately)* mejor dicho; **r. than** *(instead of)* en vez de; *(more than)* más que (**c**) **she would r. stay here** *(prefer to)* prefiere quedarse aquí

ratify ['rætɪfaɪ] VT ratificar

rating ['reɪtɪŋ] N (**a**) *(valuation)* tasación *f*; *(score)* valoración *f* (**b**) *TV (programme)* **ratings** índice *m* de audiencia (**c**) *Naut* marinero *m* sin graduación

ratio ['reɪʃɪəʊ] N razón *f*; **in the r. of** a razón de

ration ['ræʃən] 1 N (**a**) *(allowance)* ración *f* (**b**) **rations** víveres *mpl*

2 VT racionar

ration 1 N *(allowance)* ración *f*; **raciones** víveres *mpl*

2 VT racionar

rational ['ræʃənəl] ADJ racional

rationale [ræʃə'nɑːl] N base *f*

rationalize ['ræʃənəlaɪz] VT racionalizar

rattle ['rætəl] 1 N (**a**) *(of train, cart)* traqueteo *m*; *(of metal)* repiqueteo *m*; *(of glass)* tintineo *m* (**b**) *(toy)* sonajero *m*; *(instrument)* carraca *f*

2 VT (**a**) *(keys etc)* hacer sonar (**b**) *Fam (unsettle)* poner nervioso(a)

3 VI sonar; *(metal)* repiquetear; *(glass)* tintinear

rattlesnake ['rætəlsneɪk] N serpiente *f* de cascabel

raucous ['rɔːkəs] ADJ estridente

ravage ['rævɪdʒ] *Fml* 1 NPL **ravages** estragos *mpl*

2 VT asolar, devastar

rave [reɪv] 1 VI (**a**) *(be delirious)* delirar (**b**) *(be angry)* enfurecerse (**at** con) (**c**) *Fam (show enthusiasm)* entusiasmarse (**about** por)

2 ADJ *Fam* **r. review** crítica *f* muy favorable

raven ['reɪvən] N cuervo *m*

ravenous ['rævənəs] ADJ **I'm r.** tengo un hambre que no veo

ravine [rə'viːn] N barranco *m*

raving ['reɪvɪŋ] ADJ *Fam* **r. mad** loco(a) de atar

ravishing ['rævɪʃɪŋ] ADJ *(person)* encantador(a)

raw [rɔː] ADJ (**a**) *(uncooked)* crudo(a) (**b**) *(not processed)* bruto(a); **r. material** materia prima (**c**) *(emotion)* instintivo(a) (**d**) **r. deal** trato injusto (**e**) *US (inexperienced)* novato(a)

ray¹ [reɪ] N rayo *m*; *Fig* **r. of hope** rayo de esperanza

ray² [reɪ] N *(fish)* raya *f*

rayon ['reɪɒn] N rayón *m*

raze [reɪz] VT arrasar

razor ['reɪzə(r)] N *(for shaving)* maquinilla *f* de afeitar; **r. blade** hoja *f* de afeitar

R & D [ɑːrən'diː] N *(abbr* **Research and Development**) I+D

Rd *(abbr* **Road**) calle *f*, c/

re [riː] PREP respecto a, con referencia a

reach [riːtʃ] 1 VT (**a**) *(arrive at)* llegar a (**b**) *(contact)* localizar

2 VI **to r. for sth** *(tratar de)* alcanzar algo; **to r. out** extender la mano

3 N alcance *m*; **out of r.** fuera del alcance; **within r.** al alcance

react [rɪ'ækt] VI reaccionar

reaction [rɪ'ækʃən] N reacción *f*

reactionary [rɪ'ækʃənərɪ] ADJ & N reaccionario(a) *(m,f)*

reactor [rɪ'æktə(r)] N reactor *m*

read [riːd] 1 VT *(pt & pp* **read** [red]) (**a**) *(book, newspaper, letter)* leer (**b**) *Br Univ* estudiar (**c**) *(of dial)* marcar; *(of signpost, text)* decir

2 VI leer

▸ **read out** VT SEP leer en voz alta

readable ['riːdəbəl] ADJ (**a**) *(interesting)* interesante (**b**) *(legible)* legible

reader ['riːdə(r)] N (**a**) *(person)* lector(a) *m,f* (**b**) *(book)* libro *m* de lectura (**c**) *Br Univ* profesor(a) *m,f* adjunto(a)

readership ['riːdəʃɪp] N *Press* lectores *mpl*

readily ['redɪlɪ] ADV (**a**) *(easily)* fácilmente; **r. available** disponible en el acto (**b**) *(willingly)* de buena gana

readiness ['redɪnɪs] N (**a**) *(preparedness)* preparación *f* (**b**) *(willingness)* buena disposición

reading ['riːdɪŋ] N (**a**) *(action, pastime)* lectura *f* (**b**) *(interpretation)* interpretación *f* (**c**) *(of laws, bill)* presentación *f*

readjust [riːə'dʒʌst] 1 VT reajustar

2 VI *(adapt oneself)* adaptarse

ready ['redɪ] ADJ **(readier, readiest)** (**a**) *(prepared)* listo(a), preparado(a); **r., steady, go!** ¡preparados, listos, ya! (**b**) **r. to** *(about to)* a punto de (**c**) *(to hand)* a mano; **r. cash** dinero *m* en efectivo (**d**) *(willing)* dispuesto(a)

ready-cooked ['redɪ'kʊkt] ADJ precocinado(a)

ready-made ['redɪ'meɪd] ADJ confecciona-do(a); *(food)* preparado(a)

real [rɪəl] ADJ (**a**) *(danger, fear, effort)* real; *Fam* **for r.** de veras (**b**) *(genuine)* auténtico(a); **r. leather** piel legítima (**c**) *US Com* **r. estate** bienes *mpl* inmuebles; **r. estate agent** agente inmobiliario

realism ['rɪəlɪzəm] N realismo *m*

realistic ['rɪəlɪstɪk] ADJ realista

reality [rɪ'ælɪtɪ] N realidad *f*; **in r.** en realidad

realization [rɪəlaɪ'zeɪʃən] N (**a**) *(understanding)* comprensión *f* (**b**) *(of plan, assets)* realización *f*

realize ['rɪəlaɪz] VT (**a**) *(become aware of)* darse cuenta de (**b**) *(assets, plan)* realizar

really ['rɪəlɪ] ADV verdaderamente, realmente; **I r.** don't know no lo sé de verdad; **r.?** ¿de veras?

realm [relm] N *(kingdom)* reino *m*; *Fig (field)* terreno *m*

realtor ['rɪəltə(r)] N *US* agente inmobiliario(a)

ream [riːm] N *(of paper)* resma *f*

reap [riːp] VT *Agr* cosechar; *Fig* **to r. the benefits** llevarse los beneficios

reappear [riːə'pɪə(r)] VI reaparecer

reappraisal [riːə'preɪzəl] N revaluación *f*

rear¹ [rɪə(r)] **1** N (**a**) *(back part)* parte *f* de atrás (**b**) *Fam (buttocks)* trasero *m* **2** ADJ trasero(a); **r. entrance** puerta *f* de atrás

rear² [rɪə(r)] **1** VT (**a**) *(breed, raise)* criar (**b**) *(lift up)* levantar **2** VI **to r. up** *(horse)* encabritarse

rearguard ['rɪəɡɑːd] N retaguardia *f*

rearmament [riː'ɑːməmənt] N rearme *m*

rearrange [riːə'reɪndʒ] VT (**a**) *(furniture)* colocar de otra manera (**b**) *(appointment)* fijar otra fecha para

rear-view ['rɪəvjuː] ADJ **r. mirror** (espejo *m*) retrovisor *m*

reason ['riːzən] **1** N (**a**) *(cause, motive)* motivo *m*, razón *f*; **for no r.** sin razón; **for some r.** por algún motivo (**b**) *(good sense)* razón *f*; **it stands to r.** es lógico; **to listen to r.** atender a razones, *Am* atender razones **2** VI (**a**) **to r. with sb** convencer a algn (**b**) *(argue, work out)* razonar

reasonable ['riːzənəbəl] ADJ (**a**) *(fair)* razona-ble (**b**) *(sensible)* sensato(a) (**c**) *(average)* regular

reasonably ['riːzənəblɪ] ADV *(fairly)* bastante

reasoning ['riːzənɪŋ] N razonamiento *m*

reassurance [riːə'ʃʊərəns] N consuelo *m*

reassure [riːə'ʃʊə(r)] VT (**a**) *(comfort)* tranqui-lizar (**b**) *(restore confidence)* dar confianza a

reassuring [riːə'ʃʊərɪŋ] ADJ consolador(a)

rebate ['riːbeɪt] N devolución *f*; **tax r.** devolución fiscal

Note that the Spanish verb **rebatir** is a false friend and is never a translation for the English word **rebate**. In Spanish **rebatir** means "to refute".

rebel 1 ADJ & N ['rebəl] rebelde *(mf)* **2** VI [rɪ'bel] rebelarse, sublevarse (**against** contra)

rebellion [rɪ'beljən] N rebelión *f*

rebellious [rɪ'beljəs] ADJ rebelde

rebound 1 N ['riːbaʊnd] *(of ball)* rebote *m*; *Fig* **on the r.** de rebote **2** VI [rɪ'baʊnd] *(ball)* rebotar

rebuff [rɪ'bʌf] **1** N desaire *m* **2** VT desairar

rebuild [riː'bɪld] VT reconstruir

rebuke [rɪ'bjuːk] **1** N reproche *m* **2** VT reprochar

rebut [rɪ'bʌt] VT refutar

recalcitrant [rɪ'kælsɪtrənt] ADJ *Fml* recalci-trante

recall [rɪ'kɔːl] VT (**a**) *(soldiers, products)* hacer volver; *(ambassador)* retirar (**b**) *(remember)* recordar

recant [rɪ'kænt] VI *Fml* retractarse

recap 1 VT&VI [riː'kæp] resumir; **to r.** en resumen **2** N ['riːkæp] recapitulación *f*

recapitulate [riːkə'pɪtjʊleɪt] VT & VI *Fml* recapitular

recapture [riː'kæptʃə(r)] VT *Fig* recuperar

recd *Com (abbr* **received**) recibido(a)

recede [rɪ'siːd] VI retroceder; **to have a receding hairline** tener entradas

receipt [rɪ'siːt] N (**a**) *(act)* recepción *f*; **to acknowledge r. of sth** acusar recibo de algo (**b**) *Com (paper)* recibo *m* (**c**) **receipts** *(takings)* recaudación *f*

receive [rɪ'siːv] VT (**a**) *(be given, get)* recibir (**b**) *Jur (stolen goods)* ocultar (**c**) *(welcome)* acoger (**d**) *Rad & TV* captar

receiver [rɪ'siːvə(r)] N (**a**) *(person)* receptor(a) *m,f* (**b**) *Jur (of stolen goods)* perista *mf* (**c**) *(of telephone)* auricular *m*, *RP*, *Ven* tubo *m*

recent ['riːsənt] ADJ reciente; **in r. years** en los últimos años

recently ['riːsəntlɪ] ADV hace poco, reciente-mente

receptacle [rɪ'septəkəl] N receptáculo *m*

reception [rɪ'sepʃən] N (**a**) *(welcome)* recibi-miento *m* (**b**) *(party)* recepción *f*; **wedding r.** banquete *m* de boda *or Andes* matrimonio *or RP* casamiento *or RP* casamiento (**c**) **r. (desk)** recepción *f* (**d**) *Rad & TV* recepción *f*

receptionist [rɪ'sepʃənɪst] N recepcionista *mf*

receptive [rɪ'septɪv] ADJ receptivo(a)

recess ['riːses, rɪ'ses] N (**a**) *(in a wall)* hueco *m* (**b**) *(secret place)* escondrijo *m* (**c**) *US Educ* recreo *m*; *Pol* período *m* de vacaciones

recession [rɪ'seʃən] N recesión *f*

recharge [riː'tʃɑːdʒ] VT *(battery)* recargar

rechargeable [riːˈtʃɑːdʒəbəl] ADJ recargable

recipe [ˈresɪpɪ] N *Culin* receta *f*; *Fig* fórmula *f*

recipient [rɪˈsɪpɪənt] N receptor(a) *m,f*; *(of letter)* destinatario(a) *m,f*

> Note that the Spanish word **recipiente** is a false friend and is never a translation for the English word **recipient**. In Spanish **recipiente** means "receptacle, container".

reciprocate [rɪˈsɪprəkeɪt] **1** VT *(favour etc)* devolver
2 VI hacer lo mismo

recital [rɪˈsaɪtəl] N recital *m*

recite [rɪˈsaɪt] VT & VI recitar

reckless [ˈreklɪs] ADJ *(unwise)* imprudente; *(fearless)* temerario(a)

reckon [ˈrekən] **1** VT (**a**) *(calculate)* calcular; *(count)* contar (**b**) *Fam (think)* creer; *(consider)* considerar
2 VI *(calculate)* calcular; *(count)* contar
▶ **reckon on** VT INSEP contar con

reckoner [ˈrekənə(r)] N **ready r.** tabla *f* de cálculo

reckoning [ˈrekənɪŋ] N cálculo *m*; **by my r. ...** según mis cálculos ...; *Fig* **day of r.** día *m* del juicio final

reclaim [rɪˈkleɪm] VT (**a**) *(recover)* recuperar; *(demand back)* reclamar (**b**) *(marshland etc)* convertir

recline [rɪˈklaɪn] VI recostarse, reclinarse

reclining [rɪˈklaɪnɪŋ] ADJ recostado(a); **r. seat** asiento *m* abatible

recluse [rɪˈkluːs] N solitario(a) *m,f*

> Note that the Spanish word **recluso** is a false friend and is never a translation for the English word **recluse**. In Spanish **recluso** means "prisoner".

recognition [rekəgˈnɪʃən] N reconocimiento *m*; *(appreciation)* apreciación *f*; **changed beyond all r.** irreconocible

recognizable [rekəgˈnaɪzəbəl] ADJ reconocible

recognize [ˈrekəgnaɪz] VT reconocer

recoil 1 N [ˈriːkɔɪl] *(of gun)* culatazo *m*; *(of spring)* aflojamiento *m*
2 VI [rɪˈkɔɪl] (**a**) *(gun)* dar un culatazo; *(spring)* aflojarse (**b**) *(in fear)* espantarse

recollect [rekəˈlekt] VT recordar

recollection [rekəˈlekʃən] N recuerdo *m*

> Note that the Spanish word **recolección** is a false friend and is never a translation for the English word **recollection**. In Spanish **recolección** means "harvest, collection".

recommend [rekəˈmend] VT recomendar

recommendation [rekəmenˈdeɪʃən] N recomendación *f*

recompense [ˈrekəmpens] **1** N recompensa *f*; *Jur* indemnización *f*
2 VT recompensar; *Jur* indemnizar

reconcile [ˈrekənsaɪl] VT *(two people)* reconciliar; *(two ideas)* conciliar; **to r. oneself to resignarse a

recondition [riːkənˈdɪʃən] VT *(engine)* revisar

reconnaissance [rɪˈkɒnɪsəns] N *Mil* reconocimiento *m*

reconnoitre, *US* **reconnoiter** [rekəˈnɔɪtə(r)] VT *Mil* reconocer

reconsider [riːkənˈsɪdə(r)] VT reconsiderar

reconstruct [riːkənˈstrʌkt] VT reconstruir

reconstruction [riːkənˈstrʌkʃən] N reconstrucción *f*

record 1 N [ˈrekɔːd] (**a**) *(account)* relación *f*; *(of meeting)* actas *fpl* (**b**) *(document)* documento *m*; **public records** archivos *mpl* (**c**) *Mus* disco *m*; **r. player** tocadiscos *m inv* (**d**) *Sport* récord *m*
2 VT [rɪˈkɔːd] (**a**) *(relate)* hacer constar; *(note down)* apuntar (**b**) *(record, voice)* grabar

recorded [rɪˈkɔːdɪd] ADJ *Br* **r. delivery** correo certificado; **r. message** mensaje grabado

recorder [rɪˈkɔːdə(r)] N (**a**) *(person)* registrador(a) *m,f*; *Jur* magistrado(a) *m,f* (**b**) *Mus* flauta *f*

recording [rɪˈkɔːdɪŋ] N *(registering)* registro *m*; *(recorded music, message etc)* grabación *f*

recount [rɪˈkaʊnt] VT *(tell)* contar

re-count 1 VT [ˈriːˈkaʊnt] *Pol* volver a contar
2 N [ˈriːkaʊnt] *Pol* recuento *m*

recoup [rɪˈkuːp] VT *(losses etc)* recuperar

recourse [rɪˈkɔːs] N **to have r. to** recurrir a

recover [rɪˈkʌvə(r)] **1** VT *(items, lost time)* recuperar; *(consciousness)* recobrar
2 VI *(from illness etc)* reponerse

recovery [rɪˈkʌvərɪ] N (**a**) *(retrieval)* recuperación *f* (**b**) *(from illness)* restablecimiento *m*

re-create [riːkrɪˈeɪt] VT recrear

recreation [rekrɪˈeɪʃən] N (**a**) *(leisure)* ocio *m*, esparcimiento *m* (**b**) *Educ (playtime)* recreo *m*

recreational [rekrɪˈeɪʃənəl] ADJ recreativo(a); *US* **r. vehicle** autocaravana *f*, casa *f* caravana

recrimination [rɪkrɪmɪˈneɪʃən] N reproche *m*

recruit [rɪˈkruːt] **1** N recluta *m*
2 VT *(soldiers)* reclutar; *(workers)* contratar

recruitment [rɪˈkruːtmənt] N *(of soldiers)* reclutamiento *m*; *(of employees)* contratación *f*

rectangle [ˈrektæŋgəl] N rectángulo *m*

rectangular [rekˈtæŋgjʊlə(r)] ADJ rectangular

rectify [ˈrektɪfaɪ] VT rectificar

rector [ˈrektə(r)] N (**a**) *Rel* párroco *m* (**b**) *Scot Educ* director(a) *m,f*

recuperate [rɪˈkuːpəreɪt] VI reponerse

recur [rɪˈkɜː(r)] VI repetirse

> Note that the Spanish verb **recurrir** is a false friend and is never a translation for the English verb **to recur**. In Spanish **recurrir** means "to appeal, to resort".

recurrence [rɪˈkʌrəns] N repetición *f*, reaparición *f*

recurrent [rɪ'kʌrənt] ADJ constante; *Med* recurrente.

recycle [riː'saɪkəl] VT reciclar

recycling [riː'saɪklɪŋ] N reciclaje *m*; **r. bank** ecopunto *m*

red [red] **1** ADJ (**redder, reddest**) rojo(a); **r. light** semáforo *m* en rojo; **r. wine** vino tinto; **to go r.** ponerse colorado(a); **to have r. hair** ser pelirrojo(a); *Fig* **r. herring** truco *m* para despistar; *Fam* **to roll out the r. carpet for sb** recibir a algn con todos los honores; **R. Cross** Cruz Roja; **R. Indian** piel roja *mf*; **R. Riding Hood** Caperucita Roja; **R. Sea** Mar Rojo; **r. tape** papeleo *m*
2 N (**a**) (*colour*) rojo *m* (**b**) *Fin* **to be in the r.** estar en números rojos

redcurrant ['redkʌrənt] N grosella roja

redden ['redən] **1** VI (*blush*) enrojecerse, ponerse colorado(a)
2 VT (*make red*) teñir de rojo

reddish ['redɪʃ] ADJ rojizo(a)

redeem [rɪ'diːm] VT (**a**) (*regain*) recobrar; (*voucher*) canjear (**b**) (*debt*) amortizar (**c**) (*film, novel etc*) salvar (**d**) *Rel* redimir; *Fig* **to r. oneself** redimirse

redeeming [rɪ'diːmɪŋ] ADJ compensatorio(a); **his only r. feature** lo único que le salva

redemption [rɪ'dempʃən] N *Fml* (**a**) (*of debt*) amortización *f* (**b**) *Rel* redención *f*; **beyond r.** sin remedio

redeploy [riːdɪ'plɔɪ] VT redistribuir

red-handed [red'hændɪd] ADJ **he was caught r.** lo *Esp* cogieron *or Am* agarraron con las manos en la masa

redhead ['redhed] N pelirrojo(a) *m,f*

red-hot [red'hɒt] ADJ (**a**) (*very hot*) candente (**b**) *Fam* (*passionate*) ardiente (**c**) *Fam* **r. news** noticia(s) *f(pl)* de última hora

redial [riː'daɪəl] N *Tel* **r. (feature)** (botón *m* de) rellamada *f*

redirect [riːdɪ'rekt] VT (**a**) (*funds*) redistribuir (**b**) (*letter*) remitir a la nueva dirección

red-light [red'laɪt] ADJ *Fam* **r. district** *Esp* barrio chino, *Am* zona roja

redo [riː'duː] (*pt* **redid** [riː'dɪd], *pp* **redone** [riː'dʌn]) VT rehacer

redouble [riː'dʌbəl] VT redoblar

redress [rɪ'dres] *Fml* **1** N reparación *f*
2 VT reparar

redskin ['redskɪn] N piel roja *mf*

reduce [rɪ'djuːs] VT (**a**) (*make smaller, lower*) reducir; (*price, product*) rebajar (**b**) (*in rank*) degradar (**c**) *Culin* (*sauce*) espesar (**d**) *Med* recomponer

reduction [rɪ'dʌkʃən] N reducción *f*; *Com* (*in purchase price*) descuento *m*, rebaja *f*

redundancy [rɪ'dʌndənsɪ] N *Br* (*dismissal*) despido *m*

redundant [rɪ'dʌndənt] ADJ (**a**) (*superfluous*) redundante (**b**) *Br Ind* **to be made r.** perder el empleo; **to make sb r.** despedir a algn

reed [riːd] N (**a**) *Bot* caña *f* (**b**) *Mus* caramillo *m*

reef [riːf] N arrecife *m*

reek [riːk] **1** N tufo *m*
2 VI apestar

reel [riːl] **1** N (**a**) (*spool*) bobina *f*, carrete *m* (**b**) *Scot Mus* danza *f* tradicional
2 VI (*stagger*) tambalearse

re-elect [riːɪ'lekt] VT reelegir

ref [ref] N (**a**) *Fam Sport* árbitro(a) *m,f* (**b**) *Com* (*abbr* **reference**) ref

refectory [rɪ'fektərɪ] N refectorio *m*

refer [rɪ'fɜː(r)] **1** VT mandar, enviar; **to r. a matter to a tribunal** remitir un asunto a un tribunal
2 VI (**a**) (*allude*) referirse, aludir (**to** a) (**b**) **to r. to** (*consult*) consultar

referee [refə'riː] **1** N (**a**) *Sport* árbitro(a) *m,f* (**b**) *Br* (*for job application*) garante *mf*
2 VT *Sport* arbitrar

reference ['refərəns] N (**a**) (*consultation*) consulta *f*; (*source*) referencia *f*; **with r. to** referente a, con referencia a; **r. book** libro *m* de consulta; **r. library** biblioteca *f* de consulta (**b**) *Br* (*from employer*) informe *m*, referencia *f*

referendum [refə'rendəm] N referéndum *m*

refill 1 N ['riːfɪl] (**a**) (*replacement*) recambio *m*, carga *f* (**b**) *Fam* (*drink*) **a r.** otra copa
2 VT [riː'fɪl] rellenar

refine [rɪ'faɪn] VT refinar

refined [rɪ'faɪnd] ADJ refinado(a)

refinement [rɪ'faɪnmənt] N refinamiento *m*

refinery [rɪ'faɪnərɪ] N refinería *f*

reflect [rɪ'flekt] **1** VT (*light, attitude*) reflejar
2 VI (*think*) reflexionar; **to r. on sth** meditar sobre algo

reflection [rɪ'flekʃən] N (**a**) (*indication, mirror image*) reflejo *m* (**b**) (*thought*) reflexión *f*; **on r.** pensándolo bien (**c**) (*criticism*) crítica *f*

reflector [rɪ'flektə(r)] N (*of vehicle*) catafaro *m*

reflex ['riːfleks] N reflejo *m*

reflexive [rɪ'fleksɪv] ADJ reflexivo(a)

reform [rɪ'fɔːm] **1** N reforma *f*; **r. school** reformatorio *m*
2 VT reformar

reformation [refə'meɪʃən] N reforma *f*

reformatory [rɪ'fɔːmətərɪ] N reformatorio *m*

reformer [rɪ'fɔːmə(r)] N reformador(a) *m,f*

refrain [rɪ'freɪn] **1** N *Mus* estribillo *m*; *Fig* lema *m*
2 VI abstenerse (**from** de)

refresh [rɪ'freʃ] VT refrescar

refresher [rɪ'freʃə(r)] N **r. course** cursillo *m* de reciclaje

refreshing [rɪ'freʃɪŋ] ADJ refrescante; **a r. change** un cambio muy agradable

refreshment [rɪ'freʃmənt] N refresco *m*

refrigerator [rɪ'frɪdʒəreɪtə(r)] N nevera f, frigorífico m, Andes frigider m, RP heladera f

refuel [ri:'fju:əl] VI repostar combustible

refuge ['refju:dʒ] N refugio m, cobijo m; **to take r.** refugiarse

refugee [refjʊ'dʒi:] N refugiado(a) m,f

refund 1 N ['ri:fʌnd] reembolso m
2 VT [rɪ'fʌnd] reembolsar, devolver

refurbish [ri:'fɜ:bɪʃ] VT redecorar

refusal [rɪ'fju:zəl] N negativa f; **to have first r. on sth** tener la primera opción en algo

refuse¹ [rɪ'fju:z] **1** VT rechazar; **to r. sb sth** negar algo a algn
2 VI negarse

refuse² ['refju:s] N basura f; **r. collector** basurero(a) m,f

refute [rɪ'fju:t] VT refutar, rebatir

regain [rɪ'geɪn] VT recuperar; *(consciousness)* recobrar

regal ['ri:gəl] ADJ regio(a)

regard [rɪ'gɑ:d] **1** N (**a**) *(concern)* consideración f, respeto m; **with r. to** respecto a (**b**) *(esteem)* estima f (**c**) **regards** *(good wishes)* saludos mpl, CAm, Col, Ecuad saludes fpl; **give him my regards** dale recuerdos de mi parte
2 VT (**a**) *(consider)* considerar (**b**) **as regards** *(regarding)* respecto a

regarding [rɪ'gɑ:dɪŋ] PREP respecto a

regardless [rɪ'gɑ:dlɪs] **1** PREP **r. of** sin tener en cuenta; **r. of the outcome** pase lo que pase
2 ADV a toda costa

regime [reɪ'ʒi:m] N régimen m

regiment ['redʒɪmənt] **1** N regimiento m
2 VT regimentar

regimental [redʒɪ'mentəl] ADJ del regimiento

region ['ri:dʒən] N región f; **in the r. of** alrededor de, del orden de

regional ['ri:dʒənəl] ADJ regional

regionalism ['ri:dʒənəlɪzəm] N regionalismo m

register ['redʒɪstə(r)] **1** N registro m
2 VT (**a**) *(record)* registrar (**b**) *(letter)* certificar (**c**) *(show)* mostrar
3 VI *(for course)* inscribirse; Univ matricularse

registered ['redʒɪstəd] ADJ certificado(a); Br **r. letter** carta certificada; **r. trademark** marca registrada

registrar [redʒɪ'strɑ:(r), 'redʒɪstrɑ:(r)] N (**a**) *(record keeper)* registrador(a) m,f (**b**) Br Med = médico de grado superior en un hospital (**c**) Univ secretario(a) m,f general

registration [redʒɪ'streɪʃən] N inscripción f; Univ matrícula f; Br Aut **r. number** matrícula f

registry ['redʒɪstrɪ] N registro m; Br **r. office** registro civil; **to get married in a r. office** casarse por lo civil

regret [rɪ'gret] **1** N *(remorse)* remordimiento m; *(sadness)* pesar m; **regrets** *(excuses)* excusas fpl; **to have no regrets** no arrepentirse de nada
2 VT arrepentirse de, lamentar

regretful [rɪ'gretfʊl] ADJ arrepentido(a)

regrettable [rɪ'gretəbəl] ADJ lamentable

regroup [ri:'gru:p] **1** VT reagrupar
2 VI reagruparse

regular ['regjʊlə(r)] **1** ADJ (**a**) *(features, pulse, verb)* regular (**b**) *(usual)* normal (**c**) *(staff)* permanente (**d**) *(frequent)* frecuente (**e**) **r. army** tropas fpl regulares (**f**) US Fam **a r. guy** un tío legal, Am un tipo derecho
2 N *(customer)* cliente mf habitual

regularity [regjʊ'lærɪtɪ] N regularidad f

regularly ['regjʊləlɪ] ADV con regularidad

regulate ['regjʊleɪt] VT regular

regulation [regjʊ'leɪʃən] **1** N (**a**) *(control)* regulación f (**b**) *(rule)* regla f
2 ADJ reglamentario(a)

rehabilitation [ri:əbɪlɪ'teɪʃən] N rehabilitación f; **r. centre** centro m de reinserción

rehearsal [rɪ'hɜ:səl] N ensayo m

rehearse [rɪ'hɜ:s] VT & VI ensayar

reign [reɪn] **1** N reinado m
2 VI reinar

reigning ['reɪnɪŋ] ADJ **r. champion** campeón(ona) m,f actual

reimburse [ri:ɪm'bɜ:s] VT reembolsar

rein [reɪn] N *(for horse)* rienda f; Fig **he gave free r. to his emotions** dio rienda suelta a sus emociones

reindeer ['reɪndɪə(r)] N reno m

reinforce [ri:ɪn'fɔ:s] VT *(strengthen)* reforzar; *(support)* apoyar; **reinforced concrete** hormigón or Am concreto armado

reinforcement [ri:ɪn'fɔ:smənt] N (**a**) *(of wall, structure)* refuerzo m (**b**) Mil **reinforcements** refuerzos mpl

reinstate [ri:ɪn'steɪt] VT *(to job)* reincorporar

reiterate [ri:'ɪtəreɪt] VT reiterar

reject 1 N ['ri:dʒekt] (**a**) Com **rejects** artículos defectuosos (**b**) Fam Pej *(person)* desecho m
2 VT [rɪ'dʒekt] rechazar

rejection [rɪ'dʒekʃən] N rechazo m

rejoice [rɪ'dʒɔɪs] VI regocijarse (**at** or **over** de)

rejuvenate [rɪ'dʒu:vɪneɪt] VT rejuvenecer; Fig revitalizar

relapse [rɪ'læps] **1** N (**a**) Med recaída f; **to have a r.** sufrir una recaída (**b**) *(into crime, alcoholism)* reincidencia f
2 VI recaer

relate [rɪ'leɪt] **1** VT (**a**) *(connect)* relacionar (**b**) *(tell)* relatar
2 VI relacionarse

related [rɪ'leɪtɪd] ADJ (**a**) *(linked)* relacionado(a) (**to** con) (**b**) **to be r. to sb** ser pariente de algn

relation [rɪ'leɪʃən] N (**a**) *(link)* relación f; **in** or **with r. to** respecto a; **it bears no r. to what we said** no tiene nada que ver con lo que dijimos (**b**) *(member of family)* pariente mf

relationship [rɪ'leɪʃənʃɪp] N (**a**) *(link)* relación f (**b**) *(between people)* relaciones fpl; **to have a**

good/bad r. with sb llevarse bien/mal con algn

relative ['relətɪv] 1 N pariente *mf*
2 ADJ relativo(a)

relatively ['relətɪvlɪ] ADV relativamente

relax [rɪ'læks] 1 VT *(muscles, rules)* relajar
2 VI relajarse

relaxation [riːlæk'seɪʃən] N (**a**) *(rest)* descanso *m*, relajación *f* (**b**) *(of rules)* relajación *f* (**c**) *(pastime)* distracción *f*

relaxed [rɪ'lækst] ADJ relajado(a); *(peaceful)* tranquilo(a)

relaxing [rɪ'læksɪŋ] ADJ relajante

relay 1 N ['riːleɪ] (**a**) *(of workers)* relevo *m* (**b**) *Rad & TV* **r. station** repetidor *m* (**c**) *Sport* **r. (race)** carrera *f* de relevos
2 VT [rɪ'leɪ] (**a**) *(pass on)* difundir (**b**) *Rad & TV* retransmitir

release [rɪ'liːs] 1 N (**a**) *(of prisoner)* liberación *f*, puesta *f* en libertad; *(of gas)* escape *m* (**b**) *Com* puesta *f* en venta (**c**) *Cin* estreno *m* (**d**) *(record)* disco *m*
2 VT (**a**) *(let go)* soltar; *(prisoner)* poner en libertad; *(gas)* despedir (**b**) *Com* poner en venta (**c**) *Cin* estrenar (**d**) *(record)* publicar

relegate ['relɪgeɪt] VT (**a**) *(consign)* relegar (**b**) *Br Ftb* **to be relegated** bajar a una división inferior

relent [rɪ'lent] VI ceder; *(storm)* aplacarse

relentless [rɪ'lentlɪs] ADJ implacable

relevance ['reləvəns] N pertinencia *f*

relevant ['reləvənt] ADJ pertinente (**to** a); **it is not r.** no viene al caso

> Note that the Spanish word **relevante** is a false friend and is never a translation for the English word **relevant**. In Spanish **relevante** means "outstanding, important".

reliability [rɪlaɪə'bɪlɪtɪ] N (**a**) *(of person)* formalidad *f* (**b**) *(of car, machine)* fiabilidad *f*, *Am* confiabilidad *f*

reliable [rɪ'laɪəbəl] ADJ *(person, machine)* fiable, *Am* confiable; **a r. car** un coche seguro; **a r. source** una fuente fidedigna

reliably [rɪ'laɪəblɪ] ADV **to be r. informed that** saber de buena tinta que

reliant [rɪ'laɪənt] ADJ **to be r. on** depender de

relic ['relɪk] N (**a**) *Rel* reliquia *f* (**b**) *(reminder of past)* vestigio *m*

relief [rɪ'liːf] N (**a**) *(from pain, anxiety)* alivio *m* (**b**) *(help)* auxilio *m*, ayuda *f*; *US* **to be on r.** cobrar un subsidio (**c**) *Art & Geog* relieve *m*

relieve [rɪ'liːv] VT (**a**) *(alleviate)* (pain, anxiety) aliviar; *(monotony)* romper (**b**) *(take over from)* relevar (**c**) *Euph* **to r. oneself** hacer sus necesidades (**d**) **to r. sb of sth** *(burden, obligation)* quitar algo a algn

relieved [rɪ'liːvd] ADJ aliviado(a), tranquilizado(a)

religion [rɪ'lɪdʒən] N religión *f*

religious [rɪ'lɪdʒəs] ADJ religioso(a)

relinquish [rɪ'lɪŋkwɪʃ] VT renunciar a; **to r. one's hold on sth** soltar algo

relish ['relɪʃ] 1 N (**a**) *(enjoyment)* deleite *m* (**b**) *Culin* condimento *m*
2 VT agradar

relocate [riːləʊ'keɪt] VT trasladar

reluctance [rɪ'lʌktəns] N desgana *f*

reluctant [rɪ'lʌktənt] ADJ reacio(a); **to be r. to do sth** estar poco dispuesto(a) a hacer algo

reluctantly [rɪ'lʌktəntlɪ] ADV de mala gana, a regañadientes

rely [rɪ'laɪ] VI contar (**on** con), confiar (**on** en)

remain [rɪ'meɪn] 1 VI (**a**) *(stay)* permanecer, quedarse (**b**) *(be left)* quedar; **it remains to be seen** está por ver
2 NPL **remains** restos *mpl*

remainder [rɪ'meɪndə(r)] N resto *m*

remaining [rɪ'meɪnɪŋ] ADJ restante

remand [rɪ'mɑːnd] *Jur* 1 VT remitir; **remanded in custody** en prevención
2 N detención *f*; **on r.** detenido(a)

remark [rɪ'mɑːk] 1 N comentario *m*
2 VT comentar, observar

> Note that the Spanish verb **remarcar** is a false friend and is never a translation for the English word **remark**. In Spanish **remarcar** means "to stress, to underline".

remarkable [rɪ'mɑːkəbəl] ADJ extraordinario(a); *(strange)* curioso(a)

remedial [rɪ'miːdɪəl] ADJ reparador(a); **r. classes** clases *fpl* para niños atrasados en los estudios

remedy ['remɪdɪ] 1 N remedio *m*
2 VT remediar

remember [rɪ'membə(r)] 1 VT (**a**) *(recall)* acordarse de, recordar (**b**) **r. me to your mother** dale recuerdos a tu madre
2 VI acordarse, recordar; **I don't r.** no me acuerdo

remembrance [rɪ'membrəns] N **in r. of** en recuerdo de; *Br* **R. Day** *or* **Sunday** día *m* de homenaje a los caídos *(en las guerras mundiales)*

remind [rɪ'maɪnd] VT recordar; **r. me to do it** recuérdame que lo haga; **she reminds me of your sister** me recuerda a tu hermana; **that reminds me** ahora que me acuerdo

reminder [rɪ'maɪndə(r)] N recordatorio *m*, aviso *m*

reminisce [remɪ'nɪs] VI rememorar

reminiscent [remɪ'nɪsənt] ADJ *Fml* nostálgico(a); **to be r. of** recordar

remiss [rɪ'mɪs] ADJ *(negligent)* descuidado(a)

remission [rɪ'mɪʃən] N (**a**) *Med* remisión *f* (**b**) *Jur* perdón *m*

remit [rɪ'mɪt] VT (**a**) *(send)* remitir (**b**) *Jur* referir a otro tribunal

remittance [rɪˈmɪtəns] N (**a**) *(sending)* envío *m* (**b**) *(payment)* giro *m*, pago *m*

remnant [ˈremnənt] N resto *m*; **remnants** *(of cloth)* retales *mpl*

remold [ˈriːməʊld] N *US* = **remould**

remorse [rɪˈmɔːs] N remordimiento *m*

remorseful [rɪˈmɔːsfʊl] ADJ lleno(a) de remordimiento

remorseless [rɪˈmɔːslɪs] ADJ despiadado(a)

remote [rɪˈməʊt] ADJ (**a**) *(far away)* remoto(a); **r. control** mando *m* a distancia (**b**) *(isolated)* aislado(a) (**c**) *(possibility)* remoto(a); **I haven't the remotest idea** no tengo la más mínima idea

remote-controlled [rɪˈməʊtkənˈtrəʊld] ADJ teledirigido(a)

remotely [rɪˈməʊtlɪ] ADV (**a**) *(vaguely)* vagamente (**b**) *(distantly)* en lugar aislado

remould [ˈriːməʊld] N *Br Aut* neumático recauchutado, *Col, Méx* llanta *or Arg* goma recauchutada

removable [rɪˈmuːvəbəl] ADJ *(detachable)* que se puede quitar

removal [rɪˈmuːvəl] N (**a**) *Br (moving house)* mudanza *f*; **r. van** camión *m* de mudanzas (**b**) *(of stain etc)* eliminación *f*

remove [rɪˈmuːv] VT (**a**) *(move)* quitar, *Am* sacar; **to r. one's make-up** desmaquillarse; **to r. one's name from a list** tachar su nombre de una lista (**b**) *(from office)* despedir

> Note that the Spanish verb **remover** is a false friend and is never a translation for the English verb **remove**. In Spanish **remover** means "to move over, to turn over, to stir".

removed [rɪˈmuːvd] ADJ **far r. from** muy diferente de

remover [rɪˈmuːvə(r)] N **make-up r.** desmaquillador *m*; **nail varnish r.** quitaesmalte *m*; **stain r.** quitamanchas *m inv*

remuneration [rɪmjuːnəˈreɪʃən] N *Fml* remuneración *f*

renaissance [rəˈneɪsəns] **1** N renacimiento *m*; **the R.** el Renacimiento
2 ADJ renacentista

rend [rend] VT *(pt & pp rent) Fml* rasgar

render [ˈrendə(r)] VT *Fml* (**a**) *(give)* dar (**b**) *(make)* hacer (**c**) *Com* presentar (**d**) *(translate)* traducir

rendering [ˈrendərɪŋ] N (**a**) *(of song, piece of music)* interpretación *f* (**b**) *(translation)* traducción *f*

rendezvous [ˈrɒndɪvuː] **1** N (**a**) *(meeting)* cita *f* (**b**) *(place)* lugar *m* de reunión
2 VI reunirse

renegade [ˈrenɪɡeɪd] N renegado(a) *m,f*

renew [rɪˈnjuː] VT *(contract etc)* renovar; *(talks etc)* reanudar; **with renewed vigour** con renovadas fuerzas

renewal [rɪˈnjuːəl] N *(of contract etc)* renovación *f*; *(of talks etc)* reanudación *f*

renounce [rɪˈnaʊns] VT *Fml* renunciar

renovate [ˈrenəveɪt] VT renovar, hacer reformas en

renown [rɪˈnaʊn] N renombre *m*

renowned [rɪˈnaʊnd] ADJ renombrado(a)

rent¹ [rent] **1** N (**a**) *(for building, car, TV)* alquiler *m* (**b**) *(for land)* arriendo *m*
2 VT (**a**) *(building, car, TV)* alquilar, *Méx* rentar (**b**) *(land)* arrendar

rent² [rent] PT & PP of **rend**

rental [ˈrentəl] N *(of house etc)* alquiler *m*

renunciation [rɪnʌnsɪˈeɪʃən] N *Fml* renuncia *f*

reorganize [riːˈɔːɡənaɪz] VT reorganizar

rep [rep] N *Fam* (**a**) *Com* representante *mf* (**b**) *Th* teatro *m* de repertorio

repaid [riːˈpeɪd] PT & PP of **repay**

repair [rɪˈpeə(r)] **1** N reparación *f*, arreglo *m*; **in good/bad r.** en buen/mal estado
2 VT (**a**) *(shoes, clothes, road)* arreglar; *(car, machine)* reparar (**b**) *(make amends for)* reparar

repartee [repɑːˈtiː] N réplica aguda

repatriate [riːˈpætrɪeɪt] VT repatriar

repay [riːˈpeɪ] VT *(pt & pp repaid)* devolver; **to r. a debt** liquidar una deuda; **to r. a kindness** devolver un favor

repayment [riːˈpeɪmənt] N pago *m*

repeal [rɪˈpiːl] *Jur* **1** N revocación *f*
2 VT revocar

repeat [rɪˈpiːt] **1** VT repetir; **to r. oneself** repetirse
2 N *(repetition)* repetición *f*; *TV* reposición *f*

repeated [rɪˈpiːtɪd] ADJ repetido(a)

repeatedly [rɪˈpiːtɪdlɪ] ADV repetidas veces

repel [rɪˈpel] VT (**a**) *(fight off)* repeler (**b**) *(disgust)* repugnar

repellent [rɪˈpelənt] **1** ADJ repelente; **water-r.** impermeable
2 N **(insect) r.** repelente *m* (antiinsectos)

repent [rɪˈpent] VT & VI arrepentirse (de)

repentance [rɪˈpentəns] N arrepentimiento *m*

repercussion [riːpəˈkʌʃən] N repercusión *f*; **to have repercussions for** *or* **on** tener repercusiones en *or* sobre

repertoire [ˈrepətwɑː(r)] N repertorio *m*

repertory [ˈrepətərɪ] N *Th* teatro *m* de repertorio

repetition [repɪˈtɪʃən] N repetición *f*

repetitive [rɪˈpetɪtɪv] ADJ repetitivo(a)

replace [rɪˈpleɪs] VT (**a**) *(put back)* volver a poner en su sitio (**b**) *(substitute for)* sustituir, reemplazar

replacement [rɪˈpleɪsmənt] N (**a**) *(returning)* reemplazo *m* (**b**) *(person)* sustituto(a) *m,f* (**c**) *(part)* pieza *f* de recambio

replay [ˈriːpleɪ] N repetición *f*

replenish [rɪ'plenɪʃ] VT (**a**) *(fill up)* rellenar (**b**) **to r. stocks** reponer las existencias

replete [rɪ'pliːt] ADJ *Fml* repleto(a)

replica ['replɪkə] N réplica *f*

reply [rɪ'plaɪ] **1** N respuesta *f*, contestación *f*
2 VI responder, contestar

report [rɪ'pɔːt] **1** N (**a**) *(account)* informe *m*, *Andes, CAm, Méx, Ven* reporte *m*; *Br* **school r.** informe escolar (**b**) *(piece of news)* noticia *f* (**c**) *Press, Rad & TV* reportaje *m*
2 VT (**a**) **it is reported that ...** se dice que ... (**b**) *(tell authorities about)* denunciar (**c**) *Press* hacer un reportaje sobre
3 VI (**a**) *(of committee member etc)* hacer un informe (**b**) *Press* hacer un reportaje (**c**) *(for duty etc)* presentarse

reported [rɪ'pɔːtɪd] ADJ **r. speech** estilo indirecto

reportedly [rɪ'pɔːtɪdlɪ] ADV *Fml* según se dice

reporter [rɪ'pɔːtə(r)] N periodista *mf*

repose [rɪ'pəʊz] *Fml* **1** N reposo *m*
2 VT & VI reposar

repossess [riːpə'zes] VT **our house has been repossessed** el banco ha ejecutado la hipoteca de nuestra casa

reprehensible [reprɪ'hensəbəl] ADJ reprensible, censurable

represent [reprɪ'zent] VT representar

representation [reprɪzen'teɪʃən] N (**a**) *(of facts, in Parliament)* representación *f* (**b**) *Fml* **representations** protesta *f*

representative [reprɪ'zentətɪv] **1** ADJ representativo(a)
2 N (**a**) *(of company, on committee)* representante *mf* (**b**) *US Pol* diputado(a) *m,f*

repress [rɪ'pres] VT reprimir, contener

repressed [rɪ'prest] ADJ **to be r.** estar reprimido(a)

repression [rɪ'preʃən] N represión *f*

repressive [rɪ'presɪv] ADJ represivo(a)

reprieve [rɪ'priːv] **1** N (**a**) *Jur* indulto *m* (**b**) *Fig* alivio *m*
2 VT *Jur* indultar

reprimand ['reprɪmɑːnd] **1** N reprimenda *f*
2 VT reprender

reprint 1 N ['riːprɪnt] reimpresión *f*
2 VT [riː'prɪnt] reimprimir

reprisal [rɪ'praɪzəl] N represalia *f*

reproach [rɪ'prəʊtʃ] **1** N reproche *m*; **beyond r.** intachable
2 VT reprochar

reproachful [rɪ'prəʊtʃfʊl] ADJ reprobador(a)

reproduce [riːprə'djuːs] **1** VT reproducir
2 VI reproducirse

reproduction [riːprə'dʌkʃən] N reproducción *f*

reproof [rɪ'pruːf] N *Fml* reprobación *f*, censura *f*

reprove [rɪ'pruːv] VT *Fml* reprobar, censurar

reptile ['reptaɪl] N reptil *m*

republic [rɪ'pʌblɪk] N república *f*

republican [rɪ'pʌblɪkən] ADJ & N republicano(a) *(m,f)*; *US Pol* **R. Party** Partido Republicano

repudiate [rɪ'pjuːdɪeɪt] VT *Fml* (**a**) *(reject)* rechazar (**b**) *(not acknowledge)* negarse a reconocer

repugnant [rɪ'pʌgnənt] ADJ repugnante

repulse [rɪ'pʌls] VT rechazar

repulsive [rɪ'pʌlsɪv] ADJ repulsivo(a)

reputable ['repjʊtəbəl] ADJ *(company etc)* acreditado(a); *(person, products)* de toda confianza

reputation [repjʊ'teɪʃən] N reputación *f*

repute [rɪ'pjuːt] N *Fml* reputación *f*

reputed [rɪ'pjuːtɪd] ADJ supuesto(a); **to be r. to be** ser considerado(a) como

reputedly [rɪ'pjuːtɪdlɪ] ADV según se dice

request [rɪ'kwest] **1** N petición *f*, solicitud *f*, *Am* pedido *m*; **available on r.** disponible a petición de los interesados; *Br* **r. stop** *(for bus)* parada *f* discrecional
2 VT pedir, solicitar

require [rɪ'kwaɪə(r)] VT (**a**) *(need)* necesitar, requerir (**b**) *(demand)* exigir

requirement [rɪ'kwaɪəmənt] N (**a**) *(need)* necesidad *f* (**b**) *(demand)* requisito *m*

> Note that the Spanish word **requerimiento** is a false friend and is never a translation for the English word **requirement**. In Spanish **requerimiento** means both "entreaty" and "writ, injunction".

requisite ['rekwɪzɪt] *Fml* **1** ADJ requerido(a)
2 N requisito *m*

requisition [rekwɪ'zɪʃən] **1** N requisición *f*
2 VT requisar

rescind [rɪ'sɪnd] VT *Fml (contract)* rescindir; *(law)* abrogar

rescue ['reskjuː] **1** N rescate *m*; **r. team** equipo *m* de rescate
2 VT rescatar

rescuer ['reskjʊə(r)] N rescatador(a) *m,f*

research [rɪ'sɜːtʃ] **1** N investigación *f*; **R. and Development** Investigación más Desarrollo
2 VT & VI investigar

researcher [rɪ'sɜːtʃə(r)] N investigador(a) *m,f*

resemblance [rɪ'zembləns] N semejanza *f*

resemble [rɪ'zembəl] VT parecerse a

resent [rɪ'zent] VT ofenderse por

resentful [rɪ'zentfʊl] ADJ ofendido(a)

resentment [rɪ'zentmənt] N resentimiento *m*

reservation [rezə'veɪʃən] N reserva *f*, *Am* reservación *f*

reserve [rɪ'zɜːv] **1** N (**a**) *(supply)* reserva *f*; **to keep sth in r.** guardar algo de reserva (**b**) *Sport* suplente *mf* (**c**) *Mil* **reserves** reservas *fpl*
2 VT reservar

reserved [rɪ'zɜːvd] ADJ reservado(a)

reservoir ['rezəvwɑː(r)] N embalse *m*, pantano *m*; *Fig* reserva *f*

reshape [riː'ʃeɪp] VT rehacer; *Fig* reorganizar

reshuffle [riːˈʃʌfəl] N *Pol* remodelación f

reside [riˈzaid] VI *Fml* residir

residence [ˈrezidəns] N *Fml (home)* residencia f; *(address)* domicilio m; *(period of time)* permanencia f

resident [ˈrezidənt] ADJ & N residente *(mf)*; *US Med* = médico que ha cumplido la residencia y prosigue con su especialización; **to be r. in** estar domiciliado(a) en

residential [reziˈdenʃəl] ADJ residencial

residual [riˈzidjuəl] ADJ residual

residue [ˈrezidjuː] N residuo m

resign [riˈzain] 1 VT (a) *(give up)* dimitir (b) **r. oneself to sth** resignarse a algo
2 VI *(from job)* dimitir

resignation [rezigˈneiʃən] N (a) *(from a job)* dimisión f (b) *(acceptance)* resignación f

resigned [riˈzaind] ADJ resignado(a)

resilience [riˈziliəns] N resistencia f

resilient [riˈziliənt] ADJ *(strong)* resistente

resin [ˈrezin] N resina f

resist [riˈzist] 1 VT (a) *(not yield to)* resistir (b) *(oppose)* oponerse a
2 VI resistir

resistance [riˈzistəns] N resistencia f

resistant [riˈzistənt] ADJ **to be r. to sth** *(change, suggestion)* mostrarse remiso(a) a aceptar algo, mostrar resistencia a algo; *(disease)* ser resistente a algo

resit [riːˈsit] VT *Br (exam)* volver a presentarse a

resolute [ˈrezəluːt] ADJ resuelto(a), decidido(a)

resolution [rezəˈluːʃən] N resolución f

resolve [riˈzolv] 1 N resolución f
2 VT resolver; **to r. to do** resolverse a hacer
3 VI resolverse

resonant [ˈrezənənt] ADJ resonante

resort [riˈzɔːt] 1 N (a) *(place)* lugar m de vacaciones; **tourist r.** centro turístico (b) *(recourse)* recurso m; **as a last r.** como último recurso
2 VI recurrir (**to** a)

Note that the Spanish word **restorte** is a false friend and is never a translation for the English word **resort**. In Spanish **resorte** means both "spring" and "means".

resound [riˈzaund] VI resonar; *Fig* tener resonancia

resounding [riˈzaundiŋ] ADJ **a r. failure** un fracaso total; **a r. success** un éxito rotundo

resource [riˈsɔːs] N recurso m

resourceful [riˈsɔːsful] ADJ ingenioso(a)

respect [riˈspekt] 1 N (a) *(deference)* respeto m; **to pay one's respects to sb** presentar sus respetos a algn (b) *(relation, reference)* respecto m; **in that r.** a ese respecto; **with r. to** con referencia a
2 VT respetar

respectable [riˈspektəbəl] ADJ respetable; *(clothes)* decente

respectful [riˈspektful] ADJ respetuoso(a)

respective [riˈspektiv] ADJ respectivo(a)

respectively [riˈspektivli] ADV respectivamente

respite [ˈrespait] N *Fml* respiro m

resplendent [riˈsplendənt] ADJ resplandeciente

respond [riˈspond] VI responder

response [riˈspons] N (a) *(reply)* respuesta f (b) *(reaction)* reacción f

responsibility [risponsəˈbiliti] N responsabilidad f

responsible [riˈsponsəbəl] ADJ responsable (**for** de); **to be r. to sb** tener que dar cuentas a algn

responsive [riˈsponsiv] ADJ sensible

rest[1] [rest] 1 N (a) *(break)* descanso m; *US* **r. room** baño m, *Esp* servicios mpl, *CSur* toilette m (b) *(peace)* tranquilidad f; **at r.** *(object)* inmóvil (c) *(support)* apoyo m
2 VT (a) *(cause to repose)* descansar (b) *(lean)* apoyar; **to r. a ladder against a wall** apoyar una escalera contra una pared
3 VI (a) *(relax)* descansar (b) *(be calm)* quedarse tranquilo(a) (c) **it doesn't r. with me** no depende de mí

rest[2] [rest] N **the r.** *(remainder)* el resto, lo demás; **the r. of the girls** las demás chicas

restaurant [ˈrestərɒnt] N restaurante m; *Br Rail* **r. car** coche m restaurante

restful [ˈrestful] ADJ relajante

restitution [restiˈtjuːʃən] N *Fml* restitución f; **to make r.** restituir

restive [ˈrestiv] ADJ inquieto(a), nervioso(a)

restless [ˈrestlis] ADJ agitado(a), inquieto(a)

restoration [restəˈreiʃən] N (a) *(giving back)* devolución f (b) *Br Hist* **the R.** la Restauración (c) *(of building, furniture)* restauración f

restore [riˈstɔː(r)] VT (a) *(give back)* devolver (b) *(re-establish)* restablecer (c) *(building etc)* restaurar

restrain [riˈstrein] VT contener; **to r. one's anger** reprimir la cólera; **to r. oneself** contenerse

restrained [riˈstreind] ADJ *(person)* moderado(a); *(emotion)* contenido(a)

restraint [riˈstreint] N (a) *(restriction)* restricción f; *(hindrance)* traba f (b) *(moderation)* moderación f

restrict [riˈstrikt] VT restringir, limitar

restriction [riˈstrikʃən] N restricción f, limitación f

restrictive [riˈstriktiv] ADJ restrictivo(a)

result [riˈzʌlt] 1 N resultado m; **as a r. of** como consecuencia de
2 VI resultar; **to r. from** resultar de; **to r. in** causar

resume [riˈzjuːm] 1 VT *(journey, work, conversation)* reanudar; *(control)* reasumir
2 VI recomenzar

Note that the Spanish word **resumir** is a false friend and is never a translation for the English word **resume**. In Spanish **resumir** means "to sum up, to summarize".

résumé ['rezjʊmeɪ] N (**a**) *(summary)* resumen *m* (**b**) *US (curriculum vitae)* currículum (vitae) *m*

resumption [rɪ'zʌmpʃən] N *(of journey, work, conversation)* reanudación *f*

resurface [ri:'sɜ:fɪs] **1** VT *(road)* rehacer el firme de
2 VI *Fig* resurgir

resurgence [rɪ'sɜ:dʒəns] N resurgimiento *m*

resurrection [rezə'rekʃən] N resurrección *f*

resuscitate [rɪ'sʌsɪteɪt] VT *Med* reanimar

retail ['ri:teɪl] **1** N venta *f* al por menor, *Am* menoreo *m*; **r. outlet** punto *m* de venta; **r. price** precio *m* de venta al público; *Br* **r. price index** Índice *m* de Precios al Consumo
2 VT vender al por menor
3 VI venderse al por menor
4 ADV al por menor

retailer ['ri:teɪlə(r)] N detallista *mf*

retain [rɪ'teɪn] VT (**a**) *(heat)* conservar; *(personal effects)* guardar (**b**) *(water)* retener (**c**) *(facts, information)* recordar

retainer [rɪ'teɪnə(r)] N (**a**) *(payment)* anticipo *m* sobre los honorarios (**b**) *(servant)* criado(a) *m,f*

retaliate [rɪ'tælɪeɪt] VI tomar represalias (**against** contra)

retaliation [rɪtælɪ'eɪʃən] N represalias *fpl*; **in r.** en represalia

retarded [rɪ'tɑ:dɪd] ADJ retrasado(a)

retch [retʃ] VI tener náuseas

retentive [rɪ'tentɪv] ADJ retentivo(a)

rethink ['ri:θɪŋk] N *Fam* **to have a r. about sth** volver a reflexionar sobre algo

reticent ['retɪsənt] ADJ reticente

retina ['retɪnə] N retina *f*

retinue ['retɪnju:] N séquito *m*

retire [rɪ'taɪə(r)] **1** VT jubilar
2 VI (**a**) *(stop working)* jubilarse (**b**) *(from race)* retirarse; **to r. for the night** irse a la cama, acostarse

retired [rɪ'taɪəd] ADJ jubilado(a)

retiree [rɪtaɪə'ri:] N *US* retirado(a) *m,f*

retirement [rɪ'taɪəmənt] N jubilación *f*

retiring [rɪ'taɪərɪŋ] ADJ (**a**) *(reserved)* reservado(a) (**b**) *(official)* saliente

retort [rɪ'tɔ:t] **1** N réplica *f*
2 VI replicar

retrace [ri:'treɪs] VT *(recall)* reconstruir; **to r. one's steps** volver sobre sus pasos

retract [rɪ'trækt] **1** VT (**a**) *(claws)* retraer; *(landing gear)* replegar (**b**) *(statement)* retirar
2 VI (**a**) *(claws)* retraerse; *(landing gear)* replegarse (**b**) *Fml* retractarse

retread ['ri:tred] N *Aut* neumático *m* recauchutado, *Col, Méx* llanta *f* or *Arg* goma *f* recauchutada

retreat [rɪ'tri:t] **1** N (**a**) *Mil* retirada *f* (**b**) *(shelter)* refugio *m* (**c**) *Rel* retiro *m*
2 VI retirarse (**from** de)

retrial ['ri:traɪəl] N *Jur* nuevo juicio

retribution [retrɪ'bju:ʃən] N represalias *fpl*

Note that the Spanish word **retribución** is a false friend and is never a translation for the English word **retribution**. In Spanish **retribución** means "payment, reward".

retrieval [rɪ'tri:vəl] N recuperación *f*; *Comput* **information r. system** sistema *m* de recuperación de datos

retrieve [rɪ'tri:v] VT (**a**) *(recover)* recuperar; *(of dog)* cobrar; *Comput* recoger (**b**) *(rescue)* salvar

retriever [rɪ'tri:və(r)] N perro *m* cazador

retro ['retrəʊ] ADJ retro

retrograde ['retrəʊɡreɪd] ADJ retrógrado(a)

retrospect ['retrəʊspekt] N **in r.** retrospectivamente

retrospective [retrəʊ'spektɪv] **1** ADJ retrospectivo(a)
2 N *Art* (exposición *f*) retrospectiva *f*

return [rɪ'tɜ:n] **1** N (**a**) *(of person)* regreso *m*, vuelta *f*; **by r. of post** a vuelta de correo; **in r. for** a cambio de; **many happy returns!** ¡felicidades!; **r. match** partido *m* de vuelta; *Br* **r. (ticket)** billete *m* de ida y vuelta (**b**) *(of sth borrowed, stolen)* devolución *f* (**c**) *(profit)* beneficio *m*, ganancia *f* (**d**) *(interest)* interés *m*
2 VT *(give back)* devolver; **r. to sender** *(on envelope)* devuélvase al remitente; **to r. sb's love** corresponder al amor de algn
3 VI (**a**) *(come or go back)* volver, regresar (**b**) *(reappear)* reaparecer

returnable [rɪ'tɜ:nəbəl] ADJ *(bottle)* retornable

reunion [ri:'ju:njən] N reunión *f*

reunite [ri:ju:'naɪt] VT **to be reunited with** *(after separation)* reunirse con

reuse [ri:'ju:z] VT volver a utilizar, reutilizar

rev [rev] *Fam Aut* **1** N revolución *f*
2 VI **to r. (up)** acelerar el motor

revamp [ri:'væmp] VT *Fam* modernizar, renovar

reveal [rɪ'vi:l] VT *(make known)* revelar; *(show)* dejar ver

revealing [rɪ'vi:lɪŋ] ADJ revelador(a)

reveille [rɪ'vælɪ] N diana *f*

revel ['revəl] VI disfrutar (**in** con); **to r. in doing sth** gozar muchísimo haciendo algo

revelation [revə'leɪʃən] N revelación *f*

revelry ['revəlrɪ] N jarana *f*, juerga *f*

revenge [rɪ'vendʒ] N venganza *f*; **to take r. on sb for sth** vengarse de algo en algn

revenue ['revɪnju:] N renta *f*

reverberate [rɪ'vɜ:bəreɪt] VI (**a**) *(sound)* reverberar (**b**) *(ideas, news)* resonar

reverberation [rɪvɜːbəˈreɪʃən] N resonancia f
revere [rɪˈvɪə(r)] VT reverenciar
reverence [ˈrevərəns] N reverencia f
reverend [ˈrevərənd] Rel 1 ADJ reverendo(a); R. Mother reverenda madre
  2 N (Protestant) pastor m; (Catholic) padre m
reverie [ˈrevərɪ] N ensueño m
reversal [rɪˈvɜːsəl] N (a) (of order) inversión f (b) (of attitude, policy) cambio m total (c) Jur revocación f
reverse [rɪˈvɜːs] 1 ADJ inverso(a)
  2 N (a) quite the r. todo lo contrario (b) (other side) (of cloth) revés m; (of coin) cruz f; (of page) dorso m (c) Aut r. gear marcha f atrás
  3 VT (a) (order) invertir (b) (turn round) volver del revés (c) (change) cambiar totalmente (d) Br Tel to r. the charges poner una conferencia a cobro revertido
  4 VI Aut dar marcha atrás
revert [rɪˈvɜːt] VI volver (to a)
review [rɪˈvjuː] 1 N (a) (examination) examen m (b) Press crítica f, reseña f (c) (magazine) revista f
  2 VT (a) (examine) examinar (b) Mil to r. the troops pasar revista a las tropas (c) (book etc) hacer una crítica de
reviewer [rɪˈvjuːə(r)] N crítico(a) m,f
revile [rɪˈvaɪl] VT Fml injuriar
revise [rɪˈvaɪz] VT (a) (look over) revisar; Br (at school) repasar (b) (change) modificar
revision [rɪˈvɪʒən] N (a) (of text) revisión f; Br (at school) repaso m (b) (change) modificación f
revitalize [riːˈvaɪtəlaɪz] VT revivificar
revival [rɪˈvaɪvəl] N (a) (of interest) renacimiento m; (of economy, industry) reactivación f; (of a country) resurgimiento m (b) Th reestreno m (c) Med reanimación f
revive [rɪˈvaɪv] 1 VT (a) (interest) renovar; (a law) restablecer; (economy, industry) reactivar; (hopes) despertar (b) Th reestrenar (c) Med reanimar
  2 VI (a) (interest, hopes) renacer (b) Med volver en sí
revoke [rɪˈvəʊk] VT revocar; (permission) suspender
revolt [rɪˈvəʊlt] 1 N rebelión f, sublevación f
  2 VI rebelarse, sublevarse
  3 VT repugnar, dar asco a
revolting [rɪˈvəʊltɪŋ] ADJ repugnante
revolution [revəˈluːʃən] N revolución f
revolutionary [revəˈluːʃənərɪ] ADJ & N revolucionario(a) (m,f)
revolve [rɪˈvɒlv] 1 VI girar; Fig to r. around girar en torno a
  2 VT hacer girar

> Note that the Spanish verb **revolver** is a false friend and is never a translation for the English verb **to revolve**. In Spanish **revolver** means "to stir, to mix" and "to mess up".

revolver [rɪˈvɒlvə(r)] N revólver m

revolving [rɪˈvɒlvɪŋ] ADJ giratorio(a)
revue [rɪˈvjuː] N revista f
revulsion [rɪˈvʌlʃən] N repulsión f
reward [rɪˈwɔːd] 1 N recompensa f
  2 VT recompensar
rewarding [rɪˈwɔːdɪŋ] ADJ provechoso(a)
rewind [riːˈwaɪnd] (pt & pp rewound) VT (tape, film) rebobinar
rewire [riːˈwaɪə(r)] VT Elec to r. a house poner nueva instalación eléctrica a una casa
reword [riːˈwɜːd] VT expresar con otras palabras
rewound [riːˈwaʊnd] PT & PP of rewind
rewrite [riːˈraɪt] VT (pt rewrote [riːˈrəʊt]; pp rewritten [riːˈrɪtən]) escribir de nuevo
rhapsody [ˈræpsədɪ] N Mus rapsodia f
rhetoric [ˈretərɪk] N retórica f
rhetorical [rɪˈtɒrɪkəl] ADJ retórico(a)
rheumatism [ˈruːmətɪzəm] N reuma m
rheumatoid [ˈruːmətɔɪd] ADJ r. arthritis reuma m articular
Rhine [raɪn] N the R. el Rin
rhinoceros [raɪˈnɒsərəs] N rinoceronte m
rhododendron [rəʊdəˈdendrən] N rododendro m
Rhone [rəʊn] N the R. el Ródano
rhubarb [ˈruːbɑːb] N ruibarbo m
rhyme [raɪm] 1 N rima f; (poem) poema m
  2 VI rimar
rhythm [ˈrɪðəm] N ritmo m
rib [rɪb] N Anat costilla f; r. cage caja torácica
ribald [ˈrɪbəld] ADJ (humour) verde
ribbon [ˈrɪbən] N cinta f; (in hair etc) lazo m; torn to ribbons hecho(a) jirones
rice [raɪs] N arroz m; r. pudding arroz con leche
rich [rɪtʃ] 1 ADJ (person, food) rico(a); (soil) fértil; (voice) sonoro(a); (colour) vivo(a)
  2 NPL the r. los ricos
riches [ˈrɪtʃɪz] NPL riquezas fpl
richly [ˈrɪtʃlɪ] ADV ricamente; r. deserved bien merecido(a)
richness [ˈrɪtʃnɪs] N riqueza f; (of soil) fertilidad f; (of voice) sonoridad f; (of colour) viveza f
rickets [ˈrɪkɪts] N SING Med raquitismo m
rickety [ˈrɪkətɪ] ADJ (chair etc) cojo(a); (car) desvencijado(a)
ricochet [ˈrɪkəʃeɪ, ˈrɪkəʃet] 1 N rebote m.
  2 VI rebotar
rid [rɪd] VT (pt & pp rid) librar; to get r. of sth deshacerse de algo; to r. oneself of librarse de
riddance [ˈrɪdəns] N Fam good r.! ¡ya era hora!
ridden [ˈrɪdən] PP of ride
riddle¹ [ˈrɪdəl] N (a) (puzzle) acertijo m, adivinanza f (b) (mystery) enigma m
riddle² [ˈrɪdəl] VT (with bullets) acribillar
ride [raɪd] 1 N paseo m, vuelta f; a short bus r. un corto trayecto en autobús; Fam to take sb for a r. tomar el pelo a algn

2 VT (*pt* **rode**; *pp* **ridden**) *(bicycle, horse)* montar en; **can you r. a bicycle?** ¿sabes montar *or Am* andar en bicicleta?

3 VI **(a)** *(on horse)* montar *or Am* andar a caballo **(b)** *(travel)* (in bus, train etc) viajar

▸ **ride out** VT SEP sobrevivir; **to r. out the storm** capear el temporal

rider ['raɪdə(r)] N *(of horse) (man)* jinete *m*; *(woman)* amazona *f*; *(of bicycle)* ciclista *mf*; *(of motorbike)* motociclista *mf*

ridge [rɪdʒ] N *(crest of a hill)* cresta *f*; *(hillock)* loma *f*; *(of roof)* caballete *m*; *Met* área *m*

ridicule ['rɪdɪkjuːl] **1** N burla *f*
2 VT burlarse de

ridiculous [rɪ'dɪkjʊləs] ADJ ridículo(a)

riding ['raɪdɪŋ] N equitación *f*; **r. breeches** pantalones *mpl* de montar; **r. school** escuela hípica

rife [raɪf] ADJ abundante; **rumour is r. that …** corre la voz de que …; **to be r. with** abundar en

riffraff ['rɪfræf] N *Fam* chusma *f*, gentuza *f*

rifle[1] ['raɪfəl] N fusil *m*, rifle *m*; **r. range** campo *m* de tiro

rifle[2] ['raɪfəl] VT desvalijar

rift [rɪft] N **(a)** *Geol* falla *f* **(b)** *Fig (in friendship)* ruptura *f*; *Pol (in party)* escisión *f*; *(quarrel)* desavenencia *f*

rig [rɪg] **1** N **(a)** *Naut* aparejo *m* **(b)** **(oil)** **r.** *(onshore)* torre *f* de perforación; *(offshore)* plataforma petrolífera
2 VT *Pej* amañar

▸ **rig out** VT SEP *Fam* ataviar

▸ **rig up** VT SEP improvisar, *Esp* apañar

rigging ['rɪgɪŋ] N aparejo *m*, jarcia *f*

right [raɪt] **1** ADJ **(a)** *(not left)* derecho(a) **(b)** *(correct)* correcto(a); *(time)* exacto(a); **to be r.** tener razón; **r.?** ¿vale? **(c)** *(true)* cierto(a) **(d)** *(suitable)* adecuado(a); **the r. time** el momento oportuno **(e)** *(proper)* apropiado(a) **(f)** *Fam (healthy)* bien **(g)** *Br Fam (complete)* auténtico(a) **(h)** **r. angle** ángulo recto
2 N **(a)** *(right side)* derecha *f* **(b)** *(right hand)* mano derecha **(c)** *Pol* **the R.** la derecha **(d)** *(lawful claim)* derecho *m*; **in one's own r.** por derecho propio; **r. of way** *(across land)* derecho de paso; *(on roads)* prioridad *f* **(e)** **r. and wrong** el bien y el mal
3 ADV **(a)** *(correctly)* bien; **it's just r.** es justo lo que hace falta **(b)** **r. away** *(immediately)* en seguida, inmediatamente, *CAm, Méx* ahorita **(c)** *(to the right)* a la derecha; **r. and left** a diestro y siniestro **(d)** *(directly)* directamente; **go r. on** sigue recto; **r. at the top** en todo lo alto; **r. to the end** hasta el final
4 VT **(a)** *(correct)* corregir **(b)** *(put straight)* enderezar

righteous ['raɪtʃəs] ADJ *(upright)* recto(a)

rightful ['raɪtfʊl] ADJ legítimo(a)

right-hand ['raɪthænd] ADJ derecho(a); **r. drive** conducción *f* por la derecha; **r. side** lado derecho; *Fam* **r. man** brazo derecho

right-handed [raɪt'hændɪd] ADJ *(person)* que usa la mano derecha; *(tool)* para la mano derecha

rightly ['raɪtlɪ] ADV debidamente; **and r. so** y con razón

right-wing ['raɪtwɪŋ] ADJ de derechas, derechista

right-winger [raɪt'wɪŋə(r)] N derechista *mf*

rigid ['rɪdʒɪd] ADJ rígido(a)

rigidity [rɪ'dʒɪdɪtɪ] N rigidez *f*, inflexibilidad *f*

rigmarole ['rɪgmərəʊl] N *Fam (process)* engorro *m*, *Esp* latazo *m*; *(speech)* rollo *m*, galimatías *m inv*

rigor ['rɪgər] N *US* = **rigour**

rigorous ['rɪgərəs] ADJ riguroso(a)

rigour ['rɪgə(r)] N rigor *m*, severidad *f*

rile [raɪl] VT *Fam (annoy)* fastidiar, irritar, *Am* enojar

rim [rɪm] N *(edge)* borde *m*; *(of wheel)* llanta *f*; *(of spectacles)* montura *f*

rind [raɪnd] N *(of fruit, cheese)* corteza *f*

ring[1] [rɪŋ] **1** N **(a)** *(sound of bell)* toque *m*; *(of doorbell, alarm clock)* timbre *m* **(b)** *Tel* llamada *f*
2 VT *(pt* **rang**; *pp* **rung)** **(a)** *(bell)* tocar; *Fig* **it rings a bell** me suena **(b)** *Br (on phone)* llamar (por teléfono) a, *RP* hablar a
3 VI **(a)** *(bell, phone etc)* sonar **(b)** **my ears are ringing** tengo un pitido en los oídos **(c)** *Tel* llamar

▸ **ring back** VT SEP *Br Tel* volver a llamar

▸ **ring off** VI *Br Tel* colgar

▸ **ring out** VI resonar

▸ **ring up** VT SEP *Br Tel* llamar (por teléfono) a, *RP* hablar a

ring[2] [rɪŋ] **1** N **(a)** *(metal hoop)* aro *m*; **curtain r.** anilla *f*; **r. binder** archivador *m or* carpeta *f* de anillas, *RP* bibliorato *m* **(b)** *(for finger)* anillo *m*, sortija *f* **(c)** *(circle)* círculo *m*; *Br* **r. road** carretera *f* de circunvalación **(d)** *(group of people)* corro *m*; *(of spies)* red *f*; *(of thieves)* banda *f* **(e)** *(arena)* pista *f*; *(for boxing)* cuadrilátero *m*; *(for bullfights)* ruedo *m*
2 VT *(surround)* rodear

ringing ['rɪŋɪŋ] N *(of bell)* toque *m*, repique *m*; *(in ears)* pitido *m*

ringleader ['rɪŋliːdə(r)] N cabecilla *mf*

ringlet ['rɪŋlɪt] N tirabuzón *m*

ringtone ['rɪŋtəʊn] N *(of mobile phone)* melodía *f*

rink [rɪŋk] N pista *f*; **ice r.** pista de hielo

rinse [rɪns] **1** N **to give sth a r.** enjuagar *or Esp* aclarar algo
2 VT *(clothes, dishes)* enjuagar, *Esp* aclarar; **to r. one's hands** enjuagarse las manos

riot ['raɪət] **1** N **(a)** *(uprising)* disturbio *m*; **to run r.** desmandarse; **r. police** policía *f* antidisturbios **(b)** *Fig (of colour)* profusión *f*
2 VI amotinarse

rioter ['raɪətə(r)] N amotinado(a) *m,f*

riotous ['raɪətəs] ADJ **(a)** *(behaviour, mob)* descontrolado(a) **(b)** *Fam (party, living)* desenfrenado(a)

rip [rɪp] **1** N *(tear)* rasgón m
2 VT rasgar, rajar; **to r. one's trousers** rajarse los pantalones
3 VI rasgarse, rajarse
▶ **rip off** VT SEP *Fam* **to r. sb off** clavar *or Esp* timar a algn
▶ **rip up** VT SEP hacer pedacitos

ripcord ['rɪpkɔːd] N cuerda *f* de apertura

ripe [raɪp] ADJ **(a)** *(fruit)* maduro(a) **(b)** *(ready)* listo(a); **the time is r.** es el momento oportuno

ripen ['raɪpən] VT & VI madurar

rip-off ['rɪpɒf] N *Fam* timo m, *Col, RP* cagada *f*

ripple ['rɪpəl] **1** N **(a)** *(on water, fabric)* onda *f* **(b)** *(sound)* murmullo m
2 VT *(water)* ondular
3 VI **(a)** *(water)* ondularse **(b)** *(applause)* extenderse

rise [raɪz] **1** N **(a)** *(of slope, hill)* cuesta *f* **(b)** *(of waters)* crecida *f* **(c)** *(in prices, temperature)* subida *f*; *Br* **(pay) r.** aumento m *(de sueldo)* **(d)** **to give r. to** ocasionar
2 VI *(pt rose; pp risen* ['rɪzən]*)* **(a)** *(land etc)* elevarse **(b)** *(waters)* crecer; *(river)* nacer; *(tide)* subir; *(wind)* levantarse **(c)** *(sun, moon)* salir **(d)** *(voice)* alzarse **(e)** *(in rank)* ascender **(f)** *(prices, temperature)* subir; *(wages)* aumentar **(g)** *(curtain)* subir **(h)** *(from bed)* levantarse **(i)** *(stand up)* levantarse; *Fig (city, building)* erguirse
▶ **rise above** VT INSEP estar por encima de
▶ **rise up** VI *(rebel)* sublevarse

rising ['raɪzɪŋ] **1** ADJ *(sun)* naciente; *(tide)* creciente; *(prices)* en aumento; **r. damp** humedad *f*
2 N **(a)** *(of sun)* salida *f* **(b)** *(rebellion)* levantamiento m

risk [rɪsk] **1** N riesgo m; **at r.** en peligro; **at your own r.** por su cuenta y riesgo; **to take risks** arriesgarse
2 VT arriesgar; **I'll r. it** correré el riesgo

risky ['rɪskɪ] ADJ **(riskier, riskiest)** arriesgado(a)

risqué ['rɪskeɪ] ADJ atrevido(a); *(joke)* picante

rite [raɪt] N rito m; **the last rites** la extremaunción

ritual ['rɪtjʊəl] ADJ & N ritual *(m)*

rival ['raɪvəl] **1** ADJ & N rival *(mf)*
2 VT rivalizar con

rivalry ['raɪvəlrɪ] N rivalidad *f*

river ['rɪvə(r)] N río m; **down/up r.** río abajo/arriba

river-bank ['rɪvəbæŋk] N orilla *f*, ribera *f*

river-bed ['rɪvəbed] N lecho m

rivet ['rɪvɪt] **1** N *Tech* remache m, roblón m
2 VT *Tech* remachar; *Fig* cautivar

riveting ['rɪvɪtɪŋ] ADJ *Fig* fascinante

roach [rəʊtʃ] N *US Fam (cockroach)* cucaracha *f*, *Chile* barata *f*

road [rəʊd] N **(a)** *(in general)* carretera *f*; *Br* **A/B r.** carretera nacional/secundaria; **main r.** carretera principal; **r. accident** accidente m de tráfico; **r. safety** seguridad *f* vial; **r. sign** señal *f* de tráfico; *Br* **works** *or US* **work** obras *fpl* **(b)** *(in town)* calle *f* **(c)** *(path, track)* camino m

roadblock ['rəʊdblɒk] N control m policial

roadhog ['rəʊdhɒg] N *Fam* loco(a) m,f del volante, dominguero(a) m,f

roadside ['rəʊdsaɪd] N borde m de la carretera; **r. restaurant/café** restaurante m/cafetería *f* de carretera

roadway ['rəʊdweɪ] N calzada *f*

roadworthy ['rəʊdwɜːðɪ] ADJ *(vehicle)* en buen estado

roam [rəʊm] **1** VT vagar por, rondar
2 VI vagar

roar [rɔː(r)] **1** N *(of lion)* rugido m; *(of bull, sea, wind)* bramido m; *(of crowd)* clamor m
2 VI *(lion, crowd)* rugir; *(bull, sea, wind)* bramar; *(crowd)* clamar; *Fig* **to r. with laughter** reírse a carcajadas

roaring ['rɔːrɪŋ] ADJ **a r. success** un éxito clamoroso; **to do a r. trade** hacer un negocio redondo

roast [rəʊst] **1** ADJ *(meat)* asado(a); **r. beef** rosbif m
2 N *Culin* asado m
3 VT *(meat)* asar; *(coffee, nuts)* tostar
4 VI asarse

rob [rɒb] VT robar; *(bank)* atracar

robber ['rɒbə(r)] N ladrón(ona) m,f; **bank r.** atracador(a) m,f

robbery ['rɒbərɪ] N robo m

robe [rəʊb] N *(ceremonial)* toga *f*; *(dressing gown)* bata *f*

robin ['rɒbɪn] N petirrojo m

robot ['rəʊbɒt] N robot m

robust [rəʊ'bʌst] ADJ *(sturdy)* robusto(a)

rock [rɒk] **1** N **(a)** *(substance, large stone)* roca *f*; *Fig* **on the rocks** *(marriage)* a punto de fracasar; *(whisky)* con hielo **(b)** *US (stone)* piedra *f* **(c)** *Br (sweet)* **stick of r.** = barra de caramelo de menta que se vende sobre todo en localidades costeras y lleva el nombre del lugar impreso **(d)** *Mus* música *f* rock; **r. and roll** rock and roll
2 VT **(a)** *(chair)* mecer; *(baby)* acunar **(b)** *(shake)* hacer temblar; *Fig (shock)* conmover
3 VI **(a)** *(move to and fro)* mecerse **(b)** *(shake)* vibrar

rock-bottom ['rɒk'bɒtəm] ADJ bajísimo(a); **r. prices** precios regalados

rockery ['rɒkərɪ] N jardín m de rocas

rocket ['rɒkɪt] **1** N cohete m; **r. launcher** lanzacohetes m inv
2 VI *Fam (prices)* dispararse

rocking-chair ['rɒkɪŋtʃeə(r)] N mecedora *f*

rocking-horse ['rɒkɪŋhɔːs] N caballito m de balancín

rocky ['rɒkɪ] ADJ (**rockier, rockiest**) rocoso(a); *Fam Fig* (*unsteady*) inseguro(a); **the R. Mountains** las Montañas Rocosas

rod [rɒd] N (*of metal*) barra *f*; (*stick*) vara *f*; **fishing r.** caña *f* de pescar

rode [rəʊd] PT *of* **ride**

rodent ['rəʊdənt] N roedor *m*

roe¹ [rəʊ] N *Zool* **r.** (**deer**) corzo(a) *m,f*

roe² [rəʊ] N (*fish eggs*) hueva *f*

rogue [rəʊg] N granuja *m*

role, rôle [rəʊl] N papel *m*; **to play a r.** desempeñar un papel

roll [rəʊl] **1** N (**a**) (*of paper, film*) rollo *m* (**b**) (*bread*) panecillo *m*, *Méx* bolillo *m* (**c**) (*list of names*) lista *f*, nómina *f* (**d**) (*of drum*) redoble *m*; (*of thunder*) fragor *m*
2 VT (**a**) (*ball*) hacer rodar (**b**) (*cigarette*) liar (**c**) (*push*) empujar
3 VI (**a**) (*ball*) rodar (**b**) (*animal*) revolcarse (**c**) (*ship*) balancearse (**d**) (*drum*) redoblar; (*thunder*) retumbar
► **roll about, roll around** VI rodar (de acá para allá)
► **roll by** VI (*years*) pasar
► **roll in** VI *Fam* (**a**) (*arrive*) llegar (**b**) (*money*) llegar a raudales
► **roll over** VI dar una vuelta
► **roll up** VT SEP enrollar; (*blinds*) subir; **to r. up one's sleeves** (ar)remangarse
2 VI *Fam* (*arrive*) llegar

roll-call ['rəʊlkɔːl] N to have a **r.** pasar lista

roller ['rəʊlə(r)] N (**a**) *Tech* rodillo *m*; **r. blades** patines *mpl* en línea; **r. coaster** montaña rusa; **r. skates** patines *mpl* (de ruedas) (**b**) (*large wave*) ola *f* grande (**c**) (*for hair*) rulo *m*, *Chile* tubo *m*, *RP* rulero *m*

rolling ['rəʊlɪŋ] **1** ADJ (**a**) *Rail* **r. stock** material *m* rodante (**b**) (*countryside*) ondulado(a)
2 N rodamiento *m*; (*of ground*) apisonamiento *m*; **r. pin** rodillo *m* (de cocina)

ROM [rɒm] N *Comput* (*abbr* **read-only memory**) ROM *f*

Roman ['rəʊmən] ADJ & N romano(a) (*m,f*); **R. Catholic** católico(a) (romano(a)); **R. law** derecho romano; **R. numerals** números romanos

Romance [rəʊ'mæns] ADJ *Ling* romance(a), romance; **R. languages** lenguas románicas

romance [rəʊ'mæns] **1** N (**a**) (*tale*) novela romántica (**b**) (*love affair*) aventura amorosa (**c**) (*romantic quality*) lo romántico
2 VI fantasear

Romania [rəˈmeɪnɪə] N Rumanía

Romanian [rəˈmeɪnɪən] **1** ADJ rumano(a)
2 N (*person*) rumano(a) *m,f*; (*language*) rumano *m*

romantic [rəʊˈmæntɪk] ADJ & N romántico(a) (*m,f*)

Rome [rəʊm] N Roma

romp [rɒmp] **1** N jugueteo *m*
2 VI juguetear

rompers ['rɒmpəz] NPL pelele *m*

roof [ruːf] **1** N (*pl* **roofs** [ruːfs, ruːvz]) (**a**) (*of building*) tejado *m*; *Fam Fig* **to go through the r.** (*of prices*) estar por las nubes; (*with anger*) subirse por las paredes (**b**) *Aut* techo *m*; **r. rack** baca *f* (**c**) (*of mouth*) cielo *m*
2 VT techar

roofing ['ruːfɪŋ] N materiales *mpl* usados para techar

rooftop ['ruːftɒp] N tejado *m*; *Fig* **to shout sth from the rooftops** proclamar algo a los cuatro vientos

rook [rʊk] N (**a**) (*bird*) grajo *m* (**b**) (*in chess*) torre *f*

rookie ['rʊkɪ] N *US Fam* novato(a) *m,f*

room [ruːm] N (**a**) (*in house*) habitación *f*, cuarto *m*; (*in hotel*) habitación *f*; (*bedroom*) dormitorio *m*, *Am* cuarto *m*, *CAm, Col, Méx* recámara *f*; **single r.** habitación individual; **r. service** servicio *m* de habitaciones (**b**) (*space*) sitio *m*, espacio *m*, *Am* lugar *m*, *Andes* campo *m*; **to make r. (for sb)** hacer sitio *or Am* lugar *or Andes* campo (para *or* a algn)

rooming-house ['ruːmɪŋhaʊs] N *US* casa *f* de huéspedes, pensión *f*

roommate ['ruːmmeɪt] N compañero(a) *m,f* de habitación

roomy ['ruːmɪ] ADJ (**roomier, roomiest**) amplio(a)

roost [ruːst] **1** N palo *m*, percha *f*; (**hen**) **r.** gallinero *m*; *Fig* **to rule the r.** llevar la batuta
2 VI posarse

rooster ['ruːstə(r)] N *esp US* gallo *m*

root¹ [ruːt] **1** N raíz *f*; **to take r.** echar raíces
2 VT arraigar
3 VI arraigar
► **root out, root up** VT SEP arrancar de raíz

root² [ruːt] VI (*search*) buscar; **to r. about** or **around for sth** hurgar en busca de algo

root³ [ruːt] VI *Fam* **to r. for a team** animar a un equipo

rope [rəʊp] **1** N (**a**) (*thin*) cuerda *f*; (*thick*) soga *f*, *Naut* cabo *m* (**b**) *Fam Fig* **to know the ropes** estar al tanto
2 VT (*package*) atar; (*climbers*) encordar

Note that the Spanish word **ropa** is a false friend and is never a translation for the English word **rope**. In Spanish **ropa** means "clothes".rope in vt Fam enganchar rope off vt acordonar

► **rope in** VT SEP *Fam* enganchar
► **rope off** VT SEP acordonar

rop(e)y ['rəʊpɪ] ADJ (**ropier, ropiest**) *Br Fam* (*unreliable*) flojo(a); (*ill*) pachucho(a), *Am* flojo(a)

rosary ['rəʊzərɪ] N rosario *m*

rose¹ [rəʊz] PT *of* **rise**

rose² [rəʊz] N (**a**) *Bot* rosa *f*; **r. bed** rosaleda *f*; **r. bush** rosal *m* (**b**) (*colour*) rosa *m* (**c**) (*of watering can*) alcachofa *f*

rosé ['rəʊzeɪ] N (vino *m*) rosado *m*

rosebud ['rəʊzbʌd] N capullo *m* de rosa

rosemary ['rəʊzmərɪ] N romero *m*

rosette [rəʊ'zet] N (*of ribbons*) escarapela *f*

roster ['rɒstə(r)] N lista *f*

rostrum ['rɒstrəm] N estrado *m*

> Note that the Spanish word **rostro** is a false friend and is never a translation for the English word **rostrum**. In Spanish, **rostro** means "face".

rosy ['rəʊzɪ] ADJ (**rosier, rosiest**) (**a**) (*complexion*) sonrosado(a) (**b**) *Fig* (*future*) prometedor(a)

rot [rɒt] **1** N (**a**) (*decay*) putrefacción *f*; **dry r.** putrefacción de la madera (**b**) *Br Fam* (*nonsense*) sandeces *fpl*, *Am* pendejadas *fpl*
2 VT pudrir
> **rot away** VI pudrirse

rota ['rəʊtə] N *Br* lista *f*

rotary ['rəʊtərɪ] **1** N *US* (*for traffic*) rotonda *f*
2 ADJ rotatorio(a), giratorio(a)

rotate [rəʊ'teɪt] **1** VT (**a**) (*revolve*) hacer girar (**b**) (*jobs, crops*) alternar
2 VI (*revolve*) girar

rotating [rəʊ'teɪtɪŋ] ADJ rotativo(a)

rotation [rəʊ'teɪʃən] N rotación *f*

rote [rəʊt] N **by r.** de memoria

rotten ['rɒtən] ADJ (**a**) (*decayed*) podrido(a); (*tooth*) picado(a) (**b**) *Fam* (*very bad*) malísimo(a); *Fam* **I feel r.** me siento *Esp* fatal *or Am* pésimo

rouble ['ruːbəl] N rublo *m*

rouge [ruːʒ] **1** N colorete *m*
2 VT poner colorete a

rough [rʌf] **1** ADJ (**a**) (*surface, skin*) áspero(a); (*terrain*) accidentado(a); (*sea*) agitado(a); (*weather*) tempestuoso(a) (**b**) (*violent*) violento(a) (**c**) (*wine*) áspero(a) (**d**) *Fam* **to feel r.** encontrarse fatal (**e**) (*approximate*) aproximado(a); **r. draft** borrador *m* (**f**) (*harsh*) severo(a)
2 ADV duramente; *Fam Fig* **to sleep r.** dormir a la intemperie *or Am* al raso
3 VT *Fam* **we had to r. it** nos las arreglamos *or Esp* apañamos como pudimos

roughage ['rʌfɪdʒ] N (*substance*) fibra *f*

rough-and-ready ['rʌfən'redɪ] ADJ improvisado(a)

roughen ['rʌfən] VT poner áspero(a)

roughly ['rʌflɪ] ADV (**a**) (*crudely*) toscamente (**b**) (*clumsily*) torpemente (**c**) (*not gently*) bruscamente (**d**) (*approximately*) aproximadamente

roulette [ruː'let] N ruleta *f*

round [raʊnd] **1** ADJ redondo(a); **r. trip** viaje *m* de ida y vuelta
2 N (**a**) (*series*) serie *f*; **r. of talks** ronda *f* de negociaciones (**b**) (*of ammunition*) cartucho *m*; (*salvo*) salva *f* (**c**) (*of drinks*) ronda *f*, *Am* vuelta *f* (**d**) (*in golf*) partido *m* (**e**) (*in boxing*) round *m* (**f**) (*in a competition*) eliminatoria *f*
3 ADV **all year r.** durante todo el año; **to invite sb r.** invitar a algn a casa
4 PREP alrededor de; **r. here** por aquí; **it's just r. the corner** está a la vuelta de la esquina, *RP* queda a la vuelta
5 VT (*turn*) dar la vuelta a

> **round off** VT SEP acabar, concluir
> **round on** VT INSEP (*attack*) atacar
> **round up** VT SEP (*cattle*) acorralar, rodear; (*people*) reunir

roundabout ['raʊndəbaʊt] **1** N *Br* (**a**) (*merry-go-round*) tiovivo *m*, carrusel *m*, *RP* calesita *f* (**b**) (*for cars*) rotonda *f*, *Esp* glorieta *f*
2 ADJ indirecto(a)

rounders ['raʊndəz] N *Br* = juego parecido al béisbol

roundly ['raʊndlɪ] ADV completamente, totalmente

round-shouldered ['raʊnd'ʃəʊldəd] ADJ cargado(a) de espaldas

round-trip ['raʊnd'trɪp] *US* ADJ (*ticket*) de ida y vuelta

round-up ['raʊndʌp] N (**a**) (*of cattle*) rodeo *m*; (*of suspects*) redada *f* (**b**) (*summary*) resumen *m*

rouse [raʊz] VT despertar; (*stir up*) suscitar

rousing ['raʊzɪŋ] ADJ (*cheer*) entusiasta; (*applause*) caluroso(a); (*speech, song*) conmovedor(a)

rout [raʊt] **1** N aniquilación *f*
2 VT aniquilar

route [ruːt] **1** N (**a**) (*of traveller, plane, ship*) ruta *f*; (*of bus*) línea *f*; *Fig* camino *m*; **r. map** mapa *m* de carreteras (**b**) *US* **R.** ≃ carretera *f* nacional
2 VT encaminar

routine [ruː'tiːn] **1** N (**a**) (*habit*) rutina *f* (**b**) *Th* número *m*
2 ADJ rutinario(a)

roving ['rəʊvɪŋ] ADJ errante; **r. reporter** enviado(a) *m,f* especial

row¹ [rəʊ] N fila *f*, hilera *f*; *US* **r. house** casa *f* adosada; *Fig* **three times in a r.** tres veces seguidas

row² [rəʊ] VT & VI (*in a boat*) remar

row³ [raʊ] **1** N (**a**) (*quarrel*) pelea *f*, bronca *f* (**b**) (*noise*) jaleo *m*; (*protest*) escándalo *m*
2 VI pelearse

rowboat ['rəʊbəʊt] N *US* bote *m or* barca *f* de remos

rowdy ['raʊdɪ] **1** ADJ (**rowdier, rowdiest**) (**a**) (*noisy*) ruidoso(a); (*disorderly*) alborotador(a) (**b**) (*quarrelsome*) camorrista
2 N camorrista *mf*

rowing ['rəʊɪŋ] N remo *m*; *esp Br* **r. boat** bote *m* de remos

royal ['rɔɪəl] **1** ADJ real; **r. blue** azul marino; **the R. Family** la Familia Real
2 N *Fam* miembro *m* de la Familia Real

royally ['rɔɪəlɪ] ADV *Fig* magníficamente

royalty ['rɔɪəltɪ] N (**a**) *(royal persons)* miembro(s) *m(pl)* de la Familia Real (**b**) **royalties** derechos *mpl* de autor

RPI [ɑːpiːˈaɪ] N *(abbr* **Retail Price Index)** IPC *m*, Índice *m* de Precios al Consumo

rpm [ɑːpiːˈem] N *(abbr* **revolutions per minute)** r.p.m.

RSPCA [ɑːrespiːsiːˈeɪ] N *Br (abbr* **Royal Society for the Prevention of Cruelty to Animals)** ≃ Sociedad *f* Protectora de Animales

RSVP [ɑːresviːˈpiː] *(abbr* **répondez s'il vous plaît)** se ruega contestación, S.R.C.

Rt Hon *Br Pol (abbr* **(the) Right Honourable)** = tratamiento que se da a los diputados en el Parlamento británico, ≃ Su Señoría

rub [rʌb] **1** N **to give sth a r.** frotar algo
2 VT frotar; *(hard)* restregar; *(massage)* friccionar
3 VI rozar (**against** contra)
▸ **rub down** VT SEP rotar; *(horse)* almohazar; *(surface)* raspar
▸ **rub in** VT SEP (**a**) *(cream etc)* frotar con (**b**) *Fam* **don't r. it in** no me lo refriegues
▸ **rub off 1** VT SEP *(erase)* borrar
2 VI *Fig* **to r. off on sb** influir en algn
▸ **rub out** VT SEP borrar
▸ **rub up** VT SEP *Fam Fig* **to r. sb up the wrong way** fastidiar a algn

rubber¹ ['rʌbə(r)] N (**a**) *(substance)* goma *f*, *Am* hule *m*; **r. band** goma; **r. stamp** tampón *m* (**b**) *Br (eraser)* goma *f* (de borrar) (**c**) *Fam (condom)* goma *f*, *Méx* impermeable *m*, *RP* forro *m*

rubber² ['rʌbə(r)] N *(in bridge)* rubber *m*

rubbery ['rʌbərɪ] ADJ *(elastic)* elástico(a)

rubbish ['rʌbɪʃ] N (**a**) *Br (refuse)* basura *f*; *Br* **r. bin** cubo *m* or *Am* bote de la basura; **r. dump** or **tip** vertedero *m* (**b**) *Fam (worthless thing)* birria *f* (**c**) *Fam (nonsense)* tonterías *fpl*

rubble ['rʌbəl] N escombros *mpl*

rubric ['ruːbrɪk] N rúbrica *f*

ruby ['ruːbɪ] N rubí *m*

rucksack ['rʌksæk] N mochila *f*

ructions ['rʌkʃənz] NPL *Fam* jaleo *m*

rudder ['rʌdə(r)] N timón *m*

ruddy ['rʌdɪ] ADJ (**ruddier, ruddiest**) (**a**) *(complexion)* rojizo(a), colorado(a) (**b**) *Br Fam (damned)* maldito(a)

rude [ruːd] ADJ (**a**) *(impolite)* maleducado(a); *(foul-mouthed)* grosero(a); **don't be r. to your mother** no le faltes al respeto a tu madre (**b**) *(abrupt)* **a r. awakening** un despertar repentino

rudimentary [ruːdɪˈmentərɪ] ADJ rudimentario(a)

rudiments ['ruːdɪmənts] NPL rudimentos *mpl*

rue [ruː] VT arrepentirse de

rueful ['ruːfʊl] ADJ *(regretful)* arrepentido(a); *(sad)* triste

ruff [rʌf] N *(collar)* gorguera *f*

ruffian ['rʌfɪən] N canalla *m*

ruffle ['rʌfəl] VT *(water)* agitar; *(hair)* despeinar; *Fig* **to r. sb's feathers** hacer *esp Esp* enfadar or *esp Am* enojar a algn

ruffled ['rʌfəld] ADJ (**a**) *(hair)* alborotado(a); *(clothes)* en desorden (**b**) *(perturbed)* perturbado(a)

rug [rʌg] N alfombra *f*, alfombrilla *f*

rugby ['rʌgbɪ] N rugby *m*; **r. league** rugby a trece; **r. union** rugby a quince

rugged ['rʌgɪd] ADJ (**a**) *(terrain)* accidentado(a) (**b**) *(features)* marcado(a) (**c**) *(character)* vigoroso(a)

rugger ['rʌgə(r)] N *Br Fam* rugby *m*

ruin ['ruːɪn] **1** N ruina *f*; **ruins** ruinas *fpl*, restos *mpl*; **in ruins** en ruinas
2 VT arruinar; *(spoil)* estropear

ruined ['ruːɪnd] ADJ *(building)* en ruinas

rule [ruːl] **1** N (**a**) *(principle, regulation)* regla *f*, norma *f*; **to work to r.** hacer una huelga de celo; **as a r.** por regla general (**b**) *(government)* dominio *m*; *(of monarch)* reinado *m*; **r. of law** imperio *m* de la ley
2 VT & VI (**a**) *(govern)* gobernar; *(of monarch)* reinar (**b**) *(decide)* decidir; *(decree)* decretar (**c**) *(draw)* tirar
▸ **rule out** VT SEP descartar

ruled [ruːld] ADJ rayado(a)

ruler ['ruːlə(r)] N (**a**) *(of country)* gobernante *mf* (**b**) *(for measuring)* regla *f*

ruling ['ruːlɪŋ] **1** ADJ *(in charge)* dirigente; *Fig (predominant)* predominante; **the r. party** el partido en el poder
2 N *Jur* fallo *m*

rum [rʌm] N ron *m*

Rumania [ruːˈmeɪnɪə] N = **Romania**

Rumanian [ruːˈmeɪnɪən] ADJ & N = **Romanian**

rumble ['rʌmbəl] **1** N (**a**) *(of thunder, gunfire)* rugido *m*, retumbo *m* (**b**) *(of stomach)* gruñido *m*
2 VI (**a**) *(thunder)* retumbar (**b**) *(stomach)* gruñir

ruminate ['ruːmɪneɪt] VI *(chew, ponder)* rumiar

rummage ['rʌmɪdʒ] VI revolver (**through** en); *US* **r. sale** *(in store)* liquidacion *f* de saldos; *(for charity)* rastrillo benéfico

rumour, *US* **rumor** ['ruːmə(r)] **1** N rumor *m*; **r. has it that ...** se dice que ...
2 VT **it is rumoured that** se rumorea que

rump [rʌmp] N *(of animal)* ancas *fpl*, *Fam Hum (of person)* trasero *m*; **r. steak** filete *m* de lomo

rumpus ['rʌmpəs] N *Fam* jaleo *m*, bronca *f*, *Esp* follón *m*

run [rʌn] **1** N (**a**) *(act of running)* carrera *f*; **on the r.** fugado(a); **to go for a r.** hacer footing; *Fig* **in the long r.** a largo plazo (**b**) *(trip) (in car)* vuelta *f* (**c**) *(sequence)* serie *f* (**d**) *(in stocking)* carrera *f*
2 VT *(pt* **ran**; *pp* **run)** (**a**) *(distance)* correr; **to r. a race** correr en una carrera (**b**) *(drive)* llevar

(**c**) *(house, business)* llevar; *(company)* dirigir; *(organize)* organizar (**d**) *(fingers)* pasar (**e**) *Comput* **to r. a program** ejecutar un programa 3 VI (**a**) *(person)* correr (**b**) *(colour)* desteñirse (**c**) *(water, river)* correr; **to leave the tap running** dejar el grifo abierto; *Fam* **your nose is running** se te caen los mocos (**d**) *(operate) (machine)* funcionar (**on** con) (**e**) *Pol* **to r. for president** presentarse como candidato a la presidencia (**f**) *(range)* oscilar (**between** entre) (**g**) **shyness runs in the family** la timidez le viene de familia (**h**) *Cin & Th* estar en cartel

▸ **run about** VI corretear

▸ **run across** VT INSEP *(meet)* tropezar con

▸ **run away** VI fugarse; *(horse)* desbocarse

▸ **run down** VT INSEP *(stairs)* bajar corriendo
2 VT SEP (**a**) *(in car)* atropellar (**b**) *(criticize)* criticar
3 VI *(battery)* agotarse; *(clock)* pararse

▸ **run in** VT SEP *Aut* rodar

▸ **run into** VT INSEP (**a**) *(room)* entrar corriendo en (**b**) *(people, problems)* tropezar con (**c**) *(crash into)* chocar contra

▸ **run off** 1 VT SEP *(print)* tirar
2 VI escaparse

▸ **run on** 1 VT SEP *Typ* enlazar
2 VI *(meeting)* continuar

▸ **run out** VI (**a**) *(exit)* salir corriendo (**b**) *(come to an end)* agotarse; *(of contract)* vencer; **to r. out of** quedarse sin

▸ **run over** 1 VT SEP *(in car)* atropellar
2 VT INSEP *(rehearse)* ensayar
3 VI *(overflow)* rebosar

▸ **run through** VT INSEP (**a**) *(of river)* pasar por (**b**) *(read quickly)* echar un vistazo a (**c**) *(rehearse)* ensayar

▸ **run up** VT SEP (**a**) *(flag)* izar (**b**) *(debts)* acumular

▸ **run up against** VT INSEP tropezar con

runaway ['rʌnəweɪ] 1 N fugitivo(a) *m,f*
2 ADJ (**a**) *(person)* huido(a); *(horse)* desbocado(a); *(vehicle)* incontrolado(a); *(inflation)* galopante; *(success)* clamoroso(a)

rundown ['rʌndaʊn] N *Fam* **to give sb a r.** poner a algn al tanto

run-down [rʌn'daʊn] ADJ (**a**) *(exhausted)* agotado(a) (**b**) *(dilapidated)* ruinoso(a)

rung¹ [rʌŋ] PP of **ring¹**

rung² [rʌŋ] N *(of ladder)* escalón *m*, peldaño *m*

runner ['rʌnə(r)] N (**a**) *(person)* corredor(a) *m,f* (**b**) *Br* **r. bean** *Esp* judía *f* verde, *Bol, RP* chaucha *f*, *Méx* ejote *m*

runner-up [rʌnər'ʌp] N subcampeón(ona) *m,f*

running ['rʌnɪŋ] 1 N (**a**) **he likes r.** le gusta correr; *Fig* **to be in the r. for sth** tener posibilidades de conseguir algo (**b**) *(of company)* dirección *f* (**c**) *(of machine)* funcionamiento *m*
2 ADJ (**a**) **r. commentary** comentario *m* en directo; **r. costs** costos *mpl* de manteni-

miento; *Pol* **r. mate** candidato *m* a la vicepresidencia; **r. water** agua *f* corriente (**b**) **three weeks r.** tres semanas seguidas

runny ['rʌnɪ] ADJ (**runnier, runniest**) blando(a); *(egg)* crudo(a); *(butter)* derretido(a); *(nose)* que moquea

run-of-the-mill ['rʌnəvðə'mɪl] ADJ corriente y moliente

runt [rʌnt] N *Fam* enano(a) *m,f*

run-up ['rʌnʌp] N *(to elections)* preliminares *mpl*

runway ['rʌnweɪ] N *Av* pista *f* (de aterrizaje y despegue *orAm* decolaje)

rupee [ruː'piː] N rupia *f*

rupture ['rʌptʃə(r)] 1 N (**a**) *Med* hernia *f* (**b**) *Fig* ruptura *f*
2 VT (**a**) **to r. oneself** herniarse (**b**) *(break)* romper

rural ['rʊərəl] ADJ rural

ruse [ruːz] N ardid *m*, astucia *f*

rush¹ [rʌʃ] N *Bot* junco *m*

rush² [rʌʃ] 1 N (**a**) *(hurry)* prisa *f*, *Am* apuro *m*; **the r. hour** *Esp* la hora *f* punta, *Am* la hora *f* pico (**b**) *(demand)* demanda *f*
2 VT (**a**) *(task)* hacer de prisa; *(person)* meter prisa a; **to r. sb to hospital** llevar a algn urgentemente al hospital (**b**) *(attack)* abalanzarse sobre; *Mil* tomar por asalto
3 VI *(go quickly)* precipitarse

▸ **rush about** VI correr de un lado a otro

▸ **rush into** VT INSEP *Fig* **to r. into sth** hacer algo sin pensarlo bien

▸ **rush off** VI irse corriendo

rusk [rʌsk] N = galleta dura para niños

Russia ['rʌʃə] N Rusia

Russian ['rʌʃən] 1 ADJ ruso(a)
2 N (**a**) *(person)* ruso(a) *m,f* (**b**) *(language)* ruso *m*

rust [rʌst] 1 N (**a**) *(substance)* herrumbre *f* (**b**) *(colour)* pardo rojizo
2 VT oxidar
3 VI oxidarse

rustic ['rʌstɪk] ADJ rústico(a)

rustle ['rʌsəl] 1 N crujido *m*
2 VT *(papers etc)* hacer crujir
3 VI *(steal cattle)* robar ganado

rustproof ['rʌstpruːf] ADJ inoxidable

rusty ['rʌstɪ] ADJ (**rustier, rustiest**) oxidado(a); *Fam Fig* **my French is a bit r.** tengo el francés un poco oxidado

rut [rʌt] N (**a**) *(furrow)* surco *m*; *(groove)* ranura *f* (**b**) *Fig* **to be in a r.** ser esclavo de la rutina (**c**) *Zool* celo *m*

ruthless ['ruːθlɪs] ADJ despiadado(a)

RV [ɑː'viː] N *US* (*abbr* **recreational vehicle**) autocaravana *f*, casa *f* or coche *m* caravana

rye [raɪ] N centeno *m*; **r. bread** pan *m* de centeno; **r. grass** ballica *f*; *US* **r. (whiskey)** whisky *m* de centeno

S, s [es] N *(the letter)* S, s *f*

Sabbath ['sæbəθ] N *(Jewish)* sábado *m*; *(Christian)* domingo *m*

sabbatical [sə'bætɪkəl] ADJ sabático(a)

sabotage ['sæbətɑːʒ] **1** N sabotaje *m*
2 VT sabotear

saccharin ['sækərɪn] N sacarina *f*

sachet ['sæʃeɪ] N bolsita *f*, sobrecito *m*

sack [sæk] **1** N (a) *(bag)* saco *m* (b) *Fam* to get the s. ser despedido(a); *Fam* to give sb the s. despedir a algn
2 VT (a) *Fam* despedir (b) *Mil* saquear

sacking ['sækɪŋ] N *Tex* arpillera *f*

sacrament ['sækrəmənt] N sacramento *m*

sacred ['seɪkrɪd] ADJ sagrado(a)

sacrifice ['sækrɪfaɪs] **1** N sacrificio *m*
2 VT sacrificar

sacrificial [sækrɪ'fɪʃəl] ADJ s. lamb chivo expiatorio

sacrilege ['sækrɪlɪdʒ] N sacrilegio *m*

sacrosanct ['sækrəʊsæŋkt] ADJ sacrosanto(a)

sad [sæd] ADJ (**sadder, saddest**) triste; how s.! ¡qué pena!

sadden ['sædən] VT entristecer

saddle ['sædəl] **1** N *(for horse)* silla *f* (de montar); *(of bicycle etc)* sillín *m*
2 VT *(horse)* ensillar; *Fam* to s. sb with sth encajar *or Esp, Méx* encasquetar algo a algn

saddlebag ['sædəlbæg] N alforja *f*

sadist ['seɪdɪst] N sádico(a) *m,f*

sadistic [sə'dɪstɪk] ADJ sádico(a)

sadly ['sædlɪ] ADV *(reply, smile)* tristemente; **s., this is so** es así es, por desgracia

sadness ['sædnɪs] N tristeza *f*

sadomasochism [seɪdəʊ'mæsəkɪzəm] N sadomasoquismo *m*

SAE [eseɪ'iː] N *Br (abbr* **stamped addressed envelope)** sobre franqueado con la dirección del remitente

safari [sə'fɑːrɪ] N safari *m*; **s. park** reserva *f*

safe [seɪf] **1** ADJ (a) *(unharmed)* ileso(a); *(out of danger)* a salvo; **s. and sound** sano(a) y salvo(a) (b) *(not dangerous)* inocuo(a) (c) *(secure, sure)* seguro(a) (d) *(driver)* prudente
2 N *(for money etc)* caja *f* fuerte

safe-conduct [seɪf'kɒndʌkt] N salvoconducto *m*

safe-deposit [seɪfdɪ'pɒzɪt] N **s. (box)** cámara blindada

safeguard ['seɪfgɑːd] **1** N *(protection)* salvaguarda *f*; *(guarantee)* garantía *f*
2 VT proteger, salvaguardar

safekeeping [seɪf'kiːpɪŋ] N custodia *f*

safely ['seɪflɪ] ADV (a) *(without danger)* sin riesgos (b) **to arrive s.** llegar sin incidentes

safety ['seɪftɪ] N seguridad *f*; **s. first!** ¡la seguridad ante todo!; **s. belt** cinturón *m* de seguridad; **s. net** red *f* de protección; **s. pin** imperdible *m*, *Am* alfiler *m* de gancho, *CAm, Méx* seguro *m*

saffron ['sæfrən] N azafrán *m*

sag [sæg] VI (a) *(roof)* hundirse; *(wall)* pandear; *(wood, iron)* combarse; *(flesh)* colgar (b) *Fig (spirits)* flaquear

saga ['sɑːgə] N *(story)* saga *f*; *Fig* **a s. of corruption** una historia interminable de corrupción

sage¹ [seɪdʒ] **1** ADJ *(wise)* sabio(a)
2 N *(person)* sabio(a) *m,f*

sage² [seɪdʒ] N salvia *f*

Sagittarius [sædʒɪ'teərɪəs] N Sagitario *m*

Sahara [sə'hɑːrə] N **the S.** el Sahara

Saharan [sə'hɑːrən] ADJ saharaui, sahariano(a)

said [sed] **1** ADJ dicho(a)
2 PT & PP of **say**

sail [seɪl] **1** N (a) *(canvas)* vela *f*; **to set s.** zarpar (b) *(trip)* paseo *m* en barco
2 VT *(ship)* gobernar; *Literary* navegar
3 VI (a) *(ship, person)* navegar (b) *(set sail)* zarpar

▶ **sail through** VT INSEP *Fam* **he sailed through university** en la universidad todo le fue sobre ruedas

sailboat ['seɪlbəʊt] N *US* velero *m*

sailing ['seɪlɪŋ] N navegación *f*; *(yachting)* vela *f*; *Fam* **it's all plain s.** es todo coser y cantar; *Br* **s. boat** (barco *m*) velero *m*; **s. ship** barco *m* de vela

sailor ['seɪlə(r)] N marinero *m*

saint [seɪnt] N santo(a) *m,f*; *(before all masculine names except those beginning* **Do** *or* **To***)* San; *(before feminine names)* Santa; **S. Dominic** Santo Domingo; **S. Helen** Santa Elena; **S. John** San Juan; **All Saints' Day** Día *m* de Todos los Santos

saintly ['seɪntlɪ] ADJ (**saintlier, saintliest**) santo(a)

sake [seɪk] N **for the s. of** por (el bien de); **for your own s.** por tu propio bien

salad ['sæləd] N ensalada f; **potato s.** ensalada de patatas or Am papas; **s. bowl** ensaladera f; Br **s. cream** salsa f tipo mahonesa; **s. dressing** aderezo m or Esp aliño m para la ensalada

salami [sə'lɑːmɪ] N salami m, Am salame m

salary ['sælərɪ] N salario m, sueldo m

sale [seɪl] N (a) (action) venta f; **for** or **on s.** en venta; **sales department** departamento m comercial; **sales figures** cifra f de ventas; **sales manager** jefe(a) m,f de ventas; **sales tax** impuesto m de venta (b) (at low prices) rebajas fpl

salesclerk ['seɪlzklɑːk] N US dependiente(a) m,f

salesman ['seɪlzmən] N (a) (in shop) dependiente m (b) (for company) comercial m, vendedor m

salesroom ['seɪlzruːm] N sala f de subastas

saleswoman ['seɪlzwʊmən] N (a) (in shop) dependienta f (b) (for company) comercial f, vendedora f

salient ['seɪlɪənt] ADJ Fig sobresaliente

saliva [sə'laɪvə] N saliva f

sallow ['sæləʊ] ADJ cetrino(a)

salmon ['sæmən] 1 N salmón m
2 ADJ (de color) salmón

salmonella [sælmə'nelə] N Biol & Med (bacteria) salmonela f; (food poisoning) salmonelosis f

salon ['sælɒn] N salón m

saloon [sə'luːn] N (a) (on ship) cámara f (b) US (bar) taberna f, bar m; Br **s. (bar)** bar de lujo (c) Br (car) turismo m

salt [sɔːlt] 1 N sal f; Fig **to take sth with a pinch of s.** creer algo con reservas; **bath salts** sales de baño; **smelling salts** sales aromáticas
2 ADJ salado(a)
3 VT (a) (cure) salar (b) (add salt to) echar sal a

saltcellar ['sɔːltselə(r)], US **saltshaker** ['sɔːltʃeɪkə(r)] N salero m

saltwater ['sɔːltwɔːtə(r)] ADJ de agua salada

salty ['sɔːltɪ] ADJ (saltier, saltiest) salado(a)

salubrious [sə'luːbrɪəs] ADJ salubre, sano(a)

salutary ['sæljʊtərɪ] ADJ (experience) beneficioso(a); (warning) útil

salute [sə'luːt] 1 N (greeting) saludo m
2 VT (a) Mil saludar (b) Fig (achievement etc) aplaudir
3 VI Mil saludar

salvage ['sælvɪdʒ] 1 N (a) (of ship etc) salvamento m, rescate m (b) (objects recovered) objetos recuperados (c) Jur derecho m de salvamento
2 VT (from ship etc) rescatar

salvation [sæl'veɪʃən] N salvación f; **S. Army** Ejército m de Salvación

Samaritan [sə'mærɪtən] N samaritano(a) m,f; **the Samaritans** los Samaritanos, Esp ≃ el teléfono de la Esperanza

same [seɪm] 1 ADJ mismo(a); **at that very s. moment** en ese mismísimo momento; **at the s. time** (simultaneously) al mismo tiempo; (however) sin embargo; **in the s. way** del mismo modo; **the two cars are the s.** los dos coches son iguales
2 PRON **the s.** el mismo/la misma/lo mismo; Fam **the s. here** lo mismo digo yo; Fam **the s. to you!** ¡igualmente!
3 ADV del mismo modo, igual; **all the s., just the s.** sin embargo, aun así; **it's all the s. to me** (a mí) me da igual or lo mismo

sample ['sɑːmpəl] 1 N muestra f
2 VT (wines) catar; (dish) probar

sanatorium [sænə'tɔːrɪəm] N sanatorio m

sanctimonious [sæŋktɪ'məʊnɪəs] ADJ beato(a)

sanction ['sæŋkʃən] 1 N (a) (authorization) permiso m (b) (penalty) sanción f (c) Pol **sanctions** sanciones fpl
2 VT sancionar

sanctity ['sæŋktɪtɪ] N (sacredness) santidad f; (of marriage) indisolubilidad f

sanctuary ['sæŋktjʊərɪ] N (a) Rel santuario m (b) Pol asilo m (c) (for birds, animals) reserva f

sand [sænd] 1 N arena f; **s. castle** castillo m de arena; **s. dune** duna f
2 VT **to s. (down)** lijar

sandal ['sændəl] N sandalia f, Andes, CAm ojota f, Méx guarache m

sandalwood ['sændəlwʊd] N sándalo m

sandbag ['sændbæg] N saco m terrero or m de arena, RP bolsa f de arena

sandbox ['sændbɒks] N US arenal m

sandpaper ['sændpeɪpə(r)] N papel m de lija

sandpit ['sændpɪt] N Br (in playground etc) recinto m de arena

sandshoe ['sændʃuː] N Br playera f

sandstone ['sændstəʊn] N arenisca f

sandwich ['sænwɪdʒ, 'sænwɪtʃ] 1 N (with sliced bread) sándwich m; (with French bread) Esp bocadillo m, Am sándwich m, CSur sánwiche m, Méx torta; Educ **s. course** curso teórico-práctico
2 VT intercalar; **it was sandwiched between two lorries** quedó encajonado entre dos camiones

sandy ['sændɪ] ADJ (sandier, sandiest) (a) (earth, beach) arenoso(a) (b) (hair) rubio rojizo

sane [seɪn] ADJ (not mad) cuerdo(a); (sensible) sensato(a)

> Note that the Spanish word **sano** is a false friend and is never a translation for the English word **sane**. In Spanish **sano** means "healthy".

sang [sæŋ] PT of **sing**

sanitarium [sænɪ'teərɪəm] N US sanatorio m

sanitary ['sænɪtərɪ] ADJ sanitario(a); (hygienic) higiénico(a); **s.** Br **towel** or US **napkin** compresa f, Am toalla f higiénica

sanitation [sænɪ'teɪʃən] N sanidad (pública); *(plumbing)* sistema *m* de saneamiento

sanity ['sænɪtɪ] N cordura *f*, juicio *m*; *(good sense)* sensatez *f*

> Note that the Spanish word **sanidad** is a false friend and is never a translation for the English word **sanity**. In Spanish **sanidad** means "health".

sank [sæŋk] PT *of* **sink²**

Santa Claus ['sæntə'klɔːz] N Papá Noel *m*, San Nicolás *m*

sap¹ [sæp] N *Bot* savia *f*

sap² [sæp] VT *(undermine)* minar; *Fig* agotar

sap³ [sæp] N *Fam (gullible person)* papanatas *mf inv*, *Esp* pardillo(a) *m,f*

sapling ['sæplɪŋ] N *Bot* árbol *m* joven

sapphire ['sæfaɪə(r)] N zafiro *m*

sarcasm ['sɑːkæzəm] N sarcasmo *m*

sarcastic [sɑː'kæstɪk] ADJ sarcástico(a)

sardine [sɑː'diːn] N sardina *f*

Sardinia [sɑː'dmɪə] N Cerdeña *f*

sardonic [sɑː'dɒnɪk] ADJ sardónico(a)

sari ['sɑːrɪ] N sari *m*

SASE [eseɪes'iː] N *US (abbr* **self-addressed stamped envelope)** sobre franqueado con la dirección del remitente

sash¹ [sæʃ] N faja *f*

sash² [sæʃ] N **s. window** ventana *f* de guillotina

sat [sæt] PT & PP *of* **sit**

Satan ['seɪtən] N Satán *m*, Satanás *m*

satanic [sə'tænɪk] ADJ satánico(a)

satchel ['sætʃəl] N cartera *f* de colegial

satellite ['sætəlaɪt] N satélite *m*; **s. dish** antena parabólica

satin ['sætɪn] N satén *m*; **s. finish** (acabado *m*) satinado *m*

satire ['sætaɪə(r)] N sátira *f*

satirical [sə'tɪrɪkəl] ADJ satírico(a)

satisfaction [sætɪs'fækʃən] N satisfacción *f*

satisfactory [sætɪs'fæktərɪ] ADJ satisfactorio(a)

satisfied ['sætɪsfaɪd] ADJ satisfecho(a)

satisfy ['sætɪsfaɪ] VT **(a)** *(person, curiosity)* satisfacer **(b)** *(condition, demand)* cumplir **(c)** *(convince)* convencer

satisfying ['sætɪsfaɪŋ] ADJ satisfactorio(a); *(pleasing)* agradable; *(meal)* que llena

saturate ['sætʃəreɪt] VT saturar **(with** de)

Saturday ['sætədɪ] N sábado *m*

sauce [sɔːs] N **(a)** *(for food)* salsa *f* **(b)** *Br Fam (impudence)* descaro *m*

saucepan ['sɔːspən] N cacerola *f*; *(large)* olla *f*

saucer ['sɔːsə(r)] N platillo *m*

saucy ['sɔːsɪ] ADJ **(saucier, sauciest)** *Fam* fresco(a)

Saudi Arabia ['saʊdɪə'reɪbɪə] N Arabia Saudí

Saudi Arabian ['saʊdɪə'reɪbɪən] ADJ & N saudita *(mf)*, saudí *(mf)*

sauna ['sɔːnə] N sauna *f*, *Am* sauna *m or f*

saunter ['sɔːntə(r)] **1** N paseo *m*

2 VI pasearse

sausage ['sɒsɪdʒ] N *(raw)* salchicha *f*; *(cured)* salchichón *m*; *(spicy)* chorizo *m*; *Fam* **s. dog** perro *m* salchicha; *Br* **s. roll** empanada *f* de carne

sauté ['səʊteɪ] **1** ADJ salteado(a)

2 VT saltear

savage ['sævɪdʒ] **1** ADJ **(a)** *(ferocious)* feroz; *(cruel)* cruel; *(violent)* salvaje **(b)** *(primitive)* salvaje

2 N salvaje *mf*

3 VT *(attack)* embestir; *Fig (criticize)* criticar despiadadamente

save [seɪv] **1** VT **(a)** *(rescue)* salvar, rescatar; *Fig* **to s. face** salvar las apariencias **(b)** *(put by)* guardar; *(money, energy, time)* ahorrar; *(food)* almacenar; **it saved him a lot of trouble** le evitó muchos problemas

2 VI **(a)** **to s. (up)** ahorrar **(b)** **to s. on paper** *(economize)* ahorrar papel

3 N *Ftb* parada *f*

4 PREP *Literary* salvo, excepto

saving ['seɪvɪŋ] N **(a)** *(of time, money)* ahorro *m* **(b)** **savings** ahorros *mpl*; **savings account** cuenta *f* de ahorros

saviour, *US* **savior** ['seɪvjə(r)] N salvador(a) *m,f*

savour, *US* **savor** ['seɪvə(r)] **1** N sabor *m*, gusto *m*

2 VI saborear

savoury, *US* **savory** ['seɪvərɪ] ADJ *(tasty)* sabroso(a); *(salted)* salado(a); *(spicy)* picante

saw¹ [sɔː] **1** N *(tool)* sierra *f*

2 VT & VI *(pt* **sawed**; *pp* **sawed** *or* **sawn)** serrar

▶ **saw up** VT SEP serrar **(into** en)

saw² [sɔː] PT *of* **see¹**

sawdust ['sɔːdʌst] N *(a)* serrín *m*

sawed-off [sɔːd'ɒf] ADJ *US* = **sawn-off**

sawmill ['sɔːmɪl] N aserradero *m*, serrería *f*

sawn [sɔːn] PP *of* **saw¹**

sawn-off ['sɔːnɒf] ADJ recortado(a); **s. shotgun** escopeta *f* de cañones recortados

saxophone ['sæksəfəʊn] N saxofón *m*

say [seɪ] **1** VT *(pt & pp* **said)** decir; **it goes without saying that ...** huelga decir que ...; **it is said that ...** se dice que ...; **not to s. ...** por no decir ...; **that is to s.** es decir; **to s. yes/no** decir que sí/no; *Fam* **I s.!** ¡oiga!; **what does the sign s.?** ¿qué pone en el letrero?; **shall we s. Friday then?** ¿quedamos el viernes, pues?

2 N **I have no s. in the matter** no tengo ni voz ni voto en el asunto; **to have one's s.** dar su opinión

saying ['seɪɪŋ] N refrán *m*, dicho *m*

scab [skæb] N **(a)** *Med* costra *f* **(b)** *Fam* esquirol *mf*, *Am* rompehuelgas *mf inv*

scaffold ['skæfəld] N *(for execution)* patíbulo *m*

scaffolding ['skæfəldɪŋ] N *Constr* andamio *m*

scald [skɔ:ld] **1** N escaldadura f
2 VT escaldar

scale¹ [skeɪl] N *(of fish, on skin)* escama f; *(in boiler)* incrustaciones fpl

scale² [skeɪl] **1** N (**a**) *(for measuring, of pay rates)* escala f; **on a large s.** a gran escala; **to s.** a escala; **s. model** maqueta f (**b**) *(of problem, changes)* escala f, magnitud f (**c**) Mus escala f
2 VT *(climb)* escalar

▶ **scale down** VT SEP *(drawing)* reducir a escala; *(production)* reducir

scales [skeɪlz] NPL **(pair of) s.** *(shop, kitchen)* balanza f; *(bathroom)* báscula f

scallop [ˈskɒləp] N (**a**) *(mollusc)* vieira f (**b**) *(shell)* venera f

scalp [skælp] **1** N cuero cabelludo
2 VT arrancar el cuero cabelludo a

scalpel [ˈskælpəl] N bisturí m

scamper [ˈskæmpə(r)] VI corretear

scampi [ˈskæmpɪ] N gambas empanadas

scan [skæn] **1** VT (**a**) *(scrutinize)* escrutar; *(horizon)* otear (**b**) *(glance at)* ojear (**c**) *(of radar)* explorar
2 N Med exploración ultrasónica; *(in gynaecology etc)* ecografía f

scandal [ˈskændəl] N (**a**) *(outrage)* escándalo m; **what a s.!** ¡qué vergüenza! (**b**) *(gossip)* chismorreo m, Esp cotilleo m

scandalous [ˈskændələs] ADJ escandaloso(a)

Scandinavia [skændɪˈneɪvɪə] N Escandinavia

Scandinavian [skændɪˈneɪvɪən] ADJ & N escandinavo(a) *(m,f)*

scanner [ˈskænə(r)] N Med & Comput escáner m

scant [skænt] ADJ escaso(a)

scanty [ˈskæntɪ] ADJ (**scantier, scantiest**) escaso(a); *(meal)* insuficiente; *(clothes)* ligero(a)

scapegoat [ˈskeɪpgəʊt] N chivo expiatorio

scar [skɑ:(r)] N cicatriz f

scarce [skeəs] ADJ escaso(a); Fig **to make oneself s.** largarse

scarcely [ˈskeəslɪ] ADV apenas

scarcity [ˈskeəsɪtɪ] N escasez f; *(rarity)* rareza f

scare [skeə(r)] **1** N *(fright)* susto m; *(widespread alarm)* pánico m; **bomb s.** amenaza f de bomba
2 VT asustar, espantar; Fam **to be scared stiff** estar muerto(a) de miedo

▶ **scare away, scare off** VT SEP ahuyentar

scarecrow [ˈskeəkrəʊ] N espantapájaros m inv

scarf [skɑ:f] N *(pl* **scarfs** *or* **scarves)** *(long, woollen)* bufanda f; *(square)* pañuelo m; *(silk)* fular m

scarlet [ˈskɑ:lɪt] **1** ADJ escarlata
2 N escarlata f; **s. fever** escarlatina f

scarves [skɑ:vz] PL *of* **scarf**

scary [ˈskeərɪ] ADJ (**scarier, scariest**) Fam *(noise, situation)* aterrador(a), espantoso(a); *(film, book)* de miedo

scathing [ˈskeɪðɪŋ] ADJ mordaz, cáustico(a)

scatter [ˈskætə(r)] **1** VT (**a**) *(papers etc)* esparcir, desparramar (**b**) *(crowd)* dispersar
2 VI dispersarse

scatterbrained [ˈskætəbreɪnd] ADJ Fam ligero(a) de cascos; *(forgetful)* despistado(a)

scattered [ˈskætəd] ADJ **s. showers** chubascos aislados

scavenger [ˈskævɪndʒə(r)] N (**a**) *(person)* rebuscador(a) m,f, trapero m (**b**) *(animal)* *(animal m)* carroñero(a) mf

scenario [sɪˈnɑ:rɪəʊ] N (**a**) Cin guión m (**b**) *(situation)* situación f hipotética

scene [si:n] N (**a**) Th, Cin & TV escena f (**b**) *(place)* lugar m, escenario m (**c**) **to make a s.** *(fuss)* hacer una escena, Esp montar un número

scenery [ˈsi:nərɪ] N (**a**) *(landscape)* paisaje m (**b**) Th decorado m

scenic [ˈsi:nɪk] ADJ *(picturesque)* pintoresco(a)

scent [sent] **1** N (**a**) *(smell)* olor m; *(of food)* aroma m (**b**) *(perfume)* perfume m (**c**) *(in hunting)* pista f
2 VT *(add perfume to)* perfumar; *(smell)* olfatear; Fig presentir

sceptic [ˈskeptɪk] ADJ escéptico(a)

sceptical [ˈskeptɪkəl] ADJ escéptico(a)

scepticism [ˈskeptɪsɪzəm] N escepticismo m

sceptre [ˈseptə(r)] N cetro m

schedule [ˈʃedju:l, US ˈskedʒʊəl] **1** N (**a**) *(plan, agenda)* programa m; *(timetable)* horario m; **on s.** a la hora (prevista); **to be behind s.** llevar retraso (**b**) *(list)* lista f; *(inventory)* inventario m
2 VT *(plan)* programar, fijar

scheduled [ˈʃedju:ld, US ˈskedʒʊəld] ADJ previsto(a), fijo(a); **s. flight** vuelo m regular

scheme [ski:m] **1** N (**a**) *(plan)* plan m; *(project)* proyecto m; *(idea)* idea f; **colour s.** combinación f de colores m (**b**) *(plot)* intriga f; *(trick)* ardid m
2 VI *(plot)* tramar, intrigar

scheming [ˈski:mɪŋ] ADJ intrigante, maquinador(a)

schism [ˈsɪzəm] N cisma m

schizophrenic [skɪtsəʊˈfrenɪk] ADJ & N esquizofrénico(a) *(m,f)*

schmuck [ʃmʌk] N US Fam lelo(a) m,f

scholar [ˈskɒlə(r)] N *(learned person)* erudito(a) m,f; *(pupil)* alumno(a) m,f

scholarly [ˈskɒləlɪ] ADJ erudito(a)

scholarship [ˈskɒləʃɪp] N (**a**) *(learning)* erudición f (**b**) *(grant)* beca f; **s. holder** becario(a) m,f

school [sku:l] **1** N (**a**) *(for children)* *(up to 14)* colegio m, escuela f; *(from 14 to 18)* instituto m; **s. friend** amigo(a) m,f del colegio; **s. year** año m escolar (**b**) US *(university)* universidad f (**c**) *(university department)* facultad f (**d**) *(group of artists)* escuela f
2 VT *(teach)* enseñar; *(train)* formar

schoolbook ['sku:lbʊk] N libro m de texto

schoolboy ['sku:lbɔɪ] N alumno m

schoolchild ['sku:ltʃaɪld] N alumno(a) m,f

schooldays ['sku:ldeɪz] NPL años mpl de colegio

schoolgirl ['sku:lɡɜ:l] N alumna f

schooling ['sku:lɪŋ] N educación f, estudios mpl

schoolmaster ['sku:lmɑ:stə(r)] N profesor m; (primary school) maestro m

schoolmistress ['sku:lmɪstrɪs] N profesora f; (primary school) maestra f

schoolteacher ['sku:lti:tʃə(r)] N profesor(a) m,f; (primary school) maestro(a) m,f

schooner ['sku:nə(r)] N Naut goleta f

sciatica [saɪˈætɪkə] N ciática f

science ['saɪəns] N ciencia f; (school subject) ciencias; **s. fiction** ciencia-ficción f

scientific [saɪənˈtɪfɪk] ADJ científico(a)

scientist ['saɪəntɪst] N científico(a) m,f

scintillating ['sɪntɪleɪtɪŋ] ADJ brillante

scissors ['sɪzəz] NPL tijeras fpl; **a pair of s.** unas tijeras

scoff¹ [skɒf] VI (mock) mofarse (**at** de)

scoff² [skɒf] VT Br Fam (eat) zamparse

scold [skəʊld] VT regañar, reñir

scone [skəʊn, skɒn] N bollo m, pastelito m

scoop [sku:p] N (a) (for flour) pala f; (for ice cream) cucharón m; (amount) palada f, cucharada f (**b**) Press exclusiva f

▶ **scoop out** VT SEP (flour etc) sacar con pala; (water) (from boat) achicar

▶ **scoop up** VT SEP recoger

scooter ['sku:tə(r)] N (child's) patinete m; (adult's) Vespa® f

scope [skəʊp] N (a) (range) alcance m; (of undertaking) ámbito m (**b**) (freedom) libertad f

scorch [skɔ:tʃ] VT (singe) chamuscar

scorching ['skɔ:tʃɪŋ] ADJ Fam abrasador(a)

score [skɔ:(r)] N 1 (a) Sport tanteo m; Cards (in golf) puntuación f; (result) resultado m (**b**) **on that s.** a ese respecto (**c**) (twenty) veintena f (**d**) Mus (of opera) partitura f; (of film) música f 2 VT (a) (goal) marcar; (points) conseguir (**b**) (wood) hacer una muesca en; (paper) rayar 3 VI (a) Sport marcar un tanto; Ftb marcar un gol (**b**) Fam ligar (**with** con)

▶ **score out** VT SEP (word etc) tachar

scoreboard ['skɔ:bɔ:d] N marcador m

scorer ['skɔ:rə(r)] N (a) (goal striker) goleador m (**b**) (scorekeeper) encargado(a) m,f del marcador

scorn [skɔ:n] N 1 desprecio m 2 VT despreciar

scornful ['skɔ:nfʊl] ADJ desdeñoso(a)

Scorpio ['skɔ:pɪəʊ] N Escorpio m, Escorpión m

scorpion ['skɔ:pɪən] N alacrán m, escorpión m

Scot [skɒt] N escocés(esa) m,f

Scotch [skɒtʃ] 1 ADJ escocés(esa); US **S. tape®** cinta adhesiva, Esp celo® m, CAm, Méx Durex® m 2 N (whisky) whisky m escocés

scot-free ['skɒt'fri:] ADJ impune

Scotland ['skɒtlənd] N Escocia

Scots [skɒts] 1 ADJ escocés(esa) 2 N (dialecto m) escocés m

Scotsman ['skɒtsmən] N escocés m

Scotswoman ['skɒtswʊmən] N escocesa f

Scottish ['skɒtɪʃ] ADJ escocés(esa)

scoundrel ['skaʊndrəl] N sinvergüenza mf, canalla m

scour¹ [skaʊə(r)] VT (clean) fregar, restregar

scour² [skaʊə(r)] VT (search) (countryside) rastrear; (building) registrar

scourge [skɜ:dʒ] N Fig azote m

scout [skaʊt] 1 N (a) Mil explorador(a) m,f; Sport & Cin cazatalentos m inv; **boy s.** boy m scout 2 VI Mil reconocer el terreno; **to s. around for sth** andar en busca de algo

scowl [skaʊl] 1 VI fruncir el ceño; **to s. at sb** mirar a algn con ceño 2 N ceño m

scrabble ['skræbəl] VI escarbar; Fig **to s. around for sth** revolver todo para encontrar algo

scraggy ['skræɡɪ] ADJ (**scraggier, scraggiest**) delgado(a), flacucho(a)

scram [skræm] VI Fam largarse, Esp, RP pirarse; **s.!** ¡largo!

scramble ['skræmbəl] 1 VI trepar; **to s. for** pelearse por; **to s. up a tree** trepar a un árbol 2 VT (a) Culin **scrambled eggs** huevos revueltos (**b**) Rad & Tel (message) codificar; (broadcast) interferir 3 N (climb) subida f; Fig **it's going to be a s.** (rush) va a ser muy apresurado

scrap¹ [skræp] 1 N (a) (small piece) pedazo m; **there isn't a s. of truth in it** no tiene ni un ápice de verdad; **s. (metal)** chatarra f; **s. dealer** or **merchant** chatarrero(a) m,f; **s. paper** papel m de borrador; **s. yard** (for cars) cementerio m de coches (**b**) **scraps** restos mpl; (of food) sobras fpl 2 VT (discard) desechar; Fig (idea) descartar

scrap² [skræp] Fam N 1 (fight) pelea f 2 VI pelearse (**with** con)

scrapbook ['skræpbʊk] N álbum m de recortes

scrape [skreɪp] 1 VT (paint, wood) raspar; (knee) arañarse, hacerse un rasguño en 2 VI (make noise) chirriar; (rub) rozar 3 N Fam (trouble) lío m

▶ **scrape through** VI Fam (exam) aprobar por los pelos

▶ **scrape together** VT SEP reunir a duras penas

scraper ['skreɪpə(r)] N rasqueta f

scrapheap ['skræphi:p] N (dump) vertedero m

scratch [skrætʃ] 1 N (a) (on skin, paintwork) arañazo m; (on record) raya f (**b**) (noise)

chirrido *m* (**c**) *Fig* **to be up to s.** dar la talla; *Fig* **to start from s.** partir de cero
  2 ADJ **s. team** equipo improvisado
  3 VT (**a**) *(with nail, claw)* arañar, rasguñar; *(paintwork)* rayar (**b**) *(to relieve itching)* rascarse

scratchcard ['skrætʃkɑ:d] N tarjeta *f* de rasca y gana, boleto *m* de lotería instantánea, *Am* raspadito *m*

scrawl [skrɔ:l] **1** N garabatos *mpl*
  2 VT *(message etc)* garabatear
  3 VI hacer garabatos

scrawny ['skrɔ:nɪ] ADJ (**scrawnier, scrawniest**) flaco(a)

scream [skri:m] **1** N chillido *m*; **screams of laughter** carcajadas *fpl*
  2 VT *(insults etc)* gritar
  3 VI chillar; **to s. at sb** chillar a algn

scree [skri:] N pedregal *m*

screech [skri:tʃ] **1** N *(of person)* chillido *m*; *(of tyres, brakes)* chirrido *m*
  2 VI *(person)* chillar; *(tyres)* chirriar

screen [skri:n] **1** N (**a**) *(movable partition)* biombo *m* (**b**) *Fig* cortina *f* (**c**) *Cin, TV. & Comput* pantalla *f*
  2 VT (**a**) *(protect)* proteger; *(conceal)* tapar (**b**) *(candidates)* seleccionar (**c**) *(show) (film)* proyectar; *(for first time)* estrenar (**d**) *Med* examinar

screening ['skri:nɪŋ] N (**a**) *(of film)* proyección *f*; *(for first time)* estreno *m* (**b**) *Med* exploración *f*

screenplay ['skri:npleɪ] N guión *m*

screw [skru:] **1** N (**a**) *(for fixing)* tornillo *m* (**b**) *(propeller)* hélice *f*
  2 VT (**a**) *(fix)* atornillar; **to s. sth down** *or* **in** *or* **on** fijar algo con tornillos (**b**) *Vulg Esp* follar, *Am* coger
  ▶ **screw up** VT SEP (**a**) *(piece of paper)* arrugar; *(one's face)* torcer (**b**) *very Fam (ruin)* joder

screwdriver ['skru:draɪvə(r)] N destornillador *m*, *Am* desatornillador *m*

scribble ['skrɪbəl] **1** N garabatos *mpl*
  2 VT *(message etc)* garabatear
  3 VI hacer garabatos

script [skrɪpt] N (**a**) *(writing)* escritura *f*; *(handwriting)* letra *f*; *Typ* letra cursiva *f* (**b**) *(in exam)* escrito *m* (**c**) *Cin* guión *m*

Scripture ['skrɪptʃə(r)] N **Holy S.** Sagrada Escritura

scroll [skrəʊl] N rollo *m* de pergamino

scrounge [skraʊndʒ] *Fam* **1** VI gorrear, *Esp* gorronear; **to s. (around) for** buscar; **to s. off sb** vivir a costa de algn
  2 VT gorrear, *Esp* gorronear

scrounger ['skraʊndʒə(r)] N *Fam Esp, Méx* gorrón(ona) *m,f*, *RP* garronero(a) *m,f*

scrub¹ [skrʌb] N *(undergrowth)* maleza *f*

scrub² [skrʌb] **1** VT (**a**) *(floor, pots)* fregar (**b**) *Fam (cancel)* borrar
  2 N *(cleaning)* fregado *m*

scruff [skrʌf] N pescuezo *m*, cogote *m*

scruffy ['skrʌfɪ] ADJ (**scruffier, scruffiest**) *Fam* desaliñado(a)

scrum [skrʌm] N *Esp* melé *f*, *Am* scrum *f*; **s. half** *Esp* medio (de) melé *mf*, *Am* medio scrum *mf*

scruple ['skru:pəl] N escrúpulo *m*

scrupulous ['skru:pjʊləs] ADJ escrupuloso(a)

scrupulously ['skru:pjʊləslɪ] ADV **s. honest** sumamente honrado(a)

scrutinize ['skru:tɪnaɪz] VT escudriñar

scrutiny ['skru:tɪnɪ] N escrutinio *m*

scuba diving ['sku:bədaɪvɪŋ] N buceo *m*, submarinismo *m* (con botellas de oxígeno)

scuff [skʌf] VT *(floor)* rayar; *(one's feet)* arrastrar

scuffle ['skʌfəl] **1** N pelea *f*
  2 VI pelearse (**with** con)

scullery ['skʌlərɪ] N *Br* fregadero *m*, trascocina *f*

sculptor ['skʌlptə(r)] N escultor(a) *m,f*

sculpture ['skʌlptʃə(r)] N escultura *f*

scum [skʌm] N (**a**) *(on liquid)* espuma *f* (**b**) *Fig* escoria *f*

scupper ['skʌpə(r)] VT *Br Fam (plan etc)* desbaratar

scurrilous ['skʌrɪləs] ADJ *(abusive)* difamatorio(a)

scurry ['skʌrɪ] VI *(run)* corretear; *(hurry)* apresurarse; **to s. away** *or* **off** escabullirse

scuttle¹ ['skʌtəl] N cubo *m*; **coal s.** cubo del carbón

scuttle² ['skʌtəl] VT *(ship)* barrenar

scuttle³ ['skʌtəl] VI **to s. away** *or* **off** escabullirse

scythe [saɪð] **1** N guadaña *f*
  2 VT guadañar

sea [si:] N mar *m* or *f*; **by the s.** a orillas del mar; **out at s.** en alta mar; **to go by s.** ir en barco; **to put to s.** zarpar; *Fig* **to be all at s.** estar desorientado(a); **s. breeze** brisa marina; *Fig* **s. change** metamorfosis *f*; **s. level** nivel *m* del mar; **s. lion** león marino; **s. water** agua *f* de mar

seabed ['si:bed] N fondo *m* del mar

seaboard ['si:bɔ:d] N *US* costa *f*, litoral *m*

seafood ['si:fu:d] N marisco *m*, *Am* mariscos *mpl*

seafront ['si:frʌnt] N paseo marítimo

seagull ['si:gʌl] N gaviota *f*

seal¹ [si:l] N *Zool* foca *f*

seal² [si:l] **1** N (**a**) *(official stamp)* sello *m* (**b**) *(airtight closure)* cierre hermético; *(on bottle)* precinto *m*
  2 VT (**a**) *(with official stamp)* sellar; *(with wax)* lacrar (**b**) *(close)* cerrar; *(make airtight)* cerrar herméticamente (**c**) *(determine)* **this sealed his fate** esto decidío su destino
  ▶ **seal off** VT SEP *(pipe etc)* cerrar; *(area)* acordonar

seam [si:m] N (**a**) *Sewing* costura *f*; *Tech* juntura *f*; *Fam* **to be bursting at the seams** *(room)* rebosar de gente (**b**) *Geol & Min* veta *f*, filón *m*

seaman ['si:mən] N marinero m

seamy ['si:mɪ] ADJ (**seamier, seamiest**) Fig sórdido(a)

séance ['seɪɑ:ns] N sesión f de espiritismo

seaplane ['si:pleɪn] N hidroavión m

seaport ['si:pɔ:t] N puerto marítimo

search [sɜ:tʃ] **1** VT (files etc) buscar en; (building, suitcase) registrar; (person) cachear; (one's conscience) examinar
  2 VI buscar; **to s. through** registrar
  3 N búsqueda f; (of building etc) registro m; (of person) cacheo m; **in s. of** en busca de; Comput **s. engine** motor m de búsqueda; **s. party** equipo m de salvamento; **s. warrant** orden f de registro

searching ['sɜ:tʃɪŋ] ADJ (look) penetrante; (question) indagatorio(a)

searchlight ['sɜ:tʃlaɪt] N reflector m

seashell ['si:ʃel] N concha marina

seashore ['si:ʃɔ:(r)] N (beach) playa f

seasick ['si:sɪk] ADJ mareado(a); **to get s.** marearse

seaside ['si:saɪd] N playa f, costa f; **s. resort** lugar turístico de veraneo; **s. town** pueblo costero

season¹ ['si:zən] N época f; (of year) estación f; (for sport etc) temporada f; **the busy s.** la temporada alta; **the rainy s.** la estación de lluvias; **in s.** (fruit) en sazón; (animal) en celo; Br **s. ticket** abono m

season² ['si:zən] VT Culin sazonar

seasonal ['si:zənəl] ADJ estacional

seasoned ['si:zənd] ADJ (a) Culin sazonado(a) (b) Fig (campaigner) curtido(a), avezado(a)

seasoning ['si:zənɪŋ] N condimento m, aderezo m

seat [si:t] **1** N (a) (chair, in vehicle) asiento m; (in theatre, cinema) butaca f; **to take a s.** sentarse; Aut **s. belt** cinturón m de seguridad (b) (in parliament) escaño m
  2 VT (a) (guests etc) sentar (b) (accommodate) tener cabida para

seating ['si:tɪŋ] N asientos mpl

seaweed ['si:wi:d] N alga (marina)

seaworthy ['si:wɜ:ðɪ] ADJ en condiciones de navegar

sec [sek] N Fam (abbr **second**) segundo m

secede [sɪ'si:d] VI separarse (**from** de)

secluded [sɪ'klu:dɪd] ADJ retirado(a), apartado(a)

second¹ ['sekənd] **1** ADJ segundo(a); **every s. day** cada dos días; **it's the s. highest mountain** es la segunda montaña más alta; **on s. thought(s)** ... pensándolo bien ...; **to have s. thoughts about sth** dudar de algo; **to settle for s. best** conformarse con lo que hay
  2 N (a) (in series) segundo(a) m,f; **Charles the S.** Carlos Segundo; **the s. of October** el dos de octubre (b) Aut (gear) segunda f (c) Com **seconds** artículos defectuosos

  3 VT (motion) apoyar
  4 ADV **to come s.** terminar en segundo lugar

second² ['sekənd] N (time) segundo m; Fam **in a s.** enseguida; Fam **just a s.!** ¡un momentito!; **s. hand** (of watch, clock) segundero m

secondary ['sekəndərɪ] ADJ secundario(a); Br **s. school** escuela secundaria

second-class ['sekənd'klɑ:s] **1** ADJ Br (ticket, carriage) de segunda (clase)
  2 ADV **to travel s.** viajar en segunda

second-hand ['sekənd'hænd] ADJ & ADV de segunda mano

secondly ['sekəndlɪ] ADV en segundo lugar

secondment [sɪ'kɒndmənt] N Br traslado m temporal

second-rate ['sekənd'reɪt] ADJ de segunda categoría

secrecy ['si:krəsɪ] N secreto m; **in s.** en secreto

secret ['si:krɪt] **1** ADJ secreto(a); **to keep sth s.** mantener algo en secreto; **s. ballot** votación secreta
  2 N secreto m; Fig clave f; **in s.** en secreto; **to keep a s.** guardar un secreto

secretarial [sekrɪ'teərɪəl] ADJ de secretario(a)

secretary ['sekrətrɪ] N secretario(a) m,f; **S. of State** Br ministro(a) m,f con cartera; US ministro(a) m,f de Asuntos Exteriores

secretion [sɪ'kri:ʃən] N secreción f

secretive ['si:krɪtɪv] ADJ reservado(a)

secretly ['si:krɪtlɪ] ADV en secreto

sect [sekt] N secta f

sectarian [sek'teərɪən] ADJ & N sectario(a) (m,f)

section ['sekʃən] N (a) (part) sección f, parte f; (of law) artículo m; (of community) sector m; (of orchestra, department) sección (b) (cut) corte m

sector ['sektə(r)] N sector m

secular ['sekjʊlə(r)] ADJ (school, teaching) laico(a); (music, art) profano(a); (priest) seglar, secular

secure [sɪ'kjʊə(r)] **1** ADJ seguro(a); (window, door) bien cerrado(a); (ladder etc) firme
  2 VT (a) (make safe) asegurar (b) (fix) (rope, knot) sujetar, fijar; (object to floor) afianzar; (window, door) cerrar bien (c) (obtain) conseguir, obtener

security [sɪ'kjʊərɪtɪ] N (a) (stability, safety) seguridad f (b) Fin (for loan) fianza f (c) Fin **securities** valores mpl

sedan [sɪ'dæn] N (a) Hist **s. chair** silla f de manos (b) US Aut turismo m

sedate [sɪ'deɪt] **1** ADJ sosegado(a)
  2 VT sedar

sedation [sɪ'deɪʃən] N sedación f

sedative ['sedətɪv] ADJ & N sedante (m)

sediment ['sedɪmənt] N sedimento m; (of wine) poso m

seduce [sɪ'dju:s] VT seducir

seduction [sɪ'dʌkʃən] N seducción f

seductive [sɪ'dʌktɪv] ADJ seductor(a)

see¹ [siː] VT & VI (*pt* **saw**; *pp* **seen**) (**a**) (*with eyes, perceive*) ver; **let's s.** a ver; **to s. the world** recorrer el mundo; **s. you (later)/soon!** ¡hasta luego/pronto!; **s. page 10** véase la página 10; (**b**) (*meet with*) ver, tener cita con; **they are seeing each other** (*of couple*) salen juntos (**c**) (*understand*) entender; **as far as I can s.** por lo visto; **I s.** ya veo (**d**) **to s. sb home** acompañar a algn a casa

▸ **see about** VT INSEP (*deal with*) ocuparse de
▸ **see off** VT SEP (*say goodbye to*) despedirse de
▸ **see out** VT SEP (**a**) (*show out*) acompañar hasta la puerta (**b**) (*survive*) sobrevivir
▸ **see through 1** VT INSEP *Fam* **to s. through sb** verle el plumero a algn
  2 VT SEP (**a**) **I'll s. you through** puedes contar con mi ayuda; **£20 should s. me through** con 20 libras me las apaño (**b**) **to s. sth through** (*carry out*) llevar algo a cabo
▸ **see to** VT INSEP (*deal with*) ocuparse de

see² [siː] N *Rel* sede *f*; **the holy S.** la Santa Sede

seed [siːd] **1** N (**a**) *Bot* semilla *f*; (*of fruit*) pepita *f*; **to go to s.** (*of plant*) granar; *Fig* (*of person*) descuidarse (**b**) (*in tennis*) (*player*) cabeza *mf* de serie
  2 VT (**a**) (*sow with seed*) sembrar (**b**) (*grapes*) despepitar (**c**) (*in tennis*) preseleccionar

seedling ['siːdlɪŋ] N plantón *m*

seedy ['siːdɪ] ADJ (**seedier, seediest**) *Fam* (*bar etc*) sórdido(a); (*clothes*) raído(a); (*appearance*) desaseado(a)

seeing ['siːɪŋ] CONJ **s. that** visto que, dado que

seeing-eye dog ['siːɪŋaɪ'dɒg] N *US* perro *m* lazarillo

seek [siːk] **1** VT (*pt & pp* **sought**) (**a**) (*look for*) buscar (**b**) (*advice, help*) solicitar
  2 VT buscar; **to s. to do sth** procurar hacer algo
▸ **seek after** VT INSEP buscar; **much sought after** (*person*) muy solicitado(a); (*thing*) muy cotizado(a)

seem [siːm] VI parecer; **I s. to remember his name was Colin** creo recordar que su nombre era Colin; **it seems to me that** me parece que; **so it seems** eso parece

seeming ['siːmɪŋ] ADJ aparente

seemingly ['siːmɪŋlɪ] ADV aparentemente, según parece

seen [siːn] PP *of* **see**

seep [siːp] VI **to s. through/into/out** filtrarse por/en/de

seesaw ['siːsɔː] **1** N balancín *m*, subibaja *m*
  2 VI (*prices, mood*) fluctuar

seethe [siːð] VI bullir, hervir; *Fig* **to s. with anger** rabiar; **to s. with people** rebosar de gente

see-through ['siːθruː] ADJ transparente

segment ['segmənt] N segmento *m*; (*of orange*) gajo *m*

segregate ['segrɪgeɪt] VT segregar (**from** de)

segregation [segrɪ'geɪʃən] N segregación *f*

seize [siːz] VT (*grab*) agarrar, *Esp* coger; *Jur* (*property, drugs*) incautar; (*assets*) secuestrar; (*territory*) tomar; (*arrest*) detener; **to s. an opportunity** aprovechar una ocasión; **to s. power** hacerse con el poder
▸ **seize on** VT INSEP (*chance*) agarrar; (*idea*) aferrarse a
▸ **seize up** VI agarrotarse

seizure ['siːʒə(r)] N (**a**) *Jur* (*of property, drugs*) incautación *f*; (*of newspaper*) secuestro *m*; (*arrest*) detención *f* (**b**) *Med* ataque *m* (de apoplejía)

seldom ['seldəm] ADV rara vez, raramente

select [sɪ'lekt] **1** VT (*thing*) escoger, elegir; (*team*) seleccionar
  2 ADJ selecto(a)

selected [sɪ'lektɪd] ADJ escogido(a), escogido(a); (*team, player*) seleccionado(a); *Lit* **s. works** obras escogidas

selection [sɪ'lekʃən] N (*choosing*) elección *f*; (*people or things chosen*) selección *f*; (*range*) surtido *m*

selective [sɪ'lektɪv] ADJ selectivo(a)

self [self] N (*pl* **selves**) uno(a) mismo(a), sí mismo(a); *Psy* **the s.** el yo

self- [self] PREF auto-

self-addressed envelope ['selfədrest-'envələup] N sobre dirigido a uno mismo

self-adhesive [selfəd'hiːsɪv] ADJ autoadhesivo(a)

self-assured [selfə'ʃʊəd] ADJ seguro(a) de sí mismo(a)

self-catering [self'keɪtərɪŋ] ADJ sin servicio de comida

self-centred, *US* **self-centered** [self'sentəd] ADJ egocéntrico(a)

self-confessed [selfkən'fest] ADJ confeso(a)

self-confidence [self'kɒnfɪdəns] N confianza *f* en sí mismo(a)

self-confident [self'kɒnfɪdənt] ADJ seguro(a) de sí mismo(a)

self-conscious [self'kɒnʃəs] ADJ cohibido(a)

self-contained [selfkən'teɪnd] ADJ (*flat*) con entrada propia; (*person*) independiente

self-control [selfkən'trəul] N autocontrol *m*

self-defence, *US* **self-defense** [selfdɪ'fens] N autodefensa *f*

self-discipline [self'dɪsɪplɪn] N autodisciplina *f*

self-employed [selfɪm'plɔɪd] ADJ (*worker*) autónomo(a)

self-esteem [selfɪ'stiːm] N amor propio, autoestima *f*

self-evident [self'evɪdənt] ADJ evidente, patente

self-governing [self'gʌvənɪŋ] ADJ autónomo(a)

self-help [self'help] N autoayuda *f*

self-important [selfɪm'pɔːtənt] ADJ engreído(a), presumido(a)

self-indulgent [selfɪn'dʌldʒənt] ADJ inmoderado(a)

self-interest [self'ɪntrɪst] N egoísmo m

selfish ['selfɪʃ] ADJ egoísta

selfishness ['selfɪʃnɪs] N egoísmo m

selfless ['selflɪs] ADJ desinteresado(a)

self-made ['selfmeɪd] ADJ **s. man** hombre m que se ha hecho a sí mismo

self-pity [self'pɪtɪ] N autocompasión f

self-portrait [self'pɔːtreɪt] N autorretrato m

self-possessed [selfpə'zest] ADJ sereno(a), dueño(a) de sí mismo(a)

self-preservation [selfprezə'veɪʃən] N **(instinct of) s.** instinto m de conservación

self-raising ['selfreɪzɪŋ] ADJ **s. flour** Esp harina f con levadura, Am harina f con polvos de hornear, RP harina f leudante

self-reliant [selfrɪ'laɪənt] ADJ autosuficiente

self-respect [selfrɪ'spekt] N amor propio, dignidad f

self-righteous [self'raɪtʃəs] ADJ santurrón(ona)

self-rising ['selfraɪzɪŋ] ADJ US = self-raising

self-sacrifice ['self'sækrɪfaɪs] N abnegación f

self-satisfied [self'sætɪsfaɪd] ADJ satisfecho(a) de sí mismo(a)

self-service [self'sɜːvɪs] **1** N (in shop etc) autoservicio m
2 ADJ de autoservicio

self-sufficient [selfsə'fɪʃənt] ADJ autosuficiente

self-taught [self'tɔːt] ADJ autodidacta

sell [sel] **1** VT (pt & pp sold) vender
2 VI venderse; **this record is selling well** este disco se vende bien
3 N **hard/soft s.** (in advertising) publicidad f agresiva/discreta
▸ **sell off** VT SEP vender; (goods) liquidar
▸ **sell out 1** VI **to s. out to the enemy** claudicar ante el enemigo
2 VT SEP Com **we're sold out of sugar** se nos ha agotado el azúcar; Th **sold out** (sign) agotadas las localidades

sell-by date ['selbaɪdeɪt] N Com fecha f límite de venta

seller ['selə(r)] N vendedor(a) m,f

selling ['selɪŋ] N venta f; **s. point** atractivo m comercial; **s. price** precio m de venta

Sellotape® ['seləteɪp] **1** N Br cinta adhesiva, Esp celo m, CAm, Méx Durex® m
2 VT pegar o fijar con celo

sell-out ['selaʊt] N (a) Th éxito m de taquilla (b) (act of disloyalty) claudicación f

selves [selvz] PL of self

semaphore ['seməfɔː(r)] N semáforo m

semblance ['sembləns] N apariencia f; **there was some s. of truth in it** había algo de verdad en ello

semen ['siːmen] N semen m

semester [sɪ'mestə(r)] N semestre m

semi- ['semɪ] PREF semi-

semicircle ['semɪsɜːkəl] N semicírculo m

semicolon [semɪ'kəʊlən] N punto y coma m

semiconductor ['semɪkən'dʌktə(r)] N semiconductor m

semidetached [semɪdɪ'tætʃt] Br **1** ADJ adosado(a)
2 N chalé adosado, casa adosada

semifinal [semɪ'faɪnəl] N semifinal f

seminar ['semɪnɑː(r)] N seminario m

seminary ['semɪnərɪ] N seminario m

semitrailer ['semɪtreɪlə(r)] N US semirremolque m

semolina [semə'liːnə] N sémola f

senate ['senɪt] N (a) Pol senado m (b) Univ claustro m

senator ['senətə(r)] N senador(a) m,f

send [send] **1** VT (pt & pp sent) (a) (letter) enviar, mandar; (radio signal) transmitir; (rocket, ball) lanzar; **he was sent to prison** lo mandaron a la cárcel; **to s. sth flying** tirar algo (b) **to s. sb mad** (cause to become) volver loco(a) a algn
2 VI **to s. for sb** mandar llamar a algn; **to s. for sth** encargar algo
▸ **send away 1** VT SEP (dismiss) despedir
2 VI **to s. away for sth** escribir pidiendo algo
▸ **send back** VT SEP (goods etc) devolver; (person) hacer volver
▸ **send in** VT SEP (application etc) mandar; (troops) enviar
▸ **send off** VT SEP (a) (letter etc) enviar; (goods) despachar (b) Ftb (player) expulsar
▸ **send on** VT SEP (luggage) (ahead) facturar; (later) mandar (más tarde)
▸ **send out** VT SEP (a) (person) echar (b) (invitations) enviar (c) (emit) emitir
▸ **send up** VT SEP (a) (rocket) lanzar; (smoke) echar (b) Br Fam (parody) parodiar, remedar

sender ['sendə(r)] N remitente mf

sendoff ['sendɒf] N Fam despedida f

senile ['siːnaɪl] ADJ senil

senior ['siːnjə(r)] **1** ADJ (a) (in age) mayor; **William Armstrong S.** William Armstrong padre; **s. citizen** jubilado(a) m,f (b) (in rank) superior; (with longer service) más antiguo(a); Mil **s. officer** oficial mf de alta graduación
2 N (a) **she's three years my s.** (in age) me lleva tres años (b) US Educ estudiante mf del último curso

seniority [siːnɪ'ɒrɪtɪ] N antigüedad f

sensation [sen'seɪʃən] N sensación f; **to be a s.** ser un éxito; **to cause a s.** causar sensación

sensational [sen'seɪʃənəl] ADJ (marvellous) sensacional; (exaggerated) sensacionalista

sense [sens] 1 N (**a**) *(faculty)* sentido *m*; *(feeling)* sensación *f*; **s. of direction/humour** sentido *m* de la orientación/del humor (**b**) *(wisdom)* sentido *m* común, juicio *m*; **common s.** sentido común (**c**) *(meaning)* sentido *m*; *(of word)* significado *m*; **in a s.** en cierto sentido; **it doesn't make s.** no tiene sentido (**d**) **to come to one's senses** recobrar el juicio
2 VT sentir, percatarse de

senseless ['senslıs] ADJ (**a**) *(absurd)* insensato(a), absurdo(a) (**b**) *(unconscious)* sin conocimiento

sensibility [sensı'bılıtı] N (**a**) *(sensitivity)* sensibilidad *f* (**b**) **sensibilities** susceptibilidad *f*

sensible ['sensıbəl] ADJ (**a**) *(wise)* sensato(a) (**b**) *(choice)* acertado(a) (**c**) *(clothes, shoes)* práctico(a), cómodo(a)

> Note that the Spanish word **sensible** is a false friend and is never a translation for the English word **sensible**. In Spanish **sensible** means both "sensitive" and "perceptible, significant".

sensitive ['sensıtıv] ADJ (**a**) *(person)* sensible; *(touchy)* susceptible (**b**) *(skin)* delicado(a); *(document)* confidencial

sensitivity [sensı'tıvıtı] N sensibilidad *f*

sensor ['sensə(r)] N sensor *m*

sensual ['sensjʊəl] ADJ sensual

sensuous ['sensjʊəs] ADJ sensual

sent [sent] PT & PP OF **send**

sentence ['sentəns] 1 N (**a**) *Ling* oración *f*, frase *f* (**b**) *Jur* sentencia *f*; **to pass s. on sb** imponer una pena a algn; **life s.** cadena perpetua
2 VT *Jur* condenar

sentiment ['sentımənt] N (**a**) *(sentimentality)* sensiblería *f* (**b**) *(feeling)* sentimiento *m* (**c**) *(opinion)* opinión *f*

sentimental [sentı'mentəl] ADJ sentimental

sentry ['sentrı] N centinela *m*

separate 1 VT ['sepəreıt] separar (**from** de); *(divide)* dividir (**into** en); *(distinguish)* distinguir
2 VI separarse
3 ADJ ['sepərıt] separado(a); *(different)* distinto(a); *(entrance)* particular
4 NPL **separates** ['sepərıts] *(clothes)* piezas *fpl*

separately ['sepərətlı] ADV por separado

separation [sepə'reıʃən] N separación *f*

separatist ['sepərətıst] N separatista *mf*

September [sep'tembə(r)] N se(p)tiembre *m*

septic ['septık] ADJ séptico(a); **to become s.** *(of wound)* infectarse; **s. tank** fosa séptica

sequel ['si:kwəl] N secuela *f*; *(of film etc)* continuación *f*

sequence ['si:kwəns] N (**a**) *(order)* secuencia *f*, orden *m* (**b**) *(series)* serie *f*, sucesión *f*; *Cin* **film s.** secuencia *f*

Serbia ['sɜːbıə] N Serbia

Serbian ['sɜːbıən] ADJ & N Serbio(a) *(m,f)*

serenade [serı'neıd] N serenata *f*

serene [sı'ri:n] ADJ sereno(a), tranquilo(a)

sergeant ['sɑːdʒənt] N *Mil* sargento *mf*; *(of police)* ≃ oficial *mf* de policía; **s. major** sargento *mf* mayor

serial ['sıərıəl] N (**a**) *Rad & TV* serial *m*; *(soap opera)* radionovela *f*, telenovela *f* (**b**) **s. number** número *m* de serie

serialize ['sıərıəlaız] VT *(in newspaper, magazine)* publicar por entregas; *(on TV)* emitir en forma de serial

series ['sıəri:z] N *(pl* **series***)* serie *f*; *(of books)* colección *f*; *(of concerts, lectures)* ciclo *m*

serious ['sıərıəs] ADJ (**a**) *(solemn, earnest)* serio(a); **I am s.** hablo en serio (**b**) *(causing concern)* grave

seriously ['sıərıəslı] ADV (**a**) *(in earnest)* en serio (**b**) *(dangerously, severely)* gravemente

seriousness ['sıərıəsnıs] N gravedad *f*, seriedad *f*; **in all s.** hablando en serio

sermon ['sɜːmən] N sermón *m*

serpent ['sɜːpənt] N serpiente *f*

serrated [sı'reıtıd] ADJ dentado(a)

serum ['sıərəm] N suero *m*

servant ['sɜːvənt] N *(domestic)* criado(a) *m,f*; *Fig* servidor(a) *m,f*

serve [sɜːv] 1 VT (**a**) *(master, cause)* servir (**b**) *(customer)* atender a (**c**) *(in tennis)* servir (**d**) **it serves him right** bien merecido lo tiene
2 VI (**a**) *(carry out duty)* servir; **to s. on a committee** ser miembro de una comisión (**b**) *(in tennis)* servir
3 N *(in tennis)* servicio *m*

► **serve out, serve up** VT SEP servir

server ['sɜːvə(r)] N *Comput* servidor *m*

service ['sɜːvıs] 1 N (**a**) *(with army, firm)* servicio *m*; **at your s.!** ¡a sus órdenes!; **s. (charge) included** servicio incluido; **s. area** área *m* de servicio; **s. industry** sector *m* de servicios; **s. station** estación *f* de servicio (**b**) *Mil* **the Services** las Fuerzas Armadas (**c**) *(maintenance)* revisión *f* (**d**) *Rel* oficio *m*; *(mass)* misa *f* (**e**) *(in tennis)* servicio *m*
2 VT *(car, machine)* revisar

serviceable ['sɜːvısəbəl] ADJ (**a**) *(fit for use)* útil, servible (**b**) *(practical)* práctico(a)

serviceman ['sɜːvısmən] N militar *m*

serviette [sɜːvı'et] N *Br* servilleta *f*

servile ['sɜːvaıl] ADJ servil

serving ['sɜːvıŋ] N *(portion)* ración *f*; **s. spoon** cuchara *f* de servir

sesame ['sesəmı] N sésamo *m*

session ['seʃən] N (**a**) *(period of activity)* sesión *f*; **to be in s.** estar reunido(a); *(of Parliament, court)* celebrar una sesión (**b**) *Educ (academic year)* año académico

set[1] [set] 1 VT *(pt & pp* **set***)* (**a**) *(put, place)* poner, colocar; *(trap)* poner (**for** para); **the novel is s. in Moscow** la novela se desarrolla

en Moscú; **to s. fire to sth** prender fuego a algo; **to s. sb free** poner en libertad a algn (**b**) *(time, price)* fijar; *(record)* establecer; **to s. one's watch** poner el reloj en hora (**c**) *(bone)* encajar (**d**) *(arrange)* arreglar; **he s. the words to music** puso música a la letra; **to s. the table** poner la mesa (**e**) *(exam, homework)* poner; *(example)* dar; *(precedent)* sentar
 2 VI (**a**) *(sun, moon)* ponerse (**b**) *(jelly, jam)* cuajar; *(cement)* fraguar; *(bone)* encajarse (**c**) **to s. to** *(begin)* ponerse a
 3 N *(stage)* Cin plató *m*; Th escenario *m*; *(scenery)* decorado *m*
 4 ADJ (**a**) *(task, idea)* fijo(a); *(date, time)* señalado(a); *(opinion)* inflexible; **s. phrase** frase hecha; **to be s. on doing sth** estar empeñado(a) en hacer algo (**b**) *(ready)* listo(a)
► **set about** VT INSEP (**a**) *(begin)* empezar (**b**) *(attack)* agredir
► **set aside** VT SEP *(time, money)* reservar; *(differences)* dejar de lado
► **set back** VT SEP (**a**) *(delay)* retrasar; *(hinder)* entorpecer (**b**) *Fam (cost)* costar
► **set down** VT SEP *(luggage etc)* dejar (en el suelo); *Br (passengers)* dejar
► **set in** VI *(winter, rain)* comenzar; **panic s. in** cundió el pánico
► **set off 1** VI *(depart)* salir
 2 VT SEP *(bomb)* hacer estallar; *(burglar alarm)* hacer sonar; *(reaction)* desencadenar (**b**) *(enhance)* hacer resaltar
► **set out 1** VI *(depart)* salir; **to s. out for ...** partir hacia ... (**b**) **to s. out to do sth** proponerse hacer algo
 2 VT SEP *(arrange)* disponer; *(present)* presentar
► **set up 1** VT SEP (**a**) *(position)* colocar; *(statue, camp)* levantar; *(tent, stall)* montar (**b**) *(business etc)* establecer; *Fam* montar (**c**) *(committee)* constituir; *Fam* **you've been s. up!** ¡te han timado!
 2 VI establecerse

set² [set] N (**a**) *(series)* serie *f*; *(of golf clubs etc)* juego *m*; *(of tools)* estuche *m*; *(of books)* colección *f*; *(of teeth)* dentadura *f*; **chess s.** juego de ajedrez; **s. of cutlery** cubertería *f* (**b**) *(of people)* grupo *m*; *Pej (clique)* camarilla *f* (**c**) *Math* conjunto *m* (**d**) *(in tennis)* set *m* (**e**) *TV* **s.** televisor *m*

setback ['setbæk] N revés *m*, contratiempo *m*

settee [se'ti:] N sofá *m*

setting ['setɪŋ] N (**a**) *(background)* marco *m*; *(of novel, film)* escenario *m* (**b**) *(of jewel)* engaste *m*

settle ['setəl] **1** VT (**a**) *(put in position)* colocar (**b**) *(decide on)* acordar; *(date, price)* fijar; *(problem)* resolver; *(differences)* arreglar (**c**) *(debt)* pagar (**d**) *(nerves)* calmar; *(stomach)* asentar (**e**) *(establish) (person)* instalar
 2 VI (**a**) *(bird, insect)* posarse; *(dust)* depositarse; *(liquid)* asentarse; **to s. into an armchair** acomodarse en un sillón (**b**) *(put*

down roots) afincarse; *(in a colony)* asentarse (**c**) *(child, nerves)* calmarse (**d**) *(pay)* pagar; **to s. out of court** llegar a un acuerdo amistoso
► **settle down** VI (**a**) *(put down roots)* instalarse; *(marry)* casarse (**b**) **to s. down to work** ponerse a trabajar (**c**) *(child)* calmarse; *(situation)* normalizarse
► **settle for** VT INSEP conformarse con
► **settle in** VI *(move in)* instalarse; *(become adapted)* adaptarse
► **settle with** VT SEP *(pay debt to)* ajustar cuentas con

settlement ['setəlmənt] N (**a**) *(agreement)* acuerdo *m* (**b**) *(of debt)* pago *m* (**c**) *(colony)* asentamiento *m*; *(village)* poblado *m*

settler ['setlə(r)] N colono *m*

setup ['setʌp] N *(system)* sistema *m*; *(situation)* situación *f*; *Fam* Montaje *m*

seven ['sevən] ADJ & N siete *(m inv)*

seventeen [sevən'ti:n] ADJ & N diecisiete *(m inv)*, diez y siete *(m inv)*

seventeenth [sevən'ti:nθ] **1** ADJ & N decimoséptimo(a) *(m,f)*
 2 N *(fraction)* decimoséptima parte

seventh ['sevənθ] **1** ADJ & N séptimo(a) *(m,f)*
 2 N séptimo *m*

seventy ['sevəntɪ] ADJ & N setenta *(m inv)*

sever ['sevə(r)] VT *(cut)* cortar; *Fig (relations)* romper

several ['sevərəl] **1** ADJ (**a**) *(more than a few)* varios(as) (**b**) *(different)* distintos(as)
 2 PRON algunos(as)

severance ['sevərəns] N *(of relations etc)* ruptura *f*; **s. pay** indemnización *f* por despido

severe [sɪ'vɪə(r)] ADJ severo(a); *(climate, blow)* duro(a); *(illness, loss)* grave; *(pain)* intenso(a)

severity [sɪ'verɪtɪ] N *(of person, criticism, punishment)* severidad *f*; *(of climate)* rigor *m*; *(of illness)* gravedad *f*; *(of pain)* intensidad *f*; *(of style)* austeridad *f*

Seville [sə'vɪl] N Sevilla

sew [səʊ] VT & VI *(pt sewed; pp sewed or sewn)* coser
► **sew up** VT SEP *(stitch together)* coser; *(mend)* remendar

sewage ['su:ɪdʒ] N aguas *fpl* residuales

sewer ['su:ə(r)] N alcantarilla *f*, cloaca *f*

sewerage ['su:ərɪdʒ] N alcantarillado *m*

sewing ['səʊɪŋ] N costura *f*; **s. machine** máquina *f* de coser

sewn [səʊn] PP of **sew**

sex [seks] N sexo *m*; **s. education** educación *f* sexual; **to have s. with sb** tener relaciones sexuales con algn; **s. appeal** sex-appeal *m*

sexist ['seksɪst] ADJ & N sexista *(mf)*

sexual ['seksjʊəl] ADJ sexual

sexuality [seksjʊ'ælɪtɪ] N sexualidad *f*

sexy ['seksɪ] ADJ *(sexier, sexiest)* *Fam* sexi, erótico(a)

shabby ['ʃæbɪ] ADJ (**shabbier, shabbiest**) (**a**) *(garment)* raído(a); *(house)* desvencijado(a); *(person)* (*in rags*) harapiento(a); *(unkempt)* desaseado(a) (**b**) *(treatment)* mezquino(a)

shack [ʃæk] N casucha *f*, *Esp* chabola *f*, *CSur, Ven* rancho *m*

shackles ['ʃækəlz] NPL grilletes *mpl*, grillos *mpl*; *Fig* trabas *fpl*

shade [ʃeɪd] **1** N (**a**) *(shadow)* sombra *f*; **in the s.** a la sombra (**b**) *(eyeshade)* visera *f*; *(lampshade)* pantalla *f*; *US (blind)* persiana *f* (**c**) *(of colour)* tono *m*, matiz *m*; *Fig (of meaning)* matiz (**d**) *Fam* **shades** gafas *fpl* or *Am* anteojos *mpl* de sol
2 VT *(from sun)* proteger contra el sol

shadow ['ʃædəʊ] **1** N (**a**) *(shade)* sombra *f* (**b**) *Br* **the S. Cabinet** el gabinete de la oposición
2 VT *Fig* seguir la pista a

shadowy ['ʃædəʊɪ] ADJ *(dark)* oscuro(a); *(hazy)* vago(a)

shady ['ʃeɪdɪ] ADJ (**shadier, shadiest**) *(place)* a la sombra; *(suspicious) (person)* sospechoso(a); *(deal)* turbio(a)

shaft [ʃɑːft] N (**a**) *(of tool, golf club)* mango *m* (**b**) *Tech* eje *m* (**c**) *(of mine)* pozo *m*; *(of lift, elevator)* hueco *m* (**d**) *(beam of light)* rayo *m*

shaggy ['ʃægɪ] ADJ (**shaggier, shaggiest**) *(hairy)* peludo(a); *(long-haired)* melenudo(a); *(beard)* desgreñado(a)

shake [ʃeɪk] **1** N sacudida *f*
2 VT (*pt* **shook**; *pp* **shaken** ['ʃeɪkən]) *(carpet etc)* sacudir; *(bottle)* agitar; *(dice)* mover; *(building)* hacer temblar; **the news shook him** la noticia le conmocionó; **to s. hands with sb** estrechar la mano a algn; **to s. one's head** negar con la cabeza
3 VI *(person, building)* temblar; **to s. with cold** tiritar de frío

▸ **shake off** VT SEP (**a**) *(dust etc)* sacudirse (**b**) *Fig (bad habit)* librarse de; *(cough, cold)* quitarse or *Am* de encima; *(pursuer)* dar esquinazo a

▸ **shake up** VT SEP *Fig (shock)* trastornar; *(reorganize)* reorganizar

shake-up ['ʃeɪkʌp] N *Fig* reorganización *f*

shaky ['ʃeɪkɪ] ADJ (**shakier, shakiest**) *(hand, voice)* tembloroso(a); *(step)* inseguro(a); *(handwriting)* temblón(ona)

shall [ʃæl, *unstressed* ʃəl] V AUX

> En el inglés hablado, y en el escrito en estilo coloquial, el verbo **shall** se contrae de manera que **I/you/he** *etc* **shall** se transforman en **I'll/you'll/he'll** *etc*. La forma negativa **shall not** se transforma en **shan't**.

(**a**) *(used to form future tense) (first person only)* **I s.** or **I'll buy it** lo compraré; **I s. not** or **I shan't** say anything no diré nada (**b**) *(in suggestions, offers)* **s. I close the door?** ¿cierro la puerta?; **s. I mend it for you?** ¿quieres que te lo repare?; **s. we go?** ¿nos vamos? (**c**) *(emphatic, command,*

threat) (all persons) **we s. overcome** venceremos; **you s. leave immediately** te irás enseguida

shallow ['ʃæləʊ] ADJ poco profundo(a); *Fig* superficial

sham [ʃæm] **1** ADJ falso(a); *(illness etc)* fingido(a)
2 N (**a**) *(pretence)* engaño *m*, farsa *f* (**b**) *(person)* fantoche *m*
3 VT fingir, simular
4 VI fingir

shambles ['ʃæmbəlz] N SING confusión *f*; **the performance was a s.** la función fue un desastre

shame [ʃeɪm] **1** N (**a**) *(disgrace, guilt)* vergüenza *f*, *Am salvo RP* pena *f*; **to put to s.** *(far outdo)* eclipsar, sobrepasar (**b**) *(pity)* pena *f*, lástima *f*; **what a s.!** ¡qué pena!, ¡qué lástima!
2 VT avergonzar, *Am salvo RP* apenar; *(disgrace)* deshonrar

shamefaced ['ʃeɪmfeɪst] ADJ avergonzado(a), *Am salvo RP* apenado(a)

shameful ['ʃeɪmfʊl] ADJ vergonzoso(a)

shameless ['ʃeɪmlɪs] ADJ desvergonzado(a)

shampoo [ʃæm'puː] **1** N champú *m*
2 VT lavar con champú; **to s. one's hair** lavarse el pelo

shamrock ['ʃæmrɒk] N trébol *m*

shandy ['ʃændɪ] N *Br* cerveza *f* con gaseosa, *Esp* clara *f*

shan't [ʃɑːnt] = **shall not**

shantytown ['ʃæntɪtaʊn] N *Esp* barrio *m* de chabolas, *Am* barriada *f*, *Perú* pueblo *m* joven, *Arg, Bol* villa *f* miseria, *Chile* callampa *f*, *Méx* ciudad *f* perdida, *Urug* cantegril *m*

shape [ʃeɪp] **1** N (**a**) *(form)* forma *f*; *(shadow)* silueta *m*; **to take s.** tomar forma (**b**) **in good/bad s.** *(condition)* en buen/mal estado; **to be in good s.** *(health)* estar en forma
2 VT dar forma a; *(clay)* modelar; *(stone)* tallar; *(character)* formar; *(destiny)* determinar; **star-shaped** con forma de estrella
3 VI *(also* **s. up**) tomar forma; **to s. up well** *(events)* tomar buen cariz; *(person)* hacer progresos

▸ **share out** VT SEP repartir

shapeless ['ʃeɪplɪs] ADJ amorfo(a), informe

shapely ['ʃeɪplɪ] ADJ (**shapelier, shapeliest**) escultural

share ['ʃeə(r)] **1** N (**a**) *(portion)* parte *f* (**b**) *Fin* acción *f*; **s. index** índice *m* de la Bolsa; **s. prices** cotizaciones *fpl*
2 VT (**a**) *(divide)* dividir (**b**) *(have in common)* compartir
3 VI compartir

▸ **share out** VT SEP repartir

shareholder ['ʃeəhəʊldə(r)] N accionista *mf*

shark [ʃɑːk] N (**a**) *(fish)* tiburón *m* (**b**) *Fam (swindler)* estafador(a) *m,f*; **loan s.** usurero(a) *m,f*

sharp [ʃɑːp] **1** ADJ (**a**) *(razor, knife)* afilado(a), *Am* filoso(a); *(needle, pencil)* puntiagudo(a)

(**b**) *(bend)* cerrado(a) (**c**) *(contrast)* marcado(a) (**d**) *(clever)* listo(a); *(quick-witted)* avispado(a); *(cunning)* astuto(a) (**e**) *(pain, cry)* agudo(a) (**f**) *(sour)* acre (**g**) *(temper)* arisco(a); *(tone)* seco(a) (**h**) *Mus* sostenido(a)
2 ADV **at two o'clock s.** *(exactly)* a las dos en punto
3 N *Mus* sostenido *m*

sharpen ['ʃɑːpən] VT (**a**) *(knife)* afilar; *(pencil)* sacar punta a (**b**) *Fig (desire, intelligence)* agudizar

sharpener ['ʃɑːpənə(r)] N *(for knife)* afilador *m*; *(for pencil)* sacapuntas *m inv*

sharp-eyed ['ʃɑːpaɪd] ADJ con ojos de lince

sharply ['ʃɑːplɪ] ADV (**a**) *(abruptly)* bruscamente (**b**) *(clearly)* marcadamente

shat [ʃæt] PT & PP of **shit**

shatter ['ʃætə(r)] 1 VT hacer añicos; *(nerves)* destrozar; *(hopes)* frustrar
2 VI hacerse añicos

shattered ['ʃætəd] ADJ *Fam* **to be s.** *(stunned)* quedarse destrozado(a); *Br (exhausted)* estar rendido(a), *Méx* estar camotes

shave [ʃeɪv] 1 N afeitado *m*; **to have a s.** afeitarse; *Fig* **to have a close s.** escaparse por los pelos
2 VT *(pt* **shaved**; *pp* **shaved** *or* **shaven** ['ʃeɪvən]) *(person)* afeitar; *(wood)* cepillar
3 VI afeitarse

shaver ['ʃeɪvə(r)] N **(electric) s.** máquina *f* de afeitar

shaving ['ʃeɪvɪŋ] N (**a**) *(of wood)* viruta *f* (**b**) **s. brush** brocha *f* de afeitar; **s. cream** crema *f* de afeitar; **s. foam** espuma *f* de afeitar

shawl [ʃɔːl] N chal *m*, *Am* rebozo *m*

she [ʃiː] PERS PRON ella *(usually omitted in Spanish, except for contrast)*

she- [ʃiː] PREF *(of animal)* hembra; **s.-cat** gata *f*

sheaf [ʃiːf] N *(pl* **sheaves**) *Agr* gavilla *f*; *(of arrows)* haz *m*; *(of papers, banknotes)* fajo *m*

shear [ʃɪə(r)] 1 VT *(pt* **sheared**; *pp* **shorn** *or* **sheared**) *(sheep)* esquilar; **to s. off** cortar
2 VI esquilar ovejas

shears [ʃɪəz] NPL tijeras *fpl* (grandes)

sheath [ʃiːθ] N (**a**) *(for sword)* vaina *f*; *(for knife, scissors)* funda *f* (**b**) *(contraceptive)* preservativo *m*

sheaves [ʃiːvz] PL of **sheaf**

shed[1] [ʃed] N *(in garden)* cobertizo *m*; *(for cattle)* establo *m*; *(in factory)* nave *f*, *Andes, Carib, RP* galpón *m*

shed[2] [ʃed] VT *(pt & pp* **shed**) (**a**) *(clothes)* despojarse de; *(unwanted things)* deshacerse de; **the snake s. its skin** la serpiente mudó de piel (**b**) *(blood, tears)* derramar

sheen [ʃiːn] N brillo *m*

sheep [ʃiːp] N *(pl* **sheep**) oveja *f*

sheepdog ['ʃiːpdɒg] N perro *m* pastor

sheepish ['ʃiːpɪʃ] ADJ avergonzado(a)

sheepskin ['ʃiːpskɪn] N piel *f* de carnero

sheer [ʃɪə(r)] ADJ (**a**) *(utter)* total, puro(a) (**b**) *(cliff)* escarpado(a); *(drop)* vertical (**c**) *(stockings, cloth)* fino(a)

sheet [ʃiːt] N (**a**) *(on bed)* sábana *f* (**b**) *(of paper)* hoja *f*; *(of tin, glass, plastic)* lámina *f*; *(of ice)* capa *f*

sheik(h) [ʃeɪk] N jeque *m*

shelf [ʃelf] N *(pl* **shelves**) *(on bookcase)* estante *m*; *(in cupboard)* tabla *f*; **shelves** estantería *f*

shell [ʃel] 1 N (**a**) *(of egg, nut)* cáscara *f*; *(of pea)* vaina *f*; *(of tortoise etc)* caparazón *m*; *(of snail etc)* concha *f* (**b**) *(of building)* armazón *m* (**c**) *(mortar etc)* obús *m*, proyectil *m*; *(cartridge)* cartucho *m*; **s. shock** neurosis *f* de guerra
2 VT (**a**) *(peas)* desvainar; *(nuts)* pelar (**b**) *Mil* bombardear

shellfish ['ʃelfɪʃ] N *(pl* **shellfish**) marisco *m*, mariscos *mpl*

shelter ['ʃeltə(r)] 1 N (**a**) *(protection)* abrigo *m*, amparo *m*; **to take s. (from)** refugiarse (de) (**b**) *(place)* refugio *m*; *(for homeless)* asilo *m*; **bus s.** marquesina *f*
2 VT (**a**) *(protect)* abrigar, proteger (**b**) *(take into one's home)* ocultar
3 VI refugiarse

sheltered ['ʃeltəd] ADJ *(place)* abrigado(a); **to lead a s. life** vivir apartado(a) del mundo

shelve [ʃelv] VT *Fig (postpone)* dar carpetazo a

shelves [ʃelvz] PL of **shelf**

shelving ['ʃelvɪŋ] N estanterías *fpl*

shepherd ['ʃepəd] 1 N pastor *m*; **s.'s pie** = pastel de carne picada con puré de patatas *or Am* papas
2 VT *Fig* **to s. sb in** hacer entrar a algn

sheriff ['ʃerɪf] N *Br* = representante de la Corona; *Scot* ≃ juez *mf* de primera instancia; *US* sheriff *m*

sherry ['ʃerɪ] N jerez *m*

Shetland ['ʃetlənd] N **the S. Isles, S.** las Islas Shetland; **S. wool** lana *f* Shetland

shield [ʃiːld] 1 N (**a**) *(of knight)* escudo *m*; *(of policeman)* placa *f* (**b**) *(on machinery)* blindaje *m*
2 VT proteger (**from** de)

shift [ʃɪft] 1 N (**a**) *(change)* cambio *m*; *US Aut (gear)* **s.** cambio de velocidades (**b**) *(period of work, group of workers)* turno *m*; **to be on the day s.** hacer el turno de día
2 VT *(change)* cambiar; *(move)* cambiar de sitio, trasladar
3 VI *(move)* moverse; *(change place)* cambiar de sitio; *(opinion)* cambiar; *(wind)* cambiar de dirección

shiftless ['ʃɪftlɪs] N perezoso(a), vago(a)

shiftwork ['ʃɪftwɜːk] N trabajo *m* por turnos

shifty ['ʃɪftɪ] ADJ (**shiftier, shiftiest**) *(look)* furtivo(a); *(person)* sospechoso(a)

shilling ['ʃɪlɪŋ] N *Formerly* chelín *m*

shimmer ['ʃɪmə(r)] 1 VI relucir; *(shine)* brillar
2 N luz trémula, reflejo trémulo; *(shining)* brillo *m*

shin [ʃɪn] N espinilla f, RP canilla f; **s. pad** espinillera f, RP canillera f

shine [ʃaɪn] 1 VI (pt & pp **shone**) (a) (light) brillar; (metal) relucir (b) Fig (excel) sobresalir (**at** en)
2 VT (a) (lamp) dirigir (b) (pt & pp **shined**) (polish) sacar brillo a; (shoes) limpiar
3 N brillo m, lustre m

shingle ['ʃɪŋgəl] N (a) (pebbles) guijarros mpl (b) (roof tile) tablilla f

shingles ['ʃɪŋgəlz] N SING Med herpes m

shining ['ʃaɪnɪŋ] ADJ Fig (outstanding) ilustre

shiny ['ʃaɪnɪ] ADJ (**shinier, shiniest**) brillante

ship [ʃɪp] 1 N barco m, buque m
2 VT (a) (take on board) embarcar (b) (transport) transportar (en barco); (send) enviar, mandar

shipbuilding ['ʃɪpbɪldɪŋ] N construcción f naval

shipment ['ʃɪpmənt] N (a) (act) transporte m (b) (load) consignación f, envío m

shipper ['ʃɪpə(r)] N (person) cargador(a) m,f

shipping ['ʃɪpɪŋ] N (a) (ships) barcos mpl; **s. lane** vía f de navegación (b) (loading) embarque m; (transporting) transporte m (en barco); **s. company** compañía naviera

shipshape ['ʃɪpʃeɪp] ADJ & ADV en perfecto orden

shipwreck ['ʃɪprek] 1 N naufragio m
2 VT **to be shipwrecked** naufragar

shipyard ['ʃɪpjaːd] N astillero m

shire [ʃaɪə(r)] N Br condado m

shirk [ʃɜːk] 1 VT (duty) faltar a; (problem) eludir
2 VI gandulear

shirt [ʃɜːt] N camisa f; **in s. sleeves** en mangas de camisa; Fam **keep your s. on!** ¡no te sulfures!

shit [ʃɪt] Vulg 1 N (excrement) mierda f; (mess) porquería f, mierda f; **to** Br **have** or US **take a s.** cagar
2 VT (pt & pp **shitted** or **shat** [ʃæt]) **to s. oneself** (defecate) cagarse (encima); (be scared) cagarse or Esp jiñarse de miedo

shiver ['ʃɪvə(r)] 1 VI (with cold) tiritar; (with fear) temblar, estremecerse
2 N (with cold, fear) escalofrío m

shoal [ʃəʊl] N (of fish) banco m

shock [ʃɒk] 1 N (a) (jolt) choque m; **s. absorber** amortiguador m; **s. wave** onda expansiva (b) (upset) conmoción f; (scare) susto m (c) Med shock m
2 VT (upset) conmover; (startle) sobresaltar; (scandalize) escandalizar

shocking ['ʃɒkɪŋ] ADJ (a) (causing horror) espantoso(a); Fam (very bad) horroroso(a) (b) (disgraceful) escandaloso(a) (c) **s. pink** rosa chillón

shod [ʃɒd] PT & PP of **shoe**

shoddy ['ʃɒdɪ] ADJ (**shoddier, shoddiest**) (goods) de mala calidad; (work) chapucero(a)

shoe [ʃuː] 1 N (a) (for person) zapato m; **shoes** calzado m; **s. polish** betún m; **s. repair (shop)** remiendo m de zapatos; **s. shop,** US **s. store** zapatería f (b) (for horse) herradura f (c) (brake) s. zapata f
2 VT (pt & pp **shod**) (horse) herrar

shoebrush ['ʃuːbrʌʃ] N cepillo m para los zapatos

shoehorn ['ʃuːhɔːn] N calzador m

shoelace ['ʃuːleɪs] N cordón m (de zapatos)

shoestring ['ʃuːstrɪŋ] N Fig **to do sth on a s.** hacer algo con poquísimo dinero

shone [ʃɒn, US ʃəʊn] PT & PP of **shine**

shoo [ʃuː] 1 INTERJ ¡fuera!
2 VT **to s. (away)** espantar

shook [ʃʊk] PT of **shake**

shoot [ʃuːt] 1 N Bot retoño m; (of vine) sarmiento m
2 VT (pt & pp **shot**) (a) (fire at) pegar un tiro a; (kill) matar; (execute) fusilar; (hunt) cazar; **to s. dead** matar a tiros (b) (missile, glance) lanzar; (bullet, ball) disparar (c) (film) rodar, filmar; Phot fotografiar
3 VI (a) (with gun) disparar (**at sb** a algn); **to s. at a target** tirar al blanco; Ftb **to s. at the goal** chutar a puerta (b) **to s. past** or **by** pasar flechado(a)
▸ **shoot down** VT SEP (aircraft) derribar
▸ **shoot out** VI (person) salir disparado(a); (water) brotar; (flames) salir
▸ **shoot up** VI (a) (flames) salir; (water) brotar; (prices) dispararse (b) Fam (inject drugs) pincharse, Esp chutarse

shooting ['ʃuːtɪŋ] 1 N (a) (shots) tiros mpl; (murder) asesinato m; (hunting) caza f; **s. star** estrella f fugaz (b) (of film) rodaje m
2 ADJ (pain) punzante

shoot-out ['ʃuːtaʊt] N tiroteo m

shop [ʃɒp] 1 N (a) (for goods) tienda f; (large store) almacén m; **s. assistant** dependiente(a) m,f; **s. window** escaparate m, Am vidriera f, Am vitrina f (b) (workshop) taller m; **s. floor** (place) planta f; (workers) obreros mpl; **s. steward** enlace mf sindical
2 VI hacer compras; **to go shopping** ir de compras

shopkeeper ['ʃɒpkiːpə(r)] N tendero(a) m,f

shoplifter ['ʃɒplɪftə(r)] N ladrón(ona) m,f (de tiendas)

shopper ['ʃɒpə(r)] N comprador(a) m,f

shopping ['ʃɒpɪŋ] N (purchases) compra f/pl, Am compras f/pl; **s. bag/basket** bolsa f/cesta f de la compra; **s. centre** or **precinct** centro m comercial

shopsoiled ['ʃɒpsɔɪld], US **shopworn** ['ʃɒpwɔːn] ADJ deteriorado(a)

shore [ʃɔː(r)] N (of sea, lake) orilla f; US (beach) playa f; (coast) costa f; **to go on s.** desembarcar
▸ **shore up** VT SEP apuntalar

shorn [ʃɔːn] PP of **shear**

short [ʃɔːt] **1** ADJ (**a**) *(physically)* corto(a); *(person)* bajo(a), *Méx* chaparro(a), *RP* petiso(a); **in the s. term** a corto plazo; **s. circuit** cortocircuito *m*; **s. cut** atajo *m*; **s. story** relato corto, cuento *m*; **s. wave** onda corta (**b**) *(brief)* corto(a), breve; **"Bob" is s. for "Robert"** "Bob" es el diminutivo de "Robert"; **in s.** en pocas palabras (**c**) **to be s. of breath** faltarle a uno la respiración; **to be s. of food** andar escaso(a) de comida

2 ADV (**a**) **to pull up s.** pararse en seco (**b**) **to cut s.** *(holiday)* interrumpir; *(meeting)* suspender; **we're running s. of coffee** se nos está acabando el café (**c**) **s. of** *(except)* excepto, menos

shortage [ʃɔːtɪdʒ] N escasez *f*

shortbread [ʃɔːtbred] N mantecado *m*

short-change [ʃɔːtʃeɪndʒ] VT **to s. sb** no devolver el cambio completo a algn; *Fig* timar a algn

short-circuit [ʃɔːtsɜːkɪt] **1** VT provocar un cortocircuito en
2 VI tener un cortocircuito

shortcomings [ʃɔːtkʌmɪŋz] NPL defectos *mpl*

shortcrust [ʃɔːtkrʌst] N **s. pastry** pasta brisa

shorten [ʃɔːtən] VT *(skirt, visit)* acortar; *(word)* abreviar; *(text)* resumir

shortfall [ʃɔːtfɔːl] N déficit *m*

shorthand [ʃɔːthænd] N taquigrafía *f*; *Br* **s. typist** taquimecanógrafo(a) *m,f*

short-list [ʃɔːtlɪst] VT poner en la lista de seleccionados

short-lived [ʃɔːtlɪvd] ADJ efímero(a)

shortly [ʃɔːtlɪ] ADV *(soon)* dentro de poco; **s. after** poco después

short-range [ʃɔːtreɪndʒ] ADJ de corto alcance

shorts [ʃɔːts] NPL (**a**) *(short trousers)* pantalones *mpl* cortos; **a pair of s.** un pantalón corto (**b**) *US (underpants)* calzoncillos *mpl*

short-sighted [ʃɔːtsaɪtɪd] ADJ *(person)* miope; *Fig (plan etc)* sin visión de futuro

short-staffed [ʃɔːtstɑːft] ADJ escaso(a) de personal

short-tempered [ʃɔːttempəd] ADJ de mal genio

short-term [ʃɔːttɜːm] ADJ a corto plazo

shot¹ [ʃɒt] N (**a**) *(act, sound)* tiro *m*, disparo *m* (**b**) *(pellets)* perdigones *mpl* (**c**) *(person)* tirador(a) *m,f* (**d**) *Ftb (kick)* tiro *m* (a puerta); *(in billiards, cricket, golf)* golpe *m* (**e**) *(attempt)* tentativa *f*; **to have a s. at sth** intentar hacer algo (**f**) *(injection)* inyección *f*; *Fam* pinchazo *m* (**g**) *(drink)* trago *m* (**h**) *Phot* foto *f*; *Cin* toma *f*

shot² [ʃɒt] PT & PP *of* **shoot**

shotgun [ʃɒtgʌn] N escopeta *f*

should [ʃʊd, *unstressed* ʃəd] VAUX

En el inglés hablado, y en el escrito en estilo coloquial, la forma negativa **should not** se transforma en **shouldn't**.

(**a**) *(duty)* deber; **all employees s. wear helmets** todos los empleados deben llevar casco; **he s. have been an architect** debería haber sido arquitecto (**b**) *(probability)* deber de; **he s. have finished by now** ya debe de haber acabado; **this s. be interesting** esto promete ser interesante (**c**) *(conditional use)* **if anything strange s. happen** si pasara algo raro (**d**) **I s. like to ask a question** quisiera hacer una pregunta

shoulder [ʃəʊldə(r)] **1** N (**a**) *(of person)* hombro *m*; **s. blade** omóplato *m*; **s. strap** *(of garment)* tirante *m*, *CSur* bretel *m*; *(of bag)* correa *f*; *BrAut* **hard s.** arcén *m*, *Andes* berma *f*, *Méx* acotamiento *m*, *RP* banquina *f*, *Ven* hombrillo *m* (**b**) *(of meat)* paletilla *f* (**c**) *US Aut* arcén *m*, *Andes* berma *f*, *Méx* acotamiento *m*, *RP* banquina *f*, *Ven* hombrillo *m*
2 VT *Fig (responsibilities)* cargar con

shout [ʃaʊt] **1** N grito *m*
2 VT gritar
3 VI gritar; **to s. at sb** gritar a algn
▸ **shout down** VT SEP abuchear

shouting [ʃaʊtɪŋ] N gritos *mpl*, vocerío *m*

shove [ʃʌv] **1** N *Fam* empujón *m*
2 VT empujar; **to s. sth into one's pocket** meterse algo en el bolsillo a empellones
3 VI *(jostle)* dar empellones
▸ **shove off** VI *Fam* largarse
▸ **shove up** VI *Fam (move along)* correrse

shovel [ʃʌvəl] **1** N pala *f*; **mechanical s.** excavadora *f*
2 VT mover con pala *or* a paladas

show [ʃəʊ] **1** VT *(pt* **showed**; *pp* **shown** *or* **showed**) (**a**) *(ticket etc)* mostrar; *(painting etc)* exponer; *(film)* poner (**b**) *(display)* demostrar (**c**) *(explain)* explicar (**d**) *(temperature, way etc)* indicar (**e**) *(prove)* demostrar (**f**) *(conduct)* llevar; **to s. sb in** hacer pasar a algn; **to s. sb to the door** acompañar a algn hasta la puerta
2 VI *(be visible)* notarse
3 N (**a**) *(display)* demostración *f* (**b**) *(outward appearance)* apariencia *f* (**c**) *(exhibition)* exposición *f*; **on s.** expuesto(a) (**d**) *Th (entertainment)* espectáculo *m*; *(performance)* función *f*; *Rad & TV* programa *m*; **s. business** *or Fam* **biz** el mundo del espectáculo
▸ **show off** **1** VT SEP (**a**) *(highlight)* hacer resaltar (**b**) *Fam (flaunt)* hacer alarde de
2 VI *Fam* farolear
▸ **show up** **1** VT SEP (**a**) *(reveal)* sacar a luz; *(highlight)* hacer resaltar (**b**) *Fam (embarrass)* dejar en evidencia
2 VI (**a**) *(stand out)* destacarse (**b**) *Fam (arrive)* aparecer

showdown [ʃəʊdaʊn] N enfrentamiento *m*

shower [ʃaʊə(r)] **1** N (**a**) *(rain)* chubasco *m*, chaparrón *m* (**b**) *Fig (of stones, insults)* lluvia *f* (**c**) *(bath)* ducha *f*, *Col, Méx, Ven* regadera *f*; **to have a s.** ducharse
2 VT (**a**) *(spray)* rociar (**b**) *Fig* **to s. gifts/**

praise on sb colmar a algn de regalos/elogios
3 vi ducharse

showerproof ['ʃaʊəpruːf] ADJ impermeable

showery ['ʃaʊərɪ] ADJ lluvioso(a)

showing ['ʃəʊɪŋ] N (of film) proyección f

showjumping ['ʃəʊdʒʌmpɪŋ] N hípica f

shown [ʃəʊn] PP of **show**

show-off ['ʃəʊɒf] N Fam fanfarrón(ona) m,f,
Esp fantasma mf

showpiece ['ʃəʊpiːs] N (in exhibition etc) obra
maestra; Fig (at school etc) modelo m

showroom ['ʃəʊruːm] N Com exposición f; Art
galería f

showy ['ʃəʊɪ] ADJ (**showier, showiest**) llama-
tivo(a)

shrank [ʃræŋk] PT of **shrink**

shrapnel ['ʃræpnəl] N metralla f

shred [ʃred] **1** N (a) triza f; (of cloth) jirón m; (of
paper) tira f
2 VT (paper) hacer trizas; (vegetables) rallar

shredder ['ʃredə(r)] N (for waste paper)
trituradora f; (for vegetables) rallador m

shrew [ʃruː] N (a) Zool musaraña f (b) Fig
(woman) arpía f

shrewd [ʃruːd] ADJ astuto(a); (clear-sighted)
perspicaz; (wise) sabio(a); (decision) acerta-
do(a)

shriek [ʃriːk] **1** N chillido m; **shrieks of
laughter** carcajadas fpl
2 VI chillar

shrill [ʃrɪl] ADJ agudo(a), estridente

shrimp [ʃrɪmp] N Br camarón m, quisquilla f; US
(prawn) gamba f

shrine [ʃraɪn] N (tomb) sepulcro m; (chapel)
capilla f; (holy place) lugar sagrado

shrink [ʃrɪŋk] **1** VT (pt shrank; pp shrunk)
encoger
2 VI (a) (clothes) encoger(se) (b) (savings)
disminuir (c) **to s. (back)** echarse atrás; **to s.
from doing sth** no tener valor para hacer algo
3 N Fam (psychiatrist) psiquiatra mf

shrinkage ['ʃrɪŋkɪdʒ] N (a) (of cloth) encogimiento m; (of metal) contracción f (b) (of
savings etc) disminución f

shrink-wrapped ['ʃrɪŋkræpt] ADJ envuelto(a)
en plástico

shrivel ['ʃrɪvəl] **1** VT **to s. (up)** encoger; (plant)
secar; (skin) arrugar
2 VI encogerse; (plant) secarse; (skin)
arrugarse

shroud [ʃraʊd] **1** N Rel sudario m
2 VT Fig envolver

Shrove Tuesday ['ʃrəʊv'tjuːzdɪ] N martes m de
carnaval

shrub [ʃrʌb] N arbusto m

shrubbery ['ʃrʌbərɪ] N arbustos mpl

shrug [ʃrʌg] **1** VT **to s. one's shoulders**
encogerse de hombros
2 VI encogerse de hombros
3 N encogimiento m de hombros

▸ **shrug off** VT SEP no dejarse desanimar por

shrunk [ʃrʌŋk] PP of **shrink**

shrunken ['ʃrʌŋkən] ADJ encogido(a)

shudder ['ʃʌdə(r)] **1** N (a) (of person) estremecimiento m (b) (of machinery) sacudida f
2 VI (a) (person) estremecerse (b) (machinery) dar sacudidas

shuffle ['ʃʌfəl] **1** VT (a) (feet) arrastrar (b)
(papers etc) revolver; (cards) barajar
2 VI (a) (walk) andar arrastrando los pies (b)
Cards barajar

shun [ʃʌn] VT (person) esquivar; (responsibility)
rehuir

shunt [ʃʌnt] VT Rail cambiar de vía; Elec derivar

shut [ʃʌt] **1** VT (pt & pp shut) cerrar
2 VI cerrarse
3 ADJ cerrado(a)

▸ **shut down 1** VT SEP (factory) cerrar
2 VI (factory) cerrar

▸ **shut off** VT SEP (gas, water etc) cortar

▸ **shut out** VT SEP (a) (lock out) dejar fuera a (b)
(exclude) excluir

▸ **shut up 1** VT SEP (a) (close) cerrar (b)
(imprison) encerrar (c) Fam (silence) callar
2 VI Fam (keep quiet) callarse

shutdown ['ʃʌtdaʊn] N cierre m

shutter ['ʃʌtə(r)] N (a) (on window) contraventana f, postigo m (b) Phot obturador m

shuttle ['ʃʌtəl] **1** N (a) (in weaving) lanzadera f
(b) Av puente aéreo; **(space) s.** transbordador
m espacial
2 VI ir y venir

shuttlecock ['ʃʌtəlkɒk] N volante m

shy [ʃaɪ] **1** ADJ (**shyer, shyest** or **shier, shiest**)
(timid) tímido(a), Am salvo RP penoso(a); (re-
served) reservado(a)
2 VI (horse) espantarse (**at** de); Fig **to s. away
from doing sth** negarse a hacer algo

shyness ['ʃaɪnɪs] N timidez f

Siberia [saɪ'bɪərɪə] N Siberia

sibling ['sɪblɪŋ] N Fml (brother) hermano m;
(sister) hermana f; **siblings** hermanos

Sicily ['sɪsɪlɪ] N Sicilia

sick [sɪk] ADJ (a) (ill) enfermo(a); **s. leave** baja
f por enfermedad; **s. pay** subsidio m de
enfermedad (b) **to feel s.** (about to vomit) tener
ganas de devolver; **to be s.** devolver (c)
Fam (fed up) harto(a) (d) Fam (mind, joke)
morboso(a); **s. humour** humor negro

sickbay ['sɪkbeɪ] N enfermería f

sicken ['sɪkən] **1** VT (make ill) poner enfermo;
(revolt) dar asco a
2 VI (fall ill) enfermar

sickening ['sɪkənɪŋ] ADJ nauseabundo(a);
(revolting) repugnante; (horrifying) escalofriante

sickle ['sɪkəl] N hoz f

sickly ['sɪklɪ] ADJ (**sicklier, sickliest**) (a) (person)
enfermizo(a) (b) (taste) empalagoso(a) (c)
(smile) forzado(a)

sickness ['sɪknɪs] N (**a**) *(illness)* enfermedad *f* (**b**) *(nausea)* náuseas *fpl*

side [saɪd] **1** N (**a**) *(side) (of house, box, square)* lado *m*; *(of coin, sheet of paper)* cara *f*; *(of hill)* ladera *f* (**b**) *(of body)* costado *m*; *(of animal)* ijar *m*; **by my s.** a mi lado; **s. by s.** juntos (**c**) *(edge)* borde *m*; *(of lake, river)* orilla *f* (**d**) *Fig (aspect)* aspecto *m* (**e**) *(team)* equipo *m*; *Pol* partido *m*; **she's on our s.** está de nuestro lado; **to take sides with sb** ponerse de parte de algn; **s. effect** efecto secundario; **s. entrance** entrada *f* lateral; **s. street** calle *f* lateral
2 VI **to s. with sb** ponerse de parte de algn

sideboard ['saɪdbɔ:d] N aparador *m*

sideburns ['saɪdbɜ:nz], *Br* **sideboards** ['saɪdbɔ:dz] NPL patillas *fpl*

sidelight ['saɪdlaɪt] N *Aut* luz *f* lateral, piloto *m*

sideline ['saɪdlaɪn] N (**a**) *Sport* línea *f* de banda (**b**) *Com (product)* línea suplementaria; *(job)* empleo suplementario

sidelong ['saɪdlɒŋ] ADJ de reojo

side-saddle ['saɪdsædəl] **1** N silla *f* de amazona
2 ADV **to ride s.** montar a la inglesa

sideshow ['saɪdʃəʊ] N atracción secundaria

sidestep ['saɪdstep] VT *(issue)* esquivar

sidetrack ['saɪdtræk] VT *Fig (person)* despistar

sidewalk ['saɪdwɔ:k] N *US* acera *f*, *CSur* vereda *f*, *CAm, Méx* banqueta *f*

sideways ['saɪdweɪz] **1** ADJ *(movement)* lateral; *(look)* de reojo
2 ADV de lado

siding ['saɪdɪŋ] N *(on railway)* apartadero *m*; *(connected at only one end to main track)* vía *f* muerta

sidle ['saɪdəl] VI **to s. up to sb** acercarse furtivamente a algn

siege [si:dʒ] N sitio *m*, cerco *m*; **to lay s. to** sitiar

sieve [sɪv] **1** N *(fine)* tamiz *m*; *(coarse)* criba *f*
2 VT *(fine)* tamizar; *(coarse)* cribar

sift [sɪft] VT *(sieve)* tamizar; *Fig* **to s. through** examinar cuidadosamente

sigh [saɪ] **1** VI suspirar
2 N suspiro *m*

sight [saɪt] **1** N (**a**) *(faculty)* vista *f*; **at first s.** a primera vista; **to catch s. of** divisar; **to know by s.** conocer de vista; **to lose s. of sth/sb** perder algo/a algn de vista (**b**) *(range of vision)* vista *f*; **within s.** a la vista; **to come into s.** aparecer (**c**) *(spectacle)* espectáculo *m* (**d**) *(on gun)* mira *f*; *Fig* **to set one's sights on** tener la mira puesta en (**e**) **the sights** *(of city)* los lugares de interés
2 VT ver; *(land)* divisar

sightseeing ['saɪtsi:ɪŋ] N turismo *m*; **to go s.** hacer turismo

sign [saɪn] **1** N (**a**) *(symbol)* signo *m* (**b**) *(gesture)* gesto *m*, seña *f*; *(signal)* señal *f* (**c**) *(indication)* señal *f*; *(trace)* rastro *m*, huella *f* (**d**) *(notice)* anuncio *m*; *(board)* letrero *m*

2 VT (**a**) *(letter etc)* firmar (**b**) *Ftb* fichar
3 VI firmar

▸ **sign on** VI *Br (worker)* firmar un contrato; *Br Fam* = registrarse para recibir el seguro de desempleo, *Esp* apuntarse al paro; *(regularly)* ir a firmar *or Esp* sellar

▸ **sign up 1** VT SEP *(soldier)* reclutar; *(worker)* contratar
2 VI *(soldier)* alistarse; *(worker)* firmar un contrato

signal ['sɪgnəl] **1** N señal *f*; *Rad & TV* sintonía *f*; *Rail* **s. box** garita *f* de señales
2 VT (**a**) *(message)* transmitir por señales (**b**) *(direction etc)* indicar
3 VI *(with hands)* hacer señales; *(in car)* señalar

signalman ['sɪgnəlmən] N guardavía *m*

signature ['sɪgnɪtʃə(r)] N *(name)* firma *f*; *Rad & TV* **s. tune** sintonía *f*

signet ['sɪgnɪt] N **s. ring** (anillo *m* de) sello *m*

significance [sɪg'nɪfɪkəns] N *(meaning)* significado *m*; *(importance)* importancia *f*

significant [sɪg'nɪfɪkənt] ADJ *(meaningful)* significativo(a); *(important)* importante

significantly [sɪg'nɪfɪkəntlɪ] ADV *(markedly)* sensiblemente

signify ['sɪgnɪfaɪ] VT (**a**) *(mean)* significar (**b**) *(show, make known)* indicar

signpost ['saɪnpəʊst] N poste *m* indicador

Sikh [si:k] ADJ & N sij *(mf)*

silence ['saɪləns] **1** N silencio *m*
2 VT acallar; *(engine)* silenciar

silencer ['saɪlənsə(r)] N (**a**) *(on gun)* silenciador *m* (**b**) *Br (on car)* silenciador *m*

silent ['saɪlənt] ADJ silencioso(a); *(not talkative)* callado(a); *(film)* mudo(a); **be s.!** ¡cállate!; **to remain s.** guardar silencio

silently ['saɪləntlɪ] ADV silenciosamente

silhouette [sɪlu:'et] N silueta *f*

silicon ['sɪlɪkən] N silicio *m*; **s. chip** chip *m* (de silicio)

silk [sɪlk] **1** N seda *f*
2 ADJ de seda

silky ['sɪlkɪ] ADJ (**silkier, silkiest**) *(cloth)* sedoso(a); *(voice etc)* aterciopelado(a)

sill [sɪl] N *(of window)* alféizar *m*

silly ['sɪlɪ] ADJ (**sillier, silliest**) tonto(a)

silo ['saɪləʊ] N silo *m*

silt [sɪlt] N cieno *m*

▸ **silt up** VI obstruirse con cieno

silver ['sɪlvə(r)] **1** N (**a**) *(metal)* plata *f* (**b**) *Br (coins)* monedas *fpl* plateadas *(de entre 5 y 50 peniques)* (**c**) *(tableware)* vajilla *f* de plata
2 ADJ de plata; **s. foil** *(tinfoil)* papel *m* de aluminio; *Br* **s. paper** papel de plata; **s. wedding** bodas *fpl* de plata

silver-plated [sɪlvə'pleɪtɪd] ADJ plateado(a)

silversmith ['sɪlvəsmɪθ] N platero(a) *m,f*

silverware ['sɪlvəweə(r)] N vajilla *f* de plata

silvery ['sɪlvərɪ] ADJ plateado(a)

similar ['sɪmɪlə(r)] ADJ parecido(a), semejante (**to** a); **to be s.** parecerse

similarity [sɪmɪ'lærɪtɪ] N semejanza f

similarly ['sɪmɪlɪ] ADV (**a**) *(as well)* igualmente (**b**) *(likewise)* del mismo modo, asimismo

simile ['sɪmɪlɪ] N símil m

simmer ['sɪmə(r)] **1** VT cocer a fuego lento
2 VI cocerse a fuego lento
► **simmer down** VI *Fam* calmarse

simpering ['sɪmpərɪŋ] ADJ melindroso(a)

simple ['sɪmpəl] ADJ (**a**) *(uncomplicated)* sencillo(a); **s. interest** interés m simple (**b**) *(natural)* natural (**c**) *(foolish)* simple; *(naïve)* ingenuo(a); *(dim)* de pocas luces

simplicity [sɪm'plɪsɪtɪ] N (**a**) *(easiness)* sencillez f (**b**) *(naïveté)* ingenuidad f

simplify ['sɪmplɪfaɪ] VT simplificar

simply ['sɪmplɪ] ADV (**a**) *(plainly)* sencillamente (**b**) *(only)* simplemente, sólo

simulate ['sɪmjʊleɪt] VT simular

simulator ['sɪmjʊleɪtə(r)] N **flight s.** simulador m de vuelo

simultaneous [sɪməl'teɪnɪəs] ADJ simultáneo(a)

simultaneously [sɪməl'teɪnɪəslɪ] ADV simultáneamente

sin [sɪn] **1** N pecado m
2 VI pecar

since [sɪns] **1** ADV *(ever)* **s.** desde entonces; **long s.** hace mucho tiempo; **it has s. come out that ...** desde entonces se ha sabido que ...
2 PREP desde; **she has been living here s. 1975** vive aquí desde 1975
3 CONJ (**a**) *(time)* desde que; **how long is it s. you last saw him?** ¿cuánto tiempo hace que lo viste por última vez? (**b**) *(because, as)* ya que, puesto que

sincere [sɪn'sɪə(r)] ADJ sincero(a)

sincerely [sɪn'sɪəlɪ] ADV sinceramente; **Yours s.** *(in letter)* Atentamente

sincerity [sɪn'serɪtɪ] N sinceridad f

sinew ['sɪnju:] N *(tendon)* tendón m; *(in meat)* nervio m

sinful ['sɪnfʊl] ADJ *(person)* pecador(a); *(act, thought)* pecaminoso(a); *Fig (waste etc)* escandaloso(a)

sing [sɪŋ] **1** VT *(pt sang; pp sung)* cantar
2 VI *(person, bird)* cantar; *(kettle, bullets)* silbar

singe [sɪndʒ] VT chamuscar

singer ['sɪŋə(r)] N cantante mf

singing ['sɪŋɪŋ] N *(art)* canto m; *(songs)* canciones fpl; *(of kettle)* silbido m

single ['sɪŋgəl] **1** ADJ (**a**) *(solitary)* solo(a) (**b**) *(only one)* único(a) (**c**) *(not double)* sencillo(a); **s. bed/room** cama f/habitación f individual (**d**) *(unmarried)* soltero(a)
2 N (**a**) *Br Rail* billete m or *Am* boleto m or *Am*

pasaje m sencillo or de ida (**b**) *(record)* single m; *(c)* *Sport* **singles** individuales mpl
► **single out** VT SEP *(choose)* escoger; *(distinguish)* distinguir

single-breasted ['sɪŋgəl'brestɪd] ADJ *(suit, jacket)* recto(a)

single-handed ['sɪŋgəl'hændɪd] ADJ & ADV sin ayuda

single-minded ['sɪŋgəl'maɪndɪd] ADJ resuelto(a)

singlet ['sɪŋglɪt] N *Br* camiseta f (de tirantes or *Am* breteles)

singly ['sɪŋglɪ] ADV *(individually)* por separado; *(one by one)* uno por uno

singular ['sɪŋgjʊlə(r)] **1** ADJ (**a**) *Ling* singular (**b**) *Fml (outstanding)* excepcional (**c**) *Fml (unique)* único(a)
2 N *Ling* singular m

singularly ['sɪŋgjʊləlɪ] ADV excepcionalmente

sinister ['sɪnɪstə(r)] ADJ siniestro(a)

sink¹ [sɪŋk] N *(in kitchen)* fregadero m; *(in bathroom)* lavabo m, *Am* lavamanos m inv

sink² [sɪŋk] **1** VT *(pt sank; pp sunk)* (**a**) *(ship)* hundir, echar a pique; *Fig (hopes)* acabar con (**b**) *(hole, well)* cavar; *(post, knife, teeth)* hincar
2 VI (**a**) *(ship)* hundirse (**b**) *Fig* **my heart sank** se me cayó el alma a los pies (**c**) *(sun)* ponerse (**d**) **to s. to one's knees** hincarse de rodillas
► **sink in** VI *(penetrate)* penetrar; *Fig* **it hasn't sunk in yet** todavía no me he/se ha/*etc* hecho a la idea

sinner ['sɪnə(r)] N pecador(a) m,f

sinus ['saɪnəs] N seno m *(nasal)*

sip [sɪp] **1** N sorbo m
2 VT sorber, beber a sorbos

siphon ['saɪfən] N sifón m
► **siphon off** VT SEP *(liquid)* sacar con sifón; *Fig (funds, capital)* desviar

sir [sɜː(r)] N *Fml* (**a**) *(form of address)* señor m; **yes, s.** sí, señor (**b**) *(title)* **S. Walter Raleigh** Sir Walter Raleigh

siren ['saɪrən] N sirena f

sirloin ['sɜːlɔɪn] N solomillo m

sissy ['sɪsɪ] N *Fam (coward)* miedica mf

sister ['sɪstə(r)] N (**a**) *(relation)* hermana f (**b**) *Br Med* enfermera f jefe (**c**) *Rel* hermana f; **s. Teresa** sor Teresa

sister-in-law ['sɪstərɪnlɔː] N cuñada f

sit [sɪt] **1** VT *(pt & pp sat)* (**a**) *(child etc)* sentar (**in/on** en) (**b**) *Br (exam)* presentarse a
2 VI (**a**) *(action)* sentarse (**b**) *(be seated)* estar sentado(a) (**c**) *(object)* estar; *(be situated)* hallarse; *(person)* quedarse (**d**) *(assembly)* reunirse
► **sit back** VI recostarse
► **sit down** VI sentarse
► **sit in on** VT INSEP asistir sin participar a
► **sit out** VT SEP aguantar hasta el final
► **sit through** VT INSEP aguantar

▸ **sit up** VI (**a**) *(from lying position)* incorporarse (**b**) *(stay up late)* quedarse levantado(a)

sitcom ['sɪtkɒm] N *TV* telecomedia *f* (de situación)

site [saɪt] **1** N (**a**) *(area)* lugar *m*; **building s.** solar *m*; *(under construction)* obra *f* (**b**) *(location)* situación *f*; **nuclear testing s.** zona *f* de pruebas nucleares
2 VT situar

sit-in ['sɪtɪn] N *Fam (demonstration)* sentada *f*; *(strike)* huelga *f* de brazos caídos

sitting ['sɪtɪŋ] **1** N *(of committee)* sesión *f*; *(in canteen)* turno *m*
2 ADJ *Br* **s. room** sala *f* de estar

situated ['sɪtjʊeɪtɪd] ADJ situado(a), ubicado(a)

situation [sɪtjʊ'eɪʃən] N (**a**) *(circumstances)* situación *f* (**b**) *(job)* puesto *m*; *Br* **situations vacant** *(in newspaper)* ofertas de trabajo

six [sɪks] ADJ & N seis *(m inv)*

sixteen [sɪks'tiːn] ADJ & N dieciséis *(m inv)*, diez y seis *(m inv)*

sixteenth [sɪks'tiːnθ] **1** ADJ & N decimosexto(a) *(m,f)*
2 N *(fraction)* dieciseisavo *m*

sixth [sɪksθ] **1** ADJ sexto(a); *Br Educ* **the s. form** = últimos dos cursos del bachillerato británico previos a los estudios superiores; *Br Educ* **s. former** = estudiante de los dos últimos cursos del bachillerato británico
2 N (**a**) *(in series)* sexto(a) *m,f* (**b**) *(fraction)* sexto *m*, sexta parte

sixty ['sɪkstɪ] ADJ & N sesenta *(m inv)*

sizable ['saɪzəbəl] ADJ = sizeable

size [saɪz] N tamaño *m*; *(of garment)* talla *f*; *(of shoes)* número *m*; *(of person)* estatura *f*; *(scope)* alcance *m*; **what s. do you take?** *(garment)* ¿qué talla tienes?; *(shoes)* ¿qué número calzas?

▸ **size up** VT SEP *(person)* juzgar; *(situation, problem)* evaluar

sizeable ['saɪzəbəl] ADJ *(building etc)* (bastante) grande; *(sum)* considerable; *(problem)* importante

sizzle ['sɪzəl] VI chisporrotear

skate[1] [skeɪt] **1** N patín *m*
2 VI patinar

skate[2] [skeɪt] N *(fish)* raya *f*

skateboard ['skeɪtbɔːd] N monopatín *m*, *RP* skate *m*

skater ['skeɪtə(r)] N patinador(a) *m,f*

skating ['skeɪtɪŋ] N patinaje *m*; **s. rink** pista *f* de patinaje

skeleton ['skelɪtən] **1** N (**a**) *(of person)* esqueleto *m* (**b**) *(of building)* armazón *m* (**c**) *(outline)* esquema *m*
2 ADJ *(staff, service)* reducido(a); **s. key** llave maestra

skeptic ['skeptɪk] N *US* = sceptic

skeptical ['skeptɪkəl] ADJ *US* = sceptical

skepticism ['skeptɪsɪzəm] N *US* = scepticism

sketch [sketʃ] **1** N (**a**) *(preliminary drawing)* bosquejo *m*, esbozo *m*; *(drawing)* dibujo *m*; *(outline)* esquema *m*; *(rough draft)* boceto *m* (**b**) *Th & TV* sketch *m*
2 VT *(draw)* dibujar; *(preliminary drawing)* bosquejar, esbozar

sketch-book ['sketʃbʊk], **sketch-pad** ['sketʃpæd] N bloc *m* de dibujo

sketchy ['sketʃɪ] ADJ (**sketchier, sketchiest**) *(incomplete)* incompleto(a); *(not detailed)* vago(a)

skewer ['skjʊə(r)] N pincho *m*, broqueta *f*

ski [skiː] **1** N esquí *m*
2 ADJ de esquí; **s. boots** botas *fpl* de esquiar; **s. jump** *(action)* salto *m* con esquís; **s. lift** telesquí *m*; *(with seats)* telesilla *f*; **s. pants** pantalón *m* de esquiar; **s. resort** estación *f* de esquí; **s. stick** *or* **pole** bastón *m* de esquiar
3 VI esquiar; **to go skiing** ir a esquiar

skid [skɪd] **1** N patinazo *m*
2 VI patinar

skier ['skiːə(r)] N esquiador(a) *m,f*

skiing ['skiːɪŋ] N esquí *m*

skilful ['skɪlfʊl] ADJ hábil, diestro(a)

skill [skɪl] N (**a**) *(ability)* habilidad *f*, destreza *f*; *(talent)* don *m* (**b**) *(technique)* técnica *f*

skilled [skɪld] ADJ (**a**) *(dextrous)* hábil, diestro(a); *(expert)* experto(a) (**b**) *(worker)* cualificado(a)

skillet ['skɪlɪt] N *US* sartén *f*

skillful ['skɪlfʊl] ADJ *US* = skilful

skim [skɪm] **1** VT (**a**) *(milk) Esp* quitar la nata a, *Am* sacar la crema a; **skimmed milk** leche desnatada (**b**) *(brush against)* rozar; **to s. the ground** *(bird, plane)* volar a ras de suelo
2 VI *Fig* **to s. through a book** hojear un libro

skimp [skɪmp] VT & VI *(food, material)* escatimar; *(work)* chapucear

skimpy ['skɪmpɪ] ADJ (**skimpier, skimpiest**) *(shorts)* muy corto(a); *(meal)* escaso(a)

skin [skɪn] **1** N (**a**) *(of person, animal)* piel *f*; *(of face)* cutis *m*; *(complexion)* tez *f* (**b**) *(of fruit, sausage)* piel *f*; *(of lemon)* cáscara *f*, *(peeling)* mondadura *f*
2 VT (**a**) *(animal)* despellejar (**b**) *(graze)* arañar

skin-deep [skɪn'diːp] ADJ superficial

skin-diving ['skɪndaɪvɪŋ] N buceo *m*, submarinismo *m*

skinhead ['skɪnhed] N *Fam* cabeza *mf* rapada

skinny ['skɪnɪ] ADJ (**skinnier, skinniest**) *Fam* flaco(a)

skin-tight ['skɪntaɪt] ADJ *(clothing)* muy ajustado(a)

skip[1] [skɪp] **1** N *(jump)* salto *m*, brinco *m*
2 VI *(jump)* saltar, brincar; *(with rope)* saltar a la cuerda *or Esp* comba; *Fig* **to s. over sth** saltarse algo
3 VT *Fig* saltarse

skip[2] [skɪp] N *Br (for rubbish)* contenedor *m*

skipper ['skɪpə(r)] N *Naut & Sport Fam* capitán(ana) *m,f*

skipping ['skɪpɪŋ] N (saltos *mpl* a la) cuerda *f* or *Esp* comba *f; Br* **s. rope** *Esp* comba *f, Am* cuerda *f* de saltar

skirmish ['skɜːmɪʃ] N escaramuza *f*

skirt [skɜːt] **1** N falda *f, CSur* pollera *f*
2 VT *(town etc)* rodear; *(coast)* bordear; *Fig (problem)* esquivar

skirting ['skɜːtɪŋ] N *Br* **s. (board)** zócalo *m,* rodapié *m*

skit [skɪt] N sátira *f,* parodia *f*

skittle ['skɪtəl] N **(a)** *(pin)* bolo *m* **(b) skittles** *(game)* (juego *m* de los) bolos *mpl,* boliche *m*

skive [skaɪv] VI *Br Fam (avoid work)* zafarse, *Esp* escaquearse

skulk [skʌlk] VI *(hide)* esconderse; *(prowl)* merodear; *(lie in wait)* estar al acecho

skull [skʌl] N *Anat* cráneo *m; Fam* calavera *f*

skunk [skʌŋk] N mofeta *f*

sky [skaɪ] N cielo *m;* **s. blue** azul *m* celeste

skydiving ['skaɪdaɪvɪŋ] N caída *f* libre (en paracaídas)

skylight ['skaɪlaɪt] N tragaluz *m,* claraboya *f*

skyline ['skaɪlaɪn] N *(of city)* perfil *m*

skyscraper ['skaɪskreɪpə(r)] N rascacielos *m inv*

slab [slæb] N *(of stone)* losa *f; (of chocolate)* tableta *f; (of cake)* trozo *m*

slack [slæk] **1** ADJ **(a)** *(not taut)* flojo(a) **(b)** *(lax)* descuidado(a); *(lazy)* vago(a) **(c)** *(market)* flojo(a); **business is s.** hay poco negocio
2 N *(in rope)* parte floja

slacken ['slækən] **1** VT **(a)** *(rope)* aflojar **(b)** *(speed)* reducir
2 VI **(a)** *(rope)* aflojarse; *(wind)* amainar **(b)** *(trade)* aflojar
▸ **slacken off** VI disminuirse

slacker ['slækə(r)] N *Fam* vago(a) *m,f,* tirado(a) *m,f, Méx* flojo(a) *m,f*

slacks [slæks] NPL pantalones *mpl* ajustados

slag [slæg] N **(a)** *Min* escoria *f;* **s. heap** escorial *m* **(b)** *Br very Fam (woman)* fulana *f, Esp* cualquiera *f, Col, Méx* piruja *f*
▸ **slag off** VT SEP *Br Fam (criticize)* criticar, *Esp* poner a parir a, *Méx* viborear

slain [sleɪn] **1** NPL **the s.** los caídos
2 PP of **slay**

slam [slæm] **1** N *(of door)* portazo *m*
2 VT *(bang)* cerrar de golpe; **to s. sth down on the table** soltar algo sobre la mesa de un palmetazo; **to s. the door** dar un portazo; **to s. on the brakes** dar un frenazo
3 VI *(door)* cerrarse de golpe

slander ['slɑːndə(r)] **1** N difamación *f,* calumnia *f*
2 VT difamar, calumniar

slang [slæŋ] N argot *m*

slant [slɑːnt] **1** N **(a)** *(of ground)* cuesta *f,* pendiente *f; (of roof)* inclinación *f* **(b)** *Fig*

(point of view) punto *m* de vista
2 VT *Fig (problem etc)* enfocar subjetivamente
3 VI inclinarse

slanting ['slɑːntɪŋ] ADJ inclinado(a)

slap [slæp] **1** N palmada *f; (in face)* bofetada *f*
2 ADV *Fam* **he ran s. into the fence** se dio de lleno contra la valla; **s. in the middle of ...** justo en medio de ...
3 VT pegar con la mano; *(hit in face)* dar una bofetada a; **to s. sb on the back** dar a algn una palmada en la espalda

slapdash [slæp'dæʃ] ADJ *Fam* descuidado(a); *(work)* chapucero(a)

slapstick ['slæpstɪk] N bufonadas *fpl,* payasadas *fpl*

slap-up ['slæpʌp] ADJ *Br Fam* **s. meal** comilona *f*

slash [slæʃ] **1** N *Fam Typ* barra oblicua
2 VT **(a)** *(with knife; with sword)* dar un tajo a **(b)** *Fig (prices)* rebajar

slat [slæt] N tablilla *f,* listón *m*

slate [sleɪt] **1** N pizarra *f; Fig* **to wipe the s. clean** hacer borrón y cuenta nueva
2 VT *Fam* vapulear, *Esp* poner por los suelos, *Méx* viborear

slaughter ['slɔːtə(r)] **1** N *(of animals)* matanza *f; (of people)* carnicería *f*
2 VT *(animals)* matar; *(people)* matar brutalmente; *(in large numbers)* masacrar

slaughterhouse ['slɔːtəhaʊs] N matadero *m*

Slav [slɑːv] ADJ & N eslavo(a) *(m,f)*

slave [sleɪv] **1** N esclavo(a) *m,f;* **s. trade** trata *f* de esclavos
2 VI **to s. (away)** dar el callo

slavery ['sleɪvərɪ] N esclavitud *f*

Slavonic [slə'vɒnɪk] ADJ eslavo(a)

slay [sleɪ] VT *(pt* **slew;** *pp* **slain)** matar

sleazy ['sliːzɪ] ADJ **(sleazier, sleaziest)** sórdido(a)

sledge [sledʒ], *US* **sled** [sled] **1** N trineo *m*
2 VI montar en trineo

sledgehammer ['sledʒhæmə(r)] N almádena *f*

sleek [sliːk] ADJ *(hair)* lustroso(a); *(appearance)* impecable

sleep [sliːp] **1** N sueño *m;* **to go to s.** dormirse; **my foot has gone to s.** se me ha dormido el pie; *Fig* **to send to s.** (hacer) dormir
2 VI *(pt & pp* **slept)** dormir; *Fam* **to s. like a log** dormir como un lirón
▸ **sleep in** VI *Br (oversleep)* quedarse dormido(a); *(have a lie-in)* quedarse en la cama
▸ **sleep with** VT INSEP *Fam* **to s. with sb** acostarse con algn

sleeper ['sliːpə(r)] N **(a)** *(person)* durmiente *mf;* **to be a heavy s.** tener el sueño pesado **(b)** *Br Rail (on track)* traviesa *f* **(c)** *Rail (coach)* coche-cama *m; (berth)* litera *f*

sleeping ['sliːpɪŋ] ADJ **s. bag** saco *m* de dormir, *Col, Méx* sleeping *m* (bag), *RP* bolsa *f* de dormir; **S. Beauty** la Bella durmiente; **s. car** coche-cama *m*; *Br Com* **s. partner** socio(a) comanditario(a); **s. pill** somnífero *m*

sleepless ['sli:pləs] ADJ **to have a s. night** pasar la noche en blanco

sleepwalker ['sli:pwɔ:kə(r)] N sonámbulo(a) *m,f*

sleepy ['sli:pɪ] ADJ (**sleepier, sleepiest**) soñoliento(a); **to be** *or* **feel s.** tener sueño

sleet [sli:t] 1 N aguanieve *f*
2 VI **it's sleeting** cae aguanieve

sleeve [sli:v] N (*of garment*) manga *f*; (*of record*) funda *f*

sleigh [sleɪ] N trineo *m*; **s. bell** cascabel *m*

sleight [slaɪt] N **s. of hand** juego *m* de manos

slender ['slendə(r)] ADJ (a) (*thin*) delgado(a) (b) *Fig* (*hope, chance*) remoto(a)

slept [slept] PT & PP *of* **sleep**

slew [slu:] PT *of* **slay**

slice [slaɪs] 1 N (a) (*of bread*) rebanada *f*; (*of ham*) loncha *f*; (*of beef etc*) tajada *f*; (*of lemon etc*) rodaja *f*; (*of cake*) trozo *m* (b) (*utensil*) pala *f*
2 VT (*food*) cortar a rebanadas/lonchas/rodajas; (*divide*) partir

slick [slɪk] 1 ADJ (a) (*programme, show*) logrado(a) (b) (*skilful*) hábil, mañoso(a)
2 N (*oil*) **s. marea negra**

slide [slaɪd] 1 N (a) (*act*) resbalón *m* (b) (*in prices etc*) baja *f* (c) (*in playground*) tobogán *m* (d) *Phot* diapositiva *f*; **s. projector** proyector *m* de diapositivas (e) *Br* (*for hair*) pasador *m*
2 VT (*pt & pp* **slid** [slɪd]) deslizar; (*furniture*) correr
3 VI (*on purpose*) deslizarse; (*slip*) resbalar

sliding ['slaɪdɪŋ] ADJ (*door, window*) corredizo(a); *Fin* **s. scale** escala *f* móvil

slight [slaɪt] 1 ADJ (a) (*small*) pequeño(a); **not in the slightest** en absoluto (b) (*build*) menudo(a); (*slim*) delgado(a); (*frail*) delicado(a) (c) (*trivial*) leve
2 N (*affront*) desaire *m*
3 VT (a) (*scorn*) despreciar (b) (*snub*) desairar

slightly ['slaɪtlɪ] ADV (*a little*) ligeramente, algo

slim [slɪm] 1 ADJ (**slimmer, slimmest**) (a) (*person*) delgado(a) (b) *Fig* (*resources*) escaso(a); (*hope, chance*) remoto(a)
2 VI adelgazar

slime [slaɪm] N (*mud*) lodo *m*, cieno *m*; (*of snail*) baba *f*

slimming ['slɪmɪŋ] 1 ADJ (*diet, pills*) para adelgazar; (*food*) que no engorda
2 N (*process*) adelgazamiento *m*

slimy ['slaɪmɪ] ADJ (**slimier, slimiest**) (a) (*muddy*) lodoso(a); (*snail*) baboso(a) (b) *Fig* (*person*) zalamero(a)

sling [slɪŋ] 1 N (a) (*catapult*) honda *f*; (*child's*) tirador *m* (b) *Med* cabestrillo *m*
2 VT (*pt & pp* **slung**) (*throw*) tirar

slingshot ['slɪŋʃɒt] N *US* tirachinas *m inv*

slink [slɪŋk] VI (*pt & pp* **slunk**) **to s. off** escabullirse

slip [slɪp] 1 N (a) (*slide*) resbalón *m* (b) (*mistake*) error *m*; (*moral*) desliz *m*; **a s. of the tongue** un lapsus linguae (c) (*of paper*) trocito *m*
2 VI (a) (*slide*) resbalar (b) *Med* dislocarse; **slipped disc** vértebra dislocada (c) (*move quickly*) ir de prisa (d) (*standards etc*) deteriorarse
3 VT (a) (*slide*) dar a escondidas (b) **it slipped my memory** se me fue de la cabeza
▸ **slip away** VI (*person*) escabullirse
▸ **slip off** VT SEP (*clothes*) quitarse rápidamente
▸ **slip on** VT SEP (*clothes*) ponerse rápidamente
▸ **slip out** VI (a) (*leave*) salir (b) *Fig* **the secret slipped out** se le escapó el secreto
▸ **slip up** VI *Fam* (*blunder*) cometer un desliz

slipper ['slɪpə(r)] N zapatilla *f*

slippery ['slɪpərɪ] ADJ resbaladizo(a)

slip-road ['slɪprəʊd] N *Br* (*onto motorway*) carril *m* de incorporación *or* aceleración; (*out of motorway*) carril *m* de salida *or* deceleración

slipshod ['slɪpʃɒd] ADJ descuidado(a); (*work*) chapucero(a)

slip-up ['slɪpʌp] N *Fam* (*blunder*) desliz *m*

slipway ['slɪpweɪ] N grada *f*

slit [slɪt] 1 N (*opening*) hendidura *f*; (*cut*) corte *m*, raja *f*
2 VT (*pt & pp* **slit**) cortar, rajar

slither ['slɪðə(r)] VI deslizarse

sliver ['slɪvə(r)] N (*of wood, glass*) astilla *f*; (*of ham*) loncha *f*

slob [slɒb] N *Fam* (*untidy person*) cerdo(a) *m,f*, *Esp* guarro(a) *m,f*; (*lazy person*) dejado(a) *m,f*, tirado(a) *m,f*

slog [slɒg] *Fam* 1 N **it was a bit of a s.** fue un aburrimiento *or Esp* tostonazo (*de trabajo*); **it's a long s.** (*walk*) hay un buen trecho *or Esp* una buena tirada
2 VI (*pt & pp* **slogged**) (*work hard*) trabajar como un(a) negro(a), *Esp* dar el callo

slogan ['sləʊgən] N (e)slogan *m*, lema *m*

slop [slɒp] 1 VI **to s. (over)** derramarse; **to s. about** chapotear
2 VT derramar

slope [sləʊp] 1 N (*incline*) cuesta *f*, pendiente *f*; (*up*) subida *f*; (*down*) bajada *f*; (*of mountain*) ladera *f*; (*of roof*) vertiente *f*
2 VI inclinarse; **to s. up/down** subir/bajar en pendiente
▸ **slope off** VI *Br Fam* escabullirse

sloping ['sləʊpɪŋ] ADJ inclinado(a)

sloppy ['slɒpɪ] ADJ (**sloppier, sloppiest**) *Fam* descuidado(a); (*work*) chapucero(a); (*appearance*) desaliñado(a)

slot [slɒt] 1 N (a) (*for coin*) ranura *f*; (*opening*) rendija *f*; **s. machine** (*for gambling*) (máquina *f*) tragaperras *f inv*; (*vending machine*) distribuidor automático (b) *Rad & TV* espacio *m*

2 VT *(place)* meter; *(put in)* introducir

3 VI **to s. in** *or* **together** encajar

sloth [sləʊθ] N *Fml (laziness)* pereza *f*

slouch [slaʊtʃ] VI andar *or* sentarse con los hombros caídos

Slovakia [sləʊˈvækɪə] N Eslovaquia

Slovakian [sləʊˈvækɪən] ADJ & N eslovaco(a) *(m,f)*

Slovene [ˈsləʊviːn] **1** ADJ esloveno(a)

2 N **(a)** *(person)* esloveno(a) *m,f* **(b)** *(language)* esloveno *m*

Slovenia [sləʊˈviːnɪə] N Eslovenia

Slovenian [sləʊˈviːnɪən] ADJ & N = **Slovene**

slovenly [ˈslʌvənlɪ] ADJ descuidado(a); *(appearance)* desaliñado(a); *(work)* chapucero(a)

slow [sləʊ] **1** ADJ **(a)** *(not fast)* lento(a); **in s. motion** a cámara lenta; **to be s. to do sth** tardar *or Am* demorar en hacer algo **(b)** *(clock)* atrasado(a) **(c)** *(stupid)* lento(a), torpe

2 ADV despacio, lentamente

3 VT *(car)* reducir la marcha de; *(progress)* retrasar

4 VI **to s. down** *or* **up** ir más despacio; *(in car)* reducir la velocidad

slowly [ˈsləʊlɪ] ADV despacio, lentamente

sludge [slʌdʒ] N *(mud)* fango *m*, lodo *m*

slug [slʌg] **1** N **(a)** *Zool* babosa *f* **(b)** *US Fam (bullet)* posta *f* **(c)** *Fam (blow)* porrazo *m*

2 VT *Fam (hit)* aporrear

sluggish [ˈslʌgɪʃ] ADJ **(a)** *(river, engine)* lento(a); *Com* flojo(a) **(b)** *(lazy)* perezoso(a)

sluice [sluːs] N *(waterway)* canal *m*

sluicegate [ˈsluːsgeɪt] N esclusa *f*

slum [slʌm] N *(district)* barrio *m* bajo; *(on outskirts)* arrabal *m*, suburbio *m*; *(house)* tugurio *m*

slumber [ˈslʌmbə(r)] *Fml* **1** N *(sleep)* sueño *m*

2 VI dormir

slump [slʌmp] **1** N **(a)** *(drop in sales etc)* bajón *m* **(b)** *(economic depression)* crisis económica

2 VI **(a)** *(sales etc)* caer de repente; *(prices)* desplomarse; *(the economy)* hundirse; *Fig (morale)* hundirse **(b)** *(fall)* caer

slung [slʌŋ] PT & PP *of* **sling**

slunk [slʌŋk] PT & PP *of* **slink**

slur [slɜː(r)] **1** N *(stigma)* mancha *f*; *(slanderous remark)* calumnia *f*

2 VT *(word)* tragarse

slush [slʌʃ] N **(a)** *(melting snow)* nieve medio fundida **(b)** *Fam* sentimentalismo *m* **(c)** *US Fam* **s. fund** fondos *mpl* para corrupción *or Esp* corruptelas

slut [slʌt] N *very Fam Pej* **(a)** *(untidy woman)* marrana *f*, *Esp* guarra *f* **(b)** *(whore)* fulana *f*

sly [slaɪ] ADJ **(slyer, slyest** *or* **slier, sliest) (a)** *(cunning)* astuto(a) **(b)** *(secretive)* furtivo(a) **(c)** *(mischievous)* travieso(a) **(d)** *(underhand)* malicioso(a)

smack¹ [smæk] **1** N **(a)** *(slap)* bofetada *f* **(b)** *(sharp sound)* ruido sonoro

2 VT **(a)** *(slap)* dar una bofetada a **(b)** *(hit)* golpear; *Fig* **to s. one's lips** relamerse

smack² [smæk] VI *Fig* **to s. of** oler a

small [smɔːl] **1** ADJ **(a)** *(not large)* pequeño(a), *Am* chico(a); *Fig* **s. print** letra pequeña **(b)** *(in height)* bajo(a) **(c)** *(scant)* escaso(a); **s. change** cambio *m*, suelto *m*, *Am* vuelto *m* **(d)** *(minor)* insignificante; **s. businessmen** pequeños comerciantes; **s. talk** charloteo *m* **(e)** *(increase)* ligero(a)

2 N **s. of the back** región *f* lumbar

smallholder [ˈsmɔːlhəʊldə(r)] N *Br* minifundista *mf*

small-minded [smɔːlˈmaɪndɪd] ADJ mezquino(a)

smallpox [ˈsmɔːlpɒks] N viruela *f*

smarmy [ˈsmɑːmɪ] ADJ **(smarmier, smarmiest)** *Fam* cobista, zalamero(a)

smart [smɑːt] **1** ADJ **(a)** *(elegant)* elegante **(b)** *(clever)* listo(a), inteligente; *Fam* **s. alec(k)** sabelotodo *mf*, listillo(a) *m,f*, *Méx, RP* vivo(a) *m,f* **(c)** *(quick)* rápido(a); *(pace)* ligero(a)

2 VI **(a)** *(sting)* picar, escocer **(b)** *Fig* sufrir

smarten [ˈsmɑːtən] **1** VT **to s. (up)** arreglar

2 VI **to s. (oneself) up** arreglarse

smartly [ˈsmɑːtlɪ] ADV **(a)** *(elegantly)* elegantemente **(b)** *(quickly)* rápidamente, con rapidez

smash [smæʃ] **1** N **(a)** *(loud noise)* estrépito *m*; *(collision)* choque violento **(b)** *(in tennis)* smash *m*

2 VT **(a)** *(break)* romper; *(shatter)* hacer pedazos; *(crush)* aplastar **(b)** *(destroy)* destrozar; *(defeat)* aplastar **(c)** *(record)* fulminar

3 VI **(a)** *(break)* romperse; *(shatter)* hacerse pedazos; *(crash)* estrellarse; *(in tennis)* hacer un mate

▶ **smash up** VT SEP *Fam (car)* hacer pedazos; *(place)* destrozar

smashing [ˈsmæʃɪŋ] ADJ *Br Fam* genial, *Méx* padre, *RP* bárbaro(a)

smattering [ˈsmætərɪŋ] N **he had a s. of French** hablaba un poquito de francés

smear [smɪə(r)] **1** N **(a)** *(smudge)* mancha *f*; **s. (test)** citología *f* **(b)** *Fig (defamation)* calumnia *f*

2 VT **(a)** *(butter etc)* untar; *(grease)* embadurnar **(b)** *(make dirty)* manchar **(c)** *Fig (defame)* calumniar, difamar

smell [smel] **1** N **(a)** *(sense)* olfato *m* **(b)** *(odour)* olor *m*

2 VT *(pt & pp* **smelled** *or* **smelt)** oler; *Fig* olfatear

3 VI oler *(of* a); **it smells good/like lavender** huele bien/a lavanda; **he smelt of whisky** olía a whisky

smelly [ˈsmelɪ] ADJ **(smellier, smelliest)** *Fam* maloliente, apestoso(a)

smelt¹ [smelt] VT *(ore)* fundir

smelt² [smelt] PT & PP *of* **smell**

smidgen ['smɪdʒən] N *Fam* pizca f

smile [smaɪl] 1 N sonrisa f
2 VI sonreír; **to s. at sb** sonreír a algn; **to s. at sth** reírse de algo

smiling ['smaɪlɪŋ] ADJ sonriente, risueño(a)

smirk [smɜːk] 1 N *(conceited)* sonrisa satisfecha; *(foolish)* sonrisa boba
2 VI *(conceitedly)* sonreír con satisfacción; *(foolishly)* sonreír bobamente

smith [smɪθ] N herrero m

smithereens [smɪðəˈriːnz] NPL **to smash/blow sth to s.** hacer algo añicos

smithy ['smɪðɪ] N herrería f

smitten ['smɪtən] ADJ *Fam* **to be s. with sb** estar enamorado(a) de algn

smock [smɒk] N *(blouse)* blusón m; *(worn in pregnancy)* blusón de premamá; *(overall)* bata f

smog [smɒg] N niebla tóxica, smog m

smoke [sməʊk] 1 N humo m; **s. bomb** bomba f de humo; **s. screen** cortina f de humo
2 VI fumar; *(chimney)* echar humo
3 VT **(a)** *(tobacco)* fumar; **to s. a pipe** fumar en pipa **(b)** *(fish, meat)* ahumar

smoked [sməʊkt] ADJ ahumado(a)

smokeless ['sməʊklɪs] ADJ **s. fuel** combustible m sin humo; **s. zone** zona f libre de humos

smoker ['sməʊkə(r)] N **(a)** *(person)* fumador(a) m,f **(b)** *Rail* vagón m de fumadores

smoking ['sməʊkɪŋ] N **no s.** *(sign)* prohibido fumar

smoky ['sməʊkɪ] ADJ **(smokier, smokiest) (a)** *(chimney)* humeante; *(room)* lleno(a) de humo; *(atmosphere)* cargado(a) (de humo); *(taste)* ahumado(a) **(b)** *(colour)* ahumado(a)

smolder ['sməʊldə(r)] VI *US* = **smoulder**

smooth [smuːð] 1 ADJ **(a)** *(surface)* liso(a); *(skin)* suave; *(road)* llano(a) **(b)** *(beer, wine)* suave **(c)** *(flowing)* fluido(a) **(d)** *(flight)* tranquilo(a); *(transition)* sin problemas **(e)** *Pej (slick)* zalamero(a)
2 VT **(a)** *(hair etc)* alisar **(b)** *(plane down)* limar

▸ **smooth out** VT SEP *(creases)* alisar; *Fig (difficulties)* allanar; *(problems)* resolver

▸ **smooth over** VT SEP *Fig* **to s. things over** limar asperezas

smoothie ['smuːðɪ] N **(a)** *Fam Pej (person)* zalamero(a) m,f **(b)** *(drink)* = zumo de fruta con yogur o leche

smoothly ['smuːðlɪ] ADV sobre ruedas

smoothy ['smuːðɪ] N = **smoothie**

smother ['smʌðə(r)] VT **(a)** *(asphyxiate)* asfixiar; *(suffocate)* sofocar **(b)** *Fig (cover)* cubrir **(with** de)

smoulder ['sməʊldə(r)] VI *(fire)* arder sin llama; *Fig (passions)* arder; **smouldering hatred** odio m latente

smudge [smʌdʒ] 1 N *(stain)* mancha f; *(of ink)* borrón m
2 VT manchar; *(piece of writing)* emborronar

smug [smʌg] ADJ **(smugger, smuggest)** engreído(a)

smuggle ['smʌgəl] VT pasar de contrabando

smuggler ['smʌglə(r)] N contrabandista mf

smuggling ['smʌglɪŋ] N contrabando m

smutty ['smʌtɪ] ADJ **(smuttier, smuttiest)** *Fam* obsceno(a); *(joke)* verde; *(book, film etc)* pornográfico(a)

snack [snæk] N tentempié m, *Esp* piscolabis m inv, *Méx* botana f; **s. bar** cafetería f

snag [snæg] 1 N *(difficulty)* pega f, problemilla m
2 VT *(clothing)* enganchar

snail [sneɪl] N caracol m

snake [sneɪk] N *(big)* serpiente f; *(small)* culebra f

snap [snæp] 1 N **(a)** *(noise)* ruido seco; *(of branch, fingers)* chasquido m **(b)** *(bite)* mordisco m **(c)** *Phot (foto f)* instantánea f
2 ADJ *(sudden)* repentino(a)
3 VT **(a)** *(branch etc)* partir (en dos) **(b)** *(make noise)* **to s. one's fingers** chasquear los dedos; **to s. sth shut** cerrar algo de golpe **(c)** *Phot* sacar una foto de
4 VI **(a)** *(break)* romperse **(b)** *(make noise)* hacer un ruido seco **(c)** *(whip)* chasquear; **to s. shut** cerrarse de golpe **(d)** **to s. at sb** *(dog)* intentar morder a algn; *Fam (person)* hablar en mal tono a algn

▸ **snap off** 1 VT SEP *(branch etc)* arrancar
2 VI *(branch etc)* separarse

▸ **snap up** VT SEP *Fam* **to s. up a bargain** llevarse una ganga

snappy ['snæpɪ] ADJ **(snappier, snappiest)** *Fam* **(a)** *(quick)* rápido(a); **look s.!, make it s.!** ¡date prisa! **(b)** *(stylish)* elegante **(c)** *(short-tempered)* irritable

snapshot ['snæpʃɒt] N *(foto f)* instantánea f

snare [sneə(r)] 1 N trampa f
2 VT *(animal)* cazar con trampa; *Fig (person)* hacer caer en la trampa

snarl¹ [snɑːl] 1 N gruñido m
2 VI gruñir

snarl² [snɑːl] 1 N *(in wool)* maraña f
2 VT **to s. (up)** *(wool)* enmarañar; *(traffic)* atascar; *(plans)* enredar

snatch [snætʃ] 1 N **(a)** *Fam (theft)* robo m; **bag s.** tirón m **(b)** *(fragment)* fragmentos mpl
2 VT **(a)** *(grab)* arrebatar **(b)** *Fam (steal)* robar; *(kidnap)* secuestrar
3 VI **to s. at sth** intentar agarrar *or Esp* coger algo

sneak [sniːk] 1 N *Br Fam Esp* chivato(a) m,f, *Méx* hocicón(ona) m,f, *RP* buchón(ona) m,f
2 *(pt & pp* sneaked *or US* snuck) VT **to s. sth out of a place** sacar algo de un lugar a escondidas
3 VI **(a)** **to s. off** escabullirse; **to s. in/out**

entrar/salir a hurtadillas (**b**) *Fam* **to s. on sb** *(tell tales)* ir con cuentos, *Esp* chivarse

sneaker [ˈsniːkə(r)] N *US* playera *f*

sneaky [ˈsniːkɪ] ADJ (**sneakier, sneakiest**) solapado(a)

sneer [snɪə(r)] VI **to s. at** hacer un gesto de desprecio a

sneeze [sniːz] **1** N estornudo *m*
2 VI estornudar

sniff [snɪf] **1** N *(by person)* aspiración *f*; *(by dog)* husmeo *m*
2 VT *(flower etc)* oler; *(suspiciously)* husmear; *(snuff etc)* aspirar; *(glue)* esnifar
3 VI aspirar por la nariz

snigger [ˈsnɪɡə(r)] **1** N risa disimulada
2 VI reír disimuladamente; **to s. at sth** burlarse de algo

snip [snɪp] **1** N (**a**) *(cut)* tijeretada *f*; *(small piece)* recorte *m* (**b**) *Br Fam (bargain) Esp* chollo *m*, *Am* regalo *m*
2 VT cortar a tijeretazos

sniper [ˈsnaɪpə(r)] N francotirador(a) *m,f*

snippet [ˈsnɪpɪt] N *(of cloth, paper)* recorte *m*; *(of conversation)* fragmento *m*

snivel [ˈsnɪvəl] VI lloriquear

snivelling [ˈsnɪvəlɪŋ] ADJ llorica

snob [snɒb] N (e)snob *mf*

snobbery [ˈsnɒbərɪ] N (e)snobismo *m*

snobbish [ˈsnɒbɪʃ] ADJ (e)snob

snooker [ˈsnuːkə(r)] N snooker *m*, billar ruso

snoop [snuːp] VI fisgonear, *Esp* fisgar

snooty [ˈsnuːtɪ] ADJ (**snootier, snootiest**) *Fam* (e)snob

snooze [snuːz] *Fam* **1** N *Esp* siestecilla *f*, *Am* siestita *f*
2 VI echarse una *Esp* siestecilla *or Am* siestita

snore [snɔː(r)] **1** N ronquido *m*
2 VI roncar

snoring [ˈsnɔːrɪŋ] N ronquidos *mpl*

snorkel [ˈsnɔːkəl] N *(of swimmer)* tubo *m* de respiración; *(of submarine)* esnórquel *m*

snort [snɔːt] **1** N resoplido *m*
2 VI resoplar

snot [snɒt] N *Fam* mocos *mpl*

snout [snaʊt] N *(of animal, gun etc)* morro *m*

snow [snəʊ] **1** N nieve *f*; **s. shower** nevada *f*
2 VI nevar; **it's snowing** está nevando
3 VT *Fig* **to be snowed under with work** estar agobiado(a) de trabajo

snowball [ˈsnəʊbɔːl] **1** N bola *f* de nieve
2 VI *Fig* aumentar rápidamente

snowbound [ˈsnəʊbaʊnd] ADJ aislado(a) por la nieve

snowdrift [ˈsnəʊdrɪft] N ventisquero *m*

snowdrop [ˈsnəʊdrɒp] N campanilla *f* de invierno

snowfall [ˈsnəʊfɔːl] N nevada *f*

snowflake [ˈsnəʊfleɪk] N copo *m* de nieve

snowman [ˈsnəʊmæn] N hombre *m* de nieve

snowplough, *US* **snowplow** [ˈsnəʊplaʊ] N quitanieves *m inv*

snowshoe [ˈsnəʊʃuː] N raqueta *f* (de nieve)

snowstorm [ˈsnəʊstɔːm] N nevasca *f*

snowy [ˈsnəʊɪ] ADJ (**snowier, snowiest**) *(mountain)* nevado(a); *(climate)* nevoso(a); *(day)* de nieve

Snr *(abbr **Senior**)* **Neil Smith S.** Neil Smith padre

snub [snʌb] **1** N *(of person)* desaire *m*; *(of offer)* rechazo *m*
2 VT *(person)* desairar; *(offer)* rechazar

snub-nosed [ˈsnʌbnəʊzd] ADJ de nariz respingona

snuck [snʌk] *US* PT & PP *of* sneak

snuff [snʌf] N rapé *m*

snug [snʌɡ] ADJ (**snugger, snuggest**) (**a**) *(cosy)* cómodo(a) (**b**) *(tightfitting)* ajustado(a)

snuggle [ˈsnʌɡəl] VI **to s. down in bed** acurrucarse en la cama; **to s. up to sb** arrimarse a algn

snugly [ˈsnʌɡlɪ] ADV **to fit s.** *(clothes)* quedar ajustado(a); *(object in box etc)* encajar

so [səʊ] **1** ADV (**a**) *(to such an extent)* tanto; **he was so tired that ...** estaba tan cansado que ...; **it's so long since ...** hace tanto tiempo que ...; *Fam* **so long!** ¡hasta luego! (**b**) *(degree)* tanto; **a week or so** una semana más o menos; **we loved her so (much)** la queríamos tanto; *Fam* **he's ever so handsome!** ¡es tan guapo! (**c**) *(thus, in this way)* así, de esta manera; **and so on, and so forth** y así sucesivamente; **if so** en este caso; **I think/hope so** creo/espero que sí; **I told you so** ya te lo dije; **so far** hasta ahora *or* allí; **so they say** eso dicen (**d**) *(also)* **I'm going to Spain – so am I** voy a España – yo también
2 CONJ (**a**) *(expresses result)* así que; **so you like England, do you?** ¿así que te gusta Inglaterra, pues?; *Fam* **so what?** ¿y qué? (**b**) *(expresses purpose)* para que; **I'll put the key here so (that) everyone can see it** pongo la llave aquí para que todos la vean

soak [səʊk] **1** VT *(washing, food)* remojar; *(cotton, wool)* empapar (**in** en)
2 VI *(washing, food)* estar en remojo

▸ **soak in** VI penetrar

▸ **soak up** VT SEP absorber

soaking [ˈsəʊkɪŋ] ADJ *(object)* empapado(a); *(person)* calado(a) hasta los huesos

so-and-so [ˈsəʊənsəʊ] N *Fam* **Mr S.** Don Fulano (de tal); *Pej* **an old s.** un viejo imbécil

soap [səʊp] **1** N (**a**) *(for washing)* jabón *m*; **s. flakes** jabón en escamas; **s. powder** jabón en polvo (**b**) *TV* **s. (opera)** culebrón *m*
2 VT enjabonar

soapsuds [ˈsəʊpsʌdz] NPL espuma *f* (de jabón)

soapy [ˈsəʊpɪ] ADJ (**soapier, soapiest**) jabonoso(a); *(hands)* cubierto(a) de jabón

soar [sɔː(r)] VI *(bird, plane)* remontar el vuelo; *Fig (skyscraper)* elevarse; *(hopes, prices)* aumentar

sob [sɒb] **1** N sollozo *m*
2 VI sollozar

sober ['səʊbə(r)] ADJ *(not drunk, moderate)* sobrio(a); *(sensible)* sensato(a); *(serious)* serio(a); *(colour)* discreto(a)
▸ **sober up** VI he sobered up se le pasó la borrachera

so-called ['səʊkɔːld] ADJ supuesto(a), llamado(a)

soccer ['sɒkə(r)] N fútbol *m*

sociable ['səʊʃəbəl] ADJ *(gregarious)* sociable; *(friendly)* amistoso(a)

social ['səʊʃəl] ADJ social; **s. class** clase *f* social; **s. climber** arribista *mf*; **S. Democratic** socialdemócrata; *US* **s. insurance** seguro *m* social; **s. security** seguridad *f* social; **the s. services** los servicios sociales; **s. work** asistencia *f* social; **s. worker** asistente(a) *m,f* social

socialist ['səʊʃəlɪst] ADJ & N socialista *(mf)*

socialite ['səʊʃəlaɪt] N vividor(a) *m,f*

socialize ['səʊʃəlaɪz] **1** VI alternar, mezclarse con la gente
2 VT socializar

socially ['səʊʃəlɪ] ADV socialmente

society [sə'saɪətɪ] N **(a)** *(in general)* sociedad *f*; **the consumer s.** la sociedad de consumo; **(high) s.** la alta sociedad; **s. column** ecos *mpl* de sociedad **(b)** *(club)* asociación *f* **(c)** *Literary (company)* compañía *f*

sociologist [səʊsɪ'ɒlədʒɪst] N sociólogo(a) *m,f*

sociology [səʊsɪ'ɒlədʒɪ] N sociología *f*

sock [sɒk] N calcetín *m*, *CSur* zoquete *m*

socket ['sɒkɪt] N **(a)** *(of eye)* cuenca *f* **(b)** *Elec* enchufe *m*

sod[1] [sɒd] N *Fml (piece of turf)* terrón *m*

sod[2] [sɒd] *Br very Fam* **1** N **(a)** *(person)* mamón(ona) *m,f*, *Méx* mamila *mf*, *RP* choto(a) *m,f*; **the lazy s.!** ¡qué tío más vago!; **poor s.!** ¡pobre diablo! **(b)** I've done **s. all today** *(nothing)* hoy no he pegado ni golpe
2 VT **s. it!** *Esp* ¡joder!, *Méx* ¡chin!, *RP* ¡la puta!

soda ['səʊdə] N **(a)** *Chem* sosa *f*; **baking s.** bicarbonato sódico **(b)** **s. water** soda *f* **(c)** *US (fizzy drink)* gaseosa *f*

sodden ['sɒdən] ADJ empapado(a)

sodium ['səʊdɪəm] N sodio *m*

sofa ['səʊfə] N sofá *m*; **s. bed** sofá cama

soft [sɒft] ADJ **(a)** *(not hard)* blando(a); **s. drinks** refrescos *mpl*; **s. drugs** drogas blandas; **s. toy** muñeco *m* de peluche **(b)** *(skin, colour, hair, light, music)* suave; *(breeze, steps)* ligero(a) **(c)** *(lenient)* permisivo(a) **(d)** *(voice)* bajo(a)

softball ['sɒftbɔːl] N = juego parecido al béisbol jugado en un campo más pequeño y con una pelota más blanda

soften ['sɒfən] **1** VT *(leather, heart)* ablandar; *(skin)* suavizar; *Fig (blow)* amortiguar
2 VI *(leather, heart)* ablandarse; *(skin)* suavizarse

softly ['sɒftlɪ] ADV *(gently)* suavemente; *(quietly)* silenciosamente

softness ['sɒftnɪs] N **(a)** *(of ground)* blandura *f* **(b)** *(of hair, skin)* suavidad *f* **(c)** *(foolishness)* estupidez *f*

software ['sɒftweə(r)] N *Comput* software *m*; **s. package** paquete *m*

soggy ['sɒgɪ] ADJ **(soggier, soggiest)** empapado(a); *(bread)* pastoso(a)

soil [sɔɪl] **1** N *(earth)* tierra *f*
2 VT *(dirty)* ensuciar; *Fig (reputation)* manchar

soiled [sɔɪld] ADJ sucio(a)

solace ['sɒlɪs] N *Fml* consuelo *m*

solar ['səʊlə(r)] ADJ solar

sold [səʊld] PT & PP of **sell**

solder ['sɒldə(r)] **1** N soldadura *f*
2 VT soldar

soldier ['səʊldʒə(r)] N soldado *m*; *(officer)* militar *m*; **toy s.** soldadito *m* de plomo
▸ **soldier on** VI *Fig* continuar contra viento y marea

sole[1] [səʊl] N *(of foot)* planta *f*; *(of shoe, sock)* suela *f*

sole[2] [səʊl] N *(fish)* lenguado *m*

sole[3] [səʊl] ADJ *(only)* único(a)

solely ['səʊllɪ] ADV únicamente

solemn ['sɒləm] ADJ solemne

solicit [sə'lɪsɪt] **1** VT *(request)* solicitar
2 VI *(prostitute)* abordar a los clientes

solicitor [sə'lɪsɪtə(r)] N *Br* abogado(a) *m,f*

solid ['sɒlɪd] **1** ADJ **(a)** *(not liquid)* sólido(a); *(firm)* firme **(b)** *(not hollow, pure) (metal)* macizo(a) **(c)** *(of strong material)* resistente
2 N sólido *m*

solidarity [sɒlɪ'dærɪtɪ] N solidaridad *f*

solidify [sə'lɪdɪfaɪ] VI solidificarse

solidly ['sɒlɪdlɪ] ADV sólidamente; **s. built** *(house etc)* de construcción sólida; **to work s.** trabajar sin descanso

soliloquy [sə'lɪləkwɪ] N soliloquio *m*

solitaire ['sɒlɪteə(r)] N solitario *m*

solitary ['sɒlɪtərɪ] ADJ **(a)** *(alone)* solitario(a); *(secluded)* apartado(a) **(b)** *(only)* solo(a)

solitude ['sɒlɪtjuːd] N soledad *f*

solo ['səʊləʊ] N solo *m*

soloist ['səʊləʊɪst] N solista *mf*

solstice ['sɒlstɪs] N solsticio *m*

soluble ['sɒljʊbəl] ADJ soluble

solution [sə'luːʃən] N solución *f*

solve [sɒlv] VT resolver, solucionar

solvent ['sɒlvənt] ADJ & N solvente *(m)*

sombre, *US* **somber** ['sɒmbə(r)] ADJ *(dark)* sombrío(a); *(gloomy)* lúgubre; *(pessimistic)* pesimista

some [sʌm] **1** ADJ **(a)** *(with plural nouns)* unos(as), algunos(as); *(several)* varios(as); *(a* *few)* unos(as) cuantos(as); **there were s. roses** había unas rosas; **s. more peas** más guisantes (**b**) *(with singular nouns)* algún/alguna; *(a little)* un poco de; **there's s. wine left** queda un poco de vino; **would you like s. coffee?** ¿quiere café? (**c**) *(certain)* cierto(a), alguno(a); **to s. extent** hasta cierto punto; **s. people say that …** algunas personas dicen que … (**d**) *(unspecified)* algún/alguna; **for s. reason or other** por una razón o por otra; **s. day** algún día (**e**) *(quite a lot of)* bastante; **s. years ago** hace algunos años

2 PRON (**a**) *(people)* algunos(as), unos(as); **s. go by bus and s. by train** unos van en autobús y otros en tren (**b**) *(objects)* algunos(as); *(a few)* unos(as) cuantos(as); *(a little)* algo, un poco; *(certain ones)* algunos(as)

3 ADV **s. thirty cars** unos treinta coches

somebody ['sʌmbədɪ] PRON alguien; **s. else** otro(a)

somehow ['sʌmhaʊ] ADV (**a**) *(in some way)* de alguna forma (**b**) *(for some reason)* por alguna razón

someone ['sʌmwʌn] PRON = **somebody**

someplace ['sʌmpleɪs] ADV US = **somewhere**

somersault ['sʌməsɔːlt] **1** N voltereta *f*; *(by acrobat etc)* salto *m* mortal; *(by car)* vuelta *f* de campana

2 VI dar volteretas; *(acrobat etc)* dar un salto mortal; *(car)* dar una vuelta de campana

something ['sʌmθɪŋ] PRON & N algo; **s. to eat/drink** algo de comer/beber; **are you drunk or s.?** ¿estás borracho o qué?; **s. must be done** hay que hacer algo; **she has a certain s.** tiene un no sé qué; **is s. the matter?** ¿le pasa algo?; **s. else** otra cosa; **s. of the kind** algo por el estilo

sometime ['sʌmtaɪm] ADV algún día; **s. last week** un día de la semana pasada; **s. next year** durante el año que viene

sometimes ['sʌmtaɪmz] ADV a veces, de vez en cuando

somewhat ['sʌmwɒt] ADV *Fml* algo, un tanto

somewhere ['sʌmweə(r)] ADV (**a**) *(in some place)* en alguna parte; *(to some place)* a alguna parte; **s. else** *(in some other place)* en otra parte; *(to some other place)* a otra parte; **s. or other** no sé dónde (**b**) **s. in the region of** *(approximately)* más o menos

son [sʌn] N hijo *m*; **eldest/youngest s.** hijo mayor/menor

song [sɒŋ] N canción *f*; *(of bird)* canto *m*

songwriter ['sɒŋraɪtə(r)] N compositor(a) *m,f* (de canciones)

sonic ['sɒnɪk] ADJ sónico(a)

son-in-law ['sʌnɪnlɔː] N yerno *m*

sonnet ['sɒnɪt] N soneto *m*

sonny ['sʌnɪ] N *Fam* hijo *m*, hijito *m*

soon [suːn] ADV (**a**) *(within a short time)* pronto, dentro de poco; *(quickly)* rápidamente; **s. after midnight** poco después de medianoche; **s.**

afterwards poco después (**b**) **as s. as I arrived** en cuanto llegué; **as s. as possible** cuanto antes (**c**) *(preference)* **I would just as s. stay at home** prefiero quedarme en casa

sooner ['suːnə(r)] ADV (**a**) *(earlier)* más temprano; **s. or later** tarde o temprano; **the s. the better** cuanto antes mejor (**b**) **no s. had he finished than he fainted** *(immediately after)* nada más acabar se desmayó (**c**) **I would s. do it alone** *(rather)* prefiero hacerlo yo solo

soot [sʊt] N hollín *m*

soothe [suːð] VT *(calm)* tranquilizar; *(pain)* aliviar

sop [sɒp] N *(concession)* favor *m*; *(bribe)* soborno *m*

▸ **sop up** VT SEP empapar

sophisticated [sə'fɪstɪkeɪtɪd] ADJ sofisticado(a)

sophomore ['sɒfəmɔː(r)] N *US Univ* = estudiante de segundo curso

soporific [sɒpə'rɪfɪk] ADJ soporífero(a)

sopping ['sɒpɪŋ] ADJ *Fam* **s. (wet)** como una sopa

soppy ['sɒpɪ] ADJ **(soppier, soppiest)** *Fam* sensiblero(a), *Esp* ñoño(a)

soprano [sə'prɑːnəʊ] N soprano *mf*

sorcerer ['sɔːsərə(r)] N brujo *m*

sorceress ['sɔːsərɪs] N bruja *f*

sordid ['sɔːdɪd] ADJ sórdido(a)

sore [sɔː(r)] **1** ADJ (**a**) *(painful)* dolorido(a); **to have a s. throat** tener dolor de garganta (**b**) *Fam (annoyed)* esp *Esp* enfadado(a), enojado(a) *(about* por*)*; **to feel s. about sth** estar resentido(a) por algo

2 N llaga *f*

sorely ['sɔːlɪ] ADV *(greatly)* enormemente; **she will be s. missed** se la echará muchísimo de menos, *Am* se la extrañará muchísimo

sorrow ['sɒrəʊ] N pena *f*, dolor *m*

sorrowful ['sɒrəʊfʊl] ADJ afligido(a)

sorry ['sɒrɪ] **1** ADJ **(sorrier, sorriest)** (**a**) **I feel very s. for her** me da mucha pena (**b**) *(pitiful)* triste (**c**) **to be s. (about sth)** sentir (algo); **I'm s. I'm late** siento llegar tarde

2 INTERJ (**a**) *(apology)* ¡perdón! (**b**) *Br (for repetition)* ¿cómo?

sort [sɔːt] **1** N (**a**) *(kind)* clase *f*, tipo *m*; *(brand)* marca *f*; **it's a s. of teapot** es una especie de tetera (**b**) **he is a musician of sorts** tiene algo de músico; **there's an office of sorts** hay una especie de despacho (**c**) **s. of** en cierto modo

2 VT *(classify)* clasificar

▸ **sort out** VT SEP (**a**) *(classify)* clasificar; *(put in order)* ordenar (**b**) *(problem)* arreglar, solucionar

sorting ['sɔːtɪŋ] N **s. office** sala *f* de batalla

SOS [esəʊ'es] N S.O.S. *m*

so-so ['səʊsəʊ] ADV *Fam* así así, regular

soufflé ['suːfleɪ] N soufflé *m*, suflé *m*

sought [sɔːt] PT & PP *of* **seek**

soul [səʊl] N (**a**) *(spirit)* alma f (**b**) **he's a good s.** *(person)* es muy buena persona (**c**) *Mus* soul m

soul-destroying ['səʊldɪstrɔɪɪŋ] ADJ *(boring)* monótono(a); *(demoralizing)* desmoralizador(a)

soulful ['səʊlfʊl] ADJ conmovedor(a)

sound¹ [saʊnd] 1 N (**a**) *(in general)* sonido m; *(noise)* ruido m; **s. effects** efectos sonoros (**b**) *Geog* estrecho m
2 VT *(bell, trumpet)* tocar; **to s. the alarm** dar la señal de alarma
3 VI (**a**) *(trumpet, bell, alarm)* sonar (**b**) *(give an impression)* parecer; **it sounds interesting** parece interesante (**c**) *Naut & Med* sondar
▸ **sound out** VT SEP sondear

sound² [saʊnd] 1 ADJ (**a**) *(healthy)* sano(a); *(in good condition)* en buen estado (**b**) *(safe, dependable)* seguro(a); *(correct)* acertado(a); *(logical)* lógico(a) (**c**) *(basis etc)* sólido(a) (**d**) *(sleep)* profundo(a)
2 ADV **to be s. asleep** estar profundamente dormido(a)

sounding ['saʊndɪŋ] N *Naut* sondeo m

soundly ['saʊndlɪ] ADV (**a**) *(logically)* razonablemente (**b**) *(solidly)* sólidamente (**c**) **to sleep s.** dormir profundamente

soundproof ['saʊndpruːf] ADJ insonorizado(a)

soundtrack ['saʊndtræk] N banda sonora

soup [suːp] N sopa f; *(thin, clear)* caldo m; *Fam* **in the s.** en un apuro; **s. dish** plato hondo; **s. spoon** cuchara sopera

sour [saʊə(r)] ADJ (**a**) *(fruit, wine)* agrio(a); *(milk)* cortado(a); **to go s.** *(milk)* cortarse; *(wine)* agriarse; *Fig (situation)* empeorar (**b**) *Fig (person)* amargado(a)

source [sɔːs] N fuente f; *(of infection)* foco m

south [saʊθ] 1 N sur m; **in the s. of England** en el sur de Inglaterra; **to the s. of York** al sur de York
2 ADJ del sur; **S. Africa** Sudáfrica; **S. African** sudafricano(a) *(m,f)*; **S. Korea** Corea del Sur; **S. Pole** Polo m Sur
3 ADV *(location)* al sur; *(direction)* hacia el sur

southeast [saʊθ'iːst] 1 N sudeste m
2 ADJ sudeste
3 ADV *(location)* al sudeste; *(direction)* hacia el sudeste

southeasterly [saʊθ'iːstəlɪ] ADJ del sudeste

southerly ['sʌðəlɪ] ADJ *(direction)* hacia el sur; *(point)* al sur; *(wind)* del sur

southern ['sʌðən] ADJ del sur, meridional; **S. Europe** Europa del Sur; **the s. hemisphere** el hemisferio sur

southerner ['sʌðənə(r)] N sureño(a) *m,f*

southward ['saʊθwəd] ADJ & ADV hacia el sur

southwest [saʊθ'west] 1 N suroeste m
2 ADJ suroeste
3 ADV *(location)* al suroeste; *(direction)* hacia el suroeste

southwesterly [saʊθ'westəlɪ] ADJ del suroeste

souvenir [suːvə'nɪə(r)] N recuerdo m, souvenir m

sovereign ['sɒvrɪn] 1 N (**a**) *(monarch)* soberano(a) m,f (**b**) *Hist (coin)* soberano m
2 ADJ soberano(a)

sovereignty ['sɒvrəntɪ] N soberanía f

soviet ['səʊvɪət] 1 N (**a**) *(council)* soviet m (**b**) **the Soviets** los soviéticos
2 ADJ soviético(a); *Hist* **S. Union** Unión Soviética

sow¹ [səʊ] VT *(pt* **sowed**; *pp* **sowed** *or* **sown**) sembrar

sow² [saʊ] N *Zool* cerda f, puerca f, *Am* chancha f

sown [səʊn] PP *of* **sow**

soy [sɔɪ] N soja f; **s. sauce** salsa f de soja

soya ['sɔɪə] N soja f; **s. bean** semilla f de soja

spa [spaː] N balneario m

space [speɪs] 1 N (**a**) *(room)* espacio m, sitio m; **in a confined s.** en un espacio reducido (**b**) *(outer space)* espacio m; **s. age** era f espacial; **s. shuttle** transbordador m espacial; **s. station** estación f espacial
2 VT *(also* **s. out**) espaciar, separar

spacecraft ['speɪskraːft] N *(pl* **spacecraft**) nave f espacial

spaced out [speɪst'aʊt] ADJ *Fam (dazed)* atontado(a)

spaceman ['speɪsmən] N astronauta m, cosmonauta m

spaceship ['speɪsʃɪp] N nave f espacial

spacing ['speɪsɪŋ] N **double s.** doble espacio m

spacious ['speɪʃəs] ADJ espacioso(a), amplio(a)

spade¹ [speɪd] N *(for digging)* pala f

> Note that the Spanish word **espada** is a false friend and is never a translation for the English word **spade**. In Spanish **espada** means "sword".

spade² [speɪd] N *Cards* pica f

spaghetti [spə'getɪ] N espaguetis mpl

Spain [speɪn] N España

spam [spæm] *Comput* 1 N correo m basura
2 VI enviar correo basura

span [spæn] 1 N *(of wing)* envergadura f; *(of hand)* palmo m; *(of arch)* luz f; *(of road)* tramo m; *(of time)* lapso m; **life s.** vida f
2 VT *(river etc)* extenderse sobre, atravesar; *(period of time etc)* abarcar
3 PT *of* **spin**

Spaniard ['spænjəd] N español(a) m,f

spaniel ['spænjəl] N perro m de aguas

Spanish ['spænɪʃ] 1 ADJ español(a)
2 N (**a**) *(language)* español m, castellano m (**b**) PL **the S.** los españoles

Spanish-speaking ['spænɪ'spiːkɪŋ] ADJ de habla española, hispanohablante

spank [spæŋk] VT zurrar

spanner ['spænə(r)] N *Br* llave *f* plana *(herramienta)*; *Fam* **to throw a s. in the works** estropear los planes

spar¹ [spɑː(r)] N *Naut* palo *m*, verga *f*

spar² [spɑː(r)] VI (a) *(boxers)* entrenarse (b) *(argue)* discutir

spare [speə(r)] 1 VT (a) *(do without)* prescindir de; **I can't s. the time** no tengo tiempo (b) *(begrudge)* escatimar (c) *(show mercy to)* perdonar (d) **s. me the details** ahórrate los detalles

2 ADJ *(left over)* sobrante; *(surplus)* de sobra, de más; **s. part** (pieza *f* de) recambio *m*, **s. room** cuarto *m* de los invitados; **s. wheel** rueda *f* de recambio *or RP* auxilio, *Méx* llanta *f* de refacción

3 N *Aut* (pieza *f* de) recambio *m*

sparing ['speərɪŋ] ADJ **to be s. with praise** escatimar elogios; **to be s. with words** ser parco(a) en palabras

sparingly ['speərɪŋlɪ] ADV en poca cantidad

spark [spɑːk] 1 N chispa *f*; *Aut* **s. plug** bujía *f*

2 VI echar chispas

▸ **spark off** VT SEP desatar

sparking ['spɑːkɪŋ] ADJ **s. plug** bujía *f*

sparkle ['spɑːkəl] 1 VI *(diamond, glass)* centellear, destellar; *(eyes)* brillar

2 N *(of diamond, glass)* centelleo *m*, destello *m*; *(of eyes)* brillo *m*

sparkling ['spɑːklɪŋ] ADJ (a) *(diamond, glass)* centelleante; *(eyes)* brillante; **s. wine** vino espumoso (b) *Fig (person, conversation)* vivaz

sparrow ['spærəʊ] N gorrión *m*

sparse [spɑːs] ADJ *(thin)* escaso(a); *(scattered)* esparcido(a); *(hair)* ralo(a)

Spartan ['spɑːtən] ADJ & N espartano(a) *(m,f)*

spasm ['spæzəm] N (a) *Med* espasmo *m*; *(of coughing)* acceso *m* (b) *(of anger, activity)* arrebato *m*

spasmodic [spæz'mɒdɪk] ADJ (a) *Med* espasmódico(a) (b) *(irregular)* irregular

spastic ['spæstɪk] ADJ & N *Med* espástico(a) *(m,f)*

spat [spæt] PT & PP of **spit¹**

spate [speɪt] N (a) *(of letters)* avalancha *f*; *(of words)* torrente *m*; *(of accidents)* racha *f* (b) *Br (river)* desbordamiento *m*; **to be in full s.** estar crecido(a)

spatter ['spætə(r)] VT salpicar (**with** de)

spatula ['spætjʊlə] N espátula *f*

spawn [spɔːn] 1 N *(of fish, frogs)* huevas *fpl*

2 VI *(fish, frogs)* frezar

3 VT *Fig Pej* generar

speak [spiːk] 1 VT *(pt* spoke; *pp* spoken) (a) *(utter)* decir; **to s. the truth** decir la verdad (b) *(language)* hablar

2 VI (a) *(gen)* hablar, *esp Am* conversar, *Méx* platicar; **roughly speaking** a grandes rasgos; **so to s.** por así decirlo; **speaking of ...** a propósito de ...; **to s. to sb** hablar *or esp Am* conversar *or Méx* platicar con algn (b) *(make a speech)* pronunciar un discurso; *(take the*

floor) tomar la palabra (c) *Tel* hablar; **speaking!** ¡al habla!; **who's speaking, please?** ¿de parte de quién?

▸ **speak for** VT INSEP *(person, group)* hablar en nombre de; **it speaks for itself** es evidente

▸ **speak out** VI **to s. out against sth** denunciar algo

▸ **speak up** VI hablar más fuerte; *Fig* **to s. up for sb** intervenir a favor de algn

speaker ['spiːkə(r)] N (a) *(in dialogue)* interlocutor(a) *m,f*; *(at conference)* conferenciante *mf*, *Am* conferencista *mf*; **(public) s.** orador(a) *m,f* (b) *(of language)* hablante *mf* (c) *(loudspeaker)* altavoz *m*, *Am* altoparlante *m*, *Méx* bocina *f*

spear [spɪə(r)] N lanza *f*; *(javelin)* jabalina *f*; *(harpoon)* arpón *m*

spearhead ['spɪəhed] VT encabezar

spec [spek] N *Fam* **on s.** sin garantías

special ['speʃəl] 1 ADJ especial; *(specific)* específico(a); *(exceptional)* extraordinario(a); **s. delivery** envío *m* urgente; **s. effects** efectos *mpl* especiales

2 N *Rad & TV* programa *m* especial

specialist ['speʃəlɪst] N especialista *mf*

speciality [speʃɪ'ælɪtɪ] N *esp Br* especialidad *f*

specialize ['speʃəlaɪz] VI especializarse (**in** en)

specially ['speʃəlɪ] ADV *(specifically)* especialmente; *(on purpose)* a propósito

specialty ['speʃəltɪ] N *US* = **speciality**

species ['spiːʃiːz] N *(pl* species) especie *f*

specific [spɪ'sɪfɪk] ADJ específico(a); *(definite)* concreto(a); *(precise)* preciso(a); **to be s.** concretar

specifically [spɪ'sɪfɪklɪ] ADV *(exactly)* específicamente; *(expressly)* expresamente; *(namely)* en concreto

specifications [spesɪfɪ'keɪʃənz] NPL *(of machine)* especificaciones *fpl or* características *fpl* técnicas

specify ['spesɪfaɪ] VT especificar, precisar

specimen ['spesɪmɪn] N *(sample)* muestra *f*; *(example)* ejemplar *m*; **urine/tissue s.** espécimen de orina/tejido

speck [spek] N *(of dust)* mota *f*; *(stain)* manchita *f*; *(small trace)* pizca *f*

speckled ['spekəld] ADJ moteado(a)

specs [speks] NPL *Fam (spectacles)* gafas *fpl*

spectacle ['spektəkəl] N (a) *(display)* espectáculo *m* (b) **spectacles** *(glasses)* gafas *fpl*, *Am* lentes *mpl*, *Am* anteojos *mpl*

spectacular [spek'tækjʊlə(r)] 1 ADJ espectacular, impresionante

2 N *Cin & TV* (gran) espectáculo *m*

spectator [spek'teɪtə(r)] N espectador(a) *m,f*

spectre, *US* **specter** ['spektə(r)] N espectro *m*, fantasma *m*

spectrum ['spektrəm] N espectro *m*

speculate ['spekjʊleɪt] VI especular

speculation [spekjʊ'leɪʃən] N especulación *f*

sped [sped] PT & PP of **speed**

speech [spiːtʃ] N (a) (faculty) habla f; (pronunciation) pronunciación f; **freedom of s.** libertad f de expresión (b) (address) discurso m; **to give a s.** pronunciar un discurso (c) Ling **part of s.** parte f de la oración

speechless ['spiːtʃlɪs] ADJ mudo(a), boquiabierto(a)

speed [spiːd] 1 N velocidad f; (rapidity) rapidez f; **at top s.** a toda velocidad; **s. limit** límite m de velocidad
2 VI (a) (pt & pp **sped**) (go fast) ir corriendo; (hurry) apresurarse; **to s. along** (car etc) ir a toda velocidad; **to s. past** pasar volando (b) (pt & pp **speeded**) (exceed speed limit) conducir con exceso de velocidad
▸ **speed up** 1 VT SEP acelerar; (person) meter prisa a
2 VI (person) darse prisa, Am apurarse

speedboat ['spiːdbəʊt] N lancha rápida

speeding ['spiːdɪŋ] N exceso m de velocidad

speedometer [spɪˈdɒmɪtə(r)] N velocímetro m

speedway ['spiːdweɪ] N (a) (racing) carreras fpl de motos (b) (track) pista f de carreras

speedy ['spiːdɪ] ADJ (**speedier, speediest**) veloz, rápido(a)

spell¹ [spel] 1 VT (pt & pp **spelt** or **spelled**) (letter by letter) deletrear; Fig (denote) significar; **how do you s. your name?** ¿cómo se escribe su nombre?
2 VI **she can't s.** comete faltas de ortografía
▸ **spell out** VT SEP Fig explicar con detalle

spell² [spel] N (magical) hechizo m, encanto m

spell³ [spel] N (a) (period) período m; (short period) rato m; Met **cold s.** ola f de frío (b) (shift) turno m

spellbound ['spelbaʊnd] ADJ hechizado(a), embelesado(a)

spell-checker ['speltʃekə(r)] N Comput corrector m ortográfico

spelling ['spelɪŋ] N ortografía f

spelt [spelt] PT & PP of **spell¹**

spend [spend] VT (pt & pp **spent**) (a) (money) gastar (**on** en) (b) (time) pasar; **to s. time on sth** dedicar tiempo a algo

spending ['spendɪŋ] N gastos mpl; **s. money** dinero m de bolsillo; **s. power** poder adquisitivo

spendthrift ['spendθrɪft] ADJ & N derrochador(a) (m,f)

spent [spent] 1 ADJ gastado(a)
2 PT & PP of **spend**

sperm [spɜːm] N esperma m; **s. bank** banco m de esperma; **s. whale** cachalote m

spew [spjuː] VT **to s. (up)** vomitar

sphere [sfɪə(r)] N esfera f

spice [spaɪs] 1 N (a) (seasoning) especia f (b) (interest, excitement) chispa f
2 VT (a) (food) sazonar (b) **to s. (up)** (story etc) salpimentar

spick-and-span [spɪkənˈspæn] ADJ (very clean) limpísimo(a); (well-groomed) acicalado(a)

spicy ['spaɪsɪ] ADJ (**spicier, spiciest**) (a) Culin sazonado(a); (hot) picante (b) Fig (story etc) picante

spider ['spaɪdə(r)] N araña f; Br **s.'s** or US **s. web** telaraña f

spike¹ [spaɪk] N (sharp point) punta f; (metal rod) pincho m; (on railing) barrote m; Sport (on shoes) clavo m

spike² [spaɪk] N Bot espiga f

spiky ['spaɪkɪ] ADJ (**spikier, spikiest**) puntiagudo(a); (hairstyle) de punta

spill [spɪl] 1 VT (pt & pp **spilled** or **spilt** [spɪlt]) derramar
2 VI (liquid) derramarse
▸ **spill over** VI desbordarse

spin [spɪn] 1 VT (pt **span** or **spun**; pp **spun**) (a) (wheel etc) hacer girar; (washing) centrifugar (b) (cotton, wool) hilar; (spider's web) tejer
2 VI (wheel etc) girar; Av caer en barrena; Aut patinar
3 N (a) (turn) vuelta f, giro m (b) Sport efecto m (c) Br **to go for a s.** (ride) dar una vuelta (d) Pol (on news story) sesgo m; **s. doctor** asesor(a) político(a) (para dar buena prensa a un partido o político)

spinach ['spɪnɪtʃ] N espinacas fpl

spinal ['spaɪnəl] ADJ espinal, vertebral; **s. column** columna f vertebral; **s. cord** médula f espinal

spindly ['spɪndlɪ] ADJ (**spindlier, spindliest**) Fam (long-bodied) larguirucho(a); (long-legged) zanquilargo(a)

spin-dryer [spɪnˈdraɪə(r)] N secador centrífugo

spine [spaɪn] N (a) Anat columna f vertebral, espinazo m; (of book) lomo m (b) Zool púa f; Bot espina f

spineless ['spaɪnlɪs] ADJ Fig (weak) sin carácter

spinning ['spɪnɪŋ] N (a) (of cotton etc) (act) hilado m; (art) hilandería f; **s. wheel** rueca f (b) **s. top** peonza f

spin-off ['spɪnɒf] N (by-product) derivado m; Fig efecto secundario

spinster ['spɪnstə(r)] N soltera f

spiral ['spaɪərəl] 1 N espiral f
2 ADJ en espiral; **s. staircase** escalera f de caracol

spire ['spaɪə(r)] N (of church) aguja f

spirit¹ ['spɪrɪt] N (a) (soul) espíritu m, alma f; (ghost) fantasma m (b) (attitude) espíritu m; (mood) humor m (c) (courage) valor m; (liveliness) ánimo m; (vitality) vigor m (d) **spirits** (mood) humor m; **to be in good spirits** estar de buen humor

spirit² ['spɪrɪt] N (a) Chem alcohol m; **s. level** nivel m de aire (b) **spirits** (alcoholic drinks) licores mpl

spirited ['spɪrɪtɪd] ADJ (person, attempt) valiente; (horse) fogoso(a); (attack) enérgico(a)

spiritual ['spɪrɪtjʊəl] ADJ espiritual

spit¹ [spɪt] 1 VT (pt & pp **spat**) escupir
2 VI escupir; Fam **he's the spitting image of his father** es el vivo retrato de su padre
3 N (saliva) saliva f

spit² [spɪt] N Culin asador m

spite [spaɪt] 1 N (a) (ill will) rencor m, ojeriza f (b) **in s. of** a pesar de, pese a; **in s. of the fact that** a pesar de que, pese a que
2 VT (annoy) fastidiar

spiteful ['spaɪtfʊl] ADJ (person) rencoroso(a); (remark) malévolo(a); (tongue) viperino(a)

spittle ['spɪtəl] N saliva f

spittoon [spɪ'tuːn] N escupidera f

splash [splæʃ] 1 VT salpicar
2 VI (a) **to s. (about)** (in water) chapotear (b) (water etc) salpicar
3 N (a) (noise) chapoteo m (b) (spray) salpicadura f; Fig (of colour) mancha f
▸ **splash out** VI Fam tirar la casa por la ventana

spleen [spliːn] N Anat bazo m

splendid ['splendɪd] ADJ espléndido(a)

splendour, US **splendor** ['splendə(r)] N esplendor m

splint [splɪnt] N tablilla f

splinter ['splɪntə(r)] 1 N (wood) astilla f; (bone, stone) esquirla f; (glass) fragmento m; **s. group** grupo m disidente
2 VI (a) (wood etc) astillarse (b) Pol escindirse

split [splɪt] 1 N (crack) grieta f, hendidura f; (tear) desgarrón m; Fig (division) cisma m; Pol escisión f
2 ADJ partido(a); **in a s. second** en una fracción de segundo
3 VT (pt & pp **split**) (a) (crack) agrietar; (cut) partir; (tear) rajar; (atom) desintegrar (b) (divide) dividir (c) (share out) repartir (d) Pol escindir
4 VI (a) (crack) agrietarse; (into two parts) partirse; (garment) rajarse (b) (divide) dividirse (c) Pol escindirse
▸ **split up** 1 VT SEP (break up) partir; (divide up) dividir; (share out) repartir
2 VI (couple) separarse

splutter ['splʌtə(r)] VI (person) balbucear; (candle, fat) chisporrotear; (engine) petardear

spoil [spɔɪl] 1 VT (pt & pp **spoiled** or **spoilt**) (a) (ruin) estropear, echar a perder (b) (child) mimar a; **to be spoilt for choice** tener demasiadas cosas para elegir
2 VI (food) estropearse

spoilsport ['spɔɪlspɔːt] N Fam aguafiestas mf inv

spoilt [spɔɪlt] 1 ADJ (a) (food, merchandise) estropeado(a) (b) (child) mimado(a)
2 PT & PP of **spoil**

spoke¹ [spəʊk] PT of **speak**

spoke² [spəʊk] N (of wheel) radio m, rayo m

spoken ['spəʊkən] PP of **speak**

spokesman ['spəʊksmən] N portavoz m

spokeswoman ['spəʊkswʊmən] N portavoz f

sponge [spʌndʒ] 1 N esponja f; Fig **to throw in the s.** arrojar la toalla; Br **s. cake** bizcocho m
2 VT (wash) lavar con esponja
3 VI Fam vivir de gorra
▸ **sponge off, sponge on** VT INSEP vivir a costa de

sponger ['spʌndʒə(r)] Fam gorrero(a) m,f, Esp, Méx gorrón(ona) m,f, RP garronero(a) m,f

spongy ['spʌndʒɪ] ADJ (**spongier, spongiest**) esponjoso(a)

sponsor ['spɒnsə(r)] 1 VT patrocinar; Fin avalar; (support) respaldar
2 N patrocinador(a) m,f; Fin avalador(a) m,f

sponsorship ['spɒnsəʃɪp] N patrocinio m; Fin aval m; (support) respaldo m

spontaneous [spɒn'teɪnɪəs] ADJ espontáneo(a)

spoof [spuːf] N Fam (a) (parody) burla f (b) (hoax) engaño m

spooky ['spuːkɪ] ADJ (**spookier, spookiest**) Fam espeluznante

spool [spuːl] N bobina f, carrete m

spoon [spuːn] 1 N cuchara f; (small) cucharita f
2 VT sacar con cuchara; (serve) servir con cuchara

spoon-feed ['spuːnfiːd] VT (baby) dar de comer con cuchara a; Fig (spoil) mimar

spoonful ['spuːnfʊl] N cucharada f

sporadic [spə'rædɪk] ADJ esporádico(a)

sport [spɔːt] 1 N (a) (activity) deporte m (b) Fam **he's a good s.** es buena persona; **be a s.!** ¡sé amable!
2 VT (display) lucir

sporting ['spɔːtɪŋ] ADJ deportivo(a)

sports [spɔːts] ADJ **s. car** coche m or Am carro m or CSur auto m deportivo; **s. centre** polideportivo m; Br **s. jacket** chaqueta f or Am saco m de sport

sportsman ['spɔːtsmən] N deportista m

sportsmanlike ['spɔːtsmənlaɪk] ADJ deportivo(a)

sportsmanship ['spɔːtsmənʃɪp] N deportividad f

sportswear ['spɔːtsweə(r)] N (for sport) ropa f de deporte; (casual clothes) ropa (de) sport

sportswoman ['spɔːtswʊmən] N deportista f

sporty ['spɔːtɪ] ADJ (**sportier, sportiest**) Fam deportivo(a)

spot [spɒt] 1 N (a) (dot) punto m; (on fabric) lunar m (b) (stain) mancha f (c) (pimple) grano m (d) (place) sitio m, lugar m; **on the s.** (person) allí, presente; **to be in a tight s.** estar en un apuro; **to put sb on the s.** poner a algn en un aprieto (e) Br Fam (small amount) (of rain, wine) gota f; **a s. of bother** una problemilla
2 VT (notice) darse cuenta de, notar; (see) ver

spotless ['spɒtlɪs] ADJ (very clean) impecable; Fig (reputation etc) intachable

spotlight ['spɒtlaɪt] N foco m; Aut faro m auxiliar; Fig **to be in the s.** ser objeto de la atención pública

spot-on [spɒt'ɒn] ADJ Br Fam exacto(a)

spotted ['spɒtɪd] ADJ (with dots) con puntos; (fabric) con lunares; (speckled) moteado(a)

spotty ['spɒtɪ] ADJ (**spottier, spottiest**) Pej con granos

spouse [spaʊs] N cónyuge mf

spout [spaʊt] 1 N (of jug) pico m; (of teapot) pitorro m
2 VT Fam (nonsense) soltar
3 VI to s. out/up (liquid) brotar

sprain [spreɪn] 1 N esguince m
2 VT torcer; **to s. one's ankle** torcerse el tobillo

sprang [spræŋ] PT of **spring**²

sprawl [sprɔ:l] 1 VI (a) (sit, lie) tumbarse (b) (city, plant) extenderse
2 N (of city) extensión f

spray¹ [spreɪ] 1 N (a) (of water) rociada f; (from sea) espuma f; (from aerosol) pulverización f (b) (aerosol) spray m; (for plants) pulverizador m; **s. can** aerosol m
2 VT (water) rociar; (insecticide, perfume) pulverizar

spray² [spreɪ] N (of flowers) ramita f

spread [spred] 1 N (a) (of ideas) difusión f; (of disease, fire) propagación f; (of terrorism) generalización f (b) (for bread) **cheese s.** queso m para untar (c) Fam (large meal) banquetazo m
2 VT (pt & pp **spread**) (a) (unfold) desplegar; (lay out) extender (b) (butter etc) untar (c) (news) difundir; (rumour) hacer correr; (disease, fire) propagar; (panic) sembrar
3 VI (a) (stretch out) extenderse; (unfold) desplegarse (b) (news) difundirse; (rumour) correr; (disease) propagarse

spread-eagled [spred'i:gəld] ADJ despatarrado(a)

spreadsheet ['spredʃi:t] N Comput hoja f de cálculo

spree [spri:] N juerga f; **to go on a s.** ir de juerga

sprig [sprɪg] N ramita f

sprightly ['spraɪtlɪ] ADJ (**sprightlier, sprightliest**) (nimble) ágil; (energetic) enérgico(a); (lively) animado(a)

spring¹ [sprɪŋ] 1 N (season) primavera f
2 ADJ primaveral; **s. onion** cebolleta f, RP cebolla f de verdeo; **s. roll** rollo m de primavera, RP arrollado m de primavera

spring² [sprɪŋ] 1 N (a) (of water) manantial m, fuente f (b) (of watch etc) resorte m; (of mattress) muelle m; Aut ballesta f
2 VI (pt **sprang**; pp **sprung**) (a) (jump) saltar; **the lid sprang open** la tapa se abrió de golpe (b) (appear) aparecer (de repente)
3 VT (a) **to s. a leak** hacer agua (b) Fig (news, surprise) dar de golpe

▸ **spring up** VI aparecer; (plants) brotar; (buildings) elevarse; (problems) surgir

springboard ['sprɪŋbɔ:d] N trampolín m

spring-clean [sprɪŋ'kli:n] VT limpiar a fondo

springtime ['sprɪŋtaɪm] N primavera f

springy ['sprɪŋɪ] ADJ (**springier, springiest**) (bouncy) elástico(a); Fig (step) saltarín

sprinkle ['sprɪŋkəl] VT (with water) rociar (**with** de); (with sugar) espolvorear (**with** de)

sprint [sprɪnt] 1 N esprint m
2 VI esprintar

sprinter ['sprɪntə(r)] N esprínter mf, velocista mf

sprout [spraʊt] 1 VI (bud) brotar; Fig crecer rápidamente
2 N (**Brussels**) **sprouts** coles fpl or CSur repollitos mpl de Bruselas

spruce¹ [spru:s] N Bot picea f

spruce² [spru:s] ADJ (neat) pulcro(a); (smart) apuesto(a)

▸ **spruce up** VT SEP acicalar

sprung [sprʌŋ] PP of **spring**

spry [spraɪ] ADJ (**sprier, spriest**) (nimble) ágil; (active) activo(a); (lively) vivaz

spun [spʌn] PT & PP of **spin**

spur [spɜ:(r)] 1 N (a) (for riding) espuela f (b) Fig (stimulus) acicate m; **on the s. of the moment** sin pensarlo
2 VT (a) (horse) espolear (b) Fig incitar

spurious ['spjʊərɪəs] ADJ falso(a), espurio(a)

spurn [spɜ:n] VT Fml desdeñar, rechazar

spurt [spɜ:t] 1 N (a) (of liquid) chorro m (b) Fig (of activity etc) racha f; (effort) esfuerzo m
2 VI (a) (liquid) chorrear (b) (make an effort) hacer un último esfuerzo; (accelerate) acelerar

spy [spaɪ] 1 N espía mf
2 VT Fml (see) divisar
3 VI espiar (**on** a)

spyhole ['spaɪhəʊl] N mirilla f

spying ['spaɪɪŋ] N espionaje m

squabble ['skwɒbəl] 1 N riña f, pelea f
2 VI reñir, pelearse (**over** or **about** por)

squad [skwɒd] N Mil pelotón m; (of police) brigada f; Sport equipo m; **drugs s.** brigada antidroga

squadron ['skwɒdrən] N Mil escuadrón m; Av escuadrilla f; Naut escuadra f

squalid ['skwɒlɪd] ADJ (very dirty) asqueroso(a); (poor) miserable; (motive) vil

squall¹ [skwɔ:l] N (wind) ráfaga f

squall² [skwɔ:l] VI chillar, berrear

squalor ['skwɒlə(r)] N (dirtiness) mugre f; (poverty) miseria f

squander ['skwɒndə(r)] VT (money) derrochar, despilfarrar; (time) desperdiciar

square [skweə(r)] 1 N (a) (shape) cuadro m; (on chessboard, crossword) casilla f (b) (in town) plaza f (c) Math cuadrado m
2 ADJ (a) (in shape) cuadrado(a) (b) Math

(metre, root) cuadrado(a) (**c**) **a s. meal** una buena comida (**d**) *(old-fashioned)* carroza; *(conservative)* carca
  3 VT (**a**) *Math* elevar al cuadrado (**b**) *(settle)* arreglar
  4 VI *(agree)* cuadrar (**with** con)

squarely ['skweəlɪ] ADV *(directly)* directamente, de lleno

squash¹ [skwɒʃ] **1** N *Br (drink)* **orange/lemon s.** (bebida *f* a base de) concentrado *m* de naranja/limón
  2 VT *(crush)* aplastar
  3 VI aplastarse

squash² [skwɒʃ] N *Sport* squash *m*

squash³ [skwɒʃ] N *US (vegetable)* calabacín *m*

squat [skwɒt] **1** ADJ *(person)* rechoncho(a)
  2 VI (**a**) *(crouch)* agacharse, sentarse en cuclillas (**b**) *(in building)* ocupar ilegalmente
  3 N *Br (illegally occupied dwelling)* casa *f* ocupada *(ilegalmente)*

squatter ['skwɒtə(r)] N ocupante *mf* ilegal, okupa *mf*

squawk [skwɔːk] **1** N graznido *m*
  2 VI graznar

squeak [skwiːk] **1** N *(of mouse)* chillido *m*; *(of hinge, wheel)* chirrido *m*; *(of shoes)* crujido *m*
  2 VI *(mouse)* chillar; *(hinge, wheel)* chirriar, rechinar; *(shoes)* crujir

squeaky ['skwiːkɪ] ADJ (**squeakier, squeakiest**) chirriante; *(voice)* chillón(ona); *(shoes)* que crujen

squeal [skwiːl] **1** N *(of animal, person)* chillido *m*
  2 VI (**a**) *(animal, person)* chillar (**b**) *Fam (inform)* chivarse

squeamish ['skwiːmɪʃ] ADJ muy sensible

squeeze [skwiːz] **1** VT apretar; *(lemon etc)* exprimir; *(sponge)* estrujar; **to s. paste out of a tube** sacar pasta de un tubo apretando
  2 VI **to s. in** apretujarse
  3 N (**a**) *(pressure)* estrujón *m*; **a s. of lemon** unas gotas de limón (**b**) *(of hand)* apretón *m*; *(hug)* abrazo *m*; *(crush)* apiñamiento *m*; **credit s.** reducción *f* de créditos

squelch [skwɛltʃ] VI chapotear

squid [skwɪd] N calamar *m*; *(small)* chipirón *m*

squiggle ['skwɪgəl] N garabato *m*

squint [skwɪnt] **1** N (**a**) *(eye defect)* **to have a s.** tener estrabismo (**b**) *Br (quick look)* ojeada *f*, vistazo *m*
  2 VI (**a**) *(have an eye defect)* tener estrabismo (**b**) **to s. at sth** *(glance)* echar un vistazo a algo; *(with eyes half-closed)* mirar algo con los ojos entrecerrados

squirm [skwɜːm] VI retorcerse; *(with embarrassment)* ruborizarse, avergonzarse, *Am* apenarse

squirrel ['skwɪrəl] N ardilla *f*

squirt [skwɜːt] **1** N *(of liquid)* chorro *m*
  2 VT lanzar a chorro
  3 VI **to s. out** salir a chorros

Sr *(abbr* **Senior***)* **Thomas Smith, Sr** Thomas Smith, padre

Sri Lanka [sriːˈlæŋkə] N Sri Lanka

St (**a**) *(abbr* **Saint***)* S./Sto./Sta. (**b**) *(abbr* **Street***)* c/

st *Br (abbr* **stone***)* = peso que equivale a 6,348 kg

stab [stæb] **1** N *(with knife)* puñalada *f*; *(of pain)* punzada *f*
  2 VT apuñalar

stabbing ['stæbɪŋ] ADJ *(pain)* punzante

stability [stəˈbɪlɪtɪ] N estabilidad *f*

stabilize ['steɪbɪlaɪz] **1** VT estabilizar
  2 VI estabilizarse

stable¹ ['steɪbəl] ADJ estable

stable² ['steɪbəl] N cuadra *f*, caballeriza *f*

stack [stæk] **1** N *(pile)* montón *m*; *Fam* **he's got stacks of money** está forrado
  2 VT *(pile up)* amontonar, apilar; *Fig* **the odds are stacked against us** todo está en contra nuestra

stadium ['steɪdɪəm] N estadio *m*

staff [stɑːf] **1** N (**a**) *(personnel)* personal *m*; *Mil* estado *m* mayor; **s. meeting** claustro *m*; *Br* **s. nurse** enfermera cualificada (**b**) *(stick)* bastón *m*; *(of shepherd)* cayado *m*
  2 VT proveer de personal

staffroom ['stɑːfruːm] N sala *f* de profesores

stag [stæg] N ciervo *m*, venado *m*; *Fam* **s. party** despedida *f* de soltero

stage [steɪdʒ] **1** N (**a**) *(platform)* plataforma *f* (**b**) *(in theatre)* escenario *m*; **s. door** entrada *f* de artistas; **s. fright** miedo escénico; **s. manager** director(a) *m,f* de escena (**c**) *(phase)* *(of development, journey, rocket)* etapa *f*; *(of road, pipeline)* tramo *m*; **at this s. of the negotiations** a estas alturas de las negociaciones; **in stages** por etapas
  2 VT (**a**) *(play)* poner en escena, montar (**b**) *(arrange)* organizar; *(carry out)* llevar a cabo

stagecoach ['steɪdʒkəʊtʃ] N diligencia *f*

stagger ['stægə(r)] **1** VI tambalearse
  2 VT (**a**) *(amaze)* asombrar (**b**) *(hours, work)* escalonar

staggering ['stægərɪŋ] ADJ asombroso(a)

stagnant ['stægnənt] ADJ estancado(a)

stagnate [stægˈneɪt] VI estancarse

staid [steɪd] ADJ *(person)* conservador(a); *(manner, clothes)* serio(a), formal

stain [steɪn] **1** N (**a**) *(mark)* mancha *f*; **s. remover** quitamanchas *m inv* (**b**) *(dye)* tinte *m*
  2 VT (**a**) *(mark)* manchar (**b**) *(dye)* teñir
  3 VI mancharse

stained [steɪnd] ADJ **s. glass window** vidriera *f* de colores

stainless ['steɪnlɪs] ADJ *(steel)* inoxidable

stair [steə(r)] N escalón *m*, peldaño *m*; **stairs** *(flight)* escalera *f*

staircase ['steəkeɪs] N escalera *f*

stake¹ [steɪk] **1** N (*stick*) estaca *f*; (*for plant*) rodrigón *m*; (*post*) poste *m*
2 VT **to s. (out)** cercar con estacas

stake² [steɪk] **1** N (**a**) (*bet*) apuesta *f*; **the issue at s.** el tema en cuestión; **to be at s.** (*at risk*) estar en juego (**b**) (*investment*) interés *m*
2 VT (*bet*) apostar; (*invest*) invertir; **to s. a claim to sth** reivindicar algo

stale [steɪl] ADJ (*food*) pasado(a); (*bread*) duro(a)

stalemate ['steɪlmeɪt] N (*in chess*) tablas *fpl*; Fig **to reach s.** llegar a un punto muerto

stalk¹ [stɔːk] N (*of plant*) tallo *m*; (*of fruit*) rabo *m*

stalk² [stɔːk] **1** VT (*of hunter*) cazar al acecho; (*of animal*) acechar
2 VI **he stalked out of the room** salió *esp* Esp enfadado *or esp* Am enojado de la habitación

stall [stɔːl] **1** N (**a**) (*in market*) puesto *m*; (*at fair*) caseta *f* (**b**) (*stable*) establo *m*; (*stable compartment*) casilla *f* de establo (**c**) Br Cin & Th **the stalls** el patio de butacas
2 VT (*hold off*) retener
3 VI (**a**) Aut pararse, Esp calarse; Av perder velocidad (**b**) (*delay*) **to s. (for time)** intentar ganar tiempo

stallion ['stælɪən] N semental *m*

stalwart ['stɔːlwət] N incondicional *mf*

stamina ['stæmɪnə] N resistencia *f*

stammer ['stæmə(r)] **1** N tartamudeo *m*
2 VI tartamudear

stamp [stæmp] **1** N (**a**) (*postage stamp*) sello *m*, Am estampilla *f*, CAm, Méx timbre *m*; **s. album** álbum *m* de sellos; **s. collector** filatelista *mf*; **s.** Br **duty** *or* US **tax** póliza *f*, = impuesto de transmisiones patrimoniales (**b**) (*rubber stamp*) tampón *m*; (*for metals*) cuño *m* (**c**) (*with foot*) patada *f*
2 VT (**a**) (*with postage stamp*) poner el sello a; Br **stamped addressed envelope,** US **self-addressed stamped envelope** sobre franqueado con la dirección del remitente (**b**) (*with rubber stamp*) sellar (**c**) **to s. one's feet** patear; (*in dancing*) zapatear
3 VI patear

> Note that the Spanish word **estampa** is a false friend and is never a translation for the English word **stamp**. In Spanish **estampa** means "print, image".

▸ **stamp out** VT SEP Fig (*racism etc*) acabar con; (*rebellion*) sofocar

stampede [stæm'piːd] **1** N estampida *f*; Fig (*rush*) desbandada *f*
2 VI desbandarse; Fig (*rush*) precipitarse

stance [stæns] N postura *f*

stand [stænd] **1** N (**a**) (*position*) posición *f*, postura *f*; **to make a s.** resistir (**b**) (*of lamp, sculpture*) pie *m* (**c**) (*market stall*) puesto *m*; (*at fair*) caseta *f*; (*at exhibition*) stand *m* (**d**) (*platform*) plataforma *f*; (*in stadium*) gradas *fpl*, Esp graderío *m*; US (*witness box*) estrado *m*

2 VT (*pt & pp* **stood**) (**a**) (*place*) poner, colocar (**b**) (*tolerate*) aguantar, soportar
3 VI (**a**) (*be upright*) estar de pie *or* Am parado(a); (*get up*) levantarse; (*remain upright*) quedarse de pie *or* Am parado(a); **s. still!** ¡estáte quieto(a)! (**b**) (*be situated*) estar, encontrarse (**c**) (*remain valid*) seguir vigente (**d**) **as things s.** tal como están las cosas (**e**) Pol presentarse

▸ **stand back** VI (*allow sb to pass*) abrir paso

▸ **stand by** **1** VI (**a**) (*do nothing*) quedarse sin hacer nada (**b**) (*be ready*) estar listo(a)
2 VT INSEP (*person*) apoyar a; (*promise*) cumplir con; (*decision*) atenerse a

▸ **stand down** VI Fig retirarse

▸ **stand for** VT INSEP (**a**) (*mean*) significar (**b**) (*represent*) representar (**c**) (*tolerate*) aguantar

▸ **stand in** VI sustituir

▸ **stand in for** VT INSEP sustituir

▸ **stand out** VI (*mountain etc*) destacarse (**against** contra); (*person*) destacar

▸ **stand up** VI (*get up*) ponerse de pie, Am pararse; (*be standing*) estar de pie; Fig **it will s. up to wear and tear** es muy resistente; Fig **to s. up for sb** defender a algn; Fig **to s. up to sb** hacer frente a algn

standard ['stændəd] **1** N (**a**) (*level*) nivel *m*; **s. of living** nivel de vida (**b**) (*criterion*) criterio *m* (**c**) (*norm*) norma *f*, estándar *m*
2 ADJ normal, estándar; **s. lamp** lámpara *f* de pie

standardize ['stændədaɪz] VT normalizar

standby ['stændbaɪ] N (**a**) (*thing*) recurso *m* (**b**) (*person*) suplente *mf*; **to be on s.** Mil estar de retén; Av estar en la lista de espera; **s. ticket** billete *m* sin reserva

stand-in ['stændɪn] N suplente *mf*; Cin doble *mf*

standing ['stændɪŋ] **1** ADJ (**a**) (*not sitting*) de pie; (*upright*) recto(a); **to give sb a s. ovation** ovacionar a algn de pie; **there was s. room only** no quedaban asientos (**b**) (*committee, invitation*) permanente; Br **s. order** pago fijo
2 N (**a**) (*social position*) rango *m* (**b**) (*duration*) duración *f*; (*in job*) antigüedad *f*

stand-offish [stænd'ɒfɪʃ] ADJ Fam distante

standpoint ['stændpɔɪnt] N punto *m* de vista

standstill ['stændstɪl] N **at a s.** (*car, traffic*) parado(a); (*industry*) paralizado(a); **to come to a s.** (*car, traffic*) pararse; (*industry*) paralizarse

stand-up ['stændʌp] ADJ **s. comic** *or* **comedian** = humorista que basa su actuación en contar chistes al público solo desde el escenario

stank [stæŋk] PT of **stink**

staple¹ ['steɪpəl] **1** N (*fastener*) grapa *f*, Chile corchete *m*, RP ganchito *m*
2 VT grapar

staple² ['steɪpəl] **1** ADJ (*food*) básico(a); (*product*) de primera necesidad
2 N (*food*) alimento básico

stapler ['steɪplə(r)] N grapadora f, *Am* engrapadora f, *Chile* corchetera f, *RP* abrochadora f

star [stɑː(r)] **1** N estrella f
2 ADJ estelar
3 VT *Cin* tener como protagonista a
4 VI *Cin* **to s. in a movie** protagonizar una película

starboard ['stɑːbəd] N estribor m

starch [stɑːtʃ] **1** N almidón m
2 VT almidonar

stardom ['stɑːdəm] N estrellato m

stare [steə(r)] **1** N mirada fija
2 VI mirar fijamente

starfish ['stɑːfɪʃ] N estrella f de mar

stark [stɑːk] ADJ *(landscape)* desolado(a); *(décor)* austero(a); **the s. truth** la dura realidad; **s. poverty** la miseria

stark-naked ['stɑːkneɪkɪd] ADJ *Fam* en cueros

starling ['stɑːlɪŋ] N estornino m

starry ['stɑːrɪ] ADJ **(starrier, starriest)** estrellado(a)

starry-eyed [stɑːrɪ'aɪd] ADJ *(idealistic)* idealista; *(in love)* enamorado(a)

start [stɑːt] **1** N **(a)** *(beginning)* principio m, comienzo m; *(of race)* salida f; **for a s.** para empezar; **from the s.** desde el principio; **to make a fresh s.** volver a empezar **(b)** *(advantage)* ventaja f **(c)** *(jump)* sobresalto m
2 VT **(a)** *(begin)* empezar, comenzar; **to s. doing sth** empezar a hacer algo **(b)** *(cause)* causar, provocar **(c)** *(found)* fundar; **to s. a business** montar un negocio **(d)** *(set in motion)* arrancar
3 VI **(a)** *(begin)* empezar, comenzar; *(engine)* arrancar; **starting from Monday** a partir del lunes **(b)** *(take fright)* asustarse, sobresaltarse
▶ **start off** VI **(a)** *(begin)* empezar, comenzar; **to s. off by/with** empezar por/con **(b)** *(leave)* salir, ponerse en camino
▶ **start up 1** VT SEP *(engine)* arrancar
2 VI empezar; *(car)* arrancar

starter ['stɑːtə(r)] N **(a)** *Sport (official)* juez mf de salida; *(competitor)* competidor(a) m,f **(b)** *Aut* motor m de arranque **(c)** *Culin* entrada f

starting ['stɑːtɪŋ] N **s. block** taco m de salida; **s. point** punto m de partida; **s. post** línea f de salida

startle ['stɑːtəl] VT asustar

startling ['stɑːtlɪŋ] ADJ **(a)** *(frightening)* alarmante **(b)** *(news etc)* asombroso(a); *(coincidence)* extraordinario(a)

starvation [stɑː'veɪʃən] N hambre f

starve [stɑːv] **1** VT privar de comida; *Fig* **was starved of affection** fue privado de cariño
2 VI pasar hambre; **to s. to death** morirse de hambre

starving ['stɑːvɪŋ] ADJ hambriento(a); *Fam* **I'm s.!** ¡estoy muerto(a) de hambre!

state [steɪt] **1** N **(a)** *(condition, situation)* estado m; **s. of emergency** estado de emergencia; **s. of mind** estado de ánimo; **to be in no fit s. to do sth** no estar en condiciones de hacer algo **(b)** *(country, administrative region)* estado m; *Fam* **the States** los Estados Unidos; *US* **s. highway** ≃ carretera f nacional; *US* **S. Department** Departamento m de Estado, = Ministerio de Asuntos *or Am* Relaciones Exteriores estadounidense
2 ADJ **(a)** *Pol* estatal; **s. education** enseñanza pública; **s. ownership** propiedad f del Estado **(b)** *(ceremonial)* de gala; **s. visit** visita f oficial
3 VT declarar, afirmar; *(case)* exponer; *(problem)* plantear

stated ['steɪtɪd] ADJ indicado(a)

stately ['steɪtlɪ] ADJ **(statelier, stateliest)** majestuoso(a); **s. home** casa solariega

statement ['steɪtmənt] N **(a)** *(of opinion)* declaración f; **official s.** comunicado m oficial; *Jur* **to make a s.** prestar declaración **(b)** *Fin* estado m de cuenta; **monthly s.** balance m mensual

statesman ['steɪtsmən] N estadista m

static ['stætɪk] **1** ADJ estático(a)
2 N *Rad* ruido m

station ['steɪʃən] **1** N **(a)** *(for trains, buses)* estación f; *US* **s. wagon** *(car)* ranchera f, *Esp* coche m modelo familiar **(b)** *(position)* puesto m **(c)** *(social standing)* rango m
2 VT *(place)* colocar; *Mil* apostar

stationary ['steɪʃənərɪ] ADJ *(not moving)* inmóvil; *(unchanging)* estacionario(a)

stationer ['steɪʃənə(r)] N papelero(a) m,f; **s.'s (shop)** papelería f

stationery ['steɪʃənərɪ] N *(paper)* papel m de escribir; *(pens, ink etc)* artículos mpl de escritorio

stationmaster ['steɪʃənmɑːstə(r)] N jefe m de estación

statistic [stə'tɪstɪk] N estadística f

statistical [stə'tɪstɪkəl] ADJ estadístico(a)

statistics [stə'tɪstɪks] **1** N SING *(science)* estadística f
2 NPL *(data)* estadísticas fpl

statue ['stætjuː] N estatua f

stature ['stætʃə(r)] N *(physical build)* estatura f; *(reputation)* talla f, estatura f

status ['steɪtəs] N estado m; **social s.** estatus m; **s. symbol** signo m de prestigio; **s. quo** status quo m

statute ['stætjuːt] N estatuto m

statutory ['stætjʊtərɪ] ADJ reglamentario(a); *(offence)* contemplado(a) por la ley; *(right)* legal; *(holiday)* oficial

staunch [stɔːntʃ] ADJ incondicional, acérrimo

stave [steɪv] N *Mus* pentagrama m
▶ **stave off** VT SEP *(repel)* rechazar; *(avoid)* evitar; *(delay)* aplazar

stay¹ [steɪ] **1** N *Esp, Méx* estancia f, *Am* estadía f
2 VI **(a)** *(remain)* quedarse, permanecer **(b)** *(reside temporarily)* alojarse; **she's staying with us for a few days** ha venido a pasar unos días con nosotros

3 VT *Fig* **to s. the course** aguantar hasta el final; **staying power** resistencia *f*

▶ **stay in** VI quedarse en casa

▶ **stay on** VI quedarse

▶ **stay out** VI **to s. out all night** no volver a casa en toda la noche

▶ **stay up** VI no acostarse

stay² [steɪ] N *(rope)* estay *m*, viento *m*

stead [sted] N **in sb's s.** en lugar de algn; **to stand sb in good s.** resultar muy útil a algn

steadfast ['stedfəst, 'stedfɑːst] ADJ firme

steadily ['stedɪlɪ] ADV *(improve)* constantemente; *(walk)* con paso seguro; *(gaze)* fijamente; *(rain, work)* sin parar

steady ['stedɪ] 1 ADJ **(steadier, steadiest)** firme, seguro(a); *(gaze)* fijo(a); *(prices)* estable; *(demand, speed)* constante; *(pace)* regular; *(worker)* aplicado(a); **s. job** empleo fijo
2 VT *(table etc)* estabilizar; *(nerves)* calmar
3 VI *(market)* estabilizarse

steak [steɪk] N filete *m*, bistec *m*, *RP* bife *m*

steal [stiːl] *(pt* **stole;** *pp* **stolen)** 1 VT robar; **to s. a glance at sth** echar una mirada furtiva a algo; **to s. the show** llevarse todos los aplausos
2 VI **(a)** *(rob)* robar **(b)** *(move quietly)* moverse con sigilo; **to s. away** escabullirse

stealth [stelθ] N sigilo *m*

stealthily ['stelθɪlɪ] ADV a hurtadillas

stealthy ['stelθɪ] ADJ **(stealthier, stealthiest)** sigiloso(a), furtivo(a)

steam [stiːm] 1 N vapor *m*; *Fam* **to let off s.** desahogarse; **s. engine** máquina *f* de vapor
2 VT *Culin* cocer al vapor
3 VI *(give off steam)* echar vapor; *(bowl of soup etc)* humear

▶ **steam up** VI *(window etc)* empañarse

steamer ['stiːmə(r)] N *Naut* vapor *m*

steamroller ['stiːmrəʊlə(r)] N apisonadora *f*

steamship ['stiːmʃɪp] N vapor *m*

steamy ['stiːmɪ] ADJ **(steamier, steamiest)** lleno(a) de vapor

steel [stiːl] 1 N acero *m*; **s. industry** industria siderúrgica
2 VT *Fig* **to s. oneself to do sth** armarse de valor para hacer algo

steelworks ['stiːlwɜːks] NPL acería *f*

steep¹ [stiːp] ADJ *(hill etc)* empinado(a); *Fig (price, increase)* excesivo(a)

steep² [stiːp] VT *(washing)* remojar; *(food)* poner en remojo

steeple ['stiːpəl] N aguja *f*

steeplechase ['stiːpəltʃeɪs] N carrera *f* de obstáculos

steer [stɪə(r)] 1 VT dirigir; *(car)* conducir, *Am* manejar; *(ship)* gobernar
2 VI *(car)* conducir, *Am* manejar; *Fig* **to s. clear of sth** evitar algo

steering ['stɪərɪŋ] N dirección *f*; **assisted s.** dirección asistida; **s. wheel** volante *m*, *Andes* timón *m*

stem [stem] 1 N **(a)** *(of plant)* tallo *m*; *(of glass)* pie *m*; *(of pipe)* tubo *m* **(b)** *(of word)* raíz *f*
2 VI **to s. from** derivarse de
3 VT *(blood)* restañar; *(flood, attack)* contener

stench [stentʃ] N hedor *m*

stencil ['stensəl] N **(a)** *(for artwork etc)* plantilla *f* **(b)** *(for typing)* cliché *m*

step [step] 1 N **(a)** *(movement, sound)* paso *m*; **s. by s.** poco a poco **(b)** *(measure)* medida *f*; **a s. in the right direction** un paso acertado **(c)** *(stair)* peldaño *m*, escalón *m* **(d)** **steps** *(flight)* escalera *f*
2 VI dar un paso; **s. this way, please** haga el favor de pasar por aquí; **to s. aside** apartarse

▶ **step down** VI dimitir

▶ **step forward** VI *(volunteer)* ofrecerse

▶ **step in** VI intervenir

▶ **step up** VT SEP aumentar

stepbrother ['stepbrʌðə(r)] N hermanastro *m*

stepchild ['steptʃaɪld] N hijastro(a) *m,f*

stepdaughter ['stepdɔːtə(r)] N hijastra *f*

stepfather ['stepfɑːðə(r)] N padrastro *m*

stepladder ['steplædə(r)] N escalera *f* de tijera

stepmother ['stepmʌðə(r)] N madrastra *f*

stepping-stone ['stepɪŋstəʊn] N pasadera *f*; *Fig* trampolín *m*

stepsister ['stepsɪstə(r)] N hermanastra *f*

stepson ['stepsʌn] N hijastro *m*

stereo ['sterɪəʊ] 1 N estéreo *m*
2 ADJ estéreo, estereofónico(a)

stereotype ['sterɪətaɪp] N estereotipo *m*

sterile ['steraɪl] ADJ *(barren)* estéril

sterilize ['sterɪlaɪz] VT esterilizar

sterling ['stɜːlɪŋ] 1 N libras *fpl* esterlinas; **s. silver** plata *f* de ley; **the pound s.** la libra esterlina
2 ADJ *(person, quality)* excelente

stern¹ [stɜːn] ADJ *(severe)* severo(a)

stern² [stɜːn] N *Naut* popa *f*

steroid ['steroɪd] N esteroide *m*

stethoscope ['steθəskəʊp] N estetoscopio *m*

stew [stjuː] 1 N estofado *m*, cocido *m*
2 VT *(meat)* guisar, estofar; *(fruit)* cocer

steward ['stjuəd] N *(on estate)* administrador *m*; *(on ship)* camarero *m*; *(on plane)* auxiliar *m* de vuelo

stewardess ['stjuədɪs] N *(on ship)* camarera *f*; *(on plane)* auxiliar *f* de vuelo, azafata *f*, *Am* aeromoza *f*

stick¹ [stɪk] N **(a)** *(of wood)* palo *m*; *(walking stick)* bastón *m*; *(of dynamite)* cartucho *m*; *Br Fam* **to give sb s.** dar caña a algn **(b)** *Fam* **to live in the sticks** vivir en el quinto infierno or *Esp* pino

stick² [stɪk] 1 VT *(pt & pp* **stuck)** **(a)** *(push)* meter; *(knife)* clavar; **he stuck his head out of**

the window asomó la cabeza por la ventana (**b**) *Fam (put)* meter (**c**) *(with glue etc)* pegar (**d**) *Fam (tolerate)* soportar, aguantar
2 VI (**a**) *(become attached)* pegarse (**b**) *(window, drawer)* atrancarse; *(machine part)* encasquillarse
► **stick at** VT INSEP perseverar en
► **stick by** VT INSEP *(friend)* ser fiel a; *(promise)* cumplir con
► **stick out** 1 VI *(project)* sobresalir; *(be noticeable)* resaltar
2 VT SEP *(tongue)* sacar; *Fig* **to s. one's neck out** jugarse el tipo
► **stick to** VT INSEP *(principles)* atenerse a
► **stick up** 1 VI *(project)* sobresalir; *(hair)* ponerse de punta
2 VT SEP (**a**) *(poster)* fijar (**b**) *(hand etc)* levantar
► **stick up for** VT INSEP defender

sticker ['stɪkə(r)] N *(label)* etiqueta adhesiva; *(with slogan)* pegatina f

sticking-plaster ['stɪkɪŋ'plɑːstə(r)] N *Br (to cover wound)* tirita® f, *Am* curita m or f; *(to keep bandage in place)* esparadrapo m

stickler ['stɪklə(r)] N meticuloso(a) m,f; **to be a s. for detail** ser muy detallista

stick-up ['stɪkʌp] N *US Fam* atraco m, asalto m

sticky ['stɪkɪ] ADJ (**stickier, stickiest**) pegajoso(a); *(label)* engomado(a); *(weather)* bochornoso(a); *Fam (situation)* difícil

stiff [stɪf] 1 ADJ (**a**) *(rigid)* rígido(a), tieso(a); *(collar, lock)* duro(a); *(joint)* entumecido(a); *(machine part)* atascado(a); **to have a s. neck** tener tortícolis (**b**) *Fig (test)* difícil; *(punishment)* severo(a); *(price)* excesivo(a); *(drink)* fuerte; *(person) (unnatural)* estirado(a)
2 N *Fam (corpse)* fiambre m

stiffen ['stɪfən] 1 VT *(fabric)* reforzar; *(collar)* almidonar; *Fig (resistance)* fortalecer
2 VI *(person)* ponerse tieso(a); *(joints)* entumecerse; *Fig (resistance)* fortalecerse

stiffness ['stɪfnɪs] N rigidez f

stifle ['staɪfəl] 1 VT sofocar; *(yawn)* reprimir
2 VI ahogarse, sofocarse

stifling ['staɪflɪŋ] ADJ sofocante, agobiante

stigma ['stɪgmə] N estigma m

stile [staɪl] N = escalones para pasar por encima de una valla

stiletto [stɪ'letəʊ] N zapato m de tacón or *Am* taco de aguja

still [stɪl] 1 ADV (**a**) *(up to this time)* todavía, aún, *Am* siempre (**b**) *(with comp adj & adv) (even)* aún; **s. colder** aún más frío (**c**) *(nonetheless)* no obstante, con todo (**d**) *(however)* sin embargo (**e**) *(motionless)* quieto; **to stand s.** no moverse
2 ADJ *(calm)* tranquilo(a); *(peaceful)* sosegado(a); *(silent)* silencioso(a); *(motionless)* inmóvil; *Art* **s. life** naturaleza muerta

stillborn ['stɪlbɔːn] ADJ nacido(a) muerto(a)

stillness ['stɪlnɪs] N calma f; *(silence)* silencio m

stilt [stɪlt] N zanco m

stilted ['stɪltɪd] ADJ afectado(a)

stimulant ['stɪmjʊlənt] N estimulante m

stimulate ['stɪmjʊleɪt] VT estimular

stimulating ['stɪmjʊleɪtɪŋ] ADJ estimulante

stimulus ['stɪmjʊləs] N *(pl* **stimuli** ['stɪmjʊlaɪ]*)* estímulo m; *Fig* incentivo m

sting [stɪŋ] 1 N *(part of bee, wasp)* aguijón m; *(wound)* picadura f; *(burning)* escozor m; *Fig (of remorse)* punzada f; *Fig (of remark)* sarcasmo m
2 VT *(pt & pp* **stung**) picar; *Fig (of conscience)* remorder; *Fig (of remark)* herir en lo vivo
3 VI picar

stingy ['stɪndʒɪ] ADJ (**stingier, stingiest**) *Fam (person)* tacaño(a); *(amount)* escaso(a); **to be s. with** escatimar

stink [stɪŋk] 1 N peste m, hedor m
2 VI *(pt* **stank** *or* **stunk**; *pp* **stunk**) apestar, heder (**of a**)

stinking ['stɪŋkɪŋ] 1 ADJ *(smelly)* apestoso(a); *Fam* **to have a s. cold** tener un catarro bestial
2 ADV *Fam* **he's s. rich** está podrido de dinero, *Méx* tiene un chorro de lana

stint [stɪnt] 1 N *(period)* período m, temporada f; *(shift)* turno m; **he did a two-year s. in the navy** sirvió durante dos años en la Marina
2 VT escatimar

stipulate ['stɪpjʊleɪt] VT estipular

stipulation [stɪpjʊ'leɪʃən] N estipulación f

stir [stɜː(r)] 1 N *Fig* revuelo m
2 VT (**a**) *(liquid)* remover (**b**) *(move)* agitar (**c**) *Fig (curiosity, interest)* despertar; *(anger)* provocar
3 VI *(move)* rebullirse
► **stir up** VT SEP *Fig (memories, curiosity)* despertar; *(passions)* excitar; *(anger)* provocar; *(revolt)* fomentar

stirring ['stɜːrɪŋ] ADJ conmovedor(a)

stirrup ['stɪrəp] N estribo m

stitch [stɪtʃ] 1 N (**a**) *Sewing* puntada f; *(in knitting)* punto m; *Med* punto (de sutura); *Fam* **we were in stitches** nos tronchábamos de risa (**b**) *(pain)* punzada f
2 VT *Sewing* coser; *Med* suturar, dar puntos a

stoat [stəʊt] N armiño m

stock [stɒk] 1 N (**a**) *(supply)* reserva f; *Com (goods)* existencias fpl, stock m; *(selection)* surtido m; **out of s.** agotado(a); **to have sth in s.** tener existencias de algo; *Fig* **to take s. of** evaluar (**b**) *Fin* capital m social; **stocks and shares** acciones fpl, valores mpl; **S. Exchange** Bolsa f (de valores); **s. market** bolsa f (**c**) *Culin* caldo m; **s. cube** cubito m de caldo (**d**) *(descent)* estirpe f
2 ADJ *(excuse, response)* de siempre; *(phrase)* gastado(a)
3 VT (**a**) *(have in stock)* tener existencias de (**b**) *(provide)* abastecer, surtir (**with** de); *(cupboard)* llenar (**with** de)
► **stock up** VI abastecerse (**on** or **with** de)

stockbroker ['stɒkbrəʊkə(r)] N corredor(a) m,f de Bolsa

stockholder ['stɒkhəʊldə(r)] N US accionista mf

stocking ['stɒkɪŋ] N media f; **a pair of stockings** unas medias

stockist ['stɒkɪst] N distribuidor(a) m,f

stockpile ['stɒkpaɪl] **1** N reservas fpl
2 VT almacenar; (accumulate) acumular

stocks [stɒks] NPL Hist cepo m

stocktaking ['stɒkteɪkɪŋ] N Com inventario m

stocky ['stɒkɪ] ADJ (**stockier, stockiest**) (squat) rechoncho(a); (heavily built) fornido(a)

stodgy ['stɒdʒɪ] ADJ (**stodgier, stodgiest**) (food) indigesto(a); Fig (book, person) pesado(a)

stoical ['stəʊɪkəl] ADJ estoico(a)

stoke [stəʊk] VT (poke) atizar; **to s. (up)** (feed) alimentar

stole¹ [stəʊl] PT of steal

stole² [stəʊl] N estola f

stolen ['stəʊlən] PP of steal

stolid ['stɒlɪd] ADJ impasible

stomach ['stʌmək] **1** N estómago m; **s. ache** dolor m de estómago; **s. upset** trastorno gástrico
2 VT Fig aguantar

stone [stəʊn] **1** N (a) (material, piece of rock) piedra f; (on grave) lápida f (b) (of fruit) hueso m, RP carozo m (c) Br (weight) = peso que equivale a 6,348 kg
2 ADJ de piedra

stone-cold [stəʊn'kəʊld] ADJ helado(a)

stoned [stəʊnd] ADJ Fam (drugged) colocado(a); (drunk) como una cuba

stone-deaf [stəʊn'def] ADJ sordo(a) como una tapia

stonework ['stəʊnwɜːk] N mampostería f

stony ['stəʊnɪ] ADJ (**stonier, stoniest**) (ground) pedregoso(a); Fig (look, silence) glacial

stood [stʊd] PT & PP of stand

stool [stuːl] N (a) (seat) taburete m (b) Med heces fpl

stoop [stuːp] VI (a) (have a stoop) andar encorvado(a) (b) (bend) **to s. down** inclinarse, agacharse (c) Fig **to s.** rebajarse a; **he wouldn't s. so low** no se rebajaría tanto

stop [stɒp] **1** N (a) (halt) parada f, alto m; **to come to a s.** pararse; **to put a s. to sth** poner fin a algo (b) (break) pausa f; (for refuelling etc) escala f (c) (for bus, tram) parada f (d) (punctuation mark) punto m
2 VT (a) (person, vehicle) parar; (conversation) interrumpir; (pain, abuse etc) poner fin a (b) (payments) suspender; (cheque) anular (c) **to s. doing sth** dejar de hacer algo; **s. it!** ¡basta ya! (d) (prevent) evitar; **to s. sb from doing sth** impedir a algn hacer algo
3 VI (a) (person, moving vehicle) pararse, detenerse (b) (cease) acabarse, terminar

▸ **stop by** VI Fam visitar

▸ **stop off** VI pararse un rato

▸ **stop over** VI (spend the night) pasar la noche; (for refuelling etc) hacer escala

▸ **stop up** VT SEP (hole) tapar

stopgap ['stɒpgæp] N (thing) medida f provisional; (person) sustituto(a) m,f

stopover ['stɒpəʊvə(r)] N parada f; Av escala f

stoppage ['stɒpɪdʒ] N (a) (of game, payments) suspensión f; (of work) paro m; (strike) huelga f; (deduction) deducción f (b) (blockage) obstrucción f

stopper ['stɒpə(r)] N tapón m

stop-press [stɒp'pres] N noticias fpl de última hora

stopwatch ['stɒpwɒtʃ] N cronómetro m

storage ['stɔːrɪdʒ] N almacenaje m, almacenamiento m; **s. battery** acumulador m; **s. heater** placa acumuladora

store [stɔː(r)] **1** N (a) (stock) provisión f (b) **stores** víveres mpl (c) (warehouse) almacén m (d) esp US (shop) tienda f; **department s.** gran almacén m
2 VT (a) (furniture, computer data) almacenar; (keep) guardar (b) **to s. (up)** acumular

storekeeper ['stɔːkiːpə(r)] N US tendero(a) m,f

storeroom ['stɔːruːm] N despensa f

storey ['stɔːrɪ] N piso m

stork [stɔːk] N cigüeña f

storm [stɔːm] **1** N tormenta f; (with wind) vendaval m; Fig (uproar) revuelo m; Fig **she has taken New York by s.** ha cautivado a todo Nueva York
2 VT tomar por asalto
3 VI (with rage) echar pestes

stormy ['stɔːmɪ] ADJ (**stormier, stormiest**) (weather) tormentoso(a); Fig (discussion) acalorado(a); (relationship) tempestuoso(a)

story¹ ['stɔːrɪ] N historia f; (tale, account) relato m; (article) artículo m; (plot) trama f; (joke) chiste m; (rumour) rumor m; **it's a long s.** sería largo de contar; **tall s.** cuento chino

story² ['stɔːrɪ] N US = storey

storybook ['stɔːrɪbʊk] N libro m de cuentos

storyteller ['stɔːrɪtelə(r)] N cuentista mf

stout [staʊt] **1** ADJ (a) (fat) gordo(a), corpulento(a) (b) (strong) fuerte (c) (brave) valiente; (determined) firme
2 N (beer) cerveza negra

stoutly ['staʊtlɪ] ADV resueltamente

stove [stəʊv] N (a) (for heating) estufa f (b) (cooker) cocina f, Col, Méx, Ven estufa f

stow [stəʊ] VT (a) (cargo) estibar (b) (put away) guardar

▸ **stow away** VI (on ship, plane) viajar de polizón

stowaway ['stəʊəweɪ] N polizón mf

straddle ['strædəl] VT (a) (horse etc) sentarse a horcajadas sobre (b) Fig (embrace) abarcar

straggle ['strægəl] VI (a) (lag behind) rezagarse (b) (spread untidily) desparramarse

straggler ['stræglə(r)] N rezagado(a) m,f

straight [streit] **1** ADJ (**a**) (not bent) recto(a), derecho(a); (hair) liso(a) (**b**) (honest) honrado(a); (answer) sincero(a); (refusal) rotundo(a)
2 ADV (**a**) (in a straight line) en línea recta (**b**) (directly) directamente, derecho; **keep s. ahead** sigue todo recto (**c**) **s. away** en seguida

straighten ['streitən] VT (sth bent) enderezar, poner derecho; (tie, picture) poner bien; (hair) alisar
▸ **straighten out** VT SEP (problem) resolver

straight-faced ['streit'feist] ADJ con la cara seria

straightforward [streit'fɔ:wəd] ADJ (**a**) (honest) honrado(a); (sincere) franco(a) (**b**) Br (simple) sencillo(a)

strain¹ [strein] **1** VT (**a**) (rope etc) estirar; Fig crear tensiones en (**b**) Med torcer(se); (eyes, voice) forzar; (heart) cansar (**c**) (liquid) filtrar; (vegetables, tea) colar
2 VI (pull) tirar (at de)
3 N (**a**) (from pulling) tensión f; (from pushing) presión f (**b**) (mental stress) agobio m (**c**) (of ankle) torcedura f (**d**) Mus strains son m

strain² [strein] N (**a**) (breed) raza f (**b**) (streak) vena f

strained [streind] ADJ (**a**) (muscle) torcido(a); (eyes) cansado(a); (voice) forzado(a) (**b**) (atmosphere) tenso(a)

strainer ['streinə(r)] N colador m

strait [streit] N (**a**) Geog estrecho m (**b**) (difficulty) **in dire straits** en un gran aprieto

straitjacket ['streitdʒækit] N camisa f de fuerza

strait-laced ['streit'leist] ADJ remilgado(a)

strand¹ [strænd] VT Fig (person) abandonar; **to leave stranded** dejar plantado(a)

strand² [strænd] N (of thread) hebra f; (of hair) pelo m

strange [streindʒ] ADJ (**a**) (unknown) desconocido(a); (unfamiliar) nuevo(a) (**b**) (odd) raro(a), extraño(a)

stranger ['streindʒə(r)] N (unknown person) desconocido(a) m,f; (outsider) forastero(a) m,f

strangle ['stræŋgəl] VT estrangular

stranglehold ['stræŋgəlhəʊld] N **to have a s. on sb** tener a algn agarrado(a) por el cuello

strangulation [stræŋgjʊ'leiʃən] N estrangulación f

strap [stræp] **1** N (of leather) correa f; (on bag) bandolera f; (on dress, bra) tirante m, Am bretel m
2 VT atar con correa

strapping ['stræpiŋ] ADJ Fam fornido(a), robusto(a)

strata ['strɑ:tə] PL of **stratum**

strategic [strə'ti:dʒik] ADJ estratégico(a)

strategy ['strætidʒi] N estrategia f

stratosphere ['strætəsfiə(r)] N estratosfera f

stratum ['strɑ:təm] N (pl **strata**) estrato m

straw [strɔ:] N (**a**) (dry stalks) paja f; Fig **to clutch at straws** agarrarse a un clavo ardiente; Fam **that's the last s.!** ¡eso ya es el colmo! (**b**) (for drinking) pajita f, Méx popote m

strawberry ['strɔ:bəri] N fresa f, CSur frutilla f

stray [strei] **1** VI (from path) desviarse; (get lost) extraviarse
2 N animal extraviado
3 ADJ (bullet) perdido(a); (animal) callejero(a)

streak [stri:k] **1** N (**a**) (line) raya f; **s. of lightning** rayo m (**b**) (in hair) reflejo m (**c**) Fig (of genius etc) vena f; Fig (of luck) racha f
2 VT rayar (with de)
3 VI **to s. past** pasar como un rayo

stream [stri:m] **1** N (**a**) (brook) arroyo m, riachuelo m (**b**) (of water, air) flujo m; (of blood) chorro m; (of light) raudal m (**c**) (of people) oleada f
2 VI (**a**) (liquid) correr (**b**) **to s. in/out/past** (people etc) entrar/salir/pasar en tropel

streamer ['stri:mə(r)] N (paper ribbon) serpentina f

streamlined ['stri:mlaind] ADJ (**a**) (car) aerodinámico(a) (**b**) (system, method) racionalizado(a)

street [stri:t] N calle f; **the man in the s.** el hombre de la calle; **s. map, s. plan** (plano m) callejero m

streetcar ['stri:tkɑ:(r)] N US tranvía m

streetlamp ['stri:tlæmp] N farola f

streetwise ['stri:twaiz] ADJ espabilado(a)

strength [streŋθ] N (**a**) (of person) fuerza f; (of rope, nail) resistencia f; (of emotion, colour) intensidad f; (of alcohol) graduación f (**b**) (ability) punto m fuerte

strengthen ['streŋθən] **1** VT (**a**) (wall, building) reforzar; (character) fortalecer (**b**) (intensify) intensificar
2 VI (**a**) (gen) reforzarse (**b**) (intensify) intensificarse

strenuous ['strenjʊəs] ADJ (**a**) (denial) enérgico(a); (effort, life) intenso(a) (**b**) (exhausting) fatigoso(a), cansado(a)

stress [stres] **1** N (**a**) Tech tensión f (**b**) Med estrés m (**c**) (emphasis) hincapié m; (on word) acento m
2 VT (emphasize) subrayar; (word) acentuar

stressful ['stresfʊl] ADJ estresante

stretch [stretʃ] **1** VT (elastic) estirar; (wings) desplegar
2 VI (elastic) estirarse; Fig **my money won't s. to it** mi dinero no me llegará para eso
3 N (**a**) (length) trecho m, tramo m (**b**) (of land) extensión f; (of time) intervalo m

> Note that the Spanish verb **estrechar** is a false friend and is never a translation for the English verb **stretch**. In Spanish **estrechar** means "to make narrow", "to tighten".

▸ **stretch out 1** VT SEP *(arm, hand)* alargar; *(legs)* estirar

2 VI **(a)** *(person)* estirarse **(b)** *(countryside, years etc)* extenderse

stretcher ['stretʃə(r)] N camilla *f*

strew [struː] VT *(pt* **strewed**; *pp* **strewed** *or* **strewn** [struːn]) esparcir

stricken ['strɪkən] ADJ *(with grief)* afligido(a); *(with illness)* aquejado(a); *(by disaster etc)* afectado(a); *(damaged)* dañado(a)

strict [strɪkt] ADJ **(a)** *(person, discipline)* estricto(a) **(b)** *(absolute)* absoluto(a)

strictly ['strɪktlɪ] ADV **(a)** *(categorically)* terminantemente **(b)** *(precisely)* estrictamente; **s. speaking** en sentido estricto

stride [straɪd] **1** N zancada *f*, tranco *m*; *Fig (progress)* progresos *mpl*

2 VI *(pt* **strode**; *pp* **stridden** ['strɪdən]) **to s. (along)** andar a zancadas

strident ['straɪdənt] ADJ *(voice, sound)* estridente; *(protest etc)* enérgico(a)

strife [straɪf] N conflictos *mpl*

strike [straɪk] **1** VT *(pt & pp* **struck**) **(a)** *(hit)* pegar, golpear **(b)** *(collide with)* chocar contra; *(of bullet, lightning)* alcanzar **(c)** *(match)* encender, *Am* prender **(d) the clock struck three** el reloj dio las tres **(e)** *(oil, gold)* descubrir **(f)** *(impress)* impresionar; **it strikes me ...** me parece ...

2 VI **(a)** *(attack)* atacar; *(disaster)* sobrevenir **(b)** *(clock)* dar la hora **(c)** *(workers)* declararse en huelga

3 N **(a)** *(by workers)* huelga *f*; **to call a s.** convocar una huelga **(b)** *Mil* ataque *m*

▸ **strike back** VI devolver el golpe

▸ **strike down** VT SEP fulminar, abatir

▸ **strike out 1** VT SEP *(cross out)* tachar

2 VI **to s. out at sb** arremeter contra algn

▸ **strike up** VT INSEP **(a)** *(friendship)* trabar; *(conversation)* entablar **(b)** *(tune)* empezar a tocar

striker ['straɪkə(r)] N **(a)** *(worker)* huelguista *mf* **(b)** *Fam Ftb* marcador(a) *m,f*

striking ['straɪkɪŋ] ADJ *(eye-catching)* llamativo(a); *(noticeable)* notable; *(impressive)* impresionante

string [strɪŋ] **1** N **(a)** *(cord)* cuerda *f*; *Fig* **to pull strings for sb** enchufar a algn; **s. bean** judía *f* verde, *Bol, RP* chaucha *f*, *CAm* ejote *m*, *Col, Cuba* habichuela *f*, *Chile* poroto *m* verde, *Ven* vainita *f* **(b)** *(of events)* cadena *f*; *(of lies)* sarta *f* **(c)** *(of racket, guitar)* cuerda *f*; *Mus* **the strings** los instrumentos de cuerda

2 VT *(pt & pp* **strung**) **(a)** *(beads)* ensartar **(b)** *(racket etc)* encordar **(c)** *(beans)* quitar la hebra a

stringed [strɪŋd] ADJ *(instrument)* de cuerda

stringent ['strɪndʒənt] ADJ severo(a), estricto(a)

strip¹ [strɪp] **1** VT **(a)** *(person)* desnudar; *(bed)* quitar la ropa de; *(paint)* rascar, quitar, *Am*

sacar **(b)** *Tech* **to s. (down)** desmontar

2 VI *(undress)* desnudarse; *(perform striptease)* hacer un striptease

▸ **strip off 1** VT SEP quitar, *Am* sacar

2 VI *(undress)* desnudarse

strip² [strɪp] N tira *f*; *(of land)* franja *f*; *(of metal)* fleje *m*; *Br* **football s.** indumentaria *f*; **s. cartoon** historieta *f*; **s. lighting** alumbrado *m* fluorescente; **to tear sb off a s.** echar una bronca a algn

stripe [straɪp] N raya *f*; *Mil* galón *m*

striped [straɪpt] ADJ rayado(a), a rayas

stripper ['strɪpə(r)] N artista *mf* de striptease

strive [straɪv] VI *(pt* **strove**; *pp* **striven** ['strɪvən]) **to s. to do sth** esforzarse por hacer algo

strobe [strəʊb] N **s. lighting** luces estroboscópicas

strode [strəʊd] PT *of* **stride**

stroke [strəʊk] **1** N **(a) a s. of luck** un golpe de suerte **(b)** *(of pen)* trazo *m*; *(of brush)* pincelada *f* **(c)** *(caress)* caricia *f* **(d)** *Med* apoplejía *f*

2 VT acariciar

stroll [strəʊl] **1** VI dar un paseo

2 N paseo *m*

stroller ['strəʊlə(r)] N *US (for baby)* cochecito *m*

strong [strɒŋ] **1** ADJ **(a)** *(powerful)* fuerte **(b)** *(durable)* sólido(a) **(c)** *(firm, resolute)* firme **(d)** *(colour)* intenso(a); *(light)* brillante

2 ADV fuerte; **to be going s.** *(business)* ir fuerte; *(elderly person)* conservarse bien

strongbox ['strɒŋbɒks] N caja *f* fuerte

stronghold ['strɒŋhəʊld] N *Mil* fortaleza *f*; *Fig* baluarte *m*

strongly ['strɒŋlɪ] ADV fuertemente

strongroom ['strɒŋruːm] N cámara acorazada

stroppy ['strɒpɪ] ADJ *(stroppier, stroppiest) Br Fam* **to be s.** *(by nature)* tener mal genio *or Esp* mal café; *(in a mood)* estar de mal humor *or Esp* de mal café

strove [strəʊv] PT *of* **strive**

struck [strʌk] PT & PP *of* **strike**

structural ['strʌktʃərəl] ADJ estructural

structure ['strʌktʃə(r)] N estructura *f*; *(building, monument)* construcción *f*

struggle ['strʌgəl] **1** VI luchar

2 N lucha *f*; *(physical fight)* pelea *f*

strum [strʌm] VT *(guitar)* rasguear

strung [strʌŋ] PT & PP *of* **string**

strut [strʌt] VI pavonearse

stub [stʌb] **1** N *(of cigarette)* colilla *f*; *(of pencil)* cabo *m*; *(of cheque)* matriz *f*

2 VT **(a)** *(strike)* golpear **(b) to s. (out)** apagar

stubble ['stʌbəl] N *(in field)* rastrojo *m*; *(on chin)* barba *f* de tres días

stubborn ['stʌbən] ADJ **(a)** *(person)* terco(a), testarudo(a) **(b)** *(stain)* difícil **(c)** *(refusal)* rotundo(a)

stucco ['stʌkəʊ] N estuco *m*

stuck [stʌk] PT & PP *of* **stick²**

stuck-up [stʌk'ʌp] ADJ *Fam* creído(a)

stud¹ [stʌd] **1** N *(on clothing)* tachón m; *(on football boots) Esp* taco m, *RP* tapón m; *(on shirt)* botonadura f
  2 VT *(decorate)* tachonar (**with** de); *Fig (dot, cover)* salpicar (**with** de)

stud² [stʌd] N *(horse)* semental m

student ['stju:dənt] N estudiante mf; **s. teacher** profesor(a) m,f en prácticas

studio ['stju:dɪəʊ] N *TV & Cin* estudio m; *(artist's)* taller m; **s. (apartment** or *Br* **flat)** estudio

studious ['stju:dɪəs] ADJ estudioso(a)

studiously ['stju:dɪəslɪ] ADV cuidadosamente

study ['stʌdɪ] **1** VT estudiar; *(facts etc)* examinar, investigar; *(behaviour)* observar
  2 VI estudiar; **to s. to be a doctor** estudiar para médico
  3 N (**a**) *(investigation, report)* estudio m; **s. group** grupo m de trabajo (**b**) *(room)* despacho m, estudio m

stuff [stʌf] **1** VT (**a**) *(container)* llenar (**with** de); *Culin* rellenar (**with** con or de); *(animal)* disecar (**b**) *(cram)* atiborrar (**with** de)
  2 N *Fam* (**a**) *(substance)* cosa f (**b**) *(things)* cosas fpl

stuffing ['stʌfɪŋ] N *Culin* relleno m

stuffy ['stʌfɪ] ADJ (**stuffier, stuffiest**) (**a**) *(room)* mal ventilado(a); *(atmosphere)* cargado(a) (**b**) *(pompous)* estirado(a); *(narrow-minded)* de miras estrechas

stumble ['stʌmbəl] VI tropezar, dar un traspié; *Fig* **to s. across** or **on** or **upon** tropezar or dar con

stumbling ['stʌmblɪŋ] N **s. block** escollo m

stump [stʌmp] **1** N (**a**) *(of pencil)* cabo m; *(of tree)* tocón m; *(of arm, leg)* muñón m (**b**) *(in cricket)* estaca f
  2 VT *(puzzle)* confundir; **to be stumped** estar perplejo(a)

stun [stʌn] VT *(of blow)* aturdir; *Fig (of news etc)* sorprender

stung [stʌŋ] PT & PP *of* **sting**

stunk [stʌŋk] PT & PP *of* **stink**

stunning ['stʌnɪŋ] ADJ *(blow)* duro(a); *(news)* sorprendente; *Fam (woman, outfit)* fenomenal

stunt¹ [stʌnt] VT *(growth)* atrofiar

stunt² [stʌnt] N (**a**) *Av* acrobacia f (**b**) **publicity s.** truco publicitario (**c**) *Cin* escena peligrosa; **s. man** doble m

stunted ['stʌntɪd] ADJ enano(a), mal desarrollado(a)

stupefy ['stju:pɪfaɪ] VT *(of alcohol, drugs)* aturdir; *Fig (of news etc)* dejar pasmado(a)

stupendous [stju:'pendəs] ADJ *(wonderful)* estupendo(a)

stupid ['stju:pɪd] ADJ estúpido(a), imbécil

stupidity [stju:'pɪdɪtɪ] N estupidez f

stupor ['stju:pə(r)] N estupor m

sturdy ['stɜ:dɪ] ADJ (**sturdier, sturdiest**) robusto(a), fuerte; *(resistance)* enérgico(a)

stutter ['stʌtə(r)] **1** VI tartamudear
  2 N tartamudeo m

sty [staɪ] N *(pen)* pocilga f

sty(e) [staɪ] N *Med* orzuelo m

style [staɪl] **1** N (**a**) *(manner, sophistication)* estilo m; *(of dress)* modelo m (**b**) *(fashion)* moda f (**c**) **to live in s.** *(elegance)* vivir a lo grande
  2 VT *(hair)* marcar

stylish ['staɪlɪʃ] ADJ con estilo

stylist ['staɪlɪst] N *(hairdresser)* peluquero(a) mf

stylus ['staɪləs] N *(of record player)* aguja f

suave [swɑ:v] ADJ amable, afable; *Pej* zalamero(a)

> Note that the Spanish word **suave** is a false friend and is never a translation for the English word **suave**. In Spanish, **suave** means both "smooth" and "soft".

sub [sʌb] N *Fam* (**a**) *(to magazine)* suscripción f; *(to club)* cuota f (**b**) *(substitute)* suplente mf

sub- [sʌb] PREF sub-

subconscious [sʌb'kɒnʃəs] **1** ADJ subconsciente
  2 N **the s.** el subconsciente

subcontract [sʌbkən'trækt] VT subcontratar

subcontractor [sʌbkən'træktə(r)] N subcontratista mf

subdivide [sʌbdɪ'vaɪd] VT subdividir (**into** en)

subdue [səb'dju:] VT (**a**) *(nation, people)* sojuzgar (**b**) *(feelings)* dominar (**c**) *(colour, light)* atenuar

subdued [səb'dju:d] ADJ (**a**) *(person, emotion)* callado(a) (**b**) *(voice, tone)* bajo(a) (**c**) *(light)* tenue; *(colour)* apagado(a)

subject ['sʌbdʒɪkt] **1** N (**a**) *(citizen)* súbdito m (**b**) *(topic)* tema m; **s. matter** materia f; *(contents)* contenido m (**c**) *Educ* asignatura f (**d**) *Ling* sujeto m
  2 ADJ **s. to** *(law, tax)* sujeto(a) a; *(conditional upon)* previo(a)
  3 VT [səb'dʒekt] someter

subjective [səb'dʒektɪv] ADJ subjetivo(a)

subjunctive [səb'dʒʌŋktɪv] **1** ADJ subjuntivo(a)
  2 N subjuntivo m

sublet [sʌb'let] VT & VI subarrendar

sublime [sə'blaɪm] ADJ sublime

submachine-gun [sʌbmə'ʃi:ngʌn] N metralleta f

submarine ['sʌbməri:n] N submarino m

submerge [səb'mɜ:dʒ] VT sumergir; *(flood)* inundar; *Fig* **submerged in ...** sumido(a) en ...

submission [səb'mɪʃən] N (**a**) *(yielding)* sumisión f (**b**) *(of documents)* presentación f (**c**) *(report)* informe m

submissive [səb'mɪsɪv] ADJ sumiso(a)

submit [səb'mɪt] **1** VT (**a**) *(present)* presentar (**b**) *(subject)* someter (**to** a)
2 VI *(surrender)* rendirse

subnormal [sʌb'nɔːməl] ADJ subnormal

subordinate [sə'bɔːdɪnɪt] ADJ & N subordinado(a) *(m,f)*

subpoena [səb'piːnə] *Jur* **1** N citación *f*
2 VT citar

subscribe [səb'skraɪb] VI *(to magazine)* suscribirse (**to** a); *(to opinion, theory)* adherirse (**to** a)

subscriber [səb'skraɪbə(r)] N abonado(a) *m,f*

subscription [səb'skrɪpʃən] N *(to magazine)* suscripción *f*; *(to club)* cuota *f*

subsequent ['sʌbsɪkwənt] ADJ subsiguiente

subsequently ['sʌbsɪkwəntlɪ] ADV posteriormente

subside [səb'saɪd] VI *(land)* hundirse; *(floodwater)* bajar; *(wind, anger)* amainar

subsidence [səb'saɪdəns] N *(of land)* hundimiento *m*; *(of floodwater)* bajada *f*; *(of wind)* amaine *m*

subsidiary [sʌb'sɪdɪərɪ] **1** ADJ *(role)* secundario(a)
2 N *Com* sucursal *f*, filial *f*

subsidize ['sʌbsɪdaɪz] VT subvencionar

subsidy ['sʌbsɪdɪ] N subvención *f*

subsistence [səb'sɪstəns] N subsistencia *f*

substance ['sʌbstəns] N (**a**) *(matter)* sustancia *f* (**b**) *(essential element)* esencia *f* (**c**) **a woman of s.** *(wealth)* una mujer acaudalada

substantial [səb'stænʃəl] ADJ (**a**) *(solid)* sólido(a) (**b**) *(sum, loss)* importante; *(difference, improvement)* notable; *(meal)* abundante

substantiate [səb'stænʃɪeɪt] VT respaldar

substitute ['sʌbstɪtjuːt] **1** VT sustituir; **to s. X for Y** sustituir X por Y
2 N *(person)* suplente *mf*; *(thing)* sucedáneo *m*

substitution [sʌbstɪ'tjuːʃən] N sustitución *f*; *Sport* sustitución *f*, cambio *m*

subtitle ['sʌbtaɪtəl] N subtítulo *m*

subtle ['sʌtəl] ADJ sutil; *(taste)* delicado(a); *(remark)* ingenioso(a); *(irony)* fino(a)

subtlety ['sʌtəltɪ] N sutileza *f*; *(of remark)* ingeniosidad *f*; *(of irony, joke)* finura *f*

subtotal ['sʌbtəʊtəl] N subtotal *m*

subtract [səb'trækt] VT restar

subtraction [səb'trækʃən] N resta *f*

suburb ['sʌbɜːb] N barrio periférico; **the suburbs** las afueras

suburban [sə'bɜːbən] ADJ suburbano(a)

suburbia [sə'bɜːbɪə] N barrios residenciales periféricos

subversive [səb'vɜːsɪv] ADJ & N subversivo(a) *(m,f)*

subway ['sʌbweɪ] N (**a**) *Br (underpass)* paso subterráneo (**b**) *US (underground railway)* metro *m*, *RP* subte *m*

succeed [sək'siːd] **1** VI (**a**) *(person)* tener éxito; *(plan)* salir bien; **to s. in doing sth** conseguir hacer algo (**b**) *(follow after)* suceder; **to s. to** *(throne)* suceder a
2 VT *(monarch)* suceder a

succeeding [sək'siːdɪŋ] ADJ sucesivo(a)

success [sək'ses] N éxito *m*

> Note that the Spanish word **suceso** is a false friend and is never a translation for the English word **success**. In Spanish **suceso** means both "event, occurrence" and "incident".

successful [sək'sesfʊl] ADJ de éxito, exitoso(a); *(business)* próspero(a); *(marriage)* feliz; **to be s. in doing sth** lograr hacer algo

successfully [sək'sesfʊlɪ] ADV con éxito

succession [sək'seʃən] N sucesión *f*, serie *f*; **in s.** sucesivamente

successive [sək'sesɪv] ADJ sucesivo(a), consecutivo(a)

successor [sək'sesə(r)] N sucesor(a) *m,f*

succinct [sək'sɪŋkt] ADJ sucinto(a)

succumb [sə'kʌm] VI sucumbir (**to** a)

such [sʌtʃ] **1** ADJ (**a**) *(of that sort)* tal, semejante; **artists s. as Monet** artistas como Monet; **at s. and s. a time** a tal hora; **in s. a way that** de tal manera que (**b**) *(so much, so great)* tanto(a); **he's always in a hurry** siempre anda con tanta prisa; **she was in s. pain** sufría tanto
2 ADV *(so very)* tan; **it's s. a long time ago** hace tanto tiempo; **she's s. a clever woman** es una mujer tan inteligente; **s. a lot of books** tantos libros; **we had s. good weather** hizo un tiempo tan bueno

suchlike ['sʌtʃlaɪk] **1** ADJ tal
2 PRON *(things)* cosas *fpl* por el estilo; *(people)* gente *f* por el estilo

suck [sʌk] **1** VT *(by pump)* aspirar; *(liquid)* sorber; *(lollipop, blood)* chupar
2 VI *(person)* chupar; *(baby)* mamar

► **suck in** VT SEP *(of whirlpool)* tragar

sucker ['sʌkə(r)] N (**a**) *Fam* primo(a) *m,f*, bobo(a) *m,f* (**b**) *Zool* ventosa *f*; *Bot* chupón *m*

suckle ['sʌkəl] VT *(of mother)* amamantar

suction ['sʌkʃən] N succión *f*

sudden ['sʌdən] ADJ (**a**) *(hurried)* súbito(a), repentino(a) (**b**) *(unexpected)* imprevisto(a) (**c**) *(abrupt)* brusco(a); **all of a s.** de repente

suddenly ['sʌdənlɪ] ADV de repente

suds [sʌdz] NPL espuma *f* de jabón, jabonaduras *fpl*

sue [suː, sjuː] *Jur* **1** VT demandar
2 VI presentar una demanda; **to s. for divorce** solicitar el divorcio

suede [sweɪd] N ante *m*, gamuza *f*; *(for gloves)* cabritilla *f*

suet ['suːɪt] N sebo *m*

suffer ['sʌfə(r)] **1** VT (**a**) *(endure) (loss, defeat, pain)* sufrir (**b**) *(tolerate)* aguantar, soportar **2** VI sufrir; **to s. from** sufrir de

sufferer ['sʌfərə(r)] N *Med* enfermo(a) *m,f*

suffering ['sʌfərɪŋ] N *(affliction)* sufrimiento *m*; *(pain, torment)* dolor *m*

suffice [sə'faɪs] VI *Fml* bastar, ser suficiente

sufficient [sə'fɪʃənt] ADJ suficiente, bastante

sufficiently [sə'fɪʃəntlɪ] ADV suficientemente, bastante

suffix ['sʌfɪks] N sufijo *m*

suffocate ['sʌfəkeɪt] **1** VT asfixiar **2** VI asfixiarse

suffocating ['sʌfəkeɪtɪŋ] ADJ *(heat)* agobiante, sofocante

suffrage ['sʌfrɪdʒ] N sufragio *m*

suffuse [sə'fju:z] VT *Literary* bañar, cubrir (**with** de)

sugar ['ʃʊgə(r)] **1** N azúcar *m or f*; **s. beet** remolacha (azucarera), *Méx* betabel (azucarero); **s. bowl** azucarero *m*; **s. cane** caña *f* de azúcar **2** VT azucarar, echar azúcar a

sugary ['ʃʊgərɪ] ADJ *(like sugar)* azucarado(a); *Fig (insincere)* zalamero(a); *(oversentimental)* sentimentaloide

suggest [sə'dʒest] VT (**a**) *(propose)* sugerir (**b**) *(advise)* aconsejar (**c**) *(indicate, imply)* indicar

suggestion [sə'dʒestʃən] N (**a**) *(proposal)* sugerencia *f* (**b**) *(trace)* sombra *f*; *(small amount)* toque *m*

suggestive [sə'dʒestɪv] ADJ (**a**) *(reminiscent, thought-provoking)* sugerente (**b**) *(remark)* insinuante

suicidal [sjuːɪ'saɪdəl] ADJ suicida

suicide ['sjuːɪsaɪd] N suicidio *m*

suit [suːt, sjuːt] **1** N (**a**) *(clothes)* traje *m*, *Andes, RP* terno *m* (**b**) *Jur* pleito *m* (**c**) *Cards* palo *m* **2** VT (**a**) *(be convenient to)* convenir a, venir bien a (**b**) *(be right, appropriate for)* ir bien a; **red really suits you** el rojo te favorece mucho; **they are well suited** están hechos el uno para el otro (**c**) *(please)* **s. yourself!** ¡como quieras!

suitable ['sjuːtəbəl] ADJ *(convenient)* conveniente; *(appropriate)* adecuado(a); **the most s. woman for the job** la mujer más indicada para el puesto

suitably ['sjuːtəblɪ] ADV *(correctly)* correctamente; *(properly)* adecuadamente

suitcase ['suːtkeɪs] N maleta *f*, *Méx* petaca *f*, *RP* valija *f*

suite [swiːt] N (**a**) *(of furniture)* juego *m* (**b**) *(of hotel rooms, music)* suite *f*

suitor ['sjuːtə(r)] N *Literary (wooer)* pretendiente *m*

sulfur ['sʌlfə(r)] N *US* = **sulphur**

sulfuric [sʌl'fjʊərɪk] N *US* = **sulphuric**

sulk [sʌlk] VI enfurruñarse

sulky ['sʌlkɪ] ADJ (**sulkier, sulkiest**) malhumorado(a), enfurruñado(a)

sullen ['sʌlən] ADJ hosco(a); *(sky)* plomizo(a)

sulphur ['sʌlfər] N azufre *m*

sulphuric [sʌl'fjʊərɪk] ADJ sulfúrico(a)

sultan ['sʌltən] N sultán *m*

sultana [sʌl'tɑːnə] N *esp Br (raisin)* pasa *f* de Esmirna

sultry ['sʌltrɪ] ADJ (**sultrier, sultriest**) (**a**) *(muggy)* bochornoso(a) (**b**) *(seductive)* sensual

sum [sʌm] N (**a**) *(arithmetic problem, amount)* suma *f* (**b**) *(total amount)* total *m*; *(of money)* importe *m*

▶ **sum up 1** VT SEP resumir **2** VI resumir; **to s. up ...** en resumidas cuentas ...

summarize ['sʌməraɪz] VT & VI resumir

summary ['sʌmərɪ] **1** N resumen *m* **2** ADJ sumario(a)

summer ['sʌmə(r)] **1** N verano *m* **2** ADJ *(holiday etc)* de verano; *(weather)* veraniego(a); *(resort)* de veraneo

summerhouse ['sʌməhaʊs] N cenador *m*, glorieta *f*

summertime ['sʌmətaɪm] N verano *m*

summit ['sʌmɪt] N (**a**) *(of mountain)* cima *f*, cumbre *f* (**b**) *Pol* **s. (meeting)** cumbre *f*

summon ['sʌmən] VT (**a**) *(meeting, person)* convocar (**b**) *(aid)* pedir (**c**) *Jur* citar

▶ **summon up** VT SEP *(resources)* reunir; **to s. up one's courage** armarse de valor

summons ['sʌmənz] **1** N SING (**a**) *(call)* llamada *f*, llamamiento *m* (**b**) *Jur* citación *f* judicial **2** VT *Jur* citar

sumptuous ['sʌmptjʊəs] ADJ suntuoso(a)

sun [sʌn] **1** N sol *m* **2** VT **to s. oneself** tomar el sol

sunbathe ['sʌnbeɪð] VI tomar el sol

sunbed ['sʌnbed] N *(in garden)* tumbona *f*; *(with sunlamp)* solario *m*

sunburn ['sʌnbɜːn] N *(burn)* quemadura *f* de sol

sunburnt ['sʌnbɜːnt] ADJ *(burnt)* quemado(a) por el sol; *(tanned)* bronceado(a)

Sunday ['sʌndɪ] N domingo *m inv*; **S. newspaper** periódico *m* del domingo; **S. school** catequesis *f*

sundial ['sʌndaɪəl] N reloj *m* de sol

sundown ['sʌndaʊn] N *US* anochecer *m*

sundry ['sʌndrɪ] **1** ADJ diversos(as), varios(as) **2** N (**a**) *Fam* **all and s.** todos sin excepción (**b**) *Com* **sundries** artículos diversos; *(expenses)* gastos diversos

sunflower ['sʌnflaʊə(r)] N girasol *m*

sung [sʌŋ] PP of **sing**

sunglasses ['sʌnglɑːsɪz] NPL gafas *fpl or Am* anteojos *mpl* de sol

sunk [sʌŋk] PP of **sink**

sunlamp ['sʌnlæmp] N lámpara *f* solar

sunlight ['sʌnlaɪt] N sol *m*, luz *f* del sol

sunlit ['sʌnlɪt] ADJ iluminado(a) por el sol

sunny ['sʌnɪ] ADJ (**sunnier, sunniest**) (**a**) *(day)* de sol; *(place)* soleado(a); **it is s.** hace sol (**b**) *Fig (smile, disposition)* alegre; *(future)* prometedor(a)

sunrise ['sʌnraɪz] N salida *f* del sol

sunroof ['sʌnruːf] N *Aut* techo corredizo

sunset ['sʌnset] N puesta *f* del sol

sunshade ['sʌnʃeɪd] N sombrilla *f*

sunshine ['sʌnʃaɪn] N sol *m*, luz *f* del sol

sunstroke ['sʌnstrəʊk] N insolación *f*

suntan ['sʌntæn] N bronceado *m*; **s. oil** crema protectora; **s. lotion** (aceite *m*) bronceador *m*

super ['suːpə(r)] ADJ *Fam* genial, *Am salvo RP* chévere, *Méx* padre, *RP* bárbaro(a)

super- ['suːpə(r)] PREF super-, sobre-

superannuation [suːpərænjʊ'eɪʃən] N *Br* jubilación *f*, pensión *f*

superb [sʊ'pɜːb] ADJ espléndido(a)

supercilious [suːpə'sɪlɪəs] ADJ *(condescending)* altanero(a); *(disdainful)* desdeñoso(a)

superficial [suːpə'fɪʃəl] ADJ superficial

superfluous [suː'pɜːflʊəs] ADJ sobrante, superfluo(a); **to be s.** sobrar

superglue ['suːpəgluː] N pegamento rápido

superhuman [suːpə'hjuːmən] ADJ sobrehumano(a)

superimpose [suːpərɪm'pəʊz] VT sobreponer

superintendent [suːpərɪn'tendənt] N (**a**) *(police officer) (in UK)* comisario(a) *m,f*; *(in US)* comisario(a) *m,f* jefe (**b**) *US (of apartment building)* portero(a) *m,f*

superior [suː'pɪərɪə(r)] **1** ADJ (**a**) *(better, more senior)* superior (**b**) *(haughty)* altivo(a)
2 N superior *m,f*

superiority [suːpɪərɪ'ɒrɪtɪ] N superioridad *f*

superlative [suː'pɜːlətɪv] **1** ADJ superlativo(a)
2 N *Ling* superlativo *m*

superman ['suːpəmæn] N superhombre *m*, supermán *m*

supermarket ['suːpəmɑːkɪt] N supermercado *m*

supermodel ['suːpəmɒdəl] N supermodelo *f*, top model *f*

supernatural [suːpə'nætʃərəl] **1** ADJ sobrenatural
2 N **the s.** lo sobrenatural

superpower ['suːpəpaʊə(r)] N *Pol* superpotencia *f*

supersede [suːpə'siːd] VT *Fml* suplantar

supersonic [suːpə'sɒnɪk] ADJ supersónico(a)

superstar ['suːpəstɑː(r)] N superestrella *f*

superstition [suːpə'stɪʃən] N superstición *f*

superstitious [suːpə'stɪʃəs] ADJ supersticioso(a)

superstore ['suːpəstɔː(r)] N *Com* hipermercado *m*, gran superficie *f*

supertanker ['suːpətæŋkə(r)] N superpetrolero *m*

supervise ['suːpəvaɪz] VT supervisar; *(watch over)* vigilar

supervision [suːpə'vɪʒən] N supervisión *f*

supervisor ['suːpəvaɪzə(r)] N supervisor(a) *m,f*; *US (of apartment building)* portero(a) *m,f*

supper ['sʌpə(r)] N cena *f*; **to have s.** cenar

supplant [sə'plɑːnt] VT suplantar

supple ['sʌpəl] ADJ flexible

supplement 1 N ['sʌplɪmənt] suplemento *m*
2 VT ['sʌplɪment] complementar

supplementary [sʌplɪ'mentərɪ] ADJ adicional

supplier [sə'plaɪə(r)] N suministrador(a) *m,f*; *Com* proveedor(a) *m,f*

supply [sə'plaɪ] **1** N (**a**) *(provision)* abastecimiento *m*, suministro *m*; **s. and demand** oferta *f* y demanda (**b**) **supplies** *(food)* víveres *mpl*; *Mil* pertrechos *mpl*
2 VT (**a**) *(provide)* suministrar (**b**) *(with provisions)* aprovisionar (**c**) *(information)* facilitar (**d**) *Com* surtir

support [sə'pɔːt] **1** N (**a**) *(moral)* apoyo *m* (**b**) *(funding)* ayuda económica
2 VT (**a**) *(weight etc)* sostener (**b**) *Fig (back)* apoyar; *(substantiate)* respaldar (**c**) *Sport* ser (hincha) de (**d**) *(sustain)* mantener; *(feed)* alimentar

supporter [sə'pɔːtə(r)] N *Pol* partidario(a) *m,f*; *Sport* hincha *mf*

supportive [sə'pɔːtɪv] ADJ **he was s.** apoyó mucho, fue muy comprensivo

suppose [sə'pəʊz] VT suponer; *(presume)* creer; **I s. not/so** supongo que no/sí; **you're not supposed to smoke in here** no está permitido fumar aquí dentro; **you're supposed to be in bed** deberías estar acostado(a) ya

supposed [sə'pəʊzd] ADJ supuesto(a)

supposedly [sə'pəʊzdlɪ] ADV teóricamente

suppress [sə'pres] VT suprimir; *(feelings, laugh etc)* contener; *(news, truth)* callar; *(revolt)* sofocar

supremacy [sʊ'preməsɪ] N supremacía *f*

supreme [sʊ'priːm] ADJ supremo(a); **with s. indifference** con total indiferencia; *US Jur* **S. Court** Tribunal *m* Supremo, *Am* Corte *f* Suprema

supremely [sʊ'priːmlɪ] ADV sumamente

surcharge ['sɜːtʃɑːdʒ] N recargo *m*

sure [ʃʊə(r)] **1** ADJ seguro(a); **I'm s. (that) …** estoy seguro(a) de que …; **make s. that it's ready** asegúrate de que esté listo; **s. of oneself** seguro(a) de sí mismo(a); *Fam* **s. thing!** ¡claro!
2 ADV (**a**) *(of course)* claro (**b**) *(certainly)* seguro; *US* **it s. is cold** qué frío que hace (**c**) **s. enough** efectivamente

surely ['ʃʊəlɪ] ADV *(without a doubt)* sin duda; **s. not!** ¡no puede ser!

surety ['ʃʊərɪtɪ] N (**a**) *(sum)* fianza *f* (**b**) *(person)* fiador(a) *m,f*; **to stand s. for sb** ser fiador de algn

surf [sɜ:f] **1** N *(waves)* oleaje *m*; *(foam)* espuma *f*
2 VT *Comput* **to s. the Net** navegar por Internet
3 VI *Sport* hacer surf

surface ['sɜ:fɪs] **1** N superficie *f*; *(of road)* firme *m*
2 ADJ superficial; **s. area** área *f* de la superficie; **by s. mail** por vía terrestre *or* marítima
3 VT *(road)* revestir
4 VI *(submarine etc)* salir a la superficie; *Fam (wake up)* levantarse

surface-to-air ['sɜ:fɪstʊ'eə(r)] ADJ **s. missile** misil *m* tierra-aire

surfboard ['sɜ:fbɔ:d] N tabla *f* de surf

surfeit ['sɜ:fɪt] N *Fml* exceso *m*

surfer ['sɜ:fə(r)] N surfista *mf*

surfing ['sɜ:fɪŋ] N surf *m*, surfing *m*

surge [sɜ:dʒ] **1** N **(a)** *(growth)* alza *f* **(b)** *(of sea, sympathy)* oleada *f*; *Fig (of anger, energy)* arranque *m*
2 VI **to s. forward** *(people)* avanzar en tropel

surgeon ['sɜ:dʒən] N cirujano(a) *m,f*

surgery ['sɜ:dʒərɪ] N **(a)** *(operation)* cirugía *f* **(b)** *Br (consulting room)* consultorio *m*; **s. hours** horas *fpl* de consulta

surgical ['sɜ:dʒɪkəl] ADJ quirúrgico(a); **s. spirit** alcohol *m* de 90°

surly ['sɜ:lɪ] ADJ (**surlier, surliest**) *(bad-tempered)* hosco(a), malhumorado(a); *(rude)* maleducado(a)

surmount [sɜ:'maʊnt] VT superar, vencer

surname ['sɜ:neɪm] N apellido *m*

surpass [sɜ:'pɑ:s] VT superar

surplus ['sɜ:pləs] **1** N *(of goods)* excedente *m*; *(of budget)* superávit *m*
2 ADJ excedente

surprise [sə'praɪz] **1** N sorpresa *f*; **to take sb by s.** *Esp* coger *or Am* agarrar desprevenido(a) a algn
2 ADJ *(visit)* inesperado(a); **s. attack** ataque *m* sorpresa
3 VT *(astonish)* sorprender; **I'm not surprised that …** no me extraña que …

surprising [sə'praɪzɪŋ] ADJ sorprendente

surprisingly [sə'praɪzɪŋlɪ] ADV sorprendentemente, de modo sorprendente

surrealist [sə'rɪəlɪst] ADJ & N surrealista *(mf)*

surrender [sə'rendə(r)] **1** N *Mil* rendición *f*; *(of weapons)* entrega *f*; *Ins* rescate *m*
2 VT *Mil* rendir; *(right)* renunciar a
3 VI *(give in)* rendirse

surreptitious [sʌrəp'tɪʃəs] ADJ subrepticio(a)

surrogate ['sʌrəgɪt] N *Fml* sustituto(a) *m,f*; **s. mother** madre *f* de alquiler

surround [sə'raʊnd] **1** N marco *m*, borde *m*
2 VT rodear

surrounding [sə'raʊndɪŋ] **1** ADJ circundante
2 NPL **surroundings** *(of place)* alrededores *mpl*, cercanías *fpl*

surveillance [sɜ:'veɪləns] N vigilancia *f*

survey 1 N ['sɜ:veɪ] **(a)** *(of building)* inspección *f*; *(of land)* reconocimiento *m* **(b)** *(of trends etc)* encuesta *f* **(c)** *(overall view)* panorama *m*
2 VT [sə'veɪ] **(a)** *(building)* inspeccionar; *(land)* medir **(b)** *(trends etc)* hacer una encuesta sobre **(c)** *(look at)* contemplar

surveyor [sə'veɪə(r)] N agrimensor(a) *m,f*; **quantity s.** aparejador(a) *m,f*

survival [sə'vaɪvəl] N supervivencia *f*

survive [sə'vaɪv] **1** VI sobrevivir; *(remain)* perdurar
2 VT sobrevivir a

survivor [sə'vaɪvə(r)] N superviviente *mf*

susceptible [sə'septəbəl] ADJ *(to attack)* susceptible **(to** a); *(to illness)* propenso(a) **(to** a)

suspect 1 ADJ ['sʌspekt] *(dubious)* sospechoso(a)
2 N sospechoso(a) *m,f*
3 VT [sə'spekt] **(a)** *(person)* sospechar **(of** de); *(plot, motives)* recelar de **(b)** *(think likely)* imaginar, creer

suspend [sə'spend] VT suspender; *(pupil)* expulsar por un tiempo

suspended [sə'spendɪd] ADJ suspendido(a); *Jur* **s. sentence** condena *f* condicional

suspender [sə'spendə(r)] N **(a)** *Br (for stocking, sock)* liga *f*; **s. belt** liguero *m* **(b)** *US* **suspenders** *(for trousers)* tirantes *mpl*

suspense [sə'spens] N *(uncertainty)* incertidumbre *f*; *(in movie) Esp* suspense *m*, *Am* suspenso *m*; **to keep sb in s.** mantener a algn en la incertidumbre

suspension [sə'spenʃən] N **(a)** *(of car)* suspensión *f* **(b)** *(of pupil, employee)* expulsión *f* temporal **(c)** **s. bridge** puente *m* colgante

suspicion [sə'spɪʃən] N **(a)** *(belief of guilt)* sospecha *f* **(b)** *(notion, feeling)* presentimiento *m* **(c)** *(small amount)* asomo *m*

suspicious [sə'spɪʃəs] ADJ **(a)** *(arousing suspicion)* sospechoso(a) **(b)** *(distrustful)* receloso(a); **to be s. of sb** desconfiar de algn

suss out [sʌs] VT SEP *Br Fam (person)* calar; *(system) Esp* coger *or Am* agarrar el truco a; **I haven't sussed out how it works yet** todavía no me he enterado de cómo funciona

sustain [sə'steɪn] VT **(a)** *(weight, growth, life)* sostener **(b)** *(nourish)* mantener **(c)** *Jur (objection)* admitir **(d)** *(injury etc)* sufrir

sustainable [sə'steɪnəbəl] ADJ *(development)* sostenible

sustained [sə'steɪnd] ADJ sostenido(a)

sustenance ['sʌstənəns] N sustento *m*

swab [swɒb] **1** N *(cotton wool)* algodón *m*; *(for specimen)* frotis *m*
2 VT *(wound)* limpiar

swagger ['swægə(r)] **1** N pavoneo *m*
2 VI pavonearse

swallow[1] ['swɒləʊ] **1** N *(of drink, food)* trago *m*
2 VT **(a)** *(drink, food)* tragar **(b)** *Fig (believe)* tragarse
3 VI tragar

► **swallow up** VT SEP *Fig* (a) *(engulf)* tragar (b) *(eat up)* consumir

swallow² ['swɒləʊ] N *(bird)* golondrina f

swam [swæm] PT of **swim**

swamp [swɒmp] 1 N ciénaga f
2 VT (a) *(boat)* hundir (b) *Fig* inundar *(with or by* de)

swan [swɒn] 1 N cisne m
2 VI *Fam* **to s. around** pavonearse; **to s. around doing nothing** hacer el vago

swap [swɒp] 1 N *Fam* intercambio m
2 VT cambiar

► **swap round, swap over** VT SEP *(switch)* cambiar

swarm [swɔːm] 1 N enjambre m
2 VI *(bees)* enjambrar; *Fig* **Rye was swarming with tourists** Rye estaba lleno de turistas

swarthy ['swɔːðɪ] ADJ (**swarthier, swarthiest**) moreno(a)

swastika ['swɒstɪkə] N esvástica f, cruz gamada

swat [swɒt] VT aplastar

swathe [sweɪð] VT *(bind up)* envolver

sway [sweɪ] 1 N (a) *(movement)* balanceo m (b) **to hold s. over sb** dominar a algn
2 VI (a) *(swing)* balancearse, mecerse (b) *(totter)* tambalearse
3 VT *Fig (persuade)* convencer

swear [sweə(r)] 1 VT *(pt* swore; *pp* sworn) *(vow)* jurar; **to s. an oath** prestar juramento
2 VI (a) *(formally)* jurar, prestar juramento (b) *(curse)* soltar tacos, decir palabrotas; *(blaspheme)* jurar; **to s. at sb** echar pestes contra algn

swear-word ['sweəwɜːd] N palabrota f

sweat [swet] 1 N *(perspiration)* sudor m; *Fam (hard work)* trabajo duro
2 VI *(perspire)* sudar; *Fig (work hard)* sudar la gota gorda
3 VT *Fam* **to s. it out** aguantar

sweater ['swetə(r)] N suéter m, *Esp* jersey m, *RP* pulóver m

sweatshirt ['swetʃɜːt] N sudadera f, *Col, RP* buzo m

sweaty ['swetɪ] ADJ (**sweatier, sweatiest**) sudoroso(a)

Swede [swiːd] N *(person)* sueco(a) m,f

swede [swiːd] N *esp Br (vegetable)* nabo sueco

Sweden ['swiːdən] N Suecia

Swedish ['swiːdɪʃ] 1 ADJ sueco(a)
2 N (a) *(language)* sueco m (b) **the S.** los suecos

sweep [swiːp] 1 N (a) *(with broom)* barrido m, *Am* barrida f (b) **(chimney) s.** deshollinador(a) m,f
2 VT *(pt & pp* swept) *(floor etc)* barrer
3 VI (a) *(with broom)* barrer (b) **to s. in/out/past** entrar/salir/pasar rápidamente

► **sweep aside** VT SEP apartar bruscamente; *Fig (objections)* rechazar

► **sweep away** VT SEP (a) *(dust)* barrer (b) *(of storm)* arrastrar

► **sweep up** VI barrer

sweeper ['swiːpə(r)] N (a) *(machine)* barredora f (b) *Ftb* líbero m

sweeping ['swiːpɪŋ] ADJ (a) *(broad)* amplio(a); **a s. statement** una declaración demasiado general (b) *(victory)* aplastante (c) *(reforms, changes etc)* radical

sweet [swiːt] 1 ADJ (a) *(taste, wine)* dulce; *(sugary)* azucarado(a); **to have a s. tooth** ser goloso(a); **s. pea** guisante m de olor; **s. shop** confitería f (b) *(pleasant)* agradable; *(smell)* fragante; *(sound)* melodioso(a) (c) *(person, animal)* encantador(a)
2 N (a) *Br (confectionery)* dulce m; **(boiled) s.** caramelo m (b) *(dessert)* postre m

sweet-and-sour ['swiːtən'saʊə(r)] ADJ agridulce

sweetcorn ['swiːtkɔːn] N maíz tierno, *Andes, RP* choclo m, *Méx* elote m

sweeten ['swiːtən] VT (a) *(tea etc)* azucarar (b) *Fig (temper)* aplacar; **to s. the pill** suavizar el golpe

sweetener ['swiːtənə(r)] N *(for tea, coffee)* edulcorante m

sweetheart ['swiːthɑːt] N (a) *(boyfriend)* novio m; *(girlfriend)* novia f (b) *(dear, love)* cariño m, amor m

sweetness ['swiːtnɪs] N dulzura f; *(of smell)* fragancia f; *(of sound)* suavidad f

swell [swel] 1 N *(of sea)* marejada f, oleaje m
2 ADJ *US Fam* genial, *Méx* padre, *RP* bárbaro(a)
3 VI *(pt* swelled; *pp* swollen) *(part of body)* hincharse; *(river)* subir

► **swell up** VI hincharse

swelling ['swelɪŋ] N hinchazón f; *Med* tumefacción f

sweltering ['sweltərɪŋ] ADJ agobiante

swept [swept] PT & PP of **sweep**

swerve [swɜːv] 1 N (a) *(by car)* viraje m (b) *Sport (by player)* regate m
2 VI (a) *(car)* dar un viraje brusco (b) *Sport (player)* dar un regate

swift [swɪft] 1 ADJ rápido(a), veloz
2 N *(bird)* vencejo m (común)

swiftly ['swɪftlɪ] ADV rápidamente

swig [swɪg] *Fam* 1 N trago m
2 VT *Esp* pimplar, *Am* tomar

swill [swɪl] 1 N (a) *(food) (for pigs)* sobras fpl para los cerdos; *Pej (for people)* bazofia f (b) *(rinse)* enjuague m
2 VT (a) *(rinse)* enjuagar (b) *Fam (drink)* beber a grandes tragos

► **swill out** VT SEP *(rinse)* enjuagar, *Esp* aclarar

swim [swɪm] 1 VI *(pt* swam; *pp* swum) nadar; **to go swimming** ir a nadar; *Fam* **my head is swimming** la cabeza me da vueltas
2 VT *(the Channel)* pasar a nado
3 N baño m; **to go for a s.** ir a nadar *or* bañarse

swimmer ['swɪmə(r)] N nadador(a) m,f

swimming ['swɪmɪŋ] N natación f; **s. cap** gorro m de baño; **s. costume** traje m de baño, Esp bañador m, Ecuad, Perú, RP malla f; **s. pool** piscina f, Méx alberca f, RP pileta f; **s. trunks** Esp bañador m (de hombre), Ecuad, Perú, RP malla f (de hombre)

swimsuit ['swɪmsuːt] N traje m de baño, Esp bañador m, Ecuad, Perú, RP malla f

swindle ['swɪndəl] 1 N estafa f
2 VT estafar

swindler ['swɪndlə(r)] N estafador(a) m,f

swine [swaɪn] N (a) (pl swine) (pig) cerdo m, puerco m, Am chancho m (b) (pl swines) Fam (person) canalla mf, cochino(a) m,f

swing [swɪŋ] 1 N (a) (movement) (of rope, chain) balanceo m, vaivén m; Fig (in votes etc) viraje m (b) (in golf) swing m (c) (plaything) columpio m (d) (rhythm) ritmo m; **in full s.** en plena marcha
2 VI (pt & pp swung) (a) (move to and fro) balancearse; (arms, legs) menearse; (on swing) columpiarse (b) (turn) girar; **he swung round** dio media vuelta
3 VT (cause to move to and fro) balancear; (arms, legs) menear

swingeing ['swɪndʒɪŋ] ADJ Br drástico(a)

swipe [swaɪp] 1 N golpe m
2 VT (a) (hit) dar un tortazo a (b) Fam (steal) afanar, birlar

swirl [swɜːl] 1 N remolino m; (of cream, smoke) voluta f
2 VI arremolinarse

swish [swɪʃ] 1 ADJ Fam (smart) elegante
2 VT (tail) menear
3 VI (whip) dar un chasquido; (skirt) crujir

Swiss [swɪs] 1 ADJ suizo(a)
2 N (pl Swiss) (person) suizo(a) m,f

switch [swɪtʃ] 1 N (a) Elec interruptor m (b) (changeover) cambio repentino; (exchange) intercambio m (c) US Rail agujas fpl
2 VT (a) (jobs, direction) cambiar de (b) (allegiance) cambiar (to por); (attention) desviar (to hacia)
► **switch off** VT SEP apagar
► **switch on** VT SEP encender, Am prender
► **switch over** VI cambiar (to a)

switchboard ['swɪtʃbɔːd] N centralita f, Am conmutador m

Switzerland ['swɪtsələnd] N Suiza

swivel ['swɪvəl] 1 N **s. chair** silla giratoria
2 VT & VI girar

swollen ['swəʊlən] 1 ADJ (ankle, face) hinchado(a); (river, lake) crecido(a)
2 PP of swell

swoon [swuːn] 1 N desmayo m
2 VI desmayarse

swoop [swuːp] 1 N (a) (of bird) calada f; (of plane) (vuelo m en) picado m or Am picada f (b) (by police) redada f

2 VI (a) (plane, bird) volar en picado or Am picada (b) (police) hacer una redada

swop [swɒp] N & VT = swap

sword [sɔːd] N espada f

swordfish ['sɔːdfɪʃ] N pez m espada

swore [swɔː(r)] PT of swear

sworn [swɔːn] 1 ADJ jurado(a)
2 PP of swear

swot [swɒt] VI Br Fam matarse estudiando, Esp empollar, RP tragar (for para)

swum [swʌm] PP of swim

swung [swʌŋ] PT & PP of swing

sycamore ['sɪkəmɔː(r)] N (a) Br sicomoro m (b) US (plane tree) plátano m

syllable ['sɪləbəl] N sílaba f

syllabus ['sɪləbəs] N programa m de estudios

symbol ['sɪmbəl] N símbolo m

symbolic [sɪm'bɒlɪk] ADJ simbólico(a)

symbolize ['sɪmbəlaɪz] VT simbolizar

symmetry ['sɪmɪtrɪ] N simetría f

sympathetic [sɪmpə'θetɪk] ADJ (a) (showing pity) compasivo(a) (b) (understanding) comprensivo(a); (kind) amable

> Note that the Spanish word **simpático** is a false friend and is never a translation for the English word **sympathetic**. In Spanish **simpático** means "nice, likeable".

sympathize ['sɪmpəθaɪz] VI (a) (show pity) compadecerse (**with** de) (b) (understand) comprender

sympathizer ['sɪmpəθaɪzə(r)] N simpatizante mf

sympathy ['sɪmpəθɪ] N (a) (pity) compasión f (b) (condolences) pésame m; **letter of s.** pésame m; **to express one's s.** dar el pésame (c) (understanding) comprensión f

> Note that the Spanish word **simpatía** is a false friend and is never a translation for the English word **sympathy**. In Spanish **simpatía** means "liking, affection".

symphony ['sɪmfənɪ] N sinfonía f

symposium [sɪm'pəʊzɪəm] N simposio m

symptom ['sɪmptəm] N síntoma m

symptomatic [sɪmptə'mætɪk] ADJ sintomático(a)

synagogue ['sɪnəgɒg] N sinagoga f

synchronize ['sɪŋkrənaɪz] VT sincronizar

syndicate ['sɪndɪkɪt] N corporación f; **newspaper s.** sindicato periodístico

syndrome ['sɪndrəʊm] N síndrome m

synonym ['sɪnənɪm] N sinónimo m

synonymous [sɪ'nɒnɪməs] ADJ sinónimo(a) (**with** de)

synopsis [sɪ'nɒpsɪs] N sinopsis f inv

syntax ['sɪntæks] N sintaxis f inv

synthesis ['sɪnθɪsɪs] N (pl syntheses ['sɪnθɪsiːz]) síntesis f inv

synthesizer ['sɪnθɪsaɪzə(r)] N sintetizador *m*
synthetic [sɪn'θetɪk] ADJ sintético(a)
syphilis ['sɪfɪlɪs] N sífilis *f*
syphon ['saɪfən] N = **siphon**
Syria ['sɪrɪə] N Siria
Syrian ['sɪrɪən] ADJ & N sirio(a) *(m,f)*

syringe [sɪ'rɪndʒ] N jeringa *f*, jeringuilla *f*
syrup ['sɪrəp] N jarabe *m*, almíbar *m*
system ['sɪstəm] N sistema *m*; *Fam* **the s.** el orden establecido; *Comput* **systems analyst** analista *mf* de sistemas
systematic [sɪstɪ'mætɪk] ADJ sistemático(a)

T, t [tiː] N *(the letter)* T, t *f*

t *(abbr* **ton(s))** tonelada(s) *f(pl)* *(Br = 1.016 kilos; US = 907 kilos)*

ta [tɑː] INTERJ *Br Fam* gracias

tab [tæb] N (**a**) *(flap)* lengüeta *f*; *(label)* etiqueta *f*; *Fam* **to keep tabs on sb** vigilar a algn (**b**) *US Fam (bill)* cuenta *f*

tabby ['tæbɪ] N **t. (cat)** gato(a) romano(a)

table ['teɪbəl] **1** N (**a**) *(furniture)* mesa *f*; **to lay** or **set the t.** poner la mesa; **t. lamp** lámpara *f* de mesa; **t. mat** salvamanteles *m inv*; **t. tennis** ping-pong® *m*, tenis *m* de mesa; **t. wine** vino *m* de mesa (**b**) *(of figures)* tabla *f*, cuadro *m*; **t. of contents** índice *m* de materias
2 VT *(motion, proposal) Br* presentar; *US* posponer

tablecloth ['teɪbəlklɒθ] N mantel *m*

tablespoon ['teɪbəlspuːn] N cucharón *m*

tablespoonful ['teɪbəlspuːnfʊl] N cucharada *f* grande

tablet ['tæblɪt] N (**a**) *Med* pastilla *f* (**b**) *(of stone)* lápida *f*

tableware ['teɪbəlweə(r)] N vajilla *f*

tabloid ['tæblɔɪd] N periódico *m* de pequeño formato; **t. press** prensa sensacionalista

taboo [tə'buː] ADJ & N tabú *(m)*

tabulate ['tæbjʊleɪt] VT disponer en listas

tacit ['tæsɪt] ADJ tácito(a)

taciturn ['tæsɪtɜːn] ADJ taciturno(a)

tack [tæk] **1** N (**a**) *(small nail)* tachuela *f* (**b**) *Sewing* hilván *m* (**c**) *Naut* amura *f*; *(distance)* bordada *f*; *Fig* **to change t.** cambiar de rumbo
2 VT (**a**) **to t. sth down** clavar algo con tachuelas (**b**) *Sewing* hilvanar
3 VI *Naut* virar de bordo

▶ **tack on** VT SEP *(add)* añadir

tackle ['tækəl] **1** N (**a**) *(equipment)* aparejos *mpl*; **fishing t.** aparejos de pescar (**b**) *(challenge) (in football)* entrada *f*; *(in rugby, American football)* placaje *m*, *Am* tackle *m*
2 VT agarrar; *(task)* emprender; *(problem)* abordar; *(in football)* entrar a; *(in rugby, American football)* hacer un placaje a, *Am* tacklear

tacky¹ ['tækɪ] ADJ (**tackier, tackiest**) pegajoso(a)

tacky² ['tækɪ] ADJ (**tackier, tackiest**) *Fam (tasteless)* chabacano(a), ordinario(a)

tact [tækt] N tacto *m*, diplomacia *f*

tactful ['tæktfʊl] ADJ diplomático(a)

tactic ['tæktɪk] N táctica *f*; **tactics** táctica *f*

tactical ['tæktɪkəl] ADJ táctico(a)

tactless ['tæktlɪs] ADJ *(person)* poco diplomático(a); *(question)* indiscreto(a)

tadpole ['tædpəʊl] N renacuajo *m*

taffy ['tæfɪ] N *US* caramelo *m* de melaza

tag [tæg] N (**a**) *(label)* etiqueta *f* (**b**) *(saying)* coletilla *f*

▶ **tag along** VI *Fam* pegarse

▶ **tag on** VT SEP *(add to end)* añadir

tai chi [taɪ'tʃiː] N tai-chi *m*

tail [teɪl] **1** N (**a**) *(of animal, plane)* cola *f*; **t. end** cola (**b**) *(of shirt)* faldón *m*; **to wear tails** ir de frac; **t. coat** frac *m* (**c**) **tails** *(of coin)* cruz *f*, *Andes, Ven* sello *m*, *Méx* sol *m*, *RP* ceca *f*
2 VT *Fam (follow)* seguir de cerca

▶ **tail away, tail off** VI desvanecerse

tailback ['teɪlbæk] N *Br* caravana *f*

tail-gate ['teɪlgeɪt] **1** N *Aut* puerta trasera
2 VT *US* conducir or *Am* manejar pegado a, pisar los talones a

taillight ['teɪllaɪt] N *Aut* faro *m* trasero

tailor ['teɪlə(r)] **1** N sastre *m*; **t.'s (shop)** sastrería *f*
2 VT *(suit)* confeccionar; *Fig* adaptar

tailor-made [teɪlə'meɪd] ADJ hecho(a) a la medida

tailwind ['teɪlwɪnd] N viento *m* de cola

taint [teɪnt] VT contaminar; *Fig* corromper

tainted ['teɪntɪd] ADJ contaminado(a); *(reputation)* manchado(a)

take [teɪk] **1** VT *(pt* took; *pp* taken) (**a**) *(grasp)* tomar, *Esp* coger, *Am* agarrar; **to t. an opportunity** aprovechar una oportunidad; **to t. hold of sth** agarrar algo; **to t. sth from one's pocket** sacarse algo del bolsillo; **t. your time!** ¡tómate el tiempo que quieras!; **to t. a bath** bañarse; **to t. care (of oneself)** cuidarse; **his car takes six people** caben seis personas en su coche; **is this seat taken?** ¿está ocupado este asiento?; **to t. a decision** tomar una decisión; **to t. a liking/dislike to sb** tomar cariño/antipatía a algn; **to t. a photograph** sacar una fotografía; **t. the first road on the left** *esp Esp* coja la or *Am* agarre por la primera a la izquierda; **to t. the train** tomar or *esp Esp* coger el tren
(**b**) *(accept)* aceptar; *(earn)* **to t. so much per week** recaudar tanto por semana
(**c**) *(win)* ganar; *(prize)* llevarse
(**d**) *(eat, drink)* tomar; **to t. drugs** drogarse

(e) **she's taking (a degree in) law** estudia derecho; **to t. an exam (in …)** examinarse (de …)
(f) *(person to a place)* llevar
(g) *(endure)* aguantar
(h) *(consider)* considerar
(i) **I t. it that …** supongo que …; **what do you t. me for?** ¿por quién me tomas?
(j) *(require)* requerir; **it takes an hour to get there** se tarda una hora en llegar hasta allí
(k) **to be taken ill** enfermar
2 N *Cin* toma *f*

▶ **take after** VT INSEP parecerse a
▶ **take apart** VT SEP *(machine)* desmontar
▶ **take away** VT SEP (a) *(carry off)* llevarse (b) **to t. sth away from sb** quitar *or Am* sacar algo a algn (c) *Math* restar
▶ **take back** VT SEP (a) *(give back)* devolver; *(receive back)* recuperar (b) *(withdraw)* retractarse
▶ **take down** VT SEP (a) *(lower)* bajar (b) *(demolish)* derribar (c) *(write)* apuntar
▶ **take in** VT SEP (a) *(shelter, lodge)* alojar, acoger (b) *Sewing* meter (c) *(include)* abarcar (d) *(understand)* entender (e) *(deceive)* engañar
▶ **take off** 1 VT SEP (a) *(remove)* quitar, *Am* sacar; **he took off his jacket** se quitó *or Am* se sacó la chaqueta (b) *(lead or carry away)* llevarse (c) *(deduct)* descontar (d) *(imitate)* imitar burlonamente
2 VI *(plane)* despegar, *Am* decolar
▶ **take on** VT SEP (a) *(undertake)* encargarse de (b) *(acquire)* tomar (c) *(employ)* contratar (d) *(compete with)* competir con
▶ **take out** VT SEP sacar, quitar; **he's taking me out to dinner** me ha invitado a cenar fuera
▶ **take over** 1 VT SEP *Com & Pol* tomar posesión de; **the rebels took over the country** los rebeldes se apoderaron del país
2 VI **to t. over from sb** relevar a algn
▶ **take to** VT INSEP *(become fond of)* tomar *or Esp* coger cariño a; **to t. to drink** darse a la bebida
▶ **take up** VT SEP (a) *Sewing* acortar (b) *(accept)* aceptar; *(adopt)* adoptar (c) **I've taken up the piano/French** he empezado a tocar el piano/a aprender francés (d) *(occupy)* ocupar

takeaway ['teɪkəweɪ] *Br* 1 N *(food)* comida *f* para llevar; *(restaurant)* restaurante *m* que vende comida para llevar
2 ADJ *(food)* para llevar

take-home pay ['teɪkhəʊm'peɪ] N sueldo neto

taken ['teɪkən] PP *of* **take**

takeoff ['teɪkɒf] N (a) *(plane, economy)* despegue *m*, *Am* decolaje *m* (b) *(imitation)* imitación burlona

takeout ['teɪkaʊt] *US* 1 N *(food)* comida *f* para llevar
2 ADJ *(food)* para llevar

takeover ['teɪkəʊvə(r)] N *Com* absorción *f*; **military t.** golpe *m* de estado; **t. bid** oferta pública de adquisición, OPA *f*

takings ['teɪkɪŋz] NPL *Br Com* recaudación *f*

talc [tælk] N talco *m*

talcum powder ['tælkəmpaʊdə(r)] N *(polvos mpl* de) talco *m*

tale [teɪl] N cuento *m*; **to tell tales** contar chismes

talent ['tælənt] N talento *m*

talented ['tæləntɪd] ADJ dotado(a)

talk [tɔːk] 1 VI *(talk)* hablar, *CAm, Méx* platicar; *(chat)* charlar; *(gossip)* chismorrear; *Fam* **now you're talking!** ¡eso sí que me interesa!
2 VT **to t. nonsense** decir tonterías; **to t. sense** hablar con sentido común; **to t. shop** hablar del trabajo
3 N (a) *(conversation)* conversación *f*, *CAm, Méx* plática *f* (b) *(words)* palabras *fpl*; **he's all t.** no hace más que hablar (c) *(rumour)* rumor *m*; *(gossip)* chismes *mpl* (d) *(lecture)* charla *f*
▶ **talk into** VT SEP **to t. sb into sth** convencer a algn para que haga algo
▶ **talk out of** VT SEP **to t. sb out of sth** disuadir a algn de que haga algo
▶ **talk over** VT SEP discutir

talkative ['tɔːkətɪv] ADJ hablador(a)

talking ['tɔːkɪŋ] N **no t. please!** ¡silencio, por favor!; **t. book** audiolibro *m*; **t. point** tema *m* de conversación

talking-to ['tɔːkɪŋtuː] N *Fam* sermón *m*, *Esp* rapapolvo *m*

tall [tɔːl] ADJ alto(a); **a tree 10 m t.** un árbol de 10 m (de alto); **how t. are you?** ¿cuánto mides?; *Fig* **that's a t. order** eso es mucho pedir

tally ['tælɪ] 1 VI **to t. with sth** corresponderse con algo
2 N *Com* apunte *m*; **to keep a t. of** llevar la cuenta de

talon ['tælən] N garra *f*

> Note that the Spanish word **talón** is a false friend and is never a translation for the English word **talon**. In Spanish, **talón** means both "heel" and "cheque".

tambourine [tæmbə'riːn] N pandereta *f*

tame [teɪm] 1 ADJ (a) *(animal)* domado(a); *(by nature)* manso(a); *(person)* dócil (b) *(style)* soso(a)
2 VT domar

tamper ['tæmpə(r)] VI **to t. with** *(text)* adulterar; *(records, an entry)* falsificar; *(lock)* intentar forzar

tampon ['tæmpɒn] N tampón *m*

tan [tæn] 1 N (a) *(colour)* marrón rojizo (b) *(of skin)* bronceado *m*, *Esp* moreno *m*
2 ADJ *(colour)* marrón rojizo
3 VT (a) *(leather)* curtir (b) *(skin)* broncear
4 VI ponerse moreno(a)

tang [tæŋ] N sabor *m* fuerte

tangent ['tændʒənt] N tangente *f*; *Fig* **to go off at a t.** salirse por la tangente

tangerine [tændʒə'ri:n] N clementina *f*

tangible ['tændʒəbəl] ADJ tangible

tangle ['tæŋgəl] N *(of thread)* maraña *f*; *Fig* lío *m*; *Fig* **to get into a t.** hacerse un lío

tangled ['tæŋgəld] ADJ enredado(a), enmarañado(a)

tank [tæŋk] N (a) *(container)* depósito *m* (b) *Mil* tanque *m*

tanker ['tæŋkə(r)] N *Naut* tanque *m*; *(for oil)* petrolero *m*; *Aut* camión *m* cisterna

Tannoy® ['tænɔɪ] N (sistema *m*) de megafonía *f*

tantalize ['tæntəlaɪz] VT atormentar

tantalizing ['tæntəlaɪzɪŋ] ADJ atormentador(a)

tantamount ['tæntəmaʊnt] ADJ **t. to** equivalente a

tantrum ['tæntrəm] N rabieta *f*

tap¹ [tæp] 1 VT golpear suavemente; *(with hand)* dar una palmadita a

2 VI **to t. at the door** llamar suavemente a la puerta

3 N golpecito *m*; **t. dancing** claqué *m*

tap² [tæp] 1 N *Br (for water)* grifo *m*, *Chile, Col, Méx* llave *f*, *RP* canilla *f*; *Fig* **funds on t.** fondos *mpl* disponibles

2 VT (a) *(stick with tape)* pegar con cinta adhesiva; *Fig* **I've got him/it taped** lo tengo controlado (b) *(record)* grabar

tape [teɪp] 1 N (a) *(ribbon)* cinta *f*; **sticky t.** cinta adhesiva; **t. measure** cinta métrica (b) *(for recording)* cinta (magnetofónica); **t. recorder** magnetófono *m*, cassette *m*; **t. recording** grabación *f*

2 VT (a) *(stick with tape)* pegar (con cinta adhesiva) (b) *(record)* grabar (en cinta)

taper ['teɪpə(r)] 1 VI estrecharse; *(to a point)* afilarse

2 N *(candle)* vela *f*

▸ **taper off** VI ir disminuyendo

tapestry ['tæpɪstrɪ] N tapiz *m*

tapping ['tæpɪŋ] N (a) *(of tree)* sangría *f*; *(of resources)* explotación *f* (b) *Tel* intervención *f* ilegal de un teléfono

tar [tɑ:(r)] N alquitrán *m*

target ['tɑ:gɪt] N (a) *(object aimed at)* blanco *m*; **t. practice** tiro *m* al blanco (b) *(purpose)* meta *f*

tariff ['tærɪf] N tarifa *f*, arancel *m*

tarmac® ['tɑ:mæk] 1 N (a) *(substance)* alquitrán *m* (b) *Av* pista *f* de aterrizaje

2 VT alquitranar

tarnish ['tɑ:nɪʃ] VT deslustrar

tarpaulin [tɑ:'pɔ:lɪn] N lona *f*

tart¹ [tɑ:t] N *Br Culin* tarta *f*

tart² [tɑ:t] ADJ *(taste)* ácido(a), agrio(a)

tart³ [tɑ:t] *Fam* 1 N fulana *f*, *Méx* piruja *f*

2 VT *Br* **to t. oneself up** emperifollarse

tartan ['tɑ:tən] N tartán *m*

tartar ['tɑ:tə(r)] N (a) *Chem* tártaro *m* (b) *Culin* **t. sauce** salsa tártara

task [tɑ:sk] N tarea *f*; **to take sb to t.** reprender a algn; *Mil* **t. force** destacamento *m* (de fuerzas)

tassel ['tæsəl] N borla *f*

taste [teɪst] 1 N (a) *(sense)* gusto *m*; *(flavour)* sabor *m*; **it has a burnt t.** sabe a quemado (b) *(sample) (of food)* bocado *m*; *(of drink)* trago *m*; **to give sb a t. of his own medicine** pagar a algn con la misma moneda (c) *(liking)* afición *f*; **to have a t. for sth** gustarle a uno algo (d) **in bad t.** de mal gusto; **to have (good) t.** tener (buen) gusto

2 VT *(sample)* probar

3 VI **to t. of sth** saber a algo

tasteful ['teɪstfʊl] ADJ de buen gusto

tasteless ['teɪstlɪs] ADJ (a) *(food)* soso(a) (b) *(in bad taste)* de mal gusto

tasty ['teɪstɪ] ADJ (**tastier, tastiest**) sabroso(a)

tattered ['tætəd] ADJ hecho(a) jirones

tatters ['tætəz] NPL **in t.** hecho(a) jirones

tattoo¹ [tæ'tu:] N *Mil* retreta *f*

tattoo² [tæ'tu:] 1 VT tatuar

2 N *(mark)* tatuaje *m*

tatty ['tætɪ] ADJ (**tattier, tattiest**) *Fam* ajado(a), *Esp* sobado(a)

taught [tɔ:t] PT & PP of **teach**

taunt [tɔ:nt] 1 VT **to t. sb with sth** echar algo en cara a algn

2 N pulla *f*

Taurus ['tɔ:rəs] N Tauro *m*

taut [tɔ:t] ADJ tenso(a), tirante

tavern ['tævən] N taberna *f*

tawdry ['tɔ:drɪ] ADJ (**tawdrier, tawdriest**) hortera

tawn(e)y ['tɔ:nɪ] ADJ leonado(a), rojizo(a)

tax [tæks] 1 N impuesto *m*; **t. free** exento(a) de impuestos; **t. collector** recaudador(a) *m,f* (de impuestos); **t. evasion** evasión *f* fiscal; **t. return** declaración *f* de renta

2 VT (a) *(goods, income)* gravar; *(people)* cobrar impuestos a (b) *(patience etc)* poner a prueba

taxable ['tæksəbəl] ADJ imponible

taxation [tæk'seɪʃən] N impuestos *mpl*

taxi ['tæksɪ] 1 N taxi *m*; **t. driver** taxista *mf*; **t. rank** *or US* **stand** parada *f* de taxis

2 VI *(aircraft)* rodar por la pista

taxidermy ['tæksɪdɜ:mɪ] N taxidermia *f*

taxing ['tæksɪŋ] ADJ exigente

taxpayer ['tækspeɪə(r)] N contribuyente *mf*

TB [ti:'bi:] N *(abbr* **tuberculosis)** tuberculosis *f inv*

tea [ti:] N (a) *(plant, drink)* té *m*; **t. bag** bolsita *f* de té; **t. break** descanso *m*; *Br* **t. cosy** cubretetera *f*; **t. leaf** hoja *f* de té; **t. service** *or* **set** juego *m* de té; **t. towel** trapo *m* *or* paño *m* (de cocina), *RP* repasador *m* (b) *(snack)* merienda *f*; **(high) t.** merienda-cena *f*

teach [ti:tʃ] 1 VT *(pt & pp* **taught)** enseñar; *(subject)* dar clases de; **to t. sb (how) to do sth** enseñar a algn a hacer algo; *US* **to t.**

school ser profesor(a)
2 VI dar clases, ser profesor(a)

teacher ['tiːtʃə(r)] N profesor(a) m,f, (in primary school) maestro(a) m,f

teaching ['tiːtʃɪŋ] N enseñanza f

teacup ['tiːkʌp] N taza f de té

teak [tiːk] N teca f

team [tiːm] N equipo m; (of oxen) yunta f

team-mate ['tiːmmeɪt] N compañero(a) m,f de equipo

teamwork ['tiːmwɜːk] N trabajo m en equipo

teapot ['tiːpɒt] N tetera f

tear¹ [tɪə(r)] N lágrima f; **to be in tears** estar llorando; **t. gas** gas lacrimógeno

tear² [teə(r)] 1 VT (pt **tore**; pp **torn**) (a) (rip) rasgar (b) (snatch) **to t. sth out of sb's hands** arrancarle algo de las manos a algn
2 VI (a) (cloth) rajarse (b) **to t. along** ir a toda velocidad
3 N desgarrón m; (in clothes) rasgón m
► **tear down** VT SEP derribar
► **tear off** VT SEP arrancar
► **tear out** VT SEP arrancar
► **tear up** VT SEP (a) (document, photo) romper, hacer pedazos (b) (uproot) arrancar de raíz

tearful ['tɪəfʊl] ADJ lloroso(a)

tearoom ['tiːruːm] N Br = **teashop**

tease [tiːz] 1 VT tomar el pelo a
2 N bromista mf

teashop ['tiːʃɒp] N Br salón m de té

teaspoon ['tiːspuːn] N cucharilla f

teaspoonful ['tiːspuːnfʊl] N cucharadita f

teat [tiːt] N (of animal) teta f; (of bottle) tetina f

teatime ['tiːtaɪm] N esp Br hora f del té

technical ['teknɪkəl] ADJ técnico(a); Br **t. college** escuela f de formación profesional

technicality [teknɪ'kælɪtɪ] N detalle técnico

technically ['teknɪkəlɪ] ADV (theoretically) en teoría

technician [tek'nɪʃən] N técnico(a) m,f

technique [tek'niːk] N técnica f

techno ['teknəʊ] N tecno m

technological [teknə'lɒdʒɪkəl] ADJ tecnológico(a)

technology [tek'nɒlədʒɪ] N tecnología f

teddy bear ['tedɪbeə(r)] N oso m de felpa

tedious ['tiːdɪəs] ADJ tedioso(a), aburrido(a)

tee [tiː] N (in golf) tee m

teem [tiːm] VI **to t. with** rebosar de; Fam **it was teeming down** llovía a cántaros

teenage ['tiːneɪdʒ] ADJ adolescente

teenager ['tiːneɪdʒə(r)] N adolescente mf

teens [tiːnz] NPL adolescencia f

teeshirt ['tiːʃɜːt] N camiseta f, Méx playera, RP remera f

teeter ['tiːtə(r)] VI balancearse

teeth [tiːθ] PL of **tooth**

teethe [tiːð] VI echar los dientes

teething ['tiːðɪŋ] N **t. ring** chupador m; Fig **t. troubles** dificultades fpl iniciales

teetotaller [tiː'təʊtələ(r)] N abstemio(a) m,f

TEFL ['tefəl] N (abbr **Teaching of English as a Foreign Language**) enseñanza f del inglés como idioma extranjero

telecommunications ['telɪkəmjuːnɪ'keɪʃənz] N SING telecomunicaciones fpl

telegram ['telɪgræm] N telegrama m

telegraph ['telɪgrɑːf] 1 N telégrafo m; **t. pole** poste telegráfico
2 VT & VI telegrafiar

telemarketing [telɪmɑːkɪtɪŋ] N Com telemarketing m

telepathy [tɪ'lepəθɪ] N telepatía f

telephone ['telɪfəʊn] 1 N teléfono m; **t. banking** telebanca f; Br **t. booth** or **box** cabina (telefónica); **t. call** llamada telefónica, Am llamado telefónico; **t. directory** guía telefónica, Am directorio m de teléfonos; **t. number** número m de teléfono
2 VT telefonear, llamar por teléfono a, Am hablar por teléfono a

telephonist [tɪ'lefənɪst] N Br telefonista mf

telephoto ['telɪfəʊtəʊ] ADJ **t. lens** teleobjetivo m

teleprinter ['telɪprɪntə(r)] N teletipo m

telesales [telɪ'seɪlz] NPL Com televenta f, ventas fpl por teléfono

telescope ['telɪskəʊp] 1 N telescopio m
2 VI plegarse (como un catalejo)
3 VT plegar

telescopic [telɪ'skɒpɪk] ADJ (umbrella) plegable

teleshopping ['telɪʃɒpɪŋ] N Com telecompra f

televise ['telɪvaɪz] VT televisar

television ['telɪvɪʒən] N televisión f; **t. programme** programa m de televisión; **t. (set)** televisor m

teleworker ['telɪwɜːkə(r)] N teletrabajador(a) m,f

teleworking ['telɪwɜːkɪŋ] N teletrabajo m

telex ['teleks] 1 N télex m
2 VT enviar por télex

tell [tel] 1 VT (pt & pp **told**) (a) (say) decir; (relate) contar; (inform) comunicar; **to t. lies** mentir; **to t. sb about sth** contarle algo a algn; **you're telling me!** ¡a mí me lo vas a contar! (b) (order) mandar; **to t. sb to do sth** decir a algn que haga algo (c) (distinguish) distinguir; **to know how to t. the time** saber decir la hora (d) **all told** en total
2 VI (a) (reveal) reflejar (b) **who can t.?** (know) ¿quién sabe? (c) (have effect) notarse; **the pressure is telling on her** está acusando la presión
► **tell off** VT SEP Fam (scold) **to t. sb off (for)** echar una reprimenda or Esp bronca a algn (por)

teller ['telə(r)] N (in bank etc) cajero(a) m,f

telling ['telɪŋ] ADJ *(action)* eficaz; *(blow, argument)* contundente

telltale ['telteɪl] N acusica *mf*, *Esp* chivato(a) *m,f*; **t. signs** señales reveladoras

telly ['telɪ] N *Br Fam* **the t.** la tele

temp [temp] N *Fam* trabajador(a) *m,f* temporal

temper ['tempə(r)] **1** N (a) *(mood)* humor *m*; **to keep one's t.** no perder la calma; **to lose one's t.** perder los estribos (b) *(temperament)* **to have a bad t.** tener (mal) genio
2 VT *(in metallurgy)* templar; *Fig* suavizar

temperament ['tempərəmənt] N temperamento *m*

temperamental [tempərəmentəl] ADJ temperamental

temperate ['tempərɪt] ADJ (a) *(language, criticism)* moderado(a) (b) *(climate)* templado(a)

temperature ['temprɪtʃə(r)] N temperatura *f*; **to have a t.** tener fiebre

tempest ['tempɪst] N *Literary* tempestad *f*

temple¹ ['tempəl] N *Archit* templo *m*

temple² ['tempəl] N *Anat* sien *f*

tempo ['tempəʊ] N tempo *m*

temporary ['tempərərɪ] ADJ temporal, *Am* temporario(a); *(office, arrangement, repairs)* provisional, *Am* temporario(a)

tempt [tempt] VT tentar; **to t. providence** tentar la suerte; **to t. sb to do sth** incitar a algn a hacer algo

temptation [temp'teɪʃən] N tentación *f*

tempting ['temptɪŋ] ADJ tentador(a)

ten [ten] ADJ & N diez *(m inv)*

tenable ['tenəbəl] ADJ *(opinion)* sostenible

tenacious [tɪ'neɪʃəs] ADJ tenaz

tenancy ['tenənsɪ] N *(of house)* alquiler *m*; *(of land)* arrendamiento *m*

tenant ['tenənt] N *(of house)* inquilino(a) *m,f*; *(of farm)* arrendatario(a) *m,f*

tend¹ [tend] VI *(be inclined)* tender, tener tendencia (**to** a)

tend² [tend] VT *(care for)* cuidar

tendency ['tendənsɪ] N tendencia *f*

tender¹ ['tendə(r)] ADJ *(affectionate)* cariñoso(a); *(compassionate)* compasivo(a); *(meat)* tierno(a)

tender² ['tendə(r)] **1** VT ofrecer; **to t. one's resignation** presentar la dimisión
2 VI *Com* **to t. for** sacar a concurso
3 N (a) *Com* oferta *f* (b) **legal t.** moneda *f* de curso legal

tenderness ['tendənɪs] N ternura *f*

tendon ['tendən] N tendón *m*

tenement ['tenɪmənt] N **t. (building)** bloque *m* de apartamentos *or Esp* pisos *or Arg* departamentos

tenet ['tenɪt] N principio *m*

tennis ['tenɪs] N tenis *m*; **t. ball** pelota *f* de tenis; **t. court** pista *f* de tenis; **t. player** tenista *mf*; **t.**

racket raqueta *f* de tenis; **t. shoe** zapatilla *f* de tenis

tenor ['tenə(r)] N *Mus* tenor *m*

tense¹ [tens] ADJ tenso(a)

tense² [tens] N *Ling* tiempo *m*

tension ['tenʃən] N tensión *f*

tent [tent] N tienda *f* de campaña, *Am* carpa *f*; **t. peg** estaca *f*

tentacle ['tentəkəl] N tentáculo *m*

tentative ['tentətɪv] ADJ (a) *(not definite)* de prueba (b) *(hesitant)* indeciso(a)

tenterhooks ['tentəhʊks] NPL *Fig* **on t.** sobre ascuas

tenth [tenθ] **1** ADJ & N décimo(a) *(m,f)*
2 N *(fraction)* décimo *m*

tenuous ['tenjʊəs] ADJ (a) *(connection)* tenue (b) *(argument)* flojo(a)

tenure ['tenjʊə(r)] N (a) *(of office)* ocupación *f* (b) *(of property)* arrendamiento *m*

tepid ['tepɪd] ADJ tibio(a)

term [tɜːm] **1** N (a) *(period)* período *m*; *Educ* trimestre *m*; **t. of office** mandato *m*, legislatura *f*; **in the long/short t.** a largo/corto plazo (b) *(word)* término *m*; *Fig* **in terms of money** en cuanto al dinero (c) **terms** *(conditions)* condiciones *fpl*; **to come to terms with** hacerse a la idea de (d) **to be on good/bad terms with sb** tener buenas/malas relaciones con algn
2 VT calificar de

terminal ['tɜːmɪnəl] **1** ADJ terminal; **t. cancer** cáncer incurable
2 N terminal *f*

terminate ['tɜːmɪneɪt] **1** VT terminar; **to t. a pregnancy** abortar
2 VI terminarse

termini ['tɜːmɪnaɪ] PL *of* **terminus**

terminology [tɜːmɪ'nɒlədʒɪ] N terminología *f*

terminus ['tɜːmɪnəs] N *(pl* **termini**) terminal *m*

terrace ['terəs] N (a) *(on hillside)* terraza *f* (b) *(outside cafe, hotel)* terraza *f* (c) *Br (of houses)* hilera *f* de casas adosadas (d) *Br Ftb* **the terraces** las gradas

terraced ['terəst] ADJ *Br (hillside)* en terrazas; *Br (house, row)* adosado(a)

terrain [tə'reɪn] N terreno *m*

terrestrial [tɪ'restrɪəl] ADJ terrestre

terrible ['terəbəl] ADJ horrible, terrible

terribly ['terəblɪ] ADV tremendamente mal, *Esp* fatal

terrier ['terɪə(r)] N terrier *m*

terrific [tə'rɪfɪk] ADJ (a) *Fam (excellent)* estupendo, genial (b) *(extreme)* tremendo(a)

terrify ['terɪfaɪ] VT aterrorizar

terrifying ['terɪfaɪɪŋ] ADJ aterrador(a)

territory ['terɪtərɪ] N territorio *m*

terror ['terə(r)] N terror *m*

terrorism ['terərɪzəm] N terrorismo *m*

terrorist ['terərɪst] ADJ & N terrorista *(mf)*

terrorize ['terəraɪz] VT aterrorizar

terry ['terɪ] N t. towel toalla f de rizo

terse [tɜːs] ADJ *(curt)* lacónico(a)

tertiary ['tɜːʃɪərɪ] ADJ *Br Educ* superior

test [test] 1 VT probar, someter a una prueba; *(analyse)* analizar; *Med* hacer un análisis de

2 N prueba f, examen m; **to put to the t.** poner a prueba; **to stand the t.** pasar la prueba; **t. match** partido m internacional; **t. pilot** piloto m de pruebas; **t. tube** probeta f; **t.-tube baby** niño m probeta

testament ['testəmənt] N testamento m; **Old/ New T.** Antiguo/Nuevo Testamento

testicle ['testɪkəl] N testículo m

testify ['testɪfaɪ] 1 VT declarar

2 VI *Fig* **to t. to sth** atestiguar algo

testimonial [testɪ'məunɪəl] N recomendación f

testimony ['testɪmənɪ] N testimonio m, declaración f

tetanus ['tetənəs] N tétano(s) m inv

tether ['teðə(r)] 1 N ronzal m; *Fig* **to be at the end of one's t.** estar hasta la coronilla

2 VT *(animal)* atar

Texas ['teksəs] N Tejas

text [tekst] 1 N texto m

2 VT *(send text message to)* enviar un mensaje de texto a

textbook ['tekstbʊk] N libro m de texto

textile ['tekstaɪl] 1 N tejido m

2 ADJ textil

texture ['tekstʃə(r)] N textura f

Thai [taɪ] ADJ & N tailandés(esa) *(m,f)*

Thailand ['taɪlænd] N Tailandia

Thames [temz] N **the T.** el Támesis

than [ðæn, *unstressed* ðən] CONJ que; *(with numbers)* de; **he's older t. me** es mayor que yo; **I have more/less t. you** tengo más/menos que tú; **more interesting t. we thought** más interesante de lo que creíamos; **more t. once** más de una vez; **more t. ten people** más de diez personas

thank [θæŋk] VT agradecer; **t. you** gracias

thankful ['θæŋkfʊl] ADJ agradecido(a)

thankless ['θæŋklɪs] ADJ *(task)* ingrato(a)

thanks [θæŋks] NPL gracias fpl; **no t.** no gracias; **many t.** muchas gracias; **t. for phoning** gracias por llamar; **t. to** gracias a

Thanksgiving [θæŋks'gɪvɪŋ] N *US* **T. (Day)** Día m de Acción de Gracias

that [ðæt, *unstressed* ðət] 1 DEM PRON *(pl those)* **(a)** *(in near to middle distance)* ése m, ésa f; *(further away)* aquél m, aquélla f; **this one is new but t. is old** éste es nuevo pero ése es viejo **(b)** *(indefinite)* eso; *(remote)* aquello; **after t.** después de eso; **like t.** así; **t.'s right** eso es; **t.'s where I live** allí vivo yo; **what's t.?** ¿qué es eso?; **who's t.?** ¿quién es? **(c)** *(with relative)* el/la; **all those I saw** todos los que vi

2 DEM ADJ *(pl those)* *(masculine)* ese; *(feminine)* esa; *(further away)* *(masculine)* aquel;

(feminine) aquella; **at t. time** en aquella época; **t. book** ese/aquel libro; **t. one** ése/ aquél

3 REL PRON **(a)** *(subject, direct object)* que; **all (t.) you said** todo lo que dijiste; **the letter (t.) I sent you** la carta que te envié **(b)** *(governed by preposition)* que, el/la que, los/las que, el/la cual, los/las cuales; **the car (t.) they came in** el coche en el que vinieron **(c)** *(when)* que, en que; **the moment (t.) you arrived** el momento en que llegaste

---

El pronombre relativo **that** puede omitirse salvo cuando es sujeto de la oración subordinada.

---

4 CONJ que; **come here so (t.) I can see you** ven aquí (para) que te vea; **he said (t.) he would come** dijo que vendría

---

La conjunción **that** se puede omitir cuando introduce una oración subordinada.

---

5 ADV así de, tanto, tan; **cut off t. much** córteme un trozo así de grande; **I don't think it can be t. old** no creo que sea tan viejo; **we haven't got t. much money** no tenemos tanto dinero

thatched [θætʃt] ADJ cubierto(a) con paja; **t. cottage** casita f con techo de paja; **t. roof** techo m de paja

thaw [θɔː] 1 VT *(snow)* derretir; *(food, freezer)* descongelar

2 VI descongelarse; *(snow)* derretirse

3 N deshielo m

the [ðə, *before vowel sound* ðɪ, *emphatic* ðiː] 1 DEF ART **(a)** *(singular)* el/la; *(plural)* los/las; **at/ to t.** al/a la; *pl* a los/a las; **of** or **from t.** del/de la; *pl* de los/de las; **t. Alps** los Alpes; **t. right time** la hora exacta; **t. voice of t. people** la voz del pueblo **(b)** *(omitted)* George t. Sixth Jorge Sexto **(c)** **by t. day** al día; **by t. dozen** a docenas **(d)** *(with adjectives used as nouns)* **t. elderly** los ancianos **(e)** *(indicating kind)* **he's not t. person to do that** no es de los que hacen tales cosas **(f)** *(enough)* **he hasn't t. patience to wait** no tiene suficiente paciencia para esperar

2 ADV **t. more t. merrier** cuantos más mejor; **t. sooner t. better** cuanto antes mejor

theatre, *US* **theater** ['θɪətə(r)] N teatro m

theatre-goer, *US* **theater-goer** ['θɪətə-gəuə(r)] N aficionado(a) m,f al teatro

theatrical [θɪ'ætrɪkəl] ADJ teatral

theft [θeft] N robo m; **petty t.** hurto m

their [ðeə(r)] POSS ADJ su; *pl* sus

theirs [ðeəz] POSS PRON (el) suyo/(la) suya; *pl* (los) suyos/(las) suyas

them [ðem, *unstressed* ðəm] PERS PRON PL **(a)** *(direct object)* los/las; *(indirect object)* les; **I know t.** los/las conozco; **I shall tell t. so** se lo diré (a ellos/ellas); **it's t.!** ¡son ellos!; **speak to t.** hábleles **(b)** *(with preposition)* ellos/ellas; **walk in front of t.** camine delante de ellos;

they took the keys away with t. se llevaron las llaves; **both of t., the two of t.** los dos; **neither of t.** ninguno de los dos; **none of t.** ninguno de ellos

theme [θi:m] N tema *m*; **t. tune** sintonía *f*

themselves [ðəm'selvz] PERS PRON PL *(as subject)* ellos mismos/ellas mismas; *(as direct or indirect object)* se; *(after a preposition)* sí mismos/sí mismas; **they did it by t.** lo hicieron ellos solos

then [ðen] 1 ADV **(a)** *(at that time)* entonces; **since t.** desde entonces; **there and t.** en el acto; **till t.** hasta entonces **(b)** *(next, afterwards)* luego **(c)** *(anyway)* de todas formas **(d)** *(in that case)* entonces; **go t.** pues vete
2 CONJ entonces
3 ADJ **the t. president** el entonces presidente

theology [θɪ'ɒlədʒɪ] N teología *f*

theoretic(al) [θɪə'retɪk(əl)] ADJ teórico(a)

theoretically [θɪə'retɪklɪ] ADV teóricamente

theory ['θɪərɪ] N teoría *f*

therapeutic [θerə'pju:tɪk] ADJ *also Fig* terapéutico(a)

therapist ['θerəpɪst] N terapeuta *mf*

therapy ['θerəpɪ] N terapia *f*

there [ðeə(r), *unstressed* ðə(r)] 1 ADV **(a)** *(indicating place)* allí, allá; *(nearer speaker)* ahí; **here and t.** acá y allá; **in t.** ahí dentro; **is Peter t.?** ¿está Peter? **(b)** *(emphatic)* that man **t.** aquel hombre **(c)** *(unstressed)* **t. is .../t. are ...** hay ...; **t. were many cars** había muchos coches; **t. were six of us** éramos seis **(d)** *(in respect)* **t.'s the difficulty** ahí está la dificultad
2 INTERJ **so t.!** ¡ea!; **t., t.** bien, bien

thereabouts ['ðeərəbaʊts], *US* **thereabout** ['ðeərəbaʊt] ADV **in Cambridge or t.** en Cambridge o por allí cerca; **at four o'clock or t.** a las cuatro o así

thereafter [ðeər'ɑ:ftə(r)] ADV a partir de entonces

thereby ['ðeəbaɪ] ADV por eso *or* ello

therefore ['ðeəfɔ:(r)] ADV por lo tanto, por eso

thermal ['θɜ:məl] 1 ADJ *(spring)* termal; *Phys* térmico(a)
2 N *Met* corriente térmica

thermometer [θə'mɒmɪtə(r)] N termómetro *m*

Thermos® ['θɜ:məs] N **T. (flask)** termo *m*

thermostat ['θɜ:məstæt] N termostato *m*

thesaurus [θɪ'sɔ:rəs] N diccionario *m* de sinónimos

these [ði:z] 1 DEM ADJ PL estos(as)
2 DEM PRON PL éstos(as); *see* **this**

thesis ['θi:sɪs] N *(pl* **theses** ['θi:si:z]*)* tesis *f inv*

they [ðeɪ] PRON PL **(a)** *(personal use)* ellos/ellas *(usually omitted in Spanish, except for contrast);* **t. are dancing** están bailando; **t. are rich** son ricos **(b)** *(stressed)* **t. alone** ellos solos; **t. themselves told me** me lo dijeron ellos mismos **(c)** *(with relative)* los/las **(d)** *(indef-*

inite) **that's what t. say** eso es lo que se dice; **t. say that ...** se dice que ...

thick [θɪk] 1 ADJ **(a)** *(book etc)* grueso(a); **a wall 2 m t.** un muro de 2 m de espesor **(b)** *(dense)* espeso(a) **(c)** *Fam (stupid)* tonto(a)
2 ADV densamente
3 N **to be in the t. of it** estar metido(a) de lleno

thicken ['θɪkən] 1 VT espesar
2 VI espesarse; *Fig (plot)* complicarse

thickness ['θɪknɪs] N *(of wall etc)* espesor *m*; *(of wire, lips)* grueso *m*; *(of liquid, woodland)* espesura *f*

thickset [θɪk'set] ADJ *(person)* rechoncho(a)

thick-skinned [θɪk'skɪnd] ADJ *Fig* poco sensible

thief [θi:f] N *(pl* **thieves** [θi:vz]*)* ladrón(ona) *m,f*

thigh [θaɪ] N muslo *m*

thimble ['θɪmbəl] N dedal *m*

thin [θɪn] 1 ADJ **(thinner, thinnest)** **(a)** *(not thick)* delgado(a); **a t. slice** una loncha fina **(b)** *(hair, vegetation)* ralo(a); *(liquid)* claro(a); *(population)* escaso(a) **(c)** *Fig (voice)* débil; **a t. excuse** un pobre pretexto
2 VT **to t. (down)** *(paint)* diluir

thing [θɪŋ] N **(a)** *(object)* cosa *f*; **my things** *(clothing)* mi ropa *f*; *(possessions)* mis cosas *fpl*; **for one t.** en primer lugar; **the t. is ...** resulta que ...; **what with one t. and another** entre unas cosas y otras; **as things are** tal como están las cosas **(b)** **poor little t.!** ¡pobrecito(a)!

think [θɪŋk] 1 VT *(pt & pp* **thought***)* **(a)** *(believe)* pensar, creer; **I t. so/not** creo que sí/no **(b)** **I thought as much** yo me lo imaginaba
2 VI **(a)** *(reflect)* pensar (**of** *or* **about** en); **give me time to t.** dame tiempo para reflexionar; **to t. ahead** prevenir **(b)** *(have as opinion)* opinar, pensar; **to t. highly of sb** apreciar a algn; **what do you t.?** ¿a ti qué te parece? **(c)** **just t.!** ¡imagínate!

▶ **think out** VT SEP meditar; **a carefully thought-out answer** una respuesta razonada

▶ **think over** VT SEP reflexionar; **we'll have to t. it over** lo tendremos que pensar

▶ **think up** VT SEP imaginar, idear

thinking ['θɪŋkɪŋ] ADJ racional

think-tank ['θɪŋktæŋk] N *Fam* grupo *m* de expertos

thinly ['θɪnlɪ] ADV poco, ligeramente

third [θɜ:d] 1 ADJ tercero(a); *(before masculine singular noun)* tercer; **(on) the t. of March** el tres de marzo; **the T. World** el Tercer Mundo; **t. party insurance** seguro *m* a terceros
2 N **(a)** *(in series)* tercero(a) *m,f* **(b)** *(fraction)* tercio *m*, tercera parte

thirdly ['θɜ:dlɪ] ADV en tercer lugar

third-rate ['θɜ:dreɪt] ADJ de calidad inferior

thirst [θɜ:st] N sed *f*

thirsty ['θɜ:stɪ] ADJ **(thirstier, thirstiest)** sediento(a); **to be t.** tener sed

thirteen [θɜː'tiːn] ADJ & N trece (m inv)

thirteenth [θɜː'tiːnθ] **1** ADJ & N decimotercero(a) (m,f)
2 N (fraction) decimotercera parte

thirtieth ['θɜːtɪɪθ] **1** ADJ & N trigésimo(a) (m,f)
2 N (fraction) trigésima parte

thirty ['θɜːtɪ] ADJ & N treinta (m inv)

this [ðɪs] **1** DEM ADJ (pl these) (masculine) este; (feminine) esta; **t. book/these books** este libro/estos libros; **t. one** éste/ésta
2 DEM PRON (pl these) (a) (indefinite) esto; **it was like t.** fue así (b) (place) **t. is where we met** fue aquí donde nos conocimos (c) (time) **it should have come before t.** debería haber llegado ya (d) (specific person or thing) éste m, ésta f; **I prefer these to those** me gustan más éstos que aquéllos; (introduction) **t. is Mr Álvarez** le presento al Sr. Álvarez; Tel **t. is Julia (speaking)** soy Julia
3 ADV **he got t. far** llegó hasta aquí; **t. small/big** así de pequeño/grande

thistle ['θɪsəl] N cardo m

thong [θɒŋ] N (a) (for fastening) correa f (b) (underwear) tanga f (c) US, Austr (sandal) chancleta f, chancla f

thorax ['θɔːræks] N tórax m

thorn [θɔːn] N espina f

thorough ['θʌrə] ADJ (careful) minucioso(a); (work) concienzudo(a); (knowledge) profundo(a); **to carry out a t. enquiry into a matter** investigar a fondo un asunto

thoroughbred ['θʌrəbred] **1** ADJ (horse) de pura sangre
2 N (horse) pura sangre mf

thoroughfare ['θʌrəfeə(r)] N (road) carretera f; (street) calle f

thoroughly ['θʌrəlɪ] ADV (carefully) a fondo; (wholly) completamente

those [ðəʊz] **1** DEM PRON PL ésos(as); (remote) aquéllos(as); **t. who** los que/las que
2 DEM ADJ PL esos(as); (remote) aquellos(as); see **that**

though [ðəʊ] **1** CONJ aunque; **strange t. it may seem** por (muy) extraño que parezca; **as t.** como si; **it looks as t. he's gone** parece que se ha ido
2 ADV sin embargo

thought [θɔːt] **1** N (a) (act of thinking) pensamiento m; **what a tempting t.!** ¡qué idea más tentadora! (b) (reflection) reflexión f (c) **it's the t. that counts** (intention) lo que cuenta es la intención
2 PT & PP of **think**

thoughtful ['θɔːtfʊl] ADJ (pensive) pensativo(a); (considerate) atento(a)

thoughtless ['θɔːtlɪs] ADJ (person) desconsiderado(a); (action) irreflexivo(a)

thousand ['θaʊzənd] ADJ & N mil (m inv); **thousands of people** miles de personas

thousandth ['θaʊzənθ] **1** ADJ milésimo(a)
2 N (a) (in series) milésimo(a) m,f (b) (fraction) milésima parte

thrash [θræʃ] **1** VT dar una paliza a
2 VI **to t. about** or **around** agitarse
▸ **thrash out** VT SEP discutir a fondo

thrashing ['θræʃɪŋ] N (beating, defeat) paliza f

thread [θred] **1** N (a) (of cotton, nylon) hilo m; **length of t.** hebra f (b) (of screw) rosca f
2 VT (a) (needle) enhebrar (b) **to t. one's way (through)** colarse (por)

threadbare ['θredbeə(r)] ADJ raído(a)

threat [θret] N amenaza f

threaten ['θretən] VT amenazar; **to t. to do sth** amenazar con hacer algo

threatening ['θretənɪŋ] ADJ amenazador(a)

threateningly ['θretənɪŋlɪ] ADV de modo amenazador

three [θriː] ADJ & N tres (m inv)

three-dimensional ['θriːdɪ'menʃənəl] ADJ tridimensional

threefold ['θriːfəʊld] **1** ADJ triple
2 ADV tres veces; **to increase t.** triplicarse

three-piece ['θriːpiːs] ADJ **t. suit** traje m de tres piezas; **t. suite** tresillo m

three-ply ['θriːplaɪ] ADJ de tres hebras

three-wheeler [θriː'wiːlə(r)] N Aut coche m de tres ruedas; (tricycle) triciclo m

thresh [θreʃ] VT trillar

threshold ['θreʃəʊld] N umbral m; Fig **to be on the t. of** estar a las puertas or en los umbrales de

threw [θruː] PT of **throw**

thrifty ['θrɪftɪ] ADJ (thriftier, thriftiest) económico(a), ahorrador(a)

thrill [θrɪl] **1** N (a) (excitement) emoción f (b) (quiver) estremecimiento m
2 VT (excite) emocionar; (audience) entusiasmar

thriller ['θrɪlə(r)] N thriller m

thrilling ['θrɪlɪŋ] ADJ emocionante

thrive [θraɪv] VI (pt thrived or throve; pp thrived or thriven ['θrɪvən]) (a) (person) rebosar de salud (b) Fig (business) prosperar; **he thrives on it** le viene de maravilla

thriving ['θraɪvɪŋ] ADJ Fig próspero(a)

throat [θrəʊt] N garganta f

throb [θrɒb] **1** N (of heart) latido m; (of machine) zumbido m
2 VI (heart) latir; (machine) zumbar; **my head is throbbing** me va a estallar la cabeza

throes [θrəʊz] NPL **to be in one's death t.** estar agonizando; Fig **in the t. of …** en pleno(a) …

thrombosis [θrɒm'bəʊsɪs] N Med trombosis f inv

throne [θrəʊn] N trono m

throng [θrɒŋ] **1** N multitud f, gentío m
2 VI apiñarse
3 VT atestar

throttle ['θrɒtəl] 1 N t. (valve) (of engine) válvula reguladora
2 VT (person) estrangular

▶ **throttle back** VT SEP (engine) desacelerar

through [θru:] 1 PREP (a) (place) a través de, por; **to look t. the window** mirar por la ventana (b) (time) a lo largo de; **all t. his life** durante toda su vida; US **Tuesday t. Thursday** desde el martes hasta el jueves inclusive (c) (by means of) por, mediante; **I learnt of it t. Jack** me enteré por Jack (d) (because of) a or por causa de; **t. ignorance** por ignorancia
2 ADJ **a t. train** un tren directo; **t. traffic** tránsito m
3 ADV (a) (from one side to the other) de un lado a otro; **to let sb t.** dejar pasar a algn; Fig **socialist/French t. and t.** socialista/francés por los cuatro costados (b) **I'm t. with him** he terminado con él (c) Tel **to get t. to sb** comunicar con algn; **you're t.** ¡hablen!

throughout [θru:'aʊt] 1 PREP por todo(a); **t. the year** durante todo el año
2 ADV (place) en todas partes; (time) todo el tiempo

throve [θrəʊv] PT of **thrive**

throw [θrəʊ] 1 VT (pt threw; pp thrown) (a) (with hands) (in general) tirar, Am aventar; (ball, javelin) lanzar; (rider) desmontar; Fig **he threw a fit** le dio un ataque; Fig **to t. a party** dar una fiesta (b) (disconcert) desconcertar
2 N tiro m, lanzamiento m; (in wrestling) derribo m

▶ **throw away** VT SEP (rubbish) tirar, Am botar; (money) malgastar; (opportunity) perder

▶ **throw in** VT SEP (a) (ball, javelin) lanzar; Sport sacar de banda; Fig **to t. in the towel** arrojar la toalla (b) (add) añadir; (in deal) incluir (gratis)

▶ **throw off** VT SEP (person, thing) deshacerse de; (clothes) quitarse

▶ **throw out** VT SEP (rubbish) tirar; (person) echar

▶ **throw up** 1 VT SEP (a) (dust, dirt) levantar (b) (facts, information) poner de manifiesto
2 VI Fam vomitar, devolver

throwaway ['θrəʊəweɪ] ADJ desechable

throw-in ['θrəʊɪn] N Sport saque m de banda

thrown [θrəʊn] PP of **throw**

thru [θru:] PREP, ADJ & ADV US Fam = **through**

thrush [θrʌʃ] N (bird) tordo m, zorzal m

thrust [θrʌst] 1 VT (pt & pp thrust) empujar con fuerza; **he t. a letter into my hand** me puso una carta violentamente en la mano
2 N (push) empujón m; Av & Phys empuje m

thud [θʌd] N ruido sordo

thug [θʌg] N (lout) gamberro m; (criminal) criminal m

thumb [θʌm] 1 N pulgar m
2 VT (a) (book) hojear (b) Fam (hitch) **to t. a lift** hacer autostop or dedo, CAm, Méx, Perú pedir aventón

▶ **thumb through** VT INSEP (book) hojear

thumbtack ['θʌmtæk] N US Esp chincheta f, Am chinche m

thump [θʌmp] 1 N (a) (sound) ruido sordo (b) (blow) porrazo m
2 VT golpear
3 VI (a) **to t. on the table** golpear la mesa (b) (heart) latir ruidosamente

thunder ['θʌndə(r)] 1 N trueno m; **t. of applause** estruendo m de aplausos
2 VI tronar

thunderbolt ['θʌndəbəʊlt] N (lighting) rayo m; Fig (news) bomba f

thunderclap ['θʌndəklæp] N trueno m

thunderous ['θʌndərəs] ADJ Fig ensordecedor(a)

thunderstorm ['θʌndəstɔ:m] N tormenta f

thundery ['θʌndərɪ] ADJ (weather) tormentoso(a)

Thursday ['θɜ:zdɪ] N jueves m

thus [ðʌs] ADV así, de esta manera; **and t. ...** así que ...

thwart [θwɔ:t] VT frustrar, desbaratar

thyme [taɪm] N tomillo m

thyroid ['θaɪrɔɪd] N tiroides f inv

tiara [tɪ'ɑ:rə] N diadema f; Rel tiara f

tic [tɪk] N tic m

tick¹ [tɪk] 1 N (a) (sound) tic-tac m (b) Br Fam **I'll do it in a t.** ahora mismo lo hago (c) (mark) marca f de visto bueno
2 VI hacer tic-tac
3 VT marcar

▶ **tick off** VT SEP (a) (mark) marcar con una señal de visto bueno (b) Br Fam (reprimand) echar una bronca a

▶ **tick over** VI Aut funcionar al ralentí

tick² [tɪk] N (insect) garrapata f

ticket ['tɪkɪt] N (a) (for train, plane, lottery) billete m, Am boleto m; (for theatre, cinema) entrada f, Col, Méx boleto m; **t. collector** revisor(a) m,f; **t. office** taquilla f, Am boletería f; **t. tout** Br or US **scalper** reventa mf (b) (receipt) recibo m (c) (label) etiqueta f (d) Aut multa f

tickle ['tɪkəl] 1 VT hacer cosquillas a
2 VI hacer cosquillas
3 N cosquillas fpl

ticklish ['tɪklɪʃ] ADJ **to be t.** tener cosquillas

tick-tack-toe [tɪktæk'təʊ] N US tres en raya m

tidal ['taɪdəl] ADJ de la marea; **t. wave** ola f gigante

tidbit ['tɪdbɪt] N US = **titbit**

tiddlywinks ['tɪdlɪwɪŋks] N SING (game) pulga f

tide [taɪd] N (a) (of sea) marea f; **high/low t.** marea alta/baja (b) (of events) curso m; **the t. has turned** han cambiado las cosas; **to go against the t.** ir contra corriente

tidings ['taɪdɪŋz] NPL Fml noticias fpl

tidy ['taɪdɪ] 1 ADJ (tidier, tidiest) (a) (room, habits) ordenado(a) (b) (appearance) arreglado(a)

2 VT arreglar; **to t. away** poner en su sitio
3 VI **to t. (up)** ordenar las cosas

tie [taɪ] **1** VT (shoelaces etc) atar; **to t. a knot** hacer un nudo
2 VI Sport empatar (**with** con)
3 N (**a**) (link) lazo m, vínculo m (**b**) Fig (hindrance) atadura f (**c**) (item of clothing) corbata f (**d**) Sport (draw) empate m; (match) eliminatoria f, partido m de clasificación
▸ **tie down** VT SEP sujetar; Fig **to be tied down** estar atado(a); Fig **to sb down to a promise** obligar a algn a cumplir una promesa
▸ **tie up** VT SEP (**a**) (parcel, dog) atar (**b**) (deal) concluir (**c**) (capital) inmovilizar; Fig **I'm tied up just now** de momento estoy muy ocupado(a)

tiebreaker ['taɪbreɪkə(r)] N tie-break m
tiepin ['taɪpɪn] N alfiler m de corbata
tier [tɪə(r)] N (of seats) fila f; (in stadium) grada f; **four-t. cake** pastel m de cuatro pisos
tiger ['taɪgə(r)] N tigre m
tight [taɪt] **1** ADJ (**a**) (knot, screw) apretado(a); (clothing) ajustado(a); (seal) hermético(a); **my shoes are too t.** me aprietan los zapatos; Fig **to be in a t. corner** estar en un apuro (**b**) (scarce) escaso(a); **money's a bit t.** estamos escasos de dinero (**c**) (mean) agarrado(a) (**d**) Fam (drunk) alegre, Esp piripi
2 ADV estrechamente; (seal) herméticamente; **hold t.** agárrate fuerte; **shut t.** bien cerrado(a); **to sit t.** no moverse de su sitio
tighten ['taɪtən] **1** VT (screw) apretar; (rope) tensar; Fig **to t. (up) restrictions** intensificar las restricciones
2 VI apretarse; (cable) tensarse
tightfisted [taɪt'fɪstɪd] ADJ tacaño(a)
tightrope ['taɪtrəʊp] N cuerda floja; **t. walker** funámbulo(a) m,f
tights [taɪts] NPL (woollen) leotardos mpl, Col medias fpl veladas, RP cancanes mpl; Br (nylon, silk) medias fpl, pantis mpl
tile [taɪl] **1** N (of roof) teja f; (glazed) azulejo m; (for floor) baldosa f
2 VT (roof) tejar; (wall) poner azulejos en, Esp alicatar; (floor) embaldosar
tiled [taɪld] ADJ (roof) de tejas; (wall) con azulejos, Esp alicatado(a); (floor) embaldosado(a)
till[1] [tɪl] N (for cash) caja f
till[2] [tɪl] VT (field) labrar, cultivar
till[3] [tɪl] **1** PREP hasta; **from morning t. night** de la mañana a la noche; **t. then** hasta entonces
2 CONJ hasta que
tiller ['tɪlə(r)] N Naut caña f del timón
tilt [tɪlt] N (**a**) (angle) inclinación f (**b**) (at) full **t.** (speed) a toda velocidad
2 VI **to t. over** volcarse; **to t. (up)** inclinarse
3 VT inclinar
timber ['tɪmbə(r)] N (wood) madera f (de construcción); (trees) árboles mpl; (piece of) **t.** viga f

time [taɪm] **1** N (**a**) (in general) tiempo m; **all the t.** todo el tiempo; **for some t. (past)** desde hace algún tiempo; **I haven't seen him for a long t.** hace mucho (tiempo) que no lo veo; **in a short t.** en poco tiempo; **in no t.** en un abrir y cerrar de ojos; **in t.** a tiempo; **in three weeks' t.** dentro de tres semanas; **to take one's t. over sth** hacer algo con calma; Fam **to do t.** cumplir una condena; **t. bomb** bomba f de relojería; **t. limit** límite m de tiempo; (for payment etc) plazo m; **t. switch** interruptor m electrónico automático; **t. zone** huso horario
(**b**) (era) época f, tiempos mpl; **a sign of the times** un signo de los tiempos; **to be behind the times** tener ideas anticuadas
(**c**) (point in time) momento m; **at any t. (you like)** cuando quiera; **at no t.** en ningún momento; **at that t.** (en aquel) entonces; **at the same t.** al mismo tiempo; **at times** a veces; **from t. to t.** de vez en cuando; **he may turn up at any t.** puede llegar en cualquier momento
(**d**) (time of day) hora f; **and about t. too!** ¡ya era hora!; **in good t.** con anticipación; **on t.** puntualmente; **what's the t.?** ¿qué hora es?
(**e**) **t. of year** época f del año
(**f**) **to have a good/bad t.** pasarlo bien/mal
(**g**) (occasion) vez f; **four at a t.** cuatro a la vez; **next t.** la próxima vez; **several times over** varias veces; **three times running** tres veces seguidas; **t. after t.** una y otra vez
(**h**) (in multiplication) **three times four** tres (multiplicado) por cuatro; **four times as big** cuatro veces más grande
(**i**) Mus compás m; **in t.** al compás
2 VT (**a**) (speech) calcular la duración de; Sport (race) cronometrar (**b**) (choose the time of) escoger el momento oportuno para
time-consuming ['taɪmkənsjuːmɪŋ] ADJ que ocupa mucho tiempo
time-lag ['taɪmlæg] N intervalo m
timeless ['taɪmlɪs] ADJ eterno(a)
timely ['taɪmlɪ] ADJ (**timelier, timeliest**) oportuno(a)
timer ['taɪmə(r)] N (device) temporizador m
timetable ['taɪmteɪbəl] N horario m
timid ['tɪmɪd] ADJ tímido(a)
timing ['taɪmɪŋ] N (**a**) (timeliness) oportunidad f; (coordination) coordinación f; **your t. was wrong** no calculaste bien (**b**) Sport cronometraje m
tin [tɪn] **1** N (**a**) (metal) estaño m; **t. plate** hojalata f (**b**) esp Br (container) lata f, Am tarro m
2 VT (food) enlatar; **tinned food** conservas fpl
tinfoil ['tɪnfɔɪl] N papel m de estaño
tinge [tɪndʒ] **1** N tinte m, matiz m
2 VT teñir
tingle ['tɪŋgəl] VI **my feet are tingling** siento un hormigueo en los pies

tinker ['tɪŋkə(r)] **1** N *Pej* calderero(a) m,f
2 VI **stop tinkering with the radio** deja de toquetear la radio

tinkle ['tɪŋkəl] VI tintinear

tin-opener ['tɪnəupənə(r)] N abrelatas m *inv*

tinsel ['tɪnsəl] N oropel m

tint [tɪnt] **1** N tinte m, matiz m
2 VT teñir; **to t. one's hair** teñirse el pelo

tiny ['taɪnɪ] ADJ (**tinier, tiniest**) pequeñito(a); **a t. bit** un poquitín

tip¹ [tɪp] **1** N (*end*) punta f; (*of cigarette*) colilla f; **it's on the t. of my tongue** lo tengo en la punta de la lengua
2 VT poner cantera a; **tipped with steel** con punta de acero

tip² [tɪp] **1** N (**a**) (*gratuity*) propina f (**b**) (*advice*) consejo m (**c**) *Sport* (*racing*) pronóstico m
2 VT (**a**) (*give money to*) dar una propina a (**b**) *Sport* pronosticar
▶ **tip off** VT SEP (*police*) dar el chivatazo a

tip³ [tɪp] **1** N *Br* rubbish t. vertedero m
2 VT inclinar; *Br* (*rubbish*) verter
3 VI **to t. (up)** ladearse; (*cart*) bascular
▶ **tip over 1** VT SEP volcar
2 VI volcarse

tipple ['tɪpəl] *Fam* **1** VI empinar el codo, *Am* tomar
2 N bebida alcohólica; **what's your t.?** ¿qué te gusta beber?

tipsy ['tɪpsɪ] ADJ (**tipsier, tipsiest**) contentillo(a)

tiptoe ['tɪptəʊ] **1** VI caminar *or Esp* andar de puntillas; **to t. in/out** entrar/salir de puntillas
2 N **on t.** de puntillas

tiptop ['tɪptɒp] ADJ *Fam* de primera

tire¹ [taɪə(r)] N *US* = **tyre**

tire² [taɪə(r)] **1** VT cansar; **to t. sb out** agotar a algn
2 VI cansarse; **to t. of doing sth** cansarse de hacer algo

tired ['taɪəd] ADJ cansado(a); **t. out** rendido(a); **to be t.** estar cansado(a); **to be t. of sth** estar harto(a) de algo

tiredness ['taɪədnɪs] N (*fatigue*) cansancio m, fatiga f

tireless ['taɪəlɪs] ADJ incansable

tiresome ['taɪəsəm] ADJ pesado(a)

tiring ['taɪərɪŋ] ADJ agotador(a)

tissue ['tɪʃuː, 'tɪsjuː] N (**a**) *Biol* tejido m (**b**) *Tex* tisú m; **t. paper** papel m de seda (**c**) (*handkerchief*) pañuelo m de papel, kleenex® m

tit¹ [tɪt] N **to give it f. for tat** devolver la pelota

tit² [tɪt] N *very Fam* (*breast*) teta f, *Méx* chichi f, *RP* lola f

titbit ['tɪtbɪt] N tentempié m, refrigerio m

titillate ['tɪtɪleɪt] VT excitar

title ['taɪtəl] N (**a**) (*of book, chapter*) título m; *Cin* **credit titles** ficha técnica; **t. page** portada f; **t. role** papel m principal (**b**) *Jur* título m de propiedad

titter ['tɪtə(r)] **1** VI reírse nerviosamente; (*foolishly*) reírse tontamente
2 N risa ahogada; (*foolish*) risilla tonta

titular ['tɪtjʊlə(r)] ADJ titular

TM N (*abbr* **trademark**) marca registrada

to [tuː, *unstressed before vowels* tʊ, *before consonants* tə] **1** PREP (**a**) (*with place*) a; (*expressing direction*) hacia; **from town to town** de ciudad en ciudad; **he went to France/Japan** fue a Francia/Japón; **I'm going to Mary's** voy a casa de Mary; **it is 30 miles to London** Londres está a 30 millas; **the train to Madrid** el tren de Madrid; **to the east** hacia el este; **to the right** a la derecha; **what school do you go to?** ¿a qué escuela vas?
(**b**) (*time*) a; **from day to day** de día en día; **from two to four** de dos a cuatro; *Br* **it's ten to (six)** son (las seis) menos diez, *Am salvo RP* faltan diez (para las seis)
(**c**) (*as far as*) hasta; **accurate to a millimetre** exacto(a) hasta el milímetro
(**d**) (*with indirect object*) **he gave it to his cousin** se lo dio a su primo; **what's that to you?** ¿qué te importa a ti?
(**e**) (*towards a person*) **he was very kind to me** se portó muy bien conmigo
(**f**) (*of*) de; **heir to an estate** heredero m de una propiedad; **adviser to the president** consejero m del presidente
(**g**) **to come to sb's assistance** acudir en ayuda de algn; **to everyone's surprise** para sorpresa de todos; **to this end** con este fin
(**h**) (*to the best of my knowledge*) que yo sepa
(**i**) (*compared to*) **that's nothing to what I've seen** eso no es nada en comparación con lo que he visto yo
(**j**) (*in proportion*) **one house to the square kilometre** una casa por kilómetro cuadrado; **six votes to four** seis votos contra cuatro
(**k**) (*about*) **what did he say to my suggestion?** ¿qué contestó a mi sugerencia?
2 *with infin* (**a**) *with simple infinitives* **to** *is not translated but is shown by the verb endings;* **to buy** comprar; **to come** venir
(**b**) (*in order to*) para; (*with verbs of motion or purpose*) a, por; **he did it to help me** lo hizo para ayudarme; **he stopped to talk** se detuvo a hablar; **he fought to convince them** luchó por convencerlos
(**c**) *various verbs followed by dependent infinitives take particular prepositions* (a, de, en, por, con, para *etc*) *and others take no preposition; see the entry of the verb in question*
(**d**) (*with adj and infin*) a, de; **difficult to do** difícil de hacer; **ready to listen** dispuesto(a) a escuchar; **too hot to drink** demasiado caliente para bebérselo
(**e**) (*with noun and infin*) **the first to complain** el primero en quejarse; **this is the time to do it** éste es el momento de hacerlo; **to have a great deal to do** tener mucho que hacer
(**f**) (*expressing following action*) **he awoke to find the light still on** al despertarse encontró

la lámpara todavía encendida (**g**) *(with verbs of ordering, wishing etc)* **he asked me to do it** me pidió que lo hiciera (**h**) *(expressing obligation)* **fifty employees are to go** cincuenta empleados deben ser despedidos; **to have to do sth** tener que hacer algo (**i**) *(replacing infin)* **go if you want to** váyase si quiere

3 ADV **to go to and fro** ir y venir; **to push the door to** encajar la puerta

toad [təʊd] N sapo *m*

toadstool ['təʊdstuːl] N *Esp* seta venenosa, *Am* hongo (venenoso)

toast¹ [təʊst] *Culin* **1** N pan tostado; **a slice of t.** una tostada
2 VT tostar

toast² [təʊst] **1** N *(drink)* brindis *m inv*; **to drink a t.** to brindar por
2 VT brindar por

toaster ['təʊstə(r)] N tostador *m* (de pan)

tobacco [tə'bækəʊ] N tabaco *m*

tobacconist [tə'bækənɪst] N *Br* estanquero(a) *m,f*; *Br* **t.'s (shop)** estanco *m*, *CSur* quiosco *m*, *Méx* estanquillo *m*

toboggan [tə'bɒgən] N tobogán *m*

today [tə'deɪ] **1** N hoy *m*
2 ADV hoy; *(nowadays)* hoy en día; **a week t.** justo dentro de una semana

toddler ['tɒdlə(r)] N niño(a) *m,f* que empieza a andar; **the toddlers** los pequeñitos

toddy ['tɒdɪ] N *(drink)* ponche *m*

to-do [tə'duː] N lío *m*, jaleo *m*

toe [təʊ] **1** N dedo *m* del pie; **big t.** dedo gordo
2 VT **to t. the line** conformarse

toenail ['təʊneɪl] N uña *f* del dedo del pie

toffee ['tɒfɪ] N caramelo *m*

together [tə'geðə(r)] ADV junto, juntos(as); **all t.** todos juntos; **t. with** junto con; **to bring t.** reunir

toil [tɔɪl] **1** N trabajo duro
2 VI afanarse, trabajar (duro); **to t. up a hill** subir penosamente una cuesta

toilet ['tɔɪlɪt] N (**a**) *Br (in house)* cuarto *m* de baño, retrete *m*; *(in public place)* baño(s) *m(pl)*, *Esp* servicio(s) *m(pl)*, *CSur* toilette *f*; **t. paper** *or* **tissue** papel higiénico; **t. roll** rollo *m* de papel higiénico (**b**) *(washing etc)* aseo *m* (personal); **t. bag** neceser *m*; **t. soap** jabón *m* de tocador

toiletries ['tɔɪlɪtrɪz] NPL artículos *mpl* de aseo

token ['təʊkən] **1** N (**a**) *(sign)* señal *f*; **as a t. of respect** en señal de respeto (**b**) *Com* vale *m*; **book t.** vale para comprar libros
2 ADJ simbólico(a)

told [təʊld] PT & PP *of* **tell**

tolerable ['tɒlərəbəl] ADJ tolerable

tolerance ['tɒlərəns] N tolerancia *f*

tolerant ['tɒlərənt] ADJ tolerante

tolerate ['tɒləreɪt] VT tolerar

toll¹ [təʊl] **1** VT tocar
2 VI doblar

toll² [təʊl] N (**a**) *(charge)* peaje *m*, *Méx* cuota *f* (**b**) *(loss)* pérdidas *fpl*; **the death t.** el número de víctimas mortales

toll-free [təʊl'friː] *US* **1** ADJ **t. number** (número *m* de) teléfono *m* gratuito
2 ADV *(call)* gratuitamente

tomato [tə'mɑːtəʊ, *US* tə'meɪtəʊ] N *(pl* **tomatoes**) tomate *m*, *Méx* jitomate *m*

tomb [tuːm] N tumba *f*, sepulcro *m*

tomboy ['tɒmbɔɪ] N marimacho *f*

tombstone ['tuːmstəʊn] N lápida *f* sepulcral

tomcat ['tɒmkæt] N gato (macho)

tomorrow [tə'mɒrəʊ] **1** N mañana *m*; **the day after t.** pasado mañana
2 ADV mañana; **see you t.!** ¡hasta mañana!; **t. night** mañana por la noche; **t. week** dentro de ocho días a partir de mañana

ton [tʌn] N tonelada *f*; *Fam* **tons of** montones de

tone [təʊn] **1** N tono *m*
2 VI **to t. (in) with sth** armonizar con algo
▸ **tone down** VT SEP atenuar

tone-deaf ['təʊn'def] ADJ **to be t.** no tener oído musical

tongs [tɒŋz] NPL *(for sugar, hair)* tenacillas *fpl*; **(fire) t.** tenazas *fpl*

tongue [tʌŋ] N (**a**) *(in mouth)* lengua *f*; *Fig* **to say sth t. in cheek** decir algo con la boca pequeña; **t. twister** trabalenguas *m inv* (**b**) *(of shoe)* lengüeta *f*; *(of bell)* badajo *m*

tongue-tied ['tʌŋtaɪd] ADJ mudo(a) *(por la timidez)*

tonic ['tɒnɪk] **1** N (**a**) *Med* tónico *m* (**b**) *(drink)* tónica *f*
2 ADJ tónico(a)

tonight [tə'naɪt] ADV & N esta noche

tonnage ['tʌnɪdʒ] N *(of ship)* tonelaje *m*

tonne [tʌn] N = **ton**

tonsil ['tɒnsəl] N amígdala *f*; **to have one's tonsils out** ser operado(a) de las amígdalas

tonsillitis [tɒnsɪ'laɪtɪs] N amigdalitis *f*

too [tuː] ADV (**a**) *(besides)* además (**b**) *(also)* también (**c**) *(excessively)* demasiado; **t. much money** demasiado dinero; **£10 t. much** 10 libras de más; **t. frequently** con demasiada frecuencia; **t. old** demasiado viejo

took [tʊk] PT *of* **take**

tool [tuːl] N *(utensil)* herramienta *f*

toolbox ['tuːlbɒks] N caja *f* de herramientas

toot [tuːt] *Aut* **1** VT tocar
2 VI tocar la bocina

tooth [tuːθ] N *(pl* **teeth**) (**a**) *(of person)* diente *m*; *(molar)* muela *f*; *Fig* **to fight t. and nail** luchar a brazo partido (**b**) *(of saw)* diente *m*; *(of comb)* púa *f*

toothache ['tuːθeɪk] N dolor *m* de muelas

toothbrush ['tuːθbrʌʃ] N cepillo *m* de dientes

toothpaste ['tuːθpeɪst] N pasta dentífrica

toothpick ['tu:θpɪk] N mondadientes *m inv*

top¹ [tɒp] **1** N (**a**) *(upper part)* parte *f* de arriba; *(of hill)* cumbre *f*, cima *f*; *(of tree)* copa *f*; **from t. to bottom** de arriba (a) abajo; **on t. of** encima de; *Fig* **on t. of it all …** para colmo …; **t. hat** sombrero *m* de copa (**b**) *(surface)* superficie *f* (**c**) *(of list etc)* cabeza *f* (**d**) *(of bottle etc)* tapa *f*, tapón *m* (**e**) *(garment)* camiseta *f* (**f**) *(best)* lo mejor (**g**) *Fig* **at the t. of one's voice** a voz en grito

2 ADJ (**a**) *(part)* superior, de arriba; **the t. floor** el último piso; **t. coat** *(of paint)* última mano (**b**) *(highest)* más alto(a); *BrAut* **t. gear** directa *f* (**c**) *(best)* mejor

3 VT (**a**) *(place on top of)* coronar (**b**) *Th* **to t. the bill** encabezar el reparto

▸ **top up** VT SEP llenar hasta el tope; **to t. up the petrol tank** llenar el depósito; *Fig* **and to t. it all** y para colmo

top² [tɒp] N *(toy)* peonza *f*

topic ['tɒpɪk] N tema *m*

> Note that the Spanish word **tópico** is a false friend and is never a translation for the English word **topic**. In Spanish **tópico** means "cliché".

topical ['tɒpɪkəl] ADJ de actualidad

top-level ['tɒplevəl] ADJ de alto nivel

topmost ['tɒpməʊst] ADJ (el) más alto/(la) más alta

topple ['tɒpəl] **1** VI *(building)* venirse abajo; **to t. (over)** volcarse

2 VT volcar; *Fig (government)* derrocar

top-secret ['tɒp'si:krɪt] ADJ de alto secreto

topsy-turvy ['tɒpsɪ'tɜ:vɪ] ADJ & ADV al revés; *(in confusion)* en desorden, patas arriba

top-up ['tɒpʌp] N *Br* **top-up card** *(for mobile phone)* tarjeta *f* de recarga; **t. fees** *(charged by university)* = derechos de matrícula suplementarios

torch [tɔ:tʃ] N *Br (electric)* linterna *f*

tore [tɔ:(r)] PT *of* **tear**

torment 1 VT [tɔ:'ment] atormentar

2 N ['tɔ:ment] tormento *m*, suplicio *m*

torn [tɔ:n] PP *of* **tear**

tornado [tɔ:'neɪdəʊ] N tornado *m*

torpedo [tɔ:'pi:dəʊ] N torpedo *m*

torrent ['tɒrənt] N torrente *m*

torrential [tɒ'renʃəl] ADJ torrencial

torrid ['tɒrɪd] ADJ tórrido(a)

torso ['tɔ:səʊ] N torso *m*

tortoise ['tɔ:təs] N tortuga *f* (de tierra)

tortoiseshell ['tɔ:təsʃel] ADJ de carey

tortuous ['tɔ:tjʊəs] ADJ *(path)* tortuoso(a); *(explanation)* enrevesado(a)

torture ['tɔ:tʃə(r)] **1** VT torturar; *Fig* atormentar

2 N tortura *f*; *Fig* tormento *m*

Tory ['tɔ:rɪ] ADJ & N *Br Pol* conservador(a) *(m,f)*

toss [tɒs] **1** VT (**a**) *(ball)* tirar; **to t. a coin** echar a cara o cruz, *Méx* echar a águila o sol, *RP* echar

a cara o seca (**b**) *(throw about)* sacudir

2 VI (**a**) **to t. about** agitarse; **to t. and turn** dar vueltas en la cama (**b**) *Sport* **to t. (up)** sortear

3 N (**a**) *(of ball)* lanzamiento *m*; *(of coin)* sorteo *m* (a cara o cruz) (**b**) *(of head)* sacudida *f*

tot¹ [tɒt] N (**a**) **(tiny) t.** *(child)* nene(a) *m,f* (**b**) *(of whisky etc)* trago *m*

tot² [tɒt] VT *Br* **to t. up** sumar

total ['təʊtəl] **1** N total *m*; *(in bill)* importe *m*; **grand t.** suma *f* total

2 ADJ total

3 VT sumar

4 VI **to t. up to** ascender a

totalitarian [təʊtælɪ'teərɪən] ADJ totalitario(a)

totally ['təʊtəlɪ] ADV totalmente

tote [təʊt] N *Fam Sport* totalizador *m*

tote bag ['təʊtbæg] N *US* petate *m*

totem ['təʊtəm] N tótem *m*

totter ['tɒtə(r)] VI tambalearse

touch [tʌtʃ] **1** VT (**a**) *(physically)* tocar; *Fig* **to t. on a subject** tocar un tema (**b**) *(equal)* igualar (**c**) *(move)* conmover

2 VI tocarse; *Fig* **it was t. and go whether we caught the train** estuvimos a punto de perder el tren

3 N (**a**) *(act of touching)* toque *m* (**b**) *(sense of touch)* tacto *m* (**c**) **it was a nice t. of his** fue un detalle de su parte; **to put the finishing touches to sth** dar los últimos toques a algo (**d**) *(ability)* habilidad *f* (**e**) *(contact)* contacto *m*; **to be/get/keep in t. with sb** estar/ponerse/mantenerse en contacto con algn; **to be out of t. with sth** no estar al tanto de algo (**f**) *(small amount)* pizca *f* (**g**) *Sport* **in t.** fuera de banda

▸ **touch down** VI *(plane)* aterrizar

▸ **touch off** VT SEP desencadenar

▸ **touch up** VT SEP *(picture)* retocar

touchdown ['tʌtʃdaʊn] N (**a**) *(of plane)* aterrizaje *m*; *(of space capsule)* amerizaje *m* (**b**) *(in American football)* ensayo *m*

touched [tʌtʃt] ADJ (**a**) *(moved)* emocionado(a) (**b**) *Fam (crazy) Esp* tocado(a) del ala, *Am* zafado(a)

touching ['tʌtʃɪŋ] ADJ conmovedor(a)

touchline ['tʌtʃlaɪn] N línea *f* de banda

touchy ['tʌtʃɪ] ADJ (**touchier, touchiest**) *Fam (person)* susceptible; *(subject)* delicado(a)

tough [tʌf] **1** ADJ *(material, competitor etc)* fuerte, resistente; *(test, criminal, meat)* duro(a); *(punishment)* severo(a); *(problem)* difícil

2 N *(person)* matón *m*

toughen ['tʌfən] VT endurecer

toupee ['tu:peɪ] N tupé *m*

tour [tʊə(r)] **1** N (**a**) *(journey)* viaje *m*; **package t.** viaje organizado (**b**) *(of monument etc)* visita *f*; *(of city)* recorrido turístico (**c**) *Sport & Th* gira *f*; **on t.** de gira

2 VT (**a**) *(country)* viajar por (**b**) *(building)*

visitar (**c**) *Th* estar de gira en
3 *VI* estar de viaje

tourism ['tʊərɪzəm] N turismo *m*

tourist ['tʊərɪst] N turista *mf*; **t. centre** centro *m* de información turística; *Av* **t. class** clase *f* turista

tournament ['tʊənəmənt] N torneo *m*

tousled ['taʊzəld] ADJ *(hair)* despeinado(a)

tout [taʊt] **1** *VT Com* tratar de vender; *Br (tickets)* revender
2 = salir a la caza y captura de compradores
3 N *Com* gancho *m*

tow [təʊ] **1** N **to take a car in t.** remolcar un coche; *US* **t. truck** grúa *f*
2 *VT* remolcar

towards [tə'wɔːdz, tɔːdz] PREP (**a**) *(direction, time)* hacia (**b**) *(with regard to)* hacia, (para) con; **our duty to others** nuestro deber para con los demás; **what is your attitude t. religion?** ¿cuál es su actitud respecto a la religión?

towel ['taʊəl] **1** N toalla *f*; **hand t.** toallita *f*; **t. Br rail** *or US* **bar** toallero *m*
2 *VT* **to t. dry** secar con una toalla

towelling ['taʊəlɪŋ] N felpa *f*

tower ['taʊə(r)] **1** N torre *f*
2 *VI* **to t. over** *or* **above sth** dominar algo·

towering ['taʊərɪŋ] ADJ impresionante, enorme

town [taʊn] N ciudad *f*; *(small)* pueblo *m*; **to go into t.** ir al centro; *Fam* **to go to t.** tirar la casa por la ventana; *Br* **t. council** ayuntamiento *m*; *Br* **t. councillor** concejal(a) *m,f*; **t. hall** ayuntamiento *m*; **t. planning** urbanismo *m*

townspeople ['taʊnzpiːpəl] NPL ciudadanos *mpl*

towpath ['təʊpɑːθ] N sendero *m* a lo largo de un canal

towrope ['təʊrəʊp] N cable *m* de remolque

toxic ['tɒksɪk] ADJ tóxico(a)

toy [tɔɪ] **1** N juguete *m*
2 *VI* **to t. with an idea** acariciar una idea; **to t. with one's food** comer sin gana

toyshop ['tɔɪʃɒp] N juguetería *f*

trace [treɪs] **1** N (**a**) *(sign)* indicio *m*, vestigio *m* (**b**) *(tracks)* rastro *m*
2 *VT* (**a**) *(drawing)* calcar (**b**) *(plan)* bosquejar (**c**) *(locate)* seguir la pista de

tracing ['treɪsɪŋ] N **t. paper** papel *m* de calco

track [træk] **1** N (**a**) *(trail)* rastro *m*; **to keep/ lose t. of sb** no perder/perder de vista a algn (**b**) *(pathway)* camino *m*; **to be on the right/ wrong t.** ir por el buen/mal camino (**c**) *Sport* pista *f*; *(for motor racing)* circuito *m*; *Fig* **t. record** historial *m* (**d**) *Rail* vía *f*; *Fig* **he has a one-t. mind** tiene una única obsesión (**e**) *(on record, CD)* canción *f* (**f**) *US Educ* = cada una de las divisiones del alumnado en grupos por niveles de aptitud
2 *VT* seguir la pista de; *(with radar)* seguir la trayectoria de
▸ **track down** *VT SEP (locate)* localizar

tracksuit ['træksuːt] N *Esp* chándal *m*, *Méx* pants *m*, *RP* jogging *m*

tract¹ [trækt] N *(expanse)* extensión *f*

tract² [trækt] N *(treatise)* tratado *m*; *(pamphlet)* folleto *m*

traction ['trækʃən] N tracción *f*

tractor ['træktə(r)] N tractor *m*

trade [treɪd] **1** N (**a**) *(profession)* oficio *m*; **by t.** de oficio (**b**) *Com* comercio *m*; **it's good for t.** es bueno para los negocios; **the building t.** (la industria de) la construcción; **t. name** nombre *m* comercial; **t. union** sindicato *m*; **t. unionist** sindicalista *mf*
2 *VI* comerciar (**in** en)
3 *VT* **to t. sth for sth** trocar algo por algo
▸ **trade in** *VT SEP* dar como entrada

trademark ['treɪdmɑːk] N marca *f* (de fábrica); **registered t.** marca registrada

trader ['treɪdə(r)] N comerciante *mf*

tradesman ['treɪdzmən] N *(shopkeeper)* tendero *m*

trading ['treɪdɪŋ] N comercio *m*; *Br* **t. estate** polígono *m* industrial

tradition [trə'dɪʃən] N tradición *f*

traditional [trə'dɪʃənəl] ADJ tradicional

traffic ['træfɪk] **1** N (**a**) *(vehicles)* tráfico *m*; *US* **t. circle** rotonda *f*; **t. island** isleta *f*; **t. jam** atasco *m*; **t. lights** semáforo *m*; *Br* **t. warden** ≃ guardia *mf* urbano(a) (**b**) *(trade)* tráfico *m*
2 *VI (pt & pp trafficked)* **to t. in drugs** traficar con droga

trafficker ['træfɪkə(r)] N traficante *mf*

tragedy ['trædʒɪdɪ] N tragedia *f*

tragic ['trædʒɪk] ADJ trágico(a)

trail [treɪl] **1** *VT* (**a**) *(drag)* arrastrar (**b**) *(follow)* rastrear
2 *VI* (**a**) *(drag)* arrastrarse (**b**) **to t. behind** rezagarse
3 N (**a**) *(track)* pista *f*, rastro *m* (**b**) *(path)* senda *f*, camino *m* (**c**) *(of smoke)* estela *f*

trailer ['treɪlə(r)] N (**a**) *Aut* remolque *m* (**b**) *US Aut (caravan)* caravana *f* (**c**) *Cin* trailer *m*, avance *m*

train [treɪn] **1** N (**a**) *Rail* tren *m* (**b**) *(of vehicles)* convoy *m*; *(of followers)* séquito *m*; *(of events)* serie *f* (**c**) *(of dress)* cola *f*
2 *VT* (**a**) *(teach)* formar; *Sport* entrenar; *(animal)* amaestrar; *(voice etc)* educar (**b**) *(gun)* apuntar (**on** a); *(camera)* enfocar (**on** a)
3 *VI* prepararse; *Sport* entrenarse

trainee [treɪ'niː] N aprendiz(a) *m,f*

trainer ['treɪnə(r)] N (**a**) *Sport* entrenador(a) *m,f*; *(of dogs)* amaestrador(a) *m,f*; *(of lions)* domador(a) *m,f* (**b**) *Br* **trainers** *(shoes)* zapatillas *fpl* de deporte

training ['treɪnɪŋ] N *(instruction)* formación *f*; *Sport* entrenamiento *m*; *(of animals)* amaestramiento *m*; *(of lions)* doma *f*; **to go into t.** empezar el entrenamiento; **vocational t.** formación profesional

traipse [treips] VI *Fam* dar vueltas y vueltas, *Esp* estar en danza

trait [treit] N rasgo *m*

traitor ['treitə(r)] N traidor(a) *m,f*

trajectory [trə'dʒektərɪ] N trayectoria *f*

tram [træm], **tramcar** ['træmkɑ:(r)] N *Br* tranvía *m*

tramp [træmp] **1** VI caminar con pasos pesados, marchar

2 N *(person)* vagabundo(a) *m,f*; *Pej* **she's a t.** es una fulana *or Col, Méx* piruja *or RP* reventada

> Note that the Spanish word **trampa** is a false friend and is never a translation for the English word **tramp**. In Spanish **trampa** means both "trap" and "trick".

trample ['træmpəl] VT **to t. down the grass** pisotear la hierba; **to t. sth underfoot** pisotear algo

trampoline ['træmpəli:n] N cama elástica

> Note that the Spanish word **trampolín** is a false friend and is never a translation for the English word **trampoline**. In Spanish **trampoline** means both "diving board" and "ski jump".

trance [trɑ:ns] N trance *m*

tranquil ['træŋkwɪl] ADJ tranquilo(a)

tranquillity, *US* **tranquility** [træŋ'kwɪlɪtɪ] N tranquilidad *f*

tranquillizer, *US* **tranquilizer** ['træŋkwɪlaɪzə(r)] N tranquilizante *m*

transact [træn'zækt] VT negociar

transaction [træn'zækʃən] N *(procedure)* tramitación *f*; *(deal)* transacción *f*

transatlantic [trænzət'læntɪk] ADJ transatlántico(a)

transcend [træn'send] VT trascender

transcribe [træn'skraɪb] VT transcribir

transcript ['trænskrɪpt] N transcripción *f*

transcription [træn'skrɪpʃən] N transcripción *f*

transfer 1 VT [træns'fɜ:(r)] trasladar; *(funds)* transferir; *Jur* ceder; *Ftb* traspasar; *US Rail* hacer transbordo

2 N ['trænsfɜ:(r)] **(a)** *(of employee, prisoner)* traslado *m*; *(of funds)* transferencia *f*; *Jur* cesión *f*; *Ftb* traspaso *m* **(b)** *(picture, design)* calcomanía *f* **(c)** *US Rail* transbordo *m*

transform [træns'fɔ:m] VT trasformar

transformation [trænsfə'meɪʃən] N trasformación *f*

transformer [træns'fɔ:mə(r)] N *Elec* transformador *m*

transfusion [træns'fju:ʒən] N *Med* transfusión *f* (de sangre)

transgenic [trænz'dʒi:nɪk] ADJ transgénico(a)

transgress [trænz'gres] VI *Fml* transgredir

transient ['trænzɪənt] ADJ transitorio(a)

transistor [træn'zɪstə(r)] N transistor *m*

transit ['trænzɪt] N tránsito *m*; **in t.** de tránsito

transition [træn'zɪʃən] N transición *f*

transitive ['trænzɪtɪv] ADJ transitivo(a)

transitory ['trænzɪtərɪ] ADJ transitorio(a)

translate [træns'leɪt] VT traducir

translation [træns'leɪʃən] N traducción *f*

translator [træns'leɪtə(r)] N traductor(a) *m,f*

translucent [trænz'lu:sənt] ADJ translúcido(a)

transmission [trænz'mɪʃən] N transmisión *f*

transmit [trænz'mɪt] VT transmitir

transmitter [trænz'mɪtə(r)] N *Rad (set)* transmisor *m*; *Rad & TV (station)* emisora *f*

transparency [træns'pærənsɪ] N *Phot* diapositiva *f*

transparent [træns'pærənt] ADJ transparente

transpire [træn'spaɪə(r)] VI *(happen)* ocurrir; **it transpired that ...** ocurrió que ...

transplant 1 VT [træns'plɑ:nt] trasplantar

2 N ['trænsplɑ:nt] trasplante *m*

transport 1 VT [træns'pɔ:t] transportar

2 N ['trænspɔ:t] transporte *m*; **t. aircraft/ship** avión *m*/buque *m* de transporte; *Br* **t. café** bar *m* de carretera

transportation [trænspɔ:'teɪʃən] N transporte *m*

transsexual [træn(z)'seksjʊəl] N transexual *mf*

transvestite [trænz'vestaɪt] N *Fam* travestido(a) *m,f*, *Esp* travestí *mf*

trap [træp] **1** N trampa *f*; **t. door** trampilla *f*; *Th* escotillón *m*

2 VT atrapar

trapeze [trə'pi:z] N trapecio *m*

trappings ['træpɪŋz] NPL parafernalia *f*

trash [træʃ] N *(inferior goods)* bazofia *f*; *US (rubbish)* basura *f*; *Fig* **to talk a lot of t.** decir tonterías; *US* **t. can** cubo *m* de la basura

trashy ['træʃɪ] ADJ **(trashier, trashiest)** *Fam* de pacotilla, *Esp* cutre, *Méx* gacho(a)

trauma ['trɔ:mə] N trauma *m*

traumatic [trɔ:'mætɪk] ADJ traumático(a)

travel ['trævəl] **1** VI **(a)** *(person)* viajar; **to t. through** recorrer **(b)** *(vehicle)* circular; *(news, sound, electricity)* propagarse

2 VT recorrer

3 N viajar *m*; **t. agency** agencia *f* de viajes

traveller, *US* **traveler** ['trævələ(r)] N viajero(a) *m,f*; **t.'s** *Br* **cheque** *or US* **check** cheque *m* de viaje

travelling, *US* **traveling** ['trævəlɪŋ] **1** ADJ *(salesman)* ambulante

2 N viajes *mpl*, (el) viajar *m*; **I'm fond of t.** me gusta viajar; **t. expenses** gastos *mpl* de viaje

travel-sick ['trævəlsɪk] ADJ *Br* **to be** *or* **feel t.** estar mareado(a)

travesty ['trævɪstɪ] N parodia *f* burda

> Note that the Spanish word **travesti** is a false friend and is never a translation for the English word **travesty**. In Spanish **travesti** means "transvestite".

trawler ['trɔːlə(r)] N barco m de arrastre

tray [treɪ] N (for food) bandeja f; (for letters) cesta f (para la correspondencia)

treacherous ['tretʃərəs] ADJ (a) (person) traidor(a); (action) traicionero(a) (b) (dangerous) peligroso(a)

treachery ['tretʃərɪ] N traición f

treacle ['triːkəl] N Br melaza f

tread [tred] 1 VI (pt trod; pp trod or trodden) pisar; **to t. on** pisar
2 VT (a) (step on) pisar (b) **to t. water** mantenerse a flote verticalmente
3 N (a) (step) paso m; (sound) ruido m de pasos (b) (of tyre) banda f de rodadura

treadmill ['tredmɪl] N (in gym) tapiz m rodante, cinta f de footing or de correr

treason ['triːzən] N traición f

treasure ['treʒə(r)] 1 N tesoro m
2 VT (keep) guardar como oro en paño; (value) apreciar muchísimo

treasurer ['treʒərə(r)] N tesorero(a) m,f

treasury ['treʒərɪ] N tesorería f; **the T.** (in UK) el tesoro (público), ≃ (el Ministerio de) Economía; **the Department of the T.** (in US) el tesoro (público), ≃ (el Ministerio de) Hacienda; **T. bill** bono m del Tesoro

treat [triːt] 1 N (a) (present) regalo m (b) (pleasure) placer m
2 VT (a) (person, illness) tratar; **to t. badly** maltratar (b) (regard) considerar (c) **he treated them to dinner** les invitó a cenar

treatise ['triːtɪz] N tratado m

treatment ['triːtmənt] N (a) (of person) trato m (b) (of subject, patient) tratamiento m

treaty ['triːtɪ] N tratado m

treble ['trebəl] 1 ADJ (a) (triple) triple (b) Mus **t. clef** clave f de sol; **t. voice** voz f de tiple
2 VT triplicar
3 VI triplicarse

tree [triː] N árbol m; **apple/cherry t.** manzano m/cerezo m

treetop ['triːtɒp] N copa f

trek [trek] 1 N (journey) camino largo; Fam (walk) caminata f
2 VI (pt & pp trekked) hacer un viaje largo y difícil; Fam (walk) ir caminando

trellis ['trelɪs] N enrejado m

tremble ['trembəl] VI temblar, estremecerse

trembling ['tremblɪŋ] ADJ tembloroso(a)

tremendous [trɪ'mendəs] ADJ (huge) enorme; (success) arrollador(a); (shock etc) tremendo(a); Fam (marvellous) estupendo(a)

tremor ['tremə(r)] N temblor m

trench [trentʃ] N (a) (ditch) zanja f; Mil trinchera f (b) **t. coat** trinchera f

trend [trend] 1 N (tendency) tendencia f; (fashion) moda f
2 VI tender (**to** or **towards** hacia)

trendy ['trendɪ] ADJ (trendier, trendiest) Fam (person) modernillo(a) m,f, RP modernoso(a) m,f; (clothes) a la última

trepidation [trepɪ'deɪʃən] N turbación f

trespass ['trespəs] VI entrar sin autorización

> Note that the Spanish verb **traspasar** is a false friend and is never a translation for the English verb **trespass**. In Spanish **traspasar** means "to go through, to cross", "to transfer" and "to exceed".

trespasser ['trespəsə(r)] N intruso(a) m,f

trestle ['tresəl] N caballete m

trial ['traɪəl] N (a) Jur proceso m, juicio m (b) (test) prueba f; **on t.** a prueba; **by t. and error** a fuerza de equivocarse (c) **trials** (competition) concurso m (d) **trials** (suffering) sufrimiento m; **trials and tribulations** tribulaciones fpl

triangle ['traɪæŋgəl] N triángulo m

triangular [traɪ'æŋgjʊlə(r)] ADJ triangular

tribe [traɪb] N tribu f

tribunal [traɪ'bjuːnəl] N tribunal m

tributary ['trɪbjʊtərɪ] N (river) afluente m

tribute ['trɪbjuːt] N (a) (payment) tributo m (b) (mark of respect) homenaje m; **to pay t. to** rendir homenaje a

trice [traɪs] N Fam **in a t.** en un abrir y cerrar de ojos

trick [trɪk] 1 N (a) (ruse) ardid m; (dishonest) engaño m; (in question) trampa f (b) (practical joke) broma f; **to play a t. on sb** gastarle una broma a algn; (malicious) jugar una mala pasada a algn (c) (of magic, knack) truco m; **that'll do the t.!** ¡eso es exactamente lo que hace falta! (d) Cards baza f
2 VT engañar; **to t. sb out of sth** quitar or Am sacarle algo a algn a base de engaños

trickery ['trɪkərɪ] N engaños mpl, trampas fpl

trickle ['trɪkəl] 1 VI discurrir; (water) gotear
2 N hilo m

tricky ['trɪkɪ] ADJ (trickier, trickiest) (person) astuto(a); (situation, mechanism) delicado(a)

tricycle ['traɪsɪkəl] N triciclo m

tried [traɪd] PT & PP of **try**

trifle ['traɪfəl] 1 N (a) (insignificant thing) bagatela f; **he's a t. optimistic** es ligeramente optimista (b) Br Culin = postre de bizcocho, gelatina, frutas y Esp nata or Am crema de leche
2 **to t. with** tomar a la ligera

trifling ['traɪflɪŋ] ADJ insignificante, trivial

trigger ['trɪgə(r)] 1 N (of gun) gatillo m; (of mechanism) disparador m
2 VT **to t. (off)** desencadenar

trill [trɪl] N (of music, bird) trino m; Ling vibración f

trilogy ['trɪlədʒɪ] N trilogía f

trim [trɪm] 1 ADJ (trimmer, trimmest) (neat) aseado(a); **to have a t. figure** tener buen tipo
2 VT (a) (cut) recortar; Fig (expenses)

disminuir (**b**) *(decorate)* adornar
3 N (**a**) *(condition)* estado *m*; *Naut* asiento *m* (**b**) *(cut)* recorte *m*

trimming ['trımıŋ] N (**a**) *(cut)* recorte *m* (**b**) *(on clothes)* adorno *m* (**c**) *Culin* **trimmings** guarnición *f*

trinket ['trıŋkıt] N baratija *f*

trio ['triːəʊ] N trío *m*

trip [trıp] **1** N (**a**) *(journey)* viaje *m*; *(excursion)* excursión *f*; **to go on a t.** ir de excursión (**b**) *Fam* **to be on a t.** *(on drugs)* estar colocado(a)
2 VI (**a**) **to t. (up)** *(stumble)* tropezar (**over** con); *Fig (err)* equivocarse (**b**) **to t. along** ir con paso ligero
3 VT **to t. sb (up)** poner la zancadilla a algn; *Fig* hacer caer a algn

tripe [traıp] N (**a**) *Culin* mondongo *m*, *Esp* callos *mpl*, *Chile* chunchules *mpl* (**b**) *Fam (nonsense)* tonterías *fpl*, bobadas *fpl*

triple ['trıpəl] **1** ADJ triple
2 VT triplicar
3 VI triplicarse

triplet ['trıplıt] N trillizo(a) *m,f*

triplicate ['trıplıkıt] ADJ **in t.** por triplicado

tripod ['traıpɒd] N trípode *m*

trite [traıt] ADJ *(sentiment)* banal; *(subject)* trillado(a)

triumph ['traıəmf] **1** N triunfo *m*
2 VI triunfar

triumphant [traı'ʌmfənt] ADJ triunfante

trivia ['trıvıə] NPL trivialidades *fpl*

trivial ['trıvıəl] ADJ trivial, banal

trod [trɒd] PT & PP of **tread**

trodden ['trɒdən] PP of **tread**

trolley ['trɒlı] N *Br* carro *m*

trombone [trɒm'bəʊn] N trombón *m*

troop [truːp] **1** N (**a**) *(of people)* grupo *m* (**b**) *Mil* **troops** tropas *fpl*
2 VI **to t. in/out/off** entrar/salir/marcharse en tropel

trooper ['truːpə(r)] N (**a**) *(soldier)* soldado *m* *(de caballería o división acorazada)* (**b**) *US (policeman)* policía *mf*

trooping ['truːpıŋ] N *Br* **t. the colour** = ceremonia de homenaje a la bandera de un regimiento

trophy ['trəʊfı] N trofeo *m*

tropic ['trɒpık] N trópico *m*

tropical ['trɒpıkəl] ADJ tropical

trot [trɒt] **1** VI trotar
2 N trote *m*; **to go at a t.** ir al trote; *Br Fam* **on the t.** *(in succession)* seguidos(as)

trouble ['trʌbəl] **1** N (**a**) *(misfortune)* desgracia *f* (**b**) *(problems)* problemas *mpl*; **to be in t.** estar en un lío; **to cause sb t.** ocasionar problemas a algn; **to get sb out of t.** sacar a algn de un apuro; **the t. is that …** lo que pasa es que … (**c**) *(effort)* esfuerzo *m*; **it's no t.** no es ninguna molestia; **it's not worth the t.** no merece la pena; **to take the t. to do sth** molestarse en

hacer algo (**d**) *(conflict)* conflicto *m* (**e**) *Med* enfermedad *f*; **to have liver t.** tener problemas de hígado
2 VT (**a**) *(affect)* afligir; *(worry)* preocupar; **that doesn't t. him at all** eso le tiene sin cuidado (**b**) *(bother)* molestar
3 VI molestarse

troubled ['trʌbəld] ADJ agitado(a)

troublemaker ['trʌbəlmeɪkə(r)] N alborotador(a) *m,f*

troubleshooter ['trʌbəlʃuːtə(r)] N *Ind* = persona encargada de solucionar problemas

troublesome ['trʌbəlsəm] ADJ molesto(a)

trough [trɒf] N (**a**) *(drinking)* t. abrevadero *m*; **(feeding) t.** pesebre *m* (**b**) *(of wave)* seno *m* (**c**) *Geog & Met* depresión *f*

trounce [traʊns] VT dar una paliza a

troupe [truːp] N *Th* compañía *f*

trousers ['traʊzəz] NPL pantalones *mpl*; **a pair of t.** unos pantalones

trousseau ['truːsəʊ] N ajuar *m*

trout [traʊt] N trucha *f*

trowel ['traʊəl] N (**a**) *(builder's)* palustre *m* (**b**) *(for gardening)* desplantador *m*

truant ['truːənt] N *Br* **to play t.** faltar a clase, *Esp* hacer novillos, *Méx* irse de pinta

truce [truːs] N tregua *f*

truck¹ [trʌk] N (**a**) *Br Rail* vagón *m* (**b**) *Aut* camión *m*; **t. driver** camionero(a) *m,f*, *CAm, Méx* trailero(a) *m,f*; *US* **t. farm** huerta *f*; *US* **t. farmer** hortelano(a) *m,f*

truck² [trʌk] N (**a**) **to have no t. with** no estar dispuesto a tolerar (**b**) *US* verduras *fpl*; **t. farm** huerta *f*; **t. farming** cultivo *m* de hortalizas

trucker ['trʌkə(r)] N *US (lorry driver)* camionero(a) *m,f*, *CAm, Méx* trailero(a) *m,f*

truculent ['trʌkjʊlənt] ADJ agresivo(a), airado(a)

> Note that the Spanish word **truculento** is a false friend and is never a translation for the English word **truculent**. In Spanish, **truculento** means "horrifying, terrifying".

trudge [trʌdʒ] VI caminar con dificultad

true [truː] ADJ (**truer, truest**) (**a**) *(factually correct)* cierto(a), verdadero(a); **it's t. that …** es verdad que …; **to come t.** cumplirse, hacerse realidad (**b**) *(faithful)* fiel (**c**) *(aim)* acertado(a)

truffle ['trʌfəl] N trufa *f*

truly ['truːlı] ADV verdaderamente; **really and t.?** ¿de veras?; **yours t.** *(at end of letter)* atentamente

trump [trʌmp] *Cards* **1** N triunfo *m*
2 VT fallar

trumped-up ['trʌmptʌp] ADJ inventado(a)

trumpet ['trʌmpıt] N trompeta *f*

trumpeting ['trʌmpıtıŋ] N *(of elephant)* berrido *m*

truncheon ['trʌntʃən] N *Br* porra *f (de policía)*

trundle ['trʌndəl] VI rodar

trunk [trʌŋk] N (**a**) *(of tree, body)* tronco *m* (**b**) *(of elephant)* trompa *f* (**c**) *(luggage)* baúl *m* (**d**) *Br Tel* **t. call** llamada *f or Am* llamado *m* de larga distancia, *Esp* conferencia *f* (**e**) *US (of car)* maletero *m, CAm, Méx* cajuela *f, RP* baúl *m*

trunks [trʌŋks] NPL (**bathing**) **t.** bañador *m (de hombre)*

truss [trʌs] **1** VT *(tie)* atar
  2 N (**a**) *Constr* cuchillo *m* de armadura (**b**) *Med* braguero *m*

trust [trʌst] **1** N (**a**) *(belief)* confianza *f;* **breach of t.** abuso *m* de confianza (**b**) *Jur* fideicomiso *m* (**c**) *Fin* trust *m*
  2 VT (**a**) *(hope)* esperar (**b**) *(rely upon)* fiarse de; **to t. sb with sth** confiar algo a algn
  3 VI confiar (**in** en)

trusted ['trʌstɪd] ADJ de fiar

trustee [trʌs'tiː] N *Jur* fideicomisario(a) *m,f, (in bankruptcy)* síndico *m*

trustful ['trʌstfʊl], **trusting** ['trʌstɪŋ] ADJ confiado(a)

trustworthy ['trʌstwɜːðɪ] ADJ *(person)* fiable, de confianza, *Am* confiable; *(information)* fidedigno(a), fiable, *Am* confiable

trusty ['trʌstɪ] ADJ (**trustier, trustiest**) fiel, leal

truth [truːθ] N verdad *f;* **to tell the t.** decir la verdad

truthful ['truːθfʊl] ADJ *(person)* veraz, sincero(a); *(testimony)* verídico(a)

truthfully ['truːθfʊlɪ] ADV sinceramente

try [traɪ] **1** VT *(pt & pp* **tried**) (**a**) *(attempt)* intentar; **to t. to do sth** tratar de *or* intentar hacer algo (**b**) *(test)* probar, ensayar; **to t. sb's patience** poner a prueba la paciencia de algn (**c**) *Jur* juzgar
  2 VI intentar
  3 N (**a**) *(attempt)* tentativa *f,* intento *m* (**b**) *Sport* ensayo *m*
► **try on** VT SEP *(dress)* probarse
► **try out** VT SEP probar

trying ['traɪɪŋ] ADJ *(person)* molesto(a), pesado(a); **to have a t. time** pasar un mal rato

tsar [zɑː(r)] N zar *m*

T-shirt ['tiːʃɜːt] N camiseta *f, Méx* playera *f, RP* remera *f*

tub [tʌb] N (**a**) *(container)* tina *f,* cuba *f* (**b**) *(bath)* bañera *f, Am* tina *f, Am* bañadera *f*

tuba ['tjuːbə] N tuba *f*

tubby ['tʌbɪ] ADJ (**tubbier, tubbiest**) rechoncho(a)

tube [tjuːb] N (**a**) *(pipe, container)* tubo *m; (in tyre)* cámara *f* (de aire) (**b**) *Br Fam* **the t.** *(underground)* el metro, *RP* el subte

tuberculosis [tjʊbɜːkjʊ'ləʊsɪs] N tuberculosis *f*

tubing ['tjuːbɪŋ] N tubería *f;* (**piece of**) **t.** (trozo *m* de) tubo *m*

tubular ['tjuːbjʊlə(r)] ADJ tubular

tuck [tʌk] **1** VT **to t. in the bedclothes** remeter la ropa de la cama; **to t. sb in** arropar a algn; **to t. one's shirt into one's trousers** meterse la camisa por dentro (de los pantalones)
  2 N *Sewing* pliegue *m*
► **tuck in** VI *Fam* devorar

Tuesday ['tjuːzdɪ] N martes *m*

tuft [tʌft] N *(of hair)* mechón *m*

tug [tʌg] **1** VT *(pull at)* tirar de; *(haul along)* arrastrar; *Naut* remolcar
  2 N (**a**) *(pull)* tirón *m;* **t. of war** *(game)* lucha *f* de la cuerda; *Fig* lucha encarnizada (**b**) *Naut* remolcador *m*

tugboat ['tʌgbəʊt] N remolcador *m*

tuition [tjuː'ɪʃən] N instrucción *f;* **private t.** clases *fpl* particulares; **t. fees** honorarios *mpl*

tulip ['tjuːlɪp] N tulipán *m*

tumble ['tʌmbəl] **1** VI *(person)* caerse; *(acrobat)* dar volteretas; *(building)* venirse abajo
  2 VT volcar
  3 N (**a**) *(fall)* caída *f* (**b**) **t. dryer** secadora *f*

tumbledown ['tʌmbəldaʊn] ADJ en ruinas

tumbler ['tʌmblə(r)] N vaso *m*

tummy ['tʌmɪ] N *Fam* barriga *f, Chile* guata *f*

tumour, *US* **tumor** ['tjuːmə(r)] N tumor *m*

tumult ['tjuːmʌlt] N tumulto *m*

tuna ['tjuːnə] N atún *m,* bonito *m*

> Note that the Spanish word **tuna** is a false friend and is never a translation for the English word **tuna**. In Spanish **tuna** means "group of student minstrels".

tune [tjuːn] **1** N (**a**) *(melody)* melodía *f; Fig* **to change one's t.** cambiar de tono (**b**) *Mus* tono *m;* **in/out of t.** afinado/desafinado; **to sing out of t.** desafinar
  2 VT *Mus* afinar
  3 VI *Rad & TV* **to t. in to a station** sintonizar una emisora
► **tune up** VI afinar los instrumentos

tuneful ['tjuːnfʊl] ADJ melodioso(a)

tuner ['tjuːnə(r)] N (**a**) *(of pianos)* afinador(a) *m,f* (**b**) *Rad & TV (knob)* sintonizador *m*

tunic ['tjuːnɪk] N túnica *f*

tuning ['tjuːnɪŋ] N (**a**) *Mus* afinación *f;* **t. fork** diapasón *m* (**b**) *Rad & TV* **t. in** sintonización *f*

Tunisia [tjuː'nɪzɪə] N Túnez

Tunisian [tjuː'nɪzɪən] ADJ & N tunecino(a) *(m,f)*

tunnel ['tʌnəl] **1** N túnel *m; Min* galería *f*
  2 VT **to t. through** abrir un túnel a través de

turban ['tɜːbən] N turbante *m*

turbine ['tɜːbaɪn] N turbina *f*

turbulent ['tɜːbjʊlənt] ADJ turbulento(a)

tureen [tə'riːn] N sopera *f*

turf [tɜːf] N (**a**) *(grass)* césped *m; (peat)* turba *f* (**b**) *Br* **t. accountant** *(in horse racing)* corredor(a) *m,f* de apuestas
► **turf out** VT SEP *Br Fam* **to t. sb out** poner a algn de patitas en la calle

Turk [tɜːk] N turco(a) *m,f*

Turkey ['tɜːkɪ] N Turquía

turkey ['tɜːkɪ] N pavo *m*, *Méx* guajolote *m*

Turkish ['tɜːkɪʃ] **1** ADJ turco(a)
  2 N *(language)* turco *m*

turmoil ['tɜːmɔɪl] N confusión *f*

turn [tɜːn] **1** VT **(a)** *(wheel, handle)* girar; *(key, omelette)* dar la vuelta a; **to t. sth inside out** volver algo del revés; **to t. a page** volver una hoja; **to t. one's head/gaze** volver la cabeza/mirada (**towards** hacia); **to t. the corner** doblar *or Am* voltear la esquina; *Fig* **he's turned forty** ha cumplido los cuarenta **(b)** *(change)* transformar (**into** en) **(c)** *(on lathe)* tornear
  2 VI **(a)** *(rotate)* girar **(b)** *(turn round)* volverse, dar la vuelta; **to t. to sb** volverse hacia algn; *Fig (for help)* acudir a algn; **to t. upside down** volcarse; *Fig* **to t. on sb** volverse contra algn **(c)** *(become)* volverse; **the milk has turned sour** la leche se ha cortado
  3 N **(a)** *(of wheel)* vuelta *f*; **done to a t.** *(meat)* en su punto **(b)** *(change of direction)* cambio *m* de dirección; *(in road)* curva *f*; **to take a t. for the better** empezar a mejorar; **left/right t.** giro *m* a la izquierda/a la derecha; *US Aut* **t. signal** intermitente *m*, *Col, Ecuad, Méx* direccional *m or f* **(c)** *(to do sb a good t.* hacer un favor a algn **(d)** *Med* ataque *m* **(e)** *(in game, queue)* turno *m*, vez *f*; **it's your t.** te toca a ti; **to take turns (at doing sth),** *Br* **to take it in turns (to do sth)** turnarse para hacer algo **(f)** *Th* número *m* **(g)** **t. of phrase** giro *m*

▶ **turn aside 1** VT SEP desviar
  2 VI desviarse

▶ **turn away 1** VT SEP *(person)* rechazar
  2 VI volver la cabeza

▶ **turn back 1** VT SEP *(person)* hacer retroceder; *(clock)* retrasar
  2 VI volverse

▶ **turn down** VT SEP **(a)** *(gas, radio etc)* bajar **(b)** *(reject)* rechazar **(c)** *(fold)* doblar

▶ **turn in** *Fam* **1** VT SEP *(person)* entregar a la policía
  2 VI acostarse

▶ **turn off 1** VT SEP *(electricity)* desconectar; *(gas, light)* apagar; *(water)* cerrar
  2 VI desviarse

▶ **turn on** VT SEP *(electricity)* encender, *Am* prender; *(tap, gas)* abrir; *(machine)* poner en marcha; *Fam* **it turns me on** me encanta

▶ **turn out 1** VT SEP **(a)** *(extinguish)* apagar **(b)** *(eject)* echar; *(empty)* vaciar **(c)** *(produce)* producir
  2 VI **(a)** *(attend)* asistir **(b)** **it turns out that ...** resulta que ...; **things have turned out well** las cosas han salido bien

▶ **turn over 1** VT SEP *(turn upside down)* poner al revés; *(page)* dar la vuelta a
  2 VI volverse

▶ **turn round 1** VT SEP volver
  2 VI *(rotate)* girar, dar vueltas

▶ **turn up 1** VT SEP **(a)** *(collar)* levantar; **to t. up one's shirt sleeves** arremangarse; **turned-up nose** nariz respingona **(b)** *Rad & TV* subir
  2 VI **(a)** *Fig* **something is sure to t. up** algo saldrá **(b)** *(arrive)* llegar, presentarse; **no one turned up** nadie se presentó **(c)** *(attend)* asistir

turning ['tɜːnɪŋ] N **(a)** *Fig* **t. point** punto decisivo **(b)** *(in road)* salida *f*

turnip ['tɜːnɪp] N nabo *m*

turnout ['tɜːnaʊt] N asistencia *f*

turnover ['tɜːnəʊvə(r)] N *Com (sales)* facturación *f*; *(of goods)* movimiento *m*

turnpike ['tɜːnpaɪk] N *US* autopista *f* de peaje

turnstile ['tɜːnstaɪl] N torniquete *m*

turntable ['tɜːnteɪbəl] N *(for record)* plato *m* (giratorio)

turn-up ['tɜːnʌp] N *Br (of trousers)* vuelta *f*

turpentine ['tɜːpəntaɪn] N (esencia *f* de) trementina *f*

turquoise ['tɜːkwɔɪz] **1** N *(colour, stone)* turquesa *f*
  2 ADJ **t. (blue)** azul turquesa

turret ['tʌrɪt] N torrecilla *f*

turtle ['tɜːtəl] N *Br* tortuga (marina); *US (tortoise)* tortuga *f*

turtledove ['tɜːtəldʌv] N tórtola *f*

turtleneck ['tɜːtəlnek] N **a t. (sweater)** un suéter *or Esp* jersey de cuello alto

tusk [tʌsk] N colmillo *m*

tussle ['tʌsəl] N pelea *f*, lucha *f*

tutor ['tjuːtə(r)] N *Br Univ* tutor(a) *m,f*; **private t.** profesor(a) *m,f* particular

tutorial [tjuːˈtɔːrɪəl] N *Br Univ* tutoría *f*, seminario *m*

tuxedo [tʌkˈsiːdəʊ] N *US* smoking *m*

TV [tiːˈviː] N *(abbr* **television)** televisión *f*

twang [twæŋ] **1** N **(a)** *(of instrument)* sonido *m* vibrante **(b) nasal t.** gangueo *m*
  2 VT puntear
  3 VI *(string)* vibrar

tweak [twiːk] VT pellizcar

tweed [twiːd] N cheviot *m*

tweezers ['twiːzəz] NPL pinzas *fpl*

twelfth [twelfθ] **1** ADJ & N duodécimo(a) *(m,f)*
  2 N *(fraction)* duodécimo *m*

twelve [twelv] ADJ & N doce *(m inv)*

twentieth ['twentɪɪθ] **1** ADJ & N vigésimo(a) *(m,f)*
  2 N *(fraction)* vigésimo *m*

twenty ['twentɪ] ADJ & N veinte *(m inv)*

twice [twaɪs] ADV dos veces; **he's t. as old as I am** tiene el doble de años que yo

twiddle ['twɪdəl] **1** VT dar vueltas a; **to t. one's moustache** mesarse el bigote; **to t. one's thumbs** estar mano sobre mano
  2 VI **to t. with sth** juguetear con algo

twig¹ [twɪg] N ramilla *f*

twig² [twɪg] VI *Br Fam* darse cuenta

twilight ['twaɪlaɪt] N crepúsculo *m*

twin [twɪn] **1** N mellizo(a) *m,f*; **identical twins** gemelos (idénticos); **t. brother/sister** hermano gemelo/hermana gemela; **t. beds** camas *fpl* gemelas
2 VT hermanar

twine [twaɪn] **1** N bramante *m*
2 VT entretejer
3 VI **to t. round sth** enroscarse alrededor de algo

twinge [twɪndʒ] N *(of pain)* punzada *f*; *Fig* **t. of conscience** remordimiento *m*

twinkle ['twɪŋkəl] VI *(stars)* centellear; *(eyes)* brillar

twinkling ['twɪŋklɪŋ] N *(of stars)* centelleo *m*; *Fig* **in the t. of an eye** en un abrir y cerrar de ojos

twirl [twɜːl] **1** VT girar rápidamente
2 VI *(spin)* girar rápidamente; *(dancer)* piruetear
3 N *(movement)* giro rápido; *(of dancer)* pirueta *f*

twist [twɪst] **1** VT torcer; *(sense)* tergiversar; **to t. one's ankle** torcerse el tobillo
2 VI *(smoke)* formar volutas; *(path)* serpentear
3 N **(a)** *(of yarn)* torzal *m* **(b)** *(movement)* torsión *f*; *Med* torcedura *f*; *Fig* **to give a new t. to sth** dar un nuevo enfoque a algo **(c)** *(in road)* vuelta *f* **(d)** *(dance)* twist *m*

twit [twɪt] N *Br Fam* lerdo(a) *m,f*, *Esp* memo(a) *m,f*

twitch [twɪtʃ] **1** VT dar un tirón a
2 VI crisparse; **his face twitches** tiene un tic en la cara

twitter ['twɪtə(r)] **1** VI gorjear
2 N gorjeo *m*

two [tuː] **1** ADJ dos *inv*; *Fig* **to be in** or **of t. minds about sth** estar indeciso(a) respecto a algo
2 N dos *m inv*; *Fig* **to put t. and t. together** atar cabos

two-faced ['tuː'feɪst] ADJ hipócrita

twofold ['tuːfəʊld] ADJ doble

two-party ['tuːpɑːtɪ] ADJ **t. system** bipartidismo *m*

two-piece ['tuː'piːs] **1** ADJ de dos piezas
2 N *(suit)* traje *m* de dos piezas

two-seater ['tuː'siːtə(r)] ADJ & N biplaza *(m)*

twosome ['tuːsəm] N pareja *f*

two-time ['tuːtaɪm] VT *Fam* **to t. sb** engañar or *Esp* pegársela a algn

two-way ['tuːweɪ] ADJ **(a)** *(street)* de dos direcciones **(b)** **t. radio** aparato *m* emisor y receptor

tycoon [taɪ'kuːn] N magnate *m*

type [taɪp] **1** N **(a)** *(kind)* tipo *m*, clase *f*; *(brand)* marca *f*; *(of car)* modelo *m* **(b)** *Typ* carácter *m*; *(print)* caracteres *mpl*
2 VT & VI *(with typewriter)* escribir a máquina; *(with word processor)* escribir en *Esp* el ordenador or *Am* la computadora

typecast ['taɪpkɑːst] VT encasillar

typescript ['taɪpskrɪpt] N texto *m* escrito a máquina

typeset ['taɪpset] VT componer

typesetter ['taɪpsetə(r)] N **(a)** *(person)* cajista *mf* **(b)** *(machine)* máquina *f* para componer tipos

typewriter ['taɪpraɪtə(r)] N máquina *f* de escribir

typewritten ['taɪprɪtən] ADJ escrito(a) a máquina

typhoid ['taɪfɔɪd] N **t. (fever)** fiebre tifoidea

typhoon [taɪ'fuːn] N tifón *m*

typical ['tɪpɪkəl] ADJ típico(a)

typify ['tɪpɪfaɪ] VT tipificar

typing ['taɪpɪŋ] N mecanografía *f*

typist ['taɪpɪst] N mecanógrafo(a) *m,f*

tyrannical [tɪ'rænɪkəl] ADJ tiránico(a)

tyrannize ['tɪrənaɪz] VT tiranizar

tyranny ['tɪrənɪ] N tiranía *f*

tyrant ['taɪrənt] N tirano(a) *m,f*

tyre [taɪə(r)] N neumático *m*, *Am* llanta *f*; **t. pressure** presión *f* de los neumáticos

U

U, u [ju:] N *(the letter)* U, u *f*

U [ju:] ADJ *(film)* ≃ (apta) para todos los públicos

ubiquity [ju:'bɪkwɪtɪ] N ubicuidad *f*

udder ['ʌdə(r)] N ubre *f*

UFO, ufo ['ju:ef'əʊ, 'ju:fəʊ] N *(abbr* **unidentified flying object)** OVNI *m*

ugh [ʌx] INTERJ ¡uf!, ¡puf!

ugly ['ʌglɪ] ADJ *(uglier, ugliest)* feo(a); *(situation)* desagradable; *Fig* **u. duckling** patito feo

UK [ju:'keɪ] N *(abbr* **United Kingdom)** R.U. *m*

Ukraine [ju:'kreɪn] N **the U.** Ucrania

ulcer ['ʌlsə(r)] N *(sore)* llaga *f*; *(internal)* úlcera *f*

ulterior [ʌl'tɪərɪə(r)] ADJ *(motive)* oculto(a)

ultimate ['ʌltɪmɪt] ADJ **(a)** *(final)* último(a); *(aim)* final **(b)** *(basic)* esencial

ultimately ['ʌltɪmɪtlɪ] ADV **(a)** *(finally)* finalmente **(b)** *(basically)* en el fondo

ultimatum [ʌltɪ'meɪtəm] N ultimátum *m*

ultrasound ['ʌltrəsaʊnd] N ultrasonido *m*

ultraviolet [ʌltrə'vaɪəlɪt] ADJ ultravioleta

umbilical [ʌm'bɪlɪkəl] ADJ **u. cord** cordón *m* umbilical

umbrella [ʌm'brelə] N paraguas *m inv, Col* sombrilla *f*

umpire ['ʌmpaɪə(r)] **1** N árbitro *m*
2 VT arbitrar

umpteen [ʌmp'ti:n] ADJ *Fam* muchísimos(as), la tira de

umpteenth [ʌmp'ti:nθ] ADJ enésimo(a)

UN [ju:'en] N *(abbr* **United Nations (Organization))** ONU *f*

unabashed [ʌnə'bæʃt] ADJ descarado(a); **to be u. (by** *or* **at)** no sentir vergüenza *or Am* pena (de *or* por)

unable [ʌn'eɪbəl] ADJ incapaz; **to be u. to do sth/anything** no poder hacer algo/nada

unacceptable [ʌnək'septəbəl] ADJ inaceptable

unaccompanied [ʌnə'kʌmpənɪd] ADJ solo(a)

unaccountable [ʌnə'kaʊntəbəl] ADJ inexplicable

unaccounted-for [ʌnə'kaʊntɪdfɔː(r)] ADJ **to be u.** faltar

unaccustomed [ʌnə'kʌstəmd] ADJ **he's u. to this climate** no está muy acostumbrado a este clima

unaffected [ʌnə'fektɪd] ADJ **(a)** *(undamaged, untouched)* no afectado(a) **(by** por) **(b)** *(indifferent)* indiferente **(by** a) **(c)** *(natural) (person)* natural; *(style)* llano(a)

unaided [ʌn'eɪdɪd] ADJ sin ayuda, solo(a)

unanimous [ju:'nænɪməs] ADJ unánime

unannounced [ʌnə'naʊnst] ADJ sin avisar

unanswered [ʌn'ɑ:nsəd] ADJ sin contestar

unapproachable [ʌnə'prəʊtʃəbəl] ADJ inabordable, inaccesible

unarmed [ʌn'ɑ:md] ADJ desarmado(a)

unashamed [ʌnə'ʃeɪmd] ADJ descarado(a)

unasked [ʌn'ɑ:skt] ADV **u. (for)** *(unrequested)* no solicitado(a); *(spontaneous)* espontáneo(a)

unassuming [ʌnə'sju:mɪŋ] ADJ sin pretensiones

unattached [ʌnə'tætʃt] ADJ **(a)** *(independent)* libre; *(loose)* suelto(a) **(b)** *(person)* soltero(a) y sin compromiso

unattainable [ʌnə'teɪnəbəl] ADJ inalcanzable

unattended [ʌnə'tendɪd] ADJ *(counter etc)* desatendido(a); **to leave a child u.** dejar a un niño solo

unattractive [ʌnə'træktɪv] ADJ poco atractivo(a)

unauthorized [ʌn'ɔ:θəraɪzd] ADJ **(a)** *(person)* no autorizado(a) **(b)** *(trade etc)* ilícito(a), ilegal

unavailable [ʌnə'veɪləbəl] ADJ **to be u.** no estar disponible

unavoidable [ʌnə'vɔɪdəbəl] ADJ inevitable; *(accident)* imprevisible

unaware [ʌnə'weə(r)] ADJ **to be u. of sth** ignorar algo

unawares [ʌnə'weəz] ADV **(a)** *(unexpectedly)* desprevenido(a) **(b)** *(without knowing)* inconscientemente

unbalanced [ʌn'bælənst] ADJ desequilibrado(a)

unbearable [ʌn'beərəbəl] ADJ insoportable

unbeatable [ʌn'bi:təbəl] ADJ *(team)* invencible; *(price, quality)* inmejorable

unbelievable [ʌnbɪ'li:vəbəl] ADJ increíble

unbend [ʌn'bend] VI *Fam Fig* relajarse

unbia(s)sed [ʌn'baɪəst] ADJ imparcial

unblock [ʌn'blɒk] VT *(sink, pipe)* desatascar

unborn [ʌn'bɔ:n] ADJ sin nacer, nonato(a)

unbreakable [ʌn'breɪkəbəl] ADJ irrompible; *Fig* inquebrantable

unbroken [ʌn'brəʊkən] ADJ **(a)** *(whole)* intacto(a) **(b)** *(uninterrupted)* continuo(a) **(c)** *(record)* imbatido(a)

unbutton [ʌn'bʌtən] VT desabrochar

uncalled-for [ʌnˈkɔːldfɔː(r)] ADJ *(inappropriate)* insensato(a); *(unjustified)* inmerecido(a)

uncanny [ʌnˈkænɪ] ADJ misterioso(a), extraño(a)

unceasing [ʌnˈsiːsɪŋ] ADJ incesante

uncertain [ʌnˈsɜːtən] ADJ **(a)** *(not certain)* incierto(a); *(doubtful)* dudoso(a); **in no u. terms** claramente **(b)** *(hesitant)* indeciso(a)

uncertainty [ʌnˈsɜːtəntɪ] N incertidumbre f

unchanged [ʌnˈtʃeɪndʒd] ADJ igual

unchecked [ʌnˈtʃekt] ADJ **(a)** *(unrestrained)* desenfrenado(a) **(b)** *(not examined)* no comprobado(a)

uncivilized [ʌnˈsɪvɪlaɪzd] ADJ *(tribe)* incivilizado(a), salvaje; *(not cultured)* inculto(a)

uncle [ˈʌŋkəl] N tío m

unclear [ʌnˈklɪə(r)] ADJ poco claro(a)

uncomfortable [ʌnˈkʌmftəbəl] ADJ incómodo(a); **to make things u. for** complicar la vida a

uncommon [ʌnˈkɒmən] ADJ **(a)** *(rare)* poco común; *(unusual)* extraordinario(a) **(b)** *(excessive)* excesivo(a)

uncommonly [ʌnˈkɒmənlɪ] ADV **not u.** con cierta frecuencia

uncompromising [ʌnˈkɒmprəmaɪzɪŋ] ADJ intransigente; **u. honesty** sinceridad absoluta

unconcerned [ʌnkənˈsɜːnd] ADJ indiferente (**about** a)

unconditional [ʌnkənˈdɪʃənəl] ADJ incondicional; **u. refusal** negativa rotunda

unconnected [ʌnkəˈnektɪd] ADJ no relacionado(a)

unconscious [ʌnˈkɒnʃəs] 1 ADJ **(a)** *(not awake)* inconsciente **(b)** *(unintentional)* involuntario(a)

2 N **the u.** el inconsciente

unconsciousness [ʌnˈkɒnʃəsnɪs] N *Med* pérdida f del conocimiento

unconstitutional [ʌnkɒnstɪˈtjuːʃənəl] ADJ inconstitucional, anticonstitucional

uncontested [ʌnkənˈtestɪd] ADJ *Pol* **u. seat** escaño m ganado sin oposición

uncontrollable [ʌnkənˈtrəʊləbəl] ADJ incontrolable; *(desire)* irresistible

unconventional [ʌnkənˈvenʃənəl] ADJ poco convencional, original

unconvincing [ʌnkənˈvɪnsɪŋ] ADJ poco convincente

uncooperative [ʌnkəʊˈɒpərətɪv] ADJ poco cooperativo(a)

uncouth [ʌnˈkuːθ] ADJ *(rude)* grosero(a)

uncover [ʌnˈkʌvə(r)] VT destapar; *Fig* descubrir

undamaged [ʌnˈdæmɪdʒd] ADJ *(article etc)* sin desperfectos; *(person)* indemne; *(reputation)* intacto(a)

undaunted [ʌnˈdɔːntɪd] ADJ firme, impávido(a)

undecided [ʌndɪˈsaɪdɪd] ADJ **(a)** *(person)* indeciso(a) **(b)** *(issue)* pendiente; **it's still u.** está aún por decidir

undefeated [ʌndɪˈfiːtɪd] ADJ invicto(a)

undefined [ʌndɪˈfaɪnd] ADJ indeterminado(a)

undeniable [ʌndɪˈnaɪəbəl] ADJ innegable

under [ˈʌndə(r)] 1 PREP **(a)** *(beneath)* debajo de, bajo, *Am* abajo de; **u. the sun** bajo el sol **(b)** *(less than)* menos de; **incomes u. £1,000** ingresos inferiores a 1.000 libras; **u. age** menor de edad **(c)** *(of rank)* de rango inferior a **(d)** *(ruled by)* **u. Caesar** bajo César **(e)** *(subject to)* bajo; **u. arrest** detenido(a); **u. cover** a cubierto; **u. obligation to** en la obligación de; **u. the circumstances** dadas las circunstancias; *Fig* **I was u. the impression that …** tenía la impresión de que … **(f)** *(according to)* según, conforme a

2 ADV abajo, debajo

under- [ˈʌndə(r)] PREF *(below)* sub-, infra-; *(insufficiently)* insuficientemente

underarm [ˈʌndərɑːm] 1 ADJ **u. deodorant** desodorante m para las axilas

2 ADV *Sport* por debajo del hombro

undercarriage [ˈʌndəkærɪdʒ] N tren m de aterrizaje

undercharge [ʌndəˈtʃɑːdʒ] VT cobrar menos de lo debido

underclothes [ˈʌndəkləʊðz] NPL ropa f interior

undercoat [ˈʌndəkəʊt] N *(of paint)* primera mano

undercover [ʌndəˈkʌvə(r)] ADJ secreto(a)

undercurrent [ˈʌndəkʌrənt] N **(a)** *(in sea)* corriente submarina **(b)** *Fig* sentimiento m latente

undercut [ʌndəˈkʌt] VT *(pt & pp undercut)* *Com* vender más barato que

underdeveloped [ʌndədɪˈveləpt] ADJ subdesarrollado(a)

underdog [ˈʌndədɒg] N desvalido(a) m,f

underestimate [ʌndərˈestɪmeɪt] VT infravalorar

underexposure [ʌndərɪkˈspəʊʒə(r)] N *Phot* subexposición f

underfed [ʌndəˈfed] ADJ subalimentado(a)

underfoot [ʌndəˈfʊt] ADV en el suelo

undergo [ʌndəˈgəʊ] VT *(pt underwent; pp undergone* [ʌndəˈgɒn]*)* experimentar; *(change)* sufrir; *(test etc)* pasar por

undergraduate [ʌndəˈgrædjʊɪt] N estudiante mf universitario(a)

underground [ˈʌndəgraʊnd] 1 ADJ subterráneo(a); *Fig* clandestino(a)

2 N **(a)** *Pol* movimiento clandestino **(b)** *Br* **the u.** *(train)* el metro, *RP* el subte

3 ADJ [ʌndəˈgraʊnd] *Fig* **to go u.** pasar a la clandestinidad

undergrowth [ˈʌndəgrəʊθ] N maleza f

underhand 1 ADJ [ˈʌndəhænd] *(method)* ilícito(a); *(person)* solapado(a)

2 ADV [ʌndəˈhænd] bajo cuerda

underline [ʌndəˈlaɪn] VT subrayar

underling [ˈʌndəlɪŋ] N *Pej* mandado(a) m,f

underlying [ʌndə'laɪɪŋ] ADJ *(basic)* fundamental

undermine [ʌndə'maɪn] VT socavar, minar

underneath [ʌndə'ni:θ] 1 PREP debajo de, bajo
2 ADV abajo, debajo
3 ADJ de abajo
4 N parte f inferior

undernourished [ʌndə'nʌrɪʃt] ADJ desnutrido(a)

underpaid [ʌndə'peɪd] ADJ mal pagado(a)

underpants ['ʌndəpænts] NPL calzoncillos *mpl*, *Chile* fundillos *mpl*, *Méx* calzones *mpl*

underpass ['ʌndəpɑ:s] N paso subterráneo

underprivileged [ʌndə'prɪvɪlɪdʒd] 1 ADJ desfavorecido(a)
2 NPL the u. los menos favorecidos

underrate [ʌndə'reɪt] VT subestimar, infravalorar

under-secretary [ʌndə'sekrətəri] N subsecretario(a) *m,f*

undershirt ['ʌndəʃɜ:t] N *US* camiseta f

underside ['ʌndəsaɪd] N parte f inferior

underskirt ['ʌndəskɜ:t] N combinación f

understand [ʌndə'stænd] VT & VI *(pt & pp* **understood)** (a) *(comprehend)* entender, comprender; **do I make myself understood?** ¿me explico? (b) *(assume, believe)* entender; **she gave me to u. that …** me dio a entender que … (c) *(hear)* tener entendido; **to u. one another** entenderse

understandable [ʌndə'stændəbəl] ADJ comprensible

understanding [ʌndə'stændɪŋ] 1 N (a) *(intellectual grasp)* entendimiento *m*, comprensión f (b) *(interpretation)* interpretación f (c) *(agreement)* acuerdo *m* (d) **on the u. that …** a condición de que …
2 ADJ comprensivo(a)

understatement [ʌndə'steɪtmənt] N **to make an u.** minimizar, subestimar; **to say that the boy is rather clever is an u.** decir que el chico es bastante listo es quedarse corto

understood [ʌndə'stʊd] 1 ADJ (a) **I wish it to be u. that …** que conste que … (b) *(agreed on)* convenido(a) (c) *(implied)* sobreentendido(a)
2 PT & PP *of* understand

understudy ['ʌndəstʌdi] N suplente *mf*

undertake [ʌndə'teɪk] VT *(pt* **undertook**; *pp* **undertaken** [ʌndə'teɪkən]) (a) *(responsibility)* asumir; *(task, job)* encargarse de (b) *(promise)* comprometerse a

undertaker ['ʌndəteɪkə(r)] N empresario(a) *m,f* de pompas fúnebres; **u.'s** funeraria f

undertaking [ʌndə'teɪkɪŋ] N (a) *(task)* empresa f (b) *(promise)* compromiso *m*

undertone ['ʌndətəʊn] N **in an u.** en voz baja

undertook [ʌndə'tʊk] PT *of* undertake

underwater [ʌndə'wɔ:tə(r)] 1 ADJ submarino(a)
2 ADV bajo el agua

underwear ['ʌndəweə(r)] N ropa f interior

underwent [ʌndə'went] PT *of* undergo

underworld ['ʌndəwɜ:ld] N *(criminals)* hampa f, bajos fondos

underwrite [ʌndə'raɪt] VT *(pt* **underwrote**; *pp* **underwritten)** (a) *(guarantee)* garantizar, avalar (b) *(insure)* asegurar

underwriter ['ʌndəraɪtə(r)] N (a) *Fin* suscriptor(a) *m,f* (b) *(insurer)* asegurador(a) *m,f*

underwritten [ʌndə'rɪtən] PP *of* underwrite

underwrote [ʌndə'rəʊt] PT *of* underwrite

undesirable [ʌndɪ'zaɪrəbəl] ADJ & N indeseable *(mf)*

undeterred [ʌndɪ'tɜ:d] ADJ sin inmutarse; **u. by** sin arredrarse ante

undid [ʌn'dɪd] PT *of* undo

undies ['ʌndɪz] NPL *Fam* bragas *fpl*

undignified [ʌn'dɪgnɪfaɪd] ADJ *(attitude etc)* indecoroso(a)

undisciplined [ʌn'dɪsɪplɪnd] ADJ indisciplinado(a)

undisclosed [ʌndɪs'kləʊzd] ADJ sin revelar

undiscovered [ʌndɪs'kʌvəd] ADJ sin descubrir

undisguised [ʌndɪs'gaɪzd] ADJ *Fig* no disimulado(a)

undisputed [ʌndɪ'spju:tɪd] ADJ *(unchallenged)* incontestable; *(unquestionable)* indiscutible

undivided [ʌndɪ'vaɪdɪd] ADJ **to give one's u. attention** prestar toda la atención

undo [ʌn'du:] VT *(pt* **undid**; *pp* **undone)** (a) *(knot)* deshacer; *(button)* desabrochar (b) *(put right)* enmendar

undoing [ʌn'du:ɪŋ] N perdición f

undone¹ [ʌn'dʌn] ADJ *(unfinished)* inacabado(a)

undone² [ʌn'dʌn] 1 ADJ *(knot etc)* deshecho(a); **to come u.** *(shoelace)* desatarse; *(button, blouse)* desabrocharse; *(necklace etc)* soltarse
2 PP *of* undo

undoubted [ʌn'daʊtɪd] ADJ indudable

undress [ʌn'dres] 1 VT desnudar
2 VI desnudarse

undressed [ʌn'drest] ADJ *(naked)* desnudo(a)

undue [ʌn'dju:] ADJ (a) *(excessive)* excesivo(a) (b) *(improper)* indebido(a)

undulate ['ʌndjʊleɪt] VI ondular, ondear

unduly [ʌn'dju:li] ADV excesivamente

unearth [ʌn'ɜ:θ] VT desenterrar

unearthly [ʌn'ɜ:θli] ADJ (a) *(being)* sobrenatural (b) *Fam (din)* espantoso(a); **at an u. hour** a una hora intempestiva

uneasy [ʌn'i:zi] ADJ (a) *(worried)* preocupado(a); *(disturbing)* inquietante (b) *(uncomfortable)* incómodo(a)

uneconomic(al) [ʌni:kə'nɒmɪk(əl)] ADJ poco económico(a)

uneducated [ʌnˈedjʊkeɪtɪd] ADJ inculto(a)

unemployed [ʌnɪmˈplɔɪd] **1** ADJ desempleado(a), *Esp* parado(a), *Am* desocupado(a); **to be u.** estar desempleado(a) *or Esp* en (el) paro *or Am* desocupado(a)
2 NPL **the u.** los desempleados, *Esp* los parados, *Am* los desocupados

unemployment [ʌnɪmˈplɔɪmənt] N desempleo *m*, *Esp* paro *m*, *Am* desocupación *f*; **u. benefit**, *US* **u. compensation** subsidio *m* de desempleo *or Am* de desocupación

unending [ʌnˈendɪŋ] ADJ interminable

unenviable [ʌnˈenvɪəbəl] ADJ poco envidiable

unequal [ʌnˈiːkwəl] ADJ desigual

unequivocal [ʌnɪˈkwɪvəkəl] ADJ inequívoco(a)

uneven [ʌnˈiːvən] ADJ (**a**) *(not level)* desigual; *(bumpy)* accidentado(a) (**b**) *(variable)* irregular

uneventful [ʌnɪˈventfʊl] ADJ sin acontecimientos

unexceptional [ʌnɪkˈsepʃənəl] ADJ ordinario(a)

unexpected [ʌnɪkˈspektɪd] ADJ *(unhoped for)* inesperado(a); *(event)* imprevisto(a)

unexplained [ʌnɪksˈpleɪnd] ADJ inexplicado(a)

unfailing [ʌnˈfeɪlɪŋ] ADJ indefectible; *(incessant)* constante; *(patience)* inagotable

unfair [ʌnˈfeə(r)] ADJ injusto(a); *Sport* sucio(a)

unfaithful [ʌnˈfeɪθfʊl] ADJ *(friend)* desleal; *(husband, wife)* infiel

unfamiliar [ʌnfəˈmɪljə(r)] ADJ *(unknown)* desconocido(a); *(not conversant)* no familiarizado(a) (**with** con)

unfashionable [ʌnˈfæʃənəbəl] ADJ pasado(a) de moda; *(ideas etc)* poco popular

unfasten [ʌnˈfɑːsən] VT *(knot)* desatar; *(belt, clothing)* desabrochar

unfavourable, *US* **unfavorable** [ʌnˈfeɪvərəbəl] ADJ desfavorable; *(criticism)* adverso(a); *(winds)* contrario(a)

unfeeling [ʌnˈfiːlɪŋ] ADJ insensible

unfinished [ʌnˈfɪnɪʃt] ADJ inacabado(a); **u. business** un asunto pendiente

unfit [ʌnˈfɪt] ADJ (**a**) *(thing)* inadecuado(a); *(person)* no apto(a) (**for** para) (**b**) *(incompetent)* incompetente (**c**) *(physically)* incapacitado(a); **to be u.** no estar en forma

unflinching [ʌnˈflɪntʃɪŋ] ADJ (**a**) *(determined)* resuelto(a) (**b**) *(fearless)* impávido(a)

unfold [ʌnˈfəʊld] **1** VT (**a**) *(sheet)* desdoblar; *(newspaper)* abrir (**b**) *(plan, secret)* revelar
2 VI (**a**) *(open up)* abrirse; *(landscape)* extenderse (**b**) *(plot)* desarrollarse (**c**) *(secret)* descubrirse

unforeseeable [ʌnfəˈsiːəbəl] ADJ imprevisible

unforeseen [ʌnfɔːˈsiːn] ADJ imprevisto(a)

unforgettable [ʌnfəˈgetəbəl] ADJ inolvidable

unforgivable [ʌnfəˈgɪvəbəl] ADJ imperdonable

unfortunate [ʌnˈfɔːtʃənɪt] ADJ *(person, event)* desgraciado(a); *(remark)* desafortunado(a); **how u.!** ¡qué mala suerte!

unfortunately [ʌnˈfɔːtʃənɪtlɪ] ADV desgraciadamente, por desgracia

unfounded [ʌnˈfaʊndɪd] ADJ infundado(a)

unfriendly [ʌnˈfrendlɪ] ADJ (**unfriendlier, unfriendliest**) antipático(a), poco amistoso(a)

unfulfilled [ʌnfʊlˈfɪld] ADJ **to feel u.** sentirse insatisfecho(a)

unfurl [ʌnˈfɜːl] VI desplegarse

unfurnished [ʌnˈfɜːnɪʃt] ADJ sin amueblar

ungainly [ʌnˈgeɪnlɪ] ADJ *(gait)* desgarbado(a)

ungodly [ʌnˈgɒdlɪ] ADJ (**ungodlier, ungodliest**) *(behaviour)* impío(a); *Fam Fig* **at an u. hour** a una hora intempestiva

ungrateful [ʌnˈgreɪtfʊl] ADJ *(person)* desagradecido(a); *(task)* ingrato(a)

unguarded [ʌnˈgɑːdɪd] ADJ (**a**) *(unprotected)* desatendido(a); *(imprudent)* desprevenido(a) (**b**) *(frank)* franco(a)

unhappiness [ʌnˈhæpɪnɪs] N (**a**) *(sadness)* tristeza *f* (**b**) *(wretchedness)* desdicha *f*

unhappy [ʌnˈhæpɪ] ADJ (**unhappier, unhappiest**) (**a**) *(sad)* triste (**b**) *(wretched)* desgraciado(a), infeliz; *(unfortunate)* desafortunado(a)

unharmed [ʌnˈhɑːmd] ADJ ileso(a), indemne

unhealthy [ʌnˈhelθɪ] ADJ (**unhealthier, unhealthiest**) (**a**) *(ill)* enfermizo(a) (**b**) *(unwholesome)* malsano(a)

unheard [ʌnˈhɜːd] ADJ (**a**) **her request went u.** su petición no fue atendida (**b**) **u. of** *(outrageous)* inaudito(a); *(without precedent)* sin precedente

unhelpful [ʌnˈhelpfʊl] ADJ *(person)* poco servicial; *(criticism, advice)* poco constructivo(a)

unhesitating [ʌnˈhezɪteɪtɪŋ] ADJ resuelto(a)

unhook [ʌnˈhʊk] VT *(from hook)* descolgar; *(clothing)* desabrochar

unhurt [ʌnˈhɜːt] ADJ ileso(a), indemne

unhygienic [ʌnhaɪˈdʒiːnɪk] ADJ antihigiénico(a)

unidentified [ʌnaɪˈdentɪfaɪd] ADJ **u. flying object** objeto volador no identificado, ovni *m*

unification [juːnɪfɪˈkeɪʃən] N unificación *f*

uniform [ˈjuːnɪfɔːm] ADJ & N uniforme *(m)*

uniformity [juːnɪˈfɔːmɪtɪ] N uniformidad *f*

unify [ˈjuːnɪfaɪ] VT unificar

unilateral [juːnɪˈlætərəl] ADJ unilateral

unimaginative [ʌnɪˈmædʒɪnətɪv] ADJ **to be u.** *(of person)* tener poca imaginación; *(of book, choice)* ser muy poco original, no tener originalidad

unimportant [ʌnɪmˈpɔːtənt] ADJ poco importante

uninformed [ʌnɪnˈfɔːmd] ADJ *(opinion)* sin fundamento

uninhabited [ʌnɪnˈhæbɪtɪd] ADJ despoblado(a)

uninhibited [ʌnɪnˈhɪbɪtɪd] ADJ sin inhibición

uninspired [ʌnɪnˈspaɪəd] ADJ *(person)* falto(a) de inspiración; *(performance)* insulso(a)

uninspiring [ʌnɪnˈspaɪərɪŋ] ADJ que no inspira

unintelligible [ʌnɪnˈtelɪdʒəbəl] ADJ ininteligible, incomprensible

unintentional [ʌnɪnˈtenʃənəl] ADJ involuntario(a)

unintentionally [ʌnɪnˈtenʃənəlɪ] ADV sin querer

uninterested [ʌnˈɪntərestɪd] ADJ poco interesado(a)

uninteresting [ʌnˈɪntrɪstɪŋ] ADJ poco interesante

uninterrupted [ʌnɪntəˈrʌptɪd] ADJ ininterrumpido(a)

union [ˈjuːnjən] **1** N (**a**) *(of countries)* unión f (**b**) *(organization)* sindicato m (**c**) *US* **the U.** los Estados Unidos; *Br* **U. Jack** bandera f del Reino Unido
2 ADJ sindical

unique [juːˈniːk] ADJ único(a)

unison [ˈjuːnɪsən] N *Mus* unisonancia f; *Fig (harmony)* armonía f; **in u.** al unísono

unit [ˈjuːnɪt] N (**a**) *(subdivision)* unidad f; **monetary u.** unidad monetaria; *Br Fin* **u. trust** sociedad f de inversiones (**b**) *(piece of furniture)* módulo m; **kitchen u.** mueble m de cocina (**c**) *Tech* grupo m; *Comput* **central processing u.** procesador m central; **visual display u.** monitor m (**d**) *(department)* servicio m (**e**) *(team)* equipo m

unite [juːˈnaɪt] **1** VT unir
2 VI unirse

united [juːˈnaɪtɪd] ADJ unido(a); **U. Kingdom** Reino Unido; **U. States (of America)** Estados Unidos (de América); **U. Nations** Naciones Unidas

unity [ˈjuːnɪtɪ] N unidad f; *(harmony)* armonía f

universal [juːnɪˈvɜːsəl] ADJ universal

universe [ˈjuːnɪvɜːs] N universo m

university [juːnɪˈvɜːsɪtɪ] **1** N universidad f
2 ADJ universitario(a)

unjust [ʌnˈdʒʌst] ADJ injusto(a)

unkempt [ʌnˈkempt] ADJ descuidado(a); *(hair)* despeinado(a); *(appearance)* desaliñado(a)

unkind [ʌnˈkaɪnd] ADJ *(not nice)* poco amable; *(cruel)* despiadado(a)

unknowingly [ʌnˈnəʊɪŋlɪ] ADV inconscientemente, inadvertidamente

unknown [ʌnˈnəʊn] **1** ADJ desconocido(a); **u. quantity** incógnita f
2 N **the u.** lo desconocido

unlawful [ʌnˈlɔːfʊl] ADJ *(not legal)* ilegal

unleaded [ʌnˈledɪd] ADJ **u.** *Br* **petrol** or *US* **gasoline** gasolina f or *RP* nafta f sin plomo

unleash [ʌnˈliːʃ] VT (**a**) *(dog)* soltar (**b**) *Fig (release)* liberar; *(provoke)* desencadenar

unless [ʌnˈles] CONJ a menos que, a no ser que

unlike [ʌnˈlaɪk] **1** ADJ diferente, distinto(a)
2 PREP a diferencia de

unlikely [ʌnˈlaɪklɪ] ADJ (**a**) *(improbable)* poco probable (**b**) *(unusual)* raro(a)

unlimited [ʌnˈlɪmɪtɪd] ADJ ilimitado(a)

unlisted [ʌnˈlɪstɪd] ADJ *US Tel* que no figura en la guía (telefónica)

unload [ʌnˈləʊd] VT & VI descargar

unlock [ʌnˈlɒk] VT abrir (con llave)

unluckily [ʌnˈlʌkɪlɪ] ADV desafortunadamente, por desgracia

unlucky [ʌnˈlʌkɪ] ADJ (**unluckier, unluckiest**) *(unfortunate)* desgraciado(a); **to be u.** *(person)* tener mala suerte; *(thing)* traer mala suerte

unmade [ˈʌnmeɪd] ADJ *(bed)* deshecho(a), sin hacer

unmanageable [ʌnˈmænɪdʒəbəl] ADJ *(people)* ingobernable; *(child, hair)* incontrolable

unmanned [ʌnˈmænd] ADJ *(spacecraft etc)* no tripulado(a)

unmarried [ʌnˈmærɪd] ADJ soltero(a)

unmask [ʌnˈmɑːsk] VT *Fig (plot)* descubrir

unmistak(e)able [ʌnmɪsˈteɪkəbəl] ADJ inconfundible

unmistak(e)ably [ʌnmɪsˈteɪkəblɪ] ADV sin lugar a dudas

unmitigated [ʌnˈmɪtɪgeɪtɪd] ADJ (**a**) *(absolute)* absoluto(a); *(liar)* rematado(a) (**b**) *(grief)* profundo(a)

unmoved [ʌnˈmuːvd] ADV **to watch/listen u.** observar/escuchar impertérrito(a)

unnamed [ʌnˈneɪmd] ADJ *(anonymous)* anónimo(a)

unnatural [ʌnˈnætʃərəl] ADJ (**a**) *(against nature)* antinatural; *(abnormal)* anormal (**b**) *(affected)* afectado(a)

unnecessary [ʌnˈnesɪsərɪ] ADJ innecesario(a), inútil; **it's u. to add that ...** sobra añadir que ...

unnoticed [ʌnˈnəʊtɪst] ADJ desapercibido(a); **to let sth pass u.** pasar algo por alto

unobserved [ʌnɒbˈzɜːvd] ADJ inadvertido(a)

unobtainable [ʌnəbˈteɪnəbəl] ADJ inasequible, inalcanzable

unobtrusive [ʌnəbˈtruːsɪv] ADJ discreto(a)

unoccupied [ʌnˈɒkjʊpaɪd] ADJ *(house)* desocupado(a); *(seat)* libre

unofficial [ʌnəˈfɪʃəl] ADJ no oficial; *Ind* **u. strike** huelga f no apoyada por los sindicatos

unorthodox [ʌnˈɔːθədɒks] ADJ (**a**) *(behaviour etc)* poco ortodoxo(a) (**b**) *Rel* heterodoxo(a)

unpack [ʌnˈpæk] **1** VT *(boxes)* desembalar; *(suitcase)* deshacer, *Am* desempacar
2 VI deshacer la(s) maleta(s)

unpaid [ʌnˈpeɪd] ADJ (**a**) *(work, volunteer)* no retribuido(a) (**b**) *(bill, debt)* impagado(a)

unpalatable [ʌnˈpælətəbəl] ADJ desagradable

unparalleled [ʌnˈpærəleld] ADJ (**a**) *(in quality)* incomparable (**b**) *(without precedent)* sin precedente

unpardonable [ʌnˈpɑːdənəbəl] ADJ imperdonable

unperturbed [ʌnpəˈtɜːbd] ADJ impasible

unpleasant [ʌn'plezənt] ADJ desagradable (**to con**)

unpleasantness [ʌn'plezəntnɪs] N disgusto m

unplug [ʌn'plʌg] VT desenchufar

unpopular [ʌn'pɒpjʊlə(r)] ADJ impopular; **to make oneself u.** ganarse la antipatía de todos

unprecedented [ʌn'presɪdentɪd] ADJ sin precedente

unpredictable [ʌnprɪ'dɪktəbəl] ADJ imprevisible

unprepared [ʌnprɪ'peəd] ADJ (speech etc) improvisado(a); (person) desprevenido(a)

unprincipled [ʌn'prɪnsɪpəld] ADJ sin escrúpulos

unprintable [ʌn'prɪntəbəl] ADJ (word, comment) malsonante

unproductive [ʌnprə'dʌktɪv] ADJ (inefficient) improductivo(a); (fruitless) infructuoso(a)

unprofessional [ʌnprə'feʃənəl] ADJ (unethical) poco profesional; (substandard) de aficionado(a)

unprotected [ʌnprə'tektɪd] ADJ indefenso(a)

unprovoked [ʌnprə'vəʊkt] ADJ gratuito(a)

unpublished [ʌn'pʌblɪʃt] ADJ inédito(a)

unpunished [ʌn'pʌnɪʃt] ADJ impune

unqualified [ʌn'kwɒlɪfaɪd] ADJ (**a**) (without qualification) sin título; (incompetent) incompetente (**b**) (unconditional) incondicional; (denial) rotundo(a); (endorsement) sin reserva; (success) total

unquestionable [ʌn'kwestʃənəbəl] ADJ indiscutible

unquestioning [ʌn'kwestʃənɪŋ] ADJ incondicional; (obedience) ciego(a)

unravel [ʌn'rævəl] **1** VT desenmarañar
2 VI desenmarañarse

unreadable [ʌn'riːdəbəl] ADJ (**a**) (handwriting) ilegible (**b**) (book) imposible de leer

unreal [ʌn'rɪəl] ADJ irreal

unrealistic [ʌnrɪə'lɪstɪk] ADJ poco realista

unreasonable [ʌn'riːzənəbəl] ADJ poco razonable; (demands) desmedido(a); (prices) exorbitante; (hour) inoportuno(a)

unrecognizable [ʌnrekəg'naɪzəbl] ADJ irreconocible

unrefined [ʌnrɪ'faɪnd] ADJ (**a**) (sugar, oil etc) sin refinar (**b**) (person) tosco(a), basto(a)

unrelated [ʌnrɪ'leɪtɪd] ADJ (not connected) no relacionado(a)

unrelenting [ʌnrɪ'lentɪŋ] ADJ (behaviour) implacable; (struggle) encarnizado(a)

unreliable [ʌnrɪ'laɪəbəl] ADJ (**a**) (person) de poca confianza (**b**) (information) que no es de fiar; (machine) poco fiable

unrelieved [ʌnrɪ'liːvd] ADJ (boredom) total

unremitting [ʌnrɪ'mɪtɪŋ] ADJ (**a**) (efforts etc) incesante (**b**) (person) incansable

unrepentant [ʌnrɪ'pentənt] ADJ impenitente

unreserved [ʌnrɪ'zɜːvd] ADJ (praise, support) sin reserva

unreservedly [ʌnrɪ'zɜːvɪdlɪ] ADV sin reserva

unrest [ʌn'rest] N (social etc) malestar m; **political u.** agitación política

unrivalled, US **unrivaled** [ʌn'raɪvəld] ADJ sin par, sin rival

unroll [ʌn'rəʊl] VT desenrollar

unruffled [ʌn'rʌfəld] ADJ Fig tranquilo(a)

unruly [ʌn'ruːlɪ] ADJ (unrulier, unruliest) (**a**) (child) revoltoso(a) (**b**) (hair) rebelde

unsafe [ʌn'seɪf] ADJ (dangerous) peligroso(a); (risky) inseguro(a); **to feel u.** sentirse expuesto(a)

unsaid [ʌn'sed] ADJ **it's better left u.** más vale no decir nada; **much was left u.** quedó mucho por decir

unsatisfactory [ʌnsætɪs'fæktərɪ] ADJ insatisfactorio(a); **it's most u.** deja mucho que desear

unsavoury, US **unsavory** [ʌn'seɪvərɪ] ADJ desagradable

unscathed [ʌn'skeɪðd] ADJ ileso(a), indemne

unscrew [ʌn'skruː] VT destornillar

unscrupulous [ʌn'skruːpjʊləs] ADJ sin escrúpulos

unseemly [ʌn'siːmlɪ] ADJ impropio(a)

unseen [ʌn'siːn] **1** ADJ invisible; (unnoticed) inadvertido(a)
2 N Br Educ = texto no trabajado en clase

unselfish [ʌn'selfɪʃ] ADJ desinteresado(a)

unsettle [ʌn'setəl] VT perturbar

unsettled [ʌn'setəld] ADJ (**a**) (person) nervioso(a); (situation) inestable (**b**) (weather) inestable (**c**) (matter, debt) pendiente (**d**) (land) sin colonizar

unshaven [ʌn'ʃeɪvən] ADJ sin afeitar

unsightly [ʌn'saɪtlɪ] ADJ feo(a), desagradable

unskilled [ʌn'skɪld] ADJ (worker) no cualificado(a); (work) no especializado(a)

unsociable [ʌn'səʊʃəbəl] ADJ insociable, huraño(a)

unsophisticated [ʌnsə'fɪstɪkeɪtd] ADJ (**a**) (naïve) ingenuo(a) (**b**) (simple) poco sofisticado(a)

unsound [ʌn'saʊnd] ADJ (**a**) (unstable) inestable; **of u. mind** demente (**b**) (fallacious) falso(a)

unspeakable [ʌn'spiːkəbəl] ADJ (**a**) (pain) indecible (**b**) (conditions, squalor) inefable

unspoken [ʌn'spəʊkən] ADJ (**a**) (tacit) tácito(a) (**b**) (feeling) interior, secreto(a)

unstable [ʌn'steɪbəl] ADJ inestable

unsteady [ʌn'stedɪ] ADJ (not firm) inestable; (table, chair) cojo(a); (hand, voice) tembloroso(a)

unstinting [ʌn'stɪntɪŋ] ADJ pródigo(a) (**in** en)

unstuck [ʌn'stʌk] ADJ **to come u.** despegarse; Fig venirse abajo

unsuccessful [ʌnsək'sesful] ADJ (**a**) *(fruitless)* fracasado(a); *(useless)* vano(a) (**b**) *(businessman etc)* fracasado(a); *(candidate)* derrotado(a); **to be u. at sth** no tener éxito con algo

unsuccessfully [ʌnsək'sesfuli] ADV sin éxito, en vano

unsuitable [ʌn'su:təbəl] ADJ (**a**) *(person)* no apto(a) (**b**) *(thing)* inadecuado(a); *(remark)* inoportuno(a); *(time)* inconveniente

unsuited [ʌn'su:tɪd] ADJ (**a**) *(person)* no apto(a); *(thing)* impropio(a) (**to** para) (**b**) *(incompatible)* incompatible

unsure [ʌn'ʃʊə(r)] ADJ poco seguro(a)

unsuspecting [ʌnsə'spektɪŋ] ADJ confiado(a); **he went in u.** entró sin sospechar nada

unswerving [ʌn'swɜ:vɪŋ] ADJ firme

unsympathetic [ʌnsɪmpə'θetɪk] ADJ *(unfeeling)* impasible; *(not understanding)* poco comprensivo(a)

untangle [ʌn'tæŋɡəl] VT desenredar, desenmarañar

untapped [ʌn'tæpt] ADJ *(resource)* sin explotar

untarnished [ʌn'tɑ:nɪʃt] ADJ *Fig* sin mancha

untenable [ʌn'tenəbəl] ADJ insostenible

unthinkable [ʌn'θɪŋkəbəl] ADJ impensable, inconcebible

untidy [ʌn'taɪdɪ] ADJ (**untidier, untidiest**) *(room, person)* desordenado(a); *(hair)* despeinado(a); *(appearance)* desaseado(a)

untie [ʌn'taɪ] VT desatar; *(free)* soltar

until [ʌn'tɪl] **1** CONJ hasta que; **she worked u. she collapsed** trabajó hasta desfallecer; **u. she gets back** hasta que vuelva
2 PREP hasta; **u. now** hasta ahora; **u. ten o'clock** hasta las diez; **not u. Monday** hasta el lunes no

untimely [ʌn'taɪmlɪ] ADJ (**a**) *(premature)* prematuro(a) (**b**) *(inopportune)* inoportuno(a); *(hour)* intempestivo(a)

untold [ʌn'təʊld] ADJ (**a**) *(indescribable)* indecible (**b**) *Fig (loss, wealth)* incalculable (**c**) *(not told)* sin contar

untouchable [ʌn'tʌtʃəbəl] ADJ & N intocable *(mf)*

untoward [ʌntə'wɔ:d] ADJ (**a**) *(unfortunate)* desafortunado(a) (**b**) *(adverse)* adverso(a)

untrained [ʌn'treɪnd] ADJ (**a**) *(unskilled)* sin preparación profesional (**b**) *(inexpert)* inexperto(a)

untrue [ʌn'tru:] ADJ (**a**) *(false)* falso(a) (**b**) *(unfaithful)* infiel (**c**) *(inexact)* inexacto(a)

untrustworthy [ʌn'trʌstwɜ:ðɪ] ADJ (**a**) *(person)* de poca confianza (**b**) *(source)* no fidedigno(a)

untruthful [ʌn'tru:θful] ADJ *(person)* embustero(a), mentiroso(a); *(story, reply)* falso(a)

unused ADJ (**a**) [ʌn'ju:zd] *(car)* sin usar; *(flat etc)* sin estrenar; *(stamp)* sin matar (**b**) *(not in use)* que ya no se utiliza (**c**) [ʌn'ju:st] *(unaccustomed)* desacostumbrado(a) (**to** a)

unusual [ʌn'ju:ʒʊəl] ADJ *(rare)* insólito(a), poco común; *(original)* original; *(exceptional)* excepcional

unusually [ʌn'ju:ʒʊəlɪ] ADV excepcionalmente

unveil [ʌn'veɪl] VT descubrir

unwanted [ʌn'wɒntɪd] ADJ *(attentions, baby)* no deseado(a); *(clothes, trinkets)* desechado(a)

unwarranted [ʌn'wɒrəntɪd] ADJ injustificado(a); *(remark)* gratuito(a)

unwavering [ʌn'weɪvərɪŋ] ADJ *(loyalty)* constante, firme; *(courage)* inquebrantable

unwelcome [ʌn'welkəm] ADJ *(visitor)* molesto(a); *(visit)* inoportuno(a); *Fig (news etc)* desagradable

unwell [ʌn'wel] ADJ malo(a), indispuesto(a)

unwieldy [ʌn'wi:ldɪ] ADJ *(difficult to handle)* poco manejable; *(clumsy)* torpe

unwilling [ʌn'wɪlɪŋ] ADJ **to be u. to do sth** no estar dispuesto a hacer algo

unwillingly [ʌn'wɪlɪŋlɪ] ADV de mala gana

unwind [ʌn'waɪnd] **1** VT *(pt & pp* **unwound**) desenrollar
2 VI (**a**) *(string, wool)* desenrollarse (**b**) *(relax)* relajarse

unwise [ʌn'waɪz] ADJ imprudente, desaconsejable

unwitting [ʌn'wɪtɪŋ] ADJ involuntario(a)

unworkable [ʌn'wɜ:kəbəl] ADJ *(not feasible)* impracticable; *(suggestion)* irrealizable

unworthy [ʌn'wɜ:ðɪ] ADJ indigno(a)

unwound [ʌn'waʊnd] PT & PP *of* **unwind**

unwrap [ʌn'ræp] VT *(gift)* desenvolver; *(package)* deshacer

unwritten [ʌn'rɪtən] ADJ no escrito(a); *(agreement)* verbal

unyielding [ʌn'ji:ldɪŋ] ADJ inflexible

unzip [ʌnzɪp] *(pt & pp* **unzipped**) VT abrir la cremallera *or Am* el cierre de

up [ʌp] **1** PREP (**a**) *(movement)* **to climb up the mountain** escalar la montaña; **to walk up the street** caminar *or Esp* andar por la calle (**b**) *(position)* en lo alto de; **further up the street** más adelante (en la misma calle); **halfway up the ladder** a mitad de la escalera
2 ADV (**a**) *(upwards)* arriba, hacia arriba; *(position)* arriba; **from £10 up** de 10 libras para arriba; **halfway up** a medio camino; **right up (to the top)** hasta arriba (del todo); **to go/come up** subir; **this side up** *(sign)* este lado hacia arriba
(**b**) **the moon is up** ha salido la luna
(**c**) *(towards)* hacia; **to come** *or* **go up to sb** acercarse a algn; **to walk up and down** ir de un lado a otro
(**d**) *(in, to)* **he's up in Yorkshire** está en Yorkshire
(**e**) *(increased)* **bread is up** el pan ha subido
(**f**) **it's up for discussion** se está discutiendo; **up for sale** en venta
(**g**) *Fam* **something's up** pasa algo; **what's up (with you)?** ¿qué pasa (contigo)?

(**h**) **to be up against sth** enfrentarse con algo (**i**) **up to** (*as far as, until*) hasta; **I can spend up to £5** puedo gastar un máximo de 5 libras; **up to here** hasta aquí; **up to now** hasta ahora (**j**) **to be up to** (*depend on*) depender de; (*be capable of*) estar a la altura de; **I don't feel up to doing it today** hoy no me encuentro con fuerzas para hacerlo; **it's not up to much** no vale gran cosa (**k**) **he's up to sth** está tramando algo

3 ADJ (**a**) (*out of bed*) levantado(a) (**b**) (*finished*) terminado(a); **time's up** (ya) es la hora

4 VT *Fam* aumentar

5 N *Fig* **ups and downs** altibajos *mpl*

up-and-coming ['ʌpən'kʌmɪŋ] ADJ prometedor(a)

upbringing ['ʌpbrɪŋɪŋ] N educación *f*

update [ʌp'deɪt] VT actualizar, poner al día

upgrade 1 VT [ʌp'greɪd] (**a**) (*promote*) ascender (**b**) (*improve*) mejorar la calidad de (**c**) *Comput* (*software, hardware*) actualizar **2** N ['ʌpgreɪd] *Comput* actualización *f*

upheaval [ʌp'hiːvəl] N trastorno *m*

upheld [ʌp'held] PT & PP of **uphold**

uphill ADJ ['ʌphɪl] ascendente; *Fig* arduo(a) **2** ADV [ʌp'hɪl] cuesta arriba

uphold [ʌp'həʊld] VT (*pt & pp* **upheld**) sostener

upholstery [ʌp'həʊlstəri] N tapizado *m*, tapicería *f*

upkeep ['ʌpkiːp] N mantenimiento *m*

up-market ['ʌpmaːkɪt] ADJ de categoría

upon [ə'pɒn] PREP *Fml* en, sobre; **once u. a time ...** érase una vez ...; **u. my word** (mi) palabra de honor

upper ['ʌpə(r)] **1** ADJ (**a**) (*position*) superior; **u. storey** piso de arriba; *Fig* **to have the u. hand** llevar la delantera (**b**) (*in rank*) alto(a); **the u. class** la clase alta; **the U. House** la Cámara Alta **2** N (*of shoe*) pala *f*

upper-class ['ʌpə'klæs] ADJ de la clase alta

uppermost ['ʌpəməʊst] ADJ más alto(a); *Fig* **it was u. in my mind** era lo que me preocupaba más

upright ['ʌpraɪt] **1** ADJ (**a**) (*vertical*) vertical (**b**) (*honest*) honrado(a) **2** ADV derecho **3** N *Ftb* (*post*) poste *m*

uprising ['ʌpraɪzɪŋ] N sublevación *f*

uproar ['ʌprɔː(r)] N tumulto *m*, alboroto *m*

uproot [ʌp'ruːt] VT (*plant*) arrancar de raíz

upset [ʌp'set] **1** VT (*pt & pp* **upset**) (**a**) (*overturn*) volcar; (*spill*) derramar (**b**) (*shock*) trastornar; (*worry*) preocupar; (*displease*) disgustar (**c**) (*spoil*) desbaratar (**d**) (*make ill*) sentar mal a **2** ADJ (*shocked*) alterado(a); (*displeased*) disgustado(a); **to have an u. stomach** sentirse mal del estómago **3** N ['ʌpset] (**a**) (*reversal*) revés *m* (**b**) *Sport* resultado inesperado

upshot ['ʌpʃɒt] N resultado *m*

upside down ['ʌpsaɪd'daʊn] ADJ & ADV al revés

upstage [ʌp'steɪdʒ] VT *Fam* eclipsar

upstairs [ʌp'steəz] **1** ADV al piso de arriba; **she lives u.** vive en el piso de arriba **2** N piso *m* de arriba

upstart ['ʌpstaːt] N advenedizo(a) *m,f*

upstream [ʌp'striːm] ADV río arriba

uptake ['ʌpteɪk] N *Fam* **to be quick on the u.** cogerlas al vuelo

uptight [ʌp'taɪt] ADJ *Fam* nervioso(a)

up-to-date [ʌptə'deɪt] ADJ (**a**) (*current*) al día (**b**) (*modern*) moderno(a)

uptown ['ʌptaʊn] N *US* zona *f* residencial

upturn ['ʌptɜːn] N mejora *f*

upward ['ʌpwəd] ADJ ascendente

upward(s) ['ʌpwəd(z)] ADV hacia arriba; **from ten (years) u.** a partir de los diez años; *Fam* **u. of** algo más de

uranium [jʊ'reɪnɪəm] N uranio *m*

urban ['ɜːbən] ADJ urbano(a)

urbane [ɜː'beɪn] ADJ urbano(a), cortés

urchin ['ɜːtʃɪn] N (**a**) (*child*) pilluelo(a) *m,f* (**b**) **sea u.** erizo *m* de mar

urge [ɜːdʒ] **1** VT (**a**) (*encourage*) instar; (*plead*) exhortar (**b**) (*advocate*) preconizar; **to u. that sth should be done** insistir en que se haga algo **2** N impulso *m*

▸ **urge on** VT SEP animar a

urgency ['ɜːdʒənsɪ] N urgencia *f*

urgent ['ɜːdʒənt] ADJ urgente; (*need, tone*) apremiante

urinal [jʊ'raɪnəl] N (*toilet*) urinario *m*; (*bowl*) orinal *m*

urinate ['jʊərɪneɪt] VI orinar

urine ['jʊərɪn] N orina *f*

URL [juːaː'rel] N *Comput* (*abbr* **uniform resource locator**) URL *m*

urn [ɜːn] N (**a**) (*decorative, funerary*) urna *f* (**b**) **tea u.** tetera *f* grande

Uruguay ['jʊərəgwaɪ] N Uruguay

Uruguayan [jʊərə'gwaɪən] ADJ & N uruguayo(a) (*m,f*)

US [juː'es] N (*abbr* **United States**) EE.UU. *mpl*

us [ʌs, *unstressed* əs] PERS PRON (**a**) (*as object*) nos; **let's forget it** olvidémoslo (**b**) (*after prep*) nosotros(as); **both of us** nosotros dos; **he's one of us** es de los nuestros (**c**) (*after v to be*) nosotros(as); **she wouldn't believe it was us** no creía que fuéramos nosotros (**d**) *Fam* me; **give us a kiss!** ¡dame un beso!

USA [juːes'eɪ] N (*abbr* **United States of America**) EE.UU. *mpl*

usage ['juːsɪdʒ] N (**a**) (*habit, custom*) costumbre *f* (**b**) *Ling* uso *m*

use 1 VT [juːz] (**a**) (*utilize*) usar, utilizar; **what is it used for?** ¿para qué sirve?; **to u. force** hacer uso de la fuerza (**b**) (*consume*) consumir,

gastar (**c**) *(take unfair advantage of)* aprovecharse de (**d**) *Fam* **I could u. a drink** no me
vendría mal un trago
 2 N [ju:s] (**a**) *(utilization)* uso *m*; **directions for
u.** modo de empleo; **in u.** en uso; **not in u.** *(on
lift)* no funciona; **ready for u.** listo para usar;
to make (good) u. of sth aprovechar algo; **to
put to good u.** sacar partido de (**b**) *(application)* aplicación *f* (**c**) *(usefulness)* utilidad *f*;
it's no u. es inútil; **what's the u.?** ¿para qué?;
Fam **it's no u. crying** no sirve de nada llorar; **of
u.** útil; **to be of u.** servir
 3 V AUX **used to** ['ju:stə] soler, acostumbrar;
where did you u. to live? ¿dónde vivías
(antes)?

> Como verbo auxiliar, aparece siempre en la
> forma **used to**. Se traduce al español por el
> verbo principal en pretérito imperfecto, o
> por el pretérito imperfecto de **soler** más
> infinitivo.

▸ **use up** VT SEP acabar
use-by date ['ju:zbaɪdeɪt] N *Com* fecha *f* de
caducidad
used ADJ (**a**) [ju:zd] *(second-hand)* usado(a) (**b**)
[ju:st] **to be u. to** estar acostumbrado(a) a
useful ['ju:sful] ADJ útil; *(practical)* práctico(a);
Br **to come in u.** venir bien
usefulness ['ju:sfulnɪs] N utilidad *f*
useless ['ju:slɪs] ADJ inútil
user ['ju:zə(r)] N (**a**) *(of road, dictionary,
computer)* usuario(a) *m,f* (**b**) *Fam (of drugs)*
drogadicto(a) *m,f*
user-friendly [ju:zə'frendlɪ] ADJ *also Comput*
de fácil manejo
usher ['ʌʃə(r)] **1** N (**a**) *Cin & Th* acomodador(a)
m,f (**b**) *(in court etc)* ujier *m*
 2 VT **to u. in** *Cin & Th* acomodar; *(at home)*

hacer pasar; **to u. out** acompañar hasta la
puerta
USSR [ju:eses'ɑ:(r)] N *Hist (abbr* **Union of Soviet
Socialist Republics)** URSS *f*
usual ['ju:ʒʊəl] **1** ADJ corriente, normal; **as u.**
como siempre; **at the u. hour** a la hora
habitual; **earlier than u.** más pronto que de
costumbre; **the u. problems** los problemas de
siempre
 2 N lo habitual; **out of the u.** fuera de lo
común
usually ['ju:ʒʊəlɪ] ADV normalmente
usurp [ju:'zɜ:p] VT usurpar
utensil [ju:'tensəl] N utensilio *m*; **kitchen
utensils** batería *f* de cocina
uterus ['ju:tərəs] N útero *m*
utilitarian [ju:tɪlɪ'teərɪən] ADJ (**a**) *(in philosophy)* utilitarista (**b**) *(useful)* utilitario(a)
utility [ju:'tɪlɪtɪ] N (**a**) *(usefulness)* utilidad *f*; **u.
room** cuarto *m* de planchar; *(for storage)*
trascocina *f* (**b**) **(public) u.** empresa *f* de
servicio público
utilize ['ju:tɪlaɪz] VT utilizar
utmost ['ʌtməʊst] **1** ADJ sumo(a); **of the u.
importance** de suma importancia
 2 N máximo *m*; **to do** *or* **try one's u.** hacer
todo lo posible; **to the u.** al máximo, a más no
poder
utopian [ju:'təʊpɪən] ADJ utópico(a)
utter¹ ['ʌtə(r)] VT *(words)* pronunciar; *(sigh)*
dar; *(cry, threat)* lanzar
utter² ['ʌtə(r)] ADJ total, completo(a)
utterance ['ʌtərəns] N declaración *f*
utterly ['ʌtəlɪ] ADV completamente, totalmente
U-turn ['ju:tɜ:n] N cambio *m* de sentido; *Pol* giro
m de 180 grados

V

V, v [viː] N *(the letter)* V, v f

V *(abbr* **volt(s))** V

v (**a**) *(abbr* **verse**) v (**b**) *(abbr* **versus**) contra

vacancy ['veɪkənsɪ] N (**a**) *(job)* vacante f (**b**) *(room)* habitación f libre; **no vacancies** *(sign)* completo

vacant ['veɪkənt] ADJ (**a**) *(empty)* vacío(a) (**b**) *(job)* vacante; *Br* **situations v.** *(in newspaper)* ofertas de trabajo (**c**) *(free, not in use)* libre

vacate [və'keɪt] VT *(flat)* desalojar

vacation [və'keɪʃən] 1 N *Br Univ & US* vacaciones *fpl*; **on v.** de vacaciones
2 VI *US* pasar las vacaciones (**in/at** en)

vacationer [və'keɪʃənə(r)] N *US* turista *mf; (in summer)* veraneante *mf*

vaccinate ['væksɪneɪt] VT vacunar

vaccination [væksɪ'neɪʃən] N *Med* vacunación f

vaccine ['væksiːn] N vacuna f

vacuum ['vækjʊəm] 1 N vacío m; **v. cleaner** aspiradora f; *Br* **v. flask** termo m
2 VT *(carpet, room)* pasar la aspiradora por

vacuum-packed ['vækjʊəm'pækt] ADJ envasado(a) al vacío

vagina [və'dʒaɪnə] N vagina f

vagrant ['veɪgrənt] ADJ & N vagabundo(a) *(m,f)*

vague [veɪg] ADJ *(imprecise)* vago(a), impreciso(a); *(indistinct)* borroso(a)

vain [veɪn] ADJ (**a**) *(proud)* vanidoso(a), presumido(a) (**b**) *(hopeless)* vano(a); **in v.** en vano

valentine ['væləntaɪn] N (**a**) *(card)* = tarjeta que se manda el Día de los Enamorados (**b**) *(sweetheart)* novio(a) *m,f*

valet ['vælɪt, 'væleɪ] N ayuda *m* de cámara

valiant ['væljənt] ADJ valiente

valid ['vælɪd] ADJ válido(a); **no longer v.** caducado(a)

validate ['vælɪdeɪt] VT validar

valley ['vælɪ] N valle m

valour, *US* **valor** ['vælə(r)] N valor m

valuable ['væljʊəbəl] 1 ADJ valioso(a), de valor
2 NPL **valuables** objetos *mpl* de valor

valuation [væljʊ'eɪʃən] N (**a**) *(act)* valoración f (**b**) *(price)* valor m

value ['væljuː] 1 N valor m; **50 pence is good v.** 50 peniques es un buen precio; **to get good v. for money** sacarle jugo al dinero; *Br* **v.-added tax** impuesto *m* sobre el valor añadido *or Am* agregado
2 VT valorar

valve [vælv] N (**a**) *Anat & Tech* válvula f (**b**) *Rad* lámpara f

vampire ['væmpaɪə(r)] N vampiro m

van [væn] N (**a**) *Aut* furgoneta f (**b**) *Br Rail* furgón m

vandal ['vændəl] N vándalo(a) *m,f, Esp* gamberro(a) *m,f*

vandalism ['vændəlɪzəm] N vandalismo m, *Esp* gamberrismo m

vandalize ['vændəlaɪz] VT destruir, destrozar

vanguard ['vængɑːd] N vanguardia f

vanilla [və'nɪlə] N vainilla f

vanish ['vænɪʃ] VI desaparecer

vanity ['vænɪtɪ] N vanidad f; **v. bag** *or* **case** neceser m

vantage ['vɑːntɪdʒ] N ventaja f; **v. point** posición estratégica

vapor ['veɪpər] N *US* = **vapour**

vaporizer ['veɪpəraɪzə(r)] N *(device)* vaporizador m; *(spray)* pulverizador m

vapour ['veɪpə(r)] N vapor m; *(on windowpane)* vaho m; **v. trail** estela f de humo

variable ['veərɪəbəl] ADJ & N variable (f)

variance ['veərɪəns] N *Fml* **to be at v.** no concordar; **to be at v. with sb** estar en desacuerdo con algn

variant ['veərɪənt] N variante f

variation [veərɪ'eɪʃən] N variación f

varicose ['værɪkəʊs] ADJ **v. veins** varices *fpl*

varied ['veərɪd] ADJ variado(a), diverso(a)

variety [və'raɪɪtɪ] N (**a**) *(diversity)* variedad f; *(assortment)* surtido m; **for a v. of reasons** por razones diversas (**b**) **v. show** espectáculo *m* de variedades

various ['veərɪəs] ADJ diversos(as), varios(as)

varnish ['vɑːnɪʃ] 1 N barniz m; *Br* **nail v.** esmalte *m* de uñas
2 VT barnizar; *Br (nails)* esmaltar

vary ['veərɪ] VI variar; **prices v. from £2 to £4** los precios oscilan entre 2 y 4 libras; **to v. in size** variar de tamaño

varying ['veərɪɪŋ] ADJ **with v. degrees of success** con más o menos éxito

vase [*Br* vɑːz, *US* veɪs] N jarrón m

> Note that the Spanish word **vaso** is a false friend and is never a translation for the English word **vase**. In Spanish **vaso** means both "glass" and "vessel".

vasectomy [və'sektəmɪ] N *Med* vasectomía f

Vaseline® ['væsɪliːn] N vaselina f

vast [vɑːst] ADJ vasto(a); *(majority)* inmenso(a)

VAT [viːˈeɪtiː, væt] N Br *(abbr* **value-added tax)** IVA m

vat [væt] N cuba f, tina f

Vatican ['vætɪkən] N **the V.** el Vaticano

vault[1] [vɔːlt] N bóveda f; *(for wine)* bodega f; *(tomb)* cripta f; *(of bank)* cámara acorazada, *Am* bóveda f de seguridad

vault[2] [vɔːlt] **1** VT & VI saltar
2 N salto m

vaunt [vɔːnt] VT *Fml* jactarse de, hacer alarde de

VCR [viːsiːˈɑː(r)] N *(abbr* **video cassette recorder)** (aparato m de) vídeo m *or Am* video m

VD [viːˈdiː] N *(abbr* **venereal disease)** enfermedad venérea

VDU [viːdiːˈjuː] N *(abbr* **visual display unit)** monitor m

veal [viːl] N ternera f

veer [vɪə(r)] VI *(ship)* virar; *(car)* girar

vegan ['viːgən] N vegetaliano(a) m,f, vegetariano(a) m,f estricto(a)

vegeburger ['vedʒɪbɜːgə(r)] N hamburguesa vegetariana

vegetable ['vedʒtəbəl] N *(food)* verdura f, hortaliza f; **v. garden** huerta f, huerto m

vegetarian [vedʒɪˈteərɪən] ADJ & N vegetariano(a) *(m,f)*

vegetation [vedʒɪˈteɪʃən] N vegetación f

vehement ['viːɪmənt] ADJ vehemente

vehicle ['viːɪkəl] N vehículo m

veil [veɪl] **1** N velo m
2 VT velar

vein [veɪn] N vena f

velocity [vɪˈlɒsɪtɪ] N velocidad f

velvet ['velvɪt] N terciopelo m

velvety ['velvɪtɪ] ADJ aterciopelado(a)

vendetta [venˈdetə] N vendetta f

vending ['vendɪŋ] N **v. machine** máquina expendedora

vendor ['vendɔː(r)] N vendedor(a) m,f

veneer [vɪˈnɪə(r)] N **(a)** *(covering)* chapa f **(b)** *Fig* apariencia f

venerable ['venərəbəl] ADJ venerable

venereal [vɪˈnɪərɪəl] ADJ venéreo(a)

Venetian [vɪˈniːʃən] ADJ & N veneciano(a) *(m,f)*; **v. blind** persiana f graduable

Venezuela [venɪˈzweɪlə] N Venezuela

Venezuelan [venɪˈzweɪlən] ADJ & N venezolano(a) *(m,f)*

vengeance ['vendʒəns] N venganza f; *Fam* **it was raining with a v.** llovía con ganas

Venice ['venɪs] N Venecia

venison ['venɪsən] N carne f de venado

venom ['venəm] N veneno m

venomous ['venəməs] ADJ venenoso(a); *Fig* **v. tongue** lengua viperina

vent [vent] **1** N **(a)** *(opening)* abertura f, orificio m; *(grille)* rejilla f de ventilación; **air v.** respiradero m **(b)** *(of volcano)* chimenea f
2 VT *Fig (feelings)* descargar

ventilate ['ventɪleɪt] VT ventilar

ventilation [ventɪˈleɪʃən] N ventilación f

ventilator ['ventɪleɪtə(r)] N ventilador m

ventriloquist [venˈtrɪləkwɪst] N ventrílocuo(a) m,f

venture ['ventʃə(r)] **1** VT arriesgar, aventurar; **he didn't v. to ask** no se atrevió a preguntarlo
2 VI arriesgarse; **to v. out of doors** atreverse a salir
3 N empresa arriesgada, aventura f; *Com* **business/joint v.** empresa comercial/colectiva

venue ['venjuː] N **(a)** *(meeting place)* lugar m de reunión **(b)** *(for concert etc)* local m

Venus ['viːnəs] N *(goddess)* Venus f; *(planet)* Venus m

veranda(h) [vəˈrændə] N porche m, terraza f

verb [vɜːb] N verbo m

verbal ['vɜːbəl] ADJ verbal

verbatim [vəˈbeɪtɪm] **1** ADJ textual
2 ADV textualmente

verbose [vɜːˈbəʊs] ADJ pródigo(a) en palabras

verdict ['vɜːdɪkt] N **(a)** *Jur* veredicto m, fallo m **(b)** *(opinion)* opinión f, juicio m

verge [vɜːdʒ] **1** N **(a)** *(margin)* borde m; *Fig* **on the v. of** al borde de; *Fig* **to be on the v. of doing sth** estar a punto de hacer algo **(b)** *Br (of road)* arcén m, *Andes* berma f, *Méx* acotamiento m, *RP* banquina f, *Ven* hombrillo m
2 VI rayar **(on** en)

verification [verɪfɪˈkeɪʃən] N verificación f, comprobación f

verify ['verɪfaɪ] VT verificar, comprobar

veritable ['verɪtəbəl] ADJ auténtico(a)

vermicelli [vɜːmɪˈtʃelɪ] N fideos *mpl*

vermin ['vɜːmɪn] NPL **(a)** *(animals)* bichos *mpl*, sabandijas *fpl* **(b)** *Fig* gentuza f

vermouth ['vɜːməθ] N vermú m, vermut m

verruca [vəˈruːkə] N verruga f

versatile ['vɜːsətaɪl] ADJ *(person)* polifacético(a); *(object)* versátil

verse [vɜːs] N **(a)** *(stanza)* estrofa f **(b)** *(poetry)* versos *mpl*, poesía f **(c)** *(of song)* copla f **(d)** *(of Bible)* versículo m

versed [vɜːst] ADJ **to be (well) v. in** ser (muy) versado en

version ['vɜːʃən, 'vɜːʒən] N **(a)** *(account)* versión f; **stage v.** adaptación f teatral **(b)** *Aut* modelo m

versus ['vɜːsəs] PREP contra

vertebra ['vɜːtɪbrə] N *(pl* **vertebras** *or* **vertebrae** ['vɜːtɪbriː])* vértebra f

vertical ['vɜːtɪkəl] ADJ & N vertical *(f)*

vertigo ['vɜːtɪgəʊ] N vértigo m

verve [vɜːv] N vigor m, brío m

very ['verɪ] **1** ADV (**a**) *(extremely)* muy; **to be v. hungry** tener mucha hambre; **v. much** muchísimo; **v. well** muy bien (**b**) *(emphatic)* **at the v. latest** como muy tarde; **at the v. least** como mínimo; **the v. best** el mejor de todos; **the v. first/last** el primero/último de todos; **the v. same day** el mismo día
2 ADJ (**a**) **at the v. end/beginning** al final/principio de todo (**b**) *(precise)* **at this v. moment** en este mismo momento; **her v. words** sus palabras exactas; **in the v. middle** justo en medio (**c**) *(mere)* **the v. thought of it!** ¡sólo con pensarlo!

vespers ['vespəz] NPL vísperas *fpl*

vessel ['vesəl] N (**a**) *(container)* vasija *f* (**b**) *Naut* buque *m*, nave *f* (**c**) *Anat & Bot* vaso *m*

vest [vest] **1** N (**a**) *Br (undershirt)* camiseta *f* de tirantes *or Am* breteles (**b**) *US* chaleco *m*
2 VT *Jur* **by the power vested in me ...** por los poderes que se me han conferido ...

vested ['vestɪd] ADJ *Fin & Jur* **v. interests** derechos adquiridos; *Fig* intereses *mpl* creados

vestibule ['vestɪbjuːl] N vestíbulo *m*

vestige ['vestɪdʒ] N vestigio *m*

vestry ['vestrɪ] N sacristía *f*

vet [vet] **1** N veterinario(a) *m,f*
2 VT *Br* someter a investigación, examinar

veteran ['vetərən] N *Mil* ex combatiente *mf*; *Fig* veterano(a) *m,f*

veterinarian [vetərɪ'neərɪən] N *US* veterinario(a) *m,f*

veterinary ['vetərɪnərɪ] ADJ veterinario(a); **v. medicine** veterinaria *f*; *Br* **v. surgeon** veterinario(a) *m,f*

veto ['viːtəʊ] **1** N (*pl* **vetoes**) veto *m*
2 VT *Pol* vetar; *(suggestion etc)* descartar

vexed [vekst] ADJ (**a**) *(annoyed)* molesto(a), disgustado(a); *(angry) esp Esp* enfadado(a), *esp Am* enojado(a) (**b**) *(much debated)* controvertido(a)

VHF [viːeɪtʃ'ef] *(abbr* **very high frequency)** VHF

via ['vaɪə] PREP por, vía

viable ['vaɪəbəl] ADJ viable, factible

viaduct ['vaɪədʌkt] N viaducto *m*

vibrant ['vaɪbrənt] ADJ (**a**) *(sound)* vibrante (**b**) *Fig (personality)* vital; *(city)* animado(a)

vibrate [vaɪ'breɪt] VI vibrar (**with** de)

vibration [vaɪ'breɪʃən] N vibración *f*

vicar ['vɪkə(r)] N párroco *m*

vicarage ['vɪkərɪdʒ] N casa *f* del párroco

vicarious [vɪ'keərɪəs] ADJ experimentado(a) por otro; *(punishment)* sufrido(a) por otro

vice¹ [vaɪs] N vicio *m*

vice² [vaɪs] N *Br (tool)* torno *m* de banco

vice- [vaɪs] PREF vice-; **v.-chairman** vicepresidente *m*; **v.-chancellor** rector(a) *m,f*; **v.-president** vicepresidente(a) *m,f*

vice versa [vaɪsɪ'vɜːsə] ADV viceversa

vicinity [vɪ'sɪnɪtɪ] N *(area)* vecindad *f*; **in the v. of** *(geographic location)* cerca de, en las inmediaciones de; *(amount)* alrededor de

vicious ['vɪʃəs] ADJ *(violent)* violento(a); *(malicious)* malintencionado(a); *(cruel)* cruel; **v. circle** círculo vicioso

victim ['vɪktɪm] N víctima *f*

victimize ['vɪktɪmaɪz] VT perseguir, tratar injustamente

victor ['vɪktə(r)] N vencedor(a) *m,f*

victorious [vɪk'tɔːrɪəs] ADJ victorioso(a)

victory ['vɪktərɪ] N victoria *f*

video ['vɪdɪəʊ] N vídeo *m*, *Am* video *m*; **v. camera** cámara *f* de vídeo *or Am* video; **v. cassette** cinta *f* de vídeo *or Am* video; **v. game** videojuego *m*; **v. (cassette) recorder** *(aparato m de)* vídeo *or Am* video; **v. tape** cinta de vídeo *or Am* video

video-tape ['vɪdɪəʊteɪp] VT grabar (en vídeo)

vie [vaɪ] VI competir (**against** *or* **with** con)

Vienna [vɪ'enə] N Viena

Viennese [vɪə'niːz] ADJ & N vienés(esa) *(m,f)*

Vietnam [vjet'næm] N Vietnam

view [vjuː] **1** N (**a**) *(sight)* vista *f*, panorama *m*; **in full v.** completamente visible; **on v.** a la vista; **to come into v.** aparecer; *Fig* **in v. of the fact that ...** dado que ... (**b**) *(opinion)* opinión *f*; **point of v.** punto *m* de vista; **to take a dim v. of** ver con malos ojos (**c**) *(aim)* fin *m*; **with a v. to** con la intención de
2 VT (**a**) *(look at)* mirar; *(house etc)* visitar (**b**) *(consider)* contemplar; *(topic, problem)* enfocar

viewer ['vjuːə(r)] N (**a**) *TV* televidente *mf* (**b**) *Phot* visionador *m*

viewfinder ['vjuːfaɪndə(r)] N visor *m*

viewpoint ['vjuːpɔɪnt] N punto *m* de vista

vigil ['vɪdʒɪl] N vigilia *f*

vigilant ['vɪdʒɪlənt] ADJ alerta

vigilante [vɪdʒɪ'læntɪ] N **v. group** patrulla ciudadana

vigorous ['vɪgərəs] ADJ vigoroso(a), enérgico(a)

vigour, *US* **vigor** ['vɪgə(r)] N vigor *m*

vile [vaɪl] ADJ (**a**) *(evil)* vil, infame (**b**) *(disgusting)* repugnante (**c**) *Fam (awful)* horrible

vilify ['vɪlɪfaɪ] VT denigrar

villa ['vɪlə] N (**a**) *(in country)* casa *f* de campo (**b**) *Br* chalet *m*

village ['vɪlɪdʒ] N *(small)* aldea *f*; *(larger)* pueblo *m*

villager ['vɪlɪdʒə(r)] N aldeano(a) *m,f*

villain ['vɪlən] N villano(a) *m,f*; *Cin & Th* malo(a) *m,f*

vinaigrette [vɪneɪ'gret] N vinagreta *f*

vindicate ['vɪndɪkeɪt] VT justificar, vindicar

vindictive [vɪn'dɪktɪv] ADJ vengativo(a)

vine [vaɪn] N vid *f*; *(climbing)* parra *f*

vinegar ['vɪnɪgə(r)] N vinagre *m*

vineyard ['vɪnjəd] N viña *f*, viñedo *m*

vintage ['vɪntɪdʒ] 1 N (**a**) (*crop, year*) cosecha *f* (**b**) (*season*) vendimia *f* (**c**) (*era*) era *f*
2 ADJ (**a**) (*wine*) añejo(a) (**b**) (*classic*) clásico(a); **v. car** coche *m* de época

vinyl ['vaɪnɪl] N vinilo *m*

viola [vɪ'əʊlə] N viola *f*

violate ['vaɪəleɪt] VT violar

violence ['vaɪələns] N violencia *f*

violent ['vaɪələnt] ADJ violento(a)

violet ['vaɪəlɪt] 1 N (**a**) *Bot* violeta *f* (**b**) (*colour*) violeta *m*
2 ADJ violeta

violin [vaɪə'lɪn] N violín *m*

violinist [vaɪə'lɪnɪst] N violinista *mf*

VIP [viːaɪ'piː] N *Fam* (*abbr* **very important person**) VIP *mf*

viper ['vaɪpə(r)] N víbora *f*

virgin ['vɜːdʒɪn] 1 N virgen *f*; **the V. Mary** la Virgen María; **to be a v.** ser virgen
2 ADJ virgen

virginity [və'dʒɪnɪtɪ] N virginidad *f*

Virgo ['vɜːgəʊ] N Virgo *m*

virile ['vɪraɪl] ADJ viril

virtual ['vɜːtjʊəl] ADJ virtual; *Comput* **v. reality** realidad *f* virtual

virtually ['vɜːtjʊəlɪ] ADV (*almost*) prácticamente

virtue ['vɜːtjuː] N virtud *f*; **by v. of** en virtud de

virtuous ['vɜːtjʊəs] ADJ virtuoso(a)

virulent ['vɪrʊlənt] ADJ virulento(a)

virus ['vaɪrəs] N virus *m inv*; *Comput* **v. check** detección *f* de virus

visa ['viːzə] N visado *m*, *Am* visa *f*

vis-à-vis [viːzɑː'viː] PREP (**a**) (*regarding*) respecto a (**b**) (*opposite*) frente a

viscose ['vɪskəʊs] N viscosa *f*

viscount ['vaɪkaʊnt] N vizconde *m*

vise [vaɪs] N *US* = **vice**²

visibility [vɪzɪ'bɪlɪtɪ] N visibilidad *f*

visible ['vɪzɪbəl] ADJ visible

vision ['vɪʒən] N (**a**) (*apparition*) visión *f* (**b**) (*eyesight*) vista *f*

visit ['vɪzɪt] 1 VT (**a**) (*person*) visitar, hacer una visita a (**b**) (*place*) visitar
2 N visita *f*; **to pay sb a v.** hacerle una visita a algn

visiting ['vɪzɪtɪŋ] ADJ **v. card** tarjeta *f* de visita; *Med* **v. hours** horas *fpl* de visita; *Sport* **v. team** equipo *m* visitante

visitor ['vɪzɪtə(r)] N (**a**) (*guest*) invitado(a) *m,f*; **we've got visitors** tenemos visita (**b**) (*in hotel*) cliente(a) *m,f* (**c**) (*tourist*) turista *mf*

visor ['vaɪzə(r)] N visera *f*

Note that the Spanish word **visor** is a false friend and is never a translation for the English word **visor**. In Spanish **visor** means "viewfinder".

vista ['vɪstə] N vista *f*, panorama *m*

visual ['vɪʒʊəl] ADJ visual; **v. aids** medios *mpl* visuales

visualize ['vɪʒʊəlaɪz] VT (**a**) (*imagine*) imaginar(se) (**b**) (*foresee*) prever

vital ['vaɪtəl] ADJ (**a**) (*lively*) enérgico(a) (**b**) (*essential*) fundamental (**c**) (*decisive*) decisivo(a); *Fam* **v. statistics** medidas *fpl* del cuerpo de la mujer (**d**) *Med* (*function, sign*) vital

vitality [vaɪ'tælɪtɪ] N vitalidad *f*

vitally ['vaɪtəlɪ] ADV **it's v. important** es de vital importancia

vitamin ['vɪtəmɪn, *US* 'vaɪtəmɪn] N vitamina *f*

viva ['vaɪvə] N *Br* examen *m* oral

vivacious [vɪ'veɪʃəs] ADJ vivaz

vivacity [vɪ'væsɪtɪ] N viveza *f*, vivacidad *f*

vivid ['vɪvɪd] ADJ (**a**) (*bright, lively*) vivo(a), intenso(a) (**b**) (*graphic*) gráfico(a)

vivisection [vɪvɪ'sekʃən] N vivisección *f*

vixen ['vɪksən] N zorra *f*

V-neck(ed) ['viːnek(t)] ADJ de (cuello de) pico

vocabulary [və'kæbjʊlərɪ] N vocabulario *m*

vocal ['vəʊkəl] ADJ vocal; **v. cords** cuerdas *fpl* vocales

vocalist ['vəʊkəlɪst] N cantante *mf*

vocation [vəʊ'keɪʃən] N vocación *f*

vocational [vəʊ'keɪʃənəl] ADJ profesional; **v. training** formación *f* profesional

vociferous [vəʊ'sɪfərəs] ADJ (**a**) (*protest*) enérgico(a) (**b**) (*noisy*) clamoroso(a)

vodka ['vɒdkə] N vodka *m*

vogue [vəʊg] N boga *f*, moda *f*; **in v.** de moda

voice [vɔɪs] 1 N (**a**) N voz *f*; **to lose one's v.** quedarse afónico(a); *Fig* **at the top of one's v.** a voz en grito; *Comput* **v. mail** buzón *m* de voz
2 VT (**a**) (*express*) manifestar (**b**) *Ling* sonorizar

void [vɔɪd] 1 ADJ (**a**) **v. of** sin (**b**) *Jur* nulo(a), inválido(a)
2 N vacío *m*

volatile ['vɒlətaɪl] ADJ volátil

volcanic [vɒl'kænɪk] ADJ volcánico(a)

volcano [vɒl'keɪnəʊ] N (*pl* **volcanoes**) volcán *m*

volition [və'lɪʃən] N *Fml* **of one's own v.** por voluntad propia

volley ['vɒlɪ] 1 N (**a**) (*of shots*) descarga *f* (**b**) *Fig* (*of stones, insults*) lluvia *f* (**c**) (*in tennis, football*) volea *f*
2 VT (*in tennis, football*) volear

volleyball ['vɒlɪbɔːl] N voleibol *m*

volt [vəʊlt] N voltio *m*

voltage ['vəʊltɪdʒ] N voltaje *m*

voluble ['vɒljʊbəl] ADJ locuaz

Note that the Spanish word **voluble** is a false friend and is never a translation for the English word **voluble**. In Spanish, **voluble** means "fickle, changeable".

volume ['vɒljuːm] N (**a**) *(of sound)* volumen *m* (**b**) *(capacity)* capacidad *f* (**c**) *(book)* volumen *m*, tomo *m*; *Fig* **to speak volumes** decirlo todo

voluntary ['vɒləntərɪ] ADJ voluntario(a); **v. organization** organización benéfica

volunteer [vɒlən'tɪə(r)] **1** N voluntario(a) *m,f* **2** VT *(help etc)* ofrecer **3** VI (**a**) *(put self forward)* ofrecerse (**for** para) (**b**) *Mil* alistarse como voluntario

voluptuous [və'lʌptjʊəs] ADJ voluptuoso(a)

vomit ['vɒmɪt] **1** VT & VI vomitar **2** N vómito *m*

voracious [vɒ'reɪʃəs] ADJ voraz

vortex ['vɔːteks] N (*pl* **vortices** ['vɔːtɪsiːz]) vórtice *m*; *Fig* vorágine *f*

vote [vəʊt] **1** N voto *m*; *(voting)* votación *f*; **v. of confidence** voto de confianza; **to take a v. on sth** someter algo a votacíon; **to have the v.** tener derecho al voto **2** VT (**a**) *(in ballot)* votar (**b**) *(elect)* elegir (**c**)

Fam (propose) proponer **3** VI votar; **to v. for sb** votar a algn

voter ['vəʊtə(r)] N votante *mf*

voting ['vəʊtɪŋ] N votación *f*

vouch [vaʊtʃ] VI **to v. for sth/sb** responder de algo/por algn

voucher ['vaʊtʃə(r)] N *Br* vale *m*

vow [vaʊ] **1** N voto *m* **2** VT jurar

vowel ['vaʊəl] N vocal *f*

voyage ['vɔɪɪdʒ] N viaje *m*; *(crossing)* travesía *f*; **to go on a v.** hacer un viaje (en barco)

vulgar ['vʌlgə(r)] ADJ *(coarse)* vulgar, ordinario(a); *(in poor taste)* de mal gusto

vulgarity [vʌl'gærɪtɪ] N *(coarseness)* vulgaridad *f*, ordinariez *f*; *(poor taste)* mal gusto *m*

vulnerable ['vʌlnərəbəl] ADJ vulnerable

vulture ['vʌltʃə(r)] N buitre *m*

vulva ['vʌlvə] N vulva *f*

W, w ['dʌbəlju:] N *(the letter)* W, w *f*

W (**a**) *(abbr* **West**) O (**b**) *(abbr* **Watt(s)**) W

wad [wɒd] N *(of paper)* taco *m; (of cotton wool)* bolita *f; (of banknotes)* fajo *m*

waddle ['wɒdəl] VI caminar *or* andar como un pato

wade [weɪd] VI caminar por el agua; **to w. across a river** vadear un río

▶ **wade through** VT INSEP hacer con dificultad; **I'm wading through the book** me cuesta mucho terminar el libro

wading pool ['weɪdɪŋpuːl] N *US* piscina *f* para niños

wafer ['weɪfə(r)] N barquillo *m; Rel* hostia *f*

waffle¹ ['wɒfəl] N *(food) Esp* gofre *m, Am* wafle *m*

waffle² ['wɒfəl] *Br Fam* **1** VI meter mucha paja; **to w. on** parlotear
2 N paja *f*

waft [wɑːft, wɒft] **1** VT llevar por el aire
2 VI flotar (por *or* en el aire)

wag [wæg] **1** VT menear
2 VI *(tail)* menearse

wage [weɪdʒ] **1** N **wage(s)** salario *m*, sueldo *m*; **w. earner** asalariado(a) *m,f*; **w. freeze** congelación *f* salarial; **w. packet** *(envelope)* sobre *m* de la paga; *(money)* salario *m*
2 VT *(campaign)* realizar (**against** contra); **to w. war (on)** hacer la guerra a

wager ['weɪdʒə(r)] **1** N apuesta *f*
2 VT apostar

waggle ['wægəl] **1** VT menear
2 VI menearse

wa(g)gon ['wægən] N *(horse-drawn)* carro *m; Br Rail* vagón *m*

wail [weɪl] **1** N lamento *m*, gemido *m*
2 VI *(person)* lamentar, gemir

waist [weɪst] N *Anat* cintura *f; Sewing* talle *m*

waistcoat ['weɪstkəʊt] N *Br* chaleco *m*

waistline ['weɪstlaɪn] N *Anat* cintura; *Sewing* talle *m*

wait [weɪt] **1** N espera *f; (delay)* demora *f*; **to lie in w.** estar al acecho
2 VI (**a**) *(in general)* esperar; **I can't w. to see her** me muero de ganas de verla; **while you w.** en el acto; **to keep sb waiting** hacer esperar a algn (**b**) *Br* **to w. at table** servir mesas

▶ **wait about, wait around** VI esperar

▶ **wait on** VT INSEP servir

waiter ['weɪtə(r)] N camarero *m, Andes, RP* mozo *m, Chile, Ven* mesonero *m, Col, Guat, Méx, Salv* mesero *m*

waiting ['weɪtɪŋ] N **no w.** *(sign)* prohibido detenerse; **w. list** lista *f* de espera; **w. room** sala *f* de espera

waitress ['weɪtrɪs] N camarera *f, Andes, RP* moza *f, Chile, Ven* mesonera *f, Col, Guat, Méx, Salv* mesera *f*

waive [weɪv] VT *Fml (rule)* no aplicar

wake¹ [weɪk] **1** VT *(pt* **woke**; *pp* **woken**) **to w. sb (up)** despertar a algn
2 VI **to w. (up)** despertar(se)
3 N *(for dead)* velatorio *m, Am* velorio *m*

wake² [weɪk] N *(in water)* estela *f; Fig* **in the w. of** tras

waken ['weɪkən] VT *Literary* despertar

Wales [weɪlz] N (el país de) Gales

walk [wɔːk] **1** N (**a**) *(long)* caminata *f; (short)* paseo *m*; **it's an hour's w.** está a una hora de camino; **to go for a w.** dar un paseo; **to take the dog for a w.** sacar a pasear al perro (**b**) *(gait)* andares *mpl*, modo *m* de caminar *or Esp* andar (**c**) **people from all walks of life** gente *f* de toda condición
2 VT (**a**) **we walked her home** la acompañamos a casa (**b**) *(dog)* pasear
3 VI (**a**) *(move on foot)* caminar, *Esp* andar (**b**) *(as opposed to riding, driving)* ir caminando *or Esp* andando

▶ **walk away** VI irse (caminando *or Esp* andando); *Fig* **to w. away with a prize** llevarse un premio

▶ **walk into** VT INSEP (**a**) *(place)* entrar en; *Fig (trap)* caer en (**b**) *(bump into)* chocarse contra

▶ **walk out** VI salir; *Ind* declararse en huelga; **to w. out on sb** abandonar a algn

▶ **walk up** VI **to w. up to sb** abordar a algn

walkabout ['wɔːkəbaʊt] N *Br (of politician)* paseo *m* entre la multitud

walker ['wɔːkə(r)] N paseante *mf; Sport* marchador(a) *m,f*

walkie-talkie [wɔːkɪ'tɔːkɪ] N walkie-talkie *m*

walking ['wɔːkɪŋ] **1** N caminar *m, Esp* andar *m; (hiking)* excursionismo *m*
2 ADJ **at w. pace** a paso de marcha; **w. shoes** zapatos *mpl* de andar; **w. stick** bastón *m*

Walkman® ['wɔːkmən] N *(pl* **Walkmans**) walkman® *m*

walkout ['wɔːkaʊt] N *Ind* huelga *f*

walkover ['wɔːkəʊvə(r)] N **it was a w.** fue pan comido

walkway ['wɔːkweɪ] N paso m de peatones

wall [wɔːl] N (**a**) *(freestanding, exterior)* muro m; *Fig* **to have one's back to the w.** estar entre la espada y la pared; **city w.** muralla f; **garden w.** tapia f (**b**) *(interior)* pared f; **w. map** mapa m mural (**c**) *Ftb* barrera f

▸ **wall up** VT SEP *(door, fireplace)* tabicar

walled [wɔːld] ADJ *(city)* amurallado(a); *(garden)* cercado(a) con tapia

wallet ['wɒlɪt] N cartera f

wallflower ['wɔːlflaʊə(r)] N (**a**) *Bot* alhelí m (**b**) *Fam* **to be a w.** ser un convidado de piedra

wallop ['wɒləp] *Fam* **1** N tortazo m, golpetazo m, *Méx* madrazo m
2 VT (**a**) *(hit)* dar un tortazo or golpetazo a (**b**) *(defeat)* dar una buena paliza a

wallow ['wɒləʊ] VI revolcarse (**in** en); *Fig* **to w. in self-pity** sumirse en la autocompasión

wallpaper ['wɔːlpeɪpə(r)] **1** N papel pintado
2 VT empapelar

wally ['wɒlɪ] N *Br Fam* idiota mf, *Esp* chorra mf

walnut ['wɔːlnʌt] N nuez f; *(tree, wood)* nogal m

walrus ['wɔːlrəs] N morsa f

waltz [wɔːls] **1** N vals m
2 VI bailar un vals

wan [wɒn] ADJ (**wanner, wannest**) pálido(a); *(look, smile)* apagado(a)

wand [wɒnd] N (**magic**) **w.** varita (mágica)

wander ['wɒndə(r)] **1** VT **to w. the streets** vagar por las calles
2 VI (**a**) *(aimlessly)* vagar, errar; **to w. about** deambular; **to w. in/out** entrar/salir sin prisas (**b**) *(stray)* desviarse; *(mind)* divagar; **his glance wandered round the room** recorrió el cuarto con la mirada

wandering ['wɒndərɪŋ] ADJ errante; *(tribe)* nómada; *(speech)* divagador(a)

wane [weɪn] VI menguar; *(interest)* decaer

wangle ['wæŋgəl] VT *Fam* agenciarse

wank [wæŋk] *Br Vulg* **1** N paja f
2 VI hacerse una or Am la paja

wanker ['wæŋkə(r)] N *Br Vulg Esp* gilipollas mf inv, *Am* pendejo(a) m,f

want [wɒnt] **1** N (**a**) *(lack)* falta f, **for w. of** por falta de (**b**) *(poverty)* miseria f
2 VT (**a**) *(desire)* querer, desear; **to w. to do sth** querer hacer algo (**b**) *Fam (need)* necesitar; **the grass wants cutting** hace falta cortar el césped (**c**) *(seek)* buscar; **you're wanted on the phone** te llaman al teléfono

▸ **want for** VT INSEP carecer de; **to w. for nothing** tenerlo todo

wanted [wɒntɪd] ADJ *(on police poster)* se busca; **w., a good cook** *(advertisement)* se necesita buen cocinero

wanting ['wɒntɪŋ] ADJ (**a**) **she is w. in tact** le falta tacto (**b**) **he was found w.** no daba la talla

wanton ['wɒntən] ADJ (**a**) *(motiveless)* sin motivo; **w. cruelty** crueldad gratuita (**b**) *(unrestrained)* desenfrenado(a); *(licentious)* lascivo(a)

WAP [wæp] N *Comput (abbr* **Wireless Application Protocol**) WAP m; **W. phone** teléfono m WAP

war [wɔː(r)] N guerra f; **to be at w. (with)** estar en guerra (con); *Fig* **to declare/wage w. on** declarar/hacer la guerra a; **w. crime** crimen m de guerra

warble ['wɔːbəl] VI gorjear

ward [wɔːd] N (**a**) *(of hospital)* sala f (**b**) *Jur* pupilo(a) m,f; **w. of court** pupilo(a) bajo tutela judicial (**c**) *Br Pol* distrito m electoral

▸ **ward off** VT SEP *(blow)* parar, desviar; *(attack)* rechazar; *(danger)* evitar; *(illness)* prevenir

warden ['wɔːdən] N (**a**) *(of institution, hostel)* guardián(ana) m,f; **game w.** guardia m de coto (**b**) *US (of prison)* director(a) m,f, alcaide(esa) m,f

warder ['wɔːdə(r)] N *Br (in prison)* vigilante mf

wardrobe ['wɔːdrəʊb] N (**a**) *(cupboard)* armario m, ropero m (**b**) *(clothes)* guardarropa m (**c**) *Th* vestuario m

warehouse ['weəhaʊs] N almacén m

wares [weəz] NPL mercancías fpl

warfare ['wɔːfeə(r)] N guerra f

warhead ['wɔːhed] N (**nuclear**) **w.** ojiva f nuclear

warm [wɔːm] **1** ADJ (**a**) *(water)* tibio(a); *(hands)* caliente; *(climate)* cálido(a); **a w. day** un día de calor; **I am w.** tengo calor; **it is (very) w. today** hoy hace (mucho) calor; **w. clothing** ropa f de abrigo (**b**) *(welcome, applause)* cálido(a)
2 VT calentar; *Fig* alegrar
3 VI calentarse; **to w. to sb** cogerle simpatía a algn

▸ **warm up 1** VT SEP (**a**) *(food, room)* calentar (**b**) *(audience)* animar
2 VI (**a**) *(engine)* calentarse (**b**) *(dancer, athlete)* calentar, hacer calentamiento (**c**) *Fig (audience, party)* animarse

warm-blooded [wɔːm'blʌdɪd] ADJ de sangre caliente

warm-hearted [wɔːm'hɑːtɪd] ADJ afectuoso(a)

warmly ['wɔːmlɪ] ADV *Fig* calurosamente; *(thank)* con efusión

warmth [wɔːmθ] N *(heat)* calor m; *Fig* cordialidad f

warn [wɔːn] VT avisar (**of** de), advertir (**about/against** sobre/contra); **he warned me not to go** me advirtió que no fuera; **to w. sb that** advertir a algn que

warning ['wɔːnɪŋ] **1** ADJ **w. light** piloto m; **w. sign** señal f de aviso
2 N (**a**) *(of danger)* advertencia f, aviso m (**b**) *(replacing punishment)* amonestación f (**c**) *(notice)* aviso m; **without w.** sin previo aviso

warp [wɔːp] **1** VT (**a**) *(wood)* alabear, combar (**b**) *Fig (mind)* pervertir
2 VI alabearse, combarse

warrant ['wɒrənt] **1** N (**a**) *Jur* orden *f* judicial; **death w.** sentencia *f* de muerte (**b**) *(authorization note)* cédula *f*; *Com* bono *m*
2 VT (**a**) *(justify)* justificar (**b**) *(guarantee)* garantizar

warranty ['wɒrəntɪ] N *Com* garantía *f*

warren ['wɒrən] N conejera *f*; *Fig* laberinto *m*

warrior ['wɒrɪə(r)] N guerrero(a) *m,f*

Warsaw ['wɔːsɔː] N Varsovia

warship ['wɔːʃɪp] N buque *m or* barco *m* de guerra

wart [wɔːt] N verruga *f*

wartime ['wɔːtaɪm] N tiempos *mpl* de guerra

wary ['weərɪ] ADJ (**warier, wariest**) cauteloso(a); **to be w. of doing sth** dudar en hacer algo; **to be w. of sth/sb** recelar de algo/algn

was [wɒz] PT *of* be

wash [wɒʃ] **1** N (**a**) *(action)* lavado *m*; **to have a w.** lavarse (**b**) *(of ship)* estela *f*; *(sound)* chapoteo *m*
2 VT (**a**) *(clean)* lavar; *(dishes)* fregar; **to w. one's hair** lavarse el pelo (**b**) *(of sea, river)* arrastrar
3 VI (**a**) *(person)* lavarse; *(do the laundry)* hacer la colada (**b**) *(lap)* batir

▶ **wash away** VT SEP *(of sea)* llevarse; *(traces)* borrar

▶ **wash off** VI lavar, quitar *or Am* sacar lavando

▶ **wash out 1** VT SEP (**a**) *(stain)* quitar lavando (**b**) *(bottle)* enjuagar
2 VI quitarse lavando

▶ **wash up 1** VT SEP *Br (dishes)* fregar
2 VI (**a**) *Br* fregar los platos (**b**) *US* lavarse rápidamente

washable ['wɒʃəbəl] ADJ lavable

washbasin ['wɒʃbeɪsən], *US* **washbowl** ['wɒʃbəʊl] N lavabo *m*, *Am* lavamanos *m inv*

washcloth ['wɒʃklɒθ] N *US* manopla *f*

washer ['wɒʃə(r)] N *(on tap)* zapata *f*, junta *f*

washing ['wɒʃɪŋ] N *(action)* lavado *m*; *(of clothes)* colada *f*; *(dirty)* **w.** ropa sucia; **to do the w.** hacer la colada; **w. line** tendedero *m*; **w. machine** lavadora *f*, *RP* lavarropas *m inv*; **w. powder** detergente *m*

washing-up [wɒʃɪŋ'ʌp] N *Br* (**a**) *(action)* fregado *m*; **w. bowl** palangana *f or Esp* barreño *m* para lavar los platos; **w. liquid** *(detergente m)* lavavajillas *m inv* (**b**) *(dishes)* platos *mpl* (para fregar)

washout ['wɒʃaʊt] N *Fam* fracaso *m*

washroom ['wɒʃruːm] N *US* lavabo *m*, baño *m*, *Esp* servicios *mpl*, *CSur* toilette *f*

wasp [wɒsp] N avispa *f*

wastage ['weɪstɪdʒ] N pérdidas *fpl*

waste [weɪst] **1** ADJ (**a**) *(unwanted)* desechado(a); **w. food** restos *mpl* de comida; **w. products** productos *mpl* de desecho (**b**) *(ground)* baldío(a)
2 N (**a**) *(unnecessary use)* desperdicio *m*; *(of resources, effort, money)* derroche *m*; *(of time)* pérdida *f*; **to go to w.** echarse a perder (**b**) *(leftovers)* desperdicios *mpl*; *(rubbish)* basura *f*; **radioactive w.** desechos radioactivos; *Br* **w. disposal unit** trituradora *f* (de desperdicios); **w. pipe** tubo *m* de desagüe
3 VT *(squander)* desperdiciar, malgastar; *(resources)* derrochar; *(money)* despilfarrar; *(time)* perder

▶ **waste away** VI consumirse

wasteful ['weɪstfʊl] ADJ derrochador(a)

wasteland ['weɪstlænd] N baldío *m*

wastepaper [weɪst'peɪpə(r)] N **w. basket** *or* **bin** papelera *f*, *Méx* bote *m*

watch [wɒtʃ] **1** N (**a**) *(look-out)* vigilancia *f*; **to keep a close w. on sth/sb** vigilar algo/a algn muy atentamente (**b**) *Mil (body)* guardia *f*; *(individual)* centinela *m*; **to be on w.** estar de guardia (**c**) *(timepiece)* reloj *m*
2 VT (**a**) *(observe)* mirar, observar (**b**) *(keep an eye on)* vigilar; *(with suspicion)* acechar (**c**) *(be careful of)* tener cuidado con; *Fig* **to w. one's step** ir con pies de plomo
3 VI *(look)* mirar, observar; **w. out!** ¡cuidado!

▶ **watch out for** VT INSEP *(be careful of)* tener cuidado con

watchband ['wɒtʃbænd] N *US* = **watchstrap**

watchdog ['wɒtʃdɒg] N perro *m* guardián; *Fig* guardián(ana) *m,f*

watchful ['wɒtʃfʊl] ADJ vigilante

watchmaker ['wɒtʃmeɪkə(r)] N relojero(a) *m,f*

watchman ['wɒtʃmən] N vigilante *m*; **night w.** *(of site)* vigilante nocturno

watchstrap ['wɒtʃstræp] N *Br* correa *f* (de reloj)

watchtower ['wɒtʃtaʊə(r)] N atalaya *f*

water ['wɔːtə(r)] **1** N (**a**) *(liquid, element)* agua *f*; **w. bottle** cantimplora *f*; **w. lily** nenúfar *m*; **w. main** conducción *f* de aguas; **w. polo** waterpolo *m*; **w. sports** deportes acuáticos; **w. tank** depósito *m* de agua; **territorial waters** aguas jurisdiccionales; *Fig* **it's all w. under the bridge** ha llovido mucho desde entonces (**b**) **to pass w.** orinar
2 VT *(plants)* regar
3 VI **my eyes are watering** me lloran los ojos; **my mouth watered** se me hizo la boca agua

▶ **water down** VT SEP *(drink)* aguar

watercolour, *US* **watercolor** ['wɔːtəkʌlə(r)] N acuarela *f*

watercress ['wɔːtəkres] N berro *m*

waterfall ['wɔːtəfɔːl] N cascada *f*; *(very big)* catarata *f*

waterfront ['wɔːtəfrʌnt] N *(shore)* orilla *f* del agua; *(harbour)* puerto *m*

watering ['wɔːtərɪŋ] N *(of plants)* riego *m*; **w. can** regadera *f*; **w. place** abrevadero *m*

waterline ['wɔːtəlaɪn] N línea *f* de flotación

waterlogged ['wɔːtəlɒgd] ADJ anegado(a)

watermark ['wɔːtəmɑːk] N filigrana *f*

watermelon ['wɔːtəmelən] N sandía *f*

waterproof ['wɔːtəpruːf]. **1** ADJ *(material)* impermeable; *(watch)* sumergible
2 N *(coat)* impermeable *m*

watershed ['wɔːtəʃed] N *Geog* línea divisoria de aguas; *Fig* punto decisivo

water-skiing ['wɔːtəskiːɪŋ] N esquí acuático

watertight ['wɔːtətaɪt] ADJ hermético(a)

waterway ['wɔːtəweɪ] N vía *f* fluvial

waterworks ['wɔːtəwɜːks] NPL *(for treating water)* central *f* de abastecimiento de agua; *Fig* **to turn on the w.** ponerse a llorar (a voluntad)

watery ['wɔːtərɪ] ADJ **(a)** *(soup)* aguado(a); *(coffee)* flojo(a) **(b)** *(eyes)* lacrimoso(a) **(c)** *(pale)* pálido(a)

watt [wɒt] N vatio *m*

wave [weɪv] **1** N **(a)** *(at sea)* ola *f* **(b)** *(in hair)* & *Rad* onda *f* **(c)** *Fig (of anger, strikes etc)* oleada *f* **(d)** *(gesture)* saludo *m* con la mano
2 VT **(a)** *(flag, stick)* agitar; *(brandish)* blandir **(b)** *(hair)* ondular
3 VI **(a)** *(person)* **she waved (to me)** *(greeting)* me saludó con la mano; *(goodbye)* se despidió (de mí) con la mano; *(signal)* me hizo señas con la mano **(b)** *(flag)* ondear; *(corn)* ondular

wavelength ['weɪvleŋθ] N longitud *f* de onda

waver ['weɪvə(r)] VI *(hesitate)* vacilar **(between** entre)**;** *(voice)* temblar; *(courage)* flaquear

wavy ['weɪvɪ] ADJ **(wavier, waviest)** ondulado(a)

wax¹ [wæks] **1** N cera *f*
2 VT encerar

wax² [wæks] VI **(a)** *(moon)* crecer **(b)** **to w. lyrical** exaltarse

waxworks ['wækswɜːks] N SING museo *m* de cera

way [weɪ] **1** N **(a)** *(route)* camino *m*; *(road)* vía *f*, camino; **a letter is on the w.** una carta está en camino; **on the w.** en el camino; **on the w. here** de camino para aquí; **out of the w.** apartado(a); **to ask the w.** preguntar el camino; **to go the wrong w.** ir por el camino equivocado; **to lose one's w.** perderse; **to make one's w. through the crowd** abrirse camino entre la multitud; **which is the w. to the station?** ¿por dónde se va a la estación?; *Fig* **she went out of her w. to help** se desvivió por ayudar; **w. in** entrada *f*; **w. out** salida *f*; *Fig* **the easy w. out** la solución fácil; **I can't find my w. out** no encuentro la salida; **on the w. back** en el viaje de regreso; **on the w. up/down** en la subida/bajada; **there's no w. through** el paso está cerrado; **you're in the w.** estás estorbando; **(get) out of the w.!** ¡quítate de en medio!; *Fig* **to get sth/sb out of the w.** desembarazarse de algo/algn; **I kept out of the w.** me mantuve a distancia; *Aut* **right of w.** prioridad *f*; **there's a wall in the w.** hay un muro en medio; **to give w.** ceder; *Aut* ceder el paso **(b)** *(direction)* dirección *f*; **come this w.** venga por aquí; **which w. did he go?** ¿por dónde se fue?; **that w.** por allá; **the other w. round** al revés
(c) *(distance)* distancia *f*; **a long w. off** lejos; *Fig*

he'll go a long w. llegará lejos; *Fig* **we've come a long w.** hemos hecho grandes progresos
(d) **to get under w.** *(travellers, work)* ponerse en marcha; *(meeting, match)* empezar
(e) *(means, method)* método *m*, manera *f*; **do it any w. you like** hazlo como quieras; **I'll do it my w.** lo haré a mi manera
(f) *(manner)* modo *m*, manera *f*; **in a friendly w.** de modo amistoso; **one w. or another** de un modo o de otro; **the French w. of life** el estilo de vida francés; **the w. things are going** tal como van las cosas; **to my w. of thinking** a mi modo de ver; *Fam* **no w.!** ¡ni hablar!; **she has a w. with children** tiene un don para los niños; **by w. of** a modo de; **either w.** en cualquier caso; **in a w.** en cierto sentido; **in many ways** desde muchos puntos de vista; **in some ways** en algunos aspectos; **in no w.** de ninguna manera
(g) *(custom)* hábito *m*, costumbre *f*; **to be set in one's ways** tener costumbres arraigadas
(h) *(state)* estado *m*; **leave it the w. it is** déjalo tal como está; **he is in a bad w.** está bastante mal
(i) **by the w.** a propósito; **in the w. of business** en el curso de los negocios
2 ADV *Fam* mucho, muy; **it was w. off target** cayó muy desviado del blanco; **w. back in 1940** allá en 1940

waylay [weɪ'leɪ] VT *(pt & pp* **waylaid** [weɪ'leɪd]**)** **(a)** *(attack)* atacar por sorpresa **(b)** *Fig (intercept)* abordar, detener

wayside ['weɪsaɪd] N *Fig* **to fall by the w.** quedarse en el camino

wayward ['weɪwəd] ADJ rebelde; *(capricious)* caprichoso(a)

WC [dʌbljuːˈsiː] N *(abbr* **water closet)** wáter *m*, váter *m*

we [wiː] PERS PRON nosotros(as) *(usually omitted in Spanish, except for contrast)*

weak [wiːk] ADJ débil; *(argument, excuse)* pobre; *(team, piece of work, tea)* flojo(a)

weaken ['wiːkən] **1** VT debilitar; *(argument)* quitar fuerza a
2 VI debilitarse

weakling ['wiːklɪŋ] N enclenque *mf*

weakness ['wiːknɪs] N debilidad *f*; *(character flaw)* punto flaco

wealth [welθ] N riqueza *f*; *Fig* abundancia *f*

wealthy ['welθɪ] ADJ **(wealthier, wealthiest)** rico(a)

wean [wiːn] VT *(child)* destetar; *Fig* **to w. sb from** *or* **off a habit** quitar *or Am* sacarle una mala costumbre a algn

weapon ['wepən] N arma *f*

wear [weə(r)] **1** VT *(pt* **wore**; *pp* **worn)** **(a)** *(clothes)* llevar puesto, vestir; *(shoes)* llevar puestos, calzar; **he wears glasses** lleva gafas; **to w. black** vestirse de negro **(b)** *(erode)* desgastar
2 VI **to w. (thin/smooth)** desgastarse (con el roce); *Fig* **my patience is wearing thin** se me

está acabando la paciencia

3 N (**a**) (clothing) ropa f; **leisure w.** ropa de sport (**b**) (use) (of clothes) uso m (**c**) (deterioration) desgaste m; **normal w. and tear** desgaste natural

► **wear away 1** VT SEP erosionar

2 VI (stone etc) erosionarse; (inscription) borrarse

► **wear down 1** VT SEP (heels) desgastar; Fig **to w. sb down** vencer la resistencia de algn

2 VI desgastarse

► **wear off** VI (effect, pain) pasar, desaparecer

► **wear out 1** VT SEP gastar; Fig agotar

2 VI gastarse

wearily ['wɪərɪlɪ] ADV con cansancio

wearisome ['wɪərɪsəm] ADJ fatigoso(a)

weary ['wɪərɪ] **1** ADJ (**wearier, weariest**) (**a**) (tired) cansado(a) (**b**) (fed up) harto(a)

2 VT cansar

3 VI cansarse (**of** de)

weasel ['wiːzəl] N comadreja f

weather ['weðə(r)] **1** N tiempo m; **the w. is fine** hace buen tiempo; Fig **to feel under the w.** no encontrarse bien; **w. chart** mapa meteorológico; **w. forecast** parte meteorológico; **w. vane** veleta f

2 VT Fig (crisis) aguantar; Fig **to w. the storm** capear el temporal

weather-beaten ['weðəbiːtən] ADJ curtido(a)

weathercock ['weðəkɒk] N veleta f

weatherman ['weðəmæn] N hombre m del tiempo

weave [wiːv] **1** N tejido m

2 VT (pt **wove**; pp **woven**) (**a**) Tex tejer (**b**) (intertwine) entretejer (**c**) (intrigues) tramar

3 VI (person, road) zigzaguear

weaver ['wiːvə(r)] N tejedor(a) m,f

web [web] N (**a**) (of spider) telaraña f (**b**) (of lies) sarta f (**c**) Comput **the W.** la Web; **w. page** página f web; **w. site** sitio m web

webbed [webd] ADJ (foot) palmeado(a)

wed [wed] VT Literary (pt & pp **wed** or **wedded**) casarse con

wedding ['wedɪŋ] N boda f, Andes matrimonio m, RP casamiento m; **w. cake** tarta f or pastel m de boda; **w. day** día m de la boda; **w. dress** traje m de novia; **w. present** regalo m de boda; **w. ring** alianza f

wedge [wedʒ] **1** N (**a**) (for door, wheel) cuña f, calzo m (**b**) (of cake, cheese) trozo m grande

2 VT calzar; **to be wedged tight** (object) estar completamente atrancado(a)

Wednesday ['wenzdɪ] N miércoles m

wee[1] [wiː] ADJ esp Scot pequeñito(a)

wee[2] [wiː] Br Fam **1** N pipí m

2 VI hacer pipí

weed [wiːd] **1** N Bot mala hierba

2 VT (**a**) (garden) escardar (**b**) Fig **to w. out** eliminar

3 VI escardar

weedkiller ['wiːdkɪlə(r)] N herbicida m

weedy ['wiːdɪ] ADJ (**weedier, weediest**) Pej debilucho(a)

week [wiːk] N semana f; **a w. (ago) today/ yesterday** hoy hace/ayer hizo una semana; **a w. today** hoy justo dentro de una semana; **last/ next w.** la semana pasada/que viene; **once a w.** una vez por semana; **w. in, w. out** semana tras semana

weekday ['wiːkdeɪ] N día m laborable

weekend [wiːk'end] N fin m de semana

weekly ['wiːklɪ] **1** ADJ semanal

2 ADV semanalmente; **twice w.** dos veces por semana

3 N Press semanario m

weep [wiːp] **1** VI (pt & pp **wept**) llorar; **to w. with joy** llorar de alegría

2 VT (tears) derramar

weeping ['wiːpɪŋ] ADJ **w. willow** sauce m llorón

weigh [weɪ] **1** VT (**a**) (measure) pesar (**b**) (consider) ponderar (**c**) **to w. anchor** levar anclas

2 VI pesar

► **weigh down** VT SEP sobrecargar

► **weigh in** VI (**a**) Sport pesarse (**b**) Fam (join in) intervenir

► **weigh up** VT SEP (matter) evaluar; (person) formar una opinión sobre; **to w. up the pros and cons** sopesar los pros y los contras

weight [weɪt] N (**a**) (of person, object) peso m; **to lose w.** adelgazar; **to put on w.** subir de peso (**b**) (of clock, scales) pesa f (**c**) Fig **that's a w. off my mind** eso me quita or Am saca un peso de encima

weighting ['weɪtɪŋ] N Br (on salary) suplemento m de salario

weightlifter ['weɪtlɪftə(r)] N halterófilo(a) m,f

weightlifting ['weɪtlɪftɪŋ] N halterofilia f, levantamiento m de pesos

weighty ['weɪtɪ] ADJ (**weightier, weightiest**) pesado(a); Fig (problem, matter) importante, grave; (argument) de peso

weir [wɪə(r)] N presa f

weird [wɪəd] ADJ raro(a), extraño(a)

welcome ['welkəm] **1** ADJ (person) bienvenido(a); (news) grato(a); (change) oportuno(a); **to make sb w.** acoger a algn calurosamente; **you're w.!** ¡no hay de qué!

2 N (greeting) bienvenida f

3 VT acoger; (more formally) darle la bienvenida a; (news) acoger con agrado; (decision) aplaudir

welcoming ['welkəmɪŋ] ADJ (person) acogedor(a); (smile) de bienvenida

weld [weld] VT soldar

welfare ['welfeə(r)] N (**a**) (well-being) bienestar m; **animal/child w.** protección f de animales/ de menores; **w. work** asistencia f social; **w. worker** asistente mf social (**b**) US (social security) seguridad f social

well¹ [wel] N (**a**) *(for water, oil)* pozo m (**b**) *(of staircase, lift)* hueco m (**c**) *(of court, hall)* hemiciclo m

▶ **well up** VI brotar

well² [wel] **1** ADJ (**a**) *(healthy)* bien; **are you keeping w.?** ¿estás bien de salud?; **to get w.** reponerse (**b**) *(satisfactory)* bien; **all is w.** todo va bien; **it's just as w.** menos mal (**c**) **it is as w. to remember that** conviene recordar que

2 ADV (**better, best**) (**a**) *(properly)* bien; **he has done w. (for himself)** ha prosperado; **the business is doing w.** el negocio marcha bien; **she did w. in the exam** el examen le fue bien; **w. done!** ¡muy bien!; **he took it w.** lo tomó a bien (**b**) *(thoroughly)* bien; **I know it only too w.** lo sé de sobra; *Culin* **w. done** muy hecho(a) (**c**) **he's w. over thirty** tiene treinta años bien cumplidos; **w. after six o'clock** mucho después de las seis (**e**) **as w.** también; **as w. as así como**; **children as w. as adults** tanto niños como adultos

3 INTERJ (**a**) *(surprise)* ¡bueno!, ¡vaya!; **w. I never!** ¡no me digas! (**b**) *(agreement, question, resignation)* bueno; **very w.** bueno; **w.?** ¿y bien? (**c**) *(doubt)* pues; **w., I don't know** pues, no sé (**d**) *(resumption)* **w., as I was saying** pues (bien), como iba diciendo

well-behaved ['welbɪheɪvd] ADJ *(child)* formal, educado(a)

well-being ['welbiːɪŋ] N bienestar m

well-built ['welbɪlt] ADJ *(building etc)* de construcción sólida; *(person)* fornido(a)

well-earned ['welɜːnd] ADJ merecido(a)

well-educated [wel'edʊkeɪtɪd] ADJ culto(a)

well-heeled ['welhiːld] ADJ *Fam* ricachón(ona), forrado(a), *Esp* con pelas, *Am* con plata

well-informed ['welɪnfɔːmd] ADJ bien informado(a)

wellington ['welɪŋtən] N *Br* **wellingtons, w. boots** botas *fpl* de agua *or* goma *or Méx, Ven* caucho

well-known ['welnəʊn] ADJ (bien) conocido(a)

well-mannered ['welmænəd] ADJ educado(a)

well-meaning [wel'miːnɪŋ] ADJ bien intencionado(a)

well-off [wel'ɒf] ADJ *(rich)* acomodado(a)

well-read [wel'red] ADJ culto(a)

well-spoken [wel'spəʊkən] ADJ con acento culto

well-to-do [weltə'duː] ADJ acomodado(a)

well-wisher ['welwɪʃə(r)] N admirador(a) *m,f*

Welsh [welʃ] **1** ADJ galés(esa); **W. rarebit** = tostada con queso fundido

2 N (**a**) *(language)* galés m (**b**) **the W.** los galeses

Welshman ['welʃmən] N galés m

Welshwoman ['welʃwʊmən] N galesa f

welterweight ['weltəweɪt] N (peso m) wélter m

wench [wentʃ] N *Old-fashioned* moza f

went [went] PT *of* go

wept [wept] PT & PP *of* weep

were [wɜː(r), *unstressed* wə(r)] PT *of* be

west [west] **1** N oeste m, occidente m; **in/to the w.** al oeste; *Pol* **the W.** los países occidentales

2 ADJ del oeste, occidental; **the W. Indies** las Antillas; **W. Indian** antillano(a)

3 ADV al oeste, hacia el oeste

westerly ['westəlɪ] ADJ *(wind)* del oeste

western ['westən] **1** ADJ del oeste, occidental; **W. Europe** Europa Occidental

2 N *Cin* western m, película f del oeste

westward ['westwəd] ADJ **in a w. direction** hacia el oeste

westwards ['westwədz] ADV hacia el oeste

wet [wet] **1** ADJ (**wetter, wettest**) (**a**) *(soaked)* mojado(a); *(damp)* húmedo(a); *Fig* **w. blanket** aguafiestas *mf inv*; **w. paint** *(sign)* recién pintado; **w. through** *(person)* calado(a) hasta los huesos; *(thing)* empapado(a); **w. suit** traje isotérmico (**b**) *(rainy)* lluvioso(a) (**c**) *Br Fam (person)* soso(a)

2 VT *(pt & pp wet)* mojar; **to w. oneself** orinarse

whack [wæk] **1** VT *(hit hard)* dar un porrazo *or Méx* madrazo a

2 N (**a**) *(blow)* porrazo m, *Méx* madrazo m (**b**) *Fam (share)* parte f, porción f

whale [weɪl] N ballena f

wharf [wɔːf] N *(pl* **wharves** [wɔːvz]) muelle m

what [wɒt, *unstressed* wət] **1** ADJ (**a**) *(direct question)* qué; **w. (sort of) bird is that?** ¿qué tipo de ave es ésa?; **w. good is that?** ¿para qué sirve eso? (**b**) *(indirect question)* qué; **ask her w. colour she likes** pregúntale qué color le gusta

2 PRON (**a**) *(direct question)* qué; **w. are you talking about?** ¿de qué estás hablando?; **w. about your father?** ¿y tu padre (qué)?; **w. about going tomorrow?** ¿qué te parece si vamos mañana?; **w. can I do for you?** ¿en qué puedo servirle?; **w. did it cost?** ¿cuánto costó?; **w. did you do that?** ¿por qué hiciste eso?; **w. (did you say)?** ¿cómo?; **w. does it sound like?** ¿cómo suena?; **w. is happening?** ¿qué pasa?; **w. is it?** *(definition)* ¿qué es?; *(what's the matter)* ¿qué pasa?; **w.'s it called?** ¿cómo se llama?; **w.'s this for?** ¿para qué sirve esto?

(**b**) *(indirect question)* qué, lo que; **he asked me w. I thought** me preguntó lo que pensaba; **I didn't know w. to say** no sabía qué decir

(**c**) **(and) w.'s more** y además; **come w. may** pase lo que pase; **guess w.!** ¿sabes qué?; **it's just w. I need** es exactamente lo que necesito

(**d**) *(in exclamations)* **w. a goal!** ¡qué *or* vaya golazo!; **w. a lovely picture!** ¡qué cuadro más bonito!

3 INTERJ *(surprise, indignation)* ¡cómo!; **w., no dessert?** ¿cómo, no hay postre?

whatever [wɒt'evə(r), *unstressed* wət'evə(r)] 1 ADJ (a) *(any)* cualquier que; **at w. time you like** a la hora que quieras; **of w. colour** no importa de qué color (b) *(with negative)* **nothing w.** nada en absoluto; **with no interest w.** sin interés alguno

2 PRON (a) *(what)* **do w. happened?** ¿qué pasó? (b) *(anything, all that)* (todo) lo que; **do w. you like** haz lo que quieras (c) *(no matter what)* **don't tell him, w. you do** no se te ocurra decírselo; **w. (else) you find** cualquier (otra) cosa que encuentres; **he goes out w. the weather** sale haga el tiempo que haga

whatsoever [wɒtsəʊ'evə(r)] ADJ **anything w.** cualquier cosa; **nothing w.** nada en absoluto

wheat [wi:t] N trigo *m*; **w. germ** germen *m* de trigo

wheedle ['wi:dəl] VT **to w. sb into doing sth** engatusar a algn para que haga algo; **to w. sth out of sb** sonsacar algo a algn halagándole

wheel [wi:l] 1 N rueda *f*
2 VT *(bicycle)* empujar
3 VI (a) *(bird)* revolotear (b) **to w. round** girar sobre los talones

wheelbarrow ['wi:lbærəʊ] N carretilla *f*

wheelchair ['wi:ltʃeə(r)] N silla *f* de ruedas

wheeze [wi:z] VI respirar con dificultad, resollar

when [wen] 1 ADV (a) *(direct question)* cuándo; **since w.?** ¿desde cuándo?; **w. did he arrive?** ¿cuándo llegó? (b) *(indirect question)* cuándo; **tell me w. to go** dime cuándo debo irme (c) *(on which)* cuando, en que; **the days w. I work** los días en que trabajo
2 CONJ (a) *(with time)* cuando; **I'll tell you w. she comes** te lo diré cuando llegue; **w. he was a boy …** de niño … (b) *(whenever)* cuando (c) *(given that, if)* si (d) *(although)* aunque

whence [wens] ADV *Fml Literary (from where)* de dónde

whenever [wen'evə(r)] 1 CONJ *(when)* cuando; *(every time)* siempre que
2 ADV **w. that might be** sea cuando sea

where [weə(r)] ADV (a) *(direct question)* dónde; *(direction)* adónde; **w. are you going?** ¿adónde vas?; **w. did we go wrong?** ¿en qué nos equivocamos?; **w. do you come from?** ¿de dónde es usted? (b) *(indirect question)* dónde; *(direction)* adónde; **tell me w. you went** dime adónde fuiste (c) *(at, in which)* donde; *(direction)* adonde, a donde (d) *(when)* cuando

whereabouts 1 ADV [weərə'baʊts] **w. do you live?** ¿por dónde vives?
2 N ['weərəbaʊts] paradero *m*

whereas [weər'æz] CONJ (a) *(but, while)* mientras que (b) *Jur* considerando que

whereby [weə'baɪ] ADV por el/la/lo cual

whereupon [weərə'pɒn] CONJ *Fml* después de lo cual

wherever [weər'evə(r)] 1 CONJ dondequiera que; **I'll find him w. he is** le encontraré

dondequiera que esté; **sit w. you like** siéntate donde quieras
2 ADV *(direct question)* adónde

wherewithal ['weəwɪðɔ:l] N *Fam* pelas *fpl*

whet [wet] VT **to w. sb's appetite** abrir el apetito a algn

whether ['weðə(r)] CONJ (a) *(if)* si; **I don't know w. it is true** no sé si es verdad; **I doubt w. he'll win** dudo que gane (b) **w. he comes or not** venga o no

which [wɪtʃ] 1 ADJ (a) *(direct question)* qué; **w. colour do you prefer?** ¿qué color prefieres?; **w. one?** ¿cuál?; **w. way?** ¿por dónde? (b) *(indirect question)* qué; **tell me w. dress you like** dime qué vestido te gusta (c) *by w. time* y para entonces; **in w. case** en cuyo caso
2 PRON (a) *(direct question)* cuál/cuáles; **w. of you did it?** ¿quién de vosotros lo hizo? (b) *(indirect question)* cuál/cuáles; **I don't know w. I'd rather have** no sé cuál prefiero (c) *(defining relative)* que; *(after preposition)* que, el/la cual, los/las cuales, el/la que, los/las que; **here are the books (w.) I have read** aquí están los libros que he leído; **the accident (w.) I told you about** el accidente del que te hablé; **the car in w. he was travelling** el coche en (el) que viajaba; **this is the one (w.) I like** éste es el que me gusta (d) *(non-defining relative)* el/la cual, los/las cuales; **I played three sets, all of w. I lost** jugué tres sets, todos los cuales perdí (e) *(referring to a clause)* lo cual, lo que; **he won, w. made me very happy** ganó, lo cual *or* lo que me alegró mucho

whichever [wɪtʃ'evə(r)] 1 ADJ el/la que, cualquiera que; **I'll take w. books you don't want** tomaré los libros que no quieras; **w. system you choose** cualquiera que sea el sistema que elijas
2 PRON el/la que

whiff [wɪf] N (a) *(quick smell)* ráfaga *f*; *(of air, smoke)* bocanada *f* (b) *Fam (bad smell)* tufo *m*

while [waɪl] 1 N (a) *(length of time)* rato *m*, tiempo *m*; **in a little w.** dentro de poco; **once in a w.** de vez en cuando (b) **it's not worth your w. staying** no merece la pena que te quedes
2 CONJ (a) *(time)* mientras; **he fell asleep w. driving** se durmió mientras conducía (b) *(although)* aunque (c) *(whereas)* mientras que
▶ **while away** VT SEP **to w. away the time** pasar el rato

whilst [waɪlst] CONJ *Br* = **while**

whim [wɪm] N capricho *m*, antojo *m*

whimper ['wɪmpə(r)] 1 N quejido *m*
2 VI lloriquear

whine [waɪn] VI (a) *(child)* lloriquear; *(with pain)* dar quejidos (b) *(complain)* quejarse (c) *(engine)* chirriar

whip [wɪp] 1 N (a) *(for punishment)* látigo *m*; *(for riding)* fusta *f* (b) *Br Pol* = oficial encargado(a) de la disciplina de un partido

2 VT (**a**) (as punishment) azotar; (horse) fustigar (**b**) Culin batir; **whipped cream** Esp nata montada, Am crema batida (**c**) Fam (steal) mangar
▸ **whip away** VT SEP arrebatar
▸ **whip up** VT SEP (passions, enthusiasm) avivar; (support) incrementar
whipping ['wɪpɪŋ] N Fig **w. boy** cabeza f de turco
whip-round ['wɪpraʊnd] N Br Fam colecta f
whir [wɜː(r)] VI = whirr
whirl [wɜːl] **1** N giro m; Fig torbellino m
2 VT **to w. sth round** dar vueltas a or hacer girar algo
3 VI **to w. round** girar con rapidez; (leaves etc) arremolinarse; **my head's whirling** me está dando vueltas la cabeza
whirlpool ['wɜːlpuːl] N remolino m
whirlwind ['wɜːlwɪnd] N torbellino m
whirr [wɜː(r)] VI zumbar, runrunear
whisk [wɪsk] **1** N Culin batidor m; (electric) batidora f
2 VT Culin batir
▸ **whisk away, whisk off** VT SEP quitar bruscamente, llevarse de repente
whisker ['wɪskə(r)] N **whiskers** (of person) patillas fpl; (of cat) bigotes mpl
whisky, US whiskey ['wɪskɪ] N whisky m
whisper ['wɪspə(r)] **1** N (**a**) (sound) susurro m (**b**) (rumour) rumor m
2 VT decir en voz baja
3 VI susurrar
whistle ['wɪsəl] **1** N (**a**) (instrument) pito m (**b**) (sound) silbido m, pitido m
2 VT (tune) silbar
3 VI (person, kettle, wind) silbar; (train) pitar
white [waɪt] **1** ADJ blanco(a); **to go w.** (face) palidecer; (hair) encanecer; **w. coffee** café m con leche; **w. hair** pelo blanco; **a w. Christmas** una Navidad con nieve; Fig **a w. lie** una mentira piadosa; US **the W. House** la Casa Blanca; Pol **w. paper** libro blanco; **w. sauce** bechamel f, Col, CSur salsa f blanca
2 N (**a**) (colour, person, of eye) blanco m (**b**) (of egg) clara f (**c**) **whites** ropa f blanca
white-collar ['waɪtkɒlə(r)] ADJ **w. worker** empleado m de oficina
whiteness ['waɪtnɪs] N blancura f
whitewash ['waɪtwɒʃ] **1** N (**a**) (paint) cal f (**b**) Fam (cover-up) encubrimiento m
2 VT (**a**) (wall) enjalbegar, blanquear (**b**) Fam (cover up) encubrir
whiting ['waɪtɪŋ] N (pl whiting) (fish) pescadilla f
Whitsun ['wɪtsən] N Pentecostés m
whittle ['wɪtəl] VT cortar en pedazos; **to w. away at** roer; Fig **to w. down** reducir poco a poco
whiz(z) [wɪz] VI (**a**) (sound) silbar (**b**) **to w. past** pasar volando; Fam **w. kid** joven mf dinámico(a) y emprendedor(a)

who [huː] PRON (**a**) (direct question) quién/ quiénes; **w. are they?** ¿quiénes son?; **w. is it?** ¿quién es? (**b**) (indirect question) quién; **I don't know w. did it** no sé quién lo hizo (**c**) REL (defining) que; **those w. don't know** los que no saben (**d**) REL (non-defining) quien/ quienes, el/la cual, los/las cuales; **Elena's mother, w. is very rich …** la madre de Elena, la cual es muy rica …
whodun(n)it [huː'dʌnɪt] N Fam novela f/ película f de suspense
whoever [huː'evə(r)] PRON (**a**) (anyone that, no matter who) quienquiera que; **w. you are** quienquiera que seas; **give it to w.** you like dáselo a quien quieras; **w. said that is a fool** el que dijo eso es un tonto (**b**) (direct question) **w. told you that?** ¿quién te dijo eso?
whole [həʊl] **1** ADJ (**a**) (entire) entero(a), íntegro(a); **a w. week** una semana entera; **he took the w. lot** se los llevó todos (**b**) (in one piece) intacto(a)
2 N (**a**) (single unit) todo m, conjunto m; **as a w.** en su totalidad (**b**) (all) totalidad f; **the w. of London** todo Londres (**c**) **on the w.** en general
wholefood ['həʊlfuːd] N alimentos mpl integrales
wholehearted [həʊl'hɑːtɪd] ADJ (enthusiastic) entusiasta; (sincere) sincero(a); (unreserved) incondicional
wholemeal ['həʊlmiːl] ADJ Br integral
wholesale ['həʊlseɪl] Com **1** N compraventa f al por mayor, Am mayoreo m
2 ADJ al por mayor; Fig total
3 ADV al por mayor; Fig en su totalidad
wholesaler ['həʊlseɪlə(r)] N mayorista mf
wholesome ['həʊlsəm] ADJ sano(a)
wholly ['həʊllɪ] ADV enteramente, completamente
whom [huːm] PRON Fml (**a**) (direct question) (accusative) a quién; **w. did you talk to?** ¿con quién hablaste?; (after preposition) of/from **w.?** ¿de quién?; **to w. are you referring?** ¿a quién te refieres? (**b**) REL (accusative) que, a quien/a quienes; **those w. I have seen** aquéllos a quien(es) he visto (**c**) REL (after preposition) quien/quienes, el/la cual, los/las cuales; **my brothers, both of w. are miners** mis hermanos, que son mineros los dos

> En la actualidad, sólo aparece en contextos formales. **Whom** se puede sustituir por **who** en todos los casos salvo cuando va después de preposición.

whooping cough ['huːpɪŋkɒf] N tos ferina
whopping ['wɒpɪŋ] ADJ Fam enorme
whore [hɔː(r)] N very Fam Pej puta f
whose [huːz] **1** PRON (**a**) (direct question) de quién/de quiénes; **w. are these gloves?** ¿de quién son estos guantes?; **w. is this?** ¿de quién es esto? (**b**) (indirect question) de quién/de quiénes; **I don't know w. these**

coats are no sé de quién son estos abrigos (**c**) REL cuyo(s)/cuya(s); **the man w. children we saw** el hombre a cuyos hijos vimos
  2 ADJ **w. car/house is this?** ¿de quién es este coche/esta casa?

why [waɪ] **1** ADV por qué; *(for what purpose)* para qué; **w. did you do that?** ¿por qué hiciste eso?; **w. not go to bed?** ¿por qué no te acuestas?; **I don't know w. he did it** no sé por qué lo hizo; **that is w. I didn't come** por eso no vine; **there's no reason w. you shouldn't go** no hay motivo para que no vayas
  2 INTERJ (**a**) *(fancy that!)* ¡toma!, ¡vaya!; **w., it's David!** ¡sí es David! (**b**) *(protest, assertion)* sí, vamos

wick [wɪk] N mecha *f*

wicked ['wɪkɪd] ADJ (**a**) *(evil)* perverso(a), malo(a) (**b**) *Fam (appalling)* asqueroso(a); *(temper)* de perros

wicker ['wɪkə(r)] **1** N mimbre *m*
  2 ADJ de mimbre

wickerwork ['wɪkəwɜːk] N *(material)* mimbre *m*; *(articles)* artículos *mpl* de mimbre

wicket ['wɪkɪt] N *(in cricket) (stumps)* palos *mpl*

wide [waɪd] **1** ADJ (**a**) *(road, trousers)* ancho(a); *(gap, interval)* grande; **it is 10 m w.** tiene 10 m de ancho (**b**) *(area, knowledge, support, range)* amplio(a); **w. interests** intereses muy diversos (**c**) *(off target)* desviado(a)
  2 ADV **from far and w.** de todas partes; **to open one's eyes w.** abrir los ojos de par en par; **w. apart** muy separados(as); **w. awake** completamente despierto(a); **w. open** abierto(a) de par en par; **with mouth w. open** boquiabierto(a)

wide-angle ['waɪdæŋgəl] ADJ *Phot* **w. lens** gran angular *m*

widely ['waɪdlɪ] ADV *(travel etc)* extensamente; *(believed)* generalmente; **he is w. known** es muy conocido

widen ['waɪdən] **1** VT ensanchar; *(interests)* ampliar
  2 VI ensancharse

wide-ranging ['waɪd'reɪndʒɪŋ] ADJ *(interests)* muy diversos(as); *(discussion)* amplio(a); *(study)* de gran alcance

widespread ['waɪdspred] ADJ *(unrest, belief)* general; *(damage)* extenso(a); **to become w.** generalizarse

widow ['wɪdəʊ] N viuda *f*

widowed ['wɪdəʊd] ADJ enviudado(a)

widower ['wɪdəʊə(r)] N viudo *m*

width [wɪdθ] N (**a**) *(dimension)* anchura *f* (**b**) *(of material, swimming pool)* ancho *m*

wield [wiːld] VT *(weapon)* blandir; *Fig (power)* ejercer

wife [waɪf] N *(pl* **wives**) mujer *f*, esposa *f*

wig [wɪg] N peluca *f*

wiggle ['wɪgəl] **1** VT *(finger etc)* menear; **to w. one's hips** contonearse
  2 VI menearse

Wight [waɪt] N **Isle of W.** Isla *f* de Wight

wild [waɪld] **1** ADJ (**a**) *(animal, tribe)* salvaje; **w. beast** fiera *f* (**b**) *(plant)* silvestre (**c**) *(landscape)* agreste; **the W. West** el Salvaje Oeste (**d**) *(temperament, behaviour)* alocado(a); *(appearance)* desordenado(a); *(passions etc)* desenfrenado(a); *(laughter, thoughts)* loco(a); *(applause)* fervoroso(a); *Fam Fig* **she is w. about him/about tennis** está loca por él/por el tenis
  2 ADV *Fig* **to run w.** *(children)* desmandarse
  3 N **in the w.** en el estado salvaje

wildcat ['waɪldkæt] N (**a**) *(animal)* gato *m* montés (**b**) *Ind* **w. strike** huelga *f* salvaje

wilderness ['wɪldənɪs] N desierto *m*

wildfire ['waɪldfaɪə(r)] N **to spread like w.** correr como la pólvora

wildlife ['waɪldlaɪf] N fauna *f*; **w. park** parque *m* natural

wildly ['waɪldlɪ] ADV (**a**) *(rush round etc)* como un(a) loco(a); *(shoot)* sin apuntar; *(hit out)* a tontas y a locas (**b**) **w. enthusiastic** loco(a) de entusiasmo; **w. inaccurate** totalmente erróneo(a)

wilful, *US* **willful** ['wɪlfʊl] ADJ (**a**) *(stubborn)* terco(a) (**b**) *Jur* premeditado(a)

will¹ [wɪl] **1** N (**a**) *(resolve)* voluntad *f*; **good/ill w.** buena/mala voluntad; **of my own free w.** por mi propia voluntad (**b**) *Jur (testament)* testamento *m*; **to make one's w.** hacer testamento
  2 VT **fate willed that ...** el destino quiso que ...

will² [wɪl] V AUX *(pt* **would**)

En el inglés hablado, y en el escrito en estilo coloquial, el verbo **will** se contrae de manera que **I/you/he** *etc* **will** se transforman en **I'll, you'll, he'll** *etc* y el verbo **would** se contrae de manera que **I/you/he** *etc* **would** se transforman en **I'd, you'd, he'd** *etc.* Las formas negativas **will not** y **would not** se transforman en **won't** y **wouldn't**.

(**a**) *(future) (esp second & third person)* **they'll come** vendrán; **w. he be there? – yes, he w.** ¿estará allí? – sí(, estará); **you'll tell him, won't you?** se lo dirás, ¿verdad?; **don't forget, w. you!** ¡que no se te olvide, vale!; **she won't do it** no lo hará
(**b**) *(command)* **you w. be here at eleven!** ¡debes estar aquí a las once!
(**c**) *(future perfect)* **they'll have finished by tomorrow** habrán terminado para mañana
(**d**) *(willingness)* **be quiet, w. you! – no, I won't!** ¿quiere callarse? – no quiero; **I won't have it!** ¡no lo permito!; **w. you have a drink? – yes, I w.** ¿quiere tomar algo? – sí, por favor; **won't you sit down?** ¿quiere sentarse?
(**e**) *(custom)* **accidents w. happen** siempre habrá accidentes
(**f**) *(persistence)* **if you w. go out without a coat ...** si te empeñas en salir sin abrigo ...

(**g**) *(probability)* **he'll be on holiday now** ahora estará de vacaciones

(**h**) *(ability)* **the lift w. hold ten people** en el ascensor caben diez personas

willing ['wɪlɪŋ] ADJ *(obliging)* complaciente; **I'm quite w. to do it** lo haré con mucho gusto; **to be w. to do sth** estar dispuesto(a) a hacer algo

willingly ['wɪlɪŋlɪ] ADV de buena gana

willingness ['wɪlɪŋnɪs] N buena voluntad

willow ['wɪləʊ] N **w. (tree)** sauce *m*

willpower ['wɪlpaʊə(r)] N (fuerza *f* de) voluntad *f*

willy ['wɪlɪ] N *Br Fam* pito *m*, pilila *f*

willy-nilly ['wɪlɪ'nɪlɪ] ADV por gusto o por fuerza

wilt [wɪlt] VI marchitarse

wily ['waɪlɪ] ADJ (**wilier, wiliest**) astuto(a)

wimp [wɪmp] N *Fam (physically)* debilucho(a) *m,f; (lacking character)* blandengue *mf*

win [wɪn] **1** N victoria *f*
2 VT *(pt & pp* **won**) (**a**) *(battle, race, election)* ganar; *(prize)* llevarse; *(victory)* conseguir (**b**) *Fig (sympathy, friendship)* ganarse; *(praise)* cosechar; **to w. sb's love** conquistar a algn
3 VI ganar

▸ **win back** VT SEP recuperar

▸ **win over** VT SEP *(to cause, idea)* atraer (**to** a); *(voters, support)* ganarse

▸ **win through** VI conseguir triunfar

wince [wɪns] VI tener un rictus de dolor

winch [wɪntʃ] N cigüeña *f*, torno *m*

wind¹ [wɪnd] **1** N (**a**) *(air current)* viento *m; Fig* **to get w. of sth** olerse algo; **w. farm** parque eólico; **w. tunnel** túnel aerodinámico (**b**) *(breath)* aliento *m;* **to get one's second w.** recobrar el aliento (**c**) *Med* flato *m*, gases *mpl* (**d**) **w. instrument** instrumento *m* de viento
2 VT **to be winded** quedarse sin aliento

wind² [waɪnd] **1** VT *(pt & pp* **wound**) *(on to a reel)* enrollar; **to w. a bandage round one's finger** vendarse el dedo (**b**) **to w. on/back** *(film, tape)* avanzar/rebobinar (**c**) *(clock)* dar cuerda a
2 VI *(road, river)* serpentear

▸ **wind down 1** VT SEP *(window)* bajar
2 VI *Fam (person)* relajarse

▸ **wind up 1** VT SEP (**a**) *(roll up)* enrollar (**b**) *(business etc)* cerrar; *(debate)* clausurar (**c**) *(clock)* dar cuerda a
2 VI *(meeting)* terminar

windfall ['wɪndfɔːl] N *Fig* ganancia inesperada

winding ['waɪndɪŋ] ADJ *(road, river)* sinuoso(a); *(staircase)* de caracol

windmill ['wɪndmɪl] N molino *m* (de viento)

window ['wɪndəʊ] N ventana *f; (of vehicle, ticket office etc)* ventanilla *f; (shop)* **w.** escaparate *m, Am* vidriera *f, Chile, Col, Méx* vitrina *f;* **to clean the windows** limpiar los cristales; **w. box** jardinera *f;* **w. cleaner** limpiacristales *mf inv*

windowpane ['wɪndəʊpeɪn] N vidrio *m or* cristal *m*

window-shopping ['wɪndəʊʃɒpɪŋ] N **to go w.** ir a mirar escaparates

windowsill ['wɪndəʊsɪl] N alféizar *m*

windpipe ['wɪndpaɪp] N tráquea *f*

windscreen ['wɪndskriːn], *US* **windshield** ['wɪndʃiːld] N parabrisas *m inv;* **w. washer** lavaparabrisas *m inv;* **w. wiper** limpiaparabrisas *m inv*

windsurfing ['wɪndsɜːfɪŋ] N **to go w.** ir a hacer windsurf *or* tabla a vela

windswept ['wɪndswept] ADJ *(landscape)* expuesto(a) a los vientos; *(person, hair)* despeinado(a) (por el viento)

windy ['wɪndɪ] ADJ (**windier, windiest**) *(weather)* ventoso(a); *(place)* desprotegido(a) del viento; **it is very w. today** hoy hace mucho viento

wine [waɪn] N vino *m;* **w. cellar** bodega *f;* **w. list** lista *f* de vinos; **w. merchant** vinatero(a) *m,f;* **w. tasting** cata *f* de vinos; **w. vinegar** vinagre *m* de vino

wineglass ['waɪnglɑːs] N copa *f* (para vino)

wing [wɪŋ] N (**a**) *(of bird, plane)* ala *f* (**b**) *(of building)* ala *f* (**c**) *Br Aut* aleta *f;* **w. mirror** retrovisor externo (**d**) *Th* **(in the) wings** (entre) bastidores *mpl* (**e**) *Ftb* banda *f* (**f**) *Pol* ala *f;* **the left w.** la izquierda

winger ['wɪŋə(r)] N *Ftb* extremo *m*

wink [wɪŋk] **1** N guiño *m.*
2 VI (**a**) *(person)* guiñar (el ojo) (**b**) *(light)* parpadear

winner ['wɪnə(r)] N ganador(a) *m,f*

winning ['wɪnɪŋ] ADJ *(person, team)* ganador(a); *(number)* premiado(a); *(goal)* decisivo(a); **w. post** meta *f*

winnings ['wɪnɪŋz] NPL ganancias *fpl*

winter ['wɪntə(r)] **1** N invierno *m*
2 ADJ de invierno; **w. sports** deportes *mpl* de invierno
3 VI invernar

wintry ['wɪntrɪ] ADJ (**wintrier, wintriest**) invernal

wipe [waɪp] VT limpiar; **to w. one's brow** enjugarse la frente; **to w. one's feet/nose** limpiarse los pies/las narices

▸ **wipe away** VT SEP *(tear)* enjugar

▸ **wipe off** VT SEP quitar frotando; **to w. sth off the blackboard/the tape** borrar algo de la pizarra/de la cinta

▸ **wipe out** VT SEP (**a**) *(erase)* borrar (**b**) *(army)* aniquilar; *(species etc)* exterminar

▸ **wipe up** VT SEP limpiar

wiper ['waɪpə(r)] N *Aut* limpiaparabrisas *m inv*

wire [waɪə(r)] **1** N (**a**) *(in general)* alambre *m; Elec* cable *m; Tel* hilo *m;* **w. cutters** cizalla *f* (**b**) *(telegram)* telegrama *m*
2 VT (**a**) **to w. (up) a house** poner la instalación eléctrica de una casa; **to w. (up) an appliance to the mains** conectar un

aparato a la toma eléctrica (**b**) *(information)* enviar por telegrama

wireless ['waɪəlɪs] **1** N *Old-fashioned* radio *f*
2 ADJ *Comput* wireless, inalámbrico(a)

wiring ['waɪərɪŋ] N *(network)* cableado *m*; *(action)* instalación *f* del cableado

wiry ['waɪərɪ] ADJ (**wirier, wiriest**) *(hair)* basto(a) y rizado(a) *or Méx* quebrado(a); *(person)* fibroso(a)

wisdom ['wɪzdəm] N (**a**) *(learning)* sabiduría *f*, saber *m* (**b**) *(good sense) (of person)* cordura *f*; *(of action)* sensatez *f* (**c**) **w. tooth** muela *f* del juicio

wise [waɪz] ADJ (**a**) *(knowledgeable)* sabio(a); **a w. man** un sabio; **the Three W. Men** los Reyes Magos (**b**) *(remark)* juicioso(a); *(decision)* acertado(a); **it would be w. to keep quiet** sería prudente callarse

wisecrack ['waɪzkræk] N *Fam* chiste *m*, salida *f* ingeniosa

wisely ['waɪzlɪ] ADV *(with prudence)* sensatamente

wish [wɪʃ] **1** N (**a**) *(desire)* deseo *m* (**for** de); **to make a w.** pedir un deseo (**b**) **best wishes** felicitaciones *fpl*; **give your mother my best wishes** salude a su madre de mi parte; **with best wishes, Peter** *(at end of letter)* saludos cordiales, Peter
2 VT (**a**) *(want)* querer, desear; **I w. I could stay longer** me gustaría poder quedarme más tiempo; **I w. you had told me!** ¡ojalá me lo hubieras dicho!; **to w. to do sth** querer hacer algo (**b**) **to w. sb goodnight** darle las buenas noches a algn; **to w. sb well** desearle a algn mucha suerte
3 VI *(want)* desear; **as you w.** como quieras; **do as you w.** haga lo que quiera; **to w. for sth** desear algo

wishful ['wɪʃfʊl] ADJ **it's w. thinking** es hacerse ilusiones

wishy-washy ['wɪʃɪ'wɒʃɪ] ADJ *Fam* vacilante

wisp [wɪsp] N *(of wool, hair)* mechón *m*; *(of smoke)* voluta *f*

wistful ['wɪstfʊl] ADJ melancólico(a)

wit [wɪt] N (**a**) *(intelligence) (often pl)* inteligencia *f*; *Fig* **to be at one's wits' end** estar para volverse loco(a); *Fam Fig* **to have one's wits about one** ser despabilado(a) (**b**) *(humour)* ingenio *m*

witch [wɪtʃ] N bruja *f*; *Fig* **w. hunt** caza *f* de brujas

witchcraft ['wɪtʃkrɑːft] N brujería *f*

with [wɪð, wɪθ] PREP con; **a room w. a bath** un cuarto con baño; **do you have any money w. you?** ¿traes dinero?; **the man w. the glasses** el hombre de las gafas; **he went w. me/you** fue conmigo/contigo; *Fam* **w. (sugar) or without (sugar)?** ¿con o sin azúcar?; **I have six w. this one** con éste tengo seis; **w. all his faults, I admire him** le admiro con todos sus defectos; **w. your permission** con su permiso; **we're**

all w. you *(support)* todos estamos contigo; **you're not w. me, are you?** *(understand)* no me entiendes, ¿verdad?; **he's w. Lloyds** trabaja para Lloyds; **she is popular w. her colleagues** todos sus colegas · la estiman mucho; **to fill a vase w. water** llenar un jarrón de agua; **it is made w. butter** está hecho con mantequilla; **she put on weight w. so much eating** engordó de tanto comer; **to be paralyzed w. fear** estar paralizado(a) de miedo; **w. experience** con la experiencia

withdraw [wɪð'drɔː] **1** VT (**a**) *(troops, offer, support)* retirar; *(from pocket)* sacar; **to w. money from the bank** sacar dinero del banco (**b**) *(statement, accusation)* retirar; retractarse de; *(plan, claim)* renunciar a
2 VI retirarse

withdrawal [wɪð'drɔːəl] N retirada *f*; *(of statement)* retractación *f*; *(of complaint, plan)* renuncia *f*; **w. symptoms** síndrome *m* de abstinencia

withdrawn [wɪð'drɔːn] **1** ADJ *(person)* introvertido(a)
2 PP *of* **withdraw**

withdrew [wɪð'druː] PT *of* **withdraw**

wither ['wɪðə(r)] VI *(plant)* marchitarse; *(limb)* atrofiarse

withering ['wɪðərɪŋ] ADJ *(look)* fulminante; *(criticism)* mordaz

withhold [wɪð'həʊld] VT *(pt & pp* **withheld** [wɪð'held])* *(money)* retener; *(decision)* aplazar; *(consent)* negar; *(information)* ocultar

within [wɪð'ɪn] **1** PREP (**a**) *(inside)* dentro de (**b**) *(range)* **the house is w. walking distance** se puede ir andando a la casa; **situated w. 5 km of the town** situado(a) a menos de 5 km de la ciudad; **w. sight of the sea** con vistas al mar; *Fig* **w. an inch of death** a dos dedos de la muerte (**c**) *(time)* **they arrived w. a few days of each other** llegaron con pocos días de diferencia; **w. the hour** dentro de una hora; **w. the next five years** durante los cinco próximos años
2 ADV dentro; **from w.** desde dentro

with-it ['wɪðɪt] ADJ *Fam* **she is very w.** tiene ideas muy modernas; **to get w.** ponerse de moda

without [wɪð'aʊt] PREP sin; **he did it w. my knowing** lo hizo sin que lo supiera yo; *Fig* **to do** *or* **go w. sth** *(voluntarily)* prescindir de algo; *(forcibly)* pasar(se) sin algo

withstand [wɪð'stænd] VT *(pt & pp* **withstood** [wɪð'stʊd])* resistir a; *(pain)* aguantar

witness ['wɪtnɪs] **1** N (**a**) *(person)* testigo *mf*; **w. box,** *US* **w. stand** barra *f* de los testigos (**b**) *(evidence)* **to bear w. to sth** dar fe de algo
2 VT (**a**) *(see)* presenciar, ser testigo de (**b**) *Fig (notice)* notar (**c**) *Jur* **to w. a document** firmar un documento como testigo

witticism ['wɪtɪsɪzəm] N ocurrencia *f*, agudeza *f*

witty ['wɪtɪ] ADJ (**wittier, wittiest**) ingenioso(a), agudo(a)

wives [waɪvz] PL *of* **wife**

wizard ['wɪzəd] N hechicero *m*, mago *m*

wizened ['wɪzənd] ADJ marchito(a), arrugado(a)

WMD [estiː'diː] NPL (*abbr* **weapons of mass destruction**) armas *fpl* de destrucción masiva

wobble ['wɒbəl] VI (*table, ladder etc*) tambalearse; (*jelly*) temblar

wobbly ['wɒblɪ] ADJ (**wobblier, wobbliest**) (*chair, table*) cojo(a); (*shelf, ladder*) tambaleante

woe [wəʊ] N *Literary* infortunio *m*; **w. betide you if I catch you!** ¡ay de ti si te cojo!

woeful ['wəʊfʊl] ADJ (**a**) (*person*) apesadumbrado(a), afligido(a) (**b**) (*sight*) penoso(a), deplorable; **w. ignorance** una ignorancia supina

wok [wɒk] N wok *m*, = sartén china con forma de cuenco

woke [wəʊk] PT *of* **wake**

woken ['wəʊkən] PP *of* **wake**

wolf [wʊlf] N (*pl* **wolves** [wʊlvz]) lobo *m*; *Fig* **a w. in sheep's clothing** un lobo con piel de cordero

woman ['wʊmən] N (*pl* **women**) mujer *f*; **old w.** vieja *f*; *Fam* **women's libber** feminista *mf*; *Fam* **women's lib** movimiento *m* feminista; **women's rights** derechos *mpl* de la mujer

womanhood ['wʊmənhʊd] N (*adult*) edad adulta de la mujer

womanizer ['wʊmənaɪzə(r)] N mujeriego *m*

womanly ['wʊmənlɪ] ADJ femenino(a)

womb [wuːm] N matriz *f*, útero *m*

women ['wɪmɪn] PL *of* **woman**

won [wʌn] PT & PP *of* **win**

wonder ['wʌndə(r)] 1 N (**a**) (*miracle*) milagro *m*; **no w. he hasn't come** no es de extrañar que no haya venido (**b**) (*amazement*) admiración *f*, asombro *m*
  2 VT (**a**) (*be surprised*) sorprenderse (**b**) (*ask oneself*) preguntarse; **I w. why** ¿por qué será?
  3 VI (**a**) (*marvel*) maravillarse; **to w. at sth** admirarse de algo (**b**) **it makes you w.** (*reflect*) te hace pensar

wonderful ['wʌndəfʊl] ADJ maravilloso(a)

wonderfully ['wʌndəfʊlɪ] ADV maravillosamente

wont [wəʊnt] *Fml* **1** ADJ **to be w. to do sth** ser dado(a) a hacer algo
  2 N costumbre *f*; **as is his w.** como acostumbra

won't [wəʊnt] = **will not**

woo [wuː] VT *Literary* (*court*) cortejar; *Fig* intentar congraciarse con

wood [wʊd] N (**a**) (*forest*) bosque *m* (**b**) (*material*) madera *f*; (*for fire*) leña *f*

woodcarving ['wʊdkɑːvɪŋ] N (**a**) (*craft*) tallado *m* en madera (**b**) (*object*) talla *f* en madera

woodcutter ['wʊdkʌtə(r)] N leñador(a) *m,f*

wooded ['wʊdɪd] ADJ arbolado(a)

wooden ['wʊdən] ADJ (**a**) (*made of wood*) de madera; **w. spoon/leg** cuchara *f*/pata *f* de palo (**b**) *Fig* rígido(a); (*acting*) sin expresión

woodlouse ['wʊdlaʊs] N cochinilla *f*

woodpecker ['wʊdpekə(r)] N pájaro carpintero

woodwind ['wʊdwɪnd] N **w. (instruments)** instrumentos *mpl* de viento de madera

woodwork ['wʊdwɜːk] N (**a**) (*craft*) carpintería *f* (**b**) (*of building*) maderaje *m*

woodworm ['wʊdwɜːm] N carcoma *f*

wool [wʊl] **1** N lana *f*; *Fig* **to pull the w. over sb's eyes** embaucar *or* dar el pego a algn
  2 ADJ de lana

woollen, *US* **woolen** ['wʊlən] **1** ADJ (**a**) (*dress*) de lana (**b**) (*industry*) lanero(a)
  2 NPL **woollens** géneros *mpl* de lana *or* de punto

woolly, *US* **wooly** ['wʊlɪ] ADJ (**woollier, woolliest**, *US* **woolier, wooliest**) (**a**) (*made of wool*) de lana (**b**) *Fig* (*unclear*) confuso(a)

word [wɜːd] **1** N (**a**) (*spoken, written*) palabra *f*; **in other words ...** es decir ..., o sea ...; **words failed me** me quedé sin habla; *Fig* **a w. of advice** un consejo; *Fig* **I'd like a w. with you** quiero hablar contigo un momento; *Fig* **she didn't say it in so many words** no lo dijo de modo tan explícito; **in the words of the poet ...** como dice el poeta ...; *Fig* **w. for w.** palabra por palabra; **w. processing** tratamiento *m* de textos; **w. processor** procesador *m* de textos (**b**) *Fig* (*message*) recado *m*, aviso *m*; **by w. of mouth** de palabra; **is there any w. from him?** ¿hay noticias de él?; **to send w.** mandar recado (**c**) *Fig* (*rumour*) voz *f*, rumor *m* (**d**) *Fig* (*promise*) palabra *f*; **he's a man of his w.** es hombre de palabra
  2 VT (*express*) formular; **a badly worded letter** una carta mal redactada

wording ['wɜːdɪŋ] N expresión *f*; **I changed the w.** slightly cambié algunas palabras

word-perfect [wɜːd'pɜːfekt] ADJ **to be w.** saberse el papel perfectamente

wordy ['wɜːdɪ] ADJ (**wordier, wordiest**) verboso(a)

wore [wɔː(r)] PT *of* **wear**

work [wɜːk] **1** N (**a**) (*labour*) trabajo *m*; **his w. in the field of physics** su labor en el campo de la física; **it's hard w.** cuesta trabajo (**b**) (*employment*) trabajo *m*, empleo *m*; **to be out of w.** no tener trabajo, *Esp* estar parado(a) (**c**) (*action*) obra *f*, acción *f*; **keep up the good w.!** ¡que siga así! (**d**) **a piece of w.** un trabajo; **a w. of art** una obra de arte (**e**) **works** obras *fpl*; **public works** obras (públicas) (**f**) **works** (*machinery*) mecanismo *m* (**g**) *Br* **works** (*factory*) fábrica *f*
  2 VT (**a**) (*drive*) hacer trabajar; **to w. one's way up/down** subir/bajar a duras penas; *Fig* **to w. one's way up in a firm** trabajarse el ascenso en una empresa (**b**) (*machine*) manejar; (*mechanism*) accionar (**c**) (*miracles,*

changes) operar, hacer (**d**) *(land)* cultivar; *(mine)* explotar (**e**) *(wood, metal etc)* trabajar
3 VI (**a**) *(person)* trabajar (**on** *or* **at** en); **to w. as a gardener** trabajar de jardinero (**b**) *(machine)* funcionar; **it works on gas** funciona con gas (**c**) *(drug)* surtir efecto; *(system)* funcionar bien; *(plan, trick)* salir bien (**d**) *(operate)* obrar; **to w. loose** soltarse; **we have no data to w. on** no tenemos datos en que basarnos
▸ **work off** VT SEP *(fat)* eliminar trabajando; *(anger)* desahogar
▸ **work out 1** VT SEP (**a**) *(plan)* idear; *(itinerary)* planear; *(details)* desarrollar (**b**) *(problem)* solucionar; *(solution)* encontrar; *(amount)* calcular; **I can't w. out how he did it** no me explico cómo lo hizo
2 VI (**a**) **things didn't w. out for her** las cosas no le salieron bien (**b**) **it works out at five each** sale a cinco cada uno (**c**) *Sport* hacer ejercicio
▸ **work through** VI penetrar (**to** hasta)
▸ **work up** VT SEP *(excite)* acalorar; **to get worked up** excitarse; **to w. up enthusiasm (for)** entusiasmarse (con)
workable ['wɜːkəbəl] ADJ factible
workaholic [wɜːkə'hɒlɪk] N *Fam* trabajoadicto(a) *m,f*
workbench ['wɜːkbentʃ] N obrador *m*
worker ['wɜːkə(r)] N trabajador(a) *m,f*; *(manual)* obrero(a) *m,f*
workforce ['wɜːkfɔːs] N mano *f* de obra
working ['wɜːkɪŋ] **1** ADJ (**a**) *(population, capital)* activo(a); **w. class** clase obrera; **w. man** obrero *m* (**b**) *(clothes, conditions, hours)* de trabajo; **w. day** día *m* laborable; *(number of hours)* jornada *f* laboral (**c**) **it is in w. order** funciona (**d**) *(majority)* suficiente; **w. knowledge** conocimientos básicos
2 workings *(mechanics)* funcionamiento *m*; *Min* explotación *f*
workload ['wɜːkləʊd] N cantidad *f* de trabajo
workman ['wɜːkmən] N *(manual)* obrero *m*
workmanship ['wɜːkmənʃɪp] N *(appearance)* acabado *m*; *(skill)* habilidad *f*, arte *m*; **a fine piece of w.** un trabajo excelente
workmate ['wɜːkmeɪt] N compañero(a) *m,f* de trabajo
work-out ['wɜːkaʊt] N entrenamiento *m*
worksheet ['wɜːkʃiːt] N plan *m* de trabajo
workshop ['wɜːkʃɒp] N taller *m*
worktop ['wɜːktɒp] N encimera *f*
work-to-rule ['wɜːktə'ruːl] N huelga *f* de celo
world [wɜːld] N mundo *m*; **all over the w.** en todo el mundo; **the best in the w.** el mejor del mundo; *Ftb* **the W. Cup** los Mundiales; **w. record** récord *m* mundial; **w. war** guerra *f* mundial
world-class ['wɜːld'klɑːs] ADJ de categoría mundial
world-famous ['wɜːld'feɪməs] ADJ de fama mundial

worldly ['wɜːldlɪ] ADJ (**wordlier, wordliest**) mundano(a)
worldwide ['wɜːldwaɪd] ADJ mundial
worm [wɜːm] **1** N (**a**) *(in general)* gusano *m*; **(earth) w.** lombriz *f* (**b**) *Med* **worms** lombrices *fpl*
2 VT **to w. a secret out of sb** sonsacarle un secreto a algn
worn [wɔːn] **1** ADJ gastado(a), usado(a)
2 PP *of* **wear**
worn-out ['wɔːnaʊt] ADJ *(thing)* gastado(a); *(person)* rendido(a), agotado(a)
worried ['wʌrɪd] ADJ inquieto(a), preocupado(a)
worry ['wʌrɪ] **1** VT (**a**) *(cause anxiety to)* preocupar; **it doesn't w. me** me trae sin cuidado (**b**) *(pester)* molestar
2 VI preocuparse (**about** por); **don't w.** no te preocupes
3 N *(state)* inquietud *f*; *(cause)* preocupación *f*
worrying ['wʌrɪɪŋ] ADJ inquietante, preocupante
worse [wɜːs] **1** ADJ *(comp of* **bad***)* peor; **he gets w. and w.** va de mal en peor; **to get w.** empeorar; *Fam* **w. luck!** ¡mala suerte!
2 N **a change for the w.** un empeoramiento; *Fig* **to take a turn for the w.** empeorar
3 ADV *(comp of* **badly***)* peor; **w. than ever** peor que nunca
worsen ['wɜːsən] VT & VI empeorar
worship ['wɜːʃɪp] **1** VT adorar
2 N (**a**) *(of deity)* adoración *f* (**b**) *(ceremony)* culto *m* (**c**) *Br* **His W. the Mayor** el señor alcalde; *Jur* **Your W.** Su Señoría
worshipper ['wɜːʃɪpə(r)] N devoto(a) *m,f*
worst [wɜːst] **1** ADJ *(superl of* **bad***)* peor; **the w. part about it is that ...** lo peor es que ...
2 N (**a**) *(person)* el/la peor, los/las peores (**b**) **the w. of the storm is over** ya ha pasado lo peor de la tormenta
3 ADV *(superl of* **badly***)* peor; *Fig* **to come off w.** salir perdiendo
worth [wɜːθ] **1** ADJ (**a**) **to be w. £3** valer 3 libras; **a house w. £50,000** una casa que vale 50.000 libras (**b**) *(deserving of)* merecedor(a) de; **a book w. reading** un libro que merece la pena leer; **for what it's w.** por si sirve de algo; **it's w. your while, it's w. it** vale *or* merece la pena; **it's w. mentioning** es digno de mención
2 N (**a**) *(in money)* valor *m*; **£5 w. of petrol** gasolina por valor de 5 libras (**b**) *(of person)* valía *f*
worthless ['wɜːθlɪs] ADJ sin valor; *(person)* despreciable
worthwhile [wɜːθ'waɪl] ADJ valioso(a), que vale la pena
worthy ['wɜːðɪ] ADJ (**worthier, worthiest**) (**a**) *(deserving)* digno(a) (**of** de); *(winner, cause)* justo(a) (**b**) *(citizen)* respetable; *(effort, motives, action)* loable

would [wʊd, *unstressed* wəd] V AUX (a) *(conditional)* I w. go if I had time iría si tuviera tiempo; he w. have won but for that habría ganado sí no hubiera sido por eso; we w. if we could lo haríamos si pudiéramos; you w. have to choose me! ¡tenías que elegirme precisamente a mí! (b) *(reported speech)* he said that he w. come dijo que vendría (c) *(willingness)* the car wouldn't start el coche no arrancaba; they asked him to come but he wouldn't le invitaron a venir pero no quiso; w. you do me a favour? ¿quiere hacerme un favor? (d) *(wishing)* he w. like to know why quisiera saber por qué; I'd rather go home preferiría ir a casa; w. you like a cigarette? ¿quiere un cigarrillo? (e) *(custom)* we w. go for walks solíamos dar un paseo (f) *(try as I w.)* por mucho que lo intentara (g) *(conjecture)* it w. have been about three weeks ago debe haber sido hace unas tres semanas; w. this be your cousin? ¿será éste tu primo? (h) *(expectation)* so it w. appear según parece

would-be ['wʊdbiː] ADJ en potencia; a w. politician un aspirante a político; Pej a w. poet un supuesto poeta

wound[1] [waʊnd] PT & PP of **wind**[2]

wound[2] [wuːnd] 1 N herida f
2 VT herir

wove [wəʊv] PT of **weave**

woven ['wəʊvən] PP of **weave**

wow [waʊ] INTERJ Fam ¡hala!, RP ¡uau!

WP ['dʌbəljuːˈpiː] N (a) *(abbr word processor)* procesador m de textos (b) *(abbr word processing)* tratamiento m de textos

wrangle ['ræŋɡəl] 1 N disputa f
2 VI disputar (**over** por)

wrap [ræp] 1 VT to w. (up) envolver; he wrapped his arms around her la estrechó entre sus brazos; Fam we wrapped up the deal concluimos el negocio
2 VI Fam w. up well abrígate (bien)
3 N *(shawl)* chal m; *(cape)* capa f

wrapper ['ræpə(r)] N *(of sweet)* envoltorio m; *(of book)* sobrecubierta f

wrapping ['ræpɪŋ] N w. paper papel m de envolver

wreath [riːθ] N *(pl* wreaths [riːðz, riːθs]) *(of flowers)* corona f; laurel w. corona de laurel

wreck [rek] 1 N (a) *Naut* naufragio m; *(ship)* barco naufragado (b) *(of car, plane)* restos mpl; *(of building)* ruinas fpl (c) Fig *(person)* ruina f
2 VT (a) *(ship)* hacer naufragar (b) *(car, machine)* destrozar (c) Fig *(health, life)* arruinar; *(plans, hopes)* desbaratar; *(chances)* echar a perder

wreckage ['rekɪdʒ] N *(of ship, car, plane)* restos mpl; *(of building)* ruinas fpl

wren [ren] N chochín m

wrench [rentʃ] 1 N (a) *(pull)* tirón m (b) Med torcedura f (c) *(tool)* Br llave inglesa; US llave f
2 VT to w. oneself free soltarse de un tirón; to w. sth off sb arrebatarle algo a algn; to w. sth off/open quitar/abrir algo de un tirón

wrestle ['resəl] VI luchar

wrestler ['reslə(r)] N luchador(a) m,f

wrestling ['reslɪŋ] N lucha f

wretch [retʃ] N *(poor)* w. desgraciado(a) m,f

wretched ['retʃɪd] ADJ (a) *(very bad)* *(weather, state, conditions)* deplorable; *(life, childhood)* desdichado(a) (b) I feel w. *(ill)* me siento fatal (c) *(contemptible)* despreciable (d) Fam *(for emphasis)* maldito(a), condenado(a)

wriggle ['rɪɡəl] 1 VT menear
2 VI to w. (about) *(worm)* serpentear; *(restless child)* moverse nerviosamente; to w. free escapar deslizándose

wring [rɪŋ] VT *(pt & pp* wrung) (a) *(clothes)* escurrir; *(hands)* retorcer (b) Fig *(extract)* arrancar, sacar

wringing ['rɪŋɪŋ] ADJ to be w. wet estar empapado/a

wrinkle ['rɪŋkəl] 1 N arruga f
2 VT arrugar
3 VI arrugarse

wrist [rɪst] N muñeca f

wristwatch ['rɪstwɒtʃ] N reloj m de pulsera

writ [rɪt] N orden f judicial

write [raɪt] 1 VT *(pt wrote; pp written)* escribir; *(article)* redactar; *(cheque)* extender; US to w. sb escribir a algn
2 VI escribir (**about** sobre); Br to w. to sb escribir a algn; to w. for a paper colaborar en un periódico
▸ **write back** VI contestar
▸ **write down** VT SEP poner por escrito; *(note)* apuntar
▸ **write in** VI escribir
▸ **write off** 1 VT SEP *(debt)* condonar; Fam *(car)* cargarse, Méx dar en la madre, RP hacer bolsa
2 VI to w. off for sth pedir algo por escrito
▸ **write out** VT SEP *(cheque, recipe)* extender
▸ **write up** VT SEP *(notes)* redactar; *(diary, journal)* poner al día

write-off ['raɪtɒf] N the car's a w. el coche está hecho una ruina

writer ['raɪtə(r)] N *(by profession)* escritor(a) m,f; *(of book, letter)* autor(a) m,f

writhe [raɪð] VI retorcerse

writing ['raɪtɪŋ] N (a) *(script)* escritura f; *(handwriting)* letra f; in w. por escrito (b) writings escritos mpl (c) *(action)* escritura f; w. desk escritorio m

written ['rɪtən] PP of **write**

wrong [rɒŋ] 1 ADJ (a) *(person)* equivocado(a); I was w. about that boy me equivoqué con ese chico; to be w. no tener razón; you're w. in thinking that … te equivocas si piensas que …

(**b**) *(answer, way)* incorrecto(a), equivocado(a); **my watch is w.** mi reloj anda mal; **to drive on the w. side of the road** conducir *or Am* manejar por el lado contrario de la carretera; **to go the w. way** equivocarse de camino; *Tel* **I've got the w. number** me he confundido de número

(**c**) *(unsuitable)* impropio(a), inadecuado(a); *(time)* inoportuno(a); **to say the w. thing** decir algo inoportuno

(**d**) *(immoral etc)* malo(a); **there's nothing w. in that** no hay nada malo en ello; **what's w. with smoking?** ¿qué tiene de malo fumar?

(**e**) **is anything w.?** ¿pasa algo?; **something's w.** hay algo que no está bien; **what's w.?** ¿qué pasa?; **what's w. with you?** ¿qué te pasa?

2 ADV mal, incorrectamente; **to get it w.** equivocarse; *Fam* **to go w.** *(plan)* fallar, salir mal

3 N (**a**) *(evil, bad action)* mal *m*; **you did w. to hit him** hiciste mal en pegarle (**b**) *(injustice)* injusticia *f*; *(offence)* agravio *m*; **the rights and wrongs of a matter** lo justo y lo injusto de un asunto (**c**) **to be in the w.** *(be to blame)* tener la culpa

4 VT *(treat unfairly)* ser injusto(a) con; *(offend)* agraviar

wrongdoing ['rɒŋduːɪŋ] N maldad *f*

wrongful ['rɒŋfʊl] ADJ injusto(a)

wrongly ['rɒŋlɪ] ADV (**a**) *(incorrectly)* incorrectamente (**b**) *(mistakenly)* equivocadamente (**c**) *(unjustly)* injustamente

wrote [rəʊt] PT *of* **write**

wrung [rʌŋ] PT & PP *of* **wring**

wry [raɪ] ADJ (**wrier, wriest** *or* **wryer, wryest**) sardónico(a)

WTO ['dʌbəljuːtiː'eʊ] N *(abbr* **World Trade Organization)** OMC *f*

WWW N *Comput (abbr* **World Wide Web)** WWW *f*

WYSIWYG ['wɪzɪwɪg] N *Comput (abbr* **what you see is what you get)** WYSIWYG, = se imprime lo que ves

X

X, x [eks] N *(the letter)* X, x *f*

xenophobia [zenə'fəʊbɪə] N xenofobia *f*

Xerox® ['zɪərɒks] **1** N fotocopia *f*, xerocopia *f*
2 VT fotocopiar

Xmas ['krɪsməs, 'eksməs] N *(abbr* **Christmas)**
Navidad *f*

X-ray ['eksreɪ] **1** N *(radiation)* rayo *m* X; *(picture)*
radiografía *f*; **to have an X.** hacerse una
radiografía
2 VT radiografiar

xylophone ['zaɪləfəʊn] N xilófono *m*, xilofón
m

Y

Y, y [waɪ] N *(the letter)* Y, y *f*

yacht [jɒt] N yate *m*; **y. club** club náutico

yachting ['jɒtɪŋ] N *Sport* navegación *f* a vela; *(competition)* regatas *fpl*

yachtsman ['jɒtsmən] N balandrista *m*

yachtswoman ['jɒtswʊmən] N balandrista *f*

yam [jæm] N **(a)** *(vegetable)* ñame *m* **(b)** *US (sweet potato)* Esp, Arg, Col, Ven batata *f*, Esp, Cuba, Urug boniato *m*, Andes, CAm, Méx camote *m*

Yank [jæŋk] N *Fam Br (person from the USA)* yanqui *mf*; *US (person from north-eastern USA)* = estadounidense procedente del nordeste del país

yank [jæŋk] VT *Fam* tirar; *(tooth)* arrancar

Yankee ['jæŋkɪ] ADJ & N *Pej* yanqui *(mf)*

yap [jæp] VI *(dog)* aullar; *Fam (person)* darle al pico

yard¹ [jɑːd] N *(measure)* yarda *f (aprox 0,914 m)*

yard² [jɑːd] N patio *m*; *US* jardín *m*

yardstick ['jɑːdstɪk] N *Fig* criterio *m*, norma *f*

yarn [jɑːn] N **(a)** *Sewing* hilo *m* **(b)** *(story)* historia *f*, cuento *m*; **to spin a y.** *(lie)* inventarse una historia

yawn [jɔːn] VI bostezar
2 N bostezo *m*

yawning ['jɔːnɪŋ] ADJ *(gap)* profundo(a)

yd *(pl* **yds)** *(abbr* **yard)** yarda *f*

yeah [jeə] ADV *Fam* sí

year [jɪə(r)] N **(a)** *(of calendar)* año *m*; **all y. round** durante todo el año; **last y.** el año pasado; **next y.** el año que viene; **y. in, y. out** año tras año; **I'm ten years old** tengo diez años **(b)** *Educ* curso *m*; **first-y. student** estudiante *m* de primero

yearly ['jɪəlɪ] 1 ADJ anual
2 ADV anualmente, cada año

yearn [jɜːn] VI **to y. for sth** anhelar algo

yearning ['jɜːnɪŋ] N anhelo *m* **(for** de)

yeast [jiːst] N levadura *f*

yell [jel] 1 VI gritar
2 N grito *m*, alarido *m*

yellow ['jeləʊ] 1 ADJ amarillo(a); *Tel* **Y. Pages®** páginas amarillas
2 N amarillo *m*

yelp [jelp] 1 VI aullar
2 N aullido *m*

yen [jen] N **(a)** *(currency)* yen *m* **(b)** **to have a y. for sth** tener ganas de algo

yeoman ['jəʊmən] N *Br* **Y. of the Guard =** alabardero de la Casa Real británica

yes [jes] 1 ADV sí; **you said y.** dijiste que sí
2 N sí *m*

yesterday ['jestədeɪ] ADV & N ayer *m*; **the day before y.** anteayer; **y. morning** ayer por la mañana

yet [jet] 1 ADV **(a)** **not y.** aún no, todavía no; **as y.** hasta ahora; **I haven't eaten y.** no he comido todavía **(b)** *(in questions)* ya; **has he arrived y.?** ¿ha venido ya? **(c)** *(even)* más; **y. again** otra vez; **y. more** todavía más **(d)** *(eventually)* todavía, aún; **he'll win y.** todavía puede ganar
2 CONJ sin embargo

yew [juː] N tejo *m*

yield [jiːld] 1 N **(a)** *(of mine, interest)* rendimiento *m* **(b)** *Agr* cosecha *f* **(c)** *Fin* beneficio *m*
2 VT producir; *Agr* dar; *(money)* producir
3 VI **(a)** *(surrender, break)* ceder **(b)** *US Aut* ceder el paso

YMCA [waɪemsiː'eɪ] N *(abbr* **Young Men's Christian Association)** ACJ *f*, Asociación *f* Cristiana de Jóvenes *(que regenta hostales económicos)*

yob(bo) ['jɒb(əʊ)] N *Br Fam* vándalo(a) *m*, Esp gamberro(a) *m,f*, Perú, RP patotero *m*

yoga ['jəʊgə] N yoga *m*

yog(h)urt ['jɒgət] N yogur *m*

yoke [jəʊk] 1 N yugo *m*
2 VT *(oxen)* uncir; *Fig* unir

yokel ['jəʊkəl] N *Pej or Hum* palurdo(a) *m,f*, Esp paleto(a) *m,f*

yolk [jəʊk] N yema *f*

yonder ['jɒndə(r)] ADV más allá

you [juː, *unstressed* jʊ] PERS PRON

> In Spanish, the formal form **usted** takes a third person singular verb and **ustedes** takes a third person plural verb. In many Latin American countries, **ustedes** is the standard form of the second person plural and is not considered formal.

(a) *(subject) (usually omitted in Spanish, except for contrast) (singular)* tú, *esp RP* vos, *Fml* usted; *(plural) Esp* vosotros(as), *Am or Fml* ustedes; **have YOU got it?** *(singular)* ¿lo tienes tú?, *Fml* ¿lo tiene usted?; *(plural) Esp* ¿lo tenéis vosotros?, *Am or Fml* ¿lo tienen ustedes?
(b) *(direct object) (singular)* te, *Fml* lo(la); *(plural) Esp* os, *Am or Fml* los(las); **I can**

understand your son but not YOU *(singular)* a tu hijo lo entiendo, pero a ti no, *Fml* a su hijo lo entiendo, pero a usted no; *(plural) Esp* a vuestro hijo lo entiendo, pero a vosotros no, *Am or Fml* a su hijo lo entiendo, pero a ustedes no

(**c**) *(indirect object) (singular)* te, *Fml* le; *(plural) Esp* os, *Am or Fml* les; **I gave y. the book** *(singular)* te di el libro, *Fml* le di el libro; *(plural) Esp* os di el libro, *Am or Fml* les di el libro; **I told y.** *(singular)* te lo dije, *Fml* se lo dije; *(plural) Esp* os lo dije, *Am or Fml* se lo dije (**d**) *(after preposition) (singular)* ti, *Fml* usted; *(plural) Esp* vosotros(as), *Am or Fml* ustedes; **I'm thinking of y.** *(singular)* pienso en ti, *Fml* pienso en usted; *(plural) Esp* pienso en vosotros, *Am or Fml* pienso en ustedes (**e**) *(impersonal)* **y. don't do that kind of thing** esas cosas no se hacen

young [jʌŋ] **1** ADJ *(age)* joven; *(brother etc)* pequeño(a); **y. lady** señorita *f*; **y. man** joven *m* **2** NPL (**a**) *(people)* **the y.** los jóvenes, la juventud (**b**) *(animals)* crías *fpl*

youngster ['jʌŋstə(r)] N muchacho(a) *m,f*

your [jɔː(r), *unstressed* jə(r)] POSS ADJ (**a**) *(of one person)* tu, *Fml* su; **y. house** tu/su casa; **y. books** tus/sus libros; **it wasn't YOUR idea!** ¡no fue idea tuya! (**b**) *(of more than one person) Esp* vuestro(a), *Am or Fml* su; **y. house** *Esp* vuestra casa, *Am or Fml* su casa; **y. books** *Esp* vuestros libros, *Am or Fml* sus libros; **it wasn't YOUR idea!** *Esp* ¡no fue idea vuestra!, *Am or Fml* ¡no fue idea suya or de ustedes! (**c**) *(for parts of body, clothes) (translated by definite article)* **did you hit y. head?** ¿te has dado un golpe en la cabeza? (**d**) *(impersonal)* **smoking is bad for y. health** el tabaco perjudica la salud

yours [jɔːz] POSS PRON

> In Spanish, the forms **tuyo(a)**, **suyo(a)** and **vuestro(a)** require a definite article in the singular and in the plural when they are the subject of the phrase.

(**a**) *(of one person) (singular)* tuyo(a) *m,f*; *(plural)* tuyos(as) *m,fpl*; *(formal: singular)* suyo(a) *m,f*; *(formal: plural)* suyos(as) *m,fpl*; **my house is big but y. is bigger** mi casa es grande, pero la tuya/suya es mayor; **this book is y.** este libro es tuyo/suyo; **these books are y.** estos libros son tuyos/suyos; **a friend of y.** un amigo tuyo/suyo; **y. (sincerely/faithfully)** atentamente (**b**) *(of more*

than one person) (singular) Esp* vuestro(a), *Am or Fml* suyo(a); *(plural) Esp* vuestros(as), *Am or Fml* suyos(as); **this book is y.** este libro es vuestro/suyo; **these books are y.** estos libros son vuestros/suyos

yourself [jɔː'self] PRON (**a**) *(reflexive)* te; *(formal)* se; **have you hurt y.?** ¿te has hecho daño?; *(formal)* ¿se ha hecho daño? (**b**) *(emphatic)* tú mismo *m*, tú misma *f*; *(formal)* usted mismo *m*, usted misma *f*; **did you do all the work y.?** ¿has hecho todo el trabajo tú solo?; *(formal)* ¿ha hecho todo el trabajo usted solo?; **you told me y.** me lo dijiste tú mismo; *(formal)* me lo dijo usted mismo; **you're not y. today** hoy no se te nota nada bien (**c**) *(after preposition)* ti; *(formal)* usted; **did you do this by y.?** ¿lo has hecho tú solo?; *(formal)* ¿lo ha hecho usted solo?; **do you live by y.?** ¿vives solo?; **did you buy it for y.?** ¿te lo has comprado para ti?; *(formal)* ¿se lo ha comprado para usted?

yourselves [jɔː'selvz] PRON (**a**) *(reflexive) Esp* os, *Am or Fml* se; **have you hurt y.?** *Esp* ¿os habéis hecho daño?, *Am or Fml* ¿se han hecho daño? (**b**) *(emphatic) Esp* vosotros(as) mismos(as), *Am or Fml* ustedes mismos(as); **did you do all the work y.?** *Esp* ¿habéis hecho todo el trabajo vosotros solos?, *Am or Fml* ¿han hecho todo el trabajo ustedes solos? (**c**) *(after preposition) Esp* vosotros(as), *Am or Fml* ustedes; **did you do this by y.?** *Esp* ¿lo habéis hecho vosotros solos?, *Am or Fml* ¿lo han hecho ustedes solos?; **did you buy it for y.?** *Esp* ¿os lo habéis comprado para vosotros?, *Am or Fml* ¿se lo han comprado para ustedes?

youth [juːθ] N (**a**) *(period)* juventud *f* (**b**) *(young man)* joven *m*; **y. club** club *m* juvenil; **y. hostel** albergue *m* juvenil

youthful ['juːθful] ADJ juvenil, joven

Yugoslavia [juːgəʊ'slɑːvɪə] N *Formerly* Yugoslavia

Yugoslavian [juːgəʊ'slɑːvɪən] ADJ & N *Formerly* yugoslavo(a) *(m,f)*

yuppie ['jʌpɪ] N yupi *mf*; **a y. restaurant** un restaurante de yupis

YWCA ['waɪdʌbəljuːsiː'eɪ] N *(abbr* **Young Women's Christian Association)** ACJ *f*, Asociación *f* Cristiana de Jóvenes *(que regenta hostales económicos)*

Z, z [zed, *US* zi:] N *(the letter)* Z, z *f*

zany ['zeɪnɪ] ADJ (**zanier, zaniest**) *Fam* (**a**) *(mad) Esp* chiflado(a), *Am* zafado(a), *RP* rayado(a) (**b**) *(eccentric)* estrafalario(a)

zap [zæp] **1** INTERJ ¡zas!
  2 VT *Fam* (**a**) *(hit)* pegar (**b**) *(kill)* cargarse a
  3 VI *TV* hacer zapping

zeal [zi:l] N *(enthusiasm)* entusiasmo *m*

zealous ['zeləs] ADJ *(enthusiastic)* entusiasta

zebra ['zi:brə, 'zebrə] N cebra *f*; *Br* **z. crossing** paso *m* de cebra

zenith ['zenɪθ] N *Astron* cenit *m*; *Fig* apogeo *m*

zero ['zɪərəʊ] N cero *m*; **z. hour** hora *f* cero

zest [zest] N *(eagerness)* entusiasmo *m*

zigzag ['zɪgzæg] **1** N zigzag *m*
  2 VI zigzaguear

Zimbabwe [zɪm'bɑ:bweɪ] N Zimbabue

zinc [zɪŋk] N cinc *m*, zinc *m*

zip [zɪp] **1** N (**a**) *Br* **z. (fastener)** cremallera *f*, *Am* cierre *m* (**b**) *Fam* brío *m*; *US* **z. code** código *m* postal
  2 VI cerrarse con cremallera

▸ **zip by** VI pasar como un rayo

▸ **zip up** VT SEP cerrar la cremallera *or Am* el cierre de; **to z. sb up** cerrar la cremallera *or Am* el cierre a algn

zipper ['zɪpə(r)] N *US* cremallera *f*, *Am* cierre *m*

zit [zɪt] N *Fam* grano *m*

zodiac ['zəʊdɪæk] N zodiaco *m*, zodíaco *m*

zombie ['zɒmbɪ] N zombie *mf*

zone [zəʊn] **1** N zona *f*
  2 VT dividir en zonas

zoo [zu:] N zoo *m*

zoological [zu:ə'lɒdʒɪkəl] ADJ zoológico(a)

zoologist [zu:'ɒlədʒɪst] N zoólogo(a) *m,f*

zoology [zu:'ɒlədʒɪ] N zoología *f*

zoom [zu:m] **1** N (**a**) *(buzz)* zumbido *m* (**b**) **z. lens** zoom *m*, teleobjetivo *m*
  2 VI (**a**) *(buzz)* zumbar (**b**) **to z. past** pasar volando

▸ **zoom in** VI *(camera)* acercarse rápidamente

zucchini [zu:'ki:nɪ] N *US* calabacín *m*, *CSur* zapallito *m*

Zulu ['zu:lu:] ADJ & N zulú *(mf)*